Date Issued		No.	Title
April	1972	No. 24	Accounting for Income Taxes—Equity Method Investments (unchanged)
Oct.	1972	No. 25	Accounting for Stock Issued to Employees (unchanged)
Oct.	1972	No. 26	Early Extinguishment of Debt (amended)
Nov.	1972	No. 27	Accounting for Lease Transactions by Manufacturer or Dealer Lessors (superseded)
May	1973	No. 28	Interim Financial Reporting (amended and partially superseded)
May	1973	No. 29	Accounting for Nonmonetary Transactions (unchanged)
June	1973	No. 30	Reporting the Results of Operations (amended)
June	1973	No. 31	Disclosure of Lease Commitments by Lessees (superseded)

Financial Accounting Standards Board (FASB), Statements of Financial Accounting Standards (1973–1994)

Date Issued		No.	Title
Dec.	1973	No. 1	Disclosure of Foreign Currency Translation Information (superseded)
Oct.	1974	No. 2	Accounting for Research and Development Costs
Dec.	1974	No. 3	Reporting Accounting Changes in Interim Financial Statements
Mar.	1975	No. 4	Reporting Gains and Losses from Extinguishment of Debt (amended)
Mar.	1975	No. 5	Accounting for Contingencies (amended)
May	1975	No. 6	Classification of Short-term Obligations Expected to be Refinanced
June	1975	No. 7	Accounting and Reporting by Development Stage Enterprises
Oct.	1975	No. 8	Accounting for the Translation of Foreign Currency Transactions and Foreign Financial Statements (superseded)
Oct.	1975	No. 9	Accounting for Income Taxes—Oil and Gas Producing Companies (superseded)
Oct.	1975	No. 10	Extension of "Grandfather" Provisions for Business Combinations
Dec.	1975	No. 11	Accounting for Contingencies—Transition Method
Dec.	1975	No. 12	Accounting for Certain Marketable Securities
Nov.	1976	No. 13	Accounting for Leases (amended, interpreted, and partially superseded)
Dec.	1976	No. 14	Financial Reporting for Segments of a Business Enterprise (amended)
June	1977	No. 15	Accounting by Debtors and Creditors for Troubled Debt Restructurings
June	1977	No. 16	Prior Period Adjustments
Nov.	1977	No. 17	Accounting for Leases—Initial Direct Costs
Nov.	1977	No. 18	Financial Reporting for Segments of a Business Enterprise—Interim Financial Statements
Dec.	1977	No. 19	Financial Accounting and Reporting by Oil and Gas Producing Companies (amended)
Dec.	1977	No. 20	Accounting for Forward Exchange Contracts (superseded)
April	1978	No. 21	Suspension of the Reporting of Earnings per Share and Segment Information by Nonpublic Enterprises
June	1978	No. 22	Changes in the Provisions of Lease Agreements Resulting from Refundings of Tax-Exempt Debt
Aug.	1978	No. 23	Inception of the Lease
Dec.	1978	No. 24	Reporting Segment Information in Financial Statements That Are Presented in Another Enterprise's Financial Report
Feb.	1979	No. 25	Suspension of Certain Accounting Requirements for Oil and Gas Producing Companies
April	1979	No. 26	Profit Recognition on Sales-Type Leases of Real Estate
May	1979	No. 27	Classification of Renewals or Extensions of Existing Sales-Type or Direct Financing Leases
May	1979	No. 28	Accounting for Sales with Leasebacks
June	1979	No. 29	Determining Contingent Rentals
Aug.	1979	No. 30	Disclosure of Information about Major Customers
Sept.	1979	No. 31	Accounting for Tax Benefits Related to U.K. Tax Legislation Concerning Stock Relief
Sept.	1979	No. 32	Specialized Accounting and Reporting Principles and Practices in AICPA Statements of Position and Guides on Accounting and Auditing Matters (amended and partially superseded)
Sept.	1979	No. 33	Financial Reporting and Changing Prices (amended and partially superseded)
Oct.	1979	No. 34	Capitalization of Interest Cost (amended)
Mar.	1980	No. 35	Accounting and Reporting by Defined Benefit Pension Plans (amended)
May	1980	No. 36	Disclosure of Pension Information
July	1980	No. 37	Balance Sheet Classification of Deferred Income Taxes
Sept.	1980	No. 38	Accounting for Preacquisition Contingencies of Purchased Enterprises
Oct.	1980	No. 39	Financial Reporting and Changing Prices: Specialized Assets--Mining and Oil and Gas
Nov.	1980	No. 40	Financial Reporting and Changing Prices: Specialized Assets—Timberlands and Growing Timber
Nov.	1980	No. 41	Financial Reporting and Changing Prices: Specialized Assets—Income-Producing Real Estate
Nov.	1980	No. 42	Determining Materiality for Capitalization of Interest Cost
Nov.	1980	No. 43	Accounting for Compensated Absences
Dec.	1980	No. 44	Accounting for Intangible Assets of Motor Carriers

Refer to Index for page citations

Refer to Index for page citations

(Listing continued on inside of back cover.)

EIGHTH EDITION

INTERMEDIATE ACCOUNTING

Donald E. Kieso
PH.D., C.P.A.

KPMG Peat Marwick Emeritus Professor of Accounting
Northern Illinois University
DeKalb, Illinois

Jerry J. Weygandt
PH.D., C.P.A.

Arthur Andersen Alumni Professor of Accounting
University of Wisconsin
Madison, Wisconsin

John Wiley & Sons, Inc.
New York / Chichester / Brisbane / Toronto / Singapore

ACQUISITIONS EDITOR   Karen Hawkins
DEVELOPMENTAL EDITOR   Kathleen Dolan
MARKETING MANAGER   Karen Allman
SENIOR PRODUCTION EDITOR   Charlotte Hyland
TEXT DESIGNER   Karin Gerdes Kincheloe
MANUFACTURING MANAGER   Susan Stetzer
PHOTO EDITOR   Mary Ann Price
ILLUSTRATION COORDINATOR   Anna Melhorn
COVER DESIGNER   Carol C. Grobe
PROJECT MANAGEMENT   Elm Street Publishing Services, Inc.
COVER PHOTO   ©Tim Bieber/The Image Bank
All "Perspectives On" photographs provided courtesy of featured individuals.

This book was set in Palatino by CRWaldman and printed and bound by Von Hoffmann Press.
The cover was printed by Phoenix Color.

Recognizing the importance of preserving what has been written, it is a
policy of John Wiley & Sons, Inc. to have books of enduring value published
in the United States printed on acid-free paper, and we exert our best
efforts to that end.

The paper in this book was manufactured by a mill whose forest management programs include
sustained yield harvesting of its timberlands. Sustained yield harvesting principles ensure that
the number of trees cut each year does not exceed the amount of new growth.

Library of Congress Cataloging in Publication Data:
Kieso, Donald E.
    Intermediate accounting / Donald E. Kieso, Jerry J. Weygandt.—
8th ed.
        p.   cm.
    Includes bibliographical references.
    ISBN 0-471-59759-7 (cloth)
    1. Accounting.   I. Weygandt, Jerry J.   II. Title.
HF5635.K5   1995
657'.044—dc20   94-40883

Printed in the United States of America

10 9 8 7 6 5 4 3 2 1

Dedicated to

Donna and Enid

for Their
Love, Support, and Understanding

► ABOUT THE AUTHORS ◄

Donald E. Kieso, Ph.D., CPA, received his bachelors degree from Aurora University and his doctorate in accounting from the University of Illinois. He has served as chairman of the Department of Accountancy and is currently the KPMG Peat Marwick Emeritus Professor of Accountancy at Northern Illinois University. He has public accounting experience with Price Waterhouse & Co. (San Francisco and Chicago) and Arthur Andersen & Co. (Chicago) and research experience with the Research Division of the American Institute of Certified Public Accountants (New York). He has done postdoctorate work as a Visiting Scholar at the University of California at Berkeley and is a recipient of NIU's Teaching Excellence Award and four Golden Apple Teaching Awards (1986, 1990, 1992, and 1994). Professor Kieso is the author of other accounting and business books and is a member of the American Accounting Association, the American Institute of Certified Public Accountants, the Financial Executives Institute, and the Illinois CPA Society. He has served as a member of the Board of Directors of the Illinois CPA Society, the Board of Governors of the American Accounting Association's Administrators of Accounting Programs Group, the AACSB's Accounting Accreditation and Visitation Committees, the State of Illinois Comptroller's Commission, as Secretary-Treasurer of the Federation of Schools of Accountancy, and as Secretary-Treasurer of the American Accounting Association. Professor Kieso is currently serving as a member of the Board of Trustees and Executive Committee of Aurora University, the Boards of Directors of Castle BancGroup Inc. and the Sandwich State Bank, and committees of the Illinois CPA Society. From 1989 to 1993 he served as a charter member of the national Accounting Education Change Commission. In 1988 he received the Outstanding Accounting Educator Award from the Illinois CPA Society, and in 1992 he received the FSA's Joseph A. Silvoso Award of Merit and the NIU Foundation's Humanitarian Award for Service to Higher Education.

Jerry J. Weygandt, Ph.D., CPA, is Arthur Andersen Alumni Professor of Accounting at the University of Wisconsin–Madison and is President of the American Accounting Association for 1994–95. He holds a Ph.D. in accounting from the University of Illinois. Articles by Professor Weygandt have appeared in the *Accounting Review, Journal of Accounting Research*, the *Journal of Accountancy*, and other professional journals. These articles have examined such financial reporting issues as accounting for price-level adjustments, pensions, convertible securities, stock option contracts, and interim reports. He is a member of the American Accounting Association, the American Institute of Certified Public Accountants, and the Wisconsin Society of Certified Public Accountants. He has served on numerous committees of the American Accounting Association and as a member of the editorial board of the *Accounting Review*. In addition, he has been involved with the American Institute of Certified Public Accountants and has been a member of the Accounting Standards Executive Committee (AcSEC) of that organization. He has served as a consultant to a number of businesses and state agencies on financial reporting issues and served on the FASB task force that examined the reporting issues related to "accounting for income taxes." Professor Weygandt has received the Chancellor's Award for Excellence in Teaching; he also has served as Secretary-Treasurer of the American Accounting Association. In 1991 he received the Wisconsin Institute of CPA's Outstanding Educator's Award.

PREFACE

*A*ccounting is an exciting, dynamic field of study; its body of knowledge, theories, and practices as well as the methodologies of teaching these concepts are constantly evolving. In the writing of this eighth edition of *Intermediate Accounting* we have thoroughly revised and updated the text to include all the latest developments in the accounting profession as well as addressed the important recommendations of the Accounting Education Change Commission for involving students more in the learning process.

Continuing to keep pace with the complexities of the modern business enterprise and professional accounting pronouncements, we have added new topics, deleted some obsolete material, clarified some of the existing coverage, added numerous illustrations, and updated material where necessary. To provide the instructor with greater flexibility in choosing topics to cover or omit, we have continued the use of judiciously selected appendices. The appendices are concerned primarily with complex subjects, less commonly used methods, or specialized topics.

Benefiting from the comments and recommendations of adopters of our seventh edition, we have made significant revisions. Explanations have been expanded where necessary, complicated discussions and illustrations have been simplified; realism has been integrated to heighten interest and relevancy; and new topics and coverage have been added to maintain currency. We have even deleted some seventh edition coverage and condensed the coverage of other topics.

Accountants must act as well as think; therefore, we believe it is important for students to understand the *how* as well as the *why*. The study of concepts develops an understanding of procedures, and the performance of procedures enriches an understanding of the concepts. We have therefore balanced our coverage so the conceptual discussion and procedural presentation are mutually reinforcing.

We believe that individuals learn to account for financial events and phenomena best if they fully understand the nature of the business transactions and comprehend the behavioral and economic consequences of the events for which firms account and report. The ability to critically evaluate accounting alternatives and their consequences is important. Throughout this revision, we have provided coverage to help students develop a real understanding of how accounting can be used to make effective financial decisions.

▶ NEW FEATURES

Based on extensive reviews, focus groups, and interactions with other intermediate accounting instructors and students, we have developed a number of new pedagogical features designed both to help students learn more effectively and to answer the changing needs of the course.

> ▶ **Underlying Concepts:** These margin notes relate topics covered within each chapter back to the conceptual principles introduced in the beginning of the book. This continual reinforcement of underlying accounting concepts illustrates

how the concepts are applied in practice and ensures that students understand the *why* as well as the *how*.

▶ **International Insights:** Many instructors have asked for coverage of international accounting, but can't afford the time for in-depth discussion. Our "International Insights" are a series of brief paragraphs in the margin of the text containing an observation or comparison of accounting practices in other countries with the topics covered in the chapter. New international coverage is also included in examples and exhibits within the body of the text where appropriate.

▶ **Using Your Judgment:** We have created a new section of end-of-chapter assignments that go beyond the routine problem solving and calculations found in other texts. "Using Your Judgment" sections, appearing at the end of every chapter, help develop students' analytical, critical thinking, and interpersonal communication skills in the accounting environment, and include:

Financial reporting problems, usually involving analysis and interpretation of Georgia-Pacific Corporation's financial statements (Appendix 5-A).

Writing assignments that help students develop the communication skills they will need in their professional careers.

Group assignments that help students both to learn concepts cooperatively and to develop skills in working in group situations.

Ethics cases that sensitize students to the ethical considerations, situations, and dilemmas encountered by practicing accountants.

▶ **Summary of Learning Objectives:** Completely rewritten end-of-chapter summaries reinforce important ideas from each chapter and link them to the learning objectives introduced at the beginning and integrated throughout.

▶ ENHANCED FEATURES

Real-World Emphasis: To help make material relevant and readily understandable, numerous examples, many of them new, from real corporations have been used throughout the text. Virtually all of the many illustrations and exhibits are excerpts from actual financial statements of existing firms, including the 1993 annual report of the Georgia-Pacific Corporation in Appendix 5-A.

"Perspectives": Interviews with prominent accounting and business personalities on relevant accounting topics give a further real-world emphasis. Five new interviews have been added in this edition for a total of thirteen. Interviews with individuals such as Kathy Whitmire, former mayor of Houston, show students how an accounting education can be used in a wide variety of professions and how the concepts they're learning are applied and debated in the real world.

Ethics: Ethics in the accounting environment is introduced as a topic in Chapter 1 and is included in every chapter in an Ethical Case in the "Using Your Judgment" section to help students learn to identify when ethical issues are involved and how to approach ethical decision-making.

Currency and Accuracy: Accounting continually changes as its environment changes; an up-to-date book is therefore a necessity. As with past editions we have striven to make this edition the most up-to-date and accurate text available.

Readability: Adopters of previous editions have praised the readability of our text. In this edition, we have carefully reviewed each line of text to further improve clarity and directness of language, to take out unnecessary detail, and to simplify complex presentations. Our streamlining efforts have both improved user-friendliness and allowed us to add needed new material while still shortening the overall length of the text.

Flexibility: In this edition, we have further increased the flexibility of use by shifting some optional topics to Appendices. Appendices are concerned primarily with complex subjects, lesser used methods, or specialized topics.

▶ **CONTENT CHANGES**

The list below outlines the revisions and improvements of the eighth edition by chapter. The most significant changes are preceded by an asterisk (*).

Chapter 1.
Strengthened discussion of SEC.
Added "business reporting," an expansion of "financial reporting."
*Developed new "house of GAAP" (most to least authoritative levels of GAAP).
*AICPA Special Committee on Financial Reporting covered (and in Chapter 26).

Chapter 2.
Reworked the conceptual framework illustrations.

Chapter 3.
Enhanced discussion of adjusting entries.

Chapter 4.
Simplified discussion of intraperiod tax allocation.
*Added an illustration of a foreign income statement.
Revised coverage of "comprehensive income."

Chapter 5.
*New illustration of a foreign balance sheet.

Chapter 6.
Added an amortization schedule for bonds.
Deleted coverage of interpolation.

Chapter 7.
*Reorganized and simplified coverage of notes receivable.

Chapter 8.
Reorganized and expanded coverage of perpetual versus periodic inventory methods.
Streamlined coverage of cost accounting.
Moved LIFO reporting problems to Appendix 8-A.

Chapter 9.
Deleted coverage of standard cost valuation.
New coverage of hedging of purchase commitments.
*Shortened and simplified the chapter by moving coverage of LIFO retail and dollar-value LIFO retail to the appendix.

Chapter 10.
Clarified coverage of capitalization of interest.
Contributions received and made, SFAS No. 116, covered in this chapter (and in Chapter 15).

Chapter 11.
*New coverage of impairments of long-lived assets (property, plant and equipment).
Revised discussion of controversy over depletion.
Restructured depletion discussion.

Chapter 12.
*Simplified chapter by moving "valuing goodwill" to the chapter appendix.
*New coverage of goodwill impairment.

Chapter 13.
*Reorganized chapter into two main sections.
Moved coverage of employee bonus computation to an appendix.
Strengthened coverage of unearned revenue.

Chapter 14.
Reorganized and simplified coverage of notes payable.
*Post-employment benefits (SFAS No. 113) discussed.
*Discussion about the fair value of financial instruments (SFAS No. 107) covered.
*Expanded discussion of financial investments with emphasis on derivatives.
Added new graphic on defeasance.
Deleted appendix coverage of serial bonds.
*Revised appendix on restructuring of troubled debt and added impairment of a loan (SFAS No. 114).

Chapter 15.   Contributions received and made (SFAS No. 116) covered in this chapter (and in Chapter 10).

Chapter 16.   Chapter shortened by moving coverage of quasi-reorganizations to the appendix.

Chapter 17.   *Added discussion of FASB's proposed guidelines on accounting for stock options.
Added discussion on FASB's proposed standard on earnings per share.

Chapter 18.   *Completely reorganized and rewritten to take into consideration new standards (SFAS No. 115) on investments in debt and equity securities.

Chapter 19.   Strengthened coverage of the deposit method.
Simplified and shortened coverage of cost recovery method.

Chapter 20.   *Revised chapter to conform to SFAS No. 109 guidelines.

Chapter 23.   Strengthened coverage of cumulative-effect type changes to include statement presentation and explanation of proforma amounts.

Chapter 25.   Deleted appendix coverage of "fundamental analysis versus capital market analysis."

Chapter 26.   New illustration of segment reporting.
Upgraded coverage of "auditor's report."
Updated coverage on safe harbor rule.
*AICPA Special Committee on Financial Reporting (9/94) covered in this chapter (and in Chapter 1).

▶ QUESTIONS, CASES, EXERCISES, AND PROBLEMS

At the end of each chapter we have provided a comprehensive set of review and homework material consisting of questions, exercises, problems, and short cases. For this edition many exercises and problems have been revised, and a new section, "Using Your Judgment," has been added that includes financial reporting problems, writing assignments, group assignments, and ethics cases, all of which have been either class tested or double checked for accuracy and clarity.

The questions are designed for review, self-testing, and classroom discussion purposes as well as homework assignments. Typically, an exercise covers a specific topic and requires less time and effort to solve than cases and problems. The problems are designed to develop a professional level of achievement and are more challenging and time consuming to solve than the exercises. Those exercises and problems that are contained in the *Lotus Problems* supplement are identified by a blue computer disk icon in the margin. The cases generally require essay as opposed to quantitative solutions; they are intended to confront the student with situations calling for conceptual analysis and the exercise of judgment in identifying problems and evaluating alternatives. The "Using Your Judgment" assignments are designed to develop students' critical thinking, analytical, interpersonal, and communication skills.

Probably no more than one-fourth of the total case, exercise, and problem material must be used to cover the subject matter adequately; consequently, problem assignment may be varied from year to year.

▶ COLOR DESIGN

The color design not only enlivens the textbook's appearance, but, through planned and consistent usage, eases learning. Note that financial statements are presented in blue toned color with a beige header. Trial balances, work sheets, and large schedules and exhibits are presented in beige with blue headings. Most small illustrations, demonstrations, and excerpts from notes accompanying financial statements are beige colored/blue trim boxes. Significant amounts and descriptions within either blue or beige colored boxes are highlighted in solid blue color. All pages containing assignment material have a blue triangle tab to the running head, while the five interest and annuity tables in Chapter 6 have a beige triangle tab to ease locating and identifying. The names of real-world companies as part of illustrations are red. The color design is summarized as follows:

Red—Real-world company names, secondary headings, and accents.

Blue—Financial statements, highlighted amounts and descriptions in boxed illustrations.

Beige—Exhibits, schedules, trial balances, work sheets, illustrations, and lists of definitions.

► SUPPLEMENTARY MATERIALS

Accompanying this textbook is an improved and expanded package of student learning aids and instructor teaching aids.

Instructor's Manual: Chs. 1-14 (00359-X)
Instructor's Manual: Chs. 14-26 (11747-1)

► Lecture outlines keyed to text learning objectives.

► Updated Bibliography.

► Teaching Transparency Masters.

► Section on "How to assign and evaluate ethical issues in the course."

► New Sections on "How to incorporate writing" and "How to incorporate group (collaborative) work."

Solutions Manual, Vol. I: Chs. 1-14 (01366-8)
Solutions Manual, Vol. II: Chs. 14-26 (01382-X)
Solutions Manual: Chs. 1-26 (10877-4)

► Answers to all questions, exercises, problems and case material provided.

► Classification Tables categorize the end-of-chapter material by topic to assist in assigning homework.

► Assignment Tables (characteristics) describe the end-of-chapter material, its difficulty level, and estimated completion time.

► All solutions double-checked to assure accuracy.

Test Bank, Vol. I: Chs. 1-14 (04132-7)
Test Bank, Vol. II: Chs. 14-26 (11750-1)

► Essay questions with solutions help you test students' communication skills.

► Estimated completion times facilitate test planning.

► Computations for multiple choice problems assist you in giving partial credit.

Computerized Test Bank IBM 5.25" (10762-X)
Computerized Test Bank IBM 3.5" (10761-1)
Computerized Test Bank MAC (10763-8)

► A large collection of objective questions and exercises with answers for each chapter in the text.

► Generate questions randomly or manually, and modify/customize texts with your own material.

► Create multiple versions of the same text by scrambling by type, chapter, number, or Study Objective.

Test Preparation Service

Simply call Wiley's Accounting Hotline (800) 541-5602 with the questions you have selected for an exam. Wiley will provide a master exam within 24 hours.

Solution Transparencies, Vol. I: Chs. 1-14 (01431-1)
Solution Transparencies, Vol. II: Chs. 15-26 (01432-X)

▶ Provided in organizer box with chapter files folders.

▶ Large, bold type size for easier class presentation.

▶ Provided for all quantitative exercises, problems, and cases.

Checklist of Key Figures (01385-4)

Video (10765-4)
Video Instructor's Manual (10764-6)

▶ Brings accounting to life while assisting students with difficult topics.

Student Study Guide, Vol. I: Chs. 1-14 (01404-4)
Student Study Guide, Vol. II: Chs. 14-26 (01419-2)

▶ New authorship

▶ Chapter Learning Objectives

▶ Chapter Outline—a broad overview of general chapter content with space for notetaking in class

▶ Chapter Review with summary of key concepts

▶ Glossary of key terms.

▶ Review Questions and exercises—self-test items with supporting computations

Workpapers, Vol. I: Chs. 1-14 (01387-9)
Workpapers, Vol. II: Chs. 14-26 (01400-1)

Lotus Problems 3.5" (01422-2)
Lotus Problems 5.25" (01423-0)

▶ Spreadsheet requirements range in difficulty (from data entry to developing spreadsheets)

▶ Review of intermediate accounting and Lotus concepts

▶ Each chapter consists of a basic tutorial, a more advanced tutorial, and two or three problems from the text.

▶ Each problem followed by ''what-if'' questions to build students' analytical skills.

Rockford Corporation Practice Set (01427-3)
Rockford Computerized Practice Set 3.5" (01428-1)
Rockford Computerized Practice Set 5.25" (01429-X)
Solution to the Practice Set (01430-3).

▶ Shorter (income tax entry is easier with several hints offered).

▶ Check figures available in solution manual.

▶ For assignment after Chapter 3, a good review of financial accounting to get students up to speed in intermediate.

Ainsworth: Flint Hill Beauty Salon: A Case Study (57476-7)

Presents the concepts of establishing and running a business for use as review before intermediate accounting.

Teaching Transparencies

► 100 color figure illustrations and exhibits

► 90% from outside the text

Self-Study Problems/Solutions Book, Vol. I (01420-6)
Self-Study Problems/Solutions Book, Vol. II (01421-4)

► ACKNOWLEDGMENTS

We thank the many users of our seventh edition who contributed to this revision through their comments and instructive criticism. Special thanks are extended to the primary reviewers of and contributors to our eighth edition manuscript:

Primary Text Reviewers

John C. Borke, University of Wisconsin–Platteville

Myrtle Clark, University of Kentucky

Alan Davis, Community College of Philadelphia

Robert Dunlevy, Temple University

Robert Gruber, University of Wisconsin–Whitewater

Rameshwar Gupta, Jackson State University

Randall Hayes, Central Michigan University

Wayne M. Higley, Buena Vista College

Marilyn F. Hunt, University of Central Florida

Susan Kauffman, Russell Sage College

Daphne Main, University of New Orleans

Barbara Oliver, College of St. Mary

Harold Peckron, Kutztown University of Pennsylvania

Judson Stryker, Stetson University

Robert West, University of South Florida

Marilyn Young, University of Tulsa

Primary Supplement Reviewers

Taisier AlDiab, Cameron University (Lotus)

Jon Bacon, Northern Illinois University (Sol M, TB)

Eugene Cardamone, Hudson Valley Community College (TM)

Michael Chatfield, Southern Oregon State College (TB)

Douglas deVidal, University of Texas–Austin (TB)

Pamela Druger, Augustana College (Self-Study)

James M. Emig, Villanova University (Sol M)

Larry R. Falcetto, Emporia State University (Sol M, TB)

Cecelia Fewox, Trident Technical College (Prac)

Mary Fleming, California State University–Fullerton (SG)

Greg Graber, Northern Illinois University (Sol M, IM)

Mary Lee Hodge, University of Texas–Arlington (Prac)

Arthur G. Joy, Columbus College (SG)

Timothy M. Lindquist, University of Northern Iowa (Prac)

Heidi Meier, Cleveland State University (Self-Study)

Kenneth Pelfrey, Ohio State University (SG)

Sandra Pelfrey, Oakland University (TM)

John Rigsby, Mississippi State University (Lotus)

Michael Watters, New Mexico State University (TB)

Other colleagues in academe who have provided helpful criticisms and made valuable suggestions as members of a focus group or adopters of the previous edition or reviewers of selected topics include:

John B. K. Abeto, Pace University

Abdel Agami, Old Dominion University

Eli Amir, Columbia University

Anne Lee Bain, St. Cloud State University

Steven Balsam, Temple University

Judy Beckman, University of Rhode Island

Janet Cassaglo, Nassau Community College

Douglas Cloud, Pepperdine University

Patrick Delaney, Northern Illinois University

Michael Doran, Iowa State University

Dean S. Eiteman, Indiana University–Pennsylvania

Don Etnier, University of Wisconsin–Eau Claire

Kevin Feeney, Southern Connecticut State University

Robert R. Giacoletti, Eastern Kentucky University

Joseph H. Godwin, University of Georgia

Lynn Griffin, North Carolina A & T State University

Marcia L. Halvorsen, University of Cincinnati

Jerry Hamsmith, North Central College

Douglas W. Kieso, Aurora University

Lisa Koonce, University of Texas–Austin

Jeanne Lafond, University of Massachusetts–Dartmouth

Lucille Lammers, Illinois State University

Kathy Lockard, Northern Illinois University

Frank Lordi, Widener University

John E. McEnroe, DePaul University

Claudel B. McKenzie, University of North Carolina at Asheville

Janice Morris, University of Houston–Clear Lake

Curtis Norton, Northern Illinois University

Anne M. Oppegard, Augustana College

Ronald Pawliczek, Boston College

Ralph Peck, Utah State University

Patrick M. Premo, St. Bonaventure University

Charles J. Reichert, University of Wisconsin–Superior

Max Rexroad, Illinois State University

Eugene Rozanski, Illinois State University

Robert Schlosser, Rutgers University–Newark

J. Roger Selin, University of Wisconsin–Eau Claire

Sammie Smith, Stephen F. Austin State University

Norman A. Sunderman, Angelo State University

Frank F. Weinberg, Golden Gate University

Seung-Weon Yoo, University of Wisconsin–Madison

Hung Chao Yu, University of Wisconsin–Madison

Stephen A. Zeff, Rice University

Focus Group Participants

Marianne Battista, Rider College

John Cheever, California State Polytechnic University

Darrel Davis, University of Northern Iowa

Robert Dunlevy, Temple University

Hossein Shalchi, California State University–San Bernardino

Margaret Smith, North Carolina A&T State University

Charles Speer, Appalachian State University

Paul Welch, University of Central Florida

Student Focus Group Participants

Jason Choquette, Brian Corkill, Brian Hansel, Patrick Hoffman, Renata Kaczmarczyk, Valerie Lopez, Denise Meismer, Michael Papciak, Christopher Pries, Leslie Rivera, Li-Tao Tan, Daniel Wolniakowski

We would also like to thank those colleagues who contributed to several of the new features of this edition:

International Notes
Judith Ramaglia,
   Pacific Lutheran University

Underlying Concepts
John Cheever, California State Polytechnic University–Pomona

Group Cases/Assignments
Terry Warfield, University of Wisconsin–Madison

Ethics Cases
Larry Ponemon, SUNY–Binghamton;
Bruce W. Stuart and Iris Stuart, Concordia College

Writing Assignments
Susan Smith,
   Northern Illinois University

Perspectives
Stuart Weiss,
   Stuart Weiss Business Writing Inc.

From the field of corporate and public accounting we owe thanks to the following practitioners for their technical advice or for consenting to interviews:

Practicing Accountants and Business Executives

Edward N. Antoian
Delaware Management Co.

Dennis R. Beresford
Financial Accounting
Standards Board

Ted Clarke
Nike Inc.

Michael Crooch
Arthur Andersen & Co.

James F. Fitzgerald
Right Associates

Greg Graber
Deloitte & Touche

Rebecca Hoger
Coopers & Lybrand

Clark H. Johnson
Johnson & Johnson

Patricia McConnell
Bear, Stearns & Co.

George Miranda
Home Savings of America

Ronald J. Murray
Coopers & Lybrand

Robert Sack
University of Virginia

Lisa Sanborn
Ernst and Young

James C. Treadway
Paine Webber Group Inc.

Gerald L. White
New York University

Kathryn J. Whitmire
former mayor of Houston

Jerry Ulrich
Xircom

Arthur R. Wyatt
Arthur Andersen & Co. and the
University of Illinois–Urbana

Paul Kimmel of the University of Wisconsin–Milwaukee assisted in the preparation of accounting for investments in debt and equity securities. Marilyn F. Hunt of the University of Central Florida provided valued technical and consultative assistance in the writing and proofing of our coverage of deferred income taxes and other topics.

We appreciate the exemplary support and professional commitment given us by the development, marketing, production, and editorial staffs of John Wiley & Sons, including Karen Allman, Karen Hawkins, Marinita Timban, Romayne Ponleithner, Mary Ann Benson, Kathleen Dolan, Linda Muriello, Charlotte Hyland, Karin Kincheloe, and the management and staff at CRWaldman (especially Michael Klinman). A special note of thanks also to Ann Torbert (editorial and content assistance) and Elm Street Publishing Services (specifically Barb Lange and Nancy Shanahan) for facilitating the production of the manuscript. We also wish to express our special thanks to Donna R. Kieso for her 24 years of invaluable service as our compositor, proofreader, and office manager— her standards of excellence will be missed.

We appreciate the cooperation of the American Institute of Certified Public Accountants and the Financial Accounting Standards Board in permitting us to quote from their pronouncements. We thank Georgia-Pacific Corporation for permitting us to use its 1993 Annual Report for our specimen financial statements. We also acknowledge permission from the American Institute of Certified Public Accountants, the Institute of Management Accounting, and the Institute of Internal Auditors to adapt and use material from the Uniform CPA Examinations, the CMA Examinations, and the CIA Examinations, respectively.

If this book helps teachers instill in their students an appreciation for the challenges, worth, and limitations of accounting, if it encourages students to evaluate critically and understand financial accounting theory and practice, and if it prepares students for advanced study, professional examinations, and the successful and ethical pursuit of their careers in accounting or business, then we will have attained our objective.

Suggestions and comments from users of this book will be appreciated.

Somonauk, Illinois
Madison, Wisconsin
December 1994

Donald E. Kieso
Jerry J. Weygandt

CONTENTS

STANDARD SETTING

A visit with
DENNIS BERESFORD

During your senior year in college, you became president of Beta Alpha Psi, the national accounting fraternity.

Yes. It gave me an opportunity to exercise leadership. It's very important for students to have some extracurricular experiences.

What about accounting appealed to you?

I liked its precision. Back then, at least, I thought every question had a precise answer. Now I understand that that's far from how the profession actually works. Also, I worked in a grocery store from the time I was 13 through my junior year at USC—and I remember talking to the fellow who was CEO of the supermarket chain, whose office was in the store where I worked. He just impressed me as a sharp person. I probably didn't understand what an accountant did versus an actuary or a lawyer, but it just seemed that accountants were the crème de la crème of the business community. I also decided that I wanted a job where I could sit down most of the time!

How did you get to Ernst & Young?

I quit working as a grocery clerk to work in the accounting department of an oil company during the summer between my junior and senior years. At the beginning of the next school year, I needed a job to pay my bills and interviewed with accounting firms. Ernst & Young hired me to do office work and proofreading. It wasn't a professional accounting job but at least it

DENNIS R. BERESFORD received his bachelor's degree in accounting from the University of Southern California in 1961. He joined Ernst & Ernst (now Ernst & Young) upon graduation and worked his way up the audit ranks. In 1971, he transferred to the firm's Cleveland office, its headquarters, to focus on accounting and auditing standards where he became a partner. He continued in that role until January 1, 1987, when he became FASB chairman.

exposed me to office procedures. I even mastered a 10-key adding machine.

During your 10 years on the audit staff, did you specialize?

Not really. I was in charge of auditing a very large bank holding company, a large aerospace company, The Los Angeles Times, The California Angels, The Los Angeles Rams. I had a lot of variety.

Why did you go to the national office?

They had an opening for a senior manager to work in the national technical accounting and auditing group. It sounded like an opportunity to grow as an individual and to learn more about the firm and the profession. Shortly after my transfer, I became a partner and was appointed National Director of Accounting Standards.

And how did you get to the FASB?

In 1986, Don Kirk, the then-current chairman was finishing his term and was not eligible for reappointment. So the trustees of the Financial Accounting Foundation began a search both within the FASB and outside. I went through a series of interviews with the trustees and they appointed me. There have only been three chairmen since the board's inception in 1973.

How has standard setting changed since you entered the profession?

In 1961 there was really very little to read. The entirety of codified accounting standards was only about 100 pages. It was very little and very general. Most standard setting has occurred during the past 30 years.

While at Ernst & Young, what was your opinion of the FASB?

I was on record as being critical of the FASB—though I hope in a constructive way. There aren't too many people who just say the FASB is doing a wonderful job. It's the nature of standard setting. People resist change and often criticize those who are in charge of making those changes.

What were the highlights of standard setting in the 1970s?

Statement 2 on research and development was very significant and remains so. Charging all of the R&D expenditures to expense rather than capitalizing them was very controversial at the time.

Statement 8 on foreign currency translation was another major issue. The world had gone from fixed to floating exchange rates. So, new accounting was necessary. The board came out with *Statement 8*, and it wasn't well received. Not too long afterward, the board reconsidered and issued *Statement 52*, which was much better accepted. The key change was to allow companies to defer many of their foreign currency gains and losses through stockholders' equity rather than running them all through the income statement. What it did was to remove a great deal of income statement volatility associated with changes in exchange rates.

Statement 19 on oil and gas accounting was also very controversial. It was the only time the Securities and Exchange Commission overruled the FASB. The SEC was required by an act of Congress to establish accounting standards for oil and gas companies. This was during the time of the first energy crisis in the mid-1970s. The SEC asked the FASB to look into the issue on a real crash basis. The FASB issued a standard that required the so-called successful efforts method of accounting. But a number of companies had been following the full cost method, which deferred more exploration expenditures. The SEC allowed both methods to stand. That was the only time in the history of the FASB that the SEC hasn't been fully supportive of our answers.

Is it typical or common that you'll set a standard but then reconsider if the reaction is loud enough?

We don't reconsider just because a standard is unpopular. But we definitely concern ourselves with new information that may not have been available when we made the decision. And if we find that a new standard is universally opposed, which seemed to be the case with *Statement 96*, "Accounting for Income Taxes," then we will go back and reconsider, as we did for taxes. We get lots of letters asking us to reconsider other issues, and most of the time we say no.

Inflation accounting didn't stick. Do you make standards that reflect what's going on in the world at that time?

There's no question that standards relate to economic activities and events. The high inflation rates of the mid-1970s resulted in inflation accounting being pushed very hard. When rates declined, the interest in inflation accounting also declined markedly, and we decided that it wasn't worth the cost to companies to continue to prepare the information. Thus, we rescinded *Statement 33*.

What were the highlights of standard setting in the 1980s?

Pension accounting would be one of the bigger ones. The board worked on that project from 1973 to 1985. It was fought vigorously by the business community and certain compromises were made. That led to another project, "Other Post-Employment Benefits"—*Statement 106*—one of the most dramatic changes the board has ever made.

But it wasn't nearly as controversial as pensions.

That's right. I think it's primarily because people see the basic correctness of the solution. They may object to the mechanical details, but they had a hard time arguing against accrual accounting for retirement benefits. Even though the unrecorded effects of OPEB were dramatic, 106 has been relatively well received.

What were some other big topics in the 1980s?

Cash flow reporting would be another significant development—*Statement 95*, issued in 1987. We changed the focus of the sources and uses of funds statement from working capital to cash. Companies could have good working capital—with a lot tied up in receivables and inventory—but find out that they had no cash. This statement has been particularly well received by users.

What about big topics for the 1990s?

Derivatives have been in the news lately. A number of companies have taken big write-offs. Typically, a company will enter into a derivative agreement to protect against risk associated with interest rate changes, foreign currency movements, and changes in commodity prices. Currently, there just isn't enough disclosure about these contracts. They tend to be off-balance-sheet items. Market rate changes associated with them don't get recognized until the instrument is finally settled. Therefore, there can be hidden exposure. We would like to inform financial statement users as to what the companies are doing and why. In theory, a derivative is like buying insurance and ought to be a good thing. Unfortunately, some companies have entered into derivatives that have actually made their risks worse.

Another hot topic is stock options. Most companies don't want to charge earnings when they award stock options. Some of them would say, well, theoretically we agree that there ought to be a charge, but it's just so difficult to figure out that we don't want to change the current practice. The general business press has been following this issue carefully. It's kind of a general issue that the man and woman on the street can understand.

Some people worry about the effect of a change on the stock price.

That's exactly right. We're hearing that in spades. We always get those allegations in almost any project. People said that if they had to expense research and development or account for foreign currency exchange gains and losses when they occur, that the stock price would take a dive. But there just isn't any history that that's happened.

We started this conversation talking about precision. You thought accounting was a precise science 30 years ago. Now you're head of the FASB. What would be examples of lack of precision?

One would be loan loss accounting. This has been one of the big issues in the S&L crises. With 20/20 hindsight, many of those institutions have been attacked for not having sufficient reserves. But that's an area of considerable subjectivity. You don't want to have too much of a reserve—you can be accused of being overly conservative. But you certainly don't want to have too little either. *Statement 5* on loss contingencies is a very general standard that I think has worked quite well. It says that a loss should be reported when the amount is probable—probable that it has occurred already, and that the amount can be reasonably estimated. Both are very subjective judgments.

So the CPA still has to use professional judgment.

I think professional judgment is just as important as a good accounting rule. For example, the rule is to expense research and development, period. But there's still judgment because you have to determine which types of expenditures you're talking about. Is it an expenditure that should be capitalized as part of fixed assets or must it be reclassified as R&D and expensed immediately? No matter how objective or precise the rule sounds, there's still going to be some judgment. That's what makes accounting so interesting!

What is the key to success in accounting?

Analytical skills, excellent communication abilities, and perseverance are all important. However, I've always felt that a good sense of humor is essential, too. You need it to relate well to people and to keep your business and personal lives in good balance.

CHAPTER 1

FINANCIAL ACCOUNTING AND ACCOUNTING STANDARDS

LEARNING OBJECTIVES

After studying this chapter, you should be able to:

1. Define accounting and describe its essential characteristics.

2. Identify the major financial statements and other means of financial reporting.

3. Identify the objectives of financial reporting.

4. Describe the environment of financial accounting.

5. Explain the need for accounting standards.

6. Identify the major policy-setting bodies and their role in the standard-setting process.

7. Explain the meaning of generally accepted accounting principles.

8. Describe the impact of user groups on the standard-setting process.

9. Understand issues related to ethics and financial accounting.

*I*s accounting a service activity, an analytical discipline, or an information system? It is all three.

As a service activity, accounting provides interested parties with quantitative financial information that helps them to make decisions about the deployment and use of resources in business as well as nonbusiness entities. **As an analytical discipline,** it identifies the mass of events and transactions that characterize economic activity. Through measurement, classification, and summarization, it reduces those data to relatively few, highly significant, and interrelated items. When properly assembled and reported, those items describe the financial condition, results of operations, and cash flows of a specific economic entity. **As an information system,** it collects and communicates economic information about a business enterprise or other entity to a wide variety of persons whose decisions and actions are related to the activity.

Each of these three descriptions—different though they may seem—contains the three essential characteristics of accounting: (1) **identification, measurement, and communication of financial information about** (2) **economic entities to** (3) **interested persons.** These characteristics have described accounting for hundreds of years. Yet, in the last 60 years economic entities have increased so greatly in size and complexity, and the interested persons have increased so greatly in number and diversity, that the responsibility placed on the accounting profession is greater today than ever before.

OBJECTIVE 1

Define accounting and describe its essential characteristics.

▶ THE NATURE AND ENVIRONMENT OF FINANCIAL ACCOUNTING

For purposes of study and practice the discipline of accounting is commonly divided into the following areas or subsets: financial accounting, managerial (cost) accounting, tax accounting, and nonprofit or fund accounting. This textbook concentrates on financial accounting.

Financial accounting is the process that culminates in the preparation of financial reports on the enterprise as a whole for use by parties both internal and external to the enterprise. Users of these financial reports include investors, creditors, managers, unions, and government agencies. In contrast, managerial accounting is the process of identifying, measuring, analyzing, and communicating financial information needed by management to plan, evaluate, and control an organization's operations.

FINANCIAL STATEMENTS AND FINANCIAL REPORTING

OBJECTIVE 2

Identify the major financial statements and other means of financial reporting.

Financial statements are the principal means through which financial information is communicated to those outside an enterprise. These statements provide the firm's history quantified in money terms. The **financial statements** most frequently provided are (1) the balance sheet, (2) the income statement, (3) the statement of cash flows, and (4) the statement of owners' or stockholders' equity. In addition, note disclosures are an integral part of each financial statement.

Some financial information is better provided, or can be provided only, by means of **financial reporting** other than formal financial statements. Examples include the president's letter or supplementary schedules in the corporate annual report, prospectuses, reports filed with government agencies, news releases, management's forecasts, and descriptions of an enterprise's social or environmental impact. Such information may be required by authoritative pronouncement, regulatory rule, or custom; or because management wishes to disclose it voluntarily.

The primary focus of this textbook concerns the development of two types of financial information: the basic financial statements and related disclosures. Recently, a blue-ribbon committee on financial reporting indicated the possible future direction of financial reporting.[1] It recommended that financial statements in the future include the following:

Financial and nonfinancial data
- Financial statements and related disclosures.
- High-level operating data and performance measurements that management uses to manage the business.

Management's analysis
- Reasons for changes in the financial, operating, and performance-related data, and the identity and past effects of key trends.

Forward-looking information
- Opportunities and risks, including those resulting from key trends.
- Management's plans, including critical success factors.
- Comparison of actual business performance to previously disclosed forward-looking information.

Information about management and shareholders
- Directors, management, compensation, major shareholders, and transactions and relationships among related parties.

Background about the company
- Broad objectives and strategies.

---

[1]AICPA Special Committee on Financial Reporting, "Improving Business Reporting—A Customer Focus," *Journal of Accountancy,* Supplement (October 1994).

- Scope and description of business and properties.
- Impact of industry structure on the company.

These directions broaden the focus from financial reporting to business reporting.

OBJECTIVES OF FINANCIAL REPORTING

In an attempt to establish a foundation for financial accounting and reporting, the accounting profession identified a set of **objectives of financial reporting by business enterprises.** Financial reporting should provide information:

(a) that is useful to present and potential investors and creditors and other users in making rational investment, credit, and similar decisions. The information should be comprehensible to those who have a reasonable understanding of business and economic activities and are willing to study the information with reasonable diligence.

(b) to help present and potential investors and creditors and other users in assessing the amounts, timing, and uncertainty of prospective cash receipts from dividends or interest and the proceeds from the sale, redemption, or maturity of securities or loans. Since investors' and creditors' cash flows are related to enterprise cash flows, financial reporting should provide information to help investors, creditors, and others assess the amounts, timing, and uncertainty of prospective net cash inflows to the related enterprise.

(c) about the economic resources of an enterprise, the claims to those resources (obligations of the enterprise to transfer resources to other entities and owners' equity), and the effects of transactions, events, and circumstances that change its resources and claims to those resources.[2]

In summary, the objectives of financial reporting are to provide (1) information that is useful in investment and credit decisions, (2) information that is useful in assessing cash flow prospects, and (3) information about enterprise resources, claims to those resources, and changes in them.

The emphasis on "assessing cash flow prospects" might lead one to suppose that the cash basis is preferred over the accrual basis of accounting. That is not the case. Information based on **accrual accounting generally provides a better indication of an enterprise's present and continuing ability to generate favorable cash flows** than does information limited to the financial effects of cash receipts and payments.[3]

Recall from your first accounting course that the objective of **accrual basis accounting** is to ensure that events that change an entity's financial statements are recorded in the periods in which the events occur, rather than only in the periods in which the entity receives or pays cash. Using the accrual basis to determine net income means recognizing revenues when earned rather than when cash is received, and recognizing expenses when incurred rather than when paid. Under accrual accounting, revenues, for the most part, are recognized when sales are made so they can be related to the economic environment of the period in which they occurred. Over the long run, trends in revenues are generally more meaningful than trends in cash receipts.

ENVIRONMENTAL FACTORS THAT INFLUENCE ACCOUNTING

Like other human activities and disciplines, accounting is largely a product of its environment. The environment of accounting consists of social-economic-political-legal

OBJECTIVE 3
Identify the objectives of financial reporting.

INTERNATIONAL INSIGHT

The legalistic view of accounting (conformity with the law, for example) is starting to disappear in the international community. Countries like Spain, Italy, and France are moving towards an information viewpoint similar to that of the United States, the United Kingdom, and Canada. Insights into international standards will be presented throughout the text.

---

[2]"Objectives of Financial Reporting by Business Enterprises," *Statement of Financial Accounting Concepts No. 1* (Stamford, Conn.: FASB, November 1978), pars. 5–8.

[3]*SFAC No. 1*, p. iv. As used here, cash flow means "cash generated and used in operations." The term **cash flows** is frequently used also to include cash obtained by borrowing and used to repay borrowing, cash used for investments in resources and obtained from the disposal of investments, and cash contributed by or distributed to owners.

OBJECTIVE 4

Describe the environment of financial accounting.

conditions, restraints, and influences that vary from time to time. As a result, accounting objectives and practices are not the same today as they were in the past. **Accounting theory has evolved to meet changing demands and influences.** Five of these deserve special consideration.

1. **Accounting recognizes that people live in a world of scarce resources.** Because resources are limited, people try to conserve them, to use them effectively, and to identify and encourage those who can make efficient use of them. Through an efficient use of resources, the standard of living increases.

   Accounting plays an important role in obtaining a higher standard of living because it helps to identify efficient and inefficient users of resources. For example, accounting enables investors and lenders to compare the income earned and assets employed of such companies as IBM, General Motors, Apple Computer, and McDonalds. As a result, they can assess the relative return and risks associated with investment opportunities and thereby channel resources more effectively.

2. **Accounting recognizes that in our society, productive resources are generally privately owned rather than government owned.** True, the state collects taxes, pays subsidies to certain industries, and regulates others. But in general, markets, free enterprise, and competition—not a committee of social engineers—determine whether a business is to be successful and thrive. This fact places a substantial burden on the accounting profession to measure performance accurately and fairly so that the right companies are able to attract investment capital.

3. **Accounting recognizes that economic activity is conducted by separately identifiable units—business enterprises.** Enterprises consist of economic resources (assets), economic obligations (liabilities), and residual interests (owners' equity), which are increased or decreased by economic activities. Accounting accumulates and reports economic activity as it affects the elements of each business enterprise.

4. **Accounting recognizes that in complex economic systems, some (owners and investors) entrust the custodianship of and control over property to others (managers).** The corporate form of organization tends to divorce ownership from management, particularly in large organizations. In most large corporations the owners typically are the stockholders, who directly and indirectly hire managers to run the firm. Thus, the **stewardship function**—measuring and reporting data to absentee owners—has emerged as a critical role for accounting.

   This development greatly increases the need for accounting standards. Accounting has become responsible for providing standards that ensure the relevance, reliability, and comparability of information reported to absentee owners. The public accountant (auditor) plays a major role in meeting this responsibility. The auditor attests to the fairness of financial statements and their conformity to generally accepted accounting principles, thus enhancing confidence in the reliability of the statements.

5. **Accounting recognizes that economic resources, economic obligations, and residual interests should be expressed in terms of money.** In most economies, money serves as a measure of both qualitative and quantitative attributes of economic events, resources, and obligations.[4] Although this statement may seem

---

[4]Qualitative attributes, as well as quantitative ones, are measurable (valued) in money terms. For instance, in July 1994, one ounce of gold measured $385 in money terms while one ounce of silver measured $5.30. The difference in price per ounce reflected differences in qualitative attributes. A doubling of the quantity would result in doubling the amount of money measurement. A dramatic example of qualitative attributes being reflected by money measurement was the sale at auction of one of Vincent van Gogh's paintings (*Sunflowers*) for $39,921,750, while the author's brother had difficulty selling one of his paintings for $50 at an art fair. Monetary measurements reflect both quality and quantity.

obvious, recognize that at one time some companies reported their information using other measures. For example, Amoskeag Manufacturing, once the largest cotton mill in the world, had an income statement reported largely in yards rather than dollars.

HOW ACCOUNTING INFLUENCES ITS ENVIRONMENT

Accounting also shapes its environment. It plays a significant role in the conduct of economic, social, political, legal, and organizational decisions and actions. **Accounting is a system that feeds back information to organizations and individuals, which they can use to reshape their environment.** It provides information for the reevaluation of social, political, and economic objectives as well as the relative costs and benefits of the alternative means of achieving these objectives.

The accounting numbers that are reported affect the transfer of resources among companies and individuals. For example, assume that a gift of art is received by a museum. Should the gift be reported on the museum's financial statements at market value? To report this gift at market value may discourage future gifts because prospective donors will perceive the museum as prosperous and thus be less inclined to provide additional gifts.

And, eventually, nuclear power plants will have to be mothballed and their nuclear cores removed. If accountants report a portion of this expense currently, energy rates will be higher today and lower in the future. Conversely, if these costs are charged to operations after these plants are abandoned, energy rates will be lower today but higher in the future.

In summary, the accounting information that is reported affects perceptions of the enterprise's financial condition and success. These perceptions then lead to changes in economic behavior. Because behavior is affected, accounting standard setting is controversial.

▶ THE NEED TO DEVELOP STANDARDS

The main controversy in setting accounting standards is "Whose rules should we play by, and what should they be?" The answer is not immediately clear because the users of financial accounting statements have both coinciding and conflicting needs for information of various types. To meet these needs, and to satisfy the fiduciary[5] reporting responsibility of management, accountants prepare a single set of **general-purpose financial statements.** These statements are expected to present fairly, clearly, and completely the economic facts of the existence and operations of the enterprise. **In preparing financial statements, accountants are confronted with the potential dangers of bias, misinterpretation, inexactness, and ambiguity.** In order to minimize these dangers, the accounting profession has attempted to develop a set of standards that is generally accepted and universally practiced. Without these standards, each accountant or enterprise would have to develop its own standards, and readers of financial statements would have to familiarize themselves with every company's peculiar accounting and reporting practices. As a result, it would be almost impossible to prepare statements that could be compared.

The accounting profession has adopted a common set of standards and procedures called **generally accepted accounting principles (GAAP).** The term "generally accepted" can mean either that an authoritative accounting rule-making body has established a principle of reporting in a given area or that over time a given practice has been accepted as appropriate because of its universal application.[6] Although principles

OBJECTIVE 5
Explain the need for accounting standards.

INTERNATIONAL INSIGHT

Accounting practices differ widely around the world. Nations also differ in the degree to which they have developed national standards and consistent accounting practices.

---

[5]Management's responsibility to manage assets with care and trust is its **fiduciary** responsibility.

[6]The terms **principles** and **standards** are used interchangeably in practice and throughout this textbook.

and practices have provoked both debate and criticism, most accountants and members of the financial community recognize them as the standards and procedures that over time have proven to be most useful. A more extensive discussion of what constitutes GAAP is presented later in this chapter.

▶ HISTORICAL PERSPECTIVE

Before 1900 the economy of the United States required a relatively unsophisticated type of accounting function, and an accounting profession per se was virtually nonexistent. Single ownership was the predominant form of business organization in our economy. Accounting reports emphasized solvency and liquidity and were limited to internal use and scrutiny by banks and other lending institutions.

From 1900 to 1929 the growth of large corporations, with their absentee ownership and the increasing investment and speculation in corporate stocks, created a demand for greater disclosure and a change from the concern with solvency to a concern with income-producing ability. The constitutional amendment in 1913 authorizing the federal government to impose an income tax on businesses and individuals intensified the emphasis on income measurement.

As a result of the stock market crash of 1929, the Great Depression, and widespread dissatisfaction with accounting reports, the federal government, the stock exchanges, and the accounting profession made efforts to improve accounting. The needs of interested parties are the focus in the development of accounting standards. Certain professional organizations, governmental agencies, and legislative acts have exerted a significant influence in the development of these standards.

▶ PARTIES INVOLVED IN STANDARD SETTING

A number of organizations are instrumental in the development of financial accounting standards (GAAP) in the United States. The major organizations are as follows:

OBJECTIVE 6

Identify the major policy-setting bodies and their role in the standard-setting process.

1. Securities and Exchange Commission (SEC)
2. American Institute of Certified Public Accountants (AICPA)
3. Financial Accounting Standards Board (FASB)
4. Governmental Accounting Standards Board (GASB)
5. Other influential bodies

SECURITIES AND EXCHANGE COMMISSION (SEC)

INTERNATIONAL INSIGHT

Although there is no international organization with enforcement power similar to the SEC's, the International Organization of Securities Commissions (IOSCO) supports the work of such groups as the International Federation of Accountants. The SEC is a member of IOSCO.

Imagine that Associated Dry Goods reports net income in its annual report but fails to report revenue. Or Di Giorgio Fruit Corp. deducted its expenses from equity rather than from revenue. Or the publicly held Royal Baking Powder Company goes for 25 years without issuing a financial statement at all.

Such financial non-disclosure was prevalent before the creation of the **Securities and Exchange Commission (SEC)** in 1934. The SEC was created as a result of the Great Depression of the 1930s, which resulted in the widespread collapse of business and the securities market. The SEC is an agency of the federal government. It administers the Securities Exchange Act of 1934 and several other acts. Most companies that issue securities to the public or are listed on a stock exchange are required to file audited financial statements with the SEC. In addition, the SEC has broad powers to prescribe, in whatever detail it desires, the accounting practices and standards to be employed by companies that fall within its jurisdiction. As a result, the SEC exercises oversight over 12,000 companies that are listed on the major exchanges (such as the New York Stock

Exchange and the American Stock Exchange). The SEC filing requirements[7] and accounting opinions are published in: (1) its Financial Reporting Releases (FRRs),[8] (2) Regulation S-X, which contains instructions and forms for filing financial statements, and (3) decisions on cases coming before the SEC.

Public/Private Partnership

At the time the SEC was created, no group—public or private—was issuing accounting standards. The SEC encouraged the creation of a private standard-setting body because it believed that the private sector had the resources and talent to develop appropriate accounting standards. As a result, accounting standards have generally developed in the private sector either through the American Institute of Certified Public Accountants (AICPA) or the Financial Accounting Standards Board (FASB).

The SEC has affirmed its support for the FASB by indicating that financial statements conforming to standards set by the FASB will be presumed to have substantial authoritative support. In short, the SEC requires registrants to adhere to GAAP. In addition, it has indicated in its reports to Congress that "it continues to believe that the initiative for establishing and improving accounting standards should remain in the private sector, subject to Commission oversight."

SEC Oversight

The SEC's partnership with the private sector has worked well. The SEC has acted with remarkable restraint in the area of developing accounting standards. Generally, it has relied on the AICPA and FASB to regulate the accounting profession and develop and enforce accounting standards.

Over its history, however, the SEC's involvement in the development of accounting standards has varied. In some cases the private sector has attempted to establish a standard, but the SEC has refused to accept it. In other cases it has prodded the private sector into taking quicker action on certain reporting problems, such as accounting for investments in debt and equity securities and the reporting of financial derivatives. In still other situations the commission communicates problems to the FASB, responds to FASB exposure drafts, and provides the FASB with counsel and advice upon request.

The SEC has the mandate to establish accounting principles. The private sector, therefore, must listen carefully to the views of the SEC. In some sense the private sector is the formulator and the implementor of the standards.[9] The partnership appears to be a good one.

---

[7]The Securities Acts require that companies issuing securities file registration statements and periodic reports with the SEC. Most commercial and industrial companies file a *Form S-1* registration statement upon the initial issuance of securities. (Forms S-2 through S-18 are filed by companies in certain specialized industries.) *Form 10-K* is the annual report form required to be filed and *Form 10-Q* the report that must be filed for the first three quarters of each fiscal year. *Form 8-K* must be filed after the occurrence of a material event. Regulation S-K requires nonfinancial information, such as the Management Discussion and Analysis, to be reported.

[8]Prior to 1982 these pronouncements were referred to as Accounting Series Releases (ASRs). The SEC has changed the title of new releases to better reflect their nature and to differentiate FRRs (nonenforcement, nondisciplinary type releases) from the new AAERs (accounting and auditing enforcement releases, which are disciplinary in nature).

[9]One writer has described the relationship of the FASB and SEC and the development of financial reporting standards using the analogy of a pearl. The pearl (financial reporting standard) "is formed by the reaction of certain oysters (FASB) to an irritant (the SEC)—usually a grain of sand—that becomes embedded inside the shell. The oyster coats this grain with layers of nacre, and ultimately a pearl is formed. The pearl is a joint result of the irritant (SEC) and oyster (FASB); without both, it cannot be created. John C. Burton, "Government Regulation of Accounting and Information," *Journal of Accountancy* (June, 1982).

Enforcement

As indicated earlier, companies listed on a stock exchange are required to submit their financial statements to the SEC. If the SEC believes that an accounting or disclosure irregularity exists regarding the form or content of the financial statements, it sends a deficiency letter to the company. Usually these deficiency letters are resolved quickly. However, if disagreement continues, the SEC has the power to issue a "stop order," which prevents the registrant from issuing securities or trading securities on the exchanges. Criminal charges may also be brought by the Department of Justice for violations of certain laws. The SEC program, private sector initiatives, and civil and criminal litigation help to ensure the integrity of financial reporting for public companies.

AMERICAN INSTITUTE OF CERTIFIED PUBLIC ACCOUNTANTS (AICPA)

As indicated earlier, the **American Institute of Certified Public Accountants (AICPA),** the national professional organization of practicing Certified Public Accountants (CPAs), has been vital to the development of GAAP. Various committees and boards established since the founding of the AICPA have contributed to this effort.

Committee on Accounting Procedure

At the urging of the SEC, the AICPA appointed the Committee on Accounting Procedure in 1939. The **Committee on Accounting Procedure (CAP),** composed of practicing CPAs, issued 51 **Accounting Research Bulletins** (see list on inside of front cover) dealing with a variety of timely accounting problems during the years 1939 to 1959. But this problem-by-problem approach failed to provide the structured body of accounting principles that was both needed and desired. In response, in 1959 the AICPA created the Accounting Principles Board.

Accounting Principles Board

The major purposes of the **Accounting Principles Board (APB)** were (1) to advance the written expression of accounting principles, (2) to determine appropriate practices, and (3) to narrow the areas of difference and inconsistency in practice. To achieve these objectives, its mission was to develop an overall conceptual framework to assist in the resolution of problems as they become evident and to do substantive research on individual issues before pronouncements were issued.

The Board's 18 to 21 members, selected primarily from public accounting, also included representatives from industry and the academic community. The Board's official pronouncements, called **APB Opinions,** were intended to be based mainly on research studies and be supported by reasons and analysis. Between its inception in 1959 and its dissolution in 1973, the APB issued 31 opinions (see complete list inside front cover).

Unfortunately, the APB came under fire early, charged with lack of productivity and failing to act promptly to correct alleged accounting abuses. Later the APB tackled numerous thorny accounting issues, only to meet a buzz saw of industry and CPA firm opposition and occasional governmental interference. In 1971 the accounting profession's leaders, anxious to avoid governmental rule-making, appointed a Study Group on Establishment of Accounting Principles. Commonly known as the **Wheat Committee** for its chair Francis Wheat, this group was to examine the organization and operation of the APB and determine what changes would be necessary to attain better results. The Study Group's recommendations were submitted to the AICPA Council in the spring of 1972, adopted in total, and implemented by early 1973.

FINANCIAL ACCOUNTING STANDARDS BOARD (FASB)

The Wheat Committee's recommendations resulted in the demise of the APB and the creation of a new standard-setting structure composed of three organizations—the

Financial Accounting Foundation (FAF), the Financial Accounting Standards Board (FASB), and the Financial Accounting Standards Advisory Council (FASAC). The **Financial Accounting Foundation** selects the members of the FASB and the Advisory Council, funds their activities, and generally oversees the FASB's activities.

The major operating organization in this three-part structure is the **Financial Accounting Standards Board (FASB).** Its mission is to establish and improve standards of financial accounting and reporting for the guidance and education of the public, which includes issuers, auditors, and users of financial information. The expectations of success and support for the new FASB were based upon several significant differences between it and its predecessor, the APB:

1. **Smaller Membership.** The FASB is composed of seven members, replacing the relatively large 18-member APB.

2. **Full-time, Remunerated Membership.** FASB members are well-paid, full-time members appointed for renewable 5-year terms, whereas the APB members were unpaid and part-time.

3. **Greater Autonomy.** The APB was a senior committee of the AICPA, whereas the FASB is not an organ of any single professional organization. It is appointed by and answerable only to the Financial Accounting Foundation.

4. **Increased Independence.** APB members retained their private positions with firms, companies, or institutions; FASB members must sever all such ties.

5. **Broader Representation.** All APB members were required to be CPAs and members of the AICPA; currently, it is not necessary to be a CPA to be a member of the FASB.

In addition to research help from its own staff, the FASB relies on the expertise of various task force groups formed for various projects and on the **Financial Accounting Standards Advisory Council (FASAC).** FASAC has responsibility for consulting with the FASB on both major policy and technical issues and also for helping select task force members.

Due Process

Two basic premises of the FASB are that in establishing financial accounting standards: (1) it should be responsive to the needs and viewpoints of the entire economic community, not just the public accounting profession, and (2) it should operate in full view of the public through a "due process" system that gives interested persons ample opportunity to make their views known. To ensure the achievement of these goals, the following steps are taken in the evolution of a typical FASB Statement of Financial Accounting Standards:

1. A topic or project is identified and placed on the Board's agenda.

2. A task force of experts from various sectors is assembled to define problems, issues, and alternatives related to the topic.

3. Research and analysis are conducted by the FASB technical staff.

4. A **discussion memorandum** is drafted and released.

5. A public hearing is often held, usually 60 days after release of the memorandum.

6. The Board analyzes and evaluates the public response.

7. The Board deliberates on the issues and prepares an **exposure draft** for release.

8. After a 30-day (minimum) exposure period for public comment, the Board evaluates all of the responses received.

9. A committee studies the exposure draft in relation to the public responses, reevaluates its position, and revises the draft if necessary.

10. The full Board gives the revised draft final consideration and votes on issuance of a **Standards Statement.**

The passage of a new FASB Statement requires the support of five of the seven Board members. FASB Statements are considered GAAP and thereby binding in practice. All ARBs and APB Opinions that were in effect in 1973 when the FASB became effective continue to be effective until amended or superseded by FASB pronouncements. In recognition of possible misconceptions of the term "principles," the FASB uses the term **financial accounting standards** in its pronouncements.

Types of Pronouncements

The major types of pronouncements that the FASB issues are:

1. Standards and Interpretations.
2. Financial Accounting Concepts.
3. Technical Bulletins.
4. Emerging Issues Task Force Statements.

Standards and Interpretations

Financial accounting standards issued by the FASB are considered generally accepted accounting principles. In addition, the FASB also issues **interpretations** that represent modifications or extensions of existing standards. The interpretations have the same authority as standards and require the same votes for passage as standards. However, interpretations do not require the FASB to operate in full view of the public through the due process system that is required for FASB Standards. The APB also issued interpretations of APB Opinions. Both types of interpretations are now considered authoritative support for purposes of determining GAAP. Since replacing the APB, the FASB has issued 121 standards and 40 interpretations (see list inside front cover).

Financial Accounting Concepts

UNDERLYING CONCEPT

The contents of Concepts Statement No. 1, detailing the objectives of financial reporting, were presented earlier in this chapter.

As part of a long-range effort to move away from the problem-by-problem approach, the FASB in November 1978 issued the first in a series of **Statements of Financial Accounting Concepts** (see list inside back cover) as part of its conceptual framework project. The purpose of the series is to set forth fundamental objectives and concepts that the Board will use in developing future standards of financial accounting and reporting. They are intended to form a cohesive set of interrelated concepts, a conceptual framework, that will serve as tools for solving existing and emerging problems in a consistent manner. Unlike a Statement of Financial Accounting Standards, **a Statement of Financial Accounting Concepts does not establish GAAP.** Concepts statements, however, pass through the same due process system (discussion memo, public hearing, exposure draft, etc.) as do standards statements.

FASB Technical Bulletins

The FASB receives many requests from various sources for guidelines on implementing or applying FASB Standards or Interpretations, APB Opinions, and Accounting Research Bulletins. In addition, a strong need exists for timely guidance on financial accounting and reporting problems. For example, in a recent tax law, certain income taxes that companies had accrued as liabilities were forgiven. The immediate question was: How should the forgiven taxes be reported—as a reduction of income tax expense, as a prior period adjustment, or as an extraordinary item? A technical bulletin was quickly issued that required the tax reduction be reported as a reduction of the current period's income tax expense. Note that a **technical bulletin** is issued only when (1) **it is not expected to cause a major change in accounting practice for a number of enterprises,** (2) **its cost of implementation is low, and** (3) **the guidance provided by the bulletin does not conflict with any broad fundamental accounting principle.**[10]

---

[10]"Purpose and Scope of FASB Technical Bulletins and Procedures for Issuance," *FASB Technical Bulletin No. 79-1* (Revised) (Stamford, Conn.: FASB, June 1984).

Emerging Issues Task Force Statements

In 1984 the FASB created the **Emerging Issues Task Force (EITF).** The EITF is composed of 17 members, representing 11 CPA firms, 4 companies, an SEC observer, and a FASB representative. The purpose of the task force is to reach a consensus (15 of 17 members must agree) on how to account for new and unusual financial transactions that have the potential for creating differing financial reporting practices. Examples include how to account for pension plan terminations; how to account for unusual construction loans by savings and loans; and how to account for excessive amounts paid to takeover specialists.

We cannot overestimate the importance of the EITF. In one recent year, for example, the task force examined 61 emerging financial reporting issues and arrived at a consensus on approximately 75% of them. The SEC has indicated that it will view consensus solutions as preferred accounting and will require persuasive justification for departing from them.

The EITF helps the FASB in many ways. For example, emerging issues often attract public attention. If they are not resolved quickly, they can lead to financial crises and scandal and can undercut public confidence in current reporting practices. The next step, possible governmental intervention, would threaten the continuance of standard setting in the private sector. In addition, the EITF identifies controversial accounting problems as they arise and determines whether they can be quickly resolved or whether the FASB should become involved in solving them. In essence, it becomes a "problem filter" for the FASB. Thus, it is hoped that the FASB will be able to work on more pervasive long-term problems, while the EITF deals with short-term emerging issues.

GOVERNMENTAL ACCOUNTING STANDARDS BOARD (GASB)

Financial statements prepared by state and local governments are not comparable with financial reports prepared by private business organizations. For example, many state and local governments use a simple cash basis and do not include such items as depreciation in their income statements. This lack of comparability was highlighted in the 1970s when a number of large U.S. cities such as New York and Cleveland faced potential bankruptcy. As a result, a new **Governmental Accounting Standards Board (GASB),** under the oversight of the Financial Accounting Foundation, was created in 1984 to address state and local governmental reporting issues.

The operational structure of the GASB is similar to that of the FASB. That is, it has an advisory council called the Governmental Accounting Standards Advisory Council (GASAC), and it is assisted by its own technical staff and task forces.

The creation of GASB was controversial. Many believe that there should be only one standard-setting body—the FASB. It was hoped that partitioning standard setting between the GASB, which deals only with state and local government reporting, and the FASB, which reports for all other entities, would not lead to conflict. Since we are primarily concerned with financial reports prepared by profit-seeking organizations, this textbook will focus on standards issued by the FASB only.

The formal organizational structure as it currently exists for the development of financial reporting standards is presented in Illustration 1-1.

OTHER INFLUENTIAL ORGANIZATIONS

Several other organizations also have been influential in the development of accounting theory and standard setting. Illustration 1-2 provides an overview of these organizations.

In addition, the **Internal Revenue Service (IRS),** which derives its authority from the Internal Revenue Code and its amendments and legal interpretations, constitutes one of the strongest influences on accounting practice. In an effort to lessen the impact of taxes, and to avoid keeping two sets of books, business managers frequently adopt

**ILLUSTRATION 1-1
Organizational Structure
for Setting Accounting
Standards**

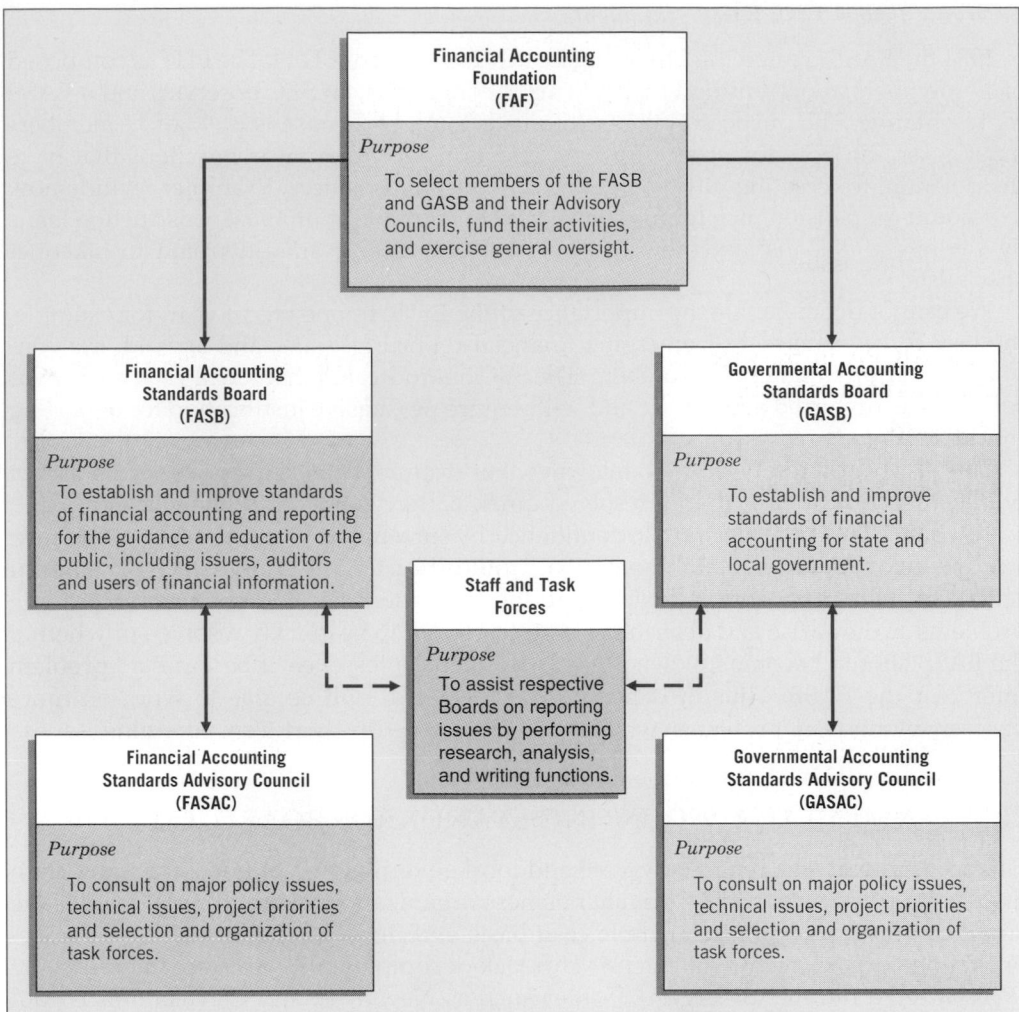

**ILLUSTRATION 1-2
Overview of Other
Influential Organizations**

Organization	Members	Purpose
American Accounting Association	Primarily accounting academics	Furthers the development of accounting theory by encouraging and sponsoring accounting research.
Institute of Management Accountants (IMA)	Primarily internal accountants	Conducts research and provides input on cost and managerial accounting issues.
Financial Executives Institute (FEI)	Financial executives generally of large corporations (treasurers, financial vice-presidents, chief financial officers)	Conducts research and makes recommendations on the impact of financial reporting at the corporate level.

"acceptable" accounting procedures that minimize taxable income. Because the objectives of the tax law differ from the objectives of financial accounting, however, "good tax accounting" is not necessarily "good financial accounting." As noted throughout this textbook, tax laws and "tax effects" are a pervasive influence in business decision making and on the selection of accounting methods. Differences between tax accounting and financial accounting are generally permissible; however, in the preparation of financial statements, tax considerations must give ground to the requirements of sound accounting.

▶ CHANGING ROLE OF THE AICPA

For several decades the AICPA provided the leadership in the development of accounting principles and rules; it regulated the accounting profession and developed and enforced accounting practice more than did any other professional organization. When the Accounting Principles Board was dissolved and replaced with the FASB, the AICPA established the Accounting Standards Division to act as its official voice on accounting and reporting issues.

The **Accounting Standards Executive Committee (AcSEC)** was established within the Division and was designated as the senior technical committee authorized to speak for the AICPA in the area of financial accounting and reporting. It does so through various written communications:

Issues Papers. A major role of AcSEC has become one of providing guidance for specific industry situations through the development of issues papers. Issues papers identify current financial reporting problems and present alternative treatments of the issue. This procedure provides the FASB with an early warning device to ensure the timely issuance of FASB Standards, Interpretations, and Technical Bulletins.

Statements of Position. In some cases, the FASB decides not to add the subject of the issues paper to its agenda; as a result, AcSEC may subsequently decide to issue a Statement of Position (SOP) on the matter. SOPs involve a reporting issue in a given industry.

Practice Bulletins. AcSEC also issues Practice Bulletins that indicate how the AICPA believes a given transaction should be reported.

Industry Accounting and Auditing Guides. Finally, the AICPA issues Industry Accounting and Auditing Guides, which provide specific guidance in a given industry. Examples are accounting for casinos, airlines, colleges and universities, banks, insurance companies, and many others.

The AICPA is still the leader in developing auditing standards through its **Auditing Standards Board,** in regulating auditing practice, in developing and enforcing professional ethics, and in providing continuing professional education programs. The AICPA also develops and grades the CPA examination, which is administered in all 50 states.

A recent initiative of the AICPA merits special attention. In 1991 the AICPA formed the Special Committee on Financial Reporting to improve the value of financial information and the public's confidence in it.[11] The initiative seeks to:

1. Enhance the utility of business reporting.
2. Improve the prevention and detection of fraud.
3. Assure the independence and objectivity of the independent auditor.
4. Discourage unwarranted litigation that inhibits innovation and undermines the profession's ability to meet evolving financial reporting needs.
5. Strengthen the auditing profession's disciplinary system.

A number of the recommendations of the Special Committee will be identified as underlying concepts in the textbook margins. Remember as you read these recommendations that the committee is not a standard-setting body. It offers its recommendations for the consideration of all who have an interest in furthering the cost-effective quality of financial reporting.

▶ GENERALLY ACCEPTED ACCOUNTING PRINCIPLES

Generally accepted accounting principles are those principles that have "substantial authoritative support." The AICPA's Code of Professional Conduct requires that mem-

---

[11]AICPA Special Committee on Financial Reporting, *op cit.*

OBJECTIVE 7

Explain the meaning of generally accepted accounting principles.

bers prepare financial statements in accordance with generally accepted accounting principles. Specifically, Rule 203 of this Code prohibits a member from expressing an opinion that financial statements conform with GAAP if those statements contain a material departure from a generally accepted accounting principle, unless the member can demonstrate that because of unusual circumstances the financial statements would otherwise have been misleading. Failure to follow Rule 203 can lead to loss of a CPA's license to practice.

The meaning of generally accepted accounting principles is defined by *Statement on Auditing Standards (SAS) No. 69,* "The Meaning of 'Present Fairly in Conformity With Generally Accepted Accounting Principles' in the Independent Auditor's Report." Under this standard, generally accepted accounting principles covered by Rule 203 are construed to be FASB Standards and Interpretations, APB Opinions, and AICPA Accounting Research Bulletins.

Oftentimes, however, a specific accounting transaction occurs that is not covered by any of these documents. In this case, other authoritative literature is used. Major examples are: FASB Technical Bulletins; AICPA Industry Accounting and Auditing Guides; and Statements of Position that have been "cleared" by the FASB.[12] These documents are considered to have substantial authoritative support because the recognized professional bodies, after giving interested and affected parties the opportunity to react to exposure drafts and respond at public hearings, have voted their issuance. If these pronouncements are lacking in guidance, then other sources might be considered. The hierarchy of these sources is presented in Illustration 1-3.[13] If the accounting treatment of an event is not specified by a category (a) pronouncement, then categories (b) through (d) should be investigated. If there is a conflict between pronouncements in (b) through (d), the higher category [for example (b) is higher than (c)] is to be followed.

**ILLUSTRATION 1-3
The House of GAAP**

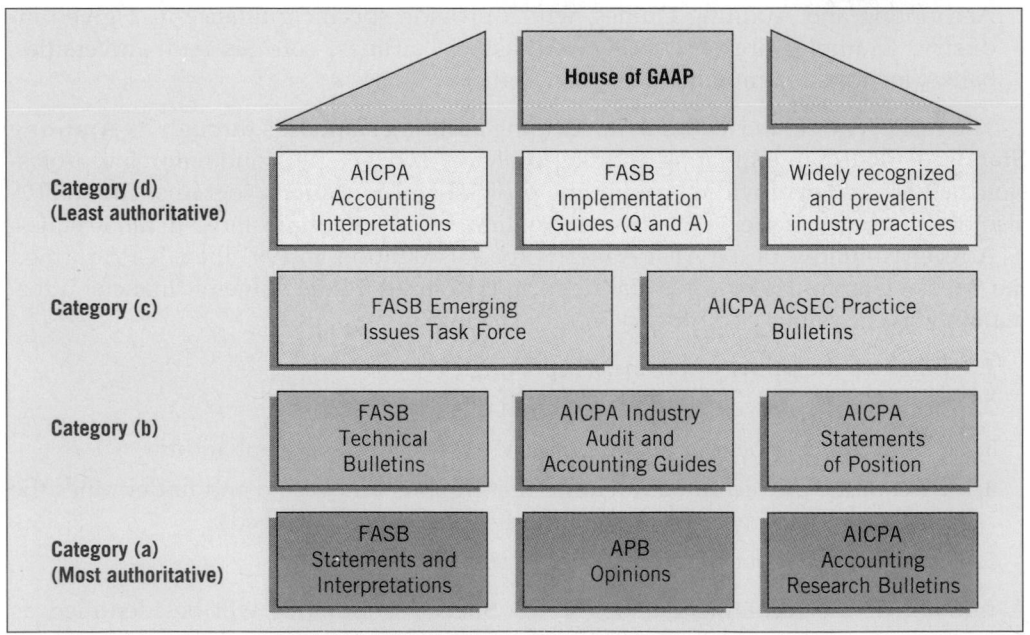

In the event that none of these pronouncements addresses the event, the accountant should seek support from other accounting literature. Examples of other accounting literature include FASB Concepts Statements, International Accounting Standards, and accounting articles.

[12]*SAS No. 69* states that Audit Guides and Statements of Position are assumed to be cleared (approved) by the FASB unless the pronouncement states otherwise.

[13]See for example, "Remodeling the House of GAAP," by Douglas Sauter, *Journal of Accountancy* (July 1991), pp. 30–37.

▶ STANDARD SETTING IN A POLITICAL ENVIRONMENT

Possibly the most powerful force influencing the development of accounting standards is user groups. User groups consist of the parties who are most interested in or affected by accounting standards, rules, and procedures. Like lobbyists in our state and national capitals, user groups play a significant role. **Accounting standards are as much a product of political action as they are of careful logic or empirical findings.**

User groups may want particular economic events accounted for or reported in a particular way, and they fight hard to get what they want. They know that the most effective way to influence the standards that dictate accounting practice is to participate in the formulation of these standards or to try to influence or persuade the formulator of them. Therefore, the FASB has become the target of many pressures and efforts to influence changes in the existing standards and the development of new ones.[14] To top it off, these pressures have been multiplying. Some influential groups demand that the accounting profession act more quickly and decisively to solve its problems and remedy its deficiencies. Other groups resist such action, preferring to implement change more slowly, if at all. Illustration 1-4 shows the various user groups that apply pressure.

OBJECTIVE 8

Describe the impact of user groups on the standard-setting process.

**ILLUSTRATION 1-4
User Groups that Influence the Formulation of Accounting Standards**

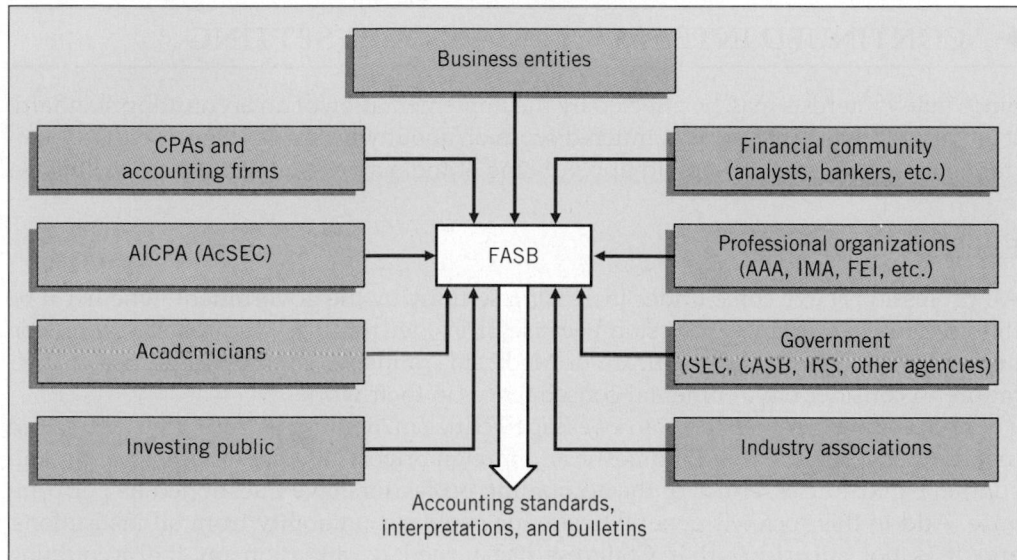

Should there be politics in setting financial accounting and reporting standards? We have politics at home; at school; at the fraternity, sorority, and dormitory; at the office; at church, temple, and mosque—politics is everywhere. The FASB does not exist in a vacuum. Standard setting is part of the real world, and it cannot escape politics and political pressures.

That is not to say that politics in standard setting is evil. Considering the **economic consequences**[15] of many accounting standards, it is not surprising that special interest groups become vocal and critical (some supporting, some opposing) when standards

---

[14]All the FASB chairmen have acknowledged that many of the Board's projects, such as "Accounting for Contingencies," "Accounting for Certain Marketable Equity Securities," "Accounting for Pensions," "Statement of Cash Flows," and "Accounting for Income Taxes," were targets of political pressure.

[15]"Economic consequences" in this context means the impact of accounting reports on the wealth positions of issuers and users of financial information and the decision-making behavior resulting from that impact. The resulting behavior of these individuals and groups could have detrimental financial effects on the providers (enterprises) of the financial information. For a more detailed discussion of this phenomenon, see Stephen A. Zeff, "The Rise of 'Economic Consequences'," *Journal of Accountancy* (December 1978), pp. 56–63. Special appreciation is extended to Professor Zeff for his insights on this chapter.

are being formulated. The Board must be attentive to the economic consequences of its actions. What the Board should *not* do is issue pronouncements that are primarily politically motivated. While paying attention to its constituencies, the Board should base its standards on sound research and a conceptual framework that has its foundation in economic reality. Even so, the FASB can continue to expect politics and special interest pressures, since as T. S. Eliot said, "Humankind cannot bear very much reality."

A current illustration of an economic consequence issue is the recent turmoil caused by the FASB's proposal that stock options granted to executives be charged as an expense on the income statement. The consequences of the proposed actions, executives argued, would be disastrous. Big companies would reduce their investment in research and development and equipment. Small companies, being cash starved, would go bankrupt. They would not be able to attract top executives because stock option plans involve too high a charge to income. Employment in the United States would plummet because small companies (who create most of the job growth) would not hire additional workers. The FASB, however, notes that options are compensation, the cost of which should be recorded. As this book goes to press, the argument still rages.

► CONTINUED INTEREST IN STANDARD SETTING

Since many interests may be affected by the implementation of an accounting standard, it is not surprising that there is much discussion about who should develop these standards and to whom they should apply. Some of the major issues are discussed below.

EXPECTATIONS GAP

All professions have come under increasing scrutiny by the government, whether it be the investment banking profession because of insider trading, the medical profession because of high costs and Medicare or Medicaid frauds, or engineers because of their failure to consider environmental consequences in their work.

The accounting profession has not escaped criticism. Because of some well-publicized instances of corporate fraud, domestic and foreign bribery, underfunded pensions, and sudden bankruptcies, critics of the accounting profession have questioned its performance. Add to this society's general desire for more accountability from all institutions, and it is not surprising that Congress has turned its attention on the accounting profession.

For example, Representative John D. Dingell's Subcommittee on Oversight and Investigation (**Dingell Committee**) has held hearings on a number of accounting and auditing matters. One of these is whether the FASB and the SEC are issuing effective and timely standards. The hearings were precipitated by massive bankruptcies and frauds involving firms such as Continental Illinois National Bank, Penn Square Bank, and Drysdale Government Securities, Inc. Some in Congress contended that such bankruptcies could have been averted if more timely information had been provided.

In addition, these hearings have highlighted a growing concern about "white collar" crime in financial reporting. In some companies, for example, the culture of a company exerts pressures on operating managers "to make things look better than they are" so as to increase short-term earnings. In other situations, greed and ego play a large role. For example, in one recent year the FBI investigated approximately 280 banks suspected of fraud, an increase of approximately 30% over the preceding year. It was estimated that banks lose eight times as much money to insiders as they do to "bank robbers."

The accounting profession recognizes that it must play an important role in combatting "white collar" fraud, and its response to criticisms in this area has been direct and immediate. For example, the AICPA established a new Accounting Firms Division with two sections: one for firms auditing SEC clients (called the **SEC Practice Section**) and the other for firms auditing privately owned, non-SEC clients (called the **Private**

Companies Section).[16] And, to help assure the public that the SEC Practice Section is meeting its responsibilities, the AICPA established as part of this structure an independent **Public Oversight Board.** The Board, composed of distinguished nonaccountants, has its own staff and is free to conduct its own inquiries and to report publicly as it wishes. The Private Companies Section also has its own quality control standards and peer review requirements.

More recently, the profession has issued new auditing standards on internal control, fraud and illegal acts, and auditors' communications. It has supported and begun to act on recommendations made by the **National Commission on Fraudulent Financial Reporting (the Treadway Commission),** chaired by former SEC Commissioner James C. Treadway. And it is developing guidelines in relation to proper disclosures of reasons why auditors resign from audit engagements, particularly when there are questions about management's integrity.

But is it enough? The **expectations gap**—what the public thinks accountants should be doing and what accountants think they can do—is a difficult one to close. The instances of fraudulent reporting have caused some to question whether the profession is doing enough. Although the profession can argue rightfully that they cannot be responsible for every financial catastrophe, it must continue to strive to meet the needs of society.

COMPETING STANDARD-SETTING BODIES

As a prominent accountant recently noted, "the FASB is literally unique: it is a private sector institution performing a public function that is defined in the federal statutes." It is not surprising therefore that the right of the FASB to establish accounting standards continues to be challenged. Some of the major challenges come not only from outside the profession, but from within as well.

AICPA

The AICPA started issuing Statements of Position because it believed that more immediate guidance was needed for specific reporting problems. Although the AICPA has reduced its issuance of SOPs, it continues to be concerned about timely financial reporting. In addition, support exists within the AICPA for two sets of GAAP—one for large companies and one for small companies. Small companies complain that the detailed reporting required by GAAP is too costly and not needed by them. This is often referred to as the BIG GAAP–LITTLE GAAP issue.

GASB

As indicated earlier, the GASB is a separate governmental accounting standards board established to regulate state and local governmental reporting. It is modeled after the FASB. The two organizations continue to debate who should set standards in certain not-for-profit accounting areas.

Congress

From time to time Congress becomes active in the standard-setting process, particularly when the issue becomes highly political. For example, Senator Joseph Lieberman (D-Connecticut) recently introduced legislation that would permit companies not to follow any FASB standard that requires a new expense charge for stock options. Senator

---

[16]CPA firms that audit SEC registered firms must join the SEC Practice Section and therefore must comply with more comprehensive practice requirements (such as compulsory peer practice review) than those of the Private Companies Section.

Lieberman believes that a standard which results in a substantial expense for stock options would be disastrous to the national economy. Such political reaction is unfortunate and raises serious issues about who should be developing accounting standards.

Business Community

Members of the business community have registered numerous complaints about accounting standards. They contend that FASB standards are too complex and costly to implement and that some standards introduce volatility into reported income numbers. Further, they contend that standards requiring disclosures put their companies at a competitive disadvantage in world markets. As a result, this group lobbied hard—and won—for a change in the voting rules of the FASB, from a simple majority (4-3) to a supermajority (5-2). By requiring a supermajority, it is hoped that standards will be less controversial and will be issued only if truly "generally accepted." In addition, the business world argues for more representation on the FASB and the Financial Accounting Foundation.

These developments are viewed by some with alarm. They believe that the supermajority will only lead to a delay in the issuances of standards. And, if the business community dominates the standard setting process, the regulated will have too much influence on the regulations (leading to a "fox in the chicken coop" situation) and, thus, undermine the credibility of financial reports.

▶ INTERNATIONAL ACCOUNTING STANDARDS

In Germany, the amortization period for an intangible asset is 5 years. In the United States, a maximum period of 40 years is allowed. In Mexico, assets are adjusted for price-level changes. In the United States, assets are generally valued at historical cost. In Japan, income smoothing is permitted because firms are allowed discretionary charges to income for such items as depreciation and bad debts. In the United States, arbitrary charges to income are not permitted. These are just some of the ways in which reporting practices in the United States differ from reporting practices in other countries.

INTERNATIONAL INSIGHT

IASC has issued thirty-one standards to date, along with a conceptual framework. Many of the earlier standards have been amended and tightened as IASC has achieved more prominence.

Most countries recognize the need for more uniform standards. As a result, the International Accounting Standards Committee (IASC) was formed in 1973—the same year the FASB was born—to attempt to narrow the areas of divergence. The objective of the IASC in terms of standard setting is "to work generally for the improvement and harmonization of regulations, accounting standards and procedures relating to the presentation of financial statements." Eliminating differences will not be easy because the objectives of financial reporting in the United States often differ from those in foreign countries, the institutional structures are often not comparable, and strong national tendencies are pervasive. Nevertheless, since IASC's inception, some headway has been made, and it is hoped that further comparability will be achieved in the future.

Interest continues to grow in the development of international accounting standards. For example, the chairman of the FASB recently noted . . . "I think the FASB would support an objective that seeks to create superior international standards that would then gradually supplant national standards as the superior standards become universally accepted."

OBJECTIVE 9

Understand issues related to ethics and financial accounting.

▶ ETHICS IN THE ENVIRONMENT OF FINANCIAL ACCOUNTING

Robert Sack, a commentator on the subject of accounting ethics, noted that "Based on my experience, new graduates tend to be idealistic . . . thank goodness for that! Still it is very dangerous to think that your armor is all in place and say to yourself 'I would have never given in to that.' The pressures don't explode on us, they build and we often don't recognize them until they have us."

These observations are particularly appropriate for anyone entering the business world. In accounting, as in other areas of business, ethical dilemmas are encountered frequently. Some of these dilemmas are simple and easy to resolve. Many, however, are complex, and solutions are not obvious. Businesses' concentration on "maximizing the bottom line," "facing the challenges of competition," and "stressing short-term results" place accountants in an environment of conflict and pressure. Basic questions such as: "Is this way of communicating financial information good or bad?" "Is it right or wrong?" "What should I do in the circumstance?" cannot always be answered by simply adhering to GAAP or following the rules of the profession. Technical competence is not enough when ethical decisions are encountered.

Doing the right thing, making the right decision, is not always easy. Right is not always evident. And, the pressures "to bend the rules," "to play the game," "to just ignore it," can be considerable. For example, "Will my decision affect my job performance negatively?" "Will my superiors be upset?" "Will my colleagues be unhappy with me?" are often questions faced in making a tough ethical decision. The decision is more difficult because a public consensus has not emerged to formulate a comprehensive ethical system to provide guidelines.

However, "applied ethics" is still necessary and possible. Here are the steps that you might apply in the process of ethical awareness and decision making:

1. **Recognize an ethical situation or ethical dilemma.** The first step is to know when you have a problem. To do that, you must develop your own personal ethics or conscience. Your ethics are a subset of society's values. They come from family, educational, and religious institutions as well as from social movements and your own reactions to all of these inputs. Being sensitive to and aware of the effects (potential harm or benefit) of one's actions and decisions on individuals or groups is a first step in resolving ethical dilemmas.

2. **Move toward an ethical resolution by identifying and analyzing the principal elements in the situation.** Seek answers to the following questions in this sequence:
    (a) What parties (*stakeholders*) may be harmed or benefited?
    (b) Whose rights or claims may be violated?
    (c) Which specific interests are in conflict?
    (d) What are my responsibilities and obligations?
    This step involves **identifying and sorting out the facts.**

3. **Identify the alternatives and weigh the impact of each alternative on various stakeholders.** For instance, in financial accounting, which alternative methods are available to measure or report the transaction, situation, or event? What is the effect of each alternative on the various stakeholders? Which stakeholders are harmed or benefited most?

4. **Select the best or most ethical alternative, considering all the circumstances and the consequences.** Some ethical issues involve one right answer; and what must be done is to identify the one right answer. Other ethical issues involve more than one right answer; these require an evaluation of each and a selection of the best or most ethical alternative.

This whole process of ethical sensitivity and selection among alternatives can be complicated by pressures that may take the form of time pressures, job pressures, client pressures, personal pressures, and peer pressures. Throughout this textbook, **ethical considerations are presented for the purpose of sensitizing you** to the type of situations you may encounter in the performance of your professional responsibility.

▶ CONCLUSION

The FASB is in its twenty-second year as this textbook is written. Will the FASB survive in its present state, or will it have to be restructured or changed as its predecessors were? As indicated, some people in government, some in the financial community, and some in the profession itself are continually challenging the accounting profession to assume more responsibility and to be more responsive to the needs of its constituencies.

At present, we believe that the accounting profession is reacting responsibly and effectively to remedy identified shortcomings. Because of its substantive resources and expertise, the private sector should be able to develop and maintain high standards. But it is a difficult process requiring time, logic, and diplomacy. By a judicious mix of these three ingredients, and a measure of luck, the profession may be able to continue to develop its own standards and regulate itself with minimal intervention.

KEY TERMS

Accounting Principles Board (APB), 12

Accounting Research Bulletins, 12

accrual basis accounting, 7

Auditing Standards Board, 17

AICPA, 12

APB Opinions, 12

Committee on Accounting Procedure (CAP), 12

discussion memorandum, 13

Emerging Issues Task Force (EITF), 15

expectations gap, 21

exposure draft, 13

financial accounting, 6

Financial Accounting Standards Board (FASB), 13

financial reporting, 6

financial statements, 6

generally accepted accounting principles (GAAP), 9

Governmental Accounting Standards Board (GASB), 15

interpretations, 14

objectives of financial reporting, 7

Public Oversight Board, 21

Securities and Exchange Commission (SEC), 10

Standards Statement, 13

▶ SUMMARY OF LEARNING OBJECTIVES ◀

1. **Define accounting and describe its essential characteristics.** Accounting is a service activity, an analytical discipline, and an information system. Its essential characteristics are: (1) identification, measurement, and communication of financial information about (2) economic entities to (3) interested persons.

2. **Identify the major financial statements and other means of financial reporting.** The financial statements most frequently provided are (1) the balance sheet, (2) the income statement, (3) the statement of cash flows, and (4) the statement of owners' or stockholders' equity. Financial reporting other than financial statements may take various forms. Examples include the president's letter or supplementary schedules in the corporate annual report, prospectuses, reports filed with government agencies, news releases, management's forecasts, and descriptions of an enterprise's social or environmental impact.

3. **Identify the objectives of financial reporting.** The objectives of financial reporting are to provide (1) information that is useful in investment and credit decisions, (2) information that is useful in assessing cash flow prospects, and (3) information about enterprise resources, claims to those resources, and changes in them.

4. **Describe the environment of financial accounting.** Modern financial accounting is the product of many influences and conditions that constitute the environment of accounting. Five of these conditions are: (1) Accounting recognizes that people live in a world of scarce resources. (2) Accounting recognizes that in our society, productive resources are generally privately owned rather than government owned. (3) Accounting recognizes that economic activity is conducted by separately identifiable units—business enterprises. (4) Accounting recognizes that in complex economic systems, some (owners and investors) entrust the custodianship of and control over property to others (managers). (5) Accounting recognizes that economic resources, economic obligations, and residual interests should be expressed in terms of money.

5. **Explain the need for accounting standards.** In preparing financial statements, accountants are confronted with the potential dangers of bias, misinterpretation, inexactness, and ambiguity. In order to minimize these dangers, the accounting profession has attempted to develop a set of standards that is generally accepted and universally practiced. Without this set of standards, each accountant or enterprise would have to develop its own standards, and readers of financial statements would have to familiarize themselves with every com-

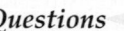

pany's peculiar accounting and reporting practices. As a result, it would be almost impossible to prepare statements that could be compared.

6. **Identify the major policy-setting bodies and their role in the standard-setting process.** The *Securities and Exchange Commission (SEC)* is an agency of the federal government that has the broad powers to prescribe, in whatever detail it desires, the accounting standards to be employed by companies that fall within its jurisdiction. The *American Institute of Certified Public Accountants (AICPA)* issued standards through its Committee on Accounting Procedure and Accounting Principles Board. The *Financial Accounting Standards Board (FASB)* establishes and improves standards of financial accounting and reporting for the guidance and education of the public. The *Governmental Accounting Standards Board (GASB)* establishes and improves standards of financial accounting for state and local governments.

7. **Explain the meaning of generally accepted accounting principles.** Generally accepted accounting principles are those principles that have substantial authoritative support, such as FASB Standards and Interpretations, APB Opinions and Interpretations, AICPA Accounting Research Bulletins, and other authoritative pronouncements.

8. **Describe the impact of user groups on the standard-setting process.** User groups may want particular economic events accounted for or reported in a particular way, and they fight hard to get what they want. Therefore, the FASB has become the target of many pressures and efforts to influence changes in the existing standards and the development of new ones. Because of the accelerated rate of change and the increased complexity of our economy, these pressures have been multiplying. As a result, accounting standards are as much a product of political action as they are of careful logic or empirical findings.

9. **Understand issues related to ethics and financial accounting.** Financial accountants in the performance of their professional duties are called on for moral discernment and ethical decision making. The decision is more difficult because a public consensus has not emerged to formulate a comprehensive ethical system that provides guidelines in making ethical judgments.

QUESTIONS

1. Differentiate broadly between financial accounting and managerial accounting.

2. Differentiate between "financial statements" and "financial reporting."

3. Accounting is an unchanging discipline independent of its environment and other influences. Comment.

4. Name several environmental conditions that shape financial accounting to a significant extent.

5. Why is it important to measure performance accurately and fairly when productive resources are privately owned?

6. Provide some examples of how accounting information influences its environment.

7. What are the major objectives of financial reporting?

8. Of what value is a common set of standards in financial accounting and reporting?

9. What is the likely limitation of "general-purpose financial statements"?

10. What are some of the developments or events that occurred between 1900 and 1930 that helped bring about changes in accounting theory or practice?

11. In what way is the Securities and Exchange Commission concerned about and supportive of accounting principles and standards?

12. What was the Committee on Accounting Procedure and what were its accomplishments and failings?

13. For what purposes did the AICPA in 1959 create the Accounting Principles Board?

14. Distinguish between Accounting Research Bulletins, Accounting Research Studies, Opinions of the Accounting Principles Board, and Statements of the Financial Accounting Standards Board.

15. If you had to explain or define "generally accepted accounting principles or standards" to a nonaccountant, what essential characteristics would you include in your explanation?

16. In what ways was it felt that the statements issued by the Financial Accounting Standards Board would carry greater weight than the opinions issued by the Accounting Principles Board?

17. How are FASB discussion memorandums and FASB exposure drafts related to FASB "statements"?

18. Distinguish between FASB "statements of financial accounting standards" and FASB "statements of financial accounting concepts."

19. What is Rule 203 of the Code of Professional Conduct and what relationship does it have to the standard-setting process?

20. Rank from the most authoritative to the least authoritative, the following three items: FASB Technical Bulletins, AICPA Practice Bulletins, and FASB Standards.

21. The chairman of the FASB at one time noted that "the flow of standards can only be slowed if (1) producers focus less on quarterly earnings per share and tax benefits and more on quality products and (2) accountants and lawyers rely less on rules and law and more on professional judgment and conduct." Explain his comment.

22. What is the purpose of FASB Technical Bulletins? How do FASB Technical Bulletins differ from FASB Interpretations?

23. Explain the role of the Emerging Issues Task Force in establishing generally accepted accounting principles.

24. What is the purpose of the Governmental Accounting Standards Board?

25. What is AcSEC and what is its relationship to the FASB? Include in your answer a discussion of AcSEC's apparent conflict with the FASB.

26. What are the sources of pressure that change and influence the development of accounting principles and standards?

27. Some individuals have indicated that the FASB must be cognizant of the economic consequences of its pronouncements. What is meant by economic consequences? What dangers exist if politics plays an important role in the development of financial reporting standards?

28. What are some possible reasons why another organization, such as the Governmental Accounting Standards Board, should not issue financial reporting standards?

29. If you were given complete authority in the matter, how would you propose that accounting principles or standards should be developed and enforced?

30. One writer recently noted that 99.4% of all companies prepare statements that are in accordance with GAAP. Why then is there such concern about fraudulent financial reporting?

31. What is the "expectations gap"? What is the profession doing to try to close this gap?

32. A number of foreign countries often have reporting standards that differ from those in the United States. What are some of the main reasons why reporting standards are often different among countries?

33. How are financial accountants challenged in their work to make ethical decisions? Is not technical mastery of GAAP sufficient to the practice of financial accounting?

34. What significant steps might one apply in the process of moral discernment and ethical decision making?

CASES

C1-1 (Financial Accounting) David Mead has recently completed his first year of studying accounting. His instructor for next semester has indicated that the primary focus will be the area of financial accounting.

Instructions

(a) Differentiate between financial accounting and managerial accounting.

(b) One part of financial accounting involves the preparation of financial statements. What are the financial statements most frequently provided?

(c) What is the difference between financial statements and financial reporting?

C1-2 (Objectives of Financial Reporting) Sam Jacobs, a recent graduate of the local state university, is presently employed by a large manufacturing company. He has been asked by Cari Peters, controller, to prepare the company's response to a current Discussion Memorandum published by the Financial Accounting Standards Board (FASB). Jacobs knows that the FASB has issued six *Statements of Financial Accounting Concepts,* and he believes that these concept statements could be used to support the company's response to the Discussion Memorandum. He has prepared a rough draft of the response citing *Statement of Financial Accounting Concepts No. 1,* "Objectives of Financial Reporting by Business Enterprises."

Instructions

(a) Identify the three objectives of financial reporting as presented in *Statement of Financial Accounting Concepts No. 1 (SFAC No. 1).*

(b) Describe the level of sophistication expected of the users of financial information by *SFAC No. 1.*

(CMA adapted)

C1-3 (Accounting Numbers and the Environment) Hardly a day goes by without an article appearing on the crises affecting many of our financial institutions in the United States. It is estimated that the Savings and Loan (S&L) debacle may end up costing $500 billion ($2,000 for every man, woman, and child in the United States). Some argue that if the S&Ls were required to report their investments at market value instead of cost, large losses would have been reported earlier, which would have signaled regulators to close those S&Ls and, therefore, minimize the losses to American taxpayers.

Instructions

Explain how reported accounting numbers might affect an individual's perceptions and actions. Cite two examples.

C1-4 (Need for Accounting Standards) Some argue that having various organizations establish accounting principles is wasteful and inefficient. Rather than mandating accounting standards, each company could voluntarily disclose the type of information it considered important. In addition, if an investor wants additional information, the investor could contact the company and pay to receive the additional information desired.

Instructions

Comment on the appropriateness of this viewpoint.

C1-5 (AICPA's Role in Standard Setting) One of the major groups involved in the standard-setting process is the American Institute of Certified Public Accountants. Initially it was the primary organization that established accounting principles in the United States. Subsequently it relinquished most of its power to the FASB.

Instructions

(a) Identify the two committees of the AICPA that established accounting principles prior to the establishment of the FASB.

(b) Speculate as to why these two organizations failed. In your answer, identify steps the FASB has taken to avoid failure.

(c) What is the present role of the AICPA in the standard-setting environment?

C1-6 (FASB Role in Standard Setting) A press release announcing the appointment of the trustees of the new Financial Accounting Foundation stated that the Financial Accounting Standards Board (to be appointed by the trustees) "... will become the established authority for setting accounting principles under which corporations report to the shareholders and others" (AICPA news release July 20, 1972).

Instructions

(a) Identify the sponsoring organization of the FASB and the process by which the FASB arrives at a decision and issues an accounting standard.

(b) Indicate the major types of pronouncements issued by the FASB and the purposes of each of these pronouncements.

C1-7 (Government Role in Standard Setting) Recently an article stated "the setting of accounting standards in the United States is now about 60 years old. It is a unique process in our society, one that has undergone numerous changes over the years. The standards are established by a private sector entity that has no dominant sponsor and is not part of any professional organization or trade association. The governmental entity that provides oversight, on the other hand, is far more a friend than a competitor or an antagonist."

Instructions

Identify the governmental entity that provides oversight and indicate its role in the standard-setting process.

C1-8 (Meaning of Generally Accepted Accounting Principles) At the completion of Taylor Company's audit, the president, Ellie Taylor, asks about the meaning of the phrase "in conformity with generally accepted accounting principles" that appears in your audit report on the management's financial statements. Ellie observes that the meaning of the phrase must include something more and different than what she thinks of as "principles."

Instructions

(a) Explain the meaning of the term "accounting principles" as used in the audit report. (Do not discuss in this part the significance of "generally accepted.")

(b) President Taylor wants to know how you determine whether or not an accounting principle is generally accepted. Discuss the sources of evidence for determining whether an accounting principle has substantial authoritative support. Do not merely list the titles of publications.

C1-9 (Politicalization of Standard Setting) Some accountants have said that politicalization in the development and acceptance of generally accepted accounting principles (i.e., standard setting) is taking place. Some use the term "politicalization" in a narrow sense to mean the influence by governmental agencies, particularly the Securities and Exchange Commission, on the development of generally accepted accounting principles. Others use it more broadly to mean the compromising that takes place in bodies responsible for developing generally accepted accounting principles because of the influence and pressure of interested groups (SEC, American Accounting Association, businesses through their various organizations, Institute of Management Accountants, financial analysts, bankers, lawyers, etc.).

Instructions

(a) The Committee on Accounting Procedures of the AICPA was established in the mid to late 1930s and functioned until 1959, at which time the Accounting Principles Board came into existence. In 1973, the Financial Accounting Standards Board was formed and the APB went out of existence. Do the reasons these groups were formed, their methods of operation while in existence, and the reasons for the demise of the first two indicate an increasing politicalization (as the term is used in the broad sense) of accounting standard setting? Explain your answer by indicating how the CAP, the APB, and the FASB operated or operate. Cite specific developments that tend to support your answer.

(b) What arguments can be raised to support the "politicalization" of accounting standard setting?

(c) What arguments can be raised against the "politicalization" of accounting standard setting?

(CMA adapted)

C1-10 (Models for Setting Accounting Standards) Presented below are three models for setting accounting standards.

1. The purely political approach, where national legislative action decrees accounting standards.
2. The private, professional approach, where financial accounting standards are set and enforced by private professional actions only.
3. The public/private mixed approach, where standards are basically set by private sector bodies that behave as though they were public agencies and whose standards to a great extent are enforced through governmental agencies.

Instructions

(a) Which of these three models best describes standard setting in the United States? Comment on your answer.

(b) Why do companies, financial analysts, labor unions, industry trade associations, and others take such an active interest in standard setting?

(c) Cite an example of a group other than the FASB that attempts to establish accounting standards. Speculate as to why another group might wish to set its own standards.

C1-11 (Standard-Setting Terminology) Marsha Hoag, a secretary at a major university, recently said, "I've got some CDs in my IRA, which I set up to beat the IRS." As elsewhere, in the world of accounting and finance, it often helps to be fluent in abbreviations and acronyms.

Instructions

Presented below is a list of common accounting acronyms. Identify the term for which each acronym stands, and provide a brief definition of each term.

(a)	FEI	(g)	FAF	(m)	CPA
(b)	IMA	(h)	FASAC	(n)	FASB
(c)	AICPA	(i)	FRR	(o)	GASB
(d)	CAP	(j)	IRS	(p)	SEC
(e)	ARB	(k)	SOP	(q)	AAA
(f)	APB	(l)	GAAP		

C1-12 (Accounting Organizations and Documents Issued) Presented below are a number of accounting organizations and type of documents they have issued. Match the appropriate document to the organization involved. Note that more than one document may be issued by the same organization. If no document is provided for an organization, write in "0."

Organization	*Document*
1. ____ Securities and Exchange Commission	**(a)** Opinions
2. ____ Accounting Standards Executive Committee	**(b)** Practice Bulletins
3. ____ Accounting Principles Board	**(c)** Accounting Research Bulletins
4. ____ Committee on Accounting Procedure	**(d)** Financial Reporting Releases
5. ____ Financial Accounting Standards Board	**(e)** Financial Accounting Standards
	(f) Statements of Position
	(g) Technical Bulletins

C1-13 (Accounting Pronouncements) A number of authoritative pronouncements have been issued by standard-setting bodies during the last 50 years. A list is provided on the left with a description of these pronouncements on the right. Match the description to the pronouncements.

____ Technical Bulletin	**(a)** Official pronouncements of the APB
____ Interpretations (of the Financial Accounting Standards Board)	**(b)** Sets forth fundamental objectives and concepts that will be used in developing future standards
____ Statement of Financial Accounting Standards	**(c)** Primary document of the FASB that establishes GAAP
____ EITF Statements	
____ Opinions	**(d)** Provides additional guidance on implementing or applying FASB Standards or Interpretations
____ Statement of Financial Accounting Concepts	**(e)** Provides guidance on how to account for new and unusual financial transactions that have the potential for creating diversity in financial reporting practices
	(f) Represent extensions or modifications of existing standards

C1-14 (Issues Involving Standard Setting) There have been a number of articles on accounting matters in the financial press. Some of the comments made in these articles are presented below. Answer the related question for each comment.

1. "In its first formal action upon commencing operations the GASB unanimously approved GASB Statement No. 1, Authoritative Status of NCGA Pronouncements and AICPA Industry Audit Guide." What is the GASB and what role does it play in the standard-setting process?
2. Some people want the FASB to deal with emerging accounting issues more promptly. But prompt resolution of issues comes at the expense of some of the elaborate due process the FASB imposes on itself. If the FASB reduces that due process, it risks undermining the acceptance of accounting rules set by a nongovernmental standard-setting body. What is meant by "due process" and how is the profession attempting to handle the problem of providing timely guidance?
3. Recently the FASB has published what it considers to be the mission of the FASB. It noted that one concept it will follow will be to weigh carefully the views of its constituents in developing standards. Who are the FASB's major constituents and what role do they play in the standard-setting process?
4. "A Securities and Exchange Commission report to Congress on the accounting profession shows that the profession has taken significant strides in regulating itself." What might be some significant strides the profession has taken to regulate itself?

C1-15 (International Accounting Standards) Michael Sharpe, Deputy Chairman, International Accounting Standards Committee made the following comments before the FEI's 63rd Annual Conference: There is an irreversible movement towards the harmonization of financial reporting throughout the world. The international capital markets require an end to:

(a) The confusion caused by international companies announcing different results depending on the set of accounting standards applied. Recent announcements by Daimler Benz highlight the confusion that this causes.

(b) Companies in some countries obtaining unfair commercial advantages from the use of particular national accounting standards.

(c) The complications in negotiating commercial arrangements for international joint ventures caused by different accounting requirements.

(d) The inefficiency of international companies having to understand and use a myriad of different accounting standards depending on the countries in which they operate and the countries in which they raise capital and debt. Executive talent is wasted on keeping up to date with numerous sets of accounting standards and the never ending changes to them.

(e) The inefficiency of investment managers, bankers and financial analysts as they seek to compare financial reporting drawn up in accordance with different sets of accounting standards.

(f) Failure of many stock exchanges and regulators to require companies subject to their jurisdiction to provide comparable, comprehensive and transparent financial reporting frameworks giving international comparability.

(g) Difficulty for developing countries and countries entering the free market economy such as China and Russia in accessing foreign capital markets because of the complexity of and differences between national standards.

(h) The restriction on the mobility of financial service providers across the world as a result of different accounting standards.

Clearly the elimination of these inefficiencies by having comparable high quality financial reporting used across the world would benefit international businesses.

Instructions

(a) What is the International Accounting Standards Committee?

(b) What stakeholders might benefit from the use of International Accounting Standards?

(c) What do you believe are some of the major obstacles to harmonization?

C1-16 (Securities and Exchange Commission) The U.S. Securities and Exchange Commission (SEC) was created in 1934 and consists of five commissioners and a large professional staff. The SEC professional staff is organized into five divisions and several principal offices. The primary objective of the SEC is to support fair securities markets. The SEC also strives to foster enlightened shareholder participation in corporate decisions of publicly-traded companies. The SEC has a significant presence in financial markets, the development of accounting practices, and corporation-shareholder relations, and has the power to exert influence on entities whose actions lie within the scope of its authority.

Instructions

(a) Explain where the Securities and Exchange Commission receives its authority.

(b) Describe the official role of the Securities and Exchange Commission in the development of financial accounting theory and practices.

(c) Discuss the interrelationship between the Securities and Exchange Commission and Financial Accounting Standards Board with respect to the development and establishment of financial accounting theory and practices.

(CMA adapted)

C1-17 (Standard-Setting Process) In 1973, the responsibility for developing and issuing rules on accounting practices was given to the Financial Accounting Foundation and, in particular, to an arm of the foundation called the Financial Accounting Standards Board (FASB). The generally accepted accounting principles established by the FASB are enunciated through a publication series entitled **Statements of Financial Accounting Standards**. These statements are issued periodically, and over 100 are currently in force. The statements have a significant influence on the way in which financial statements are prepared by U.S. corporations.

Instructions

(a) Describe the process by which a topic is selected or identified as appropriate for study by the Financial Accounting Standards Board (FASB).

(b) Once a topic is considered appropriate for consideration by the FASB, a series of steps are followed before a **Statement of Financial Accounting Standards** is issued. Describe the major steps in the process leading to the issuance of a standard.

(c) Identify at least three other organizations who influence the setting of generally accepted accounting principles (GAAP).

(CMA adapted)

▶ USING YOUR JUDGMENT ◀

▶ FINANCIAL REPORTING PROBLEM

Linda Hughes, a new staff accountant, is confused because of the complexities involving accounting standard setting. Specifically, she is confused by the number of bodies issuing financial reporting standards of one kind or another and the level of authoritative support that can be attached to these reporting standards. Linda decides that she must review the environment in which accounting standards are set, if she is to increase her understanding of the accounting profession.

Linda recalls that during her accounting education there was a chapter or two regarding the environment of financial accounting and the development of accounting standards. However, she remembers that little emphasis was placed on these chapters by her instructor.

Instructions
    (a)   Help Linda by identifying key organizations involved in accounting standard setting.
    (b)   In what ways is accounting involved in the environment as Linda refers to it? That is, what environmental factors influence accounting and how does accounting influence its environment?
    (c)   Linda asks for guidance regarding authoritative support. Please assist her by explaining what is meant by authoritative support.
    (d)   Give Linda a historical overview of how standard-setting has evolved so that she will not feel that she is the only one to be confused.
    (e)   What authority for compliance with GAAP has existed throughout the period of standard setting?

▶ WRITING ASSIGNMENT

Beta Alpha Psi, your university's accounting society, has decided to publish a brief pamphlet for seniors in high school, detailing the various facets of the accountancy profession. As a junior accountancy major, you have been asked to contribute an article for this publication. Your topic is the evolution of accounting standard-setting organizations in the United States.

Instructions
Write a 1–1.5 page article on the historical development of the organizations responsible for giving us GAAP. (The most appropriate introduction would explain the increasing need for a more standardized approach to accounting for a company's assets.)

▶ GROUP ASSIGNMENT

(Role of General Purpose Financial Statements)   Assume that your group is the investment department for a major corporation and that you have been charged with investing $1,000,000 of the company's money as an intermediate-term investment (3–5 years). Further assume that you have been approached by an investment firm to either loan money to or purchase the common stock of one of the investment firm's clients.

Instructions
Your instructor will assign one of the group members to be the group recorder and another member to be the group leader/spokesperson. For each part of the assignment, work within your group to develop responses to the following. Before moving to the next requirement, you will be asked to report your group responses to the class.
    (a)   Identify the objectives you would have as a creditor or investor in this company. For example, how does a creditor get a return from making a loan? How does the investor in common stock get a return on his or her investment?
    (b)   Generate a list of as many information items as you can that should be considered regarding the investment of $1,000,000 in *any* company. Mention any item that would be useful in making such a decision. Once the list is completed try to narrow it down to the five most important items. Identify the information items that are found in the financial statements. Where can information on the remaining items be found?
    (c)   In light of the lists generated concerning the information items that are important and where they can be found, what rules or regulations would you require concerning the quality, content, and scope of the information? That is, what qualities of this information would make it more useful in your investment decision?
    (d)   Does information found in financial statements have these qualities? What is the role of accounting standards for ensuring that information is useful to decision makers? Provide one example where accounting rules help provide more useful information.

▶ ETHICS CASE

(Early Implementation of FASB Standards) When the FASB issues new standards, the implementation date is usually 12 months from date of issuance, with early implementation encouraged. Chris Meyer, controller, discusses with her financial vice-president the need for early implementation of a standard which would result in a fairer presentation of the company's financial condition and earnings. When the financial vice-president determines that early implementation of the standard will adversely affect the reported net income for the year, he discourages Chris from implementing the standard until it is required.

Instructions
    (a) What, if any, is the ethical issue involved in this case?
    (b) Is the financial vice-president acting improperly or immorally?
    (c) What does Meyer have to gain by advocacy of early implementation?
    (d) Who might be affected by the decision against early implementation?

(CMA adapted)

CHAPTER 2

CONCEPTUAL FRAMEWORK UNDERLYING FINANCIAL ACCOUNTING

LEARNING OBJECTIVES

After studying this chapter, you should be able to:

1. Describe the usefulness of a conceptual framework.

2. Describe the FASB's efforts to construct a conceptual framework.

3. Understand the objectives of financial reporting.

4. Identify the qualitative characteristics of accounting information.

5. Define the basic elements of financial statements.

6. Describe the basic assumptions of accounting.

7. Explain the application of the basic principles of accounting.

8. Describe the impact that constraints have on reporting accounting information.

*I*n 1930, four of the largest companies in the United States (including General Electric) reported only one note to their financial statements. In the early 1990s, a survey of 25 of the largest companies in the United States indicated that they had an average of 17 pages of notes to their financial statements. Why the change?

In those sixty plus years we have seen the globalization of the economy, an explosion in technology, the impact of competition (domestic and foreign), the introduction of new and more complex financial products, and, not the least, the formation and requirements of the SEC and the FASB (and its predecessors). These innovations and organizations require changes and improvements in the type of financial information provided. As the pace of economic and financial change increases, so does the need for relevant and reliable information.

To develop the needed financial information, accountants have developed a **conceptual framework** for financial accounting and reporting. That framework, based on the objectives of financial reporting developed by the FASB (identified in Chapter 1), has been the focus of much time, talent, and expense. Many have considered the Board's real contribution—and even its continued existence—to depend upon the quality and utility of this conceptual framework.

▶ NATURE OF A CONCEPTUAL FRAMEWORK

A conceptual framework is like a **constitution:** It is "a coherent system of interrelated objectives and fundamentals that can lead to consistent standards and that prescribes the nature, function, and limits of financial accounting and financial statements."[1]

Why is a conceptual framework necessary? First, to be useful, standard setting should build on and relate to an established body of concepts and objectives. A soundly developed conceptual framework should enable the FASB to issue more useful and consistent standards in the future. **A coherent set of standards and rules should be the result,** because they would be built upon the same foundation. The framework should increase financial statement users' understanding of and confidence in financial reporting, and it should enhance comparability among companies' financial statements.

Second, new and emerging **practical problems should be more quickly solved by reference to an existing framework of basic theory.** To illustrate an emerging problem: Unique debt instruments were issued by companies in the early 1980s as a response to high interest and inflation rates. These included shared appreciation mortgages (debt in which the lender receives equity participation), zero coupon bonds (debt issued at a deep discount with no stated interest rate), and commodity-backed bonds (debt that may be repaid in a commodity). For example, in 1985 Sunshine Mining (a silver mining company) sold two issues of bonds that it would redeem either with $1,000 in cash or with 50 ounces of silver, whichever was worth more at maturity. Both bond issues matured in 1995 and both had a stated interest rate—8.5%. At what amounts should the bonds have been recorded by Sunshine or the buyers of the bonds? What is the amount of the premium or discount on the bonds and how should it be amortized, if the bond redemption payments are to be made in silver (the future value of which was unknown at the date of issuance)?

It is difficult, if not impossible, for the FASB to prescribe the proper accounting treatment quickly for situations like this. Practicing accountants, however, must resolve such problems on a day-to-day basis. Through the exercise of good judgment and with the help of a universally accepted conceptual framework, it is hoped that practitioners will be able to dismiss certain alternatives quickly and then to focus upon a logical and acceptable treatment.

▶ DEVELOPMENT OF A CONCEPTUAL FRAMEWORK

Over the years numerous organizations, committees, and interested individuals developed and published their own conceptual frameworks. But no single framework was universally accepted and relied on in practice. Perhaps the most successful was *Accounting Principles Board Statement No. 4,* "Basic Concepts and Accounting Principles Underlying Financial Statements of Business Enterprises," which described existing practice but did not prescribe what practice ought to be.[2] Recognizing the need for a generally accepted framework, the FASB in 1976 issued a massive three-part Discussion Memorandum entitled *Conceptual Framework for Financial Accounting and Reporting: Elements of Financial Statements and Their Measurement.* It set forth the major issues that must be addressed in establishing a conceptual framework that would be a basis for setting accounting standards and for resolving financial reporting controversies. Since the publication of that document, the FASB has issued five Statements of Financial

---

[1]"Conceptual Framework for Financial Accounting and Reporting: Elements of Financial Statements and Their Measurement," *FASB Discussion Memorandum* (Stamford, Conn.: FASB, 1976), page 1 of the "Scope and Implications of the Conceptual Framework Project" section.

[2]"Basic Concepts and Accounting Principles Underlying Financial Statements of Business Enterprises," *APB Statement No. 4* (New York: AICPA, 1970).

Accounting Concepts that relate to financial reporting for business enterprises.[3] They are:

1. *SFAC No. 1,* "Objectives of Financial Reporting by Business Enterprises," presents the goals and purposes of accounting.

2. *SFAC No. 2,* "Qualitative Characteristics of Accounting Information," examines the characteristics that make accounting information useful.

3. *SFAC No. 3,* "Elements of Financial Statements of Business Enterprises," provides definitions of items in financial statements, such as assets, liabilities, revenues, and expenses.

4. *SFAC No. 5,* "Recognition and Measurement in Financial Statements of Business Enterprises," sets forth fundamental recognition and measurement criteria and guidance on what information should be formally incorporated into financial statements and when.

5. *SFAC No. 6,* "Elements of Financial Statements," replaces *SFAC No. 3* and expands its scope to include not-for-profit organizations.

Illustration 2-1 provides an overview of the conceptual framework.[4] At the first level,

ILLUSTRATION 2-1
A Conceptual Framework
for Financial Reporting

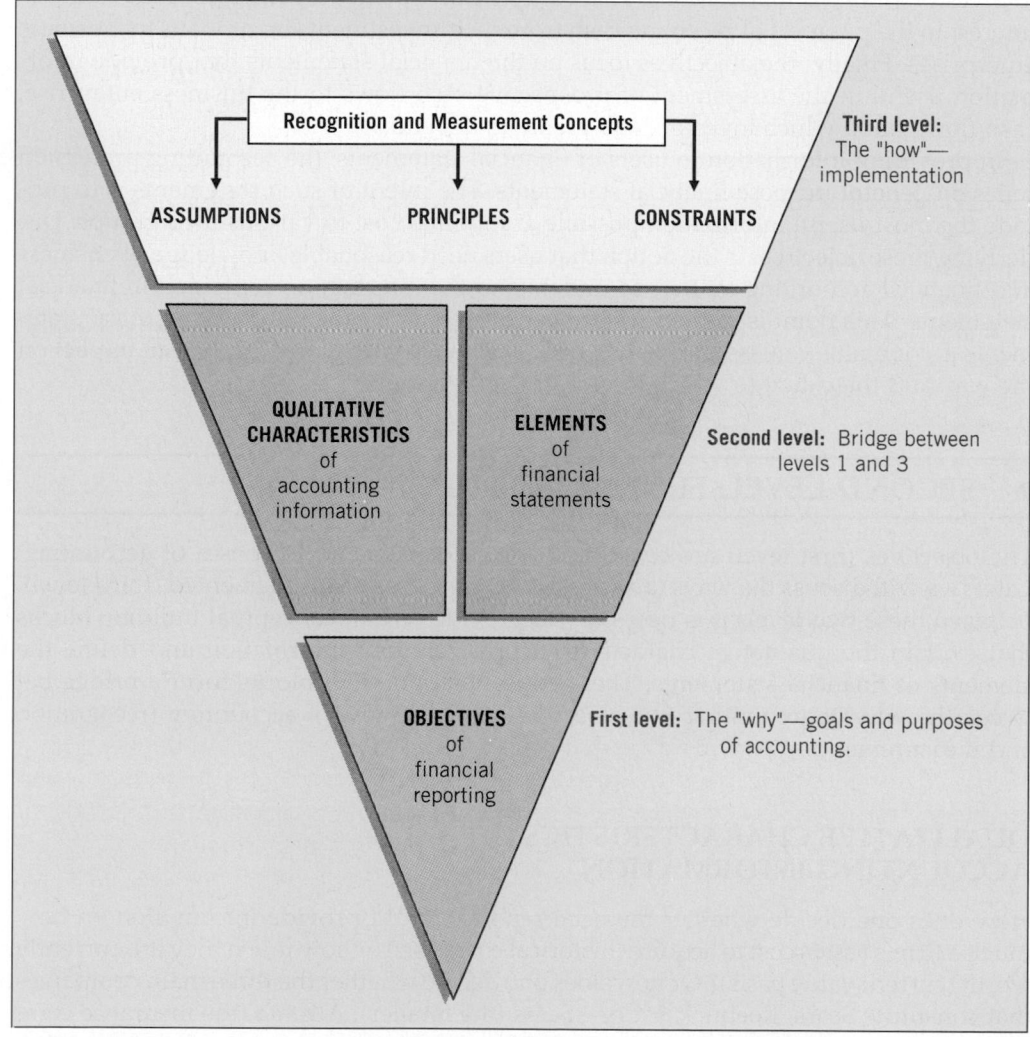

---

[3]The FASB has also issued a Statement of Financial Accounting Concepts that relates to non-business organizations: *Statement of Financial Accounting Concepts No. 4,* "Objectives of Financial Reporting by Nonbusiness Organizations" (December 1980).

[4]Adapted from William C. Norby, *The Financial Analysts Journal* (March–April, 1982), p. 22.

the **objectives** identify the goals and purposes of accounting and are the building blocks for the conceptual framework. At the second level are the **qualitative characteristics** that make accounting information useful and the **elements** of financial statements (assets, liabilities, and so on). At the final or third level are the **measurement and recognition concepts** that accountants use in establishing and applying accounting standards. These concepts include assumptions, principles, and constraints that describe the present reporting environment.

▶ FIRST LEVEL: BASIC OBJECTIVES

OBJECTIVE 3

Understand the objectives of financial reporting.

INTERNATIONAL INSIGHT

In Sweden, the government often provides capital to businesses. Swedish financial reporting is more oriented toward helping government decision makers in managing the economy.

INTERNATIONAL INSIGHT

In some nations, such as Switzerland, capital is provided to business primarily by very large banks. Creditors have very close ties to firms and can obtain information directly from them. Creditors do not need to rely on publicly available information, and financial reporting is focused on creditor protection.

As we discussed in Chapter 1, the **objectives of financial reporting** are to provide information that is: (1) useful to those making investment and credit decisions who have a reasonable understanding of business and economic activities; (2) helpful to present and potential investors, creditors, and other users in assessing the amounts, timing, and uncertainty of future cash flows; and (3) about economic resources, the claims to those resources, and the changes in them.

The objectives, therefore, begin with a broad concern about information that is useful to investor and creditor decisions. That concern narrows to the investors' and creditors' interest in the prospect of receiving cash from their investments in, or loans to, business enterprises. Finally, the objectives focus on the financial statements that provide information useful in the assessment of prospective cash flows to the business enterprise, cash flows upon which investors and creditors depend.

In providing information to users of financial statements, the accounting profession relies on general-purpose financial statements. The intent of such statements is to provide the most useful information possible at minimal cost to various user groups. Underlying these objectives is the notion that users need reasonable knowledge of business and financial accounting matters to understand the information contained in financial statements. This point is important: It means that in the preparation of financial statements accountants can assume a level of reasonable competence; this has an impact on the way and the extent to which information is reported.

▶ SECOND LEVEL: FUNDAMENTAL CONCEPTS

The objectives (first level) are concerned with the goals and purposes of accounting. Later, we will discuss the ways these goals and purposes are implemented (third level). Between these two levels it is necessary to provide certain conceptual building blocks that explain the qualitative characteristics of accounting information and define the elements of financial statements. These conceptual building blocks form a bridge between the **why** of accounting (the objectives) and the **how** of accounting (recognition and measurement).

QUALITATIVE CHARACTERISTICS OF ACCOUNTING INFORMATION

How does one decide whether financial reports should provide information on how much a firm's assets cost to acquire (historical cost basis) or how much they are currently worth (current value basis)? Or how does one decide whether the three main companies that constitute Sears, Roebuck & Co.—Sears (the retailer), Allstate (the insurance company), and Dean Witter (the brokerage firm)—should be combined and shown as one company or disaggregated and reported as three separate companies for financial reporting purposes?

Choosing an acceptable accounting method, the amount and types of information to be disclosed, and the format in which information should be presented involves determining **which alternative provides the most useful information for decision making purposes (decision usefulness)**. The FASB has identified the **qualitative characteristics** of accounting information that distinguish better (more useful) information from inferior (less useful) information for decision making purposes.[5] In addition, the FASB has identified certain constraints (cost-benefit and materiality) as part of the conceptual framework; these are discussed later in the chapter. The characteristics may be viewed as a hierarchy, as shown in Illustration 2-2 below.

Decision Makers (Users) and Understandability

Decision makers vary widely in the types of decisions they make, the methods of decision making they employ, the information they already possess or can obtain from other sources, and their ability to process the information. For information to be useful, there must be a connection (linkage) between these users and the decisions they make. This link, **understandability**, is the quality of information that permits reasonably informed users to perceive its significance. To illustrate the importance of this linkage, assume that IBM Corp. issues a three-months' earnings report (interim report) that shows interim earnings way down. This report provides relevant and reliable information for decision making purposes. Some users, upon reading the report, decide to sell their stock. Other users do not understand the report's content and significance. They are surprised when IBM declares a smaller year-end dividend and the value of the stock declines. Thus, although the information presented was highly relevant and reliable, it was useless to users who did not understand it.

OBJECTIVE 4

Identify the qualitative characteristics of accounting information.

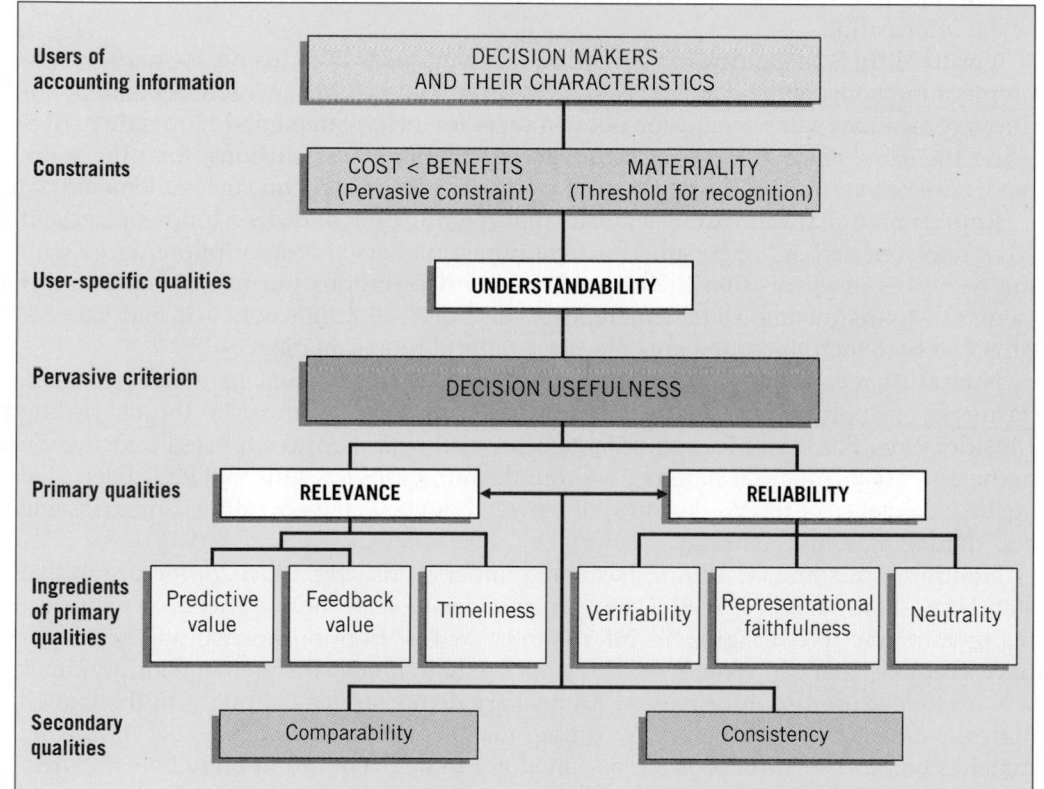

**ILLUSTRATION 2-2
A Hierarchy of
Accounting Qualities**

---

[5]"Qualitative Characteristics of Accounting Information," *Statement of Financial Accounting Concepts No. 2* (Stamford, Conn.: FASB, May 1980).

Primary Qualities: Relevance and Reliability

The FASB has indicated that **relevance and reliability are the two primary qualities that make accounting information useful for decision making.** As stated in FASB *Concepts Statement No. 2*, "the qualities that distinguish 'better' (more useful) information from 'inferior' (less useful) information are primarily the qualities of relevance and reliability, with some other characteristics that those qualities imply."[6]

Relevance

To be relevant, accounting information must be capable of making a difference in a decision.[7] If certain information has no bearing on a decision, it is irrelevant to that decision. Relevant information helps users make predictions about the ultimate outcome of past, present, and future events; that is, it has **predictive value**. Relevant information also helps users confirm or correct prior expectations; it has **feedback value**. For example, when IBM Corp. issues an interim report, this information is considered relevant because it provides a basis for forecasting annual earnings and provides feedback on past performance. For information to be relevant, it must also be available to decision makers before it loses its capacity to influence their decisions. Thus **timeliness** is a primary ingredient. If IBM Corp. did not report its interim results until six months after the end of the period, the information would be much less useful for decision making purposes. **For information to be relevant, it should have predictive or feedback value, and it must be presented on a timely basis.**

Reliability

Accounting information is reliable to the extent that **it is verifiable, is a faithful representation, and is reasonably free of error and bias.** Reliability is a necessity for individuals who have neither the time nor the expertise to evaluate the factual content of the information.

Verifiability is demonstrated when independent measurers, using the same measurement methods, obtain similar results. For example, would several independent auditors come to the same conclusion about a set of financial statements? If outside parties using the same measurement methods arrive at different conclusions, then the statements are not verifiable. Auditors could not render an opinion on such statements.

Representational faithfulness means that the numbers and descriptions represent what really existed or happened. The accounting numbers and descriptions agree with the resources or events that these numbers and descriptions purport to represent. If General Motors income statement reports sales of $150 billion when it had sales of $138.2 billion, then the statements are not a faithful representation.

Neutrality means that information cannot be selected to favor one set of interested parties over another. Factual, truthful, unbiased information must be the overriding consideration. For example, accountants cannot allow Exxon to suppress information in the notes to its financial statements about the numerous lawsuits that have been filed against it because of the Valdez oil spill—even though such disclosure is embarrassing and damaging to the company.

Neutrality in standard setting has come under increasing attack. Some argue that standards should not be issued if they cause undesirable economic effects on an industry or company. We disagree. Standards must be free from bias or we will no longer have credible financial statements. Without credible financial statements, individuals will no longer use this information. An analogy demonstrates the point: In the United States, we have both boxing and wrestling matches. Many individuals bet on boxing matches because such contests are assumed not to be fixed. But nobody bets on wrestling matches. Why? Because the public assumes that wrestling matches are rigged. If financial information is biased (rigged), the public will lose confidence and no longer use this information.

---

[6] Ibid., par. 15.

[7] Ibid., par. 47.

Secondary Qualities: Comparability and Consistency

Information about an enterprise is more useful if it can be compared with similar information about another enterprise **(comparability)** and with similar information about the same enterprise at other points in time **(consistency)**.[8]

Comparability

Information that has been measured and reported in a similar manner for different enterprises is considered comparable. Comparability enables users to identify the real similarities and differences in economic phenomena because these differences and similarities have not been obscured by the use of noncomparable accounting methods. For example, if Company A prepares its information on a historical cost basis, but Company B uses a price-level adjusted basis, it is more difficult to compare and evaluate the financial results of Companies A and B. Also, resource allocation decisions involve evaluations of alternatives; a valid evaluation can be made only if comparable information is available.

Consistency

When an entity applies the same accounting treatment to similar events, from period to period, the entity is considered to be consistent in its use of accounting standards. It does not mean that companies cannot switch from one method of accounting to another. Companies can change methods, but the changes are restricted to situations in which it can be demonstrated that the newly adopted method is preferable to the old. Then the nature and effect of the accounting change, as well as the justification for it, must be disclosed in the financial statements for the period in which the change is made.[9]

When there has been a change in accounting principles, the auditor refers to it in an explanatory paragraph of the audit report. This paragraph identifies the nature of the change and refers the reader to the note in the financial statements that discusses the change in detail.[10]

In summary, accounting reports for any given year are more useful if they can be compared with reports from other companies and with prior reports of the same entity. For example, if IBM is the only enterprise that prepares interim reports, the information is less useful because the user cannot relate it to interim reports for any other enterprise; that is, there is no comparability. Similarly, if the measurement methods used to prepare IBM's interim report change from one interim period to another, the information is considered less useful because the user cannot relate it to previous interim periods; that is, it lacks consistency.

BASIC ELEMENTS

An important aspect of developing any theoretical structure is the body of **elements** or definitions to be included in the structure. At present, accounting uses many terms that have peculiar and specific meanings. These terms constitute the language of business or the jargon of accounting.

OBJECTIVE 5
Define the basic elements of financial statements.

---

[8]As indicated in Chapter 1, the environment of accounting is continually changing; comparability and consistency are thereby made more difficult to achieve. Tax laws change, new industries (e.g., computer software) grow dramatically, new financial instruments (e.g., financial futures, collateral mortgage obligations, zero-coupon convertible bonds) are created, and mergers and divestitures occur frequently.

[9]The AICPA Special Committee on Financial Reporting noted that users highly value consistency. They note that a change tends to destroy the comparability of data before and after the change. Some companies take the time to assist users to understand the pre- and post-change data. Generally, however, users say they lose the ability to analyze over time.

[10]"Reports on Audited Financial Statements," *Statement on Auditing Standards No. 58* (New York: AICPA, April 1988), par. 34.

One such term is **asset.** Is it something we own? If the answer is yes, can we assume that any leased asset would not be shown on the balance sheet? Is an asset something we have the right to use, or is it anything of value used by the enterprise to generate revenues? If the answer is yes, then why should the management of the enterprise not be considered an asset? It seems necessary, therefore, to develop basic definitions for the elements of financial statements. *Concepts Statement No. 6* defines the ten interrelated elements that are most directly related to measuring the performance and financial status of an enterprise. We list them here for review and information purposes; you need not memorize these definitions at this point. Each of these elements will be explained and examined in more detail in subsequent chapters.

◀ ELEMENTS OF FINANCIAL STATEMENTS ▶

ASSETS. Probable future economic benefits obtained or controlled by a particular entity as a result of past transactions or events.

LIABILITIES. Probable future sacrifices of economic benefits arising from present obligations of a particular entity to transfer assets or provide services to other entities in the future as a result of past transactions or events.

EQUITY. Residual interest in the assets of an entity that remains after deducting its liabilities. In a business enterprise, the equity is the ownership interest.

INVESTMENTS BY OWNERS. Increases in net assets of a particular enterprise resulting from transfers to it from other entities of something of value to obtain or increase ownership interests (or equity) in it. Assets are most commonly received as investments by owners, but that which is received may also include services or satisfaction or conversion of liabilities of the enterprise.

DISTRIBUTIONS TO OWNERS. Decreases in net assets of a particular enterprise resulting from transferring assets, rendering services, or incurring liabilities by the enterprise to owners. Distributions to owners decrease ownership interests (or equity) in an enterprise.

COMPREHENSIVE INCOME. Change in equity (net assets) of an entity during a period from transactions and other events and circumstances from nonowner sources. It includes all changes in equity during a period except those resulting from investments by owners and distributions to owners.

REVENUES. Inflows or other enhancements of assets of an entity or settlement of its liabilities (or a combination of both) during a period from delivering or producing goods, rendering services, or other activities that constitute the entity's ongoing major or central operations.

EXPENSES. Outflows or other using up of assets or incurrences of liabilities (or a combination of both) during a period from delivering or producing goods, rendering services, or carrying out other activities that constitute the entity's ongoing major or central operations.

GAINS. Increases in equity (net assets) from peripheral or incidental transactions of an entity and from all other transactions and other events and circumstances affecting the entity during a period except those that result from revenues or investments by owners.

LOSSES. Decreases in equity (net assets) from peripheral or incidental transactions of an entity and from all other transactions and other events and circumstances affecting the entity during a period except those that result from expenses or distributions to owners.[11]

---

[11]"Elements of Financial Statements," *Statement of Financial Accounting Concepts No. 6* (Stamford, Conn.: FASB, December 1985), pp. ix and x.

Two important points should be noted about these definitions. First, the term **comprehensive income** represents a new concept. Comprehensive income is more inclusive than the traditional notion of net income; if the FASB's definition is taken literally, it includes net income and all other changes in equity exclusive of owners' investments and distributions. For example, prior period adjustments (transactions that relate to previous periods, such as corrections of errors), which are currently excluded from net income, may be included under comprehensive income. Comprehensive income, therefore, is a very broad concept that gives the FASB flexibility in defining some intermediate components of this amount. This concept is not yet being applied in practice.

Second, the FASB classifies the elements into two distinct groups. The first group of three elements—assets, liabilities, and equity—describes amounts of resources and claims to resources at a **moment in time.** The other seven elements (comprehensive income and its components—revenues, expenses, gains, and losses—as well as investments by owners and distributions to owners) describe transactions, events, and circumstances that affect an enterprise during a **period of time.** The first class—assets, liabilities, and equity—is changed by elements of the second class and at any time is the cumulative result of all changes. This interaction is referred to as "articulation." That is, key figures in one statement correspond to balances in another.

▶ THIRD LEVEL: RECOGNITION AND MEASUREMENT CONCEPTS

The third level of the framework consists of concepts that implement the basic objectives of level one. These concepts explain which, when, and how financial elements and events should be recognized, measured, and reported by the accounting system. Most of them are set forth in FASB *Statement of Financial Accounting Concepts No. 5*, "Recognition and Measurement in Financial Statements of Business Enterprises." According to *SFAC No. 5*, to be recognized, an item (event or transaction) must meet the definition of an "element of financial statements" as defined in *SFAC No. 6* and must be measurable. Most aspects of current practice are consistent with this recognition and measurement concept.

The accounting profession continues to use the concepts in *SFAC No. 5* as operational guidelines. For discussion purposes, we have chosen to identify the concepts as basic assumptions, principles, and constraints. Not everyone uses this classification system, so it is best to focus your attention more on **understanding the concepts** than on how they are classified and organized. These concepts serve as guidelines in developing rational responses to controversial financial reporting issues. They have evolved over time and are fundamental to the specific accounting principles issued by the FASB and its predecessor organizations.

BASIC ASSUMPTIONS

Four basic **assumptions** underlie the financial accounting structure: (1) **economic entity,** (2) **going concern,** (3) **monetary unit,** and (4) **periodicity.**

OBJECTIVE 6

Describe the basic assumptions of accounting.

Economic Entity Assumption

The economic entity assumption means that economic activity can be identified with a particular unit of accountability. In other words, the activity of a business enterprise can be kept separate and distinct from its owners and any other business unit.[12] For

---

[12]Surprisingly, such a distinction is not always made in practice. A *Wall Street Journal* article, for example, noted that audit committees of six publicly held companies wanted their chief executive to reimburse the companies an additional $1 million in personal expenses for such items as company yachts, speedboats, refurbishing, and rent money on personal apartments. "Posners Asked to Repay Firms $1.1 Million More" (*Wall Street Journal*, November 27, 1978), p. 6.

example, if the activities and elements of General Motors could not be distinguished from those of Ford or Chrysler, then it would be impossible to know that Ford financially outperformed the other two in recent years. If there were no meaningful way to separate all of the economic events that occur, no basis for accounting would exist.

The entity concept does not apply solely to the segregation of activities among given business enterprises. An individual, a department or division, or an entire industry could be considered a separate entity if we chose to define the unit in such a manner. Thus, **the entity concept does not necessarily refer to a legal entity.** A parent and its subsidiaries are separate **legal** entities, but merging their activities for accounting and reporting purposes does not violate the **economic entity** assumption.

Going Concern Assumption

Most accounting methods are based on the **going concern assumption—that the business enterprise will have a long life.** Experience indicates that, in spite of numerous business failures, companies have a fairly high continuance rate. Although accountants do not believe that business firms will last indefinitely, they do expect them to last long enough to fulfill their objectives and commitments.

The implications of this assumption are profound. The historical cost principle would be of limited usefulness if eventual liquidation were assumed. Under a liquidation approach, for example, asset values are better stated at net realizable value (sales price less costs of disposal) than at acquisition cost. **Depreciation and amortization policies are justifiable and appropriate only if we assume some permanence to the enterprise.** If a liquidation approach were adopted, the current-noncurrent classification of assets and liabilities would lose much of its significance. Labeling anything a fixed or long-term asset would be difficult to justify. Indeed, listing liabilities on the basis of priority in liquidation would be more reasonable.

The going concern assumption applies in most business situations. **Only where liquidation appears imminent is the assumption inapplicable.** In these cases a total revaluation of assets and liabilities can provide information that closely approximates the entity's net realizable value. Accounting problems related to an enterprise in liquidation are presented in advanced accounting courses.

Monetary Unit Assumption

The **monetary unit assumption** means that money is the common denominator of economic activity and provides an appropriate basis for accounting measurement and analysis. This assumption implies that the monetary unit is the most effective means of expressing to interested parties changes in capital and exchanges of goods and services. **The monetary unit is relevant, simple, universally available, understandable, and useful.** Application of this assumption depends on the even more basic assumption that quantitative data are useful in communicating economic information and in making rational economic decisions.

In the United States, accountants have chosen generally to ignore the phenomenon of price-level change (inflation and deflation) by assuming that **the unit of measure—the dollar—remains reasonably stable.** This assumption about the monetary unit has traditionally been used by accountants to justify adding 1968 dollars to 1995 dollars without any adjustment. The FASB in *SFAC No. 5* indicated that it expects the dollar, unadjusted for inflation or deflation, to continue to be used to measure items recognized in financial statements. Only if circumstances change dramatically (such as if the United States were to experience high inflation similar to that in many South American countries) will the Board again consider "inflation accounting."

Periodicity Assumption

The most accurate way to measure the results of enterprise activity would be to measure them at the time of the enterprise's eventual liquidation. Business, government, investors, and various other user groups, however, cannot wait that long for such information. Users need to be apprised of performance and economic status on a timely basis so that they can evaluate and compare firms. Therefore, accountants must report periodically.

The **periodicity (or time period) assumption** simply implies that the economic activities of an enterprise can be divided into artificial time periods. These time periods vary, but the most common are monthly, quarterly, and yearly.

The shorter the time period, the more difficult it becomes to determine the proper net income for the period. A month's results are usually less reliable than a quarter's results, and a quarter's results are likely to be less reliable than a year's results. Investors desire and demand that information be quickly processed and disseminated; yet the quicker the information is released, the more it is subject to error. This phenomenon provides an interesting example of the trade-off between relevance and reliability in preparing financial data.

BASIC PRINCIPLES OF ACCOUNTING

Four basic **principles of accounting** are used to record transactions: (1) **historical cost,** (2) **revenue recognition,** (3) **matching,** and (4) **full disclosure.**

Historical Cost Principle

GAAP requires that most assets and liabilities be accounted for and reported on the basis of acquisition price. This is often referred to as the **historical cost principle.**

Cost has an important advantage over other valuations: it is reliable. To illustrate the importance of this advantage, consider the problems that would arise if we adopted some other basis for keeping records. If we were to select current selling price, for instance, we might have a difficult time in attempting to establish a sales value for a given item without selling it. Every member of the accounting department might have a different opinion regarding an asset's value, and management might desire still another figure. And how often would it be necessary to establish sales value? All companies close their accounts at least annually, and some compute their net income every month. These companies would find it necessary to place a sales value on every asset each time they wished to determine income—a laborious task and one that would result in a figure of net income materially affected by opinion. Similar objections have been leveled against current cost (replacement cost, present value of future cash flows) and any other basis of valuation *except cost.*

However, the question "What is cost?" is not always easy to answer. If fixed assets are to be carried in the accounts at cost, are cash discounts to be deducted in determining cost? Does cost include freight and insurance? Does it include cost of installation as well as the cost of the machine itself? Certain assets may be acquired by the issuance of the capital stock of the acquiring company, or they may be exchanged for similar or dissimilar assets. If no money price is stated in the transaction, how is cost to be established? These questions are answered in later chapters; they are raised here to point out some of the difficulties regularly encountered in determining costs.

What about liabilities? Are they accounted for on a cost basis? Yes, they are. **If we convert the term "cost" to "exchange price," we find that it applies to liabilities as well.** Liabilities, such as bonds, notes, and accounts payable, are issued by a business enterprise in exchange for assets, or perhaps services, upon which an agreed price has usually been placed. This price, established by the exchange transaction, is the "cost" of the liability and provides the figure at which it should be recorded in the accounts and reported in financial statements.

A recent survey of users by the AICPA's Special Committee on Financial Reporting appears to support the historical cost principle in most situations. Users indicated that historical cost provides them with a stable and consistent benchmark that they can rely on to establish historical trends. They are concerned about the subjectivity and potential volatility in reported results of a model based on some type of current value.

Users also reported that they found fair value information useful for particular types of assets and liabilities and in certain types of industries. This result is not surprising

OBJECTIVE 7

Explain the application of the basic principles of accounting.

INTERNATIONAL INSIGHT

In the Netherlands, assets may be revalued at their replacement value. In fact, only one large Dutch company still revalues its assets—Heineken.

because certain assets and liabilities are already reported at current values either in the financial statements or related notes. For example, most investments in debt and equity securities are currently reported at fair value, receivables are reported at net realizable value, and inventories are reported at the lower of cost or market (usually replacement cost). At this time, certain industries such as brokerage houses and mutual funds, prepare their basic financial statements on a fair value basis.

Another concern expressed regarding the cost basis arises during a period when prices are changing substantially. At such times cost is said to "go out of date" almost as soon as it is recorded. In a period of rising or falling prices, the cost figures of the preceding years are viewed as not comparable with current cost figures. For example, assuming a rate of inflation of 8% per year, a McDonald's "quarter-pounder with cheese," which costs $1.85 today, will cost approximately $40.20 in 40 years. Chapter 26 discusses the accounting problems and benefits of reporting price-level adjusted information.

INTERNATIONAL INSIGHT

Due to their experiences with persistent inflation, South American countries do not adhere to the historical cost principle. Rather, they adjust their financial reports for inflation.

Revenue Recognition Principle

A crucial question for many enterprises is when revenue should be recognized. Revenue is generally recognized when (1) **realized** or **realizable** and (2) **earned.** This approach has often been referred to as the **revenue recognition principle**. Revenues are **realized** when products (goods or services), merchandise, or other assets are exchanged for cash or claims to cash. Revenues are **realizable** when assets received or held are readily convertible into cash or claims to cash. Assets are readily convertible when they are salable or interchangeable in an active market at readily determinable prices without significant additional cost.

In addition to the first test (realized or realizable), revenues are not recognized until earned. And revenues are considered **earned** when the entity has substantially accomplished what it must do to be entitled to the benefits represented by the revenues.[13]

Generally, an objective test—confirmation by a sale to independent interests—is used to indicate the point at which revenue is recognized. Usually, only at the date of sale is there an objective and verifiable measure of revenue—the sales price. Any basis for revenue recognition short of actual sale opens the door to wide variations in practice. To give accounting reports uniform meaning, a rule of revenue recognition comparable to the cost rule for asset valuation is essential. **Recognition at the time of sale provides a uniform and reasonable test.**

There are, however, exceptions to the rule, and at times the basic rule is difficult to apply.

During Production

Recognition of revenue is allowed before the contract is completed in certain long-term construction contracts. The main feature of this method is that revenue is recognized periodically based on the percentage that the job has been completed instead of waiting until the entire job has been finished. Although technically a transfer of ownership has not occurred, the earning process is considered substantially completed at various stages as construction progresses. Naturally, if it is not possible to obtain dependable estimates of cost and progress, then the accountant should wait and record the revenue at the completion date.

---

[13]"Recognition and Measurement in Financial Statements of Business Enterprises," *Statement of Financial Accounting Concepts No. 5* (Stamford, Conn.: FASB, December 1984), par. 83(a) and (b).

End of Production

At times, **revenue might be recognized after the production cycle has ended but before the sale takes place.** This is the case where the selling price is certain as well as the amount. For instance, if products or other assets are salable in an active market at readily determinable prices without significant additional cost, then revenue can be recognized at the completion of production. An example would be the mining of certain minerals for which, once the mineral is mined, a ready market at a standard price exists. The same holds true for some artificial price supports set by the government in establishing agricultural prices.

Receipt of Cash

Receipt of cash is another basis for revenue recognition. The cash basis approach should be used only when it is impossible to establish the revenue figure at the time of sale because of the uncertainty of collection. One form of the cash basis is the installment sales method where payment is required in periodic installments over a long period of time. Its most common use is in the retail field. Farm and home equipment and furnishings are typically sold on an installment basis. The installment method is frequently justified on the basis that the risk of not collecting an account receivable is so great that the sale is not sufficient evidence for recognition to take place. In some instances, this reasoning may be valid. Generally, though, if a sale has been completed, it should be recognized; if bad debts are expected, they should be recorded as separate estimates.

Revenue, then, is recorded in the period when realized or realizable and earned. Normally, this is the date of sale. But circumstances may dictate application of the percentage-of-completion approach, the end-of-production approach, or the receipt-of-cash approach.

Conceptually, the proper accounting treatment for revenue recognition should be apparent and should fit nicely into one of the conditions mentioned above, but often it does not. For example, how should motion picture companies such as Metro-Goldwyn-Mayer, Inc., Warner Bros., and United Artists account for the sale of rights to show motion picture films on ABC, CBS, or NBC? Should the revenue from the sale of the rights be reported when the contract is signed, when the motion picture film is delivered to the network, when the cash payment is received by the motion picture company, or when the film is shown on television? The question of revenue recognition is complicated further since the TV networks are often restricted to the number of times the film may be shown and over what period of time.

For example, Metro-Goldwyn-Mayer Film Co. (MGM) sold CBS the rights to show *Gone With the Wind* for $35 million. CBS received the right to show this classic movie 20 times over a 20-year period. MGM argued that the right to show *Gone With the Wind* 20 times over a 20-year period was a significant contract restriction and, therefore, revenue recognition should coincide with the showings. The accounting profession on the other hand argued that when (1) the sales price and cost of each film are known, (2) collectibility is assured, and (3) the film is available and accepted by the network, revenue recognition should occur immediately. The restriction that *Gone With the Wind* be shown only once a year for 20 years was not considered significant enough or appropriate justification for deferring revenue recognition. It is interesting to note that MGM, in the appropriate first quarter, reported essentially the entire $35 million in revenue in one period as the following headline in *The Wall Street Journal* reported, "MGM's Net Tripled in the First Quarter that Ended Nov. 30."

As you can see, timing revenue recognition is no simple matter. The most straightforward approach is to recognize revenue at the point of sale. Most uncertainties have usually been resolved by that time. And verifiable evidence, obtained through an exchange transaction, is available.

Matching Principle

In recognizing expenses, accountants attempt to follow the approach of "let the expense follow the revenues." Expenses are recognized not when wages are paid, or when the work is performed, or when a product is produced, but when the work (service) or the product actually makes its contribution to revenue. Thus, expense recognition is tied to revenue recognition. This practice is referred to as the **matching principle** because it dictates that **efforts (expenses) be matched with accomplishment (revenues) whenever it is reasonable and practicable to do so.**

For those costs for which it is difficult to adopt some type of rational association with revenue, some other approach must be developed. Often, the accountant must develop a "rational and systematic" allocation policy that will approximate the matching principle. This type of expense recognition pattern involves assumptions about the benefits that are being received as well as the cost associated with those benefits. The cost of a long-lived asset, for example, must be allocated over all of the accounting periods during which the asset is used because the asset contributes to the generation of revenue throughout its useful life.

Some costs are charged to the current period as expenses (or losses) simply because no connection with revenue can be determined. Examples of these types of costs are officers' salaries and other administrative expenses.

Summarizing, we might say that costs are analyzed to determine whether a relationship exists with revenue. Where this association holds, the costs are expensed and matched against the revenue in the period when the revenue is recognized. If no connection appears between costs and revenues, an allocation of cost on some systematic and rational basis might be appropriate. Where this method does not seem desirable, the cost may be expensed immediately.

Costs are generally classified into two groups: **product costs and period costs. Product costs** such as material, labor, and overhead attach to the product and are carried into future periods if the revenue from the product is recognized in subsequent periods. **Period costs** such as officers' salaries and other administrative expenses are charged off immediately, even though benefits associated with these costs occur in the future, because no direct relationship between cost and revenue can be determined.

The problem of expense recognition is as complex as that of revenue recognition. For example, at one time a large oil company spent a considerable amount of money in an introductory advertising campaign in Hawaii. The company obviously hoped that this advertising campaign would attract new customers and develop brand loyalty. Over how many years, if any, should this outlay be expensed?

For another example, Stars To Go, a major video rental company, writes off the cost of its video tapes over 3 years, 36% the first year, 36% the second, and 28% the third. Other video rental companies take a more conservative approach. They note that Class A titles (hits such as *Jurassic Park* or *Schindler's List*) average 28 rentals the first 3 months, 12 rentals the next 3 months, 12 more in the next 6 months, and 18 over the next year. As a result, they charge off these tapes in one year, or perhaps 2 years at most. As an executive of one of the major video rental companies noted, "If you ask 12 different people the useful life of a video tape, you get 12 different answers."

The conceptual validity of the matching principle has been a subject of debate. A major concern is that matching permits certain costs to be deferred and treated as assets on the balance sheet when in fact these costs may not have future benefits. If abused, this principle permits the balance sheet to become a "dumping ground" for unmatched costs. In addition, there appears to be no objective definition of "systematic and rational." For example, Hartwig, Inc. purchased an asset for $100,000 that will last 5 years. Various depreciation methods (all considered systematic and rational) might be used to allocate this cost over the 5-year period. What objective criteria should guide the accountant in determining what portion of the cost of the asset should be written off each period?[14]

Full Disclosure Principle

In deciding what information to report, accountants follow the general practice of providing information that is of sufficient importance to influence the judgment and decisions of an informed user. Often referred to as the **full disclosure principle**, it recognizes that the nature and amount of information included in financial reports reflects a series of judgmental trade-offs. These trade-offs strive for (1) sufficient detail to disclose matters that **make a difference** to users, yet (2) sufficient condensation to make the **information understandable**, keeping in mind costs of preparing and using it. The accountant can place information about financial position, income, cash flows, and investments in one of three places: (1) within the main body of financial statements, (2) in the notes to those statements, or (3) as supplementary information.

The **financial statements** are a formalized, structured means of communicating financial information. To be recognized in the main body of financial statements, **an item should meet the definition of a basic element, be measurable with sufficient certainty, and be relevant and reliable.**[15] Generally, the most useful information about assets, liabilities, revenues, expenses, and other items on financial statements and their measures (information with the best combination of relevance and reliability) should be recognized in the financial statements. The item must have been measured, recorded in the books, and passed through the double-entry system of accounting.

The **notes to financial statements** generally amplify or explain the items presented in the main body of the statements. If the information in the main body of the financial statements gives an incomplete picture of the performance and position of the enterprise, additional information that is needed to complete the picture should be included in the notes. Information in the notes does not have to be quantifiable, nor does it need to qualify as an element. Notes can be partially or totally narrative. Examples of notes are: descriptions of the accounting policies and methods used in measuring the elements reported in the statements; explanations of uncertainties and contingencies; and statistics and details too voluminous for inclusion in the statements. The notes are not only helpful but also essential to understanding the enterprise's performance and position.

Supplementary information may include details or amounts that present a different perspective from that adopted in the financial statements. It may be quantifiable information that is high in relevance but low in reliability, or information that is helpful but not essential. One example of supplementary information is the data and schedules provided by oil and gas companies: Typically they provide information on proven reserves as well as the related discounted cash flows.

Supplementary information may also include management's explanation of the financial information and its discussion of the significance of that information. For example, during the past decade many business combinations have produced innumerable conglomerate-type business organizations and financing arrangements that demand new and peculiar accounting and reporting practices and principles. In each of these situations, the accountant is faced with the problem of making sure that enough information is presented to ensure that the **reasonably prudent investor** will not be misled.

---

[14]Some would suggest that even that procedure is well nigh impossible, given that the revenue flow from any given asset is interrelated with the remaining asset structure of the enterprise. For example, see Arthur L. Thomas, "The Allocation Problem in Financial Accounting Theory," *Studies in Accounting Research No. 3* (Evanston, Ill.: American Accounting Association, 1969), and "The Allocation Problem: Part Two," *Studies in Accounting Research No. 9* (Sarasota, Fla.: American Accounting Association, 1974).

[15]*SFAC No. 5*, par. 63.

A classic illustration of the problem of determining adequate disclosure guidelines is the recent question on what banks should disclose about loans made for highly leveraged transactions such as leveraged buyouts. Investors want to know the percentage of a bank's loans that are of this risky type. The problem is what do we mean by "leveraged"? As one regulator noted: "If it looks leveraged, it probably is leveraged, but most of us would be hard-pressed to come up with a definition." Is a loan to a company with a debt to equity ratio of 4 to 1 highly leveraged? Or is 8 to 1 or 10 to 1 high leverage? The problem is complicated because some highly leveraged companies have cash flows that cover interest payments; therefore, they are not as risky as they might appear. In short, providing the appropriate disclosure to help investors and regulators differentiate risky from safe is difficult.

The content, arrangement, and display of financial statements, along with other facets of full disclosure, are discussed in Chapters 4, 5, 24, and 26.

CONSTRAINTS

OBJECTIVE 8

Describe the impact that constraints have on reporting accounting information.

In providing information with the qualitative characteristics that make it useful, two overriding **constraints** must be considered: (1) the **cost-benefit relationship** and (2) **materiality.** Two other less dominant yet important constraints that are part of the reporting environment are **industry practices** and **conservatism.**

Cost-Benefit Relationship

Too often, users assume that information is a cost-free commodity. But preparers and providers of accounting information know that it is not. Therefore, the **cost-benefit relationship** must be considered: The costs of providing the information must be weighed against the benefits that can be derived from using the information. Obviously the benefits should exceed the costs. Practicing accountants have traditionally applied this constraint through the notions of "expediency" ("it is or is not expedient") or "practicality" ("it is or is not practical"), but only recently have standard setting bodies and governmental agencies resorted to cost-benefit analysis before making their informational requirements final. In order to justify requiring a particular measurement or disclosure, the benefits perceived to be derived from it must exceed the costs perceived to be associated with it.

The following remark, made by a corporate executive about a proposed standard, was addressed to the FASB: "In all my years in the financial arena, I have never seen such an absolutely ridiculous proposal. . . . To dignify these 'actuarial' estimates by recording them as assets and liabilities would be virtually unthinkable except for the fact that the FASB has done equally stupid things in the past. . . . For God's sake, use common sense just this once."[16] Although this remark is extreme, it does indicate the frustration expressed by members of the business community about standard setting and whether the benefits of a given standard exceed the costs.

The difficulty in cost-benefit analysis is that the costs and especially the benefits are not always evident or measurable. The costs are of several kinds, including costs of collecting and processing, costs of disseminating, costs of auditing, costs of potential litigation, costs of disclosure to competitors, and costs of analysis and interpretation. Benefits accrue to preparers (in terms of greater management control and access to capital) and to users (in terms of allocation of resources, tax assessment, and rate regulation). But benefits are generally more difficult to quantify than are costs.

The FASB has attempted to address this issue. Included in its recent standard on Employers' Accounting for Postretirement Benefits Other Than Pensions is a section justifying the new rules on a cost-benefit basis. This special section was provided in response to criticisms received from the business community. As a FASB representative

---

[16]"Decision-Usefulness: The Overriding Objective," *FASB Viewpoints*, October 19, 1983, p. 4.

noted: "We may very well include such cost-benefit sections in future statements [rules], but we want to be sure they aren't just boilerplate and address each rule's specific costs and benefits."

Most recently, the AICPA Special Committee on Financial Reporting submitted the following **constraints to limit the costs of reporting:**

a. Business reporting should exclude information outside of management's expertise or for which management is not the best source, such as information about competitors.

b. Management should not be required to report information that would significantly harm the company's competitive position.

c. Management should not be required to provide forecasted financial statements. Rather, management should provide information that helps users forecast for themselves the company's financial future.

d. Other than for financial statements, management need only report the information it knows. That is, management should be under no obligation to gather information it does not have, or need, to manage the business.

e. Certain elements of business reporting should be presented only if users and management agree they should be reported—a concept of flexible reporting.

f. Companies should not have to expand reporting of forward-looking information until there are more effective deterrents to unwarranted litigation that discourages companies from doing so.

Materiality

The constraint of **materiality** relates to an item's impact on a firm's overall financial operations. An item is material if its inclusion or omission would influence or change the judgment of a reasonable person.[17] It is immaterial and, therefore, irrelevant if it would have no impact on a decision maker. In short, **it must make a difference** or it need not be disclosed. The point involved here is one of **relative size and importance.** If the amount involved is significant when compared with the other revenues and expenses, assets and liabilities, or net income of the entity, sound and acceptable standards should be followed. If the amount is so small that it is quite unimportant when compared with other items, application of a particular standard may be considered of less importance. It is difficult to provide firm guides in judging when a given item is or is not material because materiality varies both with relative amount and with relative importance. For example, the two sets of numbers presented below illustrate relative size.

	Company A	Company B
Sales	$10,000,000	$100,000
Costs and expenses	9,000,000	90,000
Income from operations	$ 1,000,000	$ 10,000
Unusual gain	$ 20,000	$ 5,000

---

[17]*SFAC No. 2* (par. 132) sets forth the essence of materiality: "The omission or misstatement of an item in a financial report is material if, in the light of surrounding circumstances, the magnitude of the item is such that it is probable that the judgement of a reasonable person relying upon the report would have been changed or influenced by the inclusion or correction of the item." This same concept of materiality has been adopted by the auditing profession. See "Audit Risk and Materiality in Conducting an Audit," *Statement on Auditing Standards No. 47* (New York: AICPA, 1983), par. 6.

During the period in question, the revenues and expenses and, therefore, the net incomes of Company A and Company B have been proportional. Each has had an unusual gain. In looking at the abbreviated income figures for Company A, it does not appear significant whether the amount of the unusual gain is set out separately or merged with the regular operating income. It is only 2% of the net income and, if merged, would not seriously distort the net income figure. Company B has had an unusual gain of only $5,000, but it is relatively much more significant than the larger gain realized by A. For Company B, an item of $5,000 amounts to 50% of its net income. Obviously, the inclusion of such an item in ordinary operating income would affect the amount of that income materially. Thus we see the importance of the **relative size** of an item in determining its materiality.

The **nature of the item may also be important.** For example, if a company is involved in a violation of a statute (Foreign Corrupt Practices Act or one of the antitrust laws), the amounts involved should be separately disclosed. Or, a $100,000 misclassification within the noncurrent section may not be considered material; but a $100,000 misclassification if it affects the current section instead of the noncurrent section may be material.

The application of the materiality constraint can be controversial. As an example, General Dynamics disclosed that at one time its Resources Group had improved its earnings by $5.8 million at the same time that its Stromberg Datagraphix subsidiary had taken writeoffs of $6.7 million. Although both numbers were far larger than the $2.5 million that General Dynamics as a whole earned for the year, neither was disclosed as an unusual or nonrecurring item in the annual report; apparently the net effect on net income was not considered material. It seems clear that General Dynamics should have disclosed each item separately since the Stromberg writeoff appeared to be a one-time charge, whereas the improvement in its Resources Group may have been ongoing.

In another case, GAC's first quarter earnings rose from 76 cents to 77 cents a share. Nowhere did the annual report disclose that a favorable tax carryforward of 4 cents a share prevented GAC's earnings from sliding to 73 cents a share. The company took the position that this carryforward should not be shown as an extraordinary item because it was not material (6%). As one executive noted, "You know that accountants have a rule of thumb which says that anything under 10% is not material." Of course, the executive's statement seems ill-advised. The firm should have considered it significant that the direction of the company's earnings was completely altered—even though 4 cents is a small amount. This information would have been of considerable importance to investors.

Materiality is a factor in a great many internal accounting decisions, too. The amount of classification required in a subsidiary expense ledger, the degree of accuracy required in prorating expenses among the departments of a business, and the extent to which adjustments should be made for accrued and deferred items, are examples of judgments that should finally be determined on a basis of reasonableness and practicability, which is the materiality constraint sensibly applied. Only by **the exercise of good judgment and professional expertise** can the accountant arrive at answers that are reasonable and appropriate.[18]

---

[18]A search for a definition of materiality based upon interpretations by the courts in cases under the securities laws reveals differing concepts of materiality; see Kenneth R. Jeffries, "Materiality as Defined by the Courts," *The CPA Journal* (October 1981), pp. 13–17. The point was recently reinforced in a Supreme Court ruling on the question of whether a company has to disclose merger talks prior to the completion of the talks (*Combustion Engineering* v. *Basic Research*). Justice Blackmun noted that materiality depends on the significance the reasonable investor would place on the withheld or misrepresented information. When the event is uncertain, such as a pending merger, materiality depends on both the importance of the event if it does transpire and the probability that the deal will be completed.

Industry Practices

Another practical consideration is **industry practices.** <u>The peculiar nature of some industries and business concerns</u> sometimes requires departure from basic theory. In the public utility industry, noncurrent assets are reported first on the balance sheet to highlight the industry's capital-intensive nature. Agricultural crops are often reported at market value because it is costly to develop accurate cost figures on individual crops. Such variations from basic theory are not many, yet they do exist. Whenever we find what appears to be a violation of basic accounting theory, we should determine whether it is explained by some peculiar feature of the type of business involved before we criticize the procedures followed.

Conservatism

Few conventions in accounting are as misunderstood as the constraint of conservatism. **Conservatism** means <u>when in doubt choose the solution that will be least likely to overstate assets and income.</u> Note that there is nothing in the conservatism convention urging the accountant to *understate* assets or income. Unfortunately it has been interpreted by some accountants to mean just that. All that conservatism does, properly applied, is to give the accountant a guide in difficult situations, and then the guide is a very reasonable one: refrain from overstatement of net income and net assets. Ex-

INTERNATIONAL INSIGHT

In Japan, capital is also provided by very large banks. Assets are often undervalued and liabilities overvalued. These practices reduce the demand for dividends and protect creditors in event of a default.

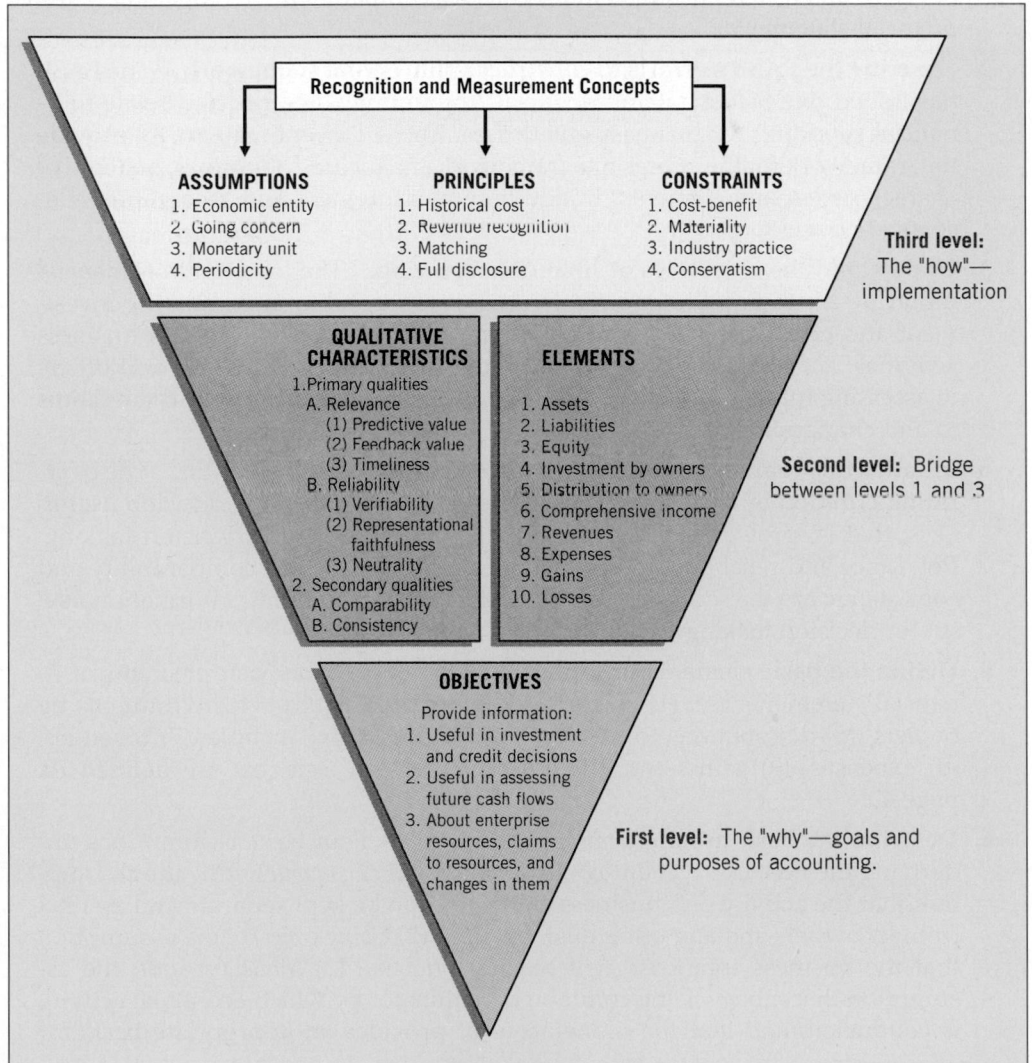

ILLUSTRATION 2-3 Conceptual Framework for Financial Reporting

amples of conservatism in accounting are the use of the lower of cost or market approach in valuing inventories and the rule that accrued net losses should be recognized on firm purchase commitments for goods for inventory. If the issue is in doubt, it is better to understate than overstate net income and net assets. Of course, if there is no doubt, there is no need to apply this constraint.

SUMMARY OF THE STRUCTURE

Illustration 2-3 presents the conceptual framework discussed in this chapter. It is similar to Illustration 2-1, except that it provides additional information for each level. We cannot overemphasize the usefulness of this conceptual framework in helping to understand many of the problem areas that are examined in subsequent chapters.

► SUMMARY OF LEARNING OBJECTIVES ◄

1. **Describe the usefulness of a conceptual framework.** A conceptual framework is needed to (1) build on and relate to an established body of concepts and objectives, (2) provide a framework for solving new and emerging practical problems, (3) increase financial statement users' understanding of and confidence in financial reporting, and (4) enhance comparability among companies' financial statements.

2. **Describe the FASB's efforts to construct a conceptual framework.** The FASB has issued five Statements of Financial Accounting Concepts that relate to financial reporting for business enterprises. These concept statements provide the framework for the conceptual framework and include objectives, qualitative characteristics, and elements. In addition, measurement and recognition concepts are developed.

3. **Understand the objectives of financial reporting.** The objectives of financial reporting are to provide information that is (1) useful to those making investment and credit decisions who have a reasonable understanding of business activities; (2) helpful to present and potential investors, creditors, and others in assessing future cash flows; and (3) about economic resources and the claims to and changes in them.

4. **Identify the qualitative characteristics of accounting information.** The overriding criterion by which accounting choices can be judged is decision usefulness; that is, providing information that is most useful for decision making. Relevance and reliability are the two primary qualities and comparability and consistency are the secondary qualities that make accounting information useful for decision making.

5. **Define the basic elements of financial statements.** The basic elements of financial statements are: (1) assets, (2) liabilities, (3) equity, (4) investments by owners, (5) distributions to owners, (6) comprehensive income, (7) revenues, (8) expenses, (9) gains, and (10) losses. These ten elements are defined on page 40.

6. **Describe the basic assumptions of accounting.** Four basic assumptions underlying the financial accounting structure are: (1) *Economic entity:* the assumption that the activity of a business enterprise can be kept separate and distinct from its owners and any other business unit. (2) *Going concern:* the assumption that the business enterprise will have a long life. (3) *Monetary unit:* the assumption that money is the common denominator by which economic activity is conducted, and that the monetary unit provides an appropriate basis for

measurement and analysis. (4) *Periodicity:* the assumption that the economic activities of an enterprise can be divided into artificial time periods.

7. **Explain the application of the basic principles of accounting.** (1) *Historical cost principle:* Existing GAAP requires that most assets and liabilities be accounted for and reported on the basis of acquisition price. (2) *Revenue recognition:* Revenue is generally recognized when (a) realized or realizable and (b) earned. (3) *Matching principle:* Expenses are recognized when the work (service) or the product actually makes its contribution to revenue. (4) *Full disclosure principle:* Accountants follow the general practice of providing information that is of sufficient importance to influence the judgment and decisions of an informed user.

8. **Describe the impact that constraints have on reporting accounting information.** The constraints and their impact are: (1) *Cost-benefit relationship:* The costs of providing the information must be weighed against the benefits that can be derived from using the information. (2) *Materiality:* Sound and acceptable standards should be followed if the amount involved is significant when compared with the other revenues and expenses, assets and liabilities, or net income of the entity. (3) *Industry practices:* Follow the general practices in the firm's industry, which sometimes requires departure from basic theory. (4) *Conservatism:* When in doubt, choose the solution that will be least likely to overstate assets and income.

qualitative characteristics, 37

realizable (revenue), 44

realized (revenue), 44

relevance, 38

reliability, 38

representational faithfulness, 38

revenue recognition principle, 44

supplementary information, 47

timeliness, 38

understandability, 37

verifiability, 38

QUESTIONS

1. What is a conceptual framework? Why is a conceptual framework necessary in financial accounting?

2. What are the primary objectives of financial reporting as indicated in *Statement of Financial Accounting Concepts No. 1?*

3. What is meant by the term "qualitative characteristics of accounting information"?

4. Briefly describe the two primary qualities of useful accounting information.

5. What is the distinction between comparability and consistency?

6. Discuss whether the changes described in each of the cases below require recognition in the CPA's report as to consistency (assume that the amounts are material).
   (a) After 3 years of computing depreciation under an accelerated method for income tax purposes and under the straight-line method for reporting purposes, the company adopted an accelerated method for reporting purposes.
   (b) The company disposed of one of the two subsidiaries that had been included in its consolidated statements for prior years.
   (c) The estimated remaining useful life of plant property was reduced because of obsolescence.
   (d) The company is using an inventory valuation method that is different from all those used by other companies in its industry.

7. Why is it necessary to develop a definitional framework for the basic elements of accounting?

8. Expenses, losses, and distributions to owners are all decreases in net assets. What are the distinctions among them?

9. Revenues, gains, and investments by owners are all increases in net assets. What are the distinctions among them?

10. What are the four basic assumptions that underlie the financial accounting structure?

11. If the going concern assumption is not made in accounting, what difference does it make in the amounts shown in the financial statements for the following items?
    (a) Land.
    (b) Unamortized bond premium.
    (c) Depreciation expense on equipment.

(d) Long-term investments in common stocks of other companies.
(e) Merchandise inventory.
(f) Prepaid insurance.

12. The life of a business is divided into specific time periods, usually a year, to measure results of operations for each such time period and to portray financial conditions at the end of each period.
(a) This practice is based on the accounting assumption that the life of the business consists of a series of time periods and that it is possible to measure accurately the results of operations for each period. Comment on the validity and necessity of this assumption.
(b) What has been the effect of this practice on accounting? What is its relation to the accrual system? What influence has it had on accounting entries and methodology?

13. What is the basic accounting problem created by the monetary unit assumption when there is significant inflation? What appears to be the FASB position on a stable monetary unit?

14. The chairman of the board of directors of the company for which you are chief accountant has told you that he is entirely out of sympathy with accounting figures based on cost. He believes that replacement values are of far more significance to the board of directors than "out-of-date costs." Present some arguments to convince him that accounting data should still be based on cost.

15. Develop an argument supporting the adjustment of cost figures in financial statements for general price-level changes, or at least, the preparation of supplementary statements adjusted for changes in the general price level.

16. When is revenue generally recognized? Why has the date of sale been chosen as the point at which to recognize the revenue resulting from the entire producing and selling process?

17. What is the difference between realized and realizable? Give an example of where the concept of realizable is used to recognize revenue.

18. What is the justification for the following deviations from recognizing revenue at the time of sale?
(a) Installment sales method of recognizing revenue.
(b) Recognition of revenue at completion of production for certain agricultural products.
(c) The percentage-of-completion basis in long-term construction contracts.

19. What accounting assumption, principle, or modifying convention does Denton Co. use in each of the situations below?
(a) Denton Co. uses the lower of cost or market basis to value inventories.
(b) Denton was involved in litigation with Loptien Co. over a product malfunction. This litigation is disclosed in the financial statements.
(c) Denton allocates the cost of its depreciable assets over the life it expects to receive revenue from these assets.
(d) Denton records the purchase of a new IBM PC at its cash equivalent price.

20. Hjelmberg Company paid $90,000 for a machine in 1995. The Accumulated Depreciation account has a balance of $31,000 at the present time. The company could sell the machine today for $101,000. The company president believes that the company has a "right to this gain." What does the president mean by this statement? Do you agree?

21. Three expense recognition methods (associating cause and effect, systematic and rational allocation, and immediate recognition) were discussed in the text under the matching principle. Indicate the basic nature of each of these types of expenses and give two examples of each.

22. Explain how you would decide whether to record each of the following expenditures as an asset or an expense. Assume all items are material.
(a) Legal fees paid in connection with the purchase of land are $1,000.
(b) Basti, Inc. paves the driveway leading to the office building at a cost of $14,000.
(c) A meat market purchases a meat-grinding machine at a cost of $230.
(d) On June 30, Elliot and Olson, medical doctors, pay six months' office rent to cover the month of June and the next five months.
(e) The Gordon's Hardware Company pays $6,000 in wages to laborers for construction on a building to be used in the business.
(f) Kat's Florists pays wages of $1,400 for November to an employee who serves as driver of their delivery truck.

23. *Statement of Financial Accounting Concepts No. 5* identifies four characteristics that an item must have before it is recognized in the financial statements. What are these four characteristics?

24. Briefly describe the types of information concerning financial position, income, and cash flows that might be provided: (a) within the main body of the financial statements, (b) in the notes to the financial statements, or (c) as supplementary information.

25. In January, 1995 Bartelli Inc. doubled the amount of its outstanding stock by selling on the market an additional 10,000 shares to finance an expansion of the business. You propose that this information be shown by a footnote on the balance sheet as of December 31, 1994. The president objects, claiming that this sale took place after December 31, 1994, and, therefore, should not be shown. Explain your position.

26. Describe the two major constraints inherent in the presentation of accounting information.

27. What are some of the costs of providing accounting information? What are some of the benefits of accounting information? Describe the cost/benefit factors that should be considered when new accounting standards are being proposed.

28. How are materiality (and immateriality) related to the proper presentation of financial statements? What factors and measures should the CPA consider in assessing the materiality of a misstatement in the presentation of a financial statement?

29. The treasurer of Lupe Co. has heard that conservatism is a doctrine that is followed in accounting and, therefore, proposes that several policies be followed that are conservative in nature. State your opinion with respect to each of the policies listed below.
    (a) A personal liability lawsuit is pending against the company. The treasurer believes there is an even chance that the company will lose the suit and have to pay damages of $140,000 to $190,000. The treasurer recommends that a loss be recorded and a liability created in the amount of $190,000.
    (b) The inventory should be valued at "cost or market whichever is lower" because the losses from price declines should be recognized in the accounts in the period in which the price decline takes place.
    (c) The company gives a 2-year warranty to its customers on all products sold. The estimated warranty costs incurred from this year's sales should be entered as an expense this year instead of an expense in the period in the future when the warranty is made good.
    (d) When sales are made on account, there is always uncertainty about whether the accounts are collectible. Therefore, the treasurer recommends recording the sale when the cash is received from the customers.

EXERCISES

E2-1 (Qualitative Characteristics)   *SFAC No. 2* identifies the qualitative characteristics that make accounting information useful. Presented below are a number of questions related to these qualitative characteristics and underlying constraints.

1. What are the two primary qualities that make accounting information useful for decision making?
2. Faulds, Inc. does not issue its first-quarter report until after the second quarter's results are reported. Which qualitative characteristic of accounting is not followed? (Do not use relevance.)
3. Predictive value is an ingredient of which of the two primary qualities that make accounting information useful for decision making purposes?
4. Rogers, Inc. is the only company in its industry to depreciate its plant assets on a straight-line basis. Which qualitative characteristic of accounting information may not be followed? (Do not use industry practices.)
5. Hines Company has attempted to determine the replacement cost of its inventory. Three different appraisers arrive at substantially different amounts for this value. The president, nevertheless, decides to report the middle value for external reporting purposes. Which qualitative characteristic of information is lacking in these data? (Do not use reliability or representational faithfulness.)
6. What is the quality of information that enables users to confirm or correct prior expectations?
7. Identify the two overall or pervasive constraints developed in *SFAC No. 2.*
8. The chairman of the SEC at one time noted that "if it becomes accepted or expected that accounting principles are determined or modified in order to secure purposes other than economic measurement—we assume a grave risk that confidence in the credibility of our financial information system will be undermined." Which qualitative characteristic of accounting information should ensure that such a situation will not occur? (Do not use reliability.)

9. Hydrogear switches from FIFO to average cost to FIFO over a 2-year period. Which qualitative characteristic of accounting information is not followed?
10. Assume that the profession permits the savings and loan industry to defer losses on investments it sells, because immediate recognition of the loss may have adverse economic consequences on the industry. Which qualitative characteristic of accounting information is not followed? (Do not use relevance or reliability.)

E2-2 (Qualitative Characteristics) The qualitative characteristics that make accounting information useful for decision-making purposes are as follows:

Relevance	Verifiability
Reliability	Neutrality
Predictive value	Representational faithfulness
Feedback value	Comparability
Timeliness	Consistency

Instructions

Identify the appropriate qualitative characteristic(s) to be used given the information provided below.

1. Predictive value is an ingredient of this primary quality of information.
2. Two qualitative characteristics that are related to both relevance and reliability.
3. Neutrality is an ingredient of this primary quality of accounting information.
4. Two primary qualities that make accounting information useful for decision making purposes.
5. Issuance of interim reports is an example of this secondary quality of financial information.
6. Qualitative characteristic being employed when companies in the same industry are using the same accounting principles.
7. Quality of information that confirms users' earlier expectations.
8. Imperative for providing comparisons of a firm from period to period.
9. Ignores the economic consequences of a standard or rule.
10. Requires a high degree of consensus among individuals on a given measurement.

E2-3 (Elements of Financial Statements) Ten interrelated elements that are most directly related to measuring the performance and financial status of an enterprise are provided below:

Assets	Comprehensive income
Liabilities	Revenues
Equity	Expenses
Investments by owners	Gains
Distributions to owners	Losses

Instructions

For each of the phrases provided below, identify the element or elements associated with the 12 items below.

1. Arises from income statement activities that constitute the entity's ongoing major or central operations.
2. Residual interest in the assets of the enterprise after deducting its liabilities.
3. Increases assets during a period through sale of product.
4. Decreases assets during the period by purchasing the company's own stock.
5. Includes all changes in equity during the period, except those resulting from investments by owners and distributions to owners.
6. Arises from peripheral or incidental transactions.
7. Obligation to transfer resources arising from past transaction.
8. Increases ownership interest.
9. Declares and pays cash dividends to owners.
10. Increases in net assets in a period from nonowner sources.
11. Items characterized by service potential or future economic benefit.
12. Equals increase in assets less liabilities during the year, after adding disinvestments by owners and subtracting investments by owners.

E2-4 (Assumptions, Principles, and Constraints) Presented below are the assumptions, principles, and constraints used in this chapter:

a. Economic entity assumption	d. Periodicity assumption
b. Going concern assumption	e. Historical cost principle
c. Monetary unit assumption	f. Matching principle

g. Full disclosure principle
h. Cost-benefit relationship
i. Materiality
j. Industry practices
k. Conservatism

Instructions

Identify by letter the accounting assumption, principle, or constraint that describes each situation below. Do not use a letter more than once.

1. Allocates expenses to revenues in the proper period.
2. Indicates that market value changes subsequent to purchase are not recorded in the accounts. (Do not use revenue recognition principle.)
3. Ensures that all relevant financial information is reported.
4. Rationale why plant assets are not reported at liquidation value. (Do not use historical cost principle.)
5. Anticipates all losses, but reports no gains.
6. Indicates that personal and business record keeping should be separately maintained.
7. Separates financial information into time periods for reporting purposes.
8. Permits the use of market value valuation in certain specific situations.
9. Requires that information significant enough to affect the decision of reasonably informed users should be disclosed. (Do not use full disclosure principle.)
10. Assumes that the dollar is the "measuring stick" used to report on financial performance.

E2-5 (Assumptions, Principles, and Constraints) Presented below are a number of operational guidelines and practices that have developed over time.

1. All important aspects of bond indentures are presented in financial statements.
2. Rationale for accrual accounting is stated.
3. The use of consolidated statements is justified.
4. Reporting must be done at defined time intervals.
5. An allowance for doubtful accounts is established.
6. All payments out of petty cash are charged to Miscellaneous Expense. (Do not use conservatism.)
7. Goodwill is recorded only at time of purchase.
8. No profits are anticipated and all possible losses are recognized.
9. A company charges its sales commission costs to expense.
10. Price-level changes are not recognized in the accounting records.
11. Lower of cost or market is used to value inventories.
12. Financial information is presented so that reasonably prudent investors will not be misled.
13. Intangibles are capitalized and amortized over periods benefited.
14. Repair tools are expensed when purchased.
15. Brokerage firms use market value for purposes of valuation of all marketable securities.
16. Each enterprise is kept as a unit distinct from its owner or owners.
17. All significant postbalance sheet events are reported.
18. Revenue is recorded at point of sale.

Instructions

Select the assumption, principle, or constraint that most appropriately justifies these procedures and practices. (Do not use qualitative characteristics.)

E2-6 (Assumptions, Principles, and Constraints) A number of operational guidelines used by accountants are described below.

1. Calvin Chemical Company "faces possible expropriation (i.e., takeover) of foreign facilities and possible losses on sums owed by various customers on the verge of bankruptcy." The company president has decided that these possibilities should not be noted on the financial statements because Calvin still hopes that these events will not take place.
2. Brenda Starr, manager of College Bookstore, Inc., bought a computer for her own use. She paid for the computer by writing a check on the bookstore checking account and charged the "Office Equipment" account.
3. Hobbs, Inc. recently completed a new 120-story office building that houses their home offices and many other tenants. All the office equipment for the building that had a per item or per unit cost of $1,000 or less was expensed as immaterial, even though the office equipment has an average life of 10 years. The total cost of such office equipment was approximately $26 million. (Do not use the matching principle.)
4. The AICPA, in an accounting guide for brokers and other dealers in securities, stated that "the trading and investment accounts ... should be valued at market or fair value for financial reporting

purposes. . . ." The brokerage firm of Winkle and Tracy, Inc. continues to value its trading and investment accounts at cost or market, whichever is lower.

5. A large lawsuit has been filed against Brunhilda Corp. by Nerwin Co. Brunhilda has recorded a loss and related estimated liability equal to the maximum possible amount it feels it might lose. Brunhilda is confident, however, that either it will win the suit or it will owe a much smaller amount.

6. The treasurer of Piestengle Co. wishes to prepare financial statements only during downturns in their wine production, which occur periodically when the rhubarb crop fails. He states that it is at such times that the statements could be most easily prepared. In no event would more than 30 months pass without statements being prepared.

7. The C. Brown Power & Light Company has purchased a large amount of property, plant, and equipment over a number of years. They have decided that because the general price level has changed materially over the years, they will issue only price-level adjusted financial statements.

8. Lockhorn Manufacturing Co. decided to manufacture its own widgets because it would be cheaper to do so than to buy them from an outside supplier. In an attempt to make their statements more comparable with those of their competitors, Lockhorn charged its inventory account for what they felt the widgets would have cost if they had been purchased from an outside supplier. (Do not use the revenue recognition principle.)

9. Zonker's Discount Centers buys its merchandise by the truck and train-carload. Zonker does not defer any transportation costs in computing the cost of its ending inventory. Such costs, although varying from period to period, are always material in amount.

10. Grab & Run, Inc., a fast-food company, sells franchises for $70,000, accepting a $1,000 down payment and a 50-year note for the remainder. Grab & Run promises for 3 years to assist in site selection, building, and management training. Grab & Run records the $70,000 franchise fee as revenue in the period in which the contract is signed.

Instructions

For each of the foregoing, list the assumption, principle, or constraint that has been violated. List only one term for each case.

CASES

C2-1 (Conceptual Framework—General) Steve MacDougall has some questions regarding the theoretical framework in which standards are set. He knows that the FASB and other predecessor organizations have attempted to develop a conceptual framework for accounting theory formulation. Yet, Steve's supervisors have indicated that these theoretical frameworks have little value in the practical sense (i.e., in the real world). Steve did notice that accounting standards seem to be established after the fact rather than before. He thought this indicated a lack of theory structure but never really questioned the process at school because he was too busy doing the homework.

Steve feels that some of his anxiety about accounting theory and accounting semantics could be alleviated by identifying the basic concepts and definitions accepted by the profession and considering them in light of his current work. By doing this, he hopes to develop an appropriate connection between theory and practice.

Instructions
   (a) Help Steve recognize the purpose of and benefit of a conceptual framework.
   (b) Identify any *Statements of Financial Accounting Concepts* issued by FASB that may be helpful to Steve in developing his theoretical background.

C2-2 (Conceptual Framework—General) The Financial Accounting Standards Board (FASB) has been working on a conceptual framework for financial accounting and reporting. The FASB has issued six *Statements of Financial Accounting Concepts.* These statements are intended to set forth objectives and fundamentals that will be the basis for developing financial accounting and reporting standards. The objectives identify the goals and purposes of financial reporting. The fundamentals are the underlying concepts of financial accounting—concepts that guide the selection of transactions, events, and circumstances to be accounted for; their recognition and measurement; and the means of summarizing and communicating them to interested parties.

The purpose of *Statement of Financial Accounting Concepts No. 2,* "Qualitative Characteristics of Accounting Information," is to examine the characteristics that make accounting information useful. The characteristics or qualities of information discussed in *SFAC No. 2* are the ingredients that make information useful and the qualities to be sought when accounting choices are made.

Instructions
   (a) Identify and discuss the benefits that can be expected to be derived from the FASB's conceptual framework study.

(b) What is the most important quality for accounting information as identified in *Statement of Financial Accounting Concepts No. 2?* Explain why it is the most important.

(c) *Statement of Financial Accounting Concepts No. 2* describes a number of key characteristics or qualities for accounting information. Briefly discuss the importance of any three of these qualities for financial reporting purposes.

(CMA adapted)

C2-3 (Objectives of Financial Reporting) Frank Pluhm and Mona Regan are discussing various aspects of the FASB's pronouncement, *Statement of Financial Accounting Concepts No. 1,* "Objectives of Financial Reporting by Business Enterprises." Frank indicates that this pronouncement provides little, if any, guidance to the practicing professional in resolving accounting controversies. He believes that the statement provides such broad guidelines that it would be impossible to apply the objectives to present-day reporting problems. Mona concedes this point but indicates that objectives are still needed to provide a starting point for the FASB in helping to improve financial reporting.

Instructions

(a) Indicate the basic objectives established in *Statement of Financial Accounting Concepts No. 1.*

(b) What do you think is the meaning of Mona's statement that the FASB needs a starting point to resolve accounting controversies?

C2-4 (Qualitative Characteristics) Accounting information provides useful information about business transactions and events. Those who provide and use financial reports must often select and evaluate accounting alternatives. *FASB Statement of Financial Accounting Concepts No. 2,* "Qualitative Characteristics of Accounting Information," examines the characteristics of accounting information that make it useful for decision making. It also points out that various limitations inherent in the measurement and reporting process may necessitate trade-offs or sacrifices among the characteristics of useful information.

Instructions

(a) Describe briefly the following characteristics of useful accounting information:

    1. Relevance.   **4.** Comparability.

    2. Reliability.   **5.** Consistency.

    3. Understandability.

(b) For each of the following pairs of information characteristics, give an example of a situation in which one of the characteristics may be sacrificed in return for a gain in the other:

    1. Relevance and reliability.   **3.** Comparability and consistency.

    2. Relevance and consistency.   **4.** Relevance and understandability.

(c) What criterion should be used to evaluate trade-offs between information characteristics?

C2-5 (Assumptions, Principles, and Constraints) You are engaged to review the accounting records of Lost Canyon Corporation prior to the closing of the revenue and expense accounts as of December 31, the end of the current fiscal year. The following information comes to your attention.

1. During the current year, Lost Canyon Corporation changed its policy in regard to expensing purchases of small tools. In the past, these purchases had always been expensed because they amounted to less than 2% of net income, but the president has decided that capitalization and subsequent depreciation should now be followed. It is expected that purchases of small tools will not fluctuate greatly from year to year.

2. Lost Canyon Corporation constructed a warehouse at a cost of $800,000. The company had been depreciating the asset on a straight-line basis over 10 years. In the current year, the controller doubled depreciation expense because the replacement cost of the warehouse had increased significantly.

3. The company decided in October of the current fiscal year to start a massive advertising campaign to enhance the marketability of their product. In November, the company paid $700,000 for advertising time on a major television network to advertise their product during the next 12 months. The controller expensed the $700,000 in the current year on the basis that "once the money is spent, it can never be recovered from the television network."

4. When the balance sheet was prepared, detailed information as to the amount of cash on deposit in each of several banks was omitted. Only the total amount of cash under a caption "Cash in banks" was presented.

5. On July 15 of the current year, Lost Canyon Corporation purchased an undeveloped tract of land at a cost of $290,000. The company spent $70,000 in subdividing the land and getting it ready for sale. An appraisal of the property at the end of the year indicated that the land was now worth $450,000. Although none of the lots were sold, the company recognized revenue of $160,000, less related expenses of $70,000, for a net income on the project of $90,000.

6. For a number of years the company used the FIFO method for inventory valuation purposes. During the current year, the president noted that all the other companies in their industry had switched to the LIFO method. The company decided not to switch to LIFO because net income would decrease $800,000.

Instructions

State whether or not you agree with the decisions made by Lost Canyon Corporation. Support your answers with reference, whenever possible, to the generally accepted principles, assumptions, and constraints applicable in the circumstances.

C2-6 (Historical Cost Principle) Presented below is a statement that appeared about Weyerhaeuser Company in a financial magazine.

The land and timber holdings are now carried on the company's books at a mere $422 million. The value of the timber alone is variously estimated at $3 billion to $7 billion and is rising all the time. "The understatement of the company is pretty severe," conceded Charles W. Bingham, a senior vice-president. Adds Robert L. Schuyler, another senior vice-president: "We have a whole stream of profit nobody sees and there is no way to show it on our books."

Instructions

(a) What does Schuyler mean when he says that "we have a whole stream of profit nobody sees and there is no way to show it on our books"?

(b) If the understatement of the company's assets is severe, why does accounting not report this information?

C2-7 (Revenue Recognition and Matching Principle) After the presentation of your report on the examination of the financial statements to the board of directors of Hagar Publishing Company, one of the new directors expresses surprise that the income statement assumes that an equal proportion of the revenue is earned with the publication of every issue of the company's magazine. She feels that the "crucial event" in the process of earning revenue in the magazine business is the cash sale of the subscription. She says that she does not understand why most of the revenue cannot be "recognized" in the period of the sale.

Instructions

(a) List the various accepted times for recognizing revenue in the accounts and explain when the methods are appropriate.

(b) Discuss the propriety of timing the recognition of revenue in Hagar Publishing Company's account with:
1. The cash sale of the magazine subscription.
2. The publication of the magazine every month.
3. Both events, by recognizing a portion of the revenue with cash sale of the magazine subscription and a portion of the revenue with the publication of the magazine every month.

(AICPA adapted)

C2-8 (Revenue Recognition and Matching Principle) On June 5, 1995, Mesa Corporation signed a contract with Cedillo Associates under which Cedillo agreed (1) to construct an office building on land owned by Mesa, (2) to accept responsibility for procuring financing for the project and finding tenants, and (3) to manage the property for 35 years. The annual net income from the project, after debt service, was to be divided equally between Mesa Corporation and Cedillo Associates. Cedillo was to accept its share of future net income as full payment for its services in construction, obtaining finances and tenants, and management of the project.

By May 31, 1996, the project was nearly completed and tenants had signed leases to occupy 90% of the available space at annual rentals aggregating $3,000,000. It is estimated that, after operating expenses and debt service, the annual net income will amount to $1,100,000. The management of Cedillo Associates believed that (a) the economic benefit derived from the contract with Mesa should be reflected on its financial statements for the fiscal year ended May 31, 1996, and directed that revenue be accrued in an amount equal to the commercial value of the services Cedillo had rendered during the year, (b) this amount be carried in contracts receivable, and (c) all related expenditures be charged against the revenue.

Instructions

(a) Explain the main difference between the economic concept of business income as reflected by Cedillo's management and the measurement of income under generally accepted accounting principles.

(b) Discuss the factors to be considered in determining when revenue should be recognized for the purpose of accounting measurement of periodic income.

(c) Is the belief of Cedillo's management in accord with generally accepted accounting principles for the measurement of revenue and expense for the year ended May 31, 1996? Support your opinion by discussing the application to this case of the factors to be considered for asset measurement and revenue and expense recognition.

(AICPA adapted)

C2-9 (Matching Principle) An accountant must be familiar with the concepts involved in determining earnings of a business entity. The amount of earnings reported for a business entity is dependent on the proper recognition, in general, of revenue and expense for a given time period. In some situations, costs are recognized as expenses at the time of product sale; in other situations, guidelines have been developed for recognizing costs as expenses or losses by other criteria.

Instructions

(a) Explain the rationale for recognizing costs as expenses at the time of product sale.

(b) What is the rationale underlying the appropriateness of treating costs as expenses of a period instead of assigning the costs to an asset? Explain.

(c) In what general circumstances would it be appropriate to treat a cost as an asset instead of as an expense? Explain.

(d) Some expenses are assigned to specific accounting periods on the basis of systematic and rational allocation of asset cost. Explain the underlying rationale for recognizing expenses on the basis of systematic and rational allocation of asset cost.

(e) Identify the conditions in which it would be appropriate to treat a cost as a loss.

(AICPA adapted)

C2-10 (Matching Principle) Accountants try to prepare income statements that are as accurate as possible. A basic requirement in preparing accurate income statements is to match costs against revenues properly. Proper matching of costs against revenues requires that costs resulting from typical business operations be recognized in the period in which they expired.

Instructions

(a) List three criteria that can be used to determine whether such costs should appear as charges in the income statement for the current period.

(b) As generally presented in financial statements, the following items or procedures have been criticized as improperly matching costs with revenues. Briefly discuss each item from the viewpoint of matching costs with revenues and suggest corrective or alternative means of presenting the financial information.

1. Receiving and handling costs.

2. Valuation of inventories at the lower of cost or market.

3. Cash discounts on purchases.

C2-11 (Matching Principle) Jason Fox sells and erects shell houses, that is, frame structures that are completely finished on the outside but are unfinished on the inside except for flooring, partition studding, and ceiling joists. Shell houses are sold chiefly to customers who are handy with tools and who have time to do the interior wiring, plumbing, wall completion and finishing, and other work necessary to make the shell houses livable dwellings.

Jason buys shell houses from a manufacturer in unassembled packages consisting of all lumber, roofing, doors, windows, and similar materials necessary to complete a shell house. Upon commencing operations in a new area, Jason buys or leases land as a site for its local warehouse, field office, and display houses. Sample display houses are erected at a total cost of $20,000 to $29,000 including the cost of the unassembled packages. The chief element of cost of the display houses is the unassembled packages, inasmuch as erection is a short, low-cost operation. Old sample models are torn down or altered into new models every 3 to 7 years. Sample display houses have little salvage value because dismantling and moving costs amount to nearly as much as the cost of an unassembled package.

Instructions

(a) A choice must be made between (1) expensing the costs of sample display houses in the periods in which the expenditure is made and (2) spreading the costs over more than one period. Discuss the advantages of each method.

(b) Would it be preferable to amortize the cost of display houses on the basis of (1) the passage of time or (2) the number of shell houses sold? Explain.

(AICPA adapted)

C2-12 (Matching Principle) The general ledger of Comic, Inc., a corporation engaged in the development and production of television programs for commercial sponsorship, contains the following accounts before amortization at the end of the current year:

Account	Balance (Debit)
Hi & Lois	$60,000
Blondie	41,000
B. Bailey	21,500
Phantom	9,000
Spiderman	4,000

An examination of contracts and records revealed the following information:

1. The first two accounts listed above represent the total cost of completed programs that were televised during the accounting period just ended. Under the terms of an existing contract Hi & Lois will be rerun during the next accounting period, at a fee equal to 50% of the fee for the first televising of the program. The contract for the first run produced $600,000 of revenue. The contract with the sponsor of Blondie provides that the program may, at the sponsor's option, be rerun during the next season at a fee of 75% of the fee on the first televising of the program.
2. The balance in the B. Bailey account is the cost of a new program that has just been completed and is being considered by several companies for commercial sponsorship.
3. The balance in the Phantom account represents the cost of a partially completed program for a projected series that has been abandoned.
4. The balance of the Spiderman account consists of payments made to a firm of engineers that prepared a report relative to the more efficient utilization of existing studio space and equipment.

Instructions
(a) State the general principle (or principles) of accounting that are applicable to the first four accounts.
(b) How would you report each of the first four accounts in the financial statements of Comic, Inc.? Explain.
(c) In what way, if at all, does the Spiderman account differ from the first four? Explain.

(AICPA adapted)

C2-13 (Full Disclosure Principle) Presented below are a number of facts related to Apgar, Inc. Assume that no mention of these facts was made in the financial statements and the related notes.
(a) The company decided that, for the sake of conciseness, only net income should be reported on the income statement. Details as to revenues, cost of goods sold, and expenses were omitted.
(b) Equipment purchases of $140,000 were partly financed during the year through the issuance of a $90,000 notes payable. The company offset the equipment against the notes payable and reported plant assets at $50,000.
(c) During the year, an assistant controller for the company embezzled $10,000. Apgar's net income for the year was $1,700,000. Neither the assistant controller nor the money have been found.
(d) Apgar has reported its ending inventory at $2,000,000 in the financial statements. No other information related to inventories is presented in the financial statements and related notes.
(e) The company changed its method of depreciating equipment from the double-declining balance to the straight-line method. No mention of this change was made in the financial statements.

Instructions
Assume that you are the auditor of Apgar, Inc. and that you have been asked to explain the appropriate accounting and related disclosure necessary for each of these items.

C2-14 (Accounting Principles—Comprehensive) Presented below are a number of business transactions that occurred during the current year for Dynagenetics, Inc.

1. Because the general level of prices increased during the current year, Dynagenetics, Inc. determined that there was a $14,000 understatement of depreciation expense on its equipment and decided to record it in its accounts. The following entry was made:

Depreciation Expense	14,000	
Accumulated Depreciation		14,000

2. Dynagenetics, Inc. has been concerned about whether intangible assets could generate cash in case of liquidation. As a consequence, goodwill arising from a purchase transaction during the current year and recorded at $900,000 was written off as follows:

Retained Earnings	900,000	
Goodwill		900,000

3. Because of a "fire sale," equipment obviously worth $190,000 was acquired at a cost of $140,000. The following entry was made:

Equipment	190,000	
Cash		140,000
Income		50,000

4. The president of Dynagenetics, Inc. used his expense account to purchase a new Saab 9000 solely for personal use. The following entry was made:

Miscellaneous Expense	35,000	
Cash		35,000

5. Merchandise inventory that cost $520,000 is reported on the balance sheet at $580,000, the expected selling price less estimated selling costs. The following entry was made to record this increase in value:

Merchandise Inventory	60,000	
Income		60,000

6. The company is being sued for $400,000 by a customer who claims damages for personal injury apparently caused by a defective product. Company attorneys feel extremely confident that the company will have no liability for damages resulting from the situation. Nevertheless, the company decides to make the following entry:

Loss from Lawsuit	400,000	
Liability for Lawsuit		400,000

Instructions

In each of the situations above, discuss the appropriateness of the journal entries in terms of generally accepted accounting principles.

C2-15 (Accounting Principles—Comprehensive) Presented below is information related to Robotics, Inc.

(a) Depreciation expense on the building for the year was $40,000. Because the building was increasing in value during the year, the controller decided to charge the depreciation expense to retained earnings instead of to net income. The following entry is recorded.

Retained Earnings	40,000	
Accumulated Depreciation—Buildings		40,000

(b) Materials were purchased on January 1, 1995 for $80,000 and this amount was entered in the Materials account. On December 31, 1995, the materials would have cost $94,000, so the following entry is made.

Inventory	14,000	
Gain on Inventories		14,000

(c) During the year, the company purchased equipment through the issuance of common stock. The stock had a par value of $90,000 and a fair market value of $300,000. The fair market value of the equipment was not easily determinable. The company recorded this transaction as follows:

Equipment	90,000	
Common Stock		90,000

(d) During the year, the company sold certain equipment for $190,000, recognizing a gain of $46,000. Because the controller believed that new equipment would be needed in the near future, the controller decided to defer the gain and amortize it over the life of any new equipment purchased.

(e) An order for $41,000 has been received from a customer for products on hand. This order was shipped on January 9, 1996. The company made the following entry in 1995.

Accounts Receivable	41,000	
Sales		41,000

Instructions

Comment on the appropriateness of the accounting procedures followed by Robotics, Inc.

▶ USING YOUR JUDGMENT ◀

▶ FINANCIAL REPORTING PROBLEM

Sara Joiner has successfully completed her first accounting course during the spring semester and is now working as a management trainee for Bluffton National Bank during the summer. One of her fellow management trainees, Rick Baker, is taking the same accounting course this summer and has been having a "lot of trouble." On the second examination, for example, Rick Baker became confused about inventory valuation methods and completely missed all the points on a problem involving LIFO and FIFO.

Rick's instructor recently indicated that the third examination will probably have a number of essay questions dealing with accounting principle's issues. Rick is quite concerned about the third examination for two reasons. First, he has never taken an accounting examination where essay questions were required. Second, Rick feels he has to do well on this examination to get an acceptable grade in the course.

Rick has therefore asked Sara to help him prepare for the next examination. Sara agrees, and suggests that Rick develop a set of possible questions on the accounting principles material that they might discuss.

Instructions

Answer the following questions that were developed by Rick.

1. What is a conceptual framework?
2. Why is there a need for a conceptual framework?
3. What are the objectives of financial reporting?
4. If you had to explain generally accepted accounting principles to a nonaccountant, what essential characteristics would you include in your explanation?
5. What are the qualitative characteristics of accounting? Explain each one.
6. Identify the basic assumptions used in accounting.
7. What are two major constraints involved in financial reporting? Explain both of them.

▶ WRITING ASSIGNMENT

Recently, your Uncle Waldo Ralph, who knows that you always have your eye out for a profitable investment, has discussed the possibility of you purchasing some corporate bonds. He suggests that you may wish to get in on the "ground floor" of this deal. The bonds being issued by the Cricket Corp. are 10-year debentures which promise a 40 percent rate of return. Cricket manufactures novelty/party items.

You have told Waldo that, unless you can take a look at Cricket's financial statements, you would not feel comfortable about such an investment. Knowing that this is the chance of a lifetime, Uncle Waldo has procured a copy of Cricket's most recent, unaudited financial statements which are a year old. These statements were prepared by Mrs. John Cricket. You peruse these statements, and they are quite impressive. The balance sheet showed a debt-to-equity ratio of .10 and, for the year shown, the company reported net income of $2,424,240.

The financial statements are not shown in comparison with amounts from other years. In addition, no significant note disclosures about inventory valuation, depreciation methods, loan agreements, etc. are available.

Instructions

Write a letter to Uncle Waldo explaining why it would be unwise to base an investment decision on the financial statements which he has provided to you. Be sure to explain why these financial statements are neither relevant nor reliable.

▶ GROUP ASSIGNMENT

(Accounting Principles—General) Your group has been engaged to review the accounting records of Siskel Flick Picks, Inc. Each of the following statements represents a decision made by the controller, on which your advice is asked.

1. A building purchased by the company 5 years ago for $150,000, including the land on which it stands, can now be sold for $200,000. The controller instructs that the new value of $200,000 be entered in the accounts.

2. Material included in the inventory that cost $120,000 has become obsolete. The controller contends that no loss can be recognized until the goods are sold, and so the material is included in the inventory at $120,000.

3. Inasmuch as profits for the year appear to be extremely small, no depreciation of fixed assets is to be recorded as an expense this year.

4. The company occupies the building in which it operates under a long-term lease requiring annual rental payments. It sublets certain office space not required for its own purposes. The controller credits rents received against rents paid, to get net rent expense.

5. A flood during the year destroyed or damaged a considerable amount of uninsured inventory. No entry was made for this loss because the controller reasons that the ending inventory will, of course, be reduced by the amount of the destroyed or damaged merchandise, and therefore, its cost will be included in cost of goods sold and the net income figure will be correct.

6. The company provides housing for certain employees and adjusts their salaries accordingly. The controller contends that the cost to the company of maintaining this housing should be charged to "Wages and Salaries."

7. The entire cost of a new delivery truck is to be charged to an expense account.

8. Siskel Flick Picks, Inc. has paid a large sum for an advertising campaign to promote a new product that will not be placed on the market until the following year. The controller has charged this amount to a prepaid expense account.

9. The company operates a cafeteria for the convenience of its employees. Sales made by the cafeteria are credited to the regular sales account for product sales; food purchased and salaries paid for the cafeteria operations are recorded in the regular purchase and payroll accounts.

10. A customer leaving the building slipped on an icy spot on the stairway and wrenched his back. He immediately entered suit against the company for permanent physical injuries and claims damages in the amount of $160,000. The suit has not yet come to trial. The controller has made an entry charging a special loss account and crediting a liability account.

Instructions

Divide the items among group members so that each member has at least one item to analyze. Considering each decision independently of all others, each member should analyze his or her item(s) individually to determine whether or not he or she agrees with the controller's decision. Also provide the reasons for agreement or disagreement.

Discuss the individual responses within the group and agree upon a single group response for each item that will be reported to the class. Your instructor will identify one member to record your group responses and one member to serve as group spokesperson.

► ETHICS CASE

(**Matching Principle—Ethical Dilemma**) A1 OK Nuclear Plant will be mothballed at the end of its useful life (approximately 20 years) at great expense. The matching principle requires that expenses be matched to revenue. Accountants Plue Tonium and Rea Ctor argue whether it is better to allocate the expense of mothballing over the next twenty years or to ignore it until mothballing occurs.

Instructions
   (a) What, if any, is the moral issue underlying the dispute?
   (b) What stakeholders should be considered?
   (c) What decision would you make?

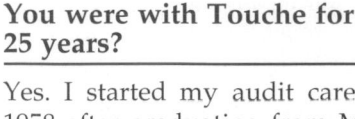

ROBERT SACK teaches accounting at the Darden Graduate School at the University of Virginia. His classes include a healthy dose of ethics—which he's pondered for nearly 30 years as a practitioner with Touche Ross & Co. (now Deloitte & Touche), and then as a member of the staff of the Securities and Exchange Commission. In contrast to what the media tells us, Mr. Sack says that business ethics seem to ebb and flow in cycles and that we are coming out of a typical down cycle.

You were with Touche for 25 years?

Yes. I started my audit career in 1958 after graduating from Miami of Ohio with a bachelor's degree in accounting. I ran audits on mid-sized private companies and small publicly-held companies.

What was the toughest ethical question you faced as an auditor?

Returning for a subsequent year's audit and finding that I had missed something in the audit last year. My client was a major subsidiary of a larger client: our office had been responsible for the subsidiary for many years. I had supervised the prior year's audit, and we told the parent that all was well. But then I came back to the client the next year and had to say, "Gee, I don't remember that inventory account being there last year." The more I looked at it, the more I realized that I had simply blown it.

So what did you do about it?

I went to see the CFO and he said, "What's the big deal? Last year is history, there is very little change in the account this year so there is no effect on this year's income. Let sleeping dogs lie." The question for the staff person in that case is whether to call the partner and admit the error. I went to mine and said, "Mea culpa."

That was exercising your accounting ethics?

It seemed to me at the time to be the only choice. It's possible that no one would ever have known. But I would have. A number of senior people in the firm thought hard about the problem, and they took it to the parent company management. The sub's financials weren't public, but the parent's were. Everyone concluded that the effect on the parent's prior year financial statements wasn't very big. On the basis of materiality, it wasn't worth going back and opening things up and correcting an error. The parent made the local CFO discontinue his funny inventory accounting, however.

It's hard to lecture someone when they're under pressure. But right is right—it doesn't matter what the pressure is.

Ethics issues have to do with people making a tough choice between conflicting interests: the firm, the client, the public, their own careers.

After a period of field experience, you went to the national office in New York. What was your job?

All the firms have people who staff the phones so that people from the field offices can call up and say, for example, that they're having trouble figuring out what the FASB means with Statement X. I was part of that group for Touche for a number of years.

What were some ethical questions in that environment?

I was working with a partner who had a not-very-nice client. It was

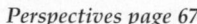

kind of a scam business, at least, in my view. However, the companies are still in business today so there must be something legitimate about them.

You wondered what the partner was doing with such a client?

Well yes, and he wasn't very proud of it either. It did present a number of interesting accounting questions, however. My field partner was concerned about revenue recognition. The company was front-ending all of their income even though they got paid over a long period of years, as the customer used the service. They claimed that they had a very good track record with collections—whether or not the customer really used the service. In our arguments about the accounting, we kept coming back to, "What kind of business is this, anyway?"

Which did you resolve first, the accounting question or the client quality question?

Well, we adopted an accounting policy for the firm which said that the front-ended revenue wasn't recognizable until it was earned, over some period of time.

That wasn't in any official standard?

No, sir. And as a result we lost the client and several similar ones.

I bet the partner in the field office was fuming.

He said, "It's easy for you guys in New York to make that kind of decision, but you don't have to make up the lost work in the office." And I said, "Yes, but that's not the kind of client this firm ought to have."

And he said, "Who the heck are you to say that?"

I am convinced the accounting was right, but I am willing to admit that my view on the accounting was strongly influenced by my value judgment of that client.

Those kinds of pressures are increased now?

The pressures must be enormous. No one wants to be associated with a shady client, much less one that has a track record of trouble. But when new clients are hard to come by, it would be tempting to shade your standards. Later you can say that you did everything according to the book, but the world is still going to ask why you were involved with those scuzzy guys.

Ethics is easy in hindsight, isn't it?

Of course. But that is why it's good to think about ethics early on in a career. Young people can't anticipate every ethics issue that they are going to confront. But we can help sensitize them to the kinds of issues that have hit others. Ethics is more than a code from the AICPA. It's dealing with the tough decisions ordinary people make every single day.

Are young people who have never been in a working situation able to appreciate this?

Based on my experience, new graduates tend to be idealistic—thank goodness for that! Still it's very dangerous to think that your armor is all in place and say to yourself "I would never have given in to that." The pressures don't explode on us; they build and we often

don't recognize them until they have us.

What were some of the ethical dilemmas facing preparers of financial statements?

The most poignant examples were companies that filed misleading financial statements because their executives—especially the financial people—gave into pressure when faced with a tough choice. In one case, a computer company had obsolete inventory on hand because they did not have adequate inventory controls. A new CEO came in, and in his first year took a hit to profits for obsolete inventory. It became increasingly clear in the next year that the charge-off was not enough. Another hit was in the offing. The CFO, faced with that dilemma, wrote a memo to the file saying that he "understands that obsolete inventory is a problem but the company can't deal with the cost of that problem now."

Had they taken the second write-off, investors would have asked why they didn't take the entire hit in the first place.

They evidently couldn't face up to it. In the following year, they really had no choice. After yet another special study they wrote off another $150 million—two years after the initial hit. The SEC brought an action challenging the first write-off and the failure to take the subsequent write-off in the earlier period. No one knows exactly how much of the second hit really belonged back earlier, but the SEC concluded that it was material.

They turned a mistake into a catastrophe.

Exactly. There are some people out there who use the marketplace to steal, and the SEC ought to go after them with hammer and tongs. Then, there are people like these computer company executives who hope that a problem will go away with the passage of time. Sometimes they get lucky, but sometimes, time catches them.

What advice would you give young people on how to be ethical?

Here are three tips. One, establish a pattern to get away from your work. People often get so caught up in the momentum of what's going on that they just lose their ethical perspective. Two, establish a network. Have people you can talk to. Have someone who can help you reestablish your perspective when things start getting tough. Three, manage your personal affairs so that your ethics are not beholden to anyone else. One CFO suggested that young people establish a "soul fund" before they get themselves financially extended—so that they can be sure that their soul is always their own. One executive told me that he always kept the notion of the family farm in his mind, as a refuge, even though the family had his independence in his head.

CHAPTER 3

A REVIEW OF THE ACCOUNTING PROCESS

LEARNING OBJECTIVES

After studying this chapter, you should be able to:

1. Understand basic accounting terminology.

2. Explain double-entry rules.

3. Identify steps in the accounting cycle.

4. Record transactions in journals, post to ledger accounts, and prepare a trial balance.

5. Explain the reasons for preparing adjusting entries.

6. Explain how inventory accounts are adjusted at year-end.

7. Prepare closing entries.

8. Identify adjusting entries that may be reversed.

9. Prepare a 10-column work sheet.

*M*aintaining a set of accounting records is not optional. The Internal Revenue Service has long required that businesses prepare and retain a set of records and documents that can be audited. And, in 1977, the U.S. Congress enacted the Foreign Corrupt Practices Act, which requires public companies to "... make and keep books, records, and accounts, which, in reasonable detail, accurately and fairly reflect the transactions and dispositions of the assets. ..." But beyond these two reasons, a company that does not keep an accurate record of its business transactions may lose revenue and is more likely to operate inefficiently.

Some companies are inefficient partly because of poor accounting procedures. Consider, for example, the Long Island Railroad,[1] once one of the nation's busiest commuter lines. The LIRR lost money because its cash position was unknown; large amounts of money owed the railroad had not been billed; some payables were erroneously paid twice; and redemptions of bonds were not recorded. And consider Gould Inc., an electronics conglomerate, where accounting and record keeping became so chaotic that results from operations had to be restated 5 of 7 years.

Similarly, when one of the largest gold and silver retailers, the International Gold Bullion Exchange (IGBE), was forced to declare bankruptcy, its records were in such a shambles that it was difficult to determine how much money it lost. The company had failed to keep track of its revenues and had written checks on uncollected funds. IGBE had even allowed its employee health insurance to lapse while continuing to collect

---

[1]"Long Island Railroad Is Said to Be Losing Revenue Due to 'Weak' Accounting System," *The Wall Street Journal*, February 19, 1971, p. 4.

premiums from workers. Although these situations are not common in large enterprises, they illustrate our point: accounts and detailed records must be kept by every business enterprise.

Even the use of computers is no assurance of accuracy and efficiency. "The conversion to a new system called MasterNet fouled up data processing records to the extent that BankAmerica is frequently unable to produce or deliver customer statements on a timely basis," said an executive at one of the country's largest banks.

▶ ACCOUNTING SYSTEMS

Accounting systems vary widely from one business to another. Factors that shape accounting systems are the **nature of the business** and the transactions in which it engages, the **size of the firm,** the **volume of data** to be handled, and the **informational demands** that management and others place on the system.

Broadly defined, accounting systems include all of the activities required to provide management with the information needed for planning, controlling, and reporting the enterprise's financial condition and operations. They help management answer such questions as:

How much and what kind of debt is outstanding?

Were our sales higher this period than last?

What assets do we have?

What were our cash inflows and outflows?

Did we make a profit last period?

Are any of our product lines or divisions operating at a loss?

Can we safely increase our dividends to stockholders?

Is our rate of return on net assets increasing?

Many other questions can be answered when there is an efficient accounting system to provide the data. A well-devised accounting system is beneficial for every business enterprise.

▶ PROCEDURES EMPLOYED IN ACCOUNTING

Financial accounting rests on a set of concepts (discussed in Chapters 1 and 2) for identifying, recording, classifying, and interpreting transactions and other events relating to enterprises. It is important to understand the **basic terminology employed in collecting accounting data.**

◀ BASIC TERMINOLOGY ▶

OBJECTIVE 1

Understand basic accounting terminology.

Cash, A/R, A/P, etc.

EVENT. A happening of consequence. An event generally is the source or cause of changes in assets, liabilities, and equity. Events may be external or internal.

TRANSACTION. An **external event** involving a transfer or exchange between two or more entities.

ACCOUNT. A systematic arrangement that shows the effect of transactions and other events on a specific asset or equity. A separate account is kept for each asset, liability, revenue, and expense, and for capital (owners' equity).

REAL AND NOMINAL ACCOUNTS. Real (permanent) accounts are asset, liability, and equity accounts; they appear on the balance sheet. Nominal (temporary) accounts are revenue, expense, and dividend accounts; except for dividends, they appear on the income statement. Nominal accounts are periodically closed; real accounts are not.

LEDGER. The book (or computer printouts) containing the accounts. Each account usually has a separate page. A **general ledger** is a collection of all the asset, liability, owners' equity, revenue, and expense accounts. A **subsidiary ledger** contains the details related to a given general ledger account.

JOURNAL. The book of original entry where transactions and selected other events are initially recorded. Various amounts are transferred to the ledger from the book of original entry, the journal.

POSTING. The process of transferring the essential facts and figures from the book of original entry to the ledger accounts.

TRIAL BALANCE. A list of all open accounts in the ledger and their balances. A trial balance taken immediately after all adjustments have been posted is called an **adjusted trial balance.** A trial balance taken immediately after closing entries have been posted is designated an **after-closing** or **post-closing trial balance.** A trial balance may be prepared at any time.

ADJUSTING ENTRIES. Entries made at the end of an accounting period to bring all accounts up to date on an accrual accounting basis so that correct financial statements can be prepared.

FINANCIAL STATEMENTS. Statements that reflect the collection, tabulation, and final summarization of the accounting data. Four statements are involved: (1) the **balance sheet,** which shows the financial condition of the enterprise at the end of a period, (2) the **income statement,** which measures the results of operations during the period, (3) the **statement of cash flows,** which reports the cash provided and used by operating, investing, and financing activities during the period, and (4) the **statement of retained earnings,** which reconciles the balance of the retained earnings account from the beginning to the end of the period.

CLOSING ENTRIES. The formal process by which all nominal accounts are reduced to zero and the net income or net loss is determined and transferred to the owners' equity account, also known as "closing the ledger," "closing the books," or merely "closing."

► DEBITS AND CREDITS

The terms debit and credit mean left and right, respectively. They are commonly abbreviated as Dr. for debit and Cr. for credit. These terms do not mean increase or decrease. The terms debit and credit are used repeatedly in the recording process. For example, the act of entering an amount on the left side of an account is called **debiting** the account, and making an entry on the right side is **crediting** the account. When the totals of the two sides are compared, an account will have a **debit balance** if the total of the debit amounts exceeds the credits. Conversely, an account will have a **credit balance** if the credit amounts exceed the debits.

OBJECTIVE 2

Explain double-entry rules.

The procedure of having debits on the left and credits on the right is an accounting custom or rule. Accountants could function just as well if debits and credits were reversed. However, the custom of having debits on the left side of an account and credits on the right side (like the custom of driving on the right-hand side of the road) has been adopted in the United States. **This rule applies to all accounts.**

The equality of debits and credits provides the basis for the double-entry system of recording transactions (sometimes referred to as double-entry bookkeeping). Under the universally used **double-entry accounting system,** the dual (two-sided) effect of each transaction is recorded in appropriate accounts. This system provides a logical method for recording transactions. It also offers a means of proving the accuracy of the recorded amounts. If every transaction is recorded with equal debits and credits, then the sum of all the debits to the accounts must equal the sum of all the credits.

All asset and expense accounts are increased on the left (or debit side) and decreased on the right (or credit side). Conversely, all liability and revenue accounts are increased on the right (or credit side) and decreased on the left (or debit side). Stockholders' equity accounts, like Common Stock and Retained Earnings, are increased on the credit side, whereas Dividends is increased on the debit side. The basic guidelines for an accounting system are presented in Illustration 3-1.

ILLUSTRATION 3-1
Double-entry (Debit and Credit) Accounting System

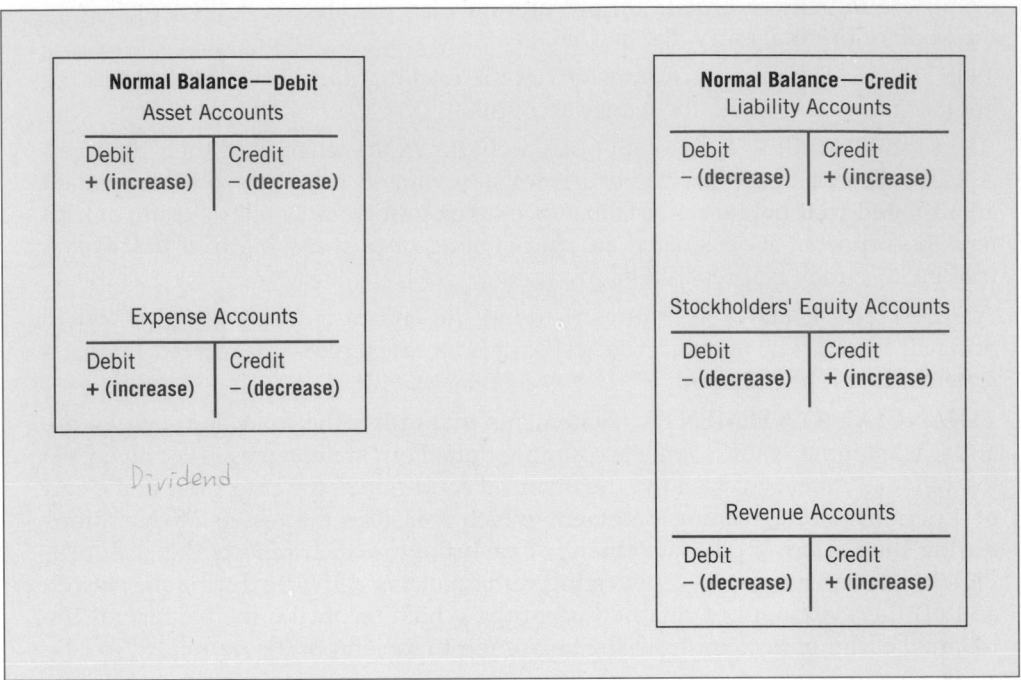

▶ BASIC EQUATION AND TRANSACTION ANALYSIS

In a double-entry system, for every debit there must be a credit and vice-versa. This leads us, then, to the basic equation in accounting (Illustration 3-2).

ILLUSTRATION 3-2
The Basic Accounting Equation

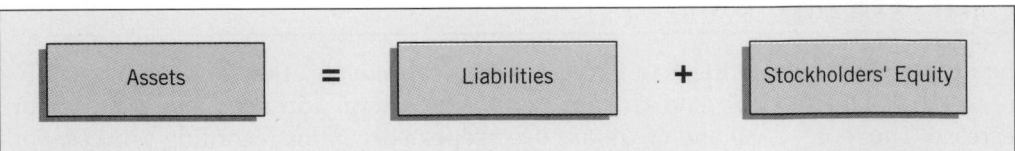

ILLUSTRATION 3-3
Expanded Basic Equation and Debit/Credit Rules and Effects

Illustration 3-3 expands this equation to show the accounts that comprise stockholders' equity. In addition, the debit/credit rules and effects on each type of account are illustrated. Study this diagram carefully. It will help you understand the fundamentals

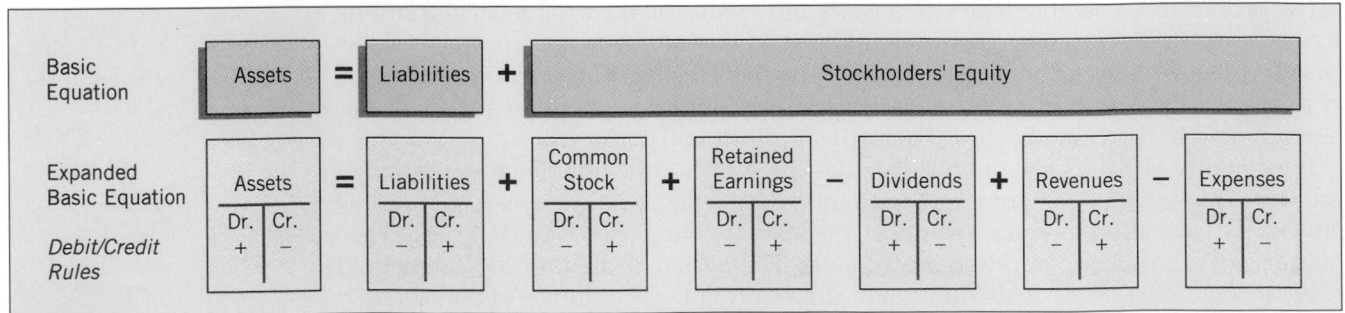

of the double-entry system. Like the basic equation, the expanded basic equation must be in balance (total debits equal total credits).

Every time a transaction occurs, the elements of the equation change, but the basic equality remains. To illustrate, here are eight different transactions for Perez Inc.

1. Owners invest $40,000 in exchange for common stock:

Assets + 40,000	=	Liabilities	+	Stockholders' Equity + 40,000

2. Disburse $600 cash for secretarial wages:

Assets − 600	=	Liabilities	+	Stockholders' Equity − 600 (expense)

3. Purchase office equipment priced at $5,200, giving a 10% promissory note in exchange:

Assets + 5,200	=	Liabilities +5,200	+	Stockholders' Equity

4. Receive $4,000 cash for services rendered:

Assets + 4,000	=	Liabilities	+	Stockholders' Equity + 4,000 (revenue)

5. Pay off a short-term liability of $7,000:

Assets − 7,000	=	Liabilities − 7,000	+	Stockholders' Equity

6. Declare a cash dividend of $5,000:

Assets	=	Liabilities + 5,000	+	Stockholders' Equity − 5,000

7. Convert a long-term liability of $80,000 into common stock:

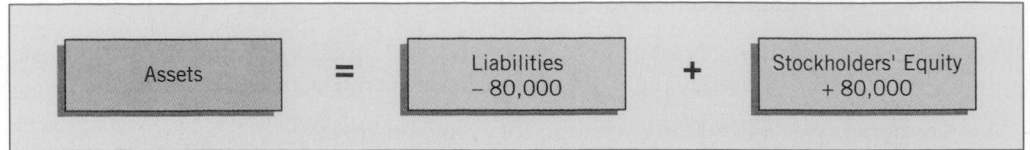

8. Pay cash of $16,000 for a delivery van:

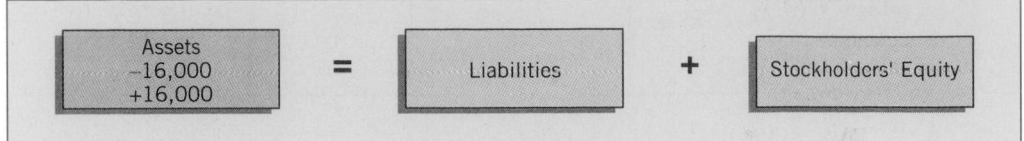

▶ FINANCIAL STATEMENTS AND OWNERSHIP STRUCTURE

Common stock and retained earnings are reported in the stockholders' equity section of the balance sheet. Dividends are reported on the statement of retained earnings. Revenues and expenses are reported on the income statement. Dividends, revenues, and expenses are eventually transferred to retained earnings at the end of the period. As a result, a change in any one of these three items affects stockholders' equity. The relationships related to stockholders' equity are shown in Illustration 3-4.

ILLUSTRATION 3-4
Financial Statements and Ownership Structure

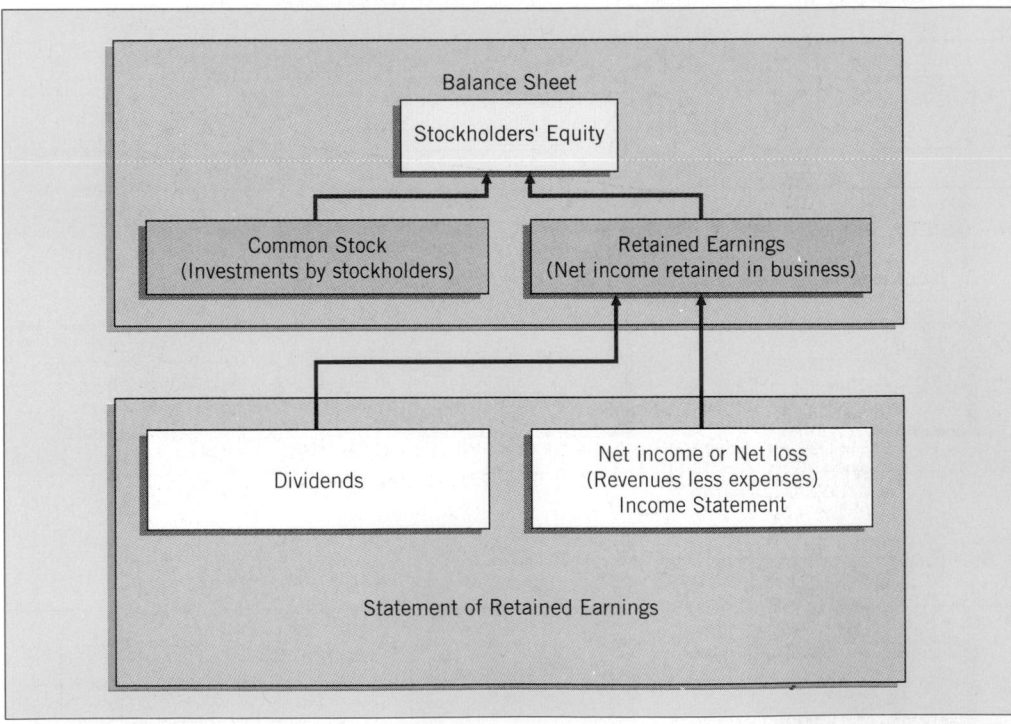

The type of ownership structure employed by a business enterprise dictates the types of accounts that are part of or affect the equity section. In a corporation, **Common Stock, Additional Paid-in Capital, Dividends,** and **Retained Earnings** are accounts commonly used. In a proprietorship or partnership, a Capital account is used to indicate the owner's or owners' investment in the company. A Drawing account is used to indicate withdrawals by the owner(s).

Illustration 3-5 summarizes and relates the transactions affecting owners' equity to the nominal (temporary) and real (permanent) classifications and to the types of business ownership.

ILLUSTRATION 3-5
Effects of Transactions on
Owners' Equity Accounts

| | | Ownership Structure | | | |
| | | Proprietorships and Partnerships | | Corporations | |
Transactions Affecting Owners' Equity	Impact on Owners' Equity	Nominal (Temporary) Accounts	Real (Permanent) Accounts	Nominal (Temporary) Accounts	Real (Permanent) Accounts
Investment by owner(s)	Increase		Capital		Common Stock and related accounts
Revenues earned	Increase	Revenue		Revenue	
Expenses incurred	Decrease	Expense	Capital	Expense	Retained Earnings
Withdrawal by owner(s)	Decrease	Drawing		Dividends	

▶ THE ACCOUNTING CYCLE

Illustration 3-6 flowcharts the steps in the **accounting cycle.** These are the accounting procedures normally used by enterprises to record transactions and prepare financial statements.

OBJECTIVE 3
Identify steps in the accounting cycle.

ILLUSTRATION 3-6
The Accounting Cycle

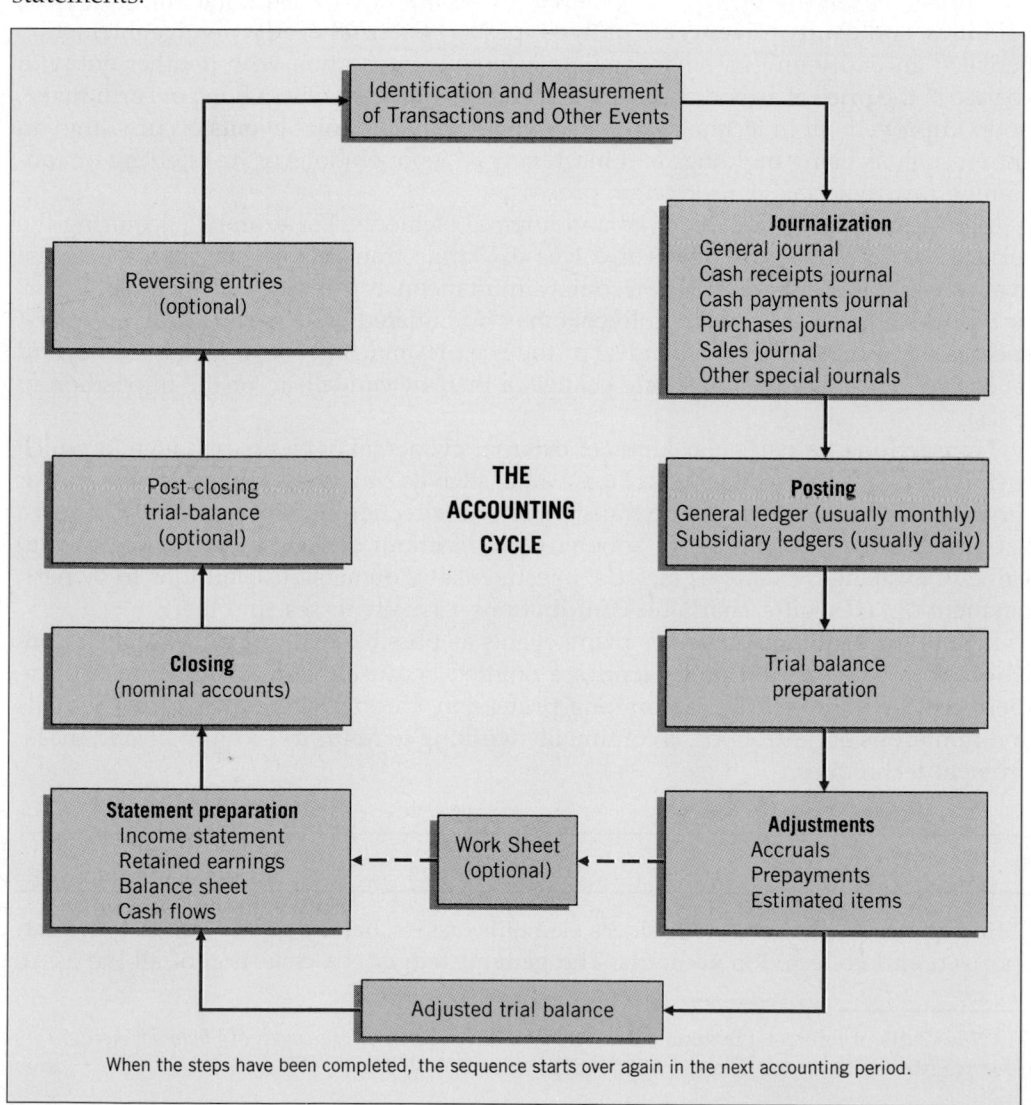

When the steps have been completed, the sequence starts over again in the next accounting period.

▶ IDENTIFICATION AND RECORDING OF TRANSACTIONS AND OTHER EVENTS

The first step in the accounting cycle is analysis of transactions and selected other events. The problem is to determine **what to record.** No simple rules exist that state whether an event should be recorded. Most accountants agree that changes in personnel, changes in managerial policies, and the value of human resources, though important, should not be recorded in the accounts. On the other hand, when the company makes a cash sale or purchase—no matter how small—it should be recorded.

The treatment relates to the accounting concepts presented in Chapter 2. **An item should be recognized in the financial statements if** it is an element, is measurable, and is relevant and reliable. Consider human resources. R. G. Barry & Co. at one time reported as supplemental data total assets of $14,055,926, including $986,094 for "net investments in human resources." AT&T and Mobil Oil Company have also experimented with human resource accounting. Should accountants value employees for balance sheet and income statement purposes? Certainly skilled employees are an important asset (highly relevant), but the problems of **determining their value and measuring it reliably have not yet been solved.** Consequently, human resources are not recorded. Perhaps when measurement techniques become more sophisticated and accepted, such information will be presented, if only in supplemental form.

The phrase "transactions and other events and circumstances that affect a business enterprise" is used to describe the sources or causes of changes in an entity's assets, liabilities, and equity.[2] **Events** are of two types: (1) **External events** involve interaction between an entity and its environment, such as a transaction with another entity, a change in the price of a good or service that an entity buys or sells, a flood or earthquake, or an improvement in technology by a competitor. (2) **Internal events** occur within an entity, such as using buildings and machinery in its operations or transferring or consuming raw materials in production processes.

Many events have both external and internal elements. For example, acquiring the services of employees or others involves exchange transactions, which are external events; using those services (labor), often simultaneously with their acquisition, is part of production, which is internal. Events may be initiated and controlled by an entity, such as the purchase of merchandise or the use of a machine, or they may be beyond its control, such as an interest rate change, a theft or vandalism, or the imposition of taxes.

Transactions, as particular kinds of external events, may be an exchange in which each entity both receives and sacrifices value, such as purchases and sales of goods or services. Or transactions may be transfers in one direction in which an entity incurs a liability or transfers an asset to another entity without directly receiving (or giving) value in exchange. Examples include investments by owners, distributions to owners, payment of taxes, gifts, charitable contributions, casualty losses, and thefts.

In short, accountants record as many events as possible that affect the **financial position** of the enterprise. Some events are omitted because the problems of measuring them are too complex. The accounting profession, through the efforts of individuals and numerous organizations, is continually working to refine its recognition and measurement techniques.

UNDERLYING CONCEPT

Assets are probable economic benefits controlled by a particular entity as a result of a past transaction or event. Do human resources of a company meet this definition?

▶ JOURNALIZATION

Differing effects on the basic business elements (assets, liabilities, and equities) are categorized and collected in **accounts.** The **general ledger** is a collection of all the asset,

---

[2]"Elements of Financial Statements of Business Enterprises," *Statement of Financial Accounting Concepts No. 6* (Stamford, Conn.: FASB, 1985), pages 259–260.

liability, stockholders' equity, revenue, and expense accounts. A **"T" account** (as shown in Illustration 3-8) is a convenient method of illustrating the effect of transactions on particular asset, liability, equity, revenue, and expense items.

In practice, transactions and selected other events are not recorded originally in the ledger because a transaction affects two or more accounts, each of which is on a different page in the ledger. To circumvent this deficiency and to have a complete record of each transaction or other event in one place, a **journal** (the book of original entry) is employed. The simplest journal form is a chronological listing of transactions and other events expressed in terms of debits and credits to particular accounts. This is called a **general journal.** It is illustrated below for the following transactions.

OBJECTIVE 4
Record transactions in journals, post to ledger accounts, and prepare a trial balance.

Nov. 1 Buys a new delivery truck on account from Auto Sales Co., $22,400.

3 Receives an invoice from the *Evening Graphic* for advertising, $280.

4 Returns merchandise to Yankee Supply for credit, $175.

16 Receives a $95 debit memo from Confederate Co., indicating that freight on a purchase from Confederate Co. was prepaid but is our obligation.

Each **general journal entry** consists of four parts: (1) the accounts and amounts to be debited (Dr.), (2) the accounts and amounts to be credited (Cr.), (3) a date, and (4) an explanation. Debits are entered first, followed by the credits, which are slightly indented. The explanation is begun below the name of the last account to be credited and may take one or more lines. The "Ref." column is completed at the time the accounts are posted.

GENERAL JOURNAL			Page 12	
Date 1996	Account Title and Explanation	Ref.	Amount Debit	Credit
Nov. 1	Delivery Equipment	8	22,400	
	Accounts Payable	34		22,400
	(Purchased delivery truck on account from Auto Sales Co.)			
3	Advertising Expense	65	280	
	Accounts Payable	34		280
	(Received invoice for advertising from *Evening Graphic*)			
4	Accounts Payable	34	175	
	Returned Purchases	53		175
	(Returned merchandise for credit to Yankee Supply)			
16	Transportation-In	55	95	
	Accounts Payable	34		95
	(Received debit memo for freight on merchandise purchased from Confederate Co.)			

ILLUSTRATION 3-7
General Journal with Sample Entries

Most businesses use **special journals** in addition to the general journal. Appendix 3-B at the end of this chapter discusses and illustrates the following special journals:

Cash receipts journal

Sales journal

Purchases journal (voucher register)

Cash payments journal (check register)

Special journals summarize transactions possessing a common characteristic, thereby reducing the time necessary to accomplish the various bookkeeping tasks.

▶ POSTING TO THE LEDGER

The items entered in a general journal must be transferred to the general ledger. This procedure, **posting,** is part of the summarizing and classifying process.

For example, the November 1 entry in the general journal in Illustration 3-7 showed a debit to Delivery Equipment of $22,400 and a credit to Accounts Payable of $22,400. The amount in the debit column is posted from the journal to the debit side of the ledger account (Delivery Equipment). The amount in the credit column is posted from the journal to the credit side of the ledger account (Accounts Payable).

The numbers in the "Ref." column of the general journal refer to the accounts in the ledger to which the respective items are posted. For example, the "34" placed in the column to the right of "Accounts Payable" indicates that this $22,400 item was posted to Account No. 34 in the ledger.

The posting of the general journal is completed when all of the posting reference numbers have been recorded opposite the account titles in the journal. Thus the number in the posting reference column serves two purposes: (1) to indicate the ledger account number of the account involved, and (2) to indicate that the posting has been completed for the particular item. Each business enterprise selects its own numbering system for its ledger accounts. One practice is to begin numbering with asset accounts and to follow with liabilities, owners' equities, revenue, and expense accounts, in that order.

The various ledger accounts appear below after the posting process is completed. The source of the data transferred to the ledger account is indicated by the reference GJ 12 (General Journal, page 12).

ILLUSTRATION 3-8
Ledger Accounts, in
T-Account Format

Delivery Equipment					No. 8
Nov. 1	GJ 12	22,400			

Accounts Payable					No. 34
Nov. 4	GJ 12	175	Nov. 1	GJ 12	22,400
			3	GJ 12	280
			16	GJ 12	95

Returned Purchases					No. 53
			Nov. 4	GJ 12	175

Transportation-In					No. 55
Nov. 16	GJ 12	95			

Advertising Expense					No. 65
Nov. 3	GJ 12	280			

▶ UNADJUSTED TRIAL BALANCE

An unadjusted trial balance should be prepared at the end of a given period after the entries have been recorded in the journal and posted to the ledger. A trial balance is a list of all open accounts in the general ledger and their balances. The trial balance accomplishes two principal purposes:

1. It proves that debits and credits of an equal amount are in the ledger.
2. It supplies a listing of open accounts and their balances; it is the basis for any adjustments; and it is used in preparing the financial statements and in supplying financial data about the concern.

But a trial balance does not prove that all transactions have been recorded or that the ledger is correct. Numerous errors may exist even though the trial balance columns agree. For example, the trial balance may balance even when (1) a transaction is not journalized, (2) a correct journal entry is not posted, (3) a journal entry is posted twice, (4) incorrect accounts are used in journalizing or posting, or (5) offsetting errors are made in recording the amount of a transaction. In other words, as long as equal debit and credits are posted, even to the wrong account or in the wrong amount, the total debits will equal the total credits.

The unadjusted trial balance for Software Sales, Inc. is shown in Illustration 3-9.

Software Sales, Inc. TRIAL BALANCE December 31, 1996		
Cash	$ 13,000	
Accounts Receivable	14,650	
Notes Receivable	8,000	
Inventory, January 1, 1996	89,500	
Office Equipment	16,000	
Furniture and Fixtures	12,300	
Accounts Payable		$ 14,100
Notes Payable		24,000
Common Stock		50,000
Retained Earnings		41,240
Sales		896,000
Returned Sales	3,760	
Sales Allowances	960	
Purchases	713,450	
Returned Purchases		4,140
Transportation-In	6,570	
Sales Salaries Expense	65,700	
Traveling Expenses	4,900	
Advertising Expense	21,200	
General Office Salaries	39,800	
Rent Expense	18,000	
Insurance Expense	2,780	
Utilities Expense	4,310	
Telephone Expense	1,260	
Auditing and Legal Expense	2,780	
Administrative Expense	2,200	
Purchase Discounts		13,500
Sales Discounts	1,860	
	$1,042,980	$1,042,980

ILLUSTRATION 3-9
Trial Balance (Unadjusted)

▶ ADJUSTMENTS

In order for revenues to be recorded in the period in which they are earned, and for expenses to be recognized in the period in which they are incurred, **adjusting entries are made at the end of the accounting period**. In short, **adjustments are needed to ensure that the revenue recognition and matching principles are followed.** The use of adjusting entries makes it possible to report on the balance sheet the appropriate assets, liabilities, and owners' equity at the statement date and to report on the income statement the proper net income (or loss) for the period. A trial balance may not contain up-to-date and complete financial statement data for the following reasons:

OBJECTIVE 5
Explain the reasons for preparing adjusting entries.

1. Some events, such as the consumption of supplies and the earning of wages by employees, are not journalized daily because it is inexpedient to do so.

2. The expiration of some costs, such as building and equipment deterioration and rent and insurance, is not journalized during the accounting period because these

costs expire with the passage of time rather than as a result of recurring daily transactions.

3. Some items, such as the cost of utility service, may be unrecorded because the bill for the service has not been received.

Adjusting entries are required every time financial statements are prepared. An essential starting point is an analysis of each account in the trial balance to determine whether it is complete and up-to-date for financial statement purposes. The analysis requires a thorough understanding of the company's operations and the interrelationship of accounts. The preparation of adjusting entries is often an involved process that requires the services of a skilled professional. In accumulating the adjustment data, the company may need to make inventory counts of supplies and repair parts. Also it may be desirable to prepare supporting schedules of insurance policies, rental agreements, and other contractual commitments. Adjustments are often prepared after the balance sheet date. However, the entries are dated as of the balance sheet date.

Normally the adjustments are classified in the following manner:

Prepaid (deferred) items:
    Prepaid expenses (e.g., prepaid insurance)
    Unearned revenues (e.g., rent received in advance)

Accrued items:
    Accrued expenses or liabilities (e.g., unpaid salaries)
    Accrued revenues or assets (e.g., interest earned but not collected)

Estimated items (e.g., depreciation)

> **UNDERLYING CONCEPT**
>
> *After adjusting entries are made, the company has the information needed to report its resources, claims to those resources, and changes in those resources.*

PREPAID EXPENSES

Payments of expenses that will benefit more than one accounting period are identified as **prepaid expenses** or **prepayments.** When a cost is incurred, an asset account is debited to show the service or benefit that will be received in the future. Prepayments often occur in regard to insurance, supplies, advertising, and rent. In addition, prepayments are made when buildings and equipment are purchased.

Prepaid expenses expire either with the passage of time (e.g., rent and insurance) or through use and consumption (e.g., supplies). The expiration of these costs does not require daily recurring entries, which would be unnecessary and impractical. Accordingly, it is customary to postpone the recognition of such cost expirations until financial statements are prepared. At each statement date, adjusting entries are made to record the expenses applicable to the current accounting period and to show the unexpired costs in the asset accounts. **An asset-expense relationship exists with prepaid expenses.** Prior to adjustment, assets are overstated and expenses are understated. Thus, **the prepaid expense adjusting entry results in a debit to an expense account and a credit to an asset account.**

Illustration

Insurance for 3 years is purchased for $1,200 cash on January 2, 1996. The business recorded the following journal entry.

Jan. 2

Unexpired Insurance	1,200	
Cash		1,200

At the end of the year, because one-third of the 3-year period has now passed, one-third of the amount paid is reported as an expense for 1996, and the asset account is reduced by the same amount. The adjusting entry required on December 31, 1996, is:

Dec. 31

Insurance Expense	400	
Unexpired Insurance		400
(To charge one-third of insurance premium to expense)		

The ledger now shows an expense for insurance of $400 and an asset, Unexpired Insurance, of $800. (Account titles synonymous with unexpired insurance are Prepaid Insurance or Prepaid Insurance Expense.)

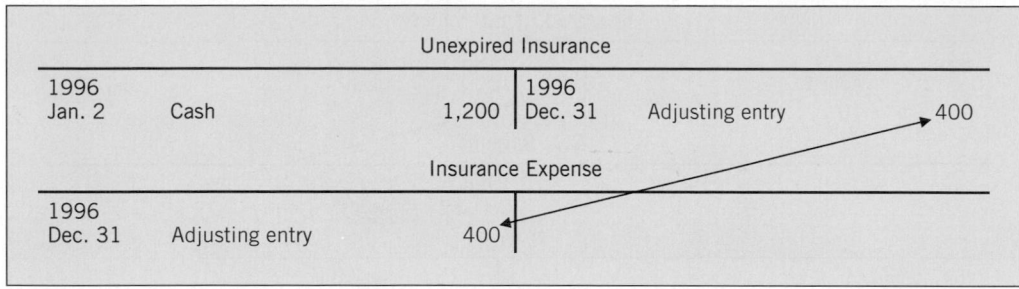

UNEARNED REVENUE

Revenues received in cash and recorded as liabilities before they are earned are called **unearned revenues.** Airlines such as United, American, and Delta, for instance, treat receipts from the sale of tickets as unearned revenue until the flight service is provided. Unearned revenues are the opposite of prepaid expenses. Indeed, unearned revenue on the books of one company is likely to be a prepayment on the books of the company that has made the advance payment. For example, if identical accounting periods are assumed, a landlord will have unearned rent revenue when a tenant has prepaid rent.

When the payment is received for services to be provided in a future accounting period, an unearned revenue (a liability) account should be credited to recognize the obligation that exists. Unearned revenues are subsequently earned through rendering service to a customer. During the accounting period it may not be practical to make daily recurring entries as the revenue is earned. In such cases, the recognition of earned revenue is delayed until the adjustment process. Then an adjusting entry is made to record the revenue that has been earned and to show the liability that remains. **A liability–revenue account relationship therefore exists with unearned revenues.** In the typical case, liabilities are overstated and revenues are understated prior to adjustment. Thus, **the adjusting entry for unearned revenues results in a debit to a liability account and a credit to a revenue account.**

Some common unearned revenue items are rent received in advance, interest received in advance on notes receivable, subscriptions and advertising received in advance by publishers, and deposits from customers in advance of delivery of merchandise.

Illustration

Assume that a business rented part of a building for a 3-year period from January 2, 1996, to a tenant who paid the full 3 years' rent, $60,000, in advance. The business made the following entry:

Jan. 2

Cash	60,000	
Unearned Rent Revenue		60,000
(To record rent received for 3 years in advance)		

At the end of 1996 one-third of this amount is earned, and an adjusting entry is made:

Dec. 31

Unearned Rent Revenue	20,000	
Rent Revenue		20,000
(To recognize as revenue one-third of $60,000)		

The entry records $20,000 in the Rent Revenue account, which represents the amount of revenue earned during the year. These two accounts now show the following balances after adjustment:

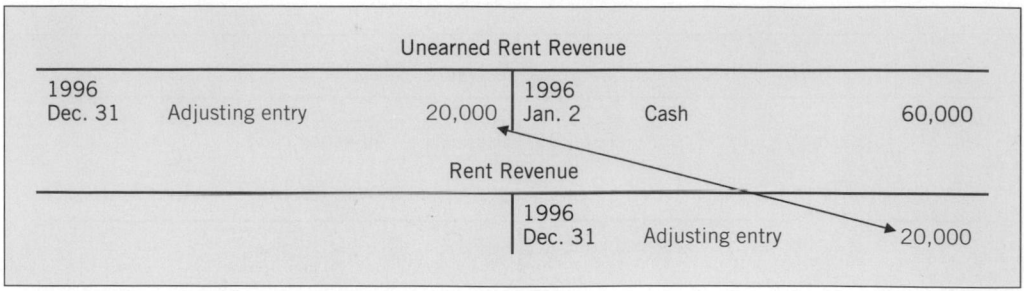

Unearned Rent Revenue					
1996 Dec. 31	Adjusting entry	20,000	1996 Jan. 2	Cash	60,000

Rent Revenue					
			1996 Dec. 31	Adjusting entry	20,000

For prepaid items, it makes no difference whether an original transaction entry is recorded in a real account (asset or liability) or in a nominal account (revenue or expense). After adjusting entries, the balances of the respective accounts are the same, regardless of the original entry.

ACCRUED LIABILITIES OR EXPENSES

accruals:
not yet paid
no receipt yet
no payment

Expenses incurred but unrecorded at the statement date are called **accrued expenses** or **accrued liabilities.** Interest, rent, taxes, and salaries are examples of accrued expenses. Accrued expenses result from the same causes as accrued revenues. In fact, an accrued expense on the books of one company is an accrued revenue to another company.

Adjustments for accrued expenses are necessary to record the obligations that exist at the balance sheet date and to recognize the expenses that are applicable to the current accounting period. **A liability–expense relationship exists with accrued expenses.** Prior to adjustment both liabilities and expenses are understated. Therefore, **the adjusting entry for accrued expenses results in a debit to an expense account and a credit to a liability account.**

Illustration

When employees are paid on the last day of the month, there are no accrued wages and salaries at the end of the month or year because all employees will have been paid all amounts due them. When they are paid on a weekly or biweekly basis, however, it is usually necessary to make an adjusting entry for wages and salaries earned but not paid at the end of the fiscal period. The reason: the reporting period's last day rarely lands on a payday.

Assume that a business pays its sales staff every Friday for a five-day week, that the total weekly payroll is $8,000, and that December 31 falls on Thursday. On December 31, the end of the fiscal period, the employees have worked four-fifths of a week for which they have not been paid and for which no entry has been made. The adjusting entry on December 31 is:

Dec. 31

Sales Salaries Expense	6,400	
Salaries Payable		6,400
(To record accrued salaries as of Dec. 31: 4/5 x $8,000)		

As a result of this entry, the income statement for the year includes the salaries earned by the sales staff during the last four days in December, and the balance sheet shows as a liability salaries payable of $6,400.

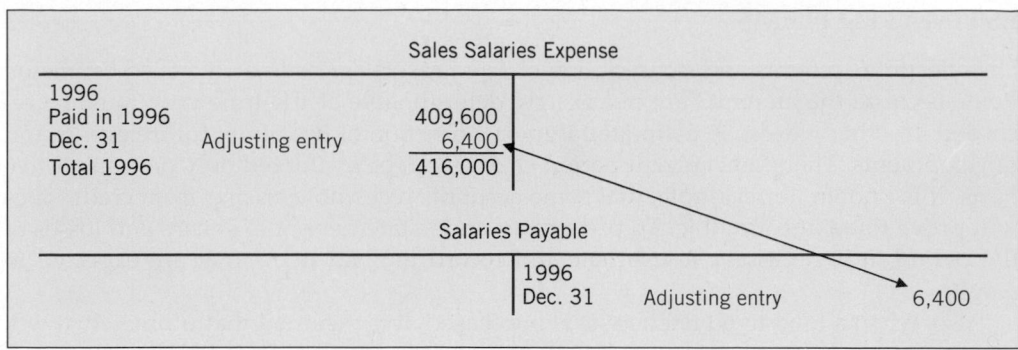

ACCRUED ASSETS OR REVENUES

Revenues earned but unrecorded at the statement date are known as **accrued revenues** or **accrued receivables.** Accrued revenues may accumulate (accrue) with the passing of time, as in the case of interest and rent. Or they may result from services that have been performed but neither billed nor collected, as in the case of commissions and fees. The former are unrecorded because the earning of interest and rent does not involve daily transactions; the latter may be unrecorded because only a portion of the total service has been provided.

An adjusting entry is required to show the receivable that exists at the balance sheet date and to record the revenue that has been earned during the period. **An asset-revenue account relationship exists with accrued revenues.** Prior to adjustment, both assets and revenues are understated. Accordingly, **an adjusting entry for accrued revenues results in a debit to an asset account and a credit to a revenue account.**

Illustration

Assume that office space is rented to a tenant at $1,000 per month, that the tenant has paid the rent for the first 11 months of the year, and that the tenant has paid no rent for December. The adjusting entry on December 31 is:

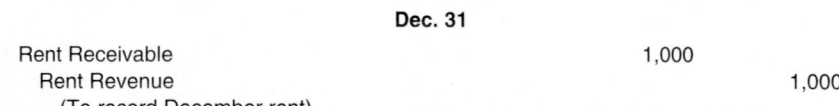

	Dec. 31		
Rent Receivable		1,000	
Rent Revenue			1,000
(To record December rent)			

As a result of this entry, an asset of $1,000, Rent Receivable, appears on the balance sheet disclosing the amount due from the tenant as of December 31. The income statement discloses rent revenue of $12,000, the $11,000 received for the first 11 months and the $1,000 for December entered by means of the adjusting entry. After adjustment, the accounts appear as shown below.

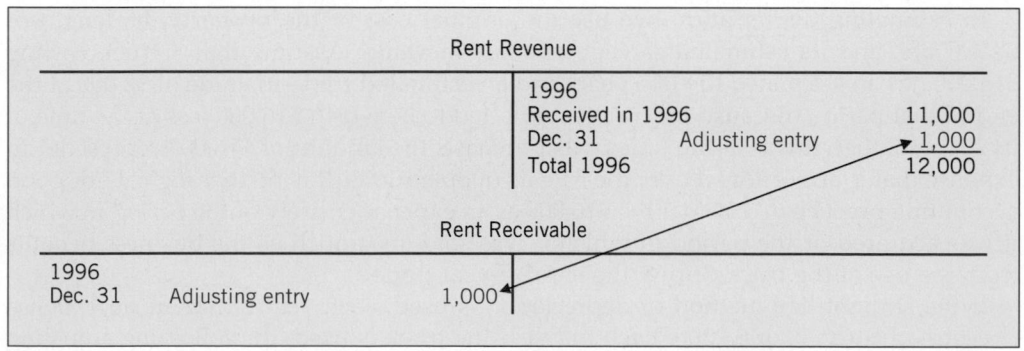

ESTIMATED ITEMS

Uncollectible accounts and depreciation of fixed assets are ordinarily called estimated items because the amounts are not exactly determinable at the time they must be recorded. In other words, an **estimated item** is a function of unknown future events and developments. Therefore, current period charges can be evaluated only on a subjective basis. It is known, for example, that some accounts receivable arising from credit sales will prove to be uncollectible. To prevent an understatement of expenses and losses of the period, it is necessary to estimate and record the bad debts that are expected to result.

Also, when a long-lived fixed asset is purchased, it is assumed that ultimately it will be scrapped or sold at a price much below the purchase price. This difference between an asset's cost and its scrap value represents an expense—depreciation—to the business that should be apportioned over the asset's useful life. We estimate the probable life of the fixed asset and its scrap value to determine the expense that is charged in each period.

Adjusting Entries for Bad Debts

Proper matching of revenues and expenses dictates recording bad debts as an expense of the period in which the sale is made instead of the period in which the accounts or notes are written off. The proper valuation of the receivable balance also requires recognition of uncollectible, worthless receivables. Proper matching and valuation require an adjusting entry.

At the end of each period an estimate is made of the amount of current period sales on account that will later prove to be uncollectible. The estimate is based on the amount of bad debts experienced in past years, general economic conditions, the age of the receivables, and other factors that indicate the element of uncollectibility. Usually it is expressed as a percent of the sales on account for the period. Or it may be computed by adjusting the Allowance for Doubtful Accounts to a certain percent of the trade accounts receivable and trade notes receivable at the end of the period.

Assume, for example, that experience reveals that bad debts usually approximate one-half of one percent of the net sales on account. If net sales on account for the year are $300,000, the adjusting entry for bad debts is:

Dec. 31

Bad Debt Expense	1,500	
Allowance for Doubtful Accounts		1,500
(To record estimated bad debts for the year:		
$300,000 x .005)		

Adjusting Entries for Depreciation

Entries for depreciation are similar to those made for reducing the prepaid expenses in which the original amount was debited to an asset account. The principal difference is that for depreciation the credit is made to a separate account, Accumulated Depreciation, instead of to the asset account.

In estimating depreciation, we use the original cost of the property, its length of useful life, and its estimated salvage or trade-in value. Assume that a truck costing $18,000 has an estimated life of 5 years and an estimated trade-in value of $2,000 at the end of that period. Because the truck is expected to be worth $16,000 less at the time of its disposal than it was at the time of its purchase, the amount of $16,000 represents an expense that is apportioned over the 5 years of operations. It is neither logical nor good accounting practice to consider the $16,000 as an expense entirely of the period in which it was acquired or the period in which it was sold, inasmuch as the business benefits from the use of the truck during the entire 5-year period.

If the straight-line method of depreciation is used, each year shows as an expense one-fifth of $16,000, or $3,200. Each full year the truck is used, the following adjusting entry is made:

Dec. 31

Depreciation Expense—Delivery Equipment	3,200	
Accumulated Depreciation—Delivery Equipment		3,200
(To record depreciation on truck for the year)		

SUMMARY OF ADJUSTMENTS SECTION

As a review, we summarize the basic adjustments and define them individually:

◄ BASIC ADJUSTMENTS ►

PREPAID EXPENSE. An expense paid in cash and recorded in an asset or expense account in advance of its use or consumption.

UNEARNED REVENUE. Cash received and recorded in a liability or revenue account before it is earned.

ACCRUED LIABILITIES (expenses). Expenses incurred but not yet paid.

ACCRUED ASSETS (revenues). Revenues earned but not yet received.

ESTIMATED ITEMS. Expenses recorded on the basis of subjective estimates of unknown future events or developments.

As soon as these adjusting entries have been recorded and posted, another trial balance is prepared before closing. The second or **adjusted trial balance** is used to prepare the financial statements. The basic set of financial statements is discussed in the next two chapters.

► INVENTORY AND RELATED ACCOUNTS

End-of-period procedures for inventory depend on what inventory system is in use. With a **perpetual inventory system**, purchases and issues are recorded directly in the inventory account as the purchases and issues occur. Therefore, the balance in the Inventory account should represent the ending inventory amount, and no adjusting entries are needed. To ensure this accuracy, a physical count of the items in the inventory is generally made annually. No Purchases account is used because the purchases are debited directly to the Inventory account. However, a Cost of Goods Sold account is used to accumulate the issuances from inventory. That is, when inventory items are sold, the cost of the sold goods is credited to Inventory and debited to Cost of Goods Sold.

With a **periodic inventory system,** a Purchases account is used and the Inventory account is unchanged during the period. The Inventory account represents the beginning inventory amount throughout the period. At the end of the accounting period the Inventory account must be adjusted by **closing out the beginning inventory** amount and **recording the ending inventory** amount. The ending inventory is determined by physically counting the items on hand and valuing them at cost or at the lower of cost or market. Under the periodic inventory system, cost of goods sold is, therefore, determined by adding the beginning inventory together with net purchases and deducting the ending inventory.

OBJECTIVE 6

Explain how inventory accounts are adjusted at year-end.

Cost of goods sold is determined as part of the closing process. It transfers the various merchandise accounts under a periodic inventory system into the Cost of Goods Sold account by use of a closing entry. To illustrate, Collegiate Apparel Shop has a beginning inventory of $30,000; Purchases $200,000; Transportation-In $6,000; Returned Purchases $1,200; Purchase Allowances $800; Purchase Discounts $2,000; and the ending inventory is $26,000.

Closing Entry

Inventory (ending)	26,000	
Purchase Discounts	2,000	
Purchase Allowances	800	
Returned Purchases	1,200	
Cost of Goods Sold	206,000	
Inventory (beginning)		30,000
Purchases		200,000
Transportation-In		6,000
(To transfer beginning inventory and net purchases to		
Cost of Goods Sold and to record the ending inventory)		

**ILLUSTRATION 3-10
Determining Cost of
Goods Sold and Closing
Related Accounts
(Periodic)**

After the foregoing entry, only the Cost of Goods Sold account remains to be closed.[3]

Illustration 3-10 illustrates in T-account form the process of determining cost of goods sold and closing the related nominal accounts.

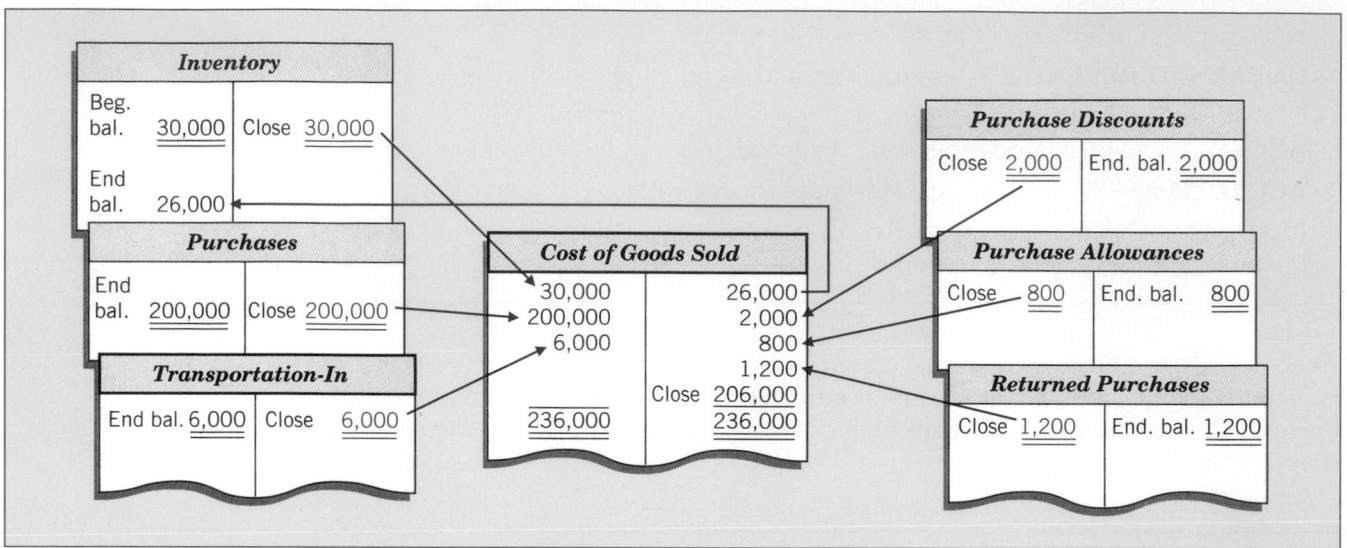

► YEAR-END CLOSING

OBJECTIVE 7

Prepare closing entries.

The procedure generally followed to reduce the balance of nominal (temporary) accounts to zero in order to prepare the accounts for the next period's transactions is known as the **closing process.** In the closing process all of the revenue and expense account balances (income statement items) are transferred to a clearing or suspense account called Income Summary, which is used only at the end of each accounting period (yearly). Revenues and expenses are matched in the Income Summary account and the net result of this matching, which represents the net income or net loss for the period, is then transferred to an owners' equity account (retained earnings for a corporation and capital accounts normally for proprietorships and partnerships). All closing entries are posted to the appropriate general ledger accounts.

For example, assume that revenue accounts of Collegiate Apparel Shop have the following balances, after adjustments, at the end of the year:

Revenue from Sales	$280,000
Rental Revenue	27,000
Interest Revenue	5,000

These **revenue accounts** would be closed and the balances transferred by the following closing journal entry:

---

[3]The change between the beginning and ending inventory balances may be made through adjusting entries rather than through closing entries. Some favor this method because they believe that changes in merchandise inventory should receive the same accounting treatment as changes in the cost of supplies on hand between two points in time. The adjusting entry method is just as acceptable as the closing entry method.

Revenue from Sales	280,000	
Rental Revenue	27,000	
Interest Revenue	5,000	
Income Summary		312,000
(To close revenue accounts to Income Summary)		

Assume that the expense accounts, including Cost of Goods Sold, have the following balances, after adjustments, at the end of the year:

Cost of Goods Sold	$206,000
Selling Expenses	25,000
General and Adm. Expenses	40,600
Interest Expense	4,400
Income Tax Expense	13,000

These **expense accounts** would be closed and the balances transferred through the following closing journal entry:

Income Summary	289,000	
Cost of Goods Sold		206,000
Selling Expenses		25,000
General and Adm. Expenses		40,600
Interest Expense		4,400
Income Tax Expense		13,000
(To close expense accounts to Income Summary)		

The Income Summary account now has a credit balance of $23,000 which is net income. The **net income is transferred to owners' equity** by closing the Income Summary account to Retained Earnings as follows:

Income Summary	23,000	
Retained Earnings		23,000
(To close Income Summary to Retained Earnings)		

Assuming that dividends of $7,000 were declared and distributed during the year, the Dividends account is closed directly to Retained Earnings as follows:

Retained Earnings	7,000	
Dividends		7,000

After the closing process is completed, each income statement (i.e., nominal) account is balanced out to zero and is ready for use in the next accounting period.

Illustration 3-11 shows the closing process in T-account form.

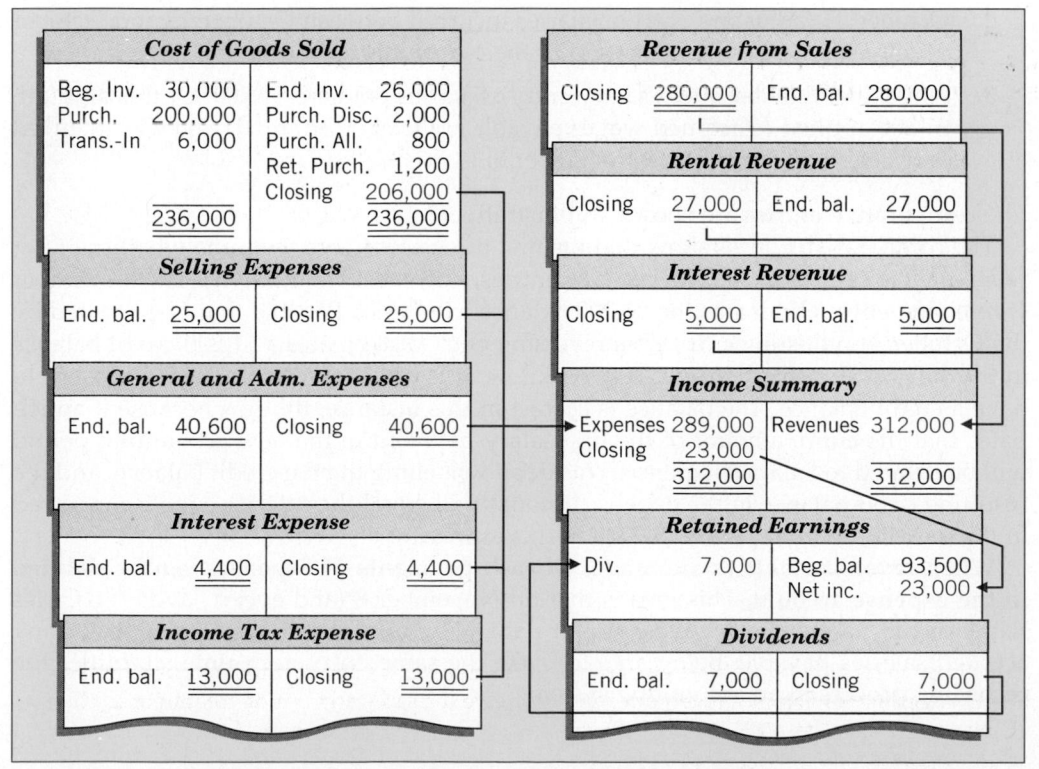

ILLUSTRATION 3-11
The Closing Process

▶ POST-CLOSING TRIAL BALANCE

We already mentioned that a trial balance is taken after the regular transactions of the period have been entered and that a second trial balance (the adjusted trial balance) is taken after the adjusting entries have been posted. A third trial balance may be taken after posting the closing entries. The trial balance after closing, often called the **post-closing trial balance,** shows that equal debits and credits have been posted to the Income Summary account. The post-closing trial balance consists only of asset, liability, and owners' equity (the real) accounts.

▶ REVERSING ENTRIES

OBJECTIVE 8

Identify adjusting entries that may be reversed.

After the financial statements have been prepared and the books have been closed, it is often helpful to reverse some of the adjusting entries before recording the regular transactions of the next period. Such entries are called **reversing entries. A reversing entry is made at the beginning of the next accounting period and is the exact opposite of the related adjusting entry made in the previous period.** The recording of reversing entries is an **optional** step in the accounting cycle that may be performed at the beginning of the next accounting period.

The purpose of reversing entries is to simplify the recording of transactions in the next accounting period. The use of reversing entries does not change the amounts reported in the financial statements for the previous period.

ILLUSTRATION OF REVERSING ENTRIES—ACCRUALS

Reversing entries are most often used to reverse two types of adjusting entries: accrued revenues and accrued expenses. To illustrate the optional use of reversing entries for accrued expenses, we will use the following transaction and adjustment data:

1. October 24 (initial salary entry): $4,000 of salaries incurred between October 1 and October 24 are paid.

2. October 31 (adjusting entry): Salaries incurred between October 25 and October 31 are $1,200. These will be paid in the November 8 payroll.

3. November 8 (subsequent salary entry): Salaries paid are $2,500. Of this amount, $1,200 applied to accrued wages payable at October 31 and $1,300 was incurred between November 1 and November 8.

The comparative entries are shown in Illustration 3-12.

The comparative entries show that the first three entries are the same whether or not reversing entries are used. The last two entries, however, are different. The November 1 reversing entry eliminates the $1,200 balance in Salaries Payable that was created by the October 31 adjusting entry. The reversing entry also creates a $1,200 credit balance in the Salaries Expense account. As you know, it is unusual for an expense account to have a credit balance. The balance is correct in this instance, though, because it anticipates that the entire amount of the first salary payment in the new accounting period will be debited to Salaries Expense. This debit will eliminate the credit balance, and the resulting debit balance in the expense account will equal the salaries expense incurred in the new accounting period ($1,300 in this example).

When reversing entries are made, all cash payments of expenses can be debited to the expense account. This means that on November 8 (and every payday) Salaries Expense can be debited for the amount paid without regard to the existence of any accrued salaries payable. Being able to make the same entry each time simplifies the recording process in an accounting system.

Reversing Entries Not Used			Reversing Entries Used		
Initial Salary Entry					
Oct. 24	Salaries Expense	4,000	Oct. 24	Salaries Expense	4,000
	Cash	4,000		Cash	4,000
Adjusting Entry					
Oct. 31	Salaries Expense	1,200	Oct. 31	Salaries Expense	1,200
	Salaries Payable	1,200		Salaries Payable	1,200
Closing Entry					
Oct. 31	Income Summary	5,200	Oct. 31	Income Summary	5,200
	Salaries Expense	5,200		Salaries Expense	5,200
Reversing Entry					
Nov. 1	No entry is made.		Nov. 1	Salaries Payable	1,200
				Salaries Expense	1,200
Subsequent Salary Entry					
Nov. 8	Salaries Payable	1,200	Nov. 8	Salaries Expense	2,500
	Salaries Expense	1,300		Cash	2,500
	Cash	2,500			

ILLUSTRATION 3-12
Comparison of Entries for Accruals, with and without Reversing Entries

ILLUSTRATION OF REVERSING ENTRIES—PREPAYMENTS

Prepayments may also be reversed if the initial entry to record the transaction is made to an expense or revenue account. To illustrate the use of reversing entries for prepaid expenses, we will use the following transaction and adjustment data:

1. December 10 (initial entry): $20,000 of office supplies are purchased with cash.
2. December 31 (adjusting entry): $5,000 of office supplies on hand.

The comparative entries are shown in Illustration 3-13.

Reversing Entries Not Used			Reversing Entries Used		
Initial Purchase of Supplies Entry					
Dec. 10	Office Supplies	20,000	Dec. 10	Office Supplies Expense	20,000
	Cash	20,000		Cash	20,000
Adjusting Entry					
Dec. 31	Office Supplies Expense	15,000	Dec. 31	Office Supplies	5,000
	Office Supplies	15,000		Office Supplies Expense	5,000
Closing Entry					
Dec. 31	Income Summary	15,000	Dec. 31	Income Summary	15,000
	Office Supplies Expense	15,000		Office Supplies Expense	15,000
Reversing Entry					
Jan. 1	No entry		Jan. 1	Office Supplies Expense	5,000
				Office Supplies	5,000

ILLUSTRATION 3-13
Comparison of Entries for Prepayments, with and without Reversing Entries

After the adjusting entry on December 31 (regardless of whether reversing entries are used), the asset account, Office Supplies, shows a balance of $5,000 and Office Supplies Expense a balance of $15,000. If Office Supplies Expense initially was debited when the supplies were purchased, a reversing entry is made to return to the expense account the cost of unconsumed supplies. The company then continues to debit Office Supplies Expense for additional purchases of office supplies during the next period.

With respect to prepaid items, why are all such items not entered originally into real accounts (assets and liabilities), thus making reversing entries unnecessary? Sometimes this practice is followed. It is particularly advantageous for items that need to be apportioned over several periods (e.g., supplies and parts inventories). However, items that do not follow this regular pattern and that may or may not involve two or more periods are ordinarily entered initially in revenue or expense accounts. The revenue and expense accounts may not require adjusting and are systematically closed to Income Summary. Using the nominal accounts adds consistency to the accounting system and makes the recording more efficient, particularly when a large number of such transactions occur during the year. For example, the bookkeeper knows that when an invoice is received for other than a capital asset acquisition, the amount is expensed. The bookkeeper need not worry at the time the invoice is received whether or not the item will result in a prepaid expense at the end of the period, because adjustments will be made at the end of the period.

SUMMARY OF REVERSING ENTRIES

A summary of guidelines for reversing entries is as follows:

1. All accrued items should be reversed.
2. All prepaid items for which the original cash transaction was debited or credited to an expense or revenue account should be reversed.
3. Adjusting entries for depreciation and bad debts are not reversed.

Recognize that reversing entries do not have to be used; therefore, some accountants avoid them entirely.

▶ THE ACCOUNTING CYCLE SUMMARIZED

A summary of the steps in the accounting cycle shows a logical sequence of the accounting procedures used during a fiscal period:

1. Enter the transactions of the period in appropriate journals.
2. Post from the journals to the ledger (or ledgers).
3. Take an unadjusted trial balance (trial balance).
4. Prepare adjusting journal entries and post to the ledger(s).
5. Take a trial balance after adjusting (adjusted trial balance).
6. Prepare the financial statements from the second trial balance.
7. Prepare closing journal entries and post to the ledger(s).
8. Take a trial balance after closing (post-closing trial balance).
9. Prepare reversing entries (optional) and post to the ledger(s).

This list of procedures constitutes a complete accounting cycle that is normally performed in every fiscal period.

▶ USING A WORK SHEET TO PREPARE FINANCIAL STATEMENTS

OBJECTIVE 9

Prepare a 10-column work sheet.

To facilitate the end-of-period (monthly, quarterly, or annually) accounting and reporting process, accountants frequently use a work sheet. A **work sheet** is a columnar sheet of paper used to adjust the account balances and prepare the financial statements. Use of a work sheet helps the accountant prepare the financial statements on a more timely basis. It is not necessary to delay preparation of the financial statements until the adjusting and closing entries are journalized and posted. The **10-column work sheet** illustrated in this chapter (Illustration 3-14) provides columns for the first trial balance, adjustments, adjusted trial balance, income statement, and balance sheet.

The work sheet does not replace the financial statements. Instead, it is the accountant's informal device for accumulating and sorting information needed for the financial statements. Completing the work sheet provides considerable assurance that all of the details related to the end-of-period accounting and statement preparation have been properly brought together.

ADJUSTMENTS ENTERED ON THE WORK SHEET

Items (a) through (f) below serve as the basis for the adjusting entries made in the work sheet shown in Illustration 3-14.

(a) Furniture and equipment is depreciated at the rate of 10% per year based on original cost of $67,000.

(b) Estimated bad debts, one-quarter of 1% of sales ($400,000).

(c) Insurance expired during the year, $360.

(d) Interest accrued on notes receivable as of December 31, $800.

(e) The Rent Expense account contains $500 rent paid in advance, which is applicable to next year.

(f) Property taxes accrued December 31, $2,000.

The adjusting entries shown on the December 31, 1996 work sheet are as follows:

(a)		
Depreciation Expense—Furniture and Equipment	6,700	
Accumulated Depreciation—Furniture and Equipment		6,700
(b)		
Bad Debts Expense	1,000	
Allowance for Doubtful Accounts		1,000
(c)		
Insurance Expense	360	
Unexpired Insurance		360
(d)		
Interest Receivable	800	
Interest Revenue		800
(e)		
Prepaid Rent Expense	500	
Rent Expense		500
(f)		
Property Tax Expense	2,000	
Property Tax Payable		2,000

These adjusting entries are transferred to the Adjustments columns of the work sheet, and each may be designated by letter. The accounts that are set up as a result of the adjusting entries and that are not already in the trial balance are listed below the totals of the trial balance, as illustrated on the work sheet. The Adjustments columns are then totaled and balanced.

The illustration does not include in the Adjustments columns the adjustments for cost of goods sold. Although these adjustments are sometimes included in these columns on a 10-column work sheet, this illustration assumes that these entries will be made during the closing process.

ADJUSTED TRIAL BALANCE COLUMNS

The amounts shown in the Trial Balance columns are combined with the Adjustments columns and are extended to the Adjusted Trial Balance columns. For example, the $2,000 shown opposite the Allowance for Doubtful Accounts in the Trial Balance Cr.

	Uptown Cabinet Corp. TEN-COLUMN WORK SHEET For the Year Ended December 31, 1996									
	Trial Balance		Adjustments		Adjusted Trial Balance		Income Statement		Balance Sheet	
Accounts	Dr.	Cr.	Dr.	Cr.	Dr.	Cr.	Dr.	Cr.	Dr.	Cr.
Cash	1,200				1,200				1,200	
Notes receivable	16,000				16,000				16,000	
Accounts receivable	41,000				41,000				41,000	
Allowance for doubtful accounts		2,000		(b) 1,000		3,000				3,000
Inventory, Jan. 1, 1996	36,000				36,000		36,000			
Unexpired insurance	900			(c) 360	540				540	
Furniture and equipment	67,000				67,000				67,000	
Accumulated depreciation— furniture and equipment		12,000		(a) 6,700		18,700				18,700
Notes payable		20,000				20,000				20,000
Accounts payable		13,500				13,500				13,500
Bonds payable		30,000				30,000				30,000
Common stock		50,000				50,000				50,000
Retained earnings, Jan. 1, 1996		14,200				14,200				14,200
Sales		400,000				400,000		400,000		
Purchases	320,000				320,000		320,000			
Sales salaries expense	20,000				20,000		20,000			
Advertising expense	2,200				2,200		2,200			
Traveling expense	8,000				8,000		8,000			
Salaries, office and general	19,000				19,000		19,000			
Telephone and telegraph expense	600				600		600			
Rent expense	4,800			(e) 500	4,300		4,300			
Property tax expense	3,300		(f) 2,000		5,300		5,300			
Interest expense	1,700				1,700		1,700			
Totals	541,700	541,700								
Depreciation expense— furniture and equipment			(a) 6,700		6,700		6,700			
Bad debts expense			(b) 1,000		1,000		1,000			
Insurance expense			(c) 360		360		360			
Interest receivable			(d) 800		800				800	
Interest revenue				(d) 800		800		800		
Prepaid rent expense			(e) 500		500				500	
Property tax payable				(f) 2,000		2,000				2,000
Totals			11,360	11,360	552,200	552,200				
Inventory, Dec. 31, 1996								40,000	40,000	
Totals							425,160	440,800		
Income before income taxes							15,640			
Totals							440,800	440,800		
Income before income taxes								15,640		
Income tax expense			(g) 3,440				3,440			
Income tax payable				(g) 3,440						3,440
Net income							12,200			12,200
Totals							15,640	15,640	167,040	167,040

ILLUSTRATION 3-14
Use of a Work Sheet

column is added to the $1,000 in the Adjustments Cr. column. The $3,000 total is then extended to the Adjusted Trial Balance Cr. column. Similarly, the $900 debit opposite Unexpired Insurance is reduced by the $360 credit in the Adjustments column. The result, $540, is shown in the Adjusted Trial Balance Dr. column. The Adjusted Trial Balance debit and credit columns are then totaled and determined to be in balance.

INCOME STATEMENT AND BALANCE SHEET COLUMNS

All the debit items in the Adjusted Trial Balance columns are extended into the balance sheet or income statement columns to the right. All the credit items in the Adjusted Trial Balance columns are similarly extended.

Note that the January 1 inventory is extended to the Income Statement Dr. column, because beginning inventory will appear as an addition in the cost of goods sold section of the income statement.

ENDING INVENTORY

The December 31 inventory, $40,000, is not in either of the trial balances but is listed as a separate item *below* the accounts already shown. It is listed in the Balance Sheet Dr. column because it is an asset at the end of the year, and in the Income Statement Cr. column because it will be used as a deduction in the cost of goods sold section of the income statement.

INCOME TAXES AND NET INCOME

The next step is to total the Income Statement columns; the figure necessary to balance the debit and credit columns is the pretax income or loss for the period. The income before income taxes of $15,640 is shown in the Income Statement Dr. column because the revenues exceeded expenses by that amount.

The federal and state income tax expense and related tax liability are then computed. The company applies an effective rate of 22% to arrive at $3,440. Because the Adjustments columns have been balanced, this adjustment is entered in the Income Statement Dr. column as Income Tax Expense and in the Balance Sheet Cr. column as Income Tax Payable. The following adjusting journal entry is recorded on December 31, 1996, and posted to the general ledger as well as entered on the work sheet.

(g)

Income Tax Expense	3,440	
Income Tax Payable		3,440

Next the Income Statement columns are balanced with the income taxes included. The $12,200 difference between the debit and credit columns in this illustration represents net income. The net income of $12,200 is entered in the Income Statement Dr. column to achieve equality and in the Balance Sheet Cr. column as the increase in retained earnings.

PREPARATION OF FINANCIAL STATEMENTS FROM WORK SHEET

The work sheet provides the information needed for preparation of the financial statements without reference to the ledger or other records. In addition, the data have been sorted into appropriate columns, which facilitates the preparation of the statements.

The financial statements prepared from the 10-column work sheet illustrated are:

Income Statement for the Year Ended December 31, 1996 (Illustration 3-15).

Statement of Retained Earnings for the Year Ended December 31, 1996 (Illustration 3-16).

Balance Sheet as of December 31, 1996 (Illustration 3-17).

STATEMENT OF INCOME

The income statement presented is that of a trading or merchandising concern; if a manufacturing concern were illustrated, three inventory accounts would be involved: raw materials, work in process, and finished goods. When these accounts are used, a supplementary statement entitled Cost of Goods Manufactured must be prepared.

ILLUSTRATION 3-15
An Income Statement

Uptown Cabinet Corp. INCOME STATEMENT For the Year Ended December 31, 1996			
Net sales			$400,000
Cost of goods sold			
Inventory, Jan. 1, 1996		$ 36,000	
Purchases		320,000	
Cost of goods available for sale		356,000	
Deduct inventory, Dec. 31, 1996		40,000	
Cost of goods sold			316,000
Gross profit on sales			84,000
Selling expenses			
Sales salaries expense		20,000	
Advertising expense		2,200	
Traveling expense		8,000	
Total selling expenses		30,200	
Administrative expenses			
Salaries, office and general	$19,000		
Telephone and telegraph expense	600		
Rent expense	4,300		
Property tax expense	5,300		
Depreciation expense—furniture and equipment	6,700		
Bad debts expense	1,000		
Insurance expense	360		
Total administrative expenses		37,260	
Total selling and administrative expenses			67,460
Income from operations			16,540
Other revenues and gains			
Interest revenue			800
			17,340
Other expenses and losses			
Interest expense			1,700
Income before income taxes			15,640
Income taxes			3,440
Net income			$ 12,200
Earnings per share			$1.22

STATEMENT OF RETAINED EARNINGS

The net income earned by a corporation may be retained in the business or it may be distributed to stockholders by payment of dividends. In the illustration the net income earned during the year was added to the balance of retained earnings on January 1, thereby increasing the balance of retained earnings to $26,400 on December 31. No dividends were declared during the year.

ILLUSTRATION 3-16
A Statement of Retained
Earnings

Uptown Cabinet Corp. STATEMENT OF RETAINED EARNINGS For the Year Ended December 31, 1996	
Retained earnings, Jan. 1, 1996	$14,200
Add net income for 1996	12,200
Retained earnings, Dec. 31, 1996	$26,400

BALANCE SHEET

The balance sheet prepared from the 10-column work sheet contains new items resulting from year-end adjusting entries. Interest receivable, unexpired insurance, and prepaid rent expense are included as current assets. These assets are considered current because they will be converted into cash or consumed in the ordinary routine of the business within a relatively short period of time. The amount of Allowance for Doubtful Accounts is deducted from the total of accounts, notes, and interest receivable because it is estimated that only $54,800 of $57,800 will be collected in cash.

In the property, plant, and equipment section the accumulated depreciation is deducted from the cost of the furniture and equipment; the difference represents the book or carrying value of the furniture and equipment.

Property tax payable is shown as a current liability because it is an obligation that is payable within a year. Other short-term accrued liabilities would also be shown as current liabilities.

The bonds payable, due in 2001, are long-term liabilities and are shown in a separate section. (Interest on the bonds was paid on December 31.)

Because Uptown Cabinet Corp. is a corporation, the capital section of the balance sheet, called the stockholders' equity section in the illustration, is somewhat different from the capital section for a proprietorship. Total stockholders' equity consists of the common stock, which is the original investment by stockholders, and the earnings retained in the business.

ILLUSTRATION 3-17
A Balance Sheet

Uptown Cabinet Corp. BALANCE SHEET As of December 31, 1996			
Assets			
Current assets			
Cash			$ 1,200
Notes receivable	$16,000		
Accounts receivable	41,000		
Interest receivable	800	$57,800	
Less allowance for doubtful accounts		3,000	54,800
Merchandise inventory on hand			40,000
Unexpired insurance			540
Prepaid rent			500
Total current assets			97,040
Property, plant, and equipment			
Furniture and equipment		67,000	
Less accumulated depreciation		18,700	
Total property, plant, and equipment			48,300
Total assets			$145,340
Liabilities and Stockholders' Equity			
Current liabilities			
Notes payable			$ 20,000
Accounts payable			13,500
Property tax payable			2,000
Income taxes payable			3,440
Total current liabilities			38,940
Long-term liabilities			
Bonds payable, due June 30, 2001			30,000
Total liabilities			68,940
Stockholders' equity			
Common stock, $1.00 par value, issued and outstanding, 50,000 shares		$50,000	
Retained earnings		26,400	
Total stockholders' equity			76,400
Total liabilities and stockholders' equity			$145,340

CLOSING AND REVERSING ENTRIES

The entries for the closing process are as follows:

General Journal
December 31, 1996

Inventory (December 31)	40,000	
Cost of Goods Sold	316,000	
Inventory (January 1)		36,000
Purchases		320,000
(To record ending inventory balance and to determine cost of goods sold)		
Interest Revenue	800	
Sales	400,000	
Cost of Goods Sold		316,000
Sales Salaries Expense		20,000
Advertising Expense		2,200
Traveling Expense		8,000
Salaries, Office and General		19,000
Telephone and Telegraph Expense		600
Rent Expense		4,300
Property Tax Expense		5,300
Depreciation Expense—Furniture and Equipment		6,700
Bad Debts Expense		1,000
Insurance Expense		360
Interest Expense		1,700
Income Tax Expense		3,440
Income Summary		12,200
(To close revenues and expenses to Income Summary)		
Income Summary	12,200	
Retained Earnings		12,200
(To close Income Summary to Retained Earnings)		

After the financial statements have been prepared, the enterprise may use reversing entries to simplify the accounting next period. The following reversing entries would be made if a reversing system were used.

January 1, 1997

(1)

Interest Revenue	800	
Interest Receivable		800

(2)

Rent Expense	500	
Prepaid Rent Expense		500

(3)

Property Tax Payable	2,000	
Property Tax Expense		2,000

Reversing entries would not appear on the 10-column work sheet because they are recorded in the next year (1997). The main object of the work sheet is to obtain the correct balances at the end of the year for financial statement presentation for the current year (1996).

MONTHLY STATEMENTS, YEARLY CLOSING

The use of a work sheet at the end of each month or quarter permits the preparation of interim financial statements even though the books are closed only at the end of each year. For example, assume that a business closes its books on December 31 but that monthly financial statements are desired. At the end of January a work sheet similar to the one illustrated in this chapter can be prepared to supply the information needed for statements for January. At the end of February a work sheet can be used again. Note that because the accounts were not closed at the end of January, the income statement taken from the work sheet on February 28 will present the net income for two months.

If an income statement for only the month of February is wanted, it can be obtained by subtracting the items in the January income statement from the corresponding items in the income statement for the two months of January and February.

A statement of retained earnings for February only also may be obtained by subtracting the January items. The balance sheet prepared from the February work sheet, however, shows assets, liabilities, and stockholders' equity as of February 28, the specific date for which a balance sheet is desired.

The March work sheet would show the revenues and expenses for three months, and the subtraction of the revenues and expenses for the first two months could be made to supply the amounts needed for an income statement for the month of March only, and so on throughout the year.

► SUMMARY OF LEARNING OBJECTIVES ◄

1. **Understand basic accounting terminology.** An understanding of the following eleven terms is important: (1) Event. (2) Transaction. (3) Account. (4) Real and nominal accounts. (5) Ledger. (6) Journal. (7) Posting. (8) Trial balance. (9) Adjusting entries. (10) Financial statements. (11) Closing entries.

2. **Explain double-entry rules.** The left side of any account is the debit side; the right side is the the credit side. All asset and expense accounts are increased on the left or debit side and decreased on the right or credit side. Conversely, all liability and revenue accounts are increased on the right or credit side and decreased on the left or debit side. Stockholders' equity accounts, Common Stock and Retained Earnings, are increased on the credit side, whereas Dividends is increased on the debit side.

3. **Identify steps in the accounting cycle.** The basic steps in the accounting cycle are (1) identification and measurement of transactions and other events; (2) journalization; (3) posting; (4) unadjusted trial balance; (5) adjustments; (6) adjusted trial balance; (7) statement presentation; and (8) closing.

4. **Record transactions in journals, post to ledger accounts, and prepare a trial balance.** The simplest journal form is a chronological listing of transactions and events expressed in terms of debits and credits to particular accounts. The items entered in a general journal must be transferred (posted) to the general ledger. An unadjusted trial balance should be prepared at the end of a given period after the entries have been recorded in the journal and posted to the ledger.

5. **Explain the reasons for preparing adjusting entries.** Adjustments are necessary to achieve a proper matching of revenues and expenses so as to determine net income for the current period and to achieve an accurate statement of end-of-the-period balances in assets, liabilities, and owners' equity accounts.

6. **Explain how inventory accounts are adjusted at year-end.** When the inventory records are maintained in a periodic inventory system, a Purchases account is used; the Inventory account is unchanged during the period. The Inventory account represents the beginning inventory amount throughout the period. At the end of the accounting period the inventory account must be adjusted by closing out the beginning inventory amount and recording the ending inventory amount. Under a perpetual inventory system the balance in the Inventory account should represent the ending inventory amount, and no adjusting entries are needed.

7. **Prepare closing entries.** In the closing process all of the revenue and expense account balances (income statement items) are transferred to a clearing account called Income Summary, which is used only at the end of each fiscal year.

KEY TERMS

account, 70
accounting cycle, 75
accrued assets (revenues), 83
accrued liabilities (expenses), 82
adjusted trial balance, 85
adjusting entry, 79
balance sheet, 71
closing entries, 71
credit, 71
debit, 71
double-entry accounting, 71
estimated item, 84
event, 70
financial statements, 71
general journal, 77
general ledger, 76
income statement, 71
journal, 71
ledger, 71
nominal accounts, 70
periodic inventory system, 85
perpetual inventory system, 85
posting, 78
prepaid expense, 80
real accounts, 70
reversing entries, 88
special journals, 77
statement of cash flows, 71
statement of retained earnings, 71
T account, 77
transaction, 70
trial balance, 78

Revenues and expenses are matched in the Income Summary account. The net result of this matching, which represents the net income or net loss for the period, is then transferred to an owners' equity account (retained earnings for a corporation and capital accounts for proprietorships and partnerships).

8. **Identify adjusting entries that may be reversed.** Reversing entries are most often used to reverse two types of adjusting entries: accrued revenues and accrued expenses. Prepayments may also be reversed if the initial entry to record the transaction is made to an expense or revenue account.

9. **Prepare a 10-column work sheet.** The 10-column work sheet provides columns for the first trial balance, adjustments, adjusted trial balance, income statement, and balance sheet. The work sheet does not replace the financial statements. Instead, it is the accountant's informal device for accumulating and sorting information needed for the financial statements.

APPENDIX 3-A

CASH BASIS ACCOUNTING VERSUS ACCRUAL BASIS ACCOUNTING

OBJECTIVE 10

After studying Appendix 3-A, you should be able to: Differentiate the cash basis of accounting from the accrual basis of accounting.

Most companies use the **accrual basis of accounting,** recognizing revenue when it is earned and recognizing expenses in the period incurred, without regard to the time of receipt or payment of cash. Some small enterprises and the average individual taxpayer, however, use a strict or modified cash basis approach. Under the **strict cash basis of accounting,** revenue is recorded only when the cash is received and expenses are recorded only when the cash is paid. The determination of income on the cash basis rests upon the collection of revenue and the payment of expenses, and the revenue recognition and the matching principle are ignored. Consequently, cash basis financial statements are not in conformity with generally accepted accounting principles.

To illustrate and contrast accrual basis accounting and cash basis accounting, assume that Quality Contractor signs an agreement to construct a garage for $22,000. In January, Quality Contractor begins construction, incurs costs of $18,000 on credit, and by the end of January delivers a finished garage to the buyer. In February, Quality Contractor collects $22,000 cash from the customer. In March, Quality pays the $18,000 due the creditors. The net incomes for each month under cash basis accounting and accrual basis accounting are as follows:

ILLUSTRATION 3A-1
Income Statement—
Cash Basis

Quality Contractor—Cash Basis Accounting INCOME STATEMENT For the Month of				
	January	February	March	Total
Cash receipts	$ –0–	$22,000	$ –0–	$22,000
Cash payments	–0–	–0–	18,000	18,000
Net income (loss)	$ –0–	$22,000	$(18,000)	$ 4,000

Quality Contractor—Accrual Basis Accounting INCOME STATEMENT For the Month of				
	January	February	March	Total
Revenues	$22,000	$ –0–	$ –0–	$22,000
Expenses	18,000	–0–	–0–	18,000
Net income (loss)	$ 4,000	$ –0–	$ –0–	$ 4,000

ILLUSTRATION 3A-2
Income Statement—
Accrual Basis

For the three months combined, total net income is the same under both cash basis accounting and accrual basis accounting; the difference is in the **timing** of net income.

The balance sheet is also affected by the basis of accounting. For instance, if cash basis accounting were used, Quality Contractor's balance sheets at each month-end would appear as follows:

Quality Contractor—Cash Basis Accounting BALANCE SHEETS As of			
	January 31	February 28	March 31
Assets			
Cash	$ –0–	$22,000	$4,000
Total assets	$ –0–	$22,000	$4,000
Liabilities and Owners' Equity			
Owners' equity	$ –0–	$22,000	$4,000
Total liabilities and owners' equity	$ –0–	$22,000	$4,000

ILLUSTRATION 3A-3
Balance Sheets—
Cash Basis

If accrual basis accounting were used, Quality Contractor's balance sheets at each month-end would appear as follows:

Quality Contractor—Accrual Basis Accounting BALANCE SHEETS As of			
	January 31	February 28	March 31
Assets			
Cash	$ –0–	$22,000	$4,000
Accounts receivable	22,000	–0–	–0–
Total assets	$22,000	$22,000	$4,000
Liabilities and Owners' Equity			
Accounts payable	$18,000	$18,000	$–0–
Owners' equity	4,000	4,000	4,000
Total liabilities and owners' equity	$22,000	$22,000	$4,000

ILLUSTRATION 3A-4
Balance Sheets—
Accrual Basis

An analysis of the preceding income statements and balance sheets shows the ways in which cash basis accounting is inconsistent with basic accounting theory:

1. The cash basis understates revenues and assets from the construction and delivery of the garage in January. It ignores the $22,000 accounts receivable, representing a near-term future cash inflow.

2. The cash basis understates expenses incurred with the construction of the garage and the liability outstanding at the end of January. It ignores the $18,000 accounts payable, representing a near-term future cash outflow.

3. The cash basis understates owners' equity in January by not recognizing the revenues and the asset until February, and it overstates owners' equity in February by not recognizing the expenses and the liability until March.

In short, cash basis accounting violates the theory underlying the elements of financial statements.

The **modified cash basis,** a mixture of cash basis and accrual basis, is the method followed by service enterprises, such as lawyers, doctors, architects, advertising agencies, and public accountants. Expenditures having an economic life of more than one year are capitalized as assets and depreciated or amortized over future years. Prepaid expenses and accrued expenses are not treated in a consistent manner: Prepayments of expenses are deferred and deducted only in the year to which they apply, but expenses paid after the year of incurrence (accrued expenses) are deducted only in the year paid. Revenue is reported in the year of receipt.[1]

▶ CONVERSION FROM CASH BASIS TO ACCRUAL BASIS

Not infrequently an accountant is required to convert a cash basis set of financial statements to the accrual basis for presentation and interpretation to a banker or for audit by an independent CPA. Illustration 3A-5 illustrates how cash basis financial data are converted to the accrual basis through various adjusting items.

ILLUSTRATION 3A-5
Conversion of Cash Basis to Accrual Basis

Cash Basis →	→	→ Accrual Basis
Receipts	− Beginning accounts receivable + Ending accounts receivable	= Net sales
Rent receipts	+ Beginning unearned rent − Ending unearned rent − Beginning rent receivable + Ending rent receivable	= Rent revenue
Payment for goods	+ Beginning inventory − Ending inventory − Beginning accounts payable + Ending accounts payable	= Cost of goods sold
Payments for expenses	+ Beginning prepaid expenses − Ending prepaid expenses − Beginning accrued expenses + Ending accrued expenses	= Operating expenses (except depreciation and similar write-offs)
Payments for property, plant, and equipment	− Cash payments for property, plant, and equipment + Periodic write-off of the asset cost through some formula(s)	= Depreciation or amortization expense

In Illustration 3A-5, cash receipts are converted to **net sales** by subtracting beginning accounts receivable and adding ending accounts receivable. This procedure takes into account any accounts receivable written off during the period. By expanding the formula to include all of the accounts related to sales, cash receipts can be converted to **gross sales,** as shown in Illustration 3A-6.

---

[1]For tax purposes individuals and personal service businesses may use modified cash basis accounting but its use by corporations (other than personal service corporations and S corporations) is prohibited if those corporations have average annual gross receipts over a 3-year period of more than $5 million. And any business in which inventory is a significant factor must use accrual accounting in reporting revenue from sales and cost of goods sold.

Cash receipts from customers		xxx
Plus: Cash discounts	xx	
Sales returns and allowances	xx	
Accounts written off	xx	
Ending accounts receivable	xx	xx
		xxx
Less: Beginning accounts receivable		xx
Gross sales		xxx

ILLUSTRATION 3A-6
Conversion of Cash Receipts to Gross Sales

Cash receipts from customers can also be converted to net sales merely by adding or subtracting the change in the balance of accounts receivable from the beginning to the end of year, as shown below.

$$\text{Cash receipts from customers} \begin{cases} + \text{ increase in accounts receivable} \\ \text{or} \\ - \text{ decrease in accounts receivable} \end{cases} = \text{Net sales}$$

ILLUSTRATION 3A-7
Conversion of Cash Receipts to Net Sales

Similarly, cash payments for goods can be converted to cost of goods sold by adding or deducting the change from the beginning to the end of the year in the accounts payable balance and in the inventory balance as follows:

$$\text{Payments for goods} \begin{cases} + \text{ increase in accounts payable} \\ \text{or} \\ - \text{ decrease in accounts payable} \end{cases} = \text{Net purchases}$$

$$\text{Net purchases} \begin{cases} + \text{ decrease in inventory} \\ \text{or} \\ - \text{ increase in inventory} \end{cases} = \text{Cost of goods sold}$$

ILLUSTRATION 3A-8
Conversion of Payments for Goods to Cost of Goods Sold

Illustration 3A-5 presents the conversion of cash payments for **all expenses** to the accrual basis operating expenses in the aggregate. That conversion involves both prepaid and accrued expenses in the conversion. Generally, each expense item is affected by a related accrual or a related prepayment, but not both. For example, the conversion of wages expense and the conversion of insurance expense are illustrated separately below.

$$\text{Wages paid during the year} \begin{cases} + \text{ Ending accrued wages} \\ - \text{ Beginning accrued wages} \end{cases} = \text{Wages expense for the year}$$

ILLUSTRATION 3A-9
Conversion of Wages Paid to Wages Expense

$$\text{Insurance premiums paid during the year} \begin{cases} - \text{ Ending prepaid insurance} \\ + \text{ Beginning prepaid insurance} \end{cases} = \text{Insurance expense for the year}$$

ILLUSTRATION 3A-10
Conversion of Insurance Paid to Insurance Expense

Nonoperating items such as selling capital stock or paying off long-term debt are increases and decreases in cash, but they are not revenues or expenses under either the cash basis or the accrual basis.

Illustration

Diana Windsor, D.D.S., keeps her accounting records on a cash basis. During 1996, Dr. Windsor collected $80,000 from her patients and paid $30,000 for operating expenses, resulting in a cash basis net income of $50,000. At January 1 and December 31, 1996, she has accounts receivable, unearned revenue, accrued expenses, and prepaid expenses as follows:

	January 1, 1996	December 31, 1996
Accounts receivable	$12,000	$5,000
Unearned revenue	–0–	1,000
Accrued expenses (liabilities)	3,800	6,800
Prepaid expenses (assets)	2,000	3,000

One approach to restatement of Diana Windsor's income statement data is presented in work sheet form below.

ILLUSTRATION 3A-11
Conversion of Statement of Cash Receipts and Disbursements to Income Statement

Diana Windsor, D.D.S.
Conversion of Income Statement Data from Cash Basis to Accrual Basis
For the Year 1996

	Cash Basis	Adjustments Add	Adjustments Deduct	Accrual Basis
Receipts for fees:	$80,000			
– Accounts receivable, Jan. 1			$12,000	
+ Accounts receivable, Dec. 31		$5,000		
– Unearned revenue, Dec. 31			1,000	
Revenue from fees				$72,000
Disbursements for expenses:	30,000			
– Accrued expenses, Jan. 1			3,800	
+ Accrued expenses, Dec. 31		6,800		
+ Prepaid expenses, Jan. 1		2,000		
– Prepaid expenses, Dec. 31			3,000	
Operating expenses				32,000
Excess of receipts over disbursements— cash basis	$50,000			
Net income—accrual basis				$40,000

Another approach to converting from the cash basis statement of receipts and disbursements to the accrual basis income statement is illustrated below.

ILLUSTRATION 3A-12
Alternative Conversion of Excess of Cash Receipts over Disbursements to Net Income

Diana Windsor, D.D.S.
Conversion of Income Statement Data from Cash Basis to Accrual Basis
For the Year 1996

Excess of receipts over disbursements	$50,000
– Decrease in accounts receivable ($12,000 to $5,000)	(7,000)
– Increase in unearned revenue ($–0– to $1,000)	(1,000)
– Increase in accrued expenses ($3,800 to $6,800)	(3,000)
+ Increase in prepaid expenses ($2,000 to $3,000)	1,000
Net income on an accrual basis	$40,000

Under the first approach, receipts and disbursements on a cash basis are adjusted to revenues and expenses on an accrual basis, along with net income. Under the second approach, only the excess of receipts over disbursements is restated to net income.

► THEORETICAL WEAKNESSES OF THE CASH BASIS

The cash basis does report exactly when cash is received and when cash is disbursed. To many people that information represents something solid, something concrete. Isn't cash what it is all about? Does it make sense to invent something, design it, produce it, market and sell it, if you aren't going to get cash for it in the end? It is frequently said, "Cash is the real bottom line." It is also said, "Cash is the oil that lubricates the economy." If so, then what is the merit of accrual accounting?

Today's economy is considerably more lubricated by credit than by cash. And the accrual basis, not the cash basis, recognizes all aspects of the credit phenomenon. Investors, creditors, and other decision makers seek timely information about an enterprise's future cash flows. Accrual basis accounting provides this information by reporting the cash inflows and outflows associated with earnings activities as soon as these cash flows can be estimated with an acceptable degree of certainty. Receivables and payables are forecasters of future cash inflows and outflows. In other words, accrual basis accounting aids in predicting future cash flows by reporting transactions and other events with cash consequences at the time the transactions and events occur, rather than when the cash is received and paid.

▶ SUMMARY OF LEARNING OBJECTIVE FOR APPENDIX 3-A ◀

KEY TERMS

accrual basis, 98

modified cash basis, 100

strict cash basis, 98

10. **Differentiate the cash basis of accounting from the accrual basis of accounting.** Accrual basis accounting provides information about cash inflows and outflows associated with earnings activities as soon as these cash flows can be estimated with an acceptable degree of certainty. That is, accrual basis accounting aids in predicting future cash flows by reporting transactions and events with cash consequences at the time the transactions and events occur, rather than when the cash is received and paid.

APPENDIX 3-B

SPECIALIZED JOURNALS AND METHODS OF PROCESSING ACCOUNTING DATA

A business constantly needs detailed information about its dealings with individual customers and creditors. Imagine a business with several thousand charge (credit) customers and the transactions with these customers are shown in only one account, Accounts Receivable, in the general ledger. It would be virtually impossible to determine the balance owed by an individual customer at a specific time. Similarly, details of transactions affecting a single creditor are needed from time to time, and a single Accounts Payable account in the general ledger cannot make this information available.

OBJECTIVE 11

After studying Appendix 3-B, you should be able to: Identify (a) the use and types of subsidiary ledgers and (b) the use and types of special journals.

▶ EXPANSION OF THE LEDGER—SUBSIDIARY LEDGERS

To provide this information, companies use a subsidiary ledger to keep track of individual balances. A **subsidiary ledger** is a group of accounts with a common characteristic, e.g., all are customer accounts, that is, all are accounts receivable. The subsidiary ledger facilitates the recording process by freeing the general ledger from the details of individual balances. Thus, a typical merchandising enterprise has subsidiary ledgers containing accounts with customers (**accounts receivable** or **customers' ledger**) and creditors (**accounts payable** or **creditors' ledger**). The enterprise maintains an account in the general ledger that summarizes the details in the accounts receivable and accounts payable ledgers. This summary account in the general ledger is called a **control account,** because the summary account controls the subsidiary ledger. **The general ledger control account balance must equal the composite balance of the individual accounts in the subsidiary ledger.**

As indicated, two common subsidiary ledgers are: (1) the accounts receivable ledger or customers' ledger, controlled by the general ledger account, Accounts Receivable; and (2) the accounts payable ledger or creditors' ledger, controlled by the general ledger account, Accounts Payable. In subsidiary ledgers, the individual accounts are usually arranged in alphabetical order.

An example of a control account and subsidiary ledger for accounts receivable is provided in Illustration 3B-1.

ILLUSTRATION 3B-1
Relationship between
General and Subsidiary
Ledgers

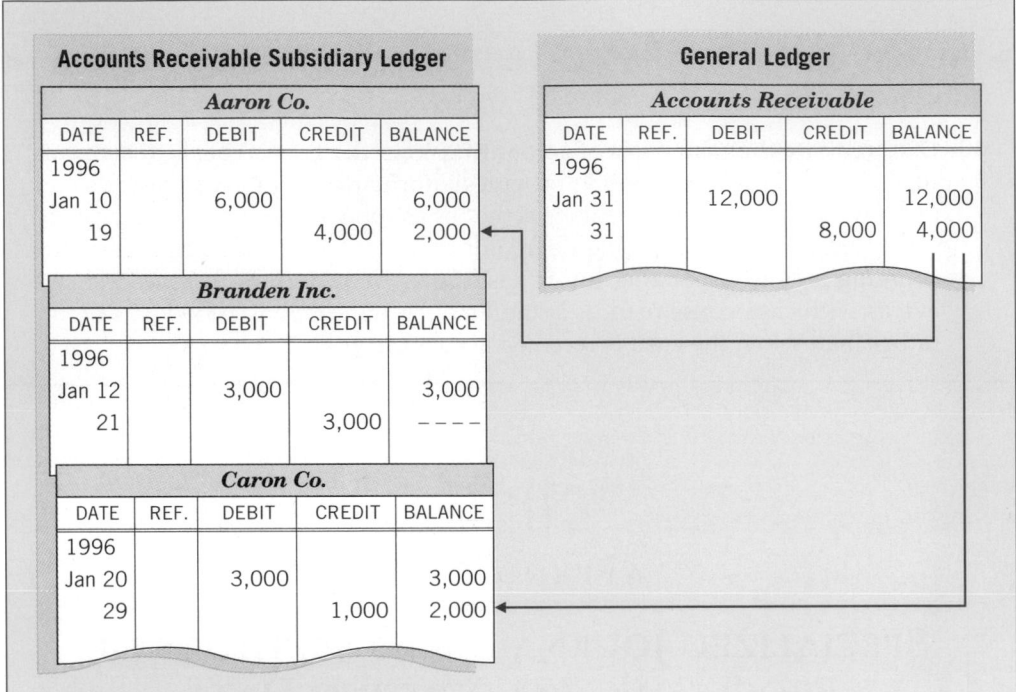

Illustration 3B-1 is based on the following transactions:

Sales and Collection Transactions					
Credit Sales			**Collections on Account**		
Jan. 10	Aaron Co.	$ 6,000	Jan. 19	Aaron Co.	$ 4,000
12	Branden Inc.	3,000	21	Branden Inc.	3,000
20	Caron Co.	3,000	29	Caron Co.	1,000
		$12,000			$ 8,000

The total debits and credits in Accounts Receivable in the general ledger are reconcilable to the detailed debits and credits in the subsidiary accounts. The balance of $4,000 in the Accounts Receivable control account agrees with the total of the balances in the individual accounts receivable accounts ($2,000 + $0 + $2,000) in the subsidiary ledger.

Postings are made to the control accounts in the general ledger **monthly** for the purpose of preparing monthly financial statements. Postings to the individual accounts in the subsidiary ledger are made **daily**. The rationale for posting daily is to ensure that current account information can be used as a basis for monitoring credit limits, for billing customers, and also to answer inquiries from customers about their account balances.

Note also in this example that postings to the control account are made in total at the end of the month, whereas each of the individual transactions is posted daily to the subsidiary ledger. Procedures used for posting entries to the subsidiary ledger and to the general ledger control account generally involve the use of special journals, discussed in the next section.

In summary, the advantages of using subsidiary ledgers are that they:

1. Show transactions affecting one customer or one creditor in a single account, thus providing necessary up-to-date information on specific account balances.
2. Free the general ledger of excessive details relating to accounts receivable and accounts payable. As a result, a trial balance of the general ledger does not contain vast numbers of individual account balances.
3. Help locate errors in individual accounts by reducing the number of accounts combined in one ledger and by using control accounts.
4. Make possible a division of labor in posting by having one employee post to the general ledger and a different employee(s) post to the subsidiary ledgers.

Note that a business may also use control accounts and subsidiary ledgers for other accounts such as inventory, equipment, and selling and administrative expenses.

► EXPANSION OF THE JOURNAL—SPECIAL JOURNALS

So far you have learned to journalize transactions in a two-column general journal and post these entries individually to the general ledger. This procedure is satisfactory in only the very smallest companies. To expedite journalizing and posting transactions, most companies use special journals in addition to the general journal.

A **special journal** is used to group similar types of transactions, such as all sales of merchandise on account, or all cash receipts. The types of special journals an enterprise uses depend largely on the types of transactions that occur frequently in its business. Most merchandising enterprises use the following journals to record transactions daily:

Sales journal—all sales of merchandise on account.

Cash receipts journal—all cash received (including cash sales).

Purchases journal—all purchases of merchandise on account.

Cash payments journal—all cash paid (including cash purchases).

If the transaction cannot be recorded in a special journal, it is recorded in the general journal. For example, if you had special journals for only the four types of transactions listed, purchase returns and allowances or sales returns and allowances would be recorded in the general journal. Similarly, correcting, adjusting, and closing entries are recorded in the general journal. Other types of special journals may be used in some situations. For example, where purchase returns and allowances or sales returns and allowances are frequent, special journals may be employed to record these transactions.

The journalization and posting process is illustrated using the sales journal and the cash receipts journal. The same procedures apply to all special journals with only the column and account names being different.

SALES JOURNAL

The **sales journal** is used to record sales of merchandise on account. Cash sales of merchandise are entered in the cash receipts journal. Similarly, credit sales of assets other than merchandise are entered in the general journal.

Journalizing Credit Sales

Each entry in the sales journal used here results in a debit to Accounts Receivable and a credit to Sales. Since each sale on account involves a debit to Accounts Receivable and a credit of equal amount to Sales, only one line is used to record the transaction.

Postings from the sales journal are made **daily** to the individual accounts receivable in the subsidiary ledger and **monthly** to the general ledger.

A check mark (√) is inserted in the reference posting column instead of an account number to indicate that the daily posting to the customer's account has been made. A check mark (√) is used when subsidiary ledger accounts are not numbered. A typical sales journal with related accounts is illustrated in Illustration 3B-2.

ILLUSTRATION 3B-2
Posting the Sales Journal

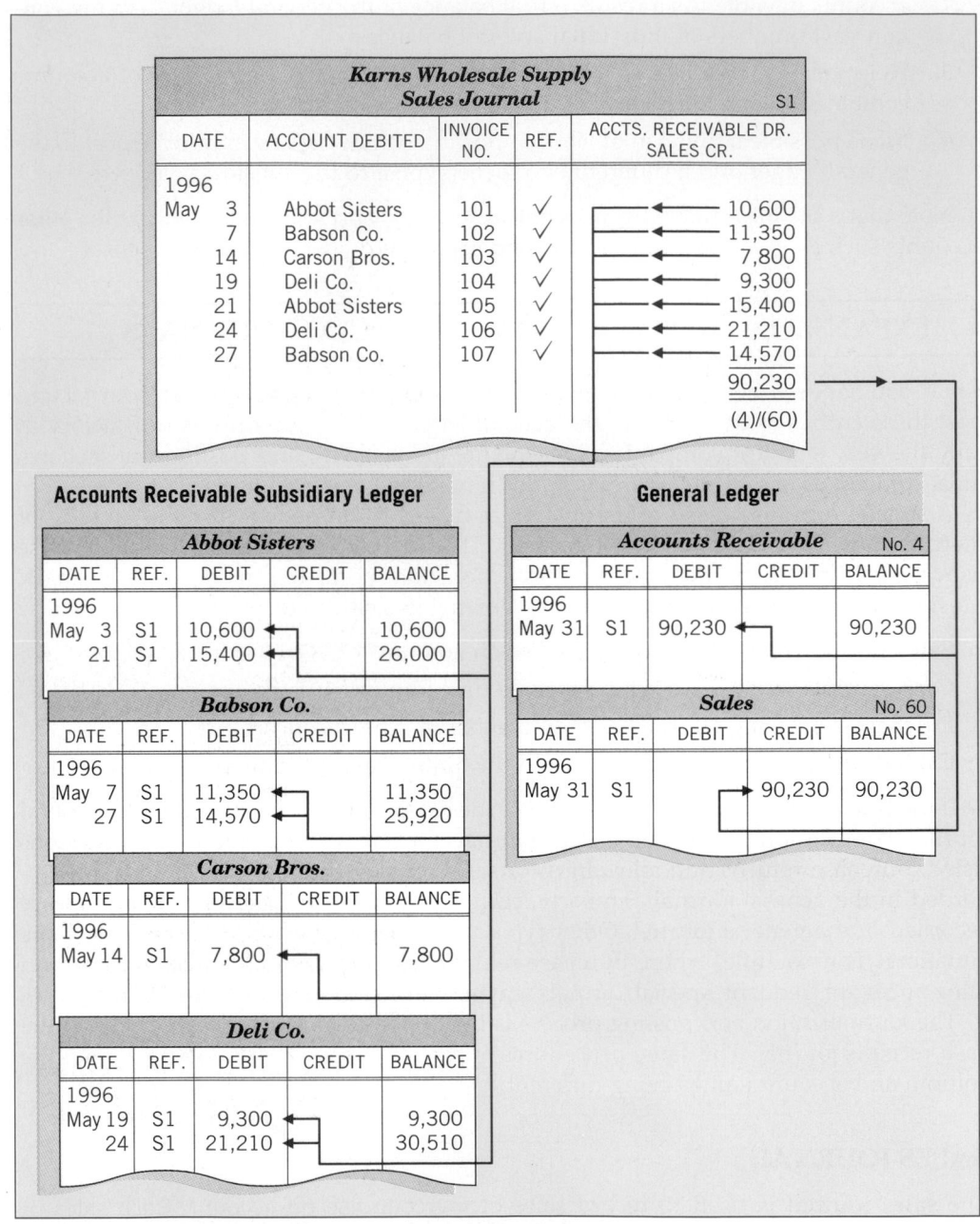

At the end of the month, the column total of the sales journal is posted to the general ledger—as a debit to Accounts Receivable (account No. 4) and as a credit to Sales (account No. 60). The insertion of the respective account numbers below the column total in the sales journal indicates that the postings have been made. In both the general ledger and subsidiary ledger accounts, the reference S1 indicates that the posting came from page 1 of the sales journal.

CASH RECEIPTS JOURNAL

All receipts of cash are recorded in the **cash receipts journal.** The most common types of cash receipts are cash sales of merchandise and collections of accounts receivable. Many other possibilities exist, however, such as receipt of money from bank loans and cash proceeds from disposals of equipment, buildings, or land. As a result, a one-column cash receipts journal is not sufficient to accommodate all possible cash receipts transactions; therefore, a multiple-column cash receipts journal is used. Generally, a cash receipts journal includes debit columns for cash and sales discounts and credit columns for accounts receivable, sales, and "other" accounts. The other accounts category is used when the cash receipt does not involve a cash sale or a collection of accounts receivable. A five-column cash receipts journal is shown in Illustration 3B-3. When a special journal has more than one column it is often referred to as a **columnar journal.**

Additional credit columns may be used if they significantly reduce postings to a specific account. For example, the cash receipts of a loan company, such as Household Finance, include thousands of collections from customers that are credited to Loans Receivable and Interest Revenue. A significant saving in posting would result from using separate credit columns for Loans Receivable and Interest Revenue. In contrast, a retailer that has only one interest collection a month would not reduce its postings by using a separate column for interest revenue.

In a columnar journal, as in a single-column journal, only one line is needed for each entry. However, in contrast to a single-column journal, **an explanation is given for each entry,** and there must be equal debit and credit amounts for each line. When the collection from Abbot Sisters on May 10 is journalized, for example, three amounts are indicated. Note also that the Accounts Credited column is used to identify both general ledger and subsidiary ledger account titles. The former is illustrated in the May 1 entry for Karns' investment; the latter is illustrated in the May 10 entry for the collection in full from Abbot Sisters.

Posting the Cash Receipts Journal

Posting a columnar journal involves the following procedures:

1. All column totals except the total for the Other Accounts column are posted once at the end of the month to the account title specified in the column heading, such as Cash or Accounts Receivable.

2. The total of the Other Accounts column is not posted. Instead, the individual amounts comprising the total are posted separately to the general ledger accounts specified in the Accounts Credited column. See, for example, the credit posting to D. A. Karns, Capital. The symbol (X) is inserted below the total of this column to indicate that the amount is not posted.

3. The individual amounts in a column, posted in total to a control account (Accounts Receivable, in this case), are posted daily to the subsidiary ledger account specified in the Accounts Credited column. See, for example, the credit posting of $10,600 to Abbot Sisters.

Therefore, cash is posted to account No. 1, accounts receivable to account No. 4, sales to account No. 60, and sales discounts to account No. 61. The symbol CR is used in the ledgers to identify postings from the cash receipts journal.

ILLUSTRATION 3B-3
Journalizing and Posting
Cash Receipts Journal

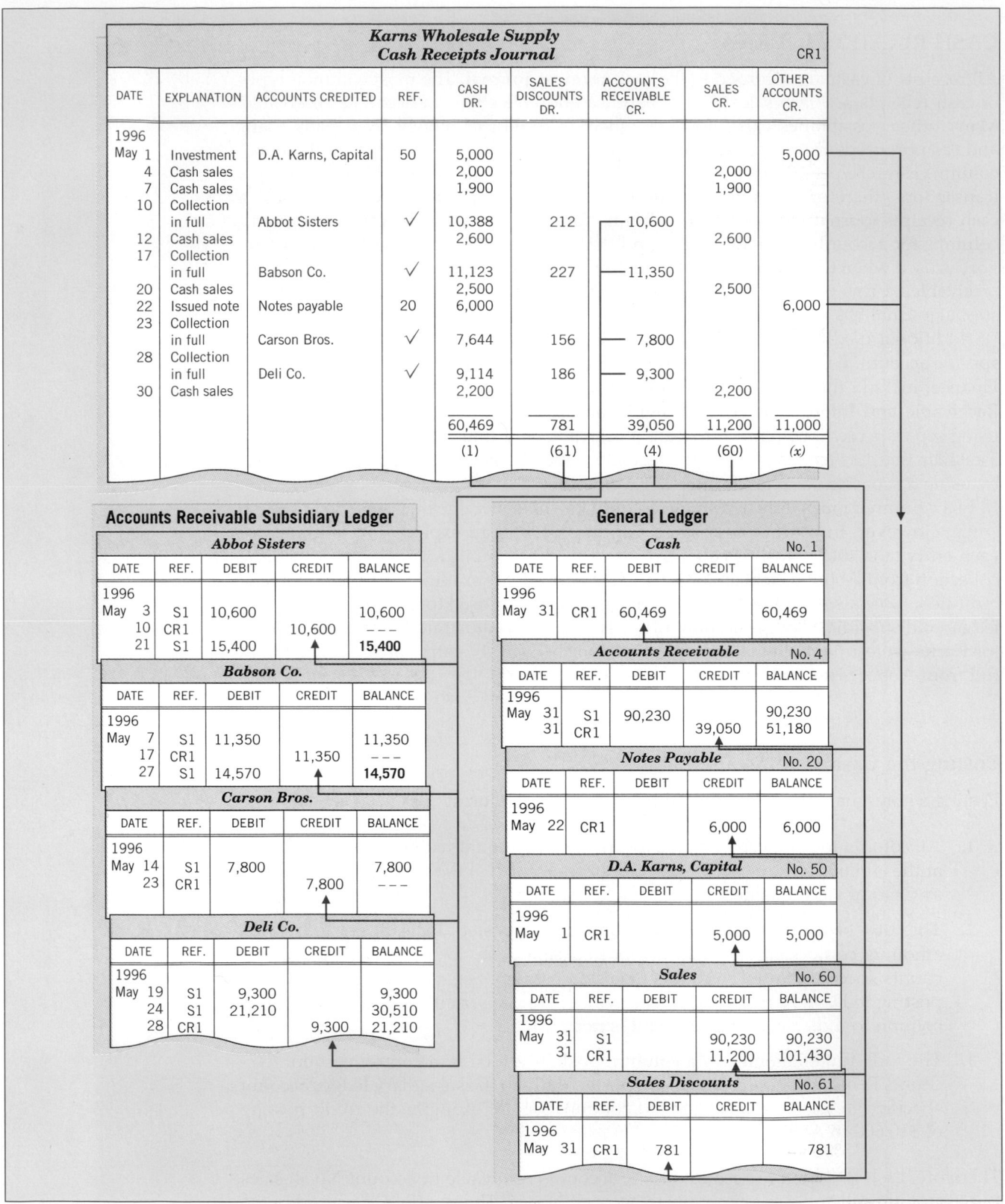

FORMAT OF PURCHASES JOURNAL AND CASH PAYMENTS JOURNAL

The column headings that might be used in a typical single-column purchases journal and a multiple-column cash payments journal are shown in Illustration 3B-4.

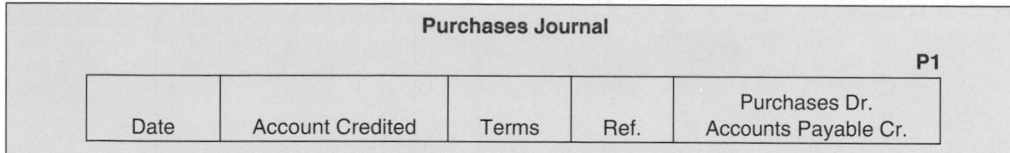

Purchases Journal

P1

Date	Account Credited	Terms	Ref.	Purchases Dr. Accounts Payable Cr.

Cash Payments Journal

CP1

Date	Ck. No.	Explanation	Accounts Debited	Ref.	Other Accounts Dr.	Accounts Payable Dr.	Store Supplies Dr.	Purchase Discounts Cr.	Cash Cr.

ILLUSTRATION 3B-4
Purchases Journal and Cash Payments Journal

► METHODS OF PROCESSING ACCOUNTING DATA

The principles of recording, classifying, and summarizing large quantities of accounting data described in this appendix are those applicable to a situation where sophisticated types of accounting machinery are not needed. In most business enterprises, the mass of data is so great that it is simply too time-consuming to post journal entries manually, add the columns, update the files, and summarize the information. For this reason, accountants have resorted to computer systems.

The computer has revolutionized data processing not only because of its speed and accuracy in processing data, but also because it can be programmed to process the data in almost any manner desired by management. One of the more interesting developments in the computer area has been the development of **on-line computer systems.** In this system, the transaction is recorded in the computer as it occurs without the use of any basic source document. The advantages of a computer are that it can take different courses of action depending on the results of data collected previously and can process data more quickly and efficiently than other types of business equipment.

Nearly every medium- or large-sized business owns or rents a computer, but until recently a computer was too expensive for a small business to own or rent. Small businesses generally avoided investing large sums of money yet gained the use of computers through **EDP service centers** or through **time-sharing arrangements.** However, with the widespread availability of inexpensive **micro-** and **mini-computers,** most small businesses now own computers and obtain the operating and record keeping efficiencies they provide.

The growth in computers is nothing short of phenomenal. From the beginning of time through 1980, there were approximately 1 million computer systems of all types. In the early 1990s, it is estimated that there were 120 million personal computers alone. This is not surprising, given the level of technological change in this area. As one executive noted, "The amount of raw computing power available at a given price has been improving 25% a year. That which cost $1,000,000 in 1970 will cost less than $10,000 in 1995." The following chart shows that in 1991, for the first time, companies spent more on computing and communication equipment than on industrial age machinery.

ILLUSTRATION 3B-6
The Rise of the
Information Economy

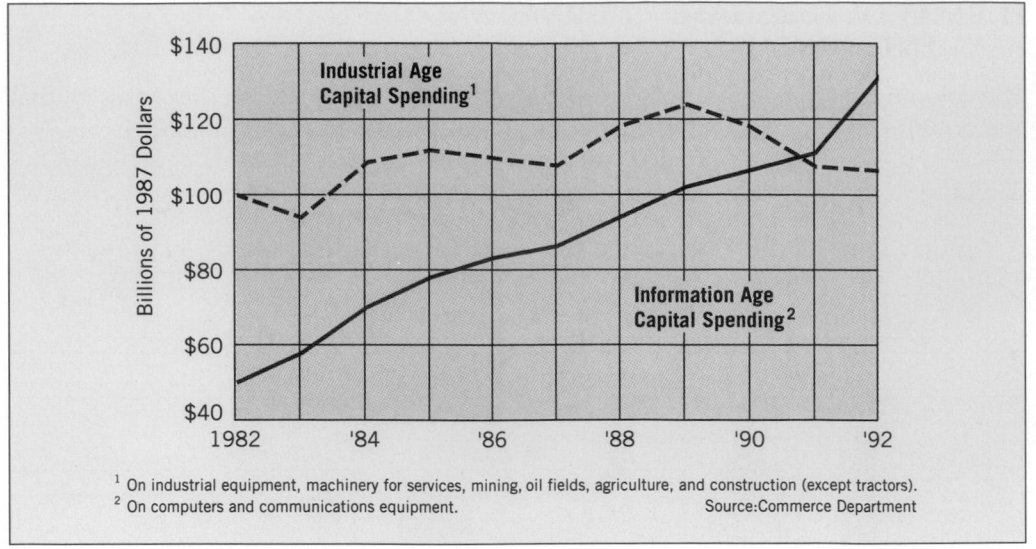

¹ On industrial equipment, machinery for services, mining, oil fields, agriculture, and construction (except tractors).
² On computers and communications equipment.   Source:Commerce Department

As one commentator recently noted, "Washington isn't pushing the National Information Infrastructure just because Al Gore likes to play with computers."

The effect this growth in home, office, and small-business computers has had on accounting is startling. Because computers are efficient and accurate at handling data, it is safe to say that most (if not all) record keeping and accounting will be performed on and by computers. Present and future accountants and auditors need to develop their computer competencies and skills in order to meet the challenges this growth brings.

KEY TERMS

accounts payable
(creditors') ledger, 103

accounts receivable
(customers') ledger, 103

cash payments
journal, 105

cash receipts journal, 105

control account, 103

purchases journal, 105

sales journal, 105

special journals, 105

subsidiary ledger, 103

▶ **SUMMARY OF LEARNING OBJECTIVES FOR APPENDIX 3-B** ◀

11. **Identify (a) the use and types of subsidiary ledgers and (b) the use and types of special journals.** Subsidiary ledgers facilitate the recording process by freeing the general ledger from the details of individual entries and balances. Subsidiary ledgers group accounts with common characteristics (e.g., customers' accounts, creditors' accounts, inventory accounts, and equipment accounts).

Special journals expedite the journalizing and posting processes for frequently occurring transactions. The most common special journals are: sales journal, purchases journal, cash receipts journal, and cash payments journal.

Note: All **asterisked** Questions, Exercises, Problems, and Cases relate to material contained in an appendix to each chapter.

QUESTIONS

1. Give an example of a transaction that results in
   (a) A decrease in an asset and a decrease in a liability.
   (b) A decrease in one asset and an increase in another asset.
   (c) A decrease in one liability and an increase in another liability.

2. Do the following events represent business transactions? Explain your answer in each case.
   (a) A computer is purchased on account.

(b) A customer returns merchandise and is given credit on account.
(c) A prospective employee is interviewed.
(d) The owner of the business withdraws cash from the business for personal use.
(e) Merchandise is ordered for delivery next month.

3. Name the accounts debited and credited for each of the following transactions:
   (a) Billing a customer for work done.
   (b) Receipt of cash from customer on account.
   (c) Purchase of office supplies on account.
   (d) Purchase of 15 gallons of gasoline for the delivery truck.

4. Why are revenue and expense accounts called temporary or nominal accounts?

5. What are the advantages of using the journal in the recording process?

6. Is it necessary that a trial balance be taken periodically? What purpose does it serve?

7. Indicate whether each of the items below is a real or nominal account and whether it appears in the balance sheet or the income statement.
(a) Prepaid Rent.	(d) Accumulated Depreciation.	(g) Office Salaries Expense.
(b) Salaries and Wages Payable.	(e) Office Equipment.	(h) Supplies on Hand.
(c) Merchandise Inventory.	(f) Income from Services.	

8. Employees are paid every Saturday for the preceding work week. If a balance sheet is prepared on Wednesday, December 31, what does the amount of wages earned during the first three days of the week (12/29, 12/30, 12/31) represent? Explain.

9. Why is the Purchases account debited both when merchandise is purchased for cash and when it is purchased on account? Why is the inventory amount as determined at the end of the fiscal period under a periodic inventory system deducted from the cost of goods available for sale?

10. What is the purpose of the Cost of Goods Sold account (assume a periodic inventory system)?

11. Under a periodic system is the amount shown for Inventory the same in a trial balance taken before closing as it is in a trial balance taken after closing? Why?

12. If the cost of a new microcomputer and printer ($2,850) purchased for office use were recorded as a debit to Purchases, what would be the effect of the error on the balance sheet and income statement in the period in which the error was made?

13. What differences are there between the trial balance before closing and the trial balance after closing with respect to the following?
(a) Accounts Payable.	(d) Retained Earnings account.
(b) Expense accounts.	(e) Cash.
(c) Revenue accounts.	

14. What are "adjusting entries" and why are they necessary?

15. What are "closing entries" and why are they necessary?

16. What are "reversing entries" and why are they necessary?

17. Billie Joel, maintenance supervisor for Columbia Insurance Co., has purchased a riding lawnmower and accessories to be used in maintaining the grounds around corporate headquarters. She has sent the following information to the accounting department:

Cost of mower and accessories	$2,400	Date purchased	7/1/95
Estimated useful life	5 yrs	Monthly salary of groundskeeper	$800
Estimated salvage value	$400	Estimated annual fuel cost	$100

    Compute the amount of depreciation expense (related to the mower and accessories) that should be reported on Columbia's December 31, 1995 income statement. Assume straight-line depreciation.

18. Gavin Bryars Enterprises made the following entry on December 31, 1995.

Dec. 31, 1995	Interest Expense	7,000	
	Interest Payable		7,000
	(To record accrued interest expense due on loan from Point National Bank.)		

    What entry would Point National Bank make regarding its outstanding loan to Gavin Bryars Enterprises? Explain why this must be the case.

*19. Distinguish between cash basis accounting and accrual basis accounting. Why for most business enterprises is accrual basis accounting acceptable and the cash basis unacceptable in the preparation of an income statement and a balance sheet?

*20. Why are beginning accrued wages subtracted from, and ending accrued wages added to, wages paid during the year when wages expense for the year is computed?

*21. List two types of transactions that would receive different accounting treatment using (a) strict cash basis accounting and (b) a modified cash basis.

*22. Why would a company use several journals instead of only a general journal? How would the company determine which special journals it should use?

*23. When the special journals illustrated in this chapter are used, how many monthly postings are made to the Cash account? Why?

*24. For each of the following transactions name the book of original entry and the accounts to be debited and credited, assuming that the five journals discussed in this chapter are used:
(a) Sale of merchandise for cash.
(b) Purchase of office equipment on account.
(c) Payment of cash to a creditor, no discount.
(d) Receipt of cash from customer on account.
(e) Loan from bank on a promissory note; interest payable at maturity date.
(f) Purchase of merchandise on account (periodic inventory system).
(g) Return of damaged merchandise to a supplier.

*25. What is a controlling account? What is its relationship to a subsidiary ledger?

*26. How does the use of controlling accounts and subsidiary ledgers affect (a) the taking of a trial balance, (b) the appearance of the trial balance, and (c) the equality of debits and credits in the trial balance?

EXERCISES

E3-1 (Transaction Analysis—Service Company) EmmiLou Harris is a licensed CPA. During the first month of operations of her business, the following events and transactions occurred.

April	1	Invested $32,000 cash and equipment valued at $11,000 in the business.
	2	Hired a secretary-receptionist at a salary of $230 per week payable monthly.
	3	Purchased supplies on account $700 (debit an asset account).
	7	Paid office rent of $550 for the month.
	11	Completed a tax assignment and billed client $1,100 for services rendered. (Use professional fees account.)
	12	Received $3,200 advance on a management consulting engagement.
	15	Purchased a new computer for $8,300 with personal funds. (The computer will be used exclusively for business purposes.)
	17	Received cash of $900 for services completed for Cowgirl Co.
	21	Paid insurance expense $110.
	30	Paid secretary-receptionist $920 for the month.
	30	A count of supplies indicated that $120 of supplies had been used.

Instructions
Journalize the transactions in the general journal (omit explanations).

E3-2 (Transaction Analysis—Merchandising Company) The Digable Planets Hardware Store completed the following merchandising transactions in the month of May. On May 1, the company had a cash balance of $5,000.

May	1	Purchased merchandise on account from Pendulum Wholesale Supply $5,200, terms 2/10, n/30.
	2	Sold merchandise on account $3,600, terms 2/10, n/30.
	5	Received credit from Pendulum Wholesale Supply for merchandise returned $100.
	9	Received collections in full, less discounts, from customers billed for $2,000 of sales on May 2.
	10	Paid Pendulum Wholesale Supply in full, less discount.
	12	Purchased merchandise for cash $2,400.
	15	Received refund for poor quality merchandise from supplier on cash purchase $230.
	17	Purchased merchandise from Hiphop Distributors $1,900, FOB shipping point, terms 3/10, n/30.
	19	Paid freight on May 17 purchase $330.
	24	Sold merchandise for cash $6,400.
	25	Purchased merchandise for cash $600.
	27	Paid Hiphop Distributors in full, less discount.
	29	Made refunds to cash customers for defective merchandise $80.
	31	Sold merchandise on account $2,100, terms n/30.

Digable Planets Hardware's chart of accounts includes the following: Cash, Accounts Receivable, Merchandise Inventory, Accounts Payable, Sales, Sales Returns and Allowances, Sales Discounts, Purchases, Purchase Returns and Allowances, Purchase Discounts, Freight-in.

Instructions

(a) Journalize the transactions.

(b) Prepare an income statement through gross profit for the month of May 1996, assuming ending inventory is $2,400, and no beginning inventory.

E3-3 (Corrected Trial Balance) The trial balance of Ella Fitzgerald Company shown below does not balance. Your review of the ledger reveals the following: (a) each account had a normal balance, (b) the debit footings in Prepaid Insurance, Accounts Payable, and Property Tax Expense were each understated $100, (c) transposition errors were made in Accounts Receivable and Fees Earned; the correct balances are $2,750 and $6,690, respectively, (d) a debit posting to Advertising Expense of $200 was omitted, and (e) a $1,000 cash drawing by the owner was debited to Ella Fitzgerald, Capital, and credited to Cash.

Ella Fitzgerald Company
TRIAL BALANCE
April 30, 1995

	Debit	Credit
Cash	$ 5,400	
Accounts Receivable	2,570	
Prepaid Insurance	700	
Equipment		$ 8,000
Accounts Payable		4,500
Property Tax Payable	560	
Ella Fitzgerald, Capital		11,700
Fees Earned	6,960	
Salaries Expense	4,200	
Advertising Expense	1,100	
Property Tax Expense		800
	$21,490	$25,000

Instructions
Prepare a correct trial balance.

E3-4 (Corrected Trial Balance) The trial balance of Sons of Soul Corporation does not balance.

Sons of Soul Corporation
TRIAL BALANCE
April 30

Cash	$ 5,912	
Accounts Receivable	5,240	
Supplies on Hand	2,967	
Furniture and Equipment	6,100	
Accounts Payable		$ 5,044
Common Stock		8,000
Retained Earnings		2,000
Revenue from Fees		5,200
Office Expense	2,320	
	$22,539	$20,244

An examination of the ledger shows these errors.

1. Cash received from a customer on account was recorded (both debit and credit) as $1,480 instead of $1,840.

2. The purchase on account of a computer costing $1,200 was recorded as a debit to Office Expense and a credit to Accounts Payable.

3. Services were performed on account for a client, $2,250, for which Accounts Receivable was debited $2,250 and Revenue from Fees was credited $225.

4. A payment of $95 for telephone charges was entered as a debit to Office Expenses and a debit to Cash.
5. The Revenue from Fees account was totaled at $5,200 instead of $5,280.

Instructions
From this information prepare a corrected trial balance.

E3-5 (Corrected Trial Balance) The trial balance of Jimmie Gilmore Co. shown below does not balance.

Jimmie Gilmore Co.
TRIAL BALANCE
June 30, 1993

	Debit	Credit
Cash		$ 2,870
Fees Receivable	$ 3,231	
Supplies	800	
Equipment	3,800	
Accounts Payable		2,666
Unearned Fees	1,200	
Common Stock		6,000
Retained Earnings		3,000
Fees Earned		2,380
Wages Expense	3,400	
Office Expense	940	
	$13,371	$16,916

Each of the listed accounts has a normal balance per the general ledger. An examination of the ledger and journal reveals the following errors.

1. Cash received from a customer on account was debited for $570 and Fees Receivable was credited for the same amount. The actual collection was for $750.
2. The purchase of a computer printer on account for $250 was recorded as a debit to Supplies for $250 and a credit to Accounts Payable for $250.
3. Services were performed on account for a client for $890. Fees Receivable was debited for $890 and Fees Earned was credited for $89.
4. A payment of $65 for telephone charges was recorded as a debit to Office Expense for $65 and a debit to Cash for $65.
5. When the Unearned Fees account was reviewed, it was found that $200 of the balance was earned prior to June 30.
6. A debit posting to Wages Expense of $670 was omitted.
7. A payment on account for $206 was credited to Cash for $206 and credited to Accounts Payable for $260.
8. A dividend of $575 was debited to Wages Expense for $575 and credited to Cash for $575.

Instructions
Prepare a correct trial balance. (Note: It may be necessary to add one or more accounts to the trial balance.)

E3-6 (Adjusting Entries) Rush Limbaugh is the new owner of Right Way Computer Services. At the end of August 1995, his first month of ownership, Rush is trying to prepare monthly financial statements. Below is some information related to unrecorded expenses that the business incurred during August.

1. At August 31, Mr. Limbaugh owed his employees $1,200 in wages that would be paid on September 1.
2. At the end of the month he had not yet received the month's utility bill. Based on past experience, he estimated the bill would be approximately $600.
3. On August 1, Mr. Limbaugh borrowed $30,000 from a local bank on a 15-year mortgage. The annual interest rate is 7%.
4. A telephone bill in the amount of $89 covering August charges is unpaid at August 31.

Instructions
Prepare the adjusting journal entries as of August 31, 1995, suggested by the information above.

E3-7 (Adjusting Entries) Selected accounts of Shana Alexander Company are shown below.

Supplies				Fees Receivable		
Beg. Bal.	800	10/31	425	10/17	2,400	
				10/31	1,488	

Salaries Expense			Salaries Payable		
10/15	550			10/31	600
10/31	600				

Unearned Fees				Supplies Expense	
10/31	400	10/20	650	10/31	425

Fees Earned		
	10/17	2,400
	10/31	1,488
	10/31	400

Instructions

From an analysis of the T-accounts, reconstruct (a) the October transaction entries, and (b) the adjusting journal entries that were made on October 31, 1995.

E3-8 (Adjusting Entries) The ledger of Reno, Inc., on March 31 of the current year includes the following selected accounts before adjusting entries have been prepared.

	Debit	Credit
Prepaid Insurance	$ 3,600	
Supplies	2,800	
Delivery Equipment	$25,000	
Accumulated Depreciation		$ 8,400
Notes Payable		20,000
Unearned Rent		9,300
Rent Revenue		$60,000
Interest Expense	–0–	
Wage Expense	14,000	

An analysis of the accounts shows the following:

1. The delivery equipment depreciates $500 per month.
2. One-third of the unearned rent was earned during the quarter.
3. Accrued wages at March 31 total $2,100.
4. Interest of $400 is accrued on the notes payable.
5. Supplies on hand total $750.
6. Insurance expires at the rate of $175 per month.

Instructions

Prepare the adjusting entries at March 31, assuming that adjusting entries are made quarterly. Additional accounts are: Depreciation Expense, Insurance Expense, Interest Payable, Supplies Expense, and Wages Payable.

E3-9 (Adjusting Entries) Susan Powter Resort opened for business on June 1 with eight air-conditioned units. Its trial balance on August 31 is as follows:

Susan Powter Resort
TRIAL BALANCE
August 31, 1995

	Debit	Credit
Cash	$ 19,600	
Prepaid Insurance	4,500	
Supplies	2,600	
Land	20,000	
Cottages	120,000	
Furniture	16,000	
Accounts Payable		$ 4,500
Advanced Rentals		4,600
Mortgage Payable		60,000
Powter, Capital		100,000
Powter, Drawing	5,000	
Rent Revenue		76,200
Salaries Expense	44,800	
Utilities Expense	9,200	
Repair Expense	3,600	
	$245,300	$245,300

Other data:

1. The balance in prepaid insurance is a 3-year premium paid on June 1, 1995.
2. An inventory count on August 31 shows $400 of supplies on hand.
3. Annual depreciation rates are cottages (4%) and furniture (10%). Salvage value is estimated to be 10% of cost.
4. Advanced rentals of $4,000 were earned prior to August 31.
5. Salaries of $200 were unpaid at August 31.
6. Rentals of $800 were due from tenants at August 31.
7. The mortgage interest rate is 8% per year.

Instructions

(a) Journalize the adjusting entries on August 31 for the 3-month period June 1–August 31.
(b) Prepare an adjusted trial balance on August 31.

E3-10 (Adjusting Entries) A review of the ledger of Holyfield Company at December 31, 1996, produces the following data pertaining to the preparation of annual adjusting entries.

1. Salaries Payable, $0. There are seven salaried employees. Payday for each month is on the fifth day of the following month. Four employees are paid salaries of $2,000 each per month, and three employees earn $3,500 each per month.
2. Sales Commissions Expense, $17,000. Salespersons are paid commissions equal to 2% of net sales payable on the tenth day of the month following the sales. Commissions have been paid in full when due. In 1996, commission payments totaled $18,500, which includes commissions payable of $1,500 on December 31, 1995. Net sales were $960,000 in 1996.
3. Unearned Rent, $276,000. The company began subleasing office space in its new building on November 1. At December 31, the company had the following rental contracts that are paid in full for the entire term of the lease.

Date	Term (in months)	Monthly Rent	Number
Nov. 1	6	$4,000	3
Dec. 1	6	$8,500	4

4. Prepaid Advertising, $13,800. This balance consists of payments on two advertising contracts. The contracts provide for monthly advertising in two trade magazines. The terms of the contracts are as follows:

Contract	Date	Amount	Issues
A650	May 1	$6,600	12
B974	Sept. 1	7,200	24

The first advertisement runs in the month in which the contract is signed.

5. Notes Payable, $81,000. There are two notes outstanding. A $45,000, 7%, one-year note was signed on May 1, and a $36,000, 6%, nine-month note was signed on November 1.

Instructions

Prepare the adjusting entries at December 31, 1996. (Show all computations.)

E3-11 (Adjusting and Reversing Entries) When the accounts of Mitch Williams Inc. are examined, the adjusting data listed below are uncovered on December 31, the end of an annual fiscal period.

1. The unexpired insurance account shows a debit of $5,280, representing the cost of a 2-year fire insurance policy dated August 1 of the current year.
2. On November 1, Rental Income was credited for $1,800, representing income from a subrental for a 3-month period beginning on that date.
3. Purchase of advertising materials for $800 during the year was recorded in the Advertising Expense account. On December 31, advertising materials of $360 are on hand.
4. Interest of $230 has accrued on notes payable.

Instructions

Prepare in general journal form: (a) the adjusting entry for each item; (b) the reversing entry for each item where appropriate.

E3-12 (Find Missing Amounts—Gross Profit) Financial information is presented below for four different companies.

	Steffi's Cosmetics	Seles Grocery	Wimbledon Wholesalers	Courier Supply Co.
Sales	$80,000	c	$144,000	$100,000
Sales returns	a	$ 8,000	12,000	15,000
Net sales	$74,000	94,000	132,000	g
Beginning inventory	16,000	d	44,000	24,000
Purchases	88,000	100,000	e	85,000
Purchase returns	6,000	10,000	8,000	h
Ending inventory	b	48,000	30,000	28,000
Cost of goods sold	64,000	72,000	f	72,000
Gross profit	10,000	22,000	20,000	i

Instructions

Determine the missing amounts (a–i). Show all computations.

E3-13 (Prepare Cost of Goods Sold Section) Information concerning the first month of operations of Cracker Jax Women's Wear is presented below. (The periodic inventory system is used.)

Transportation-in	$ 760
Total purchases on account	20,000
Purchase returns on account	700
Transportation-out	810
Total recorded as cash purchases	9,140
Purchase allowances on account	1,350
Inventory at the end of the month	4,800
Sales discounts	750
Refunds for defective items purchased for cash	400
Error made by bookkeeper debiting Supplies Expense, when in reality	
the item was a cash purchase of merchandise	790

Instructions

(a) Compute the correct amount of cost of goods sold.
(b) Prepare the cost of goods sold section of the income statement.
(c) Indicate in which section of the income statement items not used in the cost of goods sold section of this exercise should appear.

E3-14 (Prepare Cost of Goods Sold Section and Closing Entries) The trial balance of the R. Bowe Company at the end of its fiscal year, August 31, 1996 includes the following accounts: Merchandise Inventory $17,500, Purchases $142,400, Sales $190,000, Freight-in $4,000, Sales Returns and Allowances $4,000, Freight-out $1,000, and Purchase Returns and Allowances $2,000. The ending merchandise inventory is $25,000.

Instructions

(a) Prepare a cost of goods sold section for the year ending August 31.
(b) Prepare the closing entries for the above accounts. Assume R. Bowe Company is a corporation.

E3-15 (Prepare Adjusting and Reversing Entries) On December 31, adjusting information for Hannah Corporation is as follows:

1. Estimated depreciation on equipment $200.
2. Personal property taxes amounting to $300 have accrued but are unrecorded and unpaid.
3. Employees' wages earned but unpaid and unrecorded $1,200.
4. Unearned Fee Income balance includes $1,500 that has been earned.
5. Interest of $250 on $25,000 note receivable has accrued.

Instructions

(a) Prepare adjusting journal entries.
(b) Prepare reversing journal entries.

E3-16 (Closing and Reversing Entries) On December 31, the adjusted trial balance of Fleiss Co., Inc. shows the following selected data:

Commissions Receivable	$4,000	Commissions Earned	$96,000
Interest Expense	7,800	Interest Payable	2,000

Analysis shows that adjusting entries were made for (a) $4,000 of commissions earned but not billed, and (b) $2,000 of accrued but unpaid interest.

Instructions
- (a) Prepare the closing entries for the temporary accounts at December 31.
- (b) Prepare the reversing entries on January 1.
- (c) Enter the adjusted trial balance data in the four accounts. Post the entries in (a) and (b) and rule and balance the accounts. (Use T accounts.)
- (d) Prepare the entries to record (1) the collection of the accrued commissions on January 10, and (2) the payment of all interest due ($2,500) on January 15.
- (e) Post the entries in (d) to the temporary accounts.

E3-17 (Closing Entries for a Corporation) Presented below are selected account balances for Barney Co. as of December 31, 1996

Merchandise inventory 1/1/96	$ 40,000	Purchases	$205,000
Common stock	75,000	Purchase returns and	8,000
Retained earnings	45,000	allowances	
Dividends	18,000	Purchase discounts	4,000
Sales returns and allowances	12,000	Transportation-in	700
Sales discounts	15,000	Selling expenses	16,000
Sales	410,000	Administrative expenses	38,000
		Income tax expense	30,000

Instructions
Prepare closing entries for Barney Co. on December 31, 1996. Merchandise inventory was $60,000 on December 31, 1996.

E3-18 (Work Sheet Preparation) The trial balance of S. Doherty Roofing at March 31, 1996 is as follows:

S. Doherty Roofing
TRIAL BALANCE
March 31, 1996

	Debit	Credit
Cash	$ 2,300	
Fees Receivable	2,600	
Roofing Supplies	1,100	
Equipment	6,000	
Accumulated Depreciation—Equipment		$ 1,200
Accounts Payable		1,100
Unearned Fees		300
Common Stock		6,400
Retained Earnings		600
Fees Earned		3,000
Salaries Expense	500	
Miscellaneous Expense	100	
	$12,600	$12,600

Other data:

1. A physical count reveals only $620 of roofing supplies on hand.
2. Equipment is depreciated at a rate of $120 per month.
3. Unearned fees amounted to $100 on March 31.
4. Accrued salaries are $800.

Instructions
Enter the trial balance on a work sheet and complete the work sheet, assuming that the adjustments relate only to the month of March (ignore income taxes).

E3-19 (Work Sheet and Balance Sheet Presentation) The adjusted trial balance of Mandela Co. work sheet for the month ended April 30, 1995, contains the following:

Mandela Co.
WORK SHEET (PARTIAL)
For the Month Ended April 30, 1995

Account Titles	Adjusted Trial Balance Dr.	Adjusted Trial Balance Cr.	Income Statement Dr.	Income Statement Cr.	Balance Sheet Dr.	Balance Sheet Cr.
Cash	$11,980					
Marketable Securities	8,992					
Accounts Receivable	6,920					
Prepaid Rent	2,280					
Equipment	18,050					
Accumulated Depreciation		$ 4,895				
Notes Payable		5,700				
Accounts Payable		5,472				
Mandela, Capital		34,960				
Mandela, Drawing	6,650					
Fees Earned		11,590				
Salaries Expense	6,840					
Rent Expense	760					
Depreciation Expense	145					
Interest Expense	83					
Interest Payable		83				

Instructions

Complete the work sheet and prepare a balance sheet as illustrated in this chapter.

E3-20 (Partial Work Sheet Preparation) DeKlerk Co. prepares monthly financial statements from a work sheet. Selected portions of the January work sheet showed the following data:

DeKlerk Co.
WORK SHEET (PARTIAL)
For Month Ended January 31, 1996

Account Title	Trial Balance Dr.	Trial Balance Cr.	Adjustments Dr.	Adjustments Cr.	Adjusted Trial Balance Dr.	Adjusted Trial Balance Cr.
Supplies	3,256			(a) 1,200	2,056	
Accumulated Depreciation		6,682		(b) 257		6,939
Interest Payable		100		(c) 50		150
Supplies Expense			(a) 1,200		1,200	
Depreciation Expense			(b) 257		257	
Interest Expense			(c) 50		50	

During February no events occurred that affected these accounts but at the end of February the following information was available:

(a) Supplies on hand	$1,315	
(b) Monthly depreciation	$ 257	
(c) Accrued interest	$ 50	

Instructions

Reproduce the data that would appear in the February work sheet and indicate the amounts that would be shown in the February income statement.

E3-21 (Transactions of a Corporation Including Investment and Dividend) Scratch Miniature Golf and Driving Range Inc. was opened on March 1 by Jack Bogie. The following selected events and transactions occurred during March:

Mar. 1 Invested $50,000 cash in the business in exchange for common stock.
    3 Purchased Lee's Golf Land for $38,000 cash. The price consists of land, $23,000; building, $9,000; and equipment, $6,000. (Make one compound entry.)

5 Advertised the opening of the driving range and miniature golf course, paying advertising expenses of $1,600.
6 Paid cash $1,480 for a one-year insurance policy.
10 Purchased golf clubs and other equipment for $1,600 from Palmer Company payable in 30 days.
18 Received golf fees of $800 in cash.
19 Sold 100 coupon books for $15.00 each. Each book contains 10 coupons that enable the holder to one round of miniature golf or to hit one bucket of golf balls.
25 Declared and paid a $500 cash dividend.
30 Paid wages of $700.
30 Paid Palmer Company in full.
31 Received $500 of fees in cash.

Jack Bogie uses the following accounts: Cash; Prepaid Insurance; Land; Buildings; Equipment; Accounts Payable; Unearned Golf Fees; Common Stock; Dividends; Golf Fees Earned; Advertising Expense; and Wages Expense.

Instructions
Journalize the March transactions.

*E3-22 (Cash and Accrual Basis) Chita Rivera Company maintains its books on the accrual basis. The company reported insurance expense of $19,450 in its 1995 income statement. Prepaid insurance at December 31, 1995, amounted to $6,740; cash paid for insurance during the year 1995 totaled $24,100. There was no accrued insurance expense either at the beginning or at the end of 1995.

Instructions
What was the amount, if any, of prepaid insurance at January 1, 1995? Show computations.

*E3-23 (Cash to Accrual Basis) Bonnie Miller, M.D., maintains the accounting records of Miller Clinic on a cash basis. During 1995, Dr. Miller collected $142,600 from her patients and paid $55,470 in expenses. At January 1, 1995, and December 31, 1995, she had fees receivable, unearned fees, accrued expenses, and prepaid expenses as follows (all long-lived assets are rented):

	January 1, 1995	December 31, 1995
Fees receivable	$9,250	$15,927
Unearned fees	2,840	1,620
Accrued expenses	3,435	2,108
Prepaid expenses	1,917	1,775

Instructions
Prepare a schedule that converts Dr. Miller "excess of cash collected over cash disbursed" for the year 1995 to net income on an accrual basis for the year 1995.

*E3-24 (Cash and Accrual Basis) Presented below are three independent situations:

1. Horrie Co. had cash purchases of $980,000 during the past year. In addition, it had an increase in trade accounts payable of $9,000 and a decrease in merchandise inventory of $18,000. Determine purchases on an accrual basis.
2. Robert Sampson, M.D., collected $125,000 in fees during 1996. At December 31, 1995, Dr. Sampson had accounts receivable of $15,000. At December 31, 1996, Dr. Sampson had accounts receivable of $28,000 and unearned fees of $4,000. Determine Dr. Sampson's fee income on an accrual basis for 1996.
3. Kumiko Company reported revenue of $1,400,000 in its accrual basis income statement for the year ended December 31, 1996. Additional information was as follows:

> Accounts receivable December 31, 1995 $410,000
> Accounts receivable December 31, 1996   520,000
> Accounts written off during the year   45,000

Under the cash basis of accounting, determine how much revenue Kumiko should report.

*E3-25 (Cash and Accrual Basis) Hal Ketchum Corp. maintains its financial records on the cash basis of accounting. Interested in securing a long-term loan from its regular bank, Hal Ketchum Corp. requests you as its independent CPA to convert its cash basis income statement data to the accrual basis. You are provided with the following summarized data covering 1993, 1994, and 1995.

	1993	1994	1995
Cash receipts from sales:			
On 1993 sales	$290,000	$160,000	$ 30,000
On 1994 sales	–0–	350,000	90,000
On 1995 sales			408,000

	1993	1994	1995
Cash payments for expenses:			
On 1993 expenses	175,000	67,000	25,000
On 1994 expenses	30,000[a]	160,000	55,000
On 1995 expenses		45,000[b]	218,000

[a]Prepayments of 1994 expense.
[b]Prepayments of 1995 expense.

Instructions
(a) Using the data above, prepare abbreviated income statements for the years 1993 and 1994 on the cash basis.
(b) Using the data above, prepare abbreviated income statements for the years 1993 and 1994 on the accrual basis.

*E3-26 (Subsidiary Ledgers and Special Journals) Excalibur Company uses both special journals and a general journal as described in this chapter. On April 30, after all monthly postings had been completed, the Accounts Receivable controlling account in the general ledger had a debit balance of $350,000 and the Accounts Payable controlling account had a credit balance of $95,000.

The May transactions recorded in the special journals are summarized below. No entries affecting accounts receivable and accounts payable were recorded in the general journal for May.

Sales journal	Total sales, $151,500
Purchases journal	Total purchases, $58,250
Cash receipts journal	Accounts Receivable column total, $143,500
Cash payments journal	Accounts Payable column total, $55,000

Instructions
(a) What is the balance of the Accounts Receivable control account after the monthly postings on May 31?
(b) What is the balance of the Accounts Payable control account after the monthly postings on May 31?
(c) What posting would be made of the column total of $151,500 in the sales journal?
(d) What posting would be made of the accounts receivable column total of $143,500 in the cash receipts journal?

*E3-27 (Subsidiary Ledgers and Special Journals) On September 1 the balance of the Accounts Payable controlling account in the general ledger of Bertie Wooster Company was $5,460. The creditors' subsidiary ledger contained account balances as follows: Jeeves, $1,270; Glossop, $970; Bassett, $1,850; Agatha, $1,370. At the end of September the various journals contained the following information:

Purchases journal: Purchases from Jeeves, $1,500; from Glossop, $1,250; from Bassett, $1,080; from Agatha, $1,150; from Gussie, $1,365.

Cash payments journal: Cash paid to Bassett, $1,500; to Agatha, $1,070; to Jeeves, $2,746. (Jeeves allowed Bertie Wooster a $24 discount.)

General journal: An allowance from Gussie, $45; a return of merchandise to Glossop, $80; and an entry to correct a $30 overcharge that Agatha made on an invoice.

Instructions
(a) Set up control and subsidiary accounts, and enter the beginning balances. Do not construct the journals.
(b) Post the various journals. Post the items as individual items or as totals, whichever would be the appropriate procedure in the usual posting process.
(c) Prepare a list of creditors and prove the agreement of the controlling account with the subsidiary ledger.

*E3-28 (Special Journals) The Fink-Nottle Company uses the columnar cash journals illustrated in the text. In May, the following selected cash transactions occurred:

May 1 Paid cash for office equipment.
2 Received collection from customer within the 2% discount period.
3 Received cash refund from supplier for merchandise returned.
4 Made cash sales.
5 Received an advance from a customer on June sales.
6 Made cash purchases.
7 Paid a creditor within the 2% discount period.
8 Paid freight on merchandise purchased.
9 Paid dividends.
10 Made a refund to a customer for the return of damaged goods.
11 Received cash due on a non-interest-bearing note receivable.
12 Received collection from customer after the 2% discount period had expired.

Instructions
Indicate (a) the journal, and (b) the columns in the journal that should be used in recording each transaction.

*E3-29 (Special Journals)** Below are some typical transactions incurred by the Dearborn Company.

1.	Sales of merchandise on account.	9.	Collection on account from customers.
2.	Payment of creditors on account.	10.	Payment to building contractor of balance due
3.	Payment of employee wages.		on completed office building.
4.	Depreciation on building.	11.	Sold land for cash.
5.	Purchase of office supplies for cash.	12.	Close income summary to owner's capital.
6.	Return of merchandise purchased.	13.	Sales of merchandise for cash.
7.	Sales discount given on goods sold.	14.	Depreciation on machinery.
8.	Return of merchandise sold for credit.	15.	Purchase of merchandise on account.

Instructions
For each transaction, indicate whether it would normally be recorded in a cash receipts journal, cash payments journal, single-column sales journal, single-column purchases journal, or general journal.

PROBLEMS

P3-1 (Transactions, Financial Statements—Service Company) Listed below are the transactions of Laura Spencer, D.D.S., for the month of September:

Sept. 1 Laura Spencer begins practice as a dentist and invests $18,000 cash.
2 Purchases furniture and dental equipment on account from General Hospital Co. for $17,280.
4 Pays rent for office space, $680 for the month.
4 Employs a receptionist, Karen Wexler.
5 Purchases dental supplies for cash, $942.
8 Receives cash of $1,690 from patients for services performed.
10 Pays miscellaneous office expenses, $430.
14 Bills patients $4,820 for services performed.
18 Pays General Hospital Co. on account, $3,600.
19 Withdraws $3,000 cash from the business for personal use.
20 Receives $980 from patients on account.
25 Bills patients $2,110 for services performed.
30 Pays the following expenses in cash: office salaries, $1,400; miscellaneous office expenses, $85.
30 Dental supplies used during September, $330.

Instructions
(a) Enter the transactions shown above in appropriate general ledger accounts. Allow 10 lines for the Cash account and 5 lines for each of the other accounts needed. Record depreciation using an 8-year life on the furniture and equipment, the straight-line method, and no salvage value. Do not use a drawing account.
(b) Prepare a trial balance.
(c) Prepare an income statement, a balance sheet, and a statement of owner's equity.
(d) Close the ledger.
(e) Prepare a post-closing trial balance.

P3-2 (Transactions, Financial Statements—Merchandising Company) The balance sheet of Young & Restless Company as of December 31, 1995, is presented below.

Young & Restless Company
BALANCE SHEET
As of December 31, 1995

Assets		Liabilities and Stockholders' Equity		
Cash	$ 3,900	Accounts payable		$ 2,985
Accounts receivable	4,985	Notes payable		4,000
Inventory	3,300	Total liabilities		6,985
Office equipment	4,800			
Accum. depr.	(1,440)	Common stock	$10,000	
Furniture and fixtures	6,600	Retained earnings	2,960	12,960
Accum. depr.	(2,200)	Total liabilities and		
Total assets	$19,945	stockholders' equity		$19,945

The following transactions occur during the month of January 1996.

Jan. 2 Receives payment of $1,230 on accounts receivable.
    3 Purchases merchandise on account from Neil Winters Co. for $1,965, 2/30, n/60 f.o.b. shipping point (record at gross amount).
    4 Receives an invoice from *Fenmore*, a trade magazine, for advertising, $75.
    4 Sells merchandise on account to Carlton Co. for $1,034, 2/10, n/30 f.o.b. shipping point.
    4 Makes a cash sale to Nina Inc., for $1,786.
    6 Sends a letter to Neil Winters Co., regarding a slight defect in one item of merchandise received.
    9 Purchases merchandise on account from April Lynch's Novelty Company, $651.
  11 Pays freight on merchandise received from Neil Winters Co., $76.
  11 Receives a credit memo from Neil Winters Co. granting an allowance of $34 on defective merchandise (see transaction of January 6).
  15 Receives $600 on account from Carlton Co.
  19 Sells merchandise on account to Cole Howard, $812, 2/10, n/30.
  21 Pays display clerk's salary of $552.
  25 Sells merchandise for cash, $2,350.
  27 Purchases office equipment on account, $879 (begin depreciating in February).
  29 Pays Neil Winters Co. in full of account.
  30 Receives a note from Cole Howard in full of account.
  31 A count of the inventory on hand reveals $2,640 of salable merchandise.

Instructions
(a) Open ledger accounts at January 1, 1996.
(b) Enter the transactions into ledger accounts.
(c) Prepare a trial balance after adjusting for depreciation; use 10-year life, straight-line method, and no salvage for all long-term assets. Interest at 12% on the note payable is due every December 31.
(d) Prepare a balance sheet and income statement. (Ignore income taxes)
(e) Close the ledger.
(f) Take a post-closing trial balance.

P3-3 (Adjusting Entries) The accounts listed below appeared in the December 31 trial balance of the Wolftrap Theater.

	Debit	Credit
Equipment	$192,000	
Accumulated Depreciation of Equipment		$ 60,000
Notes Payable		80,000
Admissions Revenue		380,000
Concessions Revenue		36,000
Advertising Expense	13,680	
Salaries Expense	57,600	
Interest Expense	1,400	

Instructions
(a) From the account balances listed above and the information given below prepare the annual adjusting entries necessary on December 31.
  1. The equipment has an estimated life of 16 years and a trade-in value of $72,000 at the end of that time. (Use straight-line method.)
  2. The note payable is a 90-day note given to the bank October 20 and bearing interest at 10%. (Use 360 days for denominator.)
  3. In December 2,000 coupon admission books were sold at $25 each; they could be used for admission any time after January 1.
  4. The concession stand is operated by a concessionaire who pays 10% of gross receipts for the privilege of selling popcorn, candy, and soft drinks in the lobby. Sales for December were $32,700, and the 10% due for December has not yet been received or entered.
  5. Advertising expense paid in advance and included in Advertising Expense, $1,100.
  6. Salaries accrued but unpaid, $4,700.
(b) What amounts should be shown for each of the following on the income statement for the year?
  1. Interest expense.
  2. Admissions revenue.
  3. Concessions revenue.
  4. Advertising expense.
  5. Salaries expense.

P3-4 (Adjusting Entries and Financial Statements) Presented below are the trial balance and the other information related to Laura Santoro, a consulting engineer.

Laura Santoro, Consulting Engineer
TRIAL BALANCE
December 31, 1995

Cash	$ 31,500	
Accounts Receivable	49,600	
Allowance for Doubtful Accounts		$ 1,750
Engineering Supplies Inventory	1,960	
Unexpired Insurance	1,100	
Furniture and Equipment	25,000	
Accumulated Depreciation of Furniture and Equipment		5,000
Notes Payable		7,200
Laura Santoro, Capital		35,260
Revenue from Consulting Fees		100,000
Rent Expense	9,750	
Office Salaries	28,500	
Heat, Light, and Water	1,080	
Miscellaneous Office Expense	720	
	$149,210	$149,210

1. Fees received in advance from clients, $5,900.
2. Services performed for clients that were not recorded by December 31, $4,900.
3. The Allowance for Doubtful Accounts account should be adjusted to 5% of the corrected accounts receivable balance.
4. Insurance expired during the year, $480.
5. Furniture and equipment is being depreciated at 10% per year.
6. Laura Santoro gave the bank a 90-day, 10% note for $7,200 on December 1, 1995.
7. Rent of the building is $750 per month. The rent for 1995 has been paid, as has that for January 1996.
8. Office salaries earned but unpaid December 31, 1995, $2,510.

Instructions
   (a) From the trial balance and other information given, prepare annual adjusting entries as of December 31, 1995.
   (b) Prepare an income statement for 1995, a balance sheet, and a statement of owner's equity. Laura Santoro withdrew $19,000 cash for personal use during the year.

P3-5 (Adjusting Entries and Financial Statements) The Nava Advertising Corporation was founded by Tony Nava in January of 1992. Presented below are both the adjusted and unadjusted trial balances as of December 31, 1996.

Nava Advertising Corporation
TRIAL BALANCE
December 31, 1996

	Unadjusted		Adjusted	
	Dr.	Cr.	Dr.	Cr.
Cash	$ 7,000		$ 7,000	
Fees Receivable	19,000		20,000 √	
Art Supplies	8,500		5,500 √	
Prepaid Insurance	3,250		2,500 √	
Printing Equipment	60,000		60,000	
Accumulated Depreciation		$ 28,000		$ 35,000 √
Accounts Payable		5,000		5,000
Interest Payable		0		150 √
Notes Payable		5,000		5,000
Unearned Advertising Fees		7,000		5,600 √
Salaries Payable		0		1,500 √
Common Stock		10,000		10,000
Retained earnings		3,500		3,500
Advertising Fees		58,600		61,000 √

Salaries Expense	10,000		11,500 ✓	
Insurance Expense			750 ✓	
Interest Expense	350		500 ✓	
Depreciation Expense			7,000 ✓	
Art Supplies Expense	5,000		8,000 ✓	
Rent Expense	4,000		4,000	
	$117,100	$117,100	$126,750	$126,750

Instructions

(a) Journalize the annual adjusting entries that were made.

(b) Prepare an income statement and a statement of retained earnings for the year ending December 31, 1996, and a balance sheet at December 31.

(c) Answer the following questions:

    (1) If the useful life of equipment is 8 years, what is the expected salvage value?

    (2) If the note has been outstanding three months, what is the annual interest rate on that note?

    (3) If the company paid $12,500 in salaries in 1996, what was the balance in Salaries Payable on December 31, 1995?

P3-6 (Adjusting and Reversing Entries) Presented below is information related to Nicole Thompson, Realtor, at the close of the fiscal year ending December 31.

1. Nicole had paid the local newspaper $215 for an advertisement to be run in January of the next year, charging it to Advertising Expense.
2. On November 1 Nicole borrowed $6,000 from Yorkville Bank issuing a 90-day, 10% note.
3. Salaries and wages due and unpaid December 31: sales, $1,420; office clerks, $960.
4. Interest accrued to date on Mark Kluge's note, which Nicole holds, $450.
5. Estimated loss on bad debts, $980 for the period.
6. Stamps and stationery on hand, $110, charged to Stationery and Postage Expense account when purchased.
7. Nicole has not yet paid the December rent on the building her business occupies, $900.
8. Insurance paid November 1 for one year, $912, charged to Unexpired Insurance when paid.
9. Property taxes accrued, $1,670.
10. On December 1 Nicole gave Lisa Apple her (Nicole's) 60-day, 12% note for $5,000 on account.
11. On October 31 Nicole received $2,580 from Patricia Cowfer in payment of 6 months' rent for office space occupied by her in the building and credited Unearned Rent.
12. On September 1 she paid 6 months' rent in advance on a warehouse, $6,000, and debited the asset account Prepaid Rent.
13. The bill from the Storm Lake Light & Power Company for December has been received but not yet entered or paid, $460.
14. Estimated depreciation on furniture and equipment, $1,300.

Instructions

(a) Prepare annual adjusting entries as of December 31.

(b) List the numbers of the entries that would be reversed.

P3-7 (Adjusting, Closing, Reversing) Following is the trial balance of the Kishwaukee Golf Club, Inc. as of December 31. The books are closed annually on December 31.

Kishwaukee Golf Club, Inc.
TRIAL BALANCE
December 31

Cash	$ 15,000	
Dues Receivable	13,000	
Allowance for Doubtful Accounts		$ 1,100
Land	350,000	
Buildings	120,000	
Accumulated Depreciation of Buildings		48,000
Equipment	150,000	
Accumulated Depreciation of Equipment		70,000
Unexpired Insurance	9,000	
Common Stock		400,000
Retained Earnings		72,400

Revenue from Dues		200,000
Revenue from Greens Fees		8,100
Rental Revenue		15,400
Utilities Expense	54,000	
Salaries Expense	80,000	
Maintenance	24,000	
	$815,000	$815,000

Instructions

(a) Enter the balances in ledger accounts. Allow five lines for each account.

(b) From the trial balance and the information given, prepare annual adjusting entries and post to the ledger accounts.

1. The buildings have an estimated life of 20 years with no salvage value (straight-line method).
2. The equipment is depreciated at 10% per year.
3. Insurance expired during the year, $3,500.
4. The rental revenue represents the amount received for 11 months for dining facilities. The December rent has not yet been received.
5. It is estimated that 15% of the dues receivable will be uncollectible.
6. Salaries earned but not paid by December 31, $3,600.
7. Dues paid in advance by members, $7,900.

(c) Prepare an adjusted trial balance.

(d) Prepare closing entries and post.

(e) Prepare reversing entries and post.

(f) Prepare a trial balance after posting reversing entries.

P3-8 (Adjusting and Closing) Presented below is the December 31 trial balance of Madonna Boutique.

Madonna Boutique
TRIAL BALANCE
December 31

Cash	$ 18,500	
Accounts Receivable	42,000	
Allowance for Doubtful Accounts		$ 2,700
Inventory, January 1	78,000	
Furniture and Equipment	84,000	
Accumulated Depreciation of Furniture and Equipment		33,600
Prepaid Insurance	5,100	
Notes Payable		28,000
Madonna, Capital		90,000
Sales		600,000
Purchases	400,000	
Sales Salaries	50,000	
Advertising Expense	6,700	
Administrative Salaries	65,000	
Office Expense	5,000	
	$754,300	$754,300

Instructions

(a) Construct T-accounts and enter the balances shown.

(b) Prepare adjusting journal entries for the following and post to the T-accounts. Open additional T-accounts as necessary. (The books are closed yearly on December 31.)

1. Adjust the Allowance for Doubtful Accounts to 8% of the accounts receivable.
2. Furniture and equipment is depreciated at 20% per year.
3. Insurance expired during the year, $2,550.
4. Interest accrued on notes payable, $3,360.
5. Sales salaries earned but not paid, $2,400.
6. Advertising paid in advance, $700.
7. Office supplies on hand, $1,500, charged to Office Expense when purchased.

(c) Prepare closing entries and post to the accounts. The inventory on December 31 was $80,000.

P3-9 (Adjusting, Closing, Financial Statements) The balance sheet of Mattie Gibbs Company as of December 31, 1995 is presented below:

Assets		Liabilities and Capital	
Cash	$ 4,000	Accounts payable	$ 5,000
Accounts receivable	7,500	Notes payable	6,000
Inventory	5,200	Total liabilities	11,000
Office equipment	7,400		
Accumulated depreciation	(2,220)	Mattie Gibbs, capital	17,880
Furniture and fixtures	10,000		
Accumulated depreciation	(3,000)		
Total	$28,880	Total	$28,880

The following summary transactions occurred during January 1996.

Jan. 1 Sells merchandise on account, $2,800.
    2 Collects $3,210 on accounts receivable of $3,250. Sales discounts totaled $40.
    3 Sells merchandise for cash, $7,000.
    4 Receives a $1,300 note from a customer on payment of account.
    5 Purchases merchandise on account, $4,525.
    6 Pays freight on merchandise purchased, $100.
    7 Pays $3,470 on accounts payable of $3,500. Purchase discounts totaled $30.
  10 Purchases office equipment on account, $1,250.
  28 Pays expenses: advertising, $55; salaries, $840; rent, $400.

At January 31, the following information is available.
- **a.** Interest on the note payable is paid every December 31. Accrued interest for January is $60. Principal is payable December 31, 1996.
- **b.** Accrued interest on the note receivable for January is $10.
- **c.** Accrued salaries at January 31 are $125.
- **d.** Depreciation expense for January is $70 on office equipment and $80 on furniture and fixtures.
- **e.** Ending inventory is $4,225.

Instructions
- **(a)** Prepare journal entries in general journal form for the January transactions.
- **(b)** Open ledger accounts, enter the December 31 balances, and post the journal entries from (a).
- **(c)** Prepare a trial balance.
- **(d)** Prepare adjusting entries at January 31 and post.
- **(e)** Prepare an adjusted trial balance.
- **(f)** Prepare an income statement for January and a balance sheet at January 31.
- **(g)** Prepare closing entries at January 31 and post.
- **(h)** Prepare a post-closing trial balance.

P3-10 (Adjusting, Reversing) The following list of accounts and their balances represents the unadjusted trial balance of RomaLotti Corp. at December 31, 1996:

	Dr.	Cr.
Cash	$ 6,000	
Accounts Receivable	49,000	
Allowance for Doubtful Accounts		$ 750
Inventory	58,000	
Prepaid Insurance	2,940	
Prepaid Rent	13,200	
Investment in Abbott Corp. Bonds	18,000	
Land	10,000	
Plant and Equipment	104,000	
Accumulated Depreciation		18,000
Accounts Payable		9,310
Bonds Payable		50,000
Discount on Bonds Payable	1,500	
Capital Stock		100,000
Retained Earnings		80,660
Sales		213,310
Rental Revenue		10,200
Purchases	170,000	

Purchase Discounts		2,400
Transportation-Out	9,000	
Transportation-In	3,500	
Salaries and Wages	35,000	
Interest Expense	3,600	
Miscellaneous Expense	890	
	$484,630	$484,630

Additional data:

1. On November 1, 1996, RomaLotti received $10,200 rent from its lessee for a 12-month lease beginning on that date, crediting Rental Revenue.
2. RomaLotti estimates that 4% of the Accounts Receivable balances on December 31, 1996, will become uncollectible. On December 28, 1996, the bookkeeper incorrectly credited Sales for a receipt on account in the amount of $1,000. This error had not yet been corrected on December 31.
3. Per a physical inventory, inventory on hand at December 31, 1996, was $65,000. Record the adjusting entry for inventory by using a Cost of Goods Sold account.
4. Prepaid insurance contains the premium costs of two policies: Policy A, cost of $1,320, 2-year term, taken out on September 1, 1996; Policy B, cost of $1,620, 3-year term, taken out on April 1, 1996.
5. The regular rate of depreciation is 10% per year. Acquisitions and retirements during a year are depreciated at half this rate. There were no retirements during the year. On December 31, 1995, the balance of Plant and Equipment was $90,000.
6. On April 1, 1996, RomaLotti issued 50 $1,000, 11% bonds, maturing on April 1, 2006, at 97% of par value. Interest payment dates are April 1 and October 1.
7. On August 1, 1996, RomaLotti purchased 18 $1,000, 12% Abbott Corp. bonds, maturing on July 31, 1998, at par value. Interest payment dates are July 31 and January 31.
8. On May 30, 1996, RomaLotti rented a warehouse for $1,100 per month, paying $13,200 in advance, debiting Prepaid Rent.

Instructions

(a) Prepare the year-end adjusting and correcting entries in general journal form using the information above.

(b) Indicate the adjusting entries that would be reversed.

 P3-11 (Work Sheet and Financial Statement Preparation) Boffo Company closes its books only once a year, on December 31, but prepares monthly financial statements by estimating month-end inventories and by using work sheets. The company's trial balance on January 31, 1995, is presented below. Selling Expenses and Administrative Expenses are controlling accounts.

Boffo Company
TRIAL BALANCE
January 31, 1995

Cash	$ 11,000	
Accounts Receivable	23,000	
Notes Receivable	3,000	
Allowance for Doubtful Accounts		$ 720
Inventory, Jan. 1, 1995	24,000	
Furniture and Fixtures	30,000	
Accumulated Depreciation of Furniture and Fixtures		7,500
Unexpired Insurance	600	
Supplies on Hand	1,050	
Accounts Payable		6,000
Notes Payable		5,000
Common Stock		20,000
Retained Earnings		27,005
Sales		130,000
Sales Returns and Allowances	1,500	
Purchases	80,000	
Transportation-In	2,000	
Selling Expenses	11,000	
Administrative Expenses	9,000	
Interest Revenue		125
Interest Expense	200	
	$196,350	$196,350

Instructions

(a) Copy the trial balance in the first two columns of an eight-column work sheet. (Do not use adjusted trial balance columns.)

(b) Prepare adjusting entries in journal form (administrative expenses includes bad debts, depreciation, insurance, supplies, and office salaries).

    1. Estimated bad debts, .4% of net sales.

    2. Depreciation of furniture and fixtures, 10% per year.

    3. Insurance expired in January, $80.

    4. Supplies used in January, $210.

    5. Office salaries accrued, $500.

    6. Interest accrued on notes payable, $200.

    7. Interest unearned on notes receivable, $74.

(c) Transfer the adjusting entries to the work sheet.

(d) Estimate the January 31 inventory and enter it on the work sheet. The average gross profit earned by the company is 30% of net sales.

(e) Complete the work sheet.

(f) Prepare a balance sheet, an income statement, and a statement of retained earnings. Dividends of $3,000 were paid on the common stock during the month.

P3-12 (Work Sheet, Adjusting, Financial Statements) Presented below is the trial balance for Brendan Noble, proprietor.

Brendan Noble
TRIAL BALANCE
December 31, 1996

Cash	$ 13,600	
Accounts Receivable	64,800	
Allowance for Doubtful Accounts		$ 2,000
Inventory, January 1	74,000	
Land	40,000	
Building	90,000	
Accumulated Depreciation of Building		14,400
Furniture and Fixtures	22,000	
Accumulated Depreciation of Furniture and Fixtures		6,600
Unexpired Insurance	7,800	
Accounts Payable		34,200
Notes Payable		30,000
Mortgage Payable		40,000
Brendan Noble, Capital		124,730
Sales		720,000
Sales Returns and Allowances	2,800	
Purchases	540,000	
Purchase Returns and Allowances		9,500
Transportation-In	14,800	
Sales Salaries	54,000	
Advertising Expense	9,400	
Salaries, Office and General	31,000	
Heat, Light, and Water Expense	15,100	
Telephone and Telex Expense	1,700	
Miscellaneous Office Expenses	2,000	
Purchase Discounts		9,600
Sales Discounts	5,900	
Interest Expense	2,130	
	$991,030	$991,030

Instructions

(a) Copy the trial balance above in the first two columns of a 10-column work sheet.

(b) Prepare adjusting entries in journal form from the following information. (The fiscal year ends December 31.)

    1. Estimated bad debts, .25% of sales less returns and allowances.

    2. Depreciation on building, 4% per year; on furniture and fixtures, 15% per year.

3. Insurance expired during the year, $3,900.
4. Interest at 12% is payable on the mortgage on January 1 of each year.
5. Sales salaries accrued, December 31, $4,000.
6. Advertising expense paid in advance, $740.
7. Office supplies on hand December 31, $1,600. (Charged to Miscellaneous Office Expenses when purchased.)
8. Interest accrued on notes payable December 31, $1,800.

(c) Transfer the adjusting entries to the work sheet and complete it. Merchandise inventory on hand December 31, $76,000.

(d) Prepare an income statement, a balance sheet, and a statement of capital.

(e) Prepare closing journal entries.

(f) Indicate the adjusting entries that would be reversed.

P3-13 (Journalize, Post to Ledger, and Prepare Trial Balance) Gene Shumway and other student investors opened Farmers Laundromat Inc. on September 1. During the first month of operations the following transactions occurred:

Sept. 1 Stockholders invested $20,000 cash in the business.
2 Paid $1,000 cash for store rent for the month of September.
3 Purchased washers and dryers for $25,000 paying $10,000 in cash and signing a $15,000, six-month, 12% note payable.
4 Paid $1,200 for one-year accident insurance policy.
10 Received bill from the Daily News for advertising the opening of the laundromat, $200.
20 Declared and paid a cash dividend of $700 to stockholders.
30 Determined the cash receipts for laundry fees for the month were $6,200.

The chart of accounts for the company is No. 1 Cash, No. 10 Prepaid Insurance, No. 15 Laundry Equipment, No. 25 Notes Payable, No. 26 Accounts Payable, No. 40 Common Stock, No. 42 Dividends, No. 50 Fees Earned, No. 61 Advertising Expense, No. 62 Rent Expense.

Instructions

(a) Journalize the September transactions. (Use J1 for the journal page number.)

(b) Open ledger accounts and post the September transactions.

(c) Prepare a trial balance at September 30, 1996.

*P3-14 (Cash and Accrual Basis) On January 1, 1996, Deborah Brewster and Tess Wilder formed a computer sales and service enterprise in Soapsville, Arkansas by investing $90,000 cash. The new company, Micromash Sales and Service, has the following transactions during January:

1. Pays $6,000 in advance for three months' rent of office, showroom, and repair space.
2. Purchases 40 microcomputers at a cost of $1,000 each, 6 graphic computers at a cost of $2,000 each, and 25 printers at a cost of $300 each, paying cash upon delivery.
3. Sales, repair, and office employees earn $12,600 in salaries during January, of which $3,000 was still payable at the end of January.
4. Sells 30 microcomputers at $1,700 each, 4 graphic computers for $3,000 each, and 15 printers for $500 each; $50,000 is received in cash in January and $20,500 is sold on a deferred payment basis.
5. Other operating expenses of $8,400 are incurred and paid for during January; $2,000 of incurred expenses is payable at January 31.

Instructions

(a) Using the transaction data above, prepare (1) a cash basis income statement and (2) an accrual basis income statement for the month of January.

(b) Using the transaction data above, prepare (1) a cash basis balance sheet and (2) an accrual basis balance sheet as of January 31, 1996.

(c) Identify the items in the cash basis financial statements that make cash basis accounting inconsistent with the theory underlying the elements of financial statements.

*P3-15 (Cash to Accrual Basis) Presented below is information pertaining to Basler Specialty Shops, a calendar-year sole proprietorship, maintaining its books on the cash basis during the year. At year-end, however, Shirley Basler's accountant adjusts the books to the accrual basis only for sales, purchases, and cost of sales, and records depreciation to more clearly reflect the business income for income tax purposes.

Basler Speciality Shops
TRIAL BALANCE (Cash Basis)
December 31, 1996

	Dr.	Cr.
Cash	$ 18,500	
Accounts receivable, 12/31/95	4,500	
Inventory, 12/31/95	20,000	
Equipment	35,000	
Accumulated depreciation, 12/13/95		$ 9,000
Accounts payable, 12/31/95		$ 4,800
Payroll taxes withheld		850
Shirley Basler, drawings	24,000	
Shirely Basler, capital, 12/31/95		33,650
Sales		187,000
Purchases	82,700	
Salaries	29,500	
Payroll taxes	2,900	
Rent	8,400	
Miscellaneous expense	3,900	
Insurance	2,400	
Utilities	3,500	
	$235,300	$235,300

During 1996 Basler signed a new 8-year lease for the store premises and is in the process of negotiating a loan for remodeling. The bank requires Basler to present financial statements for 1996 prepared on the accrual basis. During the course of compiling information, Basler's accountant obtained the following additional information:

1. Amounts due from customers totaled $7,900 at December 31, 1996.
2. A review of the receivables at December 31, 1996, disclosed that an allowance for doubtful accounts of $1,100 should be provided. Basler had no bad debt losses from inception of the business through December 31, 1996.
3. The inventory amounted to $23,000 at December 31, 1996, based on physical counts of goods priced at cost. No reduction to market was required.
4. On signing the new lease on October 1, 1996, Basler paid $8,400, representing one year's rent in advance for the lease year ending October 1, 1997. The $7,500 annual rent under the old lease was paid on October 1, 1995, for the lease year ended October 1, 1996.
5. On April 1, 1996, Basler paid $2,400 to renew the comprehensive insurance coverage for one year. The premium was $2,160 on the old policy which expired on April 1, 1996.
6. Depreciation on equipment was computed at $5,800 for 1996.
7. Unpaid vendors' invoices for purchases totaled $8,800 at December 31, 1996.
8. Accrued expenses at December 31, 1995, and December 31, 1996, were as follows:

	12/31/95	12/31/96
Payroll taxes	$250	$400
Salaries	375	510
Utilities	275	450

Instructions

(a) Prepare a work sheet to convert the trial balance of Basler Speciality Shops to the accrual basis for the year ended December 31, 1996. Journal entries are not required to support your adjustments.
Use the following work sheet columns:

Cash Basis		Adjustments		Accrual Basis	
Dr.	Cr.	Dr.	Cr.	Dr.	Cr.

(b) Prepare the statement of changes in Shirley Basler, capital, for the year ended December 31, 1996.

(AICPA adapted)

*P3-16 **(Cash to Accrual Basis)** On January 2, 1995, Butcher-Positano, Inc., was organized with two stockholders, Tim Butcher and Jeff Positano. Butcher purchased 500 shares of $100 par value common stock for $50,000 cash; Positano received 600 shares of common stock in exchange for the assets and liabilities of a men's clothing shop that he had operated as a sole proprietorship. The trial balance immediately after incorporation appears on the work sheet.

No formal books have been kept during 1995. The following information has been gathered from the checkbooks, deposit slips, and other sources:

1. Most balance sheet account balances at December 31, 1995, have been determined and recorded on the work sheet.
2. Cash receipts for the year are summarized as follows:

Advances from customers	$ 1,100
Cash sales and collections on accounts receivable (after sales discounts	
of $1,600 and sales returns and allowances of $2,300)	132,100
Sale of equipment costing $6,000 on which $1,000 of	
depreciation had accumulated	5,800
	$139,000

3. During 1995, the depreciation expense on the building was $2,000; the depreciation expense on the equipment was $2,400.
4. Cash disbursements for the year are summarized as follows:

Insurance premiums	$ 1,400
Purchase of equipment	10,000
Addition to building	9,500
Cash purchases and payments on accounts payable (after purchase	
discounts of $2,200 and purchase returns and allowances of $1,800)	109,000
Salaries paid to employees	38,600
Utilities	3,200
Total cash disbursements	$171,700

5. Bad debts are estimated to be 1.9% of total sales for the year. The ending accounts receivable balance of $30,000 has been reduced by $760 for specific accounts that were written off as uncollectible.

Instructions

Complete the work sheet for the preparation of accrual basis financial statements. Formal financial statements and journal entries are not required. (Prepare your own work sheet because you will need additional accounts.)

(AICPA adapted)

Butcher-Positano, Inc.
WORK SHEET FOR PREPARATION OF ACCRUAL BASIS
FINANCIAL STATEMENTS
For the Year 1995

	Trial Balance January 2, 1995 Debit	Credit	Adjustments Debit	Credit	Income Statement 1995 Debit	Credit	Balance Sheet December 31, 1995 Debit	Credit
Cash	55,000							
Accounts receivable	12,000						30,000	
Merchandise inventory	31,000						51,500	
Unexpired insurance	800						900	
Land	20,000						20,000	
Buildings	30,000							
Accumulated depreciation— buildings		8,000						
Equipment	12,000							
Accumulated depreciation— equipment		3,000						25,600
Accounts payable		36,600						25,600
Advances from customers		1,100						1,700
Salaries payable		2,100						4,600
Capital stock		110,000						110,000
	160,800	160,800						

*P3-17 (Special Journals) Presented below is information related to Guiding Light Company.

Journals

Sales journal	Page 17
Purchases journal	Page 8
Cash receipts journal	Page 43
Cash payments journal	Page 44
General journal	Page 12

Ledger Accounts

Title	Balance July 1	Acct. No.
Cash	$4,000	2
Accounts Receivable	9,000	5
Delivery Equipment	8,000	8
Sales Equipment	3,000	21
Accounts Payable	7,000	35
Advertising Expense	–0–	65
Purchases	–0–	52
Purchase Returns	–0–	53
Sales	–0–	69
Transportation-In	–0–	70

The following transactions occurred during the month of July.

July	1	Sells merchandise for cash, $9,000.
	3	Buys a new delivery truck on account from Blake Thorpe Motors, $17,000.
	3	Receives an invoice from the *Daily Tattler* for a full-page advertisement, $360, which appeared in the paper on July 2.
	5	Receives a purchase requisition for display equipment from the sales manager; the equipment sells for $1,320.
	6	Returns merchandise for credit of $180 on a cash purchase.
	7	Sells merchandise on account to Tangie Hill, $18,000.
	8	Purchases merchandise on account from Joshua Lewis, $12,000, f.o.b. shipping point.
	10	Receives cash of $180 for merchandise returned July 6.
	11	Receives a debit memo for $140 from Joshua Lewis, indicating that the merchandise purchased July 8 was shipped with freight prepaid.
	13	Purchases display equipment for $1,320; the invoice is paid immediately. (See July 5 information.)
	17	Sells merchandise on account to Buzz Cooper, $3,000.
	20	Pays Joshua Lewis in full of account.
	24	Purchases merchandise on account from Fletcher Reade, $3,500.
	28	Pays the *Daily Tattler.*
	31	Receives full payment from Tangie Hill.

Instructions

Complete the following:

(a) Open ledger accounts and enter the July 1 balances.

(b) Record the July transactions in appropriate journals.

(c) Post from the journals to the ledger with posting references in good form (omit subsidiary ledger postings).

► USING YOUR JUDGMENT ◄

► FINANCIAL REPORTING PROBLEM

The financial statements of Georgia-Pacific are presented in Appendix 5-A.

Instructions

(a) Using the consolidated income statement and balance sheet, identify items that may result in adjusting entries for prepayments.

(b) Using the consolidated income statement, identify two items that may result in adjusting entries for accruals.

(c) Using the Statement of Cash Flows, what was the amount of depreciation expense for 1993 and 1992? How was depreciation expense reported in the income statement?

(d) Using Note 1 related to property, plant, and equipment, how much interest was paid in 1993? What might account for the difference between total interest costs and interest paid?

▶ WRITING ASSIGNMENT

Dr. Geoffrey S. Burnham, M.D., maintains the accounting records of Burnham Clinic on a cash basis. During 1995, Dr. Burnham collected $142,000 from his patients and paid $55,470 in expenses. At January 1, 1995 and December 31, 1995, he had fees receivable, unearned fees, accrued expenses, and prepaid expenses as follows (all long-lived assets are rented):

	January 1, 1995	December 31, 1995
Fees receivable	$9,250	$16,100
Unearned fees	2,840	1,620
Accrued expenses	3,435	2,200
Prepaid expenses	2,000	1,775

Instructions

Last week, Dr. Burnham asked you, his CPA, to help him determine his income on the accrual basis. Write a letter to him, explaining what you did to calculate net income on the accrual basis. Be sure to state net income on the accrual basis and to include a schedule of your calculations.

▶ GROUP ASSIGNMENT

(Adjusting Entries and Financial Statements) Assume your group is performing the accounting services for Denise LaGreca, a consulting engineer. Ms. LaGreca has provided the following trial balance and other information for your task.

Denise LaGreca, Consulting Engineer
TRIAL BALANCE
December 31, 1996

Cash	$ 31,500	
Accounts Receivable	49,600	
Allowance for Doubtful Accounts		$ 1,750
Engineering Supplies Inventory	1,960	
Unexpired Insurance	1,100	
Furniture and Equipment	25,000	
Accumulated Depreciation of Furniture and Equipment		5,000
Notes Payable		7,200
Denise LaGreca, Capital		35,260
Revenue from Consulting Fees		100,000
Rent Expense	9,750	
Office Salaries	28,500	
Heat, Light, and Water	1,080	
Miscellaneous Office Expense	720	
	$149,210	$149,210

1. Fees received in advance from clients, $7,000.
2. Services performed for clients that were not recorded by December 31, $5,500.
3. The Allowance for Doubtful Accounts account should be adjusted to 6% of the corrected accounts receivable balance.
4. Insurance expired during the year, $600.
5. Furniture and equipment is being depreciated at 10% per year.
6. Denise LaGreca gave the bank a 90-day, 12% note for $7,200 on December 1, 1996.

7. Rent of the building is $750 per month. The rent for 1996 has been paid, as has that for January 1997.
8. Office salaries earned but unpaid December 31, 1996, $2,600.

Instructions
Your instructor will identify one member to serve as "keeper of the trial balance" and another member to prepare financial statements; the remaining members will serve as transaction analyzers. Divide the information items among the analyzers so that each has at least one item to analyze.
  (a) From the trial balance and the other information for each item, the analyzers should prepare the entries needed for their items and report them to the keeper of the trial balance. He or she will update the trial balance for these adjusting entries as of December 31, 1996.
  (b) The "preparer" member should prepare (with the help of other members) an income statement for 1996, a balance sheet, and a statement of owner's equity. Note that Ms. LaGreca withdrew $14,740 cash during the year for personal use. The group should be prepared to report its results to the class.

▶ ETHICS CASE

While reviewing the year-end financial statements for Basler Motors Inc., chief accountant Scott Sondgeroth realizes his original estimate of bad debt expense for the current year is too high to permit the bonus payment that is linked to the company's percentage increase in earnings. Both he and his supervisor are in line for the bonus. Scott is contemplating revising downward his bad debt estimate to increase earnings.

Instructions
  (a) Should Scott lower his estimate? Who is harmed if he does lower it?
  (b) What if only his supervisor's bonus were affected and not his: should this alter Scott's decision?

CHAPTER 4

STATEMENT OF INCOME AND RETAINED EARNINGS

LEARNING OBJECTIVES

After studying this chapter, you should be able to:

1. Identify the uses and limitations of an income statement.

2. Distinguish between the capital maintenance and transaction approaches.

3. Prepare a single-step income statement.

4. Prepare a multiple-step income statement.

5. Explain how irregular items are reported.

6. Explain intraperiod tax allocation.

7. Explain where earnings per share information is reported.

8. Prepare a statement of retained earnings.

9. Explain how prior period adjustments are reported.

"*F*inancial Corp. of America restates income to show a loss of $107.5 million, stock price drops 3 points"; "Pillsbury Company's stock plunged 2⅝ on heavy volume as investors rushed to sell shares after lower earnings reported." These stories and others you can find in the financial news indicate the impact that unfavorable income numbers may have on the value of the enterprise.

The **statement of income**, often called the income statement or statement of earnings,[1] is the report that measures the success of enterprise operations for a given period of time. The business and investment community uses this report to determine profitability, investment value, and credit worthiness. It provides investors and creditors with information that helps them predict the **amounts, timing, and uncertainty of future cash flows.**

UNDERLYING CONCEPT

The measurement of income is a reflection of the many established assumptions and principles (standards) in accounting, such as the periodicity assumption, the revenue recognition principle, and the matching principle.

▶ IMPORTANCE OF STATEMENT OF INCOME

The income statement helps users of the financial statements predict future cash flows in a number of different ways. First, investors and creditors can use the information on the income statement to evaluate the past performance of the enterprise. Although

---

[1]*Accounting Trends and Techniques—1993* (New York: AICPA), indicates that for the 600 companies surveyed in 1992 the term *income* is employed in the title of 292 income statements. The term *operations* is second in acceptance with 165, while the term *earnings* is used by 132 companies.

success in the past does not necessarily mean success in the future, some important trends may be determined. It follows that if a reasonable correlation between past and future performance can be assumed, then predictions of future cash flows can be made with some confidence.

Second, the income statement helps users **determine the risk (level of uncertainty) of not achieving particular cash flows.** Information on the various components of income—revenues, expenses, gains, and losses—highlights the relationship among them. With such information one can, for example, assess better the effect of a change in demand for a company's product on revenues and expenses (and therefore income). Similarly, segregating operating performance from other aspects of performance can provide useful insights. Because operations are usually the major means by which revenues and ultimately cash are generated, results from regular continuing operations usually have greater significance than results from nonrecurring activities and events.

Sometimes, though, even "continuing operations" can mislead investors. Consider the case of National Patent Development, a company that specializes in soft contact lenses. It reported $18.6 million in income from continuing operations before taxes. A closer examination of this income, however, revealed that (1) $7.5 million of income came from a gain on the sale of stock by a subsidiary; (2) $2.4 million represented a gain on the exchange of stock; (3) $3.6 million came from a gain on the sale of stock in its investment portfolio; and, (4) $3.2 million came from settlement of lawsuits related to patent infringements. In addition, its largest revenue source, $9.9 million from royalties on its soft contact lenses, might not continue: a note indicates the company's patent on this process was about to expire. Our point here is that income, "the bottom line," doesn't tell the whole story.

Whether existing confidence in the income statement is well founded is a matter of conjecture. Because the derived income is at best a rough estimate, the reader of the statement should take care not to give it more significance than it deserves. However, taken in its entirety the income statement does, nonetheless, provide information on the nature of income and the likelihood that it will continue in the future.

▶ LIMITATIONS OF INCOME STATEMENT

Economists have often criticized accountants for their definition of income because accountants **do not include many items** that contribute to general growth and well-being of an enterprise. Economist J. R. Hicks defined income as the maximum value an entity can consume during a period and still be as well off at the end as at the beginning.[2] Any effort to measure how well-off an entity is at any point in time, however, will prove fruitless unless certain restrictive assumptions are developed and applied.

What was your net income for last year? Let us suppose that you worked during the summer and earned $4,200. Because you paid taxes and incurred tuition and living expenses for school, your income statement may show a loss for the year, if measured in terms of straight dollar value. But have you sustained a loss? How do you value the education obtained during this one year? One interpretation of Hicks's definition states that you would measure not only monetary income but also psychic income ("well-offness"). Psychic income is defined as a measure of increase in net wealth arising from qualitative factors—in this case, the value of your educational experience.

Accountants know that the recognition of such experiences might be useful, but the problem of measurement has not been solved. So, items that cannot be quantified with any degree of reliability have been discarded in determining income.

---

[2]J. R. Hicks, *Value and Capital* (Oxford: Clarendon Press, 1946), p. 172.

OBJECTIVE 1

Identify the uses and limitations of an income statement.

That's not to say that income totals are uniform and precise. **Income numbers are often affected by the accounting methods employed.**[3] For example, one company may choose to depreciate its plant assets on an accelerated basis; another may choose a straight-line basis. Assuming all other factors are equal, the income of the first company will be lower than that of the second even though the companies are essentially the same. Thus the **quality of earnings** of a given enterprise is important. Companies that use liberal (aggressive) accounting policies report higher income numbers in the short run. In such cases, we say that the quality of the earnings is low.

Other companies generate income in the short run as a result of a nonoperating or nonrecurring event that is not sustainable over a period of time. At one time Beatrice Cos. reported earnings of $4.77 per share, supposedly a 20% increase over the prior year's $3.99 per share earnings. However, $2.20 per share was earned from the sales of certain lines of business. Another $0.17 per share resulted from a nonoperating tax forgiveness granted to encourage exports. And an additional $0.19 per share of income resulted from a complicated nonrecurring exchange for its preferred stock. How real was the 20% increase? How sustainable was the reported $4.77 per share? It should not have been a surprise when Beatrice reported earnings of $2.09 per share the subsequent year, down 56%.

INTERNATIONAL INSIGHT

In some nations it is permissible to "smooth" earnings by creating balance sheet reserves. Such reserves are created by reducing income in good years. In less profitable years, previous income is "retrieved" from the reserves to increase the income in the current year.

▶ CAPITAL MAINTENANCE APPROACH VERSUS TRANSACTION APPROACH

People are sometimes surprised to learn that there are two ways to calculate net income. The first is represented by Hicks's definition of income. He subtracted beginning net assets (assets minus liabilities) from ending net assets and adjusted for any additional investments and any distributions (dividends declared or drawings made) during the period. This is the **capital maintenance approach** (sometimes referred to as the **change in equity** approach). It takes the net assets or "capital values" based on some valuation (e.g., historical cost, discounted cash flows, current cost, or fair market value) and measures income by the difference in capital values at two points in time.[4]

Suppose that a corporation had beginning net assets of $10,000 and end-of-the-year net assets of $18,000. During this same period additional owners' investments of $5,000 were made, and $1,000 of dividends were declared. Calculation of the net income for the period, employing the capital maintenance approach, is shown in Illustration 4-1.

OBJECTIVE 2
Distinguish between the capital maintenance and transaction approaches.

Net assets, December 31, 1996	$18,000
Net assets, January 1, 1996	10,000
Increase in net assets	8,000
Add:	
Dividends declared during the year	1,000
Deduct:	
Owners' investments during the year	(5,000)
Net income for 1996	$ 4,000

ILLUSTRATION 4-1
Capital Maintenance Approach to Measuring Net Income

---

[3]Experiences with Hollywood's movie producers illustrate the necessity to define net income, where possible, in advance. Numerous actors, writers, and producers signed "net profit contracts" on highly successful projects but never received a share of the profits. With the big studios' ability to allocate overhead costs creatively, "net profits" failed to materialize. Large-grossing productions like *On Golden Pond, Alien, Ghostbusters, Hart to Hart, The Rockford Files,* and *Coming to America* "never broke into net profit." Thus, several stars have brought lawsuits against the movie studios in an attempt to uncover the creative measurement of "net loss." (See *Forbes,* "Profits? What Profits?" February 19, 1990, pp. 38–40.)

[4]The Internal Revenue Service uses the capital maintenance approach to identify unreported income and refers to its approach as a "net worth check." See Joseph Karasyk, "The Net Worth Method in Tax Evasion Cases," *The CPA Journal* (Vol. XLIX, No. 4, April 1979), pp. 35–40.

The calculation is relatively straightforward. But there is one important drawback to the capital maintenance approach: Detailed information concerning the composition of the income is not evident because the revenue and expense amounts are not presented to the financial statement reader.

The alternative procedure measures the basic income-related transactions that occur during a period and summarizes them in an income statement. This method is called the **transaction approach** and is the method with which you are familiar. This approach focuses on the activities that have occurred during a given period; instead of presenting only a net change, it discloses the components of the change. Income may be classified by customer, product line, or function; by operating and nonoperating, continuing and discontinued, and regular and irregular.[5] The transaction approach to income measurement is superior to the capital maintenance approach because it provides information on the elements of income.

▶ DEVELOPING THE INCOME STATEMENT

ELEMENTS OF THE INCOME STATEMENT

The transaction approach to income measurement requires the use of revenue, expense, loss, and gain accounts, without which an income statement cannot be prepared. As indicated in Chapter 2, the major elements of the income statement are as follows:

◀ ELEMENTS OF THE INCOME STATEMENT ▶

REVENUES. Inflows or other enhancements of assets of an entity or settlements of its liabilities during a period from delivering or producing goods, rendering services, or other activities that constitute the entity's ongoing major or central operations.

EXPENSES. Outflows or other using-up of assets or incurrences of liabilities during a period from delivering or producing goods, rendering services, or carrying out other activities that constitute the entity's ongoing major or central operations.

GAINS. Increases in equity (net assets) from peripheral or incidental transactions of an entity except those that result from revenues or investments by owners.

LOSSES. Decreases in equity (net assets) from peripheral or incidental transactions of an entity except those that result from expenses or distributions to owners.[6]

Revenues take many forms, such as sales, fees, interest, dividends, and rents. Expenses also take many forms, such as cost of goods sold, depreciation, interest, rent, salaries and wages, and taxes. Gains and losses also are of many types, resulting from the sale of investments, sale of plant assets, settlement of liabilities, write-offs of assets due to obsolescence or casualty, and theft.

The distinction between revenues and gains and the distinction between expenses and losses depend to a great extent on the typical activities of the enterprise. For example, the sales price of investments sold by an insurance company such as Mutual of

---

[5]Irregular encompasses transactions and other events that are derived from developments outside the normal operations of the business.

[6]"Elements of Financial Statements," *Statement of Financial Accounting Concepts No. 6* (Stamford, Conn.: FASB, 1985), pars. 78–89.

Omaha would generally be classified as revenue, whereas the sales price less book value on the sale of an investment by a manufacturing enterprise (such as Inland Steel Co.) would be classified as a gain or loss. The different treatment results because the sale of investments by an insurance company is part of its regular operations, whereas in a manufacturing enterprise it is not.

The importance of reporting these elements should not be underestimated. For most decision makers, the parts of a financial statement will often be more useful than the whole. As indicated earlier, investors and creditors are interested in predicting the amounts, timing, and uncertainty of future income and cash flows. Having income statement elements shown in some detail and in comparison form with prior years' data, decision makers are better able to assess future income and cash flows.

INTERNATIONAL INSIGHT

In many nations financial reporting is prepared on the same bases as tax returns. In such cases, companies have incentives to minimize reported income.

SINGLE-STEP INCOME STATEMENTS

In reporting revenues, gains, expenses, and losses, many accountants prefer a format known as the **single-step income statement.** In the single-step statement, just two groupings exist: revenues and expenses. Expenses are deducted from revenues to arrive at net income or loss. The expression "single-step" is derived from the single subtraction necessary to arrive at net income. Frequently income tax is reported separately as the last item before net income to indicate their relationship to income before income tax.

OBJECTIVE 3

Prepare a single-step income statement.

For example, Illustration 4-2 shows the single-step income statement of Dan Deines Company.

ILLUSTRATION 4-2
Single-step Income Statement

Dan Deines Company INCOME STATEMENT For the Year Ended December 31, 1996	
Revenues	
Net sales	$2,972,413
Dividend revenue	98,500
Rental revenue	72,910
Total revenues	3,143,823
Expenses	
Cost of goods sold	1,982,541
Selling expenses	453,028
Administrative expenses	350,771
Interest expense	126,060
Income tax expense	66,934
Total expenses	2,979,334
Net income	$ 164,489
Earnings per common share	$1.74

The single-step form of income statement is widely used in financial reporting, although in recent years, the multiple-step form described below has regained its former popularity.[7]

The primary advantage of the single-step format lies in the simplicity of presentation and the absence of any implication that one type of revenue or expense item has priority over another. Potential classification problems are thus eliminated.

---

[7]*Accounting Trends and Techniques—1993.* Of the 600 companies surveyed by the AICPA in 1992, 389 employed the multiple-step form and 211 employed the single-step income statement format. This is a reversal from 1983, when 314 used the single-step form and 286 used the multiple-step form.

MULTIPLE-STEP INCOME STATEMENTS

OBJECTIVE 4

Prepare a multiple-step income statement.

Some accountants contend that including other important revenue and expense data makes the income statement more informative and more useful. These further classifications include:

1. A separation of operating and subordinate or nonoperating activities of the company. For example, enterprises often present an income from operations figure and then sections entitled "other revenues and gains" and "other expenses and losses." These other categories include interest revenue and expense, sales of miscellaneous items, and dividends received.

2. A classification of expenses by functions, such as merchandising or manufacturing (cost of goods sold), selling, and administration. This permits immediate comparison with costs of previous years and with the cost of other departments during the same year.

Accountants who show these additional relationships in the operating data favor what is called a **multiple-step income statement.** This statement is recommended because it recognizes a separation of operating transactions from nonoperating transactions and matches costs and expenses with related revenues. It highlights certain intermediate components of income that are used for the computation of ratios used to assess the performance of the enterprise.

To illustrate, Dan Deines Company's multiple-step statement of income is presented in Illustration 4-3. Note, for example, that in arriving at net income, three subtotals are presented: net sales revenue, gross profit, and income from operations. The disclosure of net sales revenues is useful because regular revenues are reported as a separate item. Irregular or incidental revenues are disclosed elsewhere in the income statement. As a result, trends in revenue from continuing operations should be easier to understand and analyze. Similarly, the reporting of gross profit provides a useful number for evaluating performance and assessing future earnings. A study of the trend in gross profits may show how successfully a company uses its resources; it may also be a basis for understanding how profit margins have changed as a result of competitive pressure.

Finally, disclosing income from operations highlights the difference between regular and irregular or incidental activities. This disclosure helps users recognize that incidental or irregular activities are unlikely to continue at the same level. Furthermore, disclosure of operating earnings may assist in comparing different companies and assessing operating efficiencies.

INTERMEDIATE COMPONENTS OF THE INCOME STATEMENT

When a multiple-step income statement is used, some or all of the following sections or subsections may be prepared:

◀ INCOME STATEMENT SECTIONS ▶

1. **OPERATING SECTION.** A report of the revenues and expenses of the company's principal operations.

   (a) **SALES OR REVENUE SECTION.** A subsection presenting sales, discounts, allowances, returns, and other related information. Its purpose is to arrive at the net amount of sales revenue.

   (b) **COST OF GOODS SOLD SECTION.** A subsection that shows the cost of goods that were sold to produce the sales.

(List continues on page 144.)

ILLUSTRATION 4-3
**Multiple-step Income
Statement**

Dan Deines Company
INCOME STATEMENT
For the Year Ended December 31, 1996

Sales Revenue			
Sales			$3,053,081
Less: Sales discounts		$ 24,241	
Sales returns and allowances		56,427	80,668
Net sales revenue			2,972,413
Cost of Goods Sold			
Merchandise inventory, Jan. 1, 1996		461,219	
Purchases	$1,989,693		
Less purchase discounts	19,270		
Net purchases	1,970,423		
Freight and transportation-in	40,612	2,011,035	
Total merchandise available for sale		2,472,254	
Less merchandise inventory, Dec. 31, 1996		489,713	
Cost of goods sold			1,982,541
Gross profit on sales			989,872
Operating Expenses			
Selling expenses			
Sales salaries and commissions	202,644		
Sales office salaries	59,200		
Travel and entertainment	48,940		
Advertising expense	38,315		
Freight and transportation-out	41,209		
Shipping supplies and expense	24,712		
Postage and stationery	16,788		
Depreciation of sales equipment	9,005		
Telephone and telegraph	12,215	453,028	
Administrative expenses			
Officers' salaries	186,000		
Office salaries	61,200		
Legal and professional services	23,721		
Utilities expense	23,275		
Insurance expense	17,029		
Depreciation of building	18,059		
Depreciation of office equipment	16,000		
Stationery, supplies, and postage	2,875		
Miscellaneous office expenses	2,612	350,771	803,799
Income from operations			186,073
Other Revenues and Gains			
Dividend revenue		98,500	
Rental revenue		72,910	171,410
			357,483
Other Expenses and Losses			
Interest on bonds and notes			126,060
Income before income tax			231,423
Income tax			66,934
Net income for the year			$ 164,489
Earnings per common share			$1.74

(c) **SELLING EXPENSES.** A subsection that lists expenses resulting from the company's efforts to make sales.

(d) **ADMINISTRATIVE OR GENERAL EXPENSES.** A subsection reporting expenses of general administration.

2. **NONOPERATING SECTION.** A report of revenues and expenses resulting from secondary or auxiliary activities of the company. In addition, special gains and losses that are infrequent or unusual, but not both, are normally reported in this section. Generally these items break down into two main subsections:

(a) **OTHER REVENUES AND GAINS.** A list of the revenues earned or gains incurred, generally net of related expenses, from nonoperating transactions.

(b) **OTHER EXPENSES AND LOSSES.** A list of the expenses or losses incurred, generally net of any related incomes, from nonoperating transactions.

3. **INCOME TAX.** A short section reporting federal and state taxes levied on income from continuing operations.

4. **DISCONTINUED OPERATIONS.** Material gains or losses resulting from the disposition of a segment of the business.

5. **EXTRAORDINARY ITEMS.** Unusual and infrequent material gains and losses.

6. **CUMULATIVE EFFECT OF A CHANGE IN ACCOUNTING PRINCIPLE.**

7. **EARNINGS PER SHARE.**[8]

Items 1, 2, 3, and 7 above are shown in the Dan Deines Company income statement in Illustration 4-3.

Although the content of the operating section is always the same, the organization of the material need not be as described above. The breakdown above uses a **natural expense classification** and is commonly used for manufacturing concerns and for merchandising companies in the wholesale trade. Another classification of operating expenses recommended for retail stores uses a **functional expense classification** of administrative, occupancy, publicity, buying, and selling expenses.

Usually, financial statements that are provided to external users have less detail than internal management reports. The latter tend to have more expense categories—usually grouped along lines of responsibility. This detail allows top management to judge staff performance.

Whether a single-step or a multiple-step income statement is used, irregular transactions such as discontinued operations, extraordinary items, and cumulative effect of changes in accounting principles should be reported separately following income from continuing operations.

CONDENSED INCOME STATEMENTS

In some cases it is impossible to present in a single income statement of convenient size all the desired expense detail. This problem is solved by including only the totals of expense groups in the statement of income and preparing supplementary schedules of expenses to support the totals. With this format, the income statement itself may be reduced to a few lines on a single sheet. For this reason, readers who wish to study all the reported data on operations must give their attention to the supporting schedules.

---

[8]The profession requires that earnings per share or net loss per share be included on the face of the income statement except for certain nonpublic companies.

The income statement shown in Illustration 4-4 for Dan Deines Company is a condensed version of the more detailed multiple-step statement presented earlier and is more representative of the type found in practice.

Dan Deines Company INCOME STATEMENT For the Year Ended December 31, 1996		
Net sales		$2,972,413
Cost of goods sold		1,982,541
Gross profit		989,872
Selling expense (see Note D)	$453,028	
Administrative expense	350,771	803,799
Income from operations		186,073
Other revenues and gains		171,410
		357,483
Other expenses and losses		126,060
Income before income tax		231,423
Income tax		66,934
Net income for the year		$ 164,489
Earnings per share		$1.74

ILLUSTRATION 4-4
Condensed Income Statement

An example of a supporting schedule, cross-referenced as Note D and detailing the selling expenses, is shown below in Illustration 4-5.

Note D: Selling expenses	
Sales salaries and commissions	$202,644
Sales office salaries	59,200
Travel and entertainment	48,940
Advertising expense	38,315
Freight and transportation-out	41,209
Shipping supplies and expense	24,712
Postage and stationery	16,788
Depreciation of sales equipment	9,005
Telephone and telegraph	12,215
Total selling expenses	$453,028

ILLUSTRATION 4-5
Sample Supporting Schedule

How much detail to include in the income statement is always a problem. On the one hand, we want to present a simple, summarized statement so that a reader can readily discover important facts. On the other hand, we want to disclose the results of all activities and to provide more than just a skeleton report.[9] Certain basic elements are always included, but as we'll see they can be presented in various formats.

▶ THE INCOME STATEMENT AND IRREGULAR ITEMS

The profession has not taken a position on whether the single-step or the multiple-step income statement should be employed. Flexibility in the presentation of the components of the income statement data has been permitted. In two important areas, however, guidelines have been developed. These two areas relate to what should be included in income and how certain unusual or irregular items should be reported.

OBJECTIVE 5
Explain how irregular items are reported.

---

[9]As discussed later in this chapter, the FASB has issued a statement of concepts that offers some guidance on this topic—"Recognition and Measurement in Financial Statements of Business Enterprises," *Statement of Financial Accounting Concepts No. 5* (Stamford, Conn.: FASB, 1984).

What should be included in net income has been a controversy for many years. For example, should irregular gains and losses and corrections of revenues and expenses of prior years be closed directly to Retained Earnings and therefore not be reported in the income statement? Or should they first be presented in the income statement and then carried to Retained Earnings along with the net income or loss for the period?

Advocates of the former—the **current operating performance concept**—argue that the net income figure should show only the regular, recurring earnings of the business. Irregular gains and losses do not reflect an enterprise's future earning power. Therefore, these items should not be included in computing net income but should be carried directly to Retained Earnings as special items. In addition many readers are not trained to differentiate between regular and irregular items and, therefore, would be confused if such items were included in computing net income.

Advocates of the second approach—the **all-inclusive concept**—insist that irregular items be included in net income. Any gain or loss experienced by the concern, whether directly or indirectly related to operations, contributes to its long-run profitability. Irregular gains and losses can be separated from the results of regular operations to arrive at income from operations, but net income for the year should include all transactions. Advocates believe that when judgment is allowed to determine irregular items, differences develop in treatment of questionable items and, as a result, a danger of manipulating income data arises. For example, at one time American Standard wrote off directly to Retained Earnings $17.9 million in losses from discontinued operations. This enabled the company to report earnings per share of $1.01; if the write-off had been charged to expense, American Standard would have reported a loss of 78 cents per share. As the example shows, it could be to the advantage of a corporation to run one-time losses through Retained Earnings, but gains through income. Supporters of the all-inclusive concept argue that this flexibility should not be allowed because it leads to poor financial reporting practices. In other words, Gresham's law applies; poor accounting practices drive out good ones.[10]

So, what to do? *APB Opinion No. 9* **adopted a modified all-inclusive concept and requires application of this approach in practice.** A number of subsequent pronouncements require **irregular items** to be highlighted so that the reader of financial statements can better determine the long-run earning power of the enterprise. These items fall into five general categories:

1. Discontinued operations.
2. Extraordinary items.
3. Unusual gains and losses.
4. Changes in accounting principle.
5. Changes in estimates.

DISCONTINUED OPERATIONS

One of the most common types of irregular items is the disposal of a business or a product line. Because of the increasing importance of this type of event, *APB Opinion No. 30* developed a set of classification and disclosure requirements.[11]

---

[10]A recent study noted that even within the income statement, problems exist. For example, this study noted that users believe that management sometimes reports unusual losses as non-recurring but reports unusual gains as part of regular income. Although users do not believe, in general, that managements intentionally present misleading information, they believe that much of the information that companies disseminate is too promotional and that troubled companies take great pains to convey the impression that they are not seriously troubled. AICPA Special Committee on Financial Reporting, "The Information Needs of Investors and Creditors," November 1993, p. 13.

[11]The reporting requirements for discontinued operations are complex. These complexities are discussed more fully in the appendix to this chapter. Our purpose here is to illustrate the basic presentation of this information on the income statement.

INTERNATIONAL INSIGHT

In other countries the "modified all-inclusive" income statement approach does not parallel that of the U.S. For example, some gains and losses are not reported on the income statement. Rather, they are taken directly to owners' equity accounts.

A separate income statement category for the gain or loss from **disposal of a segment of a business** must be provided. In addition, the results of operations of a segment that has been or will be disposed of is reported in conjunction with the gain or loss on disposal—separately from continuing operations. The effects of discontinued operations are shown net of tax as a separate category, after continuing operations but before extraordinary items.

To illustrate, Multiplex Products, Inc., a highly diversified company, decides to discontinue its electronics division. During the current year, the electronics division lost $300,000 (net of tax) and was sold at the end of the year at a loss of $500,000 (net of tax). The information is shown on the current year's income statement as follows:

Income from continuing operations		$20,000,000
Discontinued operations		
Loss from operation of discontinued electronics		
division (net of tax)	$300,000	
Loss from disposal of electronics division (net of tax)	500,000	800,000
Net income		$19,200,000

ILLUSTRATION 4-6
Income Statement Presentation of Discontinued Operations

Further complications of measuring and reporting discontinued operations are addressed in Appendix 4-A. Note that the phrase **"Income from continuing operations"** is only used when gains or losses on discontinued operations occur.

To qualify as discontinued operations, the assets, results of operations, and activities of a segment of a business must be clearly distinguishable, physically and operationally, from the other assets, results of operations, and activities of the entity.

Disposal of assets incidental to the evolution of the entity's business is not considered to be disposal of a segment of the business. **Disposals of assets that do *not* qualify as disposals of a segment** of a business include the following:

1. Disposal of *part* of a line of business.
2. Shifting production or marketing activities for a particular line of business from one location to another.
3. Phasing out of a product line or class of service.
4. Other changes due to a technological improvement.

Examples that would qualify as a disposal of a segment of a business are: (1) sale by a meat-packing company of a 53% interest in a professional football team, or (2) sale by a communications company of all of its radio stations but none of its television stations or publishing houses.

Conversely, examples that would not qualify are (1) discontinuance by a children's wear manufacturer of its operations in Italy but not elsewhere, or (2) sale by a diversified company of one furniture-manufacturing subsidiary but not all furniture-manufacturing subsidiaries. Judgment must be exercised in defining a disposal of a segment of a business because the criteria are difficult to apply in some cases.

EXTRAORDINARY ITEMS

Extraordinary items are defined as nonrecurring **material** items that differ significantly from the entity's typical business activities. *APB Opinion No. 30* cites the following criteria for extraordinary items:

> Extraordinary items are events and transactions that are distinguished by their unusual nature **and** by the infrequency of their occurrence. **Both** of the following criteria must be met to classify an event or transaction as an extraordinary item:
>
> (a) **Unusual Nature.** The underlying event or transaction should possess a high degree of abnormality and be of a type clearly unrelated to, or only incidentally related to, the ordinary and typical activities of the entity, taking into account the environment in which the entity operates.

(b) **Infrequency of Occurrence.** The underlying event or transaction should be of a type that would not reasonably be expected to recur in the foreseeable future, taking into account the environment in which the entity operates.[12]

For further clarification, the APB specified that the following gains and losses are **not** extraordinary items:

(a) Writedown or writeoff of receivables, inventories, equipment leased to others, deferred research and development costs, or other intangible assets.

(b) Gains or losses from exchange or translation of foreign currencies, including those relating to major devaluations and revaluations.

(c) Gains or losses on disposal of a segment of a business.

(d) Other gains or losses from sale or abandonment of property, plant, or equipment used in the business.

(e) Effects of a strike, including those against competitors and major suppliers.

(f) Adjustment of accruals on long-term contracts.[13]

The items listed above are not considered extraordinary "because they are usual in nature and may be expected to recur as a consequence of customary and continuing business activities."

Only rarely does an event or transaction clearly meet the criteria specified in *APB Opinion 30*.[14] For example, gains or losses such as (a) and (d) above would be classified as extraordinary if they are a **direct result of a major casualty** (such as an earthquake), **an expropriation,** or **a prohibition under a newly enacted law or regulation.** Such circumstances would clearly meet the criteria of unusual and infrequent. A good example of an extraordinary item is the approximately $36 million loss incurred by Weyerhaeuser Company (forest and lumber) as a result of volcanic activity at Mount St. Helens. Standing timber, logs, buildings, equipment, and transportation systems covering 68,000 acres were destroyed by the volcanic eruption.

In determining whether an item is extraordinary, **the environment in which the entity operates is of primary importance.** The environment includes such factors as industry characteristics, geographic location, and the nature and extent of governmental regulations. Thus, extraordinary item treatment is accorded the loss from hail damages to a tobacco grower's crops because severe damage from hailstorms in its locality is rare. On the other hand, frost damage to a citrus grower's crop in Florida does not qualify as extraordinary because frost damage is normally experienced every 3 or 4 years. In this environment, the criterion of infrequency is not met.

Similarly, when a company sells the only significant security investment it has ever owned, the gain or loss meets the criteria of an extraordinary item. Another company, however, that has a portfolio of securities acquired for investment purposes would not have an extraordinary item. Sale of such securities would be considered part of its ordinary and typical activities.

There are **exceptions** to the general rules provided above. The disposal of a business segment at a gain or loss [item (c) above], which is not an extraordinary item, requires special accounting treatment. In addition, **material gains and losses from extinguishment of debt** should be reported as an extraordinary item even though these gains or

INTERNATIONAL INSIGHT

Classification of items as "extraordinary" differs across nations. Even in countries in which the criteria for identifying extraordinary items are similar, they are not interpreted identically; thus, what is "extraordinary" in the U.S. is not necessarily "extraordinary" elsewhere.

---

[12]"Reporting the Results of Operations," *Opinions of the Accounting Principles Board No. 30* (New York: AICPA, 1973), par. 20.

[13]Ibid., par. 23.

[14]Some accountants have concluded that the criteria for an extraordinary item are so restrictive that only such items as a single chemist who knew the secret formula for an enterprise's mixing solution but was eaten by a tiger on a big game hunt or a plant facility that was smashed by a meteor would qualify for extraordinary item treatment.

losses do not meet the normal criteria mentioned above for extraordinary items.[15] The rationale for this position will be discussed in Chapter 14.

Unfortunately, it is often difficult to determine what is extraordinary. Firm guidelines for judging when an item is or is not material have not been established. Some companies have shown as extraordinary gains or losses items that accounted for less than 1% of income.[16] In making the materiality judgment, extraordinary items should be considered individually, and not in the aggregate.[17]

In addition, considerable judgment must be exercised in determining whether an item should be reported as extraordinary. For example, some paper companies have had their forest lands condemned by the government for state or national parks or forests. Is such an event extraordinary, or is it part of normal operations? Such determination is not easy; much depends on the frequency of previous condemnations, the expectation of future condemnations, materiality, and the like.

Extraordinary items are to be shown net of taxes in a separate section in the income statement, usually just before net income. After listing the usual revenues, costs and expenses, and income taxes, the remainder of the statement shows:

Income before extraordinary items
Extraordinary items (less applicable income tax of $_____)
Net income

ILLUSTRATION 4-7
Income Statement Placement of Extraordinary Items

For example, Keystone Consolidated Industries, Inc. presented its extraordinary loss in this manner:

Keystone Consolidated Industries, Inc.	
Income before extraordinary item	$11,638,000
Extraordinary item—flood loss (Note E)	1,216,000
Net income	$10,422,000

Note E: Extraordinary Item. The Keystone Steel and Wire Division's Steel Works experienced a flash flood on June 22. The extraordinary item represents the estimated cost, net of related income taxes of $1,279,000, to restore the steel works to full operation.

ILLUSTRATION 4-8
Income Statement Presentation of Extraordinary Items

UNUSUAL GAINS AND LOSSES

Because of the restrictive criteria for extraordinary items, financial statement users must carefully examine the financial statements for items that are **unusual or infrequent but not both.** As indicated earlier, items such as write-downs of inventories and gains and losses from fluctuation of foreign exchange are not considered extraordinary items. Thus, these items are sometimes shown with the normal, recurring revenues, costs, and expenses. If they are not material in amount, they are combined with other items in the income statement. If they are material, they must be disclosed separately, but are shown **above** "income (loss) before extraordinary items."

---

[15]"Reporting Gains and Losses from Extinguishment of Debt," *Statement of Financial Accounting Standards No. 4* (Stamford, Conn.: FASB, 1975), par. 8.

[16]Another problem deals with what is referred to as the "big-bath" approach. Many companies, if they see that a large loss is inevitable, write off as much as possible on the theory that investors do not make that great a distinction between a small loss and a larger one. Future statements are also relieved of these charges and provide a company with a quick earnings injection.

[17]"Reporting the Results of Operations," op. cit., par. 24.

For example, Meredith Corporation presented an unusual charge in the following manner in a single-step income statement:[18]

ILLUSTRATION 4-9
Income Statement
Presentation of Unusual
Charges

Meredith Corporation	
Total revenues	$718,236,000
Operating costs and expenses	
Production, distribution and editorial	334,476,000
Selling, general and administrative	343,615,000
Depreciation and amortization	17,545,000
Unusual items (Note 6)	**26,383,000**
Total operating costs and expenses	722,019,000
Loss from operations	$ (3,783,000)

Note 6: Unusual Items. In the fourth quarter, unusual items of $26,383,000 were charged to operations. These items included $12,983,000 in restructuring charges related to the Company's special voluntary early retirement program and selective job eliminations; a $10,000,000 write-off in the Book Group, due to repositioning and downsizing its direct mail operations, of inventory and deferred promotion costs; and $3,400,000 for other corporate charges.

In recent years there has been a tendency to **report unusual items in a separate section just above income from operations before income taxes and extraordinary items**, especially when there are multiple unusual items. For example, when General Electric Company experienced multiple unusual items in one year, it reported them in a separate "Unusual items" section of the income statement below "Income before unusual items and income taxes." When a multiple-step income statement is being prepared for homework purposes, unusual gains and losses should be reported in the other revenues and gains or other expenses and losses section unless you are instructed to prepare a separate unusual items section.

In dealing with events that are either unusual or nonrecurring but not both, the profession attempted to prevent a practice that many believed was misleading. Companies often reported such transactions on a net-of-tax basis and prominently displayed the earnings per share effect of these items. Although not captioned extraordinary items, they were presented in the same manner. Some had referred to these as "first cousins" to extraordinary items. As a consequence, the Board specifically **prohibited a net-of-tax treatment for such items** to ensure that users of financial statements can easily differentiate extraordinary items—which are reported net of tax—from material items that are unusual or infrequent, but not both.

CHANGES IN ACCOUNTING PRINCIPLE

Changes in accounting occur frequently in practice, because important events or conditions may be in dispute or uncertain at the statement date. One type of accounting change, therefore, comprises the normal recurring corrections and adjustments that are

---

[18]Hardly a day goes by that *The Wall Street Journal* does not announce that a well-known company has taken a restructuring charge. A restructuring charge relates to a major reorganization of company affairs, such as costs associated with employee layoffs, plant closing costs, write-offs of assets, and so on. A restructuring charge should not be reported as an extraordinary item, because these write-offs are considered part of a company's ordinary and typical activities. The SEC has expressed concern about the nature of these restructuring costs because many companies are taking future costs and lumping these costs as well into this current charge—a violation of generally accepted accounting principles.

Research in this area questions whether the "big bath" works. See, for example, Don Fried, Michael Schiff, and Ashwenpaul C. Sondhi, *Impairments and Writeoffs of Long-Lived Assets* (Montvale, NJ: NAA) and John A. Elliot and Wayne Shaw, "Write-offs as Accounting Procedures to Manage Perceptions," *Journal of Accounting Research* (Supplement—1988).

made by every business enterprise. Another accounting change results when an accounting principle is adopted that is different from the one previously used. Changes in accounting principle would include a change in the method of inventory pricing from FIFO to average cost or a change in depreciation from the double-declining to the straight-line method.[19]

Changes in accounting principle are recognized by including the cumulative effect net of tax in the current year's income statement. This amount is based on a retroactive computation of changing to a new accounting principle. **The effect on net income of adopting the new accounting principle should be disclosed as a separate item following extraordinary items in the income statement.**

To illustrate, Gaubert Inc. decided at the beginning of 1996 to change from the sum-of-the-years'-digits method of computing depreciation on its plant assets to the straight-line method. The assets originally cost $100,000 in 1994 and have a service life of 4 years. The data assumed for this illustration and the manner of reporting the change are as shown in Illustration 4-10.

ILLUSTRATION 4-10
Calculation of a Change in Accounting Principle

Year	Sum-of-the-Years'-Digits Depreciation	Straight-Line Depreciation	Excess of Sum-of-the-Years'-Digits over Straight-Line Method
1994	$40,000	$25,000	$15,000
1995	30,000	25,000	5,000
Total			$20,000

The information presented in the 1996 financial statements is shown in Illustration 4-11. (The tax rate was 30%.)

ILLUSTRATION 4-11
Income Statement Presentation of a Change in Accounting Principle

Income before extraordinary item and cumulative effect of a change in accounting principle	$120,000
Extraordinary item—casualty loss (net of $12,000 tax)	(28,000)
Cumulative effect on prior years of retroactive application of new depreciation method (net of $6,000 tax)	14,000
Net income	$106,000

CHANGE IN ESTIMATE (NORMAL, RECURRING CORRECTIONS AND ADJUSTMENTS)

Estimates are inherent in the accounting process. Estimates are made, for example, of useful lives and salvage values of depreciable assets, of uncollectible receivables, of inventory obsolescence, and of the number of periods expected to benefit from a particular expenditure. Not infrequently, as time passes, as circumstances change, or as additional information is obtained, even estimates originally made in good faith must be changed. Such **changes in estimates** are accounted for in the period of change if they affect only that period, or in the period of change and future periods if the change affects both.

To illustrate a change in estimate that affects only the period of change, assume that DuPage Materials Corp. has consistently estimated its bad debt expense at 1% of credit sales. In 1995, however, DuPage's controller determines that the estimate of bad debts for the current year's credit sales must be revised upward to 2%, or double the prior years' precentage. Using 2% results in a bad debt charge of $240,000 or double the

UNDERLYING CONCEPT

Companies can change principles, but it must be demonstrated that the newly adopted principle is preferable to the old one. Such changes mean that consistency from period to period is lost.

---

[19]"Accounting Changes," *Opinions of the Accounting Principles Board No. 20* (New York: AICPA, 1971), par. 18. Chapter 23 examines in greater detail the problems related to accounting changes; our purpose now is to provide general guidance for the major types of transactions affecting the income statement.

amount using the 1% estimate for prior years. The 2% rate is necessary to reduce accounts receivable to net realizable value. The provision is recorded at December 31, 1995, as follows:

Bad Debt Expense	240,000	
Allowance for Doubtful Accounts		240,000

The entire change in estimate is included in 1995 income because no future periods are affected by the change. **Changes in estimate are not handled retroactively**, that is, carried back to adjust prior years. Changes in estimate that affect both the current period and future periods are examined in greater detail in Chapter 23. **Changes in estimate are not considered errors (prior period adjustments) or extraordinary items.**

SUMMARY

The public accounting profession now tends to accept a modified all-inclusive income concept instead of the current operating performance concept. Except for a couple of items (discussed later in this chapter) that are charged or credited directly to retained earnings, all other irregular gains or losses or nonrecurring items are closed to Income Summary and are included in the income statement. Of these, **discontinued operations of a segment** of a business is classified as a separate item in the income statement after

ILLUSTRATION 4-12 Summary of Irregular Items in the Income Statement

Type of Situation[a]	Criteria	Examples	Placement on Financial Statements
Discontinued operations	Disposal of a segment of a business constituting a separate line of business or class of customer.	Sale by diversified company of major division that represents only activities in electronics industry. Food distributor that sells wholesale to supermarket chains and through fast-food restaurants decides to discontinue the division that sells to one of two classes of customers.	Shown in separate section of the income statement after continuing operations but before extraordinary items. (Shown net of tax.)
Extraordinary items	Material, and both unusual and infrequent (nonrecurring).	Gains or losses resulting from casualties, an expropriation, or a prohibition under a new law.[b]	Separate section in the income statement entitled extraordinary items. (Shown net of tax.)
Unusual gains or losses, not considered extraordinary	Material; character typical of the customary business activities; unusual or infrequent but not both.	Write-downs of receivables, inventories; adjustments of accrued contract prices; gains or losses from fluctuations of foreign exchange; gains or losses from sales of assets used in business.	Separate section in income statement above income before extraordinary items. Often reported in other revenues and gains or other expenses and losses section. (Not shown net of tax.)
Changes in principle[c]	Change from one generally accepted principle to another.	Changing the basis of inventory pricing from FIFO to average cost; change in the method of depreciation from accelerated to straight-line.	Cumulative effect of the change is reflected in the income statement between the captions extraordinary items and net income. (Shown net of tax.)
Changes in estimates	Normal, recurring corrections and adjustments.	Changes in the realizability of receivables and inventories; changes in estimated lives of equipment, intangible assets; changes in estimated liability for warranty costs, income taxes, and salary payments.	Change in income statement only in the account affected. (Not shown net of tax.)

[a]This summary provides only the general rules to be followed in accounting for the various situations described above. Exceptions do exist in some of these situations.
[b]Material gains and losses from extinguishment of debt are considered extraordinary, even though criteria for extraordinary items may not be met.
[c]The general rule per *APB Opinion No. 20* is to use the cumulative effect approach. However, all the recent FASB pronouncements require or permit the retroactive method whenever a new standard is adopted for the first time.

continuing operations. The **unusual, material, nonrecurring items** that are significantly different from the typical or customary business activities are shown in a separate section for **"extraordinary items"** below discontinued operations. Other items of a material amount that are of an **unusual or nonrecurring** nature and are **not considered extraordinary** are separately disclosed. In addition, the cumulative adjustment that occurs when a change in accounting principles develops is disclosed as a separate item just before net income.

Because of the numerous intermediate income figures that are created by the reporting of these irregular items, careful evaluation of information reported by the financial press is needed. For example, at one time when RCA reported its first-quarter results, *The Wall Street Journal* reported that "RCA earnings climbed by 47% in the first quarter" as compared with the first quarter of last year. Conversely, *The New York Times* reported the following regarding the same first quarter results, "RCA Slides 46%." Which article was correct? Both articles were factually correct. The difference arose because the *Times* article, in making its comparison with the quarter of the previous year, included the unusual nonrecurring gains in the income of the earlier quarter, whereas *The Wall Street Journal* did not. Such an illustration demonstrates the importance of understanding the intermediate components of net income.

Illustration 4-12 summarizes the basic concepts previously discussed. Although the chart is simplified, it provides a useful framework for determining the proper treatment of special items affecting the income statement.

UNDERLYING CONCEPT

The AICPA Special Committee on Financial Reporting indicates a company's core activities— usual and recurring events—provide the best historical data from which users determine trends and relationships and make their predictions about the future. Therefore, the effects of core and non-core activities should be separately displayed.

▶ INTRAPERIOD TAX ALLOCATION

We noted that certain irregular items are shown on the income statement net of tax. Most accountants believe that the resulting income tax effect should be directly associated with that event or item. In other words, the tax expense for the year should be related, where possible, to **specific** items on the income statement to provide a more informative disclosure to statement users. This procedure is called **intraperiod tax allocation**, that is, allocation within a period. Its main purpose is to relate the income tax expense of the fiscal period to the items that affect the amount of the tax provisions. Intraperiod tax allocation is used for the following items: (1) income from continuing operations, (2) discontinued operations, (3) extraordinary items, and (4) changes in accounting principle. The general concept is **"let the tax follow the income."**

The income tax expense attributable to "income from continuing operations" is computed by finding the income tax expense related to revenue and to expense transactions used in determining this income. In this tax computation, no effect is given to the tax consequences of the items excluded from the determination of "income from continuing operations." A separate tax effect is then associated with each irregular item.

OBJECTIVE 6
Explain intraperiod tax allocation.

EXTRAORDINARY GAINS

In applying the concept of intraperiod tax allocation, assume that Schindler Co. has income before tax and extraordinary item of $250,000 and an extraordinary gain from the sale of a single stock investment of $100,000. If the income tax rate is assumed to be 30%, the following information is presented on the income statement:

Income before income tax and extraordinary item		$250,000
Income tax		75,000
Income before extraordinary item		175,000
Extraordinary gain—sale of investment	$100,000	
Less applicable income tax	30,000	70,000
Net income		$245,000

ILLUSTRATION 4-13 Intraperiod Tax Allocation, Extraordinary Gain

The income tax of $75,000 ($250,000 × 30%) attributable to "income before income tax and extraordinary item" is determined from revenue and expense transactions related to this income. In this income tax computation, the tax consequences of items excluded from the determination of "income before income tax and extraordinary item" are not considered. The "extraordinary gain—sale of investment" then shows a separate tax effect of $30,000.

EXTRAORDINARY LOSSES

To illustrate the reporting of an extraordinary loss, assume that Schindler Co. has income before income tax and extraordinary item of $250,000 and an extraordinary loss from a major casualty of $100,000. Assuming a 30% tax rate, the presentation of income tax on the income statement would be as follows:

ILLUSTRATION 4-14
Intraperiod Tax Allocation, Extraordinary Loss

Income before income tax and extraordinary item		$250,000
Income tax		75,000
Income before extraordinary item		175,000
Extraordinary item—loss from casualty	**$100,000**	
Less applicable income tax reduction	**30,000**	70,000
Net income		$105,000

In this case, the loss provides a positive tax benefit of $30,000 and, therefore, is subtracted from the $100,000 loss.

An extraordinary item may be reported "net of tax" with note disclosure as illustrated below:

ILLUSTRATION 4-15
Note Disclosure of Intraperiod Tax Allocation

Income before income tax and extraordinary item	$250,000
Income tax	75,000
Income before extraordinary item	175,000
Extraordinary item, less applicable income tax reduction (Note 1)	70,000
Net income	$105,000

Note 1: During the year the Company suffered a major casualty loss of $70,000, net of applicable income tax reduction of $30,000.

▶ EARNINGS PER SHARE

OBJECTIVE 7

Explain where earnings per share information is reported.

The results of a company's operations are customarily summed up in one important figure: net income. As if this condensation were not enough of a simplification, the financial world has widely accepted an even more distilled and compact figure as its most significant business indicator—**earnings per share**.

The computation of earnings per share is usually straightforward. **Net income minus preferred dividends (income available to common stockholders) is divided by the weighted average of common shares outstanding to arrive at earnings per share.**[20] To illustrate, assume that Lancer, Inc. reports net income of $350,000 and declares and pays preferred dividends of $50,000 for the year. The weighted average number of common shares outstanding during the year is 100,000 shares. Earnings per share is $3.00, as computed in Illustration 4-16.

---

[20]In the calculation of earnings per share, preferred dividends are deducted from net income if declared or if cumulative though not declared.

$$\frac{\text{Net Income} - \text{Preferred Dividends}}{\text{Weighted Average of Common Shares Outstanding}} = \text{Earnings per Share}$$

$$\frac{\$350,000 - \$50,000}{100,000} = \$3.00$$

ILLUSTRATION 4-16
Equation Illustrating
Computation of Earnings
per Share

Note that the EPS figure measures the number of dollars earned by each share of common stock—but not the dollar amount paid to stockholders in the form of dividends.

"Net income per share" or "earnings per share" is a ratio commonly used in prospectuses, proxy material, and annual reports to stockholders. It is also highlighted in the financial press, by statistical services like Standard and Poor's, and by Wall Street securities analysts. Because of its importance, **earnings per share is required to be disclosed on the face of the income statement.** In addition to net income per share, per share amounts should be shown for "income from continuing operations," "income before extraordinary items and cumulative effect of changes in accounting principles," and "cumulative effect of changes in accounting principles."

To illustrate comprehensively both the income statement order of presentation and the earnings per share data, we present a comprehensive income statement for Poquito Industries, Inc. in Illustration 4-17. Notice the order in which data are shown. In addition, per share information is shown at the bottom. Assume that the company had 100,000 shares outstanding for the entire year.

ILLUSTRATION 4-17
Comprehensive Income
Statement

Poquito Industries, Inc. INCOME STATEMENT For the Year Ended December 31, 1994		
Sales revenue		$1,480,000
Cost of goods sold		600,000
Gross profit		880,000
Selling and administrative expenses		320,000
Income from operations		560,000
Other revenues and gains		
Interest revenue		10,000
Other expenses and losses		
Loss on disposal of part of Textile Division	$ (5,000)	
Unusual charge—loss on sale of investments	(45,000)	(50,000)
Income from continuing operations before income tax		520,000
Income tax		208,000
Income from continuing operations		312,000
Discontinued operations		
Income from operations of Pizza Division, less		
applicable income tax of $24,800	54,000	
Loss on disposal of Pizza Division, less		
applicable income tax of $41,000	(90,000)	(36,000)
Income before extraordinary item and cumulative		
effect of accounting change		276,000
Extraordinary item—loss from earthquake, less		
applicable income tax of $23,000		(45,000)
Cumulative effect in prior years of retroactive application of new		
depreciation method, less applicable income tax of $30,900		(60,000)
Net income		$ 171,000
Per share of common stock		
Income from continuing operations		$3.12
Income from operations of discontinued division, net of tax		.54
Loss on disposal of discontinued operation, net of tax		(.90)
Income before extraordinary item and cumulative effect		2.76
Extraordinary loss, net of tax		(.45)
Cumulative effect of change in accounting principle, net of tax		(.60)
Net income		$1.71

Reporting per share amounts for gain or loss on discontinued operations and gain or loss on extraordinary items is optional. For example, General Mills reported $1.77 earnings per share before an extraordinary item and net income of $1.83. By subtracting, readers can easily see that it had an extraordinary gain of $.06 per share net-of-income tax.

The Poquito Industries Inc. income statement, in Illustration 4-17, is highly condensed. Items such as the "Unusual Charge," "Discontinued Operations," "Extraordinary Item," and the "Change in Accounting Principle" would have to be described fully and appropriately in the statement or related notes. The 1993 statement of income of Georgia-Pacific Corporation (see Appendix 5-A, page 220) presents appropriate earnings per share amounts in much the same manner as shown for Poquito. Georgia-Pacific's Note 1 (Summary of Significant Accounting Policies) to the financial statements describes the computation of earnings per share.

The earnings per share data also may be disclosed parenthetically, as illustrated below (this form is especially applicable when only one per share amount is involved):

Net Income (per share $4.02)	$804,000

Many corporations have simple capital structures that include only common stock. For these companies, a presentation such as "earnings per common share" is appropriate on the income statement. In many instances, however, companies' earnings per share are subject to dilution (reduction) in the future because existing contingencies permit the issuance of additional common shares.[21]

In summary, the simplicity and availability of figures for per share earnings lead inevitably to their widespread use. Because of the undue importance that the public, even the well-informed public, attaches to earnings per share, accountants have an obligation to make the earnings per share figure as meaningful as possible.

▶ STATEMENT OF RETAINED EARNINGS

OBJECTIVE 8

Prepare a statement of retained earnings.

A statement of retained earnings is generally included, together with an income statement, a balance sheet, and a statement of cash flows in the financial statements of an enterprise. Actually, instead of being a statement that reports related data, **it is a reconciliation of the balance of the Retained Earnings account from the beginning to the end of the year.** A statement of retained earnings is also prepared to assist in the assessment of overall performance by providing additional information on why net assets increased or decreased during the period. This additional information relates to such items as prior period adjustments and dividend distributions.

An example of a statement of retained earnings is as follows in Illustration 4-18.

**ILLUSTRATION 4-18
Statement of Retained
Earnings**

Fieldcrest Corporation STATEMENT OF RETAINED EARNINGS For the Year Ended December 31, 1996 (000 omitted)		
Retained earnings January 1, 1996		$ 21,159
Add net income for the year		99,423
		120,582
Deduct dividends declared on:		
Preferred stock, at $5 per share	$15,000	
Common stock, at $7 per share	28,000	43,000
Retained earnings December 31, 1996		$ 77,582

---

[21]"Earnings Per Share," *Opinions of the Accounting Principles Board No. 15* (New York: AICPA, 1969), pars. 14 and 15. The computational problems involved in accounting for these dilutive securities in earnings per share computations are discussed in Chapter 17.

The association of dividend distributions with net income for the period indicates what management is doing with earnings: It may be "plowing back" into the business part or all of the earnings, distributing all current income, or distributing current income plus the accumulated earnings of prior years.

PRIOR PERIOD ADJUSTMENTS

Items of income or loss related to corrections of errors in the financial statements of a prior period are accounted for and reported in the statement of retained earnings as **prior period adjustments**. They are **excluded from the determination of net income for the current period.**

Prior period adjustments (net of tax) should be charged or credited to the opening balance of retained earnings and, thus, excluded from the determination of net income for the current period. To illustrate, assume that in 1995 Micronta Corp. determined that it had understated its depreciation expense in 1994 by $187,640 ($114,960 net of tax) owing to an error in computation. The error affected both the income statement and the tax return for 1994. Adjustment for this error is presented net of tax in the financial statements for 1995 in Illustration 4-19.

OBJECTIVE 9
Explain how prior period adjustments are reported.

Retained earnings, January 1, 1995, as previously reported	$2,767,890
Correction of an error in depreciation in prior period (net of $72,680 tax)	**114,960**
Adjusted balance of retained earnings at January 1, 1995	2,652,930
Net income	697,611
Retained earnings, December 31, 1995	$3,350,541

ILLUSTRATION 4-19
Illustration of Application of Prior Period Adjustments in Financial Statement

The accounting treatment for prior period adjustments provides an interesting illustration of the evolutionary nature of accounting principle formulation. In 1966, *APB Opinion No. 9* identified certain criteria that had to be met before an item could be classified as a prior period adjustment. These criteria permitted, for example, settlements of lawsuits in litigation to be reported as prior period adjustments but did not permit such treatment of corrections of errors. After considerable concern had been expressed about how corrections of errors should be handled, *APB Opinion No. 20,* "Accounting Changes," was issued in 1971; it required that corrections of errors related to a previous period be reported as prior period adjustments.

Subsequently, the SEC began to challenge prior period classification for litigation settlements, arguing that the outcome of litigation could not have been determined in a prior period and, therefore, these items should be run through the current year's income statement. The real concern was that adverse effects on net income could be partially hidden by direct charges to retained earnings. The FASB reconsidered this issue, but only four of the seven members voted in late 1976 to eliminate litigative suits as prior period adjustments. According to the then existing by-laws of the FASB, five votes were required to establish a new standard; therefore, no change in the accounting for prior period adjustments was made. In early 1977, the trustees of the Financial Accounting Foundation, in reviewing their operating procedures, decided that a simple majority vote of the FASB was sufficient to establish a new standard and that this change in the by-laws should be retroactive. Thus, what did not become an accounting standard in late 1976 did become an accounting standard in early 1977 **because of a change in the voting rules.** As a result, the number of prior period adjustments has been reduced, because generally only corrections of errors related to a prior period are accorded this treatment. The foregoing illustrates the tenuous nature of accounting standard setting. In 1990 the FASB reverted back to a five-vote (supermajority) requirement to establish new standards, but the prior period adjustment rule has remained as decided in 1977.

APPROPRIATIONS OF RETAINED EARNINGS

Retained earnings is often restricted—appropriated—in accordance with contract requirements, board of directors' policy, or the apparent necessity of the moment. The amounts of retained earnings appropriated are transferred to Appropriated Retained Earnings. The retained earnings section may therefore report two separate amounts— (1) retained earnings free (unrestricted) and (2) retained earnings appropriated (restricted). The total of these two amounts equals the total retained earnings.

COMBINED STATEMENT OF INCOME AND RETAINED EARNINGS

Some accountants believe that the statements of income and retained earnings are so closely related that they should be combined in one report. The principal advantage of a combined statement is that all items affecting income, including operating items and prior period adjustments, appear in one report. On the other hand, net income for the year is "buried" in the body of the statement, a feature that some find objectionable. There once was a definite trend toward this method of presentation, but it is no longer gaining in favor.

When a combined statement is prepared, the income statement is presented as if it were to be issued as an independent report. But, instead of ending that statement with net income, the reconciliation of retained earnings is shown beneath it (as shown in Illustration 4-20).

**ILLUSTRATION 4-20
Addition of
Reconciliation of
Retained Earnings to
Income Statement**

The Magnavox Company COMBINED STATEMENT OF INCOME AND RETAINED EARNINGS (lower portion only)	
Net income for the year	42,290,385
Retained earnings at beginning of year	106,734,310
	149,024,695
Cash dividends declared and paid	15,764,250
Retained earnings at end of year	$133,260,445

If the company has other capital accounts such as Additional Paid-In Capital, a good practice is to present a statement reconciling the beginning and ending balances. *APB Opinion No. 12* indicates that disclosure of changes in the separate accounts comprising stockholders' equity is required to make the financial statements sufficiently informative. Disclosure of such changes may be made in separate statements, in the basic financial statements, or in the notes.

An example of a retained earnings statement combined with changes in common stock, additional paid-in capital treasury stock, and other stockholders equity items, is Georgia-Pacific's Statement of Shareholders' Equity presented in Appendix 5-A (page 223).

► AN INTERNATIONAL PERSPECTIVE

With both commerce and capital crossing borders at an accelerated pace, attention is focusing on the significance of a growing obstacle—the language of accounting. As indicated earlier, many nations have their own individual rules of accounting sufficient to the needs of their own commerce and the maturity of their industry. In some cases, the principles and practices that guide the preparation of financial statements in various countries can be so different as to defy comparability.

Twenty years ago, this lack of uniform accounting principles was merely an inconvenience. Today it is a more significant problem since so much business is done internationally. As a result, international accounting and reporting are beginning to change. One of our purposes in this textbook is to sensitize you to some of these changes by introducing international issues and problems where appropriate. Most of this information is provided in marginal notes.

Illustration 4-21 is an adapted income statement for Guinness PLC, a British company, for a recent year. The statement is provided so that you can compare differences in terminology and accounting principles with a U.S. company. The information in the boxes to the right of the income statement highlights the difference between U.S. and British income statements.

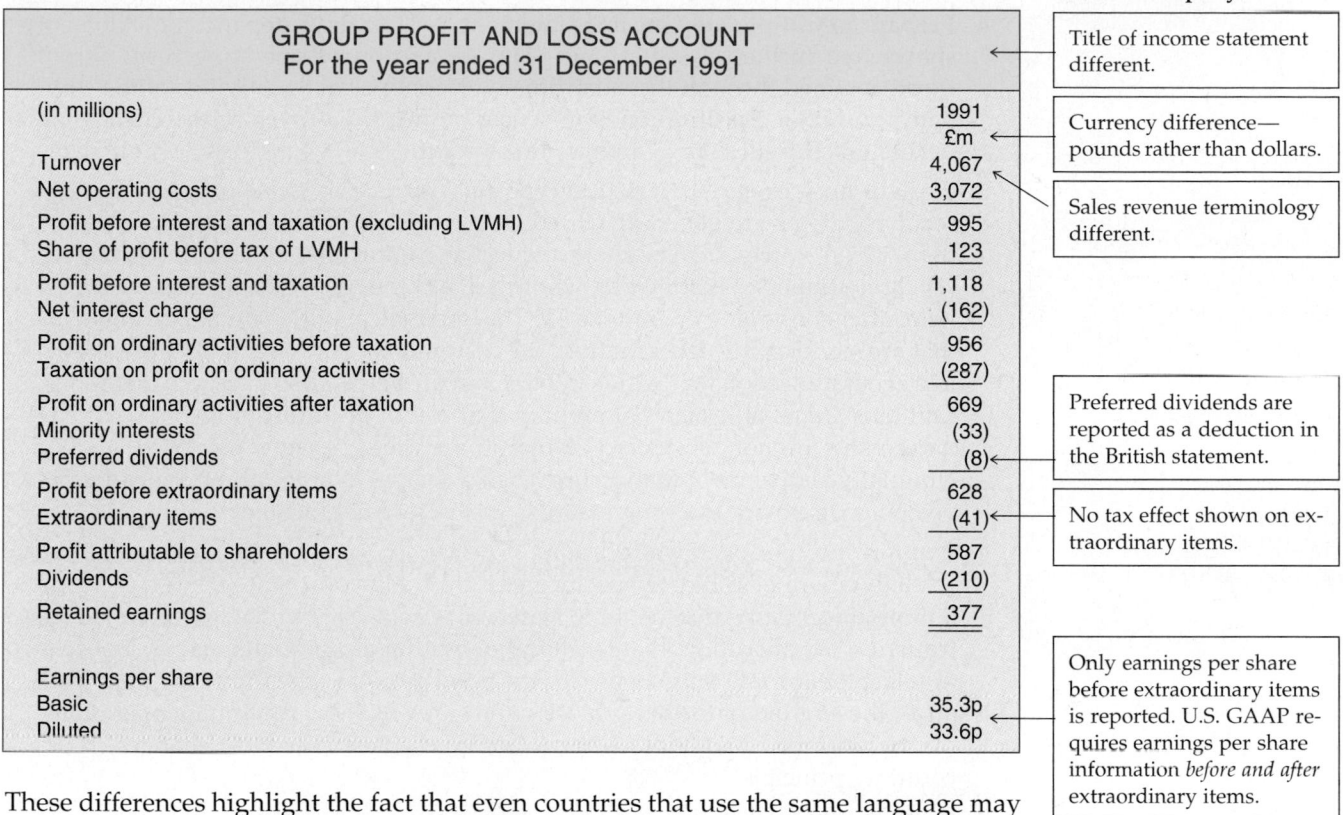

ILLUSTRATION 4-21
Income Statement for a British Company

Title of income statement different.	
Currency difference— pounds rather than dollars.	
Sales revenue terminology different.	

GROUP PROFIT AND LOSS ACCOUNT
For the year ended 31 December 1991

(in millions)	1991
	£m
Turnover	4,067
Net operating costs	3,072
Profit before interest and taxation (excluding LVMH)	995
Share of profit before tax of LVMH	123
Profit before interest and taxation	1,118
Net interest charge	(162)
Profit on ordinary activities before taxation	956
Taxation on profit on ordinary activities	(287)
Profit on ordinary activities after taxation	669
Minority interests	(33)
Preferred dividends	(8)
Profit before extraordinary items	628
Extraordinary items	(41)
Profit attributable to shareholders	587
Dividends	(210)
Retained earnings	377
Earnings per share	
Basic	35.3p
Diluted	33.6p

Preferred dividends are reported as a deduction in the British statement.

No tax effect shown on extraordinary items.

Only earnings per share before extraordinary items is reported. U.S. GAAP requires earnings per share information *before and after* extraordinary items.

These differences highlight the fact that even countries that use the same language may describe activities differently and also may use different accounting standards.

▶ **SUMMARY OF LEARNING OBJECTIVES** ◀

1. **Identify the uses and limitations of an income statement.** The income statement provides investors and creditors with information that helps them predict the amounts, timing, and uncertainty of future cash flows. Also, the income statement helps users determine the risk (level of uncertainty) of not achieving particular cash flows. The limitations of an income statement are: (1) the statement does not include many items that contribute to general growth and well-being of an enterprise; and (2) income numbers are often affected by the accounting methods used.

2. **Distinguish between the capital maintenance and transaction approaches.** The *capital maintenance approach* takes the net assets or "capital values" based on some valuation and measures income by the difference in capital values at two points in time. The *transaction approach* focuses on the activities that have occurred during a given period; instead of presenting only a net change, it discloses the components of the change. The transaction approach to income measurement requires the use of revenue, expense, loss, and gain accounts.

3. **Prepare a single-step income statement.** In a single-step income statement, just two groupings exist: revenues and expenses. Expenses are deducted from revenues to arrive at net income or loss—a single subtraction. Frequently, income tax is reported separately as the last item before net income to indicate its relationship to income before income tax.

4. **Prepare a multiple-step income statement.** A multiple-step income statement shows two further classifications: (1) a separation of operating results from those obtained through the subordinate or nonoperating activities of the company; and (2) a classification of expenses by functions, such as merchandising or manufacturing, selling, and administration.

5. **Explain how irregular items are reported.** Irregular gains or losses or non-recurring items are generally closed to Income Summary and are included in the income statement. These are treated in the income statement as follows: (1) Discontinued operation of a segment of a business is classified as a separate item, after continuing operations. (2) The unusual, material, nonrecurring items that are significantly different from the customary business activities are shown in a separate section for "extraordinary items," below discontinued operations. (3) Other items of a material amount that are of an unusual or nonrecurring nature and are not considered extraordinary are separately disclosed. (4) The cumulative adjustment that occurs when a change in accounting principles develops is disclosed as a separate item, just before net income.

6. **Explain intraperiod tax allocation.** The tax expense for the year should be related, where possible, to specific items on the income statement, to provide a more informative disclosure to statement users. This procedure is called intraperiod tax allocation, that is, allocation within a period. Its main purpose is to relate the income tax expense for the fiscal period to the following items that affect the amount of the tax provisions: (1) income from continuing operations, (2) discontinued operations, (3) extraordinary items, and (4) changes in accounting principle.

7. **Explain where earnings per share information is reported.** Because of the inherent dangers of focusing attention solely on earnings per share, the profession concluded that earnings per share must be disclosed on the face of the income statement. In addition to net income per share, per-share amounts should be shown for "income from continuing operations," "income before extraordinary items and cumulative effect of changes in accounting principles," and "cumulative effect of changes in accounting principles."

8. **Prepare a statement of retained earnings.** The statement of retained earnings should disclose net income (loss), dividends, prior period adjustments, and transfers to and from retained earnings (appropriations).

9. **Explain how prior period adjustments are reported.** Items of income or loss related to corrections of errors in the financial statements of a prior period are accounted for and reported as prior period adjustments. Prior period adjustments (net of tax) should be charged or credited to the opening balance of retained earnings and, thus, excluded from the determination of net income for the current period.

APPENDIX 4-A

ACCOUNTING FOR DISCONTINUED OPERATIONS

The chapter discussed how and where gains and losses related to discontinued operations are reported on the income statement. This appendix discusses the more technical aspects of how such a gain or loss is computed, along with related reporting issues.

Recall that the assets, results of operations, and activities of a **business segment** must be clearly distinguishable, physically and operationally, to qualify for discontinued operations treatment. Recall, too, that in the income statement, discontinued operations are classified as a separate item, net of tax, after continuing operations.

OBJECTIVE 10

After studying Appendix 4-A, you should be able to: Measure and report gains and losses from discontinued operations.

▶ FIRST ILLUSTRATION—NO PHASE-OUT PERIOD

To illustrate the accounting for a discontinued operation, assume that the Board of Directors of Heartland Inc. decided on October 1, 1994, to sell a division of their company called Record Phonograph. Record Phonograph had provided phonograph records for Heartland's 15 retail stores. Heartland's management could see that the compact disk was revolutionizing the stereo industry and would soon render its phonograph division unprofitable. Fortunately, a buyer was available immediately and the division was sold on October 1, 1994.

Heartland Inc. had income of $2,000,000 for the year 1994, not including a $150,000 loss from operations of Record Phonograph from January 1 to October 1, 1994. Heartland Inc. was able to sell the division at a gain of $400,000. Its tax rate on all items was 30%.

Heartland's accountants first must decide whether to treat the sale as a discontinued operation. The assets and operations of Record Phonograph can be easily identified, and the record business is distinct from Heartland's other lines of business. Accordingly, **the disposal of Record Phonograph does constitute the disposal of a segment of the business.**

For the period up to the time management commits itself to sell the division, the revenues and expenses of the discontinued operations are aggregated and reported as income or loss on discontinued operations, net of tax. The date at which time management formally commits itself to a formal plan to dispose of a segment of the business is referred to as the **measurement date.** In this case, it is October 1, 1994. The plan of disposal should include, as a minimum:

1. Identification of the major assets to be disposed of.
2. The expected method of disposal.
3. The period expected to be required for completion of the disposal.
4. An active program to find a buyer if disposal is to be by sale.
5. Estimated results of operations of the segment from the measurement date to the disposal date.
6. Estimated proceeds or salvage to be realized by disposal.

Because the segment has actually been sold on October 1, 1994, a gain or loss on disposal is computed. This date is referred to as the **disposal date.** Because the measurement date and the disposal date are the same, no unusual complications occur. The following diagram illustrates Heartland's situation.

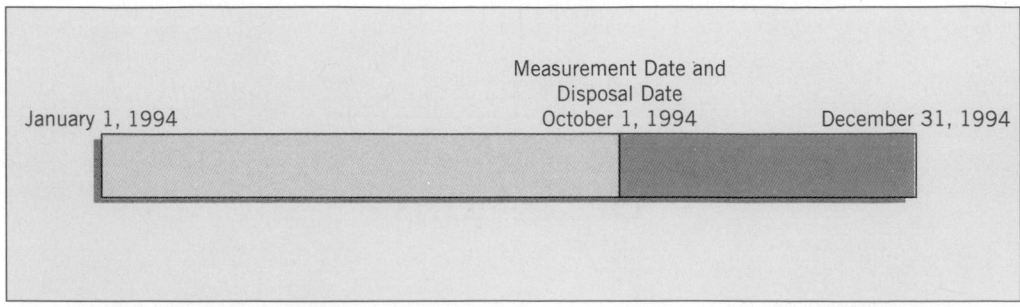

The condensed income statement presentation for Heartland Inc. for 1994 is as follows:

**ILLUSTRATION 4A-1
Presentation of
Discontinued Operations,
No Phase-Out Period**

Income from continuing operations before income taxes		$2,000,000
Income taxes		600,000
Income from continuing operations		1,400,000
Discontinued operations:		
Loss from operation of Record Phonograph, less applicable		
income taxes of $45,000	$(105,000)	
Gain on disposal of Record Phonograph, less applicable		
income taxes of $120,000	280,000	175,000
Net income		$1,575,000

► SECOND ILLUSTRATION—PHASE-OUT PERIOD

In practice the measurement date and the disposal date are rarely the same. Normally, the disposal date would be later than the measurement date. Thus, **the gain or loss on disposal would be the sum of:**

1. Income (loss) from the measurement date to the disposal date (called the **phase-out period**).
2. Gain (loss) on the disposal of the net assets.

The reason for aggregating the above two items to compute the gain (loss) on disposal is that the selling company needs a reasonable period to phase out its discontinued operations. The income (loss) from operations of the discontinued segment is part of the computation of the gain (loss) on disposal because the phase-out period often enables the seller to obtain a better selling price.

To illustrate the combination of these two components, assume that Heartland's sale of Record Phonograph does not occur until December 1, 1994, at which time it is sold at a gain of $350,000. During the period October 1, 1994, to December 1, 1994, the Record Phonograph division suffered a loss of $50,000 from operations. The following diagram illustrates Heartland's situation.

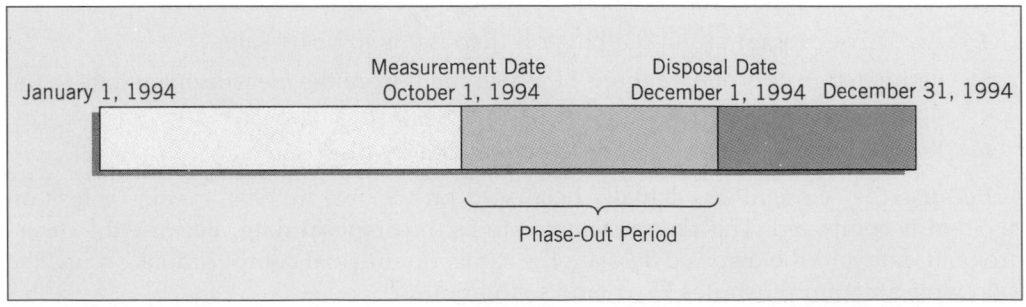

The condensed income statement presentation for Heartland Inc. for 1994 is as follows:

Income from continuing operations before income taxes		$2,000,000
Income taxes		600,000
Income from continuing operations		1,400,000
Discontinued operations:		
Loss from operation of Record Phonograph, less applicable		
income taxes of $45,000	$(105,000)	
Gain on disposal of Record Phonograph, including operating loss		
of $50,000 and gain on disposal of $350,000, less applicable		
income taxes of $90,000	210,000	105,000
Net income		$1,505,000

**ILLUSTRATION 4A-2
Presentation of
Discontinued Operations,
with Phase-Out Period**

▶ THIRD ILLUSTRATION—EXTENDED PHASE-OUT PERIOD

In the preceding illustration, the disposal of the discontinued operation occurred in the same accounting period as the measurement date. As a result, determining the proper gain or loss on the disposal of Record Phonograph at the end of year was straightforward. However, the phase-out period often extends into another year. In this case, *APB Opinion No. 30* states that **if a loss is expected on disposal, the estimated loss should be reported at the measurement date. If a gain on disposal is expected, it should be recognized when realized, which is ordinarily the disposal date.** In other words, the profession has taken a conservative position by recognizing losses immediately but deferring gains until realized.

Implementing these general rules can be troublesome. In order to determine the gain or loss on disposal of the segment, the income (loss) from operations must be estimated and then combined with the estimated gain (loss) on sale. If a net loss results, then it is recognized at the measurement date. If a net gain arises, it generally is recognized at the date of disposal. **The major exception is when realized gains exceed estimated unrealized and realized net losses. In that special case, realized gains can be recognized in the period of the measurement date.**

NET LOSS

To illustrate, assume that Heartland Inc. expects to sell its Record Phonograph division on May 1, 1995, at a gain of $350,000. In addition, from October 1, 1994, to December 31, 1994, it realized a loss of $400,000 on operations for this segment and expects to lose an additional $200,000 on it from January 1, 1995, to May 1, 1995. The following diagram illustrates Heartland's situation.

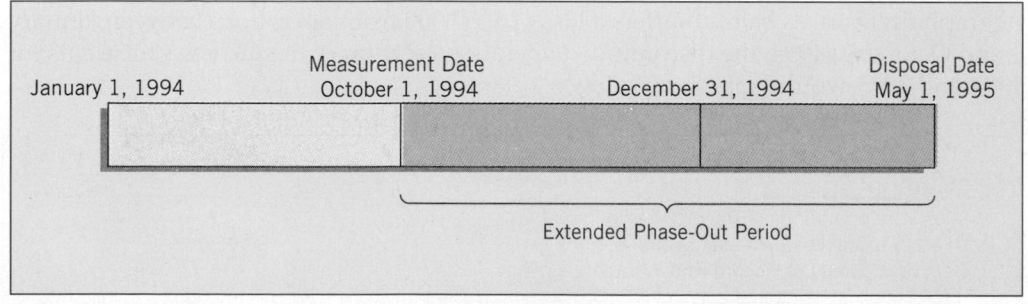

The computation of the net gain or loss on disposal is shown in Illustration 4A-3.

ILLUSTRATION 4A-3
Computation of the Net
Loss on Disposal

Realized loss on operations October 1–December 31, 1994	$(400,000)
Expected loss on operations January 1–May 1, 1995	(200,000)
Expected gain on sale of assets on May 1, 1995	350,000
Net loss on disposal	$(250,000)

Given that a net loss on disposal is expected, the loss on disposal is recognized in the period of the measurement date. The condensed income statement presentation for Heartland Inc. for 1994 is therefore reported as shown in Illustration 4A-4.

ILLUSTRATION 4A-4
Presentation of Expected
Loss from Discontinued
Operations

Income from continuing operations before income taxes		$2,000,000
Income taxes		600,000
Income from continuing operations		1,400,000
Discontinued operations:		
Loss from operation of Record Phonograph, net of applicable income taxes of $45,000	$(105,000)	

Loss on disposal of Record Phonograph, including provision
     for losses during phase-out period, $600,000, and estimated
     gain on sale of assets, $350,000, net of applicable income
     taxes of $75,000
	(175,000)	(280,000)

Net income		$1,120,000

If the estimated amounts of any of the items later prove to be incorrect, the correction should be reported in the later period when the estimate is determined to be incorrect. Prior periods should not be restated.

NET GAIN

To illustrate recognition of a realized gain and deferral of an unrealized gain in the same discontinued operation, assume that Heartland Inc. expects to sell its Record Phonograph division on May 1, 1995, at a gain of $350,000. In addition, from October 1, 1994, to December 31, 1994, it realized a gain of $200,000 on operations for this segment and expects to earn an additional $100,000 of profit on it from January 1, 1995, to May 1, 1995. The computation of the net gain or loss on disposal is as follows:

ILLUSTRATION 4A-5
Computation of Net Gain
on Disposal

Realized gain on operations October 1–December 31, 1994	$200,000
Expected gain on operations January 1–May 1, 1995	100,000
Expected gain on sale of assets on May 1, 1995	350,000
Net gain on disposal	$650,000

When a net gain on disposal is expected, the gain should be analyzed and classified into realized and unrealized amounts. In this situation, $200,000 of realized gain is recognized in 1994 from the October 1–December 31 operation and $450,000 ($100,000 + $350,000) of unrealized gain is deferred to 1995. Assuming that the phonograph division, as before, suffers a loss of $150,000 from operations between January 1 and October 1, 1994, the discontinued operations section of the income statements for 1994 and 1995 would appear as follows:

ILLUSTRATION 4A-6
Presentation of Gain
from Discontinued
Operations

	1994	
Discontinued operations		
Loss from operations of Record Phonograph, less applicable income taxes of $45,000	$(105,000)	
Gain on disposal of Record Phonograph, less applicable income taxes of $60,000	140,000	35,000

1995	
Discontinued operations	
Gain on disposal of Record Phonograph,	
less applicable income taxes of $135,000	$315,000

If a net unrealized loss of $150,000 had been expected during the 1995 portion of the extended phase-out period, instead of the $450,000 unrealized gain noted above, a net realized gain on disposal of $50,000 ($200,000 − $150,000) before income taxes would be recognized in 1994.

SUMMARY

UNDERLYING
CONCEPT

This accounting treatment is the application of conservatism: recognize all losses, but only realized gains.

All realized and estimated unrealized gains and losses related to the extended phase-out period are netted as one "event" after the measurement date. To determine the amount to be reported on the "gain or loss from disposal of a segment" line (the second line of the discontinued operations section), the following simple algorithm may be used: If an overall loss is computed for the extended phase-out period, the amount reported is the overall loss; if an overall gain is computed, the amount reported is the lesser of the overall gain or the realized gain.

▶ EXTENDED PHASE-OUT—ADDITIONAL EXAMPLES

Provided in Illustration 4A-7 are some additional cases to help you understand how the gain (loss) on disposal of a segment of a business is reported for an extended phase-out period. We will use the same measurement and disposal dates as in the previous situation. All situations are reported on a pretax basis.

ILLUSTRATION 4A-7
Gains or Losses Involving Extended Phase-Out of Discontinued Operations

	Realized Income (Loss) on Operations October 1, 1994– December 31, 1994	Expected Income (Loss) on Operations January 1, 1995– May 1, 1995	Expected Gain (Loss) on Sale of Assets	Gain (Loss) on Disposal of Segment	
Case 1	$(400,000)	$(200,000)	$350,000	1994	$ (250,000)
				1995	0
Case 2	(300,000)	(600,000)	(500,000)	1994	$(1,400,000)
				1995	0
Case 3	100,000	400,000	(600,000)	1994	$ (100,000)
				1995	0
Case 4	(500,000)	(300,000)	900,000	1994	0
				1995	$ 100,000
Case 5	400,000	300,000	250,000	1994	$ 400,000
				1995	$ 550,000
Case 6	600,000	(200,000)	(300,000)	1994	$ 100,000
				1995	0
Case 7	400,000	(300,000)	350,000	1994	$ 400,000
				1995	$ 50,000
Case 8	400,000	(350,000)	300,000	1994	$ 350,000
				1995	0

Table title: Disposals of Segments Involving Extended Phase-out of Discontinued Operations

In Case 2, all three components related to the gain (loss) on disposal were losses; therefore **a net loss of $1,400,000 is reported at the measurement date.**

In Case 3, the loss of $600,000 on the sale of the segment assets is greater than the realized $100,000 and expected $400,000 income from operations; therefore **a net loss of $100,000 is reported at the measurement date.**

In Case 4, the gain of $900,000 on the sale of the segment assets is greater than the realized $500,000 and expected $300,000 losses from operations; therefore **a net gain of $100,000 is reported at the disposal date.**

In Case 5, both components of operations report income, and a gain is expected on the sale of the segment assets. As a result, the **realized income from operations of $400,000 can be reported at the date of measurement** because there are no realized or estimated losses. **The remaining estimated gain of $550,000 ($300,000 + $250,000) is deferred and recognized at the disposal date.**

In Case 6, the realized income from operations of $600,000 exceeds the estimated losses from operations $200,000 and sale $300,000. As a result, **a realized gain of $100,000 is reported at the end of 1994, because the net gain is realized.**

In Case 7, the net gain on disposal is expected to be $450,000, of which $400,000 is realized and $50,000 is unrealized. **The realized $400,000 is recognized in 1994 and the net unrealized gain of $50,000** (the net of a $300,000 expected loss from operations in 1995 and a $350,000 expected gain from disposal in 1995) is recognized in 1995.

In Case 8, the net gain on disposal is expected to be $350,000, all of which is realized and, therefore, recognized in 1994. **The $400,000 of realized income from operations is reduced by the net expected unrealized loss of $50,000** from 1995 (the expected loss from operations of $350,000 less the expected gain on sale of $300,000).

▶ DISCLOSURE REQUIREMENTS

Amounts of income taxes applicable to the results of discontinued operations and the gain or loss from disposal of the segment should be disclosed on the face of the income statement or related notes. Revenues applicable to the discontinued operations should be separately disclosed in the related notes.

In addition to the amounts that should be reported in the financial statements, the notes to the financial statements for the period encompassing the measurement date should disclose:

1. The identity of the segment of the business that has been or will be discontinued.

2. The expected disposal date, if known.

3. The expected manner of disposition.

ILLUSTRATION 4A-8
Note Disclosure of
Discontinued Operations

Fluor Corporation		
Income from continuing operations before income taxes		$171,800,000
Income taxes		91,100,000
Income from continuing operations		80,700,000
Discontinued operations—Note G:		
Loss from operation of Distribution Group (net of income tax benefit of $22,952,000)	$(27,000,000)	
Loss on disposal of Distribution Group, including provision for estimated operating losses during phase-out period (net of income tax benefit of $15,538,000)	(26,000,000)	(53,000,000)
Net income		$27,700,000

Note G: Discontinued Operations. During the fourth quarter of the current year, the company adopted a plan to dispose of the Distribution Group through sale or liquidation. Negotiations for the sale of two of the companies are currently being conducted with the respective management groups. At October 31, the net assets of discontinued operations, consisting primarily of inventories, trade receivables, and warehouse facilities have been reclassified as current assets at estimated net realizable value.

Revenues from discontinued operations, including the Goldston Transportation Group which was sold during the year, were $368,551,000. Included in the loss on disposal is a pretax provision of $2,115,000 for estimated operating losses during the phase-out period.

4. A description of the remaining assets and liabilities of the segment at the balance sheet date.

5. The income or loss from operations and any proceeds from disposal of the segment during the period from the measurement date to the date of the balance sheet.

An example of the income statement and the note disclosure taken from the annual report of Fluor Corporation is shown in Illustration 4A-8.

Companies frequently segregate the assets and liabilities of the segment on the balance sheet into net current and net noncurrent amounts, identifying these elements as related to discontinued operations.

As previously stated, if the estimates on income or losses from operations during the phase-out period and on gains or losses on the sale of assets prove to be incorrect, the correction should be reported in the period when the estimate is determined to be incorrect; prior periods are not restated. An example of such a correction is disclosed in a note to the financial statements of BMC Industries Inc.

BMC Industries Inc.

Note 3: Discontinued Operations. In the prior year, the Company estimated a loss on the disposal of the discontinued operations of $60,000,000, which included a provision of approximately $8,000,000 for operating losses through the anticipated disposal periods. Actual operating losses exceeded the estimate by approximately $10,000,000, and the loss on the disposal of discontinued operations is expected to be approximately $5,000,000 less than the original estimate. Accordingly, the accompanying Consolidated Statement of Operations for the current year includes an additional provision for loss on disposal of $5,000,000.

ILLUSTRATION 4A-9
Example of Note Explaining Correction to Financial Statement

Note that the amount of the correction—in the case of BMC Industries, $5,000,000— is reported net of tax in the discontinued operations section of the income statement.

▶ **SUMMARY OF LEARNING OBJECTIVE FOR APPENDIX 4-A** ◀

KEY TERMS

disposal date, 161

measurement date, 161

phase-out period, 162

10. **Measure and report gains and losses from discontinued operations.** The accountant may be required to report gains and losses from discontinued operations (sale of a segment of the business) under three different situations: (1) no phase-out period, (2) a phase-out period, and (3) an extended phase-out period. The gain or loss on disposal of a segment involves the sum of: (1) income or loss from operations to the measurement date, and (2) the gain or loss on the disposal of the business segment (operating incomes or losses during the phase-out period and the gain or loss on the sale of the net assets). These two items are reported separately net of tax among the irregular items in the income statement.

Note: All **asterisked** Questions, Exercises, Problems, and Cases relate to material contained in the appendix to each chapter.

QUESTIONS

1. What is the importance of the income statement? What are its major limitations?

2. Why should caution be exercised in the use of the income figure derived in an income statement? What are the objectives of generally accepted accounting principles in their application to the income statement?

3. A *Wall Street Journal* article noted that if Canon Inc. had written off film costs in the first quarter as fast as some of its competitors, Canon would have had a loss instead of a profit. One analyst noted therefore that Canon's quality of earnings was low. What does the term "quality of earnings" mean?

4. What is the difference between the capital maintenance approach to income measurement and the transaction approach? Is the final income figure the same under both approaches?

5. What is the major distinction (a) between revenues and gains and (b) between expenses and losses?

6. What are the advantages and disadvantages of the "single-step" income statement?

7. What are the advantages and disadvantages of a combined statement of income and retained earnings? What is the basis for distinguishing between operating and nonoperating items?

8. Distinguish between the "all-inclusive" income statement and the "current operating performance" income statement. According to present generally accepted accounting principles, which is recommended? Explain.

9. What is the significance of the materiality of an item in deciding the proper placement of a nonrecurring item in the statement of retained earnings or in the income statement? Explain.

10. How should prior period adjustments be reported in the financial statements? Give an example of a prior period adjustment.

11. Discuss the appropriate treatment in the financial statements of each of the following:
   (a) An amount of $93,000 realized in excess of the cash surrender value of an insurance policy on the life of one of the founders of the company who died during the year.
   (b) A profit-sharing bonus to employees computed as a percentage of net income.
   (c) Additional depreciation on factory machinery because of an error in computing depreciation for the previous year.
   (d) Rent received from subletting a portion of the office space.
   (e) A patent infringement suit, brought two years ago against the company by another company, was settled this year by a cash payment of $685,800.
   (f) A reduction in the Allowance for Doubtful Accounts balance, because the account appears to be considerably in excess of the probable loss from uncollectible receivables.

12. Indicate where the following items would ordinarily appear on the financial statements of Obatula, Inc. for the year 1995:
   (a) The service life of certain equipment was changed from 8 to 5 years. If a 5-year life had been used previously, additional depreciation of $362,000 would have been charged.
   (b) In 1995 a flood destroyed a warehouse that had a book value of $1,475,000. Floods are rare in this locality.
   (c) In 1995 the company wrote off $1 million dollars of inventory that was considered obsolete.
   (d) An income tax refund related to the 1992 tax year was received.
   (e) In 1992, a supply warehouse with an expected useful life of 7 years was erroneously expensed.
   (f) Obatula, Inc. changed its depreciation from double-declining to straight-line on machinery in 1995. The cumulative effect of the change was $867,000 (net of tax).

13. Give the section of a multiple-step income statement in which each of the following is shown.
   (a) Loss on inventory write-down.
   (b) Loss from strike.
   (c) Bad debt expense.
   (d) Loss on disposal of a segment of the business.
   (e) Gain on sale of machinery.
   (f) Interest revenue.
   (g) Depreciation expense.
   (h) Material write-offs of notes receivable.

14. Noah Adams Land Development, Inc. purchased land for $70,000 and spent $30,000 developing it. It then sold the land for $150,000. Susan Stanburg Manufacturing purchased land for a future plant site for $100,000. Due to a change in plans, they later sold the land for $150,000. Should these two companies report the land sales, both at gains of $50,000, in a similar manner?

15. You run into Terry Gross at a party and begin discussing financial statements. Terry says "I prefer the single-step income statement because the multiple-step format generally overstates income." How should you respond to Terry?

16. Linda Worthheimer Corporation has eight expense accounts in its general ledger which could be classified as selling expenses. Should L. Worthheimer report these eight expenses separately in its income statement or simply report one total amount for selling expenses?

17. Guy Stevens Investments reported an unusual gain from the sale of certain assets in its 1995 income statement. How does intraperiod tax allocation affect the reporting of this unusual gain?

18. What effect does intraperiod tax allocation have on reported net income?

19. Cokie Roberts Company computed earnings per share as follows:

$$\frac{\text{Net Income}}{\text{Common Shares Outstanding At Year End}}$$

Cokie Roberts has a simple capital structure. What possible errors might the company have made in the computation? Explain.

20. N. Totenburg Corporation reported 1995 earnings per share of $7.21. In 1996, N. Totenburg reported earnings per share as follows:

On income before extraordinary item	$6.40
On extraordinary item	1.88
On net income	$8.28

Is the increase in earnings per share from $7.21 to $8.28 a favorable trend?

21. What is meant by "tax allocation within a period"? What is the justification for such practice?

22. When does tax allocation within a period become necessary? How should this allocation be handled?

23. During 1995, Martin Goldsmith Company earned income of $978,000 before federal income taxes and realized a gain of $421,800 on a government-forced condemnation sale of a division plant facility. The income is subject to federal income taxation at the rate of 34%; the gain on the sale of the plant is taxed at 30%. Proper accounting suggests that the unusual gain be reported as an extraordinary item. Illustrate an appropriate presentation of these items in the income statement.

24. On January 30, 1993, a suit was filed against S. Simon Corporation under the Environmental Protection Act. On August 6, 1994, S. Simon Corporation agreed to settle the action and pay $810,000 in damages to certain current and former employees. How should this settlement be reported in the 1994 financial statements? Discuss.

25. Mundt Paper Company decided to close two small pulp mills in Conway, New Hampshire, and Corvallis, Oregon. Would these closings be reported in a separate section entitled Discontinued Operations after Income from Continuing Operations? Discuss.

26. What major types of items are reported in the retained earnings statement?

27. The controller for Michael Feldman, Inc. is discussing the possibility of presenting a combined statement of income and retained earnings for the current year. Indicate a possible advantage and disadvantage of this presentation format.

28. Generally accepted accounting principles usually require the use of accrual accounting to "fairly present" income. If the cash receipts and disbursements method of accounting will "clearly reflect" taxable income, why does this method not usually also "fairly present" income?

29. State some of the more serious problems encountered in seeking to achieve the ideal measurement of periodic net income. Explain what accountants do as a practical alternative.

30. What is meant by the terms "components," "elements," and "items" as they relate to the income statement? Why might items have to be disclosed in the income statement?

*31. How are the measurement and disposal dates defined for a disposal of a segment of a business?

*32. How are gains or losses on disposal of a segment of a business determined?

*33. How should the disposal of a segment of a business be disclosed in the income statement?

EXERCISES

E4-1 (Computation of Net Income) Presented below are changes in all the account balances of Mel Gibson Furniture Co. during the current year, except for retained earnings.

	Increase (Decrease)		Increase (Decrease)
Cash	$ 79,000	Accounts payable	$(38,000)
Accounts receivable (net)	24,000	Bonds payable	82,000
Inventory	127,000	Common stock	125,000
Investments	(47,000)	Additional paid-in capital	13,000

Instructions

Compute the net income for the current year, assuming that there were no entries in the Retained Earnings account except for net income and a dividend declaration of $19,000 which was paid in the current year.

E4-2 (Capital Maintenance Approach) Presented below is selected information pertaining to the Angelica Huston Video Company:

Cash balance, January 1, 1996	$ 13,000
Accounts receivable, January 1, 1996	19,000
Collections from customers in 1996	210,000
Capital account balance, January 1, 1996	38,000
Total assets, January 1, 1996	75,000
Cash investment added, July 1, 1996	5,000
Total assets, December 31, 1996	88,000
Cash balance, December 31, 1996	16,000
Accounts receivable, December 31, 1996	36,000
Merchandise taken for personal use during 1996	11,000
Total liabilities, December 31, 1996	39,000

Instructions

Compute the net income for 1996.

E4-3 (Income Statement Items) Presented below are certain account balances of Meg Ryan Products Co.

Ending inventory	$ 48,000	Sales returns	$ 5,800
Rental revenue	6,500	Sales discounts	21,300
Interest expense	12,700	Selling expenses	99,400
Purchase allowances	10,500	Sales	390,000
Beginning retained earnings	114,400	Income tax	31,000
Ending retained earnings	134,000	Beginning inventory	45,300
Freight-in	10,100	Purchases	190,000
Dividends earned	71,000	Purchase discounts	17,300
		Administrative expenses	82,500

Instructions

From the foregoing, compute the following: (a) total net revenue; (b) cost of goods sold; (c) net income; (d) dividends declared during the current year.

E4-4 (Single-step Income Statement) The financial records of Richard Chamberlain Inc., were destroyed by fire at the end of 1996. Fortunately the controller had kept certain statistical data related to the income statement as presented below.

1. The beginning merchandise inventory was $92,000 and decreased 20% during the current year.
2. Sales discounts amount to $16,400.
3. 20,000 shares of common stock were outstanding for the entire year.
4. Interest expense was $19,560.
5. The income tax rate is 30%.
6. Cost of goods sold amounts to $450,000.
7. Administrative expenses are 20% of cost of goods sold but only 9% of gross sales.
8. Four-fifths of the operating expenses relate to sales activities.

Instructions

From the foregoing information prepare an income statement for the year 1996 in single-step form.

E4-5 (Multiple-step and Single-step) Two accountants for the firm of Cruise and Kidder are arguing about the merits of presenting an income statement in a multiple-step versus a single-step format. The discussion involves the following 1996 information related to Far and Away Company ($000 omitted).

Administrative expense	
Officers' salaries	$ 4,900
Depreciation of office furniture and equipment	3,960
Purchase returns	5,810
Purchases	59,800
Rental revenue	17,230
Selling expense	
Transportation-out	2,690
Sales commissions	7,980
Depreciation of sales equipment	6,480
Merchandise inventory, beginning inventory	15,400
Merchandise inventory, ending inventory	16,600
Sales	96,500
Transportation-in	2,780
Income tax	9,070
Interest expense on bonds payable	1,860

Instructions

(a) Prepare an income statement for the year 1996 using the multiple-step form. Common shares outstanding for 1996 total 40,000 (000 omitted).

(b) Prepare an income statement for the year 1996 using the single-step form.

(c) Which one do you prefer? Discuss.

E4-6 (Multiple-step and Extraordinary Items) The following balances were taken from the books of the Harrison Ford Corp. on December 31, 1996:

Interest revenue	$ 86,000	Accumulated depreciation—equipment	40,000
Cash	61,000	Purchases returns and allowances	125,000
Sales	1,380,000	Accumulated depreciation—building	28,000
Accounts receivable	150,000	Purchase discounts	59,000
Prepaid insurance	20,000	Notes receivable	155,000
Sales returns and allowances	150,000	Selling expenses	194,000
Allowance for doubtful accounts	7,000	Accounts payable	70,000
Sales discounts	45,000	Bonds payable	100,000
Land	100,000	Administrative and general expenses	97,000
Inventory January 1, 1996	246,000	Accrued liabilities	32,000
Equipment	200,000	Interest expense	60,000
Inventory December 31, 1996	331,000	Notes payable	100,000
Building	140,000	Loss from earthquake damage (extraordinary item)	140,000
Purchases	790,000	Common stock	500,000
		Retained earnings	21,000

Assume the total effective tax rate on all items is 34%.

Instructions

Prepare a multiple-step income statement; 50,000 shares of common stock were outstanding during the year.

E4-7 (Multiple-step and Single-step) Presented below is a trial balance for Clint Eastwood Inc. at December 31, 1996. Assume that the loss due to flood damage is an extraordinary item.

Clint Eastwood Inc.
TRIAL BALANCE
Year Ended December 31, 1996

	Debits	Credits
Administrative expenses	$ 15,600	
Equipment	20,000	
Cash	7,000	
Income tax expense	11,800	
Inventory	13,000	
Accounts payable		$ 7,200
Cash dividends	5,000	
Loss due to flood (net of $3,400 tax)	5,700	
Common stock ($2 par value)		40,000
Temporary investments	2,000	
Accrued liabilities		3,200
Accounts receivable	15,000	
Appropriation for contingencies		12,000
Notes payable		20,000
Allowance for doubtful accounts		700
Purchases	62,700	
Interest revenue		10,000
Land	9,000	
Notes receivable	17,000	
Selling expense	36,000	
Building	45,000	
Accumulated depreciation—equipment		4,000
Sales		150,000
Transportation-in	1,500	
Accumulated depreciation—building		2,800
Retained earnings		16,400
Totals	$266,300	$266,300

The December 31, 1996 inventory is $19,500.

Instructions

(a) Prepare a multiple-step income statement.
(b) Prepare a single-step income statement.
(c) Which format do you prefer? Discuss.

E4-8 (Multiple-step and Single-step) The accountant of Emma Thompson Shoe Co. has compiled the following information from the company's records as a basis for an income statement for the year ended 12/31/96.

Rental revenue	$ 29,000
Interest on notes payable	18,000
Market appreciation on temporary investments above cost	31,000
Merchandise purchases	409,000
Transportation-in—merchandise	37,000
Wages and salaries—sales	114,800
Materials and supplies—sales	17,600
Common stock outstanding (no. of shares)	10,000[a]
Income tax	66,400
Wages and salaries—administrative	135,900
Other administrative expense	51,700
Merchandise inventory, January 1, 1996	92,000
Merchandise inventory, December 31, 1996	81,000
Purchase returns and allowances	11,000
Net sales	980,000
Depreciation on plant assets (70% selling, 30% administrative)	65,000
Dividends declared	16,000

[a]Remained unchanged all year.

Instructions

(a) Prepare a multiple-step income statement.
(b) Prepare a single-step income statement.
(c) Which format do you prefer? Discuss.

E4-9 (Multiple-step and Single-step) Presented below is income statement information related to Kenneth Branagh Corporation for the year 1996.

Administrative expenses:		Transportation-in		14,000
Officers' salaries	$ 39,000	Purchase discounts		10,000
Depreciation expense—building	28,500	Inventory (beginning)		120,000
Office supplies expense	9,500	Sales returns and allowances		5,000
Inventory (ending)	137,000	Selling expenses:		
Flood damage (pretax extraordinary item)	54,000	Sales salaries		71,000
Purchases	600,000	Depreciation expense—store equipment		18,000
Sales	930,000	Store supplies expense		9,000

In addition, the corporation has other revenue from dividends received of $18,000 and other expense of interest on notes payable of $9,000. There are 30,000 shares of common stock outstanding for the year. The total effective tax rate on all income is 34%.

Instructions

(a) Prepare a multiple-step income statement for 1996.
(b) Prepare a single-step income statement for 1996.
(c) Discuss the relative merits of the two income statements.

E4-10 (Combined Statement) During 1996 Anthony Hopkins Co. had pretax earnings of $500,000 exclusive of a realized and tax deductible loss of $130,000 from the condemnation of properties (extraordinary item). In addition, the company discovered that depreciation expense was overstated by $80,000 in 1991. Retained earnings at January 1, 1996, before error correction was $640,000; dividends of $150,000 were declared on common stock during 1996. One hundred thousand shares of common stock were outstanding during 1996.

Assume that the income tax rate on income is 34% for both 1991 and 1996.

Instructions

Prepare a combined statement of income and retained earnings beginning with income before income tax and extraordinary item.

E4-11 (Combined Single-step) The following information was taken from the records of Julia Roberts Inc. for the year 1996. Income tax applicable to income from continuing operations, $187,000; income tax applicable to loss on discontinued operations, $25,000; income tax applicable to extraordinary gain, $29,000; income tax applicable to extraordinary loss, $18,000.

Extraordinary gain	$ 95,000	Cash dividends declared	70,000
Loss on discontinued operations	75,000	Retained earnings January 1, 1996	600,000
Administrative expenses	240,000	Cost of goods sold	850,000
Rent revenue	40,000	Selling expenses	300,000
Extraordinary loss	60,000	Sales	1,900,000

Shares outstanding during 1996 were 25,000.

Instructions
- **(a)** Prepare a single-step income statement for 1996. Include per share data.
- **(b)** Prepare a combined single-step income and retained earnings statement.
- **(c)** Which one do you prefer? Discuss.

E4-12 (Multiple-step Statement with Retained Earnings) Presented below is information related to Tom Hanks Corp., for the year 1996.

Net sales	$1,300,000	Writeoff of inventory due to obsolescence	80,000
Cost of goods sold	800,000	Depreciation expenses omitted by accident in 1995	40,000
Selling expenses	65,000	Casualty loss (extraordinary item) before taxes	50,000
Administrative expenses	48,000	Dividends declared	45,000
Dividend revenue	20,000	Retained earnings at December 31, 1995	2,000,000
Interest revenue	7,000	Federal tax rate of 34% on all items	

Instructions
- **(a)** Prepare a multiple-step income statement for 1996. Assume that 70,000 shares of common stock are outstanding.
- **(b)** Prepare a separate statement of retained earnings for 1996.

E4-13 (Earnings Per Share) The stockholders' equity section of Bette Midler Corporation appears below as of December 31, 1996:

8% cumulative preferred stock, $50 par value, authorized 100,000 shares, outstanding 90,000 shares		$ 4,500,000
Common stock, $1.00 par, authorized and issued 10 million shares		10,000,000
Additional paid-in capital		20,500,000
Retained earnings Dec. 31, 1995	$132,000,000	
Net income for 1996	35,000,000	167,000,000
		$202,000,000

Net income for 1996 reflects a total effective tax rate of 30%. Included in the net income figure is a loss of $18,000,000 (before tax) as a result of a major casualty.

Instructions
Compute earnings per share data as it should appear on the financial statements of Bette Midler Corporation.

E4-14 (Condensed Income Statement) Presented below are selected ledger accounts of Sean Connery Corporation at December 31, 1996:

Cash	185,000	Travel and entertainment	69,000
Merchandise inventory	535,000	Accounting and legal services	33,000
Sales	4,275,000	Insurance expense	24,000
Advances from customers	117,000	Advertising	54,000
Purchases	2,786,000	Transportation-out	93,000
Sales discounts	34,000	Depreciation of office	48,000
Purchase discounts	27,000	Depreciation of sales equipment	36,000
Sales salaries	284,000	Telephone—sales	17,000
Office salaries	346,000	Utilities—office	32,000
Purchase returns	15,000	Miscellaneous office expenses	8,000
Sales returns	79,000	Rental revenue	240,000
Transportation-in	72,000	Extraordinary loss (before tax)	70,000
Accounts receivable	142,500	Interest expense	176,000
Sales commissions	83,000	Common stock ($10 par)	950,000

Connery's effective tax rate on all items is 30%. A physical inventory indicates that the ending inventory is $686,000.

Instructions

Prepare a condensed 1996 income statement for Sean Connery Corporation.

E4-15 (Retained Earnings Statement) Michael J. Fox Corporation began operations on January 1, 1993. During its first 3 years of operations, Fox reported net income and declared dividends as follows:

	Net income	Dividends declared
1993	$ 40,000	$ –0–
1994	125,000	50,000
1995	150,000	50,000

The following information relates to 1996:

Income before income tax	$240,000
Prior period adjustment: understatement of 1994 depreciation expense (before taxes)	20,000
Cumulative decrease in income from change in inventory methods (before taxes)	35,000
Dividends declared (of this amount, $25,000 will be paid on Jan. 15, 1997)	100,000
Effective tax rate	40%

Instructions

(a) Prepare a 1996 retained earnings statement for Michael J. Fox Corporation.

(b) Assume Fox Corp. appropriated retained earnings in the amount of $70,000 on December 31, 1996. After this action, what would Fox report as total retained earnings in its December 31, 1996 balance sheet?

E4-16 (Earnings Per Share) At December 31, 1995, Denzel Washington Corporation had the following stock outstanding:

10% cumulative preferred stock, $100 par, 107,500 shares	$10,750,000
Common stock, $5 par, 4,000,000 shares	20,000,000

During 1996, Denzel Washington's only stock transaction was the issuance of 400,000 shares of common on April 1. During 1996, the following also occurred:

Income from continuing operations before taxes	$23,650,000
Discontinued operations (loss before taxes)	$ 3,225,000
Preferred dividends declared	$ 1,075,000
Common dividends declared	2,200,000
Effective tax rate	40%

Instructions

Compute earnings per share data as it should appear in the 1996 income statement of Denzel Washington Corporation.

*E4-17 (Discontinued Operations) Assume that Charles Grodin Inc. decides to sell WBTV its television subsidiary in 1995. This sale qualifies for discontinued operations treatment. Pertinent data regarding the operations of the TV subsidiary are as follows:

Loss from operations from beginning of year to measurement date, $1,000,000 (net of tax).

Realized loss from operations from measurement date to end of 1995, $600,000 (net of tax).

Estimated income from operations from end of year to disposal date of June 1, 1996, $350,000 (net of tax).

Estimated gain on sale of net assets on June 1, 1996, $150,000 (net of tax).

Instructions

(a) What is the gain (loss) on the disposal of the segment reported in 1995? In 1996?

(b) Prepare the discontinued operations section of the income statement for the year ended 1995.

(c) If the amount reported in 1995 as gain or loss from disposal of a segment by Charles Grodin Inc. proves to be materially incorrect, when and how is the correction reported, if at all?

(d) If the TV subsidiary had a realized income of $100,000 (net of tax) instead of a realized loss from the measurement date to the end of 1995, what is the gain or loss on disposal of the segment reported in 1995? In 1996?

*E4-18 (Discontinued Operations) On October 5, 1993, Doubtfire Inc.'s board of directors decided to dispose of the Spit and Polish Division. Doubtfire is a real estate firm with approximately 25% of its income from management of apartment complexes. The Spit and Polish Division contracts to clean apartments after tenants move out in the Doubtfire complexes and several others. The board decided to dispose of the division because of unfavorable operating results.

Net income for Doubtfire was $84,000 after tax (assume a 30% rate) for the fiscal year ended December 31, 1993. The Spit and Polish Division accounted for only $3,500 (after tax) of this amount and only $700 (after tax) in the fourth quarter. Spit and Polish accounted for $50,000 in revenues, of which $8,000 were earned in the last quarter. The average number of common shares outstanding was 20,000 for the year.

Because of the unfavorable results and the extreme competition, the board believes selling the business intact is impossible. Their final decision is to complete all current contracts, the last of which expires on May 3, 1995, and then auction off the cleaning equipment on May 10, 1995. This, the only asset of the division, will have a depreciated value of $25,000 at the disposal date. The board believes the sale proceeds will approximate $5,000 after the auction expenses and estimates Spit and Polish earnings in fiscal year 1994 as $3,800 (before tax), with a loss of $3,000 (before tax) in fiscal year 1995.

Instructions

Prepare the income statement and the appropriate footnotes that relate to the Spit and Polish Division for 1993. The income statement should begin with earnings from continuing operations before income taxes. Earnings per share computations are not required.

PROBLEMS

P4-1 (Combined Multiple-step) Presented below is information related to Liam Neeson Company for 1996.

Retained earnings balance, January 1, 1996	$ 880,000
Sales for the year	25,000,000
Cost of goods sold	17,000,000
Interest revenue	70,000
Selling and administrative expenses	4,900,000
Write-off of goodwill (not tax deductible)	520,000
Federal income taxes for 1996	1,100,000
Assessment for additional 1993 income taxes (normal recurring)	300,000
Gain on the sale of investments (normal recurring)	110,000
Loss due to flood damage—extraordinary item (net of tax)	90,000
Loss on the disposition of the wholesale division (net of tax)	440,000
Loss on operations of the wholesale division (net of tax)	390,000
Dividends declared on common stock	250,000
Dividends declared on preferred stock	70,000

Instructions

Prepare a combined statement of income and retained earnings using the multiple-step form. Liam Neeson Company decided to discontinue its entire wholesale operations and to retain its manufacturing operations. On September 15, Neeson sold the wholesale operations to Schindler Company. During 1996, there were 300,000 shares of common stock outstanding all year.

P4-2 (Combined Single-step) Presented below is the trial balance of Mariah Carey Corporation at December 31, 1996.

Mariah Carey Corporation
TRIAL BALANCE
Year Ended December 31, 1996

	Debits	Credits
Purchase discounts		$ 10,000
Cash	$ 210,100	
Accounts receivable	105,000	
Rent revenue		18,000
Retained earnings		260,000
Salaries payable		18,000
Sales		1,000,000
Notes receivable	110,000	
Accounts payable		49,000
Accumulated depreciation—equipment		28,000
Sales discounts	14,500	
Sales returns	17,500	
Notes payable		70,000
Selling expenses	232,000	
Administrative expenses	99,000	
Common stock		300,000
Income tax expense	38,500	
Cash dividends	60,000	

Allowance for doubtful accounts		5,000
Supplies	14,000	
Freight-in	20,000	
Land	70,000	
Equipment	140,000	
Bonds payable		100,000
Gain on sale of land		30,000
Accumulated depreciation—building		19,600
Merchandise inventory	89,000	
Building	98,000	
Purchases	590,000	
Totals	$1,907,600	$1,907,600

A physical count of inventory on December 31 resulted in an inventory amount of $124,000.

Instructions

Prepare a combined statement of income and retained earnings using the single-step form. Assume that the only changes in the retained earnings during the current year were from net income and dividends. Ten thousand shares of common stock were outstanding the entire year.

 P4-3 (Irregular Items) Aerosmith, Inc., reported income from continuing operations before taxes during 1996 of $790,000. Additional transactions occurring in 1996 but not considered in the $790,000 are as follows:

1. The corporation experienced an uninsured flood loss (extraordinary) in the amount of $60,000 during the year. The tax rate on this item is 46%.
2. At the beginning of 1994, the corporation purchased a machine for $54,000 (salvage value of $9,000) that had a useful life of six years. The bookkeeper used straight-line depreciation for 1994, 1995, and 1996 but failed to deduct the salvage value in computing the depreciation base.
3. Sale of securities held as a part of its portfolio resulted in a loss of $75,500 (pretax).
4. When its president died, the corporation realized $110,000 from an insurance policy. The cash surrender value of this policy had been carried on the books as an investment in the amount of $46,000 (the gain is nontaxable).
5. The corporation disposed of its recreational division at a loss of $115,000 before taxes. Assume that this transaction meets the criteria for discontinued operations.
6. The corporation decided to change its method of inventory pricing from average cost to the FIFO method. The effect of this change on prior years is to increase 1994 income by $60,000 and decrease 1995 income by $20,000 before taxes. The FIFO method has been used for 1996. The tax rate on these items is 40%.

Instructions

Prepare an income statement for the year 1996 starting with income from continuing operations before taxes. Compute earnings per share as it should be shown on the face of the income statement. Common shares outstanding for the year are 25,000 shares. (Assume a tax rate of 30% on all items, unless indicated otherwise.)

P4-4 (Combined Statement, Multiple- and Single-step) The following account balances were included in the trial balance of Reba McEntire Corporation at June 30, 1996.

Sales	$1,678,500	Depreciation of office furniture	
Sales discounts	31,150	and equipment	7,250
Purchases	890,000	Real estate and other local	
Freight-in	31,600	taxes	7,320
Purchase returns	5,150	Bad debt expense—selling	4,850
Purchase discounts	21,580	Building expense—prorated to	
Sales salaries	56,260	administration	9,130
Sales commissions	97,600	Miscellaneous office expenses	6,000
Travel expense—salespersons	28,930	Sales returns	62,300
Freight-out	21,400	Dividends received	38,000
Entertainment expense	14,820	Bond interest expense	18,000
Telephone and		Income taxes	133,000
telegraph—sales	9,030	Depreciation understatement	
Depreciation of sales equipment	4,980	due to error—1993 (net of	
Building expense—prorated to		tax)	6,700
sales	6,200	Dividends declared on	
Miscellaneous selling		preferred stock	9,000
expenses	4,715	Dividends declared on	
Office supplies used	3,450	common stock	32,000
Telephone and		Merchandise inventory—July	
telegraph—administration	2,820	1, 1995	250,000

The merchandise inventory at June 30, 1996, amounted to $268,100. The Unappropriated Retained Earnings account had a balance of $187,000 at June 30, 1996, before closing; the only entry in that account during the year was a debit of $41,600 to establish an Appropriation for Bonded Indebtedness. There are 70,000 shares of common stock outstanding.

Instructions

(a) Using the multiple-step form, prepare a combined statement of income and unappropriated retained earnings for the year ended June 30, 1996.

(b) Using the single-step form, prepare a combined statement of income and unappropriated retained earnings for the year ended June 30, 1996.

P4-5 (Combined Statement, Multiple- and Single-step) The president of Pearl Jam Corporation provides you with the following selected account balances as of December 31, 1996.

	Dr.	Cr.
Sales		$2,100,000
Sales office salaries	$200,000	
Officers' salaries	220,000	
Building depreciation (50% of building is directly related to sales)	70,000	
Freight-out	46,000	
Cost of goods sold	900,000	
Dividends declared and paid	75,000	
Dividends received		45,000
Interest expense—10% bonds	55,000	
Retained earnings—1/1/96		250,000
Expropriation of foreign holdings (extraordinary item)	200,000	
Damages payable from litigation		80,000

The president informs you that the damages payable from litigation arose in 1996 out of a lawsuit initiated in 1992, and the bookkeeper debited retained earnings for $80,000. Assume that the company is continually involved in litigation of this nature. The president requests your help in constructing an income statement. She advises you that the corporation has 100,000 shares of common stock outstanding, and is taxed at a tax effective rate of 35% on all income-related items.

Instructions

(a) Prepare a combined statement of income and retained earnings in multiple-step form.

(b) Prepare a combined statement of income and retained earnings in single-step form.

P4-6 (Irregular Items) Presented below is a combined single-step statement of income and retained earnings for Tina Turner Company for 1995.

		(000 omitted)
Net sales		$640,000
Cost and expenses:		
Cost of goods sold		500,000
Selling, general, and administrative expenses		66,000
Other, net		17,000
		583,000
Income before income tax		57,000
Income tax		16,800
Net income		40,200
Retained earnings at beginning of period, as previously reported	141,000	
Adjustment required for correction of error	(7,000)	
Retained earnings at beginning of period, as restated		134,000
Dividends on common stock		(12,200)
Retained earnings at end of period		$162,000

Additional facts are as follows:

1. "Selling, general, and administrative expenses" for 1995 included a usual but infrequently occurring charge of $11,000,000.

2. "Other, net" for 1995 included an extraordinary item (charge) of $10,000,000. If the extraordinary item (charge) had not occurred, income taxes for 1995 would have been $21,800,000 instead of $16,800,000.

3. "Adjustment required for correction of an error" was a result of a change in estimate (useful life of certain assets reduced to 8 years and a catch-up adjustment made).

4. Tina Turner Company disclosed earnings per common share for net income in the notes to the financial statements.

Instructions

Determine from these additional facts whether the presentation of the facts in the Tina Turner Company statements of income and retained earnings is appropriate. If the presentation is not appropriate, describe the appropriate presentation and discuss its theoretical rationale (do not prepare revised statements).

P4-7 (Statement of Retained Earnings, Prior Period Adjustment) Below is the Retained Earnings account for the year 1996 for Clay Walker Corp.

Retained earnings, January 1, 1996		$357,600
Add:		
Gain on sale of investments (net of tax)	$41,200	
Net income	84,500	
Refund on litigation with government, related to the year 1993 (net of tax)	10,800	
Recognition of income earned in 1995, but omitted from income statement in that year (net of tax)	25,400	161,900
		519,500
Deduct		
Loss on discontinued operations (net of tax)	25,000	
Write-off of goodwill	60,000	
Cumulative effect on income in changing from straight-line depreciation to accelerated depreciation in 1996 (net of tax)	18,200	
Cash dividends declared	32,000	135,200
Retained earnings, December 31, 1996		$384,300

Instructions

(a) Prepare a corrected statement of retained earnings. Clay Walker Corp. normally sells investments of the type mentioned above.

(b) State where the items that do not appear in the corrected retained earnings statement should be shown.

P4-8 (Combined Statement and Irregular Items) A condensed statement of income and retained earnings of the Wynonna Company for the year ended December 31, 1996 is presented below.

Also presented are three unrelated situations involving accounting changes and classification of certain items as ordinary or extraordinary. Each situation is based upon the condensed statements of income and retained earnings of the Wynonna Company and requires revisions of these statements.

Wynonna Company
CONDENSED STATEMENTS OF INCOME
AND RETAINED EARNINGS
For the Year Ended 1996

Sales	$5,700,000
Cost of goods sold	2,900,000
Gross margin	2,800,000
Selling, general, and administrative expenses	2,000,000
Income before extraordinary item	800,000
Extraordinary item	(540,000)
Net income	260,000
Retained earnings, January 1	700,000
Retained earnings, December 31	$ 960,000

Situation A

During the latter part of 1996, the company discontinued its retail and apparel fabric divisions. The results of such operations and the loss on sale of these two discontinued divisions amounted to a total loss of $620,000. This amount was considered part of selling, general, and administrative expenses. The transaction meets the criteria for discontinued operations.

The extraordinary item in the condensed statement of income and retained earnings for 1996 relates to a loss sustained as a result of damage to the company's merchandise caused by a tornado that struck its main warehouse in Charles City, Iowa. This natural disaster was considered an unusual and infrequent occurrence for that section of the country.

Situation B

At the end of 1996, the company's management decided that the estimated loss rate on uncollectible accounts receivable was too low. The loss rate used for the years 1995 and 1996 was 1.2% of total sales, and owing to an increase in the write-off of uncollectible accounts, the rate has been raised to 3% of total sales. The amount recorded in bad debt expense under the heading of selling, general, and administrative expenses for 1996 was $68,400 and for 1995 was $75,000.

The extraordinary item in the condensed statement of income and retained earnings for 1996 relates to a loss incurred in the abandonment of outmoded equipment formerly used in the business.

Situation C

On January 1, 1994, the company acquired machinery at a cost of $500,000. The company adopted the double-declining balance method of depreciation for this machinery, and had been recording depreciation over an estimated life of ten years, with no residual value. At the beginning of 1996, a decision was made to adopt the straight-line method of depreciation for this machinery. Owing to an oversight, however, the double-declining balance method was used for 1996. For financial reporting purposes, depreciation is included in selling, general, and administrative expenses.

The extraordinary item in the condensed statement of income and retained earnings relates to shutdown expenses incurred by the company during a major strike by its operating employees during 1996.

Instructions

For each of the three unrelated situations, prepare a revised condensed statement of income and retained earnings of Wynonna Company. Ignore income tax considerations and earnings per share computations.

(AICPA adapted)

P4-9 (Income Statement and Irregular Items) The Carlito Corporation commenced business on January 1, 1993. Recently the corporation has had several unusual accounting problems related to the presentation of their income statement for financial reporting purposes.

You have been the CPA for Carlito Corporation for several years and have been asked to examine the following data.

Carlito Corporation
STATEMENT OF INCOME
For the Year Ended December 31, 1996

Sales	$9,500,000
Cost of goods sold	5,900,000
Gross profit	3,600,000
Selling and administrative expense	1,300,000
Income before income tax	2,300,000
Income tax (30%)	690,000
Net income	$1,610,000

In addition, this information was provided:

1. The controller mentioned that the corporation has had difficulty in collecting on several of their receivables. For this reason, the bad debt write-off was increased from 1% to 2% of sales. The controller estimates that if this rate had been used in past periods, an additional $83,000 worth of expense would have been charged. The bad debt expense for the current period was calculated using the new rate and is part of selling and administrative expense.
2. Common shares outstanding at the end of 1996 totaled 500,000. No additional shares were purchased or sold during 1996.
3. Carlito noted also that the following items were not included in the income statement.
   (a) Inventory in the amount of $48,000 was obsolete.
   (b) The major casualty loss suffered by the corporation was partially uninsured and cost $77,000, net of tax (extraordinary item).
4. Retained earnings as of January 1, 1996, was $2,800,000. Cash dividends of $700,000 were paid in 1996.
5. In January, 1996, Carlito Corporation changed its method of accounting for plant assets from the straight-line method to the accelerated method (double-declining balance). The controller has prepared a schedule indicating what depreciation expense would have been in previous periods if the double-declining method had been used. (The effective tax rate for 1993, 1994, and 1995 was 30%.)

	Depreciation Expense under Straight-Line	Depreciation Expense under Double-Declining	Difference
1993	$ 75,000	$150,000	$ 75,000
1994	75,000	112,500	37,500
1995	75,000	84,375	9,375
	$225,000	$346,875	$121,875

6. In 1996, Carlito discovered that two errors were made in previous years. First, when it took a physical inventory at the end of 1993, one of the count sheets was apparently lost. The ending inventory for 1993 was therefore understated by $95,000. The inventory was correctly taken in 1994, 1995, and 1996. Also, the corporation found that in 1995 it had failed to record $20,000 as an expense for sales commissions. The effective tax rate for 1993, 1994, and 1995 was 30%. The sales commissions for 1995 are included in 1996 expenses.

Instructions

Prepare the income statement for Carlito Corporation in accordance with professional pronouncements. Do not prepare footnotes.

*P4-10 (Discontinued Operations)   Jonathan Brandis Corporation management formally decided to discontinue operation of its Electrical Switch Division on November 1, 1994. Brandis is a successful corporation with earnings in excess of $38.5 million before taxes for each of the past 5 years. The Electrical Switch Division is being discontinued because it has not contributed to this profitable performance.

The principal assets of this division are the land, plant, and equipment used to manufacture the switches. The land, plant, and equipment had a net book value of $56 million on November 1, 1994.

Brandis' management has entered into negotiations for a cash sale of the facility for $39 million. The expected date of the sale and final disposal of the segment is July 1, 1995.

Brandis Corporation has a fiscal year ending May 31. The results of operations for the Electric Switch Division for the 1994–95 fiscal year and the estimated results for June 1995 are presented below. The before-tax losses after October 31, 1994, are computed without depreciation on the plant and equipment because the net book value as of November 1, 1994, is being used as a basis of negotiation for the sale.

Period	Before-tax Income (Loss)
June 1, 1994—October 31, 1994	$(3,800,000)
November 1, 1994—May 31, 1995	$(5,900,000)
June 1—30, 1995 (estimated)	$(650,000)

The Electrical Switch Division will be accounted for as a discontinued operation on Brandis' 1994–95 fiscal year financial statements. Brandis is subject to a 30% tax rate (federal and state income taxes) on operating income and all gains and losses.

Instructions

(a) Explain how the Electrical Switch Division's assets would be reported on Jonathan Brandis Corporation's balance sheet as of May 31, 1995.

(b) Explain how the discontinued operations and pending sale of the Electrical Switch Division would be reported on Jonathan Brandis Corporation's statement of income for the year ended May 31, 1995.

(c) Explain what information ordinarily should be disclosed in the notes to the financial statements regarding discontinued operations.

(CMA adapted)

CASES

C4-1 (Identification of Income Statement Deficiencies)   Janet Jackson Corporation was incorporated and began business on January 1, 1995. It has been successful and now requires a bank loan for additional working capital to finance expansion. The bank has requested an audited income statement for the year 1995. The accountant for Janet Jackson Corporation provides you with the following income statement which Janet Jackson plans to submit to the bank:

INCOME STATEMENT

Sales		$760,000
Dividends		32,300
Gain on recovery of insurance proceeds from		
earthquake loss (extraordinary)		38,500
		830,800
Less:		
Selling expenses	$101,100	
Cost of goods sold	510,000	
Advertising expense	13,700	
Loss on obsolescence of inventories	34,000	
Loss on discontinued operations	48,600	
Administrative expense	73,400	780,800
Income before income tax		50,000
Income tax		20,000
Net income		$ 30,000

Instructions

Indicate the deficiencies in the income statement presented above. Assume that the corporation desires a single-step income statement.

C4-2 (All-inclusive vs. Current Operating) Information concerning the operations of a corporation is presented in an income statement or in a combined "statement of income and retained earnings." Income statements are prepared on a "current operating performance" basis ("earning power concept") or an "all-inclusive" basis ("historical concept"). Proponents of the two types of income statements do not agree upon the proper treatment of material nonrecurring charges and credits.

Instructions

(a) Define "current operating performance" and "all-inclusive" as used above.

(b) Explain the differences in content and organization of a "current operating performance" income statement and an "all-inclusive" income statement. Include a discussion of the proper treatment of material nonrecurring charges and credits.

(c) Give the principal arguments for the use of each of the three statements, "all-inclusive" income statement, "current operating performance" income statement, and a combined "statement of income and retained earnings."

(AICPA adapted)

C4-3 (Extraordinary Items) Michael Bolton, vice-president of finance for Timeless Company, has recently been asked to discuss with the company's division controllers the proper accounting for extraordinary items. Michael Bolton prepared the factual situations presented below as a basis for discussion.

1. An earthquake destroys one of the oil refineries owned by a large multinational oil company. Earthquakes are rare in this geographical location.
2. A publicly held company has incurred a substantial loss in the unsuccessful registration of a bond issue.
3. A large portion of a cigarette manufacturer's tobacco crops are destroyed by a hailstorm. Severe damage from hailstorms is rare in this locality.
4. A large diversified company sells a block of shares from its portfolio of securities acquired for investment purposes.
5. A company sells a block of common stock of a publicly traded company. The block of shares, which represents less than 10% of the publicly held company, is the only security investment the company has ever owned.
6. A company that operates a chain of warehouses sells the excess land surrounding one of its warehouses. When the company buys property to establish a new warehouse, it usually buys more land than it expects to use for the warehouse with the expectation that the land will appreciate in value. Twice during the past 5 years the company sold excess land.
7. A textile manufacturer with only one plant moves to another location and sustains relocation costs of $620,000.
8. A company experiences a material loss in the repurchase of a large bond issue that has been outstanding for 3 years. The company regularly repurchases bonds of this nature.

9. A railroad experiences an unusual flood loss to part of its track system. Flood losses normally occur every 3 or 4 years.

10. A machine tool company sells the only land it owns. The land was acquired 10 years ago for future expansion, but shortly thereafter the company abandoned all plans for expansion but decided to hold the land for appreciation.

Instructions

Determine whether the foregoing items should be classified as extraordinary items. Present a rationale for your position.

C4-4 (Income Reporting Items) Tracy Lawrence Corp. is a real estate firm that derives approximately 30% of its income from the Alibis Division, which manages apartment complexes. As auditor for Tracy Lawrence Corp., you have recently overheard the following discussion between the controller and financial vice-president.

VICE-PRESIDENT:	If we sell the Alibis Division, it seems ridiculous to segregate the results of the sale in the income statement. Separate categories tend to be absurd and confusing to the stockholders. I believe that we should simply report the gain on the sale as other income or expense without detail.
CONTROLLER:	Professional pronouncements would require that we disclose this information separately in the income statement. If a sale of this type is considered unusual and infrequent, it must be reported as an extraordinary item.
VICE-PRESIDENT:	What about the walkout we had last month when our employees were upset about their commission income? Would this situation not also be an extraordinary item?
CONTROLLER:	I am not sure whether this item would be reported as extraordinary or not.
VICE-PRESIDENT:	Oh well, it doesn't make any difference because the net effect of all these items is immaterial, so no disclosure is necessary.

Instructions

(a) On the basis of the foregoing discussion, answer the following questions: Who is correct about handling the sale? What would be the income statement presentation for the sale of the Alibis Division?

(b) How should the walkout by the employees be reported?

(c) What do you think about the vice-president's observation on materiality?

(d) What are the earnings per share implications of these topics?

C4-5 (Identification of Extraordinary Items) Munch Company is a major manufacturer of foodstuffs whose products are sold in grocery and convenience stores throughout the United States. The company's name is well known and respected because its products have been marketed nationally for over 50 years.

In April 1995 the company was forced to recall one of its major products. A total of 35 persons in Jefferson City were treated for severe intestinal pain, and eventually 3 people died from complications. All of the people had consumed Munch's product.

The product causing the problem was traced to one specific lot. Munch keeps samples from all lots of foodstuffs. After thorough testing, Munch and the legal authorities confirmed that the product had been tampered with after it had left the company's plant and was no longer under the company's control.

All of the product was recalled from the market—the only time a Munch product has been recalled nationally and the only time for tampering. Persons who still had the product in their homes, even though it was not from the affected lot, were encouraged to return the product for credit or refund. A media campaign was designed and implemented by the company to explain what had happened and what the company was doing to minimize any chance of recurrence. Munch decided to continue the product with the same trade name and same wholesale price. However, the packaging was redesigned completely to be tamper resistant and safety sealed. This required the purchase and installation of new equipment.

The corporate accounting staff recommended that the costs associated with the tampered product be treated as an extraordinary charge on the 1995 financial statements. Corporate accounting was asked to identify the various costs that could be associated with the tampered product and related recall. These costs ($000 omitted) are as follows.

1. Credits and refunds to stores and consumers	$30,000
2. Insurance to cover lost sales and idle plant costs for possible future recalls	5,000
3. Transportation costs and off-site warehousing of returned product	1,000
4. Future security measures for other Munch products	4,000
5. Testing of returned product and inventory	700

6. Destroying returned product and inventory	2,400
7. Public relations program to reestablish brand credibility	4,200
8. Communication program to inform customers, answer inquiries, prepare press releases, etc.	1,600
9. Higher cost arising from new packaging	700
10. Investigation of possible involvement of employees, former employees, competitors, etc.	500
11. Packaging redesign and testing	2,000
12. Purchase and installation of new packaging equipment	6,000
13. Legal costs for defense against liability suits	600
14. Lost sales revenue due to recall	32,000

Munch's estimated earnings before income taxes and before consideration of any of the above items for the year ending December 31, 1995, are $230 million.

Instructions

(a) Munch Company plans to recognize the costs associated with the product tampering and recall as an extraordinary charge.

1. Explain why Munch could classify this occurrence as an extraordinary charge.

2. Describe the placement and terminology used to present the extraordinary charge in the 1995 income statement.

(b) Refer to the 14 cost items identified by the corporate accounting staff of Munch Company.

1. Identify the cost items by number that should be included in the extraordinary charge for 1995.

2. For any item that is not included in the extraordinary charge, explain why it would not be included in the extraordinary charge.

(CMA adapted)

C4-6 (All-inclusive vs. Current Operating) Garth Brooks, controller for Chase Inc., has recently prepared an income statement for 1996. Mr. Brooks admits that he has not examined any recent professional pronouncements, but believes that the following presentation presents fairly the financial progress of this company during the current period.

Chase Inc.
INCOME STATEMENT
For the Year Ended December 31, 1996

Sales			$377,852
Less: sales returns and allowances			16,320
Net sales			361,532
Cost of goods sold:			
Inventory, January 1, 1996		$ 50,235	
Purchases	$192,143		
Less: purchase discounts	3,142	189,001	
Cost of goods available for sale		239,236	
Inventory, December 31, 1996		37,124	
Cost of goods sold			202,112
Gross profit			159,420
Selling expenses		41,850	
Administrative expenses		32,142	73,992
Income before income tax			85,428
Other revenues and gains			
Dividends received			40,000
			125,428
Income tax			43,900
Net income			$ 81,528

Chase Inc.
STATEMENT OF RETAINED EARNINGS
For the Year Ended December 31, 1996

Retained earnings, January 1, 1996			$176,000
Add			
Net income for 1996	$81,528		
Gain from casualty (net of tax)	10,000		
Gain on sale of plant assets	21,400	$112,928	
Deduct			
Loss on expropriation (net of tax)	8,000		
Cash dividends declared on common stock	30,000		
Correction of mathematical error in depreciating plant assets in 1994 (net of tax)	7,186	(45,186)	67,742
Retained earnings, December 31, 1996			$243,742

Instructions

(a) Determine whether these statements are prepared under the "current operating" or "all-inclusive" concept of income. Cite specific details.

(b) Which method do you favor and why?

(c) Which method must be used, and how should the information be presented? Common shares outstanding for the year are 100,000 shares.

For questionable items, use the classification that ordinarily would be appropriate.

C4-7 (Identification of Income Statement Weaknesses) The following financial statement was prepared by employees of Whitney Houston Corporation.

Whitney Houston Corporation
STATEMENT OF INCOME AND RETAINED EARNINGS
Year Ended December 31, 1996

Revenues	
Gross sales, including sales taxes	$1,044,300
Less returns, allowances, and cash discounts	56,200
Net sales	988,100
Dividends, interest, and purchase discounts	30,250
Recoveries of accounts written off in prior years	13,850
Total revenues	1,032,200
Costs and expenses	
Cost of goods sold, including sales taxes	425,900
Salaries and related payroll expenses	60,500
Rent	19,100
Freight-in and freight-out	3,400
Bad debt expense	24,000
Addition to reserve for possible inventory losses	3,800
Total costs and expenses	536,700
Income before extraordinary items	495,500
Extraordinary items	
Loss on discontinued styles (Note 1)	37,000
Loss on sale of marketable securities (Note 2)	39,050
Loss on sale of warehouse (Note 3)	86,350
Retroactive settlement of federal income taxes for 1995 and 1994 (Note 4)	34,500
Total extraordinary items	196,900
Net income	298,600
Retained earnings at beginning of year	310,700
Total	609,300
Less: Federal income taxes	113,468
Cash dividends on common stock	21,900
Total	135,368

Retained earnings at end of year	$ 473,932
Net income per share of common stock	$1.99

Note 1: New styles and rapidly changing consumer preferences resulted in a $37,000 loss on the disposal of discontinued styles and related accessories.

Note 2: The corporation sold an investment in marketable securities at a loss of $39,050. The corporation normally sells securities of this nature.

Note 3: The corporation sold one of its warehouses at an $86,350 loss.

Note 4: The corporation was charged $34,500 retroactively for additional income taxes resulting from a settlement in 1993. Of this amount, $17,000 was applicable to 1995, and the balance was applicable to 1994. Litigation of this nature is recurring for this company.

Instructions

Identify and discuss the weaknesses in classification and disclosure in the single-step Statement of Income and Retained Earnings above. You should explain why these treatments are weaknesses and what the proper presentation of the items would be in accordance with recent professional pronouncements.

C4-8 (Classification of Income Statement Items) As audit partner for Eric and Clapton, you are in charge of reviewing the classification of unusual items that have occurred during the current year. The following items have come to your attention:

1. A merchandising company incorrectly overstated its ending inventory 2 years ago by a material amount. Inventory for all other periods is correctly computed.
2. An automobile dealer sells for $123,000 an extremely rare 1930 S type Invicta which it purchased for $18,000 10 years ago. The Invicta is the only such display item the dealer owns.
3. A drilling company during the current year extended the estimated useful life of certain drilling equipment from 9 to 15 years. As a result, depreciation for the current year was materially lowered.
4. A retail outlet changed its computation for bad debt expense from 1% to ½ of 1% of sales because of changes in its customer clientele.
5. A mining concern sells a foreign subsidiary engaged in uranium mining, although it (the seller) continues to engage in uranium mining in other countries.
6. A steel company changes from straight-line depreciation to accelerated depreciation in accounting for its plant assets.
7. A construction company, at great expense, prepares a major proposal for a government loan. The loan is not approved.
8. A water pump manufacturer has had large losses resulting from a strike by its employees early in the year.
9. Depreciation for a prior period was incorrectly understated by $900,000. The error was discovered in the current year.
10. A large sheep rancher suffered a major loss because the state required that all sheep in the state be killed to halt the spread of a rare disease. Such a situation has not occurred in the state for 20 years.
11. A food distributor that sells wholesale to supermarket chains and to fast-food restaurants (two major classes of customers) decides to discontinue the division that sells to one of the two classes of customers.

Instructions

From the foregoing information, indicate in what section of the income statement or retained earnings statement these items should be classified. Provide a brief rationale for your position.

C4-9 (Capital Maintenance vs. Transaction Approach) In early 1981 the Peabo Bryson Company was formed when it issued 10,000 shares of common stock at $20 per share. A few years later, 3,000 additional shares were issued at $35 per share. No other common stock transactions occurred until the company was liquidated in 1995. At that time, corporate assets were sold for $1,150,000 and $100,000 of corporate liabilities were paid off. The remaining cash was distributed to stockholders. During the corporation's life, it paid total dividends of $200,000.

Instructions
(a) Discuss the two approaches to calculating income.
(b) If only the facts given above are available, which approach must be used to compute income?
(c) Compute the income of Peabo Bryson Company over its 15-year life.

*C4-10 (Discontinued Operations) You're the engagement partner on a multi-divisional, calendar year-end client with annual sales of $80 million. The company primarily sells electronic transistors to small customers and has one division that deals in acoustic transmitters for Navy submarines. The Transmitter Division has approximately $15 million in sales.

It's an evening in February, 1995, and the audit work is complete. You're working in the client's office on the report, when you overhear a conversation between the financial vice-president, the treasurer, and the controller. They're discussing the sale of the Transmitter Division, expected to take place in June of this year, and the related reporting problems.

The vice-president thinks no segregation of the sale is necessary in the income statement because separate categories tend to be abused and confuse the stockholders. The treasurer disagrees. He feels that if an item is unusual or infrequent, it should be classified as an extraordinary item, including the sale of the Transmitter Division. The controller says an item should be both infrequent and unusual to be extraordinary. He feels the sale of the Transmitter Division should be shown separately, but not as an extraordinary item.

The sale is not new to you because you read about it in the minutes of the December 16, 1994, board of directors meeting. The minutes indicated plans to sell the transmitter plant and equipment by June 30, 1995, to its major competitor, who seems interested. The board estimates that net income and sales will remain constant until the sale, on which the company expects a $700,000 profit.

You also hear the controller disagree with the vice-president that the results of the strike last year and the sale of the old transistor ovens, formerly used in manufacturing, would also be extraordinary items. In addition, the treasurer thinks the government regulation issued last month, which made much of their inventory raw material useless, would be extraordinary. The regulations set beta emission standards at levels lower than those in the raw materials supply, and there's no alternative use for materials. Finally, the controller claims the discussion is academic. Since the net effect of all three items is immaterial, no disclosure is required.

Instructions

(a) Does the Transmitter Division qualify as a segment of a business in more than one way? If so, why?

(b) Does the Transmitter Division qualify as a discontinued operation? Why?

(c) Do the minutes indicate that a formal plan has been established? If not, why?

(d) When should the gain be recognized? What if a loss were anticipated?

(e) Who is correct about reporting the sale? What would the income statement presentation be for the next fiscal year?

(f) Who is right about whether the strike, the sale of fixed assets and the imposition of a new government regulation constitute extraordinary items?

(g) What do you think about the controller's observation on materiality?

(h) What facts can you give the group about the earnings per share ramifications of these topics?

▶ USING YOUR JUDGMENT ◀

▶ FINANCIAL REPORTING PROBLEM

The financial statements of Georgia-Pacific Corporation and accompanying notes, as presented in the company's 1993 Annual Report, are contained in Appendix 5-A. Refer to Georgia-Pacific's financial statements and notes and answer the following questions.

1. What type of income statement format does Georgia-Pacific use? Name the possible advantages of this type of format.

2. What are Georgia-Pacific's primary revenue sources?

3. Identify the irregular items reported by Georgia-Pacific in its 1991, 1992, and 1993 income statements.

4. Comment on Georgia-Pacific's earnings and results of operations for 1993. What has been the trend in Georgia-Pacific's net income for the three-year period 1991–1993?

5. What three operating-financial ratios did Georgia-Pacific choose to report in its "Selected Financial Data—Operations" section covering the years 1983–1993?

▶ WRITING ASSIGNMENT

As a practicing CPA, you have just received the following letter from your client, Buy-Rite Corp., a parent corporation with a number of subsidiaries. All amounts are shown net of tax.

December 20, 1994

Dear Student Accountant:

In April of 1995, Buy-Rite is planning a bond issue to raise $3,000,000 which will allow us to expand our overseas operations. However, we have encountered two situations which may dramatically affect 1994 net income and, consequently, our ability to sell the bonds.

The first problem is that, on July 3, 1994, our Board of Directors voted unanimously to dispose of Bailey's Inns, our Southern restaurant chain (a business segment), which has become increasingly unprofitable. From January 1, 1994 until that date, Bailey's lost $400,000. With only ten days left in 1994, Bailey's has realized an additional $250,000 loss. The bright side is that we have arranged to sell Bailey's on April 1, 1995 for a gain of $400,000. We also estimate that Bailey's will bring in net operating income of $100,000 from January 1, 1995 to the date of disposal (the first quarter, peak season, being its usual profitable one).

Our greatest concern is that we must claim the entire loss of $650,000 on our 1994 income statement, deferring the recognition of the $400,000 gain and $100,000 of net operating income until the 1995 income statement. This loss may adversely affect our 1995 bond issue.

In itself, this loss would not appear so problematic if it did not also coincide with an extraordinary loss that our company took on translation of foreign currency. Last April when the Yen was very weak, Buy-Rite made several transactions with Japanese companies. Because the Yen was so weak, we did not bother to hedge. Unexpectedly, the Yen became very strong, so by the time our Japanese payables came due, we incurred a $300,000 loss.

Please explain to us how we can present these items in such a way that investors will not be reluctant to purchase our bonds.

Sincerely,

Jack O. Lantern, Chief Accountant

Instructions
Draft a letter to Mr. Lantern, explaining how Buy-Rite must account for the disposition of the segment, including what amounts will be reported in both 1994 and 1995. In addition, address the issue of the loss on translation of foreign currency.

▶ GROUP ASSIGNMENT

Depeche Mode Corp. has 100,000 shares of common stock outstanding. In 1996, the company reports income from continuing operations before taxes of $1,210,000. Additional transactions not considered in the $1,210,000 are as follows:

1. In 1996 the company reviewed its accounts receivable and determined that $26,000 of accounts receivable that had been carried for years appeared unlikely to be collected.
2. An internal audit discovered that amortization of intangible assets was understated by $35,000 (net of tax) in a prior period. The amount was charged against retained earnings.
3. The company sold its only investment in common stock during the year at a gain of $145,000. The gain is taxed at a total effective rate of 40%. Assume that the transaction meets the requirements of an extraordinary item.
4. In 1996, Depeche Mode Corp. sold equipment for $40,000. The machine had originally cost $80,000 and had accumulated depreciation of $36,000. The gain or loss is considered ordinary.
5. The company discontinued operations of one of its subsidiaries during the current year at a loss of $190,000 before taxes. Assume that this transaction meets the criteria for discontinued operations. The loss on operations of the discontinued subsidiary was $90,000 before taxes; the loss from disposal of the subsidiary was $100,000 before taxes.
6. The sum of $100,000, applicable to a breached 1992 contract, was received as a result of a lawsuit. Prior to the award, legal counsel was uncertain about the outcome of the suit and had not established a receivable.

Instructions
Your instructor will identify one member of the group to serve as a recorder and one member to serve as spokesperson. As a group, analyze the above information so that the recorder can prepare an income statement for the year 1996 starting with income from continuing operations before income taxes. Compute earnings per share as it should be shown on the face of the income statement. (Assume a total effective tax rate of 38% on all items, unless otherwise indicated.)

▶ ETHICS CASE

In the financial highlights section of its annual report, Chandra Company declares that its earnings have increased by 10% using an earnings number that includes and gives no hint of a large unusual, nonrecurring gain. The financial statements, by contrast, have correctly highlighted and classified the extraordinary items below operating income. A stockholder who has read the annual report closely asks the chief accountant, Dan Panic, to explain this apparent discrepancy, but Javid Chandra, president of Chandra suggests evading the question by saying that the highlights section is not controlled by GAAP, and anyway it is only for highlights and not details like extraordinary items.

Instructions
- **(a)** Is Javid Chandra correct about the highlights section not being controlled by GAAP? Is there an ethical issue involved in this discrepancy?
- **(b)** Who might be affected by this presentation?
- **(c)** What should Dan Panic do?

CHAPTER 5

BALANCE SHEET AND
STATEMENT OF CASH FLOWS

LEARNING OBJECTIVES

After studying this chapter, you should be able to:

1. Identify the uses and limitations of a balance sheet.

2. Identify the major classifications of the balance sheet.

3. Prepare a classified balance sheet using the report and account forms.

4. Identify balance sheet information requiring supplemental disclosure.

5. Identify major disclosure techniques for the balance sheet.

6. Indicate the purpose of the statement of cash flows.

7. Identify the content of the statement of cash flows.

8. Prepare a statement of cash flows.

*C*onsider the following: Commodore International, a microcomputer operation, reported earnings per share of $4.66 per share in one year, up approximately 63% over the prior year. Yet, its stock price dropped from a high of 60⅝ to less than 30 over this one-year period. Why? The balance sheet indicated that accounts receivable increased substantially and the composition of the inventory changed dramatically. The substantial receivable buildup indicated that the receivable collection was a problem. Furthermore, while inventory overall remained stable, finished goods inventory increased 50%. In other words, goods were piling up because sales were lagging. Savvy investors, who saw the trouble signs in the financial statements, began selling their stock. In the following year, Commodore reported a fourth quarter loss of $124 million caused by substantial inventory write-offs.

Earnings declines at Commodore could have been predicted, given the deteriorating balance sheet. And just as a deteriorating balance sheet warns of trouble, improving balance sheet quality often foreshadows long-term improvements in earnings.

Until recently, investors focused on the income statement and earnings per share. The balance sheet was skimmed and the cash flow statement all but ignored. However, many surprises in earnings per share could have been anticipated if these financial statements had not been overlooked. Liquidity and financial flexibility are necessary conditions for any profitable enterprise, and only through careful analysis of balance sheets and statements of cash flows can information about these conditions be obtained.

► SECTION 1 / BALANCE SHEET

► USEFULNESS OF THE BALANCE SHEET

OBJECTIVE 1

Identify the uses and limitations of a balance sheet.

The **balance sheet** provides information about the nature and amounts of investments in enterprise resources, obligations to creditors, and the owners' equity in net resources.[1] The balance sheet provides a basis for (1) computing rates of return, (2) evaluating the capital structure of the enterprise, and (3) assessing its liquidity and financial flexibility. In order to judge enterprise risk[2] and assess future cash flows, one must determine enterprise liquidity and financial flexibility by analyzing its balance sheet.

Liquidity describes "the amount of time that is expected to elapse until an asset is realized or otherwise converted into cash or until a liability has to be paid."[3] Both short-term and long-term credit grantors are interested in such short-term ratios as cash or near cash to current liabilities. Such ratios measure the enterprise's ability to meet current and maturing obligations. Similarly, present and prospective equity holders study liquidity to gauge future cash dividends or the possibility of expanded operations. Generally, the greater the liquidity, the lower the risk of enterprise failure.

UNDERLYING CONCEPT

The presentation of balance sheet information meets one of the objectives of financial reporting—to provide information about enterprise resources, claims to resources, and changes in them.

Financial flexibility is the "ability of an enterprise to take effective actions to alter the amounts and timing of cash flows so it can respond to unexpected needs and opportunities."[4] For example, a company may become so loaded with debt—so financially inflexible—that its sources of cash to finance expansion or to pay off maturing debt are limited or nonexistent. An enterprise with a high degree of financial flexibility is better able to survive bad times, to recover from unexpected setbacks, and to take advantage of profitable and unexpected investment opportunities. Generally, the greater the financial flexibility, the lower the risk of enterprise failure.

Lack of liquidity and inadequate financial flexibility seriously affected the U.S. airline industry in the 1980s and again in the early 1990s. American, Eastern, United, and TWA all reported quarterly operating losses that stemmed primarily from high interest costs, increased fuel costs, and price cutting resulting from deregulation. Because of operating losses and lowered liquidity, some airlines asked their employees to sign labor contracts that provided no wage increases. Other airlines, already heavily in debt and lacking financial flexibility and liquidity, had to cancel orders for new, more efficient aircraft. More recently, TWA has had to sell routes and planes to raise cash. Some of the major airlines (such as, Braniff, Continental, Eastern, Midway, and America West) have even declared bankruptcy. All of this was no secret. The airlines' balance sheets clearly revealed their financial inflexibility and low liquidity.

► LIMITATIONS OF THE BALANCE SHEET

As indicated in earlier chapters, accountants have adopted a historical cost basis in valuing and reporting most assets and liabilities. Thus, the balance sheet **does not reflect the current value** of many items. When a balance sheet is prepared in accordance with

---

[1]*Accounting Trends and Techniques—1993* indicates that approximately 93% of the companies surveyed used the term "balance sheet." The term "statement of financial position" is used infrequently, although it is conceptually appealing.

[2]Risk is an expression of the unpredictability of future events, transactions, circumstances, and results of the enterprise.

[3]"Reporting Income, Cash Flows, and Financial Position of Business Enterprises," *Proposed Statement of Financial Accounting Concepts* (Stamford, Conn.: FASB, 1981), par. 29.

[4]Ibid., par. 25.

generally accepted accounting principles, most assets are stated at cost; exceptions are receivables and most investment securities.

Many accountants believe that all assets should be restated in terms of current values; there are, however, widely differing opinions about the type of valuation basis to be employed. Some contend that **historical cost statements** should be adjusted for constant dollars (general price-level changes) when inflation is significant; others believe that a **current cost concept** (specific price-level changes) is more useful; still others believe that a **net realizable value** concept or some variant should be adopted. Regardless of the method favored, all are significantly different from the historical cost approach. Each approach has this advantage over the historical cost basis: Each presents a more accurate assessment of the current value of the enterprise, although the question of whether reliable valuations can be obtained is still unresolved.

Another basic limitation of the balance sheet is that **judgments and estimates must be used.** The collectibility of receivables, the salability of inventory, and the useful life of long-term tangible and intangible assets are difficult to determine. Although the process of depreciating long-term assets is a generally accepted practice, the recognition of an increase in asset value is generally ignored by accountants.

Because judgments and estimates used in the preparation of the balance sheet may harm or benefit particular stakeholders, ethical sensibility should come into play in the accountant's decision-making process. The accountant needs to be aware of the potential impact of these judgments and estimates on stakeholder interests (i.e., the company vs. the shareholders).

In addition, the balance sheet necessarily **omits many items that are of financial value to the business** but cannot be recorded objectively. The value of a company's human resources (employee workforce) is certainly significant, but it is omitted because such assets are difficult to quantify. Other items of value not reported are customer base, managerial skills, research superiority, and reputation. Such omissions are understandable. But many items that could and should appear on the balance sheet (most are liabilities) are reported in an "off-balance-sheet" manner, if reported at all.[5] Several of these omitted items (such as sales of receivables with recourse, leases, through-put arrangements, and take-or-pay contracts) are discussed in later chapters.

One of the most significant challenges facing the accounting profession is the limitations of financial statements. As indicated in Chapter 1, the AICPA has recently concluded a study examining the information needs of investors and creditors. Although the conclusions are still tentative, there are some major observations related to the balance sheet. Users oppose replacing the current historical-cost–based accounting model with a fair value accounting model. However, they view fair value information as useful for particular types of assets and liabilities and in certain types of industries. Also users want companies to disclose information about the estimates and assumptions used to determine material asset and liability amounts. Finally, they want more qualitative and quantitative information about the risks associated with financial instruments and off-balance-sheet financing arrangements.[6]

UNDERLYING CONCEPT

The limitations of the balance sheet section demonstrate the trade-off between relevance and reliability. On the one hand, the historical cost principle and the monetary unit assumption ensure that the information is reliable; unfortunately application of these concepts may lead to less relevant reporting because current values are not reported and significant non-quantitative information is excluded.

▶ CLASSIFICATION IN THE BALANCE SHEET

Balance sheet accounts are **classified** so that similar items are grouped together to arrive at significant subtotals. Furthermore, the material is arranged so that important relationships are shown.

The FASB has often noted that the parts and subsections of financial statements can be more informative than the whole. Therefore, as one would expect, the reporting of

OBJECTIVE 2

Identify the major classifications of the balance sheet.

---

[5]For a discussion of various methods that businesses have devised to remove debt from the balance sheet, read: "Get It Off the Balance Sheet," Richard Dieter and Arthur R. Wyatt, *Financial Executive* (Vol. 48, January 1980).

[6]"Meeting the Information Needs of Investors and Creditors," The AICPA Special Committee on Financial Reporting (Supplement to the *Journal of Accountancy*), September 1994.

summary accounts (total assets, net assets, total liabilities, etc.) alone is discouraged. Individual items should be separately reported and classified in sufficient detail to permit users to assess the amounts, timing, and uncertainty of future cash flows, as well as the evaluation of liquidity and financial flexibility, profitability, and risk.

Classification in financial statements helps analysts by grouping items with similar characteristics and separating items with different characteristics:[7]

1. Assets that differ in their **type or expected function** in the central operations or other activities of the enterprise should be reported as separate items; for example, merchandise inventories should be reported separately from property, plant, and equipment.

2. Assets and liabilities with **different implications for the financial flexibility** of the enterprise should be reported as separate items; for example, assets used in operations should be reported separately from assets held for investment, and assets subject to restrictions such as leased equipment.

3. Assets and liabilities with **different general liquidity characteristics** should be reported as separate items. For example, cash should be reported separately from inventories.

The three general classes of items included in the balance sheet are assets, liabilities, and equity. Here is how we defined them in Chapter 2:

◀ ELEMENTS OF THE BALANCE SHEET ▶

1. **ASSETS.** Probable future economic benefits obtained or controlled by a particular entity as a result of past transactions or events.

2. **LIABILITIES.** Probable future sacrifices of economic benefits arising from present obligations of a particular entity to transfer assets or provide services to other entities in the future as a result of past transactions or events.

3. **EQUITY.** Residual interest in the assets of an entity that remains after deducting its liabilities. In a business enterprise, the equity is the ownership interest.[8]

These items are then divided into several subclassifications. Illustration 5-1 indicates the general format of balance sheet presentation.

**ILLUSTRATION 5-1
Balance Sheet
Classifications**

Assets	Liabilities and Owners' Equity
Current assets	Current liabilities
Long-term investments	Long-term debt
Property, plant, and equipment	Owners' equity
Intangible assets	Capital stock
Other assets	Additional paid-in capital
	Retained earnings

---

[7]"Reporting Income, Cash Flows, and Financial Positions of Business Enterprises," *Proposed Statement of Financial Accounting Concepts* (Stamford, Conn.: FASB, 1981), par. 51.

[8]"Elements of Financial Statements of Business Enterprises," *Statement of Financial Accounting Concepts No. 6* (Stamford, Conn.: FASB, 1985), paras. 25, 35 and 49.

The balance sheet may be classified in some other manner, but there is very little departure from these major subdivisions in practice. If a proprietorship or partnership is involved, the classifications within the owners' equity section are presented a little differently, as will be shown later in the chapter.

CURRENT ASSETS

Current assets are cash and other assets expected to be converted into cash, sold, or consumed either in one year or in the operating cycle, whichever is longer. The operating cycle is the average time between the acquisition of materials and supplies and the realization of cash through sales of the product for which the materials and supplies were acquired. The cycle operates from cash through inventory, production, and receivables back to cash. When there are several operating cycles within one year, the one-year period is used. If the operating cycle is more than one year, the longer period is used.

Current assets are presented in the balance sheet in order of liquidity. The five major items found in the current asset section are cash, marketable securities, receivables, inventories, and prepayments. **Cash** is included at its stated value; **marketable securities** are generally valued at fair value; **accounts receivable** are stated at the estimated amount collectible; **inventories** generally are included at cost or the lower of cost or market; and **prepaid items** are valued at cost.

The above items are not considered current assets if they are not expected to be realized in one year or in the operating cycle, whichever is longer. For example, cash restricted for purposes other than payment of current obligations or for use in current operations is excluded from the current asset section. **Generally, the rule is that if an asset is to be turned into cash or is to be used to pay a current liability within a year or the operating cycle, whichever is longer, it is classified as current.** This requirement is subject to exceptions. An investment in common stock is classified as either a current asset or a noncurrent asset depending on management's intent. When a company has small holdings of common stocks or bonds that are going to be held long-term, they should not be classified as current.

Although a current asset is well defined, certain theoretical problems develop. One problem is justifying the inclusion of prepaid expense in the current asset section. The normal justification is that if these items had not been paid in advance, they would require the use of current assets during the operating cycle. If we follow this logic to its ultimate conclusion, however, any asset purchased previously saves the use of current assets during the operating cycle and would be considered current.

Another problem occurs in the current asset definition when fixed assets are consumed during the operating cycle. A literal interpretation of the accounting profession's position on this matter would indicate that an amount equal to the current depreciation and amortization charges on the noncurrent assets should be placed in the current asset section at the beginning of the year, because they will be consumed in the next operating cycle. This conceptual problem is generally ignored, which illustrates that the formal distinction made between current and noncurrent assets is somewhat arbitrary.[9]

INTERNATIONAL INSIGHT

Basic balance sheet formats differ across nations. For example, in Great Britain and in nations influenced by British financial reporting, the balance sheet is presented with the least liquid asset accounts appearing first and cash appearing last.

---

[9]For an interesting discussion of the shortcomings of the current and noncurrent classification framework, see Loyd Heath, "Financial Reporting and the Evaluation of Solvency," *Accounting Research Monograph No. 3* (New York: AICPA, 1978), pp. 43–69. The principal recommendation is that the current and noncurrent classification be abolished, and that assets and liabilities simply be listed without classification in their present order. This approach is justified on the basis that any classification scheme is arbitrary and that users of the financial statements can assemble the data in the manner they believe most appropriate.

Cash

Any restrictions on the general availability of cash or any commitments on its probable disposition must be disclosed. An example of such a presentation is excerpted from the Annual Report of Owens-Corning Fiberglas Corp. below:

Owens-Corning Fiberglas Corp.

Current assets

Cash	$ 3,927,000
Restricted cash (Note 22)	85,043,000

Note 22: Restricted Funds. The Company has 222,885,000 Brazilian cruzados (approximately $15,000,000) of restricted funds deposited in a Brazilian bank account representing a recent dividend payment from a Brazilian subsidiary. Those funds are expected to be available to the Company in the next year.

The Company also has 116,707,000 Swiss Francs (approximately $70,000,000) in trust and restricted for payment of the Company's maturing bonds payable in Swiss Francs.

In the example above, cash was restricted to meet an obligation due currently and, therefore, was included under current assets. If cash is restricted for purposes other than current obligations, it is excluded from current assets. An example of a noncurrent presentation is excerpted from the Annual Report of The Penn Traffic Company below:

The Penn Traffic Company

Current assets

Cash and short-term investments	$9,123,000

Other assets

Restricted funds (Note 1)	8,101,000

Note 1: Restricted Funds. During the current year, the Company entered into a long-term debt agreement for construction of a new perishables distribution center. The principal amount has been included in long-term debt, and the unexpended cash proceeds at year end have been reported as restricted funds.

Short-Term Investments

Investments in debt and equity securities are grouped into three separate portfolios for valuation and reporting purposes. These portfolios are categorized as follows:

Held-to-maturity: Debt securities that the enterprise has the positive intent and ability to hold to maturity.

Trading: Debt and equity securities bought and held primarily for sale in the near term to generate income on short-term price differences.

Available-for-sale: Debt and equity securities not classified as held-to-maturity or trading securities.

Trading securities (whether debt or equity) should be reported as current assets. Individual held-to-maturity and available-for-sale securities are classified as current or noncurrent depending upon the circumstances. All trading and available-for-sale securities are to be reported at fair value.[10]

The example on the next page is excerpted from the annual report of Anchor BanCorp Wisconsin Inc.

---

[10]"Accounting for Certain Investments in Debt and Equity Securities," *Statement of Financial Accounting Standards No. 115* (Norwalk, Conn.: FASB, 1993).

Anchor BanCorp Wisconsin Inc. (in thousands)	
Assets	
Cash and cash equivalents	$ 45,784
Securities available for sale:	
Investment securities	10,284
Mortgage-related securities	51,814
Securities held to maturity:	
Mortgage-related securities (fair value of $134.2 million and $223.7 million, respectively)	135,896
Loans receivable, net	
Held for sale	16,542
Held for investment	1,066,945
Foreclosed properties and repossessed assets, net	5,294

Receivables

Any anticipated loss due to uncollectibles, the amount and nature of any nontrade receivables, and any amounts pledged or discounted should be clearly stated. Mack Trucks, Inc. reported its receivables as follows:

Mack Trucks, Inc.	
Current assets	
Trade receivables:	
Accounts receivable	$102,212,000
Affiliated companies	1,157,000
Installment notes and contracts	625,000
Total	103,994,000
Less allowance for uncollectible accounts	8,194,000
Trade receivables—net	95,800,000
Receivable from unconsolidated financial subsidiaries	22,106,000

Inventories

For a proper presentation of inventories, the basis of valuation (i.e., lower of cost or market), and the method of pricing (FIFO or LIFO) is disclosed. For a manufacturing concern (like General Signal Corporation, shown below), the stage of completion of the inventories is also indicated.

UNDERLYING CONCEPT

The lower of cost or market valuation is an example of the use of conservatism in accounting.

General Signal Corporation		
Current assets		
Inventories—at the lower of cost (determined by the first-in, first-out method) or market		
Finished goods	$103,405,000	
Work in process	126,667,000	
Raw materials and purchased parts	167,972,000	$398,044,000

Weyerhaeuser Company, a forestry company and lumber manufacturer with several finished goods product lines, reported its inventory as follows:

Weyerhaeuser Company	
Current assets	
Inventories—at FIFO lower of cost or market	
Logs and chips	$ 68,471,000
Lumber, plywood and panels	86,741,000
Pulp, newsprint and paper	47,377,000
Containerboard, paperboard, containers and cartons	59,682,000
Other products	161,717,000
Total product inventories	423,988,000
Materials and supplies	175,540,000

Prepaid Expenses

Prepaid expenses included in current assets are expenditures already made for benefits (usually services) to be received within one year or the operating cycle, whichever is longer.[11] These items are current assets because if they had not already been paid, they would require the use of cash during the next year or the operating cycle. A common example is the payment in advance for an insurance policy. It is classified as a prepaid expense at the time of the expenditure because the payment precedes the receipt of the benefit of coverage. Prepaid expenses are reported at the amount of the unexpired or unconsumed cost. Other common prepaid expenses include prepaid rent, advertising, taxes, and office or operating supplies. Munsingwear, Inc., for example, listed its prepaid expenses in current assets as follows:

Munsingwear, Inc.	
Current assets	
Inventories	$18,013,000
Prepaid expenses	1,492,000
Net assets related to discontinued operations	5,162,000

Companies often include insurance and other prepayments for 2 or 3 years in current assets even though part of the advance payment applies to periods beyond one year or the current operating cycle.

LONG-TERM INVESTMENTS

Long-term investments often referred to simply as investments, normally consist of one of four types:

1. Investments in securities, such as bonds, common stock, or long-term notes.

2. Investments in tangible fixed assets not currently used in operations, such as land held for speculation.

3. Investments set aside in special funds such as a sinking fund, pension fund, or plant expansion fund. The cash surrender value of life insurance is included here.

4. Investments in nonconsolidated subsidiaries or affiliated companies.

---

[11]*Accounting Trends and Techniques—1993* in its survey of 600 annual reports identified 367 companies that reported prepaid expenses.

Long-term investments are to be held for many years. They are not acquired with the intention of disposing of them in the near future. They are usually presented on the balance sheet just below Current Assets in a separate section called Investments. Many securities that are properly shown among long-term investments are, in fact, readily marketable. But they are not included as current assets unless the intent is to convert them to cash in the short-term—within a year or in the operating cycle, whichever is longer. Securities classified as available-for-sale should be reported at fair value. Securities classified as held-to-maturity are reported at cost.

Alco Standard Corporation reported its investments section between Current Assets and Property, Plant, and Equipment in the following manner:

Alco Standard Corporation	
Investments	
Investment in Alco Health Services Corporation	$ 62,255,000
Other investments	37,533,000
Long-term receivables	22,191,000
Total investments	121,979,000

PROPERTY, PLANT, AND EQUIPMENT

Property, plant, and equipment are properties of a durable nature used in the regular operations of the business. These assets consist of physical property such as land, buildings, machinery, furniture, tools, and wasting resources (timberland, minerals). With the exception of land, most assets are either depreciable (such as buildings) or consumable (such as timberlands).

Mattel, Inc., a manufacturer of toys and games, presented its property, plant, and equipment in its balance sheet as follows:

Mattel, Inc.	
Property, plant, and equipment	
Land	$ 5,812,000
Buildings	46,490,000
Machinery and equipment	72,513,000
Capitalized leases	39,425,000
Leasehold improvements	19,068,000
	183,308,000
Less: Accumulated depreciation	55,496,000
	127,812,000
Tools, dies and molds, less amortization	37,053,000
Property, plant, and equipment, net	164,865,000

The basis of valuing the property, plant, and equipment, any liens against the properties, and accumulated depreciation should be disclosed—usually in notes to the statements.

INTANGIBLE ASSETS

Intangible assets lack physical substance and usually have a high degree of uncertainty concerning their future benefits. They include patents, copyrights, franchises, goodwill, trademarks, trade names, secret processes, and organization costs. Generally, all of these intangibles are written off (amortized) to expense over 5 to 40 years. Intangibles can represent significant economic resources, yet financial analysts often ignore them, and accountants write them down or off arbitrarily because valuation is difficult.

Unipack Corporation reported intangible assets in its balance sheet as follows:

Unipack Corporation	
Intangible assets	
Goodwill less $57,827 accumulated amortization	$145,617
Patents, licenses, and trademarks less $198,026 accumulated amortization	371,005
Software development costs less $46,280 accumulated amortization	120,214
Total intangibles	636,836

OTHER ASSETS

The items included in the section "Other Assets" vary widely in practice. Some of the items commonly included are deferred charges (long-term prepaid expenses), noncurrent receivables, intangible assets, assets in special funds, and advances to subsidiaries. Such a section unfortunately is too general a classification. Instead, it should be restricted to unusual items sufficiently different from assets included in specific categories. Some deferred costs such as organization costs incurred during the early life of the business are commonly classified here. Even these costs, however, are more properly placed in the intangible asset section.

CURRENT LIABILITIES

Current liabilities are the obligations that are reasonably expected to be liquidated either through the use of current assets or the creation of other current liabilities.

This concept includes:

1. Payables resulting from the acquisition of goods and services: accounts payable, wages payable, taxes payable, and so on.

2. Collections received in advance for the delivery of goods or performance of services such as unearned rent revenue or unearned subscriptions revenue.

3. Other liabilities whose liquidation will take place within the operating cycle such as the portion of long-term bonds to be paid in the current period, or short-term obligations arising from purchase of equipment.

At times, a liability payable next year is not included in the current liability section. This occurs either when the debt is expected to be refinanced through another long-term issue,[12] or when the debt is retired out of noncurrent assets. This approach is used because liquidation does not result from the use of current assets or the creation of other current liabilities.

Current liabilities are not reported in any consistent order. The items most commonly listed first are notes payable, accounts payable, or "short-term debt"; income taxes payable, current maturities of long-term debt, or "other current liabilities" are commonly listed last. An example of Dresser Industries' current liability section is shown on the following page.

---

[12]A detailed discussion of accounting for debt expected to be refinanced is found in Chapter 13 and in "Classification of Short-term Obligations Expected to Be Refinanced," *Statement of Financial Accounting Standards No. 6* (Stamford, Conn.: FASB, 1975).

Dresser Industries, Inc.	
Current liabilities	
Short-term debt	$ 22,500,000
Accounts payable—public	240,400,000
Accounts payable to unconsolidated affiliates	18,200,000
Advances from customers on contracts	161,100,000
Accrued compensation and benefits	169,400,000
Accrued warranty costs	34,100,000
Accrued taxes other than income taxes	21,900,000
Accrued interest	28,300,000
Other accrued liabilities	151,000,000
Income taxes payable	112,200,000
Current portion of long-term debt	12,400,000
Total current liabilities	971,500,000

Current liabilities include such items as trade and nontrade notes and accounts payable, advances received from customers, and current maturities of long-term debt. Income taxes and other accrued items are classified separately, if material. Any secured liability—for example, stock held as collateral on notes payable—is fully described in the notes so that the assets providing the security can be identified.

The excess of total current assets over total current liabilities is referred to as **working capital** (sometimes called net working capital). Working capital represents the net amount of a company's relatively liquid resources. That is, it is the liquid buffer available to meet the financial demands of the operating cycle. Working capital as an amount is seldom disclosed on the balance sheet, but it is computed by bankers and other creditors as an indicator of the short-run liquidity of a company. In order to determine the actual liquidity and availability of working capital to meet current obligations, however, one must analyze the composition of the current assets and their nearness to cash.[13]

LONG-TERM LIABILITIES

Long-term liabilities are obligations that are not reasonably expected to be liquidated within the normal operating cycle but, instead, are payable at some date beyond that time. Bonds payable, notes payable, deferred income taxes, lease obligations, and pension obligations are the most common examples. Generally, a great deal of supplementary disclosure is needed for this section, because most long-term debt is subject to various covenants and restrictions for the protection of lenders. Long-term liabilities that mature within the current operating cycle are classified as current liabilities if their liquidation requires the use of current assets.

Generally, long-term liabilities are of three types:

1. Obligations arising from specific financing situations, such as the issuance of bonds, long-term lease obligations, and long-term notes payable.

2. Obligations arising from the ordinary operations of the enterprise, such as pension obligations and deferred income tax liabilities.

3. Obligations that are dependent upon the occurrence or nonoccurrence of one or more future events to confirm the amount payable, or the payee, or the date payable, such as service or product warranties and other contingencies.

---

[13]The FASB in a discussion memorandum has suggested alternative classifications of assets that might help financial statement users assess the nature, amounts, and liquidity of available resources. See ''Reporting Funds Flows, Liquidity, and Financial Flexibility,'' *FASB Discussion Memorandum* (Stamford, Conn.: FASB, 1980), Chapters 8 and 9.

It is desirable to report any premium or discount separately as an addition to or subtraction from the bonds payable. The terms of all long-term liability agreements (including maturity date or dates, rates of interest, nature of obligation, and any security pledged to support the debt) are frequently described in notes to the financial statements. An example of the financial statement and accompanying note presentation is shown below in the excerpt from The Great Atlantic & Pacific Tea Company's financials.

The Great Atlantic & Pacific Tea Company, Inc.	
Total current liabilities	$978,109,000
Long-term debt (See note)	254,312,000
Obligations under capital leases	252,618,000
Deferred income taxes	57,167,000
Other non-current liabilities	127,321,000
Note: Indebtedness. Debt consists of:	
9.5% Senior notes, due in annual installments of $10,000,000	$ 40,000,000
Mortgages and other notes due through 2011 (average interest rate of 9.9%)	107,604,000
Bank borrowings at 9.7%	67,225,000
Commercial paper at 9.4%	100,102,000
	314,931,000
Less current portion	(60,619,000)
Total long-term debt	$254,312,000

OWNERS' EQUITY

The **owners' equity** (stockholders' equity) section is one of the most difficult sections to prepare and understand. This is due to the complexity of capital stock agreements and the various restrictions on residual equity imposed by state corporation laws, liability agreements, and boards of directors. The section is usually divided into three parts:

◀ STOCKHOLDERS' EQUITY SECTION ▶

1. **CAPITAL STOCK.** The par or stated value of the shares issued.
2. **ADDITIONAL PAID-IN CAPITAL.** The excess of amounts paid in over the par or stated value.
3. **RETAINED EARNINGS.** The corporation's undistributed earnings.

The major disclosure requirements for capital stock are the authorized, issued, and outstanding par value amounts. In addition, any capital stock reacquired (treasury stock) is shown as a reduction of stockholders' equity. The additional paid-in capital is usually presented in one amount, although subtotals are informative if the sources of additional capital are varied and material. The retained earnings section may be divided between the unappropriated (the amount that is usually available for dividend distribution) and any amounts that are restricted (e.g., by bond indentures or other loan agreements).

The ownership or stockholders' equity accounts in a corporation are considerably different from those in a partnership or proprietorship. Partners' permanent capital accounts and the balance in their temporary accounts (drawing accounts) are shown separately. Proprietorships ordinarily use a single capital account that handles all of the owners' equity transactions.

Presented on the following page is an example of the stockholders' equity section from Quanex Corporation.

Quanex Corporation	
	($000)
Stockholders' equity (Note 12):	
Preferred stock, no par value, 1,000,000 shares authorized; 345,000 in 1992 and none in 1991 issued and outstanding	$ 86,250
Common stock, $.50 par value, 25,000,000 shares authorized; 13,638,005 shares in 1992 and 11,735,166 shares in 1991 issued and outstanding	6,819
Additional paid-in capital	87,260
Retained earnings	57,263
	$237,592

▶ CLASSIFIED BALANCE SHEET FORM

One common arrangement followed in the presentation of a classified balance sheet is called the **account form.** It lists assets by sections on the left side and liabilities and stockholders' equity by sections on the right side. The main disadvantage is the need for two facing pages. To avoid the use of facing pages, the **report form,** shown in Illustration 5-2, lists liabilities and stockholders' equity directly below assets on the same page.[14] (Also see Georgia-Pacific's balance sheet on page 221 for the report form.)

Other balance sheet presentations are used infrequently. For example, current liabilities are sometimes deducted from current assets to arrive at working capital, or all liabilities are deducted from all assets. Caterpillar, for instance, is one of the few large companies to prepare its balance sheet in this latter unorthodox format, referred to as the **financial position form.**

OBJECTIVE 3

Prepare a classified balance sheet using the report and account forms.

▶ ADDITIONAL INFORMATION REPORTED

The balance sheet is not complete simply because the assets, liabilities, and owners' equity accounts have been listed. Great importance is given to supplemental information. It may be information not presented elsewhere in the statement, or it may be an elaboration or qualification of items in the balance sheet. There are normally four types of information that are supplemental to account titles and amounts presented in the balance sheet:

UNDERLYING CONCEPT

The basis for inclusion of additional information should meet the full disclosure principle; that is, the information should be of sufficient importance to influence the judgment of an informed user.

◀ SUPPLEMENTAL BALANCE SHEET INFORMATION ▶

1. **CONTINGENCIES.** Material events that have an uncertain outcome.
2. **VALUATIONS AND ACCOUNTING POLICIES.** Explanations of the valuation methods used or the basic assumptions made concerning inventory valuations, depreciation methods, investments in subsidiaries, etc.
3. **CONTRACTUAL SITUATIONS.** Explanations of certain restrictions or covenants attached to specific assets or, more likely, to liabilities.
4. **POST-BALANCE SHEET DISCLOSURES.** Disclosures of certain events that have occurred after the balance sheet date but before the financial statements have been issued.

OBJECTIVE 4

Identify balance sheet information requiring supplemental disclosure.

---

[14]*Accounting Trends and Techniques—1993* indicates that practically all of the 600 companies surveyed use either the "report form" (421) or the "account form" (178), sometimes collectively referred to as the "customary form."

ILLUSTRATION 5-2
Classified Report Form
Balance Sheet

Scientific Products, Inc.
BALANCE SHEET
December 31, 1994

Assets

Current assets		
Cash		$ 42,485
Available-for-sale securities—at fair value		28,250
Accounts receivable	$165,824	
Less allowance for doubtful accounts	1,850	163,974
Notes receivable		23,000
Inventories—at average cost		489,713
Supplies on hand		9,780
Prepaid expenses		16,252
Total current assets		$ 773,454
Long-term investments		
Investments in Warren Co.		87,500
Property, plant, and equipment		
Land—at cost		125,000
Buildings—at cost	975,800	
Less accumulated depreciation	341,200	634,600
Total property, plant, and equipment		759,600
Intangible assets		
Goodwill		100,000
Total assets		$1,720,554

Liabilities and Stockholders' Equity

Current liabilities		
Notes payable to banks		$ 50,000
Accounts payable		197,532
Accrued interest on notes payable		500
Income taxes payable		62,520
Accrued salaries, wages, and other liabilities		9,500
Deposits received from customers		420
Total current liabilities		$ 320,472
Long-term debt		
Twenty-year 12% debentures, due January 1, 2004		500,000
Total liabilities		820,472
Stockholders' equity		
Paid in on capital stock		
Preferred, 7%, cumulative		
Authorized, issued, and outstanding,		
30,000 shares of $10 par value	$300,000	
Common—		
Authorized, 500,000 shares of $1.00 par value;		
issued and outstanding, 400,000 shares	400,000	
Additional paid-in capital	37,500	737,500
Earnings retained in the business		162,582
Total stockholders' equity		900,082
Total liabilities and stockholders' equity		$1,720,554

CONTINGENCIES

Gain Contingencies

Gain contingencies are claims or rights to receive assets (or have a liability reduced) whose existence is uncertain but which may become valid eventually.

The typical gain contingencies are:

1. Possible receipts of monies from gifts, donations, bonuses, and so on.
2. Possible refunds from the government in tax disputes.
3. Pending court cases where the probable outcome is favorable.

Accountants have adopted a conservative policy in this area. Gain contingencies are not recorded. They are disclosed in the notes only when the probabilities are high that a gain contingency will become reality. As a result, it is unusual to find information about contingent gains in the financial statements and the accompanying notes.

Loss Contingencies

FASB Statement No. 5 requires that an estimated loss from a **loss contingency** be accrued by a charge to expense and the recording of a liability or a contra asset if both of the following conditions are met:

1. Information available prior to issuance of the financial statements indicates that it is **probable** that an asset had been impaired or that a liability had been incurred at the date of the financial statements.
2. The amount of loss can be **reasonably estimated.**[15]

A liability for service or product warranties would ordinarily meet these two conditions and thus qualify as a loss contingency that should be accrued.

In most loss contingency cases, however, one or both of the conditions are not present. For example, assume that a company is involved in a lawsuit. The company's lawyer indicates that there is a reasonable possibility that they may lose. In such a case, there is only a **reasonable possibility** of loss rather than a **probable** one. Therefore, a liability and the related loss should not be recorded. However, the nature of the contingency and, where possible, the amount involved, should be disclosed in the notes. If a reasonable estimate of the amount is not possible, disclosure is made in general terms, describing the loss contingency and explaining that no estimated amount is determinable. Because these types of contingencies are only possibilities, they should not enter into the determination of net income.

Diversity in practice exists in accounting for contingencies because varied interpretations are made of the words "probable" and "reasonably possible." As a result, the contingencies reported and disclosed vary somewhat. This area of practice requires that the accountant use professional judgment, because what constitutes full and proper accounting and disclosure is subjective.

Some of the more common sources of **loss contingencies that ordinarily will not be accrued as liabilities, but are disclosed in the notes,** are:

1. Guarantees of indebtedness of others.
2. Obligations of commercial banks under "stand-by letters of credit" (commitments to finance projects under certain circumstances).
3. Guarantees to repurchase receivables (or any related property) that have been sold or assigned.
4. Disputes over additional income taxes for prior years.
5. Pending lawsuits whose outcome is uncertain.

General risk contingencies that are inherent in business operations, such as the possibility of war, strike, uninsurable catastrophes, or a business recession, are not reported

UNDERLYING CONCEPT

Recording loss contingencies but not gain contingencies is an example of conservatism.

---

[15]"Accounting for Contingencies," *Statement of Financial Accounting Standards No. 5* (Stamford, Conn.: FASB, 1975), par. 8.

in the notes to the financial statements. The disclosure of loss contingencies is discussed in greater detail in Chapter 13.

VALUATIONS AND ACCOUNTING POLICIES

As subsequent chapters of this textbook indicate, accountants employ many different methods and bases in valuing assets and allocating costs. For instance, inventories can be computed under several cost flow assumptions (such as LIFO and FIFO); plant and equipment can be depreciated under several accepted methods of cost allocation (such as double-declining balance and straight-line); and investments can be carried at different valuations (such as cost, equity, and fair value). Sophisticated users of financial statements know of these possibilities and examine the statements closely to determine the methods used.

APB Opinion No. 22 recommends disclosure for all significant accounting principles and methods that involve selection from among alternatives or those that are peculiar to a given industry.[16] Disclosure is particularly useful if given in a separate **Summary of Significant Accounting Policies** preceding the notes to the financial statement or as the initial note. See the specimen financial statements in Appendix 5-A following this chapter for an example of such a summary (Note 1, pages 222–224) and further discussion of this topic in Chapter 26.

CONTRACTS AND NEGOTIATIONS

In addition to contingencies and different methods of valuation, any contracts and negotiations of significance should be disclosed in the notes to the financial statements. It is mandatory, for example, that the essential provisions of lease contracts, pension obligations, and stock option plans be clearly stated in the notes. The analyst who examines a set of financial statements wants to know not only the amount of the liabilities, but also how the different contractual provisions affect the company at present and in the future.

Many other items may have a significant effect on the enterprise, and this information should be disclosed. The accountant must exercise considerable judgment about whether omission of such information is misleading. The axiom is "When in doubt, disclose." It is better to disclose a little too much information than not enough.

The accountant's judgment should reflect ethical considerations, because the manner of disclosing the accounting principles, methods, and other items that have important effects on the enterprise may subtly represent the interests of a particular stakeholder (at the expense of others). A reader, for example, may benefit by the highlighting of information in comprehensive notes, whereas the company—not wishing to emphasize certain information—may choose to provide limited (rather than comprehensive) note information.

POST-BALANCE SHEET EVENTS (SUBSEQUENT EVENTS)

Notes to the financial statements should explain any significant financial events that took place after the formal balance sheet date, but before it is finally issued. These events are referred to as post-balance sheet events, events subsequent to the balance sheet date, or just plain **subsequent events.** The subsequent events period is time-diagrammed as shown in Illustration 5-3.

---

[16]"Disclosure of Accounting Policies," *Opinions of the Accounting Principles Board No. 22* (New York: AICPA, 1972).

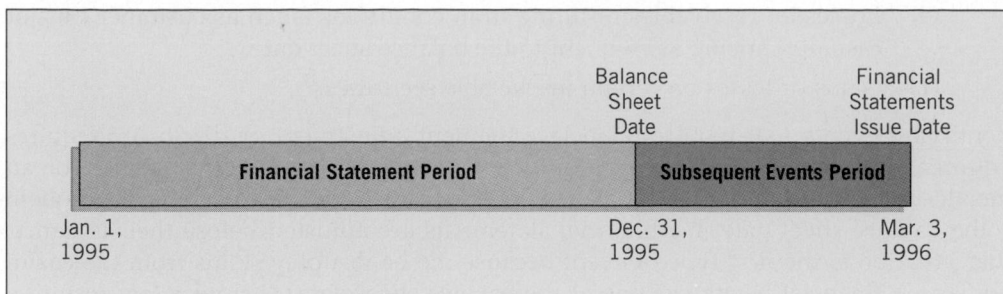

ILLUSTRATION 5-3
Time Periods for
Subsequent Events

A period of several weeks, and sometimes months, may elapse after the end of the year before the financial statements are issued. Taking and pricing the inventory, reconciling subsidiary ledgers with controlling accounts, preparing necessary adjusting entries, assuring that all transactions for the period have been entered, obtaining an audit of the financial statements by independent certified public accountants, and printing the annual report all take time. During the period between the balance sheet date and its distribution to stockholders and creditors, important transactions or other events may occur that materially affect the company's financial position or operating situation.

Many who read a recent balance sheet believe the balance sheet condition is constant and project it into the future. However, readers must be told if the company has sold one of its plants, acquired a subsidiary, suffered extraordinary losses, settled significant litigation, or experienced any other important event in the post-balance sheet period. Without an explanation in a note, the reader might be misled and draw inappropriate conclusions.

UNDERLYING CONCEPT

The periodicity or time period assumption implies that economic activities of an enterprise can be divided into artificial time periods for purpose of analysis.

Two types of events or transactions occurring after the balance sheet date may have a material effect on the financial statements or may need to be considered to interpret these statements accurately:

1. **Events that provide additional evidence about conditions that existed at the balance sheet date, affect the estimates used in preparing financial statements, and, therefore, result in needed adjustments:** The accountant must use all information available prior to the issuance of the financial statements to evaluate estimates previously made. To ignore these subsequent events is to pass up an opportunity to improve the accuracy of the financial statements. This first type encompasses information that would have been recorded in the accounts had it been available at the balance sheet date: for example, subsequent events that affect the realization of assets such as receivables and inventories or the settlement of estimated liabilities. Such events typically represent the culmination of conditions that existed for some time.

2. **Events that provide evidence about conditions that did not exist at the balance sheet date but arise subsequent to that date and do not require adjustment of the financial statements:** Some of these events may have to be disclosed to keep the financial statements from being misleading. These disclosures take the form of notes, supplemental schedules, or even pro forma "as if" financial data prepared as if the event had occurred on the balance sheet date. Below are examples of such events that require disclosure (but do not result in adjustment):

   (a) Sale of bonds or capital stock; stock splits or stock dividends.

   (b) Business combination pending or effected.

   (c) Settlement of litigation when the event giving rise to the claim took place subsequent to the balance sheet date.

   (d) Loss of plant or inventories from fire or flood.

    (e) Losses on receivables resulting from conditions (such as customer's major casualty) arising subsequent to the balance sheet date.

    (f) Gains or losses on certain marketable securities.[17]

Identifying events that require financial statement adjustment or disclosure requires judgment and knowledge of the facts and circumstances.[18] For example, if a loss on an uncollectible trade account receivable results from a customer's bankruptcy subsequent to the balance sheet date, the financial statements are adjusted before their issuance. This situation is the first type of event because the bankruptcy stems from the customer's poor financial health existing at the balance sheet date. A similar loss resulting from a customer's fire or flood after the balance sheet date is not indicative of conditions existing at that date. Thus, adjustment of the financial statements is not necessary.

The same criterion applies to settlements of litigation. The financial statements must be adjusted if the events that gave rise to the litigation, such as personal injury or patent infringement, took place prior to the balance sheet date. If the event giving rise to the claim took place subsequent to the balance sheet date, no adjustment is necessary but disclosure is. Subsequent events such as changes in the quoted market prices of securities ordinarily do not result in adjustment of the financial statements because such changes typically reflect an evaluation of new conditions.

An example of subsequent events disclosure, excerpted from Chrysler's Annual Report, is presented below.

Chrysler Corporation

Note 21: Subsequent Events. On February 10, 1993, the Company completed a public offering of 52 million shares of newly issued common stock for proceeds of approximately $1.95 billion, net of expenses. Chrysler plans to contribute approximately $1.1 billion of the net proceeds to its pension fund.

On February 1, 1993, the final stage of the sale of substantially all of the net assets of the consumer and inventory financing businesses of Chrysler First was completed for aggregate cash proceeds of $2.2 billion. On February 1, 1993, CFC also sold certain assets of its commercial leasing and lending subsidiary, Chrysler Capital Corporation, for $116 million. Proceeds from these sales approximated the net carrying value of the assets sold, and were used to reduce CFC's outstanding indebtedness.

As of February 3, 1993, the scheduled reductions of $1.35 billion under CFC's New Bank Facility and $855 million under CFC's U.S. receivable sale agreement were accomplished.

Many subsequent events or developments are not likely to require either adjustment of or disclosure in the financial statements. Typically, these are nonaccounting events or conditions that managements normally communicate by other means. These events include legislation, product changes, management changes, strikes, unionization, marketing agreements, and loss of important customers.

▶ TECHNIQUES OF DISCLOSURE

OBJECTIVE 5

Identify major disclosure techniques for the balance sheet.

The effect of various contingencies on financial condition, the methods of valuing assets, and the companies' contracts and agreements should be disclosed as completely and as intelligently as possible. These methods of disclosing pertinent information are available: parenthetical explanations, notes, cross reference and contra items, and supporting schedules. Appendix 5-A contains specimen financial statements that illustrate these methods.

---

[17]"Subsequent Events," *Statement on Auditing Standards No. 1* (New York: AICPA, 1973), pp. 123–124.

[18]*Accounting Trends and Techniques—1993* listed the following types of subsequent events and their frequency of occurrence among the 600 companies surveyed: debt incurred, reduced, or refinanced, 85; business combinations pending or effected, 56; discontinued operations, 36; litigation, 31; capital stock issued or repurchased, 14; employee benefit plans, 16; stock splits, 8.

PARENTHETICAL EXPLANATIONS

Additional information is often provided by parenthetical explanations following the item. For example, investments in available-for-sale securities are shown on the balance sheet under Investments as follows:

Investments in Available-for-Sale Securities (cost, $330,586)—at fair value	$401,500

This device permits disclosure of additional pertinent balance sheet information that adds clarity and completeness. It has an advantage over a note because it brings the additional information into the body of the statement where it is less likely to be overlooked. Of course, lengthy parenthetical explanations that might distract the reader from the balance sheet information must be used with care.

UNDERLYING CONCEPT

The user-specific quality of understandability requires accountants to be careful in describing transactions and events.

NOTES

Notes are used if additional explanations cannot be shown conveniently as parenthetical explanations. For example, inventory costing methods are reported in The Quaker Oats Company accompanying notes as follows:

The Quaker Oats Company

Inventories (Note 1)

Finished goods	$326,000,000
Grain and raw materials	114,100,000
Packaging materials and supplies	39,000,000
Total inventories	479,100,000

Note 1: Inventories. Inventories are valued at the lower of cost or market, using various cost methods, and include the cost of raw materials, labor, and overhead. The percentage of year-end inventories valued using each of the methods is as follows:

Average quarterly cost	21%
Last-in, first-out (LIFO)	65%
First-in, first-out (FIFO)	14%

If the LIFO method of valuing certain inventories was not used, total inventories would have been $60,100,000 higher than reported.

Notes are commonly used to disclose the existence and amount of any preferred stock dividends in arrears, the terms of or obligations imposed by purchase commitments, special financial arrangements and instruments, depreciation policies, any changes in the application of accounting principles, and the existence of contingencies. The following notes illustrate a common method of presenting such information:

Consolidated Papers, Inc.

Note 7: Commitments. As of December 31, 1992, the company had capital expenditure purchase commitments outstanding of approximately $17 million.

Alberto-Culver Company

Note 3: Long-Term Debt. Various borrowing arrangements impose restrictions on such items as total debt, working capital, dividend payments, treasury stock purchases and interest expense. At September 30, 1992, the company was in compliance with these arrangements and $68 million of consolidated retained earnings was not restricted as to the payment of dividends and purchases of treasury stock.

Ampco-Pittsburgh Corporation

Note 11: Change in Accounting Estimate. Effective January 1, 1992, the Corporation revised its estimate of the useful lives of certain machinery and equipment. Previously, all machinery and equipment, whether new when placed in use or not, were in one class and depreciated over 15 years. The change principally applies to assets purchased new when placed in use. Those lives are now extended to 20 years. These changes were made to better reflect the estimated periods during which such assets will remain in service. The change had the effect of reducing depreciation expense and increasing net income by approximately $991,000 ($.10 per share).

The notes must present all essential facts as completely and succinctly as possible. Careless wording may mislead rather than aid readers. Notes should add to the total information made available in the financial statements, not raise unanswered questions or contradict other portions of the statements.

CROSS REFERENCE AND CONTRA ITEMS

A direct relationship between an asset and a liability is "cross referenced" on the balance sheet. For example, on December 31, 1995, among the current assets this might be shown:

Cash on deposit with sinking fund trustee for redemption of bonds payable—see current liabilities	$800,000

Included among the current liabilities is the amount of bonds payable to be redeemed within one year:

Bonds payable to be redeemed in 1996—see current assets	$2,300,000

This cross reference points out that $2,300,000 of bonds payable are to be redeemed currently, for which only $800,000 in cash has been set aside. Therefore, the additional cash needed must come from unrestricted cash, from sales of investments, from profits, or from some other source. The same information can be shown parenthetically, if this technique is preferred.

Another common procedure is to establish contra or adjunct accounts. A **contra account** on a balance sheet is an item that reduces either an asset, liability, or owners' equity account. Examples include Accumulated Depreciation and Discount on Bonds Payable. Contra accounts provide some flexibility in presenting the financial information. With the use of the Accumulated Depreciation account, for example, a reader of the statement can see the original cost of the asset as well as the depreciation to date.

An **adjunct account,** on the other hand, increases either an asset, liability, or owners' equity account. An example is Premium on Bonds Payable, which, when added to the Bonds Payable account, describes the total liability of the enterprise.

SUPPORTING SCHEDULES

Often a separate schedule is needed to present more detailed information about certain assets or liabilities, because the balance sheet provides just a single summary item.

Property, plant, and equipment	
Land, buildings, equipment, and other fixed assets—net (see Schedule 3)	$643,300

A separate schedule then might be presented as follows:

	Total	Land	Buildings	Equip.	Other Fixed Assets
Schedule 3					
LAND, BUILDINGS, EQUIPMENT, AND OTHER FIXED ASSETS					
Balance January 1, 1996	$740,000	$46,000	$358,000	$260,000	$76,000
Additions in 1996	161,200		120,000	38,000	3,200
	901,200	46,000	478,000	298,000	79,200
Assets retired or sold in 1996	31,700			27,000	4,700
Balance December 31, 1996	869,500	46,000	478,000	271,000	74,500
Depreciation taken to January 1, 1996	196,000		102,000	78,000	16,000
Depreciation taken in 1996	56,000		28,000	24,000	4,000
	252,000		130,000	102,000	20,000
Depreciation on assets retired in 1996	25,800			22,000	3,800
Depreciation accumulated December 31, 1996	226,200		130,000	80,000	16,200
Book value of assets	$643,300	$46,000	$348,000	$191,000	$58,300

► TERMINOLOGY

The account titles in the general ledger do not necessarily represent the best terminology for balance sheet purposes. Account titles are often brief and include technical terms that are understood only by those keeping the records and by other accountants. But balance sheets are examined by many persons who are not acquainted with the technical vocabulary of accounting. Thus, they should contain descriptions that will be generally understood and not be subject to misinterpretation.

The profession has recommended that the word **reserve** be used only to describe an appropriation of retained earnings. This term had been used in several ways: to describe amounts deducted from assets (contra accounts such as accumulated depreciation and allowance for doubtful accounts), and as a part of the title of contingent or estimated liabilities. Because of the different meanings attached to this term, misinterpretation often resulted from its use. The use of "reserve" only to describe appropriated retained earnings has resulted in a better understanding of its significance when it appears in a balance sheet. However, the term "appropriated" appears more logical, and its use should be encouraged.

For years the profession has recommended that the use of the word **surplus** be discontinued in balance sheet presentations of owners' equity. The use of the terms capital surplus, paid-in surplus, and earned surplus is confusing to nonaccountants. Although condemned by the profession, these terms appear all too frequently in current financial statements.

INTERNATIONAL INSIGHT

Internationally, accounting terminology is problematic. Confusing differences arise even between nations that share a language. For example, American investors normally think of "stock" as "equity" or "ownership," but the British refer to inventory as "stocks." In the U.S. "fixed assets" generally refers to "property, plant, and equipment," while in Britain the category includes more items.

► SECTION 2 / STATEMENT OF CASH FLOWS

In Chapter 2, "assessing the amounts, timing, and uncertainty of cash flows" was presented as one of the three basic objectives of financial reporting. The balance sheet, the income statement, and the statement of retained earnings each present, to a limited extent and in a fragmented manner, information about the cash flows of an enterprise

UNDERLYING
CONCEPT

The statement of cash flows meets one of the objectives of financial reporting—to help assess the amounts, timing, and uncertainty of future cash flows.

during a period. For instance, comparative balance sheets might show what new assets have been acquired or disposed of and what liabilities have been incurred or liquidated. The income statement provides information about resources, but not exactly cash, provided by operations. The statement of retained earnings shows the amount of cash used to pay dividends. But none of these statements presents a detailed summary of all the cash inflows and outflows, or the sources and uses of cash during the period. To fill this need, the FASB requires the **statement of cash flows.**[19]

OBJECTIVE 6

Indicate the purpose of the statement of cash flows.

► PURPOSE OF THE STATEMENT OF CASH FLOWS

The primary purpose of a statement of cash flows is to provide relevant information about the cash receipts and cash payments of an enterprise during a period. To achieve this purpose, the statement of cash flows reports (1) the cash effects of operations during a period, (2) investing transactions, (3) financing transactions, and (4) the net increase or decrease in cash during the period.[20]

Reporting the sources, uses, and net increase or decrease in cash helps investors, creditors, and others know what is happening to a company's most liquid resource. Because most individuals maintain their checkbook and prepare their tax return on a cash basis, they can relate to the statement of cash flows and comprehend the causes and effects of cash inflows and outflows and the net increase or decrease in cash. The statement of cash flows provides answers to the following simple but important questions:

1. Where did the cash come from during the period?
2. What was the cash used for during the period?
3. What was the change in the cash balance during the period?

► CONTENT AND FORMAT OF THE STATEMENT OF CASH FLOWS

OBJECTIVE 7

Identify the content of the statement of cash flows.

Cash receipts and cash payments during a period are classified in the statement of cash flows into three different activities—operating, investing, and financing activities. These classifications are defined as follows:

1. **Operating activities** involve the cash effects of transactions that enter into the determination of net income.
2. **Investing activities** include making and collecting loans and acquiring and disposing of investments (both debt and equity) and property, plant, and equipment.
3. **Financing activities** involve liability and owners' equity items. They include (a) obtaining resources from owners and providing them with a return on (and a return of) their investment and (b) borrowing money from creditors and repaying the amounts borrowed.

With cash flows classified into those three categories, the statement of cash flows has assumed the following basic format:

ILLUSTRATION 5-4
Format of Cash Flow Statement

Cash flows from operating activities	$XXX
Cash flows from investing activities	XXX
Cash flows from financing activities	XXX
Net increase (decrease) in cash	XXX
Cash at beginning of year	XXX
Cash at end of year	$XXX

---

[19]"Statement of Cash Flows," *Statement of Financial Accounting Standards No. 95* (Stamford, Conn.: FASB, 1987).

[20]The basis recommended by the FASB is actually "cash and cash equivalents." Cash equivalents are short-term, highly liquid investments such as treasury bills, commercial paper, and money market funds purchased with cash that is in excess of immediate needs.

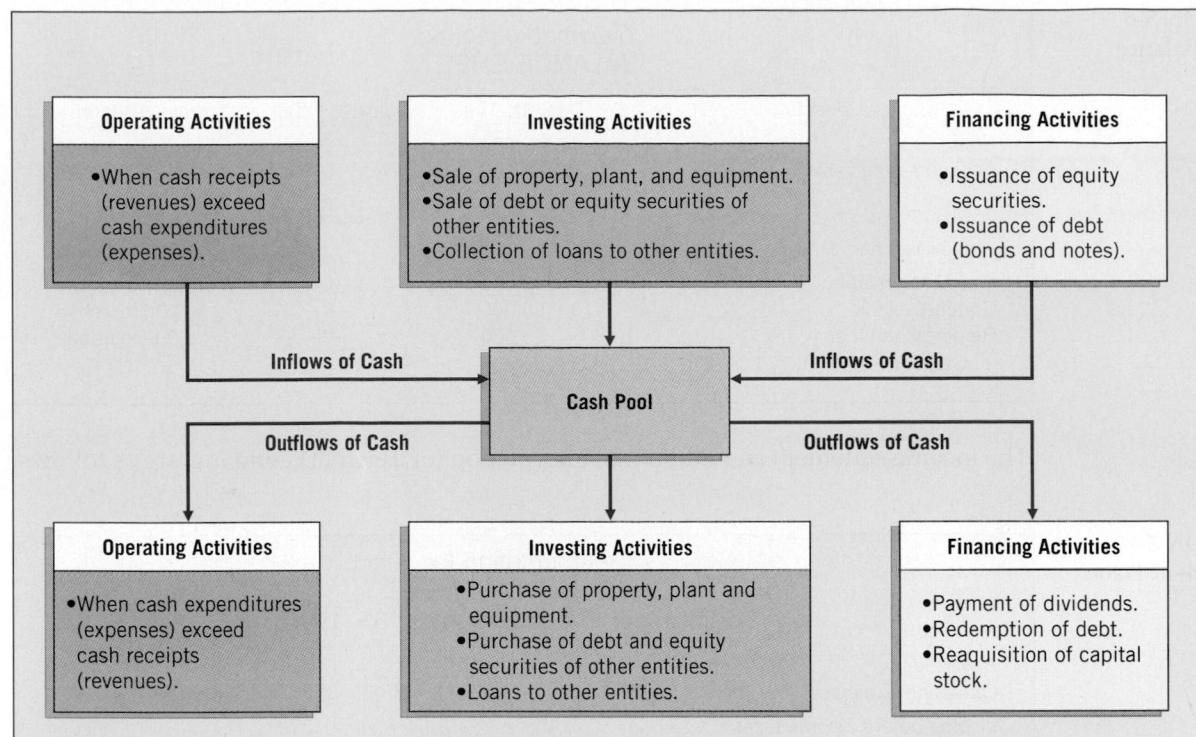

ILLUSTRATION 5-5
Cash Inflows and
Outflows

The inflows and outflows of cash classified by activity are shown in Illustration 5-5.

The statement's value is that it helps users evaluate liquidity, solvency, and financial flexibility. Liquidity refers to the "nearness to cash" of assets and liabilities. **Solvency** refers to the firm's ability to pay its debts as they mature. And **financial flexibility** refers to a firm's ability to respond and adapt to financial adversity and unexpected needs and opportunities.

We have devoted Chapter 24 entirely to the preparation and content of the statement of cash flows. Our comprehensive coverage of this topic has been deferred to that later chapter so that we can cover in the intervening chapters several elements and complex topics that make up the content of a typical statement of cash flows. The presentation in this chapter is introductory, a reminder of the existence of the statement of cash flows.

▶ PREPARATION OF THE STATEMENT OF CASH FLOWS

The information to prepare the statement of cash flows usually comes from (1) comparative balance sheets, (2) the current income statement, and (3) selected transaction data. Preparing the statement of cash flows from these sources involves the following steps:

1. Determine the cash provided by operations.
2. Determine the cash provided by or used in investing and financing activities.
3. Determine the change (increase or decrease) in cash during the period.
4. Reconcile the change in cash with the beginning and the ending cash balances.

The following simple illustration demonstrates how these steps are applied in the preparation of a statement of cash flows.

Telemarketing Inc. in its first year of operations issued on January 1, 1996, 50,000 shares of $1.00 par value common stock for $50,000 cash. The company rented its office space, furniture, and telecommunications equipment and performed surveys and marketing services throughout the first year. The comparative balance sheets at the beginning and end of the year 1996 are shown in Illustration 5-6:

OBJECTIVE 8
Prepare a statement of cash flows.

INTERNATIONAL INSIGHT

Statements of cash flows are not widely required. Some nations require a statement reporting sources and applications of "funds" (often defined as working capital); others have no requirement for either cash or funds flow statements.

**ILLUSTRATION 5-6
Comparative Balance
Sheets**

Telemarketing Inc. BALANCE SHEETS			
Assets	Dec. 31, 1996	Jan. 1, 1996	Increase/Decrease
Cash	$46,000	$ –0–	$46,000 Increase
Accounts receivable	41,000	–0–	41,000 Increase
Total	$87,000	$ –0–	
Liabilities and Stockholders' Equity			
Accounts payable	$12,000	$ –0–	12,000 Increase
Common stock	50,000	–0–	50,000 Increase
Retained earnings	25,000	–0–	25,000 Increase
Total	$87,000	$ –0–	

The income statement and additional information for Telemarketing Inc. are as follows:

**ILLUSTRATION 5-7
Income Statement Data**

Telemarketing Inc. INCOME STATEMENT For the Year Ended December 31, 1996	
Revenues	$172,000
Operating expenses	120,000
Income before income taxes	52,000
Income tax expense	13,000
Net income	$ 39,000
Additional information:	
Dividends of $14,000 were paid during the year.	

Cash provided by operations (the excess of cash receipts over cash payments) is determined by converting net income on an accrual basis to a cash basis. This is accomplished by adding to or deducting from net income those items in the income statement not affecting cash. This procedure requires an analysis not only of the current year's income statement but also of the comparative balance sheets and selected transaction data.

Analysis of Telemarketing's comparative balance sheets reveals two items that give rise to noncash credits or charges to the income statement: (1) the increase in accounts receivable reflects a noncash credit of $41,000 to revenues, and (2) the increase in accounts payable reflects a noncash charge of $12,000 to expenses. **To arrive at cash provided by operations, the increase in accounts receivable must be deducted from net income, and the increase in accounts payable must be added back to net income.**

As a result of the accounts receivable and accounts payable adjustments, cash provided by operations is determined to be $10,000, computed as follows:

**ILLUSTRATION 5-8
Computation of Net Cash
Provided by Operations**

Net income		$39,000
Adjustments to reconcile net income		
to net cash provided by operating activities		
Increase in accounts receivable	$(41,000)	
Increase in accounts payable	12,000	(29,000)
Net cash provided by operating activities		$10,000

The increase of $50,000 in common stock resulting from the issuance of 50,000 shares for cash, is classified as a financing activity. Likewise, the payment of $14,000 cash in dividends is a financing activity. Telemarketing Inc. did not engage in any investing activities during the year. The statement of cash flows for Telemarketing Inc. for 1996 is as follows:

ILLUSTRATION 5-9
Statement of Cash Flows

Telemarketing Inc.
STATEMENT OF CASH FLOWS
For the Year Ended December 31, 1996
Increase (Decrease) in Cash

Cash flows from operating activities		
Net income		$39,000
Adjustments to reconcile net income to		
net cash provided by operating activities:		
Increase in accounts receivable	$(41,000)	
Increase in accounts payable	12,000	(29,000)
Net cash provided by operating activities		10,000
Cash flows from financing activities		
Issuance of common stock	50,000	
Payment of cash dividends	(14,000)	
Net cash provided by financing activities		36,000
Net increase in cash		46,000
Cash at beginning of year		–0–
Cash at end of year		$46,000

The increase in cash of $46,000 reported in the statement of cash flows agrees with the increase of $46,000 in the Cash account calculated from the comparative balance sheets.

An illustration of a more comprehensive statement of cash flows is presented in Illustration 5-10.

ILLUSTRATION 5-10
**Comprehensive
Statement of Cash Flows**

Illustration Company
STATEMENT OF CASH FLOWS
For the Year Ended December 31, 1996
Increase (Decrease) in Cash

Cash flows from operating activities		
Net income		$320,750
Adjustments to reconcile net income to net		
cash provided by operating activities:		
Depreciation expense	$88,400	
Amortization of intangibles	16,300	
Gain on sale of plant assets	(8,700)	
Increase in accounts receivable (net)	(11,000)	
Decrease in inventory	15,500	
Decrease in accounts payable	(9,500)	91,000
Net cash provided by operating activities		411,750
Cash flows from investing activities		
Sale of plant assets	90,500	
Purchase of equipment	(182,500)	
Purchase of land	(70,000)	
Net cash used by investing activities		(162,000)
Cash flows from financing activities		
Payment of cash dividend	(19,800)	
Issuance of common stock	100,000	
Redemption of bonds	(50,000)	
Net cash provided by financing activities		30,200
Net increase in cash		279,950
Cash at beginning of year		135,000
Cash at end of year		$414,950

▶ **INTERNATIONAL PERSPECTIVE**

In this chapter, the principles and procedures used to prepare a balance sheet and a statement of cash flows are presented. The accounting principles and procedures used to prepare these financial statements are conservative, in that historical cost information is generally reported. Reliability therefore plays a key role in the type of information presented.

As indicated earlier, other countries may emphasize different approaches to presenting financial information. Illustration 5-11 is an adaptation of the balance sheet for Guiness PLC, a British company. Although many similarities exist between U.S. and British accounting, there are also many differences. First, format differences exist: In Great Britain, fixed or long-term assets are reported first on the balance sheet; assets and liabilities are netted and grouped into net current and net total assets; and within classifications such as current assets, the most liquid assets are reported last.

Second, GAAP differences exist: In Great Britain, goodwill is reported as a deduction from stockholders' equity; brands are reported as an intangible asset and may be reported at fair value; and land and buildings may be reported at fair value.

ILLUSTRATION 5-11
Balance Sheet—British
Corporation

Format differences:
1. Fixed assets reported first
2. Assets and liabilities netted
3. Liquid assets shown last

GAAP differences:
1. Brands, land, and buildings may be reported at fair value
2. Goodwill deducted from equity

Terminology differences:
1. "Stocks" means inventory
2. "Share capital" means common stock
3. Reserves used

Guiness PLC GROUP BALANCE SHEET At 31 December 1991		
(in millions)	**Net Assets**	
Fixed assets		
Acquired brands at cost		£1,395
Tangible assets		1,721
Investments		1,232
		4,348
Current assets		
Stocks	£1,661	
Debtors	1,067	
Cash deposits	475	
	3,203	
Creditors (amounts falling due within one year)		
Short-term borrowings	(779)	
Other creditors	(1,271)	
	£2,050	
Net current assets		1,153
Total assets less current liabilities		5,501
Creditors (amounts falling due after more than one year)		
Long-term borrowings		(1,493)
Other creditors		(161)
Provisions for liabilities and charges		(223)
Total net assets		£3,624
Equity		
Capital and reserves		
Share capital		£ 547
Share premium		423
		970
Other reserves		3,789
Goodwill		(1,228)
Shareholders' equity		3,531
Minority interests		93
Total equity		£3,624

Great Britain provides much more flexibility in presenting balance sheet information. As indicated, companies are permitted to present fair value information for such items as land and buildings. No rules exist about when these revaluations may occur, but they often happen when the company wishes to enhance its balance sheet for borrowing purposes or for a possible merger.

As indicated in Chapter 1, one of the most contentious issues in international accounting is the reporting of goodwill. In Great Britain, by reporting goodwill as a contra account to stockholders' equity, goodwill expense is not reported on the income statement. As a result, if a British and a U.S. company are competing to purchase a company, some contend the British company has an unfair advantage because it will not have to report goodwill expense. The U.S. company, on the other hand, has to report goodwill as an asset and amortize it against revenues. As a result the U.S. company will have to report lower earnings than its British counterpart and therefore is more reluctant to become involved in merger discussions.

The British use essentially the same type of cash flow statement as the United States. Most countries, however, use a working capital approach rather than a cash approach to report changes in liquid resources during a period.

► A LOOK AT FUTURE FINANCIAL STATEMENTS

Chapters 4 and 5 indicated the type of financial information reported in the financial statements under generally accepted accounting principles. Although it is difficult to predict how financial statements will change in the future, the FASB's conceptual framework and the AICPA Special Committee on Financial Reporting provide insights into future directions.

As indicated in Chapter 2, the FASB in its conceptual framework has identified the objectives of financial reporting and the qualitative characteristics of information, provided definitions for the elements of financial statements, and developed general recognition and measurement guidelines. And as indicated in Chapter 1, the AICPA's Special Committee on Financial Reporting has identified the types of information users need and want in the future.

Regarding the income statement, attempts at further differentiation between usual and recurring activities (core activities) and unusual and nonrecurring activities (non-core activities) will likely occur. A company's core activities provide the best information for users to determine trends and relationships and make predictions about the future. A careful distinction must therefore be made between core and non-core activities to ensure that trends and relationships are not hidden. Users, for example, do not believe that the current system provides sufficient information about nonrecurring, unusual, and infrequent items to enable them to determine core earnings.

As a result, the general format of the income statement may not change, but further subdivisions within the statement may occur. For example, in Concepts Statement No. 5 the FASB noted that new concepts of income called "earnings" and "comprehensive income" might be used. Earnings would be similar to the net income number presently reported. Comprehensive income, however, would be an all-inclusive concept of income, under which all changes in net assets (except certain transactions with owners) are reported as part of income. The advantage of such an approach is that all changes in net assets (such as unrealized gains and losses on available-for-sale investment securities) would be shown on the income statement.

Regarding the balance sheet, the historical cost valuation model seems well accepted, particularly for core assets and liabilities. Non-core assets and liabilities may, however, be reported at fair value because users can better understand the additional financial resources the company has available to sustain its core activities.

Regarding the statement of cash flows, again separation into core and non-core activities may occur. Otherwise, major changes in this statement will probably not occur. Because the statement of cash flows is relatively new, the development and evolution

UNDERLYING CONCEPT

Some of these items may not be assets at all. We can only hope that, as the recommendations of the FASB's conceptual framework project are implemented, some of these unusual deferred costs will be critically examined.

of techniques of analysis and interpretation are needed before this statement will change in any significant way.

▶ SUMMARY OF LEARNING OBJECTIVES ◀

1. **Identify the uses and limitations of a balance sheet.** The balance sheet provides information about the nature and amounts of investments in enterprise resources, obligations to creditors, and the owners' equity in net resources. The balance sheet contributes to financial reporting by providing a basis for (1) computing rates of return, (2) evaluating the capital structure of the enterprise, and (3) assessing the liquidity and financial flexibility of the enterprise. The limitations of a balance sheet are: (1) The balance sheet does not reflect current value because accountants have adopted a historical cost basis in valuing and reporting assets and liabilities. (2) Judgments and estimates must be used in preparing a balance sheet. The collectibility of receivables, the salability of inventory, and the useful life of long-term tangible and intangible assets are difficult to determine. (3) The balance sheet omits many items that are of financial value to the business but cannot be recorded objectively, such as human resources, customer base, and reputation.

2. **Identify the major classifications of the balance sheet.** The general elements of the balance sheet are assets, liabilities, and equity. The major classifications within the balance sheet on the asset side are current assets; long-term investments; property, plant, and equipment; intangible assets; and other assets. The major classifications of liabilities are current and long-term liabilities. In a corporation, owners' equity is generally classified as capital stock, additional paid-in capital, and retained earnings.

3. **Prepare a classified balance sheet using the report and account forms.** The report form lists liabilities and stockholders' equity directly below assets on the same page. The account form lists assets by sections on the left side and liabilities and stockholders' equity by sections on the right side.

4. **Identify balance sheet information requiring supplemental disclosure.** Four types of information normally are supplemental to account titles and amounts presented in the balance sheet: (1) *Contingencies:* Material events that have an uncertain outcome. (2) *Valuations and accounting policies:* Explanations of the valuation methods used or the basic assumptions made concerning inventory valuation, depreciation methods, investments in subsidiaries, etc. (3) *Contractual situations:* Explanations of certain restrictions or covenants attached to specific assets or, more likely, to liabilities. (4) *Post-balance sheet disclosures:* Disclosures of certain events that have occurred after the balance sheet date but before the financial statements have been issued.

5. **Identify major disclosure techniques for the balance sheet.** There are four methods of disclosing pertinent information in the balance sheet: (1) *Parenthetical explanations:* Additional information or description is often provided by parenthetical explanations following the item. (2) *Notes:* Notes are used if additional explanations or descriptions cannot be shown conveniently as parenthetical explanations. (3) *Cross reference and contra items:* A direct relationship between an asset and a liability is "cross referenced" on the balance sheet. (4) *Supporting schedules:* Often a separate schedule is needed to present more detailed information about certain assets or liabilities, because the balance sheet provides just a single summary item.

6. **Indicate the purpose of the statement of cash flows.** The primary purpose of a statement of cash flows is to provide relevant information about the cash receipts and cash payments of an enterprise during a period. Reporting the sources, uses, and net increase or decrease in cash enables investors, creditors, and others to know what is happening to a company's most liquid resource.

7. **Identify the content of the statement of cash flows.** Cash receipts and cash payments during a period are classified in the statement of cash flows into three different activities: (1) *Operating activities*: Involve the cash effects of transactions that enter into the determination of net income. (2) *Investing activities*: Include making and collecting loans and acquiring and disposing of investments (both debt and equity) and property, plant, and equipment. (3) *Financing activities*: Involve liability and owners' equity items and include (a) obtaining capital from owners and providing them with a return on their investment and (b) borrowing money from creditors and repaying the amounts borrowed.

8. **Prepare a statement of cash flows.** The information to prepare the statement of cash flows usually comes from (1) comparative balance sheets, (2) the current income statement, and (3) selected transaction data. Preparing the statement of cash flows from these sources involves the following steps: (1) determine the cash provided by operations; (2) determine the cash provided by or used in investing and financing activities; (3) determine the change (increase or decrease) in cash during the period; and (4) reconcile the change in cash with the beginning and the ending cash balances.

SPECIMEN FINANCIAL STATEMENTS

To the Student:

The following 18 pages contain the financial statements and accompanying notes of the world's largest forest products company and one of the U.S.'s largest manufacturers of building products— **Georgia-Pacific Corporation.** Because of the size, worldwide scope, and diversity of its operations, Georgia-Pacific's accounting and reporting practices are affected by most of the accounting topics covered in this textbook and by nearly every facet of generally accepted accounting principles. Of all U. S. industrial companies (1993), Georgia-Pacific is the 64th largest in sales ($12.3 billion) and 190th in terms of assets ($10.5 billion). As the world's largest forest products company, Georgia-Pacific employs over 50,000 people at more than 400 facilities in 49 states; it owns or controls more than 6 million acres of timberland and operates plants that manufacture lumber, plywood, pulp, paper and paperboard, and a multitude of other building products.

We do not expect that you will comprehend Georgia-Pacific's financial statements and the accompanying notes in their entirety at your first reading. But we expect that by the time you complete the coverage of the material in this text, your level of understanding and interpretive ability will have grown enormously.

At this point we recommend that you take 20 to 30 minutes to scan the statements and notes to familiarize yourself with the contents and accounting elements. Throughout the following twenty-one chapters when you are asked to refer to specific parts of Georgia-Pacific's financials, do so! Then, when you have completed reading this book, we challenge you to reread Georgia-Pacific's financials to see how much greater and more sophisticated is your understanding of them.

GEORGIA-PACIFIC CORPORATION
1993 ANNUAL REPORT HIGHLIGHTS

Courtesy of Georgia-Pacific Corporation *(Dollar amounts, except per share, and shares are in millions)*	1993	1992	Increase (Decrease)
Net sales	$12,330	$11,847	4%
Loss before extraordinary item and cumulative effect of accounting change	(18)	(60)	(70)
Loss per share before extraordinary item and cumulative effect of accounting change	(.21)	(.69)	(70)
Cash provided by operations*	489	868	(44)
Cash dividends paid	142	140	1
Total assets at year end	10,545	10,912	(3)
Total debt at year end**	5,737	5,888	(3)
Total debt to capital at year end	57.0%	57.0%	
Cash dividends paid per share of common stock	$ 1.60	$ 1.60	—%
Shares of common stock outstanding at year end	90.3	88.1	2
Shareholders of record at year end	46,000	44,000	5
Employees at year end	50,000	52,000	(4)

*T*o the Shareholders and the
Board of Directors of
Georgia-Pacific Corporation:

We have audited the accompanying balance sheets of Georgia-Pacific Corporation (a Georgia corporation) and subsidiaries as of December 31, 1993 and 1992 and the related statements of income, shareholders' equity and cash flows for each of the three years in the period ended December 31, 1993. These financial statements are the responsibility of the Corporation's management. Our responsibility is to express an opinion on these financial statements based on our audits.

We conducted our audits in accordance with generally accepted auditing standards. Those standards require that we plan and perform the audit to obtain reasonable assurance about whether the financial statements are free of material misstatement. An audit includes examining, on a test basis, evidence supporting the amounts and disclosures in the financial statements. An audit also includes assessing the accounting principles used and significant estimates made by management, as well as evaluating the overall finan-cial statement presentation. We believe that our audits provide a reasonable basis for our opinion.

In our opinion, the financial statements referred to above present fairly, in all material respects, the financial position of Georgia-Pacific Corporation and subsidiaries as of December 31, 1993 and 1992 and the results of their operations and their cash flows for each of the three years in the period ended December 31, 1993 in conformity with generally accepted accounting principles.

As explained in Note 6 to the financial statements, effective January 1, 1992, the Corporation changed its method of accounting for income taxes. Also as explained in Notes 1 and 7 to the financial statements, effective January 1, 1991, the Corporation changed its methods of accounting for certain manufacturing supplies and for postretirement health care and life insurance benefits.

Arthur Andersen & Co.

Atlanta, Georgia
February 18, 1994

Management of Georgia-Pacific Corporation is responsible for the preparation, integrity and fair presentation of the consolidated financial statements and the estimates and judgments upon which certain amounts in the financial statements are based. Management is also responsible for preparing the other financial information included in this annual report. In our opinion, the financial statements on the preceding pages have been prepared in conformity with generally accepted accounting principles, and the other financial information in this annual report is consistent with the financial statements.

Management is also responsible for establishing and maintaining a system of internal control over financial reporting, which encompasses policies, procedures and controls directly related to, and designed to provide reasonable assurance as to, the reliability of the published financial statements. An independent evaluation of the system is performed by the Corporation's internal audit staff in order to confirm that the system is adequate and operating effectively. The Corporation's independent public accountants also consider certain elements of the internal control system in order to determine their auditing procedures for the purpose of expressing an opinion on the financial statements. Management has considered any significant recommendations regarding the internal control system which have been brought to its attention by the internal audit staff or independent public accountants and has taken the steps it deems appropriate to maintain a cost-effective internal control system. The Audit Committee of the Board of Directors, consisting of five independent directors, provides oversight to the financial reporting process. The Corporation's internal auditors and independent public accountants meet regularly with the Audit Committee to discuss financial reporting and internal control issues and have full and free access to the Audit Committee.

There are inherent limitations in the effectiveness of any system of internal control, including the possibility of human error and the circumvention or overriding of controls. Accordingly, even an effective internal control system can provide only reasonable assurance with respect to financial statement preparation. Furthermore, the effectiveness of an internal control system can vary over time due to changes in conditions.

Management believes that as of December 31, 1993, the internal control system over financial reporting is adequate and effective in all material respects.

James E. Terrell

James E. Terrell
Vice President and Controller

James C. Van Meter

James C. Van Meter
Vice Chairman and Chief Financial Officer

A.D. Correll

A.D. Correll
Chairman and Chief Executive Officer

February 18, 1994

STATEMENTS OF INCOME

Georgia-Pacific Corporation and Subsidiaries

	Year ended December 31		
(Millions, except per share amounts)	**1993**	1992	1991
Net sales	**$12,330**	$11,847	$11,524
Costs and expenses			
Cost of sales	**9,814**	9,397	9,164
Selling, general and administrative	**1,190**	1,170	1,137
Depreciation and depletion	**764**	789	724
Interest	**513**	565	584
Other (income) loss	**26**	—	(344)
Total costs and expenses	**12,307**	11,921	11,265
Income (loss) before income taxes, extraordinary item and accounting changes	**23**	(74)	259
Provision (benefit) for income taxes	**41**	(14)	293
(Loss) before extraordinary item and accounting changes	**(18)**	(60)	(34)
Extraordinary item—loss from early retirement of debt, net of taxes	**(16)**	(9)	(45)
Cumulative effect of accounting changes, net of taxes	**—**	(55)	(63)
Net (loss)	**$ (34)**	$ (124)	$ (142)
Per share:			
(Loss) before extraordinary item and accounting changes	**$ (.21)**	$ (.69)	$ (.40)
Extraordinary item—loss from early retirement of debt, net of taxes	**(.18)**	(.10)	(.52)
Cumulative effect of accounting changes, net of taxes	**—**	(.64)	(.73)
Net (loss)	**$ (.39)**	$ (1.43)	$ (1.65)
Average number of shares outstanding	**87.7**	86.4	85.8

The accompanying notes are an integral part of these financial statements.

(Millions, except shares and per share amounts)	December 31 1993	December 31 1992
Assets		
Current assets		
Cash	$ 41	$ 55
Receivables, less allowances of $32 and $35	377	331
Inventories		
Raw materials	367	321
Finished goods	786	792
Supplies	262	282
LIFO reserve	(213)	(203)
Total inventories	1,202	1,192
Other current assets	26	29
Total current assets	1,646	1,607
Timber and timberlands, net	1,381	1,402
Property, plant and equipment		
Land and improvements	237	247
Buildings	1,074	1,101
Machinery and equipment	9,550	9,420
Construction in progress	125	64
Total property, plant and equipment, at cost	10,986	10,832
Accumulated depreciation	(5,538)	(5,001)
Property, plant and equipment, net	5,448	5,831
Goodwill	1,832	1,891
Other assets	238	181
Total assets	$10,545	$10,912
Liabilities and shareholders' equity		
Current liabilities		
Bank overdrafts, net	$ 173	$ 121
Commercial paper and other short-term notes	650	691
Current portion of long-term debt	57	257
Taxes payable	35	193
Accounts payable	582	563
Accrued compensation	184	179
Accrued interest	114	132
Other current liabilities	269	316
Total current liabilities	2,064	2,452
Long-term debt, excluding current portion	4,157	4,019
Other long-term liabilities	827	731
Deferred income taxes	1,095	1,202
Commitments and contingencies		
Shareholders' equity		
Common stock, par value $.80; authorized 150,000,000 shares; 90,269,000 and 88,111,000 shares issued	71	70
Additional paid-in capital	1,202	1,094
Retained earnings	1,217	1,393
Long-term incentive plan deferred compensation	(56)	(39)
Other	(32)	(10)
Total shareholders' equity	2,402	2,508
Total liabilities and shareholders' equity	$10,545	$10,912

(Millions)	Year ended December 31		
	1993	1992	1991
Cash provided by (used for) operations			
Net (loss)	$ (34)	$(124)	$ (142)
Adjustments to reconcile net (loss) to cash provided by operations:			
Depreciation	711	747	673
Depletion	53	42	51
Deferred tax benefit	(125)	(133)	(25)
Amortization of goodwill	59	59	60
Stock compensation programs	53	42	67
Gain on sales of assets	(32)	(33)	(38)
Amortization of debt issue costs, discounts and premiums	7	6	35
Other (income) loss	26	—	(344)
Extraordinary item, net of taxes	—	—	45
Cumulative effect of accounting changes, net of taxes	—	55	63
(Increase) decrease in receivables	(174)	(87)	92
(Increase) decrease in inventories	(93)	61	(43)
Change in other working capital	40	193	45
Increase (decrease) in taxes payable	(158)	13	(2)
Change in other assets and other long-term liabilities	56	27	43
Cash provided by operations	389	868	580
Cash provided by (used for) investment activities			
Capital expenditures			
Property, plant and equipment	(421)	(347)	(490)
Timber and timberlands	(46)	(37)	(38)
Total capital expenditures	(467)	(384)	(528)
Proceeds from sales of assets	260	55	1,251
Other	5	(4)	23
Cash provided by (used for) investment activities	(202)	(333)	746
Cash provided by (used for) financing activities			
Repayments of long-term debt	(576)	(566)	(2,055)
Additions of long-term debt	511	754	610
Fees paid to issue debt	(5)	(7)	(4)
Increase (decrease) in bank overdrafts	52	(50)	27
Increase (decrease) in commercial paper and other short-term notes	(41)	(519)	226
Cash dividends paid	(142)	(140)	(140)
Cash (used for) financing activities	(201)	(528)	(1,336)
Increase (decrease) in cash	(14)	7	(10)
Balance at beginning of year	55	48	58
Balance at end of year	$ 41	$ 55	$ 48

The accompanying notes are an integral part of these financial statements.
Refer to Note 11 for supplemental cash flow information.

Note 1. Summary of Significant Accounting Policies

Principles of Consolidation The consolidated financial statements include the accounts of Georgia-Pacific Corporation and subsidiaries (the Corporation). All significant intercompany balances and transactions are eliminated in consolidation.

Revenue Recognition The Corporation recognizes revenue when title to the goods sold passes to the buyer, which is generally at the time of shipment.

(Loss) Per Share (Loss) per share is computed based on net (loss) and the weighted average number of common shares outstanding (net of restricted stock). The effects of assuming issuance of common shares under long-term incentive, stock option and stock purchase plans were either insignificant or antidilutive. The number of shares used in the (loss) per share computations were 87,711,000 in 1993, 86,402,000 in 1992 and 85,837,000 in 1991.

Inventory Valuation Inventories are valued at the lower of average cost or market and include the cost of materials, labor and manufacturing overhead. The last-in, first-out (LIFO) dollar value pool method is used to value approximately 45%

(Millions, except shares)

Common stock shares issued		Total	Common stock	Additional paid-in capital	Retained earnings	Long-term incentive plan deferred compensation	Other
86,704,000	Balance at December 31, 1990	$2,975	$69	$ 995	$1,939	$(30)	$ 2
	Net loss	(142)	—	—	(142)	—	—
	Cash dividends declared—$1.60 per common share	(140)	—	—	(140)	—	—
	Common stock issued:						
145,000	Stock option plan	8	—	8	—	—	—
580,000	Employee stock purchase plans	20	1	19	—	—	—
(8,000)	Long-term incentive plan	25	—	23	—	2	—
	Other	(10)	—	—	—	—	(10)
87,421,000	Balance at December 31, 1991	2,736	70	1,045	1,657	(28)	(8)
	Net loss	(124)	—	—	(124)	—	—
	Cash dividends declared—$1.60 per common share	(140)	—	—	(140)	—	—
	Common stock issued:						
186,000	Stock option plan	12	—	12	—	—	—
112,000	Employee stock purchase plan	4	—	4	—	—	—
392,000	Long-term incentive plan	22	—	33	—	(11)	—
	Other	(2)	—	—	—	—	(2)
88,111,000	Balance at December 31, 1992	2,508	70	1,094	1,393	(39)	(10)
	Net loss	(34)	—	—	(34)	—	—
	Cash dividends declared—$1.60 per common share	(142)	—	—	(142)	—	—
	Common stock issued:						
107,000	Stock option plans	7	—	7	—	—	—
1,575,000	Employee stock purchase plans	55	1	54	—	—	—
476,000	Long-term incentive plan	26	—	43	—	(17)	—
	Other	(18)	—	4	—	—	(22)
90,269,000	**Balance at December 31, 1993**	**$2,402**	**$71**	**$1,202**	**$1,217**	**$(56)**	**$(32)**

The accompanying notes are an integral part of these financial statements.
© 1993 Georgia-Pacific Corporation. All rights reserved.

and 49%, respectively, of inventories at December 31, 1993 and 1992.

Effective January 1, 1991, the Corporation changed its accounting policy at certain manufacturing facilities to include in inventory certain supplies that were previously expensed. The Corporation believes this method is preferable because it provides a better matching of costs and related revenues and is more consistent with the Corporation's tax reporting method. The cumulative effect of this change for years prior to 1991 was to increase net income by $56 million in 1991 after related income tax expense of $35 million. This change had no effect on 1991 operating results after recording the cumulative effect for years prior to 1991. The pro forma effect of the change on years prior to 1991 was not determinable.

Property, Plant and Equipment Property, plant and equipment are recorded at cost. Lease obligations for which the Corporation assumes substantially all the property rights and risks of ownership are capitalized. Replacements of major units of property are capitalized and the replaced properties are retired. Replacements of minor components of property and repair and maintenance costs are charged to expense as incurred.

Depreciation is computed by the straight-line method over the estimated useful lives of the related assets. Upon retirement or disposition of assets, cost and accumulated depreciation are removed from the related accounts and any gain or loss is included in income.

The Corporation changed the estimated useful lives used to compute depreciation for land improvements and buildings added on or after January 1, 1993. Lives for land improvements were changed from 20 years to 25 years. Lives for buildings were changed from 20 to 33 years to 20 to 45 years. These changes were made to better reflect the estimated periods during which such assets will remain in service. Useful lives for machinery and equipment, which remain unchanged, range from 3 to 20 years.

The Corporation capitalizes interest on projects when construction takes considerable time and entails major expenditures. Such interest is charged to the property, plant and equipment accounts and amortized over the approximate life of the related assets in order to properly match costs with revenues resulting from the facilities. Interest capitalized, expensed and paid were as follows:

(Millions)	Year ended December 31		
	1993	1992	1991
Total interest costs	**$516**	$567	$598
Interest capitalized	**(3)**	(2)	(14)
Interest expense	**$513**	$565	$584
Interest paid	**$529**	$544	$585

Timber and Timberlands The Corporation depletes its investment in timber based on the total fiber that will be available during the estimated growth cycle. Timber carrying costs are expensed as incurred.

Landfills and Lagoons The Corporation accrues for landfill closure costs over the periods that benefit from the use of the landfill and accrues for lagoon clean-out costs over the useful period between clean-outs.

Goodwill The Corporation amortizes costs in excess of fair value of net assets of businesses acquired using the straight-line method over a period not to exceed 40 years. Recoverability is reviewed annually or sooner if events or changes in circumstances indicate that the carrying amount may exceed fair value. Recoverability is then determined by comparing the undiscounted net cash flows of the assets to which the goodwill applies to the net book value including goodwill of those assets.

Amortization expense was $59 million in 1993 and 1992 and $60 million in 1991. Accumulated amortization at December 31, 1993, 1992 and 1991 was $247 million, $188 million and $129 million, respectively.

Environmental Remediation and Compliance Environmental expenditures are expensed or capitalized, as appropriate.

Liabilities are recorded when assessments and/or remedial efforts are probable and the cost can be reasonably estimated.

Reclassifications Certain 1992 and 1991 amounts have been reclassified to conform with the 1993 presentation.

Note 2. Industry Segment Information

Manufactured product lines in the building products segment consist primarily of wood panels (plywood, hardboard, particleboard and oriented strand board), lumber, gypsum products, chemicals and roofing.

Manufactured product lines in the pulp and paper segment consist primarily of containerboard and packaging (linerboard, medium, bleached board, kraft paper and corrugated packaging), communication papers, market pulp, tissue and envelopes.

Timber and timberlands are managed to supply raw materials to both the pulp and paper and building products segments. Profits from sales of logs and chips to the pulp and paper segment and to outside customers in the ordinary course of business are included in the operating profits of the building products segment.

During the years 1991 through 1993, sales to foreign markets represented less than 10% of total sales to unaffiliated customers. No single customer accounted for more than 10% of total sales to unaffiliated customers in any year during that period.

Note 3. Asset Divestitures

After the acquisition of GNN in 1990, the Corporation announced plans to sell certain assets identified as not strategic to its principal operations.

The following divestitures were completed during the years 1993 and 1991. The Corporation had no major divestitures in 1992. The pretax gains and losses associated with these sales are included in other income in the accompanying statements of income.

▶ In July 1993, the Corporation completed the sale of the assets of Butler Paper Company, which operated 80 distribution centers in 31 states, to Alco Standard Corporation. The transaction resulted in after-tax cash proceeds of approximately $222 million. In addition, the Corporation recognized a $26 million pretax loss and a $7 million after-tax gain (8 cents per share) on the transaction. The large tax benefit results from the loss on the sale as well as the fact that the tax basis was significantly greater than the financial basis of stock included in the assets sold in the transaction.

▶ In December 1991, the Corporation completed the sale of an 80 percent ownership interest in two groundwood paper mills, the hydro-electric assets that power those mills, a sawmill and approximately 2.1 million acres of fee timberland for approximately $303 million in cash. A pretax gain of $52 million ($15 million after taxes) was recognized on this transaction. In July 1992, the Corporation received $22 million less working capital settlements of approximately $12 million related to the remaining 20 percent ownership interest.

▶ In June 1991, the Corporation sold 49,000 acres of fee tim-

Industry Segment Information

(Millions)	Year ended December 31					
	1993		1992		1991	
Net sales						
Building products	$ 7,067	58%	$ 6,112	52%	$ 5,405	47%
Pulp and paper	5,231	42	5,711	48	6,089	53
Other operations	32	—	24	—	30	—
Total net sales	$12,330	100%	$11,847	100%	$11,524	100%
Net (loss)						
Building products	$ 973	126%	$ 691	100%	$ 344	32%
Pulp and paper	(187)	(24)	(8)	(1)	362	34
Other operations	10	1	9	1	17	2
Other income (loss)*	(26)	(3)	—	—	344	32
Total operating profits	770	100%	692	100%	1,067	100%
General corporate	(205)		(166)		(165)	
Interest expense	(513)		(565)		(584)	
Cost of accounts receivable sale program	(29)		(35)		(59)	
(Provision) benefit for income taxes	(41)		14		(293)	
(Loss) before extraordinary item and accounting changes	(18)		(60)		(34)	
Extraordinary item—loss from early retirement of debt, net of taxes	(16)		(9)		(45)	
Cumulative effect of accounting changes, net of taxes	—		(55)		(63)	
Net (loss)	$ (34)		$ (124)		$ (142)	
Depreciation, depletion and goodwill amortization						
Building products	$ 215	26%	$ 206	24%	$ 232	30%
Pulp and paper	595	72	626	74	537	68
Other and general corporate	13	2	16	2	15	2
Total depreciation, depletion and goodwill amortization	$ 823	100%	$ 848	100%	$ 784	100%
Capital expenditures**						
Building products	$ 146	31%	$ 111	29%	$ 43	8%
Pulp and paper	261	56	217	56	436	83
Timber and timberlands	46	10	37	10	38	7
Other and general corporate	14	3	19	5	11	2
Total capital expenditures	$ 467	100%	$ 384	100%	$ 528	100%
Assets						
Building products	$ 1,726	16%	$ 1,634	15%	$ 1,681	16%
Pulp and paper	6,909	66	7,414	68	7,208	68
Timber and timberlands	1,380	13	1,402	13	1,377	13
Other and general corporate	530	5	462	4	363	3
Total assets	$10,545	100%	$10,912	100%	$10,629	100%

*Other income represents the results of various asset divestitures as described in Note 3. If these amounts had been included in segment operating profits, pulp and paper operating profits would have been $(213) million in 1993 and $546 million in 1991 and building products operating profits would have been $504 million in 1991.

**The capital expenditure amounts reported above represent additions, at cost, to property, plant and equipment and timber and timberlands.

berland in Washington for $48 million in cash. A pretax gain of $46 million ($29 million after taxes) was recognized on this transaction.

▶ In January 1991, the Corporation sold two domestic containerboard mills, 19 corrugated packaging plants and approximately 540,000 acres of fee timberland (and lease rights to 98,000 acres of timberland) for $725 million in cash and, in a separate transaction, sold its interests in a foreign containerboard mill, two corrugated packaging plants and two sheet plants for $102 million in cash. A combined pretax gain

of $246 million ($28 million after taxes) was recognized on these transactions.

Note 4. Receivables

The Corporation has a large, diversified customer base, which includes some customers who are located in foreign countries. The Corporation closely monitors extensions of credit and has not experienced significant losses related to its receivables. In addition, a majority of the receivables from foreign sales are covered by either export credit insurance or confirmed letters of credit to help ensure collectibility.

The Corporation had sold fractional ownership interests in a defined pool of trade accounts receivable for $700 million as of December 31, 1993 and $800 million as of December 31, 1992 and 1991. The $100 million reduction in the accounts receivable sale program in 1993 is reported as an increase in receivables in the accompanying statements of cash flows. The sold accounts receivable are reflected as a reduction of receivables in the accompanying balance sheets. The full amount of the allowance for doubtful accounts has been retained because the Corporation has retained substantially the same risk of credit loss as if the receivables had not been sold. A portion of the cost of the accounts receivable sale program is based on the purchasers' level of investment and borrowing costs. Additionally, the Corporation pays fees based on its senior debt ratings. The total cost of the program, which was $29 million in 1993, $35 million in 1992 and $59 million in 1991, is included in selling, general and administrative expense in the accompanying statements of income.

Under the accounts receivable sale agreement, the maximum amount of the purchasers' investment is subject to change based on the level of eligible receivables and restrictions on concentrations of receivables. The program was reduced from $800 million to $700 million, pursuant to an amendment of the agreement effective October 15, 1993. In addition, the current agreement expires in June 1994. The Corporation is currently in the process of negotiating a renewal of the program.

Supplemental information on the accounts receivable balances at December 31, 1993 and 1992 is as follows:

(Millions)	December 31	
	1993	1992
Receivables		
Trade	$358	$270
Other	51	96
	409	366
Less estimated allowances	32	35
Receivables, net	$377	$331

Note 5. Indebtedness

The Corporation's indebtedness included the following:

(Millions)	December 31	
	1993	1992
Debentures, 9.4% average rate, payable through 2023	$2,804	$2,579
Notes, 7.7% average rate, payable through 2000	974	1,238
Commercial paper and other short-term notes, 3.6% average rate	650	691
Revenue bonds, 4.0% average rate, payable through 2026	375	371
Other loans, 5.9% average rate, payable through 2009	96	121
	4,899	5,000

Less:		
Commercial paper and other short-term notes	650	691
Current portion of long-term debt	57	257
Unamortized discount	35	33
Long-term debt	$4,157	$4,019

The scheduled maturities of long-term debt for the next five years are as follows: $57 million in 1994, $55 million in 1995, $39 million in 1996, $313 million in 1997 and $446 million in 1998.

Notes and Debentures   During 1993, the Corporation issued $250 million of 8¼% Debentures Due March 1, 2023, and $250 million of 8⅛% Debentures Due June 15, 2023.

In addition, the Corporation prepaid approximately $317 million in principal of its outstanding debt during 1993 resulting in an after-tax extraordinary loss of $16 million ($27 million before taxes). During 1992, the Corporation reported an after-tax extraordinary loss of $9 million ($14 million before taxes) related to the early retirement of approximately $207 million of outstanding debt.

The estimated fair value of the Corporation's notes and debentures at December 31, 1993 was $4,172 million compared with a carrying amount of $3,778 million. At December 31, 1992, the estimated fair value of the Corporation's notes and debentures was $4,046 million compared with a carrying amount of $3,817 million. The fair value was estimated primarily by obtaining quotes from brokers for these and similar issues. For notes and debentures for which there are no quoted market prices, the fair value was estimated by calculating the present value of anticipated cash flows. The discount rate used was an estimated borrowing rate for similar debt instruments with like maturities.

Unsecured Term Loan and Revolving Credit Facility   On December 31, 1991, the Corporation entered into an agreement with Bank of America National Trust and Savings Association and 24 other domestic and international banks which provides a three-year unsecured revolving credit facility of $1.5 billion. The revolving credit facility is being used as support for commercial paper and other short-term borrowings, including bid borrowings made under the credit agreement. Effective June 30, 1993, the Corporation entered into a revised Credit Agreement with substantially the same lending group which extends the termination date until 1996, eliminates the minimum interest coverage ratio, and modifies certain representations and warranties. As of December 31, 1993, $850 million of committed credit was available in excess of all short-term borrowings outstanding under or supported by the facility.

Borrowings under the revised agreement bear interest, at the election of the Corporation, at either (A) the higher of the reference rate and the Federal Funds Rate plus ½% or (B) LIBOR plus ⅝% or (C) fixed or floating rates set by competitive bids. Fees associated with this revolving credit facility include a commitment fee of ⅛% per annum on the unused portion of the commitments and a facility fee of ⅛% per annum on the aggregate commitments of the lenders.

The revolving credit agreement contains certain restrictive covenants. The covenants include a maximum leverage ratio (funded indebtedness to operating cash flow) of 4.5 to 1.0 which is to be maintained throughout the term of the Credit Agreement. As of December 31, 1993, the leverage ratio was 3.8 to 1.0.

During 1991, the Corporation prepaid the outstanding balance of a term loan entered into in 1990 in connection with the acquisition of GNN. The prepayment of the term loan and the refinancing of the revolving credit facility in 1991 resulted in the accelerated write-off of approximately $72 million ($45 million after taxes) of capitalized debt issue costs associated with the original borrowings. This loss on early extinguishment of debt is reflected as an extraordinary item in the accompanying statements of income.

Commercial Paper and Other Short-Term Notes These borrowings are classified as current liabilities although all or a portion of them might be refinanced on a long-term basis in 1994. The carrying amounts approximate fair value because of the short maturity of these instruments.

Revenue Bonds and Other Loans The estimated fair value of the Corporation's revenue bonds and other loans at December 31, 1993 was $375 million and $96 million, respectively. The estimated fair value of the Corporation's revenue bonds and other loans at December 31, 1992 was $367 million and $121 million, respectively. The fair value was estimated by calculating the present value of anticipated cash flows. The discount rate used was an estimated borrowing rate for similar debt instruments with like maturities.

Other At December 31, 1993, the amount of long-term debt secured by property, plant and equipment and timber and timberlands was not material.

At December 31, 1993, the Corporation had outstanding interest rate exchange agreements which effectively converted $1.7 billion of floating rate obligations with a weighted average interest rate of 3.4% to fixed rate obligations with an average effective interest rate of approximately 9.0%. Under the agreements, which have a remaining average maturity of approximately 2.5 years, the Corporation makes payments to counterparties at fixed interest rates and in turn receives payments at variable rates. The differential to be paid or received is accrued as interest rates change and is recognized over the lives of the agreements. The Corporation is exposed to credit risk in the event of nonperformance by the counterparties, but does not anticipate such nonperformance. As of December 31, 1993, the Corporation's total floating rate debt, including the accounts receivable sale program, exceeded related interest rate exchange agreements by approximately $270 million.

The estimated fair value of the Corporation's liability under interest rate exchange agreements at December 31, 1993 and 1992 was $99 million and $153 million, respectively, and represents the estimated amount the Corporation might have paid to terminate the agreements. The fair value at December 31, 1993 was estimated by calculating the present value of anticipated cash flows. The discount rate used was an estimated borrowing rate for similar debt instruments with like maturities. The estimated fair value at December 31, 1992

was based on quotes obtained from brokers and calculated by them using the same methodology described above for the 1993 calculation. The Corporation accrued interest of $31 million and $37 million at December 31, 1993 and 1992, respectively, related to these agreements.

The carrying amounts of bank overdrafts at December 31, 1993 and 1992 approximate fair value.

Note 6. Income Taxes

Effective January 1992, the Corporation changed its method of accounting for income taxes from the deferred method to the liability method required by Financial Accounting Standard Number 109, "Accounting for Income Taxes" ("FAS 109"). The cumulative effect of adopting FAS 109 as of January 1, 1992 was to increase the net loss by $55 million. Prior years' financial statements were not restated to reflect the provisions of FAS 109.

The provision (benefit) for income taxes includes income taxes currently payable and those deferred because of temporary differences between the financial statement and tax bases of assets and liabilities. The provision (benefit) for income taxes consists of the following:

	Year ended December 31		
(Millions)	**1993**	1992	1991
Federal income taxes:			
Current	**$128**	$ 105	$277
Deferred	**(89)**	(117)	(21)
State income taxes:			
Current	**17**	14	41
Deferred	**(15)**	(16)	(4)
Provision (benefit) for income taxes	**$ 41**	$ (14)	$293
Income taxes paid, net of refunds	**$300**	$ 68	$273

Income taxes paid includes payments to the Internal Revenue Service (IRS) of approximately $205 million in 1993 to resolve all pending income tax issues for the years 1981 through 1988 for Georgia-Pacific Corporation and substantially all issues for the years 1982 through 1984 for Great Northern Nekoosa Corporation (GNN). Income taxes paid for 1991 include approximately $275 million of payments associated with asset sales.

Included in Taxes Payable in the accompanying balance sheet are amounts the Corporation expects to pay in 1994 to resolve the remaining income tax issues for GNN for the years 1982 through 1984 and for Georgia-Pacific Corporation for the years 1989 through 1990. These amounts are offset by the tax benefit related to the deductibility of interest paid in 1993. In addition, the IRS is currently examining GNN's federal income tax returns for the years 1985 through 1990. The IRS has proposed certain adjustments, some of which are being contested by the Corporation. In the opinion of management, adjustments resulting from these examinations will not have a material adverse effect on the Corporation's financial condition.

The difference between the statutory federal income tax rate on income (loss) before income taxes, extraordinary item and accounting changes and the Corporation's effective income tax rate is summarized as follows:

	Year ended December 31		
	1993	1992	1991
Statutory federal income tax rate	**35.0%**	(34.0)%	34.0%
State income tax, net of federal benefit	**4.0**	(4.0)	4.0
Permanent differences resulting from purchase accounting:			
Goodwill	**99.7**	30.2	8.7
Other	**—**	—	19.6
Permanent differences on assets sold	**(101.7)**	—	52.2
Foreign loss producing no tax benefit	**14.7**	—	—
Tax rate increase	**143.2**	—	—
Foreign sales corporation	**(10.1)**	(7.9)	(2.0)
Interest on tax audits	**—**	—	(5.4)
Percentage depletion	**(3.9)**	(1.5)	(.4)
Life insurance, net	**(5.0)**	(1.8)	(.5)
Dividends—nonvested LTIP shares	**(3.7)**	(1.4)	(.3)
Meals and entertainment disallowance	**4.9**	1.7	.4
Other	**1.2**	(.2)	2.8
Effective income tax rate	**178.3%**	(18.9)%	113.1%

As a result of the Revenue Reconciliation Act of 1993, the Corporation incurred after-tax charges of $34 million due to the one percent increase in the corporate income tax rate and $14 million related to the cash bonus portion of its long-term incentive program due to the increase in the marginal individual income tax rate.

FAS 109 requires recognition of deferred tax liabilities and assets for the expected future tax consequences of events that have been included in the financial statements or tax returns. The components of the net deferred tax liability are as follows:

	Year ended December 31	
(*Millions*)	**1993**	1992
Deferred tax asset:		
Compensation related accruals	**$ 303**	$ 281
Other accruals and reserves	**83**	86
Other	**81**	61
	467	428
Valuation allowance	**—**	—
	467	428
Deferred tax liability:		
Property, plant and equipment	**(1,333)**	(1,392)
Timber and timberlands	**(167)**	(161)
Other	**(62)**	(77)
	(1,562)	(1,630)
Deferred tax liability, net	**$(1,095)**	$(1,202)

As of December 31, 1993, the net deferred tax liability includes alternative minimum tax credit carryforwards of $48 million which may be utilized to offset future tax liabilities to the extent that the Corporation's regular tax liability exceeds the alternative minimum tax liability.

During 1991, the provision for income taxes was based on pretax financial income which differs from taxable income. Deferred income taxes were provided for significant timing differences between revenue and expenses for tax and financial statement purposes. Following is a summary of the significant components of the deferred tax (benefit):

	Year ended December 31
(*Millions*)	1991
Tax (under) financial depreciation and depletion	$ (5)
Liability accruals and write-down of certain assets	41
Compensation expense	(52)
Financing costs	(1)
Other	(8)
Deferred tax (benefit)	$(25)

Note 7. Retirement Plans

Defined Benefit Pension Plans Most of the Corporation's employees participate in noncontributory defined benefit pension plans. These include plans which are administered solely by the Corporation and union-administered multiemployer plans. The Corporation's funding policy for solely administered plans is based on actuarial calculations and the applicable requirements of federal law. Contributions to multiemployer plans are generally based on negotiated labor contracts.

Benefits under the majority of plans for hourly employees (including multiemployer plans) are primarily related to years of service. The Corporation has separate plans for salaried employees and officers under which benefits are primarily related to compensation and years of service. The officers' plan is not funded and is non-qualified for Federal income tax purposes.

Plan assets consist principally of common stocks, bonds, mortgage securities, interests in limited partnerships, cash equivalents and real estate. At December 31, 1993 and 1992, respectively, $57 million and $46 million of noncurrent prepaid pension cost was included in other assets. The accrued pension cost of $79 million and $56 million at December 31, 1993 and 1992, respectively, was included in other long-term liabilities.

The following table sets forth the funded status of the solely administered plans and the amounts recognized in the accompanying balance sheets.

(Millions)	Year ended December 31, 1993		Year ended December 31, 1992	
	Plans having assets in excess of accumulated benefits	Plans having accumulated benefits in excess of assets	Plans having assets in excess of accumulated benefits	Plans having accumulated benefits in excess of assets
Accumulated benefit obligation at November 30				
Vested portion	$ 896	$373	$ 918	$244
Nonvested portion	27	17	28	12
	923	390	946	256
Effect of projected future compensation levels	4	14	10	11
Projected benefit obligation at November 30	927	404	956	267
Plan assets at fair value at November 30	1,101	312	1,119	201
Plan assets in excess of (less than) projected benefit obligation	174	(92)	163	(66)
Contributions made in December	—	—	4	—
Unrecognized net (gain) loss	(80)	57	(68)	33
Unrecognized prior service cost	(17)	30	(24)	22
Unrecognized net asset from initial application of FAS 87	(20)	(15)	(29)	(15)
Adjustment required to recognize minimum liability	—	(59)	—	(30)
Prepaid (accrued) pension cost at December 31	$ 57	$ (79)	$ 46	$ (56)

Pursuant to the provisions of Financial Accounting Standard Number 87, "Employers' Accounting for Pensions," intangible assets of $30 million and $22 million were recorded as of December 31, 1993 and 1992, respectively.

Net periodic pension cost for solely and jointly administered pension plans included the following:

(Millions)	Year ended December 31		
	1993	1992	1991
Service cost of benefits earned	$ 80	$ 75	$ 73
Interest cost on projected benefit obligation	96	96	93
Actual (gain) on plan assets	(185)	(157)	(206)
Net amortization and deferral	30	11	70
Contributions to multiemployer pension plans	4	4	4
Net periodic pension cost	$ 25	$ 29	$ 34

The following assumptions were used:

	1993	1992	1991
Discount rate used to determine the projected benefit obligation	7.0%	8.0%	8.5%
Rate of increase in future compensation levels used to determine the projected benefit obligation	5.0	6.0	6.0
Expected long-term rate of return on plan assets used to determine net periodic pension cost	10.0	11.5	11.5

During 1993 and 1991, the Corporation recognized a net aggregate pretax settlement and curtailment gain of $12.7 million and $10 million, respectively, resulting from pension obligations assumed by the purchaser in certain asset divestitures (Note 3).

Defined Contribution Plans The Corporation sponsors several defined contribution plans to provide eligible employees with additional income upon retirement. The Corporation's contributions to the plans are based on employee contributions and compensation. These contributions totaled $44 million in 1993 and $43 million in 1992 and 1991.

Retiree Health Care and Life Insurance Benefits The Corporation provides certain health care and life insurance benefits to eligible retired employees. Salaried participants generally become eligible for retiree health care benefits after reaching age 55 with 10 years of service or after reaching age 65. Benefits, eligibility and cost-sharing provisions for hourly employees vary by location and/or bargaining unit. Generally, the medical plans pay a stated percentage of most medical expenses reduced for any deductible and payments made by government programs and other group coverage. The plans are unfunded.

For 1992 and 1993 the cost of providing most of these benefits has been shared with retirees. The Corporation began transferring its share of the cost of post-age 65 health care benefits to future salaried retirees in 1991. It is currently anticipated that the Corporation will continue to reduce the percentage of the cost of post-age 65 benefits that it will pay on behalf of salaried employees who retire in each of the years 1992 through 1999 and that the Corporation will continue to share the pre-age 65 cost with future salaried retirees, but will no longer pay any of the post-age 65 cost for salaried employees who retire after 1999.

The Corporation adopted Financial Accounting Standard Number 106, "Employers' Accounting for Postretirement Benefits Other Than Pensions," as of January 1, 1991. This statement requires the accrual of the cost of providing post-retirement benefits, including medical and life insurance coverage, during the active service period of the employee. The Corporation elected to immediately recognize the accumulated liability, measured as of January 1, 1991. This resulted in a one-time, after-tax charge of $119 million (after reduction for income taxes of $73 million) which does not include amounts accrued in prior years for business acquisitions. The effect of this change on 1991 operating results, after recording the cumulative effect for years prior to 1991, was to recognize additional pretax expense of $23 million. The pro forma effect of the change on years prior to 1991 was not determinable. Prior to 1991, the Corporation recognized expense in the year the benefits were provided.

The following table sets forth the funded status of the plans, reconciled to the accrued postretirement benefit cost recognized in the Corporation's balance sheet at December 31, 1993 and 1992:

	Year ended December 31	
(Millions)	**1993**	1992
Accumulated postretirement benefit obligation:		
Retirees	**$273**	$242
Fully eligible active plan participants	**33**	44
Other active participants	**135**	131
	441	417
Unrecognized net loss	**(60)**	(58)
Unrecognized prior service cost	**6**	—
Accrued postretirement benefit cost	**$387**	$359

Net periodic postretirement benefit cost for 1993, 1992 and 1991 included the following components:

	Year ended December 31		
(Millions)	**1993**	1992	1991
Service cost of benefits earned	**$ 9**	$ 6	$ 8
Interest cost on accumulated postretirement benefit obligation	**31**	27	30
Amortization of loss	**1**	—	—
Net periodic postretirement benefit cost	**$41**	$33	$38

For measuring the expected postretirement benefit obligation, a 13 percent, 14 percent and 15 percent annual rate of increase in the per capita claims cost was assumed for 1993, 1992 and 1991, respectively. The rate was assumed to decrease 1 percent per year to 7 percent in 1999 and remain at that level thereafter. The weighted-average discount rate used in determining the accumulated post-retirement benefit obligation was 6.5 percent at December 31, 1993, 7.5 percent at December 31, 1992 and 8.0 percent at December 31, 1991.

If the health care cost trend rate were increased 1 percent, the accumulated postretirement benefit obligation would have increased by 15 percent as of December 31, 1993 and 13 percent as of December 31, 1992 and 1991. The effect of this change on the aggregate of service and interest cost for 1993, 1992 and 1991 would be an increase of 17 percent, 14 percent and 15 percent, respectively.

During 1991, the Corporation recognized a pretax settlement gain of $43 million resulting from postretirement benefit obligations assumed by the purchaser in certain asset divestitures (Note 3).

Other In November 1992, the Financial Accounting Standards Board issued Financial Accounting Standard Number 112, "Employers' Accounting for Postemployment Benefits," which requires recognition of benefits provided by an employer to former or inactive employees after employment but before retirement. The Corporation will be required to adopt the new standard in the 1994 first quarter. After evaluating the Statement's requirements, the Corporation estimates that it will recognize a one-time, pretax charge of approximately $7.9 million during the 1994 first quarter. The effect of this change on 1994 operating results is not expected to be material.

Note 8. Common and Preferred Stock

The Corporation's authorized capital stock consists of 10 million shares of no par value Preferred Stock and 25 million shares of no par value Junior Preferred Stock, of which no shares were issued at December 31, 1993, and 150 million shares of Common Stock, par value $.80 per share.

At December 31, 1993, the following authorized shares of the Corporation's common stock were reserved for issue:

	1993
1993 Employee Stock Purchase Plan	1,154,000
1990 Long-Term Incentive Plan	2,912,000
1993 Employee Stock Option Plan	500,000
1984 Employee Stock Option Plan	654,000
Common stock reserved	5,220,000

Employee Stock Purchase Plans At December 31, 1993, the 1993 Employee Stock Purchase Plan (Purchase Plan) had reserved for issue 1,154,000 shares of common stock at a subscription price of $57.06. Subscribers have the option to receive a refund of their payments plus interest at the rate of 5% per annum in lieu of stock. Additional shares can no longer be subscribed under the Purchase Plan, which expires on July 31, 1995. Approximately 8,000 subscribers remained in the Purchase Plan at December 31, 1993.

Under the 1993 Purchase Plan, the Corporation issued 2,000 shares of common stock in 1993. Under the 1991 Purchase Plan (which expired on May 31, 1993), the Corporation issued 1,573,000 shares, 112,000 shares and 21,000 shares of common stock in 1993, 1992 and 1991, respectively. Under the 1989 Employee Stock Purchase Plan (which expired on April 30, 1991), the Corporation issued 559,000 shares of common stock in 1991.

Long-Term Incentive Plans   The 1990 Long-Term Incentive Plan (Incentive Plan) initially reserved 4,000,000 shares for issue. Specified portions of allocated shares under this plan are awarded as restricted stock, at no cost to the employee, based on increases in the average market value of the Corporation's common stock. At the time restricted shares are awarded, the market value of the stock is added to common stock and additional paid-in capital and an equal amount is deducted from shareholders' equity (long-term incentive plan deferred compensation). Long-term incentive plan deferred compensation is amortized over the vesting (restriction) period, generally five years, with adjustments made quarterly for market price fluctuations. At the time awarded shares become vested, the Corporation will pay on behalf of each participant a cash bonus in the amount of the estimated income tax liability to be incurred by the participant as a result of the award and cash bonus. Shares totaling 1,089,000 have been awarded under the Incentive Plan of which 925,000 restricted shares remain outstanding as of December 31, 1993.

The Incentive Plan replaced the 1988 Long-Term Incentive Plan (1988 Incentive Plan). As of December 31, 1993, 1,420,000 shares have been awarded to the plan participants under the 1988 Incentive Plan of which 689,000 restricted shares remain outstanding. These awarded shares will vest based on the provisions in the 1988 Incentive Plan.

The Corporation recognized Incentive Plan and 1988 Incentive Plan compensation expense of $69 million in 1993, $36 million in 1992 and $43 million in 1991. Additional information relating to the Incentive Plan is as follows:

	Year ended December 31		
	1993	1992	1991
Shares allocated but not awarded at January 1	**2,310,000**	2,708,000	2,733,000
Shares allocated	**483,000**	400,000	122,000
Previously allocated shares cancelled	**(235,000)**	(407,000)	(155,000)
Shares awarded	**(551,000)**	(538,000)	—
Previously awarded shares cancelled	**75,000**	147,000	8,000
Shares allocated but not awarded at December 31	**2,082,000**	2,310,000	2,708,000
Shares available for allocation at December 31	**830,000**	1,152,000	1,292,000
Total shares reserved	**2,912,000**	3,462,000	4,000,000

Employee Stock Option Plan   The 1993 Employee Stock Option Plan (1993 Option Plan) provides for the granting of stock options to certain key employees who are not officers. The 1984 Employee Stock Option Plan (1984 Option Plan) provides for the granting of stock options to certain officers and key employees.

Holders of stock options may be granted cash bonuses, payable upon exercise of an option, of an amount not to exceed the amount by which the market value of the common stock, as defined, exceeds the option price. In addition, holders may surrender all or part of the related stock option in exchange for common stock with a fair market value equal to the amount by which the market value of the shares covered by the option exceeds the aggregate option exercise price.

Compensation resulting from stock options and cash bonuses is initially measured at the grant date based on the market value of the common stock, with adjustments made quarterly for market price fluctuations. The Corporation recognized 1984 Option Plan compensation expense of $7 million in 1993, $15 million in 1992 and $31 million in 1991. The Corporation recognized 1993 Option Plan compensation expense of $7 million in 1993.

Additional information relating to the 1993 Option Plan as of December 31, 1993 is as follows:

Options outstanding at January 1	—
Options granted	472,000
Options cancelled	(71,000)
Options outstanding at December 31	401,000
Options available for grant at December 31	99,000
Total reserved shares	500,000
Options prices per share:	
Granted	$59
Cancelled	$59

Additional information relating to the 1984 Option Plan is as follows:

	Year ended December 31		
	1993	1992	1991
Options outstanding at January 1	**981,000**	1,029,000	1,191,000
Options granted	**—**	446,000	461,000
Options exercised/ surrendered	**(267,000)**	(464,000)	(570,000)
Options cancelled	**(60,000)**	(30,000)	(53,000)
Options outstanding at December 31	**654,000**	981,000	1,029,000
Options available for grant at December 31	**—**	244,000	659,000
Total reserved shares	**654,000**	1,225,000	1,688,000
Options exercisable at December 31	**654,000**	557,000	599,000
Option prices per share:			
Granted	**—**	$66	$39–$54
Exercised/surrendered	**$34–$66**	$34–$46	$26–$46
Cancelled	**$39–$66**	$34–$66	$34–$46

Shareholder Rights Plan　The Corporation has a Shareholder Rights Plan pursuant to which preferred stock purchase rights are issued at the rate of one Right for each share of common stock. The Rights expire on July 31, 1999, unless redeemed earlier. Each Right entitles the holder to buy, at an exercise price of $175, one one-hundredth of a newly issued share of Series A Junior Preferred Stock of which 5 million shares were reserved for issue at December 31, 1993. Due to the nature of its dividend, liquidation and voting rights, the economic value of one one-hundredth of a share of Junior Preferred Stock that may be acquired upon the exercise of each Right should approximate the economic value of one share of common stock. The Rights are exercisable only if a person or group acquires 15% or more of the Corporation's common stock or announces a tender offer for 30% or more of the common stock.

If a person becomes the beneficial owner of 15% or more of the Corporation's outstanding common stock, or if a holder of 15% or more of the Corporation's stock engages in certain self-dealing transactions or a merger transaction in which the Corporation is the surviving Corporation and its common stock remains outstanding, then each Right not owned by such party will entitle its holder to purchase, at the then-current exercise price, shares of the Corporation's Series A Junior Preferred Stock with a market value of twice the exercise price.

In addition, if after any person acquires 15% or more of the Corporation's outstanding common stock, the Corporation is involved in a merger or other business combination transaction with another person after which its common stock does not remain outstanding, or the Corporation sells 50% or more of its assets or earning power, each Right will entitle its holder to purchase, at the then-current exercise price, shares of the other party's common stock with a market value of twice the exercise price.

Note 9.　Commitments and Contingencies

The Corporation is a party to various legal proceedings incidental to its business and is subject to a variety of environmental and pollution control laws and regulations in all jurisdictions in which it operates. As is the case with other companies in similar industries, the Corporation faces exposure from actual or potential claims and legal proceedings involving environmental matters. The Corporation is self-insured for general liability claims up to $5 million per occurrence.

The Corporation is involved in environmental remediation activities at sites in which it has been named a potentially responsible party under the Comprehensive Environmental Response, Compensation and Liability Act or similar state "superfund" laws and at certain of its own plants. Of the known sites in which it is involved, the Corporation estimates that slightly over 50 percent are being investigated. Of the remaining sites, approximately one-half are being remediated and the other one-half are being monitored, an activity which occurs after either site investigation or remediation has been completed. The ultimate costs to the Corporation for the remediation of these sites cannot be predicted with certainty due to the often unknown magnitude

of the pollution or the necessary cleanup, the varying costs of alternative cleanup methods, the evolving nature of cleanup technologies and government regulations, and the inability to determine the Corporation's share of multi-party cleanups or the extent to which contribution will be available from other parties. The Corporation has established reserves for environmental remediation costs for these sites in amounts which it believes are probable and reasonably estimable. Based on currently available information and analysis, the Corporation believes that it is reasonably possible that costs associated with these sites may exceed current reserves by amounts that may prove insignificant or that could range, in the aggregate, up to approximately $72 million. This estimate of the range of reasonably possible additional costs is less certain than the estimates upon which reserves are based, and in order to establish the upper limit of such range, assumptions least favorable to the Corporation among the range of reasonably possible outcomes were used. In estimating both its current reserves for environmental remediation and the possible range of additional costs, the Corporation has not assumed it will bear the entire cost of remediation of every site to the exclusion of other known potentially responsible parties who may be jointly and severally liable. The ability of other potentially responsible parties to participate has been taken into account, based generally on the parties' financial condition and probable contribution on a per site basis. No amounts have been recorded for potential recoveries from insurance carriers.

In the fourth quarter of 1992, the Corporation filed suit in the State of Washington against numerous insurance carriers for coverage under comprehensive general liability insurance policies issued by those carriers. The Corporation is seeking a declaratory judgment to the effect that past and future environmental remediation and other related costs with respect to certain of the sites are within the policy provisions.

Approximately 220 suits involving approximately 9,160 plaintiffs are currently pending in Mississippi which primarily allege nuisance, trespass and infliction of emotional distress caused by the discharge of dioxin into the Leaf River prior to 1990 from a pulp mill owned by a subsidiary of the Corporation. Three of these cases have been tried. A total of $241,000 in compensatory damages and $4 million in punitive damages were awarded to three plaintiffs in two of these cases (*Ferguson* and *Simmons*) with respect to certain claims, and the jury found in favor of the Corporation with respect to a fourth plaintiff and with respect to certain claims brought by the other plaintiffs. The Corporation has appealed both judgments. On July 8, 1993, in the third of the Mississippi dioxin cases to be tried, the jury returned a verdict in favor of the Corporation on all counts, with no award being made to any of the plaintiffs. The plaintiffs have filed notice of appeal.

On November 9, 1993, the circuit court judge to whom almost all the remaining Mississippi dioxin cases have been assigned issued an Order delaying trials and other material proceedings in these cases until the Mississippi Supreme Court considers the *Ferguson* and *Simmons* appeals. The Supreme Court has advised the Corporation that it will hear the appeal of these cases on March 21, 1994.

In January 1994, one of the two dioxin-related cases pending in federal court in Mississippi, which was scheduled for trial in June 1994, was voluntarily dismissed with prejudice by the plaintiffs after testing of the plaintiffs' property indicated that no dioxin from the pulp mill was present on the property.

Although there can be no assurances as to the ultimate outcome, the Corporation, based on the opinions of counsel, believes that substantial grounds exist for reversal of the two judgments and that it has meritorious defenses to the remaining claims (the vast majority of which are principally for emotional distress as a result of consuming fish from the rivers).

On July 15, 1992, the plaintiffs in one of the pending suits moved to certify a class action. On October 20, 1992, the court issued an order certifying a class action on behalf of between 8,000 and 13,000 plaintiffs owning property and businesses on the Leaf, Pascagoula and Escatawpa Rivers as well as persons who have eaten fish from, swam in or made recreational use of the rivers. The Corporation appealed and on October 7, 1993, the Mississippi Supreme Court vacated the trial court's order. The Supreme Court ruled that the trial judge lacked authority under his special appointment to allow a class to be certified.

On January 23, 1992, the mill's primary insurance carrier took the position that the claims in these Mississippi cases are not within its coverage. Suit has been filed against the mill's carriers seeking a declaratory judgment to the effect that such claims are within the policy provisions.

Although the ultimate outcome of these environmental actions and legal proceedings cannot be determined with certainty, management believes that any liability resulting from the pending matters, after considering existing reserves, will not have a material adverse effect on the consolidated financial condition of the Corporation.

Note 10.　Related Party Transaction

The Corporation is a 50% partner in a joint venture (GA-MET) with Metropolitan Life Insurance Company (Metro-

politan). GA-MET owns and operates the Corporation's office headquarters complex in Atlanta, Georgia. The Corporation accounts for its investment in GA-MET under the equity method.

At December 31, 1993, GA-MET had an outstanding mortgage loan payable to Metropolitan in the amount of $160 million. The note bears interest at 9½%, requires monthly payments of principal and interest through 2011 and is secured by the land and building of the Atlanta headquarters complex. In the event of foreclosure, each partner has severally guaranteed payment of one-half of any shortfall of collateral value to the outstanding secured indebtedness. Based on the present market conditions and building occupancy, the likelihood of any obligation to the Corporation with respect to this guarantee is considered remote.

Note 11.　Supplemental Cash Flow Information

The noncash effect of the adoption of Financial Accounting Standard Number 109 (Note 6) as of January 1, 1992 was as follows:

(Millions)

Increase (decrease) in:	
Receivables	$　3
Inventories	25
Timber and timberlands	39
Property, plant and equipment, net	676
Other assets	(6)
(Increase) decrease in:	
Taxes payable	(177)
Other current liabilities	(9)
Long-term debt, excluding current portion	3
Other long-term liabilities	(112)
Deferred income taxes	(442)
	$　—

Note 12.　Unaudited Selected Quarterly Financial Data

	First Quarter		Second Quarter		Third Quarter		Fourth Quarter	
(Millions, except per share amounts)	**1993**	1992[1]	**1993**	1992[1]	**1993**	1992[1]	**1993**	1992
Net sales	**$2,944**	$2,830	**$3,205**	$3,046	**$2,982**	$3,061	**$3,199**	$2,910
Gross profit (net sales minus cost of sales)	**676**	630	**617**	617	**619**	635	**604**	568
Income (loss) before extraordinary item and accounting change[2]	**41**	(3)	**5**	4	**(28)**	(174)	**(36)**	113
Income (loss) per share before extraordinary item and accounting change	**.47**	(.03)	**.06**	.04	**(.33)**	(2.01)	**(.41)**	1.31
Net income (loss)[2]	**41**	(58)	**(3)**	4	**(36)**	(174)	**(36)**	104
Net income (loss) per share	**.47**	(.67)	**(.03)**	.04	**(.42)**	(2.01)	**(.41)**	1.21
Dividends declared per common share	**.40**	.40	**.40**	.40	**.40**	.40	**.40**	.40
Price range of common stock								
High	**69.50**	72.00	**69.25**	71.75	**64.13**	62.63	**75.00**	62.50
Low	**55.00**	53.50	**56.38**	57.75	**59.25**	50.13	**59.00**	48.25

[1] As restated to reflect the change in accounting for income taxes (Note 6).
[2] Includes after-tax gains (losses) on asset divestitures of $(3) million in the 1993 first quarter and $10 million in the 1993 third quarter.

(Dollar amounts, except per share, and shares are in millions)	Year ended December 31						
	1993	1992	1991	1990	1989	1988	1987
Operations							
Net sales	**$12,330**	$11,847	$11,524	$12,665	$10,171	$9,509	$8,603
Costs and expenses							
Cost of sales	**9,814**	9,397	9,164	9,738	7,621	7,452	6,777
Selling, general and administrative	**1,190**	1,170	1,137	951	689	632	583
Depreciation and depletion	**764**	789	724	699	514	450	387
Interest	**513**	565	584	606	260	197	124
Other (income) expense	**26**	—	(344)	(48)	—	—	—
Total costs and expenses	**12,307**	11,921	11,265	11,946	9,084	8,731	7,871
Income (loss) from continuing operations before unusual items, income taxes, extraordinary items and accounting changes	**23**	(74)	259	719	1,087	778	732
Unusual items	**—**	—	—	—	—	—	66
Provision (benefit) for income taxes	**41**	(14)	293	354	426	311	340
Income (loss) from continuing operations before extraordinary items and accounting changes	**(18)**	(60)	(34)	365	661	467	458
Income (loss) from discontinued operations, net of taxes	**—**	—	—	—	—	—	—
Extraordinary items and accounting changes, net of taxes	**(16)**	(64)	(108)	—	—	—	—
Net income (loss)	**$ (34)**	$ (124)	$ (142)	$ 365	$ 661	$ 467	$ 458
Cash provided by continuing operations	**$ 489**	$ 868	$ 630	$ 1,223	$ 1,358	$ 865	$ 781
Other statistical data							
Per common share							
Income (loss) from continuing operations before extraordinary items and accounting changes	**$ (.21)**	$ (.69)	$ (.40)	$ 4.28	$ 7.42	$ 4.76	$ 4.23
Income (loss) from discontinued operations	**—**	—	—	—	—	—	—
Extraordinary items and accounting changes	**(.18)**	(.74)	(1.25)	—	—	—	—
Net income (loss)	**$ (.39)**	$ (1.43)	$ (1.65)	$ 4.28	$ 7.42	$ 4.76	$ 4.23
Dividends declared	**$ 1.60**	$ 1.60	$ 1.60	$ 1.60	$ 1.45	$ 1.25	$ 1.05
Average shares of common stock outstanding	**87.7**	86.4	85.8	85.3	89.1	98.1	107.5
Shares of common stock outstanding at year end	**90.3**	88.1	87.4	86.7	86.7	94.8	104.7
Cash dividends to earnings	**100%+**	100%+	100%+	38.1%	19.7%	26.3%	25.1%
Earnings to interest	**1.0**	0.9	1.4	2.0	5.0	4.4	6.9
Cash flow to interest	**1.9**	2.4	1.9	2.7	5.9	4.8	6.8
Effective income tax rate	**178.3%**	(18.9)%	113.1%	49.2%	39.2%	40.0%	42.6%

(Dollar amounts, except per share, are in millions)	Year ended December 31						
	1993	1992	1991	1990*	1989	1988	1987
Financial position, end of year							
Current assets	$ **1,646**	$ 1,607	$ 1,562	$ 1,766	$1,829	$1,892	$1,729
Timber and timberlands, net	**1,381**	1,402	1,377	1,630	1,246	1,289	915
Property, plant and equipment, net	**5,448**	5,831	5,567	6,341	3,691	3,723	3,048
Net assets of discontinued operations	**—**	—	—	—	—	—	—
Goodwill	**1,832**	1,891	1,949	2,042	91	101	92
Other assets	**238**	181	174	284	202	113	90
Total assets	**10,545**	10,912	10,629	12,063	7,059	7,118	5,874
Current liabilities	**2,064**	2,452	2,722	2,535	924	1,013	996
Long-term debt	**4,157**	4,019	3,743	5,218	2,336	2,514	1,298
Other long-term liabilities	**827**	731	633	407	241	168	156
Deferred income taxes	**1,095**	1,202	795	928	841	788	744
Redeemable preferred stock	**—**	—	—	—	—	—	—
Shareholders' equity	$ **2,402**	$ 2,508	$ 2,736	$ 2,975	$2,717	$2,635	$2,680
Working capital	$ **(418)**	$ (845)	$(1,160)	$ (769)	$ 905	$ 879	$ 733
Other statistical data							
Capital expenditures (including acquisitions)	$ **467**	$ 384	$ 528	$ 3,789	$ 499	$1,552	$ 825
Capital expenditures (excluding acquisitions)	**467**	384	528	866	493	711	550
Per common share							
Market price: High	**75.00**	72.00	60.25	52.13	62.00	42.88	52.75
Low	**55.00**	48.25	36.25	25.38	36.63	30.75	22.75
Year-end	**68.75**	62.38	53.63	37.25	48.50	36.88	34.50
Book value	**26.60**	28.47	31.30	34.31	31.35	27.79	25.59
Total debt to capital	**57.0%**	57.0%	60.1%	63.6%	40.1%	44.1%	31.4%
Current ratio	**.8**	.7	.6	.7	2.0	1.9	1.7

QUESTIONS

1. How does information from the balance sheet help users of the financial statements?

2. A recent financial magazine indicated that a drug company had good financial flexibility. What is meant by financial flexibility and why is it important?

3. What is meant by liquidity? Rank the following assets from one to five in order of liquidity.
   (a) Goodwill   (d) Short-term investments
   (b) Inventories   (e) Accounts receivable
   (c) Buildings

4. What are the major limitations of the balance sheet as a source of information?

5. In its December 31, 1996 balance sheet Stacey McGill Corporation reported as an asset "Net Notes and Accounts Receivable, $6,800,000." What other disclosures are necessary?

6. Should marketable securities always be reported as a current asset? Explain.

7. A stock analyst recently noted that a balance sheet is more critical than the income statement. He stated "You can show beautiful profits by burying inventories." Explain the analyst's comments.

8. What is the relationship between current assets and current liabilities?

9. The Chicago Bulls, Inc. sold 10,000 season tickets at $600 each. By December 31, 1996, 18 of the 40 home games had been played. What amount should be reported as a current liability at December 31, 1996?

10. What is working capital? How does working capital relate to the operating cycle?

11. In what section of the balance sheet should the following items appear, and what balance sheet terminology would you use?
    (a) Treasury stock (recorded at cost, which is below par).
    (b) Checking account at bank.
    (c) Land (held as an investment).
    (d) Reserve for sinking fund.
    (e) Unamortized premium on bonds payable.
    (f) Investment in copyrights.
    (g) Employees' pension fund (consisting of cash and securities).
    (h) Premium on capital stock.
    (i) Long-term investments (pledged against bank loans payable).

12. Where should the following items be shown on the balance sheet, if shown at all?
    (a) Allowance for doubtful accounts receivable.
    (b) Merchandise held on consignment.
    (c) Advances received on sales contract.
    (d) Cash surrender value of life insurance.
    (e) Accommodation endorsement on note.
    (f) Merchandise out on consignment.
    (g) Pension fund on deposit with a trustee (under a trust revocable at depositor's option).
    (h) Franchises.
    (i) Accumulated depreciation of plant and equipment.
    (j) Materials in transit—purchased f.o.b. destination.

13. State the generally accepted accounting principle (standard) applicable to the balance sheet valuation of each of the following assets.
    (a) Trade accounts receivable.   (d) Marketable securities (common stock of other companies).
    (b) Land.   (e) Prepaid expenses.
    (c) Inventories.

14. Refer to the definition of assets on page 192. Discuss how a leased building might qualify as an asset of the lessee under this definition.

15. Claudia Kishi says, "Retained earnings should be reported as an asset, since it is earnings which are reinvested in the business." How would you respond to Claudia?

16. Girod Corporation is involved in a lawsuit. Its legal counsel says it is reasonably possible that Girod will lose the suit. Should the corporation record a loss and liability on this lawsuit?

17. Spencer Corporation's lawyer says the company will probably prevail in a lawsuit and win damages of $1,000,000. The bookkeeper recorded a receivable and a gain in this amount. Is this correct?

18. What is a gain contingency? A loss contingency? Give two examples of each.

19. The president of your company has recently read an article that disturbs her greatly. The author of this article stated that "although the balance sheet and income statement balance to the penny, they are full of estimates and subject to material error." Indicate items found in these statements that are based on estimates and explain why you must resort to "guessing" these amounts.

20. The creditors of Watson Brewer Company agree to accept promissory notes for the amount of its indebtedness with a proviso that two-thirds of the annual profits must be applied to their liquidation. How should these notes be reported on the balance sheet of the issuing company? Give a reason for your answer.

21. What are the major types of subsequent events? Indicate how each of the following "subsequent events" would be reported.
    (a) Collection of a note written off in a prior period.
    (b) Issuance of a large preferred stock offering.
    (c) Acquisition of a company in a different industry.
    (d) Destruction of a major plant in a flood.
    (e) Death of the company's chief executive officer (CEO).
    (f) Settlement of a four-week strike at additional wage costs.
    (g) Settlement of a federal income tax case at considerably more tax than anticipated at year-end.
    (h) Change in the product mix from consumer goods to industrial goods.

22. What are some of the techniques of disclosure for the balance sheet?

23. What is the difference between the report form and the account form for the purpose of balance sheet presentation?

24. What is a "Summary of Significant Accounting Policies"?

25. What types of contractual obligations must be disclosed in great detail in the notes to the balance sheet? Why do you think these detailed provisions should be disclosed?

26. What is the profession's recommendation in regard to the use of the term "surplus"? Explain.

27. What is the purpose of a statement of cash flows? How does it differ from a balance sheet and an income statement?

28. The net income for the year for Stoneybrook, Inc. is $750,000, but the statement of cash flows reports that the cash provided by operating activities is $890,000. What might account for the difference?

29. Differentiate between operating activities, investing activities, and financing activities.

30. Each of the following items must be considered in preparing a statement of cash flows. Indicate where each item is to be reported in the statement, if at all. Assume that net income is reported as $90,000.
    (a) Accounts receivable increased from $32,000 to $37,000 from the beginning to the end of the year.
    (b) During the year, 10,000 shares of preferred stock with a par value of $100 a share were issued at $110 per share.
    (c) Depreciation expense amounted to $14,000 and bond premium amortization amounted to $6,000.

31. British accounting practices are different from United States GAAP for certain balance sheet items. Provide rationale as to why these differences might exist.

32. The controller is asked by the financial vice president to include in the supplementary information of the annual report some comments on employee commitment to excellence which distinguishes Amstutz Motors from its competitors. The controller knows that such remarks cannot be supported objectively in the balance sheet. Should the controller comply with this request? Might this subjective material mislead some stakeholder?

EXERCISES

E5-1 (Balance Sheet Classifications) Presented below are a number of balance sheet accounts of Clara Barton, Inc.:

1. Investment in Preferred Stock
2. Treasury Stock
3. Common Stock Distributable
4. Cash Dividends Payable
5. Accumulated Depreciation
6. Warehouse in Process of Construction
7. Petty Cash
8. Accrued Interest on Notes Payable
9. Deficit
10. Marketable Securities (short-term)
11. Income Taxes Payable
12. Unearned Subscriptions
13. Work in Process
14. Accrued Vacation Pay

Instructions

For each of the accounts above, indicate the proper balance sheet classification. In the case of borderline items, indicate the additional information that would be required to determine the proper classification.

E5-2 (Classification of Balance Sheet Accounts) Presented below are the captions of Nellie Bly Company's balance sheet:

A.	Current Assets	F.	Current Liabilities
B.	Investments	G.	Noncurrent Liabilities
C.	Property, Plant, and Equipment	H.	Capital Stock
D.	Intangible Assets	I.	Additional Paid-In Capital
E.	Other Assets	J.	Retained Earnings

Instructions

Indicate by letter where each of the following items would be classified:

1.	Preferred stock	11.	Cash surrender value of life insurance
2.	Goodwill	12.	Notes payable (due next year)
3.	Wages payable	13.	Office supplies
4.	Trade accounts payable	14.	Common stock
5.	Buildings	15.	Land
6.	Marketable securities	16.	Bond sinking fund
7.	Current portion of long-term debt	17.	Merchandise inventory
8.	Premium on bonds payable	18.	Prepaid insurance
9.	Allowance for doubtful accounts	19.	Bonds payable
10.	Accounts receivable	20.	Taxes payable

E5-3 (Classification of Balance Sheet Accounts) Assume that Belva Lockwood Enterprises uses the following headings on its balance sheet:

A.	Current Assets	F.	Current Liabilities
B.	Investments	G.	Long-term Liabilities
C.	Property, Plant, and Equipment	H.	Capital Stock
D.	Intangible Assets	I.	Paid-in Capital in Excess of Par
E.	Other Assets	J.	Retained Earnings

Instructions

Indicate by letter how each of the following usually should be classified. If an item should appear in a note to the financial statements, use the letter "N" to indicate this fact. If an item need not be reported at all on the balance sheet, use the letter "X."

1.	Unexpired insurance.	13.	Machinery retired from use and held for sale.
2.	Stock owned in affiliated companies.	14.	Fully depreciated machine still in use.
3.	Unearned subscriptions.	15.	Organization costs.
4.	Advances to suppliers.	16.	Accrued interest on bonds payable.
5.	Unearned rent.	17.	Salaries that company budget shows will be paid to employees within the next year.
6.	Treasury stock.		
7.	Premium on preferred stock.	18.	Company is a defendant in a lawsuit for $1 million (possibility of loss is reasonably likely).
8.	Copyrights.		
9.	Petty cash fund.		
10.	Sale of large issue of common stock 15 days after balance sheet date.	19.	Discount on bonds payable. (Assume related to bonds payable in No. 12.)
11.	Accrued interest on notes receivable.	20.	Accumulated depreciation.
12.	Twenty-year issue of bonds payable which will mature within the next year. (No sinking fund exists and refunding is not planned.)		

E5-4 (Preparation of a Classified Balance Sheet) Assume that Gertrude Stein Inc. has the following accounts at the end of the current year.

1.	Common Stock	8.	Work in Process
2.	Discount on Bonds Payable	9.	Copyrights
3.	Treasury Stock (at cost)	10.	Buildings
4.	Common Stock Subscribed	11.	Notes Receivable (short-term)
5.	Raw Materials	12.	Cash
6.	Preferred Stock Investments—Long-term	13.	Accrued Salaries Payable
7.	Unearned Rent	14.	Accumulated Depreciation—Buildings

15. Cash Restricted for Plant Expansion
16. Land Held for Future Plant Site
17. Allowance for Doubtful Accounts—Accounts Receivable
18. Retained Earnings—Unappropriated
19. Discount on Common Stock

20. Unearned Subscriptions
21. Receivables—Officers (due in one year)
22. Finished Goods
23. Accounts Receivable
24. Bonds Payable (due in 4 years)
25. Stock Subscriptions Receivable

Instructions

Prepare a classified balance sheet in good form (no monetary amounts are necessary).

E5-5 (Preparation of a Corrected Balance Sheet) Celia Cruz Company has decided to expand their operations. The bookkeeper recently completed the balance sheet presented below in order to obtain additional funds for expansion.

Celia Cruz Company
BALANCE SHEET
For the Year Ended 1996

Current assets	
Cash (net of bank overdraft of $30,000)	$200,000
Accounts receivable (net)	340,000
Inventories at lower of average cost or market	385,000
Marketable securities—at cost (fair value $120,000)	140,000
Property, plant, and equipment	
Building (net)	570,000
Office equipment (net)	160,000
Land held for future use	175,000
Intangible assets	
Goodwill	80,000
Cash surrender value of life insurance	90,000
Prepaid expenses	5,000
Current liabilities	
Accounts payable	105,000
Notes payable (due next year)	125,000
Pension obligation	82,000
Rent payable	55,000
Premium on bonds payable	53,000
Long-term liabilities	
Bonds payable	500,000
Stockholders' equity	
Common stock, $1.00 par, authorized	
400,000 shares, issued 290,000	290,000
Additional paid-in capital	160,000
Retained earnings	?

Instructions

Prepare a revised balance sheet given the available information. Assume that the accumulated depreciation balance for the buildings is $140,000 and for the office equipment, $95,000. Marketable securities are trading securities. The allowance for doubtful accounts has a balance of $10,000. The pension obligation is considered a long-term liability.

E5-6 (Corrections of a Balance Sheet) The bookkeeper for Angeles Ochoa Company has prepared the following balance sheet as of July 31, 1996:

Angeles Ochoa Company
BALANCE SHEET
As of July 31, 1996

Cash	$ 69,000	Notes and accounts payable	$ 44,000
Accounts receivable (net)	40,500	Long-term liabilities	75,000
Inventories	60,000	Stockholders' equity	155,500
Equipment (net)	84,000		
Patents	21,000		
	$274,500		$274,500

The following additional information is provided:

1. Cash includes $1,200 in a petty cash fund and $9,000 in a bond sinking fund.
2. The net accounts receivable balance comprises the following three items: (a) accounts receivable—debit balances $50,000; (b) accounts receivable—credit balances $6,000; (c) allowance for doubtful accounts $3,500.
3. Merchandise inventory costing $5,300 was shipped out on consignment on July 31, 1996. The ending inventory balance does not include the consigned goods. Receivables in the amount of $5,300 were recognized on these consigned goods.
4. Equipment had a cost of $98,000 and an accumulated depreciation balance of $14,000.
5. Taxes payable of $6,000 were accrued on July 31. Angeles Ochoa Company, however, had set up a cash fund to meet this obligation. This cash fund was not included in the cash balance, but was offset against the taxes payable amount.

Instructions
Prepare a corrected classified balance sheet as of July 31, 1996 from the available information, adjusting the account balances using the additional information.

E5-7 (Current Asset Section of the Balance Sheet) Presented below are selected accounts of Rico Company at 12/31/96:

Finished goods	$ 52,000	Cost of goods sold	2,100,000
Revenue received in advance	90,000	Notes receivable	40,000
Bank overdraft	8,000	Accounts receivable	161,000
Equipment	253,000	Raw materials	207,000
Work-in-process	14,000	Supplies expense	60,000
Cash	37,000	Allowance for doubtful accounts	12,000
Short-term investments in stock	31,000	Licenses	18,000
Customer advances	36,000	Additional paid-in capital	88,000
Cash restricted for plant expansion	50,000	Treasury stock	22,000

The following additional information is available:

1. Inventories are valued at lower of cost or market using LIFO.
2. Equipment is recorded at cost. Accumulated depreciation, computed on a straight-line basis, is $50,600.
3. The short-term investments have a fair value of $29,000 (assume they are trading securities).
4. The notes receivable are due June 30, 1998, with interest receivable every June 30. The notes bear interest at 12% (Hint: accrue interest due on 12/31/96).
5. The allowance for doubtful accounts applies to the accounts receivable. Accounts receivable of $50,000 are pledged as collateral on a bank loan.
6. Licenses are recorded net of accumulated amortization of $14,000.
7. Treasury stock is recorded at cost.

Instructions
Prepare the current asset section of Rico Company's December 31, 1996, balance sheet, with appropriate disclosures.

E5-8 (Current vs. Long-term Liabilities) Natalie Cole Corporation is preparing its December 31, 1996, balance sheet. The following items may be reported as either a current or long-term liability.

1. On December 15, 1996, Cole declared a cash dividend of $3.00 per share to stockholders of record on December 31. The dividend is payable on January 15, 1997. Cole has issued 1,000,000 shares of common stock, of which 50,000 shares are held in treasury.
2. Also on December 15, Cole declared a 10% stock dividend to stockholders of record on December 31. The dividend will be distributed on January 15, 1997. Cole's common stock has a par value of $10 per share and a market value of $38 per share.
3. At December 31, bonds payable of $100,000,000 are outstanding. The bonds pay 12% interest every August 31 and mature in installments of $25,000,000 every August 31, beginning August 31, 1997.
4. At December 31, 1995, customer advances were $12,000,000. During 1996, Cole collected $30,000,000 of customer advances, and advances of $23,000,000 were earned.
5. At December 31, 1996, retained earnings appropriated for future inventory losses is $15,000,000.

Instructions
For each item above indicate the dollar amounts to be reported as a current liability and as a long-term liability, if any.

E5-9 (Contingencies—Entries and Disclosures) Kathleen Battle Sound Machines is involved in two contingencies at December 31, 1996.

1. The company is involved in a pending court case. Legal counsel feels it is probable the company will prevail and be awarded damages of $3,000,000.
2. Battle sells several machines under a one-year warranty. It is probable that a liability of $2,400,000 exists at December 31, 1996, because of this warranty.

Instructions

(a) Prepare all entries necessary at December 31, 1996, to record these contingencies.
(b) What disclosures would Battle make in its December 31, 1996, balance sheet?

E5-10 (Post-Balance Sheet Events) Otis Clay Corporation issued its financial statements for the year ended December 31, 1996, on March 10, 1997. The following events took place early in 1997.

1. On January 10, 10,000 shares of $5 par value common stock were issued at $70 per share.
2. On March 1, Otis Clay determined after negotiations with the Internal Revenue Service that income taxes payable for 1996 should be $1,230,000. At December 31, 1996, income taxes payable were recorded at $1,100,000.

Instructions

Discuss how the preceding post-balance sheet events should be reflected in the 1996 financial statements.

E5-11 (Current Assets and Current Liabilities) The current asset and liability sections of the balance sheet of Oliver Cromwell Company appear as follows:

Oliver Cromwell Company
PARTIAL BALANCE SHEET
December 31, 1996

Cash		$ 38,000	Accounts payable	$60,000
Accounts receivable	$86,000		Notes payable	64,000
Less allowance for doubtful accounts	7,000	79,000		
Inventories		170,000		
Prepaid expenses		9,000		
		$296,000		$124,000

The following errors in the corporation's accounting have been discovered:

1. January 1997 cash disbursements entered as of December 1996 included payments of accounts payable in the amount of $39,000, on which a cash discount of 2% was taken.
2. The inventory included $27,000 of merchandise that had been received at December 31 but for which no purchase invoices had been received or entered. Of this amount, $12,000 had been received on consignment; the remainder was purchased f.o.b. destination, terms 2/10, n/30.
3. Sales for the first four days in January 1997 in the amount of $30,000 were entered in the sales book as of December 31, 1996. Of these, $21,500 were sales on account and the remainder were cash sales.
4. Cash, not including cash sales, collected in January 1997 and entered as of December 31, 1996, totaled $35,324. Of this amount, $23,324 was received on account after cash discounts of 2% had been deducted; the remainder represented the proceeds of a bank loan.

Instructions

(a) Restate the current asset and liability sections of the balance sheet in accordance with good accounting practice. (Assume that both accounts receivable and accounts payable are recorded gross.)
(b) State the net effect of your adjustments on Oliver Cromwell Company's retained earnings balance.

E5-12 (Post-Balance Sheet Events) For each of the following subsequent (post-balance sheet) events, indicate whether a company should (a) adjust the financial statements, (b) disclose in notes to the financial statements, or (c) neither adjust nor disclose.

1. Settlement of federal tax case at a cost considerably in excess of the amount expected at year-end.
2. Introduction of a new product line.
3. Loss of assembly plant due to fire.
4. Sale of a significant portion of the company's assets.
5. Retirement of the company president.

6. Prolonged employee strike.
7. Loss of a significant customer.
8. Issuance of a significant number of shares of common stock.
9. Material loss on a year-end receivable because of a customer's bankruptcy.
10. Hiring of a new president.
11. Settlement of prior year's litigation against the company.
12. Merger with another company of comparable size.

E5-13 (Statement of Cash Flows—Classifications) The major classifications of activities reported in the statement of cash flows are operating, investing, and financing. Classify each of the transactions listed below as:

1. Operating activity—add to net income.
2. Operating activity—deduct from net income.
3. Investing activity.
4. Financing activity.
5. Not reported as a cash flow.

The transactions are as follows:

(a)	Issuance of capital stock.	**(h)**	Payment of cash dividends.
(b)	Purchase of land and building.	**(i)**	Exchange of furniture for office equipment.
(c)	Redemption of bonds.	**(j)**	Purchase of treasury stock.
(d)	Sale of equipment.	**(k)**	Loss on sale of equipment.
(e)	Depreciation of machinery.	**(l)**	Increase in accounts receivable during the year.
(f)	Amortization of patent.	**(m)**	Decrease in accounts payable during the year.
(g)	Issuance of bonds for plant assets.		

E5-14 (Preparation of a Statement of Cash Flows) The comparative balance sheets of Henry Tudor Inc. at the beginning and the end of the year 1996 appear below.

<table>
<tr><td colspan="4" align="center">Henry Tudor Inc.
Balance Sheets</td></tr>
<tr><td align="center">**Assets**</td><td align="center">Dec. 31, 1996</td><td align="center">Jan. 1, 1996</td><td align="center">Inc./Dec.</td></tr>
<tr><td>Cash</td><td>$ 45,000</td><td>$ 13,000</td><td>$32,000 Inc.</td></tr>
<tr><td>Accounts receivable</td><td>91,000</td><td>88,000</td><td>3,000 Inc.</td></tr>
<tr><td>Equipment</td><td>39,000</td><td>22,000</td><td>17,000 Inc.</td></tr>
<tr><td>Less accumulated depreciation</td><td>(17,000)</td><td>(11,000)</td><td>6,000 Inc.</td></tr>
<tr><td>Total</td><td>$158,000</td><td>$112,000</td><td></td></tr>
<tr><td>**Liabilities and Stockholders' Equity**</td><td></td><td></td><td></td></tr>
<tr><td>Accounts payable</td><td>$ 20,000</td><td>$ 15,000</td><td>5,000 Inc.</td></tr>
<tr><td>Common stock</td><td>100,000</td><td>80,000</td><td>20,000 Inc.</td></tr>
<tr><td>Retained earnings</td><td>38,000</td><td>17,000</td><td>21,000 Inc.</td></tr>
<tr><td>Total</td><td>$158,000</td><td>$112,000</td><td></td></tr>
</table>

Net income of $35,000 was reported and dividends of $14,000 were paid in 1996. New equipment was purchased and none was sold.

Instructions
Prepare a statement of cash flows for the year 1996.

E5-15 (Preparation of a Statement of Cash Flows) Presented below is a condensed version of the comparative balance sheets for Catherine Aragon Corporation for the last two years at December 31:

	1996	1995
Cash	$177,000	$ 78,000
Accounts receivable	180,000	185,000
Investments	52,000	74,000
Equipment	298,000	240,000
Less accumulated depreciation	(106,000)	(89,000)
Current liabilities	134,000	151,000
Capital stock	160,000	160,000
Retained earnings	307,000	177,000

Additional information:

Investments were sold at a loss (not extraordinary) of $9,000; no equipment was sold; cash dividends paid were $20,000; and net income was $150,000.

Instructions

Prepare a statement of cash flows for 1996 for Aragon Corporation.

E5-16 (Preparation of a Statement of Cash Flows) A comparative balance sheet for Anne Boleyn Corporation is presented below.

	December 31	
Assets	1996	1995
Cash	$ 69,000	$ 22,000
Accounts receivable	82,000	66,000
Inventories	180,000	189,000
Land	75,000	110,000
Equipment	260,000	200,000
Accumulated depreciation—equipment	(69,000)	(42,000)
Total	$597,000	$545,000
Liabilities and Stockholders' Equity		
Accounts payable	$ 34,000	$ 47,000
Bonds payable	150,000	200,000
Common stock ($1 par)	214,000	164,000
Retained earnings	199,000	134,000
Total	$597,000	$545,000

Additional information:

1. Net income for 1996 was $115,000.
2. Cash dividends of $50,000 were declared and paid.
3. Bonds payable amounting to $50,000 were retired through issuance of common stock.

Instructions

Prepare a statement of cash flows for 1996 for Anne Boleyn Corporation.

E5-17 (Preparation of a Balance Sheet) Presented below is the trial balance of Jane Seymour Corporation at December 31, 1996.

	Debits	Credits
Cash	$ 227,000	
Sales		$ 8,000,000
Marketable securities—current	153,000	
Cost of goods sold	4,800,000	
Long-term investments in bonds	269,000	
Long-term investments in stocks	277,000	
Short-term notes payable		90,000
Accounts payable		475,000
Selling expenses	2,000,000	
Investment revenue		63,000
Land	260,000	
Buildings	1,040,000	
Dividends payable		136,000
Accrued liabilities		96,000
Accounts receivable	435,000	
Accumulated depreciation—buildings		152,000
Allowance for doubtful accounts		25,000
Administrative expenses	900,000	
Interest expense	211,000	
Inventories	597,000	
Extraordinary gain		80,000
Prior period adjustment—depr. error	140,000	
Long-term notes payable		900,000
Equipment	600,000	
Bonds payable		1,100,000
Accumulated depreciation—equipment		40,000
Franchise (net of $80,000 amort.)	160,000	

Common stock ($5 par)		1,000,000
Treasury stock	191,000	
Patent (net of $30,000 amort.)	195,000	
Retained earnings		218,000
Additional paid-in capital		80,000
Totals	$12,455,000	$12,455,000

Instructions

Prepare a balance sheet at December 31, 1996, for Jane Seymour Corporation. Ignore income taxes.

E5-18 (Preparation of a Statement of Cash Flows and a Balance Sheet) Thomas More Corporation's balance sheet at the end of 1995 included the following items:

Current assets	$235,000		Current liabilities	$150,000
Land	30,000		Bonds payable	100,000
Building	120,000		Common stock	180,000
Equipment	90,000		Retained earnings	44,000
Accum. depr.—build.	(30,000)			
Accum. depr.—equip.	(11,000)			
Patents	40,000			
Total	$474,000		Total	$474,000

The following information is available for 1996.

1. Net income was $46,000.
2. Equipment (cost, $20,000 and accumulated depreciation, $8,000) was sold for $10,000.
3. Depreciation expense was $3,000 on the building and $9,000 on equipment.
4. Patent amortization was $5,000.
5. Current assets other than cash increased by $29,000. Current liabilities increased by $13,000.
6. An addition to the building was completed at a cost of $20,000.
7. A long-term investment in stock was purchased for $16,000.
8. Bonds payable of $50,000 were issued.
9. Cash dividends of $30,000 were declared and paid.
10. Treasury stock was purchased at a cost of $9,000.

Instructions
(a) Prepare a statement of cash flows for 1996.
(b) Prepare a balance sheet at December 31, 1996.

PROBLEMS

P5-1 (Preparation of a Classified Balance Sheet) Presented below is a list of accounts in alphabetical order.

Accounts Receivable	Equipment
Accrued Wages	FICA Taxes Payable
Accumulated Depreciation—Buildings	Gain on Sale of Equipment
Accumulated Depreciation—Equipment	Interest Receivable
Advances to Employees	Inventory—Beginning Inventory
Advertising Expense	Inventory—Ending Inventory
Allowance for Doubtful Accounts	Land
Bond Sinking Fund	Land for Future Plant Site
Bonds Payable	Loss from Flood
Buildings	Notes Payable
Cash in Bank	Patent (net of amortization)
Cash on Hand	Pension Obligations
Cash Surrender Value of Life Insurance	Petty Cash
Commission Expense	Preferred Stock
Common Stock	Premium on Bonds Payable
Copyright (net of amortization)	Premium on Preferred Stock
Dividends Payable	Prepaid Rent

Purchases	Sales Salaries
Purchase Returns and Allowances	Temporary Investments
Retained Earnings	Transportation-in
Sales	Treasury Stock (at cost)
Sales Discounts	Unearned Subscriptions

Instructions

Prepare a classified balance sheet in good form (no monetary amounts are to be shown).

P5-2 (Balance Sheet Preparation) Presented below are a number of balance sheet items for Santana, Inc., for the current year, 1996.

Goodwill	$ 110,000	Accumulated depreciation—equipment	$ 292,000
Payroll taxes payable	177,591	Inventories	239,800
Bonds payable	290,000	Rent payable—short-term	45,000
Discount on bonds payable	15,000	Taxes payable	98,362
Cash	260,000	Long-term rental obligations	480,000
Land	450,000	Common stock, $1 par value	200,000
Notes receivable	545,700	Preferred stock, $10 par value	150,000
Notes payable to banks	265,000	Prepaid expenses	87,920
Accounts payable	690,000	Equipment	1,470,000
Retained earnings	?	Marketable securities (short-term)	81,000
Refundable federal and state income taxes	97,630	Accumulated depreciation—building	170,200
Unsecured notes payable (long term)	1,600,000	Building	1,640,000

Instructions

Prepare a classified balance sheet in good form. Common stock authorized was 400,000 shares and preferred stock authorized was 20,000 shares. Assume that notes receivable and notes payable are short-term, unless stated otherwise. Cost and fair value of marketable securities are the same.

P5-3 (Balance Sheet Adjustment and Preparation) The trial balance of U2 Company and other related information for the year 1996 is presented below.

U2 Company
TRIAL BALANCE
December 31, 1996

Cash	$ 41,000	
Accounts Receivable	163,500	
Allowance for Doubtful Accounts		$ 6,700
Prepaid Insurance	5,900	
Inventory	308,500	
Long-term Investments	349,000	
Land	85,000	
Construction Work in Progress	124,000	
Patents	26,000	
Equipment	400,000	
Accumulated Depreciation of Equipment		142,000
Unamortized Discount on Bonds Payable	20,000	
Accounts Payable		148,000
Accrued Expenses		38,200
Notes Payable		94,000
Bonds Payable		400,000
Capital Stock		500,000
Premium on Capital Stock		45,000
Retained Earnings		149,000
	$1,522,900	$1,522,900

Additional information:

1. The inventory has a replacement market value of $353,000. The LIFO method of inventory value is used.
2. The cost and fair value of the long-term investments that consist of stocks and bonds is the same.
3. The amount of the Construction Work in Progress account represents the costs expended to date on a building in the process of construction. (The company rents factory space at the present time.) The land on which the building is being constructed cost $85,000, as shown in the trial balance.

4. The patents were purchased by the company at a cost of $36,000 and are being amortized on a straight-line basis.
5. Of the unamortized discount on bonds payable, $2,000 will be amortized in 1997.
6. The notes payable represent bank loans that are secured by long-term investments carried at $120,000. These bank loans are due in 1997.
7. The bonds payable bear interest at 11% payable every December 31 and are due January 1, 2007.
8. Six hundred thousand shares of common stock of a par value of $1 were authorized, of which 500,000 shares were issued and are outstanding.

Instructions
Prepare a balance sheet as of December 31, 1996 so that all important information is fully disclosed.

P5-4 (Preparation of a Corrected Balance Sheet) Presented below is the balance sheet of Run–D.M.C. Corporation as of December 31, 1996:

Run–D.M.C.
BALANCE SHEET
December 31, 1996

Assets

Goodwill (Note 2)	$ 120,000
Building (Note 1)	1,640,000
Inventories	312,100
Land	750,000
Accounts receivable	170,000
Treasury stock (50,000 shares, no par)	87,000
Cash on hand	193,900
Assets allocated to trustee for plant expansion	
Cash in bank	70,000
U.S. Treasury notes, at cost and fair value	$ 120,000
	$3,463,000

Equities

Notes payable (Note 3)	$ 600,000
Common stock, authorized and issued, 1,000,000 shares, no par	1,150,000
Retained earnings	648,000
Appreciation capital (Note 1)	570,000
Federal income taxes payable	75,000
Reserve for depreciation of building	420,000
	$3,463,000

Note 1: Buildings are stated at cost, except for one building that was recorded at appraised value. The excess of appraisal value over cost was $570,000. Depreciation has been recorded based on cost.
Note 2: Goodwill in the amount of $120,000 was recognized because the company believed that book value was not an accurate representation of the fair market value of the company.
Note 3: Notes payable are long-term except for the current installment due of $60,000.

Instructions
Prepare a corrected classified balance sheet in good form. The notes above are for information only.

P5-5 (Balance Sheet Adjustment and Preparation) Presented below is the balance sheet of John Lennon Corporation for the current year, 1996.

John Lennon Corporation
BALANCE SHEET
December 31, 1996

Current assets	$ 435,000	Current liabilities	$ 330,000
Investments	640,000	Long-term liabilities	1,000,000
Property, plant, and equipment	1,720,000	Stockholders' equity	1,770,000
Intangible assets	305,000		
	$3,100,000		$3,100,000

The following information is presented:

1. The current asset section includes: cash $100,000, accounts receivable $170,000 less $10,000 for allowance for doubtful accounts, inventories $180,000, and prepaid revenue $5,000. The cash balance is composed of $116,000, less a bank overdraft of $16,000. Inventories are stated on the lower of FIFO cost or market.
2. The investments section includes the cash surrender value of a life insurance contract $40,000; investments in common stock, short-term (trading) $80,000 and long-term (available-for-sale) $140,000; bond sinking fund $200,000; and organization costs $180,000. The cost and fair value of investments in common stock are the same.
3. Property, plant, and equipment includes buildings $1,040,000 less accumulated depreciation $360,000; equipment $420,000 less accumulated depreciation $180,000; land $500,000; and land held for future use $300,000.
4. Intangible assets include a franchise $165,000, goodwill $100,000, and discount on bonds payable $40,000.
5. Current liabilities include accounts payable $90,000, notes payable—short-term $120,000 and long-term $80,000, and taxes payable $40,000.
6. Long-term liabilities are composed solely of 10% bonds payable due 2004.
7. Stockholders' equity has preferred stock, no par value, authorized 200,000 shares, issued 70,000 shares for $450,000, and common stock, $1.00 par value, authorized 400,000 shares, issued 100,000 shares at an average price of $10. In addition, the corporation has retained earnings of $320,000.

Instructions
Prepare a balance sheet in good form, adjusting the amounts in each balance sheet classification as affected by the "information" given above.

P5-6 (Preparation of a Statement of Cash Flows and a Balance Sheet) Tracy Chapman Inc. had the following balance sheet at the end of operations for 1995:

Tracy Chapman Inc. BALANCE SHEET December 31, 1995			
Cash	$ 20,000	Accounts payable	$ 30,000
Accounts receivable	21,200	Long-term notes payable	41,000
Investments	32,000	Capital stock	100,000
Plant assets (net)	81,000	Retained earnings	23,200
Land	40,000		
	$194,200		$194,200

During 1996 the following occurred:

1. Tracy Chapman Inc. sold part of its investment portfolio for $16,000. This transaction resulted in a gain of $2,400 for the firm. The company often sells and buys securities of this nature.
2. A tract of land was purchased for $18,000 cash.
3. Long-term notes payable in the amount of $14,000 were retired before maturity by paying $14,000 cash.
4. An additional $25,000 in capital stock was issued at par.
5. Dividends totalling $8,200 were declared and paid to stockholders.
6. Net income for 1996 was $30,000 after allowing for depreciation of $12,000.
7. Land was purchased through the issuance of $30,000 in bonds.
8. At December 31, 1996, Cash was $40,000, Accounts Receivable was $41,600, and Accounts Payable remained at $30,000.

Instructions
(a) Prepare a statement of cash flows for 1996.
(b) Prepare the balance sheet as it would appear at December 31, 1996.
(c) How might the statement of cash flows help the user of the financial statements?

P5-7 (Income Statement and Balance Sheet Preparation) LeRoi Jones has prepared baked goods for resale since 1988. He started a baking business in his home and has been operating in a rented building with a storefront since 1993. Jones incorporated the business as B&B Inc. on January 1, 1996, with an initial stock issue of 2,500 shares of common stock at a par value of $1.00 per share. LeRoi Jones is the principal stockholder of B&B Inc..

Sales have increased 30 percent annually since operations began at the present location, and additional equipment is needed to accommodate expected continued growth. Jones wishes to purchase some additional baking equipment and to finance the equipment through a long-term note from a commercial bank. Alabama State Bank & Trust has asked Jones to submit an income statement for B&B Inc. for the first five months of 1996 and a balance sheet as of May 31, 1996.

Jones assembled the following information from the cash basis records of the corporation for use in preparing the financial statements requested by the bank.

1. The check register showed the following 1996 deposits through May 31.

Sale of common stock	$ 2,500
Cash sales	22,440
Rebates from purchases	130
Collections on credit sales	5,320
Bank loan proceeds	2,880
	$33,270

2. The following amounts were disbursed through May 31, 1996.

Baking materials	$14,300
Rent	1,800
Salaries and wages	5,500
Maintenance	110
Utilities	4,000
Insurance premium	1,680
Equipment	3,000
Principal and interest payment on bank loan	312
Advertising	424
	$31,126

3. Unpaid invoices at May 31, 1996, were as follows.

Baking materials	$256
Utilities	220
	$476

4. Customer records showed uncollected sales of $4,226 at May 31, 1996.
5. Baking materials costing $1,840 were on hand at May 31, 1996. There were no materials in process or finished goods on hand at that date. No materials were on hand or in process and no finished goods were on hand at January 1, 1996.
6. The note evidencing the 3-year bank loan is dated January 1, 1996, and states a simple interest rate of 10%. The loan requires quarterly payments on April 1, July 1, October 1, and January 1 consisting of equal principal payments plus accrued interest since the last payment.
7. LeRoi Jones receives a salary of $750 on the last day of each month. The other employees had been paid through Friday, May 25, 1996, and were due an additional $200 on May 31, 1996.
8. New display cases and equipment costing $3,000 were purchased on January 2, 1996, and have an estimated useful life of 5 years. These are the only fixed assets currently used in the business. Straight-line depreciation is to be used for book purposes.
9. Rent was paid for six months in advance on January 2, 1996.
10. A one-year insurance policy was purchased on January 2, 1996.
11. B&B Inc. is subject to an income tax rate of 20%.
12. Payments and collections pertaining to the unincorporated business through December 31, 1995, were not included in the records of the corporation, and no cash was transferred from the unincorporated business to the corporation.

Instructions

Using the accrual basis of accounting, prepare for B&B Inc.:
(a) An income statement for the five months ended May 31, 1996.
(b) A balance sheet as of May 31, 1996.

(CMA adapted)

CASES

C5-1 (Reporting Varied Transactions) The following items were brought to your attention during the course of the year-end audit:

1. The client expects to recover a substantial amount in connection with a pending refund claim for a prior year's taxes. Although the claim is being contested, counsel for the company has confirmed this expectation.
2. Your client is a defendant in a patent infringement suit involving a material amount; you have received from the client's counsel a statement that the loss can be reasonably estimated and that a reasonable possibility of a loss exists.
3. Cash includes a substantial sum specifically set aside for immediate reconstruction of plant and renewal of machinery.
4. Because of a general increase in the number of labor disputes and strikes, both within and outside the industry, it is very likely that the client will suffer a costly strike in the near future.
5. Trade accounts receivable include a large number of customers' notes, many of which had been renewed several times and may have to be renewed continually for some time in the future. The interest is settled on each maturity date and the makers are in good credit standing.
6. At the beginning of the year the client entered into a 10-year nonrenewable lease agreement. Provisions in the lease require the client to make substantial reconditioning and restoration expenditures at the termination of the lease, if necessary.
7. Inventory includes retired equipment, some at regularly depreciated book value, and some at scrap or sales value.

Instructions
For each of the situations above describe the accounting treatment you recommend for the current year. Justify your recommended treatment for each situation.

C5-2 (Post-Balance Sheet Events) At December 31, 1995, Paul Dunbar Corp. has assets of $10,000,000, liabilities of $6,000,000, common stock of $2,000,000 (representing 2,000,000 shares of $1.00 par common stock), and retained earnings of $2,000,000. Net sales for the year 1995 were $18,000,000 and net income was $800,000. As auditors of this company, you are making a review of subsequent events on February 13, 1996, and find the following.

1. On February 3, 1996, one of Dunbar's customers declared bankruptcy. At December 31, 1995, this company owed Dunbar $300,000, of which $30,000 was paid in January, 1996.
2. On January 18, 1996, one of the three major plants of the client burned.
3. On January 23, 1996, a strike was called at one of Dunbar's largest plants, which halted 30% of its production. As of today (February 13) the strike has not been settled.
4. A major electronics enterprise has introduced a line of products that would compete directly with Dunbar's primary line, now being produced in a specially designed new plant. Because of manufacturing innovations, the competitor has been able to achieve quality similar to that of Dunbar's products, but at a price 50% lower. Dunbar officials say they will meet the lower prices, which are high enough to cover variable manufacturing and selling costs but which permit recovery of only a portion of fixed costs.
5. Merchandise traded in the open market is recorded in the company's records at $1.40 per unit on December 31, 1995. This price had prevailed for two weeks, after release of an official market report that predicted vastly enlarged supplies; however, no purchases were made at $1.40. The price throughout the preceding year had been about $2.00, which was the level experienced over several years. On January 18, 1995, the price returned to $2.00, after public disclosure of an error in the official calculations of the prior December, correction of which destroyed the expectations of excessive supplies. Inventory at December 31, 1995, was on a lower of cost or market basis.
6. On February 1, 1996, the board of directors adopted a resolution accepting the offer of an investment banker to guarantee the marketing of $1,000,000 of preferred stock.

Instructions
State in each case how the 1995 financial statements would be affected, if at all.

C5-3 (Reporting the Financial Effects of Varied Transactions) In an examination of Ann Petry Corporation as of December 31, 1996, you have learned that the following situations exist. No entries have been made in the accounting records for these items.

1. The corporation erected its present factory building in 1981. Depreciation was calculated by the straight-line method, using an estimated life of 35 years. Early in 1996, the board of directors conducted a careful survey and estimated that the factory building had a remaining useful life of 25 years as of January 1, 1996.

2. An additional assessment of 1995 income taxes was levied and paid in 1996.
3. When calculating the accrual for officers' salaries at December 31, 1996, it was discovered that the accrual for officers' salaries for December 31, 1995, had been overstated.
4. On December 15, 1996, Petry Corporation declared a 1% common stock dividend on its common stock outstanding, payable February 1, 1997, to the common stockholders of record December 31, 1996.
5. Petry Corporation, which is on a calendar-year basis, changed its inventory method as of January 1, 1996. The inventory for December 31, 1995, was costed by the average method, and the inventory for December 31, 1996, was costed by the FIFO method.
6. Petry Corporation has guaranteed the payment of interest on the 20-year first mortgage bonds of Yerby Company, an affiliate. Outstanding bonds of Yerby Company amount to $150,000 with interest payable at 10% per annum, due June 1 and December 1 of each year. The bonds were issued by Yerby Company on December 1, 1992, and all interest payments have been met by the company with the exception of the payment due December 1, 1996. The Petry Corporation states that it will pay the defaulted interest to the bondholders on January 15, 1997.

Instructions

Describe fully how each of the items above should be reported in the financial statements of Petry Corporation for the year 1996.

C5-4 (Current Asset and Liability Classification) Below are the account titles of a number of debit and credit accounts as they might appear on the balance sheet of James Baldwin Corporation as of October 31, 1996.

Debits	Credits
Interest accrued on U.S. government securities	Capital stock—preferred
Notes receivable	11% first mortgage bonds due in 2003
Petty cash fund	Preferred stock dividend, payable Nov. 1, 1996
U.S. government securities	Allowance for doubtful accounts receivable
Treasury stock	Federal income taxes payable
Unamortized bond discount	Customers' advances (on contracts to be completed next year)
Cash in bank	Premium on bonds redeemable in 1996
Land	Officers' 1996 bonus accrued
Inventory of operating parts and supplies	Accrued payroll
Inventory of raw materials	Provision for renegotiation of U.S. government contracts
Patents	Notes payable
Cash and U.S. government bonds set aside for property additions	Accrued interest on bonds
Investment in subsidiary	Accumulated depreciation
Accounts receivable	Accounts payable
U.S. government contracts	Capital in excess of par
Regular	Accrued interest on notes payable
Installments—due next year	8% first mortgage bonds to be redeemed in 1996 out of current assets
Installments—due after next year	
Goodwill	
Inventory of finished goods	
Inventory of work in process	
Deficit	

Instructions

Select the current asset and current liability items from among these debits and credits. If there appear to be certain borderline cases that you are unable to classify without further information, mention them and explain your difficulty, or give your reasons for making questionable classifications, if any.

(AICPA adapted)

C5-5 (Identifying Balance Sheet Deficiencies) The assets of Jean Toomer Corporation are presented below (000s omitted):

Jean Toomer Corporation
BALANCE SHEET (Partial)
December 31, 1996

Assets

Current assets	
Cash	$ 100,000
Unclaimed payroll checks	27,500
Marketable securities (cost $30,000) at fair value	34,500

Accounts receivable (less bad debt reserve)		75,000
Inventories—at lower of cost (determined by the next-in, first-out method) or market		220,000
Total current assets		457,000
Tangible assets		
Land (less accumulated depreciation)		80,000
Buildings and equipment	$800,000	
Less accumulated depreciation	300,000	500,000
Net tangible assets		580,000
Long-term investments		
Stocks and bonds		100,000
Treasury stock		50,000
Total long-term investments		150,000
Other assets		
Discount on bonds payable		14,200
Claim against U.S. government (pending in 3rd Dist.)		975,000
Total other assets		989,200
Total assets		$2,176,200

Instructions

Indicate the deficiencies, if any, in the foregoing presentation of Jean Toomer Corporation's assets. Marketable securities are considered trading securities.

C5-6 (Critique of Balance Sheet Format and Content) Presented below is the balance sheet of Langston Hughes Corporation (000s omitted):

Langston Hughes Corporation
BALANCE SHEET
December 31, 1996

Assets

Current assets		
Cash	$30,000	
Marketable securities	18,000	
Accounts receivable	25,000	
Merchandise inventory	20,000	
Supplies inventory	4,000	
Stock investment in Subsidiary Company	20,000	$117,000
Investments		
Treasury stock		26,000
Property, plant, and equipment		
Buildings and land	91,000	
Less: Reserve for depreciation	30,000	61,000
Other assets		
Cash surrender value of life insurance		18,000
		$222,000

Liabilities and Capital

Current liabilities		
Accounts payable	$22,000	
Reserve for income taxes	14,000	
Customers' accounts with credit balances	1	$ 36,001
Deferred credits		
Unamortized premium on bonds payable		2,000
Long-term liabilities		
Bonds payable		56,000
Total liabilities		94,001
Capital stock		
Capital stock, par $5	95,000	
Earned surplus	24,999	
Cash dividends declared	8,000	127,999
		$222,000

Instructions

Criticize the balance sheet presented. State briefly the proper treatment of the item criticized.

C5-7 (Identifying Balance Sheet Deficiencies) The financial statement below was prepared by employees of your client, Ralph Ellison Co. The statement is unaccompanied by notes.

Ralph Ellison Co.
BALANCE SHEET
As of November 30, 1996

Current assets				
Cash			$ 100,000	
Accounts receivable (less allowance of $30,000 for doubtful accounts)			419,900	
Inventories			2,554,000	$3,073,900
Less current liabilities				
Accounts payable			306,400	
Accrued payroll			8,260	
Accrued interest on mortgage note			12,000	
Estimated taxes payable			66,000	392,660
Net working capital				2,681,240

Property, plant, and equipment (at cost)

	Cost	Depreciation	Value	
Land and buildings	$ 983,300	$310,000	673,300	
Machinery and equipment	1,135,700	568,699	567,001	
	$2,119,000	$878,699		1,240,301

Deferred charges				
Prepaid taxes and other expenses			22,700	
Unamortized discount on mortgage note			10,800	33,500
Total net working capital and noncurrent assets				3,955,041
Less deferred liabilities				
Mortgage note payable			300,000	
Unearned revenue			1,908,000	2,208,000
Total net assets				$1,747,041
Stockholders' equity				
10% Preferred stock at par value				$ 400,000
Common stock at par value				697,000
Paid-in surplus				210,000
Retained earnings				484,641
Treasury stock at cost (400 shares)				(44,600)
Total stockholders' equity				$1,747,041

Instructions

Indicate the deficiencies, if any, in the balance sheet above in regard to form, terminology, descriptions, content, and the like.

C5-8 (Errors and Deficiencies in a Balance Sheet and an Income Statement) The following year-end financial statements were prepared by Richard Wright Corporation's bookkeeper. Wright Corporation operates a chain of retail stores.

Richard Wright Corporation
BALANCE SHEET
June 30, 1996

Assets

Current assets	
Cash	$ 150,000
Notes receivable	50,000
Accounts receivable, less reserve for doubtful accounts	175,000

Inventories		395,500
Investment securities (at cost)		100,000
Total current assets		870,500
Property, plant, and equipment		
Land (at cost) (Note 1)	$180,000	
Buildings, at cost less accumulated depreciation of $350,000	500,000	
Equipment, at cost less accumulated depreciation of $180,000	400,000	1,080,000
Intangibles		450,000
Other assets		
Prepaid expenses		26,405
Total assets		$2,426,905

Liabilities and Owners' Equity

Current liabilities			
Accounts payable			$ 135,500
Estimated income taxes payable			160,000
Contingent liability on discounted notes receivable			50,000
Total current liabilities			345,500
Long-term liabilities			
15% serial bonds, $50,000 due annually on December 31			
Maturity value		$900,000	
Less unamortized discount		35,000	865,000
Total liabilities			1,210,500
Owners' equity			
Common stock, stated value $10		750,000	
(authorized and issued, 75,000 shares)			
Retained earnings			
Appropriated (Note 2)	$120,000		
Free	346,405	466,405	1,216,405
Total liabilities and owners' equity			$2,426,905

Richard Wright Corporation
INCOME STATEMENT
As of June 30, 1996

Sales			$2,500,000
Interest revenue			6,000
Total revenue			2,506,000
Cost of goods sold			1,780,000
Gross margin			726,000
Operating expenses			
Selling expenses			
Salaries	$105,000		
Advertising	75,000		
Sales returns and allowances	50,000	$230,000	
General and administrative expenses			
Wages	84,000		
Property taxes	38,000		
Depreciation and amortization	86,000		
Rent (Note 3)	75,000		
Interest on serial bonds	48,000	331,000	561,000
Income before income taxes			165,000
Income taxes			80,000
Net income			$ 85,000

Notes to financial statements:
Note 1: Includes a future store site acquired during the year at a cost of $90,000.
Note 2: Retained earnings of $120,000 have been set aside to finance an expansion project.
Note 3: During the year the corporation acquired certain equipment under a long-term lease.

Instructions

Identify and discuss the defects in the financial statements above with respect to terminology, disclosure, and classification. Your discussion should explain why you consider them to be defects. Do not prepare revised statements.

(AICPA adapted)

▶ USING YOUR JUDGMENT ◀

▶ FINANCIAL REPORTING PROBLEM

The financial statements of Georgia-Pacific corporation appear in Appendix 5-A. Refer to these financial statements and the accompanying notes to answer the following questions:

(a) What alternative formats could Georgia-Pacific have adopted for its balance sheet? Which format did it adopt?

(b) What alternative formats could Georgia-Pacific have adopted for its income statement presentation? Which format did it adopt?

(c) Which irregular items does Georgia-Pacific report in its financial statements covering the three years 1991–1993?

(d) Identify the various techniques of disclosure Georgia-Pacific might have used to disclose additional pertinent financial information. Which technique does it use in its financials?

(e) For which items in Georgia-Pacific's balance sheet would you expect to find notes complementing the descriptions and amounts in the balance sheet?

▶ WRITING ASSIGNMENT

During an audit of Plastics and Fibers Manufacturing Company for the year ending December 31, 1995, the following four audit points came to your attention.

1. The client recorded a receivable from the IRS in the amount of $150,000. When asked about this receivable, management claimed that, as of the balance sheet date, the client expected to recover this amount in connection with a refund claim for a prior year's taxes. The claim is being contested, but the client's attorney is confident that the company will prevail.

2. In a response to a routine attorney letter which you sent to the client's lawyer, you discovered that the client is a defendant in a patent infringement suit. Counsel for the client estimates that the amount of the loss will be $2,200,000; furthermore, she claims that the loss of this suit is reasonably possible. The financial statements fail to mention this loss contingency.

3. Through inquiry of the company's management you discovered that, included in the cash account is $2,700,000 specifically set aside for immediate plant construction and machinery overhaul.

4. Preliminary discussions with managment revealed that, in March 1996, the employees' union is going to renegotiate its contract. Due to the general increase in labor disputes and strikes both inside and outside the industry, the possibility that a costly strike will occur is becoming increasingly more likely. The client believes that this information should be disclosed in the notes to the financial statements.

Instructions

As a staff auditor, write four short memos to the audit manager describing the above audit issues and explaining the accounting treatment you have advised for each. Make sure that each memo indicates that you communicated your suggestions to your client. Each page should be headed with the client's name, the balance sheet date, and a descriptive title of the page's content. In addition, initial and date each memo in the upper right hand corner.

▶ GROUP ASSIGNMENT

Your group has been engaged to examine the financial statements of Fleetwood Mac Corporation for the year 1996. The bookkeeper who maintains the financial records has prepared all the unaudited financial statements for the corporation since its organization on January 2, 1990. The client provides you with the information below.

Fleetwood Mac Corporation
BALANCE SHEET
As of December 31, 1996

Assets		Liabilities	
Current assets	$1,881,100	Current liabilities	$ 962,400
Other assets	5,171,400	Long-term liabilities	1,439,500
		Capital	4,650,600
	$7,052,500		$7,052,500

An analysis of current assets discloses the following:

Cash (restricted in the amount of $400,000 for plant expansion)	$ 571,000
Investments in land	185,000
Accounts receivable less allowance of $30,000	480,000
Inventories (LIFO flow assumption)	645,100
	$1,881,100

Other assets include:

Prepaid expenses	$ 47,400
Plant and equipment less accumulated depreciation of $1,430,000	4,130,000
Cash surrender value of life insurance policy	84,000
Unamortized bond discount	49,500
Notes receivable (short term)	162,300
Goodwill, at cost less amortization of $63,000	252,000
Land	446,200
	$5,171,400

Current liabilities include:

Accounts payable	$ 510,000
Notes payable (due 1998)	157,400
Estimated income taxes payable	145,000
Premium on common stock	150,000
	$ 962,400

Long-term liabilities include:

Unearned revenue	$ 489,500
Dividends payable (cash)	200,000
8% bonds payable (due May 1, 2001)	750,000
	$1,439,500

Capital includes:

Retained earnings	$2,810,600
Capital stock, par value $10; authorized 200,000 shares, 184,000 shares issued	1,840,000
	$4,650,600

The supplementary information below is also provided.

1. On May 1, 1996, the corporation issued at 93.4, $750,000 of bonds to finance plant expansion. The long-term bond agreement provided for the annual payment of interest every May 1. The existing plant was pledged as security for the loan. Use straight-line method for discount amortization.
2. The bookkeeper made the following mistakes:
   (a) In 1994, the ending inventory was overstated by $183,000. The ending inventories for 1995 and 1996 were correctly computed.
   (b) In 1996, accrued wages in the amount of $275,000 were omitted from the balance sheet and these expenses were not charged on the income statement.
   (c) In 1996, a gain of $175,000 (net of tax) on the sale of certain plant assets was credited directly to retained earnings.
3. A major competitor has introduced a line of products that will compete directly with Fleetwood Mac's primary line, now being produced in a specially designed new plant. Because of manufacturing innovations, the competitor's line will be of comparable quality but priced 50% below the client's line. The competitor announced its new line on January 14, 1997. The client indicates that the company will meet the lower prices that are high enough to cover variable manufacturing and selling expenses, but permit recovery of only a portion of fixed costs.

4. You learned on January 28, 1997, prior to completion of the audit, of heavy damage because of a recent fire to one of the client's two plants; the loss will not be reimbursed by insurance. The newspapers described the event in detail.

Instructions

Your instructor will identify one member of the group to serve as a recorder and one member to serve as a spokesperson. As a group, analyze the above information so that the recorder can prepare a corrected balance sheet for Fleetwood Mac in accordance with proper accounting and reporting principles. Prepare a description of any notes that might need to be prepared (to be reported to the class). The books are closed and adjustments to income are to be made through retained earnings.

▶ ETHICS CASE

The following 1995 balance sheet for the Nagoda Corporation does not conform with generally accepted accounting principles.

The Nagoda Corporation
BALANCE SHEET [Asset Portion Only]
December 31, 1995

Current Assets	
Cash	$ 46,500
Available-for-sale securities at cost	
(Fair value $159,800)	185,800
Accounts receivable (gross value)	745,000
Inventories valued at replacement cost	
(average cost equals $1,455,000)	1,800,000
Contingent gain (the excess insurance	
proceeds on casualty loss)	310,000
Total Current Assets	3,087,300
Investments	
Treasury stock, valued using the cost method	251,540
Property, Plant & Equipment	
Land, at fair value	2,575,000
Buildings, at fair value	3,475,540
Equipment, at fair value	332,100
Total PP&E	6,382,640
Intangible assets	
Goodwill (generated by the business since	
its inception)	2,000,000
Research and development, unamortized portion	450,000
Total intangible Assets	2,450,000
Total Assets	$12,171,480

Instructions

(a) Find all the errors to the asset portion of the Nagoda Corporation's 1995 balance sheet and explain how each should be reported under generally accepted accounting principles.

(b) Comment on the ethical propriety of each accounting error indicated in part (a), keeping in mind the corporation's various stakeholders who might be harmed through erroneous, intentional, or incomplete asset reporting.

FINANCIAL ANALYSIS

A visit with
GERALD WHITE

How has the study of accounting improved your ability to manage money?

You can't make investment decisions based on a company's reported numbers without understanding how those numbers are generated. Certainly there are lots of people who invest without understanding numbers, and I'm not going to claim that the way I invest is the only way. There are people who spend a lot of time looking at a company's products, marketing, and R&D. There are people who develop a level of confidence in management. I do all of those things to some extent.

Do you have a format that you follow when examining a company?

For us, financial analysis is fundamental to the way we make investment decisions. We start by asking ourselves whether we trust this company or believe in this company enough to give our clients' money to the management. In essence, that's what you're doing when you buy a company's stock. An important part is looking at the company's financial statements and at the choices that the company made to have high debt or low debt and to adopt aggressive or conservative accounting methods. Some companies use accounting methods to make things look as good as possible; and some use conservative accounting methods, trying not to make things look as good as they could. I think those choices are a reflection of what has sometimes been called a corporate personality.

For GERALD I. WHITE, a New York–based investment counselor, the knowledge of accounting has been critical to his profession. A large part of his time is spent poring over the financial statements of the companies in which he is considering investing. Unlike many people in the money management field who have weak accounting backgrounds, he is able to spot potential business problems or opportunities in the financial statements and footnotes. And, as an adjunct professor of accounting at New York University, he is able to pass along to students the relevance of accounting to the investment process. White, who received his AB from Brown University in 1966 and his MBA from NYU in 1971, is also a Chartered Financial Analyst.

Our philosophy is to look for companies with a conservative corporate personality, on the theory that the risks are a lot lower. It's what I sometimes call the iceberg theory of investment. There's a lot about a company that you can never find out because you're on the outside, but the financial statements are the part of the iceberg that is above water, that you can look at closely, and from which you can make inferences about a company. A company that is using very aggressive accounting methods may be doing things that are very risky or even illegal.

What would be an example of conservative accounting?

For companies operating in a rising price environment, LIFO inventory accounting makes the most sense. It increases cash flow at the expense of reported earnings. There have been companies that have said "we care only about reported earnings, and therefore, we will adopt an accounting method that is, in economic terms, bad for the company, because we want things to look good." All companies that operate in rising price environments should be using LIFO. Today, at a low level of inflation, the effect isn't that great. It was more significant in the mid-1970s, when inflation was much more rapid. I remember one company in which the president decided not to use LIFO, because management didn't want to be judged by a realistic yardstick. And in fact the company was a poor investment.

But if FASB gives you a choice, why should you take the choice that makes you look bad?

There are some companies that like to be conservative. If they're taking a write-off, they'll take the maximum write-off just to make sure they don't have to come back and do it again. If they're making a provision for a lawsuit, it will be the maximum amount they can justify. There are other companies that try to get away with the minimum amount. Other examples: pensions, where the method is fixed but the company has a lot of latitude in terms of assumptions; depreciation methods and lives; capitalization of software development costs or capitalized interest. Revenue recognition is also an area where there has been a lot of abuse.

How do you boil down the investment world?

We're contrarians. We tend to look at industries and companies that are out of favor. We look for the relatively small number that we feel comfortable about in terms of staying power. If the oil drilling business is out of favor and we think that at some point it will rebound, then we'll buy a company in that industry but only if it doesn't have a lot of debt, that isn't out on a limb, so that we know that when the turn comes, they'll be around. We're definitely "value" players. We run computer screens as a starting point. Then, we'll take book value, and we'll start making adjustments to it for things that are off the balance sheet that should be on and for things that are on the balance sheet that should be off. We'll substitute replacement values for historical cost and come up with an "adjusted" book value. We'll look at the price of the company's stock relative to adjusted book value, rather than stated book value which may be completely different.

Is it a limitation of accounting that you have to make all of these adjustments, or is accounting just a starting point?

Accounting is just a starting point. You can't just take book value, net income, cash from operations and say those are the only numbers you need for making decisions. You have to go back and see how those numbers are generated, to see if those are really the numbers or whether you need to make adjustments to get numbers that are more useful for making investment decisions.

So you're interested in companies that are selling below their adjusted book value?

That's what we look for. There are times when they are very difficult to find.

What would be some examples of adjustments?

I'm a real believer in current value accounting. If it was up to me, financial statements would reflect assets and liabilities at their current value. Historical cost is largely irrelevant to me. Also, accounting goodwill is just what happens to have been put on the balance sheet because the company bought a company. What you're really interested in is *economic* goodwill. What is the real value of a company's brand names? That's not on the balance sheet. In terms of adjusted book value, you always take off the accounting goodwill.

Isn't goodwill an attempt at current value accounting since it reflects the purchase price of these other assets?

No, because it reflects the purchase price at the time of acquisition, which may have nothing to do with what it's worth today, especially since companies tend to overpay for acquisitions.

How do you factor in the new FASB 106 liability?

We started considering it in the early 1980s. I was on the FASB advisory council, and I heard somebody from General Motors talk about the amount of money they were spending on retiree health care costs. And a light went on. Even before there were disclosure requirements, we started asking companies if they had retirement plans and what it was costing them. The standard answer that we got was, "Why do you want to know that?" That was something that we could see coming a long time before it actually came. Some years before the standard, there was a disclosure requirement that gave you some basis to estimate what the liability was, and at some point, companies started disclosing their own estimate of the liability. By the time 106 was incorporated in the financial statements, it was old news. Companies overstated their earnings through the 1970s and 1980s by not accruing these liabilities.

A lot of investors ignore these one-time restructuring write-offs. Aren't these write-offs a way of manipulating the investor?

Absolutely. When you get into restructuring, you get into one of the grayest areas of financial analysis.

Companies think that by calling something a restructuring, it will be ignored. There's a line in my book (*The Analysis and Use of Financial Statements*/Wiley, 1994): "The job of analysis is to understand the past, not to forgive it." If a company writes off plant and equipment, what they are telling you is that they underdepreciated in past years, and therefore overstated earnings. Now it's good to understand that, but you can't simply ignore that and say, "I'll look at the future stream of earnings excluding that write-off." Over time, companies have found ways to manipulate the market, and this is one of those ways. The spurt of earnings that you very often get after restructuring may be artificial. If they've written off all of their fixed assets and the depreciation is gone, future earnings are going to be higher, but that's different from earnings improvements that result from better operating performance. One goal of analysis is to be able to tell operating performance from accounting performance.

On the income statement, what are the key numbers?

We look at operating income, interest expense, gains or losses on the sale of fixed assets, any other non-operating items, what happens to the tax rate—you can't look just at net income. We look at price-earnings ratios, but we try to make sure that we are applying the ratio to the right number, taking out nonrecurring items.

What about the statement of cash flows?

You can't look at one statement in isolation from the other two. The cash flow statement, once FASB changed it with *Statement 95*, became a very useful tool of analysis. Prior to that time, the funds flow statement had no value because all it did was show balance sheet changes which you already had by looking at the balance sheet. But the new cash flow statement has information that's different from what you get from the balance sheet and the income statement. And it has the categorization of cash flows among investing, operating, and financing activities. One focus is looking at cash from operations, the level as well as the trend. But one of the great fallacies is that cash flow from operations cannot be affected by accounting methods. That is not true. There are accounting methods that do affect cash from operations.

Such as?

Lease capitalization. Also, capitalization of software development costs. The capitalization/expense decision does affect cash flow from operations, so you can't just look at that number blindly. You also have to look at transactions such as the sale of receivables, which may distort cash from operations. In the same way that book value and net income are just beginning numbers, so too is cash from operations just a beginning number. If you buy a computer for $1,000 and you expense it—which many companies would do for such a small item—it's an operating expense, and that $1,000 reduces cash from operations. If you treat it as a fixed asset acquisition, then that $1,000 gets classified as an investing cash outflow, and it never affects cash from operations because depreciation is a non-cash expense. So you have a permanent reclassification away from cash from operations into cash for investing. It never reverses over time. To the extent that a company capitalizes certain expenditures rather than expensing them, cash from operations is affected.

How do you go from identifying a stock to deciding to buy it?

The first thing that we do is answer some basic questions: Is this a company that we want to own? Does it meet our general criteria of quality of balance sheet, accounting methods, management? Is it in a business that we want to invest in? There are some businesses that I won't invest in, such as tobacco. Once we have decided that we are comfortable with the company, then we get into the valuation. What is the price to adjusted book value? We look at price in relation to earnings, but not necessarily current period earnings, since we tend to buy companies that are out of favor, and current earnings may be lousy. So we'll look at past earnings as an indicator of what they might do in the future, or we'll try to construct a scenario and ask if conditions change, then what might the company earn?

ACCOUNTING AND THE TIME VALUE OF MONEY

LEARNING OBJECTIVES

After studying this chapter, you should be able to:

1. Identify accounting topics where time value of money is relevant.
2. Distinguish between simple and compound interest.
3. Learn how to use appropriate compound interest tables.
4. Identify variables fundamental to solving interest problems.
5. Solve future and present value of 1 problems.
6. Solve future amount of ordinary and annuity due problems.
7. Solve present value of ordinary and annuity due problems.

Would you like to be a millionaire? If you are 20 years old now, can save $100 every month, and can invest those savings to earn an after-tax rate of return of 1% per month (over 12% per year), you can be a millionaire before you're 59. Or if you could invest just $10,000 today at that same interest rate, you would have over a million dollars by age 59. Such is the power of **interest,** especially when it is energized with a generous dosage of **time.**[1]

Business enterprises both invest and borrow large sums of money. The common characteristic in these two types of transactions is the **time value of the money**—that is, the interest factor involved. The timing of the returns on the investment has an important effect on the worth of the investment (asset), and the timing of debt repayments has a similarly important effect on the value of the commitment (liability). Businesspeople have become acutely aware of this timing factor and invest and borrow only after carefully analyzing the relative values of the cash outflows and inflows.

The accountant also is expected to make value measurements and to understand their implications. To do so, the accountant must understand and be able to measure the **present value** of future cash inflows and outflows. This measurement requires an understanding of compound interest, annuities, and present value concepts.

---

[1]As another example of how interest can multiply dollars quickly, Sidney Homer (author of *A History of Interest Rates*) wrote, "$1,000 invested at a mere 8% for 400 years would grow to $23 quadrillion—$5 million for every human on earth." But, "the first 100 years are the hardest." (*Forbes,* July 14, 1986).

▶ **APPLICATIONS OF TIME VALUE CONCEPTS**

Financial reporting uses different measurements in different situations. Present value is one of these measurements, and its usage has been increasing.[2] Recognizing that fact, the FASB has embarked upon a project to develop a framework for applying these measurements.[3]

Some of the applications of present value-based measurements to accounting topics are listed below, several of which are required in succeeding chapters of this textbook:

◀ **PRESENT VALUE-BASED ACCOUNTING** ▶
MEASUREMENTS

OBJECTIVE 1

Identify accounting topics where the time value of money is relevant.

1. **NOTES.** Valuing noncurrent receivables and payables that carry no stated interest rate or a lower than market interest rate.

2. **LEASES.** Valuing assets and obligations to be capitalized under long-term leases and measuring the amount of the lease payments and annual leasehold amortization.

3. **AMORTIZATION OF PREMIUMS AND DISCOUNTS.** Measuring amortization of premium or discount on both bond investments and bonds payable.

4. **PENSIONS AND OTHER POSTRETIREMENT BENEFITS.** Measuring service cost components of employers' postretirement benefits expense and postretirement benefits obligation.

5. **LONG-TERM ASSETS.** Evaluating alternative long-term investments by discounting future cash flows. Determining the value of assets acquired under deferred payment contracts.

6. **SINKING FUNDS.** Determining the contributions necessary to accumulate a fund for debt retirements.

7. **BUSINESS COMBINATIONS.** Determining the value of receivables, payables, liabilities, accruals, and commitments acquired or assumed in a "purchase."

8. **DISCLOSURES.** Measuring the value of future cash flows from oil and gas reserves for disclosure in supplementary information.

9. **INSTALLMENT CONTRACTS.** Measuring periodic payments on long-term purchase contracts.[4]

In addition to accounting and business applications, compound interest, annuity, and present value concepts apply to personal finance and investment decisions. In purchasing a home or car, planning for retirement, and evaluating alternative investments, you will need to understand time value of money concepts.

▶ **THE NATURE OF INTEREST**

Interest is payment for the use of money. It is the excess cash received or repaid over and above the amount lent or borrowed (**principal**). For example, if the Corner Bank

---

[2]Since 1967, 17 financial accounting and reporting standards (4 APB Opinions and 13 FASB Statements) have dealt directly with present value-based measurements.

[3]"Present Value-Based Measurements in Accounting," *Financial Accounting Series Discussion Memorandum* (Norwalk, Ct.: FASB, Dec. 1990), 133 pages.

[4]A complete list of where GAAP specifically forbids and requires discounting is presented in an article by Roman L. Weil, "Role of the Time Value of Money in Financial Reporting," *Accounting Horizons* (December 1990), pp. 47–67.

lends you $1,000 with the understanding that you will repay $1,150, then the excess over $1,000, or $150, represents interest expense. Or if you lend your roommate $100 and then collect $110 in full payment, the $10 excess represents interest revenue.

The amount of interest to be paid is generally stated as a rate over a specific period of time. For example, if you used $1,000 for one year before repaying $1,150, the rate of interest is 15% per year ($150 ÷ $1,000). The custom of expressing interest as a rate is an established business practice.[5] In fact, business managers make investing and borrowing decisions on the basis of the rate of interest involved rather than on the actual dollar amount of interest to be received or paid.

How is the interest rate determined? One of the most important factors is the level of credit risk (risk of nonpayment) involved. Other factors being equal, the higher the credit risk, the higher the interest rate. Every borrower's risk is evaluated by the lender. A low-risk borrower like Microsoft can probably obtain a loan at or slightly below the going market rate of interest. You or the neighborhood delicatessen, on the other hand, would probably be charged several percentage points above the market rate, if you can get a loan at all!

The amount of interest involved in any financing transaction is a function of three variables:

◀ VARIABLES IN INTEREST COMPUTATION ▶

---

1. **PRINCIPAL.** The amount borrowed or invested.
2. **INTEREST RATE.** A percentage of the outstanding principal.
3. **TIME.** The number of years or fractional portion of a year that the principal is outstanding.

The larger the principal amount, or the higher the interest rate, or the longer the time period, the larger the dollar amount of interest.

▶ CHOOSING AN APPROPRIATE INTEREST RATE

A perplexing problem facing the accountant is the selection of an appropriate interest rate. Consider the following debates that have taken place in practice.

1. In oil and gas accounting, the Securities and Exchange Commission at one time recommended that the fair value of oil and gas reserves in the ground be computed at the present value of the future revenues discounted at a flat 10% rate. The SEC argued that the use of one rate leads to comparability and that a rate of this magnitude provides a reasonable representation of the present value of future oil and gas reserves. Others disagreed, noting that a 10% rate was unrealistic for two reasons. First, it ignores the current level of interest rate benchmarks such as the prime rate. Second, not all companies and situations deserve the same rate because of differences in risk.

2. In trying to resolve the problem of capitalizing interest cost incurred (recording as an asset) during construction, the profession encountered support for two different measurement bases. Some accountants favored capitalizing the interest cost associated with the specific borrowing. Others disagreed, arguing that a weighted average is preferable because the borrowing on any specific project affects the borrowing costs of the entire company as it relates to other projects.

---

[5]Federal law requires the disclosure of interest rates on an **annual basis** in all contracts. That is, instead of stating the rate as "1% per month," it must be stated as "12% per year" if it is simple interest or "12.68% per year" if it is compounded monthly.

How then should we select an interest rate for purposes of present value computations? In the past, interest rates have often been selected on the basis of expediency (availability), regulatory stipulations, and ease of auditability. No consistent approach has been adopted. This is not surprising, given the wide variety of rates from which to choose, such as the general borrowing rate (prime rate), a specific borrowing rate for a given company, opportunity cost rate, investment rate of return, cost-of-capital rate on a weighted-average basis, and so on.

An interest rate has three components:

◀ THREE COMPONENTS OF INTEREST ▶

---

1. **PURE RATE OF INTEREST** (2 to 4%). This would be the amount a lender would charge if there were no possibilities of default and no expectation of inflation.
2. **CREDIT RISK RATE OF INTEREST** (0 to 5%). The government has little or no credit risk (i.e., risk of nonpayment) when it issues bonds; a business enterprise, however, depending upon its financial stability, profitability, etc., can have a low or a high credit risk.
3. **EXPECTED INFLATION RATE OF INTEREST** (0 to ?). Lenders recognize that in an inflationary economy, they are being paid back with less valuable dollars. As a result, they increase their interest rate to compensate for this loss in purchasing power. When inflationary expectations are high, interest rates are high.

Identifying and mixing these three components in the appropriate ratio for any given company or investor at any given moment is not easy. Yet, the relevance and reliability of accounting information depend on the selection of appropriate interest rates.

Throughout the remainder of this chapter, we will focus on the mechanics of computing present values and future amounts. In most cases, interest rates will be provided. Occasionally, a problem will ask you to solve for the interest rate as the only unknown variable.

SIMPLE INTEREST

OBJECTIVE 2

Distinguish between simple and compound interest.

Simple interest is computed on the amount of the principal only. It is the return on (or growth of) the principal for one time period. Simple interest is commonly expressed as follows:[6]

$$\text{Interest} = p \times i \times n$$

where

$p = $ principal

$i = $ rate of interest for a single period

$n = $ number of periods.

To illustrate, if you borrow $1,000 for 3 years with a simple interest rate of 15% per year, the total interest you will pay is $450, computed as follows:

$$\text{Interest} = (p)(i)(n)$$
$$(\$1,000)(.15)(3)$$
$$\$450.$$

---

[6]Simple interest is traditionally expressed in textbooks in business mathematics or business finance as: I(interest) $= P$(principal) $\times R$(rate) $\times T$(time).

If you borrow $1,000 for 3 months at 15%, the interest is $37.50, computed as follows:

$$\text{Interest} = (\$1,000)(.15)(.25)$$
$$= \$37.50$$

COMPOUND INTEREST

John Maynard Keynes, the legendary English economist, supposedly called it magic. Mayer Rothschild, the founder of the famous European banking firm, is said to have proclaimed it the eighth wonder of the world. Today people continue to extol its wonder and its power. The object of their affection is compound interest.

Compound interest is computed on principal **and** on any interest earned that has not been paid or withdrawn. It is the return on (or growth of) the principal for two or more time periods. Compounding computes interest not only on the principal but also on the interest earned to date on that principal, assuming the interest is left on deposit.[7]

To illustrate the difference between simple and compound interest, assume that you deposit $1,000 in the Last National Bank, where it will earn simple interest of 9% per year, and you deposit another $1,000 in the First State Bank, where it will earn compound interest of 9% per year compounded annually. Also assume that in both cases you will not withdraw any interest until 3 years from the date of deposit. The computation of interest to be received and the accumulated year-end balance are indicated in Illustration 6-1.

ILLUSTRATION 6-1
Simple vs. Compound Interest

Last National Bank				First State Bank		
Simple Interest Calculation	Simple Interest	Accumulated Year-end Balance		Compound Interest Calculation	Compound Interest	Accumulated Year-end Balance
Year 1 $1,000.00 × 9%	$ 90.00	$1,090.00		Year 1 $1,000.00 × 9%	$ 90.00	$1,090.00
Year 2 $1,000.00 × 9%	90.00	$1,180.00		Year 2 $1,090.00 × 9%	98.10	$1,188.10
Year 3 $1,000.00 × 9%	90.00	$1,270.00		Year 3 $1,188.10 × 9%	106.93	$1,295.03
	$270.00				$295.03	

$25.03
Difference

Note in the illustration above that simple interest uses the initial principal of $1,000 to compute the interest in all 3 years. Compound interest uses the accumulated balance (principal plus interest to date) at each year-end to compute interest in the succeeding year—which explains why your compound interest account is larger.

Obviously if you had a choice between investing your money at simple interest or at compound interest, you would choose compound interest, all other things—especially risk—being equal. In the example, compounding provides $25.03 of additional interest income. For practical purposes compounding assumes that unpaid interest earned becomes a part of the principal, and the accumulated balance at the end of each year becomes the new principal sum on which interest is earned during the next year.

---

[7]Here is an illustration of the power of *time* and *compounding* interest on money. In 1626, Peter Minuit bought Manhattan Island from the Manhattoe Indians for $24 worth of trinkets and beads. If the Indians had taken a boat to Holland, invested the $24 in Dutch securities returning just 6% per year, and kept the money and interest invested at 6%, by 1971 they would have had $13 billion, enough to buy back Manhattan and still have a couple of billion dollars left for doodads (*Forbes*, June 1, 1971). By 1994, 362 years after the trade, the $24 would have grown to approximately $49 billion—or to $46 trillion had the money compounded at 8%.

Compound interest is the typical interest computation applied in business situations, particularly in our economy where large amounts of long-lived assets are used productively and financed over long periods of time. Financial managers view and evaluate their investment opportunities in terms of a series of periodic returns, each of which can be reinvested to yield additional returns. Simple interest is usually applicable only to short-term investments and debts that involve a time span of one year or less.

COMPOUND INTEREST TABLES (see pages 302–311)

OBJECTIVE 3

Learn how to use appropriate compound interest tables.

Five different types of compound interest tables are presented at the end of this chapter. These tables should help you study this chapter as well as solve later problems involving interest.[8] The titles of these five tables and their contents are:

◀ INTEREST TABLES AND CONTENTS ▶

1. **FUTURE AMOUNT OF 1** table. Contains the amounts to which 1 will accumulate if deposited now at a specified rate and left for a specified number of periods. (Table 6-1)

2. **PRESENT VALUE OF 1** table. Contains the amounts that must be deposited now at a specified rate of interest to equal 1 at the end of a specified number of periods. (Table 6-2)

3. **FUTURE AMOUNT OF AN ORDINARY ANNUITY OF 1** table. Contains the amounts to which periodic rents of 1 will accumulate if the payments (rents) are invested at the **end** of each period at a specified rate of interest for a specified number of periods. (Table 6-3)

4. **PRESENT VALUE OF AN ORDINARY ANNUITY OF 1** table. Contains the amounts that must be deposited now at a specified rate of interest to permit withdrawals of 1 at the **end** of regular periodic intervals for the specified number of periods. (Table 6-4)

5. **PRESENT VALUE OF AN ANNUITY DUE OF 1** table. Contains the amounts that must be deposited now at a specified rate of interest to permit withdrawals of 1 at the **beginning** of regular periodic intervals for the specified number of periods. (Table 6-5)

The excerpt below illustrates the general format and content of these tables. This excerpt from Table 6-1 indicates how much principal plus interest a dollar accumulates to at the end of each of five periods at three different rates of compound interest.

FUTURE AMOUNT OF 1 AT COMPOUND INTEREST (Excerpt from Table 6-1, page 303)			
Period	9%	10%	11%
1	1.09000	1.10000	1.11000
2	1.18810	1.21000	1.23210
3	1.29503	1.33100	1.36763
4	1.41158	1.46410	1.51807
5	1.53862	1.61051	1.68506

---

[8]Compound interest tables make no allowance for inflation or deflation. If you need to consider the changes in the purchasing power of the dollar, you have to do so outside the framework of these tables or by adjusting the interest rate to reflect inflation.

Interpreting the table, if $1.00 is invested for three periods at a compound interest rate of 9% per period, the $1.00 will equal the **compound future amount** of $1.30 (1.29503 × $1.00). If $1.00 is invested at 11%, at the end of four periods it equals $1.52. If the investment is $1,000 instead of $1.00, the respective amounts are:

If invested for 3 periods at 9% ($1,000 × 1.29503) = $1,295.03.

If invested for 4 periods at 11% ($1,000 × 1.51807) = $1,518.07.

Throughout the discussion of compound interest tables the use of the term **periods** instead of **years** is intentional. Interest is generally expressed in terms of an annual rate but in many business circumstances the compounding period is less than one year. In such circumstances the annual interest rate must be converted to correspond to the length of the period. The process is to convert the "annual interest rate" into the "compounding period interest rate" by **dividing the annual rate by the number of compounding periods per year.**

In addition, the number of periods is determined by **multiplying the number of years involved by the number of compounding periods per year.** To illustrate, assume that $1.00 is invested for 6 years at 8% annual interest compounded **quarterly.** Using Table 6-1, page 303, we can determine the amount to which this $1.00 will accumulate: read the factor that appears in the 2% column on the 24th row—6 years × 4 compounding periods per year, namely 1.60844, or approximately $1.61. Thus, the term **periods,** not **years,** is used in all compound interest tables to express the quantity of n.

The following schedule shows how to determine (1) the interest rate per compounding period and (2) the number of compounding periods in four situations of differing compounding frequency (f).

12% Annual Interest Rate Over 5 Years Compounded (f)	Interest Rate Per Compounding Period ($i \div f$)	Number of Compounding Periods ($i \times f$)
Annually (1)	.12 ÷ 1 = .12	5 years × 1 compounding per year = 5 periods
Semiannually (2)	.12 ÷ 2 = .06	5 years × 2 compoundings per year = 10 periods
Quarterly (4)	.12 ÷ 4 = .03	5 years × 4 compoundings per year = 20 periods
Monthly (12)	.12 ÷ 12 = .01	5 years × 12 compoundings per year = 60 periods

ILLUSTRATION 6-2
Frequency of Compounding

Because interest is theoretically earned (accruing) every second of every day, it is possible to calculate interest that is **compounded continuously.** Computations involving continuous compounding are facilitated through the use of the natural, or Napierian, system of logarithms. As a practical matter, however, most business transactions assume interest to be compounded no more frequently than daily.

How often interest is compounded can make a substantial difference in rate of return. For example, a 9% annual interest compounded **daily** provides a 9.42% yield, or a difference of .42%. The 9.42% is referred to as the **effective yield.**[9] The annual interest

---

[9]The formula for calculating the **effective rate** in situations where the compounding frequency (f) is greater than once a year is as follows:

$$\text{Effective rate} = (1 + i)^f - 1$$

To illustrate, if the stated annual rate is 8% compounded quarterly (or 2% per quarter), the effective annual rate is:

$$
\begin{aligned}
\text{Effective rate} &= (1 + .02)^4 - 1 \\
&= (1.02)^4 - 1 \\
&= 1.0824 - 1 \\
&= .0824 \\
&= 8.24\%
\end{aligned}
$$

rate (9%) is called the **stated, nominal,** or **face rate.** When the compounding frequency is greater than once a year, the effective interest rate will always be greater than the stated rate.

The schedule below shows how compounding for five different time periods affects the effective yield and the amount earned by an investment of $10,000 for one year.

ILLUSTRATION 6-3
Comparison of Different
Compounding Periods

Interest Rate	Compounding Periods				
	Annually	Semiannually	Quarterly	Monthly	Daily
8%	8.00% $800	8.16% $816	8.24% $824	8.30% $830	8.33% $833
9%	9.00% $900	9.20% $920	9.31% $931	9.38% $938	9.42% $942
10%	10.00% $1,000	10.25% $1,025	10.38% $1,038	10.47% $1,047	10.52% $1,052

▶ FUNDAMENTAL VARIABLES

OBJECTIVE 4

Identify variables .
fundamental to solving
interest problems.

The following four variables are fundamental to all compound interest problems:

◀ FUNDAMENTAL VARIABLES ▶

1. **RATE OF INTEREST.**   This rate, unless otherwise stated, is an annual rate that must be adjusted to reflect the length of the compounding period if less than a year.
2. **NUMBER OF TIME PERIODS.**   This is the number of compounding periods (a period may be equal to or less than a year).
3. **FUTURE AMOUNT.**   The value at a future date of a given sum or sums invested assuming compound interest.
4. **PRESENT VALUE.**   The value now (present time) of a future sum or sums discounted assuming compound interest.

The relationship of these four fundamental variables is depicted in the following **time diagram:**

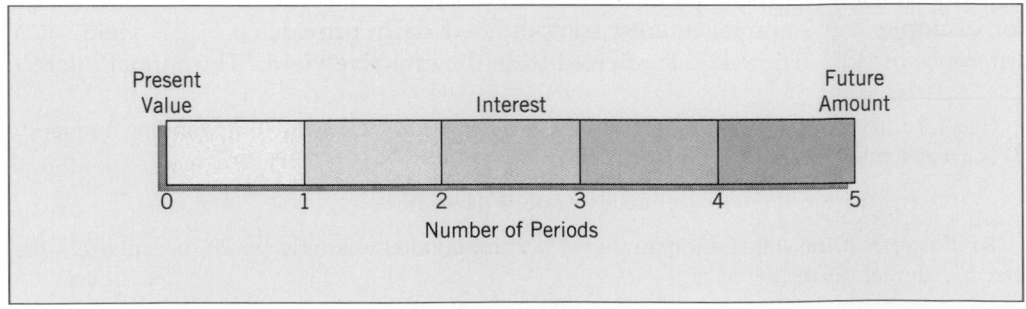

In some cases all four of these variables are known, but in many business situations at least one variable is unknown. As an aid to better understanding the problems and to finding solutions, we encourage you to sketch compound interest problems in the form of the preceding time diagram.

▶ SINGLE SUM PROBLEMS

Many business and investment decisions involve a single amount of money that either exists now or will in the future. Single sum problems can generally be classified into one of the following two categories:

OBJECTIVE 5

Solve future and present value of 1 problems.

1. Computing the **unknown future amount** of a known single sum of money that is invested now for a certain number of periods at a certain interest rate.

2. Computing the **unknown present value** of a known single sum of money in the future that is discounted for a certain number of periods at a certain interest rate.

When analyzing the problem or situation data, it is important that you determine first whether it is a future amount problem or a present value problem. **If you are solving for a future amount,** all cash flows must be *accumulated* to a future point. In this instance, the effect of interest is to increase the amounts or values over time so that the future amount is greater than the present amount. However, **if you are solving for a present value,** all cash flows must be *discounted* from the future to the present. In this case, the **discounting** reduces the amounts or values so that the present value is less than the future amount.

Preparation of time diagrams aids in identifying the unknown as an item in the future or the present. Sometimes it is neither a future amount nor a present value that is to be determined but, rather, the interest or discount rate or the number of compounding or discounting periods.

FUTURE AMOUNT OF A SINGLE SUM

The future amount to which 1 (one) will accumulate may be expressed as a formula:

$$a_{\overline{n}|i} = (1 + i)^n$$

where

$$a_{\overline{n}|i} = \text{future amount of 1}$$
$$i = \text{rate of interest for a single period}$$
$$n = \text{number of periods.}$$

The symbol $a_{\overline{n}|i}$ is expressed as "lowercase *a* angle *n* at *i*." It is the amount to which $1.00 will accumulate at *i* rate of interest per period for *n* periods.

To illustrate, assume that $1.00 is invested at 9% interest compounded annually for 3 years. The amounts to which the $1.00 will accumulate at the end of each period are:

$$a_{\overline{1}|9\%} = (1 + .09)^1 \text{ for the end of the first period}$$
$$a_{\overline{2}|9\%} = (1 + .09)^2 \text{ for the end of the second period}$$
$$a_{\overline{3}|9\%} = (1 + .09)^3 \text{ for the end of the third period.}$$

Illustrated diagrammatically, these compound amounts accumulate as follows:

Period	Beginning-of-Period Amount	×	Multiplier $(1 + i)$	=	End-of-Period Amount*	Formula $(1 + i)^n$
1	1.00000		1.09		1.09000	$(1.09)^1$
2	1.09000		1.09		1.18810	$(1.09)^2$
3	1.18810		1.09		1.29503	$(1.09)^3$

*Note that these amounts appear in Table 6-1 in the 9% column.

**ILLUSTRATION 6-4
Accumulation of
Compound Amounts**

To calculate a **future amount,** just multiply the future value factor by that amount:

$$a = p\,(a_{\overline{n}|i})$$

where

$$a = \text{future amount}$$
$$p = \text{beginning principal or sum (present value)}$$
$$a_{\overline{n}|i} = (1 + i)^n = \text{future amount of 1.}$$

To illustrate, what is the future amount of $50,000 invested for 5 years compounded annually at an interest rate of 11%? In time-diagram form, this investment situation would appear as follows:

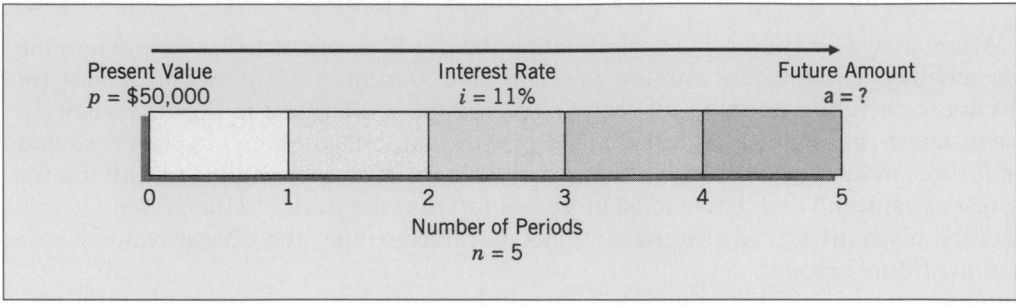

Using the formula, this investment problem is solved as follows:

$$a = p \ (a_{\overline{n}|i})$$
$$= \$50,000 \ (a_{\overline{5}|11\%})$$
$$= \$50,000 \ (1 + .11)^5$$
$$= \$50,000 \ (1.68506)$$
$$= \$84,253.$$

To determine the future amount factor of 1.68506 in the formula above, use a financial calculator or read the appropriate table, in this case Table 6-1 (11% column and the 5-period row).

This time diagram and formula approach can be applied to a routine business situation. To illustrate, Commonwealth Edison Company deposited $250 million in an escrow account with the Northern Trust Company at the beginning of 1994 as a commitment toward a power plant to be completed December 31, 1997. How much will be on deposit at the end of 4 years if interest is 10%, compounded semiannually?

With a known present value of $250 million, a total of 8 compounding periods (4 × 2), and an interest rate of 5% per compounding period (.10 ÷ 2), this problem can be time diagrammed and the future amount determined as follows:

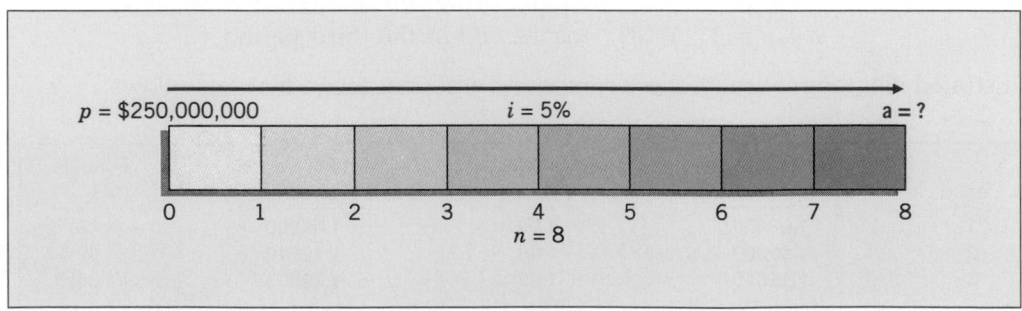

$$a = \$250,000,000 \ (a_{\overline{8}|5\%})$$
$$= \$250,000,000 \ (1 + .05)^8$$
$$= \$250,000,000 \ (1.47746)$$
$$= \$369,365,000.$$

Using a future amount factor found in Table 6-1 (5% column, 8-period row), we find that the deposit of $250 million will accumulate to $369,365,000 by December 31, 1997.

PRESENT VALUE OF A SINGLE SUM

The example on page 270 showed that $50,000 invested at an annually compounded interest rate of 11% will be worth $84,253 at the end of 5 years. It follows, then, that $84,253, 5 years in the future is worth $50,000 now; that is, $50,000 is the present value of $84,253. The **present value** is the amount that must be invested now to produce the known future amount. In the compound future amount illustrations, it was the future amount of a known present value that was determined; in present value problems, it is the present value of a known future amount that must be determined. **The present value is always a smaller amount than the known future amount because interest will be earned and accumulated on the present value to the future date.** In determining the future amount we move forward in time using a process of **accumulation**; in determining present value, we move backward in time using a process of **discounting**.

The **present value of 1** may be expressed as a formula:

$$p_{\overline{n}|i} = 1 \div a_{\overline{n}|i} = \frac{1}{(1 + i)^n}$$

where

$p_{\overline{n}|i}$ = present value of 1

$a_{\overline{n}|i} = (1 + i)^n$ = future amount of 1.

The symbol $p_{\overline{n}|i}$ is expressed as "lowercase p angle n at i." It is the present value of $1.00 discounted at i rate of interest per compounding period for n periods. To illustrate, assume that $1.00 is discounted for three periods at 9%. The present value of the $1.00 is discounted each period as follows:

$$p_{\overline{1}|9\%} = 1/(1 + .09)^1 \text{ for the first period}$$
$$p_{\overline{2}|9\%} = 1/(1 + .09)^2 \text{ for the second period}$$
$$p_{\overline{3}|9\%} = 1/(1 + .09)^3 \text{ for the third period.}$$

Illustrated diagrammatically, the $1.00 is discounted as follows:

Discount Periods	$1	÷	$(1 + i)^n$	=	Present Value*	Formula $1/(1 + i)^n$
1	$1.00000		1.09		.91743	$1/(1.09)^1$
2	1.00000		$(1.09)^2$		.84168	$1/(1.09)^2$
3	1.00000		$(1.09)^3$		.77218	$1/(1.09)^3$

*Note that these amounts appear in Table 6-2 in the 9% column.

ILLUSTRATION 6-5
Present Value of $1 Discounted at 9% for Three Periods

Quick computations of present values are frequently needed. As a result, tables have been developed from the formula above showing how much must be invested at various compound interest rates for various periods of time to equal 1 at a future date. A "present value of 1 table" appears at the end of this chapter as Table 6-2. Illustration 6-6 demonstrates the nature of such a table. It shows the present value of 1 for five different periods at three different rates of interest.

ILLUSTRATION 6-6
Excerpt from Table 6-2

PRESENT VALUE OF 1 AT COMPOUND INTEREST (Excerpt from Table 6-2, page 305)			
Period	9%	10%	11%
1	0.91743	0.90909	0.90090
2	0.84168	0.82645	0.81162
3	0.77218	0.75132	0.73119
4	0.70843	0.68301	0.65873
5	0.64993	0.62092	0.59345

The present value of 1 formula $p_{\overline{n}|i}$ can be expanded for use in computing the present value of **any single sum** as follows:

$$p = a\,(p_{\overline{n}|i}),$$

where

$$p = \text{present value of a single sum}$$

$$a = \text{future amount}$$

$$p_{\overline{n}|i} = \frac{1}{(1 + i)^n} = \text{present value of 1.}$$

To illustrate, what is the present value of \$84,253 to be received or paid in 5 years discounted at 11% compounded annually? In time-diagram form, this problem is drawn as follows:

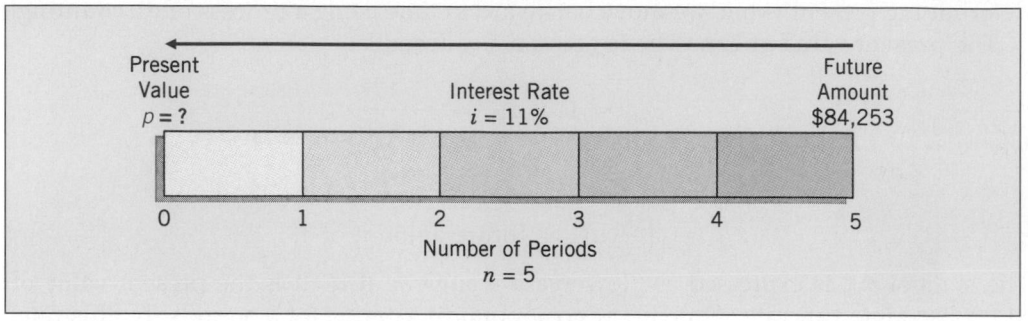

Using the formula, this problem is solved as follows:

$$p = a\,(p_{\overline{n}|i})$$

$$= \$84{,}253\,(p_{\overline{5}|11\%})$$

$$= \$84{,}253\left(\frac{1}{(1 + .11)^5}\right)$$

$$= \$84{,}253\,(.59345)$$

$$= \$50{,}000.$$

To determine the present value factor of .59345, use a financial calculator or read Table 6-2 (11% column, 5-period row).

The time diagram and formula approach can be applied in a variety of situations. For example, assume that your rich uncle proposes to give you \$2,000 for a trip to Europe when you graduate from college 3 years from now. He proposes to finance the trip by investing a sum of money now at 8% compound interest that will provide you with \$2,000 upon your graduation. The only conditions are that you graduate and that you tell him how much to invest now.

To impress your uncle, you might set up the following time diagram and solve this problem as follows:

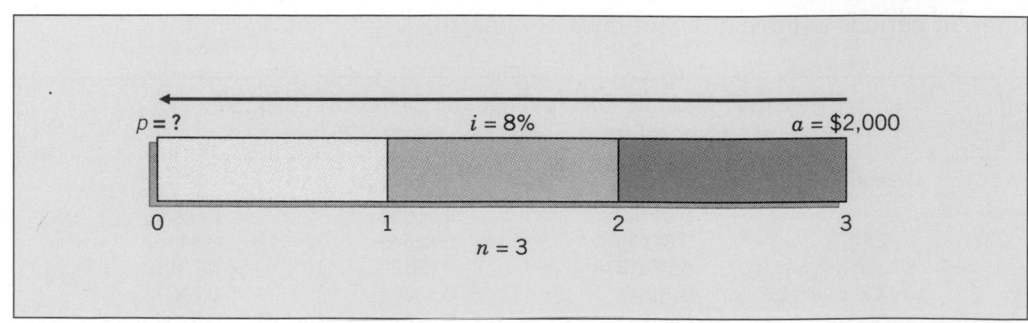

$$p = \$2,000 \ (p_{\overline{3}|8\%})$$

$$= \$2,000 \ \left(\frac{1}{(1 \ + \ .08)^3}\right)$$

$$= \$2,000 \ (.79383)$$

$$= \$1,587.66.$$

Advise your uncle to invest \$1,587.66 now to provide you with \$2,000 upon graduation. To satisfy your uncle's other condition, you must pass this course and many more.

SOLVING FOR OTHER UNKNOWNS IN SINGLE SUM PROBLEMS

In computing either the future amount or the present value in the previous single sum illustrations, both the number of periods and the interest rate were known. In many business situations, both the future amount and the present value are known, but the number of periods or the interest rate is unknown. The following two illustrations are single sum problems (future amount and present value) with either an unknown number of periods (n) or an unknown interest rate (i). These illustrations and the accompanying solutions demonstrate that if any three of the four values (future amount, a; present value, p; number of periods, n; interest rate, i) are known, the remaining unknown variable can be derived.

Illustration—Computation of the Number of Periods

The Village of Somonauk wants to accumulate \$70,000 for the construction of a veterans monument in the town square. If at the beginning of the current year the Village deposited \$47,811 in a memorial fund that earns 10% interest compounded annually, how many years will it take to accumulate \$70,000 in the memorial fund?

In this illustration, both the present value (\$47,811) and the future amount (\$70,000) are known along with the interest rate of 10%. A time diagram of this investment problem is as follows:

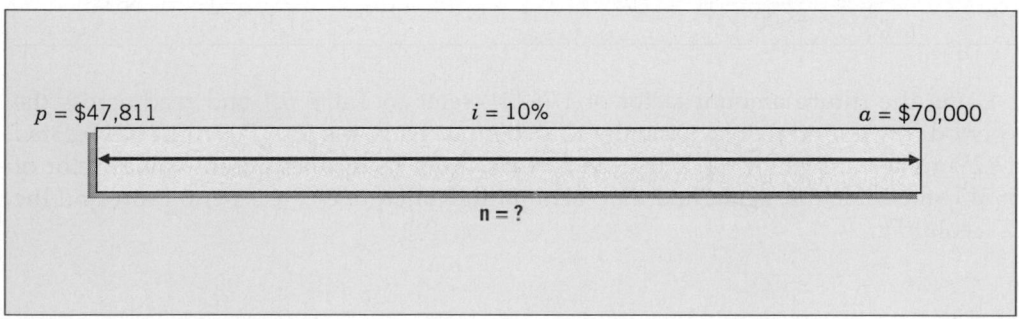

Because both the present value and the future amount are known, we can solve for the unknown number of periods using either the future amount or the present value formulas as shown below:

Future Amount Approach	Present Value Approach
$a = p \ (a_{\overline{n}|10\%})$	$p = a \ (p_{\overline{n}|10\%})$
$\$70,000 = \$47,811 \ (a_{\overline{n}|10\%})$	$\$47,811 = \$70,000 \ (p_{\overline{n}|10\%})$
$a_{\overline{n}|10\%} = \dfrac{\$70,000}{\$47,811} = 1.46410$	$p_{\overline{n}|10\%} = \dfrac{\$47,811}{\$70,000} = .68301$

ILLUSTRATION 6-7
Solving for Unknown Number of Periods

Using the future amount factor of 1.46410, refer to Table 6-1 and read down the 10% column to find that factor in the 4-period row. Thus, it will take 4 years for the \$47,811 to accumulate to $70,000 if invested at 10% interest compounded annually. Using the present value factor of .68301, refer to Table 6-2 and read down the 10% column to find again that factor in the 4-period row.

Illustration—Computation of the Interest Rate

Advanced Design, Inc. wishes to have $1,409,870 for basic research 5 years from now. The firm currently has $800,000 to invest for that purpose. At what rate of interest must the $800,000 be invested to fund basic research projects of $1,409,870, 5 years from now?

A time diagram of this investment situation is as follows:

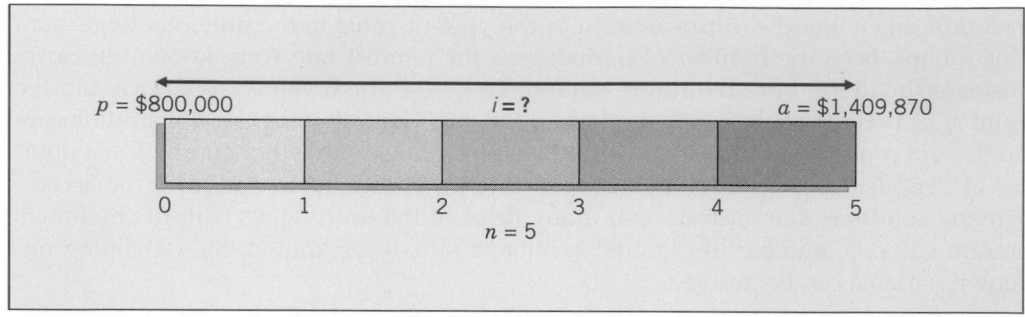

The unknown interest rate may be determined from either the future amount approach or the present value approach as shown below:

ILLUSTRATION 6-8
Solving for Unknown
Interest Rate

Future Amount Approach	Present Value Approach
$a = p\,(a_{\overline{5}|i})$	$p = a\,(p_{\overline{n}|i})$
$\$1,409,870 = \$800,000\,(a_{\overline{5}|i})$	$\$800,000 = \$1,409,870\,(p_{\overline{5}|i})$
$a_{\overline{5}|i} = \dfrac{\$1,409,870}{\$800,000} = 1.76234$	$p_{\overline{5}|i} = \dfrac{\$800,000}{\$1,409,870} = .56743$

Using the future amount factor of 1.76234, refer to Table 6-1 and read across the 5-period row to find that factor in the 12% column. Thus, the $800,000 must be invested at 12% to accumulate to $1,409,870 in 5 years. And, using the present value factor of .56743 and Table 6-2, again find that factor at the juncture of the 5-period row and the 12% column.

▶ ANNUITIES

The preceding discussion involved only the accumulation or discounting of a single principal sum. Individuals frequently encounter situations in which a series of dollar amounts are to be paid or received periodically, such as loans or sales to be repaid in installments, invested funds that will be partially recovered at regular intervals, or cost savings that are realized repeatedly. A life insurance contract is probably the most common and most familiar type of transaction involving a series of equal payments made at equal intervals of time. Such a process of periodic saving represents the accumulation of a sum of money through an annuity. An **annuity** by definition requires that (1) the periodic payments or receipts (called **rents**) always be the same amount, (2) the **interval** between such rents always be the same, and (3) the **interest be compounded** once each interval. The **future amount of an annuity** is the sum of all the rents plus the accumulated compound interest on them.

It should be noted that the rents may occur at either the beginning or the end of the periods. To distinguish annuities under these two alternatives, an annuity is classified as an **ordinary annuity** if the rents occur at the end of each period, and as an **annuity due** if the rents occur at the beginning of each period.

FUTURE AMOUNT OF AN ORDINARY ANNUITY

One approach to the problem of determining the future amount to which an annuity will accumulate is to compute the amount to which **each** of the rents in the series will accumulate and then total their individual future amounts. For example, assume that $1 is deposited at the **end** of each of 5 years (an ordinary annuity) and earns 12% interest compounded annually. The future amount can be computed as follows using the "future amount of 1" table (Table 6-1) for each of the five $1 rents:

OBJECTIVE 6

Solve future amount of ordinary and annuity due problems.

ILLUSTRATION 6-9
Solving for the Future Amount of an Ordinary Annuity

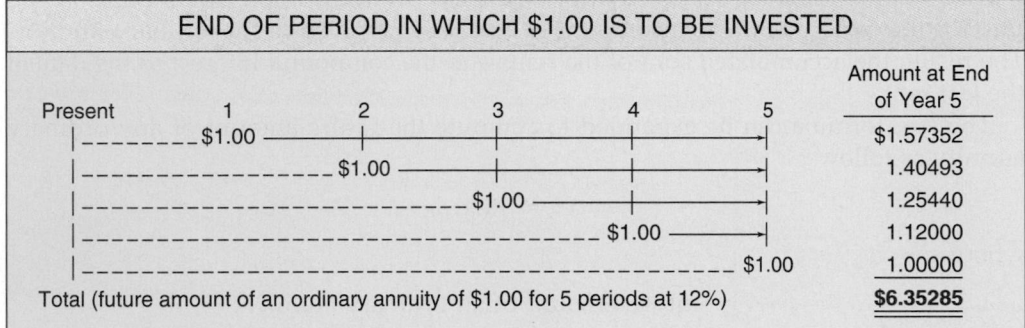

Because the rents that compose an ordinary annuity are deposited at the end of the period, they can earn no interest during the period in which they are originally deposited. For example, the third rent earns interest for only two periods (periods four and five). Obviously the third rent earns no interest for the first two periods since it is not deposited until the third period; furthermore, it can earn no interest for the third period since it is not deposited until the end of the third period. Any time the future amount of an ordinary annuity is computed, the number of compounding periods will always be **one less than the number of rents.**

Although the foregoing procedure for computing the future amount of an ordinary annuity will always produce the correct answer, it can become cumbersome if the number of rents is large. A more efficient way of expressing the future amount of an ordinary annuity of 1 is in a formula that is a summation of the individual rents plus the compound interest:

$$A_{\overline{n}|i} = \frac{(1 + i)^n - 1}{i}$$

where

$$A_{\overline{n}|i} = \text{future amount of an ordinary annuity}$$
$$\text{of 1 for } n \text{ periods at } i \text{ rate of interest}$$
$$i = \text{rate of interest per period}$$
$$n = \text{number of compounding periods.}$$

The symbol $A_{\overline{n}|i}$ is expressed "capital A angle n at i." For example, $A_{\overline{5}|12\%}$ is expressed "capital A angle 5 at 12%" and refers to the amount to which an ordinary annuity of 1 will accumulate in 5 periods at 12% interest.

Using the formula above, tables have been developed similar to those used for the "future amount of 1" and the "present value of 1" for both an ordinary annuity and an annuity due. The table in Illustration 6-10 is an excerpt from the "future amount of an ordinary annuity of 1" table.

ILLUSTRATION 6-10
Excerpt from Table 6-3

| | FUTURE AMOUNT OF AN ORDINARY ANNUITY OF 1 | | |
| | (Excerpt from Table 6-3, page 307) | | |
Period	10%	11%	12%
1	1.00000	1.00000	1.00000
2	2.10000	2.11000	2.12000
3	3.31000	3.34210	3.37440
4	4.64100	4.70973	4.77933
5	6.10510	6.22780	6.35285*

*Note that this annuity table factor is the same as the sum of the future amounts of 1 factors shown in Illustration 6-9.

Interpreting the table, if $1.00 is invested at the end of each year for 4 years at 11% interest compounded annually, the amount of the annuity at the end of the fourth year will be $4.71 (4.70973 × $1.00). Multiply the factor from the appropriate line and column of the table by the dollar amount of **one rent** involved in an ordinary annuity. The result: the accumulated sum of the rents and the compound interest to the date of the last rent.

The $A_{\overline{n}|i}$ formula can be expanded to compute the future amount of any ordinary annuity as follows:

$$A = R(A_{\overline{n}|i})$$

where

$$A = \text{future amount of an ordinary annuity}$$
$$R = \text{periodic rent}$$
$$A_{\overline{n}|i} = \frac{(1 + i)^n - 1}{i}$$

To illustrate, what is the future amount of five $5,000 deposits made at the end of each of the next 5 years, earning interest of 12%? In time-diagram form, this problem is drawn as follows:

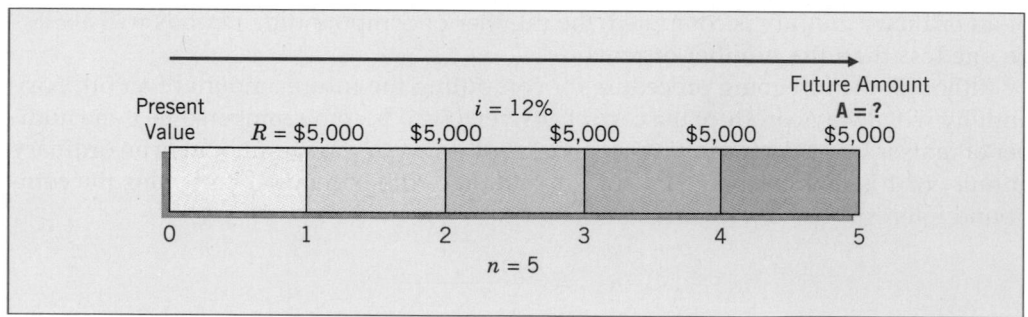

Using the formula, this investment problem is solved as follows:

$$A = R(A_{\overline{n}|i})$$
$$= \$5,000\ (A_{\overline{5}|12\%})$$
$$= \$5,000\left(\frac{(1 + .12)^5 - 1}{.12}\right)$$
$$= \$5,000\ (6.35285)$$
$$= \$31,764.25.$$

Determine the future amount of an ordinary annuity factor of 6.35285 in the formula above using a calculator or by reading the appropriate table, in this case Table 6-3 (12% column and the 5-period row).

To illustrate these computations in a business situation, assume that Hightown Electronics decides to deposit $75,000 at the end of each 6-month period for the next 3 years for the purpose of accumulating enough money to meet debts that mature in 3 years. What is the future amount that will be on deposit at the end of 3 years if the annual interest rate is 10%?

The time diagram and formula solution are as follows:

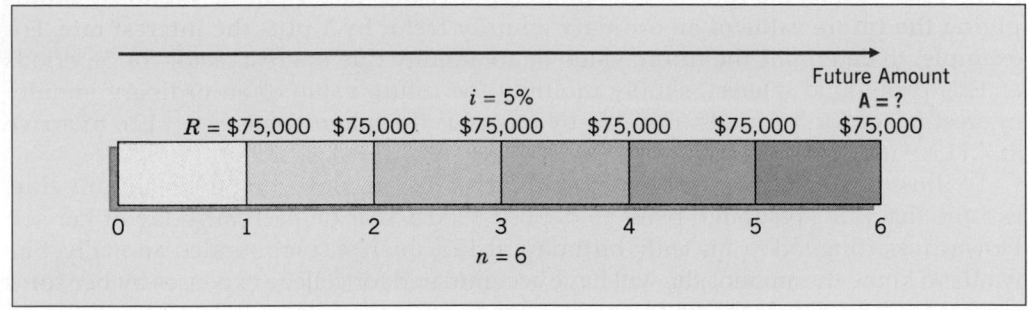

$$A = R(A_{\overline{n}|i})$$
$$= \$75{,}000 \ (A_{\overline{6}|5\%})$$
$$= \$75{,}000 \left(\frac{(1 + .05)^6 - 1}{.05} \right)$$
$$= \$75{,}000 \ (6.80191)$$
$$= \$510{,}143.25.$$

Thus, six 6-month deposits of $75,000 earning 5% per period will grow to $510,143.25.

FUTURE AMOUNT OF AN ANNUITY DUE

The preceding analysis of an ordinary annuity was based on the assumption that the periodic rents occur at the **end** of each period. An annuity due assumes periodic rents occur at the **beginning** of each period. This means an annuity due will accumulate interest during the first period, whereas an ordinary annuity rent will earn no interest during the first period because the rent is not received or paid until the end of the period. In other words, the significant difference between the two types of annuities is in the number of interest accumulation periods involved.

If rents occur at the end of a period (ordinary annuity), in determining the **future amount of an annuity** there will be one less interest period than if the rents occur at the beginning of the period (annuity due). The distinction is shown graphically below.

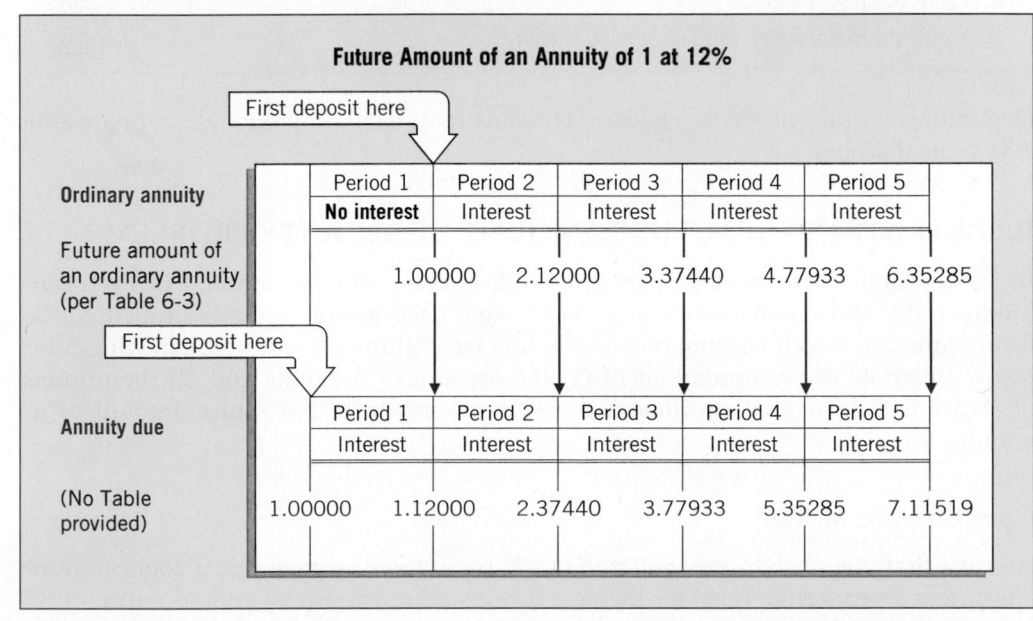

ILLUSTRATION 6-11
Comparison of the Future Amount of an Ordinary Annuity with an Annuity Due

In this example, because the cash flows from the annuity due come exactly one period earlier than for an ordinary annuity, the future value of the annuity due factor is exactly 12% higher than the ordinary annuity factor. For example, the amount of an ordinary annuity factor at the end of period one at 12% is 1.00000, whereas for an annuity due it is 1.12000. **Thus, the future value of an annuity due factor can be found by multiplying the future value of an ordinary annuity factor by 1 plus the interest rate.** For example, to determine the future value of an annuity due interest factor for 5 periods at 12% compound interest, simply multiply the future value of an ordinary annuity interest factor for 5 periods (6.35285) by one plus the interest rate $(1 + .12)$, to arrive at 7.11519 (6.35285×1.12).

To illustrate the use of the ordinary annuity tables in converting to an annuity due, assume that Sue Lotadough plans to deposit $800 a year on each birthday of her son Howard, starting today, his tenth birthday, at 12% interest compounded annually. Sue wants to know the amount she will have accumulated for college expenses by her son's eighteenth birthday. If the first deposit is made on Howard's tenth birthday, Sue will make a total of 8 deposits over the life of the annuity (assume no deposit on the eighteenth birthday). Because all the deposits will be made at the beginning of the periods, they represent an annuity due.

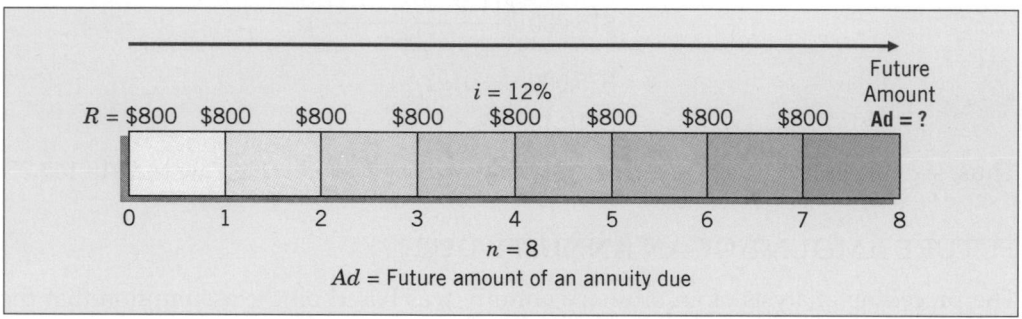

Referring to the "future amount of an ordinary annuity of 1" table for 8 periods at 12%, we find a factor of 12.29969. This factor is then multiplied by $(1 + .12)$ to arrive at the future amount of an annuity due factor. As a result, the accumulated amount on Howard's eighteenth birthday is computed as follows:

ILLUSTRATION 6-12
Computation of Accumulated Amount of Annuity Due

1. Future amount of an ordinary annuity of 1 for 8 periods at 12% (Table 6-3)	12.29969
2. Factor $(1 + .12)$	× 1.12
3. Future amount of an annuity due of 1 for 8 periods at 12%	13.77565
4. Periodic deposit (rent)	× $800
5. Accumulated amount on son's eighteenth birthday	$11,020.52

Depending on the college he chooses, Howard may have only enough to finance his first year of school.

ILLUSTRATIONS OF FUTURE AMOUNT OF ANNUITY PROBLEMS

In the foregoing annuity examples three values were known—amount of each rent, interest rate, and number of periods. They were used to determine the fourth value, future amount, which was unknown. The first two future amount problems presented below illustrate the computations of (1) the amount of the rents and (2) the number of rents. The third problem illustrates the computation of the future amount of an annuity due.

Computation of Rent

Assume that you wish to accumulate $14,000 for a down payment on a condominium apartment 5 years from now; for the next 5 years you can earn an annual return of 8%

compounded semiannually. How much should you deposit at the end of each 6-month period?

The $14,000 is the future amount of 10 (5 × 2) semiannual end-of-period payments of an unknown amount, at an interest rate of 4% (8% ÷ 2). This problem appears in the form of a time diagram as follows:

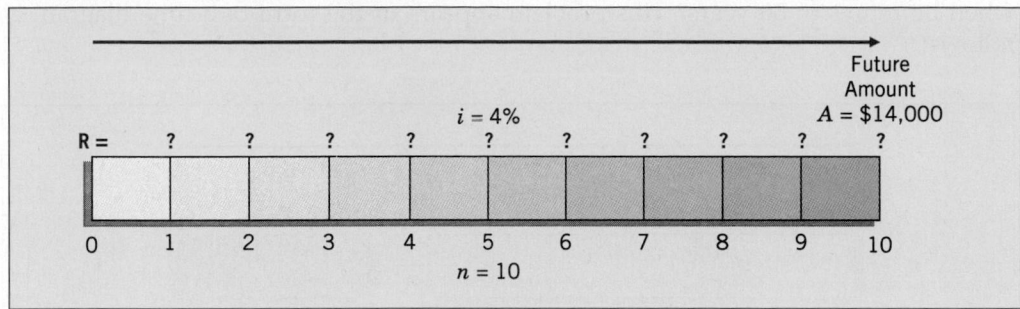

Using the formula for the future amount of an ordinary annuity, the amount of each rent is determined as follows:

$$A = R(A_{\overline{n}|i})$$

$$\$14,000 = R(A_{\overline{10}|4\%})$$

$$\$14,000 = R(12.00611)$$

$$\frac{\$14,000}{12.00611} = R$$

$$R = \$1,166.07.$$

Thus, you must make 10 semiannual deposits of $1,166.07 each in order to accumulate $14,000 for your down payment.

Computation of the Number of Periodic Rents

Suppose that your company wishes to accumulate $117,332 by making periodic deposits of $20,000 at the end of each year that will earn 8% compounded annually while accumulating. How many deposits must be made?

The $117,332 represents the future amount of n(?) $20,000 deposits, at an 8% annual rate of interest. This problem appears in the form of a time diagram as follows:

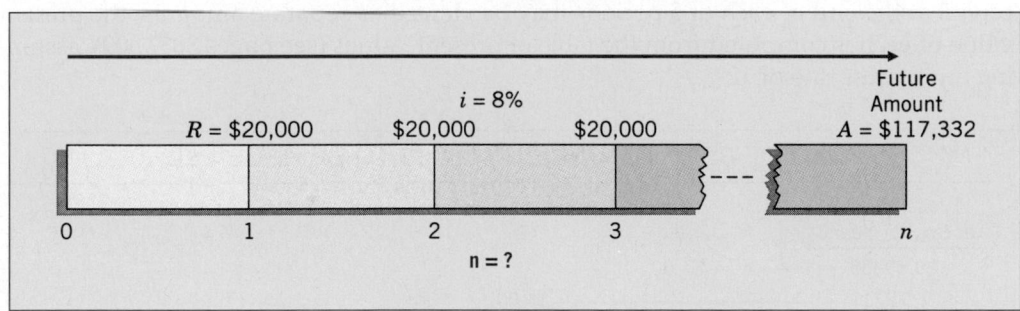

Using the future amount of an ordinary annuity formula, we obtain the following factor:

$$A = R(A_{\overline{n}|i})$$

$$\$117,332 = \$20,000 \, (A_{\overline{n}|8\%})$$

$$A_{\overline{n}|8\%} = \frac{\$117,332}{\$20,000} = 5.86660.$$

Using Table 6-3 and reading down the 8% column, we find 5.86660 in the 5-period row. Thus, five deposits of $20,000 each must be made.

Computation of the Future Amount

Walter Goodwrench, a mechanic, has taken on weekend work in the hope of creating his own retirement fund. Mr. Goodwrench deposits $2,500 today in a savings account that earns 9% interest. He plans to deposit $2,500 every year for a total of 30 years. How much cash will have accumulated in Mr. Goodwrench's retirement savings account when he retires in 30 years? This problem appears in the form of a time diagram as follows:

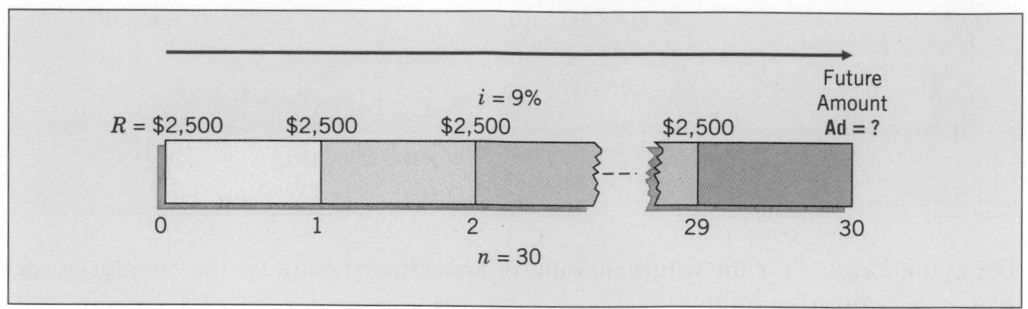

Using the "future amount of an ordinary annuity of 1" table, the solution is computed as follows:

ILLUSTRATION 6-13
Computation of Accumulated Amount of an Annuity Due

1. Future amount of an ordinary annuity of 1 for 30 periods at 9%	136.30754
2. Factor (1 + .09)	× 1.09
3. Future amount of an annuity due of 1 for 30 periods at 9%	148.57522
4. Periodic rent	× $2,500
5. Accumulated amount at end of 30 years	$371,438

PRESENT VALUE OF AN ORDINARY ANNUITY

OBJECTIVE 7

Solve present value of ordinary and annuity due problems.

The present value of an annuity is **the single sum** that, if invested at compound interest now, would provide for an annuity (a series of withdrawals) for a certain number of future periods. In other words, the present value of an ordinary annuity is the present value of a series of equal rents to be withdrawn at equal intervals.

One approach is to determine the present value of each of the rents in the series and then total their individual present values. For example, an annuity of $1.00 to be received at the **end** of each of 5 periods may be viewed as separate amounts; the present value of each is computed from the table of present values (see pages 308–309), assuming an interest rate of 12%.

ILLUSTRATION 6-14
Solving for the Present Value of an Ordinary Annuity

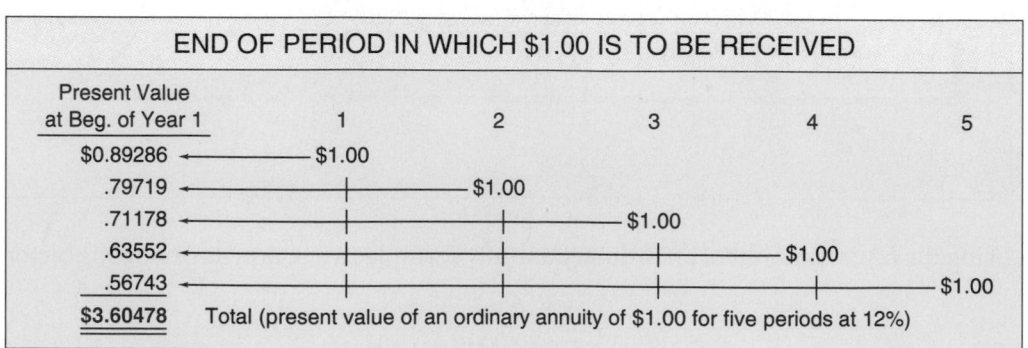

This computation tells us that if we invest the single sum of $3.60 today at 12% interest for 5 periods, we will be able to withdraw $1.00 at the end of each period for 5 periods. This cumbersome procedure can be summarized by:

$$P_{\overline{n}|i} = \frac{1 - \dfrac{1}{(1 + i)^n}}{i}.$$

The symbol $P_{\overline{n}|i}$ is expressed "capital P angle n at i"; for example, $P_{\overline{5}|12\%}$ is expressed "capital P angle 5 at 12%" and refers to the present value of an ordinary annuity of 1 for 5 periods at 12% interest. Using this formula, present value of ordinary annuity tables are prepared. An excerpt from such a table is shown below:

<table>
<tr><th colspan="4">PRESENT VALUE OF AN ORDINARY ANNUITY OF 1
(Excerpt from Table 6-4, page 309)</th></tr>
<tr><th>Period</th><th>10%</th><th>11%</th><th>12%</th></tr>
<tr><td>1</td><td>0.90909</td><td>0.90090</td><td>0.89286</td></tr>
<tr><td>2</td><td>1.73554</td><td>1.71252</td><td>1.69005</td></tr>
<tr><td>3</td><td>2.48685</td><td>2.44371</td><td>2.40183</td></tr>
<tr><td>4</td><td>3.16986</td><td>3.10245</td><td>3.03735</td></tr>
<tr><td>5</td><td>3.79079</td><td>3.69590</td><td>3.60478*</td></tr>
</table>

*Note that this annuity table factor is equal to the sum of the present value of 1 factors shown in Illustration 6-14.

ILLUSTRATION 6-15
Excerpt from Table 6-4

The general formula for the present value of any ordinary annuity is as follows:

$$P = R \, (P_{\overline{n}|i})$$

where

$$P = \text{present value of an ordinary annuity}$$
$$R = \text{periodic rent (ordinary annuity)}$$
$$P_{\overline{n}|i} = \frac{1 - \dfrac{1}{(1 + i)^n}}{i}$$

To illustrate, what is the present value of rental receipts of $6,000 each to be received at the end of each of the next 5 years when discounted at 12%? This problem may be time-diagrammed and solved as follows:

$$\begin{aligned}
P &= R \, (P_{\overline{n}|i}) \\
&= \$6{,}000 \, (P_{\overline{5}|12\%}) \\
&= \$6{,}000 \, (3.60478) \\
&= \$21{,}628.68.
\end{aligned}$$

The present value of the 5 ordinary annuity rental receipts of $6,000 each is $21,628.68. Determining the present value of the ordinary annuity factor 3.60478 in the formula above can be accomplished using a calculator or by reading the appropriate table, in this case Table 6-4 (12% column and 5-period row).

PRESENT VALUE OF AN ANNUITY DUE

In the discussion of the present value of an ordinary annuity, the final rent was discounted back the same number of periods that there were rents. In determining the present value of an annuity due, there is always one fewer discount period. This distinction is shown graphically below:

ILLUSTRATION 6-16
Comparison of Present Value of an Ordinary Annuity with an Annuity Due

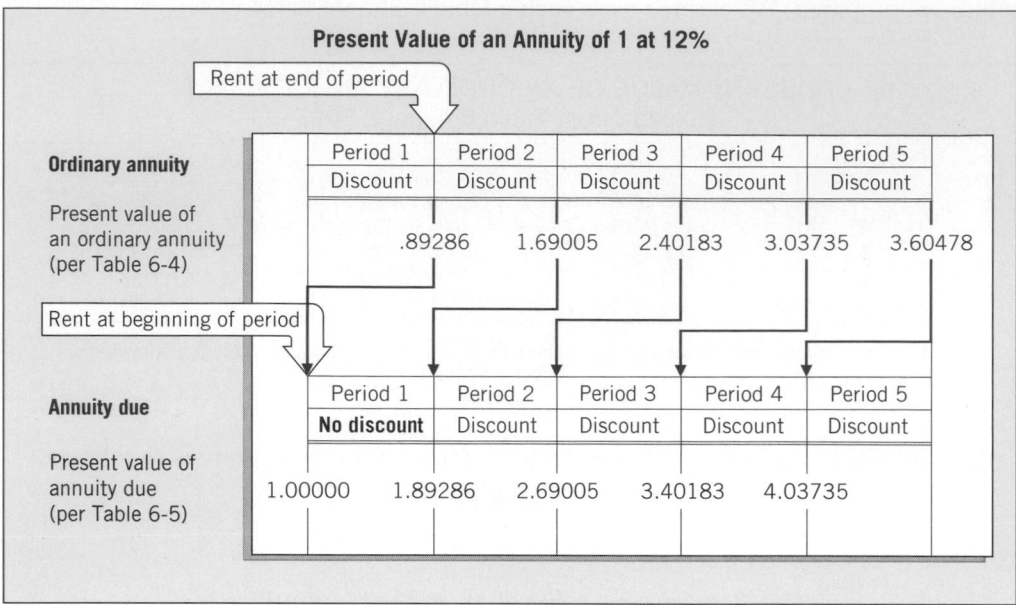

Because each cash flow comes exactly one period sooner in the present value of the annuity due, the present value of the cash flows is exactly 12% higher than the present value of an ordinary annuity. Thus, **the present value of an annuity due factor can be found by multiplying the present value of an ordinary annuity factor by 1 plus the interest rate.**

To determine the present value of an annuity due interest factor for 5 periods at 12% interest, take the present value of an ordinary annuity for 5 periods at 12% interest (3.60478) and multiply it by 1.12 to arrive at the present value of an annuity due, 4.03735 (3.60478 × 1.12). Because the payment and receipt of rentals at the beginning of periods (such as leases, insurance, and subscriptions) are as common as those at the end of the periods (referred to as "in arrears"), we have provided present value annuity due factors in the form of Table 6-5.

Space Odyssey, Inc., rents a communications satellite for 4 years with annual rental payments of $4.8 million to be made at the beginning of each year. If the relevant annual interest rate is 11%, what is the present value of the rental obligations?

This problem is time-diagrammed as follows:

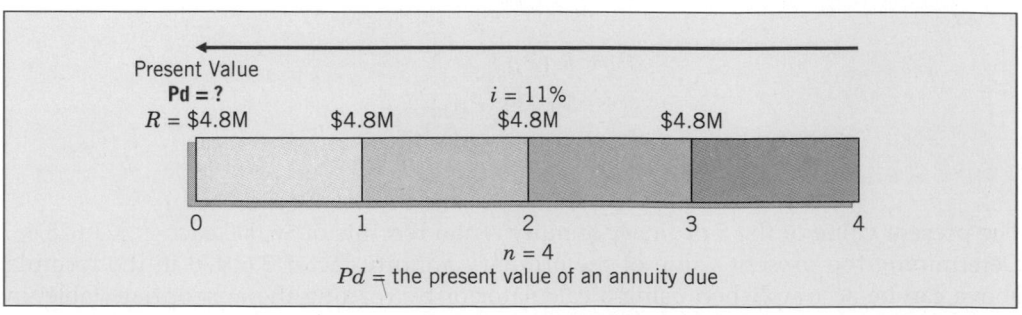

This problem is solved in the following manner.

1. Present value of an ordinary annuity of 1 for 4 periods at 11% (Table 6-4)	3.10245
2. Factor (1 + .11)	× 1.11
3. Present value of an annuity due of 1 for 4 periods at 11%	3.44372
4. Periodic deposit (rent)	× $4,800,000
5. Present value of payments	**$16,529,856**

ILLUSTRATION 6-17
Computation of Present Value of an Annuity Due

Since we have Table 6-5 for present value of an annuity due problems, we can also use $Pd_{\overline{4}|11\%}$ to locate the desired factor 3.44372 and compute the present value of the lease payments to be $16,529,856.

ILLUSTRATIONS OF PRESENT VALUE OF ANNUITY PROBLEMS

The following three illustrations demonstrate the computation of (1) the present value, (2) the interest rate, and (3) the amount of each rent.

Computation of the Present Value of an Ordinary Annuity

You have just won a lottery totaling $4,000,000 and learned that you will be paid the money by receiving a check in the amount of $200,000 at the end of each of the next 20 years. What amount have you really won? That is, what is the present value of the $200,000 checks you will receive over the next 20 years? A time diagram of this enviable situation is as follows (assuming an appropriate interest rate of 10%):

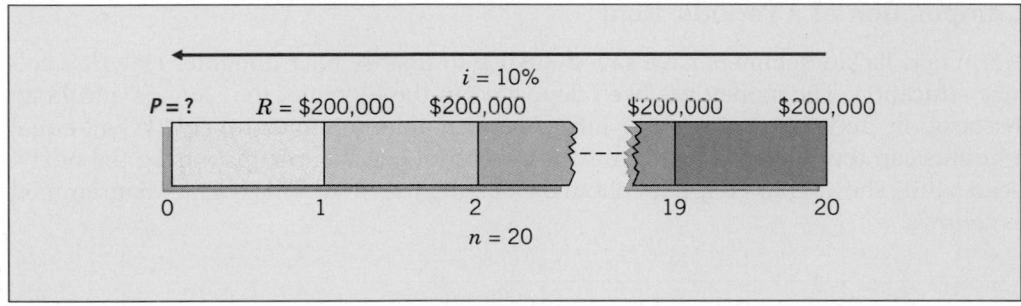

The present value is determined as follows:

$$P = R\ (P_{\overline{n}|i})$$
$$= \$200,000\ (P_{\overline{20}|10\%})$$
$$= \$200,000\ (8.51356)$$
$$= \$1,702,712.$$

As a result, if the state deposits $1,702,712 now and earns 10% interest, it can withdraw $200,000 a year for 20 years to pay you the $4,000,000.

Computation of the Interest Rate

Many shoppers make purchases by using a credit card. When you receive the invoice for payment you may pay the total amount due or you may pay the balance in a certain number of payments. For example, if you receive an invoice from VISA with a balance due of $528.77 and you are invited to pay it off in 12 equal monthly payments of $50 each with the first payment due one month from now, what rate of interest would you be paying?

The $528.77 represents the present value of the 12 payments of $50 each at an unknown rate of interest. This situation in the form of a time diagram appears as follows:

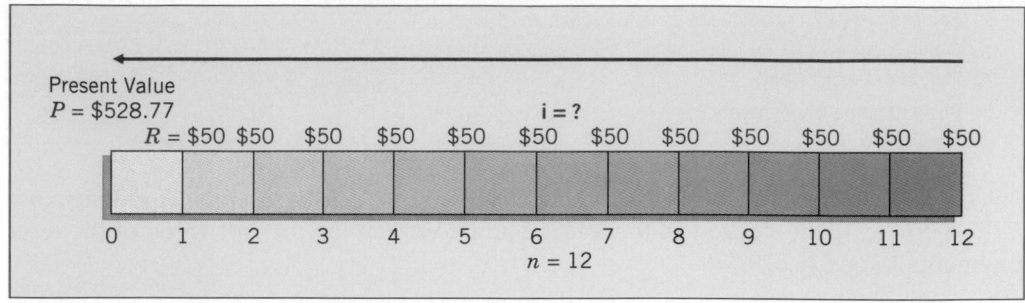

The rate is determined as follows:

$$P = R\,(P_{\overline{n}|i})$$

$$\$528.77 = \$50\,(P_{\overline{12}|i})$$

$$P_{\overline{12}|i} = \frac{\$528.77}{\$50} = 10.57540.$$

Referring to Table 6-4 and reading across the 12-period row, we find 10.57534 in the 2% column. Since 2% is a monthly rate, the nominal annual rate of interest is 24% (12 × 2%) and the effective annual rate is 26.82413% [$(1 + .02)^{12} - 1$]. Obviously, you're better off paying the entire bill now if you possibly can.

Computation of a Periodic Rent

Norm and Jackie Remmers have saved $18,000 to finance their daughter Dawna's college education. The money has been deposited in the Bloomington Savings and Loan Association and is earning 10% interest compounded semiannually. What equal amounts can their daughter withdraw at the end of every 6 months during the next 4 years while she attends college, without exhausting the fund? This is time-diagrammed as follows:

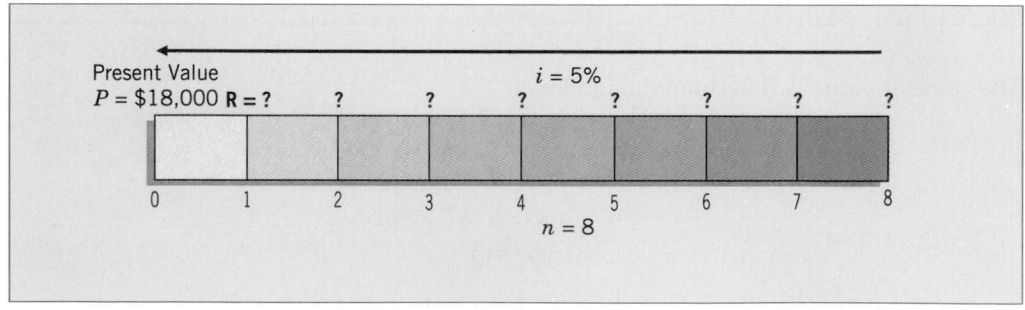

The answer is not determined simply by dividing $18,000 by 8 withdrawals because that would ignore the interest earned on the money remaining on deposit. Taking into consideration that interest is compounded semiannually at 5% (10% ÷ 2) for 8 periods (4 years × 2), and using the same present value of an ordinary annuity formula, we determine the amount of each withdrawal that she can make as follows:

$$P = R\,(P_{\overline{n}|i})$$

$$\$18,000 = R\,(P_{\overline{8}|5\%})$$

$$\$18,000 = R\,(6.46321)$$

$$R = \$2,784.99.$$

▶ MORE COMPLEX SITUATIONS

Often it is necessary to use more than one table to solve time value problems. The business problem encountered may require that computations of both present value of a single sum and present value of an annuity be made. Two common situations are:

1. Deferred annuities.
2. Bond problems.

DEFERRED ANNUITIES

A **deferred annuity** is an annuity in which the rents begin after a specified number of periods. A deferred annuity does not begin to produce rents until 2 or more periods have expired. For example, "an **ordinary annuity** of six annual rents deferred 4 years" means that no rents will occur during the first 4 years, and that the first of the six rents will occur at the end of the fifth year. "An **annuity due** of six annual rents deferred 4 years" means that no rents will occur during the first 4 years, and that the first of six rents will occur at the beginning of the fifth year.

Future Amount of a Deferred Annuity

In the case of the future amount of a deferred annuity the computations are relatively straightforward. Because there is no accumulation or investment on which interest may accrue, the future amount of a deferred annuity is the same as the future amount of an annuity not deferred. That is, the deferral period is ignored in computing the future amount.

To illustrate, assume that Sutton Corporation plans to purchase a land site in 6 years for the construction of its new corporate headquarters. Because of cash flow problems, Sutton is able to budget deposits of $80,000 that are expected to earn 12% annually only at the end of the fourth, fifth, and sixth periods. What future amount will Sutton have accumulated at the end of the sixth year?

A time diagram of this situation is as follows:

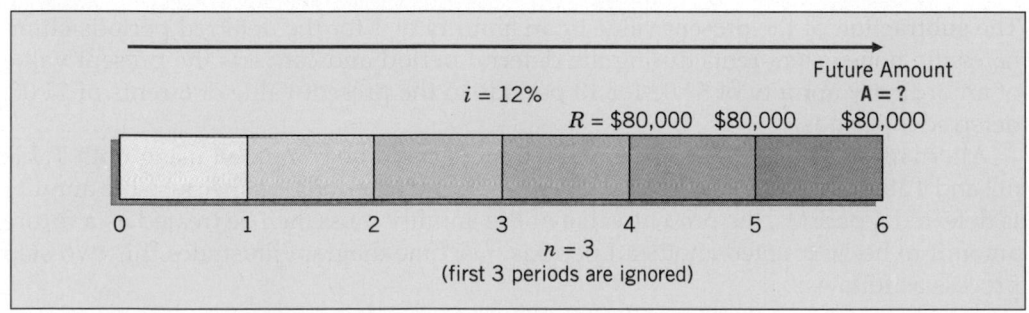

The amount accumulated is determined by using the standard formula for the future amount of an ordinary annuity:

$$A = R \, (A_{\overline{n}|i})$$
$$= \$80,000 \, (A_{\overline{3}|12\%})$$
$$= \$80,000 \, (3.37440)$$
$$= \$269,952.$$

Present Value of a Deferred Annuity

In computing the present value of a deferred annuity, the interest that accrues on the original investment during the deferral period must be recognized.

To compute the present value of a deferred annuity, we compute the present value of an ordinary annuity of 1 as if the rents had occurred for the entire period, and then subtract the present value of rents which were not received during the deferral period. We are left with the present value of the rents actually received subsequent to the deferral period.

To illustrate, Tom Bytehead has developed and copyrighted a software computer program that is a tutorial for students in advanced accounting. He agrees to sell the copyright to Campus Micro Systems for six annual payments of $5,000 each. The payments are to begin 5 years from today. Given an annual interest rate of 8%, what is the present value of the six payments?

This situation is an ordinary annuity of six payments deferred four periods. The following time diagram helps to visualize this sales agreement:

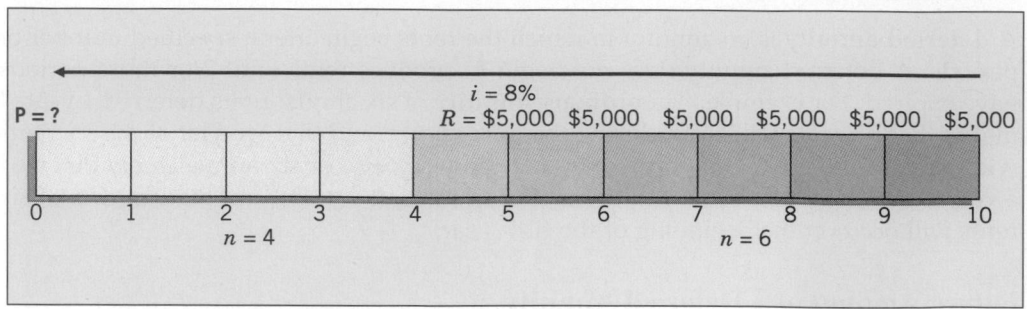

Two options are available to solve this problem. The first is to use only Table 6-4 as follows:

ILLUSTRATION 6-18
Computation of the
Present Value of a
Deferred Annuity

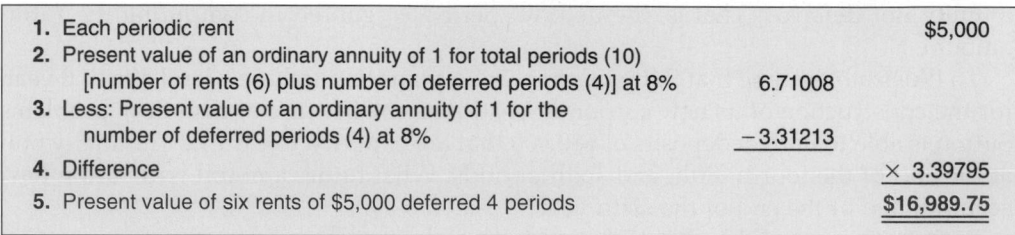

1. Each periodic rent		$5,000
2. Present value of an ordinary annuity of 1 for total periods (10) [number of rents (6) plus number of deferred periods (4)] at 8%	6.71008	
3. Less: Present value of an ordinary annuity of 1 for the number of deferred periods (4) at 8%	−3.31213	
4. Difference		× 3.39795
5. Present value of six rents of $5,000 deferred 4 periods		$16,989.75

The subtraction of the present value of an annuity of 1 for the deferred periods eliminates the nonexistent rents during the deferral period and converts the present value of an ordinary annuity of $1.00 for 10 periods to the present value of 6 rents of $1.00, deferred 4 periods.

Alternatively, the present value of the 6 rents could be computed using both Table 6-2 and Table 6-4. One can first discount the annuity 6 periods, but because the annuity is deferred 4 periods, the present value of the annuity must then be treated as a future amount to be discounted another 4 periods.[10] A time diagram illustrates this two-step process as follows:

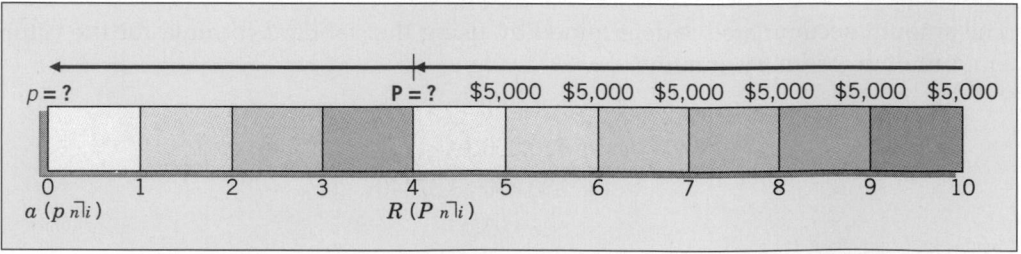

---

[10]Deferred annuity contracts are common in professional sports. Rich Gossage's old contract with the San Diego Padres (and now with the Texas Rangers), for example, in addition to salary and bonuses over the first 5 or 6 years, was to pay him at the rate of $240,000 a year from 1990 to 2006 and $125,000 from 2007 to 2016. The payouts from 1990 through 2016 total $5.33 million, but the present value of this deferred annuity is estimated at $1.5 million.

Step 1: $P = R (P_{\overline{n}|i})$

$\qquad = \$5,000 (P_{\overline{6}|8\%})$

$\qquad = \$5,000 (4.62288)$ \quad (Table 6-4 Present value of an ordinary annuity)

$\qquad = \$23,114.40$

Step 2: $p = a (p_{\overline{n}|i})$

$\qquad = \$23,114.40 (p_{\overline{4}|8\%})$

$\qquad = \$23,114.40 (.73503)$ \quad (Table 6-2 Present value of a single sum)

$\qquad = \mathbf{\$16,989.78.}$

The present value of \$16,989.78 computed above is the same result although computed differently from the first illustration.

VALUATION OF LONG-TERM BONDS

A long-term bond produces two cash flows: (1) periodic interest payments during the life of the bond, and (2) the principal (face value) paid at maturity. At the date of issue, bond buyers determine the present value of these two cash flows using the market rate of interest.

The periodic interest payments represent an annuity and the principal represents a single sum problem. The current market value of the bonds is the combined present values of the interest annuity and the principal amount.

To illustrate, Alltech Corporation on January 1, 1995, issues \$100,000 of 9% bonds due in 5 years with interest payable annually at year-end. The current market rate of interest for bonds of similar risk is 11%. What will the buyers pay for this bond issue?

The time diagram depicting both cash flows is shown below:

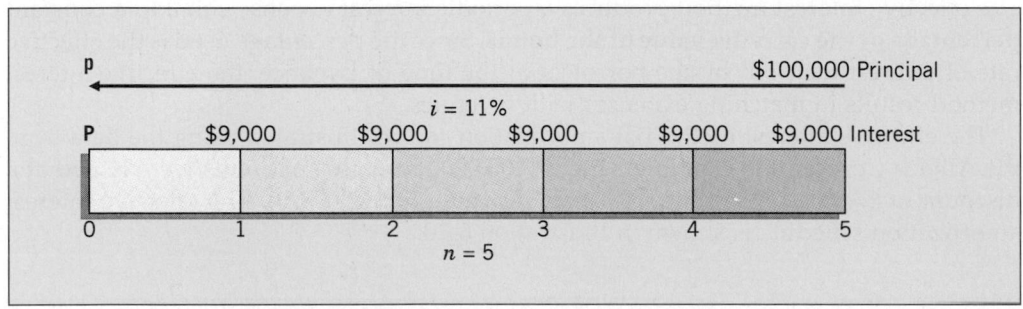

The present value of the two cash flows is computed by discounting at 11% as follows:

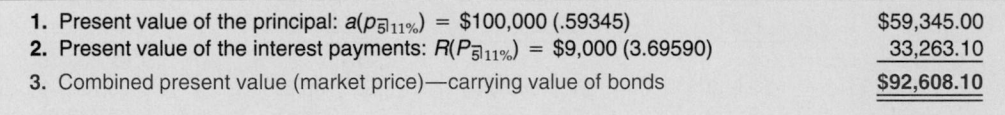

1. Present value of the principal: $a(p_{\overline{5}|11\%})$ = \$100,000 (.59345)   \$59,345.00
2. Present value of the interest payments: $R(P_{\overline{5}|11\%})$ = \$9,000 (3.69590)   33,263.10
3. Combined present value (market price)—carrying value of bonds   **\$92,608.10**

ILLUSTRATION 6-19
Computation of the Present Value of an Interest-Bearing Bond

By paying \$92,608.10 at date of issue, the buyers of the bonds will realize an effective yield of 11% over the 5-year term of the bonds. This is true because the cash flows were discounted at 11%.

EFFECTIVE INTEREST METHOD OF AMORTIZATION OF BOND DISCOUNT OR PREMIUM

In the Alltech Corporation bond issue, Illustration 6-19, the bonds were issued at a discount computed as follows:

Maturity value (face amount) of bonds		$100,000.00
Present value of the principal	$59,345.00	
Present value of the interest	33,263.10	
Proceeds (present value and cash received)		92,608.10
Discount on bonds issued		$ 7,391.90

This discount of $7,391.90 under acceptable accrual accounting is amortized (written off) over the life of the bond issue to interest expense.

The profession's preferred procedure for amortization of a discount or premium is the **effective interest method** (also called **present value amortization**). Under the effective interest method:

1. Bond interest expense is computed first by multiplying the carrying value of the bonds at the beginning of the period by the effective interest rate.

2. The bond discount or premium amortization is then determined by comparing the bond interest expense with the interest to be paid.

The computation of the amortization is depicted graphically as follows:

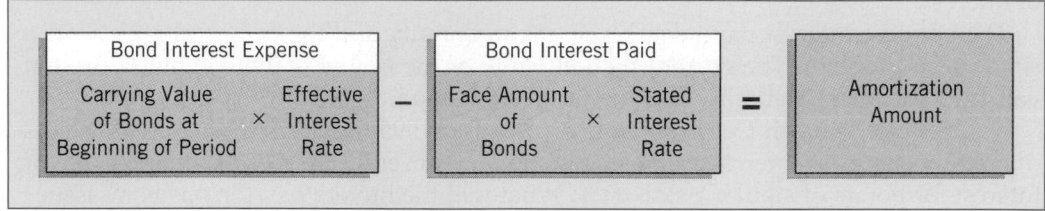

The effective interest method produces a periodic interest expense equal to **a constant percentage of the carrying value of the bonds.** Since the percentage used is the effective rate of interest incurred by the borrower at the time of issuance, the effective interest method results in matching expenses with revenues.

The effective interest method of amortization can be illustrated using the data from the Alltech Corporation example, where $100,000 face value of bonds were issued at a discount of $7,391.90 resulting in a carrying value of $92,608.10. The effective interest amortization schedule is shown in Illustration 6-20:

ILLUSTRATION 6-20
Effective Interest
Amortization Schedule

		Schedule of Bond Discount Amortization 5-Year, 9% Bonds Sold to Yield 11%		
Date	Cash Interest Paid	Interest Expense	Bond Discount Amortization	Carrying Value of Bonds
1/1/95				$ 92,608.10
12/31/95	$9,000[a]	$10,186.89[b]	$1,186.89[c]	93,794.99[d]
12/31/96	9,000	10,317.45	1,317.45	95,112.44
12/31/97	9,000	10,462.37	1,462.37	96,574.81
12/31/98	9,000	10,623.23	1,623.23	98,198.04
12/31/99	9,000	10,801.96	1,801.96	100,000.00
	$45,000	$52,391.90	$7,391.90	

[a]$100,000 × .09 = $9,000
[b]$92,608.10 × .11 = $10,186.89
[c]$10,186.89 − $9,000 = $1,186.89
[d]$92,608.10 + $1,186.89 = $93,794.99

The amortization schedule illustrated above is used for note and bond transactions in Chapters 7 and 14.

▶ SUMMARY OF LEARNING OBJECTIVES ◀

1. **Identify accounting topics where the time value of money is relevant.** Some of the applications of present value–based measurements to accounting topics are: (1) notes, (2) leases, (3) amortization of premiums and discounts, (4) pensions and other postretirement benefits, (5) capital assets, (6) sinking funds, (7) business combinations, (8) disclosures, and (9) installment contracts.

2. **Distinguish between simple and compound interest.** See Fundamental Concepts following this Summary.

3. **Learn how to use appropriate compound interest tables.** In order to identify the appropriate compound interest table to use of the five given, you must identify whether you are solving for (1) the future value of a single sum, (2) the present value of a single sum, (3) the future value of a series of sums, or (4) the present value of a series of sums (an annuity). In addition, when a series of sums (an annuity) is involved, you must identify whether these sums are received or paid (1) at the beginning of each period (ordinary annuity) or (2) at the end of each period (annuity due).

4. **Identify variables fundamental to solving interest problems.** The following four variables are fundamental to all compound interest problems: (1) *Rate of interest:* unless otherwise stated, an annual rate that must be adjusted to reflect the length of the compounding period if less than a year. (2) *Number of time periods:* the number of compounding periods (a period may be equal to or less than a year). (3) *Future amount:* the value at a future date of a given sum or sums invested assuming compound interest. (4) *Present value:* the value now (present time) of a future sum or sums discounted assuming compound interest.

5. **Solve future and present value of 1 problems.** See Fundamental Concepts following this Summary, items 5(a) and 6(a).

6. **Solve future amount of ordinary and annuity due problems.** See Fundamental Concepts following this Summary, item 5(b).

7. **Solve present values of ordinary and annuity due problems.** See Fundamental Concepts following this Summary, item 6(b).

◀ FUNDAMENTAL CONCEPTS ▶

1. **Simple Interest.** Interest on principal only, regardless of interest that may have accrued in the past.

2. **Compound Interest.** Interest accrues on the unpaid interest of past periods as well as on the principal.

3. **Rate of Interest.** Interest is usually expressed as an annual rate, but when the interest period is shorter than one year, the interest rate for the shorter period must be determined.

4. **Annuity.** A series of payments or receipts (called rents) that occur at equal intervals of time.
   Types of annuities:
   (a) **Ordinary Annuity.** Each rent is payable (receivable) at the end of the period.
   (b) **Annuity Due.** Each rent is payable (receivable) at the beginning of the period.

5. **Future Amount.** Value at a later date of a given sum that is invested at compound interest.
   (a) **Future Amount of 1** (or amount of a given sum). The future value of $1.00 (or a single given sum), a, at the end of n periods at i compound interest rate (Table 6-1).
   (b) **Future Amount of an Annuity.** The future value of a series of rents invested at compound interest; in other words, the accumulated total that results from a series of equal deposits at regular intervals invested at compound interest. Both deposits and interest increase the accumulation.
      (1) **Future Amount of an Ordinary Annuity.** The future value on the date of the last rent.
      (2) **Future Amount of an Annuity Due.** The future value one period after the date of the last rent. When an annuity due table is not available, use Table 6-3 with the following formula:

      Amount of annuity due of 1 for n rents = (Amount of ordinary annuity for n rents) × (1 + interest rate).

6. **Present Value.** The value at an earlier date (usually now) of a given future sum discounted at compound interest.
   (a) **Present Value of 1** (or present value of a single sum). The present value (worth) of $1.00 (or a given sum) p, due n periods hence, discounted at i compound interest (Table 6-2).
   (b) **Present Value of an Annuity.** The present value (worth) of a series of rents discounted at compound interest; in other words, it is the sum when invested at compound interest that will permit a series of equal withdrawals at regular intervals.
      (1) **Present Value of an Ordinary Annuity.** The value now of $1.00 to be received or paid at the end of each period (rents) for n periods, discounted at i compound interest (Table 6-4).
      (2) **Present Value of an Annuity Due.** The value now of $1.00 to be received or paid at the beginning of each period (rents) for the n periods, discounted at i compound interest (Table 6-5). To use Table 6-4 for an annuity due, apply this formula:

      Present value of annuity due of 1 for n rents = (Present value of an ordinary annuity of n rents) × (1 + interest rate).

QUESTIONS

1. What is the time value of money? Why should accountants have an understanding of compound interest, annuities, and present value concepts?

2. What is the nature of interest? Distinguish between "simple interest" and "compound interest."

3. What are the components of an interest rate? Why is it important for accountants to understand these components?

4. Presented below are a number of values taken from compound interest tables involving the same number of periods and the same rate of interest. Indicate what each of these four values represent.
   (a) 7.36009   (c) .55839
   (b) 1.79085   (d) 13.18079

5. Sondra Bassinger deposited $18,000 in a money market certificate that provides interest of 12% compounded quarterly if the amount is maintained for 3 years. How much will Sondra Bassinger have at the end of 3 years?

6. Susan Lehman will receive $30,000 on December 31, 2000 (5 years from now) from a trust fund established by her father. Assuming the appropriate interest rate for discounting is 12% (compounded semiannually), what is the present value of this amount today?

7. What are the primary characteristics of an annuity? Differentiate between an "ordinary annuity" and an "annuity due."

8. Arthur Thiessen, Inc. owes $30,000 to Wheaton Company. How much would Thiessen have to pay each year if the debt is retired through four equal payments (made at the end of the year), given an interest rate on the debt of 15%? (Round to two decimal places.)

9. The Yoders are planning for a retirement home. They estimate they will need $130,000, 4 years from now to purchase this home. Assuming an interest rate of 10%, what amount must be deposited at the end of each of the 4 years to fund the home price? (Round to two decimal places.)

10. Assume the same situation as in question 9, except that the four equal amounts are deposited at the beginning of the period rather than at the end. In this case, what amount must be deposited at the beginning of each period? (Round to two decimals.)

11. Explain how the amount of an ordinary annuity interest table is converted to the amount of an annuity due table.

12. Explain how the present value of an ordinary annuity interest table is converted to the present value of an annuity due interest table.

13. In a book named *Treasure*, the reader has to figure out where a 2.2 pound, 24 kt gold horse has been buried. If the horse is found, a prize of $25,000 a year for 20 years is provided. The actual cost of the publisher to purchase an annuity to pay for the prize is $210,000. What interest rate (to the nearest percent) was used to determine the amount of the annuity? (Assume end-of-year payments.)

14. Mark Welty Enterprises leases property to Hostetler, Inc. Because Hostetler, Inc. is experiencing financial difficulty, Welty agrees to receive five rents of $8,000 at the end of each year, with the rents deferred 3 years. What is the present value of the five rents discounted at 12%?

15. Luanna Schettler, Inc. invests $20,000 initially, which accumulates to $38,000 at the end of 5 years. What is the annual interest rate of the investment paid? (Hint: Interpolation will be needed.)

16. Answer the following questions:
    (a) On May 1, 1995, Ed Diller Company sold some machinery to Pandora Company on an installment contract basis. The contract required five equal annual payments, with the first payment due on May 1, 1995. What present value concept is appropriate for this situation?
    (b) On June 1, 1995, Schultz, Inc. purchased a new machine that it does not have to pay for until May 1, 1997. The total payment on May 1, 1997 will include both principal and interest. Assuming interest at a 12% rate, the cost of the machine would be the total payment multiplied by what time value of money concept?
    (c) Andrew Biedler, Inc. wishes to know how much money it will have available in 5 years if five equal amounts of $30,000 are invested, with the first amount invested immediately. What interest table is appropriate for this situation?
    (d) Elvira Suter invests in a "jumbo" $100,000, 3-year certificate of deposit at First Wisconsin. What table would be used to determine the amount accumulated at the end of 3 years?

17. Recently Nancy Brubaker was interested in purchasing a Honda Acura. The salesperson indicated that the price of the car was either $25,000 cash or $6,400 at the end of each of 5 years. Compute the effective interest rate to the nearest percent that Nancy would pay if she chooses to make the five annual payments.

18. Recently, property/casualty insurance companies have been criticized because they reserve for the total loss as much as 5 years before it may happen. Recently the IRS has joined the debate because they say the full reserve is unfair from a taxation viewpoint. What do you believe is the IRS position?

19. Brian Bosworth was reported to receive an $11 million contract to play linebacker for the Seattle Seahawks. The terms were a signing bonus of $500,000 in 1987 and $500,000 in 1997 through the year 2000. In addition, he was to receive a base salary of $300,000 in 1987 which was to increase $100,000 a year to the year 1991; in 1992 he was to receive $1 million which would increase $100,000 to the year 1996. Assuming that the appropriate interest rate is 9% and that each payment occurred at the end of the year, compute the present value of this contract as of December 31, 1987.

EXERCISES

(Interest rates are per annum unless otherwise indicated.)

E6-1 (Using Interest Tables) For each of the following cases, indicate (a) to what rate columns and (b) to what number of periods you would refer in looking up the interest factor.

1. In a future amount of 1 table

Annual Rate	Number of Years Invested	Compounded
a. 9%	9	Annually
b. 12%	5	Quarterly
c. 10%	15	Semiannually

2. In a present value of an annuity of 1 table

Annual Rate	Number of Years Involved	Number of Rents Involved	Frequency of Rents
a. 9%	25	25	Annually
b. 10%	15	30	Semiannually
c. 12%	7	28	Quarterly

E6-2 (Simple and Compound Interest Computations) Kriss Kross invests $10,000 at 8% annual interest, leaving the money invested without withdrawing any of the interest for 8 years. At the end of the 8 years, Kriss withdrew the accumulated amount of money.

Instructions
 (a) Compute the amount Kriss would withdraw assuming the investment earns simple interest.
 (b) Compute the amount Kriss would withdraw assuming the investment earns interest compounded annually.
 (c) Compute the amount Kriss would withdraw assuming the investment earns interest compounded semiannually.

E6-3 (Computation of Future Amounts and Present Values) Using the appropriate interest table, answer each of the following questions (each case is independent of the others).
 (a) What is the future amount of $5,000 at the end of 5 periods at 8% compounded interest?
 (b) What is the present value of $5,000 due 8 periods hence, discounted at 11%?
 (c) What is the future amount of 15 periodic payments of $5,000 each made at the end of each period and compounded at 10%?
 (d) What is the present value of $5,000 to be received at the end of each of 20 periods, discounted at 5% compound interest?

E6-4 (Computation of Future Amounts and Present Values) Using the appropriate interest table, answer the following questions (each case is independent of the others).
 (a) What is the future amount of 20 periodic payments of $2,500 each made at the beginning of each period and compounded at 8%?
 (b) What is the present value of $1,500 to be received at the beginning of each of 30 periods, discounted at 10% compound interest?
 (c) What is the future amount of 15 deposits of $1,000 each made at the beginning of each period and compounded at 10%? (Future amount as of the end of the fifteenth period.)
 (d) What is the present value of six receipts of $500 each received at the beginning of each period, discounted at 9% compounded interest?

E6-5 (Computation of Present Value) Using the appropriate interest table, compute the present values of the following periodic amounts due at the end of the designated periods.
 (a) $15,000 receivable at the end of each period for 8 periods compounded at 12%.
 (b) $15,000 payments to be made at the end of each period for 16 periods at 9%.
 (c) $15,000 payable at the end of the seventh, eighth, ninth, and tenth periods at 12%.

E6-6 (Future Amount and Present Value Problems) Presented below are three unrelated situations:
 (a) Fishbone Company recently signed a lease for a new office building, for a lease period of 10 years. Under the lease agreement, a security deposit of $10,000 is made, with the deposit to be returned at the expiration of the lease, with interest compounded at 10% per year. What amount will the company receive at the time the lease expires?

(b) Spin Doctors Corporation, having recently issued a $10 million, 15-year bond issue, is committed to make annual sinking fund deposits of $300,000. The deposits are made on the last day of each year, and yield a return of 10%. Will the fund at the end of 15 years be sufficient to retire the bonds? If not, what will the deficiency be?

(c) Under the terms of her salary agreement, President Bonnie Raitt has an option of receiving either an immediate bonus of $35,000, or a deferred bonus of $65,000, payable in 10 years. Ignoring tax considerations, and assuming a relevant interest rate of 8%, which form of settlement should President Raitt accept?

E6-7 (Computation of Bond Prices) What would you pay for a $25,000 debenture bond that matures in 15 years and pays $2,500 a year in interest if you wanted to earn a yield of:
(a) 8%?
(b) 10%?
(c) 12%?

E6-8 (Computations for a Retirement Fund) Mr. David Bowie, a super salesman contemplating retirement on his fifty-fifth birthday, decides to create a fund on an 8% basis that will enable him to withdraw $8,000 per year on June 30, beginning in 2000, and continuing through 2003. To develop this fund, David intends to make equal contributions on June 30 of each of the years 1996–1999.

Instructions
(a) How much must the balance of the fund equal on June 30, 1999, in order for David Bowie to satisfy his objective?
(b) What are each of David's contributions to the fund?

E6-9 (Unknown Periods and Unknown Interest Rate) (a) Robert Plant wishes to become a millionaire. His money market fund has a balance of $76,277.71 and has a guaranteed interest of 10%.

Instructions
How many years must Robert leave that balance in the fund in order to get his deserved $1,000,000?

(b) Assume that Oleta Adams desires to accumulate $1 million in 15 years using her money market fund balance of $122,894.51.

Instructions
At what interest rate must Oleta's investment compound annually?

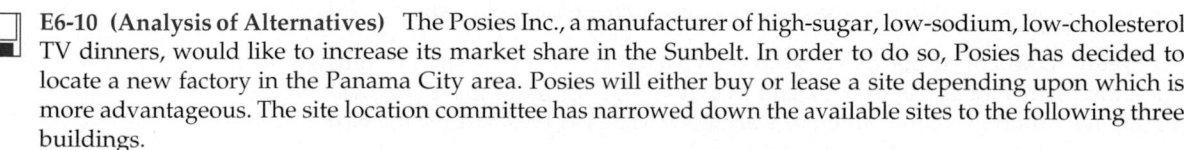

E6-10 (Analysis of Alternatives) The Posies Inc., a manufacturer of high-sugar, low-sodium, low-cholesterol TV dinners, would like to increase its market share in the Sunbelt. In order to do so, Posies has decided to locate a new factory in the Panama City area. Posies will either buy or lease a site depending upon which is more advantageous. The site location committee has narrowed down the available sites to the following three buildings.

Building A: Purchase for a cash price of $600,000, useful life 25 years.

Building B: Lease for 25 years with annual lease payments of $68,000 being made at the beginning of the year.

Building C: Purchase for $650,000 cash. This building is larger than needed; however, the excess space can be sublet for 25 years at a net annual rental of $7,000. Rental payments will be received at the end of each year. The Posies Inc. has no aversion to being a landlord.

Instructions
In which building would you recommend that The Posies Inc. locate assuming a 12% cost of funds?

E6-11 (Amount in Trust) Dianna Ross intends to invest $20,000 in a trust on January 10 of every year, 1996 to 2010, inclusive. She anticipates that interest rates will change during that period of time as follows:

1/10/96–1/10/99	10%
1/11/99–1/10/06	11%
1/11/06–1/10/10	12%

How much will Dianna have in trust on January 10, 2010?

E6-12 (Amount Needed to Retire Stock) Proclaimers Inc. is a computer software development company. In recent years, the company has experienced significant growth in sales. As a result, the board of directors has decided to raise funds by issuing redeemable preferred stock to meet the need for expansion. On January 1, 1994, the company issued 100,000 shares of 12% redeemable preferred stock with the intent to redeem this preferred stock on January 1, 2004. The redemption price per share of preferred stock will be $25.

As the controller of the company, Leith Chrysalis is asked to set up a plan to accumulate the funds that will be needed to retire the redeemable preferred stock on January 1, 2004. He expects that the company will have a surplus of funds of $120,000 each year for the next 10 years and decides to set up a sinking fund for these funds. Beginning January 1, 1995, the company will deposit $120,000 into the sinking fund annually for 10 years. The sinking fund is expected to generate 10% interest and compound annually. However, the sinking fund will not be sufficient for the redemption of preferred stock. Therefore, Leith plans to deposit on January 1, 1999 a single amount of money into a savings account which is expected to earn 9% interest.

Instructions

Help Leith Chrysalis to determine what is the amount to be deposited on January 1, 1999.

E6-13 (Computation of Bond Liability) Ned's Atomic Dustbin, Inc. publishes popular books and magazines. Recently the Vice-President of Operations of the company has requested construction of a new plant to meet the increasing needs for the company's books and magazines. After a careful evaluation of the request, the board of directors has decided to raise funds for the new plant by issuing $2,000,000 of 12% term corporate bonds on March 1, 1994, due on March 1, 2009, with interest payable each March 1 and September 1. At the time of issuance, the market interest rate for similar financial instruments is 10%.

Instructions

As the controller of the company, determine the selling price of the bonds.

E6-14 (Computation of Pension Liability) Erasure, Inc. is a furniture manufacturing company with 50 employees. Recently, after a long negotiation with the local labor union, the company decided to initiate a pension plan as a part of its compensation plan. The plan will start on January 1, 1995. Each employee covered by the plan is entitled to a pension payment each year after retirement. As required by accounting standards, the controller of the company needs to report the pension obligation (liability). On the basis of a discussion with the supervisor of the Personnel Department and an actuary from an insurance company, the controller develops the following information related to the pension plan:

Average length of time to retirement	15 years
Expected life duration after retirement	10 years
Total pension payment expected each year after retirement for all employees. Payment made at the end of the year.	$600,000 per year

The interest rate to be used is 8%.

Instructions

On the basis of the information above, determine the present value of the pension obligation (liability).

 E6-15 (Retirement of Debt) Lyle Lovett borrowed $67,000 on March 1, 1994. This amount plus accrued interest at 12% compounded semiannually is to be repaid March 1, 2004. To retire this debt, Lyle plans to contribute to a debt retirement fund five equal amounts starting on March 1, 1999 and for the next 4 years. The fund is expected to earn 10% per annum.

Instructions

How much must be contributed each year by Lyle Lovett to provide a fund sufficient to retire the debt on March 1, 2004?

E6-16 (Computation of Bond Liability) Your client, Pixies, Inc., has acquired Trompe Le Monde Manufacturing Company in a business combination that is to be accounted for as a purchase transaction (at fair market value). Along with the assets and business of Le Monde, Pixies assumed an outstanding debenture bond issue having a principal amount of $7,500,000 with interest payable semiannually at a stated rate of 8%. Le Monde received $6,800,000 in proceeds from the issuance 5 years ago. The bonds are currently 20 years from maturity. Equivalent securities command a 12% rate of interest, interest paid semiannually.

Instructions

Your client requests your advice regarding the amount to record for the acquired bond issue.

E6-17 (Computation of Amount of Rentals) Your client, Robyn Hitchcock Leasing Company, is preparing a contract to lease a machine to Egyptian Corporation for a period of 35 years. Hitchcock has an investment cost of $365,755 in the machine, which has a useful life of 35 years and no salvage value at the end of that time. Your client is interested in earning an 11% return on its investment and has agreed to accept 35 equal rental payments at the end of each of the next 35 years.

Instructions

You are requested to provide Hitchcock with the amount of each of the 35 rentals that will render an 11% return on investment.

E6-18 (Least Costly Payoff) Sonic Youth Corporation has outstanding a contractual debt. The corporation has available two means of settlement: It can either make immediate payment of $2,250,000, or it can make annual payments of $260,000 for 15 years, each payment due on the last day of the year.

Instructions

Which method of payment do you recommend, assuming an expected effective interest rate of 8% during the future period?

E6-19 (Least Costly Payoff) Assuming the same facts as those in Exercise 6–18 except that the payments must begin now and be made on the first day of each of the 15 years, what payment method would you recommend?

(To solve Exercises 6-20, 6-21, and 6-22, a calculator is needed.)

E6-20 (Determine Interest Rate) Whitney Houston wishes to invest $19,000 on July 1, 1995 and have it accumulate to $48,000 by July 1, 2005.

Instructions

At what exact annual rate of interest must Whitney invest the $19,000?

E6-21 (Determine Interest Rate) On July 17, 1994, Julia Roberts borrowed $42,000 from her grandfather to open a clothing store. Starting July 17, 1995, Julia has to make ten equal annual payments of $6,700 each to repay the loan.

Instructions

What interest rate is Julia paying?

E6-22 (Determine Interest Rate) As the purchaser of a new house, Cindy Crawford has signed a mortgage note to pay the Somonauk National Bank and Trust Co. $16,000 every six months for 20 years, at the end of which time she will own the house. At the date the mortgage is signed the purchase price was $198,000, and a down payment of $20,000 was made. The first payment will be made six months after the date the mortgage is signed.

Instructions

Compute the exact rate of interest earned on the mortgage by the bank.

PROBLEMS

(Interest rates are per annum unless otherwise indicated.)

P6-1 (Computation of Present Value) Answer each of these unrelated questions.

1. On January 1, 1995, Brokaw Corporation sold a building that cost $210,000 and that had accumulated depreciation of $100,000 on the date of sale. Brokaw received as consideration a $275,000 noninterest-bearing note due on January 1, 1998. There was no established exchange price for the building, and the note had no ready market. The prevailing rate of interest for a note of this type on January 1, 1995 was 9%. At what amount should the gain from the sale of the building be reported?

2. On January 1, 1995, Brokaw Corporation purchased 100 of the $1,000 face value, 9%, 10-year bonds of Walters Inc. The bonds mature on January 1, 2005, and pay interest annually beginning January 1, 1996. Brokaw Corporation purchased the bonds to yield 11%. How much did Brokaw pay for the bonds?

3. Brokaw Corporation bought a new machine and agreed to pay for it in equal annual installments of $3,800 at the end of each of the next 10 years. Assuming that a prevailing interest rate of 8% applies to this contract, how much should Brokaw record as the cost of the machine?

4. Brokaw Corporation purchased a special tractor on December 31, 1995. The purchase agreement stipulated that Brokaw should pay $16,000 at the time of purchase and $5,000 at the end of each of the next 8 years. The tractor should be valued on December 31, 1995 at what amount, assuming an appropriate interest rate of 12%?

5. Brokaw Corporation wants to withdraw $50,000 (including principal) from an investment fund at the end of each year for 9 years. What should be the required initial investment at the beginning of the first year if the fund earns 11%?

P6-2 (Computation of Unknown Interest Factors) Using the appropriate interest table, provide the solution to each of the following four questions by computing the unknowns.

(a) What is the amount of the payments that Diane Sawyer must make at the end of each of 8 years to accumulate a fund of $22,000 by the end of the eighth year, if the fund earns 8% interest, compounded annually?

(b) Connie Chung is 30 years old today and she wishes to accumulate $350,000 by her fifty-fifth birthday so she can retire to her summer place on Lake Hopatcong. She wishes to accumulate this amount by making equal deposits on her thirtieth through her fifty-fourth birthdays. What annual deposit must Connie make if the fund will earn 12% interest compounded annually?

(c) Dan Rather has $10,000 to invest today at 9% to pay a debt of $28,126.70. How many years will it take him to accumulate enough to liquidate the debt?

(d) Jane Pauley has a $13,800 debt that she wishes to repay 4 years from today; she has $9,090.49 that she intends to invest for the 4 years. What rate of interest will she need to earn annually in order to accumulate enough to pay the debt?

P6-3 (Future Amounts of Annuities Due) Mack Aroni, a bank robber, is worried about his retirement. He decides to start a savings account. Mack deposits annually his net share of the ''loot,'' which consists of $70,000 per year, for 3 years beginning January 1, 1988. Mack is arrested on January 4, 1990 (after making the third deposit) and spends the rest of 1990 and most of 1991 in jail. He escapes in September of 1991. He resumes his savings plan with semiannual deposits of $25,000 each beginning January 1, 1992. Assume that the bank's interest rate was 9% compounded annually from January 1, 1988 through January 1, 1991, and 12% annual rate compounded semiannually thereafter.

Instructions
When Mack retires on January 1, 1995 (6 months after his last deposit), what is the balance in his savings account?

 P6-4 (Analysis of Alternatives) R. L. Stein Inc., has decided to surface and maintain for 10 years a vacant lot next to one of its discount-retail outlets to serve as a parking lot for customers. Management is considering the following bids involving two different qualities of surfacing for a parking area of 12,000 square yards:

Bid A: A surface that costs $5.25 per square yard to install. This surface will have to be replaced at the end of 5 years. The annual maintenance cost on this surface is estimated at 15 cents per square yard for each year but the last year of its service. The replacement surface will be similar to the initial surface.

Bid B: A surface that costs $9.50 per square yard to install. This surface has a probable useful life of 10 years and will require annual maintenance in each year except the last year, at an estimated cost of 4 cents per square yard.

Instructions
Prepare computations showing which bid should be accepted by R. L. Stein Inc. You may assume that the cost of capital is 9%, that the annual maintenance expenditures are incurred at the end of each year, and that prices are not expected to change during the next 10 years.

P6-5 (Computation of Unknown Interest Factors) Solve for the unknowns in each of the following three situations using the interest tables.

(a) Mr. and Mrs. Stephen King have decided to provide for their handicapped son by investing $140,550 today in an annuity at 8% interest, compounded annually. They feel their son should receive approximately $15,000 per year beginning one year from today. The investment of the $140,550 will provide approximately $15,000 per year for how many years before being depleted?

(b) Tom Clancey wishes to invest $52,394 today to insure $6,500 payments to his son at the end of each year for the next 15 years. At what approximate interest rate must the $52,394 be invested?

(c) On June 1, 1995, Judy Bloom purchases 20 acres of farmland from her neighbor, Ann M. Martin, and agrees to pay the purchase price in five payments of $10,500 each, the first payment to be payable June 1, 1999 (Assume interest compounded annually at the rate of 9% is implicit in the payments). What is the purchase price of the 20 acres?

P6-6 (Analysis of Alternatives) Dan Quail died, leaving to his wife Murphy an insurance policy contract that provides that the beneficiary (Murphy) can choose any one of the following four options.

(a) $55,000 immediate cash.

(b) $3,700 every 3 months payable at the end of each quarter for 5 years.

(c) $20,000 immediate cash and $1,500 every 3 months for 10 years, payable at the beginning of each 3-month period.

(d) $4,000 every 3 months for 3 years and $1,200 each quarter for the following 25 quarters, all payments payable at the end of each quarter.

Instructions
If money is worth 2½% per quarter, compounded quarterly, which option would you recommend that Murphy exercise?

P6-7 (Computation of Unknown Payments) Provide a solution to each of the following situations by computing the unknowns (use the interest tables).

(a) Faith Ringold invests in a $125,000 annuity insurance policy at 9% compounded annually on February 8, 1996. The first of 20 receipts from the annuity is payable to Faith 10 years after the annuity is purchased, or on February 8, 2006. What will be the amount of each of the 20 equal annual receipts?

(b) Kendall Williams owes a debt of $20,000 from the purchase of his new sports car. The debt bears interest of 8% payable annually. Kendall wishes to pay the debt and interest in eight annual installments, beginning one year hence. What equal annual installments will pay the debt and interest?

(c) On January 1, 1996, Mike Myers offers to buy Dan Carbey's used combine for $24,600, payable in 10 equal installments, which are to include 9% interest on the unpaid balance and a portion of the principal with the first payment to be made on January 1, 1996. How much will each payment be?

P6-8 (Purchase Price of a Business (Deferred Annuities)) During the past year, Georgia O'Keefe planted a new vineyard on 150 acres of land that she leases for $27,000 a year. She has asked you as her accountant to assist her in determining the value of her vineyard operation.

The vineyard will bear no grapes for the first 5 years (1–5). In the next 5 years (6–10), Georgia estimates that the vines will bear grapes that can be sold for $55,000 each year. For the next 20 years (11–30) she expects the harvest will provide annual revenues of $100,000. But during the last 10 years (31–40) of the vineyard's life she estimates that revenues will decline to $80,000 per year.

During the first 5 years the annual cost of pruning, fertilizing, and caring for the vineyard is estimated at $9,000; during the years of production, 6–40, these costs will rise to $10,000 per year. The relevant market rate of interest for the entire period is 12%. Assume that all receipts and payments are made at the end of each year.

Instructions

Max Ernst has offered to buy Georgia's vineyard business by assuming the 40-year lease. On the basis of the current value of the business what is the minimum price Georgia should accept?

P6-9 (Annuity with Varying Interest Rates) Mrs. Whistler plans to establish an annuity arrangement whereby her four children would each receive $1,750 on December 25 of the years 1998 to 2012, inclusive. Variations in the interest rates during that period of time are estimated as follows:

12/26/97–12/25/02	12%
12/26/02–12/25/08	11%
12/26/08–12/25/12	9%

Instructions

Compute the amount that Mrs. Whistler must invest on December 26, 1997, to assure these annual payments to her children.

P6-10 (Time Value Concepts Applied to Solve Business Problems) Answer the following questions related to Grant Wood, Inc.

1. Grant Wood, Inc. has $114,400 to invest. The company is trying to decide between two alternative uses of the funds. One alternative provides $16,000 at the end of each year for 12 years, and the other is to receive a single lump sum payment of $380,000 at the end of the 12 years. Which alternative should Wood select? Assume the interest rate is constant over the entire investment.

2. Grant Wood, Inc. has completed the purchase of a new IBM computer. The fair market value of the equipment is $724,150. The purchase agreement specifies an immediate down payment of $100,000 and semiannual payments of $76,952 beginning at the end of 6 months for 5 years. What is the interest rate, to the nearest percent, used in discounting this purchase transaction?

3. Grant Wood, Inc. loans money to Renoir Corporation in the amount of $300,000. Wood accepts an 8% note due in 7 years with interest payable semiannually. After 2 years (and receipt of interest for 2 years), Wood needs money and therefore sells the note to First National Bank, which demands interest on the note of 10% compounded semiannually. What is the amount Wood will receive on the sale of the note?

4. Grant Wood, Inc. wishes to accumulate $650,000 by December 31, 2005, to retire bonds outstanding. The company deposits $150,000 on December 31, 1995, which will earn interest at 10% compounded quarterly, to help in the retirement of this debt. In addition, the company wants to know how much should be deposited at the end of each quarter for 10 years to insure that $650,000 is available at the end of 2005. (The quarterly deposits will also earn at a rate of 10%, compounded quarterly.) Round to even dollars.

P6-11 (Analysis of Alternatives) Homer Winslow Inc., a manufacturer of steel school lockers, plans to purchase a new punch press for use in its manufacturing process. After contacting the appropriate vendors, the purchasing department received differing terms and options from each vendor. The Manufacturing Engineering Department has determined that each vendor's punch press is substantially identical and each has a useful life of 20 years. In addition, Engineering has estimated that required year-end maintenance costs will be $1,000 per year for the first 5 years, $2,000 per year for the next 10 years, and $3,000 per year for the last 5 years. Following is each vendor's sale package.

Vendor A: $50,000 cash at time of delivery and 10 year-end payments of $14,000 each. Vendor A offers all its customers the right to purchase at the time of sale a separate 20-year maintenance service contract under which Vendor A will perform all year-end maintenance at a one-time initial cost of $10,000.

Vendor B: Forty semiannual payments of $8,000 each with the first installment due upon delivery. Vendor B will perform all year-end maintenance for the next 20 years at no extra charge.

Vendor C: Full cash price of $125,000 will be due upon delivery.

Instructions
Assuming that both Vendor A and B will be able to perform the required year-end maintenance, that Winslow's cost of funds is 10%, and the machine will be purchased on January 1, from which vendor should the press be purchased?

P6-12 (Analysis of Business Problems) Diego Rivera is a financial executive with El Greco Company. Although Diego has not had any formal training in finance or accounting, he has a "good sense" for numbers and has helped the company grow from a very small company ($500,000 sales) to a large operation ($45 million in sales). With the business growing steadily, however, the company needs to make a number of difficult financial decisions in which Diego feels a little "over his head." He therefore has decided to hire a new employee with facility in "numbers" to help him. As a basis for determining whom to employ, he has decided to ask each prospective employee to prepare answers to questions relating to the following situations he has encountered recently. Here are the questions.

1. In 1993 El Greco Company negotiated and closed a long-term lease contract for newly constructed truck terminals and freight storage facilities. The buildings were constructed on land owned by the company. On January 1, 1994, El Greco Company took possession of the leased property. The 20-year lease is effective for the period January 1, 1994, through December 31, 2013. Advance rental payments of $800,000 are payable to the lessor (owner of facilities) on January 1 of each of the first 10 years of the lease term. Advance payments of $240,000 are due on January 1 for each of the last 10 years of the lease term. El Greco has an option to purchase all the leased facilities for $1.00 on December 31, 2013. At the time the lease was negotiated, the fair market value of the truck terminals and freight storage facilities was approximately $7,286,896. If the company had borrowed the money to purchase the facilities, it would have to pay 10% interest. Should the company have purchased rather than leased the facilities?

2. Last year the company exchanged a piece of land for a noninterest-bearing note. The note is to be paid at the rate of $10,000 per year for 9 years, beginning one year from the date of disposal of the land. An appropriate rate of interest for the note was 11%. At the time the land was originally purchased, it cost $90,000. What is the fair value of the note?

3. The company has always followed the policy to take any cash discounts on goods purchased. Recently the company purchased a large amount of raw materials at a price of $800,000 with terms 1/10, n/30 on which it took the discount. El Greco has recently estimated its cost of funds at 10%. Should El Greco continue this policy of always taking the cash discount?

P6-13 (Analysis of Various Business Problems) Andrew Wyeth has had a difficult year as controller for Miró Inc. The company lost a considerable amount of money this year, and now the Board of Directors has decided to hire a management consulting team to review the major financial decisions made over the last 3 years. As controller, Wyeth has been asked by the Board to highlight the three major financial decisions over the last 2 years, and indicate what decisions the company made.

1. During this period, the company had to decide to replace its old equipment in the plant with automated equipment. A schedule relating to pertinent information about the old equipment and automated equipment is as follows:

	Old Equipment	Automated Equipment
Original cost (new)	$2,800,000	$2,000,000
Accumulated depreciation to date	100,000	—
Current salvage value	20,000	—
Estimated cost savings each year over old equipment (Assume that cost savings occur at the end of each year.)	—	500,000
Remaining useful life	6 years	6 years
Salvage value at end of 6 years	—	—

Miró Inc. decided to continue using the old equipment. Its cost of funds was 10%.

2. During this period, the company had $25,000,000 to invest. The company had two principal alternatives for the use of investment funds. These alternatives are provided below.

	Project I Investment	Project II Investment
Required investment	$25,000,000	$25,000,000
Annual cash inflows (Assume they will be received at the end of each year.)	9,000,000	
Cash inflows at the end of the 9th year		86,000,000
Life of the project	9 years	9 years

Miró decided to invest its funds in Project I. The cost of funds is 10%.

3. Miró has 1,000 employees. At the end of each year, it has given a bonus to its employees based on their productivity. The total bonus in a year is approximately $1 million. A number of the employees indicated that they would prefer a pension plan rather than a bonus payment each year because they have a tendency to spend the bonus immediately. Pertinent data related to a bonus plan versus a pension plan are provided below:

	Bonus Plan	Pension Plan
Number of employees	1,000	1,000
Length of time to retirement	15 years	15 years
Expected life duration after retirement	—	12 years
Bonus payment expected until retirement (paid at end of year)	$1,000,000/year	—
Pension payment expected at retirement (to be paid at the beginning of each year, starting at the beginning of the 16th year)	—	$1,600,000/year

The cost of funds in this case is assumed to be 10%. The company decided to go with the pension plan.

Instructions

Assuming that you are one of the management consultants working for the Board of Directors, would you agree with these decisions?

P6-14 (Analysis of Lease vs. Purchase) Alexander Calder Inc. owns and operates a number of hardware stores in the New England region. Recently the company has decided to locate another store in a rapidly growing area of Maryland; the company is trying to decide whether to purchase or lease the building and related facilities.

Purchase: The company can purchase the site, construct the building, and purchase all store fixtures. The cost would be $1,650,000. An immediate down payment of $400,000 is required, and the remaining $1,250,000 would be paid off over 5 years at $300,000 per year (including interest). The property is expected to have a useful life of 12 years and then it will be sold for $400,000. As the owner of the property, the company will have the following out-of-pocket expenses each period:

Property taxes (to be paid at the end of each year)	$48,000
Insurance (to be paid at the beginning of each year)	27,000
Other (primarily maintenance which occurs at the end of each year)	16,000
	$91,000

Lease: First National Bank has agreed to purchase the site, construct the building, and install the appropriate fixtures for Calder Inc. if Calder will lease the completed facility for 12 years. The annual costs for the lease would be $240,000. The lease would be a triple net lease for expenses (Calder would have no responsibility related to the facility over the 12 years). The terms of the lease are that Calder would be required to make 12 annual payments (the first payment to be made at the time the store opens and then each following year). In addition, a deposit of $100,000 is required when the store is opened which will be returned at the end of the twelfth year, assuming no unusual damage to the building structure or fixtures.

Currently the cost of funds for Calder Inc. is 10%.

Instructions

Which of the two approaches should Calder Inc. follow?

P6-15 (Business Problems) Presented below are a series of time value of money problems. Solve each of them.

(a) Your client, Kate Greenaway, wishes to provide for the payment of an obligation of $200,000 due on July 1, 2001. Kate plans to deposit $20,000 in a special fund each July 1 for 8 years, starting July 1,

1994. She also wishes to make a deposit on July 1, 1993, of an amount which, with its accumulated interest, will bring the fund up to $200,000 at the maturity of the obligation. She expects that the fund will earn interest at the rate of 4% compounded annually. Compute the amount to be deposited on July 1, 1993.

(b) Many employers establish pension plans for their employees. Accountants are often required to determine the present value of pension obligations for financial reporting. To illustrate, assume that on January 1, 1993, Chagall Corporation initiated a pension plan under which each of its employees would receive a pension annuity of $1,000 per year beginning one year after retirement and continuing until death. Employee A will retire at the end of 1999 and, according to mortality tables, is expected to live long enough to receive eight pension payments. What is the present value of Chagall Corporation's pension obligation for employee A at the beginning of 1993 if the interest rate is 10%?

(c) Gauguin Company purchases bonds from Kandinsky Corporation in the amount of $400,000. The bonds are 10-year, 12% bonds that pay interest semiannually. After 3 years (and receipt of interest for 3 years), Gauguin needs money and, therefore, sells the bonds to Yuan Ma Company, which demands interest at 16% compounded semiannually. What is the amount that Gauguin will receive on the sale of the bonds?

► USING YOUR JUDGMENT ◄

► FINANCIAL REPORTING PROBLEM

The financial statements and accompanying notes of Georgia-Pacific Corp. are presented in Appendix 5-A.

Instructions
1. Examining each item in Georgia-Pacific's balance sheet, identify those items that require present value, discounting, or interest computations in establishing the amount reported. (The accompanying notes are an additional source for this information.)
2. What interest rates are disclosed by Georgia-Pacific as being used to compute interest and present values? Why are there so many different interest rates applied to Georgia-Pacific's financial statement elements (assets, liabilities, revenues, and expenses)?

► WRITING ASSIGNMENT

Assume that you are the chief financial officer of the Orlando Magic basketball organization. You have been involved in contracting to sign Anfernee "Penny" Hardaway. You have devised the following 13-year guaranteed contract which Hardaway is willing to sign.

Salary: To accommodate salary-cap rules, Hardaway will get $1.24 million in the slot vacated by traded Brian Williams this year. In fact, Hardaway received the payment in lump sum upon signing. The salary will increase the maximum 30% a year under NBA rules for the next 12 years.

Line of credit: He can borrow $2 million this year from the Magic. In following years, he can borrow 36% more a year up to a total of $20 million. He must repay the money at the end of the contract.

Floating option: After any year in which he reaches one of 12 personal and/or team goals, he can become a restricted free agent.

A year-by-year breakdown:

Year	Salary +30%	Credit +36%	Total[1]
1993–94	$ 1.244	$ 2.000	$ 3.244
1994–95	1.617	2.720	4.337
1995–96	1.990	3.440	5.430
1996–97	2.363	4.160	6.523
1997–98	2.736	4.880	7.616
1998–99	3.109	2.800	5.909
'99–2000	3.483	—	3.483
2000–01	3.856	—	3.856
2001–02	4.229	—	4.229
2002–03	4.602	—	4.602
2003–04	4.975	—	4.975
2004–05	5.348	—	5.348
2005–06	5.722	—	5.722
Total	**$45.274**	**$20.000**	**$65.274**

[1]Figures in millions (rounded to nearest thousand)

The newspapers are reporting that the cost to the Magic is approximately $65 million. Some Board members are wondering where the club is getting $65 million to sign Hardaway.

Write a letter to members of the Board of Directors of the Orlando Magic explaining the financial arrangement and details of the contract. In your letter, be sure to include what you believe to be the real cost to the club for this contract.

▶ GROUP ASSIGNMENT

(Computation of Deposits and Benefits of a Retirement Plan) Your group has been hired as benefit consultants by Rhonda Roe, the owner of Growing Place. She wants to establish a retirement plan for her and her three employees. Rhonda has provided the following information:

The retirement plan is to be based upon annual salary for the last year before retirement and is to provide 50% of Rhonda's last year annual salary and 40% of the last year annual salary for each employee. The plan will make annual payments at the beginning of each year for 20 years from the date of retirement. Rhonda wishes to fund the plan by making 15 annual deposits beginning January 1, 1995. Invested funds will earn 12% compounded annually. Information about plan participants as of January 1, 1995 is as follows:

Rhonda Roe, owner, current annual salary of $40,000, estimated retirement date January 1, 2020.

Kenny Rogers, flower arranger, current annual salary of $30,000, estimated retirement date January 1, 2025.

Anita Baker, sales clerk, current annual salary of $15,000, estimated retirement date January 1, 2015.

Willie Nelson, part-time bookkeeper, current annual salary of $15,000, estimated retirement date January 1, 2010.

In the past, Rhonda has given herself and each employee a year-end salary increase of 4%. Rhonda plans to continue this policy in the future.

Instructions

Your instructor will identify one member of the group to serve as a recorder and one member to serve as spokesperson. As a group, provide the information for the recorder to prepare responses to the following three requirements. Upon completion of each requirement and before moving on to the next part, the spokesperson will report the group findings to the class.

(a) Based upon the above information, what will be the annual retirement benefit for each plan participant? (Round to the nearest dollar.) (Hint: Rhonda will receive raises for 24 years.)

(b) What amount must be on deposit at the end of 15 years to ensure that all benefits will be paid? (Round to the nearest dollar.)

(c) What is the amount of each annual deposit Rhonda must make to the retirement plan?

▶ ETHICS CASE

Jeb Stuart, newly appointed Controller of MBI, is considering ways to reduce his company's expenditures on annual pension costs. One way to do this is to switch MBI's pension fund assets from Prudence Life to First Fidelity. MBI is a very well respected computer manufacturer, which has recently experienced a sharp decline in its financial performance for the first time in its 25-year history. Despite fiscal problems, MBI is still committed to providing its employees with good pension and post-retirement health benefits.

Under its present plan with Prudence Life, MBI is obligated to pay $43 million dollars to meet the expected value of future pension benefits that is payable to employees as an annuity upon their retirement from the company. First Fidelity, on the other hand, requires MBI to pay only $35 million for identical future pension benefits. Prudence Life is one of the oldest and most reputable insurance companies in North America; First Fidelity has a much weaker reputation in the insurance industry. In pondering the significant difference in annual pension costs, Jeb asks himself "Is this too good to be true?"

Instructions

(a) Why might First Fidelity's pension cost requirement be $8 million less than Prudence Life's requirement for the same future value?

(b) What ethical issues should Jeb Stuart consider before switching MBI's pension fund assets.

(c) Who are the stakeholders that could be affected by Jeb Stuart's decision?

TABLE 6-1   FUTURE AMOUNT OF 1 (FUTURE AMOUNT OF A SINGLE SUM)

$$a_{\overline{n}|i} = (1 + i)^n$$

(n) Periods	2%	2½%	3%	4%	5%	6%
1	1.02000	1.02500	1.03000	1.04000	1.05000	1.06000
2	1.04040	1.05063	1.06090	1.08160	1.10250	1.12360
3	1.06121	1.07689	1.09273	1.12486	1.15763	1.19102
4	1.08243	1.10381	1.12551	1.16986	1.21551	1.26248
5	1.10408	1.13141	1.15927	1.21665	1.27628	1.33823
6	1.12616	1.15969	1.19405	1.26532	1.34010	1.41852
7	1.14869	1.18869	1.22987	1.31593	1.40710	1.50363
8	1.17166	1.21840	1.26677	1.36857	1.47746	1.59385
9	1.19509	1.24886	1.30477	1.42331	1.55133	1.68948
10	1.21899	1.28008	1.34392	1.48024	1.62889	1.79085
11	1.24337	1.31209	1.38423	1.53945	1.71034	1.89830
12	1.26824	1.34489	1.42576	1.60103	1.79586	2.01220
13	1.29361	1.37851	1.46853	1.66507	1.88565	2.13293
14	1.31948	1.41297	1.51259	1.73168	1.97993	2.26090
15	1.34587	1.44830	1.55797	1.80094	2.07893	2.39656
16	1.37279	1.48451	1.60471	1.87298	2.18287	2.54035
17	1.40024	1.52162	1.65285	1.94790	2.29202	2.69277
18	1.42825	1.55966	1.70243	2.02582	2.40662	2.85434
19	1.45681	1.59865	1.75351	2.10685	2.52695	3.02560
20	1.48595	1.63862	1.80611	2.19112	2.65330	3.20714
21	1.51567	1.67958	1.86029	2.27877	2.78596	3.39956
22	1.54598	1.72157	1.91610	2.36992	2.92526	3.60354
23	1.57690	1.76461	1.97359	2.46472	3.07152	3.81975
24	1.60844	1.80873	2.03279	2.56330	3.22510	4.04893
25	1.64061	1.85394	2.09378	2.66584	3.38635	4.29187
26	1.67342	1.90029	2.15659	2.77247	3.55567	4.54938
27	1.70689	1.94780	2.22129	2.88337	3.73346	4.82235
28	1.74102	1.99650	2.28793	2.99870	3.92013	5.11169
29	1.77584	2.04641	2.35657	3.11865	4.11614	5.41839
30	1.81136	2.09757	2.42726	3.24340	4.32194	5.74349
31	1.84759	2.15001	2.50008	3.37313	4.53804	6.08810
32	1.88454	2.20376	2.57508	3.50806	4.76494	6.45339
33	1.92223	2.25885	2.65234	3.64838	5.00319	6.84059
34	1.96068	2.31532	2.73191	3.79432	5.25335	7.25103
35	1.99989	2.37321	2.81386	3.94609	5.51602	7.68609
36	2.03989	2.43254	2.89828	4.10393	5.79182	8.14725
37	2.08069	2.49335	2.98523	4.26809	6.08141	8.63609
38	2.12230	2.55568	3.07478	4.43881	6.38548	9.15425
39	2.16474	2.61957	3.16703	4.61637	6.70475	9.70351
40	2.20804	2.68506	3.26204	4.80102	7.03999	10.28572

TABLE 6-1 FUTURE AMOUNT OF 1

8%	9%	10%	11%	12%	15%	(n) Periods
1.08000	1.09000	1.10000	1.11000	1.12000	1.15000	1
1.16640	1.18810	1.21000	1.23210	1.25440	1.32250	2
1.25971	1.29503	1.33100	1.36763	1.40493	1.52088	3
1.36049	1.41158	1.46410	1.51807	1.57352	1.74901	4
1.46933	1.53862	1.61051	1.68506	1.76234	2.01136	5
1.58687	1.67710	1.77156	1.87041	1.97382	2.31306	6
1.71382	1.82804	1.94872	2.07616	2.21068	2.66002	7
1.85093	1.99256	2.14359	2.30454	2.47596	3.05902	8
1.99900	2.17189	2.35795	2.55803	2.77308	3.51788	9
2.15892	2.36736	2.59374	2.83942	3.10585	4.04556	10
2.33164	2.58043	2.85312	3.15176	3.47855	4.65239	11
2.51817	2.81267	3.13843	3.49845	3.89598	5.35025	12
2.71962	3.06581	3.45227	3.88328	4.36349	6.15279	13
2.93719	3.34173	3.79750	4.31044	4.88711	7.07571	14
3.17217	3.64248	4.17725	4.78459	5.47357	8.13706	15
3.42594	3.97031	4.59497	5.31089	6.13039	9.35762	16
3.70002	4.32763	5.05447	5.89509	6.86604	10.76126	17
3.99602	4.71712	5.55992	6.54355	7.68997	12.37545	18
4.31570	5.14166	6.11591	7.26334	8.61276	14.23177	19
4.66096	5.60441	6.72750	8.06231	9.64629	16.36654	20
5.03383	6.10881	7.40025	8.94917	10.80385	18.82152	21
5.43654	6.65860	8.14028	9.93357	12.10031	21.64475	22
5.87146	7.25787	8.95430	11.02627	13.55235	24.89146	23
6.34118	7.91108	9.84973	12.23916	15.17863	28.62518	24
6.84847	8.62308	10.83471	13.58546	17.00000	32.91895	25
7.39635	9.39916	11.91818	15.07986	19.04007	37.85680	26
7.98806	10.24508	13.10999	16.73865	21.32488	43.53532	27
8.62711	11.16714	14.42099	18.57990	23.88387	50.06561	28
9.31727	12.17218	15.86309	20.62369	26.74993	57.57545	29
10.06266	13.26768	17.44940	22.89230	29.95992	66.21177	30
10.86767	14.46177	19.19434	25.41045	33.55511	76.14354	31
11.73708	15.76333	21.11378	28.20560	37.58173	87.56507	32
12.67605	17.18203	23.22515	31.30821	42.09153	100.69983	33
13.69013	18.72841	25.54767	34.75212	47.14252	115.80480	34
14.78534	20.41397	28.10244	38.57485	52.79962	133.17552	35
15.96817	22.25123	30.91268	42.81808	59.13557	153.15185	36
17.24563	24.25384	34.00395	47.52807	66.23184	176.12463	37
18.62528	26.43668	37.40434	52.75616	74.17966	202.54332	38
20.11530	28.81598	41.14479	58.55934	83.08122	232.92482	39
21.72452	31.40942	45.25926	65.00087	93.05097	267.86355	40

TABLE 6-2   PRESENT VALUE OF 1 (PRESENT VALUE OF A SINGLE SUM)

$$p_{\overline{n}|i} = \frac{1}{(1 + i)^n} = (1 + i)^{-n}$$

(n) Periods	2%	2½%	3%	4%	5%	6%
1	.98039	.97561	.97087	.96154	.95238	.94340
2	.96117	.95181	.94260	.92456	.90703	.89000
3	.94232	.92860	.91514	.88900	.86384	.83962
4	.92385	.90595	.88849	.85480	.82270	.79209
5	.90573	.88385	.86261	.82193	.78353	.74726
6	.88797	.86230	.83748	.79031	.74622	.70496
7	.87056	.84127	.81309	.75992	.71068	.66506
8	.85349	.82075	.78941	.73069	.67684	.62741
9	.83676	.80073	.76642	.70259	.64461	.59190
10	.82035	.78120	.74409	.67556	.61391	.55839
11	.80426	.76214	.72242	.64958	.58468	.52679
12	.78849	.74356	.70138	.62460	.55684	.49697
13	.77303	.72542	.68095	.60057	.53032	.46884
14	.75788	.70773	.66112	.57748	.50507	.44230
15	.74301	.69047	.64186	.55526	.48102	.41727
16	.72845	.67362	.62317	.53391	.45811	.39365
17	.71416	.65720	.60502	.51337	.43630	.37136
18	.70016	.64117	.58739	.49363	.41552	.35034
19	.68643	.62553	.57029	.47464	.39573	.33051
20	.67297	.61027	.55368	.45639	.37689	.31180
21	.65978	.59539	.53755	.43883	.35894	.29416
22	.64684	.58086	.52189	.42196	.34185	.27751
23	.63416	.56670	.50669	.40573	.32557	.26180
24	.62172	.55288	.49193	.39012	.31007	.24698
25	.60953	.53939	.47761	.37512	.29530	.23300
26	.59758	.52623	.46369	.36069	.28124	.21981
27	.58586	.51340	.45019	.34682	.26785	.20737
28	.57437	.50088	.43708	.33348	.25509	.19563
29	.56311	.48866	.42435	.32065	.24295	.18456
30	.55207	.47674	.41199	.30832	.23138	.17411
31	.54125	.46511	.39999	.29646	.22036	.16425
32	.53063	.45377	.38834	.28506	.20987	.15496
33	.52023	.44270	.37703	.27409	.19987	.14619
34	.51003	.43191	.36604	.26355	.19035	.13791
35	.50003	.42137	.35538	.25342	.18129	.13011
36	.49022	.41109	.34503	.24367	.17266	.12274
37	.48061	.40107	.33498	.23430	.16444	.11579
38	.47119	.39128	.32523	.22529	.15661	.10924
39	.46195	.38174	.31575	.21662	.14915	.10306
40	.45289	.37243	.30656	.20829	.14205	.09722

TABLE 6-2   PRESENT VALUE OF 1

8%	9%	10%	11%	12%	15%	(n) Periods
.92593	.91743	.90909	.90090	.89286	.86957	1
.85734	.84168	.82645	.81162	.79719	.75614	2
.79383	.77218	.75132	.73119	.71178	.65752	3
.73503	.70843	.68301	.65873	.63552	.57175	4
.68058	.64993	.62092	.59345	.56743	.49718	5
.63017	.59627	.56447	.53464	.50663	.43233	6
.58349	.54703	.51316	.48166	.45235	.37594	7
.54027	.50187	.46651	.43393	.40388	.32690	8
.50025	.46043	.42410	.39092	.36061	.28426	9
.46319	.42241	.38554	.35218	.32197	.24719	10
.42888	.38753	.35049	.31728	.28748	.21494	11
.39711	.35554	.31863	.28584	.25668	.18691	12
.36770	.32618	.28966	.25751	.22917	.16253	13
.34046	.29925	.26333	.23199	.20462	.14133	14
.31524	.27454	.23939	.20900	.18270	.12289	15
.29189	.25187	.21763	.18829	.16312	.10687	16
.27027	.23107	.19785	.16963	.14564	.09293	17
.25025	.21199	.17986	.15282	.13004	.08081	18
.23171	.19449	.16351	.13768	.11611	.07027	19
.21455	.17843	.14864	.12403	.10367	.06110	20
.19866	.16370	.13513	.11174	.09256	.05313	21
.18394	.15018	.12285	.10067	.08264	.04620	22
.17032	.13778	.11168	.09069	.07379	.04017	23
.15770	.12641	.10153	.08170	.06588	.03493	24
.14602	.11597	.09230	.07361	.05882	.03038	25
.13520	.10639	.08391	.06631	.05252	.02642	26
.12519	.09761	.07628	.05974	.04689	.02297	27
.11591	.08955	.06934	.05382	.04187	.01997	28
.10733	.08216	.06304	.04849	.03738	.01737	29
.09938	.07537	.05731	.04368	.03338	.01510	30
.09202	.06915	.05210	.03935	.02980	.01313	31
.08520	.06344	.04736	.03545	.02661	.01142	32
.07889	.05820	.04306	.03194	.02376	.00993	33
.07305	.05340	.03914	.02878	.02121	.00864	34
.06763	.04899	.03558	.02592	.01894	.00751	35
.06262	.04494	.03235	.02335	.01691	.00653	36
.05799	.04123	.02941	.02104	.01510	.00568	37
.05369	.03783	.02674	.01896	.01348	.00494	38
.04971	.03470	.02430	.01708	.01204	.00429	39
.04603	.03184	.02210	.01538	.01075	.00373	40

TABLE 6-3   FUTURE AMOUNT OF AN ORDINARY ANNUITY OF 1

$$A_{\overline{n}|i} = \frac{(1 + i)^n - 1}{i}$$

(n) Periods	2%	2½%	3%	4%	5%	6%
1	1.00000	1.00000	1.00000	1.00000	1.00000	1.00000
2	2.02000	2.02500	2.03000	2.04000	2.05000	2.06000
3	3.06040	3.07563	3.09090	3.12160	3.15250	3.18360
4	4.12161	4.15252	4.18363	4.24646	4.31013	4.37462
5	5.20404	5.25633	5.30914	5.41632	5.52563	5.63709
6	6.30812	6.38774	6.46841	6.63298	6.80191	6.97532
7	7.43428	7.54743	7.66246	7.89829	8.14201	8.39384
8	8.58297	8.73612	8.89234	9.21423	9.54911	9.89747
9	9.75463	9.95452	10.15911	10.58280	11.02656	11.49132
10	10.94972	11.20338	11.46338	12.00611	12.57789	13.18079
11	12.16872	12.48347	12.80780	13.48635	14.20679	14.97164
12	13.41209	13.79555	14.19203	15.02581	15.91713	16.86994
13	14.68033	15.14044	15.61779	16.62684	17.71298	18.88214
14	15.97394	16.51895	17.08632	18.29191	19.59863	21.01507
15	17.29342	17.93193	18.59891	20.02359	21.57856	23.27597
16	18.63929	19.38022	20.15688	21.82453	23.65749	25.67253
17	20.01207	20.86473	21.76159	23.69751	25.84037	28.21288
18	21.41231	22.38635	23.41444	25.64541	28.13238	30.90565
19	22.84056	23.94601	25.11687	27.67123	30.53900	33.75999
20	24.29737	25.54466	26.87037	29.77808	33.06595	36.78559
21	25.78332	27.18327	28.67649	31.96920	35.71925	39.99273
22	27.29898	28.86286	30.53678	34.24797	38.50521	43.39229
23	28.84496	30.58443	32.45288	36.61789	41.43048	46.99583
24	30.42186	32.34904	34.42647	39.08260	44.50200	50.81558
25	32.03030	34.15776	36.45926	41.64591	47.72710	54.86451
26	33.67091	36.01171	38.55304	44.31174	51.11345	59.15638
27	35.34432	37.91200	40.70963	47.08421	54.66913	63.70577
28	37.05121	39.85980	42.93092	49.96758	58.40258	68.52811
29	38.79223	41.85630	45.21885	52.96629	62.32271	73.63980
30	40.56808	43.90270	47.57542	56.08494	66.43885	79.05819
31	42.37944	46.00027	50.00268	59.32834	70.76079	84.80168
32	44.22703	48.15028	52.50276	62.70147	75.29883	90.88978
33	46.11157	50.35403	55.07784	66.20953	80.06377	97.34316
34	48.03380	52.61289	57.73018	69.85791	85.06696	104.18376
35	49.99448	54.92821	60.46208	73.65222	90.32031	111.43478
36	51.99437	57.30141	63.27594	77.59831	95.83632	119.12087
37	54.03425	59.73395	66.17422	81.70225	101.62814	127.26812
38	56.11494	62.22730	69.15945	85.97034	107.70955	135.90421
39	58.23724	64.78298	72.23423	90.40915	114.09502	145.05846
40	60.40198	67.40255	75.40126	95.02552	120.79977	154.76197

TABLE 6-3 FUTURE AMOUNT OF AN ORDINARY ANNUITY OF 1

8%	9%	10%	11%	12%	15%	(n) Periods
1.00000	1.00000	1.00000	1.00000	1.00000	1.00000	1
2.08000	2.09000	2.10000	2.11000	2.12000	2.15000	2
3.24640	3.27810	3.31000	3.34210	3.37440	3.47250	3
4.50611	4.57313	4.64100	4.70973	4.77933	4.99338	4
5.86660	5.98471	6.10510	6.22780	6.35285	6.74238	5
7.33592	7.52334	7.71561	7.91286	8.11519	8.75374	6
8.92280	9.20044	9.48717	9.78327	10.08901	11.06680	7
10.63663	11.02847	11.43589	11.85943	12.29969	13.72682	8
12.48756	13.02104	13.57948	14.16397	14.77566	16.78584	9
14.48656	15.19293	15.93743	16.72201	17.54874	20.30372	10
16.64549	17.56029	18.53117	19.56143	20.65458	24.34928	11
18.97713	20.14072	21.38428	22.71319	24.13313	29.00167	12
21.49530	22.95339	24.52271	26.21164	28.02911	34.35192	13
24.21492	26.01919	27.97498	30.09492	32.39260	40.50471	14
27.15211	29.36092	31.77248	34.40536	37.27972	47.58041	15
30.32428	33.00340	35.94973	39.18995	42.75328	55.71747	16
33.75023	36.97371	40.54470	44.50084	48.88367	65.07509	17
37.45024	41.30134	45.59917	50.39593	55.74972	75.83636	18
41.44626	46.01846	51.15909	56.93949	63.43968	88.21181	19
45.76196	51.16012	57.27500	64.20283	72.05244	102.44358	20
50.42292	56.76453	64.00250	72.26514	81.69874	118.81012	21
55.45676	62.87334	71.40275	81.21431	92.50258	137.63164	22
60.89330	69.53194	79.54302	91.14788	104.60289	159.27638	23
66.76476	76.78981	88.49733	102.17415	118.15524	184.16784	24
73.10594	84.70090	98.34706	114.41331	133.33387	212.79302	25
79.95442	93.32398	109.18177	127.99877	150.33393	245.71197	26
87.35077	102.72314	121.09994	143.07864	169.37401	283.56877	27
95.33883	112.96822	134.20994	159.81729	190.69889	327.10408	28
103.96594	124.13536	148.63093	178.39719	214.58275	377.16969	29
113.28321	136.30754	164.49402	199.02088	241.33268	434.74515	30
123.34587	149.57522	181.94343	221.91317	271.29261	500.95692	31
134.21354	164.03699	201.13777	247.32362	304.84772	577.10046	32
145.95062	179.80032	222.25154	275.52922	342.42945	644.66553	33
158.62667	196.98234	245.47670	306.83744	384.52098	765.36535	34
172.31680	215.71076	271.02437	341.58955	431.66350	881.17016	35
187.10215	236.12472	299.12681	380.16441	484.46312	1014.34568	36
203.07032	258.37595	330.03949	422.98249	543.59869	1167.49753	37
220.31595	282.62978	364.04343	470.51056	609.83053	1343.62216	38
238.94122	309.06646	401.44778	523.26673	684.01020	1546.16549	39
259.05652	337.88245	442.59256	581.82607	767.09142	1779.09031	40

TABLE 6-4   PRESENT VALUE OF AN ORDINARY ANNUITY OF 1

$$P_{\overline{n}|i} = \frac{1 - \dfrac{1}{(1 + i)^n}}{i} = \frac{1 - p_{\overline{n}|i}}{i}$$

(n) Periods	2%	2½%	3%	4%	5%	6%
1	.98039	.97561	.97087	.96154	.95238	.94340
2	1.94156	1.92742	1.91347	1.88609	1.85941	1.83339
3	2.88388	2.85602	2.82861	2.77509	2.72325	2.67301
4	3.80773	3.76197	3.71710	3.62990	3.54595	3.46511
5	4.71346	4.64583	4.57971	4.45182	4.32948	4.21236
6	5.60143	5.50813	5.41719	5.24214	5.07569	4.91732
7	6.47199	6.34939	6.23028	6.00205	5.78637	5.58238
8	7.32548	7.17014	7.01969	6.73274	6.46321	6.20979
9	8.16224	7.97087	7.78611	7.43533	7.10782	6.80169
10	8.98259	8.75206	8.53020	8.11090	7.72173	7.36009
11	9.78685	9.51421	9.25262	8.76048	8.30641	7.88687
12	10.57534	10.25776	9.95400	9.38507	8.86325	8.38384
13	11.34837	10.98319	10.63496	9.98565	9.39357	8.85268
14	12.10625	11.69091	11.29607	10.56312	9.89864	9.29498
15	12.84926	12.38138	11.93794	11.11839	10.37966	9.71225
16	13.57771	13.05500	12.56110	11.65230	10.83777	10.10590
17	14.29187	13.71220	13.16612	12.16567	11.27407	10.47726
18	14.99203	14.35336	13.75351	12.65930	11.68959	10.82760
19	15.67846	14.97889	14.32380	13.13394	12.08532	11.15812
20	16.35143	15.58916	14.87747	13.59033	12.46221	11.46992
21	17.01121	16.18455	15.41502	14.02916	12.82115	11.76408
22	17.65805	16.76541	15.93692	14.45112	13.16300	12.04158
23	18.29220	17.33211	16.44361	14.85684	13.48857	12.30338
24	18.91393	17.88499	16.93554	15.24696	13.79864	12.55036
25	19.52346	18.42438	17.41315	15.62208	14.09394	12.78336
26	20.12104	18.95061	17.87684	15.98277	14.37519	13.00317
27	20.70690	19.46401	18.32703	16.32959	14.64303	13.21053
28	21.28127	19.96489	18.76411	16.66306	14.89813	13.40616
29	21.84438	20.45355	19.18845	16.98371	15.14107	13.59072
30	22.39646	20.93029	19.60044	17.29203	15.37245	13.76483
31	22.93770	21.39541	20.00043	17.58849	15.59281	13.92909
32	23.46833	21.84918	20.38877	17.87355	15.80268	14.08404
33	23.98856	22.29188	20.76579	18.14765	16.00255	14.23023
34	24.49859	22.72379	21.13184	18.41120	16.19290	14.36814
35	24.99862	23.14516	21.48722	18.66461	16.37419	14.49825
36	25.48884	23.55625	21.83225	18.90828	16.54685	14.62099
37	25.96945	23.95732	22.16724	19.14258	16.71129	14.73678
38	26.44064	24.34860	22.49246	19.36786	16.86789	14.84602
39	26.90259	24.73034	22.80822	19.58448	17.01704	14.94907
40	27.35548	25.10278	23.11477	19.79277	17.15909	15.04630

TABLE 6-4   PRESENT VALUE OF AN ORDINARY ANNUITY OF 1

8%	9%	10%	11%	12%	15%	(n) Periods
.92593	.91743	.90909	.90090	.89286	.86957	1
1.78326	1.75911	1.73554	1.71252	1.69005	1.62571	2
2.57710	2.53130	2.48685	2.44371	2.40183	2.28323	3
3.31213	3.23972	3.16986	3.10245	3.03735	2.85498	4
3.99271	3.88965	3.79079	3.69590	3.60478	3.35216	5
4.62288	4.48592	4.35526	4.23054	4.11141	3.78448	6
5.20637	5.03295	4.86842	4.71220	4.56376	4.16042	7
5.74664	5.53482	5.33493	5.14612	4.96764	4.48732	8
6.24689	5.99525	5.75902	5.53705	5.32825	4.77158	9
6.71008	6.41766	6.14457	5.88923	5.65022	5.01877	10
7.13896	6.80519	6.49506	6.20652	5.93770	5.23371	11
7.53608	7.16073	6.81369	6.49236	6.19437	5.42062	12
7.90378	7.48690	7.10336	6.74987	6.42355	5.58315	13
8.24424	7.78615	7.36669	6.98187	6.62817	5.72448	14
8.55948	8.06069	7.60608	7.19087	6.81086	5.84737	15
8.85137	8.31256	7.82371	7.37916	6.97399	5.95424	16
9.12164	8.54363	8.02155	7.54879	7.11963	6.04716	17
9.37189	8.75563	8.20141	7.70162	7.24967	6.12797	18
9.60360	8.95012	8.36492	7.83929	7.36578	6.19823	19
9.81815	9.12855	8.51356	7.96333	7.46944	6.25933	20
10.01680	9.29224	8.64869	8.07507	7.56200	6.31246	21
10.20074	9.44243	8.77154	8.17574	7.64465	6.35866	22
10.37106	9.58021	8.88322	8.26643	7.71843	6.39884	23
10.52876	9.70661	8.98474	8.34814	7.78432	6.43377	24
10.67478	9.82258	9.07704	8.42174	7.84314	6.46415	25
10.80998	9.92897	9.16095	8.48806	7.89566	6.49056	26
10.93516	10.02658	9.23722	8.54780	7.94255	6.51353	27
11.05108	10.11613	9.30657	8.60162	7.98442	6.53351	28
11.15841	10.19828	9.36961	8.65011	8.02181	6.55088	29
11.25778	10.27365	9.42691	8.69379	8.05518	6.56598	30
11.34980	10.34280	9.47901	8.73315	8.08499	6.57911	31
11.43500	10.40624	0.52638	8.76860	8.11159	6.59053	32
11.51389	10.46444	9.56943	8.80054	8.13535	6.60046	33
11.58693	10.51784	9.60858	8.82932	8.15656	6.60910	34
11.65457	10.56682	9.64416	8.85524	8.17550	6.61661	35
11.71719	10.61176	9.67651	8.87859	8.19241	6.62314	36
11.77518	10.65299	9.70592	8.89963	8.20751	6.62882	37
11.82887	10.69082	9.73265	8.91859	8.22099	6.63375	38
11.87858	10.72552	9.75697	8.93567	8.23303	6.63805	39
11.92461	10.75736	9.77905	8.95105	8.24378	6.64178	40

TABLE 6-5 PRESENT VALUE OF AN ANNUITY DUE OF 1

$$Pd_{\overline{n}|i} = 1 + \frac{1 - \dfrac{1}{(1 + i)^{n-1}}}{i} = (1 + i)\left(\frac{1 - P_{\overline{n}|i}}{i}\right) = (1 + i)\, P_{\overline{n}|i}$$

(n) Periods	2%	2½%	3%	4%	5%	6%
1	1.00000	1.00000	1.00000	1.00000	1.00000	1.00000
2	1.98039	1.97561	1.97087	1.96154	1.95238	1.94340
3	2.94156	2.92742	2.91347	2.88609	2.85941	2.83339
4	3.88388	3.85602	3.82861	3.77509	3.72325	3.67301
5	4.80773	4.76197	4.71710	4.62990	4.54595	4.46511
6	5.71346	5.64583	5.57971	5.45182	5.32948	5.21236
7	6.60143	6.50813	6.41719	6.24214	6.07569	5.91732
8	7.47199	7.34939	7.23028	7.00205	6.78637	6.58238
9	8.32548	8.17014	8.01969	7.73274	7.46321	7.20979
10	9.16224	8.97087	8.78611	8.43533	8.10782	7.80169
11	9.98259	9.75206	9.53020	9.11090	8.72173	8.36009
12	10.78685	10.51421	10.25262	9.76048	9.30641	8.88687
13	11.57534	11.25776	10.95400	10.38507	9.86325	9.38384
14	12.34837	11.98319	11.63496	10.98565	10.39357	9.85268
15	13.10625	12.69091	12.29607	11.56312	10.89864	10.29498
16	13.84926	13.38138	12.93794	12.11839	11.37966	10.71225
17	14.57771	14.05500	13.56110	12.65230	11.83777	11.10590
18	15.29187	14.71220	14.16612	13.16567	12.27407	11.47726
19	15.99203	15.35336	14.75351	13.65930	12.68959	11.82760
20	16.67846	15.97889	15.32380	14.13394	13.08532	12.15812
21	17.35143	16.58916	15.87747	14.59033	13.46221	12.46992
22	18.01121	17.18455	16.41502	15.02916	13.82115	12.76408
23	18.65805	17.76541	16.93692	15.45112	14.16300	13.04158
24	19.29220	18.33211	17.44361	15.85684	14.48857	13.30338
25	19.91393	18.88499	17.93554	16.24696	14.79864	13.55036
26	20.52346	19.42438	18.41315	16.62208	15.09394	13.78336
27	21.12104	19.95061	18.87684	16.98277	15.37519	14.00317
28	21.70690	20.46401	19.32703	17.32959	15.64303	14.21053
29	22.28127	20.96489	19.76411	17.66306	15.89813	14.40616
30	22.84438	21.45355	20.18845	17.98371	16.14107	14.59072
31	23.39646	21.93029	20.60044	18.29203	16.37245	14.76483
32	23.93770	22.39541	21.00043	18.58849	16.59281	14.92909
33	24.46833	22.84918	21.38877	18.87355	16.80268	15.08404
34	24.98856	23.29188	21.76579	19.14765	17.00255	15.23023
35	25.49859	23.72379	22.13184	19.41120	17.19290	15.36814
36	25.99862	24.14516	22.48722	19.66461	17.37419	15.49825
37	26.48884	24.55625	22.83225	19.90828	17.54685	15.62099
38	26.96945	24.95732	23.16724	20.14258	17.71129	15.73678
39	27.44064	25.34860	23.49246	20.36786	17.86789	15.84602
40	27.90259	25.73034	23.80822	20.58448	18.01704	15.94907

TABLE 6-5 PRESENT VALUE OF AN ANNUITY DUE OF 1

8%	9%	10%	11%	12%	15%	(n) Periods
1.00000	1.00000	1.00000	1.00000	1.00000	1.00000	1
1.92593	1.91743	1.90909	1.90090	1.89286	1.86957	2
2.78326	2.75911	2.73554	2.71252	2.69005	2.62571	3
3.57710	3.53130	3.48685	3.44371	3.40183	3.28323	4
4.31213	4.23972	4.16986	4.10245	4.03735	3.85498	5
4.99271	4.88965	4.79079	4.69590	4.60478	4.35216	6
5.62288	5.48592	5.35526	5.23054	5.11141	4.78448	7
6.20637	6.03295	5.86842	5.71220	5.56376	5.16042	8
6.74664	6.53482	6.33493	6.14612	5.96764	5.48732	9
7.24689	6.99525	6.75902	6.53705	6.32825	5.77158	10
7.71008	7.41766	7.14457	6.88923	6.65022	6.01877	11
8.13896	7.80519	7.49506	7.20652	6.93770	6.23371	12
8.53608	8.16073	7.81369	7.49236	7.19437	6.42062	13
8.90378	8.48690	8.10336	7.74987	7.42355	6.58315	14
9.24424	8.78615	8.36669	7.98187	7.62817	6.72448	15
9.55948	9.06069	8.60608	8.19087	7.81086	6.84737	16
9.85137	9.31256	8.82371	8.37916	7.97399	6.95424	17
10.12164	9.54363	9.02155	8.54879	8.11963	7.04716	18
10.37189	9.75563	9.20141	8.70162	8.24967	7.12797	19
10.60360	9.95012	9.36492	8.83929	8.36578	7.19823	20
10.81815	10.12855	9.51356	8.96333	8.46944	7.25933	21
11.01680	10.29224	9.64869	9.07507	8.56200	7.31246	22
11.20074	10.44243	9.77154	9.17574	8.64465	7.35866	23
11.37106	10.58021	9.88322	9.26643	8.71843	7.39884	24
11.52876	10.70661	9.98474	9.34814	8.78432	7.43377	25
11.67478	10.82258	10.07704	9.42174	8.84314	7.46415	26
11.80998	10.92897	10.16095	9.48806	8.89566	7.49056	27
11.93518	11.02658	10.23722	9.54780	8.94255	7.51353	28
12.05108	11.11613	10.30657	9.60162	8.98442	7.53351	29
12.15841	11.19828	10.36961	9.65011	9.02181	7.55088	30
12.25778	11.27365	10.42691	9.69379	9.05518	7.56598	31
12.34980	11.34280	10.47901	9.73315	9.08499	7.57911	32
12.43500	11.40624	10.52638	9.76860	9.11159	7.59053	33
12.51389	11.46444	10.56943	9.80054	9.13535	7.60046	34
12.58693	11.51784	10.60858	9.82932	9.15656	7.60910	35
12.65457	11.56682	10.64416	9.85524	9.17550	7.61661	36
12.71719	11.61176	10.67651	9.87859	9.19241	7.62314	37
12.77518	11.65299	10.70592	9.89963	9.20751	7.62882	38
12.82887	11.69082	10.73265	9.91859	9.22099	7.63375	39
12.87858	11.72552	10.75697	9.93567	9.23303	7.63805	40

INTERNATIONAL ACCOUNTING AND STANDARD SETTING

A visit with
ARTHUR WYATT

ARTHUR R. WYATT has spent his entire career focusing on the principles of accounting—both in academia and in CPA practice. He received his Ph.D. from the University of Illinois in 1953 and taught there until 1966—when he joined Arthur Andersen & Co. He was soon made a partner and became head of the firm's accounting principles area. In the mid-1980s he left Arthur Andersen for a few years to become a member of the FASB. Mr. Wyatt was chairman of the International Accounting Standards Committee from 1990–1993 and is currently professor of accountancy at the University of Illinois in Champaign-Urbana.

You don't go by "Doctor?"

We discussed it when I initially went to work for Arthur Andersen, and I told them that doctor was primarily an academic designation. Since I was going to be in the practice world, I decided that I didn't want to go through the interminable explanations. I was recently in Switzerland and met with some clients there—and nearly everyone in their financial area had the title of doctor and used it. That's just a difference in the society.

How did you happen to focus on international accounting?

Arthur Andersen & Co. has a "one firm" concept, and I was responsible—in Chicago—for establishing accounting policies that must be followed around the world. In addition, I was chairman of the International Accounting Standards Committee, which represents 80 countries. My goal was to understand better why people in other countries do things the way they do.

What's a big area of disagreement?

In Germany and Switzerland, for instance, it is common practice to establish hidden reserves and to follow tax laws in financial accounting. We have never accepted such practices in the United States.

Why is international accounting a more topical subject today?

It reflects the changes in the world capital markets—which are directly related to changes in technology and communications. A company based in Peoria can raise capital around the world if it finds it difficult to raise capital in the United States. That would have been unheard of not long ago.

Does the United States have the best standards in the world?

Well, we have the most detailed disclosure standards and the most precise accounting standards. I wouldn't necessarily equate those two things to being the best. My colleagues in other countries say "If your standards were so good, how did the savings and loan fiasco arise in the United States?" There hasn't been anything like that in any other country.

The savings and loan crisis can be blamed on our accounting methods?

Very definitely. Our accounting permitted savings and loans to continue to show assets at amounts based on their historical cost when the real value was substantially lower.

In some respects, our accounting is not as conservative as some other countries, then.

Very much less conservative than Germany's or Japan's. They permit and even encourage the setting aside of reserves in good years so they never get surprised in bad years when they then return the reserves to income. In addition, labor unions in Europe are much more influential than they are in the United States. It's very common for trade unions to be represented on boards of directors. If they report high earnings and pay higher dividends, then the workers will ask for more money.

So, the politics of a country is reflected in its accounting.

No question. Accounting reflects in each country the overall philosophy of the economy and the differences in the legal system.

Should there be uniform worldwide accounting standards?

If we had a more uniform method of accounting around the world, we would have less uncertainty on the part of lenders and that might reduce borrowing costs. The fact is that market forces—not standard-setting bodies—are making accounting standards more uniform. If a lender is faced with loan requests from 20 different countries, and each of those countries follows different methods of accounting, then the burden on the lender increases—and the lender will extract a higher price for that loan. In many cases the borrower is willing to convert accounting systems to reduce the loan cost. And there is some evidence that bankers are willing to reduce their fees accordingly.

What career opportunities present themselves to accounting grads?

Not very many people deal in "international accounting," so there are opportunities there. International accounting is basically accounting between two nations. For example, if you worked for a U.S. company doing business in Germany, you would need to know something about the business conditions, the society, and the legal culture in Germany—in addition to their accounting. My thesis is that at least 50% of the next generation of students will spend at least a three-year period working for a U.S. company abroad or in the United States for a foreign-based company. We have a terrible reputation around the world for coming on the scene and trying to make everybody do things our way. That's resented. Until you understand why people do things differently, you haven't got any business telling people to do things your way.

How do we accomplish this in college?

We start the process by encouraging students to become familiar with at least one other country, its language and customs. You can't become knowledgeable about 20 languages. But you can become aware of differences in at least one other country, and that opens your horizons to the fact that not everybody thinks the same way that we think in the United States. I think that many college students should decide to take a semester and go to another country.

Of course, Japan is a major international trading partner.

Right now, Japan is in the midst of moving from a system that says don't tell the reader anything he or she doesn't need to know, to a U.S. system which is much more open. That change is the result of the Japanese becoming increasingly aware that they're going to tap into capital markets elsewhere in the world and that many people in the world don't understand their financial statements. We have about 40 Japanese companies which are listed to sell their securities in the United States. To do that, they had to meet all the SEC requirements that any U.S. company would have to meet. So, they have been increasingly willing to make disclosures. But they are still very, very conservative. What we depreciate over 30 or 40 years, they might depreciate over four or five. Goodwill is amortized over five years instead of our 40 years.

From their perspective, perhaps, maybe we're too liberal?

No question about it. They look upon what we're doing as asking for trouble. We tend to think that everything we do is fine and they're being overly conservative.

Are we the only country that uses a 40-year period for goodwill?

No, there are many others. We export a lot of things—including bad accounting. The more conservative countries use a much shorter period. But, because of the dominance of U.S. multinational companies, many countries have gradually moved toward 40 years.

Do most countries write up assets to reflect current value?

Most countries do not. Lower-of-cost or market is most prevalent. The only country that is moving toward market values more broadly is Australia. In the United Kingdom, certain assets such as real estate can be written up to market value periodically—every five years. In the Netherlands, it is common practice to account for inventory and certain long-lived assets at a replacement cost amount. But those are the rare exceptions.

Do other countries have a standard-setting body such as the FASB?

The Canadians generally use what we have. The United Kingdom established a new board that appears to be a prototype of the FASB. But in Europe, the rule makers are the tax people. It's not common to have differences between book and tax—their law provides that financial statements reflect what's on the tax return.

Are footnote disclosures as comprehensive elsewhere as here?

Footnotes are much less comprehensive in Europe or Japan. Again, I think it's tied to the capital markets. In the United States, for many years, we have found companies going broadly to get their capital. Many, many people are shareholders. Pension plans that represent many employees are shareholders. When you have an environment in which many people participate in making their money available for a price, those people want to have information. And so the demand is for open and full disclosure. When you go to Germany, almost all the capital there is provided by a handful of large banks. And they have enough clout that they can get whatever information they want. Not many people there are investors in the market.

Is that going to change now?

Yes. The demands on Germany for capital from the former Eastern bloc countries will require the Germans to turn to new sources of capital. They will find the need to make their financial statements much more open and transparent.

CHAPTER 7

CASH AND RECEIVABLES

LEARNING OBJECTIVES

After studying this chapter, you should be able to:

1. Identify items considered cash.

2. Explain common techniques employed to control cash.

3. Indicate how cash and related items are reported.

4. Define receivables and identify the different types of receivables.

5. Explain accounting issues related to recognition of accounts receivable.

6. Explain accounting issues related to valuation of accounts receivable.

7. Explain accounting issues related to recognition of notes receivable.

8. Explain accounting issues related to valuation of notes receivable.

9. Explain accounting issues related to disposition of accounts and notes receivable.

*C*onsider the Penn Central Railroad, Eastern Airlines, and Continental Illinois Bank. All were industry leaders that went bankrupt or nearly so because of lack of liquidity. **Liquidity** is the amount of time expected to elapse until an asset is converted into cash. An asset that is available for conversion into cash quickly is a *liquid asset.* Liquidity is one indication of an enterprise's ability to meet its obligations as they come due. A liquid enterprise is likely to have a lower risk of failure than an illiquid enterprise, and it generally has greater financial flexibility to accept unexpected new investment opportunities. Accountants are called upon to provide information that will help management, creditors, and investors assess an enterprise's current liquidity and prospective cash flows.

Assets are the heart of the enterprise. They generate the revenues that in turn generate the cash inflows to pay creditors, compensate employees, reward owners, and provide for growth. The primary liquid assets of most enterprises are cash, temporary investments, and receivables. This first of six asset chapters covers cash, accounts receivable, and notes receivable. Temporary investments are discussed later, in Chapter 18, along with long-term investments.

UNDERLYING CONCEPT

Providing information that will help users assess an enterprises's current liquidity and prospective cash flows is a primary objective of accounting.

315

▶ SECTION 1 / CASH

▶ NATURE AND COMPOSITION OF CASH

OBJECTIVE 1

Identify items considered cash.

Cash, the most liquid of assets, is the standard medium of exchange and the basis for measuring and accounting for all other items. It is generally classified as a current asset. To be reported as **cash,** it must be readily available for the payment of current obligations, and it must be free from any contractual restriction that limits its use in satisfying debts.

Cash consists of coin, currency, and available funds on deposit at the bank. Negotiable instruments such as money orders, certified checks, cashier's checks, personal checks, and bank drafts are also viewed as cash. Savings accounts are usually classified as cash, although the bank has the legal right to demand notice before withdrawal. But, because prior notice is rarely demanded by banks, savings accounts are considered cash.

Money market funds, money market savings certificates, certificates of deposit (CDs), and similar types of deposits and "short-term paper"[1] that provide small investors with an opportunity to earn high rates of interest are more appropriately classified as temporary investments than as cash. The reason is that these securities usually contain restrictions or penalties on their conversion to cash. Money market funds that provide checking account privileges, however, are usually classified as cash.

Certain items present classification problems: **Postdated checks and I.O.U.s** are treated as receivables. **Travel advances** are properly treated as receivables if the advances are to be collected from the employees or deducted from their salaries. Otherwise, classification of the travel advance as a prepaid expense is more appropriate. **Postage stamps on hand** are classified as part of office supplies inventory or as a prepaid expense. **Petty cash funds and change funds** are included in current assets as cash because these funds are used to meet current operating expenses and to liquidate current liabilities.

▶ MANAGEMENT AND CONTROL OF CASH

OBJECTIVE 2

Explain common techniques employed to control cash.

Cash presents special management and control problems for several reasons. The first is that cash enters into a great many transactions. Another reason is that **cash is the single asset readily convertible into any other type of asset.** It is easily concealed and transported, and it is almost universally desired. Correct accounting for cash transactions therefore requires controls to ensure that cash belonging to the enterprise is not improperly converted to personal use.

A third reason for regulating cash is that neither too much nor too little should be available at any time. An adequate supply must always be maintained without tying

---

[1]A variety of "short-term paper" is available for investment. For example, **certificates of deposit** (CDs) represent formal evidence of indebtedness, issued by a bank, subject to withdrawal under the specific terms of the instrument. Issued in $10,000 and $100,000 denominations, they mature in 30 to 360 days and generally pay interest at the short-term interest rate in effect at date of issuance. **Money market savings certificates** are issued by banks and savings and loan associations in denominations of $10,000 or more for 6-month periods (6 to 48 months). The interest rate is tied to the 26-week Treasury bill rate. In **money market funds,** a relatively recent variation of the mutual fund, the yield is determined by the mix of Treasury bills and commercial paper making up the fund's portfolio. Most money market funds require an initial minimum investment of $5,000; many allow withdrawal by check or wire transfer. **Treasury bills** are U.S. government obligations generally having 91- and 182-day maturities; they are sold in $10,000 denominations at weekly government auctions. **Commercial paper** is a short-term note (30 to 270 days) issued by corporations with good credit ratings. Issued in $5,000 and $10,000 denominations, these notes generally yield a higher rate than Treasury bills.

up too much of the firm's resources. As the medium of exchange, cash is required to pay for all assets and services purchased by the company and to meet all its obligations as they mature. The disbursement of cash is thus a daily occurrence, and a sufficient fund of cash must be kept on hand to meet these needs. On the other hand, cash, as such, is not a productive asset; it earns no return. Hence it is undesirable to keep on hand a supply of cash any larger than that necessary to meet day-to-day needs, with a reasonable margin for emergencies. Cash in excess of what is needed should be invested either in income-producing securities or in other productive assets.

Two problems of accounting for cash transactions face management: (1) Proper controls must be established to ensure that no unauthorized transactions are entered into by officers or employees; and (2) information necessary to the proper management of cash on hand and cash transactions must be provided. Yet even with sophisticated control devices errors can and do happen. *The Wall Street Journal* ran a story entitled "A $7.8 Million Error Has a Happy Ending for a Horrified Bank," which described how Manufacturers Hanover Trust Co., one of the nation's largest banks, mailed about $7.8 million too much in cash dividends to its stockholders. As implied in the headlines, most of the monies were subsequently returned.

USING BANK ACCOUNTS

A company can vary the number and location of banks and the types of bank accounts to obtain desired control objectives. For large companies operating in multiple locations, the location of bank accounts can be important. Establishing collection accounts in strategic locations can accelerate the flow of cash into the company by shortening the time between a customer's mailing of a payment and the company's use of the cash. Multiple collection centers generally are used to reduce the size of a company's **collection float,** which is the difference between the amount on deposit according to the company's records and the amount of collected cash according to the bank record.

The **general checking account** is the principal bank account in most companies and frequently the only bank account in small businesses. Cash is deposited in and disbursed from this account as all transactions are cycled through it. Deposits from and disbursements to all other bank accounts are made through the general checking account.

Imprest bank accounts are used to make a specific amount of cash available for a limited purpose. The account acts as a clearing account for a large volume of checks or for a specific type of check. The specific and intended amount to be cleared through the imprest account is deposited therein by transferring that amount from the general checking account or other source. Imprest bank accounts are often used for disbursing payroll checks, dividends, commissions, bonuses, confidential expenses (e.g., officers' salaries), and travel expenses.

Lockbox accounts are frequently used by large, multilocation companies to make collections in cities within areas of heaviest customer billing. The company rents a local post office box and authorizes a local bank to pick up the remittances mailed to that box number. The bank empties the box at least once a day and immediately credits the company's account for collections. The greatest advantage of a lockbox is that it accelerates the availability of collected cash. Generally, in a lockbox arrangement the bank microfilms the checks for record purposes and provides the company with a deposit slip, a list of collections, and any customer correspondence. If the control over cash is improved and if the income generated from accelerating the receipt of funds exceeds the cost of the lockbox system, then it is considered a worthwhile undertaking.

ELECTRONIC FUNDS TRANSFER (EFT)

Businesses and individuals use over 50 billion checks annually to pay their bills. This process is not without cost. Preparing, issuing, receiving, and clearing a check through the banking system can cost as much as $1.00 per check. It is not surprising, therefore, that in this electronic age new methods are being developed to transfer funds among

INTERNATIONAL INSIGHT

Multinational corporations often have cash accounts in more than one currency. For financial statement purposes these currencies are typically translated into U.S. dollars using the exchange rate in effect at the balance sheet date.

parties without the use and movement of paper. We are in an age of **electronic funds transfer (EFT),** a process that uses wire, telephone, telegraph, computer, satellite, or other electronic device rather than paper to make instantaneous transfers of funds.

America's major banks spent the 1980s developing national automated teller machine (ATM) networks. It is expected that most banks will be affiliated with a few national electronic banking networks that consolidate most retail banking services in much the same way that VISA and MasterCard unified consumer credit services.

But the new ATM electronic networks will be far more powerful than the credit card networks of VISA and MasterCard. They will operate with the **debit card,** which can give access to all of a customer's accounts within a bank. Using an ATM, customers are able to withdraw cash and make deposits to both their checking and savings accounts, as well as to transfer funds between accounts and make balance inquiries. By linking ATMs nationally, the new networks are building the first electronic funds transfer system capable of processing large-volume retail fund transfers between computers at different banks.

Already the use of checks has disappeared for certain funds transfers. For example, neither author of this book receives a formal payroll check from his employer; the universities send our banks a magnetic tape that transfers money from the university's account to our accounts. The services provided by ATM networks can now accommodate electronic transfers from home and retail point-of-sale terminals. Banks and consumers have the power to replace with electronic transactions many of those 50 billion checks.

THE IMPREST PETTY CASH SYSTEM

Almost every company finds it necessary to pay small amounts for a great many things such as employees' lunches, taxi fares, minor office supplies, and other miscellaneous expenses. It is frequently impractical to require that such disbursements be made by check, yet some control over them is important. A simple method of obtaining reasonable control, while adhering to the rule of disbursement by check, is the **imprest system for petty cash** disbursements.

This is how the system works:

1. Someone is designated petty cash custodian and given a small amount of currency from which to make small payments. The transfer of funds to petty cash is recorded as:

Petty Cash	300	
Cash		300

2. As disbursements are made, the petty cash custodian obtains signed receipts from each individual to whom cash is paid. If possible, evidence of the disbursement should be attached to the petty cash receipt.

   Petty cash transactions are not recorded until the fund is reimbursed and then such entries are recorded by someone other than the petty cash custodian.

3. When the supply of cash runs low, the custodian presents to the general cashier a request for reimbursement supported by the petty cash receipts and other disbursement evidence. The custodian receives a company check to replenish the fund. At this point, transactions are recorded based on petty cash receipts:

Office Supplies Expense	42	
Postage Expense	53	
Entertainment Expense	76	
Cash Over and Short	2	
Cash		173

4. If it is decided that the amount of cash in the petty cash fund is excessive, an adjustment may be made as follows (lowering the fund balance from $300 to $250):

Cash	50	
Petty Cash		50

Entries are made to the Petty Cash account only to increase or decrease the size of the fund.

A **Cash Over and Short** account is used when the petty cash fund fails to prove out. When this occurs, it is usually due to an error (failure to provide correct change, overpayment of expense, lost receipt, etc.). If cash proves out short (i.e., the sum of the receipts and cash in the fund is less than the imprest amount), the shortage is debited to the Cash Over and Short account. If it proves out over, the overage is credited to Cash Over and Short. This account is left open until the end of the year, when it is closed and generally shown on the income statement as an other expense or revenue.

There are usually expense items in the fund except immediately after reimbursement; therefore, if accurate financial statements are desired, the funds must be reimbursed at the end of each accounting period and also when nearly depleted.

Under the imprest system the petty cash custodian is responsible at all times for the amount of the fund on hand either as cash or in the form of signed receipts. These receipts provide the evidence required by the disbursing officer to issue a reimbursement check. Two additional procedures are followed to obtain more complete control over the petty cash fund:

1. Surprise counts of the fund are made from time to time by a superior of the petty cash custodian to determine that the fund is being accounted for satisfactorily.

2. Petty cash receipts are canceled or mutilated after they have been submitted for reimbursement, so that they cannot be used to secure a second reimbursement.

PHYSICAL PROTECTION OF CASH BALANCES

Not only must cash receipts and cash disbursements be safeguarded through internal control measures, but also the cash on hand and in banks must be protected. Because receipts become cash on hand and disbursements are made from cash in banks, adequate control of receipts and disbursements is a part of the protection of cash balances. Certain other procedures, however, should be given some consideration.

Physical protection of cash is so elementary a necessity that it requires little discussion. Every effort should be made to minimize the cash on hand in the office. A petty cash fund, the current day's receipts, and perhaps funds for making change should be all that is on hand at any one time. Insofar as possible, these funds should be kept in a vault, safe, or locked cash drawer. Each day's receipts should be transmitted intact to the bank as soon as practicable. Accurately stating the amount of available cash both in internal management reports and in external financial statements is also extremely important.

Every company has a record of cash received, disbursed, and the balance. Because of the many cash transactions, however, errors or omissions may be made in keeping this record. Therefore, it is necessary periodically to prove the balance shown in the general ledger. Cash actually present in the office—petty cash, change funds, and undeposited receipts—can be counted, for comparison with the company records. Cash on deposit is not available for count and is proved by preparing a bank reconciliation—a reconciliation of the company's record and the bank's record of the company's cash.

RECONCILIATION OF BANK BALANCES

At the end of each calendar month the bank supplies each customer with a **bank statement** (a copy of the bank's account with the customer) together with the customer's checks that have been paid by the bank during the month. If no errors were made by the bank or the customer, if all deposits made and all checks drawn by the customer reached the bank within the same month, and if no unusual transactions occurred that affected either the company's or the bank's record of cash, the balance of cash reported by the bank to the customer would be the same as that shown in the customer's own records. This condition seldom occurs for one or more of the following reasons:

◀ RECONCILING ITEMS ▶

1. **DEPOSITS IN TRANSIT.** End-of-month deposits of cash recorded on the depositor's books in one month are received and recorded by the bank in the following month.

2. **OUTSTANDING CHECKS.** Checks written by the depositor are recorded when written but may not be recorded by—or "clear"—the bank until the next month.

3. **BANK CHARGES.** Charges recorded by the bank against the depositor's balance for such items as bank services, printing checks, **not-sufficient-funds (NSF) checks**, and safe-deposit box rentals. The depositor may not be aware of these charges until the receipt of the bank statement.

4. **BANK CREDITS.** Collections or deposits by the bank for the benefit of the depositor that may be unknown to the depositor until receipt of the bank statement. Examples are note collection for the depositor and interest earned on interest-bearing checking accounts.

5. **BANK OR DEPOSITOR ERRORS.** Errors on either the part of the bank or the part of the depositor cause the bank balance to disagree with the depositor's book balance.

Hence, differences between the depositor's record of cash and the bank's record are usual and expected. Therefore, the two must be reconciled to determine the nature of the differences between the two amounts.

A **bank reconciliation** is a schedule explaining any differences between the bank's and the company's records of cash. If the difference results only from transactions not yet recorded by the bank, the company's record of cash is considered correct. But, if some part of the difference arises from other items, the bank's records or the company's records must be adjusted.

Two forms of bank reconciliation may be prepared. One form reconciles from the bank statement balance to the book balance or vice versa. The other form reconciles both the bank balance and the book balance to a correct cash balance. This latter form is more widely used. A sample of that form and its common reconciling items are shown in Illustration 7-1.

ILLUSTRATION 7-1
Bank Reconciliation Form and Content

Balance per bank statement (end of period)		$$$
Add: Deposits in transit	$$	
Undeposited receipts (cash on hand)	$$	
Bank errors that understate the bank statement balance	$$	$$
Deduct: Outstanding checks	$$	$$$
Bank errors that overstate the bank statement balance	$$	$$
Correct cash balance		$$$
Balance per depositor's books		$$$
Add: Bank credits and collections not yet recorded in the books	$$	
Book errors that understate the book balance	$$	$$
		$$$
Deduct: Bank charges not yet recorded in the books	$$	
Book errors that overstate the book balance	$$	$$
Correct cash balance		$$$

This form of reconciliation consists of two sections: (1) "Balance per bank statement" and (2) "Balance per depositor's books." Both sections end with the same "correct cash balance." The correct cash balance is the amount to which the books must be adjusted and is the amount reported on the balance sheet. Adjusting journal entries are prepared for all the addition and deduction items appearing in the "Balance per depositor's books" section. Any errors attributable to the bank should be called to the bank's attention immediately.

To illustrate, Nugget Mining Company's books show a cash balance at the Denver National Bank on November 30, 1995, of $20,502. The bank statement covering the month of November shows an ending balance of $22,190. An examination of Nugget's accounting records and November bank statement identified the following reconciling items:

1. A deposit of $3,680 was mailed November 30 but does not appear on the bank statement.

2. Checks written in November but not charged to the November bank statement are:

$$\begin{array}{ll} \text{Check \#7327} & \$\ 150 \\ \text{\#7348} & 4,820 \\ \text{\#7349} & 31 \end{array}$$

3. Nugget has not yet recorded the $600 of interest collected by the bank Nov. 20 on Sequoia Co. bonds held by the bank for Nugget.

4. Bank service charges of $18 are not yet recorded on Nugget's books.

5. One of Nugget's customer's checks for $220 was returned with the bank statement and marked "NSF." The bank treated this bad check as a disbursement.

6. Nugget discovered that check #7322, written in November for $131 in payment of an account payable, had been incorrectly recorded in their books as $311.

7. A check for Nugent Oil Co. in the amount of $175 accompanied the bank statement that had been incorrectly charged to Nugget Mining.

The reconciliation of bank and book balances to the correct cash balance of $21,044 would appear as follows:

Nugget Mining Company Bank Reconciliation Denver National Bank, November 30, 1995			
Balance per bank statement (end of period)			$22,190
Add: Deposit in transit	(1)	$3,680	
Bank error—incorrect check charged to account by bank	(7)	175	3,855
			26,045
Deduct: Outstanding checks	(2)		5,001
Correct cash balance			$21,044
Balance per books			$20,502
Add: Interest collected by the bank	(3)	$ 600	
Error in recording check #7322	(6)	180	780
			21,282
Deduct: Bank service charges	(4)	18	
NSF check returned	(5)	220	238
Correct cash balance			$21,044

ILLUSTRATION 7-2
Sample Bank Reconciliation

The journal entries required to adjust and correct Nugget Mining's books in early December 1995 are taken from the items in the "Balance per books" section and are as follows:

Cash	600	
Interest Revenue		600
(To record interest on Sequoia Co. bonds, collected by bank)		
Cash	180	
Accounts Payable		180
(To correct error in recording amount of check #7322)		
Office Expense—Bank Charges	18	
Cash		18
(To record bank service charges for November)		
Accounts Receivable	220	
Cash		220
(To record customer's check returned NSF)		

When the entries are posted, Nugget's cash account will have a balance of $21,044. Nugget should return the Nugent Oil Co. check to Denver National Bank, informing the bank of the error.

Another widely used form of bank reconciliation is the **four-column reconciliation** ("proof of cash"), which is discussed and illustrated in Appendix 7–A.

▶ REPORTING CASH

OBJECTIVE 3

Indicate how cash and related items are reported.

Although the reporting of cash is relatively straightforward, there are a number of issues that merit special attention. These issues relate to the reporting of:

1. Restricted cash.
2. Bank overdrafts.
3. Cash equivalents.

RESTRICTED CASH

Compensating Balances

In recent years it has become common for banks and other lending institutions to require customers to whom they lend money to maintain minimum cash balances in checking or savings accounts. These minimum balances, called **compensating balances**, are defined by the SEC as: "that portion of any demand deposit (or any time deposit or certificate of deposit) maintained by a corporation which constitutes support for existing borrowing arrangements of the corporation with a lending institution. Such arrangements would include both outstanding borrowings and the assurance of future credit availability."[2]

Compensating balances may be payment for bank services rendered to the company for which there is no direct fee, for example, check processing and lockbox management. By requiring a compensating balance, the bank achieves an effective interest rate on a loan that is higher than the stated rate because it has use of the restricted amount that must remain on deposit.

To illustrate, assume that on January 1, 1995, Biddle Co. borrowed $10,000,000 for one year from First Union Bank at an interest rate of 10%. In addition, Biddle is required to keep a compensatory balance of $2,000,000 on deposit at First Union, which will earn 6%. Normally, Biddle would deposit $1,000,000 at the bank for transaction purposes. The effective interest that Biddle pays on this loan is 10.4% computed as follows:

---

[2]*Accounting Series Release No. 148,* "Amendments to Regulations S-X and Related Interpretations and Guidelines Regarding the Disclosure of Compensating Balances and Short-Term Borrowing Arrangements," Securities and Exchange Commission (November 13, 1973). The SEC defines 15% of liquid assets (current cash balances, whether restricted or not, plus marketable securities) as being material.

Computation of Interest Cost	
$10,000,000 × 10%	$1,000,000
($2,000,000 − $1,000,000) × 4%	40,000
Total interest cost	$1,040,000

$$\frac{\text{Total interest cost}}{\text{Total principal}} = \frac{\$1,040,000}{\$10,000,000} = 10.4\%$$

Biddle pays $1,000,000 interest on the original loan of $10,000,000 and it is required to maintain an additional $1,000,000 cash balance on which it can earn only 6%. If it has to borrow this additional $1,000,000, it will be losing 4% (10% − 6%) on every dollar borrowed.

The need for the disclosure of compensating balances was highlighted in the 1970s when a number of companies were involved in a liquidity crisis. Many investors believed that the cash reported on the balance sheet was fully available to meet recurring obligations, but these funds were actually restricted because of the need for these companies to maintain minimum cash balances at various lending institutions.

The SEC recommends that **legally restricted deposits** held as compensating balances against **short-term** borrowing arrangements be stated separately among the "cash and cash equivalent items" in Current Assets. Restricted deposits held as compensating balances against **long-term** borrowing arrangements should be separately classified as noncurrent assets in either the Investments or Other Assets sections, using a caption such as "Cash on Deposit Maintained as Compensating Balance."

In cases where compensating balance arrangements exist without agreements that restrict the use of cash amounts shown on the balance sheet, the arrangements and the amounts involved should be described in the notes. Compensating balances that are maintained under an agreement to assure future credit availability also must be disclosed separately in the notes, together with the amount and duration of such agreement.

Snap-On Tools reported the following note regarding compensating balances:

Snap-On Tools

Note: Compensating Balances. At the end of the current year, the Company had total bank lines of credit available under short-term borrowing arrangements of $37.3 million. Of that amount, $35.0 million requires compensatory balances of 3% relative to these arrangements.

Other Types of Restrictions

Petty cash, payroll, and dividend funds are examples of cash set aside for a particular purpose. In most situations, these fund balances are not material and therefore are not segregated from cash when reported in the financial statements. When material in amount, restricted cash is segregated from "regular" cash for reporting purposes. The **restricted cash** is classified either in the Current Assets or in the Long-term Assets section, depending on the date of availability or disbursement. Classification in the current section is appropriate if the cash is to be used (within a year or the operating cycle, whichever is longer) for payment of existing or maturing obligations. On the other hand, if the cash is to be held for a longer period of time, the restricted cash is shown in the long-term section of the balance sheet.

Cash classified in the long-term section is frequently set aside for plant expansion, retirement of long-term debt or, in the case of Par Pharmaceutical, for self-insurance:

INTERNATIONAL INSIGHT

Among other potential restrictions, companies need to determine whether any of the cash in accounts outside the U.S. is restricted by regulations against exportation of currency.

Par Pharmaceutical	
Restricted cash and investments (See Note)	$3,000,000

Note: Restricted Cash. As a result of escalating products liability insurance premiums and in view of Par's favorable products liability experience, the Company instituted a Products Liability Self-Insurance Program effective June of the current period. Pursuant to this Program, $3,000,000 has been deposited with a financial institution and its use restricted to costs arising from such product liability claims against the Company. Such funds are invested in income-producing securities, the income from which is available to the Company for general corporate purposes.

BANK OVERDRAFTS

Bank overdrafts occur when a check is written for more than the amount in the cash account. They should be reported in the current liabilities section and are usually added to the amount reported as accounts payable. If material, these items should be separately disclosed either on the face of the balance sheet or in the related notes.[3]

Bank overdrafts are generally not offset against the cash account. A major exception is when available cash is present in another account in the same bank on which the overdraft occurred. Offsetting in this case is required.

CASH EQUIVALENTS

A current classification that has become popular is "cash and cash equivalents."[4] **Cash equivalents** are short-term, highly liquid investments that are both (a) readily convertible to known amounts of cash, and (b) so near their maturity that they present insignificant risk of changes in interest rates. Generally only investments with original maturities of 3 months or less qualify under these definitions. Examples of cash equivalents are treasury bills, commercial paper, and money market funds. Some companies combine cash with temporary investments on the balance sheet. In these cases, the amount of the temporary investments is described either parenthetically or in the notes.

▶ SUMMARY

Cash and cash equivalents includes the medium of exchange and most negotiable instruments. If the item cannot be converted to coin or currency on short notice, it is separately classified as an investment, as a receivable, or as a prepaid expense. Cash that is not available for payment of currently maturing liabilities is segregated and classified in the long-term assets section. Illustration 7-3 summarizes the classification of cash-related items.

---

[3]Bank overdrafts usually occur because of a simple oversight by the company writing the check. Banks often expect companies to have overdrafts from time to time and therefore negotiate a fee as payment for this possible occurrence. However, in the early 1980s, E. F. Hutton (a large brokerage firm) intentionally began overdrawing their accounts by astronomical amounts—on some days exceeding $1 billion—thus obtaining interest-free loans which it could invest. Because the amounts were so large and fees were not negotiated in advance, E. F. Hutton came under criminal investigation for its actions.

[4]*Accounting Trends and Techniques—1993*, indicates that approximately 16% of the companies surveyed use the caption "cash," 73% use "cash and cash equivalents," and 11% use a caption such as "cash and marketable securities" or similar terminology.

ILLUSTRATION 7-3
Classification of Cash-Related Items

Item	Classification	Comment
Cash	Cash	If unrestricted, report as cash. If restricted, identify and classify as current and noncurrent assets.
Petty cash and change funds	Cash	Report as cash.
Short-term paper	Cash equivalents	Investments with maturity of less than three months, often combined with cash.
Short-term paper	Temporary investments	Investments with maturity of 3 to 12 months.
Postdated checks and IOU's	Receivables	Assumed to be collectible.
Travel advances	Receivables	Assumed to be collected from employees or deducted from their salaries.
Postage on hand (as stamps or in postage meters)	Prepaid expenses	May also be classified as office supplies inventory.
Bank overdrafts	Current liability	If right of offset exists, reduce cash.
Compensating balances		
1. Legally restricted	Cash separately classified as a deposit maintained as compensating balance	Classify as current or noncurrent in the balance sheet.
2. Arrangement without legal restriction	Cash with note disclosure	Disclose separately in notes details of the arrangement.

(Table title: Classification of Cash, Cash Equivalent and Noncash Items)

► S E C T I O N 2 / R E C E I V A B L E S

Receivables are claims held against customers and others for money, goods, or services. For financial statement purposes, receivables are classified as either **current** (short-term) or **noncurrent** (long-term). **Current receivables** are expected to be collected within a year or during the current operating cycle, whichever is longer. All other receivables are classified as **noncurrent**. Receivables are further classified in the balance sheet as either trade or nontrade receivables.

Trade receivables are amounts owed by customers for goods sold and services rendered as part of normal business operations. Trade receivables, usually the most significant an enterprise possesses, may be subclassified into accounts receivable and notes receivable. **Accounts receivable** are oral promises of the purchaser to pay for goods and services sold. They are normally collectible within 30 to 60 days and represent "open accounts" resulting from short-term extensions of credit. **Notes receivable** are written promises to pay a certain sum of money on a specified future date. They may arise from sales, financing, or other transactions. Notes may be short-term or long-term.

Nontrade receivables arise from a variety of transactions and can be written promises either to pay or to deliver. Some examples of nontrade receivables are:

1. Advances to officers and employees.
2. Advances to subsidiaries.
3. Deposits to cover potential damages or losses.
4. Deposits as a guarantee of performance or payment.
5. Dividends and interest receivable.

OBJECTIVE 4
Define receivables and identify the different types of receivables.

6. Claims against:
   (a) Insurance companies for casualties sustained.
   (b) Defendants under suit.
   (c) Governmental bodies for tax refunds.
   (d) Common carriers for damaged or lost goods.
   (e) Creditors for returned, damaged, or lost goods.
   (f) Customers for returnable items (crates, containers, etc.).

Because of the peculiar nature of nontrade receivables, they are generally classified and reported as separate items in the balance sheet.

The basic issues in accounting for accounts and notes receivable are the same: **recognition, valuation,** and **disposition.** We will discuss these basic issues of accounts and notes receivable in the following sequence:

1. Recognition and valuation of accounts receivable.
2. Recognition and valuation of notes receivable.
3. Disposition of accounts and notes receivable.

▶ RECOGNITION OF ACCOUNTS RECEIVABLE

OBJECTIVE 5

Explain accounting issues related to recognition of accounts receivable.

In most receivables transactions, the amount to be recognized is the exchange price between the two parties. **The exchange price is the amount due from the debtor** (a customer or a borrower) and is generally evidenced by some type of business document, often an invoice. Two factors that may complicate the measurement of the exchange price are (1) the availability of discounts (trade and cash discounts) and (2) the length of time between the sale and the due date of payments (the interest element).

TRADE DISCOUNTS

Customers are often quoted prices on the basis of list or catalog prices that may be subject to a trade or quantity discount. Such **trade discounts** are used to avoid frequent changes in catalogs, to quote different prices for different quantities purchased, or to hide the true invoice price from competitors.

Trade discounts are commonly quoted in percentages. For example, if your textbook has a list price of $60.00 and the publisher sells it to college bookstores for list less a 30% trade discount, the receivable recorded by the publisher is $42.00 per textbook. The normal practice is simply to deduct the trade discount from the list price and bill the customer net.

As another example, Maxwell House at one time sold a 10 oz. jar of its instant coffee listing at $4.65 to supermarkets for $3.90, a trade discount of approximately 16%. The supermarkets in turn sold the instant coffee for $3.99 per jar. Maxwell House records the receivable and related sales revenue at $3.90 per jar, not $4.65.

CASH DISCOUNTS (SALES DISCOUNTS)

Cash discounts (**sales discounts**) are offered as an inducement for prompt payment. They are communicated in terms that read, for example, 2/10, n/30 (2% if paid within 10 days, gross amount due in 30 days), or 2/10, E.O.M. (2% if paid within 10 days of the end of the month).

Companies that fail to take sales discounts are usually not employing their money advantageously. An enterprise that receives a 1% reduction in the sales price for payment within 10 days, total payment due within 30 days, is effectively earning 18.25% (.01 ÷ [20/365]), or at least avoiding that rate of interest cost. For this reason, companies usually take the discount unless their cash is severely limited.

The easiest and most commonly used method of recording sales and related sales discount transactions is to enter the receivable and sale at the gross amount. Under this method, sales discounts are recognized in the accounts only when payment is received within the discount period. Sales discounts would then be shown in the income statement as a deduction from sales to arrive at net sales.

Some accountants contend that sales discounts not taken reflect penalties added to an established price to encourage prompt payment. That is, the seller offers sales on account at a slightly higher price than if selling for cash, and the increase is offset by the cash discount offered. Thus, customers who pay within the discount period purchase at the cash price; those who pay after expiration of the discount period are penalized because they must pay an amount in excess of the cash price. If this reasoning is used, sales and receivables are recorded net, and any discounts not taken are subsequently debited to Accounts Receivable and credited to Sales Discounts Forfeited. The following entries illustrate the difference between the gross and net methods.

Gross Method			Net Method		
Sale of $10,000, terms 2/10, n/30:					
Accounts Receivable	10,000		Accounts Receivable	9,800	
Sales		10,000	Sales		9,800
Payment of $4,000 received within discount period:					
Cash	3,920		Cash	3,920	
Sales Discounts	80		Accounts Receivable		3,920
Accounts Receivable		4,000			
Payment of $6,000 received after discount period:					
Cash	6,000		Accounts Receivable	120	
Accounts Receivable		6,000	Sales Discounts		
			Forfeited		120
			Cash	6,000	
			Accounts Receivable		6,000

ILLUSTRATION 7-4
Entries Under Gross and Net Methods of Recording Cash (Sales) Discounts

If the gross method is employed, sales discounts are reported as a deduction from sales in the income statement. Proper matching would dictate that a reasonable estimate of material amounts of expected discounts to be taken also should be charged against sales. If the net method is used, Sales Discounts Forfeited are considered as an other revenue item.

Theoretically, the recognition of Sales Discounts Forfeited is correct because the receivable is stated closer to its realizable value and the net sale figure measures the revenue earned from the sale. As a practical matter, however, the net method is seldom used because it requires additional analysis and bookkeeping. For one thing, the net method requires adjusting entries to record sales discounts forfeited on accounts receivable that have passed the discount period.

NONRECOGNITION OF INTEREST ELEMENT

Ideally, receivables should be measured in terms of their present value, that is, the discounted value of the cash to be received in the future. When expected cash receipts require a waiting period, the receivable face amount is not worth the amount that is ultimately received.

To illustrate, assume that a company makes a sale on account for $1,000 with payment due in 4 months. The applicable annual rate of interest is 12% and payment is made at the end of 4 months. The present value of that receivable is not $1,000 but $961.54 ($1,000 × .96154, Table 6–2; $n = 1$, $i = 4\%$). In other words, $1,000 to be received 4 months from now is not the same as $1,000 received today.

Theoretically, any revenue after the period of sale is interest revenue. In practice, accountants have chosen generally to ignore this for accounts receivable because the amount of the discount is not usually material in relation to the net income for the period. The profession specifically excludes from the present value considerations "re-

UNDERLYING CONCEPT

Materiality means it must make a difference to a decision maker. The FASB believes that present value concepts can be ignored for short-term notes.

ceivables arising from transactions with customers in the normal course of business which are due in customary trade terms not exceeding approximately one year."[5]

▶ VALUATION OF ACCOUNTS RECEIVABLE

OBJECTIVE 6

Explain accounting issues related to valuation of accounts receivable.

Having recorded receivables at their face value (the amount due), accountants then face the problem of financial statement presentation. Reporting of receivables involves (1) classification and (2) valuation on the balance sheet.

Classification, as already discussed, involves a determination of the length of time each receivable will be outstanding. Receivables intended to be collected within a year or the operating cycle, whichever is longer, are classified as current; all other receivables are classified as long-term.

The valuation of receivables is slightly more complex. **Short-term receivables are valued and reported at net realizable value—the net amount expected to be received in cash,** which is not necessarily the amount legally receivable. Determining net realizable value requires an estimation of both uncollectible receivables and any returns or allowances to be granted.

UNCOLLECTIBLE ACCOUNTS RECEIVABLE

As one accountant so aptly noted, the credit manager's idea of heaven probably would be a place where everyone (eventually) paid his or her debts.[6] Sales on any basis other than for cash make possible the subsequent failure to collect the account. An uncollectible account receivable is a loss of revenue that requires, through proper entry in the accounts, a decrease in the asset accounts receivable and a related decrease in income and stockholders' equity. The loss in revenue and the decrease in income are recognized by recording bad debt expense.

The chief problem in recording uncollectible accounts receivable is establishing the time at which to record the loss. Two general procedures are in use.

◀ METHODS FOR RECORDING UNCOLLECTIBLES ▶

1. **DIRECT WRITE-OFF METHOD.**   No entry is made until a specific account has definitely been established as uncollectible. Then the loss is recorded by crediting Accounts Receivable and debiting Bad Debt Expense.
2. **ALLOWANCE METHOD.**   An estimate is made of the expected uncollectible accounts from all sales made on account or from the total of outstanding receivables. This estimate is entered as an expense and an indirect reduction in accounts receivable (via an increase in the allowance account) in the period in which the sale is recorded.

---

[5]"Interest on Receivables and Payables," *Opinions of the Accounting Principles Board No. 21* (New York: AICPA, 1971), par. 3(a). According to *APB Opinion No. 21*, all receivables are subject to present value measurement techniques and interest imputation, if necessary, except for the following specifically excluded types:

1. Normal accounts receivable due within one year.
2. Security deposits, retainages, advances, or progress payments.
3. Transactions between parent and subsidiary.
4. Receivables due at some indeterminable future date.

[6]William J. Vatter, *Managerial Accounting* (Englewood Cliffs, N.J.: Prentice-Hall, 1950), p. 60.

The direct write-off method records the bad debt in the year it is determined that a specific receivable cannot be collected. The allowance method enters the expense on an estimated basis in the accounting period in which the sales on account are made.

Supporters of the **direct write-off method** contend that facts, not estimates, are recorded. It assumes that a good account receivable resulted from each sale, and that later events proved certain accounts to be uncollectible and worthless. From a practical standpoint this method is simple and convenient to apply, although receivables do not generally become worthless at an identifiable moment of time. The direct write-off method is theoretically deficient because it usually does not match costs with revenues of the period, nor does it result in receivables being stated at estimated realizable value on the balance sheet. **As a result, its use is not considered appropriate, except when the amount uncollectible is immaterial.**

Advocates of the **allowance method** believe that bad debt expense should be recorded in the same period as the sale to obtain a proper matching of expenses and revenues and to achieve a proper carrying value for accounts receivable. They support the position that although estimates are involved, the percentage of receivables that will not be collected can be predicted from past experiences, present market conditions, and an analysis of the outstanding balances. Many companies set their credit policies to provide for a certain percentage of uncollectible accounts. (In fact, many feel that failure to reach that percentage means that sales are being lost by credit policies that are too restrictive.)

Because the collectibility of receivables is considered a loss contingency, the allowance method is appropriate in situations where it is probable that an asset has been impaired and that the amount of the loss can be reasonably estimated.[7] A receivable is a prospective cash inflow, and the probability of its collection must be considered in valuing this inflow. These estimates normally are made either on (1) the basis of percentage of sales or (2) the basis of outstanding receivables.

Percentage-of-Sales (Income Statement) Approach

If there is a fairly stable relationship between previous years' charge sales and bad debts, then that relationship can be turned into a percentage and used to determine this year's bad debt expense.

The **percentage-of-sales approach** matches costs with revenues because it relates the charge to the period in which the sale is recorded. To illustrate, assume that E. T. Elsner's Inc. estimates from past experience that about 2% of charge sales become uncollectible. If Elsner's Inc. has charge sales of $400,000 in 1995, the entry to record bad debt expense using the percentage-of-sales method is as follows:

Bad Debt Expense	8,000	
Allowance for Doubtful Accounts		8,000

The Allowance for Doubtful Accounts is a valuation account (i.e., a contra asset) and is subtracted from trade receivables on the balance sheet.[8] The amount of bad debt expense and the related credit to the allowance account are unaffected by any balance currently existing in the allowance account. Because the bad debt expense estimate is related to a nominal account (Sales), and any balance in the allowance is ignored, this method is frequently referred to as the **income statement approach.** A proper matching of cost and revenues is therefore achieved.

[7]"Accounting for Contingencies," *Statement of Financial Accounting Standards No. 5* (Stamford, Conn.: FASB, 1975), par. 8.

[8]The account description employed for the allowance account is usually Allowance for Doubtful Accounts or simply Allowance. *Accounting Trends and Techniques—1993*, for example, indicates that approximately 78% of the companies surveyed used "allowance" in their description. In addition to deducting an allowance for doubtful accounts from receivables, 8% deducted amounts for unearned discounts or finance charges or sale returns.

INTERNATIONAL INSIGHT

The "allowance for doubtful accounts" is actually a "reserve" against the possibility of noncollectibility. Although, in general, the use of "reserves" is not acceptable in U.S. accounting, this is one instance where such a reserve is often mandatory. Full disclosure is, of course, also required.

UNDERLYING CONCEPT

The percentage-of-sales method is a good illustration of the use of the matching principle which relates expenses to revenues earned.

Percentage-of-Receivables (Balance Sheet) Approach

Using past experience, a company can estimate the percentage of its outstanding receivables that will become uncollectible, without identifying specific accounts. This procedure provides a reasonably accurate estimate of the receivables' realizable value, but does not fit the concept of matching cost and revenues. Rather, its objective is to report receivables in the balance sheet at net realizable values; hence it is referred to as the **percentage-of-receivables** or **balance sheet approach.**

The percentage of receivables may be applied using one **composite rate** that reflects an estimate of the uncollectible receivables. Another approach that is more sensitive to the actual status of the accounts receivable sets up an **aging schedule** and applies a different percentage based on past experience to the various age categories. An aging schedule is frequently used in practice. It indicates which accounts require special attention by providing the age of such accounts receivable. The following schedule of Wilson & Co. is an example.

ILLUSTRATION 7-5
Accounts Receivable
Aging Schedule

		Wilson & Co. AGING SCHEDULE				
Name of Customer	Balance Dec. 31	Under 60 days	61–90 days	91–120 days	Over 120 days	
Western Stainless Steel Corp.	$ 98,000	$ 80,000	$18,000			
Brockway Steel Company	320,000	320,000				
Freeport Sheet & Tube Co.	55,000				$55,000	
Allegheny Iron Works	74,000	60,000		$14,000		
	$547,000	$460,000	$18,000	$14,000	$55,000	

Summary

Age	Amount	Percentage Estimated to be Uncollectible	Required Balance in Allowance
Under 60 days old	$460,000	4%	$18,400
61–90 days old	18,000	15%	2,700
91–120 days old	14,000	20%	2,800
Over 120 days	55,000	25%	13,750
Year-end balance of allowance for doubtful accounts			$37,650

The amount $37,650 would be the bad debt expense to be reported for this year, assuming that no balance existed in the allowance account.

To change the illustration slightly, **assume that the allowance account had a credit balance of $800 before adjustment.** In this case, the amount to be added to the allowance account is $36,850 ($37,650 − $800), and the following entry is made.

Bad Debt Expense	36,850	
Allowance for Doubtful Accounts		36,850

The balance in the Allowance account is therefore stated at $37,650. **If the Allowance balance before adjustment had a debit balance of $200,** then the amount to be recorded for bad debt expense would be $37,850 ($37,650 desired balance + $200 debit balance). In the percentage-of-receivables method, the balance in the allowance account **cannot be ignored** because the percentage is related to a real account (Accounts Receivable).

An aging schedule is usually not prepared to determine the bad debt expense. Rather, it is prepared as a control device to determine the composition of receivables and to identify delinquent accounts. The estimated loss percentage developed for each category is based on previous loss experience and the advice of credit department personnel. Regardless of whether a composite rate or an aging schedule is employed, the primary objective of the percentage of outstanding receivables method for financial statement purposes is to report receivables in the balance sheet at net realizable value. However, it is deficient in that it may not match the bad debt expense to the period in which the sale takes place.

The allowance for doubtful accounts as a percentage of receivables will vary, depending upon the industry and the economic climate. Companies such as Eastman Kodak, General Electric, and Monsanto have recorded allowances ranging from $3.00 to $6.00 per $100 of accounts receivable. Others such as CPC International ($1.48), Texaco ($1.23), and U.S. Steel ($0.78) are examples of large enterprises that have had bad debt allowances of less than $1.50 per $100. At the other extreme are hospitals that allow for $15.00 to $20.00 per $100.00 of accounts receivable.[9]

In summary, the percentage-of-receivables method results in a more accurate valuation of receivables on the balance sheet. From a matching viewpoint, the percentage-of-sales approach provides the better results. The following diagram relates these methods to the basic theory:

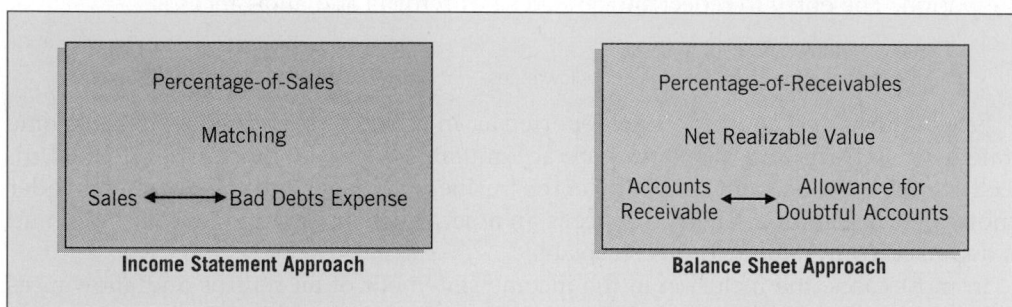

ILLUSTRATION 7-6
Comparison of Methods
for Estimating
Uncollectibles

The account title employed for the allowance account is usually Allowance for Doubtful Accounts or simply Allowance.

Collection of Accounts Receivable Written Off

When a particular account receivable is determined to be uncollectible, the balance is removed from the books by debiting Allowance for Doubtful Accounts and crediting Accounts Receivable. If a collection is made on a receivable that was previously written off, the procedure is first to reestablish the receivable by debiting Accounts Receivable and crediting Allowance for Doubtful Accounts. An entry is then made to debit Cash and credit the customer's account for the amount received.

If the direct write-off approach is employed, the amount collected is debited to Cash and credited to a revenue account entitled Uncollectible Amounts Recovered, with proper notation in the customer's account.

SPECIAL ALLOWANCE ACCOUNTS

To properly match expenses to sales revenues, it is sometimes necessary to establish additional allowance accounts. These allowance accounts are reported as contra accounts to accounts receivable, and they establish the receivables at net realizable value. The most common allowances are:

1. Allowance for sales returns and allowances.
2. Allowance for collection expenses.

---

[9]A U.S. Department of Commerce study indicated, as a general rule, the following relationships between the age of accounts receivable and their uncollectibility:

30 days or less	4% uncollectible
31–60 days	10% uncollectible
61–90 days	17% uncollectible
91–120 days	26% uncollectible

After 120 days, an approximate 3–4% increase in uncollectibles for every 30 days outstanding occurs for the remainder of the first year.

Sales Returns and Allowances

Many accountants question the soundness of recording returns and allowances in the current period when they are derived from sales made in the preceding period. Normally, however, the amount of mismatched returns and allowances is not material, if such items are handled consistently from year to year. Yet, if a company completes a few special orders involving large amounts near the end of the accounting period, **sales returns and allowances** should be anticipated in the period of the sale to avoid distorting the income statement of the current period.

As an example, Astro Turf Corporation recognizes that approximately 5% of its $1,000,000 trade receivables outstanding are returned or some adjustment made to the sale price. Omission of a $50,000 charge could have a material effect on net income for the period. The entry to reflect anticipated sales returns and allowances is:

Sales Returns and Allowances	50,000	
Allowance for Sales Returns and Allowances		50,000

Sales returns and allowances are reported as an offset to sales revenue in the income statement. Returns and allowances are accumulated separately instead of debited directly to the Sales account simply to let the business manager and the statement reader know their magnitude. The allowance is an asset valuation account (contra asset) and is deducted from total accounts receivable.

In most cases, the inclusion in the income statement of all returns and allowances made during the period, whether or not they resulted from the current period's sales, is an acceptable accounting procedure justified on the basis of practicality and immateriality.[10]

Collection Expense

A similar concept holds true for collection expense. If a significant handling and service charge is incurred to collect the open accounts receivable at the end of the year, an allowance for collection expenses should be recorded. For example, Sears, Roebuck and Co. reports its receivables net, with an attached schedule indicating the types of receivables outstanding. Sears' contra account is entitled "Allowance for Collection Expenses and Losses on Customer Accounts" as shown below:

ILLUSTRATION 7-7
Allowance for Collection Expenses and Losses on Customer Accounts

Sears, Roebuck and Co.	
Receivables	
Customer installment accounts receivable	
Easy payment accounts	$2,221,017,167
Revolving charge accounts	1,372,874,725
	3,593,891,892
Other customer accounts	101,904,882
Miscellaneous accounts and notes receivable	96,446,334
	3,792,243,108
Less allowance for collection expenses and losses on customer accounts	236,826,866
	$3,555,416,242

---

[10]An interesting sidelight to the entire problem of returns and allowances has developed in recent years. Determining when a sale **is** a sale has become difficult; because in certain circumstances the seller is exposed to such a high risk of ownership through possible return of the property that the entire transaction is nullified and the sale not recognized. Such situations have developed particularly in sales to related parties. This subject is discussed in more detail in Chapters 8 and 19.

▶ NOTES RECEIVABLE

A note receivable is supported by a formal **promissory note,** a written promise to pay a certain sum of money at a specific future date. Such a note is a negotiable instrument that is signed by a **maker** in favor of a designated **payee** who may legally and readily sell or otherwise transfer the note to others. Although notes contain an interest element because of the time value of money, notes are classified as interest-bearing or noninterest-bearing. **Interest-bearing notes** have a stated rate of interest, whereas **noninterest-bearing notes** (zero-interest-bearing) include interest as part of their face amount instead of stating it explicitly. Notes receivable are considered fairly liquid, even if long-term, because they may be easily converted to cash.

Notes receivable are frequently accepted from customers who need to extend the payment period of an outstanding receivable. Notes are also sometimes required of high-risk or new customers. In addition, notes are often used in loans to employees and subsidiaries and in the sales of property, plant, and equipment. In some industries (e.g., the pleasure and sport boat industry) all credit sales are supported by notes. The majority of notes, however, originate from lending transactions. The basic issues in accounting for notes receivable are the same as those for accounts receivable: recognition, valuation, and disposition.

RECOGNITION OF NOTES RECEIVABLE

Short-term notes are generally recorded at face value (less allowances) because the interest implicit in the maturity value is immaterial. A general rule is that notes treated as cash equivalents (maturities of 3 months or less) are not subject to premium or discount amortization. Long-term notes receivable, however, should be recorded and reported at the **present value of the cash expected to be collected.** When the interest stated on an interest-bearing note is equal to the effective (market) rate of interest, the note sells at face value.[11] When the stated rate is different from the market rate, the cash exchanged (present value) is different from the face value of the note. The difference between the face value and the cash exchanged, either a discount or a premium, is then recorded and amortized over the life of a note to approximate the effective (market) interest rate.

OBJECTIVE 7

Explain accounting issues related to recognition of notes receivable.

Note Issued at Face Value

To illustrate the discounting of a note issued at face value, assume that Bigelow Corp. lends Scandinavian Imports $10,000 in exchange for a $10,000, 3-year note bearing interest at 10% annually. The market rate of interest for a note of similar risk is also 10%. This time diagram depicting both cash flows is shown below:

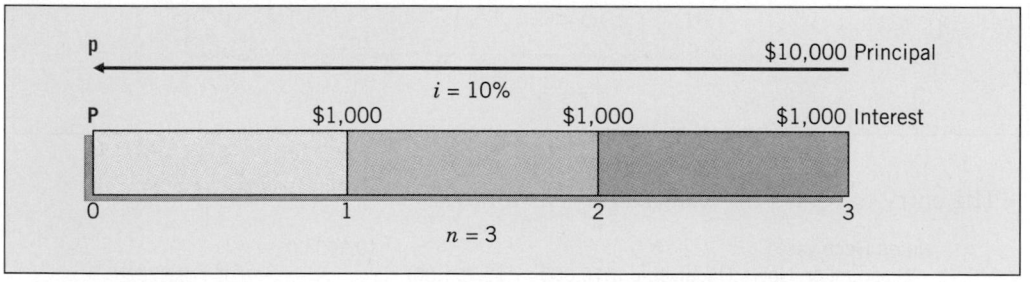

---

[11]The **stated interest rate,** also referred to as the face rate or the coupon rate, is the rate contracted as part of the note. The **effective interest rate,** also referred to as the market rate or the effective yield, is the rate used in the market to determine the value of the note—that is, the discount rate used to determine present value.

The present value or exchange price of the note is computed as follows:

ILLUSTRATION 7-8
Present Value of Note—
Stated and Market Rates
the Same

Face value of the note		$10,000
Present value of the principal:		
$10,000 ($p_{\overline{3}|10\%}$) = $10,000 (.75132)	$7,513	
Present value of the interest:		
$1,000 ($P_{\overline{3}|10\%}$) = $1,000 (2.48685)	2,487	
Present value of the note		10,000
Difference		$ –0–

In this case, the present value of the note and its face value are the same, that is, $10,000 because the effective and stated rates of interest are also the same. The receipt of the note is recorded by Bigelow Corp. as follows:

Notes Receivable	10,000	
Cash		10,000

Bigelow Corp. would recognize the interest earned each year as follows:

Cash	1,000	
Interest Revenue		1,000

Note Not Issued at Face Value

Zero-Interest-Bearing

If a zero-interest-bearing note is received solely for cash, its present value is the cash paid to the issuer. Because both the future amount and the present value of the note are known, the interest rate can be computed, i.e., it is implied. The **implicit interest rate** is the rate that equates the cash paid with the amounts receivable in the future. The difference between the future (face) amount and the present value (cash paid) is recorded as a discount or premium and amortized to interest revenue over the life of the note.

To illustrate, Jeremiah Company receives a 3-year, $10,000 zero-interest-bearing note, the present value of which is $7,721.80. The implicit rate that equates the total cash to be received ($10,000 at maturity) to the present value of the future cash flows ($7,721.80) is 9% (the present value of $1 for 3 periods at 9% is $.77218). The time diagram depicting the one cash flow is shown below.

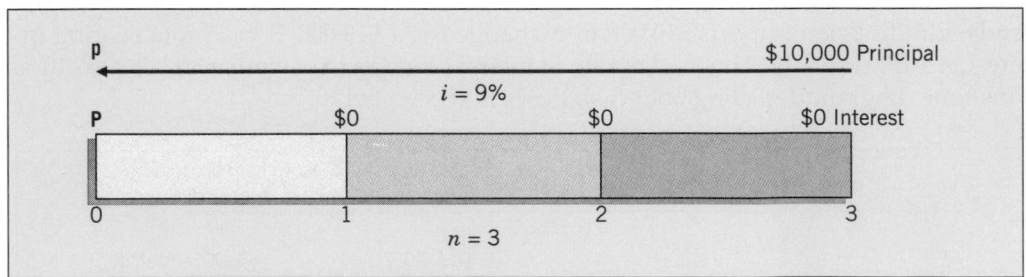

The entry to record the transaction is as follows:

Notes Receivable	10,000.00	
Discount on Notes Receivable ($10,000 − $7,721.80)		2,278.20
Cash		7,721.80

The Discount on Notes Receivable is a valuation account and is reported on the balance sheet as a contra-asset account to notes receivable. The discount is then amortized, and interest revenue is recognized annually using the **effective interest method**. The 3-year discount amortization and interest revenue schedule is shown in Illustration 7-9.

ILLUSTRATION 7-9
**Discount Amortization
Schedule—Effective
Interest Method**

	Cash Received	Interest Revenue	Discount Amortized	Carrying Amount of Note
Schedule of Note Discount Amortization				
Effective Interest Method				
0% Note Discounted at 9%				
Date of issue				$ 7,721.80
End of year 1	$-0-	$ 694.96ᵃ	$ 694.96ᵇ	8,416.76ᶜ
End of year 2	-0-	757.51	757.51	9,174.27
End of year 3	-0-	825.73ᵈ	825.73	10,000.00
	$-0-	$2,278.20	$2,278.20	

ᵃ$7,721.80 × .09 = $694.96
ᵇ$694.96 − 0 = $694.96
ᶜ$7,721.80 + $694.96 = $8,416.76
ᵈ5¢ adjustment to compensate for rounding

Interest revenue at the end of the first year using the effective interest method is recorded as follows:

Discount on Notes Receivable	694.96	
Interest Revenue ($7,721.80 × 9%)		694.96

The amount of the discount, $2,278.20 in this case, represents the revenue to be received from the note over the three years.

Interest-Bearing

Often the stated rate and the effective rate are different. The zero-interest-bearing case above is one example of such a situation.

To illustrate a more common situation, assume that Morgan Corp. lends Marie Co. $10,000 in exchange for a 3-year, $10,000 note bearing interest at 10% annually. The market rate of interest for a note of similar risk is 12%. The time diagram depicting both cash flows is shown below:

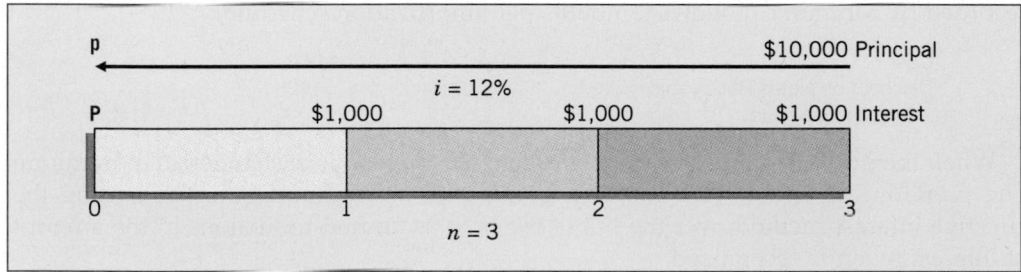

The present value of the two cash flows is computed as follows:

ILLUSTRATION 7-10
**Computation of Present
Value—Effective Rate
Different from Stated
Rate**

Face value of the note		$10,000
Present value of the principal:		
$10,000 ($p_{\overline{3}|12\%}$) = $10,000 (.71178)	$7,118	
Present value of the interest:		
$1,000 ($P_{\overline{3}|12\%}$) = $1,000 (2.40183)	2,402	
Present value of the note		9,520
Difference (Discount)		$ 480

In this case, because the effective rate of interest (12%) is greater than the stated rate (10%), the present value of the note is less than the face value; that is, the note was exchanged at a **discount**. The receipt of the note at a discount is recorded by Morgan as follows:

Notes Receivable	10,000	
Discount on Notes Receivable		480
Cash		9,520

The discount is then amortized and interest revenue is recognized annually using the **effective interest method.** The 3-year discount amortization and interest revenue schedule is shown below:

ILLUSTRATION 7-11
Discount Amortization
Schedule—Effective
Interest Method

	Schedule of Note Discount Amortization Effective Interest Method 10% Note Discounted at 12%			
	Cash Received	Interest Revenue	Discount Amortized	Carrying Amount of Note
Date of issue				$ 9,520
End of year 1	$1,000[a]	$1,142[b]	$142[c]	9,662[d]
End of year 2	1,000	1,159	159	9,821
End of year 3	1,000	1,179	179	10,000
	$3,000	$3,480	$480	

[a]$10,000 × 10% = $1,000 [c]$1,142 − $1,000 = $142
[b]$9,520 × 12% = $1,142 [d]$9,520 + $142 = $9,662

On the date of issue, the note has a present value of $9,520. Its unamortized discount—additional interest revenue to be spread over the 3-year life of the note—is $480.

At the end of year 1, Morgan receives $1,000 in cash. But its interest revenue is $1,142 ($9,520 × 12%). The difference between $1,000 and $1,142 is the amortized discount, $142. The carrying amount of the note is now $9,662 ($9,520 + $142). This process is repeated until the end of year 3.

Receipt of the annual interest and amortization of the discount for the first year are recorded by Morgan as follows (amounts per amortization schedule):

Cash	1,000	
Discount on Notes Receivable	142	
Interest Revenue		1,142

When the present value exceeds the face value, the note is exchanged at a premium. The premium on a note receivable is recorded as a debit and amortized using the effective interest method over the life of the note as annual reductions in the amount of interest revenue recognized.

Special Situations

The note transactions just discussed are the common types of situations encountered in practice. Special situations are as follows:

1. Notes received for cash and other rights.
2. Notes received for property, goods, or services.
3. Imputed interest.

Notes Received for Cash and Other Rights

The lender may also accept a **note in exchange for cash and other rights and privileges.** For example, Ideal Equipment Co. accepts a 5-year, $100,000, zero-interest-bearing note from Outland Steel Corp. plus the right to purchase 10,000 tons of steel at a bargain price in exchange for $100,000 in cash. Assume that the current rate of interest that would be charged on another note without the right to purchase at a bargain is 10%. The acceptance of the note is recorded and the present value of the note is computed as follows:

Notes Receivable	100,000	
Prepaid Purchases	37,908	
Discount on Notes Receivable		37,908*
Cash		100,000

*Present value = $100,000 \times (p_{\overline{5}|10\%}) = \$100,000 \times .62092 = \$62,092$;
Discount = $100,000 - \$62,092 = \$37,908$.

The difference between the $62,092 present value of the note and its maturity value of $100,000 represents implicit interest of $37,908. It is amortized to interest revenue over the 5-year life of the note using the effective interest method. The excess of the $100,000 over the $62,092 represents an asset, Prepaid Purchases. Prepaid Purchases is allocated to purchases or inventory in proportion to the number of tons of steel purchased each year relative to the total 10,000 tons for which a bargain price is available. For example, if 3,000 tons of steel were purchased during the first year of the 5-year bargain period, the following entry would be recorded by Ideal Equipment:

Purchases (Inventory)	11,372	
Prepaid Purchases		11,372
(3,000/10,000 $\times$ \$37,908)		

Note that although prepaid purchases and the discount on notes receivable are both recorded initially at the same amount, $37,908, they are written off differently. Prepaid purchases are written off in the ratio of tons purchased, whereas the discount is amortized using the effective interest method. The value of the right or privilege, in this case the price reduction, aids in determining the interest implicit in the transaction.

Notes Received for Property, Goods, or Services

When a **note is received in exchange for property, goods, or services** in a bargained transaction entered into at arm's length, the stated interest rate is presumed to be fair unless:

1. No interest rate is stated, or

2. The stated interest rate is unreasonable, or

3. The face amount of the note is materially different from the current cash sales price for the same or similar items or from the current market value of the debt instrument.[12]

In these circumstances, the present value of the note is measured by the fair value of the property, goods, or services or by an amount that reasonably approximates the market value of the note.

To illustrate, Oasis Development Co. sold a corner lot to Rusty Pelican as a restaurant site and accepted in exchange a 5-year note having a maturity value of $35,247 and no stated interest rate. The land originally cost Oasis $14,000 and at the date of sale had an appraised fair value of $20,000. Given the criterion above, it is acceptable to use the fair market value of the land, $20,000, as the present value of the note. The entry to record the sale therefore is:

Notes Receivable	35,247	
Discount on Notes Receivable ($35,247 - \$20,000$)		15,247
Land		14,000
Gain on Sale of Land ($20,000 - \$14,000$)		6,000

The discount is amortized to interest revenue over the 5-year life of the note using the effective interest method.

---

[12]"Interest on Receivables and Payables," *Opinions of the Accounting Principles Board No. 21* (New York: AICPA, 1971), par. 12.

Imputed Interest

In note transactions, the effective or real interest rate is either evident or determinable by other factors involved in the exchange, such as the fair market value of what is given or received. But, if the fair value of the property, goods, services, or other rights is not determinable and if the note has no ready market, the problem of determining the present value of the note is more difficult. To estimate the present value of a note under such circumstances, an applicable interest rate that may differ from the stated interest rate must be approximated. This process of interest-rate approximation is called **imputation,** and the resulting interest rate is called an **imputed interest rate.** The imputed interest rate is used to establish the present value of the note by discounting, at that rate, all future receipts (interest and principal) on the note.

> The objective for computing the appropriate interest rate is to approximate the rate which would have resulted if an independent borrower and an independent lender had negotiated a similar transaction under comparable terms and conditions with the option to pay the cash price upon purchase or to give a note for the amount of the purchase which bears the prevailing rate of interest to maturity. The rate used for valuation purposes will normally be at least equal to the rate at which the debtor can obtain financing of a similar nature from other sources at the date of the transaction.[13]

The choice of a rate is affected by the prevailing rates for similar instruments of issuers with similar credit ratings. It is also affected specifically by restrictive covenants, collateral, payment schedule, the existing prime interest rate, etc. Determination of the imputed interest rate is made when the note is received; any subsequent changes in prevailing interest rates are ignored.

To illustrate, assume that on December 31, 1995, Brown Interiors Company rendered architectural services and accepted in exchange a long-term promissory note with a face value of $550,000, a due date of December 31, 2000, and a stated interest rate of 2%, interest receivable at the end of each year. The fair value of the services is not readily determinable, and the note is not readily marketable. Given the circumstances—the maker's credit rating, the absence of collateral, the prime rate, and the prevailing interest rate on the maker's outstanding debt—an 8% interest rate is determined to be appropriate. The time diagram depicting both cash flows is shown below:

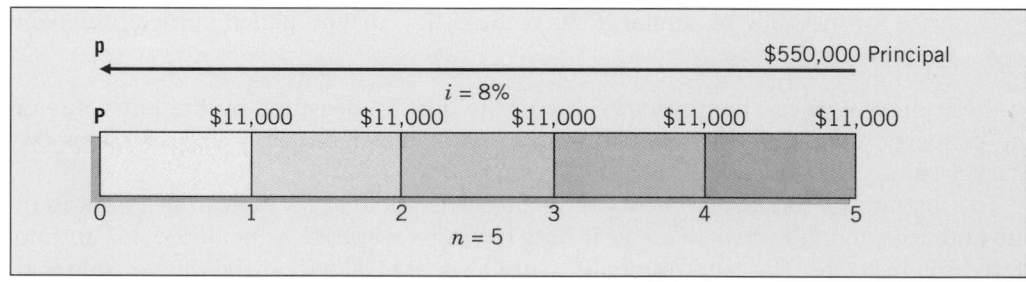

The present value of the note and the imputed fair value of the architectural services are computed as follows:

ILLUSTRATION 7-12
Computation of Present Value—Imputed Interest Rate

Face value of the note		$550,000
Present value of $550,000 due in 5 years		
at 8%—$550,000 ($p_{\overline{5}|8\%}$) = $550,000 × .68058	$374,319	
Present value of $11,000 ($550,000 × .02) payable		
annually for 5 years at 8%—		
$11,000 ($P_{\overline{5}|8\%}$) = $11,000 × 3.99271	43,920	
Present value of the note		418,239
Discount		$131,761

---

[13]Ibid., par. 13.

The value of the services is thus determined to be $418,239, the current value of the note. The receipt of the note in exchange for the services is recorded as follows:

December 31, 1995

Notes Receivable	550,000	
Discount on Notes Receivable		131,761
Revenue from Services		418,239

An amortization schedule similar to Illustration 7-11 is then prepared to help record transactions in future periods.

▶ VALUATION OF NOTES RECEIVABLE

OBJECTIVE 8
Explain accounting issues related to valuation of notes receivable.

Like accounts receivable, short-term notes receivable are recorded and reported at their net realizable value; that is, at their face amount less all necessary allowances. The primary notes receivable allowance account is Allowance for Doubtful Accounts. The computations and estimations involved in valuing short-term notes receivable and in recording bad debt expense and the related allowance are **exactly the same as for trade accounts receivable.** Either a percentage of sales revenue or an analysis of the receivables can be used to estimate the amount of uncollectibles.

Long-term notes receivable, however, pose additional estimation problems. We need only look at the problems our financial institutions, most notably money-center banks, have had in collecting receivables from energy loans, real estate loans, and loans to less-developed countries.[14]

Notes receivable that are not paid at maturity remain notes receivable and are considered notes receivable past due. These defaulted or **dishonored notes** should be separately classified on the balance sheet. If all efforts to collect fail, the note is written off as a loss.

A note receivable is considered **impaired** when it is probable that the creditor will be unable to collect all amounts due (both principal and interest) according to the contractual terms of the loan. In that case, the present value of the expected future cash flows is determined by discounting those flows at the historical effective rate. This present value amount is deducted from the carrying amount of the receivable to measure the loss. Impairments, as well as restructurings, of receivables and debts are discussed and illustrated in considerable detail in Chapter 14, Appendix A.

▶ DISPOSITION OF ACCOUNTS AND NOTES RECEIVABLE

OBJECTIVE 9
Explain accounting issues related to disposition of accounts and notes receivable.

In the normal course of events, accounts and notes receivable are collected when due and removed from the books. However, as credit sales and receivables have grown in size and significance, this "normal course of events" has evolved. **In order to accelerate the receipt of cash from receivables, the owner may transfer accounts or notes receivables to another company for cash.**

There are various reasons for this early transfer. First, for competitive reasons, providing sales financing for customers is virtually mandatory in many industries. In the sale of durable goods, such as automobiles, trucks, industrial and farm equipment, computers, and appliances, a large majority of sales are on an installment contract basis. Many major companies in these industries have created wholly-owned subsidiaries specializing in receivables financing. General Motors Corp. has General Motors Acceptance Corp. (GMAC), Sears has Sears Roebuck Acceptance Corp. (SRAC), and Chrysler Corporation has Chrysler Finance Corporation (CFC).

---

[14]A wise person once said that a bank lending money to a Third World country is like lending money to one's children: you should never expect to get the interest back, let alone the principal.

Second, the **holder** may sell receivables because money is tight and access to normal credit is not available or is prohibitively expensive. Also, a firm may have to sell its receivables, instead of borrowing to avoid violating existing lending agreements.

Finally, billing and collection of receivables are often time-consuming and costly. Credit card companies such as MasterCard, VISA, American Express, Diners Club, and others provide merchants with immediate cash.

Conversely, some **purchasers** of receivables buy them to obtain the legal protection of ownership rights afforded a purchaser of assets versus the lesser rights afforded a secured creditor. In addition, banks and other lending institutions may be forced to purchase receivables because of legal lending limits; that is, they cannot make any additional loans but they can buy receivables and charge a fee for this service.

The transfer of receivables to a third party for cash is generally accomplished in one of two ways:[15]

1. Assignment of receivables (pledging a security interest).
2. Sale (factoring) of receivables.

ASSIGNMENT OF ACCOUNTS RECEIVABLE

The owner of the receivables (the assignor) borrows cash from a lender (the assignee) by writing a promissory note designating or **pledging** the receivables as collateral. If the note is not paid when due, the assignee has the right to convert the collateral to cash, that is, to collect the receivables.

General Assignment

If the assignment is general, all receivables serve as collateral for the note. New receivables can be substituted for the ones collected. To illustrate, Machlin Motor Company assigns its accounts receivable to First City Finance Company as collateral for a loan of $946,000. The entry to record this transaction is as follows:

Cash	946,000	
Notes Payable		946,000

No special entries are made to the receivable accounts to record the assignment. Information concerning assigned receivables is disclosed in a note or in a parenthetical explanation. To illustrate, Miller Technology & Communications, Inc., reported its general assignment in the following manner:

Miller Technology & Communications, Inc.
Current Assets
Trade accounts and other receivables, net (Note 4) $3,294,888
Note 4:   Notes Payable. Under the terms of a bank credit agreement, the Corporation may borrow up to 90% of eligible trade accounts receivable and 60% of certain inventories. The principal amount is due in one year, with interest payable monthly at prime plus 1%. The Corporation's trade accounts, other receivables, and inventories are pledged as collateral. The maximum that may be borrowed under this agreement is $1,250,000.

Specific Assignment

In a specific assignment, the borrower and lender enter into an agreement as to (1) who receives the collections, (2) the finance charges (which are in addition to the interest on the note), (3) the specific accounts that serve as security, and (4) notification or non-

---

[15]*Accounting Trends and Techniques—1993* reports that of the 600 companies surveyed, 39 assigned receivables and 75 sold their receivables.

notification of account debtors. Collections on the assigned accounts are generally made by the assignor.

To illustrate, on March 1, 1995, Howat Mills, Inc., assigns $700,000 of its accounts receivable to Citizens Bank as collateral for a $500,000 note. Howat Mills will continue to collect the accounts receivable; the account debtors are not notified of the assignment. This process is referred to as "transferred on a non-notification basis." Citizens Bank assesses a finance charge of 1% of the accounts receivable assigned and interest on the note of 12%. Settlement by Howat Mills to the bank is made monthly for all cash collected on the assigned receivables.

ILLUSTRATION 7-13
Entries for Assignment of Specific Receivables

Howat Mills, Inc.			Citizens Bank		
Assignment of accounts receivable and issuance of note on March 1, 1995:					
Cash	493,000		Notes Receivable	500,000	
Finance Charge	7,000*		Finance Revenue		7,000*
Accounts Rec. Assigned	700,000		Cash		493,000
Notes Payable		500,000			
Accounts Receivable		700,000	*(1% × $700,000)		
Collection in March of $440,000 of assigned accounts less cash discounts of $6,000. In addition, sales returns of $14,000 were received:					
Cash	434,000				
Sales Discounts	6,000				
Sales Returns	14,000		(No entry)		
Accts. Rec. Assigned		454,000			
($440,000 + $14,000 = $454,000)					
Remitted March collections plus accrued interest to the bank on April 1:					
Interest Expense	5,000*		Cash	439,000	
Notes Payable	434,000		Interest Revenue		5,000*
Cash		439,000	Notes Receivable		434,000
*($500,000 × .12 × 1/12)					
Collection in April of the balance of assigned accounts less $2,000 written off as uncollectible:					
Cash	244,000				
Allow. for Doubtful Accts.	2,000		(No entry)		
Accts. Rec. Assigned		246,000*			
*($700,000 − $454,000)					
Remitted the balance due of $66,000 ($500,000 − $434,000) on the note plus interest on May 1:					
Interest Expense	660*		Cash	66,660	
Notes Payable	66,000		Interest Revenue		660*
Cash		66,660	Notes Receivable		66,000
*($66,000 × .12 × 1/12)					

Receivables assigned are identified by recording them in an Accounts Receivable Assigned account. An alternative is to indicate in the notes to the financial statements the accounts receivable assigned. In addition to recording the collection of receivables, all discounts, returns and allowances, and bad debts must be recognized. Each month the proceeds from the collection of the assigned accounts receivable are used to retire the note obligation. In addition, interest on the note is paid.

If material, specifically assigned accounts receivable should be reported in Howat Mills' financial statements as a separate asset account. Its equity in the assigned accounts should be disclosed. For instance, Howat Mills, Inc., has equity of $200,000 ($700,000 − $500,000) in its assigned receivables at March 1.

SALES (TRANSFERS) OF ACCOUNTS AND NOTES RECEIVABLE

Sales of receivables have increased substantially in recent years. A common type is a sale to a factor. **Factors** are finance companies or banks that buy receivables from businesses for a fee and then collect the remittances directly from the customers. **Factoring receivables** is traditionally associated with the textile, apparel, footwear, furniture, and home furnishing industries.[16]

A recent phenomenon in the sale (transfer) of receivables is "securitization." **Securitization** takes a pool of assets such as credit card receivables, mortgage receivables, or car loan receivables and sells shares in these pools of interest and principal payments (in effect, creating securities backed by these pools of assets). Virtually every asset with a payment stream and a long-term payment history is a candidate for securitization.

The differences between factoring and securitization are that factoring usually involves sale to only one company, fees are high, the quality of the receivables is low, and the seller afterward does not service the receivable. In a securitization, many investors are involved, margins are tight, the receivables are of high quality, and the seller usually continues to service the receivable.

For an illustration of a factoring arrangement, see Illustration 7-14.

ILLUSTRATION 7-14
Basic Procedures in
Factoring

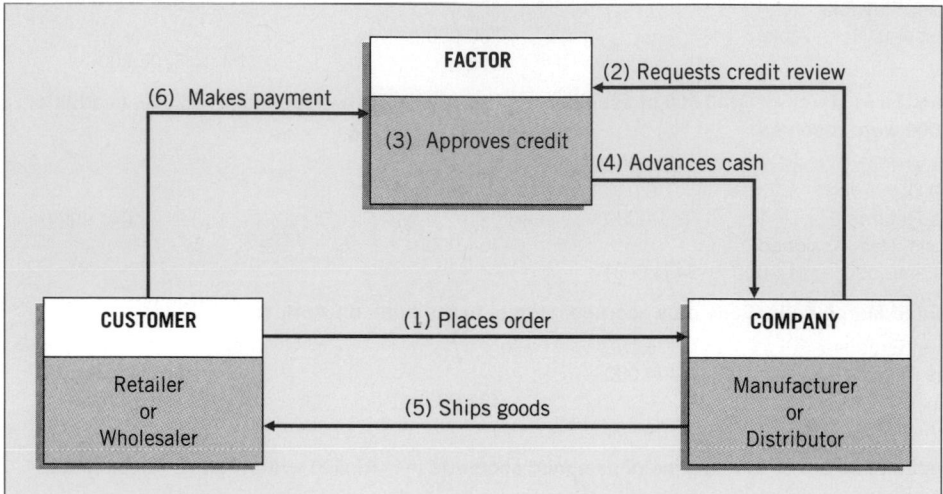

In either a factoring or a securitization transaction, receivables are sold on either a **without recourse** or a **with recourse** basis.[17]

Transfer without Recourse

When receivables are sold **without recourse,** the purchaser assumes the risk of collectibility and absorbs any credit losses. The transfer of accounts receivable in a nonrecourse transaction is an outright sale of the receivables both in form (transfer of title) and substance (transfer of the risk and reward). In nonrecourse transactions, as in any sale of assets, Cash is debited for the proceeds. Accounts Receivable is credited for the face value of the receivables. The difference, reduced by any provision for probable

---

[16]Credit cards like MasterCard and VISA are a type of factoring arrangement. Typically the purchaser of the receivable charges a ¾% to 1½% commission of the receivables purchased (the commission is 4–5% for credit card factoring).

[17]**Recourse** is the right of a transferee of receivables to receive payment from the transferor of those receivables for (1) failure of the debtors to pay when due, (2) the effects of prepayments, or (3) adjustments resulting from defects in the eligibility of the transferred receivables. See "Reporting by Transferors for Transfers of Receivables with Recourse," *Statement of Financial Accounting Standards No. 77* (Stamford, Conn.: FASB, 1983), p. 7.

adjustments (discounts, returns, allowances, etc.), is recognized as a Loss on the Sale of Receivables. The seller uses a Due from Factor account (reported as a receivable) to account for the proceeds retained by the factor to cover probable sales discounts, sales returns, and sales allowances.

To illustrate, Crest Textiles, Inc. factors $500,000 of accounts receivable with Commercial Factors, Inc., on a **without recourse** basis. The receivable records are transferred to Commercial Factors, Inc., which will receive the collections. Commercial Factors assesses a finance charge of 3% of the amount of accounts receivable and retains an amount equal to 5% of the accounts receivable. The journal entries for both Crest Textiles and Commercial Factors for the receivables transferred without recourse are as follows:

ILLUSTRATION 7-15
Entries for Sale of Receivables Without Recourse

Crest Textiles, Inc.			Commercial Factors, Inc.		
Cash	460,000		Accounts (Notes) Receivable	500,000	
Due from Factor	25,000*		Due to Crest Textiles		25,000
Loss on Sale of Rec.	15,000**		Financing Revenue		15,000
Accounts (Notes) Receivable		500,000	Cash		460,000
*(5% × $500,000)					
**(3% × $500,000)					

In recognition of the sale of receivables, Crest Textiles records a loss of $15,000. The factor's net income will be the difference between the financing revenue of $15,000 and the amount of any uncollectible receivables.

A comprehensive illustration of all the entries involved in the sale, collection, and final settlement of these receivables for both Crest Textiles and Commercial Factors is presented in Appendix 7–B, page 351.

Transfer with Recourse

If receivables are sold **with recourse,** the seller guarantees payment to the purchaser in the event the debtor fails to pay. With this method, many contend that a sale has not occurred because the transferor retains the same risk of collection after the deal as before. Others disagree, noting that most of the risks and benefits have transferred and therefore a sale should be recorded.

The question is: Is it a **sale transaction** in which a gain or loss should be recognized immediately? Or, is the sale of receivables with recourse a **borrowing transaction,** in which the difference between the proceeds and the receivables is a financing cost (interest) that should be amortized over the term of the receivables?

The FASB requires that a transfer of receivables with recourse be accounted for as a sale, recognizing any gain or loss, if **all three** of the following conditions are met:[18]

1. The transferor surrenders control of the future economic benefits of the receivables.

2. The transferor's obligation under the recourse provisions can be reasonably estimated.

3. The transferee cannot require the transferor to repurchase the receivables.[19]

---

[18]Ibid., par. 5.

[19]The transferor's ability to initiate repurchase, however, does not violate a sale accounting. For example, because Motorola wishes to maintain long-term service relationships with its customers, it reserves the unlimited right to repurchase receivables contracts that it has sold to its factor, Associates Capital Services Corporation. This arrangement allows Motorola to restructure existing receivables contracts, to accept customer prepayments, and to trade in or reconfigure customer products and still account for the receivables transfer as a sale.

If the transfer with recourse does not meet these three conditions, the proceeds from the transfer of the receivables is accounted for as a borrowing. That is, instead of crediting receivables, a current liability titled Liability on Transferred Accounts (Notes) Receivable is credited.

The journal entries for Crest Textiles treating the transfer of receivables **with recourse** both as a sale and as a borrowing are as follows:

Treated as a Sale by Crest			Treated as a Borrowing by Crest		
Cash	460,000		Cash	460,000	
Due from Factor	25,000*		Due from Factor	25,000	
Loss on Sale of Rec.	15,000**		Discount on Transferred		
Accounts (Notes) Receivable		500,000	Accts. (Notes) Rec.	15,000	
			Liability on Transferred		
			Accts. (Notes) Rec.		500,000
*(5% × $500,000)					
**(3% × $500,000)					

ILLUSTRATION 7-16
Entries by Crest Textiles, Inc., for Receivables Transferred With Recourse

Note two differences: First, when the transaction is classified as a borrowing, Crest Textiles recognizes a liability instead of crediting Accounts (Notes) Receivable. Second, instead of recording a loss of $15,000 on the transfer, Crest Textiles records a discount under the borrowing of $15,000, which is amortized to interest expense over the borrowing period.

The rules of accounting for sales of receivable with and without recourse are illustrated below.

ILLUSTRATION 7-17
Accounting for Sales of Receivables With and Without Recourse

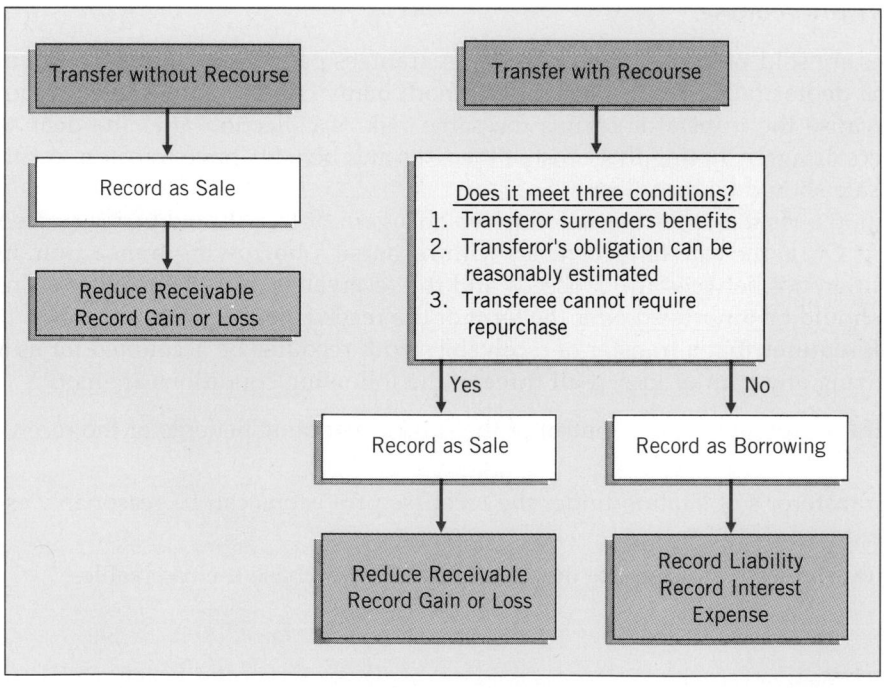

A comprehensive illustration of all Crest's entries involved in the transfer, collection, and final settlement, both as a sale and as a borrowing, is presented in Appendix 7–B, page 351.

▶ CONCEPTUAL ISSUES RELATED TO THE TRANSFER OF RECEIVABLES

As indicated from the chapter discussion, the transfer of accounts or notes receivables to a third party for cash takes one of three forms.[20]

1. One form is to borrow from a third party and **assign or pledge the receivables** as collateral. Both the form of this transaction and its substance suggest that it be accounted for and reported as a **borrowing.**

2. A second form is to **transfer the receivables without recourse** to a third party in exchange for cash. Both the form of this transaction and its substance suggest that it be accounted for and reported as a **sale.**

3. A third form is to **transfer the receivables with recourse** to a third party in exchange for cash. In this case the form of the transaction may either be a sale or a borrowing, depending on the facts.

At one extreme are outright sales of assets. At the other extreme are borrowings collateralized by assets (pledges). In between are sales of assets with recourse. The transactions at the two extremes are easy to account for—the ones in the middle create accounting problems.

Regarding the in-between situation, the authors believe that the proceeds from the transfer of receivables with recourse should be reported as a liability. The transfer should not be treated as a sale of receivables unless and until both the future economic benefits embodied in the receivables and the related inherent risks of uncollectibility are transferred.[21] The transferor's retention of credit risk through the recourse provision generally leaves the transferor in a position undistinguishable from that of any other borrower. We believe, therefore, that the FASB's position often legitimatizes what is actually a form of **"off-balance-sheet financing."**[22]

▶ BALANCE SHEET PRESENTATION OF ACCOUNTS AND NOTES RECEIVABLE

The general rules in classifying the receivable section are: (1) segregate the different types of receivables that an enterprise possesses, if material; (2) insure that the valuation accounts are appropriately offset against the proper receivable accounts; (3) determine that receivables classified in the current assets section will be converted into cash within the year or the operating cycle, whichever is longer; (4) disclose any loss contingencies

INTERNATIONAL INSIGHT

Holding receivables payable in a foreign currency represents risk in that the exchange rate may move against the company, causing a decrease in the amount collected in terms of U.S. dollars. Companies engaged in cross-border transactions often "hedge" these receivables by buying contracts to exchange currencies at specified amounts at future dates.

---

[20]Understanding these transactions is made more difficult by the inconsistent use of terms to describe these transactions in practice. When you encounter such transactions in practice, we recommend that you attempt to classify them in accordance with their basic nature as one of the foregoing three types.

[21]See for example Eugene A. Imhoff, "Asset Securitizations: Economic Effects and Accounting Issues," *Accounting Horizons,* March, 1992, and Raymond E. Perry "Accounting for Securitizations," *Accounting Horizons,* September 1993, for interesting ideas in determining when ownership risks and rewards transfer.

[22]We are particularly distressed by advertisements in *The Wall Street Journal,* which state "Cash without a liability"—it sounds like the answer to every treasurer's dream, or "Meet your short-term needs off the balance sheet"—suggesting the use of the transfer of receivables approach. Standards need to be tightened in this area.

that exist on the receivables; (5) disclose any receivables assigned or pledged as collateral; (6) disclose all significant concentrations of credit risk arising from receivables.[23]

The asset sections of Colton Corporation's balance sheet shown below illustrate many of the disclosures required for receivables:

ILLUSTRATION 7-18
Disclosure of Receivables

Colton Corporation PARTIAL BALANCE SHEET As of December 31, 1995			
Current assets			
Cash and cash equivalents			$ 1,870,250
Accounts receivable (Note 2)	$8,977,673		
Less allowance for doubtful accounts	500,226		
	8,477,447		
Advances to subsidiaries due 9/30/96	2,090,000		
Notes receivable—trade (Note 2)	1,532,000		
Federal income taxes refundable	146,704		
Dividends and interest receivable	75,500		
Other receivables and claims (including debit balances			
in accounts payable)	174,620	12,496,271	
Total current assets		14,366,521	
Noncurrent receivables			
Notes receivable from officers and key employees		376,090	
Claims receivable (litigation settlement to be collected			
over four years)		585,000	

Note 2: Accounts and Notes Receivable

In November 1995, the Company arranged with a finance company to refinance a part of its indebtedness. The loan is evidenced by a 12% note payable. The note is payable on demand and is secured by substantially all the accounts receivable.

In May 1995, the Company entered into an agreement with a financial institution whereby the Company had the right to sell designated receivables, with recourse, not to exceed $3,000,000 at any time. During the period May 1 through September 30, 1995, proceeds totaling $2,480,000 were received from such sales. Losses totaling $202,640 were recognized on these sales during 1995. As of December 31, 1995, $171,500 of transferred receivables remain uncollected.

In several countries outside the United States, notes receivable are sold with recourse. The contingent liability under such arrangements amounted to $751,000 at December 31, 1995.

---

[23]Concentrations of credit risk exist when receivables have common characteristics that may affect their collection. These common characteristics might be companies in the same industry or same region of the country. For example, financial statements users want to know if a substantial amount of receivables are with defense contractors or with companies in the Middle East. No numerical guidelines are provided as to what is meant by a "concentration of credit risk." When a concentration is identified, three items should be disclosed: (1) information on the characteristic that determines the concentration should be identified, (2) the amount of loss that could occur upon nonperformance, and (3) information on any collateral related to the receivable. "Disclosure of Information About Financial Instruments with Off-Balance-Sheet Risk and Financial Instruments with Concentrations of Credit Risk," *Statement of Financial Accounting Standards No. 105* (Norwalk, CT: FASB, 1990).

▶ SUMMARY OF LEARNING OBJECTIVES ◀

1. **Identify items considered cash.**   To be reported as "cash," an asset must be readily available for the payment of current obligations and free from contractual restrictions that limit its use in satisfying debts. Cash consists of coin, currency, and available funds on deposit at the bank. Negotiable instruments such as money orders, certified checks, cashier's checks, personal checks, and bank drafts are also viewed as cash. Savings accounts are usually classified as cash.

2. **Explain common techniques employed to control cash.**   The common techniques employed to control cash are: (1) *Using bank accounts:* a company can vary the number and location of banks and the types of accounts to obtain desired control objectives. (2) *Electronic funds transfer (EFT):* Electronic funds transfer uses wire, telephone, telegraph, computer, satellite, or other electronic device to make instantaneous transfers of funds. (3) *The imprest petty cash system:* It may be impractical to require small amounts of various expenses be paid by check, yet some control over them is important. (4) *Physical protection of cash balances:* Adequate control of receipts and disbursements is a part of the protection of cash balances. Every effort should be made to minimize the cash on hand in the office. (5) *Reconciliation of bank balances:* Cash on deposit is not available for count and is proved by preparing a bank reconciliation.

3. **Indicate how cash and related items are reported.**   Cash is reported as a current asset in the balance sheet. The reporting of other related items are: (1) *Restricted cash:* The SEC recommends that legally restricted deposits held as compensating balances against short-term borrowing be stated separately among the "cash and cash equivalent items" in Current Assets. Restricted deposits held against long-term borrowing arrangements should be separately classified as noncurrent assets in either the Investments or Other assets sections. (2) *Bank overdrafts:* They should be reported in the current liabilities section and are usually added to the amount reported as accounts payable. If material, these items should be separately disclosed either on the face of the balance sheet or in the related notes. (3) *Cash equivalents:* This item is often reported together with cash as "cash and cash equivalents."

4. **Define receivables and identify the different types of receivables.**   Receivables are claims held against customers and others for money, goods, or services. The receivables are classified into three types: (1) current or noncurrent; (2) trade or nontrade; (3) accounts receivable or notes receivable.

5. **Explain accounting issues related to recognition of accounts receivable.**   Two issues that may complicate the measurement of accounts receivable are: (1) The availability of discounts (trade and cash discounts) and (2) the length of time between the sale and the payment due dates (the interest element).

    Ideally, receivables should be measured in terms of their present value—that is, the discounted value of the cash to be received in the future. The profession specifically excludes from the present value considerations receivables arising from normal business transactions that are due in customary trade terms within approximately one year.

6. **Explain accounting issues related to valuation of accounts receivable.**   Short-term receivables are valued and reported at net realizable value—the net amount expected to be received in cash, which is not necessarily the amount legally receivable. Determining net realizable value requires an estimation of both uncollectible receivables and any returns or allowances.

7. **Explain accounting issues related to recognition of notes receivable.** Short-term notes are recorded at face value. Long-term notes receivable are recorded at the present value of the cash expected to be collected. When the interest stated on an interest-bearing note is equal to the effective (market) rate of interest, the note sells at face value. When the stated rate is different from the effective rate, either a discount or premium is recorded.

8. **Explain accounting issues related to valuation of notes receivable.** Like accounts receivable, short-term notes receivable are recorded and reported at their net realizable value. The same is also true of long-term receivables. Special issues relate to impairments and notes receivable past due.

9. **Explain accounting issues related to disposition of accounts and notes receivable.** To accelerate the receipt of cash from receivables, the owner may transfer the receivables to another company for cash. The transfer of receivables to a third party for cash may be accomplished in one of two ways: (1) *Assignment of receivables:* The owner of the receivables borrows cash from a lender by writing a promissory note pledging the receivables as collateral. (2) *Sale (factoring) of receivables:* Factors are finance companies or banks that buy receivables from businesses and then collect the remittances directly from the customers. Receivables are sold on either a with recourse or a without recourse basis.

APPENDIX 7-A

FOUR-COLUMN
BANK RECONCILIATION

▶ RECONCILIATION OF RECEIPTS AND DISBURSEMENTS

OBJECTIVE 10

After studying Appendix 7-A, you should be able to: Prepare a proof of cash (four-column bank reconciliation).

In addition to the form presented in the body of the chapter, another form of reconciliation is frequently used by auditors (and typically illustrated in auditing textbooks). That is the so-called **proof of cash** or **four-column bank reconciliation.** It is an expanded version of the bank reconciliation shown in Illustration 7-2.

The proof-of-cash form of reconciliation is actually four reconciliations in one (see Illustration 7A-1):

1. Reconciliation of the **beginning-of-the-period cash balances** per the bank statement and the books (first column).

2. Reconciliation of the **current period cash receipts** (deposits) per the bank statement to receipts recorded in the books (second column).

3. Reconciliation of the **current period cash disbursements** per the bank statement to disbursements recorded in the books (third column).

4. Reconciliation of the **end-of-the-period cash balances** per the bank statement and the books (fourth column).

The top row ("Per bank statement") is a summary of transactions for the period as taken from the bank statement. The beginning and ending bank balances are shown on

Nugget Mining Company Proof of Cash for November 1995 Denver National Bank—Checking Account				
	Balance October 31	November		Balance November 30
		Receipts	Disbursements	
Per bank statement	$17,520	$96,450	$91,780	$22,190
Deposits in transit				
at October 31	4,200	(4,200)		
at November 30		3,680		3,680
Outstanding checks				
at October 31	(3,700)		(3,700)	
at November 30			5,001	(5,001)
Bank error—incorrect check				
charged by bank			(175)	175
Correct amounts	$18,020	$95,930	$92,906	$21,044
Per books	$18,020	$95,330	$92,848	$20,502
Interest collected by bank		600		600
Error in recording check #7322			(180)	180
Unrecorded service charges				
at November 30			18	(18)
NSF check returned			220	(220)
Correct amounts	$18,020	$95,930	$92,906	$21,044

ILLUSTRATION 7A-1
Four-column Bank
Reconciliation—Bank
and Book Balance to
Corrected Balance Form

the bank statement as are the bank receipts (as shown in the "deposits" column) and the bank disbursements (as shown in the "charges" or "checks cashed" column).

The "Per books" line is a summary of the cash transactions as recorded in the books. These totals should be taken directly from the books, preferably from the Cash account itself, which should, of course, show receipts and disbursements as debit and credit entries and the beginning and ending cash balances.

The left-hand and right-hand columns are simply **end-of-the-prior-period** and **end-of-the-current-period** reconciliations, the preparation of which was illustrated on page 321. The two center columns, receipts and disbursements, tie the left-hand column and right-hand column reconciliations together. With few exceptions, the amounts needed to complete these center columns may be found in the figures included in either the top or bottom rows or in the left- and right-hand columns; no new data need be added.[1]

The four-column proof of cash is preferred by auditors as a means of identifying all differences between the books and the bank statement during the period covered by the reconciliation. It is generally prepared by auditors when a company has weak internal control over cash; it assists in identifying unauthorized and unrecorded transfers of cash.

To illustrate the four-column reconciliation, the data provided for the Nugget Mining Company at November 30 in Illustration 7-2 will be used, along with the following information:

1. The cash balance as of October 31, 1995, per the bank statement (the beginning of November balance) was $17,520.

2. The cash balance as of October 31, 1995, per Nugget's books was $18,020.

---

[1] An exception would be a customer's check deposited, returned NSF, and redeposited without entry in the same period. In this situation, receipts and disbursements per bank would be higher than the receipts and disbursements per books. Deposits would have been reported twice in the bank statement but only recorded once for books' purposes. Also, the bank would have shown a disbursement when the check bounced. No disbursement has been recorded in the accounting records.

3. The total cash receipts (deposits) per the November bank statement are $96,450. These receipts include a deposit in transit of $4,200 at October 31.

4. The total cash receipts per Nugget's books during November are $95,330.

5. The total cash disbursements per the bank statement for November are $91,780. These disbursements include $3,700 of checks outstanding at October 31.

6. The total cash disbursements per the books during November are $92,848.

The completed reconciliation, reconciling to the corrected balance, is shown in Illustration 7A-1.

An alternative procedure for preparing a proof-of-cash reconciliation involves reconciling from the bank balance to the book balance rather than reconciling both amounts to a correct cash balance. This alternative is shown in Illustration 7A-2.

ILLUSTRATION 7A-2
Four-column Bank
Reconciliation—Bank to
Book Form

Nugget Mining Company
Proof of Cash for November 1995
Denver National Bank—Checking Account

	Balance October 31	November Receipts	November Disbursements	Balance November 30
Per bank statement	$17,520	$96,450	$91,780	$22,190
Deposits in transit				
at October 31	4,200	(4,200)		
at November 30		3,680		3,680
Outstanding checks				
at October 31	(3,700)		(3,700)	
at November 30			5,001	(5,001)
Bank error—incorrect check			(175)	175
Interest collected by bank		(600)		(600)
Error per books—check #7322			180	(180)
Unrecorded service charges				
at November 30			(18)	18
NSF check returned by bank			(220)	220
Per books	$18,020	$95,330	$92,848	$20,502

The "bank to book" reconciliation form in Illustration 7A-2 is generally illustrated in auditing textbooks. Auditors frequently use this form because their main objective is to identify all of the items that make up the difference between the bank's records and the depositor's records. Preparation of the adjusting entries is secondary. This form is usually more difficult to prepare because each of the reconciling items must be analyzed carefully to determine whether an addition or subtraction from the top of the column "Per bank" amount is the correct reconciliation treatment.

KEY TERMS

proof of cash, 348

▶ SUMMARY OF LEARNING OBJECTIVE FOR APPENDIX 7-A ◀

10. **Prepare a proof of cash (four-column bank reconciliation).** The proof of cash reconciles four items per the bank statement to four items per the company's books: (1) the beginning-of-the-period cash balances, (2) the current period cash receipts, (3) the current period cash disbursements, and (4) the end-of-the-period cash balances.

APPENDIX 7-B

COMPREHENSIVE ILLUSTRATIONS OF TRANSFERS OF RECEIVABLES

In order to free the foregoing chapter from the complexities and details of recording all the journal entries related to the transfer, collection, and final settlement of transferred receivables, we are presenting that coverage in this appendix. The first illustration (7B-1) below is for the transfer of receivables **without recourse** and the second illustration (7B-2) is for the transfer of receivables **with recourse,** both as a **sale** transaction and as a **borrowing** transaction.

OBJECTIVE 11

After studying Appendix 7-B, you should be able to: Prepare entries for the transfer of receivables with and without recourse in a complex situation.

▶ TRANSFER OF RECEIVABLES WITHOUT RECOURSE

Crest Textiles, Inc., factors $500,000 of accounts receivable with Commercial Factors, Inc., on a **without recourse** basis. On May 1, the receivable records are transferred to Commercial Factors, Inc., which will receive the collections. Commercial Factors assesses a finance charge of 3% and retains an amount equal to 5% of the accounts receivable. Crest Textiles handles returned goods, claims for defective goods (allowances), and disputes concerning shipments. Crest has not recorded any bad debt expense relative to these receivables. In the process of collecting the cash, Commercial Factors acknowledges sales discounts but charges the cost of such discounts to Crest Textiles by debiting the Due to Crest Textiles account. Credit losses (uncollectible accounts) are absorbed by Commercial Factors, and on the basis of an analysis of the accounts purchased, Commercial Factors allows $4,100 for uncollectible accounts.

Crest Textiles, Inc.			Commercial Factors, Inc.		
Sale of accounts receivable without recourse on May 1:					
Cash	460,000		Accounts Receivable	500,000	
Due from Factor	25,000*		Due to Crest Textiles		25,000
Loss on Sale of Rec.	15,000**		Financing Revenue		15,000
Accounts Receivable		500,000	Cash		460,000
			Bad Debt Expense	4,100	
			Allow. for Doubtful		
			Accounts		4,100

*(5% × $500,000)
**(3% × $500,000)

Transactions in May and June—collections of $483,800 by factor; sales returns and allowances of $9,500; sales discounts taken of $2,600; and uncollectibles of $4,100 are written off by the factor.

Sales Ret. and Allow.	9,500		Cash	483,800	
Sales Discounts	2,600		Due to Crest Textiles	12,100	
Due from Factor		12,100	Accounts Receivable		495,900
			Allow. for Doubtful		
			Accounts	4,100	
			Accounts Receivable		4,100

Final settlement between Crest Textiles and Commercial Factors:

Cash	12,900		Due to Crest Textiles	12,900	
Due from Factor		12,900	Cash		12,900
($25,000 − $9,500 − $2,600)					

**ILLUSTRATION 7B-1
Entries for Factored Receivables Without Recourse**

Note from the entries in this illustration that the factor's income is the difference between the financing revenue of $15,000 and the bad debt expense of $4,100. As indicated earlier, the factor absorbs the loss from uncollectibles in a without recourse transfer of receivables. Crest Textiles absorbs the cost of sales discounts and sales returns and allowances.

▶ TRANSFER OF RECEIVABLES WITH RECOURSE

To illustrate the differences between the two methods of accounting for a transfer of receivables with recourse—in one case a sale and in another case a borrowing—we will use the same data previously used in the Crest Textiles/Commercial Factors illustration. (We have chosen to use the same data for purposes of comparability even though the situations in real life would dictate different rates, risks, etc.) One different piece of information is Crest's estimate that $4,100 of the accounts transferred to Commercial Factors will not be paid by the debtors. The entries for both a sale and a borrowing by Crest Textiles appear below.

ILLUSTRATION 7B-2
Entries for Factored Receivables With Recourse

Crest Textiles, Inc.

Treated as a Sale by Crest			Treated as a Borrowing by Crest		
Transfer of accounts receivable on May 1:					
Cash	460,000		Cash	460,000	
Due from Factor	25,000*		Due from Factor	25,000*	
Loss on Sale of Rec.	15,000**		Discount on Transferred		
Accounts Receivable		500,000	Accts. Rec.	15,000**	
			Liability on Transferred		
			Accts. Rec.		500,000
*(5% × $500,000)					
**(3% × $500,000)					
Recognition of doubtful accounts on May 1:					
Bad Debt Expense	4,100		Bad Debt Expense	4,100	
Due from Factor		4,100	Allow. for Doubtful		
			Accounts		4,100

Transactions in May and June—collections of $483,800 by the factor; sales returns and allowances of $9,500; sales discounts taken of $2,600; and uncollectibles of $4,100 materialize:

Sales Ret. and Allow.	9,500		Same entry.		
Sales Discounts	2,600				
Due from Factor		12,100			
			Allow. for Doubtful Accts.	4,100	
			Due from Factor		4,100
			Liability on Transferred		
			Accts. Rec.	500,000	
			Accounts Receivable		500,000
			($483,800 + $9,500 + $2,600 + $4,100)		
			Interest Expense	15,000	
			Discount on Trans-		
			ferred Accts. Rec.		15,000

Final settlement between Crest Textiles and the factor:

Cash	8,800		Same entry.		
Due from Factor		8,800*			
*($25,000 − $9,500 − $2,600 − $4,100)					

First, note that in the with recourse borrowing example Crest Textiles credited a liability on May 1 instead of crediting Accounts Receivable. Second, in both with-recourse cases Crest Textiles reimburses the factor for the $4,100 of uncollectible accounts and records the bad debt expense on its books. In the without recourse illustration shown in Illustration 7B-1, Commercial Factors absorbed the loss due to uncollectibility.

However, because accounts receivable are removed from the books when the transfer is treated as a sale, it is meaningless to credit an allowance account when recognizing the bad debt expense. Therefore, Crest immediately credited Due from Factor for the $4,100, thereby crediting the factor for the bad debts anticipated. Third, Crest recognized interest expense of $15,000 over the two months the receivables were outstanding (borrowing situation) instead of recording the loss on sale of $15,000 at May 1.

▶ SUMMARY OF LEARNING OBJECTIVE FOR APPENDIX 7-B ◀

11. **Prepare entries for the transfer of receivables with and without recourse in a complex situation.** These factoring transactions are complicated by the inclusion of finance charges, retainers for returns and allowances, and bad debts. Transfers of receivables with recourse may, under differing conditions, be treated as a sale or as a borrowing.

Note: All **asterisked** Questions, Exercises, Problems, and Cases relate to material contained in the appendix to each chapter.

QUESTIONS

1. What may be included under the heading of "cash"?

2. In what accounts should the following items be classified?
   (a) Coins and currency.
   (b) U.S. Treasury (Government) bonds.
   (c) Certificate of deposit.
   (d) Cash in a bank that is in receivership.
   (e) NSF check (returned with bank statement).
   (f) Deposit in foreign bank (exchangeability limited).
   (g) Postdated checks.
   (h) Cash (to be used for retirement of long-term bonds).
   (i) Deposits in transit.
   (j) Three shares of General Motors stock (intention is to sell in one year or less).
   (k) Savings and checking accounts.
   (l) Petty cash.
   (m) Stamps.
   (n) Travel advances.

3. Distinguish among the following: (1) a general checking account, (2) an imprest bank account, and (3) a lockbox account.

4. What is electronic funds transfer, and what effect is its widespread use likely to have on record keeping and accounting?

5. Define a "compensating balance." How should a compensating balance be reported?

6. Chris Spear Inc. reported in a recent annual report "Restricted cash for debt redemption." What section of the balance sheet would report this item?

7. What are the reasons that a company gives trade discounts? Why are trade discounts not recorded in the accounts like cash discounts?

8. What are two methods of recording accounts receivable transactions when a cash discount situation is involved? Which is the most theoretically correct? Which is used in practice most of the time? Why?

9. What are the basic problems that occur in the valuation of accounts receivable?

10. Why is the account "Allowance for Sales Returns and Allowances" sometimes used? What other types of allowance accounts (similar to Allowance for Sales Returns and Allowances) are employed? What is their purpose?

11. What is the theoretical justification of the allowance method as contrasted with the direct write-off method of accounting for bad debts?

12. Indicate how well the percentage-of-sales method and the aging method accomplish the objectives of the allowance method of accounting for bad debts.

13. Of what merit is the contention that the allowance method lacks the objectivity of the direct write-off method? Discuss in terms of accounting's measurement function.

14. Because of calamitous earthquake losses, Kehoe Company, one of your client's oldest and largest customers, suddenly and unexpectedly became bankrupt. Approximately 30% of your client's total sales have been made to Kehoe Company during each of the past several years. The amount due from Kehoe Company—none of which is collectible—equals 22% of total accounts receivable, an amount that is considerably in excess of what was determined to be an adequate provision for doubtful accounts at the close of the preceding year. How would your client record the write-off of the Kehoe Company receivable if it is using the allowance method of accounting for bad debts? Justify your suggested treatment.

15. What is the normal procedure for handling the collection of accounts receivable previously written off using the direct write-off method? The allowance method?

16. Steenwyk, Inc., shows a balance in Accounts Receivable on December 31, 1995 of $300,000. Of this amount $100,000 is assigned to the First Finance Co. as security for a loan of $82,000. Illustrate three satisfactory methods for showing this information on the balance sheet for December 31, 1995.

17. Identify three forms by which receivables can be transferred to a third party for cash. Conceptually, what is the nature or substance of each form?

18. What is "imputed interest"? In what situations is it necessary to impute an interest rate for notes receivable? What are the considerations in imputing an appropriate interest rate?

19. On January 1, 1993, Rolanda Co. sells property for which it had paid $490,000 to Travaris Company receiving in return Travaris' zero-interest-bearing note for $800,000 payable in 5 years. What entry would Rolanda make to record the sale, assuming that Rolanda frequently sells similar items of property for a cash sales price of $655,000?

20. The Meers Company includes in its trial balance for December 31 an item for "Accounts Receivable, $700,000." This balance consists of the following items:

Due from regular customers	$523,000
Refund receivable on prior year's income taxes (an established claim)	10,000
Loans to officers	22,000
Loan to wholly owned subsidiary	45,500
Advances to creditors for goods ordered	61,000
Accounts receivable assigned as security for loans payable	21,500
Notes receivable past due plus interest on these notes	17,000
Total	$700,000

Illustrate how these items should be shown in the balance sheet as of December 31.

EXERCISES

E7-1 (Determining Cash Balance) The controller for AMC Co. is attempting to determine the amount of cash to be reported on its December 31, 1995, balance sheet. The following information is provided:

1. Commercial savings account of $1,000,000 and a commercial checking account balance of $900,000 are held at First Nebraska Bank.

2. Money market fund account held at Anton Lange Co. (a mutual fund organization) that permits AMC to write checks on this balance, $6,000,000.

3. Travel advances of $180,000 for executive travel for the first quarter of next year (employee to reimburse through salary reduction).

4. A separate cash fund in the amount of $1,500,000 is restricted for the retirement of long-term debt.

5. Petty cash fund of $1,000.

6. An I.O.U. from Adam Chandler, a company officer, in the amount of $190,000.

7. A bank overdraft of $110,000 has occurred at one of the banks the company uses to deposit its cash receipts. At the present time, the company has no deposits at this bank.

8. The company has two certificates of deposit, each totaling $500,000. These certificates of deposit have a maturity of 120 days.

9. AMC has received a check that is dated January 12, 1996, in the amount of $125,000.
10. AMC has agreed to maintain a cash balance of $500,000 at all times at First Nebraska Bank to insure future credit availability.
11. AMC has purchased $2,100,000 of commercial paper of Hector Santos Co. which is due in 60 days.
12. Currency and coin on hand amounted to $5,300.

Instructions

(a) Compute the amount of cash to be reported on AMC Co.'s balance sheet at December 31, 1995.
(b) Indicate the proper reporting for items that are not reported as cash on the December 31, 1995, balance sheet.

E7-2 (Determine Cash Balance) Presented below are a number of independent situations. For each individual situation, determine the amount that should be reported as cash. If the item(s) is not reported as cash, explain the rationale.

1. Checking account balance $950,000; certificate of deposit $1,400,000; cash advance to subsidiary of $980,000; utility deposit paid to gas company $180.
2. Checking account balance $600,000; an overdraft in special checking account at same bank as normal checking account of $10,000; cash held in a bond sinking fund $200,000; petty cash fund $300; coins and currency on hand $1,350.
3. Checking account balance $600,000; postdated check from customer $11,000; cash restricted due to maintaining compensating balance requirement of $100,000; certified check from customer $9,800; postage stamps on hand $620.
4. Checking account balance at bank $35,000; money market balance at mutual fund (has checking privileges) $48,000; NSF check received from customer $800.
5. Checking account balance $800,000; cash restricted for future plant expansion $500,000; short-term treasury bills $180,000; cash advance received from customer $900 (not included in checking account balance); cash advance of $7,000 to company executive, payable on demand; refundable deposit of $26,000 paid to federal government to guarantee performance on construction contract.

E7-3 (Petty Cash) Alvarez, Inc. decided to establish a petty cash fund to help insure internal control over its small cash expenditures. The following information is available for the month of April.

1. On April 1, it established a petty cash fund in the amount of $200.
2. A summary of the petty cash expenditures made by the petty cash custodian as of April 10, is as follows:

Delivery charges paid on merchandise purchased	$70.00
Supplies purchased and used	15.00
Postage expense	33.00
I.O.U. from employees	17.00
Miscellaneous expense	36.00

The petty cash fund was replenished on April 10. The balance in the fund was $27.
3. The petty cash fund balance was increased $50 to $250 on April 20.

Instructions
Prepare the journal entries to record transactions related to petty cash for the month of April.

E7-4 (Petty Cash) The petty cash fund of Montgomery's Auto Repair Service, a sole proprietorship, contains the following:

1. Coins and currency		$ 15.20
2. Postage stamps		2.90
3. An I.O.U. from Felicity La Fortune, an employee, for cash advance		40.00
4. Check payable to Montgomery's Auto Repair from B. Dharan, an employee, marked NSF		34.00
5. Vouchers for the following:		
Stamps	$20.00	
Two Rose Bowl tickets for Laurel Montgomery	70.00	
Typewriter repairs	14.35	104.35
		$196.45

The general ledger account Petty Cash has a balance of $200.00.

Instructions
Prepare the journal entry to record the reimbursement of the petty cash fund.

E7-5 (Bank Reconciliation and Adjusting Entries) Acadian Company deposits all receipts and makes all payments by check. The following information is available from the cash records.

June 30 Bank Reconciliation

Balance per bank	$7,000
Add: Deposits in transit	1,540
Deduct: Outstanding checks	(2,000)
Balance per books	$6,540

Month of July Results

	Per Bank	Per Books
Balance July 31	$8,550	$9,150
July deposits	5,000	5,710
July checks	4,100	3,100
July note collected (not included in July deposits)	900	—
July bank service charge	15	—
July NSF check of a customer returned by the bank (recorded by bank as a charge)	235	—

Instructions

(a) Prepare a bank reconciliation going from balance per bank and balance per book to correct cash balance.

(b) Prepare the general journal entry or entries to correct the Cash account.

E7-6 (Bank Reconciliation and Adjusting Entries) Monie Love Company has just received the August 31, 1995, bank statement, which is summarized below:

County National Bank	Disbursements	Receipts	Balance
Balance, August 1			$ 9,369
Deposits during August		$32,000	41,369
Note collected for depositor, including $36 interest		1,036	42,405
Checks cleared during August	$34,400		8,005
Bank service charges	25		7,980
Balance, August 31			7,980

The general ledger Cash account contained the following entries for the month of August:

Cash

Balance, August 1	10,050	Disbursements in August	34,903
Receipts during August	35,000		

Deposits in transit at August 31 are $4,000 and checks outstanding at August 31 are determined to total $1,150. Cash on hand at August 31 is $310. The bookkeeper improperly entered one check in the books at $146.50 which was written for $164.50 for supplies (expense); it cleared the bank during the month of August.

Instructions

(a) Prepare a bank reconciliation dated August 31, 1995, proceeding to a correct balance.

(b) Prepare any entries necessary to make the books correct and complete.

(c) What amount of cash should be reported in the August 31 balance sheet?

E7-7 (Financial Statement Presentation of Receivables) Leontine Price Company shows a balance of $181,140 in the Accounts Receivable account on December 31, 1995. The balance consists of the following:

Installment accounts due in 1996	$23,000
Installment accounts due after 1996	24,000
Overpayments to creditors	2,640
Due from regular customers, of which $40,000 represents accounts pledged as security for a bank loan	79,000
Advances to employees	1,500
Advance to subsidiary company (made in 1990)	51,000

Instructions

Illustrate how the information above should be shown on the balance sheet of the Leontine Price Company on December 31, 1995.

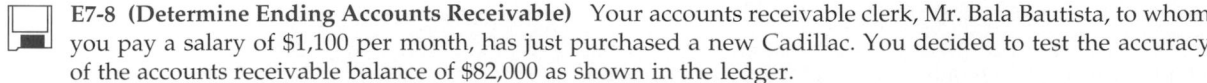

E7-8 (Determine Ending Accounts Receivable) Your accounts receivable clerk, Mr. Bala Bautista, to whom you pay a salary of $1,100 per month, has just purchased a new Cadillac. You decided to test the accuracy of the accounts receivable balance of $82,000 as shown in the ledger.

The following information is available for your *first year* in business:

(1)	Collections from customers	$198,000
(2)	Merchandise purchased	310,000
(3)	Ending merchandise inventory	90,000
(4)	Goods are marked to sell at 40% above cost	

Instructions

Compute an estimate of the ending balance of accounts receivable from customers that should appear in the ledger and any apparent shortages. Assume that all sales are made on account.

E7-9 (Record Sales Gross and Net) On June 3, Igneous Company sold to Opal Moonstone merchandise having a sale price of $2,000 with terms of 2/10, n/60, f.o.b. shipping point. An invoice totaling $90, terms n/30, was received by Opal on June 8 from the Obsidian Transport Service for the freight cost. On receipt of the goods, June 5, Opal notified the Igneous Company that merchandise costing $400 contained flaws that rendered it worthless; the same day Igneous Company issued a credit memo covering the worthless merchandise and asked that it be returned at company expense. The freight on the returned merchandise was $25, paid by Igneous Company on June 7. On June 12, the company received a check for the balance due from Opal Moonstone.

Instructions

(a) Prepare journal entries on the Igneous Company books to record all the events noted above under each of the following bases:

  1. Sales and receivables are entered at gross selling price.
  2. Sales and receivables are entered at net of cash discounts.

(b) Prepare the journal entry under basis 2, assuming that Opal Moonstone did not remit payment until July 29.

E7-10 (Computing Bad Debts) At January 1, 1996, the credit balance in the Allowance for Doubtful Accounts of the Sunchi Company was $400,000. For 1996, the provision for doubtful accounts is based on a percentage of net sales. Net sales for 1996 were $70,000,000. On the basis of the latest available facts, the 1996 provision for doubtful accounts is estimated to be 0.7% of net sales. During 1996, uncollectible receivables amounting to $480,000 were written off against the allowance for doubtful accounts.

Instructions

Prepare a schedule computing the balance in Sunchi's Allowance for Doubtful Accounts at December 31, 1996.

E7-11 (Computing Bad Debts and Preparing Journal Entries) The trial balance before adjustment of G. Washington Inc. shows the following balances:

	Dr.	Cr.
Accounts Receivable	$90,000	
Allowance for Doubtful Accounts	1,750	
Sales (all on credit)		$680,000
Sales Returns and Allowances	30,000	

Instructions

Give the entry for estimated bad debts assuming that the allowance is to provide for doubtful accounts on the basis of (a) 4% of gross accounts receivable and (b) 3% of net sales.

E7-12 (Bad Debt Reporting) The chief accountant for J. Adams Corporation provides you with the following list of accounts receivable written off in the current year.

Date	Customer	Amount
March 31	Creative Constitution	$7,800
June 30	Hamilton Associates	6,700
September 30	Abigail's Dress Shop	7,000
December 31	Federalist Corporation	8,730

J. Adams Corporation follows the policy of debiting Bad Debt Expense as accounts are written off. The chief accountant maintains that this procedure is appropriate for financial statement purposes because the Internal Revenue Service will not accept other methods for recognizing bad debts.

All of J. Adams Corporation's sales are on a 30-day credit basis. Sales for the current year total $2,100,000 and research has determined that bad debt losses approximate 2% of sales.

Instructions

(a) Do you agree or disagree with J. Adams Corporation policy concerning recognition of bad debt expense? Why or why not?

(b) By what amount would net income differ if bad debt expense was computed using the percentage-of-sales approach?

E7-13 (Bad Debts—Aging) Amy Liu, Inc. includes the following account among its trade receivables.

	Avery Brooks				
1/1	Balance forward	700	1/28	Cash (#1710)	1,100
1/20	Invoice #1710	1,100	4/2	Cash (#2116)	1,350
3/14	Invoice #2116	1,350	4/10	Cash (1/1 Balance)	145
4/12	Invoice #2412	1,680	4/30	Cash (#2412)	1,000
9/5	Invoice #3614	490	9/20	Cash (#3614 and	
10/17	Invoice #4912	860		part of #2412)	790
11/18	Invoice #5681	2,000	10/31	Cash (#4912)	860
12/20	Invoice #6347	800	12/1	Cash (#5681)	1,200
			12/29	Cash (#6347)	800

Instructions

Age the balance and specify any items that apparently require particular attention at year-end.

E7-14 (Journalizing Various Receivable Transactions) Presented below is information related to Madison Corp.

July 1 Madison Corp. sold to Hamilton Co. merchandise having a sales price of $7,000 with terms 2/10, net/60. Madison records its sales and receivables net.

      3 Hamilton Co. returned merchandise having a sales price of $700 that was defective.

      5 Accounts receivable of $9,000 (gross) are factored with Collazo Credit Corp. without recourse at a financing charge of 10%. Cash is received for the proceeds; collections are handled by the finance company. (These accounts were all past the discount period.)

      9 Specific accounts receivable of $9,000 (gross) are assigned to Monteiro Credit Corp. as security for a loan of $6,000 at a finance charge of 6% of the amount of the loan. The finance company will make the collections. (All the accounts receivable are past the discount period.)

Dec. 29 Hamilton Co. notifies Madison that it is bankrupt and will pay only 10% of its account. Give the entry to write off the uncollectible balance using the allowance method. (Note: First record the increase in the receivable on July 11 when the discount period passed.)

Instructions

Prepare all necessary entries in general journal form for Madison Corp.

E7-15 (Assigned Accounts Receivable) Presented below is information related to Monroe Co.

1. Customers' accounts in the amount of $40,000 are assigned to the Quincy Adams Finance Company as security for a loan of $30,000. The finance charge is 3% of the amount borrowed.
2. Cash collections on assigned accounts amount to $17,000.
3. Collections on assigned accounts to date, plus a $400 check for interest on the loan, are forwarded to Quincy Adams Finance Company.
4. Additional collections on assigned accounts amount to $16,200.
5. The loan is paid in full plus additional interest of $150.
6. Uncollected balances of the assigned accounts are returned to the regular customers' ledger.

Instructions

Prepare entries in journal form for Monroe Co.

E7-16 (Journalizing Various Receivable Transactions) The trial balance before adjustment for Jackson Company shows the following balances:

	Dr.	Cr.
Accounts Receivable	$82,000	
Allowance for Doubtful Accounts	2,120	
Sales		$430,000
Sales Returns and Allowances	7,600	

Instructions

Using the data above, give the journal entries required to record each of the following cases (each situation is independent):

1. To obtain additional cash, Jackson factors, without recourse, $24,000 of accounts receivable with Old Hickory Finance. The finance charge is 10% of the amount factored.
2. To obtain a one-year loan of $54,000, Jackson assigns $65,000 of specific receivable accounts to Tennessee Financial. The finance charge is 8% of the loan; the cash is received and the accounts turned over to Tennessee Financial.

3. The company wants to maintain the Allowance for Doubtful Accounts at 4% of gross accounts receivable.
4. The company wishes to increase the allowance by 1½% of net sales.

E7-17 (Transfer of Receivables with Recourse) Monteray Inc. factors receivables with a carrying amount of $187,000 to Wm. Ortega Company for $150,000 on a with recourse basis.

Instructions
(a) Assuming that this transaction should be reported as a sale, prepare the appropriate journal entry.
(b) Assuming that this transaction should be reported as a borrowing, prepare the appropriate journal entry.

E7-18 (Transfer of Receivables with Recourse) William Henry Corporation factors $150,000 of accounts receivable with Harrison Financing, Inc. on a with recourse basis. Harrison Financing will collect the receivables. The receivable records are transferred to Harrison Financing on August 15, 1995. Harrison Financing assesses a finance charge of 2% of the amount of accounts receivable and also reserves an amount equal to 4% of accounts receivable to cover probable adjustments.

Instructions
(a) What conditions must be met for a transfer of receivables with recourse to be accounted for as a sale?
(b) Assume the conditions from part (a) are met. Prepare the journal entry on August 15, 1995, for William Henry to record the sale of receivables.
(c) Assume that not all the conditions from part (a) are met. Prepare the journal entry on August 15, 1995, for William Henry to record the transfer of receivables.

E7-19 (Transfer of Receivables Without Recourse) Tyler Corp. factors $250,000 of accounts receivable with Tippecanoe Finance Corporation on a without recourse basis on July 1, 1995. The receivable records are transferred to Krafty Finance, which will receive the collections. Tippecanoe Finance assesses a finance charge of 1½% of the amount of accounts receivable and retains an amount equal to 4% of accounts receivable to cover sales discounts, returns, and allowances.

Instructions
(a) Prepare the journal entry on July 1, 1995, for Tyler Corp. to record the sale of receivables without recourse.
(b) Prepare the journal entry on July 1, 1995, for Tippecanoe Finance Corporation to record the purchase of receivables without recourse.

E7-20 (Note Transactions at Unrealistic Interest Rates) On July 1, 1996, Zachary Taylor Company made two sales:

1. It sold land having a fair market value of $700,000 in exchange for a 4-year noninterest-bearing promissory note in the face amount of $1,101,460. The land is carried on Zachary Taylor Company's books at a cost of $620,000.
2. It rendered services in exchange for a 3%, 8-year promissory note having a face value of $300,000 (interest payable annually).

Zachary Taylor Company recently had to pay 8% interest for money that it borrowed from Buena Vista National Bank. The customers in these two transactions have credit ratings that require them to borrow money at 12% interest.

Instructions
Record the two journal entries that should be recorded by Zachary Taylor Company for the sales transactions above that took place on July 1, 1996.

E7-21 (Note Receivable at Unrealistic Interest Rates) On December 31, 1996, Fillmore Company sold some of its product to Millard Company, accepting a $340,000 noninterest-bearing note, receivable in full on December 31, 1999. Fillmore Company enjoys a high credit rating and, therefore, borrows funds from its several lines of credit at 9%. Millard Company, however, pays 12% for its borrowed funds. The product sold is carried on the books of Fillmore Company at a manufactured cost of $190,000. Assume that the effective interest method is used for discount amortization.

Instructions
(a) Prepare the journal entry to record the sale on December 31, 1996, by Fillmore Company. Assume that a perpetual inventory system is used.
(b) Prepare the journal entries on the books of Fillmore Company for the year 1997 that are necessitated by the sales transaction of December 31, 1996. Preparation of an amortization schedule may be of assistance.
(c) Prepare the journal entries on the books of Fillmore Company for the year 1998 that are necessitated by the sale on December 31, 1996.

*E7-22 (Proof of Cash)** Following is the general format of a four-column bank reconciliation with the various categories and operations numbered (1) through (8):

	Balance 10/31	November Receipts	November Disbursements	Balance 11/30
Per Bank Statement	$XXXXX	$XXXXX	$XXXXX	$XXXXX
Items to be *added:*	(1)	(3)	(5)	(7)
Items to be *deducted:*	(2)	(4)	(6)	(8)
Per Books	$XXXXX	$XXXXX	$XXXXX	$XXXXX

Instructions

(a) For each of the following items indicate in which columns the reconciling items would appear. Question 1 is answered as an example.

   6   7   **1.** November service charge of $20 is included on bank statement.

             2. The bank collected a $500 note receivable for the firm in November plus $40 interest. The firm has not yet recorded this receipt.

             3. An "NSF" check in the amount of $320 was returned with the November bank statement. This check will be redeposited in December. The firm has not yet made an entry for this "NSF" check.

             4. All $9,000 of checks written in October, which had not cleared the bank at October 31, cleared the bank in November.

             5. October service charge of $20 is included in book disbursements for November.

             6. A $5,000 deposit in transit is included in book receipts for November.

             7. The bank, in error, credited the firm's account for $400 in November for another firm's deposit.

             8. A check written in November for $670 was written in the check register in error in the amount of $760. This check cleared the bank in November for $670. Both the debit to Utilities Expense and the credit were overstated as a result of this error in the books.

             9. The initial $4,500 deposit shown on the November bank statement was included in October's book receipts.

             10. $8,000 of checks written in November have not cleared the bank by November 30.

(b) Prepare the entries that should be recorded to make the books complete and accurate at November 30.

PROBLEMS

P7-1 (Cash Related Issues) Presented below are five independent situations:

1. The bank reconciliation for April 1996 of NYPD Co. was as follows:

Balance per bank statement 4/30/96	$80,000
Add deposits in transit	6,000
	86,000
Less outstanding checks	15,000
Balance per books 4/30/96	$71,000

During May 1996, the bank recorded $74,000 of cash receipts and $31,900 of cash disbursements. All deposits in transit and outstanding checks from April cleared the bank in May. Outstanding checks at May 31, 1996 totaled $13,300. There were no deposits in transit. Determine the cash balance per books as of May 31, 1996.

2. Caruso Enterprises owns the following assets at December 31, 1996.

Cash in bank—savings account	82,000
Cash on hand	9,300
Cash refund due from IRS	31,400
Checking account balance	17,000
Postdated checks	750
Certificates of deposit (180 day)	90,000

What amount should be reported as cash?

3. The June 30 bank reconciliation of John Kelly Inc. indicated that deposits in transit totaled $475. During July the general ledger account Cash in Bank shows deposits of $15,250, but the bank statement indicates that only $15,100 in deposits were received during the month. What were the deposits in transit at July 31?

4. In September, cash disbursements per books for Sipowiez Co. were $22,900, checks clearing the bank were $24,000, and outstanding checks at September 30 were $2,000. What were the outstanding checks at August 31?

5. Medavoy Corporation on July 1, 1995 obtained a $4,000,000, 6-month loan at an annual rate of 11% from Blue's Bank. As part of the loan agreement, Medavoy is required to maintain a $500,000 compensating balance in a checking account at Blue's Bank. Normally Medavoy would maintain only a balance of $200,000 in this checking account. The checking account pays 5% interest. Determine the effective interest rate paid by Medavoy for this loan.

Instructions
Answer the questions relating to each of the five independent situations as requested.

P7-2 (Determine Proper Cash Balance) Larry King Equipment Co. closes its books regularly on December 31, but at the end of 1995 it held its cash book open so that a more favorable balance sheet could be prepared for credit purposes. Cash receipts and disbursements for the first 10 days of January were recorded as December transactions. The following information is given.

1. January cash receipts recorded in the December cash book totaled $38,640, of which $21,000 represents cash sales and $17,640 represents collections on account for which cash discounts of $360 were given.
2. January cash disbursements recorded in the December check register liquidated accounts payable of $26,450 on which discounts of $159 were taken.
3. The ledger has not been closed for 1995.
4. The amount shown as inventory was determined by physical count on December 31, 1995.

Instructions
(a) Prepare any entries you consider necessary to correct King's accounts at December 31.
(b) To what extent was Larry King Equipment Co. able to show a more favorable balance sheet at December 31 by holding its cash book open? Assume that the balance sheet that was prepared by the company showed the following amounts:

	Dr.	Cr.
Cash	$39,000	
Receivables	42,000	
Inventories	67,000	
Accounts payable		$45,000
Other current liabilities		14,200

P7-3 (Bank Reconciliation and Adjusting Entries) The cash account of Dr. Quinn Co. showed a ledger balance of $5,588.35 on June 30, 1995. The bank statement as of that date showed a balance of $3,950. Upon comparing the statement with the cash records, the following facts were determined:

1. There were bank service charges for June of $25.00.
2. A bank memo stated that John McLaughlin's note for $800 and interest of $36 had been collected on June 29, and the bank had made a charge of $5.50 on the collection. (No entry had been made on Quinn's books when John McLaughlin's note was sent to the bank for collection.)
3. Receipts for June 30 for $2,890 were not deposited until July 2.
4. Checks outstanding on June 30 totaled $1,936.05.
5. The bank had charged the Quinn Co.'s account for a customer's uncollectible check amounting to $453.20 on June 29.
6. A 60-day, 6%, $1,500 customer's note dated April 25, and discounted by Quinn on June 12, remained unpaid by the customer on the due date. On June 28 the bank charged the Quinn Co. for $1,518.50, which included a protest fee of $3.50. (Quinn discloses discounted notes receivable by use of a note to the financial statements.)
7. A customer's check for $90 had been entered as $60 in the cash receipts journal by Quinn on June 15.
8. Check no. 742 in the amount of $491 had been entered in the cashbook as $419, and check no. 747 in the amount of $58.20 had been entered as $582. Both checks had been issued to pay for purchases of equipment.

Instructions
(a) Prepare a bank reconciliation dated June 30, 1995, proceeding to a correct cash balance.
(b) Prepare any entries necessary to make the books correct and complete.

P7-4 (Bank Reconciliation and Adjusting Entries) Presented below is information related to Doug Inc. Balance per books at October 31, $41,847.85; receipts, $173,523.91; disbursements, $166,193.54. Balance per bank statement November 30, $56,274.20.

The following checks were outstanding at November 30:

1224	$1,635.29
1230	2,468.30
1232	3,625.15
1233	482.17

Included with the November bank statement and not recorded by the company were a bank debit ticket for $27.40 covering bank charges for the month, a debit ticket for $372.13 for a customer's check returned and marked NSF, and a credit ticket for $1,200 representing bond interest collected by the bank in the name of Doug Inc. Cash on hand at November 30 recorded and awaiting deposit amounted to $1,915.40.

Instructions
(a) Prepare a bank reconciliation (to the correct balance) at November 30, 1995, for Doug Inc. from the information above.
(b) Prepare any journal entries required to adjust the cash account at November 30.

P7-5 (Bank Reconciliation) Presented below is information related to Clarissa Industries.

Clarissa Industries
BANK RECONCILIATION
May 31, 1995

Balance per bank statement		$30,928.46
Less outstanding checks		
No. 6124	$2,125.00	
No. 6138	932.65	
No. 6139	960.57	
No. 6140	1,420.00	5,438.22
		25,490.24
Add deposit in transit		4,710.56
Balance per books (correct balance)		$30,200.80

CHECK REGISTER—JUNE

Date	Payee	No.	V. Pay	Discount	Cash
June 1	Ren Mfg.	6141	$ 237.50		$ 237.50
1	Stimpy Mfg.	6142	915.00	$ 9.15	905.85
8	Rugrats Co., Inc.	6143	122.90	2.45	120.45
9	Ren Mfg.	6144	306.40		306.40
10	Petty Cash	6145	89.93		89.93
17	Muppet Babies Photo	6146	706.00	14.12	691.88
22	Hey Dude Publishing	6147	447.50		447.50
23	Payroll Account	6148	4,130.00		4,130.00
25	Dragnet Tools, Inc.	6149	390.75	3.91	386.84
28	Double Dare Insurance Agency	6150	1,050.00		1,050.00
28	Get Smart Construction	6151	2,250.00		2,250.00
29	MMT, Inc.	6152	750.00		750.00
30	Lassie Co.	6153	295.25	5.90	289.35
			$11,691.23	$35.53	$11,655.70

STATEMENT
Nickelodeon State Bank
General Checking Account of Clarissa Industries—June 1995

Debits			Date	Credits	Balance
					$30,928.46
$2,125.00	$ 237.50	$ 905.85	June 1	$4,710.56	32,370.67
932.65	120.45		12	1,507.06	32,824.63
1,420.00	447.50	306.40	23	1,458.55	32,109.28
4,130.00		11.05 (BC)	26		27,968.23
89.93	2,250.00	1,050.00	28	4,157.48	28,735.78

Cash received June 29 and 30 and deposited in the mail for the general checking account June 30 amounted to $4,407.96. Because the cash account balance at June 30 is not given, it must be calculated from other information in the problem.

Instructions

From the information above, prepare a bank reconciliation (to the correct balance) as of June 30, 1995, for Clarissa Industries.

P7-6 (Bad Debt Reporting) Presented below are a series of unrelated situations.

1. Beau Bridges Company's unadjusted trial balance at December 31, 1995 included the following accounts:

	Debit	Credit
Allowance for doubtful accounts	$ 4,000	
Sales		$1,500,000
Sales returns and allowances	100,000	

Bridges Company estimates its bad debt expense to be 1½% of net sales. Determine its bad debt expense for 1995.

2. An analysis and aging of Candice Bergen Corp. accounts receivable at December 31, 1995 disclosed the following:

Amounts estimated to be uncollectible	$ 180,000
Accounts receivable	1,700,000
Allowance for doubtful accounts (per books)	125,000

What is the net realizable value of Bergen's receivables at December 31, 1995?

3. Kevin Costner Co. provides for doubtful accounts based on 3% of credit sales. The following data are available for 1995.

Credit sales during 1995	$2,100,000
Allowance for doubtful accounts 1/1/95	17,000
Collection of accounts written off in prior years	
(customer credit was reestablished)	9,000
Customer accounts written off as uncollectible during 1995	30,000

What is the balance in the Allowance for Doubtful Accounts at December 31, 1995?

4. At the end of its first year of operations, December 31, 1995, Devito Inc. reported the following information:

Accounts receivable, net of allowance for doubtful accounts	$950,000
Customer accounts written off as uncollectible during 1995	24,000
Bad debt expense for 1995	74,000

What should be the balance in accounts receivable at December 31, 1995 before subtracting the allowance for doubtful accounts?

5. The following accounts were taken from Morgan Freeman Inc.'s balance sheet at December 31, 1995.

	Debit	Credit
Net credit sales		$750,000
Allowance for doubtful accounts	$ 16,000	
Accounts receivable	410,000	

If doubtful accounts are 3% of accounts receivable, determine the bad debt expense to be reported for 1995.

Instructions

Answer the questions relating to each of the five independent situations as requested.

P7-7 (Bad Debt Reporting—Aging) Whoopi Goldberg Corporation operates in an industry that has a high rate of bad debts. On December 31, 1995, before any year-end adjustments, the balance in Goldberg Accounts Receivable account was $555,000 and the Allowance for Doubtful Accounts had a credit balance of $35,000. The year-end balance reported in the statement of financial position for the Allowance for Doubtful Accounts will be based on the aging schedule shown below.

Days Account Outstanding	Amount	Probability of Collection
Less than 15 days	$300,000	.98
Between 16 and 30 days	100,000	.90
Between 31 and 45 days	80,000	.80
Between 46 and 60 days	40,000	.70
Between 61 and 75 days	20,000	.40
Over 75 days	15,000	.00

Instructions

(a) What is the appropriate balance for the Allowance for Doubtful Accounts on December 31, 1995?

(b) Show how accounts receivable would be presented on the balance sheet prepared on December 31, 1995.

(c) What is the dollar effect of the year-end bad debt adjustment on the before-tax income for 1995?

(CMA adapted)

P7-8 (Bad Debt Reporting) From inception of operations to December 31, 1995, Dustin Hoffman Corporation provided for uncollectible accounts receivable under the allowance method: provisions were made monthly at 2% of credit sales; bad debts written off were charged to the Allowance account; recoveries of bad debts previously written off were credited to the allowance account; and no year-end adjustments to the allowance account were made. Hoffman's usual credit terms are net 30 days.

The balance in the Allowance for Doubtful Accounts was $130,000 at January 1, 1996. During 1996 credit sales totaled $9,000,000, interim provisions for doubtful accounts were made at 2% of credit sales, $90,000 of bad debts were written off, and recoveries of accounts previously written off amounted to $15,000. Hoffman installed a computer facility in November 1996 and an aging of accounts receivable was prepared for the first time as of December 31, 1996. A summary of the aging is as follows:

Classification by Month of Sale	Balance in Each Category	Estimated % Uncollectible
November–December 1996	$1,080,000	2%
July–October	650,000	10%
January–June	420,000	25%
Prior to 1/1/96	150,000	80%
	$2,300,000	

Based on the review of collectibility of the account balances in the "prior to 1/1/96" aging category, additional receivables totaling $60,000 were written off as of December 31, 1996. The 80% uncollectible estimate applies to the remaining $90,000 in the category. Effective with the year ended December 31, 1996, Hoffman adopted a new accounting method for estimating the allowance for doubtful accounts at the amount indicated by the year-end aging analysis of accounts receivable.

Instructions

(a) Prepare a schedule analyzing the changes in the Allowance for Doubtful Accounts for the year ended December 31, 1996. Show supporting computations in good form. (Hint: In computing the 12/31/96 allowance, subtract the $60,000 writeoff.)

(b) Prepare the journal entry for the year-end adjustment to the Allowance for Doubtful Accounts balance as of December 31, 1996.

(AICPA adapted)

P7-9 (Bad Debt Reporting) Presented below is information related to the Accounts Receivable accounts of Paul Newman Inc. during the current year 1996.

1. An aging schedule of the accounts receivable as of December 31, 1996 is as follows:

Age	Net Debit Balance	% to Be Applied After Correction Made
Under 60 days	$172,342	1%
61–90 days	136,490	3%
91–120 days	39,924*	6%
Over 120 days	23,644	$4,200 definitely uncollectible; estimated remainder uncollectible is 25%
	$372,400	

*The $2,520 write-off of receivables is related to the 91-to-120 day category.

2. The Accounts Receivable control account has a debit balance of $372,400 on December 31, 1996.

3. Two entries were made in the Bad Debt Expense account during the year: (1) a debit on December 31 for the amount credited to Allowance for Doubtful Accounts, and (2) a credit for $2,520 on November 3, 1996 and a debit to Allowance for Doubtful Accounts because of a bankruptcy.

4. The Allowance for Doubtful Accounts is as follows for 1996:

Allowance for Doubtful Accounts			
Nov. 3 Uncollectible accounts written off	2,520	Jan. 1 Beginning balance	8,750
		Dec. 31 5% of $372,400	18,620

5. A credit balance exists in the Accounts Receivable (61–90 days) of $4,840, which represents an advance on a sales contract.

Instructions

Assuming that the books have not been closed for 1996, make the necessary correcting entries.

P7-10 (Journalize Various Account and Notes Receivable Transactions) The balance sheet of Jane Seymour Company at December 31, 1995 includes the following:

Notes receivable	$ 36,000	
Accounts receivable	182,100	
Less: Allowance for doubtful accounts	17,300	200,800

Transactions in 1996 include the following:

1. A note receivable sold on a with recourse basis was unable to be collected by the purchaser. The purchaser now requires payment of $5,060 which includes $60 of interest. Recovery is expected in 1996. (Use Notes Receivable Past Due account.)
2. Accounts receivable of $138,000 were collected including accounts of $30,000 on which 2% sales discounts were allowed.
3. $6,200 was received in payment of an account which was written off the books as worthless in 1993. (Hint: Reestablish the receivable account.)
4. Customer accounts of $19,500 were written off during the year.
5. At year-end the Allowance for Doubtful Accounts was estimated to need a balance of $20,000. This estimate is based on an analysis of aged accounts receivable.

Instructions

Prepare all journal entries necessary to reflect the transactions above.

P7-11 (Assigned Accounts Receivable—Journal Entries) Bruce Willis Company finances some of its current operations by assigning accounts receivable to a finance company. On July 1, 1996, it assigned, under guarantee, specific accounts amounting to $70,000, the finance company advancing to Bruce Willis 80% of the accounts assigned (20% of the total to be withheld until the finance company has made its full recovery), less a finance charge of ½% of the total accounts assigned.

On July 31, Bruce Willis Company received a statement that the finance company had collected $38,000 of these accounts, and had made an additional charge of ½% of the total accounts outstanding as of July 31, this charge to be deducted at the time of the first remittance due Bruce Willis Company from the finance company. (Hint: Make entries at this time.) On August 31, 1996, Bruce Willis Company received a second statement from the finance company, together with a check for the amount due. The statement indicated that the finance company had collected an additional $20,000 and had made a further charge of ½% of the balance outstanding as of August 31.

Instructions

(a) Make all entries on the books of Bruce Willis Company that are involved in the transactions above.

(b) Explain how these accounts should be presented in the balance sheet of Bruce Willis Company at July 31 and at August 31.

(AICPA adapted)

P7-12 (Notes Receivable Journal Entries) Bo Jackson Sports Company produces soccer, football, and track shoes. The treasurer has recently completed negotiations in which Bo Jackson Sports agrees to loan Payton Company, a leather supplier, $400,000. Payton Company will issue a noninterest-bearing note due in five years (a 12% interest rate is appropriate), and has agreed to furnish Bo Jackson Sports with leather at prices that are 10% lower than those usually charged.

Instructions

(a) Prepare the accounting entry to record this transaction on Bo Jackson Sports Company's books.

(b) Determine the balances at the end of each year the note is outstanding for the following accounts for Bo Jackson Sports Company:
  Notes receivable
  Unamortized discount
  Interest revenue

P7-13 (Notes Receivable Journal Entries) On December 31, 1996, La Tourette Inc. rendered services to Husky Corporation at an agreed price of $73,844.10, accepting $18,000 down and agreeing to accept the balance in four equal installments of $18,000 receivable each December 31. An assumed interest rate of 11% is imputed.

Instructions

Prepare the journal entries that would be recorded by La Tourette Inc. for the sale and for the receipts and interest on the following dates (assume that the effective interest method is used for amortization purposes):

(a) December 31, 1996.
(b) December 31, 1997.
(c) December 31, 1998.
(d) December 31, 1999.
(e) December 31, 2000.

P7-14 (Sale of Notes Receivable) Gregor Wholesalers Co. sells industrial equipment for a standard three-year note receivable. Revenue is recognized at time of sale. Each note is secured by a lien on the equipment and has a face amount equal to the equipment's list price. Each note's stated interest rate is below the customer's market rate at date of sale. All notes are to be collected in three equal annual installments beginning one year after sale. Some of the notes are subsequently sold to a bank with recourse, some are subsequently sold without recourse, and some are retained by Gregor. At year end, Gregor evaluates all outstanding notes receivable and provides for estimated losses arising from defaults.

Instructions

(a) What is the appropriate valuation basis for Gregor's notes receivable at the date it sells equipment?
(b) How should Gregor account for the sale, without recourse, of a February 1, 1995, note receivable sold on May 1, 1995? Why is it appropriate to account for it in this way?
(c) At December 31, 1995, how should Gregor measure and account for the impact of estimated losses resulting from notes receivable that it
    1. Retained and did **not** sell?
    2. Sold to bank with recourse?

(CPA adapted)

P7-15 (Comprehensive Accounts Receivable) Ritter Supply produces paints and related products for sale to the construction industry throughout the southwest United States. While sales have remained relatively stable despite a decline in the amount of new construction, there has been a noticeable change in the timeliness with which Ritter's customers are paying their bills.

Ritter sells its products on payment terms of 2/10, n/30. In the past, over 75 percent of the credit customers have taken advantage of the discount by paying within ten days of the invoice date. During the fiscal year ended November 30, 1995, the number of customers taking the full 30 days to pay has increased. Current indications are that less than 60 percent of the customers are now taking the discount. Uncollectible accounts as a percentage of total credit sales have risen from the 1.5 percent provided in past years to 4.0 percent in the current year.

In response to a request for more information on the deterioration of accounts receivable collections, Ritter's controller has prepared the following report.

Ritter Supply
Accounts Receivable Collections
November 30, 1995

The fact that some credit accounts will prove uncollectible is normal, and annual bad debt write-offs had been 1.5 percent of total credit sales for many years. However, during the 1993–94 fiscal year, this percentage increased to 4.0 percent. The current accounts receivable balance is $1,500,000, and the condition of this balance in terms of age and probability of collection is shown below.

Proportion of Total	Age Categories	Probability of Collection
64.0%	1 to 10 days	99.0%
18.0	11 to 30 days	97.5
8.5	Past due 31 to 60 days	95.0
5.0	Past due 61 to 120 days	80.0
3.0	Past due 121 to 180 days	65.0
1.5	Past due over 180 days	20.0

At the beginning of the fiscal year, December 1, 1994, the Allowance for Doubtful Accounts had a credit balance of $26,300. Ritter has provided for a monthly bad debt expense accrual during the fiscal year just ended based on the assumption that four percent of total credit sales will be uncollectible. Total credit sales for the 1994–95 fiscal year amounted to $8,000,000, and write-offs of uncollectible accounts during the year totaled $292,500.

Instructions
  (a) Prepare an accounts receivable aging schedule at November 30, 1995, for Ritter Supply using the age categories identified in the controller's report showing
    1. the amount of accounts receivable outstanding for each age category and in total.
    2. the estimated amount that is uncollectible for each category and in total.
  (b) Compute the amount of the year-end adjustment necessary to bring Ritter Supply's Allowance for Doubtful Accounts to the balance indicated by the aging analysis.
  (c) Calculate the net realizable value of Ritter Supply's accounts receivable at November 30, 1995. Ignore any discounts that may be applicable to the accounts not yet due.
  (d) Describe the accounting to be performed for subsequent collections of previously written-off accounts receivable.

(CMA adapted)

P7-16 (Noninterest-Bearing Note Receivable) On September 30, 1995, B. Hoger Machinery Co. sold a machine and accepted the customer's noninterest-bearing note. Hoger normally makes sales on a cash basis. Since the machine was unique, its sales price was not determinable using Hoger's normal pricing practices.

After receiving the first of two equal annual installments on September 30, 1996 Hoger immediately sold the note with recourse. On October 9, 1997, Hoger received notice that the note was dishonored, and it paid all amounts due. At all times prior to default, the note was reasonably expected to be paid in full.

Instructions
  (a) **1.** How should Hoger determine the sales price of the machine?
    2. How should Hoger report the effects of the noninterest-bearing note on its income statement for the year ended December 31, 1995? Why is this accounting presentation appropriate?
  (b) What are the effects of the sale of the note receivable with recourse on Hoger's income statement for the year ended December 31, 1996, and its balance sheet at December 31, 1996?
  (c) How should Hoger account for the effects of the note being dishonored?

(CPA adapted)

P7-17 (Comprehensive Receivables Problem) Weaver, Inc., had the following long-term receivable account balances at December 31, 1995:

Note receivable from sale of division	$1,500,000
Note receivable from officer	400,000

Transactions during 1996 and other information relating to Weaver's long-term receivables were as follows:

  1. The $1,500,000 note receivable is dated May 1, 1995, bears interest at 9%, and represents the balance of the consideration received from the sale of Weaver's electronics division to Kodiac Company. Principal payments of $500,000 plus appropriate interest are due on May 1, 1996, 1997, and 1998. The first principal and interest payment was made on May 1, 1996. Collection of the note installments is reasonably assured.
  2. The $400,000 note receivable is dated December 31, 1995, bears interest at 8%, and is due on December 31, 1998. The note is due from George Weaver, president of Weaver, Inc., and is collateralized by 10,000 shares of Weaver's common stock. Interest is payable annually on December 31 and all interest payments were paid on their due dates through December 31, 1996. The quoted market price of Weaver's common stock was $45 per share on December 31, 1996.
  3. On April 1, 1996, Weaver sold a patent to Zhao Company in exchange for a $100,000 noninterest-bearing note due on April 1, 1998. There was no established exchange price for the patent, and the note had no ready market. The prevailing rate of interest for a note of this type at April 1, 1996, was 12%. The present value of $1 for two periods at 12% is 0.797 (use this factor). The patent had a carrying value of $40,000 at January 1, 1993, and the amortization for the year ended December 31, 1996, would have been $8,000. The collection of the note receivable from Zhao is reasonably assured.
  4. On July 1, 1996, Weaver sold a parcel of land to Sbarboro Company for $200,000 under an installment sale contract. Sbarboro made a $60,000 cash down payment on July 1, 1996, and signed a 4-year 11% note for the $140,000 balance. The equal annual payments of principal and interest on the note will be $45,125 payable on July 1, 1997, through July 1, 2000. The land could have been sold at an established cash price of $200,000. The cost of the land to Weaver was $150,000. Circumstances are such that the collection of the installments on the note is reasonably assured.

Instructions
  (a) Prepare the long-term receivables section of Weaver's balance sheet at December 31, 1996.
  (b) Prepare a schedule showing the current portion of the long-term receivables and accrued interest receivable that would appear in Weaver's balance sheet at December 31, 1996.

(c)   Prepare a schedule showing interest revenue from the long-term receivables that would appear on Weaver's income statement for the year ended December 31, 1996.

*P7-18 (Proof of Cash)   You have been hired as the new assistant controller of Lilja Inc. and assigned the task of proving the cash account balance. As of December 31, 1995, you have obtained the following information relative to the December cash operations.

1. Balance per bank

11/30/95	$137,600
12/31/95	115,666

2. Balance per books

11/30/95	101,162
12/31/95	105,046

3. Receipts for the month of December, 1995

per bank	714,280
per books	742,415

4. Outstanding checks

11/30/95	37,258
12/31/95	45,297

5. Dishonored checks returned by the bank and recorded by Lilja Inc. amounted to $3,125 during the month of December 1995; according to the books $2,500 was redeposited. Dishonored checks, recorded on the bank statement but not on the books until the following months, amounted to $820 at November 30, 1995, and $1,150 at December 31, 1995.

6. On December 31, 1995, a $1,162 check of the Hakala Company was charged to Lilja Inc. account by the bank in error.

7. Proceeds of a note of Cherese Company collected by the bank for Lilja on December 10, 1995, were not entered on the books:

Principal	$2,000
Interest	20
	2,020
Less collection charge	5
	$2,015

8. Interest on a bank loan for the month of December charged by the bank but not recorded on the books amounted to $4,230.

9. Deposit in transit:

12/31/95	$30,150

Instructions
Prepare bank reconciliations as of November 30, 1995, and December 31, 1995, using a four-column "proof of cash" with the following column headings for amounts:

11/30/95 Beginning Reconciliation	Receipts	Disbursements	12/31/95 Ending Reconciliation

Proceed from "balance per bank statement" to "balance per books."

*P7-19 (Proof of Cash)   Using the data given in Problem 7–18, prepare (a) a four-column bank reconciliation proceeding from "balance per bank statement" to "correct balance" and "balance per books" to "correct balance," and (b) accompanying entries to adjust the books at December 31.

*P7-20 (Proof of Cash)   You have been hired by Mark Kaleel Manufacturing Company as an internal auditor. One of your first assignments is to reconcile the bank account for the Montana Division.
The bank statement shows the following:

Beginning Balance, August 1, 1996	$ 90,125
Deposits—(20)	915,376
Checks—(64) plus debit memos	(851,415)
Service charges—new checks	(44)
Ending Balance, August 31, 1996	$ 154,042

The cash account on the books of the Montana Division is as follows:

		Cash		
July 1	64,192	July 31—Cash Disbursements	665,441
July 31—Cash Receipts	682,429	August 1—Bank Reconciliation	375
August 31—Cash Receipts	919,872	August 31—Cash Disbursements	856,446

Your review of last month's bank reconciliation and the current bank statement reveals the following:

1. Outstanding checks

July 31, 1996	$25,742
August 31, 1996	33,561

2. Deposits in transit

July 31, 1996	16,422
August 31, 1996	20,918

3. Check #216 for office furniture was written for $695 but recorded in the cash disbursements journal as $965. The bank deducted the check as $695.
4. A check written on the account of Mark Kaleel Manufacturing Co. for $583 was deducted by the bank from the Montana Division account.
5. Included with the bank statement was a debit memorandum dated August 31 for $2,475 for interest on a note taken out by the Montana Division on July 30.
6. The service charge for new checks has not been recorded.
7. The July 31, 1996 bank reconciliation showed as reconciling items a service charge of $26 and an NSF check for $349.

Instructions

(a) Prepare a four-column proof of cash reconciling the balance per bank to the balance per book.
(b) Prepare a four-column proof of cash reconciling balance per bank to the "correct balance" and balance per books to the "correct balance."
(c) Prepare any adjusting journal entries necessary to correct the cash account per the books of the Montana Division.

*P7-21 (Comprehensive Journal Entries for Seller and Factor) Hrubec Corp. factors $400,000 of accounts receivable with Waubonsee Factors, Inc. on a without recourse basis. The finance charge is 2¾% of the amount of receivables, and an additional 4% is retained to cover probable adjustments. Per the terms of the factoring agreement, Hrubec handles returned goods, allowances, and shipping disputes. Waubonsee collects the cash and acknowledges sales discounts, but such discounts are charged to Hrubec. Credit losses are absorbed by Waubonsee. Hrubec has not recorded any bad debt expense related to the factored receivables. The following transactions pertain to this factoring:

Aug. 1 The receivable records are transferred to Waubonsee Factors. Waubonsee estimates that $2,900 of the accounts will prove to be uncollectible.

31 Waubonsee collects $234,000 during August after allowing for $9,000 of sales discounts. Sales returns and allowances during August totaled $2,400.

Sept. 20 Waubonsee writes off a $2,000 account after learning of the company's bankruptcy.

30 Waubonsee collects $151,720 during September. Sales returns and allowances during September totaled $880.

Oct. 10 Hrubec and Waubonsee make a final cash settlement.

Instructions

(a) Prepare all journal entries for both companies on the above dates.
(b) Compute the net cash proceeds Hrubec ultimately realizes from the factoring.
(c) Compute the factor's net income from the factoring.

*P7-22 (Comprehensive Journal Entries for Seller and Factor) Frippery Furnishings, Inc. factors $700,000 of accounts receivable with Boyd, Dewey, Cheetum, and Howe Financing Corporation on a with recourse basis. The situation indicates that Frippery should account for the factoring as a borrowing activity. The finance charge is 2½% of the amount of accounts receivable; an additional 3½% is withheld to cover sales discounts, returns, and allowances. Frippery handles returns, allowances, and shipping disputes. Howe handles cash collections, acknowledging sales discounts that are charged to Frippery. The receivable records are transferred to Howe on February 2, at which time uncollectible accounts are estimated to be $10,000. During February and March, Howe collects $673,900; sales returns and allowances are $9,500; sales discounts are $6,600; and bad debts of $10,000 materialize. On April 7, Frippery and Howe make a final cash settlement.

Instructions

(a) Prepare all journal entries for Frippery Furnishings, Inc. that result from the above transactions.

(b) Indicate how the above transactions would be reflected on Frippery's February 2 balance sheet.

*P7-23 (Comprehensive Journal Entries—Factoring) Green Mountain Woolens, Inc. factors $1,000,000 of accounts receivable with Bennington Credit Corp. on a without-recourse basis. On June 1, the receivable records are transferred to Bennington Credit, which will make the collections. Bennington Credit assesses a finance charge of 5% of the total accounts receivable factored and retains an amount equal to 6% of the total receivables to cover sales discounts, returns, and allowances. Green Mountain Woolens handles any returned goods, claims and allowances for defective goods, and disputes concerning shipments. Bennington handles the sale discounts and absorbs the credit losses.

During the month of June, the factor collects $650,000; merchandise totaling $14,300 is returned; sales discounts of $9,500 are taken; and allowances of $5,600 are granted.

During the month of July, the factor collects $237,000; merchandise totaling $2,300 is returned; no sales discounts are allowed; and allowances of $3,800 for defective goods are granted.

On August 1, Green Mountain Woolens and Bennington Credit agree that any further returns, discounts, and allowance will be absorbed by Green Mountain Woolens; Bennington therefore returns the balance of the retainer held for such events. Uncollectibles are estimated to be $6,200.

Instructions

(a) Prepare the entries on Green Mountain Woolens' books at June 1, for the June transactions, for the July transactions, and at August 1.

(b) Prepare the entries on Bennington Credit's books at June 1, for the June transactions, for the July transactions, and at August 1.

CASES

C7-1 (Cash Reporting) Presented below are two financial statement excerpts. Answer the question(s) that follow each of these excerpts.

1. Spinal Tap Inc. reported the following information:

	Current Year	Prior Year
	(in thousands)	
Current Assets:		
Cash and short-term investments (Note 2)	$9,123	$5,227

Note 2: Cash and Short-term Investments
Cash and short-term investments consisted of the following:

	Current Year	Prior Year
	(in thousands)	
Cash on hand and demand deposits	$ 554	$1,809
Temporary cash investments	8,569	3,418
	$9,123	$5,227

Spinal Tap Inc. does not maintain any significant formal or informal compensating balance arrangements with financial institutions. Short-term investments are stated at cost that approximates market value.

Instructions

(a) Why does the company report the amount of the short-term investments in the notes to the financial statements?

(b) What are compensating balance arrangements and how should they be reported in the financial statements?

(c) Indicate the possible differences between cash equivalents and short-term investments.

2. Gin Blossoms Corporation presented the following information:

	Current Year	Prior Year
	($000)	
Cash (including time deposits of $3,799 in the current year, and $2,846 in the prior year) (Note 3)	$7,957	$6,588

Note 3: In connection with the Chapter 11 proceedings the company has placed certain funds in escrowed accounts and segregated other accounts on the books and records of the company. These funds totaled approximately $278,379,000 in the current period and $220,358,000 in the preceding period.

Instructions

(a) What is the difference between a demand deposit and a time deposit?

(b) Why are the amounts of the time deposits reported separately?

(c) Why are the funds in escrow not reported as part of cash? Provide examples of why cash might be restricted.

(d) Why is Petty Cash not reported in the financial statements?

C7-2 (Bad Debt Accounting) En Vogue Company has significant amounts of trade accounts receivable. En Vogue uses the allowance method to estimate bad debts instead of the direct writeoff method. During the year, some specific accounts were written off as uncollectible, and some that were previously written off as uncollectible were collected.

Instructions

(a) What are the deficiencies of the direct writeoff method?

(b) What are the two basic allowance methods used to estimate bad debts, and what is the theoretical justification for each?

(c) How should En Vogue account for the collection of the specific accounts previously written off as uncollectible?

C7-3 (Various Receivable Accounting Issues) Ween Company uses the net method of accounting for sales discounts. Ween also offers trade discounts to various groups of buyers.

On August 1, 1995, Ween factored some accounts receivable on a without recourse basis. Ween incurred a finance charge.

Ween also has some notes receivable bearing an appropriate rate of interest. The principal and total interest are due at maturity. The notes were received on October 1, 1995, and mature on September 30, 1997. Ween's operating cycle is less than one year.

Instructions

(a) 1. Using the net method, how should Ween account for the sales discounts at the date of sale? What is the rationale for the amount recorded as sales under the net method?

2. Using the net method, what is the effect on Ween's sales revenues and net income when customers do not take the sales discounts?

(b) What is the effect of trade discounts on sales revenues and accounts receivable? Why?

(c) How should Ween account for the accounts receivable factored on August 1, 1995? Why?

(d) How should Ween account for the note receivable and the related interest on December 31, 1995? Why?

C7-4 (Bad Debt Reporting Issues) Jay Hawks conducts a wholesale merchandising business that sells approximately 5,000 items per month with a total monthly average sales value of $200,000. Its annual bad debt ratio has been approximately 1½% of sales. In recent discussions with his bookkeeper, Mr. Hawks has become confused by all the alternatives apparently available in handling the Allowance for Doubtful Accounts balance. The following information has been shown.

1. An allowance can be set up (a) on the basis of a percentage of sales or (b) on the basis of a valuation of all past due or otherwise questionable accounts receivable—those considered uncollectible being charged to such allowance at the close of the accounting period or specific items charged off directly against (1) Gross Sales, or to (2) Bad Debt Expense in the year in which they are determined to be uncollectible.

2. Collection agency and legal fees, and so on, incurred in connection with the attempted recovery of bad debts can be charged to (a) Bad Debt Expense, (b) Allowance for Doubtful Accounts, (c) Legal Expense, or (d) General Expense.

3. Debts previously written off in whole or in part but currently recovered can be credited to (a) other revenue, (b) bad debt expense, or (c) allowance for doubtful accounts.

Instructions

Which of the foregoing methods would you recommend to Mr. Hawks in regard to (1) allowances and charge-offs, (2) collection expenses, and (3) recoveries? State briefly and clearly the reasons supporting your recommendations.

C7-5 (Basic Note and Accounts Receivable Transactions)

Part 1

On July 1, 1996, DADAY Company, a calendar-year company, sold special-order merchandise on credit and received in return an interest-bearing note receivable from the customer. DADAY Company will receive interest at the prevailing rate for a note of this type. Both the principal and interest are due in one lump sum on June 30, 1997.

Instructions

When should DADAY Company report interest income from the note receivable? Discuss the rationale for your answer.

Part 2

On December 31, 1996, DADAY Company had significant amounts of accounts receivable as a result of credit sales to its customers. DADAY Company uses the allowance method based on credit sales to estimate bad debts. Past experience indicates that 2% of credit sales normally will not be collected. This pattern is expected to continue.

Instructions

(a) Discuss the rationale for using the allowance method based on credit sales to estimate bad debts. Contrast this method with the allowance method based on the balance in the trade receivables accounts.

(b) How should DADAY Company report the allowance for bad debts account on its balance sheet at December 31, 1996? Also, describe the alternatives, if any, for presentation of bad debt expense in DADAY Company's 1996 income statement.

(AICPA adapted)

C7-6 (Bad Debt Reporting Issues) The Primus Company sells office equipment and supplies to many organizations in the city and surrounding area on contract terms of 2/10, n/30. In the past, over 75% of the credit customers have taken advantage of the discount by paying within 10 days of the invoice date.

The number of customers taking the full 30 days to pay has increased within the last year. Current indications are that less than 60% of the customers are now taking the discount. Bad debts as a percentage of gross credit sales have risen from the 1.5% provided in past years to about 4% in the current year.

The controller has responded to a request for more information on the deterioration in collections of accounts receivable with the report reproduced below.

The Primus Company
Finance Committee Report—Accounts Receivable Collections
May 31, 1996

The fact that some credit accounts will prove uncollectible is normal. Annual bad debt write-offs have been 1.5% of gross credit sales over the past five years. During the last fiscal year, this percentage increased to slightly less than 4%. The current Accounts Receivable balance is $1,600,000. The condition of this balance in terms of age and probability of collection is as follows:

Proportion of Total	Age Categories	Probability of Collection
68%	not yet due	99%
15%	less than 30 days past due	96½%
8%	30 to 60 days past due	95%
5%	61 to 120 days past due	91%
2½%	121 to 180 days past due	75%
1½%	over 180 days past due	20%

The Allowance for Doubtful Accounts had a credit balance of $40,300 on June 1, 1995. The Primus Company has provided for a monthly bad debts expense accrual during the current fiscal year based on the assumption that 4% of gross credit sales will be uncollectible. Total gross credit sales for the 1995–96 fiscal year amounted to $4,000,000. Write-offs of bad accounts during the year totaled $145,000.

Instructions

(a) Prepare an accounts receivable aging schedule for The Primus Company using the age categories identified in the controller's report to the Finance Committee showing:

  1. The amount of accounts receivable outstanding for each age category and in total.

  2. The estimated amount that is uncollectible for each category and in total.

(b) Compute the amount of the year-end adjustment necessary to bring Allowance for Doubtful Accounts to the balance indicated by the age analysis. Then prepare the necessary journal entry to adjust the accounting records.

(c) In a recessionary environment with tight credit and high interest rates:
    1. Identify steps The Primus Company might consider to improve the accounts receivable situation.
    2. Then evaluate each step identified in terms of the risks and costs involved.

(CMA adapted)

C7-7 (Reporting of Notes Receivable, Interest, and Sale of Receivables) On July 1, 1996, Wayne Company sold special-order merchandise on credit and received in return an interest-bearing note receivable from the customer. Wayne will receive interest at the prevailing rate for a note of this type. Both the principal and interest are due in one lump sum on June 30, 1997.

On September 1, 1996, Wayne sold special-order merchandise on credit and received in return a noninterest-bearing note receivable from the customer. The prevailing rate of interest for a note of this type is determinable. The note receivable is due in one lump sum on August 31, 1998.

Wayne also has significant amounts of trade accounts receivable as a result of credit sales to its customers. On October 1, 1996, some trade accounts receivable were assigned to Garth Finance Company on a with recourse, non-notification (Wayne handles collections) basis for an advance of 75% of their amount at an interest charge of 20% on the balance outstanding.

On November 1, 1996, other trade accounts receivable were factored on a without recourse basis. The factor withheld 5% of the trade accounts receivable factored as protection against sales returns and allowances and charged a finance charge of 3%.

Instructions
(a) How should Wayne determine the interest income for 1996 on the
    1. Interest-bearing note receivable? Why?
    2. Noninterest-bearing note receivable? Why?
(b) How should Wayne report the interest-bearing note receivable and the noninterest-bearing note receivable on its balance sheet at December 31, 1996?
(c) How should Wayne account for subsequent collections on the trade accounts receivable assigned on October 1, 1996, and the payments to Garth Finance? Why?
(d) How should Wayne account for the trade accounts receivable factored on November 1, 1996? Why?

(AICPA adapted)

C7-8 (Accounting for Non-interest Note) Soon after beginning the year-end audit work on March 10 at Elvis Company, the auditor has the following conversation with the controller.

CONTROLLER:	The year ended March 31st should be our most profitable in history and, as a consequence, the Board of Directors has just awarded the officers generous bonuses.
AUDITOR:	I thought profits were down this year in the industry, according to your latest interim report.
CONTROLLER:	Well, they were down but 10 days ago we closed a deal that will give us a substantial increase for the year.
AUDITOR:	Oh, what was it?
CONTROLLER:	Well, you remember a few years ago our former president bought stock in Graceland Enterprises because he had those grandiose ideas about becoming a conglomerate. For 6 years we have not been able to sell this stock, which cost us $3,000,000 and has not paid a nickel in dividends. Thursday we sold this stock to Houn'dog, Inc. for $4,000,000. So, we will have a gain of $700,000 ($1,000,000 pretax) which will increase our net income for the year to $4,000,000, compared with last year's $3,800,000. As far as I know, we'll be the only company in the industry to register an increase in net income this year. That should help the market value of the stock!
AUDITOR:	Do you expect to receive the $4,000,000 in cash by March 31st, your fiscal year-end?
CONTROLLER:	No. Although Houn'dog, Inc. is an excellent company, they are a little tight for cash because of their rapid growth. Consequently, they are going to give us a $4,000,000 noninterest-bearing note due $400,000 per year for the next 10 years. The first payment is due on March 31 of next year.
AUDITOR:	Why is the note noninterest-bearing?
CONTROLLER:	Because that's what everybody agreed to. Since we don't have any interest-bearing debt, the funds invested in the note do not cost us anything and besides, we were not getting any dividends on the Graceland Enterprises stock.

Instructions

Do you agree with the way the controller has accounted for the transaction? If not, how should the transaction be accounted for?

C7-9 (Financial and Accounting Impacts of Credit Cards) Houseall, Inc. operates a full-line department store that is dominant in its market area, is easily accessible to public and private transportation, has adequate parking facilities, and is near a large permanent military base. The president of the company, Josi Brandt, seeks your advice on a recently received proposal.

A local bank in which your client has an account recently affiliated with a popular national credit card plan and has extended an invitation to your client to participate in the plan. Under the plan, affiliated banks mail credit card applications to persons in the community who have good credit ratings regardless of whether they are bank customers. If the recipients wish to receive a credit card, they complete, sign, and return the application and installment credit agreement. Holders of cards thus activated may charge merchandise or services at any participating establishment throughout the nation.

The bank guarantees payment to all participating merchants on all presented invoices that have been properly completed, signed, and validated with the impression of credit cards that have not expired or been reported stolen or otherwise canceled. Local merchants including your client may turn in all card-validated sales tickets or invoices to their affiliated local bank at any time and receive immediate credits to their checking accounts of 96.5% of the face value of the invoices. If card users pay the bank in full within 30 days for amounts billed, the bank levies no added charges against the customer. If they elect to make their payments under a deferred payment plan, the bank adds a service charge that amounts to an effective interest rate of 18% per annum on unpaid balances. Only the local affiliated banks and the franchiser of the credit card plan share in these revenues.

The 18% service charge approximates what your client has been billing customers who pay their accounts over an extended period on a schedule similar to that offered under the credit card plan. Participation in the plan does not prevent your client from continuing to carry on its credit business as in the past.

Instructions

(a) What are (1) the positive and (2) the negative financial and accounting-related factors that Houseall, Inc. should consider in deciding whether to participate in the described credit card plan? Explain.

(b) If Houseall, Inc. does participate in the plan, which income statement and balance sheet accounts may change materially as the plan becomes fully operative? (Such factors as market position, sales mix, prices, markup, etc., are expected to remain about the same as in the past.) Explain.

(AICPA adapted)

▶ Using Your Judgment ◀

▶ FINANCIAL REPORTING PROBLEM

Refer to the financial statements and other documents of Georgia-Pacific Corporation presented in Appendix 5-A and answer the following questions.

(a) In the Financial Strategy section of Georgia-Pacific Corporation 1993 annual report, the management stated that "we believe it is more important to focus on the cash flow generated by our business than on net income." Do you agree with management's comment? Explain.

(b) In 1993, Georgia-Pacific sold part of its accounts receivable. What was the amount received from the sale of receivables? In which statements did the management report the transaction and how? Had the portion of allowance for doubtful accounts related to the receivables sold been removed and why? What kind of agreement existed between the purchasers and Georgia-Pacific?

▶ WRITING ASSIGNMENT

As the manager of the accounts receivable department for Lord Byron Leather Goods, Ltd., you recently noticed that Percy Shelley, your accounts receivable clerk who is paid $1,200 per month, has been wearing unusually tasteful and expensive clothing. (This is Lord Byron's first year in business.) This morning, Shelley drove up to work in a brand new Cadillac.

Naturally suspicious by nature, you decide to test the accuracy of the accounts receivable balance of $132,000 as shown in the ledger. The following information is available for your first year (precisely nine months ended September 30, 1995) in business:

(1)	Collections from customers	$198,000
(2)	Merchandise purchased	360,000
(3)	Ending merchandise inventory	90,000
(4)	Goods are marked to sell at 40% above cost.	

Instructions

Assuming all sales were made on account, compute the ending accounts receivable balance that should appear in the ledger, noting any apparent shortage. Then, draft a memo dated October 3, 1995, to John Keats, the branch manager, explaining the facts in this situation. Remember that this problem is serious, and you do not want to make hasty accusations.

▶ GROUP ASSIGNMENT

(Compute Income Effect of Various Transfers of Receivables) Radisson Company requires additional cash for its business. Radisson has decided to use its accounts receivable to raise the additional cash and has asked your group to determine the income statement effects of the following contemplated transactions.

1. On July 1, 1996, Radisson assigned $400,000 of accounts receivable to Stickum Finance Company. Radisson received an advance from Stickum of 85% of the assigned accounts receivable less a commission on the advance of 3%. Prior to December 31, 1996, Radisson collected $220,000 on the assigned accounts receivable, and remitted $232,720 to Stickum, $12,720 of which represented interest on the advance from Stickum.

2. On December 1, 1996, Radisson sold $300,000 of net accounts receivable to Wunsch Company for $250,000. The receivables were sold outright on a nonrecourse basis.

3. On December 31, 1996, an advance of $120,000 was received from the First Bank by pledging $160,000 of Radisson's accounts receivable. Radisson's first payment to First Bank is due on January 30, 1997.

Instructions

Your instructor will identify one member of the group to serve as a recorder and one member to serve as spokesperson. Work within your group to provide information for the recorder to prepare a schedule showing the income statement effect for the year ended December 31, 1996, as a result of the above facts. The spokesperson will report the group findings to the class and be prepared to show supporting computations.

▶ ETHICS CASES

EC7-1 (Ethical Issues—Bad Debt Reporting) Little Bear Company is a subsidiary of Big Bear Corp. The controller believes that the yearly allowance for doubtful accounts for Little Bear should be 2% of net credit sales. The president, nervous that the parent company might expect the subsidiary to sustain its 10% growth rate, suggests that the controller increase the allowance for doubtful accounts to 3% yearly. The supervisor thinks that the lower net income, which reflects a 6% growth rate, will be a more sustainable rate for Little Bear Company (a fast-food company).

Instructions
(a) Should the controller be concerned with Little Bear Company's growth rate in estimating the allowance? Explain your answer.
(b) Does the president's request pose an ethical dilemma for the controller? Give your reasons.

EC7-2 (Ethical Issues—Classification of Notes Receivable) Venghaus Corporation has several current notes receivable on its year-end balance sheet. While collection seems certain, it may be delayed beyond one year. Because of this, the controller wants to re-classify these notes as non-current. The treasurer of Venghaus also thinks that collection will be delayed, but does not favor re-classification because this will reduce the current ratio from 1.5:1 to .8:1. This reduction in current ratio is detrimental to company prospects for securing a major loan.

Instructions
(a) Should the controller re-classify the notes? Give your reasons.
(b) Considering the possible harm to stakeholders, what is the ethical dilemma for the controller and the treasurer?

CHAPTER 8

VALUATION OF INVENTORIES:
A COST BASIS APPROACH

LEARNING OBJECTIVES

After studying this chapter, you should be able to:

1. Identify major classifications of inventory.
2. Distinguish between the perpetual and periodic inventory systems.
3. Identify the effects of inventory errors on the financial statements.
4. Identify the items that should be included as inventory cost.
5. Describe and compare the flow assumptions used in accounting for inventories.
6. Explain the effect of LIFO liquidations.
7. Explain the dollar-value LIFO method.
8. Identify the major advantages and disadvantages of LIFO.
9. Identify the reasons why a given inventory method is selected.

UNDERLYING CONCEPT

Because inventory provides future economic benefits to the company (revenue from sales), it meets the definition of an asset. Inventory costs will be matched against revenue in the period that sales occur.

*I*nventories are asset items held for sale in the ordinary course of business or goods that will be used or consumed in the production of goods to be sold. The description and measurement of inventory require careful attention because the investment in inventories is frequently the largest current asset in manufacturing and retail businesses. Indeed, inventories may be a significant portion of the company's total assets. The sale of inventory at a price greater than total cost is the primary source of revenue for both manufacturing and retailing enterprises. Inventories are particularly significant because they may materially affect both the income statement and the balance sheet.

Recent cases of fraudulent financial reporting have emphasized the importance of inventory. According to *The Wall Street Journal*, "creating phantom inventory instantly benefits a company's bottom line."[1] For example, it is alleged that Phar-Mor Inc., a deep-discount drugstore chain, overstated its profits by $50 million by keeping in its inventory records items that had already been sold, maintaining secret inventory records, and creating phantom inventory at many of the chain's stores.[2]

Similarly, Crazy Eddie's new management alleged that previous management had created phantom inventory and profits. The company said its former management inflated the inventory count by $10 million by drafting phony count sheets and improp-

---

[1]"Inventory Chicanery Tempts More Firms, Fools More Auditors," *The Wall Street Journal*, December 12, 1992, p. A1.

[2]Overstatement of ending inventory reduces cost of sales and thus increases profits.

erly including merchandise that was being returned to suppliers. The total shortfall for the company was later revised to $65 million.[3] In short, Crazy Eddie went crazy.

► MAJOR CLASSIFICATIONS OF INVENTORY

A **merchandising concern,** such as Wal-Mart, ordinarily purchases its merchandise in a form ready for sale. It reports the cost assigned to unsold units left on hand as **merchandise inventory.** Only one inventory account, Merchandise Inventory, appears in the financial statements. **Manufacturing concerns,** on the other hand, produce goods to be sold to the merchandising firms. Many of the largest U.S. businesses are manufacturers—Boeing, IBM, Exxon, Procter and Gamble, Ford, Motorola, to name only a few. Although the products they produce may be quite different, manufacturers normally have three inventory accounts—Raw Materials, Work in Process, and Finished Goods.

OBJECTIVE 1

Identify major classifications of inventory.

The cost assigned to goods and materials on hand but not yet placed into production is reported as **raw materials inventory.** Raw materials include the wood to make a baseball bat or the steel to make a car. These materials ultimately can be traced directly to the end product.

At any point in a continuous production process some units are not completely processed. The cost of the raw material on which production has been started but not completed, plus the direct labor cost applied specifically to this material and a ratable share of manufacturing overhead costs, constitute the **work in process inventory.**

The costs identified with the completed but unsold units on hand at the end of the fiscal period are reported as **finished goods inventory.** The current asset sections presented in Illustration 8-1 contrast the financial statement presentation of inventories of a merchandising company and those of a manufacturing company. The remainder of the balance sheet is essentially similar for the two types of companies.

ILLUSTRATION 8-1 Comparison of Current Asset Presentation for Merchandising and Manufacturing Companies

Merchandising Company BALANCE SHEET December 31, 1996		Manufacturing Company BALANCE SHEET December 31, 1996		
Current assets		Current assets		
Cash	$100,000	Cash		$180,000
Receivables (net)	210,000	Receivables (net)		210,000
Merchandise inventory	**400,000**	**Inventories:**		
Prepaid expenses	22,000	**Finished goods**	**$ 80,000**	
Total	$732,000	**Work in process**	**95,000**	
		Raw materials	**160,000**	335,000
		Prepaid expenses		18,000
		Total		$743,000

A manufacturing company also might include a **manufacturing or factory supplies inventory** account. In it would be items such as machine oils, nails, cleaning materials, and the like that are used in production but are not the primary materials being processed. The flow of costs through a merchandising company is different from that of a manufacturing company, as shown in Illustration 8-2.

---

[3]"Short Circuit: How Mounting Woes at Crazy Eddie Sank a Turnaround Effort," *The Wall Street Journal,* July 10, 1989, p. A1.

ILLUSTRATION 8-2
Flow of Costs through Manufacturing and Merchandising Companies

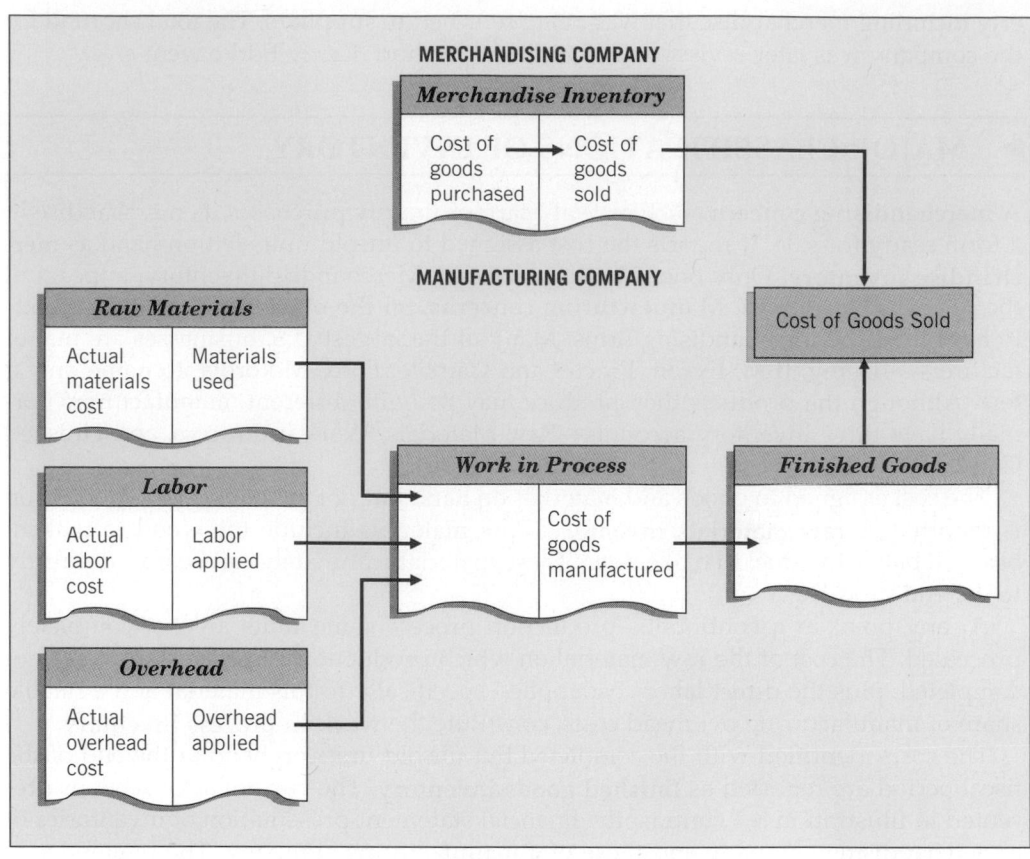

▶ INVENTORY MANAGEMENT AND CONTROL

OBJECTIVE 2

Distinguish between the perpetual and periodic inventory systems.

For various reasons, management is vitally interested in inventory planning and control. An accurate accounting system with up-to-date records is essential. If unsalable items have accumulated in the inventory, a potential loss exists. Sales and customers may be lost if products ordered by customers are not available in the desired style, quality, and quantity. Also, businesses must monitor inventory levels carefully to limit the financing costs of carrying large inventories. In recent years, with the introduction and use of "just-in-time" (JIT) inventory order systems and better supplier relationships, inventory levels have become leaner for many enterprises.[4]

PERPETUAL SYSTEM

As indicated in Chapter 3, inventory records may be maintained on a perpetual or periodic basis. Under a **perpetual inventory system,** a continuous record of changes in inventory is maintained in the Inventory account. That is, all purchases and sales (issues) of goods are recorded directly in the Inventory account **as they occur.** The accounting features of a perpetual inventory system are:

1. Purchases of merchandise for resale or raw materials for production are debited to Inventory rather than to Purchases.

2. Freight-in, purchase returns and allowances, and purchase discounts are recorded in Inventory rather than in separate accounts.

3. Cost of goods sold is recognized for each sale by debiting the account, Cost of Goods Sold, and crediting Inventory.

---

[4]On the other hand, Lands' End, a catalogue clothier, flouts just-in-time—it builds inventory. The reason: a complete inventory is vital to cementing customer loyalty.

4. Inventory is a control account that is supported by a subsidiary ledger of individual inventory records. The subsidiary records show the quantity and cost of each type of inventory on hand.

The perpetual inventory system provides a continuous record of the balances in both the inventory account and the cost of goods sold account.

Under a computerized recordkeeping system, additions to and issuances from inventory can be recorded nearly instantaneously. The popularity and affordability of computerized accounting software have made the perpetual system cost-effective for all sizes and kinds of businesses. Recording sales with optical scanners at the cash register has been incorporated into perpetual inventory systems at many retail stores.

PERIODIC SYSTEM

Under a **periodic inventory system,** the quantity of inventory on hand is determined, as its name implies, only periodically. All acquisitions of inventory during the accounting period are recorded by debits to a Purchases account. The total in the Purchases account at the end of the accounting period is added to the cost of the inventory on hand at the beginning of the period to determine the total cost of the goods available for sale during the period. Ending inventory is subtracted from the cost of goods available for sale to compute the cost of goods sold. Note that under a periodic inventory system, the cost of goods sold is a residual amount that is dependent upon a physically counted ending inventory.

The **physical inventory count** required by a periodic system is taken once a year at the end of the year.[5] However, most companies need more current information regarding their inventory levels to protect against stockouts or overpurchasing and to aid in the preparation of monthly or quarterly financial data. As a consequence, many companies use a **modified perpetual inventory system** in which increases and decreases in quantities only—not dollar amounts—are kept in a detailed inventory record. It is merely a memorandum device outside the double-entry system which helps in determining the level of inventory at any point in time.

Whether a company maintains a perpetual inventory in quantities and dollars, quantities only, or has no perpetual inventory record at all, it probably takes a physical inventory once a year. No matter what type of inventory records are in use or how well organized the procedures for recording purchases and requisitions, the danger of loss and error is always present. Waste, breakage, theft, improper entry, failure to prepare or record requisitions, and any number of similar possibilities may cause the inventory records to differ from the actual inventory on hand. This requires periodic verification of the inventory records by actual count, weight, or measurement. These counts are compared with the detailed inventory records. The records are corrected to agree with the quantities actually on hand.

Insofar as possible, the physical inventory should be taken near the end of the concern's fiscal year so that correct inventory quantities are available for use in preparing annual accounting reports and statements. Because this is not always possible, however, physical inventories taken within two or three months of the year's end are satisfactory, if the detailed inventory records are maintained with a fair degree of accuracy.

To illustrate the difference between a perpetual and a periodic system, assume that Fesmire Company had the following transactions during the current year:

Beginning inventory	100 units at $ 6 =	$ 600
Purchases	900 units at $ 6 =	$5,400
Sales	600 units at $12 =	$7,200
Ending inventory	400 units at $ 6 =	$2,400

---

[5]In recent years, some companies have developed methods of determining inventories, including statistical sampling, that are sufficiently reliable to make unnecessary an annual physical count of each item of inventory.

The entries to record these transactions during the current year are shown in Illustration 8-3.

ILLUSTRATION 8-3
Comparative Entries—
Perpetual vs. Periodic

Perpetual Inventory System			Periodic Inventory System		
1. Beginning inventory, 100 units at $6:					
The inventory account shows the inventory on hand at $600.			The inventory account shows the inventory on hand at $600.		
2. Purchase 900 units at $6:					
Inventory	5,400		Purchases	5,400	
Accounts Payable		5,400	Accounts Payable		5,400
3. Sale of 600 units at $12:					
Accounts Receivable	7,200		Accounts Receivable	7,200	
Sales		7,200	Sales		7,200
Cost of Goods Sold	3,600			(No entry)	
(600 at $6)					
Inventory		3,600			
4. End-of-period entries for inventory accounts, 400 units at $6:					
No entry necessary.			Inventory (ending, by count)	2,400	
The account, Inventory, shows the ending			Cost of Goods Sold	3,600	
balance of $2,400			Purchases		5,400
($600 + $5,400 − $3,600).			Inventory (beginning)		600

When a perpetual inventory system is used and a difference exists between the perpetual inventory balance and the physical inventory count, a separate entry is needed to adjust the perpetual inventory account. To illustrate, assume that at the end of the reporting period, the perpetual inventory account reported an inventory balance of $4,000, but a physical count indicated $3,800 was actually on hand. The entry to record the necessary writedown is as follows:

Inventory Over and Short	200	
Inventory		200

Perpetual inventory overages and shortages generally represent a misstatement of cost of goods sold. The difference is a result of normal and expected shrinkage, breakage, shoplifting, incorrect record keeping, and the like. Inventory Over and Short would therefore be an adjustment of cost of goods sold. In practice, the account Inventory Over and Short is sometimes reported in the other revenues and gains or other expenses and losses section, depending on its balance. Note that in a periodic inventory system the account Inventory Over and Short does not arise because there are no accounting records available against which to compare the physical count. Thus, inventory overages and shortages are buried in cost of goods sold.

▶ BASIC ISSUES IN INVENTORY VALUATION

Because the goods sold or used during an accounting period seldom correspond exactly to the goods bought or produced during that period, the physical inventory either increases or decreases. The cost of all the goods available for sale or use should be allocated between the goods that were sold or used and those that are still on hand. The **cost of goods available for sale or use** is the sum of (1) the cost of the goods on hand at the beginning of the period and (2) the cost of the goods acquired or produced during the period. The **cost of goods sold** is the difference between the cost of goods available for sale during the period and the cost of goods on hand at the end of the period.

Beginning inventory, Jan. 1	$100,000
Cost of goods acquired or produced during the year	800,000
Total cost of goods available for sale	900,000
Ending inventory, Dec. 31	200,000
Cost of goods sold during the year	$700,000

The valuation of inventories can be a complex process that requires determination of:

1. **The physical goods to be included in inventory** (who owns the goods?—goods in transit, consigned goods, special sales agreements).

2. **The costs to be included in inventory** (product vs. period costs, variable costing vs. absorption costing).

3. **The cost flow assumption to be adopted** (specific identification, average cost, FIFO, LIFO, retail, etc.).

We will explore these basic issues in the next three sections of the chapter.

▶ PHYSICAL GOODS TO BE INCLUDED IN INVENTORY

Technically, purchases should be recorded when legal title to the goods passes to the buyer. General practice, however, is to record acquisitions when the goods are received, because it is difficult for the buyer to determine the exact time of legal passage of title for every purchase. In addition, no material error is likely to result from such a practice if it is consistently applied.

GOODS IN TRANSIT

Sometimes purchased merchandise is in transit—not yet received—at the end of a fiscal period. The accounting for these shipped goods depends on who owns them. That can be determined by application of the "passage of title" rule. If the goods are shipped **f.o.b. shipping point,** title passes to the buyer when the seller delivers the goods to the common carrier, who acts as an agent for the buyer. (The abbreviation f.o.b. stands for free on board.) If the goods are shipped **f.o.b. destination,** title does not pass until the buyer receives the goods from the common carrier. "Shipping point" and "destination" are often designated by a particular location, for example, f.o.b. Denver.

The accounting rule is that goods to which legal title has passed should be recorded as purchases of the fiscal period. Goods shipped f.o.b. shipping point that are in transit at the end of the period belong to the buyer and should be shown in the buyer's records. Legal title to these goods passed to the buyer when the goods were shipped. To disregard such purchases would result in an understatement of inventories and accounts payable in the balance sheet and an understatement of purchases and ending inventories in the income statement.

The accountant normally prepares a purchase cut-off schedule at the end of the period to ensure that the purchases and inventories are recorded in the proper period. The passage of title rule determines what goods are included in the purchase cut-off. In cases where there is some question as to whether title has passed, the accountant exercises judgment, taking into consideration industry practices, the intent of the sales agreement, the policies of the parties involved, and any other available information.

CONSIGNED GOODS

A specialized method of marketing certain products uses a device known as a **consignment** shipment. Under this arrangement, one party (the consignor) ships merchandise to another (the consignee), who acts as the consignor's agent in selling the **consigned goods.** The consignee agrees to accept the goods without any liability, except to exercise due care and reasonable protection from loss or damage, until the goods are sold to a third party. When the consignee sells the goods, the revenue less a selling commission and expenses incurred in accomplishing the sale is remitted to the consignor.

Goods out on consignment remain the property of the consignor and are included in the consignor's inventory at purchase price or production cost. Occasionally, the inventory out on consignment is shown as a separate item, but unless the amount is large there is little need for this. Sometimes the inventory on consignment is reported in the notes to the financial statements. For example, Eagle Clothes, Inc. reported the following related to consigned goods: "Inventories consist of finished goods shipped on consignment to customers of the Company's subsidiary April-Marcus, Inc."

The consignee makes no entry to the inventory account for goods received because they are the property of the consignor. The consignee should be extremely careful *not* to include any of the goods consigned as a part of inventory.

SPECIAL SALE AGREEMENTS

As indicated earlier, transfer of legal title is the general guideline used to determine whether an item should be included in inventory. Unfortunately, transfer of legal title and the underlying substance of the transaction often do not match. For example, it is possible that legal title has passed to the purchaser but the seller of the goods retains the risks of ownership. Conversely, transfer of legal title may not occur, but the economic substance of the transaction is such that the seller no longer retains the risks of ownership. Three special sale situations are illustrated here to indicate the types of problems encountered in practice. These are:

1. Sales with buyback agreement.
2. Sales with high rates of return.
3. Sales on installment.

Sales with Buyback Agreement

Sometimes an enterprise finances its inventory without reporting either the liability or the inventory on its balance sheet. Such an approach—often referred to as a **product financing arrangement**—usually involves a "sale" with either an implicit or explicit "buyback" agreement. To illustrate, Hill Enterprises transfers ("sells") inventory to Chase, Inc. and simultaneously agrees to repurchase this merchandise at a specified price over a specified period of time. Chase then uses the inventory as collateral and borrows against it. Chase uses the loan proceeds to pay Hill. Hill repurchases the inventory in the future, and Chase employs the proceeds from repayment to meet its loan obligation.

The essence of this transaction is that Hill Enterprises is financing its inventory—and retaining risk of ownership—even though technical legal title to the merchandise was transferred to Chase. The advantage to Hill Enterprises for structuring a transaction in this manner is the avoidance of personal property taxes in certain states, the removal of the current liability from its balance sheet, and the ability to manipulate income. The advantages to Chase are that the purchase of the goods may solve a LIFO liquidation problem (discussed later), or that Chase may be interested in a reciprocal agreement at a later date.

These arrangements are often described as "**parking transactions**" in practice, because the seller simply parks the inventory on another enterprise's balance sheet for a short period of time. When a repurchase agreement exists at a set price and this price covers all costs of the inventory plus related holding costs, the accounting profession now requires that the inventory and related liability remain on the seller's books.[6]

Sales with High Rates of Return

Formal or informal agreements often exist in industries such as publishing, music, and toys and sporting goods that permit inventory to be returned for a full or partial refund. To illustrate, Quality Publishing Company sells textbooks to Campus Bookstores with an agreement that any books not sold may be returned for full credit. In the past,

---

[6]"Accounting for Product Financing Arrangements," *Statement of Financial Accounting Standards No. 49* (Stamford, Conn.: FASB, 1981).

approximately 25% of the textbooks sold to Campus Bookstores were returned. How should Quality Publishing report its sales transactions? One alternative is to record the sale at the full amount and establish an estimated sales returns and allowances account. A second possibility is to not record any sale until circumstances indicate the amount of inventory the buyer will return. The key question is: Under what circumstances should the inventory be considered sold and removed from Quality's inventory? The answer is that when the amount of returns can be reasonably estimated, the goods should be considered sold. Conversely, if returns are unpredictable, removal of these goods from the inventory of the seller is inappropriate.[7]

Sales on Installment

"Goods sold on installment" describes any type of sale in which payment is required in periodic installments over an extended period of time. Because the risk of loss from uncollectibles is higher in installment sale situations than in other sales transactions, the seller often withholds legal title to the merchandise until all the payments have been made. The question is whether the inventory should be considered sold, even though legal title has not passed. The answer is that **the goods should be excluded from the seller's inventory if the percentage of bad debts can be reasonably estimated.** Installment sales are discussed here to show that in some cases, the goods should be removed from inventory, although legal title may not have passed.

UNDERLYING CONCEPT

Revenues should be recognized because they have been substantially earned and are reasonably estimable. Collection is not the most critical event because bad debts can be reasonably estimated.

EFFECT OF INVENTORY ERRORS

Items incorrectly included or excluded in determining cost of goods sold will result in errors in the financial statements. Let's look at two cases:

OBJECTIVE 3

Identify the effects of inventory errors on the financial statements.

Ending Inventory Misstated

What would happen if the beginning inventory and purchases are recorded correctly, but some items are not included in ending inventory? In this situation, we would have the following effect on the financial statements at the end of the period:

Balance Sheet		Income Statement	
Inventory	Understated	Cost of goods sold	Overstated
Retained earnings	Understated		
Working capital	Understated	Net income	Understated
(current assets less current liabilities)			
Current ratio	Understated		
(current assets divided by current liabilities)			

ILLUSTRATION 8-4 Financial Statement Effects of Misstated Ending Inventory

Working capital and the current ratio are understated because ending inventory is understated; net income is understated because cost of goods sold is overstated.

To illustrate the effect on net income over a 2-year period, assume that the ending inventory of Jay Weiseman Corp. is understated by $10,000 and that all other items are correctly stated. The effect of this error will be to decrease net income in the current year and to increase net income in the following year. The error will be counterbalanced (offset) in the next period because beginning inventory will be understated and net income will be overstated. Both net income figures are misstated, but the total for the two years is correct as shown in Illustration 8-5.

UNDERLYING CONCEPT

When inventory is misstated, its presentation lacks representational faithfulness.

[7]"Revenue Recognition When Right of Return Exists," *Statement of Financial Accounting Standards No. 48* (Stamford, Conn.: FASB, 1981).

ILLUSTRATION 8-5
Effect of Ending Inventory Error on Two Periods

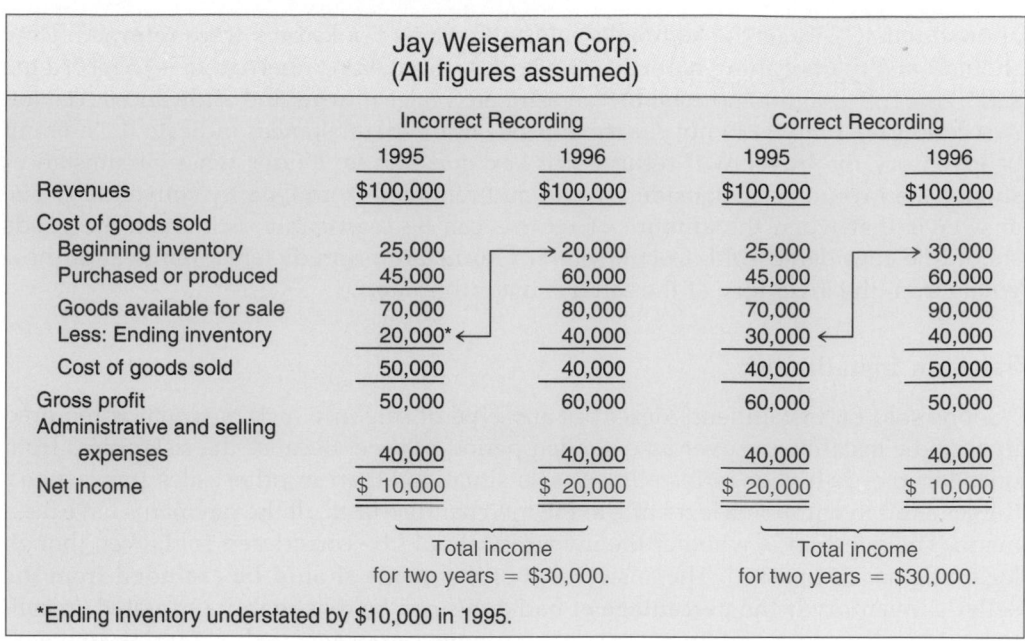

Jay Weiseman Corp.
(All figures assumed)

	Incorrect Recording		Correct Recording	
	1995	1996	1995	1996
Revenues	$100,000	$100,000	$100,000	$100,000
Cost of goods sold				
Beginning inventory	25,000	→ 20,000	25,000	→ 30,000
Purchased or produced	45,000	60,000	45,000	60,000
Goods available for sale	70,000	80,000	70,000	90,000
Less: Ending inventory	20,000*←	40,000	30,000 ←	40,000
Cost of goods sold	50,000	40,000	40,000	50,000
Gross profit	50,000	60,000	60,000	50,000
Administrative and selling				
expenses	40,000	40,000	40,000	40,000
Net income	$ 10,000	$ 20,000	$ 20,000	$ 10,000

Total income
for two years = $30,000.

Total income
for two years = $30,000.

*Ending inventory understated by $10,000 in 1995.

If ending inventory is *overstated*, the reverse effect occurs. Inventory, working capital, current ratio, and net income are overstated and cost of goods sold is understated. The effect of the error on net income will be counterbalanced in the next year, but both years' net income figures will be misstated.

Purchases and Inventory Misstated

Suppose that certain goods that the company owns are not recorded as a purchase and are not counted in ending inventory. The effect on the financial statements (assuming this is a purchase on account) is as follows:

ILLUSTRATION 8-6
Financial Statement Effects of Misstated Purchases and Inventory

Balance Sheet		Income Statement	
Inventory	Understated	Purchases	Understated
Retained earnings	No effect	Cost of goods sold	No effect
Accounts payable	Understated	Net income	No effect
Working capital	No effect	Inventory (ending)	Understated
Current ratio	Overstated		

To omit goods from purchases and inventory results in an understatement of inventory and accounts payable in the balance sheet and an understatement of purchases and ending inventory in the income statement. Net income for the period is not affected by the omission of such goods because purchases and ending inventory are both understated by the same amount—the error thereby offsetting itself in cost of goods sold. Total working capital is unchanged, but the **current ratio** is overstated because of the omission of equal amounts from inventory and accounts payable.

To illustrate the effect on the current ratio, assume that Larry Mall Company understated accounts payable and ending inventory by $40,000. The understated and correct data are shown below.

ILLUSTRATION 8-7
Effects of Purchases and Ending Inventory Errors

Purchases and Ending Inventory Understated		Purchases and Ending Inventory Correct	
Current assets	$120,000	Current assets	$160,000
Current liabilities	$ 40,000	Current liabilities	$ 80,000
Current ratio	3 to 1	Current ratio	2 to 1

The correct ratio is 2 to 1 rather than 3 to 1. Thus, understatement of accounts payable and ending inventory can lead to a "window dressing" of the current ratio (make it appear better than it is).

If both purchases (on account) and ending inventory are overstated, then the effects on the balance sheet are exactly the reverse. Inventory and accounts payable are overstated and the current ratio is understated; working capital is not affected. Cost of goods sold and net income are not affected because the errors offset one another.

We cannot overemphasize the importance of proper inventory computation in presenting accurate financial statements. For example, Leslie Fay, a women's apparel maker, recently had accounting irregularities that wiped out 1992 net income and caused a restatement of 1991's earnings. One reason, it inflated inventory and deflated cost of goods sold. Or remember Phar-Mor Inc. mentioned earlier. Or, Anixter Bros. Inc. had to restate its income by $1.7 million because an accountant in the antenna manufacturing division overstated the ending inventory, thereby reducing its cost of sales. Similarly, AM International allegedly recorded as sold products that were only being rented. As a result, inaccurate inventory figures added $7.9 million to pretax income.

▶ COSTS TO BE INCLUDED IN INVENTORY

One of the most important problems in dealing with inventories concerns the amount at which the inventory should be carried in the accounts and stated in the accounting reports. **The acquisition of inventories, like other assets, is generally accounted for on a basis of cost.** (Other bases are discussed in Chapter 9.)

OBJECTIVE 4
Identify the items that should be included as inventory cost.

PRODUCT COSTS

Product costs are those costs that "attach" to the inventory and are recorded in the inventory account. These costs are directly connected with the bringing of goods to the place of business of the buyer and converting such goods to a salable condition. Such charges would include freight charges on goods purchased, other direct costs of acquisition, and labor and other production costs incurred in processing the goods up to the time of sale.

It would seem proper also to allocate to inventories a share of any buying costs or expenses of a purchasing department, storage costs, and other costs incurred in storing or handling the goods before they are sold. Because of the practical difficulties involved in allocating such costs and expenses, however, these items are not ordinarily included in valuing inventories.

PERIOD COSTS

Selling expenses and, under ordinary circumstances, **general and administrative expenses** are not considered to be directly related to the acquisition or production of goods and, therefore, are not considered to be a part of inventories. Such costs are **period costs.**

Conceptually, these expenses are as much a cost of the product as the initial purchase price and related freight charges attached to the product. Why then are these costs not considered inventoriable items? Selling expenses are generally considered as more directly related to the cost of goods sold than to the unsold inventory. In most cases, though, the costs, especially administrative expenses, are so unrelated or indirectly related to the immediate production process that any allocation is purely arbitrary.

Interest costs associated with getting inventories ready for sale usually are expensed as incurred. A major argument for this approach is that interest costs are really a cost of financing. Others have argued, however, that interest costs incurred to finance activities associated with bringing inventories to a condition and place ready for sale are as much a cost of the asset as materials, labor, and overhead and, therefore, should be capitalized.[8] **The FASB has ruled that interest costs related to assets constructed for**

---

[8]The reporting rules related to interest cost capitalization have their greatest impact in accounting for long-term assets and, therefore, are discussed in detail in Chapter 10.

internal use or assets produced as discrete projects (such as ships or real estate projects) for sale or lease should be capitalized.[9] The FASB emphasized that these discrete projects should take considerable time, entail substantial expenditures, and be likely to involve significant amounts of interest cost. Interest costs should not be capitalized for inventories that are routinely manufactured or otherwise produced in large quantities on a repetitive basis because the informational benefit does not justify the cost.

MANUFACTURING COSTS

As previously indicated, a business that manufactures goods utilizes three inventory accounts—Raw Materials, Work in Process, and Finished Goods. Work in process and finished goods include materials, direct labor, and manufacturing overhead costs. Manufacturing overhead costs include indirect material, indirect labor, and such items as depreciation, taxes, insurance, heat, and electricity incurred in the manufacturing process.

VARIABLE COSTING VERSUS ABSORPTION COSTING

In a **variable costing system** (frequently called a direct costing system), all costs must be classified as variable or fixed. **Variable costs** are those that fluctuate in direct proportion to changes in output, and **fixed costs** are those that remain constant in spite of changes in output. Under variable costing only costs that vary directly with the production volume are charged to products as manufacturing takes place. Because variable costing is so useful to management in decision making, cost control, and budget preparation, it is widely used internally. However, it is not acceptable for tax purposes or for use in published financial reports (external reporting) because it understates the firm's investment in inventories.

Under **absorption costing** (often referred to as full costing), all manufacturing costs, variable and fixed, direct and indirect, that are incurred in the factory or production process attach to the product and are included in the cost of inventory. Absorption costing (full costing) is required by GAAP as the basis of inventory valuation for financial statements. A modified version of absorption costing is required for tax purposes too.[10]

TREATMENT OF PURCHASE DISCOUNTS

The use of a **Purchase Discounts** account indicates that the company is reporting its purchases and accounts payable at the gross amount. Another approach is to record the purchases and accounts payable at an amount **net** of the cash discounts. This treatment is considered to be better because (1) it provides a correct reporting of the cost of the asset and related liability and (2) it presents the opportunity to measure inefficiency of management if the discount is not taken. In the net approach, the failure to take a purchase discount within the discount period is recorded in a Purchase Discounts Lost

---

[9]"Capitalization of Interest Cost," *Statement of Financial Accounting Standards No. 34* (Stamford, Conn.: FASB, 1979).

[10]The Tax Reform Act of 1986 requires that all manufacturers and most wholesalers and retailers replace the previously existing full absorption costing provisions with the following new rules related to costs to be capitalized as inventory. **The new tax rules require that in addition to direct material and direct labor, indirect costs that directly benefit or are incurred by reason of the performance of a production or resale activity must be capitalized.**

In December 1986, the FASB's Emerging Issues Task Force concluded that the fact that a cost (such as bidding, warehousing, purchasing, officer salaries, and administrative and selling expenses) is capitalizable for tax purposes does not, in itself, indicate that capitalizing the cost for financial reporting is preferable—or even appropriate. Task Force members, however, indicated that certain of the additional costs that now have to be capitalized for tax purposes **may be** capitalizable for financial reporting purposes, but only after the individual facts and circumstances have been analyzed.

account (for which someone, probably the treasurer, is held responsible). To illustrate the difference between the gross and net method, assume the following transactions:

ILLUSTRATION 8-8
Entries under Gross and Net Methods

Gross Method			Net Method		
Purchase cost $10,000, terms 2/10, net 30:					
Purchases	10,000		Purchases	9,800	
Accounts Payable		10,000	Accounts Payable		9,800
Invoices of $4,000 are paid within discount period:					
Accounts Payable	4,000		Accounts Payable	3,920	
Purchase Discounts		80	Cash		3,920
Cash		3,920			
Invoices of $6,000 are paid after discount period:					
Accounts Payable	6,000		Accounts Payable	5,880	
Cash		6,000	Purchase Discounts Lost	120	
			Cash		6,000

If the **gross method** is employed, purchase discounts should be reported as a deduction from purchases on the income statement. If the **net method** is used, purchase discounts lost should be considered a financial expense and reported in the other expense and loss section of the income statement. Many believe that the difficulty involved in using the somewhat more complicated net method is not justified considering the resulting benefits. This could account for the widespread use of the less logical but simpler gross method. In addition, some contend that management is reluctant to report the amount of purchase discounts lost in the financial statements.

UNDERLYING CONCEPT

Not using the net method because of resultant difficulties is an example of the application of the cost-benefit constraint.

▶ WHAT COST FLOW ASSUMPTION SHOULD BE ADOPTED?

During any given fiscal period it is very likely that merchandise will be purchased at several different prices. If inventories are to be priced at cost and numerous purchases have been made at different unit costs, which of the various cost prices should be used? Conceptually, a specific identification of the given items sold and unsold seems optimal, but this measure is often not only expensive but impossible to achieve. Consequently, the accountant must turn to one of several systematic inventory **cost flow assumptions.** Indeed, the actual physical flow of goods and the cost flow assumption are often quite different. **There is no requirement that the cost flow assumption adopted be consistent with the physical movement of goods.** The major objective in selecting a method should be to choose the one which, under the circumstances, most clearly reflects periodic income.[11]

To illustrate, assume that Call-Mart Inc. had the following transactions in its first month of operations.

OBJECTIVE 5
Describe and compare the flow assumptions used in accounting for inventories.

Date	Purchases	Sold or Issued	Balance
March 2	2,000 @ $4.00		2,000 units
March 15	6,000 @ $4.40		8,000 units
March 19		4,000 units	4,000 units
March 30	2,000 @ $4.75		6,000 units

From this information, we can compute the ending inventory of 6,000 units and the cost of goods available for sale (beginning inventory + purchases) of $43,900 [(2,000 @ $4.00) + (6,000 @ $4.40) + (2,000 @ $4.75)]. The question is, which price or prices should be assigned to the 6,000 units of ending inventory? The answer depends on which cost flow assumption is employed.

---

[11]"Restatement and Revision of Accounting Research Bulletins," *Accounting Research Bulletin No. 43* (New York: AICPA, 1953), Ch. 4, Statement 4.

SPECIFIC IDENTIFICATION

Specific identification calls for identifying each item sold and each item in inventory. The costs of the specific items sold are included in the cost of goods sold, and the costs of the specific items on hand are included in the inventory. This method may be used only in instances where it is practical to separate physically the different purchases made. It can be successfully applied in situations where a relatively small number of costly, easily distinguishable items are handled. In the retail trade this includes some types of jewelry, fur coats, automobiles, and some furniture. In manufacturing it includes special orders and many products manufactured under a job cost system.

To illustrate the specific identification method, assume that Call-Mart Inc.'s 6,000 units of inventory is composed of 1,000 units from the March 2 purchase, 3,000 from the March 15 purchase, and 2,000 from the March 30 purchase. The ending inventory and cost of goods sold would be computed as shown in Illustration 8-9.

ILLUSTRATION 8-9
Specific Identification Method

Date	No. of Units	Unit Cost	Total Cost
March 2	1,000	$4.00	$ 4,000
March 15	3,000	4.40	13,200
March 30	2,000	4.75	9,500
Ending inventory	**6,000**		**$26,700**

Cost of goods available for sale (computed in previous section)	$43,900	
Deduct ending inventory	26,700	
Cost of goods sold	**$17,200**	

Conceptually, this method appears ideal because actual costs are matched against actual revenue, and ending inventory is reported at actual cost. In other words, under specific identification the cost flow matches the physical flow of the goods. On closer observation, however, this method has certain deficiencies.

One argument against specific identification is that it makes it possible to manipulate net income. For example, assume that a wholesaler purchases otherwise identical plywood early in the year at three different prices. When the plywood is sold, the wholesaler can select either the lowest or the highest price to charge to expense simply by selecting the plywood from a specific lot for delivery to the customer. A business manager, therefore, can manipulate net income simply by delivering to the customer the higher- or lower-priced item, depending on whether higher or lower reported earnings is desired for the period.

Another problem relates to the arbitrary allocation of costs that sometimes occurs with specific inventory items. In certain circumstances, it is difficult to relate adequately, for example, shipping charges, storage costs, and discounts directly to a given inventory item. The alternative, then, is to allocate these costs somewhat arbitrarily, which leads to a "breakdown" in the precision of the specific identification method.[12]

AVERAGE COST

As the name implies, the **average cost method** prices items in the inventory on the basis of the average cost of all similar goods available during the period. To illustrate, assuming that Call-Mart Inc. used the periodic inventory method, the ending inventory

---

[12]A good illustration of the cost allocation problem arises in the motion picture industry. Often actors and actresses receive a percentage of net income for a given movie or television program. Some actors such as James Garner and Fess Parker, who had these arrangements, have alleged that their programs have been extremely profitable to the motion picture studios but they have received little in the way of profit sharing. Actors contend that the studios allocate additional costs to successful projects to insure that there will be no profits to share.

and cost of goods sold would be computed as follows using a **weighted average method:**

ILLUSTRATION 8-10
Weighted-Average Method—Periodic Inventory

Date of Invoice	No. Units	Unit Cost	Total Cost
March 2	2,000	$4.00	$ 8,000
March 15	6,000	4.40	26,400
March 30	2,000	4.75	9,500
Total goods available	10,000		$43,900

Weighted-average cost per unit $\dfrac{\$43,900}{10,000} = \$4.39$

Inventory in units   6,000 units

Ending inventory   6,000 × $4.39 = $26,340

Cost of goods available for sale	$43,900
Deduct ending inventory	26,340
Cost of goods sold	**$17,560**

If the company has a beginning inventory, it is included both in the total units available and in the total cost of goods available in computing the average cost per unit.

Another average cost method is the **moving-average method,** which is used with perpetual inventory records. The application of the average cost method for perpetual records is shown in Illustration 8-11.

ILLUSTRATION 8-11
Moving-Average Method—Perpetual Inventory

Date	Purchased		Sold or Issued		Balance	
March 2	(2,000 @ $4.00)	$ 8,000			(2,000 @ $4.00)	$ 8,000
March 15	(6,000 @ 4.40)	26,400			(8,000 @ 4.30)	34,400
March 19			(4,000 @ $4.30)			
				$17,200	(4,000 @ 4.30)	$17,200
March 30	(2,000 @ 4.75)	9,500			(6,000 @ 4.45)	26,700

In this method, a new average unit cost is computed each time a purchase is made. On March 15, after 6,000 units are purchased for $26,400, 8,000 units costing $34,400 ($8,000 plus $26,400) are on hand. The average unit cost is $34,400 divided by 8,000, or $4.30. This unit cost is used in costing withdrawals until another purchase is made, when a new average unit cost is computed. Accordingly, the cost of the 4,000 units withdrawn on March 19 is shown at $4.30, a total cost of goods sold of $17,200. On March 30, following the purchase of 2,000 units for $9,500, a new unit cost of $4.45 is determined for an ending inventory of $26,700.

The use of the average cost methods is usually justified on the basis of practical rather than conceptual reasons. These methods are simple to apply, objective, and not as subject to income manipulation as some of the other inventory pricing methods. In addition, proponents of the average cost methods argue that it is often impossible to measure a specific physical flow of inventory and therefore it is better to cost items on an average price basis. This argument is particularly persuasive when the inventory involved is relatively homogeneous in nature.

FIRST-IN, FIRST-OUT (FIFO)

The **FIFO method** assumes that goods are used in the order in which they are purchased. In other words, it assumes that **the first goods purchased are the first used** (in a manufacturing concern) **or sold** (in a merchandising concern). The inventory remaining must therefore represent the most recent purchases.

To illustrate, assume that Call-Mart Inc. uses the periodic inventory system (amount of inventory computed only at the end of the month). The cost of the ending inventory is computed by taking the cost of the most recent purchase and working back until all units in the inventory are accounted for. The ending inventory and cost of goods sold are determined as shown in Illustration 8-12.

**ILLUSTRATION 8-12
FIFO Method—Periodic
Inventory**

Date	No. Units	Unit Cost	Total Cost
March 30	2,000	$4.75	$ 9,500
March 15	4,000	4.40	17,600
Ending inventory	6,000		$27,100

Cost of goods available for sale	$43,900	
Deduct ending inventory	27,100	
Cost of goods sold	$16,800	

If a perpetual inventory system in quantities and dollars is used, a cost figure is attached to each withdrawal. Then the cost of the 4,000 units removed on March 19 would be made up of the items purchased on March 2 and March 15. The inventory on a FIFO basis perpetual system for Call-Mart Inc. is shown in Illustration 8-13.

**ILLUSTRATION 8-13
FIFO Method—Perpetual
Inventory**

Date	Purchased		Sold or Issued	Balance	
March 2	(2,000 @ $4.00)	$ 8,000		2,000 @ $4.00	$ 8,000
March 15	(6,000 @ 4.40)	26,400		2,000 @ 4.00 ⎫ 6,000 @ 4.40 ⎬	34,400
March 19			2,000 @ $4.00 ⎫ 2,000 @ 4.40 ⎬ ($16,800)	4,000 @ 4.40	17,600
March 30	(2,000 @ 4.75)	9,500		4,000 @ 4.40 ⎫ 2,000 @ 4.75 ⎬	27,100

The ending inventory in this situation is $27,100, and the cost of goods sold is $16,800 [(2,000 @ 4.00) + (2,000 @ $4.40)].

Notice that in these two FIFO examples, the cost of goods sold and ending inventory are the same. **In all cases where FIFO is used, the inventory and cost of goods sold would be the same at the end of the month whether a perpetual or periodic system is used.** This is true because the same costs will always be first in and, therefore, first out whether cost of goods sold is computed as goods are sold throughout the accounting period (the perpetual system) or as a residual at the end of the accounting period (the periodic system).

One objective of FIFO is to approximate the physical flow of goods. When the physical flow of goods is actually first-in, first-out, the FIFO method very nearly represents specific identification. At the same time, it does not permit manipulation of income because the enterprise is not free to pick a certain cost item to be charged to expense.

Another **advantage** of the FIFO method is that the ending inventory is close to current cost. Because the first goods in are the first goods out, the ending inventory amount will be composed of the most recent purchases. This is particularly true where the inventory turnover is rapid. This approach generally provides a reasonable approximation of replacement cost on the balance sheet when price changes have not occurred since the most recent purchases.

The basic **disadvantage** of the FIFO method is that current costs are not matched against current revenues on the income statement. The oldest costs are charged against the more current revenue, which can lead to distortions in gross profit and net income.

LAST-IN, FIRST-OUT (LIFO)

The **LIFO method** first matches the cost of the last goods purchased against revenue. If a periodic inventory is used, then it would be assumed that **the cost of the total quantity sold or issued during the month would have come from the most recent purchases.** The ending inventory would be priced by using the total units as a basis of computation and disregarding the exact dates involved. The example below assumes that the cost of the 4,000 units withdrawn absorbed the 2,000 units purchased on March 30 and 2,000 of the 6,000 units purchased on March 15. The inventory and related cost of goods sold would then be computed as shown in Illustration 8-14.

Date of Invoice	No. Units	Unit Cost	Total Cost
March 2	2,000	$4.00	$ 8,000
March 15	4,000	4.40	17,600
Ending inventory	6,000		$25,600
	Goods available for sale	$43,900	
	Deduct ending inventory	25,600	
	Cost of goods sold	$18,300	

ILLUSTRATION 8-14
LIFO Method—Periodic Inventory

If a perpetual inventory record is kept in quantities and dollars, application of the last-in, first-out method will result in **different ending inventory and cost of goods sold amounts,** as shown in Illustration 8-15.

Date	Purchased		Sold or Issued		Balance		
March 2	(2,000 @ $4.00)	$ 8,000			2,000 @ $4.00		$ 8,000
March 15	(6,000 @ 4.40)	26,400			2,000 @ 4.00 ⎱ 6,000 @ 4.40 ⎰		34,400
March 19			(4,000 @ $4.40) $17,600		2,000 @ 4.00 ⎱ 2,000 @ 4.40 ⎰		16,800
March 30	(2,000 @ 4.75)	9,500			2,000 @ 4.00 ⎱ 2,000 @ 4.40 ⎬ 2,000 @ 4.75 ⎰		26,300

ILLUSTRATION 8-15
LIFO Method—Perpetual Inventory

Notice that the month-end periodic inventory computation illustrated above (inventory $25,600 and cost of goods sold $18,300) shows a different amount from the perpetual inventory computation (inventory $26,300 and cost of goods sold $17,600). This is because the periodic system matches the total withdrawals for the month with the total purchases for the month in applying the last-in, first-out method, whereas the perpetual system matches each withdrawal with the immediately preceding purchases. In effect, the first computation assumed that the cost of the goods that were purchased on March 30 were included in the sale or issue on March 19.

► ## SPECIAL ISSUES RELATED TO LIFO

LIFO LIQUIDATION

Up to this point, we have emphasized a **specific goods approach** to costing LIFO inventories (also called traditional LIFO or unit LIFO). This approach is often unrealistic for two reasons:

OBJECTIVE 6
Explain the effect of LIFO liquidations.

1. When a company has many different inventory items, the accounting cost of keeping track of each inventory item is expensive.

2. Erosion of the LIFO inventory can easily occur (referred to as **LIFO liquidation**). This often leads to distortions of net income and substantial tax payments.

To understand the LIFO liquidation problem, assume that Basler Co. has 30,000 pounds of steel in its inventory on December 31, 1996, costed on a specific goods LIFO approach.

	Ending Inventory (1996)		
	Pounds	Unit Cost	LIFO Cost
1993	8,000	$ 4	$ 32,000
1994	10,000	6	60,000
1995	7,000	9	63,000
1996	5,000	10	50,000
	30,000		$205,000

As indicated, the ending 1996 inventory for Basler Co. comprises costs from past periods. These costs are called layers (increases from period to period), with the first layer identified as the base layer. An illustration of the layers for Basler is as follows:

ILLUSTRATION 8-16
Layers of LIFO Inventory

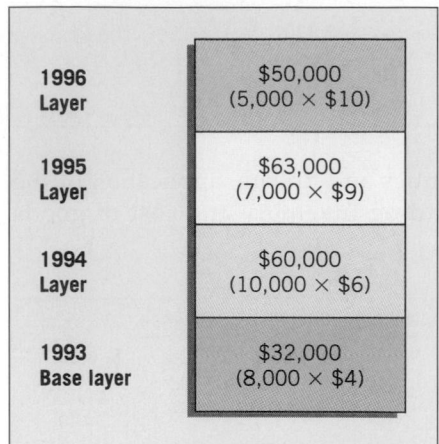

The price of steel has increased over the 4-year period. In 1997, Basler Co. experienced metal shortages and had to liquidate much of its inventory (a LIFO liquidation). At the end of 1997, only 6,000 pounds of steel remained in inventory. Because the company is using LIFO, the most recent layer, 1996, is liquidated first, followed by the 1995 layer, and so on. The result: costs from preceding periods are matched against sales revenues reported in current dollars; this leads to a distortion in net income and a substantial tax bill in the current period. These effects are shown in Illustration 8-17.

ILLUSTRATION 8-17
LIFO Liquidation

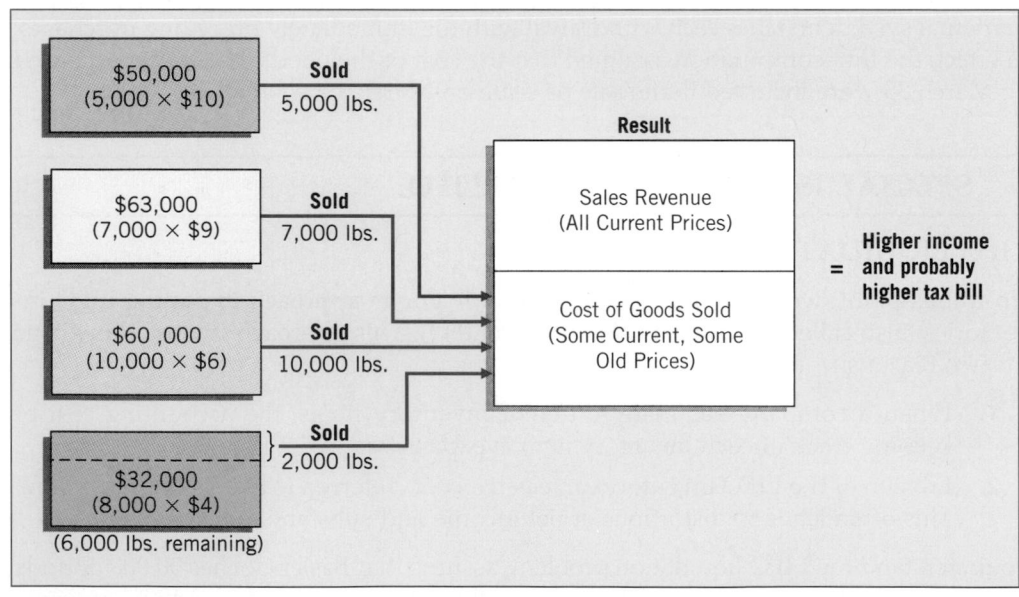

Unfortunately LIFO liquidations can occur frequently when a specific goods LIFO approach is employed.

To alleviate the LIFO liquidation problems and to simplify the accounting, goods can be combined into pools. A **pool** is defined as a group of items of a similar nature. Thus, instead of only identical units, a number of similar units or products are combined and accounted for together. This method is referred to as the **specific goods pooled approach.** Using the specific goods pooled LIFO approach, LIFO liquidations are less likely to happen because the reduction of one quantity in the pool may be offset by an increase in another.

The specific goods pooled LIFO approach eliminates some of the disadvantages of the specific goods (traditional) accounting for LIFO inventories. This pooled approach, using quantities as its measurement basis, however, creates other problems.

First, most companies are continually changing the mix of their products, materials, and production methods. A business once engaged in manufacturing train locomotives may now be involved in the automobile or aircraft business. A business that had used cotton fabric in its clothing now uses synthetic fabric (dacron, nylon, etc.). If a pooled approach using quantities is employed, it means that the pools must be continually redefined; this can be time consuming and costly.

Second, even when such an approach is practical, an erosion ("LIFO liquidation") of the layers often results, and much of the LIFO costing benefit is lost. An erosion of the layers results because a specific good or material in the pool may be replaced by another good or material either temporarily or permanently. This replacement may occur for competitive reasons or simply because a shortage of a certain material exists. Whatever the reason, the new item may not be similar enough to be treated as part of the old pool. Therefore any inflationary profit deferred on the old goods may have to be recognized as the old goods are replaced.

DOLLAR-VALUE LIFO

To overcome the problems of redefining pools and eroding layers, the dollar-value LIFO method was developed. **An important feature of the dollar-value LIFO method is that increases and decreases in a pool are determined and measured in terms of total dollar value, not the physical quantity of the goods in the inventory pool.**

OBJECTIVE 7

Explain the dollar-value LIFO method.

Such an approach has two important advantages over the specific goods pooled approach. First, a broader range of goods may be included in a dollar-value LIFO pool. Second, in a dollar-value LIFO pool, replacement is permitted if it is a similar material, or similar in use, or interchangeable. (In contrast, in a specific goods LIFO pool, an item may be replaced only with an item that is substantially identical.)

Thus, dollar-value LIFO techniques help protect LIFO layers from erosion. Because of this advantage, the dollar-value LIFO method is frequently used in practice.[13] Only in situations where few goods are employed and little change in product mix is predicted would the more traditional LIFO approaches be used.

Under the dollar-value LIFO method, it is possible to have the entire inventory in only one pool, although several pools are commonly employed.[14] In general, the more goods included in a pool, the more likely that decreases in the quantities of some goods will be offset by increases in the quantities of other goods in the same pool; thus liquidation of the LIFO layers is avoided. It follows that fewer pools means less cost and less chance of a reduction of a LIFO layer.[15]

---

[13]A study by James M. Reeve and Keith G. Stanga disclosed that the vast majority of respondent companies applying LIFO use the dollar-value method or the dollar-value retail method (explained in Chapter 9) to apply LIFO. Only a small minority of companies use the specific goods (unit LIFO) approach or the specific goods pooling approach. See "The LIFO Pooling Decision," *Accounting Horizons* (June 1987), p. 27.

[14]The Reeve and Stanga study (ibid.,) reports that most companies have only a few pools (the median is six for retailers and three for nonretailers), but the distributions are highly skewed; some companies have 100 or more pools. Retailers that use LIFO have significantly more pools than nonretailers. About a third of the nonretailers (mostly manufacturers) use a single pool for their entire LIFO inventory.

[15]In a later study, William R. Coon and Randall B. Hayes point out that when quantities are increasing, multiple pools over a period of time may produce (under rather general conditions) significantly higher cost of goods sold deductions than a single pool approach. When a stock-out occurs, a single pool approach may lessen the layer liquidation for that year, but it may not erase the cumulative cost of goods sold advantage accruing to the use of multiple pools built up over the preceding years. See "The Dollar Value LIFO Pooling Decision: The Conventional Wisdom Is Too General," *Accounting Horizons* (December 1989), pp. 57–70.

Dollar-Value LIFO Illustration

To illustrate how the dollar-value LIFO method works, assume that dollar-value LIFO was first adopted (base period) on December 31, 1995, that the inventory at current prices on that date was $20,000, and that the inventory on December 31, 1996 at current prices is $26,400. We should not conclude that the quantity has increased 32% during the year ($26,400 ÷ $20,000 = 132%). First, we need to ask: What is the value of the ending inventory in terms of beginning-of-the-year prices? Assuming that prices have increased 20% during the year, the ending inventory at beginning-of-the-year prices amounts to $22,000 ($26,400 ÷ 120%). Therefore, the inventory quantity has increased 10%, or from $20,000 to $22,000 in terms of beginning-of-the-year prices.

The next step is to price this real dollar quantity increase. This real dollar quantity increase of $2,000 valued at year-end prices is $2,400 (120% × $2,000). This increment (layer) of $2,400, when added to the beginning inventory of $20,000, gives a total of $22,400 for the December 31, 1996, inventory, as shown below:

First layer—(beginning inventory) in terms of 100	$20,000
Second layer—(1996 increase) in terms of 120	2,400
Dollar-value LIFO inventory, December 31, 1996	$22,400

It should be emphasized that **a layer is formed only when the ending inventory at base-year prices exceeds the beginning inventory at base-year prices.** And only when a new layer is formed must a new index be computed.

Comprehensive Dollar-Value LIFO Illustration

To illustrate the use of the dollar-value LIFO method in a more complex situation, assume that Bismark Company develops the following information:

December 31	Inventory at End-of-Year Prices	÷	Price Index (percentage)	=	End-of-Year Inventory at Base-Year Prices
(Base year) 1993	$200,000		100		$200,000
1994	299,000		115		260,000
1995	300,000		120		250,000
1996	351,000		130		270,000

At December 31, 1993, the ending inventory under dollar-value LIFO is simply the $200,000 computed as shown in Illustration 8-18.

ILLUSTRATION 8-18
Computation of 1993 Inventory at LIFO Cost

Ending Inventory at Base-Year Prices	Layer at Base-Year Prices		Price Index (percentage)		Ending Inventory at LIFO Cost
$200,000	$200,000	×	100	=	$200,000

At December 31, 1994, a comparison of the ending inventory at base-year prices ($260,000) with the beginning inventory at base-year prices ($200,000), indicates that the quantity of goods has increased $60,000 ($260,000 − $200,000). This increment (layer) is then priced at the 1994 index of 115% to arrive at a new layer of $69,000. Ending inventory for 1994 is $269,000, composed of the beginning inventory of $200,000 and the new layer of $69,000. These computations are shown in Illustration 8-19.

ILLUSTRATION 8-19
Computation of 1994 Inventory at LIFO Cost

Ending Inventory at Base-Year Prices	Layers at Base-Year Prices		Price Index (percentage)		Ending Inventory at LIFO Cost
$260,000	1993	$200,000 × 100	=		$200,000
	1994	60,000 × 115	=		69,000
		$260,000			$269,000

At December 31, 1995, a comparison of the ending inventory at base-year prices ($250,000) with the beginning inventory at base-year prices ($260,000) indicates that the quantity of goods has decreased $10,000 ($250,000 − $260,000). If the ending inventory at base-year prices is less than the beginning inventory at base-year prices, **the decrease must be subtracted from the most recently added layer. When a decrease occurs, previous layers must be "peeled off" at the prices in existence when the layers were added.** In Bismark Company's situation, this means that $10,000 in base-year prices must be removed from the 1994 layer of $60,000 at base-year prices. The balance of $50,000 ($60,000 − $10,000) at base-year prices must be valued at the 1994 price index of 115% so that this 1994 layer now is valued at $57,500 ($50,000 × 115%). The ending inventory is therefore computed at $257,500, consisting of the beginning inventory of $200,000 and the second layer, $57,500. The computations for 1995 are shown in Illustration 8-20.

Ending Inventory at Base-Year Prices	Layers at Base-Year Prices		Price Index (percentage)		Ending Inventory at LIFO Cost
$250,000	1993 $200,000	×	100	=	$200,000
	1994 50,000	×	115	=	57,500
	$250,000				$257,500

ILLUSTRATION 8-20
Computation of 1995 Inventory at LIFO Cost

Note that if a layer or base (or portion thereof) has been eliminated, it cannot be rebuilt in future periods. That is, it is gone forever.

At December 31, 1996, a comparison of the ending inventory at base-year prices ($270,000) with the beginning inventory at base-year prices ($250,000) indicates that the dollar quantity of goods has increased $20,000 ($270,000 − $250,000) in terms of base-year prices. After converting the $20,000 increase to the 1996 price index, the ending inventory is $283,500, composed of the beginning layer of $200,000, a 1994 layer of $57,500, and a 1996 layer of $26,000 ($20,000 × 130%). This computation is shown in Illustration 8-21.

Ending Inventory at Base-Year Prices	Layers at Base-Year Prices		Price Index (percentage)		Ending Inventory at LIFO Cost
$270,000	1993 $200,000	×	100	=	$200,000
	1994 50,000	×	115	=	57,500
	1996 20,000	×	130	=	26,000
	$270,000				$283,500

ILLUSTRATION 8-21
Computation of 1996 Inventory at LIFO Cost

The ending inventory at base-year prices must always equal the total of the layers at base-year prices; checking that this situation exists will help to ensure that the dollar-value computation is made correctly.

Selecting a Price Index

Obviously, price changes are critical in dollar-value LIFO. How are the price indexes determined? Many companies use the general price-level index prepared and published monthly by the federal government; the most popular general external price-level index is the Consumers Price Index for Urban Consumers (CPI-U).[16] Specific external price indexes are also widely used. For instance, specific indexes are computed and published daily for most commodities (gold, silver, other metals, corn, wheat, and other farm

---

[16]Indexes may be **general** (composed of several commodities, goods, or services) or **specific** (for one commodity, good, or service) and **external** (computed by an outside party, such as the government, or commodity exchange, or trade association) or **internal** (computed by the enterprise for its own product or service).

products). Many trade associations prepare indexes for specific product lines or industries. Any of these indexes may be used for dollar-value LIFO purposes.

When a specific external price index is not readily available or relevant, a company may compute its own specific internal price index. The desired approach is to price ending inventory at the most current cost. Current cost is ordinarily determined by referring to the actual cost of those goods most recently purchased. The price index provides a measure of the change in price or cost levels between the base year and the current year. An index is computed for each year after the base year. The general formula for computing the index is as follows:

ILLUSTRATION 8-22
Formula for Computing a Price Index

$$\frac{\text{Ending Inventory for the Period at Current Cost}}{\text{Ending Inventory for the Period at Base-Year Cost}} = \text{Price Index for Current Year}$$

This approach is generally referred to as the **double-extension method** because the value of the units in inventory is extended at both base-year prices and current-year prices. To illustrate this computation, assume that Toledo Company's base-year inventory (January 1, 1996) was composed of the following:

Items	Quantity	Cost per Unit	Total Cost
A	1,000	$ 6	$ 6,000
B	2,000	20	40,000
(January 1, 1996 inventory at base-year costs)			$46,000

Examination of the ending inventory indicates that 3,000 units of Item A and 6,000 units of Item B are held on December 31, 1996. The most recent actual purchases related to these items were as follows:

Items	Purchase Date	Quantity Purchased	Cost per Unit
A	December 1, 1996	4,000	$ 7
B	December 15, 1996	5,000	25
B	November 16, 1996	1,000	22

We double-extend the inventory as shown in Illustration 8-23.

ILLUSTRATION 8-23
Double-Extension Method of Selecting a Price Index

	12/31/96 Inventory at Base-Year Costs			12/31/96 Inventory at Current-Year Costs		
Items	Units	Base-Year Cost per Unit	Total	Units	Current-Year Cost per Unit	Total
A	3,000	$ 6	$ 18,000	3,000	$ 7	$ 21,000
B	6,000	20	120,000	5,000	25	125,000
B				1,000	22	22,000
			$138,000			$168,000

After the inventories are double-extended, the formula above is used to develop the index for the current year (1996) as shown in Illustration 8-24.

ILLUSTRATION 8-24
Computation of 1996 Index

$$\frac{\text{Ending Inventory for the Period at Current Cost}}{\text{Ending Inventory for the Period at Base-Year Cost}} = \frac{\$168,000}{\$138,000} = 121.74\%$$

This index (121.74%) is then applied to the layer added in 1996. Note in this illustration that Toledo Company used the most recent actual purchases to determine current cost; other approaches such as FIFO and average cost may also be used. Whichever flow assumption is adopted, consistent use from one period to another is required.[17]

Use of the double-extension method is time consuming and difficult where substantial technological change has occurred or where a large number of items is involved. That is, as time passes, a new base-year cost must be determined for new products and a base-year cost must be kept for each inventory item.[18]

LIFO APPROACHES—A COMPARISON

Three different approaches to computing LIFO inventories are presented in this chapter—specific goods LIFO, specific goods pooled LIFO, and dollar-value LIFO. As indicated earlier, the use of the specific goods LIFO is unrealistic because most enterprises have numerous goods in inventory at the end of a period, and costing (pricing) them on a unit basis is extremely expensive and time consuming.

The specific goods pooled LIFO approach is better in that it reduces record keeping and clerical costs. In addition, it is more difficult to erode the layers because the reduction of one quantity in the pool may be offset by an increase in another. Nonetheless, the pooled approach using quantities as its measurement basis can lead to untimely LIFO liquidations.

As a result, **dollar-value LIFO is the method employed by most companies that currently use a LIFO system.** Although the approach appears complex, the logic and the computations are actually quite simple, once an appropriate index is determined.

This is not to suggest that problems do not exist with the dollar-value LIFO method. The selection of the items to be put in a pool can be subjective.[19] Such a determination, however, is extremely important because manipulation of the items in a pool without conceptual justification can affect reported net income. For example, the SEC recently noted that some companies are setting up pools that are easy to liquidate. As a result, when the company wants to increase its income, it decreases inventory, thereby matching low-cost inventory items to current revenues.

To curb this practice, the SEC has taken a much harder line on the number of pools that companies may establish. In the well-publicized Stauffer Chemical Company case,

---

[17]Another approach to finding an index is the **link-chain method.** Under the link-chain method the base cost of ending inventory is determined by applying a cumulative index to the dollar value of the ending inventory. The cumulative index is the relationship of the current-year prices to those of the prior year (based on either double-extension or an index) multiplied by the prior year's cumulative index. Thus each year's index may be characterized as a link in a chain of indexes back to the base year. It is not illustrated here because it is permitted only in limited circumstances. For a more detailed discussion of the link-chain method, read C. Paul Jannis, Carl H. Poedtke, Jr., and Donald R. Ziegler, *Managing and Accounting for Inventories* 3rd ed., New York: John Wiley & Sons, Inc., 1980.

[18]Another approach, which was initially sanctioned by the Internal Revenue Service for tax purposes, may be used to simplify the analysis. Under this method, an index is obtained by reference to an outside source or by double-extending only a sample portion of the inventory. For example, all companies are allowed to use 80% of the inflation rate reported by the appropriate consumer or producer price indexes prepared by the Bureau of Labor Statistics (BLS) as their inflation rate for a LIFO pool. Small companies (less than $2 million in sales) can use 100% of the inflation rate reported by such indexes as their inflation rate. Once the index is obtained, the ending inventory at current cost is divided by the index to find the base-year cost. Using generally available external indexes greatly simplifies LIFO computations as internal indexes need not be computed. Although this approach was initially established for reporting taxable income, it is permissible to use this method for financial reporting as well.

[19]It is suggested that companies analyze how inventory purchases are affected by price changes, how goods are stocked, how goods are used, and if future liquidations are likely. See William R. Cron and Randall Hayes, "The Dollar Value LIFO Pooling Decision: The Conventional Wisdom is Too General," *Accounting Horizons* (December 1989), p. 57.

Stauffer had increased the number of LIFO pools from eight to 280, boosting its net income by $16,515,000 or approximately 13%.[20] Stauffer justified the change in its Annual Report on the basis of "achieving a better matching of cost and revenue." The SEC required Stauffer to reduce the number of its inventory pools, contending that some pools were inappropriate and alleging income manipulation.

MAJOR ADVANTAGES OF LIFO APPROACHES

OBJECTIVE 8

Identify the major advantages and disadvantages of LIFO.

One obvious advantage of LIFO approaches is that in certain situations the LIFO cost flow actually approximates the physical flow of the goods in and out of inventory. For instance, in the case of a coal pile, the last coal in is the first coal out because it is on the top of the pile. The coal remover is not going to take the coal from the bottom of the pile! The coal that is going to be taken first is the coal that was placed on the pile last.

However, the coal pile situation is one of only a few situations where the actual physical flow corresponds to LIFO. Therefore most adherents of LIFO use other arguments for its widespread employment, as follows:

Matching

In LIFO, the more recent costs are matched against current revenues to provide a better measure of current earnings. During periods of inflation, many challenge the quality of non-LIFO earnings, noting that by failing to match current costs against current revenues, **transitory or "paper" profits ("inventory profits") are created.** Inventory profits occur when the inventory costs matched against sales are less than the inventory replacement cost. The cost of goods sold therefore is understated and profit is overstated. Using LIFO (rather than a method such as FIFO), current costs are matched against revenues and inventory profits are thereby reduced.

Tax Benefits

INTERNATIONAL INSIGHT

To the degree that they do allow LIFO, other nations often permit it only in limited circumstances. Further, outside the United States, LIFO is often disallowed for tax purposes. Thus, incentives for its use are reduced.

Tax benefits are the major reason why LIFO has become popular. As long as the price level increases and inventory quantities do not decrease, a deferral of income tax occurs, because the items most recently purchased at the higher price level are matched against revenues. For example, when Fuqua Industries decided to switch to LIFO, it had a resultant tax savings of about $4 million. Even if the price level decreases later, the company has been given a temporary deferral of its income taxes.[21] The tax law requires that if a company uses LIFO for tax purposes, it must also use LIFO for financial accounting purposes[22] (although neither tax law nor GAAP requires a company to pool its inventories in the same manner for book and tax purposes). This requirement is often referred to as the **LIFO conformity rule.** Other inventory valuation methods do not have this requirement. Unfortunately, the general attitude too frequently is: "Whatever is good for tax is good for financial reporting."

---

[20]Commerce Clearing House, *SEC Accounting Rules* (Chicago: CCH, 1983), par. 4035.

[21]In periods of rising prices, the use of fewer pools will translate into greater income tax benefits through the use of LIFO. The use of fewer pools allows inventory reductions of some items to be offset by inventory increases in others. In contrast, the use of more pools increases the likelihood that old, low-cost inventory layers will be liquidated and tax consequences will be negative. See Reeve and Stanga, *Accounting Horizons*, pp. 28–29.

[22]Management often selects an accounting procedure because a lower tax results from its use, instead of an accounting method that is conceptually more appealing. Throughout this textbook, an effort has been made to identify accounting procedures that provide income tax benefits to the user.

Improved Cash Flow

Improved cash flow is related to the tax benefits, because taxes must be paid in cash. As a consequence, some companies not receiving LIFO tax benefits are forced to borrow to finance replacement of existing inventory levels, and interest costs can be staggering. Fuqua Industries expected to save approximately $400,000 in interest costs by switching to LIFO. Even if the company has plenty of cash to pay its taxes, LIFO permits management to invest these funds and earn a return unavailable to those using FIFO.[23]

Future Earnings Hedge

With LIFO, a company's future reported earnings will not be affected substantially by future price declines. LIFO eliminates or substantially minimizes write-downs to market as a result of price decreases. The reason: since the most recent inventory is sold first, there isn't much ending inventory sitting around at high prices vulnerable to a price decline. In contrast, inventory costed under FIFO is more vulnerable to price declines, which can reduce net income substantially.

MAJOR DISADVANTAGES OF LIFO APPROACHES

Despite its advantages, LIFO has the following drawbacks:

Reduced Earnings

Many corporate managers view the lower profits reported under the LIFO method in inflationary times as a distinct disadvantage and would rather have higher reported profits than lower taxes. Some fear that an accounting change to LIFO may be misunderstood by investors and that, as a result of the lower profits, the price of the company's stock will fall. In fact, though, there is some evidence to refute this contention. Non-LIFO earnings are now highly suspect and may be severely penalized by Wall Street.

Inventory Understated

LIFO may have a distorting effect on a company's balance sheet. The inventory valuation is normally outdated because the oldest costs remain in inventory. This understatement makes the working capital position of the company appear worse than it really is.

The magnitude and direction of this variation between the carrying amount of inventory and its current price depend on the degree and direction of the price changes and the amount of inventory turnover.[24] The combined effect of rising product prices and avoidance of inventory liquidations increases the difference between the inventory carrying value at LIFO and current prices of that inventory, thereby magnifying the balance sheet distortion attributed to the use of LIFO.[25]

---

[23]Note that, even though some would receive substantial tax benefits if they switched to LIFO, they have chosen not to. Some of the reasons for not changing to LIFO are presented in Gary C. Biddle, "Accounting Methods and Management Decisions: The Case of Inventory Costing and Inventory Policy," *The Journal of Accounting Research*, Supplement 1980.

[24]In 1986, the Accounting Standards Executive Committee (AcSEC) of the AICPA considered but voted down (by 8 to 6) a draft issues paper that explored an intriguing alternative to the way some companies report inventories in their financial statements. Under the suggested method, dubbed LIFO/FIFO, a company would use LIFO to measure cost of goods sold in its income statement and FIFO to report inventories in its balance sheet. See M. P. Bohan and S. Rubin, "LIFO/FIFO: How Would It Work?" *Journal of Accountancy* (September 1986), p. 106.

[25]This position is supported by the findings of James M. Reeve and Keith G. Stanga, "Balance Sheet Impact of Using LIFO: An Empirical Study," *Accounting Horizons* (September 1987), pp. 9–15.

Physical Flow

LIFO does not approximate the physical flow of the items except in peculiar situations (such as the coal pile). Originally LIFO could be used only in certain circumstances. This situation has changed over the years to the point where physical flow characteristics no longer play an important role in determining whether LIFO may be employed.

Current Cost Income Not Measured

LIFO falls short of measuring current cost (replacement cost) income though not as far as FIFO. When measuring current cost income, the cost of goods sold should consist not of the most recently incurred costs but rather of the cost that will be incurred to replace the goods that have been sold. Using replacement cost is referred to as the next-in, first-out method, which is not currently acceptable for purposes of inventory valuation.

Involuntary Liquidation

If the base or layers of old costs are eliminated, strange results can occur because old, irrelevant costs can be matched against current revenues. A distortion in reported income for a given period may result, as well as consequences that are detrimental from an income tax point of view.[26]

For example, Allied Corporation reported net earnings of $.09 per share in a year in which its inventory reductions resulted in liquidations of LIFO inventory quantities. The effect of the inventory reduction was to increase income by $13 million or $.17 per share. The income tax problem is particularly severe when the involuntary liquidation results from a strike or a shortage of materials. In these situations, companies may incur high tax bills when they can least afford to pay taxes.

Poor Buying Habits

Because of the liquidation problem, LIFO may cause poor buying habits. A company may simply purchase more goods and match these goods against revenue to ensure that the old costs are not charged to expense. Furthermore, the possibility always exists with LIFO that a company will attempt to manipulate its net income at the end of the year simply by altering its pattern of purchases.[27]

Because price rises have been the way of life in the U.S. economy during the last four decades, LIFO has provided a tax advantage over FIFO. During periods of price decreases, this tax advantage could become a disadvantage. And during periods of stable prices, FIFO and LIFO methods of inventory costing would generally produce identical results.

One survey uncovered the following reasons why companies reject LIFO:[28]

---

[26]The AICPA Task Force on LIFO Inventory Problems recommends that the effects on income of LIFO inventory liquidations be disclosed in the notes to the financial statements but that the effects not receive special treatment in the income statement, *Issues Paper* (New York: AICPA, 1984), pp. 36–37.

[27]For example, one reason why General Tire and Rubber at one time accelerated raw material purchases at the end of the year was to minimize the book profit from a liquidation of LIFO inventories and to minimize income taxes for the year.

[28]Granof, Michael H. and Daniel Short, "Why Do Companies Reject LIFO," *Journal of Accounting, Auditing, and Finance* (Summer 1984), pp. 323–333, Table 1, p. 327.

Explanation	Number	% of Total*
No expected tax benefits		
No required tax payment	34	16%
Declining prices	31	15
Rapid inventory turnover	30	14
Immaterial inventory	26	12
Miscellaneous tax related	38	17
	159	74%
Regulatory or other restrictions	26	12%
Excessive cost		
High administrative costs	29	14
LIFO liquidation–related costs	12	6
	41	20%
Other adverse consequences		
Lower reported earnings	18	8
Bad accounting	7	3
	25	11%

*Percentage totals more than 100% as some companies offered more than one explanation.

ILLUSTRATION 8-25
Why Do Companies Reject LIFO? Summary of Responses

▶ BASIS FOR SELECTION

How does one choose among the various inventory methods? Although no absolute rules can be stated, preferability for LIFO can ordinarily be established in either of the following circumstances: (1) if selling prices and revenues have been increasing faster than costs, thereby distorting income, and (2) in situations where LIFO has been traditional, such as department stores and industries where a fairly constant "base stock" is present such as refining, chemicals, and glass.

Conversely, LIFO would probably not be appropriate: (1) where prices tend to lag behind costs; (2) in situations where specific identification is traditional, such as in the sale of automobiles, farm equipment, art, and antique jewelry; or (3) where unit costs tend to decrease as production increases, thereby nullifying the tax benefit that LIFO might provide.[29]

Tax consequences are another consideration. Switching from FIFO to LIFO usually results in an immediate tax benefit. However, switching from LIFO to FIFO can result in a substantial tax burden. For example, when Chrysler changed from LIFO to FIFO, it became responsible for an additional $53 million in taxes that had been deferred over 14 years of LIFO inventory valuation. Why, then, would Chrysler, and other companies, change to LIFO? The major reason was the profit crunch of that era. Although Chrysler showed a loss of $7.6 million dollars after the switch, the loss would have been $20 million *more* if the company had not changed its inventory valuation back to FIFO from LIFO.

It is questionable whether companies should switch from LIFO to FIFO for the sole purpose of increasing reported earnings.[30] Intuitively one would assume that companies with higher reported earnings would have a higher share (common stock price) valuation. Some studies have indicated, however, that the users of financial data exhibit

OBJECTIVE 9
Identify the reasons why a given inventory method is selected.

---

[29]See Barry E. Cushing and Marc J. LeClere, "Evidence on the Determinants of Inventory Accounting Policy Choice," *The Accounting Review* (April 1992), pp. 355–366, Table 4, p. 363, for a list of factors hypothesized to affect FIFO–LIFO choices.

[30]*Accounting Trends and Techniques—1993* reports that of 1,011 inventory method disclosures, 358 used LIFO, 415 used FIFO, 193 used average cost, and 45 used other methods.

a much higher sophistication than might be expected. Share prices are the same and, in some cases, even higher under LIFO in spite of lower reported earnings.[31]

The concern about reduced income resulting from adoption of LIFO has even less substance now because the IRS has relaxed the LIFO conformity rule which required a company that employed LIFO for tax purposes to use it for book purposes as well. In addition, the IRS recently relaxed restrictions against providing non-LIFO income numbers as supplementary information. As a result, the profession now permits supplemental non-LIFO disclosures but not on the face of the income statement. The supplemental disclosure, while not intended to override the basic LIFO method adopted for financial reporting, may be useful in comparing operating income and working capital with companies not on LIFO.

For example, J. C. Penney, Inc. (a LIFO user) in its annual report presented the following information.

ILLUSTRATION 8-26
Supplemental Non-LIFO Disclosure

J. C. Penney, Inc.
Some companies in the retail industry use the FIFO method in valuing part or all of their inventories. Had J. C. Penney used the FIFO method and made no other assumptions with respect to changes in income resulting therefrom, income and income per share from continuing operations would have been:

Income from continuing operations (in millions)	$ 325
Income from continuing operations per share	$4.63

Another user of LIFO, Weyerhaeuser Company, made the following disclosure in its Annual Report relative to product inventories carried in its balance sheet at $423,988,000 (current period) and $379,399,000 (prior period):

ILLUSTRATION 8-27
Supplemental Non-LIFO Disclosure

Weyerhaeuser Company
Had the FIFO method been used to cost all inventories, the amounts at which product inventories are stated would have been $178,122,000 and $183,001,000 greater during the current and prior period, respectively.

Relaxation of the LIFO conformity rule will probably lead more companies to select LIFO as their inventory valuation method because they will be able to disclose FIFO income numbers in the financial reports if they so desire.[32]

Often the inventory methods are used in combination with other methods. For example, most companies never use LIFO totally, but rather use it in combination with other valuation approaches. One reason is that certain product lines can be highly susceptible to deflation instead of inflation. In addition, if the level of inventory is unstable, unwanted involuntary liquidations may result in certain product lines if LIFO is used. Finally, where inventory turnover in certain product lines is high, the additional

---

[31]See, for example, Shyam Sunder, "Relationship Between Accounting Changes and Stock Prices: Problems of Measurement and Some Empirical Evidence," *Empirical Research in Accounting: Selected Studies, 1973* (Chicago: University of Chicago), pp. 1–40; but see Robert Moren Brown, "Short-Range Market Reaction to Changes to LIFO Accounting Using Preliminary Earnings Announcement Dates," *The Journal of Accounting Research* (Spring 1980), which found that companies that do change to LIFO suffer a short-run decline in the price of their stock; see also William E. Ricks, "Market's Response to the 1974 LIFO Adoptions," *The Journal of Accounting Research* (Autumn 1982), pp. 367–387.

[32]Note that a company can use one variation of LIFO for financial reporting purposes and another for tax without violating the LIFO conformity rule. Such a relaxation will undoubtedly involve many problems for accountants because the general approach to accounting for LIFO has been "whatever is good for tax is good for financial reporting." The AICPA published a useful paper on this subject entitled "Identification and Discussion of Certain Financial Accounting and Reporting Issues Concerning LIFO Inventories," (New York: AICPA, November 30, 1984).

recordkeeping and expense are not justified by LIFO. Average cost is often used in such cases because it is easy to compute.[33]

This variety of inventory methods has been devised to assist in accurate computation of net income rather than to permit manipulation of reported income. Hence, it is recommended that the pricing method most suitable to a company be selected and, once selected, be applied consistently thereafter. If conditions indicate that the inventory pricing method in use is unsuitable, serious consideration should be given to all other possibilities before selecting another method. Any change should be clearly explained and its effect disclosed in the financial statements.

INVENTORY VALUATION METHOD—SUMMARY ANALYSIS

A number of inventory valuation methods are described in the preceding sections of this chapter. A brief summary of the three major inventory methods, assuming periodic inventory procedures, is presented below to show the differing effects these valuation methods have on the financial statements. The first schedule provides selected data for the comparison as follows:

Selected Data		
Given		
Beginning cash balance		$ 7,000
Beginning retained earnings		$10,000
Beginning inventory	4,000 units @ $3	$12,000
Purchases	6,000 units @ $4	$24,000
Sales	5,000 units @ $12	$60,000
Operating expenses		$10,000
Income tax rate		40%

The comparative results of using average cost, FIFO, and LIFO on net income are computed as shown in Illustration 8-28.

	Average Cost	FIFO	LIFO
Sales	$60,000	$60,000	$60,000
Cost of goods sold	18,000[a]	16,000[b]	20,000[c]
Gross profit	42,000	44,000	40,000
Operating expenses	10,000	10,000	10,000
Income before taxes	32,000	34,000	30,000
Income taxes (40%)	12,800	13,600	12,000
Net income	$19,200	$20,400	$18,000

[a] 4,000 @ $3 = $12,000
   6,000 @ $4 = 24,000
              $36,000

   $36,000 ÷ 10,000 = $3.60
   $3.60 × 5,000 = $18,000

[b] 4,000 @ $3 = $12,000
   1,000 @ $4 = 4,000
              $16,000

[c] 5,000 = $4 = $20,000

**ILLUSTRATION 8-28
Comparative Results of Average Cost, FIFO, and LIFO Methods**

Notice that gross profit and net income are lowest under LIFO, highest under FIFO and somewhere in the middle under Average Cost.

---

[33]For an interesting discussion of the reasons for and against the use of FIFO and average cost, see: Michael H. Granof and Daniel G. Short "For Some Companies, FIFO Accounting Makes Sense," *The Wall Street Journal* (August 30, 1982) and the subsequent rebuttal by Gary C. Biddle "Taking Stock of Inventory Accounting Choices," *The Wall Street Journal* (September 15, 1982).

The table below then shows the final balances of selected items at the end of the period:

ILLUSTRATION 8-29
Balances of Selected Items Under Alternative Inventory Valuation Methods

	Inventory	Gross Profit	Taxes	Net Income	Retained Earnings	Cash
Average Cost	$18,000 (5,000 × $3.60)	$42,000	$12,800	$19,200	$29,200 ($10,000 + $19,200)	$20,200[a]
FIFO	$20,000 (5,000 × $4)	$44,000	$13,600	$20,400	$30,400 ($10,000 + $20,400)	$19,400[a]
LIFO	$16,000 (4,000 × $3) (1,000 × $4)	$40,000	$12,000	$18,000	$28,000 ($10,000 + $18,000)	$21,000[a]

[a]Cash at year-end	=	Beg. balance	+	sales	−	purchases	−	operating expenses	−	taxes
Average cost—$20,200	=	$7,000	+	$60,000	−	$24,000	−	$10,000	−	$12,800
FIFO—$19,400	=	$7,000	+	$60,000	−	$24,000	−	$10,000	−	$13,600
LIFO—$21,000	=	$7,000	+	$60,000	−	$24,000	−	$10,000	−	$12,000

LIFO results in the highest cash balance at year-end because taxes are lower. This example assumes prices are rising; the opposite result occurs if prices are declining.

KEY TERMS

absorption costing, 386

average cost method, 388

consigned goods, 381

cost flow assumptions, 387

current ratio, 384

dollar-value LIFO, 393

double-extension method, 396

finished goods inventory, 377

first-in, first-out (FIFO) method, 389

fixed costs, 386

f.o.b. destination, 381

f.o.b. shipping point, 381

gross method, 387

inventories, 376

last-in, first-out (LIFO) method, 390

LIFO liquidation, 391

merchandise inventory, 377

moving-average method, 389

net method, 387

period costs, 385

periodic inventory system, 379

perpetual inventory system, 378

product costs, 385

purchase discounts, 386

▶ SUMMARY OF LEARNING OBJECTIVES ◀

1. **Identify major classifications of inventory.** Only one inventory account, Merchandise Inventory, appears in the financial statements of a merchandising concern. A manufacturer normally has three inventory accounts: Raw Materials, Work in Process, and Finished Goods. The cost assigned to goods and materials on hand but not yet placed into production is reported as raw materials inventory. The cost of the raw materials on which production has been started but not completed, plus the direct labor cost applied specifically to this material and a ratable share of manufacturing overhead costs, constitute the work in process inventory. The costs identified with the completed but unsold units on hand at the end of the fiscal period are reported as finished goods inventory.

2. **Distinguish between the perpetual and periodic inventory systems.** Under a perpetual inventory system, a continuous record of changes in inventory is maintained in the Inventory account. That is, all purchases and sales (issues) of goods are recorded directly in the Inventory account as they occur. Under a periodic inventory system, the quantity of inventory on hand is determined only periodically. The Inventory account remains the same and a Purchases account is debited. Cost of goods sold is determined at the end of the period using a formula. Ending inventory is ascertained by physical count.

3. **Identify the effects of inventory errors on the financial statements.** *If the ending inventory is misstated,* (1) the inventory, retained earnings, working capital, and current ratio in the balance sheet will be misstated, and (2) the cost of goods sold and net income in the income statement will be misstated. *If purchases and inventory are misstated,* (1) the inventory, accounts payable, and current ratio will be misstated, and (2) purchases, and ending inventory in the income statement will be misstated.

4. **Identify the items that should be included as inventory cost.** Product costs are directly connected with the bringing of goods to the place of business of the buyer and converting such goods to a salable condition. Such charges would include freight charges on goods purchased, other direct costs of acquisition, and labor and other production costs incurred in processing the goods up to the time of sale. Manufacturing overhead costs that include indirect material,

indirect labor, and such items as depreciation, taxes, insurance, heat, and electricity incurred in the manufacturing process are also allocated to inventory.

5. **Describe and compare the flow assumptions used in accounting for inventories.** (1) *Average cost* prices items in the inventory on the basis of the average cost of all similar goods available during the period. (2) *First-in, first-out (FIFO)* assumes that goods are used in the order in which they are purchased. The inventory remaining must therefore represent the most recent purchases. (3) *Last-in, first-out (LIFO)* matches the cost of the last goods purchased against revenue.

6. **Explain the effect of LIFO liquidations.** The effect of LIFO liquidations is that costs from preceding periods are matched against sales revenues reported in current dollars. This leads to a distortion in net income and a substantial tax bill in the current period. LIFO liquidations can occur frequently when a specific goods LIFO approach is employed.

7. **Explain the dollar-value LIFO method.** An important feature of the dollar-value LIFO method is that increases and decreases in a pool are determined and measured in terms of total dollar value, not the physical quantity of the goods in the inventory pool.

8. **Identify the major advantages and disadvantages of LIFO.** The major advantages of LIFO are: (1) recent costs are matched against current revenues to provide a better measure of current earnings; (2) as long as the price level increases and inventory quantities do not decrease, a deferral of income tax occurs in LIFO; (3) because of the deferral of income tax, there is improvement of cash flow; (4) a company's future reported earnings will not be affected substantially by future price declines (future earnings hedge). Major disadvantages are: (1) reduced earnings, (2) understated inventory, (3) no approximated physical flow of the items except in peculiar situations.

9. **Identify the reasons why a given inventory method is selected.** Preferability for LIFO can ordinarily be established if: (1) selling prices and revenues have been increasing faster than costs, and (2) LIFO has been traditional, such as department stores and industries like refining, chemicals, and glass where a fairly constant "base stock" is present. Conversely, LIFO would probably not be appropriate: (1) where prices tend to lag behind costs; (2) in situations where specific identification is traditional, such as in the sales of automobiles, farm equipment, art, and antique jewelry; and (3) where unit costs tend to decrease as production increases, thereby nullifying the tax benefit that LIFO might provide.

APPENDIX 8-A

SPECIAL LIFO REPORTING PROBLEMS

OBJECTIVE 10

After studying Appendix 8-A, you should be able to: Understand the LIFO reporting problems related to the initial adoption of LIFO, the LIFO reserve, and interim LIFO reporting.

The LIFO discussion in this chapter has emphasized the basic issues and procedures related to this inventory valuation technique. This appendix introduces a number of special LIFO reporting problems that may occur. They are generally classified as follows:

1. Initial adoption of LIFO.
2. LIFO reserve.
3. Interim reporting problems.

▶ INITIAL ADOPTION OF LIFO

The initial adoption of LIFO presents a reporting problem: It is difficult if not impossible to reconstruct the accounting records to determine what net income would have been in prior years had LIFO been used. As a result, **when changing to LIFO, neither a cumulative effect nor a retroactive adjustment can be made.** The base-year inventory for all subsequent LIFO computations is the opening inventory of the year the method is adopted. The effect that the change to LIFO has on **current net income** must be disclosed in a note.

Revere Copper and Brass Incorporated's annual report provides a good example of the type of information disclosed:

ILLUSTRATION 8A-1
Inventory Valuation Disclosure

> ### Revere Copper and Brass
>
> **Inventory Pricing.** In the fourth quarter the Company expanded its use of the last-in, first-out (LIFO) method of inventory valuation to a substantial additional portion of its inventories in order to more closely match current costs with current revenues. The effect of this change was to reduce net income for the current year by $2,804,000 or $.49 per share. It is not practicable to restate prior years or determine the cumulative effect of the change. As of December 31, inventories valued on a LIFO basis amounted to $74,166,000. If valued on a first-in, first-out basis, such inventories would be increased to $90,551,000.

Formal journal entries are not required in adopting LIFO except when the inventory is restored to a cost basis from the lower of cost or market approach. Because LIFO is considered a cost approach, the inventory must be restated to a cost basis if market is lower than cost at the time of LIFO adoption. To illustrate, assume that Ramos, Inc. decided to switch **from FIFO to LIFO.** The inventory under FIFO has a cost basis of $100,000 but is reported at $90,000 because market is lower than cost. The following entry is made to restate the inventory to a cost basis (ignoring tax effects):

Inventory	10,000	
Adjustment to Record Inventory at Cost		10,000

The Adjustment to Record Inventory at Cost should be reported on the income statement in the Other Revenues and Gains section.

▶ LIFO RESERVE

Many companies use LIFO for tax and external reporting purposes, but maintain a FIFO, average cost, or standard cost system for internal reporting purposes. There are several reasons to do so: (1) Companies often base their pricing decisions on a FIFO, average, or standard cost assumption, rather than on a LIFO basis. (2) Record keeping is easier because the LIFO assumption usually does not approximate the physical flow of the product. (3) Profit-sharing and other bonus arrangements are often not based on a LIFO inventory assumption. Finally, (4) the use of a pure LIFO system is troublesome for interim periods, for which estimates must be made of year-end quantities and prices.

The difference between the inventory method used for internal reporting purposes and LIFO is referred to as the Allowance to Reduce Inventory to LIFO or the **LIFO reserve.** The change in the allowance balance from one period to the next is called the **LIFO effect.** The LIFO effect is the adjustment that must be made to the accounting records in a given year. To illustrate, assume that Acme Boot Company uses the FIFO method for internal reporting purposes and LIFO for external reporting purposes. At January 1, 1996, the Allowance to Reduce Inventory to LIFO balance was $20,000 and the ending balance should be $50,000. The LIFO effect is, therefore, $30,000 and the following entry is made at year-end:

Cost of Goods Sold	30,000	
Allowance to Reduce Inventory to LIFO		30,000

The Allowance to Reduce Inventory to LIFO would be deducted from inventory to ensure that the inventory is stated on a LIFO basis at year-end.

The AICPA Task Force on LIFO Inventory Problems concluded that either the LIFO reserve or the replacement cost of the inventory should be disclosed.[1] Two types of this kind of disclosure are shown below.

American Maize-Products Company

Inventories (Note 3)	$80,320,000

Note 3: Inventories. At December 31, $31,516,000 of inventories were valued using the LIFO method. This amount is less than the corresponding replacement value by $3,765,000.

Brown Group, Inc.

Inventories, net of adjustment to last-in, first-out cost of $68,736,000 (Note D)	$309,426,000

Note D: Inventories. Inventories are valued at the lower of cost or market determined principally by the last-in, first-out (LIFO) method. If the first-in, first-out (FIFO) cost method had been used, inventories would have been $68,736,000 higher.

Georgia-Pacific Corporation chose to report its LIFO reserve as a deduction from its average cost inventory total as part of its inventory on the balance sheet (see balance sheet in the Specimen Financial Statements, page 221, Appendix 5-A).

▶ INTERIM REPORTING PROBLEMS

The use of LIFO in interim periods is complicated because LIFO is an annual, not an interim, computation. *APB Opinion No. 28,* however, specifies that accounting principles must be consistently applied among interim periods and that the same principles used for annual purposes must be used for interim periods.[2] This situation presents difficulties because at an interim period the future prices of the inventory and the quantity on hand at year-end are not known. The accountant, therefore, must **estimate the total LIFO effect and allocate this LIFO effect** in some reasonable and consistent fashion. This is not an easy task and it often results in substantial fourth-quarter adjustments. The LIFO effect may be allocated on the basis of estimated sales or estimated production costs, or it may be allocated equally over the four periods.

A special problem develops in interim periods when the temporary liquidation of a LIFO layer occurs. A temporary liquidation occurs when a layer would be liquidated for interim purposes but is expected to be reinstated by year-end. In such a situation, the inventory at the interim period should not give effect to the LIFO liquidation. Instead, the cost of goods sold for the interim period affected should include the expected cost of the replacement of the liquidated LIFO layer.

---

[1]The AICPA Task Force on LIFO Inventory Problems defined **LIFO reserve** for its purposes as "the difference between (a) inventory at the lower of LIFO cost or market and (b) inventory at replacement cost or at the lower of cost determined by some acceptable inventory accounting method (such as FIFO or average cost) or market." *Issues Paper* (New York: AICPA, November 30, 1984), par. 2–24.

[2]"Interim Financial Reporting," *APB Opinion No. 28* (New York: AICPA, 1973).

To illustrate, assume that in the second quarter Trident Manufacturing Co. experiences a temporary reduction in its LIFO inventory of 1,000 units that cost $40.00 per unit. Trident expects to replace the entire reduction in the third quarter at a cost of $55.00 per unit. The entry to record the second-quarter reduction is as follows:

Cost of Goods Sold	55,000	
Inventory		40,000
Excess of Replacement Cost of LIFO		
Temporarily Liquidated		15,000

When the inventory is replenished in the third quarter, the following entry is made:

Inventory	40,000	
Excess of Replacement Cost of LIFO		
Temporarily Liquidated	15,000	
Accounts Payable (Cash)		55,000

The Excess of Replacement Cost of LIFO Temporarily Liquidated is reported as a current liability and **is reported only in interim reports.**

Any part of the LIFO base liquidated at year-end represents a permanent reduction. Because a permanent reduction may have a substantive impact on net income when low-cost items are matched against current revenues, disclosure is required in the annual report. Burlington Industries, Inc. reported a year-end LIFO liquidation in its Annual Report as follows:

Burlington Industries, Inc.

Note C: Inventories. The decrease in excess of average cost over LIFO was due to the liquidation of LIFO inventory quantities carried at lower costs prevailing in prior years, principally due to the sale of the company's Domestics division, and lower cotton prices. The effect of the liquidation of LIFO inventory quantities was to increase net earnings by approximately $8,875,000 or 32 cents per share of which $6,003,000 or 21 cents per share was related to the sale of the company's Domestics division.

KEY TERMS

LIFO reserve, 406

▶ **SUMMARY OF LEARNING OBJECTIVE FOR APPENDIX 8-A** ◀

10. **Understand the LIFO reporting problems related to the initial adoption of LIFO, the LIFO reserve, and interim LIFO reporting.** When changing to LIFO, neither a cumulative effect nor a retroactive adjustment can be made. The base-year inventory is the opening inventory of the year the method is adopted. The difference between the inventory method used for internal reporting purposes and LIFO is referred to as the Allowance to Reduce Inventory to LIFO. In interim periods, the LIFO effect may be allocated on the basis of estimated sales or estimated production costs, or it may be allocated equally over the four periods.

Note: All **asterisked** Questions, Exercises, Problems, and Cases relate to material contained in the appendix to each chapter.

QUESTIONS

1. In what ways are the inventory accounts of a retailing concern different from those of a manufacturing enterprise?

2. Why should inventories be included in (a) a statement of financial position and (b) the computation of net income?

3. What is the difference between a perpetual inventory and a physical inventory? If a company maintains a perpetual inventory, should its physical inventory at any date be equal to the amount indicated by the perpetual inventory records? Why?

4. Ansel Adams, Inc. indicated in a recent annual report that approximately $8 million of merchandise was received on consignment. Should Ansel Adams, Inc. report this amount on their balance sheet? Explain.

5. What is a product financing arrangement? How should product financing arrangements be reported in the financial statements?

6. Where, if at all, should the following items be classified on a balance sheet?
   (a) Goods out on approval to customers.   (d) Raw materials.
   (b) Goods in transit that were recently   (e) Goods received on consignment.
       purchased f.o.b. destination.   (f) Manufacturing supplies.
   (c) Land held by a realty firm for sale.

7. At the balance sheet date Richard Avedon Company held title to goods in transit amounting to $110,100. This amount was omitted from the purchases figure for the year and also from the ending inventory. What is the effect of this omission on the net income for the year as calculated when the books are closed? On the company's financial position as shown in its balance sheet? Is materiality a factor in determining whether an adjustment for this item should be made?

8. Define "cost" as applied to the valuation of inventories.

9. What is the difference between variable costing and conventional absorption costing? Is variable costing acceptable for external financial reporting and for income tax purposes? Why?

10. Stieglitz Corp. is considering alternate methods of accounting for the cash discounts it takes when paying suppliers promptly. One method suggested was to report these discounts as financial income when payments are made. Comment on the propriety of this approach.

11. Dorothea Lange Inc. purchases 300 units of an item at an invoice cost of $30,000. What is the cost per unit? If the goods are shipped f.o.b. shipping point and the freight bill was $3,000, what is the cost per unit if Lange Inc. pays the freight charges? If these items were bought on 2/10, n/30 terms and the invoice and the freight bill were paid within the 10-day period, what would be the cost per unit?

12. Specific identification is sometimes said to be the ideal method of assigning cost to inventory and to cost of goods sold. Briefly indicate the arguments for and against this method of inventory valuation.

13. First-in, first-out; weighted average; and last-in, first-out methods are often used instead of specific identification for inventory valuation purposes. Compare these methods with the specific identification method, discussing the theoretical propriety of each method in the determination of income and asset valuation.

14. How might a company obtain a price index in order to apply dollar-value LIFO?

15. Describe the LIFO double-extension method. Using the following information, compute the index at December 31, 1996, applying the double-extension method to a LIFO pool consisting of 25,500 units of product A and 10,350 units of product B: the base-year cost of product A is $10.20 and of product B is $37.00; the price at December 31, 1996, for product A is $21.00 and for product B is $45.60.

16. As compared with the FIFO method of costing inventories, does the LIFO method result in a larger or smaller net income in a period of rising prices? What is the comparative effect on net income in a period of falling prices?

17. What is the dollar-value method of LIFO inventory valuation? What advantage does the dollar-value method have over the specific goods approach of LIFO inventory valuation? Why will the traditional LIFO inventory costing method and the dollar-value LIFO inventory costing method produce different inventory valuations if the composition of the inventory base changes?

18. What is the LIFO conformity rule? How has the LIFO conformity rule been relaxed?

19. On December 31, 1995, the inventory of Alvarado Company amounts to $800,000. During 1996, the company decides to use the dollar-value LIFO method of costing inventories. On December 31, 1996, the inventory is $1,020,000 at December 31, 1996 prices. Using the December 31, 1995, price level of 100 and the December 31, 1996 price level of 108, compute the inventory value at December 31, 1996, under the dollar-value LIFO method.

20. In an article that appeared in the *Wall Street Journal*, the phrases "phantom (paper) profits" and "high LIFO profits" through involuntary liquidation were used. Explain these phrases.

*21. Salvador Company switched from the FIFO to the LIFO method of inventory valuation. As a result, the beginning inventory was increased $365,700 in order to report it on the cost basis. What is the appropriate journal entry to record this adjustment?

*22. Your instructor has noted that some special problems are associated with the use of LIFO. In particular, in interim reports, the allocation of LIFO reserves and the possibility of temporary liquidation present difficulties. Why do these items present difficulties in interim reports?

*23. Companies using LIFO sometimes establish an "Excess of Replacement Cost of LIFO Temporarily Liquidated" account. Explain why and how this account is established and where it should be reported on the balance sheet.

EXERCISES

E8-1 (Inventoriable Costs) Presented below is a list of items that may or may not be reported as inventory in a company's December 31 balance sheet.

1. Goods out on consignment at another company's store.
2. Goods sold on an installment basis.
3. Goods purchased f.o.b. shipping point that are in transit at December 31.
4. Goods purchased f.o.b. destination that are in transit at December 31.
5. Goods sold to another company, for which our company has signed an agreement to repurchase at a set price that covers all costs related to the inventory.
6. Goods sold where returns are unpredictable.
7. Goods sold f.o.b. shipping point that are in transit at December 31.
8. Freight charges on goods purchased.
9. Factory labor costs incurred on goods still unsold.
10. Interest costs incurred for inventories that are routinely manufactured.
11. Costs incurred to advertise goods held for resale.
12. Materials on hand not yet placed into production by a manufacturing firm.
13. Office supplies.
14. Raw materials on which a manufacturing firm has started production, but which are not completely processed.
15. Factory supplies.
16. Goods held on consignment from another company.
17. Costs identified with units completed by a manufacturing firm, but not yet sold.
18. Goods sold f.o.b. destination that are in transit at December 31.
19. Temporary investments in stocks and bonds that will be resold in the near future.

Instructions
Indicate which of these items would typically be reported as inventory in the financial statements. If an item should **not** be reported as inventory, indicate how it should be reported in the financial statements.

E8-2 (Inventoriable Costs) In your audit of the Muddy Waters Company, you find that a physical inventory on December 31, 1994 showed merchandise with a cost of $430,000 was on hand at that date. You also discover the following items were all excluded from the $430,000.

1. Merchandise of $55,000 which is held by Waters on consignment. The consignor is the CeDell Davis Company.
2. Merchandise costing $38,000 which was shipped by Waters f.o.b. destination to a customer on December 31, 1994. The customer was expected to receive the merchandise on January 6, 1995.
3. Merchandise costing $46,000 which was shipped by Waters f.o.b. shipping point to a customer on December 29, 1994. The customer was scheduled to receive the merchandise on January 2, 1995.
4. Merchandise costing $78,000 shipped by a vendor f.o.b. destination on December 30, 1994, and received by Waters on January 4, 1995.
5. Merchandise costing $51,000 shipped by a vendor f.o.b. seller on December 31, 1994, and received by Waters on January 5, 1995.

Instructions
Based on the above information, calculate the amount that should appear on Waters' balance sheet at December 31, 1994, for inventory.

E8-3 (Inventoriable Costs) In an annual audit of Fat Possum Company at December 31, 1996, you find the following transactions near the closing date.

1. A special machine, fabricated to order for a customer, was finished and specifically segregated in the back part of the shipping room on December 31, 1996. The customer was billed on that date and the machine excluded from inventory although it was shipped on January 4, 1997.
2. Merchandise costing $2,800 was received on January 3, 1997, and the related purchase invoice recorded January 5. The invoice showed the shipment was made on December 29, 1996, f.o.b. destination.
3. A packing case containing a product costing $1,500 was standing in the shipping room when the physical inventory was taken. It was not included in the inventory because it was marked "Hold for shipping instructions." Your investigation revealed that the customer's order was dated December 18,

1996, but that the case was shipped and the customer billed on January 10, 1997. The product was a stock item of your client.

4. Merchandise received on January 6, 1997, costing $680 was entered in the purchase journal on January 7, 1997. The invoice showed shipment was made f.o.b. supplier's warehouse on December 31, 1996. Because it was not on hand at December 31, it was not included in inventory.

5. Merchandise costing $720 was received on December 28, 1996, and the invoice was not recorded. You located it in the hands of the purchasing agent; it was marked on consignment.

Instructions

Assuming that each of the amounts is material, state whether the merchandise should be included in the client's inventory and give your reason for your decision on each item.

E8-4 (Inventoriable Costs) Junior Kimbrough Machine Company maintains a general ledger account for each class of inventory, debiting such accounts for increases during the period and crediting them for decreases. The transactions below relate to the Raw Materials inventory account, which is debited for materials purchased and credited for materials requisitioned for use.

1. An invoice for $6,400, terms f.o.b. destination, was received and entered January 2, 1996. The receiving report shows that the materials were received December 28, 1995.

2. Materials costing $28,000, shipped f.o.b. destination, were not entered by December 31, 1995, "because they were in a railroad car on the company's siding on that date and had not been unloaded."

3. Materials costing $7,300 were returned on December 29, 1995, to the creditor, and were shipped f.o.b. shipping point. The return was entered on that date, even though the materials are not expected to reach the creditor's place of business until January 6, 1996.

4. An invoice for $9,200, terms f.o.b. shipping point, was received and entered December 30, 1995. The receiving report shows that the materials were received January 4, 1996, and the bill of lading shows that they were shipped January 2, 1996.

5. Materials costing $19,800 were received December 30, 1995, but no entry was made for them because "they were ordered with a specified delivery of no earlier than January 10, 1996."

Instructions

Prepare correcting general journal entries required at December 31, 1995, assuming that the books have not been closed.

E8-5 (Inventoriable Costs—Error Adjustments) The following purchase transactions occurred during the last few days of R. L. Burnside Company's business year, which ends October 31, or in the first few days after that date. A periodic inventory system is used.

1. An invoice for $3,000, terms f.o.b. shipping point, was received and entered November 1. The invoice shows that the material was shipped October 29, but the receiving report indicates receipt of goods on November 3.

2. An invoice for $2,700, terms f.o.b. destination, was received and entered November 2. The receiving report indicates that the goods were received October 29.

3. An invoice for $3,150, terms f.o.b. shipping point, was received October 15 but never entered. Attached to it is a receiving report indicating that the goods were received October 18. Across the face of the receiving report is the following notation: "Merchandise not of same quality as ordered—returned for credit October 19."

4. An invoice for $3,600, terms f.o.b. shipping point, was received and entered October 27. The receiving report attached to the invoice indicates that the shipment was received October 27 in satisfactory condition.

5. An invoice for $5,100, terms f.o.b. destination, was received and entered October 28. The receiving report indicates that the merchandise was received November 2.

Before preparing financial statements for the year, you are instructed to review these transactions and to determine whether any correcting entries are required and whether the inventory of $77,500 determined by physical count on October 31 should be changed.

Instructions

Complete the following schedule, and state the correct inventory at October 31. Assume that the books have not been closed.

Transaction	Purchase and Related Payable Should Be Recognized in (month)	Purchase and Related Payable Were Recognized in (month)	Correcting Journal Entries Needed	Should Inventory Be Included in October Ending Inventory?	Was Inventory Included in October Ending Inventory?	Dollar Adjustments Needed to October Ending Inventory

E8-6 (Determining Merchandise Amounts) Two or more items are omitted in each of the following tabulations of income statement data. Fill in the amounts that are missing.

	1994	1995	1996
Sales	$290,000	$ _____	$400,000
Sales Returns	11,000	13,000	_____
Net Sales	_____	347,000	_____
Beginning Inventory	20,000	30,000	_____
Ending Inventory	_____	_____	_____
Purchases	_____	260,000	298,000
Purchase Returns and Allowances	5,000	8,000	10,000
Transportation-in	8,000	9,000	12,000
Cost of Goods Sold	233,000	_____	293,000
Gross Profit on Sales	46,000	91,000	97,000

E8-7 (Financial Statement Presentation of Manufacturing Amounts) Linda Yu Company is a manufacturing firm. Presented below is selected information from their 1995 accounting records.

Raw materials inventory, 1/1/95	$ 30,800	Transportation-out	8,000
Raw materials inventory, 12/31/95	37,400	Selling expenses	300,000
Work-in-process inventory, 1/1/95	72,600	Administrative expenses	180,000
Work-in-process inventory, 12/31/95	61,600	Purchase discounts	10,640
Finished goods inventory, 1/1/95	35,200	Purchase returns and allowances	3,960
Finished goods inventory, 12/31/95	22,000	Interest expense	15,000
Purchases	278,600	Direct labor	440,000
Transportation-in	6,600	Manufacturing overhead	330,000

Instructions

(a) Compute raw materials used.
(b) Compute the cost of goods manufactured.
(c) Compute cost of goods sold.
(d) Indicate how inventories would be reported in the 12/31/95 balance sheet.

E8-8 (Manufacturing Closing Entries) The following accounts, among others, appear on the trial balance of Leno Corporation at the end of the year 1996:

Raw Materials Inventory 1/1/96	$ 28,000
Goods in Process Inventory 1/1/96	50,000
Finished Goods Inventory 1/1/96	60,000
Raw Materials Purchased	75,000
Direct Labor	87,000
Manufacturing Overhead	98,000
Sales	400,000
General and Administrative Expense	65,000

Instructions

Assuming that no other nominal accounts existed, give the closing entries that would be made at the end of the year. Inventories on December 31, 1996, are: raw materials, $36,000; goods in process, $65,000; finished goods, $80,000. Ignore income tax effects.

E8-9 (Purchases Recorded Net) Presented below are transactions related to Johnny Carson, Inc.

May 10 Purchased goods billed at $14,600 subject to cash discount terms of 2/10, n/60.
    11 Purchased goods billed at $13,200 subject to terms of 1/15, n/30.
    19 Paid invoice of May 10.
    24 Purchased goods billed at $11,500 subject to cash discount terms of 2/10, n/30.

Instructions

(a) Prepare general journal entries for the transactions above under the assumption that purchases are to be recorded at net amounts after cash discounts and that discounts lost are to be treated as financial expense.
(b) Assuming no purchase or payment transactions other than those given above, prepare the adjusting entry required on May 31 if financial statements are to be prepared as of that date.

E8-10 (Periodic Versus Perpetual Entries) The Letterman Company sells one product. Presented below is information for January for the Letterman Company.

Jan. 1 Inventory   100 units at $5 each
      4 Sale   80 units at $8 each
   11 Purchase   150 units at $6 each
   13 Sale   120 units at $8.50 each

	20 Purchase	150 units at $7 each
	27 Sale	100 units at $9 each

Letterman uses the FIFO cost flow assumption. All purchases and sales are on account.

Instructions
  (a) Assume Letterman uses a periodic system. Prepare all necessary journal entries, including the end-of-month closing entry to record cost of goods sold. A physical count indicates that the ending inventory for January is 100 units.
  (b) Compute gross profit using the periodic system.
  (c) Assume Letterman uses a perpetual system. Prepare all necessary journal entries.
  (d) Compute gross profit using the perpetual system.

E8-11 (Inventory Errors) Chevy Chase Company makes the following errors during the current year.

1. Ending inventory is overstated, but purchases are recorded correctly.
2. Both ending inventory and purchases on account are understated (Assume this purchase was recorded in the following year).
3. Ending inventory is correct, but a purchase on account was not recorded (Assume this purchase was recorded in the following year).

Instructions
Indicate the effect of each of these errors on working capital, current ratio (assume that the current ratio is positive), retained earnings, and net income for the current year and the subsequent year.

E8-12 (Inventory Errors) Clive James Company has a calendar-year accounting period. The following errors have been discovered in 1996.

1. The December 31, 1994, merchandise inventory had been understated by $14,000.
2. Merchandise purchased on account during 1995 was recorded on the books for the first time in February 1996, when the original invoice for the correct amount of $5,430 arrived. The merchandise had arrived December 28, 1995, and was included in the December 31, 1995, merchandise inventory. The invoice arrived late because of a mixup on the wholesaler's part.
3. Accrued interest of $632 at December 31, 1995, on notes receivable had not been recorded until the cash for the interest was received in March 1996.

Instructions
  (a) Compute the effect each error had on the 1995 net income.
  (b) Compute the effect, if any, each error had on the related December 31, 1995, balance sheet items.

E8-13 (Inventory Errors) At December 31, 1995, Arsenio Hall Corporation reported current assets of $350,000 and current liabilities of $200,000. The following items may have been recorded incorrectly.

1. Goods purchased costing $22,000 were shipped f.o.b. shipping point by a supplier on December 28. Hall received and recorded the invoice on December 29, but the goods were not included in Hall's physical count of inventory because they were not received until January 4.
2. Goods purchased costing $15,000 were shipped f.o.b. destination by a supplier on December 26. Hall received and recorded the invoice on December 31, but the goods were not included in Hall's physical count of inventory because they were not received until January 2.
3. Goods held on consignment from Number One Company were included in Hall's physical count of inventory at $13,000.
4. Freight-in of $3,000 was debited to advertising expense on December 28.

Instructions
  (a) Compute the current ratio based on Hall's balance sheet.
  (b) Recompute the current ratio after corrections are made.
  (c) By what amount will income (before taxes) be adjusted up or down as a result of the corrections?

E8-14 (Inventory Errors) The net income per books of Joan Rivers Company was determined without knowledge of the errors indicated.

Year	Net Income per Books	Error in Ending Inventory	
1991	$50,000	Overstated	$ 3,000
1992	52,000	Overstated	7,000
1993	54,000	Understated	11,000
1994	56,000	No error	
1995	58,000	Understated	4,000
1996	60,000	Overstated	8,000

Instructions
Prepare a work sheet to show the adjusted net income figure for each of the 6 years after taking into account the inventory errors.

E8-15 (FIFO and LIFO—Periodic and Perpetual) Inventory information for Part 311 of Betts Siwy Corp. discloses the following information for the month of June:

June 1:	Balance	300 units @ $10	June 10:	Sold	200 units @ $24
11:	Purchased	800 units @ $12	15:	Sold	500 units @ $25
20:	Purchased	500 units @ $14	27:	Sold	300 units @ $26

Instructions
(a) Assuming that the periodic inventory method is used, compute the cost of goods sold and ending inventory under (1) LIFO; (2) FIFO.
(b) Assuming that the perpetual inventory record is kept in dollars, and costs are computed at the time of each withdrawal, what is the value of the ending inventory at LIFO?
(c) Assuming that the perpetual inventory record is kept in dollars, and costs are computed at the time of each withdrawal, what is the gross profit if the inventory is valued at FIFO?
(d) Why is it stated that LIFO usually produces a lower gross profit than FIFO?

E8-16 (FIFO, LIFO and Average Cost Determination) Tod Pietens Company's record of transactions for the month of April was as follows:

Purchases			Sales		
April 1 (balance on hand)	600 @ $6.20		April 3	500 @ $10.00	
4	1,500 @ 6.00		9	1,400 @ 10.00	
8	800 @ 6.40		11	600 @ 11.00	
13	1,200 @ 6.50		23	1,200 @ 11.00	
21	700 @ 6.60		27	900 @ 12.00	
29	500 @ 6.79			4,600	
	5,300				

Instructions
(a) Assuming that perpetual inventory records are kept in units only, compute the inventory at April 30 using (1) LIFO; (2) average cost.
(b) Assuming that perpetual inventory records are kept in dollars, determine the inventory using (1) FIFO; (2) LIFO.
(c) Compute cost of goods sold assuming periodic inventory procedures and inventory priced at FIFO.
(d) In an inflationary period, which of the following inventory methods (FIFO, LIFO, average cost) will show the highest net income?

E8-17 (FIFO, LIFO, Average Cost Inventory) A. C Neher Company was formed on December 1, 1994. The following information is available from Neher's inventory records for Product BAP:

	Units	Unit Cost
January 1, 1995 (beginning inventory)	600	$ 8.00
Purchases:		
January 5, 1995	1,200	$ 9.00
January 25, 1995	1,300	$10.00
February 16, 1995	800	$11.00
March 26, 1995	600	$12.00

A physical inventory on March 31, 1995 shows 1,500 units on hand.

Instructions
Prepare schedules to compute the ending inventory at March 31, 1995 under each of the following inventory methods:
(a) FIFO.
(b) LIFO.
(c) Weighted average.

(AICPA adapted)

E8-18 (Compute FIFO, LIFO, Average Cost—Periodic) Presented below is information related to Product G of Kent Adamson Company for the month of July:

Date	Transaction	Units In	Unit Cost	Total	Units Sold	Selling Price	Total
July 1	Balance	100	$4.10	$ 410			
6	Purchase	800	4.20	3,360			

7	Sale				300	$7.00	$ 2,100
10	Sale				300	$7.30	2,190
12	Purchase	400	4.50	1,800			
15	Sale				200	7.40	1,480
18	Purchase	300	4.60	1,380			
22	Sale				400	7.40	2,960
25	Purchase	500	4.70	2,350			
30	Sale				200	7.50	1,500
	Totals	2,100		$9,300	1,400		$10,230

Instructions

(a) Assuming that the periodic inventory method is used, compute the inventory cost at July 31 under each of the following cost flow assumptions:

    1. FIFO.

    2. LIFO.

    3. Weighted-average (round the weighted-average unit cost to the nearest one-tenth of one cent).

(b) Answer the following questions:

    1. Which of the methods used above will yield the lowest figure for gross profit for the income statement? Explain why.

    2. Which of the methods used above will yield the lowest figure for ending inventory for the balance sheet? Explain why.

E8-19 (FIFO and LIFO; Periodic and Perpetual) The following is a record of Kaster Company's transactions for transistor radios for the month of May 1996:

May 1 Balance 400 units @ $20	May 10 Sale 300 units @ $38
12 Purchase 600 units @ $25	20 Sale 500 units @ $38
28 Purchase 400 units @ $30	

Instructions

(a) Assuming that perpetual inventories are **not** maintained and that a physical count at the end of the month shows 600 units on hand, what is the cost of the ending inventory using (1) FIFO? and (2) LIFO?

(b) Assuming that perpetual records are maintained and they tie into the general ledger, calculate the ending inventory using (1) FIFO; (2) LIFO.

E8-20 (FIFO and LIFO; Income Statement Presentation) The board of directors of Burke Corporation is considering whether or not it should instruct the accounting department to shift from a first-in, first-out (FIFO) basis of pricing inventories to a last-in, first-out (LIFO) basis. The following information is available.

Sales	20,000 units @ $50
Inventory January 1	6,000 units @ 20
Purchases	6,000 units @ 22
	10,000 units @ 25
	7,000 units @ 30
Inventory December 31	9,000 units @ ?
Operating expenses	$200,000

Instructions

Prepare a condensed income statement for the year on both bases for comparative purposes.

E8-21 (FIFO and LIFO Effects) You are the vice-president of finance of Gleason Corporation, a retail company that prepared two different schedules of gross margin for the first quarter ended March 31, 1996. These schedules appear below.

	Sales ($5 per unit)	Cost of Goods Sold	Gross Margin
Schedule 1	$150,000	$124,900	$25,100
Schedule 2	150,000	126,100	23,900

The computation of cost of goods sold in each schedule is based on the following data:

	Units	Cost per Unit	Total Cost
Beginning inventory, January 1	10,000	$4.00	$40,000
Purchase, January 10	8,000	4.20	33,600
Purchase, January 30	6,000	4.25	25,500
Purchase, February 11	9,000	4.30	38,700
Purchase, March 17	11,000	4.10	45,100

Linda Dizburg, the president of the corporation, cannot understand how two different gross margins can be computed from the same set of data. As the vice-president of finance you have explained to Ms. Dizburg that the two schedules are based on different assumptions concerning the flow of inventory costs, i.e., first-in, first-out; and last-in, first-out. Schedules 1 and 2 were not necessarily prepared in this sequence of cost flow assumptions.

Instructions

Prepare two separate schedules computing cost of goods sold and supporting schedules showing the composition of the ending inventory under both cost flow assumptions.

E8-22 (FIFO and LIFO—Periodic) Amos Stagg Shop began operations on January 1, 1996. The following stock record card for footballs was taken from the records at the end of the year.

Date	Voucher	Terms	Units Received	Unit Invoice Cost	Gross Invoice Amount
1/15	10624	Net 30	50	$20.00	$1,000.00
3/15	11437	1/5, net 30	65	16.00	1,040.00
6/20	21332	1/10, net 30	90	15.00	1,350.00
9/12	27644	1/10, net 30	84	12.00	1,008.00
11/24	31269	1/10, net 30	76	11.00	836.00
	Totals		365		$5,234.00

A physical inventory on December 31, 1996 reveals that 130 footballs were in stock. The bookkeeper informs you that all the discounts were taken. Assume that Stagg Shop uses the invoice price less discount for recording purchases.

Instructions

(a) Compute the 12/31/96 inventory using the FIFO method.

(b) Compute the 1996 cost of goods sold using the LIFO method.

(c) What method would you recommend to the owner to minimize income taxes in 1996, using the inventory information for footballs as a guide?

E8-23 (Specific Goods and Specific Goods Pooled LIFO Contrasted) Presented below is inventory, purchases and sales data for Mario Lemieux Inc. for 1996.

	Material X		**Material Y**	
	Units	Price	Units	Price
Inventory, January 1	100	$3	300	$2
Purchases	1,000	6	600	5
Sales	900		700	

Mario Lemieux Inc. uses the periodic method of inventory valuation.

Instructions

(a) Determine the ending inventory of these two products using specific goods LIFO.

(b) Determine the ending inventory of these two products using specific goods pooled LIFO; that is, assume that Material X and Material Y are one pool.

(c) Determine which of these two methods will result in Lemieux Inc. reporting higher net income in 1996. Provide an explanation for this result.

E8-24 (Alternative Inventory Methods—Comprehensive) Brett Hull Corporation began operations on December 1, 1995. The only inventory transaction in 1995 was the purchase of inventory on December 10, 1995 at a cost of $20 per unit. None of this inventory was sold in 1995. Relevant information is as follows:

Ending inventory units		
December 31, 1995		100
December 31, 1996, by purchase data		
December 2, 1996	100	
July 20, 1996	50	150

During the year the following purchases and sales were made:

	Purchases		**Sales**	
March 15	300 units at $24		April 10	200
July 20	300 units at $25		August 20	300
September 4	200 units at $28		November 18	150
December 2	100 units at $32		Dec. 12	200

The company uses the periodic inventory method.

Instructions
(a) Determine ending inventory under (1) specific identification, (2) FIFO, (3) LIFO periodic, and (4) average cost.
(b) Determine ending inventory using dollar-value LIFO. Assume that the December 2, 1996 purchase cost is the current cost of inventory (Hint: The beginning inventory is the base layer priced at $20 per unit).

E8-25 (Dollar-Value LIFO)   Stan Mitira Company has used the dollar-value LIFO method for inventory cost determination for many years. The following data were extracted from Hatter's records:

Date	Price Index	Ending Inventory at Base Prices	Ending Inventory at Dollar-value LIFO
December 31, 1994	105	$92,000	$92,600
December 31, 1995	?	97,000	98,600

Instructions
Calculate the index used for 1995 which yielded the above results.

E8-26 (Dollar-Value LIFO)   The dollar-value LIFO method was adopted by Bobby Orr Corp. on January 1, 1996. Its inventory on that date was $160,000. On December 31, 1996, the inventory at prices existing on that date amounted to $140,000. The price level at January 1, 1996, was 100, and the price level at December 31, 1996, was 112.

Instructions
(a) Compute the amount of the inventory at December 31, 1996, under the dollar-value LIFO method.
(b) On December 31, 1997, the inventory at prices existing on that date was $180,000, and the price level was 120. Compute the inventory on that date under the dollar-value LIFO method.

E8-27 (Dollar-Value LIFO)   Presented below is information related to Wayne Gretzky Company.

Date	Ending Inventory (End-of-Year Prices)	Price Index
December 31, 1993	$ 80,000	100
December 31, 1994	115,500	105
December 31, 1995	108,000	120
December 31, 1996	123,500	130
December 31, 1997	154,000	140
December 31, 1998	174,000	145

Instructions
Compute the ending inventory for Wayne Gretzky Company for 1993 through 1998 using the dollar-value LIFO method.

E8-28 (Dollar-Value LIFO)   The following information relates to the Jerome Jagger Company.

Date	Ending Inventory (End-of-Year Prices)	Price Index
December 31, 1992	$ 70,000	100
December 31, 1993	90,300	105
December 31, 1994	95,120	116
December 31, 1995	108,000	120
December 31, 1996	95,000	125

Instructions
Use the dollar-value LIFO method to compute the ending inventory for Jagger Company for 1992 through 1996.

*E8-29 (Change to LIFO Retail)   The Casey Stengel Ltd., a local retailing concern in the Bronx, N.Y., has decided to change from the conventional retail inventory method to the LIFO retail method starting on January 1, 1996. The company recomputed its ending inventory for 1995 in accordance with the procedures necessary to switch to LIFO retail. The inventory computed was $210,300.

Instructions
Assuming that The Casey Stengel Ltd.'s ending inventory for 1995 under the conventional retail inventory method was $205,000, prepare the appropriate journal entry on January 1, 1996.

PROBLEMS

P8-1 (Various Inventory Issues) The following independent situations relate to inventory accounting.

1. Temptations Co. purchased goods with a list price of $100,000, subject to trade discounts of 20% and 10%, with no cash discounts allowable. How much should Temptations Co. record as the cost of these goods?

2. Four Tops Company's inventory of $1,100,000 at December 31, 1995, was based on a physical count of goods priced at cost and before any year-end adjustments relating to the following items:
   a. Goods shipped f.o.b. shipping point on December 24, 1995 from a vendor at an invoice cost of $75,000 to Four Tops Company were received on January 4, 1996.
   b. The physical count included $29,000 of goods billed to Righteous Brothers Corp. f.o.b. shipping point on December 31, 1995. The carrier picked up these goods on January 3, 1996.
   What amount should Four Tops report as inventory on its balance sheet?

3. Supreme Corp. had 1,500 units of Part M.O. on hand May 1, 1995, costing $21 each. Purchases of Part M.O. during May were as follows:

	Units	Unit Cost
May 9	2,000	$22.00
17	3,500	23.00
26	1,000	24.00

   A physical count on May 31, 1995, shows 2,500 units of Part M.O. on hand. Using the FIFO method, what is the cost of Part M.O. inventory at May 31, 1995? Using the LIFO method, what is the inventory cost? Using the average cost method, what is the inventory cost?

4. Ross Company adopted the dollar-value LIFO method on January 1, 1995 (using internal price indexes and multiple pools). The following data are available for Inventory Pool A for the 2 years following adoption of LIFO:

Inventory	At Base-Year Cost	At Current-Year Cost
1/1/95	$200,000	$200,000
12/31/95	240,000	252,000
12/31/96	256,000	281,600

   Computing an internal price index and using the dollar-value LIFO method, at what amount should the inventory be reported at December 31, 1996?

5. Platters Inc., a retail store chain, had the following information in its general ledger for the year 1996:

Merchandise purchased for resale	$909,400
Interest on notes payable to vendors	8,700
Purchase returns	16,500
Freight-in	21,000
Freight-out	17,100
Cash discounts on purchases	6,800

   What is Platters' inventoriable cost for 1996?

Instructions
Answer each of the questions above about inventories and explain your answer.

P8-2 (Inventory Adjustments) Fats Domino Company, a manufacturer of small tools, provided the following information from its accounting records for the year ended December 31, 1996:

Inventory at December 31, 1996 (based on physical count of goods in Domino's plant at cost on December 31, 1996)	$1,520,000
Accounts payable at December 31, 1996	1,200,000
Net sales (sales less sales returns)	8,150,000

Additional information is as follows:

1. Included in the physical count were tools billed to a customer f.o.b. shipping point on December 31, 1996. These tools had a cost of $31,000 and were billed at $40,000. The shipment was on Domino's loading dock waiting to be picked up by the common carrier.

2. Goods were in transit from a vendor to Domino on December 31, 1996. The invoice cost was $65,000, and the goods were shipped f.o.b. shipping point on December 29, 1996.

3. Work-in-process inventory costing $30,000 was sent to an outside processor for plating on December 30, 1996.

4. Tools returned by customers and held pending inspection in the returned goods area on December 31, 1996 were not included in the physical count. On January 8, 1997, the tools costing $32,000 were

inspected and returned to inventory. Credit memos totaling $43,000 were issued to the customers on the same date.

5. Tools shipped to a customer f.o.b. destination on December 26, 1996, were in transit at December 31, 1996, and had a cost of $21,000. Upon notification of receipt by the customer on January 2, 1997, Michael issued a sales invoice for $42,000.

6. Goods, with an invoice cost of $27,000, received from a vendor at 5:00 p.m. on December 31, 1996, were recorded on a receiving report dated January 2, 1997. The goods were not included in the physical count, but the invoice was included in accounts payable at December 31, 1996.

7. Goods received from a vendor on December 26, 1996, were included in the physical count. However, the related $56,000 vendor invoice was not included in accounts payable at December 31, 1996, because the accounts payable copy of the receiving report was lost.

8. On January 3, 1997, a monthly freight bill in the amount of $6,000 was received. The bill specifically related to merchandise purchased in December 1996, one-half of which was still in the inventory at December 31, 1996. The freight charges were not included in either the inventory or in accounts payable at December 31, 1996.

Instructions

Using the format shown below, prepare a schedule of adjustments as of December 31, 1996, to the initial amounts per Domino's accounting records. Show separately the effect, if any, of each of the eight transactions on the December 31, 1996 amounts. If the transactions would have no effect on the initial amount shown, state NONE.

	Inventory	Accounts Payable	Net Sales
Initial amounts	$1,520,000	$1,200,000	$8,150,000
Adjustments—increase (decrease)			
1			
2			
3			
4			
5			
6			
7			
8			
Total adjustments			
Adjusted amounts	$	$	$

(AICPA adapted)

P8-3 (Inventory Adjustments) McGuire Sisters Company is a wholesale distributor of automotive replacement parts. Initial amounts taken from McGuire's accounting records are as follows:

Inventory at December 31, 1996 (based on physical count of goods in McGuire's warehouse on December 31, 1996)	$1,240,000

Accounts payable at December 31, 1996:

Vendor	Terms	Amount
Sonny James Company	2%, 10 days, net 30	$ 260,000
Frankie Avalon Corporation	Net 30	290,000
Big Bopper Company	Net 30	205,000
Mindy Carson Enterprises	Net 30	220,000
Pat Boone Products	Net 30	—
Perry Como Company	Net 30	—
		$ 975,000
Sales in 1996		$8,600,000

Additional information is as follows:

1. Parts received on consignment from Avalon Corporation by McGuire, the consignee, amounting to $150,000, were included in the physical count of goods in McGuire's warehouse on December 31, 1996, and in accounts payable at December 31, 1996.

2. Parts costing $20,000 that were purchased from Boone and paid for in December 1996 were sold in the last week of 1996 and appropriately recorded as sales of $28,000. The parts were included in the physical count of goods in McGuire's warehouse on December 31, 1996, because the parts were on the loading dock waiting to be picked up by customers.

3. Parts in transit on December 31, 1996, to customers, shipped f.o.b. shipping point, on December 28, 1996, amounted to $34,000. The customers received the parts on January 6, 1997. Sales of $50,000 to the customers for the parts were recorded by McGuire on January 2, 1997.

4. Retailers were holding $210,000 at cost ($260,000 at retail), of goods on consignment from McGuire, the consignor, at their stores on December 31, 1996.

5. Goods were in transit from Como to McGuire on December 31, 1996. The cost of the goods was $36,000, and they were shipped f.o.b. shipping point on December 29, 1996.

6. A quarterly freight bill in the amount of $4,700 specifically relating to merchandise purchases in December 1996, all of which was still in the inventory at December 31, 1996, was received on January 3, 1997. The freight bill was not included in the inventory or in accounts payable at December 31, 1996.

7. All of the purchases from James occurred during the last seven days of the year. These items have been recorded in accounts payable and accounted for in the physical inventory at cost before discount. McGuire's policy is to pay invoices in time to take advantage of all cash discounts, adjust inventory accordingly, and record accounts payable, net of cash discounts.

Instructions

Prepare a schedule of adjustments to the initial amounts using the format shown below. Show the effect, if any, of each of the transactions separately and if the transactions would have no effect on the amount shown, state **NONE**.

	Inventory	Accounts Payable	Sales
Initial amounts	$1,240,000	$975,000	$8,600,000
Adjustments—increase (decrease)			
1			
2			
3			
4			
5			
6			
7			
Total adjustments			
Adjusted amounts	$	$	$

(AICPA adapted)

P8-4 (Purchases Recorded Gross and Net) Some of the transactions of Conway Twitty Company during August are listed below. Twitty uses the periodic inventory method.

August 10 Purchased merchandise on account, $9,000, terms 2/10, n/30.
13 Returned part of the purchase of August 10, $800, and received credit on account.
15 Purchased merchandise on account, $12,000, terms 1/10, n/60.
25 Purchased merchandise on account, $10,000, terms 2/10, n/30.
28 Paid invoice of August 15 in full.

Instructions

(a) Assuming that purchases are recorded at gross amounts and that discounts are to be recorded when taken:
  1. Prepare general journal entries to record the transactions.
  2. Describe how the various items would be shown in the financial statements.
(b) Assuming that purchases are recorded at net amounts and that discounts lost are treated as financial expenses:
  1. Prepare general journal entries to enter the transactions.
  2. Prepare the adjusting entry necessary on August 31 if financial statements are to be prepared at that time.
  3. Describe how the various items would be shown in the financial statements.
(c) Which of the two methods do you prefer and why?

P8-5 (Compute FIFO, LIFO, and Average Cost—Periodic and Perpetual) Dolly Parton Company's record of transactions concerning Part X for the month of April was as follows:

Purchases		Sales	
April 1 (balance on hand)	100 @ $5.00	April 5	300
April 4	400 @ 5.10	April 12	200
April 11	300 @ 5.20	April 27	800
April 18	200 @ 5.35	April 28	100
April 26	500 @ 5.60		
April 30	200 @ 5.80		

Instructions

(a) Compute the inventory at April 30 on each of the following bases. Assume that perpetual inventory records are kept in units only. Carry unit costs to the nearest cent.

1. First-in, first-out (FIFO).

2. Last-in, first-out (LIFO).

3. Average cost.

(b) If the perpetual inventory record is kept in dollars, and costs are computed at the time of each withdrawal, what amount would be shown as ending inventory in 1, 2, and 3 above? Carry average unit costs to four decimal places.

P8-6 (Compute FIFO, LIFO and Average Cost—Periodic and Perpetual) Here is some of the information found on a detail inventory card for Randy Travis Inc., for the first month of operations.

| | Received | | Issued, | Balance, |
Date	No. of Units	Unit Cost	No. of Units	No. of Units
January 2	1,200	$3.00		1,200
7			700	500
10	600	3.20		1,100
13			500	600
18	1,000	3.30	300	1,300
20			1,100	200
23	1,300	3.40		1,500
26			800	700
28	1,500	3.50		2,200
31			1,300	900

Instructions

(a) From these data compute the ending inventory on each of the following bases (assume that perpetual inventory records are kept in units only; carry unit costs to the nearest cent and ending inventory to the nearest dollar):

1. First-in, first-out (FIFO).

2. Last-in, first-out (LIFO).

3. Average cost.

(b) If the perpetual inventory record is kept in dollars, and costs are computed at the time of each withdrawal, would the amounts shown as ending inventory in 1, 2, and 3 above be the same? Explain and compute.

P8-7 (Compute FIFO, LIFO and Average Cost—Periodic) Summarized below are certain quarterly data relative to Connie Francis Company. Assume that there was no inventory on hand at the beginning of the first quarter.

	Purchases	Sales
First quarter	8,000 @ $3.00	7,000 @ $6.00
	5,000 @ 3.20	3,000 @ 6.10
Second quarter	7,000 @ 3.40	5,000 @ 6.30
	6,000 @ 3.50	4,000 @ 6.50
Third quarter	9,000 @ 3.60	10,000 @ 6.60
	3,000 @ 3.70	3,000 @ 6.70
Fourth quarter	8,000 @ 3.80	5,000 @ 6.80
	6,000 @ 4.00	7,000 @ 7.00

Instructions

(a) Compute the gross profit for Connie Francis Company by quarters under each of the following methods of inventory pricing, assuming that inventory costs are determined only at the end of each quarter.

1. First-in, first-out (FIFO).

2. Last-in, first-out (LIFO).

3. Average cost (carry unit costs to the nearest cent).

(b) Evaluate the effect of each of these three methods on gross profit in a period of rising prices as presented above.

P8-8 (Compute FIFO, LIFO and Average Cost—Periodic) As the controller of Shirelles Inc., a retail company, you made three different schedules of gross margin for the third quarter ended September 30, 1996. These schedules appear below.

	Sales ($10 per Unit)	Cost of Goods Sold	Gross Margin
Schedule A	$570,000	$319,600	$250,400
Schedule B	570,000	312,480	257,520
Schedule C	570,000	305,700	264,300

The computation of cost of goods sold in each schedule is based on the following data:

	Units	Cost per Unit	Total Cost
Beginning inventory, July 1	12,000	$5.00	$ 60,000
Purchase, July 25	18,000	5.40	97,200
Purchase, August 15	32,000	5.50	176,000
Purchase, September 5	13,000	5.60	72,800
Purchase, September 25	16,000	5.80	92,800

Donna Summer, president of the corporation, cannot understand how three different gross margins can be computed from the same set of data. As controller, you have explained that the three schedules are based on three different assumptions concerning the flow of inventory costs, that is, first-in, first-out; last-in, first-out; and weighted average. Schedules A, B, and C were not necessarily prepared in this sequence of cost flow assumptions.

Instructions

Prepare three separate schedules computing cost of goods sold and supporting schedules showing the composition of the ending inventory under each of the three cost flow assumptions.

P8-9 (Compute FIFO, LIFO, Average Cost—Periodic and Perpetual) Jan & Dean Company is a multi-product firm. Presented below is information concerning one of their products, Pasadena 59:

Date	Transaction	Quantity	Price/Cost
1/1	Beginning inventory	1,000	$12
2/4	Purchase	2,000	18
2/20	Sale	2,500	30
4/2	Purchase	3,000	22
11/4	Sale	2,000	33

Instructions

Compute cost of goods sold, assuming Jan & Dean uses:
   (a) Periodic system, FIFO cost flow.
   (b) Perpetual system, FIFO cost flow.
   (c) Periodic system, LIFO cost flow.
   (d) Perpetual system, LIFO cost flow.
   (e) Periodic system, weighted-average cost flow.
   (f) Perpetual system, moving-average cost flow.

P8-10 (Financial Statement Effects of FIFO and LIFO) The management of Oscar Wilde Company has asked its accounting department to describe the effect upon the company's financial position and its income statements of accounting for inventories on the LIFO rather than the FIFO basis during 1996 and 1997. The accounting department is to assume that the change to LIFO would have been effective on January 1, 1996, and that the initial LIFO base would have been the inventory value on December 31, 1995. Presented below are the company's financial statements and other data for the years 1996 and 1997 when the FIFO method was in fact employed.

Financial Position as of	12/31/95	12/31/96	12/31/97
Cash	$ 90,000	$130,000	$ 154,000
Accounts receivable	80,000	100,000	120,000
Inventory	120,000	140,000	176,000
Other assets	160,000	170,000	200,000
Total assets	$450,000	$540,000	$ 650,000
Accounts payable	$ 40,000	$ 60,000	$ 80,000
Other liabilities	70,000	80,000	110,000
Common stock	200,000	200,000	200,000
Retained earnings	140,000	200,000	260,000
Total equities	$450,000	$540,000	$ 650,000

Income for Years Ended		12/31/96	12/31/97
Sales		$900,000	$1,350,000
Less: Cost of goods sold		505,000	756,000
Other expenses		205,000	304,000
		710,000	1,060,000
Net income before income taxes		190,000	290,000
Income taxes (40%)		76,000	116,000
Net income		$114,000	$ 174,000

Other data:

1. Inventory on hand at 12/31/95 consisted of 40,000 units valued at $3.00 each.
2. Sales (all units sold at the same price in a given year):

   1996—150,000 units @ $6.00 each   1997—180,000 units @ $7.50 each.

3. Purchases (all units purchased at the same price in given year):

   1996—150,000 units @ $3.50 each   1997—180,000 units @ $4.40 each.

4. Income taxes at the effective rate of 40% are paid on December 31 each year.

Instructions
Name the account(s) presented in the financial statement that would have different amounts for 1997 if LIFO rather than FIFO had been used and state the new amount for each account that is named. Show computations.

(CMA adapted)

P8-11 (Dollar-Value LIFO) A. E. Housman's Televisions produces television sets in three categories: portable, midsize, and console. On January 1, 1995, Housman adopted dollar-value LIFO and decided to use a single inventory pool. The company's January 1 inventory consists of:

Category	Quantity	Cost per Unit	Total Cost
Portable	6,000	$100	$ 600,000
Midsize	8,000	250	2,000,000
Console	3,000	400	1,200,000
	17,000		$3,800,000

During 1995, the company had the following purchases and sales:

Category	Quantity Purchased	Cost per Unit	Quantity Sold	Selling Price per Unit
Portable	15,000	$120	14,000	$150
Midsize	20,000	275	24,000	$370
Console	10,000	460	6,000	$600
	45,000		44,000	

Instructions
(Round to four decimals)
(a) Compute ending inventory, cost of goods sold, and gross profit.
(b) Assume the company uses three inventory pools instead of one. Repeat instruction (a).

P8-12 (LIFO Effect on Income) Dr. Seuss Inc. sells two products: Horton the Elephant and The Cat in the Hat. At December 31, 1996, Seuss used the first-in, first-out (FIFO) inventory method. Effective January 1, 1997, Seuss changed to the last-in, first-out (LIFO) inventory method. The cumulative effect of this change is not determinable and, as a result, the ending inventory of 1996 for which the FIFO method was used is also the beginning inventory for 1997 for the LIFO method. Any layers added during 1997 should be costed by reference to the first acquisitions of 1997 and any layers liquidated during 1997 should be considered a permanent liquidation.

The following information was available from Seuss' inventory records for the 2 most recent years:

	Horton the Elephant		The Cat in the Hat	
	Units	Unit Cost	Units	Unit Cost
1996 purchases				
January 7	7,000	$4.00	22,000	$2.00
April 16	12,000	4.50		
November 8	17,000	5.40	18,500	3.40
December 13	9,000	6.20		
1997 purchases				
February 11	3,000	6.60	23,000	3.60
May 20	8,000	7.50		
October 15	20,000	8.10		
December 23			15,500	4.20
Units on hand				
December 31, 1996	15,100		15,000	
December 31, 1997	18,000		13,200	

Instructions

Compute the effect on income before income taxes for the year ended December 31, 1997, resulting from the change from the FIFO to the LIFO inventory method.

(AICPA adapted)

P8-13 (Internal Indexes—Dollar-Value LIFO) On January 1, 1995, Edith Sitwell Wholesalers Inc. adopted the dollar-value LIFO inventory method for income tax and external financial reporting purposes. However, Sitwell continued to use the FIFO inventory method for internal accounting and management purposes. In applying the LIFO method, Sitwell uses internal conversion price indexes and the multiple pools approach under which substantially identical inventory items are grouped into LIFO inventory pools. The following data were available for Inventory Pool No. 1, which comprises products A and B, for the two years following the adoption of LIFO:

| | **FIFO Basis per Records** | | |
	Units	Unit Cost	Total Cost
Inventory, 1/1/95			
Product A	10,000	$30	$300,000
Product B	9,000	25	225,000
			$525,000
Inventory, 12/31/95			
Product A	17,000	35	$595,000
Product B	9,000	28	252,000
			$847,000
Inventory, 12/31/96			
Product A	13,000	40	$520,000
Product B	10,000	32	320,000
			$840,000

Instructions

(a) Prepare a schedule to compute the internal conversion price indexes for 1995 and 1996. Round indexes to two decimal places.

(b) Prepare a schedule to compute the inventory amounts at December 31, 1995 and 1996, using the dollar-value LIFO inventory method.

(AICPA adapted)

P8-14 (Internal Indexes—Dollar-Value LIFO) Presented below is information related to Rudyard Kipling Corporation for the last three years:

Item	Quantities in Ending Inventories	Base-Year Cost		Current-Year Cost	
		Unit Cost	Amount	Unit Cost	Amount
December 31, 1994					
A	9,000	$2.00	$18,000	$2.40	$21,600
B	6,000	3.00	18,000	3.55	21,300
C	4,000	5.00	20,000	5.40	21,600
		Totals	$56,000		$64,500
December 31, 1995					
A	9,000	$2.00	$18,000	$2.60	$23,400
B	6,800	3.00	20,400	3.75	25,500
C	6,000	5.00	30,000	6.10	36,600
		Totals	$68,400		$85,500
December 31, 1996					
A	8,000	$2.00	$16,000	$2.70	$21,600
B	8,000	3.00	24,000	4.00	32,000
C	6,000	5.00	30,000	6.23	37,380
		Totals	$70,000		$90,980

Instructions

Compute the ending inventories under the dollar-value method for 1994, 1995, and 1996. The base period is January 1, 1994, and the beginning inventory cost at that date was $45,000. Compute indexes to two decimal places.

P8-15 (Comprehensive Inventory Adjustment Problem) Thomas Hardy Corp. cans two food commodities that it stores at various warehouses. The company employs a perpetual inventory accounting system under which the finished-goods inventory is charged with production and credited for sales at standard cost. The detail of the finished-goods inventory is maintained on punched cards by the tabulating department in units and dollars for the various warehouses.

Company procedures call for the accounting department to receive copies of daily production reports and sales invoices. Units are then extended at standard cost and a summary of the day's activity is posted to the Finished Goods Inventory general ledger control account. Next the sales invoices and production reports are sent to the tabulating department for processing. Every month the control account and detailed tab records are reconciled and adjustments recorded. The last reconciliation and adjustments were made at November 30, 1996.

Your CPA firm, Robert & Stevenson, observed the taking of the physical inventory at all locations on December 31, 1996. The inventory count began at 3:00 p.m. and was completed at 8:00 p.m. The company's figure for the physical inventory is $401,200. The general ledger control account balance at December 31 was $466,900, and the final "tab" run of the inventory punched cards showed a total of $465,100.

Unit cost data for the company's two products are as follows:

Product	Standard Cost
A	$4.00
B	5.00

A review of December transactions disclosed the following:

1. Sales invoice #1603, 12/2/96, was priced at standard cost for $16,400 but was listed on the accounting department's daily summary at $14,600.
2. A production report for $11,600, 12/15/96, was processed twice in error by the tabulating department.
3. Sales invoice #1481, 12/9/96, for 1,400 units of product A, was priced at a standard cost of $2.00 per unit by the accounting department. The tabulating department noticed and corrected the error but did not notify the accounting department of the error.
4. A shipment of 2,500 units of product A was invoiced by the billing department as 2,000 units on sales invoice #1703, 12/27/96. The error was discovered by your review of transactions.
5. On December 27 the Boise warehouse notified the tabulating department to remove 2,200 unsalable units of product A from the finished-goods inventory, which it did without receiving a special invoice from the accounting department. The accounting department received a copy of the Boise warehouse notification on December 29 and made up a special invoice that was processed in the normal manner. The units were not included in the physical inventory.
6. A production report for the production on January 3 of 3,200 units of product B was processed for the Columbus plant as of December 31.
7. A shipment of 500 units of product B was made from the Goshen warehouse to Yeats Markets, Inc., at 8:30 p.m. on December 31 as an emergency service. The sales invoice was processed as of December 31. The client prefers to treat the transactions as a sale in 1996.
8. The working papers of the auditor observing the physical count at the Bangor warehouse revealed that 600 units of product B were omitted from the client's physical count. The client concurred that the units were omitted in error.
9. A sales invoice for 400 units of product A shipped from the Providence warehouse was mislaid and was not processed until January 5. The units involved were shipped on December 30.
10. The physical inventory of the Omaha warehouse excluded 250 units of product A that were marked "reserved." Upon investigation it was ascertained that this merchandise was being stored as a convenience for Dylan Thomas Grocery, a customer. This merchandise, which has not been recorded as a sale, is billed as it is shipped.
11. A shipment of 8,000 units of product B was made on December 27 from the Providence warehouse to the Bangor warehouse. The shipment arrived on January 6 but had been excluded from the physical inventories.

Instructions

Prepare a work sheet to reconcile the balances for the physical inventory, Finished Goods Inventory general ledger control account, and tabulating department's detail of finished-goods inventory ("Tab Run").

The following format is suggested for the work sheet.

	Physical Inventory	General Ledger Control Account	Tabulating Department's Detail of Inventory
Balance per client	$401,200	$466,900	$465,100

(AICPA adapted)

CASES

C8-1 (Inventoriable Costs) You are asked to travel to Milwaukee to observe and verify the inventory of the Milwaukee branch of one of your clients. You arrive on Thursday, December 30, and find that the inventory procedures have just been started. You spot a railway car on the sidetrack at the unloading door and ask the warehouse superintendent Rob Sanborn how he plans to inventory the contents of the car. Rob responds: "We are not going to include the contents in the inventory."

Later in the day, you ask the bookkeeper for the invoice on the carload and the related freight bill. The invoice lists the various items, prices, and extensions of the goods in the car. You note that the carload was shipped December 24 from Albuquerque f.o.b. Albuquerque, and that the total invoice price of the goods in the car was $34,200. The freight bill called for a payment of $1,200. Terms were net 30 days. The bookkeeper affirms the fact that this invoice is to be held for recording in January.

Instructions
- **(a)** Does your client have a liability that should be recorded at December 31? Discuss.
- **(b)** Prepare a journal entry(ies), if required, to reflect any accounting adjustment required.
- **(c)** For what possible reason(s) might your client wish to postpone recording the transaction?

C8-2 (Inventoriable Costs) Jerry Springer, an inventory control specialist, is interested in better understanding the accounting for inventories. Although Jerry understands the more sophisticated computer inventory control systems, he has little knowledge of how inventory cost is determined. In studying the records of Geraldo Enterprises, which sells normal brand-name goods from its own store and on consignment through Oprah Inc., he asks you to answer the following questions.

Instructions
- **(a)** Should Geraldo Enterprises include in its inventory normal brand-name goods purchased from its suppliers but not yet received if the terms of purchase are f.o.b. shipping point (manufacturer's plant)? Why?
- **(b)** Should Geraldo Enterprises include freight-in expenditures as an inventory cost? Why?
- **(c)** If Geraldo Enterprises purchases its goods on terms 2/10, net 30, should the purchases be recorded gross or net? Why?
- **(d)** What are products on consignment? How should they be reported in the financial statements?

(AICPA adapted)

C8-3 (Inventoriable Costs—Complex) Sally J. Raphael, the controller for Raphael Lumber Company, has recently hired you as assistant controller. She wishes to determine your expertise in the area of inventory accounting and therefore asks you to answer the following unrelated questions:
- **(a)** A company is involved in the wholesaling and retailing of automobile tires for foreign cars. Most of the inventory is imported, and it is valued on the company's records at the actual inventory cost plus freight-in. At year-end, the warehousing costs are prorated over cost of goods sold and ending inventory. Are warehousing costs considered a product cost or a period cost?
- **(b)** A certain portion of a company's "inventory" is composed of obsolete items. Should obsolete items that are not currently consumed in the production of "goods or services to be available for sale" be classified as part of inventory?
- **(c)** A company purchases airplanes for sale to others. However, until they are sold, the company charters and services the planes. What is the proper way to report these airplanes in the company's financial statements?
- **(d)** A company wants to buy coal deposits but does not want the financing for the purchase to be reported on its financial statements. The company therefore establishes a trust to acquire the coal deposits. The company agrees to buy the coal over a certain period of time at specified prices. The trust is able to finance the coal purchase and pay off the loan as it is paid by the company for the minerals. How should this transaction be reported?

C8-4 (Accounting Treatment of Purchase Discounts) Donahue Corp., a household appliances dealer, purchases its inventories from various suppliers. Donahue has consistently stated its inventories at the lower of cost (FIFO) or market.

Instructions
Donahue is considering alternate methods of accounting for the cash discounts it takes when paying its suppliers promptly. From a theoretical standpoint, discuss the acceptability of each of the following methods:
1. Financial income when payments are made.
2. Reduction of cost of goods sold for period when payments are made.
3. Direct reduction of purchase cost.

(AICPA adapted)

C8-5 (General Inventory Issues) In January 1996, Jenny Jones Inc. requested and secured permission from the Commissioner of the Internal Revenue Service to compute inventories under the last-in, first-out (LIFO) method and elected to determine inventory cost under the dollar-value method. Jones Inc. satisfied the Commissioner that cost could be accurately determined by use of an index number computed from a representative sample selected from the company's single inventory pool.

Instructions
- **(a)** Why should inventories be included in (1) a balance sheet and (2) the computation of net income?
- **(b)** The Internal Revenue Code allows some accountable events to be considered differently for income tax reporting purposes and financial accounting purposes, while other accountable events must be reported the same for both purposes. Discuss why it might be desirable to report some accountable events differently for financial accounting purposes than for income tax reporting purposes.
- **(c)** Discuss the ways and conditions under which the FIFO and LIFO inventory costing methods produce different inventory valuations. Do not discuss procedures for computing inventory cost.

(AICPA adapted)

C8-6 (Variable Costing and Financial Statement Presentation) Teresa Lopez Co. is a manufacturing business with relatively heavy fixed costs and large inventories of finished goods. These inventories constitute a very material item on the balance sheet. The company has a departmental cost accounting system that assigns all manufacturing costs to the product each period.

Aubrey Beardsley, controller of the company, has informed you that the management is giving serious consideration to the adoption of variable (direct) costing as a method of accounting for plant operations and inventory valuation. The management wishes to have your opinion of the effect, if any, that such a change would have on: (1) the year-end financial position, and (2) the net income for the year.

Instructions
State your reply to the request and the reasons for your conclusions.

(AICPA adapted)

C8-7 (LIFO Inventory Advantages) Emily Carr, president of Titian Co., recently read an article that claimed that at least 100 of the country's largest 500 companies were either adopting or considering adopting the last-in, first-out (LIFO) method for valuing inventories. The article stated that the firms were switching to LIFO to (1) neutralize the effect of inflation in their financial statements, (2) eliminate inventory profits, and (3) reduce income taxes. Ms. Carr wonders if the switch would benefit her company.

Titian currently uses the first-in, first-out (FIFO) method of inventory valuation in its periodic inventory system. The company has a high inventory turnover rate, and inventories represent a significant proportion of the assets.

In discussing this trend toward LIFO inventory with business friends, Ms. Carr has been told that the LIFO system is more costly to operate and will provide little benefit to companies with high turnover. She intends to use the inventory method that is best for the company in the long run rather than selecting a method just because it is the current fad.

Instructions
- **(a)** Explain to Ms. Carr what "inventory profits" are and how the LIFO method of inventory valuation could reduce them.
- **(b)** Explain to Ms. Carr the conditions that must exist for Titian Co. to receive tax benefits from a switch to the LIFO method.

C8-8 (Average Cost, FIFO, and LIFO) Presented below are three independent situations.
- **(a)** Describe the cost flow assumptions used in average cost, FIFO, and LIFO methods of inventory valuation.
- **(b)** Distinguish between weighted average cost and moving average cost for inventory costing purposes.
- **(c)** Identify the effects on both the balance sheet and the income statement of using the LIFO method instead of the FIFO method for inventory costing purposes over a substantial time period when purchase prices of inventoriable items are rising. State why these effects take place.

C8-9 (LIFO Application and Advantages) The Jen Li Corporation is a medium-sized manufacturing company with two divisions and three subsidiaries, all located in the United States. The Metallic Division manufactures metal castings for the automotive industry, and the Plastic Division produces small plastic items for electrical products and other uses. The three subsidiaries manufacture various products for other industrial users.

The Jen Li Corporation plans to change from the lower of first-in, first-out (FIFO) cost or market method of inventory valuation to the last-in, first-out (LIFO) method of inventory valuation to obtain tax benefits. To make the method acceptable for tax purposes, the change also will be made for its annual financial statements.

Instructions

    (a) Describe the establishment of and subsequent pricing procedures for each of the following LIFO inventory methods:

        1. LIFO applied to units of product when the periodic inventory system is used.

        2. Application of the dollar-value method to LIFO units of product.

    (b) Discuss the specific advantages and disadvantages of using the dollar-value LIFO application as compared to specific goods LIFO (unit LIFO). Ignore income tax considerations.

    (c) Discuss the general advantages and disadvantages claimed for LIFO methods.

C8-10 (Dollar-Value LIFO Issues) Gainsborough Co. is considering switching from the specific goods LIFO approach to the dollar value LIFO approach. Because the financial personnel at Gainsborough know very little about dollar value LIFO, they ask you to answer the following questions.

    (a) What is a LIFO pool?

    (b) Is it possible to use a LIFO pool concept and not use dollar-value LIFO? Explain.

    (c) What is a LIFO liquidation?

    (d) How are price indexes used in the dollar-value LIFO method?

    (e) What are the advantages of dollar-value LIFO over specific goods LIFO?

C8-11 (Cost Determination) Brueghel Company has been growing rapidly, but during this period of rapid growth the accounting records have not been properly maintained. You were recently employed to correct the accounting records and to assist in the preparation of the financial statements for the fiscal year ended February 28, 1996. One of the accounts you have been analyzing is entitled "Merchandise." That account in summary form follows. Numbers in parentheses following each entry correspond to related numbered explanations and additional information that you have accumulated during your analysis.

Merchandise				
Balance, March 1, 1995	(1)	Merchandise sold		(5)
Purchases	(2)	Consigned merchandise		(6)
Freight-in	(3)			
Insurance	(4)			
Freight-out on consigned merchandise	(7)			
Freight-out on merchandise sold	(8)			

Explanations and Additional Information:

    1. You have satisfied yourself that the March 1, 1995, inventory balance represents the approximate cost of the few units in inventory at the beginning of the year. Brueghel employs the FIFO method of accounting for inventories.

    2. The merchandise purchased was recorded in the account at the sellers' catalog list price, which is the price appearing on the face of each vendor's invoice. All purchased merchandise is subject to a trade (chain) discount of 20%–10%. These discounts have been accounted for as revenue when the merchandise was paid for.

        All merchandise purchased was also subject to cash terms of 2/15, n/30. During the fiscal year Brueghel recorded $4,000 in purchase discounts as revenue when the merchandise was paid for. Some purchase discounts were lost because payment was made after the discount period ended. All purchases of merchandise were paid for in the fiscal year they were recorded as purchased.

    3. All merchandise is purchased f.o.b. sellers' business locations. The freight-in amount is the cost of transporting the merchandise from the sellers' business locations to Brueghel.

    4. The insurance charge is for an all-perils policy to cover merchandise in transit to Brueghel from sellers.

    5. The credit to this account for merchandise sold represents the sellers' catalog list price of merchandise sold plus the cost of the beginning inventory; the debit side of the entry was made to the cost of goods sold account.

    6. Consigned merchandise represents goods that were shipped to Isamu Noguchi Co. during January 1996, priced at the sellers' catalog list price. The offsetting debit was made to accounts receivable when the merchandise was shipped to Isamu Noguchi Co.

    7. The freight-out on consigned goods is the cost of trucking the consigned goods to Isamu Noguchi Co. from Brueghel.

    8. Freight-out on merchandise sold is the amount paid trucking companies to deliver merchandise sold to Brueghel's customers.

Instructions

Consider each of the eight (8) numbered items independently and explain specifically how and why each item should have (if correctly accounted for) affected (a) the amount of cost of goods sold to be included in Brueghel's earnings statement, and (b) the amount of any other account to be included in Brueghel's February 28, 1996, financial statements.

Organize your answer in the following format:

Item Number	How and Why the Amount of Cost of Goods Sold Should Have Been Affected	How and Why the Amount of Any Other Account Should Have Been Affected

C8-12 (FIFO and LIFO) Albrecht Durer Company is considering changing its inventory valuation method from FIFO to LIFO because of the potential tax savings. However, the management wishes to consider all of the effects on the company, including its reported performance, before making the final decision.

The inventory account, currently valued on the FIFO basis, consists of 1,000,000 units at $7 per unit on January 1, 1996. There are 1,000,000 shares of common stock outstanding as of January 1, 1996, and the cash balance is $400,000.

The company has made the following forecasts for the period 1996–1998.

	1996	1997	1998
Unit sales (in millions of units)	1.1	1.0	1.3
Sales price per unit	$10	$10	$12
Unit purchases (in millions of units)	1.0	1.1	1.2
Purchase price per unit	$7	$8	$9
Annual depreciation (in thousands of dollars)	$300	$300	$300
Cash dividends per share	$.15	$.15	$.15
Cash payments for additions to and replacement of plant and equipment (in thousands of dollars)	$350	$350	$350
Income tax rate	40%	40%	40%
Operating expense (exclusive of depreciation) as a percent of sales	15%	15%	15%
Common shares outstanding (in millions)	1	1	1

Instructions

(a) Prepare a schedule that illustrates and compares the following data for Durer Company under the FIFO and the LIFO inventory method for 1996–1998. Assume the company would begin LIFO at the beginning of 1996.

1. Year-end inventory balances. **3.** Earnings per share.
2. Annual net income after taxes. **4.** Cash balance.

Assume all sales are collected in the year of sale and all purchases, operating expenses, and taxes are paid during the year incurred.

(b) Using the data above, your answer to (a), and any additional issues you believe need to be considered, prepare a report that recommends whether or not Durer Company should change to the LIFO inventory method. Support your conclusions with appropriate arguments.

(CMA adapted)

▶ USING YOUR JUDGMENT ◀

▶ FINANCIAL REPORTING PROBLEM

Refer to the financial statements and other documents of Georgia-Pacific Corporation presented in Appendix 5-A and answer the following questions.

(a) How does Georgia-Pacific value its inventories? Which inventory costing method does Georgia-Pacific use to value the majority of its inventories?

(b) In the Letter to Shareholder section, the management claimed that "our building products business extended a string of record setting quarters," and "our building products business achieved a record year." Compute the percentages of cost of sales to net sales for the years from 1989 to 1993. Was the trend of these ratios consistent with the above statement? Were these statements consistent with Georgia-Pacific's reported net income for 1993?

▶ WRITING ASSIGNMENT

Carrie Bemis Company cans a variety of vegetable-type soups. Recently, the company decided to value its inventories using dollar-value LIFO pools. The clerk who accounts for inventories does not understand how to value the inventory pools using this new method, so, as a private consultant, you have been asked to teach her how this new method works.

She has provided you with the following information about purchases made over a 6-year period:

Date	Ending Inventory (End-of-Year Prices)	Price Index
Dec. 31, 1990	$ 80,000	100
Dec. 31, 1991	115,500	105
Dec. 31, 1992	108,000	120
Dec. 31, 1993	131,300	130
Dec. 31, 1994	154,000	140
Dec. 31, 1995	174,000	145

You have already explained to her how this inventory method is maintained, but she would feel better about it if you were to leave her detailed instructions explaining how these calculations are done and why she needs to put all inventories at a base-year value.

Instructions

Compute the ending inventory for Carrie Bemis Company for 1990 through 1995 using dollar-value LIFO. Using your computation schedules as your illustration, write a step-by-step set of instructions explaining how the calculations are done. Begin your explanation by briefly explaining the theory behind this inventory method, including the purpose of putting all amounts into base-year price levels.

▶ GROUP ASSIGNMENT

(Compute FIFO, LIFO, Average Cost—Periodic and Perpetual) Presented below is information related to Product A of Prince Co. for the month of July:

Date	Transaction	Units In	Unit Cost	Total	Units Sold	Selling Price	Total
July 1	Balance	100	$4.10	$ 410			
6	Purchase	800	4.21	3,368			
7	Sale				300	$7.00	$ 2,100
10	Sale				300	7.30	2,190
12	Purchase	400	4.54	1,816			
15	Sale				200	7.40	1,480
18	Purchase	300	4.60	1,380			
22	Sale				400	7.40	2,960
25	Purchase	500	4.70	2,350			
30	Sale				200	7.50	1,500
	Totals	2,100		$9,324	1,400		$10,230

Instructions

Work within your group to address the following requirements related to the above data (you may want to divide the items among group members). Your instructor will assign one member to record your group responses and one member to serve as group spokesperson.

(a) Assuming that the periodic inventory method is used, compute the inventory cost at July 31 under each of the following cost flow assumptions:
   1. FIFO.
   2. LIFO.
   3. Weighted-average (round the weighted-average unit cost to the nearest one-tenth of one cent).
(b) Answer the following questions:
   1. Which of the methods used above will yield the lowest figure for gross profit for the income statement? Explain why.
   2. Which of the methods used above will yield the lowest figure for ending inventory for the balance sheet? Explain why.
(c) Discuss how use of a perpetual inventory system would change the responses to parts (a) and (b).

▶ ETHICS CASES

EC8-1 (Ethical Issues—Year-End Inventory Purchase) H. Frankenthaler Company uses the LIFO method for inventory costing. In an effort to lower net income, the president tells the plant accountant to take the unusual step of recommending to the purchasing department a large purchase of inventory at year end. The price of the item has nearly doubled during the year, and the item represents a major portion of inventory value.

Instructions
   (a) Should the plant accountant recommend the inventory purchase to lower income? Who will benefit?
   (b) If H. Frankenthaler had been using the FIFO method of inventory costing, would the president give the same order? Why?

EC8-2 (Ethical Issues—Manipulation of Inventory Amounts) Pollock Corporation manufactures and distributes a line of toys for adolescent boys and girls, preschool children, and infants. As a consequence, the corporation has large seasonal variations in sales. The company issues quarterly financial statements, and first quarter earnings were down from the same period last year.

During a visit to the Preschool and Infant Division, Pollock's president expressed dissatisfaction with the division's first quarter performance. As a result, Paul Klee, division manager, felt pressure to report higher earnings in the second quarter. Klee was aware that Pollock Corporation uses the LIFO inventory method so he had the purchasing manager postpone several large inventory orders scheduled for delivery in the second quarter. Klee knew that the use of older inventory costs during the second quarter would cause a decline in the cost of goods sold and thus increase earnings.

During a review of the preliminary second quarter income statement, Isabel Bishop, division controller, noticed that the cost of goods sold was low relative to sales. Bishop analyzed the inventory account and discovered that the scheduled second quarter material purchases had been delayed until the third quarter. Bishop prepared a revised income statement using current replacement costs to calculate cost of goods sold and submitted the income statement to Paul Klee, her superior, for review. Klee was not pleased with these results and insisted that the second quarter income statement remain unchanged. Bishop tried to explain to Klee that the interim inventory should reflect the expected cost of the replacement of the liquidated layers when the inventory is expected to be replaced before the end of the year. Klee did not relent and told Bishop to issue the income statement using the LIFO costs. Bishop is concerned about Klee's response, and is contemplating what her next action should be.

Instructions
   (a) Determine whether or not the actions of Paul Klee, division manager, are ethical and explain why.
   (b) Recommend a course of action that Isabel Bishop should take in proceeding to resolve this situation.

(CMA adapted)

CHAPTER 9

INVENTORIES: ADDITIONAL VALUATION PROBLEMS

LEARNING OBJECTIVES

After studying this chapter, you should be able to:

1. Explain and apply the lower of cost or market rule.

2. Identify when inventories are valued at net realizable value.

3. Explain when the relative sales value method is used to value inventories.

4. Explain accounting issues related to purchase commitments.

5. Determine ending inventory by applying the gross profit method.

6. Determine ending inventory by applying the retail inventory method.

7. Describe financial statement presentation of inventories.

---

*I*n Chapter 8, we examined the various flow assumptions used in accounting to explain the different methods for computing the unit cost for inventories. But, the inventory costing and valuation methods learned so far do not adequately cover all situations. For example, what happens if the value of the inventory increases or decreases after the initial purchase date? Does the accountant recognize these increases or decreases in value before the point of sale? If there is a fire and physical count cannot be made, how does the accountant determine the ending inventory for insurance purposes? Or, what happens in large department stores where monthly inventory figures are needed but monthly physical counts are not feasible?

These questions involve the development and use of **estimation techniques** to value the ending inventory without a physical count. Estimation methods that are widely used are discussed in this chapter. First, though, we will examine a method used to account for declining inventory values.

► LOWER OF COST OR MARKET

OBJECTIVE 1

Explain and apply the lower of cost or market rule.

As noted in Chapter 8, inventories are recorded at their original cost. However, a major departure from the historical cost principle is made in the area of inventory valuation if inventory declines in value below its original cost. Whatever the reason for a decline— obsolescence, price-level changes, damaged goods, and so forth—the inventory should be written down to reflect this loss. **The general rule is that the historical cost principle is abandoned when the future utility (revenue-producing ability) of the asset is no longer as great as its original cost.**

Inventories that experience a decline in utility are valued therefore on the basis of the lower of cost or market, instead of on an original cost basis. **Cost** is the acquisition price of inventory computed using one of the historical cost-based methods—specific identification, average cost, FIFO, or LIFO. The term **market** in the phrase "the lower of cost or market" (LCM) generally means the cost to replace the item by purchase or reproduction. In a retailing business the term "market" refers to the market in which goods were purchased, not the market in which they are sold; in manufacturing, the term "market" refers to the cost to reproduce. Thus the rule really means that **goods are to be valued at cost or cost to replace, whichever is lower.** For example, a Casio calculator wristwatch that costs a retailer $30.00 when purchased, that can be sold for $48.95, and that can be replaced for $25.00 should be valued at $25.00 for inventory purposes under the lower of cost or market rule. The lower of cost or market rule of valuation can be used after any of the cost flow methods discussed in Chapter 8 have been applied to determine the inventory cost.

A departure from cost is justified because **a loss of utility should be charged against revenues in the period in which the loss occurs,** not in the period in which it is sold. In addition, the lower of cost or market method is **a conservative approach to inventory valuation.** That is, when doubt exists about the value of an asset, it is preferable to undervalue rather than to overvalue it.

> **UNDERLYING CONCEPT**
>
> *The use of the lower of cost or market method is an excellent example of the conservatism constraint.*

LOWER OF COST OR MARKET—CEILING AND FLOOR

Why use replacement cost to represent market value? The reason is that a decline in the replacement cost of an item usually reflects or predicts a decline in selling price. Using replacement cost allows a company to maintain a consistent rate of gross profit on sales (normal profit margin). Sometimes, however, a reduction in the replacement cost of an item does not indicate a corresponding reduction in its utility. Then, two additional valuation limitations are used to value ending inventory—net realizable value and net realizable value less a normal profit margin.

Net realizable value (NRV) is defined as the estimated selling price in the ordinary course of business less reasonably predictable costs of completion and disposal. A normal profit margin is subtracted from that amount to arrive at **net realizable value less a normal profit margin.**

To illustrate, assuming that Jerry Mander Corp. has unfinished inventory with a sales value of $1,000, estimated cost of completion of $300, and a normal profit margin of 10% of sales, the following can be determined:

Inventory—sales value	$1,000
Less: Estimated cost of completion and disposal	300
Net realizable value	700
Less: Allowance for normal profit margin (10% of sales)	100
Net realizable value less a normal profit margin	$ 600

**ILLUSTRATION 9-1
Computation of Net Realizable Value**

The general rule of lower of cost or market is: **inventory is valued at the lower of cost or market, with market limited to an amount that is not more than net realizable value or less than net realizable value less a normal profit margin.**[1]

What is the rationale for these two limitations? The **upper (ceiling)** and **lower (floor) limits** for the value of the inventory are intended to prevent the inventory from being reported at an amount in excess of the net selling price or at an amount less than the net selling price less a normal profit margin. The maximum limitation, **not to exceed the net realizable value (ceiling),** covers obsolete, damaged, or shopworn material and prevents overstatement of inventories and understatement of the loss in the current period. That is, if the replacement cost of an item is greater than its net realizable value, inventory should not be reported at replacement cost because the company can only receive the selling price less cost of disposal. To report the inventory at replacement cost would result in an overstatement of inventory and an understated loss in the current period. To illustrate, assume that Computerland paid $2,500 for a laser printer that

---

[1]"Restatement and Revision of Accounting Research Bulletins," *Accounting Research Bulletin No. 43* (New York: AICPA, 1953), Ch. 4, par. 8.

can now be replaced for $2,200 and whose net realizable value is $1,800. At what amount should the laser printer be reported in the financial statements? To report the replacement cost of $2,200 overstates the ending inventory and understates the loss for the period. The printer should, therefore, be reported at $1,800.

The minimum limitation, **not to be less than net realizable value reduced by an allowance for an approximately normal profit margin (floor),** deters understatement of inventory and overstatement of the loss in the current period. It establishes a floor below which the inventory should not be priced regardless of replacement cost. It makes no sense to price inventory below net realizable value less a normal margin because this minimum amount (floor) measures what the company can receive for the inventory and still earn a normal profit. These guidelines are illustrated graphically in Illustration 9-2.

**ILLUSTRATION 9-2
Inventory Valuation—
Lower of Cost or Market**

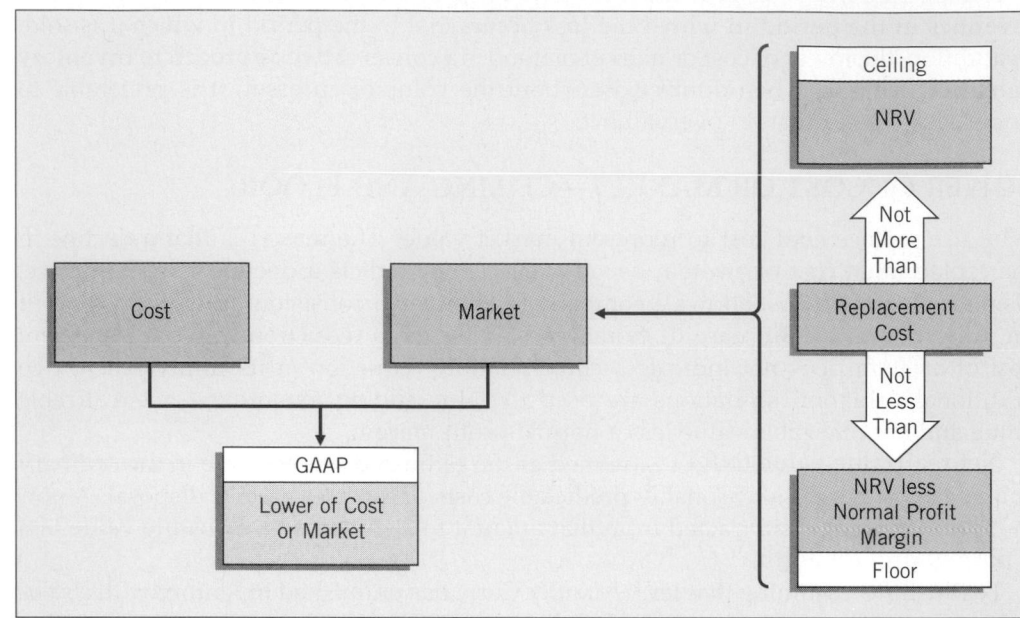

HOW LOWER OF COST OR MARKET WORKS

The amount that is compared to cost, often referred to as **designated market value,** is **always the middle value of three amounts:** replacement cost, net realizable value, and net realizable value less a normal profit margin. To illustrate how designated market value is computed, assume the following information relative to the inventory of Regner Foods, Inc.

**ILLUSTRATION 9-3
Computation of
Designated Market Value**

Food	Replacement Cost	Net Realizable Value (Ceiling)	Net Realizable Value Less a Normal Profit Margin (Floor)	Designated Market Value
Spinach	$ 88,000	$120,000	$104,000	$104,000
Carrots	90,000	100,000	70,000	90,000
Cut Beans	45,000	40,000	27,500	40,000
Peas	36,000	72,000	48,000	48,000
Mixed Vegetables	105,000	92,000	80,000	92,000

Designated Market Value Decision:

Spinach	Net realizable value less a normal profit margin is selected because it is the middle value.
Carrots	Replacement cost is selected because it is the middle value.
Cut Beans	Net realizable value is selected because it is the middle value.
Peas	Net realizable value less a normal profit margin is selected because it is the middle value.
Mixed Vegetables	Net realizable value is selected because it is the middle value.

Designated market value is then compared to cost to determine the lower of cost or market. To illustrate, the final inventory value for Regner Foods is determined as follows:

Food	Cost	Replacement Cost	Net Realizable Value (Ceiling)	Net Realizable Value Less a Normal Profit Margin (Floor)	Designated Market Value	Final Inventory Value
Spinach	$ 80,000	$ 88,000	$120,000	$104,000	$104,000	$ 80,000
Carrots	100,000	90,000	100,000	70,000	90,000	90,000
Cut Beans	50,000	45,000	40,000	27,500	40,000	40,000
Peas	90,000	36,000	72,000	48,000	48,000	48,000
Mixed Vegetables	95,000	105,000	92,000	80,000	92,000	92,000
						$350,000

Final Inventory Value:

Spinach	Cost ($80,000) is selected because it is lower than designated market value (net realizable value less a normal profit margin).
Carrots	Designated market value (replacement cost, $90,000) is selected because it is lower than cost.
Cut Beans	Designated market value (net realizable value, $40,000) is selected because it is lower than cost.
Peas	Designated market value (net realizable value less a normal profit margin, $48,000) is selected because it is lower than cost.
Mixed Vegetables	Designated market value (net realizable value, $92,000) is selected because it is lower than cost.

**ILLUSTRATION 9-4
Determining Final
Inventory Value**

The application of the lower of cost or market rule incorporates only losses in value that occur in the normal course of business from such causes as style changes, shift in demand, or regular shop wear. Damaged or deteriorated goods are reduced to net realizable value. When material, such goods may be carried in separate inventory accounts.

METHODS OF APPLYING LOWER OF COST OR MARKET

In the previous illustration for Regner Foods, we assumed that the lower of cost or market rule was applied to each individual type of food. However, the lower of cost or market rule may be "applied either directly to each item, to each category, or to the total of the inventory." Increases in market prices tend to offset decreases in market prices, if a major category or total inventory approach is followed in applying the lower of cost or market rule. To illustrate, assume that Regner Foods separates its food products into frozen and canned for purposes of designating major categories.

Regner Foods, Inc.

	Cost	Designated Market	Lower of Cost or Market By: Individual Items	Lower of Cost or Market By: Major Categories	Lower of Cost or Market By: Total Inventory
Frozen					
Spinach	$ 80,000	$104,000	$ 80,000		
Carrots	100,000	90,000	90,000		
Cut Beans	50,000	40,000	40,000		
Total frozen	230,000	234,000		$230,000	
Canned					
Peas	90,000	48,000	48,000		
Mixed Vegetables	95,000	92,000	92,000		
Total canned	185,000	140,000		140,000	
Total	$415,000	$374,000	$350,000	$370,000	$374,000

**ILLUSTRATION 9-5
Alternative Applications
of Lower of Cost
or Market**

If the lower of cost or market rule is applied to individual items, the amount of inventory is $350,000; if applied to major categories, it is $370,000; if applied to the total inventory, it is $374,000. The reason for the difference is that market values higher than cost are offset against market values lower than cost when the major categories or total inventory approach is adopted. For Regner Foods, the high market value for spinach is partially offset when the major categories approach is adopted and is totally offset when the total inventory approach is used.

The most common practice is to price the inventory on an item-by-item basis. For one thing, tax rules require that an individual item basis be used unless it involves practical difficulties. In addition, the individual item approach gives the most conservative valuation for balance sheet purposes.[2] Inventory is often priced on a total inventory basis when there is only one end product (comprised of many different raw materials) because the main concern is the pricing of the final inventory. If several end products are produced, a category approach might be used. The method selected should be the one that most clearly reflects income. **Whichever method is selected, it should be applied consistently from one period to another.**[3]

RECORDING "MARKET" INSTEAD OF COST

Two methods are used for recording inventory at market. One method, referred to as the **direct method,** substitutes the market value figure for cost when valuing the inventory. As a result, no loss is reported in the income statement because the loss is buried in cost of goods sold. The second method, referred to as the **indirect method** or **allowance method,** does not change the cost amount, but establishes a separate contra asset account and a loss account to record the writeoff.

The following illustrations of entries under both methods are based on the following inventory data:

---

[2]If a company uses dollar-value LIFO, determining the LIFO cost of an individual item may be more difficult. The company might decide that it is more appropriate to apply the lower of cost or market rule to the total amount of each pool. The AICPA Task Force on LIFO Inventory Problems concluded that the most reasonable approach to applying the lower of cost or market provisions to LIFO inventories is to base the determination on reasonable groupings of items and that a pool constitutes a reasonable grouping. Both the Task Force and AcSEC, however, support the use of the item-by-item approach for identifying product obsolescence and product discontinuance writedowns and writeoffs.

[3]Inventory accounting for financial statement purposes can be different from income tax purposes. For example, the lower of cost or market rule cannot be used with LIFO for tax purposes. There is nothing, however, to prevent the use of the lower of cost or market and LIFO for financial accounting purposes. In addition, for financial accounting purposes, companies often write down slow-moving inventory because experience indicates that some of it will not be sold for many years, if at all. However, to be deductible for tax purposes a writedown in inventory value resulting from the application of lower of cost or market rule can be taken only in the year in which the actual decline in the sale price of the item occurs, and the writedown must be computed on an individual item basis rather than on classes of inventory or on the inventory as a whole. The important tax case *Thor Power Tool Company* v. *Commissioner of Internal Revenue* provides guidelines. In this case, the IRS negated Thor's practice of writing down the value of its spare parts inventory which it held to cover future warranty commitments. Thor contended that, although the sales price on the individual parts did not decline over the years, the probability of all the parts being sold decreased as time passed, and thus so did the net realizable value of the inventory as a whole. The IRS contended that a decline in inventory values for tax purposes must await actual decline in the sales price of the individual parts. The Supreme Court indicated that for tax purposes, the lower of cost or market method was to be applied on an individual item basis and that if no decline in sales price occurred, no loss should be permitted. The Court did indicate that for financial accounting purposes, the writedown to lower of cost or market for the parts inventory is consistent with the accounting principle of matching current costs and revenues.

The importance of the Thor Tool case should not be underestimated. Many businesses that maintain large inventories over extended periods of time, such as book publishers and auto and appliance replacement part distributors, have complained that they may be forced to destroy their inventory to receive their tax deductions. Such a situation then would lead to less inventory of old books and replacement parts.

Inventory	At Cost	At Market
Beginning of the period	$65,000	$65,000
End of the period	82,000	70,000

The following entries assume the use of a **periodic** inventory system.

Ending Inventory Recorded at Market (Direct Method)		Ending Inventory Recorded at Cost and Reduced to Market (Indirect or Allowance Method)	
To close beginning inventory:			
Cost of Goods Sold		Cost of Goods Sold	
(or Income Summary) 65,000		(or Income Summary) 65,000	
Inventory	65,000	Inventory	65,000
To record ending inventory:			
Inventory 70,000		Inventory 82,000	
Cost of Goods Sold		Cost of Goods Sold	
(or Income Summary)	70,000	(or Income Summary)	82,000
To write down inventory to market:			
No entry		Loss Due to Market	
		Decline of Inventory 12,000	
		Allowance to Reduce	
		Inventory to Market	12,000

ILLUSTRATION 9-6
Accounting for the
Reduction of Inventory
to Market—Periodic
Inventory System

If the company had used a **perpetual** inventory system, the entries would be as follows:

(No inventory closing entries are necessary under the perpetual method; only the reduction to market is recorded.)			
Direct Method		Indirect or Allowance Method	
To reduce inventory from cost to market:			
Cost of Goods Sold 12,000		Loss Due to Market	
Inventory	12,000	Decline of Inventory 12,000	
		Allowance to Reduce	
		Inventory to Market	12,000

ILLUSTRATION 9-7
Accounting for the
Reduction of Inventory
to Market—Perpetual
Inventory System

The advantage of identifying the loss due to market decline is that it is shown separately from cost of goods sold in the income statement (not as an extraordinary item); the cost of goods sold for the year is not distorted. The data from the preceding illustration are used to contrast the differing amounts reported in the income statements below.

Direct Method		
Revenue from sales		$200,000
Cost of goods sold		
Inventory Jan. 1	$ 65,000	
Purchases	125,000	
Goods available	190,000	
Inventory Dec. 31 (at market which is lower than cost)	70,000	
Cost of goods sold		120,000
Gross profit on sales		$ 80,000
Indirect or Allowance Method		
Revenue from sales		$200,000
Cost of goods sold		
Inventory Jan. 1	$ 65,000	
Purchases	125,000	
Goods available	190,000	
Inventory Dec. 31 (at cost)	82,000	
Cost of goods sold		108,000
Gross profit on sales		92,000
Loss due to market decline of inventory		12,000
		$ 80,000

ILLUSTRATION 9-8
Income Statement
Presentation—Direct
and Indirect Methods
of Reducing Inventory
to Market

UNDERLYING
CONCEPT

*The income statement under
the first presentation
lacks representational
faithfulness. The cost of
goods sold does not represent
what it purports to
represent. However, allowing
the first presentation
illustrates the concept of
materiality. The presentation
does not affect net income
and would not "change the
judgment of a reasonable
person."*

The second presentation is preferable, because it clearly discloses the loss resulting from the market decline of inventory prices. The first presentation buries the loss in the cost of goods sold. The Allowance to Reduce Inventory to Market would be reported on the balance sheet as a $12,000 deduction from the inventory. This deduction permits both the income statement and the balance sheet to show the ending inventory of $82,000, although the balance sheet shows a net amount of $70,000. It also keeps subsidiary inventory ledgers and records in correspondence with the control account without changing unit prices.

Although use of an allowance account permits balance sheet disclosure of the inventory at cost and the lower of cost or market, it raises the problem of how to dispose of the balance of the new account in the following period. If the merchandise in question is still on hand, the allowance account should be retained. Otherwise, beginning inventory and cost of goods are overstated. But if the goods have been sold, then the account should be closed. A "new allowance account" is then established for any decline in inventory value that has taken place in the current year.[4]

Some accountants leave this account on the books and merely adjust the balance at the next year-end to agree with the discrepancy between cost and the lower of cost or market at that balance sheet date. Thus, if prices are falling, a loss is recorded. If prices are rising, a loss recorded in prior years is recovered and a "gain" (which is not really a gain, but a recovery of a previously recognized loss) is recorded, as illustrated in the example below.

**ILLUSTRATION 9-9
Effect on Net Income
of Reducing Inventory
to Market**

Date	Inventory at Cost	Inventory at Market	Amount Required in Valuation Account	Adjustment of Valuation Account Balance	Effect on Net Income
Dec. 31, 1995	$188,000	$176,000	$12,000	$12,000 inc.	Loss
Dec. 31, 1996	194,000	187,000	7,000	5,000 dec.	Gain
Dec. 31, 1997	173,000	174,000	0	7,000 dec.	Gain
Dec. 31, 1998	182,000	180,000	2,000	2,000 inc.	Loss

This net "gain" can be thought of as the excess of the credit effect of closing the beginning allowance balance over the debit effect of setting up the current year-end allowance account. Recognition of gain or loss has the same effect on net income as closing the allowance balance to beginning inventory or to cost of goods sold. Recovery of the loss up to the original cost is permitted, **but it may not exceed original cost.**

UNDERLYING
CONCEPT

*The inconsistency in the
presentation of inventory is
an example of the trade-off
between relevancy and
reliability. Market is more
relevant than cost, and cost
is more reliable than market.
Apparently, the profession
believes relevancy is more
important than reliability in
a down market and reliability
is more important than
relevancy in an up market.*

EVALUATION OF THE LOWER OF COST OR MARKET RULE

The lower of cost or market rule suffers some conceptual deficiencies:

1. Decreases in the value of the asset and the charge to expense are recognized in the period in which the loss in utility occurs—not in the period of sale. On the other hand, increases in the value of the asset are recognized only at the point of sale. This treatment is inconsistent and can lead to distortions in income data.

2. Application of the rule results in inconsistency because the inventory of a company may be valued at cost in one year and at market in the next year.

3. Lower of cost or market values the inventory in the balance sheet conservatively, but its effect on the income statement may or may not be conservative. Net income for the year in which the loss is taken is definitely lower; net income of the subsequent period may be higher than normal if the expected reductions in sales price do not materialize.

---

[4]The AICPA Task Force on LIFO Inventory Problems concluded that for LIFO inventories the allowance from the prior year should be closed and that the allowance at the end of the year should be based on a new lower of cost or market computation. *Issues Paper* (New York: AICPA, November 30, 1984), pp. 50–55.

4. Application of the lower of cost or market rule uses a "normal profit" in determining inventory values. Since "normal profit" is an estimated figure based upon past experience (and might not be attained in the future), it is not objective in nature and presents an opportunity for income manipulation.

Many financial statement users appreciate the lower of cost or market rule because they at least know that the inventory is not overstated. In addition, recognizing all losses but anticipating no gains generally results in lower income.

▶ VALUATION AT NET REALIZABLE VALUE

For the most part, inventory is recorded at cost or the lower of cost or market.[5] However, many believe that market should always be defined as net realizable value (rather than replacement cost) for purposes of applying the lower of cost or market rule. This argument is based on the fact that net realizable value is the amount that will be collected from this inventory in the future.[6] Under limited circumstances, support exists for **recording inventory at net realizable value (selling price less estimated costs to complete and sell)** even if that amount is above cost. This exception to the normal recognition rule is permitted where (1) there is a controlled market with a quoted price applicable to all quantities and (2) no significant costs of disposal are involved. Inventories of certain minerals (rare metals especially), are ordinarily reported at selling prices because there is often a controlled market without significant costs of disposal. A similar treatment is given agricultural products that are immediately marketable at quoted prices.

Another reason for allowing this method of valuation is that sometimes the cost figures are too difficult to obtain. In a manufacturing plant, various raw materials and purchased parts are put together to create a finished product. The various items in inventory, whether completely or partially finished, can be accounted for on a basis of cost because the cost of each individual component part is known. In a meat-packing house, however, a different situation prevails. The "raw material" consists of cattle, hogs, or sheep, each unit of which is purchased as a whole and then divided into parts that are the products. Instead of one product out of many raw materials or parts, many products are made from one "unit" of raw material. To allocate the cost of the animal "on the hoof" into the cost of ribs, chucks, and shoulders, for instance, is a practical impossibility. It is much easier and more useful to determine the market price of the various products and value them in the inventory at selling price less the various costs,

OBJECTIVE 2

Identify when inventories are valued at net realizable value.

INTERNATIONAL INSIGHT

In the Netherlands and the United Kingdom, inventory is valued at "lower of cost or market," but in contrast to the U.S., market in these nations is defined as "net realizable value."

---

[5]Manufacturing companies frequently employ a **standardized cost system** that predetermines the unit costs for material, labor, and manufacturing overhead and values raw materials, work in process, and finished goods inventories at their standard costs. For financial reporting purposes the pricing of inventories at standard costs is acceptable if there is no significant difference between the actual costs and standard costs. If there is a significant difference, the inventory amounts should be adjusted to actual cost. In *Accounting Research and Terminology Bulletin, Final Edition* the profession takes a long-standing position that **"standard costs are acceptable if adjusted at reasonable intervals to reflect current conditions."** Burlington Industries, Syntex, Hewlett-Packard, and Westinghouse Electric are just a few of the many companies that use standard costs for valuing at least a portion of their inventory.

[6]*Accounting Research Study No. 13*, "The Accounting Basis of Inventories" (New York: AICPA, 1973) recommends that net realizable value be adopted. It also should be noted that a literal interpretation of the rules of lower of cost or market is frequently not applied in practice. For example, the lower limit, net realizable value less a normal markup, is rarely computed and applied because it results in an extremely conservative inventory valuation approach. In addition, inventory is often not reduced to market unless its disposition is expected to result in a loss. Furthermore, if the net realizable value of finished goods exceeds cost, it is usually assumed that both work in process and raw materials do as well. In practice, therefore, *ARB No. 43* is considered a guide, and professional judgment is often exercised in lieu of following this pronouncement literally.

such as shipping and handling, necessary to get them to market. Hence, because of a peculiarity of the meat-packing industry, **inventories are sometimes carried at sales price less distribution costs.**

▶ VALUATION USING RELATIVE SALES VALUE

OBJECTIVE 3

Explain when the relative sales value method is used to value inventories.

A special problem arises when a group of varying units is purchased at a single **lump sum price,** a so-called **basket purchase.** Assume that Woodland Developers purchases land for $1 million that can be subdivided in 400 lots. These lots are of different sizes and shapes but can be roughly sorted into three groups graded A, B, and C. As lots are sold, the purchase cost of $1 million is apportioned among the lots sold and the lots remaining on hand.

It is inappropriate to divide 400 lots into the total cost of $1 million to get a cost of $2,500 for each lot, because they vary in size, shape, and attractiveness. When such a situation is encountered—and it is not at all unusual—the common and most logical practice is to allocate the total cost among the various units on the basis of their relative sales value. For the example given, the allocation works out as follows:

**ILLUSTRATION 9-10
Allocation of Costs,
Using Relative Sales
Value**

Lots	Number of Lots	Sales Price Per Lot	Total Sales Price	Relative Sales Price	Total Cost	Cost Allocated to Lots	Cost Per Lot
A	100	$10,000	$1,000,000	100/250	$1,000,000	$ 400,000	$4,000
B	100	6,000	600,000	60/250	1,000,000	240,000	2,400
C	200	4,500	900,000	90/250	1,000,000	360,000	1,800
			$2,500,000			$1,000,000	

The cost of lots sold can be computed by using the amounts given in the column for "Cost Per Lot," and the gross profit is determined as follows:

**ILLUSTRATION 9-11
Determination of Gross
Profit, Using Relative
Sales Value**

Lots	Number of Lots Sold	Cost Per Lot	Cost of Lots Sold	Sales	Gross Profit
A	77	$4,000	$308,000	$ 770,000	$ 462,000
B	80	2,400	192,000	480,000	288,000
C	100	1,800	180,000	450,000	270,000
			$680,000	$1,700,000	$1,020,000

The ending inventory is therefore $320,000 ($1,000,000 − $680,000). This inventory amount can also be computed in another manner. The ratio of cost to selling price for all the lots is $1 million divided by $2,500,000, or 40%. Accordingly, if the total sales price of lots sold is, say $1,700,000, then the cost of these lots sold is 40% of $1,700,000, or $680,000. The inventory of lots on hand is then $1 million less $680,000, or $320,000.

The relative sales value method is used throughout the petroleum industry to value (at cost) the many products and by-products obtained from a barrel of crude oil.

▶ PURCHASE COMMITMENTS—A SPECIAL PROBLEM

OBJECTIVE 4

Explain accounting issues related to purchase commitments.

In many lines of business, the survival and continued profitability of a firm depends on it having a sufficient stock of merchandise to meet all customer demands. Consequently, it is quite common for a company to agree to buy inventory weeks, months, or even years in advance. Such arrangements may be made on the basis of estimated or firm sales commitments by the company's customers. Generally, title to the merchandise or materials described in these **purchase commitments** has not passed to the buyer. Indeed, the goods may exist only as natural resources or, in the case of commodities, as unplanted seed, or in the case of a product, as work in process.

Usually it is neither necessary nor proper for the buyer to make any entries to reflect commitments for purchases of goods that have not been shipped by the seller. Ordinary orders, for which the prices are determined at the time of shipment and **which are subject to cancellation** by the buyer or seller, do not represent either an asset or a liability to the buyer. Therefore they need not be recorded in the books or reported in the financial statements.

Even with formal, noncancelable purchase contracts, no asset or liability is recognized at the date of inception, **because the contract is "executory" in nature:** neither party has fulfilled its part of the contract. However, if material, such contract details should be disclosed in the buyer's balance sheet in a note:

Note 1: Contracts for the purchase of raw materials in 1996 have been executed in the amount of $600,000. The market price of such raw materials on December 31, 1995, is $640,000.

In the foregoing illustration the contracted price was less than the market price at the balance sheet date. **If the contracted price is in excess of market and it is expected that losses will occur when the purchase is effected, losses should be recognized in the period during which such declines in market prices take place.**[7]

In the early 1980s, many Northwest forest product companies such as Boise Cascade, Georgia-Pacific, Weyerhaeuser, and St. Regis signed long-term timber-cutting contracts with the United States Forest Service. These contracts required that the companies pay $310 per thousand board feet for timber-cutting rights. Unfortunately, the market price for timber-cutting rights in late 1984 dropped to $80 per thousand board feet. As a result, a number of these companies had long-term contracts that, if fulfilled, projected substantial future losses.

To illustrate the accounting problem, assume that St. Regis Paper Co. signed timber-cutting contracts to be executed in 1996 at a firm price of $10,000,000 and that the market price of the timber cutting rights on December 31, 1995, dropped to $7,000,000. The following entry is made on December 31, 1995:

Estimated Loss on Purchase Commitments	3,000,000	
Estimated Liability on Purchase Commitments		3,000,000

This loss would be reported in the income statement under Other Expenses and Losses. The Estimated Liability on Purchase Commitments is reported in the current liability section of the balance sheet because the contract is to be executed within the next fiscal year. When St. Regis cuts the timber at a cost of $10 million, the following entry would be made:

Purchases (Inventory)	7,000,000	
Estimated Liability on Purchase Commitments	3,000,000	
Cash		10,000,000

The company paid $10 million for a contract worth only $7 million. The loss was recorded in the previous period—when the price actually declined.

If the price is partially or fully recovered before the timber is cut, the Estimated Liability on Purchase Commitments is reduced. A resulting gain (Recovery of Loss) is then reported in the period of the price increase for the amount of the partial or full recovery. For example, Congress permitted some of these companies to buy out of their contracts at reduced prices in order to avoid some potential bankruptcies. To illustrate, assume that St. Regis is permitted to reduce its contract price and therefore its commitment by $1,000,000. The entry to record this transaction is as follows:

Estimated Liability on Purchase Commitments	1,000,000	
Recovery of Loss on Purchase Commitments		1,000,000

If the market price at the time the timber is cut is more than $3,000,000 below the contract price, St. Regis will have to recognize an additional loss in the period of cutting and record the purchase at the lower of cost or market.

UNDERLYING CONCEPT

Reporting the loss is conservative. However, reporting the decline in market price is debatable because no asset is recorded. This area demonstrates the need for good definitions of assets and liabilities.

---

[7]*Accounting Research Bulletin No. 43*, op. cit., par. 16.

The purchasers in purchase commitments can protect themselves against the possibility of market price declines of goods under contract by **hedging.** Hedging is accomplished through a futures contract in which the purchaser in the purchase commitment simultaneously contracts to a future sale of the same quantity of the same or similar goods at a fixed price. When a company holds a buy position in a purchase commitment and a sell position in a futures contract in the same commodity, it will be better off under one contract by approximately (maybe exactly) the same amount by which it is worse off under the other contract. That is, a loss on one will be offset by a gain on the other. For example, if St. Regis Paper Co. had hedged its purchase commitment contract by selling futures contracts for timber rights of the same amount, its loss of $3,000,000 on the purchase commitment would have been offset by a $3,000,000 gain on the futures contract.

The FASB in *Statement No. 80* requires that in hedging of purchase commitments "the accounting for the futures contract shall be related to the accounting for the hedged item so that changes in the market value of the futures contract are recognized in income when the effects of related changes in the price of the hedged item are recognized."[8]

Accounting for purchase commitments (and, for that matter, all commitments) is unsettled and controversial. Some argue that these contracts should be reported as assets and liabilities at the time the contract is signed.[9] Others believe that the present recognition at the delivery date is more appropriate. *FASB Concepts Statement No. 6* states that "a purchase commitment involves both an item that might be recorded as an asset and an item that might be recorded as a liability. That is, it involves both a right to receive assets and an obligation to pay.... If both the right to receive assets and the obligation to pay were recorded at the time of the purchase commitment, the nature of the loss and the valuation account that records it when the price falls would be clearly seen." Although the discussion in *Concepts Statement No. 6* does not exclude the possibility of recording assets and liabilities for purchase commitments, it contains no conclusions or implications about whether they should be recorded.[10]

▶ THE GROSS PROFIT METHOD OF ESTIMATING INVENTORY

OBJECTIVE 5

Determine ending inventory by applying the gross profit method.

Recall that the basic purpose of taking a physical inventory is to verify the accuracy of the perpetual inventory records or, if no records exist, to arrive at an inventory amount. Sometimes, taking a physical inventory is impractical. Then, substitute measures are used to approximate inventory on hand. One substitute method of verifying or determining the inventory amount is called the gross profit method (often called the gross margin method). This method is widely used by auditors in situations (e.g., interim reports) where only an estimate of the company's inventory is needed. It is also used where either inventory or inventory records have been destroyed by fire or other catastrophe.

---

[8]"Accounting for Futures Contracts," *Statement of Financial Accounting Standards No. 80* (Norwalk, Conn.: FASB, 1984), par. 3.

[9]See, for example, Yuji Ijiri; *Recognition of Contractual Rights and Obligations, Research Report* (Stamford, Conn.: FASB, 1980), who argues that firm purchase commitments might be capitalized. "Firm" means that it is unlikely that performance under the contract can be avoided without a severe penalty.

Also, see Mahendra R. Gujarathi and Stanley F. Biggs, "Accounting for Purchase Commitments: Some Issues and Recommendations," *Accounting Horizons*, September 1988, pages 75–78, who conclude, "Recording an asset and liability on the date of inception for the noncancelable purchase commitments is suggested as the first significant step towards alleviating the accounting problems associated with the issue. At year-end, the potential gains and losses should be treated as contingencies under FASB 5 which provides a coherent structure for the accounting and informative disclosure for such gains and losses."

[10]"Elements of Financial Statements," *Statement of Financial Accounting Concepts No. 6* (Stamford, Conn.: FASB, 1985), pars. 251–253.

The **gross profit method** is based on three assumptions: (1) the beginning inventory plus purchases equal total goods to be accounted for; (2) goods not sold must be on hand; and (3) if the sales, reduced to cost, are deducted from the sum of the opening inventory plus purchases, the result is the ending inventory.

To illustrate, assume that Cetus Corp. has a beginning inventory of $60,000 and purchases of $200,000, both at cost. Sales at selling price amount to $280,000. The gross profit on selling price is 30%. The gross margin method is applied as follows:

			ILLUSTRATION 9-12
Beginning inventory (at cost)		$ 60,000	**Application of Gross**
Purchases (at cost)		200,000	**Profit Method**
Goods available (at cost)		260,000	
Sales (at selling price)	$280,000		
Less gross profit (30% of $280,000)	84,000		
Sales (at cost)		196,000	
Approximate inventory (at cost)		$ 64,000	

All the information needed to compute Cetus' inventory at cost, except for the gross profit percentage, is available in the current period's records. The gross profit percentage is determined by reviewing company policies or prior period records. In some cases, this percentage must be adjusted if prior periods are not considered representative of the current period.[11]

COMPUTATION OF GROSS PROFIT PERCENTAGE

In most situations, the **gross profit percentage** is given as a percentage of selling price. The previous illustration, for example, used a 30% gross profit on sales. Gross profit on selling price is the common method for quoting the profit for several reasons: (1) Most goods are stated on a retail basis, not a cost basis. (2) A profit quoted on selling price is lower than one based on cost, and this lower rate gives a favorable impression to the consumer. (3) The gross profit based on selling price can never exceed 100%.[12]

In the previous example, the gross profit was a given. But how was that figure derived? To see how gross profit percentage is computed, assume that an article cost $15.00 and sells for $20.00, a gross profit of $5.00. This markup is ¼ or 25% of retail and ⅓ or 33⅓% of cost:

	ILLUSTRATION 9-13
$\dfrac{\text{Markup}}{\text{Retail}} = \dfrac{\$5.00}{\$20.00} = 25\%$ at retail $\qquad \dfrac{\text{Markup}}{\text{Cost}} = \dfrac{\$5.00}{\$15.00} = 33\frac{1}{3}\%$ on cost	**Computation of Gross** **Profit Percentage**

---

[11]An alternative method of estimating inventory using the gross profit percentage, considered by some to be less complicated than the traditional method illustrated above, uses the standard income statement format as follows (assume the same data as in the Cetus Corp. illustration above):

Sales		$280,000		$280,000
Cost of sales				
Beginning inventory	$ 60,000		$ 60,000	
Purchases	200,000		200,000	
Goods available for sale	260,000		260,000	
Ending inventory	(3) ?		(3) **64,000** Est.	
Cost of goods sold		(2) ?		(2)**196,000** Est.
Gross profit on sales (30%)		(1) ?		(1) **84,000** Est.

Compute the unknowns as follows: first the gross profit amount, then cost of goods sold, and then the ending inventory.
(1) $280,000 × 30% = $84,000 (gross profit on sales).
(2) $280,000 − $84,000 = $196,000 (cost of goods sold).
(3) $260,000 − $196,000 = $64,000 (ending inventory).

[12]The terms "gross margin percentage," "rate of gross profit," and "percentage markup" are synonymous, although it sounds more acceptable to use "markup" in reference to cost and "gross profit" in reference to sales.

Although it is normal to compute the gross profit on the basis of selling price, the accountant should understand the basic relationship between markup on cost and markup on selling price.

For example, assume that you were told that the markup on cost for a given item is 25%. What, then, is the **gross profit on selling price?** To find the answer, assume that the sale price of the item is $1.00. In this case, the following formula applies:

$$\text{Cost} + \text{Gross profit} = \text{Selling price}$$
$$C + .25C = SP$$
$$(1 + .25)C = SP$$
$$1.25C = \$1.00$$
$$C = \$0.80$$

The gross profit equals $0.20 ($1.00 − $0.80), and the rate of gross profit on selling price is therefore 20% ($0.20/$1.00).

Conversely, assume that you were told that the gross profit on selling price is 20%. What is the **markup on cost?** To find the answer, again assume that the sales price is $1.00. Again, the same formula holds:

$$\text{Cost} + \text{Gross profit} = \text{Selling price}$$
$$C + .20SP = SP$$
$$C = (1 - .20)SP$$
$$C = .80SP$$
$$C = .80(\$1.00)$$
$$C = \$0.80$$

Here, as in the example above, the markup equals $0.20 ($1.00 − $0.80) and the markup on cost is 25% ($0.20/$0.80).

Retailers use the following formulas to express these relationships:

**ILLUSTRATION 9-14
Formulas Relating
to Gross Profit**

1. $\text{Gross profit on selling price} = \dfrac{\text{Percentage markup on cost}}{100\% + \text{Percentage markup on cost}}$

2. $\text{Percentage markup on cost} = \dfrac{\text{Gross profit on selling price}}{100\% - \text{Gross profit on selling price}}$

To understand how these formulas are employed, consider the following calculations:

**ILLUSTRATION 9-15
Application of Gross
Profit Formulas**

Gross Profit on Selling Price	Percentage Markup on Cost
Given: 20% ⟶	$\dfrac{.20}{1.00 - .20} = 25\%$
Given: 25% ⟶	$\dfrac{.25}{1.00 - .25} = 33\frac{1}{3}\%$
$\dfrac{.25}{1.00 + .25} = 20\%$ ⟵	Given: 25%
$\dfrac{.50}{1.00 + .50} = 33\frac{1}{3}\%$ ⟵	Given: 50%

Because selling price is greater than cost, and with the gross profit amount the same for both, **gross profit on selling price will always be less than the related percentage based on cost.** It should be emphasized that sales may not be multiplied by a cost-based markup percentage; the gross profit percentage must be converted to a percentage based on selling price.

Gross profits are closely followed by managements and analysts. A small change in the gross profit rate can have a significant effect on the bottom line. In 1993, Apple

Computer suffered a textbook case of shrinking gross profits. In response to pricing wars in the personal computer market, Apple was forced to quickly reduce the price of its signature Macintosh computers—reducing prices more quickly than it could reduce its costs. As a result its gross profit rate fell from 44% in 1992 to 40% in 1993. While the drop of 4% may appear small, its impact on the bottom line caused Apple's stock price to drop from $57 per share on June 1, 1993, to $27.50 by mid-July 1993. A similar effect (a 40% plummet in stock price) occurred when Woolworth Corp. disclosed a "correction of gross profits" due to a reporting of inaccurate gross profits in at least three of the company's quarterly reports during the fiscal year ended January 29, 1994.[13]

APPRAISAL OF GROSS PROFIT METHOD

The gross profit method is not normally acceptable for financial reporting purposes because it provides only an estimate. A physical inventory is needed as additional verification that the inventory indicated in the records is actually on hand. Nevertheless, the gross profit method is permitted to determine ending inventory for interim (generally quarterly) reporting purposes provided the use of this method is disclosed. Note that the gross profit method will follow closely the inventory method used (FIFO, LIFO, average cost) because it is based on historical records.

What are the major disadvantages of the gross profit method? One major disadvantage is that **it provides an estimate;** as a result, a physical inventory must be taken once a year to verify that the inventory is actually on hand. Second, the gross profit method **uses past percentages** in determining the markup. Although the past can often provide answers to the future, a current rate is more appropriate. It is important to emphasize that whenever significant fluctuations occur, the percentage should be adjusted as appropriate. Third, **care must be taken in applying a blanket gross profit rate.** Frequently, a store or department handles merchandise with widely varying rates of gross profit. In these situations, the gross profit method may have to be applied by subsections, lines of merchandise, or a similar basis that classifies merchandise according to their respective rates of gross profit.

▶ RETAIL INVENTORY METHOD

OBJECTIVE 6

Determine ending inventory by applying the retail inventory method.

Accounting for inventory in a retail operation presents several challenges. Retailers with certain types of inventory may use the specific identification method to value their inventories. Such an approach makes sense when individual inventory units are significant, such as automobiles, pianos, or fur coats. However, imagine attempting to use such an approach at Kmart, True-Value Hardware, Sears, or Bloomingdales—high-volume retailers that have many different types of merchandise. It would be extremely difficult to determine the cost of each sale, to enter cost codes on the tickets, to change the codes to reflect declines in value of the merchandise, to allocate costs such as transportation, and so on.

An alternative is to compile the inventories at retail prices. In most retail concerns, an observable pattern between cost and price exists. Retail prices can therefore be converted to cost through formula. This method, called **the retail inventory method, requires that a record be kept of (1) the total cost and retail value of goods purchased, (2) the total cost and retail value of the goods available for sale, and (3) the sales for the period.**

Here is how it works: The sales for the period are deducted from the retail value of the goods available for sale, to produce an estimated inventory (goods on hand) at retail. The ratio of cost to retail for all goods passing through a department or firm is then determined by dividing the total goods available for sale at cost by the total goods available at retail. The inventory valued at retail is converted to ending inventory at cost by applying the cost-to-retail ratio. Use of the retail inventory method is very

---

[13]"Two Top Woolworth Officers Step Down Amid Probe of Accounting Irregularities," *The Wall Street Journal*, April 4, 1994, p. A3.

common. Safeway and Giant supermarkets both use the retail inventory method as do the department store chains of Dayton Hudson Corp. and Marshall Field and Company. The retail inventory method is illustrated below for Jordan-Guess Inc.

ILLUSTRATION 9-16
Retail Inventory Method

Jordan-Guess Inc. (current period)	Cost	Retail
Beginning inventory	$14,000	$ 20,000
Purchases	63,000	90,000
Goods available for sale	$77,000	110,000
Deduct sales		85,000
Ending inventory, at retail		$ 25,000
Ratio of cost to retail ($77,000 ÷ $110,000)		70%
Ending inventory at cost (70% of $25,000)		$ 17,500

To avoid a potential overstatement of the inventory, periodic inventory counts are made, especially in retail operations where loss due to shoplifting and breakage is common.

There are different versions of the retail inventory method—the conventional (lower of average cost or market) method, the cost method, the LIFO retail method, and the dollar-value LIFO retail method. Regardless of which version is used, the retail inventory method is sanctioned by the IRS, various retail associations, and the accounting profession. One of its advantages is that the inventory balance **can be approximated without a physical count**.

The retail inventory method is particularly useful for any type of interim report, because a fairly quick and reliable measure of the inventory value is usually needed. Insurance adjusters often use this approach to estimate losses from fire, flood, or other type of casualty. This method also acts as a **control device** because any deviations from a physical count at the end of the year have to be explained. In addition, the retail method **expedites the physical inventory count** at the end of the year. The crew taking the physical inventory need record only the retail price of each item; there is no need to look up each item's invoice cost, thereby saving time and expense.

RETAIL METHOD TERMINOLOGY

The amounts shown in the Retail column of Illustration 9-16 represent the original retail prices, assuming no price changes. Sales prices are frequently marked up or down. For retailers, the term **markup** means an additional markup of the original retail price. (In another context, such as the gross profit discussion on page 443, we often think of markup on the basis of cost.) **Markup cancellations** are decreases in prices of merchandise that had been marked up above the original retail price.

Markdowns below the original sale prices may be necessary because of a decrease in the general level of prices, special sales, soiled or damaged goods, overstocking, and competition. Markdowns are common in retailing these days. **Markdown cancellations** occur when the markdowns are later offset by increases in the prices of goods that had been marked down—such as after a one-day sale, for example. Neither a markup cancellation nor a markdown cancellation can exceed the original markup or markdown.

To illustrate these different concepts, assume that the Designer Clothing Store recently purchased 100 dress shirts from Marroway, Inc. The cost for these shirts was $1,500, or $15.00 a shirt. Designer Clothing established the selling price on these shirts at $30.00 a shirt. The manager noted that the shirts were selling quickly, so he added a markup of $5.00 per shirt. This markup made the price too high for customers and sales lagged. The manager then reduced the price to $32.00. At this point we would say that Designer Clothing has had a markup of $5.00 and a markup cancellation of $3.00. As soon as the major marketing season passed, the manager marked the remaining shirts down to a sales price of $23.00. At this point, an additional markup cancellation of $2.00

has taken place and a $7.00 markdown has occurred. If the shirts are later written up to $24.00, a markdown cancellation of $1.00 would occur.

RETAIL INVENTORY METHOD WITH MARKUPS AND MARKDOWNS—CONVENTIONAL METHOD

Retailers use markup and markdown concepts in developing the proper inventory valuation at the end of the accounting period. To obtain the appropriate inventory figures, proper treatment must be given to markups, markup cancellations, markdowns, and markdown cancellations.

To illustrate the different possibilities, consider the data for In-Fashion Stores Inc., shown in Illustration 9-17. In-Fashion's ending inventory at cost can be calculated under two assumptions, A and B (the reasons for the two will be explained later):

Assumption A: Computes a cost ratio after markups (and markup cancellations) but before markdowns.

Assumption B: Computes a cost ratio after both markups and markdowns (and cancellations).

	Cost	Retail
Beginning inventory	$ 500	$ 1,000
Purchases (net)	20,000	35,000
Markups		3,000
Markup cancellations		1,000
Markdowns		2,500
Markdown cancellations		2,000
Sales (net)		25,000

ILLUSTRATION 9-17
Retail Inventory Method with Markups and Markdowns

In-Fashion Stores Inc.

	Cost	Retail	
Beginning inventory	$ 500	$ 1,000	
Purchases (net)	20,000	35,000	
Merchandise available for sale	20,500	36,000	
Add:			
Markups	$3,000		
Less markup cancellations	(1,000)		
Net markups		2,000	
	20,500	38,000	
Cost-to-retail ratio $\frac{\$20,500}{\$38,000}$ = 53.9%			**(A)**
Deduct:			
Markdowns	2,500		
Less markdown cancellations	(2,000)		
Net markdowns		500	
	$20,500	37,500	
Cost-to-retail ratio $\frac{\$20,500}{\$37,500}$ = 54.7%			**(B)**
Deduct sales (net)		25,000	
Ending inventory at retail		$12,500	

The computations for In-Fashion Stores are:

Ending inventory at retail × cost ratio = Value of ending inventory
Assumption A: $12,500 × 53.9% = $6,737.50
Assumption B: 12,500 × 54.7% = 6,837.50

The question becomes: Which assumption and which percentage should be employed to compute the ending inventory valuation?

The answer depends on the retail inventory method chosen. **The conventional retail inventory method uses assumption A only. It is designed to approximate the lower of average cost or market.** We will refer to this approach as the **lower of cost or market approach** or **the conventional retail inventory method.** To understand why the markups but not the markdowns are considered in the cost percentage, we must understand how a retail outlet operates. Markup normally indicates that the market value of that item has increased. On the other hand, a markdown means that a decline in the utility of that item has occurred. Therefore, if we attempt to approximate the lower of cost or market, markdowns are considered a current loss and are not involved in the calculation of the cost-to-retail ratio. Thus, the cost-to-retail ratio is lower, which leads to an approximate lower of cost or market.

An example will make this clear. Two items were purchased for $5.00 apiece, and the original sales price was established at $10.00 each. One item was subsequently written down to $2.00. Assuming no sales for the period, **if markdowns are considered** in the cost-to-retail ratio (assumption B, above), we compute the ending inventory in the following manner:

Markdowns Included in Cost-to-Retail Ratio	Cost	Retail
Purchases	$10.00	$20.00
Deduct markdowns		8.00
Ending inventory, at retail		$12.00
Cost-to-retail ratio $\dfrac{\$10.00}{\$12.00}$ = 83.3%		
Ending inventory at cost ($12.00 × .833) = $10.00		

This approach is the **cost method.** It reflects an average cost of the two items of the commodity without considering the loss on the one item.

If markdowns are not considered, the result is the lower of cost or market method (assumption A). The calculation is made as shown below.

Markdowns Not Included in Cost-to-Retail Ratio	Cost	Retail
Purchases	$10.00	$20.00
Cost-to-retail ratio $\dfrac{\$10.00}{\$20.00}$ = 50%		
Deduct markdowns		8.00
Ending inventory, at retail		$12.00
Ending inventory, at cost ($12 × .50) = $6.00		

Under the conventional retail inventory method (when markdowns are **not** considered in computing the cost-to-retail ratio), the ratio would be 50% ($10.00/$20.00) and ending inventory would be $6.00 ($12.00 × .50).

The inventory valuation of $6.00 reflects two inventory items, one inventoried at $5.00, the other at $1.00. Basically, the sale price was reduced from $10.00 to $2.00 and the cost reduced from $5.00 to $1.00.[14] To approximate the lower of cost or market, therefore, the **cost-to-retail ratio** must be established by dividing the cost of goods available by the sum of the original retail price of these goods plus the net markups; the markdowns and markdown cancellations are excluded. The basic format for the retail inventory method using the lower of cost or market approach is shown in Illustration 9-20 using the In-Fashion Stores information.

---

[14]This figure is really not market (replacement cost), but is net realizable value less the normal margin that is allowed. In other words, the sale price of the goods written down is $2.00, but subtracting a normal margin of 50% ($5.00 cost, $10 price), the figure becomes $1.00.

ILLUSTRATION 9-20
Comprehensive
Conventional Retail
Inventory Method Format

In-Fashion Stores Inc.			
		Cost	Retail
Beginning inventory		$ 500.00	$ 1,000.00
Purchases (net)		20,000.00	35,000.00
Totals		20,500.00	36,000.00
Add net markups—			
Markups	$3,000.00		
Markup cancellations	1,000.00		2,000.00
Totals		$20,500.00 ⟵ ⟶	38,000.00
Deduct net markdowns—			
Markdowns	2,500.00		
Markdown cancellations	2,000.00		500.00
Sales price of goods available			37,500.00
Deduct sales (net)			25,000.00
Ending inventory, at retail			$12,500.00

Cost-to-retail ratio $= \dfrac{\text{cost of goods available}}{\text{original retail price of goods available, plus net markups}}$

$= \dfrac{\$20,500}{\$38,000} = 53.9\%$

Ending inventory at lower of cost or market (53.9% × $12,500.00) $ 6,737.50

Because an averaging effect occurs, an exact lower of cost or market inventory valuation is ordinarily not obtained, but an adequate approximation can be achieved. In contrast, adding net markups **and** deducting net markdowns yields **approximate cost.**

SPECIAL ITEMS RELATING TO RETAIL METHOD

The retail inventory method becomes more complicated when such items as freight-in, purchase returns and allowances, and purchase discounts are involved. **Freight costs** are treated as a part of the purchase cost; **purchase returns and allowances** are ordinarily considered both as a reduction of the price at cost and retail; and **purchase discounts** usually are considered as a reduction of the cost of purchases. When the purchase allowance is not reflected by a reduction in the selling price, no adjustment is made to the retail column. In short, the treatment for the items affecting the cost column of the retail inventory approach follows the computation for cost of goods available for sale.

Note also that **sales returns and allowances** are considered as proper adjustments to gross sales; **sales discounts,** however, are not recognized when sales are recorded gross. To adjust for the sales discount account in such a situation would provide an ending inventory figure at retail that would be overvalued.

In addition, a number of special items require careful analysis. **Transfers-in** from another department, for example, should be reported in the same way as purchases from an outside enterprise. **Normal shortages** (breakage, damage, theft, shrinkage) should reduce the retail column because these goods are no longer available for sale. Such costs are reflected in the selling price because a certain amount of shortage is considered normal in a retail enterprise. As a result, this amount is not considered in computing the cost to retail percentage. Rather, it is shown as a deduction similar to sales to arrive at ending inventory at retail. **Abnormal shortages** should be deducted from both the cost and retail columns and reported as a special inventory amount or as a loss. To do otherwise distorts the cost-to-retail ratio and overstates ending inventory. Finally, companies often provide their employees with special discounts to encourage loyalty, better performance, and so on. **Employee discounts** should be deducted from the retail column in the same way as sales. These discounts should not be considered in the cost-to-retail percentage because they do not reflect an overall change in the selling price.

Illustration 9-21 shows some of these concepts. The company, Feminine Executive Apparel, determines its inventory using the conventional retail inventory method.

ILLUSTRATION 9-21
Conventional Retail
Inventory Method—
Special Items Included

Feminine Executive Apparel		
	Cost	Retail
Beginning inventory	$ 1,000	$ 1,800
Purchases	30,000	60,000
Freight-in	600	—
Purchase returns	(1,500)	(3,000)
Totals	30,100	58,800
Net markups		9,000
Abnormal shortage	(1,200)	(2,000)
Totals	$28,900 ⟷	65,800
Deduct:		
Net markdowns		1,400
Sales	$36,000	
Sales returns	(900)	35,100
Employee discounts		800
Normal shortage		1,300
		$27,200

Cost-to-retail ratio $= \dfrac{\$28,900}{\$65,800} = 43.9\%$

Ending inventory at lower of cost or market (43.9% × $27,200) = $\underline{\$11,940.80}$

APPRAISAL OF RETAIL INVENTORY METHOD

The retail inventory method of computing inventory is used widely (1) to permit the computation of net income without a physical count of inventory, (2) as a control measure in determining inventory shortages, (3) in regulating quantities of merchandise on hand, and (4) for insurance information.

One characteristic of the retail inventory method is that it **has an averaging effect on varying rates of gross profit.** When applied to an entire business where rates of gross profit vary among departments, no allowance is made for possible distortion of results because of such differences. Some companies refine the retail method under such conditions by computing inventory separately by departments or by classes of merchandise with similar gross profits. In addition, the reliability of this method assumes that the distribution of items in inventory is similar to the "mix" in the total goods available for sale.

▶ FINANCIAL STATEMENT PRESENTATION OF INVENTORIES

OBJECTIVE 7

Describe financial statement presentation of inventories.

Accounting standards require financial statement disclosure of the composition of the inventory, the inventory financing, and the inventory costing methods employed. The standards also require the consistent application of costing methods from one period to another.

Manufacturers should report the inventory composition either in the balance sheet or in a separate schedule in the notes. The relative mix of raw materials, work in process, and finished goods is important in assessing liquidity and in computing the stage of inventory completion.

Significant or unusual financing arrangements relating to inventories may require note disclosure. Examples are: transactions with related parties, product financing arrangements, firm purchase commitments, involuntary liquidation of LIFO inventories, and pledging of inventories as collateral. Inventories pledged as collateral for a loan should be presented in the Current Asset section rather than as an offset to the liability.

The basis upon which inventory amounts are stated (lower of cost or market) and the method used in determining cost (LIFO, FIFO, average cost, etc.) should also be reported. For example, the annual report of Mumford of Wyoming contains the following disclosures:

Mumford of Wyoming	
Note A: Significant Accounting Policies	
Live feeder cattle and feed—last-in, first-out (LIFO) cost, which is below approximate market	$854,800
Live range cattle—lower of principally identified cost or market	$1,240,500
Live sheep and supplies—lower of first-in, first-out (FIFO) cost or market	$674,000
Dressed meat and by-products—principally at market less allowances for distribution and selling expenses	$362,630

The preceding illustration shows that a company can use different pricing methods for different elements of its inventory. If Mumford changes the method of pricing any of its inventory elements, a change in accounting principle must be reported. For example, if Mumford changes its method of accounting for live sheep from FIFO to average cost, this change, along with the effect on income, should be separately reported in the financial statements. Changes in accounting principle require an explanatory paragraph in the auditor's report describing the change in method.

American Brands, Inc. reported its inventories in its Annual Report as follows (note the "trade practice" followed in classifying inventories among the current assets):

INTERNATIONAL INSIGHT

In Switzerland inventory may be reported on the balance sheet at amounts substantially (one-third or more) below cost or market due to provisions of the tax code. Further, Swiss accounting principles do not require any specific disclosures related to inventories.

American Brands, Inc.	
Current assets	
Inventories (Note 2)	
Leaf tobacco	$ 563,424,000
Bulk whiskey	232,759,000
Other raw materials, supplies and work in process	238,906,000
Finished products	658,326,000
	1,693,415,000
Note 2: Inventories	
Inventories are priced at the lower of cost (average; first-in, first-out; and minor amounts at last-in, first-out) or market. In accordance with generally recognized trade practice, the leaf tobacco and bulk whiskey inventories are classified as current assets, although part of such inventories due to the duration of the aging process, ordinarily will not be sold within one year.	

The following inventory disclosures by Newmont Gold Company reveal the application of different bases of valuation, including market value, for different classifications of inventory.

Newmont Gold Company		
Current assets		
Inventories (Note 2)		$44,303,000
Noncurrent assets		
Inventories—ore in stockpiles (Note 2)		$5,250,000
Note 2: Inventories		
Inventories included in current assets at December 31 were:		
Ore and in-process inventory	$11,303,000	
Gold bullion and gold precipitates	24,209,000	
Materials and supplies	8,791,000	
	$44,303,000	

Ore and in-process inventory and materials and supplies are stated at the lower of average cost or net realizable value. Gold bullion and gold precipitates are stated at market value, less a provision for estimated refining and delivery charges. Expenditures capitalized as ore and in-process inventory include labor, material and other production costs.

Noncurrent inventories are stated at the lower of average cost or net realizable value and represent ore in stockpiles anticipated to be processed in future years.

Georgia-Pacific Corporation chose to report in its balance sheet the dollar amounts for the major inventory classes and to disclose information relative to the inventory basis of valuation and the primary assumed flow method in its note "Summary of Significant Accounting Policies" (see balance sheet on page 221 and Note 1 on pages 222–223 of the Specimen Financial Statements, Appendix 5–A).

KEY TERMS

conventional retail inventory method, 448

cost-to-retail ratio, 448

designated market value, 434

gross profit method, 443

gross profit percentage, 443

hedging, 442

lower (floor) limit, 433

lower of cost or market (LCM), 433

lump sum (basket) purchase, 440

markdown cancellations, 446

markdowns, 446

market (for LCM), 433

markup, 446

markup cancellations, 446

net realizable value (NRV), 433

net realizable value less a normal profit margin, 433

purchase commitments, 440

retail inventory method, 445

upper (ceiling) limit, 433

▶ SUMMARY OF LEARNING OBJECTIVES ◀

1. **Explain and apply the lower of cost or market rule.** If inventory declines in value below its original cost for whatever reason, the inventory should be written down to reflect this loss. The general rule is that the historical cost principle is abandoned when the future utility (revenue-producing ability) of the asset is no longer as great as its original cost.

2. **Identify when inventories are valued at net realizable value.** Inventories are valued at net realizable value when (1) there is a controlled market with a quoted price applicable to all quantities, (2) no significant costs of disposal are involved, and (3) the cost figures are too difficult to obtain.

3. **Explain when the relative sales value method is used to value inventories.** When a group of varying units is purchased at a single lump sum price, a so-called basket purchase, the total purchase price may be allocated to the individual items on the basis of relative sales value.

4. **Explain accounting issues related to purchase commitments.** Accounting for purchase commitments is controversial. Some argue that these contracts should be reported as assets and liabilities at the time the contract is signed; others believe that the present recognition at the delivery date is most appropriate. The FASB neither excludes nor recommends the recording of assets and liabilities for purchase commitments but notes that if they were recorded at the time of commitment, "the nature of the loss and the valuation account that records it when the price falls would be clearly seen."

5. **Determine ending inventory by applying the gross profit method.** The steps to determine ending inventory by applying the gross profit method are as follows: (1) Compute the gross profit percentage on selling price; (2) compute gross profit by multiplying total sales by the gross profit percentage; (3) compute cost of goods sold by subtracting gross profit from total goods available for sale; (4) compute ending inventory by subtracting cost of goods sold from total goods available for sale.

6. **Determine ending inventory by applying the retail inventory method.** The steps to determine ending inventory by applying the conventional retail method are: (1) the sales for the period are deducted from the retail value of the goods available for sale to produce an estimated inventory at retail; (2) the ratio of cost to retail for all goods passing through a department or firm is then determined by dividing the total goods available for sale at cost by the total goods available at retail; (3) the inventory valued at retail is converted to approximate cost by applying the cost-to-retail ratio.

7. **Describe financial statement presentation of inventories.** Accounting standards require financial statement disclosure of: (1) the composition of the inventory (in a balance sheet or a separate schedule in the notes); (2) significant or unusual inventory financing arrangements; and (3) inventory costing methods employed (which may differ for different elements of inventory). Accounting standards also require the consistent application of costing methods from one period to another.

APPENDIX 9-A

LIFO RETAIL METHODS

Many retailers and accounting theorists have argued that the conventional retail method follows a flow assumption that does not match current cost against current revenues. They suggest that a LIFO assumption be adopted to obtain a better matching of costs and revenues.

▶ LIFO RETAIL METHODS

Many retail establishments have already changed from the more conventional treatment to the **LIFO retail method** simply for the tax advantages associated with valuing inventories on a LIFO basis.

The application of LIFO retail is made under two assumptions: (1) stable prices and (2) fluctuating prices.

STABLE PRICES—LIFO RETAIL METHOD

Computing the final inventory balance assuming a LIFO flow is much more complex than the calculation for the conventional retail method. Because the LIFO method is a cost method, not a cost or market approach, **both the markups and the markdowns must be considered** in obtaining the proper cost-to-retail percentage. Furthermore, since the LIFO method is concerned only with the additional layer, or the amount that should be subtracted from the previous layer, the beginning inventory is excluded from the cost-to-retail percentage. **A major assumption of the LIFO retail method—one that is debatable—is that the markups and markdowns apply only to the goods purchased during the current period and not to the beginning inventory.** In addition, to simplify the accounting, we have assumed that the price level has remained unchanged. The concepts are presented in Illustration 9A-1.

OBJECTIVE 8

After studying Appendix 9-A, you should be able to: Determine ending inventory by applying the LIFO retail method.

	Cost	Retail
Beginning inventory—1995	$ 27,000	$ 45,000
Net purchases during the period	346,500	480,000
Net markups		20,000
Net markdowns		(5,000)
Total (excluding beginning inventory)	346,500 ⟷	495,000
Total (including beginning inventory)	$373,500	540,000
Net sales during the period		(484,000)
Ending inventory at retail		$ 56,000
Establishment of cost-to-retail percentage under assumptions of LIFO retail ($346,500 ÷ $495,000)		70%

ILLUSTRATION 9A-1
LIFO Retail Method— Stable Prices

Illustration 9A-2 indicates that the inventory is composed of two layers: the beginning inventory and the additional increase that occurred in the inventory this period (1995). If we start the next period (1996), the beginning inventory will be composed of those two layers, and if an increase in inventory occurs again, an additional layer will be added.

ILLUSTRATION 9A-2
Ending Inventory at LIFO Cost, 1995—Stable Prices

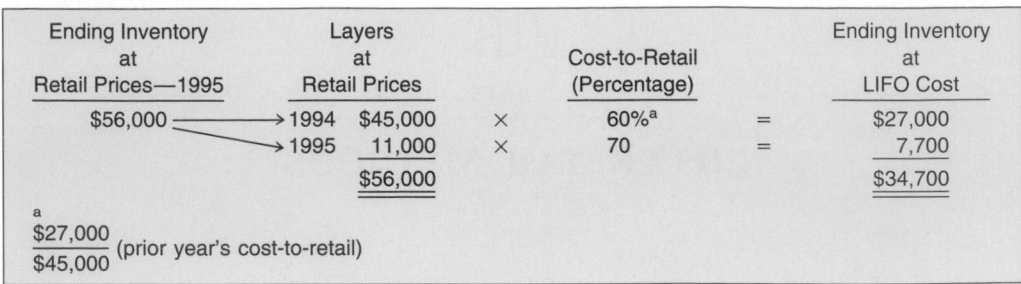

Ending Inventory at Retail Prices—1995	Layers at Retail Prices			Cost-to-Retail (Percentage)		Ending Inventory at LIFO Cost
$56,000	→ 1994	$45,000	×	60%[a]	=	$27,000
	→ 1995	11,000	×	70	=	7,700
		$56,000				$34,700

a
$\dfrac{\$27,000}{\$45,000}$ (prior year's cost-to-retail)

However, if the final inventory figure is below the beginning inventory, it is necessary to reduce the beginning inventory starting with the most recent layer. For example, assume that the ending inventory for 1996 at retail is $50,000. The computation of the ending inventory at cost is shown below.

ILLUSTRATION 9A-3
Ending Inventory at LIFO Cost, 1996—Stable Prices

Ending Inventory at Retail Prices—1996	Layers at Retail Prices			Cost-to-Retail (Percentage)		Ending Inventory at LIFO Cost
$50,000	→ 1994	$45,000	×	60%	=	$27,000
	→ 1995	5,000	×	70	=	3,500
		$50,000				$30,500

Notice that the 1995 layer is reduced from $11,000 to $5,000.

FLUCTUATING PRICES—DOLLAR-VALUE LIFO RETAIL METHOD

The computation of the LIFO retail method was simplified in the previous illustration because changes in the selling price of the inventory were ignored. Let us now assume that a change in the price level of the inventories occurs (as is usual). If the price level does change, **the price change must be eliminated** because we are measuring the real increase in inventory, not the dollar increase.

To illustrate, assume that the beginning inventory had a retail market value of $10,000 and the ending inventory a retail market value of $15,000. If the price level has risen from 100 to 125, it is inappropriate to suggest that a real increase in inventory of $5,000 has occurred. Instead, the ending inventory at retail should be deflated as indicated by the computation shown below.

ILLUSTRATION 9A-4
Ending Inventory at Retail—Deflated and Restated

Ending inventory at retail (deflated) $15,000 ÷ 1.25*	$12,000	
Beginning inventory at retail	10,000	
Real increase in inventory at retail	$ 2,000	
Ending inventory at retail on LIFO basis:		
First layer	$10,000	
Second layer ($2,000 × 1.25)	2,500	$12,500
*1.25 = 125 ÷ 100		

This approach is essentially the dollar-value LIFO method previously discussed in Chapter 8. In computing the LIFO inventory under a dollar-value LIFO approach, the dollar increase in inventory is found and deflated to beginning-of-the-year prices to determine whether actual increases or decreases in quantity have occurred. If an increase in quantities occurs, this increase is priced at the new index to compute the value of the new layer. If a decrease in quantities happens, it is subtracted from the most recent layers to the extent necessary.

The following computations, taken from Illustration 9A-4, illustrate the differences between the **dollar-value LIFO retail method** and the regular LIFO retail approach. Assume that the current 1995 price index is 112 (prior year = 100) and that the inventory ($56,000) has remained unchanged. In comparing these two illustrations, note that the computations involved in finding the cost-to-retail percentage are exactly the same. However, the dollar-value method determines the increase that has occurred in the inventory in terms of base-year prices.

	Cost	Retail
Beginning inventory—1995	$ 27,000	$ 45,000
Net purchases during the period	346,500	480,000
Net markups		20,000
Net markdowns		(5,000)
Total (excluding beginning inventory)	346,500 ⟶	⟶ 495,000
Total (including beginning inventory)	$373,500	540,000
Net sales during the period at retail		(484,000)
Ending inventory at retail		$ 56,000
Establishment of cost-to-retail percentage under assumptions of LIFO retail ($346,500 ÷ $495,000)		70%
A. Ending inventory at retail prices deflated to base year prices $56,000 ÷ 112 =		$50,000
B. Beginning inventory (retail) at base-year prices		45,000
C. Inventory increase (retail) from beginning of period		$ 5,000

ILLUSTRATION 9A-5
Dollar-Value LIFO Retail Method—Fluctuating Prices

From this information, we compute the inventory amount at cost:

Ending Inventory at Base-Year Retail Prices—1995	Layers at Base-Year Retail Prices			Price Index (percentage)		Cost-to-Retail (percentage)		Ending Inventory at LIFO Cost
$50,000 ⟶	1994	$45,000	×	100%	×	60%	=	$27,000
⟶	1995	5,000	×	112	×	70	=	3,920
		$50,000						$30,920

ILLUSTRATION 9A-6
Ending Inventory at LIFO Cost, 1995—Fluctuating Prices

As illustrated above, layers of a particular year must be restated to the prices in effect in the year when the layer was added before the conversion to cost takes place.

Note the difference between the LIFO approach (stable prices) and the dollar-value LIFO method as indicated below:

	LIFO (stable prices)	LIFO (fluctuating prices)
Beginning inventory	$27,000	$27,000
Increment	7,700	3,920
Ending inventory	$34,700	$30,920

ILLUSTRATION 9A-7
Comparison of Effect of Price Assumptions

The difference of $3,780 ($34,700 − $30,920) is a result of an increase in the price of goods, not of an increase in the quantity of goods.

SUBSEQUENT ADJUSTMENTS UNDER DOLLAR-VALUE LIFO RETAIL

The dollar-value LIFO retail method follows the same procedures in subsequent periods as the traditional dollar-value method discussed in Chapter 8. That is, when a real increase in inventory occurs, a new layer is added. Using the data from the previous illustration, assume that the retail value of the 1996 ending inventory at current prices is $64,800, the 1996 price index is 120% of base-year, and the cost-to-retail percentage is 75%. In base-year dollars, the ending inventory is therefore $54,000 ($64,800/120%). The computation of the ending inventory at LIFO cost is as follows:

ILLUSTRATION 9A-8
Ending Inventory at LIFO Cost, 1996—Fluctuating Prices

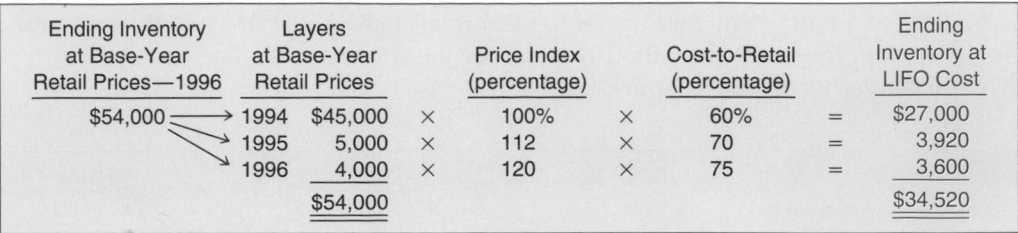

Ending Inventory at Base-Year Retail Prices—1996	Layers at Base-Year Retail Prices		Price Index (percentage)		Cost-to-Retail (percentage)		Ending Inventory at LIFO Cost
$54,000 →	1994	$45,000	×	100%	×	60%	=	$27,000
	1995	5,000	×	112	×	70	=	3,920
	1996	4,000	×	120	×	75	=	3,600
		$54,000						$34,520

Conversely, when a real decrease in inventory develops, previous layers are "peeled off" at prices in existence when the layers were added. To illustrate, assume that in 1996 the ending inventory in base-year prices is $48,000. The computation of the LIFO inventory is as follows:

ILLUSTRATION 9A-9
Ending Inventory at LIFO Cost, 1996, Fluctuating Prices

Ending Inventory at Base-Year Retail Prices—1996	Layers at Base-Year Retail Prices		Price Index (percentage)		Cost-to-Retail (percentage)		Ending Inventory at LIFO Cost
$48,000 →	1994	$45,000	×	100%	×	60%	=	$27,000
	1995	3,000	×	112	×	70	=	2,352
		$48,000						$29,352

The advantages and disadvantages of the lower of cost or market method (conventional retail) versus LIFO retail are the same for retail as for nonretail operations. As a practical matter, the selection of the retail inventory method to be used often involves determining which method provides a lower taxable income. Although it might appear that retail LIFO will provide the lower taxable income in a period of rising prices, such is not always the case. LIFO will provide an approximate current cost matching, but the ending inventory is stated at cost. The conventional retail method may have a large write-off because of the use of the lower of cost or market approach which may offset the LIFO current cost matching.

► CHANGING FROM CONVENTIONAL RETAIL TO LIFO

As discussed in Chapter 8, Appendix 8-A, the initial adoption of LIFO is problematic. When changing from the conventional retail method to LIFO retail, neither a cumulative adjustment nor a retroactive adjustment can be made easily. Because conventional retail is a lower of cost or market approach, the beginning inventory must be restated to a cost basis. The usual approach is to compute the cost basis from the purchases of the prior year, adjusted for both markups and markdowns.[1] To illustrate, assume that Clark Clothing Store employs the conventional retail method but wishes to change to the LIFO retail method beginning in 1996. The amounts shown by the firm's books are as follows:

	At Cost	At Retail
Inventory, January 1, 1995	$ 5,210	$ 15,000
Net purchases in 1995	47,250	100,000
Net markups in 1995		7,000
Net markdowns in 1995		2,000
Sales in 1995		95,000

Ending inventory under the **conventional retail method** for 1995 is computed as shown in Illustration 9A-10.

---

[1]A logical question to ask is, "Why are only the purchases from the prior period considered and not also the beginning inventory?" Apparently the IRS believes that "the purchases only approach" provides a more reasonable cost basis. The IRS position is debatable. However, for our purposes, it seems appropriate to use the purchases only approach.

	Cost	Retail
Inventory January 1, 1995	$ 5,210	$ 15,000
Net purchases	47,250	100,000
Net additional markups		7,000
	$52,460	122,000
Net markdowns		(2,000)
Sales		(95,000)
Ending inventory at retail		$ 25,000
Establishment of cost-to-retail percentage ($52,460 ÷ $122,000)	43%	
December 31, 1995, inventory at cost		
Inventory at retail		$ 25,000
Cost-to-retail ratio		43%
Inventory at cost under conventional retail		$ 10,750

The ending inventory for 1995 under the **LIFO retail method** can then be quickly approximated in the following way.

December 31, 1995 inventory at LIFO cost

	Retail	Ratio	LIFO
Ending inventory	$25,000 ×	45%[a] =	$11,250

[a]The cost-to-retail ratio was computed as follows:

$$\frac{\text{Net purchases at cost}}{\text{Net purchases at retail plus markups less markdowns}} = \frac{\$47,250}{\$100,000 + \$7,000 - \$2,000} = 45\%$$

The difference of $500 ($11,250 − $10,750) between the LIFO retail method and the conventional retail method in the ending inventory for 1995 is the amount by which the beginning inventory for 1996 must be adjusted. The entry to adjust the inventory to a cost basis is as follows:

Inventory	500	
Adjustment to Record Inventory at Cost		500

► **SUMMARY OF LEARNING OBJECTIVE FOR APPENDIX 9-A** ◄

8. **Determine ending inventory by applying the LIFO retail methods.** The application of LIFO retail is made under two assumptions: stable prices and fluctuating prices. *Procedures under stable prices:* (a) Because the LIFO method is a cost method, both the markups and the markdowns must be considered in obtaining the proper cost-to-retail percentage. (b) Since the LIFO method is concerned only with the additional layer, or the amount that should be subtracted from the previous layer, the beginning inventory is excluded from the cost-to-retail percentage. (c) The markups and markdowns apply only to the goods purchased during the current period and not to the beginning inventory. *Procedures under fluctuating prices:* The steps are the same as for stable prices except that in computing the LIFO inventory under a dollar-value LIFO approach, the dollar increase in inventory is found and deflated to beginning-of-the-year prices to determine whether actual increases or decreases in quantity have occurred. If quantities increase, this increase is priced at the new index to compute the new layer. If quantities decrease, the decrease is subtracted from the most recent layers to the extent necessary.

Note: All **asterisked** Questions, Exercises, Problems, and Cases relate to material contained in the appendix to each chapter.

QUESTIONS

1. Where there is evidence that the utility of inventory goods, as part of their disposal in the ordinary course of business, will be less than cost, what is the proper accounting treatment?

2. Why are inventories valued at the lower of cost or market? What are the arguments against the use of the lower of cost or market method of valuing inventories?

3. What approaches may the accountant employ in applying the lower of cost or market procedure? Which approach is normally used and why?

4. In some instances accounting principles require a departure from valuing inventories at cost alone. Determine the proper unit inventory price in the following cases:

	Cases				
	1	2	3	4	5
Cost	$15.90	$15.90	$15.90	$15.90	$15.90
Net realizable value	14.40	19.20	15.20	10.40	16.40
Net realizable value less normal profit	12.80	17.60	13.60	8.80	14.80
Market (replacement cost)	14.80	17.20	12.80	9.60	16.80

5. What method(s) might be used in the accounts to record a loss due to a price decline in the inventories? Discuss.

6. What factors might call for inventory valuation at sales prices (net realizable value or market price)?

7. Under what circumstances is relative sales value an appropriate basis for determining the price assigned to inventory?

8. Define standard costs. What are the advantages of a standard cost system? Present arguments in support of each of the following three methods of treating standard cost variances (actual costs— standard costs) for purposes of financial reporting:
   (a) They may be allocated between inventories and cost of goods sold.
   (b) They may be carried as deferred charges or credits on the balance sheet.
   (c) They may appear as charges or credits on the income statement.

9. At December 31, 1996, Jose Hernandez Co. has outstanding purchase commitments for purchase of 150,000 gallons, at $6.40 per gallon, of a raw material to be used in its manufacturing process. The company prices its raw material inventory at cost or market, whichever is lower. Assuming that the market price as of December 31, 1996 is $5.80, how would you treat this situation in the accounts?

10. What are the major uses of the gross margin method?

11. Distinguish between gross profit as a percentage of cost and gross profit as a percentage of sales price. Convert the following gross profit percentages based on cost to gross profit percentages based on sales price: 20% and 33⅓%. Convert the following gross profit percentages based on sales price to gross profit percentages based on cost: 33⅓% and 60%.

12. Bart Taylor Co. with annual net sales of $5 million maintains a markup of 25% based on cost. Taylor's expenses average 15% of net sales. What is Taylor's gross profit and net profit in dollars?

13. A fire destroys all of the merchandise of Pike Company on February 10, 1996. Presented below is information compiled up to the date of the fire.

Inventory January 1, 1996	$ 400,000
Sales to February 10, 1996	1,700,000
Purchases to February 10, 1996	1,140,000
Freight-in to February 10, 1996	60,000
Rate of gross profit on selling price	40%

What is the approximate inventory on February 10, 1996?

14. What conditions must exist for the retail inventory method to provide valid results?

15. The retail inventory method yields results that are essentially the same as those yielded by the lower of cost or market method. Explain. Prepare an illustration of how the retail inventory method reduces inventory to market.

16. (a) Determine the ending inventory under the conventional retail method for the furniture department of Logan Department Stores from the following data.

	Cost	Retail
Inventory Jan. 1	$ 149,000	$ 283,500
Purchases	1,400,000	2,160,000
Freight-in	70,000	
Markups, net		92,000
Markdowns, net		48,000
Sales		2,244,000

(b) If the results of a physical inventory indicated an inventory at retail of $240,000, what inferences would you draw?

17. Gringo Company reported inventory in its balance sheet as follows:

Inventories $140,800,506

What additional disclosures might be necessary to present the inventory fairly?

*18. What modifications to the conventional retail method are necessary to approximate a LIFO retail flow?

EXERCISES

E9-1 (Lower of Cost or Market) The inventory of Boitano Company on December 31, 1996, consists of these items:

Part No.	Quantity	Cost per Unit	Cost to Replace per Unit
110	1,000	$ 90	$100
111	600	60	52
112	500	80	76
113	200	170	180
120	400	205	208
121ᵃ	1,600	16	14
122	200	240	235

ᵃPart No. 121 is obsolete and has a realizable value of $0.20 each as scrap.

Instructions
(a) Determine the inventory as of December 31, 1996, by the method of cost or market, whichever is lower, applying this method directly to each item.
(b) Determine the inventory by cost or market, whichever is lower, applying the method to the total of the inventory.

E9-2 (Lower of Cost or Market) N. Kerrigan Company uses the lower of cost or market method, on an individual-item basis, in pricing its inventory items. The inventory at December 31, 1996, consists of products D, E, F, G, H, and I. Relevant per-unit data for these products appear below:

	Item D	Item E	Item F	Item G	Item H	Item I
Estimated selling price	$120	$110	$90	$90	$110	$90
Cost	80	80	80	80	50	36
Replacement cost	120	70	70	30	70	30
Estimated selling expense	30	30	30	30	30	30
Normal profit	20	20	20	20	20	20

Instructions
Using the lower of cost or market rule, determine the proper unit value for balance sheet reporting purposes at December 31, 1996, for each of the inventory items above.

E9-3 (Lower of Cost or Market) Sonja Henie Company follows the practice of pricing its inventory at the lower of cost or market, on an individual-item basis.

Item No.	Quantity	Cost per Unit	Cost to Replace	Estimated Selling Price	Cost of Completion and Disposal	Normal Profit
1320	900	$3.20	$3.00	$4.50	$.35	$1.25
1333	1,200	2.70	2.30	3.50	.50	.50
1426	800	4.50	3.70	5.00	.40	1.00
1437	1,000	3.60	3.10	3.20	.25	.90
1510	700	2.25	2.00	3.25	.80	.60
1522	500	3.00	2.70	3.80	.40	.50
1573	3,000	1.80	1.60	2.50	.75	.50
1626	1,100	4.70	5.20	6.00	.50	1.00

Instructions
From the information above, determine the amount of Henie Company inventory.

E9-4 (Lower of Cost or Market—Journal Entries) Eric Heiden Company determined its ending inventory at cost and at lower of cost or market at December 31, 1995, and December 31, 1996. This information is presented below:

	Cost	Lower of cost or market
12/31/95	$346,000	$325,000
12/31/96	410,000	395,000

Instructions
(a) Prepare the journal entries required at 12/31/95 and 12/31/96, assuming that the inventory is recorded at market, and a periodic inventory system (direct method) is used.
(b) Prepare journal entries required at 12/31/95 and 12/31/96, assuming that the inventory is recorded at cost and an allowance account is adjusted at each year-end under a periodic system.
(c) Which of the two methods above provides the higher net income in each year?

E9-5 (Lower of Cost or Market—Valuation Account) Presented below is information related to Bonnie Blair Enterprises:

	Jan. 31	Feb. 28	Mar. 31	Apr. 30
Inventory at cost	$15,000	$15,100	$17,000	$13,000
Inventory at the lower of cost or market	14,500	13,600	15,600	12,300
Purchases for the month		20,000	24,000	26,000
Sales for the month		29,000	35,000	40,000

Instructions
(a) From the information prepare (as far as the data permit) monthly income statements in columnar form for February, March, and April. The inventory is to be shown in the statement at cost, the gain or loss due to market fluctuations is to be shown separately, and a valuation account is to be set up for the difference between cost and the lower of cost or market.
(b) Prepare the journal entry required to establish the valuation account at January 31 and entries to adjust it monthly thereafter.

E9-6 (Lower of Cost or Market—Error Effect) Fleming Company uses the lower of cost or market method, on an individual-item basis, in pricing its inventory items. The inventory at December 31, 1995, included Product X. Relevant per-unit data for Product X appear below:

Estimated selling price	$45
Cost	40
Replacement cost	35
Estimated selling expense	15
Normal profit	10

There were 1,000 units of Product X on hand at December 31, 1995. Product X was incorrectly valued at $35 per unit for reporting purposes. All 1,000 units were sold in 1996.

Instructions
Compute the effect of this error on net income for 1995 and the effect on net income for 1996 and indicate the direction of the misstatement for each year.

E9-7 (Relative Sales Value Method) Corbett Realty Corporation purchased a tract of unimproved land for $55,000. This land was improved and subdivided into building lots at an additional cost of $28,070. These building lots were all of the same size but owing to differences in location were offered for sale at different prices as follows:

Group	No. of Lots	Price per Lot
1	9	$3,000
2	15	4,000
3	17	2,400

Operating expenses for the year allocated to this project total $18,200. Lots unsold at the year-end were as follows:

Group 1	5 lots
Group 2	7 lots
Group 3	2 lots

Instructions

At the end of the fiscal year Corbett Realty Corporation instructs you to arrive at the net income realized on this operation to date.

E9-8 (Relative Sales Value Method) Sullivan Furniture Company purchases, during 1996, a carload of wicker chairs. The manufacturer sells the chairs to Sullivan for a lump sum of $58,900, because it is discontinuing manufacturing operations and wishes to dispose of its entire stock. Three types of chairs are included in the carload. The three types and the estimated selling price for each are listed below.

Type	No. of Chairs	Estimated Selling Price Each
Lounge chairs	400	$90
Armchairs	300	80
Straight chairs	700	50

During 1996 Sullivan sells 200 lounge chairs, 100 armchairs, and 120 straight chairs.

Instructions

What is the amount of gross profit realized during 1996? What is the amount of inventory of unsold wicker chairs on December 31, 1996?

E9-9 (Purchase Commitments) George Foreman Company has been having difficulty obtaining key raw materials for its manufacturing process. The company therefore signed a long-term noncancelable purchase commitment with its largest supplier of this raw material on November 30, 1996, at an agreed price of $400,000. At December 31, 1996, the raw material had declined in price to $370,000.

Instructions

What entries would you make on December 31, 1996 to recognize these facts?

E9-10 (Purchase Commitments) At December 31, 1996, Gene Tunney Company has outstanding noncancelable purchase commitments for 40,000 gallons, at $3.00 per gallon, of raw material to be used in its manufacturing process. The company prices its raw material inventory at cost or market, whichever is lower.

Instructions

(a) Assuming that the market price as of December 31, 1996, is $3.30, how would this matter be treated in the accounts and statements? Explain.

(b) Assuming that the market price as of December 31, 1996, is $2.70, instead of $3.30, how would you treat this situation in the accounts and statements?

(c) Give the entry in January 1997, when the 40,000-gallon shipment is received, assuming that the situation given in (b) above existed at December 31, 1996, and that the market price in January 1997 was $2.70 per gallon. Give an explanation of your treatment.

E9-11 (Gross Profit Method) Each of the following gross profit percentages is expressed in terms of cost.

1. 20%.
2. 25%.
3. 33⅓%.
4. 50%.

Instructions

Indicate the gross profit percentage in terms of sales for each of the above.

E9-12 (Gross Profit Method) Floyd Patterson Company uses the gross profit method to estimate inventory for monthly reporting purposes. Presented below is information for the month of May:

Inventory, May 1	$ 160,000
Purchases (gross)	640,000
Freight-in	30,000
Sales	1,000,000
Sales returns	70,000
Purchase discounts	12,000

Instructions

(a) Compute the estimated inventory at May 31, assuming that the gross profit is 25% of sales.

(b) Compute the estimated inventory at May 31, assuming that the gross profit is 25% of cost.

E9-13 (Gross Profit Method) John Queensberry requires an estimate of the cost of goods lost by fire on March 9. Merchandise on hand on January 1 was $38,000. Purchases since January 1 were $72,000; freight-in, $3,400; purchase returns and allowances, $2,400. Sales are made at 33⅓% above cost and totaled $100,000 to March 9. Goods costing $7,700 were left undamaged by the fire; remaining goods were destroyed.

Instructions

(a) Compute the cost of goods destroyed.

(b) Compute the cost of goods destroyed, assuming that the gross profit is 33⅓% of sales.

E9-14 (Gross Profit Method) Sugar Ray Company lost most of its inventory in a fire in December just before the year-end physical inventory was taken. The corporation's books disclosed the following:

Beginning inventory	$170,000	Sales	$650,000
Purchases for the year	390,000	Sales returns	24,000
Purchase returns	30,000	Rate of gross margin on sales	40%

Merchandise with a selling price of $20,000 remained undamaged after the fire. Damaged merchandise with an original selling price of $15,000 had a net realizable value of $6,000.

Instructions

Compute the amount of the loss as a result of the fire, assuming that the corporation had no insurance coverage.

E9-15 (Gross Profit Method) You are called by Nadia Comaneci of Trampolines Inc. on July 16 and asked to prepare a claim for insurance as a result of a theft that took place the night before. You suggest that an inventory be taken immediately. The following data are available:

Inventory, July 1	$ 38,000
Purchases—goods placed in stock July 1–15	85,000
Sales—goods delivered to customers (gross)	116,000
Sales returns—goods returned to stock	4,000

Your client reports that the goods on hand on July 16 cost $29,000, but you determine that this figure includes goods of $6,000 received on a consignment basis. Your past records show that sales are made at approximately 40% over cost.

Instructions

Compute the claim against the insurance company.

E9-16 (Gross Profit Method) Becker Lumber Company handles three principal lines of merchandise with these varying rates of gross profit on cost:

Lumber	30%
Millwork	25%
Hardware and fittings	40%

On August 18, a fire destroyed the office, lumber shed, and a considerable portion of the lumber stacked in the yard. To file a report of loss for insurance purposes, the company must know what the inventories were immediately preceding the fire. No detail or perpetual inventory records of any kind were maintained. The only pertinent information you are able to obtain are the following facts from the general ledger, which was kept in a fireproof vault and thus escaped destruction.

	Lumber	Millwork	Hardware
Inventory, Jan. 1, 1996	$ 250,000	$ 90,000	$ 45,000
Purchases to Aug. 18, 1996	1,500,000	375,000	160,000
Sales to Aug. 18, 1996	2,080,000	500,000	210,000

Instructions

Submit your estimate of the inventory amounts immediately preceding the fire.

E9-17 (Gross Profit Method) Presented below is information related to Aggassi Corporation for the current year:

Beginning inventory	$ 600,000	
Purchases	1,500,000	
Total goods available for sale		$2,100,000
Sales		2,500,000

Instructions

Compute the ending inventory, assuming that (1) gross profit is 35% of sales; (2) gross profit is 25% of cost; (3) gross profit is 60% of cost; and (4) gross profit is 45% of sales.

E9-18 (Retail Inventory Method) Presented below is information related to Jimmy Conners Company:

	Cost	Retail
Beginning inventory	$ 58,000	$100,000
Purchases (net)	122,000	200,000

Net markups	10,345
Net markdowns	26,135
Sales	190,000

Instructions

(a) Compute the ending inventory at retail.

(b) Compute a cost-to-retail percentage (round to two decimals).
  1. Excluding both markups and markdowns.
  2. Excluding markups but including markdowns.
  3. Excluding markdowns but including markups.
  4. Including both markdowns and markups.

(c) Which of the methods in (b) above (1, 2, 3, or 4)
  1. Provides the most conservative estimate of ending inventory?
  2. Provides an approximation of lower of cost or market?
  3. Is used in the conventional retail method?

(d) Compute ending inventory at lower of cost or market (round to nearest dollar).

(e) Compute cost of goods sold based on (d).

(f) Compute gross margin based on (d).

E9-19 (Retail Inventory Method) Presented below is information related to Chris Evert Company.

	Cost	Retail
Beginning inventory	$ 200,000	$ 280,000
Purchases	1,400,000	2,140,000
Markups		95,000
Markup cancellations		15,000
Markdowns		35,000
Markdown cancellations		5,000
Sales		2,200,000

Instructions

Compute the inventory by the conventional retail inventory method.

E9-20 (Retail Inventory Method) The records of Lendl's Boutique report the following data for the month of April.

Sales	$99,000	Purchases (at cost)	$48,000
Sales returns	1,000	Purchases (at sales price)	88,000
Additional markups	10,000	Purchase returns (at cost)	2,000
Markup cancellations	1,500	Purchase returns (at sales price)	3,000
Markdowns	9,300	Beginning inventory (at cost)	30,000
Markdown cancellations	2,800	Beginning inventory (at sales price)	46,500
Freight on purchases	2,400		

Instructions

Compute the ending inventory by the conventional retail inventory method.

***E9-21 (Retail Inventory Method—Conventional and LIFO)** Helen Wills Company began operations on January 1, 1994, adopting the conventional retail inventory system. None of its merchandise was marked down in 1994 and, because there was no beginning inventory, its ending inventory for 1994 of $38,100 would have been the same under either the conventional retail system or the LIFO retail system. On December 31, 1995, the store management considers adopting the LIFO retail system, and desires to know how the December 31, 1995, inventory would appear under both systems. All pertinent data regarding purchases, sales, markups, and markdowns are shown below. There has been no change in the price level.

	Cost	Retail
Inventory, Jan. 1, 1995	$ 38,100	$ 60,000
Markdowns (net)		13,000
Markups (net)		22,000
Purchases (net)	130,900	178,000
Sales (net)		165,000

Instructions

Determine the cost of the 1995 ending inventory under both (1) the conventional retail method and (2) the LIFO retail method.

***E9-22 (Retail Inventory Method—Conventional and LIFO)** McEnroe Company began operations late in 1994 and adopted the conventional retail inventory method. Because there was no beginning inventory for 1994 and no markdowns during 1994, the ending inventory for 1994 was $14,000 under both the conventional retail method and the LIFO retail method. At the end of 1995, management wants to compare the results of applying the conventional and LIFO retail methods. There was no change in the price level during 1995. The following data are available for computations:

	Cost	Retail
Inventory, January 1, 1995	$14,000	$20,000
Sales		80,000
Net markups		9,000
Net markdowns		1,600
Purchases	58,800	81,000
Freight-in	7,500	
Estimated theft		3,000

Instructions

Compute the cost of the 1995 ending inventory under both (1) the conventional retail method and (2) the LIFO retail method.

*E9-23 (Dollar-Value LIFO Retail) You assemble the following information for Ashe Department Store, which computes its inventory under the dollar-value LIFO method.

	Cost	Retail
Inventory on January 1, 1996	$216,000	$300,000
Purchases	364,800	480,000
Increase in price level for year		9%

Instructions

Compute the cost of the inventory on December 31, 1996, assuming that the inventory at retail is (1) $288,850, (2) $354,250.

*E9-24 (Dollar-Value LIFO Retail) Presented below is information related to Althea Gibson Corporation:

	Price Index	LIFO Cost	Retail
Inventory on December 31, 1996 when dollar-value LIFO is adopted	100	$36,000	$74,500
Inventory, December 31, 1997	110	?	97,900

Instructions

Compute the ending inventory under the dollar-value LIFO method at December 31, 1997. The cost-to-retail ratio for 1997 was 60%.

*E9-25 (Conventional Retail and Dollar-Value LIFO Retail) Red Barber Corporation began operations on January 1, 1995, with a beginning inventory of $30,000 at cost and $50,000 at retail. The following information relates to 1995:

	Retail
Net purchases ($108,500 at cost)	$150,000
Net markups	10,000
Net markdowns	5,000
Sales	128,000

Instructions

(a) Assume Barber decided to adopt the conventional retail method. Compute the ending inventory to be reported in the balance sheet.

(b) Assume instead that Barber decides to adopt the dollar-value LIFO retail method. The appropriate price indexes are 100 at January 1 and 110 at December 31. Compute the ending inventory to be reported in the balance sheet.

(c) On the basis of the information in part (b), compute cost of goods sold.

*E9-26 (Dollar-Value LIFO Retail) The DiMaggio Corporation adopted the dollar-value LIFO retail inventory method on January 1, 1994. At that time the inventory had a cost of $55,000 and a retail price of $100,000. The following information is available:

	Year-End Inventory at Retail	Current Year Cost—Retail %	Year-End Price Index
1994	$118,720	57%	106
1995	138,750	60%	111
1996	124,200	61%	115
1997	162,500	58%	125

The price index at January 1, 1994 is 100.

Instructions

Compute the ending inventory at December 31 of the years 1994–1997. Round to the nearest dollar.

PROBLEMS

P9-1 (Lower of Cost or Market) Pete Company manufactures desks. Most of the company's desks are standard models and are sold on the basis of catalog prices. At December 31, 1996, the following finished desks appear in the company's inventory:

Finished desks	A	B	C	D
1996 catalog selling price	$450	$480	$900	$1,050
FIFO cost per inventory list 12/31/96	470	450	830	960
Estimated current cost to manufacture (at December 31, 1996, and early 1997)	460	440	720	1,000
Sales commissions and estimated other costs of disposal	50	60	90	130
1997 catalog selling price	500	550	900	1,200

The 1996 catalog was in effect through November, 1996, and the 1997 catalog is effective as of December 1, 1996. All catalog prices are net of the usual discounts. Generally, the company attempts to obtain a 20% gross margin on selling price and has usually been successful in doing so.

Instructions
At what amount should each of the four desks appear in the company's December 31, 1996, inventory, assuming that the company has adopted a lower of FIFO cost or market approach for valuation of inventories on an individual-item basis?

P9-2 (Lower of Cost or Market) Lombardi Home Improvement Company installs replacement siding, windows, and louvered glass doors for single family homes and condominium complexes in northern New Jersey and southern New York. The company is in the process of preparing its annual financial statements for the fiscal year ended May 31, 1995, and Dick Wolfe, controller for Lombardi, has gathered the following data concerning inventory.

At May 31, 1995, the balance in Lombardi's Raw Material Inventory account was $408,000, and the Allowance to Reduce Inventory to Market had a credit balance of $29,500. Wolfe summarized the relevant inventory cost and market data at May 31, 1995, in the schedule below.

Wolfe assigned Laura Salem, an intern from a local college, the task of calculating the amount that should appear on Lombardi's May 31, 1995, financial statements for inventory under the lower of cost or market rule as applied to each item in inventory. Salem expressed concern over departing from the cost principle.

	Cost	Replacement Cost	Sales Price	Net Realizable Value	Normal Profit
Aluminum siding	$ 70,000	$ 62,500	$ 64,000	$ 56,000	$ 5,100
Cedar shake siding	86,000	79,400	94,000	84,800	7,400
Louvered glass doors	112,000	124,000	186,400	168,300	18,500
Thermal windows	140,000	126,400	154,800	140,000	15,400
Total	$408,000	$392,300	$499,200	$449,100	$46,400

Instructions
(a) 1. Determine the proper balance in the Allowance to Reduce Inventory to Market at May 31, 1995.
    2. For the fiscal year ended May 31, 1995, determine the amount of the gain or loss that would be recorded due to the change in the Allowance to Reduce Inventory to Market.
(b) Explain the rationale for the use of the lower of cost or market rule as it applies to inventories.

(CMA adapted)

P9-3 (Lower of Cost or Market—Errors) Puebla Corporation, which began operations in 1993, always values its inventories at the current replacement cost. Its annual inventory figure is arrived at by taking a physical inventory and then pricing each item in the physical inventory at current prices determined from recent vendors' invoices or catalogs. Here is the condensed income statement for this company for the last four years.

	1993	1994	1995	1996
Sales	$850,000	$880,000	$950,000	$990,000
Cost of goods sold	560,000	590,000	630,000	650,000
Gross profit	290,000	290,000	320,000	340,000
Operating expenses	190,000	180,000	200,000	210,000
Income before income taxes	$100,000	$110,000	$120,000	$130,000

Instructions

(a) Do you see any objections to their procedure for valuing inventories?

(b) Assuming that the inventory at cost and as determined by the corporation at the end of each of the 4 years is as follows, restate the condensed income statements, using cost for inventories.

Ending Inventory	At Cost	As Determined by Company
1993	$130,000	$106,000
1994	140,000	110,000
1995	135,000	103,000
1996	150,000	129,000

P9-4 (Lower of Cost or Market) J. Weissmuller Company is a food wholesaler that supplies independent grocery stores in the immediate region. The company has a perpetual inventory system for all of its food products. The first-in, first-out (FIFO) method of inventory valuation is used to determine the cost of the inventory at the end of each month. Transactions and other related information regarding two of the items (instant coffee and sugar) carried by Weissmuller are given below for October 1995, the last month of Weissmuller's fiscal year.

	Instant Coffee	Sugar
Standard unit of packaging:	Case containing 24, one-pound jars	Baler containing 12, five-pound bags
Inventory, 10/1/95:	1,000 cases @ $60.20 per case	500 balers @ $6.50 per baler
Purchases:	1. 10/10/95—1,600 cases @ $62.10 per case plus freight of $480.	1. 10/5/95—850 balers @ $5.76 per baler plus freight of $320.
	2. 10/20/95—2,400 cases @ $64.00 per case plus freight of $480.	2. 10/16/95—640 balers @ $6.00 per baler plus freight of $320.
		3. 10/24/95—600 balers @ $6.20 per baler plus freight of $360.
Purchase terms:	2/10, net/30, f.o.b. shipping point	Net 30 days, f.o.b. shipping point
October sales:	3,700 cases @ $76.00 per case	2,000 balers @ $8.00 per baler
Returns and allowances:	A customer returned 50 cases that had been shipped by error. The customer's account was credited for $3,800.	As the October 16 purchase was unloaded, 20 balers were discovered damaged. A representative of the trucking firm confirmed the damage and the balers were discarded. Credit of $120 for the merchandise and $10 for the freight was received by Weissmuller.
Inventory values 10/31/95:		
• Net realizable value	$66.00 per case	$6.60 per baler
• Net realizable value less a normal profit of 15%	$56.10 per case	$5.61 per baler

Weissmuller's sales terms are 1/10, net/30, f.o.b. shipping point. Weissmuller records all purchases net of purchase discounts and takes all purchase discounts. The most recent quoted price for coffee is $60 per case and for sugar $6.10 per baler before freight and purchase discounts.

Instructions

(a) Calculate the number of units in inventory and the FIFO unit cost for instant coffee and sugar as of October 31, 1995.

(b) Weissmuller Company applies the lower of cost or market rule in valuing its year-end inventory. Calculate the total dollar amount of the inventory for instant coffee and sugar applying the lower of cost or market rule on an individual-product basis.

(c) Could Weissmuller Company apply the lower of cost or market rule to groups of products or the inventory as a whole rather than on an individual product basis? Explain your answer.

(CMA adapted)

P9-5 (Entries for Lower of Cost or Market—Direct and Allowance) Edmund Hillary Company determined its ending inventory at cost and at lower of cost or market at December 31, 1994, December 31, 1995, and December 31, 1996, as shown below:

	Cost	Lower of Cost or Market
12/31/94	$650,000	$650,000
12/31/95	780,000	725,000
12/31/96	900,000	830,000

Instructions

(a) Prepare the journal entries required at 12/31/95 and 12/31/96 assuming that a periodic inventory system and the direct method of adjusting to market is used.

(b) Prepare the journal entries required at 12/31/95 and 12/31/96 assuming that a periodic inventory is recorded at cost and reduced to market through the use of an allowance account (indirect method).

P9-6 (Gross Profit Method) Tenzing Company lost most of its inventory in a fire in December just before the year-end physical inventory was taken. Corporate records disclose the following:

Inventory (beginning)	$ 80,000	Sales	$415,000
Purchases	280,000	Sales returns	21,000
Purchase returns	28,000	Gross profit % based on	
		selling price	30%

Merchandise with a selling price of $30,000 remained undamaged after the fire, and damaged merchandise has a salvage value of $7,150. The company does not carry fire insurance on its inventory.

Instructions

Prepare a formal labeled schedule computing the fire loss incurred. (Do not use the retail inventory method.)

P9-7 (Gross Profit Method) Jim Thorpe Corporation is an importer and wholesaler. It purchases its merchandise from several suppliers and warehouses it until it is sold to consumers.

In conducting her audit for the year ended June 30, 1996, the corporation's CPA determined that the system of internal control was good. Accordingly, she observed the physical inventory at an interim date, May 31, 1996, instead of at year-end.

The following information was obtained from the general ledger.

Inventory, July 1, 1995	$ 120,000
Physical inventory, May 31, 1996	98,500
Sales for 11 months ended May 31, 1996	970,000
Sales for year ended June 30, 1996	1,060,000
Purchases for 11 months ended May 31, 1996 (before audit adjustments)	650,000
Purchases for year ended June 30, 1996 (before audit adjustments)	755,000

The CPA's audit disclosed the following information.

Shipments received in May and included in the physical inventory but recorded as June purchases	12,000
Shipments received in unsalable condition and excluded from physical inventory; credit memos had not been received nor had chargebacks to vendors been recorded:	
Total at May 31, 1996.	1,500
Total at June 30, 1996 (including the May unrecorded chargebacks).	2,000
Deposit made with vendor and charged to purchases in April, 1996. Product was shipped in July, 1996.	3,000
Deposit made with vendor and charged to purchases in May, 1996. Product was shipped, f.o.b. destination, on May 29, 1996, and was included in May 31, 1996, physical inventory as goods in transit.	6,500
Through the carelessness of the receiving department, a June shipment was damaged by rain. This shipment was later sold in June at its cost of $8,000.	

Instructions

In audit engagements in which interim physical inventories are observed, a frequently used auditing procedure is to test the reasonableness of the year-end inventory by the application of gross profit ratios.

Prepare in good form the following schedules:

(a) Computation of the gross profit ratio for 11 months ended May 31, 1996.

(b) Computation by the gross profit method of cost of goods sold during June, 1996.

(c) Computation by the gross profit method of June 30, 1996, inventory.

(AICPA adapted)

P9-8 (Gross Profit Method) On April 15, 1996, fire damaged the office and warehouse of Flojo Corporation. The only accounting record saved was the general ledger, from which the trial balance below was prepared.

Flojo Corporation
TRIAL BALANCE
March 31, 1996

Cash	$ 20,000
Accounts receivable	40,000
Inventory, December 31, 1995	75,000
Land	35,000

Building and equipment	110,000	
Accumulated depreciation		$ 41,300
Other assets	3,600	
Accounts payable		23,700
Other expense accruals		10,200
Capital stock		100,000
Retained earnings		52,000
Sales		135,000
Purchases	52,000	
Other expenses	26,600	
	$362,200	$362,200

The following data and information have been gathered:

1. The fiscal year of the corporation ends on December 31.
2. An examination of the April bank statement and canceled checks revealed that checks written during the period April 1–15 totaled $13,000: $5,700 paid to accounts payable as of March 31, $3,400 for April merchandise shipments, and $3,900 paid for other expenses. Deposits during the same period amounted to $12,950, which consisted of receipts on account from customers with the exception of a $950 refund from a vendor for merchandise returned in April.
3. Correspondence with suppliers revealed unrecorded obligations at April 15 of $10,600 for April merchandise shipments, including $2,300 for shipments in transit (FOB Shipping Point) on that date.
4. Customers acknowledged indebtedness of $36,000 at April 15, 1996. It was also estimated that customers owed another $8,000 that will never be acknowledged or recovered. Of the acknowledged indebtedness, $600 will probably be uncollectible.
5. The companies insuring the inventory agreed that the corporation's fire-loss claim should be based on the assumption that the overall gross profit ratio for the past 2 years was in effect during the current year. The corporation's audited financial statements disclosed this information:

	Year Ended December 31	
	1995	**1994**
Net sales	$530,000	$390,000
Net purchases	280,000	235,000
Beginning inventory	50,000	66,000
Ending inventory	75,000	50,000

6. Inventory with a cost of $7,000 was salvaged and sold for $3,500. The balance of the inventory was a total loss.

Instructions

Prepare a schedule computing the amount of inventory fire loss. The supporting schedule of the computation of the gross profit should be in good form.

(AICPA adapted)

P9-9 (Retail Inventory Method) The records for Clothing Department of Albert Spalding's Discount Store are summarized below for the month of January.

Inventory; January 1:   at retail, $25,000; at cost, $17,000
Purchases in January: at retail, $137,000; at cost, $86,500
Freight-in: $7,000
Purchase returns: at retail, $3,000; at cost, $2,300
Purchase allowances: $2,200
Transfers in from suburb branch: at retail, $13,000; at cost, $11,000
Net markups: $8,000
Net markdowns: $4,000
Inventory losses due to normal breakage, etc.:   at retail, $400
Sales at retail: $85,000
Sales returns: $2,400

Instructions

Compute the inventory for this department as of January 31, at (1) sales price and (2) lower of average cost or market.

P9-10 (Retail Inventory Method) Presented below is information related to Yamaguchi Inc.

	Cost	Retail
Inventory 12/31/1995	$250,000	$ 390,000
Purchases	970,000	1,460,000

Purchase returns	60,000	80,000
Purchase discounts	18,000	—
Gross sales (after employee discounts)	—	1,460,000
Sales returns	—	97,500
Markups	—	120,000
Markup cancellations	—	40,000
Markdowns	—	45,000
Markdown cancellations	—	20,000
Freight-in	79,000	—
Employee discounts granted	—	8,000
Loss from breakage (normal)	—	2,500

Instructions

Assuming that Yamaguchi Inc., uses the conventional retail inventory method, compute the cost of their ending inventory at December 31, 1996.

P9-11 (Retail Inventory Method) Richard Petty, Inc., uses the retail inventory method to estimate ending inventory for its monthly financial statements. The following data pertain to a single department for the month of October 1996.

Inventory, October 1, 1996	
At cost	$ 52,000
At retail	78,000
Purchases (exclusive of freight and returns):	
At cost	272,000
At retail	423,000
Freight-in	16,600
Purchase returns	
At cost	5,600
At retail	8,000
Additional markups	9,000
Markup cancellations	2,000
Markdowns (net)	3,600
Normal spoilage and breakage	10,000
Sales	380,000

Instructions

(a) Using the conventional retail method, prepare a schedule computing estimated lower of cost or market inventory for October 31, 1996.

(b) A department store using the conventional retail inventory method estimates the cost of its ending inventory as $60,000. An accurate physical count reveals only $44,000 of inventory at lower of cost or market. List the factors that may have caused the difference between the computed inventory and the physical count.

P9-12 (Statement and Note Disclosure, LCM, and Purchase Commitment) LeMonde Specialty Company, a division of Gregg Inc., manufactures three models of gear shift components for bicycles that are sold to bicycle manufacturers, retailers, and catalog outlets. Since beginning operations in 1966, LeMonde has used normal absorption costing and has assumed a first-in, first-out cost flow in its perpetual inventory system. Except for overhead, manufacturing costs are accumulated using actual costs. Overhead is applied to production using predetermined overhead rates. The balances of the inventory accounts at the end of LeMonde's fiscal year, November 30, 1995, are shown below. The inventories are stated at cost before any year-end adjustments.

Finished goods	$645,000
Work-in-process	112,500
Raw materials	240,000
Factory supplies	69,000

The following information relates to LeMonde's inventory and operations.

1. The finished goods inventory consists of the items analyzed below.

	Cost	Market
Down tube shifter		
Standard model	$ 67,500	$67,000
Click adjustment model	94,500	89,000
Deluxe model	108,000	110,000
Total down tube shifters	270,000	266,000

Bar end shifter		
Standard model	83,000	90,050
Click adjustment model	99,000	97,550
Total bar end shifters	182,000	187,600
Head tube shifter		
Standard model	78,000	77,650
Click adjustment model	117,000	119,300
Total head tube shifters	195,000	196,950
Total finished goods	$645,000	$647,550

2. One-half of the head tube shifter finished goods inventory is held by catalog outlets on consignment.
3. Three-quarters of the bar end shifter finished goods inventory has been pledged as collateral for a bank loan.
4. One-half of the raw materials balance represents derailleurs acquired at a contracted price 20 percent above the current market price. The market value of the rest of the raw materials is $127,400.
5. The total market value of the work-in-process inventory is $108,700.
6. Included in the cost of factory supplies are obsolete items with an historical cost of $4,200. The market value of the remaining factory supplies is $65,900.
7. LeMonde applies the lower of cost or market method to each of the three types of shifters in finished goods inventory. For each of the other three inventory accounts, LeMonde applies the lower of cost or market method to the total of each inventory account.
8. Consider all amounts presented above to be material in relation to LeMonde's financial statements taken as a whole.

Instructions

(a) Prepare the inventory section of LeMonde's Statement of Financial Position as of November 30, 1995, including any required note(s).

(b) Without prejudice to your answer to Requirement A, assume that the market value of LeMonde's inventories is less than cost. Explain how this decline would be presented in LeMonde's income statement for the fiscal year ended November 30, 1995.

(c) Assume that LeMonde has a firm purchase commitment for the same type of derailleur included in the raw materials inventory as of November 30, 1995, and that the purchase commitment is at a contracted price 15 percent greater than the current market price. These derailleurs are to be delivered to LeMonde after November 30, 1995. Discuss the impact, if any, that this purchase commitment would have on LeMonde's financial statements prepared for the fiscal year ended November 30, 1995.

(CMA adapted)

*P9-13 (Conventional and Dollar-Value LIFO Retail) As of January 1, 1996, Unser Inc. installed the retail method of accounting for its merchandise inventory.

To prepare the store's financial statements at June 30, 1996, you obtain these data.

	Cost	Selling Price
Inventory, January 1	$ 30,000	$ 43,000
Markdowns		10,500
Markups		9,200
Markdown cancellations		6,500
Markup cancellations		3,200
Purchases	112,800	155,000
Sales		159,000
Purchase returns and allowances	2,800	4,000
Sales returns and allowances		8,000

Instructions

(a) Prepare a schedule to compute Unser's June 30, 1996, inventory under the conventional retail method of accounting for inventories.

(b) Without prejudice to your solution to part (a), assume that you computed the June 30, 1996, inventory to be $99,360 at retail and the ratio of cost to retail to be 65%. The general price level has increased from 100 at January 1, 1996, to 108 at June 30, 1996. Prepare a schedule to compute the June 30, 1996, inventory at the June 30 price level under the dollar-value LIFO retail method.

(AICPA adapted)

*P9-14 (Retail, LIFO Retail, and Inventory Shortage) Late in 1992, Babe Didrikson and four other investors took the chain of Sprint Department Stores private, and the company has just completed its third year of operations under the ownership of the investment group. Jim Ryun, controller of Sprint Department Stores, is in the process of preparing the year-end financial statements. Based on the preliminary financial statements, Didrikson has expressed concern over inventory shortages, and she has asked Ryun to determine whether an abnormal amount of theft and breakage has occurred. The accounting records of Sprint Department Stores contain the following amounts on November 30, 1995, the end of the fiscal year.

	Cost	Retail
Beginning inventory	$ 68,000	$100,000
Purchases	261,800	400,000
Net markups		50,000
Net markdowns		110,000
Sales		330,000

According to the November 30, 1995, physical inventory, the actual inventory at retail is $106,000.

Instructions
- **(a)** Describe the circumstances under which the retail inventory method would be applied, and the advantages of using the retail inventory method.
- **(b)** Assuming that prices have been stable, calculate the value, at cost, of Sprint Department Stores' ending inventory using the last-in, first-out (LIFO) retail method. Be sure to furnish supporting calculations.
- **(c)** Estimate the amount of shortage, at retail, that has occurred at Sprint Department Stores during the year ended November 30, 1995.
- **(d)** Complications in the retail method can be caused by such items as (1) freight-in expense, (2) purchase returns and allowances, (3) sales returns and allowances, and (4) employee discounts. Explain how each of these four special items is handled in the retail inventory method.

(CMA adapted)

*P9-15 (Change to LIFO Retail; Dollar-Value LIFO Retail) Aquarius Shoppe uses the conventional retail method and is now considering converting to the retail LIFO method for the period beginning 1/1/1995. Available information consists of the following:

	1994		1995	
	Cost	Retail	Cost	Retail
Inventory 1/1/1994	$ 20,850	$ 43,000	$?	$?
Purchases (net)	329,150	442,000	321,192	467,000
Net additional markups	—	15,000	—	12,840
Net markdowns	—	4,249	—	4,000
Sales (net)	—	453,000	—	460,024
Loss from breakage	—	1,751	—	–0–
Applicable price index	—	100	—	106

Following is a schedule showing the computation of the cost of inventory on hand at 12/31/1994 based on the conventional retail method.

	Cost	Retail
Inventory 1/1/1994	$ 20,850	$ 43,000
Purchases (net)	329,150	442,000
Net additional markups	—	15,000
Goods available	$350,000	500,000
(Ratio: $350,000 ÷ $500,000 = 70%)		
Less:		
Sales		453,000
Net markdowns		4,249
Loss from breakage		1,751
Inventory 12/31/1994 at retail		$ 41,000
Inventory 12/31/1994 at lower of cost or market		
Cost ($41,000 × 70%)	$ 28,700	

Instructions
- **(a)** Prepare a schedule showing the recomputation of the inventory on hand at 12/31/1994 in accordance with the procedures necessary to convert from the conventional retail method to the LIFO retail method beginning January 1, 1995.
- **(b)** Prepare the journal entry necessary to restate the 1/1/1995 inventory to LIFO retail.
- **(c)** Prepare a schedule showing the computation of the 12/31/1995 inventory by the LIFO retail method as adjusted for fluctuating prices. Without prejudice to your answers to parts (a) or (b) above, assume

that you computed the 12/31/1994 inventory (retail value $41,000) under the LIFO retail method at a cost of $30,000. Round your answer to the nearest dollar.

*P9-16 (Change to LIFO Retail)   Bett's Stores Inc., which uses the conventional retail inventory method, wishes to change to the LIFO retail method beginning with the accounting year ending December 31, 1995. Amounts as shown below appear on the store's books before adjustment:

	At Cost	At Retail
Inventory, January 1, 1995	$ 13,600	$ 24,000
Purchases in 1995	116,200	184,000
Markups in 1995		12,000
Markdowns in 1995		5,500
Sales in 1995		165,000

You are to assume that all markups and markdowns apply to 1995 purchases, and that it is appropriate to treat the entire inventory as a single department.

Instructions

Compute the inventory at December 31, 1995, under:
- (a)   Conventional retail method.
- (b)   Last-in, first-out retail method, effecting the change in method as of January 1, 1995. Assume that the cost-to-retail percentage for 1994 was recomputed correctly in accordance with procedures necessary to change to LIFO. This ratio was 58%.

(AICPA adapted)

*P9-17 (Change to LIFO Retail; Dollar-Value LIFO Retail)   Shoreline Department Store converted from the conventional retail method to the LIFO retail method on January 1, 1994, and is now considering converting to the dollar-value LIFO inventory method. During your examination of the financial statements for the year ended December 31, 1995, management requested that you furnish a summary showing certain computations of inventory cost for the past three years.
Here is the available information.

1.   The inventory at January 1, 1993, had a retail value of $56,000 and cost of $29,800 based on the conventional retail method.
2.   Transactions during 1993 were as follows:

	Cost	Retail
Gross purchases	$311,000	$554,000
Purchase returns	5,200	10,000
Purchase discounts	6,000	
Gross sales (after employee discounts)		551,000
Sales returns		9,000
Employee discounts		3,000
Freight-in	17,600	
Net markups		20,000
Net markdowns		12,000

3.   The retail value of the December 31, 1994, inventory was $75,600, the cost ratio for 1994 under the LIFO retail method was 62%, and the regional price index was 105% of the January 1, 1994, price level.
4.   The retail value of the December 31, 1995, inventory was $54,000, the cost ratio for 1995 under the LIFO retail method was 61%, and the regional price index was 108% of the January 1, 1994, price level.

Instructions
- (a)   Prepare a schedule showing the computation of the cost of inventory on hand at December 31, 1993, based on the conventional retail method.
- (b)   Prepare a schedule showing the recomputation of the inventory to be reported on December 31, 1993, in accordance with procedures necessary to convert from the conventional retail method to the LIFO retail method beginning January 1, 1994. Assume that the retail value of the December 31, 1993, inventory was $63,000.
- (c)   Without prejudice to your solution to part (b), assume that you computed the December 31, 1993, inventory (retail value $63,000) under the LIFO retail method at a cost of $36,225. Prepare a schedule showing the computations of the cost of the store's 1994 and 1995 year-end inventories under the dollar-value LIFO method.

(AICPA adapted)

CASES

C9-1 (Lower of Cost or Market) You have been asked by the financial vice-president to develop a short presentation on the lower of cost or market method for inventory purposes. The financial VP needs to explain this method to the president, because it appears that a portion of the company's inventory has declined in value.

Instructions
The financial VP asks you to answer the following questions.

1. What is the purpose of the lower of cost or market method?
2. What is meant by market? (Hint: discuss the ceiling and floor constraints.)
3. Do you apply the lower of cost or market method to each individual item, to a category, or to the total of the inventory? Explain.
4. What are the potential disadvantages of the lower of cost or market method?

C9-2 (Lower of Cost or Market) Power Rangers Inc. manufactures and sells four products, the inventories of which are priced at cost or market, whichever is lower. A normal profit margin rate of 30% is usually maintained on each of the four products.

The following information was compiled as of December 31, 1995.

Product	Original Cost	Cost to Replace	Estimated Cost to Dispose	Expected Selling Price[a]
A	$17.50	$15.00	$ 5.00	$ 30.00
B	45.00	78.00	26.00	100.00
C	35.00	42.00	15.00	80.00
D	47.50	45.00	20.50	95.00

[a]Normal margin is 30% of selling price.

Instructions
(a) Why are expected selling prices important in the application of the lower of cost or market rule?
(b) Prepare a schedule containing unit values (including "floor" and "ceiling") for determining the lower of cost or market on an individual-product basis. The last column of the schedule should contain for each product the unit value for the purpose of inventory valuation resulting from the application of the lower of cost or market rule.

C9-3 (Lower of Cost or Market) Sonic Corporation purchased a significant amount of raw materials inventory for a new product that it is manufacturing.

Sonic uses the lower of cost or market rule for these raw materials. The replacement cost of the raw materials is above the net realizable value and both are below the original cost.

Sonic uses the average cost inventory method for these raw materials. In the last 2 years, each purchase has been at a lower price than the previous purchase, and the ending inventory quantity for each period has been higher than the beginning inventory quantity for that period.

Instructions
(a) 1. At which amount should Sonic's raw materials inventory be reported on the balance sheet? Why?
    2. In general, why is the lower of cost or market rule used to report inventory?
(b) What would have been the effect on ending inventory and cost of goods sold had Sonic used the LIFO inventory method instead of the average cost inventory method for the raw materials? Why?

C9-4 (Lower of Cost or Market) You are in charge of the audit of Seinfeld Company. The following items were in Seinfeld's inventory at November 30, 1995 (fiscal year-end).

Product number	075936	078310	079104	081111
Selling price per unit November 30, 1995	$15.00	$23.00	$28.00	$13.00
Standard cost, per unit, as included in inventory at November 30, 1995	$ 8.00	$11.25	$14.26	$ 7.40

In discussions with Seinfeld's marketing and sales personnel, you were told that there will be a general 9% (rounded to the next highest nickel) increase in selling prices, effective December 1, 1995. This increase will affect all garments except those that have 081 as the first three digits of the product code. The 081 codes are assigned to new apparel introductions, and for product code 081111, the selling price will be $9.00 effective December 1, 1995.

In addition, you were told by the controller that Seinfeld's attempts to earn a 40% gross profit on selling price for all their hosiery.

From the cost department you obtained the following standard costs, which will be used for fiscal 1996:

Product number	1996 Standard
075936	$ 8.25
078310	$10.75
079104	$14.71
081111	$ 7.51

Sales commissions and estimates of other costs of disposal approximate 25% of fiscal 1996 standard costs to manufacture. Assume that standard costs for fiscal 1996 provide an accurate assessment of the replacement cost of the product.

Instructions
(a) Compute the value at which each of the items should be reported in the November 30, 1995, inventory.
(b) When should inventories be reported at market?
(c) Does the literal interpretation of the rule of lower of cost or market always apply? Could you cite in this case where a possible exception to the lower of cost or market might be employed?

C9-5 (Retail Inventory Method) Easyclean Company, your client, manufactures paint. The company's president, Ms. Marcia Tennyson, has decided to open a retail store to sell Easyclean paint as well as wallpaper and other supplies that would be purchased from other suppliers. She has asked you for information about the conventional retail method of pricing inventories at the retail store.

Instructions
Prepare a report to the president explaining the retail method of pricing inventories. Your report should include these points:
(a) Description and accounting features of the method.
(b) The conditions that may distort the results under the method.
(c) A comparison of the advantages of using the retail method with those of using cost methods of inventory pricing.
(d) The accounting theory underlying the treatment of net markdowns and net markups under the method.

(AICPA adapted)

C9-6 (Cost Determination, LCM, Retail Method) Edy Son Corporation, a retailer and wholesaler of national brand-name household lighting fixtures, purchases its inventories from various suppliers.

Instructions
(a) 1. What criteria should be used to determine which of Son's costs are inventoriable?
  2. Are Son's administrative costs inventoriable? Defend your answer.
(b) 1. Son uses the lower of cost or market rule for its wholesale inventories. What are the theoretical arguments for that rule?
  2. The replacement cost of the inventories is below the net realizable value less a normal profit margin, which, in turn, is below the original cost. What amount should be used to value the inventories? Why?
(c) Son calculates the estimated cost of its ending inventories held for sale at retail using the conventional retail inventory method. How would Son treat the beginning inventories and net markdowns in calculating the cost ratio used to determine its ending inventories? Why?

(AICPA adapted)

*C9-7 (Retail Inventory Method) Presented below are a number of items that may be encountered in computing the cost to retail percentage when using the conventional retail method or the LIFO retail method.

1. Markdowns.
2. Markdown cancellations.
3. Cost of items transferred in from other departments.
4. Retail value of items transferred in from other departments.
5. Sales discounts.
6. Purchases discounts (purchases recorded gross).
7. Estimated retail value of goods broken or stolen.
8. Cost of beginning inventory.
9. Retail value of beginning inventory.
10. Cost of purchases.
11. Retail value of purchases.
12. Markups.
13. Markup cancellations.
14. Employee discounts (sales recorded net).

Instructions
For each of the items listed above, indicate whether this item would be considered in the cost to retail percentage under (1) conventional retail, (2) LIFO retail.

▶ USING YOUR JUDGMENT ◀

▶ FINANCIAL REPORTING PROBLEM

Prab Robots, Inc., reported the following information regarding 1991–1992 inventory:

Prab Robots, Inc.

	1992	1991
Current Assets		
Cash	$ 153,010	$ 538,489
Accounts receivable, net of allowance for doubtful accounts		
of $46,000 in 1992 and $160,000 in 1991	1,627,980	2,596,291
Inventories (Note 2)	1,340,494	1,734,873
Other current assets	123,388	90,592
Assets of discontinued operations	—	32,815
Total current assets	3,244,872	4,993,060

Notes to Consolidated Financial Statements

Note 1: (In Part): Nature of Business and Significant Accounting Policies

Inventories—Inventories are stated at the lower of cost or market. Cost is determined by the last-in, first-out (LIFO) method by the parent company and by the first-in, first-out (FIFO) method by its subsidiaries.

Note 2: Inventories

Inventories consist of the following:

	1992	1991
Raw materials	$1,264,646	$2,321,178
Work in process	240,988	171,222
Finished goods and display units	129,406	711,252
Total inventories	1,635,040	3,203,652
Less amount classified as long-term	294,546	1,468,779
Current portion	$1,340,494	$1,734,873

Inventories are stated at the lower of cost determined by the LIFO method or market for Prab Robots, Inc. Inventories for the two wholly-owned subsidiaries, Prab Command, Inc. (U.S.) and Prab Limited (U.K.) are stated on the FIFO method which amounted to $566,000 at October 31, 1991. No inventory is stated on the FIFO method at October 31, 1992. Included in inventory stated at FIFO cost was $32,815 at October 31, 1991 of Prab Command inventory classified as an asset from discontinued operations (see Note 14). If the FIFO method had been used for the entire consolidated group, inventories after an adjustment to the lower of cost or market, would have been approximately $2,000,000 and $3,800,000 at October 31, 1992 and 1991, respectively.

Inventory has been written down to estimated net realizable value, and results of operations for 1992, 1991 and 1990 include a corresponding charge of approximately $868,000, $960,000, and $273,000, respectively, which represents the excess of LIFO cost over market.

Inventory of $294,546 and $1,468,779 at October 31, 1992 and 1991, respectively, shown on the balance sheet as a noncurrent asset represents that portion of the inventory that is not expected to be sold currently.

Reduction in inventory quantities during the years ended October 31, 1992, 1991 and 1990 resulted in liquidation of LIFO inventory quantities carried at a lower cost prevailing in prior years as compared with the cost of fiscal 1992 purchases. The effect of these reductions was to decrease the net loss by approximately $24,000, $157,000 and $90,000 at October 31, 1992, 1991 and 1990, respectively.

Instructions
- **(a)** Why might Prab Robots, Inc., use two different methods for valuing inventory?
- **(b)** Comment on why Prab Robots, Inc., might disclose how its LIFO inventories would be valued under FIFO.
- **(c)** Why does the LIFO liquidation reduce operating costs?
- **(d)** Comment on whether Prab Robots would report more or less income if it had been on a FIFO basis for all its inventory.

▶ WRITING ASSIGNMENT

Jones Co. follows the practice of valuing its inventory at the lower of cost or market. The following information is available from the company's inventory records as of December 31, 1993:

Item	Quantity	Unit Cost	Replacement Cost/Unit	Estimated Selling Price/Unit	Completion & Disposal Cost/Unit	Normal Profit Margin/Unit
A	1,100	$7.50	$8.40	$10.50	$1.50	$1.80
B	800	8.20	8.00	9.40	.90	1.20
C	1,000	5.60	5.40	7.20	1.10	.60
D	1,000	3.80	4.20	6.30	.80	1.50
E	1,400	6.40	6.30	6.80	.70	1.00

Instructions
Marcia Marzec is an accounting clerk in the accounting department of Jones Co., and she cannot understand why the market value keeps changing from replacement cost to net realizable value to something that she cannot even figure out. Marcia is very confused, and she is the one who records inventory purchases and calculates ending inventory.

You are the manager of the department and an accountant. Calculate the lower of cost or market using the "individual item" approach. Then write a memo to Marcia explaining what designated market value is as well as how it is computed. Use your calculations to aid in your explanation. Finally, include the journal entry she will need to make in order to write down the ending inventory from cost to market.

▶ GROUP ASSIGNMENT

(General Inventory Estimation Issues) Your group has been engaged as accountants for the accounting firm of Check and Doublecheck. The manager of the office is interested in your collective formal educations and describes the following factual situations that were recently encountered in their practice. Work within your group to analyze each situation and develop a group response for each item. Your instructor will assign one member of the group to serve as a recorder and one member to serve as spokesperson. The spokesperson will be asked to report your group findings to the class before moving on to the next situation.

Situation 1: In December 1995, one of our clients underwent a major management change and a new president was hired. After reviewing the various policies of the company, the president's opinion was that prior systems employed by the company did not allow for adequate testing of obsolescence (including discontinued products) and overstocks in inventories. Accordingly, the president changed the mechanics of the procedures of reviewing for obsolete and excess stock and determining the amount. These reviews resulted in a significant increase between years in the amount of inventory that was written off. You are satisfied that these procedures are accurate and provide reliable results. The amounts charged against operations for excess and obsolete stock for the last 3 years were: 1995—$500,000; 1994—$120,000; and 1993—$115,000. Net income for 1995 before adjustment for these additional obsolescence charges was $600,000.

Instructions
How should these charges be reported in the financial statements, if at all?

Situation 2: Another of our clients, Sunset Foods, was upset because we forced them to write down their inventory on an item-by-item basis. For example, our computation resulted in a write-down of approximately $380,000 as follows:

	Frozen	Cans
Spinach	$183,000	$ 8,000
Carrots	12,000	7,000
Cut beans	—	25,000
Peas	—	45,000
Mixed vegetables	75,000	25,000
	$270,000	$110,000

The company argued that the products are sold on a line basis (frozen or canned) with customers taking all varieties, and only rarely are sales made on an individual product basis. As a result, they argued that the application of the lower of cost or market rule to the total product line would result in the proper determination of income (loss). A pricing of the inventory on this basis would result in a $140,000 write-off.

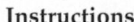

Instructions
Why do you believe our accounting firm argued for the item-by-item approach? Which method should be used, given the information in this case?

Situation 3: One of our client's major business activities is the purchase and resale of used heavy mining and construction equipment, including trucks, cranes, shovels, conveyors, crushers, etc. The company was organized in 1981. In its earlier years it purchased individual items of heavy equipment and resold them to customers throughout the United States. In the late-1980s, the company began negotiating the "package" purchase of all the existing euqipment at mine sites, concurrent with the closing down of several of the large iron mines in Minnesota and exhausted coal mines in Ohio. The mine operators preferred to liquidate their mine assets on that basis rather than holding auctions or leaving the mine site open until all of the equipment could be liquidated. As there were numerous pieces of equipment in these package purchases, the client found it dificult to assign costs to each individual item. As a result, the company followed the policy of valuing these "package" purchases by the cost recovery method. Under this method, the company recognized no income until the entire cost had been recovered through sales revenues. This produced a desirable tax answer by deferring income to later periods and represented, for financial reporting purposes, a "conservative" valuation of inventories in what was essentially a new field for the company.

Instructions
Comment on the propriety of this approach.

► ETHICS CASES

EC9-1. (Ethical Issue: Disclosure of Inventory Write Down) The market value of Lake Corporation's inventory has declined significantly below its cost. Sharon Groves, the Controller, wants to use the direct method to write down inventory without calling attention to the decline in market value. Her supervisor, Financial Vice-President Ann Thoms, prefers the allowance method because it more clearly discloses the decline in market value and it does not distort the cost of goods sold.

Instructions
  (a) What, if any, is the ethical issue in this decision?
  (b) Is any stakeholder harmed if Controller Groves' direct method is used?
  (c) What should Sharon Groves do?

EC9-2. (Ethical Issues: Purchase Commitments) LogaLot signed a long-term purchase contract to buy timber from The United States Forest Service at $250 per thousand board feet. Under these terms, LogaLot must cut and pay $5,000,000 for this timber during the next year. Currently the market value is $200 per thousand board feet. At this rate, the market price is $4,000,000. Jim Sanders, the Controller, wants to recognize the loss in value on the year-end financial statements; but the Financial Vice-President, John Smith, argues that the loss is temporary and it should be ignored. Sanders notes, however, that market value has remained near $200 for many months, and he sees no sign of significant change.

Instructions
  (a) What are the ethical issues, if any?
  (b) Is any particular stakeholder harmed by the financial vice-president's decision?
  (c) What would you do if you were the controller?

FINANCIAL ACCOUNTING: A PREPARER'S VIEWPOINT

A visit with
TED CLARKE

TED CLARKE, 35, is corporate controller of Nike, the $4 billion shoe and apparel company based in Beaverton, Oregon, near Portland. It's a very young age to have the top accounting job in such a major company. But Nike, whose award-winning television commercials feature the likes of Michael Jordan and Charles Barkley, is supportive of accountants: it's a company founded by a CPA and run by many others.

What got you interested in accounting?

I started out as a pre-law/political science major at Portland State University. My adviser suggested that I also take some accounting because it would help me wherever I went. It turned out that I really liked it and decided that if I didn't go to law school, then accounting would be more useful than political science.

You didn't go to law school. Why not?

During my junior year, a friend of a friend was a partner at a big accounting firm downtown. He said it wouldn't hurt to get into public accounting. It could open more doors. So I went to work for Price Waterhouse, working in the audit department for three and one-half years. I was an audit senior when I left.

What made you leave Price Waterhouse?

Nike was a client of the Portland office. A position became open, and they offered me the job. Plus, I had been married about six months after I started at PW, and I was traveling close to half of the year. But I got superior training at PW, and I'm not sure I would have left if it had been a company other than Nike.

Nike provides a good opportunity for accountants.

There are so many there. While they're the first ones to call you a bean counter, they also recognize the abilities of CPAs. When I started in 1984, half the vice-presidents were accountants.

The company founder is a CPA.

Phil Knight graduated from the University of Oregon. He was a track runner. Then he went to Stanford Business School and wrote his thesis on how we can go overseas and produce shoes cheaper and better. He worked for Price Waterhouse in Portland, and during that time he was also selling shoes out of the trunk of his car.

And he hired more accountants?

A lot of his contacts were through Price Waterhouse. Those people became vice-presidents, and they recognized the capability of people with accounting backgrounds. In many companies, there's a barrier to accountants moving up: You're an accountant, and you are going to stay an accountant. At Nike, the barrier isn't there. Besides, in the early days, everybody did everything.

What was your first job?

Corporate General Ledger Supervisor was the title. I had eight people reporting to me. We did the consolidated financial statements and prepared the internal statements for top management. It was a good introductory, supervisory position.

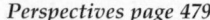
You weren't worried that you were going to get pigeonholed?

No, because there were a lot of other opportunities. Remember, this is a company that has grown from $460 million in sales to $4 billion in under 15 years.

How long were you in that first job?

About three years. During that period, the assistant corporate controller left to become European controller. My boss, who was the corporate accounting manager, and I split up the remaining duties. Then he became assistant corporate controller, and I became accounting manager. Then, he became internal audit manager, reporting to the vice-president of finance and the board of directors, and I moved to assistant corporate controller. About three years ago, the corporate controller moved on, so I moved up.

Where might this take you?

I report directly to the vice-president of finance. One would hope that my next step would be that job. Or, perhaps a line function.

Give me some examples of accountants who have nonaccounting jobs.

Sure. We've got one guy who says he's escaped accounting to be a vice-president of marketing. Our CFO formerly was director of human resources. The country managers in Korea and Thailand are accountants.

Is Nike on LIFO?

We're on LIFO for all of our domestic inventories. We had been on LIFO for our foreign inventories, but it just didn't make sense because of the difficulty of obtaining this information overseas and because of the immaterial balance. In 1994 our LIFO reserve was $19.4 million on a total inventory of $470 million.

What about *Statement 106* on "Other Post-Employment Benefits"?

We don't have a current program to continue medical benefits past retirement. However, we are looking at implementing such a plan, and our benefits people are aware of the potential costs there. Our work force is very young. The average age is about 30. We've only been around for 20 years, so we don't have too many retirees.

What other FASB statement would affect you?

Certainly stock options. We typically have an annual stock option grant to upper management. If you have to recognize compensation expense, then that would have an impact on us. The concern is how to value these options. Right now, the methodology doesn't seem to be consistent. It's hard to argue that they don't have value when people are issuing them as part of compensation.

Have you ever met Michael Jordan?

Yes, I have. During the NBA Finals in 1992, he came over to Nike to work out. He comes and plays pickup basketball games. Everyone says, "I think I'll take Michael on my team." Actually, he has an office upstairs. Charles Barkley shows up, too. When basketball teams are in town to play the Portland Trailblazers, they will practice here because it is off-limits to the media. People around here are instructed not to ask for autographs. Our new headquarters campus has a world-class workout facility open to all employees for a nominal fee. Working out at lunchtime is perhaps one of the finest benefits.

I'd imagine that the accounting for some athlete contracts can get complex.

Agents are always coming up with new compensation methods. For example, we have some contracts in which compensation is tied to our stock price. They earn an amount that equals the increase in value. You account for it by marking the shares they've earned to market at the end of the accounting period. The debit is to compensation expense, and the credit is to a payable or to a deferred liability.

If it turned out that an athlete suddenly lost his or her value as an endorsement property, what would the accounting impact be?

Say you had a guaranteed amount due over future periods, but it turned out that he or she was not going to provide any future benefit to you. Then, you would probably take the present value of the guaranteed amount and expense it in the current year.

You have an unusual year-end, May. What's the advantage of that?

January, February, and March are big shipping times for us. So is June through August. May is a slowdown period. But it sure makes a busy summer for me.

CHAPTER 10

ACQUISITION AND DISPOSITION OF PROPERTY, PLANT, AND EQUIPMENT

LEARNING OBJECTIVES

After studying this chapter, you should be able to:

1. Describe the major characteristics of property, plant, and equipment.

2. Identify the costs included in the initial valuation of land, buildings, and equipment.

3. Describe the accounting problems associated with self-constructed assets.

4. Describe the accounting problems associated with interest capitalization.

5. Understand accounting issues related to acquiring and valuing plant assets.

6. Describe the accounting treatment for costs subsequent to acquisition.

7. Describe the accounting treatment for the disposal of property, plant, and equipment.

*I*n 1991, Chambers Development Co., the developer and operator of landfills based in Pittsburgh, reported that earnings rose 45 percent. Net sales approached $322 million, a ten-fold increase in just five years. This amazing growth was powered by the acquisition and rapid development of new landfills. During 1991, its stock price rose from $16.13 to $37. Unfortunately, on March 17, 1992, in a tersely worded statement, Chambers revealed that its profit growth had been greatly overstated. The highly profitable company was not so profitable after all. In October 1992, Chambers restated income for 1991 and several prior years, wiping out $362 million in earnings and retained earnings. Not surprisingly, the next day, Chamber's stock plunged 63%—from $30.50 to $11.13 in one day!

What happened? As Chambers' stockholders would learn, the company had been deferring recognition of certain "indirect" landfill development expenses and writing them off over the life of the landfills (3 to 10 years). The deferred expenses included executives' salaries and travel, legal and public relations costs, and security guard contracts. These capitalized costs were tucked near the bottom of the balance sheet under the heading "other assets" on a line described "deferred costs." As one Wall Street analyst remarked, "whenever you see an asset called 'deferred anything' hold on to your pocketbook." This chapter discusses the basic accounting problems associated with (1) the incurrence of costs related to property, plant, and equipment and (2) the accounting methods used to record the retirement or disposal of these costs. Depreciation—allocating costs of property, plant, and equipment to accounting periods—is presented in Chapter 11.

▶ CHARACTERISTICS OF PROPERTY, PLANT, AND EQUIPMENT

Almost every business enterprise of any size or activity uses assets of a durable nature. Such assets, commonly referred to as **property, plant, and equipment; plant assets;** or **fixed assets,** include land, building structures (offices, factories, warehouses), and equipment (machinery, furniture, tools). These terms are used interchangeably throughout this textbook. The major characteristics of property, plant, and equipment are:

1. **They are acquired for use in operations and not for resale.** Only assets used in normal business operations should be classified as property, plant, and equipment. An idle building is more appropriately classified separately as an investment; land held by land developers or subdividers is classified as inventory.

2. **They are long-term in nature and usually subject to depreciation.** Property, plant, and equipment yield services over a number of years. The investment in these assets is assigned to future periods through periodic depreciation charges. The exception is land, which is not depreciated unless a material decrease in value occurs, such as a loss in fertility of agricultural land because of poor crop rotation, drought, or soil erosion.

3. **They possess physical substance.** Property, plant, and equipment are characterized by physical existence or substance and thus are differentiated from intangible assets, such as patents or goodwill. Unlike raw material, however, property, plant, and equipment do not physically become part of a product held for resale.

OBJECTIVE 1
Describe the major characteristics of property, plant, and equipment.

▶ ACQUISITION OF PROPERTY, PLANT, AND EQUIPMENT

Historical cost is the usual basis for valuing property, plant, and equipment. **Historical cost is measured by the cash or cash equivalent price of obtaining the asset and bringing it to the location and condition necessary for its intended use.** The purchase price, freight costs, sales taxes, and installation costs of a productive asset are considered part of the asset's cost. These costs are allocated to future periods through depreciation. Any related costs incurred **after the asset's acquisition,** such as additions, improvements, or replacements, are **added to the asset's cost if they provide future service potential.** Otherwise they are expensed immediately.

Cost should be the basis used at the acquisition date because the cash or cash equivalent price best measures the asset's value at that time. Disagreement does exist concerning differences between historical cost and other valuation methods (such as replacement cost or fair market value) arising after acquisition. *APB Opinion No. 6* states that "property, plant, and equipment should not be written up to reflect appraisal, market, or current values which are above cost." Although minor exceptions are noted, current standards indicate that departures from historical cost are rare.

The main reasons for this position are (1) at the date of acquisition, cost reflects fair value; (2) historical cost involves actual, not hypothetical transactions, and as a result is the most reliable; and (3) gains and losses should not be anticipated but should be recognized when the asset is sold.

Several other valuation methods have been considered, such as (1) constant dollar accounting (adjustments for general price-level changes), (2) current cost accounting (adjustments for specific price-level changes), (3) net realizable value, or (4) a combination of constant dollar accounting and current cost or net realizable value. These alternative valuation concepts are discussed in Chapter 26.

OBJECTIVE 2
Identify the costs included in the initial valuation of land, buildings, and equipment.

UNDERLYING CONCEPT

Market value is relevant to inventory but less so for property, plant, and equipment which, consistent with the going concern assumption, are held for use in the business, not for sale like inventory.

COST OF LAND

All expenditures made to acquire land and to ready it for use are considered part of the land cost. Land costs typically include (1) the purchase price, (2) closing costs, such as title to the land, attorney's fees, and recording fees, (3) costs incurred in getting the land in condition for its intended use, such as grading, filling, draining, and clearing, (4) assumption of any liens, mortgages, or encumbrances on the property, and (5) any additional land improvements that have an indefinite life.

When land has been purchased for the purpose of constructing a building, all costs incurred up to the excavation for the new building are considered land costs. **Removal of old buildings—clearing, grading, and filling—are considered land costs because these costs are necessary to get the land in condition for its intended purpose.** Any proceeds obtained in the process of getting the land ready for its intended use, such as salvage receipts on the demolition of an old building or the sale of cleared timber are treated as **reductions in the price of the land.**

In some cases, the purchaser of land has to assume certain obligations on the land such as back taxes or liens. In such situations, the cost of the land is the cash paid for it, plus the encumbrances. In other words, if the purchase price of the land is $50,000 cash, but accrued property taxes of $5,000 and liens of $10,000 are assumed, the cost of the land is $65,000.

Special assessments for local improvements, such as pavements, street lights, sewers, and drainage systems, are usually charged to the Land account because they are relatively permanent in nature and are maintained and replaced by the local government body. In addition, permanent improvements made by the owner, such as landscaping, are properly chargeable to the Land account. **Improvements with limited lives,** such as private driveways, walks, fences, and parking lots, are recorded separately as Land Improvements so they can be depreciated over their estimated lives.

Generally, land is part of property, plant, and equipment. If the major purpose of acquiring and holding land is speculative, however, it is more appropriately classified as an investment. If the land is held by a real estate concern for resale, it should be classified as inventory.

In cases where land is held as an investment, what accounting treatment should be given taxes, insurance, and other direct costs incurred while holding the land? Many believe these costs should be capitalized because the revenue from the investment still has not been received. This approach is reasonable and seems justified except in cases where the asset is currently producing revenue (such as rental property).

COST OF BUILDINGS

The cost of buildings should include all expenditures related directly to their acquisition or construction. These costs include (1) materials, labor, and overhead costs incurred during construction and (2) professional fees and building permits. Generally, companies contract to have their buildings constructed. All costs incurred, from excavation to completion, are considered part of the building costs.

One accounting problem is deciding what to do about an old building that is on the site of a newly proposed building. Is the cost of removal of the old building a cost of the land or a cost of the new building? The answer is that if land is purchased with an old building on it, then the cost of demolition less its salvage value is a cost of getting the land ready for its intended use and relates to the land rather than to the new building. As indicated earlier, all costs of getting an asset ready for its intended use are costs of that asset.

COST OF EQUIPMENT

The term "equipment" in accounting includes delivery equipment, office equipment, machinery, furniture and fixtures, furnishings, factory equipment, and similar fixed assets. The cost of such assets includes the purchase price, freight and handling charges incurred, insurance on the equipment while in transit, cost of special foundations if required, assembling and installation costs, and costs of conducting trial runs. Costs thus include all expenditures incurred in acquiring the equipment and preparing it for use.

SELF-CONSTRUCTED ASSETS

Occasionally companies (particularly in the railroad and utility industries) construct their own assets. Determining the cost of such machinery and other fixed assets can be a problem. Without a purchase price or contract price, the company must allocate costs and expenses to arrive at the cost of the **self-constructed asset.** Materials and direct labor used in construction pose no problem; these costs can be traced directly to work and material orders related to the fixed assets constructed.

OBJECTIVE 3
Describe the accounting problems associated with self-constructed assets.

However, the assignment of indirect costs of manufacturing creates special problems. These indirect costs, called overhead or burden, include power, heat, light, insurance, property taxes on factory buildings and equipment, factory supervisory labor, depreciation of fixed assets, and supplies.

These costs might be handled in one of three ways:

1. **Assign No Fixed Overhead to the Cost of the Constructed Asset.** The major argument for this treatment is that indirect overhead is generally fixed in nature and does not increase as a result of constructing one's own plant or equipment. This approach assumes that the company will have the same costs regardless of whether the company constructs the asset or not, so to charge a portion of the overhead costs to the equipment will normally relieve current expenses and consequently overstate income of the current period. In contrast, variable overhead costs that increase as a result of the construction are assigned to the cost of the asset.

2. **Assign a Portion of All Overhead to the Construction Process.** This approach, a full costing concept, is appropriate if one believes that costs attach to all products and assets manufactured or constructed. This procedure assigns overhead costs to construction as it would to normal production. Advocates say that failure to allocate overhead costs understates the initial cost of the asset and results in an inaccurate future allocation.

3. **Allocate on the Basis of Lost Production.** A third alternative is to allocate to the construction project the cost of any curtailed production that occurs because the asset is built instead of purchased. This method is conceptually appealing, but is based on "what might have occurred"—an opportunity cost concept—which is difficult to measure.

A pro rata portion of the fixed overhead should be assigned to the asset to obtain its cost. This treatment is employed extensively because most accountants believe a better matching of costs with revenues is obtained. If the allocated overhead results in recording construction costs in excess of the costs that would be charged by an outside independent producer, the excess overhead should be recorded as a period loss rather than be capitalized to avoid capitalizing the asset at more than its probable market value.

INTEREST COSTS DURING CONSTRUCTION

The proper accounting for interest costs has been a long-standing controversy. Three approaches have been suggested to account for the interest incurred in financing the construction or acquisition of property, plant, and equipment:

OBJECTIVE 4
Describe the accounting problems associated with interest capitalization.

1. **Capitalize No Interest Charges During Construction.** Under this approach interest is considered a cost of financing and not a cost of construction. It is contended that if the company had used stock financing rather than debt financing, this expense would not have been incurred. The major argument against this approach is that an implicit interest cost is associated with the use of cash regardless of its source; if stock financing is employed, a real cost exists to the stockholders although a contractual claim does not take place.

2. **Capitalize Only the Actual Interest Costs Incurred During Construction.** This approach relies on the historical cost concept that only actual transactions are

recorded. It is argued that interest incurred is as much a cost of acquiring the asset as the cost of the materials, labor, and other resources used. As a result, a company that uses debt financing will have an asset of higher cost than an enterprise that uses stock financing. The results achieved by this approach are considered unsatisfactory by some because the cost of an asset should be the same whether cash, debt financing, or stock financing is employed.

3. **Charge Construction with All Costs of Funds Employed, Whether Identifiable or Not.** This method maintains that one part of the cost of construction is the cost of financing, whether by debt, cash, or stock financing. An asset should be charged with all costs necessary to get it ready for its intended use. Interest, whether actual or imputed, is a cost of building, just as labor, materials, and overhead are costs. A major criticism of this approach is that imputation of a cost of equity capital is subjective and outside the framework of an historical cost system.

The profession generally adopts the second approach: **Actual interest (with modification) should be capitalized,** in accordance with the concept that the historical cost of acquiring an asset includes all costs (including interest) incurred to bring the asset to the condition and location necessary for its intended use. The rationale for this approach is that during construction the asset is not generating revenues, and therefore interest costs should be deferred (capitalized).[1] Once construction is completed, the asset is ready for its intended use and revenues can be earned. At this point interest should be reported as an expense and matched to these revenues. It follows that any interest cost incurred in purchasing an asset that is ready for its intended use should be expensed. To implement this general approach, three items must be considered:

1. Qualifying assets.
2. Capitalization period.
3. Amount to capitalize.

Qualifying Assets

To qualify for interest capitalization, assets must require a period of time to get them ready for their intended use. Interest costs are capitalized starting with the first expenditure related to the asset, and capitalization continues until the asset is substantially completed and ready for its intended use.

Assets that qualify for interest cost capitalization include assets under construction for an enterprise's own use (including buildings, plants, and large machinery) and assets intended for sale or lease that are constructed or otherwise produced as discrete projects (e.g., ships or real estate developments).

Examples of assets that do not qualify for interest capitalization are (1) assets that are in use or ready for their intended use, and (2) assets that are not being used in the earnings activities of the enterprise and that are not undergoing the activities necessary to get them ready for use (such as land that is not being developed and assets not being used because of obsolescence, excess capacity, or need for repair).

Capitalization Period

INTERNATIONAL INSIGHT

In Japan and Brazil, companies are not permitted to capitalize interest as part of the cost of an asset.

The **capitalization period** is the period of time during which interest must be capitalized. It begins when three conditions are present:

1. Expenditures for the asset have been made.
2. Activities that are necessary to get the asset ready for its intended use are in progress.
3. Interest cost is being incurred.

---

[1]"Capitalization of Interest Cost," *Statement of Financial Accounting Standards No. 34* (Stamford, Conn.: FASB, 1979).

Interest capitalization **continues as long as these three conditions are present.** The capitalization period ends when the asset is substantially complete and ready for its intended use.

Amount to Capitalize

The amount of interest to be capitalized is limited to the lower of actual interest cost incurred during the period or avoidable interest. **Avoidable interest** is the amount of interest cost during the period that theoretically could have been avoided if expenditures for the asset had not been made. If the actual interest cost for the period is $90,000 and the avoidable interest is $80,000, only $80,000 is capitalized. Or, if the actual interest cost is $80,000 and the avoidable interest is $90,000, only $80,000 is capitalized. In no situation should interest cost include a cost of capital charge for stockholders' equity. And, interest capitalization is required for a qualifying asset only if its effect, compared with the effect of expensing interest, is material.[2]

To apply the avoidable interest concept, the potential amount of interest that may be capitalized during an accounting period is determined by multiplying an interest rate(s) by the **weighted-average amount of accumulated expenditures** for qualifying assets during the period.

Weighted-Average Accumulated Expenditures

In computing the weighted-average accumulated expenditures, the construction expenditures are weighted by the amount of time (fraction of a year or accounting period) that interest cost could be incurred on the expenditure. To illustrate, assume a 17-month bridge construction project with current-year payments to the contractor of $240,000 on March 1, $480,000 on July 1, and $360,000 on November 1. The weighted-average accumulated expenditure for the year ended December 31 is computed as follows:

Date	Expenditures Amount		Capitalization Period*		Weighted-Average Accumulated Expenditures
March 1	$ 240,000	×	10/12	=	$200,000
July 1	480,000		6/12		240,000
November 1	360,000		2/12		60,000
	$1,080,000				$500,000

*Months between date of expenditure and date interest capitalization stops or end of year, whichever comes first (in this case December 31).

ILLUSTRATION 10-1
Computation of Weighted-Average Accumulated Expenditures

To compute the weighted-average accumulated expenditures, we weight the expenditures by the amount of time that interest cost could be incurred on each one. For the March 1 expenditure a 10 months' interest cost can be associated with the expenditure, whereas for the expenditure on July 1, only 6 months' interest costs can be incurred, and for the expenditure made on November 1, only 2 months of interest cost is incurred.

Interest Rates

The principles to be used in selecting the appropriate interest rates to be applied to the weighted-average accumulated expenditures are:

1. For the portion of weighted-average accumulated expenditures that is less than or equal to any amounts borrowed specifically to finance construction of the assets, **use the interest rate incurred on the specific borrowings.**

2. For the portion of weighted-average accumulated expenditures that is greater than any debt incurred specifically to finance construction of the assets, **use a**

[2]Ibid., summary paragraph.

weighted average of interest rates incurred on all other outstanding debt during the period.[3]

An illustration of the computation of a weighted-average interest rate for debt greater than the amount incurred specifically to finance construction of the assets is shown below:

ILLUSTRATION 10-2
Computation of
Weighted-Average
Interest Rate

	Principal	Interest
12%, 2-year note	$ 600,000	$ 72,000
9%, 10-year bonds	2,000,000	180,000
7.5%, 20-year bonds	5,000,000	375,000
	$7,600,000	$627,000

$$\text{Weighted-average interest rate} = \frac{\text{Total interest}}{\text{Total principal}} = \frac{\$627,000}{\$7,600,000} = 8.25\%$$

Comprehensive Illustration of Interest Capitalization

To illustrate the issues related to interest capitalization, assume that on November 1, 1994 Shalla Company contracted with Pfeifer Construction Co. to have a building constructed for $1,400,000 on land costing $100,000 (purchased from the contractor and included in the first payment). Shalla made the following payments to the construction company during 1995:

January 1	March 1	May 1	December 31	Total
$210,000	$300,000	$540,000	$450,000	$1,500,000

Construction was completed and the building was ready for occupancy on December 31, 1995. Shalla Company had the following debt outstanding at December 31, 1995:

Specific Construction Debt

1. 15%, 3-year note to finance purchase of land and construction of the building, dated December 31, 1994, with interest payable annually on December 31 $750,000

Other Debt

2. 10%, 5-year note payable, dated December 31, 1991, with interest payable annually on December 31 $550,000
3. 12%, 10-year bonds issued December 31, 1990, with interest payable annually on December 31 $600,000

The weighted-average accumulated expenditures during 1995 are computed as follows:

ILLUSTRATION 10-3
Computation of
Weighted-Average
Accumulated
Expenditures

Expenditures			Current Year Capitalization		Weighted-Average
Date	Amount	×	Period	=	Accumulated Expenditures
January 1	$ 210,000		12/12		$210,000
March 1	300,000		10/12		250,000
May 1	540,000		8/12		360,000
December 31	450,000		0		0
	$1,500,000				$820,000

---

[3]The interest rate to be used may be based exclusively on an average rate of all the borrowings, if desired. For our purposes, we will use the specific borrowing rate followed by the average interest rate because we believe it to be more conceptually consistent. Either method can be used; *FASB Statement No. 34* does not provide explicit guidance on this measurement. For a discussion of this issue and others related to interest capitalization see Kathryn M. Means and Paul M. Kazenski, "SFAS 34: Receipt for Diversity," *Accounting Horizons,* September 1988; and, Wendy A. Duffy, "A Graphical Analysis of Interest Capitalization," *Journal of Accounting Education,* Fall 1990. Also, Appendix 10–A discusses interest capitalization in a more complex environment where debt is issued during the year.

Note that the expenditure made on December 31, the last day of the year, does not have any interest cost.

The avoidable interest is computed as follows:

Weighted-Average Accumulated Expenditures		Interest Rate	=	Avoidable Interest
$750,000	×	.15 (construction note)		$112,500
70,000ᵃ		.1104 (weighted average of		
$820,000		other debt)ᵇ		7,728
				$120,228

ᵃThe amount by which the weighted-average accumulated expenditures exceeds the specific construction loan.

ᵇWeighted-average interest rate computation:

	Principal	Interest
10%, 5-year note	$ 550,000	$ 55,000
12%, 10-year bonds	600,000	72,000
	$1,150,000	$127,000

Weighted-average interest rate $= \dfrac{\text{Total interest}}{\text{Total principal}} = \dfrac{\$127,000}{\$1,150,000} = 11.04\%$

ILLUSTRATION 10-4
Computation of Avoidable Interest

The actual interest cost, which represents the maximum amount of interest that may be capitalized during 1995, is computed as shown below.

Construction note	$750,000 × .15	=	$112,500
5-year note	$550,000 × .10	=	55,000
10-year bonds	$600,000 × .12	=	72,000
Actual interest			$239,500

ILLUSTRATION 10-5
Computation of Actual Interest Cost

The interest cost to be capitalized is the lesser of $120,228 (avoidable interest) or $239,500 (actual interest), which is **$120,228.**

The journal entries to be made by Shalla Company during 1995 would be as follows:

January 1

Land	100,000	
Building (or Construction in Process)	110,000	
Cash		210,000

March 1

Building	300,000	
Cash		300,000

May 1

Building	540,000	
Cash		540,000

December 31

Building	450,000	
Cash		450,000

Building (Capitalized interest)	120,228	
Interest Expense ($239,500 − $120,228)	119,272	
Cash ($112,500 + $55,000 + $72,000)		239,500

Capitalized interest cost should be written off as part of depreciation over the useful life of the assets involved and not over the term of the debt. The total interest cost incurred during the period should be disclosed, with the portion charged to expense and the portion capitalized indicated.

At December 31, 1995, Shalla would disclose the amount of interest capitalized either as part of the nonoperating section of the income statement or in the notes accompanying the financial statements. Both forms of disclosure are illustrated on page 488.

ILLUSTRATION 10-6
Capitalized Interest
Reported in the Income
Statement

Income from operations		XXXX
Other expenses and losses:		
Interest expense	$239,500	
Less capitalized interest	120,228	119,272
Income before taxes on income		XXXX
Income taxes		XXX
Net income		XXXX

ILLUSTRATION 10-7
Capitalized Interest
Disclosed in a Note

Note 1: Accounting Policies. *Capitalized interest.* During 1995 total interest cost was $239,500, of which $120,228 was capitalized and $119,272 was charged to expense.

Special Issues Related to Interest Capitalization

Three issues related to interest capitalization merit special attention:

1. Expenditures for land.
2. Interest revenue.
3. Significance of interest capitalization.

Expenditures for Land

When land is purchased with the intention of developing it for a particular use, interest costs associated with those expenditures qualify for interest capitalization. If land is purchased as a site for a structure (such as a plant site), interest costs capitalized during the period of construction are part of the cost of the plant, not the land. In the Shalla illustration where land was acquired for a structure, all interest costs capitalized (including those related to land expenditures) should be allocated to the cost of the building. Conversely, if land is being developed for lot sales, any capitalized interest cost should be part of the acquisition cost of the developed land. However, interest costs involved in purchasing land held **for speculation** should **not** be capitalized because the asset is ready for its intended use.

Interest Revenue

Companies frequently borrow money to finance construction of assets and temporarily invest the excess borrowed funds in interest-bearing securities until the funds are needed to pay for construction. During the early stages of construction, interest revenue earned may exceed the interest cost incurred on the borrowed funds.

The question is whether it is appropriate to offset interest revenue against interest cost when determining the amount of interest to be capitalized as a part of the construction cost of assets? According to *FASB Statement No. 62* on capitalization of interest cost, **interest revenue should not be netted or offset against interest cost,** except in cases involving externally restricted tax exempt borrowings. Temporary or short-term investment decisions are not related to the interest incurred as part of the acquisition cost of assets. Therefore, the interest incurred on qualifying assets should be capitalized whether or not excess funds are temporarily invested in short term securities. Some accountants are critical of this accounting because a company can defer the interest cost but report the interest revenue in the current period.

Significance of Interest Capitalization

The requirement of interest capitalization can have a substantive impact on the financial statements of business enterprises. When Jim Walter Corporation's earnings dropped from $1.51 to $1.17 per share, the building materials manufacturer, looking for ways to regain its profitability, was able to pick up an additional 11 cents per share by capitalizing the interest on coal mining projects and several plants under construction.

Public utilities have been permitted to capitalize interest during construction (whether actual or imputed) for many years.[4] For example, at one time it was estimated that Duke Power's net income of $58.5 million would be reduced by more than 85% if capitalized interest costs were shown as an expense.

The interest capitalization requirement, while now universally adopted, is still debated. From a conceptual viewpoint, many believe that either no interest cost should be capitalized or all interest costs, actual or imputed, should be capitalized for the reasons mentioned earlier in this section.

▶ ACQUISITION AND VALUATION

We have seen that **an asset should be recorded at the fair market value of what is given up to acquire it or at its own fair market value, whichever is more clearly evident.** Fair market value, however, is sometimes obscured by the process through which the asset is acquired. As an example, assume that land and buildings are bought together for one price. How are separate values for the land and building determined? A number of accounting problems of this nature are examined in the following sections.

OBJECTIVE 5

Understand accounting issues related to acquiring and valuing plant assets.

CASH DISCOUNT

When plant assets are purchased subject to cash discounts for prompt payment, how should the discount be reported? If the discount is taken, it should be considered a reduction in the purchase price of the asset. What is not clear, however, is whether a reduction in the asset cost should occur even if the discount is not taken.

Two points of view exist on this matter. Under one approach, the discount, whether taken or not, is considered a reduction in the cost of the asset. The rationale for this approach is that the real cost of the asset is the cash or cash equivalent price of the asset. In addition, some argue that the terms of cash discounts are so attractive that failure to take them indicates management error or inefficiency. Proponents of the other approach argue that the discount should not always be considered a loss because the terms may be unfavorable or because it might not be prudent for the company to take the discount. At present, both methods are employed in practice. The former method is generally preferred.

DEFERRED PAYMENT CONTRACTS

Plant assets are purchased frequently on long-term credit contracts through the use of notes, mortgages, bonds, or equipment obligations. **To properly reflect cost, assets purchased on long-term credit contracts should be accounted for at the present value of the consideration exchanged between the contracting parties at the date of the transaction.** For example, an asset purchased today in exchange for a $10,000 noninterest-bearing note payable 4 years from now should not be recorded at $10,000. The present value of the $10,000 note establishes the exchange price of the transaction (the purchase price of the asset). Assuming an appropriate interest rate of 12% at which to

---

[4]Nonutility companies traditionally had not capitalized any interest cost during construction, whether actual or imputed. In the early 1970s, however, a number of companies decided to do so. The reason for this switch was to prevent the decline in earnings that resulted when an enterprise expensed these interest costs. In 1974, the SEC in *ASR No. 163* declared a temporary moratorium on the capitalization of interest costs for most nonutility companies, indicating that these practices were leading to noncomparability of financial data. In 1979, the FASB finally standardized accounting for interest costs during construction.

Public utility companies are allowed to include in the costs of additions to plant and equipment an "allowance for funds used during construction" (AFUDC) in conformity with Federal Energy Regulatory Commission pronouncements. AFUDC includes not only interest on borrowed funds but also an **imputed interest on equity funds** used during construction.

discount this single payment of $10,000 due 4 years from now, this asset should be recorded at $6,355.20 [$10,000 × .63552; see Table 6–2 for the present value of an amount, p = $10,000 $(p_{\overline{4}|12\%})$].

When no interest rate is stated, or if the specified rate is unreasonable, an appropriate interest rate must be imputed. The objective is to approximate the interest rate that the buyer and seller would negotiate at arm's length in a similar borrowing transaction. Factors to be considered in imputing an interest rate are the borrower's credit rating, the amount and maturity date of the note, and prevailing interest rates. If determinable, the cash exchange price of the asset acquired should be used as the basis for recording the asset and measuring the interest element.

To illustrate, Sutter Company purchases a specially built robot spray painter for its production line. The company issues a $100,000, 5-year, noninterest-bearing note to Wrigley Robotics, Inc. for the new equipment when the prevailing market rate of interest for obligations of this nature is 10%. Sutter is to pay off the note in five $20,000 installments made at the end of each year. The fair market value of this specially built robot is not readily determinable and must therefore be approximated by establishing the market value (present value) of the note. Computation of the present value of the note and the date of purchase and dates of payment entries are as follows:

Date of Purchase

Equipment	75,816*	
Discount on Notes Payable	24,184	
Notes Payable		100,000

*Present value of note = $20,000 $(P_{\overline{5}|10\%})$
= $20,000 (3.79079) Table 6-4
= $75,816

End of First Year

Interest Expense	7,582	
Notes Payable	20,000	
Cash		20,000
Discount on Notes Payable		7,582

Interest expense in the first year under the effective interest approach is $7,582 [($100,000 − $24,184) × 10%]. The entry at the end of the second year to record interest and principal payment is as follows:

End of Second Year

Interest Expense	6,340	
Notes Payable	20,000	
Cash		20,000
Discount on Notes Payable		6,340

Interest expense in the second year under the effective interest approach is $6,340 [($100,000 − $24,184) − ($20,000 − $7,582)] × 10%.

If an interest rate were not imputed for such deferred payment contracts, the asset would be recorded at an amount greater than its fair value. In addition, interest expense reported in the income statement would be understated for all periods involved.

LUMP SUM PURCHASE

A special problem of pricing fixed assets arises when a group of plant assets is purchased at a single **lump sum price.** When such a situation occurs, and it is not at all unusual, the practice is to allocate the total cost among the various assets on the basis of their relative fair market values. The assumption is that costs will vary in direct proportion to sales value. This is the same principle that is applied to allocate a lump sum cost among different inventory items.

To determine fair market value, any of the following might be used: an appraisal for insurance purposes, the assessed valuation for property taxes, or simply an independent appraisal by an engineer or other appraiser.

To illustrate, Norduct Homes, Inc. decides to purchase several assets of a small heating concern, Comfort Heating, for $80,000. Comfort Heating is in the process of liquidation, and its assets sold are:

	Book Value	Fair Market Value
Inventory	$30,000	$ 25,000
Land	20,000	25,000
Building	35,000	50,000
	$85,000	$100,000

The $80,000 purchase price would be allocated on the basis of the relative fair market values (assuming specific identification of costs is not practicable) in the following manner:

Inventory $\dfrac{\$25,000}{\$100,000} \times \$80,000 = \$20,000$

Land $\dfrac{\$25,000}{\$100,000} \times \$80,000 = \$20,000$

Building $\dfrac{\$50,000}{\$100,000} \times \$80,000 = \$40,000$

ILLUSTRATION 10-8
Allocation of Purchase Price—Relative Fair Market Value Basis

ISSUANCE OF STOCK

When property is acquired by issuance of securities, such as common stock, the cost of the property is not properly measured by the par or stated value of such stock. If the stock is being actively traded, **the market value of the stock issued is a fair indication of the cost of the property acquired because the stock is a good measure of the current cash equivalent price.**

For example, Upgrade Living Co. decides to purchase some adjacent land for expansion of its carpeting and cabinet operation. In lieu of paying cash for the land, the company issues to Deedland Company 5,000 shares of common stock (par value $10) that have a fair market value of $12 per share. Upgrade Living Co. would make the following entry.

Land (5,000 × $12)	60,000	
Common Stock		50,000
Additional Paid-In Capital		10,000

If the market value of the common stock exchanged is not determinable, the market value of the property should be established and used as the basis for recording the asset and issuance of the common stock.[5]

EXCHANGES OF PROPERTY, PLANT, AND EQUIPMENT (NONMONETARY ASSETS)

The proper accounting for exchanges of nonmonetary assets (such as inventories and property, plant, and equipment) is controversial.[6] Some accountants argue that the ac-

---

[5]When the fair market value of the stock is used as the basis of valuation, careful consideration must be given to the effect that the issuance of additional shares will have on the existing market price. Where the effect on market price appears significant, an independent appraisal of the asset received should be made. This valuation should be employed as the basis for valuation of the asset as well as for the stock issued. In the unusual case where the fair market value of the stock or the fair market value of the asset cannot be determined objectively, the board of directors of the corporation may set the value.

[6]Nonmonetary assets are items whose price in terms of the monetary unit may change over time, whereas monetary assets—cash and short- or long-term accounts and notes receivable—are fixed in terms of units of currency by contract or otherwise.

counting for these types of exchanges should be based on the fair value of the asset given up or the fair value of the asset received with a gain or loss recognized. Others believe that the accounting should be based on the recorded amount (book value) of the asset given up, with no gain or loss recognized. Still others favor an approach that would recognize losses in all cases, but defer gains in special situations.

Ordinarily accounting for the exchange of **nonmonetary assets** should be based on **the fair value of the asset given up or the fair value of the asset received, whichever is clearly more evident.**[7] Thus, any gains or losses on the exchange **should be recognized immediately.** The rationale for such immediate recognition is that the earnings process related to these assets is completed and, therefore, a gain or loss should be recognized. This approach is always employed when the assets are **dissimilar** in nature, such as the exchange of land for a building, or the exchange of equipment for inventory. If the fair value of either asset is not reasonably determinable, the book value of the asset given up is usually used as the basis for recording the nonmonetary exchange.

The general rule of immediate recognition is modified when exchanges of **similar** nonmonetary assets occur for gain situations. For example, when a company exchanges its inventory items with inventory of another company because of color, size, etc. to facilitate sale to an outside customer, the earnings process is not considered completed and a **gain** should not be recognized. Likewise if a company trades **similar productive assets** such as land for land or equipment for equipment, the earnings process is not considered complete and, therefore, **a gain should not be recognized.** However, if the exchange transaction involving **similar assets** would result in a loss, **the loss is recognized immediately.**

In certain situations, gains on exchange of similar nonmonetary assets may be recognized where **monetary consideration (boot)** is received. When monetary consideration such as cash is received in addition to the nonmonetary asset, it is assumed that a portion of the earnings process is completed and, therefore, a partial gain is recognized.[8]

In summary, losses on nonmonetary transactions are always recognized whether the exchange involves dissimilar or similar assets. Gains on nonmonetary transactions are recognized if the exchange involves dissimilar assets; gains are deferred if the exchange involves similar assets, unless cash or some other form of monetary consideration is received, in which case a partial gain is recognized. Any gain or loss on disposal of nonmonetary assets is computed by comparing the book value with the fair value of the asset given up.

To illustrate the accounting for these different types of transactions, we will look at the following three situations: **1.** Accounting for dissimilar assets. **2.** Accounting for similar assets—loss situation. **3.** Accounting for similar assets—gain situation.

Dissimilar Assets

The cost of a nonmonetary asset acquired in exchange for a **dissimilar nonmonetary asset** is usually recorded at the **fair value of the asset given up,** and a gain or loss is recognized. The **fair value of the asset received** should be used only if it is more clearly evident than the fair value of the asset given up.

To illustrate, Interstate Transportation Company exchanged a number of used trucks plus cash for vacant land that might be used for a future plant site. The trucks have a combined book value of $42,000 (cost $64,000 less $22,000 accumulated depreciation). Interstate's purchasing agent, who has had previous dealings in the second-hand market, indicates that the trucks have a fair market value of $49,000. In addition to the trucks, Interstate must pay $17,000 cash for the land. The cost of the land to Interstate is $66,000 computed as follows:

---

[7]"Accounting for Nonmonetary Transactions," *Opinions of the Accounting Principles Board No. 29* (Stamford, Conn.: FASB, 1973), par. 18.

[8]When the monetary consideration is significant, i.e., **25% or more** of the fair value of the exchange, the transaction is considered a **monetary exchange** by both parties. In such "monetary" exchanges the fair values are used to measure the gains or losses that are recognized in their entirety. *EITF Issue No. 86-29,* "Nonmonetary Transactions: Magnitude of Boot and the Exception to the Use of Fair Value," *Emerging Issues Task Force Abstracts* (October 1, 1987).

Fair value of trucks exchanged	$49,000
Cash paid	17,000
Cost of land	$66,000

ILLUSTRATION 10-9
Computation of
Land Cost

The journal entry to record the exchange transaction is:

Land	66,000	
Accumulated Depreciation—Trucks	22,000	
Trucks		64,000
Gain on Disposal of Trucks		7,000
Cash		17,000

The gain is the difference between the fair value of the trucks and their book value. It is verified as follows:

Fair value of trucks		$49,000
Cost of trucks	$64,000	
Less accumulated depreciation	22,000	
Book value of trucks		42,000
Gain on disposal of used trucks		$ 7,000

ILLUSTRATION 10-10
Computation of Gain on
Disposal of Used Trucks

It follows that if the fair value of the trucks was $39,000 instead of $49,000, a loss on the exchange of $3,000 ($42,000 − $39,000) would be reported. In either case, as a result of the exchange of dissimilar assets, the earnings process on the used trucks has been completed and **a gain or loss should be recognized.**

Similar Assets—Loss Situation

Similar nonmonetary assets are those that are of the same general type, or that perform the same function, or that are employed in the same line of business. When similar nonmonetary assets are exchanged and a loss results, the loss should be recognized immediately. For example, Information Processing, Inc. trades its used accounting machine for a new model. The accounting machine given up has a book value of $8,000 (original cost $12,000 less $4,000 accumulated depreciation) and a fair value of $6,000. It is traded for a new model that has a list price of $16,000. In negotiations with the seller, a trade-in allowance of $9,000 is finally agreed on for the used machine. The cash payment that must be made for the new asset and the cost of the new machine are computed as follows:

List price of new machine	$16,000
Less trade-in allowance for used machine	9,000
Cash payment due	7,000
Fair value of used machine	6,000
Cost of new machine	$13,000

ILLUSTRATION 10-11
Computation of Cost
of New Machine

The journal entry to record this transaction is:

Equipment	13,000	
Accumulated Depreciation—Equipment	4,000	
Loss on Disposal of Equipment	2,000	
Equipment		12,000
Cash		7,000

The loss on the disposal of the used machine can be verified as follows:

Fair value of used machine	$6,000
Book value of used machine	8,000
Loss on disposal of used machine	$2,000

ILLUSTRATION 10-12
Computation of Loss on
Disposal of Used
Machine

Why was the trade-in allowance or the book value of the old asset not used as a basis for the new equipment? The trade-in allowance is not used because it included a price concession (similar to a price discount) to the purchaser. Few individuals pay list price for a new car. Trade-in allowances on the used car are often inflated so that actual selling prices are below list prices. To record the car at list price would state it at an amount in excess of its cash equivalent price because the new car's list price is usually inflated. Use of book value in this situation would overstate the value of the new accounting machine by $2,000. Because assets should not be valued at more than their cash equivalent price, the loss should be recognized immediately rather than added to the cost of the newly acquired asset.

Similar Assets—Gain Situation (No Cash Received)

The accounting treatment for exchanges of **similar** nonmonetary assets when a gain develops is more complex. If the exchange does not complete the earnings process, then any **gain should be deferred.**

The real estate industry provides a good example of why the accounting profession decided not to recognize gains on exchanges of similar nonmonetary assets. In this industry, it is common practice for companies to "swap" real estate holdings. Assume that Landmark Company and Hillfarm, Inc. each had undeveloped land on which they intended to build shopping centers. Appraisals indicated that the land of both companies had increased significantly in value. The companies decided to exchange (swap) their undeveloped land, record a gain, and report their new parcels of land at current fair values. But, should gains be recognized at this point? No: the earnings process is not completed because the companies remain in the same economic position after the swap as before. Therefore, the asset acquired should be recorded at book value with no gain recognized. In contrast, had book value exceeded fair value, a loss would be recognized immediately.

Davis Rent-A-Car has a rental fleet of automobiles consisting primarily of Ford Motor Company products. Davis's management is interested in increasing the variety of automobiles in its rental fleet by adding numerous General Motors models. Davis arranges with Nertz Rent-A-Car to exchange a group of Ford automobiles with a fair value of $160,000 and a book value of $135,000 (cost $150,000 less accumulated depreciation $15,000) for a number of Chevy and Pontiac models with a fair value of $170,000; Davis pays $10,000 in cash in addition to the Ford automobiles exchanged. The total gain to Davis Rent-A-Car is computed as shown in the schedule below:

ILLUSTRATION 10-13
Computation of Gain (Unrecognized)

Fair value of Ford automobiles exchanged	$160,000
Book value of Ford automobiles exchanged	135,000
Total gain (unrecognized)	$ 25,000

But the earnings process is not considered completed in this transaction. The company still has a fleet of cars, although different models. Therefore, the total gain is deferred and the basis of the General Motors automobiles is reduced via two different but acceptable computations as shown below:

ILLUSTRATION 10-14
Basis of New Automobiles—Fair Value vs. Book Value

Fair value of GM automobiles	$170,000		Book value of Ford automobiles	$135,000
Less gain deferred	(25,000)	OR	Cash paid	10,000
Basis of GM automobiles	$145,000		Basis of GM automobiles	$145,000

The entry by Davis to record this transaction is as follows:

Automobiles (GM)	145,000	
Accumulated Depreciation—Automobiles	15,000	
Automobiles (Ford)		150,000
Cash		10,000

The gain that reduced the basis of the new automobiles will be recognized when those automobiles are sold to an outside party. While these automobiles are held, depreciation charges will be lower and net income will be higher in subsequent periods because of the reduced basis.

Similar Assets—Gain Situation (Some Cash Received)

The accounting issue of gain recognition becomes more difficult if monetary consideration such as cash is **received** in an exchange of similar nonmonetary assets. When cash is received, part of the nonmonetary asset is considered sold and part exchanged; therefore, only a portion of the gain is deferred. The general formula for gain recognition when some cash is received is as follows:

$$\frac{\text{Cash Received (Boot)}}{\text{Cash Received (Boot)} + \text{Fair Value of Other Assets Received}} \times \text{Total Gain} = \frac{\text{Recognized}}{\text{Gain}}$$

ILLUSTRATION 10-15
Formula for Gain Recognition, Some Cash Received

If the book value of Nertz's Chevy and Pontiac automobiles exchanged in the foregoing example is $136,000 (cost $200,000 less accumulated depreciation $64,000), then the total gain on the exchange to Nertz would be computed as follows:

Fair value of GM automobiles exchanged	$170,000
Book value of GM automobiles exchanged	136,000
Total gain	$ 34,000

ILLUSTRATION 10-16
Computation of Total Gain

But, because Nertz received $10,000 in cash, the recognized gain on this transaction is computed as follows:

$$\frac{\$10,000}{\$10,000 + \$160,000} \times \$34,000 = \$2,000$$

ILLUSTRATION 10-17
Computation of Recognized Gain Based on Ratio of Cash Received

The ratio of monetary assets ($10,000) to the total consideration received ($10,000 + $160,000) is the portion of the total gain ($34,000) to be recognized—that is, $2,000. Because only a gain of $2,000 is recognized on this transaction, the remaining $32,000 ($34,000 − $2,000) is deferred and reduces the basis (recorded cost) of the new automobiles. The computation of the basis is as follows:

Fair value of Ford automobiles	$160,000		Book value of GM automobiles	$136,000
Less gain deferred	(32,000)	OR	Portion of book value	
Basis of Ford automobiles	$128,000		presumed sold	(8,000)*
			Basis of Ford automobiles	$128,000

$$* \frac{\$10,000}{\$170,000} \times \$136,000 = \$8,000$$

ILLUSTRATION 10-18
Basis of New Automobiles—Fair Value vs. Book Value

The entry by Nertz to record this transaction is as follows:

Cash	10,000	
Automobiles (Ford)	128,000	
Accumulated Depreciation—Automobiles (GM)	64,000	
Automobiles (GM)		200,000
Gain on Disposal of GM Automobiles		2,000

The rationale for this treatment is as follows: Before the exchange, Nertz Rent-A-Car had an unrecognized gain of $34,000, as evidenced by the difference between the book value ($136,000) and the fair value ($170,000) of its GM automobiles. When the exchange occurred, a portion ($10,000/$170,000 or 1/17) of the fair value was converted to a more liquid asset. The ratio of this liquid asset ($10,000) to the total consideration received ($160,000 + $10,000) is the portion of the gain ($34,000) realized. Thus, a gain of $2,000 (1/17 × $34,000) is recognized and recorded.

Presented below in summary form are the accounting requirements for recognizing gains and losses on exchanges of nonmonetary assets.[9]

ILLUSTRATION 10-19
Summary of Gain and
Loss Recognition on
Exchanges of
Nonmonetary Assets

1. Compute the total gain or loss on the transaction, which is equal to the difference between the fair value of the asset given up and the book value of the asset given up.
2. If a loss is computed in 1, always recognize the entire loss.
3. If a gain is computed in 1,
   (a) and the earnings process is considered completed, the entire gain is recognized (dissimilar assets).
   (b) and the earnings process is not considered completed (similar assets),
     (1) and no cash is involved, no gain is recognized.
     (2) and some cash is given, no gain is recognized.
     (3) and some cash is received, the following portion of the gain is recognized:

$$\frac{\text{Cash Received (Boot)}}{\text{Cash Received (Boot)} + \text{Fair Value of Other Assets Received}} \times \text{Total Gain.}$$

An enterprise that engages in one or more nonmonetary exchanges during a period should disclose in financial statements for the period the nature of the transactions, the method of accounting for the assets transferred, and gains or losses recognized on transfers.[10]

ACCOUNTING FOR CONTRIBUTIONS

Companies sometimes receive or make contributions (donations or gifts). Such contributions are referred to as **nonreciprocal transfers** because they are transfers of assets in one direction. Contributions are often some type of asset (such as cash, securities, land, buildings, or use of facilities), but it also could be the foregiveness of a debt.

When assets are acquired as a donation, a strict cost concept dictates that the valuation of the asset should be zero. A departure from the cost principle seems justified, however, because the only costs incurred (legal fees and other relatively minor expenditures) do not constitute a reasonable basis of accounting for the assets acquired. To record nothing is to ignore the economic realities of an increase in wealth and assets. Therefore, **the fair value of the asset should be used to establish its value on the books.**

Two general approaches have been used to record the credit for the asset received. Some believe the credit should be to Donated Capital (an additional paid-in capital account). The increase in assets is viewed more as contributed capital than as earned revenue. To illustrate, Max Wayer Meat Packing, Inc. has recently accepted a donation of land with a fair value of $150,000 from the city of Burke in return for a promise to build a packing plant in Burke. Max Wayer's entry is:

Land	150,000	
Donated Capital		150,000

Others argue that capital is contributed only by the owners of the business and that donations are benefits to the enterprise that should be reported as revenues from contributions. At issue is whether the revenue should be reported immediately or over the period that the asset is employed. To attract new industry a city may offer land, but the receiving enterprise may incur additional costs in the future (transportation, higher state income taxes, etc.) because the location is not the most desirable. As a consequence,

---

[9]Adapted from an article by Robert Capettini and Thomas E. King, "Exchanges of Nonmonetary Assets: Some Changes," *The Accounting Review* (January 1976).

[10]"Accounting for Nonmonetary Transactions," op. cit., par. 28.

some argue that the revenue should be deferred and recognized as the costs are incurred.

In a recent standard, the FASB has taken the position that, **in general, contributions received should be recognized as revenues in the period received.**[11] Contributions would be measured at the fair value of the assets received.[12]

When a nonmonetary asset is contributed, the amount of the donation should be recorded as an expense at the fair value of the donated asset. If a difference exists between the fair value of the asset and its book value, a gain or loss should be recognized. To illustrate, Kline Industries donates land that cost $80,000 and has a fair market value of $110,000 to the city of Los Angeles for a city park. The entry to record this donation would be:

Contribution Expense	110,000	
Land		80,000
Gain on Disposal of Land		30,000

In some cases, companies will promise (pledge) some type of asset in the future. The question is whether this promise should be recorded immediately or at the time the assets are given. If the promise is **unconditional** (depends only on the passage of time or on demand by the recipient for performance), the contribution and related payable should be reported. If the promise is **conditional,** the expense is recognized in the period benefited by the contribution, which is generally when the asset is transferred.

▶ COSTS SUBSEQUENT TO ACQUISITION

After plant assets are installed and ready for use, additional costs are incurred that range from ordinary repair to significant additions. The major problem is allocating these costs to the proper time periods. **In general, costs incurred to achieve greater future benefits should be capitalized, whereas expenditures that simply maintain a given level of services should be expensed.** In order for costs to be capitalized, one of three conditions must be present:

1. The useful life of the asset must be increased.
2. The quantity of units produced from the asset must be increased.
3. The quality of the units produced must be enhanced.

Expenditures that do not increase an asset's future benefits should be expensed. Ordinary repairs are expenditures that maintain the existing condition of the asset or restore it to normal operating efficiency and should be expensed immediately.

Most expenditures below an established arbitrary minimum amount are expensed rather than capitalized. Many enterprises have adopted the rule that expenditures below, say, $100 or $500, should always be expensed. Although conceptually this treatment may not be correct, expediency demands it. Otherwise, accountants would have to set up depreciation schedules for such items as wastepaper baskets and ash trays.

The distinction between a **capital (asset)** and **revenue (expense) expenditure** is not always clear-cut. Determining the **property unit** with which costs should be associated is critical. If a fully equipped steamship is considered a property unit, then replacement of the engine might be considered an expense. On the other hand, if the ship's engine is considered a property unit, then its replacement would be capitalized. AT&T at one time argued that it should be permitted to expense its station connectors (wires that

OBJECTIVE 6

Describe the accounting treatment for costs subsequent to acquisition.

UNDERLYING CONCEPT

Expensing long-lived ash trays and waste baskets is an application of the materiality constraint.

---

[11]"Accounting for Contributions Received and Contributions Made," *Statement of Financial Accounting Standards No. 116* (Norwalk, CT: FASB, 1993). Transfers of assets from governmental units to business enterprises are excluded from the scope of this standard. However, we believe that the basic requirements should hold also for these types of contributions and, therefore, all assets should be recorded at fair value and all credits should be recorded as revenue.

[12]"Accounting for Nonmonetary Transactions," op. cit., par. 18. Also, *FASB No. 116* indicates that expenses on contributions made should be recorded at the fair value of the assets given up.

connect your telephone to the outside wall). Previously, these wires had been capitalized and depreciated over an 8-year period. AT&T argued that continual home occupancy changes resulted in so much rewiring that expensing these wires was more appropriate. The Federal Communications Commission approved this request, and, the cost of wiring is now expensed. This decision is significant: it was at one time estimated that the cost of phone installation in Illinois would triple as a result of this accounting change. In most cases, **consistent application of a capital/expense policy** is justified as more important than attempting to provide general theoretical guidelines for each transaction.

Generally, four major types of expenditures are incurred relative to existing assets.

◀ MAJOR TYPES OF EXPENDITURES ▶

ADDITIONS.   Increase or extension of existing assets.

IMPROVEMENTS AND REPLACEMENTS.   Substitution of an improved asset for an existing one.

REARRANGEMENT AND REINSTALLATION.   Movement of assets from one location to another.

REPAIRS.   Expenditures that maintain assets in condition for operation.

ADDITIONS

Additions should present no major accounting problems. By definition, **any addition to plant assets is capitalized** because a new asset has been created. The addition of a wing to a hospital or the addition of an air conditioning system to an office, for example, increases the service potential of that facility. Such expenditures should be capitalized and matched against the revenues that will result in future periods.

The most difficult problem that develops in this area is accounting for any changes related to the existing structure as a result of the addition. Is the cost that is incurred to tear down a wall of the old structure to make room for the addition a cost of the addition or an expense or loss of the period? The answer is that it depends on the original intent. If the company had anticipated that an addition was going to be added later, then this cost of removal is a proper cost of the addition. But if the company had not anticipated this development, it should properly be reported as a loss in the current period on the basis that the company was inefficient in its planning. Normally, the carrying amount of the old wall remains in the accounts, although theoretically it should be removed.

IMPROVEMENTS AND REPLACEMENTS

Improvements (often referred to as betterments) and **replacements** are substitutions of one asset for another. What is the difference between an improvement and a replacement? An improvement is the substitution of a **better asset** for the one currently used (say, a concrete floor for a wooden floor). A replacement, on the other hand, is the substitution of a **similar asset** (a wooden floor for a wooden floor).

Many times improvements and replacements result from a general policy to modernize or rehabilitate an older building or piece of equipment. The problem is differentiating these types of expenditure from normal repairs. Does the expenditure increase the **future service potential** of the asset, or does it merely **maintain the existing level** of service? Frequently, the answer is not clear-cut, and good judgment must be used in order to classify these expenditures.

If it is determined that the expenditure increases the future service potential of the asset and, therefore, should be capitalized, the accounting is handled in one of three ways, depending on the circumstances.

1. **Substitution Approach.** Conceptually, the substitution approach is the correct procedure if the carrying amount of the old asset is available. If the carrying amount of the old asset can be determined, it is a simple matter to remove the cost of the old asset and replace it with the cost of the new asset.

   To illustrate, Instinct Enterprises decides to replace the pipes in its plumbing system. A plumber suggests that in place of the cast iron pipes and copper tubing, a newly developed plastic tubing be used. The old pipe and tubing have a book value of $15,000 (cost of $150,000 less accumulated depreciation of $135,000), and a scrap value of $1,000. The plastic tubing system has a cost of $125,000. Assuming that Instinct has to pay $124,000 for the new tubing after exchanging the old tubing, the entry is:

Plumbing System	125,000	
Accumulated Depreciation	135,000	
Loss on Disposal of Plant Assets	14,000	
Plumbing System		150,000
Cash ($125,000 − $1,000)		124,000

   The problem is determining the book value of the old asset. Generally, the components of a given asset depreciate at different rates, but no separate accounting is made. As an example, the tires, motor, and body of a truck depreciate at different rates, but most concerns use only one depreciation rate for the entire truck. Separate depreciation rates could be set for each component, but it would be impractical. If the carrying amount of the old asset cannot be determined, one of two other approaches is adopted.

2. **Capitalizing the New Cost.** The justification for capitalizing the cost of the improvement or replacement is that even though the carrying amount of the old asset is not removed from the accounts, sufficient depreciation was taken on the item to reduce the carrying amount almost to zero. Although this assumption may not be true in every case, the differences are not often significant. Improvements are usually handled in this manner.

3. **Charging to Accumulated Depreciation.** There are times when the quantity or quality of the asset itself has not been improved, but its useful life has been extended. Replacements, particularly, may extend the useful life of the asset, yet may not improve its quality or quantity. In these circumstances, the expenditure may be debited to Accumulated Depreciation rather than to an asset account. The theory behind this approach is that the replacement extends the useful life of the asset and thereby recaptures some or all of the past depreciation. The net carrying amount of the asset is the same whether the asset is debited or the accumulated depreciation is debited.

REARRANGEMENT AND REINSTALLATION

Rearrangement and reinstallation costs, which are expenditures intended to benefit future periods, are different from additions, replacements, and improvements. An example is the rearrangement and reinstallation of a group of machines to facilitate future production. If the original installation cost and the accumulated depreciation taken to date can be determined or estimated, the rearrangement and reinstallation cost is handled as a replacement. If not, which is generally the case, the new costs (if material in amount) should be capitalized as an asset to be amortized over those future periods expected to benefit.[13] If these costs are not material, if they cannot be separated from

---

[13]Another cost of this nature is relocation costs. For example, when Shell Oil moved its headquarters from New York to Houston, it amortized the cost of relocating over 4 years. Conversely, estimated relocation costs of $15 million were charged to expense at GAF Corp. The point is that no definitive guidelines have been established in this area, and generally costs are deferred over some arbitrary period in the future. Some writers have argued that these costs should generally be expensed as incurred. See, for example, Charles W. Lamden, Dale L. Gerboth, and Thomas W. McRae, "Accounting for Depreciable Assets," *Accounting Research Monograph No. 1* (New York: AICPA, 1975), pp. 54–61.

other operating expenses, or if their future benefit is questionable, they should be immediately expensed.

REPAIRS

Ordinary repairs are expenditures made to maintain plant assets in operating condition; they are charged to an expense account in the period in which they are incurred on the basis that **it is the primary period benefited.** Replacement of minor parts, lubricating and adjusting of equipment, repainting, and cleaning are examples of maintenance charges that occur regularly and are treated as ordinary operating expenses.

It is often difficult to distinguish a repair from an improvement or replacement. The major consideration is whether the expenditure benefits more than one year or one operating cycle, whichever is longer. If a **major repair,** such as an overhaul, occurs, several periods will benefit and the cost should be handled as an addition, improvement, or replacement.

If income statements are prepared for short periods of time, say, monthly or quarterly, the same principles apply. Ordinary repairs and other regular maintenance charges for an annual period may benefit several quarters, and allocation of the cost among the periods concerned might be required. A concern will often find it advantageous to concentrate its repair program at a certain time of the year, perhaps during the period of least activity or when the plant is shut down for vacation. Short-term comparative statements might be misleading if such expenditures were shown as expenses of the quarter in which they were incurred. To give comparability to monthly or quarterly income statements, an account such as Allowance for Repairs might be used so that repair costs could be better assigned to periods benefited.

To illustrate, Cricket Tractor Company estimated that its total repair expense for the year would be $720,000. It decided to charge each quarter for a portion of the repair cost even though the total cost for the year would occur only in two quarters.

End of First Quarter (zero repair costs incurred):

Repair Expense	180,000	
Allowance for Repairs (¼ × 720,000)		180,000

End of Second Quarter ($344,000 repair costs incurred):

Allowance for Repairs	344,000	
Cash, Wages Payable, Inventory, etc.		344,000
Repair Expense	180,000	
Allowance for Repairs (¼ × $720,000)		180,000

End of Third Quarter (zero repair costs incurred):

Repair Expense	180,000	
Allowance for Repairs (¼ × $720,000)		180,000

End of Fourth Quarter ($380,800 repair costs incurred):

Allowance for Repairs	380,800	
Cash, Wages Payable, Inventory, etc.		380,800
Repair Expense	184,800	
Allowance for Repairs		184,800
($344,000 + $380,800 − $180,000 − $180,000 − $180,000)		

Ordinarily, no balance in the Allowance for Repairs account should be carried over to the following year. The fourth quarter would normally absorb the variation from estimates. If balance sheets are prepared during the year, the Allowance account should be added to or subtracted from the property, plant, and equipment section to obtain a proper valuation.

Some accountants advocate accruing estimated repair costs beyond one year on the assumption that depreciation does not take into consideration the incurrence of repair costs. For example, in aircraft overhaul and open hearth furnace rebuilding, an allowance for repairs is sometimes established because the amount of repairs can be estimated with a high degree of certainty. Although conceptually appealing, it is difficult to justify the Allowance for Repairs account as a liability because one might ask, To whom do you owe the liability? Placement in the stockholders' equity section is also illogical because no addition to the stockholders' investment has taken place. One possibility might be to treat allowance for repairs as an addition to or subtraction from the asset on the basis that the value has changed. In general, expenses should not be anticipated before they arise unless estimates of the future are reasonably predictable.

SUMMARY

The following schedule summarizes the accounting treatment for various costs incurred subsequent to the acquisition of capitalized assets.

Type of Expenditure	Normal Accounting Treatment
Additions	Capitalize cost of addition to asset account.
Improvements and Replacements	(a) **Carrying value known:** Remove cost of and accumulated depreciation on old asset, recognizing any gain or loss. Capitalize cost of improvement/replacement. (b) **Carrying value unknown:** 1. If the asset's useful life is extended, debit accumulated depreciation for cost of improvement/replacement. 2. If the quantity or quality of the asset's productivity is increased, capitalized cost of improvement/replacement to asset account.
Rearrangement and Reinstallation	(a) If original installation cost is **known,** account for cost of rearrangement/reinstallation as a replacement (carrying value known). (b) If original installation cost is **unknown** and rearrangement/reinstallation cost is **material** in amount and benefits future periods, capitalize as an asset. (c) If original installation cost is **unknown** and rearrangement/reinstallation cost is **not material or future benefit is questionable,** expense the cost when incurred.
Repairs	(a) **Ordinary:** Expense cost of repairs when incurred. (b) **Major:** As appropriate, treat as an addition, improvement, or replacement.

ILLUSTRATION 10-20
Summary of Costs Subsequent to Acquisition of Property, Plant, and Equipment

▶ DISPOSITIONS OF PLANT ASSETS

Plant assets may be retired voluntarily or disposed of by sale, exchange, involuntary conversion, or abandonment. Regardless of the time of disposal, depreciation must be taken up to the date of disposition, and then all accounts related to the retired asset should be removed. Ideally, the book value of the specific plant asset would be equal to its disposal value. But this is generally not the case. As a result, a gain or loss develops. The reason: depreciation is an estimate of cost allocation and not a process of valuation. **The gain or loss is really a correction of net income** for the years during which the fixed asset was used. If it had been possible at the time of acquisition to forecast the exact date of disposal and the amount to be realized at disposition, then a more accurate estimate of depreciation could have been recorded and no gain or loss would be incurred.

Gains or losses on the retirement of plant assets should be shown in the income statement along with other items that arise from customary business activities. If, however, the "operations of a segment of a business" are sold, abandoned, spun off, or otherwise disposed of, then the results of "continuing operations" should be reported separately from "discontinued operations." Any gain or loss from disposal of a segment of a business should be reported with the related results of discontinued operations and not as an extraordinary item.

OBJECTIVE 7
Describe the accounting treatment for the disposal of property, plant, and equipment.

SALE OF PLANT ASSETS

Depreciation must be recorded for the period of time between the date of the last depreciation entry and the date of sale. To illustrate, assume that depreciation on a machine costing $18,000 has been recorded for nine years at the rate of $1,200 per year. If the machine is sold in the middle of the tenth year for $7,000, the entry to record depreciation to the date of sale is:

Depreciation Expense	600	
Accumulated Depreciation—Machinery		600

This separate entry ordinarily is not made because most companies enter all depreciation, including this amount, in one entry at the end of the year. In either case the entry for the sale of the asset is:

Cash	7,000	
Accumulated Depreciation—Machinery	11,400	
[($1,200 × 9) + $600]		
Machinery		18,000
Gain on Disposal of Machinery		400

The book value of the machinery at the time of the sale is $6,600 ($18,000 − $11,400); because it is sold for $7,000, the amount of the gain on the sale is $400.

INVOLUNTARY CONVERSION

Sometimes, an asset's service is terminated through some type of **involuntary conversion** such as fire, flood, theft, or condemnation. The gains or losses are treated no differently from those in any other type of disposition except that **they are often reported in the extraordinary items section of the income statement.**

To illustrate, Camel Transport Corp. was forced to sell a plant located on company property that stood directly in the path of an interstate highway. For a number of years the state had sought to purchase the land on which the plant stood, but the company resisted. The state ultimately exercised its right of eminent domain and was upheld by the courts. In settlement, Camel received $500,000, which was substantially in excess of the $200,000 book value of the plant and land (cost of $400,000 less accumulated depreciation of $200,000). The following entry was made:

Cash	500,000	
Accumulated Depreciation—Plant Assets	200,000	
Plant Assets		400,000
Gain on Disposal of Plant Assets		300,000

However, some object to the recognition of a gain or loss in certain involuntary conversions. For example, the federal government often condemns forests for national parks; as a result, the paper companies that owned these forests are required to report a gain or loss on the condemnation. However, companies such as Georgia-Pacific contend that because they must replace this condemned forest land immediately, they are in the same economic position as they were before and no gain or loss should be reported. The issue is whether the condemnation and subsequent purchase should be viewed as one or two transactions. *FASB Interpretation No. 30* rules against the companies by requiring "that gain or loss be recognized when a nonmonetary asset is involuntarily converted to monetary assets even though an enterprise reinvests or is obligated to reinvest the monetary assets in replacement nonmonetary assets."[14]

The gain or loss that develops on these types of unusual, nonrecurring transactions should be shown as an extraordinary item. Similar treatment is given to other types of involuntary conversions such as those resulting from a major casualty (such as an earthquake) or an expropriation, assuming that it meets other conditions for extraordinary item treatment. The difference between the amount recovered (condemnation award or insurance recovery), if any, and the asset's book value is reported as a gain or loss.

---

[14]"Accounting for Involuntary Conversions of Nonmonetary Assets to Monetary Assets," *FASB Interpretation No. 30* (Stamford, Conn.: FASB, 1979), summary paragraph.

MISCELLANEOUS PROBLEMS

If an asset is scrapped or abandoned without any cash recovery, a loss should be recognized equal to the asset's book value. If scrap value exists, the gain or loss that occurs is the difference between the asset's scrap value and its book value. If an asset still can be used even though it is fully depreciated, it may be kept on the books at historical cost less depreciation, or the asset may be carried at scrap value.

Disclosure of the amount of fully depreciated assets in service should be made in notes to the financial statements. For example, Petroleum Equipment Tools Inc. in its annual report disclosed: "The amount of fully depreciated assets included in property, plant, and equipment at December 31 amounted to approximately $98,900,000."

▶ OTHER ASSET VALUATION METHODS

We have generally assumed that cost is the appropriate basis for valuing assets at acquisition. An exception is the acquisition of plant assets through donation, in which case valuation is based on fair value. Another approach that is sometimes allowed and not considered a violation of historical cost is a concept often referred to as **prudent cost.** This concept states that if for some reason you were ignorant about a certain price and paid too much for the asset originally, it is theoretically preferable to charge a loss immediately.

As an example, assume that a company constructs an asset at a cost substantially in excess of its present economic usefulness. In this case, it would be appropriate to charge these excess costs as a loss to the current period, rather than capitalize them as part of the cost of the asset. This problem seldom develops because at the outset individuals either use good reasoning in paying a given price or fail to recognize any such errors.

On the other hand, a purchase that is obtained at a bargain, or a piece of equipment internally constructed at a cost savings, should not result in immediate recognition of a gain under any circumstances. Although immediate recognition of a gain is conceptually appealing, the implications of such a treatment would be to change completely the entire basis of accounting.

> **INTERNATIONAL INSIGHT**
>
> *In the European Union, the Fourth Directive (standard) permits alternative valuation bases. Current cost and other bases may be used as long as historical cost information is also provided.*

▶ SUMMARY OF LEARNING OBJECTIVES ◀

1. **Describe the major characteristics of property, plant, and equipment.** The major characteristics of property, plant, and equipment are: (1) They are acquired for use in operations and not for resale; (2) they are long-term in nature and usually subject to depreciation; and (3) they possess physical substance.

2. **Identify the costs included in the initial valuation of land, buildings, and equipment.** *Cost of land:* Includes all expenditures made to acquire land and to ready it for use. Land costs typically include (1) the purchase price; (2) closing costs, such as title to the land, attorney's fees, and recording fees; (3) costs incurred in getting the land in condition for its intended use, such as grading, filling, draining, and clearing; (4) assumption of any liens, mortgages or encumbrances on the property; and (5) any additional land improvements that have an indefinite life.

   Cost of buildings: Includes all expenditures related directly to their acquisition or construction. These costs include (1) materials, labor, and overhead costs incurred during construction and (2) professional fees and building permits.

   Cost of equipment: Includes the purchase price, freight and handling charges incurred, insurance on the equipment while in transit, cost of special foundations if required, assembling and installation costs, and costs of conducting trial runs.

KEY TERMS

additions, 498

avoidable interest, 485

capital expenditure, 497

capitalization period, 484

dissimilar nonmonetary asset, 492

historical cost, 481

improvements (betterments), 498

involuntary conversion, 502

lump sum price, 490

major repairs, 500

nonmonetary assets, 492

nonreciprocal transfers, 496

ordinary repairs, 500

property, plant, and equipment, 481

3. **Describe the accounting problems associated with self-constructed assets.** The assignment of indirect costs of manufacturing creates special problems because these costs cannot be traced directly to work and material orders related to the fixed assets constructed. These costs might be handled in one of three ways: (1) Assign no fixed overhead to the cost of the constructed asset, (2) assign a portion of all overhead to the construction process, or (3) allocate on the basis of lost production. The second method is used extensively in practice.

4. **Describe the accounting problems associated with interest capitalization.** Only actual interest (with modifications) should be capitalized. The rationale for this approach is that during construction, the asset is not generating revenue and therefore interest cost should be deferred (capitalized); once construction is completed, the asset is ready for its intended use and revenues can be earned. Any interest cost incurred in purchasing an asset that is ready for its intended use should be expensed.

5. **Understand accounting issues related to acquiring and valuing plant assets.** The following issues relate to acquiring and valuing plant assets: (1) *Cash discounts:* Whether taken or not, they are generally considered a reduction in the cost of the asset; the real cost of the asset is the cash or cash equivalent price of the asset. (2) *Assets purchased on long-term credit contracts:* Are accounted for at the present value of the consideration exchanged between the contracting parties. (3) *Lump sum purchase:* Allocate the total cost among the various assets on the basis of their relative fair market values. (4) *Issuance of stock:* If the stock is being actively traded, the market value of the stock issued is a fair indication of the cost of the property acquired; if the market value of the common stock exchanged is not determinable, the value of the property should be established and used as the basis for recording the asset and issuance of the common stock. (5) *Exchanges of property, plant, and equipment.* See Illustration 10-19 for a summary of how to account for exchanges. (6) *Contributions:* Should be recorded at the fair value of the asset received and a related credit should be made to revenue for the same amount.

6. **Describe the accounting treatment for costs subsequent to acquisition.** See Illustration 10-20 for a summary of how to account for costs subsequent to acquisition.

7. **Describe the accounting treatment for the disposal of property, plant, and equipment.** Regardless of the time of disposal, depreciation must be taken up to the date of disposition, and then all accounts related to the retired asset should be removed. Gains or losses on the retirement of plant assets should be shown in the income statement along with other items that arise from customary business activities. Gains or losses on involuntary conversions should be reported as extraordinary items. If an asset is scrapped or abandoned without any cash recovery, a loss should be recognized equal to the asset's book value. If scrap value exists, the gain or loss that occurs is the difference between the asset's scrap value and its book value.

APPENDIX 10-A

INTEREST CAPITALIZATION— SPECIAL SITUATIONS

Three special problems associated with interest capitalization, as previously discussed within the chapter, are as follows:

1. Noninterest-bearing liabilities.
2. Interim computations.
3. Interest compounding.

▶ NONINTEREST-BEARING LIABILITIES

In defining expenditures to which interest capitalization rates should be applied, only expenditures that involve the payment of cash, the transfer of other assets, or the incurrence of a liability on which interest is recognized should be considered. Therefore, in determining expenditures to which interest cost is associated (average accumulated expenditures), amounts related to liabilities that recognize no interest should be excluded.[1] The primary examples of these types of liabilities are trade payables or accruals such as wages payable, utilities payable, and so on.

To illustrate this concept, assume that Aucoin Co. is in the process of building a complex machine. At the end of the period, the company has outstanding $350,000 of trade payables related to the machine. The entire $350,000 should be excluded in determining average accumulated expenditures for the period. The rationale for this approach is that noninterest-bearing short-term liabilities do not create interest cost for the company. Only after payment has been made does a company incur a cost, which is the interest lost (opportunity cost) on the funds used.

OBJECTIVE 8

After studying Appendix 10-A, you should be able to: Understand interest capitalization involving noninterest-bearing liabilities, interim period computations, and interest compounding.

▶ INTERIM (MONTHLY) COMPUTATIONS

The example provided in this chapter assumed that the interest capitalization computation was made at the end of the year. Many companies, however, compute the amount of interest to be capitalized on a monthly or quarterly basis. For example, assume that Chaisson Co. has the following expenditures and related debt outstanding for the month of March:

Expenditures	
Accumulated expenditures (March 1)	$100,000
Accumulated expenditures (March 31)	200,000

Debt Outstanding	
Construction note, 10%, borrowed specifically for construction of machine	$120,000
Short-term loan, 12%	300,000

The weighted-average accumulated expenditures are computed as follows:

Accumulated expenditures (March 1)	$100,000
Accumulated expenditures (March 31)	200,000
Total	300,000
	÷ 2
Weighted-average accumulated expenditures outstanding during the month of March	$150,000

**ILLUSTRATION 10A-1
Computation of Weighted-Average Accumulated Expenditures for One Month**

---

[1]Note that long-term noninterest-bearing liabilities must recognize an interest element and, therefore, this interest element is capitalized.

Avoidable interest is then computed as follows:

ILLUSTRATION 10A-2
Computation of
Avoidable Interest
for One Month

Weighted-Average Accumulated Expenditures	× Interest Rate =	Avoidable Interest
$120,000	(10% × 1/12)	$1,000
30,000	(12% × 1/12)	300
Avoidable interest for the month of March		$1,300

Assuming that avoidable interest is lower than actual interest, $1,300 is capitalized for the month of March.

If the construction note (the specific borrowing) is not outstanding during March, it is not used in the computation of avoidable interest. In the illustration in the chapter, we made the simplifying assumption that all of the debt was outstanding at the beginning of the year; therefore, all interest cost associated with the debt was capitalized.

Debt issued during the year, however, needs to be weighted by the fraction of the year that it is outstanding. By using a monthly computation, this procedure is easily accomplished because only the debt outstanding during the month is considered. Debt issued in subsequent months is ignored.

▶ INTEREST COMPOUNDING

The compounding of interest is conceptually consistent with the notion of determining the proper cost of an asset. That is, interest added to the cost of an asset should be considered as part of accumulated expenditures for the next period under consideration. For example, in the previous illustration, Chaisson Co. capitalized $1,300 of interest at the end of March. As a result, at the beginning of April, accumulated expenditures are $201,300 ($200,000 + $1,300).

▶ A COMPREHENSIVE ILLUSTRATION OF INTEREST CAPITALIZATION

To illustrate the concepts in this appendix, assume that Inboard Marine Co. had the following expenditures and debt outstanding:

Accumulated expenditures

Accumulated expenditures (February 1)	$100,000
Expenditures during February	200,000
Expenditures during March	100,000

Debt outstanding during February

Trade payables at Feb. 1	$ 30,000
Trade payables at Feb. 28 (noninterest-bearing)	30,000
Mortgage note, 12% (not a specific borrowing)	400,000

Debt outstanding during March

Trade payables at March 31 (noninterest-bearing)	$ 20,000
Mortgage note, 12%, (not a specific borrowing)	400,000
Bank loan, 9%, borrowed specifically for financing construction	600,000

The weighted-average accumulated expenditures for February are computed as follows:

ILLUSTRATION 10A-3
Weighted-Average
Accumulated
Expenditures Excluding
Trade Payables—
February

Accumulated expenditures (February 1)	$100,000	
Less: trade payables (February 1)	30,000	$ 70,000
Accumulated expenditures (February 28) ($100,000 + $200,000)	300,000	
Less: trade payables (February 28)	30,000	270,000
Total		340,000
		÷ 2
Weighted-average accumulated expenditures outstanding during the month of February		$170,000

The avoidable interest for February is then computed as follows:

Weighted-Average Accumulated Expenditures	× Interest Rate	=	Avoidable Interest
$170,000	(12% × ¹⁄₁₂)		$1,700

ILLUSTRATION 10A-4
Computation of
Avoidable Interest for
February

Assuming that avoidable interest is lower than actual interest, interest of $1,700 is capitalized. Accumulated expenditures at the end of March are computed as follows:

Accumulated expenditures (March 1)	$301,700
Expenditures during March	100,000
Accumulated expenditures (March 31)	$401,700

ILLUSTRATION 10A-5
**Accumulated
Expenditures Including
Prior Month's Capitalized
Interest**

The weighted-average accumulated expenditures for March is computed as follows:

Accumulated expenditures (March 1)	$301,700	
Less: trade payables (March 1)	30,000	$271,700
Accumulated expenditures (March 31)	401,700	
Less: trade payables (March 31)	20,000	381,700
Total		653,400
		÷ 2
Weighted-average accumulated expenditures outstanding during the month of March		$326,700

ILLUSTRATION 10A-6
**Weighted-Average
Accumulated
Expenditures Excluding
Trade Payables—March**

The avoidable interest for March is then computed as follows:

Weighted-Average Accumulated expenditures	× Interest rate	=	Avoidable Interest
$326,700	(9% × ¹⁄₁₂)		$2,450 (Rounded)

ILLUSTRATION 10A-7
**Computation of
Avoidable Interest for
March**

Assuming that avoidable interest is lower than actual interest, the accumulated expenditures at the beginning of April would be $404,150 ($401,700 + $2,450).

▶ SUMMARY OF LEARNING OBJECTIVE FOR APP. 10-A ◀

8. Understand interest capitalization involving noninterest-bearing liabilities, interim period computations, and interest compounding. Noninterest-bearing liabilities, such as trade payables and short-term accruals, should be excluded from the computation of average accumulated expenditures. When computing weighted-average accumulated expenditures on an interim basis, the capitalized interest for the prior periods must be included.

Note: All **asterisked** Questions, Exercises, Problems, and Cases relate to material contained in the appendix to each chapter.

QUESTIONS

1. What are the major characteristics of plant assets?

2. DuBois Inc. owns land that it purchased on January 1, 1988, for $400,000. At December 31, 1995, its current value is $750,000 as determined by appraisal. At what amount should DuBois report this asset on its December 31, 1995, balance sheet? Explain.

3. Name the items, in addition to the amount paid to the former owner or contractor, that may properly be included as part of the acquisition cost of the following plant assets:
   (a) Land.
   (b) Machinery and equipment.
   (c) Buildings.

4. Indicate where the following items would be shown on a balance sheet.
   (a) A lien that was attached to the land when purchased.
   (b) Landscaping costs.
   (c) Attorney's fees and recording fees related to purchasing land.
   (d) Variable overhead related to construction of machinery.
   (e) A parking lot servicing employees in the building.
   (f) Cost of temporary building for workers during construction of building.
   (g) Interest expense on bonds payable incurred during construction of a building.
   (h) Assessments for sidewalks that are maintained by the city.
   (i) The cost of demolishing an old building that was on the land when purchased.

5. Three positions have normally been taken with respect to the recording of fixed manufacturing overhead as an element of the cost of plant assets constructed by a company for its own use:
   (a) It should be excluded completely.
   (b) It should be included at the same rate as is charged to normal operations.
   (c) It should be allocated on the basis of the lost production that occurs from normal operations.
   What are the circumstances or rationale that support or deny the application of these methods?

6. The Buildings account of James Alan McPherson Inc. includes the following items that were used in determining the basis for depreciating the cost of a building:
   (a) Organization and promotion expenses.
   (b) Architect's fees.
   (c) Interest and taxes during construction.
   (d) Commission paid on the sale of capital stock.
   (e) Bond discount and expenses.
   Do you agree with these charges? If not, how would you deal with each of the items above in the corporation's books and in its annual financial statements?

7. One financial accounting issue encountered when a company constructs its own plant is whether the interest cost on funds borrowed to finance construction should be capitalized and then amortized over the life of the assets constructed. What is a common accounting justification for capitalizing such interest?

8. What interest rates should be used in determining the amount of interest to be capitalized? How should the amount of interest to be capitalized be determined?

9. How should the amount of interest capitalized be disclosed in the footnotes to the financial statements? How should interest revenue from temporarily invested excess funds borrowed to finance the construction of assets be accounted for?

10. Discuss the basic accounting problem that arises in handling each of the following situations.
    (a) Assets purchased by issuance of capital stock.
    (b) Acquisition of plant assets by gift or donation.
    (c) Purchase of a plant asset subject to a cash discount.
    (d) Assets purchased on a long-term credit basis.
    (e) A group of assets acquired for a lump sum.
    (f) An asset traded in or exchanged for another asset.

11. Bontemps Industries acquired equipment this year to be used in its operations. The equipment was delivered by the suppliers, installed by Bontemps, and placed into operation. Some of it was purchased for cash with discounts available for prompt payment. Some of it was purchased under long-term payment plans for which the interest charges approximated prevailing rates. What costs should Bontemps capitalize for the new equipment purchased this year? Explain.

12. Sterling Brown Co. purchased for $1 million property that included both land and a building to be used in operations. The seller's book value was $300,000 for the land and $900,000 for the building. By appraisal, the fair market value was estimated to be $500,000 for the land and $2,000,000 for the building. At what amount should Brown report the land and the building at the end of the year?

13. Claude McKay is studying for an accounting examination. He is having difficulty with the topic of exchanging plant assets. Explain to Claude what steps should be followed when accounting for an exchange of plant assets.

14. Zora Hurston Company purchased a heavy-duty truck on July 1, 1992, for $30,000. It was estimated that it would have a useful life of 10 years and then would have a trade-in value of $6,000. It was traded on October 1, 1996, for a similar truck costing $39,000; $13,000 was allowed as trade-in value (also fair value) on the old truck and $26,000 was paid in cash. What is the entry to record the trade-in? The company uses the straight-line method.

15. Once equipment has been installed and placed in operation, subsequent expenditures relating to this equipment are frequently thought of as repairs or general maintenance and, hence, chargeable to operations in the period in which the expenditure is made. Actually, determination of whether such an expenditure should be charged to operations or capitalized involves a much more careful analysis of the character of the expenditure. What are the factors that should be considered in making such a decision? Discuss fully.

16. What accounting treatment is normally given to the following items in accounting for plant assets?
    (a) Additions.
    (b) Major repairs.
    (c) Improvements and replacements.

17. New machinery, which replaced a number of employees, was installed and put in operation in the last month of the fiscal year. The employees had been dismissed after payment of an extra month's wages and this amount was added to the cost of the machinery. Discuss the propriety of the charge and, if it was improper, describe the proper treatment.

18. To what extent do you consider the following items to be proper costs of the fixed asset? Give reasons for your opinions.
    (a) Overhead of a business that builds its own equipment.
    (b) Cost of constructing new models of machinery.
    (c) Cash discounts on purchases of equipment.
    (d) Interest paid during construction of a building.
    (e) Cost of a safety device installed on a machine.
    (f) Freight on equipment returned before installation, for replacement by other equipment of greater capacity.
    (g) Cost of moving machinery to a new location.
    (h) Cost of plywood partitions erected as part of the remodeling of the office.
    (i) Replastering of a section of the building.
    (j) Cost of a new motor for one of the trucks.

19. Recently, James C. Lyman Manufacturing Co. presented the account "Allowance for Repairs" in the long-term liability section. Evaluate this procedure.

20. Fisher Enterprises has a number of fully depreciated assets that are still being used in the main operations of the business. Because the assets are fully depreciated, the president of the company decides not to show them on the balance sheet or disclose this information in the footnotes. Evaluate this procedure.

21. Recently, William Kelley, Inc. decided to discontinue production of one of its product lines because demand for it had fallen substantially. Although it is highly unlikely that the plant may be used for this type of production in the future, the controller is reluctant to write the plant down to its net realizable value. Why might the controller be reluctant to write the asset down?

*22. Is any interest capitalized relative to noninterest-bearing debts and accrued liabilities? Explain. Identify three noninterest-bearing liabilities.

*23. John Clarke Company began the month of March with accumulated expenditures of $280,000 on its construction project and made $120,000 additional expenditures during March. Clarke's debt outstanding during March consisted of a $100,000, 12% construction bank loan and $500,000 of 9.6% bonds. Its trade payables and accrued liabilities (noninterest-bearing) on March 1 were $50,000 and on March 31 were $40,000. What is the amount of interest capitalized by Clarke Company for March?

EXERCISES

E10-1 (Acquisition Costs of Realty) The following expenditures and receipts are related to land, land improvements, and buildings acquired for use in a business enterprise. The receipts are enclosed in parentheses.

(a)	Money borrowed to pay building contractor (signed a note)	$(250,000)
(b)	Payment for construction from note proceeds	250,000
(c)	Cost of land fill and clearing	8,000

(d)	Delinquent real estate taxes on property assumed by purchaser	7,000
(e)	Premium on six-month insurance policy during construction	6,000
(f)	Refund of one-month insurance premium because construction	
	completed early	(1,000)
(g)	Architect's fee on building	22,000
(h)	Cost of real estate purchased as a plant site (land $200,000 and	
	building $50,000)	250,000
(i)	Commission fee paid to real estate agency	9,000
(j)	Installation of fences around property	4,000
(k)	Cost of razing and removing building	11,000
(l)	Proceeds from salvage of demolished building	(5,000)
(m)	Interest paid during construction on money borrowed for construction	13,000
(n)	Cost of parking lots and driveways	21,000
(o)	Cost of trees and shrubbery planted (permanent in nature)	12,000
(p)	Excavation costs for new building	3,000

Instructions

Identify each item by letter and list the items in columnar form, as shown below. All receipt amounts should be reported in parentheses. For any amounts entered in the Other Accounts column also indicate the account title.

Item	Land	Land Improvements	Building	Other Accounts

E10-2 (Acquisition Costs of Realty) Paton Co. purchased land as a factory site for $500,000. The process of tearing down two old buildings on the site and constructing the factory required 6 months.

The company paid $42,000 to raze the old buildings and sold salvaged lumber and brick for $4,300. Legal fees of $1,850 were paid for title investigation and drawing the purchase contract. Payment to an engineering firm was made for a land survey, $2,200, and for drawing the factory plans, $68,000. The land survey had to be made before definitive plans could be drawn. Title insurance on the property cost $1,500, and a liability insurance premium paid during construction was $900. The contractor's charge for construction was $2,840,000. The company paid the contractor in two installments: $1,200,000 at the end of 3 months and $1,640,000 upon completion. Interest costs of $170,000 were incurred to finance the construction.

Instructions

Determine the cost of the land and the cost of the building as they should be recorded on the books of Paton Co. Assume that the land survey was for the building.

E10-3 (Acquisition Costs of Trucks) McArthur Corporation operates a retail computer store. To improve delivery services to customers, the company purchases four new trucks on April 1, 1995. The terms of acquisition for each truck are described below:

1. Truck #1 has a list price of $15,000 and is acquired for a cash payment of $14,200.
2. Truck #2 has a list price of $16,000 and is acquired for a down payment of $3,000 cash and a noninterest-bearing note with a face amount of $13,000. The note is due April 1, 1996. McArther would normally have to pay interest at a rate of 10% for such a borrowing, and the dealership has an incremental borrowing rate of 8%.
3. Truck #3 has a list price of $16,000. It is acquired in exchange for a computer system that McArthur carries in inventory. The computer system cost $12,000 and is normally sold by McArthur for $15,500. McArthur uses a perpetual inventory system.
4. Truck #4 has a list price of $14,000. It is acquired in exchange for 1,000 shares of common stock in McArthur Corporation. The stock has a par value per share of $10 and a market value of $13 per share.

Instructions

Prepare the appropriate journal entries for the foregoing transactions for McArthur Corporation.

E10-4 (Purchase and Self-Constructed Cost of Assets) Montgomery Co. both purchases and constructs various equipment it uses in its operations. The following items for two different types of equipment were recorded in random order during the calendar year 1996.

Purchase

Cash paid for equipment, including sales tax of $6,000	$106,000
Freight and insurance cost while in transit	2,000
Cost of moving equipment into place at factory	3,100
Wage cost for technicians to test equipment	4,000
Insurance premium paid during first year of operation on this equipment	1,500
Special plumbing fixtures required for new equipment	8,000
Repair cost incurred in first year of operations related to this equipment	1,300

Construction

Material and purchased parts (gross cost $200,000; failed to take 3% cash discount)	$200,000
Imputed interest on funds used during construction (stock financing)	14,000
Labor costs	190,000
Overhead costs (fixed—$20,000; variable—$30,000)	50,000
Profit on self-construction	30,000
Cost of installing equipment	4,400

Instructions

Compute the total cost for each of these two pieces of equipment. If an item is not capitalized as a cost of the equipment, indicate how it should be reported.

E10-5 (Treatment of Various Costs) Rommel Supply Company, a newly formed corporation, incurred the following expenditures related to Land, to Buildings, and to Machinery and Equipment.

Abstract company's fee for title search		$ 520
Architect's fees		2,800
Cash paid for land and dilapidated building thereon		100,000
Removal of old building	$20,000	
Less salvage	5,500	14,500
Surveying before construction		370
Interest on short-term loans during construction		7,400
Excavation before construction for basement		19,000
Machinery purchased (subject to 3% cash discount, which was not taken)		55,000
Freight on machinery purchased		1,340
Storage charges on machinery, necessitated by noncompletion of		
building when machinery was delivered		2,180
New building constructed (building construction took 6 months from		
date of purchase of land and old building)		500,000
Assessment by city for drainage project		1,600
Hauling charges for delivery of machinery from storage to new building		620
Installation of machinery		2,000
Trees, shrubs, and other landscaping after completion of building		
(permanent in nature)		5,400

Instructions

Determine the amounts that should be debited to Land, to Buildings, and to Machinery and Equipment. Assume the benefits of capitalizing interest during construction exceed the cost of implementation. Indicate how any costs not debited to these accounts should be recorded.

E10-6 (Correction of Improper Cost Entries) Plant acquisitions for selected companies are as follows:

1. Napoleon Industries, Inc. acquired land, buildings, and equipment from a bankrupt company, S. Grant Co., for a lump sum price of $600,000. At the time of purchase, Grant assets had the following book and appraisal values:

	Book Values	Appraisal Values
Land	$200,000	$150,000
Buildings	250,000	350,000
Equipment	200,000	300,000

To be conservative, the company decided to take the lower of the two values for each asset acquired. The following entry was made:

Land	150,000	
Buildings	250,000	
Equipment	200,000	
Cash		600,000

2. Bismarck Enterprises purchased store equipment by making a $2,000 cash down payment and signing a 1-year $23,000, 10% note payable. The purchase was recorded as follows:

Store Equipment	27,300	
Cash		2,000
Note Payable		23,000
Interest Payable		2,300

3. Omar Bradley Company purchased office equipment for $30,000, terms 2/10, n/30. Because the company intended to take the discount, it made no entry until it paid for the acquisition. The entry was:

Office Equipment	30,000	
Cash		29,400
Purchase Discounts		600

4. Schwartzkopf Inc. recently received at zero cost land from the Village of Desert Hills as an inducement to locate their business in the Village. The appraised value of the land is $28,000. The company made no entry to record the land because it had no cost basis.

5. Wellington Company built a warehouse for $600,000. It could have purchased the building for $720,000. The controller made the following entry:

Warehouse	720,000	
Cash		600,000
Profit on Construction		120,000

Instructions

Prepare the entry that should have been made at the date of each acquisition.

E10-7 (Capitalization of Interest) Accardo Furniture Company started construction of a combination office and warehouse building for its own use at an estimated cost of $5,000,000 on January 1, 1995. Accardo expected to complete the building by December 31, 1995. Accardo has the following debt obligations outstanding during the construction period.

Construction loan—12% interest, payable semiannually, issued December 31, 1994	$2,000,000
Short-term loan—10% interest, payable monthly, and principal payable at maturity on May 30, 1996	1,400,000
Long-term loan—11% interest, payable on January 1 of each year. Principal payable on January 1, 1999	1,000,000

Instructions (Carry all computations to two decimal places.)

(a) Assume that Accardo completed the office and warehouse building on December 31, 1995, as planned at a total cost of $5,200,000 and the weighted average of accumulated expenditures was $4,000,000. Compute the avoidable interest on this project.

(b) Compute the depreciation expense for the year ended December 31, 1996. Accardo elected to depreciate the building on a straight-line basis and determined that the asset has a useful life of 10 years and a salvage value of $10,000.

E10-8 (Capitalization of Interest) On December 31, 1994, Jared Jones Inc. borrowed $3,000,000 at 12% payable annually to finance the construction of a new building. In 1995, the company made the following expenditures related to this building: March 1, $360,000; June 1, $600,000; July 1, $1,500,000; December 1, $1,200,000. Additional information is provided as follows:

1. Other debt outstanding

Ten-year, 13% bond, December 31, 1988, interest payable annually	$4,000,000
Six-year, 10% note, dated December 31, 1992, interest payable annually	$1,600,000

2. March 1, 1995, expenditure included land costs of $150,000.
3. Interest revenue earned in 1995 $49,000

Instructions

(a) Determine the amount of interest to be capitalized in 1995 in relation to the construction of the building.

(b) Prepare the journal entry to record the capitalization of interest and the recognition of interest expense, if any, at December 31, 1995.

E10-9 (Capitalization of Interest) On July 31, 1995, Lauren Hutton Company engaged Brinkley Tooling Company to construct a special-purpose piece of factory machinery. Construction was begun immediately and was completed on November 1, 1995. To help finance construction, on July 31, Lauren Hutton issued a $300,000, 3-year, 12% note payable at Sugar Grove National Bank, on which interest is payable each July 31. $100,000 of the proceeds of the note was paid to Brinkley on July 31. The remainder of the proceeds was temporarily invested in short-term marketable securities at 10% until November 1. On November 1, Lauren Hutton made a final $200,000 payment to Brinkley. Other than the note to Sugar Grove, Lauren Hutton's only outstanding liability at December 31, 1995, is a $30,000, 8%, 6-year note payable, dated January 1, 1992, on which interest is payable each December 31.

Instructions

(a) Calculate the interest revenue, weighted-average accumulated expenditures, avoidable interest, and total interest cost to be capitalized during 1995. Round all computations to the nearest dollar.

(b) Prepare the journal entries needed on the books of Lauren Hutton Company at each of the following dates:
1. July 31, 1995.
2. November 1, 1995.
3. December 31, 1995.

E10-10 (Capitalization of Interest) The following three situations involve the capitalization of interest:

Situation I.

On January 1, 1995, Robert Duval, Inc., signed a fixed-price contract to have Builder Associates construct a major plant facility at a cost of $4,000,000. It was estimated that it would take 3 years to complete the project. Also on January 1, 1995, to finance the construction cost, Robert Duval borrowed $4,000,000 payable in 10 annual installments of $400,000, plus interest at the rate of 10%. During 1995 Robert Duval made deposit and progress payments totaling $1,500,000 under the contract; the weighted-average amount of accumulated expenditures was $650,000 for the year. The excess borrowed funds were invested in short-term securities, from which Robert Duval realized investment income of $250,000.

Instructions

What amount should Robert Duval report as capitalized interest at December 31, 1995?

Situation II.

During 1995, Brando Corporation constructed and manufactured certain assets and incurred the following interest costs in connection with those activities:

	Interest costs incurred
Warehouse constructed for Brando's own use	$30,000
Special-order machine for sale to unrelated customer, produced according to customer's specifications	11,000
Inventories routinely manufactured, produced on a repetitive basis	8,000

All of these assets required an extended period of time for completion.

Instructions

Assuming the effect of interest capitalization is material, what is the total amount of interest costs to be capitalized?

Situation III.

Debra Winger, Inc. has a fiscal year ending April 30. On May 1, 1995, Debra Winger borrowed $10,000,000 at 11% to finance construction of its own building. Repayments of the loan are to commence the month following completion of the building. During the year ended April 30, 1996, expenditures for the partially completed structure totaled $6,000,000. These expenditures were incurred evenly throughout the year. Interest earned on the unexpended portion of the loan amounted to $360,000 for the year.

Instructions

How much should be shown as capitalized interest on Debra Winger's financial statements at April 30, 1996?

(CPA adapted)

E10-11 (Entries for Equipment Acquisitions) Allegro Engineering Corporation purchased conveyor equipment with a list price of $7,000. The vendor's credit terms were 2/10, n/30. Presented below are three independent cases related to the equipment. Assume that the purchases of equipment are recorded gross. (Round to nearest dollar.)
- **(a)** Allegro paid cash for the equipment eight days after the purchase.
- **(b)** Allegro traded in equipment with a book value of $450 (initial cost, $800), and paid $6,500 in cash one month after the purchase. The old equipment could have been sold for $400 at the date of trade (assume similar equipment).
- **(c)** Allegro gave the vendor an $8,502 noninterest-bearing note for the equipment on the date of purchase. The note was due in one year and was paid on time. Assume that the effective interest rate in the market was 9%.

Instructions

Prepare the general journal entries required to record the acquisition and payment in each of the independent cases above. Round to the nearest dollar.

E10-12 (Entries for Asset Acquisition, Including Self-Construction) Below are transactions related to Andante Company.
- **(a)** The City of Vienna gives the company 5 acres of land as a plant site. The market value of this land is determined to be $58,000.
- **(b)** 13,000 shares of common stock with a par value of $50 per share are issued in exchange for land and buildings. The property has been appraised at a fair market value of $820,000, of which $190,000 has been allocated to land and $630,000 to buildings. The stock of Andante Company is not listed on any exchange, but a block of 100 shares was sold by a stockholder 12 months ago at $65 per share, and a block of 200 shares was sold by another stockholder 18 months ago at $58 per share.

(c)   No entry has been made to remove from the accounts for Materials, Direct Labor, and Overhead the amounts properly chargeable to plant asset accounts for machinery constructed during the year. The following information is given relative to costs of the machinery constructed.

Materials used	$12,500
Factory supplies used	900
Direct labor incurred	15,000
Additional overhead (over regular) caused by construction of machinery, excluding factory supplies used	2,200
Fixed overhead rate applied to regular manufacturing operations	60% of direct labor cost
Cost of similar machinery if it had been purchased from outside suppliers	44,000

Instructions

Prepare journal entries on the books of Andante Company to record these transactions.

E10-13 (Entries for Acquisition of Assets) Presented below is information related to Vivace Company.

1.   On July 6 Vivace Company acquired the plant assets of Saraband Company, which had discontinued operations. The appraised value of the property is:

Land	$ 400,000
Building	1,200,000
Machinery and equipment	800,000
Total	$2,400,000

Vivace Company gave 12,500 shares of its $100 par value common stock in exchange. The stock had a market value of $144 per share on the date of the purchase of the property.

2.   Vivace Company expended the following amounts in cash between July 6 and December 15, the date when it first occupied the building:

Repairs to building	$105,000
Construction of bases for machinery to be installed later	135,000
Driveways and parking lots	122,000
Remodeling of office space in building, including new partitions and walls	130,000
Special assessment by city on land	18,000

3.   On December 20, the company paid cash for machinery, $250,000, subject to a 2% cash discount, and freight on machinery of $10,500.

Instructions

Prepare entries on the books of Vivace Company for these transactions.

E10-14 (Purchase of Equipment with Noninterest-Bearing Debt) Sebastian Bach, Inc. has decided to purchase equipment from Karl Phillip Industries on January 2, 1995, to expand its production capacity to meet customers' demand for its product. Sebastian Bach issues a $700,000, five-year, noninterest-bearing note to Karl Phillip for the new equipment when the prevailing market rate of interest for obligations of this nature is 12%. The company will pay off the note in five $140,000 installments due at the end of each year over the life of the note.

Instructions

(a)   Prepare the journal entry(ies) at the date of purchase. (Round to nearest dollar in all computations.)
(b)   Prepare the journal entry(ies) at the end of the first year to record the payment and interest, assuming that the company employs the effective interest method.
(c)   Prepare the journal entry(ies) at the end of the second year to record the payment and interest.
(d)   Assuming that the equipment had a 10-year life and no salvage value, prepare the journal entry necessary to record depreciation in the first year. (Straight-line depreciation is employed.)

E10-15 (Purchase of Computer with Noninterest-Bearing Debt) Hollerith, Inc. purchased a computer on December 31, 1994, for $90,000, paying $15,000 down and agreeing to pay the balance in five equal installments of $15,000 payable each December 31 beginning in 1995. An assumed interest of 10% is implicit in the purchase price.

Instructions

(a)   Prepare the journal entry(ies) at the date of purchase. (Round to two decimal places.)
(b)   Prepare the journal entry(ies) at December 31, 1995, to record the payment and interest (effective interest method employed).
(c)   Prepare the journal entry(ies) at December 31, 1996, to record the payment and interest (effective interest method employed).

E10-16 (Nonmonetary Exchange With Boot) Imelda Corporation, which manufactures shoes, hired a recent college graduate to work in their accounting department. On the first day of work, the accountant was assigned to total a batch of invoices with the use of an adding machine. Before long, the accountant, who had never before seen such a machine, managed to break the machine. Imelda Corporation gave the machine plus $680 to Capek Business Machine Company (dealer) in exchange for a new machine. Assume the following information about the machines:

	Imelda Corp. (Old Machine)	Capek Co. (New Machine)
Machine cost	$580	$540
Accumulated depreciation	280	–0–
Fair value	170	850

Instructions

For each company, prepare the necessary journal entry to record the exchange.

E10-17 (Exchange With Boot) Dupré Company purchased an electric wax melter on 6/30/96 by trading in their old gas model and paying the balance in cash. The following data relate to the purchase:

List price of new melter	$15,800
Cash paid	10,000
Cost of old melter (5-year life, $700 residual value)	11,200
Accumulated depreciation—old melter (straight-line)	6,300
Second-hand market value of old melter	5,200

Instructions

Prepare the journal entry(ies) necessary to record this exchange, assuming that the melters exchanged are (1) similar in nature; (2) dissimilar in nature. Dupré's fiscal year ends on 12/31 and depreciation has been recorded through 12/31/95.

E10-18 (Nonmonetary Exchange with Boot) Dvořák Company exchanged equipment used in its manufacturing operations plus $5,000 in cash for similar equipment used in the operations of Franz Liszt Company. The following information pertains to the exchange:

	Dvořák Co.	Franz Liszt Co.
Equipment (cost)	$28,000	$28,000
Accumulated depreciation	19,000	10,000
Fair value of equipment	13,500	15,500
Cash given up	2,000	

Instructions

Prepare the journal entries to record the exchange on the books of both companies.

E10-19 (Nonmonetary Exchange with Boot) Beethoven Inc. has negotiated the purchase of a new piece of automatic equipment at a price of $8,000 plus trade-in, f.o.b. factory. Beethoven Inc. paid $8,000 cash and traded in used equipment. The used equipment has originally cost $62,000; it had a book value of $42,000 and a secondhand market value of $46,800, as indicated by recent transactions involving similar equipment. Freight and installation charges for the new equipment required a cash payment of $1,100.

Instructions

(a) Prepare the general journal entry to record this transaction, assuming that the assets Beethoven Inc. exchanged are similar in nature.

(b) Assuming the same facts as in (a) except that the asset traded in are dissimilar in nature, prepare the general journal entry to record this transaction.

E10-20 (Analysis of Subsequent Expenditures) Elgar Resources Group has been in its plant facility for 15 years. Although the plant is quite functional, numerous repair costs are incurred to maintain it in sound working order. The company plant asset book value is currently $800,000, as indicated below:

Original cost	$1,200,000
Accumulated depreciation	400,000
	$ 800,000

During the current year, the following expenditures were made to the plant facility:

(a) Because of increased demands for its product, the company increased its plant capacity by building a new addition at a cost of $210,000.

(b) The entire plant was repainted at a cost of $18,000.

(c) The roof was an asbestos cement slate; for safety purposes it was removed and replaced with a wood shingle roof at a cost of $58,000. Book value of the old roof was $39,000.

(d) The electrical system was completely updated at a cost of $21,000. The cost of the old electrical system was not known. It is estimated that the useful life of the building will not change as a result of this updating.

(e) A series of major repairs were made at a cost of $45,000, because parts of the wood structure were rotting. The cost of the old wood structure was not known. These extensive repairs are estimated to increase the useful life of the building.

Instructions

Indicate how each of these transactions would be recorded in the accounting records.

E10-21 (Analysis of Subsequent Expenditures) The following transactions occurred during 1996. Assume that depreciation of 10% per year is charged on all machinery and 5% per year on buildings, on a straight-line basis, with no estimated salvage value. Depreciation is charged for a full year on all fixed assets acquired during the year, and no depreciation is charged on fixed assets disposed of during the year.

Jan. 30   A building that cost $92,000 in 1979 is torn down to make room for a new building. The wrecking contractor was paid $5,100 and was permitted to keep all materials salvaged.

Mar. 10   Machinery that was purchased in 1989 for $16,000 is sold for $2,500 cash, f.o.b. purchaser's plant. Freight of $300 is paid on this machinery.

Mar. 20   A gear breaks on a machine that cost $9,000 in 1991, and the gear is replaced at a cost of $370.

May 18   A special base installed for a machine in 1990 when the machine was purchased has to be replaced at a cost of $5,400 because of defective workmanship on the original base. The cost of the machinery was $14,200 in 1990; the cost of the base was $3,500, and this amount was charged to the Machinery account in 1990.

June 23   One of the buildings is repainted at a cost of $7,300. It had not been painted since it was constructed in 1992.

Instructions

Prepare general journal entries for the transactions. (Round to nearest dollar.)

E10-22 (Analysis of Subsequent Expenditures) Plant assets often require expenditures subsequent to acquisition. It is important that they be accounted for properly. Any errors will affect both the balance sheets and income statements for a number of years.

Instructions

For each of the following items, indicate whether the expenditure should be capitalized (C) or expensed (E) in the period incurred.

_____ 1. Betterment.

_____ 2. Replacement of a broken part on a machine.

_____ 3. Expenditure that increases the useful life of an existing asset.

_____ 4. Expenditure that increases the efficiency and effectiveness of a productive asset but does not increase its salvage value.

_____ 5. Expenditure that increases the efficiency and effectiveness of a productive asset and increases the asset's salvage value.

_____ 6. Expenditure that increases the quality of the output of the productive asset.

_____ 7. Improvement to a machine that increased its fair market value and its production capacity by 30% without extending the machine's useful life.

_____ 8. Ordinary repairs.

_____ 9. Improvement.

_____ 10. Interest on borrowing necessary to finance a major overhaul of machinery. The overhaul extended the life of the machinery.

E10-23 (Entries for Disposition of Assets) On December 31, 1995, Grieg Inc. has a machine with a book value of $940,000. The original cost and related accumulated depreciation at this date are as follows:

Machine	$1,300,000
Accumulated depreciation	360,000
	$ 940,000

Depreciation is computed at $60,000 per year on a straight-line basis.

Instructions

Presented below is a set of independent situations. For each independent situation, indicate the journal entry to be made to record the transaction. Make sure that depreciation entries are made to update the book value of the machine prior to its disposal.

(a) A fire completely destroys the machine on June 30, 1996. An insurance settlement of $430,000 was received for this casualty. Assume the settlement was received immediately.

(b) On March 1, 1996, Grieg sold the machine for $1,040,000 to Peer Gynt Company.

(c) On July 31, 1996, the company donated this machine to the Mountain King City Council. The fair market value of the machine at the time of the donation was estimated to be $1,000,000.

E10-24 (Disposition of Assets) On April 1, 1995, Joplin Company received a condemnation award of $400,000 cash as compensation for the forced sale of the company's land and building, which stood in the path of a new state highway. The land and building cost $60,000 and $280,000, respectively, when they were acquired. At April 1, 1995, the accumulated depreciation relating to the building amounted to $160,000. On August 1, 1995, Alba purchased a piece of replacement property for cash. The new land cost $80,000, and the new building cost $300,000.

Instructions

Prepare the journal entries to record the transactions on April 1 and August 1, 1995.

*E10-25 (Capitalization of Interest) Chopin Inc. is in the process of starting construction on a new machine it intends to use in its operations. Its expenditures to date and related debt outstanding for the month of May are as follows:

Accumulated expenditures (May 1)		$600,000
Expenditures during May		100,000
Trade payables (noninterest-bearing)		
Outstanding May 1	$30,000	
May 31	20,000	
Bank loan at 12%	$700,000	

Instructions

Determine the amount of interest to capitalize on Chopin's machine for the month of May.

*E10-26 (Capitalization of Interest) Brahms Company is constructing an asset for its own use and has been capitalizing interest on expenditures for the asset since development activities began. The following details are necessary for the current month's entry:

Expenditures

Accumulated expenditures (July 1)	$2,000,000
Accumulated expenditures (July 31)	2,200,000

Debt (Outstanding during July)

A short-term, 15% note payable of $1,000,000
A note of $900,000, bearing interest at 12%, specifically for financing construction of the asset
A 9% mortgage note of $700,000

Instructions

(a) Compute the weighted-average accumulated expenditures, avoidable interest, and interest to be capitalized for the month of July.
(b) Determine the accumulated expenditure balance at the start of the next month (August 1).

PROBLEMS

P10-1 (Classification of Acquisition and Other Asset Costs) At December 31, 1994, certain accounts included in the property, plant, and equipment section of Stefano DiMera Company's balance sheet had the following balances:

Land	$230,000
Buildings	890,000
Leasehold improvements	660,000
Machinery and equipment	875,000

During 1995 the following transactions occurred:

Land site number 621 was acquired for $850,000. In addition, to acquire the land DiMera paid a $60,000 commission to a real estate agent. Costs of $35,000 were incurred to clear the land. During the course of clearing the land, timber and gravel were recovered and sold for $13,000.

A second tract of land (site number 622) with a building was acquired for $420,000. The closing statement indicated that the land value was $300,000 and the building value was $120,000. Shortly after acquisition, the building was demolished at a cost of $45,000. A new building was constructed for $230,000 plus the following costs:

Excavation fees	$38,000
Architectural design fees	11,000
Building permit fee	2,500
Imputed interest on funds used	
during construction (stock financing)	8,500

The building was completed and occupied on September 30, 1995.

A third tract of land (site number 623) was acquired for $650,000 and was put on the market for resale. During December 1995 costs of $92,000 were incurred to improve leased office space. The related lease will terminate on December 31, 1997, and is not expected to be renewed. (Hint: Leasehold improvements should be handled in the same manner as land improvements.)

A group of new machines was purchased under a royalty agreement that provides for payment of royalties based on units of production for the machines. The invoice price of the machines was $87,000, freight costs were $3,800, installation costs were $2,400, and royalty payments for 1995 were $17,500.

Instructions

(a) Prepare a detailed analysis of the changes in each of the following balance sheet accounts for 1995:

Land	Leasehold improvements
Buildings	Machinery and equipment

Disregard the related accumulated depreciation accounts.

(b) List the items in the situation that were not used to determine the answer to (a) above, and indicate where, or if, these items should be included in DiMera's financial statements.

(AICPA adapted)

P10-2 (Classification of Acquisition Costs) Selected accounts included in the property, plant, and equipment section of John Black Corporation's balance sheet at December 31, 1994, had the following balances:

Land	$ 300,000
Land improvements	140,000
Buildings	1,100,000
Machinery and equipment	960,000

During 1995 the following transactions occurred:

1. A tract of land was acquired for $150,000 as a potential future building site.
2. A plant facility consisting of land and building was acquired from Wendy Reardon Company in exchange for 20,000 shares of Black's common stock. On the acquisition date, Black's stock had a closing market price of $36 per share on a national stock exchange. The plant facility was carried on Reardon's books at $110,000 for land and $320,000 for the building at the exchange date. Current appraised values for the land and building, respectively, are $230,000 and $690,000.
3. Items of machinery and equipment were purchased at a total cost of $400,000. Additional costs were incurred as follows:

Freight and unloading	$17,000
Sales taxes	20,000
Installation	26,000

4. Expenditures totaling $90,000 were made for new parking lots, streets, and sidewalks at the corporation's various plant locations. These expenditures had an estimated useful life of 15 years.
5. A machine costing $80,000 on January 1, 1987, was scrapped on June 30, 1995. Double-declining-balance depreciation has been recorded on the basis of a 10-year life.
6. A machine was sold for $20,000 on July 1, 1995. Original cost of the machine was $44,000 on January 1, 1992, and it was depreciated on the straight-line basis over an estimated useful life of 7 years and a salvage value of $2,000.

Instructions

(a) Prepare a detailed analysis of the changes in each of the following balance sheet accounts for 1995:

Land
Land improvements
Buildings
Machinery and equipment

(Hint: Disregard the related accumulated depreciation accounts.)

(b) List the items in the fact situation that were not used to determine the answer to (a), showing the pertinent amounts and supporting computations in good form for each item. In addition, indicate where, or if, these items should be included in John Black's financial statements.

(AICPA adapted)

P10-3 (Classification of Land and Building Costs) Deveraux Company was incorporated on January 2, 1996, but was unable to begin manufacturing activities until July 1, 1996, because new factory facilities were not completed until that date.

The Land and Building account at December 31, 1996, was as follows:

January 31, 1996	Land and building	$160,000
February 28, 1996	Cost of removal of building	4,800

May 1, 1996	Partial payment of new construction	60,000
May 1, 1996	Legal fees paid	3,770
June 1, 1996	Second payment on new construction	40,000
June 1, 1996	Insurance premium	2,280
June 1, 1996	Special tax assessment	4,000
June 30, 1996	General expenses	16,300
July 1, 1996	Final payment on new construction	40,000
December 31, 1996	Asset write-up	18,200
		349,350
December 31, 1996	Depreciation—1996 at 1%	3,494
	Account balance	$345,856

The following additional information is to be considered.

1. To acquire land and building the company paid $80,000 cash and 800 shares of its 8% cumulative preferred stock, par value $100 per share. Fair market value of the stock is $105 per share.
2. Cost of removal of old buildings amounted to $4,800, and the demolition company retained all materials of the building.
3. Legal fees covered the following:

Cost of organization	$ 610
Examination of title covering purchase of land	1,300
Legal work in connection with construction contract	1,860
	$3,770

4. Insurance premium covered the building for a two-year term beginning May 1, 1996.
5. The special tax assessment covered street improvements that are permanent in nature.
6. General expenses covered the following for the period from January 2, 1996, to June 30, 1996.

President's salary	$12,100
Plant superintendent covering supervision of new building	4,200
	$16,300

7. Because of a general increase in construction costs after entering into the building contract, the Board of Directors increased the value of the building $18,200, believing that such an increase was justified to reflect the current market at the time the building was completed. Retained earnings was credited for this amount.
8. Estimated life of building—50 years.
   Writeoff for 1996—1% of asset value (1% of $349,350, or $3,494).

Instructions

(a) Prepare entries to reflect correct land, building, and depreciation allowance accounts at December 31, 1996.
(b) Show the proper presentation of land, building, and depreciation on the balance sheet at December 31, 1996.

(AICPA adapted)

P10-4 (Analysis of Machinery Costs) During 1996, Abe Carver Company manufactured a machine for its own use. At December 31, 1996, the account related to that machine is as follows:

Machinery				
Old machine cost	$ 9,200	Old machine cost	$9,200
Cost of dismantling old machine	1,500	Cash proceeds from sale of old machine	800
Raw materials used in construction of new machine	27,000	Depreciation for 1996, 10% of $76,400	7,640
Labor in construction of new machine	32,000		
Cost of installation	2,600		
Materials used in trial runs	1,500		
Profit on construction	12,600		

An analysis of the detail in the account discloses the following:

1. The old machine, which was removed during installation of the new one, has been fully depreciated.
2. Cash discounts received on the payments for materials used in construction totaled $950 and were reported in the "purchase discount" account.

3. The factory overhead account shows a balance of $300,000, which includes variable overhead and total fixed overhead, for the year ended December 31, 1996. $11,300 of the variable overhead is attributable to the production of the machine. Fixed overhead is normally priced to operations at $5 per direct-labor hour; 3,000 direct-labor hours were consumed in the production of the machine.
4. A profit was recognized on construction for the difference between costs incurred and the price at which the machine could have been purchased. The profit was credited to "self-construction gains."
5. Machinery has an estimated life of 10 years with no salvage value. The new machine was used for production beginning July 1, 1996.

Instructions

Prepare the entries necessary to correct the Machinery account as of December 31, 1996, and to record depreciation expense for the year 1996.

P10-5 (Dispositions, Including Condemnation, Demolition, and Trade-in) Presented below is a schedule of property dispositions for Billie Reed Co.

SCHEDULE OF PROPERTY DISPOSITIONS

	Cost	Accumulated Depreciation	Cash Proceeds	Fair Market Value	Nature of Disposition
Land	$40,000	—	$32,000	$32,000	Condemnation
Building	15,000	—	3,600	—	Demolition
Warehouse	65,000	$11,000	74,000	74,000	Destruction by fire
Machine	8,000	3,200	900	7,200	Trade-in
Furniture	10,000	7,850	—	2,800	Contribution
Automobile	8,000	3,460	2,960	2,960	Sale

The following additional information is available:

Land

On February 15, a condemnation award was received as consideration for unimproved land held primarily as an investment, and on March 31, another parcel of unimproved land to be held as an investment was purchased at a cost of $35,000.

Building

On April 2, land and building were purchased at a total cost of $75,000, of which 20% was allocated to the building on the corporate books. The real estate was acquired with the intention of demolishing the building, and this was accomplished during the month of November. Cash proceeds received in November represent the net proceeds from demolition of the building.

Warehouse

On June 30, the warehouse was destroyed by fire. The warehouse was purchased January 2, 1982, and had depreciated $11,000. On December 27, part of the insurance proceeds was used to purchase a replacement warehouse at a cost of $65,000.

Machine

On December 26, the machine was exchanged for another machine having a fair market value of $6,300 and cash of $900 was received.

Furniture

On August 15, furniture was contributed to a qualified charitable organization. No other contributions were made or pledged during the year.

Automobile

On November 3, the automobile was sold to Victor Kiriakis, a stockholder.

Instructions

Indicate how these items would be reported on the income statement of Billie Reed Co.

(AICPA adapted)

P10-6 (Classification of Costs and Interest Capitalization) On January 1, 1995, Spitfire Corporation purchased a tract of land (site number 101) with a building for $600,000. Spitfire paid a real estate broker's commission of $36,000, legal fees of $6,000, and title guarantee insurance of $18,000. The closing statement indicated that the land value was $500,000 and the building value was $100,000. Shortly after acquisition, the building was razed at a cost of $75,000.

Spitfire entered into a $3,000,000 fixed-price contract with Phaeton Builders, Inc. on March 1, 1995, for the construction of an office building on land site number 101. The building was completed and occupied on September 30, 1996. Additional construction costs were incurred as follows:

Plans, specifications, and blueprints	$14,000
Architects' fees for design and supervision	82,000

The building is estimated to have a 40-year life from date of completion and will be depreciated using the 150% declining balance method.

To finance the construction cost, Spitfire borrowed $3,000,000 on March 1, 1995. The loan is payable in ten annual installments of $300,000 plus interest at the rate of 10%. Spitfire's weighted-average amounts of accumulated building construction expenditures were as follows:

For the period March 1 to December 31, 1995	$1,200,000
For the period January 1 to September 30, 1996	1,800,000

Instructions

(a) Prepare a schedule that discloses the individual costs making up the balance in the land account in respect of land site number 101 as of September 30, 1996.

(b) Prepare a schedule that discloses the individual costs that should be capitalized in the office building account as of September 30, 1996. Show supporting computations in good form.

(AICPA adapted)

P10-7 (Exchanges with Boot) Studebaker Corporation wishes to exchange a machine used in its operations. Studebaker has received the following offers from other companies in the industry:

1. Lark Company offered to exchange a similar machine plus $22,000.
2. Nash Company offered to exchange a similar machine.
3. Avanti Company offered to exchange a similar machine, but wanted $15,000 in addition to Studebaker's machine.

In addition, Studebaker contacted Hawk Corporation, a dealer in machines. To obtain a new machine, Studebaker must pay $93,000 in addition to trading in its old machine.

	Studebaker	Lark	Nash	Avanti	Hawk
Machine cost	$160,000	$120,000	$147,000	$160,000	$130,000
Accumulated depreciation	50,000	45,000	72,000	75,000	–0–
Fair value	92,000	70,000	92,000	107,000	185,000

Instructions

For each of the four independent situations, prepare the journal entries to record the exchange on the books of each company. (Round to nearest dollar.)

P10-8 (Nonmonetary Exchanges with Boot) On August 1, 1996, Chrysler, Inc. exchanged productive assets with Belvidere, Inc. Chrysler's asset is referred to below as "Asset A" and Belvidere's is referred to as "Asset B." The following facts pertain to these assets:

	Asset A	Asset B
Original cost	$96,000	$110,000
Accumulated depreciation (to date of exchange)	40,000	52,000
Fair market value at date of exchange	60,000	75,000
Cash paid by Chrysler, Inc.	15,000	
Cash received by Belvidere, Inc.		15,000

Instructions

(a) Assume that Assets A and B are dissimilar, and record the exchange for both Chrysler, Inc. and Belvidere, Inc. in accordance with generally accepted accounting principles.

(b) Assume that Assets A and B are similar, and record the exchange for both Chrysler, Inc. and Belvidere, Inc. in accordance with generally accepted accounting principles.

P10-9 (Monetary Exchanges with Boot) During the current year, BelAir Construction trades an old crane that has a book value of $86,000 (original cost $140,000 less accumulated depreciation $54,000) for a new crane from Impala Manufacturing Co. The new crane cost Impala $165,000 to manufacture and is classified as inventory. The following information is also available.

	BelAir Const.	Impala Mfg. Co.
Fair market value of old crane	$ 72,000	
Fair market value of new crane		$190,000
Cash paid	118,000	
Cash received		118,000

Instructions

(a) Assume that this exchange is considered to involve dissimilar assets, and prepare the journal entries on the books of (1) BelAir Construction, and (2) Impala Manufacturing.

(b) Assume that this exchange is considered to involve similar assets and prepare the journal entries on the books of (1) BelAir Construction, and (2) Impala Manufacturing.

(c) Assuming the same facts as those in (a), except that the fair market value of the old crane is $98,000 and the cash paid $92,000, prepare the journal entries on the books of (1) BelAir Construction, and (2) Impala Manufacturing.

(d) Assuming the same facts as those in (b), except that the fair market value of the old crane is $87,000 and the cash paid $103,000, prepare the journal entries on the books of (1) BelAir Construction, and (2) Impala Manufacturing.

P10-10 (Costs of Self-Constructed Assets) Bronco Mining Co. received a $740,000 low bid from a reputable manufacturer for the construction of special production equipment needed by Bronco in an expansion program. Because the company's own plant was not operating at capacity, Bronco decided to construct the equipment there and recorded the following production costs related to the construction:

Services of consulting engineer	$ 32,000
Work subcontracted	28,000
Materials	300,000
Plant labor normally assigned to production	114,000
Plant labor normally assigned to maintenance	160,000
Total	$634,000

Management prefers to record the cost of the equipment under the incremental cost method. Approximately 40% of the company's production is devoted to government supply contracts which are all based in some way on cost. The contracts require that any self-constructed equipment be allocated its full share of all costs related to the construction.

The following information is also available:

(a) The production labor was for partial fabrication of the equipment in the plant. Skilled personnel were required and were assigned from other projects. The maintenance labor would have been idle time of nonproduction plant employees who would have been retained on the payroll whether or not their services were utilized.

(b) Payroll taxes and employee fringe benefits are approximately 35% of labor cost and are included in manufacturing overhead cost. Total manufacturing overhead for the year was $6,084,000, including the $160,000 maintenance labor used to construct the equipment.

(c) Manufacturing overhead is approximately 60% variable and is applied on the basis of production labor cost. Production labor cost for the year for the corporation's normal products totaled $8,286,000.

(d) General and administrative expenses include $27,000 of allocated executive salary cost and $13,750 of postage, telephone, supplies, and miscellaneous expenses identifiable with this equipment construction.

Instructions

(a) Prepare a schedule computing the amount that should be reported as the full cost of the constructed equipment to meet the requirements of the government contracts. Any supporting computations should be in good form.

(b) Prepare a schedule computing the incremental cost of the constructed equipment.

(c) What is the greatest amount that should be capitalized as the cost of the equipment? Why?

(AICPA adapted)

P10-11 (Purchases by Deferred Payment, Lump-sum, and Nonmonetary Exchanges) Pavlova Company is a manufacturer of ballet shoes and is experiencing a period of sustained growth. In an effort to expand its production capacity to meet the increased demand for its product, the company recently made several acquisitions of plant and equipment. Robert Joffrey, newly hired in the position of Fixed Asset Accountant, requested that Rudolf Nureyev, Pavlova's Controller, review the following transactions.

Transaction 1

On June 1, 1995, Pavlova Company purchased equipment from Twyla Corporation. Pavlova issued a $20,000 four-year noninterest-bearing note to Twyla for the new equipment. Pavlova will pay off the note in four equal installments due at the end of each of the next four years. At the date of the transaction, the prevailing market rate of interest for obligations of this nature was 10 percent. Freight costs of $300 and installation costs of $500 were incurred in completing this transaction. The appropriate factors for the time value of money at a 10 percent rate of interest are given in the next column.

Future value of $1 for four (4) periods	1.46
Future value of an ordinary annuity for four (4) periods	4.64
Present value of $1 for four (4) periods	0.68
Present value of an ordinary annuity for four (4) periods	3.17

Transaction 2

On December 1, 1995, Pavlova Company purchased several assets of Misha Shoes Inc., a small shoe manufacturer whose owner was retiring. The purchase amounted to $160,000 and included the assets listed below. Pavlova Company engaged the services of Bolshoi Appraisal Inc., an independent appraiser, to determine the fair market values of the assets which are also presented below.

	Misha Book Value	Fair Market Value
Inventory	$ 60,000	$ 50,000
Land	40,000	80,000
Building	70,000	120,000
	$170,000	$250,000

During its fiscal year ended May 31, 1996, Pavlova incurred $8,000 for interest expense in connection with the financing of these assets.

Transaction 3

On March 1, 1996, Pavlova Company exchanged a number of used trucks plus cash for vacant land adjacent to its plant site. Pavlova intends to use the land for a parking lot. The trucks had a combined book value of $30,000, as Pavlova had recorded $20,000 of accumulated depreciation against these assets. Pavlova's purchasing agent, who has had previous dealings in the second-hand market, indicated that the trucks had a fair market value of $40,000 at the time of the transaction. In addition to the trucks, Pavlova Company paid $18,000 cash for the land.

Instructions

(a) Plant assets such as land, buildings, and equipment receive special accounting treatment. Describe the major characteristics of these assets that differentiate them from other types of assets.

(b) For each of the three transactions described above, determine the value at which Pavlova Company should record the acquired assets. Support your calculations with an explanation of the underlying rationale.

(c) The books of Pavlova Company show the following additional transactions for the fiscal year ended May 31, 1995.

    1. Acquisition of a building for speculative purposes.

    2. Purchase of a two-year insurance policy covering plant equipment.

    3. Purchase of the rights for the exclusive use of a process used in the manufacture of ballet shoes.

    For each of these transactions, indicate whether the asset should be classified as a plant asset. If it is

    a. a plant asset, explain why.

    b. not a plant asset, explain why and identify the proper classification.

(CMA adapted)

CASES

C10-1 (Options to Purchase Property) Your client, Nick Nolte Plastics Co., found three suitable sites, each having certain unique advantages, for a new plant facility. In order to thoroughly investigate the advantages and disadvantages of each site, 1-year options were purchased for an amount equal to 6% of the contract price of each site. The costs of the options cannot be applied against the contracts. Before the options expired, one of the sites was purchased at the contract price of $300,000. The option on this site had cost $18,000. The two options not exercised had cost $12,000 each.

Instructions

Present arguments in support of recording the cost of the land at each of the following amounts.

(a) $300,000

(b) $318,000

(c) $342,000.

(AICPA adapted)

C10-2 (Acquisition, Improvements, and Sale of Realty) Danny DeVito Company purchased land for use as its corporate headquarters. A small factory that was on the land when it was purchased was torn down before construction of the office building began. Furthermore, a substantial amount of rock blasting and removal had to be done to the site before construction of the building foundation began. Because the office building was set back on the land far from the public road, DeVito Company had the contractor construct a paved road that led from the public road to the parking lot of the office building.

Three years after the office building was occupied, DeVito Company added four stories to the office building. The four stories had an estimated useful life of 5 years more than the remaining estimated useful life of the original office building.

Ten years later the land and building were sold at an amount more than their net book value and Devito Company had a new office building constructed in another state for use as its new corporate headquarters.

Instructions

(a) Which of the expenditures above should be capitalized? How should each be depreciated or amortized? Discuss the rationale for your answers.

(b) How would the sale of the land and building be accounted for? Include in your answer an explanation of how to determine the net book value at the date of sale. Discuss the rationale for your answer.

C10-3 (Accounting for Self-Constructed Assets) Rodham Medical Labs, Inc., began operations 5 years ago producing stetrics, a new type of instrument it hoped to sell to doctors, dentists, and hospitals. The demand for stetrics far exceeded initial expectations, and the company was unable to produce enough stetrics to meet demand.

The company was manufacturing its product on equipment that it built at the start of its operations. To meet demand, more efficient equipment was needed. The company decided to design and build the equipment, because the equipment currently available on the market was unsuitable for producing stetrics.

In 1995 a section of the plant was devoted to development of the new equipment and a special staff was hired. Within six months a machine developed at a cost of $510,000 increased production dramatically and reduced labor costs substantially. Elated by the success of the new machine, the company built three more machines of the same type at a cost of $315,000 each.

Instructions

(a) In general, what costs should be capitalized for self-constructed equipment?

(b) Discuss the propriety of including in the capitalized cost of self-constructed assets:
  1. The increase in overhead caused by the self-construction of fixed assets.
  2. A proportionate share of overhead on the same basis as that applied to goods manufactured for sale.

(c) Discuss the proper accounting treatment of the $195,000 ($510,000 − $315,000) by which the cost of the first machine exceeded the cost of the subsequent machines. This additional cost should not be considered research and development costs.

C10-4 (Capitalization of Interest) Tinfoil Airline is converting from piston-type planes to jets. Delivery time for the jets is 3 years, during which substantial progress payments must be made. The multimillion-dollar cost of the planes cannot be financed from working capital; Tinfoil must borrow funds for the payments.

Because of high interest rates and the large sum to be borrowed, management estimates that interest costs in the second year of the period will be equal to one-third of income before interest and taxes, and one-half of such income in the third year.

After conversion, Tinfoil's passenger-carrying capacity will be doubled with no increase in the number of planes, although the investment in planes would be substantially increased. The jet planes have a 7-year service life.

Instructions

Give your recommendation concerning the proper accounting for interest during the conversion period. Support your recommendation with reasons and suggested accounting treatment. (Disregard income tax implications.)

(AICPA adapted)

C10-5 (Assets Acquired through Issuance of Stock) You have been engaged to examine the financial statements of LeMew Corporation for the year ending December 31, 1995. LeMew was organized in January, 1995, by Messrs. Morris and Garfield, original owners of options to acquire oil leases on 5,000 acres of land for $900,000. They expected that (1) the oil leases would be acquired by the corporation and (2) subsequently 180,000 shares of the corporation's common stock would be sold to the public at $15 per share. In February 1996, they exchanged their options, $300,000 cash, and $125,000 of other assets for 75,000 shares of common stock of the corporation. The corporation's board of directors appraised the leases at $1,600,000, basing its appraisal on the price of other acreage recently leased in the same area. The options were, therefore, recorded at $700,000 ($1,600,000 − $900,000 option price).

The options were exercised by the corporation in March, 1996, prior to the sale of common stock to the public in April, 1995. Leases on approximately 500 acres of land were abandoned as worthless during the year.

Instructions

(a) Why is the valuation of assets acquired by a corporation in exchange for its own common stock sometimes difficult?

(b) 1. What reasoning might LeMew Corporation use to support valuing the leases at $1,600,000, the amount of the appraisal by the board of directors?

2. Assuming that the board's appraisal was sincere, what steps might LeMew Corporation have taken to strengthen its position to use the $1,600,000 value and to provide additional information if questions were raised about possible overvaluation of the leases?

(c) Discuss the propriety of charging one-tenth of the recorded value of the leases to expense at December 31, 1996, because leases on 500 acres of land were abandoned during the year.

(AICPA adapted)

C10-6 (Costs of Acquisition) The invoice price of a machine is $40,000. Various other costs relating to the acquisition and installation of the machine including transportation, electrical wiring, special base, and so on amount to $7,000. The machine has an estimated life of 10 years, with no residual value at the end of that period.

The owner of the business suggests that the incidental costs of $7,000 be charged to expense immediately for the following reasons.

1. If the machine should be sold, these costs cannot be recovered in the sales price;
2. The inclusion of the $7,000 in the machinery account on the books will not necessarily result in a closer approximation of the market price of this asset over the years, because of the possibility of changing demand and supply levels; and
3. Charging the $7,000 to expense immediately will reduce federal income taxes.

Instructions
Discuss each of the points raised by the owner of the business.

(AICPA adapted)

C10-7 (Acquisition Costs of Long-Term Assets) You have recently been hired as a junior accountant in the firm of Restin and Peace. Mr. Peace is an alumnus of the same school from which you graduated and, therefore, is quite interested in your accounting training. He therefore presents the following situations and asks for your response.

Situation I
Every few years, one of our clients publishes a new catalog for distribution to its sales outlets and customers. The latest catalog was published in 1994. Periodically, current price lists and new product brochures are issued. The company is now contemplating the issue of a new catalog during the latter part of 1997. The cost of the new catalog has been accounted for as follows:

(a) Estimated total cost of the catalog is accounted for over a period beginning with the initial planning (1995) and is expected to end at time of publication.
(b) Estimated costs are accumulated in an accrued liability account through monthly charges to selling expenses.
(c) Monthly charges were based upon the estimated total cost of the guide and the estimated number of months remaining before publication; periodic revisions were made to the estimates as current information became available.
(d) Actual costs were recorded as charges to the accrued liability account as they were accrued.

In summary, the company accrues the entire estimated cost (including anticipated costs to be incurred) of a contemplated catalog through charges to operations prior to the expected publication date.

Instructions
Comment on the propriety of this treatment.

Situation II
Recently a construction company agreed to construct a new hospital for its client at the construction company's cost; that is, the contractor was to realize no profit. The construction company was interested in performing this service because it had substantial interests in the community and wanted to make the community more attractive. The building was completed in 1995 at a cost of $24,000,000. An appraisal firm indicated, however, that the fair market value of the properties was $26,000,000; the difference was due to the $2,000,000 profit that the company did not charge the hospital.

Instructions
At what amount should the hospital value the asset? A related question is whether the donated profit on the hospital should be reported as revenue or as a capital contribution. What is your answer to this question?

Situation III
Recently, one of our clients asked whether it would be appropriate to capitalize a portion of the salaries of the corporate officers for time spent on construction activities. During construction, one of the officers devotes full time to the supervision of construction projects. Her activities are similar to those of a construction superintendent for a general contractor. During periods of heavy construction activity, this officer also employs several assistants to help with administrative matters related to construction. All other officers are general corporate officers.

The compensation and other costs related to the construction officer are not dependent upon the level of construction activity in a particular period (except to the extent that additional assistants are employed on a short-term basis). These expenses would continue to be incurred even if there was no construction activity unless the company decided to discontinue permanently, or for the foreseeable future, all construction activity. In that case, it could well reach the decision to terminate the construction officer. The company has, however, aggressive expansion plans that entail continuing construction of shopping center properties.

Instructions
What salary costs, if any, should be capitalized to the cost of properties?

► USING YOUR JUDGMENT ◄

► FINANCIAL REPORTING PROBLEM

Refer to the financial statements and other documents of Georgia-Pacific Corporation presented in Appendix 5-A and answer the following questions:

(a) In one of the notes to its financial statements, Georgia-Pacific indicated that it capitalizes interest on projects when construction takes considerable time and entails major expenditures. What was the amount of interest capitalized for each of the years 1991, 1992, and 1993?

(b) As part of its strategic restructuring, Georgia-Pacific sold some assets in 1993. What kinds of assets were sold? What was the amount of net gain or loss recognized from the sale of assets? How was the net gain or loss reported in Georgia-Pacific's financial statements?

► WRITING ASSIGNMENT

Murphy Brown Magazine Company started construction of a warehouse building for its own use at an estimated cost of $6,000,000 on January 1, 1993, and completed the building on December 31, 1993. During the construction period, Murphy Brown has the following debt obligations outstanding:

Construction loan—12% interest, payable semiannually, issued December 31, 1992.	$2,000,000
Short-term loan—10% interest, payable monthly, and principal payable at maturity, on May 30, 1994.	1,400,000
Long-term loan—11% interest, payable on January 1 of each year. Principal payable on January 1, 1996.	2,000,000

Total cost amounted to $6,200,000 and the weighted average of accumulated expenditures was $4,000,000.

William Brown, the president of the company, has been shown the costs associated with this construction project and capitalized on the balance sheet. He is bothered by the "avoidable interest" included in the cost. He argues that, first, all the interest is unavoidable—no one lends money without expecting to be compensated for it. Second, why can't the company use all the interest on all the loans when computing this avoidable interest? Finally, why can't his company capitalize all the annual interest which accrued over the period of construction?

Instructions
You are the manager of accounting for the company. In a memo, explain what avoidable interest is, how you computed it (being especially careful to explain why you used the interest rates which you did), and why the company cannot capitalize all its interest for the year. Attach a schedule supporting any computations which you use.

► GROUP ASSIGNMENT

GA10-1 (Capitalization of Interest) Wordcrafters Inc. is a book distributor that had been operating in its original facility since 1970. The increase in certification programs and continuing education requirements in several professions has contributed to an annual growth rate of 15% for Wordcrafters since 1990. Wordcrafters' original facility became obsolete by early 1995 because of the increased sales volume and the fact that Wordcrafters now carries tapes and disks in addition to books.

On June 1, 1995, Wordcrafters contracted with Ezra Pound Construction to have a new building constructed for $5,000,000 on land owned by Wordcrafters. The payments made by Wordcrafters to Pound Construction are shown in the schedule below.

Date	Amount
July 30, 1995	$1,200,000
January 30, 1996	1,500,000
May 30, 1996	1,300,000
Total payments	$4,000,000

Construction was completed and the building was ready for occupancy on May 27, 1996. Wordcrafters had no new borrowings directly associated with the new building but had the following debt outstanding at May 31, 1996, the end of its fiscal year:

14½%, 5-year note payable of $2,000,000, dated April 1, 1992, with interest payable annually on April 1.

12%, 10-year bond issue of $3,000,000 sold at par on June 30, 1988, with interest payable annually on June 30.

The new building qualifies for interest capitalization. The effect of capitalizing the interest on the new building, compared with the effect of expensing the interest, is material.

Instructions

Work within your group to answer the following questions. Your instructor will assign one member of the group to serve as a recorder and one member to serve as spokesperson. Upon completion of each requirement, the spokesperson should be prepared to report the group findings to the class.

(a) Compute the weighted-average accumulated expenditures on Wordcrafters' new building during the capitalization period.

(b) Compute the avoidable interest on Wordcrafters' new building.

(c) Some interest cost of Wordcrafters Inc. is capitalized for the year ended May 31, 1996.

    1. Identify the items relating to interest cost that must be disclosed in Wordcrafters' financial statements.

    2. Compute the amount of each of the items that must be disclosed.

(CMA adapted)

▶ ETHICS CASE

(Classification of Land and Building Costs) Glamour Company purchased a warehouse in a downtown district where land values are rapidly increasing. Richard Gere, Controller, and Cindy Crawford, Financial Vice-President, are trying to allocate the cost of the purchase between the land and the building. The Controller, noting that depreciation can only be taken on the building, favors under-valuing the land and placing a very high proportion of the cost on the warehouse itself, thus reducing taxable income and income taxes. Crawford, his supervisor, argues that the allocation should recognize the increasing value of the land, regardless of the depreciation potential of the warehouse. Besides, she says, net income is negatively impacted by additional depreciation and the company's stock price goes down.

Instructions

(a) What are the ethical issues, if any?

(b) What stakeholder interests are in conflict?

(c) How should these costs be allocated? Why?

CHAPTER 11

DEPRECIATION AND DEPLETION

LEARNING OBJECTIVES

After studying this chapter, you should be able to:

1. Explain the concept of depreciation.
2. Identify the factors involved in the depreciation process.
3. Compare activity, straight-line, and decreasing charge methods of depreciation.
4. Explain special depreciation methods.
5. Identify reasons why depreciation methods are selected.
6. Describe income tax methods of depreciation.

7. Explain the accounting issues related to asset impairment.
8. Describe financial statement disclosures for property, plant, and equipment.
9. Explain the accounting procedures for depletion of natural resources.
10. Describe financial statement disclosures for natural resources.

*A*lthough accountants, engineers, appraisers, and economists define depreciation differently, they all agree that most assets are on an inevitable "march to the rubbish heap." As a result, some type of writeoff of cost is needed to indicate that the usefulness of an asset has declined.

However, some disagree that certain assets should be depreciated. For example, the FASB proposed that not-for-profit organizations, such as churches, should depreciate the cost of houses of worship, monuments, and historical treasures. Opponents argued that "depreciating cathedrals and churches is stupid. . . . It would be like trying to compare the cost per soul saved among the churches." Others argued that "depreciating churches would be like depreciating the Pyramids and the Sphinx of Egypt, and the Sistine Chapel of the Vatican. Figuring such depreciation is the acme of futility!" The FASB countered by noting that "the Parthenon may still be there but its roof has fallen in. Physical assets that are exhaustible should be depreciated."[1]

When long-lived assets are written off, the term **depreciation** is most often used to indicate that tangible plant assets have declined in value. Where natural resources, such as timber, gravel, oil, and coal, are involved, the term **depletion** is employed. The expiration of intangible assets, such as patents or goodwill, is called **amortization**.

---

[1]*The Wall Street Journal,* April 10, 1987, pp. 1 and 10. Subsequently the FASB decided not to require the recognition of depreciation on historical works of art or historical treasures whose economic benefits diminish very slowly over long periods of time. "Recognition of Depreciation for Not-for-Profit Organizations," *Statement of Financial Accounting Standards No. 93* (Norwalk, Conn.: FASB, 1987).

▶ DEPRECIATION—A METHOD OF COST ALLOCATION

Most individuals at one time or another purchase and trade-in an automobile. In discussions with the automobile dealer, depreciation is a consideration on two points. First, how much has the old car "depreciated"? That is, what is the trade-in value? Second, how fast will the new car depreciate? That is, what will its trade-in value be? In both cases depreciation is thought of as a loss in value.

To accountants, however, **depreciation is not a matter of valuation but a means of cost allocation.** Assets are not depreciated on the basis of a decline in their fair market value, but on the basis of systematic charges to expense. **Depreciation is defined as the accounting process of allocating the cost of tangible assets to expense in a systematic and rational manner to those periods expected to benefit from the use of the asset.**

This approach is employed because the value of the asset may fluctuate between the time the asset is purchased and the time it is sold or junked. Attempts to measure these interim value changes have not been well received by accountants because values are difficult to measure objectively. Therefore, the asset's cost is charged to depreciation expense over its estimated life, making no attempts to value the asset at fair market value between acquisition and disposition. The cost allocation approach is used because a matching of costs with revenues occurs and because fluctuations in market value are tenuous and difficult to measure.

OBJECTIVE 1
Explain the concept of depreciation.

▶ FACTORS INVOLVED IN THE DEPRECIATION PROCESS

Before a pattern of charges to revenue can be established, three basic questions must be answered:

1. What depreciable base is to be used for the asset?
2. What is the asset's useful life?
3. What method of cost apportionment is best for this asset?

The answers to these questions involve the distillation of several estimates into one single figure. The calculations on which depreciation is based assume perfect knowledge of the future, which is never attainable.

OBJECTIVE 2
Identify the factors involved in the depreciation process.

DEPRECIABLE BASE FOR THE ASSET

The base established for depreciation is a function of two factors: the original cost and salvage or disposal value. We discussed historical cost in Chapter 10. **Salvage value** is the estimated amount that will be received at the time the asset is sold or removed from service. It is the amount to which the asset must be written down or depreciated during its useful life. To illustrate, if an asset has a cost of $10,000 and a salvage value of $1,000, its depreciation base is $9,000.

Original cost	$10,000
Less salvage value	1,000
Depreciation base	$ 9,000

**ILLUSTRATION 11-1
Computation of
Depreciation Base**

From a practical standpoint, salvage value is often considered to be zero because its valuation is small. Some long-lived assets, however, have substantial salvage values.

Companies also differ as to their estimate of salvage value. At one time Leasco, Greyhound Corp., and Boothe Computer all depreciated the same IBM computer equipment on a straight-line basis, but Leasco and Greyhound assumed a 10% salvage value, whereas Boothe assumed zero.

ESTIMATION OF SERVICE LIVES

The service life of an asset and its physical life are often not the same. A piece of machinery may be physically capable of producing a given product for many years beyond its service life, but the equipment is not used for all of those years because the cost of producing the product in later years may be too high. For example, the old Slater cotton mill in Pawtucket, Rhode Island is preserved in remarkable physical condition as an historic landmark in American industrial development, although its service life was terminated many years ago.[2]

Assets are retired for two reasons: **physical factors** (such as casualty or expiration of physical life) and **economic factors** (obsolescence). Physical factors are the wear and tear, decay, and casualties that make it difficult for the asset to perform indefinitely. These physical factors set the outside limit for the service life of an asset.

The economic or functional factors can be classified into three categories: inadequacy, supersession, and obsolescence. **Inadequacy** results when an asset ceases to be useful to a given enterprise because the demands of the firm have increased. Example: the need for a larger building to handle increased production. Although the old building may still be sound, it may have become inadequate for that enterprise's purposes. **Supersession** is the replacement of one asset with another more efficient and economical asset. Example: the replacement of the mainframe computer with a PC network, or the replacement of the Boeing 767 with the Boeing 777. **Obsolescence** is the catchall for situations not involving inadequacy and supersession. Because the distinction between these categories appears artificial, it is probably best to consider economic factors totally instead of trying to make distinctions that are not clear-cut.

INTERNATIONAL
INSIGHT

In the U.S., depreciation must take into account any expected obsolescence. In many nations this is not required.

To illustrate the concepts of physical and economic factors, consider a new nuclear power plant. Which do you think would be more important in determining the useful life of a nuclear power plant—physical factors or economic factors? The limiting factors seem to be (1) ecological considerations, (2) competition from other power sources (non-nuclear), and (3) safety concerns. Physical life does not appear to be the primary factor affecting useful life. Although the plant's physical life may be far from over, the plant may become obsolete in 10 years.

For a house, physical factors undoubtedly are more important than the economic or functional factors relative to useful life. Whenever the physical nature of the asset is the primary determinant of useful life, maintenance plays an extremely vital role. The better the maintenance, the longer the life of the asset.[3]

In some cases, arbitrary service lives are selected; in others, sophisticated statistical methods are employed to establish a useful life for accounting purposes. In many cases, the primary basis for estimating the useful life of an asset is the enterprise's past experience with the same or similar assets. In a highly industrial economy such as that of the United States, where research and innovation are so prominent, technological factors have as much effect, if not more, on service lives of tangible plant assets as physical factors do.

▶ METHODS OF COST APPORTIONMENT (DEPRECIATION)

The third factor involved in the depreciation process is the method of cost apportionment. The profession requires that the depreciation method employed be "systematic and rational."

---

[2]Taken from J. D. Coughlan and W. K. Strand, *Depreciation Accounting, Taxes and Business Decisions* (New York: The Ronald Press, 1969), pp. 10–12.

[3]The airline industry also illustrates the type of problem involved in estimation. In the past, aircraft were assumed not to wear out—they just became obsolete. However, some jets have been in service as long as 20 years, and maintenance of these aircraft has become increasingly expensive. In addition, the public's concern about worn-out aircraft has been heightened by some recent air disasters. As a result, some airlines are finding it necessary to replace aircraft not because of obsolescence but because of physical deterioration.

A number of depreciation methods are used. They may be classified as follows.

1. Activity method (units of use or production).
2. Straight-line method.
3. Decreasing charge methods.
   (a) Sum-of-the-years'-digits.
   (b) Declining-balance method.
4. Special depreciation methods.
   (a) Inventory method.
   (b) Retirement and replacement methods.
   (c) Group and composite methods.
   (d) Compound interest methods.[4]

To illustrate some of these depreciation methods, assume that Stanley Coal Mines recently purchased an additional crane for digging purposes. Pertinent data concerning the purchase of the crane are:

Cost of crane	$500,000
Estimated useful life	5 years
Estimated salvage value	$ 50,000
Productive life in hours	30,000 hours

ILLUSTRATION 11-2
Data Used to Illustrate Depreciation Methods

ACTIVITY METHOD

The **activity method** (also called the variable charge approach) assumes that depreciation is **a function of use or productivity instead of the passage of time.** The life of the asset is considered in terms of either the **output** it provides (units it produces), or an **input** measure such as the number of hours it works. Conceptually, the proper cost association is established in terms of output instead of hours used, but often the output is not easily measurable. In such cases, an input measure such as machine hours is a more appropriate method of measuring the dollar amount of depreciation charges for a given accounting period.

The crane poses no particular problem because the usage (hours) is relatively easy to measure. If the crane is used 4,000 hours the first year, the depreciation charge is:

OBJECTIVE 3
Compare activity, straight-line, and decreasing charge methods of depreciation.

$$\frac{\text{(Cost less salvage)} \times \text{Hours this year}}{\text{Total estimated hours}} = \text{Depreciation charge}$$

$$\frac{(\$500,000 - \$50,000) \times 4,000}{30,000} = \$60,000$$

ILLUSTRATION 11-3
Depreciation Calculation, Activity Method—Crane Example

The major limitation of this method is that it is not appropriate in situations in which depreciation is a function of time instead of activity. For example, a building is subject to a great deal of steady deterioration from the elements (time) regardless of its use. In addition, where an asset is subject to economic or functional factors, independent of its use, the activity method loses much of its significance. For example, if a company is expanding rapidly, a particular building may soon become obsolete for its intended purposes. In both cases, activity is irrelevant. Another problem in using an activity method is that an estimate of units of output or service hours received is often difficult to determine.

Where loss of services is a result of activity or productivity, the activity method will best match costs and revenues. Companies that desire low depreciation during periods

---

[4]*Accounting Trends and Techniques—1993* reports that of its 600 surveyed companies various depreciation methods were used for financial reporting purposes: straight-line, 564; declining-balance, 26; sum-of-the-years'-digits, 12; accelerated method (not specified), 62; units of production, 47. No utility or transportation companies (the ones that use the "special depreciation methods") are included in the AICPA's survey.

of low productivity and high depreciation during high productivity either adopt or switch to an activity method. In this way, a plant running at 40% of capacity generates 60% lower depreciation charges. Inland Steel, for example, switched to units-of-production depreciation at one time and reduced its losses by $43 million, or $1.20 per share.[5]

UNDERLYING
CONCEPT

If those benefits flow on a "straight-line" basis, then justification exists for matching the cost of the asset on a straight-line basis with these benefits.

STRAIGHT-LINE METHOD

The **straight-line method** considers depreciation a **function of time rather than a function of usage.** This method is widely employed in practice because of its simplicity. The straight-line procedure is often the most conceptually appropriate, too. When creeping obsolescence is the primary reason for a limited service life, a decline in usefulness may be constant from period to period. The depreciation charge for the crane is computed as follows:

**ILLUSTRATION 11-4
Depreciation
Calculations, Straight-
Line Method—Crane
Example**

$$\frac{\text{Cost less salvage}}{\text{Estimated service life}} = \text{Depreciation charge}$$

$$\frac{\$500,000 - \$50,000}{5} = \$90,000$$

The major objection to the straight-line method is that it rests on two unrealistic assumptions: (1) the asset's economic usefulness is the same each year, and (2) the repair and maintenance expense is essentially the same each period.

One additional problem that occurs in using the straight-line—as well as some others—is that distortions in the rate of return analysis (income/assets) develop. Illustration 11-5 indicates how the rate of return increases, given constant revenue flows, because the asset's book value decreases.

**ILLUSTRATION 11-5
Depreciation and Rate of
Return Analysis—Crane
Example**

Year	(1) Depreciation Expense	(2) Undepreciated Asset Balance (book value)	(3) Income (after depreciation expense)	(4) Rate of Return (income ÷ assets)
0		$500,000		
1	$90,000	410,000	$100,000	24.4%
2	90,000	320,000	100,000	31.2%
3	90,000	230,000	100,000	43.5%
4	90,000	140,000	100,000	71.4%
5	90,000	50,000	100,000	200.0%

DECREASING CHARGE METHODS

UNDERLYING
CONCEPT

The matching concept does not justify a constant charge to income. If the benefits from the asset decline as the asset gets older, then a decreasing charge to income would better match cost to benefits.

The **decreasing charge methods** (often called accelerated depreciation) provide for a higher depreciation cost in the earlier years and lower charges in later periods. The main justification for this approach is that more depreciation should be charged in earlier years inasmuch as the asset suffers the greatest loss of services in those years. Another argument presented is that the accelerated methods provide a constant cost because the depreciation charge is lower in the later periods, at the time when the repair and maintenance costs are often higher. Generally, one of two decreasing charge methods is employed: the sum-of-the-years'-digits method or the declining-balance method.

Sum-of-the-Years'-Digits

The **sum-of-the-years'-digits method** results in a decreasing depreciation charge based on a decreasing fraction of depreciable cost (original cost less salvage value). Each fraction uses the sum of the years as a denominator (5 + 4 + 3 + 2 + 1 = 15) and

---

[5]"Double Standard," *Forbes* (November 22, 1982), p. 178.

the number of years of estimated life remaining as of the beginning of the year as a numerator. In this method, the numerator decreases year by year and the denominator remains constant (5/15, 4/15, 3/15, 2/15, and 1/15). At the end of the asset's useful life, the balance remaining should be equal to the salvage value. This method of computation is shown in Illustration 11-6 below.[6]

Year	Depreciation Base	Remaining Life in Years	Depreciation Fraction	Depreciation Expense	Book Value, End of Year
1	$450,000	5	5/15	$150,000	$350,000
2	450,000	4	4/15	120,000	230,000
3	450,000	3	3/15	90,000	140,000
4	450,000	2	2/15	60,000	80,000
5	450,000	1	1/15	30,000	50,000[a]
		15	15/15	$450,000	

[a]Salvage value.

ILLUSTRATION 11-6
Sum-of-the-Years'-Digits Depreciation Schedule— Crane Example

Declining-Balance Method

Another decreasing charge method is the **declining-balance method,** which utilizes a depreciation rate (expressed as a percentage) that is some multiple of the straight-line method. For example, the double-declining rate for a 10-year asset would be 20% (double the straight-line rate, which is 1/10 or 10%). The declining-balance rate remains constant and is applied to the reducing book value each year. Unlike other methods, in the declining-balance method the salvage value is not deducted in computing the depreciation base. The declining-balance rate is multiplied by the book value of the asset at the beginning of each period. Since the book value of the asset is reduced each period by the depreciation charge, the constant-declining-balance rate is applied to a successively lower book value which results in lower depreciation charges each year. This process continues until the book value of the asset is reduced to its estimated salvage value, at which time depreciation is discontinued.

As indicated above, various multiples are used in practice, such as twice (200%) the straight-line rate **(double-declining-balance method)** and 150% of the straight-line rate. Using the double-declining approach in the crane example, Stanley Coal Mines would have the depreciation charges shown in Illustration 11-7 below.

Year	Book Value of Asset First of Year	Rate on Declining Balance[a]	Debit Depreciation Expense	Balance Accumulated Depreciation	Book Value, End of Year
1	$500,000	40%	$200,000	$200,000	$300,000
2	300,000	40%	120,000	320,000	180,000
3	180,000	40%	72,000	392,000	108,000
4	108,000	40%	43,200	435,200	64,800
5	64,800	40%	14,800[b]	450,000	50,000

[a]Based on twice the straight-line rate of 20% ($90,000/$450,000 = 20%; 20% × 2 = 40%).
[b]Limited to $14,800 because book value should not be less than salvage value.

ILLUSTRATION 11-7
Double-Declining Depreciation Schedule— Crane Example

---

[6]What happens if the estimated service life of the asset is, let us say, 51 years? How would you calculate the sum-of-the-years'-digits? Fortunately the mathematicians have developed a formula that permits easy computation as follows. It is:

$$\frac{n(n + 1)}{2} = \frac{51(51 + 1)}{2} = 1,326.$$

Enterprises often switch from the declining-balance method to the sum-of-the-years'-digits or straight-line method near the end of the asset's useful life to ensure that the asset is depreciated only to its salvage value.[7]

▶ SPECIAL DEPRECIATION METHODS

OBJECTIVE 4

Explain special depreciation methods.

Sometimes an enterprise does not select one of the more popular depreciation methods because the assets involved have unique characteristics, or the nature of the industry dictates that a special depreciation method be adopted. Generally, these special methods can be classified into five groups:

1. Inventory method.
2. Retirement and replacement methods.
3. Group and composite methods.
4. Compound interest methods.
5. Hybrid or combination methods.

INVENTORY METHOD

The **inventory method** (often called the appraisal system) is used to value small tangible assets such as hand tools or utensils. A tool inventory, for example, might be taken at the beginning and the end of the year. Then, the amount of depreciation expense could be calculated by using the value of the beginning inventory plus the cost of tools acquired for the year less the value of the ending inventory. This method is appealing because separate depreciation schedules for the assets in use are impractical.

The major objection to this depreciation method is that it is not "systematic and rational." No set formula is involved, and a great deal of subjectivity may occur. In many situations, a market or liquidation value is used, a practice that is criticized as a violation of the historical cost principle.

RETIREMENT AND REPLACEMENT METHODS

The **retirement and replacement methods** are used principally by public utilities and railroads that own many similar units of small value such as poles, ties, conductors, and telephones. The purpose of these approaches is to avoid elaborate depreciation schedules for individual assets.

The distinction between the two methods is that **the retirement method charges the cost of the retired asset (less salvage value) to depreciation expense; the replacement method charges the cost of the asset purchased (less salvage value from the asset retired) to depreciation expense.** The retirement method therefore follows a FIFO flow because the first asset purchased is the first asset expensed. The replacement method follows a LIFO flow because the last asset purchased is the first asset expensed.[8]

---

[7]A pure form of the declining-balance method (sometimes appropriately called the "fixed percentage of book value method") has also been suggested as a possibility. This approach finds a rate that depreciates the asset exactly to salvage value at the end of its expected useful life. The formula for determination of this rate is as follows:

$$\text{Depreciation rate} = 1 - \sqrt[n]{\frac{\text{Salvage value}}{\text{Acquisition cost}}}$$

The life in years is n. Once the depreciation rate is computed, it is applied on the declining book value of the asset from period to period, which means that depreciation expense will be successively lower. This method is not used extensively in practice because the computations are cumbersome and it is not permitted for tax purposes.

[8]In the replacement method the original cost (sometimes called aboriginal cost) of the old asset is maintained in the accounts indefinitely. For example, railroad companies, which only recently switched to a more traditional method of depreciating railroad track, have had track costs in their accounts from as early as 1887.

To illustrate these two methods, let us assume that the transmission lines of Hi-Test Utility, Inc. originally cost $1,000,000 and that 8 years later lines costing $150,000 are replaced with lines having a cost of $200,000. Under both methods any salvage value from the old transmission lines is considered a reduction of the depreciation expense in the period of retirement or replacement. Neither makes use of an accumulated depreciation account.

Retirement Method			Replacement Method		
Installation of lines—1993:					
Plant Assets—Lines	1,000,000		Plant Assets—Lines	1,000,000	
Cash		1,000,000	Cash		1,000,000
Retirement of old asset—2001:					
Depreciation Expense	150,000		(no entry)		
Plant Assets—Lines		150,000			
Cost of new asset—2001:					
Plant Assets—Lines	200,000		Depreciation Expense	200,000	
Cash		200,000	Cash		200,000

ILLUSTRATION 11-8
Entries Under Retirement and Replacement Depreciation Methods

Both methods are subject to the criticism that a proper allocation of costs to all periods, particularly in the early years, does not occur. (Depreciation expense is understated and net income is overstated.) To overcome this objection, a special allowance account may be established in the earlier years so that an assumed depreciation charge can be provided. The probability of retirements or replacements being fairly constant is essential to the validity of this concept; otherwise, depreciation is simply a function of when retirement and replacement occur.

GROUP AND COMPOSITE METHODS

Depreciation methods are usually applied to a single asset. In certain circumstances, however, multiple-asset accounts are depreciated using one rate. For example, an enterprise such as American Telephone and Telegraph Co. might depreciate telephone poles, microwave systems, or switchboards by groups.

Two methods of depreciating multiple-asset accounts are employed: the group method and the composite method. The term **group refers to a collection of assets that are similar in nature; composite refers to a collection of assets that are dissimilar in nature.** The group method is frequently used when the assets are fairly homogeneous and have approximately the same useful lives. The **composite approach** is used when the assets are heterogeneous and have different lives. The group method more closely approximates a single-unit cost procedure because the dispersion from the average is not as great. The method of computation for group or composite is essentially the same: find an average and depreciate on that basis.

To illustrate, Ahrens Motors depreciates its fleet of cars, trucks, and campers on a composite basis. The depreciation rate is established in this manner:

Asset	Original Cost	Residual Value	Depreciable Cost	Estimated Life (yrs.)	Depreciation Per Year (straight-line)
Cars	$145,000	$25,000	$120,000	3	$40,000
Trucks	44,000	4,000	40,000	4	10,000
Campers	35,000	5,000	30,000	5	6,000
	$224,000	$34,000	$190,000		$56,000

$$\text{Composite depreciation rate} = \frac{\$56,000}{\$224,000} = 25\%$$

Composite life = 3.39 years ($190,000 ÷ $56,000)

ILLUSTRATION 11-9
Depreciation Calculation, Composite Basis

The **composite depreciation rate** is determined by dividing the depreciation per year by the total cost of the assets. If there are no changes in the asset account, the group of assets will be depreciated to the residual or salvage value at the rate of $56,000 ($224,000 × 25%) a year. As a result, it will take Ahrens 3.39 years (composite life as indicated above) to depreciate these assets.

The differences between the group or composite method and the single-unit depreciation method become accentuated when we look at asset retirements. If an asset is retired before, or after, the average service life of the group is reached, the resulting gain or loss is buried in the Accumulated Depreciation account. This practice is justified because some assets will be retired before the average service life and others after the average life. For this reason, the debit to Accumulated Depreciation is the difference between original cost and cash received. No gain or loss on disposition is recorded. To illustrate, suppose that one of the campers with a cost of $5,000 was sold for $2,600 at the end of the third year. The entry is:

Accumulated Depreciation	2,400	
Cash	2,600	
Cars, Trucks, and Campers		5,000

If a new type of asset is purchased (mopeds, for example), a new depreciation rate must be computed and applied in subsequent periods.

A typical financial statement disclosure of the group depreciation method is shown for Ampco-Pittsburg Corporation as follows:

ILLUSTRATION 11-10
Disclosure of Group
Depreciation Method

Ampco-Pittsburg Corporation

Depreciation rates are based on estimated useful lives of the asset groups. Gains or losses on normal retirements or replacements of depreciable assets, subject to composite depreciation methods, are not recognized; the difference between the cost of the assets retired or replaced and the related salvage value is charged or credited to the accumulated depreciation.

The group or composite method simplifies the bookkeeping process and tends to average out errors caused by over- or underdepreciation. As a result, periodic income is not distorted by gains or losses on disposals of assets.

On the other hand, the unit method has several advantages over the group or composite methods: (1) it simplifies the computation mathematically; (2) it identifies gains and losses on disposal; (3) it isolates depreciation on idle equipment; and (4) it represents the best estimate of the depreciation of each asset, not the result of averaging the cost over a longer period of time. As a consequence, the unit method is generally used in practice and is generally assumed to be used in homework problems unless stated otherwise.

COMPOUND INTEREST METHODS

Unlike most depreciation methods, the **compound interest methods** ("sinking fund method" and "annuity method") are **increasing charge methods** that result in lower depreciation charges in the early years and higher depreciation charges in the later years. Conceptually, these methods have much to offer, but they have found limited acceptance. At the present time, their use is limited primarily to companies in the public utility industry. Other industries, such as the real estate industry, also have argued for such an approach. The compound interest methods are not illustrated in this textbook.

HYBRID OR COMBINATION METHODS

In addition to the aforementioned depreciation methods, companies are free to develop their own special or tailor-made depreciation methods. GAAP requires only that the method result in the allocation of an asset's cost over the asset's life in a systematic and rational manner.

A hybrid depreciation method widely used in the steel industry is a combination straight-line/activity approach referred to as the **production variable method.** The following note from Wheeling-Pittsburgh Corporation's 1993 Annual Report explains one variation of this method:

Wheeling-Pittsburgh Corporation

The Company utilizes the modified units of production method of depreciation which recognizes that the depreciation of steelmaking machinery is related to the physical wear of the equipment as well as a time factor. The modified units of production method provides for straight-line depreciation charges modified (adjusted) by the level of raw steel production. In 1991 and 1992 depreciation under the modified units of production method was $2.6 million or 7.8% and $1.2 million or 3.2%, respectively, less than straight-line depreciation.

ILLUSTRATION 11-11
Disclosure of Hybrid Depreciation Method

▶ SELECTING A DEPRECIATION METHOD

Which depreciation method should be selected? Many believe that the **method which best matches revenues and expenses** should be used. For example, if revenues generated by the asset are constant over the asset's useful life, straight-line depreciation is employed. On the other hand, if revenues are higher (or lower) at the beginning, some form of decreasing (or increasing) charge method of depreciation appears justified. Others argue that it is difficult in most cases to project future revenues and therefore **simplicity** (the straight-line method) should govern. Similarly, others argue that whatever is used for tax purposes should be used for book purposes because it **eliminates some record-keeping costs.**

Because it is difficult to defend one approach as more useful than another on a conceptual basis, the selection of the depreciation method is often made on more practical grounds. Many companies use the straight-line method for book purposes and adopt the accelerated depreciation method for tax purposes. This provides the best of both worlds—a **lower tax** and usually a **higher net income** for financial reporting purposes. At one time, U.S. Steel (now USX) changed its method of depreciation from an accelerated to a straight-line method for financial reporting purposes. Many observers note that the reason for the change was to report higher income so that it would be less susceptible to takeover by another enterprise. In effect, U.S. Steel wanted to report higher income so that the market value of its stock would rise.[9]

The real estate industry is frustrated with depreciation accounting because it argues that real estate often does not decline in value. In addition, because real estate is highly debt financed, most real estate concerns report losses in earlier years when the sum of depreciation and interest charges exceeds the revenues from the real estate project. The industry argues for some form of increasing charge method of depreciation (lower depreciation at the beginning and higher depreciation at the end), so that higher total assets and net income are reported in the earlier years of the project.

Tax policy also has an impact. In the 1980s railroads changed from the retirement-replacement method of accounting for railroad tracks to the more traditional method of capitalizing these track costs and depreciating them. Although the railroads had argued for the traditional method for many years, they had been reluctant to switch because higher tax deductions were achieved through the retirement-replacement approach. The railroads feared that changing to a more traditional method of depreciating

OBJECTIVE 5
Identify reasons why depreciation methods are selected.

INTERNATIONAL INSIGHT

In most non-Anglo-Saxon nations, companies are not permitted to use one depreciation method for financial statements and a different method for tax returns. The financial statements must conform to the tax return.

INTERNATIONAL INSIGHT

Some even use an economic consequences argument that Canadian real estate companies (which may use an increasing charge method) have a competitive edge over U.S. real estate companies.

---

[9]This assumption is highly tenuous. It is based on the belief that stock market analysts will not be able to recognize that the change in depreciation methods is purely cosmetic and therefore will give more value to the stock after the change. In fact, research in this area reports just the opposite. One study showed that companies that switched from accelerated to straight-line (which increased income) experienced declines in stock value after the change; see Robert J. Kaplan and Richard Roll, "Investor Evaluation of Accounting Information: Some Empirical Evidence," *The Journal of Business* (April 1972), pp. 225–257. Others have noted that switches to more liberal accounting policies (generating higher income numbers) have resulted in lower stock market performance. One rationale is that such changes signal that the company is in trouble and also leads to skepticism about management's attitudes and behavior.

for financial reporting purposes might suggest to Congress that this method be used for tax purposes. Ultimately, Congress provided favorable tax legislation to the industry and the concern was alleviated. As a result, many companies have since changed to more traditional methods of depreciation.

To summarize, the selection of a depreciation method involves factors such as the nature and uncertainty of revenue flows, matching costs and revenues, effect on income and asset book values, tax considerations, and record-keeping costs.

▶ SPECIAL DEPRECIATION ISSUES

Several special issues related to depreciation remain to be discussed. The major issues are:

1. How should depreciation be computed for partial periods?
2. Does depreciation provide for the replacement of assets?
3. How are revisions in depreciation rates handled?
4. How is depreciation computed for income tax purposes?

DEPRECIATION AND PARTIAL PERIODS

Plant assets are seldom purchased on the first day of a fiscal period or disposed of on the last day of a fiscal period. A practical question is: How much depreciation should be charged for the partial periods involved? Assume, for example, that an automated drill machine with a 5-year life is purchased by Steeltex Company for $45,000 (no salvage value) on June 10, 1994. The company's fiscal year ends December 31 and depreciation is charged for $6\frac{2}{3}$ months during that year. The total depreciation for a full year (assuming straight-line depreciation) is $9,000 ($45,000/5), and the depreciation for the first, partial year is:

$$\frac{6\frac{2}{3}}{12} \times \$9,000 = \$5,000$$

The partial-period calculation is relatively simple when straight-line depreciation is used. But how is partial period depreciation handled when an accelerated method such as sum-of-the-years'-digits or double-declining balance is used when partial periods are involved? As an illustration, assume that an asset was purchased for $10,000 on July 1, 1994, with an estimated useful life of 5 years; the depreciation figures for 1994, 1995, and 1996 are shown in Illustration 11-12.

ILLUSTRATION 11-12
Calculation of Partial-Period Depreciation, Two Methods

	Sum-of-the-Years'-Digits	Double-Declining Balance
1st full year	(5/15 × $10,000) = $3,333.33	(40% × $10,000) = $4,000
2nd full year	(4/15 × 10,000) = 2,666.67	(40% × 6,000) = 2,400
3rd full year	(3/15 × 10,000) = 2,000.00	(40% × 3,600) = 1,440

Depreciation from July 1, 1994 to December 31, 1994

	Sum-of-the-Years'-Digits	Double-Declining Balance
6/12 × $3,333.33 =	$1,666.67	6/12 × $4,000 = $2,000

Depreciation for 1995

	Sum-of-the-Years'-Digits	Double-Declining Balance
6/12 × $3,333.33 =	$1,666.67	6/12 × $4,000 = $2,000
6/12 × 2,666.67 =	1,333.33	6/12 × 2,400 = 1,200
	$3,000.00	$3,200
		or ($10,000 − $2,000) × 40% = $3,200

Depreciation for 1996

	Sum-of-the-Years'-Digits	Double-Declining Balance
6/12 × $2,666.67 =	$1,333.33	6/12 × $2,400 = $1,200
6/12 × 2,000.00 =	1,000.00	6/12 × 1,440 = 720
	$2,333.33	$1,920
		or ($10,000 − $5,200) × 40% = $1,920

In computing depreciation expense for partial periods, it is necessary to determine the depreciation expense for the full year and then to prorate this depreciation expense between the two periods involved. This process should continue throughout the useful life of the asset.

Sometimes the process of allocating costs to a partial period is modified to handle acquisitions and disposals of plant assets more simply. Depreciation may be computed for the full period on the opening balance in the asset account and no depreciation is charged on acquisitions during the year. Other variations charge a full year's depreciation on assets used for a full year, charge one-half year's depreciation in the year of acquisition and in the year of disposal, or charge a full year in the year of acquisition and none in the year of disposal.

A company is at liberty to adopt any one of these several fractional-year policies in allocating cost to the first and last years of an asset's life so long as the method is applied consistently. However, **unless otherwise stipulated, depreciation is normally computed on the basis of the nearest full month.** The schedule below shows depreciation allocated under five different fractional-year policies using the straight-line method on the $45,000 automated drill machine purchased on June 10, 1994, by Steeltex Company discussed earlier.

Machine Cost = $45,000	Depreciation Allocated Per Period Over 5-Year Life*					
Fractional-Year Policy	1994	1995	1996	1997	1998	1999
1. Nearest fraction of a year.	$5,000[a]	$9,000	$9,000	$9,000	$9,000	$4,000[b]
2. Nearest full month.	5,250[c]	9,000	9,000	9,000	9,000	3,750[d]
3. Half year in period of acquisition and disposal.	4,500	9,000	9,000	9,000	9,000	4,500
4. Full year in period of acquisition, none in period of disposal.	9,000	9,000	9,000	9,000	9,000	–0–
5. None in period of acquisition, full year in period of disposal.	–0–	9,000	9,000	9,000	9,000	9,000

[a]6.667/12 ($9,000) [b]5.333/12 ($9,000) [c]7/12 ($9,000) [d]5/12 ($9,000)
*(Rounded to nearest dollar)

ILLUSTRATION 11-13
Fractional-Year Depreciation Policies

DEPRECIATION AND REPLACEMENT OF FIXED ASSETS

A common misconception about depreciation is that it provides funds for the replacement of fixed assets. Depreciation is similar to any other expense in that it reduces net income, but it differs in that **it does not involve a current cash outflow.**

To illustrate why depreciation does not provide funds for replacement of plant assets, assume that a business starts operating with plant assets of $500,000, which have a useful life of 5 years. The company's balance sheet at the beginning of the period is:

Plant Assets	$500,000	Owners' Equity	$500,000

Now if we assume that the enterprise earned no revenue over the 5 years, the income statements are:

	Year 1	Year 2	Year 3	Year 4	Year 5
Revenue	$ –0–	$ –0–	$ –0–	$ –0–	$ –0–
Depreciation	(100,000)	(100,000)	(100,000)	(100,000)	(100,000)
Loss	$(100,000)	$(100,000)	$(100,000)	$(100,000)	$(100,000)

The balance sheet at the end of the 5 years is:

Plant Assets	–0–	Owners' Equity	–0–

This extreme example illustrates that depreciation in no way provides funds for the replacement of assets. **The funds for the replacement of the assets come from the** revenues; without the revenues no income materializes and no cash inflow results. A separate decision must be made by management to set aside cash to accumulate asset replacement funds.

REVISION OF DEPRECIATION RATES

When a plant asset is purchased, depreciation rates are carefully determined based on past experience with similar assets and other pertinent information. The provisions for depreciation are only estimates, however, and it may be necessary to revise them during the life of the asset. Unexpected physical deterioration or unforeseen obsolescence may make the useful life of the asset less than originally estimated. Improved maintenance procedures, revision of operating procedures, or similar developments may prolong the life of the asset beyond the expected period.[10]

For example, assume that machinery originally costing $90,000 is estimated to have a 20-year life with no salvage value. However, at the end of year 10 it is estimated that the machine will be used an additional 20 years. Its total life, therefore, will be 30 years instead of 20. Depreciation has been recorded at the rate of 1/20 of $90,000, or $4,500 per year by the straight-line method. On the basis of a 30-year life, depreciation should have been 1/30 of $90,000, or $3,000 per year. Depreciation, therefore, has been over-estimated, and net income has been understated by $1,500 for each of the past 10 years, or a total amount of $15,000. The amount of the difference can be computed as shown below.

ILLUSTRATION 11-14
Computation of
Accumulated Difference
Due to Revisions

	Per Year	For 10 Years
Depreciation charged per books (1/20 × $90,000)	$4,500	$45,000
Depreciation based on a 30-year life (1/30 × $90,000)	3,000	30,000
Excess depreciation charged	$1,500	$15,000

Changes in estimate should be handled in the current and prospective periods. No changes should be made in previously reported results. Opening balances are not adjusted and no attempt is made to "catch up" for prior periods. The reason is that changes in estimates are a continual and inherent part of any estimation process, and continual restatement of prior periods would occur for revisions of estimates unless they are handled prospectively. Therefore, no entry is made at the time the change in estimate occurs, and charges for depreciation in subsequent periods (assuming use of the straight-line method) are based on **dividing the remaining book value less any salvage value by the remaining estimated life:**

ILLUSTRATION 11-15
Computing Depreciation
after Revision of
Estimated Life

Machinery	$90,000
Less: Accumulated depreciation	45,000
Book value of machinery at end of 10th year	$45,000

Depreciation (future periods) = $45,000 book value ÷ 20 years remaining life = $2,250

The entry to record depreciation for each of the remaining 20 years is:

Depreciation Expense	2,250	
Accumulated Depreciation—Machinery		2,250

---

[10]As an example of a change in operating procedures, General Motors (GM) used to write off its tools—such as dies and equipment used to manufacture car bodies—over the life of the body type. Through this procedure, it expensed tools twice as fast as Ford and three times as fast as Chrysler. Now it has slowed the depreciation process on these tools and lengthened the lives on its plant and equipment. These revisions had the effect of reducing depreciation and amortization charges by approximately $1.23 billion, or $2.55 per share in the year of the change.

INCOME TAX DEPRECIATION

For the most part, issues related to the computation of income taxes are not discussed in a financial accounting course. However, because the concepts of tax depreciation are similar to those of book depreciation, and because tax depreciation methods are sometimes adopted for book purposes, an overview of this subject is presented.

OBJECTIVE 6
Describe income tax methods of depreciation.

Efforts to stimulate capital investment through faster writeoffs and to bring more uniformity to the writeoff period resulted in enactment of the Accelerated Cost Recovery System (ACRS) as part of the Economic Recovery Tax Act of 1981. For assets purchased in the years 1981 through 1986, ACRS and its preestablished "cost recovery periods" for various classes of assets are used.

A **Modified Accelerated Cost Recovery System,** known as **MACRS,** was enacted by Congress in the Tax Reform Act of 1986. It applies to depreciable assets placed in service in 1987 and later. The following discussion is based on these latest MACRS rules.

The computation of depreciation under MACRS differs from the computation under GAAP in three respects: (1) a mandated tax life, which is generally shorter than the economic life; (2) cost recovery on an accelerated basis; and (3) an assigned salvage value of zero.

Tax Lives (Recovery Periods)

Each item of depreciable property is assigned to a property class. The recovery period (depreciable tax life) of an asset depends on the property class.[11] The MACRS property classes are presented below:

ILLUSTRATION 11-16
MACRS Property Classes

3-year property—includes small tools, horses, and assets used in research and development activities

5-year property—includes automobiles, trucks, computers and peripheral equipment, and office machines

7-year property—includes office furniture and fixtures, agriculture equipment, oil exploration and development equipment, railroad track, manufacturing equipment, and any property not designated by law as being in any other class

10-year property—includes railroad tank cars, mobile homes, boilers, and certain public utility property

15-year property—includes roads, shrubbery, and certain low-income housing

20-year property—includes waste-water treatment plants and sewer systems

27.5-year property—includes residential rental property

39-year property—includes nonresidential real property

Tax Depreciation Methods

The depreciation expense is computed based on the tax basis, usually the cost, of the asset. The depreciation method depends on the life of the assets as mandated by the MACRS property class, as shown below:

ILLUSTRATION 11-17
Depreciation Method for Various MACRS Property Classes

MACRS Property Class	Depreciation Method
3-, 5-, 7-, and 10-year property	Double-declining balance
15- and 20-year property	150% declining balance
27.5- and 39-year property	Straight-line

When one of the accelerated methods is used, a change is made to the straight-line method in the first year in which straight-line depreciation exceeds the accelerated depreciation. Depreciation computations for income tax purposes are based on the half-

---

[11]Tax depreciation has changed numerous times during the 1980s. For example, since 1980, six different depreciation requirements have been enacted. The tax life of certain real property has moved from 35 years in 1980 to 15 in 1981, 18 in 1982, 19 in 1984, 31.5 in 1986, and 39 in 1993. As one writer noted, "It appears that the useful life of a depreciation law is 2.2 years."

year convention; that is, a half year of depreciation is allowable in the year of acquisition and in the year of disposition.[12] An asset is depreciated to a zero value so that there is no salvage value at the end of its MACRS life.

The application of these depreciation methods is simplified by using IRS published tables as shown below:

**ILLUSTRATION 11-18
IRS Table of MACRS
Depreciation Rates, by
Property Class**

MACRS DEPRECIATION RATES BY CLASS OF PROPERTY						
Recovery Year	3-year (200% DB)	5-year (200% DB)	7-year (200% DB)	10-year (200% DB)	15-year (150% DB)	20-year (150% DB)
1	33.33	20.00	14.29	10.00	5.00	3.750
2	44.45	32.00	24.49	18.00	9.50	7.219
3	14.81*	19.20	17.49	14.40	8.55	6.677
4	7.41	11.52*	12.49	11.52	7.70	6.177
5		11.52	8.93*	9.22	6.93	5.713
6	....	5.76	8.92	7.37	6.23	5.285
7			8.93	6.55*	5.90*	4.888
8			4.46	6.55	5.90	4.522
9				6.56	5.91	4.462*
10				6.55	5.90	4.461
11	....			3.28	5.91	4.462
12					5.90	4.461
13					5.91	4.462
14					5.90	4.461
15					5.91	4.462
16					2.95	4.461
17						4.462
18						4.461
19						4.462
20						4.461
21						2.231

*Switchover to straight-line depreciation.

**INTERNATIONAL
INSIGHT**

In Korea, companies are allowed to take additional depreciation (in excess of declining balance) on machinery and equipment for such reasons as energy saving, implementation of new technology, and antipollution measures. Companies that record such additional special depreciation report it as an extraordinary loss.

Illustration—MACRS System

To illustrate depreciation computations under both the MACRS system and GAAP straight-line accounting, assume the following facts for a computer and peripheral equipment purchased by Rotos Company on January 1, 1996:

Acquisition date	January 1, 1996
Cost	$100,000
Estimated useful life	7 years
Estimated salvage value	$16,000
MACRS class life	5 years
MACRS method	200% declining balance
GAAP method	Straight-line
Disposal proceeds—January 2, 2003	$11,000

Using the rates from the MACRS depreciation rate schedule for a 5-year class of property, depreciation is computed as follows for tax purposes:

**ILLUSTRATION 11-19
Computation of MACRS
Depreciation**

MACRS Depreciation			
1996	$100,000 × .20	=	$ 20,000
1997	$100,000 × .32	=	32,000
1998	$100,000 × .192	=	19,200
1999	$100,000 × .1152	=	11,520
2000	$100,000 × .1152	=	11,520
2001	$100,000 × .576	=	5,760
Total Depreciation			$100,000

[12]Mid-quarter and mid-month conventions are required for MACRS purposes in certain circumstances.

The depreciation under GAAP straight-line method with $16,000 of estimated salvage value and an estimated useful life of 7 years is computed as follows:

GAAP Depreciation
($100,000 − $16,000) ÷ 7 = $12,000 annual depreciation
× 7 years
1/1/96–1/2/2003 $84,000 total depreciation

ILLUSTRATION 11-20
Computation of GAAP Depreciation

The MACRS depreciation recovers the total cost of the asset on an accelerated basis. But, a taxable gain of $11,000 results from the sale of the asset at January 2, 2003. Therefore, the net effect on taxable income for the years 1996 through 2003 is $89,000 ($100,000 depreciation minus $11,000 gain).

Under GAAP, a loss on disposal of $5,000 ($16,000 book value − $11,000 disposal proceeds) is recognized. The net effect on income before income taxes for the years 1996 through 2003 is $89,000 ($84,000 depreciation plus $5,000 loss), the same as the net effect of MACRS on taxable income.

Even though the net effects are equal in amount, the deferral of income tax payments under MACRS from early in the life of the asset to later in life is desirable when considering present value concepts. The different amounts of depreciation for income tax reporting and financial GAAP reporting in each year are a matter of timing and result in temporary differences, which require interperiod tax allocation (see Chapter 20 for an extended treatment of this topic).

Optional Straight-line Method

An alternate MACRS method to determine depreciation deductions is based on the straight-line method. Often referred to as the optional (elective) straight-line method, it applies to the six classes of property described earlier. Under the alternate MACRS, the straight-line method is generally applied to the MACRS recovery periods. Salvage value is ignored. Under the optional straight-line method, in the first year the property is placed in service, half of the amount of depreciation that would be permitted for a full year is generally deducted (half-year convention). Use the half-year convention for homework problems.

Tax Versus Book Depreciation

GAAP requires that the cost of depreciable assets be allocated to expense over the expected useful life of the asset in a systematic and rational manner. Some argue that from a cost-benefit perspective it would be better for the accounting profession to adopt the MACRS approach to eliminate the necessity of maintaining two different sets of records. However, because the objectives of the tax laws and financial reporting are different, the adoption of one method for both tax and book purposes in all cases would be unfortunate. The purpose of taxation is to raise revenue from constituents in an equitable manner; the purpose of financial reporting is to reflect the economic substance of a transaction as closely as possible and to help predict the amounts, timing, and uncertainty of future cash flows.

INTERNATIONAL INSIGHT

In Switzerland depreciation in the financial statements must conform to that on the tax returns. As a consequence, companies may depreciate as much as 80% of the cost of assets in the first year.

► IMPAIRMENTS

The general accounting standard of **lower of cost or market for inventories does not apply to property, plant, and equipment.** Even when property, plant, and equipment has suffered partial obsolescence, accountants have been reluctant to reduce the carrying amount of the asset. This reluctance occurs because, unlike inventories, it is difficult to arrive at a fair value for property, plant, and equipment that is not subjective and arbitrary. For example, Falconbridge Nickel Mines had to decide whether all or a part of its property, plant, and equipment in a nickel-mining operation in the Dominican

OBJECTIVE 7

Explain the accounting issues related to asset impairment.

Republic should be written off. The project had been incurring losses because nickel prices were low and operating costs were high. Only if nickel prices increased by approximately 33% would the project be reasonably profitable. Whether a writeoff was appropriate depended on the future price of nickel. Even if the decision were made to write off the asset, another important question would be: How much should be written off?[13]

Recognizing that guidance was needed in this area, "Accounting for Impairments of Long-Lived Assets" was issued in 1994.[14] In this standard, an **impairment** occurs when the carrying amount of an asset is not recoverable and, therefore, a writeoff is needed. Various events and changes in circumstances might lead to an impairment. Examples are:

Underlying Concept

The going concern *concept assumes that the firm can recover the cost of the investment in its assets. Under GAAP the fair value of long-lived assets is not reported because a* going concern *does not plan to sell such assets. However, if the assumption of being able to recover the cost of the investment is not valid, then a reduction in value should be reported.*

a. A significant decrease in the market value of an asset.

b. A significant change in the extent or manner in which an asset is used.

c. A significant adverse change in legal factors or in the business climate that affects the value of an asset.

d. An accumulation of costs significantly in excess of the amount originally expected to acquire or construct an asset.

e. A projection or forecast that demonstrates continuing losses associated with an asset.

If these events or changes in circumstances indicate that the carrying amount of the asset may not be recoverable, a **recoverability test** is used to determine whether an impairment has occurred. To apply the first step of the recoverability test, you estimate the future net cash flows expected from the **use of that asset and its eventual disposition.** If the sum of the expected future net cash flows (undiscounted) is **less than the carrying amount** of the asset, the asset has been impaired. Conversely, if the sum of the expected future net cash flows (undiscounted) is **greater than the carrying amount** of the asset, no impairment has occurred. The recoverability test is a screening device to determine whether an impairment has occurred. For example, if the expected future net cash flows from an asset are $400,000 and its carrying amount is $350,000, no impairment has occurred. However, if the expected future net cash flows are $300,000, an impairment has occurred. The rationale for the recoverability test is the basic presumption that a balance sheet should report long-lived assets at no more than the carrying amounts that are recoverable.

If the recoverability test indicates that an impairment has occurred, a loss is computed. **The impairment loss is the amount by which the carrying amount of the asset exceeds its fair value.** The fair value of an asset is measured by its market value if an active market for it exists. If no active market exists, the **present value of expected future net cash flows** should be used. The company's market rate of interest should be used in discounting to present value. To summarize, the process of determining an impairment loss is as follows:

1. Review events or changes in circumstances for possible impairment.

2. If the review indicates impairment, apply the recoverability test. If the sum of the expected future net cash flows from the long-lived asset is less than the carrying amount of the asset, an impairment has occurred.

3. Assuming an impairment, the impairment loss is the amount by which the carrying amount of the asset is greater than the fair value of the asset. The fair value is the market value or the present value.

---

[13]Even given these difficult valuation problems, many companies during the earlier part of the 1990s have taken a number of large writeoffs. One study, for example, noted that writeoffs of long-lived assets during a recent 5-year period totaled over $50 billion. Also it has been estimated that over one-third of the largest companies in the United States have recently taken restructuring losses of some amount.

[14]"Accounting for Impairments of Long-Lived Assets," *Statement of Financial Accounting Standards* (Norwalk, Conn.: 1994).

Illustration One

M. Alou Inc. has an asset that, due to changes in its use, is reviewed for possible impairment. The asset's carrying amount is $600,000 ($800,000 cost less $200,000 accumulated depreciation). The expected future net cash flows (undiscounted) from the use of the asset and its eventual disposition are determined to be $650,000.

The recoverability test indicates that the $650,000 of expected future net cash flows from the asset's use exceed its carrying amount of $600,000. As a result, no impairment is assumed to have occurred. The undiscounted future net cash flows must be less than the carrying amount for an asset to be deemed impaired and for the impairment loss to be measured. M. Alou Inc. will thus not recognize an impairment loss in this case.

Illustration Two

Assume the same facts as Illustration One, except that the expected future net cash flows from Alou's equipment is $580,000 (instead of $650,000). The recoverability test indicates that the expected future net cash flows of $580,000 from the use of the asset are less than its carrying amount of $600,000. Therefore an impairment has occurred. The difference between the carrying amount of Alou's asset and its fair value is the impairment loss. This asset has a market value of $525,000. The computation of the loss is:

Carrying amount of the equipment	$600,000
Fair value of equipment (market value)	525,000
Loss on impairment	$ 75,000

ILLUSTRATION 11-21
Computation of Impairment Loss

The entry to record the impairment loss is as follows:

Loss on Impairment	75,000	
Accumulated Depreciation		75,000

The impairment loss is reported as part of income from continuing operations, generally in the other expenses and losses section. This loss should **not be reported as an extraordinary item.** Costs associated with an impairment loss are the same costs that would flow through operations and be reported as part of continuing operations. These assets will continue to be used in operations and, therefore, the loss should not be reported below income from continuing operations.

A company that recognizes an impairment loss should disclose the asset(s) impaired, the events leading to the impairment, the amount of the loss, and how fair value was determined (disclosing the interest rate used, if appropriate).

SPECIAL ISSUES

Two special issues relate to impairments. They are:

1. Restoration of impairment loss
2. Assets to be disposed of

Restoration of Impairment Loss

Once an impairment loss is recorded, the reduced carrying amount of an asset held for use becomes its new cost basis. As a result, the new cost basis is not changed except for depreciation in future periods or for additional impairments. To illustrate, assume that Ortiz Company at December 31, 1995, has equipment with a carrying amount of $500,000, which is impaired and is written down to its fair value of $400,000. At the end of 1996, assume that the fair value of this asset is $480,000. The carrying amount of the asset should not change in 1996 except for the depreciation taken in 1996. **The**

INTERNATIONAL INSIGHT

Australia, France, Germany, Mexico, and the United Kingdom, for example, permit restoration of the impairment loss. Canada and New Zealand follow the U.S. approach.

impairment loss may not be restored for an asset held for use. The rationale for not writing the asset up in value is that the new cost basis puts the impaired asset on an equal basis with other assets that are not impaired.

Assets To Be Disposed Of

What happens if the impaired asset is intended to be disposed of instead of held for use? In this case, the impaired asset is reported at the lower of cost or fair value less cost to sell (net realizable value). Because the asset is intended to be disposed of in a short period of time, net realizable value is used in order to provide a better measure of the net cash flows that will be received from this asset.

Assets that are being held for disposal are not depreciated during the period they are held. The rationale is that depreciation is inconsistent with the notion of assets to be disposed of and with the use of the lower of cost or net realizable value. In other words, **assets held for disposal are like inventory and should be reported at the lower of cost or net realizable value.**

Because assets held for disposal will be recovered through sale rather than through operations, they are continually revalued. Each period they are reported at the lower of cost or net realizable value. Thus **an asset held for disposal can be written up or down in future periods, as long as the write-up is never greater than the carrying amount of the asset before the impairment.** Losses or gains related to these impaired assets should be reported as part of **income from continuing operations.** The disclosure requirements for these assets are complex; we leave that issue for an advanced course. A summary of the key concepts in accounting for impairments is presented in Illustration 11-22.

ILLUSTRATION 11-22
Graphic of Accounting for Impairments

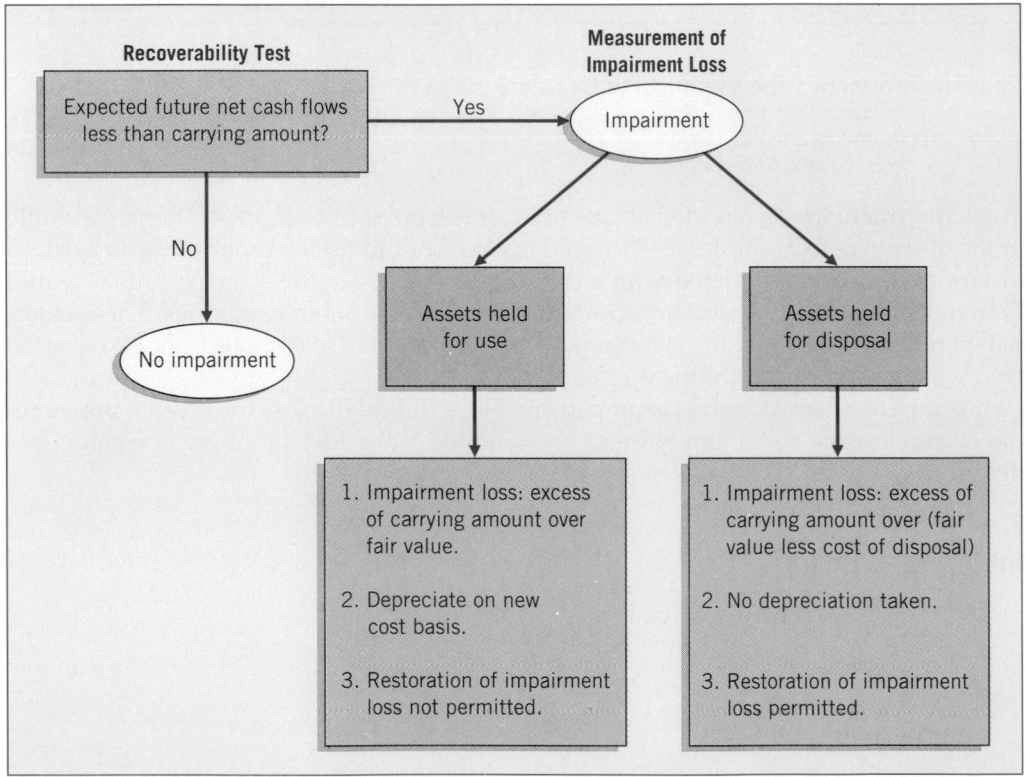

▶ ## DISCLOSURE OF PROPERTY, PLANT, AND EQUIPMENT, AND DEPRECIATION

OBJECTIVE 8

Describe financial statement disclosures for property, plant, and equipment.

The basis of valuation—usually historical cost—for property, plant, and equipment should be disclosed along with pledges, liens, and other commitments related to these assets. Any liability secured by property, plant, and equipment should not be offset against these assets, but should be reported in the liability section. Property, plant, and equipment not currently employed as producing assets in the business (such as idle facilities or land held as an investment) should be segregated from assets used in operations.

When assets are depreciated, a valuation account normally called Accumulated Depreciation or Allowance for Depreciation is credited. The employment of an Accumulated Depreciation account permits the user of the financial statements to see the original cost of the asset and the amount of depreciation that has been charged to expense in past years.

In the presentation of depreciation, the following disclosures should be made:

a. Depreciation expense for the period.

b. Balances of major classes of depreciable assets, by nature and function.

c. Accumulated depreciation, either by major classes of depreciable assets or in total.

d. A general description of the method or methods used in computing depreciation with respect to major classes of depreciable assets.[15]

Many individuals argue that the disclosure requirements are not sufficient. Some accountants believe that the average useful life of the assets or the range of years for asset life is significant information that should be disclosed.[16]

The financial statements of Georgia-Pacific Corporation (see Appendix 5-A, page 221) present property, plant, and equipment in a very condensed manner in the balance sheet. The company discloses depreciation expense for the year in the income statement (page 220), annual expenditures for property, plant, and equipment in the statement of cash flows (page 222), and provides detailed information and accounting policies in the notes (pages 223–224) regarding its interest capitalization policy. Note that Georgia-Pacific uses the straight-line method.

The financial report of The Clorox Company in Illustration 11-23 illustrates an acceptable disclosure using condensed balance sheet data supplemented with details and policies in notes to the financial statements.

UNDERLYING CONCEPT

Disclosing such information would make the statements more relevant. Management would probably argue that the cost-benefit relationship does not justify such additional disclosure.

ILLUSTRATION 11-23
Disclosure of Property, Plant, and Equipment and Depreciation

The Clorox Company		
	1992	1991
	($000)	
Total current assets	$418,250	$502,448
Property, plant and equipment, net	581,460	521,778
Brands, trademarks, patents and other intangibles	479,377	523,967
Investment in affiliates	90,599	73,610
Other assets	45,139	46,449

Notes to Financial Statements

Note 5:   Property, Plant and Equipment.   The major classes are (in thousands):

	1992	1991
Land and improvements	$ 53,996	$ 48,453
Buildings	267,599	255,141
Machinery and equipment	430,746	397,536
Construction in progress	113,031	59,421
Total	865,372	760,551
Less accumulated depreciation	283,912	238,773
Net	$581,460	$521,778

Property, plant and equipment are stated at cost, reduced in certain cases by valuation allowances. Depreciation is calculated by the straight-line method over the estimated useful lives of the depreciable assets. Depreciation expense was $55,316,000 in 1992, $56,708,000 in 1991 and $43,559,000 in 1990.

INTERNATIONAL INSIGHT

In Australia, Denmark, the Netherlands, and New Zealand, companies must disclose the current value of land and buildings.

---

[15]"Omnibus Opinion—1967," *Opinions of the Accounting Principles Board No. 12* (New York: AICPA, 1967), par. 5.

[16]Charles W. Lamden, Dale L. Gerboth, and Thomas W. McRae, "Accounting for Depreciable Assets," *Accounting Research Monograph No. 1* (New York: AICPA, 1975), p. 111. Also, one writer found that variances in useful life had a greater impact than the depreciation methods selected. See Robert R. Sterling, "A Test of the Uniformity Hypothesis," *Abacus* (September 1969), pp. 39–47.

In addition, many believe some form of price-level adjustment should be made for depreciation expense. At one time the Department of Commerce noted that if depreciation based on the replacement cost of aging assets were correctly measured, corporate net income for U.S. companies would decrease $18 billion. The subject of price-level adjustments is discussed in Chapter 26.

▶ DEPLETION

OBJECTIVE 9

Explain the accounting procedures for depletion of natural resources.

Natural resources, often called wasting assets, include petroleum, minerals, and timber. They are characterized by two main features: (1) the complete removal (consumption) of the asset, and (2) replacement of the asset only by an act of nature. Unlike plant and equipment, natural resources are consumed physically over the period of use and do not maintain their physical characteristics. Still, the accounting problems associated with natural resources are similar to those encountered with fixed assets. The questions to be answered are:

1. How is the cost basis for writeoff (depletion) established?
2. What pattern of allocation should be employed?

ESTABLISHING A DEPLETION BASE

How do we determine the depletion base for natural resources? Sizable expenditures are needed to find these natural resources, and for every successful discovery there are many "failures." Furthermore, long delays are encountered between the time the costs are incurred and the benefits are obtained from the extracted resources. As a result, a conservative policy frequently is adopted in accounting for the expenditures incurred in finding and extracting natural resources. The computation of the depreciation base involves four factors: (1) acquisition cost of the deposit, (2) exploration costs, (3) development costs, and (4) restoration costs.

Acquisition Costs

Acquisition cost is the price paid to obtain the property right to search and find an undiscovered natural resource or the price paid for an already discovered resource. In some cases, property is leased and special royalty payments paid to the owner if a productive natural resource is found and is commercially profitable. Generally, the acquisition cost is placed in an account titled Undeveloped Property and assigned to the natural resource if exploration efforts are successful. If they are unsuccessful, the cost is written off as a loss.

Exploration Costs

As soon as a company has the right to use the property, **exploration costs** are often needed to find the resource. In most cases, these costs are expensed as incurred. When these costs are substantial and the risks of finding the resource uncertain (such as in the oil and gas industry), capitalization may occur. The unique issues related to the oil and gas industry are examined on page 550.

Development Costs

Development costs are divided into: (1) tangible equipment and (2) intangible development costs. Tangible equipment includes all of the transportation and other heavy equipment necessary to extract the resource and get it ready for production or shipment. Because the asset can be moved from one drilling or mining site to another, **tangible equipment costs are normally not considered in the depletion base.** Instead, separate depreciation charges are employed. Tangible assets that cannot be moved should be depreciated over their useful life or the life of the resource, whichever is shorter. **Intan-**

gible development costs, on the other hand, are considered part of the depletion base. These costs are for such items as the drilling costs, tunnels, shafts, and wells, which have no tangible characteristics but are needed for the production of the natural resource.

Restoration Costs

Companies sometimes incur substantial costs to restore property to its natural state after extraction has occurred. These **restoration costs** should be added to the depletion base for purposes of computing the depletion cost per unit. It follows that any salvage value received on the property should be deducted from the depletion base.

WRITEOFF OF RESOURCE COST

As soon as the depletion base is established, the next problem is determining how the cost of the natural resource should be allocated to accounting periods. Normally, depletion is computed on the units of production method (activity approach), which means that depletion is a function of the number of units withdrawn during the period. In adopting this approach, the total cost of the natural resource less salvage value is divided by the number of units estimated to be in the resource deposit, to obtain a cost per unit of product. This cost per unit is multiplied by the number of units extracted to compute depletion.

For example, MaClede Co. has acquired the right to use 1,000 acres of land in Alaska to mine for gold. The lease cost is $50,000; the related exploration costs on the property are $100,000; and intangible development costs incurred in opening the mine are $850,000. Total costs related to the mine before the first ounce of gold is extracted are, therefore, $1,000,000. MaClede estimates that the mine will provide approximately 100,000 ounces of gold. The depletion rate established is computed in the following manner:

$$\frac{\text{Total cost} - \text{Salvage value}}{\text{Total estimated units available}} = \text{Depletion cost per unit}$$

$$\frac{\$1,000,000}{100,000} = \$10.00 \text{ per ounce}$$

ILLUSTRATION 11-24
Computation of Depletion Rate

If 25,000 ounces are extracted in the first year, then the depletion for the year is $250,000 (25,000 ounces at $10.00). The entry to record the depletion is:

Inventory	250,000	
Accumulated Depletion		250,000

Inventory is first debited for the total depletion for the year, and then is credited for the cost of materials sold during the year. The amount not sold remains in inventory and is reported in the current asset section.

In some instances an Accumulated Depletion account is not used, and the credit goes directly to the natural resources asset account. The balance sheet presents the cost of the property and the amount of accumulated depletion entered to date as follows:

Gold mine (at cost)	$1,000,000	
Less accumulated depletion	250,000	$750,000

ILLUSTRATION 11-25
Balance Sheet Presentation of Natural Resource

In the income statement the depletion cost is part of the cost of goods sold.

The tangible equipment used in extracting the gold may also be depreciated on a units of production basis, especially if the estimated lives of the equipment can be directly assigned to one given resource deposit. If the equipment is used on more than one job, other cost allocation methods such as straight-line or accelerated depreciation methods would be more appropriate.

CONTINUING CONTROVERSY

A major controversy relates to the accounting for exploration costs in the oil and gas industry. Conceptually, the question is whether unsuccessful exploration costs are a cost of those that are successful. Some believe that unsuccessful ventures are a cost of those that are successful (**full cost concept**) because the cost of drilling a dry hole is a cost that is needed to find the commercially profitable wells. Those who believe that only the costs of successful projects should be capitalized (**successful efforts concept**) contend that an unsuccessful company will end up capitalizing many costs that will make it, over a short period of time, show no less income than does one that is successful.[17] In addition, the only relevant measure for a single property unit is the cost directly related to that unit. The remainder of the costs should be reported as period charges.

The FASB has attempted to narrow the available alternatives but has met with little success. Here is a brief history of the debate.

1. **1977—The FASB issued *Statement No. 19*, which required oil and gas companies to follow successful efforts accounting.** However, after small oil and gas producers, voicing strong opposition, lobbied extensively in Congress, governmental agencies assessed the implications of this standard from a public interest perspective and reacted contrary to the FASB's position.[18]

2. **1978—In response to criticisms of the FASB's actions, the SEC reexamined the issue and found both successful efforts and full-cost accounting inadequate because neither reflects the economic substance of oil and gas exploration.** As a substitute, the SEC argued in favor of a yet-to-be developed method, **Reserve Recognition Accounting (RRA),** which it believed would provide more useful information. Under RRA, as soon as a company discovers oil, it reports the value of the oil on the balance sheet and in the income statement. Thus, RRA is a current value approach as opposed to full costing and successful efforts, which are historical cost approaches.[19]

3. **1979–1981—As a result of the SEC's actions, the FASB had no choice but to issue another standard that suspended the requirement that companies follow successful efforts accounting.** Therefore, full costing again became permissible. In attempting to implement RRA, however, the SEC encountered practical problems in estimating **(1) the amount of the reserves, (2) the future production costs, (3) the periods of expected disposal, (4) the discount rate, and (5) the selling price.** An estimate for each of these elements is necessary to arrive at an accurate valuation of the existing oil or gas reserve. If the oil or gas reserve is not to be extracted and sold for several years, estimating the future selling price, the appropriate discount rate, and the future costs of extraction and delivery can each be a formidable task.

---

[17]Large international oil companies such as Exxon, Mobil, and Gulf use the successful efforts approach. Full-cost accounting is used by most of the smaller, exploration-oriented companies. The differences in net income figures under the two methods can be staggering. It was estimated that Texaco's full-cost accounting increased its reported profits by $500 million over a 10-year period.

[18]The Department of Energy indicated that companies now using the full-cost method would reduce their exploration activities because of the unfavorable earnings impact associated with successful efforts accounting. The Justice Department asked the SEC to postpone adoption of one uniform method of accounting in the oil and gas industry until the SEC could determine whether the information reported to investors would be enhanced and competition constrained by adoption of the successful efforts method.

[19]The use of RRA would make a substantial difference in the balance sheets and income statements of oil companies. For example, Atlantic Richfield Co. at one time reported net producing property of $2.6 billion. If RRA were adopted, the same properties would be valued at $11.8 billion. Similarly, Standard Oil of Ohio, which reported net producing properties of $1.7 billion, would have reported approximately $10.7 billion under RRA.

4. **1981—The SEC announced that it had abandoned RRA as a potential accounting method in the primary financial statements of oil and gas producers.** Because of the inherent uncertainty of determining recoverable quantities of proved oil and gas reserves, the SEC indicated that RRA does not currently possess the required degree of reliability for use as a primary method of financial reporting. However, the SEC continued to stress that some form of value-based disclosure was needed for oil and gas reserves. As a result, the FASB issued *Statement No. 69,* "Disclosure about Oil and Gas Producing Activities," which requires current value disclosures.

5. **1986—One requirement of full-cost accounting is that costs can only be capitalized up to a ceiling, the height of which is determined by the present value of company reserves.** Capitalized costs above that ceiling have to be expensed. In 1986 the price of oil plummeted and as a result a number of companies faced massive writeoffs of their reserves because capitalized costs exceeded the present value of the companies' reserves. Companies lobbied for leniency, but the SEC decided that the writeoffs had to be taken. As a result, Mesa Limited Partnerships' $31 million profit was restated to a $169 million loss and Pacific Lighting's $44.5 million profit was changed to a $70.5 million loss.

Either the full-cost approach or the successful efforts approach is currently acceptable. It does seem ironic that Congress directed the FASB to develop one method of accounting for the oil and gas industry, and when the FASB did so, the government chose not to accept it. Subsequently, the government (SEC) attempted to develop a new approach, failed, and then urged the FASB to develop the disclosure requirements in this area. After all these changes, alternatives still exist in the oil and gas industry.

This controversy in the oil and gas industry provides a number of lessons to the student in accounting. First, it demonstrates the strong influence that the federal government has in financial reporting matters. Second, the concern for economic consequences places considerable pressure on the FASB to weigh the economic effects of any required standard. Third, the experience with RRA highlights the problems that are encountered when a change from an historical cost to a current value approach is proposed. Fourth, this controversy illustrates the difficulty of establishing standards when affected groups have differing viewpoints. And finally, it reinforces the need for a conceptual framework with carefully developed guidelines for recognition, measurement, and reporting, so that issues of this nature hopefully may be more easily resolved in the future.

UNDERLYING CONCEPT

Failure to consider the economic consequences of accounting principles is a frequent criticism of the profession. However, the neutrality concept requires that the statements be free from bias. Freedom from bias requires that the statements reflect economic reality, even if undesirable effects occur.

SPECIAL PROBLEMS IN DEPLETION ACCOUNTING

Accounting for natural resources has some interesting problems that are uncommon to most other types of assets. For purposes of discussion we have divided these problems into four categories:

1. Difficulty of estimating recoverable reserves.
2. Problems of discovery value.
3. Tax aspects of natural resources.
4. Accounting for liquidating dividends.

Estimating Recoverable Reserves

Not infrequently the estimate of recoverable reserves has to be changed either because new information has become available or because production processes have become more sophisticated. Natural resources such as oil and gas deposits and some rare metals have recently provided the greatest challenges. Estimates of these reserves are in large measure "knowledgeable guesses."

This problem is the **same as accounting for changes in estimates of the useful lives of plant and equipment.** The procedure is to revise the depletion rate on a prospective basis by dividing the remaining cost by the estimate of the new recoverable reserves. This approach has much merit because the required estimates are so tenuous.

Discovery Value

Discovery value accounting and reserve recognition accounting are similar. RRA is specifically related to the oil and gas industry, whereas **discovery value** is a broader term associated with the whole natural resources area. As indicated earlier, accountants do not recognize discovery values. However, if discovery value were to be recorded, an asset account would be debited and an Unrealized Appreciation account would be credited. Unrealized Appreciation is part of stockholders' equity. Unrealized Appreciation would then be transferred to revenue as the natural resources are sold.

A similar issue arises with resources such as growing timber, aging liquor, and maturing livestock that increase in value over time. One method is to record the increase in value as the accretion occurs. Debit the asset account and credit revenue or an unrealized revenue account. These increases can be substantial. Boise Cascade's timber resources were at one time valued at $1.7 billion, whereas its book value was approximately $289 million. Accountants have been hesitant to record these increases because of the uncertainty regarding the final sales price and the problem of estimating the costs involved in getting the resources ready for sale.

Tax Aspects of Natural Resources

The tax aspects of accounting for most natural resources have comprised some of the most controversial provisions of the Internal Revenue Code (IRC). The tax law has long provided a deduction for the greater of **cost** or **percentage depletion** against revenue from oil, gas, and most minerals. The percentage or statutory depletion allows a writeoff ranging from 5% to 22% (depending on the natural resource) of gross revenue received. As a result, the amount of depletion may exceed the cost assigned to a given natural resource. An asset's carrying amount may be zero, but a depletion deduction may still be taken if the enterprise has gross revenue. The significance of the percentage depletion allowance is now greatly reduced because it has been repealed for most oil and gas companies and is of only limited use in most other situations.

Liquidating Dividends

A company often owns as its only major asset a certain property from which it intends to extract natural resources. If the company does not expect to purchase additional properties, it may distribute gradually to stockholders their capital investments by paying dividends equal to the amount of accumulated net income. The major accounting problem is to distinguish between dividends that are a return of capital and those that are not. The company issuing a **liquidating dividend** should debit Paid-in Capital in Excess of Par for that portion related to the original investment instead of Retained Earnings, because the dividend is a return of part of the investor's original contribution.

To illustrate, at December 31, 1993, Callahan Mining has a retained earnings balance of $1,650,000, accumulated depletion on mineral properties of $2,100,000, and paid-in capital in excess of par of $5,435,493. Callahan's board declares a dividend of $3.00 a share on the 1,000,000 shares outstanding. The entry to record the $3,000,000 cash dividend is as follows:

Retained Earnings	1,650,000	
Paid-in Capital in Excess of Par	1,350,000	
Cash		3,000,000

Stockholders must be informed that each $3.00 dividend per share represents a $1.65 ($1,650,000 ÷ 1,000,000 shares) per share return on investment and a $1.35 ($1,350,000 ÷ 1,000,000 shares) per share liquidating dividend.

▶ FINANCIAL REPORTING OF NATURAL RESOURCES AND DEPLETION

The FASB requires both publicly traded and privately held companies engaged in significant oil and gas producing activities to disclose in their financial statements (1) the basic method of accounting for those costs incurred in oil and gas producing activities (e.g., full cost versus successful efforts) and (2) the manner of disposing of costs relating to oil and gas producing activities (e.g., expensing immediately versus depreciation and depletion).[20] Public companies, in addition to these two required disclosures, must include as supplementary information numerous schedules reporting reserve quantities; capitalized costs; acquisition, exploration, and development activities; and a standardized measure of discounted future net cash flows related to proved oil and gas reserve quantities.

OBJECTIVE 10
Describe financial statement disclosures for natural resources.

The following cost classifications and descriptions are from the Annual Report of Quaker State Corporation. (Also, see the financials of Georgia-Pacific in Appendix 5-A pages 221 and 224.)

ILLUSTRATION 11-26
Presentation and Disclosure of Natural Resources and Depletion

Quaker State Corporation		
	1992	1991
	($000)	
Total current assets	$205,445	$143,059
Property, plant and equipment, net of accumulated depreciation and depletion (Note 6)	227,935	308,372
Other assets	75,428	25,484
Total assets other than insurance	508,808	476,915

Notes to Consolidated Financial Statements

Note 1 (In Part): Summary of Significant Accounting Policies.

c. Property, plant and equipment, at cost.   Costs of buildings and equipment, other than oil and gas producing properties, are charged against income over their estimated useful lives, using the straight-line method of depreciation. Repairs and maintenance, which are not considered betterments and do not extend the useful life of property, are charged to expense as incurred. When property, plant and equipment are retired or otherwise disposed of, the asset and accumulated depreciation are removed from the accounts and the resulting profit or loss is reflected in income.

Costs of oil and gas producing properties are accounted for under the successful efforts method. Lease acquisition costs are capitalized and amortized by the unit of production method based on proved reserves, and equipment and intangible drilling costs are capitalized and amortized by the unit of production method based on proved developed reserves. An additional provision for depreciation and depletion is provided if the net capitalized costs of production properties exceed the discounted future net revenues for proved oil and gas reserves on a company-wide basis, using year-end prices and an annual discount rate of 10%.

Costs of individual oil and gas wells determined to be uneconomical are charged to the allowance for accumulated depreciation and depletion when abandoned, with no gain or loss being recognized until the property group is abandoned. Exploratory costs, associated with dry holes, geological and geophysical costs and annual delay rentals are charged to expense.

Some companies do not record depletion expense because the number of recoverable units is considered not determinable with enough certainty to avoid distortions. In addition, it is argued that as long as resources are being discovered, there is no need for depletion. This approach has no validity in theory and should not be considered appropriate.

---

[20]"Disclosure about Oil and Gas Producing Activities," *Statement of Financial Accounting Standards Board No. 69* (Stamford, Conn.: FASB, 1982).

▶ SUMMARY OF LEARNING OBJECTIVES ◀

1. **Explain the concept of depreciation.** Depreciation is the accounting process of allocating the cost of tangible assets to expense in a systematic and rational manner to those periods expected to benefit from the use of the asset.

2. **Identify the factors involved in the depreciation process.** Three factors involved in the depreciation process are: (1) determining the depreciation base for the asset, (2) estimating service lives, and (3) selecting a method of cost apportionment (depreciation).

3. **Compare activity, straight-line, and decreasing charge methods of depreciation.** (1) *Activity method:* Assumes that depreciation is a function of use or productivity instead of the passage of time. The life of the asset is considered in terms of either the output it provides, or an input measure such as the number of hours it works. (2) *Straight-line method:* Considers depreciation a function of time instead of a function of usage. This method is widely employed in practice because of its simplicity. The straight-line procedure is often the most conceptually appropriate when a decline in usefulness is constant from period to period. (3) *Decreasing charge methods:* Provide for a higher depreciation cost in the earlier years and lower charges in later periods. The main justification for this approach is that the asset suffers the greatest loss of services in those years.

4. **Explain special depreciation methods.** There are five special depreciation methods: (1) *Inventory method:* Used to value small tangible assets such as hand tools or utensils. (2) *Retirement and replacement methods:* Used principally by public utilities and railroads that own many similar units of small value such as poles, ties, conductors, and telephones. The purpose of these approaches is to avoid elaborate depreciation schedules for individual assets. (3) *Group and composite methods:* The term group refers to a collection of assets that are similar in nature; composite refers to a collection of assets that are dissimilar in nature. The group method is frequently used where the assets are fairly homogeneous and have approximately the same useful lives. The composite approach is used when the assets are heterogeneous and have different lives. (4) *Compound interest methods:* Unlike most depreciation methods, the compound interest methods are increasing charge methods that result in lower depreciation charges in the early years and higher depreciation charges in the later years. (5) *Hybrid or combination methods:* A hybrid depreciation method widely used in the steel industry is a combination straight-line/activity approach referred to as the production variable method.

5. **Identify reasons why depreciation methods are selected.** The selection of a depreciation method involves factors such as the nature and uncertainty of revenue flows, matching costs and revenues, effect on income and asset book values, tax considerations, and record-keeping costs.

6. **Describe income tax methods of depreciation.** A Modified Accelerated Cost Recovery System (MACRS) was enacted by Congress in the Tax Reform Act of 1986. It applies to depreciable assets placed in service in 1987 and later. The computation of depreciation under MACRS differs from the computation under GAAP in three respects: (1) a mandated tax life, which is generally shorter than the economic life; (2) cost recovery on an accelerated basis; and (3) an assigned salvage value of zero.

7. **Explain the accounting issues related to asset impairment.** The process to determine an impairment loss is as follows: (1) Review events and changes in circumstances for possible impairment. (2) If events or changes suggest impairment, determine if the sum of the expected future net cash flows from the long-lived asset is less than the carrying amount of the asset. If less, measure

the impairment loss. (3) The impairment loss is the amount by which the carrying amount of the asset is greater than the fair value of the asset. After an impairment loss is recorded, the reduced carrying amount of the long-lived asset is now considered its new cost basis. Impairment losses may not be restored for assets held for use. If the asset is expected to be disposed of, the impaired asset should be reported at the lower of cost or net realizable value. It is not depreciated. It can be continuously revalued, as long as the write-up is never greater than the carrying amount before impairment.

8. **Describe financial statement disclosures for property, plant, and equipment.** The basis of valuation for property, plant, and equipment should be disclosed along with pledges, liens, and other commitments related to these assets. Any liability secured by property, plant, and equipment should not be offset against these assets, but should be reported in the liability section. Property, plant, and equipment not currently employed as producing assets in the business should be segregated from assets used in operations. When assets are depreciated, a valuation account normally called Accumulated Depreciation is credited.

9. **Explain the accounting procedures for depletion of natural resources.** The accounting procedures for depletion of nature resources are (1) establishment of depletion base, and (2) writeoff of resource cost. Four factors are involved in establishing the depletion base: (a) *acquisition costs*, (b) *exploration costs*, (c) *development costs*, and (d) *restoration costs*. To write off resource cost, normally, depletion is computed on the units of production method, which means that depletion is a function of the number of units withdrawn during the period. In adopting this approach, the total cost of the natural resource less salvage value is divided by the number of units estimated to be in the resource deposit, to obtain a cost per unit of product. This cost per unit is multiplied by the number of units withdrawn to compute depletion.

10. **Describe financial statement disclosures for natural resources.** The FASB requires both publicly traded and privately held companies engaged in significant oil and gas producing activities to disclose in their financial statements (1) the basic method of accounting for those costs incurred in oil and gas producing activities and (2) the manner of disposing of costs relating to oil and gas producing activities. Public companies, in addition to these two required disclosures, must include as supplementary information numerous schedules reporting reserve quantities; capitalized costs; acquisition, exploration, and development activities; and a standardized measure of discounted future net cash flows related to proved oil and gas reserve quantities.

QUESTIONS

1. Distinguish between depreciation, depletion, and amortization.

2. Identify the factors that are relevant in determining the annual depreciation charge and explain whether these factors are determined objectively or whether they are based on judgment.

3. Recently, a trustee of a state college noted that "depreciation of assets for any college is nonsensical. We're not public companies. Forcing colleges to depreciate would only boost our bookkeeping costs for no good reason." Do you agree? Discuss.

4. The plant manager of a manufacturing firm suggested in a conference of the company's executives that accountants should speed up depreciation on the machinery in the finishing department because improvements were rapidly making those machines obsolete and a depreciation fund big enough to cover their replacement is needed. Discuss the accounting concept of depreciation and the effect on a business concern of the depreciation recorded for plant assets, paying particular attention to the issues raised by the plant manager.

5. For what reasons are plant assets retired? Define inadequacy, supersession, and obsolescence.

6. What basic questions must be answered before the amount of the depreciation charge can be computed?

7. Walt Whitman Company purchased a machine on January 2, 1994 for $500,000. The machine has an estimated useful life of 5 years and a salvage value of $100,000. Depreciation was computed by the 150% declining balance method. What is the amount of accumulated depreciation at the end of December 31, 1995?

8. Emily Dickinson Company purchased machinery for $120,000 on January 1, 1995. It is estimated that the machinery will have a useful life of 20 years, scrap value of $20,000, production of 84,000 units, and working hours of 42,000. During 1995 the company uses the machinery for 14,300 hours, and the machinery produces 20,000 units. Compute depreciation under the straight-line, units-of-output, working-hours, sum-of-the-years'-digits, and declining-balance (use 10% as the annual rate) methods.

9. What are the major factors considered in determining what depreciation method to use?

10. Under what conditions is it appropriate for a business to use the composite method of depreciation for its plant assets? What are the advantages and disadvantages of this method?

11. If Bala, Inc., uses the composite method and its composite rate is 7.5% per year, what entry should it make when plant assets that originally cost $50,000 and have been used for 10 years are sold for $13,000?

12. Under what conditions is it appropriate for a concern to use the retirement method of depreciation for plant assets? What are the advantages of this method?

13. If a business that uses the retirement method sells for $14,000 plant assets originally costing $32,000 5 years ago, what entry should be made? The assets sold consist of 500 small motors, which usually last about 7 years.

14. A building that was purchased December 31, 1970, for $1,200,000 was originally estimated to have a life of 50 years with no salvage value at the end of that time. Depreciation has been recorded through 1994. During 1995 an examination of the building by an engineering firm discloses that its estimated useful life is 15 years after 1994. What should be the amount of depreciation for 1995?

15. T. S. Elliot, president of Cats Company, has recently noted that depreciation increases cash provided by operations and, therefore, depreciation is a good source of funds. Do you agree? Discuss.

16. Amy Lowell purchased a computer for $5,000 on July 1, 1995. She intends to depreciate it over 4 years using the double-declining balance method. Salvage value is $1,000. Compute depreciation for 1996.

17. Hernandez is considering the writedown of its long-term plant because of a lack of profitability. Explain to the management of Hernandez how to determine whether a writeoff is permitted.

18. Ahmid Gupta Co. has equipment with a carrying amount of $700,000. The expected future net cash flows from the equipment is $705,000 and its fair value is $604,000. The equipment is expected to be used in operations in the future. What amount (if any) should Gupta report as an impairment to its equipment?

19. What is a modified accelerated cost recovery system (MACRS)? Speculate as to why this system is now required.

20. It has been suggested that plant and equipment could be replaced more quickly if depreciation rates for income tax and accounting purposes were substantially increased. As a result, business operations would receive the benefit of more modern and more efficient plant facilities. Discuss the merits of this proposition.

21. Neither depreciation on replacement cost nor depreciation adjusted for changes in the purchasing power of the dollar has been recognized as generally accepted accounting practice for inclusion in the primary financial statements. Briefly present the accounting treatment that might be used to assist in the maintenance of the ability of a company to replace its productive capacity.

22. List (a) the similarities and (b) the differences in the accounting treatments of depreciation and cost depletion.

23. Describe cost depletion and percentage depletion. Why is the percentage depletion method permitted?

24. In what way may the use of percentage depletion violate sound accounting theory?

25. In the extractive industries, businesses may pay dividends in excess of net income. What is the maximum permissible? How can this practice be justified?

26. The following statement appeared in a financial magazine: "RRA—or Rah-Rah, as it's sometimes dubbed—has kicked up quite a storm. Oil companies, for example, are convinced that the approach

is misleading. Major accounting firms agree." What is RRA? Why might oil companies believe that this approach is misleading?

27. Generic Oil uses successful efforts accounting and also provides full-cost results as well. Under full-cost, Generic Oil would have reported retained earnings of $42 million and net income of $4 million. Under successful efforts, retained earnings were $29 million and net $4 million. Explain the difference between full costing and successful efforts accounting.

EXERCISES

 E11-1 (Depreciation Computations—SL, SYD, DDB) Patsy Cline Company purchases equipment on January 1, Year 1, at a cost of $430,000. The asset is expected to have a service life of 12 years and a salvage value of $40,000.

Instructions
(a) Compute the amount of depreciation for each of Years 1 through 3 using the straight-line depreciation method.
(b) Compute the amount of depreciation for each of Years 1 through 3 using the sum-of-the-years'-digits method.
(c) Compute the amount of depreciation for each of Years 1 through 3 using the double-declining balance method. (In performing your calculations, round constant percentage to the nearest one-hundredth of a point and round answers to the nearest dollar.)

E11-2 (Depreciation—Conceptual Understanding) The Everly Brothers Company acquired a plant asset at the beginning of Year 1. The asset has an estimated service life of 5 years. An employee has prepared depreciation schedules for this asset using three different methods to compare the results of using one method with the results of using other methods. You are to assume that the following schedules have been correctly prepared for this asset using (1) the straight-line method, (2) the sum-of-the-years'-digits method, and (3) the double-declining balance method.

Year	Straight-line	Sum-of-the-Years'-Digits	Double-declining Balance
1	$ 6,000	$10,000	$13,200
2	6,000	8,000	7,920
3	6,000	6,000	4,752
4	6,000	4,000	2,851
5	6,000	2,000	1,277
Total	$30,000	$30,000	$30,000

Instructions
Answer the following questions:
(a) What is the cost of the asset being depreciated?
(b) What amount, if any, was used in the depreciation calculations for the salvage value for this asset?
(c) Which method will produce the highest charge to income in Year 1?
(d) Which method will produce the highest charge to income in Year 4?
(e) Which method will produce the highest book value for the asset at the end of Year 3?
(f) If the asset is sold at the end of Year 3, which method would yield the highest gain (or lowest loss) on disposal of the asset?

E11-3 (Depreciation Computations—SYD, DDB—Partial Periods) LaVern Baker Company purchased a new plant asset on April 1, 1995, at a cost of $690,000. It was estimated to have a service life of 20 years and a salvage value of $60,000. Hunter's accounting period is the calendar year.

Instructions
(a) Compute the depreciation for this asset for 1995 and 1996 using the sum-of-the-years'-digits method.
(b) Compute the depreciation for this asset for 1995 and 1996 using the double-declining balance method.

E11-4 (Depreciation Computations—Five Methods) Skeeter Davis Furnace Corp. purchased machinery for $195,000 on May 1, 1995. It is estimated that it will have a useful life of 10 years, scrap value of $15,000, production of 240,000 units, and working hours of 25,000. During 1996 Davis Corp. uses the machinery for 2,650 hours, and the machinery produces 25,500 units.

Instructions

From the information given, compute the depreciation charge for 1996 under each of the following methods (round to three decimal places):

- **(a)** Straight-line.
- **(b)** Units-of-output.
- **(c)** Working hours.
- **(d)** Sum-of-the-years'-digits.
- **(e)** Declining-balance (use 20% as the annual rate).

E11-5 (Depreciation Computations—Four Methods) The Drifters Corporation purchased a new machine for its assembly process on October 1, 1995. The cost of this machine was $117,900. The company estimated that the machine would have a trade-in value of $12,900 at the end of its service life. Its life is estimated at 5 years and its working hours are estimated at 21,000 hours. Year-end is December 31.

Instructions

Compute the depreciation expense under the following methods: (1) straight-line depreciation for 1995, (2) activity method for 1995, assuming that machine usage was 800 hours, (3) sum-of-the-years'-digits for 1996, and (4) double-declining balance for 1996. Each of the foregoing should be considered unrelated.

E11-6 (Depreciation Computations—Five Methods, Partial Periods) Ben E. King Winery Company purchased equipment for $212,000 on April 1, 1994. It is estimated that the equipment will have a useful life of 8 years and a salvage value of $12,000. Estimated production is 40,000 units and estimated working hours 20,000. During 1994 King Winery uses the equipment for 1,600 hours and the equipment produces 3,000 units.

Instructions

Compute depreciation expense under each of the following methods. King Winery is on a calendar-year basis ending December 31.

- **(a)** Straight-line method for 1994.
- **(b)** Activity method (units of output) for 1994.
- **(c)** Activity method (working hours) for 1994.
- **(d)** Sum-of-the-years'-digits method for 1996.
- **(e)** Double-declining balance method for 1995.

E11-7 (Depreciation Computations, SYD) The Five Satins Company purchased a piece of equipment at the beginning of 1995. The equipment cost $430,000. It has an estimated service life of 8 years and an expected salvage value of $70,000. The sum-of-the-years'-digits method of depreciation is being used. Someone has already correctly prepared a depreciation schedule for this asset. This schedule shows that $60,000 will be depreciated for a particular calendar year.

Instructions

Show calculations to determine for what particular year the depreciation amount for this asset will be $60,000.

E11-8 (Depreciation Computation—Replacement, Nonmonetary Exchange) Connie Francis Corporation bought a machine on June 1, 1993, for $31,000, f.o.b. the place of manufacture. Freight to the point where it was set up was $200, and $500 was expended to install it. The machine's useful life was estimated at 10 years, with a scrap value of $2,500. On June 1, 1994, an essential part of the machine is replaced, at a cost of $1,980, with one designed to reduce the cost of operating the machine. On June 1, 1997, the company buys a new machine of greater capacity for $35,000, delivered, trading in the old machine which has a fair market value and trade-in allowance of $20,000. To prepare the old machine for removal from the plant cost $75, and expenditures to install the new one were $1,200. It is estimated that the new machine has a useful life of 10 years, with a scrap value of $3,000 at the end of that time.

Instructions

Assuming that depreciation is to be computed on the straight-line basis, prepare schedules showing the annual depreciation on the new equipment that should be provided for the fiscal year beginning June 1, 1997. (Round to the nearest dollar.)

E11-9 (Composite Depreciation) Presented below is information related to Marcy Walker Manufacturing Corporation:

Asset	Cost	Estimated Scrap	Estimated Life (in years)
A	$40,500	$5,500	10
B	33,600	4,800	9
C	36,000	3,600	8
D	19,000	1,500	7
E	23,500	2,500	6

Instructions

- **(a)** Compute the rate of depreciation per year to be applied to the plant assets under the composite method.
- **(b)** Prepare the adjusting entry necessary at the end of the year to record depreciation for the year.
- **(c)** Prepare the entry to record the sale of fixed asset D for cash of $5,000. It was used for 6 years, and depreciation was entered under the composite method.

E11-10 (Retirement and Replacement Methods) In 1996 Side Kicks Co. replaced 22,000 utility poles at a cost of $200 each. The old poles originally cost $150 apiece.

Instructions
   (a) Prepare the entry(ies) assuming that Side Kicks Co. uses the retirement method for depreciating their utility poles.
   (b) Prepare the entry(ies) assuming that Side Kicks Co. uses the replacement method for depreciating their utility poles.

E11-11 (Retirement Method) Alan Alda Company decides to use the retirement method in accounting for house meters that it installs, because they are of small value and replaced frequently. The life of the meters is from 1 to 15 years, with the average life about 12 years.
   Below are the transactions related to the house meters for 1996.

Jan. 10, 1996	Purchases 13,000 meters at $130 each.
Apr. 15, 1996	Discards 40 of the meters purchased January 10, 1996, as worthless.
June 20, 1996	Sells 80 of the meters purchased January 10, 1996, for $1,000.
Dec. 12, 1996	Replaces 1,200 meters at $140 each.

Instructions
Using the retirement method, prepare entries to record the transactions for 1996.

E11-12 (Depreciating Small Tools) Wayne Rodgers Company has approximately 3,000 hand tools, which it uses in its operations. Each is of relatively small value and is frequently replaced. The total cost of such tools is approximately $21,000.
   Because of the characteristics of this asset, the company prefers not to keep detailed records of each tool and depreciate it. You are asked to suggest some reasonably simple method of accounting for these tools so that the asset is carried at a fair amount and operating expenses are charged with a fair amount. What do you suggest?

Instructions
Illustrate your suggestion with pro forma entries for the various types of transactions that might occur.

E11-13 (Depreciation—Change in Estimate) Machinery purchased for $52,000 by Alistair Cooke Co. in 1991 was originally estimated to have a life of 8 years with a salvage value of $4,000 at the end of that time. Depreciation has been entered for 5 years on this basis. In 1996, it is determined that the total estimated life (including 1996) should be 10 years with a salvage value of $4,500 at the end of that time. Assume straight-line depreciation.

Instructions
   (a) Prepare the entry to correct the prior years' depreciation, if necessary.
   (b) Prepare the entry to record depreciation for 1996.

E11-14 (Depreciation Computation—Addition, Change in Estimate) In 1968, Angela Lansbury Company completed the construction of a building at a cost of $1,860,000 and first occupied it in January, 1969. It was estimated that the building will have a useful life of 40 years, and a salvage value of $60,000 at the end of that time.
   Early in 1979, an addition to the building was constructed at a cost of $375,000. At that time it was estimated that the remaining life of the building would be, as originally estimated, an additional 30 years, and that the addition would have a life of 30 years, and a salvage value of $15,000.
   In 1997, it is determined that the probable life of the building and addition will extend to the end of 2029, or 20 years beyond the original estimate.

Instructions
   (a) Using the straight-line method, compute the annual depreciation that would have been charged from 1969 through 1978.
   (b) Compute the annual depreciation that would have been charged from 1979 through 1996.
   (c) Prepare the entry, if necessary, to adjust the account balances because of the revision of the estimated life in 1997.
   (d) Compute the annual depreciation to be charged beginning with 1997.

E11-15 (Depreciation—Replacement, Change in Estimate) Kate Jackson Company constructed a building at a cost of $2,100,000 and occupied it beginning in January, 1976. It was estimated at that time that its life would be 40 years, with no salvage value.
   In January 1996, a new roof was installed at a cost of $300,000, and it was estimated then that the building would have a useful life of 25 years from that date. The cost of the old roof was $150,000.

Instructions
   (a) What amount of depreciation should have been charged annually from the years 1976 to 1995? (Assume straight-line depreciation.)

(b) What entry should be made in 1996 to record the replacement of the roof?

(c) Prepare the entry in January, 1996, to record the revision in the estimated life of the building, if necessary.

(d) What amount of depreciation should be charged for the year 1996?

E11-16 (Error Analysis and Depreciation, SL and SYD) Victoria Principal Company shows the following entries in its Equipment account for 1996; all amounts are based on historical cost.

Equipment						
1996				**1996**		
Jan. 1	Balance	134,750		June 30	Cost of equipment sold	
Aug. 10	Purchases	32,000			(purchased prior	
12	Freight on equipment				to 1996)	22,000
	purchased	700				
25	Installation costs	2,700				
Nov. 10	Repairs	400				

Instructions

(a) Prepare any correcting entries necessary.

(b) Assuming that depreciation is to be charged for a full year on the ending balance in the asset account, compute the proper depreciation charge for 1996 under each of the methods listed below. Assume an estimated life of 10 years, with no salvage value. The machinery included in the January 1, 1996, balance was purchased in 1994.

    1. Straight-line.

    2. Sum-of-the-years'-digits.

E11-17 (Depreciation for Fractional Periods) On April 10, 1996, Jurassic Company sells equipment that it purchased for $192,000 on August 20, 1989. It was originally estimated that the equipment would have a life of 12 years and a scrap value of $16,800 at the end of that time, and depreciation has been computed on that basis. The company uses the straight-line method of depreciation.

Instructions

(a) Compute the depreciation charge on this equipment for 1989, for 1996, and the total charge for the period from 1990 to 1995, inclusive, under each of the six following assumptions with respect to partial periods.

    1. Depreciation is computed for the exact period of time during which the asset is owned. (Use 365 days for base.)

    2. Depreciation is computed for the full year on the January 1 balance in the asset account.

    3. Depreciation is computed for the full year on the December 31 balance in the asset account.

    4. Depreciation for one-half year is charged on plant assets acquired or disposed of during the year.

    5. Depreciation is computed on additions from the beginning of the month following acquisition and on disposals to the beginning of the month following disposal.

    6. Depreciation is computed for a full period on all assets in use for over one-half year, and no depreciation is charged on assets in use for less than one-half year. (Use 365 days for base.)

(b) Briefly evaluate the methods above, considering them from the point of view of basic accounting theory as well as simplicity of application.

E11-18 (Impairment) Presented below is information related to equipment owned by Fernandez Company at December 31, 1996.

Cost	$9,000,000
Accumulated depreciation to date	1,000,000
Expected future net cash flows	7,000,000
Fair value	5,000,000

Assume that Fernandez will continue to use this asset in the future. As of December 31, 1996, the equipment has a remaining useful life of 4 years.

Instructions

(a) Prepare the journal entry (if any) to record the impairment of the asset at December 31, 1996.

(b) Prepare the journal entry to record depreciation expense for 1997.

(c) The fair value of the equipment at December 31, 1997, is $5,300,000. Prepare the journal entry (if any) necessary to record this increase in fair value.

E11-19 (Impairment) Assume the same information as Exercise 11-18, except that Fernandez intends to dispose of the equipment in the coming year. It is expected that the cost of disposal will be $20,000.

Instructions

(a) Prepare the journal entry (if any) to record the impairment of the asset at December 31, 1995.

(b) Prepare the journal entry (if any) to record depreciation expense for 1996.

(c) The asset was not sold by December 31, 1996. The fair value of the equipment on that date is $5,300,000. Prepare the journal entry (if any) necessary to record this increase in fair value. It is expected that the cost of disposal is still $20,000.

E11-20 (Impairment) The management of Trassic Inc. was discussing whether certain equipment should be written off as a charge to current operations because of obsolescence. This equipment has a cost of $900,000 with depreciation to date of $400,000 as of December 31, 1995. On December 31, 1995, management projected its future net cash flows from this equipment to be $300,000 and its fair value to be $280,000. The company intends to use this equipment in the future.

Instructions

(a) Prepare the journal entry (if any) to record the impairment at December 31, 1995.

(b) Where should the gain or loss (if any) on the writedown be reported in the income statement?

(c) At December 31, 1996, the equipment's fair value increased to $290,000. Prepare the journal entry (if any) to record this increase in fair value.

(d) What accounting issues did management face in accounting for this writedown?

E11-21 (Book vs. Tax (MACRS) Depreciation) Paleozoic Enterprises purchased a delivery truck on January 1, 1996, at a cost of $26,000. The truck has a useful life of 7 years with an estimated salvage value of $5,000. The straight-line method is used for book purposes. For tax purposes the truck, having an MACRS class life of 7 years, is classified as 5-year property; the optional MACRS tax rate tables are used to compute depreciation. In addition, assume that for 1996 and 1997 the company has revenues of $200,000 and operating expenses (excluding depreciation) of $130,000.

Instructions

(a) Prepare income statements for 1996 and 1997 (the final amount reported on the income statement should be income before income taxes).

(b) Compute taxable income for 1996 and 1997.

(c) Determine the total depreciation to be taken over the useful life of the delivery truck for both book and tax purposes.

(d) Explain why depreciation for book and tax purposes will generally be different over the useful life of a depreciable asset.

E11-22 (Book vs. Tax (MACRS) Depreciation) Pliocene Inc. purchased computer equipment on March 1, 1995, for $25,000. The computer equipment has a useful life of 10 years and a salvage value of $1,000. For tax purposes, the MACRS class life is 5 years.

Instructions

(a) Assuming that the company uses the straight-line method for book and tax purposes, what is the depreciation expense reported in (1) the financial statements for 1995 and (2) the tax return for 1995?

(b) Assuming that the company uses the double-declining balance method for both book and tax purposes, what is the depreciation expense reported in (1) the financial statements for 1995 and (2) the tax return for 1995?

(c) Why is depreciation for tax purposes different from depreciation for book purposes even if the company uses the same depreciation method to compute them both?

E11-23 (Depletion Computations—Timber) Kate Lockard Timber Company owns 9,000 acres of timberland purchased in 1984 at a cost of $1,400 per acre. At the time of purchase the land without the timber was valued at $400 per acre. In 1985, Lockard built fire lanes and roads, with a life of 30 years, at a cost of $81,000. Every year Lockard sprays to prevent disease at a cost of $2,000 per year and spends $6,000 to maintain the fire lanes and roads. During 1986, Lockard selectively logged and sold 700,000 board feet of timber, of the estimated 3,500,000 board feet. In 1987, Lockard planted new seedlings to replace the trees cut at a cost of $100,000.

Instructions

(a) Determine the depreciation expense and the cost of timber sold related to depletion for 1986.

(b) Lockard has not logged since 1986. If Lockard logged and sold 1,000,000 board feet of timber in 1997, when the timber cruise (appraiser) estimated 5,000,000 board feet, determine the cost of timber sold related to depletion for 1997.

E11-24 (Depletion Computations—Oil) Marin Bosley Drilling Company has leased property on which oil has been discovered. Wells on this property produced 18,000 barrels of oil during the past year that sold at an average sales price of $15 per barrel. Total oil resources of this property are estimated to be 250,000 barrels. The lease provided for an outright payment of $600,000 to the lessor before drilling could be commenced and an annual rental of $27,000. A premium of 5% of the sales price of every barrel of oil removed is to be paid annually to the lessor. In addition, the lessee is to clean up all the waste and debris from drilling and to bear the costs of reconditioning the land for farming when the wells are abandoned. It is estimated that this clean-up and reconditioning will cost $30,000.

Instructions
From the provisions of the lease agreement, you are to compute the cost per barrel for the past year, exclusive of operating costs, to Marin Bosley Drilling Company.

E11-25 (Depletion Computations—Timber) Paul Wenger Lumber Company owns a 7,000-acre tract of timber purchased in 1989 at a cost of $1,300 per acre. At the time of purchase the land was estimated to have a value of $300 per acre without the timber. Wenger Lumber Company has not logged this tract since it was purchased. In 1996, Wenger had the timber cruised. The cruise (appraiser) estimated that each acre contained 8,000 board feet of timber. In 1996, Wenger built 10 miles of roads at a cost of $6,120 per mile. After the roads were completed, Wenger logged and sold 3,500 trees containing 840,000 board feet.

Instructions
- **(a)** Determine the cost of timber sold related to depletion for 1996.
- **(b)** If Wenger depreciates the logging roads on the basis of timber cut, determine the depreciation expense for 1996.
- **(c)** If Wenger plants five seedlings at a cost of $4 per seedling for each tree cut, how should Wenger treat the reforestation?

E11-26 (Depletion Computations—Mining) Carrie Mosiman Mining Company purchased land on February 1, 1995, at a cost of $1,190,000. It estimated that a total of 60,000 tons of mineral was available for mining. After it has removed all the natural resources, the company will be required to restore the property to its previous state because of strict environmental protection laws. It estimates the cost of this restoration at $90,000. It believes it will be able to sell the property afterwards for $100,000. It incurred developmental costs of $180,000 before it was able to do any mining. In 1995 resources removed totaled 30,000 tons. It sold 22,000 tons.

Instructions (Round to two decimals)
Compute the following information for 1995: (1) per unit material cost; (2) total material cost of 12/31/95 inventory; and (3) total material cost in cost of goods sold at 12/31/95.

E11-27 (Depletion Computations—Minerals) At the beginning of 1995, Nathan Burkhalter Company acquired a mine for $850,000. Of this amount, $100,000 was ascribed to the land value and the remaining portion to the minerals in the mine. Surveys conducted by geologists have indicated that approximately 12,000,000 units of the ore appear to be in the mine. Burkhalter incurred $170,000 of development costs associated with this mine prior to any extraction of minerals and estimates that it will require $40,000 to prepare the land for an alternative use when all of the mineral has been removed. During 1995, 2,500,000 units of ore were extracted and 2,100,000 of these units were sold.

Instructions
Compute (1) the total amount of depletion for 1995, and (2) the amount that is charged as an expense for 1995 for the cost of the minerals sold during 1995.

PROBLEMS

P11-1 (Depreciation for Partial Period—SL, SYD, and DDB) Boyz II Men purchased Machine #201 on May 1, 1995. The following information relating to Machine #201 was gathered at the end of May.

Price	$71,500
Credit terms	2/10, n/30
Freight-in costs	$ 1,130
Preparation and installation costs	$ 3,800
Labor costs during regular production operations	$10,500

It was expected that the machine could be used for 10 years, after which the salvage value would be zero. Boyz II Men intends to use the machine for only 8 years, however, after which it expects to be able to sell it for $1,200. The invoice for Machine #201 was paid May 5, 1995. Men uses the calendar year as the basis for the preparation of financial statements.

Instructions
- **(a)** Compute the depreciation expense for the years indicated using the following methods. (Round to the nearest cent.)
  1. Straight-line method for 1995.
  2. Sum-of-the-years'-digits method for 1996.
  3. Double-declining balance method for 1995.

(b) Suppose Latoya Jones, the president of Boyz II Men, tells you that because the company is a new organization, she expects it will be several years before production and sales reach optimum levels. She asks you to recommend a depreciation method that will allocate less of the company's depreciation expense to the early years and more to later years of the assets' lives. What method would you recommend?

P11-2 (Depreciation for Partial Periods—SL, Act., SYD, and DDB) The cost of equipment purchased by Blind Melon, Inc. on April 1, 1995, is $67,000. It is estimated that the machine will have a $4,000 salvage value at the end of its service life. Its service life is estimated at 7 years; its total working hours are estimated at 42,000 and its total production is estimated at 525,000 units. During 1995 the machine was operated 6,000 hours and produced 55,000 units. During 1996 the machine was operated 5,500 hours and produced 48,000 units.

Instructions
Compute depreciation expense on the machine for the year ending December 31, 1995, and the year ending December 31, 1996, using the following methods: (1) straight-line; (2) units-of-output; (3) working hours; (4) sum-of-the-years'-digits; and (5) declining balance (twice the straight-line rate).

 P11-3 (Depreciation—SL, DDB, SYD, Act., and MACRS) On January 1, 1993, Vanessa Williams Company, a small machine-tool manufacturer, acquired for $980,000 a piece of new industrial equipment. The new equipment had a useful life of 5 years and the salvage value was estimated to be $80,000. Williams estimates that the new equipment can produce 12,000 machine tools in its first year. It estimates that production will decline by 1,000 units per year over the remaining useful life of the equipment.

The following depreciation methods may be used: (1) straight-line; (2) double-declining balance; (3) sum-of-the-years'-digits; and (4) units-of-output. For tax purposes, the class life is 7 years. Use the MACRS tables for computing depreciation.

Instructions
(a) Which depreciation method would maximize net income for financial statement reporting for the 3-year period ending December 31, 1995? Prepare a schedule showing the amount of accumulated depreciation at December 31, 1995, under the method selected. Ignore present value, income tax, and deferred income tax considerations.
(b) Which depreciation method (MACRS or optional straight-line) would minimize net income for income tax reporting for the 3-year period ending December 31, 1995? Determine the amount of accumulated depreciation at December 31, 1995. Ignore present value considerations.

(AICPA adapted)

P11-4 (Depreciation—Partial Periods, Machinery) Red Hot Tool Company records depreciation annually at the end of the year. Its policy is to take a full year's depreciation on all assets used throughout the year and depreciation for one-half a year on all machines acquired or disposed of during the year. The depreciation rate for the machinery is 10% applied on a straight-line basis, with no estimated scrap value.

The balance of the Machinery account at the beginning of 1996 was $162,300; the Accumulated Depreciation on Machinery account had a balance of $72,900. The following transactions affecting the machinery accounts took place during the year.

Jan. 15 Machine No. 38, which cost $9,600 when acquired June 3, 1989, was retired and sold as scrap metal for $600.

Feb. 27 Machine No. 81 was purchased. The fair market value of this machine was $12,500. It replaces Machines No. 12 and No. 27, which were traded in on the new machine. Machine No. 12 was acquired Feb. 4, 1984, at a cost of $5,500 and is still carried in the accounts although fully depreciated and not in use; Machine No. 27 was acquired June 11, 1989, at a cost of $8,200. In addition to these two used machines, $9,000 was paid in cash. (Assume exchange of similar assets.)

Apr. 7 Machine No. 54 was equipped with electric control equipment at a cost of $840. This machine, originally equipped with simple hand controls, was purchased Dec. 11, 1992, for $1,800. The new electric controls can be attached to any one of several machines in the shop.

12 Machine No. 24 was repaired at a cost of $750 after a fire caused by a short circuit in the wiring burned out the motor and damaged certain essential parts.

July 22 Machines No. 25, 26, and 41 are sold for $2,700 cash. The purchase dates and cost of these machines are:

No. 25	$4,000	May 8, 1988
No. 26	3,200	May 8, 1988
No. 41	2,800	June 1, 1990

Nov. 17 Rearrangement and reinstallation of several machines to facilitate material handling and to speed up production are completed at a cost of $12,400.

Instructions
(a) Record each transaction in general journal entry form.
(b) Compute and record depreciation for the year. No machines now included in the balance of the account were acquired before Jan. 1, 1987.

P11-5 (Depreciation—SYD, Act., SL, and DDB) The following data relate to the Plant Asset account of Magdalena Aguilar, Inc. at December 31, 1995:

Plant Asset

	A	B	C	D
Original cost	$35,000	$51,000	$80,000	$75,000
Year purchased	1990	1991	1992	1994
Useful life	10 years	15,000 hours	15 years	10 years
Salvage value	$ 3,100	$ 3,000	$ 5,000	$ 5,000
Depreciation method	Sum-of-the-years'-digits	Activity	Straight-line	Double-declining balance
Accum. Depr. through 1995[a]	$23,200	$35,200	$15,000	$15,000

[a]In the year an asset is purchased, Aguilar, Inc. does not record any depreciation expense on the asset. In the year an asset is retired or traded in, Aguilar, Inc. takes a full year's depreciation on the asset.

The following transactions occurred during 1996:

(a) On May 5, Asset A was sold for $12,000 cash. The company's bookkeeper recorded this retirement in the following manner in the cash receipts journal:

Cash	12,000	
Asset A		12,000

(b) On December 31, it was determined that Asset B had been used 2,000 hours during 1996.

(c) On December 31, before computing depreciation expense on Asset C, the management of Aguilar, Inc. decided the useful life remaining from 1/1/96 was 10 years.

(d) On December 31, it was discovered that a plant asset purchased in 1995 had been expensed completely in that year. This asset cost $21,000 and has a useful life of 10 years and no salvage value. Management has decided to use the double-declining balance method for this asset, which can be referred to as "Asset E."

Instructions

Prepare the necessary correcting entries for the year 1996. Record the appropriate depreciation expense on the above-mentioned assets.

P11-6 (Depreciation and Error Analysis) A depreciation schedule for semitrucks of LaShon Baily Manufacturing Company was requested by your auditor soon after December 31, 1996, showing the additions, retirements, depreciation, and other data affecting the income of the company in the four-year period 1993 to 1996, inclusive. The following data were ascertained:

Balance of Semitrucks account, Jan. 1, 1993:	
Truck No. 1 purchased Jan. 1, 1990, cost	$18,000
Truck No. 2 purchased July 1, 1990, cost	22,000
Truck No. 3 purchased Jan. 1, 1992, cost	30,000
Truck No. 4 purchased July 1, 1992, cost	24,000
Balance, Jan. 1, 1993	$94,000

The Semitrucks-Accumulated Depreciation account previously adjusted to January 1, 1993, and duly entered in the ledger, had a balance on that date of $30,200 (depreciation on the four trucks from the respective dates of purchase, based on a 5-year life, no salvage value). No charges had been made against the account before January 1, 1993.

Transactions between January 1, 1993, and December 31, 1996, and their record in the ledger were as follows:

July 1, 1993 Truck No. 3 was traded for a larger one (No. 5), the agreed purchase price of which was $32,000. Baily Mfg. Co. paid the automobile dealer $13,000 cash on the transaction. The entry was a debit to Semitrucks and a credit to Cash, $13,000.

Jan. 1, 1994 Truck No. 1 was sold for $3,500 cash; entry debited Cash and credited Semitrucks, $3,500.

July 1, 1995 A new truck (No. 6) was acquired for $23,000 cash and was charged at that amount to the Semitrucks account. (Assume truck No. 2 was not retired.)

July 1, 1995 Truck No. 4 was damaged in a wreck to such an extent that it was sold as junk for $700 cash. Baily Mfg. Co. received $2,500 from the insurance company. The entry made by the bookkeeper was a debit to Cash, $3,200, and credits to Miscellaneous Income, $700, and Semitrucks, $2,500.

Entries for depreciation had been made at the close of each year as follows: 1993, $20,320; 1994, $21,220; 1995, $23,270; 1996, $25,320.

Instructions

(a) For each of the 4 years compute separately the increase or decrease in net income arising from the company's errors in determining or entering depreciation or in recording transactions affecting trucks, ignoring income tax considerations.

(b) Prepare one compound journal entry as of December 31, 1996, for adjustment of the Semitrucks account to reflect the correct balances as revealed by your schedule, assuming that the books have not been closed for 1996.

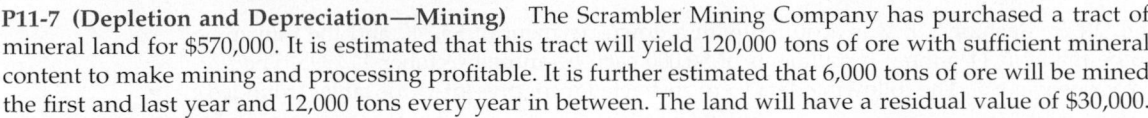

P11-7 (Depletion and Depreciation—Mining) The Scrambler Mining Company has purchased a tract of mineral land for $570,000. It is estimated that this tract will yield 120,000 tons of ore with sufficient mineral content to make mining and processing profitable. It is further estimated that 6,000 tons of ore will be mined the first and last year and 12,000 tons every year in between. The land will have a residual value of $30,000.

The company builds necessary structures and sheds on the site at a cost of $36,000. It is estimated that these structures can serve 15 years but, because they must be dismantled if they are to be moved, they have no scrap value. The company does not intend to use the buildings elsewhere. Mining machinery installed at the mine was purchased second-hand at a cost of $48,000. This machinery cost the former owner $100,000 and was 50% depreciated when purchased. The Scrambler Mining Company estimates that about half of this machinery will still be useful when the present mineral resources have been exhausted but that dismantling and removal costs will just about offset its value at that time. The company does not intend to use the machinery elsewhere. The remaining machinery will last until about one-half the present estimated mineral ore has been removed and will then be worthless. Cost is to be allocated equally between these two classes of machinery.

Instructions

(a) As chief accountant for the company, you are to prepare a schedule showing estimated depletion and depreciation costs for each year of the expected life of the mine.

(b) Also compute the depreciation and depletion for the first year assuming actual production of 7,000 tons. Nothing occurred during the year to cause the company engineers to change their estimates of either the mineral resources or the life of the structures and equipment.

P11-8 (Depletion, Timber, and Extraordinary Loss) Splinter Logging and Lumber Company owns 3,000 acres of timberland on the north side of Mount St. Helens, which was purchased in 1968 at a cost of $500 per acre. In 1980, Splinter began selectively logging this timber tract. In May of 1980, Mount St. Helens erupted, burying the timberland of Splinter under a foot of ash. All of the timber on the Splinter tract was downed. In addition, the logging roads, built at a cost of $150,000, were destroyed, as well as the logging equipment, with a net book value of $300,000.

At the time of the eruption, Splinter had logged 20% of the estimated 500,000 board feet of timber. Prior to the eruption, Splinter estimated the land to have a value of $200 per acre after the timber was harvested. Splinter includes the logging roads in the depletion base.

Splinter estimates it will take 3 years to salvage the downed timber at a cost of $700,000. The timber can be sold for pulp wood at an estimated price of $3 per board foot. The value of the land is unknown, but must be considered nominal due to future uncertainties.

Instructions

(a) Determine the depletion cost per board foot for the timber harvested prior to the eruption of Mount St. Helens.

(b) Prepare the journal entry to record the depletion prior to the eruption.

(c) If this tract represents approximately half of the timber holdings of Splinter, determine the amount of the estimated loss and show how the losses of roads, machinery, and timber and the salvage of the timber should be reported in the financial statements of Splinter for the year ended December 31, 1980.

P11-9 (Comprehensive Depreciation Computations) Dorothea Dix Corporation, a manufacturer of steel products, began operations on October 1, 1994. The accounting department of Dix has started the fixed-asset and depreciation schedule presented below. You have been asked to assist in completing this schedule. In addition to ascertaining that the data already on the schedule are correct, you have obtained the following information from the company's records and personnel:

1. Depreciation is computed from the first of the month of acquisition to the first of the month of disposition.

2. Land A and Building A were acquired from a predecessor corporation. Dix paid $800,000 for the land and building together. At the time of acquisition, the land had an appraised value of $90,000, and the building had an appraised value of $810,000.

3. Land B was acquired on October 2, 1994, in exchange for 2,500 newly issued shares of Dix's common stock. At the date of acquisition, the stock had a par value of $5 per share and a fair value of $30 per share. During October 1994, Dix paid $13,000 to demolish an existing building on this land so it could construct a new building.

4. Construction of Building B on the newly acquired land began on October 1, 1995. By September 30, 1996, Dix had paid $320,000 of the estimated total construction costs of $450,000. It is estimated that the building will be completed and occupied by July, 1997.

5. Certain equipment was donated to the corporation by a local university. An independent appraisal of the equipment when donated placed the fair market value at $40,000 and the salvage value at $3,000.

6. Machinery A's total cost of $164,900 includes installation expense of $600 and normal repairs and maintenance of $14,900. Salvage value is estimated at $6,000. Machinery A was sold on February 1, 1996.

7. On October 1, 1995, Machinery B was acquired with a down payment of $5,740 and the remaining payments to be made in 11 annual installments of $6,000 each beginning October 1, 1995. The prevailing interest rate was 8%. The following data were abstracted from present-value tables (rounded):

Present value of $1.00 at 8%		Present value of an ordinary annuity of $1.00 at 8%	
10 years	.463	10 years	6.710
11 years	.429	11 years	7.139
15 years	.315	15 years	8.559

Dorothea Dix Corporation
FIXED ASSET AND DEPRECIATION SCHEDULE
For Fiscal Years Ended September 30, 1995, and September 30, 1996

Assets	Acquisition Date	Cost	Salvage	Depreciation Method	Estimated Life in Years	Depreciation Expense Year Ended September 30 1995	1996
Land A	October 1, 1994	$ (1)	N/A	N/A	N/A	N/A	N/A
Building A	October 1, 1994	(2)	$40,000	Straight-Line	(3)	$17,000	(4)
Land B	October 2, 1994	(5)	N/A	N/A	N/A	N/A	N/A
Building B	Under Construction	320,000 to date	—	Straight-Line 150%	30	—	(6)
Donated Equipment	October 2, 1994	(7)	3,000	Declining Balance	10	(8)	(9)
Machinery A	October 2, 1994	(10)	6,000	Sum-of-the-Years'-Digits	8	(11)	(12)
Machinery B	October 1, 1995	(13)	—	Straight-Line	20	—	(14)

N/A—Not applicable

Instructions

For each numbered item on the foregoing schedule, supply the correct amount. Round each answer to the nearest dollar.

(AICPA adapted)

P11-10 (Comprehensive Depreciation and Error Analysis) You are engaged in the examination of the financial statements of the Jose Amaro Corporation for the year ended December 31, 1996. The schedules below for the property, plant, and equipment, and related accumulated depreciation accounts have been prepared by the client. You have checked the opening balances to your prior year's audit workpapers.

Your examination reveals the following information:

1. All plant and equipment is depreciated on the straight-line basis (no salvage value taken into consideration) using the following estimated lives: buildings, 25 years; all other items, 10 years. The company's policy is to take one-half year's depreciation on all asset acquisitions and disposals during the year.

2. On April 1, the company entered into a 10-year lease contract for a die-casting machine with annual rentals of $8,000 payable in advance every April 1. The lease can be canceled by either party (60 days written notice is required) and there is no option to renew the lease or buy the equipment at the end of the lease. The estimated useful life of the machine is 10 years with no salvage value. The company recorded the die-casting machine in the Machinery and Equipment account at $55,962, the present discounted value at the date of the lease, and $2,798, applicable to the machine, has been included in depreciation expense for the year. (Hint: Leases with these conditions should not be capitalized nor should a liability be recognized.)

3. The company completed the construction of a wing on the plant building on June 30. The useful life of the building was not extended by this addition. The lowest construction bid received was $51,000,

the amount recorded in the Buildings account. Corporation personnel were used to construct the addition at a cost of $48,000 (materials, $24,000; labor, $15,000; and overhead, $9,000).

4. On August 18, $15,000 was paid for paving and fencing a portion of land owned by the company and used as a parking lot for employees. The expenditure was charged to the Land account.

5. The amount shown in the machinery and equipment asset retirement column represents cash received on September 5 upon disposal of a machine purchased in July, 1992, for $60,000. The bookkeeper recorded depreciation expense of $4,500 on this machine in 1996.

6. Carson City donated land and building appraised at $20,000 and $69,000, respectively, to Amaro Corporation for a plant. On September 1, the company began operating the plant. Because no costs were involved, the bookkeeper made no entry to record the transaction.

Jose Amaro Corp.
ANALYSIS OF PROPERTY, PLANT AND EQUIPMENT, AND RELATED ACCUMULATED DEPRECIATION ACCOUNTS
Year Ended December 31, 1996

Assets

Description	Final 12/31/95	Additions	Retirements	Per Books 12/31/96
Land	$ 70,000	$ 15,000		$ 85,000
Buildings	160,000	51,000		211,000
Machinery and equipment	390,000	55,962	$30,000	415,962
	$620,000	$121,962	$30,000	$711,962

Accumulated Depreciation

Description	Final 12/31/95	Additions[a]	Retirements	Per Books 12/31/96
Buildings	$ 80,000	$ 7,420		$ 87,420
Machinery and equipment	156,000	40,298		196,298
	$236,000	$ 47,718		$283,718

[a]Depreciation expense for the year.

Instructions
Prepare the formal journal entries that you would suggest at December 31, 1996, to adjust the accounts for the transactions noted above. Disregard income tax implications. The books have not been closed. Computations should be rounded off to the nearest dollar.

(AICPA adapted)

P11-11 (Depreciation for Partial Periods—SL, Act., SYD, and DDB) On January 1, 1993, a machine was purchased for $75,000. The machine has an estimated salvage value of $5,000 and an estimated useful life of 5 years. The machine can operate for 100,000 hours before it needs to be replaced. The company closed its books on December 31 and operates the machine as follows: 1993, 20,000 hrs; 1994, 25,000 hrs; 1995, 15,000 hrs; 1996, 30,000 hrs; 1997, 10,000 hrs.

Instructions
(a) Compute the annual depreciation charges over the machine's life assuming a December 31 year-end for each of the following depreciation methods:
  1. Straight-line method.
  2. Activity method.
  3. Sum-of-the-years'-digits method.
  4. Double-declining balance method.
(b) Assume a fiscal year-end of September 30. Compute the annual depreciation charges over the asset's life applying
  1. Straight-line method.
  2. Sum-of-the-years'-digits method.
  3. Double-declining balance method.

CASES

C11-1 (Depreciation Basic Concepts) Blue Velvet Manufacturing Company was organized January 1, 1996. During 1996, it has used in its reports to management the straight-line method of depreciating its plant assets.

On November 8 you are having a conference with Velvet's officers to discuss the depreciation method to be used for income tax and stockholder reporting. Bobby Vinton, president of Velvet, has suggested the use of a new method, which he feels is more suitable than the straight-line method for the needs of the company during the period of rapid expansion of production and capacity that he foresees. Following is an example in which the proposed method is applied to a fixed asset with an original cost of $248,000, an estimated useful life of 5 years, and a scrap value of approximately $8,000.

Year	Years of Life Used	Fraction Rate	Depreciation Expense	Accumulated Depreciation at End of Year	Book Value at End of Year
1	1	1/15	$16,000	$ 16,000	$232,000
2	2	2/15	32,000	48,000	200,000
3	3	3/15	48,000	96,000	152,000
4	4	4/15	64,000	160,000	88,000
5	5	5/15	80,000	240,000	8,000

The president favors the new method because he has heard that

1. It will increase the funds recovered during the years near the end of the assets' useful lives when maintenance and replacement disbursements are high.
2. It will result in increased writeoffs in later years and thereby will reduce taxes.

Instructions
(a) What is the purpose of accounting for depreciation?
(b) Is the president's proposal within the scope of generally accepted accounting principles? In making your decision discuss the circumstances, if any, under which use of the method would be reasonable and those, if any, under which it would not be reasonable.
(c) The president wants your advice.
   1. Do depreciation charges recover or create funds? Explain.
   2. Assume that the Internal Revenue Service accepts the proposed depreciation method in this case. If the proposed method were used for stockholder and tax reporting purposes, how would it affect the availability of funds generated by operations?

C11-2 (Unit, Group, and Composite Depreciation) The certified public accountant is frequently called upon by management for advice regarding methods of computing depreciation. Of comparable importance, although it arises less frequently, is the question of whether the depreciation method should be based on consideration of the assets as units, as a group, or as having a composite life.

Instructions
(a) Briefly describe the depreciation methods based on treating assets as (1) units and (2) a group or as having a composite life.
(b) Present the arguments for and against the use of each of the two methods.
(c) Describe how retirements are recorded under each of the two methods.

(AICPA adapted)

C11-3 (Depreciation—Strike, Units-of-Production, Obsolescence) Presented below are three different and unrelated situations involving depreciation accounting. Answer the question(s) at the end of each case situation.

Situation I
Recently, Jonny Mathis Company experienced a strike that affected a number of its operating plants. The controller of this company indicated that it was not appropriate to report depreciation expense during this period because the equipment did not depreciate and an improper matching of costs and revenues would result. She based her position on the following points:

1. It is inappropriate to charge the period with costs for which there are no related revenues arising from production.
2. The basic factor of depreciation in this instance is wear and tear, and because equipment was idle, no wear and tear occurred.

Instructions
Comment on the appropriateness of the controller's comments.

Situation II
Paul Anka Company manufactures electrical appliances, most of which are used in homes. Company engineers have designed a new type of blender which, through the use of a few attachments, will perform more functions than any blender currently on the market. Demand for the new blender can be projected with reasonable probability. In order to make the blenders, Anka needs a specialized machine that is not available from outside sources. It has been decided to make such a machine in Anka's own plant.

Instructions

(a) Discuss the effect of projected demand in units for the new blenders (which may be steady, decreasing, or increasing) on the determination of a depreciation method for the machine.

(b) What other matters should be considered in determining the depreciation method? Ignore income tax considerations.

Situation III

Conway Twitty Paper Company operates a 300-ton-per-day kraft pulp mill and four sawmills in Wisconsin. The company is in the process of expanding its pulp mill facilities to a capacity of 1,000 tons per day and plans to replace three of its older, less efficient sawmills with an expanded facility. One of the mills to be replaced did not operate for most of 1995 (current year), and there are no plans to reopen it before the new sawmill facility becomes operational.

In reviewing the depreciation rates and in discussing the residual values of the sawmills that were to be replaced, it was noted that if present depreciation rates were not adjusted, substantial amounts of plant costs on these three mills would not be depreciated by the time the new mill came on stream.

Instructions

What is the proper accounting for the four sawmills at the end of 1995?

▶ FINANCIAL REPORTING PROBLEM

Refer to the financial statements and other documents of Georgia-Pacific Corporation presented in Appendix 5-A and answer the following questions.

1. What method or methods does Georgia-Pacific use to depreciate its property, plant, and equipment? How does Georgia-Pacific report the disposition of assets in its financial statements?

2. What is Georgia-Pacific's policy relative to the replacement of property, plant, and equipment?

3. Explain the reason why Georgia-Pacific changed its estimates on the useful life of certain assets in 1993.

4. What is the amount of avoidable interest reported by Georgia-Pacific for the year 1993? What is the amount of actual interest incurred by Georgia-Pacific in 1993? What is the amount of interest capitalized by Georgia-Pacific in 1993?

5. What basis does Georgia-Pacific use to record the depletion of its approximately 6 million acres of timber?

6. What was Georgia-Pacific's major asset divestiture during 1993?

▶ WRITING ASSIGNMENT

As a cost accountant for Mont Delli Cannery, you have been approached by Chris Laskewicz, canning room supervisor, about the 1994 costs charged to his department. In particular, he is concerned about the line item "depreciation." Laskewicz is very proud of the excellent condition of his canning room equipment. He has always been vigilant about keeping all equipment serviced and well oiled. He is sure that the huge charge to depreciation is a mistake: it does not at all reflect the cost of minimal wear and tear that the machines have experienced over the last year. He believes that the charge should be considerably lower.

The machines being depreciated are six automatic canning machines. All were put into use on January 1, 1994. Each cost $469,000, having a salvage value of $40,000 and a useful life of 12 years. Mont Delli depreciates this and similar assets using double-declining balance. Laskewicz has also pointed out that if you used straight-line depreciation the charge to his department would not be so great.

Instructions

Write a memo to Chris Laskewicz to clear up his misunderstanding of the term "depreciation." Also, calculate year 1 depreciation on all machines using both methods. Explain the theoretical justification for double-declining balance and why, in the long run, the aggregate charge to depreciation will be the same under both methods.

▶ GROUP ASSIGNMENT

(Comprehensive Asset and Interest Capitalization with Depreciation Computations) Cominsky Sporting Goods Inc. has been experiencing growth in the demand for its products over the last several years. The last two Olympic Games greatly increased the popularity of basketball around the world. As a result, a European sports retailing consortium entered into an agreement with Cominsky's Roundball Division to purchase basketballs and other accessories on an increasing basis over the next 5 years.

To be able to meet the quantity commitments of this agreement, Cominksy had to obtain additional manufacturing capacity. A real estate firm located an available factory in close proximity to Cominsky's Roundball manufacturing facility, and Cominsky agreed to purchase the factory and used machinery from Jabbar Athletic Equipment Company on October 1, 1994. Renovations were necessary to convert the factory for Cominsky's manufacturing use.

The terms of the agreement required Cominsky to pay Jabbar $50,000 when renovations started on January 1, 1995, with the balance to be paid as renovations were completed. The overall purchase price for the factory and machinery was $400,000. The building renovations were contracted to Patrick Ewing Construction at $100,000. The payments made, as renovations progressed during 1995, are shown below. The factory was placed in service on January 1, 1996.

	1/1	4/1	10/1	12/31
Jabbar	$50,000	$100,000	$100,000	$150,000
Ewing		30,000	30,000	40,000

On January 1, 1995, Cominsky secured a $500,000 line-of-credit with a 12% interest rate to finance the purchase cost of the factory and machinery, and the renovation costs. Cominsky drew down on the line-of-credit to meet the payment schedule shown above; this was Cominsky's only outstanding loan during 1995.

Charles Barkley, Cominsky's controller, will capitalize the maximum allowable interest costs for this project. Cominsky's policy regarding purchases of this nature is to use the appraisal value of the land for book purposes and prorate the balance of the purchase price over the remaining items. The building had originally cost Jabbar $300,000 and had a net book value of $50,000, while the machinery originally cost $125,000 and had a net book value of $40,000 on the date of sale. The land was recorded on Jabbar's books at $40,000. An appraisal, conducted by independent appraisers at the time of acquisition, valued the land at $280,000, the building at $105,000, and the machinery at $45,000.

Lew Aleindor, chief engineer, estimated that the renovated plant would be used for 15 years, with an estimated salvage value of $30,000. Aleindor estimated that the productive machinery would have a remaining useful life of five years and a salvage value of $3,000. Cominsky depreciation policy specifies the 200% declining-balance method for machinery and the 150% declining-balance method for the plant. One-half year's depreciation is taken in the year the plant is placed in service and one-half is allowed when the property is disposed of or retired. Cominsky uses a 360-day year for calculating interest costs.

Instructions
Your instructor will assign one member of the group to serve as a recorder and one member to serve as spokesperson. As a group, provide the information for the recorder to prepare responses to following three requirements. Upon completion of each requirement and before moving on to the next part, the spokesperson will report the group findings to the class.
- **(a)** Determine the amounts to be recorded on the books of Cominsky Sporting Goods Inc. as of December 31, 1995, for each of the following properties acquired from Jabbar Athletic Equipment Company.
  1. Land. **2.** Building. **3.** Machinery.
- **(b)** Calculate Cominsky Sporting Goods Inc.'s 1996 depreciation expense, for book purposes, for each of the properties acquired from Jabbar Athletic Equipment Company.
- **(c)** Discuss the arguments for and against the capitalization of interest costs.

(CMA adapted)

▶ ETHICS CASE

(Ethical Issue: Depreciation—Change in Estimate) Sunshine Manufacturing Company faces a decline in sales of their principal product, an automatic sprinkler system for high-rise buildings. The financial vice-president, Jeanie Moyer, suggests lengthening asset lives to reduce depreciation expense. Machinery purchased for $905,000 in January 1993 was originally estimated to have a life of 9 years with a salvage value of $50,000 at the end of the period. Depreciation has been recorded for 3 years on this basis. Moyer wants to change the estimated life of the machinery to 12 years (assume straight-line depreciation). The controller, Mike Locke, disagrees with Moyer and says it would be unethical to increase net income in this manner.

Instructions
- **(a)** Is the change in asset lives unethical, or simply a good business practice by a far-sighted vice-president?
- **(b)** Assume that the change in asset lives is made according to Moyer's suggestion. Prepare the entry to record depreciation for 1996, assuming no change in salvage value.

CHAPTER 12

INTANGIBLE ASSETS

LEARNING OBJECTIVES

After studying this chapter, you should be able to:

1. Describe the characteristics of intangible assets.

2. Explain the procedure for valuing and amortizing intangible assets.

3. Identify the types of specifically identifiable intangible assets.

4. Explain the conceptual issues related to goodwill.

5. Describe the accounting procedures for recording goodwill.

6. Identify the conceptual issues related to research and development costs.

7. Describe the accounting procedures for research and development costs.

*I*ntangible assets are generally characterized by a lack of physical existence and a high degree of uncertainty concerning future benefits. These criteria are not so clear-cut as they may seem. The following discussion by a well-noted accountant typifies some of the major problems encountered in attempting to define intangibles.

Q. I infer, Mr. May, from your experience . . . that you know what in ordinary speech the word tangible means, don't you?

A. Yes.

Q. Well, what do you understand it to mean in ordinary speech?

A. Something that can be touched, I imagine.

Q. Like merchandise?

A. Yes.

Q. You can touch merchandise or horses?

A. Yes.

Q. Can you touch an account receivable?

A. You can touch the debtor.

Q. Is that the basis on which you include the debtor's debt as tangible?

A. It had not occurred to me before, but possibly it is.[1]

---

[1]From testimony given to referee, *In the Matter of the Estate of E. P. Hatch Deceased (1912).* Reprinted in Bishop Carleton Hunt, ed., *Twenty-five Years of Accounting Responsibility, 1911–1936* (New York: Price Waterhouse and Company, 1936), I, p. 246. Selected essays and discussions of George O. May.

OBJECTIVE 1

*Describe the
characteristics of
intangible assets.*

This discussion indicates that the **lack of physical existence** is not by itself a satisfactory criterion for distinguishing a tangible from an intangible asset. Such assets as bank deposits, accounts receivable, and long-term investments lack physical substance, yet accountants classify them as tangible assets.

Some accountants believe that an intangible asset's major characteristic is the **high degree of uncertainty concerning the future benefits** that are to be received from its employment. For example, many intangibles (1) have value only to a given enterprise, (2) have indeterminate lives, and (3) are subject to large fluctuations in value because their benefits are based on a competitive advantage. The determination and timing of future benefits are extremely difficult and pose serious valuation problems. True, some tangible assets possess similar characteristics but they are not so pronounced.

Other accountants, finding the problem of defining intangibles insurmountable, prefer simply to present them in financial statements on the basis of tradition. The more common types of intangibles are patents, copyrights, franchises, goodwill, organization costs, and trademarks or trade names. Intangibles may be further subdivided on the basis of the following characteristics.

1. **Identifiability.** Separately identifiable or lacking specific identification.
2. **Manner of Acquisition.** Acquired singly, in groups, or in business combinations, or developed internally.
3. **Expected Period of Benefit.** Limited by law or contract, related to human or economic factors, or indefinite or indeterminate duration.
4. **Separability from an Entire Enterprise.** Rights transferable without title, salable, or inseparable from the enterprise or a substantial part of it.[2]

These subdivisions provide insight into how the reporting requirements for intangibles have developed.

▶ VALUATION OF PURCHASED INTANGIBLES

OBJECTIVE 2

*Explain the procedure for
valuing and amortizing
intangible assets.*

**UNDERLYING
CONCEPT**

*The basic attributes of
intangibles, their uncertainty
as to future benefits, and
their uniqueness, have
discouraged valuation in
excess of cost.*

Intangibles, like tangible assets, are **recorded at cost.** Cost includes all costs of acquisition and expenditures necessary to make the intangible asset ready for its intended use—for example, purchase price, legal fees and other incidental expenses.

If intangibles are acquired for stock or in exchange for other assets, **the cost of the intangible is the fair market value of the consideration given or the fair market value of the intangible received, whichever is more clearly evident.** When several intangibles, or a combination of intangibles and tangibles, are bought in a "basket purchase," the cost should be allocated on the basis of fair market values or on the basis of relative sales values. Essentially the accounting treatment for intangibles closely parallels that followed for tangible assets. The profession has resisted employment of some other basis of valuation, such as current replacement costs or appraisal value for intangible assets.[3]

▶ AMORTIZATION OF INTANGIBLE ASSETS

As we learned in Chapter 11, the expiration of intangible assets is called **amortization.** Intangible assets should be amortized by systematic charges to expense over their useful lives. *APB Opinion No. 17* lists the factors that might be considered in determining useful life:

---

[2]"Intangible Assets," *Opinions of the Accounting Principles Board No. 17* (New York: AICPA, 1970), par. 10.

[3]For example, Sprouse and Moonitz in *AICPA Accounting Research Study No. 3*, "A Tentative Set of Broad Accounting Principles for a Business Enterprise," advocate abandonment of historical cost in favor of replacement cost for most asset items, but suggest that intangibles should normally be carried at acquisition cost less amortization because valuation problems are so difficult.

1. Legal, regulatory, or contractual provisions.
2. Provisions for renewal or extension.
3. Effects of obsolescence, demand, competition, and other economic factors.
4. A useful life may parallel the service life expectancies of individuals or groups of employees.
5. Expected actions of competitors and others may restrict competitive advantages.
6. An apparently unlimited useful life may in fact be indefinite and benefits cannot be reasonably projected.
7. An intangible asset may be a composite of many individual factors with varying effective lives.[4]

One problem relating to the amortization of intangibles is that some intangibles have indeterminable useful lives. In this case, **intangible assets must be amortized over a period not exceeding 40 years.**[5] The 40-year requirement is based on the premise that only a few, if any, intangibles last forever. Sometimes, because useful life is difficult to determine, a 40-year period is employed because it is practical, although admittedly arbitrary. Another reason for this 40-year limitation is simply that it ensures that companies eventually write off their intangibles. Prior to the 40-year rule, there was evidence that some companies retained their intangibles (notably goodwill) indefinitely on their balance sheet for only one reason—to avoid the charge to expense that occurs when goodwill is written off.

Intangible assets acquired from other enterprises (notably goodwill) should not be written off at acquisition. Some accountants contend that certain intangibles should not be carried as assets on the balance sheet under any circumstances but should be written off directly to retained earnings or additional paid-in capital. However, the immediate writeoff to retained earnings and additional paid-in capital is not acceptable because this approach denies the existence of an asset that has just been purchased.

Intangible assets are generally amortized on a straight-line basis (tax practice requires a straight-line approach), although there is no reason why another systematic approach might not be employed if the firm demonstrates that another method is more appropriate. In any case the method and period of amortization should be disclosed.

When intangible assets are amortized, the charges should be shown as expenses, and the credits should be made either to the appropriate asset accounts or to separate accumulated amortization accounts.

INTERNATIONAL INSIGHT

Although in many nations it is standard practice to capitalize and amortize goodwill, practice varies widely. In a few countries goodwill is capitalized but not amortized, thus remaining as a permanent asset. In other nations goodwill is written off immediately.

► SPECIFICALLY IDENTIFIABLE INTANGIBLE ASSETS

Originally, the accounting profession recognized two types of classification for intangibles: (a) intangibles that had a limited life and (b) intangibles that had an unlimited life. This classification framework was subsequently changed to intangibles that are specifically identifiable, as contrasted to "goodwill type" intangible assets (unidentifiable values). **Specifically identifiable** means that costs associated with obtaining a given intangible asset can be identified as a part of the cost of that intangible asset. In contrast, a **goodwill type** intangible may create some right or privilege, but it is not specifically identifiable and it has an indeterminable life. The accounting treatments accorded these two types of intangibles are shown in Illustration 12-1.

OBJECTIVE 3

Identify the types of specifically identifiable intangible assets.

Type of Intangible	Manner Acquired	
	Purchased	Generated Internally
Specifically Identifiable Intangibles	Capitalize	Expense, except certain costs
Goodwill Type Intangibles	Capitalize	Expense

ILLUSTRATION 12-1 Accounting for the Costs of Intangibles

The accounting for intangibles is discussed on the following pages.

[4]*APB Opinion No. 17, op. cit.,* par. 27.

[5]Ibid., par. 10.

PATENTS

Patents are granted by the U.S. Patent Office. The two principal kinds of patents are **product patents,** which cover actual physical products, and **process patents,** which govern the process by which products are made. A **patent** gives the holder exclusive right to use, manufacture, and sell a product or process **for a period of 17 years** without interference or infringement by others. With this exclusive right, fortunes can be made. For example: companies such as Merck, Polaroid, and Xerox were founded on patents.[6] If a patent is purchased from an inventor (or other owner), the purchase price represents its cost. Other costs incurred in connection with securing a patent, as well as attorneys' fees and other unrecovered costs of a successful legal suit to protect the patent, can be capitalized as part of the patent cost. Research and development costs related to the **development** of the product, process, or idea that is subsequently patented **must be expensed as incurred,** however. See pages 586–589 for a more complete presentation of accounting for research and development costs.

The cost of a patent should be amortized over its legal life or its useful life (the period benefits are received), whichever is shorter. If a patent is owned from the date it is granted, and it is expected to be useful during its entire legal life, it should be amortized over 17 years. If it appears that the patent will be useful for a shorter period of time, say, for 5 years, its cost should be amortized to expense over 5 years. Changing demand, new inventions superseding old ones, inadequacy, and other factors often limit the useful life of a patent to less than the legal life. For example, the useful life of patents in the pharmaceutical and drug industry is frequently less than the legal life because of the testing and approval period that follows their issuance. A typical drug patent has 5 to 11 years knocked off its 17-year legal life because 1 to 4 years must be spent on tests on animals, 4 to 6 years on human tests, and 2 to 3 years for the Food and Drug Administration to review the tests—all after the patent is issued but before the product goes on a pharmacist's shelves.

From bioengineering to software design, battles over patents are heating up as global competition intensifies. Consider *Hughes Tool* vs. *Smith International* with a judgment of $205 million against Smith which caused it to declare bankruptcy, or *Lemelson* vs. *Mattel, Inc.,* in which Lemelson was awarded $71 million because Mattel infringed on his flexible track invention in marketing Hot Wheels miniature cars; or *Polaroid* vs. *Kodak* with Kodak permanently withdrawing from the U.S. instant photography market and paying damages of $900 million.[7] Texas Instruments has 35 patent lawyers on its payroll, which is only one of the costs it incurs to obtain and defend its many patents. **Legal fees and other costs incurred in successfully defending a patent suit are debited to Patents,** an asset account, because such a suit establishes the legal rights of the holder of the patent. Such costs should be amortized along with acquisition cost over the remaining useful life of the patent.

Amortization of patents may be computed on a time basis or on a basis of units produced and may be credited directly to the Patents account. It is acceptable also, although less common, to credit an Accumulated Patent Amortization account. To illustrate, assume that Harcott Co. incurs $170,000 in legal costs on January 1, 1994, to successfully defend a patent. The patent has a useful life of 17 years, and is amortized

---

[6]Consider the opposite result: Sir Alexander Fleming, who discovered penicillin, decided not to use a patent to protect his discovery. He hoped that companies would produce it more quickly to help save sufferers. Companies, however, refused to develop it because they did not have the patent shield and, therefore, were afraid to make the investment.

[7]In a 1988 suit, Apple Computer sued Hewlett-Packard and Microsoft, the major supplier of software for IBM desktop computers, charging that they copied the "look and feel" of the Macintosh's distinctive user-friendly programming. Determining exactly what the "look and feel" of a piece of software amounts to is a tricky legal question, but suing over patent and copyright infringement has become increasingly successful and necessary. See "New Profits from Patents," *Fortune,* April 25, 1988; "Loophole Closing Time," *Forbes,* May 4, 1987; and "The Surprising New Power of Patents," *Fortune,* June 23, 1986.

on a straight-line basis. The entries to record the legal fees and the amortization at the end of each year are as follows:

January 1, 1994

Patents	170,000	
Cash		170,000
(To record legal fees related to patent)		

December 31, 1994

Patent Amortization Expense	10,000	
Patents (or Accumulated Patent Amortization)		10,000
(To record amortization of patent)		

Amortization on a units-of-production basis would be computed in a manner similar to that described for depreciation on property, plant, and equipment in Chapter 11, pages 531–532.

Although a patent's useful life should not extend beyond its legal life of 17 years, small modifications or additions may lead to a new patent. The effect may be to extend the life of the old patent. In that case it is permissible to apply the unamortized costs of the old patent to the new patent if the new patent provides essentially the same benefits. Alternatively, if a patent becomes worthless (impairment) because demand drops for the product produced, the asset should be written down or written off immediately to expense.

COPYRIGHTS

A **copyright** is a federally granted right that all authors, painters, musicians, sculptors, and other artists have in their creations and expressions. A copyright is granted for the **life of the creator plus 50 years,** and gives the owner, or heirs, the exclusive right to reproduce and sell an artistic or published work. Copyrights are not renewable. Like patents, they may be assigned or sold to other individuals. The costs of acquiring and defending a copyright may be capitalized, but the research and development costs involved must be expensed as incurred.

Generally, the useful life of the copyright is less than its legal life (life in being plus 50 years). The costs of the copyright should be allocated to the years in which the benefits are expected to be received, not to exceed 40 years. The difficulty of determining the number of years over which benefits will be received normally encourages the company to write these costs off over a fairly short period of time.

Copyrights can be valuable. Really Useful Group is a company that consists of copyrights on the musicals of Andrew Lloyd Webber—*Cats, Phantom of the Opera, Jesus Christ-Superstar*, and others. It has little in the way of hard assets, yet it was recently valued at $300 million.[8]

TRADEMARKS AND TRADE NAMES

A **trademark** or **trade name** is a word, phrase, or symbol that distinguishes or identifies a particular enterprise or product. The right to use a trademark or trade name under common law, whether it is registered or not, rests exclusively with the original user as long as the original user continues to use it. Registration with the U.S. Patent Office provides legal protection for an **indefinite number of renewals for periods of 20 years each,** so a business that uses an established trademark or trade name may properly consider it to have an unlimited life. Trade names like Kleenex, Pepsi-Cola, Oldsmobile, Excedrin, Wheaties, and Sunkist create immediate product identification in our minds, thereby enhancing marketability.

The value of a trademark or trade name can be substantial. For example, of all Philip Morris Corporation's many assets, none surpasses in value the most intangible of in-

---

[8]Russell L. Parr, *Investing in Intangible Assets*, (New York: John Wiley & Sons, Inc., 1991), p. 47.

tangibles, the appeal of the Marlboro Cowboy. At one time it was estimated that the value of that image was $10 billion, or ½ of the company's value.[9]

Company names themselves identify qualities and characteristics that the companies have worked hard and spent much to develop. In a recent year an estimated 1,230 companies took on new names in an attempt to forge new identities and paid over $250 million to corporate-identity consultants. Among these were Primerica (formerly American Can), Navistar (formerly International Harvester), Nissan (formerly Datsun), and USX (U.S. Steel).

If a trademark or trade name is acquired, its capitalizable cost is the purchase price. If a trademark or trade name is developed by the enterprise itself, the capitalizable cost includes attorney fees, registration fees, design costs, consulting fees, successful legal defense costs, and other expenditures directly related to securing it (excluding research and development costs). When the total cost of a trademark or trade name is insignificant, it can be expensed rather than capitalized.

Although the life of a trademark, trade name, or company name may be unlimited, for accounting purposes the cost must be amortized over the periods benefited, not to exceed 40 years. However, because of the uncertainty involved in estimating their useful life, the cost of trademarks and trade names is frequently amortized over a much shorter period of time.[10]

LEASEHOLDS

A leasehold is a contractual understanding between a lessor (owner of property) and a lessee (renter of property) that grants the lessee **the right to use specific property, owned by the lessor, for a specific period of time in return for stipulated, and generally periodic, cash payments.** In most cases, the rent is included as an expense on the books of the lessee. Special problems, however, develop in the following situations.

Lease Prepayments

If the rent for the period of the lease is paid in advance, or if a lump sum payment is made in advance in addition to periodic rental payments, it is necessary to allocate this prepaid rent to the proper periods. The lessee has purchased the exclusive right to use the property for an extended period of time. These prepayments should be reported as a prepaid expense and not as an intangible asset.

Leasehold Improvements

Long-term leases ordinarily provide that any **leasehold improvements,** improvements made to the leased property, revert to the lessor at the end of the life of the lease. If the lessee constructs new buildings on leased land or reconstructs and improves existing buildings, **the lessee has the right to use such facilities during the life of the lease, but they become the property of the lessor when the lease expires.**

The lessee should charge the cost of the facilities to the Leasehold Improvements account and **depreciate the cost as operating expense over the remaining life of the lease, or the useful life of the improvements, whichever is shorter.** If a building with an estimated useful life of 25 years is constructed on land leased for 35 years, the cost of the building should be depreciated over 25 years. On the other hand, if the building has an estimated life of 50 years, it should be depreciated over 35 years, the life of the lease.

INTERNATIONAL INSIGHT

Traditionally, when brand names are included in the acquisition of another company, the value of the brand name has been included in goodwill. Recently, however, a number of firms in Great Britain have begun to separately value brand names in their balance sheets. This practice is highly controversial.

UNDERLYING CONCEPT

The treatment of leases is an example of the importance of the definition of an asset. The definition does not require ownership but it does require that the benefits of an asset flow to and be under the control of the entity.

---

[9]"Here's One Tough Cowboy," *Forbes* (February 9, 1987), p. 110.

[10]To illustrate how various intangibles might arise from a given product, consider what the creators of the highly successful game, Trivial Pursuit, did to protect their creation. First, they copyrighted the 6,000 questions that are at the heart of the game. Then they shielded the Trivial Pursuit name by applying for a registered trademark. As a third mode of protection, the creators obtained a design patent on the playing board's design because it represents a unique graphic creation.

If the lease contains an option to renew for a period of additional years and the likelihood of renewal is too uncertain to warrant apportioning the cost over the longer period of time, the leasehold improvements are generally written off over the original term of the lease (assuming that the life of the lease is shorter than the useful life of the improvements). **Leasehold improvements are generally shown in the tangible property, plant, and equipment section,** although some accountants classify them as intangible assets. The rationale for intangible asset treatment is that the improvements revert to the lessor at the end of the lease and are therefore more of a right than a tangible asset.

Capital Leases

In some cases, the lease agreement transfers substantially all of the benefits and risks incident to ownership of the property so that the economic effect on the parties is similar to that of an installment purchase. As a result, the asset value recognized when a lease is capitalized is classified as a tangible rather than an intangible asset. Such a lease is referred to as a **capital lease.** We will cover the accounting for leases in more detail in Chapter 22.

ORGANIZATION COSTS

Costs incurred in the formation of a corporation such as fees to underwriters (investment bankers) for handling stock or bond issues, legal fees, state fees of various sorts, and certain promotional expenditures are classified as **organization costs.**

These items are usually charged to an account called Organization Costs and may be carried as an asset on the balance sheet as expenditures that will benefit the company over its life. These costs are amortized over an arbitrary period of time (maximum 40 years), since the life of the corporation is indeterminate. However, the amortization period is frequently short (5–10 years) because of the assumption that the early years of a business benefit most from organization costs and that these costs lose their significance once the business becomes fully established. In addition, because income tax regulations require the amortization of organization costs over a period of at least 5 years, some find it convenient to use the same period for accounting purposes.

It is sometimes difficult to draw a line between organization costs, normal operating expenses, and losses. Some accountants contend that **operating losses incurred in the start-up of a business** should be capitalized, since they are unavoidable and are a cost of starting a business. This approach seems unsound, however, since losses have no future service potential and cannot be considered an asset.

Our position that operating losses should not be capitalized during the early years is supported by *Statement of Financial Accounting Standards No. 7*, which clarifies the accounting and reporting practices for **development stage enterprises.** The FASB concludes that the accounting practices and reporting standards should be no different for an enterprise trying to establish a new business than they are for other enterprises. The same "generally accepted accounting principles that apply to established operating enterprises shall govern the recognition of revenue by a development stage enterprise and shall determine whether a cost incurred by a development stage enterprise is to be charged to expense when incurred or is to be capitalized or deferred."[11]

---

[11]"Accounting and Reporting by Development Stage Enterprises," *Statement of Financial Accounting Standards No. 7* (Stamford, Conn.: FASB, 1975), par. 10. A company is considered to be in the developing stages when its efforts are directed toward establishing a new business and either the principal operations have not started or no significant revenue has been earned. To evaluate the economic impact of applying the same accounting principles to development stage enterprises that apply to established operating enterprises, the FASB interviewed officers of fifteen venture capital companies. The consensus was that whether a development stage enterprise defers or expenses preoperating costs has little effect on the amount of, or the terms under which venture capital is provided. According to these officers, venture capital investors instead rely on an evaluation of potential cash flows resulting from an investigation of the technological, marketing, management, and financial aspects of the enterprise.

FRANCHISES AND LICENSES

When you drive down the street in an automobile purchased from a Chrysler dealer, fill your tank at the corner Texaco station, eat lunch at McDonald's, cool off with one of Baskin-Robbins' 31 flavors, work at a Coca-Cola bottling plant, live in a home purchased through a Century 21 real estate broker, or vacation at a Holiday Inn resort, you are dealing with franchises. A **franchise** is a contractual arrangement under which the franchisor grants the franchisee the right to sell certain products or services, to use certain trademarks or trade names, or to perform certain functions, usually within a designated geographical area.

The franchisor, having developed a unique concept or product, protects its concept or product through a patent, copyright, or trademark or trade name. The franchisee acquires the right to exploit the franchisor's idea or product by signing a franchise agreement.

Another type of franchise is the arrangement commonly entered into by a municipality (or other governmental body) and a business enterprise that uses public property. In such cases, a privately owned enterprise is permitted to use public property in performing its services. Examples are the use of public waterways for a ferry service, the use of public land for telephone or electric lines, the use of phone lines for cable TV, the use of city streets for a bus line, or the use of the airwaves for radio or TV broadcasting. Such operating rights, obtained through agreements with governmental units or agencies, are frequently referred to as **licenses** or **permits.**

Franchises and licenses may be for a definite period of time, for an indefinite period of time, or perpetual. The enterprise securing the franchise or license carries an intangible asset account entitled Franchise or License on its books only when there are costs (such as a lump sum payment in advance or legal fees and other expenditures) that are identified with the acquisition of the operating right. **The cost of a franchise (or license) with a limited life should be amortized as operating expense over the life of the franchise.** A franchise with an indefinite life, or a perpetual franchise, should be carried at cost and amortized over a reasonable period not to exceed 40 years.

If a franchise is deemed to be worthless, it should be written off immediately. For example, in 1980, Congress deregulated the trucking industry and opened to competition long-protected routes covered by franchises. Because these franchise rights were substantial, approximately 15% of the trucking industry's equity was eliminated; as a result, losses instead of profits were reported in the period of write-off.[12] For example, Roadway Express wrote off all $26.8 million worth of these assets, changing a $16.4 million profit for the quarter to a $10.4 million loss.

Annual payments made under a franchise agreement should be entered as operating expenses in the period in which they are incurred. They do not represent an asset to the concern since they do not relate to future rights to use public property.

PROPERTY RIGHTS

Most of the above-discussed identifiable intangibles represent **rights**—rights to use, produce, sell, or operate something. Other rights that appear to be growing in significance, and therefore in value, are water, mineral, solar and wind (the legal right to free flow of light and air across one's property), and other types of property rights. Although these rights have a value of their own, they are generally attached to a particular parcel of property. Therefore, the value of such property rights, if **inseparable** from the property, is accounted for as part of the capitalized land cost.

If the right is separable from the property, as in the case of mineral rights, its cost may be capitalized separately. If minerals are later discovered or developed, the cost of the rights should be reclassified and capitalized as part of the cost of the minerals and written off as the mineral deposit is depleted.

---

[12]"Accounting for Intangible Assets of Motor Carriers," *Statement of Financial Accounting Standards No. 44* (Stamford, Conn.: FASB, 1980).

▶ GOODWILL

Goodwill is often referred to as the most "intangible" of the intangibles. It is undoubtedly one of the most complex and controversial assets presented in financial statements. Goodwill is unique because unlike receivables, inventories, and patents that can be sold or exchanged individually in the marketplace, goodwill can be identified only with the business as a whole. For example, a substantial list of regular customers and an established reputation are unrecorded assets that give the enterprise a valuation greater than the sum of the fair market value of the individual identifiable assets. Goodwill is comprised of many advantageous factors and conditions that might contribute to the value and the earning power of an enterprise:[13]

OBJECTIVE 4

Explain the conceptual issues related to goodwill.

1. Superior management team
2. Outstanding sales organization
3. Effective advertising
4. Secret process or formula
5. Good labor relations
6. Outstanding credit rating
7. Top-flight training program
8. High standing in the community
9. Discovery of talents or resources
10. Favorable tax conditions
11. Favorable government regulation
12. Favorable association with another company
13. Strategic location
14. Weakness in management of a competitor
15. Unfavorable developments in the operations of a competitor[14]

Goodwill is recorded only when an entire business is purchased because goodwill is a "going-concern" valuation and cannot be separated from the business as a whole.[15] Goodwill generated internally should **not** be capitalized in the accounts, because measuring the components of goodwill (as listed above) is simply too complex and associating any costs with future benefits too difficult. The future benefits of goodwill may have no relationship to the costs incurred in the development of that goodwill. To add to the mystery, goodwill may even exist in the absence of specific costs to develop it. In addition, because no objective transaction with outside parties has taken place, a great deal of subjectivity—even misrepresentation—might be involved.

UNDERLYING CONCEPT

Capitalizing goodwill only when it is purchased in an arm's-length transaction and not capitalizing any goodwill generated internally is another example of reliability winning out over relevance.

RECORDING GOODWILL

To record goodwill, the fair market value of the net tangible and identifiable intangible assets are compared with the purchase price of the acquired business. The difference is considered goodwill, which is why goodwill is sometimes referred to as a "plug" or

OBJECTIVE 5

Describe the accounting procedures for recording goodwill.

---

[13]George R. Catlett and Norman O. Olson, "Accounting for Goodwill," *Accounting Research Study No. 10* (New York: AICPA, 1968), pp. 17–18.

[14]Another study clustered 17 specific characteristics of goodwill into four more general categories as follows:

Increasing Short-Run Cash Flows	Human Factor
Production economies	Managerial talent
Raise more funds	Good labor relations
Cash reserves	Good training programs
Low cost of funds	Organizational structure
Reduce inventory holding cost	Good public relations
Avoiding transaction cost	
Tax benefits	Stability
	Assurance of supply
Exclusiveness	Reducing fluctuations
	Good government relations
Access to technology	
Brand name	

See Haim Falk and L. A. Gordon, "Imperfect Markets and the Nature of Goodwill," *Journal of Business Finance and Accounting* (April 1977), pp. 443–463.

[15]See "Conceptual Framework for Financial Accounting and Reporting Elements of Financial Statements and Their Measurement," *FASB Discussion Memorandum* (Stamford, Conn.: FASB, 1976), p. 235.

"gap filler" or **"master valuation"** account. **Goodwill is the residual: the excess of cost over fair value of the identifiable net assets acquired.**

To illustrate, Multi-Diversified, Inc. decides that it needs a parts division to supplement its existing tractor distributorship. The president of Multi-Diversified is interested in buying a small concern in Chicago (Tractorling Company) that has an established reputation and is seeking a merger candidate. The balance sheet of Tractorling Company is presented below.

ILLUSTRATION 12-2
Tractorling Balance Sheet

Tractorling Co. BALANCE SHEET as of Dec. 31, 1995			
Assets		**Equities**	
Cash	$ 25,000	Current liabilities	$ 55,000
Receivables	35,000	Capital stock	100,000
Inventories	42,000	Retained earnings	100,000
Property, plant, and equipment, net	153,000		
Total assets	$255,000	Total equities	$255,000

After considerable negotiation, Tractorling Company decides to accept Multi-Diversified's offer of $400,000. What then is the value of the goodwill, if any?

The answer is not obvious. The fair market values of Tractorling's identifiable assets are not disclosed in its historical cost-based balance sheet. Suppose, though, that as the negotiations progressed, Multi-Diversified conducted an investigation of the underlying assets of Tractorling to determine the fair market value of the assets. Such an investigation may be accomplished either through a purchase audit undertaken by Multi-Diversified's auditors in order to estimate the values of the seller's assets, or an independent appraisal from some other source. The following valuations are determined.

ILLUSTRATION 12-3
Fair Market Value of Tractorling's Assets

Fair Market Values	
Cash	$ 25,000
Receivables	35,000
Inventories	122,000
Property, plant, and equipment, net	205,000
Patents	18,000
Liabilities	(55,000)
Fair market value of net assets	$350,000

Normally, differences between current fair market value and book value are more common among long-term assets, although significant differences can also develop in the current asset category. Cash obviously poses no problems, and receivables normally are fairly close to current valuation, although at times certain adjustments need to be made because of inadequate bad debt provisions. Liabilities usually are stated at book value, although if interest rates have changed since the liabilities were incurred, a different valuation (such as present value) might be appropriate. Careful analysis must be made to determine that no unrecorded liabilities are present.

The $80,000 difference in inventories ($122,000 − $42,000) could result from a number of factors, the most likely being that Tractorling Company uses LIFO. Recall that during periods of inflation, LIFO better matches expenses against revenues, but in doing so creates a balance sheet distortion. Ending inventory is comprised of older layers costed at lower valuations.

In many cases, the values of long-term assets such as property, plant, and equipment, and intangibles may have increased substantially over the years. This difference could be due to inaccurate estimates of useful lives, continual expensing of small expenditures (say, less than $300), inaccurate estimates of salvage values and the discovery of some unrecorded assets (as in Tractorling's case where Patents are discovered to have a fair value of $18,000). Or, replacement costs may have substantially increased.

Since the fair market value of net assets is now determined to be $350,000, why did Multi-Diversified pay $400,000? Undoubtedly, the seller pointed to an established reputation, good credit rating, top management team, well-trained employees, and so on, as factors that make the value of the business greater than $350,000.[16] At the same time, Multi-Diversified placed a premium on the future earning power of these attributes as well as the basic asset structure of the enterprise today. At this point in the negotiations, price can be a function of many factors: the most important is probably sheer skill at the bargaining table.

The difference between the purchase price of $400,000 and the fair market value of $350,000 is labeled goodwill. Goodwill is viewed as one or a group of unidentifiable values (intangible assets) the cost of which "is measured by the difference between the cost of the group of assets or enterprise acquired and the sum of the assigned costs of individual tangible and identifiable intangible assets acquired less liabilities assumed."[17] This procedure for valuation is referred to as a **master valuation approach** because goodwill is assumed to cover all the values that cannot be specifically identified with any identifiable tangible or intangible asset; this approach is shown in Illustration 12-4.

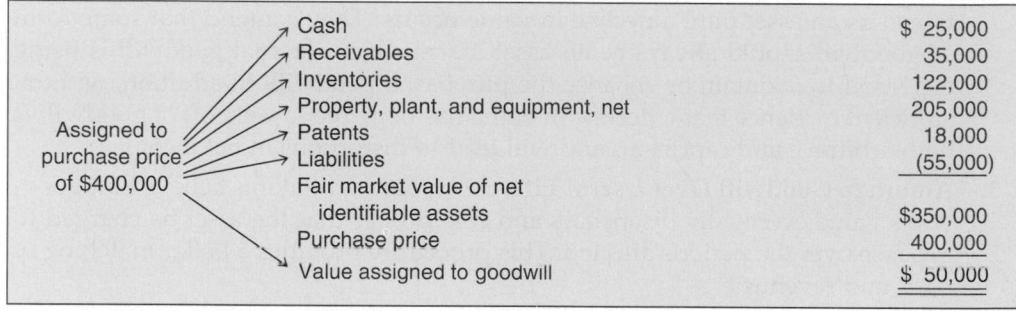

ILLUSTRATION 12-4
Determination of
Goodwill—Master
Valuation Approach

The entry to record this transaction would be as follows:

Cash	25,000	
Receivables	35,000	
Inventories	122,000	
Property, plant, and equipment	205,000	
Patents	18,000	
Goodwill	50,000	
Liabilities		55,000
Cash		400,000

Goodwill is often identified on the balance sheet as the **excess of cost over the fair value** of the net assets acquired.

AMORTIZATION OF GOODWILL

Once goodwill has been recognized in the accounts, the next question is how it should be amortized (if at all). Three basic approaches have been suggested.

---

[16]As another example of valuation criteria, the National Economic Research Associates of New York ranked "the quality of assets" of the 24 U.S.-based major league baseball teams in the early 1980s: At the high end were the Detroit Tigers at $36.2 million, Philadelphia Phillies at $35.3 million and Boston Red Sox at $34.3 million. At the low end were the Chicago Cubs and the Chicago White Sox at $20.6 million each, and the San Francisco Giants and the Oakland A's at $19 million each. Research Associates based their estimates on what the baseball franchises could be worth if they were "reasonably well managed," on the population and per capita income of the area in which a team plays, and on the number of local professional sports franchises it competes with. Surprisingly, the valuation did not include the team's recent attendance, local radio and TV revenue, and past profits.

[17]*APB Opinion No. 17*, op. cit., par. 26.

1. **Charge Goodwill Off Immediately to Stockholders' Equity.** *Accounting Research Study No. 10,* "Accounting for Goodwill," takes the position that goodwill differs from other types of assets and demands special attention.[18] Unlike other assets, it is not separable and distinct from the business as a whole and therefore is not an asset in the same sense as cash, receivables, or plant assets. In other words, goodwill cannot be sold without selling the business.

   Furthermore, say proponents of this approach, the accounting treatment for purchased goodwill and goodwill internally created should be consistent. Goodwill created internally is immediately expensed and does not appear as an asset: the same treatment should be accorded purchased goodwill. Amortization of purchased goodwill leads to double counting, because net income is reduced by amortization of the purchased goodwill as well as by the internal expenditure made to maintain or enhance the value of assets.

   Perhaps the best rationale for direct writeoff is that determining the periods over which the future benefits are to be received is so difficult that immediate charging to stockholders' equity is justified.

2. **Retain Goodwill Indefinitely Unless Reduction in Value Occurs.** Many accountants believe that goodwill can have an indefinite life and should be maintained as an asset until a decline in value occurs. They contend that some form of goodwill should always be an asset inasmuch as internal goodwill is being expensed to maintain or enhance the purchased goodwill. In addition, without sufficient evidence that a decline in value has occurred, a writeoff of goodwill is both arbitrary and capricious and will lead to distortions in net income.

3. **Amortize Goodwill Over Useful Life.** Still other accountants believe that goodwill's value eventually disappears and it is proper that the asset be charged to expense over the periods affected. This procedure provides a better matching of costs and revenues.

APB Opinion No. 17 takes the position that goodwill should be written off over its useful life, which is dependent on a number of factors such as regulatory restrictions, demand, competition, and obsolescence. **The profession did note that goodwill should never be written off immediately or amortized over more than 40 years.**

INTERNATIONAL INSIGHT

In the United Kingdom companies are allowed to write off goodwill immediately against equity. This, of course, makes the earnings subsequently reported by U.K. companies higher than they would otherwise have been.

Immediate writeoff was not considered proper, because it would lead to the untenable conclusion that goodwill has no future service potential. The profession merely prohibits the writing off of goodwill in the period of purchase and over a period exceeding 40 years; no other mention is made regarding another period. Some believe that a 5-year period for amortization would be appropriate unless a shorter period is obviously justified.[19] Such circumstances would include continuous losses or an exodus of managerial talent. A single loss year or a combination of loss years does not automatically necessitate a charge-off of the goodwill.

Goodwill amortization should be computed using the straight-line method unless another method is deemed more appropriate. It should be treated as a regular operating expense. Where the amortization is material, a disclosure of the charge is necessary, as well as the method and period of amortization. Goodwill amortization is now deductible for tax purposes.

The amortization practices associated with goodwill sometimes lead to major disagreements. When Ted Turner of Turner Broadcasting attempted to take over CBS, he was required to file income statements on what a combined Turner-CBS company would look like in subsequent years. Turner assigned the difference between what he

---

[18]Catlett and Olson, op. cit., pp. 89–95.

[19]A recent study of goodwill reached the following conclusion: "Thus, the 40-year amortization period used in current practice is too long and cannot be supported on either theoretical or technical grounds. Consequently, a rapid amortization (specifically if the use of the present value amortization method is permitted by the FASB) of capitalized goodwill over a relatively short period of time should occur. J. Ron Colley and Ara G. Volkan, "Accounting for Goodwill," *Accounting Horizons* (March 1988), p. 40.

proposed to pay and the book value of CBS entirely to goodwill and amortized this amount over 40 years. CBS disagreed, noting that some of CBS's assets should have been revalued and a smaller amount assigned to goodwill. These revalued assets have a shorter life than goodwill and would lower the net income of the combined Turner-CBS Company. Thus the merger would be supposedly less attractive to stockholders of CBS. Questions of valuation and amortization of goodwill were important considerations in this takeover battle.[20]

NEGATIVE GOODWILL—BADWILL

Negative goodwill, often appropriately dubbed badwill, or bargain purchase, arises when the fair market value of the assets acquired is higher than the purchase price of the assets. This situation is a result of market imperfection because the seller would be better off to sell the assets individually than in total. Situations do occur in which the purchase price is less than the value of the net identifiable assets and therefore a credit develops; this credit is referred to as negative goodwill or **excess of fair value over the cost of assets acquired.** Companies that have negative goodwill are in a very interesting position because the amortization of this negative goodwill to revenue increases earnings.

APB Opinion No. 16 **takes the position that an excess of fair value over purchase price should be allocated to reduce proportionately the values assigned to noncurrent assets** of the acquired company (except long-term investments in marketable securities). If the allocation reduces the noncurrent assets to zero, the remainder of the excess over cost should be classified as a deferred credit and should be amortized systematically to revenue over the period estimated to be benefited but not in excess of 40 years. The method and period of amortization should be disclosed.[21]

Negative goodwill most frequently develops in a depressed securities market when the market value of a company's stock sells at less than book value. For example, Emhart Corp. offered $23 a share (a premium over market) for U.S.M. Corp. stock that had a per-share book value of $43. Emhart Corp. (in consolidation) was able to write down its newly acquired plant assets by more than $49 million and thereby effect a reduction in annual depreciation charges of $5.8 million and add 50 cents annually to its earnings per share (on top of the $2.00 a share it would gain from consolidating U.S.M.'s reported profits—this extra $2.50 per share represented a 90% increase over Emhart's prior year earnings).

▶ IMPAIRMENT OF INTANGIBLES

The general rules that apply to **impairments of long-lived assets also apply to intangibles.** As indicated in Chapter 11, long-lived assets to be held and used by a company are to be reviewed for impairment whenever events or changes in circumstances indicate that **the carrying amount of the assets may not be recoverable.** In performing the review for recoverability, the company would estimate the future cash flows expected to result from the use of the asset and its eventual disposition. If the sum of the expected future net cash flows (undiscounted) is less than the carrying amount of the asset, an impairment loss would be measured and recognized. Otherwise, an impairment loss would not be recognized.[22]

The impairment loss is the amount by which the carrying amount of the asset exceeds the fair value of the impaired asset. Illustrations of impairment for specifically identifiable and goodwill type intangibles are shown on the next page.

---

[20]*The Wall Street Journal*, May 9, 1985.

[21]"Business Combinations," *Opinions of the Accounting Principles Board No. 16* (New York: AICPA, 1970), par. 91.

[22]"Accounting for the Impairment of Long-Lived Assets," *Statement of Financial Accounting Standards* (Norwalk, CT: FASB, 1994).

SPECIFICALLY IDENTIFIABLE INTANGIBLES

Assume that Lerch, Inc. has a patent on how to extract oil from shale rock. Unfortunately, reduced oil prices have made the shale oil technology somewhat unprofitable, and the patent has provided little income to date. As a result, a recoverability test is performed, and it is found that the expected net future cash flows from this patent are $35 million. Lerch's patent has a carrying amount of $60 million. Because the expected future net cash flows of $35 million are less than the carrying amount of $60 million, an impairment loss must be measured. Discounting the expected net future cash flows at its market rate of interest, Lerch determines the fair value of its patent to be $20 million. The impairment loss computation is shown in Illustration 12-5:

ILLUSTRATION 12-5
Computation of Loss on Impairment of Patent

Carrying amount of patent	$60,000,000
Fair value (based on present value computation)	20,000,000
Loss on impairment	$40,000,000

The journal entry to record this loss is:

Loss on Impairment	40,000,000	
Patents		40,000,000

After the impairment is recognized, the reduced carrying amount of the patents is its new cost basis. The patent's new cost should be amortized over its useful life or legal life, whichever is shorter. Even if oil prices increase in subsequent periods, and the value of the patent increases, **restoration of the previously recognized impairment loss is not permitted.**

GOODWILL TYPE INTANGIBLES

Goodwill is a "going concern" valuation and cannot be separated from the other assets and liabilities which give it value. As a result, goodwill impairments involve a grouping of net assets.

To illustrate an impairment loss when goodwill is involved, assume that Kohlberg Corporation has three divisions in its company. One division, Pritt Products, was purchased four years ago for $2 million. Unfortunately, it has experienced operating losses over the last three quarters and management is reviewing the division for purposes of recognizing an impairment. The Pritt Division's net assets including the associated goodwill of $1,200,000 are listed in Illustration 12-6:

ILLUSTRATION 12-6
Pritt Division Net Assets

Cash	$ 200,000
Receivables	300,000
Inventory	400,000
Property, plant, and equipment (net)	800,000
Goodwill	1,200,000
Less: Accounts and notes payable	(500,000)
Net assets	$2,400,000

A recoverability test is performed and it is found that the expected net future cash flows from Pritt Division are $2,000,000. The fair value of the division is estimated to be $1,300,000, the present value of the expected future net cash flows. The impairment loss is computed as follows:

ILLUSTRATION 12-7
Computation of Impairment Loss on Pritt Division

Carrying amount of Pritt Division	$2,400,000
Fair value	1,300,000
Loss on impairment	$1,100,000

How should the impairment loss be allocated to the net assets of the Pritt Division? Various allocation approaches might be used. The FASB requires that where goodwill is associated with assets that are subject to the impairment loss, the carrying amount of the associated goodwill should be eliminated *before* the carrying amounts of impaired long-lived assets and identifiable intangibles are reduced to their fair values.

For Pritt Division, therefore, the total loss on impairment reduces only goodwill. The entry to record the impairment is:

Loss on Impairment	1,100,000	
Goodwill		1,100,000

If the impairment loss were greater than the carrying amount of goodwill, the additional loss would be used to reduce the remaining long-lived assets to fair value.[23]

► REPORTING INTANGIBLES

The reporting of intangibles differs from the reporting of property, plant, and equipment in that contra accounts are not normally shown. The amortization of intangibles is frequently credited directly to the intangible asset.[24]

The financial statements should disclose the method and period of amortization. Intangible assets shown net of amortization might appear on the balance sheet as follows:

Intangible assets (Note 3)		
Patents	$ 98,000	
Franchises	115,000	
Goodwill	342,000	$555,000

Note 3: The patents are amortized on a unit-of-production approach over a period of 6 years. The franchises are perpetual in nature, but in accordance with *APB Opinion No. 17* are being written off over the maximum period allowable (40 years) on a straight-line basis. The goodwill arose from the purchase of Multi-Media and is being amortized over a 10-year period on a straight-line basis.

ILLUSTRATION 12-8
Balance Sheet Presentation of Intangible Assets, Net of Amortization

The following example, taken from the 1992 annual report of Crystal Brands, Inc., illustrates the reporting of intangibles net using a contra valuation account in the notes:

Crystal Brands, Inc.	1992	1991
	($000)	
Total current assets	$238,308	$350,048
Property, plant and equipment, net	48,294	87,479
Goodwill, net	120,806	139,047
Trademarks, trade names and patents, net	59,517	73,146
Other noncurrent assets	11,948	9,717
Total assets	$478,873	$659,437

Note 1 (in part): Amortization of Intangibles
Goodwill and trademarks, trade names and patents are as follows:

ILLUSTRATION 12-9
Balance Sheet Presentation of Intangibles with Contra Valuation Account in Notes

---

[23]Once the goodwill is completely eliminated, the remaining loss would probably be allocated pro-rata, based on relative fair values, to those long-lived assets and identifiable intangible assets that had fair values less than their carrying amounts.

[24]*Accounting Trends and Techniques—1993* reports that the most common type of intangible is goodwill followed by patents; trademarks, brand names, and copyrights; and then noncompete covenants, licenses, franchises, and memberships.

	December 31, 1992	($000)	December 28, 1991	
	Goodwill	Trademarks, trade names & patents	Goodwill	Trademarks, trade names & patents
Subject to 40 yr. straight-line amortization	$103,648	$ 64,797	$119,219	$ 76,266
Subject to 15 yr. straight-line amortization	—	2,773	—	2,773
Subject to 5 yr. straight-line amortization	—	5,463	—	5,463
Not amortized	27,896	—	29,146	—
	131,544	73,033	148,365	84,502
Less: Accumulated amortization	(10,738)	(13,516)	(9,318)	(11,356)
	$120,806	$ 59,517	$139,047	$ 73,146
Amortization expense	$ 2,894	$ 3,264	$ 2,986	$ 3,289

Discontinued operations and the sale of assets resulted in the write-off of goodwill and trademarks, trade names and patents of $15,332 and $10,365, (net of accumulated amortization of $1,489 and $1,104), respectively in 1992 and 1991.

Some companies follow the practice of writing their intangibles down to $1.00 to indicate that they have intangibles of uncertain value. This practice is not good accounting. It would be much better to disclose the nature of the intangible, its original cost, and other relevant information such as competition, danger of obsolescence, and so on.

▶ RESEARCH AND DEVELOPMENT COSTS

OBJECTIVE 6

Identify the conceptual issues related to research and development costs.

Research and development (R & D) costs are not in themselves intangible assets. The accounting for R & D costs is presented here, however, because research and development activities frequently result in the development of something that is patented or copyrighted (such as a new product, process, idea, formula, composition, or literary work).

Many businesses spend considerable sums of money on research and development to create new products or processes, to improve present products, and to discover new knowledge that may be valuable at some future date. The following schedule shows the outlays for R & D made by selected American companies:[25]

ILLUSTRATION 12-10 R & D Outlays, as Percent of Sales and Profits

INTERNATIONAL INSIGHT

Contrary to U.S. practice, in most other nations (the Netherlands, Canada, and Japan, for example) the capitalization of research and development costs is allowed under specified circumstances.

Company	Dollars	% of Sales	% of Profits
Amoco Corporation	$ 292,000,000	1.2%	16%
Bristol-Myers-Squibb Company	1,100,000,000	9.6	56
Kellogg Company	39,800,000	0.1	6
Eastman Kodak Company	1,301,000,000	8.0	(Loss)
IBM	5,558,000,000	18.2	(Loss)
PepsiCo, Inc.	113,000,000	0.05	7

The difficulties in accounting for these research and development (R & D) expenditures are (1) identifying the costs associated with particular activities, projects, or achievements and (2) determining the magnitude of the future benefits and length of time over which such benefits may be realized. Because of these latter uncertainties, the accounting profession, through *FASB Statement No. 2,* has standardized and simplified accounting practice in this area by requiring that **all research and development costs be charged to expense when incurred.**[26]

---

[25]As presented in the companies' 1993 annual reports.

[26]"Accounting for Research and Development Costs," *Statement of Financial Accounting Standards No. 2* (Stamford, Conn.: FASB, 1974), par. 12.

To differentiate research and development costs from **other similar costs,** the FASB issued the following definitions:

RESEARCH is planned search or critical investigation aimed at discovery of new knowledge with the hope that such knowledge will be useful in developing a new product or service . . . or a new process or technique . . . or in bringing about a significant improvement to an existing product or process.

DEVELOPMENT is the translation of research findings or other knowledge into a plan or design for a new product or process or for a significant improvement to an existing product or process whether intended for sale or use. It includes the conceptual formulation, design, and testing of product alternatives, construction of prototypes, and operation of pilot plants. It does not include routine or periodic alterations to existing products, production lines, manufacturing processes, and other on-going operations even though those alterations may represent improvements and it does not include market research or market testing activities.[27]

Many costs have characteristics similar to those of research and development costs. Examples are costs of relocation and rearrangement of facilities, start-up costs for a new plant or new retail outlet, marketing research costs, promotion costs of a new product or service, and costs of training new personnel. To distinguish between R & D and these other similar costs, the following schedule provides (1) examples of activities that typically would be **included** in research and development, and (2) examples of activities that typically would be **excluded** from research and development.[28]

1. R & D Activities

(a) Laboratory research aimed at discovery of new knowledge.

(b) Searching for applications of new research findings.

(c) Conceptual formulation and design of possible product or process alternatives.

(d) Testing in search for or evaluation of product or process alternatives.

(e) Modification of the design of a product or process.

(f) Design, construction, and testing of preproduction prototypes and models.

(g) Design of tools, jigs, molds, and dies involving new technology.

(h) Design, construction, and operation of a pilot plant not useful for commercial production.

(i) Engineering activity required to advance the design of a product to the manufacturing stage.

2. Activities Not Considered R & D

(a) Engineering follow-through in an early phase of commercial production.

(b) Quality control during commercial production including routine testing.

(c) Trouble-shooting breakdowns during production.

(d) Routine, on-going efforts to refine, enrich, or improve the qualities of an existing product.

(e) Adaptation of an existing capability to a particular requirement or customer's need.

(f) Periodic design changes to existing products.

(g) Routine design of tools, jigs, molds, and dies.

(h) Activity, including design and construction engineering related to the construction, relocation, rearrangement, or start-up of facilities or equipment.

(i) Legal work on patent applications, sale, licensing, or litigation.

COSTS ASSOCIATED WITH R & D

The costs associated with R & D activities and the accounting treatment accorded them are as follows:

OBJECTIVE 7

Describe the accounting procedures for research and development costs.

(a) **Materials, Equipment, and Facilities.** Expense the entire costs, **unless the items have alternative future uses** (in other R & D projects or otherwise), then carry as inventory and allocate as consumed or capitalize and depreciate as used.

[27]Ibid., par. 8.

[28]Ibid., pars. 9 and 10.

(b) Personnel. Salaries, wages, and other related costs of personnel engaged in R & D should be expensed as incurred.

(c) Purchased Intangibles. Expense the entire cost, **unless the items have alternative future uses** (in other R & D projects or otherwise), then capitalize and amortize.

(d) Contract Services. The costs of services performed by others in connection with the reporting company's R & D should be expensed as incurred.

(e) Indirect Costs. A reasonable allocation of indirect costs shall be included in R & D costs, except for general and administrative cost, which must be clearly related in order to be included and expensed.[29]

Consistent with item (a) above, if an enterprise owns a research facility consisting of buildings, laboratories, and equipment that conducts R & D activities and that has alternative future uses (in other R & D projects or otherwise), the facility should be accounted for as a capitalized operational asset. The depreciation and other costs related to such research facilities are accounted for as R & D expenses.

Sometimes enterprises conduct R & D activities for other entities under a **contractual arrangement.** In this case, the contract usually specifies that all direct costs, certain specific indirect costs, plus a profit element, should be reimbursed to the enterprise performing the R & D work. Because reimbursement is expected, such R & D costs should be recorded as a receivable. It is the company for whom the work has been performed that reports these costs as R & D and expenses them as incurred.[30]

To illustrate the identification of R & D activities and the accounting treatment of related costs, assume that Next Century Incorporated develops, produces, and markets laser machines for medical, industrial, and defense uses. The types of expenditures related to its laser machine activities, along with the recommended accounting treatment, are listed below.

ILLUSTRATION 12-11
Sample R & D
Expenditures and Their
Accounting Treatment

| **Next Century Incorporated** | |
Type of Expenditure	Accounting Treatment
1. Construction of long-range research facility for use in current and future projects (three-story, 400,000-square-foot building).	Capitalize and depreciate as R & D expense.
2. Acquisition of R & D equipment for use on current project only.	Expense immediately as R & D.
3. Acquisition of machinery to be used on current and future R & D projects.	Capitalize and depreciate as R & D expense.
4. Purchase of materials to be used on current and future R & D projects.	Inventory and allocate to R & D projects; expense as consumed.
5. Salaries of research staff designing new laser bone scanner.	Expense immediately as R & D.
6. Research costs incurred under contract with New Horizon, Inc., and billable monthly.	Record as a receivable (reimbursable expenses).
7. Material, labor, and overhead costs of prototype laser scanner.	Expense immediately as R & D.
8. Costs of testing prototype and design modifications.	Expense immediately as R & D.
9. Legal fees to obtain patent on new laser scanner.	Capitalize as patent and amortize to overhead as part of cost of goods manufactured.
10. Executive salaries.	Expense as operating expense (general and administrative).

---

[29]Ibid., par. 11.

[30]For a more complete discussion of how an enterprise should account for its obligation under an arrangement for the funding of its research and development by others, see "Research and Development Arrangements," *Statement of Financial Accounting Standards No. 68* (Stamford, Conn.: FASB, 1982).

11. Cost of marketing research to promote new laser scanner.	Expense as operating expense (selling).
12. Engineering costs incurred to advance the laser scanner to full production stage.	Expense immediately as R & D.
13. Costs of successfully defending patent on laser scanner.	Capitalize as patent and amortize to overhead as part of cost of goods manufactured.
14. Commissions to sales staff marketing new laser scanner.	Expense as operating expense (selling).

A special problem arises in distinguishing R & D costs from selling and administrative activities. The FASB's intent was that the acquisition, development, or improvement of a product or process by an enterprise **for use in its selling or administrative activities** be excluded from the definition of research and development activities. For example, the costs of software incurred by an airline in acquiring, developing, or improving its computerized reservation system, or the costs incurred during the development of a general management information system, are not research and development costs. Accounting for computer software costs is a specialized and complicated new accounting topic that is discussed and illustrated in an appendix to this chapter (Appendix 12-A).

FINANCIAL STATEMENT PRESENTATION

Acceptable accounting practice requires that disclosure be made in the financial statements (generally in the notes) of the total R & D costs charged to expense in each period for which an income statement is presented. An example of an R & D disclosure in the income statement and in an accompanying note is the excerpt from the 1993 annual report of Oncogene Science, Inc.

Oncogene Science, Inc.			
	Years Ended September 30,		
	1993	1992	1991
Expenses:			
Research and development—Note 1(d)	$10,659,806	$ 8,127,466	$4,860,226
Production	1,443,649	1,420,686	748,927
Selling, general and administrative	6,429,701	5,219,606	4,130,777
Amortization of intangibles—Note 1(c)	1,745,713	1,745,694	—
	20,278,869	16,513,452	9,739,930

Note 1: Summary of Significant Accounting Policies
   (d) Research and Development Costs
   Research and development costs are charged to operations as incurred and include direct costs of research scientists and equipment and an allocation of laboratory facility and central service. In fiscal years 1993, 1992, and 1991 R & D activities include approximately $3,012,000, $2,701,000, and $2,122,000 of independent R & D, respectively. Independent R & D represents those research and development activities, including research and development activities funded by government research grants, the results of which the Company retains substantially all rights. The balance of research and development represents research and development expenses under the collaborative agreements funded by Pfizer Inc., Becton Dickinson and Co., Wyeth-Ayerst, a division of American Home Products, Marion Merrell Dow Inc., and Hoechst AG.

**ILLUSTRATION 12-12
Income Statement and
Note Disclosure of R & D
Costs**

Costs of research, exploration, and development activities that are unique to companies in the **extractive industries** (e.g., prospecting, acquisition of mineral rights, exploration, drilling, mining, and related mineral development) and those costs discussed above which are similar to but not classified as R & D costs may be:

1. expensed as incurred,
2. capitalized and either depreciated or amortized over an appropriate period of time, or
3. accumulated as part of inventoriable costs.

Choice of the appropriate accounting treatment for such costs should be guided by the degree of certainty of future benefits and the principle of matching revenues and expenses.

CONCEPTUAL QUESTIONS

UNDERLYING
CONCEPT

*The requirement that all
R & D costs be expensed as
incurred is an example of the
conflict between relevance
and reliability, with this
requirement leaning strongly
in support of reliability, as
well as conservatism,
consistency, and
comparability. No attempt is
made to match costs and
revenues.*

The requirement that all R & D costs incurred internally be expensed immediately is a conservative, practical solution that ensures consistency in practice and uniformity among companies. But the practice of immediately writing off expenditures made in the expectation of benefiting future periods cannot be justified on the grounds that it is good accounting theory.[31]

Defendants of immediate expensing contend that from an income statement standpoint, long-run application of this standard frequently makes little difference. They contend that the amount of R & D cost charged to expense each accounting period would be about the same whether there is immediate expensing or capitalization and subsequent amortization because of the ongoing nature of most companies' R & D activities. Critics of this practice argue that the balance sheet should report an intangible asset related to expenditures that have future benefit. To preclude capitalization of all R & D expenditures removes from the balance sheet what may be a company's most valuable asset.[32] This standard represents one of the many trade-offs made among relevance, reliability, and cost-benefit considerations.[33]

▶ OTHER ASSETS

Other assets (sometimes referred to as **deferred charges**) is a classification often used to describe a number of different items that have debit balances, among them certain types of intangibles. How do these items happen to be classified in this section and not in a separate intangible section? In truth, the other asset section serves as a dumping ground for a number of small items. Some of these items are: property held for sale, prepaid pension costs, segregated cash or securities, cash surrender value of life insurance, and deferred income taxes. In many cases, deferred income taxes are separately identified.

KEY TERMS

capital lease, 577

copyright, 575

deferred charges, 590

development
activities, 587

development stage
enterprises, 577

franchise, 578

goodwill, 579

intangible assets, 572

▶ SUMMARY OF LEARNING OBJECTIVES ◀

1. **Describe the characteristics of intangible assets.** A major characteristic of intangible assets is the high degree of uncertainty concerning the *future benefits* that are to be received from their employment. Intangibles may be subdivided on the basis of the following characteristics: (1) *Identifiability:* separately identifiable or lacking specific identification. (2) *Manner of acquisition:* acquired singly, in groups, or in business combinations, or developed internally. (3) *Expected period of benefit:* limited by law or contract, related to human or economic factors, or indefinite or indeterminate duration. (4) *Separability from the enterprise:* rights

---

[31]The International Accounting Standards Committee issued a standard that is in disagreement with the FASB's standard on accounting for R & D costs. The International Committee identified certain circumstances that justify the capitalization and deferral of development costs. See "Accounting for Research and Development Activities," *International Accounting Standard No. 9* (London, England: International Accounting Standards Committee, 1978), par. 17.

[32]Bertrand Horwitz and Richard Kolodmy, "The FASB, the SEC, and R & D," *Bell Journal of Economics* (Spring 1981), who argue that expensing R & D has economic consequences.

[33]For a discussion of the position that R & D should be capitalized in certain situations, see Harold Bierman, Jr., and Roland E. Dukes, "Accounting for Research and Development Costs, *The Journal of Accountancy* (April, 1975).

transferable without title, salable, or inseparable from the enterprise or a substantial part of it.

2. **Explain the procedure for valuing and amortizing intangible assets.** Intangibles are recorded at cost. Cost includes all costs of acquisition and expenditures necessary to make the intangible asset ready for its intended use. If intangibles are acquired for stock or in exchange for other assets, the cost of the intangible is the fair market value of the consideration given or the fair market value of the intangible received, whichever is more clearly evident. When several intangibles, or a combination of intangibles and tangibles, are bought in a "basket purchase," the cost should be allocated on the basis of fair market values or on the basis of relative sales values. Intangible assets should be amortized by systematic charges to expense over their useful lives. Intangible assets must be amortized over a period not exceeding 40 years.

3. **Identify the types of specifically identifiable intangible assets.** The major identifiable assets are: (1) *Patents:* give the holder exclusive right to use, manufacture, and sell a product or process for a period of 17 years without interference or infringement by others. (2) *Copyrights:* a federally granted right that all authors, painters, musicians, sculptors, and other artists have in their creations and expressions. (3) *Trademarks and trade names:* a word, phrase, or symbol that distinguishes or identifies a particular enterprise or product. (4) *Leaseholds:* a contractual understanding between a lessor (owner of property) and a lessee (renter of property) that grants the lessee the right to use specific property, owned by the lessor, for a specific period of time in return for stipulated, and generally periodic, cash payments. (5) *Organization costs:* costs incurred in the formation of a corporation such as fees to underwriters for handling stock or bond issues, legal fees, state fees of various sorts, and certain promotional expenditures. (6) *Franchises and licenses:* a contractual arrangement under which the franchisor grants the franchisee the right to sell certain products or services, to use certain trademarks or trade names, or to perform certain functions, usually within a designated geographical area. (7) *Property rights:* such as water, mineral, solar, and wind, generally attached to a particular parcel of property.

4. **Explain the conceptual issues related to goodwill.** Goodwill is unique because unlike receivables, inventories, and patents that can be sold or exchanged individually in the marketplace, goodwill can be identified only with the business as a whole. Goodwill is a "going-concern" valuation and is recorded only when an entire business is purchased. Goodwill generated internally should not be capitalized in the accounts, because measuring the components of goodwill is simply too complex and associating any costs with future benefits too difficult. The future benefits of goodwill may have no relationship to the costs incurred in the development of that goodwill. Goodwill may exist even in the absence of specific costs to develop it.

5. **Describe the accounting procedures for recording goodwill.** To record goodwill, the fair market value of the net tangible and identifiable intangible assets are compared with the purchase price of the acquired business. The difference is considered goodwill. Goodwill is the residual—the excess of cost over fair value of the identifiable net assets acquired. Goodwill is often identified on the balance sheet as the excess of cost over the fair value of the net assets acquired.

6. **Identify the conceptual issues related to research and development costs.** R & D costs are not in themselves intangible assets, but research and development activities frequently result in the development of something that is patented or copyrighted. The difficulties in accounting for R & D expenditures are (1) identifying the costs associated with particular activities, projects, or achievements and (2) determining the magnitude of the future benefits and length of time over which such benefits may be realized. Because of these latter uncertainties, the FASB has standardized and simplified accounting practice

by requiring that all research and development costs be charged to expense when incurred.

7. **Describe the accounting procedures for research and development costs.** The costs associated with R & D activities and the accounting treatment accorded them are as follows: (1) *Materials, equipment, and facilities:* Expense the entire costs, unless the items have alternative future uses, then carry as inventory and allocate as consumed or capitalize and depreciate as used. (2) *Personnel:* Salaries, wages, and other related costs of personnel engaged in R & D should be expensed as incurred. (3) *Purchased intangibles:* Expense the entire cost, unless the items have alternative future uses, then capitalize and amortize. (4) *Contract services:* The costs of services performed by others in connection with the reporting company's R & D should be expensed as incurred. (5) *Indirect costs:* A reasonable allocation of indirect costs shall be included in R & D costs, except for general and administrative costs, which must be related to be included and expensed.

APPENDIX 12-A

ACCOUNTING FOR COMPUTER SOFTWARE COSTS

OBJECTIVE 8

After studying Appendix 12-A, you should be able to: Identify the accounting treatment for computer software costs.

The development of computer software products takes on increasing importance as our economy continues to change from a manufacturing process orientation (tangible outputs) to an information flow society (intangible outputs).[1] This short appendix discusses the basic issues involved in accounting for computer software.

▶ DIVERSITY IN PRACTICE

Computer software may be either **purchased** or **created** by a company. It may be purchased or created for **external use** (such as spreadsheet applications like Excel or Lotus 1-2-3) or for **internal use** (e.g., to establish a better internal accounting system). Should costs incurred in developing the computer software be expensed immediately or capitalized and amortized in the future? Prior to 1985, some companies expensed all software costs, and others capitalized such costs. Still others differentiated such costs on the basis of whether the computer software was purchased or created or whether it was used for external or internal purposes.

The issue is controversial because some companies' major assets are computer software programs. For example, Comserve (maker of software systems for manufacturing companies) at one time reported net income of $2.2 million. However, if Comserve were forced to expense the costs it incurred to develop software, this $2.2 million would become a loss of $1 million. And, if IBM had been forced to expense its $785 million

---

[1]A major contributing factor was IBM's decision in 1969 to "unbundle" its hardware and software, that is, to state the cost of the hardware and software separately. Prior to the unbundling, most applications software was provided free with the hardware. This unbundling led to the creation of a whole new industry, the software industry, whose members began selling software to hardware users. Today, there are more than 4,000 companies in the United States that develop software for sale.

"investment in program products" in 1985, its earnings would have been decreased by $443 million.

▶ THE PROFESSION'S POSITION

A major question is whether the costs involved in developing computer software are research and development costs. If they are actually R & D, then the profession requires that they be expensed as incurred. If they are not research and development costs, then a strong case can be made for capitalization. As one financial executive of a computer software company who argues for capitalization noted: "The key distinction between our spending and R & D is recoverability. We know we are developing something we can sell."

In an attempt to resolve this issue (at least for companies that sell computer software), the FASB issued *Statement of Financial Accounting Standards No. 86*, "Accounting for the Costs of Computer Software to Be Sold, Leased, or Otherwise Marketed."[2] The major recommendations of this pronouncement are:

(a) Costs incurred in creating a computer software product should be charged to research and development expense when incurred until **technological feasibility** has been established for the product.

(b) Technological feasibility is established upon completion of a detailed program design or working model.

In short, the FASB has taken a conservative position in regard to computer software costs. All costs must be expensed until the company has completed planning, designing, coding, and testing activities necessary to establish that the product can be produced to meet its design specifications. Subsequent costs incurred should be capitalized and amortized to current and future periods.

Two additional points should be emphasized. First, **if the computer software is purchased and it has alternative future uses, then it may be capitalized.** Second, **this standard applies only to the development of computer software that is to be sold, leased, or otherwise marketed to third parties** (i.e., for external use). Accounting for the costs of developing computer software for internal purposes is still open to question. The Board's position was that because most of the costs associated with developing computer software for internal purposes are already being expensed, there is no need for a standard in this area.[3]

▶ ACCOUNTING FOR CAPITALIZED COMPUTER SOFTWARE COSTS

If computer software costs are capitalized, then a proper amortization pattern for these costs must be established. **Companies are required to use the greater of (1) the ratio of current revenues to current and anticipated revenues (percent of revenue approach) or (2) the straight-line method over the remaining useful life of the asset (straight-line approach) as a basis for amortization.** These rules can result in the use of the ratio method one year and the straight-line method in another.

To illustrate, assume that AT&T has capitalized computer software costs of $10 million and its current (first-year) revenues from sales of this product are $4 million. AT&T anticipates earning $16 million in additional future revenues from this product, which

---

[2]"Accounting for the Cost of Computer Software to Be Sold, Leased, or Otherwise Marketed," *Statement of Financial Accounting Standards No. 86* (Stamford, Conn.: FASB, 1985).

[3]Although the FASB did not address accounting for computer software **purchased or created for internal use,** a committee of the Institute of Management Accountants published an issues paper of "suggested accounting treatment" on the topic: The Management Accounting Practices Committee, "Accounting for Software Used Internally," *Issues Paper* (Montvale, NJ: NAA, 1985), 24 pp.

is estimated to have an economic life of 4 years. Using the percent of revenue approach, the current (first) year's amortization would be $2 million ($10,000,000 × $4,000,000/$20,000,000). Using the straight-line approach, the amortization would be $2.5 million ($10,000,000/4 years). Thus the straight-line approach would be employed because it results in the greater amortization charge.

▶ REPORTING COMPUTER SOFTWARE COSTS

Because much concern exists about the reliability of an asset such as computer software, the Board indicated that capitalized computer software costs should be valued at the **lower of unamortized cost or net realizable value.** If net realizable value is lower, then the capitalized computer software costs should be written down to this value. Once written down, it **may not be written back up.** In addition to the regular disclosures for R & D costs, the following should be reported in the financial statements:

(a) Unamortized computer software costs.

(b) The total amount charged to expense and amounts, if any, written down to net realizable value.

Once again these accounting and reporting requirements apply only to computer software **developed for external purposes.**

An example of software development cost disclosure, taken from the annual report of Moscom Corporation, is shown below.

ILLUSTRATION 12A-1
Disclosure of Software
Development Costs

Moscom Corporation

Balance Sheet	1989	($000)	1988
Other Assets:			
License fees (net of accumulated amortization of $652,013 and $319,878, respectively)	501		736
Software development costs (net of accumulated amortization of $1,567,330 and $814,500, respectively) (Note D)	1,038		1,163
Excess purchase price over net assets acquired (net of accumulated amortization of $318,391, and $63,678, respectively) (Note K)	2,228		2,483
Deposits and other assets	88		84

	Year Ended December 31,		
Income Statement	1989	1988	1987
Sales	$13,619	$10,595	$8,530
Costs and Operating Expenses:			
Cost of sales	5,112	3,344	2,738
Engineering and software development (Note D)	958	855	1,498

Significant Accounting Policies

Software development costs meeting recoverability tests are capitalized under *Statement of Financial Accounting Standards No. 86.* The cost of software capitalized is amortized on a product-by-product basis over its economic life, generally three years, or the ratio of current revenues to current and anticipated revenues from such software, whichever provides the greater amortization. There were no amounts written down to net realizable value during the years ended December 31, 1989, 1988 and 1987.

Note D: Engineering and Software Development Costs

	Year Ended December 31,		
	1989	1988	1987
Total expenditures for engineering and software development	$1,750,563	$1,797,495	$1,916,428
Less:			
Amounts capitalized under Statement of Financial Accounting Standards No. 86	(792,295)	(942,470)	(418,059)
Engineering and software development expense	$ 958,268	$ 855,025	$1,498,369

Amortization expense of software development costs was approximately $917,000, $528,000 and $185,000 for the years ended December 31, 1989, 1988 and 1987, respectively.

▶ SETTING STANDARDS FOR SOFTWARE ACCOUNTING

"It's unreasonable to expense all software costs, and it's unreasonable to capitalize all software costs," says Joseph Smith, IBM's director of financial reporting. "If you subscribe to those two statements, then it follows that there is somewhere in between where development ends and capitalization begins. Now you have to define that point."[4] The FASB defined that point as "technological feasibility," which is established upon completion of a detailed program design or working model. The difficulty of applying this criterion to software is that, "there is no such thing as a real, specific, baseline design. But you could make it look like you have one as early or as late as you like," says Osman Erlop of Hambrecht & Quist.[5] That is, if you wish to capitalize, draw up a detailed program design quickly. If you want to expense lots of development costs, simply hold off writing a detailed program design. And, once capitalized, the costs are amortized over the useful life specified by the developer, which because of either constant redesign or supersession is generally quite short (2 to 4 years).

As another example, some companies "manage by the numbers"; that is, they are very careful to identify projects that are worthwhile and capitalize the computer software costs associated with them. They believe that good projects must be capitalized and amortized in the future; otherwise, the concept of properly matching expense and revenues is abused.

Other companies choose not to manage by the numbers and simply expense all these costs. Companies that expense all these costs have no use for a standard that requires capitalization. In their view, it would mean only that a more complex, more expensive cost accounting system would be required, one that would provide little if any benefit.

Financial analysts have reacted almost uniformly against any capitalization. They believe computer software costs should be expensed because of the rapid obsolescence of computer software and the potential for abuse that may result from capitalizing costs inappropriately. As Donald Kirk, former chairman of the FASB stated: "The Board is now faced with the problem of balancing what it thought was good theory with the costs for some companies of implementing a new accounting system with the concerns of users about the potential for abuse of the standard."[6]

Resolving the computer software accounting problem again demonstrates the difficulty of establishing reporting standards.

▶ SUMMARY OF LEARNING OBJECTIVE FOR APP. 12-A ◀

8. **Identify the accounting treatment for computer software costs.**   Costs incurred in creating a computer software product should be charged to R & D expense when incurred until technological feasibility has been established for the product. Subsequent costs should be capitalized and amortized to current and future periods. Computer software that is purchased for sale or lease to third parties and has alternative future uses may be capitalized and amortized using the greater of the percent of revenue approach or the straight-line approach.

---

[4]"When Does Life Begin?" *Forbes,* June 16, 1986, pp. 72–74.

[5]Ibid.

[6]Donald J. Kirk, "Growing Temptation & Rising Expectation = Accelerating Regulation," *FASB Viewpoints,* June 12, 1985, p. 7.

APPENDIX 12-B

VALUING GOODWILL

OBJECTIVE 9

After studying Appendix 12-B, you should be able to: Explain various approaches to valuing goodwill.

In this chapter we discussed the generally accepted method of measuring and recording goodwill as the excess of cost over fair value of the identifiable net assets acquired in a business acquisition. Accountants are frequently asked to participate in the valuation of businesses as part of a planned business acquisition.

To determine the purchase price for a business and the resulting goodwill is a difficult and inexact process. As indicated, it is often possible to determine the fair value of identifiable assets. But how does a buyer value intangible factors like good management, good credit rating, and so on?

▶ EXCESS EARNINGS APPROACH

One method is called the **excess earnings approach**. Using this approach, the total earning power that the company commands is computed. The next step is to calculate "normal earnings" by determining the normal rate of return on assets in that industry. **The difference between what the firm earns and what is normal in the industry is referred to as the excess earning power.** This extra earning power indicates that there are unidentifiable values (intangible assets) that provide this increased earning power. Finding the value of goodwill then is a matter of discounting these excess future earnings to the present.

This approach appears to be a systematic and logical way of determining goodwill. However, each factor necessary to compute a value under this approach is subject to question. Generally, the problems relate to getting answers to the following questions:

1. What is a normal rate of return?
2. How does one determine the future earnings?
3. What discount rate should be applied to the excess earnings?
4. Over what period should the excess earnings be discounted?

FINDING A NORMAL RATE OF RETURN

Determining the normal rate of return for tangible and identifiable intangible assets requires analysis of companies similar to the enterprise in question. An industry average may be determined by examining annual reports or data from statistical services. Suppose that a rate of 15% is decided as normal for a concern such as Tractorling (see page 580). In this case, the normal earnings are calculated in the following manner.[1]

ILLUSTRATION 12B-1
Calculation of Normal Earnings

Fair market value of Tractorling's net identifiable assets	$350,000
Normal rate of return	15%
Normal earnings	$ 52,500

---

[1]The fair value of Tractorling's assets (rather than historical cost) is used to compute the normal profit, because fair value is closer to the true value of the company's assets exclusive of goodwill.

DETERMINING FUTURE EARNINGS

The starting point for determining future earnings is normally the past earnings of the enterprise. Although estimates of future earnings are needed, the past often provides useful information concerning the enterprise's future earnings potential. Past earnings—generally 3 to 6 years—are also useful because estimates of the future are usually overly optimistic; the hard facts of previous periods bring a sobering reality to the negotiations.

Tractorling's net earnings for the last 5 years are as follows:

ILLUSTRATION 12B-2
Calculation of Average
Earnings

Earnings History—Tractorling		
1991	$ 60,000	Average Earnings
1992	55,000	
1993	110,000[a]	$\dfrac{\$375,000}{5} = \$75,000$
1994	70,000	
1995	80,000	
	$375,000	

[a]Includes extraordinary gain of $25,000.

The average net earnings for the last 5 years is $75,000 or a rate of return of approximately 21.4% on the current value of the assets excluding goodwill ($75,000 ÷ $350,000). Before we go further, however, we need to know whether $75,000 is representative of the future earnings of this enterprise.

Often past earnings of a company to be acquired need to be evaluated on the basis of the acquirer's own accounting procedures. Suppose, that in determining earning power, Multi-Diversified measures earnings in relation to a FIFO inventory valuation figure rather than LIFO, which Tractorling employs, and that the use of LIFO reduced Tractorling's net income by $2,000 per year. In addition, Tractorling uses accelerated depreciation while Multi-Diversified uses straight-line. As a result, Tractorling's earnings were lower by $3,000.

Also, assets discovered on examination that might affect the earnings flow should be considered. Patent costs not previously recorded should be amortized, say, at the rate of $1,000 per period. Finally because the estimate of the future earnings is what we are attempting to determine, some items, like the extraordinary gain of $25,000, probably should not be considered. An analysis can now be made as follows:

ILLUSTRATION 12B-3
Calculation of Adjusted
Net Earnings

Average net earnings per Tractorling computation		$75,000
Add		
Adjustment for switch from LIFO to FIFO	$2,000	
Adjustment for change from accelerated to		
straight-line approach	3,000	5,000
		80,000
Deduct		
Extraordinary gain ($25,000 ÷ 5)	5,000	
Patent amortization on straight-line basis	1,000	6,000
Adjusted average net earnings of Tractorling		$74,000

The excess earnings would be determined to be $21,500 ($74,000 − $52,500).

CHOOSING A DISCOUNT RATE TO APPLY TO EXCESS EARNINGS

Determining the discount rate is a fairly subjective estimate.[2] **The lower the discount rate, the higher the value of the goodwill and vice versa.** To illustrate, assume that the excess earnings are $21,500 and that these earnings will continue indefinitely. If the excess earnings are capitalized at, say, a rate of 25% in perpetuity,[3] the results are:

ILLUSTRATION 12B-4
Capitalization of Excess Earnings at 25% in Perpetuity

Capitalization at 25%
$\dfrac{\text{Excess earnings}}{\text{Capitalization rate}} \quad \dfrac{\$21,500}{.25} = \$86,000$

If the excess earnings are capitalized in perpetuity at a somewhat lower rate, say 15%, a much higher goodwill figure results.

ILLUSTRATION 12B-5
Capitalization of Excess Earnings at 15% in Perpetuity

Capitalization at 15%
$\dfrac{\text{Excess earnings}}{\text{Capitalization rate}} \quad \dfrac{\$21,500}{.15} = \$143,333$

Because the continuance of excess profits is uncertain, a conservative rate (higher than the normal rate) is usually employed. Factors that are considered in determining the rate are the stability of past earnings, the speculative nature of the business, and general economic conditions.

CHOOSING A DISCOUNTING PERIOD FOR EXCESS EARNINGS

Determining the period over which excess earnings will exist is perhaps the most difficult problem associated with computing goodwill. If it is assumed that the excess earnings will last indefinitely, then goodwill is $143,333 as computed in the previous section (assuming a rate of 15%).

Another method of computing goodwill that gives the same answer, using the normal return of 15%, is to discount the total average earnings of the company and subtract the fair market value of the net identifiable assets as shown in Illustration 12B-6.

---

[2]The following illustration shows how the capitalization rate might be computed for a small business:

A Method of Selecting a Capitalization Rate

Long-term U.S. government bond rate	10%
Plus: Average premium return on small stocks over U.S. government bonds	<u>10</u>
Expected total rate of return on small publicly held stocks	20
Plus: Premium for greater risk and illiquidity	<u>6</u>
Total required expected rate of return, including inflation component	26
Less: Consensus long-term inflation expectation	<u>6</u>
Capitalization rate to apply to current earnings	<u><u>20%</u></u>

From Warren Kissin and Ronald Zulli, "Valuation of a Closely Held Business," *The Journal of Accountancy* (June 1988), p. 42.

[3]Why do we divide by the capitalization rate to arrive at the goodwill amount? Recall that the present value of an ordinary annuity is equal to:

$$P_{\overline{n}|i} = \frac{1 - \dfrac{1}{(1 + i)^n}}{i}$$

When a number is capitalized into perpetuity, $(1 + i)^n$ becomes so large that $1/(1 + i)^n$ essentially equals zero, which leaves $1/i$ or, as in the case above, $21,500/.25$.

Average earnings capitalized at 15% in perpetuity		
($74,000 ÷ 15%)		$493,333
Less fair market value of net identifiable assets		350,000
Present value of estimated earnings (goodwill)		$143,333

ILLUSTRATION 12B-6
Capitalization of Average Earnings Less Fair Value of Net Assets

Frequently, however, the excess earnings are assumed to last a limited number of years, say 10, and then it is necessary to discount these earnings only over that time. Assume that Multi-Diversified believes that the excess earnings of Tractorling will last 10 years and, because of the uncertainty surrounding this earning power, uses 25% as an appropriate rate of return. The present value of an annuity of $21,500 ($74,000 − $52,500) discounted at 25% for 10 years is $76,766.[4] That is the amount that Multi-Diversified should be willing to pay above the fair value of net identifiable assets.

▶ OTHER METHODS OF VALUATION[5]

Some accountants fail to discount but simply multiply the excess earnings by the number of years they believe the excess earnings will continue. This approach, often referred to as the **number of years method,** is used to provide a rough measure for the goodwill factor. The approach has only the advantage of simplicity; it is sounder to recognize the discount factor.

An even simpler method is one that relies on multiples of average yearly earnings that are paid for other companies in the same industry. If Skyward Airlines was recently acquired for five times its average yearly earnings of $50 million, or $250 million, then Worldwide Airways, a close competitor, with $80 million in average yearly earnings would be worth $400 million.

Another method (similar to discounting excess earnings) is the **discounted free cash flow method,** which involves a projection of the acquired company's free cash flow over a long period, typically 10 or 20 years. The method first projects into the future a dozen or so important financial variables, including production, prices, noncash expenses (such as depreciation and amortization), taxes, and capital outlays, all adjusted for inflation. The objective is to determine the amount of cash that will accumulate over a specified number of years. The present value of the free cash flows is then computed. This amount represents the price to be paid for the business.[6]

For example, if Magnaputer Company is expected to generate $1 million a year for 20 years, and the buyer's rate-of-return objective is 15%, the buyer would be willing to pay about $6.26 million for Magnaputer Company. (The present value of $1 million to be received for 20 years discounted at 15% is $6,259,330.)

In practice, prospective buyers use a variety of methods to produce a "valuation curve" or range of prices. But the actual price paid may be more a factor of the buyer's or seller's ego and horse-trading acumen.

Valuation of goodwill is at best a highly uncertain process. The estimated value of goodwill depends on a number of factors, all of which are extremely tenuous and subject to bargaining.

---

[4]The present value of an annuity of one dollar received in a steady stream for 10 years in the future discounted at 25% is 3.57050, (3.57050 × $21,500 = $76,766).

[5]One article lists three "asset-based approaches" (tangible net worth, adjusted book value, and price-book value ratio methods) and three "earnings-based approaches" (capitalization of earnings, capitalization of excess earnings, and discounted cash flow methods) as the popular methods for valuing closely held businesses. See Warren Rissin and Ronald Zulli, "Valuation of a Closely Held Business," *The Journal of Accountancy* (June 1988), pp. 38–44.

[6]Tim Metz, "Deciding How Much a Company Is Worth Often Depends on Whose Side You're On," *The Wall Street Journal,* March 18, 1981.

► **SUMMARY OF LEARNING OBJECTIVE FOR APP. 12-B** ◄

9. Explain various approaches to valuing goodwill. One method of valuing goodwill is the excess earnings approach. Using this approach, the total earning power that the company commands is computed. The next step is to calculate "normal earnings" by determining the normal rate of return on assets in that industry. The difference between what the firm earns and what is normal in the industry is referred to as the excess earning power. This excess earning power indicates that there are unidentifiable values that provide the increased earning power. Finding the value of goodwill then is a matter of discounting these excess future earnings to the present. The number of years method of valuing goodwill, which simply multiplies the excess earnings by the number of years of expected excess earnings, is used to provide a rough measure for the goodwill factor. A third method of valuing goodwill is the discounted free cash flow method, which projects the amount of cash that will accumulate over a specified number of years and then finds the present value of that amount as today's value of the firm.

Note: All **asterisked** Questions, Exercises, Problems, and Cases relate to material contained in the appendix to each chapter.

QUESTIONS

1. What are the major accounting problems related to accounting for intangibles?

2. Accounting authors and practitioners have proposed various solutions to the problems of accounting in terms of historical cost for goodwill and similar intangibles. What problems of accounting for goodwill and similar intangibles are comparable to those of accounting for plant assets? What problems are different?

3. Many accountants advocate the abandonment of historical cost for plant assets but argue that historical cost should be used in accounting for intangible assets. Are the two viewpoints inconsistent?

4. Intangible assets may be classified on a number of different bases. Indicate three different bases and illustrate how intangibles could be subdivided into these groupings.

5. What are some examples of internally created intangibles? Why does the accounting profession make a distinction between internally created "goodwill type" intangibles and other intangibles?

6. In 1994, Navajo Corp. spent $400,000 for "goodwill" visits by sales personnel to key customers. The purpose of these visits was to build a solid, friendly relationship for the future and to gain insight into the problems and needs of the companies served. How should this expenditure be reported?

7. State the generally accepted accounting procedures for the amortization and writedown or writeoff of capitalized intangible assets.

8. It has been argued, on the grounds of conservatism, that all intangible assets should be written off immediately after acquisition. Give the accounting arguments against this treatment.

9. Hopi Company spent $175,000 developing a new process, $40,000 in legal fees to obtain a patent, and $87,000 to market the process that was patented, all in the year 1995. How should these costs be accounted for in 1995?

10. Indicate the period of time over which each of the following should be amortized.
    (a) Research and development costs.
    (b) Trademarks.
    (c) Goodwill.
    (d) A 25-year lease with payments of $75,000 per year on property with an estimated useful life of 50 years. The lessee has the option to renew the lease for 25 additional years at $5,000 per year.
    (e) Franchises.
    (f) Patents.
    (g) Leasehold improvements.
    (h) Copyrights.

11. What is a lease prepayment? What are property rights capitalized by the lessee? What are leasehold improvements? Should any of these items be classified as an intangible asset?

12. On January 1, 1989, an intangible asset with a 35-year estimated useful life was acquired. On January 1, 1994, a review was made of the estimated useful life, and it was determined that the intangible asset had an estimated useful life of 45 more years. Assuming that the company wants to amortize this intangible over the maximum period possible, how many more years may this intangible be amortized?

13. Recently Paunee Corporation entered into a lease agreement with Eagle Developers, Inc. to lease some land for 25 years in southwest New Mexico. Paunee Corporation as lessee then built on this site a number of apartment buildings having a useful life of 35 years. The lease agreement states that the lessee has the option to renew the lease for another 20 years. Over what period should the apartments be depreciated?

14. Recently, a group of university students decided to incorporate for the purposes of selling a process to recycle the waste product from manufacturing cheese. Some of the initial costs involved were legal fees and office expenses incurred in starting the business, state incorporation fees, and stamp taxes. One student wishes to charge these costs against revenue in the current period; another wishes to defer these costs and amortize them in the future; and another believes these costs should be netted against common stock. Which student is correct?

15. What is goodwill? What is negative goodwill?

16. Under what circumstances is it appropriate to record goodwill in the accounts? How should goodwill, properly recorded on the books, be amortized in order to conform with generally accepted accounting principles?

17. In examining financial statements, financial analysts often write off goodwill immediately. Evaluate this procedure.

18. What is the nature of research and development costs? What other costs have similar characteristics?

19. Research and development activities may include (a) personnel costs, (b) materials and equipment costs, and (c) indirect costs. What is the recommended accounting treatment for these three types of R & D costs?

20. Which of the following activities should be expensed currently as R & D costs:
    (a) Testing in search for or evaluation of product or process alternatives.
    (b) Engineering follow-through in an early phase of commercial production.
    (c) Legal work in connection with patent applications or litigation, and the sale or licensing of patents.
    (d) Adaptation of an existing capability to a particular requirement or customer's need as a part of continuing commercial activity.

21. During the current year R&D Railroad spent $600,000 to develop a computer program that will assist in identifying and locating all of its rolling equipment. How should R&D account for this expenditure?

22. In 1994, Iroquois Corporation developed a new product that will be marketed in 1995. In connection with the development of this product, the following costs were incurred in 1994: research and development departmental costs, $400,000; materials and supplies consumed, $50,000; compensation paid to research consultants, $80,000. It is anticipated that these costs will be recovered in 1997. What is the amount of research and development costs that Iroquois should record in 1994 as a charge to expense?

23. An intangible asset with an estimated useful life of 30 years was acquired on January 1, 1985 for $360,000. On January 1, 1995, a review was made of intangible assets and their expected service lives and it was determined that this asset had an estimated useful life of 35 more years from the date of the review. What is the amount of amortization for this intangible asset for 1995?

*24. An article in the financial press stated "More than half of software maker Comserve's net worth is in a pile of tapes and ring-bound books. That raises some accountants' eyebrows." What is the profession's position regarding the incurrence of costs for computer software that will be sold?

*25. Osage, Inc. has incurred $3 million in developing a computer software product for sale to third parties. Of the $3 million costs incurred, $2 million is capitalized. The product produced from this development work has generated $1 million in 1995 and is anticipated to generate another $4 million in future years. The estimated useful life of the project is 4 years. How much of the capitalized costs should be amortized in 1995?

*26. In 1995 Teton Software developed a software package for assisting calculus instruction in business colleges, at a cost of $1,000,000. Although there are tens of thousands of calculus students in the market, college instructors seem to change their minds frequently on the use of teaching aids. And, not one package has yet been ordered or delivered. Prepare an argument to advocate expensing the development cost in the current year. Offer an argument for capitalizing the development cost over its estimated useful life. Which stakeholders are harmed or benefited by either approach?

*27. Explain how "average excess earnings" are determined. What is the justification for the use of this method of estimating goodwill?

*28. Discuss two methods for estimating the value of goodwill in determining the amount that should properly be paid for it.

EXERCISES

E12-1 (Classification Issues—Intangibles) Presented below is a list of items that could be included in the intangible asset section of the balance sheet.

1. Investment in a subsidiary company.
2. Timberland.
3. Cost of engineering activity required to advance the design of a product to the manufacturing stage.
4. Lease prepayment (6 months' rent paid in advance).
5. Cost of equipment obtained under a capital lease.
6. Retained earnings appropriation.
7. Costs incurred in the formation of a corporation.
8. Operating losses incurred in the start-up of a business.
9. Sinking fund for repayment of bonds.
10. Cost of a franchise.
11. Goodwill generated internally.
12. Cost of testing in search for product alternatives.
13. Cost of developing computer software for internal use.
14. Goodwill acquired in the purchase of a business.
15. Cost of developing a patent.
16. Cost of purchasing a patent from an inventor.
17. Legal costs incurred in securing a patent.
18. Unrecovered costs of a successful legal suit to protect the patent.
19. Cost of modifying the design of a product or process.
20. Cost of acquiring a copyright.
21. Research and development costs.
22. Long-term receivables.
23. Cost of developing a trademark.
24. Cost of securing a trademark.

Instructions

(a) Indicate which items on the list above would generally be reported as intangible assets in the balance sheet.

(b) Indicate how, if at all, the items not reportable as intangible assets would be reported in the financial statements.

E12-2 (Classification Issues—Intangibles) Presented below is selected account information related to Nez Perce Inc. as of December 31, 1995. All these accounts have debit balances.

Cable television franchises	Film contract rights
Music copyrights	Customer lists
Research and development costs	Prepaid expenses
Goodwill	Covenants not to compete
Cash	Brand names
Discount on notes payable	Notes receivable
Accounts receivable	Investments in affiliated companies
Property, plant, and equipment	Organization cost
Leasehold improvements	Land

Instructions

Identify which items should be classified as an intangible asset. For those items not classified as an intangible asset, indicate where they would be reported in the financial statements.

E12-3 (Classification Issues—Intangible Asset) Mohegan Inc. has the following amounts included in its general ledger at December 31, 1995:

Organization costs	$22,000
Trademarks	15,000
Discount on bonds payable	40,000
Deposits with advertising agency for ads to promote goodwill of company	10,000
Excess of cost over book value of net assets of acquired subsidiary	75,000
Cost of equipment acquired for research and development projects	90,000
Costs of developing a secret formula for a product	
that is expected to be marketed for at least 20 years	80,000

Instructions

(a) On the basis of the information above, compute the total amount to be reported by Mohegan for intangible assets on its balance sheet at December 31, 1995. Equipment has alternative future use.

(b) If an item is not to be included in intangible assets, explain its proper treatment for reporting purposes.

E12-4 (Intangible Amortization) Presented below is selected information for Arawak Company. Answer each of the factual situations.

1. Arawak purchased a patent from Huron Co. for $900,000 on January 1, 1992. The patent is being amortized over its remaining legal life of 10 years, expiring on January 1, 2002. During 1994, Arawak determined that the economic benefits of the patent would not last longer than 5 years from the date of acquisition. What amount should be reported in the balance sheet for the patent, net of accumulated amortization, at December 31, 1994?

2. Arawak bought a franchise from Kansa Co. on January 1, 1993 for $300,000. It is estimated that the franchise has a useful life of 60 years. Its carrying amount on Kansa's books at January 1, 1993 was $400,000. Arawak has decided to amortize the franchise over the maximum period permitted. What amount should be amortized for the year ended December 31, 1994?

3. On January 1, 1990, Arawak incurred organization costs of $250,000. Arawak is amortizing these costs on the same basis as the maximum allowable for federal income tax purposes. What amount should be reported as unamortized organization costs as of December 31, 1994?

E12-5 (Correct Intangible Asset Account) As the recently appointed auditor for Pequot Corporation, you have been asked to examine selected accounts before the 6-month financial statements of June 30, 1995, are prepared. The controller for Pequot Corporation mentions that only one account (shown below) is kept for Intangible Assets.

Intangible Assets

		Debit	Credit	Balance
January 4	Research and development costs	920,000		920,000
January 5	Legal costs to obtain patent	75,000		995,000
January 31	Payment of 7 months' rent on property			
	leased by Pequot	77,000		1,072,000
February 1	Stock issue costs	36,000		1,108,000
February 11	Premium on common stock		250,000	858,000
March 31	Unamortized bond discount on bonds			
	due March 31, 2015	84,000		942,000
April 30	Promotional expenses related to			
	start-up of business	207,000		1,149,000
June 30	Operating losses for first 6 months	241,000		1,390,000

Instructions

Prepare the entry or entries necessary to correct this account. Assume that the patent has a useful life of 10 years, and that organization costs are being amortized over a 5-year period.

E12-6 (Recording and Amortization of Intangibles) Wyandot Company, organized in 1995, has set up a single account for all intangible assets. The following summary discloses the debit entries that have been recorded during 1996.

1/2/96	Purchased patent (7-year life)	$ 350,000
4/1/96	Goodwill purchased (indefinite life)	360,000
7/1/96	10-year franchise; expiration date 7/1/2006	450,000
8/1/96	Payment for copyright (4-year life)	160,000
9/1/96	Research and development costs	185,000
		$1,505,000

Instructions

Prepare the necessary entries to clear the Intangible Asset account and to set up separate accounts for distinct types of intangibles. Make the entries as of December 31, 1996, recording any necessary amortization and reflecting all balances accurately as of that date.

E12-7 (Accounting for Trade Name) In early January of 1995, Drastic Plastic Corporation applied for a trade name, incurring legal costs of $12,000. In January of 1996, Drastic Plastic incurred $7,800 of legal fees in a successful defense of its trade name.

Instructions
   (a) Compute 1995 amortization, 12/31/95 book value, 1996 amortization, and 12/31/96 book value if the company amortizes the tradename over the maximum allowable life.
   (b) Repeat part (a), assuming a useful life of 5 years.

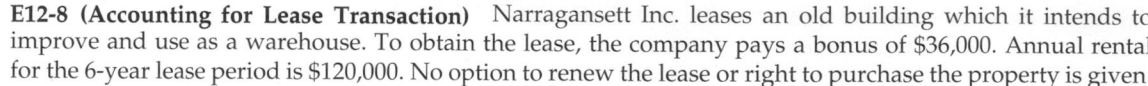

E12-8 (Accounting for Lease Transaction) Narragansett Inc. leases an old building which it intends to improve and use as a warehouse. To obtain the lease, the company pays a bonus of $36,000. Annual rental for the 6-year lease period is $120,000. No option to renew the lease or right to purchase the property is given.

   After the lease is obtained, improvements costing $150,000 are made. The building has an estimated remaining useful life of 17 years.

Instructions
   (a) What is the annual cost (excluding depreciation) of this lease to Narragansett Inc.?
   (b) What amount of annual depreciation, if any, on a straight-line basis should Narragansett record?

E12-9 (Accounting for Organization Costs) Erie Corporation was organized in 1994 and began operations at the beginning of 1995. The company is involved in interior design consulting services. The following costs were incurred prior to the start of operations:

Attorney's fees in connection with organization of the company	$15,000
Improvements to leased offices prior to occupancy	25,000
Fees to underwriters for handling stock issue	4,000
Costs of meetings of incorporators to discuss organizational activities	5,000
State filing fees to incorporate	1,000
	$50,000

Instructions
   (a) Compute the total amount of organization costs incurred by Erie.
   (b) Assuming Erie Corporation is amortizing organization costs for financial reporting purposes on the same basis as the maximum amount allowable for federal income tax purposes, prepare the journal entry to amortize organization costs for 1995.

E12-10 (Accounting for Patents, Franchises, and R&D) Inuit Company has provided information on intangible assets as follows:

   A patent was purchased from Zuni Company for $1,800,000 on January 1, 1995. Inuit estimated the remaining useful life of the patent to be 10 years. The patent was carried in Zuni's accounting records at a net book value of $2,000,000 when Zuni sold it to Inuit.

   During 1996, a franchise was purchased from the Laguna Company for $480,000. In addition, 5% of revenue from the franchise must be paid to Laguna. Revenue from the franchise for 1996 was $2,500,000. Inuit estimates the useful life of the franchise to be 10 years and takes a full year's amortization in the year of purchase.

   Inuit incurred research and development costs in 1996 as follows:

Materials and equipment	$142,000
Personnel	176,000
Indirect costs	102,000
	$420,000

Inuit estimates that these costs will be recouped by December 31, 1999.

   On January 1, 1996, Inuit, because of recent events in the field, estimates that the remaining life of the patent purchased on January 1, 1995, is only 5 years from January 1, 1996.

Instructions
   (a) Prepare a schedule showing the intangibles section of Inuit's balance sheet at December 31, 1996. Show supporting computations in good form.
   (b) Prepare a schedule showing the income statement effect for the year ended December 31, 1996, as a result of the facts above. Show supporting computations in good form.

(AICPA adapted)

E12-11 (Accounting for Patents) Pueblo Inc. has its own research department. In addition, the company purchases patents from time to time. The following statements summarize the transactions involving all patents now owned by the company.

During 1989 and 1990, $153,000 was spent developing a new process that was patented (No. 1) on March 18, 1991; additional legal and other costs were $16,320. A patent (No. 2) developed by Ben Franklin, an inventor, was purchased for $60,000 on November 30, 1992, on which date it had 12½ years yet to run.

During 1991, 1992, and 1993, research and development activities cost $170,000. No additional patents resulted from these activities.

A patent infringement suit brought by the company against a competitor because of the manufacture of articles infringing on Patent No. 2 was successfully prosecuted at a cost of $14,200. A decision in the case was rendered in July, 1993.

A competing patent (No. 3) was purchased for $57,600 on July 1, 1994. This patent had 16 years yet to run. During 1995, $60,000 has been expended on patent development: $20,000 of this amount represents the cost of a device for which a patent application has been filed, but no notification of acceptance or rejection by the Patent Office has been received. The other $40,000 represents costs incurred on uncompleted development projects.

Instructions
- **(a)** Compute the carrying value of these patents as of December 31, 1995, assuming that the legal life and useful life of each patent is the same and that each patent is to be amortized from the first day of the month following its acquisition.
- **(b)** Prepare a journal entry to record amortization for 1995.

E12-12 (Accounting for Patents) During 1992, the Yakima Corporation spent $90,000 in research and development costs. As a result, a new product called the Barney was patented at additional legal and other costs of $15,000. The patent was obtained on October 1, 1992, and had a legal life of 17 years and a useful life of 10 years.

Instructions
- **(a)** Prepare all journal entries required in 1992 and 1993 as a result of the transactions above.
- **(b)** On June 1, 1994, Yakima spent $11,500 to successfully prosecute a patent infringement. As a result, the estimate of useful life was extended to 12 years from June 1, 1994. Prepare all journal entries required in 1994 and 1995.
- **(c)** In 1996, Yakima determined that a competitor's product would make the Barney obsolete and the patent worthless by December 31, 1997. Prepare all journal entries required in 1996 and 1997.

E12-13 (Accounting for Goodwill) On July 1, 1995, Mohave Corporation purchased Hupa Company by paying $200,000 cash and issuing a $100,000 note payable to Sam Hupa. At July 1, 1995, the balance sheet of Hupa Company was as follows:

Cash	$ 50,000	Accounts payable	$200,000
Receivables	90,000	Hupa, capital	235,000
Inventory	100,000		$435,000
Land	40,000		
Buildings (net)	75,000		
Equipment (net)	70,000		
Trademarks	10,000		
	$435,000		

The recorded amounts all approximate current values except for land (worth $60,000), inventory (worth $125,000), and trademarks (worthless).

Instructions
- **(a)** Prepare the July 1 entry for Mohave Corporation to record the purchase.
- **(b)** Prepare the December 31 entry for Mohave Corporation to record amortization of goodwill. The goodwill is estimated to have a useful life of 50 years.

E12-14 (Intangible Impairment) Presented below is information related to copyrights owned by Who Company at December 31, 1996.

Cost	$8,600,000
Carrying amount	4,300,000
Expected future net cash flows	4,000,000
Fair value	3,400,000

Assume that Who Company will continue to use this copyright in the future. As of December 31, 1996, the copyright is estimated to have a remaining useful life of 10 years.

Instructions

(a) Prepare the journal entry (if any) to record the impairment of the asset at December 31, 1996. The company does not use accumulated amortization accounts.

(b) Prepare the journal entry to record amortization expense for 1997 related to the copyrights.

(c) The fair value of the copyright at December 31, 1997 is $3,700,000. Prepare the journal entry (if any) necessary to record the increase in fair value.

E12-15 (Goodwill Impairment) Presented below is net asset information (including associated goodwill of $200 million) related to the Nuc-Air Division of Pearl, Inc.

Nuc-Air Division
NET ASSETS
as of December 31, 1996
(in millions)

Cash	$ 50,000
Receivables	200,000
Property, plant, and equipment (net)	2,600,000
Goodwill	200,000
Less: Notes payable	(2,700,000)
Net assets	$ 350,000

The purpose of this division is to develop a nuclear-powered aircraft. If successful, traveling delays associated with refueling could be substantially reduced. Many other benefits would also occur. To date, management has not had much success and is deciding whether a writedown at this time is appropriate. Management estimated its future net cash flows from the project to be $300 million. Management has also received an offer to purchase the division for $210 million.

Instructions

(a) Prepare the journal entry (if any) to record the impairment at December 31, 1996.

(b) At December 31, 1997, it is estimated that the division's fair value increased to $240 million. Prepare the journal entry (if any) to record this increase in fair value.

E12-16 (Accounting for R & D Costs) Blackfoot Company from time to time embarks on a research program when a special project seems to offer possibilities. In 1995 the company expends $300,000 on a research project, but by the end of 1995 it is impossible to determine whether any benefit will be derived from it.

Instructions

(a) What account should be charged for the $300,000, and how should it be shown in the financial statements?

(b) The project is completed in 1996, and a successful patent is obtained. The R & D costs to complete the project are $100,000. The administrative and legal expenses incurred in obtaining patent number 472-1001-84 in 1996 total $14,000. The patent has an expected useful life of 5 years. Record these costs in journal entry form. Also, record patent amortization (full year) in 1996.

(c) In 1997 the company successfully defends the patent in extended litigation at a cost of $48,000, thereby extending the patent life to 12/31/04. What is the proper way to account for this cost? Also, record patent amortization (full year) in 1997.

(d) Additional engineering and consulting costs incurred in 1997 required to advance the design of a product to the manufacturing stage total $60,000. These costs enhance the design of the product considerably. Discuss the proper accounting treatment for this cost.

E12-17 (Accounting for R & D Costs) The Winnebago Company incurred the following costs during 1995:

Quality control during commercial production, including routine testing of products	$58,000
Laboratory research aimed at discovery of new knowledge	68,000
Testing for evaluation of new products	24,000
Modification of the formulation of a plastics product	6,000
Engineering follow-through in an early phase of commercial production	15,000

Adaptation of an existing capability to a particular
   requirement or customer's need as a part of continuing
   commercial activity
	13,000

Trouble-shooting in connection with breakdowns during commercial production	29,000
Searching for applications of new research findings	19,000

Instructions

Compute the total amount Winnebago should classify and expense as research and development costs for 1995.

E12-18 (Accounting for R & D Costs) Crow Company incurred the following costs during 1995 in connection with its research and development activities:

Cost of equipment acquired that will have alternative uses in future research and development projects over the next 5 years (uses straight-line depreciation)	$280,000
Materials consumed in research and development projects	59,000
Consulting fees paid to outsiders for research and development projects	100,000
Personnel costs of persons involved in research and development projects	98,000
Indirect costs reasonably allocable to research and development projects	50,000
Materials purchased for future research and development projects	34,000

Instructions

Compute the amount to be reported as research and development expense by Crow on its income statement for 1995. Assume equipment purchased at beginning of year.

E12-19 (Accounting for R & D Costs) Listed below are four independent situations involving research and development costs:

1. During 1996 Susquehanna Co. incurred the following costs:

Research and development services performed by Cayuse Company for Susquehanna	$350,000
Testing for evaluation of new products	300,000
Laboratory research aimed at discovery of new knowledge	400,000

For the year ended December 31, 1996, Susquehanna should report research and development expense of how much?

2. Creek Corp. incurred the following costs during the year ended December 31, 1996:

Design, construction, and testing of preproduction prototypes and models	$270,000
Routine, on-going efforts to refine, enrich, or otherwise improve upon the qualities of an existing product	250,000
Quality control during commercial production including routine testing of products	300,000
Laboratory research aimed at discovery of new knowledge	420,000

What is the total amount to be classified and expensed as research and development for 1996?

3. Tonkawa Company incurred costs in 1996 as follows:

Equipment acquired for use in various research and development projects	$900,000
Depreciation on the equipment above	210,000
Materials used in R & D	300,000
Compensation costs of personnel in R & D	400,000
Outside consulting fees for R & D work	180,000
Indirect costs appropriately allocated to R & D	260,000

What is the total amount of research and development that should be reported in Tonkawa's 1996 income statement?

4. Klamath Inc. incurred the following costs during the year ended December 31, 1996:

Laboratory research aimed at discovery of new knowledge	$200,000
Radical modification to the formulation of a chemical product	130,000
Research and development costs reimbursable under a contract to perform research and development for Quapaw Inc.	350,000
Testing for evaluation of new products	225,000

What is the total amount to be classified and expensed as research and development for 1996?

Instructions

Provide the correct answer to each of the four situations.

*E12-20 (Accounting for Computer Software Costs) Scioto Inc. has capitalized computer software costs of $3,000,000 on its new "Bitbyte" software package. Revenues from 1995 (first year) sales are $2,000,000; additional future revenues from "Bitbyte" for the remainder of its economic life, through 1999, are estimated to be $10,000,000.

Instructions

(a) What method or methods of amortization are to be applied in the writeoff of capitalized computer software costs?

(b) Compute the amount of amortization for 1995 for "Bitbyte."

*E12-21 (Accounting for Computer Software Costs) During 1995, Olentangy Enterprises spent $5,000,000 developing its new Data Find software package. Of this amount, $2,000,000 was spent before technological feasibility was established for the product, which is to be marketed to third parties. The package was completed at December 31, 1995. Olentangy expects a useful life of 8 years for this product with total revenues of $16,000,000. During the first year (1996), Olentangy realizes revenues of $3,200,000.

Instructions

(a) Prepare journal entries required in 1995 for the foregoing facts.

(b) Prepare the entry to record amortization at December 31, 1996.

(c) At what amount should the computer software costs be reported in the December 31, 1996, balance sheet? Could the net realizable value of this asset affect your answer?

(d) What disclosures are required in the December 31, 1996, financial statements for the computer software costs?

(e) How would your answers for (a), (b), and (c) be different if the computer software was developed for internal use?

*E12-22 (Compute Goodwill) The net worth of Ojibwa Company excluding goodwill totals $800,000 and earnings for the last 5 years total $890,000. Included in the latter figure are extraordinary gains of $60,000, nonrecurring losses of $40,000, and sales commissions of $15,000. In developing a sales price for the business a 14% return on net worth is considered normal for the industry, and annual excess earnings are to be capitalized at 20% in arriving at goodwill.

Instructions

Compute estimated goodwill.

*E12-23 (Compute Normal Earnings) Sahaptin Petroleum Corporation's pretax accounting income for the year 1995 was $850,000 and included the following items:

Amortization of goodwill	$ 60,000
Amortization of identifiable intangibles	57,000
Depreciation on building	80,000
Extraordinary losses	44,000
Extraordinary gains	135,000
Profit-sharing payments to employees	65,000

Delaware Oil Industries is seeking to purchase Sahaptin Petroleum Corporation. In attempting to measure Sahaptin's normal earnings for 1995, Delaware determines that the fair value of the building is triple the book value and that the remaining economic life is double that used by Sahaptin. Delaware would continue the profit-sharing payments to employees; such payments are based on income before depreciation and amortization.

Instructions

Compute the normal earnings (for purposes of computing goodwill) of Sahaptin Petroleum Corporation for the year 1995.

*E12-24 (Compute Goodwill) Algonquin News Inc. is considering acquiring Ottawa Company in total as a going concern. Algonquin makes the following computations and conclusions:

1. The fair value of the identifiable assets of Ottawa Company is $720,000.
2. The liabilities of Ottawa Company are $380,000.
3. A fair estimate of annual earnings for the indefinite future is $120,000 per year.
4. Considering the risk and potential of Ottawa Company, Algonquin feels that it must earn a 24% return on its investment.

Instructions

(a) How much should Algonquin be willing to pay for Ottawa Company?

(b) How much of the purchase price would be goodwill?

*E12-25 (Compute Goodwill) As the president of Chippewa Records Corp., you are considering purchasing Mohican Tape Corp., whose balance sheet is summarized as follows:

Current assets	$ 300,000		Current liabilities	$ 300,000
Fixed assets (net of depreciation)	700,000		Long-term liabilities	500,000
Other assets	300,000		Common stock	400,000
			Retained earnings	100,000
Total	$1,300,000		Total	$1,300,000

The fair market value of current assets is $600,000 because of the undervaluation of inventory. The normal rate of return on net assets for the industry is 15%. The average expected annual earnings projected for Mohican Tape Corp. is $140,000.

Instructions
Assuming that the excess earnings continue for 5 years, how much would you be willing to pay for goodwill? (Estimate goodwill by the present-value method.)

*E12-26 (Compute Goodwill) Net income figures for Menominee Company are as follows:

1991—$64,000	1994—$80,000
1992—$50,000	1995—$70,000
1993—$81,000	

Tangible net assets of this company are appraised at $400,000 on December 31, 1995. This business is to be acquired by Pontiac Co. early in 1996.

Instructions
What amount should be paid for goodwill if:
   (a) 14% is assumed to be a normal rate of return on net tangible assets, and average excess earnings for the last 5 years are to be capitalized at 25%?
   (b) 12% is assumed to be a normal rate of return on net tangible assets, and payment is to be made for excess earnings for the last 4 years?

*E12-27 (Compute Goodwill) Comanche Corporation is interested in acquiring Kiowa Plastics Company. It has determined that Kiowa Company's excess earnings have averaged approximately $120,000 annually over the last 6 years. Kiowa Company agrees with the computation of $120,000 as the approximate excess earnings and feels that such amount should be capitalized over an unlimited period at a 20% rate. Comanche Corporation feels that because of increased competition the excess earnings of Kiowa Company will continue for 7 more years at best and that a 15% discount rate is appropriate.

Instructions
   (a) How far apart are the positions of these two parties?
   (b) Is there really any difference in the two approaches used by the two parties in evaluating Kiowa Company's goodwill? Explain.

*E12-28 (Compute Goodwill) Natchez Corporation is contemplating the purchase of Apache Industries and evaluating the amount of goodwill to be recognized in the purchase.
   Apache reported the following net incomes:

1990	$170,000
1991	200,000
1992	240,000
1993	250,000
1994	380,000

Apache has indicated that 1994 net income included the sale of one of its warehouses at a gain of $140,000 (net of tax). Net identifiable assets of Apache have a total fair market value of $850,000.

Instructions
Calculate goodwill in the following cases, assuming that expected income is to be a simple average of **normal income** for the past 5 years.
   (a) Goodwill is determined by capitalizing average net earnings at 16%.
   (b) Goodwill is determined by presuming a 16% return on identifiable net assets and capitalizing excess earnings at 25%.

*E12-29 (Compute Fair Value of Identifiable Assets) Kishwaukee Company bought a business that would yield exactly a 20% annual rate of return on its investment. Of the total amount paid for the business, $80,000 was deemed to be goodwill, and the remaining value was attributable to the identifiable net assets.
   Kishwaukee Company projected that the estimated annual future earnings of the new business would be equal to its average annual ordinary earnings over the past 4 years. The total net income over the past 4 years was $380,000, which included an extraordinary loss of $35,000 in one year and an extraordinary gain of $95,000 in one of the other 3 years.

Instructions
Compute the fair market value of the identifiable net assets that Kishwaukee Company purchased in this transaction.

PROBLEMS

P12-1 (Correct Intangible Asset Account) Colin Davis Co., organized in 1994, has set up a single account for all intangible assets. The following summary discloses the debit entries that have been recorded during 1994 and 1995.

Intangible Assets

7/1/94	5-year franchise; expiration date 6/30/99	$ 42,000
10/1/94	Advance payment on leasehold (4-year lease)	28,000
12/31/94	Net loss for 1994 including state incorporation fee, $1,000, and related legal fees of organizing, $5,000 (all fees incurred in 1994)	16,000
1/2/95	Patent purchased (8-year life)	74,000
3/1/95	Cost of developing a secret formula (indefinite life)	75,000
4/1/95	Goodwill purchased (indefinite life)	278,400
6/1/95	Legal fee for successful defense of patent purchased above	12,350
9/1/95	Research and development costs	160,000

Instructions

Prepare the necessary entries to clear the Intangible Assets account and to set up separate accounts for distinct types of intangibles. Make the entries as of December 31, 1995, recording any necessary amortization and reflecting all balances accurately as of that date. (Assume a 40-year amortization for intangibles unless specified. Ignore income tax effects.)

P12-2 (Accounting for Patents) Eric Leinsdorf Laboratories holds a valuable patent (No. 758-6002-1A) on a precipitator that prevents certain types of air pollution. Leinsdorf does not manufacture or sell the products and processes it develops; it conducts research and develops products and processes which it patents, and then assigns the patents to manufacturers on a royalty basis. Occasionally it sells a patent. The history of Leinsdorf patent number 758-6002-1A is as follows:

Date	Activity	Cost
1985–1986	Research conducted to develop precipitator	$384,000
Jan. 1987	Design and construction of a prototype	87,600
March 1987	Testing of models	42,000
Jan. 1988	Fees paid engineers and lawyers to prepare patent application; patent granted July 1, 1988	61,880
Nov. 1989	Engineering activity necessary to advance the design of the precipitator to the manufacturing stage	81,500
Dec. 1990	Legal fees paid to successfully defend precipitator patent	35,000
April 1991	Research aimed at modifying the design of the patented precipitator	43,000
July 1995	Legal fees paid in unsuccessful patent infringement suit against a competitor	34,000

Leinsdorf assumed a useful life of 17 years when it received the initial precipitator patent. On January 1, 1993, it revised its useful life estimate downward to 5 remaining years. Amortization is computed for a full year if the cost is incurred prior to July 1, and no amortization for the year if the cost is incurred after June 30. The company's year ends December 31.

Instructions

Compute the carrying value of patent No. 758-6002-1A on each of the following dates:
- **(a)** December 31, 1988.
- **(b)** December 31, 1992.
- **(c)** December 31, 1995.

P12-3 (Accounting for Franchise, Patents, and Tradename) Information concerning George Solti Corporation's intangible assets is as follows:

1. On January 1, 1996, Solti signed an agreement to operate as a franchisee of Rapid Copy Service, Inc. for an initial franchise fee of $75,000. Of this amount, $15,000 was paid when the agreement was signed and the balance is payable in 4 annual payments of $15,000 each, beginning January 1, 1997. The agreement provides that the down payment is not refundable and no future services are required of the franchisor. The present value at January 1, 1996, of the 4 annual payments discounted at 14% (the implicit rate for a loan of this type) is $43,700. The agreement also provides that 5% of the revenue from the franchise must be paid to the franchisor annually. Solti's revenue from the franchise for 1996 was $900,000. Solti estimates the useful life of the franchise to be 10 years. (Hint: You may refer to Appendix 19–A to determine the proper accounting treatment for the franchise fee and payments.)

2. Solti incurred $65,000 of experimental and development costs in its laboratory to develop a patent which was granted on January 2, 1996. Legal fees and other costs associated with registration of the patent totaled $13,200. Solti estimates that the useful life of the patent will be 8 years.
3. A trademark was purchased from Chicago Company for $32,000 on July 1, 1993. Expenditures for successful litigation in defense of the trademark totaling $8,000 were paid on July 1, 1996. Solti estimates that the useful life of the trademark will be 20 years from the date of acquisition.

Instructions

(a) Prepare a schedule showing the intangible section of Solti's balance sheet at December 31, 1996. Show supporting computations in good form.
(b) Prepare a schedule showing all expenses resulting from the transactions that would appear on Solti's income statement for the year ended December 31, 1996. Show supporting computations in good form.

(AICPA adapted)

P12-4 (Amortization of Various Intangibles) The following information relates to the intangible assets of Inventa Product Company:

	Organization Costs	Goodwill	Purchased Patent Costs
Original cost at 1/1/1995	$76,000	$280,000	$48,000
Useful life at 1/1/1995 (estimated)	Indefinite[a]	50 years	6 years

[a]The company has decided to write off for accounting and tax purposes the organization costs as quickly as the tax law allows.

Instructions

(a) Assuming straight-line amortization, compute the amount of the amortization of **each** item for 1995 in accordance with generally accepted accounting principles.
(b) Prepare the journal entries for the amortization of organization costs and goodwill for 1995.
(c) Assume that at January 1, 1996, Inventa Product Company incurred $5,000 of legal fees in successfully defending the rights to the patents. Prepare the entry for the year 1996 to amortize the patents.
(d) Assume that at the beginning of year 1997 the company decided that the patent costs would be applicable only for the years 1997 and 1998. (A competitor has developed a product that will eventually make Inventa Product's obsolete.) Record the amortization of the patent costs at the end of 1997.

P12-5 (Accounting for Purchase of a Business) Slatkin Inc. has recently become interested in acquiring a South American plant to handle many of its production functions in that market. One possible candidate is Bernstein, Inc., a closely held corporation, whose owners have decided to sell their business if a proper settlement can be obtained. Bernstein's balance sheet appears as follows:

Current assets	$150,000	Current liabilities	$ 80,000
Investments	50,000	Long-term debt	100,000
Plant assets (net)	400,000	Capital stock	50,000
Total assets	$600,000	Additional paid-in capital	170,000
		Retained earnings	200,000
		Total equities	$600,000

Slatkin has hired Michael Tilson Thomas Appraisal Corporation to determine the proper price to pay for Bernstein, Inc. The appraisal firm finds that the investments have a fair market value of $150,000 and that inventory is understated by $75,000. All other assets and equities are properly stated. An examination of the company's income for the last 4 years indicates that the net income has steadily increased. In 1995, the company had a net operating income of $100,000, and this income should increase 20% each year over the next 4 years. Slatkin believes that a normal return in this type of business is 18% on net assets. The asset investment in the South American plant is expected to stay the same for the next 4 years.

Instructions

(a) Thomas Appraisal Corporation has indicated that the fair value of the company can be estimated in a number of ways. Prepare an estimate of the value of Bernstein, Inc., assuming that any goodwill will be computed as:
   1. The capitalization of the average excess earnings of Bernstein, Inc. at 18%.
   2. The purchase of average excess earnings over the next 4 years.
   3. The capitalization of average excess earnings of Bernstein, Inc. at 24%.
   4. The present value of the average excess earnings over the next four years discounted at 15%.
(b) Bernstein, Inc. is willing to sell the business for $1,000,000. How do you believe Thomas Appraisal should advise Slatkin?
(c) If Slatkin were to pay $750,000 to purchase the assets and assume the liabilities of Bernstein, Inc., how would this transaction be reflected on Slatkin's books?

P12-6 (Accounting for R & D Costs) During 1993, Joffrey Tool Company purchased a building site for its proposed research and development laboratory at a cost of $60,000. Construction of the building was started in 1993. The building was completed on December 31, 1994, at a cost of $280,000 and was placed in service on January 2, 1995. The estimated useful life of the building for depreciation purposes was 20 years; the straight-line method of depreciation was to be employed and there was no estimated net salvage value.

Management estimates that about 50% of the projects of the research and development group will result in long-term benefits (i.e., at least 10 years) to the corporation. The remaining projects either benefit the current period or are abandoned before completion. A summary of the number of projects and the direct costs incurred in conjunction with the research and development activities for 1995 appears below.

Upon recommendation of the research and development group Joffrey Tool Company acquired a patent for manufacturing rights at a cost of $100,000. The patent was acquired on April 1, 1994, and has an economic life of 10 years.

	Number of Projects	Salaries and Employee Benefits	Other Expenses (excluding Building Depreciation Charges)
Completed projects with long-term benefits	15	$ 90,000	$50,000
Abandoned projects or projects that benefit the current period	10	60,000	15,000
Projects in process—results indeterminate	5	40,000	12,000
Total	30	$190,000	$77,000

Instructions

If generally accepted accounting principles were followed, how would the items above relating to research and development activities be reported on the company's

(a) Income statement for 1995?

(b) Balance sheet as of December 31, 1995?

Be sure to give account titles and amounts, and briefly justify your presentation.

(CMA adapted)

P12-7 (Comprehensive Problem on Intangibles) Sara Cheng Corporation was incorporated on January 3, 1994. The corporation's financial statements for its first year's operations were not examined by a CPA. You have been engaged to audit the financial statements for the year ended December 31, 1995, and your audit is substantially completed. The corporation's trial balance appears below.

Sara Cheng Corporation
TRIAL BALANCE
December 31, 1995

	Debit	Credit
Cash	$ 15,000	
Accounts Receivable	73,000	
Allowance for Doubtful Accounts		$ 1,460
Inventories	50,200	
Machinery	82,000	
Equipment	37,000	
Accumulated Depreciation		26,200
Patents	128,200	
Leasehold Improvements	36,100	
Prepaid Expenses	13,000	
Organization Costs	32,000	
Goodwill	30,000	
Licensing Agreement No. 1	60,000	
Licensing Agreement No. 2	57,000	
Accounts Payable		73,000
Unearned Revenue		17,280
Capital Stock		300,000
Retained Earnings, January 1, 1995		159,060
Sales		720,000
Cost of Goods Sold	475,000	
Selling and General Expenses	180,000	
Interest Expense	8,500	
Extraordinary Losses	20,000	
Totals	$1,297,000	$1,297,000

The following information relates to accounts that may yet require adjustment.

1. Patents for Cheng's manufacturing process were acquired January 2, 1995, at a cost of $95,200. An additional $33,000 was spent in December, 1995, to improve machinery covered by the patents and charged to the Patents account. Depreciation on fixed assets has been properly recorded for 1995 in accordance with Cheng's practice, which provides a full year's depreciation for property on hand June 30 and no depreciation otherwise. Cheng uses the straight-line method for all depreciation and amortization and the legal life on its patents.

2. On January 3, 1994, Cheng purchased licensing agreement No. 1, which was believed to have an unlimited useful life. The balance in the Licensing Agreement No. 1 account includes its purchase price of $57,000 and expenses of $3,000 related to the acquisition. On January 1, 1995, Cheng purchases licensing agreement No. 2, which has a life expectancy of 10 years. The balance in the Licensing Agreement No. 2 account includes its $54,000 purchase price and $6,000 in acquisition expenses, but it has been reduced by a credit of $3,000 for the advance collection of 1996 revenue from the agreement.

   In late December, 1994, an explosion caused a permanent 70% reduction in the expected revenue-producing value of licensing agreement No. 1 and in January, 1996, a flood caused additional damage that rendered the agreement worthless.

3. The balance in the Goodwill account includes (a) $16,000 paid December 30, 1994, for an advertising program it is estimated will assist in increasing Cheng's sales over a period of 4 years following the disbursement, and (b) legal expenses of $14,000 incurred for Cheng's incorporation on January 3, 1994.

4. The Leasehold Improvements account includes (a) the $15,000 cost of improvements with a total estimated useful life of 12 years, which Cheng, as tenant, made to leased premises in January, 1994, (b) movable assembly line equipment costing $15,000 that was installed in the leased premises in December, 1995, and (c) real estate taxes of $6,100 paid by Cheng in 1995, which under the terms of the lease should have been paid by the landlord. Cheng paid its rent in full during 1995. A 10-year nonrenewable lease was signed January 3, 1994, for the leased building that Cheng used in manufacturing operations.

5. The balance in the Organization Costs account properly includes costs incurred during the organizational period. The corporation has exercised its option to amortize organization costs over a 60-month period for federal income tax purposes and wishes to amortize these for accounting purposes on the same basis.

Instructions
Prepare an 8-column worksheet to adjust accounts that require adjustment and include columns for an income statement and a balance sheet.

A separate account should be used for the accumulation of each type of amortization and for each prior period adjustment. Formal adjusting journal entries and financial statements are **not** required. (Hint: Make sure that Licensing Agreement No. 1 is amortized over the maximum life required in *APB Opinion No. 17* before the explosion damage loss is determined.)

(AICPA adapted)

*P12-8 (Compute Goodwill) Presented below are financial forecasts related to Neville Mariner Company for the next 10 years.

Forecasted average earnings (per year)	$ 65,000
Forecasted market value of net assets, exclusive of goodwill (average over 10 years)	340,000

Instructions
You have been asked to compute goodwill under the following methods. The normal rate of return on net assets for the industry is 15%.

  (a) Goodwill is equal to 5 years' excess earnings.
  (b) Goodwill is equal to the present value of 5 years' excess earnings discounted at 12%.
  (c) Goodwill is equal to the average excess earnings capitalized at 16%.
  (d) Goodwill is equal to average excess earnings capitalized at the normal rate of return for the industry of 15%.

*P12-9 (Compute Goodwill) Presented below is information related to Fritz Reiner Company for 1996, its first year of operation.

Income Summary

Raw Material Purchased	$145,900	Sales		$544,000
Productive Labor	41,250	Closing Inventories		
Factory Overhead	29,750	Raw Material		32,400
Selling Expenses	39,400	Goods in Process		32,000
Adm. Expenses	24,950	Finished Goods		39,000
Interest Expense	8,650	Appreciation of Land		4,500
Opening Inventories		Profit on Sale of Forfeited Stock		7,200
Raw Material	34,500			
Goods in Process	20,000			
Finished Goods	35,000			
Extraordinary Loss (net)	9,700			
Income Taxes	85,000			
Net Income	185,000			
	$659,100			$659,100

Instructions

Reiner is negotiating to sell the business after one full year of operation. Compute the amount of goodwill as 200% of the income before extraordinary items and before taxes that is in excess of $150,000; $150,000 is considered to be a normal return on investment.

*P12-10 (Compute Goodwill) Zubin Mehta Corp., a high-flying conglomerate, has recently been involved in discussions with Arthur Fiedler, Inc. As its CPA, you have been instructed by Mehta to conduct a purchase audit of Fiedler's books to determine a possible purchase price for Fiedler's net assets. The following information is found.

Total identifiable assets of Fiedler's (fair market value)	$250,000
Liabilities	60,000
Average rate of return on net assets for Fiedler's industry	15%
Forecasted earnings per year based on past earnings figures	34,500

Instructions

(a) Mehta asked you to determine the purchase price on the basis of the following assumptions:
  1. Goodwill is equal to 3 years' excess earnings.
  2. Goodwill is equal to the present value of excess earnings discounted at 15% for 3 years.
  3. Goodwill is equal to the capitalization of excess earnings at 15%.
  4. Goodwill is equal to the capitalization of excess earnings at 25%.
(b) Mehta asks you which of the methods above is the most theoretically sound. Justify your answer. Any assumptions made should be clearly indicated.

*P12-11 (Compute Goodwill) André Previn Inc. has contracted to purchase Beverly Sills Company including the goodwill of the latter company. The agreement between purchaser and seller on the price to be paid for goodwill is as follows: "The value of the goodwill to be paid for is to be determined by capitalizing at 18% the average annual earnings from ordinary operations for the last 5 years in excess of 16% on the net worth, which, for purposes of this computation, is to be considered $300,000."

The net income per books for the last 5 years is:

1992	$43,150
1993	49,680
1994	64,320
1995	51,250
1996	68,580

As assistant to the treasurer of André Previn, you are instructed to review the accounts of Beverly Sills Company and determine the amount to be paid for goodwill in accordance with the terms of the contract. In your review of the accounts you discover the following:

1. An additional assessment of federal income taxes in the amount of $10,120 for the year 1994 was made and paid in 1996. The amount was charged against Retained Earnings.
2. In 1992 the company reviewed its accounts receivable and wrote off as an expense of that year $18,180 of accounts receivable that had been carried for years and appeared very unlikely to be collected.
3. In 1993 an account for $2,100 included in the 1992 writeoff above was collected and credited to "Miscellaneous Income."
4. A fire in 1995 caused a loss, charged to Income, as follows:

Book value of property destroyed	$29,400
Recovery from insurance company	10,000
Net loss	$19,400

5. Expropriation of property in 1995 resulted in a gain of $9,080 credited to income.
6. Amounts paid out under the company's product guarantee plan and charged to expense in each of the 5 years were as follows:

1992	$1,000
1993	1,300
1994	950
1995	1,100
1996	1,400

7. In 1996, the president of the company died, and the company realized $75,000 on an insurance policy on his life. The cash surrender value of this policy had been carried on the books as an investment in the amount of $62,240. The excess of proceeds over cash surrender value was credited to income.

Instructions

What is the price to be paid for the goodwill in accordance with the contract agreement? Prepare your computations in good form so that you can answer any questions asked by the treasurer in regard to your conclusions.

CASES

C12-1 (Patent Cost) In examining the books of Seminole Mfg. Company, you find on the December 31, 1995, balance sheet, the item, "Costs of patents, $822,000."

Referring to the ledger accounts, you note the following items regarding one patent acquired in 1992.

1992 Legal costs incurred in defending the validity of the patent	$ 35,000
1994 Legal costs in prosecuting an infringement suit	74,000
1995 Legal costs (additional expenses) in the infringement suit	24,500
1995 Cost of improvements (unpatented) on the patented device	131,200

There are no credits in the account, and no allowance for amortization has been set up on the books for any of the patents. Three other patents issued in 1989, 1991, and 1992 were developed by the staff of the client. The patented articles are currently very marketable, but it is estimated that they will be in demand only for the next few years.

Instructions

Discuss the items included in the Patent account from an accounting standpoint.

(AICPA adapted)

C12-2 (Accounting for Intangible-Type Expenditures) Taos Inc. is a large, publicly held corporation. Listed below are six selected expenditures made by the company during the current fiscal year ended April 30, 1995. The proper accounting treatment of these transactions must be determined in order that Taos' annual financial statements will be prepared in accordance with generally accepted accounting principles.

1. Taos Inc. spent $3,000,000 on a program designed to improve relations with its dealers. This project was favorably received by the dealers and Taos' management believes that significant future benefits should be received from this program. The program was conducted during the fourth quarter of the current fiscal year.
2. A pilot plant was constructed during 1994–95 at a cost of $5,000,000 to test a new production process. The plant will be operated for approximately 5 years. At that time, the company will make a decision regarding the economic value of the process. The pilot plant is too small for commercial production, so it will be dismantled when the test is over.
3. A new product will be introduced next year. The company spent $4,000,000 during the current year for design of tools, jigs, molds, and dies for this product.
4. Taos Inc. purchased Shoshone Company for $6,000,000 in cash in early August 1994. The fair market value of the identifiable assets of Shoshone was $5,000,000.
5. A large advertising campaign was conducted during April 1995 to introduce a new product to be released during the first quarter of the 1995–96 fiscal year. The advertising campaign cost $3,500,000.
6. During the first six months of the 1994–95 fiscal year, $500,000 was expended for legal work in connection with a successful patent application. The patent became effective November 1, 1994. The legal life of the patent is 17 years and the economic life of the patent is expected to be approximately 10 years.

Instructions

For each of the six expenditures presented, determine and justify:

(a) The amount, if any, that should be capitalized and be included on Taos' statement of financial position prepared as of April 30, 1995.

(b) The amount that should be included in Taos' statement of income for the year ended April 30, 1995.

(CMA adapted)

C12-3 (Accounting for Pollution Expenditure) Sioux Company operates several plants at which limestone is processed into quicklime and hydrated lime. The Alta plant, where most of the equipment was installed many years ago, continually deposits a dusty white substance over the surrounding countryside. Citing the unsanitary condition of the neighboring community of Primghar, the pollution of the Raccoon River, and the high incidence of lung disease among workers at Alta, the state's Pollution Control Agency has ordered the installation of air pollution control equipment. Also, the Agency has assessed a substantial penalty, which will be used to clean up Primghar. After considering the costs involved (which could not have been reasonably estimated prior to the Agency's action), Sioux Company decides to comply with the Agency's orders, the alternative being to cease operations at Alta at the end of the current fiscal year. The officers of Sioux agree that the air pollution control equipment should be capitalized and depreciated over its useful life, but they disagree over the period(s) to which the penalty should be charged.

Instructions
Discuss the conceptual merits and reporting requirements of accounting for the penalty as a
  (a) Charge to the current period.
  (b) Correction of prior periods.
  (c) Capitalizable item to be amortized over future periods.

(AICPA adapted)

C12-4 (Accounting for Pre-Opening Costs) After securing lease commitments from several major stores, Cherokee Shopping Center, Inc. was organized and built a shopping center in a growing suburb.

The shopping center would have opened on schedule on January 1, 1995, if it had not been struck by a severe tornado in December; it opened for business on October 1, 1995. All of the additional construction costs that were incurred as a result of the tornado were covered by insurance.

In July, 1994, in anticipation of the scheduled January opening, a permanent staff had been hired to promote the shopping center, obtain tenants for the uncommitted space, and manage the property.

A summary of some of the costs incurred in 1994 and the first nine months of 1995 follows.

	1994	January 1, 1995 through September 30, 1995
Interest on mortgage bonds	$360,000	$270,000
Cost of obtaining tenants	150,000	180,000
Promotional advertising	270,000	278,500

The promotional advertising campaign was designed to familiarize shoppers with the center. Had it been known in time that the center would not open until October, 1995, the 1994 expenditure for promotional advertising would not have been made. The advertising had to be repeated in 1995.

All of the tenants who had leased space in the shopping center at the time of the tornado accepted the October occupancy date on condition that the monthly rental charges for the first nine months of 1995 be canceled.

Instructions
Explain how each of the costs for 1994 and the first nine months of 1995 should be treated in the accounts of the shopping center corporation. Give the reasons for each treatment.

(AICPA adapted)

C12-5 (Accounting for Patents) On June 30, 1995, your client, Choctaw Company, was granted two patents covering plastic cartons that it has been producing and marketing profitably for the past 3 years. One patent covers the manufacturing process and the other covers the related products.

Choctaw executives tell you that these patents represent the most significant breakthrough in the industry in the past 30 years. The products have been marketed under the registered trademarks Evertight, Duratainer, and Sealrite. Licenses under the patents have already been granted by your client to other manufacturers in the United States and abroad and are producing substantial royalties.

On July 1, Choctaw commenced patent infringement actions against several companies whose names you recognize as those of substantial and prominent competitors. Choctaw's management is optimistic that these suits will result in a permanent injunction against the manufacture and sale of the infringing products and collection of damages for loss of profits caused by the alleged infringement.

The financial vice-president has suggested that the patents be recorded at the discounted value of expected net royalty receipts.

Instructions
  (a) What is the meaning of "discounted value of expected net receipts"? Explain.
  (b) How would such a value be calculated for net royalty receipts?

(c) What basis of valuation for Choctaw's patents would be generally accepted in accounting? Give supporting reasons for this basis.

(d) Assuming no practical problems of implementation and ignoring generally accepted accounting principles, what is the preferable basis of valuation for patents? Explain.

(e) What would be the preferable theoretical basis of amortization? Explain.

(f) What recognition, if any, should be made of the infringement litigation in the financial statements for the year ending September 30, 1995? Discuss.

(AICPA adapted)

C12-6 (Accounting for Goodwill) After extended negotiations, Powhatan Corporation bought from Shawnee Company most of the latter's assets on June 30, 1995. At the time of the sale, Shawnee's accounts (adjusted to June 30, 1995) reflected the following descriptions and amounts for the assets transferred.

	Cost	Contra (Valuation) Account	Book Value
Receivables	$ 86,600	$ 2,500	$ 84,100
Inventory	107,000	5,400	101,600
Land	18,000	—	18,000
Buildings	208,600	73,000	135,600
Fixtures and equipment	203,900	42,000	161,900
Goodwill	50,000	—	50,000
	$674,100	$122,900	$551,200

You ascertain that the contra (valuation) accounts were allowance for doubtful accounts, allowance to reduce inventory to market, and accumulated depreciation.

During the extended negotiations Shawnee held out for a consideration of approximately $700,000 (depending on the level of the receivables and inventory). As of June 30, 1995, however, Shawnee agreed to accept Powhatan's offer of $500,000 cash plus 1% of the net sales (as defined in the contract) of the next 5 years with payments at the end of each year. Shawnee expects that Powhatan's total net sales during this period will exceed $15,000,000.

Instructions

(a) How should Powhatan Corporation record this transaction? Explain.

(b) Discuss the propriety of recording goodwill in the accounts of Powhatan Corporation for this transaction.

(AICPA adapted)

C12-7 (Accounting for Goodwill) Cree Co., a retail propane gas distributor, has increased its annual sales volume to a level three times greater than the annual sales of a dealer it purchased in 1992 in order to begin operations.

The Board of Directors of Cree Co. recently received an offer to negotiate the sale of Cree to a large competitor. As a result, the majority of the Board wants to increase the stated value of goodwill on the balance sheet to reflect the larger sales volume developed through intensive promotion and the current market price of sales gallonage. A few of the Board members, however, would prefer to eliminate goodwill altogether from the balance sheet in order to prevent "possible misinterpretations." Goodwill was recorded properly in 1992.

Instructions

(a) Discuss the meaning of the term "goodwill."

*(b) List the techniques used to calculate the tentative value of goodwill in negotiations to purchase a going concern.

(c) Why are the book and market values of the goodwill of Cree Co. different?

(d) Discuss the propriety of
  1. Increasing the stated value of goodwill prior to the negotiations.
  2. Eliminating goodwill completely from the balance sheet prior to negotiations.

(AICPA adapted)

C12-8 (Accounting for Research and Development Costs) Seneca Co. is in the process of developing a revolutionary new product. A new division of the company was formed to develop, manufacture, and market this new product. As of year-end (December 31, 1995) the new product has not been manufactured for resale; however, a prototype unit was built and is in operation.

Throughout 1995 the new division incurred certain costs. These costs include design and engineering studies, prototype manufacturing costs, administrative expenses (including salaries of administrative personnel), and market research costs. In addition, approximately $800,000 in equipment (estimated useful life—10 years) was purchased for use in developing and manufacturing the new product. Approximately $300,000 of this equipment was built specifically for the design development of the new product; the remaining $500,000 of equipment was used to manufacture the pre-production prototype and will be used to manufacture the new product once it is in commercial production.

Instructions

    (a) How are "research" and "development" defined in *Statement of Financial Accounting Standards No. 2?*

    (b) Briefly indicate the practical and conceptual reasons for the conclusion reached by the Financial Accounting Standards Board on accounting and reporting practices for research and development costs.

    (c) In accordance with *Statement of Financial Accounting Standards No. 2,* how should the various costs of Seneca described above be recorded on the financial statements for the year ended December 31, 1995?

(AICPA adapted)

*C12-9 **(Computer Software Costs)** During the examination of the financial statements of Shabbona Corp., your assistant calls attention to significant costs incurred in the development of the computer software for major segments of the sales and inventory scheduling systems (internal use).

    The computer software development costs will benefit future periods to the extent that the systems change slowly and the program instructions are compatible with new equipment acquired at 3- to 6-year intervals. The service value of the software is affected almost entirely by changes in the technology of systems and EDP equipment and does not decline with the number of times the program is used. Because many system changes are minor, program instructions frequently can be modified with only minor losses in program efficiency. The frequency of such changes tends to increase with the passage of time.

Instructions

    (a) Discuss the propriety of classifying the unamortized computer software development costs as
        1. A prepaid expense.
        2. An intangible asset.
        3. A tangible fixed asset.

    (b) Discuss the propriety of amortizing the computer software development costs by means of
        1. The straight-line method.
        2. A decreasing-charge method (e.g., the sum-of-the-years'-digits method).
        3. A variable-charge method (e.g., the units-of-production method).

    (c) If the computer software had been developed for sale (external use), how should the development cost be accounted for and amortized?

(AICPA adapted)

▶ USING YOUR JUDGMENT ◀

▶ FINANCIAL REPORTING PROBLEM

Refer to the financial statements and other documents of Georgia-Pacific Corporation presented in Appendix 5-A and answer the following questions.

    1. In its 1993 balance sheet, Georgia-Pacific reported $1,832 million of goodwill compared to $1,891 million in 1992. How does Georgia-Pacific amortize its goodwill? What is the amount of goodwill amortization expense in 1993? What is the amount of accumulated goodwill amortization at December 31, 1993?

    2. Can you estimate the age or remaining life of Georgia-Pacific's property, plant, and equipment from the information provided for 1993 in the financial statements or accompanying notes? What role does "recoverability" play in valuing goodwill annually?

▶ WRITING ASSIGNMENT

The president of Dane Co., Ms. Joyce Pollachek, is considering purchasing Balloon Bunch Company. She thinks that the offer sounds pretty good, but she wants to consult a public accountant to be sure. Balloon Bunch Company is asking $78,000 over the fair market value of the net identifiable assets. Balloon Bunch's net income figures for the last 5 years are as follows:

1991—$64,000	1994—$80,000
1992—$50,000	1995—$70,000
1993—$81,000	

The tangible net assets of this company were appraised at $400,000 on December 31, 1995.

You have done some initial research on the balloon industry and discovered that the normal rate of return on net tangible assets is 13%. After analyzing variables such as stability of past earnings, the nature of the business, and general economic conditions, you have decided that the average excess earnings for the last 5 years should be capitalized at 25%.

Instructions

Determine a fair amount to pay for goodwill in this situation. Then, write a letter to Ms. Pollachek explaining what goodwill is, what amount is appropriate in this case, and how you determined this amount. (You need not explain the operations which you performed on all the numbers; simply include a separate page with your calculations.)

▶ GROUP ASSIGNMENT

(Accounting for Various Intangible Assets and R & D Costs) The following situations relate to the accounting for intangible assets and research and development costs.

1. Warfield Corporation, a development stage company, deferred all its preoperating and R & D costs. Its 1995 financial statements consisted only of statements of cash receipts and disbursements, capital shares, and assets and unrecovered preoperating costs and liabilities. The officers indicate that operations should start June 30, 1996, and complete financials will be issued December 31, 1996.
2. Hanson Components Corp. develops computer software to be used internally for its management information systems. The corporation incurred $290,000 in developing this new software package.
3. Williams Research Company is developing a new space station under contract for Star Search Corp. The contract, signed January 4, requires payments to Williams Research of $600,000 on December 31 and $1,000,000 at the completion of the project. At December 31, Williams has recorded an account receivable of $600,000 and has deferred R & D costs of $400,000.
4. Wild Co. purchased two patents directly from the inventors. Patent No. 1 can be used only in its listening device development research project. Patent No. 2 can be used in many different projects and currently is being used in a research project.
5. Green Golf Company deferred all of its 1994 R & D costs, which totaled $360,000. In November 1995, you are hired as controller and informed that an additional $450,000 has been deferred thus far in 1995. The company wants to issue comparative financial statements in accordance with generally accepted accounting principles for the first time this year.

Instructions

Your instructor will assign one member of the group to serve as a recorder and one member to serve as spokesperson. As a group, provide the information for the recorder to prepare a recommended accounting treatment for each of the items above (you may wish to divide the parts among the members). Upon completion, the spokesperson will report the group findings to the class and be prepared to provide justifications for the recommendations.

▶ ETHICS CASE

Health Drug Company has purchased from Bristol Pharmaceuticals a cancer research laboratory, including some personnel, in Orlando, Florida where land values are increasing rapidly. John Cunning, controller, and Larry Beatem, financial vice-president of Health Drug are attempting to allocate the $40 million purchase price among the four types of assets included in the acquired research operation: building, special equipment, land, and goodwill. The controller, noting that depreciation and amortization can be taken only on the building, special equipment, and goodwill, favors undervaluing the land and placing a very high proportion of the cost on the shortest-lived assets, namely special equipment (7-year tax life), and goodwill (15-year tax life), thus reducing taxable income and income taxes. The financial vice-president argues just the opposite: "a very high proportion of the cost should be placed on the land in order to relieve net income of some depreciation and amortization charge. We must minimize the negative impact of this purchase on net income in order to keep the company's stock price up." Neither suggests allocating any cost to the personnel.

Instructions

(a) Whose interests are affected by the controller's and the financial vice-president's contrary positions?
(b) What are the ethical issues in this case?
(c) How should the purchase cost be allocated? Why?

How has the background in accounting been helpful to you in the investment business?

It's been a tremendous help. We all wish that the scorecard of business could be as easy as a baseball game, but financial scorecards are a lot more complicated than that. Being able to understand what goes into all the varying issues that end up in a financial report is invaluable in your understanding of what these numbers really do mean. In the stocks that I follow—small- to mid-sized companies that are growing rapidly—everybody is constantly focused on earnings and earnings estimates. But quality of earnings is also important. If you understand what goes into the earnings, you're able to determine the quality of earnings. The issues really become evident when you look at the most basic tenet of accounting: matching expenses with revenues.

Can you give me an example, say, in technology?

Capitalization of software R&D—a widely abused accounting principle, which allows management to determine on a quarterly basis what percent of their R&D expense should be capitalized, and what percent of their capitalized R&D expense should be amortized. In the old days, you knew you had an expense when you spent the money. Now, accrual accounting gives flexibility in estimating—and this is the difficult part—what portion of those expenses should be attributed to future revenues.

One of the boom industries of the 1990s is the mutual fund industry. The number of mutual funds—close to 5,000—is beginning to rival the number of public companies in which the funds invest. **EDWARD N. ANTOIAN** is a senior portfolio manager with the Delaware Management Company, based in Philadelphia. Mr. Antoian holds a bachelor of science degree from the State University of New York at Albany and earned an MBA in finance from the University of Pennsylvania's Wharton School in 1982. Prior to entering the MBA program, Antoian became a CPA, beginning his career with Price Waterhouse. Antoian believes that his accounting background gives him a big advantage in the investment management field.

Are there companies whose growth rate in earnings actually hinges on this?

Without a doubt. Here's our little axiom: today's balance sheet ultimately must enter into tomorrow's P&L. We spend a lot of time analyzing balance sheets to determine if the growth rate as currently reported is an accurate depiction of the company's true results. We look for disproportionate increases in asset categories compared to the revenue growth of the business. Ultimately that tells you they're spending money at a much higher rate than the company's revenues were growing in the past. If you can't project a higher growth rate in revenues in the future, then margins must come down. Capitalized software is a big abuse.

Where else might you find an example where assets become expenses later on?

Inventory balances in the retail industry. In retail accounting, once you've reduced the sales price of an item, you're required to write off that portion in your inventory. If inventories are growing faster than sales, it is typically a sign that you're not managing your inventory well or that you have planned your inventory for a higher level of sales, which didn't occur. What typically happens is that you lower prices, and your gross profit margin should decline. If the inventory balance is continually rising and the gross profit margins *haven't* declined, then we'll argue that gross profit margins are likely to decline in the future, because of that excess inventory currently on the books.

I remember when Blockbuster Entertainment had an issue of how fast to write off movie rentals.

That's a good example. Clearly, the company has come around. It's a great case study. When they initially were in business, they would write off their rental tape inventory over a five-year period of time. For one thing, Blockbuster was a rapidly growing company that needed a tremendous amount of capital. The last thing they wanted to do was to depress reported earnings. When you first bring in a title, say *Beauty and the Beast*, for the first number of weeks, a store will need ten copies of that title. Let's make the math easy: Say you spend $50 per copy for the title, and you're going to amortize that over five years. When month six comes along and the rental volume of *Beauty and the Beast* declines precipitously, you no longer need ten copies of that title in your store. You probably need only two. Blockbuster was growing so quickly that all they did was take those excess eight copies and transfer them to new stores. They literally were growing that fast. And they would transfer those copies out at current book value. So if the title is only six months old, it's now only a tenth written off, and they would transfer it out at a $45 book value. If they had attempted to dispose of the title because they didn't have another shelf to stick it on, they probably would have received somewhere between $10-$15 a copy for that title. There would have been a huge accounting write-off of $30 if they would have sold that tape with a book value of $45. And they surely couldn't have af-forded to do that for reported accounting purposes. So their growth benefited them tremendously, although clearly, the accounting didn't represent the true economics of that tape. Currently, Blockbuster depreciates all tapes over a six-month period of time.

That was because of the controversy or because they got more conservative?

Two reasons: One, they weren't growing their store base as rapidly, so they didn't have a place to put those titles. And two, they had the luxury of taking a more conservative approach since they were through with their real growth and capital-raising activity.

Is there another entertainment company that comes to mind where these issues come into play?

Orion Pictures went bankrupt with hundreds of millions of dollars of film inventory. In motion picture accounting, you absorb into inventory all of your costs during production. The day you start to receive a dollar of revenue from a film, you are supposed to predict the total revenues for it over its useful life. For example, let's predict that a $50 million film is going to generate revenue of $100 million. If I receive $1 million of revenue, I'm supposed to take 1% of my total costs accumulated on the balance sheet into the P&L, because I have received 1% of the total expected revenues. The quandary here is that we know what the costs of the film are—we've already made it—but we have to predict what the revenues are going to be. That's a rather difficult task. Even more important, the numbers are easily manipu-lated. Who's going to argue with management? This is reasonable accounting in theory, but it's poor accounting in practice. Orion went bankrupt even though their earnings were fine. They had a balance sheet that showed they had a book value of hundreds of millions of dollars, but it was overstated.

My criticism of movie industry accounting is overstated inventory: You spend $100 million on a movie, and then after it's released for six months and you've realized only $20 million in revenue—and there's no way in heaven you're going to break even—you're still carrying an internal estimate that you're going to make money on it, and the inventory is still residing on the balance sheet.

Management can always say that they're going to make it up on home video or foreign sales.

They sure can. And trust me, that's what Orion said.

Do you look at cash flow more closely than earnings?

For large established companies, cash flow can be more indicative of performance. But that's not necessarily the case with the growth companies that I follow. Here's an example: If I am spending $10 million for a movie or a piece of software that I'm developing in 1994, and I can't sell it until it's finished, why should those expenses be incurred on the P&L in 1994? Then, when I sell it in 1995, I'd have a 100% profit margin. I don't think that's representative of the true scenario. But that's the view of investors who look merely at cash flow. Many growing companies don't have positive cash flows.

CHAPTER 13

CURRENT LIABILITIES AND CONTINGENCIES

LEARNING OBJECTIVES

After studying this chapter, you should be able to:

1. Define current liabilities and describe how they are valued.

2. Identify the nature and types of current liabilities.

3. Explain the classification issues of short-term debt expected to be refinanced.

4. Identify types of employee-related liabilities.

5. Indicate how current liabilities are disclosed.

6. Identify the criteria used to account for and disclose loss contingencies.

7. Explain the accounting for different types of contingent liabilities.

---

*T*he credit quality of many corporations has substantially declined. For U.S. nonfinancial corporations over a recent 7-year period, liabilities increased from 34% to 47% of total capital, and interest payments increased from 22% to 34% of pretax income. The reason: American corporations—in a manner similar to the federal government—went on an unprecedented debt-binge. Companies borrowed money to expand in a booming economy. They also borrowed heavily to fend off takeovers by other companies. Currently many companies are paying off or refinancing much of that debt. As a result investors as well as the accounting profession are paying more attention to liabilities.

▶ SECTION 1 / CURRENT LIABILITIES

▶ WHAT IS A LIABILITY?

The question, "What is a liability?" is not easy to answer. The acquisition of goods or services on credit terms gives rise to liabilities. But it seems clear that liabilities include more than debts arising from borrowings. Less similar are liabilities resulting from taxes, withholdings from employees' wages and salaries, dividend declarations, pension plans and employee benefits, and product warranties.

To illustrate the complexity of this issue, one might ask whether preferred stock is a liability or an ownership claim. The first reaction is to say that preferred stock is in fact an ownership claim and should be reported as part of stockholders' equity. In fact, preferred stock has many elements of debt as well.[1] The issuer (and in some cases the holder) often has the right to call the stock within a specific period of time—making it similar to a repayment of principal. The dividend is in many cases almost guaranteed (cumulative provision)—making it look like interest. And preferred stock is but one of many financial instruments that are difficult to classify.[2]

To help resolve some of these controversies, the FASB, as part of its conceptual framework study, defined **liabilities** as **"probable future sacrifices of economic benefits arising from present obligations of a particular entity to transfer assets or provide services to other entities in the future as a result of past transactions or events."**[3] In other words, a liability has three essential characteristics:

UNDERLYING CONCEPT

To determine the appropriate classification of specific financial instruments, proper definitions of assets, liabilities, and equities are needed. The conceptual framework definitions are often used as the basis for resolving controversial classification issues.

1. It is a present obligation that entails settlement by probable future transfer or use of cash, goods, or services.

2. It is an unavoidable obligation.

3. The transaction or other event creating the obligation has already occurred.

Because liabilities involve future disbursements of assets or services, one of their most important features is the date on which they are payable. Currently maturing obligations represent a demand on the current assets of the enterprise—a demand that must be satisfied promptly and in the ordinary course of business if operations are to be continued. Liabilities with a more distant due date do not, as a rule, represent a claim on the enterprise's current resources and are therefore in a slightly different category. This feature gives rise to the basic division of liabilities into (1) current liabilities and (2) long-term debt.

The distinction between current liabilities and long-term debt is important because it provides information about the liquidity of the company. Liquidity regarding a liability is the time that is expected to elapse until a liability has to be paid. In other words, a liability soon to be paid is a current liability. A liquid company—one that has more liquid assets than current liabilities—is less likely to fail. A liquid company is better able to withstand a financial downturn. Also, it has a better chance to take advantage of investment opportunities that develop.

▶ WHAT IS A CURRENT LIABILITY?

Current assets are cash or other assets that can reasonably be expected to be converted into cash, sold, or consumed in operations within a single operating cycle or within a year if more than one cycle is completed each year. **Current liabilities are "obligations whose liquidation is reasonably expected to require use of existing resources prop-**

OBJECTIVE 1

Define current liabilities and describe how they are valued.

---

[1]It should be noted that this illustration is not just a theoretical exercise. In practice, there are a number of preferred stock issues that have all the characteristics of a debt instrument, except that they are called and legally classified preferred stock. In some cases, the IRS has even permitted the dividend payments to be treated as interest expense for tax purposes. This issue is discussed further in Chapter 15.

[2]As examples of the diversity within preferred stock, companies now issue (1) mandatorily redeemable preferred stock (redeemable at a specified price and time), (2) Dutch auction preferred stock (holders have the right to change the rate at defined intervals through a bidding process), (3) increasing rate (exploding rate) preferred stock (holder receives an increasing dividend rate each period with the issuer having the right to call the stock at a certain date in the future). In all three cases the issuer either has to redeem the stock per the contract or has a strong economic reason for calling the stock. These securities are more like debt than equity. The FASB has issued a discussion memorandum addressing these issues: "Distinguishing between Liability and Equity Instruments and Accounting for Instruments with Characteristics of Both," Discussion Memorandum (Norwalk, Conn.: FASB, 1990).

[3]"Elements of Financial Statements of Business Enterprises," *Statement of Financial Accounting Concepts No. 6* (Stamford, Conn.: FASB, 1980).

INTERNATIONAL
INSIGHT

In France, the balance sheet does not show current liabilities in a separate category. Rather, debts are disclosed separately by maturity in the notes.

OBJECTIVE 2

Identify the nature and types of current liabilities.

erly classified as current assets, or the creation of other current liabilities."[4] This definition has gained wide acceptance because it recognizes operating cycles of varying lengths in different industries and takes into consideration the important relationship between current assets and current liabilities. The FASB affirmed this concept of **"maturity within one year or the operating cycle whichever is longer"** in its definition of short-term obligations in *Statement No. 6*.[5]

The **operating cycle** is the period of time elapsing between the acquisition of goods and services involved in the manufacturing process and the final cash realization resulting from sales and subsequent collections. Industries that manufacture products requiring an aging process and certain capital-intensive industries have an operating cycle of considerably more than one year. On the other hand, most retail and service establishments have several operating cycles within a year.

There are many different types of current liabilities. The following ones are covered in this chapter in this order.

1. Accounts payable.	6. Returnable deposits.
2. Notes payable.	7. Unearned revenues.
3. Current maturities of long-term debt.	8. Sales taxes payable.
4. Short-term obligations expected to be refinanced.	9. Property taxes payable.
	10. Income taxes payable.
5. Dividends payable.	11. Employee related liabilities.

ACCOUNTS PAYABLE

Accounts payable, or **trade accounts payable,** are balances owed to others for goods, supplies, or services purchased on open account. Accounts payable arise because of the time lag between the receipt of services or acquisition of title to assets and the payment for them. This period of extended credit is usually found in the terms of the sale (e.g., 2/10, n/30 or 1/10, E.O.M.) and is commonly 30 to 60 days.

Most accounting systems are designed to record liabilities for purchases of goods when the goods are received or, practically, when the invoices are received. Frequently there is some delay in recording the goods and the related liability on the books. If title has passed to the purchaser before the goods are received, the transaction should be recorded at the time of title passage. Attention must be paid to transactions occurring near the end of one accounting period and at the beginning of the next to ascertain that the record of goods received (the inventory) is in agreement with the liability (accounts payable) and that both are recorded in the proper period.

Measuring the amount of an account payable poses no particular difficulty because the invoice received from the creditor specifies the due date and the exact outlay in money that is necessary to settle the account. The only calculation that may be necessary concerns the amount of cash discount. See Chapter 8 for illustrations of entries related to accounts payable and purchase discounts.

NOTES PAYABLE

Notes payable are written promises to pay a certain sum of money on a specified future date and may arise from sales, financing, or other transactions. In some industries, notes (often referred to as **trade notes payable**) are required as part of the sales/purchases transaction in lieu of the normal extension of open account credit. Notes payable to banks or loan companies generally arise from cash loans. Notes may be classified as short-term or long-term, depending upon the payment due date. Notes may also be interest-bearing or zero-interest-bearing.

---

[4]Committee on Accounting Procedure, American Institute of Certified Public Accountants, "Accounting Research and Terminology Bulletins," Final Edition (New York: AICPA, 1961), p. 21.

[5]"Classification of Short-term Obligations Expected to Be Refinanced," *Statement of Financial Accounting Standards No. 6* (Stamford, Conn.: FASB, 1975), par. 2.

Interest-Bearing Note Issued

Assume that the Castle National Bank agrees to lend $100,000 on March 1, 1996, to Landscape Co. if Landscape Co. signs a $100,000, 12%, 4-month note. The entry to record the cash received by Landscape Co. on March 1 is:

March 1

Cash	100,000	
Notes Payable		100,000
(To record issuance of 12%, 4-month note to Castle		
National Bank)		

If Landscape Co. prepares financial statements semiannually, an adjusting entry is required to recognize interest expense and interest payable of $4,000 ($100,000 × 12% × 4/12) at June 30. The adjusting entry is:

June 30

Interest Expense	4,000	
Interest Payable		4,000
(To accrue interest for 4 months on Castle National		
Bank note)		

If Landscape prepared financial statements monthly, the adjusting entry at the end of each month would have been $1,000 ($100,000 × 12% × 1/12).

At maturity (July 1), Landscape Co. must pay the face value of the note ($100,000) plus $4,000 interest ($100,000 × 12% × 4/12).

The entry to record payment of the note and accrued interest is as follows:

July 1

Notes Payable	100,000	
Interest Payable	4,000	
Cash		104,000
(To record payment of Castle National Bank interest-		
bearing note and accrued interest at maturity)		

Zero-Interest-Bearing Note Issued

A zero-interest-bearing note may be issued instead of an interest-bearing note. A zero-interest-bearing note does not explicitly state an interest rate on the face of the note. Interest is still charged, however, because the borrower is required at maturity to pay back an amount greater than the cash received at the issuance date. In other words, the borrower receives in cash the present value of the note. The present value equals the face value of the note at maturity minus the interest or discount charged by the lender for the term of the note. In essence, the bank takes its fee "up front" rather than on the date the note matures.

To illustrate, we will assume that Landscape Co. issues a $104,000 4-month, zero-interest-bearing note to the Castle National Bank. The present value of the note is $100,000.[6] The entry to record this transaction for Landscape Co. is as follows:

March 1

Cash	100,000	
Discount on Notes Payable	4,000	
Notes Payable		104,000
(To record issuance of 4-month, zero-interest-bearing		
note to Castle National Bank)		

The Notes Payable account is credited for the face value of the note, which is $4,000 more than the actual cash received. The difference between the cash received and the face value of the note is debited to Discount on Notes Payable. **Discount on Notes Payable is a contra account to Notes Payable and therefore is subtracted from Notes Payable on the balance sheet.** The balance sheet presentation on March 1 is as follows:

---

[6]The bank discount rate used in this example to find the present value is 11.538%.

ILLUSTRATION 13-1
Balance Sheet
Presentation of Discount

Current liabilities		
Notes Payable	104,000	
Less: Discount on notes payable	4,000	100,000

The amount of the discount, $4,000 in this case, represents the cost of borrowing $100,000 for 4 months. Accordingly, the discount is charged to interest expense over the life of the note. That is, the Discount on Notes Payable balance **represents interest expense chargeable to future periods.** Thus, it would be incorrect to debit Interest Expense for $4,000 at the time the loan is obtained. Additional accounting issues related to notes payable are discussed in Chapter 14.

CURRENT MATURITIES OF LONG-TERM DEBTS

The portion of bonds, mortgage notes, and other long-term indebtedness that matures within the next fiscal year—**current maturities of long-term debt**—is reported as a current liability. When only a part of a long-term debt is to be paid within the next 12 months, as in the case of serial bonds that are to be retired through a series of annual installments, **the maturing portion of long-term debt is reported as a current liability,** the balance as a long-term debt.

Long-term debts maturing currently should not be included as current liabilities if they are to be:

1. retired by assets accumulated for this purpose that properly have not been shown as current assets,

2. refinanced, or retired from the proceeds of a new debt issue (see next topic), or

3. converted into capital stock.

In these situations, the use of current assets or the creation of other current liabilities does not occur. Therefore, classification as a current liability is inappropriate. The plan for liquidation of such a debt should be disclosed either parenthetically or by a note to the financial statements.

However, a liability that is **due on demand** (callable by the creditor) or will be due on demand within a year (or operating cycle, if longer) should be classified as a current liability. Liabilities often become callable by the creditor when there is a violation of the debt agreement. For example, most debt agreements specify a given level of equity to debt be maintained, or specify that working capital be of a minimum amount. If an agreement is violated, classification of the debt as current is required because it is a reasonable expectation that existing working capital will be used to satisfy the debt. Only if it can be shown that it is **probable** that the violation will be cured (satisfied) within the grace period usually given in these agreements can the debt be classified as noncurrent.[7]

SHORT-TERM OBLIGATIONS EXPECTED TO BE REFINANCED

OBJECTIVE 3

Explain the classification issues of short-term debt expected to be refinanced.

Short-term obligations are those debts that are scheduled to mature within one year after the date of an enterprise's balance sheet or within an enterprise's operating cycle, whichever is longer. Some **short-term obligations** are **expected to be refinanced** on a long-term basis and, therefore, are not expected to require the use of working capital during the next year (or operating cycle).[8]

At one time, the accounting profession generally supported the exclusion of short-term obligations from current liabilities if they were "expected to be refinanced." Be-

---

[7]"Classification of Obligations That Are Callable by the Creditor," *Statement of Financial Accounting Standards No. 78* (Stamford, Conn.: FASB, 1983).

[8]*Refinancing a short-term obligation on a long-term basis* means either replacing it with a long-term obligation or with equity securities, or renewing, extending, or replacing it with short-term obligations for an uninterrupted period extending beyond one year (or the operating cycle, if longer) from the date of the enterprise's balance sheet.

cause the profession provided no specific guidelines, however, determining whether a short-term obligation was "expected to be refinanced" was usually based solely on management's **intent** to refinance on a long-term basis. A company may obtain a 5-year bank loan but, because the bank prefers it, handle the actual financing with 90-day notes, which it must keep turning over (renewing). So what is the loan—a long-term debt or a current liability? Another example of this problem of classification was the Penn Central Railroad before it went bankrupt. The railroad was deep into short-term debt and commercial paper but classified it as long-term debt. Why? Because the railroad believed it had commitments from lenders to keep refinancing the short-term debt. When those commitments suddenly disappeared, it was good-bye Pennsy. As the Greek philosopher Epictetus once said, "Some things in this world are not and yet appear to be."

Refinancing Criteria

As a result of these classification problems, the profession set forth authoritative criteria for determining the circumstances under which short-term obligations may properly be excluded from current liabilities. An enterprise is required to exclude a short-term obligation from current liabilities only if **both** of the following conditions are met:

1. It must **intend to refinance** the obligation on a long-term basis, and
2. It must **demonstrate an ability** to consummate the refinancing.[9]

Intention to refinance on a long-term basis means the enterprise intends to refinance the short-term obligation so that the use of working capital will not be required during the ensuing fiscal year or operating cycle, if longer. The **ability** to consummate the refinancing may be demonstrated by:

(a) **Actually refinancing** the short-term obligation by issuing a long-term obligation or equity securities after the date of the balance sheet but before it is issued; or

(b) Entering into a **financing agreement** that clearly permits the enterprise to re-finance the debt on a long-term basis on terms that are readily determinable.

If an actual refinancing occurs, the portion of the short-term obligation to be excluded from current liabilities may not exceed the proceeds from the new obligation or equity securities that are applied to retire the short-term obligation. For example, Montavon Winery with $3,000,000 of short-term debt issued 100,000 shares of common stock subsequent to the balance sheet date but before the balance sheet was issued, intending to use the proceeds to liquidate the short-term debt at its maturity. If the net proceeds from the sale of the 100,000 shares totaled $2,000,000, only that amount of the short-term debt could be excluded from current liabilities.

When a financing agreement is relied upon to demonstrate ability to refinance a short-term obligation on a long-term basis, the agreement must meet **all** of the following conditions:

(a) The agreement must be noncancelable as to all parties and must extend beyond the normal operating cycle of the company or one year, whichever is longer.

(b) At the balance sheet date and at the date of its issuance, the company must not be in violation of the agreement.

(c) The lender or investor is expected to be financially capable of honoring the agreement.

There are limits on the amount of short-term debt that can be excluded from current liabilities. Such debt:

1. Cannot exceed the amount available for refinancing under the agreement.

---

[9]"Classification of Short-term Obligations Expected to Be Refinanced," *Statement of Financial Accounting Standards No. 6* (Stamford, Conn.: FASB, 1975), pars. 10 and 11.

2. Must be adjusted for any limitations or restrictions in the agreement that indicate that the full amount obtainable will not be available to retire the short-term obligations.

3. Cannot exceed a reasonable estimate of the **minimum** amount expected to be available, if the amount available for refinancing will fluctuate. (That is, the most conservative estimate must be used.)

If any of these three amounts **cannot be reasonably estimated, the entire amount of the short-term debt must be included in current liabilities.**

As an illustration of a fluctuating amount (item 3 above), consider the following:

Chicago Casket Company enters into an agreement with Continental Bank to borrow up to 80% of the amount of its trade receivables. During the next fiscal year, the receivables are expected to range between a low of $900,000 in the first quarter and a high of $1,700,000 in the third quarter. The minimum amount expected to be available to refinance the short-term obligations that mature during the first quarter of the next year is $720,000 (80% of the expected low for receivables during the first quarter). Consequently, no more than $720,000 of short-term obligations may be excluded from current liabilities at the balance sheet date.

An additional question relates to whether a short-term obligation should be excluded from current liabilities if it is paid off after the balance sheet date and subsequently replaced by long-term debt before the balance sheet is issued. To illustrate, Marquardt Company pays off short-term debt of $40,000 on January 17, 1996, and issues long-term debt of $100,000 on February 3, 1996. Marquardt's financial statements dated December 31, 1995, are to be issued March 1, 1996. Because repayment of the short-term obligation **before** funds were obtained through long-term financing required the use of **existing** current assets, the profession requires that the short-term obligation be included in current liabilities at the balance sheet date (see graphical presentation below).[10]

ILLUSTRATION 13-2
Short-Term Debt Paid Off after Balance Sheet Date and Later Replaced by Long-Term Debt

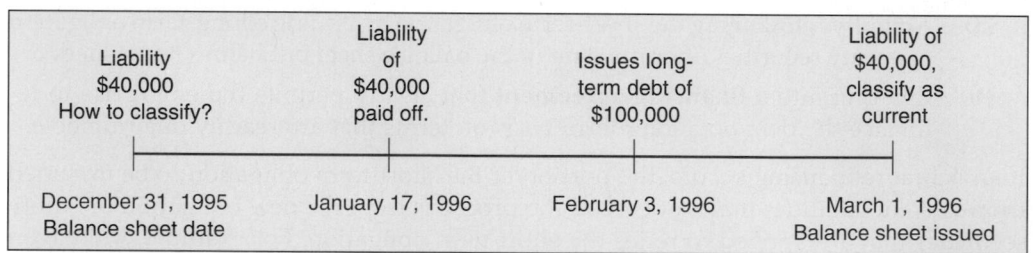

Disclosure

If a short-term obligation is excluded from current liabilities because of refinancing, the note to the financial statements should include:

1. A general description of the financing agreement.
2. The terms of any new obligation incurred or to be incurred.
3. The terms of any equity security issued or to be issued.

When refinancing on a long-term basis is expected to be accomplished through the issuance of equity securities, it is not appropriate to include the short-term obligation in owners' equity. At the date of the balance sheet, the obligation is a liability and not owners' equity.

Short-term obligations expected to be refinanced may be shown in captions distinct from both current liabilities and long-term debt, such as "Interim Debt," "Short-term Debt Expected to Be Refinanced," or "Intermediate Debt." The disclosure requirements are shown in Illustrations 13-3 and 13-4 for an actual refinancing situation and a financing agreement situation.

---

[10]"Classification of a Short-term Obligation Repaid Prior to Being Replaced by a Long-term Security" (an interpretation of *FASB Statement No. 6*), *FASB Interpretation No. 8* (Stamford, Conn.: FASB, 1976), par. 3.

ILLUSTRATION 13-3
Actual Refinancing of Short-Term Debt

	December 31, 1994
Current liabilities:	
Accounts payable	$ 3,600,000
Accrued payables	2,500,000
Income taxes payable	1,100,000
Current portion of long-term debt	1,000,000
Total current liabilities	$ 8,200,000
Long-term debt:	
Notes payable refinanced in January 1995 (Note 1)	$ 2,000,000
11% bonds due serially through 2005	15,000,000
Total long-term debt	$17,000,000

Note 1: On January 19, 1995, the Company issued 50,000 shares of Common Stock and received proceeds totaling $2,385,000 of which $2,000,000 was used to liquidate notes payable that matured on February 1, 1995. Accordingly, such notes payable have been classified as long-term debt at December 31, 1994.

ILLUSTRATION 13-4
Disclosure of Financing Agreement

	December 31, 1994
Current liabilities:	
Accounts payable	$ 3,600,000
Accrued payables	2,500,000
Income taxes payable	1,100,000
Current portion on long-term debt	1,000,000
Total current liabilities	$ 8,200,000
Long-term debt:	
Notes payable expected to be refinanced in 1995 (Note 1)	$ 2,000,000
11% bonds due serially through 2005	15,000,000
Total long-term debt	$17,000,000

Note 1: Under a financing agreement with a major New York bank, the Company may borrow up to $4,000,000 at any time through 1996. Amounts borrowed under the agreement bear interest at 1% above the bank's prime interest rate and mature 3 years from the date of the loan. The agreement requires the Company to maintain a working capital level of $9,000,000 and prohibits the payment of dividends on common stock without prior approval of the bank. The notes have been classified as long-term debt because the Company intends to borrow $2,000,000 under the agreement to liquidate its notes payable which mature on May 1, 1995.

DIVIDENDS PAYABLE

A **cash dividend payable** is an amount owed by a corporation to its stockholders as a result of board of directors' authorization. At the date of declaration the corporation assumes a liability that places the stockholders in the position of creditors in the amount of dividends declared. Because cash dividends are always paid within one year of declaration (generally within 3 months), they are classified as current liabilities.

Accumulated but undeclared dividends on cumulative preferred stock are not a recognized liability because **preferred dividends in arrears** are not an obligation until formal action is taken by the board of directors authorizing the distribution of earnings. Nevertheless, the amount of cumulative dividends unpaid should be disclosed in a note or it may be shown parenthetically in the capital stock section.

Dividends payable in the form of additional shares of stock are not recognized as a liability. Such **stock dividends** (as discussed in Chapter 16) do not require future outlays of assets or services and are revocable by the board of directors at any time prior to issuance. Even so, such undistributed stock dividends are generally reported in the stockholders' equity section because they represent retained earnings in the process of transfer to paid-in capital.

UNDERLYING
CONCEPT

Preferred dividends in arrears do represent a probable future economic sacrifice, but the expected sacrifice does not result from a past transaction or past event. The sacrifice will result from a future event (declaration by the board of directors). Note disclosure improves the predictive value of the financial statements.

RETURNABLE DEPOSITS

Current liabilities of a company may include **returnable cash deposits** received from customers and employees. Deposits may be received from customers to guarantee performance of a contract or service or as guarantees to cover payment of expected future obligations. For example, telephone companies often require a deposit upon installation of a phone. Deposits may also be received from customers as guarantees for possible damage to property left with the customer. Some companies require their employees to make deposits for the return of keys or other company property. The classification of these items as current or noncurrent liabilities is dependent on the time between the date of the deposit and the termination of the relationship that required the deposit.

UNEARNED REVENUES

A magazine publisher such as Golf Digest may receive a customer's check when magazines are ordered, and an airline company, such as American Airlines, often sells tickets for future flights. Restaurants may issue meal tickets that can be exchanged or used for future meals. Who hasn't received or given a McDonald's gift certificate? Retail stores issue gift certificates that are redeemable in merchandise. How do these companies account for **unearned revenues** that are received before goods are delivered or services are rendered?

1. When the advance is received, Cash is debited, and a current liability account identifying the source of the unearned revenue is credited.

2. When the revenue is earned, the unearned revenue account is debited, and an earned revenue account is credited.

To illustrate, assume that Allstate University sells 10,000 season football tickets at $50 each for its five-game home schedule. The entry for the sales of season tickets is:

August 6

Cash	500,000	
Unearned Football Ticket Revenue		500,000
(To record sale of 10,000 season tickets)		

As each game is completed, the following entry is made:

September 7

Unearned Football Ticket Revenue	100,000	
Football Ticket Revenue		100,000
(To record football ticket revenues earned)		

Unearned Football Ticket Revenue is, therefore, unearned revenue and is reported as a current liability in the balance sheet. As revenue is earned, a transfer from unearned revenue to earned revenue occurs. Unearned revenue is material for some companies: In the airline industry, tickets sold for future flights represent almost 50% of total current liabilities. At United Air Lines, unearned ticket revenue is the largest current liability, recently amounting to over $882 million.

Illustration 13-5 shows specific unearned and earned revenue accounts used in selected types of businesses.

ILLUSTRATION 13-5
Unearned and Earned Revenue Accounts

Type of Business	Account Title	
	Unearned Revenue	Earned Revenue
Airline	Unearned Passenger Ticket Revenue	Passenger Revenue
Magazine Publisher	Unearned Subscription Revenue	Subscription Revenue
Hotel	Unearned Rental Revenue	Rental Revenue
Auto Dealer	Unearned Warranty Revenue	Warranty Revenue

The balance sheet should report obligations for any commitments that are redeemable in goods and services; the income statement should report revenues earned during the period.

SALES TAXES PAYABLE

Sales taxes on transfers of tangible personal property and on certain services must be collected from customers and remitted to the proper governmental authority. A liability is set up to provide for taxes collected from customers but not yet remitted to the tax authority. The Sales Taxes Payable account should reflect the liability for sales taxes due various governments. The entry below is the proper one for a sale of $3,000 when a 4% sales tax is in effect.

Cash or Accounts Receivable	3,120	
Sales		3,000
Sales Taxes Payable		120

When the sales tax collections credited to the liability account are not equal to the liability as computed by the governmental formula, an adjustment of the liability account may be made by recognizing a gain or a loss on sales tax collections.

In many companies, however, the sales tax and the amount of the sale are not segregated at the time of sale; both are credited in total in the Sales account. In that case, to reflect correctly the actual amount of sales and the liability for sales taxes, the Sales account must be debited for the amount of the sales taxes due the government on these sales and the Sales Taxes Payable account credited for the same amount. As an illustration, assume that the Sales account balance of $150,000 includes sales taxes of 4%. Because the amount recorded in the Sales account is equal to sales plus 4% of sales, or 1.04 times the sales total, sales are $150,000 ÷ 1.04, or $144,230.77. The sales tax liability is $5,769.23 ($144,230.77 × 0.04; or $150,000 − $144,230.77), and the following entry would be made to record the amount due the taxing unit:

Sales	5,769.23	
Sales Taxes Payable		5,769.23

PROPERTY TAXES PAYABLE

Local governmental units generally depend on property taxes as their primary source of revenue. Such taxes are based on the assessed value of both real and personal property and become a lien against the property at a date determined by law, usually the assessment date. This lien is a liability of the property owner and is a cost of the services of such property. The accounting questions that arise from property taxes are:

1. When should property owners record the liability?
2. To which accounting period should the cost be charged?

The accounting profession, in considering the various periods to which property taxes might be charged and how the liability should be reported, contends that "generally, the most acceptable basis of providing for property taxes is monthly accrual on the taxpayer's books during the fiscal period of the taxing authority for which the taxes are levied."[11] Charging the taxes to the period subsequent to the levy **relates the expense to the period in which the taxes are used by the governmental unit to provide benefits to the property owner.**

Assume that Seaboard Company, which closes its books each year on December 31, receives its property tax bill in May each year. The fiscal year for the city and county in which Seaboard Company is located begins on May 1 and ends on the following April 30. Property taxes of $36,000 are assessed against Seaboard Company property on January 1, 1995, and become a lien on May 1, 1995. Tax bills are sent out in May and are payable in equal installments on July 1 and September 1.

Entries to record the liability, monthly tax charges, and the tax payments for taxes becoming a lien on May 1, 1995 are shown on the next page.

---

[11]Possible alternatives are: (a) year in which paid, (b) year ending on assessment (or lien) date, (c) year beginning on assessment (or lien) date, (d) calendar or fiscal year of taxpayer prior to assessment (or lien) date, (e) calendar or fiscal year of taxpayer including assessment (or lien) date, (f) calendar or fiscal year of taxpayer prior to payment date, (g) fiscal year of governing body levying the tax, and (h) year appearing on tax bill. Committee on Accounting Procedure, American Institute of Certified Public Accountants, *Accounting Research and Terminology Bulletin, Final Edition* (New York: AICPA, 1961), ch. 10, sec. A, par. 10.

May 1, 1995 (lien date):

No entry

May 31 and June 30, 1995 (monthly expense accrual):

Property Tax Expense	3,000	
Property Taxes Payable		3,000

July 1, 1995 (first tax payment):

Property Taxes Payable	6,000	
Prepaid Property Taxes	12,000	
Cash		18,000

July 31 and August 31, 1995 (monthly expense accrual):

Property Tax Expense	3,000	
Prepaid Property Taxes		3,000

September 1, 1995 (second tax payment):

Prepaid Property Taxes	18,000	
Cash		18,000

Sept. 30, Oct. 31, Nov. 30, and Dec. 31, 1995, and Jan. 31, Feb. 29, March 31, and April 30, 1996 (monthly expense accrual):

Property Tax Expense	3,000	
Prepaid Property Taxes		3,000

Prepaid Property Taxes of $12,000 on July 1 represents a 4-month prepayment and $18,000 on September 1 represents a 6-month prepayment. At December 31, the account has 4 months of unexpired tax.[12]

Some accountants advocate accruing property taxes by charges to expense during the fiscal year **ending on the lien date,** rather than during the fiscal year beginning on the lien date (the fiscal year of the tax authority). In such instances the property tax for the coming fiscal year must be estimated and charged monthly to Property Tax Expense and must be credited to Property Tax Payable. Under this method the entire amount of the tax is accrued by the lien date and the expense is therefore charged to the fiscal period preceding payment of the tax. Justification for this method exists when the assessment date precedes the lien date by a year or more, as is the case in some taxing units. Since, in such instances, the amount is estimated and accrued by the property owner before receipt of the tax bill, it is theoretically proper to categorize property taxes as an **estimated** rather than as a **determinable** current liability.

Recognizing that special circumstances can suggest the use of alternative accrual periods, the profession supports the view that **"consistency of application from year to year is the important consideration and selection of any of the periods mentioned is a matter for individual judgment."**[13]

INCOME TAX PAYABLE

Any federal or state income tax varies in proportion to the amount of annual income. Some accountants consider the amount of income tax on annual income as an estimate because the computation of income (and the tax thereon) is subject to IRS review and approval. The meaning and application of numerous tax rules, especially new ones, are debatable and often dependent on a court's interpretation. Using the best information and advice available, a business must prepare an income tax return and compute the income tax payable resulting from the operations of the current period. The taxes pay-

---

[12]Some accountants have argued that the entire liability of $36,000 should be recorded on the lien date with a related debit to a Deferred Charge account. These individuals contend that the company has a legal liability at that date and therefore the full amount of the liability should be reported. We disagree. To report the full liability at the lien date necessitates the recording of a Deferred Property Tax Asset for unpaid property taxes—a dubious asset. In addition, the liability accrues as the property is used—if the property is sold, the buyer has the responsibility for the property taxes subsequent to purchase—not the seller.

[13]*Accounting Research and Terminology Bulletin,* Final Edition, par. 3.

able on the income of a corporation, as computed per the tax return, should be classified as a current liability.[14]

Unlike the corporation, the proprietorship and the partnership are not taxable entities. Because the individual proprietor and the members of a partnership are subject to personal income taxes on their share of the business's taxable income, income tax liabilities do not appear on the financial statements of proprietorships and partnerships.

Most corporations must make periodic tax payments in an authorized bank depository or a Federal Reserve bank throughout the year. These payments are based upon estimates of the total annual tax liability. As the estimated total tax liability changes, the periodic contributions also change. If in a later year an additional tax is assessed on the income of an earlier year, Income Taxes Payable should be credited. The related debit should be charged to current operations.

Differences between taxable income under the tax laws and accounting income under generally accepted accounting principles have become greater in recent years. Because of these differences, the amount of income tax payable to the government in any given year may differ substantially from income tax expense, as reported on the financial statements. Chapter 20 is devoted solely to income tax matters and presents an extensive discussion of this complex and controversial problem.

EMPLOYEE-RELATED LIABILITIES

Amounts owed to employees for salaries or wages at the end of an accounting period are reported as a current liability. In addition, the following items related to employee compensation are often reported as current liabilities:

OBJECTIVE 4
Identify types of employee-related liabilities.

1. Payroll deductions.
2. Compensated absences.
3. Postretirement benefits.
4. Bonuses. (Accounting for bonuses is covered in Appendix 13-A.)

Payroll Deductions

The most common types of payroll deductions are taxes and miscellaneous items such as insurance premiums, employee savings, and union dues. To the extent the amounts deducted have not been remitted to the proper authority at the end of the accounting period, they should be recognized as current liabilities.

Social Security Taxes

Since January 1, 1937, social security legislation has provided federal old-age, survivor, and disability insurance (O.A.S.D.I.) benefits for certain individuals and their families through taxes levied on both the employer and the employee. All employers covered are required to collect the employee's share of this tax, by deducting it from the employee's gross pay, and to remit it to the government along with the employer's share. Both the employer and the employee are taxed at the same rate, currently 6.2% (1994) based on the employee's gross pay up to a $60,600 annual limit.

---

[14]The four-step progressive tax rate structure on corporate income applies:

Corporate Taxable Income	1994 Tax Rate
$50,000 or less	15%
$50,001–$75,000	25%
$75,001–$10,000,000	34%
Above $10,000,000	35%

If a corporation has taxable income in excess of $100,000 for any taxable year, the amount of tax is increased by the lesser of 5% of such excess or $11,750. This surtax phases out the benefits of the 15% and 25% rates. A similar phaseout applies for taxable incomes above $15,000,000. In such cases, a 3% surtax is imposed, up to a maximum tax of $100,000.

In 1965 Congress passed the first federal health insurance program for the aged—popularly known as Medicare. It is a two-part program designed to alleviate the high cost of medical care for those over age 65. The Basic Plan, which provides hospital and other institutional services, is financed by a separate Hospital Insurance tax paid by both the employee and the employer at the rate of 1.45% on the employee's total compensation. The Voluntary Plan takes care of the major part of doctors' bills and other medical and health services and is financed by monthly payments from all who enroll plus matching funds from the federal government.

The combination of the O.A.S.D.I. tax, often called Federal Insurance Contribution Act (F.I.C.A.) tax, and the federal Hospital Insurance Tax is commonly referred to as the **social security tax.** The combined rate for these taxes, 7.65% on an employee's wages to $60,600 and 1.45% in excess of $60,600, is changed intermittently by acts of Congress. The amount of unremitted employee and employer social security tax on gross wages paid should be reported by the employer as a current liability.

Unemployment Taxes

Another payroll tax levied by the federal government in cooperation with state governments provides a system of unemployment insurance. All employers who (1) paid wages of $1,500 or more during any calendar quarter in the year or preceding year or (2) employed at least one individual on at least one day in each of 20 weeks during the current or preceding calendar year are subject to the Federal Unemployment Tax Act (F.U.T.A.). This tax is levied only on the employer at a rate of 6.2% (1994) on the first $7,000 of compensation paid to each employee during the calendar year. The employer is allowed a tax credit not to exceed 5.4% for contributions paid to a state plan for unemployment compensation. Thus, if an employer is subject to a state unemployment tax of 5.4% or more, only 0.8% tax is due the federal government.

State unemployment compensation laws differ from the federal law and differ among various states. Therefore, employers must be familiar with the unemployment tax laws in each state in which they pay wages and salaries. Although the normal state tax may range from 3% to 7% or higher, all states provide for some form of merit rating under which a reduction in the state contribution rate is allowed. Employers who display by their benefit and contribution experience that they have provided steady employment may be entitled to this reduction—if the size of the state fund is adequate to provide the reduction. In order not to penalize an employer who has earned a reduction in the state contribution rate, the federal law allows a credit of 5.4% even though the effective state contribution rate is less than 5.4%.

To illustrate, Appliance Repair Co., which has a taxable payroll of $100,000, is subject to a federal rate of 6.2% and a state contribution rate of 5.7%. But because of stable employment experience, the company's state rate has been reduced to 1%. The computation of the federal and state unemployment taxes for Appliance Repair Co. is:

ILLUSTRATION 13-6
Computation of
Unemployment Taxes

State unemployment tax payment (1%)($100,000)	$1,000
Federal unemployment tax (6.2% − 5.4%)($100,000)	800
Total federal and state unemployment tax	$1,800

The federal unemployment tax is paid annually, on or before January 31 following the taxable calendar year. State contributions generally are required to be paid quarterly. Because both the federal and the state unemployment taxes accrue on earned compensation, the amount of accrued but unpaid employer contributions should be recorded as an operating expense and as a current liability when financial statements are prepared at year-end.

Income Tax Withholding

Federal and some state income tax laws require employers to withhold from the pay of each employee the applicable income tax due on those wages. The amount of income tax withheld is computed by the employer according to a government-prescribed formula or withholding tax table. That amount depends on the length of the pay period and each employee's taxable wages, marital status, and claimed dependents.

If the income tax withheld plus the employee and the employer social security taxes exceeds specified amounts per month, the employer is required to make remittances to the government during the month. Monthly deposits are not required if the employer's liability for the calendar quarter is less than $500. Instead, the tax liability is remitted with the employer's quarterly payroll tax return.

Illustration

Assume a weekly payroll of $10,000 entirely subject to F.I.C.A. and Medicare (7.65%), federal (0.8%) and state (4%) unemployment taxes with income tax withholding of $1,320 and union dues of $88 deducted.

The entry to record the wages and salaries paid and the employee payroll deductions would be:

Wages and Salaries	10,000	
Withholding Taxes Payable		1,320
F.I.C.A. Taxes Payable		765
Union Dues Payable to Local No. 257		88
Cash		7,827

The entry to record the employer payroll taxes would be:

Payroll Tax Expense	1,245	
F.I.C.A. Taxes Payable		765
Federal Unemployment Tax Payable		80
State Unemployment Tax Payable		400

The employer is required to remit to the government its share of F.I.C.A. tax along with the amount of F.I.C.A. tax deducted from each employee's gross compensation. All unremitted employer F.I.C.A. taxes should be recorded as payroll tax expense and payroll tax payable. In a manufacturing enterprise, all of the payroll costs (wages, payroll taxes, and fringe benefits) are allocated to appropriate cost accounts such as Direct Labor, Indirect Labor, Sales Salaries, Administrative Salaries, and the like. This abbreviated and somewhat simplified discussion of payroll costs and deductions is not indicative of the volume of records and clerical work that may be involved in maintaining a sound and accurate payroll system.

Compensated Absences

Compensated absences are absences from employment—such as vacation, illness, and holidays—for which employees are paid anyway. Prior to the issuance of *FASB Statement No. 43*, "Accounting for Compensated Absences," employers used alternative methods to account for compensated absences. Some accrued the cost. Some recorded the cost in the period when paid. *FASB No. 43* was issued to eliminate the latter alternative and to reduce the potential for significant unrecorded or understated liabilities. It requires that a liability be accrued for the cost of compensation for future absences if **all** of the following conditions are met:[15]

(a) The employer's obligation relating to employees' rights to receive compensation for future absences is attributable to employees' services **already rendered,**

(b) The obligation relates to the rights that **vest or accumulate,**

(c) Payment of the compensation is **probable,** and

(d) The amount can be **reasonably estimated.**[16]

UNDERLYING
CONCEPT

When these four conditions exist, all elements in the definition of a liability exist. In addition, the matching concept requires that the period receiving the services also should report the related expense.

---

[15]"Accounting for Compensated Absences," *Statement of Financial Accounting Standards No. 43* (Stamford, Conn.: FASB, 1980), par. 6.

[16]These same four conditions are to be applied to accounting for **postemployment benefits. Postemployment benefits** are benefits provided by an enterprise to past or inactive employees **after employment but prior to retirement.** Examples include salary continuation, supplemental unemployment benefits, severance pay, job training, and continuation of health and life insurance coverage. The FASB recently issued *Statement No. 112*, "Employers' Accounting for Postemployment Benefits" which requires that the accounting treatment for compensated absences described in *FASB Statement No. 43* should be applied to postemployment benefits. "Employers' Accounting for Postemployment Benefits," *Statement of Financial Accounting Standards No. 112* (Norwalk, CT: FASB, November 1992), par. 18.

An example of an accrual for compensated absences is shown below in an excerpt from the balance sheet of Clarcor Inc. presented in its Annual Report.

ILLUSTRATION 13-7
Balance Sheet
Presentation of Accrual
for Compensated
Absences

Clarcor Inc.	
Current Liabilities	
Accounts payable	$ 6,308
Accrued salaries, wages and commissions	2,278
Compensated absences	2,271
Accrued pension liabilities	1,023
Other accrued liabilities	4,572
	$16,452

If an employer meets conditions (a), (b), and (c) on the previous page, but does not accrue a liability because of a failure to meet condition (d), that fact should be disclosed. An example of such a disclosure is the following note from the financial statements of Gotham Utility Company:

ILLUSTRATION 13-8
Disclosure of Policy for
Compensated Absences

> **Gotham Utility Company**
>
> Employees of the Company are entitled to paid vacation, personal, and sick days off, depending on job status, length of service, and other factors. Due to numerous differing union contracts and other agreements with nonunion employees, it is impractical to estimate the amount of compensation for future absences, and, accordingly, no liability has been reported in the accompanying financial statements. The Company's policy is to recognize the cost of compensated absences when actually paid to employees; compensated absence payments to employees totaled $2,786,000.

Vested rights exist when an employer has an obligation to make payment to an employee even if his or her employment is terminated; thus, vested rights are not contingent on an employee's future service. **Accumulated rights** are those that can be carried forward to future periods if not used in the period in which earned. For example, assume that you have earned 4 days of vacation pay as of December 31, the end of your employer's fiscal year, and that you will be paid for this vacation time even if you terminate employment. In this situation, your 4 days of vacation pay are considered vested and must be accrued. Now assume that your vacation days are not vested, but that you can carry the 4 days over into later periods. Although the rights are not vested, they are accumulated rights for which the employer must provide an accrual, allowing for estimated forfeitures due to turnover.

A modification of the general rules relates to the issue of **sick pay.** If sick pay benefits vest, accrual is required. If sick pay benefits accumulate but do not vest, accrual is permitted but not required. The reason for this distinction is that compensation that is designated as sick pay may be administered in one of two ways. In some companies, employees receive sick pay only if they are absent because of illness. Accrual of a liability is permitted but not required because its payment is contingent upon future employee illness. In other companies, employees are allowed to accumulate unused sick pay and take compensated time off from work even though they are not ill. For this type of sick pay, a liability must be accrued because it will be paid whether or not employees ever become ill.

The expense and related liability for compensated absences should be recognized in the year earned by employees. For example, if new employees receive rights to 2 weeks' paid vacation at the beginning of their second year of employment, the vacation pay is considered to be earned during the first year of employment.

What rate should be used to accrue the compensated absence cost—the current rate or an estimated future rate? *FASB Statement No. 43* is silent on this subject; therefore, it is likely that companies will use the current rather than future rate. The future rate is less certain and raises issues concerning the time value of money. To illustrate, assume that Amutron Inc. began operations on January 1, 1994. The company employs 10 individuals who are paid $480 per week. Vacation weeks earned by all employees in 1994 were 20 weeks, but none were used during this period. In 1995, the vacation weeks were used when the current rate of pay was $540 per week for each employee. The entry at December 31, 1994 to accrue the accumulated vacation pay is as follows:

Wages Expense	9,600	
Vacation Wages Payable ($480 × 20)		9,600

At December 31, 1994 the company would report on its balance sheet a liability of $9,600. In 1995, the vacation pay related to 1994 would be recorded as follows:

Vacation Wages Payable	9,600	
Wages Expense	1,200	
Cash ($540 × 20)		10,800

In 1995 the vacation weeks were used; therefore, the liability is extinguished. Note that the difference between the amount of cash paid and the reduction in the liability account is recorded as an adjustment to Wages Expense in the period when paid. This difference arises because the liability account was accrued at the rates of pay in effect during the period when compensated time was earned. The cash paid, however, is based on the rates in effect during the period when compensated time is used. If the future rates of pay had been used to compute the accrual in 1994, then the cash paid in 1995 would have been equal to the liability.

Postretirement Benefits

The accounting and reporting standards for postretirement benefit payments are complex. These standards relate to two different types of **postretirement benefits:** (1) pensions and (2) postretirement health care and life insurance benefits. These issues are discussed extensively in Chapter 21.

Bonus Agreements

For various reasons, many companies give a **bonus** to certain or all officers and employees in addition to their regular salary or wage. Frequently the bonus amount is dependent on the company's yearly profit. For example, Ford Motor Company has a plan whereby employees share in the success of the company's operations on the basis of a complicated formula using net income as its primary basis for computation. From the standpoint of the enterprise, **bonus payments to employees** may be considered additional wages and should be included as a deduction in determining the net income for the year.

To illustrate the entries for an employee bonus, assume a company whose income for the year 1995 is $100,000 will pay out bonuses of $10,714.29 in January 1996. (Computations of this and other bonuses are illustrated in Appendix 13-A.) An adjusting entry dated December 31, 1995, is made to record the bonus as follows:

Employees' Bonus Expense	10,714.29	
Profit-Sharing Bonus Payable		10,714.29

In January 1996, when the bonus is paid, the journal entry would be:

Profit-Sharing Bonus Payable	10,714.29	
Cash		10,714.29

The expense account should appear in the income statement as an operating expense. The liability, accrued profit-sharing bonus payable, is usually payable within a short period of time and should be included as a current liability in the balance sheet.

Similar to bonus arrangements are contractual agreements covering rents or royalty payments conditional on the amount of revenues earned or the quantity of product produced or extracted. Conditional expenses based on revenues or units produced are usually less difficult to compute than bonus arrangements. For example, if a lease calls for a fixed rent payment of $500 per month and 1% of all sales over $300,000 per year, the annual rent obligation would amount to $6,000 plus $.01 of each dollar of revenue over $300,000. Or, a royalty agreement may accrue to the patent owner $1.00 for every ton of product resulting from the patented process, or accrue to the mineral rights owner

$.50 on every barrel of oil extracted. As each additional unit of product is produced or extracted, an additional obligation, usually a current liability, is created.

▶ DISCLOSURE OF CURRENT LIABILITIES IN THE FINANCIAL STATEMENTS

OBJECTIVE 5

Indicate how current liabilities are disclosed.

Theoretically, liabilities should be measured by the present value of the future outlay of cash required to liquidate them. But, in practice, current liabilities are usually recorded in accounting records and reported in financial statements at their full maturity value. Because of the short time periods involved, frequently less than one year, the difference between the present value of a current liability and the maturity value is not usually large. The slight overstatement of liabilities that results from carrying current liabilities at maturity value is accepted as immaterial. *APB Opinion No. 21,* "Interest on Receivables and Payables," specifically exempts from present value measurements those payables arising from transactions with suppliers in the normal course of business that do not exceed approximately one year.[17]

The current liability accounts are commonly presented as the first classification in the liabilities and stockholders' equity section of the balance sheet. In some instances, current liabilities are presented as a group immediately below current assets with the total of the current liabilities deducted from the total current assets to obtain "working capital" or "current assets in excess of current liabilities."

Within the current liability section the accounts may be listed in order of maturity, in descending order of amount, or in order of liquidation preference. The authors' review of published financial statements in 1992–93 disclosed that a significant majority of the companies examined listed "notes payable" first (sometimes called "commercial paper" or "bank loans" or "short-term debt"), regardless of relative amount, followed most often with "accounts payable," and ended the current liability section with "current portion of long-term debt." Georgia-Pacific's current liability section on page 221 begins with a less typical account—"Bank overdrafts, net, $173 million."

INTERNATIONAL INSIGHT

In Brazil, material current liabilities due in foreign currencies are presented separately.

Detail and supplemental information concerning current liabilities should be sufficient to meet the requirement of full disclosure. Secured liabilities should be identified clearly, and the related assets pledged as collateral indicated. If the due date of any liability can be extended, the details should be disclosed. Current liabilities should not be offset against assets that are to be applied to their liquidation. Current maturities of long-term debt should be classified as current liabilities.

A major exception exists when a currently maturing obligation is to be paid from assets classified as long-term. For example, if payments to retire a bond payable are made from a bond sinking fund classified as a long-term asset, the bonds payable should be reported in the long-term liability section. Presentation of this debt in the current liability section would distort the working capital position of the enterprise.

Existing commitments that will result in obligations in succeeding periods that are material in amount may require disclosure. For example, commitments to purchase goods or services, or for the construction, purchase, or lease of equipment or properties may require disclosure in notes accompanying the balance sheet.

Presented in Illustration 13-9 is an excerpt of the Albertson's, Inc. (a large grocery store chain) published financial statements, which is a representative presentation of the current liabilities as found in the reports of large corporations:

---

[17]"Interest on Receivables and Payables," *Opinions of the Accounting Principles Board No. 21* (New York: AICPA, 1971), par. 3.

Albertson's, Inc.		
	1993	1992
	($000)	
Current Liabilities		
Accounts payable	$518,614	$400,417
Notes payable	5,000	30,000
Salaries and related liabilities	95,820	80,719
Taxes other than income taxes	41,522	37,807
Income taxes	29,592	9,589
Unearned income	15,567	16,429
Other	77,903	68,164
Current maturities of long-term debt	25,757	3,588
Current obligations under capital leases	6,044	5,634
Total current liabilities	815,819	652,247

ILLUSTRATION 13-9
Balance Sheet Presentation of Current Liabilities

▶ SECTION 2 / CONTINGENCIES

A **contingency** is defined in *FASB Statement No. 5* "as an existing condition, situation, or set of circumstances involving uncertainty as to possible gain (**gain contingency**) or loss (**loss contingency**) to an enterprise that will ultimately be resolved when one or more future events occur or fail to occur."[18] As discussed in Chapter 5, gain contingencies are not recorded and are disclosed in the notes only when the probabilities are high that a gain contingency will be realized. As a result, it is unusual to find information about contingent gains in the financial statements and the accompanying notes. A liability incurred as a result of a "loss contingency" is by definition a **contingent liability.** **Contingent liabilities** are obligations that are dependent upon the occurrence or non-occurrence of one or more future events to confirm either the amount payable, the payee, the date payable, or its existence. That is, one or more of these factors depend upon a contingency.

▶ ACCOUNTING FOR LOSS CONTINGENCIES

When a loss contingency exists, the likelihood that the future event or events will confirm the incurrence of a liability can range from probable to remote. As previously discussed in Chapter 5, the FASB uses the terms **probable, reasonably possible,** and **remote** to identify three areas within that range and assigns the following meanings:

OBJECTIVE 6
Identify the criteria used to account for and disclose loss contingencies.

Probable. The future event or events are likely to occur.

Reasonably Possible. The chance of the future event or events occurring is more than remote but less than likely.

Remote. The chance of the future event or events occurring is slight.

An estimated loss from a loss contingency should be accrued by a charge to expense and a liability recorded only if **both** of the following conditions are met:[19]

1. Information available prior to the issuance of the financial statements indicates that it is **probable that a liability has been incurred** at the date of the financial statements.

2. The amount of the loss can be **reasonably estimated.**

---

[18]"Accounting for Contingencies," *Statement of Financial Accounting Standards No. 5* (Stamford, Conn.: FASB, 1975), par. 1.

[19]Those loss contingencies that result in the incurrence of a liability are most relevant to the discussion in this chapter. Loss contingencies that result in the impairment of an asset (e.g., collectibility of receivables or threat of expropriation of assets) are discussed more fully in other sections of this textbook.

Neither the exact payee nor the exact date payable need be known to record a liability. **What must be known is whether it is probable that a liability has been incurred.**

The second criterion indicates that an amount for the liability can be reasonably determined; otherwise, it should not be accrued as a liability. Evidence to determine a reasonable estimate of the liability may be based on the company's own experience, experience of other companies in the industry, engineering or research studies, legal advice, or educated guesses by personnel in the best position to know. The following excerpt from the annual report of Quaker State Oil Refining Corp. is an example of an accrual recorded for a loss contingency.

ILLUSTRATION 13-10
Disclosure of Accrual for Loss Contingency

Quaker State Oil Refining Corp.
Note 5: Contingencies. During the period from November 13 to December 23, a change in an additive component purchased from one of its suppliers caused certain oil refined and shipped to fail to meet the Company's low-temperature performance requirements. The Company has recalled this product and has arranged for reimbursement to its customers and the ultimate consumers of all costs associated with the product. Estimated cost of the recall program, net of estimated third party reimbursement, in the amount of $3,500,000 has been charged to current operations.

Use of the terms probable, reasonably possible, and remote as guidelines for classifying contingencies involves judgment and subjectivity. The items in Illustration 13-11 are examples of loss contingencies and the general accounting treatment accorded them.[20]

ILLUSTRATION 13-11
Accounting Treatment of Loss Contingencies

Loss Related to	Usually Accrued	Not Accrued	May Be Accrued*
1. Collectibility of receivables	X		
2. Obligations related to product warranties and product defects	X		
3. Premiums offered to customers	X		
4. Risk of loss or damage of enterprise property by fire, explosion, or other hazards		X	
5. General or unspecified business risks		X	
6. Risk of loss from catastrophes assumed by property and casualty insurance companies including reinsurance companies		X	
7. Threat of expropriation of assets			X
8. Pending or threatened litigation			X
9. Actual or possible claims and assessments**			X
10. Guarantees of indebtedness of others			X
11. Obligations of commercial banks under "standby letters of credit"			X
12. Agreements to repurchase receivables (or the related property) that have been sold			X

*Should be accrued when both criteria are met (probable and reasonably estimable).
**Estimated amounts of losses incurred prior to the balance sheet date but settled subsequently should be accrued as of the balance sheet date.

INTERNATIONAL INSIGHT

The European Directives (Standards) do not specify accounting treatments for contingencies.

The accounting concepts and procedures relating to contingent items are relatively new and unsettled. Practicing accountants express concern over the diversity that now exists in the interpretation of "probable," "reasonably possible," and "remote." Current practice relies heavily on the exact language used in responses received from lawyers (such language is necessarily biased and protective rather than predictive). As a result,

---

[20]Adapted from Ernst & Ernst, *Financial Reporting Developments*—No. 38353 (August 1975), p. 4.

accruals and disclosures of contingencies vary considerably in practice. Some of the more common loss contingencies discussed in this chapter are:[21]

1. Litigation, claims, and assessments.
2. Guarantee and warranty costs.
3. Premiums and coupons.
4. Environmental liabilities.
5. Self-insurance risks.

LITIGATION, CLAIMS, AND ASSESSMENTS

The following factors, among others, must be considered in determining whether a liability should be recorded with respect to **pending or threatened litigation** and actual or possible **claims** and **assessments:**

OBJECTIVE 7
Explain the accounting for different types of loss contingencies.

1. The **time period** in which the underlying cause for action occurred.
2. The **probability** of an unfavorable outcome.
3. The ability to make a **reasonable estimate** of the amount of loss.

To report a loss and a liability in the financial statements, the cause for litigation must have occurred on or before the date of the financial statements. It does not matter that the company did not become aware of the existence or possibility of the lawsuit or claims until after the date of the financial statements but before they are issued. To evaluate the probability of an unfavorable outcome, consider: the nature of the litigation; the progress of the case; the opinion of legal counsel; the experience of your company and others in similar cases; and any management response to the lawsuit.

The outcome of pending litigation, however, can seldom be predicted with any assurance. And, even if the evidence available at the balance sheet date does not favor the defendant, it is hardly reasonable to expect the company to publish in its financial statements a dollar estimate of the probable negative outcome. Such specific disclosures could weaken the company's position in the dispute and encourage the plaintiff to intensify its efforts. A typical example of the wording of such a disclosure is the note to the financial statements of The Quaker Oats Company relating to its litigation with Sands, Taylor & Wood Co. shown in Illustration 13-12.

ILLUSTRATION 13-12
Disclosure of Litigation

The Quaker Oats Company

Note 19: Litigation. On December 19, 1990, the Court for the Northern District of Illinois found that the use of the words "thirst aid" in advertising *Gatorade* thirst quencher infringed the Plaintiff's rights in the trademark THIRST-AID. On July 9, 1991, District Court Judge Marshall entered a judgment of $42.6 million, composed of $31.4 million in principal, plus prejudgment interest of $10.6 million and fees, expenses and costs of $0.6 million. The order enjoined use of the phrase "THIRST-AID" in connection with the advertising or sale of *Gatorade* thirst quencher. On September 2, 1992, the appellate court affirmed the finding of infringement, but found that the monetary award was an inequitable "windfall" to the Plaintiff. Further appeal or request for rehearing is possible and the Company is reviewing its options. The amount of any liability which might finally exist cannot reasonably be estimated and no provision for loss has been made in the accompanying financial statements.

The Company is not a party to any other pending legal proceedings which it believes will have a material adverse effect on its financial position or results of operations.

With respect to **unfiled suits** and **unasserted claims and assessments,** a company must determine (1) the degree of **probability** that a suit may be filed or a claim or assessment may be asserted and (2) the **probability** of an unfavorable outcome. For example, assume that Nawtee Company is being investigated by the Federal Trade Commission for restraint of trade, and enforcement proceedings have been instituted.

---

[21]*Accounting Trends and Techniques—1993* reports that of the 600 companies surveyed, loss contingencies of the following nature and number were reported: litigation, 366; environmental, 233; possible tax assessments, 57; insurance, 47; governmental investigation, 30; and others, 52.

Such proceedings are often followed by private claims of triple damages for redress. In this case, Nawtee Company must determine the probability of the claims being asserted **and** the probability of triple damages being awarded. If both are probable, if the loss is reasonably estimable, and if the cause for action is dated on or before the date of the financial statements, then the liability should be accrued.

GUARANTEE AND WARRANTY COSTS

A **warranty (product guarantee)** is a promise made by a seller to a buyer to make good on a deficiency of quantity, quality, or performance in a product. It is commonly used by manufacturers as a sales promotion technique. Automakers, for instance, recently "hyped" their sales by extending their new-car warranty to 7 years or 70,000 miles. For a specified period of time following the date of sale to the consumer, the manufacturer may promise to bear all or part of the cost of replacing defective parts, to perform any necessary repairs or servicing without charge, to refund the purchase price, or even to "double your money back."

Warranties and guarantees entail future costs, frequently significant additional costs, which are sometimes called "after costs" or "post-sale costs." Although the future cost is indefinite as to amount, due date, and even customer, a liability is probable in most cases and should be recognized in the accounts if it can be reasonably estimated. The amount of the liability is an estimate of all the costs that will be incurred after sale and delivery and that are incident to the correction of defects or deficiencies required under the warranty provisions. Warranty costs are a classic example of a loss contingency. There are two basic methods of accounting for warranty costs: (1) the cash basis method and (2) the accrual method.

Cash Basis

Under the **cash basis method,** warranty costs are charged to expense as they are incurred. In other words, **warranty costs are charged to the period in which the seller or manufacturer complies with the warranty.** No liability is recorded for future costs arising from warranties, nor is the period in which the sale is recorded necessarily charged with the costs of making good on outstanding warranties. Use of this method, the only one recognized for income tax purposes, is frequently justified for accounting on the basis of expediency when warranty costs are immaterial or when the warranty period is relatively short. The cash basis method is required when a warranty liability is not accrued in the year of sale either because

1. It is not probable that a liability has been incurred; or
2. The amount of the liability cannot be reasonably estimated.

Accrual Basis

If it is probable that customers will make claims under warranties relating to goods or services that have been sold and a reasonable estimate of the costs involved can be made, the accrual method must be used. Under the **accrual method,** warranty costs are charged to operating expense **in the year of sale.** It is the generally accepted method and should be used whenever the warranty is an integral and inseparable part of the sale and is viewed as a loss contingency. We refer to this approach as the **expense warranty approach.**

Illustration of Expense Warranty Approach

To illustrate the expense warranty method, assume that the Denson Machinery Company begins production on a new machine in July 1995, and sells 100 units at $5,000 each by its year-end, December 31, 1995. Each machine is under warranty for one year and the company has estimated, from past experience with a similar machine, that the warranty cost will probably average $200 per unit. Further, as a result of parts replacements and services rendered in compliance with machinery warranties, the company incurs $4,000 in warranty costs in 1995 and $16,000 in 1996.

Sale of 100 machines at $5,000 each, July through December 1995

Cash or Accounts Receivable	500,000	
Sales		500,000

Recognition of warranty expense, July through December 1995

Warranty Expense	4,000	
Cash, Inventory, or Accrued Payroll		4,000
(Warranty costs incurred)		
Warranty Expense	16,000	
Estimated Liability Under Warranties		16,000
(To accrue estimated warranty costs)		

The 12/31/95 balance sheet would report Estimated Liability Under Warranties as a current liability of $16,000, and the income statement for 1995 would report Warranty Expense of $20,000.

Recognition of warranty costs incurred in 1996 (on 1995 machinery sales)

Estimated Liability Under Warranties	16,000	
Cash, Inventory, or Accrued Payroll		16,000
(Warranty costs incurred)		

If the cash basis method were applied to the facts in the Denson Machinery Company example, $4,000 would be recorded as warranty expense in 1995 and $16,000 as warranty expense in 1996 with all of the sale price being recorded as revenue in 1995. In many instances, application of the cash basis method does not match the warranty costs relating to the products sold during a given period with the revenues derived from such products, and therefore it violates the matching principle. Where ongoing warranty policies exist year after year, the differences between the cash and the expense warranty basis probably would not be so great.

Sales Warranty Approach

A warranty is sometimes **sold separately from the product.** For example, when you purchase a television set or VCR, you will be entitled to the manufacturer's warranty. You also will undoubtedly be offered an extended warranty on the product at an additional cost.[22]

In this case, the seller should recognize separately the sale of the television or VCR with the manufacturer's warranty and the sale of the extended warranty.[23] This approach is referred to as the **sales warranty approach. Revenue on the sale of the extended warranty is deferred** and is generally recognized on a straight-line basis over the life of the contract. Revenue is deferred because the seller of the warranty has an obligation to perform services over the life of the contract. Only costs that vary with and are directly related to the sale of the contracts (mainly commissions) should be deferred and amortized. Costs such as employees' salaries, advertising, and general and administrative expenses that would have been incurred even if no contract were sold should be expensed as incurred.

To illustrate, assume you have just purchased a new automobile from Hanlin Auto for $20,000. In addition to the regular warranty on the auto (all repairs will be paid by the manufacturer for the first 36,000 miles or 3 years, whichever comes first), you purchase at a cost of $600 an extended warranty that protects you for an additional 3 years or 36,000 miles. The entry to record the sale of the automobile (with the regular

---

[22]A contract is separately priced **if the customer has the option to purchase** the services provided under the contract for an expressly stated amount separate from the price of the product. An extended warranty or product maintenance contract usually meets these conditions.

[23]"Accounting for Separately Extended Warranty and Product Maintenance Contracts," *FASB Technical Bulletin No. 90–1* (Stamford, Conn.: FASB, 1990).

warranty) and the sale of the extended warranty on January 2, 1995, on Hanlin Auto's books is:

Cash	20,600	
Sales		20,000
Unearned Warranty Revenue		600

The entry to recognize revenue at the end of the fourth year (using straight-line amortization) would be as follows:

Unearned Warranty Revenue	200	
Warranty Revenue		200

Because the extended warranty contract does not start until after the regular warranty expires, revenue is not recognized until the fourth year. If the costs of performing services under the extended warranty contract are incurred on other than a straight-line basis (as historical evidence might indicate), revenue should be recognized over the contract period in proportion to the costs expected to be incurred in performing services under the contract.[24]

PREMIUMS AND COUPONS

Numerous companies offer (either on a limited or continuing basis) premiums to customers in return for boxtops, certificates, coupons, labels, or wrappers. The **premium** may be silverware, dishes, a small appliance, a toy, other goods, or free transportation.[25] Also, **printed coupons** that can be redeemed for a cash discount on items purchased are extremely popular.[26] A more recent marketing innovation is the **cash rebate,** which the buyer can obtain by returning the store receipt, a rebate coupon, and Universal Product Code (UPC label) or "bar code" to the manufacturer. These premiums, coupon offers, and rebates are made to stimulate sales, and their **costs should be charged to expense in the period of the sale** that benefits from the premium plan. At the end of the accounting period many of these premium offers may be outstanding and, when presented in subsequent periods, must be redeemed. **The number of outstanding premium offers that will be presented for redemption must be estimated in order to reflect the existing current liability and to match costs with revenues.** The cost of

---

[24]Ibid, par. 3.

[25]Recent premium plans that have gained momentum and widespread adoption are the **frequent-flier programs** used by nearly every major airline. On the basis of mileage accumulated, frequent-flier members are awarded discounted or free airline tickets. Although the frequent-flier concept, begun in 1981 by American Airlines, was little more than a takeoff on green stamps, its success in generating repeat business stunned the airline industry. Today, especially with the advent of triple-mileage bonuses, frequent-flier programs are so popular that airlines now owe participants more than 3 million round-trip domestic tickets. That's enough to fly at least 5.4 billion miles—free. And therein lies the accounting problem. Those free tickets represent an enormous potential liability because people using them may displace paying passengers.

When airlines first started offering frequent-flier bonuses, everyone assumed that they could accommodate the free-ticket holders with otherwise-empty seats. That made the additional cost of the program so minimal that airlines didn't accrue it or report the small liability. But, as more and more paying passengers have been crowded off of flights by frequent-flier awardees, the loss of revenues has grown enormously. One investment analyst estimated in a recent year the loss in airline profits due to the frequent-flier plan at $150 million.

Although the accounting for this transaction has been studied by the profession, no authoritative guidelines have been issued.

[26]Approximately 4% of coupons are redeemed. Redeemed coupons eventually make their way to the corporate headquarters of the stores that accept them. From there they are shipped in 50-pound boxes to Mexico's border towns (Juárez, Tijuana, Nuevo Laredo), where clearinghouses operated by A. C. Nielsen Company (of TV rating fame) count them and report back to the manufacturers who, in turn, reimburse the stores.

premium offers should be charged to Premium Expense, and the outstanding obligations should be credited to an account titled Estimated Liability for Premiums.

Although the FASB did not include premium offers in its list of loss contingencies, the authors believe that **premium offers result in the probable existence of a liability at the date of the financial statements, can be reasonably estimated in amount, are contingent upon the occurrence of a future event (redemption), and, therefore, are a loss contingency** within the guidelines of *FASB Statement No. 5.*

The following example illustrates the accounting treatment accorded a premium offer. Fluffy Cakemix Company offered its customers a large nonbreakable mixing bowl in exchange for 25 cents and 10 boxtops. The mixing bowl costs Fluffy Cakemix Company 75 cents, and the company estimates that 60% of the boxtops will be redeemed. The premium offer began in June 1995 and resulted in the following transactions and entries during 1995.

UNDERLYING CONCEPT

Warranties and coupons are loss contingencies that satisfy the conditions necessary for a liability. Regarding the income statement, the matching principle *requires that the related expense be reported in the period that the sale occurs.*

1. To record purchase of 20,000 mixing bowls at 75 cents each:

Inventory of Premium Mixing Bowls	15,000	
Cash		15,000

2. To record sales of 300,000 boxes of cake mix at 80 cents:

Cash	240,000	
Sales		240,000

3. To record the actual redemption of 60,000 boxtops, the receipt of 25 cents per 10 boxtops, and the delivery of the mixing bowls:

Cash [(60,000 ÷ 10) × $0.25]	1,500	
Premium Expense	3,000	
Inventory of Premium Mixing Bowls		4,500
(Computation: [60,000 ÷ 10] × $0.75 = $4,500)		

4. To record end-of-period adjusting entry for estimated liability for outstanding premium offers (boxtops):

Premium Expense	6,000	
Estimated Liability for Premiums		6,000

Computation:

Total boxtops sold in 1995	300,000
Total estimated redemptions (60%)	180,000
Boxtops redeemed in 1995	60,000
Estimated future redemptions	120,000

Cost of estimated claims outstanding
(120,000 ÷ 10) × ($0.75 − $0.25) = $6,000

The December 31, 1995, balance sheet of Fluffy Cakemix Company will report an Inventory of Premium Mixing Bowls of $10,500 as a current asset and Estimated Liability for Premiums of $6,000 as a current liability. The 1995 income statement will report a $9,000 Premium Expense among the selling expenses.

In the illustration above, the company establishes its own premium plan, issues its own boxtops, and assumes complete redemption responsibilities. Another very common premium plan, also used to stimulate sales, is the issuance of trading stamps. Generally the trading stamp company sells its stamps to consumer-type businesses (commonly grocery stores and gasoline stations) and assumes full responsibility for the redemption of the stamps. The trading stamp company records the sale of stamps, the purchase of premiums (all sorts of consumer articles), the distribution of the premiums at gift centers, and the estimated premium claims outstanding. For instance, the Sperry and Hutchinson Company (licensor of S & H Green Stamps) reported "Liability for Stamp Redemptions—$117,599,000" as a current liability with a like amount as a long-term liability and made the following note disclosure:

ILLUSTRATION 13-13
Disclosure of Liability for
Premium Redemptions

> ### Sperry and Hutchinson Company
>
> **Liability for Stamp Redemptions.** The Company records stamp service revenue and provides for cost of redemptions at the time stamps are furnished to licensees. The liability for stamp redemptions is adjusted each year based upon current operating experience and includes the cost of merchandise and related redemption service expenses required to redeem 95% of the stamps issued.
>
> Company studies have indicated that approximately 50% of the stamps outstanding are not presented for redemption within one year; consequently this portion of the liability for stamp redemptions is classified as a long-term liability.

The businesses that buy the trading stamps merely record the purchase and the issuance of the stamps; stamps on hand are reported as an asset and stamps issued as a selling expense.

ENVIRONMENTAL LIABILITIES

Estimates to clean up existing toxic waste sites run to upward of $752 billion over a 30-year period. In addition, the cost of cleaning up our air and preventing future deterioration of the environment is estimated to cost even more. The average environmental cost per firm in various industries is: high-tech firms, $2 million (6.1% of revenues); utilities, $340 million (6.1% of revenues); steel and metals, $50 million (2.9% of revenues); and oil companies, $430 million (1.9% of revenues). Given that the average pretax profit of the 500 largest U.S. manufacturing companies recently was 7.7 percent of sales, these figures are staggering!

These costs will only grow when one considers "superfund legislation": it provides not only a government-supported fund to clean up pollution, but a mandate to clean up existing waste sites. Further it provided the Environmental Protection Agency (EPA) with the power to clean up waste sites and charge the clean-up costs to parties the EPA deems responsible for contaminating the site. These potentially responsible parties have an onerous liability. The EPA estimates that it will likely cost an average of $25 million to clean up each polluted site. For the most troublesome sites, the cost could easily reach $100 million or more. It is estimated that $65 billion will be required nationwide by the year 2000 to clean up contaminated land.

Presently **companies infrequently record any liability for these potential costs.** They note that the liability is a contingent liability that is not estimable. As a result, generally only a description regarding the possible liability is disclosed in the financial statements. An example of one company that did report a liability is provided in Illustration 13-14.

ILLUSTRATION 13-14
Disclosure of a Recorded
Liability for
Environmental Costs

> ### Crown Central Petroleum Corporation
>
> **Note G (in part): Contingencies—Environmental.** Like other petroleum refiners and marketers, the Company's operations are subject to extensive and rapidly changing federal and state environmental regulations governing air emissions, waste water discharges, and solid and hazardous waste management activities. The Company's policy is to accrue environmental and clean-up related costs of a non-capital nature when it is both probable that a liability has been incurred and the amount can be reasonably estimated. While it is often extremely difficult to reasonably quantify future environmental related expenditures, the Company anticipates a substantial capital investment will be required over the next several years to comply with existing regulations. The Company had recorded a liability of approximately $10,485,000 as of December 31, 1992 to cover the estimated costs of compliance with environmental regulations which are not anticipated to be of a capital nature.

More extensive disclosure is needed regarding environmental liabilities. In addition, more of these liabilities should be recorded. The SEC believes that managements should not delay recognition of a liability due to significant uncertainty. The SEC argues that if the liability is within a range and no amount within the range is the best estimate, then management should recognize the minimum amount of the range; that is in accordance with *FASB Interpretation No. 14*, "Reasonable Estimation of a Loss." The SEC also believes that environmental liabilities should be reported in the balance sheet independent of recoveries from third parties. Thus, possible insurance recoveries are not permitted to be netted against liabilities but must be shown separately. Because there is much litigation regarding recovery of insurance proceeds, these "assets" appear to be gain contingencies and, therefore, companies will not be reporting these on the balance sheet.[27]

RISK OF LOSS DUE TO LACK OF INSURANCE COVERAGE

Uninsured risks may arise in a number of ways, including **noninsurance** of certain risks or **coinsurance** or **deductible clauses** in an insurance contract. But **the absence of insurance** (frequently referred to as **self-insurance**) **does not mean that a liability has been incurred at the date of the financial statements.** For example, fires, explosions, and other similar events that may cause damage to a company's own property are random in occurrence and unrelated to the activities of the company prior to their occurrence. The conditions for accrual stated in *FASB Statement No. 5* are not satisfied prior to the occurrence of the event; until that time there is no diminution in the value of the property. And, unlike an insurance company, which has contractual obligations to reimburse policyholders for losses, a company can have no such obligations to itself and, hence, **no liability either before or after the occurrence of damage.**[28]

Exposure to **risks of loss resulting from uninsured past injury to others,** however, is an existing condition involving uncertainty about the amount and timing of losses that may develop, in which case a contingency exists. A company with a fleet of vehicles would have to accrue uninsured losses resulting from injury to others or damage to the property of others that took place prior to the date of the financial statements (if the experience of the company or other information enables it to make a reasonable estimate of the liability). However, it should not establish a liability for **expected future injury** to others or damage to the property of others even if the amount of losses is reasonably estimable.

DISCLOSURE OF LOSS CONTINGENCIES

A loss contingency and a liability is recorded if the loss is both probable and estimable. But, if the loss is **either probable or estimable but not both** and if there is at least a **reasonable possibility** that a liability may have been incurred, the following disclosure in the notes is required:

1. The nature of the contingency.
2. An estimate of the possible loss or range of loss or a statement that an estimate cannot be made.

Presented in Illustration 13-15 is an extensive litigation disclosure note (taken from the financial statements of Raymark Corporation), which shows that although actual losses have been charged to operations and further liability possibly exists, no estimate of this liability is possible.

Contingencies involving an unasserted claim or assessment need not be disclosed when no claimant has come forward unless (1) it is considered **probable** that a claim will be asserted **and** (2) there is a **reasonable possibility** that the outcome will be unfavorable.

UNDERLYING CONCEPT

Even if the amount of losses is estimable with a high degree of certainty, the losses are not liabilities because they result from a future event and not from a past event.

INTERNATIONAL INSIGHT

In Switzerland, companies may make provisions for general (non-specified) contingencies to the extent allowed by tax regulations.

---

[27]As indicated earlier, the FASB pronouncements on this topic require that, when some amount within the range appears at the time to be a better estimate than any other amount within the range, that amount is accrued. When no amount within the range is a better estimate than any other amount, the dollar amount at the low end of the range is **accrued** and the dollar amount of the high end of the range is **disclosed**. See *FASB Interpretation No. 14*, "Reasonable Estimation of the Amount of a Loss" (Stamford, Conn.: FASB, 1976), par. 3, and *FASB Statement No. 5*, "Accounting for Contingencies" (Stamford, Conn.: FASB, 1975).

[28]"Accounting for Contingencies," *FASB Statement No. 5*, op. cit., par. 28.

ILLUSTRATION 13-15
Disclosure of Loss
Contingency through
Litigation

Raymark Corporation

Note I: Litigation. Raymark is a defendant or co-defendant in a substantial number of lawsuits alleging wrongful injury and/or death from exposure to asbestos fibers in the air. The following table summarizes the activity in these lawsuits:

Claims	
Pending at beginning of year	8,719
Received during year	4,494
Settled or otherwise disposed of	(1,445)
Pending at end of year	11,768
Average indemnification cost	$3,364
Average cost per case, including defense costs	$6,499
Trial activity	
Verdicts for the Company	23
Total trials	36

The following table presents the cost of defending asbestos litigation, together with related insurance and workers' compensation expenses.

Included in operating profit	$ 1,872,000
Nonoperating expense	9,077,000
Total	$10,949,000

The Company is seeking to reasonably determine its liability. However, it is not possible to predict which theory of insurance will apply, the number of lawsuits still to be filed, the cost of settling and defending the existing and unfiled cases, or the ultimate impact of these lawsuits on the Company's consolidated financial statements.

An example of an accrual resulting from the probability that claims will be asserted and a reasonable possibility that the outcome will be unfavorable is Wickes Co.'s establishment of a $20 million contingent liability and loss related to substandard carpeting products. Wickes acknowledged the loss/liability resulting from an acquired company that had marketed $360 million of polyvinyl chloride-backed carpet that did not meet some local building-code flammability and smoke-density standards. A sizable portion of the $20 million charge to income related to future legal fees, the cost of tracing and dealing with specific customers, and the cost of inventory writeoffs.

Certain other contingent liabilities that should be disclosed even though the possibility of loss may be remote are the following:

1. Guarantees of indebtedness of others.

2. Obligations of commercial banks under "stand-by letters of credit."

3. Guarantees to repurchase receivables (or any related property) that have been sold or assigned.

Disclosure should include the nature and amount of the guarantee and, if estimable, the amount that could be recovered from outside parties. Cities Service Company disclosed its guarantees of indebtedness of others in the following note:

ILLUSTRATION 13-16
Disclosure of Guarantees
of Indebtedness

Cities Service Company

Note 10: Contingent Liabilities. The Company and certain subsidiaries have guaranteed debt obligations of approximately $62 million of companies in which substantial stock investments are held. Also, under long-term agreements with certain pipeline companies in which stock interests are held, the Company and its subsidiaries have agreed to provide minimum revenue for product shipments. The Company has guaranteed mortgage debt ($80 million) incurred by a 50 percent owned tanker affiliate for construction of tankers which are under long-term charter contracts to the Company and others. It is not anticipated that any loss will result from any of the above described agreements.

► SUMMARY OF LEARNING OBJECTIVES ◄

1. **Define current liabilities and describe how they are valued.** Current liabilities are obligations whose liquidation is reasonably expected to require the use of current assets or the creation of other current liabilities. Theoretically, liabilities should be measured by the present value of the future outlay of cash required to liquidate them. In practice, current liabilities are usually recorded in accounting records and reported in financial statements at their full maturity value.

2. **Identify the nature and types of current liabilities.** There are several types of liabilities: (1) accounts payable, (2) notes payable, (3) current maturities of long-term debts, (4) dividends payable, (5) returnable deposits, (6) unearned revenue, (7) taxes payable, and (8) employee-related liabilities.

3. **Explain the classification issues of short-term debt expected to be refinanced.** An enterprise is required to exclude a short-term obligation from current liabilities if both of the following conditions are met: (1) It must intend to refinance the obligation on a long-term basis, *and* (2) it must demonstrate an ability to consummate the refinancing.

4. **Identify types of employee-related liabilities.** The employee-related liabilities are: (1) payroll deductions; (2) compensated absences; (3) postretirement benefits, which consist of pensions and postretirement health care and life insurance benefits; and (4) bonus agreements.

5. **Indicate how current liabilities are disclosed.** The current liability accounts are commonly presented as the first classification in the liabilities and stockholders' equity section of the balance sheet. Within the current liability section the accounts may be listed in order of maturity, in descending order of amount, or in order of liquidation preference. Detail and supplemental information concerning current liabilities should be sufficient to meet the requirement of full disclosure.

6. **Identify the criteria used to account for and disclose loss contingencies.** An estimated loss from a loss contingency should be accrued by a charge to expense and a liability recorded only if both of the following conditions are met: (1) Information available prior to the issuance of the financial statements indicates that it is probable that a liability has been incurred at the date of the financial statements, and (2) the amount of the loss can be reasonably estimated. If the loss is either probable or estimable but not both, and if there is at least a reasonable possibility that a liability may have been incurred, disclosure should be made in the notes of the nature of the contingency and an estimate of the possible loss.

7. **Explain the accounting for different types of loss contingencies.** (1) The following factors must be considered in determining whether a liability should be recorded with respect to pending or threatened litigation and actual or possible claims and assessments: (a) the time period in which the underlying cause for action occurred; (b) the probability of an unfavorable outcome; and (c) the ability to make a reasonable estimate of the amount of loss.

    (2) If it is probable that customers will make claims under warranties relating to goods or services that have been sold and a reasonable estimate of the costs involved can be made, the accrual method must be used. Warranty costs under the accrual basis are charged to operating expense in the year of sale.

    (3) Premiums, coupon offers, and rebates are made to stimulate sales, and their costs should be charged to expense in the period of the sale that benefits from the premium plan.

KEY TERMS

accumulated rights, 636

bonus, 637

compensated absences, 635

contingency, 639

contingent liabilities, 639

current liabilities, 623

current maturities of long-term debts, 626

expense warranty method, 642

liabilities, 623

litigation, claims, and assessments, 641

operating cycle, 624

postretirement benefits, 637

premiums, 644

probable (contingency), 639

reasonably possible (contingency), 639

returnable cash deposits, 629

sales warranty method, 643

self-insurance, 647

short-term obligations expected to be refinanced, 626

trade accounts payable, 624

trade notes payable, 624

unearned revenues, 630

vested rights, 636

warranty, 642

APPENDIX 13-A

COMPUTATION OF EMPLOYEES' BONUSES

OBJECTIVE 8

After studying Appendix 13-A, you should be able to: Compute employee bonuses under differing arrangements.

Because the amount of a bonus is an expense of the business, the problem of computing the amount of bonus based on income becomes more difficult. Say a company has income of $100,000 determined before considering the bonus expense. According to the terms of the bonus agreement, 20% of the income is to be set aside for distribution among the employees. If the bonus were not itself an expense to be deducted in determining net income, the amount of the bonus could be computed very simply as 20% of the income before bonus of $100,000. However, the bonus itself is an expense that must be deducted in arriving at the amount of income on which the bonus is to be based. Hence, $100,000 reduced by the bonus is the figure on which the bonus is to be computed. That is, the bonus is equal to 20% of $100,000 less the bonus. Stated algebraically:

$$B = 0.20\ (\$100{,}000 - B)$$
$$B = \$20{,}000 - 0.2B$$
$$1.2B = \$20{,}000$$
$$B = \$16{,}666.67$$

A similar problem results from the relationship of bonus payments to federal income taxes. Assume income of $100,000 computed without subtracting either the employees' bonus or taxes on income. The bonus is to be based on income **after deducting income taxes but before deducting the bonus.** The rate of income tax is 40% and the bonus of 20% is a deductible expense for tax purposes. The bonus is, therefore, equal to 20% of $100,000 minus the tax, and the tax is equal to 40% of $100,000 minus the bonus. Thus we have two simultaneous equations that, using B as the symbol for the bonus and T for the tax, may be stated algebraically as follows:

$$B = 0.20\ (\$100{,}000 - T)$$
$$T = 0.40\ (\$100{,}000 - B)$$

These may be solved by substituting the value of T as indicated in the second equation for T in the first equation.

$$B = 0.20\ [\$100{,}000 - 0.40(\$100{,}000 - B)]$$
$$B = 0.20\ (\$100{,}000 - \$40{,}000 + 0.4B)$$
$$B = 0.20\ (\$60{,}000 + 0.4B)$$
$$B = \$12{,}000 + 0.08B$$
$$0.92B = \$12{,}000$$
$$B = \$13{,}043.48$$

Substituting this value for B into the second equation allows us to solve for T:

$$T = 0.40\ (\$100{,}000 - \$13{,}043.48)$$
$$T = 0.40\ (\$86{,}956.52)$$
$$T = \$34{,}782.61$$

To prove these amounts, both should be worked back into the original equation.

$$B = 0.20\ (\$100,000 - T)$$
$$\$13,043.48 = 0.20\ (\$100,000 - \$34,782.61)$$
$$\$13,043.48 = 0.20\ (\$65,217.39)$$
$$\$13,043.48 = \$13,043.48$$

If the terms of the agreement provide for deducting both the tax and the bonus to arrive at the income figure on which the bonus is computed, the equations would be:

$$B = 0.20\ (\$100,000 - B - T)$$
$$T = 0.40\ (\$100,000 - B)$$

Substituting the value of T from the second equation into the first equation enables us to solve for B:

$$B = 0.20\ [\$100,000 - B - 0.40\ (\$100,000 - B)]$$
$$B = 0.20\ (\$100,000 - B - \$40,000 + 0.4B)$$
$$B = 0.20\ (\$60,000 - 0.6B)$$
$$B = \$12,000 - 0.12B$$
$$1.12B = \$12,000$$
$$B = \$10,714.29$$

The value for B may then be substituted in the second equation above, and that equation solved for T:

$$T = 0.40\ (\$100,000 - \$10,714.29)$$
$$T = 0.40\ (\$89,285.71)$$
$$T = \$35,714.28$$

If these values are then substituted in the original bonus equation, they prove themselves as follows:

$$B = 0.20\ (\$100,000 - B - T)$$
$$\$10,714.29 = 0.20\ (\$100,000 - \$10,714.29 - \$35,714.28)$$
$$\$10,714.29 = 0.20\ (\$53,571.43)$$
$$\$10,714.29 = \$10,714.29$$

Drawing up a legal document such as a bonus agreement is a task for a lawyer, not an accountant, although accountants are frequently called on to express an opinion on the agreement's feasibility. In this respect, one should always insist that the agreement state specifically whether income taxes and the bonus itself are expenses deductible in determining income for purposes of the bonus computation.

▶ SUMMARY OF LEARNING OBJECTIVE FOR APP. 13-A ◀

8. Compute employee bonuses under differing arrangements. Because the bonus is based on net income and is deductible in determining net income, the bonus may have to be determined algebraically. Its computation is made more difficult by the bonus being deductible for tax purposes and the taxes being deductible from the income on which the bonus is based.

Note: All **asterisked** Questions, Exercises, Problems, and Cases relate to material contained in the appendix to each chapter.

QUESTIONS

1. Distinguish between a current liability and a long-term debt.

2. Assume that your friend Erin Copeland, who is a music major, asks you to define and discuss the nature of a liability. Assist her by preparing a definition of a liability and by explaining to her what you believe are the elements or factors inherent in the concept of a liability.

3. Why is the liability section of the balance sheet of primary significance to bankers?

4. How are current liabilities related by definition to current assets? How are current liabilities related to a company's operating cycle?

5. How is present value related to the concept of a liability?

6. What is the nature of a "discount" on notes payable?

7. How should a debt callable by the creditor be reported in the debtor's financial statements?

8. Under what conditions should a short-term obligation be excluded from current liabilities?

9. (a) What evidence is necessary to demonstrate the ability to consummate the refinancing of short-term debt?
   (b) When a financing agreement is relied upon to demonstrate ability to consummate refinancing, what amount of short-term debt may be excluded from current liabilities?

10. Discuss the accounting treatment or disclosure that should be accorded a declared but unpaid cash dividend; an accumulated but undeclared dividend on cumulative preferred stock; a stock dividend distributable.

11. How does deferred or unearned revenue arise? Why can it be classified properly as a current liability? Give several examples of business activities that result in unearned revenues.

12. What are compensated absences?

13. Under what conditions must an employer accrue a liability for the cost of compensated absences?

14. What are postretirement benefits? What is the proper reporting for postretirement benefits?

15. Under what conditions is an employer required to accrue a liability for sick pay? Under what conditions is an employer permitted but not required to accrue a liability for sick pay?

16. Over which two periods of time is the property tax most commonly allocated? Under what circumstances might each of these periods be justified as the period of expense?

17. Define (a) a contingency and (b) a contingent liability.

18. Under what conditions should a contingent liability be recorded?

19. Distinguish between a "current liability" and a "contingent liability." Give two examples of each type.

20. How are the terms "probable," "reasonably possible," and "remote" related to contingent liabilities?

21. Contrast the cash basis method and the accrual method of accounting for warranty costs.

22. How does the expense warranty treatment differ from the sales warranty method?

23. Wright Airlines Inc. awards members of its Flightline program a second ticket at half price, valid for 2 years anywhere on its flight system, when a full-price ticket is purchased. How would you account for the full-fare and half-fare tickets?

24. Kitty Hawk Airlines Co. awards members of its Frequent Fliers Club one free round-trip ticket, anywhere on its flight system, for every 50,000 miles flown on its planes. How would you account for the free ticket award?

25. Should a liability be recorded for risk of loss due to lack of insurance coverage? Discuss.

26. What factors must be considered in determining whether or not to record a liability for pending litigation? For threatened litigation?

27. Within the current liability section, how do you believe the accounts should be listed? Defend your position.

28. When should liabilities for each of the following items be recorded on the books of an ordinary business corporation?
    (a) Acquisition of goods by purchase on credit.
    (b) Officers' salaries.
    (c) Special bonus to employees.
    (d) Dividends.
    (e) Purchase commitments.

EXERCISES

E13-1 (Balance Sheet Classification of Various Liabilities) How would each of the following items be reported on the balance sheet?

(a) Accrued vacation pay.
(b) Estimated taxes payable.
(c) Service warranties on appliance sales.
(d) Bank overdraft.
(e) Employee payroll deductions unremitted.
(f) Unpaid bonus to officers.
(g) Deposit received from customer to guarantee performance of a contract.
(h) Sales taxes payable.
(i) Gift certificates sold to customers but not yet redeemed.
(j) Premium offers outstanding.
(k) Discount on notes payable.
(l) Personal injury claim pending.
(m) Current maturities of long-term debts to be paid from current assets.
(n) Cash dividends declared but unpaid.
(o) Dividends in arrears on preferred stock.
(p) Loans from officers.

E13-2 (Accounts and Notes Payable) The following are selected 1995 transactions of Alpha Romero Corporation:

Sept. 1 Purchased inventory from Corto Company on account for $50,000. Romero records purchases gross and uses a periodic inventory system.
Oct. 1   Issued a $50,000, 12-month, 10% note to Corto in payment of account.
Oct. 1   Borrowed $50,000 from the Giulia Bank by signing a 12-month, noninterest-bearing $55,000 note.

Instructions
(a) Prepare journal entries for the selected transactions above.
(b) Prepare adjusting entries at December 31.
(c) Compute the total net liability to be reported on the December 31 balance sheet for:
    (1) the interest-bearing note.
    (2) the noninterest-bearing note.

E13-3 (Refinancing of Short-Term Debt) On December 31, 1995, Campari Company had $1,200,000 of short-term debt in the form of notes payable due February 2, 1996. On January 21, 1996, the company issued 25,000 shares of its common stock for $39 per share, receiving $975,000 proceeds after brokerage fees and other costs of issuance. On February 2, 1996, the proceeds from the stock sale, supplemented by an additional $225,000 cash, are used to liquidate the $1,200,000 debt. The December 31, 1995, balance sheet is issued on February 23, 1996.

Instructions
Show how the $1,200,000 of short-term debt should be presented on the December 31, 1995, balance sheet, including note disclosure.

E13-4 (Refinancing of Short-Term Debt) On December 31, 1995, Austin Healy Company has $7,000,000 of short-term debt in the form of notes payable to Lancia State Bank due periodically in 1996. On January 28, 1996, Healy enters into a refinancing agreement with Lancia that will permit it to borrow up to 60% of the gross amount of its accounts receivable. Receivables are expected to range between a low of $5,000,000 in May to a high of $6,000,000 in October during the year 1996. The interest cost of the maturing short-term debt is 15%, and the new agreement calls for a fluctuating interest at 1% above the prime rate on notes due in 2000. Healy's December 31, 1995, balance sheet is issued on February 15, 1996.

Instructions
Prepare a partial balance sheet for Healy at December 31, 1995, showing how its $7,000,000 of short-term debt should be presented, including footnote disclosures.

E13-5 (Compensated Absences) Mercer Company began operations on January 2, 1994. It employs 9 individuals who work 8-hour days and are paid hourly. Each employee earns 10 paid vacation days and 6 paid sick days annually. Vacation days may be taken after January 15 of the year following the year in which they are earned. Sick days may be taken as soon as they are earned; unused sick days accumulate. Additional information is as follows:

	Actual Hourly Wage Rate		Vacation Days Used by Each Employee		Sick Days Used by Each Employee	
	1994	1995	1994	1995	1994	1995
	$6.00	$7.00	0	9	4	5

Mercer Company has chosen to accrue the cost of compensated absences at rates of pay in effect during the period when earned and to accrue sick pay when earned.

Instructions

(a) Prepare journal entries to record transactions related to compensated absences during 1994 and 1995.

(b) Compute the amounts of any liability for compensated absences that should be reported on the balance sheet at December 31, 1994 and 1995.

E13-6 (Compensated Absences) Assume the facts in the preceding exercise, except that Mercer Company has chosen not to accrue paid sick leave until used, and has chosen to accrue vacation time at expected future rates of pay without discounting. The company used the following projected rates to accrue vacation time:

Year in Which Vacation Time Was Earned	Projected Future Pay Rates Used to Accrue Vacation Pay
1994	$6.90
1995	7.60

Instructions

(a) Prepare journal entries to record transactions related to compensated absences during 1994 and 1995.

(b) Compute the amounts of any liability for compensated absences that should be reported on the balance sheet at December 31, 1994, and 1995.

E13-7 (Adjusting Entry for Sales Tax) During the month of June, Hispano-Suiza Boutique had cash sales of $234,000 and credit sales of $137,000, both of which include the 6% sales tax that must be remitted to the state by July 15.

Instructions

Prepare the adjusting entry that should be recorded to fairly present the June 30 financial statements.

E13-8 (Payroll Tax Entries) The payroll of Bently Company for September 1994 is as follows:

Total payroll was $480,000, of which $120,000 is exempt from social security tax because it represented amounts paid in excess of $60,600 to certain employees. The amount paid to employees in excess of $7,000 was $400,000. Income taxes in the amount of $90,000 were withheld, as was $9,000 in union dues. The state unemployment tax is 3.5%, but Bently Company is allowed a credit of 2.3% by the state for its unemployment experience. Also, assume that the current F.I.C.A. tax is 7.65% on an employee's wages to $60,600 and 1.45% in excess of $60,600. No employee for Bently makes more than $125,000. The federal unemployment tax rate is .5% after state credit.

Instructions

Prepare the necessary journal entries if the wages and salaries paid and the employer payroll taxes are recorded separately.

E13-9 (Payroll Tax Entries) Triumph Hardware Company's payroll for November, 1995, is summarized below.

			Amount Subject to Payroll Taxes		
				Unemployment Tax	
Payroll	Wages Due	F.I.C.A.	Federal	State
---	---	---	---	---
Factory	$120,000	$120,000	$40,000	$40,000
Sales	44,000	32,000	4,000	4,000
Administrative	36,000	36,000	—	—
Total	$200,000	$188,000	$44,000	$44,000

At this point in the year some employees have already received wages in excess of those to which payroll taxes apply. Assume that the state unemployment tax is 2.5%. The F.I.C.A. rate is 7.65% on an employee's wages to $60,600 and 1.45% in excess of $60,600. Of the $188,000 wages subject to F.I.C.A. tax, $20,000 is in excess of $60,600 related to the sales wages. Federal unemployment tax rate is .6% after credits. Income tax withheld amounts to $14,000 for factory, $6,000 for sales, and $7,000 for administrative.

Instructions
   (a) Prepare a schedule showing the employer's total cost of wages for November by function. (Round all computations to nearest dollar.)
   (b) Prepare the journal entries to record the factory, sales, and administrative payrolls including the employer's payroll taxes.

E13-10 (Warranties) Doppleganger Company sold 200 copymaking machines in 1995 for $4,000 apiece, together with a one-year warranty. Maintenance on each machine during the warranty period averages $320.

Instructions
   (a) Prepare entries to record the sale of the machines and the related warranty costs, assuming that the accrual method is used. Actual warranty costs incurred in 1995 were $51,300.
   (b) On the basis of the data above, prepare the appropriate entries, assuming that the cash basis (i.e., "tax") method is used.

E13-11 (Warranties) The Delage Equipment Company sold 500 Rollomatics during 1995 at $6,000 each. During 1995, Delage spent $30,000 servicing the 2-year warranties that accompany the Rollomatic. All applicable transactions are on a cash basis.

Instructions
   (a) Prepare 1995 entries for Delage using the expense warranty treatment. Assume that Delage estimates the total cost of servicing the warranties will be $120,000 for 2 years.
   (b) Prepare 1995 entries for Delage assuming that the warranties are not an integral part of the sale. Assume that of the sales total, $160,000 relates to sales of warranty contracts. Delage estimates the total cost of servicing the warranties will be $120,000 for 2 years. Estimate revenues earned on the basis of costs incurred and estimated costs.

E13-12 (Liability for Returnable Containers) Vauxhall Company sells its products in expensive, reusable containers. The customer is charged a deposit for each container delivered and receives a refund for each container returned within two years after the year of delivery. Vauxhall accounts for the containers not returned within the time limit as being sold at the deposit amount. Information for 1995 is as follows:

Containers held by customers at December 31, 1994,			
from deliveries in:	1993	$170,000	
	1994	480,000	$650,000
Containers delivered in 1995			860,000
Containers returned in 1995 from deliveries in:	1993	$100,000	
	1994	280,000	
	1995	314,000	694,000

Instructions
   (a) Prepare all journal entries required for Vauxhall Company during 1995 for the returnable containers.
   (b) Compute the total amount Vauxhall should report as a liability for returnable containers at December 31, 1995.
   (c) Should the liability computed in (b) above be reported as current or long-term?

(AICPA adapted)

E13-13 (Premium Entries) Tucker Company includes 1 coupon in each box of soap powder that it packs, and 10 coupons are redeemable for a premium (a kitchen utensil). In 1995, Tucker Company purchased 8,800 premiums at 88 cents each and sold 110,000 boxes of soap powder @ $3.30 per box; 44,000 coupons were presented for redemption in 1995. It is estimated that 60% of the coupons will eventually be presented for redemption.

Instructions
Prepare all the entries that would be made relative to sales of soap powder and to the premium plan in 1995.

E13-14 (Contingencies) Presented below are three independent situations. Answer the question at the end of each situation.

   1. During 1995, Peugeot Inc. became involved in a tax dispute with the IRS. Peugeot's attorneys have indicated that they believe it is probable that Peugeot will lose this dispute. They also believe that Peugeot will have to pay the IRS between $800,000 and $1,400,000. After the 1995 financial statements were issued, the case was settled with the IRS for $1,100,000. What amount, if any, should be reported as a liability for this contingency as of December 31, 1995?
   2. On October 1, 1995, Schmutz Chemical was identified as a potentially responsible party by the Environmental Protection Agency. Schmutz' management along with its counsel have concluded that it is probable that Schmutz will be responsible for damages, and a reasonable estimate of these damages is $5,000,000. Schmutz' insurance policy of $9,000,000 has a deductible clause of $600,000. How should Schmutz Chemical report this information in its financial statements at December 31, 1995?

3. Bugatti Inc. had a manufacturing plant in Kuwait, which was destroyed in the Gulf War. It is not certain who will compensate Bugatti for this destruction, but Bugatti has been assured by governmental officials that it will receive a definite amount for this plant. The amount of the compensation will be less than the fair value of the plant, but more than its book value. How should the contingency be reported in the financial statements of Bugatti Inc.?

E13-15 (Premiums) Presented below are three independent situations.

1. Invicta Stamp Company records stamp service revenue and provides for the cost of redemptions in the year stamps are sold to licensees. Invicta's past experience indicates that only 80% of the stamps sold to licensees will be redeemed. Invicta's liability for stamp redemptions was $13,000,000 at December 31, 1994. Additional information for 1995 is as follows:

Stamp service revenue from stamps sold to licensees	$9,500,000
Cost of redemptions (stamps sold prior to 1/1/95)	6,000,000

If all the stamps sold in 1995 were presented for redemption in 1996, the redemption cost would be $5,000,000. What amount should Invicta report as a liability for stamp redemptions at December 31, 1995?

2. In packages of its products, Daimler Inc. includes coupons that may be presented at retail stores to obtain discounts on other Daimler products. Retailers are reimbursed for the face amount of coupons redeemed plus 10% of that amount for handling costs. Daimler honors requests for coupon redemption by retailers up to 3 months after the consumer expiration date. Daimler estimates that 60% of all coupons issued will ultimately be redeemed. Information relating to coupons issued by Daimler during 1995 is as follows:

Consumer expiration date	12/31/95
Total face amount of coupons issued	$800,000
Total payments to retailers as of 12/31/95	290,000

What amount should Daimler report as a liability for unredeemed coupons at December 31, 1995?

3. Cord Company sold 700,000 boxes of pie mix under a new sales promotional program. Each box contains one coupon, which submitted with $5.00, entitles the customer to a baking pan. Cord pays $6.00 per pan and $0.50 for handling and shipping. Cord estimates that 70% of the coupons will be redeemed, even though only 250,000 coupons had been processed during 1995. What amount should Cord report as a liability for unredeemed coupons at December 31, 1995?

(AICPA adapted)

E13-16 (Financial Statement Impact of Liability Transactions) Presented below is a list of possible transactions.

1. Purchased inventory for $75,000 on account (assume perpetual system is used).
2. Issued an $80,000 note payable in payment on account (see item 1 above).
3. Recorded accrued interest on the note from item 2 above.
4. Borrowed $100,000 from the bank by signing a 6-month, $110,000 noninterest-bearing note.
5. Recognized four months' interest expense on the note from item 4 above.
6. Recorded cash sales of $74,500, which includes 6% sales tax.
7. Recorded wage expense of $35,000. The cash paid was $25,000; the difference was due to various amounts withheld.
8. Recorded employer's payroll taxes.
9. Accrued accumulated vacation pay.
10. Recorded accrued property taxes payable.
11. Recorded bonuses due to employees.
12. Recorded a contingent loss on a lawsuit that the company will probably lose.
13. Accrued warranty expense (assume expense warranty treatment).
14. Paid warranty costs that were accrued in item 13 above.
15. Recorded sales of product and related warranties (assume sales warranty treatment).
16. Paid warranty costs under contracts from item 15 above.
17. Recognized warranty revenue (see item 15 above).
18. Recorded estimated liability for premium claims outstanding.

Instructions
Set up a table using the format shown on the next page and analyze the effect of the 18 transactions on the financial statement categories indicated.

#	Assets	Liabilities	Owners' Equity	Net Income
1				

Use the following code:

I: Increase   D: Decrease   NE: No net effect

*E13-17 **(Bonus Computation)** Charles Rolls, president of the Rolls-Royce Company, has a bonus arrangement with the company under which he receives 15% of the net income (after deducting taxes and bonuses) each year. For the current year, the net income before deducting either the provision for income taxes or the bonus is $239,800. The bonus is deductible for tax purposes, and the effective tax rate may be assumed to be 40%.

Instructions
- **(a)** Compute the amount of Charles Rolls' bonus.
- **(b)** Compute the appropriate provision for federal income taxes for the year.
- **(c)** Prepare the December 31 journal entry to record the bonus (which will not be paid until next year).

*E13-18 **(Bonus Computation and Income Statement Preparation)** The incomplete income statement of Duesenberg Company appears below:

Duesenberg Company
INCOME STATEMENT
For the Year 1995

Revenue		$5,000,000
Cost of goods sold		3,500,000
Gross profit		1,500,000
Administrative and selling expenses	$500,000	
Profit-sharing bonus to employees	?	?
Income before income taxes		?
Income taxes		?
Net income		$?

The employee profit-sharing plan requires that 20% of all profits remaining after the deduction of the bonus and income taxes be distributed to the employees by the first day of the fourth month following each year end. The federal income tax is 45%, and the bonus is tax-deductible.

Instructions
Complete the condensed income statement of Duesenberg Company for the year 1995.

*E13-19 **(Bonus Compensation)** Maserati Company has a profit-sharing agreement with its employees that provides for deposit in a pension trust for the benefit of the employees of 20% of the net income after deducting (1) federal taxes on income, (2) the amount of the annual pension contribution, and (3) a return of 10% on the stockholders' equity as of the end of the year 1995.

Instructions
Compute the amount of the pension contribution under the assumption that the stockholders' equity at the end of the year before adding the net income for the year is $700,000; that net income for the year before either the pension contribution or tax is $300,000; and that the pension contribution is deductible for tax purposes. Use 40% as the applicable rate of tax.

PROBLEMS

P13-1 **(Current Liability Entries and Adjustments)** Described below are certain transactions of Shao Yu Corporation.

1. On February 2, the corporation purchased goods from Lan Jiang Company for $50,000 subject to cash discount terms of 2/10, n/30. Purchases and accounts payable are recorded by the corporation at net amounts after cash discounts. The invoice was paid on February 26.
2. On April 1, the corporation bought a truck for $30,000 from General Motors Company, paying $4,000 in cash and signing a one-year, 12% note for the balance of the purchase price.

3. On May 1, the corporation borrowed $80,000 from Lima National Bank by signing a $90,200 noninterest bearing note due one year from May 1.
4. On August 1, the Board of Directors declared a $200,000 cash dividend that was payable on September 10 to stockholders of record on August 31.

Instructions

(a) Make all the journal entries necessary to record the transactions above using appropriate dates.

(b) Shao Yu Corporation's year-end is December 31. Assuming that no adjusting entries relative to the transactions above have been recorded, prepare any adjusting journal entries concerning interest that are necessary to present fair financial statements at December 31. Assume straight-line amortization of discounts.

P13-2 (Current Liability Entries and Adjustments) Listed below are selected transactions of Bono Department Store for the current year ending December 31.

1. On December 5, the store received $1,000 from the Bob Marley Players as a deposit to be returned after certain furniture to be used in stage production was returned on January 15.
2. During December, cash sales totaled $819,000, which includes the 5% sales tax that must be remitted to the state by the fifteenth day of the following month.
3. On December 10, the store purchased for cash three delivery trucks for $66,000. The trucks were purchased in a state that applies no sales tax, but the store is located in and must register the trucks in a state that applies a use tax of 5% to nonsalable goods bought outside of its sales tax authority.
4. The store follows the practice of accruing its property tax liability from the lien date. Property taxes of $84,000 became a lien on May 1 and were paid in two equal installments on July 1 and October 1.

Instructions

Prepare all the journal entries necessary to record the transactions noted above as they occurred and any adjusting journal entries relative to the transactions that would be required to present fair financial statements at December 31. Date each entry. For simplicity, assume that adjusting entries are recorded only once a year on December 31.

P13-3 (Payroll Tax Entries) Liverpool Company pays its office employee payroll weekly. Below is a partial list of employees and their payroll data for August. Because August is their vacation period, vacation pay is also listed.

Employee		Earnings to July 31	Weekly Pay	Vacation Pay to Be Received in August
Ringo Starr		$4,200	$180	—
George Harrison		3,500	150	$300
Yoko Ono		2,700	110	220
Paul McCartney		6,400	250	—
John Lennon		8,000	290	580

Assume that the federal income tax withheld is 10% of wages. Union dues withheld are 3% of wages. Vacations are taken the second and third weeks of August by Harrison, Ono, and Lennon. The state unemployment tax rate is 2% and the federal is .6%, both on a $6,000 maximum. The F.I.C.A. rate is 7.65% on employee and employer on a maximum of $60,600 per employee. In addition, a 1.45% rate is charged both employer and employee for an employee's wage in excess of $60,600.

Instructions

Make the journal entries necessary for each of the four August payrolls. The entries for the payroll and for the company's liability are made separately. Also make the entry to record the monthly payment of accrued payroll liabilities.

P13-4 (Payroll Tax Entries) This is a payroll sheet for Hasselback Import Company for the month of September 1995. The company is allowed a 1% unemployment compensation rate by the state; the federal unemployment tax rate is .6% and the maximum for both is $6,000. Assume a 10% federal income tax rate for all employees and a 7.65% F.I.C.A. tax on employee and employer on a maximum of $60,600. In addition, 1.45% is charged both employer and employee for an employee's wage in excess of $60,600 per employee.

Name	Earnings to Aug. 31	September Earnings	Income Tax Withholding	F.I.C.A.	State U.C.	Federal U.C.
J. Icerman	$ 5,800	$ 700				
W. Heck	5,300	500				
K. Lorek	7,600	800				
T. Schaefer	13,600	1,700				
S. Baginski	120,000	15,000				
A. Nichols	130,000	16,000				

Instructions

(a) Complete the payroll sheet and make the necessary entry to record the payment of the payroll.

(b) Make the entry to record the payroll tax expenses of Hasselback Import Company.

(c) Make the entry to record the payment of the payroll liabilities created. Assume that the company pays all payroll liabilities at the end of each month.

P13-5 (Warranties, Accrual, and Cash Basis) Duane Eddy Corporation sells portable computers under a 2-year warranty contract that requires the corporation to replace defective parts and to provide the necessary repair labor. During 1995 the corporation sells for cash 300 computers at a unit price of $2,500. On the basis of past experience, the 2-year warranty costs are estimated to be $110 for parts and $130 for labor per unit. (For simplicity, assume that all sales occurred on December 31, 1995.) The warranty is not sold separately from the computer.

Instructions

(a) Record any necessary journal entries in 1995, applying the cash basis method.

(b) Record any necessary journal entries in 1995, applying the expense warranty accrual method.

(c) What liability relative to these transactions would appear on the December 31, 1995 balance sheet and how would it be classified if the cash basis method is applied?

(d) What liability relative to these transactions would appear on the December 31, 1995 balance sheet and how would it be classified if the expense warranty accrual method is applied?

   In 1996 the actual warranty costs to Duane Eddy Corporation were $15,300 for parts and $17,800 for labor.

(e) Record any necessary journal entries in 1996, applying the cash basis method.

(f) Record any necessary journal entries in 1996, applying the expense warranty accrual method.

P13-6 (Extended Warranties) Mind Benders Company sells televisions at an average price of $700 and also offers to each customer a separate 3-year warranty contract for $75 that requires the company to perform periodic services and to replace defective parts. During 1995, the company sold 300 televisions and 250 warranty contracts for cash. It estimates the 3-year warranty costs as $20 for parts and $40 for labor and accounts for warranties separately. Assume sales occurred on December 31, 1995, income is recognized on the warranties, and straight-line recognition of warranty revenues occurs.

Instructions

(a) Record any necessary journal entries in 1995.

(b) What liability relative to these transactions would appear on the December 31, 1995, balance sheet and how would it be classified?

   In 1996, Mind Benders Company incurred actual costs relative to 1995 television warranty sales of $2,000 for parts and $3,000 for labor.

(c) Record any necessary journal entries in 1996 relative to 1995 television warranties.

(d) What amounts relative to the 1995 television warranties would appear on the December 31, 1996, balance sheet and how would they be classified?

P13-7 (Warranties, Accrual, and Cash Basis) Willie Dixon Company sells a machine for $7,400 under a 12-month warranty agreement that requires the company to replace all defective parts and to provide the repair labor at no cost to the customers. With sales being made evenly throughout the year, the company sells 650 machines in 1996 (warranty expense is incurred half in 1996 and half in 1997). As a result of product testing, the company estimates that the warranty cost is $240 per machine ($110 parts and $130 labor).

Instructions

Assuming that actual warranty costs are incurred exactly as estimated, what journal entries would be made relative to these facts:

(a) Under application of the expense warranty accrual method for:
   1. Sale of machinery in 1996?
   2. Warranty costs incurred in 1996?
   3. Warranty expense charged against 1996 revenues?
   4. Warranty costs incurred in 1997?

(b) Under application of the cash basis method for:
   1. Sale of machinery in 1996?
   2. Warranty costs incurred in 1996?
   3. Warranty expense charged against 1996 revenues?
   4. Warranty costs incurred in 1997?

(c) What amount, if any, is disclosed in the balance sheet as a liability for future warranty cost as of December 31, 1996, under each method?

(d) Which method best reflects the income in 1996 and 1997 of Willie Dixon Company? Why?

P13-8 (Premium Entries) To stimulate the sales of its Captain Kanga Roo breakfast cereal, the Greenjeans Company places 1 coupon in each box. Five coupons are redeemable for a premium consisting of a children's hand puppet. In 1996, the company purchases 40,000 puppets at $1.50 each and sells 400,000 boxes of Captain Kanga Roo at $3.75 a box. From its experience with other similar premium offers, the company estimates that 40% of the coupons issued will be mailed back for redemption. During 1996, 95,000 coupons are presented for redemption.

Instructions
Prepare the journal entries that should be recorded in 1996 relative to the premium plan.

P13-9 (Premium Entries and Financial Statement Presentation) Yummy Candy Company offers a CD single as a premium for every five candy bar wrappers presented by customers together with $1.00. The candy bars are sold by the company to distributors for 30 cents each. The purchase price of each CD to the company is 90 cents; in addition it costs 25 cents to mail each record. The results of the premium plan for the years 1995 and 1996 are as follows (all purchases and sales are for cash):

	1995	1996
CDs purchased	250,000	330,000
Candy bars sold	2,895,400	2,743,600
Wrappers redeemed	1,200,000	1,500,000
1995 wrappers expected to be redeemed in 1996	290,000	
1996 wrappers expected to be redeemed in 1997		350,000

Instructions
(a) Prepare the journal entries that should be made in 1995 and 1996 to record the transactions related to the premium plan of the Yummy Candy Company.
(b) Indicate the account names, amounts, and classifications of the items related to the premium plan that would appear on the balance sheet and the income statement at the end of 1995 and 1996.

P13-10 (Loss Contingencies: Entries and Essay) On November 24, 1995, 26 passengers on Flutterbye Airlines Flight No. 901 were injured upon landing when the plane skidded off the runway. Personal injury suits for damages totaling $4,000,000 were filed on January 11, 1996, against the airline by 18 injured passengers. The airline carries no insurance. Legal counsel has studied each suit and advised Flutterbye that it can reasonably expect to pay 60% of the damages claimed. The financial statements for the year ended December 31, 1995, were issued February 27, 1996.

Instructions
(a) Prepare any disclosures and journal entries required by the airline in preparation of the December 31, 1995, financial statements.
(b) Ignoring the Nov. 24, 1995, accident, what liability due to the risk of loss from lack of insurance coverage should Flutterbye Airlines record or disclose? During the past decade the company has experienced at least one accident per year and incurred average damages of $2,500,000. Discuss fully.

P13-11 (Loss Contingencies: Entries and Essays) Ruby Lillian Corporation, in preparation of its December 31, 1995, financial statements, is attempting to determine the proper accounting treatment for each of the following situations:

1. As a result of uninsured accidents during the year, personal injury suits for $350,000 and $60,000 have been filed against the company. It is the judgment of Lillian's legal counsel that an unfavorable outcome is unlikely in the $60,000 case but that an unfavorable verdict approximating $200,000 will probably result in the $350,000 case.
2. Ruby Lillian Corporation owns a subsidiary in a foreign country that has a book value of $5,690,000 and an estimated fair value of $8,700,000. The foreign government has communicated to Lillian its intention to expropriate the assets and business of all foreign investors. On the basis of settlements other firms have received from this same country, Lillian expects to receive 40% of the fair value of its properties as final settlement.
3. Lillian's chemical product division consisting of five plants is uninsurable because of the special risk of injury to employees and losses due to fire and explosion. The year 1995 is considered one of the safest (luckiest) in the division's history because no loss due to injury or casualty was suffered. Having suffered an average of three casualties a year during the rest of the past decade (ranging from $60,000 to $700,000), management is certain that next year the company will probably not be so fortunate.

Instructions
(a) Prepare the journal entries that should be recorded as of December 31, 1995, to recognize each of the situations above.
(b) Indicate what should be reported relative to each situation in the financial statements and accompanying notes. Explain why.

P13-12 (Warranties and Premiums) Charlie Parker's Music Emporium carries a wide variety of musical instruments, sound reproduction equipment, recorded music, and sheet music. Parker's uses two sales pro-motion techniques—warranties and premiums—to attract customers.

Musical instruments and sound equipment are sold with a one-year warranty for replacement of parts and labor. The estimated warranty cost, based on past experience, is 1% of sales.

The premium is offered on the recorded and sheet music. Customers receive a coupon for each dollar spent on recorded music or sheet music. Customers may exchange 200 coupons and $20 for a cassette player. Parker's pays $32 for each cassette player and estimates that 60% of the coupons given to customers will be redeemed.

Parker's total sales for 1995 were $7,200,000—$5,400,000 from musical instruments and sound reproduc-tion equipment and $1,800,000 from recorded music and sheet music. Replacement parts and labor for war-ranty work totaled $82,000 during 1995. A total of 6,500 cassette players used in the premium program were purchased during the year and there were 1,200,000 coupons redeemed in 1995.

The accrual method is used by Parker's to account for the warranty and premium costs for financial reporting purposes. The balances in the accounts related to warranties and premiums on January 1, 1995, were as shown below.

Inventory of Premium Cassette Players	$37,600
Estimated Premium Claims Outstanding	38,400
Estimated Liability from Warranties	68,000

Instructions
Charlie Parker's Music Emporium is preparing its financial statements for the year ended December 31, 1995. Determine the amounts that will be shown on the 1995 financial statements for the following:

1. Warranty Expense.
2. Estimated Liability from Warranties.
3. Premium Expense.
4. Inventory of Premium Cassette Players.
5. Estimated Premium Claims Outstanding.

(CMA adapted)

*P13-13 (Bonus Computation) Dick Clark Inc. has a contract with its president, Kimberly Aiken, to pay her a bonus during each of the years 1994, 1995, 1996, and 1997. The federal income tax rate is 40% during the 4 years. The profit before deductions for bonus and federal income taxes was $250,000 in 1994, $300,000 in 1995, $350,000 in 1996, and $380,000 in 1997. The president's bonus of 12% is deductible for tax purposes in each year and is to be computed as follows:

(a) In 1994 the bonus is to be based on profit before deductions for bonus and income tax.
(b) In 1995 the bonus is to be based on profit after deduction of bonus but before deduction of income tax.
(c) In 1996 the bonus is to be based on profit before deduction of bonus but after deduction of income tax.
(d) In 1997 the bonus is to be based on profit after deductions for bonus and income tax.

Instructions
Compute the amounts of the bonus and the income tax for each of the 4 years.

*P13-14 (Warranty, Bonus, and Coupon Computation) Jann Wenner Company must make computations and adjusting entries for the following independent situations at December 31, 1995:

1. Its line of amplifiers carries a 3-year warranty against defects. On the basis of past experience the estimated warranty costs related to dollar sales are: first year after sale—2% of sales; second year after sale—3% of sales; and third year after sale—4% of sales. Sales and actual warranty expenditures for the first 3 years of business were:

	Sales	Warranty Expenditures
1993	$ 800,000	$ 5,800
1994	1,100,000	17,000
1995	1,200,000	61,200

Instructions
Compute the amount that Wenner Company should report as a liability in its December 31, 1995, balance sheet. Assume that all sales are made evenly throughout each year with warranty expenses also evenly spaced relative to the rates above.

2. Wenner Company's profit-sharing plan provides that the company will contribute to a fund an amount equal to one-fourth of its net income each year. Income before deducting the profit-sharing

contribution and taxes for 1995 is $1,000,000. The applicable income tax rate is 40%, and the profit-sharing contribution is deductible for tax purposes.

Instructions
Compute the amount to be contributed to the profit-sharing fund for 1995.

3. With some of its products, Wenner Company includes coupons that are redeemable in merchandise. The coupons have no expiration date and, in the company's experience, 40% of them are redeemed. The liability for unredeemed coupons at December 31, 1994, was $9,000. During 1995, coupons worth $23,000 were issued, and merchandise worth $8,000 was distributed in exchange for coupons redeemed.

Instructions
Compute the amount of the liability that should appear on the December 31, 1995, balance sheet.

(AICPA adapted)

CASES

C13-1 (Nature of Liabilities) Presented below is the current liability section of Maytag Corporation.

	($000)	
	1993	1992
Current Liabilities		
Notes payable	$ 68,713	$ 7,700
Accounts payable	179,496	101,379
Compensation to employees	60,312	31,649
Accrued liabilities	158,198	77,621
Income taxes payable	5,486	21,491
Current maturities of long-term debt	16,592	6,649
Total current liabilities	$488,797	$246,489

Instructions
Answer the following questions.
(a) What are the essential characteristics that make an item a liability?
(b) How does one distinguish between a current liability and a long-term liability?
(c) What are accrued liabilities? Give three examples of accrued liabilities that Maytag might have.
(d) What is the theoretically correct way to value liabilities? How are current liabilities usually valued?
(e) Why are notes payable reported first in the current liability section?
(f) What might be the items that comprise Maytag's liability for "Compensation to employees"?

C13-2 (Current versus Noncurrent Classification) A. Torbert Corporation includes the following items in their liabilities at December 31, 1995:

1. Notes payable, $20,000,000, due June 30, 1996.
2. Deposits from customers on equipment ordered by them from A. Torbert, $5,000,000.
3. Salaries payable, $3,000,000, due January 14, 1996.

Instructions
Indicate in what circumstances, if any, each of the three liabilities above would be excluded from current liabilities.

C13-3 (Current versus Noncurrent Classification) The following items are listed as liabilities on the balance sheet of Bing Crosby Company on December 31, 1995:

Accounts payable	$ 280,000
Notes payable	500,000
Bonds payable	1,500,000

The accounts payable represent obligations to suppliers that were due in January 1996. The notes payable mature on various dates during 1996. The bonds payable mature on July 1, 1996.

These liabilities must be reported on the balance sheet in accordance with generally accepted accounting principles governing the classification of liabilities as current and noncurrent.

Instructions
(a) What is the general rule for determining whether a liability is classified as current or noncurrent?
(b) Under what conditions may any of Crosby Company's liabilities be classified as noncurrent? Explain your answer.

(CMA adapted)

C13-4 (Refinancing of Short-Term Debt) Spinners Corporation reflects in the current liability section of its balance sheet at December 31, 1995 (its year-end), short-term obligations of $15,000,000, which includes the current portion of 12% long-term debt in the amount of $10,000,000 (matures in March 1996). Management has stated its intention to refinance the 12% debt whereby no portion of it will mature during 1996. The date of issuance of the financial statements is March 25, 1996.

Instructions
    (a) Is management's intent enough to support long-term classification of the obligation in this situation?
    (b) Assume that Spinners Corporation issues $12,000,000 of 10-year debentures to the public in January 1996 and that management intends to use the proceeds to liquidate the $10,000,000 debt maturing in March 1996. Furthermore, assume that the debt maturing in March 1996 is paid from these proceeds prior to the issuance of the financial statements. Will this have any impact on the balance sheet classification at December 31, 1995? Explain your answer.
    (c) Assume that Spinners Corporation issues common stock to the public in January and that management intends to entirely liquidate the $10,000,000 debt maturing in March 1996 with the proceeds of this equity securities issue. In light of these events, should the $10,000,000 debt maturing in March 1996 be included in current liabilities at December 31, 1995?
    (d) Assume that Spinners Corporation, on February 15, 1996, entered into a financing agreement with a commercial bank that permits Spinners Corporation to borrow at any time through 1997 up to $15,000,000 at the bank's prime rate of interest. Borrowings under the financing agreement mature three years after the date of the loan. The agreement is not cancelable except for violation of a provision with which compliance is objectively determinable. No violation of any provision exists at the date of issuance of the financial statements. Assume further that the current portion of long-term debt does not mature until August 1996. In addition, management intends to refinance the $10,000,000 obligation under the terms of the financial agreement with the bank, which is expected to be financially capable of honoring the agreement.
        1. Given these facts, should the $10,000,000 be classified as current on the balance sheet at December 31, 1995?
        2. Is disclosure of the refinancing method required?

C13-5 (Refinancing of Short-Term Debt) Sammy Kaye Inc. issued $9,000,000 of short-term commercial paper during the year 1994 to finance construction of a plant. At December 31, 1994, the corporation's year-end, Sammy Kaye intends to refinance the commercial paper by issuing long-term debt. However, because the corporation temporarily has excess cash, in January 1995 it liquidates $3,000,000 of the commercial paper as the paper matures. In February 1995, Sammy Kaye completes an $18,000,000 long-term debt offering. Later during the month of February, it issues its December 31, 1994, financial statements. The proceeds of the long-term debt offering are to be used to replenish $3,000,000 in working capital, to pay $6,000,000 of commercial paper as it matures in March 1995, and to pay $9,000,000 of construction costs expected to be incurred later that year to complete the plant.

Instructions
    (a) How should the $9,000,000 of commercial paper be classified on the December 31, 1994; January 31, 1995; and February 28, 1995, balance sheets? Give support for your answer and also consider the cash element.
    (b) What would your answer be if, instead of a completed financing at the date of issuance of the financial statements, a financing agreement existed at that date?

C13-6 (Loss Contingencies) Ink Spots Company is a manufacturer of toys. During the year, the following situations arose:

    1. A safety hazard related to one of its toy products was discovered. It is considered probable that liabilities have been incurred. On the basis of past experience, a reasonable estimate of the amount of loss can be made.
    2. One of its small warehouses is located on the bank of a river and could no longer be insured against flood losses. No flood losses have occurred after the date that the insurance became unavailable.
    3. This year, Ink Spots began promoting a new toy by including a coupon, redeemable for a movie ticket, in each toy's carton. The movie ticket, which cost Ink Spots $3, is purchased in advance and then mailed to the customer when the coupon is received by Ink Spots. Ink Spots estimated, based on past experience, that 60% of the coupons would be redeemed. Forty percent of the coupons were actually redeemed this year, and the remaining 20% of the coupons are expected to be redeemed next year.

Instructions
    (a) How should Ink Spots report the safety hazard? Why? Do not discuss deferred income tax implications.
    (b) How should Ink Spots report the noninsurable flood risk? Why?
    (c) How should Ink Spots account for the toy promotion campaign in this year?

                                                         (AICPA adapted)

C13-7 (Gain and Loss Contingencies)
   (a)   What is the meaning of the term "contingency" as used in accounting?
   (b)   Distinguish between accounting for a gain contingency and accounting for a loss contingency.
   (c)   How should the following situations be recognized in the calendar year-end financial statements of Nitro Chemical Company? Explain.
       1.   Pending in a federal district court is a suit against Nitro Chemical. The suit, which asks for token damages, alleges that Nitro has infringed on a 15-year-old patent. Briefs will be heard on March 31.
       2.   The TUF Union, sole bargaining agent of Nitro's production employees, has threatened a strike unless Nitro agrees to a proposed profit-sharing plan. Negotiations begin on March 1.
       3.   A recently completed (during the calendar year in question) government contract is subject to renegotiation. Although Nitro suspects that a refund of approximately $175,000 may be required by the government, the company does not wish, for obvious reasons, to publicize this fact.
       4.   Nitro has a $200,000, 9% note receivable due next May 1 from TNT Company, its largest customer. Nitro sold the note on December 20, with recourse, to raise needed cash. TNT Company has never defaulted on a debt and possesses a high credit rating. (Treated as a sale on December 20.)

C13-8 (Loss Contingencies) On February 1, 1995, one of the huge storage tanks of Sturm Manufacturing Company exploded. Windows in houses and other buildings within a one-mile radius of the explosion were severely damaged, and a number of people were injured. As of February 15, 1995 (when the December 31, 1994, financial statements were completed and sent to the publisher for printing and public distribution), no suits had been filed or claims asserted against the company as a consequence of the explosion. The company fully anticipates that suits will be filed and claims asserted for injuries and damages. Because the casualty was uninsured and the company considered at fault, Sturm Manufacturing will have to cover the damages from its own resources.

Instructions
Discuss fully the accounting treatment and disclosures that should be accorded the casualty and related contingent losses in the financial statements dated December 31, 1994.

C13-9 (Loss Contingency) Presented below is a note disclosure for Shumway Corporation:

> **Litigation and Environmental:** The Company has been notified, or is a named or a potentially responsible party in a number of governmental (federal, state and local) and private actions associated with environmental matters, such as those relating to hazardous wastes, including certain sites which are on the United States EPA National Priorities List ("Superfund"). These actions seek cleanup costs, penalties and/or damages for personal injury or to property or natural resources.
>
> In 1993, the Company recorded a pre-tax charge of $51,229,000, included in the "Other Expense (Income)—Net" caption of the Company's Consolidated Statements of Income, as an additional provision for environmental matters. These expenditures are expected to take place over the next several years and are indicative of the Company's commitment to improve and maintain the environment in which it operates. At December 31, 1993, environmental accruals amounted to $63,931,000, of which $56,535,000 are considered noncurrent and are included in the "Deferred Credits and Other Liabilities" caption of the Company's Consolidated Balance Sheets.
>
> While it is impossible at this time to determine with certainty the ultimate outcome of environmental matters, it is management's opinion, based in part on the advice of independent counsel (after taking into account accruals and insurance coverage applicable to such actions) that when the costs are finally determined they will not have a material adverse effect on the financial position of the Company.

Instructions
Answer the following questions.
   (a)   What conditions must exist before a loss contingency can be recorded in the accounts?
   (b)   Suppose that Shumway Corporation could not reasonably estimate the amount of the loss, although it could establish with a high degree of probability the minimum and maximum loss possible. How should this information be reported in the financial statements?
   (c)   If the amount of the loss is uncertain, how would the loss contingency be reported in the financial statements?

C13-10 (Loss Contingencies) The following three independent sets of facts relate to (1) the possible accrual or (2) the possible disclosure of a loss contingency.

Situation I
Subsequent to the date of a set of financial statements, but prior to the issuance of the financial statements, a company enters into a contract that will probably result in a significant loss to the company. The amount of the loss can be reasonably estimated.

Situation II

A company offers a one-year warranty for the product that it manufactures. A history of warranty claims has been compiled and the probable amount of claims related to sales for a given period can be determined.

Situation III

A company has adopted a policy of recording self-insurance for any possible losses resulting from injury to others by the company's vehicles. The premium for an insurance policy for the same risk from an independent insurance company would have an annual cost of $3,000. During the period covered by the financial statements, there were no accidents involving the company's vehicles that resulted in injury to others.

Instructions

Discuss the accrual or type of disclosure necessary (if any) and the reason(s) why such disclosure is appropriate for each of the three independent sets of facts above.

(AICPA adapted)

C13-11 (Warranties and Loss Contingencies) The following two independent situations involve loss contingencies:

Part 1

Phil Remmers Company sells two types of merchandise, Type A and Type B. Each carries a one-year warranty.

1. Type A merchandise—Product warranty costs, based on past experience, will normally be 1% of sales.
2. Type B merchandise—Product warranty costs cannot be reasonably estimated because this is a new product line. However, the chief engineer believes that product warranty costs are likely to be incurred.

Instructions

How should Phil Remmers report the estimated product warranty costs for each of the two types of merchandise above? Discuss the rationale for your answer. Do not discuss deferred income tax implications, or disclosures that should be made in Phil Remmers's financial statements or notes.

Part 2

Russ Morgan Company is being sued for $3,000,000 for an injury caused to a child as a result of alleged negligence while the child was visiting the Russ Morgan Company plant in March 1995. The suit was filed in July 1995. Russ Morgan's lawyer states that it is probable that Russ Morgan will lose the suit and be found liable for a judgment costing anywhere from $300,000 to $1,500,000. However, the lawyer states that the most probable judgment is $600,000.

Instructions

How should Russ Morgan report the suit in its 1995 financial statements? Discuss the rationale for your answer. Include in your answer disclosures, if any, that should be made in Russ Morgan's financial statements or notes.

(AICPA adapted)

C13-12 (Warranties) Presented below is the current liability section and related note of the Toro Company.

	1993	1992
	(dollars in thousands)	
Current Liabilities		
Current portion of long-term debt	$ 15,000	$ 10,000
Short-term debt	2,668	405
Accounts payable	29,495	42,427
Accrued warranty	16,843	16,741
Accrued marketing programs	17,512	16,585
Other accrued liabilities	35,653	33,290
Accrued and deferred income taxes	6,206	7,348
Total current liabilities	$123,377	$126,796

Notes to Consolidated Financial Statements

1(in part): Summary of Significant Accounting Policies and Related Data

Accrued Warranty—The company provides an accrual for future warranty costs based upon the relationship of prior years' sales to actual warranty costs.

Instructions

Answer the following questions.

(a) What is the difference between the cash basis and the accrual basis of accounting for warranty costs?

(b) Under what circumstance, if any, would it be appropriate for Toro Company to recognize deferred revenue on warranty contracts?

(c) If Toro Company recognized deferred revenue on warranty contracts, how would it recognize this revenue in subsequent periods?

► USING YOUR JUDGMENT ◄

► FINANCIAL REPORTING PROBLEM

Refer to the financial statements and other documents of Georgia-Pacific Corporation presented in Appendix 5-A and answer the following questions.

1. What were Georgia-Pacific's current portion of long-term debt at December 31, 1992 and 1993? What are the amounts of the remaining scheduled maturities of long-term debt for the years 1994 to 1998?
2. What were the contingencies mentioned in Georgia-Pacific's Notes to Financial Statements? What was the management's reaction and conclusion relative to these contingencies?
3. Are there any unusual items listed among the current liabilities of Georgia-Pacific? Describe the item or items and explain the circumstances surrounding each.

► WRITING ASSIGNMENT

You are the independent auditor engaged to audit Dorothy Segrt Corporation's December 31, 1994, financial statements. Dorothy Segrt manufactures household appliances. During the course of your audit, you discovered the following contingent liabilities:

1. Dorothy Segrt began production on a new dishwasher in June 1994 and, by December 31, 1994, sold 100,000 to various retailers for $500 each. Each dishwasher is under a one-year warranty. The company estimates that its warranty expense per dishwasher will amount to $25. At year-end, the company had already paid out $1,000,000 in warranty expenses. Dorothy Segrt's income statement shows warranty expense of $1,000,000 for 1994. Segrt accounts for warranty costs on the accrual basis.
2. In response to your attorney's letter, Robert Sklodowski, Esq., has informed you that Dorothy Segrt has been cited for dumping toxic waste into the Kishwaukee River. Clean-up costs and fines amount to $3,330,000. Although the case is still being contested, Sklodowski is certain that Dorothy Segrt will most probably have to pay the fine and clean-up costs. No disclosure of this situation was found in the financial statements.
3. Dorothy Segrt is the defendant in a patent infringement lawsuit by Heidi Silverman over Segrt's use of a hydraulic compressor in several of its products. Sklodowski claims that, if the suit goes against Segrt, the loss may be as much as $5,000,000; however, Sklodowski believes the loss of this suit to be only reasonably possible. Again, no mention of this suit occurs in the financial statements.

As presented, these contingencies are not reported in accordance with GAAP which may create problems in issuing a clean audit report. You feel the need to note these problems in the work papers.

Instructions

Heading each page with the name of the company, balance sheet date, and a brief description of the problem, write a brief narrative for each of the above issues in the form of **a memorandum** to be incorporated in the audit work papers. Explain what led to the discovery of each problem, what the problem really is, and what you advised your client to do (along with any appropriate journal entries) in order to bring these contingencies in accordance with GAAP.

► GROUP ASSIGNMENT

(Entries for Liabilities and Loss Contingencies) Andrew Wyeth Inc., a publishing company, is preparing its December 31, 1995, financial statements and must determine the proper accounting treatment for the following situations; they have retained your group to assist them in this task.

1. Wyeth sells subscriptions to several magazines for a 1-year, 2-year, or 3-year period. Cash receipts from subscribers are credited to magazine subscriptions collected in advance, and this account had a balance of $2,300,000 at December 31, 1995. Outstanding subscriptions at December 31, 1995, expire as follows:

During 1996—$600,000
During 1997— 500,000
During 1998— 800,000

2. On January 2, 1995, Wyeth discontinued collision, fire, and theft coverage on its delivery vehicles and became self-insured for these risks. Actual losses of $50,000 during 1995 were charged to delivery expense. The 1994 premium for the discontinued coverage amounted to $80,000 and the controller wants to set up a reserve for self-insurance by a debit to delivery expense of $30,000 and a credit to the reserve for self-insurance of $30,000.

3. A suit for breach of contract seeking damages of $1,000,000 was filed by an author against Wyeth on July 1, 1995. The company's legal counsel believes that an unfavorable outcome is probable. A reasonable estimate of the court's award to the plaintiff is in the range between $300,000 and $700,000. No amount within this range is a better estimate of potential damages than any other amount.

4. During December 1995, a competitor company filed suit against Wyeth for industrial espionage claiming $1,500,000 in damages. In the opinion of management and company counsel, it is reasonably possible that damages will be awarded to the plaintiff. However, the amount of potential damages awarded to the plaintiff cannot be reasonably estimated.

Instructions

Your instructor will assign one group member to serve as a recorder and one member to serve as spokesperson. As a group, provide the information for the recorder to prepare, for each of the above situations, the journal entry that should be recorded as of December 31, 1995, or explain why an entry should not be recorded (you may wish to divide the parts among the members). Upon completion, the spokesperson will report the group findings to the class and be prepared to show supporting computations in good form.

(AICPA adapted)

► ETHICS CASES

EC13-1 (Ethical Issues: Bonus Compensation) Mail Order Company has a bonus arrangement which grants the Financial Vice-President and other executives a $15,000 bonus if net income exceeds the previous year's by $1,000,000. Noting that the current financial statements report an increase of $950,000 in net income, Vice-President Glenn Close asks Christopher Walkin, the controller, to reduce the estimate of warranty expense by $60,000. The present estimate of warranty expense is $500,000 and is known by both Glenn and Christopher to be a fairly "soft" amount.

Instructions

(a) Should Walkin lower his estimate?
(b) What ethical issue is at stake? Is anyone harmed?
(c) Is Vice-President Close acting unethically?

EC13-2 (Ethical Issues: Contingent Rent Expense) Old Kentucky Company, the owner of Camptown Mall, charges "Old Folks" Home Store a rental fee of $600 per month plus 5% of yearly profits over $500,000. Stephen Foster, the owner of the store, directs his accountant, Osue Sanna, to increase the estimate of bad debt expense, warranty costs, and depreciation on the computerized inventory system in order to keep profits at $475,000.

Instructions

(a) Should Sanna follow her boss' directive?
(b) Who is harmed, if her estimates are increased?
(c) Is Foster's directive unethical?

EC13-3 (Ethical Issues: Environmental Contingencies) On January 2, 1995, Workman Steel Company received notice from the Environmental Protection Agency that the Prior Lake Toxic Disposal Site needs to be cleaned up and that Workman Steel will be assessed 1/25 of the $25,000,000 cost. The clean-up will begin in 1998 and will take an estimated 5 years. Workman Steel has been using this disposal site for several decades. The Vice-President and the controller discuss the proper recording of the environmental liability. Vice-President Renea Rhodes advocates recording the entire liability in 1995. Controller Jared Wagner suggests footnote disclosure at most and prefers nondisclosure until cleanup begins in 1998.

Instructions

(a) What is the appropriate manner of reporting?
(b) Is there an ethical issue involved in this discussion?
(c) Who is harmed by nondisclosure?

GOVERNMENT ACCOUNTING

A visit with
KATHY WHITMIRE

For ten years, KATHRYN J. WHITMIRE had one of the toughest jobs in America—mayor of a major metropolitan city. From 1982 to 1992 she was mayor of Houston, Texas, serving five two-year terms. During her tenure, she is credited with helping diversify the Houston economy beyond the oil industry as well as making major improvements in the city's public transportation, emergency medical services, police services, and wastewater treatment facilities. Prior to serving as mayor, she was elected city controller in 1977 and was re-elected to a second term in 1979. Mayor Whitmire is the first woman to be elected to any city office in Houston. Another rarity among politicians: she is a CPA, having spent eight years with a national CPA firm in Houston prior to entering public life.

What is your educational background?

I received a bachelor's degree from the University of Houston in business administration with a major in accounting. And then I went on and got a Master of Science in accountancy, also from the University of Houston. After I graduated, I went to work for what was then called Haskins & Sells (now Deloitte & Touche), where I worked for three years, and then went to work for Coopers & Lybrand, also on the audit staff. While at Coopers, I was promoted to manager. All of the partners gathered into the office and had a bouquet of yellow roses for me because I was the first woman ever to join the management team in the Houston office.

What did you do after you left Coopers?

I took a job teaching accounting at the University of Houston for one year; then I decided to run for city controller. There was a vacancy—the man who had the job was appointed to a job in the new Carter administration. At that time, no woman had ever been elected to an office in Houston government. I tried to convince the city council to appoint me—they had the right to fill the position when the incumbent left to go to Washington—but they decided not to. By then, I had gotten so involved in envisioning myself as the city's chief financial officer that I just decided to go ahead and run for the office.

When you were at the accounting firms, had you done any audits of government entities?

No, but I did audits of regulated public utilities. The electric utility here in Houston was the first big client that I was responsible for at Haskins & Sells. At Coopers & Lybrand I supervised the audit of the power company that serves Southeastern Texas and Louisiana. So I had a great deal of experience with regulated public utilities and in fact had been talking with the former city controller about the city's regulatory role and approaches that I felt the city could take to do a better job in regulating the public utility industry.

What made you decide to run for mayor of Houston?

As city controller I had a chance to observe the city management from the inside, and I felt that the management itself was not carried out in a businesslike fashion. The mayor was a real estate developer, and I felt that he didn't give the level of attention that he should to basic issues of planning and management. As an example, each January, the finance office that worked for the mayor would just be starting to put together budget proposals. By the time they finished and the city council argued over it, half the year would have gone by without an adopted budget. Another issue was the fact that the mayor would usually meet with employee organizations around November and talk with them about their pay situation. Around December he would come to the city council and suggest that employees' pay be raised across the board by a certain amount. Usually it would be a large amount because inflation was running rampant at the time. Economic growth in Houston was running rampant then, too, so there was lots of money to spend. It seemed to me that there was a complete lack of planning, and the only thing that was keeping us afloat was that the economy was so strong and that our revenues were going up 15%–20% per year.

What types of issues in government would relate to financial accounting?

As I mentioned before, my background in auditing public utility financial statements helped a lot. Another issue that I became interested in was accounting for pension plans. Even before I ran for city controller, reviewing the city's financial statement brought to my attention the fact that the auditors took exception to the financial reporting of the pension plan, mainly because it was not being funded on an actuarially acceptable basis. I tried to make that an issue in my controller's campaign, but the terms "actuarial" and "pension funding" seemed not to have much political appeal. I made it a major cause of mine while I was city controller, and was actually able to get some legislation passed that required our local pension plans to be funded on an actuarially sound basis. We were also grappling with the issue of other post-retirement benefits. I got involved in things that seemed to be arcane issues like the city's policy of allowing employees to accumulate and be paid

for their unused sick time, which resulted in retirees getting checks for $100,000 when they walked out the door because they had accumulated so many days of sick time. That was a policy that I had to ultimately take to the state legislature because it had been written into state law. I got that changed in my third term as mayor because it had accumulated a $200 million unreported, unrecorded, unfunded liability. And who, but an accountant, would understand that as mayor? That's why nobody had done anything about it.

I remember when you were elected that it made big news nationally. Were you prepared for all that limelight?

No, not at all. My goodness. That was when they started talking about me having the soul of an accountant. I went to the inaugural ball that my supporters had organized, and I was so unprepared for the crush of television cameras that I got up and left. That became part of the folklore in Houston.

In a position of leadership, you have to have some communication skills.

I tell my MBA students that it doesn't matter how much you know if you can't communicate it. I recommend that everyone take public speaking because no matter what field you go into, you're going to need verbal communication skills. Even though I took one public speaking course as an undergraduate, I was still afraid to stand up in front of a group. However, the thing that caused me to overcome that and to be comfortable enough as a public speaker to run for office was when I was a graduate student and suddenly found myself with a room full of sopho-

mores to whom I was supposed to teach introductory accounting. I immediately had to get over my fear of public speaking.

You were mayor for ten years. What accomplishments are you most proud of?

The most important one is bringing the city successfully through its economic downturn—getting the economy growing again, keeping the city out of bankruptcy, and maintaining a AA bond rating during that time. We had a very very bad recession in Houston in the mid-1980s, beginning right at the end of my first term and continuing until about 1988.

And you ran for re-election how many times?

Five two-year terms. I ran for re-election five times, which means I ran six times altogether. But I was defeated the last time, in fall of 1991, because the major issue by then was not the economy or the budget—it was the horrible crime wave going through the city, for which I was perceived as not doing enough.

Financial matters are more concrete, but social problems are very difficult to deal with.

Well, I don't know. It is the duty of the mayor to get out in front of whatever the issues are that people are concerned about. I don't subscribe to the theory that government ought to take care of everything. But I learned somewhere along the way that the job of mayor is not just what it says it is in the city charter, but to see what the issues are and make sure that they are addressed.

CHAPTER 14

LONG-TERM LIABILITIES

LEARNING OBJECTIVES

After studying this chapter, you should be able to:

1. Describe the formal procedures associated with issuing long-term debt.
2. Identify various types of bond issues.
3. Describe the accounting valuation for bonds at date of issuance.
4. Apply the methods of bond discount and premium amortization.
5. Describe the accounting procedures for the extinguishment of debt.
6. Explain the accounting procedures for long-term notes payable.
7. Describe off-balance-sheet financing arrangements.
8. Describe disclosure requirements for long-term debt.

*A*pparently, the motto of the 1980s was "Let us all be happy and live within our means, even if we have to borrow the money to do it with."[1] Companies and consumers took on increasing levels of debt to finance expansion, take over companies, and satisfy consumption needs.[2] Unfortunately as the recession continued into 1991, many of the companies that greatly increased their debt loads found it difficult to survive. They responded by selling off assets, restructuring, cutting dividends, laying off workers, and selling new equity. As interest rates decreased dramatically and the economy and earnings improved in 1992–94, much of that debt has been refinanced at lower rates and some has been paid down.

▶ ISSUING LONG-TERM DEBT

Long-term debt consists of probable future sacrifices of economic benefits arising from present obligations that are not payable within a year or the operating cycle of the business, whichever is longer. Bonds payable, long-term notes payable, mortgages payable, pension liabilities, and lease liabilities are examples of long-term liabilities.

Incurring long-term debt is often accompanied by considerable formality. For example, the bylaws of corporations usually require approval by the board of directors and the stockholders before bonds can be issued or other long-term debt arrangements can be contracted.

---

[1]A comment by Artemus Ward in *Investment Vision,* September/October 1990.

[2]Anne B. Fisher, "Don't Be Afraid of the Big Bad Debt," *Fortune,* April 22, 1991, p. 124.

Generally, long-term debt has various **covenants or restrictions** for the protection of both lenders and borrowers. The covenants and other terms of the agreement between the borrower and the lender are stated in the bond indenture or note agreement. Items often mentioned in the indenture or agreement include the amounts authorized to be issued, interest rate, due date or dates, call provisions, property pledged as security, sinking fund requirements, working capital and dividend restrictions, and limitations concerning the assumption of additional debt. Whenever these stipulations are important for a complete understanding of the financial position and the results of operations, they should be described in the body of the financial statements or the notes thereto. In many cases, the loan instrument or contract is held by a trustee, usually a bank or trust company, that acts as an independent third party to protect the interests of the lender and the borrower.

Although it would seem that these covenants provide adequate protection to the long-term debt holder, many bondholders suffer considerable losses when additional debt is added to the capital structure. Consider what happened to bondholders in the leveraged buyout of RJR Nabisco. Solidly rated 9⅜% bonds due in 2016 plunged 20% in value when management announced the leveraged buyout. Such a loss in value occurs because the additional debt added to the capital structure increases the likelihood of default. Although bondholders have covenants to protect them, they often are written in a manner that can be interpreted in a number of different ways.

OBJECTIVE 1

Describe the formal procedures associated with issuing long-term debt.

► BONDS PAYABLE

Bonds are the most common type of long-term debt reported on a company's balance sheet. The main purpose of bonds is to borrow for the long term when the amount of capital needed is too large for one lender to supply. By issuing bonds in $100, $1,000, or $10,000 denominations, a large amount of long-term indebtedness can be divided into many small investing units, thus enabling more than one lender to participate in the loan.

A bond arises from a contract known as a **bond indenture** and represents a promise to pay: (1) a sum of money at a designated maturity date, plus (2) periodic interest at a specified rate on the maturity amount (face value). Individual bonds are evidenced by a paper certificate and typically have a $1,000 face value. Bond interest payments usually are made semiannually, although the interest rate is generally expressed as an annual rate.

An entire bond issue may be sold to an investment banker who acts as a selling agent in the process of marketing the bonds. In such arrangements, investment bankers may either underwrite the entire issue by guaranteeing a certain sum to the corporation, thus taking the risk of selling the bonds for whatever price they can get (firm underwriting), or they may sell the bond issue for a commission to be deducted from the proceeds of the sale (best efforts underwriting). Alternatively, the issuing company may choose to place privately a bond issue by selling the bonds directly to a large institution, financial or otherwise, without the aid of an underwriter (private placement).

► TYPES AND RATINGS OF BONDS

Some of the more common types of bonds found in practice are:

OBJECTIVE 2

Identify various types of bond issues.

◄ TYPES OF BONDS ►

SECURED AND UNSECURED BONDS. Secured bonds are backed by a pledge of some sort of collateral. Mortgage bonds are secured by a claim on real estate. Collateral trust bonds are secured by stocks and bonds of other corporations. Bonds not backed by collateral are **unsecured.** A debenture bond is unsecured. A "junk bond" is unsecured and also very risky, and therefore pays a high interest rate. These bonds are often used to finance leveraged buyouts.

TERM, SERIAL BONDS, AND CALLABLE BONDS. Bond issues that mature on a single date are called **term bonds,** and issues that mature in installments are called **serial bonds.** Serially maturing bonds are frequently used by school or sanitary districts, municipalities, or other local taxing bodies that borrow money through a special levy. **Callable bonds** give the issuer the right to call and retire the bonds prior to maturity.

CONVERTIBLE, COMMODITY-BACKED, AND DEEP DISCOUNT BONDS. If bonds are convertible into other securities of the corporation for a specified time after issuance, they are called **convertible bonds.** Accounting for bond conversions is discussed in Chapter 17. Two new types of bonds have been developed in an attempt to attract capital in a tight money market—commodity-backed bonds and deep discount bonds.

Commodity-backed bonds (also called **asset-linked bonds**) are redeemable in measures of a commodity, such as barrels of oil, tons of coal, or ounces of rare metal. In the early 1980s Sunshine Mining, a silver mining producer, sold two issues of bonds redeemable with either $1,000 in cash or 50 ounces of silver, whichever is greater at maturity. The issues are due in 1995 and have a stated interest rate of 8½%. The accounting problem is one of projecting the maturity value, especially since silver has fluctuated between $4 and $40 an ounce since issuance.

J. C. Penney Company sold the first publicly marketed long-term debt securities in the United States that do not bear interest. These **deep discount bonds,** also referred to as **zero interest debenture bonds,** are sold at a discount that provides the buyer's total interest payoff at maturity. Caesar's World Inc., a Las Vegas/Lake Tahoe gambling casino operator proposed a unique version of the zero interest bond.[3] Caesar's World proposed to issue 5,000 of $15,000 face amount bonds that would entitle each bondholder to spend two weeks a year at its Lake Tahoe resort in lieu of interest.

REGISTERED AND BEARER (COUPON) BONDS. Bonds issued in the name of the owner are **registered bonds** and require surrender of the certificate and issuance of a new certificate to complete a sale. A **bearer** or **coupon bond,** however, is not recorded in the name of the owner and may be transferred from one owner to another by mere delivery.

INCOME AND REVENUE BONDS. **Income bonds** pay no interest unless the issuing company is profitable. **Revenue bonds,** so called because the interest on them is paid from specified revenue sources, are most frequently issued by airports, school districts, counties, toll-road authorities, and governmental bodies.

Two major investment publication companies, Moody's Investors Service and Standard & Poor's Corporation issue quality ratings on every public bond issue. The bond quality designations and rating symbols of these two firms are as follows:

ILLUSTRATION 14-1
Bond Quality Ratings

Quality	Symbols	
	Moody's	Standard & Poor's
Prime	Aaa	AAA
Excellent	Aa	AA
Upper medium	A	A
Lower medium	Baa	BBB
Marginally speculative	Ba	BB
Very speculative	B, Caa	B
Default	Ca, C	D

[3]"Caesar's World May Try Bond Issue Paying in Vacations," *The Wall Street Journal* (January 22, 1982), p. 32.

A quality rating is assigned to each new public bond issue and is a current assessment of the company's ability to pay with respect to a specific borrowing. The rating may be changed up or down during the issue's outstanding life because the quality is constantly monitored. The debt rating is not a recommendation to purchase, sell, or hold a security, because it does not comment on market prices or suitability for particular investors.[4]

▶ VALUATION OF BONDS PAYABLE— DISCOUNT AND PREMIUM

The issuance and marketing of bonds to the public does not happen overnight. It usually takes weeks or even months. Underwriters must be arranged, Securities and Exchange Commission approval must be obtained, audits and issuance of a prospectus may be required, and certificates must be printed. Frequently, the terms in a bond indenture are established well in advance of the sale of the bonds. Between the time the terms are set and the bonds are issued, the market conditions and the financial position of the issuing corporation may change significantly. Such changes affect the marketability of the bonds and thus their selling price.

The selling price of a bond issue is set by such familiar phenomena as supply and demand of buyers and sellers, relative risk, market conditions, and the state of the economy. The investment community values a bond at the present value of its future cash flows, which consist of (1) interest and (2) principal. The rate used to compute the present value of these cash flows is the interest rate that provides an acceptable return on an investment commensurate with the issuer's risk characteristics.

The interest rate written in the terms of the bond indenture (and ordinarily printed on the bond certificate) is known as the **stated, coupon,** or **nominal rate.** This rate, which is set by the issuer of the bonds, is expressed as a percentage of the **face value,** also called the **par value, principal amount,** or **maturity value,** of the bonds. If the rate employed by the investment community (buyers) differs from the stated rate, the present value of the bonds computed by the buyers (and the current purchase price) will differ from the face value of the bonds. The difference between the face value and the present value of the bonds is either a discount or premium.[5] If the bonds sell for less than face value, they are sold at a **discount.** If the bonds sell for more than face value, they are sold at **a premium.**

The rate of interest actually earned by the bondholders is called the **effective yield,** or **market rate.** If bonds sell at a discount, the effective rate is higher than the stated rate. Conversely, if bonds sell at a premium, the effective rate or yield is lower than the stated rate. While the bond is outstanding, its price is affected by several variables, most notably the market rate of interest. There is an inverse relationship between the market interest rate and the price of the bond. The proof of this is graphically portrayed in Illustration 14-2. These huge bond principal losses are due primarily to the Federal Reserve's 1.5% increase in the short-term interest rate in the first half of 1994.

OBJECTIVE 3

Describe the accounting valuation for bonds at date of issuance.

INTERNATIONAL INSIGHT

Valuation of long-term debt varies internationally. In the U.S. discount and premium are booked and amortized over the life of the debt. In some countries (e.g., Sweden, Japan, Belgium) it is permissible to write off the discount and premium immediately.

[4]As indicated previously, the credit quality of American business declined during the 1980s. In 1990, Dun & Bradstreet reported that 60,432 companies failed. Meanwhile, Standard & Poor's reported 766 downgrades in 1990, approximately twice as many as 1988. As of April 1991, only 40 companies are rated AAA by Standard and Poor's, an approximate 40% drop from 1980. Anne B. Fisher, "Don't Be Afraid of the Big Bad Debt," *Fortune,* April 1991, p. 121.

[5]Until the 1950s it was common for corporations to issue bonds with low, even-percentage coupons (such as 4%) to demonstrate their financial solidity. Frequently, the result was large discounts. More recently, it has become acceptable to set the stated rate of interest on bonds in rather precise fractions (such as 10⅞%). Companies usually attempt to align the stated rate as closely as possible with the market or effective rate at the time of issue. While discounts and premiums continue to occur, their absolute magnitude tends to be much smaller; many times it is immaterial. Professor Bill N. Schwartz (Virginia Commonwealth University) studied the 685 new debt offerings in 1985. Of these, none were issued at a premium. Approximately 95% were issued either with no discount or at a price above 98. Now, however, zero interest (deep discount) bonds are more popular.

ILLUSTRATION 14-2
Effects of Interest Rate
Change on Various Types
of Outstanding Bonds

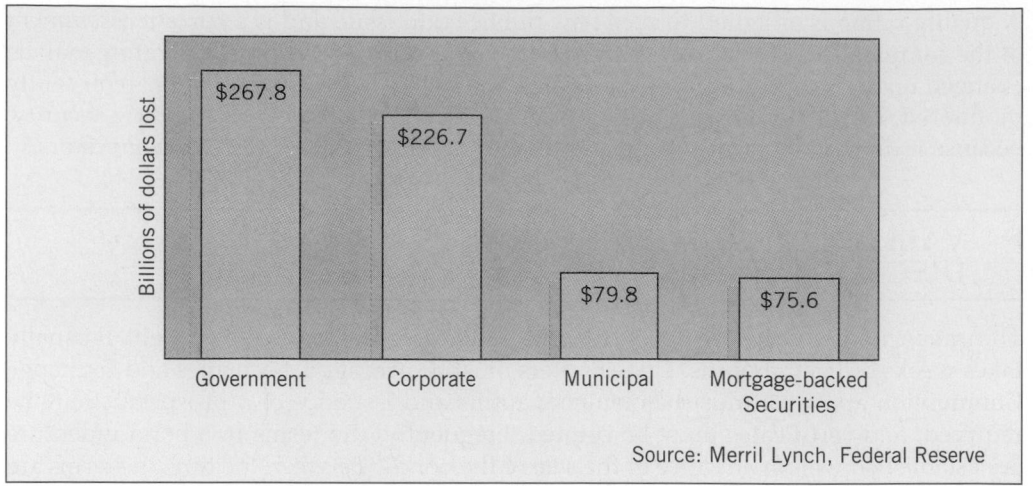

To illustrate the computation of the **present value of a bond issue,** consider ServiceMaster which issues $100,000 in bonds, due in 5 years with 9% interest payable annually at year-end. At the time of issue, the market rate for such bonds is 11%. The following time diagram depicts both the interest and the principal cash flows:

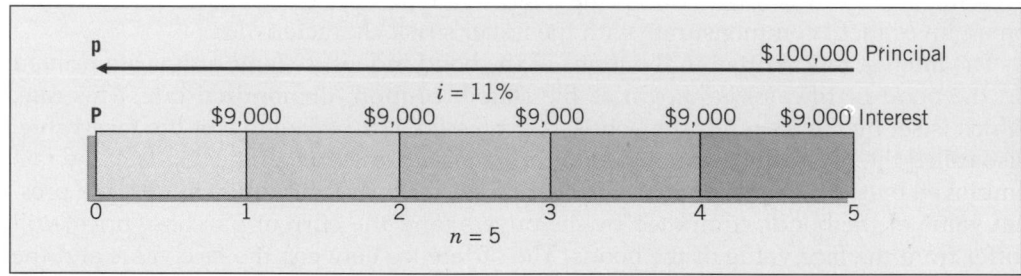

The actual principal and interest cash flows are discounted at an 11% rate as follows:

ILLUSTRATION 14-3
Present Value
Computation of Bond
Selling at a Discount

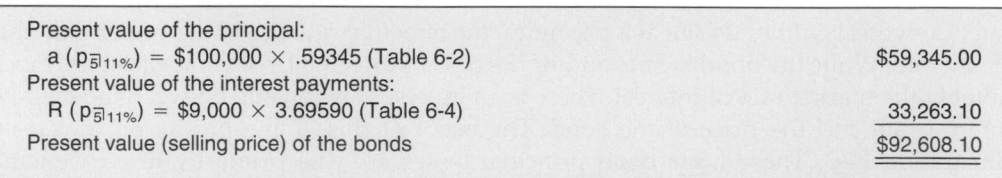

By paying $92,608.10 at the date of issue, the investors will realize an effective rate or yield of 11% over the 5-year term of the bonds. These bonds would sell at a discount of $7,391.90 ($100,000 − $92,608.10). The price at which the bonds sell is typically stated as a percentage of the face or par value of the bonds. For example, the ServiceMaster bonds sold for 92.6 (92.6% of par). If ServiceMaster had received $102,000, we would say the bonds sold for 102 (102% of par).

When bonds sell below face value, it means that investors demand a rate of interest higher than the stated rate. The investors are not satisfied with the stated rate because they can earn a greater rate on alternative investments of equal risk. They cannot change the stated rate, so they refuse to pay face value for the bonds. Thus, by changing the amount invested they alter the effective rate of interest. The investors receive interest at the stated rate computed on the face value, but they are earning at **an effective rate that is higher than the stated rate because they paid less than face value for the bonds.** (An illustration of a bond that sells at a premium is shown in Illustrations 14-7 and 14-8.)

► BONDS ISSUED AT PAR ON INTEREST DATE

When bonds are issued on an interest payment date at par (face value), no interest has accrued and no premium or discount exists. The accounting entry is made simply for the cash proceeds and the face value of the bonds. To illustrate, if 10-year term bonds with a par value of $800,000, dated January 1, 1995, and bearing interest at an annual rate of 10% payable semiannually on January 1 and July 1, are issued on January 1 at par, the entry on the books of the issuing corporation would be:

Cash	800,000	
Bonds Payable		800,000

The entry to record the first semiannual interest payment of $40,000 ($800,000 × .10 × 1/2) on July 1, 1995, would be as follows:

Bond Interest Expense	40,000	
Cash		40,000

The entry to record accrued interest expense at December 31, 1995 (year-end) would be as follows:

Bond Interest Expense	40,000	
Bond Interest Payable		40,000

► BONDS ISSUED AT DISCOUNT OR PREMIUM ON INTEREST DATE

If the $800,000 of bonds illustrated above were issued on January 1, 1995, at 97 (meaning 97% of par), the issuance would be recorded as follows:

OBJECTIVE 4

Apply the methods of bond discount and premium amortization.

Cash ($800,000 × .97)	776,000	
Discount on Bonds Payable	24,000	
Bonds Payable		800,000

Because of its relation to interest, as previously discussed, **the discount is amortized and charged to interest expense over the period of time that the bonds are outstanding.** Under the **straight-line method,**[6] the amount amortized each year is a constant amount. For example, using the bond discount above of $24,000, the amount amortized to interest expense each year for 10 years is $2,400 ($24,000 ÷ 10 years) and, if amortization is recorded annually, it is recorded as follows:

Bond Interest Expense	2,400	
Discount on Bonds Payable		2,400

At the end of the first year, 1995, as a result of the amortization entry above, the unamortized balance in Discount on Bonds Payable is $21,600, ($24,000 − $2,400).

If the bonds were dated and sold on October 1, 1995, and if the fiscal year of the corporation ended on December 31, the discount amortized during 1995 would be only 3/12 of 1/10 of $24,000, or $600. Three months of accrued interest must also be recorded on December 31.

Premium on Bonds Payable is accounted for in a manner similar to that for Discount on Bonds Payable. If the 10-year bonds of a par value of $800,000 are dated and sold on January 1, 1995, at 103, the following entry is made to record the issuance:

Cash ($800,000 × 1.03)	824,000	
Premium on Bonds Payable		24,000
Bonds Payable		800,000

---

[6]Although the effective interest method is preferred for amortization of discount or premium, to keep these initial illustrations simple, we have chosen to use the straight–line method (which is acceptable if the results obtained are not materially different from those produced by the effective interest method).

At the end of 1995 and for each year the bonds are outstanding, the entry to amortize the premium on a straight-line basis is:

Premium on Bonds Payable	2,400	
Bond Interest Expense		2,400

Bond interest expense is increased by amortization of a discount and decreased by amortization of a premium. Amortization of a discount or premium under the effective interest method is discussed later.

Some bonds are callable by the issuer after a certain date at a stated price so that the issuing corporation may have the opportunity to reduce its bonded indebtedness or take advantage of lower interest rates. **Whether callable or not, any premium or discount must be amortized over the life to maturity date because early redemption (call of the bond) is not a certainty.**

▶ BONDS ISSUED BETWEEN INTEREST DATES

Bond interest payments are usually made semiannually on dates specified in the bond indenture. When bonds are issued on other than the interest payment dates, **buyers of the bonds will pay the seller the interest accrued from the last interest payment date to the date of issue.** The purchasers of the bonds, in effect, pay the bond issuer in advance for that portion of the full 6-months' interest payment to which they are not entitled, not having held the bonds during that period. **The purchasers will receive the full 6-months' interest payment on the next semiannual interest payment date.**

To illustrate, if 10-year bonds of a par value of $800,000, dated January 1, 1995, and bearing interest at an annual rate of 10% payable semiannually on January 1 and July 1, are issued on March 1, 1995, at **par plus accrued interest,** the entry on the books of the issuing corporation is:

Cash	813,333	
Bonds Payable		800,000
Bond Interest Expense ($800,000 × .10 × 2/12)		13,333
(Interest Payable might be credited instead)		

The purchaser advances 2 months' interest, because on July 1, 1995, 4 months after the date of purchase, 6 months' interest will be received from the issuing company. The company makes the following entry on July 1, 1995:

Bond Interest Expense	40,000	
Cash		40,000

The expense account now contains a debit balance of $26,667, which represents the proper amount of interest expense, 4 months at 10% on $800,000.

The illustration above was simplified by having the January 1, 1995, bonds issued on March 1, 1995, **at par.** If, however, the 10% bonds were issued at 102, the entry on March 1 on the books of the issuing corporation would be:

Cash [($800,000 × 1.02) + ($800,000 × .10 × 2/12)]	829,333	
Bonds Payable		800,000
Premium on Bonds Payable ($800,000 × .02)		16,000
Bond Interest Expense		13,333

The premium would be amortized from the date of sale, March 1, 1995, not from the date of the bonds, January 1, 1995.

▶ EFFECTIVE INTEREST METHOD

The profession's preferred procedure for amortization of a discount or premium is the **effective interest method** (also called **present value amortization**). Under the effective interest method:

1. Bond interest expense is computed first by multiplying the **carrying value**[7] of the bonds at the beginning of the period by the effective interest rate.

2. The bond discount or premium amortization is then determined by comparing the bond interest expense with the interest to be paid.

The computation of the amortization is depicted graphically as follows:

ILLUSTRATION 14-4
Bond Discount and Premium Amortization Computation

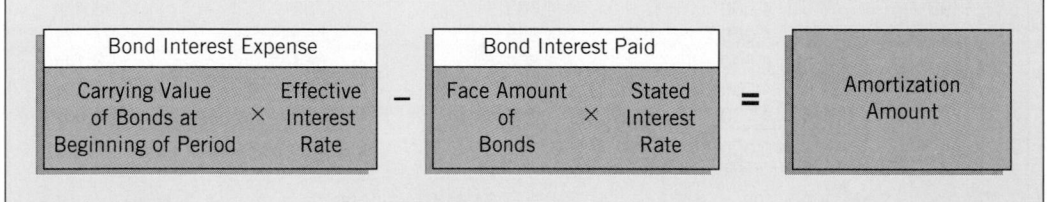

The effective interest method produces a periodic interest expense equal to **a constant percentage of the carrying value of the bonds.** Since the percentage is the effective rate of interest incurred by the borrower at the time of issuance, the effective interest method results in a better matching of expenses with revenues than the straight-line method.

Both the effective interest and straight-line methods result in the **same total amount of interest expense over the term of the bonds,** and the annual amounts of interest expense are generally quite similar. However, **when the annual amounts are materially different, the effective interest method is required under generally accepted accounting principles.**

BONDS ISSUED AT A DISCOUNT

To illustrate amortization of a discount, Evermaster Corporation issued $100,000 of 8% term bonds on January 1, 1995, due on January 1, 2000, with interest payable each July 1 and January 1. Because the investors required an effective interest rate of 10%, they paid $92,278 for the $100,000 of bonds, creating a $7,722 discount. The $7,722 discount is computed as follows:[8]

Maturity value of bonds payable		$100,000
Present value of $100,000 due in 5 years at 10%, interest payable semiannually (Table 6-2); a ($p_{\overline{10}|5\%}$); ($100,000 × .61391)	$61,391	
Present value of $4,000 interest payable semiannually for 5 years at 10% annually (Table 6-4); R ($P_{\overline{10}|5\%}$); ($4,000 × 7.72173)	30,887	
Proceeds from sale of bonds		92,278
Discount on bonds payable		$ 7,722

ILLUSTRATION 14-5
Computation of Discount on Bonds Payable

---

[7]The **book value,** also called the **carrying value,** equals the face amount minus any unamortized discount or plus any unamortized premium.

[8]Because interest is paid semiannually, the interest rate used is 5% (10% × 6/12). The number of periods is 10 (5 years × 2).

The 5-year amortization schedule appears below.

ILLUSTRATION 14-6
Bond Discount
Amortization Schedule

		SCHEDULE OF BOND DISCOUNT AMORTIZATION EFFECTIVE INTEREST METHOD—SEMIANNUAL INTEREST PAYMENTS 5-YEAR, 8% BONDS SOLD TO YIELD 10%		
Date	Cash Paid	Interest Expense	Discount Amortized	Carrying Amount of Bonds
1/1/95				$ 92,278
7/1/95	$ 4,000ᵃ	$ 4,614ᵇ	$ 614ᶜ	92,892ᵈ
1/1/96	4,000	4,645	645	93,537
7/1/96	4,000	4,677	677	94,214
1/1/97	4,000	4,711	711	94,925
7/1/97	4,000	4,746	746	95,671
1/1/98	4,000	4,783	783	96,454
7/1/98	4,000	4,823	823	97,277
1/1/99	4,000	4,864	864	98,141
7/1/99	4,000	4,907	907	99,048
1/1/00	4,000	4,952	952	100,000
	$40,000	$47,722	$7,722	

ᵃ$4,000 = $100,000 × .08 × 6/12   ᶜ$614 = $4,614 − $4,000
ᵇ$4,614 = $92,278 × .10 × 6/12   ᵈ$92,892 = $92,278 + $614

The entry to record the issuance of Evermaster Corporation's bonds at a discount on January 1, 1995, is:

Cash	92,278	
Discount on Bonds Payable	7,722	
Bonds Payable		100,000

The journal entry to record the first interest payment on July 1, 1995, and amortization of the discount is:

Bond Interest Expense	4,614	
Discount on Bonds Payable		614
Cash		4,000

The journal entry to record the interest expense accrued at December 31, 1995 (year-end) and amortization of the discount is:

Bond Interest Expense	4,645	
Bond Interest Payable		4,000
Discount on Bonds Payable		645

BONDS ISSUED AT A PREMIUM

If the market had been such that the investors were willing to accept an effective interest rate of 6% on the bond issue described above, they would have paid $108,530 or a premium of $8,530, computed as follows:

ILLUSTRATION 14-7
Computation of Premium
on Bonds Payable

Maturity value of bonds payable		$100,000
Present value of $100,000 due in 5 years at 6%, interest payable semiannually (Table 6-2); a ($p_{\overline{10}|3\%}$); ($100,000 × .74409)	$74,409	
Present value of $4,000 interest payable semiannually for 5 years at 6% annually (Table 6-4); R ($P_{\overline{10}|3\%}$); ($4,000 × 8.53020)	34,121	
Proceeds from sale of bonds		108,530
Premium on bonds payable		$ 8,530

The 5-year amortization schedule appears below.

ILLUSTRATION 14-8
**Bond Premium
Amortization Schedule**

		SCHEDULE OF BOND PREMIUM AMORTIZATION EFFECTIVE INTEREST METHOD—SEMIANNUAL INTEREST PAYMENTS 5-YEAR, 8% BONDS SOLD TO YIELD 6%		
Date	Cash Paid	Interest Expense	Premium Amortized	Carrying Amount of Bonds
1/1/95				$108,530
7/1/95	$ 4,000[a]	$ 3,256[b]	$ 744[c]	107,786[d]
1/1/96	4,000	3,234	766	107,020
7/1/96	4,000	3,211	789	106,231
1/1/97	4,000	3,187	813	105,418
7/1/97	4,000	3,162	838	104,580
1/1/98	4,000	3,137	863	103,717
7/1/98	4,000	3,112	888	102,829
1/1/99	4,000	3,085	915	101,914
7/1/99	4,000	3,057	943	100,971
1/1/00	4,000	3,029	971	100,000
	$40,000	$31,470	$8,530	

[a]$4,000 = $100,000 × .08 × 6/12   [c]$744 = $4,000 − $3,256
[b]$3,256 = $108,530 × .06 × 6/12   [d]$107,786 = $108,530 − $744

The entry to record the issuance of Evermaster bonds at a premium on January 1, 1995, is:

Cash	108,530	
Premium on Bonds Payable		8,530
Bonds Payable		100,000

The journal entry to record the first interest payment on July 1, 1995, and amortization of the premium is:

Bond Interest Expense	3,256	
Premium on Bonds Payable	744	
Cash		4,000

The discount or premium should be amortized as an adjustment to interest expense over the life of the bond in such a way as to result in a **constant rate of interest** when applied to the carrying amount of debt outstanding at the beginning of any given period.[9] Although the effective interest method is recommended, other methods are permitted if the results obtained are not materially different from those produced by the effective interest method.

▶ ACCRUING INTEREST

In our previous examples, the interest payment dates and the date the financial statements were issued were the same. For example, when Evermaster sold bonds at a premium (page 677), the two interest payment dates coincided with the financial reporting dates. However, what happens if Evermaster wishes to report financial statements at the end of February 1995? In this case, the premium is prorated by the appropriate number of months to arrive at the proper interest expense as follows:

ILLUSTRATION 14-9
**Computation of Interest
Expense**

Interest accrual ($4,000 × 2/6)	$1,333.33
Premium amortized ($744 × 2/6)	(248.00)
Interest expense (Jan.–Feb.)	$1,085.33

---

[9]"Interest on Receivables and Payables," *Opinions of the Accounting Principles Board No. 21* (New York: AICPA, 1971), par. 16.

The journal entry to record this accrual is as follows:

Interest Expense	1,085.33	
Premium on Bonds Payable	248.00	
Interest Payable		1,333.33

If the company prepares financial statements 6 months later, the same procedure is followed; that is, the premium amortized would be as follows:

ILLUSTRATION 14-10
Computation of Premium Amortization

Premium amortized (March–June) ($744 × 4⁄6)	$496.00
Premium amortized (July–August) ($766 × 2⁄6)	255.33
Premium amortized (March–August, 1995)	$751.33

The computation is much simpler if the straight-line method is employed. For example, in the Evermaster situation, the total premium is $8,530, which is allocated evenly over the 5-year period. Thus, premium amortization per month is $142.17 ($8,530 ÷ 60 months).

► CLASSIFICATION OF DISCOUNT AND PREMIUM

Discount on bonds payable is not an asset because it does not provide any future economic benefit. The enterprise has the use of the borrowed funds, but for that use it must pay interest. A bond discount means that the company borrowed less than the face or maturity value of the bond and therefore is faced with an actual (effective) interest rate higher than the stated (nominal) rate. Conceptually, discount on bonds payable is a liability valuation account; that is, it is a reduction of the face or maturity amount of the related liability.[10] This account is referred to as a **contra** account.

Premium on bonds payable has no existence apart from the related debt. The lower interest cost results because the proceeds of borrowing exceed the face or maturity amount of the debt. Conceptually, premium on bonds payable is a liability valuation account; that is, it is an addition to the face or maturity amount of the related liability.[11] This account is referred to as an **adjunct** account. As a result, the profession requires that **bond discount and bond premium be reported as a direct deduction from or addition to the face amount of the bond.**

When a corporation has numerous bond issues outstanding, each with its own related discount or premium, the total unamortized discount or premium is typically shown net at the bottom of a schedule of listed bond issuances. Illustration 14-11 is an example of such a disclosure for SCE Corp., the parent company of the nation's second largest utility company, Southern California Edison:

ILLUSTRATION 14-11
Disclosure of Net Unamortized Discount

SCE Corp. (Southern California Edison)		
Note 3: Long-Term Debt		
	December 31,	
In millions	1993	1992
First and refunding mortgage bonds		
1994–1997 (5.55% to 6.125%)	$ 700	$1,050
1998–2002 (5.45% to 7.5%)	725	650
2003–2026 (5.875% to 10%)	2,118	2,025
Pollution-control bonds		
1999–2027 (5.585% to 7.2% and variable)	1,208	1,209
Funds held by trustees	(2)	(2)
Debentures and notes		
1994–2017 (4.875% to 10.364% and variable)	1,758	1,259

---

[10]"Elements of Financial Statements of Business Enterprises," *Statement of Financial Accounting Concepts No. 3* (Stamford, Conn.: FASB, 1980), par. 160.

[11]Ibid., par. 162.

Commercial paper	252	245
Spent nuclear fuel obligation	—	6
Capital lease obligation	128	153
Current portion of capital lease obligation	(13)	(19)
Long-term debt due within one year	(336)	(195)
Unamortized debt discount—net	(79)	(61)
Total	$6,459	$6,320
Fair value*	$6,915	$6,682

*The fair value estimates were based on brokers' quotes.

▶ COSTS OF ISSUING BONDS

The issuance of bonds involves engraving and printing costs, legal and accounting fees, commissions, promotion costs, and other similar charges. According to *APB Opinion No. 21*, these items should be debited to a **deferred charge** account for Unamortized Bond Issue Costs and amortized over the life of the debt, in a manner similar to that used for discount on bonds.[12]

The FASB, however, in *Concepts Statement No. 3* takes the position that debt issue cost can be treated as either an expense or a reduction of the related debt liability. Debt issue cost is not considered an asset because it provides no future economic benefit. The cost of issuing bonds in effect reduces the proceeds of the bonds issued and increases the effective interest rate and thus may be accounted for the same as the unamortized discount.

There is an obvious difference between GAAP and *Concepts Statement No. 3*'s view of debt issue costs. Until a standard is issued to supersede *Opinion No. 21*, however, **acceptable GAAP for debt issue costs is to treat them as a deferred charge and amortize them over the life of the debt.**

To illustrate the accounting for costs of issuing bonds, assume that Microchip Corporation sold $20,000,000 of 10-year debenture bonds for $20,795,000 on January 1, 1996 (also the date of the bonds). Costs of issuing the bonds were $245,000. The entries at January 1, 1996, and December 31, 1996, for issuance of the bonds and amortization of the bond issue costs would be as follows:

January 1, 1996

Cash	20,550,000	
Unamortized Bond Issue Costs	245,000	
Premium on Bonds Payable		795,000
Bonds Payable		20,000,000
(To record issuance of bonds)		

December 31, 1996

Bond Issue Expense	24,500	
Unamortized Bond Issue Costs		24,500
(To amortize one year of bond issue costs—straight-line method)		

While the bond issue costs should be amortized using the effective interest method, the straight-line method is generally used in practice because it is easier and the results are not materially different.

▶ TREASURY BONDS

Bonds payable that have been reacquired by the issuing corporation or its agent or trustee and have not been canceled are known as **treasury bonds.** They should be shown on the balance sheet at par value—as a deduction from the bonds payable issued to arrive at a net figure representing bonds payable outstanding. When they are sold or canceled, the Treasury Bonds account should be credited.

[12]"Interest on Receivables and Payables," op. cit., par. 15.

▶ EXTINGUISHMENT OF DEBT

How is the payment of debt—often referred to as **extinguishment of debt**—recorded? If the bonds (or any other form of debt security) are held to maturity, the answer is relatively straightforward—no gain or loss is computed. Any premium or discount and any issue costs will be fully amortized at the date the bonds mature. As a result, the carrying amount will be equal to the maturity (face) value of the bond. As the maturity or face value is also equal to the bond's market value at that time, no gain or loss exists.

The problems, however, become more complex when the debt is extinguished prior to maturity. Two types of early extinguishments are:

1. Reacquisition of debt.

2. In-substance (or economic) defeasance.

REACQUISITION OF DEBT

A reacquisition of debt can occur either by payment to the creditor or by reacquisition in the open market. At the time of reacquisition, **the unamortized premium or discount, and any costs of issue applicable to the bonds, must be amortized up to the reacquisition date.**

The issuer of callable bonds is generally required to exercise the call on an interest date. Therefore, the amortization of any discount or premium will be up to date and there will be no accrued interest. However, early extinguishments through purchases of bonds in the open market are more likely to be on other than an interest date. If the purchase is not made on an interest date, the discount or premium must be amortized and the interest payable must be accrued from the last interest date to the date of purchase.

The amount paid on extinguishment or redemption before maturity, including any call premium and expense of reacquisition, is called the **reacquisition price.** On any specified date, the **net carrying amount** of the bonds is the amount payable at maturity, adjusted for unamortized premium, discount, and cost of issuance. Any excess of the net carrying amount over the reacquisition price is a **gain from extinguishment,** whereas the excess of the reacquisition price over the net carrying amount is a **loss from extinguishment.**

To illustrate, assume that on January 1, 1986, General Bell Corp. issued at 97 bonds with a par value of $800,000, due in 20 years. Bond issue costs totaling $16,000 were incurred. Ten years after the issue date, the entire issue is called at 101 and canceled. The loss on redemption (extinguishment) is computed as follows (straight-line amortization is used for simplicity):

**ILLUSTRATION 14-12
Computation of Loss on
Redemption of Bonds**

Reacquisition price ($800,000 × 1.01)		$808,000
Net carrying amount of bonds redeemed:		
Face value	$800,000	
Unamortized discount ($24,000* × 10/20)	(12,000)	
Unamortized issue costs ($16,000 × 10/20)		
(both amortized using straight-line basis)	(8,000)	780,000
Loss on redemption		$ 28,000

*[$800,000 × (1 − .97)]

The entry to record the reacquisition and cancellation of the bonds is:

Bonds Payable	800,000	
Loss on Redemption of Bonds (Extraordinary)	28,000	
Discount on Bonds Payable		12,000
Unamortized Bond Issue Costs		8,000
Cash		808,000

Note that it is often advantageous for the issuing corporation to acquire the entire outstanding bond issue and replace it with a new bond issue bearing a lower rate of interest. The replacement of an existing issuance with a new one is called **refunding.** Whether the early redemption or other extinguishment of outstanding bonds is a non-refunding or a refunding situation, the difference (gain or loss) between the reacquisition price and the net carrying amount of the redeemed bonds should be recognized currently in income of the period of redemption, and **classified as an extraordinary item.**[13] The impact of decreasing interest rates (1991–1993) on corporate bond redemptions is graphically shown in Illustration 14-13.

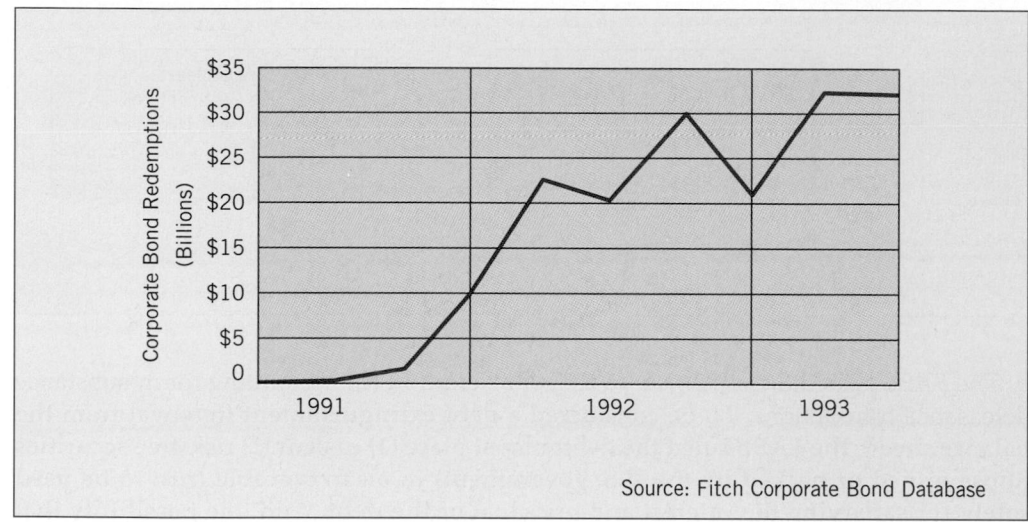

ILLUSTRATION 14-13 Increase in Corporate Bond Redemptions Caused by Decreasing Interest Rates

Source: Fitch Corporate Bond Database

IN-SUBSTANCE DEFEASANCE

Another form of extinguishment is referred to as in-substance defeasance. **In-substance defeasance** is an arrangement whereby a company provides for the future repayment of one or more of its long-term debt issues by placing purchased securities in an irrevocable trust, the principal and interest of which are pledged to pay off the principal and interest of its own debt securities as they mature. The company, however, is not legally released from being the primary obligor under the debt that is still outstanding.[14] In some cases, debt holders are not even aware of the transaction and continue to look to the company for repayment.

There are two key reasons for arranging such an extinguishment. **First, the debt is removed from the balance sheet without actually being repurchased.** Actual repurchase is sometimes a problem because (1) it may be costly if a high call premium is required to be paid or (2) much of the debt may be publicly held and may therefore be difficult to buy back in large quantities. **Second, the company is usually able to record a gain on its income statement from extinguishment of the debt. The reason this is so is that the cost of the purchased securities is usually less than the book value of the company's debt in times of rising interest rates (as interest rates rise, the fair value of the outstanding debt falls below book value).** The gain usually does not result in a tax liability because for tax purposes the debt is not considered retired.

To illustrate one of the first of these transactions, Exxon placed in a trust six of its own bond issues totaling $515 million; the trust purchased $313 million in government securities to service the bond interest and principal. Exxon needed only $313 million to extinguish the large debt because interest rates had risen substantially since the issue of the original debt. The following entry would, therefore, be made (assuming the trust—a separate entity—purchased the government bonds):

Bonds Payable	515,000,000	
Gain on Redemption of Bonds (Extraordinary)		202,000,000
Cash		313,000,000

---

[13]It is no longer acceptable practice to amortize a refunding loss either over the remaining life of the old issue being canceled or over the life of the new issue.

[14]In contrast, legal defeasance is the release of a debtor from legal liability.

Exxon was thus able to remove the $515 million bond debt from its balance sheet and reported a sizable gain, and the government securities generated sufficient interest to pay the accrued interest and maturing principal on the bonds. Illustration 14-14 indicates how the defeasance process worked for Exxon:

ILLUSTRATION 14-14
Defeasance by Exxon

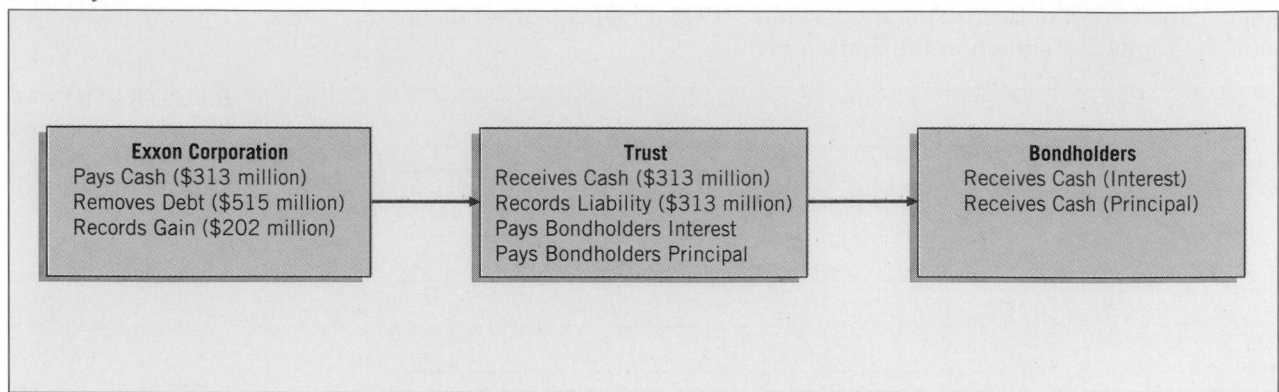

Exxon Corporation
Pays Cash ($313 million)
Removes Debt ($515 million)
Records Gain ($202 million)

Trust
Receives Cash ($313 million)
Records Liability ($313 million)
Pays Bondholders Interest
Pays Bondholders Principal

Bondholders
Receives Cash (Interest)
Receives Cash (Principal)

UNDERLYING CONCEPT

The profession's conditions for removal of such debt from the balance sheet require the situation to be as close to a sure thing (assured future payoff) as possible in order to achieve representational faithfulness.

The FASB issued *Statement No. 76* as its prescription for accounting for in-substance defeasance transactions. **To be considered a debt extinguishment (removal from the balance sheet), the FASB ruled the debtor must place (1) cash or (2) risk-free securities (those issued or backed by the U.S. government) in an irrevocable trust to be used solely for satisfying the interest and principal of the debt. And, the possibility that the debtor will be required to make any future payments with respect to the debt must be remote.**[15]

This standard is controversial and has been subjected to much criticism. Dissenters from *Statement No. 76* believe that gain or loss recognition should not be extended to situations wherein the debtor is not legally released from being the primary obligor under the debt. They contend that "the setting aside of assets in trust does not, in and of itself, constitute either the disposition of assets with potential gain or loss recognition or the satisfaction of a liability with potential gain or loss recognition."[16] In other words, while committing the assets to a single purpose might ensure that the debt is serviced in a timely fashion, this event alone merely matches up cash flow. It does not satisfy, eliminate, or extinguish the obligation. For a debt to be satisfied, the creditor must be satisfied. This is not the case in an in-substance defeasance.

On the other hand, supporters of *Statement No. 76* believe that the effect of an in-substance defeasance is essentially the same as a cash settlement. They further believe that the liability should be removed from the balance sheet because placing sufficient risk-free assets irrevocably in trust ensures that the possibility of the debtor having to make additional future payments is remote.

Where in-substance defeasance is permitted, accounting for the extinguishment is the same as it is for other types of reacquisition. **Differing reasons for extinguishment, or differing means by which the bonds are redeemed, have no bearing on how to account for the loss or gain.**[17]

---

[15]Because of differences in interest rates in different world financing markets, it is possible for a company to borrow at one interest rate and concurrently invest in essentially risk-free assets that yield a higher rate. Immediately placing such assets in an irrevocable trust effects what is referred to as "instantaneous in-substance defeasance." The profession does not permit extinguishment of debt through instantaneous defeasance. *FASB Statement No. 76* applies only to the in-substance defeasance of previously oustanding debt, not to newly issued debt. Instantaneous defeasance is accounted for as a borrowing and an investment, not an extinguishment. See "In-Substance Defeasance of Debt," *FASB Technical Bulletin No. 84-4* (Stamford, Conn.: FASB, 1984).

[16]"Extinguishment of Debt," *Statement of Financial Accounting Standards No. 76* (Stamford, Conn.: FASB, 1983), p. 5.

[17]"Early Extinguishment of Debt," *Opinions of the Accounting Principles Board No. 26* (New York: AICPA, 1972), par. 19.

REPORTING GAINS AND LOSSES

Because of soaring interest rates in the 1970s and early 1980s, many companies were able to buy back long-term debt securities, issued in the 1960s, at prices well below face value. For instance, United Brands at one time extinguished $125 million (face value) of 5½% convertible subordinate debentures due in 1994 (with a market value of $87.5 million) by exchanging $12.5 million in cash and $75 million in 9⅛% debenture bonds (nonconvertible). The company thus realized a gain of approximately $37.5 million, which was taken entirely into earnings. These large gains were being reported as operating income before extraordinary items.

This was considered misleading. The FASB therefore issued *Statement No. 4*, which requires that **gains or losses from extinguishment of debt should be aggregated and, if material, classified in the income statement as an extraordinary item, net of related income tax effect.**[18] That treatment shall apply whether an extinguishment is early or at scheduled maturity date or later without regard to the criteria of "unusual nature" and "infrequency of occurrence."

The following types of extinguishment result in **classification of the gains or losses as extraordinary items:**[19]

1. Extinguishment of debt at less than the net carrying amount (resulting in a gain).
2. Extinguishment of debt at more than the net carrying amount (resulting in a loss).
3. Extinguishment of debt by exchanging common or preferred stock.
4. Refinancing existing debt with new debt.
5. Retirement of debt maturing serially.
6. In-substance defeasance of previously outstanding debt.

Gains or losses from extinguishment of debt that are reported as extraordinary items should be described in such a way that readers of the financial statements can evaluate their significance. The following disclosures are required:

1. A description of the extinguishment transactions, including the sources of any funds used to extinguish debt if it is practicable to identify the sources.
2. The income tax effect in the period of extinguishment.
3. The per-share amount of the aggregate gain or loss net of related tax effect.[20]
4. A general description of any in-substance defeasance transaction and disclosure of the amount of debt that is considered extinguished for as long as the debt remains outstanding.[21]

The preceding information, to the extent that it is not shown separately on the face of the income statement, must be disclosed in a single note or adequately cross-referenced if in more than one note. The following illustration presents disclosure on the face of the income statement and in a note to the financial statements.

Digital Computer Corp. purchased for $5,000,000 cash its outstanding 5% debenture bonds having a face or maturity value, as well as net carrying amount, of $6,000,000. Disclosure was appropriately made in its annual report as follows:

---

[18]"Reporting Gains and Losses from Extinguishment of Debt," *Statement of Financial Accounting Standards No. 4* (Stamford, Conn.: FASB, 1975), par. 8.

[19]Two types of extinguishment that are not reported as extraordinary items are (1) gains and losses that result from a conversion agreement that is part of the original debt covenant and (2) gains and losses from cash purchases of debt made to satisfy current or future sinking fund requirements.

[20]Disclosure of earnings per share applicable to extraordinary items is optional under the provisions of *APB Opinion No. 15*; however, *FASB Statement No. 4* requires disclosure of the per-share effect of gains and losses from extinguishment of debt.

[21]"Extinguishment of Debt," op. cit., par. 6.

ILLUSTRATION 14-15
Disclosure of Debt
Extinguishment

Digital Computer Corp.

Income before extraordinary item	$4,200,000
Extraordinary item—gain from liquidation of debt, net of income tax effect of $480,000—Note 3	520,000
Net income	$4,720,000
Per share of common stock:	
Income before extraordinary item	$1.62
Extraordinary item, net of tax	.20
Net income	$1.82

Note 3: Extraordinary Item. The extraordinary item represents a gain of $1,000,000 less related income tax effect from the redemption and retirement of the company's outstanding 5% debenture bonds pursuant to an offer made by the company. The funds used to purchase the debentures represent a portion of the proceeds from the sale of 300,000 shares of the company's common stock.

▶ LONG-TERM NOTES PAYABLE

OBJECTIVE 6

Explain the accounting procedures for long-term notes payable.

The difference between current notes payable and **long-term notes payable** is the maturity date. As discussed in Chapter 13, short-term notes payable are expected to be paid within a year or the operating cycle—whichever is longer. Long-term notes are similar in substance to bonds in that both have fixed maturity dates and carry either a stated or implicit interest rate. However, notes do not trade as readily as bonds in the organized public securities markets. Noncorporate and small corporate enterprises issue notes as their long-term instruments, whereas larger corporations issue both long-term notes and bonds.

Accounting for notes and bonds is quite similar. **Like a bond, a note is valued at the present value of its future interest and principal cash flows, with any discount or premium being similarly amortized over the life of the note.**[22] The computation of the present value of an **interest-bearing note,** the recording of its issuance, and the amortization of any discount or premium and accrual of interest are as shown for bonds on pages 673–680 of this chapter.

As you might expect, accounting for long-term notes payable parallels accounting for long-term notes receivable as was presented in Chapter 7.

NOTE ISSUED AT FACE VALUE

In Chapter 7, we discussed the discounting and recognition of a $10,000, 3-year note issued at face value by Scandinavian Imports to Bigelow Corp. In this transaction, the stated rate and the effective rate were both 10%. The time diagram and present value computation on page 333 of Chapter 7 (see Illustration 7-8) for Bigelow Corp. would be the same for the issuer of the note, Scandinavian Imports, in recognizing a note payable. Because the present value of the note and its face value are the same, $10,000, no premium or discount is recognized. The issuance of the note is recorded by Scandinavian Imports as follows:

Cash	10,000	
Notes Payable		10,000

---

[22]According to *APB Opinion No. 21,* all payables that represent commitments to pay money at a determinable future date are subject to present value measurement techniques, except for the following specifically excluded types:
1. Normal accounts payable due within one year.
2. Security deposits, retainages, advances, or progress payments.
3. Transactions between parent and subsidiary.
4. Convertible debt securities.
5. Obligations payable at some indeterminable future date.

Scandinavian Imports would recognize the interest incurred each year as follows:

Interest Expense	1,000	
Cash		1,000

NOTE NOT ISSUED AT FACE VALUE

Zero Interest-Bearing Note[23]

If a noninterest-bearing note (zero coupon) is issued solely for cash, its present value is measured by the cash received by the issuer of the note. The implicit interest rate is the **rate that equates the cash received with the amounts received in the future.** The difference between the face amount and the present value (cash received) is recorded as **a discount or premium and amortized to interest expense over the life of the note.**

An example of such a transaction is Beneficial Corporation's offering of $150 million of zero-coupon notes (deep discount bonds) having an 8-year life. With a face value of $1,000 each, these notes sold for $327—a deep discount of $673 each. The present value of each note is the cash proceeds of $327. The interest rate can be calculated by determining the interest rate that equates the amount currently paid by the investor with those amounts to be received in the future. Thus, Beneficial amortized the discount over the 8-year life of the notes using an effective interest rate of 15%.[24]

To illustrate the entries and the amortization schedule, assume that your company is the one that issued the 3-year, $10,000, zero interest-bearing note to Jeremiah Company as illustrated on page 335 of Chapter 7 (notes receivable). The implicit rate that equated the total cash to be paid ($10,000 at maturity) to the present value of the future cash flows ($7,721.80 cash proceeds at date of issuance) was 9%. (The present value of $1 for 3 periods at 9% is $.77218.) The time diagram depicting the one cash flow is shown below:

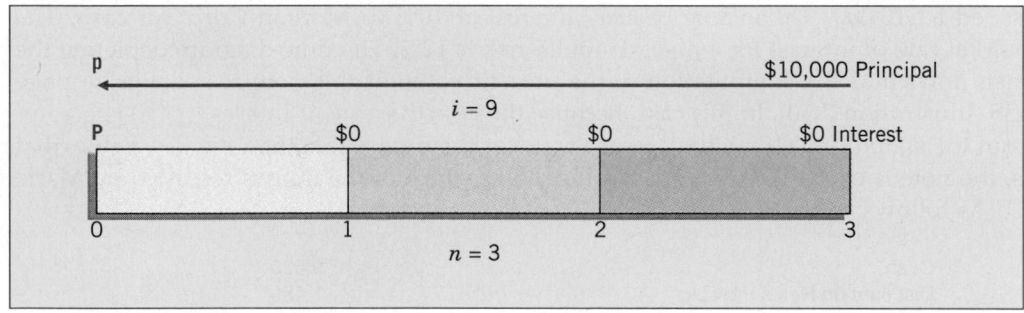

Your entry to record issuance of the note is as follows:

Cash	7,721.80	
Discount on Notes Payable	2,278.20	
Notes Payable		10,000.00

The discount is amortized and interest revenue is recognized annually using the **effective interest method.** The 3-year discount amortization and interest expense schedule is shown in Illustration 14-16. (This schedule is similar to the note receivable schedule of Jeremiah Company in Illustration 7-9.)

---

[23]Although the term "note" is used throughout this discussion, the basic principles and methodology are equally applicable to other long-term debt instruments, such as bonds.

[24]$327 = $1,000 ($p_{\overline{8}|i}$)

$$p_{\overline{8}|i}) = \frac{\$327}{\$1,000} = .327$$

.327 = 15% (in Table 6-2 locate .32690).

ILLUSTRATION 14-16
Schedule of Note
Discount Amortization

	Schedule of Note Discount Amortization Effective Interest Method 0% Note Discounted at 9%			
	Cash Paid	Interest Expense	Discount Amortized	Carrying Amount of Note
Date of issue				$ 7,721.80
End of year 1	$–0–	$ 694.96[a]	$ 694.96[b]	8,416.76[c]
End of year 2	–0–	757.51	757.51	9,174.27
End of year 3	–0–	825.73[d]	825.73	10,000.00
	$–0–	$2,278.20	$2,278.20	

[a]$7,721.80 × .09 = $694.96 [c]$7,721.80 + $694.96 = $8,416.76
[b]$694.96 − 0 = $694.96 [d]5¢ adjustment to compensate for rounding

Interest expense at the end of the first year using the effective interest method is recorded as follows:

Interest Expense ($7,721.80 × 9%)	694.96	
Discount on Notes Payable		694.96

The total amount of the discount, $2,278.20 in this case, represents the expense to be incurred on the note over the three years.

Interest-Bearing Note

The zero interest-bearing note above is an example of the extreme difference between the stated rate and the effective rate. In many cases, the difference between these rates is not so great. Take, for example, the illustration from Chapter 7 where Marie Co. issued a $10,000, 3-year note bearing interest at 10% to Morgan Corp. for cash. The market rate of interest for a note of similar risk is 12%. The time diagram depicting the cash flows and the computation of the present value of this note are shown on page 335 (Illustration 7-10). In this case, because the effective rate of interest (12%) is greater than the stated rate (10%), the present value of the note is less than the face value; that is, the note is exchanged at a **discount.**. The issuance of the note is recorded by Marie Co. as follows:

Cash	9,520	
Discount on Notes Payable	480	
Notes Payable		10,000

The discount is then amortized and interest expense is recognized annually using the **effective interest method.** The 3-year discount amortization and interest expense schedule is shown in Illustration 14-17.

ILLUSTRATION 14-17
Schedule of Note
Discount Amortization

	Schedule of Note Discount Amortization Effective Interest Method 10% Note Discounted at 12%			
	Cash Paid	Interest Expense	Discount Amortized	Carrying Amount of Note
Date of issue				$ 9,520
End of year 1	$1,000[a]	$1,142[b]	$142[c]	9,662[d]
End of year 2	1,000	1,159	159	9,821
End of year 3	1,000	1,179	179	10,000
	$3,000	$3,480	$480	

[a]$10,000 × 10% = $1,000 [c]$1,142 − $1,000 = $142
[b]$9,520 × 12% = $1,142 [d]$9,520 + $142 = $9,662

Payment of the annual interest and amortization of the discount for the first year are recorded by Marie Co. as follows (amounts per amortization schedule):

Interest Expense	1,142	
Discount on Bonds Payable		142
Cash		1,000

When the present value exceeds the face value, the note is exchanged at a premium. The premium on a note payable is recorded as a credit and amortized using the effective interest method over the life of the note as annual reductions in the amount of interest expense recognized.

SPECIAL NOTE PAYABLE SITUATIONS

The note payable transactions just discussed are the common types of transactions encountered in practice. Three special situations are as follows:

1. Notes issued for cash and other rights.
2. Notes issued for property, goods, and services.
3. Imputed interest.

Notes Issued for Cash and Other Rights

Sometimes when a note is issued, additional rights or privileges are given to the recipient of the note. For example, a corporation issues at face value a noninterest-bearing note payable that is to be repaid over 5 years with no stated interest. In exchange it agrees to sell merchandise to the lender at less than prevailing prices. In this circumstance, the difference between the present value of the payable and the amount of **cash received should be recorded by the issuer of the note (borrower/supplier) simultaneously as a discount (debit) on the note and an unearned revenue (credit) on the future sales.** The discount should be amortized as a charge to interest expense over the life of the note. The unearned revenue, equal in amount to the discount, reflects a partial prepayment for sales transactions that will occur over the next 5 years. This unearned revenue should be recognized as revenue when sales are made to the lender over the next 5 years.

To illustrate, assume that the face or maturity value of a 5-year, noninterest-bearing note is $100,000, that it is issued at face value, and that the appropriate rate of interest is 10%. The conditions of the note provide that the recipient of the note (lender/customer) can purchase $500,000 of merchandise from the issuer of the note (borrower/supplier) at something less than regular selling price over the next 5 years. To record the loan, the issuer of the note records a discount of $37,908, the difference between the $100,000 face amount of the loan and its present value of $62,092 ($100,000 × $p_{\overline{5}|10\%}$ = $100,000 x .62092); as the supplier of the merchandise, the issuer also records a credit to unearned revenue of $37,908. The issuer's journal entry is:

UNDERLYING CONCEPT

Nonrecognition of the discount and the unearned revenue would understate specific liabilities and future interest (both expense and revenue), thus lacking representational faithfulness.

Cash	100,000	
Discount on Notes Payable	37,908	
Notes Payable		100,000
Unearned Revenue		37,908

The Discount on Notes Payable is subsequently amortized to interest expense using the effective interest method. The Unearned Revenue is recognized as revenue from the sale of merchandise and is prorated on the same basis that each period's sales to the lender-customer bear to the total sales to that customer for the term of the note. In this situation the writeoff of the discount and the recognition of the unearned revenue are at different rates.

Notes Issued for Property, Goods, and Services

The second type of situation involves the issuance of a note for some noncash consideration such as property, goods, or services. When the debt instrument is exchanged for property, goods, or services in a bargained transaction entered into at arm's length, the stated interest rate is presumed to be fair unless:

1. No interest rate is stated, or

2. The stated interest rate is unreasonable, or

3. The stated face amount of the debt instrument is materially different from the current cash sales price for the same or similar items or from current market value of the debt instrument.

In these circumstances the present value of the debt instrument is measured by the fair value of the property, goods, or services or by an amount that reasonably approximates the market value of the note.[25] **The interest element other than that evidenced by any stated rate of interest is the difference between the face amount of the note and the fair value of the property.**

For example, assume that Scenic Development Company sold land having a cash sale price of $200,000 to Health Spa, Inc. in exchange for Health Spa's 5-year, $293,860 noninterest-bearing note. The $200,000 cash sale price represents the present value of the $293,860 note discounted at 8% for 5 years. If the transaction is recorded on the sale date at the face amount of the note, $293,860, by both parties, Health Spa's Land account and Scenic's sales would be overstated by $93,860, because the $93,860 represents the interest for 5 years at an effective rate of 8%. Interest revenue to Scenic and interest expense to Health Spa for the 5-year period correspondingly would be understated by $93,860.

Because the difference between the cash sale price of $200,000 and the face amount of the note, $293,860, represents interest at an effective rate of 8%, the transaction is recorded at the exchange date as follows:

ILLUSTRATION 14-18
Entries for Noncash Note Transactions

Health Spa, Inc. Books			Scenic Development Company Books		
Land	200,000		Notes Receivable	293,860	
Discount on Notes Payable	93,860		Discount on Notes Rec.		93,860
Notes Payable		293,860	Sales		200,000

During the 5-year life of the note, Health Spa amortizes annually a portion of the discount of $93,860 as a charge to interest expense. Scenic Development records interest revenue totaling $93,860 over the 5-year period by also amortizing the discount. The effective interest method is required, although other approaches to amortization may be used if the results obtained are not materially different from those that result from the effective interest method.

Imputed Interest

In instances when the stated rate is known to be unreasonable, the effective rate must be imputed (as explained in Chapter 7). Whenever the **imputed interest rate** is different from the stated rate at the date the note is issued, a discount or premium must be recognized and amortized in subsequent periods. Using the illustration from Chapter 7, assume that on December 31, 1995, Wunderlich Company issued a promissory note to Brown Interiors Company for architectural services. The note has a face value of $550,000, a due date of December 31, 2000, and bears a stated interest rate of 2%, payable at the end of each year. The fair value of the architectural services is not readily determinable, nor is the note readily marketable. On the basis of the credit rating of Wunderlich Company, the absence of collateral, the prime interest rate at that date, and the prevailing interest on Wunderlich's other outstanding debt, an 8% interest rate is imputed as appropriate in this circumstance. The time diagram depicting both cash flows is shown as follows.

---

[25]"Interest on Receivables and Payables," op. cit., par. 12.

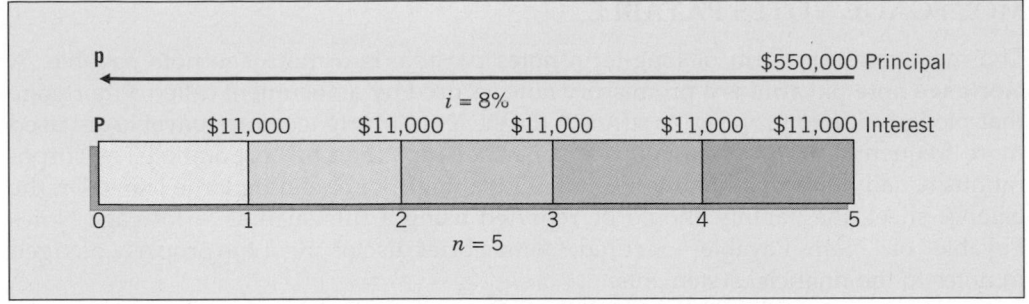

The present value of the note and the imputed fair value of the architectural services are determined as follows:

Face value of the note		$550,000
Present value of $550,000 due in 5 years at 8% interest payable annually (Table 6-2); a ($p_{\overline{5}|8\%}$); ($550,000 × .68058)	$374,319	
Present value of $11,000 interest payable annually for 5 years at 8%; R ($P_{\overline{5}|8\%}$); ($11,000 × 3.99271)	43,920	
Present value of the note		418,239
Discount on notes payable		$131,761

ILLUSTRATION 14-19 Computation of Imputed Fair Value and Note Discount

The issuance of the note and receipt of the architectural services are recorded as follows:

December 31, 1995

Building (or Construction in Process)	418,239	
Discount on Notes Payable	131,761	
Notes Payable		550,000

The 5-year amortization schedule appears below.

**SCHEDULE OF NOTE DISCOUNT AMORTIZATION
EFFECTIVE INTEREST METHOD
2% NOTE DISCOUNTED AT 8% (IMPUTED)**

Date	Cash Paid (2%)	Interest Expense (8%)	Discount Amortized	Carrying Amount of Note
12/31/95				$418,239
12/31/96	$11,000[a]	$ 33,459[b]	$ 22,459[c]	440,698[d]
12/31/97	11,000	35,256	24,256	464,954
12/31/98	11,000	37,196	26,196	491,150
12/31/99	11,000	39,292	28,292	519,442
12/31/00	11,000	41,558[e]	30,558	550,000
	$55,000	$186,761	$131,761	

[a]$550,000 × 2% = $11,000
[b]$418,239 × 8% = $33,459
[c]$33,459 − $11,000 = $22,459
[d]$418,239 + $22,459 = $440,698
[e]$3 adjustment to compensate for rounding.

ILLUSTRATION 14-20 Schedule of Discount Amortization Using Imputed Interest Rate

Payment of the first year's interest and amortization of the discount is recorded as follows:

December 31, 1996

Interest Expense	33,459	
Discount on Notes Payable		22,459
Cash		11,000

MORTGAGE NOTES PAYABLE

The most common form of long-term notes payable is a mortgage note payable. A **mortgage note payable** is a promissory note secured by a document called a mortgage that pledges title to property as security for the loan. Mortgage notes payable are used more frequently by proprietorships and partnerships than by corporations, as corporations usually find that bond issues offer advantages in obtaining large loans. On the balance sheet, the liability should be reported using a title such as "Mortgage Notes Payable" or "Notes Payable—Secured," with a brief disclosure of the property pledged in notes to the financial statements.

The borrower usually receives cash in the face amount of the mortgage note. In that case, the face amount of the note is the true liability and no discount or premium is involved. When "points" are assessed by the lender, however, the total amount paid by the borrower exceeds the face amount of the note.[26] Points raise the effective interest rate above the rate specified in the note. A point is 1% of the face of the note. For example, assume that a 20-year mortgage note in the amount of $100,000 with a stated interest rate of 10.75% is given by you to Local Savings and Loan Association as part of the financing of your new house. If Local Savings demands 4 points to close the financing, you will receive 4% less than $100,000—or $96,000—but you will be obligated to repay the entire $100,000 at the rate of $1,015 per month. Because you received only $96,000, and must repay $100,000, your effective interest rate is increased to approximately 11.3% on the money you actually borrowed.

Mortgages may be payable in full at maturity or in installments over the life of the loan. If payable at maturity, the mortgage payable is shown as a long-term liability on the balance sheet until such time as the approaching maturity date warrants showing it as a current liability. If it is payable in installments, the current installments due are shown as current liabilities, with the remainder shown as a long-term liability.

Because of unusually high, unstable interest rates and a tight money supply, the traditional **fixed-rate mortgage** recently has been partially supplanted with new and unique mortgage arrangements. Most lenders offer **variable-rate mortgages** (also called floating-rate or adjustable rate mortgages) featuring interest rates tied to changes in the fluctuating market rate. Generally the variable-rate lenders adjust the interest rate at either 1- or 3-year intervals, pegging the adjustments to changes in the prime rate or the U.S. Treasury bond rate.

▶ OFF-BALANCE-SHEET FINANCING

OBJECTIVE 7

Describe off-balance-sheet financing arrangements.

Off-balance-sheet financing is an attempt to borrow monies in such a way that the obligations are not recorded. It is an issue of extreme importance to accountants (as well as general management). As one writer noted, "The basic drives of humans are few: to get enough food, to find shelter, and to keep debt off the balance sheet."

We have already discussed some off-balance-sheet financing techniques. In Chapter 7, for example, transfers of receivables to third parties with recourse may be either reported as sales of the receivables or as a borrowing, depending on the facts. When it is deemed to be a sale, no liability is recorded on the balance sheet. In this chapter, in-substance defeasance is viewed as an off-balance-sheet financing transaction because the debt is not reported on the balance sheet even though it is not legally retired.

Two additional off-balance-sheet approaches are covered below:

1. Interest rate swaps.
2. Project financing arrangements.

In subsequent chapters, other off-balance-sheet financing transactions (leasing and pensions) are examined.

---

[26]Points, in mortgage financing, are analogous to the original issue discount of bonds.

INTEREST RATE SWAPS

Comments similar to the following continue to appear in the financial press:

> With today's volatile interest rates, you can be certain of one thing. Nothing is certain. However, you have one option that could considerably lessen the risks involved.
>
> Hedging flourishes as rates fluctuate.
>
> If you're confused about the timing of economic recovery and how that affects the nation's credit markets, you might want to hedge your bet. Whether interest rates are headed up or down, diversify now, and you can ride out the storm safely.

As these comments indicate, interest rates are volatile and companies often want protection against their fluctuations. As a result, many companies use sophisticated types of financial instruments such as interest rate futures, forward rate agreements, and interest rate swaps to hedge their bets.

A corporation in the 1990s went to its investment banker and presented the following problem: It wanted to borrow at a fixed rate for protection, but either such borrowing was too expensive or no suitable market existed. The investment banker found a borrower who had a fixed-rate loan but wanted a floating rate. The match was made, the two companies swapped interest payments (just interest, not principal), and the **interest rate swap** was born.

Many companies find interest rate swaps a convenient way to limit interest rate exposure. A company with a substantial amount of variable rate debt may wish to swap into fixed-rate debt to limit its exposure to rising interest rates. Or a company with a high fixed rate may want to swap to a floating rate if it expects interest rates to fall. Second, some companies with lower credit ratings often cannot borrow in the fixed-rate market but can swap into it.

Swap participants report on their balance sheets only their original borrowings. As a result, swaps are considered off-balance-sheet financing because the right to receive interest payments and the obligation to make interest payments per the swap agreement are not reported on the balance sheet. The FASB requires extensive disclosures of financial instruments with off-balance-sheet risk.[27] These disclosures include:

1. The face, or contract principal amount.

2. The nature and terms of the instruments and a discussion of their credit and market risk, cash requirements, and related accounting policies.

3. The **accounting loss** the entity would incur if any party to the financial instrument failed completely to perform according to the terms of the contract and the collateral or other security, if any, for the amount due proved to be of no value to the entity.

4. The entity's policy for requiring collateral or other security on financial instruments it accepts and a description of collateral on instruments presently held.[28]

These disclosures will become even more important as Wall Street continues to develop new and different types of financial instruments.

PROJECT FINANCING ARRANGEMENTS

Project financing arrangements arise when (1) two or more entities form a new entity to construct an operating plant that will be used by both parties; (2) the new entity borrows funds to construct the project and repays the debt from the proceeds received

---

[27]"Disclosure of Information about Financial Instruments with Off-Balance Sheet Risk and Financial Instruments with Concentrations of Credit Risk," *Statement of Financial Accounting Standards No. 105* (Norwalk, Conn.: FASB, 1990).

[28]This standard was recently amended to include all derivative financial instruments. Only the first two of the disclosure requirements would apply to all derivative financial instruments "Disclosure about Derivative Financial Instruments and Fair Value of Financial Instruments," *Statement of Financial Accounting Standards No. 119* (Norwalk, Conn.: FASB, 1994).

from the project; (3) payment of the debt is guaranteed by the companies that formed the new entity. The advantage of such an arrangement is that **the companies that formed the new entity do not have to report the liability on their books.** To illustrate, assume that Dow Chemical and Mobil Oil each put up $1 million and form a separate company to build a chemical plant to be used by both companies. The newly formed company borrows $48 million to construct the plant. The arrangement is illustrated below:

ILLUSTRATION 14-21 Project Financing Arrangement

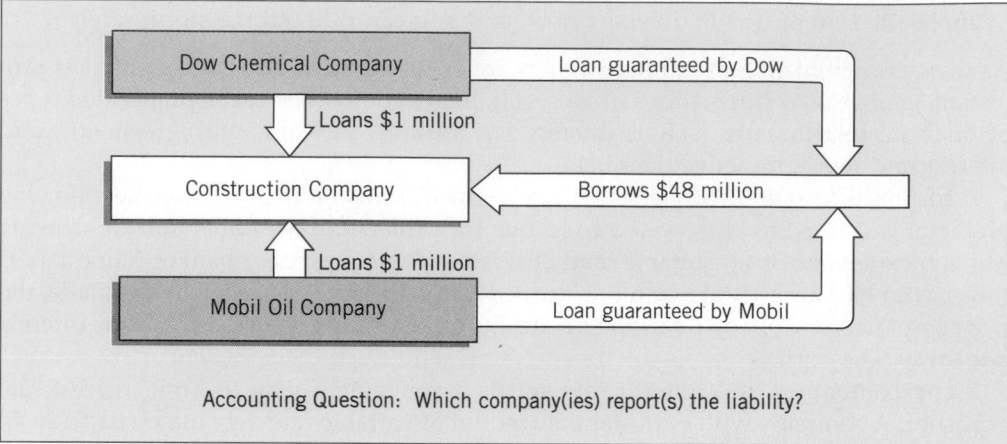

Accounting Question: Which company(ies) report(s) the liability?

The answer is that each needs to disclose only that they guarantee debt repayment if the project's proceeds are inadequate to pay off the loan.[29]

In some cases, project financing arrangements become more formalized through the use of a variety of contracts. In a simple **take-or-pay contract,** a purchaser of goods signs an agreement with a seller to pay specified amounts periodically in return for an option to receive products. The purchaser must make specified minimum payments even if delivery of the contracted products is not taken. Often these take-or-pay contracts are associated with project financing arrangements. For example, in the illustration above, Dow Chemical and Mobil Oil sign an agreement that they will purchase products from this new plant and that they will make certain minimum payments **even if they do not take delivery of the goods.**

Through-put agreements are similar in concept to take-or-pay contracts, except that a service instead of a product is provided by the asset under construction. Assume that Dow and Mobil become involved in a project financing arrangement to build a pipeline to transport their various products. They sign an agreement that requires them to pay specified amounts in return for the transportation of the product. In addition, these companies are required to make cash payments **even if they do not provide the minimum quantities to be transported.**

Inconsistent methods have been used in practice to account for and disclose the unconditional obligation in a take-or-pay or through-put contract involved in a project financing arrangement. In general, most companies have attempted to develop these types of contracts to "get the debt off the balance sheet."

RATIONALE FOR OFF-BALANCE-SHEET FINANCING

Companies attempt to arrange off-balance-sheet financing for several reasons. First, many believe that removing debt enhances the quality of the balance sheet and permits credit to be obtained more readily and at less cost.

Second, loan covenants often impose a limitation on the amount of debt a company may have. As a result, off-balance-sheet financing is used because these types of commitments might not be considered in computing the debt limitation.

---

[29]"Accounting for Contingencies," *Statement of Financial Accounting Standards No. 5* (Stamford, Conn.: FASB, 1975), par. 12.

Third, it is argued by some that the asset side of the balance sheet is severely understated. For example, companies that use LIFO costing for inventories and depreciate assets on an accelerated basis will often have carrying amounts for inventories and property, plant, and equipment that are much lower than their current values. As an offset to these lower values, some managements believe that part of the debt does not have to be reported. In other words, if assets were reported at current values, less pressure would undoubtedly exist for off-balance-sheet financing arrangements.

Whether the arguments above have merit is debatable. The general idea "out of sight, out of mind" may not be true in accounting. Many users of financial statements indicate that they factor these off-balance-sheet financing arrangements into their computations when assessing debt to equity relationships. Similarly, many loan covenants also attempt to take these complex arrangements into account. Nevertheless, many companies still believe that benefits will accrue if certain obligations are not reported on the balance sheet.

The FASB response to these off-balance-sheet financing arrangements has been increased disclosure (note) requirements. This response is consistent with an "efficient markets" philosophy: the important question is not whether the presentation is off-balance sheet or not, but whether the items are disclosed at all.[30]

▶ REPORTING LONG-TERM DEBT

CLASSIFICATION AND DISCLOSURES

Companies that have large amounts and numerous issues of long-term debt frequently report only one amount in the balance sheet and support this with comments and schedules in the accompanying notes. These note disclosures generally indicate the nature of the liabilities, maturity dates, interest rates, call provisions, conversion privileges, restrictions imposed by the borrower, and assets pledged as security. Any assets pledged as security for the debt should be shown in the asset section of the balance sheet.

OBJECTIVE 8
Describe disclosure requirements for long-term debt.

Long-term debt that matures within one year should be reported as a current liability, unless retirement is to be accomplished with other than current assets. If the debt is to be refinanced, converted into stock, or is to be retired from a bond retirement fund, it should continue to be reported as noncurrent and accompanied with a note explaining the method to be used in its liquidation.[31] For example, Georgia-Pacific discloses details of its long-term debt in notes to the financial statements (see Note 5, pages 226–227).

Disclosure is required of future payments for sinking fund requirements and maturity amounts of long-term debt during each of the next 5 years.[32] The purpose of the disclosures is to aid financial statement users in evaluating the amounts and timing of future cash flows. For example, assume that Percy Corporation has two long-term borrowings outstanding at December 31, 1995. The first borrowing is a $50 million sinking fund debenture with annual sinking fund payments of $5 million in 1996, 1997, and 1998, $10 million in 1999 and 2000, and $15 million in 2001. The second borrowing is a $75 million bond issue that matures in 1998. Percy's disclosures would be as follows:

[30]It is unlikely that the FASB will be able to stop all types of off-balance-sheet transactions. Financial information is the Holy Grail of Wall Street. Developing new financial instruments and arrangements to sell and market to customers is not only profitable, but also adds to the prestige of the investment firms that create them. Thus, new financial products will continue to appear that will test the ability of the FASB to develop appropriate accounting standards for them.

[31]"Balance Sheet Classification of Short-Term Obligations Expected to Be Refinanced," *FASB Statement of Financial Accounting Standards No. 6* (Stamford, Conn.: FASB, 1975), par. 15.

[32]"Disclosure of Long-Term Obligations," *Statement of Financial Accounting Standards No. 47* (Stamford, Conn.: FASB, 1981), par. 10.

ILLUSTRATION 14-22
Disclosure of Long-Term Debt Maturing in Next 5 Years

Maturities and sinking fund requirements on long-term debt for the next 5 years are as follows:	
1996	$ 5,000,000
1997	5,000,000
1998	80,000,000
1999	10,000,000
2000	10,000,000

In addition, any unconditional long-term obligations (such as project financing arrangements) must be disclosed.

For **unconditional purchase obligations** recorded on the purchaser's balance sheet, disclosure must be made of the payments to be made under the obligation for each of the next 5 years. In addition, the following disclosures are required for those unconditional purchase obligations **not recorded** on the purchaser's balance sheet:

1. The nature and term of the obligations.

2. The total amount of the fixed and determinable portion of the obligations at the balance sheet date and for each of the next 5 years.

3. The nature of any variable portions of the obligations.

4. The amounts purchased under the obligations (as in take-or-pay contracts or through-put contracts) for each period for which an income statement is presented.

With respect to requirement (2) above, it is recommended, but not required, that the amount of imputed interest necessary to reduce the total amount of the obligation to its present value be disclosed.[33] The discount rate to be used should be the effective interest rate, if known, of the borrowings that financed the facility that will provide the contracted goods or services. If not known, the discount rate should be the purchaser's incremental borrowing rate when the obligation is entered into—the rate the purchaser would have incurred to borrow the funds necessary to discharge the unconditional purchase obligation. An example of a through-put agreement involving a project financing arrangement is reported below for Hewlett Chemical Company:

ILLUSTRATION 14-23
Disclosure of a Project Financing Arrangement

Hewlett Chemical Company

To secure access to facilities to process the chemical phenoxyethanol, the company has signed a processing agreement with a chemical company allowing Hewlett to submit 100,000 tons for processing annually for 15 years. Under the terms of the agreement, Hewlett may be required to advance funds if the chemical company is unable to meet its financial obligations. The aggregate amount of required payments at December 31, 1990 is as follows:

1991	$ 20,000,000
1992	15,000,000
1993	10,000,000
1994	9,000,000
1995	8,000,000
Later years	78,000,000
Total	140,000,000
Less: Amount representing interest	(79,791,510)
Total at present value	$ 60,208,490

In addition, the company is required to pay a proportional share of the variable operating expenses of the plant. The company's total processing charges under the agreement for each of the preceding 5 years were: 1986 and 1987, $27,000,000; 1988 and 1989, $29,000,000; and 1990, $28,000,000.

Determination of the proper accounting for off-balance-sheet financing has been called the major financial reporting issue facing the accounting profession today. Resolving this controversy will not be easy. The definition of a liability established in *Concepts Statement No. 6* and the recognition criteria established in *Concepts Statement*

---

[33]Ibid., par. 7.

No. 5 are sufficiently imprecise that arguments still can be made for either recognition or nonrecognition of such obligations. We believe it is imperative that the accounting profession address this issue and determine when these obligations are effectively liabilities. Even though the profession has already attempted to develop guidelines in certain areas, much still needs to be done. The authors believe that financial reporting would be enhanced if more obligations were recorded on the balance sheet instead of merely disclosed in the notes to the financial statements.

▶ ACCOUNTING FOR DERIVATIVE FINANCIAL INSTRUMENTS

It has been said that until the early 1970s most financial managers worked in a cozy, if unthrilling world. Since then, however, constant change caused by volatile markets, new technology, and deregulation has increased the risks to businesses. For example, in 1971 currencies were allowed to float freely. After that came oil price shocks, high inflation, and wide swings in interest rates. The response from the financial community was to develop products to manage these risks due to changes. These products—often referred to as financial instruments[34]—are aided by the development of powerful computing and communications technology which provides new ways to analyze information about markets as well as the power to process high volumes of payments.[35]

In a general sense, **financial instruments** are defined as cash, an ownership interest in an entity, or a contractual right to receive or deliver cash or another financial instrument on potentially favorable or unfavorable terms. By this definition, traditional assets and liabilities such as accounts and notes receivable, accounts and notes payable, investment in debt and equity securities, and bonds payable are considered financial instruments. But the definition also includes many innovative and complex financial instruments such as futures, options, forwards, swaps and caps.

These innovative financial instruments are referred to as **derivative financial instruments** (or just simply "derivatives") because their value is derived from the value of some underlying asset, (i.e., stocks, bonds, or commodities) or is tied to a basic indicator (i.e., interest rates, Dow-Jones averages). Illustration 14-24 highlights some of the most common financial instruments.

Traditional	Derivatives
Accounts receivable and payable	Interest-rate swaps and options
Corporate bonds and notes	Currency futures and options
Municipal bonds	Stock-index futures and options
Treasury bonds, bills, and notes	Caps, floors, and collars
Bank certificates of deposit	Commodity futures and options
Mortgages	Swaptions and leaps
Currencies	Collateralized mortgage obligations

ILLUSTRATION 14-24 Traditional and Derivative Financial Instruments

DERIVATIVES

Derivative financial instruments "keep bursting into the news" as they did recently when the Federal Reserve raised interest rates and securities prices sank, costing traders and holders of derivatives huge amounts. "These things," says one Wall Streeter, "are

---

[34]*SFAS No. 105* defines a financial instrument as "cash, evidence of ownership interest in an entity, or a contract that both:

   a. Imposes on one entity a contractual obligation (1) to deliver cash or another financial instrument to a second entity or (2) to exchange financial instruments on potentially unfavorable terms with the second entity.
   b. Conveys to that second entity a contractual right (1) to receive cash or another financial instrument from the first entity or (2) to exchange other financial instruments on potentially favorable terms with the first entity."

[35]"A Comedy of Errors," *The Economist*, Survey of International Banking, April 10, 1993.

metastasizing." They demand superlatives, are measured in trillions of dollars, are quintessentially global, and are positioned on what some call the bleeding edge of technology. Innovative financial instruments, especially derivatives, are causing problems for accountants and regulators. These instruments raise questions about off-balance-sheet financing, unjustifiable deferrals of losses, premature recognition of gains, inadequate disclosure of information about risks, fair values, and other attributes of these instruments.[36] One of the earliest and most popular derivatives, interest rate swaps, was discussed earlier in this chapter.

The proper accounting and reporting for innovative financial instruments has taken on an urgency because of the lack of understanding about these instruments among investors and creditors. Also gaining attention is the fact that a number of companies have reported sizable losses as a result of trading these instruments. Illustration 14-25 shows ten companies that recently experienced substantial losses in the derivatives market.

ILLUSTRATION 14-25
Companies with Losses from Derivatives

Company	Pretax Loss (in millions)	Type of Derivative	Who Pays
Showa Shell Sekiyu (Japan)	$1,580	Currency derivatives	Stockholders
Metaligesellschaft (Germany)	$1,340	Oil derivatives	Stockholders
Codelco (Chile)	$200	Metals derivatives	Taxpayers
Procter & Gamble (U.S.)	$157	Leveraged currency swaps	Stockholders
Air Prod. & Chemicals (U.S.)	$113	Leveraged interest rate and currency swaps	Stockholders
Dell Computer (U.S.)	$35*	Leveraged interest rate swaps	Stockholders
Louisiana state retirees (U.S.)	$25	Mortgage derivatives	Pensioners
Arco employees savings (U.S.)	$22	Money market derivatives	Pensioners
Gibson Greetings (U.S.)	$20	Leveraged interest rate swaps	Stockholders
Mead (U.S.)	$12	Leveraged interest rate swaps	Stockholders

*Estimate
Source: *Fortune*, July 25, 1994, p. 107.

Although these losses are substantial, derivatives do not introduce risks that are fundamentally different from the risks already present in the financial markets. Therefore, companies will continue to use these derivatives because they provide a powerful tool in managing risks. The accounting profession is attempting to develop the appropriate information for investors, creditors, managers, and regulators. Only recently have we determined what should be disclosed and how various kinds of derivatives should be accounted for.

ACCOUNTING PROFESSION PRONOUNCEMENTS

The FASB has issued three pronouncements related to financial instruments. These three pronouncements are as follows:

1. "Disclosure of Information about Financial Instruments with Off-Balance-Sheet Risk and Financial Instruments with Concentration of Credit Risk" (*Statement No. 105*), addressed the issue of how to account for financial instruments that were not reported in the financial statements but which could affect the financial

---

[36]"The Risk that Won't Go Away," *Fortune*, March 7, 1994, pp. 40–55. The article also states that the total notional value of all derivative contracts outstanding in 1994 was $16 trillion. This may be compared to the gross domestic product of the United States which was $6.4 trillion in 1994.

position of the company. Interest rate swaps, for example, are covered in this pronouncement.

2. "Disclosures About Fair Value of Financial Instruments" (*Statement No. 107*) requires disclosure of the fair values of financial instruments, both assets and liabilities recognized and not recognized in the balance sheet, for which it is practicable to estimate fair value.

3. "Disclosure about Derivative Financial Instruments and Fair Values of Financial Instruments" (*Statement No. 119*) requires that all entities disclose information about derivative financial instruments and changes the way they disclose fair value of financial instruments.

As a consequence of these three recent pronouncements, the acceptable accounting and reporting practices for financial instruments are as summarized below:

1. A company should disclose the fair value and related carrying value of its financial instruments in the body of the financial statements, a single note, or in a summary table in a form that makes it clear whether the amounts represent assets and liabilities.

2. The fair value disclosures should distinguish between financial instruments held or issued for trading purposes and financial instruments held or issued for purposes other than trading. Also specific disclosures related to the nature of each classification are required.

3. In disclosing the fair value of derivative financial instruments, an entity should not combine, aggregate, or net the fair value of separate financial instruments of a different class, even if those instruments are considered to be related.

4. For financial instruments with off-balance-sheet risk and for all derivative financial instruments, specific disclosures are required as shown on page 693.

5. Companies are encouraged, but not required, to provide quantitative information about market risks of derivative financial instruments, and also of the other assets and liabilities, that is consistent with the way the company manages or adjusts risks and that is useful for comparing the results of applying the entity's strategies to its objectives for holding or issuing the derivative financial instruments.

UNDERLYING CONCEPT

The AICPA Special Committee on Financial Reporting indicates that the following questions need answering: What is the company's objective in using innovative financial instruments? What is the company's policy with respect to hedging certain risks? What instruments has the company entered into and what are their terms? How has the company accounted for those instruments, and how has that accounting impacted the financial statements? What risks has the company transferred or assumed?

▶ DISCLOSURES ABOUT FAIR VALUE OF FINANCIAL INSTRUMENTS

If a reporting entity is unable to arrive at an estimate of fair value,[37] it must disclose information relevant to the estimate of fair value (such as the terms of the instrument), and the reason why it was unable to disclose fair value information. While these additional disclosures of fair value may provide useful information to financial statement users, it is important to note that **these fair values are provided as supplemental information only.** The balance sheet continues to rely primarily on historical cost.

One exception to traditional reliance on historical cost is the FASB's requirement that companies report most investment securities at fair value.[38] An example of fair value of financial instruments disclosure is reported in Illustration 14-26 for Lowe's Companies, Inc.

---

[37]*FASB Statement No. 107* lists many exceptions to the requirement. Most of these exceptions are covered under other standards. This exception list includes: obligations for pension and other postretirement benefits; employee stock option and deferred compensation plans; substantively extinguished debt and the related assets in trust; many insurance contracts; lease contracts; obligations and rights resulting from warranties; unconditional purchase obligations; equity method investments; minority interests in consolidated subsidiaries; and instruments classified as stockholders' equity in the entity's balance sheet.

[38]*FASB Statement No. 115.* See our discussion of this new standard in Chapter 18.

**ILLUSTRATION 14-26
Disclosures about Fair
Values of Financial
Instruments**

Lowe's Companies, Inc.

Note 7: Disclosures about Fair Values of Financial Instruments. The following disclosure of the estimated fair value of financial instruments is made in accordance with the requirements of SFAS No. 107, Disclosures about Fair Value of Financial Instruments. The estimated fair value amounts have been determined by the Company, using available market information and appropriate valuation methodologies. However, considerable judgment is necessarily required in interpreting market data to develop the estimates of fair value. Accordingly, the estimates presented herein are not necessarily indicative of the amounts that the Company could realize in a current market exchange. The use of different market assumptions and/or estimation methodologies may have a material effect on the estimated fair value amounts.

	January 31, 1993	
	Carrying Amount	Fair Value
Assets		
Cash and Short-Term Investments	$ 54,849	$ 54,849
Net Receivables	53,288	53,288
Long-Term Investments	23,270	23,664
Liabilities:		
Accounts Payable	330,584	330,584
Short-Term Debt	3,193	3,193
Long-Term Debt	$335,283	336,286
Off-Balance Sheet Financial Instruments—		
Unrealized Gains:		
Interest Rate Swaps Agreements	—	$ 2,434

Cash and short-term investments, receivables, accounts payable, and short-term debt—The carrying amounts of these items are a reasonable estimate of their fair value due to their short-term nature.

Long-term investments—The fair value is estimated from quoted market prices for these or similar investments.

Long-term debt—Interest rates that are currently available to the Company for issuance of debt with similar terms and remaining maturities are used to estimate fair value for debt issues that are not quoted on an exchange.

Interest rate swap agreements—The fair value of interest rate swaps is the amount at which they could be settled, based on estimates obtained from dealers.

KEY TERMS

bearer (coupon) bonds, 672

bond discount, 673

bond premium, 673

bond indenture, 671

callable bonds, 672

carrying value, 677

commodity-backed bonds, 672

convertible bonds, 672

debenture bonds, 671

deep discount (zero interest) debenture bonds, 672

derivative financial instruments, 697

effective interest method, 677

effective, yield, or market rate, 673

extinguishment of debt, 682

▶ SUMMARY OF LEARNING OBJECTIVES ◀

1. **Describe the formal procedures associated with issuing long-term debt.** Incurring long-term debt is often a formal procedure. The bylaws of corporations usually require approval by the board of directors and the stockholders before bonds can be issued or other long-term debt arrangements can be contracted. Generally, long-term debt has various convenants or restrictions. The covenants and other terms of the agreement between the borrower and the lender are stated in the bond indenture or note agreement. In many cases, the loan instrument or contract is held by a trustee that acts as an independent third party to protect the interests of the lenders and the borrower.

2. **Identify various types of bond issues.** (1) *Secured and unsecured bonds.* (2) *Term, serial bonds, and callable bonds.* (3) *Convertible, commodity-backed, and deep discount bonds.* (4) *Registered and bearer (coupon) bonds.* (5) *Income and revenue bonds.* The variety in the types of bonds is a result of attempts to attract capital from different investors and risk takers and to satisfy the cash flow needs of the issuers.

3. **Describe the accounting valuation for bonds at date of issuance.** The investment community values a bond at the present value of its future cash flows, which consist of interest and principal. The rate used to compute the present value of these cash flows is the interest rate that provides an acceptable return on an investment commensurate with the issuer's risk characteristics. The in-

terest rate written in the terms of the bond indenture and ordinarily appearing on the bond certificate is the stated, coupon, or nominal rate. This rate, which is set by the issuer of the bonds, is expressed as a percentage of the face value, also called the par value, principal amount, or maturity value, of the bonds. If the rate employed by the buyers differs from the stated rate, the present value of the bonds computed by the buyers will differ from the face value of the bonds. The difference between the face value and the present value of the bonds is either a discount or premium.

4. **Apply the methods of bond discount and premium amortization.** The discount (premium) is amortized and charged (credited) to interest expense over the period of time that the bonds are outstanding. Bond interest expense is increased by amortization of a discount and decreased by amortization of a premium. The profession's preferred procedure for amortization of a discount or premium is the effective interest method. Under the effective interest method, (1) bond interest expense is computed by multiplying the carrying value of the bonds at the beginning of the period by the effective interest rate, and (2) the bond discount or premium amortization is then determined by comparing the bond interest expense with the interest to be paid.

5. **Describe the accounting procedures for the extinguishment of debt.** There are two types of extinguishment: (1) *Reacquisition of debt:* At the time of reacquisition, the unamortized premium or discount and any costs of issue applicable to the bonds, must be amortized up to the reacquisition date. The amount paid on extinguishment or redemption before maturity, including any call premium and expense of reacquisition, is the reacquisition price. On any specified date, the net carrying amount of the bonds is the amount payable at maturity, adjusted for unamortized premium, discount, and cost of issuance. Any excess of the net carrying amount over the reacquisition price is a gain from extinguishment, whereas the excess of the reacquisition price over the net carrying amount is a loss from extinguishment. (2) *In-substance defeasance:* For an in-substance defeasance transaction to be considered a debt extinguishment, the debtor must place cash or risk-free securities in an irrevocable trust to be used solely for satisfying the interest and principal of the debt. When debt is extinguished, any difference between its net carrying amount and its reacquisition price is treated as an extraordinary gain or loss.

6. **Explain the accounting procedures for long-term notes payable.** Accounting procedures for notes and bonds are quite similar. Like a bond, a note is valued at the present value of its future interest and principal cash flows, with any discount or premium being similarly amortized over the life of the note. Whenever the face amount of the note does not reasonably represent the present value of the consideration given or received in the exchange, the entire arrangement must be evaluated to properly record the exchange and the subsequent interest.

7. **Describe off-balance-sheet financing arrangements.** Off-balance-sheet financing is an attempt to borrow funds in such a way that the obligations are not recorded. In-substance defeasance is viewed as an off-balance-sheet financing transaction because the debt is not reported on the balance sheet even though it is not legally retired. Two additional off-balance-sheet approaches are interest rate swaps and project financing arrangements.

8. **Describe disclosure requirements for long-term debt.** Companies that have large amounts and numerous issues of long-term debt frequently report only one amount in the balance sheet and support this with comments and schedules in the accompanying notes. Any assets pledged as security for the debt should be shown in the asset section of the balance sheet. Long-term debt that matures within one year should be reported as a current liability, unless retirement is to be accomplished with other than current assets. If the debt is to be refinanced,

converted into stock, or is to be retired from a bond retirement fund, it should continue to be reported as noncurrent and accompanied with a note explaining the method to be used in its liquidation. Disclosure is required of future payments for sinking fund requirements and maturity amounts of long-term debt during each of the next 5 years.

|||||

APPENDIX 14-A

ACCOUNTING FOR TROUBLED DEBT

OBJECTIVE 9

After studying Appendix 14-A, you should be able to: Distinguish between and account for (1) a loss on loan impairment, (2) a troubled debt restructuring that results in the settlement of a debt, and (3) a troubled debt restructuring that results in a continuation of debt with modification of terms.

During periods of depressed economic conditions or other financial hardship, some debtors have difficulty meeting their financial obligations. For example, owing to rising interest rates and corporate mismanagement, the savings and loan industry has experienced a decade of financial crises. The banking industry also faced credit concerns: During the late 1980s bad energy loans and the rescheduling of loans between "less developed countries," such as Argentina, Brazil, and Mexico, and major U.S. banks created considerable uncertainty about the soundness of our banking system. Electric utilities with large nuclear plant construction programs suffered from the financial strains of illiquidity. Companies such as Public Service of New Hampshire, Continental Illinois Bank, Lions Capital, and Braniff Airlines had to restructure their debts or in some other way be bailed out of negative cash flow situations.

▶ ACCOUNTING ISSUES

The major accounting issues related to troubled debt situations involve recognition and measurement. In other words, when should a loss be recognized and at what amount?

To illustrate the major issue related to recognition, assume that Citicorp has a $10,000,000, 5-year, 10% loan to Brazil with interest receivable annually. At the end of the third year, Citicorp has determined that it probably will be able to collect $7,000,000 of this loan at maturity. Should it wait until the loan becomes uncollectible, or should it record a loss immediately? The general recognition principle is: **Losses should be recorded immediately if it is probable that the loss will occur.**

Assuming that Citicorp decides to record a loss, at what amount should the loss be recorded? Three alternatives are:

1. **Aggregate Cash Flows.** Some argue that a loss should not be recorded unless the aggregate cash flows from the loan are less than its carrying amount. In the Citicorp example, the aggregate cash flows expected are $7,000,000 of principal and $2,000,000 of interest ($10,000,000 × 10% × 2), for a total of $9,000,000. Thus, a loss of only $1,000,000 ($10,000,000 − $9,000,000) would be reported.

   Advocates of this position argue that Citicorp will recover $9,000,000 of the $10,000,000 and, therefore, its loss is only $1,000,000. Others disagree, noting that this approach ignores present values. That is, the present value of the future cash flows is much less than $9,000,000 and, therefore, the loss is much greater than $1,000,000.

2. **Present Value—Historical Effective Rate.** Those who argue for the use of present value, however, disagree about the interest rate to use to discount the ex-

pected future cash flows. The two rates discussed are the historical (original) effective rate and the market rate at the time the loan is recognized as troubled. Those who favor the historical effective rate believe that losses should reflect only a deterioration in credit quality. When the historical effective loan rate is used, the value of the investment will change only if some of the legally contracted cash flows are reduced. A loss in this case is recognized because the expected future cash flows have changed. Interest rate changes caused by current economic events that affect the fair value of the loan are ignored.

3. **Present Value—Market Rate.** Others believe that expected future cash flows of a troubled loan should be discounted at market interest rates, which reflect current economic events and conditions that are commensurate with the risks involved. The historical effective interest rate reflects the risk characteristics of the loan at the time it was originated or acquired, but not at the time it is troubled. In short, proponents of the market rate believe that a fair value measure should be used.

This appendix addresses issues concerning the accounting by debtors and creditors for troubled debt. Two different types of situations result with troubled debt:

1. Impairments.
2. Restructurings:
    a. Settlements.
    b. Modification of terms.

In a troubled debt situation, the creditor usually first recognizes a loss on impairment. Subsequently the terms of the loan are either modified or the loan is settled on terms unfavorable to the creditor. In unusual cases, the creditor forces the debtor into bankruptcy in order to ensure the highest possible collection on the loan. Illustration 14A-1 shows this continuum:

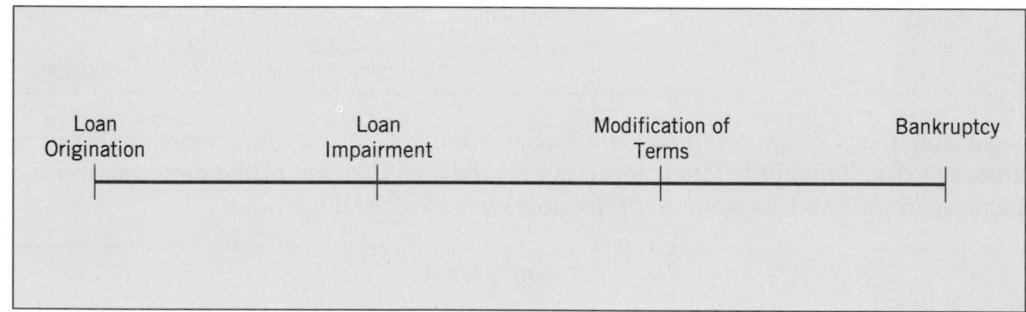

**ILLUSTRATION 14A-1
Usual Progression in
Troubled Debt Situations**

▶ IMPAIRMENTS

A loan[1] is considered **impaired** when it is **probable**,[2] based on current information and events, that the creditor will be unable to collect all amounts due (both principal and interest) according to the contractual terms of the loan. Creditors should apply their normal review procedures in making the judgment as to the probability of collection.[3]

---

[1]*FASB Statement No. 114*, "Accounting by Creditors for Impairment of a Loan," (Norwalk, CT: FASB, May 1993), defines a loan as "a contractual right to receive money on demand or on fixed and determinable dates that is recognized as an asset in the creditor's statement of financial position." For example, accounts receivable with terms exceeding one year would be considered loans.

[2]Recall the definitions of probable, reasonably possible, and remote with respect to contingencies, as defined in *FASB Statement No. 5*.

[3]Normal review procedures include examination of "watch lists," review of regulatory reports of examination, and examination of management reports of total loan amounts by borrower.

If a loan is considered impaired, the loss due to the **impairment** should be measured as the difference between the investment in the loan (generally the principal plus accrued interest) and the expected future cash flows discounted at the loan's historical effective interest rate.[4] In estimating future cash flows the creditor should employ all reasonable and supportable assumptions and projections.[5]

ILLUSTRATION OF LOSS ON IMPAIRMENT

On December 31, 1995, Prospect Inc. issued a $500,000, 5-year, noninterest-bearing note to Community Bank. The note was issued to yield 10% annual interest. As a result, Prospect received and Community Bank paid $310,460 ($500,000 × .62092) on December 31, 1995.[6] A time diagram illustrates the factors involved:

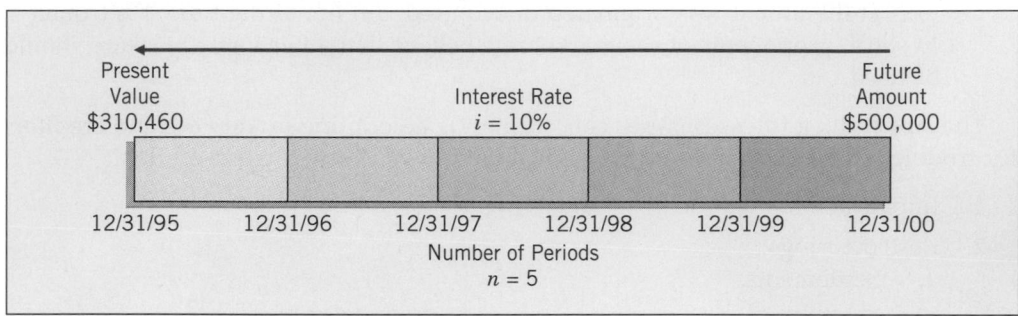

The entries to record this transaction on the books of Community Bank (creditor) and Prospect Inc. (debtor) are as follows:

ILLUSTRATION 14A-2
Creditor and Debtor
Entries to Record Note

December 31, 1995				
Community Bank (Creditor)			**Prospect Inc. (Debtor)**	
Notes Receivable	500,000		Cash	310,460	
Discount on Notes Receivable		189,540	Discount on Notes		
Cash		310,460	Payable	189,540	
			Notes Payable		500,000

Assuming that Community Bank and Prospect Inc. use the effective interest method to amortize discounts, Illustration 14A-3 shows the amortization of the discount and the increase in the carrying amount of the note over the life of the note.

ILLUSTRATION 14A-3
Schedule of Interest and
Discount Amortization
(Before Impairment)

	Community Bank			
Date	Cash Received (0%)	Interest Revenue (10%)	Discount Amortized	Carrying Amount of Note
12/31/95				$310,460
12/31/96	$0	$ 31,046[a]	$ 31,046	341,506[b]
12/31/97	0	34,151	34,151	375,657
12/31/98	0	37,566	37,566	413,223
12/31/99	0	41,322	41,322	454,545
12/31/00	0	45,455	45,455	500,000
Total	$0	$189,540	$189,540	

[a]$31,046 = $310,460 × .10
[b]$341,506 = $310,460 + $31,046

---

[4]The creditor may also, for the sake of expediency, use the market price of the loan (if such a price is available) or the fair value of collateral if it is a collateralized loan. *FASB Statement No. 114*, par. 13.

[5]*FASB Statement No. 114*, par. 15.

[6]Present value of $500,000 due in 5 years at 10%, annual compounding (Table 6-2) equals $500,000 × .62092.

Unfortunately, during 1997 Prospect's business deteriorated due to increased competition and a faltering regional economy. After reviewing all available evidence at December 31, 1997, Community Bank determined that it was probable that Prospect would pay back only $300,000 of the principal at maturity. As a result, Community Bank decided that the loan was impaired, and that a loss should be recorded immediately.

To determine the loss, the first step is to compute the present value of the expected cash flows discounted at the historical effective rate of interest. This amount is $225,396. The time diagram highlights the factors involved in this computation.

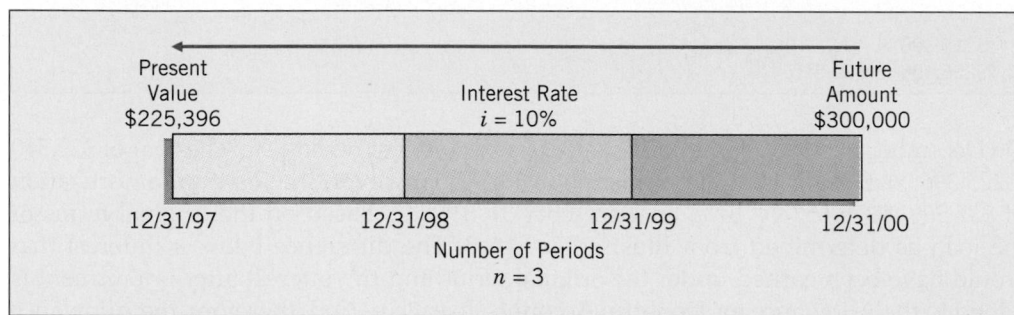

ILLUSTRATION 14A-4
Time Diagram, Factors for Loss on Note

The loss due to impairment is equal to the difference between the present value of the expected future cash flows and the recorded carrying amount of the investment in the loan. The calculation of the loss is shown in Illustration 14A-5:

Carrying amount of investment (12/31/97)—Illustration 14A-3	$375,657
Less: Present value of $300,000 due in 3 years at 10% interest compounded annually (Table 6-2); a ($p_{\overline{3}|10\%}$);	
($300,000 × .75132)	225,396
Loss due to impairment	$150,261

ILLUSTRATION 14A-5
Computation of Loss Due to Impairment

The loss due to the impairment is $150,261 not $200,000 ($500,000 − $300,000). The reason is that the loss is measured at a present value amount, not an undiscounted amount, at the time the loss is recorded.

The entry to record the loss is as follows:

December 31, 1997			
Community Bank (Creditor)		**Prospect Inc. (Debtor)**	
Bad Debt Expense	150,261	No entry	
Allowance for Doubtful Accounts	150,261		

ILLUSTRATION 14A-6
Creditor and Debtor Entries to Record Loss on Note

Community Bank (creditor) debits Bad Debt Expense for the expected loss. At the same time, it reduces the overall value of its loan receivable by crediting Allowance for Doubtful Accounts.[7] On the other hand, Prospect Inc. (debtor) makes no entry because it still legally owes $500,000.

In subsequent periods, Community Bank records interest revenue on the note based upon the new carrying amount of $225,396.[8] Illustration 14A-7 shows the computation of the amortization of the discount and the annual increase in the carrying amount.

---

[7]In the event that the loan is written off, the loss is charged against the allowance. In subsequent periods, if the estimated expected cash flows are revised based on new information, the allowance account and loss account would be adjusted (either increased or decreased depending whether conditions improved or worsened) in the same fashion as the original impairment.

[8]Many alternatives are permitted to recognize income. For problem purposes, use the method shown here. See *FASB Statement No. 118*," Accounting by Creditors for Impairment of a Loan—Income Recognition and Disclosures," (Norwalk, Ct: FASB, October 1994).

	Community Bank			
Date	Interest Received (0%)	Interest Revenue (10%)	Discount Amortized	Carrying Amount of Note
12/31/97				$225,396
12/31/98	$0	$22,540[a]	$22,540	247,936[b]
12/31/99	0	24,794	24,794	272,730
12/31/00	0	27,270	27,270	300,000
Total	$0	$74,604	$74,604	

[a]$225,396 × 10%.
[b]$225,396 + $22,540.

On December 31, 1998, Community Bank records interest revenue for the year of $22,540 ($225,396 × 10%) as shown in Illustration 14A-7. However, the discount amortization of $37,566 ($375,657 × 10%) on December 31, 1998, is based on the original terms of the loan as determined from Illustration 14A-3. The difference between interest that would have been earned under the original terms and the interest after impairment is added to the Allowance for Doubtful Accounts. In each period, therefore, the Allowance for Doubtful Accounts is increased to ensure that at maturity the appropriate amount is reported in the allowance account. The entry is as follows.

December 31, 1998			
Community Bank (Creditor)		**Prospect Inc. (Debtor)**	
Discount on Notes Receivable	37,566	Interest Expense	37,566
Interest Revenue	22,540	Discount on Notes Payable	37,566
Allowance for Doubtful Accounts	15,026		

On January 1, 2001, assuming that Prospect pays only $300,000, the entries are as follows:[9]

January 1, 2001			
Community Bank (Creditor)		**Prospect Inc. (Debtor)**	
Cash	300,000	Notes Payable	500,000
Allowance for Doubtful Accounts	200,000	Gain on Extinguishment	200,000
Notes Receivable	500,000	Cash	300,000

Community Bank has a credit balance in its Allowance for Doubtful Accounts of $200,000 on January 1, 2001. The allowance account is then debited for the deficiency of $200,000. Prospect, Inc., on the other hand, records a gain on extinguishment of debt (extraordinary). Its total obligation was $500,000 but Community Bank accepted $300,000 in full payment. In most cases, Community Bank will attempt some restructuring of the note to ensure additional payment.

---

[9]On the other hand, if Community Bank receives $500,000, on January 1, 2001, it should make the following entry:

Cash	500,000	
Allowance for Doubtful Accounts	200,000	
Notes Receivable		500,000
Bad Debt Expense		150,261
Interest Revenue		49,739

This represents a change in estimate and is an adjustment to bad debts expense and interest revenue in the current period.

▶ TROUBLED DEBT RESTRUCTURINGS

A **troubled debt restructuring** occurs when a creditor "for economic or legal reasons related to the debtor's financial difficulties grants a concession to the debtor that it would not otherwise consider."[10] Thus **troubled** debt restructuring does not apply to modifications of a debt obligation that reflect general economic conditions that dictate a reduction in interest rates. Nor does it apply to the refunding of an old debt with new debt having an effective interest rate approximately equal to that of similar debt issued by nontroubled debtors.

A troubled debt restructuring involves one of two basic types of transactions:

1. Settlement of debt at less than its carrying amount.
2. Continuation of debt with a modification of terms.

SETTLEMENT OF DEBT

A transfer of noncash assets (real estate, receivables, or other assets) or the issuance of the debtor's stock can be used to settle a debt obligation in a troubled debt restructuring. In these situations, **the noncash assets or equity interest given should be accounted for at their fair market value.** The debtor is required to determine the excess of the carrying amount of the payable over the fair value of the assets or equity transferred (gain). Likewise, the creditor is required to determine the excess of the receivable over the fair value of those same assets or equity interests transferred (loss). The debtor recognizes an extraordinary gain equal to the amount of the excess, and the creditor normally would charge the excess (loss) against Allowance for Doubtful Accounts. In addition, the debtor recognizes a gain or loss on disposition of assets to the extent that the fair value of those assets differs from their carrying amount (book value).

To illustrate a transfer of assets, assume that American City Bank has loaned $20,000,000 to Union Mortgage Company. Union Mortgage in turn has invested these monies in residential apartment buildings, but because of low occupancy rates it cannot meet its loan obligations. American City Bank agrees to accept from Union Mortgage real estate with a fair market value of $16,000,000 in full settlement of the $20,000,000 loan obligation. The real estate has a recorded value of $21,000,000 on the books of Union Mortgage Company. The entry to record this transaction on the books of American City Bank (creditor) is as follows:

Real Estate	16,000,000	
Allowance for Doubtful Accounts	4,000,000	
Note Receivable from Union Mortgage Company		20,000,000

The real estate is recorded at fair market value, and a charge is made to the Allowance for Doubtful Accounts to reflect the bad debt writeoff. If no allowance were available to absorb the charge of $4,000,000, the debit would be to a loss (ordinary) account.

The entry to record this transaction on the books of Union Mortgage Company (debtor) is as follows:

Note Payable to American City Bank	20,000,000	
Loss on Disposition of Real Estate	5,000,000	
Real Estate		21,000,000
Gain on Restructuring of Debt (Extraordinary)		4,000,000

Union Mortgage Company has a loss on the disposition of real estate in the amount of $5,000,000 (the difference between the $21,000,000 book value and the $16,000,000 fair market value), which should be shown as an ordinary loss on the income statement in accordance with *APB Opinion No. 30*. In addition, it has a gain on restructuring of debt of $4,000,000 (the difference between the $20,000,000 carrying amount of the note payable and the $16,000,000 fair market value of the real estate). **The gain on restruc-**

---

[10]*FASB Statement No. 15*, par. 1.

turing should be shown as an extraordinary item in accordance with *FASB Statement No. 4.*

To illustrate the granting of an equity interest, assume that American City Bank had agreed to accept from Union Mortgage Company 320,000 shares of Union's common stock ($10 par) that has a fair market value of $16,000,000 in full settlement of the $20,000,000 loan obligation. The entry to record this transaction on the books of American City Bank (creditor) is as follows:

Investment	16,000,000	
Allowance for Doubtful Accounts	4,000,000	
Note Receivable from Union Mortgage Company		20,000,000

The stock received by American City Bank is recorded as an investment at the fair market value at the date of restructure.

The entry to record this transaction on the books of Union Mortgage Company (debtor) is as follows:

Note Payable to American City Bank	20,000,000	
Common Stock		3,200,000
Additional Paid-in Capital		12,800,000
Gain on Restructuring of Debt (Extraordinary)		4,000,000

The stock issued by Union Mortgage Company is recorded in the normal manner with the difference between the par value and the fair value of the stock recorded as additional paid-in capital.

MODIFICATION OF TERMS

In some cases, a debtor will have serious short-run cash flow problems that lead it to request one or a combination of the following modifications:

1. Reduction of the stated interest rate.

2. Extension of the maturity date of the face amount of the debt.

3. Reduction of the face amount of the debt.

4. Reduction or deferral of any accrued interest.

Prior to *FASB Statement No. 114,* debtors and creditors computed the gain or loss on restructuring based upon the undiscounted restructured cash flows. Under *FASB Statement No. 114,* the creditor's loss is based upon cash flows discounted at the historical effective rate of the loan. The FASB recently concluded that, "because loans are recorded originally at discounted amounts, the ongoing assessment for impairment should be made in a similar manner."[11] The debtor's gain will continue to be calculated based upon **undiscounted amounts,** as described in *FASB Statement No. 15.* As a consequence, **the gain recorded by the debtor will not equal the loss recorded by the creditor under many circumstances.**[12]

Two illustrations demonstrate the accounting for a troubled debt restructuring by debtors and creditors:

1. The debtor does not record a gain.

2. The debtor does record a gain.

In both instances the creditor has a loss.

---

[11]*FASB Statement No. 114,* par. 42.

[12]In response to concerns expressed about this nonsymmetric treatment the FASB stated that *Statement No. 114* does not address debtor accounting because the FASB was concerned that expansion of the scope of the statement would delay its issuance.

Illustration 1—No Gain for Debtor

This illustration demonstrates a restructuring in which no gain is recorded by the debtor.[13] On December 31, 1995, Morgan National Bank enters into a debt restructuring agreement with Resorts Development Company, which is experiencing financial difficulties. The bank restructures a $10,500,000 loan receivable issued at par (interest paid to date) by:

1. Reducing the principal obligation from $10,500,000 to $9,000,000,
2. Extending the maturity date from December 31, 1995, to December 31, 1999, and
3. Reducing the interest rate from 12% to 8%.

Debtor Calculations

The total future cash flow after restructuring of $11,880,000 ($9,000,000 of principal plus $2,880,000 of interest payments[14]) exceeds the total pre-restructuring carrying amount of the debt of $10,500,000. Consequently, **no gain is recorded and no adjustment is made by the debtor** to the carrying amount of the payable. As a result, no entry is made by Resorts Development Co. (debtor) at the date of restructuring.

A new effective interest rate must be computed by the debtor in order to record interest expense in future periods. The new effective interest rate equates the present value of the future cash flows specified by the new terms with the pre-restructuring carrying amount of the debt. In this case, the new rate is computed by relating the pre-restructure carrying amount ($10,500,000) to the total future cash flow ($11,880,000). The rate necessary to discount the total future cash flow ($11,880,000) to a present value equal to the remaining balance ($10,500,000) is 3.46613%.[15]

On the basis of the effective rate of 3.46613%, the schedule shown in Illustration 14A-10 is prepared:

Resorts Development Co. (Debtor)					
Date	Interest Paid (8%)	Interest Expense (3.46613%)	Reduction of Carrying Amount	Carrying Amount of Note	
12/31/95				$10,500,000	
12/31/96	$ 720,000[a]	$ 363,944[b]	$ 356,056[c]	10,143,944	
12/31/97	720,000	351,602	368,398	9,775,546	
12/31/98	720,000	338,833	381,167	9,394,379	
12/31/99	720,000	325,621	394,379	9,000,000	
	$2,880,000	$1,380,000	$1,500,000		

[a]$720,000 = $9,000,000 × .08
[b]$363,944 = $10,500,000 × 3.46613%
[c]$356,056 = $720,000 − $363,944

ILLUSTRATION 14A-10
Schedule Showing Reduction of Carrying Amount of Note

---

[13]Note that the examples given for restructuring assume no previous entries were made by the creditor for impairment. In actuality it is likely that, in accordance with *Statement No. 114,* the creditor would have already made an entry when the loan initially became impaired, and restructuring would simply require an adjustment of the initial estimated loss by the creditor. Recall, however, that the debtor makes no entry upon impairment.

[14]Total interest payments are: $9,000,000 × .08 × 4 years = $2,880,000.

[15]An accurate interest rate i can be found by using the formulas given at the tops of Tables 6-2 and 6-4 to set up the following equation:

$$\$10,500,000 = \underbrace{\frac{1}{(1 + i)^4} \times \$9,000,000}_{\text{(from Table 6-2)}} + \underbrace{\frac{1 - \frac{1}{(1 + i)^4}}{i} \times \$720,000}_{\text{(from Table 6-4)}}$$

Solving algebraically for i, we find that i = 3.46613%.

In practice a computer program is frequently used to find the implicit interest rate.

Thus, on December 31, 1996 (date of first interest payment after restructure), the debtor makes the following entry:

December 31, 1996

Notes Payable	356,056	
Interest Expense	363,944	
Cash		720,000

A similar entry (except for different amounts for debits to Notes Payable and Interest Expense) is made each year until maturity. At maturity, the following entry is made:

December 31, 1999

Notes Payable	9,000,000	
Cash		9,000,000

Creditor Calculations

Morgan National Bank (creditor) is required to calculate its loss based upon the expected future cash flows discounted at the historical effective rate of the loan. This loss is calculated as follows:

**ILLUSTRATION 14A-11
Computation of Loss to
Creditor on Restructuring**

Pre-restructure carrying amount		$10,500,000
Present value of restructured cash flows:		
Present value of $9,000,000 due in 4 years at 12%, interest payable annually (Table 6-2); a ($p_{\overline{4}|12\%}$); ($9,000,000 × .63552).	$5,719,680	
Present value of $720,000 interest payable annually for 4 years at 12% (Table 6-4); R($P_{\overline{4}|12\%}$); ($720,000 × 3.03735).	2,186,892	
Present value of restructured cash flows		7,906,572
Loss on restructuring		$ 2,593,428

As a result, Morgan National Bank records the write-off against its allowance account as follows:

Allowance for Doubtful Accounts	2,593,428	
Notes Receivable		2,593,428

In subsequent periods, interest revenue is reported based on the historical effective rate. Illustration 14A-12 provides the following interest information:

**ILLUSTRATION 14A-12
Schedule of Interest and
Amortization after Debt
Restructuring**

Morgan National Bank (Creditor)				
Date	Interest Received (8%)	Interest Revenue (12%)	Discount Amortized	Carrying Amount of Note
12/31/95				$7,906,572
12/31/96	$ 720,000ᵃ	$ 948,789ᵇ	$ 228,789ᶜ	8,135,361
12/31/97	720,000	976,243	256,243	8,391,604
12/31/98	720,000	1,006,992	286,992	8,678,596
12/31/99	720,000	1,041,404ᵈ	321,404ᵈ	9,000,000
Total	$2,880,000	$3,973,428	$1,093,428	

[a]$720,000 = $9,000,000 × .08
[b]$948,789 = $7,906,572 × .12
[c]$228,789 = $948,789 − $720,000
[d]$28 adjustment to compensate for rounding.

On December 31, 1996, Morgan National Bank would make the following entry:

December 31, 1996

Cash	720,000	
Notes Receivable	228,789	
Interest Revenue		948,789

A similar entry (except for different amounts debited to Notes Receivable and credited to Interest Revenue) is made each year until maturity. At maturity, the following entry is made:

December 31, 1999

Cash	9,000,000	
Notes Receivable		9,000,000

Illustration 2—Gain for Debtor

If the pre-restructure carrying amount exceeds the total future cash flows as a result of a modification of the terms, the debtor records a gain. To illustrate, assume the facts in the previous example except that Morgan National Bank reduced the principal to $7,000,000 (and extended the maturity date to December 31, 1999, and reduced the interest from 12% to 8%). The total future cash flow is now $9,240,000 ($7,000,000 of principal plus $2,240,000 of interest[16]), which is $1,260,000 less than the pre-restructure carrying amount of $10,500,000. Under these circumstances, Resorts Development Company (debtor) would reduce the carrying amount of its payable $1,260,000 and record an extraordinary gain of $1,260,000. On the other hand, Morgan National Bank (creditor) would debit its allowance account for $4,350,444. This computation is shown in Illustration 14A-13.

Pre-restructure carrying amount		$10,500,000
Present value of restructured cash flows:		
Present value of $7,000,000 due in 4 years at 12%, interest payable annually (Table 6-2); a ($p_{\overline{4}|12\%}$); ($7,000,000 × .63552).	$4,448,640	
Present value of $560,000 interest payable annually for 4 years at 12% (Table 6-4); R($P_{\overline{4}|12\%}$); ($560,000 × 3.03735).	1,700,916	6,149,556
Creditor's loss on restructuring		$ 4,350,444

ILLUSTRATION 14A-13
Computation of Loss to Creditor on Restructuring

Entries to record the gain and loss on the debtor's and creditor's books at the date of restructure, December 31, 1995, are as follows:

ILLUSTRATION 14A-14
Debtor and Creditor Entries to Record Gain and Loss on Note

December 31, 1995 (date of restructure)					
Resorts Development Co. (Debtor)			**Morgan National Bank (Creditor)**		
Notes Payable	1,260,000		Allowance for Doubtful Accounts	4,350,444	
Gain on Restructuring of			Notes Receivable		3,500,000
Debt (Extraordinary)		1,260,000	Discount on Notes Receivable		850,444

For Resorts Development (debtor), because the new carrying value of the note ($10,500,000 − $1,260,000 = $9,240,000) equals the sum of the undiscounted cash flows ($9,240,000), the imputed interest rate is 0%. Consequently, all of the future cash flows reduce the principal balance, and no interest expense is recognized. For Morgan National the interest revenue would be reported in the same fashion as the previous example, that is, using the historical effective interest rate applied toward the newly discounted value of the note. Interest computations are shown in Illustration 14A-15.

---

[16]Total interest payments are: $7,000,000 × .08 × 4 years = $2,240,000.

ILLUSTRATION 14A-15
Schedule of Interest and Amortization after Debt Restructuring

		Morgan National Bank (Creditor)		
Date	Cash Received 8%	Interest Revenue 12%	Increase in Carrying Amount	Carrying Amount of Note
12/31/95				$6,149,556
12/31/96	$ 560,000[a]	$ 737,947[b]	$177,947[c]	6,327,503
12/31/97	560,000	759,300	199,300	6,526,803
12/31/98	560,000	783,216	223,216	6,750,019
12/31/99	560,000	809,981[d]	249,981[d]	7,000,000
Total	$2,240,000	$3,090,444	$850,444	

[a]$560,000 = $7,000,000 × .08
[b]$737,947 = $6,149,556 × .12
[c]$177,947 = $737,947 − $560,000
[d]$21 adjustment to compensate for rounding.

ILLUSTRATION 14A-16
Debtor and Creditor Entries to Record Periodic Interest and Final Principal Payments

The following journal entries illustrate the accounting by debtor and creditor for periodic interest payments and final principal payment:

Resorts Development Co. (Debtor)			Morgan National Bank (Creditor)		
December 31, 1996 (date of first interest payment following restructure):					
Notes Payable	560,000		Cash	560,000	
Cash		560,000	Discount on Notes Receivable	177,947	
			Interest Revenue		737,947
December 31, 1997, 1998, and 1999 (dates of 2nd, 3rd, and last interest payments.)					
		(Debit and credit same accounts as 12/31/96 using applicable amounts from appropriate amortization schedules.)			
December 31, 1999 (date of principal payment):					
Notes Payable	7,000,000		Cash	7,000,000	
Cash		7,000,000	Notes Receivable		7,000,000

▶ SUMMARY COMMENT

Under *Statement No. 15*, the FASB justified accounting for troubled debt restructurings at undiscounted values by saying that a restructuring involving a modification of terms is a continuation of an existing debt and is not a business transaction involving transfers of resources and obligations. Many accountants challenged this approach. If a company has a $1,000,000 loan receivable earning interest at 10% and the interest rate is lowered to 5% because the debtor has financial problems, they believed that a loss should be recognized immediately to reflect the change in the economic relationship between the debtor and the creditor. The FASB contended that the creditor's primary objective is to recover its investment—as long as this is accomplished a loss should not be recognized.

The position taken by the FASB under *Statement No. 15* was the position lobbied for by financial institutions. They argued that the economic consequences of loss recognition would be devastating to their industry. During the troubled economic times of the early and mid-1970s and the late 1980s, many financial institutions would have had to take substantial losses if the usual present value techniques had been employed. They argued that the recognition of these losses might cause individuals to lose confidence in the financial system, which would make it more difficult for financial institutions to raise capital and to grant credit to marginal or small borrowers. They argued that some bankruptcies, perhaps even a recession, would result.

With the gift of hindsight, in light of the savings-and-loan crisis, it appears that the nonrecognition of losses under *Statement No. 15* hid the extent to which financial institutions had many bad loans on their books. In the aftermath of the savings-and-loan clean-up, bank regulators and accounting regulators have taken considerable steps toward improving the accounting and disclosure for loans.

► SUMMARY OF ACCOUNTING FOR IMPAIRMENT AND TROUBLED DEBT RESTRUCTURINGS

Event	Accounting Procedure
1. Impairment	**Creditor:** Loss based upon difference between present value of future cash flows discounted at historical effective interest rate and carrying amount of note. Recognize interest revenue based upon new carrying amount and original effective rate. **Debtor:** No recognition.
2. Restructurings—Settlement of Debt a. Transfer of noncash assets.	**Creditor:** Recognize loss on restructure. **Debtor:** Recognize gain on restructure and recognize gain or loss on asset transfer.
b. Granting of equity interest.	**Creditor:** Recognize loss on restructure. **Debtor:** Recognize gain on restructure.
3. Restructurings—Continuation of Debt with Modified Terms a. Carrying amount of debt is less than future cash flows (no gain for debtor).	**Creditor:** Recognize loss based upon present value of restructured cash flows. Recognize interest revenue based upon new recorded value and original effective rate. **Debtor:** Recognize no gain on restructure. Determine new effective interest rate to be used in recording interest expense.
b. Carrying amount of debt is greater than total future cash flows (gain for debtor).	**Creditor:** Recognize loss based upon present value of restructured cash flows. Recognize interest revenue based upon new recorded value and original effective rate. **Debtor:** Recognize gain on restructure and reduce carrying amount to the sum of the undiscounted cash flows. Recognize no interest expense over the remaining life of the debt.

ILLUSTRATION 14A-17
Procedures for Impairments and Troubled Debt Restructurings

The following disclosures for loan impairment and restructurings are required of creditors:[17]

DISCLOSURES OF CREDITORS

1. As of the date of each balance sheet presented, the total recorded investment in the impaired loans at the end of each period and (1) the amount of that recorded investment for which there is a related allowance for doubtful accounts determined in accordance with this Statement and the amount of that allowance and (2) the amount of that recorded investment for which there is no related allowance for doubtful accounts determined in accordance with this Statement

2. The creditor's policy for recognizing interest revenue on impaired loans, including how cash receipts are recorded

3. For each period for which results of operations are presented, the average recorded investment in the impaired loans during each period, the related amount of interest revenue recognized during the time within that period that the loans were impaired, and, unless not practicable, the amount of interest revenue recognized using a cash-basis method of accounting during the time within that period that the loans were impaired.

4. Activity in allowance for doubtful accounts, including beginning and ending balances.

ILLUSTRATION 14A-18
Disclosures of Creditors for Loan Impairment and Restructurings

---

[17]*FASB Statement No. 118*, par. 6.i.

The following disclosures for troubled debt restructures as of the date of each balance sheet presented are required of debtors:

ILLUSTRATION 14A-19
Disclosures of Debtors
for Restructurings

DISCLOSURES OF DEBTORS
1. A description of the changes in terms or major features of settlement.
2. The aggregate gain on restructuring and the related tax effect.
3. The per-share amount of the aggregate gain on restructuring.
4. The aggregate gain or loss on transfers of assets.
5. Information on any contingent payments.

KEY TERMS

impairments, 704

troubled debt
restructuring, 707

► **SUMMARY OF LEARNING OBJECTIVE FOR APP. 14-A** ◄

9. **Distinguish between and account for (1) a loss on loan impairment, (2) a troubled debt restructuring that results in the settlement of a debt, and (3) a troubled debt restructuring that results in a continuation of debt with modification of terms.** An impairment loan loss is based on the difference between the present value of the future cash flows and the carrying amount of the note. There are two types of settlement of debt restructurings: (1) transfer of noncash assets and (2) granting of equity interest. For accounting purposes there are also two types of restructurings with continuation of debt with modified terms: (1) the carrying amount of debt is less than the future cash flows, and (2) the carrying amount of debt is greater than the total future cash flows.

Note: All **asterisked** Questions, Exercises, Problems, and Cases relate to material contained in the appendix to each chapter.

QUESTIONS

1. (a) From what sources might a corporation obtain funds through long-term debt? (b) What is a bond indenture? What does it contain? (c) What is a mortgage?

2. Differentiate between term bonds, mortgage bonds, collateral trust bonds, debenture bonds, income bonds, callable bonds, registered bonds, bearer or coupon bonds, convertible bonds, commodity-backed bonds, and deep discount bonds.

3. (a) What is the typical denomination of corporate bonds? (b) How often is bond interest typically payable?

4. Distinguish between the following interest rates for bonds payable:
   (a) yield rate   (d) market rate
   (b) nominal rate   (e) effective rate
   (c) stated rate

5. Distinguish between the following values relative to bonds payable:
   (a) maturity value   (c) market value
   (b) face value   (d) par value

6. Under what conditions of bond issuance does a discount on bonds payable arise? Under what conditions of bond issuance does a premium on bonds payable arise?

7. How should unamortized discount on bonds payable be reported on the financial statements? Unamortized premium on bonds payable?

8. What are the two methods of amortizing discount and premium on bonds payable? Explain each.

9. Lopez Company sells its bonds at a premium and applies the effective interest method in amortizing the premium. Will the annual interest expense increase or decrease over the life of the bonds? Explain.

10. How should the costs of issuing bonds be accounted for and classified in the financial statements?

11. Where should treasury bonds be shown on the balance sheet? Should treasury bonds be carried at par or at reacquisition cost?

12. What is the "call" feature of a bond issue? How does the call feature affect the amortization of bond premium or discount?

13. Why would a company wish to reduce its bond indebtedness before its bonds reach maturity? Indicate how this can be done and the correct accounting treatment for such a transaction.

14. How are gains and losses from extinguishment of debt classified in the income statement? What disclosures are required of such transactions by *FASB Statement No. 4*?

15. What is in-substance defeasance? What is the advantage of this technique?

16. What must the accountant do to record properly a transaction involving the issuance of a noninterest-bearing long-term note in exchange for property?

17. How is the present value of a noninterest-bearing note computed?

18. When is the stated interest rate of a debt instrument presumed to be fair?

19. What types of payables are exempted from the provisions of *APB Opinion No. 21?*

20. What are the considerations in imputing an appropriate interest rate?

21. B. Crystal Inc. recently became involved in an interest rate swap. What is an interest rate swap and how is it reported in the financial statements?

22. Differentiate between a fixed-rate mortgage and a variable-rate mortgage.

23. According to *FASB Statement No. 47*, "Disclosure of Long-Term Obligations," what disclosures are required relative to long-term debt and sinking fund requirements?

24. What are project financing arrangements?

25. What are take-or-pay contracts and through-put contracts?

26. What conditions must be met in order for a contractual obligation to be disclosed as an unconditional purchase obligation?

27. What disclosures are required relative to unconditional purchase obligations that have been recognized as balance sheet liabilities?

28. What disclosures are required relative to unconditional purchase obligations that have been disclosed only in the notes to the financial statements?

*29. What are three measurement bases that might be used to value troubled debt? What are the advantages of each method?

*30. What are the general rules for measuring and recognizing gain or loss by both the debtor and the creditor in an impairment?

*31. What are the general rules for measuring gain or loss by both creditor and debtor in a troubled debt restructuring involving a settlement?

*32. (a) In a troubled debt situation, why might the creditor grant concessions to the debtor?
 (b) What type of concessions might a creditor grant the debtor in a troubled debt situation?
 (c) What is meant by "impairment" of a loan? Under what circumstances should a creditor or debtor recognize an impaired loan?

*33. What are the general rules for measuring and recognizing gain or loss by both the debtor and the creditor in a troubled debt restructuring involving a modification of terms?

*34. What is meant by "accounting symmetry" between the entries recorded by the debtor and creditor in a troubled debt restructuring involving a modification of terms? In what ways is the accounting for troubled debt restructurings and impairments non-symmetrical?

*35. Under what circumstances would a transaction be recorded as a troubled debt restructuring by only one of the two parties to the transaction?

*36. Lodi Bank agrees to restructure Green Company's troubled debt situation by reducing the interest rate from 14% to 8% and extending the maturity date of the debt 5 additional years. Explain how Green Company should account for this modification of terms in the restructuring of its debt to Lodi Bank.

*37. What is the major difference between *FASB Statement No. 114* and *No. 15* when debtors and creditors want to compute the gain or loss on debt restructuring?

*38. Assume that on January 1, 1994, the National First Bank enters into a debt restructuring agreement with Dallas Sports Co., which is experiencing financial difficulties. The bank agrees to reduce both the principal obligation and interest rate. In this situation, what are the general rules for both debtor and creditor to measure and recognize gain or loss resulting from the debt restructuring?

*39. Assume that Chrysis Company has recently fallen into financial difficulties. By reviewing all available evidence on December 31, 1994, one creditor of Chrysis, the National American Bank, determined that Chrysis would pay back only 65% of the principal at maturity. As a result, the bank decided that the loan was impaired. If the loss is estimated to be $195,000, what entries should both Chrysis and National American Bank make to record this loss?

EXERCISES

E14-1 (Classification of Liabilities) Presented below are various account balances of Enrico Caruso Inc.:

1. Unamortized premium on bonds payable, of which $1,500 will be amortized during the next year.
2. Bank loans payable of a winery, due March 10, 1999. (The product requires aging for 5 years before sale.)
3. Serial bonds payable, $500,000, of which $100,000 are due each July 31.
4. Dividends payable in shares of stock on January 20, 1997.
5. Amounts withheld from employees' wages for income taxes.
6. Notes payable due January 15, 1998.
7. Credit balances in customers' accounts arising from returns and allowances after collection in full of account.
8. Bonds payable of $1,000,000 maturing June 30, 1997.
9. Overdraft of $500 in a bank account. (No other balances are carried at this bank.)
10. Deposits made by customers who have ordered goods.

Instructions

Indicate whether each of the items above should be classified on December 31, 1996, as a current liability, a long-term liability, or under some other classification. Consider each one independently from all others; that is, do not assume that all of them relate to one particular business. If the classification of some of the items is doubtful, explain why in each case.

E14-2 (Classification) The following items are found in the financial statements:
  (a) Discount on bonds payable
  (b) Interest expense (credit balance)
  (c) Unamortized bond issue costs
  (d) Gain on repurchase of debt
  (e) Mortgage payable (payable in equal amounts over next 3 years)
  (f) Gain on defeased debt
  (g) Debenture bonds payable (maturing in 5 years)
  (h) Notes payable (due in 4 years)
  (i) Premium on bonds payable
  (j) Treasury bonds
  (k) Income bonds payable (due in 3 years)

Instructions

Indicate how each of these items should be classified in the financial statements.

E14-3 (Entries for Bond Transactions) Presented below are two independent situations:

1. On January 1, 1995, Carmen Company issued $200,000, of 10%, 10-year bonds at par. Interest is payable quarterly on April 1, July 1, October 1, and January 1.
2. On June 1, 1995, Bizet Company issued $100,000 of 9%, 10-year bonds dated January 1 at par plus accrued interest. Interest is payable semiannually on July 1 and January 1.

Instructions

For each of these two independent situations, present journal entries to record:
  (a) The issuance of the bonds.
  (b) The payment of interest on July 1.
  (c) The accrual of interest on December 31.

E14-4 (Entries for Bond Transactions) Maria Callas Company issued $500,000 of 10%, 20-year bonds on January 1, 1996, at 102. Interest is payable semiannually on July 1 and January 1. Callas Company uses the straight-line method of amortization for bond premium or discount.

Instructions

  (a) Prepare the journal entries to record
    1. The issuance of the bonds.

2. The payment of interest and the related amortization on July 1, 1996.
3. The accrual of interest and the related amortization on December 31, 1996.
(b) If the effective interest method of amortization was used, what would be the (1) interest expense recorded on July 1, 1996; (2) premium or discount amortization for the 6-month period July 1 to December 31, 1996. Assume an effective yield of 9.75%.

E14-5 (Determine Proper Amounts in Account Balances) Presented below are three independent situations:
(a) Renata Corporation incurred the following cost in connection with the issuance of bonds: (1) printing and engraving costs, $12,000; (2) legal fees, $37,000, and (3) commissions paid to underwriter, $60,000. What amount should be reported as Unamortized Bond Issue Costs and where should this amount be reported on the balance sheet?
(b) Scotto Co. sold $2,000,000 of 10%, 10-year bonds at 103 on January 1, 1995. The bonds were dated January 1, 1995, and pay interest on July 1 and January 1. If Scotto uses the straight-line method to amortize bond premium or discount, determine the amount of interest expense to be reported on July 1, 1995, and December 31, 1995.
(c) Sutherland Inc. issued $480,000 of 9%, 10-year bonds on June 30, 1995 for $450,000. This price provided a yield of 10% on the bonds. Interest is payable semiannually on December 31 and June 30. If Sutherland uses the effective interest method, determine the amount of interest expense to record if financial statements are issued on October 31, 1995.

E14-6 (Entries and Questions for Bond Transactions) On June 30, 1996, Beverly Sills Company issued $3,000,000 face value of 13%, 20-year bonds at $3,225,690, a yield of 12%. Sills uses the effective interest method to amortize bond premium or discount. The bonds pay semiannual interest on June 30 and December 31.

Instructions
(a) Prepare the journal entries to record the following transactions.
1. The issuance of the bonds on June 30, 1996.
2. The payment of interest and the amortization of the premium on December 31, 1996.
3. The payment of interest and the amortization of the premium on June 30, 1997.
4. The payment of interest and the amortization of the premium on December 31, 1997.
(b) Show the proper balance sheet presentation for the liability for bonds payable on the December 31, 1997 balance sheet.
(c) Provide the answers to the following questions.
1. What amount of interest expense is reported for 1997?
2. Will the bond interest expense reported in 1997 be the same as, greater than, or less than the amount that would be reported if the straight-line method of amortization were used?
3. Determine the total cost of borrowing over the life of the bond.
4. Will the total bond interest expense for the life of the bond be greater than, the same as, or less than the total interest expense if the straight-line method of amortization were used?

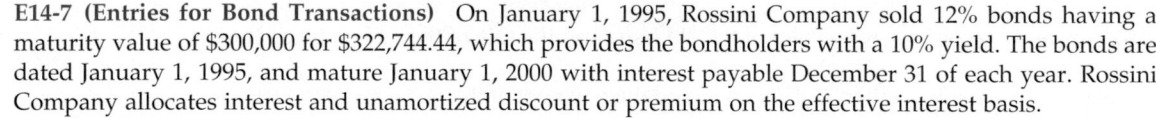 **E14-7 (Entries for Bond Transactions)** On January 1, 1995, Rossini Company sold 12% bonds having a maturity value of $300,000 for $322,744.44, which provides the bondholders with a 10% yield. The bonds are dated January 1, 1995, and mature January 1, 2000 with interest payable December 31 of each year. Rossini Company allocates interest and unamortized discount or premium on the effective interest basis.

Instructions
(a) Prepare the journal entry at the date of the bond issuance.
(b) Prepare a schedule of interest expense and bond amortization for 1995–97.
(c) Prepare the journal entry to record the interest payment and the amortization for 1995.
(d) Prepare the journal entry to record the interest payment and the amortization for 1997.

E14-8 (Entries for Subscribed Bonds) Puccini Company authorized the issuance of 10% coupon bonds in the amount of $1,000,000, with interest coupons payable semiannually, and the bonds to be dated January 1, 1996. The financial events are as follows:

1. The authorization of 1,000 bonds of $1,000 each.
2. Subscriptions received for 800 bonds, at par.
3. Cash received in full on January 1, 1996, from subscribers to 600 bonds; bonds are issued.
4. On April 1, 1996, cash is received from subscribers to 200 bonds in the amount of the par value of the bonds plus accrued interest. The bonds are issued.
5. On July 1, 1996, 6 months' interest is paid on the bonds outstanding.

Instructions
Prepare entries to record the events listed above.

E14-9 (Information Related to Various Bond Issues) Turandot Inc. has issued three types of debt on January 1, 1995, the start of the company's fiscal year.

1. $10 million, 10-year, 15% unsecured bonds, interest payable quarterly. Bonds were priced to yield 12%.
2. $30 million par of 10-year zero-coupon bonds at a price to yield 12% per year.
3. $20 million, 10-year, 10% mortgage bonds, interest payable annually to yield 12%.

Instructions
Prepare a schedule that identifies the following items for each bond: (1) maturity value, (2) number of interest periods over life of bond, (3) stated rate per each interest period, (4) effective interest rate per each interest period, (5) payment amount per period, and (6) present value of bonds at date of issue.

E14-10 (Entry for Retirement of Bond; Bond Issue Costs) On January 2, 1990, Tosca Corporation issued $1,500,000 of 10% bonds at 96 due December 31, 1999. Legal and other costs of $24,000 were incurred in connection with the issue. Interest on the bonds is payable annually each December 31. The $24,000 issue costs are being deferred and amortized on a straight-line basis over the 10-year term of the bonds. The discount on the bonds is also being amortized on a straight-line basis over the 10 years. (Straight-line is not materially different in effect from the preferable "interest method".)

The bonds are callable at 101 (i.e., at 101% of face amount), and on January 2, 1995, Tosca called $900,000 face amount of the bonds and retired them.

Instructions
Ignoring income taxes, compute the amount of loss, if any, to be recognized by Tosca as a result of retiring the $900,000 of bonds in 1995 and prepare the journal entry to record the retirement.

(AICPA adapted)

E14-11 (Entries for Retirement and Issuance of Bonds) M. Butterfly, Inc. had outstanding $6,000,000 of 11% bonds (interest payable July 31 and January 31) due in 10 years. On July 1, it issued $9,000,000 of 10%, 15-year bonds (interest payable July 1 and January 1) at 97. A portion of the proceeds was used to call the 11% bonds at 102 on August 1. Unamortized bond discount and issue cost applicable to the 11% bonds were $90,000 and $30,000, respectively.

Instructions
Prepare the journal entries necessary to record issue of the new bonds and the refunding of the bonds.

E14-12 (Entries for Retirement and Issuance of Bonds) On June 30, 1987, Aida Company issued 12% bonds with a par value of $700,000 due in 20 years. They were issued at 98 and were callable at 104 at any date after June 30, 1995. Because of lower interest rates and a significant change in the company's credit rating, it was decided to call the entire issue on June 30, 1996, and to issue new bonds. New 10% bonds were sold in the amount of $800,000 at 102; they mature in 20 years. Aida Company uses straight-line amortization. Interest payment dates are December 31 and June 30.

Instructions
(a) Prepare journal entries to record the retirement of the old issue and the sale of the new issue on June 30, 1996.
(b) Prepare the entry required on December 31, 1996, to record the payment of the first 6 months' interest and the amortization of premium on the bonds.

E14-13 (Entries for Retirement and Issuance of Bonds) Verdi Company had bonds outstanding with a maturity value of $300,000. On April 30, 1996, when these bonds had an unamortized discount of $5,000, they were called in at 104. To pay for these bonds, Verdi had issued other bonds a month earlier bearing a lower interest rate. The newly issued bonds had a life of 10 years. The new bonds were issued at 102 (face value $300,000). Issue costs related to the new bonds were $3,000.

Instructions
Ignoring interest, compute the gain or loss and record this refunding transaction.

(AICPA adapted)

E14-14 (Entries for Retirement of Bonds By Trustee) Under the terms of its 9% bonds (interest payable June 30 and December 31), Traviata Company must pay $3,000,000 to a trustee each year. The funds are to be used to retire as many bonds as possible in the open market. (*Hint:* Establish a bond retirement fund.)

On July 1, 1995, the company paid $3,000,000 to the trustee, who purchased $3,300,000 par value of bonds with the $3,000,000. Unamortized bond discount applicable to the bonds purchased was $66,000.

Instructions
Record the payment and purchase of the bonds on the Traviata Company's books.

E14-15 (Entries for Noninterest-Bearing Debt) On January 1, 1996, Rigoletto Company makes the two following acquisitions:

1. Purchases land having a fair market value of $200,000 by issuing a 5-year noninterest-bearing promissory note in the face amount of $337,012.
2. Purchases equipment by issuing a 6%, 8-year promissory note having a maturity value of $180,000 (interest payable annually).

The Company has to pay 11% interest for funds from its bank.

Instructions
(a) Record the two journal entries that should be recorded by Rigoletto Company for the two purchases on January 1, 1996.
(b) Record the interest at the end of the first year on both notes using the effective interest method.

E14-16 (Imputation of Interest) Presented below are two independent situations:
(a) On January 1, 1996, Parsifal Inc. purchased land that had an assessed value of $325,000 at the time of purchase. A $500,000 noninterest-bearing note due January 1, 1999, was given in exchange. There was no established exchange price for the land, nor a ready market value for the note. The interest rate charged on a note of this type is 12%. Determine at what amount the land should be recorded at January 1, 1996, and the interest expense to be reported in 1996 related to this transaction.
(b) On January 1, 1996, Tristan Furniture Co. borrowed $4,000,000 (face value) from Isolde Co., a major customer, through a noninterest-bearing note due in 4 years. Because the note was noninterest-bearing, Tristan Furniture agreed to sell furniture to this customer at lower than market price. A 10% rate of interest is normally charged on this type of loan. Prepare the journal entry to record this transaction and determine the amount of interest expense to report for 1996.

E14-17 (Imputation of Interest with Right) On January 1, 1994, Lohengrin Co. borrowed and received $360,000 from a major customer evidenced by a noninterest-bearing note due in 3 years. As consideration for the noninterest-bearing feature, Lohengrin agrees to supply the customer's inventory needs for the loan period at lower than the market price. The appropriate rate at which to impute interest is 12%.

Instructions
(a) Prepare the journal entry to record the initial transaction on January 1, 1994. (Round all computations to the nearest dollar.)
(b) Prepare the journal entry to record any adjusting entries needed at December 31, 1994. Assume that the sales of Lohengrin's product to this customer occur evenly over the 3-year period.

E14-18 (Long-Term Debt Disclosure) At December 31, 1994, Seville Company has outstanding three long-term debt issues. The first is a $2,000,000 note payable which matures June 30, 1997. The second is a $6,000,000 bond issue which matures September 30, 1998. The third is a $20,000,000 sinking fund debenture with annual sinking fund payments of $4,000,000 in each of the years 1996 through 2000.

Instructions
Prepare the note disclosure required by *FASB Statement No. 47*, "Disclosure of Long-term Obligations," for the long-term debt at December 31, 1994.

E14-19 (Long-Term Debt Disclosure) To secure a long-term supply, Lalo Company entered into a take-or-pay contract with an aluminum recycling plant on January 1, 1994. Lalo is obligated to purchase 40% of the output of the plant each period while the debt incurred to finance the plant remains outstanding. The annual cost of the aluminum to Lalo will be the sum of 40% of the raw material costs, operating expenses, depreciation, interest on the debt used to finance the plant, and return on the owner's investment. The minimum amount payable to the plant under the contract, whether or not Lalo is able to take delivery, is $6 million annually through December 31, 2013. Lalo's total purchases under the agreement were $7 million in 1994 and $7.5 million in 1995. Funds to construct the plant were borrowed at an effective interest rate of 9%. Lalo's incremental borrowing rate was 10% at January 1, 1994 and is 11% at December 31, 1995. Lalo intends to disclose the contract in the footnotes to its financial statements at December 31, 1995.

Instructions
Assuming that the contract is an "unconditional purchase obligation" as specified by *FASB Statement No. 47*, "Disclosure of Long-term Obligations," prepare the note disclosure required for the contract at December 31, 1995.

*E14-20 (Settlement of Debt)** American Store Company owes $199,000 plus $18,700 of accrued interest to First State Bank. The debt is a 10-year, 10% note. During 1995 American Store's business deteriorated due to a faltering regional economy. On December 31, 1995, First State Bank agrees to accept an old machine and cancel the entire debt. The machine has a cost of $389,000, accumulated depreciation of $220,000, and a fair market value of $190,000.

Instructions

(a) Prepare journal entries for American Store Company and First State Bank to record this debt settlement.

(b) How should American Store report the gain or loss on the disposition of machine and on restructuring of debt in its 1995 income statement?

(c) Assume that, instead of transferring the machine, American Store decides to grant 15,000 shares of its common stock ($10 par) which has a fair market value of $200,000 in full settlement of the loan obligation. If First State Bank treats American Store's stock as a trading investment, prepare the entries to record the transaction for both parties.

*E14-21 (Term Modification without Gain—Debtor's Entries) On December 31, 1995, the Firstar Bank enters into a debt restructuring agreement with Robinson Company, which is now experiencing financial trouble. The bank agrees to restructure a 12%, issued at par, $1,950,000 note receivable by the following modifications:

1. Reducing the principal obligation from $1,950,000 to $1,550,000.
2. Extending the maturity date from December 31, 1995 to December 31, 1998.
3. Reducing the interest rate from 12% to 10%.

Robinson pays interest at the end of each year. On January 1, 1999, Robinson Company pays $1,550,000 in cash to Firstar Bank.

Instructions

(a) Based on *FASB Statement No. 114*, will the gain recorded by Robinson be equal to the loss recorded by Firstar Bank under the debt restructuring?

(b) Can Robinson Company record a gain under the term modification mentioned above? Explain.

(c) Assuming that the interest rate Robinson should use to compute interest expense in future periods is 1.1931%, prepare the interest payment schedule of the note for Robinson Company after the debt restructuring.

(d) Prepare the interest payment entry for Robinson Company on December 31, 1997.

(e) What entry should Robinson make on January 1, 1999?

*E14-22 (Term Modification without Gain—Creditor's Entries) Using the same information as in E14-21 above, answer the following questions related to Firstar Bank (creditor).

Instructions

(a) What interest rate should Firstar Bank use to calculate the loss on the debt restructuring?

(b) Compute the loss that Firstar Bank will suffer from the debt restructuring. Prepare the journal entry to record the loss.

(c) Prepare the interest receipt schedule for Firstar Bank after the debt restructuring.

(d) Prepare the interest receipt entry for Firstar Bank on December 31, 1997.

(e) What entry should Firstar Bank make on January 1, 1999?

*E14-23 (Term Modification with Gain—Debtor's Entries) Use the same information as in E14-21 above except that Firstar Bank reduced the principal to $1,250,000 rather than $1,550,000. On January 1, 1999, Robinson pays $1,250,000 in cash to Firstar Bank for the principal.

Instructions

(a) Can Robinson Company record a gain under this term modification? If yes, compute the gain for Robinson Company.

(b) Prepare the journal entries to record the gain on Robinson's books.

(c) What interest rate should Robinson use to compute its interest expense in future periods? Will your answer be the same as in E14-21 above? Why or why not?

(d) Prepare the interest payment schedule of the note for Robinson Company after the debt restructuring.

(e) Prepare the interest payment entries for Robinson Company on December 31 of 1996, 1997, and 1998.

(f) What entry should Robinson make on January 1, 1999?

*E14-24 (Term Modification with Gain—Creditor's Entries) Using the same information as in E14-21 and E14-23 above, answer the following questions related to Firstar Bank (creditor).

Instructions

(a) Compute the loss Firstar Bank will suffer under this new term modification. Prepare the journal entry to record the loss on Firstar's books.

(b) Prepare the interest receipt schedule for Firstar Bank after the debt restructuring.

(c) Prepare the interest receipt entry for Firstar Bank on December 31, 1996, 1997, and 1998.

(d) What entry should Firstar Bank make on January 1, 1999?

*E14-25 (Debtor/Creditor Entries for Settlement of Troubled Debt) Toshiba Co. owes $199,800 to Zimmer Inc. The debt is a 10-year, 11% note. Because Toshiba Co. is in financial trouble, Zimmer Inc. agrees to accept

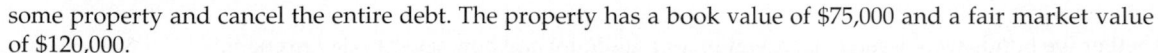

some property and cancel the entire debt. The property has a book value of $75,000 and a fair market value of $120,000.

Instructions

   (a) Prepare the journal entry on Toshiba's books for debt restructure.

   (b) Prepare the journal entry on Zimmer's books for debt restructure.

*E14-26 (Debtor/Creditor Entries for Modification of Troubled Debt) Eaton Corp. owes $224,000 to First Trust. The debt is a 10-year, 12% note due December 31, 1995. Because Eaton Corp. is in financial trouble, First Trust agrees to extend the maturity date to December 31, 1997, reduce the principal to $200,000, and reduce the interest rate to 5%, payable annually on December 31.

Instructions

   (a) Prepare the journal entries on Eaton's books on December 31, 1995, 1996, 1997.

   (b) Prepare the journal entries on First Trust's books on December 31, 1995, 1996, 1997.

*E14-27 (Impairments) On December 31, 1994, D. Honan Company borrowed $62,092 from Kinney Bank, signing a 5-year, $100,000 noninterest bearing note. The note was issued to yield 10% interest. Unfortunately, during 1996, Honan began to experience financial difficulty. As a result, at December 31, 1996, Kinney Bank determined that is was probable that it would receive back only $80,000 at maturity. The market rate of interest on loans of this nature is now 11%.

Instructions

   (a) Prepare the entry to record the issuance of the loan by Kinney Bank on December 31, 1994.

   (b) Prepare the entry (if any) to record the impairment of the loan on December 31, 1996 by Kinney Bank.

   (c) Prepare the entry (if any) to record the impairment of the loan on December 31, 1996 by Honan Company.

*E14-28 (Impairments) On December 31, 1993, American Realty Company signed a $1,000,000 note to Sauk City Bank. The market interest rate at that time was 12%. The stated interest rate on the note was 10%, payable annually. The note matures in 5 years. Unfortunately, because of lower sales, American Realty's financial situation worsened. On December 31, 1995, Sauk City Bank determined that it was probable that the company would pay back only $700,000 of the principal at maturity. However, it was considered likely that interest would continue to be paid, based on the $1,000,000 loan.

Instructions

   (a) Determine the amount of cash American Realty received from the loan on December 31, 1993.

   (b) Prepare a note amortization schedule for Sauk City Bank up to December 31, 1995.

   (c) Determine the loss on impairment that Sauk City Bank should recognize on December 31, 1995.

PROBLEMS

P14-1 (Analysis of Amortization Schedule and Interest Entries) The following amortization and interest schedule reflects the issuance of 10-year bonds by Roadmaster Corporation on January 1, 1988, and the subsequent interest payments and charges. The company's year-end is December 31, and financial statements are prepared once yearly.

AMORTIZATION SCHEDULE

Year	Cash	Interest	Amount Unamortized	Book Value
1/1/88			$5,651	$ 94,349
1988	$11,000	$11,322	5,329	94,671
1989	11,000	11,361	4,968	95,032
1990	11,000	11,404	4,564	95,436
1991	11,000	11,452	4,112	95,888
1992	11,000	11,507	3,605	96,395
1993	11,000	11,567	3,038	96,962
1994	11,000	11,635	2,403	97,597
1995	11,000	11,712	1,691	98,309
1996	11,000	11,797	894	99,106
1997	11,000	11,894		100,000

Instructions

(a) Indicate whether the bonds were issued at a premium or a discount and how you can determine this fact from the schedule.

(b) Indicate whether the amortization schedule is based on the straight-line method or the effective interest method and how you can determine which method is used.

(c) Determine the stated interest rate and the effective interest rate.

(d) On the basis of the schedule above, prepare the journal entry to record the issuance of the bonds on January 1, 1988.

(e) On the basis of the schedule above, prepare the journal entry or entries to reflect the bond transactions and accruals for 1988.

(f) On the basis of the schedule above, prepare the journal entry or entries to reflect the bond transactions and accruals for 1995.

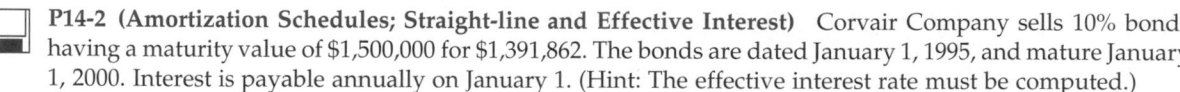 **P14-2 (Amortization Schedules; Straight-line and Effective Interest)** Corvair Company sells 10% bonds having a maturity value of $1,500,000 for $1,391,862. The bonds are dated January 1, 1995, and mature January 1, 2000. Interest is payable annually on January 1. (Hint: The effective interest rate must be computed.)

Instructions

(a) Set up a schedule of interest expense and discount amortization under the straight-line method.

(b) Set up a schedule of interest expense and discount amortization under the effective interest method.

P14-3 (Entries for Bonds Issued at Discount; Bond Issued at Par with Premium at Maturity Provision) In 1995, Riviera Co. was considering the issuance of bonds as of January 1, 1996, as follows:

Plan 1:

$2,000,000 par value 11%, first mortgage, 20-year bonds, due Dec. 31, 2015, at 95, with interest payable annually, or

Plan 2:

$2,000,000 par value 11%, first mortgage, 20-year bonds, due Dec. 31, 2015, at 100, with provision for payment of a 5% ($100,000) premium at maturity, interest payable annually.

Costs of issue such as printing and lawyers' fees may be ignored for the purpose of answering this question. Discount and premium are to be allocated to accounting periods on a straight-line basis.

Instructions

Give two separate sets of journal entries with appropriate explanations showing the accounting treatment that the foregoing bond issues would necessitate, respectively:

(a) At time of issue.

(b) Yearly thereafter.

(c) On payment at date of maturity.

P14-4 (Issuance and Retirement of Bonds; Income Statement Presentation) Eldorado Company issued its 9%, 25-year mortgage bonds in the principal amount of $5,000,000 on January 2, 1981, at a discount of $200,000, which it proceeded to amortize by charges to expense over the life of the issue on a straight-line basis. The indenture securing the issue provided that the bonds could be called for redemption in total but not in part at any time before maturity at 104% of the principal amount, but it did not provide for any sinking fund.

On December 18, 1995, the company issued its 11%, 20-year debenture bonds in the principal amount of $6,000,000 at 101, and the proceeds were used to redeem the 9%, 25-year mortgage bonds on January 2, 1996. The indenture securing the new issue did not provide for any sinking fund or for retirement before maturity.

Instructions

(a) Prepare journal entries to record the issuance of the 11% bonds and the retirement of the 9% bonds.

(b) Indicate the income statement treatment of the gain or loss from retirement and the note disclosure required. Assume 1996 income before extraordinary items of $3,200,000, a weighted number of shares outstanding of 1,500,000, and an income tax rate of 40%.

P14-5 (Comprehensive Bond Problem) In each of the following independent cases the company closes its books on December 31.

1. Brougham Co. sells $250,000 of 10% bonds on March 1, 1995. The bonds pay interest on September 1 and March 1. The due date of the bonds is September 1, 1998. The bonds yield 12%. Give entries through December 31, 1996.

2. Biarritz Co. sells $600,000 of 12% bonds on June 1, 1995. The bonds pay interest on December 1 and June 1. The due date of the bonds is June 1, 1999. The bonds yield 10%. On September 1, 1996, Biarritz buys back $120,000 worth of bonds for $126,000 (includes accrued interest). Give entries through December 1, 1997.

Instructions
(Round to the nearest dollar.)
For the two cases above prepare all of the relevant journal entries from the time of sale until the date indicated. Use the effective interest method for discount and premium amortization (construct amortization tables where applicable). Amortize premium or discount on interest dates and at year-end. (Assume that no reversing entries were made.)

P14-6 (Issuance of Bonds Between Interest Dates, Straight-line, Retirement) Presented below are selected transactions on the books of FleetLine Powerglide Corporation.

May 1, 1995	Bonds payable with a par value of $700,000, which are dated January 1, 1995, are sold at 105 plus accrued interest. They are coupon bonds, bear interest at 12% (payable annually at January 1), and mature January 1, 2005. (Use interest expense account for accrued interest.)
Dec. 31	Adjusting entries are made to record the accrued interest on the bonds, and the amortization of the proper amount of premium. (Use straight-line amortization.)
Jan. 1, 1996	Interest on the bonds is paid.
April 1	Bonds of par value of $420,000 are purchased at 102 plus accrued interest, and retired. (Bond premium is to be amortized only at the end of each year.)
Dec. 31	Adjusting entries are made to record the accrued interest on the bonds, and the proper amount of premium amortized.

Instructions
Prepare journal entries for the transactions above.

P14-7 (Entries for Life Cycle of Bonds) On April 1, 1995, Impala Company sold 12,000 of its 12%, 15-year, $1,000 face value bonds at 97. Interest payment dates are April 1 and October 1, and the company uses the straight-line method of bond discount amortization. On March 1, 1996, Impala took advantage of favorable prices of its stock to extinguish 3,000 of the bonds by issuing 100,000 shares of its $10 par value common stock. At this time, the accrued interest was paid in cash. The company's stock was selling for $31 per share on March 1, 1996.

Instructions
Prepare the journal entries needed on the books of Impala Company to record the following:
 (a) April 1, 1995: issuance of the bonds.
 (b) October 1, 1995: payment of semiannual interest.
 (c) December 31, 1995: accrual of interest expense.
 (d) March 1, 1996: extinguishment of 3,000 bonds. (No reversing entries made.)

P14-8 (Analysis of Amortization Schedule, Issue Costs; Retirement) On January 1, 1993, Malibu Co. sold $150,000 (face value) of bonds. The bonds are dated January 1, 1993, and will mature on January 1, 1998. Interest is paid annually on December 31. The bonds are callable after December 31, 1995, at 101. Issue costs related to these bonds amounted to $3,000, and these costs are being amortized by the straight-line method. The following amortization schedule was prepared by the accountant for the first 2 years of the life of the bonds:

Date	Cash	Interest	Amortization	Carrying Value of Bonds
1/ 1/93				$139,186
12/31/93	$15,000	$16,702	$1,702	140,888
12/31/94	15,000	16,907	1,907	142,795

Instructions
On the basis of the information above, answer the following questions (round your answers to the nearest dollar or percent):
 (a) What is the nominal or stated rate of interest for this bond issue?
 (b) What is the effective or market rate of interest for this bond issue?
 (c) Present the journal entry to record the sale of the bond issue, including the issue costs.
 (d) Present the appropriate entry(ies) at December 31, 1995.
 (e) Present the disclosure of this bond issue on the December 31, 1995, balance sheet. Proper balance sheet subheadings must be indicated.
 (f) On June 30, 1996, $100,000 of the bond issue was redeemed at the call price. Present the journal entry for this redemption. Amortization of the discount is recorded only at the end of the year.
 (g) Present the effects of the bond redemption on the 1996 income statement and proper note disclosure. Proper income statement subheadings must be indicated. The income tax rate is 40%; 1996 income before extraordinary items is $30,000 with a weighted number of common shares outstanding during the year of 10,000. Working capital funds were used to redeem the bonds.

P14-9 (Entries for Life Cycle of Bonds—Trustee Pays Interest) Here are transactions of Crosley Hotshot Company:

Jan. 1, 1995	Bonds payable (coupon bonds) in the amount of $1,500,000, and bearing interest at the rate of 10% payable semiannually on January 1 and July 1, due January 1, 2011, are issued at 96.
June 15	The First Bank and Trust Co. has been engaged as trustee to handle the payment of interest to individual bondholders. A check for the interest due July 1, 1995, is sent to the trustee.
30	Record the interest expense for the first 6 months of 1995. Bond discount is to be amortized only at the end of each year and by the straight-line method.
July 20	The trustee returns to the company canceled interest coupons paid in the amount of $68,000 and reports that trustee's expenses charged against the account amounted to $645.
Dec. 15	A check for the interest due January 1, 1996, and for reported expenses is sent to the trustee.
31	Record the interest expense for the 6 months ended December 31, and amortize the proper amount of discount for the year.
Jan. 21, 1996	The trustee returns to the company canceled interest coupons paid in the amount of $73,000.
Mar. 1	Bonds of par value of $200,000 are bought on the market at 95 plus accrued interest, and retired. All interest coupons dated before July 1, 1996, have been removed.

Instructions
   (a) Prepare entries in journal form on the books of Crosley Co. for the transactions given above.
   (b) What will be the amount of the check to the trustee for the interest for the first 6 months of 1996?
   (c) What will be the amount of the discount amortized on December 31, 1996?

P14-10 (Account Balances When Trustee Pays Interest) Crest Liner Company issued 10-year coupon bonds in the amount of $2,000,000 on July 1, 1994. They were issued at par and bear interest at 12%, payable semiannually on July 1 and January 1. The Ford State Bank is to act as trustee to handle the payment of interest.

On December 10, 1994, Crest Liner Company sent the Ford State Bank a check for the interest due January 1, 1995, none of which was paid to bondholders before January 1, 1995.

Instructions
   (a) What balances will be shown in the ledger of Crest Liner Company on December 31, 1994, relating to the bonds and the interest on the bonds? How will these balances be shown in the financial statements? Establish a fund account for the trustee payment.
   (b) Assume that in 1995 Crest Liner Company sends the Ford State Bank checks for the interest due July 1, 1995, and January 1, 1996, and that the Ford State Bank returns to the company canceled interest coupons in the amount of $205,000. Crest Liner Company sent the Ford State Bank a check for $2,000 to cover the trustee expenses.
      What balances will be shown in the ledger of Crest Liner Company on December 31, 1995, relating to the bonds and the interest on the bonds? How will these balances be shown in financial statements?

P14-11 (Entries for Noninterest-Bearing Debt) On December 31, 1995, Falcon Company acquired a computer from Galaxie Corporation by issuing a $400,000 noninterest-bearing note, payable in full on December 31, 1999. Falcon Company's credit rating permits it to borrow funds from its several lines of credit at 10%. The computer is expected to have a 5-year life and a $40,000 salvage value.

Instructions
   (a) Prepare the journal entry for the purchase on December 31, 1995.
   (b) Prepare any necessary adjusting entries relative to depreciation (use straight-line) and amortization (use effective interest method) on December 31, 1996.
   (c) Prepare any necessary adjusting entries relative to depreciation and amortization on December 31, 1997.

P14-12 (Entries for Noninterest-Bearing Debt; Payable in Installments) Electia Cosmetics Co. purchased machinery on December 31, 1994, paying $10,000 down and agreeing to pay the balance in four equal installments of $30,000 payable each December 31. An assumed interest of 12% is implicit in the purchase price.

Instructions
Prepare the journal entries that would be recorded for the purchase and for the payments and interest on the following dates:
   (a) December 31, 1994.
   (b) December 31, 1995.
   (c) December 31, 1996.
   (d) December 31, 1997.
   (e) December 31, 1998.

P14-13 (Comprehensive Problem; Issuance, Classification, Defeasance, Reporting) Presented below are five independent situations:
   (a) On March 1, 1996, Invicta Co. issued at 104 plus accrued interest $3,000,000, 9% bonds. The bonds are dated January 1, 1996, and pay interest semiannually on July 1 and January 1. In addition, Invicta

Co. incurred $27,000 of bond issuance costs. Compute the net amount of cash received by Invicta Co. as a result of the issuance of these bonds.

(b) On January 1, 1995, Lesabre Co. issued 9% bonds with a face value of $500,000 for $469,280 to yield 10%. The bonds are dated January 1, 1995, and pay interest annually. What amount is reported for interest expense in 1995 related to these bonds, assuming that Lesabre used the effective interest method for amortizing bond premium and discount?

(c) Wildcat Building Co. has a number of long-term bonds outstanding at December 31, 1996. These long-term bonds have the following sinking fund requirements and maturities for the next 6 years.

	Sinking Fund	Maturities
1997	$100,000	$100,000
1998	200,000	250,000
1999	300,000	100,000
2000	200,000	—
2001	200,000	150,000
2002	200,000	100,000

Indicate how this information should be reported in the financial statements at December 31, 1996.

(d) Centurion Co. on February 1, 1993, issued at 98 plus accrued interest, 12%, $4,000,000 face amount, 10-year bonds. The bonds are dated November 1, 1992, and interest is payable on May 1 and November 1. On May 1, 1996, Centurion decided to defease this debt because interest rates had risen, and the bonds are defeased at a cost of $3,650,000. Ignoring the income tax effect, at what amount and where would Centurion's defeasance be reported on the financial statements? (Use straight-line amortization.)

(e) In the long-term debt structure of Skylark Inc., the following three bonds were reported: mortgage bonds payable $10,000,000; collateral trust bonds $5,000,000; bonds maturing in installments, secured by plant equipment $4,000,000. Determine the total amount, if any, of debenture bonds outstanding.

P14-14 (Comprehensive Liability Problem; Balance Sheet Presentation) DeVille Inc. has been producing quality children's apparel for more than 25 years. The company's fiscal year runs from April 1 to March 31. The following information relates to the obligations of DeVille as of March 31, 1996.

Bonds Payable
DeVille issued $5,000,000 of 11% bonds on July 1, 1990 at 96 which yielded proceeds of $4,800,000. The bonds will mature on July 1, 2000. Interest is paid semiannually on July 1 and January 1. DeVille uses the straight-line method to amortize the bond discount.

Notes Payable
DeVille has signed several long-term notes with financial institutions and insurance companies. The maturities of these notes are given in the schedule below. The total unpaid interest for all of these notes amounts to $210,000 on March 31, 1996.

Due Date	Amount Due
April 1, 1996	$ 200,000
July 1, 1996	150,000
October 1, 1996	150,000
January 1, 1997	150,000
April 1, 1997–March 31, 1998	500,000
April 1, 1998–March 31, 1999	500,000
April 1, 1999–March 31, 2000	700,000
April 1, 2000–March 31, 2001	400,000
April 1, 2001–March 31, 2002	500,000
	$3,250,000

Estimated Warranties
DeVille has a one-year product warranty on some selected items in its product line. The estimated warranty liability on sales made during the 1994–95 fiscal year and still outstanding as of March 31, 1995 amounted to $84,000. The warranty costs on sales made from April 1, 1995 through March 31, 1996 are estimated at $200,000. The actual warranty costs incurred during the current 1995–96 fiscal year are as follows:

Warranty claims honored on 1994–95 sales	$ 84,000
Warranty claims honored on 1995–96 sales	95,000
Total warranty claims honored	$179,000

Other Information
1. *Trade payables.* Accounts payable for supplies, goods and services purchased on open account amount to $350,000 as of March 31, 1996.

2. *Payroll related items.* Outstanding obligations related to DeVille's payroll as of March 31, 1996 are:

Accrued salaries and wages	$150,000
FICA taxes	18,000
State and federal income taxes withheld from employees	25,000
Other payroll deductions	5,000

3. *Taxes.* The following taxes incurred but not due until the next fiscal year are:

State and federal income taxes	$305,000
Property taxes	125,000
Sales and use taxes	182,000

4. *Miscellaneous accruals.* Other accruals not separately classified amount to $75,000 as of March 31, 1996.
5. *Dividends.* On March 15, 1996 DeVille's Board of Directors declared a cash dividend of $.40 per common share and a 10% common stock dividend. Both dividends were to be distributed on April 12, 1996 to the common stockholders of record at the close of business on March 31, 1996. Data regarding DeVille common stock are as follows:

Par value	$5 per share
Number of shares issued and outstanding	3,000,000 shares
Market values of common stock:	
March 15, 1996	$22.00 per share
March 31, 1996	21.50 per share
April 12, 1996	22.50 per share

Instructions
Prepare the liability section of the balance sheet and appropriate notes to the statement for DeVille Inc. as of March 31, 1996, as they should appear in its annual report to the stockholders.

(CMA adapted)

*P14-15 **(Loan Impairment Entries)** On January 1, 1995, Ashland Company issued a $1,200,000, 5-year, non-interest-bearing note to National Organization Bank. The note was issued to yield 8% annual interest. Unfortunately, during 1996, Ashland fell into financial trouble due to increased competition. After reviewing all available evidence on December 31, 1996, National Organization Bank decided that the loan was impaired. Ashland will probably pay back only $900,000 of the principal at maturity.

Instructions
(a) Prepare journal entries for both Ashland Company and National Organization Bank to record the issuance of the note on January 1, 1995.
(b) Assuming that both Ashland Company and National Organization Bank use the effective interest method to amortize the discount, prepare the amortization schedule for the note.
(c) Under what circumstances can National Organization Bank consider Ashland's note to be "impaired"?
(d) Compute the loss National Organization Bank will suffer from Ashland's financial distress on December 31, 1996. What journal entries should be made to record this loss?
(e) Prepare the amortization schedule for National Organization Bank after the note impairment. What journal entries should National Organization Bank make to record the interest revenue on December 31, 1997?
(f) Prepare the journal entry to record Ashland's payment on January 1, 2000. Assume that the payment is $1,200,000.

*P14-16 **(Debtor/Creditor Entries for Continuation of Troubled Debt)** Mark Covaleski is the sole shareholder of Covaleski Inc., which is currently under protection of the United States bankruptcy court. As a "debtor in possession," he has negotiated the following revised loan agreement with Valley Bank. Covaleski Inc.'s $372,000, 12%, 10-year note was refinanced with a $372,000, 5%, 10-year note.

Instructions
(a) What is the accounting nature of this transaction?
(b) Prepare the journal entry to record this refinancing.
   1. On the books of Covaleski Inc.
   2. On the books of Valley Bank.
(c) Discuss whether generally accepted accounting principles provide the proper information useful to managers and investors in this situation.

*P14-17 **(Restructure of Note Under Different Circumstances)** Downunder Corporation is having financial difficulty and therefore has asked Second National Bank to restructure its $3 million note outstanding. The present note has 3 years remaining and pays a current rate of interest of 10%. The present market rate for a loan of this nature is 12%. The note was issued at its face value.

Instructions

Presented below are four independent situations. Prepare the journal entry that Downunder and Second National Bank would make for each of these restructurings.

(a) Second National Bank agrees to take an equity interest in Downunder by accepting common stock valued at $2,500,000 in exchange for relinquishing its claim on this note. The common stock has a par value of $2,100,000.

(b) Second National Bank agrees to accept land in exchange for relinquishing its claim on this note. The land has a book value of $1,900,000 and a fair value of $2,300,000.

(c) Second National Bank agrees to modify the terms of the note, indicating that Downunder does not have to pay any interest on the note over the 3-year period.

(d) Second National Bank agrees to reduce the principal balance due to $2,500,000 and require interest only in the second and third year at a rate of 10%.

*P14-18 (Debtor/Creditor Entries for Continuation of Troubled Debt) New York Inc. owes Parsons Bank a 10-year, 15% note in the amount of $250,000 plus $37,500 of accrued interest. The note is due today, 12/31/95. Because New York Inc. is in financial trouble, Parsons agrees to accept 60,000 shares of New York's $1.00 par value common stock, which is selling for $1.30, forgive the accrued interest, reduce the face amount of the note to $150,000, extend the maturity date to 12/31/99, and reduce the interest rate to 6%. Interest will continue to be due on December 31 each year.

Instructions

(a) Prepare all the necessary journal entries on the books of New York Inc. from restructure through maturity.

(b) Prepare all the necessary journal entries on the books of Parsons Bank from restructure through maturity.

*P14-19 (Entries for Troubled Debt Restructurings) At December 31, 1994, Menlow Manufacturing Company had outstanding a $300,000, 12% note payable to Janesville National Bank. Dated January 1, 1992, the note was due December 31, 1995, with interest payable each December 31. During 1995 Menlow notified Janesville that it might be unable to meet the scheduled December 31, 1995 payment of principal and interest because of financial difficulties. On September 30, 1995, Janesville sold the note, including interest accrued since December 31, 1994, for $290,000 to Wampum Foundry, one of Menlow's oldest and largest customers. On December 31, 1995, Wampum agreed to accept inventory costing $240,000 and worth $320,000 from Menlow in full settlement of the note.

Instructions

(a) Prepare the journal entry to record the September 30, 1995, transaction on the books of Janesville, Menlow, and Wampum. For each, indicate whether the transaction is a troubled debt restructuring.

(b) Prepare the journal entries to record the December 31, 1995, transaction on the books of Menlow and Wampum. For each, indicate whether the transaction is a troubled debt restructuring.

*P14-20 (Debtor/Creditor Entries for Continuation of Troubled Debt with New Effective Interest) Crooch Corp. owes Jenkins Corp. a 10-year, 10% note in the amount of $220,000 plus $22,000 of accrued interest. The note is due today, December 31, 1995. Because Crooch Corp. is in financial trouble, Jenkins Corp. agrees to forgive the accrued interest, $20,000 of the principal, and to extend the maturity date to December 31, 1998. Interest at 10% of revised principal will continue to be due on 12/31 each year.

Assume the following present value factors for 3 periods:

	2¼%	2⅜%	2½%	2⅝%	2¾%	3%
Single sum	.93543	.93201	.92859	.92521	.92184	.91514
Ord. Annuity of 1	2.86989	2.86295	2.85602	2.84913	2.84226	2.82861

Instructions

(a) Compute the new effective interest rate for Crooch Corp. following restructure. (Hint: Find the interest rate that establishes approximately $242,000 as the present value of the total future cash flows.)

(b) Prepare a schedule of debt reduction and interest expense for the years 1995 through 1998.

(c) Compute Jenkins Corp. gain or loss and prepare a schedule of receivable reduction and interest revenue for the years 1995 through 1998.

(d) Prepare all the necessary journal entries on the books of Crooch Corp. for the years 1995, 1996, and 1997.

(e) Prepare all the necessary journal entries on the books of Jenkins Corp. for the years 1995, 1996, and 1997.

CASES

C14-1 (Bond Theory: Balance Sheet Presentations, Interest Rate, Premium) On January 1, 1996, Placido Company issued for $1,075,230 its 20-year, 13% bonds that have a maturity value of $1,000,000 and pay interest semiannually on January 1 and July 1. Bond issue costs were not material in amount. Below are three presentations of the long-term liability section of the balance sheet that might be used for these bonds at the issue date:

1.	Bonds payable (maturing January 1, 2016)	$1,000,000
	Unamortized premium on bonds payable	75,230
	Total bond liability	$1,075,230

2.	Bonds payable—principal (face value $1,000,000 maturing January 1, 2016)	$ 97,220[a]
	Bonds payable—interest (semiannual payment $65,000)	978,010[b]
	Total bond liability	$1,075,230

3.	Bonds payable—principal (maturing January 1, 2016)	$1,000,000
	Bonds payable—interest ($65,000 per period for 40 periods)	2,600,000
	Total bond liability	$3,600,000

[a]The present value of $1,000,000 due at the end of 40 (6-month) periods at the yield rate of 6% per period.
[b]The present value of $65,000 per period for 40 (6-month) periods at the yield rate of 6% per period.

Instructions
(a) Discuss the conceptual merit(s) of each of the date-of-issue balance sheet presentations shown above for these bonds.
(b) Explain why investors would pay $1,075,230 for bonds that have a maturity value of only $1,000,000.
(c) Assuming that a discount rate is needed to compute the carrying value of the obligations arising from a bond issue at any date during the life of the bonds, discuss the conceptual merit(s) of using for this purpose:
   1. The coupon or nominal rate.
   2. The effective or yield rate at date of issue.
(d) If the obligations arising from these bonds are to be carried at their present value computed by means of the current market rate of interest, how would the bond valuation at dates subsequent to the date of issue be affected by an increase or a decrease in the market rate of interest?

(AICPA adapted)

C14-2 (Various Long-Term Liability Conceptual Issues) The Elly Ameling Company has completed a number of transactions during 1995. In January the company purchased under contract a machine at a total price of $1,000,000, payable over 5 years with installments of $200,000 per year. The seller has considered the transaction as an installment sale with the title transferring to Ameling at the time of the final payment.

On March 1, 1995, Ameling issued $10 million of general revenue bonds priced at 99 with a coupon of 10% payable July 1 and January 1 of each of the next 10 years. The July 1 interest was paid and on December 30 the company transferred $1,000,000 to the trustee, La Scala Trust Company, for payment of the January 1, 1996, interest.

Due to the depressed market for the company's stock, Ameling purchased $500,000 par value of their 6% convertible bonds for a price of $450,000. They expect to resell the bonds when the price of their stock has recovered.

As the accountant for Elly Ameling Company, you have prepared the balance sheet as of December 31, 1995, and have presented it to the president of the company. You are asked the following questions about it:
1. Why has depreciation been charged on equipment being purchased under contract? Title has not passed to the company as yet and, therefore, they are not our assets. Why should the company not show on the left side of the balance sheet only the amount paid to date instead of showing the full contract price on the left side and the unpaid portion on the right side? After all the seller considers the transaction an installment sale.
2. What is bond discount? As a debit balance, why is it not classified among the assets?
3. Bond interest is shown as a current liability. Did we not pay our trustee, La Scala Trust Company, the full amount of interest due this period?
4. Treasury bonds are shown as a deduction from bonds payable issued. Why should they not be shown as an asset, since they can be sold again? Are they the same as bonds of other companies that we hold as investments?

Instructions
Outline your answers to these questions by writing a brief paragraph that will justify your treatment.

C14-3 (Effect of Market Condition on Bond Issue) The following article appeared in *The Wall Street Journal:*

Bond Markets

Giant Commonwealth Edison Issue Hits Resale Market With $70 Million Left Over

NEW YORK—Commonwealth Edison Co.'s slow-selling new 9¼% bonds were tossed onto the resale market at a reduced price with about $70 million still available from the $200 million offered Thursday, dealers said.

The Chicago utility's bonds, rated double-A by Moody's and double-A-minus by Standard & Poor's, originally had been priced at 99.803, to yield 9.3% in 5 years. They were marked down yesterday the equivalent of about $5.50 for each $1,000 face amount, to about 99.25, where their yield jumped to 9.45%.

Instructions

    (a) How will the development above affect the accounting for Commonwealth Edison's bond issue?

    (b) Provide several possible explanations for the markdown and the slow sale of Commonwealth Edison's bonds.

C14-4 (Bond Theory: Price, Presentation, and Retirement) On March 1, 1996, Pavarotti Company sold its 5-year, $1,000 face value, 9% bonds dated March 1, 1996, at an effective annual interest rate (yield) of 11%. Interest is payable semiannually, and the first interest payment date is September 1, 1996. Pavarotti uses the interest method of amortization. Bond issue costs were incurred in preparing and selling the bond issue. The bonds can be called by Pavarotti at 101 at any time on or after March 1, 1997.

Instructions

    (a)   **1.** How would the selling price of the bond be determined?

           2. Specify how all items related to the bonds would be presented in a balance sheet prepared immediately after the bond issue was sold.

    (b) What items related to the bond issue would be included in Pavarotti's 1996 income statement, and how would each be determined?

    (c) Would the amount of bond discount amortization using the effective interest method of amortization be lower in the second or third year of the life of the bond issue? Why?

    (d) Assuming that the bonds were called in and retired on March 1, 1997, how should Pavarotti report the retirement of the bonds on the 1997 income statement?

                                                                (AICPA adapted)

C14-5 (Bond Theory: Amortization and Gain or Loss Recognition) **Part I.** The appropriate method of amortizing a premium or discount on issuance of bonds is the effective interest method.

Instructions

    (a) What is the effective interest method of amortization and how is it different from and similar to the straight-line method of amortization?

    (b) How is amortization computed using the effective interest method, and why and how do amounts obtained using the effective interest method differ from amounts computed under the straight-line method?

Part II. Gains or losses from the early extinguishment of debt that is refunded can theoretically be accounted for in three ways:

    1. Amortized over remaining life of old debt.

    2. Amortized over the life of the new debt issue.

    3. Recognized in the period of extinguishment.

Instructions

    (a) Develop supporting arguments for each of the three theoretical methods of accounting for gains and losses from the early extinguishment of debt.

    (b) Which of the methods above is generally accepted and how should the appropriate amount of gain or loss be shown in a company's financial statements?

                                                                  (AICPA adapted)

C14-6 (Defeasance of Bonds) Tannhauser is a Delaware corporation with its corporate offices located in Connecticut. Tannhauser's products are sold throughout the United States and in Western Europe through a sales office in Germany.

Tannhauser issued a $20 million, 15-year bond on December 1, 1996, that will mature in 10 years. The bonds have an interest rate of 9⅞%, meaning that Tannhauser's interest payments on this issue total $1,975,000 annually.

Richard Wagner, Tannhauser's Vice-President of Finance, would like to remove this debt from Tannhauser's Statement of Financial Position because of the high interest rate. He knows that he can accomplish this through in-substance defeasance of debt but that he must comply with *Statement of Financial Accounting Standards (SFAS) No. 76,* ''Extinguishment of Debt.''

International Bank is the clearing agent for the 1996 bond issue. Birgit Nilsson, the bank representative assigned to Tannhauser's account, has approached Wagner with a financing proposal. International could obtain, on Tannhauser's behalf, a 10-year, $26 million, 5½% long-term note from a bank in Germany. The proceeds from this loan could then be used to purchase $26 million of 10-year, U.S. treasury notes at an annual interest rate of 7.9% to yield $2,054,000 in annual interest income. The timing of the interest payments from the treasury notes would satisfy the time schedule and fees of the 1996 bond issue.

Instructions

(a) Explain in general terms what is meant by in-substance defeasance of debt.

(b) Richard Wagner believes that he can use in-substance defeasance of debt to remove the 1996 bond issue from Tannhauser's Statement of Financial Position. He also believes that Birgit Nilsson's proposal will satisfy the requirements of *SFAS No. 76*.

    1. Explain why the 1996 bond issue qualifies for in-substance defeasance of debt.

    2. Explain why Nilsson's proposal satisfies the requirements of in-substance defeasance of debt.

    3. Explain what additional steps or procedures that are not mentioned in the situation, if any, that Wagner must take to assure that the in-substance defeasance of debt proposal will comply with *SFAS No. 76*.

(c) Are there any debt instruments, other than debt similar to Tannhauser's 1996 bond issue, that qualify for in-substance defeasance of debt? Explain your answer.

(d) Explain what financial disclosures must be made in Tannhauser's financial statements regarding in-substance defeasance of debt in the

    1. year that the transaction takes place.

    2. years subsequent to the transaction year.

(CMA adapted)

C14-7 (In-Substance Defeasance) Following is a footnote prepared by Domingo Corporation for its 1995 annual report:

> On December 30, 1995, the Bank entered into agreements with a trustee which facilitated in-substance defeasance of the 5% and 5¼% capital note issues.
>
> On December 30, 1995, U.S. Government securities costing $10,063,000 were deposited in an irrevocable trust, the principal and interest of which will be sufficient to pay the scheduled principal and interest on the 5% and 5¼% capital note issues of the Bank. Proceeds from the sale of certain short-term liquid assets of the Bank were used to purchase these securities. The 5% capital notes require principal payments of $500,000 on January 1 in each of the years 1996 through 2000 and the balance of $7,500,000 in 2001. The 5¼% capital notes require principal payments of $262,500 in each of the years 1996 through 2002 and the balance of $1,750,000 due in 2003. Interest on both issues is payable on January 1, and July 1 of each year that the notes remain outstanding. In December 1995, the Bank prepaid the principal and interest payments on both issues due January 1, 1996.
>
> The Corporation recognized a gain calculated as the excess of the current principal outstanding on the note issues over the cost of the securities placed in the defeasance trusts, plus related trustee costs. The gain on the in-substance defeasance of both note issues of $2,732,000 equivalent to a gain of $0.57 per common share, is presented in the Corporation's consolidated statement of income as an extraordinary gain.

Instructions

    1. What is in-substance defeasance?

    2. Discuss alternative accounting methods that might be used for this type of transaction.

    3. What is the treatment under GAAP?

C14-8 (Off-Balance Sheet Financing) The HeartLand Sparkle Corporation is interested in building its own soda can manufacturing plant adjacent to its existing plant in Partyville, Kansas. The objective would be to ensure a steady supply of cans at a stable price and to minimize transportation costs. However, the company has been experiencing some financial problems and has been reluctant to borrow any additional cash to fund the project. The company is not concerned with the cash flow problems of making payments, but rather with the impact of adding additional long-term debt to their balance sheet.

The president of HeartLand, Bill Crawford, approached the president of the Aluminum Can Company (ACC), their major supplier, to see if some agreement could be reached. ACC was anxious to work out an arrangement, since it seemed inevitable that HeartLand would begin their own can production. The Aluminum Can Company could not afford to lose the account.

After some discussion a two part plan was worked out. First ACC was to construct the plant on HeartLand's land adjacent to the existing plant. Second, HeartLand would sign a 20-year purchase agreement. Under the purchase agreement, HeartLand would express its intention to buy all of its cans from ACC, paying a unit price which at normal capacity would cover labor and material, an operating management fee, and the debt service requirements on the plant. The expected unit price, if transportation costs are taken into consideration, is lower than current market. If HeartLand did not take enough production in any one year and if the excess cans could not be sold at a high enough price on the open market, HeartLand agrees to make up any cash shortfall so that ACC could make the payments on its debt. The bank will be willing to make a 20-year loan for the plant, taking the plant and the purchase agreement as collateral. At the end of 20 years the plant is to become the property of HeartLand.

Instructions

1. What are project financing arrangements?
2. What are take-or-pay contracts?
3. What conditions must be met in order for a contractual obligation to be disclosed as an unconditional purchase obligation?
4. Should HeartLand record the plant as an asset together with the related obligation?
5. If not, should HeartLand record an asset relating to the future commitment?
6. What is meant by off-balance-sheet financing?

*C14-9 (Restructured Debt) Chrysis Corp. has recently fallen into financial difficulties. To help Chrysis avert bankruptcy, two creditors of Chrysis have agreed to restructure the terms of some loans they have made to the company.

First National Bank has agreed to accept 80,000 shares of Chrysis common stock in full payment of a $1,000,000 loan due in 5 years from Chrysis. The interest terms of the loan are 10% per year. Chrysis common stock has recently been trading for $11 per share. Its par value is $10.

Mr. Audrey, controller of First National, intends to record the transaction as follows:

Investment in Chrysis Common	1,000,000	
10% Loan Receivable from Chrysis		1,000,000

This would imply that Chrysis should record the transaction in this manner:

10% Loan payable to First National	1,000,000	
Common Stock		800,000
Paid-In Capital in Excess of Par		200,000

Chrysis, however, has a different view. Lee Cocamocha, controller at Chrysis, is desperate for any sweeteners he can find to improve the financial statements of Chrysis. He would like to record the transaction as follows:

10% Loan Payable to First National	1,000,000	
Common Stock		800,000
Paid-In Capital in Excess of Par		80,000
Gain on Restructuring of Loan		120,000

If Mr. Cocamocha's view is correct, this would mean that the bank should record the transaction as below:

Investment in Chrysis Stock	880,000	
Loss on Restructuring of Loan	120,000	
10% Loan Receivable from Chrysis		1,000,000

Mr. Cocamocha likes this approach because of the gain it produces. Naturally, Mr. Audrey does not favor this method because of the loss which the bank must show.

Southeast Bank has also given Chrysis a break. Chrysis owes Southeast Bank $2,000,000, payable in 10 years. The interest rate on this loan is 10%. Southeast, wishing to minimize its losses, has agreed to reduce the interest rate to 5% per year.

Mr. Walters, Southeast's controller, sees no need for making any journal entries to record this deal. Since Chrysis still owes $2,000,000 he feels that there is no need for a writedown of this loan and a recognition of a loss. Likewise, he would see no need for a journal entry on the books of Chrysis in recognition of this event.

Mr. Cocamocha, however, would not do it this way. He points out that the present value of Chrysis's restructured obligations to Southeast (discounted at the original 10% interest rate) is considerably less than the present value of the obligation before the interest rate was reduced. He feels that this provides a basis for recognition of a gain by Chrysis. He would record the transaction as follows:

10% Loan Payable to Southeast	2,000,000	
Discount on 5% Loan Payable to Southeast	614,463	
5% Loan Payable to Southeast		2,000,000
Gain on Restructuring of Debt		614,463

Thus he would carry the restructured debt at $1,385,537 (face value less discount). His calculations were as follows:

Present value of principal ($2,000,000 received 10 years from now)	$ 771,080
Present value of interest ($100,000 per year for 10 years)	614,457
Total present value of loan (using a 10% discount rate above)	$1,385,537

If we accept this view, then the bank's entry would look like this:

5% Loan Receivable from Chrysis	2,000,000	
Loss on Restructuring of Loan	614,463	
10% Loan Receivable from Chrysis		2,000,000
Discount on 5% Loan Receivable		614,463

Instructions

(a) What are some arguments that First National and Chrysis would use to support their respective views of the first restructuring? Which is the correct method, according to GAAP?

(b) What are some of the arguments that you would expect from Southeast and Chrysis to support their respective views of the second restructuring agreement? Which method is correct, according to GAAP?

(c) How would the debtor and the creditor present the appropriate gains or losses, if any, in their financial statements?

▶ USING YOUR JUDGMENT ◀

▶ FINANCIAL REPORTING PROBLEM

Refer to the financial statements and other documents of Georgia-Pacific Corporation presented in Appendix 5-A and answer the following questions.

1. What is the difference among term bonds, serial bonds, mortgage bonds, collateral trust bonds, debentures, registered bonds, and bearer bonds?

2. Speculate as to why certain debt is classified as current even though it is expected to be refinanced on a long-term basis in the near future.

3. In 1993, Georgia-Pacific's total debt to capital ratio is 57% and its current ratio is 0.8. Should these ratios be a concern to its investors and creditors? Why?

4. As indicated in the Notes to Financial Statements, Georgia-Pacific faces certain restrictive covenants in the credit agreement with its lending banks. What is the major limit in the agreement regarding Georgia-Pacific's indebtedness? Where is Georgia-Pacific's indebtedness relative to this restriction?

5. At December 31, 1993, Georgia-Pacific had outstanding interest rate exchange agreements (interest rate swaps). What was the amount of debt affected by these agreements? What are the terms in these agreements? Why might Georgia-Pacific be involved in these types of transactions?

▶ WRITING ASSIGNMENT

Candy Paul, an intermediate accounting student, is having difficulty amortizing bond premiums and discounts using the effective interest method. Furthermore, she cannot understand why the accountancy profession prefers that this method be used instead of the straight-line method. She has come to you with the following problem, looking for help.

On June 30, 1995, Oregon Company issued $3,000,000 face value of 13%, 20-year bonds at $3,225,690, a yield of 12%. Oregon uses the effective interest method to amortize bond premiums or discounts. The bonds pay semiannual interest on June 30 and December 31. Compute the amortization schedule for four periods.

Instructions

Write a short paper (1–1.5 pages double-spaced) to Candy, explaining what the effective interest method is, why it is preferable, and how it is computed. As an illustration, use the data from the foregoing problem. (Do not forget to include an amortization schedule, referring to it whenever necessary.)

▶ GROUP ASSIGNMENT

GA14-1 Use the data provided in P14-14 for this group project. Your instructor will assign one group member to serve as a recorder and one member to serve as spokesperson. As a group, provide the information for the recorder to prepare the liability section of the balance sheet and appropriate notes to the statement for DeVille Inc. as of March 31, 1996, as they should appear in its annual report to the stockholders. Upon completion, the spokesperson will report the group findings to the class and be prepared to provide justification for your solution.

(CMA adapted)

GA14-2 Use the data in P14-8 to work this group project. Your instructor will assign one group member to serve as a recorder and one member to serve as spokesperson. As a group, provide the information for the recorder to prepare responses for each of the requirements below. (You may wish to divide the parts among the members.) Upon completion, the spokesperson will report the group findings to the class and be prepared to show supporting computations in good form (round answers to the nearest dollar or percent).

- **(a)** What is the nominal or stated rate of interest for this bond issue?
- **(b)** What is the effective or market rate of interest for this bond issue?
- **(c)** Present the journal entry to record the sale of the bond issue, including the issue costs.
- **(d)** Present the appropriate entry(ies) at December 31, 1995.
- **(e)** Present the disclosure of this bond issue on the December 31, 1995, balance sheet. Proper balance sheet subheadings must be indicated.
- **(f)** On June 30, 1996, $100,000 of the bond issue was redeemed at the call price. Present the journal entry for this redemption. Amortization of the discount is recorded only at the end of the year.
- **(g)** Present the effects of the bond redemption on the 1996 income statement and proper note disclosure. Proper income statement subheadings must be indicated. The income tax rate is 40%; 1996 income before extraordinary items is $30,000 with a weighted number of common shares outstanding during the year of 10,000. Working capital funds were used to redeem the bonds.

▶ ETHICS CASE

(In-substance defeasance and off-balance sheet financing) In-substance defeasance allows a company to remove debt from the balance sheet as long as it places risk-free securities or cash in an irrevocable trust, such that these new assets will be used to satisfy the full value of the original debt. Following this accounting rule, Exxon was permitted to remove $515 million of its bonds payable by placing only $313 million of government securities in an irrevocable trust, which resulted in a large extraordinary gain on the "supposed" redemption of bonds, recorded as follows:

Bonds Payable	$515,000,000	
Gain on Redemption of Bonds (Extraordinary)		$202,000,000
Cash		$313,000,000

Instructions
- **(a)** What are the ethical implications of in-substance defeasance and off-balance sheet financing to users of financial statement information?
- **(b)** How does Exxon benefit from the accounting rule on in-substance defeasance and, in particular, its ability to remove long-term liabilities from the balance sheet?
- **(c)** Who could be harmed by Exxon's ability to remove $515 million of bonds payable from the balance sheet (keeping in mind that it is still legally obligated to pay the original debtors)?

CHAPTER 15

STOCKHOLDERS' EQUITY: CONTRIBUTED CAPITAL

LEARNING OBJECTIVES

After studying this chapter, you should be able to:

1. Explain the key components of stockholders' equity.
2. Discuss the characteristics of the corporate form of organization.
3. Identify the rights of stockholders.
4. Explain the accounting procedures for issuing shares of stock.
5. Identify the major reasons for purchasing treasury stock.
6. Contrast the cost and par value methods of accounting for treasury stock.
7. Describe the major features of preferred stock.
8. Distinguish between debt and preferred stock.
9. Identify items reported as additional paid-in capital.
10. Describe the classifications of additional equity items.

*T*he distinction between liabilities and equities is more than a matter of form.[1] Obviously, whether a particular financial instrument is classified as a liability or an equity affects the content of the balance sheet and the ratios of assets to equity and of debt to equity. But, more critically, the line between liabilities and equity affects the measurement of income. Income is defined to include changes in equity during a period other than those resulting from transactions with owners of an enterprise's equity instruments. Income is a return **on** equity capital and includes only inflows in excess of the amount needed to maintain capital. Without a distinction between the claims of creditors and those of owners, measurement of income is not possible.

The coverage in this chapter and Chapter 16 is based on the current concepts of liabilities and equity, the essential distinction being: a liability embodies an obligation to sacrifice future economic benefits—due dates for principal and interest—whereas an equity instrument does not. Like several other areas of financial accounting, the equity/liability area has become more complicated and is under intense study. Thus, in the near future that basic distinction could change.

OBJECTIVE 1

Explain the key components of stockholders' equity.

▶ THE NATURE OF STOCKHOLDERS' EQUITY

The owners of an enterprise bear the ultimate risks and uncertainties and receive the benefits of enterprise operations. Their interest in the enterprise is measured by the

[1]See *Distinguishing Between Liability and Equity Instruments and Accounting for Instruments with Characteristics of Both,* FASB Discussion Memorandum (Norwalk, Conn.: FASB, 1990), 93 pages.

difference between the assets and the liabilities of the enterprise. Therefore, **the owners' or stockholders' interest in a business enterprise is a residual interest.**[2] **Stockholders' (owners') equity** represents the cumulative net contributions by stockholders plus recorded earnings that have been retained. As a residual interest, stockholders' equity has no existence apart from the assets and liabilities of the enterprise—**stockholders' equity equals net assets.** Stockholders' equity is not a claim to specific assets but a claim against a portion of the total assets. Its amount is not specified or fixed; it depends on the enterprise's profitability. Stockholders' equity grows if the enterprise is profitable, and it shrinks or may disappear entirely if the enterprise is unprofitable.

SOURCES OF EQUITY

Accounting for stockholders' equity is greatly influenced by tradition and by corporate law. Although the legal aspects of equity must be respected and disclosed, legal requirements need not be the accounting basis for classifying and reporting the components of equity.[3] **The two primary sources from which equity is derived are (1) contributions by stockholders (paid-in capital) and (2) income retained** by a corporation—called **retained earnings.** These two components should be accounted for and reported by every corporation. The diagram in Illustration 15-1 depicts the sources of changes in equity.[4]

**ILLUSTRATION 15-1
Sources of Changes in Equity**

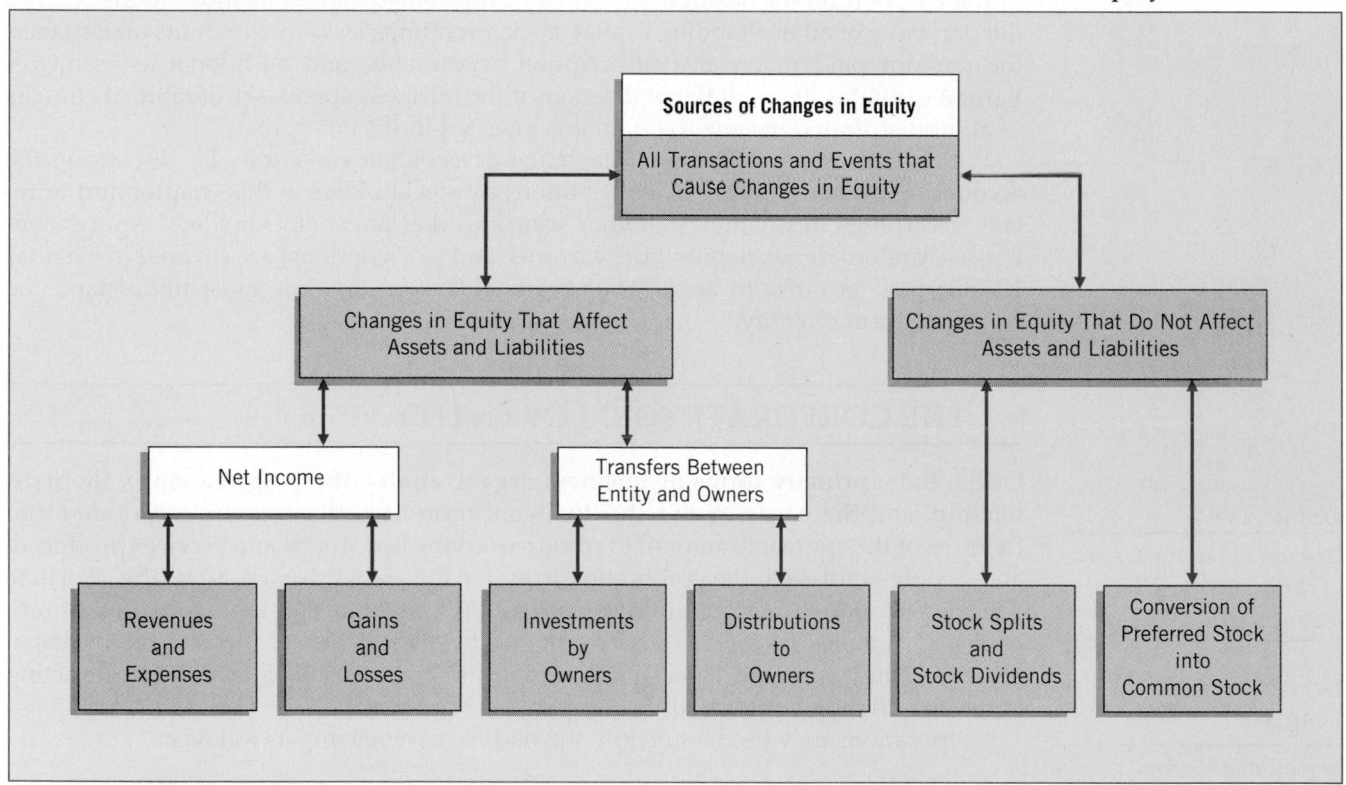

Changes in equity are also brought about by conversions of debt into equity. In addition, changes within equity are brought about by stock dividends, stock conversions, and recapitalizations (quasi reorganizations).

---

[2]"Elements of Financial Statements," *Statement of Financial Accounting Concepts No. 6* (Stamford, Conn.: FASB, 1985), par. 60.

[3]Beatrice Melcher, "Stockholders' Equity," *Accounting Research Study No. 15* (New York: AICPA, 1973), p. 2. Melcher's study is the most comprehensive pronouncement published on this topic.

[4]Adapted from "Elements of Financial Statements," *FASB Statement of Accounting Concepts No. 6,* (FASB, 1985), p. 23.

WHAT IS CAPITAL?

Up to this point we have used the term stockholders' or owners' equity to denote the total capital of the enterprise. It is important to understand the many different meanings that are attached to the word **capital,** because the word often is construed differently by various user groups. **In corporation finance,** for example, capital commonly represents the total assets of the enterprise. **In law,** capital is considered that portion of stockholders' equity that is required by statute to be retained in the business for the protection of creditors. Generally, **legal capital (stated capital)** is the par value of all capital stock issued, but when shares without par value are issued, it may be:

1. Total consideration paid in for the shares.
2. A minimum amount stated in the applicable state incorporation law.
3. An arbitrary amount established by the board of directors at its discretion.

Accountants for the most part define capital more narrowly than total assets but more broadly than legal capital. **When accountants refer to capital they mean stockholders' equity or owners' equity.** They then classify stockholders' or owners' equity into two further categories—contributed capital and earned capital. **Contributed capital** (paid-in capital) is the term used to describe the total amount paid in on capital stock at any given time. Put another way, it is the amount advanced by stockholders to the corporation for use in the business. Contributed capital includes items such as the par value of all outstanding capital stock, premiums less any discounts on issuance, the amount paid in on any subscription agreements, and additional assessments. **Earned capital** is the capital that develops if the business operates profitably; it consists of all undistributed income that remains invested in the enterprise.

We have chosen to divide our coverage of stockholders' equity by discussing the accounting matters relating to contributions by stockholders in this chapter and to retained earnings in Chapter 16. Other securities that affect stockholders' equity (convertible preferreds, stock purchase warrants, and stock options) are covered in Chapter 17. But first, in order to account for stockholders' equity, one must understand the corporate form of entity.

▶ THE CORPORATE FORM OF ENTITY

OBJECTIVE 2

Discuss the characteristics of the corporate form of organization.

INTERNATIONAL INSIGHT

In the United States, stockholders are treated equally as far as access to financial information. That is not always the case in other countries. For example, in Mexico foreign investors as well as minority investors often have difficulty obtaining financial data. These restrictions are rooted in the habits of companies that for many years have been tightly controlled by a few stockholders and managers.

Of the three **primary forms of business organization—the proprietorship, the partnership, and the corporation**—the dominant form of business is the corporate form. In terms of the aggregate amount of resources controlled, goods and services produced, and people employed, the corporation is by far the leader. Nearly all of the "Fortune 500" largest industrial firms are corporations. Although the corporate form has a number of advantages (as well as disadvantages) over the other two forms, the principal attribute that has helped it reach its present dominant role is its facility for attracting and accumulating large amounts of capital.

Corporations may be classified by the nature of ownership as follows:

1. **Public sector corporations:** governmental units or business operations owned by governmental units (such as the Federal Deposit Insurance Corporation).
2. **Private sector corporations:**
   a. **Nonstock:** nonprofit in nature and no stock issued (such as churches, charities, and colleges).
   b. **Stock:** companies that operate for profit and issue stock.
      (i) **Closed corporations (nonpublic or private enterprises):** stock held by a few stockholders (perhaps a family) and not available for public purchase.
      (ii) **Open corporations (public companies):** stock widely held and available for purchase by the public.
          (a) **Listed corporation:** stock traded on an organized stock exchange.
          (b) **Unlisted or over-the-counter corporation:** stock traded in a market in which securities dealers buy from and sell to the public.

Among the special characteristics of the corporate form that affect accounting are:

1. Influence of state corporate law.
2. Use of the capital stock or share system.
3. Development of a variety of ownership interests.
4. Limited liability of stockholders.
5. Formality of profit distribution.

STATE CORPORATE LAW

Anyone who wishes to establish a corporation must submit **articles of incorporation** to the state in which incorporation is desired. Assuming the requirements are properly fulfilled, the corporation charter is issued, and the corporation is recognized as a legal entity subject to state law. To some extent its actions are circumscribed by the laws of any state in which it seeks to carry on business, but, insofar as stockholders' equity accounting is concerned, the business corporation act of the state of incorporation governs.

The importance of this condition to accountants lies in the fact that **each of the 50 states has its own business corporation act.** Some of these laws are uniform; others vary considerably, which means that permissible transactions may vary from state to state and that accounting must reflect these differences. State laws usually prescribe the requirements for issuing stock, the treatment of proceeds of issued stock, the distributions permitted to stockholders, the effects of retiring stock, the regulations for and restrictions on acquiring treasury stock, as well as other procedures and restrictions.

Many states have adopted the principles contained in the Model Business Corporation Act and its numerous subsequent revisions that were prepared by the Committee on Corporate Laws of the American Bar Association. But some states have corporate legislation with contrary features, including elaborate and unusual provisions. The state laws are complex and vary not only in their provisions but also in their definitions of certain terms. Some laws fail to define technical terms, so that terms often mean one thing in one state and another in a different state. And the problems are compounded because legal authorities often interpret the effects and restrictions of the laws differently.[5]

CAPITAL STOCK OR SHARE SYSTEM

OBJECTIVE 3

Identify the rights of stockholders.

Stockholders' equity in a corporation is generally made up of a large number of units or shares. Within a given class of stock each share is exactly equal to every other share. Each owner's interest is determined by the number of shares possessed. If a company has but one class of stock divided into 1,000 shares, a person owning 500 shares controls one-half of the ownership interest of the corporation; one holding 10 shares has a one-hundredth interest.

Each share of stock has certain rights and privileges that can be restricted only by special contract at the time the shares are issued. One must examine the articles of incorporation, stock certificates, and the provisions of the state law to ascertain such restrictions on or variations from the standard rights and privileges. In the absence of restrictive provisions, each share carries the following rights:

1. To share proportionately in profits and losses.
2. To share proportionately in management (the right to vote for directors).
3. To share proportionately in corporate assets upon liquidation.
4. To share proportionately in any new issues of stock of the same class (called the **preemptive right**).

The first three rights are to be expected in the ownership of any business; the last may be used in a corporation to protect each stockholder's proportional interest in the en-

---

[5]*Accounting Research Study No. 15*, p. 8.

terprise. **The preemptive right protects an existing stockholder from involuntary dilution of ownership interest.** Without this right, stockholders with a given percentage interest might find their interest reduced by the issuance of additional stock without their knowledge and at prices that were not favorable to them. Because the preemptive right that attaches to existing shares makes it inconvenient for corporations to make large issuances of additional stock, as they frequently do in acquiring other companies, it has been eliminated by many corporations.

The great advantage of the share system is the ease with which an interest in the business may be transferred from one individual to another. **Individuals owning shares in a corporation may sell them to others at any time and at any price without obtaining the consent of the company or other stockholders.** Each share is personal property of the owner and may be disposed of at will. All that is required of the corporation is that it maintain a list or subsidiary ledger of stockholders as a guide to dividend payments, issuance of stock rights, voting proxies, and the like. Because shares are freely and frequently transferred, it is necessary for the corporation to revise the subsidiary ledger of stockholders periodically, generally in advance of every dividend payment or stockholders' meeting. As the number of stockholders grows, the need may develop for a more efficient system that can handle large numbers of stock transactions. Also, the major stock exchanges require controls that the typical corporation finds uneconomic to provide. Thus **registrars and transfer agents** who specialize in providing services for recording and transferring stock are usually used. The negotiability of stock certificates is governed by the Uniform Stock Transfer Act and the Uniform Commercial Code.

VARIETY OF OWNERSHIP INTERESTS

In every corporation one class of stock must represent the basic ownership interest. That class is called common stock. **Common stock** is the residual corporate interest that bears the ultimate risks of loss and receives the benefits of success. It is guaranteed neither dividends nor assets upon dissolution. But common stockholders generally control the management of the corporation and tend to profit most if the company is successful. In the event that a corporation has only one authorized issue of capital stock, that issue is by definition common stock, whether so designated in the charter or not.

In an effort to appeal to all types of investors, corporations may offer two or more classes of stock each with different rights or privileges. In the preceding section it was pointed out that each share of stock of a given issue has the same rights as other shares of the same issue and that there are four rights inherent in every share. By special stock contracts between the corporation and its stockholders, certain of these rights may be sacrificed by the stockholder in return for other special rights or privileges. Thus special classes of stock are created. Because they have certain preferential rights, they are usually called **preferred stock**. In return for any special preference, the preferred stockholder is always called on to sacrifice some of the inherent rights of capital stock interests.

A common type of preference is to give the preferred stockholders a prior claim on earnings. They are assured a dividend, usually at a stated rate, before any amount may be distributed to the common stockholders. In return for this preference the preferred stock may sacrifice its right to a voice in management or its right to share in profits beyond the stated rate.

A company may accomplish much the same thing by issuing two classes of common stock, Class A stock and Class B stock. In this case one of the issues is the common stock and the other issue has some preference or restriction of basic rights. For example, DeKalb Genetics Corporation was organized with two classes of common stock, Class A and Class B. Both Class A and Class B participate equally (per share) in all dividend payments and have the same claim on assets in dissolution. The differences are that Class A is voting and Class B is not; Class B is traded publicly over the counter while Class A, which is "family owned," must be sold privately (Class A shares are convertible, one for one, into Class B shares but not vice versa). By issuing two classes of common stock, the Class A owners of DeKalb Genetics have obtained a ready market for the company's stock and yet provided an effective shield against outside takeover.[6]

LIMITED LIABILITY OF STOCKHOLDERS

Those who "own" a corporation, the stockholders, contribute either property or services to the enterprise in return for ownership shares. **The property or service invested in the enterprise is the extent of a stockholder's possible loss.** That is, if the corporation sustains losses to such an extent that remaining assets are insufficient to pay creditors, no recourse can be had by the creditors against personal assets of the individual stockholders. In a partnership or proprietorship, personal assets of the owners can be attached to satisfy unpaid claims against the enterprise. Ownership interests in a corporation are legally protected against such a contingency. **The stockholders have limited liability—they may lose their investment but they cannot lose more than their investment.**

Stock that has a fixed per-share amount printed on each stock certificate is called **par value stock.** Par value has but one real significance: it establishes the maximum responsibility of a stockholder in the event of insolvency or other involuntary dissolution. Par value is thus not "value" in the ordinary sense of the word. It is merely an amount per share determined by the incorporators of the company and stated in the corporation charter or certificate of incorporation. Par value establishes the nominal value per share and is the minimum amount that must be paid in by each stockholder if the stock is to be fully paid when issued. A corporation may, however, issue its capital stock either above or below par, in which case the stock is said to be issued at a **premium or a discount,** respectively.[7]

If par value stock is issued at par or at a price above par and the corporation subsequently suffers losses so that assets to repay stockholders upon dissolution are insufficient, stockholders may lose their entire investment. If, however, the stock is issued at a price below par and the losses prove to be of such magnitude as to consume not only the stockholders' investments but also a portion of the assets required to repay creditors, the creditors can force the stockholders to pay in to the corporation the amount of the discount on their capital shares. Thus the original purchasers of stock issued at a price below par are contingently liable to creditors of the corporation. In other words, stockholders may lose their entire investment in a corporation if the investments are equal to or in excess of the par value of the shares they own, or, if the investments are less than their par value, they may lose the amount of their investment plus an additional amount equal to the discount at which they purchased the stock. The limited liability feature of corporate capital stock prevents them from losing any more than the par value of their stock plus any premium paid upon purchase.

It should be emphasized that **the contingent liability of a stockholder for stock purchased at a price below par:**

1. Is an obligation to the corporation's creditors, not to the corporation itself.
2. Becomes a real liability only if the amount below par must be collected in order to pay the creditors upon dissolution of the company.
3. Is the responsibility of the original certificate holder at the time of dissolution unless by contract such responsibility is transferred to a subsequent holder.

While the corporate form of organization grants the protective feature of limited liability to the stockholders, the corporation must guarantee not to distribute the amount of stockholders' investment unless all prior claims on corporate assets have been paid. **The corporation must maintain the corporate legal capital until dissolu-**

---

[6]Ironically, the voting class (which would necessarily be concerned about an unfriendly takeover) often gains the most if an acquisition does take place. That is, the acquirer is willing to pay a substantial premium for the voting shares, but not for the nonvoting ones.

[7]In most states capital stock may not be issued below par; California and Maryland are among the few that allow corporations to issue stock below par.

tion, and upon dissolution it must satisfy all prior claims before distributing any amounts to the stockholders.

In a proprietorship or partnership the owners can withdraw amounts at will because all their personal assets may be called on to protect creditors from loss. In a corporation, however, the owners cannot withdraw any amounts paid in because the only protection creditors have against loss is the amount paid in plus any discount below par.

FORMALITY OF PROFIT DISTRIBUTION

Essentially the owners of an enterprise may determine what is to be done with profits realized through operations. Profits may be left in the business to permit expansion or merely to provide a margin of safety, or they may be withdrawn and divided among the owners. In a proprietorship or partnership this decision is made by the owner or owners informally and requires no specific action. In a corporation, however, profit distribution is controlled by certain legal restrictions.

First, **distributions to owners must be in compliance with the state laws governing corporations.** Currently, the 50 states may be classified into one of three groups for purposes of comparing restrictions on distributions to owners.[8] Generally, in the largest group (22 states) distribution of dividends has to come from retained earnings or from current earnings. Chapter 16 covers this topic in more detail.

Second, **distributions to stockholders must be formally approved by the board of directors** and recorded in the minutes of their meetings. As the top executive body in the corporation, the board of directors must make certain that no distributions are made to stockholders that are not justified by profits, and directors are generally held personally liable to creditors if liabilities cannot be paid because company assets have been illegally paid out to stockholders.

Third, **dividends must be in full agreement with the capital stock contracts as to preferences, participation, and the like.** Once the corporation has entered into contracts with various classes of stockholders, the stipulations of such contracts must be observed.

▶ ACCOUNTING FOR THE ISSUANCE OF STOCK

OBJECTIVE 4

Explain the accounting procedures for issuing shares of stock.

In issuing stock, the following procedures are followed. First, the stock must be authorized by the state, generally in a certificate of incorporation or charter; next, shares are offered for sale and contracts to sell stock are entered into; then, amounts to be received for the stock are collected and the shares issued. The accounting problems involved in the issuance of stock are discussed under the following topics:

1. Accounting for par value stock.
2. Accounting for no-par stock.
3. Accounting for stock sold on a subscription basis.
4. Accounting for stock issued in combination with other securities (lump sum sales).
5. Accounting for stock issued in noncash transactions.
6. Accounting for assessments on stock.
7. Accounting for costs of issuing stock.

PAR VALUE STOCK

As indicated earlier, the par value of a stock has no relationship to its fair market value. At present, the par value associated with most capital stock issuances is very low ($1, $5, $10), which contrasts dramatically with the situation in the early 1900s when prac-

---

[8]See Michael L. Roberts, William D. Samson, and Michael T. Dugan, ''The Stockholders' Equity Section: Form Without Substance,'' *Accounting Horizons,* December 1990, pp. 35–46.

tically all stock issued had a par value of $100. The reason for this change is to permit the original sale of stock at low amounts per share and to avoid the contingent liability associated with stock sold below par. Stock with a low par value is rarely, if ever, sold below par value. In addition, in states that charge a transfer tax based on the par value of the stock, a low par value may result in lower taxes.

To show the required information for issuance of par value stock, accounts must be kept for each class of stock as follows:

1. **Preferred Stock or Common Stock.** Reflects the par value of the corporation's issued shares. These accounts are credited when the shares are originally issued. No additional entries are made in these accounts unless additional shares are issued or shares are retired.

2. **Paid-in Capital in Excess of Par or Additional Paid-in Capital.** Indicates any excess over par value paid in by stockholders in return for the shares issued to them. Once paid in, the excess over par becomes a part of the corporation's additional paid-in capital, and the individual stockholder has no greater claim on the excess paid in than all other holders of the same class of shares.

3. **Discount on Stock.** Indicates that the stock has been issued at less than par. The original purchaser or the current holder of shares issued below par may be called on to pay in the amount of the discount if necessary to prevent creditors from sustaining loss upon liquidation of the corporation.

To illustrate how these accounts are used, assume that Colonial Corporation sold, for $1,100, one hundred shares of stock with a par value of $5 per share. The entry to record the issuance is:

Cash	1,100	
Common Stock		500
Paid-in Capital in Excess of Par (Premium on Common Stock)		600

If the stock had been issued in return for $300, the entry would have been recorded as follows:

Cash	300	
Paid-in Capital in Excess of Par (Discount on Common Stock)	200	
Common Stock		500

Usually no entry would be made in the general ledger accounts at the time the corporation receives its stock authorization from the state of incorporation. In case a formal journal entry is to be made for the authorization of stock, the following separate accounts would be used for authorized stock and for unissued stock:

1. **Authorized Preferred or Common Stock.** Shows the total amount of capital stock authorized. This account is credited at the time authorization from the state is received. No additional entries are made in this account unless the charter is amended to authorize the issuance of additional shares or to reduce the present authorized shares.

2. **Unissued Preferred or Common Stock.** Shows the total authorized shares not yet issued. When the unissued stock is subtracted from the amount authorized, the stock already issued is obtained. This account is debited at the time of recording the stock authorized, and is credited for the par value of stock issued.

NO-PAR STOCK

Many states permit the issuance of capital stock without par value. **No-par stock** is shares issued with no per-share amount printed on the stock certificate. The reasons for issuance of no-par stock are twofold. First, issuance of no-par stock **avoids the contingent liability** that might occur if par value stock were issued at a discount. Second, some confusion still exists over the relationship (or rather the absence of a relationship) between the par value and fair market value. If shares have no par value, **the questionable treatment of using par value as a basis for fair value never arises.** This circumstance is particularly advantageous whenever stock is issued for property items such as tangible or intangible fixed assets. The major disadvantages of no-par stock are that some states levy a high tax on these issues, and the total may be considered legal capital.

No-par shares, like par value shares, are sold for what they will bring, but unlike par value shares, they are issued without a premium or a discount. Therefore, no contingent liability accrues to the stockholders. The exact amount received represents the credit to common or preferred stock. For example, Video Electronics Corporation is organized with authorized common stock of 10,000 shares without par value. No entry, other than a memorandum entry, need be made for the authorization inasmuch as no amount is involved. If 500 shares are then issued for cash at $10 per share, the entry should be:

Cash	5,000	
Common Stock—No-Par Value		5,000

If another 500 shares are issued for $11 per share, the entry should be:

Cash	5,500	
Common Stock—No-Par Value		5,500

True no-par stock should be carried in the accounts at issue price without any complications due to additional paid-in capital or discount. But some states permit the issuance of no-par stock and then proceed either to require or, in some cases, to permit such stock to have a **stated value;** that is, a minimum value below which it cannot be issued. Thus, instead of becoming no-par stock it becomes, in effect, stock with a very low par value, open to all the criticisms and abuses that first encouraged the development of no-par stock.[9]

If no-par stock is required to have a minimum issue price of $5 per share and no provision is made as to how amounts in excess of $5 per share are to be handled, the inclination is for the board of directors to declare all such amounts to be additional paid-in capital, which in many states is fully or partially available for dividends. Thus, no-par value stock with either a minimum stated value or a stated value assigned by the board of directors permits a new corporation to commence its operations with additional paid-in capital that may be in excess of its stated capital. For example, if 1,000 of the shares with a $5 stated value were issued at $15 per share for cash, the entry could be either

Cash	15,000	
Common Stock		15,000

or

Cash	15,000	
Common Stock		5,000
Paid-in Capital in Excess of Stated Value		10,000

In most instances the obvious advantages to the corporation of setting up an initial Additional Paid-in Capital account will influence the board of directors to require the latter entry. Whether for this or for other reasons, the prevailing tendency is to account for no-par stock with stated value as if it were par value stock with par equal to the stated value.

STOCK SOLD ON A SUBSCRIPTION BASIS

The preceding discussion assumed that the stock was sold for cash, but stock may also be sold on a subscription basis. Sale of **subscribed stock** generally occurs when new, small companies "go public" or when corporations offer stock to employees to obtain

---

[9]*Accounting Trends and Techniques—1993* indicates that its 600 surveyed companies reported 656 issues of outstanding common stock, 570 par value issues, and 62 no-par issues; 13 of the no-par issues were shown at their stated (assigned) values.

employee participation in the ownership of the business. When stock is sold on a subscription basis, the full price of the stock is not received initially. Normally only a partial payment is made, and the stock is not issued until the full subscription price is received.

Accounting for Subscribed Stock

Two new accounts are used when stock is sold on a subscription basis. The first, **Common or Preferred Stock Subscribed,** indicates the corporation's obligation to issue shares of its stock upon payment of final subscription balances by those who have subscribed for stock. This account thus signifies a commitment against the unissued capital stock. Once the subscription price is fully paid, the Common or Preferred Stock Subscribed account is debited and the Common or Preferred Stock account is credited. Common or Preferred Stock Subscribed should be presented in the stockholders' equity section below Common or Preferred Stock.

The second account, **Subscriptions Receivable,** indicates the amount yet to be collected before subscribed stock will be issued. Controversy exists concerning the presentation of Subscriptions Receivable on the balance sheet. Some argue that Subscriptions Receivable should be reported in the current assets section (assuming, of course, that payment on the receivable will be received within the operating cycle or one year, whichever is longer). They note that it is similar to trade accounts receivable. Trade accounts receivable grow out of sales transactions in the ordinary course of business; subscriptions receivable relate to the issuance of a concern's own stock and in a sense represent funds (capital contributions) not yet paid the corporation.

Others argue that Subscriptions Receivable should be reported as **a deduction from stockholders' equity** (similar to treasury stock recorded at cost). Their reasoning is that in most states no deficiency judgment can be sought for failure of a subscriber to pay the unpaid balance of a subscription receivable. Given the risk of collectibility, the SEC requires companies to use the **contra equity approach.**[10] For example, in the prospectus of Morlan International, Inc., its subscriptions receivable was reported as a contra equity in the following manner (common stock subscribed is included in the Common Stock rather than shown separately):

UNDERLYING
CONCEPT

Subscriptions Receivable would appear to fulfill all the requirements for an asset. *As a result of a past transaction the company expects to receive a future economic benefit. An Allowance for Doubtful Accounts would disclose the collection risk in the same manner as for Accounts Receivable.*

Morlan International, Inc.	
Stockholders' equity	
Common stock, par value $.01 a share:	
Authorized 9,000,000 shares	
Issued 3,547,638 shares	$ 35,500
Additional capital	2,146,700
Retained earnings	3,878,600
Less subscriptions receivable	(148,500)
Total stockholders' equity	$5,912,300

ILLUSTRATION 15-2
**Treatment of
Subscriptions Receivable**

Practice now generally follows the contra equity approach. Therefore, unless stated otherwise, this practice should be followed in working homework problems.

Most states consider common or preferred stock subscribed to be similar to outstanding common or preferred stock, which means that **individuals who have signed a valid subscription contract normally have the same rights and privileges as a stockholder who holds outstanding shares of stock.**

The journal entries for handling stock sold on a subscription basis are illustrated by the following example. Lubradite Corp. offers stock on a subscription basis to selected individuals, giving them the right to purchase 10 shares of stock (par value $5) at a price of $20 per share. Fifty individuals accept the company's offer and agree to pay 50% down and to pay the remaining 50% at the end of 6 months.

---

[10]The SEC has specified that subscriptions receivable may be shown as an asset only if collected prior to the publication of the financial statements.

At date of issuance

Subscriptions Receivable	10,000	
Common Stock Subscribed		2,500
Paid-in Capital in Excess of Par		7,500
(To record receipt of subscriptions for 500 shares)		
Cash	5,000	
Subscriptions Receivable		5,000
(To record receipt of first installment representing		
50% of total due on subscribed stock)		

When the final payment is received and the stock is issued, the entries are:

Six months later

Cash	5,000	
Subscriptions Receivable		5,000
(To record receipt of final installment on		
subscribed stock)		
Common Stock Subscribed	2,500	
Common Stock		2,500
(To record issuance of 500 shares upon receipt of		
final installment from subscribers)		

Defaulted Subscription Accounts

Sometimes a subscriber is unable to pay all installments and defaults on the agreement. The question is what to do with the balance of the subscription account as well as the amount already paid in. The answer is a function of applicable state law. Some states permit the corporation to retain any amounts paid in on defaulted subscription accounts; other states require that any amount realized on the resale in excess of the amount due from the original subscriber be returned.

STOCK ISSUED IN COMBINATION WITH OTHER SECURITIES (LUMP SUM SALES)

Generally, corporations sell classes of stock separately from one another so that the proceeds relative to each class, and ordinarily even relative to each lot, are known. Occasionally, two or more classes of securities are issued for a single payment or lump sum. It is not uncommon, for example, for more than one type or class of security to be issued in the acquisition of another company. The accounting problem in such **lump sum sales** is the allocation of the proceeds among the several classes of securities. The two methods of allocation available for accountants are (1) the proportional method and (2) the incremental method.

Proportional Method

If the fair market value or other sound basis for determining relative value is available for each class of security, **the lump sum received is allocated among the classes of securities on a proportional basis,** that is, the ratio that each is to the total. For instance, if 1,000 shares of $10 stated value common stock having a market value of $20 a share and 1,000 shares of $10 par value preferred stock having a market value of $12 a share are issued for a lump sum of $30,000, the allocation of the $30,000 to the two classes would be as shown below.

ILLUSTRATION 15-3
Allocation in Lump-Sum Securities Issuance—Proportional Method

Fair market value of common (1,000 × $20) =	$20,000
Fair market value of preferred (1,000 × $12) =	12,000
Aggregate fair market value	$32,000
Allocated to common: $\dfrac{\$20,000}{\$32,000} \times \$30,000 =$	$18,750
Allocated to preferred: $\dfrac{\$12,000}{\$32,000} \times \$30,000 =$	11,250
Total allocation	$30,000

Incremental Method

In instances where the fair market value of all classes of securities is not determinable, the incremental method may be used. The market value of the securities is used as a basis for those classes that are known and the remainder of the lump sum is allocated to the class for which the market value is not known. For instance, if 1,000 shares of $10 stated value common stock having a market value of $20 and 1,000 shares of $10 par value preferred stock having no established market value are issued for a lump sum of $30,000, the allocation of the $30,000 to the two classes would be as follows:

Lump sum receipt	$30,000
Allocated to common (1,000 × $20)	20,000
Balance allocated to preferred	$10,000

ILLUSTRATION 15-4
Allocation in Lump-Sum Securities Issuance—Incremental Method

If no fair market value is determinable for any of the classes of stock involved in a lump sum exchange, the allocation may have to be arbitrary. An expert's appraisal may be used. Or, if it is known that one or more of the classes of securities issued will have a determinable market value in the near future, the arbitrary basis may be used with the intent to make an adjustment when the future market value is established.

STOCK ISSUED IN NONCASH TRANSACTIONS

It is not uncommon for some paid-in capital of a corporation to be the result of stock issued in exchange for property, services, or any form of asset other than cash. Accounting for the issuance of shares of stock for property or services may involve a problem of valuation. **The general rule to be applied when stock is issued for services or property other than cash is that the property or services be recorded at either the fair market value of the stock issued or the fair market value of the noncash consideration received, whichever is more clearly determinable.**

If both are readily determinable and the transaction is the result of an arm's-length exchange, there will probably be little difference in their fair market values. In such cases it should not matter which value is regarded as the basis for valuing the exchange.

If the fair market value of the stock being issued and the property or services being received are not readily determinable, the value to be assigned is generally established by the board of directors or management at an amount that they consider fair and that is not controverted by available evidence. Independent appraisals usually serve as dependable bases. The use of the book, par, or stated values as a basis of valuation for these transactions should be avoided.

Unissued stock or treasury stock (issued shares that have been reacquired but not retired) may be exchanged for the property or services. If treasury shares are used, their cost should not be regarded as the decisive factor in establishing the fair market value of the property or services. Instead, the fair market value of the treasury stock, if known, should be used to value the property or services. If the fair market value of the treasury stock is not known, the fair market value of the property or services should be used, if determinable.

The following series of transactions illustrates the procedure for recording the issuance of 10,000 shares of $10 par value common stock for a patent, in various circumstances:

1. The fair market value of the patent is not readily determinable but the fair market value of the stock is known to be $140,000.

Patent	140,000	
Common Stock		100,000
Paid-in Capital in Excess of Par		40,000

2. The fair market value of the stock is not readily determinable, but the fair market value of the patent is determined to be $150,000.

Patent	150,000	
Common Stock		100,000
Paid-in Capital in Excess of Par		50,000

3. Neither the fair market value of the stock nor the fair market value of the patent is readily determinable. An independent consultant values the patent at $125,000, and the board of directors agrees with that valuation.

Patent	125,000	
Common Stock		100,000
Paid-in Capital in Excess of Par		25,000

In corporate law, the Board of Directors is granted the power to set the value of noncash transactions. This power has been abused. The issuance of stock for property or services has resulted in cases of overstated corporate capital through intentional overvaluation of the property or services received. The overvaluation of the stockholders' equity resulting from inflated asset values creates what is referred to as **watered stock.** The "water" can be eliminated from the corporate structure by simply writing down the overvalued assets.

If as a result of the issuance of stock for property or services the recorded assets are undervalued, **secret reserves** are created. An understated corporate structure or secret reserve may also be achieved by other methods: excessive depreciation or amortization charges, expensing capital expenditures, excessive writedowns of inventories or receivables, or any other understatement of assets or overstatement of liabilities. An example of a liability overstatement is an excessive provision for estimated product warranties that ultimately results in an understatement of owners' equity, thereby creating a secret reserve.

ASSESSMENTS ON STOCK

The laws of some states provide that a corporation may assess stockholders an additional amount above their original contribution. Although this situation occurs infrequently, when stockholders are assessed, they must either pay or possibly forfeit their existing shares. Upon receiving the assessments from the stockholders, the corporation should determine whether the original stock was sold at a discount or a premium. If the stock was originally sold at a discount, the additional proceeds are credited to the discount account. If the stock was originally issued at a premium, the account Additional Paid-in Capital Arising from Assessments is credited.

COSTS OF ISSUING STOCK

The costs associated with the acquisition of corporate capital resulting from the issuance of securities include the following:

1. Attorneys' fees.
2. Certified public accountants' fees.
3. Underwriters' fees and commissions.
4. Expenses of printing and mailing certificates and registration statements.
5. Expenses of filing with the SEC.
6. Clerical and administrative expenses of preparation.
7. Costs of advertising the issue.

In practice there are two primary methods of accounting for initial issue costs. **The first method treats issue costs as a reduction of the amounts paid in.** In effect, such costs are debited to the Paid-in Capital in Excess of Par or Stated Value. This treatment is based on the premise that issue costs are unrelated to corporate operations and thus are not properly chargeable to expense. In this view, issue costs are a reduction of proceeds of the financing activity.

The second method treats issue costs as an organization cost that is not charged off immediately to expense or to corporate capital. Instead, such costs are capitalized and classified as an intangible asset and written off as expense over an arbitrary time period not to exceed 40 years. This treatment is based on the premise that amounts paid in as invested capital should not be violated, and that issue costs benefit the corporation over a long period of time or so long as the invested capital is utilized.

Although both treatments are applied in practice, the first method of **charging issue costs to paid-in capital predominates.** The Securities and Exchange Commission permits the use of either method. In addition to the costs of initial issuance of stock, corporations annually incur costs of maintaining the stockholders' records and handling ownership transfers. These recurring costs, primarily registrar and transfer agents' fees, are normally charged as expense to the period in which incurred.

► REACQUISITION OF SHARES

It is not unusual for companies to buy back their own shares. Merrill Lynch & Co. estimated that in a recent year more than 1,400 corporations announced buyback programs totaling over $80 billion and 2.4 billion shares. Two of the biggest stock buyback programs were General Motors' purchase of 20% (64 million shares) of its stock for $4.8 billion and Santa Fe Southern Pacific's buyback of 38% (60 million shares) of its stock for $3.4 billion. The following table lists some of the companies that made purchases of their own stock.

Company	Shares Purchased	% of Shares Outstanding
Georgia-Pacific Corporation	6,182,000	5.8%
Prime Computer Inc.	2,400,000	4.9
Circus Circus	3,790,000	10.0
Ford Motor Co.	42,700,000	14.1
Exxon Corp.	153,700,000	18.0

ILLUSTRATION 15-5
Companies that Purchased Back Their Own Stock

The reasons corporations purchase their outstanding stock are varied. Some major reasons are:

OBJECTIVE 5
Identify the major reasons for purchasing treasury stock.

1. **To meet employee stock compensation contracts or meet potential merger needs.** Honeywell Inc. reported that part of its purchase of one million common shares was to be used for employee stock option contracts. Other companies acquire shares to have them available for business acquisitions.

2. **To increase earnings per share by reducing the shares outstanding.** For example, Levi Strauss and Co. increased its earnings per share by more than 10% through a common stock repurchase.

3. **To thwart takeover attempts or to reduce the number of stockholders.** By reducing the number of shares held by the public, existing owners and managements can keep "outsiders" from gaining control or significant influence. When Ted Turner attempted to acquire CBS, CBS started a substantial buyback of its stock. Stock purchases may also be used to eliminate dissident stockholders.

4. **To make a market in the stock.** As one company executive noted, "Our company is trying to establish a floor for the stock." By purchasing stock in the marketplace, a demand is created which may stabilize the stock price or, in fact, increase it.

5. **To contract operations.** Although management is often reluctant to contract operations, it may do so when it believes that the stock price is low enough. For example, oil companies have purchased their shares because the stock price was low in relation to the dollar value of their oil reserves. Specifically, Exxon at one time acquired a great number of its own shares because oil cost $7 to $9 a barrel to find but only $2.42 a barrel when buying from existing stockholders through stock repurchases.

Numerous publicly held corporations have recently chosen to "go private," that is, to eliminate public (outside) ownership entirely by purchasing all of their outstanding stock. Such a procedure is often accomplished through a **leveraged buyout (LBO),** in

INTERNATIONAL
INSIGHT

In the U.S. and several other nations, treasury stock is shown as a reduction of shareholder equity. This, however, is not the practice in a number of countries, including Germany, Japan, Belgium, and Italy.

UNDERLYING
CONCEPT

As indicated in Chapter 2, an asset should have probable future economic benefits. Treasury stock simply reduces common stock outstanding.

OBJECTIVE 6

Contrast the cost and par value methods of accounting for treasury stock.

which management or another employee group purchases the stock of the company and finances the purchase by using the assets of the company as collateral.

Once shares are reacquired, they may either be retired or held in the treasury for reissue. If not retired, such shares are referred to as **treasury shares** or **treasury stock.** Technically treasury stock is a corporation's own stock that has been reacquired after having been issued and fully paid. Stock originally issued at a discount and then reacquired is not properly treasury stock, but the distinction is of such little practical importance that it is commonly ignored.

Treasury stock is not an asset. When treasury stock is purchased, a reduction occurs in both assets and stockholders' equity. It is inappropriate to imply that a corporation can own a part of itself. Treasury stock may be sold to obtain funds, but that possibility does not make treasury stock a balance sheet asset. When a corporation buys back some of its own outstanding stock, it has reduced its capitalization but has not acquired an asset. The possession of treasury stock does not give the corporation the right to vote, to exercise preemptive rights as a stockholder, to receive cash dividends, or to receive assets upon corporate liquidation. **Treasury stock is essentially the same as unissued capital stock,** and no one advocates classifying unissued capital stock as an asset in the balance sheet.[11]

METHODS OF ACCOUNTING FOR TREASURY STOCK

Two general methods of handling treasury stock in the accounts are the cost method and the par value method. Both methods are considered generally acceptable and are applied in practice. The **cost method,** which enjoys more widespread use,[12] results in debiting the Treasury Stock account for the reacquisition cost and in reporting this account as a deduction from the total paid-in capital **and** retained earnings on the balance sheet. The **par** or **stated value method,** which is theoretically more justifiable, records all transactions in treasury shares at their par value and reports the treasury stock as a deduction from capital stock only. No matter which method is used, the cost of the treasury shares acquired is considered a restriction on retained earnings in most states.

Cost Method

Under the cost method, acquisition of treasury stock is viewed as the initial step in a two-part transaction. Its reissuance is the second step and completes the transaction. The acquisition is a temporary contraction of total capital, and reissuance is a restoration of the total capital. Between acquisition and reissuance, treasury shares are held in suspense by the corporation.

Under the cost method, **the Treasury Stock account is debited for the cost of the shares acquired and is credited upon reissuance for this same cost,** in a manner similar to that used in an inventory account. In fact, if numerous acquisitions of blocks of treasury shares are made at different prices, inventory costing methods, such as specific identification, average, or FIFO, may be used to identify the cost at date of reissuance. **Under the cost method, the price received for the stock when originally issued does not affect the entries to record the acquisition and reissuance of the treasury stock.**

---

[11]In some special circumstances treasury stock is presented as an asset in the balance sheet. For example, in its 1984 balance sheet, General Motors Corporation reported treasury stock as a separate asset item entitled "Common Stocks Held for the Incentive Program." At December 31, 1984, 2,053,560 shares of GM's common stock at a cost of $144,200,000 were included among the long-term assets between "Investments" and "Property." The justification for classifying these shares as assets is that they will be used to liquidate a specific liability that appears on the balance sheet. *Accounting Trends and Techniques—1993* reported that out of 600 companies surveyed, 381 disclosed treasury stock but none classified it among the noncurrent assets.

[12]*Accounting Trends and Techniques—1993* indicates that of its selected list of 600 companies, 341 carried common stock in treasury at cost and only 24 at par or stated value; 5 companies carried preferred stock in treasury at cost and none at par or stated value.

If the treasury shares are reissued at a price in excess of the acquisition cost, the excess is credited to an account titled Paid-in Capital from Treasury Stock. If the treasury shares are reissued at less than acquisition cost, the deficiency is treated first as a reduction of any paid-in capital related to previous reissuances or retirements of treasury stock of the same class. If the balance in Paid-in Capital from Treasury Stock is insufficient to absorb the deficiency, the remainder is recorded as a reduction of retained earnings.[13] The following sequence of transactions with accompanying journal entries illustrates the cost method:

Cost Method

1. **One thousand shares of common stock of $100 par value are originally issued at $110.**

Cash	110,000	
Common Stock		100,000
Paid-in Capital in Excess of Par		10,000

2. **One hundred shares of common stock are reacquired at $112.**

Treasury Stock	11,200	
Cash		11,200

3. **Ten shares of treasury stock are reissued at $112.**

Cash	1,120	
Treasury Stock (10 shares at $112 per share)		1,120

4. **Ten shares of treasury stock are reissued at $130.**

Cash	1,300	
Treasury Stock (10 shares at $112 per share)		1,120
Paid-in Capital from Treasury Stock		180

5. **Ten shares of treasury stock are reissued at $98.**

Cash	980	
Paid-in Capital from Treasury Stock	140	
Treasury Stock (10 shares at $112 per share)		1,120

Even though the treasury stock was reissued at less than par in transaction 5 above, no consideration is given to this because the legal capital requirements were satisfied when the stock was originally issued in transaction 1. Only the difference between the cost of the treasury stock and its reissue price affects paid-in capital. Note also that the difference of $140 between the cost of the treasury shares and the reissue price is charged against Paid-in Capital from Treasury Stock, reducing the credit balance in that account to $40.[14] If no Paid-in Capital from Treasury Stock existed at the time of reissuance at $98, the entire $140 would be charged to Retained Earnings.

6. **Ten shares of treasury stock are reissued at $105.**

Cash	1,050	
Paid-in Capital from Treasury Stock	40	
Retained Earnings	30	
Treasury Stock (10 shares at $112 per share)		1,120

---

[13]"Status of Accounting Research Bulletins," *Opinions of the Accounting Principles Board No. 6* (New York: AICPA, 1965), par. 12.

[14]Accounting practice frequently applies a slight variation to the cost treatment of the reissuance transaction. The excess of cost over the reissuance price is charged to Paid-in Capital in Excess of Par for a pro rata amount per share of any premium on the original sale of the stock, and any remaining excess is charged to Paid-in Capital from Treasury Stock and then to Retained Earnings. For example, in transaction 5—reissuance at $98—Paid-in Capital in Excess of Par would be debited for $100 (10 shares at original premium of $10 per share) and Paid-in Capital from Treasury Stock debited for the remainder, $40.

In transaction 6 the reissuance of 10 additional shares at a price below cost more than eliminated the remaining balance of $40 in Paid-in Capital from Treasury Stock. When Paid-in Capital from Treasury Stock is reduced to zero, any remaining deficiency is charged to Retained Earnings. In each of the reissuing transactions illustrated above, the Treasury Stock account was credited for its reacquisition cost regardless of the reissuance price.

Par Value Method

Those who advocate accounting for treasury shares at par (or stated value) adhere to the theory that **the purchase or other acquisition of treasury shares is, in effect, a constructive retirement of those shares.** Inasmuch as the shares cannot be an asset, they must represent a retirement or at least a reduction of outstanding stock. Because shares outstanding are shown at par, the reacquired shares must be carried at par to indicate the proper reduction in stock outstanding.

Under the par value method, **the acquisition cost of treasury shares is compared with the amount received at the time of their original issue.** The Treasury Stock account is debited for the par value (or stated value) of the shares, and a pro rata amount of any excess over par (or stated value) on original issuance is charged to the related Paid-in Capital account per transaction 2 below. **Any excess of the acquisition cost over the original issue price is charged to Retained Earnings** and may be viewed as a dividend to the retiring stockholder. **If, however, the original issue price exceeds the acquisition price of the treasury stock, this difference is credited to Paid-in Capital from Treasury Stock** and may be viewed as a capital contribution from the retiring stockholder. This accounting treatment offsets (through the use of a contra account) all original capital balances identifiable with the treasury shares. If the treasury shares are reissued, the accounting treatment is similar to that accorded any original issuance of stock. A series of transactions with accompanying journal entries illustrates the par value method.

Par Value Method

1. **One thousand shares of common stock of $100 par value are originally issued at $110.**

Cash	110,000	
Common Stock		100,000
Paid-in Capital in Excess of Par		10,000

2. **One hundred shares of common stock are reacquired at $112.**

Treasury Stock (100 shares at $100 par)	10,000	
Paid-in Capital in Excess of Par (100 at $10)[15]	1,000	
Retained Earnings	200*	
Cash		11,200

   *This amount could be charged to Paid-in Capital from Treasury Stock if a balance existed in that account from previous transactions.

3. **One hundred shares of common stock are reacquired at $98.**

Treasury Stock (100 shares at $100 par)	10,000	
Paid-in Capital in Excess of Par (100 at $10)	1,000	
Cash		9,800
Paid-in Capital from Treasury Stock		1,200

4. **One hundred shares of common stock are reacquired at $105.**

Treasury Stock (100 shares at $100 par)	10,000	
Paid-in Capital in Excess of Par (100 at $10)	1,000	
Cash		10,500
Paid-in Capital from Treasury Stock		500

---

[15]Because there was only one previous issuance of common stock (at $110 per share), the average price received is the same as the original issue price. Therefore, the $10 original excess over par per share is used to determine the total reduction in Paid-in Capital in Excess of Par. More typically, the average excess over par originally received per share is computed by dividing the total paid-in capital in excess of par from all original issuances of common stock by the number of common shares issued.

5. **One hundred shares of treasury stock are reissued at $115.**

Cash	11,500	
Treasury Stock (100 shares at $100 par)		10,000
Paid-in Capital in Excess of Par		1,500

6. **One hundred shares of treasury stock are reissued at $104.**

Cash	10,400	
Treasury Stock (100 shares at $100 par)		10,000
Paid-in Capital in Excess of Par		400

Note that when the treasury stock is reissued, the accounting treatment is similar to that accorded any original issuance of stock. Any balance in Paid-in Capital from Treasury Stock would be reduced by any reissuances of treasury stock at less than par value; when that balance is exhausted, Retained Earnings would be debited.

7. **One hundred shares of treasury stock are reissued at $94.**

Cash	9,400	
Paid-in Capital from Treasury Stock	600	
Treasury Stock (100 shares at $100 par)		10,000

A Discount on Capital Stock account would not be debited because no contingent liability exists on the part of the stockholders of the reissued shares.

Comparison of Cost and Par Value Methods

The cost method avoids identifying and accounting for the premiums, discounts, and other amounts related to the original issue of the specific shares acquired. For that reason, it is the simpler, more popular method. The par value method, however, maintains the integrity of the sources of the various components of capital. Thus, the par value method, although more complex in application, is conceptually superior. The profession takes the position that the cost method is acceptable when a corporation acquires its own stock for purposes other than retirement (formal or constructive), or when ultimate disposition has not yet been decided.[16]

Other Methods of Accounting for Treasury Stock

INTERNATIONAL INSIGHT

In some states the purchase of treasury stock must be handled by methods other than the two previously described. For example, the applicable state law may require a permanent reduction of retained earnings, in which case the cost of the shares purchased in excess of the stated or par value would be charged to retained earnings. Many companies use the balance in Additional Paid-in Capital, regardless of its source, to absorb all charges resulting from treasury stock transactions. Although not theoretically sound, this method is acceptable under *APB Opinion No. 6,* and it avoids reclassification of premiums and discounts because only one Additional Paid-in Capital account is used. Care should always be exercised in recording treasury stock transactions because of the considerable variety of possible requirements. The advice of an attorney is frequently desirable in this connection.[17]

In Austria, Germany, and Japan, profits (losses) on transactions in a company's own stock must be included in income. This is not allowed in Canada, Colombia, Korea, or the Netherlands.

RETIREMENT OF TREASURY STOCK

A corporation may retire treasury stock. Retired treasury shares have the status of **authorized and unissued shares.** The accounting treatment for retired treasury stock depends on whether the cost or the par value method was used to record the acquisition.

---

[16]*APB Opinion No. 6,* par. 12.

[17]An interesting accounting question has arisen in regard to "greenmail payments" to repurchase shares held by investors to avert a hostile takeover attempt. Some argue that when shares are repurchased at an amount significantly higher than the current market price, the premium paid (greenmail) should be recorded as an expense rather than debited to treasury stock. For example, Phillips Petroleum paid $466.7 million to T. Boone Pickens (a takeover specialist) to buy back 8.9 million of Phillips' shares. Some estimate that if the accounting profession had a rule requiring that these greenmail payments be expensed, it would have reduced Phillips' quarterly earnings by at least 10%.

Using data from the previous cost method and par value method illustrations, the following entries would be made for the retirement of 10 shares of common stock of $100 par value issued at $110.

ILLUSTRATION 15-6
Entries to Record Retirement of Treasury Stock Under the Cost and Par Value Methods

Cost Method			Par Value Method		
If the treasury shares were acquired at $112:					
Common Stock	1,000		Common Stock	1,000	
Paid-in Capital in Excess of Par	100		Treasury Stock		1,000
Retained Earnings	20				
Treasury Stock		1,120			
If the treasury shares were acquired at $98:					
Common Stock	1,000		Common Stock	1,000	
Paid-in Capital in Excess of Par	100		Treasury Stock		1,000
Paid-in Capital from Retirement of					
Common Stock		120			
Treasury Stock		980			

There are two types of treasury stock retirements—actual and constructive. Cancellation of treasury shares through formal application to the secretary of state's office is an actual retirement. Constructive retirement is effecting the retirement on the financial statements by board authorization without formal cancellation through the secretary of state. The accounting is the same for actual and constructive retirements.

TREASURY STOCK IN THE BALANCE SHEET

The two acceptable methods of reporting treasury stock in the balance sheet are related to the two bases of accounting for treasury stock. If the treasury stock is accounted for **at cost,** it is customary to report the cost as an unallocated reduction of the stockholders' equity. The cost of the treasury stock is subtracted from the total of capital stock, additional paid-in capital, and retained earnings as shown below:

ILLUSTRATION 15-7
Cost Method of Reporting Treasury Stock

Stockholders' equity	
Common stock, $1 par; authorized 2,000,000 shares;	
issued 1,500,000 shares	$1,500,000
Additional paid-in capital	3,600,000
Total paid-in capital	5,100,000
Retained earnings (see note)	4,781,484
Total paid-in capital and retained earnings	9,881,484
Less cost of treasury stock (80,000 shares)	480,000
Total stockholders' equity	$9,401,484

Note: Retained earnings are restricted for dividends in the amount of $480,000, the cost of the treasury stock.

Under the **par value method,** treasury stock is reported in the balance sheet as a deduction—at par value of $80,000—from issued shares of the same class. In the illustration below, note that additional paid-in capital is $400,000 less than it is under the cost method.

ILLUSTRATION 15-8
Par Value Method of Reporting Treasury Stock

Stockholders' equity	
Common stock, $1 par; authorized 2,000,000 shares;	
issued 1,500,000 shares	$1,500,000
Less: Treasury stock (80,000 shares at par)	80,000
Common stock outstanding	1,420,000
Additional paid-in capital	3,200,000
Total paid-in capital	4,620,000
Retained earnings (see note)	4,781,484
Total stockholders' equity	$9,401,484

Note: Retained earnings are restricted for dividends in the amount of $480,000, the cost of the treasury stock.

Under both methods, the total stockholders' equity is the same, although the components are different in amount. **Retained earnings is restricted by many state laws in the amount of the cost of the treasury stock under both methods.**

► PREFERRED STOCK

Preferred stock is a special class of shares that is designated "preferred" because it possesses certain preferences or features not possessed by the common stock.[18] The following features are those most often associated with preferred stock issues:

1. Preference as to dividends.
2. Preference as to assets in the event of liquidation.
3. Convertible into common stock.
4. Callable at the option of the corporation.
5. Nonvoting.

OBJECTIVE 7
Describe the major features of preferred stock.

The features that distinguish preferred from common stock may be of a more restrictive and negative nature than preferences; for example, the preferred stock may be nonvoting, noncumulative, and nonparticipating.

Preferred stock is usually issued with a par value, and the dividend preference is expressed as a **percentage of the par value.** Thus, holders of 8% preferred stock, with a $100 par value are entitled to an annual dividend of $8 per share. This stock is commonly referred to as 8% preferred stock. In the case of no-par preferred stock, a dividend preference is expressed as a **specific dollar amount** per share, for example, $7 per share. This stock is commonly referred to as $7 preferred stock. A preference as to dividends is not assurance that dividends will be paid; it is merely assurance that the stated dividend rate or amount applicable to the preferred stock must be paid before any dividends can be paid on the common stock.

FEATURES OF PREFERRED STOCK

A corporation may attach whatever preferences or restrictions in whatever combination it desires to a preferred stock issue so long as it does not specifically violate its state incorporation law, and it may issue more than one class of preferred stock. For example, The New York Times Company reported the following:

> 5½% Cumulative prior preference stock of $100 par value, redeemable at company option at par.
>
> Serial preferred stock of $1 par value, issuable for at least $100 per share.

The most common features attributed to preferred stock are discussed below:

1. **Cumulative Preferred Stock.** Dividends not paid in any year must be made up in a later year before any profits can be distributed to common stockholders. If the directors fail to declare a dividend at the normal date for dividend action, the dividend is said to have been "passed." Any passed dividend on cumulative preferred stock constitutes a **dividend in arrears.** Because no liability exists until the board of directors declares a dividend, a dividend in arrears is not recorded as a liability but is disclosed in a note to the financial statements. (At common law, if the corporate charter is silent about the cumulative feature, the preferred stock is considered to be cumulative.) Noncumulative preferred stock is seldom issued because a passed dividend is lost forever to the preferred stockholder and so this stock issue would be less marketable.

---

[18]*Accounting Trends and Techniques—1993* reports that of its 600 surveyed companies, 150 had preferred stock outstanding; 112 had one class of preferred, 31 had two classes, and 7 had three classes.

2. **Participating Preferred Stock.** Holders of participating preferred stock share ratably with the common stockholders in any profit distributions beyond the prescribed rate. That is, 5% preferred stock, if fully participating, will receive not only its 5% return, but also dividends at the same rates as those paid to common stockholders if amounts in excess of 5% of par or stated value are paid to common stockholders. Also, participating preferred stock may not always be fully participating as described, but partially participating. For example, provision may be made that 5% preferred stock will be participating up to a maximum total rate of 10%, after which it ceases to participate in additional profit distributions; or 5% preferred stock may participate only in additional profit distributions that are in excess of a 9% dividend rate on the common stock. Although participating preferreds are not used extensively (unlike the cumulative provision), examples of companies that have used participating preferreds recently are ENSTAR Corporation, LTV Corporation, Southern California Edison, and Allied Products Corporation.

3. **Convertible Preferred Stock.** The stockholders may at their option exchange their preferred shares for common stock at a predetermined ratio. The convertible preferred stockholder not only enjoys a preferred claim on dividends but also has the option of converting into a common stockholder with unlimited participation in earnings. Convertible preferred stock has been widely used in the past two decades, especially in consummating business combinations, and is favored by investors. The accounting problems related to convertible securities are discussed in Chapter 17.

4. **Callable Preferred Stock.** The issuing corporation can call or redeem at its option the outstanding preferred shares at specified future dates and at stipulated prices. Many preferred issues are callable. The call or redemption price is ordinarily set slightly above the original issuance price and is commonly stated in terms related to the par value. The callable feature permits the corporation to use the capital obtained through the issuance of such stock until the need has passed or it is no longer advantageous. The existence of a call price or prices tends to set a ceiling on the market value of the preferred shares unless they are convertible into common stock. When a preferred stock is called for redemption, any dividends in arrears must be paid. For many decades some preferred stock issues have contained provisions for redemption at some future date, through sinking funds or other means. More recently, some preferred stock issues have provided for mandatory redemption within 5 or 10 years of issuance.

Preferred stock is often issued instead of debt because a company's debt-to-equity ratio has become too high. In other instances, issuances are made through private placements with other corporations at a lower than market dividend rate because the acquiring corporation receives dividends that are largely tax free (owing to the IRS's 70% or 80% dividends received deduction).

DEBT CHARACTERISTICS OF PREFERRED STOCK

OBJECTIVE 8

Distinguish between debt and preferred stock.

With the right combination of features (i.e., fixed return, no vote, redeemable), a preferred stockholder may possess more of the characteristics of a creditor than those of an owner. Preferred shares generally have no maturity date, but the preferred stockholder's relationship with the company may be terminated if the corporation exercises its call privilege. At present GAAP does not distinguish between preferred stocks (not even mandatorily redeemable preferred stock[19]) and other classes of capital stock for

---

[19]**Redeemable preferred stock** is subject to mandatory redemption requirements or has a redemption feature that is outside the control of the issuer. It includes preferred stock that (1) has a fixed or determinable redemption date, (2) is redeemable at the option of the holder, or (3) has conditions for redemption that are not solely within the control of the issuer.

Nonredeemable preferred stock is not redeemable or is redeemable solely at the option of the issuer. *Securities and Exchange Commission Release No. 33-6097* (Washington, D.C.: SEC, July 27, 1979).

balance sheet classification purposes.[20] But the FASB in *Statement No. 47* does require disclosure in the notes of any redemption features of a preferred stock issued and a schedule of redemptions required within the next 5 years.[21] For example, at one time Reliance Group, Inc., which might otherwise have reported only the $4 million par value of its preferred issue, was required to disclose the $116 million redemption price due within 5 years.

The SEC, however, has issued a rule that prohibits companies from combining preferred stock with common stock in financial statements. Amounts must be presented separately for redeemable preferred stock,[22] nonredeemable preferred stock, and common stock. The amounts applicable to these three categories of equity items cannot be totaled or combined for SEC reporting purposes. The general heading, **stockholders' equity, should not include redeemable preferred stock.**

The proposal was triggered by an SEC concern about the increasing issuance of preferred stock specifying redemption over relatively short periods such as 5 to 10 years; such stock issues are called **transient preferreds.** According to the SEC, such stock involves a commitment to use future resources of the company to redeem the issue, giving the holder a claim against prospective cash flows and hence a unique status different from that of holders of equity securities that represent permanent capital investments. This new type of preferred is nothing but thinly disguised debt. The roster of issuers of transient preferreds includes The Gillette Company, National Distillers, Revlon, Inc., Westinghouse Electric, Occidental Petroleum, TWA, and Tenneco. Shown in Illustration 15-9 is an excerpt from the BFGoodrich Company balance sheet and accompanying notes, which is typical of how redeemable preferred stock is being reported.

INTERNATIONAL INSIGHT

In Switzerland, there are no specific disclosure requirements for shareholders' equity. However, companies typically disclose separate categories of capital on the balance sheet.

The BFGoodrich Company

(Partial Balance Sheet)

	1992	1991
	($ Millions)	
Redeemable Preferred Stock (Note 5)	$ 6.3	$ 7.5
Shareholders' equity		
$3.50 Cumulative convertible preferred stock, Series D (stated at involuntary liquidation value of $50 per share) 2,200,000 shares issued and outstanding	110.0	110.0
Common stock—$5 par value		
Authorized 100,000,000 shares; issued 25,646,866 shares in 1992 and 25,554,627 shares in 1991	128.2	127.8
Additional capital	391.5	385.9
Income retained in the business	230.9	591.3
Cumulative unrealized translation adjustments	(7.8)	7.5
Amount related to recording minimum pension liability	(10.9)	(1.9)
Unearned portion of restricted stock awards	(11.9)	(1.2)

ILLUSTRATION 15-9
Balance Sheet Presentation with Note, of Redeemable Preferred Stock

UNDERLYING CONCEPT

Even though present GAAP does not dictate (or prohibit) separate classification, application of the FASB's qualitative characteristic of representational faithfulness would require that economic substance rather than the legal form or description of such securities dictate their financial statement classification.

---

[20]Several accounting standards, however, have recognized the difference between redeemable and nonredeemable preferred stock (not necessarily using those terms). These include *FASB Statement No. 47* (which requires for capital stock redeemable at fixed or determinable prices the same disclosures required for long-term debt), *FASB Statement No. 12* (which excludes redeemable preferred stock from the definition of "equity security"), and *APB Opinion No. 16* (which requires that the cost of a company acquired by issuing senior equity securities having characteristics of redeemable preferred stock be determined on the same basis as that used in the case of debt securities). This topic receives in-depth analysis in the FASB's 1990 Discussion Memorandum "Distinguishing between Liability and Equity Instruments and Accounting for Instruments with Characteristics of Both."

[21]"Disclosure of Long-Term Obligations," *Statement of Financial Accounting Standards No. 47* (Stamford, Conn.: FASB, 1981), par. 10 c.

[22]*SEC Release No. 33-6097,* op. cit.

Common stock held in treasury, at cost (27,777 shares in 1992 and 156,679 shares in 1991)	(1.2)	(5.4)
Total shareholders' equity	828.8	1,214.0

Note 5: Preferred Stock (in part). Redeemable Preferred Stock—Series A (stated at involuntary liquidation value of $100 per share). BFGoodrich has issued 250,000 shares of $7.85 Cumulative Preferred Stock, Series A. In order to comply with sinking-fund requirements, each year on August 15, BFGoodrich must redeem 12,500 shares of the Series A Stock. The redemption price is $100 per share, plus dividends accrued at the redemption date. BFGoodrich may redeem, at such price, up to an additional 12,500 shares in each year. The sinking-fund requirements may also be satisfied with shares acquired on the open market. At December 31, 1992, 1991 and 1990, BFGoodrich held 880, 12,160 and 13,500 shares, respectively, for future sinking-fund requirements. After giving effect to the shares held for future sinking-fund requirements, there were 74,120, 75,340 and 86,500 shares of Series A Stock outstanding at December 31, 1992, 1991, and 1990, respectively. The aggregate amount of redemption requirement for the Series A Stock is $1.2 for 1993 and $1.3 in each of the years 1994 through 1997.

The initial carrying amount of redeemable preferred stock should be its fair market value at the date of issuance. If the fair value is less than the mandatory redemption amount, **periodic amortizations** using the interest method should be recorded so that the carrying value will equal the redemption amount on the mandatory redemption date. The initial carrying value should also be **periodically increased by dividends** that are not currently declared or paid but that will be due under the redemption agreement. In practice, the corresponding debit has been made to retained earnings (or to additional paid-in capital in the absence of retained earnings). This accounting treatment also applies when the redeemable preferred stock may be voluntarily redeemed by the issuer before the mandatory redemption date and when such preferred stock may be converted into another class of securities by the holder.

A phenomenon in the preferred stock market is the issuance of the **auction-rate preferred,** also called remarketed preferred, or adjustable-rate preferred. This preferred security is designed to allow corporations to sell equity to buyers of short-term debt. To keep the principal price from fluctuating, the dividend rate is re-set regularly, usually every 7 weeks, either through auction or other remarketing efforts, so that the investors have a chance to get rid of the stock if they don't like the new rate. Because the preferred pays dividends not interest, corporate buyers pay taxes on only 30% or 20% of their earnings (due to the 70% and 80% dividends received deductions), so they are willing to take a lower yield than they do on debt. Issuers love the low rate, and the market for this product has grown explosively. The security is classified as an equity rather than a debt security because investors cannot look to the issuer for repayment; instead, a buyer must be found for the security.

▶ ADDITIONAL PAID-IN CAPITAL

OBJECTIVE 9

Identify items reported as additional paid-in capital.

As indicated throughout this chapter, additional paid-in capital arises from the issuance of capital stock. In addition, a number of other types of transactions affect additional paid-in capital. The basic transactions affecting additional paid-in capital are expressed in account form below:

ILLUSTRATION 15-10
Transactions that Affect Paid-in Capital

Additional Paid-in Capital	
1. Discounts on capital stock issued.	1. Premiums on capital stock issued.
2. Sale of treasury stock below cost.	2. Sale of treasury stock above cost.
3. Absorption of a deficit in a recapitalization (quasi-reorganization).*	3. Additional capital arising in recapitalizations or revisions in the capital structure (quasi-reorganizations).
4. Declaration of a liquidating dividend.	4. Additional assessments on stockholders.
	5. Conversion of convertible bonds or preferred stock.
	6. Declaration of a "small" (ordinary) stock dividend.

*Discussed in Chapter 16.

In balance sheet presentation, **only one amount need appear,** Additional Paid-in Capital, to summarize all of these possible transactions.[23] A subsidiary ledger or separate general ledger accounts may be kept of the different sources of additional paid-in capital because certain state laws permit dividend distributions out of designated additional paid-in capital.

No operating gains or losses or extraordinary gains and losses may be debited or credited to Additional Paid-in Capital. The profession has long discouraged bypassing net income and retained earnings through the direct writeoff of losses (e.g., writeoffs of bond discount, goodwill, or obsolete plant and equipment) to additional paid-in capital accounts or other capital accounts.

▶ ADDITIONAL EQUITY ITEMS

Two other items that may be reported in the stockholders' equity section as a form of additional capital are **donated capital and revaluation or unrealized appreciation capital.** Donated capital results from donations to the company **by governmental units**— for example, land received by a corporation from a municipality as an incentive to locate its plant in that municipality. The donated asset should be recorded at fair value.[24] Revaluation capital results from the writeup or writedown of assets from cost. Because of adherence to the cost principle and the concept of conservatism, assets are generally not written up from cost. Revaluation or unrealized appreciation capital having a credit balance, therefore, rarely appears on financial statements.

Because donated capital and revaluation capital (writeups or writedowns not reported in the income statement) are such unique items, they warrant special attention when they occur. For this reason, the following stockholders' equity classifications should be distinguished.

Capital Stock

Additional Paid-in Capital

Donated Capital

Revaluation Capital

Retained Earnings

In addition to treasury stock, other amounts are required to be reported as contra or adjunct equity items; generally these items are presented as adjustments to or below retained earnings in the stockholders' equity section of the balance sheet.[25]

OBJECTIVE 10
Describe the classifications of additional equity items.

---

[23]*Accounting Trends and Techniques—1993* reports that of its 600 surveyed companies, 531 had additional paid-in capital; 242 used the caption "Additional paid-in capital"; 148 used "Capital in excess of par or stated value" as the caption; 34 used "Capital surplus"; and 107 used some other variation or combination of those three captions.

[24]As indicated in Chapter 10, donations from parties other than governmental units must be recognized as revenues or gains in the period received. See "Accounting for Contributions Received and Contributions Made," *Statement of Financial Accounting Standards No. 116* (Norwalk, Conn.: FASB, 1993). The Board was silent on how donations from stockholders should be reported. In rare situations, stockholders might donate some of their stock to the corporation (donated treasury stock). In a recent survey of over 4,000 companies, the authors did not find any examples of this practice. As a result, discussion of accounting procedures for such a transaction is not provided in this chapter.

[25]Among these items are "foreign currency translation adjustments" (covered in advanced accounting), "unrealized holding gains and losses for available-for-sale securities" (covered in Chapter 18), "excess of additional pension liability over unrecognized prior service cost" (covered in Chapter 21), "guarantees of employee stock option plan (ESOP) debt," "unearned or deferred compensation related to employee stock award plans," and others. *Accounting Trends and Techniques—1993* reports that of its 600 surveyed companies reporting other items in the equity section, 367 reported cumulative translation adjustments, 98 reported guarantees of ESOP debt, 86 reported unearned compensation, 63 reported minimum pension liability adjustments, 18 reported unrealized losses/gains on equity securities, and 14 reported receivables from sale of stock.

▶ SUMMARY OF LEARNING OBJECTIVES ◀

1. **Explain the key components of stockholders' equity.** Stockholders' or owners' equity is classified into two categories: contributed capital and earned capital. Contributed capital (paid-in capital) is the term used to describe the total amount paid in on capital stock; put another way, it is the amount advanced by stockholders to the corporation for use in the business. Contributed capital includes items such as the par value of all outstanding capital stock, premiums less any discounts on issuance, the amount paid in on any subscription agreements, and additional assessments. Earned capital is the capital that develops if the business operates profitably; it consists of all undistributed income that remains invested in the enterprise.

2. **Discuss the characteristics of the corporate form of organization.** Among the specific characteristics of the corporate form that affect accounting are: (1) influence of state corporate law; (2) use of the capital stock or share system; (3) development of a variety of ownership interests; (4) limited liability of stockholders; (5) formality of profit distribution.

3. **Identify the rights of stockholders.** In the absence of restrictive provisions, each share of stock carries the following rights: (1) to share proportionately in profits and losses; (2) to share proportionately in management (the right to vote for directors); (3) to share proportionately in corporate assets upon liquidation; (4) to share proportionately in any new issues of stock of the same class (called the preemptive right).

4. **Explain the accounting procedures for issuing shares of stock.** Accounts required to be kept for different types of stock are: (1) *Par value stock:* (a) preferred stock or common stock; (b) paid-in capital in excess of par or additional paid-in capital; and (c) discount on stock. (2) *No-par stock:* common stock or common stock and additional paid-in capital, if stated value used. (3) *Stock sold on a subscription basis:* (a) common or preferred stock subscribed; and (b) subscriptions receivable. (4) *Stock issued in combination with other securities (lump sum sales).* The two methods of allocation available for accountants are (a) the proportional method; and (b) the incremental method. (5) *Stock issued in noncash transactions:* When stock is issued for services or property other than cash, the property or services should be recorded at either the fair market value of the stock issued or the fair market value of the noncash consideration received, whichever is more clearly determinable.

5. **Identify the major reasons for purchasing treasury stock.** The reasons corporations purchase their outstanding stock are varied. Some major reasons are: (1) to meet employee stock compensation contracts or meet potential merger needs; (2) to increase earnings per share by reducing the shares outstanding; (3) to thwart takeover attempts or to reduce the number of stockholders; (4) to make a market in the stock; (5) to contract operations.

6. **Contrast the cost and par value methods of accounting for treasury stock.** The cost method avoids identifying and accounting for the premiums, discounts, and other amounts related to the original issue of the specific shares acquired and is the simpler, more popular method. The par value method, however, maintains the integrity of the sources of the various components of capital. Thus, the par value method, although more complex in application, is conceptually the superior method. The profession takes the position that the cost method is acceptable when a corporation acquires its own stock for purposes other than retirement, or when ultimate disposition has not yet been decided.

7. **Describe the major features of preferred stock.** Preferred stock is a special class of shares that possesses certain preferences or features not possessed by

the common stock. The features that are most often associated with preferred stock issues are: (1) preference as to dividends; (2) preference as to assets in the event of liquidation; (3) convertible into common stock; (4) callable at the option of the corporation; (5) nonvoting.

8. **Distinguish between debt and preferred stock.** With the right combination of features (i.e., fixed return, no vote, redeemable), a preferred stockholder may possess more of the characteristics of a creditor than those of an owner. Preferred shares generally have no maturity date, but the preferred stockholder's relationship with the company may be terminated if the corporation exercises its call privilege.

9. **Identify items reported as additional paid-in capital.** Items reported as additional paid-in capital are: (1) discounts (premiums) on capital stock issued; (2) sale of treasury stock below (above) cost; (3) absorption of a deficit in a recapitalization or additional capital arising in recapitalizations or revisions in the capital structure (quasi-reorganization); (4) declaration of a liquidating dividend; (5) additional assessments on stockholders; (6) conversion of convertible bonds or preferred stock; (7) declaration of a "small" (ordinary) stock dividend.

10. **Describe the classifications of additional equity items.** Two items that may be reported in the stockholders' equity section as a form of additional capital are donated capital and revaluation capital. Some other items that may be reported as contra or adjunct to equity are: (1) unrealized holding gains and losses on available-for-sale securities; (2) accumulated foreign currency translation adjustments; (3) excess of additional pension liability over unrecognized prior service cost; (4) guarantees of employee stock option plan (ESOP) debt; (5) unearned or deferred compensation related to employee stock award plans; and (6) amounts owed to a company by employees for loans to buy company stock.

QUESTIONS

1. Differentiate between capital in a legal sense, capital in a corporate finance sense, and capital in an accounting sense.

2. Distinguish between the following types of corporations:
   (a) Public sector vs. private sector.
   (b) Nonstock vs. stock.
   (c) Closed vs. open.
   (d) Listed vs. unlisted.

3. Discuss the special characteristics of the corporate form of business that have a direct effect on owners' equity accounting.

4. In the absence of restrictive provisions, what are the basic rights of stockholders of a corporation?

5. Distinguish between common and preferred stock.

6. What are the legal restrictions that control the distribution of profit of a corporation?

7. Explain each of the following terms: authorized capital stock, unissued capital stock, issued capital stock, outstanding capital stock, subscribed stock, and treasury stock.

8. Distinguish between paid-in capital and stated capital.

9. What is meant by par value, and what is its significance to stockholders?

10. Describe the accounting for the issuance for cash of no-par value common stock at a price in excess of the stated value of the common stock.

11. When might the Stock Subscription Receivable account be classified as a current asset? As a deduction in the stockholders' equity section?

12. Describe the accounting for the subscription of common stock at a price in excess of the par value of the common stock.

13. Explain the difference between the proportional method and the incremental method of allocating the proceeds of lump sum sales of capital stock.

14. What are the different bases for stock valuation when assets other than cash are received for issued shares of stock?

15. Discuss the two methods of accounting for initial issue costs. Which do you support and why?

16. For what reasons might a corporation purchase its own stock?

17. Distinguish between the cost method and the par value method of accounting for treasury stock.

18. How is stockholders' equity affected differently by using the cost method instead of the par value method for treasury stock purchases?

19. Discuss the propriety of showing:
    (a) Treasury stock as an asset.
    (b) "Gain" or "loss" on sale of treasury stock as additions to or deductions from income.
    (c) Dividends received on treasury stock as income.

20. What features or rights may alter the character of preferred stock?

21. Raul Julia Inc. recently noted that its 4% preferred stock and 4% participating second preferred stock, which are both cumulative, have priority as to dividends up to 4% of their par value; its participating preferred stock participates equally with the common stock in any dividends in excess of 4%. What is meant by the term participating? Cumulative?

22. (a) In what ways may preferred stock be more like a debt security than an equity security? (b) How should preferred stock be classified in the financial statements?

23. List possible sources of additional paid-in capital.

24. Indicate the ways in which revaluation and donated capital originate.

25. Leguizamo Inc. purchases 10,000 shares of its own previously issued $5 par common stock for $280,000. Assuming the shares are held in the treasury with intent to reissue, what effect does this transaction have on (a) net income, (b) total assets, (c) total paid-in capital, and (d) total stockholders' equity?

26. Indicate how each of the following accounts should be classified in the stockholders' equity section.
    (a) Common Stock   (e) Paid-in Capital from Treasury Stock
    (b) Retained Earnings   (f) Paid-in Capital in Excess of Stated Value
    (c) Paid-in Capital in Excess of Par Value   (g) Donated Capital
    (d) Treasury Stock   (h) Preferred Stock

EXERCISES

E15-1 (Recording the Issuances of Common Stock) During its first year of operations, Esai Morales Corporation had the following transactions pertaining to its common stock.

Jan. 10 Issued 80,000 shares for cash at $6 per share.
Mar. 1 Issued 5,000 shares to attorneys in payment of a bill for $35,000 for services rendered in helping the company to incorporate.
July 1 Issued 30,000 shares for cash at $8 per share.
Sept. 1 Issued 60,000 shares for cash at $10 per share.

Instructions
(a) Prepare the journal entries for these transactions, assuming that the common stock has a par value of $6 per share.
(b) Prepare the journal entries for these transactions, assuming that the common stock is no par with a stated value of $2 per share.

E15-2 (Recording the Issuance of Common and Preferred Stock) Carmen Miranda Corporation was organized on January 1, 1995. It is authorized to issue 10,000 shares of 8%, $100 par value preferred stock, and 500,000 shares of no par common stock with a stated value of $2 per share. The following stock transactions were completed during the first year.

Jan. 10 Issued 80,000 shares of common stock for cash at $5 per share.
Mar. 1 Issued 5,000 shares of preferred stock for cash at $108 per share.

Apr. 1 Issued 24,000 shares of common stock for land. The asking price of the land was $90,000; the fair market value
of the land was $80,000.
May 1 Issued 80,000 shares of common stock for cash at $7 per share.
Aug. 1 Issued 10,000 shares of common stock to attorneys in payment of their bill of $50,000 for services rendered in
helping the company organize.
Sept. 1 Issued 10,000 shares of common stock for cash at $9 per share.
Nov. 1 Issued 1,000 shares of preferred stock for cash at $112 per share.

Instructions
Prepare the journal entries to record the above transactions.

E15-3 (Subscribed Stock) Jose Santana Inc. intends to sell capital stock to raise additional capital to allow for expansion in the rapidly growing service industry. The corporation decides to sell this stock through a subscription basis and publicly notifies the investment world. The stock is a $10 par value issue and 30,000 shares are offered at $25 a share. The terms of the subscription are 40% down and the balance at the end of six months. All shares are subscribed for during the offering period.

Instructions
Give the journal entry for the original subscription, the collection of the down payments, the collection of the balance of the subscription price, and the issuance of the common stock.

E15-4 (Stock Issued for Nonmonetary Assets) Freddie Prinze Products, Inc., was formed to operate a manufacturing plant in Milagro. The events for the formation of the corporation include the following:

1. 5,000 shares of no-par common stock were issued to investors at $20 per share.
2. 8,000 shares were issued to acquire used equipment that has a depreciated book value to the seller of $120,000.
3. The city of Milagro conveys title to land and buildings to Prinze. Concurrently Prinze has agreed to accept full responsibility for the $75,000 first mortgage held by Chico State Bank. The recent appraised value of the property is $45,000 for the land and $90,000 for the building.

Instructions
Prepare journal entries for the transactions above.

E15-5 (Treasury Stock—Par Value and Cost Methods) La Bamba Corporation reacquired 40,000 of its common shares in the market at $54 per share. The per share par value is $1; the average issue price was $30 per share.

Instructions
(a) Record the purchase assuming:
  1. The par value method.
  2. The cost method.
(b) Which of the methods will provide the financial statement reader with more useful information? Briefly explain.

E15-6 (Stock Issued for Land) Twenty-five thousand shares reacquired by La Bamba Corporation in Exercise 15–5 were exchanged for undeveloped land that has an appraised value of $1,700,000. At the time of the exchange the common stock was trading at $62 per share on an organized exchange.

Instructions
(a) Prepare the journal entry to record the acquisition of land assuming the stock was originally recorded on the:
  1. Par value method.
  2. Cost method.
(b) Briefly identify the possible alternatives (including those that are totally unacceptable) for quantifying the cost of the land and briefly support your choice.

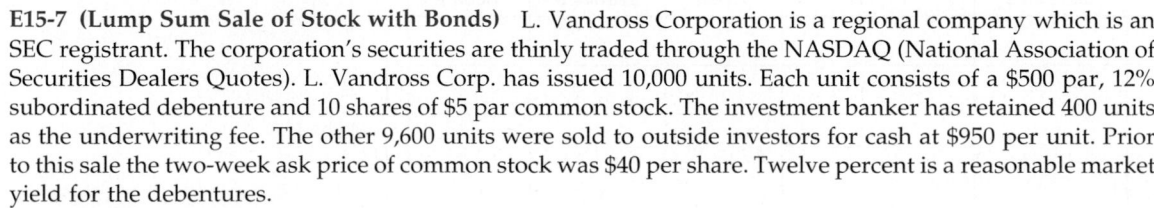 **E15-7 (Lump Sum Sale of Stock with Bonds)** L. Vandross Corporation is a regional company which is an SEC registrant. The corporation's securities are thinly traded through the NASDAQ (National Association of Securities Dealers Quotes). L. Vandross Corp. has issued 10,000 units. Each unit consists of a $500 par, 12% subordinated debenture and 10 shares of $5 par common stock. The investment banker has retained 400 units as the underwriting fee. The other 9,600 units were sold to outside investors for cash at $950 per unit. Prior to this sale the two-week ask price of common stock was $40 per share. Twelve percent is a reasonable market yield for the debentures.

Instructions
(a) Prepare the journal entry to record the transaction above:
  1. Employing the incremental method assuming the interest rate on the debentures is the best market measure.
  2. Employing the proportional method using the recent price quotes on the common stock.
(b) Briefly explain which method is, in your opinion, the better method.

E15-8 (Lump Sum Sales of Stock with Preferred Stock) Dionne Warwick Inc. issues 500 shares of $10 par value common stock and 100 shares of $100 par value preferred stock for a lump sum of $100,000.

Instructions

(a) Prepare the journal entry for the issuance when the market value of the common shares is $170 each and market value of the preferred is $230 each.

(b) Prepare the journal entry for the issuance when only the market value of the common stock is known and it is $175 per share.

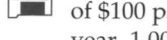

E15-9 (Lump Sum Sale of Stock with Preferred) Diana Ross Company was organized with 50,000 shares of $100 par value 9% preferred stock and 100,000 shares of common stock without par value. During the first year, 1,000 shares of preferred and 1,000 shares of common were issued for a lump sum price of $180,000.

Instructions

What entry should be made to record this transaction under each of the following independent conditions:

(a) Shortly after the transaction described above, 500 shares of preferred stock were sold at $115.

(b) The directors have established a stated value of $95 a share for the common stock.

(c) At the date of issuance, the preferred stock had a market price of $135 per share and the common stock had a market price of $45 per share.

E15-10 (Stock Issuances and Repurchase) Leon Russell Corporation is authorized to issue 50,000 shares of $10 par value common stock. During 1995, Leon Russell took part in the following selected transactions:

1. Issued 5,000 shares of stock at $45 per share, less costs related to the issuance of the stock totaling $7,000.

2. Issued 1,000 shares of stock for land appraised at $50,000. The stock was actively traded on a national stock exchange at approximately $46 per share on the date of issuance.

3. Purchased 500 shares of treasury stock at $43 per share. The treasury shares purchased were issued in 1994 at $40 per share.

Instructions

(a) Prepare a journal entry to record item 1:
1. Treating the issue costs as a reduction of amounts paid in.
2. Treating the issue costs as organization costs.

(b) Prepare a journal entry to record item 2.

(c) Prepare a journal entry to record item 3:
1. Using the cost method.
2. Using the par value method.

(d) Discuss the subsequent accounting treatment of the organization costs recorded in (a) 2.

E15-11 (Effect of Treasury Stock Transactions on Financials) Lena Horn Company has outstanding 40,000 shares of $5 par common stock which had been issued at $30 per share. Lena Horn then entered into the following transactions:

1. Purchased 5,000 treasury shares at $40 per share.
2. Resold 2,000 of the treasury shares at $44 per share.
3. Resold 500 of the treasury shares at $35 per share.
4. Retired the remaining treasury shares.

Instructions

Use the following code (I = Increase; D = Decrease; NE = No effect) to indicate the effect each of the four transactions has on the financial statement categories listed in the table below, first for the cost method and then for the par value method.

#	Assets	Liabilities	Stockholders' Equity	Paid-in Capital	Retained Earnings	Net Income	
1							
2							Cost Method
3							
4							
1							
2							Par Value Method
3							
4							

E15-12 (Treasury Stock—Par Value and Cost Methods) Frankie Beverly Inc. has outstanding 35,000 shares of $10 par common stock which has been issued at $25 per share. On July 5, 1995, Frankie Beverly repurchased 1,000 of these shares at $39 per share. The company then retired the treasury shares.

Instructions
Give the appropriate journal entries for the acquisition and retirement of the treasury stock under:
- **(a)** The cost method.
- **(b)** The par value method.

E15-13 (Preferred Stock Entries and Dividends) Ron Simmons Corporation has 10,000 shares of $100 par value, 9%, preferred stock and 50,000 shares of $10 par value common stock outstanding at December 31, 1995.

Instructions
Answer the questions in each of the following independent situations:

1. If the preferred stock is cumulative and dividends were last paid on the preferred stock on December 31, 1992, what are the dividends in arrears that should be reported on the December 31, 1995 balance sheet? How should these dividends be reported?
2. If the preferred stock is fully participating (but not cumulative) and a cash dividend of $450,000 is declared at December 31, 1995, how is the total dividend distributed between the preferred and common stock?
3. If the preferred stock is convertible into seven shares of $10 par value common stock and 5,000 shares are converted, what entry is required for the conversion assuming the preferred stock was issued at par value?
4. If the preferred stock was issued at $108 per share, how should the preferred stock be reported in the stockholders' equity section?

E15-14 (Stockholders' Equity Section) Aragonite Corporation's charter authorized 100,000 shares of $10 par value common stock, and 30,000 shares of 6% cumulative and nonparticipating preferred stock, par value $100 per share. The corporation engaged in the following stock transactions through December 31, 1995: 30,000 shares of common stock were issued for $350,000 and 12,000 shares of preferred stock for machinery valued at $1,450,000. Subscriptions for 4,500 shares of common have been taken, and 30% of the subscription price of $16 per share has been collected. The stock will be issued upon collection of the subscription price in full. Treasury stock of 1,000 shares of common has been purchased for $15 and accounted for under the cost method. The Retained Earnings balance is $180,000.

Instructions
Prepare the stockholders' equity section of the balance sheet in good form. Assume that state law requires that the amount of retained earnings available for dividends be restricted by an amount equal to the cost of treasury shares acquired.

E15-15 (Correcting Entries for Equity Transactions) Basalt Inc. recently hired a new accountant with extensive experience in accounting for partnerships. Because of the pressure of the new job, the accountant was unable to review what he had learned earlier about corporation accounting. During the first month, he made the following entries for the corporation's capital stock.

May 2	Cash	192,000	
	Capital Stock		192,000
	(Issued 12,000 shares of $10 par value common stock at $16 per share)		
10	Cash	600,000	
	Capital Stock		600,000
	(Issued 10,000 shares of $50 par value preferred stock at $60 per share)		
15	Capital Stock	15,000	
	Cash		15,000
	(Purchased 1,000 shares of common stock for the treasury at $15 per share)		
31	Cash	8,500	
	Capital Stock		5,000
	Gain on Sale of Stock		3,500
	(Sold 500 shares of treasury stock at $17 per share)		

Instructions
On the basis of the explanation for each entry, prepare the entries that should have been made for the capital stock transactions.

E15-16 (Analysis of Equity Data and Equity Section Preparation) For a recent 2-year period, the balance sheet of Cinnabar Company showed the following stockholders' equity data in millions.

	1996	1995
Additional paid-in capital	$ 923	$ 817
Common stock-par	545	540
Retained earnings	7,167	5,226
Treasury stock	1,562	910
Total stockholders' equity	7,073	5,674
Common stock shares issued	218	216
Common stock shares authorized	500	500
Treasury stock shares	34	27

Instructions

(a) Answer the following questions.
   (1) What is the par value of the common stock?
   (2) Was the cost per share of acquiring treasury stock higher in 1996 or in 1995?
(b) Prepare the stockholders' equity section for 1996.

PROBLEMS

P15-1 (Stockholders' Equity Classifications) The accounts shown below appear in the December 31 trial balance of Libby Riddles Company:

Preferred Stock Authorized ($100 par value)	$640,000
Common Stock Authorized ($10 par value)	380,000
Unissued Preferred Stock	300,000
Unissued Common Stock	180,000
Subscriptions Receivable, Common	18,000
Subscriptions Receivable, Preferred	21,500
Preferred Stock Subscribed	28,000
Common Stock Subscribed	43,000
Treasury Stock, Preferred (1230 shares at cost)	120,540
Paid-in Capital (excess of amount paid in over par value of common stock)	153,400

Instructions

Assuming that it is reasonably assured that the subscriptions will be collected, use the accounts above to determine the following:
1. Total authorized capital stock.
2. Total unissued capital stock.
3. Total issued capital stock.
4. Capital stock subscribed.
5. Capital stock available for subscription.
6. Net paid-in capital. (*Hint:* Assume that capital stock subscribed accounts and related receivables are not considered part of net paid-in capital.)

P15-2 (Subscribed Stock with Defaulting Subscriber) Stock transactions of Iditarod Corporation are as follows:

Apr. 1 Subscriptions to 500 shares of its $100 par value capital stock are received, together with checks from the various subscribers to cover a 25% down payment. The stock was subscribed at 120. The remainder of the subscription price is to be paid in three equal monthly installments.

May 1 First installments are collected from all subscribers.

June 1 Second installments are received from all subscribers except Susan Butcher, who had subscribed for 100 shares.

5 In reply to correspondence, Ms. Butcher states that she is unable to complete her installment payments and authorizes the company to dispose of the shares subscribed for her.

17 The shares subscribed for Ms. Butcher are sold for cash at 105. Expenses of $125 were incurred in disposing of this stock. (*Hint:* Expenses and deficiencies are charged against the amount due to the subscriber.)

25 A check is mailed to Ms. Butcher equal to the refund due her.

July 1 The final installments are collected on all open subscription accounts, and the stock is issued.

Instructions

Prepare entries in general journal form for the transactions above. Assume that defaulting subscribers are to receive refunds for the amount related to par value but any premium subscribed and paid in is refunded only if it is collected on resale.

P15-3 (Equity Transactions and Statement Preparation) On January 5, 1995, Masek Corporation received a charter granting the right to issue 5,000 shares of $100 par value, 8% cumulative and nonparticipating preferred stock and 50,000 shares of $10 par value common stock. It then completed these transactions:

Jan. 11 Accepted subscriptions to 20,000 shares of common stock at $16 per share; 40% down payments accompanied the subscription.

Feb. 1 Issued Kate Persons Corp. 4,000 shares of preferred stock for the following assets: machinery with a fair market value of $50,000; a factory building with a fair market value of $110,000; and land with an appraised value of $270,000.

Mar. 16 Land, with a fair market value of $210,000, was donated to the company by Gotham City.

Apr. 15 Collected the balance of the subscription price on the common shares and issued the stock.

July 29 Purchased 1,800 shares of common stock at $19 per share (use cost method).

Aug. 10 Sold the 1,800 treasury shares at $14 per share.

Dec. 31 Declared a $0.25 per share cash dividend on the common stock and declared the preferred dividend.

Dec. 31 Closed the Income Summary account. There was a $125,300 net income.

Instructions

(a) Record the journal entries for the transactions listed above.

(b) Prepare the stockholders' equity section of Masek Corporation's balance sheet as of December 31, 1995.

P15-4 (Equity Transactions and Statement Preparation) Mary Ellen Shea Company has two classes of capital stock outstanding: 8%, $20 par preferred and $5 par common. At December 31, 1994, the following accounts were included in stockholders' equity:

Preferred Stock, 100,000 shares	$ 2,000,000
Common Stock, 2,000,000 shares	10,000,000
Paid-in Capital in Excess of Par—Preferred	100,000
Paid-in Capital in Excess of Par—Common	28,000,000
Retained Earnings	3,500,000

The following transactions affected stockholders' equity during 1995:

Jan. 1 25,000 shares of preferred stock issued at $22 per share.

Feb. 1 40,000 shares of common stock issued at $20 per share.

June 1 2-for-1 stock split (par value reduced to $2.50).

July 1 30,000 shares of common treasury stock purchased at $8 per share. Shea uses the cost method.

Sept. 15 10,000 shares of treasury stock reissued at $11 per share.

Dec. 31 Net income is $2,100,000.

Dec. 31 The preferred dividend is declared, and a common dividend of 50¢ per share is declared.

Instructions

Prepare the stockholders' equity section for Mary Ellen Shea Company at December 31, 1995. Show all supporting computations.

P15-5 (Stock Transactions—Assessment and Lump Sum) Karen Schmidt Corporation's charter authorized issuance of 100,000 shares of $10 par value common stock and 50,000 shares of $50 preferred stock. The following transactions involving the issuance of shares of stock were completed. Each transaction is independent of the others.

1. Issued a $10,000, 9% bond payable at par and gave as a bonus one share of preferred stock, which at that time was selling for $105 a share.

2. Issued 500 shares of common stock for machinery. The machinery had been appraised at $6,700; the seller's book value was $6,200. The most recent market price of the common stock is $15 a share.

3. Voted a 10% assessment on both the 10,000 shares of outstanding common and the 1,000 shares of outstanding preferred. The assessment was paid in full.

4. Issued 375 shares of common and 100 shares of preferred for a lump sum amounting to $12,625. The common had been selling at $14 and the preferred at $65.

5. Issued 200 shares of common and 50 shares of preferred for furniture and fixtures. The common had a fair market value of $16 per share and the furniture and fixtures were appraised at $6,100.

Instructions

Record the transactions listed above in journal entry form.

P15-6 (Treasury Stock—Par Value and Cost Methods) Before Jonrowe Corporation engages in the treasury stock transactions listed below, its general ledger reflects, among others, the following account balances (par value of its stock is $30 per share).

Paid-in Capital in Excess of Par	Common Stock	Retained Earnings
Balance $90,000	Balance $270,000	Balance $80,000

Instructions

Record the treasury stock transactions (given below) under the two generally accepted methods of handling treasury stock; use the FIFO method for purchase-sale purposes.

(a) Bought 380 shares of treasury stock at $39 per share.
(b) Bought 300 shares of treasury stock at $43 per share.
(c) Sold 350 shares of treasury stock at $42 per share.
(d) Sold 120 shares of treasury stock at $38 per share.
(e) Retired the remaining shares in the treasury.

P15-7 (Treasury Stock Analysis) The stockholders' equity section of Dolomite Company's balance sheet at December 31, 1996, was as follows:

Common stock—$100 par (authorized 50,000 shares,	
issued and outstanding 15,000 shares)	$1,500,000
Paid-in capital in excess of par	150,000
Retained earnings	210,000
Total stockholders' equity	$1,860,000

On January 2, 1997, having idle cash, the company repurchased 800 shares of its stock for $89,600. During the year it sold 150 of the reacquired shares at $117 per share, another 150 at $110 per share, and legally retired the remaining 500 shares.

Instructions

(a) Discuss the possible alternatives in handling these transactions.
(b) Prepare journal entries for each transaction in accordance with the method that you believe should be applied.

P15-8 (Stock Transaction and Equity Section Preparation) Transactions of Gypsum Company are as follows:

1. The company is granted a charter that authorizes issuance of 15,000 shares of $100 par value preferred stock and 15,000 shares of common stock without par value.
2. 8,000 shares of common stock are issued to founders of the corporation for land valued by the Board of Directors at $210,000. The Board establishes a par value of $10 a share for the common stock.
3. 4,200 shares of preferred stock are sold for cash at 110.
4. 600 shares of common stock are sold to an officer of the corporation for $42 a share.
5. 300 shares of outstanding preferred stock are purchased for cash at par.
6. 400 shares of outstanding preferred stock are purchased for cash at 98.
7. 500 shares of the outstanding common stock issued in No. 2 above are purchased at $49 a share.
8. 200 shares of repurchased preferred stock are reissued at 102.
9. 2,100 shares of preferred stock are issued at 99.
10. 400 shares of reacquired common stock are reissued for $39 a share.
11. 200 shares of the common stock sold in No. 10 above are repurchased for $30 a share.

Instructions

(a) Prepare entries in journal form to record the transactions listed above. No other transactions affecting the capital stock accounts have occurred. Treasury stock is to be entered in the Treasury Stock accounts at par.
(b) Assuming that the company has retained earnings from operations of $112,000, prepare the stockholders' equity section of its balance sheet after considering all the transactions given.

P15-9 (Reacquisition of Stock—FIFO and Weighted Average) Magic Thangs Inc. (MTI) is a closely held toy manufacturer in the Southwest. You have been engaged as the independent public accountant to perform the first audit of MTI. It is agreed that only current-year (1996) financial statements will be prepared.

The following stockholder's equity information has been developed from MTI records on December 31, 1995:

Common stock, no par value; no stated value;	
authorized 30,000 shares; issued 9,000 shares	$405,000
Retained earnings	180,000

The following stock transactions took place during 1996:

1. On March 15, MTI issued 7,000 shares of common stock to Mary Lyon for $62 per share.
2. On March 31, MTI reacquired 4,000 shares of common stock from Emma Goldman (MTI's founder) for $75 per share. These shares were canceled and retired upon receipt.

For the year 1996, MTI reported net income of $110,000.

Instructions

(a) How should the stockholders' equity information be reported in the MTI financial statements for the year ended December 31, 1996 (1) assuming specific identification of the shares is impossible and (2) assuming application of the FIFO method?

(b) How would your answer in part (a) have been altered if MTI had treated the reacquired shares as treasury stock carried at cost rather than retired?

(c) On December 30, 1997, MTI's Board of Directors changed the common stock from no par, no stated value to no par with a $10 stated value per share. How will the stockholders' equity section be affected if comparative financial statements are prepared at December 31, 1997? (Apply the method used in (a)(1).)

P15-10 (Treasury Stock Transactions) During May 1993 Sardonyx Inc. was organized with 4,000,000 authorized shares of $10 par value common stock, and 400,000 shares of its common stock were issued for $4,600,000. Net income through December 31, 1993, was $690,000.

On July 13, 1994, Sardonyx issued 500,000 shares of its common stock for $6,250,000. A 10% stock dividend was declared on October 2, 1994, and issued on November 6, 1994, to stockholders of record on October 23, 1994. The market value of the common stock was $12 per share on the declaration date. Sardonyx's net income for the year ended December 31, 1994, was $470,000. (*Hint:* Retained earnings should be reduced by the fair market value of the stock dividend.)

During 1995 Sardonyx had the following transactions:

1. In February, Sardonyx reacquired 50,000 shares of its common stock for $9 per share. Sardonyx uses the cost method to account for treasury stock.
2. In June, Sardonyx sold 15,000 shares of its treasury stock for $12 per share.
3. On December 15, 1995, Sardonyx declared its first cash dividend to stockholders of $0.10 per share, payable on January 10, 1996, to stockholders of record on December 31, 1995.
4. On December 21, 1995, in accordance with the applicable state law, Sardonyx formally retired 25,000 shares of its treasury stock and had them revert to an unissued basis. The market value of the common stock was $11 per share on this date.
5. Net income for 1995 was $640,000.

Instructions

Prepare a schedule of all transactions affecting the capital stock (shares and dollar amounts), additional paid-in capital, retained earnings, and the treasury stock (shares and dollar amounts) and the amounts that would be included in Sardonyx's balance sheet at December 31, 1993, 1994, and 1995, as a result of the facts above. Show supporting computations in good form.

(AICPA adapted)

P15-11 (Treasury Stock—Cost Method—Equity Section Preparation) Taconite Company has the following owners' equity accounts at December 31, 1994:

Common Stock—$100 par value, authorized 8,000 shares	$480,000
Retained Earnings	294,000

Instructions

(a) Prepare entries in journal form to record the following transactions, which took place during 1995. (*Hint:* Debit retained earnings in transaction 6.)

1. 240 shares of outstanding stock were purchased at 96. (These are to be accounted for using the cost method.)
2. A $20 per share cash dividend was declared.
3. The dividend declared in No. 2 above was paid.
4. The treasury shares purchased in No. 1 above were resold at 102.
5. 500 shares of outstanding stock were purchased at 103.
6. 120 shares of outstanding stock were purchased at 105 and retired.
7. 330 of the shares purchased in No. 5 above were resold at 96.

(b) Prepare the stockholders' equity section of Taconite Company's balance sheet after giving effect to these transactions, assuming that the net income for 1995 was $72,000.

P15-12 (Comprehensive Stockholders' Equity—Work Sheet) Mica Corporation is a publicly owned company whose shares are traded on a national stock exchange. At December 31, 1994, Mica had 60,000,000 shares of $10 par value common stock authorized, of which 30,000,000 shares were issued and 26,000,000 shares were outstanding.

The stockholders' equity accounts at December 31, 1994, had the following balances:

Common Stock	$300,000,000
Additional Paid-in Capital	240,000,000
Retained Earnings	150,000,000
Treasury Stock	36,000,000

During 1995, Mica had the following transactions:

1. On February 1, 1995, a secondary distribution of 4,000,000 shares of $10 par value common stock was completed. The stock was sold to the public at $21 per share, net of offering costs.

2. On February 15, 1995, Mica issued at $120 per share, 100,000 shares of $100 par value, 8% cumulative preferred stock.

3. On March 1, 1995, Mica reacquired 40,000 shares of its common stock for $23 per share. Mica uses the cost method to account for treasury stock.

4. On March 31, 1995, Mica declared a semiannual cash dividend on common stock of $0.15 per share, payable on April 30, 1995, to stockholders of record on April 10, 1995. The appropriate state law prohibits cash dividends on treasury stock.

5. On April 30, 1995, employees exercised 200,000 options that were granted in 1993 under a noncompensatory stock option plan. When the options were granted, each option had a preemptive right and entitled the employee to purchase one share of common stock for $25 per share. On April 30, 1995, the market price of the common stock was $25 per share. Mica issued new shares to settle the transaction.

6. On May 31, 1995, when the market price of the common stock was $25 per share, Mica declared a 10% stock dividend distributable on July 1, 1995, to stockholders of record on June 1, 1995. The appropriate state law prohibits stock dividends on treasury stock. The stock dividend is recorded using the market price.

7. On June 30, 1995, Mica sold the 40,000 treasury shares reacquired on March 1, 1995, and an additional 560,000 treasury shares costing $14,400,000 that were on hand at the beginning of the year. The selling price was $36 per share.

8. On September 30, 1995, Mica declared a semiannual cash dividend on common stock of 25 cents per share and the yearly dividend on preferred stock, both payable on October 30, 1995, to stockholders of record on October 10, 1995. The appropriate state law prohibits cash dividends on treasury stock.

Net income for 1995 was $90,000,000.

Instructions

Prepare a work sheet to be used to summarize, for each transaction, the changes in Mica's stockholders' equity accounts for 1995. The columns on this work sheet should have the following headings:

Date of transaction (or beginning date)

Common stock—number of shares

Common stock—amount

Preferred stock—number of shares

Preferred stock—amount

Additional paid-in capital

Retained earnings

Treasury stock—number of shares

Treasury stock—amount

Show supporting computations in good form.

(AICPA adapted)

CASES

C15-1 (Preemptive Rights and Dilution of Ownership) Garcia Computer Company is a small closely held corporation. Eighty percent of the stock is held by Andy Garcia, President; of the remainder, 10% is held by members of his family and 10% by Rosie Perez, a former officer who is now retired. The balance sheet of the company at June 30, 1995, was substantially as shown below:

Assets		Liabilities and Capital	
Cash	$ 22,000	Current liabilities	$150,000
Other	600,000	Capital stock	300,000
		Retained earnings	172,000
	$622,000		$622,000

Additional authorized capital stock of $300,000 par value had never been issued. To strengthen the cash position of the company, Andy Garcia issued capital stock of a par value of $100,000 to himself at par for cash. At the next stockholders' meeting, Perez objected and claimed that her interests had been injured.

Instructions
- **(a)** Which stockholder's right was ignored in the issue of shares to Andy Garcia?
- **(b)** How may the damage to Perez's interests be repaired most simply?
- **(c)** If Andy Garcia offered Perez a personal cash settlement and they agreed to employ you as an impartial arbitrator to determine the amount, what settlement would you propose? Present your calculations with sufficient explanation to satisfy both parties.

C15-2 (Subscribed Stock and Subscription Receivable) Jesus Trevino Corporation sold 50,000 shares of its $10 par value common stock on a subscription basis for $40 per share. By December 31, 1995, collections on these subscriptions totaled $1,200,000. No subscriptions have yet been paid in full.

Instructions
- **(a)** Discuss the meaning of the account Common Stock Subscribed and indicate how it is reported in the financial statements.
- **(b)** Discuss the arguments in favor of reporting Subscriptions Receivable as a current asset.
- **(c)** Discuss the arguments in favor of reporting Subscriptions Receivable as a contra equity account.
- **(d)** Indicate how these 50,000 shares would be presented on Trevino's December 31, 1995, balance sheet under the method discussed in (c) above.

C15-3 (Issuance of Stock for Land) Jimmy Smits Corporation is planning to issue 3,000 shares of its own $10 par value common stock for 2 acres of land to be used as a building site.

Instructions
- **(a)** What general rule should be applied to determine the amount at which the land should be recorded?
- **(b)** Under what circumstances should this transaction be recorded at the fair market value of the land?
- **(c)** Under what circumstances should this transaction be recorded at the fair market value of the stock issued?
- **(d)** Assume Smits intentionally records this transaction at an amount greater than the fair market value of the land and the stock. Discuss this situation.

C15-4 (Equipment Purchase with Treasury Stock) Olmos Corporation purchased $160,000 worth of equipment in 1993 for $100,000 cash and a promise to deliver an indeterminate number of treasury shares of its $5 par common stock, with a market value of $20,000 on January 1 of each year for the next 4 years. Hence $80,000 in "market value" of treasury shares will be required to discharge the $60,000 balance due on the equipment.

The corporation then acquired 5,000 shares of its own stock in the expectation that the market value of the stock would increase substantially before the delivery dates.

Instructions
- **(a)** Discuss the propriety of recording the equipment at
  1. $100,000 (the cash payment).
  2. $160,000 (the cash price of the equipment).
  3. $180,000 (the $100,000 cash payment plus the $80,000 market value of treasury stock that must be transferred to the vendor in order to settle the obligation according to the terms of the agreement).
- **(b)** Discuss the arguments for treating the balance due as
  1. A liability.
  2. Treasury stock subscribed.
- **(c)** Assuming that legal requirements do not affect the decision, discuss the arguments for treating the corporation's treasury shares as
  1. An asset awaiting ultimate disposition.
  2. A capital element awaiting ultimate disposition.
- **(d)** Compare and contrast the cost method with the par value method for each of the following:
  1. Purchase of shares at a price less than par value.
  2. Purchase of shares at a price greater than par value.
  3. Subsequent resale of treasury shares at a price less than purchase price, but more than par value.
  4. Subsequent resale of treasury shares at a price greater than both purchase price and par value.
  5. Effect on net income.

(AICPA adapted)

C15-5 (Secret Reserves and Watered Stock) It has been said that (1) the use of the LIFO inventory method during an extended period of rising prices and (2) the expensing of all human-resource costs are among the accepted accounting practices that help create "secret reserves."

Instructions
- **(a)** What is a "secret reserve"? How can "secret reserves" be created or enlarged?
- **(b)** What is the basis for saying that the two specific practices cited above tend to create "secret reserves"?

(c) Is it possible to create a "secret reserve" in connection with accounting for a liability? If so, explain or give an example.

(d) What are the objections to the creation of "secret reserves"?

(e) It has also been said that "watered stock" is the opposite of a "secret reserve." What is "watered stock"?

(f) Describe the general circumstances in which "watered stock" can arise.

(g) What steps can be taken to eliminate "water" from a capital structure?

(AICPA adapted)

▶ USING YOUR JUDGMENT ◀

▶ FINANCIAL REPORTING PROBLEM

The stockholders' equity section of Georgia-Pacific Corporation is shown in its Balance Sheet on page 221 of Appendix 5-A. You will also find data relative to this problem on other pages of the Appendix.

Instructions

Answer the following questions.

1. What is the par or stated value of Georgia-Pacific's common stock?
2. What percentage of Georgia-Pacific's authorized common stock was issued at December 31, 1993? (Round to the nearest full percentage)
3. How many shares of common stock were outstanding at December 31, 1993 and December 31, 1992?
4. What was book value per share at December 31, 1993 and at December 31, 1992?
5. Explain what has happened to Georgia-Pacific's capital structure over the last ten years.
6. What was the closing market price per share at December 31, 1993, and at December 31, 1983?

▶ WRITING ASSIGNMENT

(Treasury Stock—Par Value and Cost Methods) John Uteg International, a relatively new corporation, has just become liquid enough to reacquire some of its own $1 par common stock in the market for $45 per share. It decided to repurchase 40,000 shares. The company has 200,000 shares of common stock authorized and 100,000 outstanding. All shares were originally issued at $30 per share. Retained Earnings amounts to $2,420,000. Since John Uteg is only beginning to reacquire its own stock, it has not yet decided how to account for this treasury stock.

As the company's independent auditor, you have been asked by the president, Douglas Pierce, to compare the cost and par value methods, indicating which would provide more valuable, theoretically sound financial information to financial statement users.

Instructions

Using the foregoing data, draft a memo comparing the two methods. Include separate appendixes illustrating the journal entries under each method and the stockholders' equity portion of the balance sheet, referring to these in your memo whenever necessary. Include the balance sheet effect of each method in your discussion. Which would you recommend as the more useful method? Might other considerations enter into your choice?

▶ GROUP ASSIGNMENT

(Redeemable Preferred Stock) The following information relates to Altoona Industries Inc.:

Altoona Industries, Inc.

	1993	1992
($000)		
Series A first preferred stock—subject to mandatory redemption ($4,062,500 liquidation value in 1993 and 1992); $1.00 par value; authorized 100,000 shares; issued 40,625 shares in 1993 and 1992 (note 6)	$ 3,473	$ 3,425

Common stockholders' equity:
Common stock, $.10 par value; authorized 20,000,000 shares;

issued 5,522,602 shares in 1993 and 5,280,602 in 1992	552	528
Additional paid-in capital	10,463	6,014
Valuation allowance for investments	(675)	(1,773)
Retained earnings	25,286	17,110
Common stockholders' equity	35,626	21,879

Notes to Consolidated Financial Statements   Note 6:   Redeemable Preferred Stock.   The Company's preferred stock consists of 250,000 authorized shares of $1.00 par value First Preferred Stock of which 40,625 shares of Series A First Preferred Stock were outstanding at December 31, 1993. The Series A First Preferred Stock, which is not convertible, has a carrying value of $80.00 per share representing fair value at date of issuance based upon an independent appraisal and sales to third parties, plus accumulated accretion. The shares are entitled to cumulative dividends of $12.70 annually ($3.175 per quarter) per share and must be redeemed at 10% per year commencing on December 31, 1996, at $100.00 per share plus accrued and unpaid dividends. The Company, at its option, may redeem at that price in each year in which mandatory redemption is required an additional number of shares not exceeding the mandatory redemption and may redeem all or any part of the shares at that price plus a premium amounting to $3.55 in 1994 and declining proportionately thereafter through 2002 after which there will be no premium.

Altoona had total debt of $85,979 in 1993. A restrictive covenant on some of the debt prohibits Altoona from additional borrowing if the debt/equity ratio exceeds 2.5 or if retained earnings falls below $17,000.

Instructions
Your instructor will assign one group member to serve as a recorder and one member to serve as spokesperson. As a group, provide the information for the recorder to prepare responses to the following questions based on the above information. Upon completion, the spokesperson will report the group findings to the class and be prepared to provide justification for your responses.
   (a)   Does the series A preferred stock have characteristics more like common stock or like debt? Explain.
   (b)   What are the present GAAP requirements for redeemable preferred stock?
   (c)   Is Altoona in violation of its debt covenants in 1993, based upon the reported numbers above? Would your answer change if Altoona classifies the redeemable stock as debt?
   (d)   How should redeemable preferred stock be reported?

▶ ETHICS CASE

(Ethical Issue: Watered Stock).   Morris Lester is the accounting manager of LBC, which is a closely held and rapidly growing retail sporting equipment concern with 60 stores located throughout New York and New England. Morris has been asked by the CFO, Kathy Morgan, to review two agreed-upon alternatives for the purchase of a newly constructed warehouse facility located in Pittsfield, Massachusetts (defined as follows):

Option 1:

New Building	$1,500,000	
LBC Common Stock (100 Par Value)		$1,000,000
Paid-in Capital in Excess of Par		500,000

Option 2:

New Building	$1,350,000	
Notes Payable (with Contractor)		$1,200,000
Cash		150,000

In addition to the above facts and figures, Morris knows that LBC would probably prefer the first option because Kathy Morgan told him earlier that, ". . . the company is experiencing tough working capital problems due to its rapid expansion in recent years."

Instructions
   (a)   Assuming that the value of the new warehouse was independently appraised by a real estate consulting firm at $1.5 million, what are the ethical implications that should be considered by Morris when considering both options?
   (b)   Assuming that the value of the new warehouse was independently appraised by a real estate consulting firm at $1.35 million, what are the ethical implications that should be considered by Morris when considering both options?
   (c)   Who could be harmed if LBC chose to inflate its asset values in a "watered stock" transaction?
   (d)   Explain how your answers to the above questions would change if LBC were a publicly traded corporation.

CHAPTER 16

STOCKHOLDERS' EQUITY: RETAINED EARNINGS

LEARNING OBJECTIVES

After studying this chapter, you should be able to:

1. Identify the major categories of stockholders' equity.

2. Describe the policies used in distributing dividends.

3. Identify the various forms of dividend distributions.

4. Explain the accounting for small and large stock dividends.

5. Distinguish between stock dividends and stock splits.

6. Explain the effect of different types of preferred stock dividends.

7. Identify the reasons for appropriating retained earnings.

8. Explain accounting and reporting for appropriated retained earnings.

9. Prepare a statement of stockholders' equity.

OBJECTIVE 1

Identify the major categories of stockholders' equity.

The following three categories normally appear as part of stockholders' equity:

1. Capital stock (legal capital).

2. Additional paid-in capital (capital in excess of par or stated value).

3. Retained earnings or deficit.

The first two categories, capital stock and additional paid-in capital, constitute **contributed (or paid-in) capital;** retained earnings represents the **earned capital** of the enterprise. The distinction between contributed capital and earned capital has a legal origin, but at present it serves the useful purpose of indicating the different sources from which the corporation has obtained its **equity capital.**

Contributed capital consisting of preferred and common stock along with additional paid-in capital was discussed in Chapter 15. Retained earnings, dividends, and appropriations are discussed in this chapter.

▶ RETAINED EARNINGS

The basic source of **retained earnings**—earnings retained for use in the business—is income from operations. Stockholders assume the greatest risk in enterprise operations and stand any losses or share in any profits resulting from enterprise activities. Any income not distributed among the stockholders thus becomes additional stockholders' equity. Net income includes a considerable variety of income sources. These include the main operation of the enterprise (such as manufacturing and selling a given product), plus any ancillary activities (such as disposing of scrap or renting out unused space), plus the results of extraordinary and unusual items. All give rise to net income that increases retained earnings. The more common items that either increase or decrease retained earnings are expressed in account form below.

Retained Earnings	
1. Net loss	1. Net income
2. Prior period adjustments (error corrections) and certain changes in accounting principle	2. Prior period adjustments (error corrections) and certain changes in accounting principle
3. Cash or scrip dividends	3. Adjustments due to quasi-reorganization
4. Stock dividends	
5. Property dividends	
6. Some treasury stock transactions	

**ILLUSTRATION 16-1
Transactions that Affect
Retained Earnings**

Chapter 4 pointed out that under the modified all-inclusive concept of income, the results of irregular transactions should be reported in the income statement, not the retained earnings statement. However, prior period adjustments (error corrections) should be reported as adjustments to beginning retained earnings, bypassing completely the current income statement.

► DIVIDEND POLICY

As soon as retained earnings is recorded, two alternatives exist: the credit balance can be (1) reduced by a distribution of assets—a **dividend**—to the stockholders, or (2) left intact and the offsetting assets used in the operations of the business.

Very few companies pay dividends in amounts equal to their legally available retained earnings. The major reasons are as follows:

OBJECTIVE 2
Describe the policies used in distributing dividends.

1. Agreements (bond covenants) with specific creditors to retain all or a portion of the earnings, in the form of assets, to build up additional protection against possible loss.

2. Some state corporation laws require that earnings equivalent to the cost of treasury shares purchased be restricted against dividend declarations.

3. Desire to retain assets that would otherwise be paid out as dividends, to finance growth or expansion. This is sometimes called internal financing, reinvesting earnings, or "plowing" the profits back into the business.

4. Desire to smooth out dividend payments from year to year by accumulating earnings in good years and using such accumulated earnings as a basis for dividends in bad years.

5. Desire to build up a cushion or buffer against possible losses or errors in the calculation of profits.

The reasons above are probably self-explanatory except for the second. The laws of some states require that the corporation's legal capital be restricted from distribution to stockholders so that it may serve as a protection against loss to creditors.[1]

If a company is considering declaring a dividend, two preliminary questions must be asked:

1. Is the condition of the corporation such that a dividend is **legally permissible?**

2. Is the condition of the corporation such that a dividend is **economically sound?**

---

[1] If the corporation buys its own outstanding stock, it has reduced its legal capital and distributed assets to stockholders. If this were permitted, the corporation could, by purchasing treasury stock at any price desired, return to the stockholders their investments and leave creditors with little or no protection against loss.

LEGALITY OF DIVIDENDS

The legality of a dividend can be determined only by reviewing the applicable state law. Currently, the 50 states may be classified into one of three groups for purposes of comparing restrictions on dividends and other distributions to owners.[2] The largest group, consisting of 22 states, operates under the 1950 Model Business Corporation Act, which permits distributions to stockholders as long as the corporation is not insolvent. Insolvency is defined as the inability to pay debts as they come due in the normal course of business. Generally, in these states distribution in the form of dividends has to come from retained earnings or from current earnings.

Another 18 states either follow the 1984 Revised Model Business Corporation Act or have distribution restrictions similar to it. That is, (1) the corporation must be solvent, and (2) distributions must not exceed the fair value of net assets. Under the latter criterion, distributions are not limited to retained earnings or GAAP determined current earnings. Instead of being tied to the book value of the assets, distributions are linked to the fair (appraised) value of the assets—a notable new criterion.

The remaining states use a variety of hybrid restrictions that consist of solvency and balance sheet tests of liquidity and risk. To avoid illegal distribution of corporate assets to stockholders, the relevant state corporation act should be examined and legal advice obtained.

Unfortunately, current financial statement disclosures do not include basic information such as: whether a corporation is in compliance with state legal requirements; the corporation's capacity to make distributions; or, occasionally, what legal restrictions exist regarding distributions to stockholders.

An example of the inadequacies of such disclosures is the 1987–88 stockholders' equity balance sheet sections of Holiday Corporation (owner of Holiday Inns of America). Its 1987 balance sheet reported total stockholders' equity of $639 million. The 1988 balance sheet, however, revealed a **$770 million deficit** in Holiday's total stockholders' equity. How did this deficit develop? During the year, Holiday distributed a $65 per share dividend to prevent a hostile takeover. This $1.55 billion dividend to stockholders, financed with borrowed money, not only exceeded Holiday's retained earnings (then about $400 million), but exceeded total stockholders' equity as well by $770 million.

Holiday was allowed to distribute the $1.55 billion dividend (legally, under Delaware law) because the fair value of its assets exceeded its liabilities after the distribution; that is, on a fair value basis it had positive equity. Yet, the traditional balance sheet disclosures in the equity section or the accompanying notes do not contain any information (either before or after the dividend distribution), enabling financial statement readers to assess Holiday's capacity for making such distributions.

Because the traditional equivalency of minimum legal capital and par value no longer holds in many states, the stockholders' equity accounting presentation of par value, additional paid-in capital, and retained earnings is being eroded. It implies that some amount, represented by a portion of stockholders' equity, exists to protect creditors, when in many instances, it may not.

FINANCIAL CONDITION AND DIVIDEND DISTRIBUTIONS

Good management of a business requires attention to more than the legality of dividend distributions. Consideration must be given to economic conditions, most importantly, liquidity. Assume an extreme situation as follows:

ILLUSTRATION 16-2
Balance Sheet, Showing a Lack of Liquidity

BALANCE SHEET			
Plant assets	$500,000	Capital stock	$400,000
		Retained earnings	100,000
	$500,000		$500,000

---

[2]Michael L. Roberts, William D. Samson, and Michael T. Dugan, "The Stockholders' Equity Section: Form Without Substance," *Accounting Horizons*, December 1990, pp. 35–46.

The depicted company has a retained earnings credit balance and generally, unless it is restricted, can declare a dividend of $100,000. But because all its assets are plant assets and used in operations, payment of a cash dividend of $100,000 would require the sale of plant assets or borrowing.

Even if we assume a balance sheet showing current assets, the question remains as to whether those assets are needed for other purposes.

ILLUSTRATION 16-3
Balance Sheet, Showing Cash but Minimal Working Capital

BALANCE SHEET				
Cash	$100,000	Current liabilities		$ 60,000
Plant assets	460,000	Capital stock	$400,000	
		Retained earnings	100,000	500,000
	$560,000			$560,000

The existence of current liabilities implies very strongly that some of the cash is needed to meet current debts as they mature. In addition, day-by-day cash requirements for payrolls and other expenditures not included in current liabilities also require cash.

Thus, before a dividend is declared, management must consider **availability of funds to pay the dividend.** Other demands for cash should perhaps be investigated by preparing a cash forecast. A dividend should not be paid unless both the present and future financial position appear to warrant the distribution.

Directors must also consider the effect of inflation and replacement costs before making a dividend commitment. During a period of significant inflation, some costs charged to expense under historical cost accounting are understated in terms of comparative purchasing power. Income is thereby overstated because certain costs have not been adjusted for inflation. For example, St. Regis Paper Company reported historical cost net income of $179 million, but when it was adjusted for general inflation, net income was only $68 million. Yet St. Regis paid cash dividends of $72 million. Were cash dividends excessive? This subject is discussed more in Chapter 26.

The SEC encourages companies to disclose their dividend policy in their annual report. Those that (1) have earnings but fail to pay dividends or (2) do not expect to pay dividends in the forseeable future are encouraged to report this information. In addition, companies that have had a consistent pattern of paying dividends are encouraged to indicate whether they intend to continue this practice in the future.

Two disclosures relative to the policy of payment or nonpayment of dividends are those of Kellogg Company (Annual Report) and Atmel Corporation presented below.

ILLUSTRATION 16-4
Disclosures about Dividend Payment Policy

Kellogg Corporation
37 Years of Dividend Increase. Dividend payments for the year totaled $1.32, up 10 percent from 1992, marking the 37th consecutive year of increase. The trend of increased dividends is expected to continue in 1994.

Atmel Corporation
Dividend Policy. The Company has not paid any dividends on its capital stock. The Company presently intends to retain any earnings for use in business and therefore does not anticipate paying cash dividends on its outstanding shares in the foreseeable future. In addition, the Company's bank credit agreement restricts the Company's ability to pay cash dividends without the bank's consent.

TYPES OF DIVIDENDS

Dividend distributions generally are based either on accumulated profits, that is, retained earnings, or on some other capital item such as additional paid-in capital. The natural expectation of any stockholder who receives a dividend is that the corporation has operated successfully and that he or she is receiving a share of its profits. A **liquidating dividend**—that is, a dividend not based on retained earnings—should be

OBJECTIVE 3

Identify the various forms of dividend distributions.

adequately described in the accompanying message to the stockholders so that there will be no misunderstanding about its source. Dividends are of the following types:

1. Cash dividends.
2. Property dividends.
3. Scrip dividends.
4. Liquidating dividends.
5. Stock dividends.

Dividends are commonly paid in cash but occasionally are paid in stock, scrip, or some other asset.[3] **All dividends, except for stock dividends, reduce the stockholders' equity in the corporation,** because the equity is reduced either through an immediate or promised future distribution of assets. When a stock dividend is declared, the corporation does not pay out assets or incur a liability. It issues additional shares of stock to each stockholder and nothing more.

Cash Dividends

The board of directors votes on the declaration of **cash dividends,** and if the resolution is properly approved, the dividend is declared. Before it is paid, a current list of stockholders must be prepared. For this reason there is usually a time lag between declaration and payment. A resolution approved at the January 10 (**date of declaration**) meeting of the board of directors might be declared payable February 5 (**date of payment**) to all stockholders of record January 25 (**date of record**).[4]

The period from January 10 to January 25 gives time for any transfers in process to be completed and registered with the transfer agent. The time from January 25 to February 5 provides an opportunity for the transfer agent or accounting department, depending on who does this work, to prepare a list of stockholders as of January 25 and to prepare and mail dividend checks.

A declared cash dividend is a liability and, because payment is generally required very soon, is usually a current liability. The following entries are required to record the declaration and payment of an ordinary dividend payable in cash. For example, Roadway Freight Corp. on June 10 declared a cash dividend of 50 cents a share on 1.8 million shares payable July 16 to all stockholders of record June 24.

At date of declaration (June 10)

Retained Earnings (Cash Dividends Declared)	900,000	
Dividends Payable		900,000

At date of record (June 24)

    No entry

At date of payment (July 16)

Dividends Payable	900,000	
Cash		900,000

To set up a ledger account that shows the amount of dividends declared during the year, Cash Dividends Declared might be debited instead of Retained Earnings at the time of declaration. This account is then closed to Retained Earnings at year end.

Dividends may be declared either as a certain percent of par, such as a 6% dividend on preferred stock, or as an amount per share, such as 60 cents per share on no-par

---

[3]*Accounting Trends and Techniques—1993* reported that of its 600 surveyed companies, 452 paid a cash dividend on common stock, 130 paid a cash dividend on preferred stock, 10 issued stock dividends, and 12 issued or paid dividends in kind.

[4]Theoretically, the ex-dividend date is the day after the date of record. However, to allow time for transfer of the shares, the stock exchanges generally advance the ex-dividend date 2 to 4 days. Therefore, the party who owns the stock on the day prior to the expressed ex-dividend date receives the dividends, and the party who buys the stock on and after the ex-dividend date does not receive the dividend. Between the declaration date and the ex-dividend date, the market price of the stock includes the dividend.

common stock. In the first case, the rate is multiplied by the par value of outstanding shares to get the total dividend; in the second, the amount per share is multiplied by the number of shares outstanding. **Cash dividends are not declared and paid on treasury stock.**

Dividend policies vary among corporations. Some older, well-established firms take pride in a long, unbroken string of quarterly dividend payments. They would lower or pass the dividend only if forced to do so by a sustained decline in earnings or a critical shortage of cash.

The percentage of annual earnings distributed as cash dividends ("payout ratio") depends somewhat on the stability and trend of earnings, with 25 to 75% of earnings being paid out by many well-established corporations. For example, Emerson Electric Co. of St. Louis continues its policy of paying dividends equivalent to 45 to 50% of the prior year's earnings. "Growth" companies, on the other hand, pay little or no cash dividends because their policy is to expand as rapidly as internal and external financing permit. Neither Quest Medical, Inc., a small growth company, nor Federal Express Corporation, a large growth company, has ever paid cash dividends to their common stockholders. These investors hope that the price of their shares will appreciate in value and that they will realize a profit when they sell their shares. The graphic in Illustration 16-5 shows the dividend payout as a percentage of profits for the Standard and Poor's 500 stocks during the past decade.

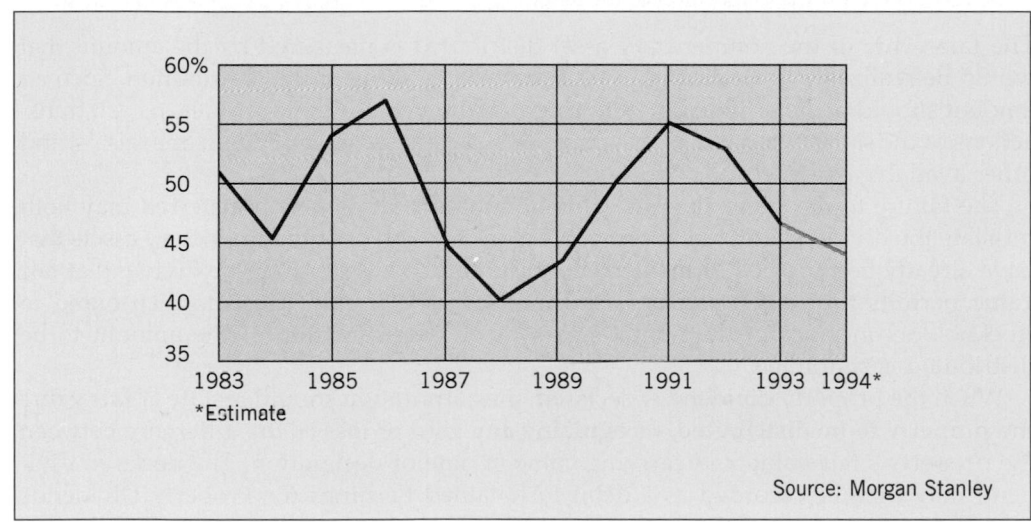

**ILLUSTRATION 16-5
Dividend Payout as a
Percentage of Profits**

Source: Morgan Stanley

Property Dividends

Dividends payable in assets of the corporation other than cash are called **property dividends** or **dividends in kind.** Property dividends may be merchandise, real estate, or investments, or whatever form the board of directors designates. Ranchers Exploration and Development Corp. reported one year that it would pay a fourth-quarter dividend in gold bars instead of cash. Because of the obvious difficulties of divisibility of units and delivery to stockholders, the usual property dividend is in the form of securities of other companies that the distributing corporation holds as an investment.

For example, when DuPont's 23% stock interest in General Motors was held by the Supreme Court to be in violation of antitrust laws. DuPont was ordered to divest itself of the GM stock within 10 years. The stock represented 63 million shares of GM's 281 million shares then outstanding. DuPont couldn't sell the shares in one block of 63 million, nor could it sell 6 million shares annually for the next 10 years without severely depressing the value of the GM stock. At that time the entire yearly trading volume in GM stock did not exceed 6 million shares. DuPont solved its problem by declaring a property dividend and distributing the GM shares as a dividend to its own stockholders.

Dresser Industries, Inc., distributed a dividend in kind and reported its accounting for the distribution as follows:

ILLUSTRATION 16-6
Disclosure of a Dividend
in Kind

Dresser Industries, Inc.

Notes to Consolidated Financial Statements

Note B: Dividend in Kind. The Company divested its industrial products and equipment businesses effective August 1, 1992. The divestiture/spin-off was accomplished by a distribution of one INDRESCO share for every five shares of the Company's common stock. The distribution is included as charges totaling $413.9 million to retained earnings and accumulated translation adjustment in the 1992 statement of shareholders' investment.

A property dividend is a nonreciprocal transfer[5] of nonmonetary assets between an enterprise and its owners. Prior to the issuance of *APB Opinion No. 29*, the accounting for such transfers was based on the carrying amount (book value) of the nonmonetary assets transferred. This practice was based on the rationale that there is no sale or arm's-length transaction on which to base a gain or loss and that only this method is consistent with the historical cost basis of accounting. However, the profession's current position is quite clear on this matter:

> A transfer of a nonmonetary asset to a stockholder or to another entity in a nonreciprocal transfer should be recorded at the fair value of the asset transferred, and a gain or loss should be recognized on the disposition of the asset.[6]

The **fair value** of the nonmonetary asset distributed is measured by the amount that would be realizable in an outright sale at or near the time of the distribution. Such an amount should be determined by referring to estimated realizable values in cash transactions of the same or similar assets, quoted market prices, independent appraisals, and other available evidence.[7]

The failure to recognize the fair value of nonmonetary assets transferred may both misstate the dividend and fail to recognize gains and losses on nonmonetary assets that have already been earned or incurred by the enterprise. Recording the dividend at fair value permits future comparisons of dividend rates. If cash must be distributed to stockholders in place of the nonmonetary asset, determination of the amount to be distributed is simplified.

When the property dividend is declared, the corporation should **restate at fair value the property to be distributed, recognizing any gain or loss** as the difference between the property's fair value and carrying value at date of declaration. The declared dividend may then be recorded as a debit to Retained Earnings (or Property Dividends Declared) and a credit to Property Dividends Payable at an amount equal to the fair value of the property to be distributed. Upon distribution of the dividend, Property Dividends Payable is debited, and the account containing the distributed asset (restated at fair value) is credited.

For example, Trendler, Inc., transferred to stockholders some of its investments in marketable securities costing $1,250,000 by declaring a property dividend on December 28, 1994, to be distributed on January 30, 1995, to stockholders of record on January 15, 1995. At the date of declaration the securities have a market value of $2,000,000. The entries are shown at the top of page 779:

---

[5]A nonreciprocal transfer of assets or services is in one direction, either from or to an enterprise.

[6]"Accounting for Nonmonetary Transactions," *Opinions of the Accounting Principles Board No. 29* (New York: AICPA, 1973), par. 18.

[7]According to *APB Opinion No. 29*, accounting for the distribution of nonmonetary assets to owners of an enterprise in a spin-off or other form of reorganization or liquidation should be based on the **book value** (after reduction, if appropriate, for an indicated impairment of value) of the nonmonetary assets distributed. This is an exception to the fair value treatment prescribed for nonmonetary distributions.

At date of declaration (December 28, 1994)

Investments in Securities	750,000	
Gain on Appreciation of Securities		750,000
Retained Earnings (Property Dividends Declared)	2,000,000	
Property Dividends Payable		2,000,000

At date of distribution (January 30, 1995)

Property Dividends Payable	2,000,000	
Investments in Securities		2,000,000

Scrip Dividends

A **scrip dividend**—dividend payable in scrip—means that instead of paying the dividend now, the corporation has elected to pay it at some later date. **The scrip issued to stockholders as a dividend is merely a special form of note payable.** For example, in 1980 the Bank of Puerto Rico issued a $9 million note as a dividend that matured in 1990, at which time each holder of the corporation's three million common shares received $3 a share. Scrip dividends may be declared when the corporation has a sufficient retained earnings balance but is short of cash. The recipient of the scrip dividend may hold it until the due date, if one is specified, and collect the dividend or may sell it to obtain immediate cash.

When a scrip dividend is declared, the corporation debits Retained Earnings (or Scrip Dividend Declared) and credits Scrip Dividend Payable or Notes Payable to Stockholders, **reporting the payable as a liability** on the balance sheet. Upon payment, Scrip Dividend Payable is debited and Cash credited. If the scrip bears interest, the interest portion of the cash payment should be debited to Interest Expense and not treated as part of the dividend. For example, Berg Canning Company avoided missing its 84th consecutive quarterly dividend by declaring on May 27, 1992 a scrip dividend in the form of two-month promissory notes amounting to 80 cents a share on 2,545,000 shares outstanding and payable at the date of record, June 5, 1992. The notes paid interest of 10% per annum and matured on July 27, 1992. The entries are as follows:

At date of declaration (May 27, 1992)

Retained Earnings (Scrip Dividend Declared)	2,036,000	
Notes Payable to Stockholders ($.80 × 2,545,000)		2,036,000

At date of payment (July 27, 1992)

Notes Payable to Stockholders	2,036,000	
Interest Expense ($2,036,000 × 2/12 × .10)[a]	33,933	
Cash		2,069,933

[a]The interest runs from the date of declaration to the date of payment.

Liquidating Dividends

Some corporations use paid-in capital as a basis for dividends. Without proper disclosure of this fact, stockholders may erroneously believe the corporation has been operating at a profit. A further result could be subsequent sale of additional shares at a higher price than is warranted. This type of deception, intentional or unintentional, can be avoided by requiring that a clear statement of the source of every dividend accompany the dividend check.

Dividends based on other than retained earnings are sometimes described as **liquidating dividends,** thus implying that they are a return of the stockholder's investment rather than of profits. In fact, the distribution may be based on capital that resulted from donations by outsiders or other stockholders and not be a return of the given stockholder's contribution. But, in a more general sense, **any dividend not based on earnings must be a reduction of corporate paid-in capital and, to that extent, it is a liquidating dividend.** We noted in Chapter 11 that companies in the extractive industries may pay dividends equal to the total of accumulated income and depletion. The portion of these dividends in excess of accumulated income represents a return of part of the stockholder's investment.

For example, McChesney Mines Inc. issued a "dividend" to its common stockholders of $1,200,000. The cash dividend announcement noted that $900,000 should be considered income and the remainder a return of capital. The entries are:

At date of declaration

Retained Earnings	900,000	
Additional Paid-in Capital	300,000	
Dividends Payable		1,200,000

At date of payment

Dividends Payable	1,200,000	
Cash		1,200,000

In some cases, management may simply decide to cease business and declare a liquidating dividend. In these cases, liquidation may take place over a number of years to ensure an orderly and fair sale of assets. For example, when Overseas National Airways was dissolved in 1980, it agreed to pay a liquidating dividend to its stockholders over a period of years equivalent to $8.60 per share. Each liquidating dividend payment in such cases reduces paid-in capital.

Stock Dividends

If the management wishes to "capitalize" part of the earnings (i.e., reclassify amounts from earned to contributed capital), and thus retain earnings in the business on a permanent basis, it may issue a stock dividend. In this case, **no assets are distributed,** and each stockholder has exactly the same proportionate interest in the corporation and the same total book value after the stock dividend was issued as before it was declared. Of course, the book value per share is lower because an increased number of shares is held.

While accountants agree that a **stock dividend** is the nonreciprocal issuance by a corporation of its own stock to its stockholders on a pro rata basis, they do not agree on the proper entries to be made at the time of a stock dividend. Some believe that the **par value** of the stock issued as a dividend should be transferred from retained earnings to capital stock. Others believe that the **fair value** of the stock issued—its market value at the declaration date—should be transferred from retained earnings to capital stock and additional paid-in capital.

The fair value position was originally adopted in this country, at least in part, in order to influence the stock dividend policies of corporations. Evidently in 1941 both the New York Stock Exchange and a majority of the Committee on Accounting Procedure regarded periodic stock dividends as objectionable. The Committee therefore acted to make it more difficult for corporations to sustain a series of such stock dividends out of their accumulated earnings by requiring the use of fair market value when it was substantially in excess of book value.[8]

When the stock dividend is less than 20–25% of the common shares outstanding at the time of the dividend declaration, the accounting profession requires that the **fair market value** of the stock issued be transferred from retained earnings.[9] Stock dividends of less than 20–25% are often referred to as **small (ordinary) stock dividends.** This method of handling stock dividends is justified on the grounds that "many recipients of stock dividends look upon them as distributions of corporate earnings and

---

UNDERLYING CONCEPT

If the intent of the CAP was to punish companies that used stock dividends by requiring fair value, it violated the neutrality concept; that is, that standard-selling should be even-handed.

OBJECTIVE 4

Explain the accounting for small and large stock dividends.

---

[8]This represented perhaps the earliest instance of an accounting pronouncement being affected by "economic consequences," because the Committee on Accounting Procedure described its action as being required by "proper accounting and corporate policy." See *Proceedings on the Conference on the Impact of Rule Making on Intermediate Financial Accounting Textbooks,* paper presented by Stephen A. Zeff, The Ohio State University, Columbus, Ohio, June 4, 1982. Also see, Stephen A. Zeff, "The Rise of 'Economic Consequences,'" *The Journal of Accountancy* (December 1978), pp. 53–66.

[9]American Institute of Certified Public Accountants, *Accounting Research and Terminology Bulletins,* No. 43 (New York: AICPA, 1961), Ch. 7, par. 10.

usually in an amount equivalent to the fair value of the additional shares received."[10] We do not consider this a convincing argument. It is generally agreed that stock dividends are not income to the recipients, and, therefore, sound accounting should not recommend procedures simply because some recipients think they are income.[11]

To illustrate a small stock dividend, assume that a corporation has outstanding 1,000 shares of $100 par value capital stock and retained earnings of $50,000. If the corporation declares a 10% stock dividend, it issues 100 additional shares to current stockholders. If it is assumed that the fair value of the stock at the time of the stock dividend is $130 per share, the entry is:

INTERNATIONAL INSIGHT

Revaluation of assets is likely to result in revaluation capital. Such capital is available as the basis for stock dividends in some nations and for cash dividends in others. Some nations require the accumulation of such capital but do not permit it to be used as the basis for either form of dividend.

At date of declaration

Retained Earnings (Stock Dividend Declared)	13,000	
Common Stock Dividend Distributable		10,000
Paid-in Capital in Excess of Par		3,000

Note that no asset or liability has been affected. The entry merely reflects a reclassification of stockholders' equity. If a balance sheet is prepared between the dates of declaration and distribution, the common stock dividend distributable should be shown in the stockholders' equity section as an addition to capital stock (whereas cash or property dividends payable are shown as current liabilities).

When the stock is issued, the entry is:

At date of distribution

Common Stock Dividend Distributable	10,000	
Common Stock		10,000

No matter what the fair value is at the time of the stock dividend, each stockholder retains the same proportionate interest in the corporation.

Some state statutes specifically prohibit the issuance of stock dividends on treasury stock. In those states that permit treasury shares to participate in the distribution accompanying a stock dividend or stock split, practice is influenced by the planned use of the treasury shares. For example, if the treasury shares are intended for issuance in connection with employee stock options, the treasury shares may participate in the distribution because the number of shares under option is usually adjusted for any stock dividends or splits. But unless there are specific uses for the treasury stock, no useful purpose is served by issuing additional shares to the treasury stock since they are essentially equivalent to authorized but unissued shares.

To continue with our example of the effect of the small stock dividend, note in Illustration 16-7 that the total stockholders' equity has not changed as a result of the stock dividend. Also note that the proportion of the total shares outstanding held by each stockholder is unchanged.

---

[10]Ibid., par. 10. One study concluded that *small* stock dividends do not always produce significant amounts of extra value on the date after issuance (ex date) and that *large* stock dividends almost always fail to generate extra value on the ex-dividend date. Taylor W. Foster III and Don Vickrey, "The Information Content of Stock Dividend Announcements," *The Accounting Review*, Vol. LIII, No. 2 (April, 1978), pp. 360–370.

[11]The case against treating an ordinary stock dividend as income is supported under either an **entity** or **proprietary assumption** regarding the business enterprise. If the corporation is considered an entity separate from the stockholders, the income of the corporation is corporate income and not income to the stockholders, although the equity of the stockholders in the corporation increases. This position argues that a dividend is not income to the recipients until it is realized by them as a result of a division or severance of corporate assets. The stock dividend merely distributes the "recipients'" equity over a larger number of shares. Under this interpretation, selling the stock received as a dividend has the effect of reducing the recipients' proportionate share of the corporation's equity. Under the proprietary assumption, income of the corporation is considered income to the owners, and, hence, a stock dividend represents only a reclassification of equity, inasmuch as there is no change in total proprietorship.

ILLUSTRATION 16-7
Effects of a Small (10%)
Stock Dividend

Before dividend:	
Capital stock, 1,000 shares of $100 par	$100,000
Retained earnings	50,000
Total stockholders' equity	$150,000
Stockholders' interests:	
A. 400 shares, 40% interest, book value	$ 60,000
B. 500 shares, 50% interest, book value	75,000
C. 100 shares, 10% interest, book value	15,000
	$150,000
After declaration but before distribution of 10% stock dividend:	
If fair value ($130) is used as basis for entry	
Capital stock, 1,000 shares at $100 par	$100,000
Common stock distributable, 100 shares at $100 par	10,000
Paid-in capital in excess of par	3,000
Retained earnings ($50,000 − $13,000)	37,000
Total stockholders' equity	$150,000
After declaration and distribution of 10% stock dividend:	
If fair value ($130) is used as basis for entry	
Capital stock, 1,100 shares at $100 par	$110,000
Paid-in capital in excess of par	3,000
Retained earnings ($50,000 − $13,000)	37,000
Total stockholders' equity	$150,000
Stockholders' interest:	
A. 440 shares, 40% interest, book value	$ 60,000
B. 550 shares, 50% interest, book value	75,000
C. 110 shares, 10% interest, book value	15,000
	$150,000

STOCK SPLIT

If a company has undistributed earnings over several years and a sizable balance in retained earnings has accumulated, the market value of its outstanding shares is likely to increase. Stock that was issued at prices less than $50 a share can easily attain a market value in excess of $200 a share. The higher the market price of a stock, the less readily it can be purchased by most people. The managements of many corporations believe that for better public relations, wider ownership of the corporation stock is desirable. They wish, therefore, to have a market price sufficiently low to be within range of the majority of potential investors. To reduce the market value of shares, the common device of a **stock split** is employed.[12] For example, when IBM's stock was selling at $304 a share, the company split its common stock 4-for-1. The day after IBM's split (involving 583,268,480 shares) was effective, the stock sold for $76 a share, exactly one quarter of its price per share before the split. IBM's intent was to obtain a wider distribution of its stock by improving the marketability of the shares.[13]

---

[12]The *DH&S Review*, May 12, 1986, page 7, listed the following as reasons behind a stock split:

1. To adjust the market price of the company's shares to a level where more individuals can afford to invest in the stock.
2. To spread the stockholder base by increasing the number of shares outstanding and making them more marketable.
3. To benefit existing stockholders by allowing them to take advantage of an imperfect market adjustment following the split.

[13]Some companies use reverse stock splits. A **reverse stock split** reduces the number of shares outstanding and increases the per share price. This technique is used when the stock price is unusually low or when management wishes to take control of the company. For example, two officers of Metropolitan Maintenance Co. took their company private by forcing a 1 for 3,000 reverse stock split on their stockholders. For every 3,000 old shares, one new share was issued. But anyone who had fewer than 3,000 shares received only cash for his or her stock. Only the two officers owned more than 3,000 shares, so they now own all the stock. A nice squeeze play! (*Forbes*, November 19, 1984, p. 54.)

From an accounting standpoint, **no entry is recorded for a stock split;** a memorandum note, however, is made to indicate that the par value of the shares has changed, and that the number of shares has increased. The lack of change in stockholders' equity is portrayed in Illustration 16-8 of a 2-for-1 stock split on 1,000 shares of $100 par value stock with the par being halved upon issuance of the additional shares:

Stockholders' Equity Before 2-for-1 Split		Stockholders' Equity After 2-for-1 Split	
Common stock, 1,000 shares		Common stock, 2,000 shares	
at $100 par	$100,000	at $50 par	$100,000
Retained earnings	50,000	Retained earnings	50,000
	$150,000		$150,000

ILLUSTRATION 16-8
Effect of Stock Split

Stock Split and Stock Dividend Differentiated

From a legal standpoint a stock split is distinguished from a stock dividend, because a stock split results in an increase in the number of shares outstanding and a corresponding decrease in the par or stated value per share. **A stock dividend, although it results in an increase in the number of shares outstanding, does not decrease the par value; thus it increases the total par value of outstanding shares.**

OBJECTIVE 5
Distinguish between stock dividends and stock splits.

The reasons for issuing a stock dividend are numerous and varied. Stock dividends can be more of a publicity gesture, because they are considered by many as dividends and, consequently, the corporation is not criticized for retention of profits. Some corporations even lead their stockholders to believe that a stock dividend is equivalent to a cash dividend. For instance, the Board of Directors of Wickes Companies Inc. declared a 2½% stock dividend "in lieu of the quarterly cash dividend, which had been 26¢ per share." E. L. McNeely, chairman of Wickes said, "This dividend continues Wickes' 88-year record of uninterrupted dividend payments." More defensible perhaps, the corporation may simply wish to retain profits in the business by capitalizing a part of retained earnings. In such a situation, a transfer is made on declaration of a stock dividend from earned capital to contributed or permanent capital.

A stock dividend, like a stock split, also may be used to increase the marketability of the stock, although marketability is often a secondary consideration. If the stock dividend is large, it has the same effect on market price as a stock split. The profession has taken the position that **whenever additional shares are issued for the purpose of reducing the unit market price, then the distribution more closely resembles a stock split than a stock dividend. This effect usually results only if the number of shares issued is more than 20–25% of the number of shares previously outstanding.**[14] A stock dividend of more than 20–25% of the number of shares previously outstanding is called a **large stock dividend.**[15] The profession also recommends that such a distribution not be called a stock dividend, but it might properly be called "a split-up effected in the form of a dividend" or "stock split." Also, since the par value of the outstanding shares is not altered, the transfer from retained earnings is only in the amount required by statute. Ordinarily this means a transfer from retained earnings to capital stock **for the par value of the stock issued** as opposed to a transfer of the market value of the shares issued as in the case of a small stock dividend. For example, Brown Group, Inc. recently authorized a 2-for-1 split, effected in the form of a stock dividend. As a result of this authorization, approximately 10.5 million shares were distributed and more than $39 million representing the par value of the shares issued was transferred from Retained Earnings to the Common Stock account.

To illustrate a large stock dividend (stock split-up effected in the form of a dividend), Rockland Steel, Inc. declared a 30% stock dividend on November 20, payable December 29 to stockholders of record December 12. At the date of declaration, 1,000,000 shares,

---

[14]*Accounting Research and Terminology Bulletin No. 43,* par. 13.

[15]The SEC has added more precision to the 20–25% rule. Specifically, the SEC indicates that distributions of 25% or more should be considered a "split-up effected in the form of a dividend." Distributions of less than 25% should be accounted for as a stock dividend. The SEC more precisely defined GAAP here, and as a result the SEC rule is followed by public companies.

par value $10, are outstanding and with a fair market value of $200 per share. The entries are:

At date of declaration (November 20)

Retained Earnings	3,000,000	
Common Stock Dividend Distributable		3,000,000

Computation: 1,000,000 shares   300,000 Additional shares
              × 30%   × $10 Par value
               300,000 $3,000,000

At date of distribution (December 29)

Common Stock Dividend Distributable	3,000,000	
Common Stock		3,000,000

The following table summarizes and compares the effects of various types of dividends and stock splits on various elements of the financial statements.

**ILLUSTRATION 16-9
Effects of Dividends and
Stock Splits on Financial
Statement Elements**

			Declaration and Distribution of		
Effect on:	Declaration of Cash Dividend	Payment of Cash Dividend	Small Stock Dividend	Large Stock Dividend	Stock Split
Retained earnings	Decrease	–0–	Decrease[a]	Decrease[b]	–0–
Capital stock	–0–	–0–	Increase[b]	Increase[b]	–0–
Additional paid-in capital	–0–	–0–	Increase[c]	–0–	–0–
Total stockholders' equity	Decrease	–0–	–0–	–0–	–0–
Working capital	Decrease	–0–	–0–	–0–	–0–
Total assets	–0–	Decrease	–0–	–0–	–0–
Number of shares outstanding	–0–	–0–	Increase	Increase	Increase

[a]Market value of shares.
[b]Par or stated value of shares.
[c]Excess of market value over par.

EFFECTS OF DIVIDEND PREFERENCES

OBJECTIVE 6

*Explain the effect of
different types of preferred
stock dividends.*

The examples given below illustrate the **effects of** various **dividend preferences** on dividend distributions to common and preferred stockholders. Assume that in a given year, $50,000 is to be distributed as cash dividends, outstanding common stock has a par value of $400,000, and 6% preferred stock has a par value of $100,000. Dividends would be distributed to each class as shown below, employing the assumptions given.

1. If the preferred stock is noncumulative and nonparticipating:

**ILLUSTRATION 16-10
Dividend Distribution,
Noncumulative and
Nonparticipating
Preferred**

	Preferred	Common	Total
6% of $100,000	$6,000		$ 6,000
The remainder to common		$44,000	44,000
Totals	$6,000	$44,000	$50,000

2. If the preferred stock is cumulative and nonparticipating, and dividends were not paid on the preferred stock in the preceding 2 years:

**ILLUSTRATION 16-11
Dividend Distribution,
Cumulative and
Nonparticipating
Preferred, with Dividends
in Arrears**

	Preferred	Common	Total
Dividends in arrears, 6% of $100,000 for 2 years	$12,000		$12,000
Current year's dividend, 6% of $100,000	6,000		6,000
The remainder to common		$32,000	32,000
Totals	$18,000	$32,000	$50,000

3. If the preferred stock is noncumulative and is fully participating:[16]

	Preferred	Common	Total
Current year's dividend, 6%	$ 6,000	$24,000	$30,000
Participating dividend of 4%	4,000	16,000	20,000
Totals	$10,000	$40,000	$50,000

The participating dividend was determined as follows:

Current year's dividend:	
Preferred, 6% of $100,000 = $ 6,000	
Common, 6% of $400,000 = 24,000	$ 30,000
Amount available for participation	
($50,000 − $30,000)	$ 20,000
Par value of stock that is to participate	
($100,000 + $400,000)	$500,000
Rate of participation	
($20,000 ÷ $500,000)	4%
Participating dividend:	
Preferred, 4% of $100,000	$ 4,000
Common, 4% of $400,000	16,000
	$ 20,000

ILLUSTRATION 16-12
Dividend Distribution, Noncumulative and Fully Participating Preferred

4. If the preferred stock is cumulative and is fully participating, and if dividends were not paid on the preferred stock in the preceding 2 years (The same procedure as described in example (3) is used in this example to effect the participation feature):

	Preferred	Common	Total
Dividends in arrears, 6% of $100,000 for 2 years	$12,000		$12,000
Current year's dividend, 6%	6,000	$24,000	30,000
Participating dividend, 1.6% ($8,000 ÷ $500,000)	1,600	6,400	8,000
Totals	$19,600	$30,400	$50,000

ILLUSTRATION 16-13
Dividend Distribution, Cumulative and Fully Participating Preferred, with Dividends in Arrears

---

▶ **APPROPRIATIONS OF RETAINED EARNINGS**

The act of appropriating retained earnings is a policy matter requiring approval by the board of directors. According to *FASB Statement No. 5*, the appropriation of retained earnings is acceptable practice, "provided that it is shown within the stockholders' equity section of the balance sheet and is clearly identified as an appropriation of retained earnings."[17]

OBJECTIVE 7
Identify the reasons for appropriating retained earnings.

---

[16]When preferred stock is participating, there may be different agreements as to how the participation feature is to be executed. However, in the absence of any specific agreement the following procedure is recommended:

a. After the preferred stock is assigned its current year's dividend, the common stock will receive a "like" percentage of par value outstanding. In example (3), this amounts to 6% of $400,000.

b. If there is a remainder of declared dividends for participation by the preferred and common stock, this remainder will be shared in proportion to the par value dollars outstanding in each class of stock. In example (3) this proportion is:

$$\text{Preferred } \frac{\$100,000}{\$500,000} \times \$20,000 = \$4,000$$

$$\text{Common } \frac{\$400,000}{\$500,000} \times \$20,000 = \$16,000$$

[17]"Accounting for Contingencies," *Statement of Financial Accounting Standards No. 5* (Stamford, Conn.: FASB, March 1975), par. 15.

INTERNATIONAL
INSIGHT

In some nations (Germany, Japan, and France, for example) companies are legally required to create reserves (appropriations) for creditor protection. They must allocate profits to reserves at a specified annual rate until the amount of the required reserve is accumulated.

Appropriations of retained earnings are regarded as **nothing more than reclassifications of retained earnings for a specific purpose.** It should be emphasized that an appropriation does not set aside cash. The appropriation discloses that management does not intend to distribute assets as a dividend up to the amount of the appropriation because these assets are needed by the corporation for a specified purpose. The unappropriated retained earnings is debited (reduced) by the amount of the appropriation, and a new account for the specific purpose is established and credited for the transferred amount. When the appropriation is no longer necessary, either because the specific purpose has been accomplished or the loss has occurred or because it no longer appears as a possibility, the appropriation should be returned to retained earnings. In accordance with *FASB Statement No. 5,* **"costs or losses shall not be charged to an appropriation of retained earnings, and no part of the appropriation shall be transferred to income."**[18]

Various reasons are advanced for appropriations of retained earnings. These include:

1. **Legal restrictions.** As indicated earlier, some state laws prohibit the purchase of treasury stock by the corporation unless earnings available for dividends are present. Retained earnings in an amount equal to the cost of any treasury stock acquired are restricted. Earnings must be retained to substitute for capital stock temporarily acquired as treasury stock.

2. **Contractual restrictions.** Bond indentures frequently contain a requirement that retained earnings in specified amounts be appropriated each year during the life of the bonds. The appropriation created under such a provision is commonly called Appropriation for Sinking Fund or Appropriation for Bonded Indebtedness.

3. **Existence of possible or expected loss.** Appropriations might be established for estimated losses due to lawsuits, unfavorable contractual obligations, and other contingencies.

4. **Protection of working capital position.** The board of directors may authorize the creation of an "Appropriation for Working Capital" out of retained earnings in order to indicate that the amount specified is not available for dividends because it is desirable to maintain a strong current position. Another example involves a decision made to finance a building program by internal financing. An "Appropriation for Plant Expansion" is created to indicate that retained earnings in the amount appropriated will not be considered by the directors as available for dividends.

Some corporations establish appropriations for general contingencies, or appropriate retained earnings for unspecified purposes. In some cases this is justified by statutory or contractual restrictions. In other cases no adequate explanation for such actions is available. The FASB does not encourage the establishment of general or unspecified appropriations.

RECORDING APPROPRIATIONS OF RETAINED EARNINGS

OBJECTIVE 8

Explain accounting and reporting for appropriated retained earnings.

When a company records an appropriation in the accounts, the unappropriated retained earnings must be reduced by the amount of the appropriation and a new account must be established to receive the amount transferred. The new account Appropriated Retained Earnings is simply a subclassification of total retained earnings. If the appropriation merely augments a previously established amount, the account already in use should receive the credit. The appropriation is recorded as a debit to Retained Earnings and a credit to an appropriately named account that itself is just a subdivision of retained earnings. For example:

(a) An Appropriation for Plant Expansion is to be created by transfer from Retained Earnings of $400,000 a year for 5 years. The entry for each year would be:

---

[18]Ibid., par. 15.

Retained Earnings	400,000	
Retained Earnings Appropriated for		
Plant Expansion		400,000

(b) At the end of 5 years the appropriation would have a balance of $2,000,000. If we assume that the expansion plan has been completed, the appropriation is no longer required and can be returned to retained earnings.

Retained Earnings Appropriated for		
Plant Expansion	2,000,000	
Retained Earnings		2,000,000

Return of such an appropriation to retained earnings has the effect of increasing unappropriated retained earnings considerably without affecting the assets or current position. In effect, over the 5 years the company has expanded by reinvesting assets acquired through the earnings process.

DISCLOSURE OF RESTRICTIONS ON RETAINED EARNINGS

In many corporations restrictions on retained earnings or dividends exist, but no appropriation resulting in a debit to Retained Earnings and a credit to an appropriation account is recorded.[19] In such cases the accountant must weigh the significance of the restriction and decide whether to disclose it in some manner other than through debits and credits in the equity accounts. Bond indentures and loan agreements may make appropriations of retained earnings mandatory.[20]

Most restrictions for which journal entries are not made are of a contractual nature resulting from agreements with creditors and are **best disclosed by note.** Parenthetical notations are sometimes used, but restrictions imposed by bond indentures and loan agreements commonly require an extended explanation; notes provide a medium for more complete explanations and free the financial statements from abbreviated notations. The note disclosure should reveal the source of the restriction, pertinent provisions, and the amount of retained earnings subject to restriction, or the amount not restricted.

Restrictions may be based on the retention of a certain retained earnings balance, the corporation's ability to observe certain working capital requirements, additional borrowing, and on other considerations. The following example from the 1992 annual report of Dean Foods Company illustrates a note disclosing multiple restrictions on retained earnings and dividends.

Dean Foods Company

Notes to Consolidated Financial Statements

Borrowing Arrangements (in part). At May 31, 1992, under the most restrictive provisions of the Company's borrowing arrangements: tangible net worth of at least $175 million, working capital of at least $60 million, and a current ratio of at least 1.25 were required to be maintained; approximately $63 million of retained earnings was unrestricted for the payment of cash dividends and repurchase of common stock; and the Company could not incur total long-term debt in excess of 40% of its total capital.

**ILLUSTRATION 16-14
Disclosure of Restrictions on Retained Earnings and Dividends**

DISCLOSURES FOR SELF-INSURANCE

A company may insure against many contingencies such as fire, flood, storm, and accident by taking out insurance policies and paying premiums to insurance companies. Some contingencies are, however, not insurable or the rates are prohibitive (e.g., earth-

---

[19]In recent years the use of appropriations to indicate retained earnings restrictions has declined. In its 1950 survey of the annual report of 600 companies, the AICPA noted approximately 100 appropriations of various types; a similar survey in 1971 revealed that only 10 balance sheets contained such appropriations; and in 1975 the AICPA ceased tabulating this bit of data because of its infrequency.

[20]*Accounting Trends and Techniques—1993* reports that of its list of 600 selected companies, 379 disclosed dividend or retained earnings restrictions.

quakes and riots). Even though insurance is available, some businesses may adopt a policy of **self-insurance.**[21] Self-insurance appears especially valid when a company's physical or operating characteristics permit application of the law of large numbers as utilized by insurance companies. Whenever the risk of loss can be spread over a large number of possible loss events that individually would be small in relation to the total potential loss, self-insurance is a temptation. It is based on the belief that the losses will cost fewer dollars over an extended period of time than the premiums that would be paid to insure against such losses. The company thus avoids paying the insurance company's overhead costs, including the insurance agent's commission. Examples of such self-insurance situations are a truck line with hundreds of trucks in different locations or a grocery chain with hundreds of stores scattered geographically. At one time Shell Oil Company decided that it was paying too much for insurance while incurring few losses. Therefore, it decided against insuring its offshore drilling rigs and many of its onshore facilities as well; instead, it set up a self-insurance appropriation classified as a liability.

The accounting treatment for self-insurance can take one of three forms:

1. **Record Losses as Incurred.** No accounting recognition is given to the fact that self-insurance is the mode of operation or that uninsured losses may have to be absorbed in some future period. Losses are charged to expense in the period in which "it is probable that an asset has been impaired or a liability has been incurred at the date of the financial statements" and "the amount of loss can be reasonably estimated."[22] **This approach is permitted under GAAP.**

2. **Appropriate Retained Earnings and Record Losses as Incurred.** Uninsured losses are charged entirely to expense of the period in which they are sustained. Recognition is given to contingent losses in periods other than their incurrence, however, by appropriations of retained earnings. The amount of the annual appropriation may approximate the premium cost of adequate insurance covering the risk, or it may be a prorated allocation of an estimated and anticipated future loss. The appropriation account normally does not exceed the maximum expected loss at any one time and is never charged with actual losses. The effect of this and the first method is a varying charge for actual losses instead of a stable charge to expense that would result from premium payments to an insurance company. **This approach is also permitted under GAAP.**

3. **Accrue Expense.**[23] This approach avoids the erratic effects on net income resulting from irregularly occurring uninsured losses and makes the income statement of a company that does not insure appear to be comparable to those of firms carrying insurance. This method accrues the estimated losses by charging operations each year with a hypothetical amount of insurance expense and crediting a similar amount to a liability account entitled Liability for Self-Insured Risks or Liability for Uninsured Losses. When the casualty losses occur, they are charged against the liability account instead of an expense account. The liability account absorbs the impact of the loss; each year's income statement absorbs only a portion of the loss. Before 1975 the liability for self-insurance was acceptable and widely used by many large companies, especially in the airlines, insurance, and oil industries. **At present, this approach is not permitted under GAAP.**

Despite its name, **self-insurance is no insurance,** and any company that assumes its own risks puts itself in the position of incurring expenses or losses as the casualties

---

[21]The American Management Association advertises its popular 2½-day course on "Self-insurance and Risk Retention" as follows: "There comes a point where sky-high insurance rates no longer make sense. The dollars you're investing in premiums could be building your corporate assets. Find out how more and more companies are using self-insurance to cut down premium costs."

[22]"Accounting for Contingencies," op. cit., par. 8.

[23]Although unacceptable today, this method is presented because of its previous widespread usage and appeal.

occur. The improper application of the accrual method (third method) to self-insurance obscures a fundamental difference in circumstances between companies that transfer risks to others through insurance and those that do not. There is little theoretical justification for the establishment of a liability based on a hypothetical charge to insurance expense. This is "as if" accounting.[24] Can there be an expense, in advance of the actual occurrence of a casualty, or a liability to incur a casualty loss in the future? The FASB's answer to that question is:

INTERNATIONAL INSIGHT

In Switzerland companies are allowed to create income reserves. That is, they reduce income in years with good profits by allocating it to reserves on the balance sheet. In less profitable years, they are able to reallocate from the reserves to improve income. This "smoothes" income across years.

> Fires, explosions, and other similar events that may cause loss or damage of an enterprise's property are random in their occurrence. With respect to events of that type, the condition for accrual is not satisfied prior to the occurrence of the event because until that time there is no diminution in the value of the property. There is no relationship of those events to the activities of the enterprise prior to their occurrence, and no asset is impaired prior to their occurrence. Further, unlike an insurance company, which has a contractual obligation under policies in force to reimburse insureds for losses, an enterprise can have no such obligation to itself, and, hence, no liability.[25]

With respect to uninsured losses that may result from injury to others, damage to the property of others, or business interruptions that may occur after the balance sheet date, premature accrual is similarly objectionable. The following note from the annual report of Adolph Coors Company is typical of the self-insurance disclosure.

Adolph Coors Company

Notes to Financial Statements

Note 4: Commitments and Contingencies. It is generally the policy of the Company to act as a self-insurer for certain insurable risks consisting primarily of physical loss to corporate property, business interruption resulting from such loss, employee health insurance programs, and workmen's compensation. Losses and claims are accrued as incurred.

ILLUSTRATION 16-15 Disclosure of Self-Insurance

▶ STATEMENT OF STOCKHOLDERS' EQUITY

Statements of stockholders' equity are frequently presented in the following basic format:

1. Balance at the beginning of the period.
2. Additions.
3. Deductions.
4. Balance at the end of the period.

OBJECTIVE 9
Prepare a statement of stockholders' equity.

The disclosure of changes in the separate accounts comprising stockholders' equity is required to make the financial statements sufficiently informative.[26] Disclosure of such changes may take the form of separate statements or may be made in the basic financial statements or notes thereto.[27]

---

[24]A commentary in *Forbes* (June 15, 1974, p. 42) stated its position on this matter quite succinctly: "The simple and unquestionable fact of life is this: Business is cyclical and full of unexpected surprises. Is it the role of accounting to disguise this unpleasant fact and create a fairyland of smoothly rising earnings? Or, should accounting reflect reality, warts and all—floods, expropriations and all manner of rude shocks?"

[25]"Accounting for Contingencies," op. cit., par. 28.

[26]"Omnibus Opinion—1967 (Capital Changes)," *APB Opinion No. 12* (New York: AICPA, 1967), par. 10.

[27]*Accounting Trends and Techniques—1993* reports that of the 600 companies surveyed, 481 presented statements of stockholders' equity, 48 presented separate statements of retained earnings only, 27 presented combined statements of income and retained earnings, and 44 presented changes in equity items in the notes only.

ILLUSTRATION 16-16
Columnar Format for
Statement of
Stockholders' Equity

A **columnar format** for the presentation of changes in stockholders' equity items in published annual reports is gaining in popularity; an example is Bassett Furniture Industries' Statement of Stockholders' Equity shown below.

	Common Stock		Additional Capital	Retained Earnings	Treasury Stock at Cost	
	Shares	Amount			Shares	Amount
Bassett Furniture Industries, Incorporated STATEMENT OF STOCKHOLDERS' EQUITY For the Year Ended November 30, 1992						
Balance, November 30, 1991	9,572,968	47,864,840	7,993,618	250,798,846	1,894,944	51,551,707
Net income	—	—	—	27,492,698	—	—
Cash dividends	—	—	—	(9,205,978)	—	—
Purchase of treasury stock	—	—	—	—	3	92
Contribution of treasury stock to Employee Savings/Retirement Plan	—	—	232,780	—	(10,929)	(148,369)
Exercise of stock options	—	—	38,837	—	(1,642)	(9,233)
Retire treasury stock	(1,882,376)	(9,411,880)	(8,265,235)	(33,717,082)	(1,882,376)	(51,394,197)
3 for 2 stock split distributed April, 1992	3,844,750	19,223,750	—	(19,223,750)	—	—
Balance, November 30, 1992	11,535,342	$57,676,710	$ 0	$216,144,734	0	$ 0

The annual report of Georgia-Pacific in the Appendix to Chapter 5, page 223 includes a 3-year comprehensive illustration of the various items that commonly appear as either additions or deductions in a "Statements of Shareholders' Equity."

▶ TRENDS IN TERMINOLOGY

As discussed in Chapter 5, the profession's recommendations relating to changes in terminology have been directed primarily to the balance sheet presentation of stockholders' equity so that words or phrases used will more accurately describe the nature of the amounts shown.

The accounting profession has suggested the term "surplus" not be used in financial statements. Substitute terminology is recommended because the term "surplus" connotes a residue or "something not needed." The use of the term is gradually decreasing. **"Retained earnings"** or some similar phrase has generally replaced "earned surplus." Apparently, consensus regarding the terminology to replace "capital surplus" and "paid-in surplus" has not yet been reached, inasmuch as these two terms still appear in many financial statements. **"Capital in excess of par (or stated value)"** or **"additional paid-in capital"** are gaining favor over the term "paid-in surplus."[28] The persistent use of "surplus" terms by many leading corporations can perhaps be attributed to the numerous state incorporation acts that still contain antiquated terminology in their provisions regulating the issuance of stock and other equity transactions.

Formerly, the term "reserve" was used in accounting to describe such diverse items as accumulated depreciation, accumulated allowances for doubtful accounts, current liabilities, and segregations of retained earnings. **The profession recommends that use of the word "reserve" be confined to appropriations of retained earnings if it is to be used at all.** The general adoption of this recommendation could help to clear up one of the most troublesome terminology areas in accounting.[29]

---

[28]*Accounting Trends and Techniques—1993* reports that the use of the term "surplus" is gradually declining. In its survey of 600 companies, 34 out of 531 companies reporting additional paid-in capital used either "capital surplus" or "paid-in surplus" for the caption. Only 2 companies used the term "earned surplus," while 470 used the caption "retained earnings."

[29]*Accounting Trends and Techniques—1993* reports that of its list of 600 selected companies, 122 continued incorrectly to use the term "reserve" in the asset or liability section of the balance sheet.

The presentation below is an example of a comprehensive stockholders' equity section taken from a balance sheet that includes most of the equity items discussed in Chapters 15 and 16.

ILLUSTRATION 16-17
**Comprehensive
Stockholders' Equity
Presentation**

Model Corporation STOCKHOLDERS' EQUITY December 31, 1994		
Capital stock		

Preferred stock, $100 par value, 7% cumulative,
     100,000 shares authorized, 30,000 shares issued
     and outstanding
		$ 3,000,000

Common stock, no par, stated value $10 per share, 500,000 shares authorized, 400,000 shares issued		4,000,000
Common stock dividend distributable, 20,000 shares		200,000
Total capital stock		7,200,000
Additional paid-in capital		
Excess over par—preferred	$ 150,000	
Excess over stated value—common	840,000	990,000
Total paid-in capital		8,190,000
Donated capital		100,000
Retained earnings		
Appropriated for plant expansion	2,100,000	
Unappropriated	2,160,000	4,260,000
Total paid-in capital and retained earnings		12,550,000
Less cost of treasury stock (2,000 shares, common)		(190,000)
Total stockholders' equity		$12,360,000

▶ SUMMARY OF LEARNING OBJECTIVES ◀

1. **Identify the major categories of stockholders' equity.** Stockholders' equity is composed of three categories: (1) capital stock (legal capital), (2) additional paid-in capital, and (3) retained earnings or deficit. Capital stock and additional paid-in capital represent contributed capital, and retained earnings represents earned capital.

2. **Describe the policies used in distributing dividends.** The state incorporation laws normally provide information concerning the legal restrictions related to the payment of dividends. Corporations rarely pay dividends in an amount equal to the legal limit. This is due, in part, to the fact that assets represented by undistributed earnings are used to finance future operations of the business. If a company is considering declaring a dividend, two preliminary questions must be asked: (1) Is the condition of the corporation such that the dividend is **legally permissible?** (2) Is the condition of the corporation such that a dividend is **economically sound?**

3. **Identify the various forms of dividend distributions.** Dividends are of the following types: (1) cash dividends, (2) property dividends, (3) scrip dividends (instead of paying a dividend now, the corporation has elected to pay it at some later date; the scrip issued to stockholders as a dividend is merely a special form of note payable), (4) liquidating dividends (dividends based on other than retained earnings are sometimes described as liquidating dividends), (5) stock dividends (the nonreciprocal issuance by a corporation of its own stock to its stockholders on a pro rata basis).

4. **Explain the accounting for small and large stock dividends.** Generally accepted accounting principles require that the accounting for small stock dividends (less than 20 or 25%) be based on the fair market value of the stock issued. When a stock dividend is declared, retained earnings is debited at the fair market value of the stock to be distributed. The entry includes a credit to Common Stock Dividend Distributable at par value times the number of shares, with any excess credited to Paid-in Capital in Excess of Par. Common stock dividend distributable is reported in the stockholders' equity section between the declaration date and the date of issuance. If the number of shares issued exceeds 20 or 25% of the shares outstanding (large stock dividend), Retained Earnings is debited at par value, and there is no additional paid-in capital.

5. **Distinguish between stock dividends and stock splits.** A stock dividend is a capitalization of retained earnings that results in a reduction in retained earnings and a corresponding increase in certain contributed capital accounts. The par value and total stockholders' equity remain unchanged with a stock dividend. Also, all stockholders retain their same proportionate share of ownership in the corporation. A stock split results in an increase or decrease in the number of shares outstanding, with a corresponding decrease or increase in the par or stated value per share. No accounting entry is required for a stock split. Similar to a stock dividend, the total dollar amount of all stockholders' equity accounts remains unchanged. A stock split is usually intended to improve the marketability of the shares by reducing the market price of the stock being split.

6. **Explain the effect of different types of preferred stock dividends.** Dividends paid to shareholders are affected by the dividend preferences of the preferred stock. Preferred stock can be: (1) cumulative or noncumulative, and (2) fully participating, partially participating, or nonparticipating.

7. **Identify the reasons for appropriating retained earnings.** An appropriation of retained earnings serves to restrict for a specific purpose the payout of retained earnings. In general, the reason for retained earnings appropriations is the corporation's desire to reduce the basis upon which dividends are declared (unappropriated credit balance in retained earnings).

8. **Explain accounting and reporting for appropriated retained earnings.** To establish an appropriation of retained earnings, a corporation prepares a journal entry, debiting unappropriated retained earnings and crediting a specific appropriations account (for example, Retained Earnings Appropriated for Sinking Fund). The entry is confined to stockholders' equity accounts and does not directly affect corporate assets or liabilities. The only way to dispose of an appropriation of retained earnings is to reverse the entry that created the appropriation. Appropriations of retained earnings are more often disclosed in the notes to the financial statements as an alternative to making a formal entry against retained earnings.

9. **Prepare a statement of stockholders' equity.** A presentation of stockholders' equity items and changes in those items often appears in published financial statements. A reconciliation format is generally reported starting with balances at the beginning of the period, additions, deductions, and the balances at the end of the period.

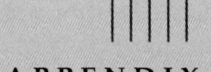

APPENDIX 16-A

QUASI-REORGANIZATION

A corporation that consistently suffers net losses accumulates negative retained earnings, or a deficit. The laws of many states provide that no dividends may be declared and paid so long as a corporation's paid-in capital has been reduced by a deficit. In these states, a corporation with a debit balance of retained earnings must accumulate sufficient profits to offset the deficit before dividends may be paid.

This situation may be a real hardship on a corporation and its stockholders. A company that has operated unsuccessfully for several years and accumulated a deficit may have finally "turned the corner." Development of new products and new markets, a new management group, or improved economic conditions may point to much improved operating results. But, if the state law prohibits dividends until the deficit has been replaced by earnings, the stockholders must wait until such profits have been earned, which may take a considerable period of time. Furthermore, future success may depend on obtaining additional funds through the sale of stock. If no dividends can be paid for some time, the market price of any new stock issue is likely to be low, if such stock can be marketed at all.

Thus, a company with excellent prospects may be prevented from accomplishing its plans because of a deficit, although present management may have had nothing whatever to do with the years over which the deficit was accumulated. To permit the corporation to proceed with its plans might well be to the advantage of all interests in the enterprise; to require it to eliminate the deficit through profits might actually force it to liquidate.

A procedure provided for in some state laws eliminates an accumulated deficit and permits the company to proceed on much the same basis as if it had been legally reorganized, without the difficulty and expenses generally connected with a legal reorganization. This procedure, known as a **quasi-reorganization,** is justified under the concept of an accounting "fresh start."

A quasi-reorganization may be accomplished under two accounting procedures. The simpler procedure, referred to as a **deficit reclassification,** results solely in eliminating a deficit in retained earnings without restating assets or liabilities. The accounting procedure is limited to a reclassification of a deficit in reported retained earnings as a reduction of paid-in capital.

The more complex accounting procedure, referred to as an **accounting reorganization** type of quasi-reorganization, involves restating the assets of the enterprise to their fair values and the liabilities to their present values with the net amount of these adjustments added to or deducted from the deficit.[1] The balance in the retained earnings account (debit or credit) is then closed to other capital accounts, usually Additional Paid-in Capital, so that the company has a "fresh start" with a zero balance in retained earnings.

OBJECTIVE 10

After studying Appendix 16-A, you should be able to: Describe the accounting for a quasi-reorganization.

UNDERLYING CONCEPT

No net asset write-up is permitted in a quasi-reorganization. The reason: Conservatism as indicated in Chapter 2.

---

[1]The SEC states in SAB78, *Quasi-Reorganization* (Topic 5.S), dated August 25, 1988, that write-ups of assets or reductions of liabilities to fair and present values in a quasi-reorganization are limited to an amount sufficient to offset decreases in other assets or increases in other liabilities in their fair and present values. Therefore, there should be **no net asset writeup** in a quasi-reorganization.

Also, the SEC does not allow the "deficit reclassification" type quasi-reorganization (the simpler form) to be used by publicly held companies; thus, it may be used only by privately held companies. Both public and private companies may use the accounting reorganization type (i.e., restating assets and liabilities and eliminating the deficit).

The series of entries shown below illustrates the accounting procedures applied in an "accounting reorganization" type of quasi-reorganization. Assume New Horizons Inc. shows a deficit of $1,000,000 before a quasi-reorganization is effected on June 30, 1995.

Restatement of assets and liabilities to recognize unrecorded gains and losses

Plant Assets (gain on writeup)	400,000	
Long-term Liabilities (gain on writedown)	150,000	
Retained Earnings (net adjustment)	200,000	
Intangible Assets (loss or writedown)		525,000
Inventories (loss or writedown)		225,000

Reduction in par value of 60,000 shares of common stock outstanding from $100 per share to $75 per share (this procedure creates sufficient additional paid-in capital to absorb the deficit)

Common Stock	1,500,000	
Additional Paid-in Capital		1,500,000

Elimination of deficit against additional paid-in capital

Additional Paid-in Capital	1,200,000	
Retained Earnings ($1,000,000 + $200,000)		1,200,000

In connection with the foregoing accounting procedures, the following requirements must be fulfilled:

1. The proposed quasi-reorganization procedure should be submitted to and receive the approval of the corporation's stockholders before it is put into effect.

2. The new asset and liability valuations should be fair and not deliberately understate or overstate assets, liabilities, and earnings.

3. After the quasi-reorganization the corporation must have a zero balance of retained earnings, although it may have additional paid-in capital arising from the quasi-reorganization.

4. In subsequent reports the retained earnings must be "dated" (1) for a period of approximately 10 years to show the fact and the date of the quasi-reorganization, and (2) for a period of at least 3 years from the quasi-reorganization date, the amount of accumulated deficit eliminated should be disclosed as illustrated in the following excerpt from the 1994 balance sheet of Stumble, Inc.[2]

ILLUSTRATION 16A-1
Disclosure of Quasi-Reorganization in the Balance Sheet

Stumble, Inc.	
Stockholders' equity	
Common stock, $75 par value, 60,000 shares authorized and issued	$4,500,000
Additional paid-in capital arising from reduction in par value of common stock	300,000
Retained earnings since June 30, 1992, when a deficit of $1,000,000 was eliminated through a quasi-reorganization	593,640
	$5,393,640

In times of general economic or specific industry recession or depression, the use of the quasi-reorganization procedure becomes more common as companies attempt to turn around and get a fresh start. For example, First Wisconsin Mortgage Trust, because of severe real estate losses, effected a quasi-reorganization. Similarly, Lockheed Corporation, given its large losses on the L-1011 Tri Star program, decided to use the quasi-reorganization approach to offset a large deficit balance in retained earnings. And Astrotech International Corporation eliminated a $28 million deficit in Retained Earnings as it changed from an investment company to an operating company through the quasi-reorganization approach.

---

[2]*Regulation S-X*, Securities and Exchange Commission, Rule 5-02(31)6.

An example of a quasi-reorganization disclosure, shown below, is excerpted from the Annual Report of Information Science Incorporated.

ILLUSTRATION 16A-2
Disclosure of Quasi-Reorganization in the Balance Sheet and in the Notes

Information Science Incorporated

Shareholders' equity (000 omitted)	1989	1988
Common stock, par value $.01 per share—authorized 25,000,000 shares; issued and outstanding 11,186,785 in 1989 and 8,710,500 in 1988	$ 112	$ 87
Class B Common stock, par value $.01 per share—authorized, issued and outstanding, 6,100,000 shares	61	61
Additional paid-in capital	6,080	30,506
Retained earnings (deficit), 1989, accumulated since May 1, 1988	107	(25,759)
Treasury stock	(51)	(51)
Total shareholders' equity	$6,309	$ 4,844

Note 11: Quasi-Reorganization. The Board of Directors determined that it would be in the best interest of the Company to implement a quasi-reorganization effective May 1, 1988. The effect of this quasi-reorganization is that certain assets, primarily fixed assets, have been written down to their estimated fair value. This adjustment ($918,000) was charged to accumulated deficit and the total deficit ($26,677,700) was then applied to additional paid-in capital. The quasi-reorganization adjustments have no effect on the Company's cash flow or tax basis but result in a balance sheet that better reflects the Company's financial position.

The above action, which involved the application of additional paid-in capital to the elimination of a deficit, required shareholder approval which was obtained at the Company's annual meeting of shareholders held on November 16, 1988.

The authoritative literature and accounting standards on quasi-reorganizations are generally antiquated and are permissive rather than mandatory. Moreover, "there are financial accounting and reporting issues concerning quasi-reorganizations for which the authoritative accounting literature provides no guidance or for which the guidance provided is unclear or conflicting."[3] As a result, accounting for quasi-reorganizations is in need of study and clarification.

▶ SUMMARY OF LEARNING OBJECTIVE FOR APP. 16-A ◀

KEY TERM

quasi-reorganization, 793

10. **Describe the accounting for a quasi-reorganization.** A corporation that has accumulated a large debit balance (deficit) in retained earnings may, under the laws of certain states, enter into a process known as a quasi-reorganization. This procedure consists of the following steps: (1) All assets are revalued at appropriate current values so the company will not be burdened with excessive inventory or fixed asset valuations in following years. Any loss on revaluation increases the deficit. (2) Paid-in or other types of capital must be available or must be created, at least equal in amount to the deficit. If no such capital exists, it is created through donation of outstanding stock, or by some similar means. (3) The deficit is then eliminated by a charge against paid-in capital. In addition to the steps above, a quasi-reorganization requires: (1) approval by stockholders, (2) fair and unbiased valuation of assets, (3) a zero balance in retained earnings at the conclusion of the reorganization, (4) the date of the quasi-reorganization shown with retained earnings for the succeeding 10 years, and (5) balance sheet disclosure of the amount of the deficit eliminated, for 3 years.

[3]"Quasi-Reorganization," *Issues Paper 88-1* (New York: AICPA, September 22, 1988), 75 pp. This issues paper prepared by an AICPA Accounting Standards Division task force identified 46 issues that need to be resolved relative to accounting and reporting for quasi-reorganizations.

Note: All **asterisked** Questions, Exercises, Problems, and Cases relate to material contained in the appendix to each chapter.

QUESTIONS

1. Distinguish among: contributed capital, earned capital, and equity capital.

2. What are some of the common items that increase or decrease retained earnings?

3. What factors influence the dividend policy of a company?

4. What are the characteristics of state incorporation laws relative to the legality of dividend payments?

5. Very few companies pay dividends in amounts equal to their retained earnings legally available for dividends. Why?

6. What are the principal considerations of a board of directors in making decisions involving dividend declarations? Discuss briefly.

7. In a report from the FASB, it was noted that on a price-level basis (adjusted for specific prices), dividends exceeded profits. As a result, some industries, such as primary and fabricated metals, are in effect undergoing gradual liquidation. Explain what this statement means.

8. Dividends are sometimes said to have been paid "out of retained earnings." What is the error in that statement?

9. Distinguish among: cash dividends, property dividends, scrip dividends, liquidating dividends, and stock dividends.

10. Describe the accounting entry for a stock dividend. Describe the accounting entry for a stock split.

11. Stock splits and stock dividends may be used by a corporation to change the number of shares of its stock outstanding.
    (a) What is meant by a stock split effected in the form of a dividend?
    (b) From an accounting viewpoint, explain how the stock split effected in the form of a dividend differs from an ordinary stock dividend.
    (c) How should a stock dividend that has been declared but not yet issued be classified in a statement of financial position? Why?

12. The following comment appeared in the notes of Saskatchewan Battery Corporation's annual report: "Such distributions, representing proceeds from the sale of Regina, Inc. were paid in the form of partial liquidating dividends and were in lieu of a portion of the Company's ordinary cash dividends." How would a partial liquidating dividend be accounted for in the financial records?

13. This comment appeared in the annual report of Manitoba Inc.: "The Company could pay cash or property dividends on the Class A common stock without paying cash or property dividends on the Class B common stock, but if the Company pays any cash or property dividends on the Class B Common Stock, it would be required to pay at least the same dividend on the Class A Common Stock." How is a property dividend accounted for in the financial records?

14. St. Pierre Corporation has consistently reported a significant amount of income and has accumulated a large balance of retained earnings. At a recent stockholders' meeting, the company's policy of declaring little or no dividends caused some controversy.
    (a) Why might St. Pierre Corporation establish such a conservative dividend policy?
    (b) What steps might St. Pierre take to reduce the amount of retained earnings available for dividends?

15. Miquelon Corp. had $100,000 of 10%, $20 par value preferred stock and 12,000 shares of $25 par value common stock outstanding throughout 1995.
    (a) Assuming that total dividends declared in 1995 were $80,000, and that the preferred stock is not cumulative but is fully participating, each common share should receive 1995 dividends of what amount?
    (b) Assuming that total dividends declared in 1995 were $80,000, and that the preferred stock is fully participating and cumulative with preferred dividends in arrears for 1994, preferred stockholders should receive 1995 dividends totaling what amount?
    (c) Assuming that total dividends declared in 1995 were $30,000, that cumulative non-participating preferred stock was issued on January 1, 1994, and that $5,000 of preferred dividends were declared and paid in 1994, the common stockholders should receive 1995 dividends totaling what amount?

16. For what reasons might a company appropriate a portion of its retained earnings?

17. How should appropriations of retained earnings be created and written off?

18. Comment on the propriety of Yukon Company reporting "paid-in surplus" and "earned surplus" in the equity section of its balance sheet.

19. Indicate the misuse and the proper use of the term "reserve."

20. What are some of the ways in which retained earnings may be restricted?

21. Is there a duplication of charges to current year's costs or expenses where a sinking fund appropriation is created for the retirement of bonds, as well as accumulated depreciation with respect to the capital assets by which such bonds are secured? Discuss briefly the point raised by this question.

22. What is self-insurance? What are the two acceptable forms that the accounting treatment for self-insurance may take?

*23. Outline the accounting steps involved in accomplishing a quasi-reorganization.

*24. Under what circumstances would a corporation consider submitting itself to a quasi-reorganization?

*25. What disclosures are required in the balance sheet for years subsequent to a quasi-reorganization?

EXERCISES

E16-1 (Equity Items on the Balance Sheet) The following are selected transactions that may affect stockholders' equity.

1. Recorded accrued interest earned on a note receivable.
2. Declared a cash dividend.
3. Declared and distributed a stock split.
4. Recorded a retained earnings appropriation.
5. Recorded the expiration of insurance coverage that was previously recorded as prepaid insurance.
6. Paid the cash dividend declared in item 2 above.
7. Recorded accrued interest expense on a note payable.
8. Recorded an increase in value of an investment that will be distributed as a property dividend.
9. Declared a property dividend (see item 8 above).
10. Distributed the investment to stockholders (see items 8 and 9 above).
11. Declared a stock dividend.
12. Distributed the stock dividend declared in item 11.

Instructions
In the table below, indicate the effect each of the twelve transactions has on the financial statement elements listed. Use the following code:

I = Increase   D = Decrease   NE = No effect

Item	Assets	Liabilities	Stockholders' Equity	Paid-in Capital	Retained Earnings	Net Income

E16-2 (Classification of Equity Items) Stockholders' equity on the balance sheet of Wexford Corp. is composed of three major sections. They are: A. Capital stock; B. Additional paid-in capital; and C. Retained earnings.

Instructions

Classify each of the following items as affecting one of the three sections above or as D, an item not to be included in stockholders' equity.

1. Net income
2. Subscriptions receivable
3. Stock split
4. Property dividends declared
5. Preferred stock
6. Common stock subscribed
7. Retained earnings appropriated
8. Sinking fund
9. Treasury stock
10. Paid-in capital in excess of par—common

E16-3 (Cash Dividend and Liquidating Dividend) Dwarfie Stone Corporation has ten million shares of common stock issued and outstanding. On June 1 the board of directors voted a 75 cents per share cash dividend to stockholders of record as of June 14, payable June 30.

Instructions

(a) Prepare the journal entry for each of the dates above assuming the dividend represents a distribution of earnings.

(b) How would the entry differ if the dividend were a liquidating dividend?

(c) Assume Dwarfie Stone Corporation holds 300,000 common shares in the treasury and as a matter of administrative convenience dividends are paid on treasury shares. How should this cash receipt be recorded?

E16-4 (Preferred Dividends) The outstanding capital stock of Lochmaben Corporation consists of 2,000 shares of $100 par value, 8% preferred, and 5,000 shares of $50 par value common.

Instructions

Assuming that the company has retained earnings of $86,000, all of which is to be paid out in dividends, and that preferred dividends were not paid during the two years preceding the current year, state how much each class of stock should receive under each of the following conditions:

(a) The preferred stock is noncumulative and nonparticipating.

(b) The preferred stock is cumulative and nonparticipating.

(c) The preferred stock is cumulative and participating.

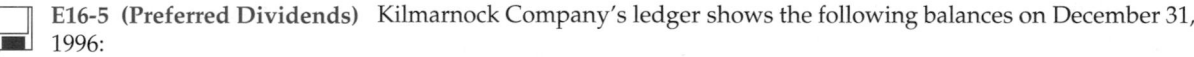

E16-5 (Preferred Dividends) Kilmarnock Company's ledger shows the following balances on December 31, 1996:

7% Preferred stock—$10 par value, outstanding 20,000 shares	$ 200,000
Common stock—$100 par value, outstanding 30,000 shares	3,000,000
Retained earnings	630,000

Instructions

Assuming that the directors decide to declare total dividends in the amount of $334,000, determine how much each class of stock should receive under each of the conditions stated below. One year's dividends are in arrears on the preferred stock.

(a) The preferred stock is cumulative and fully participating.

(b) The preferred stock is noncumulative and nonparticipating.

(c) The preferred stock is noncumulative and is participating in distributions in excess of a 10% dividend rate on the common stock.

E16-6 (Stock Split and Stock Dividend) The common stock of Troon Inc. is currently selling at $120 per share. The directors wish to reduce the share price and increase share volume prior to a new issue. The per share par value is $10; book value is $70. Eight million shares are issued and outstanding.

Instructions

Prepare the necessary journal entries assuming:

(a) The board votes a 2-for-1 stock split.

(b) The board votes a 100% stock dividend.

(c) Briefly discuss the accounting and securities market differences between these two methods of increasing the number of shares outstanding.

E16-7 (Stock Dividends) Swansea Inc. has 5 million shares issued and outstanding. The per share par value is $1, book value is $32 and market value is $39.

Instructions

Prepare the necessary journal entry for the date of declaration and date of issue assuming:

(a) A 10% stock dividend is declared.

(b) A 50% stock dividend is declared.

(c) If Swansea has 500,000 shares of treasury stock, should the stock dividend be applied to the treasury shares? Explain.

(d) What is the amount of the corporation's liability for the period from the declaration date to the distribution date?

E16-8 (Entries for Stock Dividends and Stock Splits) The stockholders' equity accounts of Crymmych Company have the following balances on December 31, 1996:

Common stock, $10 par, 300,000 shares issued and outstanding	$3,000,000
Paid-in capital in excess of par	1,200,000
Retained earnings	5,600,000

Shares of Crymmych Company stock are currently selling on the Midwest Stock Exchange at $34.

Instructions
Prepare the appropriate journal entries for each of the following cases:

(a) A stock dividend of 5% is declared and issued.

(b) A stock dividend of 100% is declared and issued.

(c) A 2-for-1 stock split is declared and issued.

E16-9 (Dividend Entries) The following data were taken from the balance sheet accounts of Tiverton Corporation on December 31, 1995:

Current assets	$540,000
Investments	624,000
Common stock (par value $10)	500,000
Paid-in capital in excess of par	150,000
Retained earnings	840,000

Instructions
Prepare the required journal entries for the following unrelated items:

(a) A 5% stock dividend is declared and distributed at a time when the market value of the shares is $38 per share.

(b) A scrip dividend of $75,000 is declared.

(c) The par value of the capital stock is reduced to $2 and the stock is split 5 for 1.

(d) A dividend is declared January 5, 1996, and paid January 25, 1996, in bonds held as an investment; the bonds have a book value of $100,000 and a fair market value of $130,000.

E16-10 (Computation of Retained Earnings) The following information has been taken from the ledger accounts of St. Albans Corporation:

Total income since incorporation	$300,000
Total cash dividends paid	60,000
Proceeds from sale of donated stock	40,000
Total value of stock dividends distributed	30,000
Gains on treasury stock transactions	18,000
Unamortized discount on bonds payable	32,000
Appropriated for plant expansion	70,000

Instructions
Determine the current balance of unappropriated retained earnings.

E16-11 (Retained Earnings Appropriations and Disclosures) At December 31, 1994, the retained earnings account of Thrapston Inc. had a balance of $320,000. There was no appropriation at this time. During 1995, net income was $235,000. Cash dividends declared during the year were $50,000 on preferred stock and $68,000 on common stock. A stock dividend on common stock resulted in a $70,000 charge to retained earnings. At December 31, 1995, the board of directors decided to create an appropriation for contingencies of $100,000 because of an outstanding lawsuit that does not meet the criteria for accrual.

Instructions

(a) Prepare the journal entry to record the appropriation at December 31, 1995.

(b) Prepare a statement of unappropriated retained earnings for 1995.

(c) Prepare the retained earnings section of the December 31, 1995, balance sheet.

(d) Assume that in May 1996, the lawsuit is settled and Thrapston agrees to pay $88,000. At this time, the board of directors also decides to eliminate the appropriation. Prepare all necessary entries.

(e) Return to part (a), but assume that Thrapston decided to disclose the appropriation through a footnote at December 31, 1995, instead of preparing a formal journal entry. Prepare the necessary footnote.

E16-12 (Appropriations for Self-Insurance) Colin Booth, as president of Redcar Inc. has decided against purchasing casualty insurance to cover the company's four plants. Recognizing the possibility of casualty losses, he has $60,000 a year appropriated as a reserve for such contingencies; the first appropriation is made in 1995. In 1998 a fire completely destroys one of his plants. The plant had a 30-year life, no salvage value, and an original cost of $270,000 when it was constructed 12 years ago (straight-line depreciation). After the fire in 1998, Colin Booth changes his mind, buys insurance and pays an annual premium of $25,000 on January 2, 1999, and eliminates his casualty reserve.

Instructions
Prepare the entries to journalize the insurance and casualty transactions of 1995, 1998, and 1999.

E16-13 (Stockholders' Equity Section) Bordeaux Corporation's post-closing trial balance at December 31, 1995, was as follows:

Bordeaux Corporation
POST-CLOSING TRIAL BALANCE
December 31, 1995

	Dr.	Cr.
Accounts payable		$ 310,000
Accounts receivable	$ 480,000	
Accumulated depreciation—building and equipment		185,000
Additional paid-in capital—common		
In excess of par value		1,350,000
From sale of treasury stock		180,000
Allowance for doubtful accounts		30,000
Bonds payable		300,000
Building and equipment	1,450,000	
Cash	190,000	
Common stock ($1 par value)		150,000
Dividends payable on preferred stock—cash		4,000
Inventories	560,000	
Land	400,000	
Preferred stock ($50 par value)		500,000
Prepaid expenses	40,000	
Retained earnings		281,000
Treasury stock—common at cost	170,000	
Totals	$3,290,000	$3,290,000

At December 31, 1995, Bordeaux had the following number of common and preferred shares:

	Common	Preferred
Authorized	600,000	60,000
Issued	150,000	10,000
Outstanding	140,000	10,000

The dividends on preferred stock are $4 cumulative. In addition, the preferred stock has a preference in liquidation of $50 per share.

Instructions
Prepare the stockholders' equity section of Bordeaux' balance sheet at December 31, 1995.

(AICPA adapted)

E16-14 (Participating Preferred, Stock Dividend, and Treasury Stock Retirement) The following is the stockholders' equity section of Rennes Corp. at December 31, 1995:

Common stock, $20 par; authorized 200,000 shares;	
issued 90,000 shares	$ 1,800,000
Preferred stock,* $50 par; authorized 100,000 shares;	
issued 15,000 shares	750,000
Additional paid-in capital	3,150,000
Total paid-in capital	5,700,000
Retained Earnings	5,213,000
Total paid-in capital and retained earnings	10,913,000
Less cost of treasury stock (7,500 common shares)	(742,500)
Total stockholders' equity	$10,170,500

*The preferred stock has a 12% dividend rate, is cumulative, and is participating in distribution in excess of a 15% dividend rate on the common stock.

Instructions

(a) No dividends have been paid in 1993 or 1994. On December 31, 1995, Rennes wants to pay a cash dividend of $4.00 a share to common stockholders. How much cash would be needed for the **total amount paid** to preferred and common stockholders?

(b) Instead, Rennes will declare a 10% stock dividend on the outstanding common stock. The market value of the stock is $103 per share. Prepare the entry on the date of declaration.

(c) Instead, Rennes will retire the treasury stock. It was originally issued at $51 a share. The current market value is $103 per share. Prepare the entry to record the retirement.

E16-15 (Dividends and Stockholders' Equity Section) Moulins Company reported the following amounts in the stockholders' equity section of its December 31, 1994, balance sheet:

Preferred stock, 10%, $100 par (10,000 shares authorized, 2,000 shares issued)	$200,000
Common stock, $5 par (100,000 shares authorized, 20,000 shares issued)	100,000
Additional paid-in capital	125,000
Retained earnings	450,000
Total	$875,000

During 1995, Moulins took part in the following transactions concerning stockholders' equity.

1. Paid the annual 1994 $10 per share dividend on preferred stock and a $1 per share dividend on common stock. These dividends had been declared on December 31, 1994.

2. Purchased 1,700 shares of its own outstanding common stock for $35 per share. Moulins uses the cost method.

3. Reissued 700 treasury shares for land valued at $30,000.

4. Issued 500 shares of preferred stock at $106 per share.

5. Declared a 10% stock dividend on the outstanding common stock when the stock is selling for $39 per share.

6. Issued the stock dividend.

7. Declared the annual 1995 $10 per share dividend on preferred stock and the $1 per share dividend on common stock. These dividends are payable in 1996.

8. Appropriated retained earnings for plant expansion, $150,000.

Instructions

(a) Prepare journal entries to record the transactions described above.

(b) Prepare the December 31, 1995, stockholders' equity section. Assume 1995 net income was $305,000.

*E16-16 (Quasi-Reorganization) The following account balances are available from the ledger of Glamorgan Corporation on December 31, 1995:

Common Stock—$50 par value, 20,000 shares authorized and outstanding	$1,000,000
Retained Earnings (deficit)	(190,000)

As of January 2, 1996, the corporation gave effect to a stockholder-approved quasi-reorganization by reducing the par value of the stock to $35 a share, writing down plant assets by $85,600, and eliminating the deficit.

Instructions

Prepare the required journal entries for the quasi-reorganization of Glamorgan Corporation.

*E16-17 (Quasi-Reorganization) The condensed balance sheets of Morecambe Company immediately before and one year after it had completed a quasi-reorganization appear below:

	Before Quasi	One Year After		Before Quasi	One Year After
Current assets	$ 300,000	$ 420,000	Common stock	$2,400,000	$1,550,000
Plant assets (net)	1,700,000	1,290,000	Premium on common	220,000	
			Retained earnings	(620,000)	160,000
	$2,000,000	$1,710,000		$2,000,000	$1,710,000

For the year following the quasi-reorganization, Morecambe Company reported net income of $190,000, depreciation expense of $80,000, and paid a cash dividend of $30,000. As part of the quasi-reorganization, the company wrote down inventories by $120,000. No purchases or sales of plant assets and no stock transactions occurred in the year following the quasi-reorganization.

Instructions

Prepare all the journal entries made at the time of the quasi-reorganization.

*E16-18 (Quasi-Reorganization) Cognac Corporation is under protection of the bankruptcy court and has the following account balances at June 30, 1995.

Cash	$ (5,000)	Accounts payable	$ 450,000
Accounts receivable	320,000	Notes payable	605,000
Inventory	450,000	Taxes and wages	60,000
Equipment	860,000	Mortgage payable	150,000
Accumulated depreciation	(525,000)	Common stock	50,000
Intangibles	80,000	Retained earnings	(135,000)
Total	$1,180,000	Total	$1,180,000

The court has accepted the following proposed settlement of the company's affairs. Write down the assets by the following amounts:

Accounts receivable	$ 40,000
Inventory	$160,000
Intangibles	$ 80,000

The trade creditors (accounts payable) will reduce their claim by 30%, will accept one-year notes for 50%, and retain their current claim for the remaining 20%. The tax, wage, and mortgage claims will remain unchanged. The current common stock will be surrendered to the corporation and cancelled. In consideration thereof, the current stockholders shall be held harmless from any possible personal liability. The current holder of the note payable shall receive 1,000 shares of no par common stock in full satisfaction of the note payable. After these adjustments have been made the retained earnings shall be raised to zero by a charge against invested capital.

Instructions
 (a) Prepare a balance sheet at June 30, 1995, that reflects the events listed above.
 (b) Briefly discuss the nature of a quasi-reorganization.

PROBLEMS

P16-1 (Correction of Equity Items) As the newly appointed controller in 1996 for Zeeland Company, you are interested in analyzing the "Additional Capital" account of the company in order to present an accurate balance sheet. Your assistant, Kevin Utrecht, who has analyzed the account from the inception of the company, submits the following summary:

	Debits	Credits
Cash dividends—preferred	$ 114,000	
Cash dividends—common	340,000	
Excess of amount paid in over par value of common stock		400,000
Discount on preferred stock	60,000	
Net income		780,000
Contra to appraisal increase of land		430,000
Additional assessments of prior years' income taxes	91,000	
Extraordinary gain		22,500
Donated treasury stock, preferred; issued and reacquired, at par	270,000	
Extraordinary loss	98,500	
Correction of a prior period error	55,000	
	1,028,500	1,632,500
Credit balance of additional capital account	604,000	
	$1,632,500	$1,632,500

Instructions
 (a) Prepare a journal entry to close the single "Additional Capital" account now used and to establish appropriately classified accounts. Indicate how you derive the balance of each new account.
 (b) If generally accepted accounting principles had been followed, what amount should have been shown as total net income?

P16-2 (Equity Shortage and Treasury Stock Settlement) The balance sheet of Jambes Inc. shows $400,000 capital stock consisting of 4,000 shares of $100 each, and retained earnings of $144,000. As controller of the company, you find that Ann Twerp, the assistant treasurer, is $83,000 short in her accounts and had concealed this shortage by adding the amount to the inventory. She owns 740 shares of the company's stock and, in settlement of the shortage, offers this stock at its book value. The offer is accepted; the company pays her the excess value and distributes the 740 shares thus acquired to the other stockholders.

Instructions
   (a) What amount should Jambes Inc. pay the assistant treasurer?
   (b) By what journal entries should the foregoing transactions be recorded? (Treasury stock is recorded using the cost method.)
   (c) What is the total stockholders' equity after the distribution noted above?
   (d) What would have been done if Jambes Inc. had had a deficit of $85,000 and the 740 shares had been accepted at par?

P16-3 (Preferred Stock Dividends) Andorra Inc. began operations in January 1992 and had the following reported net income or loss for each of its five years of operations:

1992	$ 225,000 loss
1993	140,000 loss
1994	180,000 loss
1995	422,500 income
1996	1,500,000 income

At December 31, 1996, Andorra capital accounts were as follows:

Common stock, par value $15 per share; authorized 200,000 shares; issued and outstanding 50,000 shares	$ 750,000
8% nonparticipating noncumulative preferred stock, par value $100 per share; authorized, issued and outstanding 5,000 shares	500,000
5% fully participating cumulative preferred stock, par value $150 per share; authorized, issued and outstanding 10,000 shares	1,500,000

Andorra has never paid a cash or stock dividend. There has been no change in the capital accounts since Andorra began operations. The appropriate state law permits dividends only from retained earnings.

Instructions
Prepare a work sheet showing the maximum amount available for cash dividends on December 31, 1996, and how it would be distributable to the holders of the common shares and each of the preferred shares. Show supporting computations in good form.

(AICPA adapted)

P16-4 (Stock Dividend Involving Exchangeable Shares and Cash in Lieu of Fractional Shares) The Board of Directors of Nyborg Corporation on December 1, 1996 declared a 4% stock dividend on the common stock of the corporation, payable on December 28, 1996, only to the holders of record at the close of business December 15, 1996. They stipulated that cash dividends were to be paid in lieu of issuing any fractional shares. They also directed that the amount to be charged against Retained Earnings should be an amount equal to the market value of the stock on the record date multiplied by the total of (a) the number of shares issued as a stock dividend, and (b) the number of shares on which cash is paid in place of the issuance of fractional shares. The following facts are given:

   1. At the dividend record date:
       (a) Shares of Nyborg common issued 3,048,750
       (b) Shares of Nyborg common held in treasury 1,100
       (c) Shares of Nyborg common included in (a) above held by persons who will receive cash in lieu of fractional shares 222,750
   2. Values of Nyborg common were:
       Par value .... $ 5
       Market value at December 1st and 15th $20
       Book value at December 1st and 15th $14

Instructions
Prepare entries and explanations to record the payment of the dividend.

(AICPA adapted)

P16-5 (Cash Dividend Entries) The books of Tisvildeleje Corporation carried the following account balances as of December 31, 1995:

Cash	$ 195,000
Preferred stock, 6% cumulative, nonparticipating, $50 par	750,000
Common stock, no par value, 300,000 shares issued	1,500,000
Paid-in capital in excess of par (preferred)	150,000
Treasury stock (common 4,200 shares at cost)	33,600
Retained earnings	105,000

The preferred stock has dividends in arrears for the past year (1995).

The board of directors, at their annual meeting on December 21, 1996, declared the following: "The current year dividends shall be 6% on the preferred and $.25 per share on the common; the dividends in arrears shall be paid by issuing one share of treasury stock for each ten shares of preferred held."

The preferred is currently selling at $80 per share and the common at $8 per share. Net income for 1996 is estimated at $64,000.

Instructions
- **(a)** Prepare the journal entries required for the dividend declaration and payment, assuming that they occur simultaneously.
- **(b)** Could Tisvildeleje Corporation give the preferred stockholders 2 years' dividends and common stockholders a 25 cents per share dividend, all in cash?

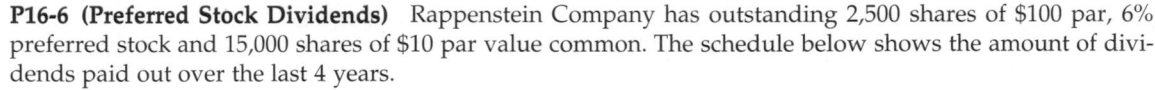

P16-6 (Preferred Stock Dividends) Rappenstein Company has outstanding 2,500 shares of $100 par, 6% preferred stock and 15,000 shares of $10 par value common. The schedule below shows the amount of dividends paid out over the last 4 years.

Instructions
Allocate the dividends to each type of stock under assumptions (a) and (b). Express your answers in per-share amounts using the following format.

		Assumptions			
		(a) Preferred, noncumulative, and nonparticipating		(b) Preferred, cumulative, and fully participating	
Year	Paid-out	Preferred	Common	Preferred	Common
1993	$12,500				
1994	$26,000				
1995	$57,000				
1996	$72,000				

P16-7 (Stock and Cash Dividends) Zabbar Company has these stockholders' equity accounts:

	Shares	Amount
Preferred stock, $100 par value	2,200	$220,000
Treasury shares, preferred (at cost)	160	22,000
Common stock without par value (at issue price)	3,600	118,800
Retained earnings		494,640

In view of the large retained earnings, the board of directors resolves: (1) "to pay a 100% stock dividend on all shares outstanding, capitalizing amounts of retained earnings equal to the par value and the issue price of the preferred and common stock outstanding, respectively," and thereafter (2) "to pay a cash dividend of 6% on preferred stock and a cash dividend of $2 a share on common stock."

Instructions
- **(a)** Prepare entries in journal form to record declaration of these dividends.
- **(b)** Prepare the stockholders' equity section of a balance sheet for Zabbar Company after declaration but before distribution of these dividends.

P16-8 (Entries for Stockholders' Equity Transactions) Some of the account balances of Portalegre Company at December 31, 1995, are shown below:

6% Preferred Stock ($100 par, 2,000 shares authorized)	$ 20,000
Paid-in Capital in Excess of Par—Preferred Stock	3,000
Common Stock ($10 par, 100,000 shares authorized)	500,000
Paid-in Capital in Excess of Par—Common Stock	100,000

Unappropriated Retained Earnings	304,000
Treasury Stock—Preferred (50 shares at cost)	5,500
Treasury Stock—Common (1,000 shares at cost)	16,000
Retained Earnings Appropriated for Contingencies	75,000
Retained Earnings Appropriated for Fire Insurance	95,000

The price of the company's common stock has been increasing steadily on the market; it was $21 on January 1, 1996, advanced to $23 by July 1, and to $27 at the end of the year 1996. The preferred stock is not openly traded but was appraised at $120 per share during 1996.

Instructions

Give the proper journal entries for each of the following:

(a) The company incurred a fire loss of $54,000 to its warehouse.

(b) The company declared a property dividend on April 1. Each common stockholder was to receive one share of Beja for every 10 shares outstanding. Portalegre had 8,000 shares of Beja (2% of total outstanding stock) which was purchased in 1993 for $68,400. The market value of Beja stock was $16 per share on April 1. Record appreciation only on the shares distributed.

(c) The company resold the 50 shares of preferred stock held in the treasury for $115 per share.

(d) On July 1, the company declared a 5% stock dividend to the common (outstanding) stockholders.

(e) The city of Lisbon, in an effort to persuade the company to expand into that city, donated to Portalegre Company a plot of land with an appraised value of $36,000 (credit to Donated Capital).

(f) At the annual board of directors meeting, the board decided to "Set up an appropriation in retained earnings for the future construction of a new plant. Such appropriation to be for $124,000 per year. Also, to increase the appropriation for possible contingencies by $25,000 and to eliminate the appropriation for fire insurance and begin purchasing such insurance from Chaves Insurance Company."

P16-9 (Equity Entries and Retained Earnings Statement) The stockholders' equity section of Cartagena Company balance sheet on January 1 of the current year is as follows:

Paid-in Capital		
Common stock, par $100, 20,000 shares authorized,		
10,000 shares issued	$1,000,000	
Paid-in capital in excess of par	400,000	
Total paid-in capital		$1,400,000
Retained Earnings:		
Unappropriated	$ 300,000	
Appropriated for plant expansion	120,000	
Appropriated for treasury stock	90,000	
Total retained earnings		510,000
		$1,910,000
Less cost of treasury stock (600 shares)		90,000
Total stockholders' equity		$1,820,000

The following selected transactions occurred during the year:

1. Paid cash dividends of $1.20 per share on the common stock. The dividend had been properly recorded when declared last year. (State law prohibits cash or stock dividends on treasury shares.)

2. Declared a 10% stock dividend on the common stock when the shares were selling at $112 each in the market.

3. Made a prior period adjustment to correct an error of $60,000 which overstated net income in the previous year. The error was the result of an overstatement of ending inventory.

4. Sold all of the treasury shares for $105,000.

5. Issued the certificates for the stock dividend.

6. The board appropriated $40,000 of retained earnings for plant expansion, eliminated the appropriation for treasury stock, and declared a cash dividend of $1.65 per share on the common stock.

7. The company reported net income of $210,000 for the year.

Instructions

(a) Prepare journal entries for the selected transactions above (ignore income taxes).

(b) Prepare a retained earnings statement for the current year.

P16-10 (Equity Entries and Balance Sheet Presentation) On December 15, 1995, the directors of Malaga Corporation voted to appropriate $90,000 of retained earnings and to retain in the business assets equal to the appropriation for use in expanding the corporation's factory building. This was the fourth of such appropriations; after it was recorded, the stockholders' equity section of Malaga's balance sheet appeared as follows:

Stockholders' equity:
Common stock, $10 par value, 300,000 shares
    authorized, 200,000 shares issued and outstanding $2,000,000
Paid-in capital in excess of par   3,600,000

    Total paid-in capital   5,600,000
Retained earnings—
Unappropriated $1,800,000
Appropriated for plant expansion   360,000

    Total retained earnings   2,160,000
Total stockholders' equity $7,760,000

On January 9, 1996, the corporation entered into a contract for the construction of the factory addition for which the retained earnings were appropriated. On November 1, 1996, the addition was completed and the contractor was paid the contract price of $322,500.

On December 14, 1996, the Board of Directors voted to return the balance of the Retained Earnings Appropriated for Plant Expansion account to Unappropriated Retained Earnings. They also voted a 25,000 share stock dividend distributable on January 23, 1997, to the January 15, 1997, stockholders of record. The stock dividend was paid per the Board's resolution. The corporation's stock was selling at $46 in the market on December 14, 1996. Malaga reported net income for 1995 of $525,000 and for 1996 of $600,000.

Instructions

  (a) Prepare the appropriate journal entries for Malaga Corporation for the information above (December 15, 1995, to January 23, 1997, inclusive).

  (b) Prepare the stockholders' equity section of the balance sheet for Malaga at December 31, 1996, in proper accounting form.

P16-11 (Stockholders' Equity Section of Balance Sheet) The following is a summary of all relevant transactions of Marbella Corporation since it was organized in 1990:

In 1993, 15,000 shares were authorized and 7,000 shares of common stock ($50 par value) were issued at a price of $56. In 1994, 1,000 shares were issued as a stock dividend when the stock was selling for $62. Three hundred shares of common stock were bought in 1995 at a cost of $65 per share. These 300 shares are still in the company treasury. (State law requires an appropriation of retained earnings equal to cost of treasury stock.)

In 1994, 10,000 preferred shares were authorized and the company issued 4,000 of them ($100 par value) at $112. Some of the preferred stock was reacquired by the company and later reissued for $4,300 more than it cost the company.

The corporation has earned a total of $600,000 in net income after income taxes and paid out a total of $312,600 in cash dividends since incorporation. An appropriation was made in 1995 by the Board of Directors from retained earnings in the amount of $75,000 for Fixed Asset Replacements.

Instructions

Prepare the stockholders' equity section of the balance sheet in proper form for Marbella Corporation as of December 31, 1995. Account for treasury stock using the cost method.

P16-12 (Stock and Cash Dividends) Burgos Corporation has outstanding 2,000,000 shares of common stock of a par value of $10 each. The balance in its retained earnings account at January 1, 1995, was $24,000,000, and it then had Additional Paid-in Capital of $5,000,000. During 1995, the company's net income was $5,600,000. A cash dividend of 50¢ a share was paid June 30, 1995, and a 6% stock dividend was distributed to stockholders of record at the close of business on December 31, 1995. You have been asked to advise on the proper accounting treatment of the stock dividend.

The existing stock of the company is quoted on a national stock exchange. The market price of the stock has been as follows:

October 31, 1995	$31
November 30, 1995	33
December 31, 1995	38
Average price over the two-month period	35

Instructions

  (a) Prepare a journal entry to record the cash dividend.

  (b) Prepare a journal entry to record the stock dividend.

  (c) Prepare the stockholders' equity section (including schedules of retained earnings and additional paid-in capital) of the balance sheet of Burgos Corporation for the year 1995 on the basis of the foregoing information. Draft a note to the financial statements setting forth the basis of the accounting for the stock dividend and add separately appropriate comments or explanations regarding the basis chosen.

P16-13 (Analysis and Classification of Equity Transactions) Ludvika Company was formed on July 1, 1992. It was authorized to issue 300,000 shares of $10 par value common stock and 100,000 shares of 8 percent $25 par value, cumulative and nonparticipating preferred stock. Ludvika Company has a July 1–June 30 fiscal year.

The following information relates to the stockholders' equity accounts of Ludvika Company:

Common Stock

Prior to the 1994–95 fiscal year, Ludvika Company had 110,000 shares of outstanding common stock issued as follows:

1. 95,000 shares were issued for cash on July 1, 1992, at $30 per share.
2. On July 24, 1992, 5,000 shares were exchanged for a plot of land which cost the seller $70,000 in 1986 and had an estimated market value of $220,000 on July 24, 1992.
3. 10,000 shares were issued on March 1, 1994; the shares had been subscribed for $42 per share on October 31, 1993.

During the 1994–95 fiscal year, the following transactions regarding common stock took place:

October 1, 1994	Subscriptions were received for 10,000 shares at $46 per share. Cash of $92,000 was received in full payment for 2,000 shares and stock certificates were issued. The remaining subscription for 8,000 shares were to be paid in full by September 30, 1995, at which time the certificates were to be issued.
November 30, 1994	Ludvika purchased 2,000 shares of its own stock on the open market at $38 per share. Ludvika uses the cost method for treasury stock.
December 15, 1994	Ludvika declared a 5% stock dividend for stockholders of record on January 15, 1995, to be issued on January 31, 1995. Ludvika was having a liquidity problem and could not afford a cash dividend at the time. Ludvika's common stock was selling at $52 per share on December 15, 1994.
June 20, 1995	Ludvika sold 500 shares of its own common stock that it had purchased on November 30, 1994, for $21,000.

Preferred Stock

Ludvika issued 50,000 shares of preferred stock at $43 per share on July 1, 1993.

Cash Dividends

Ludvika has followed a schedule of declaring cash dividends in December and June with payment being made to stockholders of record in the following month. The cash dividends which have been declared since inception of the company through June 30, 1995, are shown below:

Declaration Date	Common Stock	Preferred Stock
12/15/93	$.30 per share	$1.00 per share
6/15/94	$.30 per share	$1.00 per share
12/15/94	—	$1.00 per share

No cash dividends were declared during June 1995 due to the company's liquidity problems.

Retained Earnings

As of June 30, 1994, Ludvika's retained earnings account had a balance of $670,000. For the fiscal year ending June 30, 1995, Ludvika reported net income of $40,000.

In March of 1994, Ludvika received a term loan from Skovde National Bank. The bank requires Ludvika to establish a sinking fund and restrict retained earnings for an amount equal to the sinking fund deposit. The annual sinking fund payment of $50,000 is due on April 30 each year; the first payment was made on schedule on April 30, 1995.

Instructions

Prepare the stockholders' equity section of the Balance Sheet, including appropriate notes, for Ludvika Company as of June 30, 1995, as it should appear in its annual report to the shareholders.

(CMA adapted)

P16-14 (Retained Earnings and Dividend Policy) Bjorli Corporation is a publisher of children's books. The company was started as a family business in 1947 and is still closely held. For its fiscal year ended May 31, 1995, Bjorli had net income of $900,000 on sales of $10,625,000. The net income included a loss of $350,000, net of tax, that resulted from the disposal of an unprofitable segment of the business. The Board of Directors of Bjorli will be meeting on June 25, 1995, to review the company's financial condition. One of the agenda items for this meeting is to reexamine Bjorli's dividend policy and draft the dividend plans for the 1995–96 fiscal year.

Joanne Dillman, Assistant Controller of Bjorli Corporation, is responsible for the preparation of the company's financial statements for both internal and external reporting purposes. She also is responsible for preparing any reports and statements to be reviewed by the Board of Directors. Of the material specifically requested by the Board for its June 25 meeting, the only report that has not been prepared is the Statement of Retained Earnings. To assist in this preparation, Dillman has listed the account balances for Bjorli's equity accounts as of May 31, 1994, and has accumulated, from the Corporation's books, pertinent information that affected Bjorli's equity accounts during the 1994–95 fiscal year. These data are presented below.

Account Balances as of May 31, 1994

Unappropriated retained earnings	$1,255,000
Appropriation for plant expansion (appropriation is 100 percent of cost)	425,000
Appropriation for bond sinking fund	300,000
Appropriation for treasury stock transactions	360,000
Preferred stock, 8% cumulative, $100 par value, 20,000 shares authorized, 10,000 shares issued and outstanding	1,000,000
Common stock, $10 stated value, 220,000 shares authorized, 190,000 shares issued, 174,000 outstanding	1,900,000
Contributed capital in excess of par, preferred	40,000
Contributed capital in excess of stated value, common	1,520,000
Contributed capital from treasury stock transactions, common	11,000
Treasury stock (at cost)	320,000

Additional Information

1. Dividend activity for the year was as follows.
   —A cash dividend of $.50 per share was paid June 10, 1994. The dividend was declared May 10, 1994, to all common shareholders of record May 25, 1994.
   —A cash dividend of $1.25 per share was declared on November 1, 1994, to all common shareholders of record on November 15, 1994. This dividend was paid November 25, 1994.
   —A 10 percent stock dividend was declared May 15, 1995, to all common stockholders of record on May 25, 1995. This dividend is to be paid from authorized but unissued shares of common stock on June 15, 1995. The per share market price on May 15, 1995, was $27.
   —The required preferred dividend was paid on May 31, 1995, to all preferred stockholders of record.
2. On June 1, 1994, Bjorli sold an additional 5,000 shares of preferred stock at $102 per share.
3. The fiscal year addition to the bond sinking fund and the appropriation for the sinking fund was $25,000.
4. On January 1, 1995, 10,000 shares of treasury stock were sold for $24 per share.
5. Bjorli's plant expansion program is now 60 percent complete, and a proportionate share of the appropriation for this purpose will be returned to retained earnings at May 31, 1995.
6. During the year, depreciation expense for the fiscal year ended May 31, 1994, was discovered to be understated by $25,000. This is considered an error that requires an adjustment to the previous year's earnings.
7. Bjorli Corporation was subject to an effective income tax rate of 30 percent for the fiscal years ended May 31, 1994 and 1995.

Instructions

(a) Bjorli Corporation's Board of Directors has requested the Statement of Retained Earnings in order to determine the retained earnings available for dividends as of May 31, 1995. Prepare the Statement of Retained Earnings in good form for the year ended May 31, 1995, showing:
   1. total retained earnings as of May 31, 1994.
   2. adjustments, additions, and deductions that occurred during the 1994–95 fiscal year.
   3. total retained earnings as of May 31, 1995.
   4. appropriations of retained earnings by restriction as of May 31, 1995.
   5. retained earnings available for dividends as of May 31, 1995.

(b) Discuss how each of the following items would impact the Board of Directors' decision regarding Bjorli Corporation's dividend policy.
   1. The disposal of the segment during the 1994–95 fiscal year that resulted in a $350,000 net-of-tax loss.
   2. The forecasted earnings for the next three fiscal years.
   3. The declaration of the stock dividends to all common stockholders of record that took place on May 15, 1995, and the declaration of any additional stock dividends to common stockholders in the future.

(c) Explain why many companies do not distribute all their available retained earnings.

CASES

C16-1 (Conceptual Issues—Equity) Statements of Financial Accounting Concepts set forth financial accounting and reporting objectives and fundamentals that will be used by the Financial Accounting Standards Board in developing standards. *Concepts Statement No. 6* was issued to replace *Concepts Statement No. 3,* and it defines various elements of financial statements.

Instructions

Answer the following questions based on *SFAC No. 6*.

    (a)   Define and discuss the term "equity."

    (b)   What transactions or events change owners' equity?

    (c)   Define "investments by owners" and provide examples of this type of transaction. What financial statement element other than equity is typically affected by owner investments?

    (d)   Define "distributions to owners" and provide examples of this type of transaction. What financial statement element other than equity is typically affected by distributions?

    (e)   What are examples of changes within owners' equity that do not change the total amount of owners' equity?

C16-2 (Stock Dividends and Splits) The directors of Chinandega Corporation are considering the issuance of a stock dividend. They have asked you to discuss the proposed action by answering the following questions.

Instructions

    (a)   What is a stock dividend? How is a stock dividend distinguished from a stock split-up (1) From a legal standpoint? (2) From an accounting standpoint?

    (b)   For what reasons does a corporation usually declare a stock dividend? A stock split-up?

    (c)   Discuss the amount, if any, of retained earnings to be capitalized in connection with a stock dividend.

(AICPA adapted)

C16-3 (Stock Dividends) Montserrat Inc., a client, is considering the authorization of a 10% common stock dividend to common stockholders. The financial vice-president of Montserrat wishes to discuss the accounting implications of such an authorization with you before the next meeting of the board of directors.

Instructions

    (a)   The first topic the vice-president wishes to discuss is the nature of the stock dividend to the recipient. Discuss the case against considering the stock dividend as income to the recipient.

    (b)   The other topic for discussion is the propriety of issuing the stock dividend to all "stockholders of record" or to "stockholders of record exclusive of shares held in the name of the corporation as treasury stock." Discuss the case against issuing stock dividends on treasury shares.

(AICPA adapted)

C16-4 (Self-Insurance) Half Moon Bay, a large retail chain store company, has stores throughout the United States. Because of the stores' many different locations, Half Moon Bay's president thinks it would be advantageous to self-insure the company's stores against the risk of any future loss or damage from fire or other natural causes. From past experience and by applying appropriate statistical and actuarial techniques, the president feels the amount of future losses can be predicted with reasonable accuracy.

Instructions

The president has asked you how Half Moon Bay should record this type of contingency and on what basis the current period should be allocated a portion of the estimated losses. What would you tell the president?

C16-5 (Stock Dividend, Cash Dividend, and Treasury Stock) Tralee Company has 30,000 shares of $10 par value common stock authorized and 20,000 shares issued and outstanding. On August 15, 1995, Tralee purchased 1,000 shares of treasury stock for $15 per share. Tralee uses the cost method to account for treasury stock. On September 14, 1995, Tralee sold 500 shares of the treasury stock for $18 per share.

In October 1995, Tralee declared and distributed 1,950 shares as a stock dividend from unissued shares when the market value of the common stock was $20 per share.

On December 20, 1995, Tralee declared a $1 per share cash dividend, payable on January 10, 1996, to shareholders of record on December 31, 1995.

Instructions

    (a)   How should Tralee account for the purchase and sale of the treasury stock, and how should the treasury stock be presented in the balance sheet at December 31, 1995?

    (b)   How should Tralee account for the stock dividend, and how would it affect the stockholders' equity at December 31, 1995? Why?

    (c)   How should Tralee account for the cash dividend, and how would it affect the balance sheet at December 31, 1995? Why?

(AICPA adapted)

*C16-6 (Quasi-Reorganization) Basse-Terre Company, a medium-sized manufacturer, has been experiencing losses for the 5 years that it has been doing business. Although the operations for the year just ended resulted in a loss, several important changes resulted in a profitable fourth quarter, and the future operations of the company are expected to be profitable. The treasurer, Van Johnson, suggests that there be a quasi-reorganization to eliminate the accumulated deficit of $650,000.

Instructions

  (a) What are the characteristics of a quasi-reorganization? In other words, of what does it consist?

  (b) List the conditions under which a quasi-reorganization generally is justified.

  (c) Discuss the propriety of the treasurer's proposals to eliminate the deficit of $650,000.

(AICPA adapted)

*C16-7 (Quasi-Reorganization) After operating several years, Sperrin Corporation showed a net worth of $1,500,000, of which $300,000 was represented by 3,000 shares of $100 each, and $1,200,000 was retained earnings. Subsequently, three additional shares were issued for each share held, which made the capital stock $1,200,000 and retained earnings $300,000. The operations of later years showed an aggregate loss of $840,000, leaving a deficit of $540,000.

    The corporation then reduced the par value of each share of stock to 25% of its former value, thus restoring the capital to the original amount of $300,000. The deficit was absorbed and the retained earnings shown as $360,000. It is argued that this amount represents the net operating results since organization and is, therefore, retained earnings.

Instructions

Give your opinion of these transactions; disregard their legal aspects.

▶ USING YOUR JUDGMENT ◀

▶ FINANCIAL REPORTING PROBLEM

Refer to the financial statements and other documents of Georgia-Pacific Corporation presented in Appendix 5-A and answer the following questions.

  (a) In the Financial Strategy section of Georgia-Pacific's 1993 Annual Report, the management indicated that "our policy is to pay regular dividends at a rate of approximately one-third of sustainable earnings—the average earnings expected over a cycle. Recognizing the cyclical nature of our business, we do not intend to adjust dividends based on short-term swings in earnings." What were the Corporation's cash dividends to earnings ratios for the years from 1989 to 1993? Were these ratios consistent with the management's statement? What factors influence the dividend policy of a company?

  (b) In one of its Notes to the Financial Statements, Georgia-Pacific indicated that "the Corporation is self-insured for general liability claims up to $5 million per occurrence." What does "self-insurance" mean? What are the two acceptable forms that the accounting treatment for self-insurance may take?

▶ WRITING ASSIGNMENT

Jenny Durdil Inc. is selling its $10 par common stock for $120 per share. Five million shares are currently issued and outstanding. The Board of Directors wishes to stimulate interest in Jenny Durdil common stock before a forthcoming stock issue but does not wish to distribute capital at this time. The Board also believes that too many adjustments to the Stockholders' Equity section, especially Retained Earnings, might discourage potential investors.

    The Board has considered three options for stimulating interest in the stock:

  1. A 20% stock dividend

  2. A 100% stock dividend

  3. A 2-for-1 stock split.

Acting as financial advisor to the Board, you have been asked to report briefly on each option and, considering the Board's wishes, make a recommendation. Discuss the effects of each of the foregoing options.

▶ GROUP ASSIGNMENT

GA16-1 (Preparation of Retained Earnings Statement and Equity Section) Navajo Company is a public enterprise whose shares are traded in the over-the-counter market. At December 31, 1994, Navajo had

5,000,000 authorized shares of $10 par value common stock, of which 1,500,000 shares were issued and outstanding. The stockholders' equity accounts at December 31, 1994, had the following balances:

Common stock	$15,000,000
Additional paid-in capital	7,000,000
Retained earnings	5,700,000

Transactions during 1995 and other information relating to the stockholders' equity accounts were as follows:

1. On January 5, 1995, Navajo issued at $108 per share, 100,000 shares of $100 par value, 8% cumulative preferred stock. Navajo had 600,000 authorized shares of preferred stock. The preferred stock has a liquidation value equal to its par value.
2. On February 1, 1995, Navajo reacquired 20,000 shares of its common stock for $16 per share. Navajo uses the cost method to account for treasury stock.
3. On April 30, 1995, Navajo sold 500,000 shares (previously unissued) of $10 par value common stock to the public at $17 per share.
4. On June 18, 1995, Navajo declared a cash dividend of $1 per share of common stock, payable on July 12, 1995, to stockholders of record on July 1, 1995.
5. On November 10, 1995, Navajo sold 10,000 shares of treasury stock for $21 per share.
6. On December 14, 1995, Navajo declared the yearly cash dividend on preferred stock, payable on January 14, 1996, to stockholders of record on December 31, 1995.
7. On January 20, 1996, before the books were closed for 1995, Navajo became aware that the ending inventories at December 31, 1994, were understated by $300,000 (after tax effect on 1994 net income was $180,000). The appropriate correction entry was recorded the same day.
8. After correcting the beginning inventory, net income for 1995 was $3,600,000.

Instructions

Your instructor will assign one group member to serve as a recorder and one member to serve as spokesperson. As a group, provide the information for the recorder to prepare (show supporting computations in good form):

(a) a statement of retained earnings for the year ended December 31, 1995. Assume that only single-period financial statements for 1995 are presented.

(b) the stockholders' equity section of Navajo's balance sheet at December 31, 1995.

Upon completion, the spokesperson will report the group findings to the class and be prepared to provide supporting computations.

(AICPA adapted)

*GA16-2 (Quasi-Reorganization) On June 30, 1995, the stockholders' equity section of the balance sheet of Pima Company, appears as follows:

Stockholders' Equity:			
8% cumulative preferred stock			
Authorized and issued, 3,000 shares			
of $100 par value	$300,000		
Common stock			
Authorized 30,000 shares of $50 par value,			
issued, 13,600 shares	680,000	$980,000	
Retained earnings (deficit)		(320,000)	$660,000

A footnote to the balance sheet points out that preferred stock dividends are in arrears in the amount of $96,000.

At a stockholders' meeting, a new group of officers was voted into power, and a quasi-reorganization plan proposed by the new officers was accepted by the stockholders. The terms of this plan are as follows:

1. Preferred stockholders to cancel their claim against the corporation for accrued dividends.
2. The par value of the common stock to be reduced from $50 a share to $15 in order to create "capital in excess of par."
3. Certain depreciable properties and inventories owned by the company to be revalued downward $90,000 and $30,000, respectively.
4. The deficit to be written off against capital in excess of par created by reduction of the par value of common stock.

Instructions

Your instructor will assign one member of the group to serve as a recorder and one member to serve as spokesperson. As a group, provide the information for the recorder to prepare responses to the following two requirements. Upon completion of each requirement and before moving on to the next part, the spokesperson will report the group findings to the class.

(a) Assuming that the various steps in the reorganization plan are carried out as of June 30, prepare journal entries to record the effect of the reorganization.

(b) Assuming that the company earns a net income of $60,000 for the year ended June 30, 1996, prepare the stockholders' equity section of the balance sheet as of that date.

▶ ETHICS CASE

"You can't write-up assets," said Al Schick, Internal Audit Director of Ruland International, to his boss, Jim Gaa, Vice President and Chief Financial Officer. "Nonsense," said Jim, "I can do this as part of a quasi-reorganization of our company." For the last 3 years, Ruland International, a farm equipment manufacturing firm, has experienced a downturn in its profits resulting from stiff competition with overseas firms and increasing direct labor costs. Though the prospects are still gloomy, the company is hoping to turn a profit by modernizing its property, plant, and equipment (PP&E). This will require Ruland International to raise serious money.

Over the past few months, Jim tried to raise funds from various financial institutions. They are unwilling to consider lending capital, however, because the company's net book value of fixed assets on the balance sheet, based on historic cost, was not ample to sustain major funding. Jim attempted to explain to bankers and investors that these assets were more valuable than their recorded amounts, given that the company used accelerated depreciation methods and tended to underestimate the useful lives of assets. Jim also believes that the company's land and buildings are substantially undervalued because of rising real estate prices over the past several years.

Jim's idea is a simple one: First, declare a large dividend to shareholders of the company, such that Retained Earnings would have a large debit balance. Then, write-up the fixed assets of Ruland International to an amount equal to the deficit in the Retained Earnings account.

Instructions

(a) What are the ethical implications of Jim Gaa's creative accounting scheme?

(b) Who could be harmed if the accounting reorganization were implemented and Ruland International received additional funding?

(c) Why can't a company write-up assets when the fair value of these assets exceed their original cost?

CHAPTER 17

DILUTIVE SECURITIES AND EARNINGS PER SHARE CALCULATIONS

LEARNING OBJECTIVES

After studying this chapter, you should be able to:

1. Describe the accounting for the issuance, conversion, and retirement of convertible securities.

2. Explain the accounting for convertible preferred stock.

3. Contrast the accounting for stock warrants and stock warrants issued with other securities.

4. Explain the controversy involving stock compensation plans.

5. Describe the accounting for stock compensation plans under generally accepted accounting principles.

6. Compute earnings per share in a simple capital structure.

7. Compute earnings per share in a complex capital structure.

*T*he "urge to merge" that predominated on the business scene in the 1960s developed into merger mania in the 1980s.[1] One consequence of heavy merger activity is an increase in the use of securities such as convertible bonds, convertible preferred stocks, stock warrants, and contingent shares to structure these deals. Although not common stock in form, these securities enable their holders to obtain common stock upon exercise or conversion. They are called **dilutive securities** because a reduction—dilution—in earnings per share often results when these securities become common stock.

During the 1960s, corporate officers recognized that the issuance of dilutive securities in a merger did not have the same immediate adverse effect on earnings per share as the issuance of common stock. In addition, many companies found that issuance of convertible securities did not seem to upset common stockholders, even though the common stockholders' interests were substantially diluted when these securities were later converted or exercised.

---

[1]The 1990s have seen fewer mergers than the 1980s, except among information and entertainment-type companies. Cable, movie, telephone, television, and computer companies are all talking merger, to create some large multi-media companies. For example, Time acquired Warner Communications for $10.1 billion, and Matsushita Electric Industries acquired MCA for $7.41 billion. QVC, CBS, Viacom, Blockbuster Entertainment, Tele-Communications, and Liberty Media all have been involved in serious merger discussions. The mergers are generally huge. To appreciate the significance of "just" a billion-dollar merger, consider this fact: If a company started in the year A.D. 1 with $1 billion in capital, it could have lost $1,000 a day and still be in business today. In fact, the company would not go broke for another 750 years.

As a consequence of the step-up in merger activity in the 1980s, the presence of dilutive securities on corporate balance sheets is now very prevalent. Also increasing is the usage of stock option plans, which are dilutive in nature. These option plans are used mainly to attract and retain executive talent and to provide tax relief for executives in high tax brackets.

The widespread use of dilutive securities has led the accounting profession to examine the area closely. Specifically, the profession has directed its attention to accounting for these securities at date of issuance and to the presentation of earnings per share figures that recognize their effect. The following section discusses convertible securities, warrants, stock options, and contingent shares. The second section of the chapter indicates how these securities are used in earnings per share computations.

▶ SECTION 1 / DILUTIVE SECURITIES AND COMPENSATION PLANS

▶ ACCOUNTING FOR CONVERTIBLE DEBT

OBJECTIVE 1

Describe the accounting for the issuance, conversion, and retirement of convertible securities.

If bonds can be converted into other corporate securities during some specified period of time after issuance, they are called **convertible bonds**. A **convertible bond combines the benefits of a bond with the privilege of exchanging it for stock at the holder's option.** It is purchased by investors who desire the security of a bond holding—guaranteed interest—plus the added option of conversion if the value of the stock appreciates significantly.

Corporations issue convertibles for two main reasons. One is the desire to raise equity capital without giving up more ownership control than necessary. To illustrate, assume that a company wants to raise $1,000,000 at a time when its common stock is selling at $45 per share. Such an issue would require sale of 22,222 shares (ignoring issue costs). By selling 1,000 bonds at $1,000 par, each convertible into 20 shares of common stock, the enterprise may raise $1,000,000 by committing only 20,000 shares of its common stock.

A second reason why companies issue convertible securities is to obtain common stock financing at cheaper rates. Many enterprises could issue debt only at high interest rates unless a convertible covenant were attached. The conversion privilege entices the investor to accept a lower interest rate than would normally be the case on a straight debt issue. A company might have to pay 12% for a straight debt obligation, but it can issue a convertible at 9%. For this lower interest rate, the investor receives the right to buy the company's common stock at a fixed price until maturity, which is often 10 years.

Accounting for convertible debt involves reporting issues at the time of (1) issuance, (2) conversion, and (3) retirement.

AT TIME OF ISSUANCE

The method for recording convertible bonds **at the date of issue follows the method used to record straight debt issues.** Any discount or premium that results from the issuance of convertible bonds is amortized to its maturity date because it is difficult to predict when, if at all, conversion will occur. However, the accounting for convertible debt as a straight debt issue is controversial; we discuss it more fully later in this chapter.

AT TIME OF CONVERSION

If bonds are converted into other securities, the principal accounting problem is to determine the amount at which to record the securities exchanged for the bond. Assume Hilton, Inc. issued at a premium of $60 a $1,000 bond convertible into 10 shares of common stock (par value $10). At the time of conversion the unamortized premium is $50, the market value of the bond is $1,200, and the stock is quoted on the market at $120. Two possible methods of determining the issue price of the stock could be used:

1. The **market price** of the stocks or bonds ($1,200).
2. The **book value** of the bonds ($1,050).

Market Value Approach

Recording the stock using its **market price at the issue date** is a theoretically sound method. If 10 shares of $10 par value common stock could be sold for $1,200, paid-in capital in excess of par of $1,100 ($1,200 − $100) should be recorded. Since bonds having a book value of $1,050 are converted, a $150 ($1,200 − $1,050) loss on the bond conversion occurs.[2] The entry would be:

Bonds Payable	1,000	
Premium on Bonds Payable	50	
Loss on Redemption of Bonds Payable	150	
Common Stock		100
Paid-in Capital in Excess of Par		1,100

Using the bonds' market price can be supported on similar grounds. If the market price of the stock is not determinable, but the bonds can be purchased at $1,200, a good argument can be made that the stock has an issue price of $1,200.

Book Value Approach

From a practical point of view, if the market price of the stock or bonds is not determinable, then the **book value of the bonds** offers the best available measurement of the issue price. Indeed, many accountants contend that even if market quotations are available, they should not be used. The common stock is merely substituted for the bonds and should be recorded at the carrying amount of the converted bonds.

Supporters of this view argue that an agreement was established at the date of issuance to pay either a stated amount of cash at maturity or to issue a stated number of shares of equity securities. Therefore, when the debt is converted to equity in accordance with preexisting contract terms, no gain or loss should be recognized upon conversion.

To illustrate the specifics of this approach, the entry for the foregoing transaction of Hilton, Inc. would be:

Bonds Payable	1,000	
Premium on Bonds Payable	50	
Common Stock		100
Paid-in Capital in Excess of Par		950

The book value method of recording convertible bonds is the method most commonly used in practice[3] and should be used on homework unless the problem specifies otherwise.

---

[2]Because the conversion described above is initiated by the holder of the debt instrument (rather than the issuer), it is not an "early extinguishment of debt." As a result, the gain or loss would not be classified as an extraordinary item.

[3]As with any investment, a buyer has to be careful. For example, Wherehouse Entertainment Inc., which had 6¼% convertibles outstanding, was taken private in a leveraged buyout. As a result, the convertible was suddenly as risky as a junk bond of a highly leveraged company with a coupon of only 6¼%. As one holder of the convertibles noted, "What's even worse is that the company will be so loaded down with debt that it probably won't have enough cash flow to make its interest payments. And the convertible debt we hold is subordinated to the rest of Wherehouse's debt." These types of situations have made convertibles less attractive and has led to the introduction of takeover protection covenants in some convertible bond offerings. Or, sometimes convertibles are permitted to be called at par and therefore the conversion premium may be lost.

INDUCED CONVERSIONS

Sometimes the issuer wishes to induce prompt conversion of its convertible debt to equity securities in order to reduce interest costs or to improve its debt to equity ratio. As a result, the issuer may offer some form of additional consideration (such as cash or common stock), called a "sweetener," to **induce conversion.** The sweetener should be reported as an expense of the current period at an amount equal to the fair value of the additional securities or other consideration given.

Assume that Helloid, Inc. has outstanding $1,000,000 par value convertible debentures convertible into 100,000 shares of $1 par value common stock. Helloid wishes to reduce its annual interest cost. To do so, Helloid agrees to pay the holders of its convertible debentures an additional $80,000 if they will convert. Assuming conversion occurs, the following entry is made:

Debt Conversion Expense	80,000	
Bonds Payable	1,000,000	
Common Stock		100,000
Additional Paid-in Capital		900,000
Cash		80,000

The additional $80,000 is recorded as **an expense of the current period** and not as a reduction of equity. Some argue that the cost of a conversion inducement is a cost of obtaining equity capital. As a result, they contend, it should be recognized as a cost of—a reduction of—the equity capital acquired and not as an expense. However, the FASB indicated that when an additional payment is needed to make bondholders convert, the payment is for a service (bondholders converting at a given time) and should be reported as an expense. This expense is not reported as an extraordinary item.[4]

RETIREMENT OF CONVERTIBLE DEBT

Should the retirement of convertible debt be considered a debt transaction or an equity transaction? In theory, it could be either. If it is treated as a debt transaction, the difference between the carrying amount of the retired convertible debt and the cash paid should result in a charge or credit to income. If it is an equity transaction, the difference should go to additional paid-in capital.

To answer the question, we need to remember that the method for recording the **issuance** of convertible bonds follows that used in recording straight debt issues. Specifically this means that no portion of the proceeds should be attributable to the conversion feature and credited to Additional Paid-in Capital. Although theoretical objections to this approach can be raised, to be consistent, a gain or loss on **retiring convertible debt needs to be recognized in the same way as a gain or loss on retiring debt** that is not convertible. For this reason, differences between the cash acquisition price of debt and its carrying amount should be reported **currently in income as a gain or loss.**[5] As indicated in Chapter 14, material gains or losses on extinguishment of debt are considered extraordinary items.

Nevertheless, failure to recognize the equity feature of convertible debt when issued creates problems upon early extinguishment. Assume that URL issues convertible debt at a time when the investment community attaches value to the conversion feature. Subsequently the price of URL stock decreases so sharply that the conversion feature has little or no value. If URL extinguishes its convertible debt early, a large gain develops because the book value of the debt will exceed the retirement price. Many accountants consider this treatment incorrect, because the reduction in value of the

---

[4]"Induced Conversions of Convertible Debt," *Statement of Financial Accounting Standards No. 84* (Stamford, Conn.: FASB, 1985).

[5]"Early Extinguishment of Debt," *Opinions of the Accounting Principles Board No. 26* (New York: AICPA, 1972).

convertible debt relates to its equity features, not its debt features. Therefore, they argue, an adjustment to Additional Paid-in Capital should be made. However, present practice requires that an extraordinary gain or loss be recognized at the time of early extinguishment.

▶ CONVERTIBLE PREFERRED STOCK

The major difference in accounting for a convertible bond and a **convertible preferred stock** at the date of issue is that convertible bonds are considered liabilities, whereas convertible preferreds (unless mandatory redemption exists) are considered a part of stockholders' equity.

OBJECTIVE 2
Explain the accounting for convertible preferred stock.

In addition, when convertible preferred stocks are exercised, there is no theoretical justification for recognition of a gain or loss. No gain or loss is recognized when the entity deals with stockholders in their capacity as business owners. **The book value method is employed:** Preferred Stock, along with any related Additional Paid-in Capital, is debited; Common Stock and Additional Paid-in Capital (if an excess exists) are credited.

A different treatment develops when the par value of the common stock issued exceeds the book value of the preferred stock. In that case, Retained Earnings is usually debited for the difference.

Assume Host Enterprises issued 1,000 shares of common stock (par value $2) upon conversion of 1,000 shares of preferred stock (par value $1) that was originally issued for a $200 premium. The entry would be:

Convertible Preferred Stock	1,000	
Paid-in Capital in Excess of Par (Premium on Preferred Stock)	200	
Retained Earnings	800	
Common Stock		2,000

The rationale for the debit to Retained Earnings is that the preferred stockholders are offered an additional return to facilitate their conversion to common stock. In this example, the additional return is charged to retained earnings. Many states, however, require that this charge simply reduce additional paid-in capital from other sources.

▶ STOCK WARRANTS

Warrants are certificates entitling the holder to acquire shares of stock at a certain price within a stated period. This option is similar to the conversion privilege because warrants, if exercised, become common stock and usually have a dilutive effect (reduce earnings per share) similar to that of the conversion of convertible securities. However, a substantial difference between convertible securities and stock warrants is that upon exercise of the warrants, the holder has to pay a certain amount of money to obtain the shares.

OBJECTIVE 3
Contrast the accounting for stock warrants and stock warrants issued with other securities.

The issuance of warrants or options to buy additional shares normally arises under three situations:

1. When issuing different types of securities, such as bonds or preferred stock, warrants are often included to make the **security more attractive**—to provide an "equity kicker."

2. Upon the issuance of additional common stock, existing stockholders have a **preemptive right to purchase common stock** first. Warrants may be issued to evidence that right.

3. Warrants, often referred to as stock options, are given as **compensation to executives and employees.**

The problems in accounting for stock warrants are complex and present many difficulties—some of which remain unresolved.

STOCK WARRANTS ISSUED WITH OTHER SECURITIES

Warrants issued with other securities are basically long-term options to buy common stock at a fixed price. Although some perpetual warrants are traded, generally their life is 5 years, occasionally 10.

A warrant works like this: Tenneco, Inc. offered a unit comprising one share of stock and one detachable warrant exercisable at $24.25 per share and good for 5 years. The unit sold for 22¾ ($22.75) and, since the price of the common the day before the sale was 19⅞ ($19.88), it suggests a price of 2⅞ ($2.87) for the warrants.

In this situation, the warrants had an apparent value of 2⅞ ($2.87), even though it would not be profitable at present for the purchaser to exercise the warrant and buy the stock, because the price of the stock is much below the exercise price of $24.25.[6] The investor pays for the warrant to receive a possible future call on the stock at a fixed price when the price has risen significantly. For example, if the price of the stock rises to $30, the investor has gained $2.88 ($30 minus $24.25 minus $2.87) on an investment of $2.87, a 100% increase! But, if the price never rises, the investor loses the full $2.87.[7]

The proceeds from the sale of debt with **detachable stock warrants** should be allocated between the two securities.[8] The profession takes the position that two separable instruments are involved, that is, (1) a bond and (2) a warrant giving the holder the right to purchase common stock at a certain price. Warrants that are detachable can be traded separately from the debt and, therefore, a market value can be determined. The two methods of allocation available are:

1. The proportional method.
2. The incremental method.

Proportional Method

AT&T's offering of detachable 5-year warrants to buy one share of common stock (par value $5) at $25 (at a time when a share was selling for approximately $50) enabled it to price its offering of bonds at par with a moderate 8¾% yield. To place a value on the two securities one would determine (1) the value of the bonds without the warrants and (2) the value of the warrants. For example, assume that AT&T's bonds (par $1,000) sold for 99 without the warrants soon after they were issued. The market value of the warrants at that time was $30. Prior to sale the warrants will not have a market value. The allocation is based on an estimate of market value, generally as established by an investment banker, or on the relative market value of the bonds and the warrants soon after they are issued and traded. The price paid for 10,000, $1,000 bonds with the warrants attached was par, or $10,000,000. The allocation between the bonds and warrants would be made in this manner:

ILLUSTRATION 17-1
Proportional Allocation of Proceeds between Bonds and Warrants

Fair market value of bonds (without warrants) ($10,000,000 × .99)	=	$ 9,900,000
Fair market value of warrants (10,000 × $30)	=	300,000
Aggregate fair market value		$10,200,000
Allocated to bonds:	$\dfrac{\$9,900,000}{\$10,200,000} \times \$10,000,000 =$	$ 9,705,882
Allocated to warrants:	$\dfrac{\$300,000}{\$10,200,000} \times \$10,000,000 =$	294,118
Total allocation		$10,000,000

---

[6]Later in this discussion it will be shown that the value of the warrant is normally determined on the basis of a relative market value approach because of the difficulty of imputing a warrant value in any other manner.

[7]Trading in warrants is often referred to as licensed gambling. From the illustration, it is apparent that buying warrants can be an "all or nothing" proposition.

[8]A detachable warrant means that the warrant can sell separately from the bond. *APB Opinion No. 14* makes a distinction between detachable and nondetachable warrants because nondetachable warrants must be sold with the security as a complete package; thus, no allocation is permitted.

In this situation the bonds sell at a discount and are recorded as follows:

Cash	9,705,882	
Discount on Bonds Payable	294,118	
Bonds Payable		10,000,000

In addition, the company sells warrants that are credited to paid-in capital. The entry is as follows:

Cash	294,118	
Paid-in Capital—Stock Warrants		294,118

The entries may be combined if desired; they are shown separately here to indicate that the purchaser of the bond is buying not only a bond, but also a possible future claim on common stock.

Assuming that all 10,000 warrants are exercised (one warrant per one share of stock), the following entry would be made:

Cash (10,000 × $25)	250,000	
Paid-in Capital—Stock Warrants	294,118	
Common Stock (10,000 × $5)		50,000
Paid-in Capital in Excess of Par		494,118

What if the warrants are not exercised? In that case, Paid-in Capital—Stock Warrants is debited for $294,118 and Paid-in Capital from Expired Warrants is credited for a like amount. The additional paid-in capital reverts to the former stockholders.

Incremental Method

In instances where the fair value of either the warrants or the bonds is not determinable, the incremental method used in lump sum security purchases (explained in Chapter 15, page 745) may be used. That is, the security for which the market value is determinable is used and the remainder of the purchase price is allocated to the security for which the market value is not known. Assume that the market price of the AT&T warrants was known to be $300,000, but the market price of the bonds without the warrants could not be determined. In this case, the amount allocated to the warrants and the stock would be as follows:

Lump sum receipt	$10,000,000
Allocated to the warrants	300,000
Balance allocated to bonds	$ 9,700,000

ILLUSTRATION 17-2
Incremental Allocation of Proceeds by the Incremental Method

CONCEPTUAL QUESTIONS

The question arises whether the allocation of value to the warrants is consistent with the handling accorded convertible debt, in which no value is allocated to the conversion privilege. The Board stated that the features of a convertible security are **inseparable** in the sense that choices are mutually exclusive: the holder either converts or redeems the bonds for cash, but cannot do both. No basis, therefore, exists for recognizing the conversion value in the accounts. The Board, however, indicated that the issuance of bonds with **detachable warrants** involves two securities, one a debt security, which will remain outstanding until maturity, and the other a warrant to purchase common stock. At the time of issuance, separable instruments exist, and therefore separate treatment is justified. **Nondetachable warrants,** however, **do not require an allocation of the proceeds between the bonds and the warrants.** The entire proceeds are recorded as debt.

Many argue that the conversion feature is not significantly different in nature from the call represented by a warrant. The question is whether, although the legal forms are different, sufficient similarities of substance exist to support the same accounting treatment. Some contend that inseparability per se is not a sufficient basis for restricting allocation between identifiable components of a transaction. Examples of allocation

UNDERLYING CONCEPT

Reporting a convertible bond solely as debt is not representationally faithful. However, the cost-benefit constraint is used to justify the failure to allocate between debt and equity.

between assets of value in a single transaction are not uncommon. Such transactions as allocation of values in basket purchases, and separation of principal and interest in capitalizing long-term leases, indicate that the accountant has attempted to allocate values in a single transaction. Critics of the current accounting for convertibles say that to deny recognition of value to the conversion feature merely looks to the form of the instrument and does not deal with the substance of the transaction.

The authors disagree with the FASB as well. In both situations (convertible debt and debt issued with warrants), the investor has made a payment to the firm for an equity feature, that is, the right to acquire an equity instrument in the future. The only real distinction between them is that the additional payment made when the equity instrument is formally acquired takes different forms. The warrant holder pays additional cash to the issuing firm; the convertible debt holder pays for stock by forgoing the receipt of interest from conversion date until maturity date and by forgoing the receipt of the maturity value itself. Thus, it is argued that the difference is one of method or form of payment only, rather than one of substance. **Until the profession officially reverses its stand in regard to accounting for convertible debt, however, only bonds issued with detachable stock warrants will result in accounting recognition of the equity feature.**[9]

RIGHTS TO SUBSCRIBE TO ADDITIONAL SHARES

If the directors of a corporation decide to issue new shares of stock, the old stockholders generally have the right (preemptive privilege) to purchase newly issued shares in proportion to their holdings. The privilege, referred to as a **stock right,** saves existing stockholders from suffering a dilution of voting rights without their consent, and it may allow them to purchase stock somewhat below its market value. The warrants issued in these situations are of short duration, unlike the warrants issued with other securities.

The certificate representing the stock right states the number of shares the holder of the right may purchase, as well as the price at which the new shares may be purchased. Each share owned ordinarily gives the owner one stock right. The price is normally less than the current market value of such shares, which gives the rights a value in themselves. From the time they are issued until they expire, they may be purchased and sold like any other security.

No entry is required when rights are issued to existing stockholders. Only a memorandum entry is needed to indicate the number of rights issued to existing stockholders and to insure that the company has additional unissued stock registered for issuance in case the rights are exercised. No formal entry is made at this time because no stock has been issued and no cash has been received.

If the rights are exercised, usually a cash payment of some type is involved. If the cash received is equal to the par value, an entry crediting Common Stock at par value is made. If it is in excess of par value, a credit to Paid-in Capital in Excess of Par develops; if it is less than par value, a charge to Paid-in Capital is appropriate.

▶ STOCK COMPENSATION PLANS

OBJECTIVE 4

Explain the controversy involving stock compensation plans.

Another form of warrant arises in stock compensation plans used to pay and motivate employees. This warrant is a **stock option,** which gives selected employees the option to purchase common stock at a given price over an extended period of time. Stock options are very popular because they meet the objectives of an effective compensation program.

---

[9]The FASB issued a discussion memorandum that considered (among other issues) how to account for convertible securities and other financial instruments that have both debt and equity characteristics. ''Distinguishing between Liability and Equity Instruments and Accounting for Instruments with Characteristics of Both,'' *FASB Discussion Memorandum* (Norwalk, Conn.: FASB, 1990).

Effective compensation has been a subject of considerable interest lately. A consensus of opinion is that effective compensation programs are ones that (1) motivate employees to high levels of performance, (2) help retain executives and allow for recruitment of new talent, (3) base compensation on employee and company performance, (4) maximize the employee's after-tax benefit and minimize the employee's after-tax cost, and (5) use performance criteria over which the employee has control. Although straight cash compensation plans (salary and, perhaps, bonus) are an important part of any compensation program, they are oriented to the short run. Many companies recognize that a more long-run compensation plan is often needed in addition to a cash component.

Long-term compensation plans attempt to develop in the executive a strong loyalty toward the company. An effective way to accomplish this goal is to give the employees "a piece of the action"—that is, an equity interest based on changes in long-term measures such as increases in earnings per share, revenues, stock price, or market share. These plans, generally referred to as **stock option plans,** come in many different forms. Essentially, they provide the executive with the opportunity to receive stock or cash in the future if the performance of the company (however measured) is satisfactory.

Stock options are the fastest-growing segment of executive pay. Executives want stock option contracts because options can make them instant millionaires if the company is successful. For example, the average large-company CEO earned approximately $3.2 million, with stock options comprising the major share of their compensation. The top ten success stories from the largest 200 companies for 1993 are shown in Illustration 17-3. Notice that eight of the ten earn more in long-term incentives and stock grants than in salary and bonus.

ILLUSTRATION 17-3
Executive Compensation

Pay Rank	CEO/Company	In Thousands			Value of Long-Term Incentives and Stock Grants	Total	Company-Stock Owned	
		Salary	Bonus	Other			Value in Millions	As a Multiple of Salary
1	SANFORD I. WEILL Travelers Inc.	$1,019	$3,030	$ 245	$41,367	$45,660	$174.6	171.3
2	GEORGE M.C. FISHER Eastman Kodak	331	154	5,000	19,908	25,392	7.2	21.7
3	GERALD M. LEVIN Time Warner	1,050	4,000	244	15,870	21,164	102.2	97.3
4	JAMES R. MELLOR General Dynamics	670	1,350	12,879	5,380	20,279	52.1	77.7
5	JAMES E. CAYNE Bear Stearns	200	8,137	0	7,578	15,915	76.8	384.1
6	LOUIS V. GERSTNER International Business Machines	1,500	1,125	5,085	7,542	15,252	8.8	5.9
7	JOHN S. REED Citicorp	1,150	3,000	69	8,906	13,125	40.3	35.0
8	REUBEN MARK Colgate-Palmolive	901	1,264	94	10,658	12,916	115.1	127.7
9	HARVEY GOLUB American Express	777	1,850	335	8,878	11,840	19.5	25.1
10	ALSTON D. CORRELL Georgia-Pacific	817	550	667	9,625	11,659	5.4	6.6

THE MAJOR ACCOUNTING ISSUE

To illustrate the most contentious accounting issue related to stock option plans, suppose that you are an employee for Hurdle Inc. and you are granted options to purchase 10,000 shares of the firm's common stock as part of your compensation. The date you receive the options is referred to as the **grant date.** The options are good for 10 years; the market price and the exercise price for the stock are both $20 at the grant date. What is the value of the compensation you just received?

Some believe you have not received anything; that is, the difference between the market price and the exercise price is zero and therefore no compensation results. Others argue these options have value: if the stock price goes above $20 any time over the next 10 years and you exercise these options, substantial compensation results. For example, if at the end of the fourth year, the market price of the stock is $30 and you exercise your options, you will have earned $100,000 [10,000 options × ($30 − $20)], ignoring income taxes.

How should the granting of these options be reported by Hurdle Inc.? In most situations, GAAP requires that compensation cost be measured by the excess of the market price of the stock over its exercise price at the grant date. Hurdle would therefore not recognize any compensation expense related to your options because at the grant date the market price and exercise price were the same.

Recently the FASB issued an exposure draft on accounting for stock option plans which would require companies to use sophisticated option pricing models to value these options at the grant date.[10] If the exposure draft requirements are implemented, many companies will have substantial compensation costs that up to this time have not been reported. The effect that the new standard might have on earnings per share for selected companies is shown in Illustration 17-4.

**ILLUSTRATION 17-4
FASB Proposal's Effect
on EPS for Selected
Companies**

Company	1992 EPS Reported	% Decline	Company	1992 EPS Reported	% Decline
Allied Signal	$3.91	− 6.3%	McDonald's	$2.60	− 5.4%
Alcoa	0.89	−10.0	Merck	3.12	− 1.6
American Express	0.83	− 7.0	Microsoft	2.41	−18.9
Amgen	2.42	− 8.7	Minn. Min. & Mfg.	5.65	− 2.0
AT&T	2.86	− 0.9	Morgan, J.P.	6.93	− 3.2
Boeing	4.57	− 2.5	Novell	0.81	−15.0
Chevron	6.32	− 0.4	Paramount Commun.	2.27	− 6.9
Coca-Cola	1.73	− 1.7	Philip Morris	5.45	− 1.4
Disney	2.55	− 4.7	Pogo Producing	0.66	− 3.3
DuPont	1.82	− 0.9	Procter & Gamble	3.22	− 2.2

Source: Bear, Stearns & Co.; R. G. Associates Inc. of Baltimore.

UNDERLYING CONCEPT

The stock option controversy involves economic consequences issues. The FASB believes the neutrality concept should be followed; others disagree, noting that factors other than accounting theory should be considered.

It is an understatement to say that corporate America is unhappy with the tentative requirements of this exposure draft. Many small high-technology companies have been particularly vocal in their opposition, arguing that only through offering stock options can they attract top professional management. They contend that if they are forced to recognize large amounts of compensation expense under these plans, they will be at a competitive disadvantage with larger companies that can withstand higher compensation charges. As one high-tech executive stated: "If your goal is to attack fat-cat executive compensation in multi-billion dollar firms, then please do so! But not at the expense of the people who are 'running lean and mean,' trying to build businesses and creating jobs in the process."

A LOOK AT THE DEBATE

A chronology of events related to this exposure draft demonstrates the difficulty in standard-setting when various stakeholders believe they are adversely affected.

1. **In 1984 the FASB embarked on a major project to determine if compensation should be reported for stock options.** The business community objected to this project, noting that the present accounting was appropriate. In other words, "if it ain't broke, don't fix it." Many alleged that the reason for the business community's objection was the fear that additional compensation cost would have to be reported. The FASB eventually put the project on hold until it completed a study on more fundamental questions related to debt and equity.

2. **Option plans continued to proliferate.** Sizable grants were given to executives; in some cases, the company did not report compensation expense for these awards. In addition, the relationship between the level of pay and the performance of the company, in some cases, was not well correlated. The SEC received criticism from legislators and the press about the lack of disclosure and reporting on these options. The SEC prodded the FASB to move more quickly on their project on stock option accounting.

---

[10]"Accounting for Stock-base Compensation," *Exposure Draft of Proposed Statement of Financial Accounting Standards* (Norwalk, Conn.: FASB, June 30, 1993).

3. **In January 1992 Senator Carl Levin (Michigan) introduced a bill in Congress that would mandate more disclosure on stock options. It also would require the SEC to issue regulations requiring publicly traded companies to recognize an expense based on the fair value of options granted to employees.** Senator Levin stated that the FASB had indicated that the rules related to stock options *were broken* and needed to be fixed. He agreed to delay action on the bill, provided the FASB fix the stock option problem.

4. **In late 1992 the SEC issued new disclosure guidelines on executive compensation.** The disclosure included four charts spelling out compensation for a company's five highest-paid executives. The disclosures were favorably accepted, although limited in scope.

5. **In June 1993 the FASB issued an exposure draft on stock options.** The recommendations were that the value of stock options issued to employers is compensation which should be recognized in the financial statements. Nonrecognition of these costs results in financial statements that are neither credible nor representationally faithful. The draft recommended that sophisticated option pricing models be used to estimate the value of stock options. In addition, disclosures related to these plans would be enhanced.

6. **The exposure draft met a blizzard of opposition from the business community.** Some argued stock option plans were not compensation expense; some contended that it was impossible to develop appropriate option pricing models; others said that these standards would be disastrous to American business. The economic consequences argument was used extensively. In mid-1993 Congresswoman Anna Eshoo (California) submitted a congressional resolution calling for the FASB *not* to change its current accounting rules. Eshoo stated that the FASB proposal "poses a threat to economic recovery and entrepreneurship in the United States. . . . (it) hurts low- and mid-level employees and stunts the growth of new-growth sectors, such as high technology which relies heavily on entrepreneurship."

7. **On June 30, 1993, the Equity Expansion Act of 1993 was introduced by Senator Joseph Lieberman (Connecticut).** The bill mandates that the SEC require that no compensation expense be reported on the income statement for stock option plans. To make the bill appeal to various constituencies, it would exclude 50% of the tax on any gain if the employees held their stock for two years after exercise. In addition, the bill requires that 50% of the stock in the new plan would be awarded to 80% of the workplace designated as "not highly compensated." It therefore took the "fat cats" label off the legislation and made it more saleable. In other words, if Senator Levin could put a bill together that forces the FASB to do something (and thereby set a precedent for interfering in the operations of the Board), then some other bill could tell the FASB *not* to do the same thing.

8. **During the latter part of 1993, the FASB looked for political support but found few supporters.** The SEC commissioners all expressed reservations about the FASB's proposed ruling. However, the chief accountant of the SEC spoke in opposition to much of the lobbying effort directed against the FASB.

9. **In early 1994 a group of senators wrote to the SEC.** They expressed concern "that the credibility of the financial reporting process may be harmed significantly if Congress, in order to further economic or political goals, either discourages the FASB from revising what the FASB believes to a deficient standard or overrules the FASB by writing an accounting standard directly into the Federal securities laws."

10. **In mid 1994 the FASB agreed to delay, by one year, the exposure draft requirement that companies disclose additional information related to stock options.** In addition, it appears that compensation expense will be reported at lower amounts on the income statement than originally recommended. An alternative scenario is that the Board will not be able to require any charge for many option contracts.

The stock option saga is a classic example of the difficulty the FASB faces in issuing an accounting standard. Many powerful interests have aligned against the Board; even some who initially appeared to support the Board's actions later reversed themselves. The whole incident is troubling because the debate for the most part has not been about the **proper accounting** but more about the **economic consequences** of the standards. If we continue to write standards so that some social, economic, or public policy goal is achieved, it will not be too long before financial reporting will lose its credibility.

▶ CURRENT ACCOUNTING FOR STOCK COMPENSATION PLANS

OBJECTIVE 5

Describe the accounting for stock compensation plans under generally accepted accounting principles.

What will happen regarding the accounting for stock options is anyone's guess at this point. Dennis Beresford, chair of the FASB, indicated recently that all aspects of the stock option controversy are still being considered. To understand the significance of the possible changes, you need to understand the current accounting for stock compensation plans. We illustrate the current GAAP in this section. In the next, we'll examine the FASB's proposed changes.

Stock option plans involve three main issues:

1. How should compensation expense be determined?
2. Over what periods should compensation expense be allocated?
3. What types of plans are used to compensate officers and key executives?

DETERMINING COMPENSATION EXPENSE

UNDERLYING CONCEPT

GAAP can be characterized as conservative when compensation is measured at the grant date, using the excess of the market price of the stock over the exercise price. GAAP in this case is reliable, but many question the relevance of the compensation reported.

Total compensation expense is computed as the **excess of the market price of the stock over the option price on the measurement date.**[11] The **measurement date** is the first date on which are known both (1) the number of shares that an individual employee is entitled to receive and (2) the option or purchase price. The measurement date for many plans is the date an **option is granted** to an employee (i.e., the grant date). The measurement date may be later than the grant date in plans with variable terms (either number of shares or option price or both not known) that depend on events after date of grant. Usually the measurement date for plans with variable terms is the **date of exercise.**

If the number of shares or the option price, or both, are unknown, compensation expense may have to be estimated on the basis of assumptions as to what will be the final number of shares and the option price.

ALLOCATING COMPENSATION EXPENSE

Compensation expense is recognized **in the period(s) in which the employee performs the services** (often referred to as the **service period**). The total compensation expense is determined at the measurement date and allocated to the appropriate periods benefited by the employee's services. In practice, it is often difficult to specify the period of service, and considerable judgment is exercised in this determination. If the service period cannot be clearly defined, the general rule followed is that any method that is systematic and rational is appropriate. Assuming the measurement date is the date of grant, many enterprises recognize the compensation expense over an arbitrary period; others amortize it from the grant date to the date the option may be first exercised; still others record it as a current expense.

---

[11]"Accounting for Stock Issued to Employees," *Opinions of the Accounting Principles Board No. 25* (New York: AICPA, 1972).

TYPES OF PLANS

Many different types of plans are used to compensate key executives. In all these plans the amount of the reward depends upon future events. Consequently, continued employment is a necessary element in almost all types of plans. The popularity of a given plan usually depends on prospects in the stock market and tax considerations. For example, if it appears that appreciation will occur in a company's stock, a plan that offers the option to purchase stock is attractive to an executive. Conversely, if it appears that price appreciation is unlikely, then compensation might be tied to some performance measure such as an increase in book value or earnings per share.

Three common plans that illustrate different accounting issues are:

1. Stock option plans (incentive or nonqualified).
2. Stock appreciation rights plans.
3. Performance-type plans.

We'll look at the accounting for each type of plan.

STOCK OPTION PLANS

A stock option plan can be either an **incentive stock option plan** or a **nonqualified (or nonstatutory) stock option plan.** The distinction between an incentive and a nonqualified stock option plan is based on the IRS Code and relates to the tax treatment afforded the plan.

From the perspective of the executive, the incentive stock option provides a greater tax advantage. In these plans, an executive pays no tax on the difference between the market price of the stock and the option price when the stock is purchased. Subsequently, when the shares are sold, the executive pays tax on that difference at either capital gains rates (28%) or ordinary income tax rates (usually higher than 28%), depending upon the executive's holding period. Conversely, an executive who receives a nonqualified stock option must pay taxes, at ordinary income tax rates, on the difference between the market price of the stock and the option price at the time the stock is purchased. Thus, under an incentive stock option, the payment of the tax is deferred and may be less.

From the perspective of the company, the nonqualified option plan provides greater tax advantages. No tax deduction is received in an incentive stock option plan, whereas in a nonqualified stock option plan the company receives a tax deduction equal to the difference between the market price and option price at the date the employee purchases the stock. To illustrate, assume that Hubbard, Inc. grants options to purchase 10,000 shares at an option price of $10 when the current market price of the stock is $10; the shares are purchased at a time when the market price is $20; and the executive sells the shares one year later at $20. A comparison of the effect of both plans on the executive and on the company is shown in Illustration 17-5.

	Incentive Stock Option[12]	Nonqualified Stock Option
Effect on Executive: (assuming 36% tax bracket)		
Profit on exercise [10,000 × ($20 − $10)]	$100,000	$100,000
Tax on exercise ($100,000 × 36%)	–0–	$ 36,000
Tax on sale ($100,000 × 36%)	$ 36,000	–0–
After tax benefit	$ 64,000	$ 64,000
Effect on Company: (assuming 34% corporate rate)	Zero tax deduction resulting in no tax benefit.	$100,000 tax deduction resulting in a $34,000 tax benefit.

ILLUSTRATION 17-5
Comparison of Incentive and Nonqualified Stock Option Plans

---

[12]For an ISO, the executive has an alternative minimum tax (AMT) preference upon exercise, which may lead to tax payments under AMT rules. The illustration also assumes that the executive receiving an ISO receives favorable capital gains treatment.

In effect, the executive in Hubbard, Inc.'s, case would incur a $64,000 benefit under the incentive stock option plan and a $64,000 benefit under the nonqualified stock option plan. The tax is also deferred until the stock is sold under the incentive stock option plan. The company receives no benefit from an incentive stock option but a $100,000 tax deduction (which becomes a $34,000 tax benefit) for the nonqualified stock option.

Incentive Stock Option Plans

Why would companies want to issue incentive stock options? The major reason is to attract high-quality personnel, and many companies believe that incentive stock options are a greater attraction than nonqualified plans. Incentive stock options are particularly helpful to smaller high-technology enterprises that have little cash and perhaps so little taxable income that the tax deduction is not important. Granting such options helps them attract and retain key personnel for whom they must compete against larger, established companies.

In an incentive stock option plan the tax laws require that the market price of the stock and the option price at the date of grant be equal. The tax laws do not require this equality in nonqualified plans. **No compensation expense is, therefore, recorded for an incentive stock option** because no excess of market price over the option price exists at the date of grant (the measurement date in this case).

Nonqualified Stock Option Plans

Nonqualified stock option plans usually involve compensation expense because the market price exceeds the option price **at the date of grant** (the measurement date). Total compensation cost is measured by this difference and then allocated to the periods benefited. The option price is set by the terms of the grant and generally remains the same throughout the option period. The market price of the shares under option, however, may vary materially in the extended period during which the option is outstanding.

To illustrate the accounting for a nonqualified plan, assume that on November 1, 1994, the stockholders of Scott Company approve a plan that grants the company's five executives options to purchase 2,000 shares each of the company's $1 par value common stock. The options are granted on January 1, 1995, and may be exercised at any time within the next 10 years. The option price per share is $60, and the market price of the stock at the date of grant is $70 per share. The total compensation expense is computed below. (Note that January 1, 1995, is the measurement date because the number of shares each executive can purchase and the option price are known on this date.)

**ILLUSTRATION 17-6
Compensation Expense,
Nonqualified Plan**

Market value of 10,000 shares at date of grant ($70 per share)	$700,000
Option price of 10,000 shares at date of grant ($60 per share)	600,000
Total compensation expense	$100,000

As indicated earlier, the value of the option must be recognized as an expense in the period(s) in which the employee performs services. In the case of Scott Company, assume that documents associated with issuance of the options indicate that the expected period of benefit is 2 years, starting with the grant date. The entry to record the total compensation expense at the date of grant is as follows:

Deferred Compensation Expense	100,000	
Paid-in Capital—Stock Options		100,000

The deferred compensation expense (a contra stockholders' equity account) then is amortized to expense over the period of service involved (2 years).[13] The credit balance

---

[13]The rationale for using a contra equity account is that deferred compensation expense represents an unearned compensation amount and is better reported as contra equity than as an asset. An alternative to this entry is to record no formal entry at the date of grant, but to accrue compensation expense at the end of each period as incurred. We will use the approach illustrated above for problem material because this method formalizes in the records the compensation element of these plans.

in the Paid-in Capital—Stock Options account is treated as an element of stockholders' equity (additional paid-in capital). On December 31, 1995, and on December 31, 1996, the following journal entry is recorded to recognize the compensation cost for the year attributable to the stock option plan.

Compensation Expense	50,000	
Deferred Compensation Expense		50,000

At December 31, 1995, the stockholders' equity section would be presented as follows, assuming that 1,000,000 shares were issued at $1 par value and retained earnings were $400,000.

Stockholders' equity	
Common stock, $1.00 par, 1,000,000 shares	
issued and outstanding	$1,000,000
Paid-in capital—stock options	100,000
Retained earnings	400,000
	1,500,000
Less deferred compensation expense	50,000
Total stockholders' equity	$1,450,000

ILLUSTRATION 17-7
Balance Sheet Presentation of Deferred Compensation Expense

If 20% or 2,000 of the 10,000 options were exercised on June 1, 1998 (3 years and 5 months after date of grant), the following journal entry would be recorded:

Cash (2,000 × $60)	120,000	
Paid-in Capital—Stock Options (20% × $100,000)	20,000	
Common Stock (2,000 × $1.00)		2,000
Paid-in Capital in Excess of Par		138,000

If the remaining stock options are not exercised before their expiration date, the balance in the Paid-in Capital—Stock Options account should be transferred to a more properly titled paid-in capital account, such as Paid-in Capital from Expired Stock Options. The entry to record this transaction at the date of expiration would be as follows:

Paid-in Capital—Stock Options (80% × $100,000)	80,000	
Paid-in Capital from Expired Stock Options		80,000

The fact that a stock option is not exercised does not nullify the propriety of recording the costs of services received from executives and attributable to the stock option plan. Under GAAP, compensation expense is, therefore, not adjusted upon expiration of the options. However, if a stock option is forfeited because **an employee fails to fulfill an obligation** (e.g., leaves employment), the estimate of compensation expense recorded in the current period should be adjusted (as a change in estimate). This change in estimate would be recorded by debiting Paid-in Capital—Stock Options and crediting Compensation Expense, thereby decreasing compensation expense in the period of forfeiture.

STOCK APPRECIATION RIGHTS

One of the main advantages of a **nonqualified stock option** plan is that an executive may acquire shares of stock having a market price substantially above the option price. A major disadvantage is that an executive must pay income tax on the difference between the market price of the stock and the option price at the **date of exercise.** This can be a big financial hardship for an executive who wishes to keep the stock (rather than sell it immediately) because he or she would have to pay not only income tax but the option price as well. Note that for **incentive stock options,** much the same problem exists; that is, the executive may have to borrow to finance the exercise price, which leads to related interest costs.

One solution to this problem was the creation of **stock appreciation rights (SARs).** In this type of plan, the executive is given the right to receive **share appreciation,** which is defined as the excess of the market price of the stock at the date of exercise over a pre-established price. This share appreciation may be paid in cash, shares, or a combination of both. The major advantage of SARs is that the executive often does not have to make a cash outlay at the date of exercise, but receives a payment for the share appreciation. Unlike shares acquired under a stock option plan, the shares that constitute the basis for computing the appreciation in a SARs plan are not issued. The executive is awarded only cash or stock having a market value equivalent to the appreciation.

As indicated earlier, the usual date for measuring compensation related to stock compensation plans is the date of grant. However, with SARs, the final amount of cash or shares (or a combination of the two) to be distributed is not known until the date of exercise—the measurement date. Therefore total compensation cannot be measured until this date.

How then should compensation expense be recorded during the interim periods from the date of grant to the date of exercise? Such a determination is not easy because it is impossible to know what total compensation cost will be until the date of exercise, and the service period will probably not coincide with the exercise date. The best estimate of total compensation cost for the plan at any interim period is the difference between the **current market price** of the stock and the **option price** multiplied by the number of stock appreciation rights outstanding. This total estimated compensation cost is then allocated over the service period, to record an expense (or a decrease in expense if market price falls) in each period.[14] At the end of each interim period, total compensation expense reported to date should equal the percentage of the total service period that has elapsed multiplied by the estimated compensation cost.

For example, if at an interim period the service period is 40% complete and total estimated compensation is $100,000, then cumulative compensation expense reported to date should equal $40,000 ($100,000 × .40). As another illustration, in the first year of a 4-year plan, the company charges one-fourth of the appreciation to date. In the second year, it charges off two-fourths or 50% of the appreciation to date less the amount already recognized in the first year. In the third year, it charges off three-fourths of the appreciation to date less the amount recognized previously, and in the fourth year it charges off the remaining compensation expense. We will refer to this method as the **percentage approach** for allocating compensation expense.

A special problem arises when the exercise date is later than the service period. In the previous example, if the SARs were not exercised at the end of 4 years it would be necessary to account for the difference in the market price and the option price in the fifth year. In this case, compensation expense is adjusted whenever a change in the market price of the stock **occurs in subsequent reporting periods until the rights expire or are exercised, whichever comes first.**

Increases or decreases in the market value of those shares between the date of grant and the exercise date, therefore, result in a change in the measure of compensation. Some periods will have credits to compensation expense if the quoted market price of the stock falls from one period to the next; the credit to compensation expense, however, cannot exceed previously recognized compensation expense. In other words, **cumulative compensation expense cannot be negative.**

To illustrate, assume that American Hotels, Inc. establishes a SARs program on January 1, 1995, which entitles executives to receive cash at the date of exercise (anytime in the next 5 years) for the difference between the market price of the stock and the preestablished price of $10 on 10,000 SARs; the market price of the stock on December 31, 1995, is $13, and the service period runs for 2 years (1995–1996). Illustration 17-8 indicates the amount of compensation expense to be recorded each period, assuming that the executives hold the SARs for 3 years, at which time the rights are exercised.

---

[14]"Accounting for Stock Appreciation Rights and Other Variable Stock Option or Award Plans," *FASB Interpretation No. 28* (Stamford, Conn.: FASB, 1978), par. 2.

| | | | | | STOCK APPRECIATION RIGHTS | | | |
| | | | | | Schedule of Compensation Expense | | | |

(1)	(2)	(3)	(4)	(5)	(6)			
		Pre-established	Cumulative		Cumulative Compensation			
	Market	Price	Compensation	Percentage	Accrued	Expense	Expense	Expense
Date	Price	(10,000 SARs)	Recognizable[a]	Accrued[b]	to Date	1995	1996	1997
12/31/95	$13	$10	$30,000	50%	$ 15,000	$15,000		
					55,000		$55,000	
12/31/96	17	10	70,000	100%	70,000			
					(20,000)			$(20,000)
12/31/97	15	10	50,000	100%	$ 50,000			

[a]Cumulative compensation for unexercised SARs to be allocated to periods of service.
[b]The percentage accrued is based upon a 2-year service period (1995–1996).

ILLUSTRATION 17-8
Compensation Expense, Stock Appreciation Rights

In 1995 American Hotels would record compensation expense of $15,000 because 50% of the $30,000 total of compensation cost estimated at December 31, 1995, is allocable to 1995.

In 1996 the market price increased to $17 per share; therefore, the additional compensation expense of $55,000 ($70,000 minus $15,000) was recorded. The SARs were held through 1997, during which time the stock decreased to $15. The decrease is recognized by recording a $20,000 credit to compensation expense and a debit to Liability Under Stock Appreciation Plan. Note that after the service period ends, since the rights are still outstanding, the rights are adjusted to market at December 31, 1997. Any such credit to compensation expense cannot exceed previous charges to expense attributable to that plan.

As the compensation expense is recorded each period, the corresponding credit should be to a liability account if the stock appreciation is to be paid in cash. If stock is to be issued, then a more appropriate credit would be to Paid-in Capital. The entry to record compensation expense in the first year, assuming that the SARs ultimately will be paid in cash, is as follows:

Compensation Expense	15,000	
Liability Under Stock Appreciation Plan		15,000

The liability account would be credited again in 1996 for $55,000 and debited for $20,000 in 1997 when the negative compensation expense is recorded. The entry to record the negative compensation expense is as follows:

Liability Under Stock Appreciation Plan	20,000	
Compensation Expense		20,000

At December 31, 1997 the executives receive $50,000; the entry removing the liability is as follows:

Liability Under Stock Appreciation Plan	50,000	
Cash		50,000

Because compensation expense is measured by the difference between market prices of the stock from period to period, multiplied by the number of SARs, compensation expense can increase or decrease substantially from one period to the next.

Many accountants are disturbed about the accounting for SARs because the amount of compensation expense to be reported each period is subject to fluctuations in the stock market. Shouldn't earnings determine stock prices, rather than stock prices determine earnings?, ask some accountants.[15] Even with this drawback, though, this type

---

[15]For this reason, companies are reluctant to measure compensation expense other than at the date of grant for nonqualified option plans, because a very high compensation cost can develop that must be reported as an expense on the income statement. Few nonqualified option plans are, therefore, adopted in which the measurement date is other than the date of the grant.

of plan is gaining in popularity because executives are required to make little, if any, cash outlay under these programs.

SARs are often issued in combination with compensatory stock options (referred to as **tandem** or **combination plans**) and the executive must then select which of the two sets of terms to exercise, thereby canceling the other. The existence of alternative plans running concurrently poses additional problems from an accounting standpoint because the accountant must determine, on the basis of the facts available each period, which of the two plans has the higher probability of exercise and then account for this plan and ignore the other.

PERFORMANCE-TYPE PLANS

Many executives have become disenchanted with stock compensation plans whose ultimate payment depends on an increase in the market price of the common stock. They do not like having their compensation and judgment of performance at the mercy of the stock market's erratic behavior. As a result, there has been a substantial increase in the use of plans whereby executives receive common stock (or cash) if specified performance criteria are attained during the performance period (generally 3 to 5 years). Most of the 200 largest companies now have some type of plan that does not rely on stock price appreciation.

The **performance criteria** employed usually are increases in return on assets or equity, growth in sales, growth in earnings per share (EPS), or a combination of these factors. A good illustration of this type of plan is that of Atlantic Richfield, which at one time offered performance units valued in excess of $700,000 to the chairman of the board. These performance units are payable in 5 years, contingent upon the company's meeting certain levels of return on stockholders' equity and cash dividends.

As another example, Honeywell uses growth in EPS as its performance criterion. When certain levels of EPS are achieved, executives receive shares of stock. If the company achieves an average annual EPS growth of 13%, the executive will earn 100% of the shares. The maximum allowable is 130%, which would require a 17% growth rate; below 9% the executives receive nothing.

A performance-type plan's measurement date is the date of exercise because the number of shares that will be issued or cash that will be paid out when performance is achieved are not known at the date of grant. The compensation cost is allocated to the periods involved in the same manner as with stock appreciation rights; that is, the percentage approach is used.

Tandem or combination awards are popular with these plans. The executive has the choice of selecting between a performance or stock option award. Companies such as Bristol-Myers, General Electric, Sperry, and Xerox have adopted plans of this nature. In these cases the executive has the best of both worlds: if either the stock price increases or the performance goal is achieved, the executive gains. Sometimes, the executive receives both types of plans, so that the monies received from the performance plan can finance the exercise price on the stock option plan.

NONCOMPENSATORY PLANS

In some companies, stock purchase plans permit all employees to purchase stock at a discounted price over a short period of time. These plans are usually classified as **noncompensatory.** Noncompensatory means that the primary purpose of the plan was not to compensate the employees but, rather, to enable the employer to secure equity capital or to induce widespread ownership of an enterprise's common stock among employees. Specifically, the profession has concluded that noncompensatory plans have the following characteristics:

1. Participation by all employees who meet limited employment qualifications.

2. Equal offers of stock to all eligible employees.

3. Limitation to a reasonable period of time permitted for exercise of an option or purchase right.

4. Discount from the market price of the stock no greater than would be reasonable in an offer of stock to stockholders or others.

For example, IBM has a stock purchase plan under which employees who meet minimal employment qualifications are entitled to purchase IBM stock at a 15% reduction from market price for a short period of time. Such a reduction from market price is not considered compensatory because the employer's objectives appear to be either to raise additional equity capital or to expand ownership of the enterprise's stock among the employees as a means of enhancing loyalty to the enterprise. This position is debatable because the employee is receiving a valuable fringe benefit. However, because it is difficult to determine the company's objectives, in practice, the foregoing type of stock purchase plan is considered noncompensatory if the discount is in the amount of 10–15% of the market price. **It should be emphasized that plans that do not possess all of the above-mentioned four characteristics are classified as compensatory.**

DISCLOSURE OF COMPENSATION PLANS

Disclosure plays an important role in helping users of the financial statements better understand compensation plans and their possible effects. Regardless of the basis used in valuing stock options, rights, and other types of awards, **full disclosure should be made** about the status of these plans at the end of the period, including the number of shares under option and the option price. As to options exercised during the period, disclosure should be made of the number of shares involved and the option price used for exercise. Illustration 17-9 indicates how this disclosure is presented.

ILLUSTRATION 17-9
Disclosure of Stock Option Plan

Clorox Company

The Company has a stock option plan under which options to purchase shares of common stock may be granted to key employees. The plan provides that the option price shall not be less than the fair market value of the shares on the date of grant and that no portion of the option may be exercised beyond ten years from that date.

Options which are outstanding at June 30, 1992 become exercisable cumulatively over the first two, three or five years from the grant date. At June 30, 1992, 1,487,093 shares were available for the granting of additional options or other stock compensation awards.

A summary of changes in common stock options during 1992 and 1991 is:

	Number of Shares	Price Per Share
Outstanding at June 30, 1990	1,796,019	$ 5.56–$40.94
Granted	417,144	34.56
Exercised	(258,832)	5.56– 31.75
Cancelled	(46,600)	24.34– 40.94
Outstanding at June 30, 1991	1,907,731	$ 5.59– 40.94
Granted	388,848	40.50
Exercised	(395,904)	5.59– 40.74
Cancelled	(47,717)	30.69– 40.94
Outstanding (held by 206 optionees) at June 30, 1992	1,852,958	$ 7.28–$40.94
Options exercisable at:		
June 30, 1992	1,133,991	
June 30, 1991	1,230,064	

SUMMARY

A summary of these compensation plans and their major characteristics is provided in Illustration 17-10.

ILLUSTRATION 17-10
Summary of
Compensation Plans

Type of Plan	Measurement Date	Measurement of Compensation	Allocation Period	Allocation Method
Incentive stock option	Grant	Market price less exercise price	N/A (no compensation expense)	N/A (no compensation expense)
Nonqualified stock option	Grant	Market price less exercise price	Service	Straight-line
Stock appreciation rights	Exercise	Market price less exercise price	Service	Percentage approach for service period, then mark to market
Performance-type plan	Exercise	Market value of shares issued	Service	Percentage approach for service period, then mark to market

► WHAT IS THE FASB PROPOSAL?

As indicated earlier, much debate has taken place concerning the proper accounting for stock compensation plans. The FASB has wrestled with this issue for such an extended period of time that one financial writer noted: "The FASB ought to have an actuary to determine if a standard is possible in the lifetime of the members of the board." The basics of the FASB proposal are as follows:

1. **Measurement Date.** Generally, the FASB proposes that employee stock options be treated like all other types of compensation and that their value be included in financial statements as part of the cost of employing people. The Exposure Draft proposes that all types of stock options, fixed or variable, be recognized as **compensation based on the fair value of the options.** Fair value for public companies would be estimated using an option-pricing model **at the date of grant,**[16] with some adjustments for the unique characteristics of employee stock options. **No adjustments after the grant date** would be made for changes in the stock price—either up or down. Nonpublic companies would be permitted to use a "minimum value" method to estimate the value of their options. That method does not consider the volatility of the stock for which the employee is granted an option.

2. **Allocation Period.** For both public and nonpublic companies, the value of the award would be charged to expense (net of tax) over the period in which employees provide the related service, which is usually the vesting period.

3. **Implementation of Proposal.** The proposed standard would level the playing field for different types of plans, and companies would be able to select compensation programs that achieve their desired economic objectives without overriding concerns about accounting results.

   Because existing compensation plans were developed with the current accounting requirements in mind, the proposal would apply prospectively to grants made after December 31, 1996. That will give companies time to rethink their compensation programs and time to work with option pricing methods. During that time, from 1994 to 1996, the income statement and earnings-per-share effects would be disclosed in the notes to financial statements.

---

[16]The date the option becomes vested is favored by some because at that date the employee has performed the option contract, and the company is obligated to issue shares at the option price.

Others state that the excess of the market price over the option price at the date the option becomes vested is still an incomplete valuation that understates the value of the option, particularly when this option may be held for several years before expiring. They believe that only at the date that **the option is exercised** is the final value of the employee's services recognizable. In short, the commitment to transfer cash or stock to employees under a plan is only a contingency until the date of exercise, when the amount of the transfer will be known.

4. **Disclosures.** The proposed disclosures are consistent with current disclosures under *APB Opinion No. 25* but would be enhanced—principally by describing the assumptions used to calculate fair value.

In summary, the FASB proposal will determine compensation cost at the date of grant using an option pricing model. This compensation cost will be allocated over the expected service period of the employee. Disclosures will be enhanced.

▶ SECTION 2 / COMPUTING EARNINGS PER SHARE

Earnings per share data are frequently reported in the financial press and are widely used by stockholders and potential investors in evaluating the profitability of a company. **Earnings per share** indicates the income earned by each share of common stock. Thus, **earnings per share is reported only for common stock.** For example, if Oscar Co. has net income of $300,000 and a weighted average of 100,000 shares of common stock outstanding for the year, earnings per share is $3 ($300,000 ÷ 100,000).

Because of the importance of earnings per share information, most companies are required to report this information on the face of the income statement.[17] The exception is nonpublic companies; because of cost-benefit considerations they do not have to report this information.[18] Generally, earnings per share information is reported below net income in the income statement. For Oscar Co. the presentation would be as follows:

INTERNATIONAL INSIGHT

In many nations (e.g., Switzerland, Sweden, Spain, and Mexico) there is no requirement to disclose earnings per share.

Net income	$300,000
Earnings per share	$3.00

ILLUSTRATION 17-11
Income Statement Presentation of EPS

When the income statement contains intermediate components of income, earnings per share should be disclosed for each component. The following is representative:

Earnings per share:	
Income from continuing operations	$4.00
Loss from discontinued operations, net of tax	.60
Income before extraordinary item and	
cumulative effect of change in accounting principle	3.40
Extraordinary gain, net of tax	1.00
Cumulative effect of change in accounting principle, net of tax	.50
Net income	$4.90

ILLUSTRATION 17-12
Income Statement Presentation of EPS Components

These disclosures enable the user of the financial statements to recognize the effects of income from continuing operations on EPS, as distinguished from income or loss from irregular items.[19]

---

[17]"Earnings per Share," *Opinions of the Accounting Principles Board No. 15* (New York: AICPA, 1969). For an article on the usefulness of EPS reported data and the application of the qualitative characteristics of accounting information to EPS data, see Lola W. Dudley, "A Critical Look at EPS," *Journal of Accountancy* (August 1985), pp. 102–111.

[18]A nonpublic enterprise is an enterprise other than (1) whose debt or equity securities are traded in a public market on a foreign or domestic stock exchange or in the over-the-counter market (including securities quoted locally or regionally) or (2) that is required to file financial statements with the SEC. An enterprise is no longer considered a nonpublic enterprise when its financial statements are issued in preparation for the sale of any class of securities in a public market.

[19]Reporting per share amounts for gain or loss on discontinued operations and gain or loss on extraordinary items is optional. The reason is that a financial statement user can determine these amounts if the other per share data are provided.

▶ EARNINGS PER SHARE—SIMPLE CAPITAL STRUCTURE

OBJECTIVE 6

Compute earnings per share in a simple capital structure.

A corporation's capital structure is **simple** if it consists only of common stock or includes no potentially dilutive convertible securities, options, warrants, or other rights that upon conversion or exercise could in the aggregate dilute earnings per common share. (A capital structure is **complex** if it includes securities that could have a dilutive effect on earnings per common share.) The computation of earnings per share for a simple capital structure involves two items (other than net income)—preferred stock dividends and weighted average number of shares outstanding.

PREFERRED STOCK DIVIDENDS

As indicated earlier, earnings per share relates to earnings per common share. When a company has both common and preferred stock outstanding, **the current year preferred stock dividend is subtracted from net income to arrive at income available to common stockholders.** The formula for computing earnings per share is then as follows:

$$\frac{\text{Net Income} - \text{Preferred Dividends}}{\text{Weighted Average Number of Shares Outstanding}} = \text{Earnings Per Share}$$

In reporting earnings per share information, dividends on preferred stock should be subtracted from each of the intermediate components of income (income from continuing operations and income before extraordinary items) and finally from net income to arrive at income available to common stockholders. If dividends on preferred stock are declared and a net loss occurs, **the preferred dividend is added to the loss** for purposes of computing the loss per share. If the preferred stock is cumulative and the dividend is not declared in the current year, **an amount equal to the dividend that should have been declared for the current year only** should be subtracted from net income or added to the net loss. Dividends in arrears for previous years should have been included in the previous years' computations.

INTERNATIONAL INSIGHT

Where EPS disclosure is prevalent, it is usually based on the weighted average of shares outstanding. Some countries such as Australia, France, Japan, and Mexico use the number of shares outstanding at year-end.

WEIGHTED AVERAGE NUMBER OF SHARES OUTSTANDING

In all computations of earnings per share, the **weighted average number of shares outstanding** during the period constitutes the basis for the per share amounts reported. Shares issued or purchased during the period affect the amount outstanding and must be **weighted by the fraction of the period they are outstanding.** The rationale for this approach is to find the equivalent number of whole shares outstanding for the year. To illustrate, assume that Stallone Inc. has the following changes in its common stock shares outstanding for the period.

ILLUSTRATION 17-13
Shares Outstanding, Ending Balance—Stallone Inc.

Date	Share Changes	Shares Outstanding
January 1	Beginning balance	90,000
April 1	Issued 30,000 shares for cash	30,000
		120,000
July 1	Purchased 39,000 shares	39,000
		81,000
November 1	Issued 60,000 shares for cash	60,000
December 31	Ending balance	141,000

To compute the weighted average number of shares outstanding, the following computation is made.

ILLUSTRATION 17-14
**Weighted Average
Number of Shares
Outstanding**

Dates Outstanding	(A) Shares Outstanding	(B) Fraction of Year	(C) Weighted Shares (A × B)
Jan. 1—Apr. 1	90,000	3/12	22,500
Apr. 1—July 1	120,000	3/12	30,000
July 1—Nov. 1	81,000	4/12	27,000
Nov. 1—Dec. 31	141,000	2/12	23,500
Weighted average number of shares outstanding			103,000

As illustrated, 90,000 shares were outstanding for 3 months, which translates to 22,500 whole shares for the entire year. Because additional shares were issued on April 1, the shares outstanding change and these shares must be weighted for the time outstanding. When 39,000 shares were purchased on July 1, the shares outstanding were reduced and again a new computation must be made to determine the proper weighted shares outstanding.

Stock Dividends and Stock Splits

When **stock dividends** or **stock splits** occur, computation of the weighted average number of shares requires restatement of the shares outstanding before the stock dividend or split. For example, assume that a corporation had 100,000 shares outstanding on January 1 and issued a 25% stock dividend on June 30. For purposes of computing a weighted average for the current year, the additional 25,000 shares outstanding as a result of the stock dividend are assumed to have been **outstanding since the beginning of the year.** Thus the weighted average for the year would be 125,000 shares.

The issuance of a stock dividend or stock split is restated, but the issuance or repurchase of stock for cash is not. Why? The reason is that stock splits and stock dividends do not increase or decrease the net assets of the enterprise; only additional shares of stock are issued and, therefore, the weighted average shares must be restated. Conversely, the issuance or purchase of stock for cash changes the amount of net assets. As a result, the company either earns more or less in the future as a result of this change in net assets. Stated another way, **a stock dividend or split does not change the shareholders' total investment**—it only increases (unless it is a reverse stock split) the number of common shares representing this investment.

To illustrate how a stock dividend affects the computation of the weighted average number of shares outstanding, assume that Rambo Company has the following changes in its common stock shares during the year.

ILLUSTRATION 17-15
**Shares Outstanding,
Ending Balance—Rambo
Company**

Date	Share Changes	Shares Outstanding
January 1	Beginning balance	100,000
March 1	Issued 20,000 shares for cash	20,000
		120,000
June 1	60,000 additional shares (50% stock dividend)	60,000
		180,000
November 1	Issued 30,000 shares for cash	30,000
December 31	Ending balance	210,000

The computation of the weighted average number of shares outstanding would be as follows:

ILLUSTRATION 17-16
Weighted Average
Number of Shares
Outstanding—Stock
Issue and Stock Dividend

Dates Outstanding	(A) Shares Outstanding	(B) Restatement	(C) Fraction of Year	(D) Weighted Shares (A × B × C)
Jan. 1—Mar. 1	100,000	1.50	2/12	25,000
Mar. 1—June 1	120,000	1.50	3/12	45,000
June 1—Nov. 1	180,000		5/12	75,000
Nov. 1—Dec. 31	210,000		2/12	35,000
Weighted average number of shares outstanding				180,000

The shares outstanding prior to the stock dividend must be restated. The shares outstanding from January 1 to June 1 are adjusted for the stock dividend, so that these shares are stated on the same basis as shares issued subsequent to the stock dividend. Shares issued after the stock dividend do not have to be restated because they are on the new basis. The stock dividend simply restates existing shares. The same type of treatment occurs for a stock split.

If a stock dividend or stock split occurs after the end of the year, but before the financial statements are issued, the weighted average number of shares outstanding for the year (and any other years presented in comparative form) must be restated. For example, assume that Hendricks Company computes its weighted average number of shares to be 100,000 for the year ended December 31, 1995. On January 15, 1996, before the financial statements are issued, the company splits its stock 3 for 1. In this case, the weighted average number of shares used in computing earnings per share for 1995 would be 300,000 shares. If earnings per share information for 1994 is provided as comparative information, it also must be adjusted for the stock split.

COMPREHENSIVE ILLUSTRATION

Sylvester Corporation has income before extraordinary item of $580,000 and an extraordinary gain, net of tax of $240,000. In addition, it has declared preferred dividends of $1 per share on 100,000 shares of preferred stock outstanding. Sylvester Corporation also has the following changes in its common stock shares outstanding during 1995:

ILLUSTRATION 17-17
Shares Outstanding,
Ending Balance—
Sylvester Corp.

Dates	Share Changes	Shares Outstanding
January 1	Beginning balance	180,000
May 1	Purchased 30,000 treasury shares	30,000
		150,000
July 1	300,000 additional shares (3 for 1 stock split)	300,000
		450,000
December 31	Issued 50,000 shares for cash	50,000
December 31	Ending balance	500,000

To compute the earnings per share information, the weighted average number of shares outstanding is determined as follows:

ILLUSTRATION 17-18
Weighted Average
Number of Shares
Outstanding

Dates Outstanding	(A) Shares Outstanding	(B) Restatement	(C) Fraction of Year	(D) Weighted Shares (A × B × C)
Jan. 1—May 1	180,000	3	4/12	180,000
May 1—Dec. 31	150,000	3	8/12	300,000
Weighted average number of shares outstanding				480,000

In computing the weighted average number of shares, the shares sold on December 31, 1995, are ignored because they have not been outstanding during the year. The weighted average number of shares is then divided into income before extraordinary item and net income to determine earnings per share. Sylvester Corporation's preferred dividends of $100,000 are subtracted from income before extraordinary item ($580,000) to arrive at income before extraordinary item available to common stockholders of $480,000 ($580,000 − $100,000). Deducting the preferred dividends from the income before extraordinary item has the effect of also reducing net income without affecting the amount of the extraordinary item. The final amount is referred to as **income available to common stockholders.**

INTERNATIONAL INSIGHT

In most Commonwealth countries (such as Australia, Malaysia, Singapore, South Africa, and the U.K.), EPS is computed before extraordinary items.

ILLUSTRATION 17-19
Computation of Income Available to Common Stockholders

	(A) Income Information	(B) Weighted Shares	(C) Earnings Per Share (A ÷ B)
Income before extraordinary item available to common stockholders	$480,000*	480,000	$1.00
Extraordinary gain (net of tax)	240,000	480,000	.50
Income available to common stockholders	$720,000	480,000	$1.50

*$580,000 − $100,000

Disclosure of the per share amount for the extraordinary item is optional. Income and per share information reported on the face of the income statement would be as follows:

ILLUSTRATION 17-20
Earnings per Share, with Extraordinary Item

Income before extraordinary item	$580,000
Extraordinary gain, net of tax	240,000
Net income	$820,000
Earnings per share:	
Income before extraordinary item	$1.00
Extraordinary item, net of tax	.50
Net income	$1.50

► EARNINGS PER SHARE—COMPLEX CAPITAL STRUCTURE

One problem with a simple EPS computation is that it fails to recognize the potentially dilutive impact on outstanding stock when a corporation has dilutive securities in its capital structure. Dilutive securities present a serious problem because conversion or exercise often has an adverse effect on earnings per share. This adverse effect can be significant and, more important, unexpected unless financial statements call attention to the potential dilutive effect in some manner.

Because of the increasing use of dilutive securities in the 1960s, the profession could no longer ignore the significance of these securities. *APB Opinion No. 15* was therefore issued, which developed the concept of a complex capital structure. A **complex capital structure** exists when a corporation has convertible securities, options, warrants, or other rights that upon conversion or exercise could in the aggregate dilute earnings per share. Roughly one-third of all public companies have these types of securities outstanding.

A complex capital structure requires a **dual presentation** of earnings per share, each with equal prominence on the face of the income statement. These two presentations are referred to as "primary earnings per share" and "fully diluted earnings per share." **Primary earnings per share** is based on the number of common shares outstanding plus the shares referred to as common stock equivalents—securities that are in substance equivalent to common shares. **Fully diluted earnings per share** indicates the dilution of earnings per share that would have occurred if **all** contingent issuances of common stock that would have reduced earnings per share had taken place. Because of computational rules, fully diluted earnings per share are always less than or equal to primary EPS.

OBJECTIVE 7
Compute earnings per share in a complex capital structure.

In contrast to the formula for computing EPS for a simple capital structure, the following formula portrays the computation of EPS for a complex capital structure:

ILLUSTRATION 17-21
**Formula for Computing
EPS for a Complex
Capital Structure**

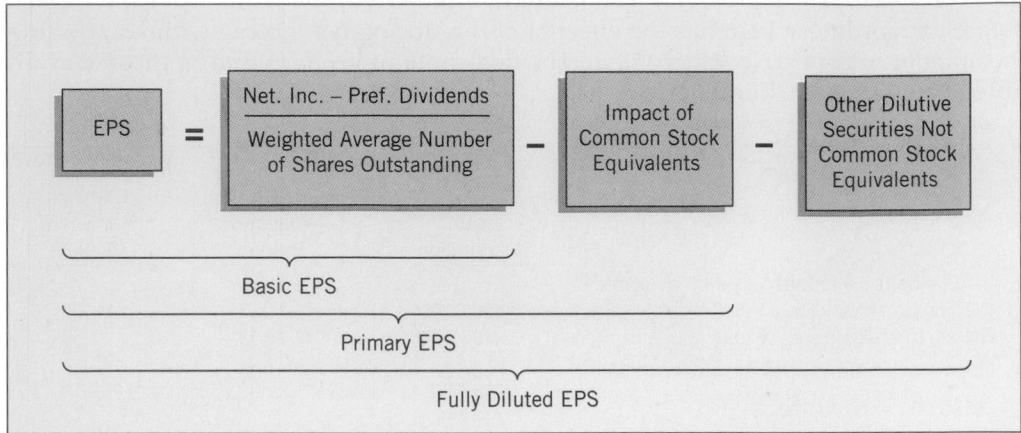

MATERIALITY AND ANTIDILUTION

A company may have dilutive securities but still not have to report primary and fully diluted earnings per share. The reason: Many corporations have dilution that is not material. In defining materiality, the profession uses a **3% materiality test.** Any corporation whose capital structure has potential dilution of less than 3% of earnings per share is considered to have a simple capital structure.

To illustrate, Streeter Company has earnings per share of $2, ignoring all dilutive securities in its capital structure. If the possible conversion or exercise of the dilutive securities in the aggregate reduces earnings per share to $1.94 (97% × $2) or below, a dual presentation is required. Otherwise the company reports earnings per share at $2 without additional disclosure. **In computing the 3% dilution factor, the aggregate of all dilutive securities is considered.**

Another reason why some companies with complex capital structures do not report primary or fully diluted earnings per share is that the securities in their capital structure are antidilutive. **Antidilutive securities** are securities which upon conversion or exercise increase earnings per share (or reduce the loss per share). Companies that have only antidilutive securities are not permitted to increase earnings per share and are required to report only a simple EPS number. The purpose of the dual presentation is to inform financial statement users of situations that will likely occur and to provide "worst case" dilutive situations. If the securities are antidilutive, the likelihood of conversion or exercise is remote.

PRIMARY EARNINGS PER SHARE—CONVERTIBLE SECURITIES

We have seen that the basis for primary earnings per share is the outstanding common stock plus common stock equivalents. To determine whether a convertible security is a common stock equivalent, a special test is performed, called the effective yield test.

Effective Yield Test

The **effective yield test** considers convertible securities to be common stock equivalents if the effective yield to the holder at the time of issuance is significantly below the yield for a similar security of the issuer without the conversion option. More specifically, a convertible security, whether bonds or preferred stock, is a common stock equivalent if at the time of issuance it has an **effective yield of less than 66⅔%** of the current average Aa corporate bond yield.[20] The "effective yield" is based on the security's stated annual interest or dividend payments, any original issuance premium or discount, and the yield to maturity.[21] The rationale for the effective yield test is that **the investor would not be willing to accept an effective yield less than ⅔ of the average Aa corporate bond yield unless the convertible security contains significant common stock characteristics.**

To illustrate this test, assume that Clayton Corp. purchased a 5-year convertible bond (face amount $1,000) with a coupon rate of 11% and a market price of $1,120. It would have an effective yield to the purchaser of 8%.[22] If the average Aa corporate bond yield were 15% at the **date of issuance,** this security would be considered a common stock equivalent because the effective yield is less than ⅔ of the average Aa corporate bond yield:

⅔ of average Aa corporate bond yield rate of 15%	=	10%
Effective yield	=	8%
Common stock equivalent?		Yes

ILLUSTRATION 17-22
Example of Effective Yield Test

The effective yield test is an arbitrary rule but it provides a simple and objective criterion that is easily applied. There is a weakness in this approach, however. The effective yield test is applied **only at the date of issuance** to determine whether the convertible is a common stock equivalent. As a result, if the security is determined to be a common stock equivalent at date of issuance, it is considered always a common stock equivalent. Conversely if it is not a common stock equivalent at the date of issuance, it can never be a common stock equivalent. If market conditions change, this initial classification may not report results in the most useful manner. Recognize that even if a convertible is a common stock equivalent, it enters into the computation of primary earnings per share only if it is dilutive. That is, a common stock equivalent may enter into the computation in one period and not in another, depending on whether it is dilutive or antidilutive.

If-Converted Method

If a convertible is deemed a common stock equivalent, it is then necessary to measure its dilutive effect. The method used to measure the dilutive effect is called the **if-converted method.** The if-converted method for a convertible bond assumes (1) the conversion of the convertible securities at the beginning of the period (or at the time of issuance of the security, if issued during the period), and (2) the elimination of interest, net of tax. Thus the denominator—the weighted average number of shares outstanding—is increased by the additional shares assumed converted and the numerator—the net income—is increased by the amount of interest expense, net of tax.

---

[20]"Determining Whether a Convertible Security is a Common Stock Equivalent," *Statement of Financial Accounting Standards No. 55* (Stamford, Conn.: FASB, 1982), par. 7. The test used is a trade-off between reliability and relevance. The test itself is objective, and has some conceptual justification. However, there appear to be much more useful approaches to measuring common stock equivalency. See, for example, Bruce R. Gaumnitz and Joel E. Thompson, "Establishing the Common Stock Equivalence of Convertible Bonds," *The Accounting Review* (July 1987).

[21]"Yield Test for Determining Whether a Convertible Security Is a Common Stock Equivalent," *Statement of Financial Accounting Standards No. 85* (Stamford, Conn.: FASB, 1985), par. 3. The yield test was changed in 1985 from a cash yield test to an effective yield test as a result of the emergence of zero and low coupon convertible securities.

If the convertible securities have a call premium or discount, the effective yield shall be the lowest of the yield to maturity or the yields to all call dates.

[22]$1,120 = \dfrac{1}{(1 + i)^5} \times \$1,000 + \dfrac{1 - \dfrac{1}{(1 + i)^5}}{i} \times \$110$; solving for i results in an effective yield of 8%.

As an example, Marshy Field Corporation has net income for the year of $210,000 and a weighted average number of common shares outstanding during the period of 100,000 shares. The simple or basic earnings per share is, therefore, $2.10 ($210,000 ÷ 100,000). The company has two convertible debenture bond issues outstanding. One is a 6% issue sold at 100 (total $1,000,000) in a prior year when the average Aa corporate bond yield was 11% and convertible into 20,000 common shares. The other is a 10% issue sold at 100 (total $1,000,000) on April 1 of the current year when the average Aa corporate bond yield was 11% and convertible into 32,000 common shares. The tax rate is 40%. Each of the convertible securities issuances is tested to determine whether it is a common stock equivalent as follows:

ILLUSTRATION 17-23
Tests for Common Stock Equivalency

$1,000,000, 6%, convertible bond	
⅔ of average Aa corporate bond yield of 11%	= 7⅓%
Effective yield	= 6%
Common stock equivalent?	Yes

$1,000,000, 10%, convertible bond	
⅔ of average Aa corporate bond yield of 11%	= 7⅓%
Effective yield	= 10%
Common stock equivalent?	No

Primary earnings per share includes only one dilutive security—the 6% convertible debentures. The 6% effective yield rate at date of issue is less than ⅔ of the average Aa corporate bond yield of 11%. The 10% convertible is not considered in the primary earnings per share calculation because the effective yield (10%) at date of issue was higher than ⅔ of the Aa corporate bond yield.

To determine the numerator, we add back the interest on the if-converted securities less the related tax effect. Because the if-converted method assumes conversion as of the beginning of the year, no interest on the convertibles is assumed to be paid during the year. The interest on the convertibles is $60,000 for the year ($1,000,000 × 6%). The increased tax expense is $24,000 ($60,000 × .40), and the interest added back net of taxes is $36,000 [$60,000 − $24,000 or simply $60,000 × (1 − .40)]. The primary earnings per share computation is shown as follows:

ILLUSTRATION 17-24
Computation of Primary Earnings per Share

Net income for the year	$210,000	Average number of shares outstanding	100,000
Add: Adjustment for interest (net of tax) on 6% debentures		Add: Shares assumed to be issued upon conversion of 6%	
$60,000 × (1 − .40)	36,000	debentures as of the beginning of	
Adjusted net income	$246,000	the year	20,000
	A		
		Average number of common and common equivalent shares	120,000
			B

PRIMARY EARNINGS PER SHARE (A ÷ B) = $2.05

Note: Assumed conversion is dilutive because primary EPS is less than EPS of $2.10 ($210,000 ÷ 100,000 shares).

This example assumed that Marshy Field's bonds were sold at face amount. If the bonds are sold at a premium or discount, interest expense must be adjusted each period to account for this occurrence. Therefore, the amount of interest expense added back, net of tax, to net income is the **interest expense reported on the income statement,** not the interest paid in cash during the period.

If the 6% convertible debentures were instead 6% convertible preferred stock, the convertible preferred would be classified as common stock equivalents. Preferred dividends are not subtracted from net income in computing the numerator because it is assumed that the convertible preferreds are converted and are outstanding as common stock for purposes of computing EPS. Net income is used as the numerator—no tax effect is implied because preferred dividends are not deductible for tax purposes.

FULLY DILUTED EARNINGS PER SHARE— CONVERTIBLE SECURITIES

Fully diluted earnings per share includes not only the 6% debentures but also the 10% debentures. The interest charges (net of tax) for both issuances are added back to arrive at adjusted net income. A determination is made of the weighted average number of shares outstanding. Because the date of issuance is subsequent to the beginning of the year in the case of the 10% convertibles, the shares assumed to have been issued on that date, April 1, are weighted as outstanding from then to the end of the period.

Net income for the year	$210,000	Average number of common shares outstanding	100,000
Add: Adjustment for interest (net of tax)–6% debentures (previously computed)	36,000	Add: Shares assumed to be issued upon conversion of debentures	
10% debentures ($1,000,000 × 10% × ¾ year × [1 − 40% tax rate])	45,000	6% (as of beginning of year) 10% (as of date of issue, Apr. 1; ¾ × 32,000)	20,000 24,000
Adjusted net income	$291,000	Average number of common and common equivalent shares	144,000
	A		B

FULLY DILUTED EARNINGS PER SHARE (A ÷ B) = $2.02

Note: Assumed conversion of bonds is dilutive because EPS with conversion ($2.02) is less than EPS without conversion ($2.10).

ILLUSTRATION 17-25 Computation of Fully Diluted Earnings per Share

Marshy Field Corporation would then present a dual presentation for earnings per share. Primary and fully diluted earnings per share are reported because fully diluted earnings per share exceeds the 3% materiality test. The presentation is shown in Illustration 17-26.

(Bottom of income statement)	
Net income	$210,000
Earnings per share:	
On common and common equivalent shares (Note X)	$2.05
On a fully diluted basis (Note X)	$2.02

Note X: Earnings per common share and common equivalent share are computed by dividing net income by the weighted average number of shares of common stock and common stock equivalents outstanding during the year. The 6% convertible debentures are considered to be common stock equivalents. Consequently, the number of shares issuable, assuming full conversion of these debentures as of the beginning of the year is added to the number of common shares, and net income is adjusted to eliminate the interest on these debentures, net of the applicable tax effect. Fully diluted earnings per share is computed assuming conversion of all debentures.

ILLUSTRATION 17-26 Dual Presentation of Earnings per Share

When the if-converted method is employed, the **conversion rate in effect during the period** is used in computing primary earnings per share. It is not uncommon, however, for bond agreements to have a conversion rate that changes over the period the bond issue is outstanding. In this situation, the **earliest conversion rate** is used for computation of primary earnings per share. For fully diluted earnings per share, the **most advantageous conversion** rate available to the holder within 10 years is used.

Assume that a convertible bond was issued January 1, 1994, with a conversion rate of 10 common shares for each bond starting January 1, 1996; beginning January 1, 1999, the conversion rate is 12 common shares for each bond, and beginning January 1, 2003, it is 15 common shares for each bond. In computing primary EPS in 1994, the conversion rate of 10 shares to one bond is used; in computing fully diluted EPS in 1994, the conversion rate of 15 shares to one bond is used.

PRIMARY AND FULLY DILUTED EARNINGS PER SHARE—OPTIONS, WARRANTS, AND THEIR EQUIVALENTS

Stock options and warrants outstanding and their equivalents (whether or not presently exercisable) are considered common stock equivalents and are included in primary earnings per share computations unless they are antidilutive.[23] Options, warrants, and their equivalents are included in earnings per share computations through the **treasury stock method.**

Treasury Stock Method

The treasury stock method assumes that the options or warrants are exercised at the beginning of the year (or date of issue if later) and the proceeds from the exercise of options and warrants are used to purchase common stock for the treasury. If the exercise price is lower than the market price of the stock, then the proceeds from exercise are not sufficient to buy back all the shares. The incremental shares remaining are added to the weighted average number of shares outstanding for purposes of computing primary and fully diluted earnings per share.

For example, if the exercise price of a warrant is $5 and the fair market value of the stock is $15, the treasury stock method would increase the shares outstanding. Exercise of the warrant would result in one additional share outstanding, but the $5 received for the one share issued is not sufficient to purchase one share in the market at $15. Three warrants would have to be exercised (and three additional shares issued) to produce enough money ($15) to acquire one share in the market. Thus, a net increase of two shares outstanding would result.

In terms of larger numbers, assume 1,500 options outstanding at an exercise price of $30 for a common share and a common stock market price per share of $50. Through application of the treasury stock method there would be 600 **incremental shares** outstanding, computed as follows:[24]

ILLUSTRATION 17-27
Computation of Incremental Shares

Proceeds from exercise of 1,500 options (1,500 × $30)	$45,000
Shares issued upon exercise of options	1,500
Treasury shares purchasable with proceeds ($45,000 ÷ $50)	900
Incremental shares outstanding (considered common stock equivalents)	600

Thus, if the exercise price of the option or warrant is **lower** than the market price of the stock, dilution occurs. If the exercise price of the option or warrant is **higher** than the market price of the stock, common shares are reduced. In this case, the options or warrants are **antidilutive** because their assumed exercise leads to an increase in earnings per share.

For both options and warrants,[25] exercise may not be assumed until the market price of the stock is above the exercise price for substantially[26] all of 3 consecutive months,

---

[23]If exercise of options or warrants cannot take place within 5 years, these securities cannot be considered common stock equivalents. For fully diluted EPS, options and warrants are excluded if antidilutive or if the exercise period is beyond 10 years.

[24]The incremental number of shares may be more simply computed:

$$\frac{\text{Market Price} - \text{Option Price}}{\text{Market Price}} \times \text{Number of Options} = \text{Number of Shares}$$

$$\frac{\$50 - \$30}{\$50} \times 1{,}500 \text{ Options} = 600 \text{ Shares}$$

[25]It might be noted that options and warrants have essentially the same assumptions and computational problems, although the warrants may allow or require the tendering of some other security such as debt in lieu of cash upon exercise. In such situations, the accounting becomes quite complex, and the reader should refer to *Opinion No. 15* for its proper disposition.

[26]"Substantially" is assumed to mean 11 of 13 weeks.

with the latest month being the last month of the period to which earnings per share data relate. Once this 3-month criterion has been satisfied, the **average market price** of the common stock for the period should be used in computing primary earnings per share. In computing fully diluted earnings per share, it is assumed that the **closing market price** (if it is higher than the average price) is used in computing the incremental shares.

Comprehensive Illustration

To illustrate application of the treasury stock method, assume that Kubitz Industries, Inc. has net income for the period of $220,000. The average number of shares outstanding for the period was 100,000 shares. Hence, EPS—ignoring all dilutive securities—is $2.20. The average number of shares under outstanding options (although not exercisable at this time), at an option price of $20 per share, is 5,000 shares. The average market price of the common stock during the year was $24 and the closing price at the end of the year is $28. The computation is shown below.

Kubitz Industries, Inc.		
Options		
	Primary Earnings Per Share	Fully Diluted Earnings Per Share
Average number of shares under options outstanding	5,000	5,000
Option price per share	×$20	×$20
Proceeds upon exercise of options	$100,000	$100,000
Market price of common stock:		
Average	$24	
Closing		$28
Treasury shares that could be repurchased with proceeds		
($100,000 ÷ $24)	4,166	
($100,000 ÷ $28)		3,571
Excess of shares under option over treasury shares that could be repurchased (5,000 − 4,166);	834	
(5,000 − 3,571)		1,429
Common stock equivalent shares (Incremental shares)	834	1,429
Average number of common shares outstanding	100,000	100,000
Total average number of common and common equivalent shares	100,834 (A)	101,429 (C)
Net income for the year	$220,000 (B)	$220,000 (D)
Earnings per share	$2.18 (B ÷ A)	$2.17 (D ÷ C)

ILLUSTRATION 17-28
Computation of Earnings per Share—Treasury Stock Method

In this example potential dilution is less than 3% for both primary and fully diluted, and, therefore, the options can be ignored. As discussed previously, if fully diluted earnings per share is more than 97% of earnings per common share outstanding, earnings per share need be based only on the weighted average of the common shares outstanding, which would be $220,000 ÷ 100,000 shares or $2.20. In this illustration, fully diluted would have to be $2.13 ($2.20 × 97%) or below before a dual presentation would be required. Primary earnings per share was computed to be $2.18 ($220,000 ÷ 100,834 shares) and fully diluted earnings per share was $2.17

($220,000 ÷ 101,429 shares). Therefore, a simple capital structure is assumed and a single presentation of $2.20 per share is appropriate.[27]

CONTINGENT ISSUANCE AGREEMENT

In business combinations, the acquirer may promise to issue additional shares—referred to as **contingent shares**—if certain conditions are met. If these shares are issuable upon the **mere passage of time or upon the attainment of a certain earnings or market price level, and this level is met at the end of the year,** they should be considered as outstanding for the computation of both primary and fully diluted earnings per share.[28]

For example, assume that Walz Corporation purchased Cardella Company and agreed to give the stockholders of Cardella Company 20,000 additional shares in 1997 if Cardella Company's net income in 1996 is $90,000; in 1995 Cardella Company's net income is $100,000. Both primary and fully diluted earnings per share of Walz for 1995 would reflect the 20,000 contingent shares because the 1996 stipulated earnings of $90,000 are already being attained.

If attainment of increased earnings above the present level is the condition, the additional shares should be considered as outstanding only for the purpose of computing fully diluted earnings per share (but only if dilution results). For this computation, current earnings should be adjusted to give effect to the increase in earnings necessary to reach the specified level.

To illustrate, assume the same facts as those above for Walz and Cardella except that the 20,000 shares are contingent upon Cardella Company's attaining a net income of $110,000 in 1996. Inasmuch as the earnings level is not being attained currently in 1995, no computation for Walz's primary earnings per share other than the traditional one need be made. In computing Walz's fully diluted earnings per share, however, the 20,000 shares would be considered outstanding. In addition, in computing fully diluted earnings per share, the 1995 net income of $100,000 would be increased by $10,000 to achieve an assumed earnings level of $110,000.

ANTIDILUTION REVISITED

In computing the 3% dilution factor, the aggregate of **all dilutive securities** must be considered. But first we must determine which potentially dilutive securities are in fact individually dilutive and which are antidilutive. Any security that is antidilutive should be excluded and cannot be used to offset dilutive securities.

Recall that **antidilutive securities** are securities whose inclusion in earnings per share computations would increase earnings per share (or reduce net loss per share). Convertible debt is antidilutive if the addition to income of the interest net of tax causes a greater percentage increase in income (numerator) than conversion of the bonds causes a percentage increase in common and common equivalent shares (denominator). In other words, convertible debt is antidilutive if conversion of the security causes common stock earnings to **increase by a greater amount per additional common share than earnings per share was before the conversion.**

---

[27]If upon exercise of options and warrants, the number of shares assumed to be repurchased would exceed 20% of the already outstanding common stock, the treasury stock approach is modified. Once the proceeds have been applied to purchase common stock up to 20% of the outstanding common stock (for either primary or fully diluted EPS or both), the balance of the proceeds is assumed to be used to reduce short-term or long-term borrowings, with any remaining funds invested in government securities. The rationale for the 20% cutoff is that the purchase of this amount of stock would have a significant impact on the market price of the stock and make the use of the treasury stock method questionable.

[28]In addition to contingent issuances of stock, other types of situations that might lead to dilution are the issuance of participating securities and two-class common. The reporting of these types of securities in EPS computation is complex and beyond the scope of this textbook.

To illustrate, assume that Kohl Corporation has a 6%, $1,000,000 debt issue that is convertible into 10,000 common shares. Net income for the year is $210,000, the weighted average number of common shares outstanding is 100,000 shares, and the tax rate is 40%. In this case assumed conversion of the debt into common stock at the beginning of the year requires the following adjustments of net income and the weighted average number of shares outstanding:

Net income for the year	$210,000	Average number of shares outstanding	100,000
Add: Adjustment for interest (net of tax) on 6% debentures		Add: Shares issued upon assumed conversion of debt	10,000
$60,000 × (1 − .40)	36,000	Average number of common and	
Adjusted net income	$246,000	common equivalent shares	110,000

EPS = $210,000 ÷ 100,000 = $2.10
Primary EPS = $246,000 ÷ 110,000 = $2.24 = **Antidilutive.**

ILLUSTRATION 17-29
Test for Antidilution

As a short cut, the convertible debt also can be identified as antidilutive by comparing the EPS resulting from conversion, $3.60 ($36,000 additional earnings ÷ 10,000 additional shares), with EPS before inclusion of the convertible debt ($2.10).

With options or warrants, whenever the exercise price is higher than the market price, the security is antidilutive. **Antidilutive securities should be ignored in all calculations and should not be considered in computing either primary or fully diluted earnings per share.** This approach is reasonable because the profession's intent was to inform the investor of the **possible dilution** that might occur in reported earnings per share and not to be concerned with securities that, if converted or exercised, would result in an increase in earnings per share. The appendix to this chapter provides an extended example of how antidilution is considered in a complex situation with multiple securities.

After identifying individually the dilutive and antidilutive securities, the 3% test is performed by comparing fully diluted EPS to basic EPS, to determine if 3% dilution in the aggregate exists.

EARNINGS PER SHARE PRESENTATIONS AND DISCLOSURES

If a corporation's capital structure is complex but contains no securities classified as common stock equivalents, the earnings per share presentation would be as follows:

Earnings per common share	
Assuming no dilution	$3.30
Assuming full dilution	$2.70

ILLUSTRATION 17-30
EPS Presentation, Complex Capital Structure, No Common Stock Equivalents

Another approach would be to identify these amounts as primary and fully diluted earnings per share, respectively.

If common stock equivalents are present and dilutive, the earnings per share presentation should be as follows:

Earnings per share	
On a common and common equivalent share	$3.00
On a fully diluted basis	$2.70

ILLUSTRATION 17-31
EPS Presentation, Complex Capital Structure, with Common Stock Equivalents

When the earnings of a period include irregular items, per share amounts (where applicable) should be shown for income from continuing operations, income before extraordinary items, cumulative effect of changes in accounting principles, and net income. As indicated previously, reporting per share amounts for gain or loss on discontinued operations and gain or loss on extraordinary items is optional. A presentation reporting extraordinary items only is presented below.

ILLUSTRATION 17-32
EPS Presentation, with
Extraordinary Item

Earnings per common and common equivalent share	
Income before extraordinary item	$3.80
Extraordinary item	.80
Net income	$3.00
Earnings per share—assuming full dilution	
Income before extraordinary item	$3.35
Extraordinary item	.65
Net income	$2.70

INTERNATIONAL INSIGHT

In most Commonwealth countries (such as Australia, Malaysia, Singapore, South Africa, and the U.K.), EPS is computed before extraordinary items.

Earnings per share amounts must be shown for all periods presented and all prior period earnings per share amounts presented should be restated for stock dividends and stock splits. When results of operations of a prior period have been restated as a result of a prior period adjustment, the earnings per share data shown for the prior periods should also be restated. The effect of the restatement should be disclosed in the year of the restatement.

Complex capital structures and dual presentation of earnings require the following additional disclosures in note form:

1. Description of pertinent rights and privileges of the various securities outstanding.

2. Bases on which both primary and fully diluted earnings per share were computed.
    (a) Identify securities included in common stock equivalents.
    (b) Identify securities included in fully diluted earnings per share computation.
    (c) Describe all assumptions made.
    (d) Disclose the number of shares issued upon conversion, exercise, or satisfaction of required conditions.

3. Effect of conversions subsequent to year-end.

Illustration 17-33, excerpted from Marcor Inc.'s annual report, illustrates the use of the columnar format for disclosing the required information clearly and concisely.

ILLUSTRATION 17-33
Sample EPS Disclosure

Marcor, Inc.	Common and Common Equivalent Shares	Assuming Full Dilution
Average number of common shares outstanding	12,692,190	12,692,190
Common stock equivalents due to assumed exercise of options	99,636	114,612
Average number of Series A preferred shares outstanding	—	6,513,378
Series A preferred stock equivalents due to assumed exercise of options	—	175,154
Total shares	12,791,826	19,495,334
Net earnings	$66,950,000	$66,950,000
Less: Preferred dividend requirements based on average number of preferred shares and preferred equivalent shares outstanding during year	13,372,000	—
Net earnings used in per share calculations	$53,578,000	$66,950,000
Net earnings per share	$4.19	$3.43

SUMMARY

As you can see, computation of earnings per share has become a complex issue. Many accountants take strong exception to some of the arbitrary rules contained in *APB Opinion No. 15* and similar pronouncements. It is a controversial area because many securities, although technically not common stock, have many of its basic characteristics. Many companies have issued these types of securities rather than common stock in order to avoid an adverse effect on earnings per share. *APB Opinion No. 15* and related pronouncements were issued as an attempt to develop credibility in reporting earnings per share data.

Illustration 17-34 displays graphically the elementary points of calculating earnings per share in a simple capital structure.

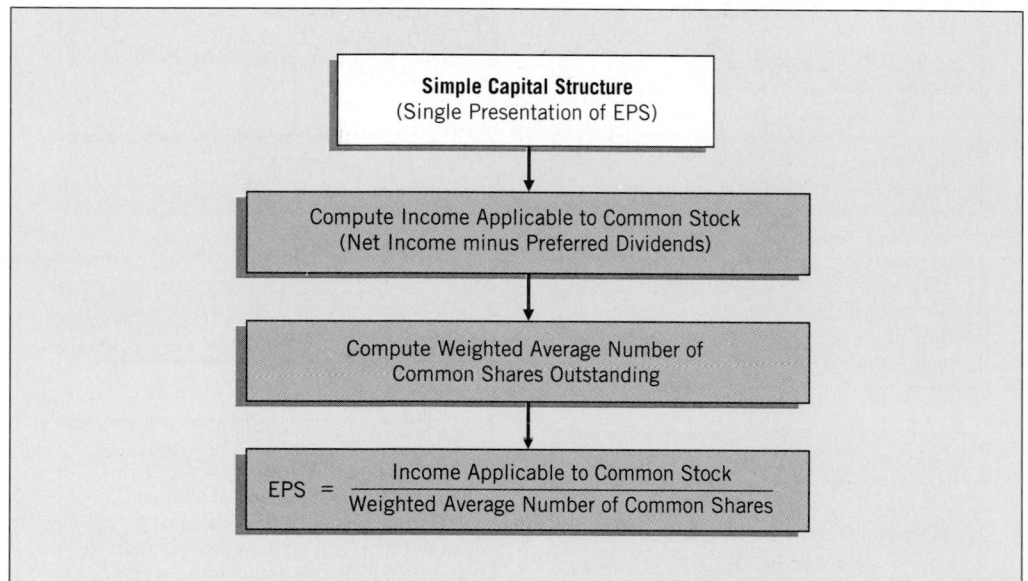

**ILLUSTRATION 17-34
Calculating EPS, Simple
Capital Structure**

Illustration 17-35 shows the calculation of earnings per share for a complex capital structure.

Some accountants argue that presenting earnings per share adjusted for dilutive securities obscures the one real fact available—earnings per outstanding shares. In addition, many small companies complain that they are overburdened with the required information because it is often costly to prepare and precludes providing other, more helpful information.[29] As a result, the FASB has chosen in *Statement No. 21*, to suspend the reporting requirements related to earnings per share for nonpublic companies.[30]

In addition, the Board plans to issue a new standard on EPS which will simplify the present computations. Tentatively, the FASB is recommending that a simple and fully diluted earnings per share be computed. The primary earnings per share computation would be eliminated. Thus, the major changes will relate solely to the denominator in the calculation of EPS. It is the authors' opinion that these changes will be readily accepted and that changes in the calculation of EPS will result.

INTERNATIONAL INSIGHT

The FASB is coordinating its project on EPS with a similar project currently under way by the ISAC. It appears likely that both organizations will issue an exposure draft concurrently on the issue sometime in 1995. Co-operation suggests that harmonization of accounting standards is starting to occur.

---

[29]See an article by R. David Mautz, Jr. and Thomas Jeffrey Hogan, "Earnings per Share Reporting: Time for an Overhaul?" *Accounting Horizons* (September, 1989), pp. 21–27 which recommends expanded disclosure format but elimination of many of the computational procedures used in determining earnings per share.

[30]"Suspension of the Reporting of Earnings per Share and Segment Information by Nonpublic Enterprises," *Statement of Financial Accounting Standards No. 21* (Stamford, Conn.: FASB, 1978).

ILLUSTRATION 17-35
Calculating EPS, Complex Capital Structure

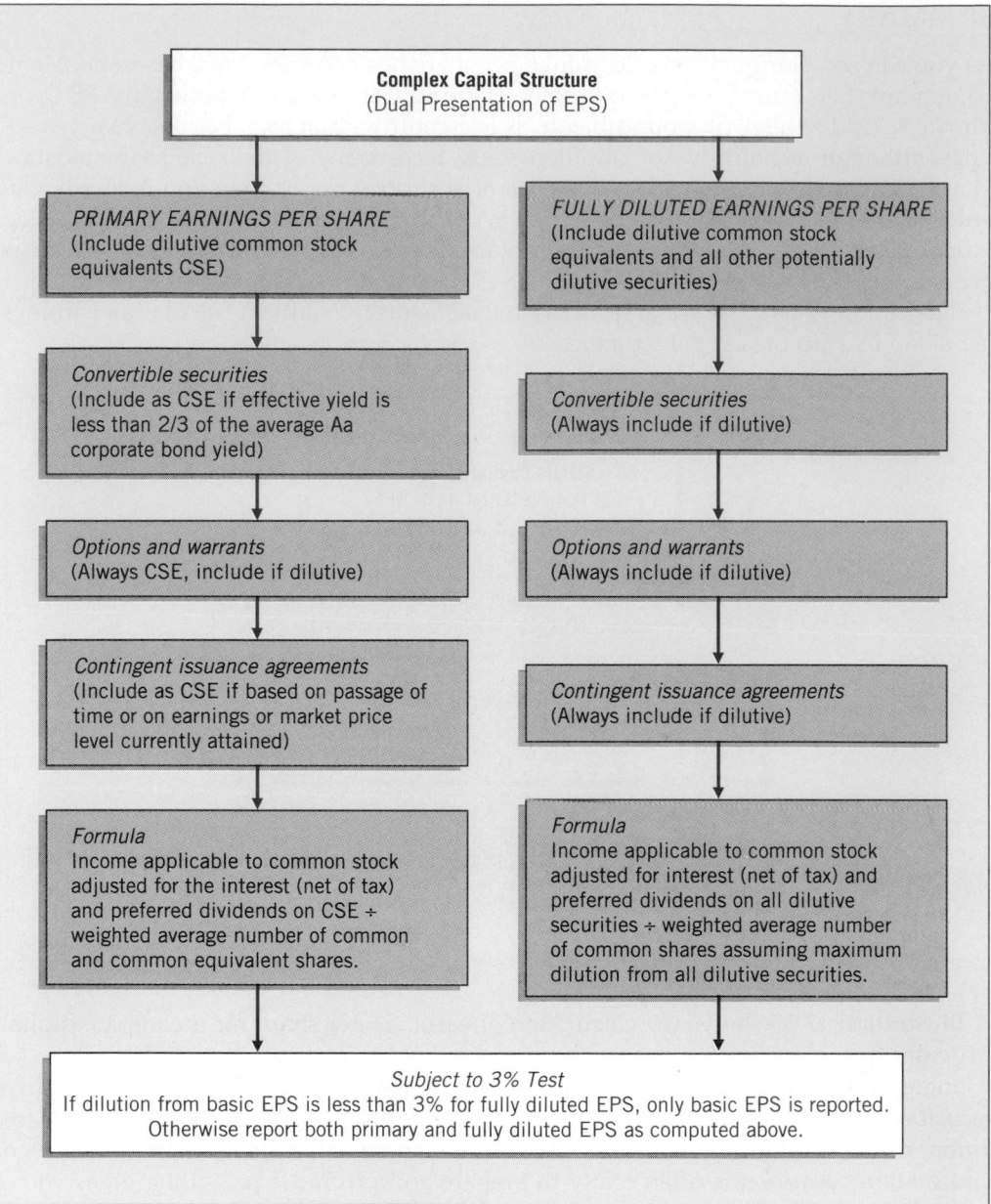

▶ SUMMARY OF LEARNING OBJECTIVES ◀

1. Describe the accounting for the issuance, conversion, and retirement of convertible securities. The method for recording convertible bonds at the date of issuance follows that used to record straight debt issues. Any discount or premium that results from the issuance of convertible bonds is amortized assuming the bonds will be held to maturity. If bonds are converted into other securities, the principal accounting problem is to determine the amount at which to record the securities exchanged for the bond. Two possible methods of determining the issue price of the stock could be used: (1) the market value approach or (2) book value approach. The book value of the bonds is the method used in practice. Under GAAP, the retirement of convertible debt, is considered a debt retirement, and the difference between the carrying amount of the retired convertible debt and the cash paid should result in a charge or credit to income.

2. **Explain the accounting for convertible preferred stock.** When convertible preferred stock is converted, the book value method is employed; Preferred Stock, along with any related Additional Paid-in Capital, is debited, and Common Stock and Additional Paid-in Capital (if an excess exists) are credited.

3. **Contrast the accounting for stock warrants and stock warrants issued with other securities.** *Stock rights:* No entry is required when rights are issued to existing stockholders. Only a memorandum entry is needed to indicate the number of rights issued to existing stockholders and to ensure that the company has additional unissued stock registered for issuance in case the rights are exercised. *Stock warrants:* The proceeds from the sale of debt with detachable stock warrants should be allocated between the two securities. Warrants that are detachable can be traded separately from the debt, and therefore, a market value can be determined. The two methods of allocation available are the proportional method and the incremental method. Nondetachable warrants do not require an allocation of the proceeds between the bonds and the warrants. The entire proceeds are recorded as debt.

4. **Explain the controversy involving stock compensation plans.** If the new FASB exposure draft is implemented, many companies will have substantial compensation costs that up to this time have not been reported. Corporate America is unhappy with the tentative requirements of this exposure draft. Many small high-technology companies are particularly vocal in their opposition. They believe they will be placed at a competitive disadvantage with larger companies that can withstand higher compensation charges. Some in the business community enlisted the help of politicians in fighting to keep the exposure draft from being implemented, while others have pointed out the need to keep the financial accounting process free of political taint. In mid-1994, the FASB agreed to delay the exposure draft changes by one year.

5. **Describe the accounting for stock compensation plans under generally accepted accounting principles.** (1) *Incentive stock option plans:* The market price and exercise price on the grant date must be equal. Because there is no compensation expense, there is no allocation problem. (2) *Nonqualified stock option plans:* Compensation is the difference between the market price and exercise price on the grant date. Compensation expense is allocated by the straight-line method during the service period. (3) *Stock appreciation rights:* The compensation is measured by the difference between market price and exercise price on the exercise date. The compensation expense is allocated by the percentage approach over the service period, then marked to market. (4) *Performance-type plan:* Compensation is measured by the market value of shares issued on the exercise date. Compensation expense is allocated by the percentage approach over the service period, then marked to market. See also Illustration 17-10.

6. **Compute earnings per share in a simple capital structure.** When a company has both common and preferred stock outstanding, the current year preferred stock dividend is subtracted from net income to arrive at income available to common stockholders. The formula for computing earnings per share is net income less preferred stock dividends divided by the weighted average of shares outstanding.

7. **Compute earnings per share in a complex capital structure.** A complex capital structure requires a dual presentation of earnings per share, each with equal prominence on the face of the income statement. These two presentations are referred to as primary earnings per share and fully diluted earnings per share. Primary earnings per share is based on the number of common shares outstanding plus the shares referred to as common stock equivalents (i.e., equivalent to common shares). Fully diluted earnings per share indicates the dilution of earnings per share that would have occurred if all contingent issuances of common stock that would have reduced earnings per share had taken place.

|||||

APPENDIX 17-A

COMPREHENSIVE EARNINGS PER SHARE ILLUSTRATION

The purpose of this appendix is to illustrate the method of computing dilution when many securities are involved. The following section of the balance sheet of Webster Corporation is presented for analysis; assumptions related to the capital structure follow:

ILLUSTRATION 17A-1
Balance Sheet for Comprehensive Illustration

Webster Corporation SELECTED BALANCE SHEET INFORMATION At December 31, 1995	
Long-term debt:	
Notes payable, 14%	$ 1,000,000
8% convertible bonds payable	2,500,000
10% convertible bonds payable	2,500,000
Total long-term debt	$ 6,000,000
Stockholders' equity:	
10% cumulative, convertible preferred stock, par value $100;	
100,000 shares authorized, 25,000 shares issued and outstanding	$ 2,500,000
Common stock, par value $1, 5,000,000 shares authorized,	
500,000 shares issued and outstanding	500,000
Additional paid-in capital	2,000,000
Retained earnings	9,000,000
Total stockholders' equity	$14,000,000

Notes and Assumptions
December 31, 1995

OBJECTIVE 8

After studying Appendix 17-A, you should be able to: Compute earnings per share in a complex situation.

1. Options were granted in July, 1993 to purchase 50,000 shares of common stock at $20 per share. The average market price of Webster's common stock during 1995 was $25. The market price at December 31, 1995 was $30 per share. No options were exercised during 1995.

2. Both the 8% and 10% convertible bonds were issued in 1994 at face value. The 8% issue was sold when the average Aa corporate bond yield was 13%, and the 10% issue was sold when the average Aa corporate bond yield was 14%. Each convertible bond is convertible into 40 shares of common stock (each bond has a face value of $1,000).

3. The 10% cumulative, convertible preferred stock was issued at the beginning of 1995 at par. Each share of preferred is convertible into four shares of common stock. The average Aa bond yield was 16% when the preferred stock was issued.

4. The average income tax rate is 40%.

5. The 500,000 shares of common stock were outstanding during the entire year.

6. Preferred dividends were not declared in 1995.

7. Net income was $1,750,000 in 1995.

8. No bonds or preferred stock were converted during 1995.

The computation of primary earnings per share for 1995 starts with the amount based upon the weighted average of common shares outstanding. See Illustration 17A-2.

Net income	$1,750,000
Less: 10% cumulative, convertible preferred stock dividend requirements	250,000
Income applicable to common stockholders	$1,500,000
Weighted average number of common shares outstanding	500,000
Earnings per common share	$3.00

ILLUSTRATION 17A-2
Computation of Earnings Per Share—Simple Capital Structure

Note the following points concerning the calculation above.

1. When preferred stock is cumulative, the preferred dividend is subtracted to arrive at income applicable to common stock whether the dividend is declared or not.

2. The earnings per share of $3 must be computed as a starting point, because it is the per share amount that is subject to reduction due to the existence of convertible securities and options.

3. The earnings per share of $3 must also be computed because, if fully diluted earnings per share is $2.91 or less (.97 × $3), a dual EPS presentation is required.

The steps for computing primary earnings per share are:

1. Determine which securities are common stock equivalents.

2. Determine, for each common stock equivalent, the per share effect assuming exercise/conversion.

3. Rank the results from step 2 from smallest to largest earnings effect per share; that is, rank the results from most dilutive to least dilutive.

4. Beginning with the earnings per share based upon the weighted average of common shares outstanding ($3), recalculate earnings per share by adding the smallest per share effects from step 3. If the results from this recalculation are less than $3, proceed to the next smallest per share effect and recalculate earnings per share. This process is continued so long as each recalculated earnings per share is smaller than the previous amount. The process will end either because there are no more securities to test or a particular security maintains or increases earnings per share (is antidilutive).

The 4 steps are now applied to the Webster Corporation. (Note that net income and income available to common stockholders are not the same if preferred dividends are declared or in arrears.)

► PRIMARY EARNINGS PER SHARE

The Webster Corporation has four securities (options, 8% and 10% convertible bonds, and the convertible preferred stock) that could reduce EPS. The first step in computing primary earnings per share is to determine, for each of the securities above, whether or not each is a common stock equivalent. Illustration 17A-3 shows this determination for each security.

Security	Test	CSE (Yes/No)
Options	None	Yes (always)
8% Bonds	Effective Yield = 8% 2/3 (13%) = 8⅔%	Yes (8% < 8⅔%)
10% Bonds	Effective Yield = 10% 2/3 (14%) = 9⅓%	No (10% > 9⅓%)
10% Preferred	Effective Yield = 10% 2/3 (16%) = 10⅔%	Yes (10% < 10⅔%)

ILLUSTRATION 17A-3
Determination of Common Stock Equivalents, Primary Earnings Per Share

The second step in the computation of primary earnings per share is to determine a per share effect for each common stock equivalent noted in the preceding illustration. Illustrations 17A-4 through 17A-6 illustrate these computations.

ILLUSTRATION 17A-4
Per Share Effect of Options (Treasury Stock Method), Primary Earnings Per Share

Number of shares under options	50,000
Option price per share	× $20
Proceeds upon assumed exercise of options	$1,000,000
Average market price of common during 1995	$25
Treasury shares that could be acquired with proceeds ($1,000,000 ÷ $25)	40,000
Excess of shares under option over treasury shares that could be repurchased (50,000 − 40,000)	10,000

Per share effect:

$$\frac{\text{Incremental Numerator Effect:}\quad \text{None}}{\text{Incremental Denominator Effect: 10,000 shares}} = \$0$$

ILLUSTRATION 17A-5
Per Share Effect of 8% Bonds (If-Converted Method), Primary Earnings Per Share

Interest expense for year .08($2,500,000)	$200,000
Income tax reduction due to interest (40% × $200,000)	80,000
Interest expense avoided (net of tax)	$120,000
Number of common shares issued assuming conversion of bonds (2,500 bonds × 40 shares)	100,000

Per share effect:

$$\frac{\text{Incremental Numerator Effect:}\quad \$120,000}{\text{Incremental Denominator Effect: 100,000 shares}} = \$1.20$$

ILLUSTRATION 17A-6
Per Share Effect of 10% Convertible Preferred (If-Converted Method), Primary Earnings Per Share

Dividend requirement on cumulative preferred (25,000 shares × $10)	$250,000
Income tax effect (dividends not a tax deduction)	none
Dividend requirement avoided	$250,000
Number of common shares issued assuming conversion of preferred (4 × 25,000 shares)	100,000

Per share effect:

$$\frac{\text{Incremental Numerator Effect:}\quad \$250,000}{\text{Incremental Denominator Effect: 100,000 shares}} = \$2.50$$

The earnings per share effects for all common stock equivalents are ranked from smallest to largest in step 3. This is shown in Illustration 17A-7.

ILLUSTRATION 17A-7
Ranking of Per Share Effects (Smallest to Largest), Primary Earnings Per Share

	Effect Per Share
1. Options	$ 0
2. 8% convertible bonds	1.20
3. 10% convertible preferred	2.50

The fourth step in the computation of primary earnings per share is the recalculation of earnings per share giving effect to the ranking in Illustration 17A-7. Starting with the earnings per share of $3 computed previously, add the incremental numerator and denominator effects of the options to the original calculation, as shown below.

ILLUSTRATION 17A-8
Recomputation of EPS Using Incremental Effects of Options

Options	
Income applicable to common stockholders	$1,500,000
Add: Incremental numerator effect of options	none
Total	$1,500,000
Weighted average number of common shares outstanding	500,000
Add: Incremental denominator effect of options	10,000
Total	510,000
Recomputed earnings per share ($1,500,000 ÷ 510,000 shares)	$2.94

Since the recomputed earnings per share is reduced (from $3 to $2.94), the effect of the options is dilutive—a predictable outcome since the average market price ($25) is greater than the option price ($20).

The next security to enter the primary EPS calculation is the 8% convertible bond issue. Starting with the earnings per share of $2.94 as shown in Illustration 17A-8, add the incremental numerator and denominator effects from Illustration 17A-5, as follows:

ILLUSTRATION 17A-9
Recomputation of EPS Using Incremental Effects of 8% Convertible Bonds

8% Convertible Bonds	
Numerator from previous calculation	$1,500,000
Add: Interest expense avoided (net of tax)	120,000
Total	$1,620,000
Denominator from previous calculation (shares)	510,000
Add: Number of common shares assumed issued upon conversion of bonds	100,000
Total	610,000
Recomputed earnings per share ($1,620,000 ÷ 610,000 shares)	$2.66

Since the recomputed earnings per share is reduced (from $2.94 to $2.66), the effect of the 8% convertible bonds is dilutive.

The last security to enter the primary EPS computation is the 10% convertible preferred stock. Starting with the recomputed earnings per share of $2.66, add the incremental numerator and denominator effects from Illustration 17A-6, as shown below.

ILLUSTRATION 17A-10
Recomputation of EPS Using Incremental Effect of Convertible 10% Preferred Stock

Convertible 10% Preferred Stock	
Numerator from previous calculation	$1,620,000
Add: Dividend requirement avoided	250,000
Total	$1,870,000
Denominator from previous calculation (shares)	610,000
Add: Number of common shares assumed issued upon conversion of preferred	100,000
Total	710,000
Recomputed earnings per share ($1,870,000 ÷ 710,000 shares)	$2.63

Since the recomputed earnings per share is reduced (from $2.66 to $2.63), the effect of the 10% preferred stock is dilutive. This would appear to be an immaterial reduction in EPS. However, the 3% test is only applied cumulatively. **Since there are no more common stock equivalents to test, the $2.63 is primary earnings per share.**

If the recomputed earnings per share, after adding the effects of the preferred stock, had been $2.66 or higher, the preferred stock would have been antidilutive. The primary earnings per share would have been $2.66 under this circumstance.

▶ FULLY DILUTED EARNINGS PER SHARE

The steps for computing fully diluted earnings per share follow the same approach as that for primary earnings per share. In general, most of the information gathered in the primary calculation is usable in the fully diluted computation. The per share effects for the 8% bonds and the 10% preferred stock remain the same. However, a per share effect has to be determined for the 10% bonds, which were not a common stock equivalent. In addition, the treasury stock method for the options has to be altered because of a higher end-of-period market price. Illustrations 17A-11 and 12 show these new computations.

ILLUSTRATION 17A-11
Per Share Effect of Options (Treasury Stock Method), Fully Diluted Earnings Per Share

Number of shares under option	50,000
Option price per share	× $20
Proceeds upon assumed exercise of options	$1,000,000
December 31, 1995 market price of common	$30
Treasury shares that could be acquired with proceeds ($1,000,000 ÷ $30)	33,333
Excess of shares under option over treasury shares that could be repurchased (50,000 − 33,333)	16,667

Per share effect:

$$\frac{\text{Incremental Numerator Effect:} \quad \text{None}}{\text{Incremental Denominator Effect: 16,667 shares}} = \underline{\$0}$$

ILLUSTRATION 17A-12
Per Share Effect of 10% Bonds (If-Converted Method), Fully Diluted Earnings Per Share

Interest expense for year (10% × $2,500,000)	$250,000
Income tax reduction due to interest (40% × $250,000)	100,000
Interest expense avoided (net of tax)	$150,000
Number of common shares issued assuming conversion of bonds (2,500 bonds × 40 shares)	100,000

Per share effect:

$$\frac{\text{Incremental Numerator Effect:} \quad \$150,000}{\text{Incremental Denominator Effect: 100,000 shares}} = \underline{\$1.50}$$

Illustration 17A-13 shows the ranking of all four potentially dilutive securities.

ILLUSTRATION 17A-13
Ranking of Per Share Effects (Smallest to Largest), Fully Diluted Earnings Per Share

	Effect Per Share
1. Options	$ 0
2. 8% convertible bonds	1.20
3. 10% convertible bonds	1.50
4. 10% convertible preferred	2.50

The next step is to determine earnings per share giving effect to the ranking in Illustraton 17A-13. Starting with the earnings per share of $3 computed previously, add the incremental effects of the options to the original calculation, as follows:

ILLUSTRATION 17A-14
Recomputation of EPS Using Incremental Effect of Options

Options	
Income applicable to common stockholders	$1,500,000
Add: Incremental numerator effect of options	none
Total	$1,500,000
Weighted average number of common shares outstanding	500,000
Add: Incremental denominator effect of options—Illustration 17A-11	16,667
Total	516,667
Recomputed earnings per share ($1,500,000 ÷ 516,667 shares)	$2.90

Since the recomputed earnings per share is reduced (from $3 to $2.90), the effect of the options is dilutive. Again, this effect could have been anticipated because the market price at year end ($30) exceeded the option price ($20).

Recomputed earnings per share, assuming the 8% bonds are converted, is as follows:

ILLUSTRATION 17A-15
Recomputation of EPS Using Incremental Effect of 8% Convertible Bonds

8% Convertible Bonds	
Numerator from previous calculation	$1,500,000
Add: Interest expense avoided (net of tax)	120,000
Total	$1,620,000
Denominator from previous calculation (shares)	516,667
Add: Number of common shares assumed issued upon conversion of bonds	100,000
Total	616,667
Recomputed earnings per share ($1,620,000 ÷ 616,667 shares)	$2.63

Since the recomputed earnings per share is reduced (from $2.90 to $2.63), the effect of the 8% bonds is dilutive.

Next, earnings per share is recomputed assuming the conversion of the 10% bonds. This is shown below:

10% Convertible Bonds	
Numerator from previous computation	$1,620,000
Add: Interest expense avoided (net of tax)	150,000
Total	$1,770,000
Denominator from previous calculation (shares)	616,667
Add: Number of common shares assumed issued upon conversion of bonds	100,000
Total	716,667
Recomputed earnings per share ($1,770,000 ÷ 716,667 shares)	$2.47

ILLUSTRATION 17A-16
Recomputation of EPS Using Incremental Effect of 10% Convertible Bonds

Since the recomputed earnings per share is reduced (from $2.63 to $2.47), the effect of the 10% convertible bonds is dilutive.

The final step is the recomputation that includes the 10% preferred stock. This is shown below.

10% Convertible Preferred	
Numerator from previous calculation	$1,770,000
Add: Dividend requirement avoided	250,000
Total	$2,020,000
Denominator from previous calculation (shares)	716,667
Add: Number of common shares assumed issued upon conversion of preferred	100,000
Total	816,667
Recomputed earnings per share ($2,020,000 ÷ 816,667 shares)	$2.47

ILLUSTRATION 17A-17
Recomputation of EPS Using Incremental Effect of 10% Convertible Preferred

Since the recomputed earnings per share is not reduced, the effect of the 10% convertible preferred is not dilutive. Fully dilutive earnings per share is $2.47, and the per share effects of the preferred are not used in the computation.

Finally, the disclosure of earnings per share for Webster Corporation is shown below. Note that the 3% materiality test is satisfied because primary and fully diluted earnings per share are well below $2.91 (.97 × $3).

Net income	$1,750,000
Earnings per common share and common equivalent share (Note X)	$2.63
Earnings per common share, assuming full dilution	$2.47

Note X: Earnings per common share and common equivalent share were computed by dividing net income by the weighted average number of shares of common stock and common stock equivalents outstanding during the year. The 8% convertible bonds and the 10% convertible preferred have been considered to be common stock equivalents. Consequently, the number of shares issuable, assuming full conversion of these bonds and preferred shares as of the beginning of the year, was added to the number of common shares, and net income was adjusted to eliminate the interest on these bonds (net of applicable tax) and the dividend requirement on the preferred stock. Options were also considered in the computation of earnings per common and common equivalent shares.

Fully diluted earnings per share was computed assuming conversion of all debentures and exercise of all options and warrants.

ILLUSTRATION 17A-18
Income Statement Presentation, EPS

▶ SUMMARY OF LEARNING OBJECTIVE FOR APP. 17-A ◀

8. **Compute earnings per share in a complex situation.** For primary EPS, (1) determine which securities are common stock equivalents; (2) determine, for each common stock equivalent, the per share effect assuming exercise/ conversion; (3) rank from most dilutive to least dilutive. Recalculate EPS starting with the most dilutive, and continue adding securities until EPS increases (is antidilutive). The steps for computing fully diluted EPS follow the same approach as that for primary EPS.

Note: All **asterisked** Questions, Exercises, Problems, and Cases relate to material contained in the appendix to each chapter.

QUESTIONS

1. What are some of the major reasons for increased merger activity in the 1980s? Why might this increased activity lead to the issuance of dilutive securities?

2. Discuss the similarities and the differences between convertible debt and debt issued with stock purchase warrants.

3. What accounting treatment is required for convertible debt? What accounting treatment is required for debt issued with stock purchase warrants?

4. Plantagenet Corp. offered holders of its 1,000 convertible bonds a premium of $150 per bond to induce conversion into shares of its common stock. Upon conversion of all the bonds, Plantagenet Corp. recorded the $150,000 premium as a reduction of paid-in capital. Comment on Plantagenet's treatment of the $150,000 "sweetener."

5. Explain how the conversion feature of convertible debt has a value (a) to the issuer and (b) to the purchaser.

6. What are the arguments for giving separate accounting recognition to the conversion feature of debentures?

7. Assume that no value is assigned to the conversion feature upon issue of the debentures. Assume further that 4 years after issue, debentures with a face value of $1,000,000 and book value of $960,000 are tendered for conversion into 80,000 shares of common stock immediately after an interest payment date when the market price of the debentures is 104 and the common stock is selling at $14 per share (par value $10). The company records the conversion as follows:

Bonds Payable	1,000,000	
Discount on Bonds Payable		40,000
Common Stock		800,000
Paid-in Capital in Excess of Par		160,000

Discuss the propriety of this accounting treatment.

8. On July 1, 1994, Beaufort Corporation issued $3,000,000 of 9% bonds payable in 20 years. The bonds include detachable warrants giving the bondholder the right to purchase for $30 one share of $1 par value common stock at any time during the next 10 years. The bonds were sold for $3,000,000. The value of the warrants at the time of issuance was $200,000. Prepare the journal entry to record this transaction.

9. What are stock rights? How does the issuing company account for them?

10. What are the advantages to an executive of receiving an incentive stock option? Why do some accountants believe that the present accounting for these options is inappropriate?

11. Warwick Corporation has an employee stock purchase plan which permits all full-time employees to purchase 10 shares of common stock on the third anniversary of their employment and an additional 15 shares on each subsequent anniversary date. The purchase price is set at the market price on the date purchased and no commission is charged. Discuss whether this plan would be considered compensatory.

12. What date or event does the profession believe should be used in determining the value of a stock option? What arguments support this position? What criticism may be brought against the date or event advocated by the profession?

13. Why are companies objecting to the new FASB exposure draft on stock options?

14. What is the advantage to an executive of a stock appreciation right (SAR) plan? How is compensation expense measured in a SAR plan?

15. At December 31, 1995, the Mortimer Company had 600,000 shares of common stock issued and outstanding, 400,000 of which had been issued and outstanding throughout the year, and 200,000 of which were issued on October 1, 1995. Net income for 1995 was $3,000,000 and dividends declared on preferred stock were $400,000. Compute Mortimer's earnings per common share (round to the nearest penny).

16. Define the following terms.
    (a) Common stock equivalent.
    (b) Potentially dilutive security.
    (c) Fully diluted earnings per share.
    (d) 3% test for dilution.
    (e) Complex capital structure.
    (f) Primary earnings per share.

17. What are the computational guidelines for determining whether a convertible security is a common stock equivalent?

18. Discuss the reasons why securities other than common stock may be considered common stock equivalents for the computation of primary earnings per share.

19. Explain how convertible securities are determined to be common stock equivalents and how those convertible senior securities that are not considered to be common stock equivalents enter into the determination of earnings per share data.

20. Explain the treasury stock method as it applies to options and warrants in computing primary earnings per share data.

21. Earnings per share can affect market prices of common stock. Can market prices affect earnings per share? Explain.

22. What is meant by the term antidilution? Give an example.

*23. How is antidilution determined when multiple securities are involved?

EXERCISES

E17-1 (Conversion of Bonds) Proteus Inc. issued $4,000,000 of 10%, 10-year convertible bonds on June 1, 1995, at 98 plus accrued interest. The bonds were dated April 1, 1995, with interest payable April 1 and October 1. Bond discount is amortized semiannually on a straight-line basis.

On April 1, 1996, $1,500,000 of these bonds were converted into 30,000 shares of $20 par value common stock. Accrued interest was paid in cash at the time of conversion.

Instructions
(a) Prepare the entry to record the interest expense at October 1, 1995. Assume that accrued interest payable was credited when the bonds were issued. (Round to nearest dollar.)
(b) Prepare the entry(ies) to record the conversion on April 1, 1996. (Book value method is used.) Assume that the entry to record amortization of the bond discount and interest payment has been made.

E17-2 (Issuance and Conversion of Bonds) For each of the unrelated transactions described below, present the entry(ies) required to record each transaction.

1. Thurio Corp. issued $20,000,000 par value 10% convertible bonds at 99. If the bonds had not been convertible, the company's investment banker estimates they would have been sold at 95. Expenses of issuing the bonds were $70,000.

2. Valentine Company issued $20,000,000 par value 10% bonds at 98. One detachable stock purchase warrant was issued with each $100 par value bond. At the time of issuance, the warrants were selling for $4.

3. On July 1, 1995, Silvia Company called its 11% convertible debentures for conversion. The $10,000,000 par value bonds were converted into 1,000,000 shares of $1 par value common stock. On July 1, there was $150,000 of unamortized discount applicable to the bonds, and the company paid an additional $75,000 to the bondholders to induce conversion of all the bonds. The company records the conversion using the book value method.

E17-3 (Conversion of Bonds) Lysander Company has bonds payable outstanding in the amount of $500,000 and the Premium on Bonds Payable account has a balance of $7,500. Each $1,000 bond is convertible into 20 shares of preferred stock of par value of $50 per share.

Instructions

(a) Assuming that the bonds are quoted on the market at 102 and that the preferred stock may be sold on the market at $50⅞, make the entry to record the conversion of the bonds to preferred stock. (Use the market value approach.)

(b) Assuming that the book value method was used, what entry would be made?

E17-4 (Conversion of Bonds) On January 1, 1994, when its $30 par value common stock was selling for $80 per share, Demetrius Corp. issued $10,000,000 of 8% convertible debentures due in 20 years. The conversion option allowed the holder of each $1,000 bond to convert the bond into five shares of the corporation's common stock. The debentures were issued for $10,800,000. The present value of the bond payments at the time of issuance was $8,500,000 and the corporation believes the difference between the present value and the amount paid is attributable to the conversion feature. On January 1, 1995, the corporation's $30 par value common stock was split 2 for 1, and the conversion rate for the bonds was adjusted accordingly. On January 1, 1996, when the corporation's $15 par value common stock was selling for $135 per share, holders of 30% of the convertible debentures exercised their conversion options. The corporation uses the straight-line method for amortizing any bond discounts or premiums.

Instructions

(a) Prepare in general journal form the entry to record the original issuance of the convertible debentures.

(b) Prepare in general journal form the entry to record the exercise of the conversion option, using the book value method. Show supporting computations in good form.

E17-5 (Conversion of Bonds) The December 31, 1995 balance sheet of Hermia Corp. is as follows:

10% Callable, Convertible Bonds Payable (semiannual interest dates April 30 and October 31; convertible into 6 shares of $25 par value common stock per $1,000 of bond principal; maturity date April 30, 2001)	$500,000	
Discount on Bonds Payable	10,240	$489,760

On March 5, 1996, Hermia Corp. called all of the bonds as of April 30 for the principal plus interest through April 30. By April 30 all bondholders had exercised their conversion to common stock as of the interest payment date. Consequently, on April 30, Hermia Corp. paid the semiannual interest and issued shares of common stock for the bonds. The discount is amortized on a straight-line basis. Hermia uses the book value method.

Instructions

Prepare the entry(ies) to record the interest expense and conversion on April 30, 1996. Reversing entries were made on January 1, 1996. (Round to the nearest dollar.)

E17-6 (Conversion of Bonds) On January 1, 1995, Helena Corporation issued $4,000,000 of 10-year, 8% convertible debentures at 102. Interest is to be paid semiannually on June 30 and December 31. Each $1,000 debenture can be converted into eight shares of Helena Corporation $100 par value common stock after December 31, 1996.

On January 1, 1997, $400,000 of debentures are converted into common stock, which is then selling at $110. An additional $400,000 of debentures are converted on March 31, 1997. The market price of the common stock is then $115. Accrued interest at March 31 will be paid on the next interest date.

Bond premium is amortized on a straight-line basis.

Instructions

Make the necessary journal entries for:

(a) December 31, 1996. (c) March 31, 1997.

(b) January 1, 1997. (d) June 30, 1997.

Record the conversions under both the fair market value method and the book value method.

E17-7 (Issuance of Bonds with Warrants) Theseus Inc. has decided to raise additional capital by issuing $170,000 face value of bonds with a coupon rate of 10%. In discussions with their investment bankers, it was determined that to help the sale of the bonds, detachable stock warrants should be issued at the rate of one warrant for each $100 bond sold. The value of the bonds without the warrants is considered to be $136,000, and the value of the warrants in the market is $24,000. The bonds sold in the market at issuance for $152,000.

Instructions

(a) What entry should be made at the time of the issuance of the bonds and warrants?

(b) If the warrants were nondetachable, would the entries be different? Discuss.

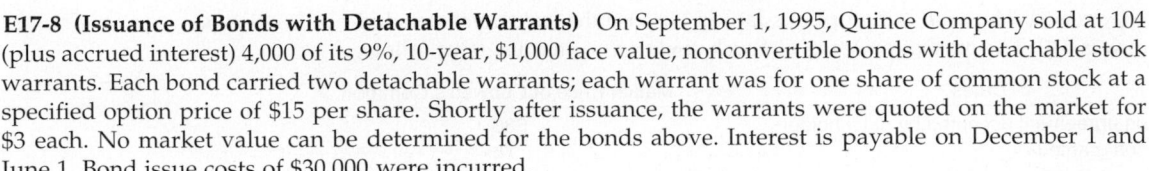

E17-8 (Issuance of Bonds with Detachable Warrants) On September 1, 1995, Quince Company sold at 104 (plus accrued interest) 4,000 of its 9%, 10-year, $1,000 face value, nonconvertible bonds with detachable stock warrants. Each bond carried two detachable warrants; each warrant was for one share of common stock at a specified option price of $15 per share. Shortly after issuance, the warrants were quoted on the market for $3 each. No market value can be determined for the bonds above. Interest is payable on December 1 and June 1. Bond issue costs of $30,000 were incurred.

Instructions
Prepare in general journal format the entry to record the issuance of the bonds.

(AICPA adapted)

E17-9 (Use of Proportional and Incremental Method) Presented below are two independent situations:

1. On March 15, 1996, Flute Corporation issued $3,000,000 of 11% nonconvertible bonds at 105; the bonds are due on March 15, 2011. Each $1,000 bond was issued with 50 detachable stock warrants, each of which entitled the bondholder to purchase, for $48, one share of Flute's common stock, $25 par. On March 15, 1996, the market value of Flute's common stock was $41 per share and the market value of each warrant was $5. Prepare the journal to record this transaction.
2. On February 1, 1996, Snug Inc. issued $4,000,000, 10-year, 12% bonds for $4,080,000. Each $1,000 bond had a detachable warrant for the purchase of one share of Snug's $40 common stock for $62. Immediately after the bonds were issued, Snug's securities had the following market values:

Common stock, $40 par	$58
Warrant	10
12% bond without warrant	1,040

Instructions
Prepare the journal entry to record this transaction. (Round all computations to nearest dollar.)

E17-10 (Issuance and Exercise of Stock Options) On November 1, 1993, Oberon Company adopted a stock option plan that granted options to key executives to purchase 30,000 shares of the company's $10 par value common stock. The options were granted on January 2, 1994, and were exercisable 2 years after the date of grant if the grantee was still an employee of the company; the options expired 6 years from date of grant. The option price was set at $40; market price at the date of the grant was $47 a share.

All of the options were exercised during the year 1996; 20,000 on January 3 when the market price was $67, and 10,000 on May 1 when the market price was $77 a share.

Instructions
(a) Compute the total compensation cost to be recognized for accounting purposes.
(b) Prepare journal entries relating to the stock option plan for the years 1994, 1995, and 1996. Assume that the employee performs services equally in 1994 and 1995.

E17-11 (Issuance, Exercise, and Termination of Stock Options) On January 1, 1993, Titania Inc. granted stock options to officers and key employees for the purchase of 20,000 shares of the company's $10 par common stock at $25 per share. The options were exercisable within a 5-year period beginning January 1, 1995, by grantees still in the employ of the company, and expiring December 31, 1999. The market price of Titania's common stock was $33 per share at the date of grant. Titania prepares a formal journal entry to record this award. The service period for this award is 2 years.

On April 1, 1994, 2,000 option shares were terminated when the employees resigned from the company. The market value of the common stock was $35 per share on this date.

On March 31, 1995, 12,000 option shares were exercised when the market value of the common stock was $40 per share.

Instructions
Prepare journal entries to record issuance of the stock options, termination of the stock options, exercise of the stock options, and charges to compensation expense, for the years ended December 31, 1993, 1994, and 1995.

(AICPA adapted)

E17-12 (Issuance, Exercise, and Termination of Stock Options) On November 2, 1992, the stockholders of Cobweb Company voted to adopt a stock option plan for Cobweb's key officers. According to terms of the option agreement, the officers of the company can purchase 40,000 shares of common stock during 1995 and 54,000 shares during 1996. The shares that are purchasable during 1995 represent executive compensation for 1993 and 1994, and those purchasable during 1996 represent such compensation for 1993, 1994, and 1995. If options for shares are not exercised during either year, they lapse as of the end of that year.

Options were granted to the officers of Cobweb on January 1, 1993, and at that time the option price was set for all shares at $30. During 1995, all options were exercised. During 1996, however, options for only

27,000 shares were exercised. The remaining options lapsed because the executives decided not to exercise. Par value of the stock is $10. The market prices of Cobweb common at various dates follow:

Dates	Market Price of Cobweb's Common
Option agreement accepted by stockholders	$33
Options granted	36
Options exercised in 1995	38
Options exercised in 1996	34

Instructions

Make any necessary journal entries related to this stock option for the years 1992 through 1996 (Cobweb closes its books on December 31).

E17-13 (Stock Appreciation Rights) On December 31, 1994, Paris Company issues 150,000 stock appreciation rights to its officers entitling them to receive cash for the difference between the market price of its stock and a preestablished price of $10. The market price fluctuates as follows: 12/31/95—$14; 12/31/96—$8; 12/31/97—$20; 12/31/98—$19. The service period is 4 years and the exercise period is 7 years.

Instructions

(a) Prepare a schedule that shows the amount of compensation expense allocable to each year affected by the stock appreciation rights plan.

(b) Prepare the entry at 12/31/98 to record compensation expense, if any, in 1998.

(c) Prepare the entry on 12/31/98 assuming that all 150,000 SARs are exercised.

E17-14 (Stock Appreciation Rights) Capulet Company establishes a stock appreciation rights program that entitles its new president Ben Tybalt to receive cash for the difference between the market price of the stock and a preestablished price of $30 (also market price) on December 31, 1995 on 30,000 SARs. The date of grant is December 31, 1995 and the required employment (service) period is 4 years. President Tybalt exercises all of the SARs in 2001. The market value of the stock fluctuates as follows: 12/31/96—$36; 12/31/97—$39; 12/31/98—$45; 12/31/99—$36; 12/31/00—$48.

Instructions

(a) Prepare a 5-year (1996–2000) schedule of compensation expense pertaining to the 30,000 SARs granted President Tybalt.

(b) Prepare the journal entry for compensation expense in 1996, 1999, and 2000 relative to the 30,000 SARs.

E17-15 (Weighted Average Number of Shares) Montague Inc. uses a calendar year for financial reporting. The company is authorized to issue 9,000,000 shares of $10 par common stock. At no time has Montague issued any potentially dilutive securities. Listed below is a summary of Montague's common stock activities.

1. Number of common shares issued and outstanding at December 31, 1993	2,000,000
2. Shares issued as a result of a 10% stock dividend on September 30, 1994	200,000
3. Shares issued for cash on March 31, 1995	2,000,000
Number of common shares issued and outstanding at December 31, 1995	4,200,000
4. A 2-for-1 stock split of Montague's common stock took place on March 31, 1996.	

Instructions

(a) Compute the weighted average number of common shares used in computing earnings per common share for 1994 on the 1995 comparative income statement.

(b) Compute the weighted average number of common shares used in computing earnings per common share for 1995 on the 1995 comparative income statement.

(c) Compute the weighted average number of common shares to be used in computing earnings per common share for 1995 on the 1996 comparative income statement.

(d) Compute the weighted average number of common shares to be used in computing earnings per common share for 1996 on the 1996 comparative income statement.

(CMA adapted)

E17-16 (EPS: Simple Capital Structure) On January 1, 1996, the Romeo Corp. had 480,000 shares of common stock outstanding. During 1996, it had the following transactions that affected the common stock account.

February 1	Issued 120,000 shares
March 1	Issued a 10% stock dividend
May 1	Acquired 100,000 shares of treasury stock
June 1	Issued a 3-for-1 stock split
October 1	Reissued 60,000 shares of treasury stock

Instructions

(a) Determine the weighted average number of shares outstanding as of December 31, 1996.

(b) Assume that Romeo Corp. earned net income of $3,456,000 during 1996. In addition, it had 100,000 of shares of 9%, $100 par nonconvertible, noncumulative preferred stock outstanding for the entire year. Because of liquidity considerations, however, the company did not declare and pay a preferred dividend in 1996. Compute earnings per share for 1996, using the weighted average number of shares determined in part (a).

(c) Assume the same facts as in part (b), except that the preferred stock was cumulative. Compute earnings per share for 1996.

(d) Assume the same facts as in part (b), except that net income included an extraordinary gain of $864,000 and a loss from discontinued operations of $432,000. Both items are net of applicable income taxes. Compute earnings per share for 1996.

E17-17 (EPS: Simple Capital Structure) Juliet Company had 200,000 shares of common stock outstanding on December 31, 1996. During the year 1997 the company issued 8,000 shares on May 1 and retired 14,000 shares on October 31. For the year 1997 Juliet Company reported net income of $249,690 after a casualty loss of $40,600 (net of tax).

Instructions
What earnings per share data should be reported at the bottom of its income statement, assuming that the casualty loss is extraordinary?

E17-18 (EPS: Simple Capital Structure) F. Laurence Inc. presented the following data:

Net income	$2,500,000
Preferred stock: 50,000 shares outstanding,	
$100 par, 8% cumulative, not convertible	5,000,000
Common stock: Shares outstanding 1/1	750,000
Issued for cash, 5/1	300,000
Acquired treasury stock for cash, 8/1	150,000
2-for-1 stock split, 10/1	

Instructions
Compute earnings per share.

E17-19 (EPS: Simple Capital Structure) A portion of the combined statement of income and retained earnings of Mercutio Inc. for the current year follows:

Income before extraordinary item		$15,000,000
Extraordinary loss, net of applicable		
income tax (Note 1)		1,340,000
Net income		13,660,000
Retained earnings at the beginning of the year		83,250,000
		96,910,000
Dividends declared:		
On preferred stock—$6.00 per share	$ 300,000	
On common stock—$1.75 per share	14,875,000	15,175,000
Retained earnings at the end of the year		$81,735,000

Note 1. During the year, Mercutio Inc. suffered a major casualty loss of $1,340,000 after applicable income tax reduction of $1,200,000.

At the end of the current year, Mercutio Inc. has outstanding 8,500,000 shares of $10 par common stock and 50,000 shares of 6% preferred.

On April 1 of the current year, Mercutio Inc. issued 1,000,000 shares of common stock for $32 per share to help finance the casualty.

Instructions
Compute the earnings per share on common stock for the current year as it should be reported to stockholders.

E17-20 (EPS: Simple Capital Structure) On January 1, 1996, John Gaunt Industries had stock outstanding as follows:

6% Cumulative preferred stock, $100 par value,	
issued and outstanding 10,000 shares.	$1,000,000
Common stock, $10 par value, issued and	
outstanding 200,000 shares.	2,000,000

To acquire the net assets of three smaller companies, Gaunt authorized the issuance of an additional 160,000 common shares. The acquisitions took place as follows:

Date of Acquisition		Shares Issued
Company A	April 1, 1996	50,000
Company B	July 1, 1996	80,000
Company C	October 1, 1996	30,000

On May 14, 1996, Gaunt realized a $90,000 (before taxes) insurance gain on the expropriation of investments originally purchased in 1985.

On December 31, 1996, Gaunt recorded net income of $300,000 before tax and exclusive of the gain.

Instructions

Assuming a 50% tax rate, compute the earnings per share data that should appear on the financial statements of John Gaunt Industries as of December 31, 1996. Assume that the expropriation is extraordinary.

E17-21 (EPS: Simple Capital Structure) At January 1, 1996 Langley Company's outstanding shares included:

> 280,000 shares of $50 par value, 7% cumulative preferred stock
> 900,000 shares of $1 par value common stock

Net income for 1996 was $2,530,000. No cash dividends were declared or paid during 1996. On February 15, 1997, however, all preferred dividends in arrears were paid, together with a 5% stock dividend on common shares. There were no dividends in arrears prior to 1996.

On April 1, 1996, 450,000 shares of common stock were sold for $10 per share and on October 1, 1996, 110,000 shares of common stock were purchased for $20 per share and held as treasury stock.

Instructions

Compute earnings per share for 1996. Assume that financial statements for 1996 were issued in March 1997.

E17-22 (EPS with Convertible Bonds, Various Situations) In 1995 Bolingbroke Enterprises issued, at par, 60, $1,000, 8% bonds, each convertible into 100 shares of common stock. At the time the bonds were issued, the average Aa corporate bond yield was 10%. Bolingbroke had revenues of $15,750 and expenses other than interest and taxes of $8,400 for 1996 (assume that the tax rate is 40%). Throughout 1996, 2,000 shares of common stock were outstanding; none of the bonds was converted or redeemed.

Instructions

   (a) Compute earnings per share for 1996.

   (b) Assume the same facts as those assumed for Part (a), except that the 60 bonds were issued on September 1, 1996 (rather than in 1995), and none have been converted or redeemed.

   (c) Assume the same facts as assumed for Part (a), except that 20 of the 60 bonds were actually converted on July 1, 1996.

E17-23 (EPS with Convertible Bonds) On June 1, 1993, Mowbray Company and Surrey Company merged to form Lancaster Inc. A total of 800,000 shares were issued to complete the merger. The new corporation reports on a calendar-year basis.

On April 1, 1995, the company issued an additional 400,000 shares of stock for cash. All 1,200,000 shares were outstanding on December 31, 1995.

Lancaster Inc. also issued $600,000 of 20-year, 8% convertible bonds at par on July 1, 1995, when the average Aa corporate bond yield was 10%. Each $1,000 bond converts to 40 shares of common at any interest date. None of the bonds have been converted to date.

Lancaster Inc. is preparing its annual report for the fiscal year ending December 31, 1995. The annual report will show earnings per share figures based upon a reported after-tax net income of $1,430,000 (the tax rate is 40%).

Instructions

   (a) Should Lancaster Inc. convertible bonds be treated as common stock equivalents for the calculation of earnings per share? Explain your answer.

   (b) Disregarding your answer in Part (a), assume that the convertible bonds are not to be treated as common stock equivalents. (*Hint:* Ignore 3% test.) Determine for 1995:

      1. The number of shares to be used for calculating:
         a. Primary earnings per share.
         b. Fully diluted earnings per share.
      2. The earnings figures to be used for calculating:
         a. Primary earnings per share.
         b. Fully diluted earnings per share.

(CMA adapted)

E17-24 (Determine Common Stock Equivalency for Bond and Preferred Stock) The Scroop Corporation issued 10-year, $5,000,000 par, 8% callable convertible subordinated debentures on January 2, 1996. The bonds have a par value of $1,000, with interest payable annually. The current conversion ratio is 14:1, and in 2 years it will increase to 18:1. At the date of issue, the bonds were sold at 98. Bond discount is amortized on a straight-line basis. The yield on Aa grade corporate bonds was 12.76% and the effective yield on the bonds was computed to be 8.16%. Scroop's effective tax was 35%. Net income in 1996 was $9,500,000, and the company had 2,000,000 shares outstanding during the entire year.

Instructions

(a) Are these bonds common stock equivalents for purposes of computing primary earnings per share? Explain.

(b) Prepare a schedule to compute both primary and fully diluted earnings per share.

(c) Discuss how the schedule would differ if the security was convertible preferred stock.

E17-25 (EPS with Options, Various Situations) Portia Company's net income for 1996 is $60,000. The only potentially dilutive securities outstanding were 1,000 options issued during 1995, each exercisable for one share at $6. None has been exercised, and 10,000 shares of common were outstanding during 1996. The average market price of Portia's stock during all quarters of 1996 was $12; the December 31, 1996 price was $20.

Instructions

(a) Compute the earnings per share (round to nearest cent).

(b) Assume the same facts as those assumed for Part (a), except that the 1,000 options were issued on October 1, 1996 (rather than in 1995). The average market price during the last three months of 1996 was $18. The 1996 closing price was $20.

E17-26 (EPS with Options) Shylock Inc. indicates that its net income for 1996 is $17,748,000, which includes a gain on casualty (net of tax) of $1,566,000. Its capital structure includes some common stock reserved under employee stock options (109,000 shares). The common shares outstanding for the year remained at 5,800,000. The controller, Lance Gobbo, asks your advice concerning the earnings per share figure that they should present. The common stock price has remained fairly stable during the year at $39 per share and the option price for the stock options is $33 per share.

Instructions

What would you tell the controller? (Assume that the gain is extraordinary.)

E17-27 (EPS with Contingent Issuance Agreement) Petruchio Inc. recently purchased Verona Corp., a large midwestern home painting corporation. One of the terms of the merger was that if Verona's income for 1996 was $110,000 or more, 10,000 additional shares would be paid to Verona's stockholders in 1997. Verona's income for 1995 was $120,000.

Instructions

(a) Would the contingent shares have to be considered in Petruchio's 1995 earnings per share computations?

(b) Assume the same facts, except that the 10,000 shares are contingent on Verona's achieving a net income of $130,000 in 1996. Would the contingent shares have to be considered in Petruchio's earnings per share computations?

E17-28 (EPS with Warrants) Baptista Corporation earned $360,000 during a period when it had an average of 100,000 shares of common stock outstanding. The common stock sold at an average market price of $15 per share during the period and sold at $25 at the end of the period. Also outstanding were 15,000 warrants that could be exercised to purchase one share of common stock for $10 for each warrant exercised.

Instructions

(a) Are the warrants dilutive?

(b) Compute primary earnings per share.

(c) Compute fully diluted earnings per share.

PROBLEMS

P17-1 (Entries for Various Dilutive Securities) The stockholders' equity section of Falstaff Inc. at the beginning of the current year appears below:

Common stock, $10 par value, authorized 1,000,000 shares, 300,000 shares issued and outstanding	$3,000,000
Paid-in capital in excess of par	600,000
Retained earnings	570,000

During the current year the following transactions occurred:

1. The company issued to the stockholders 100,000 rights. Ten rights are needed to buy one share of stock at $32. The rights were void after 30 days. The market price of the stock at this time was $34 per share.

2. The company sold to the public a $200,000, 10% bond issue at par. The company also issued with each $100 bond one detachable stock purchase warrant, which provided for the purchase of common stock at $30 per share. Shortly after issuance, similar bonds without warrants were selling at 96 and the warrants at $8.

3. All but 10,000 of the rights issued in (1) were exercised in 30 days.

4. At the end of the year, 80% of the warrants in (2) had been exercised, and the remaining were outstanding and in good standing.

5. During the current year, the company granted stock options for 5,000 shares of common stock to company executives. The market price of the stock on that date was $40 and the option price was $30. The options were to expire at year-end and were considered compensation for the current year.

6. All but 1,000 shares related to the stock option plan were exercised by year-end. The expiration resulted because one of the executives failed to fulfill an obligation related to the employment contract.

Instructions

(a) Prepare general journal entries for the current year to record the transactions listed above.

(b) Prepare the stockholders' equity section of the balance sheet at the end of the current year. Assume that retained earnings at the end of the current year is $750,000.

P17-2 (Entries for Conversion, Amortization, and Interest of Bonds) Windsor Inc. issued $1,500,000 of convertible 10-year bonds on July 1, 1995. The bonds provide for 12% interest payable semiannually on January 1 and July 1. Expense and discount in connection with the issue was $34,000, which is being amortized monthly on a straight-line basis.

The bonds are convertible after one year into 8 shares of Windsor Inc.'s $100 par value common stock for each $1,000 of bonds.

On August 1, 1996, $150,000 of bonds were turned in for conversion into common. Interest has been accrued monthly and paid as due. At the time of conversion any accrued interest on bonds being converted is paid in cash.

Instructions (Round to nearest dollar)

Prepare the journal entries to record the conversion, amortization, and interest in connection with the bonds as of:

(a) August 1, 1996 (assume the book value method is used).

(b) August 31, 1996.

(c) December 31, 1996, including closing entries for end-of-year.

(AICPA adapted)

P17-3 (Stock Option Plan) MAAN Company adopted a stock option plan on November 30, 1994, that provided that 70,000 shares of $5 par value stock be designated as available for the granting of options to officers of the corporation at a price of $8 a share. The market value was $12 a share on November 30, 1994.

On January 2, 1995, options to purchase 28,000 shares were granted to President Don Pedro—15,000 for services to be rendered in 1995 and 13,000 for services to be rendered in 1996. Also on that date, options to purchase 14,000 shares were granted to Vice-President Beatrice Leonato—7,000 for services to be rendered in 1995 and 7,000 for services to be rendered in 1996. The market value of the stock was $14 a share on January 2, 1995. The options were exercisable for a period of one year following the year in which the services were rendered.

In 1996 neither the president nor the vice-president exercised their options because the market price of the stock was below the exercise price. The market value of the stock was $7 a share on December 31, 1996, when the options for 1995 services lapsed.

On December 31, 1997, both President Pedro and Vice-President Leonato exercised their options for 13,000 and 7,000 shares, respectively, when the market price was $16 a share.

Instructions

(a) Prepare the necessary journal entries in 1994 when the stock option plan was adopted, in 1995 when options were granted, in 1996 when options lapsed and in 1997 when options were exercised.

(b) What disclosure of the stock option plan should appear in the financial statements at December 31, 1994? At December 31, 1995? Assume that the stock options outstanding or exercised at any time are a significant financial item.

P17-4 (EPS with Complex Capital Structure) Marion Tess, controller, at Norris Pharmaceutical Industries, a public company, is currently preparing the calculation for primary and fully diluted earnings per share and the related disclosure for Norris' external financial statements. Below is selected financial information for the fiscal year ended June 30, 1995.

Norris Pharmaceutical Industries
Selected Statement of
Financial Position Information
June 30, 1995

Long-term debt	
Notes payable, 10%	$ 1,000,000
7% convertible bonds payable	5,000,000
10% bonds payable	6,000,000
Total long-term debt	$12,000,000
Shareholders' equity	
Preferred stock, 8.5% cumulative, $50 par value,	
100,000 shares authorized, 25,000 shares issued	
and outstanding	$ 1,250,000
Common stock, $1 par, 10,000,000 shares authorized,	
1,000,000 shares issued and outstanding	1,000,000
Additional paid-in capital	4,000,000
Retained earnings	6,000,000
Total shareholders' equity	$12,250,000

The following transactions have also occurred at Norris.

1. Options were granted in 1993 to purchase 100,000 shares at $15 per share. Although no options were exercised during 1995, the average price per common share during fiscal year 1995 was $20 per share, and the market price on June 30, 1995, was $25 per common share.
2. Each bond was issued at face value. The 7% convertible debenture will convert into common stock at 50 shares per $1,000 bond. It is exercisable after 5 years and was issued in 1994 when the average Aa corporate bond yield was 10%.
3. The 8.5% preferred stock was issued in 1993.
4. There are no preferred dividends in arrears; however, preferred dividends were not declared in fiscal year 1995.
5. The 1,000,000 shares of common stock were outstanding for the entire 1995 fiscal year.
6. Net income for fiscal year 1995 was $1,500,000, and the average income tax rate is 40%.

Instructions
(a) For the fiscal year ended June 30, 1995, calculate Norris Pharmaceutical Industries':
   1. primary earnings per share.
   2. fully diluted earnings per share.
(b) Describe the appropriate disclosure required for earnings per share for Norris Pharmaceutical Industries for the fiscal year ended June 30, 1995.

(CMA adapted)

P17-5 (Simple EPS and EPS with Stock Options) As auditor for Banquo & Associates, you have been assigned to check Duncan Corporation's computation of earnings per share for the current year. The controller, Mac Beth, has supplied you with the following computations:

Net income	$3,374,960
Common shares issued and outstanding:	
Beginning of year	1,285,000
End of year	1,200,000
Average	1,242,500

Earnings per share

$$\frac{\$3,374,960}{1,242,500} = \$2.72 \text{ per share}$$

You have developed the following additional information:

1. There are no other equity securities in addition to the common shares.
2. There are no options or warrants outstanding to purchase common shares.
3. There are no convertible debt securities.
4. Activity in common shares during the year was as follows:

Outstanding, Jan. 1	1,285,000
Treasury shares acquired, Oct. 1	(250,000)
	1,035,000
Shares reissued, Dec. 1	165,000
Outstanding, Dec. 31	1,200,000

Instructions

(a) On the basis of the information above, do you agree with the controller's computation of earnings per share for the year? If you disagree, prepare a revised computation of earnings per share.

(b) Assume the same facts as those in (a), except that options had been issued to purchase 140,000 shares of common stock at $10 per share. These options were outstanding at the beginning of the year and none had been exercised or canceled during the year. The average market price of the common shares during the year was $25 and the ending market price was $35. Prepare a computation of earnings per share.

P17-6 (Simple EPS: Two-Year Presentation) Hecate Corporation is preparing the comparative financial statements for the annual report to its shareholders for fiscal years ended May 31, 1994, and May 31, 1995. The income from operations for each year was $1,800,000 and $2,500,000, respectively. In both years, the company incurred a 10% interest expense on $2,400,000 of debt, an obligation that requires interest-only payments for 5 years. The company experienced a loss of $500,000 from a fire in its Scotsland facility in February 1995, which was determined to be an extraordinary loss. The company uses a 40% effective tax rate for income taxes.

The capital structure of Hecate Corporation on June 1, 1993, consisted of 2 million shares of common stock outstanding and 20,000 shares of $50 par value, 8%, cumulative preferred stock. There were no preferred dividends in arrears, and the company had not issued any convertible securities, options, or warrants.

On October 1, 1993, Hecate sold an additional 500,000 shares of the common stock at $20 per share. Hecate distributed a 20% stock dividend on the common shares outstanding on January 1, 1994. On December 1, 1994, Hecate was able to sell an additional 800,000 shares of the common stock at $22 per share. These were the only common stock transactions that occurred during the two fiscal years.

Instructions

(a) Identify whether the capital structure at Hecate Corporation is a simple or complex capital structure, and explain why.

(b) Determine the weighted average number of shares that Hecate Corporation would use in calculating earnings per share for the fiscal year ended
  1. May 31, 1994.
  2. May 31, 1995.

(c) Prepare, in good form, a Comparative Income Statement, beginning with income from operations, for Hecate Corporation for the fiscal years ended May 31, 1994, and May 31, 1995. This statement will be included in Hecate's annual report and should display the appropriate earnings per share presentations.

(CMA adapted)

P17-7 (EPS Computation of Primary and Fully Diluted EPS) Edmund Gloucester of the controller's office of Lear Corporation was given the assignment of determining the primary and fully diluted earnings per share values for the year ending December 31, 1995. Gloucester has compiled the information listed below.

1. The company is authorized to issue 8,000,000 shares of $10 par value common stock. As of December 31, 1994, 3,000,000 shares had been issued and were outstanding.

2. The per share market price of the common stock and the average Aa corporate bond yield on selected dates were as follows:

	Price per Share	Average Aa Corporate Bond Yield
July 1, 1994	$20.00	17%
January 1, 1995	21.00	18
April 1, 1995	25.00	20
July 1, 1995	11.00	21
August 1, 1995	10.50	21
November 1, 1995	9.00	20
December 31, 1995	10.00	18

3. A total of 700,000 shares of an authorized 1,200,000 shares of convertible preferred stock had been issued on July 1, 1994. The stock was issued at its par value of $25, and it has a cumulative dividend of $3 per share. The stock is convertible into common stock at the rate of one share of convertible

preferred for one share of common. The rate of conversion is to be automatically adjusted for stock splits and stock dividends. Dividends are paid quarterly on September 30, December 31, March 31, and June 30.

4. Lear Corporation is subject to a 40% income tax rate.
5. The after-tax net income for the year ended December 31, 1995 was $13,550,000.

The following specific activities took place during 1995.

1. January 1—A 5% common stock dividend was issued. The dividend had been declared on December 1, 1994, to all stockholders of record on December 29, 1994.
2. April 1—A total of 200,000 shares of the $3 convertible preferred stock was converted into common stock. The company issued new common stock and retired the preferred stock. This was the only conversion of the preferred stock during 1995.
3. July 1—A 2-for-1 split of the common stock became effective on this date. The Board of Directors had authorized the split on June 1.
4. August 1—A total of 300,000 shares of common stock were issued to acquire a factory building.
5. November 1—A total of 24,000 shares of common stock were purchased on the open market at $9 per share. These shares were to be held as treasury stock and were still in the treasury as of December 31, 1995.
6. Common stock cash dividends—Cash dividends to common stockholders were declared and paid as follows:
   April 15—$.30 per share
   October 15—$.20 per share
7. Preferred stock cash dividends—Cash dividends to preferred stockholders were declared and paid as scheduled.

Instructions
(a) Determine the number of shares used to compute primary earnings per share for the year ended December 31, 1995.
(b) Determine the number of shares used to compute fully diluted earnings per share for the year ended December 31, 1995.
(c) Compute the adjusted net income to be used as the numerator in the primary earnings per share calculation for the year ended December 31, 1995.

P17-8 (EPS with Stock Dividend and Extraordinary Items) Cordelia Corporation is preparing the comparative financial statements to be included in the annual report to stockholders. Cordelia employs a fiscal year ending May 31.

Income from operations before income taxes for Cordelia was $1,400,000 and $660,000, respectively, for fiscal years ended May 31, 1996 and 1995. Cordelia experienced an extraordinary loss of $500,000 because of an earthquake on March 3, 1996. A 40% combined income tax rate pertains to any and all of Cordelia Corporation's profits, gains, and losses.

Cordelia's capital structure consists of preferred stock and common stock. The company has not issued any convertible securities or warrants and there are no outstanding stock options.

Cordelia issued 50,000 shares of $100 par value, 6% cumulative preferred stock in 1982. All of this stock is outstanding, and no preferred dividends are in arrears.

There were 1,500,000 shares of $1 par common stock outstanding on June 1, 1994. On September 1, 1994, Cordelia sold an additional 400,000 shares of the common stock at $17 per share. Cordelia distributed a 20% stock dividend on the common shares outstanding on December 1, 1995. These were the only common stock transactions during the past two fiscal years.

Instructions
(a) Determine the weighted average number of common shares that would be used in computing earnings per share on the current comparative income statement for:
   1. The year ended May 31, 1995.
   2. The year ended May 31, 1996.
(b) Starting with income from operations before income taxes, prepare a comparative income statement for the years ended May 31, 1996 and 1995. The statement will be part of Cordelia Corporation's annual report to stockholders and should include appropriate earnings per share presentation.
(c) The capital structure of a corporation is the result of its past financing decisions. Furthermore, the earnings per share data presented on a corporation's financial statements is dependent upon the capital structure.
   1. Explain why Cordelia Corporation is considered to have a simple capital structure.
   2. Describe how earnings per share data would be presented for a corporation that has a complex capital structure.

(CMA adapted)

P17-9 (Comprehensive EPS Calculation with Complicating Features) The controller of Polonius Corporation has requested assistance in determining income, primary earnings per share, and fully diluted earnings per share for presentation in the company's income statement for the year ended September 30, 1997. As currently calculated, the company's net income is $830,000 for fiscal year 1996–1997. The controller has indicated that the income figure might be adjusted for the following transactions that were recorded by charges or credits directly to retained earnings (the amounts are net of applicable income taxes):

1. The sum of $300,000, applicable to a breached 1993 contract, was received as a result of a lawsuit. Prior to the award, legal counsel was uncertain about the outcome of the suit.
2. A gain of $270,000 was realized from a condemnation sale (extraordinary).
3. A "gain" of $165,000 was realized on the sale of treasury stock.
4. A special inventory writeoff of $200,000 was made, of which $140,000 applied to goods manufactured prior to October 1, 1996.

Your working papers disclose the following opening balances and transactions in the company's capital stock accounts during the year:

1. Common stock (at October 1, 1996, stated value $10, authorized 450,000 shares; effective December 1, 1996, stated value $5, authorized 900,000 shares):

   > Balance, October 1, 1996—issued and outstanding 100,000 shares
   > December 1, 1996—100,000 shares issued in a 2-for-1 stock split.
   > December 1, 1996—420,000 shares (stated value $5) issued at $39 per share.

2. Treasury stock—common:

   > March 1, 1997—purchased 60,000 shares at $37.25 per share.
   > April 1, 1997—sold 60,000 shares at $40 per share.

3. Stock purchase warrants, Series A (initially, each warrant was exchangeable with $60 for one common share; effective December 1, 1996, each warrant became exchangeable for two common shares at $30 per share):

   > October 1, 1996—40,000 warrants issued at $6 each.

4. Stock purchase warrants, Series B (each warrant is exchangeable with $45 for one common share):

   > April 1, 1997—30,000 warrants authorized and issued at $10 each.

5. First mortgage bonds, 9%, due 2009 (nonconvertible; priced to yield 8% when issued):

   > Balance, October 1, 1996—authorized, issued, and outstanding—the face value of $2,100,000.

6. Convertible debentures, 7%, due 2013 (initially, each $1,000 bond was convertible at any time until maturity into 12½ common shares; effective December 1, 1996, the conversion rate became 25 shares for each bond):

   > October 1, 1996—authorized and issued at their face value (no premium or discount) of $3,600,000.

The following table shows market prices for the company's securities and the assumed average Aa corporate bond yield rate during 1996–1997:

	Price (or Rate) at			Average for Year
	10/1/96	4/1/97	9/30/97	Ended 9/30/97
Common stock	66	40	36¼	37½[a]
First mortgage bonds	88½	87	86	87
Convertible debentures	100	120	119	115
Series A Warrants	6	22	19½	15
Series B Warrants	—	10	9	9½
Avg. Aa corp. bond yield	8%	7¾%	7½%	7¾%

[a]Adjusted for stock split.

Instructions

(a) Prepare a schedule computing net income as it should be presented in the company's income statement for the year ended September 30, 1997.

(b) Assuming that net income after income taxes for the year was $1,125,000 and that there were no extraordinary items, prepare a schedule computing (1) the primary earnings per share and (2) the fully diluted earnings per share that should be presented in the company's income statement for the year ended September 30, 1997. A supporting schedule computing the numbers of shares to be used in these computations should also be prepared. (Because of the relative stability of the market price for its common shares, the annual average market price may be used where appropriate in your calculations. Assume an income tax rate of 48%.)

(AICPA adapted)

P17-10 (Comprehensive EPS Calculation with Complicating Features) The stockholders' equity section of Rosencrantz Company's balance sheet as of December 31, 1996, contains the following:

$2 cumulative convertible preferred stock (par value $25 a share; authorized 1,500,000 shares, issued 1,400,000, converted to common 750,000, and outstanding 650,000 shares; liquidation value, $30 a share, aggregating $19,500,000)	$16,250,000
Common stock (par value $.25 a share; authorized 15,000,000 shares, issued and outstanding 9,200,000 shares)	2,300,000
Additional paid-in capital	30,500,000
Retained earnings	45,050,000
Total stockholders' equity	$94,100,000

On April 1, 1996, Rosencrantz Company acquired the business and assets and assumed the liabilities of Gildenstern Corporation in a transaction accounted for as a pooling of interests. For each of Gildenstern Corporation's 2,400,000 shares of $.25 par value common stock outstanding, the owner received one share of common stock of Rosencrantz Company. (*Hint:* In a pooling of interests, shares are considered outstanding for the entire year.)

Included in the liabilities of Rosencrantz Company are 10% convertible subordinated debentures issued at their face value of $20,000,000 in 1995. The debentures are due in 2012 and until then are convertible into the common stock of Rosencrantz Company at the rate of five shares of common stock for each $100 debenture. To date none of these has been converted.

On April 2, 1996, Rosencrantz Company issued 1,400,000 shares of convertible preferred stock at $40 per share. Assume an effective yield to the preferred stockholders of approximately 5%. Quarterly dividends to December 31, 1996 have been paid on these shares. The preferred stock is convertible into common stock at the rate of two shares of common for each share of preferred. On October 1, 1996, 150,000 shares and on November 1, 1996, 600,000 shares of the preferred stock were converted into common stock.

During July, 1995, Rosencrantz Company granted options to its officers and key employees to purchase 610,000 shares of the company's common stock at a price of $20 a share. The options do not become exercisable until 1997.

During 1996, dividend payments and average market prices of the Rosencrantz common stock were:

	Dividend Per Share	Average Market Price Per Share
First quarter	$.10	$25
Second quarter	.13	30
Third quarter	.15	20
Fourth quarter	.12	25
Average for the year		25

The December 31, 1996 closing price of the common stock was $25 a share.

Assume that the average Aa corporate bond yield was 14% throughout 1995 and 1996. Rosencrantz Company's consolidated net income for the year ended December 31, 1996, was $11,360,000. The provision for income taxes was computed at a rate of 48%.

Instructions

(a) Prepare a schedule that shows the evaluation of the common stock equivalency status of the (1) convertible debentures, (2) convertible preferred stock, and (3) employee stock options.

*(b) Prepare a schedule that shows for 1996 the computation of:
1. The weighted-average number of shares for computing primary earnings per share.
2. The weighted-average number of shares for computing fully diluted earnings per share.

*(c) Prepare a schedule that shows for 1996 the computation to the nearest cent of:
1. Primary earnings per share.
2. Fully diluted earnings per share.
   *(*Hint:* Parts (b) and (c) may be more efficiently prepared if done simultaneously.)

(AICPA adapted)

P17-11 (Various Equity, Dividend, and EPS Calculations) On February 1, 1996, when your audit and report are nearly complete, Gertrude Queen, the president of Hamlet Corporation asks you to prepare statistical schedules of comparative financial data for the past five years for inclusion in the company's annual report. Your working papers reveal the following information.

1. Income statements show net income amounts as follows:

$$
\begin{array}{ll}
1991— & \$ \ 40,000 \\
1992— & (39,000) \ (loss) \\
1993— & 49,000 \\
1994— & 76,000 \\
1995— & 100,000 \\
\end{array}
$$

2. On January 1, 1991, there were outstanding 2,000 shares of common stock, par value $100 and 1,000 shares of 6% cumulative preferred stock, par value $50.
3. A 6% dividend was paid in common stock to common stockholders on December 31, 1992. The fair market value of the stock was $145 per share at the time.
4. Nine hundred shares of common stock were issued on March 31, 1993, to purchase another company. (The transaction was accounted for as a purchase, not a pooling of interests: use weighted average approach for purchase of a business.)
5. A dividend of cumulative preferred stock was distributed to common stockholders on July 1, 1993. One share of preferred stock was distributed for every five shares of common stock held. The fair market value of the preferred stock was $57 per share before the distribution and $54 per share immediately after the distribution.
6. The common stock was split 2-for-1 on December 31, 1994, and again on December 31, 1995.
7. Cash dividends are paid on the preferred stock on June 30 and December 31. Preferred stock dividends were paid in each year except 1992; the 1992 and 1993 dividends were paid in 1993.
8. Cash dividends on common stock are paid on June 30 and December 31. Dividends paid per share of stock outstanding at the respective dates were:

	June 30	Dec. 31
1991	$ .50	$.50
1992	None	None
1993	.50	.75
1994	1.00	.50[a]
1995	.75	.75[b]

[a]After 2-for-1 split.
[b]Before 2-for-1 split.

Instructions

(a) In connection with your preparation of the statistical schedule of comparative financial data for the past 5 years:
   1. Prepare a schedule computing the number of shares of common stock and preferred stock outstanding as of the respective year-end dates.
   2. Prepare a schedule computing the current equivalent number of shares of common stock outstanding as of the respective year-end dates. The current equivalent shares means the weighted-average number of shares outstanding in the respective prior periods after restatement for stock splits and stock dividends.
   3. Compute the total cash dividends paid to holders of preferred stock and to holders of common stock for each of the 5 years.

(b) Prepare a 5-year summary of financial statistics to be included in the annual report. The summary should show by years "Net Income (or Loss)," "Earnings Per Share of Common Stock," and "Cash Dividends Per Share of Common Stock." The per share figures should be computed on the basis of current equivalent shares.

(AICPA adapted)

CASES

C17-1 (Warrants Issued with Bonds and Convertible Bonds) Incurring long-term debt with an arrangement whereby lenders receive an option to buy common stock during all or a portion of the time the debt is outstanding is a frequent corporate financing practice. In some situations the result is achieved through the issuance of convertible bonds; in others the debt instruments and the warrants to buy stock are separate.

Instructions

(a) 1. Describe the differences that exist in current accounting for original proceeds of the issuance of convertible bonds and of debt instruments with separate warrants to purchase common stock.
   2. Discuss the underlying rationale for the differences described in (a)1 above.
   3. Summarize the arguments that have been presented in favor of accounting for convertible bonds in the same manner as accounting for debt with separate warrants.

(b) At the start of the year Biron Company issued $18,000,000 of 12% notes along with warrants to buy 1,200,000 shares of its $10 par value common stock at $18 per share. The notes mature over the next 10 years starting one year from date of issuance with annual maturities of $1,800,000. At the time, Biron had 9,600,000 shares of common stock outstanding and the market price was $23 per share. The company received $20,040,000 for the notes and the warrants. For Biron Company, 12% was a relatively low borrowing rate. If offered alone, at this time, the notes would have been issued at a

22% discount. Prepare the journal entry (or entries) for the issuance of the notes and warrants for the cash consideration received.

(AICPA adapted)

C17-2 (Convertible Bonds)   On February 1, 1992, Armado Company sold its 5-year, $1,000 par value, 8% bonds, which were convertible at the option of the investor into Armado Company common stock at a ratio of 10 shares of common stock for each bond. The convertible bonds were sold by Armado Company at a discount. Interest is payable annually each February 1. On February 1, 1995, Holofernes Company, an investor in the Armado Company convertible bonds, tendered 1,000 bonds for conversion into 10,000 shares of Armado Company common stock that had a market value of $120 per share at the date of the conversion.

Instructions

How should Armado Company account for the conversion of the convertible bonds into common stock under both the book value and market value methods? Discuss the rationale for each method.

(AICPA adapted)

C17-3 (Stock Warrants—Various Types)   For various reasons a corporation may issue warrants to purchase shares of its common stock at specified prices that, depending on the circumstances, may be less than, equal to, or greater than the current market price. For example, warrants may be issued:

1. To existing stockholders on a pro rata basis.
2. To certain key employees under an incentive stock option plan.
3. To purchasers of the corporation's bonds.

Instructions

For each of the three examples of how stock warrants are used:
   (a) Explain why they are used.
   (b) Discuss the significance of the price (or prices) at which the warrants are issued (or granted) in relation to (1) the current market price of the company's stock, and (2) the length of time over which they can be exercised.
   (c) Describe the information that should be disclosed in financial statements, or notes thereto, that are prepared when stock warrants are outstanding in the hands of the three groups listed above.

(AICPA adapted)

C17-4 (Stock Options and Stock Appreciation Rights)   In 1993 Costard Co. adopted a plan to give additional incentive compensation to its dealers to sell its principal product, fire extinguishers. Under the plan Costard transferred 9,000 shares of its $1 par value stock to a trust with the provision that Costard would have to forfeit interest in the trust and no part of the trust fund could ever revert to Costard. Shares were to be distributed to dealers on the basis of their shares of fire extinguisher purchases from Costard (above certain minimum levels) over the 3-year period ending June 30, 1996.

In 1993 the stock was closely held. The book value of the stock was $7.90 per share as of June 30, 1993, and in 1993 additional shares were sold to existing stockholders for $8 per share. On the basis of this information, market value of the stock was determined to be $8 per share.

In 1993 when the shares were transferred to the trust, Costard charged prepaid expenses for $72,000 ($8 per share market value) and credited capital stock for $9,000 and additional paid-in capital for $63,000. The prepaid expense was charged to operations over a 3-year period ended June 30, 1996.

Costard sold a substantial number of shares of its stock to the public in 1995 at $60 per share.

In July 1996 all shares of the stock in the trust were distributed to the dealers. The market value of the shares at date of distribution of the stock from the trust had risen to $110 per share. Costard obtained a tax deduction equal to that market value for the tax year ended June 30, 1997.

Instructions

   (a) How much should be reported as selling expense in each of the years noted above?
   (b) Costard is also considering other types of option plans. One such plan is a stock appreciation right (SAR) plan. What is a stock appreciation right plan? What is a potential disadvantage of a SAR plan from the viewpoint of the company?

C17-5 (Exposure Draft on Stock Compensation Plans)   Presented below is an excerpt from a speech given by SEC Commissioner J. Carter Beese, Jr., in December 1993.

> . . . I believe investors will be far better off if the value of stock options is reported in a footnote rather than on the face of the income statement. By allowing footnote disclosures, we will protect shareholders' current and future investments by not raising the cost of capital for the innovative, growth companies that depend on stock options to attract and retain key employees. I've said it before and I'll say it again: the stock option accounting debate essentially boils down to one thing—the cost of capital. And as long as we can adequately protect investors without raising the cost of capital to such a vital segment of our economy, why would we want to do it any other way?

The FASB has made the assertion that when it comes to public policy, they lack the competence to weigh various national goals. I also agree with the sentiment that, as a general matter, Congress should not be in the business of writing accounting standards.

But the SEC has the experience and the capability to determine exactly where to draw the regulatory lines to best serve investors and our capital markets. That is our mandate, and that is what we do, day in and day out.

But we may have to act sooner rather than later. As we speak, the FASB's proposals are raising the cost of venture capital. That's because venture capitalists are pricing deals based on their exit strategies, which usually include cashing out in public offerings. The FASB's proposals, however, provide incentives for companies to stay private longer—they are able to use options more freely to attract and retain key employees, and they avoid the earnings hit that going public would entail. Even worse, as venture capital deals become profitable because of the FASB's proposed actions, venture capitalists are starting to look overseas for alternative investment opportunities that lack the investment drag now associated with certain American ventures.

I acknowledge that the FASB deserves some degree of freedom to determine what they believe is the best accounting approach. At the same time, however, I cannot stand by idly for long and watch venture capital increase in price or even flee this country because of a myopic search for an accounting holy grail. At some point, I believe that the SEC must inject itself into this debate, and help the FASB determine what accounting approach is ultimately in the best interests of investors as a whole.

We owe it to shareholders, issuers and all market participants, and indeed our country, to make the best decision in accordance with the public good, not just technical accounting theory.

Instructions

(a) What are the major recommendations of the FASB's exposure draft on "Accounting for Stock-Based Compensation Plans"?

(b) Write a response to Commissioner Beese, defending the use of the concept of neutrality in financial accounting and reporting.

C17-6 (EPS: Preferred Dividends, Options, and Convertible Debt) "Earnings per share" (EPS) is the most featured single financial statistic about modern corporations. Daily published quotations of stock prices have recently been expanded to include for many securities a "times earnings" figure that is based on EPS. Stock analysts often focus their discussions on the EPS of the corporations they study.

Instructions

(a) Explain how dividends or dividend requirements on any class of preferred stock that may be outstanding affect the computation of EPS.

(b) One of the technical procedures applicable in EPS computations is the "treasury stock method."
  1. Briefly describe the circumstances under which it might be appropriate to apply the treasury stock method.
  2. There is a limit to the extent to which the treasury stock method is applicable. Indicate what this limit is and give a succinct summary of the procedures that should be followed beyond the treasury stock limits.

(c) Under some circumstances, convertible debentures would be considered "common stock equivalents"; under other circumstances they would not.
  1. When is it proper to treat convertible debentures as common stock equivalents? What is the effect on computation of EPS in such cases?
  2. In case convertible debentures are not considered as common stock equivalents, explain how they are handled for purposes of EPS computations.

(AICPA adapted)

C17-7 (EPS Concepts and Professional Pronouncements) Earnings per share (EPS) amounts were calculated and reported in various ways on an optional basis prior to 1969. *APB Opinion No. 15,* "Earnings per Share," issued in 1969, required that EPS be reported and prescribed how these amounts would be computed and disclosed.

The Accounting Principles Board defined a simple capital structure for which it prescribed a single EPS presentation, and a complex capital structure for which it prescribed a dual EPS presentation. Although some of the definitions within *APB Opinion No. 15* have been amended by statements of the Financial Accounting Standards Board, the overall scheme for the computation and disclosure of EPS has remained unchanged since 1969.

Instructions

(a) Explain why the existence of convertible securities and other financing instruments necessitated the reporting requirements for EPS prescribed by *APB Opinion No. 15.*

(b) Much of the effort involved in reporting EPS concerns the identification of common stock equivalents.
  1. In addition to convertible securities that meet the yield test for common stock equivalence, what other items are considered common stock equivalents?

2. Describe the circumstances under which a convertible security that meets the yield test for common stock equivalence would not be assumed to be converted in the computation of EPS.

(c) *Statement of Financial Accounting Standards No. 55,* "Determining Whether a Convertible Security is a Common Stock Equivalent," which was adopted in 1982, changed the test for common stock equivalence from, "a cash yield of less than 66⅔ percent of the then current bank prime interest rate" as prescribed in *APB Opinion No. 15,* to "a cash yield of less than 66⅔ percent of the then current average Aa corporate bond yield." Explain the reason for this change.

(d) *Statement of Financial Accounting Standards No. 85,* "Yield Test for Determining Whether a Convertible Security is a Common Stock Equivalent," which was adopted in 1985, changed the test for common stock equivalence from the "cash yield test" as prescribed in *APB Opinion No. 15* and continued in *Statement of Financial Accounting Standards No. 55,* to the "effective yield test." Explain the reason for this change.

(CMA adapted)

C17-8 (EPS Concepts and Effect of Transactions on EPS) Dromio Corporation, a new audit client of yours, has not reported earnings per share data in its annual reports to stockholders in the past. The treasurer, Angelo Balthazar, requested that you furnish information about the reporting of earnings per share data in the current year's annual report in accordance with generally accepted accounting principles.

Instructions

(a) Define the term "earnings per share" as it applies to a corporation with a capitalization structure composed of only one class of common stock and explain how earnings per share should be computed and how the information should be disclosed in the corporation's financial statements.

(b) Discuss the treatment, if any, that should be given to each of the following items in computing earnings per share of common stock for financial statement reporting.

1. Outstanding preferred stock issued at a premium with a par value liquidation right.
2. The exercise at a price below market value but above book value of a common stock option issued during the current fiscal year to officers of the corporation.
3. The replacement of a machine immediately prior to the close of the current fiscal year at a cost 20% above the original cost of the replaced machine. The new machine will perform the same function as the old machine that was sold for its book value.
4. The declaration of current dividends on cumulative preferred stock.
5. The acquisition of some of the corporation's outstanding common stock during the current fiscal year. The stock was classified as treasury stock.
6. A 2-for-1 stock split of common stock during the current fiscal year.
7. A provision created out of retained earnings for a contingent liability from a possible lawsuit.

▶ USING YOUR JUDGMENT ◀

▶ FINANCIAL REPORTING PROBLEMS

Refer to the financial statements and other documents of Georgia-Pacific Corporation presented in Appendix 5-A and answer the following questions.

1. At December 31, 1993, Georgia-Pacific's Employee Stock Purchase Plan had reserved for issue 1,154,000 shares of common stock. How many shares were issued to employees in 1993 as a result of this plan?
2. At December 31, 1990, Georgia-Pacific reserved 4 million shares of common stock for its Long-Term Incentive Plan. How does Georgia-Pacific account for the shares awarded? What was the amount of Incentive Plan compensation expense recognized for the years 1991, 1992, and 1993?
3. In addition to its Long-Term Incentive Plan, Georgia-Pacific has an Employee Stock Option Plan for certain officers and key employees. How does the corporation account for the stock options granted? What was the Option Plan compensation expense (income) for the years 1991, 1992, and 1993?
4. In computing its 1993 earnings per share, what kind of shares were excluded by Georgia-Pacific from the computation of weighted average number of common shares outstanding?

▶ WRITING ASSIGNMENT

Matt Kacskos, a stockholder of Howat Corporation, has asked you, the firm's accountant, to explain why his stock warrants were not included in fully diluted EPS. In order to explain this situation, you must briefly explain what dilutive securities are, why they are included in the EPS calculation, and why some securities are antidilutive and thus not included in this calculation.

Instructions

Write Mr. Kacskos a 1–1.5 page letter explaining why the warrants are not included in the calculation. Use the following data to help you explain:

Howat Corporation earned $228,000 during the period, when it had an average of 100,000 shares of common stock outstanding. The common stock sold at an average market price of $15 per share during the period and $25 at the end of the period. Also outstanding were 15,000 warrants that could be exercised to purchased one share of common stock for $30 each warrant.

▶ GROUP ASSIGNMENT

On December 12, 1993, the Board of Directors of McClure Company authorized a grant of nonqualified options to company executives for the purchase of 20,000 shares of common stock at $50 any time during 1996 if the executives still are employed by the company. The closing price of McClure common stock was $55 on December 12, 1993, $51 on January 2, 1996, and $49⅛ on December 31, 1996. None of the options were exercised.

Instructions

Your instructor will assign one member of the group to serve as recorder and one member to serve as spokesperson. As a group, provide the information for the recorder to prepare responses to the following three requirements. Upon completion of each requirement and before moving on to the next part, the spokesperson will report the group findings to the class.

- **(a)** Prepare a schedule presenting the computation of the compensation cost that should be attributed to the options of McClure Company.
- **(b)** Assume that the market price of McClure common stock rose to $58 (instead of declining to $51) on January 2, 1996, and that all options were exercised on that date. Would the company incur a cost for executive compensation? Why?
- **(c)** Discuss the arguments for measuring compensation from executive stock options in terms of the spread between the
  1. Market price and option price when the grant is made.
  2. Market price and option price when the options are first exercisable.
  3. Market price and option price when the options are exercised.
  4. Cash value of the executives' services estimated at date of grant and the amount of their salaries.

(AICPA adapted)

▶ ETHICS CASE

The executive officers of Veryshrewd Corporation have a performance-based compensation plan. The performance criteria of this plan is linked to growth in earnings per share. When annual earnings per share growth is 12%, executives earn 100% of the shares; if growth is 16%, executives earn 125%. If earnings per share growth is lower than 8%, executives receive no additional compensation.

In 1995, Kate Padua, the controller of Veryshrewd, reviews year end estimates of bad debt expense and warranty expense. She calculates the EPS growth at 15%. Vince Lucentio, a member of the executive group, remarks over lunch that the estimate of bad debt expense might be decreased so that EPS growth will be 16.1%. Padua is not sure that she should do this because she believes that the current estimate of bad debts is sound. On the other hand, she recognizes that a great deal of subjectivity is involved in the computation.

Instructions

- **(a)** What, if any, is the ethical dilemma for Padua?
- **(b)** Should Padua's knowledge of the compensation plan be a factor that influences her estimate?
- **(c)** How would you respond to Lucentio's request?

ACCOUNTING ISSUES FOR HIGH-TECH FIRMS

A visit with
JERRY ULRICH

How did you make the transition from accounting to finance?

When I was at Arthur Young, right out of college, I was on the audit staff, but I also interfaced a fair amount with the management services group because I was the resident microcomputer specialist. The transition to finance was accomplished when I went to AST Research, which was a company that had a single location but was on the verge of expanding geometrically. When I left, five years later, we had a dozen locations around the world. As the controller, I had the responsibility for everything from cash management to insurance to sales forecasting as well as traditional accounting and financial reporting. When I became vice president of finance and treasurer, I took over the responsibility for the banking relationship. Early on, I was managing cash as the controller, so I got my initial treasury experience that way. I joined Xircom in March of 1992 just prior to the company going public.

So you think that accounting is as good a background as any to becoming a chief financial officer?

Absolutely. I think public accounting lends itself to broadening your views. You have to go into companies and take a fairly broad view of what's going on with their business as opposed to just making debit and credit entries. You see a wide variety of companies. You see com-

Working in the public accounting field turned out to be a route to chief financial officer for JERRY ULRICH, CFO of Xircom, a fast-growing high technology company based near Los Angeles. Xircom, which makes products that connect portable computers to local area networks, has grown well beyond $100 million in revenues from a start-up in the late 1980s. Such a fast-paced environment has proven to be an excellent career opportunity for Ulrich, who began his career as a CPA in the mid-1970s after graduating from Ohio State University with a major in accounting and an emphasis in computer science.

panies that are very profitable and companies that are losing money. Also, you gain experience in dealing with top management and boards of directors.

What are some of the technical issues that you deal with today?

I think the first one is accounting for acquired software. We're actually a company with products that are a combination of hardware and software. The hardware is in many cases the easier part to build, but the software is what makes the products unique. Sometimes, when we're looking at product development, we get into situations where there is software that someone else has developed that would become a key part of our product. If we were to go out and acquire the rights to that software, we would have to expense it upon acquisition. The alternative to doing that would be to have a license agreement with that software company that would allow us to use it with our hardware in exchange for a royalty.

Why does it matter whether you purchase the software outright or acquire it on a royalty basis?

In many cases, a royalty may be the better way to go if you're uncertain about how successful the product will be. When you purchase the software outright, you're going to have to make some prediction about the sales of your product. Then you calculate the present value of what would normally be a royalty stream in the future and pay that up front as a nonrefundable payment to the software developer. On a royalty basis, payment typically is based on sales in the future, so it's more closely tied to the success of the product. If the product ends up being very successful in the market, you may wind up paying more than you like, and you wish you had paid for it up front because you probably could have saved money. In some cases, we look hard at whether we want to develop a portion of the software internally, which would mean that we would develop it over several quarters as opposed to purchasing something outright, and having to expense it all in one quarter. You always have that make-or-buy decision.

Anything you develop internally has to be expensed right away.

Generally, it is expensed right away. *FASB 86* says that once you reach a certain point in your software development, you have to capitalize those development costs. If you look at software companies in general, they have huge expenditures up front, and when they actually start selling the product, they have very high gross margins. It's not atypical to see 80% gross profit margins because at that point in time, the cost of duplicating disks and manuals is insignificant. The purpose of *FASB 86* is to more closely match the cost of goods with the sale of product. Once you have reached technological feasibility—in other words you know that this product is going to work and it is just a matter of completing the software coding and marketing the product—then you should capitalize those expenses and write them

off over some life of the product. This is another area that's very gray in many cases.

It must be tempting to try to find accountants who will give you the answer that you want to hear.

I've had heated arguments with a chief operating officer who thought that he could get a different technical answer from a different office of our accounting firm. I will challenge our accounting firm to properly interpret what gray areas there might be in the accounting literature for various transactions. But you can't just call up another office, ask for the technical opinion and say, "by the way, your L.A. office audits us."

Do you offer your employees stock options?

Yes, we do. We utilize stock options as a motivational tool. Our business is very risky. Technologies come and go very quickly. Product life cycles are very short. It results in less stability for your product developer, product manager and engineers. To compensate for the risk, we view stock options as a critical element in total compensation.

I don't think anyone quarrels with the use of stock options. The question is whether a company's earnings should be charged for offering them.

The best argument I've read against the notion that you should put an accounting charge on the books for the stock options is that there's really no economic impact to the company for issuing them. In fact, the gain is completely the result of the performance of the company in the eyes of Wall Street. Because of certain tax ramifications of how

long employees may hold the stock that they acquire as a result of stock options, the company may actually benefit. In addition, in an industry that has such tremendous fluctuation in not only business results but share prices in general, the ability to gauge the value of a stock option at a particular point in time is extremely difficult.

What drives FASB to proceed with this?

I think the underlying reason is the public outcry against executive compensation. The media hyped all of the gains that were occurring in the chief executive ranks, and by far the majority of those compensation figures that seemed excessive were related to stock options. The overall value of these options increased dramatically. Of course, all of the shareholders were benefiting, but the CEOs got the most press. That caused the Washington contingent to jump on the bandwagon. We all hear about the success stories, but there are many more situations in which the stock option grants never have any value.

You're in a fast-growing company. Regarding Wall Street, should you promise as little as possible and overdeliver?

As a general rule, you like to keep expectations in line so that you can at least meet them if not exceed them. We try to provide guidance to analysts in terms of what the underlying market is and some of the dynamics that are affecting us in terms of competition and so forth. We can't tell them what to publish. It's really their job to try to figure out where the company is going to be. We try to give guidance to make sure that expectations are not falsely based.

CHAPTER 18

INVESTMENTS

LEARNING OBJECTIVES

After studying this chapter, you should be able to:

1. Identify the three categories of debt securities and describe the accounting and reporting treatment for each category.

2. Identify the categories of equity securities and describe the accounting and reporting treatment for each category.

3. Explain the equity method of accounting and compare it to the fair value method for equity securities.

4. Describe the disclosure requirements for investments in debt and equity securities.

5. Discuss the accounting for impairments of debt and equity investments.

6. Describe the accounting for transfer of investment securities between categories.

*I*n one corner were the head of the SEC, Richard Breeden; Comptroller General Charles Bowsher, head of the Government Accounting Office; and many influential accounting practitioners and academics. In the other corner were Alan Greenspan, head of the Federal Reserve; Treasury Secretary Nicholas Brady; Federal Deposit Insurance Corp. Chair William Taylor; and practically every banker and bank regulator in the country. At issue: whether investments in debt and equity securities should be reported at fair value.

"Fairy-tale" accounting was how the SEC's Breeden described existing historical cost rules for investments in debt and equity securities. Or as a noted academic expert on the savings & loan fiasco noted: "Historical cost practices for investments allowed zombie institutions to conceal the depth of their insolvency." Fed Chairman Greenspan countered that forcing financial institutions to carry bonds, loans, and stock at fair value would undermine investors' and depositors' confidence. And one corporate controller noted: "These fair values represent 'fire sale' valuation that will gyrate up and down as interest rates and credit factors change. This doomsday portrayal can be very damaging to the uneducated user." The final result: a compromise that will move financial reporting closer to fair value for certain debt and equity securities.

As indicated, accounting for investments is controversial. The accounting problems involve measurement, recognition, and disclosure. This chapter on investments is divided into two sections: (1) accounting for debt securities, and (2) accounting for equity securities. Appendices to this chapter cover changes from and to the equity method of accounting for investments in stock and special issues related to investments.

► **S ECTION 1 / I NVESTMENTS IN D EBT S ECURITIES**

Debt securities are instruments representing a creditor relationship with an enterprise. Debt securities include U.S. government securities, municipal securities, corporate bonds, convertible debt, commercial paper, and all securitized debt instruments. Trade accounts receivable and loans receivable are not debt securities because they do not meet the definition of a security.[1]

OBJECTIVE 1

Identify the three categories of debt securities and describe the accounting and reporting treatment for each category.

Investments in debt securities are grouped into three separate categories for accounting and reporting purposes. These categories are as follows:

Held-to-maturity: Debt securities that the enterprise has the positive intent and ability to hold to maturity.

Trading: Debt securities bought and held primarily for sale in the near term to generate income on short-term price differences.

Available-for-sale: Debt securities not classified as held-to-maturity or trading securities.

Illustration 18-1 identifies these categories, along with the accounting and reporting treatments required for each.

**ILLUSTRATION 18-1
Accounting for Debt
Securities by Category**

Category	Valuation	Unrealized Holding Gains or Losses	Other Income Effects
Held-to-maturity	Amortized cost	Not recognized	Interest when earned; gains and losses from sale.
Trading securities	Fair value	Recognized in income	Interest when earned; gains and losses from sale.
Available-for-sale	Fair value	Recognized but included as separate component of stockholders' equity	Interest when earned; gains and losses from sale.

**UNDERLYING
CONCEPT**

Debt securities are reported at fair value not only because the information is relevant but also because it is reliable.

Amortized cost is the acquisition cost adjusted for the amortization of discount or premium, if appropriate. **Fair value** is the amount at which a financial instrument could be exchanged in a current transaction between willing parties, other than in a forced or liquidation sale.[2]

► **HELD-TO-MATURITY SECURITIES**

Only debt securities can be classified as held-to-maturity because, by definition, equity securities have no maturity date. A debt security should be classified as **held-to-maturity** only if the reporting entity has **both (1) the positive intent** and **(2) the ability**

---

[1]A **security** is a share, participation, or other interest in property or in an enterprise of the issuer or an obligation of the issuer that: (a) either is represented by an instrument issued in bearer or registered form or, if not represented by an instrument, is registered in books maintained to record transfers by or on behalf of the issuer; (b) is of a type commonly dealt in on securities exchanges or markets or, when represented by an instrument, is commonly recognized in any area in which it is issued or dealt in as a medium for investment; and (c) either is one of a class or series or by its terms is divisible into a class or series of shares, participations, interests, or obligations. From "Accounting for Certain Investments in Debt and Equity Securities," *Statement of Financial Accounting Standards No. 115* (Norwalk, CT: FASB, 1993), p. 48, par. 137.

[2]Ibid., pp. 47–48. The fair value is **readily determinable** if its sale price or other quotations are available on SEC registered exchanges, or, for over the counter securities, are published by recognized national publication systems. Foreign shares have readily determinable fair values if they trade in markets comparable in breadth and scope to the described U.S. markets.

to hold those securities to maturity. A company should not classify a debt security as held-to-maturity if the company intends to hold the security for an indefinite period of time. Likewise, if the enterprise anticipates that a sale may be necessary due to changes in interest rates, foreign currency risk, liquidity needs, or other asset-liability management reasons, the security should not be classified as held-to-maturity.[3]

Held-to-maturity securities are accounted for at amortized cost, not fair value. If management intends to hold certain investment securities to maturity and has no plans to sell them, fair values (selling prices) are not relevant for measuring and evaluating the cash flows associated with these securities. Finally, because held-to-maturity securities are not adjusted to fair value, they do not increase the volatility of either reported earnings or reported capital as do trading securities and available-for-sale securities.

To illustrate the accounting for held-to-maturity debt securities, assume that Robinson Company purchased $100,000 of 8% bonds of Evermaster Corporation on January 1, 1995, paying $92,278. The bonds mature January 1, 2000; interest is payable each July 1 and January 1. The discount of $7,722 ($100,000 − $92,278) provided an effective interest yield of 10%. The entry to record the investment is:[4]

January 1, 1995

Held-to-Maturity Securities	92,278	
Cash		92,278

A Held-to-Maturity Securities account is used to indicate the type of debt security purchased. Discounts and premiums on long-term investments in bonds are amortized in a manner similar to discounts and premiums on bonds payable, discussed in Chapter 14. Illustration 18-2 shows the effect of the discount amortization on the interest revenue recorded each period for the investment in Evermaster Corporation bonds.

ILLUSTRATION 18-2
Schedule of Interest Revenue and Bond Discount Amortization— Effective Interest Method

	8% Bonds Purchased to Yield 10%			
Date	Cash Received	Interest Revenue	Bond Discount Amortization	Carrying Amount of Bonds
1/1/95				$ 92,278
7/1/95	$ 4,000[a]	$ 4,614[b]	$ 614[c]	92,892[d]
1/1/96	4,000	4,645	645	93,537
7/1/96	4,000	4,677	677	94,214
1/1/97	4,000	4,711	711	94,925
7/1/97	4,000	4,746	746	95,671
1/1/98	4,000	4,783	783	96,454
7/1/98	4,000	4,823	823	97,277
1/1/99	4,000	4,864	864	98,141
7/1/99	4,000	4,907	907	99,048
1/1/00	4,000	4,952	952	100,000
	$40,000	$47,722	$7,722	

[a]$4,000 = $100,000 × .08 × 6/12
[b]$4,614 = $92,278 × .10 × 6/12
[c]$614 = $4,614 − $4,000
[d]$92,892 = $92,278 + $614

---

[3]The FASB defines situations where, even though a security is sold before maturity, it has constructively been held to maturity, and thus does not represent a violation of the held-to-maturity requirement. These include selling a security close enough to maturity (such as three months) so that interest rate risk is no longer an important pricing factor. Additionally, if the enterprise has already collected a substantial portion of the principal of the security (at least 85%) it is considered to have been held to its maturity date.

[4]Investments acquired at par, at a discount, or at a premium are generally recorded in the accounts at cost, including brokerage and other fees but excluding the accrued interest; generally they are not recorded at maturity value. The use of a separate discount or premium account as a valuation account is acceptable procedure for investments, but in practice it has not been widely used. This traditional exclusion of a separate discount or premium account has not yet changed even though *APB Opinion No. 21* recommends the disclosure of unamortized discount or premium on notes and bonds receivable.

As indicated in Chapter 14, the **effective interest method** is required unless some other method—such as the straight-line method—yields a similar result. The effective interest method is applied to bond investments in a fashion similar to that described for bonds payable. The effective interest rate or yield is computed at the time of investment and is applied to its beginning carrying amount (book value) for each interest period to compute interest revenue. The investment carrying amount is increased by the amortized discount or decreased by the amortized premium in each period.

The journal entry to record the receipt of the first semiannual interest payment on July 1, 1995 (using the data in Illustration 18-2), is:

July 1, 1995

Cash	4,000	
Held-to-Maturity Securities	614	
Interest Revenue		4,614

Because Robinson Company is on a calendar-year basis, it accrues interest and amortizes the discount at December 31, 1995, as follows:

December 31, 1995

Interest Receivable	4,000	
Held-to-Maturity Securities	645	
Interest Revenue		4,645

Again, the interest and amortization amounts are provided in Illustration 18-2.

Robinson Company would report the following items related to its investment in Evermaster bonds in its December 31, 1995, financial statements:

ILLUSTRATION 18-3
Reporting of Held-to-Maturity Securities

Balance Sheet	
Current assets	
Interest receivable	$ 4,000
Long-term investments	
Held-to-maturity securities, at amortized cost	$93,537
Income Statement	
Other revenues and gains	
Interest revenue	$ 9,259

The sale of a held-to-maturity debt security close enough to its maturity date that a change in the market interest rates would not significantly affect the security's fair value may be considered a sale at maturity. If Robinson Company sells its investment in Evermaster bonds on November 1, 1999, for example, at 99¾ plus accrued interest, the following computations and entries would be made. The discount amortization from July 1, 1999, to November 1, 1999, is $635 (⁴⁄₆ × $952). The entry to record this discount amortization is as follows:

November 1, 1999

Held-to-Maturity Securities	635	
Interest Revenue		635

The computation of the realized gain on the sale is shown in Illustration 18-4.

ILLUSTRATION 18-4
Computation of Gain on Sale of Bonds

Selling price of bonds (exclusive of accrued interest)		$99,750
Less: Book value of bonds on November 1, 1999:		
Amortized cost, July 1, 1999	$99,048	
Add: Discount amortized for the period July 1, 1999,		
to November 1, 1999	635	
		99,683
Gain on sale of bonds		$ 67

The entry to record the sale of the bonds is:

November 1, 1999

Cash	102,417	
Interest Revenue (⅘ × $4,000)		2,667
Held-to-Maturity Securities		99,683
Gain on Sale of Securities		67

The credit to Interest Revenue represents accrued interest for 4 months, for which the purchaser pays cash. The debit to Cash represents the selling price of the bonds, $99,750, plus accrued interest of $2,667. The credit to the Held-to-Maturity Securities account represents the book value of the bonds on the date of sale, and the credit to Gain on Sale of Securities represents the excess of the selling price over the book value of the bonds.

▶ AVAILABLE-FOR-SALE SECURITIES

Investments in debt securities that are in the **available-for-sale** category are reported at fair value. The unrealized gains and losses related to changes in the fair value of available-for-sale debt securities are recorded in an unrealized holding gain or loss account. This account is reported as a separate component of stockholders' equity until realized. Thus, **changes in fair value are not reported as part of net income until the security is sold.** This approach reduces the volatility of net income.

UNDERLYING
CONCEPT

Recognizing unrealized gains and losses is moving the profession closer to the concept of comprehensive income.

ILLUSTRATION: SINGLE SECURITY

To illustrate the accounting for available-for-sale securities, assume that Graff Corporation purchases $100,000, 10%, 5-year bonds on January 1, 1995, with interest payable on July 1 and January 1. The bonds sell for $108,111 which results in a bond premium of $8,111 and an effective interest rate of 8%.

The entry to record the purchase of the bonds is as follows:

January 1, 1995

Available-for-Sale Securities	108,111	
Cash		108,111

Illustration 18-5 discloses the effect of the premium amortization on the interest revenue recorded each period using the effective interest method.

ILLUSTRATION 18-5
Schedule of Interest Revenue and Bond Premium Amortization— Effective Interest Method

10% Bonds Purchased to Yield 8%				
Date	Cash Received	Interest Revenue	Bond Premium Amortization	Carrying Amount of Bonds
1/1/95				$108,111
7/1/95	$ 5,000[a]	$ 4,324[b]	$ 676[c]	107,435[d]
1/1/96	5,000	4,297	703	106,732
7/1/96	5,000	4,269	731	106,001
1/1/97	5,000	4,240	760	105,241
7/1/97	5,000	4,210	790	104,451
1/1/98	5,000	4,178	822	103,629
7/1/98	5,000	4,145	855	102,774
1/1/99	5,000	4,111	889	101,885
7/1/99	5,000	4,075	925	100,960
1/1/2000	5,000	4,040	960	100,000
	$50,000	$41,899	$8,111	

[a]$5,000 = $100,000 × .10 × 6/12
[b]$4,324 = $108,111 × .08 × 6/12
[c]$676 = $5,000 − $4,324
[d]$107,435 = $108,111 − $676

The entry to record interest revenue on July 1, 1995, would be as follows:

July 1, 1995

Cash	5,000	
Available-for-Sale Securities		676
Interest Revenue		4,324

At December 31, 1995, Graff would make the following entry to recognize interest revenue:

December 31, 1995

Interest Receivable	5,000	
Available-for-Sale Securities		703
Interest Revenue		4,297

As a result, Graff would report interest revenue for 1995 of $8,621 ($4,324 + $4,297).

To apply the fair value method to these debt securities, assume that at year-end the fair value of the bonds is $105,000. Comparing this fair value with the carrying amount (amortized cost) of the bonds at December 31, 1995, as shown in Illustration 18-5, Graff recognizes an unrealized holding loss of $1,732 ($106,732 − $105,000). This loss is reported as a separate component of stockholders' equity. The entry is as follows:

December 31, 1995

Unrealized Holding Gain or Loss—Equity	1,732	
Securities Fair Value Adjustment (Available-for-Sale)		1,732

A valuation account is used instead of crediting the Available-for-Sale Securities account. The use of the **Securities Fair Value Adjustment (Available-for-Sale)** account enables the company to maintain a record of its amortized cost. Because the adjustment account has a credit balance in this case, it is subtracted from the balance of the Available-for-Sale Securities account to arrive at fair value. The fair value is the amount reported on the balance sheet. At each reporting date, the bonds would be reported at fair value with an adjustment to the Unrealized Holding Gain or Loss—Equity account.

ILLUSTRATION: PORTFOLIO

To illustrate the accounting for a portfolio of securities, assume that Webb Corporation has two debt securities that are classified as available-for-sale. Illustration 18-6 provides information on amortized cost, fair value, and the amount of the unrealized gain or loss.

ILLUSTRATION 18-6
Computation of Securities Fair Value Adjustment—Available-for-Sale Securities (1996)

Available-for-Sale Debt Security Portfolio December 31, 1996			
Investments	Amortized Cost	Fair Value	Unrealized Gain (Loss)
Watson Corporation 8% bonds	$ 93,537	$103,600	$ 10,063
Anacomp Corporation 10% bonds	200,000	180,400	(19,600)
Total of portfolio	$293,537	$284,000	(9,537)
Previous securities fair value adjustment balance			0
Securities fair value adjustment—Cr.			$ (9,537)

The total fair value of Webb's available-for-sale portfolio is $284,000. The gross unrealized gains are $10,063 and the gross unrealized losses are $19,600 resulting in a net unrealized loss of $9,537. That is, the fair value of available-for-sale securities is $9,537 lower than its amortized cost. An adjusting entry is made to a valuation allowance to record the decrease in value and to record the loss as follows:

December 31, 1996

Unrealized Holding Gain or Loss—Equity	9,537	
Securities Fair Value Adjustment (Available-for-Sale)		9,537

The unrealized holding loss of $9,537 is reported as a reduction of stockholders' equity. As indicated earlier, unrealized holding gains and losses related to investments that are classified in the available-for-sale category are not included in net income.

SALE OF AVAILABLE-FOR-SALE SECURITIES

If bonds carried as investments in available-for-sale securities are sold before the maturity date, entries must be made to amortize the discount or premium to the date of sale and to remove from the Available-for-Sale Securities account the amortized cost of bonds sold. To illustrate, assume that the Webb Corporation sold the Watson bonds (from Illustration 18-6) on July 1, 1997, for $90,000. Assume that the entry to recognize the discount amortization and the receipt of interest through July 1, 1997, has been recorded and the amortized cost is $94,214. The computation of the realized loss is as follows:

Amortized cost (Watson bonds)	$94,214
Less: Selling price of bonds	90,000
Loss on sale of bonds	$ 4,214

ILLUSTRATION 18-7
Computation of Loss on Sale of Bonds

The entry to record the sale of the Watson bonds is as follows:

July 1, 1997

Cash	90,000	
Loss on Sale of Securities	4,214	
Available-for-Sale Securities		94,214

This realized loss is reported in the Other Expenses and Losses section of the income statement. Assuming no other purchases and sales of bonds in 1997, Webb Corporation prepares the following information on December 31, 1997:

ILLUSTRATION 18-8
Computation of Securities Fair Value Adjustment—Available-for-Sale (1997)

Available-for-Sale Debt Security Portfolio December 31, 1997			
Investments	Amortized Cost	Fair Value	Unrealized Gain (Loss)
Anacomp Corporation 10% bonds (total portfolio)	$200,000	$195,000	$(5,000)
Previous securities fair value adjustment balance—Cr.			(9,537)
Securities fair value adjustment—Dr.			$ 4,537

As shown in Illustration 18-8, Webb Corporation has an unrealized holding loss of $5,000. However, the Securities Fair Value Adjustment account already has a credit balance of $9,537. To reduce the adjustment account balance to $5,000, it is debited for $4,537, as follows:

December 31, 1997

Securities Fair Value Adjustment (Available-for-Sale)	4,537	
Unrealized Holding Gain or Loss—Equity		4,537

FINANCIAL STATEMENT PRESENTATION

Webb Corporation's December 31, 1997 balance sheet and the 1997 income statement would contain the following items and amounts (the Anacomp bonds are long-term investments but are not intended to be held-to-maturity):

ILLUSTRATION 18-9
Reporting of Available-
for-Sale Securities

Balance Sheet	
Current assets	
Interest receivable	$ xxx
Investments	
Available-for-sale securities, at fair value	$195,000
Stockholders' equity	
Unrealized holding loss on securities	$ 5,000
Income Statement	
Other revenues and gains	
Interest revenue	$ xxx
Other expenses and losses	
Loss on sale of securities	$ 4,214

Prior to the issuance of *SFAS No. 115*, the FASB appeared to favor including the unrealized holding gain or loss in income rather than showing it as a separate component of stockholders' equity. However, some companies, particularly financial institutions, noted that recognizing gains and losses on assets, but not liabilities, would introduce substantial volatility in income. They argued that often hedges exist between assets and liabilities so that gains in assets are offset by losses in liabilities, and vice versa. In short, to recognize gains and losses only on the asset side is unfair and not representative of the economic activities of the company.

This argument was convincing to the FASB. As a result, these unrealized gains and losses are **not included in income.** However, even this approach does not solve some of the problems, because volatility of capital still results. This is of concern to financial institutions because regulators restrict financial institutions' operations based upon their level of capital. In addition, companies can still manage their income by engaging in **gains trading** (i.e., selling the winners and holding the losers).

▶ TRADING SECURITIES

Trading securities are held with the intention of selling them in a short period of time. Trading in this context means frequent buying and selling, and trading securities are used to generate profits from short-term differences in price. The holding period for these securities is generally less than 3 months and more probably is measured in days or hours. **These securities are reported at fair value, with unrealized holding gains and losses reported as part of net income. Any discount or premium is not amortized.** A **holding gain or loss** is the net change in the fair value of a security from one period to another, exclusive of dividend or interest revenue recognized but not received. In short, the FASB says to adjust the trading securities to fair value, at each reporting date. In addition, the change in value is reported as part of net income, not equity.

To illustrate, assume that on December 31, 1996, Western Publishing Corporation determined its trading securities portfolio to be as shown in Illustration 18-10 (assume that 1996 is the first year that Western Publishing held trading securities). At the date of acquisition, these trading securities were recorded at cost, including brokerage commissions and taxes, in the account entitled Trading Securities. This is the first valuation of this recently purchased portfolio.

ILLUSTRATION 18-10
Computation of
Securities Fair Value
Adjustment—Trading
Securities Portfolio (1996)

Trading Debt Security Portfolio December 31, 1996			
Investments	Cost	Fair Value	Unrealized Gain (Loss)
Burlington Northern 10% bonds	$ 43,860	$ 51,500	$ 7,640
Chrysler Corporation 11% bonds	184,230	175,200	(9,030)
Time Warner 8% bonds	86,360	91,500	5,140
Total of portfolio	$314,450	$318,200	3,750
Previous securities fair value adjustment balance			0
Securities fair value adjustment—Dr.			$ 3,750

The total cost of Western's trading portfolio is $314,450. The gross unrealized gains are $12,780 ($7,640 + $5,140) and the gross unrealized losses are $9,030, resulting in a net unrealized gain of $3,750. The fair value of trading securities is $3,750 greater than its cost.

At December 31, an adjusting entry is made to a valuation allowance, referred to as Securities Fair Value Adjustment (Trading), to record the increase in value and to record the unrealized holding gain:

December 31, 1996

Securities Fair Value Adjustment (Trading)	3,750	
Unrealized Holding Gain or Loss—Income		3,750

Because the Securities Fair Value Adjustment account balance is a debit, it is added to the cost of the Trading Securities account to arrive at a fair value for the trading securities. The fair value of the securities is the amount reported on the balance sheet.

When securities are actively traded, the FASB believes that financial reporting is improved when the economic events affecting the company (changes in fair value) and related unrealized gains and losses are reported in the same period. Including changes in fair value in income provides more relevant information to current stockholders whose composition may be different next period.

▶ SECTION 2 / INVESTMENT IN EQUITY SECURITIES

Equity securities are described as securities representing ownership interests such as common, preferred, or other capital stock. They also include rights to acquire or dispose of ownership interests at an agreed upon or determinable price such as warrants, rights, and call options or put options. Convertible debt securities and redeemable preferred stocks are not treated as equity securities. When equity securities are purchased, their cost includes the purchase price of the security plus broker's commissions and other fees incidental to the purchase.

The degree to which one corporation (**investor**) acquires an interest in the common stock of another corporation (**investee**) generally determines the accounting treatment for the investment subsequent to acquisition. Investments by one corporation in the common stock of another can be classified according to the percentage of the voting stock of the investee held by the investor:

1. Holdings of less than 20% (fair value method)—investor has passive interest.
2. Holdings between 20% and 50% (equity method)—investor has significant influence.
3. Holdings of more than 50% (consolidated statements)—investor has controlling interest.

These levels of interest or influence and the corresponding valuation and reporting method that must be applied to the investment are graphically displayed in Illustration 18-11.

OBJECTIVE 2

Identify the categories of equity securities and describe the accounting and reporting treatment for each category.

INTERNATIONAL INSIGHT

Historically, consolidation practices in Europe differ in terms of how the group of companies is determined. The U.K. approach focuses on ownership and the legal right to control; in contrast, the German approach focuses on management control.

ILLUSTRATION 18-11
Levels of Influence Determine Accounting Methods

Percentage of Ownership	0% ⟵⟶	20% ⟵⟶	50% ⟵⟶	100%
Level of Influence	Little or None	Significant	Control	
Valuation Method	Fair Value Method	Equity Method	Consolidation	

The accounting and reporting for equity securities therefore depends upon the level of influence and the type of security involved, as shown in Illustration 18-12.

ILLUSTRATION 18-12
Accounting and
Reporting for Equity
Securities by Category

Category	Valuation	Unrealized Holding Gains or Losses	Other Income Effects
Holdings less than 20%			
1. Available-for-sale	Fair value	Recognized but included as separate component of stockholders' equity	Dividends declared; gains and losses from sale.
2. Trading	Fair value	Recognized in income	Dividends declared; gains and losses from sale.
Holdings between 20% and 50%	Equity	Not recognized	Proportionate shares of investee's net income (adjusted for appropriate amortization).
Holdings more than 50%	Consolidation	Not recognized	Not applicable

► HOLDINGS OF LESS THAN 20%

As mentioned earlier, equity securities are recorded at cost. In some cases, cost is difficult to determine. For example, equity securities acquired in **exchange for noncash consideration** (property or services) should be recorded at (1) the fair value of the consideration given or (2) the fair value of the security received, whichever is more clearly determinable. The absence of clearly determinable values for the property or services or a market price for the security acquired may require the use of appraisals or estimates to arrive at a cost.

The purchase of two or more classes of securities for a lump sum price calls for the allocation of the cost to the different classes in some equitable manner. If fair values (market prices) are available for each class of security, the lump sum cost may be apportioned on the basis of the **relative fair values.** If the market price is available for one security but not for the other, the **incremental method** may be used and the market price assigned to the one and the cost excess to the other. If market prices are not available at the date of acquisition of several securities, it may be necessary to defer cost apportionment until evidence of at least one value becomes available. In some instances cost apportionment may have to wait until one of the securities is sold. In such cases, the proceeds from the sale of the one security may be subtracted from the lump sum cost, leaving the residual cost to be assigned as the cost of the other.[5]

When an investor has an interest of less than 20%, it is presumed that the investor has little or no influence over the investee. In such cases, if market prices are available, the investment is valued and reported subsequent to acquisition using the **fair value method.**[6] The fair value method requires that companies classify equity securities at

---

[5]Accounting for numerous purchases of securities requires that information regarding the cost of individual purchases be preserved, as well as the dates of purchases and sales. If **specific identification** is not possible, the use of an **average cost** may be used for multiple purchases of the same class of security. The **first-in, first-out method** of assigning costs to investments at the time of sale is also acceptable and is normally employed.

[6]When market prices are not available, the investment is valued and reported at cost in periods subsequent to acquisition. This approach is often referred to as the **cost method.** Dividends are recognized as dividend revenue when received, and the portfolio is valued and reported at acquisition cost. No gains or losses are recognized until the securities are sold.

acquisition as **available-for-sale securities** or **trading securities.** Because equity securities have no maturity date, they cannot be classified as held-to-maturity.

AVAILABLE-FOR-SALE SECURITIES

Available-for-sale securities when acquired are recorded at cost. To illustrate, assume that on November 3, 1996, Republic Corporation purchased common stock of three companies, each investment representing less than a 20% interest:

	Cost
Northwest Industries, Inc.	$259,700
Campbell Soup Co.	317,500
St. Regis Pulp Co.	141,350
Total cost	$718,550

These investments would be recorded as follows:

November 3, 1996

Available-for-Sale Securities	718,550	
Cash		718,550

On December 6, 1996, Republic receives a cash dividend of $4,200 on its investment in the common stock of Campbell Soup Co. The cash dividend is recorded as follows:

December 6, 1996

Cash	4,200	
Dividend Revenue		4,200

All three of the investee companies reported net income for the year but only Campbell Soup declared and paid a dividend to Republic. But, as indicated before, when an investor owns less than 20% of the common stock of another corporation, it is presumed that the investor has relatively little influence on the investee. As a result, **net income earned by the investee is not considered a proper basis for recognizing income from the investment by the investor.** The reason is that the investee may choose to retain for use in the business increased net assets resulting from profitable operations. Therefore, **net income is not considered earned by the investor until cash dividends are declared by the investee.**

At December 31, 1996, Republic's available-for-sale equity security portfolio has the following cost and fair value:

Available-for-Sale Equity Security Portfolio December 31, 1996			
Investments	Cost	Fair Value	Unrealized Gain (Loss)
Northwest Industries, Inc.	$259,700	$275,000	$15,300
Campbell Soup Co.	317,500	304,000	(13,500)
St. Regis Pulp Co.	141,350	104,000	(37,350)
Total of portfolio	$718,550	$683,000	(35,550)
Previous securities fair value adjustment balance			0
Securities fair value adjustment—Cr.			$(35,550)

**ILLUSTRATION 18-13
Computation of
Securities Fair Value
Adjustment—Available-
for-Sale Equity Security
Portfolio (1996)**

For Republic's available-for-sale equity securities portfolio the gross unrealized gains are $15,300 and the gross unrealized losses are $50,850 ($13,500 + $37,350), resulting in a net unrealized loss of $35,550. The fair value of the available-for-sale securities portfolio is $35,550 less than its cost. As with available-for-sale **debt** securities, the net unrealized gains and losses related to changes in the fair value of available-for-sale **equity** securities are recorded in an Unrealized Holding Gain or Loss—Equity account that is reported as a **separate component of stockholders' equity until realized.** In this case, Republic prepares an adjusting entry debiting the Unrealized Holding Gain or Loss—Equity account and crediting the Securities Fair Value Adjustment account to record the decrease in fair value and to record the loss as follows:

December 31, 1996

Unrealized Holding Gain or Loss—Equity	35,550	
Securities Fair Value Adjustment		35,550

On January 23, 1997, Republic sold all of its Northwest Industries, Inc. common stock receiving net proceeds of $287,220. The realized gain on the sale is computed as follows:

**ILLUSTRATION 18-14
Computation of Gain on
Sale of Stock**

Net proceeds from sale	$287,220
Cost of Northwest shares	259,700
Gain on sale of stock	$ 27,520

The sale is recorded as follows:

January 23, 1997

Cash	287,220	
Available-for-Sale Securities		259,700
Gain on Sale of Stock		27,520

In addition, assume that on February 10, 1997, Republic purchased 20,000 shares of Continental Trucking at a market price of $12.75 per share plus brokerage commissions of $1,850 (total cost, $256,850).

On March 31, 1997, Republic's portfolio of available-for-sale securities is as follows:

**ILLUSTRATION 18-15
Computation of
Securities Fair Value
Adjustment—Available-
for-Sale Equity Security
Portfolio (1997)**

**Available-for-Sale Equity Security Portfolio
December 31, 1997**

Investments	Cost	Fair Value	Unrealized Gain (Loss)
Continental Trucking	$256,850	$278,350	$ 21,500
Campbell Soup Co.	317,500	362,550	45,050
St. Regis Pulp Co.	141,350	139,050	(2,300)
Total of portfolio	$715,700	$779,950	64,250
Previous securities fair value adjustment balance—Cr.			(35,550)
Securities fair value adjustment—Dr.			$ 99,800

At March 31, 1997, the fair value of Republic's available-for-sale equity securities portfolio exceeds cost by $64,250 (unrealized gain). The Securities Fair Value Adjustment account had a credit balance of $35,550 at December 31, 1996. To adjust Republic's December 31, 1997, available-for-sale portfolio to fair value requires that the Securities Fair Value Adjustment account be debited for $99,800 ($35,550 + $64,250). The entry to record this adjustment is as follows:

December 31, 1997

Securities Fair Value Adjustment (Available-for-Sale)	99,800	
Unrealized Holding Gain or Loss—Equity		99,800

TRADING SECURITIES

The accounting entries to record trading equity securities are the same as for available-for-sale equity securities except for recording the unrealized holding gain or loss. For trading equity securities, the unrealized holding gain or loss is **reported as part of net income.** Thus, the account title Unrealized Holding Gain or Loss—Income is used.

▶ HOLDINGS BETWEEN 20% AND 50%

Although an investor corporation may hold an interest of less than 50% in an investee corporation and thus not possess legal control, its "investment in voting stock gives it the ability to exercise **significant influence** over operating and financial policies of an investee."[7] To provide a guide for accounting for investors when 50% or less of the common voting stock is held and to develop an operational definition of "significant influence," the APB in *Opinion No. 18* noted that ability to exercise influence may be indicated in several ways. Examples would be: representation on the board of directors, participation in policy making processes, material intercompany transactions, interchange of managerial personnel, or technological dependency. Another important consideration is the extent of ownership by an investor in relation to the concentration of other shareholdings. However, substantial or majority ownership of the voting stock of an investee by another investor does not necessarily preclude the ability to exercise significant influence by the investor.[8]

Judgment is frequently required in determining whether an investment of 20% or more results in "significant influence" over the policies of an investee. In the late 1970s and early 1980s an increased number of "hostile" merger and takeover attempts created situations where "significant influence" over investees was difficult to determine. The FASB therefore provided examples of cases in which an investment of 20% or more might not enable an investor to exercise **significant influence:**

(a) The investee opposes the investor's acquisition of its stock. For example, the investee files suit against the investor, or files a complaint with a governmental regulatory agency.

(b) The investor and investee sign an agreement under which the investor surrenders significant shareholder rights. This commonly occurs when an investee is resisting a takeover attempt by the investor, and the investor agrees to limit its shareholding in the investee.

(c) The investor's ownership share does not result in "significant influence" because majority ownership of the investee is concentrated among a small group of shareholders who operate the investee without regard to the views of the investor.

(d) The investor needs or wants more financial information than that which is publicly issued by the investee, tries to obtain it from the investee, and fails.

(e) The investor tries and fails to obtain representation on the investee's board of directors.[9]

The FASB says this list of examples is not all-inclusive. It is meant to provide examples of the types of evidence requiring further analysis when determining whether or not an investor is able to exert "significant influence" over an investee.

---

[7]"The Equity Method of Accounting for Investments in Common Stock," *Opinions of the Accounting Principles Board No. 18* (New York: AICPA, 1971), par. 17.

[8]Ibid.

[9]"Criteria for Applying the Equity Method of Accounting for Investments in Common Stock," *Interpretations of the Financial Accounting Standards Board No. 35* (Stamford, Conn.: FASB, 1981).

To achieve a reasonable degree of uniformity in application of the "significant influence" criterion, the profession concluded that an investment (direct or indirect) of 20% or more of the voting stock of an investee should lead to a presumption that in the absence of evidence to the contrary, an investor has the ability to exercise significant influence over an investee.

In instances of "significant influence" (generally an investment of 20% or more), the investor is required to account for the investment using the **equity method.**

EQUITY METHOD

OBJECTIVE 3

Explain the equity method of accounting and compare it to the fair value method for equity securities.

Under the **equity method** a substantive economic relationship is acknowledged between the investor and the investee. The investment is originally recorded at the cost of the shares acquired but is subsequently adjusted each period for changes in the net assets of the investee. That is, the **investment's carrying amount is periodically increased (decreased) by the investor's proportionate share of the earnings (losses) of the investee and decreased by all dividends received by the investor from the investee.** The equity method recognizes that investee earnings increase investee net assets, and that investee losses and dividends decrease these net assets.

To illustrate the equity method and compare it with the fair value method, assume that Maxi Company purchases a 20% interest in Mini Company. To apply the fair value method in this example, assume that Maxi does not have the ability to exercise significant influence and the securities are classified as available-for-sale. Where the equity method is applied in this example, assume that the 20% interest permits Maxi to exercise significant influence. The entries are shown in Illustration 18-16.

**ILLUSTRATION 18-16
Comparison of Fair Value
Method and Equity
Methods**

**INTERNATIONAL
INSIGHT**

In the European Community the Seventh Directive requires the use of the equity method of accounting for investments in affiliates. However, there is still strong disagreement internationally concerning accounting for such investments. Currently, some nations (U.S., U.K., Japan) require the use of the equity method; others (Sweden, Switzerland) do not.

Entries by Maxi Company

Fair Value Method		Equity Method	

On January 2, 1996, Maxi Company acquired 48,000 shares (20% of Mini Company common stock) at a cost of $10 a share.

Available-for-Sale			Investment in		
Securities	480,000		Mini Stock	480,000	
Cash		480,000	Cash		480,000

For the year 1996, Mini Company reported net income of $200,000; Maxi Company's share is 20% or $40,000.

No entry			Investment in		
			Mini Stock	40,000	
			Revenue from investment		40,000

At December 31, 1996, the 48,000 shares of Mini Company have a fair value (market price) of $12 a share, or $576,000.

Securities Fair Value Adjustment			No entry	
(Available-for-Sale)	96,000			
Unrealized Holding Gain				
or Loss—Equity		96,000		

On January 28, 1997, Mini Company announced and paid a cash dividend of $100,000; Maxi Company received 20% or $20,000.

Cash	20,000		Cash	20,000	
Dividend Revenue		20,000	Investment in		
			Mini Stock		20,000

For the year 1997, Mini reported a net loss of $50,000; Maxi Company's share is 20% or $10,000.

No entry			Loss on Investment	10,000	
			Investment in Mini		
			Stock		10,000

At December 31, 1997, the Mini Company 48,000 shares have a fair value (market price) of $11 a share, or $528,000.

Unrealized Holding				
Gain or Loss—Equity	48,000		No entry	
Securities Fair Value Adjustment				
(Available-for-Sale)		48,000		

Note that under the fair value method only the cash dividends received from Mini Company are reported as revenue by Maxi Company. **The earning of net income by the investee is not considered a proper basis for recognition of income from the investment by the investor.** The reason is that increased net assets resulting from the investee's profitable operation may be permanently retained in the business by the investee. Therefore, revenue is not considered earned by the investor until dividends are received from the investee.

Under the equity method, Maxi Company reports as revenue its share of the net income reported by Mini Company; the cash dividends received from Mini Company are recorded as a decrease in the investment carrying value. As a result, the investor records its share of the net income of the investee in the year when it is earned. In this case, the investor can ensure that any net asset increases of the investee resulting from net income will be paid in dividends if desired. To wait until a dividend is received ignores the fact that the investor is better off if the investee has earned income.

Using dividends as a basis for recognizing income poses an additional problem. For example, assume that the investee reports a net loss, but the investor exerts influence to force a dividend payment from the investee. In this case, the investor reports income, even though the investee is experiencing a loss. **In other words, if dividends are used as a basis for recognizing income, the economics of the situation are not properly reported.**

UNDERLYING
CONCEPT

Revenue to be recognized should be earned and realized and realizable. A low level of ownership indicates that the income from an investee should be deferred until cash is received.

Expanded Illustration of the Equity Method

Under the equity method, periodic investor revenue consists of the investor's proportionate share of investee earnings (adjusted to eliminate intercompany gains and losses) and **amortization of the difference between the investor's initial cost and the investor's proportionate share of the underlying book value of the investee at date of acquisition.** And, if the investee's net income includes extraordinary items, the investor treats a proportionate share of the extraordinary items as an extraordinary item, rather than as ordinary investment revenue before extraordinary items.

Assume that on January 1, 1996, Investor Company purchased 250,000 shares of Investee Company's 1,000,000 shares of outstanding common stock for $8,500,000. Investee Company's total net worth or book value was $30,000,000 at the date of Investor Company's 25% investment. Investor Company thereby paid $1,000,000 [$8,500,000 − .25($30,000,000)] in excess of book value. It was determined that $600,000 of this is attributable to its share of **undervalued depreciable assets** of Investee Company and $400,000 to **unrecorded goodwill.** Investor Company estimated the average remaining life of the undervalued assets to be 10 years and decided upon a 40-year amortization period for goodwill (the maximum length of time allowed). For the year 1996, Investee Company reported net income of $2,800,000 including an extraordinary loss of $400,000, and paid dividends at June 30, 1996 of $500,000 and at December 31, 1996 of $900,000. The following entries would be recorded on the books of Investor Company to report its long-term investment using the equity method.

January 1, 1996

Investment in Investee Stock	8,500,000	
Cash		8,500,000
(To record the acquisition of 250,000 shares of Investee Company common stock)		

June 30, 1996

Cash	125,000	
Investment in Investee Stock		125,000
[To record dividend received ($500,000 × .25) from Investee Company]		

The entries on December 31, however, are more complex. In addition to the dividend received, Investor Company must recognize its share of Investee Company's income. **Both an ordinary and extraordinary component must be recorded** by Investor Company, because Investee Company's income includes both. Furthermore, Investor Company paid more than the book value for an interest in Investee Company's net assets. As a result, this additional cost must be allocated to the proper accounting period.

December 31, 1996

Investment in Investee Stock	700,000	
Loss from Investment (extraordinary)	100,000	
Revenue from Investment (ordinary)		800,000
[To record share of Investee Company ordinary		
income ($3,200,000 × .25) and extraordinary loss		
($400,000 × .25)]		

December 31, 1996

Cash	225,000	
Investment in Investee Stock		225,000
[To record dividend received ($900,000 × .25) from		
Investee Company]		

December 31, 1996

Revenue from Investment (ordinary)	70,000	
Investment in Investee Stock		70,000
(To record amortization of investment cost in excess		
of book value represented by:		

      Undervalued depreciable assets—$600,000 ÷ 10 = $60,000
      Unrecorded goodwill—$400,000 ÷ 40   =   10,000
         Total $70,000)

The investment in Investee Company is presented in the balance sheet of Investor Company at a carrying amount of $8,780,000 computed as shown below.

ILLUSTRATION 18-17
Computation of Investment Carrying Amount

Investment in Investee Company		
Acquisition cost, 1/1/96	$8,500,000	
Plus: Share of 1996 income before extraordinary item	800,000	$9,300,000
Less: Share of extraordinary loss	100,000	
Dividends received 6/30 and 12/31	350,000	
Amortization of undervalued depreciable assets	60,000	
Amortization of unrecorded goodwill	10,000	520,000
Carrying amount, 12/31/96		$8,780,000

In the preceding illustration the investment cost exceeded the underlying book value. In some cases, an investor may acquire an investment at a **cost less than the underlying book value.** In such cases specific assets are assumed to be **overvalued** and, if depreciable, the excess of the investee's book value over the investor's acquisition cost is amortized into investment revenue over the remaining lives of the assets. Investment revenue is increased under the presumption that the investee's net income as reported is actually understated because the investee is charging depreciation on overstated asset values.

Investee Losses Exceed Carrying Amount

If an investor's share of the investee's losses exceeds the carrying amount of the investment, should the investor recognize additional losses? Ordinarily the investor should discontinue applying the equity method and not recognize additional losses.

If the investor's potential loss is not limited to the amount of its original investment (by guarantee of the investee's obligations or other commitment to provide further financial support), however, or if imminent return to profitable operations by the investee appears to be assured, it is appropriate for the investor to recognize additional losses.[10]

---

[10]"The Equity Method of Accounting for Investments in Common Stock," op. cit., par. 19(i).

Changing From and To the Equity Method

If the investor level of influence of ownership falls below that necessary for continued use of the equity method, a change must be made to the fair value method. And an investment in common stock of an investee that has been accounted for by other than the equity method may become qualified for use of the equity method by an increase in the level of ownership. Both of these situations are discussed and illustrated in the appendix to this chapter.

Disclosures Required Under the Equity Method

The significance of an investment to the investor's financial position and operating results should determine the extent of disclosures. The following disclosures in the investor's financial statements generally apply to the equity method:

1. The name of each investee and the percentage of ownership of common stock.
2. The accounting policies of the investor with respect to investments in common stock.
3. The difference, if any, between the amount in the investment account and the amount of underlying equity in the net assets of the investee.
4. The aggregate value of each identified investment based on quoted market price (if available).
5. When investments of 20% or more interest are in the aggregate material in relation to the financial position and operating results of an investor, it may be necessary to present summarized information concerning assets, liabilities, and results of operations of the investees, either individually or in groups, as appropriate.

In addition, the investor is expected to disclose the reasons for **not** using the equity method in cases of 20% or more ownership interest and **for** using the equity method in cases of less than 20% ownership interest.

▶ HOLDINGS OF MORE THAN 50%

When one corporation acquires a voting interest of more than 50%—**controlling interest**—in another corporation, the investor corporation is referred to as the **parent** and the investee corporation as the **subsidiary.** The investment in the common stock of the subsidiary is presented as a long-term investment on the separate financial statements of the parent.

When the parent treats the subsidiary as an investment, **consolidated financial statements** are generally prepared instead of separate financial statements for the parent and the subsidiary. Consolidated financial statements disregard the distinction between separate legal entities and treat the parent and subsidiary corporations as a single economic entity. The subject of when and how to prepare consolidated financial statements is discussed extensively in advanced accounting. Whether or not consolidated financial statements are prepared, the investment in the subsidiary is generally accounted for on the parent's books **using the equity method** as explained in this chapter.

▶ FINANCIAL STATEMENT PRESENTATION OF INVESTMENTS

BALANCE SHEET

Companies are required to present individual amounts for the three categories of investments either on the balance sheet or in the related notes. Trading securities should be reported at aggregate fair value as current assets. Individual held-to-maturity and available-for-sale securities are classified as current or noncurrent depending upon the circumstances.

Held-to-maturity securities should be classified as current or noncurrent, based on the maturity date of the individual securities. Debt securities identified as available-for-sale should be classified as current or noncurrent, based on maturities and expectations as to sales and redemptions in the following year. Equity securities identified as available-for-sale should be classified as current if these securities are available for use in current operations. Thus, if the invested cash used to purchase the equity securities is considered a contingency fund to be used whenever a need arises, then the securities should be classified as current.

For securities classified as available-for-sale and separately for securities classified as held-to-maturity, a company should describe:

(a) Aggregate fair value, gross unrealized holding gains, gross unrealized losses, and amortized cost basis by major security type (debt and equity).

(b) Information about the contractual maturities of debt securities. Maturity information may be combined in appropriate groupings such as (1) within 1 year, (2) after 1 year through 5 years, (3) after 5 years through 10 years, and (4) after 10 years.

INCOME STATEMENT

For each period for which an income statement is presented, a company must disclose:

(a) The proceeds from sales of available-for-sale securities and the gross realized gains and gross realized losses on those sales.

(b) The basis on which cost was determined in computing realized gain or loss (that is, specific identification, average cost, or other method used).

(c) The gross gains and gross losses included in earnings from transfers of securities from the available-for-sale category into the trading category. Additional disclosure is also required for held-to-maturity securities sold or transferred.

(d) The change in net unrealized holding gain or loss on available-for-sale securities that has been included in the separate component of shareholders' equity during the period.

(e) The change in net unrealized holding gain or loss on trading securities that has been included in earnings during the period.

In classifying investments, management's expressed intent should be supported by evidence, such as the history of the company's investment activities, events subsequent to the balance sheet date, and the nature and purpose of the investment.

Companies have to be extremely careful with debt securities held-to-maturity. If a debt security in this category is sold prematurely, the sale may "taint" the entire held-to-maturity portfolio. That is, a management's statement regarding "intent" is no longer as credible and, therefore, the securities might have to be reclassified; this could lead to unfortunate consequences. An interesting by-product of this situation is that companies that wish to retire their debt securities early are finding it difficult to do so; the holder will not sell because the securities are classified as held-to-maturity.

Illustration 18-18 shows a financial statement presentation of debt and equity securities along with relevant note disclosures.

Mall Corporation

Excerpts from Balance Sheet
(in thousands)

Current assets		
Held-to-maturity securities, at amortized cost (Note 4)		$130,000
Available-for-sale securities, at fair value (Note 4)		710,000
Long-term investments		
Held-to-maturity securities, at amortized cost (Note 4)		$195,000
Available-for-sale securities, at fair value (Note 4)		785,000
Stockholders' equity		
Common stock	$500,000	
Additional paid-in capital	100,000	
Retained earnings	80,000	$680,000
Less: Unrealized holding loss on securities (Note 4)		16,250
Total stockholders' equity		$663,750

Excerpts from Income Statement

Income from operations	$600,000
Other revenue and gains	
Gain on sale of securities	50,000
Income before income tax	$650,000

Note 4: Investments.
The following is a summary of available-for-sale securities and held-to-maturity securities:

		Available-for-Sale Securities		
(in thousands)	Cost	Gross Unrealized Gains	Gross Unrealized Losses	Fair Value
December 31, 1996				
U.S. corporate securities	$850	$70	$20	$900
Other debt securities	250	25	5	270
Total debt securities	1,100	95	25	1,170
Equity securities	300	40	15	325
	$1,400	$135	$40	$1,495

		Held-to-Maturity Securities		
(in thousands)	Cost	Gross Unrealized Gains	Gross Unrealized Losses	Estimated Fair Value
December 31, 1996				
U.S. corporate securities	$250	$30	$15	$265
Other debt securities	75	5	10	70
	$325	$35	$25	$335

The gross realized gains on sales of available-for-sale securities totaled $50,000, $35,500, and $15,800 in 1996, 1995, and 1994, respectively. No gross realized losses occurred over this 3-year period. The net adjustment to unrealized holding gains (losses) on available-for-sale securities included as a separate component of shareholders' equity totaled $16,250, $10,000, and $8,500, in 1996, 1995, and 1994, respectively.

The amortized cost and estimated fair value of debt and marketable equity securities at December 31, 1996, by contractual maturity, are shown below.

(in thousands)	Cost	Fair Value
Available-for-Sale		
Due in one year or less	$700	$710
Due after one year through 3 years	275	320
Due after 3 years	125	140
	1,100	1,170
Equity securities	300	325
	$1,400	$1,495
Held-to-Maturity		
Due in one year or less	$130	$135
Due after one year through 3 years	110	115
Due after 3 years through 5 years	60	65
Due after 5 years	25	20
	$325	$335

▶ IMPAIRMENT OF VALUE

OBJECTIVE 5

Discuss the accounting for impairments of debt and equity investments.

Every investment should be evaluated at each reporting date to determine if it has suffered a loss in value that is other than temporary (**impairment**). A bankruptcy or a significant liquidity crisis being experienced by an investee are examples of situations in which a loss in value to the investor may be permanent. **If the decline is judged to be other than temporary, the cost basis of the individual security is written down to a new cost basis.** The amount of the writedown is accounted for as a realized loss and, therefore, included in net income.

For debt securities, the impairment test is to determine whether "it is probable that the investor will be unable to collect all amounts due according to the contractual terms." **For equity securities,** the guideline is less precise. Any time realizable value is lower than the carrying amount of the investment, an impairment must be considered. Factors involved are the length of time and the extent to which the fair value has been less than cost, the financial condition and near-term prospects of the issuer, and the intent and ability of the investor company to retain its investment to allow for any anticipated recovery in fair value.

To illustrate an impairment, assume that Strickler Company holds available-for-sale bond securities with a par value and amortized cost of $1 million. The fair value of these securities is $800,000. Strickler has previously reported an unrealized loss on these securities of $200,000 as a separate component of stockholder's equity. In evaluating the securities, Strickler now determines it probable that it will not be able to collect all amounts due. In this case, the unrealized loss of $200,000 will be reported as a loss on impairment of $200,000 and included in income, with the bonds stated at their new cost basis. The journal entry to record this impairment would be as follows:

Loss on Impairment	200,000	
Securities Fair Value Adjustment (Available-for-Sale)	200,000	
Unrealized Holding Gain or Loss—Equity		200,000
Available-for-Sale Securities		200,000

The new cost basis of the investment in debt securities is $800,000. Subsequent increases and decreases in the fair value of impaired available-for-sale securities are included as a separate component of stockholders' equity.[11]

The impairment test used for debt and equity securities is based on a fair value test. This test is slightly different from the impairment test for loans discussed in Appendix 14-A, which was based on discounted cash flows using the historical effective interest rate. The FASB rejected the discounted cash flow alternative for securities because of the availability of market price information.

▶ TRANSFERS BETWEEN CATEGORIES

OBJECTIVE 6

Describe the accounting for transfer of investment securities between categories.

Transfers between any of the categories are accounted for at fair value. Thus, if trading securities are transferred to held-to-maturity investments, the new investment (held-to-maturity) is recorded at the date of transfer at fair value in the new category. Similarly, if held-to-maturity investments are transferred to available-for-sale investments, the new investments (available-for-sale) are recorded at fair value. This "fair value" rule assures that a company cannot escape recognition of fair value simply by transferring securities to the held-to-maturity category. Illustration 18-19 summarizes the accounting treatment for transfers.

---

[11]Amortization of any discount related to the debt securities is not permitted after recording the impairment. The new cost basis of impaired held-to-maturity securities would not change unless additional impairment occurred.

Type of Transfer	Measurement Basis	Impact of Transfer on Stockholders' Equity	Impact of Transfer on Income
Transfer from Trading to Available-for-Sale*	Security transferred at fair value at the date of transfer, which is the new cost basis of the security.	None	None
Transfer from Available-for-Sale to Trading*	Security transferred at fair value at the date of transfer, which is the new cost basis of the security.	The unrealized gain or loss at the date of transfer carried as a separate component of stockholders' equity is reversed.	The unrealized gain or loss at the date of transfer is recognized in income.
Transfer from Held-to-Maturity to Available-for-Sale*	Security transferred at fair value at the date of transfer.	The separate component of stockholders' equity is increased or decreased by the unrealized gain or loss at the date of transfer.	None
Transfer from Available-for-Sale to Held-to-Maturity	Security transferred at fair value at the date of transfer.	The unrealized gain or loss at the date of transfer carried as a separate component of stockholders' equity is amortized over the remaining life of the security.	None

Statement No. 115 states that these types of transfers should be rare.

ILLUSTRATION 18-19
Accounting for Transfers

Four examples are provided below to illustrate the accounting entries necessary to record the transfer of securities.

EXAMPLE 1: TRANSFER FROM TRADING TO AVAILABLE-FOR-SALE

Assume that Morgan Bank decides to transfer its municipal bonds held in its trading portfolio to its available-for-sale portfolio as of December 31, 1995. Its portfolios before and after the transfer are as follows:

ILLUSTRATION 18-20
Transfer from Trading to Available-for-Sale Category

	Before Transfer					
	Trading Securities			Available-for-Sale Securities		
	Cost	Fair Value			Cost	Fair Value
U.S. government bonds	$100,000	$110,000	Equity securities		$110,000	$80,000
Municipal bonds	70,000	85,000				
	$170,000	$195,000				

	After Transfer					
	Trading Securities			Available-for-Sale Securities		
	Cost	Fair Value			Cost	Fair Value
U.S. government bonds	$100,000	$110,000	Equity securities		$110,000	$80,000
			Municipal bonds		85,000	85,000
					$195,000	$165,000

The municipal bonds are transferred to the available-for-sale category at fair value, which is the new cost basis of the security. When this transfer occurs, stockholders' equity and net income are not affected. Because the new cost basis of the transferred securities is now recorded at fair value, it is necessary to debit the Available-for-Sale Securities account to recognize the transfer. In addition, the Trading Securities account and related fair value adjustment balance are eliminated. The entry to record this transfer is as follows:

Available-for-Sale Securities	85,000	
Securities Fair Value Adjustment (Trading)		15,000
Trading Securities		70,000

EXAMPLE 2: TRANSFER FROM AVAILABLE-FOR-SALE TO TRADING

Assume that Halson Bank decided to transfer its municipal bonds held in its available-for-sale portfolio to its trading securities portfolio. Its portfolios before and after the transfer are as follows:

ILLUSTRATION 18-21 Transfer from Available-for-Sale to Trading Category

	Before Transfer					
	Available-for-Sale Securities				Trading Securities	
	Cost	Fair Value			Cost	Fair Value
Equity securities	$90,000	$100,000	(No securities in portfolio)			
Municipal bonds	80,000	75,000				
	$170,000	$175,000				

	After Transfer					
	Available-for-Sale Securities				Trading Securities	
	Cost	Fair Value			Cost	Fair Value
Equity securities	$90,000	$100,000	Municipal bonds		$75,000	$75,000

The municipal bonds are transferred to the trading security category at fair value, which is the new cost basis of the security. When this transfer occurs, the unrealized holding loss reported in stockholders' equity related to the municipal bonds is reversed, and the loss is recognized in income. The journal entry to record the unrealized holding loss in income is as follows:

Unrealized Holding Gain or Loss—Income	5,000	
Unrealized Holding Gain or Loss—Equity		5,000

In addition, it is necessary to increase the Trading Securities account and record the new cost basis. The journal entry is as follows:

Trading Securities	75,000	
Securities Fair Value Adjustment (Available-for-Sale)	5,000	
Available-for-Sale Securities		80,000

EXAMPLE 3: TRANSFER FROM HELD-TO-MATURITY TO AVAILABLE-FOR-SALE

Assume that Leisenring Corporation decides to transfer its corporate bonds in its held-to-maturity portfolio to its available-for-sale portfolio. The fair value of its corporate bonds is $90,000. Its portfolios before and after transfer are as follows:

Before Transfer

Held-to-Maturity Securities	Cost		Available-for-Sale Securities	Cost	Fair Value
Municipal bonds	$60,000	Equity securities		$100,000	$130,000
Corporate bonds	80,000				
	$140,000				

After Transfer

Held-to-Maturity Securities	Cost		Available-for-Sale Securities	Cost	Fair Value
Municipal bonds	$60,000	Equity securities		$100,000	$130,000
		Corporate bonds		90,000	90,000
				$190,000	$220,000

The corporate bonds are transferred to the available-for-sale category at fair value. When this transfer occurs, a Securities Fair Value Adjustment account is used to record the difference between cost and fair value. In addition, stockholders' equity is increased due to the recognition of the unrealized holding gain, but net income is not affected. The entry to record this transaction is as follows:

Securities Fair Value Adjustment (Available-for-Sale)	10,000	
Available-for-Sale Securities	80,000	
Unrealized Holding Gain or Loss—Equity		10,000
Held-to-Maturity Securities		80,000

Note that a Securities Fair Value Adjustment account is used here unlike the first two transfer situations. The reason: this account must equal the Unrealized Holding Gain or Loss-Equity account. In the first two transfers that situation does not result because the Unrealized Holding Gain or Loss—Income account is closed each reporting period.

EXAMPLE 4: TRANSFER FROM AVAILABLE-FOR-SALE TO HELD-TO-MATURITY

Assume that Fields Corporation decides to transfer its corporate bonds from available-for-sale to held-to-maturity as of December 31, 1995. The corporate bonds were sold at par of $100,000 and mature in 10 years. Fields' portfolios before and after the transfer are as follows:

Before Transfer

Available-for-Sale Securities	Cost	Fair Value		Held-to-Maturity Securities	Cost	Fair Value
Corporate bonds	$100,000	$104,000	(No securities in portfolio)			

After Transfer

Available-for-Sale Securities	Cost	Fair Value		Held-to-Maturity Securities	Cost	Fair Value
(No securities in portfolio)			Corporate bonds		$100,000	$104,000

The entry to record the transfer is as follows:

Securities Fair Value Adjustment (Held-to-Maturity)	4,000	
Held-to-Maturity Securities	100,000	
Securities Fair Value Adjustment (Available-for-Sale)		4,000
Available-for-Sale Securities		100,000

Upon transfer, the carrying value in the balance sheet and the unrealized holding gain of $4,000 reported in stockholders' equity will remain the same. Both the Securities Fair Value Adjustment (Held-to-Maturity) balance of $4,000 and the Unrealized Holding Gain—Equity of $4,000 are amortized over the remaining life of the bonds.

To illustrate this computation (assuming the straight-line method for amortization purposes), the financial statement effect is as follows:

ILLUSTRATION 18-24
Amortization
Adjustments

	Increase (Decrease) Income*
Amortization of fair value adjustment ($14,000 ÷ 10 years)	$(1,400)
Amortization of unrealized holding gain ($14,000 ÷ 10 years)	1,400
Net adjustment	$ –0–

*If the bonds originally sold at a premium or a discount, the premium or discount would have to be amortized over the remaining life of the bonds.

As a result, at maturity, the investment in corporate bonds is reported at $100,000 (its maturity value), and the unrealized holding gain is eliminated. Although held-to-maturity investments are generally reported at amortized cost, in this case due to the transfer, they are presented at an amount above cost. As a result, this presentation may be misleading to investors who assume that the balance sheet amounts are at amortized cost for held-to-maturity securities.

▶ FAIR VALUE ACCOUNTING CONTROVERSY

FASB Statement No. 115 leaves many issues unresolved. Many parties are dissatisfied with its results: some think it goes too far, others think it does not go far enough. In this section we look at some of the major unresolved issues.

MEASUREMENT BASED ON INTENT

Debt securities can be classified as held-to-maturity, available-for-sale, or trading. As a result, three identical debt securities could be reported in three different ways in the financial statements. Some argue such treatment is confusing. Furthermore, the held-to-maturity category is based solely on intent, which is a subjective evaluation. What is not subjective is the market price of the debt instrument, which is observable in the marketplace. In other words, the three classifications are subjective, and therefore arbitrary classifications will result.

GAINS TRADING

Certain debt securities can be classified as held-to-maturity and therefore reported at amortized cost; other debt and equity securities can be classified as available-for-sale and reported at fair value with the unrealized gain or loss reported as a component of stockholders' equity. In either case, a company can become involved in "gains trading" (also referred to as "cherry picking"). In gains trading, companies sell their "winners," reporting the gains in income, and hold on to the losers.

LIABILITIES NOT FAIRLY VALUED

Many argue that if the investments securities are going to be reported at fair value, so also should liabilities. They note that by recognizing changes in value on only one side (the asset side), a high degree of volatility can occur in the income and stockholders' equity amounts. It is further argued that financial institutions are involved in asset and liability management (not just asset management) and that viewing only one side may lead managers to make uneconomic decisions as a result of the accounting. Although the Board was sympathetic with this view, it noted that certain debt securities were still reported at amortized cost and that other types of securities were excluded from the scope of this standard. In addition, serious valuation issues arose in relation to some types of liabilities. As a result, liabilities were excluded from consideration.

SUBJECTIVITY OF FAIR VALUES

Some people question the relevance of fair value measures for investments in securities, arguing in favor of reporting based on amortized cost. They believe that amortized cost provides relevant information because it focuses on the decision to acquire the asset, the earning effects of that decision that will be realized over time, and the ultimate recoverable value of the asset. They argue that fair value ignores those concepts and focuses instead on the effects of transactions and events that do not involve the enterprise, reflecting opportunity gains and losses whose recognition in the financial statements is, in their view, not appropriate until they are realized.

► SUMMARY

The major debt and equity securities and their reporting treatment are summarized below.

Category	Balance Sheet	Income Statement
Trading (debt and equity securities)	Investments shown at fair value. Current assets.	Interest and dividends are recognized as revenue. Unrealized holding gains and losses are included in income.
Available-for-sale (debt and equity securities)	Investments shown at fair value. Current or long-term assets. Unrealized holding gains and losses are a separate component of stockholders' equity.	Interest and dividends are recognized as revenue. Unrealized holding gains and losses are **not** included in net income.
Held-to-maturity (debt securities)	Investments shown at amortized cost. Current or long-term assets.	Interest is recognized as revenue.
Equity method and/or consolidation (equity securities)	Investments are carried at cost, are periodically adjusted by the investor's share of the investee's earnings or losses, and are decreased by all dividends received from the investee. Classified long term.	Revenue is recognized to the extent of the investee's earnings or losses reported subsequent to the date of investment (adjusted by amortization of the difference between cost and underlying book value).

ILLUSTRATION 18-25 Summary of Treatment of Major Debt and Equity Securities

► SUMMARY OF LEARNING OBJECTIVES ◄

1. **Identify the three categories of debt securities and describe the accounting and reporting treatment for each category.** (1) *Held-to-maturity debt securities* are carried and reported at amortized cost. (2) *Trading debt securities* are valued for reporting purposes at fair value, with unrealized holding gains or losses included in income. (3) *Available-for-sale debt securities* are valued for reporting purposes at fair value, with unrealized holding gains or losses reported as a separate component of stockholders' equity.

2. **Identify the categories of equity securities and describe the accounting and reporting treatment for each category.** The degree to which one corporation (investor) acquires an interest in the common stock of another corporation (in-

vestee) generally determines the accounting treatment for the investment. Long-term investments by one corporation in the common stock of another can be classified according to the percentage of the voting stock of the investee held by the investor.

3. **Explain the equity method of accounting and compare it to the fair value method for equity securities.** Under the equity method a substantive economic relationship is acknowledged between the investor and the investee. The investment is originally recorded at cost but is subsequently adjusted each period for changes in the net assets of the investee. That is, the investment's carrying amount is periodically increased (decreased) by the investor's proportionate share of the earnings (losses) of the investee and decreased by all dividends received by the investor from the investee. Under the fair value method the equity investment is reported by the investor at fair value each reporting period irrespective of the investee's earnings or dividends paid to the investor. The equity method is applied to investment holdings between 20% and 50% of ownership, whereas the fair value method is applied to holdings below 20%.

4. **Describe the disclosure requirements for investments in debt and equity securities.** Trading securities should be reported at aggregate fair value as current assets. Individual held-to-maturity and available-for-sale securities are classified as current or noncurrent depending upon the circumstances. For available-for-sale and held-to-maturity securities, a company should describe: aggregate fair value, gross unrealized holding gains, gross unrealized losses, amortized cost basis by type (debt and equity), and information about the contractual maturity of debt securities. For the income statement, a company must disclose information about realized gains and losses and changes in unrealized holding gains and losses. In addition, proceeds from sales and the basis on which cost is determined should be reported.

5. **Discuss the accounting for impairments of debt and equity investments.** Impairments of debt and equity securities are losses in value that are determined to be other than temporary, are based on a fair value test, and are charged to income.

6. **Describe the accounting for transfer of investment securities between categories.** Transfers of securities between categories of investments are accounted for at fair value, with unrealized holding gains or losses treated in accordance with the nature of the transfer.

APPENDIX 18-A

CHANGING FROM AND TO THE EQUITY METHOD

▶ CHANGE FROM THE EQUITY METHOD

If the investor level of influence or ownership falls below that necessary for continued use of the equity method, a change must be made to the fair value method. The earnings or losses that were previously recognized by the investor under the equity method should **remain as part of the carrying amount** of the investment with no retroactive restatement to the new method.

When a change is made from the equity method to the fair value method, the cost basis for accounting purposes is the carrying amount of the investment at the date of the change. In addition, amortizing the excess of acquisition price over the proportionate share of book value acquired attributable to undervalued depreciable assets and unrecorded goodwill ceases when the change of methods occurs. In other words, the new method is applied in its entirety once the equity method is no longer appropriate. At the next reporting date, the investor should record the unrealized holding gain or loss to recognize the difference between the carrying amount and fair value.

OBJECTIVE 7

After studying Appendix 18-A, you should be able to: Make the computations and prepare the entries necessary to record a change from or to the equity method of accounting.

DIVIDENDS IN EXCESS OF EARNINGS

To the extent that dividends received by the investor in subsequent periods exceed its share of the investee's earnings for such periods (all periods following the change in method), they should be accounted for as a **reduction of the investment carrying amount**, rather than as revenue.

For example, using the data from the Investee/Investor illustration on pages 893–894, assume that on January 2, 1997, Investee Company sold 1,500,000 additional shares of its own common stock to the public, thereby reducing Investor Company's ownership from 25% to 10%. The net income (or loss) and dividends of Investee Company for the years 1997 through 1999 are as shown below.

Year	Investor's Share of Investee Income (Loss)	Investee Dividends Received by Investor
1997	$600,000	$ 400,000
1998	350,000	400,000
1999	–0–	210,000
Totals	$950,000	$1,010,000

ILLUSTRATION 18A-1
Income Earned and Dividends Received

Assuming a change from the equity method to the fair value method as of January 2, 1997, Investor Company's reported investment in Investee Company and its reported income would be as shown below.

Year	Dividend Revenue Recognized	Cumulative Excess of Share of Earnings Over Dividends Received	Investment at December 31
1997	$400,000	$200,000[a]	$8,780,000
1998	400,000	150,000[b]	8,780,000
1999	150,000	(60,000)[c]	8,780,000 − $60,000 = $8,720,000

[a]$600,000 − $400,000 = $200,000
[b]($350,000 − $400,000) + $200,000 = $150,000
[c]$150,000 − $210,000 = $(60,000)

ILLUSTRATION 18A-2
Impact on Investment Carrying Amount

The following entries would be recorded by Investor Company to recognize the above dividends and earnings data for the 3 years subsequent to the change in methods.

1997 and 1998

Cash	400,000	
Revenue from Investment		400,000
(To record dividend received from Investee Company)		

1999

Cash	210,000	
Available-for-Sale Securities		60,000
Revenue from Investment		150,000
(To record dividend revenue from Investee Company in 1999 and to recognize cumulative excess of dividends received over share of Investee earnings in periods subsequent to change from equity method.)		

▶ CHANGE TO THE EQUITY METHOD

When converting to the equity method, a retroactive adjustment is necessary. Such a change involves **adjusting retroactively** the carrying amount of the investment, results of current and prior operations, and retained earnings of the investor as if the equity method has been in effect during all of the preivous periods in which this investment was held.[1] When changing from the fair value method to the equity method, it is also necessary to eliminate any balances in the Unrealized Holding Gain or Loss—Equity account and the Securities Fair Value Adjustment account. In addition, the available-for-sale classification for this investment is eliminated, and the investment in stock under the equity method is recorded.

For example, on January 2, 1995, Amsted Corp. purchased for $500,000 cash 10% of the outstanding shares of Cable Company common stock. On that date, the net assets of Cable Company had a book value of $3,000,000. The excess of cost over the underlying equity in net assets of Cable Company is attributed to goodwill, which is amortized over 40 years. On January 2, 1997, Amsted Corp. purchased an additional 20% of Cable Company's stock for $1,200,000 cash when the book value of Cable's net assets was $4,000,000. Now having a 30% interest, Amsted Corp. must use the equity method. From January 2, 1995, to January 2, 1997, Amsted Corp. used the fair value method and categorized these securities as available-for-sale. At January 2, 1997, Amsted has a credit balance of $92,000 in its Unrealized Holding Gain or Loss—Equity account and a debit balance in its Securities Fair Value Adjustment account of the same amount. Assume that this adjustment was made on December 31, 1995. The net income reported by Cable Company and the Cable Company dividends received by Amsted during the period 1995 thorugh 1997 were as follows:

ILLUSTRATION 18A-3
Income Earned and
Dividends Received

Year	Cable Company Net Income	Cable Co. Dividends Paid to Amsted
1995	$ 500,000	$ 20,000
1996	1,000,000	30,000
1997	1,200,000	120,000

The journal entries recorded from January 2, 1995, through December 31, 1997, relative to Amsted Corp.'s investment in Cable Company, reflecting the data above and a change from the fair value method to the equity method, are as follows.[2]

January 2, 1995

Available-for-Sale Securities	500,000	
Cash		500,000
(To record the purchase of a 10% interest in Cable Company)		

December 31, 1995

Cash	20,000	
Dividend Revenue		20,000
(To record the receipt of cash dividends from Cable Company)		
Securities Fair Value Adjustment (Available-for-Sale)	92,000	
Unrealized Holding Gain or Loss-Equity		92,000
(To record increase in fair value of securities)		

December 31, 1996

Cash	30,000	
Dividend Revenue		30,000
(To record the receipt of cash dividends from Cable Company)		

---

[1]Ibid., par. 19(m).

[2]Adapted from Paul A. Pacter, "Applying APB Opinion No. 18—Equity Method," *Journal of Accountancy* (September 1971), pp. 59–60.

January 2, 1997

Investment in Cable Stock	1,290,000	
Cash		1,200,000
Retained Earnings		90,000

(To record the purchase of an additional interest in Cable Company and to reflect retroactively a change from the fair value method to the equity method of accounting for the investment. The $90,000 adjustment is computed as follows:

	1995	1996	Total
Amsted Corp. equity in earnings of Cable Company (10%)	$50,000	$100,000	$150,000
Amortization of excess of acquisition price over underlying equity [$500,000 − (10% × $3,000,000)] ÷ 40 years = $5,000 per year.	(5,000)	(5,000)	(10,000)
Dividend received	(20,000)	(30,000)	(50,000)
Prior period adjustment	$25,000	$ 65,000	$ 90,000

January 2, 1997

Investment in Cable Stock	500,000	
Available-for-Sale Securities		500,000

(To reclassify initial 10% interest to equity method)

January 2, 1997

Unrealized Holding Gain or Loss—Equity	92,000	
Securities Fair Value Adjustment (Available-for-Sale)		92,000

(To eliminate fair value accounts for change to equity method)

December 31, 1997

Investment in Cable Stock	345,000	
Revenue from Investment		345,000

[To record equity in earnings of Cable Company (30% of $1,200,000) less $15,000 amortization of goodwill[a]]

[a]Goodwill amortization includes $5,000 [$500,000 − (10% × $3,000,000) ÷ 40 years] from 1995 purchase of 10% interest plus $10,000 [$1,200,000 (20% × $4,000,000) ÷ 40 years] from 1997 purchase of 20% interest.

Cash	120,000	
Investment in Cable Stock		120,000

(To record the receipt of cash dividends from Cable Company)

Changing to the equity method is accomplished by placing the accounts related to and affected by the investment on the same basis as if the equity method had always been the basis of accounting for that investment.

▶ SUMMARY OF LEARNING OBJECTIVE FOR APP. 18-A ◀

7. Make the computations and prepare the entries necessary to record a change from or to the equity method of accounting. When changing from the equity method to the fair value method, the cost basis for accounting purposes is the carrying amount used for the investment at the date of change. The new method is applied in its entirety once the equity method is no longer appropriate. When changing to the equity method, a retroactive adjustment of the carrying amount, of results of current and past operations, and of retained earnings is necessary to make the accounts as if the equity method has been in effect during all of the periods in which the investment was held.

APPENDIX 18-B

SPECIAL ISSUES RELATED TO INVESTMENTS

Special issues relate to accounting for investments: (1) revenue from investments in equity securities; (2) dividends received in stock; (3) stock rights; (4) cash surrender value of life insurance; and (5) accounting for funds.

▶ REVENUE FROM INVESTMENTS IN EQUITY SECURITIES

OBJECTIVE 8

After studying Appendix 18-B, you should be able to: Discuss the special issues that relate to accounting for investments.

Revenue recognized from investments—whether under the equity, or the fair value methods—should be included in the income statement of the investor. Under the fair value method, the dividends received (or receivable if declared but unpaid) are reported as dividend revenue. Under the equity method, if the investee has extraordinary and prior period items reported during the period, the investor should report in a similar manner its **proportionate share** of the ordinary income, of the extraordinary items, and prior period adjustments unless separation into these components is considered immaterial.

The gains or losses on sales of investments also are factors in determining the net income for the period. The gain or loss resulting from the sale of long-term investments, unless it is the result of a major casualty, an expropriation, or the introduction of a new law prohibiting its ownership (which may be viewed as unusual and nonrecurring), is reported as **part of current income from operations** and is not an extraordinary item.

Dividends that are paid in some form of assets other than cash are called **property dividends.** In such instances, the fair market value of the property received becomes the basis for debiting an appropriate asset account and crediting Dividend Revenue.

Occasionally an investor receives a dividend that is in part, or entirely, a **liquidating dividend.**[1] The investor should reduce the investment account for the amount of the liquidating portion of the dividend and credit Dividend Revenue for the balance. To illustrate, assume that Donley Inc. purchases a 1% investment in Rodriguez Co. for $60,000 on December 31, 1995. In 1996, Rodriguez has no income but declares and pays a dividend of $3,000 to Donley. The entry by Donley to record this transaction is as follows:

Cash	3,000	
Available-for-Sale Securities		3,000

▶ DIVIDENDS RECEIVED IN STOCK

If the investee corporation declares a dividend distributable in its own stock of the same class, instead of in cash, each stockholder owns a larger number of shares but retains the same proportionate interest in the firm as before. The issuing corporation has distributed no assets; it has merely transferred a specified amount of retained earnings to paid-in capital, thus indicating that this amount will not provide a basis in the future for cash dividends.

---

[1]A company can receive a dividend from preacquisition retained earnings of the investee, which the investor should treat as a liquidating dividend. From the investee's point of view, however, it is not a liquidating dividend.

Shares received as a result of a stock dividend or stock split do not constitute revenue to the recipients. The reason they do not is that the recipients' interest in the issuing corporation is unchanged and the issuing corporation has not distributed any of its assets. The **recipient of such additional shares would make no formal entry,** but should make a memorandum entry and record a notation in the investments account to show that additional shares have been received.

Although no dollar amount is entered at the time of the receipt of stock dividends, the fact that additional shares have been received must be considered in computing the carrying amount of any shares sold. The cost of the original shares purchased (plus the effect of any adjustments under the equity method) now constitutes the total carrying amount of both those shares plus the additional shares received, because no price was paid for the additional shares. The carrying amount per share is computed by dividing the total shares into the carrying amount of the original shares purchased.

To illustrate, assume that 100 shares of Flemal Company common stock are purchased for $9,600, and that 2 years later the company issues to stockholders one additional share for every two shares held; 150 shares of stock that cost a total of $9,600 are then held. Therefore, if 60 shares are sold for $4,300, the carrying amount of the 60 shares would be computed as shown below, assuming that the investment has been accounted for under the fair value method.

Cost of 100 shares originally purchased	$9,600
Cost of 50 shares received as stock dividend	0
Carrying amount of 150 shares held	$9,600
Carrying amount per share is $9,600/150, or $64.	
Carrying amount of 60 shares sold is 60 × $64, or $3,840.	

ILLUSTRATION 18B-1
Computation of the Carrying Amount of Shares Received in a Stock Dividend

The entry to record the sale is:

Cash	4,300	
Available-for-Sale Securities		3,840
Gain on Sale of Stock		460

A total of 90 shares is still retained, and they are carried in the Available-for-Sale Securities account at $9,600 − $3,840, or $5,760. Thus the carrying amount for those shares remaining is also $64 per share, or a total of $5,760 for the 90 shares.

▶ STOCK RIGHTS

When a corporation is about to offer for sale additional shares of an issue already outstanding, it may forward to present holders of that issue certificates permitting them to purchase **additional shares in proportion to their present holdings.** These certificates represent rights to purchase additional shares and are called **stock rights.** In rights offerings, rights generally are issued on the basis of one right per share, but it may take many rights to purchase one new share.

The certificate representing the stock rights, called a **warrant,** states the number of shares that the holder of the right may purchase and also the price at which they may be purchased. If this price is less than the current market value of such shares, the rights have an intrinsic value, and from the time they are issued until they expire they may be purchased and sold like any other security.

Stock rights have three important dates:

1. The date the rights offering is announced.
2. The date as of which the certificates or rights are issued.
3. The date the rights expire.

From the date the right is announced until it is issued, the share of stock and the right are not separable, and the share is described as **rights-on.** After the certificate or right is received and up to the time it expires, the share and right can be sold separately. A share sold separately from an effective stock right is sold **ex-rights.**

When a right is received, the stockholders have actually received nothing that they did not have before, because the shares already owned brought them the right; they have received no distribution of the corporation assets. The carrying amount of the original shares held is now the carrying amount of those shares plus the rights, and it should be allocated between the two on the basis of their total market values at the time the rights are received. If the value allocated to the rights is maintained in a separate account, an entry would be made debiting Available-for-Sale Securities (Stock Rights) and crediting Available-for-Sale Securities.

DISPOSITION OF RIGHTS

The investor who receives rights to purchase additional shares has three alternatives:

1. To exercise the rights by purchasing additional stock.
2. To sell the rights.
3. To permit them to expire without selling or using them.

If the investor buys additional stock, the carrying amount of the original shares allocated to the rights becomes a part of the carrying amount of the new shares purchased. If the investor sells the rights, the allocated carrying amount compared with the selling price determines the gain or loss on sale. If the investor permits the rights to expire, a loss is suffered, and the investment should be reduced accordingly. The following example illustrates the problem involved.

ILLUSTRATION 18B-2
Cost Allocations to Stock
and to Rights

Shares owned before issuance of rights—100.
Cost of shares owned—$50 a share for a total cost of $5,000.
Rights received—one right for every share owned, or 100 rights; two
   rights are required to purchase one new share at $50.
Market value at date rights issued: Shares $60 a share
                                    Rights $3 a right

Total market value of shares (100 × $60)	$6,000
Total market value of rights (100 × $3)	300
Combined market value	$6,300

Cost allocated to stock: $\dfrac{\$6,000}{\$6,300} \times \$5,000 = \$4,761.90$

Cost allocated to rights: $\dfrac{\$300}{\$6,300} \times \$5,000 = \underline{\quad 238.10\quad}$

$\$5,000.00$

Cost allocated to each share of stock: $\dfrac{\$4,761.90}{100} = \$47.619$

Cost allocated to each right: $\dfrac{\$238.10}{100} = \$2.381$

The reduction in the carrying amount of the stock from $5,000 to $4,761.90 and the acquisition of the rights with an allocated cost of $238.10 would be recorded as follows:

Available-for-Sale Securities (Stock Rights)	238.10	
Available-for-Sale Securities		238.10

If some of the original shares are later sold, their cost for purposes of determining gain or loss on sale is $47.619 per share, as computed above. If 10 of the original shares are sold at $58 per share, the entry would be:

Cash	580.00	
Available-for-Sale Securities		476.19
Gain on Sale of Stock		103.81

ENTRIES FOR STOCK RIGHTS

Rights may be sold or used to purchase additional stock or permitted to expire. If 40 rights to purchase 20 shares of stock are sold at $3.00 each, the entry is:

Cash	120.00	
Available-for-Sale Securities (Stock Rights)		95.24
Gain on Sale of Stock Rights		24.76

The amount removed from the stock rights account is the amount allocated to 40 rights, 40 × $2.381.

If rights to purchase 20 shares of stock are exercised and 20 additional shares are purchased at the offer price of $50, the entry is:

Available-for-Sale Securities	1,095.24	
Cash		1,000.00
Available-for-Sale Securities (Stock Rights)		95.24

If these shares are sold in the future, their cost should be considered to be $1,095.24, or $54.762 per share—the price paid of $50 per share plus the amount allocated to two rights of $4.762.

If the remaining 20 rights are permitted to expire, the amount allocated to these rights should be removed from the general ledger account by this entry:

Loss on Expiration of Stock Rights	47.62	
Available-for-Sale Securities (Stock Rights)		47.62

The balances of the general ledger investment accounts are shown below.

Available-for-Sale Securities (Stock)

Purchase of original 100 shares @ $50 per share	5,000.00	Cost allocated to 100 rights received		238.10
Purchase of 20 shares by exercise of rights	1,095.24	Sale of 10 shares of original purchase		476.19
		Balance		5,380.95
	6,095.24			6,095.24
Balance	5,380.95*			

*Analysis of Balance:

90 shares of original purchase, at allocated cost of $47.619 per share	$4,285.71
20 shares purchased through exercise of rights, carried at $54.762 per share (cash paid of $50.00, plus $4.762 for allocated cost of two rights)	1,095.24
Balance of account, as above	$5,380.95

Available-for-Sale Securities (Stock Rights)

Cost allocated to 100 rights received	238.10	Sale of 40 rights		95.24
		Exercise of 40 rights		95.24
		Expiration of 20 rights		47.62
	238.10			238.10
Balance	–0–			

ILLUSTRATION 18B-3
Balances of General Ledger Investment Accounts

▶ CASH SURRENDER VALUE OF LIFE INSURANCE

There are many different kinds of insurance. The kinds usually carried by businesses include (1) casualty insurance, (2) liability insurance, and (3) life insurance. Certain types of **life insurance** constitute an investment, whereas casualty insurance and liability insurance do not. The three common types of life insurance policies that companies often carry on the lives of their principal officers are (a) **ordinary life,** (b) **limited payment,** and (c) **term insurance.** During the period that ordinary life and limited payment policies are in force, there is a cash surrender value and a loan value. Term insurance ordinarily has no cash surrender value or loan value.

If the insured officers or their heirs are the beneficiaries of the policy, the premiums paid by the company represent expense to the company and, for income tax purposes, income (excluding the first $50,000) to the officer insured. In this case the cash surrender value of the policy does not represent an asset to the company.

If the company, however, is the beneficiary and has the right to cancel the policy at its own option, the cash surrender value of the policy or policies is an asset of the company. Accordingly, part of the premiums paid is not an expense, because the cash surrender value increases each year. Only the difference between the premium paid and the increase in cash surrender value represents expense to the company.

For example, if Zima Corporation pays an insurance premium of $2,300 on a $100,000 policy covering its president and, as a result, the cash surrender value of the policy increases from $15,000 to $16,400 during the period, the entry to record the premium payment is:

Life Insurance Expense	900	
Cash Surrender Value of Life Insurance	1,400	
Cash		2,300

If the insured officer were to die halfway through the most recent period of coverage for which the $2,300 premium payment was made, the following entry would be made (assuming cash surrender value of $15,700 and refund of a pro rata share of the premium paid):

Cash [$100,000 + (1/2 of $2,300)]	101,150	
Cash Surrender Value of Life Insurance		16,400
Life Insurance Expense (1/2 × $900)		450
Gain on Life Insurance Coverage ($100,000 − $15,700)		84,300

The gain on life insurance coverage is not generally reported as an extraordinary item because it is considered to be a "normal" business transaction.

The cash surrender value of such life insurance policies should be reported in the balance sheet as a **long-term investment,** inasmuch as it is unlikely that the policies will be surrendered and canceled in the immediate future. The premium is not deductible for tax purposes, however, and the proceeds of such policies are not taxable as income.

To illustrate such a disclosure, Alico Inc. reported information related to its cash surrender value as follows:

ILLUSTRATION 18B-4 Disclosure of Cash Surrender Value

Alico Inc.

Other investments (Note 4)	
Cash surrender value of life insurance	$448,000

Note 4. The company purchased as owner and beneficiary, individual life insurance policies on the lives of such officers and employees as a means of funding substantially all of such additional benefits. The company's accounting policy with respect to such insurance coverage is to charge operations with the annual premium cost, net of increase in cash surrender value.

▶ FUNDS

Assets may be set aside in special funds for specific purposes and, therefore, become unavailable for ordinary operations of the business. Assets segregated in the special funds are then available when needed for the intended purposes.

There are two general types of funds: (1) those in which cash is set aside to meet specific current obligations, and (2) those that are not directly related to current operations and are therefore in the nature of long-term investments.

Several funds of the first type, discussed in preceding chapters, include the following:

Fund	Purpose
Petty Cash Fund	Payment of small expenditures, in currency
Payroll Cash Account	Payment of salaries and wages
Dividend Cash Account	Payment of dividends
Interest Fund	Payment of interest on long-term debt

In general, these funds are used to handle more expeditiously the payments of certain current obligations, to maintain better control over such expenditures, and to divide adequately the responsibility for cash disbursements. They are ordinarily shown as current assets (as part of Cash if immaterial), because the obligations to which they relate are ordinarily current liabilities.

Funds of the second type are similar to long-term investments, as they do not relate directly to current operations. They are ordinarily shown in the long-term investments section of the balance sheet or in a separate section if relatively large in amount. The more common funds of this type and the purpose of each are listed below:

Fund	Purpose
Sinking Fund	Payment of long-term debt
Plant Expansion Fund	Purchase or construction of additional plant
Stock Redemption Fund	Retirement of capital stock (usually preferred stock)
Contingency Fund	Payment of unforeseen obligations

Because the cash set aside will not be needed until some time in the future, it is usually invested in securities so that revenue may be earned on the fund assets. The assets of a fund may or may not be placed in the hands of a trustee. If appointed, the trustee becomes the custodian of the assets, accounts to the company for them, and reports fund revenues and expenses.

ENTRIES FOR FUNDS

To keep track of the assets, revenues, and expenses of funds, it is desirable to maintain separate accounts. For example, if a fund is kept for the redemption of a preferred stock issue that was issued with a redemption provision at par after a certain date, the following accounts relating to that fund might be kept:

Stock Redemption Fund Cash

Stock Redemption Fund Investments

Stock Redemption Fund Revenue

Stock Redemption Fund Expense

Gain on Sale of Stock Redemption Fund Investments

Loss on Sale of Stock Redemption Fund Investments

When cash is transferred from the regular cash account, perhaps periodically, the entry is:

Stock Redemption Fund Cash	30,000	
Cash		30,000

Securities purchased by the fund are recorded at cost:

Stock Redemption Fund Investments	27,000	
Stock Redemption Fund Cash		27,000

If securities purchased for the fund are to be held temporarily, they would be treated in the accounts in the same manner as temporary investments, described earlier in this chapter. If they are to be held for a long period of time, they are treated in accordance with the entries described for long-term investments. In both cases the securities purchased are recorded at cost when acquired, but if bonds are purchased as long-term investments for the fund, premium or discount should be amortized.

If we assume that the entry above records the purchase at a premium of 10-year bonds of a par value of $25,000 on April 1, the issue date, and that the bonds bear interest at 8%, the entry for the receipt of semiannual interest on October 1 is:

Stock Redemption Fund Cash	1,000	
Stock Redemption Fund Revenue		1,000

At December 31, entries are made to record amortization of premium for 9 months and to accrue interest on the bonds for 3 months:

Stock Redemption Fund Revenue	150	
Stock Redemption Fund Investments		150
(To record amortization of premium for 9 months, 9/12 of 1/10 of $2,000)		

Interest Receivable on Stock Redemption		
Fund Investments	500	
Stock Redemption Fund Revenue		500
(To record accrued interest for		
3 months, 3/12 of 8% of $25,000)		

Expenses of the fund paid are recorded by debiting Stock Redemption Fund Expenses and crediting Stock Redemption Fund Cash.

When the investments held by the fund are disposed of, the entries to record the sale are similar to regular stock sales. Any revenue and expense accounts set up to record fund transactions should be closed to Income Summary at the end of the accounting period and reflected in earnings of the current period.

The entry for retirement of the preferred stock is:

Preferred Stock	500,000	
Stock Redemption Fund Cash		500,000

Any balance remaining in the Stock Redemption Fund Cash account is transferred back to a general cash account.

In some cases, a company purchases its own stock or bonds when it is using a stock redemption fund or sinking fund. In these situations, the treasury stock should be deducted from common stock (or the Stockholders' Equity section), and treasury bonds should be deducted from bonds payable. Dividend revenue or interest revenue should not be recorded for these securities.

DISTINCTION BETWEEN FUNDS AND RESERVES

Although funds and reserves (appropriations) are not similar, they are sometimes confused because they may be related and often have similar titles. A simple distinction may be drawn: **A fund is always an asset and always has a debit balance; a reserve (if used only in the limited sense recommended) is an appropriation of retained earnings, always has a credit balance, and is never an asset.**

This distinction is illustrated by reconsidering the entries made in connection with a stock redemption fund discussed earlier. The fund was originally established by the entry:

Stock Redemption Fund Cash	30,000	
Cash		30,000

Some of this cash was used to purchase investments; the assets of the fund were then cash and investments. Ultimately the investments were sold, and the stock redemption fund cash was used to retire the preferred stock.

If the company chose to do so, it could establish an appropriation for stock redemption at the same time to reduce the retained earnings apparently available for dividends. Appropriated retained earnings is established by periodic transfers from retained earnings, as follows:

Retained Earnings	30,000	
Appropriation for Stock Redemption		30,000

It will have a credit balance and will be shown in the stockholders' equity section of the balance sheet. When the stock is retired by payment of cash from the stock redemption fund, the appropriation is transferred back to retained earnings:

Appropriation for Stock Redemption	500,000	
Retained Earnings		500,000

The fund was an asset accumulated to retire stock and had a debit balance; the appropriation was a subdivision of retained earnings and had a credit balance. The fund was used to redeem the stock; the appropriation was transferred back to retained earnings.

> ▶ **SUMMARY OF LEARNING OBJECTIVE FOR APP. 18-B** ◀
>
> 8. **Discuss the special issues that relate to accounting for investments.** The special issues that relate to investments are: recognizing revenue from investments in equity securities; recognizing dividends received in shares of stock (stock dividends and stock splits); allocating cost between stocks and stock rights; accounting for changes in the cash surrender value of life insurance; and accounting for assets set aside in special funds.

Note: All **asterisked** Questions, Exercises, Problems, and Cases relate to material contained in the appendix to each chapter.

QUESTIONS

1. Distinguish between a debt security and an equity security.

2. What purpose does the variety in bond features (types and characteristics) serve?

3. What is the cost of a long-term investment in bonds?

4. What are the problems of accounting for bond investments between interest dates?

5. Identify and explain the three types of classifications for investments in debt securities.

6. At what amount should trading, available-for-sale, and held-to-maturity securities be reported on the balance sheet?

7. Indicate how unrealized holding gains and losses should be reported for investment securities classified as trading, available-for-sale, and held-to-maturity.

8. (a) Assuming no Securities Fair Value Adjustment (Available-for-Sale) account balance at the beginning of the year, prepare the adjusting entry at the end of the year if Sharp Company has an unrealized holding loss of $60,000 on its available-for-sale securities. (b) Assume the same information as part (a), except that Sharp Company has a debit balance in its Securities Fair Value Adjustment (Available-for-Sale) account of $10,000 at the beginning of the year. Prepare the adjusting entry at year-end.

9. On July 1, 1996, Chen Company purchased $1,000,000 of Swift Company's 8% bonds, due on July 1, 2003. The bonds, which pay interest semiannually on January 1 and July 1, were purchased for $875,000 to yield 10%. Determine the amount of interest revenue Chen should report on its income statement for year ended December 31, 1996.

10. If the bonds in question 9 are classified as available-for-sale and they have a fair value at December 31, 1996, of $901,000, prepare the journal entry (if any) at December 31, 1996, to record this transaction.

11. How is the premium or discount handled relative to a trading debt security?

12. On what basis should stock acquired or exchanged for noncash consideration be recorded?

13. Identify and explain the different types of classifications for investment in equity securities.

14. Why are held-to-maturity investments applicable only to debt securities?

15. Box Hunter Company sold 10,000 shares of Gibbons Co. common stock for $26.50 per share, incurring $1,770 in brokerage commissions. These securities were classified as trading and originally cost $250,000. Prepare the entry to record the sale of these securities.

16. Distinguish between the accounting treatment for available-for-sale equity securities and trading equity securities.

17. What constitutes "significant influence" when an investor's financial interest is below the 50% level?

18. Distinguish between the fair value and equity method of accounting for long-term investments in stocks subsequent to the date of acquisition.

19. When the equity method is applied, what disclosures should be made in the investor's financial statements?

20. Sack Co. uses the equity method to account for investments in common stock. What accounting should be made for dividends received in excess of Sack's share of investee's earnings subsequent to the date of investment?

21. Patrick Inc. uses the equity method to account for investments in Kennedy common stock. The purchase price paid by Patrick implies a fair value of Kennedy's depreciable assets in excess of Kennedy's net asset carrying values. How should Patrick account for this excess?

22. In applying the equity method, what recognition, if any, does the investor give to the excess of its investment cost over its proportionate share of the investee book value at the date of acquisition? What recognition, if any, is given if the investment cost is less than the underlying book value?

23. Delaney Corp. has an investment carrying value (equity method) on its books of $170,000 representing a 40% interest in Norton Company, which suffered a $600,000 loss this year. How should Delaney Corp. handle its proportionate share of Norton's loss?

24. Where on the balance sheet are trading securities, available-for-sale securities, and held-to-maturity securities reported? Explain.

25. When an income statement is prepared, what types of disclosures are required for debt and equity securities?

26. When is a debt security considered impaired? Explain how to account for the impairment of an available-for-sale debt security.

27. Frank Company reclassifies a bond currently included in the trading security category to the available-for-sale category. Prepare the journal entry (if any) to record this transfer, assuming that the bond has a cost of $45,000 and a fair value of $40,000.

28. Thomas Company transfers bond investments costing $850,000 (fair value $890,000) from the available-for-sale category to the held-to-maturity category. Prepare the journal entry to record this transfer.

*29. Mohs Inc. gradually acquired stock in Stein Corp. (a nonsubsidiary) until its ownership exceeded 20%. How is this investment recorded and reported after the last purchase?

*30. How is a stock dividend accounted for by the recipient? How is a stock split accounted for by the recipient?

*31. What three dates are significant in relation to stock rights? What are the alternatives available to the recipient of stock rights?

*32. Henshaw Co. owns 300 shares of Warren Corporation common stock acquired on June 10, 1996 at a total cost of $11,000. On December 2, 1997, Henshaw received 300 stock rights from Warren. Each right entitles the holder to acquire one share of stock for $45. The market price of Warren's stock on this date, ex-rights, was $50, and the market price of each right was $5. Henshaw sold its rights the same date for $5 a right less a $90 commission. Determine the gain on sale of the rights by Henshaw.

*33. Distinguish between a fund and a reserve.

*34. What are the two general types of funds? Give three examples of each type of fund.

EXERCISES

E18-1 (Entries for Debt Securities) Presented below are two independent situations:

Situation I
On January 1, 1995, the Brown Company purchased at par $200,000 of 10%, 10-year bonds. Interest is received quarterly on April 1, July 1, September 1, and January 1. Brown does not intend to hold these bonds to maturity.

Situation II
On June 1, 1995, the Northcutt Company purchased at par plus accrued interest $100,000 of 9%, 10-year bonds dated January 1. Interest is received annually on July 1 and January 1. Northcutt intends to hold these bonds to maturity.

Instructions
For each of these two situations, present journal entries to record:
  (a) The purchase of the bonds.
  (b) The receipt of interest on July 1.
  (c) The accrual of interest on December 31.

E18-2 (Entries for Held-to-Maturity Securities) On January 1, 1995, Sampson Company purchased 12% bonds, having a maturity value of $300,000, for $322,744.44. The bonds provide the bondholders with a 10% yield. They are dated January 1, 1995, and mature January 1, 2000, with interest receivable December 31 of each year. Sampson uses the effective interest method to allocate unamortized discount or premium. The bonds are classified in the held-to-maturity category.

Instructions
(a) Prepare the journal entry at the date of the bond purchase.
(b) Prepare a bond amortization schedule.
(c) Prepare the journal entry to record the interest received and the amortization for 1995.
(d) Prepare the journal entry to record the interest received and the amortization for 1997.

E18-3 (Entries for Available-for-Sale Securities) Assume the same information as in Exercise 18-2 except that the securities are classified as available-for-sale. The fair value of the bonds at December 31 of each year-end is as follows:

1995	$321,000	1998	$310,000
1996	$309,000	1999	$300,000
1997	$308,000		

Instructions
(a) Prepare the journal entry at the date of the bond purchase.
(b) Prepare the journal entries to record the interest received and recognition of fair value for 1995.
(c) Prepare the journal entry to record the recognition of fair value for 1996.

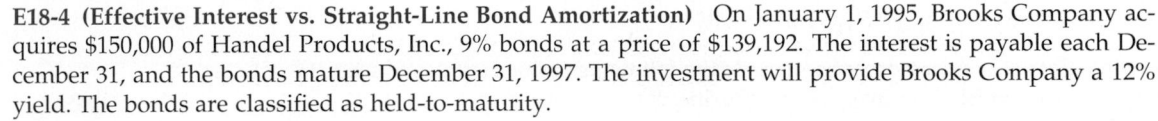

E18-4 (Effective Interest vs. Straight-Line Bond Amortization) On January 1, 1995, Brooks Company acquires $150,000 of Handel Products, Inc., 9% bonds at a price of $139,192. The interest is payable each December 31, and the bonds mature December 31, 1997. The investment will provide Brooks Company a 12% yield. The bonds are classified as held-to-maturity.

Instructions
(a) Prepare a 3-year schedule of interest revenue and bond discount amortization, applying the straight-line method.
(b) Prepare a 3-year schedule of interest revenue and bond discount amortization, applying the effective interest method.
(c) Prepare the journal entry for the interest receipt of December 31, 1996, and the discount amortization under the straight-line method.
(d) Prepare the journal entry for the interest receipt of December 31, 1996, and the discount amortization under the effective interest method.

E18-5 (Trading Securities Entries and Reporting) Cost and fair value data for the trading debt and equity securities portfolio of the Michelle Company at December 31 are $62,000 and $65,000, respectively.

Instructions
(a) Prepare the adjusting entry to report the securities properly.
(b) Prepare the balance sheet and income statement presentations with the accompanying note for these securities investments.

E18-6 (Trading Securities Entries) On December 31, 1995, Wildcat Company provided you with the following information regarding its trading securities.

December 31, 1995

Investments (Trading)	Cost	Fair Value	Unrealized Gain (Loss)
Mendota Corp. stock	$20,000	$19,000	$(1,000)
Waubesa Co. stock	10,000	9,000	(1,000)
Wantco stock	20,000	20,600	600
Total of portfolio	$50,000	$48,600	(1,400)
Previous securities fair value adjustment balance			–0–
Securities Fair Value adjustment—Cr.			$(1,400)

During 1996, Waubesa Company stock was sold for $9,200. The fair value of the stock on December 31, 1996, was: Mendota Corp. stock—$19,000; Wantco Co. stock—$20,500.

Instructions
(a) Prepare the adjusting journal entry needed on December 31, 1995.
(b) Prepare the journal entry to record the sale of the Waubesa Company stock during 1996.
(c) Prepare the adjusting journal entry needed on December 31, 1996.

E18-7 (Available-for-Sale Securities Entries and Reporting) The Duggen Corporation purchases equity securities costing $72,000 and classifies them as available-for-sale securities. At December 31, the fair value of the portfolio is $65,000.

Instructions
Prepare the adjusting entry to report the securities properly. Indicate the statement presentation of the accounts in your entry.

E18-8 (Available-for-Sale Securities Entries and Financial Statement Presentation) At December 31, 1994, the available-for-sale equity security portfolio for Nielson, Inc., is as follows:

Security	Cost	Fair Value	Unrealized Gain(Loss)
A	$17,500	$15,000	($2,500)
B	12,500	14,000	1,500
C	23,000	25,500	2,500
Total	$53,000	$54,500	1,500
Previous securities fair value adjustment balance—Dr.			500
Securities fair value adjustment account—Dr.			$1,000

On January 20, 1995, Nielson, Inc. sold security A for $14,900. The sale proceeds are net of brokerage fees.

Instructions
   (a) Prepare the adjusting entry at December 31, 1994, to report the portfolio at fair value.
   (b) Show the proper financial statement presentation of the investment related accounts at December 31, 1994. (Ignore notes presentation)
   (c) Prepare the journal entry for the 1995 sale of security A.

E18-9 (Equity Securities Entries) Acer Corporation made the following cash purchases of securities during 1995, which is the first year in which Acer invested in securities:

   1. On January 15, purchased 10,000 shares of Ellis Company's common stock at $32.50 per share plus commission $1,980.
   2. On April 1, purchased 5,000 shares of Cambridge Co.'s common stock at $52.00 per share plus commission $3,370.
   3. On September 10, purchased 7,000 shares of Forest Co.'s preferred stock at $26.50 per share plus commission $4,910.

On May 20, 1995, Acer sold 4,000 shares of Ellis Company's common stock at a market price of $35 per share less brokerage commissions, taxes, and fees of $3,850. The year-end fair values per share were: Ellis $30, Cambridge $55, and Forest $28. In addition, the chief accountant of Acer told you that Acer Corporation holds these securities with the intention of selling them in order to earn profits from appreciation in prices.

Instructions
   (a) Prepare the journal entries to record the above three security purchases.
   (b) Prepare the journal entry for the security sale on May 20.
   (c) Compute the unrealized gains or losses and prepare the adjusting entries for Acer on December 31, 1995.

E18-10 (Journal Entries for Fair Value and Equity Methods) Presented below are two independent situations:

Situation I
Karen Cosmetics acquired 10% of the 200,000 shares of common stock of Bell Fashion at a total cost of $12 per share on March 18, 1995. On June 30, Bell declared and paid a $75,000 cash dividend. On December 31, Bell reported net income of $122,000 for the year. At December 31, the market price of Bell Fashion was $15 per share. The securities are classified as available-for-sale.

Situation II
Barb, Inc., obtained significant influence over Diner Corporation by buying 30% of Diner's 30,000 outstanding shares of common stock at a total cost of $9 per share on January 1, 1995. On June 15, Diner declared and paid a cash dividend of $35,000. On December 31, Diner reported a net income of $80,000 for the year.

Instructions
Prepare all necessary journal entries in 1995 for both situations.

E18-11 (Equity Method with Revalued Assets) On January 1, 1996, Filley Company purchased 2,500 shares (25%) of the common stock of Pricer Co. for $350,000. Additional information related to the identifiable assets and liabilities of Pricer Co. at the date of acquisition is as follows:

	Cost	Fair Value
Assets not subject to depreciation	$ 500,000	$ 500,000
Assets subject to depreciation (10 years remaining)	800,000	860,000
Total identifiable assets	$1,300,000	$1,360,000
Liabilities	$ 100,000	$ 100,000

During 1996, Pricer Co. reported the following information on its income statement:

Income before extraordinary item	$200,000
Extraordinary gain (net of tax)	80,000
Net income	$280,000
Dividends declared and paid by Pricer Co. during 1996 were	$120,000

Instructions

(a) Prepare the journal entry to record the purchase by Filley Company of Pricer Co. on January 1, 1996.

(b) Prepare the journal entries to record Filley's equity in the net income and dividends of Pricer Co. for 1996. Depreciable assets are depreciated on a straight-line basis, and goodwill is amortized over 20 years.

E18-12 (Securities Entries—Buy, Sale, Transfer) Godfrey Company has the following securities in its trading portfolio of securities on December 31, 1995:

Investments (Trading)	Cost	Fair Value
1,500 shares of General Motors, Common	$ 75,000	$ 69,000
5,000 shares of GTE, Common	180,000	175,000
400 shares of CBS, Preferred	60,000	61,600
	$315,000	$305,600

All of the securities were purchased in 1995.
In 1996, Godfrey completed the following securities transactions:

March	1	Sold the 1,500 shares of General Motors, Common, @ $45 less fees of $1,200.
April	1	Bought 700 shares of Dow Chemical, Common, @ $75 plus fees of $1,300.
December 31		Transferred the CBS, Preferred, from the trading portfolio to the available-for-sale portfolio; the stock was selling at $145 per share.

Godfrey Company's portfolio of trading securities appeared as follows on December 31, 1996:

Investments (Trading)	Cost	Fair Value
5,000 shares of GTE, Common	$180,000	$175,000
700 shares of Dow Chemical, Common	53,800	50,400
400 shares of CBS, Preferred	60,000	58,000
	$293,800	$283,400

Instructions
Prepare the general journal entries for Godfrey Company for:

(a) The 1995 adjusting entry.

(b) The sale of the GM stock.

(c) The purchase of the Dow Chemical stock.

(d) The 1996 adjusting entry for the trading portfolio (including the CBS preferred).

(e) The transfer of the CBS stock from the trading portfolio to the available-for-sale portfolio.

E18-13 (Fair Value and Equity Method Compared) Cardinal Concrete Inc. acquired 20% of the outstanding common stock of Edra Inc. on December 31, 1994. The purchase price was $1,200,000 for 50,000 shares. Edra Inc. declared and paid an $0.80 per share cash dividend on June 30 and on December 31, 1995. Edra reported net income of $700,000 for 1995. The fair value of Edra's stock was $28 per share at December 31, 1995.

Instructions

(a) Prepare the journal entries for Cardinal Concrete Inc. for 1995, assuming that Cardinal cannot exercise significant influence over Edra. The securities should be classified as available-for-sale.

(b) Prepare the journal entries for Cardinal Concrete Inc. for 1995, assuming that Cardinal can exercise significant influence over Edra.

(c) At what amount is the investment in securities reported on the balance sheet under each of these methods at December 31, 1995? What is the total income reported in 1995 under each of these methods?

E18-14 (Equity Method with Revalued Assets) On January 1, 1996, Fernandez Inc. purchased 40% of the common stock of Erin Company for $400,000. The balance sheet reported the following information related to Erin Company at the date of acquisition.

Assets not subject to depreciation	$200,000
Assets subject to depreciation (10 year-life remaining)	600,000
Liabilities	100,000

Additional information:

1. Both book value and fair value are the same for assets not subject to depreciation and the liabilities.

2. The fair market value of the assets subject to depreciation is $680,000.
3. The company depreciates its assets on a straight-line basis; intangible assets are amortized over 5 years.
4. Erin Company reports net income of $150,000 and declares and pays dividends of $100,000 in 1996.

Instructions
(a) Prepare the journal entry to record Fernandez's purchase of Erin Company.
(b) Prepare the journal entries to record Fernandez's equity in the net income and dividends of Erin Company for 1996.
(c) Assume the same facts as above, except that Erin's net income included an extraordinary loss (net of tax) of $30,000. Prepare the journal entries to record Fernandez's equity in the net income of Erin Company for 1996.

E18-15 (Impairment of Debt Securities) Selig Corporation has municipal bonds classified as available-for-sale at December 31, 1995. These bonds have a par value of $800,000, an amortized cost of $800,000, and a fair value of $710,000. The unrealized loss of $90,000 previously recognized as a separate component of stockholders' equity is now determined to be other than temporary; that is, the company believes that impairment accounting is now appropriate for these bonds.

Instructions
(a) Prepare the journal entry to recognize the impairment.
(b) What is the new cost basis of the municipal bonds? Given that the maturity value of the bonds is $800,000, should Selig Corporation accrete the difference between the carrying amount and the maturity value over the life of the bonds?
(c) At December 31, 1996, the fair value of the municipal bonds is $760,000. Prepare the entry (if any) to record this information.

E18-16 (Reclassification of Securities) Presented below is the available-for-sale securities portfolio for Beresford Company as of December 31, 1995:

Available-for-Sale Securities
December 31, 1995

	Cost	Fair Value
U.S. government securities	$110,000	$112,000
Equity securities	300,000	408,000
Corporate bonds	80,000	70,000
	$490,000	$590,000

Instructions
(a) Assume that Beresford Company decides to transfer its U.S. government securities to the trading portfolio on December 31, 1995. Prepare the journal entry(ies) necessary to record this transfer.
(b) Assume that Beresford Company decides to transfer its corporate bonds to the held-to-maturity portfolio. Prepare the journal entry(ies) necessary to record this transfer.
(c) Indicate the accounting procedure used to ensure that the held-to-maturity securities will be reported at their maturity value at the maturity date if the maturity value is $80,000.

E18-17 (Reclassification of Securities) Presented below are three independent situations:

Situation I
Coopers transfers its trading securities portfolio to the available-for-sale securities portfolio. The cost and fair value of the trading securities portfolio are $700,000 and $800,000, respectively. Prepare the entry(ies) to record this transfer.

Situation II
Beth Kinney Company transfers its held-to-maturity securities portfolio to its available-for-sale portfolio. The cost and fair value of the held-to-maturity portfolio are $900,000 and $860,000, respectively. Prepare the journal entry(ies) to record the transfer.

Situation III
D. Joseph Co. transfers its available-for-sale portfolio to its trading portfolio. The cost and fair value of the available-for-sale portfolio are $600,000 and $620,000, respectively. Prepare the journal entry(ies) to record the transfer.

*E18-18 (Change from Fair Value to Equity) On January 1, 1995, Poley Co. purchased 25,000 shares (a 10% interest) in Lindsay Corp. for $1,400,000. At the time, the book value and the fair value of Lindsay's net assets were $13,000,000.

On July 1, 1996, Poley paid $3,040,000 for 50,000 additional shares of Lindsay common stock, which represented a 20% investment in Lindsay. The fair value of Lindsay's identifiable assets net of liabilities was equal to their carrying amount of $14,200,000. As a result of this transaction, Poley owns 30% of Lindsay and can exercise significant influence over Lindsay's operating and financial policies. Intangible assets are amortized over 20 years.

Lindsay reported the following net income and declared and paid the following dividends:

	Net Income	Dividend Per Share
Year ended 12/31/95	$700,000	None
Six months ended 6/30/96	500,000	None
Six months ended 12/31/96	740,000	$1.40

Instructions
Determine the ending balance that Poley Co. should report as its investment in Lindsay Corp. at the end of 1996.

*E18-19 (Change from Equity to Fair Value) Land Corp. was a 30% owner of Jersey Company, holding 210,000 shares of Jersey's common stock on December 31, 1994. The investment account had the following entries:

Investment in Jersey

1/1/93 Cost	$3,180,000	12/6/93 Dividend received	$150,000
12/31/93 Share of income	390,000	12/31/93 Amortization of under-	
12/31/94 Share of income	510,000	valued assets	30,000
		12/5/94 Dividend received	240,000
		12/31/94 Amortization of under-	
		valued assets	30,000

On January 2, 1995, Land sold 119,000 shares of Jersey for $3,250,000, thereby losing its significant influence. During the year 1995 Jersey experienced the following results of operations and paid the following dividends to Land.

	Jersey Income (Loss)	Dividends Paid to Land
1995	$300,000	$54,600

At December 31, 1995, the fair value of Jersey shares held by Land is $1,700,000. This is the first reporting date since the January 2 sale.

Instructions
(a) What effect does the January 2, 1995, transaction have upon Land's accounting treatment for its investment in Jersey?
(b) Compute the carrying amount in Jersey as of December 31, 1995.
(c) Prepare the adjusting entry on December 31, 1995, applying the fair value method to Land's long-term investment in Jersey Company securities.

*E18-20 (Determine Proper Income Reporting) Presented below are three independent situations that you are to solve:
1. Village Green Inc. received dividends from its common stock investments during the year ended December 31, 1996, as follows:
    (a) A cash dividend of $10,000 is received from Gary Corporation. (Village Green owns a 2% interest in Gary.)
    (b) A cash dividend of $60,000 is received from Mid-Plains Corporation. (Village Green owns a 30% interest in Mid-Plains.) A majority of Village Green's directors are also directors of Mid-Plains Corporation.
    (c) A stock dividend of 300 shares from Petty Inc. was received on December 10, 1996, on which date the quoted market value of Petty's shares was $10 per share. Village Green owns less than 1% of Petty's common stock.
    Determine how much dividend income Village Green should report in its 1996 income statement.
2. On January 3, 1996, Perly Co. purchased as a long-term investment 5,000 shares of Bonton Co. common stock for $79 per share, which represents a 2% interest. On December 31, 1996, the market price of the stock was $83 per share. On March 3, 1997, it sold all 5,000 shares of Bonton stock for $100 per share. The company regularly sells securities of this type. The income tax rate is 35%. Determine the amount of gain or loss on disposal that should be reported on the income statement in 1997.

3. Morgan owns a 5% interest in Canton Corporation, which declared a cash dividend of $600,000 on November 27, 1996, to shareholders of record on December 16, 1996, payable on January 6, 1997. In addition, on October 15, 1996, Morgan received a liquidating dividend of $9,000 from Silver Mining Company. Morgan owns 6% of Silver Mining Co. Determine the amount of dividend income Morgan should report in its financial statements for 1996.

*E18-21 (Entries for Stock Rights) On January 10, 1995, Missle Company purchased 240 shares, $50 par value (a 3% interest), of common stock of Patriot Corporation for $24,000 as a long-term investment. On July 12, 1995, Patriot Corporation announced that one right would be issued for every two shares of stock held.

July 30, 1995	Rights to purchase 120 shares of stock at $100 per share are received. The market value of the stock is $120 per share and the market value of the rights is $30 per right.
Aug. 10	The rights to purchase 50 shares of stock are sold at $28 per right.
Aug. 11	The additional 70 rights are exercised, and 70 shares of stock are purchased at $100 per share.
Nov. 15	50 shares of those purchased on January 10, 1995, are sold at $130 per share.

Instructions
Prepare general journal entries on the books of Missle Company for each of the foregoing transactions.

*E18-22 (Entries for Stock Rights) Voss Company purchases 240 shares of common stock of Cadlac Inc. on February 17. The $100 par stock, costing $27,300, is to be a long-term investment for Voss Company.

1. On June 30, Cadlac Inc. announces that rights are to be issued. One right will be received for every two shares owned.
2. The rights mentioned in (1) are received on July 15; 120 shares of $100 par stock may be purchased with these rights at par. The stock is currently selling for $120 per share. Market value of the stock rights is $20 per right.
3. On August 5, 70 rights are exercised, and 70 shares of stock are purchased at par.
4. On August 12, the remaining stock rights are sold at $22 per right.
5. On September 28, Voss Company sells 50 shares of those purchased February 17, at $125 a share.

Instructions
Prepare necessary journal entries for the five numbered items above.

*E18-23 (Investment in Life Insurance Policy) Mall Company pays the premiums on two insurance policies on the life of its president, Jean Mall. Information concerning premiums paid in 1996 is given below.

Beneficiary	Face	Prem.	Dividends Cr. to Prem.	Net Prem.	Cash Surrender Value 1/1/96	12/31/96
1. Mall Co.	$250,000	$8,500	$2,940	$5,560	$35,000	$37,700
2. President's spouse	75,000	3,000		3,000	9,000	9,750

Instructions
(a) Prepare entries in journal form to record the payment of premiums in 1996.
(b) If the president died in January, 1997, and the beneficiaries are paid the face amounts of the policies, what entry would the Mall Company make?

*E18-24 (Entries and Disclosure for Bond Sinking Fund) The general ledger of Norm Rogers Company shows an account for Bonds Payable with a balance of $2,000,000. Interest is payable on these bonds semi-annually. Of the $2,000,000, bonds in the amount of $400,000 were recently purchased at par by the sinking fund trustee and are held in the sinking fund as an investment of the fund. The annual rate of interest is 11%.

Instructions
(a) What entry or entries should be made by Norm Rogers Company to record payment of the semi-annual interest? (The company makes interest payments directly to bondholders.)
(b) Illustrate how the bonds payable and the sinking fund accounts should be shown in the balance sheet. Assume that the sinking fund investments other than Norm Rogers Company's bonds amount to $506,000, and that the sinking fund cash amounts to $21,000.

*E18-25 (Entries for Plant Expansion Fund, Numbers Omitted) The transactions given below relate to a fund being accumulated by John Spoor Electrical Company over a period of 20 years for the construction of additional buildings.

1. Cash is transferred from the general cash account to the fund.
2. Preferred stock of Habitat Company is purchased as an investment of the fund.
3. Bonds of Jerry Huber Corporation are purchased between interest dates at a discount as an investment of the fund.
4. Expenses of the fund are paid from the fund cash.
5. Interest is collected on Jerry Huber Corporation bonds.
6. Bonds held in the fund are sold at a gain between interest dates.

7. Dividends are received on Habitat Company preferred stock.
8. Common stocks held in the fund are sold at a loss.
9. Cash is paid from the fund for building construction.
10. The cash balance remaining in the fund is transferred to general cash.

Instructions
Prepare journal entries to record the miscellaneous transactions listed above with amounts omitted.

PROBLEMS

P18-1 (Debt Securities) Presented below is an amortization schedule related to Thomas Company's 5-year, $100,000 bond with a 7% interest rate and a 5% yield, purchased on December 31, 1993, for $108,660.

Date	Cash Received	Interest Revenue	Bond Premium Amortization	Carry Amount of Bonds
12/31/93				$108,660
12/31/94	$7,000	$5,433	$1,567	107,093
12/31/95	7,000	5,354	1,646	105,447
12/31/96	7,000	5,272	1,728	103,719
12/31/97	7,000	5,186	1,814	101,905
12/31/98	7,000	5,095	1,905	100,000

The following schedule presents a comparison of the amortized cost and fair value of the bonds at year-end:

	12/31/94	12/31/95	12/31/96	12/31/97	12/31/98
Amortized cost	$107,093	$105,447	$103,719	$101,905	$100,000
Fair value	$106,000	$107,500	$105,500	$103,000	$100,000

Instructions
(a) Prepare the journal entry to record the purchase of these bonds on December 31, 1993, assuming the bonds are classified as held-to-maturity securities.
(b) Prepare the journal entry(ies) related to the held-to-maturity bonds for 1994.
(c) Prepare the journal entry(ies) related to the held-to-maturity bonds for 1996.
(d) Prepare the journal entry(ies) to record the purchase of these bonds, assuming they are classified as available-for-sale.
(e) Prepare the journal entry(ies) related to the available-for-sale bonds for 1994.
(f) Prepare the journal entry(ies) related to the available-for-sale bonds for 1996.

P18-2 (Debt Securities Available-for-Sale) On January 1, 1996, Brock Company purchased $200,000, 8% bonds of Universal Co. for $184,557. The bonds were purchased to yield 10% interest. Interest is payable semiannually on July 1 and January 1. The bonds mature on January 1, 2000. Brock Company uses the effective interest method to amortize discount or premium. On January 1, 1998, Brock Company sold the bonds for $185,363 after receiving interest to meet its liquidity needs.

Instructions
(a) Prepare the journal entry to record the purchase of bonds on January 1. Assume that the bonds are classified as available-for-sale.
(b) Prepare the amortization schedule for the bonds.
(c) Prepare the journal entries to record the semiannual interest on July 1, 1996 and December 31, 1996.
(d) If the fair value of Universal bonds is $185,363 on December 31, 1997, prepare the necessary adjusting entry. (Assume the securities fair value adjustment balance on January 1, 1997, is a debit of $3,375.)
(e) Prepare the journal entry to record the sale of the bonds on January 1, 1998.
(f) According to *SFAS No. 115*, what other information should be disclosed on Brock's 1996 and 1998 financial statements?

P18-3 (Available-for-Sale Debt Securities) Presented below is information taken from a bond investment amortization schedule with related fair values provided. These bonds are classified as available-for-sale.

	12/31/95	12/31/96	12/31/97
Amortized cost	$491,150	$519,442	$550,000
Fair value	$495,000	$506,000	$550,000

Instructions
(a) Indicate whether the bonds were purchased at a discount or at a premium.
(b) Indicate whether the amortization schedule is based on the effective interest method and how you can determine which method is used.

(c) Prepare the adjusting entry to record the bonds at fair value at December 31, 1995. The Securities Fair Value Adjustment account has a debit balance of $1,000 prior to adjustment.

(d) Prepare the adjusting entry to record the bonds at fair value at December 31, 1996.

P18-4 (Equity Securities Entries and Disclosures) Bolex Company has the following securities in its investment portfolio on December 31, 1995 (all securities were purchased in 1995): (1) 3,000 shares of Chrysler Co. common stock which cost $58,500, (2) 10,000 shares of Logan Ltd. common stock which cost $580,000, and (3) 6,000 shares of Bascom Company preferred stock which cost $255,000. The Securities Fair Value Adjustment account shows a credit of $9,500 at the end of 1995.

In 1996, Bolex completed the following securities transactions:

1. On January 15, sold 3,000 shares of Chrysler's common stock at $22 per share less fees of $2,150.
2. On April 17, purchased 1,000 shares of Gordon's common stock at $31.50 per share plus fees of $1,980.

On December 31, 1996, the market values per share of these securities were: Chrysler $20, Logan $62, Bascom $40, and Gordon $29. In addition, the accounting supervisor of Bolex told you that, even though all these securities have readily determinable fair values, Bolex will not actively trade these securities because the top management intends to hold them for more than one year.

Instructions

(a) Prepare the entry for the security sale on January 15, 1996.

(b) Prepare the journal entry to record the security purchase on April 17, 1996.

(c) Compute the unrealized gains or losses and prepare the adjusting entry for Bolex on December 31, 1996.

(d) How should the realized and unrealized gains or losses be reported on Bolex's financial statements?

P18-5 (Trading and Available-for-Sale Securities Entries) Colonial Company has the following portfolio of investment securities at September 30, 1995, its last reporting date.

Trading Securities	Cost	Fair Value
London common (5,000 shares)	$225,000	$200,000
Fontaine, Inc. preferred (3,500 shares)	133,000	140,000
Monty common (1,000 shares)	180,000	179,000

On October 10, 1995, the London shares were sold at a price of $53 per share. In addition, 3,000 shares of Forrest common stock were acquired at $59.50 per share on November 2, 1995. The December 31, 1995 fair values were: Fontaine $96,000; Forrest $132,000, and the Monty common $190,000. All the securities are classified as trading.

Instructions

(a) Prepare the journal entries to record the sale, purchase, and adjusting entries related to the trading securities in the last quarter of 1995.

(b) How would the entries in part (a) change if the securities were classified as available-for-sale?

P18-6 (Available-for-Sale and Held-to-Maturity Debt Securities Entries) The following information relates to the debt securities investments of the Lakeside Company.

1. On February 1, the company purchased 9% bonds of Crandall Co. having a par value of $500,000 at 100 plus accrued interest. Interest is payable April 1 and October 1.
2. On April 1, semiannual interest is received.
3. On July 1, 12% bonds of Quincy, Inc. were purchased. These bonds with a par value of $200,000 were purchased at 100 plus accrued interest. Interest dates are June 1 and December 1.
4. On September 1, bonds of a par value of $100,000, purchased on February 1, are sold at 99 plus accrued interest.
5. On October 1, semiannual interest is received.
6. On December 1, semiannual interest is received.
7. On December 31, the fair value of the bonds purchased February 1 and July 1 are 95 and 94, respectively.

Instructions

(a) Prepare any journal entries you consider necessary, including year-end entries (December 31), assuming these are available-for-sale securities.

(b) If Lakeside classified these as held-to-maturity securities, explain how the journal entries would differ from those in part (a).

P18-7 (Applying Fair Value Method) GraNite is a medium-sized corporation specializing in quarrying stone for building construction. The company has long dominated the market, at one time achieving a 70% market penetration. During prosperous years, the company's profits, coupled with a conservative dividend policy, resulted in funds available for outside investment. Over the years, GraNite has had a policy of investing idle cash in equity securities. In particular, GraNite has made periodic investments in the company's principal supplier, Mark Industries. Although the firm currently owns 12 percent of the outstanding common stock of Mark Industries, GraNite does not have significant influence over the operations of Mark Industries.

Marcia Blake has recently joined GraNite as Assistant Controller, and her first assignment is to prepare the 1994 year-end adjusting entries for the accounts that are valued by the "fair value" rule for financial reporting purposes. Blake has gathered the following information about GraNite's pertinent accounts.

1. GraNite has trading securities related to Ajax Motors and Morgan Electric. During this fiscal year, GraNite purchased 100,000 shares of Ajax Motors for $1,400,000; these shares currently have a market value of $1,600,000. GraNite's investment in Morgan Electric has not been as profitable; the company acquired 50,000 shares of Morgan in April 1994 at $20 per share, a purchase that currently has a value of $600,000.

2. Prior to 1994, GraNite invested $22,500,000 in Mark Industries and has not changed its holdings this year. This investment in Mark Industries was valued at $21,500,000 on December 31, 1993. GraNite's 12% ownership of Mark Industries has a current market value of $22,200,000.

Instructions

(a) Prepare the appropriate adjusting entries for GraNite as of December 31, 1994, to reflect the application of the "fair value" rule for both classes of securities described above.

(b) For both classes of securities presented above, describe how the results of the valuation adjustments made in Instruction (a) would be reflected in the body of and/or notes to GraNite's 1994 financial statements.

P18-8 (Financial Statement Presentation of Available-for-Sale Investments) Arnold Company has the following portfolio of available-for-sale securities at December 31, 1995.

Security	Quantity	Percent Interest	Per Share Cost	Per Share Market
Microtape, Inc.	2,000 shares	8%	$11	$16
Surley Corp.	5,000 shares	14%	23	17
Terminator Company	4,000 shares	2%	31	25

Instructions

(a) What should be reported on Arnold's December 31, 1995, balance sheet relative to these long-term available-for-sale securities?

On December 31, 1996, Arnold's portfolio of available-for-sale securities consisted of the following common stocks.

Security	Quantity	Percent Interest	Per Share Cost	Per Share Market
Surley Corp.	5,000 shares	14%	$23	$30
Terminator Company	4,000 shares	2%	31	24
Terminator Company	2,000 shares	1%	25	24

At the end of year 1996, Arnold Company changed its intent relative to its investment in Microtape, Inc. and reclassified the shares to trading securities status when the shares were selling for $9 per share.

(b) What should be reported on the face of Arnold's December 31, 1996, balance sheet relative to available-for-sale securities investments? What should be reported to reflect the transactions above in Arnold's 1996 income statement?

(c) Assuming that comparative financial statements for 1995 and 1996 are presented, draft the footnote necessary for full disclosure of Arnold's transactions and position in equity securities.

P18-9 (Entries for Equity Investments) Kentucky Wildcats Corp. makes the following long-term investments during 1995.

Security	Quantity	Percent Interest	Per Share Cost
Paduca Forms Company	3,000 shares	2%	$80
Lexington Grader Corp.	8,000 shares	16%	20
Knoblett Development Inc.	3,000 shares	4%	36

The following information concerning these investments relates to 1995 and 1996:

1. For the year 1995—Cash dividends received:
   Paduca Forms $4.00 per share
   Lexington Grader $1.00 per share
   Knoblett Development $1.50 per share

2. Market values per share, 12/31/95:

    Paduca Forms $74

    Lexington Grader $23

    Knoblett Development $28

3. For the year 1996—Cash dividends received:

    Paduca Forms $4.00 per share

    Lexington Grader $ .50 per share

    Knoblett Development $1.70 per share

4. On Sept. 30, 1996, the investment in Lexington Grader was reclassified as trading when its market value per share was $17.

5. Market value per share, 12/31/96:

    Paduca Forms $68

    Knoblett Development $46

Instructions

(a) Prepare all of the journal entries to reflect the transactions above for 1995 and 1996.

(b) Prepare the descriptions and amounts that should be reported on the face of Kentucky Wildcat Corp.'s comparative financial statements for 1995 and 1996 relative to these long-term investments.

(c) Draft the footnote that should accompany the 1995–96 comparative statements relative to these securities.

P18-10 (Entries for Long-Term Investments) Curtis Strange Corp. carries an account in its general ledger called "Investments," which contained the following debits for investment purchases, and no credits.

Feb. 1, 1995	Player Company common stock, $100 par, 200 shares	$ 36,400
April 1	U.S. Government bonds, 11%, due April 1, 2005, interest payable April 1 and October 1, 100 bonds of $1,000 par each	100,000
July 1	Nicklaus Company 12% bonds, par $50,000, dated March 1, 1995 purchased at 104 plus accrued interest, interest payable annually on March 1, due March 1, 2015	54,000

Instructions

(a) Prepare entries necessary to classify the amounts into proper accounts, assuming that all the securities are classified as available-for-sale.

(b) Prepare the entry to record the accrued interest and amortization of premium on December 31, 1995, using the straight-line method.

(c) The fair values of the securities on December 31, 1995, were:

Player Company common stock	$ 33,800 (1% interest)
U.S. Government bonds	124,700
Nicklaus Company bonds	58,600

What entry or entries, if any, would you recommend be made?

(d) The U.S. Government bonds were sold on July 1, 1996, for $114,200 plus accrued interest. Give the proper entry.

P18-11 (Available-for-Sale and Equity Method) Zoe Incorporated is a publicly traded company that manufactures products to clean and demagnetize video and audio tape recorders and players. The company grew rapidly during its first 10 years and made three public offerings during this period. During its rapid growth period, Zoe acquired common stock in Guttman Inc. and Cairo Importers. In 1985 Zoe acquired 25% of Guttman's common stock for $588,000 and properly accounts for this investment using the equity method. For its fiscal year ended November 30, 1993, Guttman Inc. reported net income of $240,000 and paid dividends of $100,000. In 1987 Zoe acquired 10% of Cario Importers' common stock for $204,000, and properly accounts for this investment using the fair value method. Zoe has a policy of investing idle cash in equity securities. The following data pertain to the securities in Zoe's investment portfolio.

Available-for-Sale Securities at November 30, 1995

Security	Cost	Fair Value
Horton Electric	$326,000	$314,000
Edwards Inc.	184,000	181,000
Evert Company	96,000	98,000
	$606,000	593,000
Cairo Importers	204,000	198,000
	$810,000	$791,000

Available-for-Sale Securities at November 30, 1996

Security	Cost	Fair Value
Horton Electric	$326,000	$323,000
Edwards Inc.	184,000	180,000
Rogers Limited	105,000	108,000
	$615,000	611,000
Cairo Importers	204,000	205,000
	$819,000	$816,000

On November 14, 1996, Amanda McElroy was hired by Zoe as assistant controller. Her first assignment was to propose the entries to record the November activity and the November 30, 1996, year-end adjusting entries for the investments in available-for-sale securities and the long-term investment in common stock. Using Zoe's ledger of investment transactions and the data given above, McElroy proposed the following entries and submitted them to Able Gance, controller, for review.

Entry 1 (November 8, 1996)

Cash	99,500	
Available-for-Sale Securities		98,000
Gain on Sale of Securities		1,500
To record the sale of Evert Company stock for $99,500.		

Entry 2 (November 26, 1996)

Available-for-Sale Securities	105,000	
Cash		105,000
To record the purchase of Rogers Limited common stock for $102,200 plus brokerage fees of $2,800.		

Entry 3 (November 30, 1996)

Unrealized Holding Gain or Loss—Equity	3,000	
Securities Fair Value Adjustment (Available-for-Sale)		3,000
To recognize a loss equal to the excess of cost over market value of equity securities.		

Entry 4 (November 30, 1996)

Cash	37,000	
Dividend Revenue		37,000
To record dividends received from securities.		
Guttman Inc. $25,000		
Cairo Importers 9,000		
Horton Electric 3,000		

Entry 5 (November 30, 1996)

Investment in Guttman Inc.	60,000	
Revenue from Investment		60,000
To record share of Guttman Inc. income under the equity method, $240,000 × .25.		

Instructions

(a) Distinguish between the characteristics of available-for-sale investments and held-to-maturity investments.

(b) The journal entries proposed by Amanda McElroy will establish the value of Zoe Incorporated's equity investments to be reported on the company's external financial statements. Review each of the journal entries proposed by McElroy and indicate whether or not it is in accordance with the applicable reporting standards. If an entry is incorrect, prepare the correct entry or entries that should have been made.

(c) Because Zoe Incorporated owns more than 20% of Guttman Inc., Able Gance has adopted the equity method to account for the investment in Guttman Inc. Under what circumstances would it be inappropriate to use the equity method to account for a 25% interest in the common stock of Guttman Inc.?

(AICPA adapted)

P18-12 (Available-for-Sale Securities—Statement Presentation) Oakwood Corp. invested its excess cash in available-for-sale securities during 1994. As of December 31, 1994, the portfolio of available-for-sale securities consisted of the following common stocks:

Security	Quantity	Cost	Fair Value
Tinkers, Inc.	1,000 shares	$ 15,000	$ 19,000
Evers Corp.	2,000 shares	50,000	42,000
Chance Aircraft	2,000 shares	72,000	60,000
	Totals	$137,000	$121,000

Instructions

(a) What should be reported on Oakwood's December 31, 1994, balance sheet relative to these securities?

On December 31, 1995, Oakwood's portfolio of available-for-sale securities consisted of the following common stocks:

Security	Quantity	Cost	Fair Value
Tinkers, Inc.	1,000 shares	$ 15,000	$20,000
Tinkers, Inc.	2,000 shares	38,000	40,000
Lakeshore Company	1,000 shares	16,000	12,000
Chance Aircraft	2,000 shares	72,000	22,000
	Totals	$141,000	$94,000

During the year 1995, Oakwood Corp. sold 2,000 shares of Evers Corp. for $37,000 and purchased 1,000 more shares of Tinkers, Inc. and 1,000 shares of Lakeshore Company.

(b) What should be reported on Oakwood's December 31, 1995, balance sheet? What should be reported to Oakwood's 1995 income statement?

On December 31, 1996, Oakwood's portfolio of available-for-sale securities consisted of the following common stocks:

Security	Quantity	Cost	Fair Value
Chance Aircraft	2,000 shares	$72,000	$82,000
Lakeshore Company	500 shares	8,000	6,000
	Totals	$80,000	$88,000

During the year 1996, Oakwood Corp. sold 3,000 shares of Tinkers, Inc. for $39,500 and 500 shares of Lakeshore Company at a loss of $2,500.

(c) What should be reported on the face of Oakwood's December 31, 1996, balance sheet? What should be reported on Oakwood's 1996 income statement?

(d) Draft the footnote necessary for full disclosure of Oakwood's transactions and position in available-for-sale securities for 1996.

P18-13 (Debt and Equity Securities) Demo, Inc., a calendar-year corporation, had the following transactions in debt and equity securities during 1994:

Jan. 1   Purchased various securities for cash and classified them as follows:

Trading Securities

10,000 common shares of Timidity Co. at $48 per share	$ 480,000
5,000 warrants on the common shares of Timidity Co. at $12 each	60,000
10,000 $5 convertible preferred shares of Timidity Co. at $87 each	870,000
Total	$1,410,000

Available-for-Sale Securities

5,000 common shares of Alpha, Inc. at $8 per share	$ 40,000
100 8% convertible debentures of Alpha, Inc., at 99; the bonds have a $1,000 face value, mature on 12/31/98, and pay interest on June 30 and Dec. 31	99,000
600,000 common shares of Amtek, Inc., at $1 each	600,000
200,000 common shares of Geneswitch, Inc., at $3 each	600,000
Total	$1,339,000

Held-to-Maturity Securities

200 10% debentures of Risky Business, Inc., at 74.9; the bonds have a $1,000 face value, mature on 12/31/03, and pay interest annually on Dec. 31. The purchase price provides a yield of 15% on the investment	$ 149,800

March 1   Received the $2.50 semiannual dividend on the preferred shares of Timidity Co. for $25,000.

April 1   Sold 5,000 common shares of Timidity Co. at $68 per share for $340,000.

June 30   Received the 4% semiannual interest on the Alpha, Inc., bonds for $4,000 and recorded straight-line amortization of the discount for 6 months. The difference between straight-line and effective interest is considered to be immaterial.

Aug. 15   Changed intention regarding the 200,000 common shares of Geneswitch, Inc., and reclassified them as Trading Securities when the shares were trading at $2 each.

Sep. 1   Received the $25,000 semiannual dividend on the Timidity preferred shares.

Dec. 31   Received the 4% semiannual interest on the Alpha, Inc., bonds for $4,000 and recorded straight-line amortization of the discount for 6 months.

Dec. 31   Received the 10% annual interest on the Risky Business, Inc., bonds for $20,000 and recorded 12 months' amortization of the discount using the effective interest method and a rate of 15%.

Dec. 31   The market values of the various securities are:

Timidity Co.

Common stock	$ 88
Warrants	$ 22
Convertible preferred	$147

Geneswitch

Common stock	$ 1

Alpha, Inc.

Common stock	$ 7
Convertible bonds	99.2

Amtek, Inc.

Common stock	$ 3

Risky Business

Bonds	80.0

Instructions

(a) Prepare general journal entries for all of the above transactions and year-end adjustments. For the initial purchase, you need only record one debit for each security category.

(b) What descriptions and amounts should be reported on Demo, Inc.'s, 1994 income statement?

(c) What descriptions and amounts should be reported on the face of Demo, Inc.'s, classified balance sheet for December 31, 1994? (Demo, Inc., has no intention to sell the "Securities Available-for-Sale" within one year.)

(d) Draft the note necessary for full disclosure of Demo, Inc.'s, transactions and position in various securities.

*P18-14 (Fair Value to Equity Method with Goodwill) On January 1, 1994, Feiner Inc. paid $700,000 for 10,000 shares of Wolf Company's voting common stock, which was a 10% interest in Wolf. At that date the net assets of Wolf totaled $6,000,000. The fair values of all of Wolf's identifiable assets and liabilities were equal to their book values. Feiner does not have the ability to exercise significant influence over the operating and financial policies of Wolf. Feiner received dividends of $1.00 per share from Wolf on October 1, 1994. Wolf reported net income of $500,000 for the year ended December 31, 1994.

On July 1, 1995, Feiner paid $2,325,000 for 30,000 additional shares of Wolf Company's voting common stock which represents a 30% investment in Wolf. The fair values of all of Wolf's identifiable assets net of liabilities were equal to their book values of $6,550,000. As a result of this transaction, Feiner has the ability to exercise significant influence over the operating and financial policies of Wolf. Feiner received dividends of $1.00 per share from Wolf on April 1, 1995, and $1.50 per share on October 1, 1995. Wolf reported net income of $550,000 for the year ended December 31, 1995, and $300,000 for the 6 months ended December 31, 1995. Feiner amortizes goodwill over a 40-year period.

Instructions

(a) Prepare a schedule showing the income or loss before income taxes for the year ended December 31, 1994, that Feiner should report from its investment in Wolf in its income statement issued in March 1995.

(b) During March 1996, Feiner issues comparative financial statements for 1994 and 1995. Prepare schedules showing the income or loss before income taxes for the years ended December 31, 1994 and 1995, that Feiner should report from its investment in Wolf.

(AICPA adapted)

*P18-15 (Change from Fair Value to Equity Method) On January 3, 1993, Cajun Company purchased for $500,000 cash a 10% interest in Summerset Corp. On that date the net assets of Summerset had a book value of $3,750,000. The excess of cost over the underlying equity in net assets is attributable to undervalued depreciable assets having a remaining life of 10 years from the date of Cajun's purchase.

The fair value of Cajun's investment in Summerset securities is as follows: December 31, 1993, $570,000; December 31, 1994, $610,000.

On January 2, 1995, Cajun purchased an additional 30% of Summerset's stock for $1,545,000 cash when the book value of Summerset's net assets was $4,150,000. The excess was attributable to depreciable assets having a remaining life of 8 years.

During 1993, 1994, and 1995 the following occurred:

	Summerset Net Income	Dividends Paid by Summerset to Cajun
1993	$350,000	$15,000
1994	400,000	20,000
1995	500,000	60,000

Instructions

On the books of Cajun Company prepare all journal entries in 1993, 1994, and 1995 that relate to its investment in Summerset Corp., reflecting the data above and a change from the fair value method to the equity method.

*P18-16 (Stock Rights—Comprehensive) Jeff Grandgeorge Company holds 300 shares of common stock of Rick's Decorating Inc. that it purchased for $32,589 as a long-term investment. On January 15, 1996, it is announced that one right will be issued for every 4 shares of Rick's Decorating Inc. stock held.

Instructions

(a) Prepare entries on Jeff Grandgeorge Company's books for the transactions below that occurred after the date of this announcement. Show all computations in good form.
   1. 100 shares of stock are sold rights-on for $11,500.
   2. Rights to purchase 50 additional shares of stock at par value of $100 per share are received. The market value of the stock on this date is $105 per share and the market value of the rights is $6 per right.
   3. The rights are exercised, and 50 additional shares are purchased at $100 per share.
   4. 100 shares of the stock originally held are sold at $106 per share.

(b) If the rights had not been exercised but instead had been sold at $6 per right, what would have been the amount of the gain or loss on the sale of the rights?

(c) If the stock purchased through the exercise of the rights is later sold at $107 per share, what is the amount of the gain or loss on the sale?

(d) If the rights had not been exercised, but had been allowed to expire, what would be the proper entry?

*P18-17 (Entries for Sinking Fund) The transactions given below relate to a sinking fund for retirement of long-term bonds of Castleman Roofing:

1. In accordance with the terms of the bond indenture, cash in the amount of $150,000 is transferred at the end of the first year, from the regular cash account to the sinking fund.
2. Joe Briel Siding Company 10% bonds of a par value of $50,000, maturing in 5 years, are purchased for $48,000.
3. 500 shares of Mankato Company 8% preferred stock ($50 par value) are purchased at $53 per share.
4. Annual interest of $5,000 is received on Joe Briel Siding Company bonds. (Amortize a full year of discount using straight-line amortization.)
5. Sinking fund expenses of $450 are paid from sinking fund cash.
6. O'Neil Glass Company 9% bonds with interest payable February 1 and August 1 are purchased on April 15 at par value of $60,000 plus accrued interest.
7. Dividends of $2,000 are received on Mankato Company preferred stock.
8. All the O'Neil Glass Company bonds are sold on September 1 at 101 plus accrued interest. Assume interest collected August 1 was properly recorded.
9. Investments carried in the fund at $1,583,000 are sold for $1,528,000.
10. The fund contains cash of $1,622,000 after disposing of all investments and paying all expenses. $1,600,000 of this amount is used to retire the bonds payable at maturity date.
11. The remaining cash balance is returned to the general account.

Instructions

Prepare the journal entries required by Castleman Roofing for the transactions above.

CASES

C18-1 (Issues Raised About Investment Securities) You have just started work for Duff Co. as part of the controller's group involved in current financial reporting problems. Teresa Chavez, controller for Duff, is interested in your accounting background because the company has experienced a series of financial reporting surprises over the last few years. Recently, the controller has learned from the company's auditors that an FASB *Statement* may apply to its investment in securities. She assumes that you are familiar with this pronouncement and asks how the following situations should be reported in the financial statements.

Situation I

Trading securities in the current asset section have a fair value of $3,000 lower than cost.

Situation II

A trading security whose fair value is currently less than cost is transferred as to the available-for-sale category.

Situation III

An available-for-sale security, whose fair value is currently less than cost, is classified as noncurrent but is to be reclassified as current.

Situation IV

A company's portfolio of available-for-sale securities consists of the common stock of one company. At the end of the prior year the fair value of the security was 50% of original cost, and this reduction in market value was reported as an other than temporary impairment. However, at the end of the current year the fair value of the security had appreciated to twice the original cost.

Situation V

The company has purchased some convertible debentures that it plans to hold for less than a year. The fair value of the convertible debenture is $8,000 below its cost.

Instructions

What is the effect upon carrying value and earnings for each of the situations above? Assume that these situations are unrelated.

C18-2 (Equity Securities) Badger Co. has the following available-for-sale securities outstanding on December 31, 1994:

	Cost	Fair Value
Mendota Corp. Stock	$20,000	$19,000
Waubesa Company Stock	10,000	9,000
Monona Company Stock	20,000	20,600
	$50,000	$48,600

During 1995 Waubesa Company stock was sold for $9,200, the difference between the $9,200 and the "fair value" of $9,000 being recorded as a "Gain on Sale of Securities." The market price of the stock on December 31, 1995, was: Mendota Corp. stock—$19,900; Monona Company stock—$20,500.

Instructions

(a) What justification is there for valuing available-for-sale securities at fair value and reporting the unrealized gain or loss as part of stockholders' equity?
(b) How should Badger Company apply this rule on December 31, 1994? Explain.
(c) Did Badger Company properly account for the sale of the Waubesa Company stock? Explain.
(d) Are there any additional entries necessary for Badger Company at December 31, 1995, to reflect the facts on the balance sheet and income statement in accordance with generally accepted accounting principles? Explain.

(AICPA adapted)

C18-3 (Financial Statement Effect of Equity Securities) Presented below are three unrelated situations involving equity securities:

Situation I

An equity security, whose market value is currently less than cost, is classified as available-for-sale but is to be reclassified as trading.

Situation II

A noncurrent portfolio with an aggregate market value in excess of cost includes one particular security whose market value has declined to less than one-half of the original cost. The decline in value is considered to be other than temporary.

Situation III

The portfolio of trading securities has a cost in excess of fair value of $12,000. The available-for-sale portfolio has a fair value in excess of cost of $29,000.

Instructions

What is the effect upon carrying value and earnings for each of the situations above? Complete your response to each situation before proceeding to the next situation.

C18-4 (Equity Securities, Current and Noncurrent) The Financial Accounting Standards Board issued its *Statement No. 115* to clarify accounting methods and procedures with respect to certain debt and all equity securities. An important part of the statement concerns the distinction between held-to-maturity, available-for-sale, and trading securities.

Instructions

(a) Why does a company maintain an investment portfolio of held-to-maturity, available-for-sale, and trading securities?
(b) What factors should be considered in determining whether investments in securities should be classified as held-to-maturity, available-for-sale, and trading, and how do these factors affect the accounting treatment for unrealized losses?

C18-5 (Economic Consequences of Standard Setting) Alan Greenspan, chairman of the Federal Reserve Board, recently commented:

> Jettisoning established accounting conventions for new, untested rules depending upon highly subjective estimates of market values will undermine investors' and depositors' confidence in banks. Such a change could also encourage bankers to abandon their traditional role as providers of long-term credit and holders of long-term securities.

Instructions

Prepare a one-page letter to Mr. Greenspan, indicating the role you believe "economic consequences" should play in accounting standard-setting.

C18-6 (Investment Accounted for Under the Equity Method) On July 1, 1996, N. Rogers Company purchased for cash 40% of the outstanding capital stock of J. Huber Company. Both N. Rogers Company and J. Huber Company have a December 31 year-end. Huber Company, whose common stock is actively traded in the over-the-counter market, reported its total net income for the year to Rogers Company and also paid cash dividends on November 15, 1996, to Rogers Company and its other stockholders.

Instructions

How should Rogers Company report the above facts in its December 31, 1996, balance sheet and its income statement for the year then ended? Discuss the rationale for your answer.

(AICPA adapted)

*C18-7 (Change from Fair Value to Equity) For the past 5 years RMT, Inc. has maintained an investment (properly accounted for and reported upon) in Beloit Co. amounting to a 10% interest in the voting common stock of Beloit Co. The purchase price was $1,050,000 and the underlying net equity in Beloit at the date of purchase was $930,000. On January 2 of the current year, RMT purchased an additional 20% of the voting common stock of Beloit for $2,400,000; the underlying net equity of the additional investment at January 2 was $2,000,000. Beloit has been profitable and has paid dividends annually since RMT's initial acquisition.

Instructions

Discuss how this increase in ownership affects the accounting for and reporting upon the investment in Beloit Co. Include in your discussion adjustments, if any, to the amount shown prior to the increase in investment to bring the amount into conformity with generally accepted accounting principles. Also include how current and subsequent periods would be reported upon.

(AICPA adapted)

*C18-8 (Investment in Life Insurance Policy) In the course of your examination of the financial statements of Bartlett Corporation as of December 31, 1996, the following entry came to your attention.

January 4, 1996

Receivable from Insurance Company	1,000,000	
Cash Surrender Value of Life Insurance Policies		136,000
Retained Earnings		159,000
Donated Capital from Life Insurance Proceeds		705,000
(Disposition of the proceeds of the life insurance policy on		
Mr. Bartlett's life. Mr. Bartlett died on January 1, 1996.)		

You are aware that Mr. Tom Bartlett, an officer-stockholder in the small manufacturing firm, insisted that the corporation's Board of Directors authorize the purchase of an insurance policy to compensate for any loss of earning potential upon his death. The corporation paid $295,000 in premiums prior to Mr. Bartlett's death, and was the sole beneficiary of the policy. At the date of death there had been no premium prepayment and no rebate was due. In prior years cash surrender value in the amount of $136,000 had been recorded in the accounts.

Instructions

(a) What is the cash surrender value of a life insurance policy?

(b) How should the cash surrender value of a life insurance policy be classified in the financial statements while the policy is in force? Why?

(c) Comment on the propriety of the entry recording the insurance receivable.

*C18-9 (Basic Investment Concepts and Classification of Sinking Fund)

Part A

To manufacture and sell its products, a company must invest in inventories, plant and equipment, and other operating assets. In addition, a manufacturing company often finds it desirable or necessary to invest a portion of its available resources, either directly or through the operation of special funds, in stocks, bonds, and other securities.

Instructions

(a) List the reasons why a manufacturing company might invest funds in stocks, bonds, and other securities.

(b) What are the criteria for classifying investments as current or noncurrent assets?

Part B

Because of favorable market prices, the trustee of Gail Anderson Company's bond sinking fund invested the current year's contribution to the fund in the company's own bonds. The bonds are being held in the fund without cancellation. The fund also includes cash and securities of other companies.

Instructions

Describe three methods of classifying the bond sinking fund on the balance sheet of Gail Anderson Company. Include a discussion of the propriety of using each method.

*C18-10 (Classification of Sinking Fund)** Gibson Inc. administers the sinking fund applicable to its own outstanding long-term bonds. The following four proposals relate to the accounting treatment of sinking fund cash and securities.

1. To mingle sinking fund cash with general cash and sinking fund securities with other securities, and to show both as current assets on the balance sheet.

2. To keep sinking fund cash in a separate bank account and sinking fund securities separate from other securities, but on the balance sheet to treat cash as a part of the general cash and the securities as part of general investments, both being shown as current assets.

3. To keep sinking fund cash in a separate bank account and sinking fund securities separate from other securities, but to combine the two accounts on the balance sheet under one caption, such as "Sinking Fund Cash and Investments," to be listed as a noncurrent asset.

4. To keep sinking fund cash in a separate bank account and sinking fund securities separate from other securities, and to identify each separately on the balance sheet among the current assets.

Instructions

Identify the proposal that is most appropriate. Give the reasons for your selection.

▶ USING YOUR JUDGMENT ◀

▶ FINANCIAL REPORTING PROBLEM

Strand Inc., a chemical processing company, has been operating profitably for many years. On March 1, 1995, Strand purchased 50,000 shares of First Executive Company stock for $2,000,000. The 50,000 shares represented 40% of First's outstanding stock. Both Strand and First operate on a fiscal year ending August 31.

For the fiscal year ended August 31, 1995, First reported net income of $900,000 earned ratably throughout the year. During November, 1994, February, May, and August, 1995, First Executive paid its regular quarterly cash dividend of $125,000.

Instructions

(a) What criteria should Strand consider in determining whether its investment in First should be classified as (1) a current asset (available-for-sale) or (2) a noncurrent asset (investment) in Strand's August 31, 1995, balance sheet? Confine your discussion to the decision criteria for determining the balance sheet classification of the investment.

(b) Assume that the securities should be classified as a long-term investment in the noncurrent asset section of Strand's balance sheet. The cost of Strand's investment equaled its equity in the recorded values of First's net assets; recorded values were not materially different from fair values (individually or collectively). For the fiscal year ended August 31, 1995, how did the net income reported and dividends paid by First affect the accounts of Strand? (Ignore income tax considerations.) Indicate each account affected, whether it increased or decreased, and explain the reason for the change in the account balance (such as Cash, Investment in First, etc.). Organize your answer in the following format:

Account Name	Increase or Decrease	Reason for Change in Account Balance

▶ WRITING ASSIGNMENT

On July 1, 1996, N. Rogers Company purchased for cash 40% of the outstanding capital stock of H. Huber Corporation. Both Rogers and Huber have a December 31 year-end. Huber Corporation, whose common stock is actively traded on the American Stock Exchange, paid a cash dividend on November 15, 1996, to N. Rogers Company and its other stockholders. It also reported its total net income for the year of $920,000 to N. Rogers Company.

Instructions

Prepare a one-page memorandum of instructions on how N. Rogers Company should report the above facts in its December 31, 1996, balance sheet and its 1996 income statement. In your memo, identify and describe the method of valuation you recommend. Provide rationale where you can. Address your memo to the Chief Accountant at N. Rogers Company.

▶ GROUP ASSIGNMENT

(Equity vs. Fair Value Method of Accounting for Investments) On December 31, 1994, Steve Zeff Company acquired 75,000 shares of Lassie Corporation common stock as a long-term investment at a cost of $30 a share. The cost of the shares to Steve Zeff Company represented 30% of the book value of Lassie's net assets, which was also 30% of the fair value of the net assets taken separately.

On May 1, 1995, Lassie Corporation paid a cash dividend of $1.50 a common share.

For the year 1995, Lassie Corporation reported net income of $450,000; the fair value of the investment was $2,025,000 at December 31, 1995.

On May 1, 1996, Lassie Corporation paid a dividend of $0.50 a share. For the year 1996, Lassie Corporation reported net income of $600,000; the fair value of the investment was $2,175,000 at December 31, 1996.

Instructions

Your instructor will assign one member of the group to serve as recorder and one member to serve as spokesperson. As a group, provide the information for the recorder to prepare responses to the following three requirements. Upon completion of each requirement and before moving on to the next part, the spokesperson will report the group findings to the class.

- **(a)** Prepare the journal entries necessary to record the transactions listed above on Steve Zeff Company's books, assuming that the investment in Lassie Corporation does not represent a significant influence and, therefore, is carried as an available-for-sale security investment. December 31 is Steve Zeff Company's year-end.
- **(b)** Prepare the journal entries necessary to record the transactions listed above on Steve Zeff Company's books, assuming that the investment in Lassie Corporation is carried on the equity basis.
- **(c)** What is the carrying value of the investment in Lassie Corporation stock on January 1, 1997 (1) under the fair value (available-for-sale) method, and (2) under the equity method?

▶ ETHICS CASE

Clark Manufacturing holds a large portfolio of debt and equity securities as an investment. The fair value of the portfolio is greater than its original cost, even though some securities have decreased in value. John Hartman, the financial vice president, and Larry Castleman, the controller, are near year-end in the process of classifying for the first time this securities portfolio in accordance with *FASB Statement No. 115*. Hartman wants to classify those securities that have increased in value during the period as trading securities in order to increase net income this year. He wants to classify all the securities that have decreased in value as available-for-sale (the equity securities) and as held-to-maturity (the debt securities). Castleman disagrees and wants to classify those securities that have decreased in value as trading securities and those that have increased in value as available-for-sale (equity) and held-to-maturity (debt). He contends that the company is having a good earnings year and that recognizing the losses will help to smooth the income this year. As a result, the company will have built-in gains for future periods when the company may not be as profitable.

Instructions

- **(a)** Will classifying the portfolio as each proposes actually have the effect on earnings that each says it will?

(b) Is there anything unethical in what each of them proposes? Who are the stakeholders affected by their proposals?

(c) Assume that Hartman and Castleman properly classify the entire portfolio into trading, available-for-sale, and held-to-maturity categories, but then each proposes to sell just before year-end the securities with gains or with losses, as the case may be, to accomplish their effect on earnings. Is this unethical?

THRIFT ACCOUNTING

A visit with
GEORGE MIRANDA

Where did you go to college, and what jobs have you had?

I went to Pasadena City College for two years and then transfered to Cal State University at Los Angeles where I graduated with a B.S. degree in accounting. After college, I went to work as a staff accountant for Pacific Holding Corporation, a company that manufactured clay and paint products. I worked there for almost two years and in 1972 came to work for H.F. Ahmanson & Company as a consolidation accountant. During the next five years, I specialized in public reporting and accounting issues related to Home Savings, our savings & loan subsidiary. In 1977, I transferred to Home Savings as its assistant controller in charge of daily accounting operations, and in 1981 became controller and treasurer. In 1989, I was named first vice president and principal accounting officer of H.F. Ahmanson & Co.

What was it like to work in the industry during the 1980s when so many thrifts were failing?

Those were very interesting times that saw a tremendous number of mergers and acquisitions. From our company's perspective, they were exciting and challenging times because we were able to expand our operations to states outside California and work toward our goal to be a dominant adjustable-rate lender. Obviously, there were some negatives which caused us a great deal of pain, such as an increase in loan delinquencies and foreclosures.

One of the most harrowing periods in American business history occurred in the 1980s, when the savings and loan crisis led to the failure of hundreds of institutions. Fortunately for **GEORGE MIRANDA,** Principal Accounting Officer of Home Savings of America, his employer was not one of them. Home Savings, a subsidiary of H.F. Ahmanson, has been one of the strongest financial institutions in the nation for many years. Miranda, as the top accounting officer for Ahmanson, has been an industry leader in implementing several new FASB statements designed to improve disclosure in the financial services industry.

What is your daily routine as principal accounting officer?

My principal responsibility is to oversee the company's accounting and financial reporting functions to ensure that financial information is completed accurately and on time for filing with various regulatory agencies such as the Office of Thrift Supervision, the Securities & Exchange Commission, the IRS, and so on. I am involved daily in company decisions that relate to operations or financial matters. I am also actively involved in various committees throughout the company relating to internal controls and compliance, finance, information systems, asset quality review, and many others.

How have some recent FASB pronouncements affected you?

During the past few years, the FASB has issued various pronouncements affecting the thrift and banking industries. Three of these come to mind easily because our company has adopted all of them. First, there is *FASB 107*, "Disclosures about Fair Value of Financial Instruments," which was effective for 1992 financial statements. *FASB 107* requires market value disclosures for all of the company's interest-sensitive assets such as loans and investment portfolios, as well as interest-bearing liabilities such as deposits. The SEC has put a lot of pressure on the FASB to require these market-value disclosures. Second, there is *FASB 115*, "Accounting for Certain Investments in Debt and Equity Securities," which is effective for fiscal years beginning after December 15, 1993. *FASB 115* requires a company to classify debt and equity securities into three categories: held-to-maturity, available-for-sale, or trading. The accounting treatment of these assets varies depending on their categories. Our company elected to adopt *FASB 115* in 1993. Last but not least is *FASB 114*, "Accounting by Creditors for Impairment of a Loan," which is effective for fiscal years beginning after December 15, 1994. *FASB 114* is a very complex document, yet we adopted it early because we had been using that accounting method for years.

What was the impact of *FASB 115*?

The impact to our company was to formally document the process of classifying our portfolio of debt and equity securities into the categories of held-to-maturity or available-for-sale. We don't use the third category because we don't have a trading portfolio. Assets classified as held-to-maturity are measured at amortized cost, whereas assets classified as available-for-sale are measured at market value. Unrealized gains or losses are reported in a separate component of the company's stockholders' equity account until actually realized. The trading category would measure these assets at market value, with the unrealized gains or losses reported in earnings.

Do you get the benefit of market fluctuations as well as the downside?

Absolutely. For example, during the first quarter of 1994 we saw the change in the market value of assets classified as available-for-sale go south on us. As a result, we reported a significant reduction in

our stockholders' equity. This is the very reason the industry fought so hard with FASB to have this market value fluctuation not go through the statement of operations, since it would result in very volatile earnings.

What about *FASB 114*, the statement on loan impairment?

That's a very complex document to interpret and to implement. *FASB 114* defines when a loan is impaired and what methods should be used to value impaired loans. A loan is impaired when it is probable that a creditor will be unable to collect all amounts due according to the contractual terms of the loan agreement. These rules are subjective in nature and open to different interpretations.

What is FASB trying to accomplish with all of this?

I think they are trying to make more and more information available to the investment community. They are trying to deal with some very complex valuation issues related to these so-called problem assets, and also with the sensitivity of various assets to market fluctuations. There is a school of thought out there that believes that historical accounting is really not meaningful for banks and thrifts, because too many of our assets and liabilities reprice frequently. And there is a lot of truth to that. However, you've got to look at both sides of the balance sheet, and the FASB has elected to look only at the asset side for the time being.

Historically, hasn't thrift accounting been considered rather poor?

You read that the fall of the thrift industry was because the account-

ing was poor. I think that thrifts that were publicly held such as Ahmanson, Golden West, and others had accounting that was as good as the major banks such as Bank of America or Chase Manhattan. The problem, in my opinion, was that the regulators overseeing the thrift industry were a little more liberal with regulatory accounting rules than their bank counterparts. Some of the thrifts that were not publicly held were able to record certain transactions under regulatory thrift accounting, which they would not have been able to do under GAAP. But now you see the OTS, the FDIC, and the Federal Reserve all moving a lot closer to using the same accounting practices.

Does the investment community give you credit for early adoption of these pronouncements?

I guess you do get a little credit from the point of view that the investment community may look at the company's adequacy of its loan loss reserve and realize that even after adopting such a complex pronouncement as *FASB 114*, the company's earnings stream potential was not significantly affected.

What advice would you give a college student who is thinking about following in your footsteps?

The old saying that "being in the right place at the right time" helps a great deal. I was fortunate to be there. Being prepared and getting ready for whatever the next step may be is also very important.

CHAPTER 19

REVENUE RECOGNITION

LEARNING OBJECTIVES

After studying this chapter, you should be able to:

1. Apply the revenue recognition principle.
2. Describe accounting issues involved with revenue recognition at point of sale.
3. Apply the percentage-of-completion method for long-term contracts.
4. Apply the completed-contract method for long-term contracts.
5. Identify the proper accounting for losses on long-term contracts.
6. Identify alternative revenue recognition bases before delivery.
7. Describe the installment method of accounting.
8. Explain the cost recovery method of accounting.

*F*requent-flier programs are so popular that airlines at one time owed participants more than 34.6 billion miles of free travel. If all these miles were cashed in, it could cost the airlines $2.3 billion. Currently, each airline determines its own frequent-flier revenues and liabilities; the airlines take into account the rates at which the frequent-flier coupons are redeemed. Up to this point, airlines have recognized as revenue the entire sales price of the ticket at the time the ticket is purchased. The incremental costs expected to be incurred when the free transportation is provided are accrued at the time a free travel award is reached. Some disagree with this accounting. As one expert noted: "You can no longer say that the revenue process is substantially complete when the ticket is sold. Passengers are purchasing tickets with the expectation of a free flight, and we have to account for that liability." Therefore, such critics argue, a portion of the revenue from the tickets sold should be deferred and reported as a liability.

The accounting question is, "When should revenue be recognized?" It's a complex question for which no easy answers exist. Revenue recognition is one of the most difficult and pressing problems facing the accounting profession. The many methods of marketing products and services make it extremely difficult to develop guidelines that will apply to all situations. Major lawsuits involving revenue recognition problems[1] illustrate the complexity of determining when and at what amount revenue should be recognized. Nevertheless, accountants have developed certain general guidelines to record such transactions. These guidelines are the subject of this chapter.

---

[1]Lawsuits such as U.S. Financial (related-party transactions), National Student Marketing (revenue that did not materialize), and Equity Funding (sales that never were).

▶ GUIDELINES FOR REVENUE RECOGNITION

OBJECTIVE 1

Apply the revenue recognition principle.

The **revenue recognition principle** provides that revenue is recognized[2] when (1) it is realized or realizable and (2) it is earned.[3] Revenues are **realized** when goods and services are exchanged for cash or claims to cash (receivables). Revenues are **realizable** when assets received in exchange are readily convertible to known amounts of cash or claims to cash. Revenues are **earned** when the entity has substantially accomplished what it must do to be entitled to the benefits represented by the revenues, that is, when the earnings process is complete or virtually complete.[4]

Four revenue transactions are recognized in accordance with this principle:

1. Revenue from selling products is recognized at the date of sale, usually interpreted to mean the date of delivery to customers.

2. Revenue from services rendered is recognized when services have been performed and are billable.

3. Revenue from permitting others to use enterprise assets, such as interest, rent, and royalties, is recognized as time passes or as the assets are used.

4. Revenue from disposing of assets other than products is recognized at the date of sale.

These revenue transactions are diagrammed in Illustration 19-1.

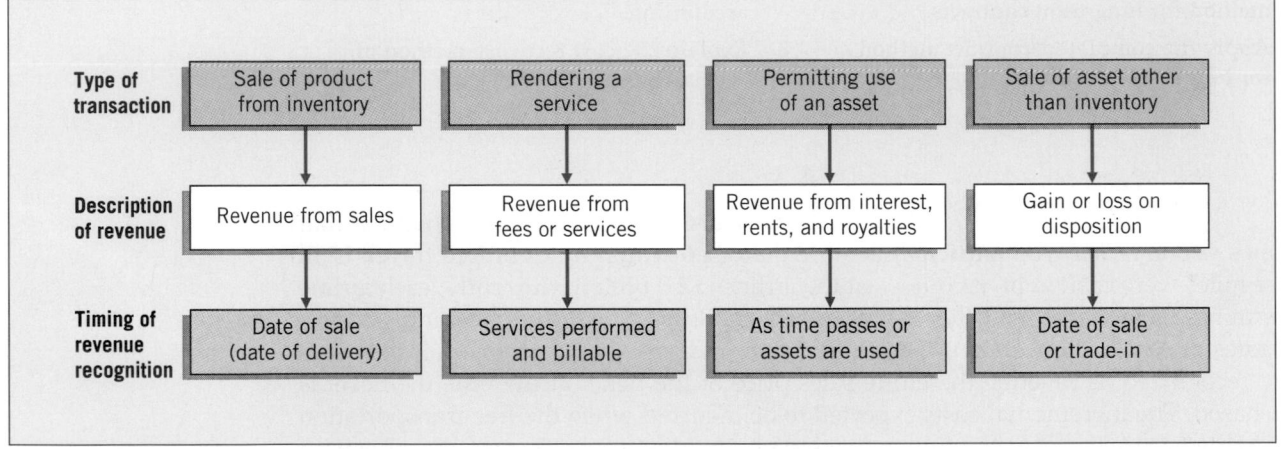

**ILLUSTRATION 19-1
Revenue Recognition
Classified by Nature of
Transaction**

The preceding statements describe the conceptual nature of revenue and are the basis of accounting for revenue transactions. Yet, in practice, there are departures from the revenue recognition principle (the full accrual method). Revenue is sometimes recog-

---

[2]Recognition is "the process of formally recording or incorporating an item in the accounts and financial statements of an entity" (*SFAC No. 3*, par. 83). "Recognition includes depiction of an item in both words and numbers, with the amount included in the totals of the financial statements" (*SFAC No. 5*, par. 6). For an asset or liability, recognition involves recording not only acquisition or incurrence of the item but also later changes in it, including removal from the financial statements previously recognized.

Recognition is not the same as realization, although the two are sometimes used interchangeably in accounting literature and practice. *Realization* is "the process of converting noncash resources and rights into money and is most precisely used in accounting and financial reporting to refer to sales of assets for cash or claims to cash" (*SFAC No. 3*, par. 83).

[3]"Recognition and Measurement in Financial Statements of Business Enterprises," *Statement of Financial Accounting Concepts No. 5* (Stamford, Conn.: FASB, 1984), par. 83.

[4]Gains (as contrasted to revenues) commonly result from transactions and other events that do not involve an "earning process." For gain recognition, being earned is generally less significant than being realized or realizable. Gains are commonly recognized at the time of sale of an asset, disposition of a liability, or when prices of certain assets change.

nized at other points in the earning process, owing in great measure to the considerable variety of revenue transactions.

For example, many revenue recognition problems develop because the ultimate collection of the selling price is not reasonably assured or because it is difficult to determine when the earning process is complete. Real estate land sales provide a good example. At one time General Development recognized the entire sales price of real estate as revenue as soon as it received 5% of the purchase price or a minimum down payment and two monthly payments. Cavanaugh Industries indicated that the percentage collected need be only 3%. Dart Industries required a 10% down payment, as did Boise Cascade, yet McCulloch demanded 15%. The issuance of *FASB Statement No. 66* provides a definitive schedule for determining the "minimum initial investment" (down payment) required for full accrual (sale) accounting in real estate transactions. The initial investment may range from 5% to 25% of the sales value of the property, depending on the type of real estate, with 13 types encompassing the range.[5]

INTERNATIONAL INSIGHT

Accounting principles in some nations (e.g., Mexico, Sweden, Switzerland) do not specifically address the issue of revenue recognition.

The profession is continually developing criteria that should be met before a departure from the sale basis is acceptable. An FASB study found some common **reasons for departures from the sale basis.**[6] One reason is a desire to **recognize earlier** in the earning process than the time of sale the effect of earning activities (revenue) if there is a high degree of certainty about the amount of revenue earned. A second reason is a desire to **delay recognition** of revenue beyond the time of sale if the degree of uncertainty concerning the amount of either revenue or costs is sufficiently high or if the sale does not represent substantial completion of the earnings process. That same study concluded that there are significant inconsistencies in accounting pronouncements and, consequently, in practice for recognizing revenue.

This chapter is devoted exclusively to the discussion and illustration of two of the four general types of revenue transactions described earlier, namely, (1) selling products and (2) rendering services—both of which are **sales transactions.** The other two types of revenue transactions—(3) revenue from permitting others to use enterprise assets and (4) revenue from disposing of assets other than products—are discussed in several other sections of the textbook. Our discussion of product sales transactions is organized around the following topics:

1. Revenue recognition at point of sale (delivery).
2. Revenue recognition before delivery.
3. Revenue recognition after delivery.
4. Revenue recognition for special sales transactions—franchises and consignments.

This organization of revenue recognition topics is depicted graphically below.

**ILLUSTRATION 19-2
Revenue Recognition
Alternatives**

At date of delivery (point of sale)	Before delivery			After delivery		Special sales	
"The General Rule"	Before production	During production	At completion of production	As cash is collected	After costs are recovered	Franchises	Consignments

---

[5]AICPA Industry Accounting Guide, "Accounting for Profit Recognition on Sales of Real Estate," 1973; and "Accounting for Sales of Real Estate," *Statement of Financial Accounting Standards No. 66* (Stamford, Conn.: FASB, 1982).

[6]Henry R. Jaenicke, *Survey of Present Practices in Recognizing Revenues, Expenses, Gains, and Losses,* A Research Report (Stamford, Conn.: FASB, 1981), p. 11.

OBJECTIVE 2

Describe accounting issues involved with revenue recognition at point of sale.

► REVENUE RECOGNITION AT POINT OF SALE (DELIVERY)

According to the FASB in *Concepts Statement No. 5*, the two conditions for recognizing revenue (being realized or realizable and being earned) are usually met by the time product or merchandise is delivered or services are rendered to customers. Revenues from manufacturing and selling activities are commonly recognized at **point of sale** (usually meaning delivery).[7] Problems of implementation, however, can arise; three such situations are discussed below: (1) sales with buyback agreements, (2) sales when right of return exists, and (3) trade loading and channel stuffing.

SALES WITH BUYBACK AGREEMENTS

If a company sells a product in one period and agrees to buy it back in the next accounting period, has the company sold the product? As indicated in Chapter 8, legal title has transferred in this situation, but the economic substance of the transaction is that retention of risks of ownership are retained by the seller. The profession has taken steps to curtail the recognition of revenue from this practice. When a repurchase agreement exists at a set price and this price covers all costs of the inventory plus related holding costs, the inventory and related liability remain on the seller's books.[8] In other words, no sale.

SALES WHEN RIGHT OF RETURN EXISTS

UNDERLYING CONCEPT

This is an example of realized *but* unearned revenue. *When high rates of return exist and cannot be reasonably estimated, a question arises as to whether the earnings process has been substantially completed.*

Whether cash or credit sales are involved, a special problem arises with claims for returns and allowances. In Chapter 7, the accounting treatment for normal returns and allowances was presented. However, certain companies experience such a **high rate of returns**—a high ratio of returned merchandise to sales—that they find it necessary to postpone reporting sales until the return privilege has substantially expired. For example, in the publishing industry the rate of return approaches 25% for hardcover books and 65% for some magazines. Other types of companies that experience high return rates are perishable food dealers, rack jobbers or distributors who sell to retail outlets, record and tape companies, and some toy and sporting goods manufacturers. Returns in these industries are frequently made either through a right of contract or as a matter of practice involving "guaranteed sales" agreements or consignments.

Three alternative revenue recognition methods are available when the seller is exposed to continued risks of ownership through return of the product. These are: (1) not recording a sale until all return privileges have expired; (2) recording the sale, but reducing sales by an estimate of future returns; and (3) recording the sale and accounting for the returns as they occur. The FASB concluded that if a company sells its product but gives the buyer the right to return it, then revenue from the sales transaction shall be recognized at the time of sale only if **all** of the following six conditions have been met:[9]

1. The seller's price to the buyer is substantially fixed or determinable at the date of sale.

2. The buyer has paid the seller, or the buyer is obligated to pay the seller and the obligation is not contingent on resale of the product.

3. The buyer's obligation to the seller would not be changed in the event of theft or physical destruction or damage of the product.

4. The buyer acquiring the product for resale has economic substance apart from that provided by the seller.

---

[7]*Statement of Financial Accounting Concepts No. 5*, op. cit., par. 84.

[8]"Accounting for Product Financing Arrangements," *Statement of Financial Accounting Standards No. 49* (Stamford, Conn.: FASB, 1981).

[9]"Revenue Recognition When Right of Return Exists," *Statement of Financial Accounting Standards No. 48* (Stamford, Conn.: FASB, 1981), par. 6.

5. The seller does not have significant obligations for future performance to directly bring about resale of the product by the buyer.

6. The amount of future returns can be reasonably estimated.

What if revenue cannot be recognized at the time of sale because the six conditions are not met? In that case sales revenue and cost of sales that are not recognized at the time of sale because the six conditions above are not met should be recognized either when the return privilege has substantially expired or when those six conditions subsequently are met (whichever occurs first). Sales revenue and cost of sales reported in the income statement should be reduced to report estimated returns.[10]

TRADE LOADING AND CHANNEL STUFFING

Some companies record revenues at date of delivery with neither buyback nor unlimited return provisions. Although they appear to be following acceptable point of sale revenue recognition, they are recognizing revenues and earnings prematurely. The domestic cigarette industry until very recently engaged in a distribution practice known as "trade loading." "Trade loading is a crazy, uneconomic, insidious practice through which manufacturers—trying to show sales, profits, and market share they don't actually have—induce their wholesale customers, known as the trade, to buy more product than they can promptly resell."[11] In total, the cigarette industry appears to have exaggerated a couple years' operating profits by as much as $600 million by taking the profits from future years.

In the computer software industry this same practice is referred to as "channel stuffing." When Ashton-Tate, a software maker, needed to make its financial results look good, it offered deep discounts to its distributors to overbuy and recorded revenue when the software left the loading dock.[12] Of course, the distributors' inventories become bloated and the marketing channel gets stuffed but the software maker's financials are improved—but only to the detriment of future periods' results, unless the process is repeated.

Trade loading and channel stuffing are management and marketing policy decisions and actions that hype sales, distort operating results, and window dress financial statements. End-of-period accounting adjustments are not made to reduce the impact of these types of sales on operating results. The practices of trade loading and channel stuffing need to be discouraged. Business managers need to be aware of the ethical dangers of misleading the financial community by engaging in such practices to improve their financial statements.

▶ REVENUE RECOGNITION BEFORE DELIVERY

For the most part, recognition at the point of sale (delivery) is used because most of the uncertainties concerning the earning process are removed and the exchange price is known. Under certain circumstances, however, revenue is recognized prior to completion and delivery. The most notable example is long-term construction contract accounting where the percentage-of-completion method is applicable.

REVENUE RECOGNITION DURING PRODUCTION

Long-term contracts such as construction-type contracts, development of military and commercial aircraft, weapons delivery systems, and space exploration hardware frequently provide that the seller (builder) may bill the purchaser at intervals, as various points in the project are reached. When the project consists of separable units such as

---

[10]Ibid., pars. 6 and 7.

[11]"The $600 Million Cigarette Scam," *Fortune* (December 4, 1989), p. 89.

[12]"Software's Dirty Little Secret," *Forbes* (May 15, 1989), p. 128.

a group of buildings or miles of roadway, passage of title and billing may take place at stated stages of completion, such as the completion of each building unit or every 10 miles of road. Such contract provisions provide for delivery in installments, and the accounting records should report this by recording sales when installments are "delivered."[13]

Two distinctly different methods of accounting for long-term construction contracts are recognized by the accounting profession:[14]

INTERNATIONAL INSIGHT

The European Directives (standards) do not specify accounting for long-term contracts.

1. **Percentage-of-Completion Method.** Revenues and gross profit are recognized each period based upon the progress of the construction, that is, the percentage of completion. Construction costs **plus gross profit earned to date** are accumulated in an inventory account (Construction in Process), and progress billings are accumulated in a contra inventory account (Billings on Construction in Process).

2. **Completed-Contract Method.** Revenues and gross profit are recognized only when the contract is completed. Construction costs are accumulated in an inventory account (Construction in Process), and progress billings are accumulated in a contra inventory account (Billings on Construction in Process).

The rationale for using percentage-of-completion accounting is that under most of these contracts the buyer and seller have obtained enforceable rights. The buyer has the legal right to require specific performance on the contract; the seller has the right to require progress payments that provide evidence of the buyer's ownership interest. As a result, a continuous sale occurs as the work progresses, and revenue should be recognized accordingly.

The profession requires that the percentage-of-completion method be used when estimates of progress toward completion, revenues, and costs are reasonably dependable and **all** the following conditions exist:[15]

UNDERLYING CONCEPT

The percentage-of-completion method recognizes revenue from long-term contracts in the periods that the revenue is earned. The firm contract fixes the selling price. And, if costs are estimable and collection reasonably assured, the revenue recognition concept is not violated.

1. The contract clearly specifies the enforceable rights regarding goods or services to be provided and received by the parties, the consideration to be exchanged, and the manner and terms of settlement.

2. The buyer can be expected to satisfy all obligations under the contract.

3. The contractor can be expected to perform the contractual obligation.

The completed-contract method should be used only (1) when an entity has primarily short-term contracts, or (2) when the conditions for using the percentage-of-completion method cannot be met, or (3) when there are inherent hazards in the contract beyond the normal, recurring business risks. The presumption is that **percentage-of-completion is the better method and that the completed-contract method should be used only when the percentage-of-completion method is inappropriate.**

PERCENTAGE-OF-COMPLETION METHOD

OBJECTIVE 3

Apply the percentage-of-completion method for long-term contracts.

The **percentage-of-completion method** recognizes revenues, costs, and gross profit as progress is made toward completion on a long-term contract. To defer recognition of these items until completion of the entire contract is to misrepresent the efforts (costs) and accomplishments (revenues) of the interim accounting periods. In order to apply the percentage-of-completion method, one must have some basis or standard for measuring the progress toward completion at particular interim dates.

---

[13]*Statement of Financial Accounting Concepts No. 5*, par. 84, item c.

[14]*Accounting Trends and Techniques—1993* reports that, of the 135 of its 600 sample companies that referred to long-term construction contracts, 129 used the percentage-of-completion method and 5 used the completed-contract method (1 was not determinable).

[15]"Accounting for Performance of Construction-Type and Certain Production-Type Contracts," *Statement of Position 81-1* (New York: AICPA, 1981), par. 23.

Measuring the Progress Toward Completion

As one practicing accountant wrote, "The big problem in applying the percentage-of-completion method that cannot be demonstrated in an example has to do with the ability to make reasonably accurate estimates of completion and the final gross profit."[16] Various methods are used in practice to determine the **extent of progress toward completion;** the most common are "cost-to-cost method," "efforts expended methods," and "units of work performed method."

The objective of all the methods is to measure the extent of progress in terms of costs, units, or value added. The various measures (costs incurred, labor hours worked, tons produced, stories completed, etc.) are identified and classified as input and output measures. **Input measures** (costs incurred, labor hours worked) are made in terms of efforts devoted to a contract. **Output measures** (tons produced, stories of a building completed, miles of a highway completed) are made in terms of results. Neither are universally applicable to all long-term projects; their use requires careful tailoring to the circumstances and the exercise of judgment.

Both input and output measures have certain disadvantages. The input measure is based on an established relationship between a unit of input and productivity. If inefficiencies cause the productivity relationship to change, inaccurate measurements result. Another potential problem, called "front-end loading," produces higher estimates of completion by virtue of incurring significant costs up front. Some early-stage construction costs should be disregarded if they do not relate to contract performance, for example, costs of uninstalled materials or costs of subcontracts not yet performed.

Output measures can result in inaccurate measures if the units used are not comparable in time, effort, or cost to complete. For example, using stories completed can be deceiving; completing the first story of an eight-story building may require more than one-eighth the total cost because of the substructure and foundation construction.

One of the more popular input measures used to determine the progress toward completion is the **cost-to-cost basis.** Under the cost-to-cost basis, the percentage of completion is measured by comparing costs incurred to date with the most recent estimate of the total costs to complete the contract, as shown in the following formula:

$$\frac{\text{Costs incurred to date}}{\text{Most recent estimate of total costs}} = \text{Percent complete}$$

ILLUSTRATION 19-3
Formula for Percentage of Completion, Cost-to-Cost Basis

The percentage that costs incurred bear to total estimated costs is applied to the total revenue or the estimated total gross profit on the contract in arriving at the revenue or the gross profit amounts to be recognized to date.

$$\text{Percent complete} \times \begin{array}{c}\text{Estimated total}\\\text{revenue (or gross}\\\text{profit)}\end{array} = \begin{array}{c}\text{Revenue (or gross}\\\text{profit) to be}\\\text{recognized to date}\end{array}$$

ILLUSTRATION 19-4
Formula for Total Revenue to be Recognized to Date

To find the amounts of revenue and gross profit recognized each period, we would need to subtract total revenue or gross profit recognized in prior periods, as shown in the following formula:

$$\begin{array}{c}\text{Revenue (or gross}\\\text{profit) to be}\\\text{recognized to date}\end{array} - \begin{array}{c}\text{Revenue (or gross}\\\text{profit) recognized}\\\text{in prior periods}\end{array} = \begin{array}{c}\text{Current period}\\\text{revenue (or}\\\text{gross profit)}\end{array}$$

ILLUSTRATION 19-5
Formula for Amount of Current Period Revenue, Cost-to-Cost Basis

---

[16]Richard S. Hickok, "New Guidance for Construction Contractors: 'A Credit Plus,'" *The Journal of Accountancy* (March 1982), p. 46.

Because **the profession specifically recommends the cost-to-cost method** (without excluding other bases for measuring progress toward completion), we have adopted it for use in our illustrations.[17]

Illustration of Percentage-of-Completion Method—Cost-to-Cost Basis

To illustrate the percentage-of-completion method, assume that the Hardhat Construction Company has a contract starting July 1995, to construct a $4,500,000 bridge that is expected to be completed in October 1997, at an estimated cost of $4,000,000. The following data pertain to the construction period (note that by the end of 1996 the estimated total cost has increased from $4,000,000 to $4,050,000):

	1995	1996	1997
Costs to date	$1,000,000	$2,916,000	$4,050,000
Estimated costs to complete	3,000,000	1,134,000	—
Progress billings during the year	900,000	2,400,000	1,200,000
Cash collected during the year	750,000	1,750,000	2,000,000

The percent complete would be computed as follows:

ILLUSTRATION 19-6
Application of Percentage-of-Completion Method, Cost-to-Cost Basis

Hardhat Construction Company			
	1995	1996	1997
Contract price	$4,500,000	$4,500,000	$4,500,000
Less estimated cost:			
Costs to date	1,000,000	2,916,000	4,050,000
Estimated costs to complete	3,000,000	1,134,000	—
Estimated total costs	4,000,000	4,050,000	4,050,000
Estimated total gross profit	$ 500,000	$ 450,000	$ 450,000
Percent complete:	25%	72%	100%
	$\left(\dfrac{\$1,000,000}{\$4,000,000}\right)$	$\left(\dfrac{\$2,916,000}{\$4,050,000}\right)$	$\left(\dfrac{\$4,050,000}{\$4,050,000}\right)$

On the basis of the data above, the following entries would be prepared to record (1) the costs of construction, (2) progress billings, and (3) collections. These entries appear as summaries of the many transactions that would be entered individually as they occur during the year:

ILLUSTRATION 19-7
Journal Entries—Percentage-of-Completion Method, Cost-to-Cost Basis

	1995		1996		1997	
To record cost of construction						
Construction in Process	1,000,000		1,916,000		1,134,000	
Materials, cash,						
payables, etc.		1,000,000		1,916,000		1,134,000
To record progress billings						
Accounts Receivable	900,000		2,400,000		1,200,000	
Billings on Construction						
in Process		900,000		2,400,000		1,200,000
To record collections						
Cash	750,000		1,750,000		2,000,000	
Accounts Receivable		750,000		1,750,000		2,000,000

In this illustration, the costs incurred to date as a proportion of the estimated total costs to be incurred on the project are a measure of the extent of progress toward

---

[17]Committee on Accounting Procedure, "Long-Term Construction-Type Contracts," *Accounting Research Bulletin No. 45* (New York: AICPA, 1955), p. 7.

completion. The estimated revenue and gross profit to be recognized for each year are calculated as follows:

	1995	1996	1997
Revenue recognized in:			
1995 $4,500,000 × 25%	$1,125,000		
1996 $4,500,000 × 72%		$3,240,000	
Less revenue recognized in 1995		1,125,000	
Revenue in 1996		$2,115,000	
1997 $4,500,000 × 100%			$4,500,000
Less revenue recognized in 1995 and 1996			3,240,000
Revenue in 1997			$1,260,000
Gross profit recognized in:			
1995 $500,000 × 25%	$ 125,000		
1996 $450,000 × 72%		$ 324,000	
Less gross profit recognized in 1995		125,000	
Gross profit in 1996		$ 199,000	
1997 $450,000 × 100%			$ 450,000
Less gross profit recognized in 1995 and 1996			324,000
Gross profit in 1997			$ 126,000

ILLUSTRATION 19-8
Percentage-of-Completion, Revenue and Gross Profit, by Year

The entries to recognize revenue and gross profit each year and to record completion and final approval of the contract are shown below.

	1995		1996		1997	
To recognize revenue and gross profit						
Construction in Process (gross profit)	125,000		199,000		126,000	
Construction Expenses	1,000,000		1,916,000		1,134,000	
Revenue from Long-Term Contract		1,125,000		2,115,000		1,260,000
To record completion of the contract						
Billings on Construction in Process					4,500,000	
Construction in Process						4,500,000

ILLUSTRATION 19-9
Journal Entries to Recognize Revenue and Gross Profit and to Record Contract Completion—Percentage-of-Completion Method, Cost-to-Cost Basis

Note that gross profit as computed above is debited to Construction in Process, while Revenue from Long-Term Contract is credited for the amounts as computed above. The difference between the amounts recognized each year for revenue and gross profit is debited to a nominal account, Construction Expenses (similar to cost of goods sold in a manufacturing enterprise), which is reported in the income statement. That amount is the actual cost of construction incurred in that period. For example, in the Hardhat Construction Company cost-to-cost illustration the actual costs of $1,000,000 in 1995 are used to compute both the gross profit of $125,000 and the percent complete (25%).

Costs must continue to be accumulated in the Construction in Process account to maintain a record of total costs incurred (plus recognized profit) to date. Although theoretically a series of "sales" takes place using the percentage-of-completion method, the inventory cost cannot be removed until the construction is completed and transferred to the new owner. The Construction in Process account would include the following summarized entries over the term of the construction project.

Construction in Process				
1995 construction costs	$1,000,000	12/31/97	to close	
1995 recognized gross profit	125,000		completed	
1996 construction costs	1,916,000		project	$4,500,000
1996 recognized gross profit	199,000			
1997 construction costs	1,134,000			
1997 recognized gross profit	126,000			
Total	$4,500,000	Total		$4,500,000

The Hardhat Construction Company illustration contained a **change in estimate** in the second year, 1996, when the estimated total costs increased from $4,000,000 to $4,050,000. By adjusting the percent completed to the new estimate of total costs and then deducting the amount of revenues and gross profit recognized in prior periods from revenues and gross profit computed for progress to date, the change in estimate is accounted for in a **cumulative catch-up manner.** That is, the change in estimate is accounted for **in the period of change** so that the balance sheet at the end of the period of change and the accounting in subsequent periods are as they would have been if the revised estimate had been the original estimate.

Financial Statement Presentation—Percentage of Completion

Generally when a receivable from a sale is recorded, the Inventory account is reduced. In this case, however, both the receivable and the inventory continue to be carried. Subtracting the balance in the **Billings** account from Construction in Process avoids double-counting the inventory. During the life of the contract, the difference between the Construction in Process and the Billings on Construction in Process accounts is reported in the balance sheet **as a current asset if a debit, and as a current liability if a credit.**

When the costs incurred plus the gross profit recognized to date (the balance in Construction in Process) exceed the billings, this excess is reported as a current asset entitled "Costs and Recognized Profit in Excess of Billings." The unbilled portion of revenue recognized to date can be calculated at any time by subtracting the billings to date from the revenue recognized to date as illustrated below for 1995 for Hardhat Construction:

**ILLUSTRATION 19-10
Computation of Unbilled
Contract Price at 12/31/95**

Hardhat Construction Company	
Contract revenue recognized to date: $4,500,000 \times \dfrac{\$1,000,000}{\$4,000,000} =	$1,125,000
Billings to date	900,000
Unbilled revenue	$ 225,000

When the billings exceed costs incurred and gross profit to date, this excess is reported as a current liability entitled "Billings in Excess of Costs and Recognized Profit."

When a company has a number of projects, and costs exceed billings on some contracts and billings exceed costs on others, the contracts should be segregated. The asset side should include only those contracts on which costs and recognized profit exceed billings, and the liability side includes only those on which billings exceed costs and recognized profit. Separate disclosures of the dollar volume of billings and costs are preferable to a summary presentation of the net difference.

Using data from the previous illustration, the Hardhat Construction Company would report the status and results of its long-term construction activities under the percentage-of-completion method as follows:

Hardhat Construction Company

		1995	1996	1997
Income Statement				
Revenue from long-term contracts		$1,125,000	$2,115,000	$1,260,000
Costs of construction		1,000,000	1,916,000	1,134,000
Gross profit		$ 125,000	$ 199,000	$ 126,000

Balance Sheet (12/31)				
Current assets:				
Accounts receivable			$ 150,000	$ 800,000
Inventories				
Construction in process	$1,125,000			
Less: Billings	900,000			
Costs and recognized profit				
in excess of billings			$ 225,000	
Current liabilities:				
Billings ($3,300,000) in excess of costs and				
recognized profit ($3,240,000)				$ 60,000

Note 1. Summary of significant accounting policies.
Long-Term Construction Contracts. The company recognizes revenues and reports profits from long-term construction contracts, its principal business, under the percentage-of-completion method of accounting. These contracts generally extend for periods in excess of one year. The amounts of revenues and profits recognized each year are based on the ratio of costs incurred to the total estimated costs. Costs included in construction in process include direct material, direct labor, and project-related overhead. Corporate general and administrative expenses are charged to the periods as incurred and are not allocated to construction contracts.

COMPLETED-CONTRACT METHOD

Under the **completed-contract method,** revenue and gross profit are recognized only at point of sale, that is, when the contract is completed. Costs of long-term contracts in process and current billings are accumulated, but there are **no interim charges or credits to income statement accounts for revenues, costs, and gross profit.**

The principal advantage of the completed-contract method is that reported revenue is based on final results rather than on estimates of unperformed work. Its major disadvantage is that it does not reflect current performance when the period of a contract extends into more than one accounting period. Although operations may be fairly uniform during the period of the contract, revenue is not reported until the year of completion, creating a distortion of earnings.

The **annual entries** to record costs of construction, progress billings, and collections from customers would be identical to those illustrated under the percentage-of-completion method with the significant exclusion of the recognition of revenue and gross profit. For the bridge project of Hardhat Construction Company illustrated on the preceding pages, the following entries are made in 1997 under the completed-contract method to recognize revenue and costs and to close out the inventory and billing accounts:

Billings on Construction in Process	4,500,000	
Revenue from Long-Term Contracts		4,500,000
Costs of Construction	4,050,000	
Construction in Process		4,050,000

Comparing the two methods in relation to the same bridge project, the Hardhat Construction Company would have recognized gross profit as follows:

	Percentage-of-Completion	Completed-Contract
1995	$125,000	$ 0
1996	199,000	0
1997	126,000	450,000

OBJECTIVE 4
Apply the completed-contract method for long-term contracts.

UNDERLYING CONCEPT

The completed-contract method does not violate the matching concept *because the costs are also deferred until the completion of the contract.*

INTERNATIONAL INSIGHT

Internationally, some nations (e.g., U.K., Mexico, Hong Kong) require use of percentage-of-completion accounting; others (e.g., Germany, the Netherlands) require accounting on a completed-contract basis.

ILLUSTRATION 19-12
Comparison of Gross Profit Recognized under Different Methods

Hardhat Construction would report its long-term construction activities as follows:

Hardhat Construction Company			
	1995	1996	1997
Income Statement			
Revenue from long-term contracts	—	—	$4,500,000
Costs of construction	—	—	4,050,000
Gross profit	—	—	$ 450,000

Balance Sheet (12/31)			
Current assets:			
Accounts receivable		$150,000	$800,000
Inventories			
Construction in process	$1,000,000		
Less: Billings	900,000		
Unbilled contract costs		$100,000	
Current liabilities:			
Billings ($3,300,000) in excess of contract			
costs ($2,916,000)			$384,000

Note 1. Summary of significant accounting policies.
Long-Term Construction Contracts. The company recognizes revenues and reports profits from long-term construction contracts, its principal business, under the completed-contract method. These contracts generally extend for periods in excess of one year. Contract costs and billings are accumulated during the periods of construction, but no revenues or profits are recognized until completion of the contract. Costs included in construction in process include direct material, direct labor, and project-related overhead. Corporate general and administrative expenses are charged to the periods as incurred.

ACCOUNTING FOR LONG-TERM CONTRACT LOSSES

Two types of losses can become evident under long-term contracts:[18]

1. **Loss in Current Period on a Profitable Contract.** This condition arises when, during construction, there is a significant increase in the estimated total contract costs but the increase does not eliminate all profit on the contract. Under the percentage-of-completion method only, the estimated cost increase requires a current period adjustment of excess gross profit recognized on the project in prior periods. This adjustment is recorded as a loss in the current period because it is a **change in accounting estimate** (discussed in Chapter 23).

UNDERLYING
CONCEPT

Conservatism justifies recognizing the losses immediately. Loss recognition does not require realization; it only requires evidence that an impairment of asset value has occurred.

2. **Loss on an Unprofitable Contract.** Cost estimates at the end of the current period may indicate that a loss will result on completion of the entire contract. Under both the percentage-of-completion and the completed-contract methods, the entire expected contract loss must be recognized in the current period.

The treatment described for unprofitable contracts is consistent with the accounting custom of anticipating foreseeable losses to avoid overstatement of current and future income (conservatism).

Loss in Current Period

To illustrate a loss in the current period on a contract expected to be profitable upon completion, assume that on December 31, 1996, Hardhat Construction Company estimates the costs to complete the bridge contract at $1,468,962 instead of $1,134,000 (refer to page 946). Assuming all other data are the same as before, Hardhat would compute the percent complete and recognize the loss as shown in Illustration 19-14. Compare

---

[18]Sak Bhamornsiri, "Losses from Construction Contracts," *The Journal of Accountancy* (April 1982), p. 26.

these computations with those for 1996 in Illustration 19-6. The "percent complete" has dropped from 72% to 66½% due to the increase in estimated future costs to complete the contract.

The 1996 loss of $48,500 is a cumulative adjustment of the "excessive" gross profit recognized on the contract in 1995. **Instead of restating the prior period, the prior period misstatement is absorbed entirely in the current period.** In this illustration, the adjustment was large enough to result in recognition of a loss.

Costs to date (12/31/96)	$2,916,000
Estimated costs to complete (revised)	1,468,962
Estimated total costs	$4,384,962
Percent complete ($2,916,000 ÷ $4,384,962)	66½%
Revenue recognized in 1996	
($4,500,000 × 66½% − $1,125,000)	$1,867,500
Costs incurred in 1996	1,916,000
Loss recognized in 1996	$ 48,500

ILLUSTRATION 19-14
Computation of Recognizable Loss, 1996—Loss in Current Period

Hardhat Construction would record the loss in 1996 as follows:

Construction Expenses	1,916,000	
Construction in Process (loss)		48,500
Revenue from Long-Term Contract		1,867,500

The loss of $48,500 will be reported on the 1996 income statement as the difference between the reported revenues of $1,867,500 and the costs of $1,916,000.[19] **Under the completed-contract method, no loss is recognized in 1996 because the contract is still expected to result in a profit** to be recognized in the year of completion.

Loss on an Unprofitable Contract

To illustrate the accounting for an overall loss on a long-term contract, assume that at December 31, 1996, Hardhat Construction Company estimates the costs to complete the bridge contract at $1,640,250 instead of $1,134,000. Revised estimates relative to the bridge contract appear as follows:

	1995 Original Estimates	1996 Revised Estimates
Contract price	$4,500,000	$4,500,000
Estimated total cost	4,000,000	4,556,250*
Estimated gross profit	$ 500,000	
Estimated loss		$ (56,250)

*($2,916,000 + $1,640,250)

Under the percentage-of-completion method, $125,000 of gross profit was recognized in 1995 (see Illustration 19-8). This $125,000 must be offset in 1996 because it is no longer expected to be realized. In addition, the total estimated loss of $56,250 must be recognized in 1996 since losses must be recognized as soon as estimable. Therefore, a total loss of $181,250 ($125,000 + $56,250) must be recognized in 1996.

---

[19]In 1997 Hardhat Construction will recognize the remaining 33½% of the revenue, $1,507,500, with costs of $1,468,962 as expected, and report a gross profit of $38,538. The total gross profit over the 3 years of the contract would be $115,038 [$125,000 (1995) − $48,500 (1996) + $38,538 (1997)], which is the difference between the total contract revenue of $4,500,000 and the total contract costs of $4,384,962.

The revenue recognized in 1996 is computed as follows:

ILLUSTRATION 19-15
Computation of Revenue Recognizable, 1996—Unprofitable Contract

Revenue recognized in 1996:		
Contract price		$4,500,000
Percent complete		× 64%*
Revenue recognizable to date		2,880,000
Less revenue recognized prior to 1996		1,125,000
Revenue recognized in 1996		$1,755,000
*Cost to date (12/31/96)	$2,916,000	
Estimated cost to complete	1,640,250	
Estimated total costs	$4,556,250	
Percent complete: $2,916,000 ÷ $4,556,250 = 64%		

To compute the construction costs to be expensed in 1996 we add the total loss to be recognized in 1996 ($125,000 + $56,250) to the revenue to be recognized in 1996. This computation is shown below:

ILLUSTRATION 19-16
Computation of Construction Expense, 1996—Unprofitable Contract

Revenue recognized in 1996 (computed above)		$1,755,000
Total loss recognized in 1996:		
Reversal of 1995 gross profit	$125,000	
Total estimated loss on the contract	56,250	181,250
Construction cost expensed in 1996		$1,936,250

Hardhat Construction would record the long-term contract revenues, expenses, and loss in 1996 as follows:

Construction Expenses	1,936,250	
Construction in Process (Loss)		181,250
Revenue from Long-Term Contracts		1,755,000

At the end of 1996, Construction in Process has a balance of $2,859,750 as shown below:[20]

ILLUSTRATION 19-17
Content of Construction in Process Account at End of 1996—Unprofitable Contract

Construction in Process			
1995 Construction costs	1,000,000		
1995 Recognized gross profit	125,000		
1996 Construction costs	1,916,000	1996 Recognized loss	181,250
Balance, 2,859,750			

Under the completed-contract method, the contract loss of $56,250 is also recognized in the year in which it first became evident through the following entry in 1996:

Loss from Long-Term Contracts	56,250	
Construction in Process (Loss)		56,250

Just as the Billings account balance cannot exceed the contract price, neither can the balance in Construction in Process exceed the contract price. In circumstances where the Construction in Process balance exceeds the billings, the recognized loss may be deducted on the balance sheet from such accumulated costs. That is, under both the percentage-of-completion and the completed-contract methods, the provision for the

---

[20]If the costs in 1997 are $1,640,250 as projected, at the end of 1997 the Construction in Process account will have a balance of $1,640,250 + $2,859,790, or $4,500,000, equal to the contract price. When the revenue remaining to be recognized in 1997 of $1,620,000 [$4,500,000 (total contract price) − $1,125,000 (1995) − $1,755,000 (1996)] is matched with the construction expense to be recognized in 1997 of $1,620,000 [total costs of $4,556,250 less the total costs recognized in prior years of $2,936,250 (1995, $1,000,000; 1996, $1,936,250)], a zero profit results. Thus the total loss has been recognized in 1996, the year in which it first became evident.

loss (the credit) may be combined with Construction in Process, thereby reducing the inventory balance. In those circumstances, however (as in the 1996 illustration above), where the billings exceed the accumulated costs, the amount of the estimated loss must be reported separately on the balance sheet as a current liability. That is, under both the percentage-of-completion and the completed-contract methods, the amount of the loss of $56,250, as estimated in 1996, would be taken from the Construction in Process account and reported separately as a current liability entitled Estimated Liability from Long-Term Contracts.[21]

DISCLOSURES IN FINANCIAL STATEMENTS

In addition to making the financial statement disclosures required of all businesses, construction contractors usually make some unique disclosures. Generally these additional disclosures are made in the notes to the financial statements. For example, a construction contractor should disclose the method of recognizing revenue,[22] the basis used to classify assets and liabilities as current (the nature and length of the operating cycle), the basis for recording inventory, the effects of any revision of estimates, the amount of backlog on uncompleted contracts, and the details about receivables (billed and unbilled, maturity, interest rates, retainage provisions, and significant individual or group concentrations of credit risk).

OTHER REVENUE RECOGNITION BASES BEFORE DELIVERY

Three additional revenue recognition bases that have been suggested as appropriate in certain circumstances are: (1) the **completion of production basis,** (2) the **accretion basis,** and (3) the **discovery basis.** Only the completion of production basis is permitted by GAAP. The other two methods have conceptual merit, but because of practical problems and economic and tax consequences, neither the accounting profession nor the affected industries have pressed for their implementation.

OBJECTIVE 6

Identify alternative revenue recognition bases before delivery.

Completion of Production

In certain cases revenue is recognized at the completion of production even though no sale has been made. Examples of such situations involve precious metals or agricultural products with assured prices. Revenue is recognized when these metals are mined or agricultural crops harvested because the sales price is reasonably assured, the units are interchangeable, and no significant costs are involved in distributing the product (see discussion in Chapter 9, page 439, "Valuation at Net Realizable Value").[23] When sale or cash receipt precedes production and delivery, as in the case of magazine subscriptions, revenues may be recognized as earned by production and delivery.[24]

UNDERLYING CONCEPT

These are not exceptions to the revenue recognition principle. At the completion of production, realization is virtually assured and the earning process is substantially completed.

Accretion Basis

Accretion is the increase in value resulting from natural growth or aging processes. Farmers experience accretion by growing crops and breeding animals. Timberland and nursery stock increase in value as the trees and plants grow. Some wines improve with age. Is accretion revenue? Should it be recognized as revenue? Periodic recognition of accretion as revenue has not been adopted in practice.

Accounting theoreticians are somewhat divided on the nature of accretion. Some reject recognition of accretion as revenue. They contend that while there is no doubt

---

[21]*Construction Contractors,* Audit and Accounting Guide (New York: AICPA, 1981), pp. 148–149.

[22]Ibid., p. 30.

[23]Such revenue satisfies the criteria of *Concepts Statement No. 5* since the assets are readily realizable and the earning process is virtually complete (see par. 84, item c).

[24]*Statement of Financial Accounting Concepts No. 5,* par. 84, item b.

that assets have increased, the technical process of production remains to be undertaken, followed by conversion into liquid assets.[25] Others conclude that from an economic point of view, recognition of accretion may be justified. However, the present discounted value (required to make the necessary comparative inventory valuations) is dependent upon future market prices and future costs of providing for growth, harvesting, and getting the product ready for market, all of which are uncertain.[26]

The profession permits recognition of revenue at the completion of production for certain agricultural products that possess "immediate marketability at quoted prices that cannot be influenced by the producer."[27] The accounting profession's official pronouncements, however, are silent on the possible extension of that principle to agricultural products still in the growth or production stage even if they are readily marketable at quoted prices.

Discovery Basis

The SEC's proposal for reserve recognition accounting (RRA) for oil and gas producers, as discussed in Chapter 11, revived interest in the use of some form of discovery basis accounting in the extractive industries. As noted above in regard to accretion, there is no doubt that an enterprise's assets may be greatly increased and enhanced by exploration and discovery. Many contend that the financial reporting of companies in the extractive industries would be vastly improved if discovered resources were recognized as assets and changes in oil and gas reserves were included in earnings. Their arguments for the discovery basis are based on the significance of discovery in the earning process and the view that the product's market price can be reasonably estimated.

The arguments against revenue recognition at the time of discovery focus on the uncertainties surrounding the assumptions needed to determine discovery values, the cost of obtaining the necessary data, and the departure from historical cost-based accounting.[28] Except for the SEC's requirement that RRA be used in supplemental data, the discovery basis of revenue recognition is sanctioned currently neither by current practice nor by official accounting pronouncements.

▶ REVENUE RECOGNITION AFTER DELIVERY

In some cases, the collection of the sales price is not reasonably assured and revenue recognition is deferred. One of two methods is generally employed to defer revenue recognition until the cash is received, that is, **the installment sales method** or **the cost recovery method.** In some situations cash is received prior to delivery or transfer of the property and is recorded as a deposit because the sale transaction is incomplete. This is referred to as the **deposit method.**

INSTALLMENT SALES ACCOUNTING METHOD

OBJECTIVE 7

Describe the installment method of accounting.

The installment sales method emphasizes collection rather than sale. It recognizes income in the periods of collection rather than in the period of sale. The installment basis of accounting is justified on the basis that when there is no reasonable basis for estimating the degree of collectibility, revenue should not be recognized until cash is collected.

The expression "installment sales" is generally used by accountants and others to describe any type of sale for which payment is required in periodic installments over

---

[25]W. A. Paton and A. C. Littleton, *An Introduction to Corporate Accounting Standards* (Sarasota, Fla.: American Accounting Association, 1940), p. 52.

[26]E. S. Hendricksen, *Accounting Theory,* 4th ed. (Homewood, Ill.: Richard D. Irwin, 1982).

[27]"Basic Concepts and Accounting Principles Underlying Financial Statements of Business Enterprises," *APB Statement No. 4* (New York: AICPA, 1970), par. 184.

[28]*Survey of Present Practices in Recognizing Revenues, Expenses, Gains, and Losses,* op. cit., p. 80.

an extended period of time. It is used in retailing where all types of farm and home equipment and furnishings are sold on an installment basis. It is also sometimes used in the heavy equipment industry in which machine installations are paid for over a long period. A more recent application of the method is in land development sales.

Because payment for the product or property sold is spread over a relatively long period, the risk of loss resulting from uncollectible accounts is greater in installment sales transactions than in ordinary sales. Consequently, various devices are used to protect the seller. In merchandising, the two most common are (1) the use of a conditional sales contract that provides that title to the item sold does not pass to the purchaser until all payments have been made, and (2) use of notes secured by a chattel (personal property) mortgage on the article sold. Either of these permits the seller to "repossess" the goods sold if the purchaser defaults on one or more payments. The repossessed merchandise is then resold at whatever price it will bring to compensate the seller for the uncollected installments and the expense of repossession.

Under the installment method of accounting, income recognition is deferred until the period of cash collection. Both revenues and costs of sales are recognized in the period of sale but the related gross profit is deferred to those periods in which cash is collected. Thus, **instead of the sale being deferred to the future periods of anticipated collection and then related costs and expenses being deferred, only the proportional gross profit is deferred,** which is equivalent to deferring both sales and cost of sales. Other expenses, that is, selling expense, administrative expense, and so on, are not deferred.

Thus, the theory that cost and expenses should be matched against sales is applied in installment sales transactions through the gross profit figure but no further. Companies using the installment sales method of accounting generally record operating expenses without regard to the fact that some portion of the year's gross profit is to be deferred. This practice is often justified on the basis that (1) these expenses do not follow sales as closely as does the cost of goods sold, and (2) accurate apportionment among periods would be so difficult that it could not be justified by the benefits gained.[29]

Underlying Concept

Realization is a critical part of revenue recognition. Thus, if a high degree of uncertainty exists about collectibility, revenue recognition must be deferred.

Acceptability of the Installment Sales Method

The use of the installment method for revenue recognition has fluctuated widely. Until the early 1960s it was widely used and accepted for installment sales transactions. As installment sales transactions increased during the sixties, somewhat paradoxically, acceptance and application of the installment method for financial accounting purposes decreased. In 1966 the APB concluded that except in special circumstances, "the installment method of recognizing revenue is not acceptable."[30]

The rationale for this position is that because the installment method of accounting recognizes no income until cash is collected, it is not in accordance with the accrual accounting concept. On the other hand, the installment method is frequently justified on the grounds that the risk of not collecting an account receivable may be so great that the sale itself is not sufficient evidence that recognition should occur. In some cases, this reasoning may be valid but not in a majority of cases. The general approach is that if a sale has been completed, it should be recognized; if bad debts are expected, they should be recorded as separate estimates of uncollectibles. Although collection expenses, repossession expenses, and bad debts are an unavoidable part of installment sales activities, the incurrence of these costs and the collectibility of the receivables are reasonably predictable.

We study this topic in financial accounting because the method is acceptable in cases where a reasonable basis of estimating the degree of collectibility is deemed not to exist. In addition, weaknesses in the sales method of revenue recognition became very ap-

[29]In addition, other theoretical deficiencies of the installment method could be cited. For example, see Richard A. Scott and Rita K. Scott, "Installment Accounting: Is It Inconsistent?" *The Journal of Accountancy* (November 1979).

[30]"Omnibus Opinion," *Opinions of the Accounting Principles Board No. 10* (New York: AICPA, 1966), par. 12.

parent when the franchise and land development booms of the 1960s and 1970s produced many failures and disillusioned investors. Application of the sales method to **franchise and license operations** resulted in the abuse described earlier as "front-end loading" (recognizing revenue prematurely, such as when the franchise is granted or the license issued rather than as it is earned or as the cash is received). Many **land development** ventures were susceptible to the same abuses. As a result, the FASB prescribes application of the installment method of accounting for sales of real estate under certain circumstances.[31]

Procedure for Deferring Revenue and Cost of Sales of Merchandise

One could easily work out a procedure that deferred both the uncollected portion of the sales price and the proportionate part of the cost of the goods sold. Instead of apportioning both sales price and cost over the period of collection, however, **only the gross profit is deferred.** This procedure has exactly the same effect as deferring both sales and cost of sales but requires only one deferred account rather than two.

The steps to be used are as follows:

For the sales in any one year:

1. During the year, record both sales and cost of sales in the regular way, using the special accounts described later, and compute the rate of gross profit on installment sales transactions.

2. At the end of the year, apply the rate of gross profit to the cash collections of the current year's installment sales to arrive at the realized gross profit.

3. The gross profit not realized should be deferred to future years.

For sales made in prior years:

1. The gross profit rate of each year's sales must be applied against cash collections of accounts receivable resulting from that year's sales to arrive at the realized gross profit.

From the preceding discussion of the general practice followed in taking up income from installment sales, it is apparent that special accounts must be used. These accounts provide certain special information required to determine the realized and unrealized gross profit in each year of operations. The requirements for special accounts are as follows:

1. Installment sales transactions must be kept separate in the accounts from all other sales.

2. Gross profit on sales sold on installment must be determinable.

3. The amount of cash collected on installment sales accounts receivable must be known, and, further, the total collected on the current year's and on each preceding year's sales must be determinable.

4. Provision must be made for carrying forward each year's deferred gross profit.

In each year, ordinary operating expenses are charged to expense accounts and are closed to the Income Summary account as under customary accounting procedure. Thus, the only peculiarity in computing net income under the installment sales method as generally applied is **the deferment of gross profit until realized by accounts receivable collection.**

---

[31]"Accounting for Sales of Real Estate," *Statement of Financial Accounting Standards No. 66* (Norwalk, Conn.: FASB, 1982), pars. 45–47. The installment method of accounting must be applied to a retail land sale that meets **all** of the following criteria: (1) the period of cancellation of the sale with refund of the down payment and any subsequent payments has expired; (2) cumulative cash payments equal or exceed 10% of the sales value; and (3) the seller is financially capable of providing all promised contract representations (e.g., land improvements, off-site facilities).

To illustrate the installment sales method in accounting for the sales of merchandise, assume the following data:

	1995	1996	1997
Installment sales	$200,000	$250,000	$240,000
Cost of installment sales	150,000	190,000	168,000
Gross profit	$ 50,000	$ 60,000	$ 72,000
Rate of gross profit on sales	25%[a]	24%[b]	30%[c]
Cash receipts			
1995 sales	$ 60,000	$100,000	$ 40,000
1996 sales		100,000	125,000
1997 sales			80,000

[a] $\dfrac{\$\ 50,000}{\$200,000}$ [b] $\dfrac{\$\ 60,000}{\$250,000}$ [c] $\dfrac{\$\ 72,000}{\$240,000}$

To simplify the illustration, interest charges have been excluded. Summary entries in general journal form for year 1995 are shown below.

1995

Installment Accounts Receivable, 1995	200,000	
Installment Sales		200,000
(To record sales made on installment in 1995)		
Cash	60,000	
Installment Accounts Receivable, 1995		60,000
(To record cash collected on installment receivables)		
Cost of Installment Sales	150,000	
Inventory (or Purchases)		150,000
(To record cost of goods sold on installment in 1995 on either a perpetual or a periodic inventory basis)		
Installment Sales	200,000	
Cost of Installment Sales		150,000
Deferred Gross Profit, 1995		50,000
(To close installment sales and cost of installment sales for the year)		
Deferred Gross Profit, 1995	15,000	
Realized Gross Profit on Installment Sales		15,000
(To remove from deferred gross profit the profit realized through cash collections; $60,000 × 25%)		
Realized Gross Profit on Installment Sales	15,000	
Income Summary		15,000
(To close profits realized by collections)		

The realized and deferred gross profit is computed for the year 1995 as follows:

1995	
Rate of gross profit current year	25%
Cash collected on current year's sales	$60,000
Realized gross profit (25% of $60,000)	15,000
Gross profit to be deferred ($50,000 − $15,000)	35,000

ILLUSTRATION 19-18
Computation of Realized and Deferred Gross Profit, Year 1

Summary entries in journal form for year 2 (1996) are shown below.

1996

Installment Accounts Receivable, 1996	250,000	
Installment Sales		250,000
(To record sales per account sales)		
Cash	200,000	
Installment Accounts Receivable, 1995		100,000
Installment Accounts Receivable, 1996		100,000
(To record cash collected on installment receivables)		

Cost of Installment Sales	190,000	
Inventory (or Purchases)		190,000
(To record cost of goods sold on installment in 1996)		
Installment Sales	250,000	
Cost of Installment Sales		190,000
Deferred Gross Profit, 1996		60,000
(To close installment sales and cost of installment sales for the year)		
Deferred Gross Profit, 1995 ($100,000 × 25%)	25,000	
Deferred Gross Profit, 1996 ($100,000 × 24%)	24,000	
Realized Gross Profit on Installment Sales		49,000
(To remove from deferred gross profit the profit realized through collections)		
Realized Gross Profit on Installment Sales	49,000	
Income Summary		49,000
(To close profits realized by collections)		

The realized and deferred gross profit is computed for the year 1996 as follows:

ILLUSTRATION 19-19
Computation of Realized and Deferred Gross Profit, Year 2

1996	
Current year's sales	
Rate of gross profit	24%
Cash collected on current year's sales	$100,000
Realized gross profit (24% of $100,000)	24,000
Gross profit to be deferred ($60,000 − $24,000)	36,000
Prior year's sales	
Rate of gross profit—1995	25%
Cash collected on 1995 sales	$100,000
Gross profit realized in 1996 on 1995 sales (25% of $100,000)	25,000
Total gross profit realized in 1996	
Realized on collections of 1995 sales	$ 25,000
Realized on collections of 1996 sales	24,000
Total	$ 49,000

The entries in 1997 would be similar to those of 1996, and the total gross profit taken up or realized would be $64,000, as shown by the computations below.

ILLUSTRATION 19-20
Computation of Realized and Deferred Gross Profit, Year 3

1997	
Current year's sales	
Rate of gross profit	30%
Cash collected on current year's sales	$ 80,000
Gross profit realized on 1997 sales (30% of $80,000)	24,000
Gross profit to be deferred ($72,000 − $24,000)	48,000
Prior years' sales	
1995 sales	
Rate of gross profit	25%
Cash collected	$ 40,000
Gross profit realized in 1997 on 1995 sales (25% of $40,000)	10,000
1996 sales	
Rate of gross profit	24%
Cash collected	$125,000
Gross profit realized in 1997 on 1996 sales (24% of $125,000)	30,000
Total gross profit realized in 1997	
Realized on collections of 1995 sales	$ 10,000
Realized on collections of 1996 sales	30,000
Realized on collections of 1997 sales	24,000
Total	$ 64,000

Additional Problems of Installment Sales Accounting

In addition to computing realized and deferred gross profit currently, other problems are involved in accounting for installment sales transactions. These problems are related to:

1. Interest on installment contracts.
2. Uncollectible accounts.
3. Defaults and repossessions.

Interest on Installment Contracts

Because the collection of installment receivables is spread over a long period, it is customary to charge the buyer interest on the unpaid balance. A schedule of equal payments consisting of interest and principal is set up. Each successive payment is attributable to a smaller amount of interest and a correspondingly larger amount attributable to principal, as shown in Illustration 19-21. This illustration assumes that an asset costing $2,400 is sold for $3,000 with interest of 8% included in the three installments of $1,164.10.

Date	Cash (Debit)	Interest Earned (Credit)	Installment Receivables (Credit)	Installment Unpaid Balance	Realized Gross Profit (20%)
1/2/95	—	—	—	$3,000.00	—
1/2/96	$1,164.10ᵃ	$240.00ᵇ	$ 924.10ᶜ	2,075.90ᵈ	$184.82ᵉ
1/2/97	1,164.10	166.07	998.03	1,077.87	199.61
1/2/98	1,164.10	86.23	1,077.87	–0–	215.57
					$600.00

ᵃPeriodic payment = Original unpaid balance ÷ PV of an annuity of $1.00 for three periods at 8%;
$1,164.10 = $3,000 ÷ 2.57710.
ᵇ$3,000.00 × .08 = $240.
ᶜ$1,164.10 − $240.00 = $924.10.
ᵈ$3,000.00 − $924.10 = $2,075.90.
ᵉ$924.10 × .20 = $184.82.

ILLUSTRATION 19-21
Installment Payment Schedule

Interest should be accounted for separately from the gross profit recognized on the installment sales collections during the period. It is recognized as interest revenue at the time of the cash receipt. Also, interest accrued since the last collection date on the installment receivables should be recorded as an adjusting entry at year-end.

Uncollectible Accounts

The problem of bad debts or uncollectible accounts receivable is somewhat different for concerns selling on an installment basis because of a repossession feature commonly incorporated in the sales agreement. This feature gives the selling company an opportunity to recoup any uncollectible accounts through repossession and resale of repossessed merchandise. If the experience of the company indicates that repossessions do not, as a rule, compensate for uncollectible balances, it may be advisable to provide for such losses through charges to a special bad debts expense account just as is done for other credit sales.

Defaults and Repossessions

Depending on the terms of the sales contract and the policy of the credit department, the seller can repossess merchandise sold under an installment arrangement if the purchaser fails to meet payment requirements. Repossessed merchandise may be reconditioned before being offered for sale. It may be resold for cash or installment payments.

The accounting for **repossessions** recognizes that the related installment receivable account is not collectible and that it should be written off. Along with the account receivable, the applicable deferred gross profit must be removed from the ledger using the following entry:

Repossessed Merchandise (an inventory account)	xx	
Deferred Gross Profit	xx	
Installment Accounts Receivable		xx

The entry above assumes that the repossessed merchandise is to be recorded on the books at exactly the amount of the uncollected account less the deferred gross profit applicable. This assumption may or may not be proper. The condition of the merchandise repossessed, the cost of reconditioning, and the market for second-hand merchandise of that particular type must all be considered. **The objective should be to put any asset acquired on the books at its fair value or, when fair value is not ascertainable, at the best possible approximation of fair value.** If the fair value of the merchandise repossessed is less than the uncollected balance less the deferred gross profit, a "loss on repossession" should be recorded at the date of repossession.

Some accountants contend that repossessed merchandise should be entered at a valuation that will permit the company to make its regular rate of gross profit on resale. If it is entered at its approximated cost to purchase, the regular rate of gross profit could be provided for upon its ultimate sale, but that is completely a secondary consideration. It is more important that the asset acquired by repossession be recorded at fair value in accordance with the general practice of carrying assets at acquisition price as represented by the fair market value at the date of acquisition.

To illustrate the required entry, assume that a refrigerator was sold to Marilyn Hunt for $500 on September 1, 1995. Terms require a down payment of $200 and $20 on the first of every month for 15 months thereafter. It is further assumed that the refrigerator cost $300 and that it is sold to provide a 40% rate of gross profit on selling price. At the year-end, December 31, 1995, a total of $60 should have been collected in addition to the original down payment.

If Hunt makes her January and February payments in 1996 and then defaults, the account balances applicable to Hunt at time of default would be:

Installment Account Receivable ($500 − $200 − $20 − $20 − $20 − $20 − $20)	200 (dr.)
Deferred Gross Profit (40% × $240)	96 (cr.)

The deferred gross profit applicable to the Hunt account still has the December 31, 1995, balance because no entry has yet been made to take up gross profit realized by 1996 cash collections. The regular entry at the end of 1996, however, will take up the gross profit realized by all cash collections including amounts received from Hunt. Hence, the balance of deferred gross profit applicable to Hunt's account may be computed by applying the gross profit rate for the year of sale to the balance of Hunt's account receivable, 40% of $200, or $80. The account balances should therefore be considered as:

Installment Account Receivable (Hunt)	200 (dr.)
Deferred Gross Profit (applicable to Hunt after	
recognition of $16 of profit in January and February)	80 (cr.)

If the estimated fair value of the article repossessed is set at $70, the following entry would be required to record the repossession:

Deferred Gross Profit	80	
Repossessed Merchandise	70	
Loss on Repossession	50	
Installment Account Receivable (Hunt)		200

The amount of the loss is determined by (1) subtracting the deferred gross profit from the amount of the account receivable, to determine the unrecovered cost (or book value) of the merchandise repossessed, and (2) subtracting the estimated fair value of the merchandise repossessed from the unrecovered cost to get the amount of the loss on repossession. The loss on the refrigerator in our example is computed as shown in Illustration 19-22.

**ILLUSTRATION 19-22
Computation of Loss
on Repossession**

Balance of account receivable (representing uncollected selling price)	$200
Less deferred gross profit	80
Unrecovered cost	120
Less estimated fair value of merchandise repossessed	70
Loss (Gain) on repossession	$ 50

As pointed out earlier, the loss on repossession may be charged to Allowance for Doubtful Accounts if such an account is carried.

Financial Statement Presentation of Installment Sales Transactions

If installment sales transactions represent a significant part of total sales, full disclosure of installment sales, the cost of installment sales, and any expenses allocable to installment sales is desirable. If, however, installment sales transactions constitute an insignificant part of total sales, it may be satisfactory to include only the realized gross profit in the income statement as a special item following the gross profit on sales, as shown below.

Health Machine Company STATEMENT OF INCOME For the Year Ended December 31, 1996	
Sales	$620,000
Cost of goods sold	490,000
Gross profit on sales	130,000
Gross profit realized on installment sales	51,000
Total gross profit on sales	$181,000

ILLUSTRATION 19-23
Disclosure of Installment Sales Transactions— Insignificant Amount

If more complete disclosure of installment sales transactions is desired, a presentation similar to the following may be used:

Health Machine Company STATEMENT OF INCOME For the Year Ended December 31, 1996			
	Installment Sales	Other Sales	Total
Sales	$248,000	$620,000	$868,000
Cost of goods sold	182,000	490,000	672,000
Gross profit on sales	66,000	130,000	196,000
Less deferred gross profit on installment sales of this year	47,000		47,000
Realized gross profit on this year's sales	19,000	130,000	149,000
Add gross profit realized on installment sales of prior years	32,000		32,000
Gross profit realized this year	$ 51,000	$130,000	$181,000

ILLUSTRATION 19-24
Disclosure of Installment Sales Transactions— Significant Amount

The apparent awkwardness of this method of presentation is difficult to avoid if full disclosure of installment sales transactions is to be provided in the income statement. One solution, of course, is to prepare a separate schedule showing installment sales transactions with only the final figure carried into the income statement.

In the balance sheet it is generally considered desirable to classify installment accounts receivable by year of collectibility. There is some question as to whether installment accounts that are not collectible for two or more years should be included in current assets. If installment sales are part of normal operations, they may be considered as current assets because they are collectible within the operating cycle of the business. Little confusion should result from this practice if maturity dates are fully disclosed, as illustrated in the following example:

Current Assets		
Notes and accounts receivable		
Trade customers	$78,800	
Less allowance for doubtful accounts	3,700	
	75,100	
Installment accounts collectible in 1996	22,600	
Installment accounts collectible in 1997	47,200	$144,900

ILLUSTRATION 19-25
Disclosure of Installment Accounts Receivable, by Year

On the other hand, receivables from an installment contract, or contracts, resulting from a transaction **not** related to normal operations should be reported in the Other Assets section if due beyond one year.

Repossessed merchandise is a part of inventory and should be included as such in the Current Asset section of the balance sheet. Any gain or loss on repossessions should be included in the income statement in the Other Revenues and Gains or Other Expenses and Losses section.

Deferred gross profit on installment sales is generally treated as unearned revenue and is classified as a current liability. Theoretically, deferred gross profit consists of three elements: (1) income tax liability to be paid when the sales are reported as realized revenue (current liability); (2) allowance for collection expense, bad debts, and repossession losses (deduction from installment accounts receivable); and (3) net income (retained earnings, restricted as to dividend availability). Because of the difficulty in allocating deferred gross profit among these three elements, however, the whole amount is frequently reported as unearned revenue.

In contrast, the FASB in *SFAC No. 3* states that "no matter how it is displayed in financial statements, deferred gross profit on installment sales is conceptually an asset valuation—that is, a reduction of an asset."[32] We support the FASB position but we recognize that until an official standard on this topic is issued, financial statements will probably continue to report such deferred gross profit as a current liability.

COST RECOVERY METHOD

OBJECTIVE 8

Explain the cost recovery method of accounting.

Under the cost recovery method, no profit is recognized until cash payments by the buyer exceed the seller's cost of the merchandise sold. After all costs have been recovered, any additional cash collections are included in income. The income statement for the period of sale reports sales revenue, the cost of goods sold, and the gross profit— both the amount (if any) that is recognized during the period and the amount that is deferred. The deferred gross profit is offset against the related receivable—reduced by collections—on the balance sheet. Subsequent income statements report the gross profit as a separate item of revenue when it is recognized as earned.

APB Opinion No. 10 allows a seller to use the cost recovery method to account for sales in which "there is no reasonable basis for estimating collectibility." This method is required under *FASB Statements No. 45* (franchises) and *No. 66* (real estate) where a high degree of uncertainty exists related to the collection of receivables.[33]

To illustrate the cost recovery method, assume that early in 1995, Fesmire Manufacturing sells inventory with a cost of $25,000 to Higley Company for $36,000 with payments receivable of $18,000 in 1995, $12,000 in 1996, and $6,000 in 1997. If the cost recovery method applies to this sale transaction and the cash is collected on schedule, cash collections, revenue, cost, and gross profit are recognized as follows:[34]

---

[32]See *Statement of Financial Accounting Concepts No. 3*, pars. 156–158.

[33]"Omnibus Opinion—1966," *Opinions of the Accounting Principles Board No. 10* (New York: AICPA, 1969), footnote 8, page 149; "Accounting for Franchise Fee Revenue," *Statement of Financial Accounting Standards No. 45* (Stamford, Conn.: FASB, 1981), par. 6; *Statement of Financial Accounting Standards No. 66*, pars. 62 and 63.

[34]An alternative format for computing the amount of gross profit recognized annually is shown below:

Year	Cash Received	Original Cost Recovered	Balance of Unrecovered Cost	Gross Profit Realized
Beginning balance	—	—	$25,000	—
12/31/95	$18,000	$18,000	7,000	$–0–
12/31/96	12,000	7,000	–0–	5,000
12/31/97	6,000	–0–	–0–	6,000

	1995	1996	1997
Cash collected	$18,000	$12,000	$6,000
Revenue recognized	$36,000	–0–	–0–
Cost of goods sold	25,000	–0–	–0–
Deferred gross profit	11,000	$11,000	$6,000
Recognized gross profit	–0–	5,000*	6,000
Deferred gross profit balance (end of period)	$11,000	$ 6,000	$–0–

*$25,000 – $18,000 = $7,000 of unrecovered cost at the end of 1995; $12,000 – $7,000 = $5,000, the excess of cash received in 1996 over unrecovered cost.

ILLUSTRATION 19-26
Computation of Gross Profit—Cost Recovery Method

Under the cost recovery method, total revenue and cost of goods sold are reported in the period of sale similar to the installment sales method. However, unlike the installment sales method, which recognizes income as cash is collected, the cost recovery method recognizes profit only when cash collections exceed the total cost of the goods sold.

The journal entry to record the deferred gross profit on this transaction (after the sale and the cost of sale were recorded in the normal manner) at the end of 1995 is as follows:

1995

Sales	36,000	
Cost of Sales		25,000
Deferred Gross Profit		11,000
(To close sales and cost of sales and to record deferred gross profit on sales accounted for under the cost recovery method)		

In 1996 and 1997, the deferred gross profit becomes realized gross profit as the cumulative cash collections exceed the total costs by recording the following entries:

1996

Deferred Gross Profit	5,000	
Realized Gross Profit		5,000
(To recognize gross profit to the extent that cash collections in 1996 exceed costs)		

1997

Deferred Gross Profit	6,000	
Realized Gross Profit		6,000
(To recognize gross profit to the extent that cash collections in 1997 exceed costs)		

DEPOSIT METHOD

In some cases, cash is received from the buyer before transfer of the goods or property. There is not sufficient transfer of the risks and rewards of ownership for a sale to be recorded. In such cases the seller has not performed under the contract and has no claim against the purchaser. The method of accounting for these incomplete transactions is the **deposit method.** Under the deposit method the seller reports the cash received from the buyer as a deposit on the contract and classifies it as a liability (refundable deposit or customer advance) on the balance sheet. The seller continues to report the property as an asset on its balance sheet, along with any related existing debt. Also, the seller continues to charge depreciation expense as a period cost for the property. **No revenue or income should be recognized until the sale is complete.**[35] At that time, the deposit account is closed and one of the revenue recognition methods discussed in this chapter is applied to the sale.

The **major difference between the installment and cost recovery methods and the deposit method** is that in the installment and cost recovery methods it is assumed that

---

[35]*Statement of Financial Accounting Standards No. 66,* par. 65.

the seller has performed on the contract, but cash collection is highly uncertain. In the deposit method, the seller has not performed and no legitimate claim exists. The **deposit method** postpones recognizing a sale until a determination can be made as to whether a sale has occurred for accounting purposes. Revenue recognition is delayed until a future event occurs. If there has not been sufficient transfer of risks and rewards of ownership, even if a deposit has been received, recognition of the sale should be postponed until sufficient transfer has occurred. In that sense, the deposit method is not a revenue recognition method as are the installment and cost recovery methods.

SUMMARY OF PRODUCT REVENUE RECOGNITION BASES

ILLUSTRATION 19-27
Revenue Recognition
Bases Other Than the
Sale Basis for Products[36]

The revenue recognition bases or methods, the criteria for their use, and the reasons for departing from the sale basis are summarized in Illustration 19-27.

Recognition Basis (or Method of Applying a Basis)	Criteria for Use	Reason(s) for Departing from Sale Basis
Percentage-of-completion method	Long-term construction of property; dependable estimates of extent of progress and cost to complete; reasonable assurance of collectibility of contract price; expectation that both contractor and buyer can meet obligations; and absence of inherent hazards that make estimates doubtful.	Availability of evidence of ultimate proceeds; better measure of periodic income; avoidance of fluctuations in revenues, expenses, and income; performance is a "continuous sale" and therefore not a departure from the sale basis.
Completed-contract method	Use on short-term contracts, and whenever percentage-of-completion cannot be used on long-term contracts.	Existence of inherent hazards in the contract beyond the normal, recurring business risks; conditions for using the percentage-of-completion method are absent.
Completion-of-production basis	Immediate marketability at quoted prices; unit interchangeability; difficulty of determining costs; and no significant distribution costs.	Known or determinable revenues; inability to determine costs and thereby defer expense recognition until sale.
Accretion basis	Criteria unspecified because accretion basis is not permitted by authoritative literature.	Possible support for recognizing accretion as revenue includes product marketability at known prices and desirability of recognizing changes in assets.
Discovery basis	Criteria unspecified because discovery basis is not permitted by authoritative literature.	Possible support for recognizing revenue at time natural resources are discovered includes the significance of discovery in the earning process and the view that sales prices can be estimated.
Installment sales method and cost recovery method	Absence of reasonable basis for estimating degree of collectibility and costs of collection.	Collectibility of the receivable is so uncertain that gross profit (or income) is not recognized until cash is actually received.
Deposit method	Cash received before the sales transaction is completed.	No recognition of revenue and income because there is not sufficient transfer of the risks and rewards of ownership.

---

[36]Adapted from *Survey of Present Practices in Recognizing Revenues, Expenses, Gains, and Losses,* op. cit., pp. 12 and 13.

► **CONCLUDING REMARKS**

Some "common threads" underlie the rationale for particular revenue recognition methods. Revenue recognition issues are frequently resolved by reference to concepts such as probability of collection, transfer of benefits and risks of ownership, measurability of revenues and costs, completion of the earnings process, and substance over form. In some cases, however, these concepts are used inconsistently or inappropriately.

► **SUMMARY OF LEARNING OBJECTIVES** ◀

1. **Apply the revenue recognition principle.** The revenue recognition principle provides that revenue is recognized (1) when it is realized or realizable and (2) when it is earned. Revenues are realized when goods and services are exchanged for cash or claims to cash. Revenues are realizable when assets received in exchanges are readily convertible to known amounts of cash or claims to cash. Revenues are earned when the entity has substantially accomplished what it must do to be entitled to the benefits represented by the revenues, that is, when the earnings process is complete or virtually complete.

2. **Describe accounting issues involved with revenue recognition at point of sale.** The two conditions for recognizing revenue are usually met by the time product or merchandise is delivered or services are rendered to customers. Revenues from manufacturing and selling activities are commonly recognized at time of sale. Problems of implementation can arise because of (1) sales with buyback agreements, (2) revenue recognition when right of return exists, and (3) trade loading and channel stuffing.

3. **Apply the percentage-of-completion method for long-term contracts.** To apply the percentage-of-completion method to long-term contracts, one must have some basis for measuring the progress toward completion at particular interim dates. One of the most popular input measures used to determine the progress toward completion is the cost-to-cost basis. Using this basis, the percentage of completion is measured by comparing costs incurred to date with the most recent estimate of the total costs to complete the contract. The percentage that costs incurred bear to total estimated costs is applied to the total revenue or the estimated total gross profit on the contract in arriving at the revenue or the gross profit amounts to be recognized to date.

4. **Apply the completed-contract method for long-term contracts.** Under this method, revenue and gross profit are recognized only at point of sale, that is, when the contract is completed. Costs of long-term contracts in process and current billings are accumulated, but there are no interim charges or credits to income statement accounts for revenues, costs, and gross profit. The annual entries to record costs of construction, progress billings, and collections from customers would be identical to those for the percentage-of-completion method with the significant exclusion of the recognition of revenue and gross profit.

5. **Identify the proper accounting for losses on long-term contracts.** Two types of losses can become evident under long-term contracts: (1) *Loss in current period on a profitable contract:* Under the percentage-of-completion method only, the estimated cost increase requires a current period adjustment of excess gross profit recognized on the project in prior periods. This adjustment is recorded as a loss in the current period because it is a change in accounting estimate. (2) *Loss on an unprofitable contract:* Under both the percentage-of-completion and the completed-contract methods, the entire expected contract loss must be recognized in the current period.

6. **Identify alternative revenue recognition bases before delivery.** Three additional revenue recognition bases are: (1) *The completion of production basis:* Revenue is recognized at the completion of production even though no sale has been made. (2) *The accretion basis:* Accretion is the increase in value resulting from natural growth or aging processes. (3) *The discovery basis:* It is based on the significance of discovery in the earning process and the view that the product's market price can be reasonably estimated. Only the completion of production basis is permitted by GAAP.

7. **Describe the installment method of accounting.** The installment method recognizes income in the periods of collection rather than in the period of sale. The installment basis of accounting is justified on the basis that when there is no reasonable basis for estimating the degree of collectibility, revenue should not be recognized until cash is collected.

8. **Explain the cost recovery method of accounting.** Under the cost recovery method, no profit is recognized until cash payments by the buyer exceed the seller's cost of the merchandise sold. After all costs have been recovered, any additional cash collections are included in income. The income statement for the period of sale reports sales revenue, the cost of goods sold, and the gross profit—both the amount that is recognized during the period and the amount that is deferred. The deferred gross profit is offset against the related receivable on the balance sheet. Subsequent income statements report the gross profit as a separate item of revenue when it is recognized as earned.

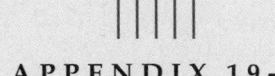

APPENDIX 19-A

REVENUE RECOGNITION FOR SPECIAL SALES TRANSACTIONS

To supplement our presentation of revenue recognition, we have chosen to cover two common yet unique types of business transactions—**franchises** and **consignments.**

▶ FRANCHISES

OBJECTIVE 9

After studying Appendix 19-A, you should be able to: Explain revenue recognition for franchises and consignment sales.

Accounting for franchise sales was chosen because of its popularity, complexity, and applicability to many of the previously discussed revenue recognition bases. In accounting for franchise sales, the accountant must analyze the transaction and, considering all the circumstances, must use judgment in selecting and applying one or more of the revenue recognition bases and then, possibly, monitor the situation over a long period of time.

THE FRANCHISE SALES PHENOMENON

Franchised operations in the United States now employ 8 million people and account for one of every three retail sales. Revenues through franchises totaled $860 billion in 1991 and are growing at a 10% annual rate. The U.S. Commerce Department reports that since the 1950s more millionaires have been created through franchising than any other way. Twenty years ago you could get a McDonald's or Aamco transmission outlet in a prime location for an initial fee of around $10,000. Today McDonald's won't talk to you about a franchise unless you can come up with $435,000 to $450,000, depending on location.

As indicated throughout this chapter, the accountant determines when revenue is recognized essentially on the basis of two criteria: (1) when it is realized or realizable (occurrence of an exchange for cash or claims to cash), and (2) when it is earned (completion or virtual completion of the earning process). These criteria are appropriate for most business activities, but for some sales transactions they simply do not adequately define when revenue should be recognized. In some situations, the accountant is forced to look to the circumstances surrounding the contract to ascertain when to recognize revenue and income. Sales transactions in some industries (for example, land development, leasing, and franchising) require closer scrutiny. The fast-growing franchise industry has given accountants special concern and challenge.

Four types of franchising arrangements have evolved: (1) manufacturer-retailer, (2) manufacturer-wholesaler, (3) service sponsor-retailer, and (4) wholesaler-retailer. The fastest growing category of franchising, and the one that caused a reexamination of appropriate accounting, has been the third category, **service sponsor-retailer.** Included in this category are such industries and businesses as:

Soft ice cream/frozen yogurt stores (Tastee Freeze, TCBY, Dairy Queen)

Food drive-ins (McDonald's, Kentucky Fried Chicken, Burger King)

Restaurants (Perkins, Pizza Hut, Denny's)

Motels (Holiday Inn, Marriott, Best Western)

Auto rentals (Avis, Hertz, National)

Part-time help (Manpower, Kelly Girl)

Others (H & R Block, Meineke Mufflers, 7-Eleven Stores)

Franchise companies derive their revenue from one or both of two sources: (1) from the sale of initial franchises and related assets or services, and (2) from continuing fees based on the operations of franchises. The **franchisor** (the party who grants business rights under the franchise) normally provides the **franchisee** (the party who operates the franchised business) with the following services:

1. Assistance in site selection.
   (a) Analyzing location.
   (b) Negotiating lease.
2. Evaluation of potential income.
3. Supervision of construction activity.
   (a) Obtaining financing.
   (b) Designing building.
   (c) Supervising contractor while building.
4. Assistance in the acquisition of signs, fixtures, and equipment.
5. Bookkeeping and advisory services.
   (a) Setting up franchisee's records.
   (b) Advising on income, real estate, and other taxes.
   (c) Advising on local regulations of the franchisee's business.
6. Employee and management training.
7. Quality control.
8. Advertising and promotion.[1]

During the 1960s and early 1970s it was standard practice for franchisors to recognize the entire franchise fee at the date of sale whether the fee was received then or was collectible over a long period of time. Frequently, franchisors recorded the entire amount as revenue in the year of sale even though many of the services were yet to be

---

[1]Archibald E. MacKay, "Accounting for Initial Franchise Fee Revenue," *The Journal of Accountancy* (January 1970), pp. 66–67.

performed and uncertainty existed regarding the collection of the entire fee.[2] In effect the franchisors were counting their fried chickens before they were hatched.

However, a **franchise agreement** may provide for refunds to the franchisee if certain conditions are not met, and franchise fee profit can be reduced sharply by future costs of obligations and services to be rendered by the franchisor. To curb the abuses in revenue recognition that existed and to standardize the accounting and reporting practices in the franchise industry, the FASB issued *Statement No. 45*.

INITIAL FRANCHISE FEES

The **initial franchise fee** is consideration for establishing the franchise relationship and providing some initial services. Initial franchise fees are to be recorded as revenue only when and as the franchisor makes "substantial performance" of the services it is obligated to perform and collection of the fee is reasonably assured. **Substantial performance** occurs when the franchisor has no remaining obligation to refund any cash received or excuse any nonpayment of a note and has performed all the initial services required under the contract. According to FASB No. 45 "commencement of operations by the franchisee shall be presumed to be the earliest point at which substantial performance has occurred, unless it can be demonstrated that substantial performance of all obligations, including services rendered voluntarily, has occurred before that time."[3]

ILLUSTRATION OF ENTRIES FOR INITIAL FRANCHISE FEE

To illustrate, assume that Tum's Pizza, Inc. charges an initial franchise fee of $50,000 for the right to operate as a franchisee of Tum's Pizza. Of this amount, $10,000 is payable when the agreement is signed and the balance is payable in five annual payments of $8,000 each. In return for the initial franchise fee, the franchisor will help locate the site, negotiate the lease or purchase of the site, supervise the construction activity, and provide the bookkeeping services. The credit rating of the franchisee indicates that money can be borrowed at 8%. The present value of an ordinary annuity of five annual receipts of $8,000 each discounted at 8% is $31,941.68. The discount of $8,058.32 represents the interest revenue to be accrued by the franchisor over the payment period.

1. If there is reasonable expectation that the down payment may be refunded and if substantial future services remain to be performed by Tum's Pizza, Inc., the entry should be:

Cash	10,000.00	
Notes Receivable	40,000.00	
Discount on Notes Receivable		8,058.32
Unearned Franchise Fees		41,941.68

2. If the probability of refunding the initial franchise fee is extremely low, the amount of future services to be provided to the franchisee is minimal, collectibility of the note is reasonably assured, and substantial performance has occurred, the entry should be:

Cash	10,000.00	
Notes Receivable	40,000.00	
Discount on Notes Receivable		8,058.32
Revenue from Franchise Fees		41,941.68

3. If the initial down payment is not refundable, represents a fair measure of the services already provided, with a significant amount of services still to be per-

---

[2]In 1987 and 1988 the SEC ordered a half-dozen fast-growing startup franchisors, including Jiffy Lube International, Moto Photo, Inc., Swensen's, Inc., and LePeep Restaurants, Inc., to defer their initial franchise fee recognition until earned. See "Claiming Tomorrow's Profits Today," *Forbes,* October 17, 1988, p. 78.

[3]"Accounting for Franchise Fee Revenue," *Statement of Financial Accounting Standards No. 45* (Stamford, Conn.: FASB, 1981), par. 5.

formed by the franchisor in future periods, and collectibility of the note is reasonably assured, the entry should be:

Cash	10,000.00	
Notes Receivable	40,000.00	
Discount on Notes Receivable		8,058.32
Revenue from Franchise Fees		10,000.00
Unearned Franchise Fees		31,941.68

4. If the initial down payment is not refundable and no future services are required by the franchisor, but collection of the note is so uncertain that recognition of the note as an asset is unwarranted, the entry should be:

Cash	10,000	
Revenue from Franchise Fees		10,000

5. Under the same conditions as those listed under 4 except that the down payment is refundable or substantial services are yet to be performed, the entry should be:

Cash	10,000	
Unearned Franchise Fees		10,000

In cases 4 and 5—where collection of the note is extremely uncertain—cash collections may be recognized using the installment method or the cost recovery method.[4]

CONTINUING FRANCHISE FEES

Continuing franchise fees are received in return for the continuing rights granted by the franchise agreement and for providing such services as management training, advertising and promotion, legal assistance, and other support. Continuing fees should be reported as revenue when they are earned and receivable from the franchisee, unless a portion of them has been designated for a particular purpose, such as providing a specified amount for building maintenance or local advertising. In that case, the portion deferred shall be an amount sufficient to cover the estimated cost in excess of continuing franchise fees and provide a reasonable profit on the continuing services.

BARGAIN PURCHASES

In addition to paying continuing franchise fees, franchisees frequently purchase some or all of their equipment and supplies from the franchisor. The franchisor would account for these sales as it would for any other product sales. Sometimes, however, the franchise agreement grants the franchisee the right to make **bargain purchases** of equipment or supplies after the initial franchise fee is paid. If the bargain price is lower than the normal selling price of the same product, or if it does not provide the franchisor a reasonable profit, then a portion of the initial franchise fee should be deferred. The deferred portion would be accounted for as an adjustment of the selling price when the franchisee subsequently purchases the equipment or supplies.

OPTIONS TO PURCHASE

A franchise agreement may give the franchisor an **option to purchase** the franchisee's business. As a matter of management policy, the franchisor may reserve the right to purchase a profitable franchised outlet, or to purchase one that is in financial difficulty.

---

[4]A study that compared four revenue recognition procedures—installment sales basis, spreading recognition over the contract life, percentage-of-completion basis, and substantial performance—for franchise sales concluded that the percentage-of-completion method is the most acceptable revenue recognition method; the substantial performance method was found sometimes to yield ultra-conservative results. See Charles H. Calhoun III, "Accounting for Initial Franchise Fees: Is It a Dead Issue?" *The Journal of Accountancy* (February 1975), pp. 60–67.

If it is probable at the time the option is given that the franchisor will ultimately purchase the outlet, then the initial franchise fee should not be recognized as revenue but should be recorded as a liability. When the option is exercised, the liability would reduce the franchisor's investment in the outlet.

FRANCHISOR'S COSTS

Franchise accounting also involves proper accounting for the **franchisor's costs.** The objective is to match related costs and revenues by reporting them as components of income in the same accounting period. Franchisors should ordinarily defer **direct costs** (usually incremental costs) relating to specific franchise sales for which revenue has not yet been recognized. Costs should not be deferred, however, without reference to anticipated revenue and its realizability.[5] **Indirect costs** of a regular and recurring nature such as selling and administrative expenses that are incurred irrespective of the level of franchise sales should be expensed as incurred.

DISCLOSURES OF FRANCHISORS

Disclosure of all significant commitments and obligations resulting from franchise agreements, including a description of services that have not yet been substantially performed, is required. Any resolution of uncertainties regarding the collectibility of franchise fees should be disclosed. Initial franchise fees should be segregated from other franchise fee revenue if they are significant. Where possible, revenues and costs related to franchisor-owned outlets should be distinguished from those related to franchised outlets.

▶ CONSIGNMENTS

In some arrangements the delivery of the goods by the manufacturer (or wholesaler) to the dealer (or retailer) is not considered to be full performance and a sale because the manufacturer retains title to the goods. This specialized method of marketing certain types of products makes use of a device known as a **consignment.** Under this arrangement, the **consignor** (manufacturer) ships merchandise to the **consignee** (dealer), who is to act as an agent for the consignor in selling the merchandise. Both consignor and consignee are interested in selling—the former to make a profit or develop a market, the latter to make a commission on the sales.

The consignee accepts the merchandise and agrees to exercise due diligence in caring for and selling it. Cash received from customers is remitted to the consignor by the consignee, after deducting a sales commission and any chargeable expenses.

A modified version of the sale basis of revenue recognition is used by the consignor. That is, revenue is recognized only after the consignor receives notification of sale and the cash remittance from the consignee. The merchandise is carried throughout the consignment as the inventory of the consignor, separately classified as Merchandise on Consignment. It is not recorded as an asset on the consignee's books. Upon sale of the merchandise, the consignee has a liability for the net amount due the consignor. The consignor periodically receives from the consignee an **account sales** that shows the merchandise received, merchandise sold, expenses chargeable to the consignment, and the cash remitted. Revenue is then recognized by the consignor.

To illustrate consignment accounting entries, assume that Nelba Manufacturing Co. ships merchandise costing $36,000 on consignment to Best Value Stores. Nelba pays $3,750 of freight costs and Best Value pays $2,250 for local advertising costs that are reimbursable from Nelba. By the end of the period, two-thirds of the consigned merchandise has been sold for $40,000 cash. Best Value notifies Nelba of the sales, retains a 10% commission, and remits the cash due Nelba. The following journal entries would be made by the consignor (Nelba) and the consignee (Best Value):

---

[5]"Accounting for Franchise Fee Revenue," p. 17.

ILLUSTRATION 19A-1
Entries for Consignment Sales

Nelba Mfg. Co. (Consignor)			Best Value Stores (Consignee)		
Shipment of consigned merchandise:					
Inventory on Consignment	36,000		No entry (record memo of merchandise		
Finished Goods Inventory		36,000	received).		
Payment of freight costs by consignor:					
Inventory on Consignment	3,750		No entry.		
Cash		3,750			
Payment of advertising by consignee:					
No entry until notified.			Receivable from Consignor	2,250	
			Cash		2,250
Sales of consigned merchandise:					
No entry until notified.			Cash	40,000	
			Payable to Consignor		40,000
Notification of sales and expenses and remittance of amount due:					
Cash	33,750		Payable to Consignor	40,000	
Advertising Expense	2,250		Receivable from		
Commission Expense	4,000		Consignor		2,250
Revenue from			Commission Revenue		4,000
Consignment Sales		40,000	Cash		33,750
Adjustment of inventory on consignment for cost of sales:					
Cost of Goods Sold	26,500		No entry.		
Inventory on Consignment		26,500			
[2/3 ($36,000 + $3,750) = $26,500]					

Under the consignment arrangement, the manufacturer (consignor) accepts the risk that the merchandise might not sell and relieves the dealer (consignee) of the need to commit part of its working capital to inventory. A variety of different systems and account titles are used to record consignments, but they all share the common goal of postponing the recognition of revenue until it is known that a sale to a third party has occurred.

▶ **SUMMARY OF LEARNING OBJECTIVE FOR APP. 19-A** ◀

9. **Explain revenue recognition for franchises and consignment sales.** In a franchise arrangement, the initial franchise fee is recorded as revenue only when and as the franchisor makes substantial performance of the services it is obligated to perform and collection of the fee is reasonably assured. Continuing franchise fees are recognized as revenue when they are earned and receivable from the franchisee. Revenue is recognized by the consignor when an account sales and the cash are received from the consignee.

KEY TERMS

account sales, 970

consignee, 970

consignment, 970

consignor, 970

continuing franchise fee, 969

franchisee, 967

franchisor, 967

initial franchise fee, 968

substantial performance, 968

Note: All **asterisked** Questions, Exercises, Problems, and Cases relate to material contained in the appendix to each chapter.

QUESTIONS

1. When is revenue conventionally recognized? What conditions should exist for the recognition at date of sale of all or part of the revenue and income of any sale transaction?

2. When is revenue recognized in the following situations:
(a) Revenue from selling products? (b) Revenue from services rendered? (c) Revenue from permitting others to use enterprise assets? (d) Revenue from disposing of assets other than products?

3. Identify several types of sales transactions and indicate the types of business for which that type of transaction is common.

4. What are the three alternative accounting methods available to a seller that is exposed to continued risks of ownership through return of the product?

5. Under what conditions may a seller who is exposed to continued risks of a high rate of return of the product sold recognize sales transactions as current revenue?

6. How does the accounting for a "contract of sale" differ from the accounting for a "contract to sell"?

7. What are the two basic methods of accounting for long-term construction contracts? Indicate the circumstances that determine when one or the other of these methods should be used.

8. Tonya Construction Co. has a $50 million contract to construct a highway overpass and cloverleaf. The total estimated cost for the project is $42.5 million. Costs incurred in the first year of the project are $8.5 million. Tonya Construction Co. appropriately uses the percentage-of-completion method. How much revenue and gross profit should Tonya recognize in the first year of the project?

9. For what reasons should the percentage-of-completion method be used over the completed-contract method whenever possible?

10. What methods are used in practice to determine the extent of progress toward completion? Identify some "input measures" and some "output measures" that might be used to determine the extent of progress.

11. What are the two types of losses that can become evident in accounting for long-term contracts? What is the nature of each type of loss? How is each type accounted for?

12. What is accretion? Why isn't accretion generally recognized as revenue?

13. What are the current arguments for and against using some form of discovery basis accounting in the extractive industries?

14. Identify and briefly describe the two methods generally employed to account for the cash received in situations where the collection of the sales price is not reasonably assured.

15. What is the deposit method and when might it be applied?

16. What is the nature of an installment sale? How do installment sales differ from ordinary credit sales?

17. Describe the installment sales method of accounting.

18. How are operating expenses (not included in cost of goods sold) handled under the installment method of accounting? What is the justification for such treatment?

19. Tommy Moe sold his condominium for $500,000 on September 14, 1994; he had paid $350,000 for it in 1986. Moe collected the selling price as follows: 1994, $80,000; 1995, $320,000; and 1996, $100,000. Moe appropriately uses the installment method. Prepare a schedule to determine the gross profit for 1994, 1995, and 1996 from the installment sale.

20. When interest is involved in installment sales transactions, how should it be treated for accounting purposes?

21. How should the results of installment sales be reported on the income statement?

22. At what time is it proper to recognize income in the following cases:
(a) installment sales with no reasonable basis for estimating the degree of collectibility; (b) sales for future delivery; (c) merchandise shipped on consignment; (d) profit on incomplete construction contracts; and (e) subscriptions to publications?

23. When is revenue recognized under the cost recovery method?

24. When is revenue recognized under the deposit method? How does the deposit method differ from the installment and cost recovery methods?

*25. Why in franchise arrangements may it not be proper to recognize the entire franchise fee as revenue at the date of sale?

*26. How does the concept of "substantial performance" apply to accounting for franchise sales?

*27. How should a franchisor account for continuing franchise fees and routine sales of equipment and supplies to franchisees?

*28. What changes are made in the franchisor's recording of the initial franchise fee when the franchise agreement:
(a) Contains an option allowing the franchisor to purchase the franchised outlet, and it is likely that the option will be exercised?
(b) Allows the franchisee to purchase equipment and supplies from the franchisor at bargain prices?

*29. What is the nature of a sale on consignment? When is revenue recognized from a consignment sale?

EXERCISES

E19-1 (Revenue Recognition on Book Sales with High Returns) Picabo Street Publishing Co. publishes college textbooks that are sold to bookstores on the following terms. Each title has a fixed wholesale price, terms f.o.b. shipping point, and payment is due 60 days after shipment. The retailer may return a maximum of 30% of an order at the retailer's expense. Sales are made only to retailers who have good credit ratings. Past experience indicates that the normal return rate is 12% and the average collection period is 72 days.

Instructions
  (a) Identify alternative revenue recognition tests that Picabo could employ concerning textbook sales.
  (b) Briefly discuss the reasoning for your answers in (a) above.
  (c) In late July, Picabo shipped books invoiced at $15,000,000. Prepare the journal entry to record this event that best conforms to generally accepted accounting principles and your answer to part (b).
  (d) In October, $2 million of the invoiced July sales were returned according to the return policy, and the remaining $13 million was paid; prepare the entry recording the return and payment.

E19-2 (Sales Recorded Both Gross and Net) On June 3, Schuss Company sold to Diann Roffe-Steinrotter merchandise having a sale price of $4,800 with terms of 2/10, n/60, f.o.b. shipping point. An invoice totaling $120, terms n/30, was received by Steinrotter on June 8 from the Potsdam Transport Service for the freight cost. Upon receipt of the goods, June 5, Steinrotter notified Schuss Company that merchandise costing $400 contained flaws that rendered it worthless; the same day Schuss Company issued a credit memo covering the worthless merchandise and asked that it be returned at company expense. The freight on the returned merchandise was $24, paid by Schuss Company on June 7. On June 12, the company received a check for the balance due from Steinrotter.

Instructions
  (a) Prepare journal entries on Schuss Company books to record all the events noted above under each of the following bases:
    1. Sales and receivables are entered at gross selling price.
    2. Sales and receivables are entered net of cash discounts.
  (b) Prepare the journal entry under basis 2, assuming that Diann Roffe-Steinrotter did not remit payment until August 5.

E19-3 (Revenue Recognition on Marina Sales with Discounts) Wasmeier Marina has 300 available slips that rent for $850 per season. Payments must be made in full at the start of the boating season, April 1. Slips for the next season may be reserved if paid for by December 31. Under a new policy, if payment is made by December 31, a 5% discount is allowed. The boating season ends October 31, and the marina has a December 31 year-end. To provide cash flow for major dock repairs, the marina operator is also offering a 25% discount to slip renters who pay for the second season following the current December 31.

For the fiscal year ended December 31, 1995, all 300 slips were rented at full price. Two hundred slips were reserved and paid for for the 1996 boating season, and 60 slips were reserved and paid for for the 1997 boating season.

Instructions
  (a) Prepare the appropriate journal entries for fiscal 1995.
  (b) Assume the marina operator is unsophisticated in business. Explain the managerial significance of the accounting above to this person.

E19-4 (Analysis of Percentage-of-Completion Financial Statements) In 1995, Soft Hat Construction Corp. began construction work under a 3-year contract. The contract price was $1,000,000. Soft Hat uses the percentage-of-completion method for financial accounting purposes. The income to be recognized each year is based on the proportion of cost incurred to total estimated costs for completing the contract. The financial statement presentations relating to this contract at December 31, 1995, follow:

Balance Sheet

Accounts receivable—construction contract billings		$21,500
Construction in progress	$65,000	
Less contract billings	61,500	
Cost of uncompleted contract in excess of billings		3,500

Income Statement

Income (before tax) on the contract recognized in 1995	$19,500

Instructions
  (a) How much cash was collected in 1995 on this contract?
  (b) What was the initial estimated total income before tax on this contract?

(AICPA adapted)

E19-5 (Gross Profit on Uncompleted Contract) On April 1, 1995, Tomba, Inc., entered into a cost-plus-fixed-fee contract to construct an electric generator for Alberto Corporation. At the contract date, Tomba estimated that it would take 2 years to complete the project at a cost of $2,000,000. The fixed fee stipulated in the contract is $400,000. Tomba appropriately accounts for this contract under the percentage-of-completion method. During 1995 Tomba incurred costs of $700,000 related to the project. The estimated cost at December 31, 1995, to complete the contract is $1,300,000. Alberto was billed $600,000 under the contract.

Instructions

Prepare a schedule to compute the amount of gross profit to be recognized by Tomba under the contract for the year ended December 31, 1995. Show supporting computations in good form.

(AICPA adapted)

E19-6 (Recognition of Profit, Percentage-of-Completion) In 1995, Liz McIntyre Construction Company agreed to construct an apartment building at a price of $1,000,000. The information relating to the costs and billings for this contract is as follows:

	1995	1996	1997
Costs incurred to date	$320,000	$600,000	$ 780,000
Estimated costs yet to be incurred	480,000	200,000	–0–
Customer billings to date	150,000	400,000	1,000,000
Collection of billings to date	120,000	320,000	940,000

Instructions
- **(a)** Assuming that the percentage-of-completion method is used: (1) compute the amount of gross profit to be recognized in 1995 and 1996, and (2) prepare journal entries for 1996.
- **(b)** For 1996, show how the details related to this construction contract would be disclosed on the balance sheet and on the income statement.

E19-7 (Recognition of Revenue on Long-Term Contract and Entries) Aamodt Construction Company uses the percentage-of-completion method of accounting. In 1995, Aamodt began work under contract #E2-D2, which provided for a contract price of $2,200,000. Other details follow:

	1995	1996
Costs incurred during the year	$ 400,000	$1,425,000
Estimated costs to complete, as of December 31	1,200,000	–0–
Billings during the year	420,000	1,680,000
Collections during the year	350,000	1,500,000

Instructions
- **(a)** What portion of the total contract price would be recognized as revenue in 1995? In 1996?
- **(b)** Assuming the same facts as those above except that Aamodt uses the completed-contract method of accounting, what portion of the total contract price would be recognized as revenue in 1996?
- **(c)** Prepare a complete set of journal entries for 1995 (using percentage-of-completion).

E19-8 (Recognition of Profit and Balance Sheet Amounts for Long-Term Contracts) Fabrik Construction Company began operations January 1, 1995. During the year, Fabrik Construction entered into a contract with Lloyd Eisler Corp. to construct a manufacturing facility. At that time, Fabrik estimated that it would take 5 years to complete the facility at a total cost of $4,500,000. The total contract price for construction of the facility is $6,300,000. During the year, Fabrik incurred $1,190,000 in construction costs related to the construction project. The estimated cost to complete the contract is $4,200,000. Lloyd Eisler Corp. was billed and paid 30% of the contract price.

Instructions

Prepare schedules to compute the amount of gross profit to be recognized for the year ended December 31, 1995, and the amount to be shown as "cost of uncompleted contract in excess of related billings" or "billings on uncompleted contract in excess of related costs" at December 31, 1995, under each of the following methods:
- **(a)** Completed-contract method.
- **(b)** Percentage-of-completion method.

Show supporting computations in good form.

(AICPA adapted)

E19-9 (Long-Term Contract Reporting) Gothic Construction Company began operations in 1995. Construction activity for the first year is shown below. All contracts are with different customers, and any work remaining at December 31, 1995, is expected to be completed in 1996.

Project	Total Contract Price	Billings Through 12/31/95	Cash Collections Through 12/31/95	Contract Costs Incurred Through 12/31/95	Estimated Additional Costs to Complete
1	$ 560,000	$ 360,000	$340,000	$450,000	$130,000
2	670,000	220,000	210,000	126,000	504,000
3	490,000	490,000	440,000	330,000	–0–
	$1,720,000	$1,070,000	$990,000	$906,000	$634,000

Instructions
Prepare a partial income statement and balance sheet to indicate how the above information would be reported for financial statement purposes. Gothic Construction Company uses the completed-contract method.

E19-10 (Analysis of Installment Sales Accounts) Slow-Go Co. appropriately uses the installment sales method of accounting. On December 31, 1997, the books show balances as follows:

Installment Receivables		Deferred Gross Profit		Gross Profit on Sales	
1995	$12,000	1995	$ 7,000	1995	35%
1996	40,000	1996	26,000	1996	34%
1997	80,000	1997	95,000	1997	32%

Instructions
   (a) Prepare the adjusting entry or entries required on December 31, 1997 to recognize 1997 realized gross profit. (Installment receivables have already been credited for cash receipts during 1997.)
   (b) Compute the amount of cash collected in 1997 on accounts receivable each year.

E19-11 (Gross Profit Calculations and Repossessed Merchandise) Torvill & Dean Corporation, which began business on January 1, 1995, appropriately uses the installment sales method of accounting. The following data were obtained for the years 1995 and 1996:

	1995	1996
Installment sales	$750,000	$840,000
Cost of installment sales	600,000	630,000
General & administrative expenses	70,000	84,000
Cash collections on sales of 1995	310,000	300,000
Cash collections on sales of 1996	–0–	400,000

Instructions
   (a) Compute the balance in the deferred gross profit accounts on December 31, 1995 and on December 31, 1996.
   (b) A 1995 sale resulted in default in 1997. At the date of default, the balance on the installment receivable was $12,000, and the repossessed merchandise had a fair value of $8,000. Prepare the entry to record the repossession.

(AICPA adapted)

E19-12 (Interest Revenue from Installment Sale) Oksana Baiul Corporation sells farm machinery on the installment plan. On July 1, 1995, Baiul entered into an installment sale contract with Ukraine Inc. for a 10-year period. Equal annual payments under the installment sale are $100,000 and are due on July 1. The first payment was made on July 1, 1995.

Additional Information

   1. The amount that would be realized on an outright sale of similar farm machinery is $575,000.
   2. The cost of the farm machinery sold to Ukraine Inc. is $423,000.
   3. The finance charges relating to the installment period are $225,000 based on a stated interest rate of 10%, which is appropriate.
   4. Circumstances are such that the collection of the installments due under the contract is reasonably assured.

Instructions
What income or loss before income taxes should Baiul record for the year ended December 31, 1995, as a result of the transaction above?

(AICPA adapted)

E19-13 (Installment Method and Cost Recovery) Cathy Turner Corp., a capital goods manufacturing business that started on January 4, 1995, and operates on a calendar-year basis, uses the installment method of profit recognition in accounting for all its sales. The following data were taken from the 1995 and 1996 records:

	1995	1996
Installment sales	$480,000	$620,000
Gross profit as a percent of costs	25%	20%
Cash collections on sales of 1995	$140,000	$240,000
Cash collections on sales of 1996	–0–	$180,000

The amounts given for cash collections exclude amounts collected for interest charges.

Instructions

(a) Compute the amount of realized gross profit to be recognized on the 1996 income statement, prepared using the installment method.

(b) State where the balance of Deferred Gross Profit would be reported on the financial statements for 1996.

(c) Compute the amount of realized gross profit to be recognized on the income statement, prepared using the cost recovery method.

(CIA adapted)

E19-14 (Cost Recovery Method) On January 1, 1996, Lasse Kjus Company sold real estate that cost $108,000 to Harald Nilsen for $120,000. Harald agreed to pay for the purchase over 3 years by making three end-of-year equal payments of $52,557 that included 15% interest. Shortly after the sale, Lasse Kjus Company learns distressing news about Harald's financial circumstances and because collection is so uncertain decides to account for the sale using the cost recovery method.

Instructions

Applying the cost recovery method, prepare a schedule showing the amounts of cash collected, the increase (decrease) in deferred interest revenue, the balance of the receivable, the balance of the unrecovered cost, the gross profit realized, and the interest revenue realized for each of the 3 years assuming the payments are made as agreed.

E19-15 (Installment Sales—Default and Repossession) Pechstein Imports Inc. was involved in two default and repossession cases during the year:

1. A refrigerator was sold to Espen Bredesen for $1,800, including a 40% markup on selling price. Bredesen made a down payment of 20%, four of the remaining 16 equal payments, and then defaulted on further payments. The refrigerator was repossessed, at which time the fair value was determined to be $800.

2. An oven that cost $1,200 was sold to Hiromi Yamamoto for $1,500 on the installment basis. Yamamoto made a down payment of $225 and paid $75 a month for six months, after which she defaulted. The oven was repossessed and the estimated value at time of repossession was determined to be $750.

Instructions

Prepare journal entries to record each of these repossessions (ignore interest charges).

E19-16 (Installment Sales—Default and Repossession) Andy Gabel Company uses the installment sales method in accounting for its installment sales. On January 1, 1996, Gabel Company had an installment account receivable from Eric Flaim with a balance of $1,800. During 1996, $300 was collected from Flaim. When no further collection could be made, the merchandise sold to Flaim was repossessed. The merchandise had a fair market value of $650 after the company spent $60 for reconditioning of the merchandise. The merchandise was originally sold with a gross profit rate of 40%.

Instructions

Prepare the entries on the books of Gabel Company to record all transactions related to Flaim during 1996 (ignore interest charges).

E19-17 (Cost Recovery Method) On January 1, 1996, Randy Bartz sells 200 acres of farmland for $600,000, taking in exchange a 10% interest-bearing note. Randy Bartz purchased the farmland in 1981 at a cost of $490,000. The note will be paid in three installments of $241,269 each on December 31, 1996, 1997, and 1998. Collectibility of the note is uncertain; Randy, therefore, uses the cost recovery method.

Instructions

Prepare for Randy a 3-year installment payment schedule (under the cost recovery method) that shows cash collections, deferred interest revenue, installment receivable balances, unrecovered cost, realized gross profit, and realized interest revenue by year.

*E19-18 (Franchise Entries) Bungi Burger Inc. charges an initial franchise fee of $80,000. Upon the signing of the agreement, a payment of $50,000 is due; thereafter, three annual payments of $10,000 are required. The credit rating of the franchisee is such that it would have to pay interest at 10% to borrow money.

Instructions

Prepare the entries to record the initial franchise fee on the books of the franchisor under the following assumptions:

(a) The down payment is not refundable, no future services are required by the franchisor, and collection of the note is reasonably assured.

(b) The franchisor has substantial services to perform, the down payment is refundable, and the collection of the note is very uncertain.

(c) The down payment is not refundable, collection of the note is reasonably certain, the franchisor has yet to perform a substantial amount of services, and the down payment represents a fair measure of the services already performed.

*E19-19 (Franchise Fee, Initial Down Payment) On January 1, 1995, Nathalie Lambert signed an agreement to operate as a franchisee of Short-Track, Inc., for an initial franchise fee of $60,000. The amount of $30,000 was paid when the agreement was signed, and the balance is payable in five annual payments of $6,000 each, beginning January 1, 1996. The agreement provides that the down payment is not refundable and that no future services are required of the franchisor. Nathalie Lambert's credit rating indicates that she can borrow money at 11% for a loan of this type.

Instructions

(a) How much should Short-Track record as revenue from franchise fees on January 1, 1995? At what amount should Nathalie Lambert record the acquisition cost of the franchise on January 1, 1995?

(b) What entry would be made by Short-Track on January 1, 1995, if the down payment is refundable and substantial future services remain to be performed by Short-Track?

(c) How much revenue from franchise fees would be recorded by Short-Track on January 1, 1995, if:

1. The initial down payment is not refundable, it represents a fair measure of the services already provided, a significant amount of services is still to be performed by Short-Track in future periods, and collectibility of the note is reasonably assured?

2. The initial down payment is not refundable and no future services are required by the franchisor, but collection of the note is so uncertain that recognition of the note as an asset is unwarranted?

3. The initial down payment has not been earned and collection of the note is so uncertain that recognition of the note as an asset is unwarranted?

*E19-20 (Consignment Computations) On May 3, 1995, Chae Ji-Hoon Company consigned 70 freezers, costing $600 each, to Nicholas Gooch Company. The cost of shipping the freezers amounted to $800 and was paid by Ji-Hoon Company. On December 30, 1995, an account sales was received from the consignee, reporting that 35 freezers had been sold for $700 each. Remittance was made by the consignee for the amount due, after deducting a commission of 6%, advertising of $200, and total installation costs of $300 on the freezers sold.

Instructions

(a) Compute the inventory value of the units unsold in the hands of the consignee.

(b) Compute the profit for the consignor for the units sold.

(c) Compute the amount of cash that will be remitted by the consignee.

PROBLEMS

P19-1 (Comprehensive Three-Part Revenue Recognition) J. Coyle Industries has three operating divisions—Bo-Dyn Construction Division, Lutz Publishing Division, and Gillooly Securities Division. Each division maintains its own accounting system and method of revenue recognition.

Bo-Dyn Construction Division

During the fiscal year ended November 30, 1995, Bo-Dyn Construction Division had one construction project in process. A $30,000,000 contract for construction of a civic center was granted on June 19, 1995, and construction began on August 1, 1995. Estimated costs of completion at the contract date were $26,000,000 over a 2-year time period from the date of the contract. On November 30, 1995, construction costs of $8,000,000 had been incurred and progress billings of $9,500,000 had been made. The construction costs to complete the remainder of the project were reviewed on November 30, 1995, and were estimated to amount to only $16,000,000 because of an expected decline in raw materials costs. Revenue recognition is based upon a percentage-of-completion method.

Lutz Publishing Division

The Lutz Publishing Division sells large volumes of novels to a few book distributors, which in turn sell to several national chains of bookstores. Lutz allows distributors to return up to 30% of sales, and distributors give the same terms to bookstores. While returns from individual titles fluctuate greatly, the returns from distributors have averaged 20% in each of the past 5 years. A total of $8,000,000 of paperback novel sales were made to distributors during fiscal 1995. On November 30, 1995, $3,000,000 of fiscal 1995 sales were still subject to return privileges over the next six months. The remaining $5,000,000 of fiscal 1995 sales had actual returns of 21%. Sales from fiscal 1994 totaling $2,000,000 were collected in fiscal 1995 less 18% returns. This division records revenue according to the method referred to as revenue recognition when the right of return exists.

Gillooly Securities Division

Gillooly Securities Division works through manufacturers' agents in various cities. Orders for alarm systems and down payments are forwarded from agents, and the Division ships the goods f.o.b. factory directly to customers (usually police departments and security guard companies). Customers are billed directly for the balance due plus actual shipping costs. The company received orders for $6,000,000 of goods during the fiscal year ended November 30, 1995. Down payments of $600,000 were received and $5,000,000 of goods were billed and shipped. Actual freight costs of $100,000 were also billed. Commissions of 10% on product price are paid manufacturing agents after goods are shipped to customers. Such goods are warranted for 90 days after shipment, and warranty returns have been about 1% of sales. Revenue is recognized at the point of sale by this division.

Instructions

(a) There are a variety of methods of revenue recognition. Define and describe each of the following methods of revenue recognition and indicate whether each is in accordance with generally accepted accounting principles.
   1. Point of sale.
   2. Completion of production.
   3. Percentage of completion.
   4. Installment contract.

(b) Compute the revenue to be recognized in fiscal year 1995 for each of the three operating divisions of J. Coyle Industries in accordance with generally accepted accounting principles.

P19-2 (Recognition of Profit on Long-Term Contract) Tim Taylor Construction Company has entered into a contract beginning January 1, 1995, to build a parking complex. It has been estimated that the complex will cost $600,000 and will take three years to construct. The complex will be billed to the purchasing company at $900,000. The following data pertain to the construction period.

	1995	1996	1997
Costs to date	$300,000	$420,000	$600,000
Estimated costs to complete	300,000	180,000	–0–
Progress billings to date	270,000	550,000	900,000
Cash collected to date	240,000	500,000	900,000

Instructions

(a) Using the percentage-of-completion method, compute the estimated gross profit that would be recognized during each year of the construction period.
(b) Using the completed-contract method, compute the estimated gross profit that would be recognized during each year of the construction period.

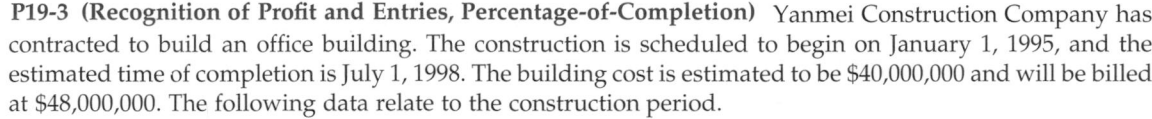

P19-3 (Recognition of Profit and Entries, Percentage-of-Completion) Yanmei Construction Company has contracted to build an office building. The construction is scheduled to begin on January 1, 1995, and the estimated time of completion is July 1, 1998. The building cost is estimated to be $40,000,000 and will be billed at $48,000,000. The following data relate to the construction period.

	1995	1996	1997	1998
Costs to date	$12,000,000	$20,000,000	$28,000,000	$40,000,000
Estimated cost to complete	28,000,000	20,000,000	12,000,000	–0–
Progress billings to date	6,000,000	18,000,000	28,000,000	48,000,000
Cash collected to date	6,000,000	15,000,000	25,000,000	48,000,000

Instructions

(a) Compute the estimated gross profit for 1995, 1996, 1997, and 1998 assuming that the percentage-of-completion method is used. (Ignore income taxes.)
(b) Prepare the necessary journal entries for Yanmei Construction Company for the years 1997 and 1998.

P19-4 (Recognition of Profit and Balance Sheet Presentation, Percentage-of-Completion) On February 1, 1995, Tchepikov Construction Company obtained a contract to build an athletic stadium. The stadium was to be built at a total cost of $5,400,000 and was scheduled for completion by September 1, 1997. One clause of the contract stated that Tchepikov was to deduct $10,000 from the $6,600,000 billing price for each week that completion was delayed. Completion was delayed six weeks, which resulted in a $60,000 penalty. Below are the data pertaining to the construction period.

	1995	1996	1997
Costs to date	$1,800,000	$3,850,000	$5,500,000
Estimated costs to complete	3,600,000	1,650,000	–0–
Progress billings to date	1,200,000	3,000,000	6,540,000
Cash collected to date	1,000,000	2,800,000	6,540,000

Instructions
(a) Using the percentage-of-completion method, compute the estimated gross profit recognized in the years 1995–1997.
(b) Prepare a partial balance sheet for December 31, 1996, showing the balances in the receivable and inventory accounts.

P19-5 (Completed Contract and Percentage of Completion with Interim Loss) Rockland Custom Builders (RCB) was established in 1966 by Thomas Johnston and initially built high quality customized homes under contract with specific buyers. In the 1980s, Johnston's two sons joined the firm and expanded RCB's activities into the high-rise apartment and industrial plant markets. Upon the retirement of RCB's long-time financial manager, Johnston's sons recently hired Joe Gurney as controller for RCB. Gurney, a former college friend of Johnston's sons, has been associated with a public accounting firm for the last six years.

Upon reviewing RCB's accounting practices, Gurney observed that RCB followed the completed-contract method of revenue recognition, a carryover from the years when individual home building was the majority of RCB's operations. Several years ago, the predominant portion of RCB's activities shifted to the high-rise and industrial building areas. From land acquisition to the completion of construction, most building contracts cover several years. Under the circumstances, Gurney believes that RCB should follow the percentage-of-completion method of accounting. From a typical building contract, Gurney developed the following data.

Allweather Tractor Plant

Contract price: $8,000,000

	1994	1995	1996
Estimated costs	$1,675,000	$3,015,000	$2,010,000
Progress billings	1,000,000	2,500,000	4,500,000
Cash collections	800,000	2,300,000	4,900,000

Instructions
(a) Explain the difference between completed-contract revenue recognition and percentage-of-completion revenue recognition.
(b) Using the data provided for the Allweather Tractor Plant and assuming the percentage-of-completion method of revenue recognition is used, calculate RCB's revenue and gross profit for 1994, 1995, and 1996, under **each** of the following circumstances.
1. Assume that all costs are incurred, all billings to customers are made, and all collections from customers are received within 30 days of billing, as planned.
2. Further assume that, as a result of unforeseen local ordinances and the fact that the building site was in a wetlands area, RCB experienced cost overruns of $800,000 in 1994 to bring the site into compliance with the ordinances and to overcome wetlands barriers to construction.
3. Futher assume that, in addition to the cost overruns of $800,000 for this contract incurred under Instruction (b)2., inflationary factors over and above those anticipated in the development of the original contract cost have caused an additional cost overrun of $540,000 in 1995. It is not anticipated that any cost overruns will occur in 1996.

(CMA adapted)

P19-6 (Long-Term Contract with Interim Loss) On March 1, 1995, Gumbel Construction Company contracted to construct a factory building for Scot Hamilton Manufacturing, Inc., for a total contract price of $8,500,000. The building was completed by October 31, 1997. The annual contract costs incurred, estimated costs to complete the contract, and accumulated billings to Hamilton for 1995, 1996, and 1997 are given below:

	1995	1996	1997
Contract costs incurred during the year	$3,200,000	$2,600,000	$1,450,000
Estimated costs to complete the contract at 12/31	3,200,000	1,450,000	–0–
Billings to Hamilton during the year	3,200,000	3,500,000	1,800,000

Instructions
(a) Using the percentage-of-completion method, prepare schedules to compute the profit or loss to be recognized as a result of this contract for the years ended December 31, 1995, 1996, and 1997. Ignore income taxes.
(b) Using the completed-contract method, prepare schedules to compute the profit or loss to be recognized as a result of this contract for the years ended December 1995, 1996, and 1997. Ignore income taxes.

P19-7 (Long-Term Contract With an Overall Loss) On July 1, 1995, DiCenta Construction Company, Inc. contracted to build an office building for Laroche Corp. for a total contract price of $1,900,000. On July 1, DiCenta estimated that it would take between 2 and 3 years to complete the building. On December 31, 1997, the building was deemed substantially completed. Following are accumulated contract costs incurred, estimated costs to complete the contract, and accumulated billings to Laroche for 1995, 1996, and 1997.

	At 12/31/95	At 12/31/96	At 12/31/97
Contract costs incurred to date	$ 150,000	$1,200,000	$2,100,000
Estimated costs to complete the contract	1,350,000	800,000	–0–
Billings to Laroche	300,000	1,100,000	1,800,000

Instructions

(a) Using the percentage-of-completion method, prepare schedules to compute the profit or loss to be recognized as a result of this contract for the years ended December 31, 1995, 1996, and 1997. Ignore income taxes.

(b) Using the completed-contract method, prepare schedules to compute the profit or loss to be recognized as a result of this contract for the years ended December 1995, 1996, and 1997. Ignore income taxes.

P19-8 (Installment Sales Computations and Entries) Presented below is summarized information for Myriam Bedard Co., which sells merchandise on the installment basis:

	1995	1996	1997
Sales (on installment plan)	$250,000	$260,000	$280,000
Cost of sales	150,000	169,000	196,000
Gross profit	$100,000	$ 91,000	$ 84,000
Collections from customers on:			
1995 installment sales	$ 75,000	$100,000	$ 50,000
1996 installment sales		100,000	120,000
1997 installment sales			110,000

Instructions

(a) Compute the realized gross profit for each of the years 1995, 1996, and 1997.

(b) Prepare in journal form all entries required in 1997, applying the installment method of accounting (ignore interest charges).

P19-9 (Installment Sales Income Statements) Urs Kaelin Stores sells merchandise on open account as well as on installment terms.

	1995	1996	1997
Sales on account	$385,000	$426,000	$525,000
Installment sales	320,000	275,000	380,000
Collections on installment sales			
Made in 1995	110,000	90,000	40,000
Made in 1996		110,000	140,000
Made in 1997			125,000
Cost of sales			
Sold on account	264,000	297,000	389,600
Sold on installment	214,400	165,000	224,200
Selling expenses	77,000	87,000	92,000
Administrative expenses	50,000	51,000	52,000

Instructions

From the data above, which cover the 3 years since Urs Kaelin Stores commenced operations, determine the net income for each year, applying the installment method of accounting (ignore interest charges).

P19-10 (Installment Sales Computations and Entries) Brian O'Neil Stores sell appliances for cash and also on the installment plan. Entries to record cost of sales are made monthly.

Brian O'Neil Stores
TRIAL BALANCE
December 31, 1997

Cash	$153,000	
Installment Accounts Receivable, 1996	48,000	
Installment Accounts Receivable, 1997	91,000	
Inventory—New Merchandise	131,200	
Inventory—Repossessed Merchandise	24,000	
Accounts Payable		$ 98,500
Deferred Gross Profit, 1996		45,600
Capital Stock		170,000
Retained Earnings		93,900
Sales		343,000
Installment Sales		200,000
Cost of Sales	255,000	
Cost of Installment Sales	120,000	
Gain or Loss on Repossessions	800	
Selling and Administrative Expenses	128,000	
	$951,000	$951,000

The accounting department has prepared the following analysis of cash receipts for the year:

Cash sales (including repossessed merchandise)	$424,000
Installment accounts receivable, 1996	104,000
Installment accounts receivable, 1997	109,000
Other	36,000
Total	$673,000

Repossessions recorded during the year are summarized as follows:

	1996
Uncollected balance	$8,000
Loss on repossession	800
Repossessed merchandise	4,800

Instructions

From the trial balance and accompanying information:
- **(a)** Compute the rate of gross profit for 1996 and 1997.
- **(b)** Prepare closing entries as of December 31, 1997, under the installment method of accounting.
- **(c)** Prepare a statement of income for the year ended December 31, 1997. Include only the realized gross profit in the income statement.

P19-11 (Installment Sales Entries) The following summarized information relates to the installment sales activity of Chantal Bailey Stores, Inc. for the year 1995:

Installment sales during 1995	$500,000
Costs of goods sold on installment basis	350,000
Collections from customers	200,000
Unpaid balances on merchandise repossessed	24,000
Estimated value of merchandise repossessed	9,200

Instructions
- **(a)** Prepare journal entries at the end of 1995 to record on the books of Chantal Bailey Stores, Inc. the summarized data above.
- **(b)** Prepare the entry to record the gross profit realized during 1995.

P19-12 (Installment Sales Computation and Entries) Harper Phillips Inc. sells merchandise for cash and also on the installment plan. Entries to record cost of goods sold are made at the end of each year.

Repossessions of merchandise (sold in 1996) were made in 1997 and were recorded correctly as follows:

Deferred Gross Profit, 1996	7,200	
Repossessed Merchandise	8,000	
Loss on Repossessions	2,800	
Installment Accounts Receivable, 1996		18,000

Part of this repossessed merchandise was sold for cash during 1997, and the sale was recorded by a debit to Cash and a credit to Sales.

The inventory of repossessed merchandise on hand December 31, 1997, is $4,000; of new merchandise, $122,000. There was no repossessed merchandise on hand January 1, 1997.

Collections on accounts receivable during 1997 were:

Installment Accounts Receivable, 1996	$80,000
Installment Accounts Receivable, 1997	50,000

The cost of the merchandise sold under the installment plan during 1997 was $122,400.

The rate of gross profit on 1996 and on 1997 installment sales can be computed from the information given above.

Harper Phillips
TRIAL BALANCE
December 31, 1997

	Dr.	Cr.
Cash	$ 98,400	
Installment Accounts Receivable, 1996	80,000	
Installment Accounts Receivable, 1997	110,000	
Inventory, Jan. 1, 1997	120,000	
Repossessed Merchandise	8,000	
Accounts Payable		$ 47,200
Deferred Gross Profit, 1996		64,000
Capital Stock, Common		200,000
Retained Earnings		40,000
Sales		380,000
Installment Sales		180,000
Purchases	380,000	
Loss on Repossessions	2,800	
Operating Expenses	112,000	
	$911,200	$911,200

Instructions

(a) From the trial balance and other information given above, prepare adjusting and closing entries as of December 31, 1997.

(b) Prepare an income statement for the year ended December 31, 1997. Include only the realized gross profit in the income statement.

P19-13 (Installment Repossession Entries) Selected transactions of Lundquist TV Sales Company are presented below:

1. A television set costing $560 is sold to Duncan Douglas on November 1, 1996 for $800. Douglas makes a down payment of $200 and agrees to pay $25 on the first of each month for 24 months thereafter.
2. Douglas pays the $25 installment due December 1, 1996.
3. On December 31, 1996, the appropriate entries are made to record profit realized on the installment sales.
4. The first seven 1997 installments of $25 each are paid by Douglas. (Make one entry.)
5. In August 1997, the set is repossessed, after Douglas fails to pay the August 1 installment and indicates that he will be unable to continue the payments. The estimated fair value of the repossessed set is $100.

Instructions

Prepare journal entries to record on the books of Lundquist TV Sales Company the transactions above. Closing entries should not be made.

P19-14 (Installment Sales Computations and Schedules) Amy Peterson Company, on January 2, 1995, entered into a contract with a manufacturing company to purchase room-size air conditioners and to sell the units on an installment plan with collections over approximately 30 months with no carrying charge.

For income tax purposes Amy Peterson Company elected to report income from its sales of air conditioners according to the installment method.

Purchases and sales of new units were as follows:

	Units Purchased			Units Sold	
Year	Quantity	Price Each		Quantity	Price Each
1995	1,400	$130		1,100	$200
1996	1,200	112		1,500	170
1997	900	136		800	182

Collections on installment sales were as follows:

	Collections Received		
	1995	1996	1997
1995 sales	$42,000	$98,000	$ 80,000
1996 sales		84,000	138,000
1997 sales			34,600

In 1997, 50 units from the 1996 sales were repossessed and sold for $80 each on the installment plan. At the time of repossession, $1,440 had been collected from the original purchasers and the units had a fair value of $3,000.

General and administrative expenses for 1997 were $60,000. No charge has been made against current income for the applicable insurance expense from a 3-year policy expiring June 30, 1998 costing $3,600, and for an advance payment of $12,000 on a new contract to purchase air conditioners beginning January 2, 1998.

Instructions

Assuming that the weighted-average method is used for determining the inventory cost, including repossessed merchandise, prepare schedules computing for 1995, 1996, and 1997:

(a) 1. The cost of goods sold on installments.
    2. The average unit cost of goods sold on installments for each year.
(b) The gross profit percentages for 1995, 1996, and 1997.
(c) The gain or loss on repossessions in 1997.
(d) The net income from installment sales for 1997 (ignore income taxes).

(AICPA adapted)

P19-15 (Completed-Contract Method) Ferraro Construction Company, Inc., entered into a firm fixed-price contract with Lazaro Clinic on July 1, 1993, to construct a four-story office building. At that time, Ferraro estimated that it would take between 2 and 3 years to complete the project. The total contract price for construction of the building is $4,500,000. Ferraro appropriately accounts for this contract under the completed-contract method in its financial statements and for income tax reporting. The building was deemed substantially completed on December 31, 1995. Estimated percentage of completion, accumulated contract costs incurred, estimated costs to complete the contract, and accumulated billings to the Lazaro Clinic under the contract were as follows:

	At December 31, 1993	At December 31, 1994	At December 31, 1995
Percentage of completion	30%	60%	100%
Contract costs incurred	$1,140,000	$2,820,000	$4,800,000
Estimated costs to complete the contract	$2,660,000	$1,880,000	–0–
Billings to Lazaro Clinic	$1,500,000	$2,500,000	$4,300,000

Instructions

(a) Prepare schedules to compute the amount to be shown as "cost of uncompleted contract in excess of related billings" or "billings on uncompleted contract in excess of related costs" at December 31, 1993, 1994, and 1995. Ignore income taxes. Show supporting computations in good form.
(b) Prepare schedules to compute the profit or loss to be recognized as a result of this contract for the years ended December 31, 1993, 1994, and 1995. Ignore income taxes. Show supporting computations in good form.

(AICPA adapted)

CASES

C19-1 (Revenue Recognition—Alternative Methods) Archer Industries has three operating divisions— Barwood Mining, Winston Paperbacks, and Quality Protection Devices. Each division maintains its own accounting system and method of revenue recognition.

Barwood Mining

Barwood Mining specializes in the extraction of precious metals such as silver, gold, and platinum. During the fiscal year ended November 30, 1995, Barwood entered into contracts worth $2,250,000 and shipped metals worth $2,000,000. A quarter of the shipments were made from inventories on hand at the beginning of the fiscal year while the remainder were made from metals that were mined during the year. Mining totals for the year, valued at market prices, were: silver at $750,000, gold at $1,300,000, and platinum at $430,000.

Barwood uses the completion-of-production method to recognize revenue, because its operations meet the specified criteria, i.e., reasonably assured sales prices, interchangeable units, and insignificant distribution costs.

Winston Paperbacks

Winston Paperbacks sells large quantities of novels to a few book distributors that in turn sell to several national chains of bookstores. Winston allows distributors to return up to 30 percent of sales, and distributors give the same terms to bookstores. While returns from individual titles fluctuate greatly, the returns from distributors have averaged 20 percent in each of the past five years. A total of $8,000,000 of paperback novel sales were made to distributors during the fiscal year. On November 30, 1995, $3,000,000 of fiscal 1995 sales were still subject to return privileges over the next six months. The remaining $5,000,000 of fiscal 1995 sales had actual returns of 21 percent. Sales from fiscal 1994 totaling $2,500,000 were collected in fiscal 1995, with less than 18 percent of sales returned. Winston records revenue according to the method referred to as revenue recognition when the right of return exists, because all applicable criteria for use of this method are met by Winston's operations.

Quality Protection Devices

Quality Protection Devices works through manufacturers' agents in various cities. Orders for alarm systems and down payments are forwarded from agents, and Quality ships the goods f.o.b. shipping point. Customers are billed for the balance due plus actual shipping costs. The firm received orders for $6,000,000 of goods during the fiscal year ended November 30, 1995. Down payments of $600,000 were received, and $5,000,000 of goods were billed and shipped. Actual freight costs of $100,000 were also billed. Commissions of 10 percent on product price were paid to manufacturers' agents after the goods were shipped to customers. Such goods are warranted for 90 days after shipment, and warranty returns have been about one percent of sales. Revenue is recognized at the point of sale by Quality.

Instructions

(a) There are a variety of methods for revenue recognition. Define and describe each of the following methods of revenue recognition and indicate whether each is in accordance with generally accepted accounting principles.
    1. Completion-of-production method.
    2. Percentage-of-completion method.
    3. Installment sales method.
(b) Compute the revenue to be recognized in the fiscal year ended November 30, 1995, for
    1. Barwood Mining.
    2. Winston Paperbacks.
    3. Quality Protection Devices.

(CMA adapted)

C19-2 (Recognition of Revenue—Theory) Revenue is usually recognized at the point of sale. Under special circumstances, however, bases other than the point of sale are used for the timing of revenue recognition.

Instructions

(a) Why is the point of sale usually used as the basis for the timing of revenue recognition?
(b) Disregarding the special circumstances when bases other than the point of sale are used, discuss the merits of each of the following objections to the sales basis of revenue recognition:
    1. It is too conservative because revenue is earned throughout the entire process of production.
    2. It is not conservative enough because accounts receivable do not represent disposable funds, sales returns and allowances may be made, and collection and bad debt expenses may be incurred in a later period.
(c) Revenue may also be recognized (1) during production and (2) when cash is received. For each of these two bases of timing revenue recognition, give an example of the circumstances in which it is properly used and discuss the accounting merits of its use in lieu of the sales basis.

(AICPA adapted)

C19-3 (Recognition of Revenue—Theory) The earning of revenue by a business enterprise is recognized for accounting purposes when the transaction is recorded. In some situations, revenue is recognized approximately as it is earned in the economic sense. In other situations, however, accountants have developed guidelines for recognizing revenue by other criteria, such as at the point of sale.

Instructions (Ignore income taxes.)

(a) Explain and justify why revenue is often recognized as earned at time of sale.
(b) Explain in what situations it would be appropriate to recognize revenue as the productive activity takes place.
(c) At what times, other than those included in (a) and (b) above, may it be appropriate to recognize revenue? Explain.

C19-4 (Recognition of Revenue—Trading Stamps) Gordeeva & Grinkov Stamps, Inc., was formed early this year to sell trading stamps throughout the Southwest to retailers who distribute the stamps free to their customers. Books for accumulating the stamps and catalogs illustrating the merchandise for which the stamps may be exchanged are given free to retailers for distribution to stamp recipients. Centers with inventories of merchandise premiums have been established for redemption of the stamps. Retailers may not return unused stamps to Gordeeva & Grinkov.

The following schedule expresses Gordeeva & Grinkov's expectations as to percentages of a normal month's activity that will be attained. For this purpose, a "normal month's activity" is defined as the level of operations expected when expansion of activities ceases or tapers off to a stable rate. The company expects that this level will be attained in the third year and that sales of stamps will average $5,000,000 per month throughout the third year.

Month	Actual Stamp Sales Percent	Merchandise Premium Purchases Percent	Stamp Redemptions Percent
6th	30%	40%	10%
12th	60	60	45
18th	80	80	70
24th	90	90	80
30th	100	100	95

Gordeeva & Grinkov plans to adopt an annual closing date at the end of each 12 months of operation.

Instructions
  (a) Discuss the factors to be considered in determining when revenue should be recognized in measuring the income of a business enterprise.
  (b) Discuss the accounting alternatives that should be considered by Gordeeva & Grinkov Stamps, Inc., for the recognition of its revenues and related expenses.
  (c) For each accounting alternative discussed in (b), give balance sheet accounts that should be used and indicate how each should be classified.

(AICPA adapted)

C19-5 (Recognition of Revenue from Subscriptions) *Cutting Edge* is a monthly magazine that has been on the market for 18 months. It currently has a circulation of 1.4 million copies. Currently negotiations are underway to obtain a bank loan in order to update their facilities. They are producing close to capacity and expect to grow at an average of 20% per year over the next 3 years.

After reviewing the financial statements of *Cutting Edge*, Chen Lu, the bank loan officer, has indicated that a loan could be offered to *Cutting Edge* only if they could increase their current ratio and decrease their debt to equity ratio to a specified level.

Victor Petrenko, the marketing manager of *Cutting Edge*, has devised a plan to meet these requirements. Petrenko indicates that an advertising campaign can be initiated to immediately increase their circulation. The potential customers would be contacted after the purchase of another magazine's mailing list. The campaign would include:

  1. An offer to subscribe to *Cutting Edge* at 3/4 the normal price.
  2. A special offer to all new subscribers to receive the most current world atlas whenever requested at a guaranteed price of $1.00.
  3. An unconditional guarantee that any subscriber will receive a full refund if dissatisfied with the magazine.

Although the offer of a full refund is risky, Petrenko claims that few people will ask for a refund after receiving half of their subscription issues. Petrenko notes that other magazine companies have tried this sales promotion technique and experienced great success. Their average cancellation rate was 25%. On the average, each company increased their initial circulation threefold and in the long run had increased circulation to twice that which existed before the promotion. In addition, 70% of the new subscribers are expected to take advantage of the atlas premium. Petrenko feels confident that the increased subscriptions from the advertising campaign will increase the current ratio and decrease the debt to equity ratio.

You are the controller of *Cutting Edge* and must give your opinion of the proposed plan.

Instructions
  (a) When should revenue from the new subscriptions be recognized?
  (b) How would you classify the estimated sales returns stemming from the unconditional guarantee?
  (c) How should the atlas premium be recorded? Is the estimated premium claims a liability? Explain.
  (d) Does the proposed plan achieve the goals of increasing the current ratio and decreasing the debt to equity ratio?

C19-6 (Long-Term Contract—Percentage-of-Completion) Dan Jansen Company is accounting for a long-term construction contract using the percentage-of-completion method. It is a 4-year contract that is currently in its second year. The latest estimates of total contract costs indicate that the contract will be completed at a profit to Dan Jansen Company.

Instructions

(a) What theoretical justification is there for Dan Jansen Company's use of the percentage-of-completion method?

(b) How would progress billings be accounted for? Include in your discussion the classification of progress billings in Dan Jansen Company financial statements.

(c) How would the income recognized in the second year of the 4-year contract be determined using the cost-to-cost method of determining percentage of completion?

(d) What would be the effect on earnings per share in the second year of the 4-year contract of using the percentage-of-completion method instead of the completed-contract method? Discuss.

(AICPA adapted)

C19-7 (Revenue Recognition—Real Estate Development) Lillehammer Lakes is a new recreational real estate development which consists of 500 lake-front and lake-view lots. As a special incentive to the first 100 buyers of lake-view lots, the developer is offering 3 years of free financing on 10-year, 12% notes, no down payment, and one week at a nearby established resort—"a $1,200 value." The normal price per lot is $10,000. The cost per lake-view lot to the developer is an estimated average of $2,000. The development costs continue to be incurred, the actual average cost per lot is not known at this time. The resort promotion cost is $700 per lot. The notes are held by Golden Committee Corp., a wholly owned subsidiary.

Instructions

(a) Discuss the revenue recognition and gross profit measurement issues raised by this situation.

(b) How would the developer's past financial and business experience influence your decision concerning the recording of these transactions?

(c) Assume 50 persons have accepted the offer, signed 10-year notes, and have stayed at the local resort. Prepare the journal entries that you believe are proper.

(d) What should be disclosed in the notes to the financial statements?

*C19-8 (Franchise Revenue) Frozen Delight Inc. sells franchises to independent operators throughout the northwestern part of the United States. The contract with the franchisee includes the following provisions:

1. The franchisee is charged an initial fee of $70,000. Of this amount, $20,000 is payable when the agreement is signed, and a $10,000 non-interest-bearing note is payable at the end of each of the five subsequent years.

2. All of the initial franchise fee collected by Frozen Delight Inc. is to be refunded and the remaining obligation canceled if, for any reason, the franchisee fails to open his or her franchise.

3. In return for the initial franchise fee, Frozen Delight Inc. agrees to (a) assist the franchisee in selecting the location for the business, (b) negotiate the lease for the land, (c) obtain financing and assist with building design, (d) supervise construction, (e) establish accounting and tax records, and (f) provide expert advice over a 5-year period relating to such matters as employee and management training, quality control, and promotion.

4. In addition to the initial franchise fee, the franchisee is required to pay to Frozen Delight Inc. a monthly fee of 2% of sales for menu planning, recipe innovations, and the privilege of purchasing ingredients from Frozen Delight Inc. at or below prevailing market prices.

Management of Frozen Delight Inc. estimates that the value of the services rendered to the franchisee at the time the contract is signed amounts to at least $20,000. All franchisees to date have opened their locations at the scheduled time and none have defaulted on any of the notes receivable.

The credit ratings of all franchisees would entitle them to borrow at the current interest rate of 10%. The present value of an ordinary annuity of five annual receipts of $10,000 each discounted at 10% is $37,908.

Instructions

(a) Discuss the alternatives that Frozen Delight Inc. might use to account for the initial franchise fee, evaluate each by applying generally accepted accounting principles, and give illustrative entries for each alternative.

(b) Given the nature of Frozen Delight Inc.'s agreement with its franchisees, when should revenue be recognized? Discuss the question of revenue recognition for both the initial franchise fee and the additional monthly fee of 2% of sales and give illustrative entries for both types of revenue.

(c) Assuming that Frozen Delight Inc. sells some franchises for $90,000, which includes a charge of $20,000 for the rental of equipment for its useful life of 10 years, that $40,000 of the fee is payable immediately and the balance on non-interest-bearing notes at $10,000 per year, that no portion of the $20,000 rental payment is refundable in case the franchisee goes out of business, and that title to the equipment remains with the franchisor, what would be the preferable method of accounting for the rental portion of the initial franchise fee? Explain.

(AICPA adapted)

▶ USING YOUR JUDGMENT ◀

▶ FINANCIAL REPORTING PROBLEM

The following note appears in the "Summary of Significant Accounting Policies" section of the Annual Report of Westinghouse Electric Corporation.

> **Note 1 (in Part): Revenue Recognition.**   Sales are primarily recorded as products are shipped and services are rendered. The percentage-of-completion method of accounting is used for nuclear steam supply system orders with delivery schedules generally in excess of five years and for certain construction projects where this method of accounting is consistent with industry practice.
>
> WFSI revenues are generally recognized on the accrual method. When accounts become delinquent for more than two payment periods, usually 60 days, income is recognized only as payments are received. Such delinquent accounts for which no payments are received in the current month, and other accounts on which income is not being recognized because the receipt of either principal or interest is questionable, are classified as nonearning receivables.

Instructions
1. Identify the revenue recognition methods used by Westinghouse Electric as discussed in its note on significant accounting policies.
2. Under what conditions are the revenue recognition methods identified in the first paragraph of Westinghouse's note above acceptable?
3. From the information provided in the second paragraph of Westinghouse's note, identify the type of operation being described and defend the acceptability of the revenue recognition method.

▶ WRITING ASSIGNMENT

Honest John's Construction is in its fourth year of business. John performs long-term construction projects and accounts for them using the completed contract method. Honest John built an apartment building at a price of $1,000,000. The costs and billings for this contract for the first three years are as follows:

	1995	1996	1997
Costs incurred to date	$320,000	$600,000	$ 790,000
Estimated costs yet to be incurred	480,000	200,000	–0–
Customer billings to date	150,000	410,000	1,000,000
Collection of billings to date	120,000	340,000	950,000

John has contacted you, a certified public accountant, about the following concern. He would like to attract some investors, but he believes that, in order to recognize revenue, he must first "deliver" the product. Therefore, on his balance sheet, he did not recognize any gross profits from the above contract until 1997, when he recognized the entire $210,000. That looked good for 1997, but the preceding years looked grim by comparison. He wants to know about an alternative to this completed contract revenue recognition.

Instructions
Draft a letter to John, telling him about the percentage-of-completion method of recognizing revenue. Compare it to the completed-contract method. Explain the idea behind the percentage-of-completion method. In addition, illustrate how much revenue he could have recognized in 1995, 1996, and 1997 if he had used this method.

▶ GROUP ASSIGNMENT

(Long-Term Contracts)   Your group has been engaged by Rich Mathre Construction Company to advise it concerning the proper accounting for a series of long-term contracts. Rich Mathre Construction Company commenced doing business on January 1, 1996. Construction activities for the first year of operations are shown below. All contract costs are with different customers, and any work remaining at December 31, 1996, is expected to be completed in 1997.

Project	Total Contract Price	Billings Through 12/31/96	Cash Collections Through 12/31/96	Contract Costs Incurred Through 12/31/96	Estimated Additional Costs to Complete
A	$ 300,000	$200,000	$180,000	$248,000	$ 67,000
B	350,000	110,000	105,000	67,800	271,200
C	280,000	280,000	255,000	186,000	–0–
D	200,000	35,000	25,000	123,000	87,000
E	240,000	205,000	200,000	185,000	15,000
	$1,370,000	$830,000	$765,000	$809,800	$440,200

Instructions

Your instructor will assign one member of the group to serve as recorder and one member to serve as spokesperson. As a group, provide the information for the recorder to prepare responses to the following four requirements. Upon completion of each requirement and before moving on to the next part, the spokesperson will report the group findings to the class.

(a) Prepare a schedule to compute gross profit (loss) to be reported, unbilled contract costs and recognized profit, and billings in excess of costs and recognized profit using the percentage-of-completion method.

(b) Prepare a partial income statement and balance sheet to indicate how the information would be reported for financial statement purposes.

(c) Repeat the requirements for part (a) assuming Rich Mathre uses the completed-contract method.

(d) Using the responses above for illustrative purposes, prepare a brief report comparing the conceptual merits (both positive and negative) of the two revenue recognition approaches.

▶ ETHICS CASE

Nimble Health and Racquet Club (NHRC), which operates eight clubs in the Chicago metropolitan area, offers one-year memberships. The members may use any of the eight facilities but must reserve racquetball court time and pay a separate fee before using the court. As an incentive to new customers, NHRC advertised that any customers not satisfied for any reason could receive a refund of the remaining portion of unused membership fees. Membership fees are due at the beginning of the individual membership period; however, customers are given the option of financing the membership fee over the membership period at a 15 percent interest rate.

Some customers have expressed a desire to take only the regularly scheduled aerobic classes without paying for a full membership. During the current fiscal year, NHRC began selling coupon books for aerobic classes only to accommodate these customers. Each book is dated and contains 50 coupons that may be redeemed for any regularly scheduled aerobic class over a one-year period. After the one-year period, unused coupons are no longer valid.

During 1990, NHRC expanded into the health equipment market by purchasing a local company that manufactures rowing machines and cross-country ski machines. These machines are used in NHRC's facilities and are sold through the clubs and mail order catalogs. Customers must make a 20 percent down payment when placing an equipment order; delivery is 60-90 days after order placement. The machines are sold with a two-year unconditional guarantee. Based on past experience, NHRC expects the costs to repair machines under guarantee to be 4 percent of sales.

NHRC is in the process of preparing financial statements as of May 31, 1996, the end of its fiscal year. James Hogan, corporate controller, expressed concern over the company's performance for the year and decided to review the preliminary financial statements prepared by Barbara Hardy, NHRC's assistant controller. After reviewing the statements, Hogan proposed that the following changes be reflected in the May 31, 1996, published financial statements.

1. Membership revenue should be recognized when the membership fee is collected.
2. Revenue from the coupon books should be recognized when the books are sold.
3. Down payments on equipment purchases and expenses associated with the guarantee on the rowing and cross-country machines should be recognized when paid.

Barbara indicated to Hogan that the proposed changes are not in accordance with generally accepted accounting principles, but Hogan insisted that the changes be made. Barbara believes that Hogan wants to manipulate income to forestall any potential financial problems and increase his year-end bonus. At this point, Barbara is unsure what action to take.

Instructions

(a) 1. Describe when Nimble Health and Racquet Club (NHRC) should recognize revenue from membership fees, court rentals, and coupon book sales.

2. Describe how NHRC should account for the down payments on equipment sales, explaining when this revenue should be recognized.

3. Indicate when NHRC should recognize the expense associated with the guarantee of the rowing and cross-country machines.

(b) Discuss why James Hogan's proposed changes and his insistence that the financial statement changes be made is unethical. Structure your answer around or to include the following aspects of ethical conduct: competence, confidentiality, integrity, and/or objectivity.

(c) Identify some specific actions Barbara Hardy could take to resolve this situation.

(CMA adapted)

CHAPTER 20

ACCOUNTING FOR INCOME TAXES

LEARNING OBJECTIVES

After studying this chapter, you should be able to:

1. Identify differences between pretax financial income and taxable income.

2. Describe a temporary difference that results in future taxable amounts.

3. Describe a temporary difference that results in future deductible amounts.

4. Explain the purpose of a deferred tax asset valuation account.

5. Describe the presentation of income tax expense in the income statement.

6. Describe various temporary and permanent differences.

7. Explain the effect of various tax rates and tax rate changes on deferred income taxes.

8. Apply accounting procedures for a loss carryback and a loss carryforward.

9. Describe the presentation of deferred income taxes in financial statements.

10. Identify special issues related to deferred income taxes.

11. Indicate the basic principles of the asset-liability approach.

"FASB Proposal Provides Income Boost to Many Companies"
"Board Issues Another Pronouncement on Income Taxes"
"Deferred Tax Assets Increase Under Deferred Tax Proposal"

What these headlines from the financial press indicate is the most recent FASB pronouncement on accounting for income taxes, *SFAS No. 109*, is having a material impact on the assets, liabilities, and income of many companies.[1] This latest effort represents the culmination of almost 10 years of work on this subject, and it supersedes or amends more than 37 different, previously issued GAAP pronouncements. It is complex and has caused companies to incur substantial cost in its implementation. This chapter discusses the basic guidelines that companies must follow in reporting income taxes under this pronouncement.

---

[1]*Statement of Financial Accounting Standards No. 109*, "Accounting for Income Taxes," was issued by the Financial Accounting Standards Board in February 1992. Five years earlier the Board had issued *Statement of Financial Accounting Standards No. 96*, "Accounting for Income Taxes." No. 96 met with opposition from the business community because of its complexity and failure to recognize certain future tax benefits. As a result, the Board issued *SFAS No. 109*.

► PRETAX FINANCIAL INCOME AND TAXABLE INCOME

Before we discuss this latest FASB pronouncement on income taxes, a number of fundamental points need clarification. **Pretax financial income** is a financial accounting term often referred to as income before income taxes, income for financial reporting purposes, or income for book purposes. **Taxable income** (or income for tax purposes) is a tax accounting term used to indicate the amount upon which a company's income tax payable is computed. Taxable income is determined by following the rules of the Internal Revenue Code. Because GAAP and tax regulations are different in many ways, pretax financial income and taxable income frequently differ. Examples of differences are:

1. Depreciation is computed on a straight-line basis for financial reporting purposes, but by an accelerated method **(MACRS)** for tax purposes. The MACRS method was discussed in Chapter 11.

2. Income is recognized on the accrual (sale) basis for financial reporting purposes, but may be recognized on the installment basis for tax purposes.

3. Warranty costs are recognized in the period incurred (matched with the sales revenue) for financial reporting purposes, but recognized when paid for tax purposes.

To illustrate how these differences affect pretax financial income and taxable income, assume that Chelsea Inc. in 1996 (its first year of operations) has revenues of $130,000 for book purposes and $100,000 for tax purposes. It also has expenses of $60,000 for both book and tax purposes. The $30,000 difference in revenues results because Chelsea recognizes revenue on the accrual basis for book purposes, but reports revenues as cash is collected for tax purposes. Chelsea's pretax financial income and taxable income for 1996 would be reported as follows:

ILLUSTRATION 20-1
Pretax Financial Income and Taxable Income, Chelsea Inc.

	Financial Income	Taxable Income
Revenues	$130,000	$100,000
Expenses	60,000	60,000
Pretax financial income for 1996	**$ 70,000**	
Taxable income for 1996		**$ 40,000**

The computation of **income tax payable** (assuming a 40% tax rate) would then be as follows:

ILLUSTRATION 20-2
Computation of Income Tax Payable

Taxable income for 1996	$40,000
Tax rate	40%
Income tax payable for 1996	**$16,000**

Income tax payable is classified as a current liability on the balance sheet.

► FUTURE TAXABLE AMOUNTS AND DEFERRED TAXES

After income tax payable (the amount owed the government) is computed, the next question is whether any other income taxes have to be recognized for book purposes. The answer depends on whether there are any temporary differences between the amounts reported for tax purposes and those reported for book purposes. A **temporary difference** is the difference between the tax basis of an asset or liability and its reported (carrying or book) amount in the financial statements that will result in taxable amounts or deductible amounts in future years. **Taxable amounts** increase taxable income, and **deductible amounts** decrease taxable income.

In Chelsea Inc.'s situation, the only difference between the book basis and tax basis of the assets and liabilities relates to accounts receivable that arose from revenue recognized for book purposes. As a result, the asset difference at the end of 1996 would be as follows:

Chelsea Inc.			
Per Books	12/31/96	Per Tax Return	12/31/96
Accounts Receivable	$30,000	Accounts Receivable	$-0-

ILLUSTRATION 20-3
Temporary Difference, Sales Revenue

What will happen to this $30,000 temporary difference that originated in 1996 for Chelsea Inc.? Assuming that Chelsea expects to collect $20,000 of the receivables in 1997 and $10,000 in 1998, this collection will result in future taxable amounts of $20,000 in 1997 and $10,000 in 1998. These future taxable amounts will cause taxable income to exceed pretax financial income in both 1997 and 1998.

Illustration 20-3 indicates that Accounts Receivable are reported at $30,000 in the December 31, 1996, GAAP-basis balance sheet but the receivables have a zero tax basis. In the FASB's view, an assumption inherent in a company's GAAP balance sheet is that the assets and liabilities will be recovered and settled at their reported amounts (carrying amounts). The FASB believes that this assumption creates a requirement under accrual accounting to recognize currently the deferred tax consequences of temporary differences, that is, the amount of income taxes that would be payable (or refundable) when the reported amounts of the assets are recovered and the liabilities are settled, respectively. The following diagram illustrates the reversal or turn around of the temporary difference described in Illustration 20-3 and the resulting taxable amounts in future periods.

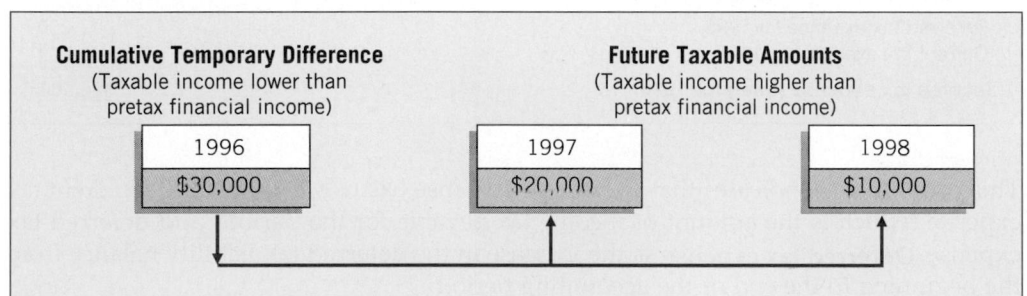

ILLUSTRATION 20-4
Reversal of Temporary Difference, Chelsea Inc.

We have assumed that Chelsea will collect the accounts receivable and report the $30,000 collection as taxable revenues in future tax returns. A payment of income tax in both 1997 and 1998 will therefore occur. We therefore should record in Chelsea's books in 1996 the deferred tax consequences of the revenue and related receivables reflected in the 1996 financial statements. This necessitates the recording of a deferred tax liability.

► DEFERRED TAX LIABILITY

A **deferred tax liability** is the deferred tax consequences attributable to taxable temporary differences. In other words, **a deferred tax liability represents the increase in taxes payable in future years as a result of taxable temporary differences existing at the end of the current year.** Recall from the Chelsea example that income tax payable is $16,000 ($40,000 × 40%) in 1996 (Illustration 20-2). In addition, a temporary difference exists at year-end because the revenue and related accounts receivable are reported differently for book and tax purposes. The book basis of accounts receivable is $30,000 and the tax basis is zero. Thus, the total deferred tax liability at the end of 1996 is $12,000, computed as follows:

**ILLUSTRATION 20-5
Computation of Deferred
Tax Liability, End of 1996**

Chelsea Inc.	
Book basis of accounts receivable	$30,000
Tax basis of accounts receivable	–0–
Cumulative temporary difference at the end of 1996	30,000
Tax rate	40%
Deferred tax liability at the end of 1996	**$12,000**

Another way to compute the deferred tax liability is to prepare a schedule that indicates the taxable amounts scheduled for the future as a result of existing temporary differences. Such a schedule is particularly useful when the computations become more complex.

**ILLUSTRATION 20-6
Schedule of Future
Taxable Amount**

	Future Years	
	1997	1998
Future taxable amounts	$20,000	$10,000
Tax rate	40%	40%
Deferred tax liability at the end of 1996	$ 8,000	$ 4,000

Because it is the first year of operations for Chelsea, there is no deferred tax liability at the beginning of the year. The income tax expense for 1996 is computed as follows:

**ILLUSTRATION 20-7
Computation of Income
Tax Expense, 1996**

Chelsea Inc.	
Deferred tax liability at end of 1996	$12,000
Deferred tax liability at beginning of 1996	–0–
Deferred tax expense for 1996	12,000
Current tax expense for 1996	16,000
Income tax expense (total) for 1996	**$28,000**

This computation indicates that income tax expense has two components—current tax expense (which is the amount of income tax payable for the period) and deferred tax expense. **Deferred tax expense** is the increase in the deferred tax liability balance from the beginning to the end of the accounting period.

Taxes due and payable are credited to Income Tax Payable; the increase in deferred taxes is credited to Deferred Tax Liability; and the sum of those two items is debited to Income Tax Expense. For Chelsea Inc. the following entry is made at the end of 1996:

Income Tax Expense	28,000	
Income Tax Payable		16,000
Deferred Tax Liability		12,000

At the end of 1997 (the second year) the difference between the book basis and the tax basis of the accounts receivable is $10,000. This difference is multiplied by the applicable tax rate to arrive at the deferred tax liability of $4,000 ($10,000 × 40%) to be reported at the end of 1997. Assuming that income tax payable for 1997 is $19,000, the income tax expense for 1997 is as follows:

**ILLUSTRATION 20-8
Computation of Income
Tax Expense, 1997**

Chelsea Inc.	
Deferred tax liability at end of 1997	$ 4,000
Deferred tax liability at beginning of 1997	12,000
Deferred tax expense (benefit) for 1997	(8,000)
Current tax expense for 1997	19,000
Income tax expense (total) for 1997	**$11,000**

The journal entry to record income tax expense, the change in the deferred tax liability, and income tax payable for 1997 is as follows:

Income Tax Expense	11,000	
Deferred Tax Liability	8,000	
Income Tax Payable		19,000

In the entry to record income taxes at the end of 1998, the Deferred Tax Liability is reduced by $4,000. The Deferred Tax Liability account appears as follows at the end of 1998:

ILLUSTRATION 20-9
Deferred Tax Liability Account after Reversals

Deferred Tax Liability			
1997	8,000	1996	12,000
1998	4,000		

The Deferred Tax Liability account has a zero balance at the end of 1998.

Some analysts dismiss deferred tax liabilities when assessing the financial strength of a company. But the FASB indicates that the deferred tax liability meets the definition of a liability established in *Statement of Financial Accounting Concepts No. 6*, "Elements of Financial Statements" because:

1. **It results from a past transaction.** In the Chelsea example, services were performed for customers and revenue was recognized in 1996 for financial reporting purposes but was deferred for tax purposes.

2. **It is a present obligation.** Taxable income in future periods will be higher than pretax financial income as a result of this temporary difference. Thus, a present obligation exists.

3. **It represents a future sacrifice.** Taxable income and taxes due in future periods will result from events that have already occurred. The payment of these taxes when they come due is the future sacrifice.

► SUMMARY OF OBJECTIVES

One objective of accounting for income taxes is to recognize the amount of taxes payable or refundable for the current year. In Chelsea's case, income tax payable is $16,000 for 1996.

A **second objective** is to recognize deferred tax liabilities and assets for the future tax consequences of events that have already been recognized in the financial statements or tax returns. Chelsea sold services to customers that resulted in accounts receivable of $30,000 in 1996; the $30,000 was reported on the 1996 income statement—it was not reported on the tax return as income. It will appear on future tax returns as income when it is collected. As a result, a $30,000 temporary difference exists at the end of 1996 which will cause future taxable amounts. A deferred tax liability of $12,000 is reported on the balance sheet at the end of 1996, which represents the increase in taxes payable in future years ($8,000 in 1997 and $4,000 in 1998) as a result of a temporary difference existing at the end of the current year. The related deferred tax liability is reduced by $8,000 at the end of 1997 and by another $4,000 at the end of 1998.

In addition to affecting the balance sheet, deferred taxes have an impact on income tax expense in each of the three years affected. In 1996, taxable income ($40,000) is less than pretax financial income ($70,000). Income tax payable for 1996 is therefore $16,000 (based on taxable income). Deferred tax expense of $12,000 is caused by the increase in the Deferred Tax Liability account on the balance sheet. Income tax expense is then $28,000 for 1996.

In 1997 and 1998, however, taxable income will be more than pretax financial income due to the reversal of the temporary difference ($20,000 in 1997 and $10,000 in 1998).

INTERNATIONAL INSIGHT

In Japan and Korea deferred taxes are not recognized; in Sweden they are generally recognized only through consolidation.

Income tax payable will therefore be higher than income tax expense in 1997 and 1998. The Deferred Tax Liability account will be debited for $8,000 in 1997 and $4,000 in 1998. Credits for these amounts are recorded in Income Tax Expense (often referred to as a **deferred tax benefit**).

▶ FUTURE DEDUCTIBLE AMOUNTS AND DEFERRED TAXES

OBJECTIVE 3

Describe a temporary difference that results in future deductible amounts.

Assume that during 1996, Cunningham Inc. estimated its warranty costs related to the sale of microwave ovens to be $500,000 paid evenly over the next 2 years. For book purposes, in 1996 Cunningham reported warranty expense and a related estimated liability for warranties of $500,000 in its financial statements. For tax purposes, **the warranty tax deduction is not allowed until paid;** therefore, no warranty liability is recognized on a tax basis balance sheet. Thus, the balance sheet difference at the end of 1996 is as follows:

ILLUSTRATION 20-10
Temporary Difference, Warranty Expense

	Cunningham Inc.			
Per Books	12/31/96	Per Tax Return		12/31/96
Estimated liability for warranties	$500,000	Estimated liability for warranties		$–0–

When the warranty liability is paid, an expense (deductible amount) will be reported for tax purposes. Because of this temporary difference, Cunningham Inc. should recognize in 1996 the tax benefits (positive tax consequences) for the tax deductions that will result from the future settlement of the liability. This future tax benefit is reported in the December 31, 1996, balance sheet as a **deferred tax asset.**

Another way to think about this situation is as follows: Deductible amounts will occur in future tax returns. These **future deductible amounts** will cause taxable income to be less than pretax financial income in the future as a result of an existing temporary difference. Cunningham's temporary difference originates (arises) in one period (1996) and reverses over two periods (1997 and 1998). This situation is diagramed as follows:

ILLUSTRATION 20-11
Reversal of Temporary Difference, Cunningham Inc.

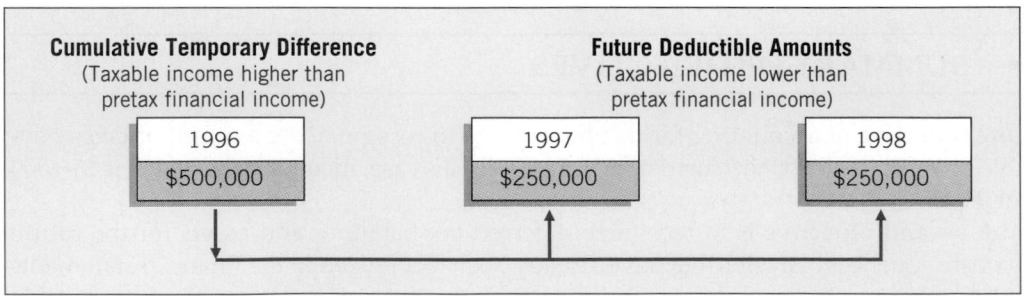

▶ DEFERRED TAX ASSET

A **deferred tax asset** is the deferred tax consequence attributable to deductible temporary differences. In other words, a **deferred tax asset represents the increase in taxes refundable (or saved) in future years as a result of deductible temporary differences existing at the end of the current year.**[2]

---

[2]In *Statement of Financial Accounting Standards No. 96,* the FASB took a strong position against recording deferred tax assets. It noted that future deductible amounts are beneficial only if the company has sufficient taxable amounts to offset them in the future. That is, if there are no taxable amounts in the future, then there is no benefit from the deductible amounts in the future and therefore no deferred tax asset. However, **the Board reversed its position** in *SFAS No. 109,* noting that deferred tax assets meet the definition of an asset and therefore should be reported in the financial statements.

To illustrate, assume that Hunt Co. accrues a loss of $50,000 in 1996 for financial reporting purposes because of pending litigation. This amount is not deductible for tax purposes until the period the loss is realized, which is expected to be 1997. As a result, a deductible amount will occur in 1997 when the liability (Estimated Litigation Liability) is settled, causing taxable income to be lower than pretax financial income. The computation of the deferred tax asset at the end of 1996 (assuming a 40% tax rate) is as follows:

Hunt Co.	
Book basis of litigation liability	$50,000
Tax basis of litigation liability	–0–
Cumulative temporary difference at the end of 1996	50,000
Tax rate	40%
Deferred tax asset at the end of 1996	$20,000

ILLUSTRATION 20-12
Computation of Deferred Tax Asset, End of 1996

Another way to compute the deferred tax asset is to prepare a schedule that indicates the deductible amounts scheduled for the future as a result of deductible temporary differences. Such a schedule is presented below:

	Future Years
Future deductible amounts	$50,000
Tax rate	40%
Deferred tax asset at the end of 1996	$20,000

ILLUSTRATION 20-13
Schedule of Future Deductible Amounts

Assuming that 1996 is Hunt's first year of operations, and income tax payable is $100,000, the income tax expense is computed as follows:

Hunt Co.	
Deferred tax asset at end of 1996	$ 20,000
Deferred tax asset at beginning of 1996	–0–
Deferred tax expense (benefit) for 1996	(20,000)
Current tax expense for 1996	100,000
Income tax expense (total) for 1996	$ 80,000

ILLUSTRATION 20-14
Computation of Income Tax Expense, 1996

The **deferred tax benefit** results from the increase in the deferred tax asset from the beginning to the end of the accounting period. The deferred tax benefit is a negative component of income tax expense. The total income tax expense of $80,000 on the income statement for 1996 is then comprised of two elements—current tax expense of $100,000 and deferred tax benefit of $20,000. For Hunt Co. the following journal entry is made at the end of 1996 to record income tax expense, deferred income taxes, and income tax payable.

Income Tax Expense	80,000	
Deferred Tax Asset	20,000	
Income Tax Payable		100,000

At the end of 1997 (the second year) the difference between the book value and the tax basis of the litigation liability is zero. Therefore, there is no deferred tax asset at this date. Assuming that income tax payable for 1997 is $140,000, the computation of income tax expense for 1997 is as follows:

Hunt Co.	
Deferred tax asset at the end of 1997	$ –0–
Deferred tax asset at the beginning of 1997	20,000
Deferred tax expense (benefit) for 1997	20,000
Current tax expense for 1997	140,000
Income tax expense (total) for 1997	$160,000

ILLUSTRATION 20-15
Computation of Income Tax Expense, 1997

The journal entry to record income taxes for 1997 is as follows:

Income Tax Expense	160,000	
Deferred Tax Asset		20,000
Income Tax Payable		140,000

The total income tax expense of $160,000 on the income statement for 1997 is then comprised of two elements—current tax expense of $140,000 and deferred tax expense of $20,000.

The Deferred Tax Asset account would appear as follows at the end of 1997:

ILLUSTRATION 20-16
Deferred Tax Asset
Account after Reversals

Deferred Tax Asset			
1996	20,000	1997	20,000

A key issue in accounting for income taxes is whether a deferred tax asset should be recognized in the financial records. We believe that a deferred tax asset meets the three main conditions for an item to be reported as an asset:

1. **It results from a past transaction.** In the Hunt Co. example, the accrual of the loss contingency is the past event that gives rise to a future deductible temporary difference.

2. **It gives rise to a probable benefit in the future.** Taxable income is higher than pretax financial income in the current year (1996). However, in the next year the exact opposite occurs; that is, taxable income is lower than pretax financial income. Because this deductible temporary difference reduces taxes payable in the future, a probable future benefit exists at the end of the current period.

3. **It controls access to the benefits.** Hunt Co. has the ability to obtain the benefit of existing deductible temporary differences by reducing its taxes payable in the future. Hunt Co. has the exclusive right to that benefit and can control others' access to it.

▶ DEFERRED TAX ASSET—VALUATION ACCOUNT

OBJECTIVE 4

Explain the purpose of a deferred tax asset valuation account.

A deferred tax asset is recognized for all deductible temporary differences. However, a deferred tax asset should be reduced by a valuation allowance if, based on all available evidence, **it is more likely than not** that some portion or all of the deferred tax asset **will not be realized.** More likely than not means a level of likelihood that is at least slightly more than 50%.

Assume that Jensen Co. has a deductible temporary difference of $1,000,000 at the end of its first year of operations. Its tax rate is 40%, which means a deferred tax asset of $400,000 ($1,000,000 × 40%) is recorded. Assuming that income taxes payable are $900,000, the journal entry to record income tax expense, the deferred tax asset, and income tax payable is as follows:

Income Tax Expense	500,000	
Deferred Tax Asset	400,000	
Income Tax Payable		900,000

After careful review of all available evidence, it is determined that it is more likely than not that $100,000 of this deferred tax asset will not be realized. The journal entry to record this reduction in asset value is as follows:

Income Tax Expense	100,000	
Allowance to Reduce Deferred Tax Asset		
to Expected Realizable Value		100,000

In this journal entry, income tax expense is increased in the current period because a favorable tax benefit is not expected to be realized for a portion of the deductible temporary difference. **A valuation account is simultaneously established to recognize the reduction in the carrying amount of the deferred tax asset.** This valuation account is a contra account and may be reported on the financial statements in the following manner:

Jensen Co.	
Deferred Tax Asset	$400,000
Less: Allowance to Reduce Deferred Tax	
Asset to Expected Realizable Value	100,000
Deferred Tax Asset (Net)	$300,000

ILLUSTRATION 20-17
Balance Sheet Presentation of Valuation Allowance Account

This allowance account is evaluated at the end of each accounting period. If, at the end of the next period, the deferred tax asset is still $400,000, but now $350,000 of this asset is expected to be realized, then the following entry is made to adjust the valuation account:

Allowance to Reduce Deferred Tax Asset		
to Expected Realizable Value	50,000	
Income Tax Expense		50,000

All available evidence, both positive and negative, should be carefully considered to determine whether, based on the weight of available evidence, a valuation allowance is needed. For example, if the company has been experiencing a series of loss years, a reasonable assumption is that these losses will continue and the benefit of the future deductible amounts will be lost. The use of a valuation account under other conditions will be discussed later in the chapter.

▶ INCOME STATEMENT PRESENTATION

Whether the change in deferred income taxes should be added to or subtracted from income tax payable in computing income tax expense depends on the circumstances. For example, an increase in a deferred tax liability would be added to income tax payable. On the other hand, an increase in a deferred tax asset would be subtracted from income tax payable. The formula to compute income tax expense (benefit) is as follows:

OBJECTIVE 5
Describe the presentation of income tax expense in the income statement.

ILLUSTRATION 20-18
Formula to Compute Income Tax Expense

In the income statement or in the notes to the financial statements, the significant components of income tax expense attributable to continuing operations should be disclosed. Given the information related to Chelsea Inc. on page 994, Chelsea's income statement might be reported as follows:

ILLUSTRATION 20-19
Income Statement Presentation of Income Tax Expense

Chelsea Inc. Income Statement For the Year Ending December 31, 1996		
Revenues		$130,000
Expenses		60,000
Income before income taxes		70,000
Income tax expense		
Current	$16,000	
Deferred	12,000	28,000
Net income		$ 42,000

As illustrated, both the current portion (amount of income tax payable for the period) and the deferred portion of income tax expense are reported. Another option is to simply report the total income tax expense on the income statement, and then in the notes to the financial statements indicate the current and deferred portions. Income tax expense is often referred to as "Provision for Income Taxes." Using this terminology, the current provision is $16,000 and the provision for deferred taxes is $12,000.

▶ SPECIFIC DIFFERENCES

OBJECTIVE 6

Describe various temporary and permanent differences.

Numerous items create differences between pretax financial income and taxable income. For purposes of accounting recognition, these differences are of two types: (1) temporary differences, and (2) permanent differences.

TEMPORARY DIFFERENCES

Temporary differences that will result in taxable amounts in future years when the related assets are recovered are often called **taxable temporary differences;** temporary differences that will result in deductible amounts in future years when the related book liabilities are settled are often called **deductible temporary differences.** Taxable temporary differences give rise to recording deferred tax liabilities; deductible temporary differences give rise to recording deferred tax assets. Examples of temporary differences are provided below.[3]

ILLUSTRATION 20-20
Examples of Temporary Differences

A. **Revenues or gains are taxable after they are recognized in financial income.** An asset (e.g., accounts receivable or investment) may be recognized for revenues or gains that will result in **taxable amounts in future years** when the asset is recovered. Examples:
1. Installment sale accounted for on the accrual basis for financial reporting purposes and on the installment (cash) basis for tax purposes.
2. Contracts accounted for under the percentage-of-completion method for financial reporting purposes and a portion of related gross profit deferred for tax purposes.
3. Investments accounted for under the equity method for financial reporting purposes and under the cost method for tax purposes.
4. Gain on involuntary conversion of nonmonetary asset which is recognized for financial reporting purposes but deferred for tax purposes.

B. **Expenses or losses are deductible after they are recognized in financial income.** A liability (or contra asset) may be recognized for expenses or losses that will result in **deductible amounts in future years** when the liability is settled. Examples:
1. Product warranty liabilities.
2. Estimated liabilities related to discontinued operations or restructurings.
3. Litigation accruals.
4. Bad debt expense recognized using the allowance method for financial reporting purposes; direct write-off method used for tax purposes.

C. **Revenues or gains are taxable before they are recognized in financial income.** A liability may be recognized for an advance payment for goods or services to be provided in future years. For tax purposes, the advance payment is included in taxable income upon the receipt of cash. Future sacrifices to provide goods or services (or future refunds to those who cancel their orders) that settle the liability will result in **deductible amounts in future years.** Examples:
1. Subscriptions received in advance.
2. Advance rental receipts.
3. Sales and leasebacks for financial reporting purposes (income deferral) and reported as sales for tax purposes.
4. Prepaid contracts and royalties received in advance.

D. **Expenses or losses are deductible before they are recognized in financial income.** The cost of an asset may have been deducted for tax purposes faster than it was expensed for financial reporting purposes. Amounts received upon future recovery of the amount of the asset for financial reporting (through use or sale) will exceed the remaining tax basis of the asset and thereby result in **taxable amounts in future years.** Examples:
1. Depreciable property, depletable resources, and intangibles.
2. Deductible pension funding exceeding expense.
3. Prepaid expenses that are deducted on the tax return in the period paid.

---

[3]*SFAS No. 109* gives more examples of temporary differences. We have presented the most common types.

Determining a company's temporary differences may prove difficult. A company should prepare a balance sheet for tax purposes that can be compared with its GAAP balance sheet; many of the differences between the two balance sheets would be temporary differences.

Originating and Reversing Aspects of Temporary Differences

An **originating temporary difference** is the initial difference between the book basis and the tax basis of an asset or liability, regardless of whether the tax basis of the asset or liability exceeds or is exceeded by the book basis of the asset or liability. A **reversing difference,** on the other hand, occurs when a temporary difference that originated in prior periods is eliminated and the related tax effect is removed from the deferred tax account.

For example, assume that Sharp Co. has tax depreciation in excess of book depreciation of $2,000 in 1992, 1993, and 1994, and that it has an excess of book depreciation over tax depreciation of $3,000 in 1995 and 1996 for the same asset. Assuming a tax rate of 30% for all years involved, the Deferred Tax Liability account would reflect the following:

	Deferred Tax Liability					
Tax Effects	1995	900	1992	600	Tax Effects	
of	1996	900	1993	600	of	
Reversing Differences			1994	600	Originating Differences	

ILLUSTRATION 20-21
Tax Effects of Originating and Reversing Differences

The originating differences for Sharp in each of the first three years would be $2,000, and the related tax effect of each originating difference would be $600. The reversing differences in 1995 and 1996 would each be $3,000, and the related tax effect of each would be $900.

PERMANENT DIFFERENCES

Some differences between taxable income and pretax financial income are permanent. **Permanent differences** are caused by items that (1) enter into pretax financial income but **never** into taxable income or (2) enter into taxable income but **never** into pretax financial income.

Congress has enacted a variety of tax law provisions in an effort to attain certain political, economic, and social objectives. Some of these provisions exclude certain revenues from taxation, limit the deductibility of certain expenses, and permit the deduction of certain other expenses in excess of costs incurred. A corporation that has tax-free income, nondeductible expenses, or allowable deductions in excess of cost has an effective tax rate that is different from the statutory (regular) tax rate.

Since permanent differences affect only the period in which they occur, they do not give rise to future taxable or deductible amounts. As a result, **there are no deferred tax consequences to be recognized.** Examples of permanent differences are shown in Illustration 20-22.

A. **Items are recognized for financial reporting purposes but not for tax purposes.**
Examples:
1. Interest received on state and municipal obligations.
2. Proceeds from life insurance carried by the company on key officers or employees.
3. Compensation expense associated with certain employee stock options.
4. Premiums paid for life insurance carried by the company on key officers or employees (company is beneficiary).
5. Fines and expenses resulting from a violation of law.
6. Expenses incurred in obtaining tax-exempt income.

B. **Items are recognized for tax purposes but not for financial reporting purposes.**
Examples:
1. "Percentage depletion" of natural resources in excess of their cost.
2. The deduction for dividends received from U.S. corporations, generally 70% to 80%.

ILLUSTRATION 20-22
Examples of Permanent Differences

TEMPORARY AND PERMANENT DIFFERENCES ILLUSTRATED

To illustrate the computations used when both temporary and permanent differences exist, assume that the Bio-Tech Company reports pretax financial income of $200,000 in each of the years 1994, 1995, and 1996. The company is subject to a 30% tax rate, and has the following differences between pretax financial income and taxable income:

1. An installment sale of $18,000 in 1994 is reported for tax purposes over an 18-month period at a constant amount per month beginning January 1, 1995. The entire sale is recognized for book purposes in 1994.

2. Premium paid for life insurance carried by the company on key officers is $5,000 in 1995 and 1996. This is not deductible for tax purposes, but is expensed for book purposes.

The first item is a temporary difference and the second is a permanent difference. The reconciliation of Bio-Tech Company's pretax financial income to taxable income and the computation of income tax payable appear below.

ILLUSTRATION 20-23
Reconciliation and Computation of Income Taxes Payable

Bio-Tech Company			
	1994	1995	1996
Pretax financial income	$200,000	$200,000	$200,000
Permanent difference			
Nondeductible expense		5,000	5,000
Temporary difference			
Installment sale	(18,000)	12,000	6,000
Taxable income	182,000	217,000	211,000
Tax rate	30%	30%	30%
Income tax payable	$ 54,600	$ 65,100	$ 63,300

Note that differences causing pretax financial income to exceed taxable income are deducted from pretax financial income when determining taxable income. Conversely, differences causing pretax financial income to be less than taxable income are added to pretax financial income in determining taxable income.

Both permanent and temporary differences are considered in reconciling pretax financial income to taxable income. Since the permanent difference (nondeductible expense) does not result in future taxable or deductible amounts, deferred income taxes are not recorded for this difference.

The journal entries to record income taxes for Bio-Tech for 1994, 1995, and 1996 are as follows:

December 31, 1994

Income Tax Expense ($54,600 + $5,400)	60,000	
Income Tax Payable ($182,000 × 30%)		54,600
Deferred Tax Liability ($18,000 × 30%)		5,400

December 31, 1995

Income Tax Expense ($65,100 − $3,600)	61,500	
Deferred Tax Liability ($12,000 × 30%)	3,600	
Income Tax Payable ($217,000 × 30%)		65,100

December 31, 1996

Income Tax Expense ($63,300 − $1,800)	61,500	
Deferred Tax Liability ($6,000 × 30%)	1,800	
Income Tax Payable ($211,000 × 30%)		63,300

Bio-Tech has one temporary difference which originates in 1994 and reverses in 1995 and 1996. A deferred tax liability is recognized at the end of 1994 because the temporary difference causes future taxable amounts. As the temporary difference reverses, the deferred tax liability is reduced. There is no deferred tax amount associated with the difference caused by the nondeductible insurance expense because it is a permanent difference.

Although a statutory (enacted) tax rate of 30% applies for all three years, the effective rate is 30% for 1994 ($60,000 ÷ $200,000 = 30%) and 30.75% for 1995 and 1996 ($61,500 ÷ $200,000 = 30.75%). The **effective tax rate** is computed by dividing total income tax expense for the period by pretax financial income.

► TAX RATE CONSIDERATIONS

In our previous illustrations, the enacted tax rate did not change from one year to the next. Thus, to compute the deferred income tax amount to be reported on the balance sheet, the cumulative temporary difference is simply multiplied by the current tax rate. Using Bio-Tech as an example, the cumulative temporary difference of $18,000 is multiplied by the enacted tax rate, 30% in this case, to arrive at a deferred tax liability of $5,400 ($18,000 × 30%) at the end of 1994.

OBJECTIVE 7
Explain the effect of various tax rates and tax rate changes on deferred income taxes.

FUTURE TAX RATES

What happens if tax rates are different for future years? In this case, the **enacted tax rate** expected to apply should be used. Therefore presently enacted changes in the tax rate that become effective for a particular future year(s) must be considered when determining the tax rate to apply to existing temporary differences. For example, assume that Warlen Co. at the end of 1993 has the following cumulative temporary difference of $300,000 computed as follows:

Warlen Co.	
Book basis of depreciable assets	$1,000,000
Tax basis of depreciable assets	700,000
Cumulative temporary difference	$ 300,000

ILLUSTRATION 20-24
Computation of Cumulative Temporary Difference

Furthermore, assume that the $300,000 will reverse and result in taxable amounts in the following years when the enacted tax rates are as follows:

	1994	1995	1996	1997	1998	Total
Future taxable amounts	$80,000	$70,000	$60,000	$50,000	$40,000	$300,000
Tax rate	40%	40%	35%	30%	30%	
Deferred tax liability	$32,000	$28,000	$21,000	$15,000	$12,000	$108,000

ILLUSTRATION 20-25
Deferred Tax Liability Based on Future Rates

The total deferred tax liability at the end of 1993 is $108,000. Tax rates other than the current rate may be used only when the future tax rates have been enacted into law, as is apparently the case in this example. **If new rates are not yet enacted into law for future years, the current rate should be used.**

In determining the appropriate enacted tax rate for a given year, companies are required to use the **average tax rate.** The Internal Revenue Service and other taxing jurisdictions tax income on a graduated tax basis. For a U.S. corporation, the first $50,000 of taxable income is taxed at 15%, the next $25,000 at 25%, and from $75,001 to $10 million at 34%. An additional 5% tax up to $11,750 is imposed on corporate taxable income between $100,000 and $335,000. This surtax phases out the benefits of the 15% and 25% rates. Corporations with taxable income of over $10 million pay a tax rate of 35%. A similar phaseout surtax of 3%, up to a maximum of $100,000, applies for taxable income above $15 million. In computing deferred income taxes, companies for which graduated tax rates are a significant factor are therefore required to **determine the average tax rate and use that rate.**

REVISION OF FUTURE TAX RATES

When a change in the tax rate is enacted into law, its effect on the existing deferred income tax accounts should be recorded immediately. **The effect is reported as an adjustment to income tax expense in the period of the change.**

Assume that on December 10, 1993, a new income tax act is signed into law that lowers the corporate tax rate from 40% to 35%, effective January 1, 1995. If Hostel Co. has one temporary difference at the beginning of 1993 related to $3 million of excess tax depreciation, then it has a Deferred Tax Liability account with a balance of $1,200,000 ($3,000,000 × 40%) at January 1, 1993. If taxable amounts related to this difference are scheduled to occur equally in 1994, 1995, and 1996, the deferred tax liability at the end of 1993 should be $1,100,000 computed as follows:

ILLUSTRATION 20-26
Schedule of Future Taxable Amounts and Related Tax Rates

Hostel Co.				
	1994	1995	1996	Total
Future taxable amounts	$1,000,000	$1,000,000	$1,000,000	$3,000,000
Tax rate	40%	35%	35%	
Deferred tax liability	$ 400,000	$ 350,000	$ 350,000	$1,100,000

An entry, therefore, would be made at the end of 1993 to recognize the decrease of $100,000 ($1,200,000 − $1,100,000) in the deferred tax liability as follows:

Deferred Tax Liability	100,000	
Income Tax Expense		100,000

Corporate tax rates do not change often and, therefore, the current rate will usually be employed. However, state and foreign tax rates change more frequently and they require adjustments in deferred income taxes accordingly.[4]

▶ ACCOUNTING FOR NET OPERATING LOSSES

OBJECTIVE 8

Apply accounting procedures for a loss carryback and a loss carryforward.

A **net operating loss (NOL)** occurs for tax purposes in a year when tax-deductible expenses exceed taxable revenues. An inequitable tax burden would result if companies were taxed during profitable periods without receiving any tax relief during periods of net operating losses. Under certain circumstances, therefore, the federal tax laws permit taxpayers to use the losses of one year to offset the profits of other years. This income-averaging provision is accomplished through the **carryback and carryforward of net operating losses.** Under this provision, a company pays no income taxes for a year in which it incurs a net operating loss. In addition, it may select one of the two options discussed below.

LOSS CARRYBACK

Through use of a **loss carryback,** a company may carry the net operating loss back 3 years and receive refunds for income taxes paid in those years. The loss must be applied to the earliest year first and then sequentially to the second and third years. Any loss remaining after the 3-year carryback may be **carried forward** up to 15 years to offset future taxable income. The following diagram illustrates the loss carryback procedure, assuming a loss in 1996.

---

[4]Tax rate changes nearly always will have a substantial impact on income numbers and the reporting of deferred income taxes on the balance sheet. As a result, you can expect to hear an economic consequences argument every time that Congress decides to change the tax rates. For example, when Congress raised the corporate rate from 34% to 35% in 1993, companies took an additional "hit" to earnings if they were in a deferred tax liability position. For example, expected decreases in 1993 third quarter earnings were Alcoa 27.9%, Allied Signal 11.1%, and CSX 40%.

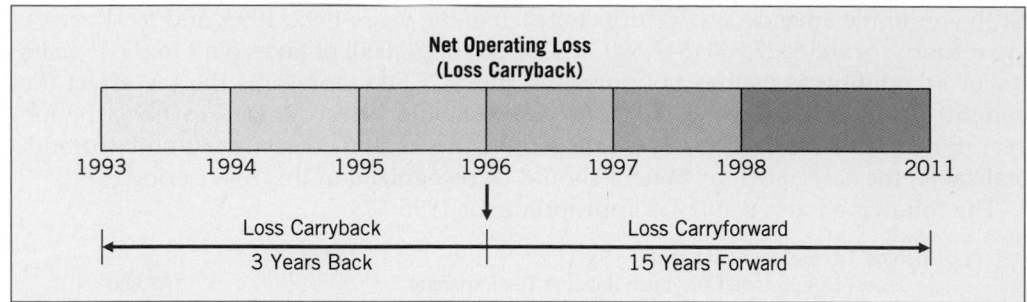

ILLUSTRATION 20-27
Loss Carryback Procedure

LOSS CARRYFORWARD

A company may elect to forgo the loss carryback and use only the **loss carryforward option,** offsetting future taxable income for up to 15 years.[5] The following diagram illustrates this approach.

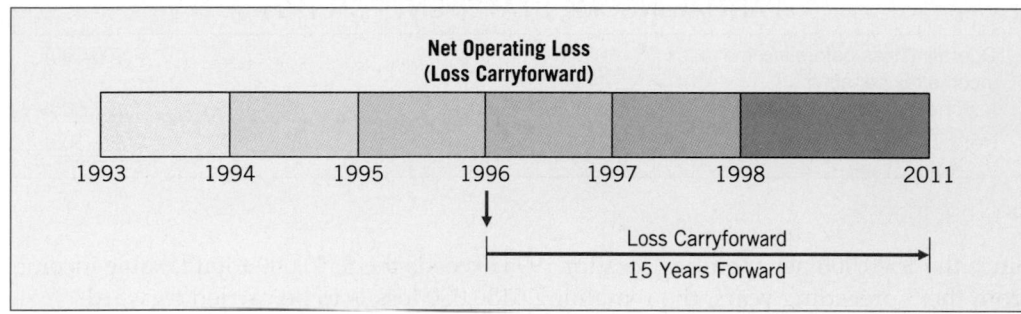

ILLUSTRATION 20-28
Loss Carryforward
Procedure

Operating losses can be substantial. IBM Corporation's total losses exceeded $15 billion dollars for the years 1992 and 1993, representing billions of dollars in potential tax savings. Companies that have suffered substantial losses are often attractive merger candidates because in certain cases the acquirer may use these losses to reduce its own income taxes.

LOSS CARRYBACK ILLUSTRATED

To illustrate the accounting procedures for a net operating loss carryback, assume that Groh Inc. has no temporary or permanent differences. Groh experiences the following:

Year	Taxable Income or Loss	Tax Rate	Tax Paid
1991	$ 75,000	30%	$22,500
1992	50,000	35%	17,500
1993	100,000	30%	30,000
1994	200,000	40%	80,000
1995	(500,000)	—	–0–

In 1995, Groh Inc. incurs a net operating loss that it decides to carry back. Under the law, the carryback must be applied first to the **third year preceding the loss year.** Therefore, the loss would be carried back first to 1992. Any unused loss would then be carried back to 1993; the remainder would finally be applied against 1994. Accordingly,

---

[5]The election to forgo the 3-year carryback period might be advantageous when a taxpayer had tax credit carryovers that might be wiped out and lost because of the carryback of the net operating loss. However, use of the carryback option provides an immediate inflow of cash at a time when alternate sources of cash may not be available. For this reason many companies with net operating losses, including companies that do not expect to return to profitable operations for a period of time, choose to carry their losses back.

Groh would file amended tax returns for each of the years 1992, 1993, and 1994, receiving refunds for the $127,500 ($17,500 + $30,000 + $80,000) of taxes paid in those years.

For accounting as well as tax purposes, the $127,500 represents the **tax effect (tax benefit) of the loss carryback.** This tax effect should be recognized in 1995, the loss year. Since the tax loss gives rise to a refund that is both measurable and currently realizable, the associated tax benefit should be recognized in this loss period.

The following journal entry is appropriate for 1995:

Income Tax Refund Receivable	127,500	
Benefit Due to Loss Carryback (Income Tax Expense)		127,500

The account debited, **Income Tax Refund Receivable,** is reported on the balance sheet as a current asset at December 31, 1995. The account credited is reported on the income statement for 1995 as follows:

ILLUSTRATION 20-29
Recognition of Benefit of the Loss Carryback in the Loss Year

Groh Inc. PARTIAL INCOME STATEMENT FOR 1995	
Operating loss before income taxes	$(500,000)
Income tax benefit	
Benefit due to loss carryback	127,500
Net loss	$(372,500)

Since the $500,000 net operating loss for 1995 exceeds the $350,000 total taxable income from the 3 preceding years, the remaining $150,000 loss is to be carried forward.

LOSS CARRYFORWARD ILLUSTRATED

If a net operating loss is not fully absorbed through a carryback or if the company decides not to carry the loss back, then it can be carried forward for up to 15 years.[6] Because carryforwards are used to offset future taxable income, the **tax effect of a loss carryforward** represents **future tax savings.** Realization of the future tax benefit is dependent upon future earnings, the prospect of which may be highly uncertain.

The key accounting issue is whether there should be different requirements for recognition of a deferred tax asset for (a) deductible temporary differences and (b) operating loss carryforwards. The FASB's position is that in substance these items are the same—both are amounts that are deductible on tax returns in the future years. As a result, the Board concluded that there should not be different requirements for recognition of a deferred tax asset from deductible temporary differences and operating loss carryforwards.[7]

Carryforward Without Valuation Account

To illustrate the accounting for an operating loss carryforward, return to the Groh Inc. example from the preceding section. In 1995 the company would record the tax effect of the $150,000 loss carryforward as a deferred tax asset of $60,000 ($150,000 × 40%) assuming that the enacted future tax rate is 40%. The journal entries to record the benefits of the carryback and the carryforward in 1995 would be as follows:

---

[6]The length of the carryforward period has varied. It was increased from 7 years to 15 years by the Economic Recovery Tax Act of 1981.

[7]This requirement is controversial because many do not believe it is appropriate to recognize deferred tax assets except when they are assured beyond a reasonable doubt. Others argue that deferred tax assets for loss carryforwards should never be recognized until income is realized in the future.

To recognize benefit of loss carryback

Income Tax Refund Receivable	127,500	
Benefit Due to Loss Carryback (Income Tax Expense)		127,500

To recognize benefit of loss carryforward

Deferred Tax Asset	60,000	
Benefit Due to Loss Carryforward (Income Tax Expense)		60,000

The income tax refund receivable of $127,500 will be realized immediately as a refund of taxes paid in the past. A Deferred Tax Asset is established for the benefits of future tax savings. The two accounts credited are contra income tax expense items, which would be presented on the 1995 income statement as follows:

Groh Inc.
PARTIAL INCOME STATEMENT FOR 1995

Operating loss before income taxes		$(500,000)
Income tax benefit		
Benefit due to loss carryback	$127,500	
Benefit due to loss carryforward	60,000	187,500
Net loss		$(312,500)

ILLUSTRATION 20-30
Recognition of the Benefit of the Loss Carryback and Carryforward in the Loss Year

The $127,500 **current tax benefit** is the income tax refundable for the year, which is determined by applying the carryback provisions of the tax law to the taxable loss for 1995. The $60,000 is the **deferred tax benefit** for the year, which results from an increase in the deferred tax asset.

For 1996, assume that Groh Inc. returns to profitable operations and has taxable income of $200,000 (prior to adjustment for the NOL carryforward) subject to a 40% tax rate. Groh Inc. would then realize the benefits of the carryforward for tax purposes in 1996 which were recognized for accounting purposes in 1995. The income tax payable for 1996 is computed as follows:

Taxable income prior to loss carryforward	$200,000
Loss carryforward deduction	(150,000)
Taxable income for 1996	50,000
Tax rate	40%
Income tax payable for 1996	$ 20,000

ILLUSTRATION 20-31
Computation of Income Tax Payable with Realized Loss Carryforward

The journal entry to record income taxes in 1996 would be as follows:

Income Tax Expense	80,000	
Deferred Tax Asset		60,000
Income Tax Payable		20,000

The Deferred Tax Asset account is reduced because the benefits of the NOL carryforward are realized in 1996.

The 1996 income statement that appears below would **not report** the tax effects of either the loss carryback or the loss carryforward, because both had been reported previously.

Groh Inc.
PARTIAL INCOME STATEMENT FOR 1996

Income before income taxes		$200,000
Income tax expense		
Current	$20,000	
Deferred	60,000	80,000
Net income		$120,000

ILLUSTRATION 20-32
Presentation of the Benefit of Loss Carryforward Realized in 1996, Recognized in 1995

Carryforward with Valuation Account

Return to the Groh Inc. example. Assume that it is more likely than not that the entire NOL carryforward will not be realized in future years. In this situation, Groh Inc. records the tax benefits of $127,500 associated with the $350,000 NOL carryback, as previously described. In addition, it records a Deferred Tax Asset of $60,000 ($150,000 × 40%) for the potential benefits related to the loss carryforward and an allowance to reduce the deferred tax asset by the same amount. The journal entries in 1995 are as follows:

To recognize benefit of loss carryback

Income Tax Refund Receivable	127,500	
Benefit Due to Loss Carryback (Income Tax Expense)		127,500

To recognize benefit of loss carryforward

Deferred Tax Asset	60,000	
Benefit Due to Loss Carryforward (Income Tax Expense)		60,000

To record allowance amount

Benefit Due to Loss Carryforward (Income Tax Expense)	60,000	
Allowance to Reduce Deferred Tax Asset to		
Expected Realizable Value		60,000

The latter entry indicates that because positive evidence of sufficient quality and quantity is not available to counteract the negative evidence—a valuation allowance is needed.

The presentation in the 1995 income statement would be as follows:

ILLUSTRATION 20-33
Recognition of Benefit of Loss Carryback Only

Groh Inc. PARTIAL INCOME STATEMENT FOR 1995	
Operating loss before income taxes	$(500,000)
Income tax benefit	
Benefit due to loss carryback	127,500
Net loss	$(372,500)

In 1996, assuming that the company has taxable income of $200,000 (before considering the carryforward) subject to a tax rate of 40%, the deferred tax asset is realized and the allowance is no longer needed. The following entries would be made:

To record current and deferred income taxes

Income Tax Expense	80,000	
Deferred Tax Asset		60,000
Income Tax Payable		20,000

To eliminate allowance and recognize loss carryforward

Allowance to Reduce Deferred Tax Asset to		
Expected Realizable Value	60,000	
Benefit Due to Loss Carryforward (Income Tax Expense)		60,000

The $60,000 Benefit Due to the Loss Carryforward is computed by multiplying the $150,000 loss carryforward by the 40% tax rate. This amount is reported on the 1996 income statement because it was not recognized in 1995. Assuming that the income for 1996 is derived from continuing operations, the income statement would be presented as follows:

ILLUSTRATION 20-34
Recognition of Benefit of Loss Carryforward When Realized

Groh Inc. PARTIAL INCOME STATEMENT FOR 1996		
Income before income taxes		$200,000
Income tax expense		
Current	$20,000	
Deferred	60,000	
Benefit due to loss carryforward	(60,000)	20,000
Net income		$180,000

Another method is to report only one line for total income tax expense of $20,000 on the face of the income statement and disclose the components of income tax expense in the notes to the financial statements.

► FINANCIAL STATEMENT PRESENTATION

The proper presentation of income taxes in the financial statements is illustrated below.

BALANCE SHEET PRESENTATION

Deferred tax accounts are reported on the balance sheet as assets and liabilities. They should be classified in a net current amount and a net noncurrent amount. An individual deferred tax liability or asset is classified as current or noncurrent based on the classification of the related asset or liability for financial reporting purposes. A deferred tax asset or liability is considered to be related to an asset or liability if reduction of the asset or liability will cause the temporary difference to reverse or turn around. A deferred tax liability or asset that is not related to an asset or liability for financial reporting, including a deferred tax asset related to a loss carryforward, shall be classified according to the expected reversal date of the temporary difference.

To illustrate, assume that Morgan Inc. records bad debt expense using the allowance method for accounting purposes and the direct write-off method for tax purposes. The company currently has Accounts Receivable and Allowance for Doubtful Accounts balances of $2 million and $100,000, respectively. In addition, given a 40% tax rate, it has a debit balance in the Deferred Tax Asset account of $40,000 (40% × $100,000). The $40,000 debit balance in the Deferred Tax Asset is considered to be related to the Accounts Receivable and the Allowance for Doubtful Accounts balances because collection or write-off of the receivables will cause the temporary difference to reverse. Therefore, the Deferred Tax Asset account is classified as current, the same as the Accounts Receivable and Allowance for Doubtful Accounts balances.

In practice, most companies engage in a large number of transactions that give rise to deferred taxes. The balances in the deferred tax accounts should be analyzed and classified on the balance sheet in two categories: one for the **net current amount,** and one for the **net noncurrent amount.** This procedure is summarized as indicated below.

1. **Classify the amounts as current or noncurrent.** If they are related to a specific asset or liability, they should be classified in the same manner as the related asset or liability. If not so related, they should be classified on the basis of the expected reversal date.

2. **Determine the net current amount** by summing the various deferred tax assets and liabilities classified as current. If the net result is an asset, report on the balance sheet as a current asset; if a liability, report as a current liability.

3. **Determine the net noncurrent amount** by summing the various deferred tax assets and liabilities classified as noncurrent. If the net result is an asset, report on the balance sheet as a noncurrent asset; if a liability, report as a long-term liability.

To illustrate, assume that K. Scott Company has four deferred tax items at December 31, 1996. An analysis reveals the following:

OBJECTIVE 9

Describe the presentation of deferred income taxes in financial statements.

ILLUSTRATION 20-35
Classification of Temporary Differences as Current or Noncurrent

	K. Scott Company			
Temporary Difference	Resulting Deferred Tax (Asset)	Liability	Related Balance Sheet Account	Classification
1. Rent collected in advance: recognized when earned for accounting purposes and when received for tax purposes.	$(42,000)		Unearned Rent	Current

ILLUSTRATION 20-35
(*Continued*)

2. Use of straight-line depreciation for accounting purposes and accelerated depreciation for tax purposes.	$214,000	Equipment	Noncurrent
3. Recognition of profits on installment sales during period of sale for accounting purposes and during period of collection for tax purposes.	45,000	Installment Accounts Receivable	Current
4. Warranty liabilities: recognized for accounting purposes at time of sale; for tax purposes at time paid.	(12,000)	Estimated Liability Under Warranties	Current
Totals	$(54,000)	$259,000	

The deferred taxes to be classified as current net to a $9,000 asset ($42,000 + $12,000 − $45,000), and the deferred taxes to be classified as noncurrent net to a $214,000 liability. Consequently, deferred income taxes would appear as follows on K. Scott's December 31, 1996, balance sheet:

ILLUSTRATION 20-36
Balance Sheet
Presentation of Deferred
Income Taxes

K. Scott Company	
Current assets	
Deferred tax asset	$ 9,000
Long-term liabilities	
Deferred tax liability	$214,000

As indicated earlier, a deferred tax asset or liability **may not be related** to an asset or liability for financial reporting purposes. One example is organizational costs, that are sometimes recognized as expenses when incurred for financial reporting purposes but for tax purposes are deferred and deducted in later years. Another example is an operating loss carryforward. In both cases, a deferred tax asset is recorded, but there is no related, identifiable asset or liability for financial reporting purposes. In these limited situations, deferred income taxes should be classified according to the **expected reversal date** of the temporary difference. That is, the tax effect of any temporary difference reversing next year should be reported as current and the remainder should be reported as noncurrent. If a deferred tax asset is noncurrent, it should be classified in the "Other assets" section.

The total of all deferred tax liabilities, the total of all deferred tax assets, and the total valuation allowance should be disclosed. In addition, (1) any net change during the year in the total valuation allowance and (2) the types of temporary differences, carryforwards, or carrybacks that give rise to significant portions of deferred tax liabilities and assets should be disclosed.

Income tax payable is shown as a current liability on the balance sheet. Corporations are required to make estimated tax payments to the Internal Revenue Service quarterly. These estimated payments are recorded by a debit to Prepaid Income Taxes. As a result, the balance of the Income Tax Payable is offset by the balance of the Prepaid Income Taxes account when reporting income taxes on the balance sheet.

INCOME STATEMENT PRESENTATION

Income tax expense (or benefit) should be allocated to continuing operations, discontinued operations, extraordinary items, the cumulative effect of accounting changes, and prior period adjustments. This approach is referred to as intraperiod tax allocation and is illustrated later in the chapter.

In addition, the significant components of income tax expense attributable to continuing operations should be disclosed:

1. Current tax expense or benefit.

2. Deferred tax expense or benefit, exclusive of other components listed below.

3. Investment tax credits.

4. Government grants (to the extent they are recognized as a reduction of income tax expense).

5. The benefits of operating loss carryforwards (resulting in a reduction of income tax expense).

6. Tax expense that results from allocating certain tax benefits either directly to paid-in capital or to reduce goodwill or other noncurrent intangible assets of an acquired entity.

7. Adjustments of a deferred tax liability or asset for enacted changes in tax laws or rates or a change in the tax status of an enterprise.

8. Adjustments of the beginning-of-the-year balance of a valuation allowance because of a change in circumstances that causes a change in judgment about the realizability of the related deferred tax asset in future years.

In the notes, companies are also required to reconcile (using percentages or dollar amounts) income tax expense attributable to continuing operations with the amount that results from applying domestic federal statutory tax rates to pretax income from continuing operations. The estimated amount and the nature of each significant reconciling item should be disclosed. An example from the 1993 Annual Report of PepsiCo, Inc., is presented in Illustration 20-37.

For another example, refer to Georgia-Pacific Corporation's Annual Report at the end of Chapter 5. (See Note 6 on page 227.)

These income tax disclosures are required for several reasons. Some of the reasons are:

1. **Assessment of Quality of Earnings.** Many investors seeking to assess the quality of a company's earnings are interested in the reconciliation of pretax financial income to taxable income. Earnings that are enhanced by a favorable tax effect should be examined carefully, particularly if the tax effect is nonrecurring. For example, one year Wang Laboratories reported net income of $3.3 million, or 82 cents a share, versus $3.1 million, or 77 cents a share, in the preceding period. The entire increase in net income and then some resulted from a lower effective tax rate.

2. **Better Predictions of Future Cash Flows.** Examination of the deferred portion of income tax expense provides information as to whether taxes payable are likely to be higher or lower in the future. A close examination may disclose the company's policy regarding capitalization of costs, recognition of revenue, and other policies giving rise to a difference between pretax financial income and taxable income. As a result, it may be possible to predict future reductions in deferred tax liabilities leading to a loss of liquidity because actual tax payments will be higher than the tax expense reported on the income statement.

3. **Helpful in Setting Governmental Policy.** Understanding the amount companies currently pay and the effective tax rate is helpful to government policymakers. In the early 1970s; when the oil companies were believed to have earned excess profits, many politicians and other interested parties attempted to determine their effective tax rates. Unfortunately, at that time such information was not available in published annual reports.

DISCLOSURE OF OPERATING LOSS CARRYFORWARDS

The amounts and expiration dates of any operating loss carryforwards for tax purposes should be disclosed. From this disclosure, the reader can determine the amount of income that may be recognized in the future on which no income tax will be paid. For example, Chrysler generated $3 billion in tax losses between 1978–1981, which were used to offset future income. Its executive vice president of finance at one time remarked that "it still had approximately $650 million loss carryforwards going into 1985."

ILLUSTRATION 20-37
Disclosure of Income Taxes—PepsiCo, Inc.

PepsiCo, Inc.

Note 13: Income Taxes

Effective December 29, 1991, PepsiCo adopted Statement of Financial Accounting Standards No. 109 (SFAS 109), "Accounting for Income Taxes." PepsiCo elected to adopt SFAS 109 on a prospective basis as a change in accounting principle, resulting in a noncash tax charge in 1992 of $570.7 million ($0.71 per share) for the cumulative effect of the change related to years prior to 1992.

Detail of the provision for income taxes on income from continuing operations before cumulative effect of accounting changes:

	1993	1992	1991
Current— Federal	$466.8	$413.0	$315.5
Foreign	195.5	170.4	114.3
State	89.0	65.7	51.5
	751.3	649.1	481.3
Deferred—Federal	78.2	(18.8)	63.5
Foreign	(12.5)	(33.5)	25.3
State	17.6	0.3	9.4
	83.3	(52.0)	98.2
	$834.6	$597.1	$579.5

U.S. and foreign income before income taxes and cumulative effect of accounting changes:

	1993	1992	1991
U.S.	$1,633.0	$1,196.8	$1,054.3
Foreign	789.5	702.0	605.4
	$2,422.5	$1,898.8	$1,659.7

Reconciliation of the U.S. federal statutory tax rate to PepsiCo's effective tax rate on pretax income, based on the dollar impact of these major components on the provision for income taxes:

	1993	1992	1991
U.S. federal statutory tax rate	35.0%	34.0%	34.0%
State income tax, net of federal tax benefit	2.9	2.3	2.4
Effect of lower taxes on foreign income (including Puerto Rico and Ireland)	(3.3)	(5.0)	(2.7)
Reduction of prior year foreign accruals	(2.0)	—	—
Effect of 1993 tax legislation on deferred income taxes	1.1	—	—
Nondeductible amortization of domestic goodwill (all years) and other intangible assets (1991 only)	0.8	0.9	1.8
Other, net	—	(0.8)	(0.6)
Effective tax rate	34.5%	31.4%	34.9%

Detail of the 1993 and 1992 deferred tax liabilities (assets):

	1993	1992
Liabilities		
Intangible assets other than nondeductible goodwill	$ 1,551.0	$1,292.2
Property, plant and equipment	552.3	526.8
Safe Harbor Leases	177.5	185.6
Zero coupon notes	103.5	96.0
Other	549.0	233.2
Gross deferred tax liabilities	2,933.3	2,333.8
Assets		
Postretirement benefits	(268.0)	(238.4)
Net operating loss carryforwards	(241.5)	(138.6)
Restructuring accruals	(42.0)	(73.2)
Deferred state income taxes	(39.9)	(63.3)
Various accrued liabilities and other	(697.6)	(383.0)
Gross deferred tax assets	(1,289.0)	(896.5)
Deferred tax assets valuation allowance	249.0	181.3
Net deferred tax liability	$ 1,893.3	$1,618.6
Included in:		
"Prepaid expenses, taxes and other current assets"	$ (138.2)	$ (107.9)
"Other current liabilities"	23.9	44.2
"Deferred Income Taxes"	2,007.6	1,682.3
	$ 1,893.3	$1,618.6

	1993	1992	1991
Income taxes paid	$675.6	$519.7	$385.9

Loss carryforwards can be extremely valuable to a potential acquirer. At one time, Dalfort Company received nearly $360 million in operating loss carryforwards and other credits as a result of its ownership of Braniff Airlines. Many speculate that Dalfort bought Levitz Furniture Corp. (a large discounter of quality furniture) so that it could offset its carryforward losses from Braniff against Levitz's earnings. Companies that have suffered substantial losses may find themselves worth more "dead" than alive because their tax losses have little value to themselves but great value to other enterprises. In short, substantial tax carryforwards can have real economic value.[8]

▶ SPECIAL ISSUES

A number of issues merit special attention when accounting for deferred income taxes. These are as follows:

1. Multiple temporary differences.
2. Necessity for a valuation allowance.
3. Multiple tax rates.
4. Pattern of taxable and deductible amounts.
5. Alternative minimum tax.
6. Intraperiod tax allocation.

OBJECTIVE 10

Identify special issues related to deferred income taxes.

MULTIPLE TEMPORARY DIFFERENCES

To simplify the accounting when multiple temporary differences are involved, the following schedules should prove useful. Assume that Griggs Co. has two temporary differences in its first year of operation, one involving an installment sale and the other involving warranty costs. Other assumptions made should be apparent from the presentation of the scheduled material.

	Future Years		
	1997	1998	Total
Future taxable (deductible) amounts:			
Installment sale	$100,000	$100,000	$200,000
Warranty costs	(40,000)	(50,000)	(90,000)

ILLUSTRATION 20-38
Schedule of Future Taxable and Deductible Amounts

The deferred income taxes to be reported at the end of 1996 are computed as follows:

Temporary Differences	Future Taxable (Deductible) Amounts	Tax Rate	Deferred Tax (Asset)	Liability
Installment sale	$200,000	40%		$80,000
Warranty costs	(90,000)	40%	$(36,000)	
	$110,000		$(36,000)	$80,000

Because of a flat rate, these totals can be reconciled: $110,000 × 40% = ($36,000) + $80,000

ILLUSTRATION 20-39
Computation of Deferred Income Taxes

---

[8]The IRS frowns on acquisitions done solely to obtain operating loss carryforwards. If the merger is determined to be solely tax motivated, then the deductions will be disallowed. But because it is very difficult to determine whether a merger is or is not tax motivated, the "purchase of operating loss carryforwards" continues. A recent study by the GAO indicates that ⅔ of all corporations had amassed at least $246 billion in NOL carryovers in 1989.

The journal entry to record income tax expense for the period, assuming income tax payable is $500,000 is as follows:

Income Tax Expense	544,000	
Deferred Tax Asset	36,000	
Income Tax Payable		500,000
Deferred Tax Liability		80,000

NECESSITY FOR VALUATION ALLOWANCE

All positive and negative information should be considered in determining whether a valuation allowance is needed. Whether a deferred tax asset will be realized depends on whether sufficient taxable income exists or will exist within the carryback or carryforward period available under tax law. The following possible sources of taxable income may be available under the tax law to realize a tax benefit for deductible temporary differences and carryforwards:

**ILLUSTRATION 20-40
Possible Sources of
Taxable Income**

> ### Taxable Income Sources
> a. Future reversals of existing taxable temporary differences
> b. Future taxable income exclusive of reversing temporary differences and carryforwards
> c. Taxable income in prior carryback year(s) if carryback is permitted under the tax law
> d. **Tax-planning strategies** that would, if necessary, be implemented to:
>   (1) Accelerate taxable amounts to utilize expiring carryforwards
>   (2) Change the character of taxable or deductible amounts from ordinary income or loss to capital gain or loss
>   (3) Switch from tax-exempt to taxable investments.[9]

If any one of these sources is sufficient to support a conclusion that a valuation allowance is not necessary, other sources need not be considered.

Forming a conclusion that a valuation allowance is not needed is difficult when there is negative evidence such as cumulative losses in recent years. Other examples of negative evidence include (but are not limited to) the following:

**ILLUSTRATION 20-41
Negative Evidence to
Support Need for
Valuation Account**

> ### Negative Evidence
> a. A history of operating loss or tax credit carryforwards expiring unused
> b. Losses expected in early future years (by a presently profitable entity)
> c. Unsettled circumstances that, if unfavorably resolved, would adversely affect future operations and profit levels on a continuing basis in future years
> d. A carryback, carryforward period that is so brief that it would limit realization of tax benefits if (1) a significant deductible temporary difference is expected to reverse in a single year or (2) the enterprise operates in a traditionally cyclical business.

Examples (not prerequisites) of positive evidence that might support a conclusion that a valuation allowance is not needed when there is negative evidence include the following:

---

[9]"Accounting for Income Taxes," *Statement of Financial Accounting Standards No. 109* (Norwalk, Conn.: FASB, 1992). A tax planning strategy is an action that would be implemented to realize a tax benefit for an operating loss or tax credit carryforward before it expires. Tax planning stategies are considered when assessing the need for and amount of a valuation allowance for deferred tax assets.

ILLUSTRATION 20-42
Positive Evidence Against Need for Valuation Account

> **Positive Evidence**
> a. Existing contracts or firm sales backlog that will produce more than enough taxable income to realize the deferred tax asset based on existing sale prices and cost structures
> b. An excess of appreciated asset value over the tax basis of the entity's net assets in an amount sufficient to realize the deferred tax asset
> c. A strong earnings history exclusive of the loss that created the future deductible amount (tax loss carryforward or deductible temporary difference) coupled with evidence indicating that the loss (for example, an unusual, infrequent, or extraordinary item) is an aberration rather than a continuing condition.[10]

The use of this valuation account provides management with an opportunity to manage its earnings. As one accounting expert noted: "The 'more likely than not' provision is perhaps the most judgmental clause in accounting." What some companies will do is set up valuation accounts and then use the valuation account to increase income as needed. Others will take the income immediately to increase capital or to offset large negative charges to income.

MULTIPLE TAX RATES

As indicated previously, **the enacted future tax rate** should be used to measure deferred taxes. This rate is applied to future taxable and deductible amounts arising from temporary differences. If there is a phased-in change in tax rates, selection of the future tax rate used to apply to a particular temporary difference requires some knowledge of when related taxable or deductible amounts will occur.

Deferred Tax Liability

Assume that Crandall Inc. at the end of 1996 (its third year of operations) has $2,400,000 of taxable temporary differences that are expected to result in taxable amounts of $800,000 in each of the following 3 years, 1997–1999. Enacted tax rates are 35% for 1994–1996, 40% for 1997–1999, and 45% for 2000 and thereafter. Assuming that taxable income is expected in 1997–1999, the deferred tax liability at December 31, 1996, is $960,000 which is computed as follows:

ILLUSTRATION 20-43
Computation of Deferred Tax Liability

| | Future Years | | | |
	1997	1998	1999	Total
Future taxable amounts	$800,000	$800,000	$800,000	$2,400,000
Enacted future tax rate	40%	40%	40%	
Deferred tax liability at 12/31/96	$320,000	$320,000	$320,000	$ 960,000

Now assume that Crandall Inc. is expected to incur **losses** for tax purposes in 1997–1999. The tax rate to use to compute the deferred tax liability is 35% if realization of the tax benefit for those losses in years 1997–1999 will be by loss carryback to 1994–1996. The deferred tax liability at December 31, 1996, under this assumption is $840,000 ($2,400,000 × 35%).

If, on the other hand, realization of the tax benefit for those tax losses in 1997–1999 will be by loss carryforward to 2000 and thereafter, the tax rate to be used is 45%. In this situation, the deferred tax liability is $1,080,000 ($2,400,000 × 45%) at December 31, 1996.

Deferred Tax Asset

To illustrate the measurement of a deferred tax asset, assume that Gateway Co. has a $9,000,000 deductible temporary difference at the end of 1996 (its third year of opera-

---

[10]Ibid., par. 23 and 24.

tions). The $9,000,000 is expected to result in tax deductions of $3,000,000 in each of the next three years (1997–1999). Enacted tax rates are 30% for 1994–1996 and 40% for 1997 and thereafter. The tax rate to be used to measure the deferred tax asset is 40% if Gateway expects to realize a tax benefit for the deductible temporary differences by offsetting taxable income earned in future years. Under this assumption, the amount of the deferred tax asset at December 31, 1996, is $3,600,000 ($9,000,000 × 40%).

Alternatively, the tax rate to be used is 30% if Gateway expects to realize a tax benefit for the deductible temporary differences by loss carryback refund (that is, if Gateway expects tax losses rather than taxable income in the future). In this case, the deferred tax asset at December 31, 1996, is $2,700,000 ($9,000,000 × 30%).

Valuation Allowance

Assume that Gateway reports a $3,600,000 ($9,000,000 × 40%) deferred tax asset at December 31, 1996, which is expected to be realized by offsetting taxable income in future years. Also assume that taxable income and taxes payable in each of the 3 years 1994–1996 were $3,000,000 and $900,000, respectively. Realization of a tax benefit of, at least, $2,700,000 is assured because carryback refunds totalling $2,700,000 ($9,000,000 × 30%) can be used even if no taxable income is earned in future years. Recognition of a valuation allowance for the other $900,000 ($3,600,000 − $2,700,000) of the deferred tax asset depends on management's assessment of whether, based on the weight of available evidence, a portion or all of the tax benefit of the deductible temporary differences will be realized in future years.

PATTERN OF TAXABLE OR DEDUCTIBLE AMOUNTS

Temporary differences may accumulate over several years and then reverse over several years. That pattern is common for depreciable assets. It is sometimes important that all future originating differences for existing depreciable assets and all reversals be scheduled to determine in what future periods taxable or deductible amounts will occur. To illustrate, assume that DeVall Inc. acquired $150,000 of depreciable assets at the beginning of 1996. The assets have a 5-year useful life, and depreciation is computed on a straight-line basis for financial reporting purposes. Depreciation deductions are accelerated for tax purposes using a 3-year class life. The depreciation pattern is as follows:

ILLUSTRATION 20-44
Depreciation Schedules and Temporary Differences

Year	Book Depreciation	Tax Depreciation	Temporary Difference
1996	$ 30,000	$ 49,500	$(19,500)
1997	30,000	67,500	(37,500)
1998	30,000	22,500	7,500
1999	30,000	10,500	19,500
2000	30,000	–0–	30,000
	$150,000	$150,000	$ –0–

At the end of 1996 the cumulative temporary difference is $19,500, and the pattern of future taxable and deductible amounts for 1997–2000 is as follows:

ILLUSTRATION 20-45
Schedule of Future Taxable and Deductible Amounts

	Future Years				
	1997	1998	1999	2000	Total
Future taxable (deductible) amounts	$(37,500)	$7,500	$19,500	$30,000	$19,500

At the end of 1996, the temporary difference of $19,500 will result in a net future taxable amount of $19,500. However, for DeVall more originating differences in 1997 (due to assets existing at the end of 1996) will cause deductible amounts to occur in 1997 before the temporary difference reverses and results in taxable amounts in 1998–2000. In other words, there will be a **deductible amount** of $37,500 in 1997 because depreciation for tax purposes exceeds depreciation for book purposes by that amount.

This schedule also can be important in determining whether a valuation allowance might be needed for a deferred tax asset. In addition, this schedule is useful for computing deferred taxes when the enacted tax rates vary for individual future years.

ALTERNATIVE MINIMUM TAX

The current tax law requires a corporation to compute its potential tax liability using the regular tax system and an alternative minimum tax (AMT) system.[11] The **alternative minimum tax system** is used to insure that corporations do not avoid paying a fair share of income taxes through various tax avoidance approaches.[12]

For any given year, a corporation's annual income tax liability is the greater of the regular tax or the alternative minimum tax. Any deferred income taxes are computed using the regular tax rate(s), without regard to whether the company is subject to the alternative minimum tax now or is expected to be affected by it in the future. A company that pays the alternative minimum tax is entitled to a credit against its regular tax liability in subsequent years. Thus, paying the AMT gives the entity a tax credit carryforward.

A **tax credit carryforward** is similar to a future deductible amount with one major difference. A future deductible amount will offset **future taxable income** and a tax credit carryforward will offset **income taxes payable** in the future. If a tax rate of 40% applies, a tax credit of $1,000 is more valuable than a deduction of $1,000. The former will save $1,000 in tax and the latter will save only $400 in tax.

A deferred tax asset is recognized for an AMT credit carryforward. The need for a related valuation allowance must then be assessed. The AMT computations and considerations are extremely complex and require a background in income tax accounting. We will generalize here to say that unless there is a significant amount of tax preference items (determined by a set of complex income tax rules), total taxes paid over the entire life of a company will be based on the regular tax system, not the AMT system; thus, an AMT credit carryforward will usually be judged to be realizable in the future and a related valuation account will not be necessary.

INTRAPERIOD TAX ALLOCATION

As we learned in Chapter 4, the amount of income tax expense (or benefit) should be allocated to the following items:

Continuing operations

Discontinued operations

Extraordinary items

Cumulative effect of accounting changes

Prior period adjustments.

This approach is referred to as **intraperiod tax allocation**

If there is only one item other than continuing operations, the portion remaining after allocation to continuing operations is allocated to that item. To illustrate, assume that Copy Doctor Inc. has an ordinary loss from continuing operations of $500,000. Its tax rate on ordinary income is 40%. In addition, it has an extraordinary gain of $900,000 which is taxed at a capital gain rate of 30%. Pretax financial income and taxable income

---

[11]Companies most likely to be affected by the AMT are capital-intensive companies subject to significant depreciation deductions. Also companies that significantly reduce regular tax liabilities by using the completed-contract method, or by using the installment method for reporting sales of certain real property often pay taxes at AMT rates.

[12]The reason for the alternative minimum tax is quite simple: During the 1981–1984 period many of the nation's largest corporations paid little if any income tax, and few paid at the full statutory rate. The alternative minimum tax now ensures that most corporations will pay a certain base amount.

are the same (no permanent or temporary differences). In this case, taxable income and income tax payable are computed as follows:

ILLUSTRATION 20-46
Computation of Income
Tax Payable

Loss from continuing operations	($500,000)
Extraordinary gain	900,000
Taxable income	400,000
Tax rate	30%
Income tax payable	$120,000

The $500,000 loss from continuing operations offsets an equal amount of capital gains that otherwise would be taxed at a 30% rate. Thus, $150,000 ($500,000 × 30%) of the tax benefit is allocated to continuing operations. This computation is as follows:

ILLUSTRATION 20-47
Allocation of Incremental
Tax to Extraordinary Gain

Total income tax expense	$120,000
Tax benefit allocated to the loss from continuing operations	(150,000)
Incremental tax expense allocated to the extraordinary gain	$270,000

The $270,000 incremental tax effect allocated to the extraordinary gain is the sum of the $120,000 of total tax expense and the $150,000 tax benefit from continuing operations. Income taxes would be reported in the income statement as follows:

Copy Doctor Inc.	
Loss before income taxes and extraordinary item	($500,000)
Income tax benefit from operating loss	150,000
Loss before extraordinary item	(350,000)
Extraordinary gain (net of $270,000 tax)	630,000
Net income	$280,000

Intraperiod tax allocation procedures for two or more items other than continuing operations are complex and beyond the scope of this textbook.

▶ PRINCIPLES OF THE ASSET-LIABILITY APPROACH

The Board believes that the **asset-liability method** (sometimes referred to as the liability approach) is the most consistent method for accounting for income taxes. One objective of this approach is to recognize the amount of taxes payable or refundable for the current year. A second objective is to recognize **deferred tax liabilities and assets** for the **future tax consequences** of events that have been recognized in the financial statements or tax returns.

To implement the objectives, the following basic principles are applied in accounting for income taxes at the date of the financial statements:

INTERNATIONAL INSIGHT

Nations that recognize deferred taxes using the liability method include, among others, Australia, Germany, the United Kingdom, and Spain. The European Directives do not specify the accounting for deferred taxes.

a. A current tax liability or asset is recognized for the estimated taxes payable or refundable on the tax return for the current year.

b. A deferred tax liability or asset is recognized for the estimated future tax effects attributable to temporary differences and carryforwards.

c. The measurement of current and deferred tax liabilities and assets is based on provisions of the enacted tax law; the effects of future changes in tax laws or rates are not anticipated.

d. The measurement of deferred tax assets is reduced, if necessary, by the amount of any tax benefits that, based on available evidence, are not expected to be realized.[13]

---

[13]"Accounting for Income Taxes," par. 6 and 8, 1992.

▶ ANNUAL COMPUTATION OF DEFERRED TAX LIABILITIES AND ASSETS

The procedures for the computation of deferred income taxes are as follows:

ILLUSTRATION 20-49
Procedures for Computation of Deferred Income Taxes

Annual Procedures

a. Identify (1) the types and amounts of existing temporary differences and (2) the nature and amount of each type of operating loss and tax credit carryforward and the remaining length of the carryforward period.

b. Measure the total deferred tax liability for taxable temporary differences using the applicable tax rate.

c. Measure the total deferred tax asset for deductible temporary differences and operating loss carryforwards using the applicable tax rate.

d. Measure deferred tax assets for each type of tax credit carryforward.

e. Reduce deferred tax assets by a **valuation allowance** if, based on the weight of available evidence, it is *more likely than not* that some portion or all of the deferred tax assets will not be realized. The valuation allowance should be sufficient to reduce the deferred tax assets to the amount that is more likely than not to be realized.[14]

These procedures are illustrated graphically in Illustration 20-50.

ILLUSTRATION 20-50
Procedures for Computing and Reporting Deferred Income Taxes

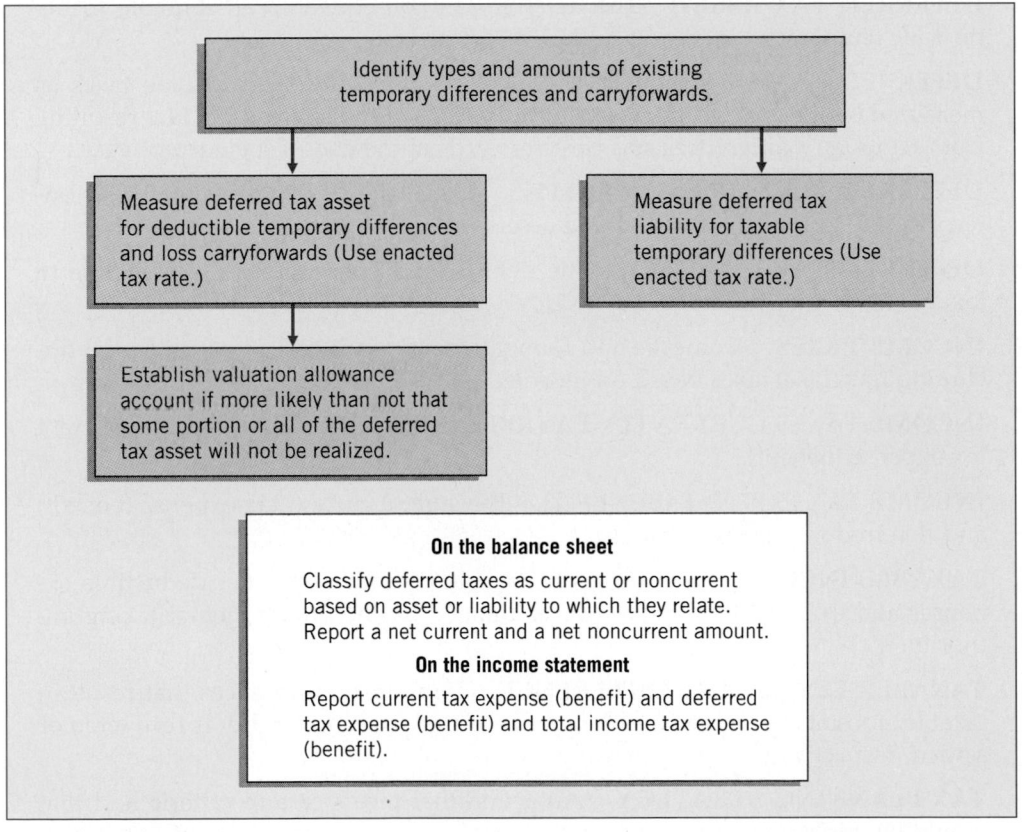

As an aid to understanding deferred income taxes, the following glossary[15] is provided:

---

[14]"Accounting for Income Taxes," par. 17.

[15]Ibid., Appendix E.

◀ KEY DEFERRED INCOME TAX TERMS ▶

CARRYBACKS. Deductions or credits that cannot be utilized on the tax return during a year and that may be carried back to reduce taxable income or taxes paid in a prior year. An **operating loss carryback** is an excess of tax deductions over gross income in a year; a **tax credit carryback** is the amount by which tax credits available for utilization exceed statutory limitations.

CARRYFORWARDS. Deductions or credits that cannot be utilized on the tax return during a year and that may be carried forward to reduce taxable income or taxes payable in a future year. An **operating loss carryforward** is an excess of tax deductions over gross income in a year; a **tax credit carryforward** is the amount by which tax credits available for utilization exceed statutory limitations.

CURRENT TAX EXPENSE (BENEFIT). The amount of income taxes paid or payable (or refundable) for a year as determined by applying the provisions of the enacted tax law to the taxable income or excess of deductions over revenues for that year.

DEDUCTIBLE TEMPORARY DIFFERENCE. Temporary differences that result in deductible amounts in future years when the related asset or liability is recovered or settled, respectively.

DEFERRED TAX ASSET. The deferred tax consequences attributable to deductible temporary differences and carryforwards.

DEFERRED TAX CONSEQUENCES. The future effects on income taxes as measured by the enacted tax rate and provisions of the enacted tax law resulting from temporary differences and carryforwards at the end of the current year.

DEFERRED TAX EXPENSE (BENEFIT). The change during the year in an enterprise's deferred tax liabilities and assets.

DEFERRED TAX LIABILITY. The deferred tax consequences attributable to taxable temporary differences.

INCOME TAXES. Domestic and foreign federal (national), state, and local (including franchise) taxes based on income.

INCOME TAXES CURRENTLY PAYABLE (REFUNDABLE). Refer to current tax expense (benefit).

INCOME TAX EXPENSE (BENEFIT). The sum of current tax expense (benefit) and deferred tax expense (benefit).

TAXABLE INCOME. The excess of taxable revenues over tax deductible expenses and exemptions for the year as defined by the governmental taxing authority.

TAXABLE TEMPORARY DIFFERENCE. Temporary differences that result in taxable amounts in future years when the related asset or liability is recovered or settled, respectively.

TAX-PLANNING STRATEGY. An action that meets certain criteria and that would be implemented to realize a tax benefit for an operating loss or tax credit carryforward before it expires. Tax-planning strategies are considered when assessing the need for and amount of a valuation allowance for deferred tax assets.

TEMPORARY DIFFERENCE. A difference between the tax basis of an asset or liability and its reported amount in the financial statements that will result in taxable or deductible amounts in future years when the reported amount of the asset or liability is recovered or settled, respectively.

VALUATION ALLOWANCE. The portion of a deferred tax asset for which it is more likely than not that a tax benefit will not be realized.

▶ SOME CONCEPTUAL QUESTIONS

The asset-liability method is the approach that the Board deemed most appropriate to record deferred income taxes. However, some conceptual questions remain. Presented below are three important issues.

1. **Failure to Discount.** Without discounting the asset or liability (that is, failing to consider its present value), financial statements do not indicate the appropriate benefit of tax deferral or the burden of tax prepayment. Thus, comparability of the financial statements is impaired because a dollar related to short-term deferral appears to be of the same value as a dollar of longer-term deferral.

2. **Classification Issue.** Consistent with the asset-liability approach, deferred tax assets and liabilities should be classified on the balance sheet based on when they will be realized or settled. Previously, the Board took the position that deferred taxes related to temporary differences reversing next period should be reported as current. Many believe this approach is correct and therefore disagree with the present requirements.

3. **Dual Criteria for Recognition of Deferred Tax Asset.** Many believe that future deductible amounts arising from net operating loss carryforwards are different from future deductible amounts arising from normal operations. One rationale provided is that a deferred tax asset arising from normal operations results in a tax prepayment—a prepaid tax asset. In the case of loss carryforwards, no tax prepayment has been made.

    Others argue that realization of a loss carryforward is less likely—and thus should require a more severe test—than for a net deductible amount arising from normal operations. Some have suggested that the test be changed from "more likely than not" to "probable" realization. Still others have indicated that because of the nature of net operating losses, deferred tax assets should never be established for these items.

The above controversies assume that the asset-liability approach is used. Others argue that completely different types of approaches should be used to report deferred income taxes. These approaches are covered in Appendix 20-B to this chapter.

▶ SUMMARY OF LEARNING OBJECTIVES ◀

1. **Identify differences between pretax financial income and taxable income.** Pretax financial income (or income for book purposes) is computed in accordance with generally accepted accounting principles. Taxable income (or income for tax purposes) is computed in accordance with prescribed tax regulations. Because tax regulations and GAAP are different in many ways, pretax financial income and taxable income frequently differ. Differences may exist, for example, in the timing of revenue recognition and the timing of expense recognition.

2. **Describe a temporary difference that results in future taxable amounts.** A credit sale that is recognized as revenue for book purposes in the period it is earned but is deferred and reported as revenue for tax purposes in the period it is collected will result in future taxable amounts. The future taxable amounts will occur in the periods the receivable is recovered and the collections are reported as revenue for tax purposes. This results in a deferred tax liability.

3. **Describe a temporary difference that results in future deductible amounts.** An accrued warranty expense that is paid for and is deductible for tax purposes in a period later than the period in which it is incurred and recognized

KEY TERMS

alternative minimum tax system, 1017

asset-liability method, 1018

average tax rate, 1003

current tax expense or benefit, 1007

deductible amounts, 992

deductible temporary difference, 1000

deferred tax asset, 996

deferred tax expense (benefit), 994, 996

deferred tax liability, 993

effective tax rate, 1003

enacted tax rate, 1003

income tax benefit, 1006

income tax payable (refundable), 992, 1006

for book purposes will result in future deductible amounts. The future deductible amounts will occur in the periods during which the related liability for book purposes is settled. This results in a deferred tax asset.

4. **Explain the purpose of a deferred tax asset valuation account.** A deferred tax asset should be reduced by a valuation allowance if, based on all available evidence, it is more likely than not (a level of likelihood that is at least slightly more than 50%) that some portion or all of the deferred tax asset will not be realized. All available evidence, both positive and negative, should be carefully considered to determine whether, based on the weight of available evidence, a valuation allowance is needed.

5. **Describe the presentation of income tax expense in the income statement.** The significant components of income tax expense should be disclosed in the income statement or in the notes to the financial statements. The most commonly encountered components are the current expense (or benefit) and the deferred expense (or benefit).

6. **Describe various temporary and permanent differences.** Examples of temporary differences are: (1) revenue or gains that are taxable after they are recognized in financial income; (2) expenses or losses that are deductible after they are recognized in financial income; (3) revenues or gains that are taxable before they are recognized in financial income; (4) expenses or losses that are deductible before they are recognized in financial income. Examples of permanent differences are: (1) items recognized for financial reporting purposes but not for tax purposes; and (2) items recognized for tax purposes but not for financial reporting purposes.

7. **Explain the effect of various tax rates and tax rate changes on deferred income taxes.** Tax rates other than the current rate may be used only when the future tax rates have been enacted into law. When a change in the tax rate is enacted into law, its effect on the deferred income tax accounts should be recorded immediately. The effects are reported as an adjustment to income tax expense in the period of the change.

8. **Apply accounting procedures for a loss carryback and a loss carryforward.** A company may carry a net operating loss back 3 years and receive refunds for income taxes paid in those years. The loss must be applied to the earliest year first and then sequentially to the second and third years. Any loss remaining after the 3-year carryback may be carried forward up to 15 years to offset future taxable income. A company may forgo the loss carryback and use the loss carryforward, offsetting future taxable income for up to 15 years.

9. **Describe the presentation of deferred income taxes in financial statements.** Deferred tax accounts are reported on the balance sheet as assets and liabilities. They should be classified as a net current and a net noncurrent amount. An individual deferred tax liability or asset is classified as current or noncurrent based on the classification of the related asset or liability for financial reporting. A deferred tax liability or asset that is not related to an asset or liability for financial reporting, including a deferred tax asset related to a loss carryforward, shall be classified according to the expected reversal date of the temporary difference.

10. **Identify special issues related to deferred income taxes.** A number of issues related to deferred income taxes are special: (1) multiple temporary differences; (2) necessity for a valuation allowance; (3) multiple tax rates; (4) pattern of taxable and deductible amounts; (5) alternative minimum tax; (6) intraperiod tax allocation.

11. **Indicate the basic principles of the asset-liability approach.** The following basic principles are applied in accounting for income taxes at the date of the

financial statements: (1) a current tax liability or asset is recognized for the estimated taxes payable or refundable on the tax return for the current year; (2) a deferred tax liability or asset is recognized for the estimated future tax effects attributable to temporary differences and carryforwards using the enacted tax rate; (3) the measurement of current and deferred tax liabilities and assets is based on provisions of the enacted tax law; (4) the measurement of deferred tax assets is adjusted, if necessary, by the amount of any tax benefits that, based on available evidence, are not expected to be realized.

APPENDIX 20-A

COMPREHENSIVE ILLUSTRATION OF INTERPERIOD TAX ALLOCATION

This appendix presents a comprehensive illustration of a deferred income tax problem with several temporary and permanent differences. The illustration follows one company through two complete years (1995 and 1996). **Study it carefully.** It should help you understand the concepts and procedures presented in the chapter.

OBJECTIVE 12
After studying Appendix 20-A, you should be able to: Understand and apply the concepts and procedures of interperiod tax allocation.

▶ FIRST YEAR—1995

Allman Company, which began operations at the beginning of 1995, produces various products on a contract basis. Each contract generates a gross profit of $80,000. Some of Allman's contracts provide for the customer to pay on an installment basis whereby one-fifth of the contract revenue is collected in each of the following four years. Gross profit is recognized in the year of completion for financial reporting purposes (accrual basis) and in the year cash is collected for tax purposes (installment basis).

Presented below is information related to Allman's operations for 1995:

1. In 1995, the company completed seven contracts that allow for the customer to pay on an installment basis. The related gross profit amount of $560,000 was recognized for financial reporting purposes, whereas only $112,000 of gross profit on installment sales was reported on the 1995 tax return. The future collections on the related installment receivables are expected to result in taxable amounts of $112,000 in each of the next four years.

2. At the beginning of 1995, Allman Company purchased depreciable assets with a cost of $540,000. For financial reporting purposes, Allman depreciates these assets using the straight-line method over a 6-year service life. For tax purposes, the assets fall in the 5-year recovery class and Allman uses the MACRS system. The depreciation schedules for both financial reporting and tax purposes follow:

Year	Depreciation for Financial Reporting Purposes	Depreciation for Tax Purposes	Difference
1995	$ 90,000	$108,000	$(18,000)
1996	90,000	172,800	(82,800)
1997	90,000	103,680	(13,680)
1998	90,000	62,208	27,792
1999	90,000	62,208	27,792
2000	90,000	31,104	58,896
	$540,000	$540,000	$ –0–

3. The company warrants their product for 2 years from the date of completion of a contract. During 1995 product warranty liability accrued for financial reporting purposes was $200,000, and the amount paid for the satisfaction of warranty liability was $44,000. The remaining $156,000 is expected to be settled by expenditures of $56,000 in 1996 and $100,000 in 1997.

4. In 1995 nontaxable municipal bond interest revenue was $28,000.

5. During 1995 nondeductible fines and penalties of $26,000 were paid.

6. Pretax financial income for 1995 amounts to $412,000.

7. Tax rates enacted before the end of 1995:

1995	50%
1996 and later years	40%

8. The accounting period is the calendar year.

9. The company is expected to have taxable income in all future years.

TAXABLE INCOME AND INCOME TAX PAYABLE—1995

The first step to determine Allman Company's income tax payable for 1995 is to calculate its taxable income. This computation is as follows:

ILLUSTRATION 20A-1
Computation of Taxable Income, 1995

Pretax financial income for 1995	$412,000
Permanent differences:	
Nontaxable revenue—municipal bond interest	(28,000)
Nondeductible expenses—fines and penalties	26,000
Temporary differences:	
Excess gross profit per books ($560,000 − $112,000)	(448,000)
Excess depreciation per tax ($108,000 − $90,000)	(18,000)
Excess warranty expense per books ($200,000 − $44,000)	156,000
Taxable income for 1995	$100,000

Income tax payable is computed on taxable income of $100,000 as follows:

ILLUSTRATION 20A-2
Computation of Income Tax Payable, End of 1995

Taxable income for 1995	$100,000
Tax rate	50%
Income tax payable (current tax expense) for 1995	$ 50,000

COMPUTING DEFERRED INCOME TAXES—END OF 1995

The following schedule is helpful in summarizing the temporary differences and the resulting future taxable and deductible amounts:

ILLUSTRATION 20A-3
Schedule of Future Taxable and Deductible Amounts, End of 1995

	Future Years					
	1996	1997	1998	1999	2000	Total
Future taxable (deductible) amounts:						
Installment sales	$112,000	$112,000	$112,000	$112,000		$448,000
Depreciation	(82,800)	(13,680)	27,792	27,792	$58,896	18,000
Warranty costs	(56,000)	(100,000)				(156,000)

The amounts of deferred income taxes to be reported at the end of 1995 are computed as follows:

Temporary Difference	Future Taxable (Deductible) Amounts	Tax Rate	Deferred Tax (Asset)	Liability
Installment sales	$448,000	40%		$179,200
Depreciation	18,000	40%		7,200
Warranty costs	(156,000)	40%	$(62,400)	
Totals	$310,000		$(62,400)	$186,400*

*Because only a single tax rate is involved in all relevant years, these totals can be reconciled: $310,000 × 40% = ($62,400) + $186,400.

ILLUSTRATION 20A-4
Computation of Deferred Income Taxes, End of 1995

The temporary difference caused by the use of the accrual basis for financial reporting purposes and the installment method for tax purposes will result in future taxable amounts; hence, a deferred tax liability will arise. Because of the installment contracts completed in 1995, a temporary difference of $448,000 originates that will reverse in equal amounts over the next 4 years. The company is expected to have taxable income in all future years, and there is only one enacted tax rate applicable to all future years. Therefore, that rate (40%) is used to compute the entire deferred tax liability resulting from this temporary difference.

The temporary difference caused by different depreciation policies for books and for tax purposes originates over 3 years and then reverses over 3 years. This difference will cause deductible amounts in 1996 and 1997 and taxable amounts in 1998, 1999, and 2000, which sum to a net future taxable amount of $18,000 (which is the cumulative temporary difference at the end of 1995). Because the company is expected to have taxable income in all future years and because there is only one tax rate enacted for all of the relevant future years, that rate is applied to the net future taxable amount to determine the related net deferred tax liability.

The third temporary difference, caused by different methods of accounting for warranties, will result in deductible amounts in each of the 2 future years it takes to reverse. Because the company expects to report a positive income on all future tax returns and because there is only one tax rate enacted for each of the relevant future years, that 40% rate is used to calculate the resulting deferred tax asset.

DEFERRED TAX EXPENSE (BENEFIT) AND THE JOURNAL ENTRY TO RECORD INCOME TAXES—1995

To determine the deferred tax expense (benefit), the beginning and ending balances of the deferred income tax accounts must be compared.

Deferred tax asset at the end of 1995	$ 62,400
Deferred tax asset at the beginning of 1995	–0–
Deferred tax expense (benefit)	$ (62,400)
Deferred tax liability at the end of 1995	$186,400
Deferred tax liability at the beginning of 1995	–0–
Deferred tax expense (benefit)	$186,400

ILLUSTRATION 20A-5
Computation of Deferred Tax Expense (Benefit), 1995

The $62,400 increase in the deferred tax asset causes a deferred tax benefit to be reflected in the income statement. The $186,400 increase in the deferred tax liability during 1995 results in a deferred tax expense. These two amounts **net** to a deferred tax expense of $124,000 for 1995.

Deferred tax expense (benefit)	$ (62,400)
Deferred tax expense (benefit)	186,400
Net deferred tax expense for 1995	$124,000

ILLUSTRATION 20A-6
Computation of Net Deferred Tax Expense, 1995

The total income tax expense is then computed as follows:

ILLUSTRATION 20A-7
Computation of Total
Income Tax Expense, 1995

Current tax expense for 1995	$ 50,000
Deferred tax expense for 1995	124,000
Income tax expense (total) for 1995	$174,000

The journal entry to record income tax payable, deferred income taxes, and income tax expense is as follows:

Income Tax Expense	174,000	
Deferred Tax Asset	62,400	
Income Tax Payable		50,000
Deferred Tax Liability		186,400

FINANCIAL STATEMENT PRESENTATION—1995

Deferred tax assets and liabilities are to be classified as current and noncurrent on the balance sheet based on the classifications of related assets and liabilities. When there is more than one category of deferred taxes, they are classified into a net current amount and a net noncurrent amount. The classification of Allman's deferred tax accounts at the end of 1995 is as follows:

ILLUSTRATION 20A-8
Classification of Deferred
Tax Accounts, End of
1995

	Resulting Deferred Tax		Related Balance	
Temporary Difference	(Asset)	Liability	Sheet Account	Classification
Installment sales		$179,200	Installment Receivable	Current
Depreciation		7,200	Plant Assets	Noncurrent
Warranty costs	$(62,400)		Warranty Obligation	Current
Totals	$(62,400)	$186,400		

For the first temporary difference, there is a related asset on the balance sheet, installment accounts receivable. That asset is classified as a current asset because the company has a trade practice of selling to customers on an installment basis; hence, the resulting deferred tax liability is classified as a current liability. There are assets on the balance sheet that are related to the depreciation difference—the property, plant, and equipment being depreciated. The plant assets are classified as noncurrent; therefore, the resulting deferred tax liability is to be classified as noncurrent. Since Allman's operating cycle is at least 4 years in length, the entire $156,000 warranty obligation is classified as a current liability. Thus, the related deferred tax asset of $62,400 is classified as current.[1]

The balance sheet at the end of 1995 reports the following amounts:

ILLUSTRATION 20A-9
Balance Sheet
Presentation of Deferred
Taxes, 1995

Current liabilities	
Income tax payable	$ 50,000
Deferred tax liability ($179,200 − $62,400)	116,800
Long-term liabilities	
Deferred tax liability	$ 7,200

---

[1]If Allman's operating cycle was less than one year in length, $56,000 of the warranty obligation would be expected to be settled within one year of the December 31, 1995 balance sheet and would require the use of current assets to settle it; thus $56,000 of the warranty obligation would be a current liability and the remaining $100,000 warranty obligation would be classified as a long-term (noncurrent) liability. This would mean $22,400 ($56,000 × 40%) of the related deferred tax asset would be classified as a current asset and $40,000 ($100,000 × 40%) of the deferred tax asset would be classified as a noncurrent asset. In doing homework problems, unless it is evident otherwise, assume a company's operating cycle is not longer than a year.

The income statement for 1995 reports the following:

Income before income taxes		$412,000
Income tax expense		
Current	$ 50,000	
Deferred	124,000	174,000
Net income		$238,000

ILLUSTRATION 20A-10
Income Statement
Presentation of Income
Tax Expense, 1995

▶ **SECOND YEAR—1996**

---

1. During 1996 the company collected $112,000 from customers for the receivables arising from contracts completed in 1995. Recovery of the remaining receivables is expected to result in taxable amounts of $112,000 in each of the following 3 years.

2. In 1996 the company completed four new contracts that allow for the customer to pay on an installment basis. These installment sales created new installment receivables. Future collections of these receivables will result in reporting gross profit of $64,000 for tax purposes in each of the next four years.

3. During 1996 Allman continued to depreciate the assets acquired in 1995 according to the depreciation schedules appearing on page 1023. Thus, depreciation amounted to $90,000 for financial reporting purposes and $172,800 for tax purposes.

4. An analysis at the end of 1996 of the product warranty liability account showed the following details:

Balance of liability at beginning of 1996	$156,000
Expense for 1996 income statement purposes	180,000
Amount paid for contracts completed in 1995	(56,000)
Amount paid for contracts completed in 1996	(50,000)
Balance of liability at end of 1996	$230,000

The balance of the liability is expected to require expenditures in the future as follows:

$100,000 in 1997 due to 1995 contracts	
$ 50,000 in 1997 due to 1996 contracts	
$ 80,000 in 1998 due to 1996 contracts	
$230,000	

5. During 1996 nontaxable municipal bond interest revenue was $24,000.

6. A loss of $172,000 was accrued for financial reporting purposes because of pending litigation. This amount is not tax deductible until the period the loss is realized, which is estimated to be 2004.

7. Pretax financial income for 1996 amounts to $504,800.

8. The enacted tax rates still in effect are:

1995	50%
1996 and later years	40%

TAXABLE INCOME AND INCOME TAX PAYABLE—1996

The computation of taxable income for 1996 is as follows:

**ILLUSTRATION 20A-11
Computation of Taxable
Income, 1996**

Pretax financial income for 1996	$504,800
Permanent difference:	
Nontaxable revenue—municipal bond interest	(24,000)
Reversing temporary differences:	
Collection on 1995 installment sales	112,000
Payments on warranties from 1995 contracts	(56,000)
Originating temporary differences:	
Excess gross profit per books—1996 contracts	(256,000)
Excess depreciation per tax	(82,800)
Excess warranty expense per books—1996 contracts	130,000
Loss accrual per books	172,000
Taxable income for 1996	$500,000

Income tax payable for 1996 is computed as follows:

**ILLUSTRATION 20A-12
Computation of Income
Tax Payable, End of 1996**

Taxable income for 1996	$500,000
Tax rate	40%
Income tax payable (current tax expense) for 1996	$200,000

COMPUTING DEFERRED INCOME TAXES—END OF 1996

**ILLUSTRATION 20A-13
Schedule of Future
Taxable and Deductible
Amounts, End of 1996**

The following schedule is helpful in summarizing the temporary differences existing at the end of 1996 and the resulting future taxable and deductible amounts.

	Future Years					
	1997	1998	1999	2000	2004	Total
Future taxable (deductible) amounts:						
Installment sales—1995	$112,000	$112,000	$112,000			$336,000
Installment sales—1996	64,000	64,000	64,000	$64,000		256,000
Depreciation	(13,680)	27,792	27,792	58,896		100,800
Warranty costs	(150,000)	(80,000)				(230,000)
Loss accrual					$(172,000)	(172,000)

The amounts of deferred income taxes to be reported at the end of 1996 are computed as follows:

**ILLUSTRATION 20A-14
Computation of Deferred
Income Taxes, End of 1996**

Temporary Difference	Future Taxable (Deductible) Amounts	Tax Rate	Deferred Tax (Asset)	Liability
Installment sales	$592,000*	40%		$236,800
Depreciation	100,800	40%		40,320
Warranty costs	(230,000)	40%	$ (92,000)	
Loss accrual	(172,000)	40%	(68,800)	
Totals	$290,800		$(160,800)	$277,120**

*Cumulative temporary difference = $336,000 + $256,000
**Because of a flat tax rate, these totals can be reconciled: $290,800 × 40% = $(160,800) + $277,120

DEFERRED TAX EXPENSE (BENEFIT) AND THE JOURNAL ENTRY TO RECORD INCOME TAXES—1996

To determine the deferred tax expense (benefit), the beginning and ending balances of the deferred income tax accounts must be compared.

Deferred tax asset at the end of 1996	$160,800
Deferred tax asset at the beginning of 1996	62,400
Deferred tax expense (benefit)	$ (98,400)
Deferred tax liability at the end of 1996	$277,120
Deferred tax liability at the beginning of 1996	186,400
Deferred tax expense (benefit)	$ 90,720

ILLUSTRATION 20A-15
Computation of Deferred Tax Expense (Benefit), 1996

The deferred tax expense (benefit) and the total income tax expense for 1996 are, therefore, as follows:

Deferred tax expense (benefit)	$ (98,400)
Deferred tax expense (benefit)	90,720
Deferred tax benefit for 1996	(7,680)
Current tax expense for 1996	200,000
Income tax expense (total) for 1996	$192,320

ILLUSTRATION 20A-16
Computation of Total Income Tax Expense, 1996

The deferred tax expense of $90,720 and the deferred tax benefit of $98,400 net to a deferred tax benefit of $7,680 for 1996.

The journal entry to record income taxes for 1996 is as follows:

Income Tax Expense	192,320	
Deferred Tax Asset	98,400	
Income Tax Payable		200,000
Deferred Tax Liability		90,720

FINANCIAL STATEMENT PRESENTATION

The classification of Allman's deferred tax accounts at the end of 1996 is as follows:

Temporary Difference	Resulting Deferred Tax (Asset)	Liability	Related Balance Sheet Account	Classification
Installment sales		$236,800	Installment Receivables	Current
Depreciation		40,320	Plant Assets	Noncurrent
Warranty costs	$ (92,000)		Warranty Obligation	Current
Loss accrual	(68,800)		Litigation Obligation	Noncurrent
Totals	$(160,800)	$277,120		

ILLUSTRATION 20A-17
Classification of Deferred Tax Accounts, End of 1996

The new temporary difference introduced in 1996 (due to the litigation loss accrual) results in a litigation obligation that is classified as a long-term liability. Thus, the related deferred tax asset is noncurrent.

The balance sheet at the end of 1996 reports the following amounts:

Other assets (noncurrent)	
Deferred tax asset ($68,800 − $40,320)	$ 28,480
Current liabilities	
Income tax payable	$200,000
Deferred tax liability ($236,800 − $92,000)	144,800

ILLUSTRATION 20A-18
Balance Sheet Presentation of Deferred Taxes, End of 1996

The income statement for 1996 reports the following:

Income before income taxes		$504,800
Income tax expense		
Current	$200,000	
Deferred	(7,680)	192,320
Net income		$312,480

ILLUSTRATION 20A-19
Income Statement Presentation of Income Tax Expense, 1996

> ▶ SUMMARY OF LEARNING OBJECTIVE FOR APP. 20-A ◀

12. **Understand and apply the concepts and procedures of interperiod tax allocation.** Accounting for deferred taxes includes calculating taxable income and income tax payable for the year, computing deferred income taxes at the end of the year, determining deferred tax expense (benefit) and making the journal entry to record income taxes, and classifying deferred tax assets and liabilities as current and noncurrent in the financial statements.

APPENDIX 20-B

CONCEPTUAL ASPECTS OF INTERPERIOD TAX ALLOCATION

OBJECTIVE 13

After studying Appendix 20-B, you should be able to: Understand the arguments for and against interperiod tax allocation and the alternative approaches.

The desirability of using **interperiod tax allocation** is not unanimously agreed upon. Some believe that the appropriate tax to be reported on the income statement is the tax actually levied in that year. In short, this group, often referred to as the **non-allocation** (or flow-through) **proponents,** does not believe that the recognition of deferred income taxes provides useful information, or at least benefits in excess of cost. They note that the nature of the Deferred Tax Liability account is not clear. They contend that it is not a liability at the time the account is established because it is not payable to anyone. The payment of additional tax in the future is contingent upon the earning of future taxable income. If taxable income does not occur in the future, there is no liability. Similarly, others note that if there is no taxable income in the future, a deferred tax asset should not be recognized.

Others argue that income taxes are similar to a dividend, not an expense. As a result, allocation between accounting periods is inappropriate because taxes are considered to be an involuntary distribution of income, rather than a determinant of income.

Despite these arguments, the profession justified the recognition of deferred income taxes on the basis of asset-liability recognition concepts. Income taxes are seldom paid completely in the period to which they relate. However, the operations of a business entity are expected to continue on a going-concern basis in the absence of evidence to the contrary, and income taxes are expected to continue to be assessed in the future. Recognition of deferred taxes is needed to report the future taxes expected to be paid or recovered because the tax return treatment for various items is different from their financial statement treatment.

Although the predominant view holds that recognition of deferred taxes is appropriate, there are two concepts regarding the extent to which it should be applied: (1) comprehensive allocation and (2) partial allocation.

▶ COMPREHENSIVE ALLOCATION VERSUS PARTIAL ALLOCATION

Under **comprehensive allocation,** recognition of deferred taxes is applied to **all temporary differences.**[1] Supporters of this view believe that reported deferred income taxes should reflect the tax effects of all temporary differences included in pretax financial income, regardless of the period in which the related income taxes are actually paid or

---

[1]Note that under the asset-liability approach (present GAAP) all temporary differences are tax affected.

recovered. This view recognizes that the amount of income tax currently payable is not necessarily the income tax reported in the financial statements relating to the current period. Consequently, deferred taxes should be recognized when temporary differences originate, even if it is virtually certain that their reversal in future periods will be offset by new originating differences at that time. As a practical matter, therefore, recurring differences between taxable income and pretax financial income give rise to an indefinite postponement of tax.

An example of a recurring temporary difference is the use of accelerated depreciation for tax purposes by a company that uses straight-line depreciation for financial reporting purposes. This results in the accumulation of deferred tax liabilities that will not be paid as long as the company is acquiring depreciable assets faster than it is retiring them. Although the deferred taxes associated with specific assets do indeed reverse, the aggregate balance in deferred taxes remains stable or continues to grow because of the recurring purchases of additional assets.

Supporters of **partial allocation** contend that unless deferred tax amounts are expected to be paid or recovered within a relevant period of time, they should not affect reported income. Consequently, recognition of deferred income taxes is not considered appropriate for recurring temporary differences that result in an indefinite postponement of tax. Under this view, the presumption is that reported tax expense for a period should be the same as the tax payable for the period. Accordingly, only **nonrecurring,** material temporary differences should give rise to the recognition of deferred taxes. Deferred taxes should be recognized only if they are reasonably expected to be paid or recovered within a relatively short period of time not exceeding, for example, 3 years. An example is an **isolated** installment sale in which the receivable and related gross profit are reported for financial reporting purposes at the date of sale and for tax purposes when collected.

The supporters of comprehensive allocation contend that partial allocation is a departure from accrual accounting because it emphasizes cash outlays, whereas comprehensive allocation results in a more thorough and consistent recognition of assets and liabilities. **Present GAAP requires application of comprehensive allocation.**

▶ CONCEPTUAL APPROACHES TO DEFERRED INCOME TAXES

The preceding viewpoints involving no allocation, partial allocation, and comprehensive allocation represent different approaches to the problem of identifying those transactions for which the recognition of deferred income taxes is appropriate. The three views differ as to **whether accounting recognition should be given to the deferred tax effects of temporary differences.** Because tax rates change over time, additional questions relate to what method of tax allocation should be used in accounting for tax effects and how those effects should be presented in the financial statements. Three different methods of tax allocation have been proposed: (1) the deferred method, (2) the asset-liability method, and (3) the net-of-tax method.

DEFERRED METHOD

Under the deferred method, the amount of deferred income tax is based on tax rates in effect when temporary differences originate. The balance in deferred taxes is not adjusted to reflect subsequent changes in tax rates or the imposition of new taxes. Consequently, the balance in deferred income taxes may not be representative of the actual amount of additional taxes payable or receivable in the periods that temporary differences reverse. Under this method, deferred charges and credits relating to temporary differences "represent the cumulative recognition given to their tax effects and as such do not represent receivables or payables" in the usual economic sense.[2] It is an

---

[2]"Accounting for Income Taxes," *Opinions of the Accounting Principles Board No. 11* (New York: AICPA, 1967), par. 56.

income statement-oriented approach that emphasizes proper matching of expenses with revenue in the periods that temporary differences originate. **This method is not acceptable for financial reporting purposes.**

ASSET-LIABILITY METHOD

Under the asset-liability method, the amount of deferred income tax is based on the tax rates expected to be in effect during the periods in which the temporary differences reverse. The most reasonable assumption about future tax rates is that the current tax rate will continue. However, if a rate change is enacted into law, the new rate will be used under the asset-liability method—one of many reasons why companies will fight a boost in tax rates. Under this method, deferred taxes are viewed as economic liabilities for taxes payable or assets for prepaid tax. This method is a **balance sheet-oriented approach** that emphasizes the usefulness of financial statements in evaluating financial position and predicting future cash flows. **Present GAAP requires that the asset-liability method be used for interperiod tax allocation.**

NET-OF-TAX METHOD

Under the **net-of-tax method,** no deferred tax account is reported on the balance sheet. Further, the amount of income tax expense reported on the income statement is the same as the taxes currently payable. The tax effects of temporary differences (determined by either the deferred or asset-liability methods) are not reported separately. Instead, they are reported as **adjustments to the carrying amounts of specific assets or liabilities and the related revenues or expenses.** This view recognizes that future taxability and tax deductibility are important factors in the valuation of individual assets and liabilities.

For example, depreciation is said to reduce the value of an asset both because of a decline in economic usefulness and because of the loss of a portion of future tax deductibility; accelerated depreciation uses up this portion of the asset value more rapidly than does straight-line depreciation. Under this view, depreciation expense reported on the income statement would include, in addition to an amount for straight-line depreciation, an amount equal to the current tax effect of the excess of tax depreciation over accounting depreciation. On the balance sheet the related cumulative deferred tax effect would be reported as a reduction of the specific asset rather than as a credit balance in a Deferred Tax Liability account. The asset, liability, revenue, and expense accounts would be presented "net-of-tax" under this method. **The net-of-tax method is not accepted currently for financial accounting purposes.**

AN ILLUSTRATION OF THE DIFFERENT METHODS OF TAX ALLOCATION

To illustrate the difference in these three methods of interperiod tax allocation, assume that on January 1, 1995, Orange Inc. acquires for $100,000 equipment that has a 5-year useful life and no salvage value. Straight-line depreciation is used for financial reporting purposes. Depreciation for tax purposes is $25,000. The tax rate for 1995 is 40%, but the tax rate (enacted into law) for future years is 50%. Income tax payable for 1995, assuming that income before depreciation and taxes is $200,000, is computed below.

ILLUSTRATION 20B-1
Computation of Income
Tax Payable, End of 1995

Income before depreciation and income taxes	$200,000
Depreciation for tax purposes	25,000
Taxable income	175,000
Tax rate	40%
Income tax payable	$ 70,000

An abbreviated income statement for 1995 under the three methods is as follows:

	Deferred	Asset-Liability	Net-of-Tax
Income before depreciation and income taxes	$200,000	$200,000	$200,000
Depreciation	20,000	20,000	22,000
Income before income taxes	180,000	180,000	178,000
Current tax expense	70,000	70,000	70,000
Deferred tax expense	2,000	2,500	—
Total income tax expense	72,000	72,500	70,000
Net income	$108,000	$107,500	$108,000

ILLUSTRATION 20B-2
Income Statement Presentation of Income Tax Expense for Three Methods

Under the deferred method, the deferred portion of income taxes is computed as follows:

Depreciation for tax purposes	$25,000
Depreciation for book purposes (20% × $100,000)	20,000
Difference	5,000
Tax rate	40%
Deferred income tax credit	$ 2,000

ILLUSTRATION 20B-3
Computation of Deferred Income Taxes—Deferred Method

Under the asset-liability method, the computation of the deferred portion of income taxes is essentially the same except that the future rate is used instead of the current rate.

Depreciation for tax purposes	$25,000
Depreciation for book purposes (20% × $100,000)	20,000
Difference	5,000
Tax rate	50%
Deferred tax liability	$ 2,500

ILLUSTRATION 20B-4
Computation of Deferred Income Taxes—Asset-Liability Method

Under **the net-of-tax method** the computation is more complicated. As indicated earlier, depreciation expense reported on the income statement would include, in addition to an amount for straight-line depreciation, an amount equal to the current tax effect of the excess of tax depreciation over book depreciation. This computation is as follows:[3]

Depreciation for book purposes (20% × $100,000)	$20,000
Tax effect of excess depreciation [($25,000 − $20,000) × 40%]	2,000
Depreciation expense	$22,000

ILLUSTRATION 20B-5
Computation of Deferred Income Taxes—Net-of-Tax Method

Thus, under the net-of-tax method, depreciation expense and accumulated depreciation are higher by $2,000.

---

[3]Conceptually, under the net-of-tax method we assume that a company purchases two items when it purchases an asset: one item is its service potential and the other is its tax deductibility feature. In the case above, the service potential feature is $60,000 ($100,000 × 60%), and the tax deductibility feature is $40,000 ($100,000 × 40%). In the first year, the service potential feature depreciates at a 20% rate, whereas the tax deductibility feature depreciates at a 25% rate. Total depreciation would, therefore, be computed as follows:

Depreciation of service potential feature ($60,000 × 20%)	$12,000
Depreciation of tax deductibility feature ($40,000 × 25%)	10,000
Depreciation expense	$22,000

Note that the depreciation amount of $22,000 is the same as the computation reported above under net-of-tax.

Note that both the deferred method and the net-of-tax method report the same net income. The difference between these two methods relates to the classification of the expense and whether a deferred tax account is created. The asset-liability method uses a different—and, in this case, higher—tax rate than the deferred and net-of-tax methods; net income is thereby lower.

<table>
<tr><td>

KEY TERMS

asset-liability method, 1032

comprehensive allocation, 1030

deferred method, 1031

interperiod tax allocation, 1030

net-of-tax method, 1032

non-allocation, 1030

partial allocation, 1031

</td><td>

▶ SUMMARY OF LEARNING OBJECTIVE FOR APP. 20-B ◀

13. Understand the arguments for and against interperiod tax allocation and the alternative approaches. Although the predominant view holds that comprehensive tax allocation is appropriate, there are those who support no allocation or partial allocation. Of those who support allocation, three different methods of tax allocation have been proposed: (1) the deferred method, (2) the asset-liability method, and (3) the net-of-tax method.

</td></tr>
</table>

Note: All **asterisked** Questions, Exercises, Problems, and Cases relate to material contained in the appendix to each chapter.

QUESTIONS

1. As controller for Buchanan Co., you are asked to meet with the Board of Directors to discuss the company's income tax situation. Several members of the board express concern because the company is reporting a larger amount of income tax expense on its published income statement than is to be paid to the federal government with the company's income tax return for that same year.
   (a) Explain to the Board members the accounting rationale for this discrepancy.
   (b) How might this difference between tax paid and tax expense have arisen?

2. Interest on municipal bonds is referred to as a permanent difference when determining the proper amount to report for deferred taxes. Explain the meaning of permanent differences and give two other examples.

3. Explain the meaning of a temporary difference as it relates to deferred tax computations and give three examples.

4. The book basis of depreciable assets for Hillsborough Co. is $900,000, and the tax basis is $800,000 at the end of 1996. The enacted tax rate is 34% for all periods. Determine the amount of deferred taxes to be reported on the balance sheet at the end of 1996.

5. Bowdoin Inc. has a deferred tax liability of $68,000 at the beginning of 1996. At the end of 1996, it reports accounts receivable on the books at $100,000 and the tax basis at zero (its only temporary difference). If the enacted tax rate is 34% for all periods, and income tax payable for the period is $230,000, determine the amount of total income tax expense to report for 1996.

6. What is the difference between a future taxable amount and a future deductible amount? When is it appropriate to record a valuation account for a deferred tax asset?

7. Pretax financial income for Appleton Inc. is $300,000, and its taxable income is $100,000 for 1996. Its only temporary difference at the end of the period relates to a $90,000 difference due to excess depreciation for tax purposes. If the tax rate is 30% for all periods, compute the amount of income tax expense to report in 1996. No deferred income taxes existed at the beginning of the year.

8. How are deferred tax assets and deferred tax liabilities reported on the balance sheet?

9. Describe the procedures involved in segregating various deferred tax amounts into current and non-current categories.

10. How is it determined whether deferred tax amounts are considered to be "related" to specific assets or liability amounts?

11. At the end of the year, William King Co. has pretax financial income of $550,000. Included in the $550,000 is $70,000 interest income on municipal bonds, $35,000 fine for dumping hazardous waste, and depreciation of $60,000. Depreciation for tax purposes is $45,000. Compute income taxes payable, assuming the tax rate is 30% for all periods.

12. Franklin Co. has one temporary difference at the beginning of 1996 of $500,000. The deferred tax liability established for this amount is $150,000, based on a tax rate of 30%. The temporary difference will provide the following taxable amounts: $100,000 in 1997; $200,000 in 1998; and $200,000 in 1999. If a new tax rate for 1999 of 20% is enacted into law at the end of 1996, what is the journal entry necessary in 1996 (if any) to adjust deferred taxes?

13. What are some of the reasons that the components of income tax expense should be disclosed and a reconciliation between the effective tax rate and the statutory tax rate be provided?

14. Differentiate between "carryback" and "carryforward." Which can be accounted for with the greater certainty when it arises? Why?

15. What are the possible treatments for tax purposes of a net operating loss? What are the circumstances that determine the option to be applied? What is the proper treatment of a net operating loss for financial reporting purposes?

16. What is intraperiod tax allocation and how are taxes allocated under this concept?

17. What is the alternative minimum tax and how does it affect the computation of deferred income taxes?

18. What controversy relates to the accounting for net operating loss carryforwards?

*19. What method of accounting for income taxes has the profession adopted? Speculate as to why this approach is required.

*20. Explain the following terms: net-of-tax method; partial tax allocation; and comprehensive tax allocation.

EXERCISES

E20-1 (One Temporary Difference, Future Taxable Amounts, One Rate, No Beginning Deferred Taxes) U.S. Grant Corporation has one temporary difference at the end of 1996 that will reverse and cause taxable amounts of $55,000 in 1997, $60,000 in 1998, and $60,000 in 1999. Grant's pretax financial income for 1996 is $300,000 and the tax rate is 30% for all years. There are no deferred taxes at the beginning of 1996.

Instructions
- **(a)** Compute taxable income and income taxes payable for 1996.
- **(b)** Prepare the journal entry to record income tax expense, deferred income taxes, and income taxes payable for 1996.
- **(c)** Prepare the income tax expense section of the income statement for 1996, beginning with the line "Income before income taxes."

E20-2 (One Temporary Difference, Future Deductible Amounts, One Rate, No Beginning Deferred Taxes) Schuyler Colfax Corporation has one temporary difference at the end of 1996 that will reverse and cause deductible amounts of $50,000 in 1997, $65,000 in 1998, and $40,000 in 1999. Schuyler Colfax's pretax financial income for 1996 is $200,000, and the tax rate is 30% for all years. There are no deferred taxes at the beginning of 1996. Schuyler Colfax expects profitable operations to continue in the future.

Instructions
- **(a)** Compute taxable income and income taxes payable for 1996.
- **(b)** Prepare the journal entry to record income tax expense, deferred income taxes, and income taxes payable for 1996.
- **(c)** Prepare the income tax expense section of the income statement for 1996, beginning with the line "Income before income taxes."

E20-3 (One Temporary Difference, Future Taxable Amounts, One Rate, Beginning Deferred Taxes) Julia Dent Corporation began 1996 with a $90,000 balance in the Deferred Tax Liability account. At the end of 1996, the related cumulative temporary difference amounts to $350,000, and it will reverse evenly over the next two years. Pretax accounting income for 1996 is $525,000, the tax rate for all years is 40%, and taxable income for 1996 is $400,000.

Instructions
- **(a)** Compute income taxes payable for 1996.
- **(b)** Prepare the journal entry to record income tax expense, deferred income taxes, and income taxes payable for 1996.
- **(c)** Prepare the income tax expense section of the income statement for 1996, beginning with the line "Income before income taxes."

E20-4 (Three Differences, Compute Taxable Income, Entry for Taxes) Ruther Ford B. Hayes Company reports pretax financial income of $70,000 for 1996. The following items cause taxable income to be different than pretax financial income:

1. Depreciation on the tax return is greater than depreciation on the income statement by $18,000.
2. Rent collected on the tax return is greater than rent earned on the income statement by $22,000.
3. Fines for pollution appear as an expense of $11,000 on the income statement.

Hayes' tax rate is 30% for all years and the company expects to report taxable income in all future years. There are no deferred taxes at the beginning of 1996.

Instructions
(a) Compute taxable income and income taxes payable for 1996.
(b) Prepare the journal entry to record income tax expense, deferred income taxes, and income taxes payable for 1996.
(c) Prepare the income tax expense section of the income statement for 1996, beginning with the line "Income before income taxes."
(d) Compute the effective income tax rate for 1996.

E20-5 (Two Temporary Differences, One Rate, Beginning Deferred Taxes) The following facts relate to William Wheeler Corporation:

1. Deferred tax liability, January 1, 1996, $40,000.
2. Deferred tax asset, January 1, 1996, $0.
3. Taxable income for 1996, $95,000.
4. Pretax financial income for 1996, $180,000.
5. Cumulative temporary difference at December 31, 1996, giving rise to future taxable amounts, $220,000.
6. Cumulative temporary difference at December 31, 1996, giving rise to future deductible amounts, $35,000.
7. Tax rate for all years, 40%.
8. The company is expected to operate profitably in the future.

Instructions
(a) Compute income taxes payable for 1996.
(b) Prepare the journal entry to record income tax expense, deferred income taxes, and income taxes payable for 1996.
(c) Prepare the income tax expense section of the income statement for 1996, beginning with the line "Income before income taxes."

E20-6 (Identify Temporary or Permanent Differences) Listed below are items that are commonly accounted for differently for financial reporting purposes than they are for tax purposes.

Instructions
For each item below, indicate whether it involves
(a) A temporary difference that will result in future deductible amounts and, therefore, will usually give rise to a deferred income tax asset.
(b) A temporary difference that will result in future taxable amounts and, therefore, will usually give rise to a deferred income tax liability.
(c) A permanent difference.

Use the appropriate letter to indicate your answer for each.

_____ 1. The MACRS depreciation system is used for tax purposes, and the straight-line depreciation method is used for financial reporting purposes for some plant assets.
_____ 2. A landlord collects some rents in advance. Rents received are taxable in the period when they are received.
_____ 3. Expenses are incurred in obtaining tax-exempt income.
_____ 4. Costs of guarantees and warranties are estimated and accrued for financial reporting purposes.
_____ 5. Installment sales of investments are accounted for by the accrual method for financial reporting purposes and the installment method for tax purposes.
_____ 6. For some assets, straight-line depreciation is used for both financial reporting purposes and tax purposes but the assets' lives are shorter for tax purposes.
_____ 7. Interest is received on an investment in tax-exempt municipal obligations.
_____ 8. Proceeds are received from a life insurance company because of the death of a key officer (the company carries a policy on key officers).

_____ 9. The tax return reports a deduction for 80% of the dividends received from U.S. corporations. The cost method is used in accounting for the related investments for financial reporting purposes.

_____ 10. Estimated losses on pending lawsuits and claims are accrued for books. These losses are tax deductible in the period(s) when the related liabilities are settled.

E20-7 (Terminology, Relationships, Computations, Entries)

Instructions

Complete the following statements by filling in the blanks:

1. In a period in which a taxable temporary difference reverses, the reversal will cause taxable income to be _____ (less than, greater than) pretax financial income.

2. If a $60,000 balance in Deferred Tax Asset was computed by use of a 40% rate, the underlying cumulative temporary difference amounts to $_____.

3. Deferred taxes _____ (are, are not) recorded to account for permanent differences.

4. If a taxable temporary difference originates in 1996, it will cause taxable income of 1996 to be _____ (less than, greater than) pretax financial income for 1996.

5. If total tax expense is $50,000 and deferred tax expense is $70,000, then the current portion of the expense computation is referred to as current tax _____ (expense, benefit) of $_____.

6. If a corporation's tax return shows taxable income of $100,000 for Year 2 and a tax rate of 40%, how much will appear on the December 31, Year 2 balance sheet for "Income tax payable" if the company has made estimated tax payments of $37,000 for Year 2? $_____

7. An increase in the Deferred Tax Liability account on the balance sheet is recorded by a _____ (debit, credit) to the Income Tax Expense account.

8. An income statement that reports current tax expense of $82,000 and deferred tax benefit of $21,000 will report total income tax expense of $_____

9. A valuation account is needed whenever it is judged to be _____ that a portion of a deferred tax asset _____ (will be, will not be) realized.

10. If the tax return shows total taxes due for the period of $75,000 but the income statement shows total income tax expense of $55,000, the difference of $20,000 is referred to as deferred tax _____ (expense, benefit).

E20-8 (One Temporary Difference Through Three Years, One Rate) Kenyon Company reports the following amounts in its first three years of operations:

	1996	1997	1998
Taxable income	160,000	142,000	140,000
Pretax financial income	200,000	120,000	125,000

The difference between taxable income and pretax financial income is due to one temporary difference. The tax rate is 40% for all years and the company expects to continue with profitable operations in the future.

Instructions

(a) For each year, (1) identify the amount of the temporary difference originating or reversing during that year, and (2) indicate the amount of the cumulative temporary difference at the end of the year.

(b) Indicate the balance in the related deferred tax account at the end of each year and identify it as either a deferred tax asset or liability.

E20-9 (Carryback and Carryforward of NOL, No Valuation Account, No Temporary Differences) The pretax financial income (or loss) figures for the Lucy Webb Company are as follows:

1991	$160,000
1992	250,000
1993	80,000
1994	(160,000)
1995	(380,000)
1996	120,000
1997	100,000

Pretax financial income (or loss) and taxable income (loss) were the same for all years involved. Assume a 50% tax rate for 1991 and 1992 and a 40% tax rate for the remaining years.

Instructions

Prepare the journal entries for the years 1993 to 1997 to record income tax expense and the effects of the net operating loss carrybacks and carryforwards assuming Lucy Webb Company uses the carryback provision. All income and losses relate to normal operations. (In recording the benefits of a loss carryforward, assume that no valuation account is deemed necessary.)

E20-10 (2 NOLs, No Temporary Differences, No Valuation Account, Entries and Income Statement) James Garfield Corporation has pretax financial income (or loss) equal to taxable income (or loss) from 1988 through 1996 as follows:

	Income (Loss)	Tax Rate
1988	$ 29,000	30%
1989	40,000	30%
1990	17,000	20%
1991	48,000	50%
1992	(150,000)	40%
1993	60,000	40%
1994	30,000	40%
1995	105,000	40%
1996	(60,000)	45%

Pretax financial income (loss) and taxable income (loss) were the same for all years since Garfield has been in business. Assume the carryback provision is employed for net operating losses. In recording the benefits of a loss carryforward, assume that it is more likely than not that the related benefits will be realized.

Instructions

(a) What entry(ies) for income taxes should be recorded for 1992?

(b) Indicate what the income tax expense portion of the income statement for 1992 should look like. Assume all income (loss) relates to continuing operations.

(c) What entry for income taxes should be recorded in 1993?

(d) How should the income tax expense section of the income statement for 1993 appear?

(e) What entry for income taxes should be recorded in 1996?

(f) How should the income tax expense section of the income statement for 1996 appear?

E20-11 (Three Differences, Classify Deferred Taxes) At December 31, 1995, Orange Company had a net deferred tax liability of $350,000. An explanation of the items that compose this balance is as follows:

Temporary Differences	Resulting Balances in Deferred Taxes
1. Excess of tax depreciation over book depreciation	$200,000
2. Accrual, for book purposes, of estimated loss contingency from pending lawsuit that is expected to be settled in 1996. The loss will be deducted on the tax return when paid.	(50,000)
3. Accrual method used for book purposes and installment method used for tax purposes for an isolated installment sale of an investment.	200,000
	$350,000

In analyzing the temporary differences, you find that $10,000 of the depreciation temporary difference will reverse in 1996 and $100,000 of the temporary difference due to the installment sale will reverse in 1996. The tax rate for all years is 40%.

Instructions

Indicate the manner in which deferred taxes should be presented on Orange Company's December 31, 1995, balance sheet.

E20-12 (Two Temporary Differences, One Rate, Beginning Deferred Taxes, Compute Pretax Financial Income) The following facts relate to Hiram Corporation:

1. Deferred tax liability, January 1, 1996, $60,000.
2. Deferred tax asset, January 1, 1996, $20,000.
3. Taxable income for 1996, $105,000.
4. Cumulative temporary difference at December 31, 1996, giving rise to future taxable amounts, $225,000.
5. Cumulative temporary difference at December 31, 1996, giving rise to future deductible amounts, $80,000.
6. Tax rate for all years, 40%. No permanent differences exist.
7. The company is expected to operate profitably in the future.

Instructions

(a) Compute the amount of pretax financial income for 1996.

(b) Prepare the journal entry to record income tax expense, deferred income taxes, and income taxes payable for 1996.

(c) Prepare the income tax expense section of the income statement for 1996, beginning with the line "Income before income taxes."

(d) Compute the effective tax rate for 1996.

E20-13 (One Difference, Multiple Rates, Effect of Beginning Balance Versus No Beginning Deferred Taxes)   At the end of 1995, Lucretia Rudolph Company has $180,000 of cumulative temporary differences that will result in reporting future taxable amounts as follows:

1996	$ 60,000
1997	20,000
1998	70,000
1999	30,000
	$180,000

Tax rates enacted as of the beginning of 1994 are:

1994 and 1995	40%
1996 and 1997	30%
1998 and later	25%

Rudolph's taxable income for 1995 is $320,000. Taxable income is expected in all future years.

Instructions
   (a)   Prepare the journal entry for Rudolph to record income taxes payable, deferred income taxes, and income tax expense for 1995, assuming that there were no deferred taxes at the end of 1994.
   (b)   Prepare the journal entry for Rudolph to record income taxes payable, deferred income taxes, and income tax expense for 1995, assuming that there was a balance of $22,000 in a Deferred Tax Liability account at the end of 1994.

E20-14 (Deferred Tax Asset With and Without Valuation Account)   C. J. Guiteau Corp. has a deferred tax asset account with a balance of $150,000 at the end of 1995 due to a single cumulative temporary difference of $375,000. At the end of 1996 this same temporary difference has increased to a cumulative amount of $450,000. Taxable income for 1996 is $850,000. The tax rate is 40% for all years. No valuation account related to the deferred tax asset is in existence at the end of 1995.

Instructions
   (a)   Record income tax expense, deferred income taxes, and income taxes payable for 1996, assuming that it is more likely than not that the deferred tax asset will be realized.
   (b)   Assuming that it is more likely than not that $20,000 of the deferred tax asset will not be realized, prepare the journal entry at the end of 1996 to record the valuation account.

E20-15 (Deferred Tax Asset with Previous Valuation Account)   Assume the same information as E20-14, except that at the end of 1995, C. J. Guiteau Corp. had a valuation account related to its deferred tax asset of $40,000.

Instructions
   (a)   Record income tax expense, deferred income taxes, and income taxes payable for 1996, assuming that it is more likely than not that the deferred tax asset will be realized in full.
   (b)   Record income tax expense, deferred income taxes, and income taxes payable for 1996, assuming that it is more likely than not that none of the deferred tax asset will be realized.

E20-16 (Deferred Tax Liability, Change in Tax Rate, Prepare Section of Income Statement)   Chester Arthur Inc.'s only temporary difference at the beginning and end of 1995 is caused by a $3 million deferred gain for tax purposes for an installment sale of a plant asset, and the related receivable (only one-half of which is classified as a current asset) is due in equal installments in 1996 and 1997. The related deferred tax liability at the beginning of the year is $1,200,000. In the third quarter of 1995, a new tax rate of 30% is enacted into law and is scheduled to become effective for 1997. Taxable income for 1995 is $5,000,000 and taxable income is expected in all future years.

Instructions
   (a)   Determine the amount reported as a deferred tax liability at the end of 1995. Indicate proper classification(s).
   (b)   Prepare the journal entry (if any) necessary to adjust the deferred tax liability when the new tax rate is enacted into law.
   (c)   Draft the income tax expense portion of the income statement for 1995. Begin with the line "Income before income taxes." Assume no permanent differences exist.

E20-17 (Two Temporary Differences, Tracked Through 3 Years, Multiple Rates)   Taxable income and pretax financial income would be identical for Fairfield Co. except for its treatments of gross profit on installment sales and estimated costs of warranties. The following income computations have been prepared:

Taxable income	1995	1996	1997
Excess of revenues over expenses			
(excluding two temporary differences)	$160,000	$210,000	$90,000
Installment gross profit collected	7,000	7,000	7,000
Expenditures for warranties	(5,000)	(5,000)	(5,000)
Taxable income	$162,000	$212,000	$92,000

Pretax financial income	1995	1996	1997
Excess of revenues over expenses			
(excluding two temporary differences)	$160,000	$210,000	$90,000
Installment gross profit earned	21,000	–0–	–0–
Estimated cost of warranties	(15,000)	–0–	–0–
Income before taxes	$166,000	$210,000	$90,000

The tax rates in effect are: 1995, 40%; 1996 and 1997, 45%. All tax rates were enacted into law on January 1, 1995. No deferred income taxes existed at the beginning of 1995. Taxable income is expected in all future years.

Instructions
Prepare the journal entry to record income tax expense, deferred income taxes, and income tax payable for 1995, 1996, and 1997.

E20-18 (Two Differences, No Beginning Deferred Taxes, Multiple Rates, Compute Pretax Financial Income) The following data pertain to the Ellen Herndon Company.

1. At December 31, 1995, the company has a $30,000 liability reported for estimated litigation claims. This $30,000 balance represents amounts that have been charged to income but that are not tax deductible until they are paid. The company expects to pay the claims and thus have tax-deductible amounts in the future in the following manner:

Year	Payments
1998	$ 5,000
1999	23,000
2000	2,000
	$30,000

2. The company uses different depreciation methods for financial reporting and tax purposes. Consequently, at December 31, 1995, the company has a cumulative temporary difference due to depreciable property of $80,000. This $80,000 cumulative temporary difference due to depreciation is to result in taxable amounts in future years in the following manner:

Year	Amount
1996	$16,000
1997	16,000
1998	16,000
1999	16,000
2000	16,000
	$80,000

3. The tax rates enacted at the beginning of 1994 are as follows:

1995 and 1996	50%
1997 and 1998	40%
1999 and later	30%

4. Taxable income for 1995 is $80,000. Herndon expects to report taxable income for at least the next five years.
5. No temporary differences existed at the end of 1994.

Instructions
(a) Prepare the journal entry for Herndon to record income tax payable, deferred income taxes, and income tax expense for 1995.
(b) Prepare the income tax expense section of the income statement, beginning with the line "Income before income taxes."

E20-19 (Two Differences, One Rate, Pretax Financial Loss) Grover Cleveland Inc., in its first year of operations, has a pretax financial loss even though it has taxable income. A reconciliation between these two amounts for the calendar year 1996 is as follows:

Pretax financial loss	$ (50,000)
Estimated expenses that will be deductible	
for tax purposes when paid	2,000,000
Additional depreciation taken for tax purposes	(1,200,000)
Taxable income	$ 750,000

At the end of 1996, the reported amount of Cleveland's depreciable assets in the financial statements is $3 million, and the tax basis of these assets is $1.8 million. Future recovery of the depreciable assets will result in $1,200,000 of taxable amounts ($300,000 per year in years 1997–2000) over the 4-year remaining life of the assets. Also, a $2,000,000 estimated liability for litigation expenses has been recognized in the financial statements in 1996, but the related expenses will be deductible on the tax return in 1999 when the liability is expected to be settled. Cleveland expects to report taxable income in the next few years.

Instructions
Prepare the journal entry (if any) to record income tax expense, income tax payable, and deferred income taxes for 1996, assuming a tax rate of 30% for all periods.

 E20-20 (Depreciation Difference, Effect of Expectation for Future Income Versus Future Losses) Thomas Hendricks Inc. began operations at the beginning of 1996. Plant assets costing $2,400,000 were placed into service on January 2, 1996. Presented below is a schedule of depreciation for book and tax purposes to be taken by Hendricks Inc.

	Book Depreciation	Tax Depreciation	Difference
1996	$ 240,000	$ 300,000	$ (60,000)
1997	240,000	510,000	(270,000)
1998	240,000	530,000	(290,000)
1999	240,000	530,000	(290,000)
2000	240,000	530,000	(290,000)
2001	240,000		240,000
2002	240,000		240,000
2003	240,000		240,000
2004	240,000		240,000
2005	240,000		240,000
	$2,400,000	$2,400,000	$ –0–

Assume that the tax rates are 50% for 1996 through 2000, 40% in 2001, and 30% in 2002 and later years. All rates were enacted by the end of 1996.

Instructions
(a) Compute the deferred taxes to be reported for Thomas Hendricks Inc. at the end of 1996, 1997, and 1998 assuming taxable income is expected in each of the next 10 years. Explain how they would appear on the balance sheet.
(b) Compute the deferred taxes to be reported for Thomas Hendricks Inc. at the end of 1996, 1997, and 1998. Assume there is zero taxable income for 1996, net operating losses are expected for the next 5 years, and large amounts of taxable income are expected for all subsequent years.

E20-21 (Three Differences, Multiple Rates, Future Taxable Income) During 1996, James Blaine Co.'s first year of operations, the company reports pretax financial income at $250,000. Blaine's enacted tax rate is 50% for 1996 and 40% for all later years. Blaine expects to have taxable income in each of the next 5 years. The effects on future tax returns of temporary differences existing at December 31, 1996, are summarized below:

	Future Years					
	1997	1998	1999	2000	2001	Total
Future taxable (deductible) amounts:						
Installment sales	$32,000	$32,000	$32,000			$ 96,000
Depreciation	(30,000)	(30,000)	30,000	$30,000	$30,000	30,000
Unearned rent	(50,000)	(50,000)				(100,000)

Instructions
(a) Complete the schedule below to compute deferred taxes at December 31, 1996.
(b) Compute taxable income for 1996.

(c) Prepare the journal entry to record income tax payable, deferred taxes, and income tax expense for 1996.

Temporary Difference	Future Taxable (Deductible) Amounts	Tax Rate	December 31, 1996 Deferred Tax (Asset)	December 31, 1996 Deferred Tax Liability
Installment sales	$ 96,000			
Depreciation	30,000			
Unearned rent	(100,000)			
Totals	$			

E20-22 (One Temporary Difference, Multiple Rates, Beginning Deferred Tax Balance) Frances Folsom Company's taxable income for 1995 is $350,000. Folsom's noncurrent deferred tax liability balance at December 31, 1994, was $85,000. At the end of 1995, Folsom Company has a $220,000 cumulative temporary difference that will result in reporting future taxable amounts as follows:

1996	$ 50,000
1997	40,000
1998	60,000
1999	70,000
	$220,000

Tax rates enacted at the beginning of 1994 are as follows:

1994 and 1995	50%
1996 and 1997	40%
1998 and later	30%

Folsom is expected to report taxable income through 1999. All deferred taxes relate to a single temporary difference.

Instructions
(a) Calculate the amount of deferred income taxes that should be reported on Folsom's balance sheet at December 31, 1995.
(b) Prepare the journal entry to record income tax expense, deferred income taxes, and income taxes payable for 1995.
(c) Draft the income tax expense section of the income statement beginning with the line "Income before income taxes," assuming pretax financial income for 1995 is $354,000.

E20-23 (Two Differences, One Rate, Beginning Deferred Balance, Compute Pretax Financial Income) Benjamin Harrison Co. establishes a $100 million liability at the end of 1996 for the estimated costs of closing of two of its manufacturing facilities. All related closing costs will be paid and deducted on the tax return in 1997. Also, at the end of 1996, the company has $50 million of temporary differences due to excess depreciation for tax purposes, $7 million of which will reverse in 1997.

The enacted tax rate for all years is 40%, and the company pays taxes of $60 million on $150 million of taxable income in 1996. Harrison expects to have taxable income in 1997.

Instructions
(a) Determine the deferred taxes to be reported at the end of 1996.
(b) Indicate how the deferred taxes computed in (a) are to be reported on the balance sheet.
(c) Assuming that the only deferred tax account at the beginning of 1996 was a deferred tax liability of $10,000,000, draft the income tax expense portion of the income statement for 1996 beginning with the line "Income before income taxes." (*Hint:* You must first compute (1) the amount of temporary difference underlying the beginning $10,000,000 deferred tax liability, then (2) the amount of temporary differences originating or reversing during the year, then (3) the amount of pretax financial income.)

E20-24 (Two Differences, No Beginning Deferred Taxes, Multiple Rates) Levi Morton Inc., in its first year of operations, has the following differences between the book basis and tax basis of its assets and liabilities at the end of 1995.

	Book Basis	Tax Basis
Equipment (net)	$400,000	$340,000
Estimated warranty liability	$200,000	$ –0–

It is estimated that the warranty liability will be settled in 1996. The difference in equipment (net) will result in taxable amounts of $20,000 in 1996, $30,000 in 1997, and $10,000 in 1998. The company has taxable income of $550,000 in 1995. As of the beginning of 1995, its enacted tax rate is 34% for 1995–1997, and 30% for 1998. Morton expects to report taxable income through 1998.

Instructions
  (a) Prepare the journal entry to record income tax expense, deferred income taxes, and income tax payable for 1995.
  (b) Indicate how deferred income taxes will be reported on the balance sheet at the end of 1995.

E20-25 (Depreciation, Temporary Difference Tracked over 5 Years) Caroline Scott Co. purchased depreciable assets costing $900,000 on January 2, 1994. For tax purposes, the company uses the elective straight-line depreciation method over the recovery period of 3 years. (*Hint:* The half-year convention must be used on these assets.) For financial reporting purposes, the company uses straight-line depreciation over 5 years. The enacted tax rate is 34% for all years. This depreciation difference is the only temporary difference the company has. Assume that Scott has taxable income of $240,000 in each of the years 1994–1998.

Instructions
Determine the amount of deferred income taxes and indicate where it should be reported in the balance sheet for each year from 1994 to 1998.

E20-26 (Two Temporary Differences, Multiple Rates, Future Taxable Income) Garret Hobart Inc. has two temporary differences at the end of 1995. The first difference stems from installment sales and the second one results from the accrual of a loss contingency. Hobart's accounting department has developed a schedule of future taxable and deductible amounts related to these temporary differences as follows:

	1996	1997	1998	1999
Taxable amounts	$40,000	$50,000	$60,000	$80,000
Deductible amounts		(15,000)	(19,000)	
	$40,000	$35,000	$41,000	$80,000

As of the beginning of 1995, the enacted tax rate is 34% for 1995 and 1996 and 40% for 1997–2000. At the beginning of 1995 the company had no deferred income taxes on its balance sheet. Taxable income for 1995 is $500,000. Taxable income is expected in all future years.

Instructions
  (a) Prepare the journal entry to record income tax expense, deferred income taxes, and income taxes payable for 1995.
  (b) Indicate how deferred income taxes would be classified on the balance sheet at the end of 1995.

E20-27 (Two Differences, One Rate, First Year) The differences between the book basis and tax basis of the assets and liabilities of Niles Corporation at the end of 1995 are presented below:

	Book Basis	Tax Basis
Accounts receivable	$50,000	$-0-
Litigation liability	10,000	-0-

It is estimated that the litigation liability will be settled in 1996. The difference in accounts receivable will result in taxable amounts of $30,000 in 1996 and $20,000 in 1997. The company has taxable income of $350,000 in 1995 and is expected to have taxable income in each of the following 2 years. Its enacted tax rate is 34% for all years. This is the company's first year of operations. The operating cycle of the business is two years.

Instructions
  (a) Prepare the journal entry to record income tax expense, deferred income taxes, and income tax payable for 1995.
  (b) Indicate how deferred income taxes will be reported on the balance sheet at the end of 1995.

E20-28 (NOL Carryback and Carryforward, Valuation Account Versus No Valuation Account) Ida Saxton Inc. reports the following pretax income (loss) for both financial reporting purposes and tax purposes (assume the carryback provision is used for a net operating loss):

Year	Pretax Income (Loss)	Tax Rate
1994	$120,000	34%
1995	90,000	34%
1996	(280,000)	40%
1997	220,000	40%

The tax rates listed were all enacted by the beginning of 1994.

Instructions
  (a) Prepare the journal entries for the years 1994–1997 to record income tax expense (benefit) and income tax payable (refundable) and the tax effects of the loss carryback and carryforward, assuming that

at the end of 1996 the benefits of the loss carryforward are judged more likely than not to be realized in the future.

(b) Using the assumption in (a), prepare the income tax section of the 1996 income statement beginning with the line "Operating loss before income taxes."

(c) Prepare the journal entries for 1996 and 1997, assuming that based on the weight of available evidence, it is more likely than not that one-fourth of the benefits of the carryforward will not be realized.

(d) Using the assumption in (c), prepare the income tax section of the 1996 income statement beginning with the line "Operating loss before income taxes."

E20-29 (NOL Carryback and Carryforward, Valuation Account Needed) William Jennings Bryan Inc. reports the following pretax income (loss) for both book and tax purposes (assume the carryback provision is used where possible for a net operating loss):

Year	Pretax Income (Loss)	Tax Rate
1994	$120,000	40%
1995	90,000	40%
1996	(280,000)	50%
1997	120,000	50%

The tax rates listed were all enacted by the beginning of 1994.

Instructions

(a) Prepare the journal entries for years 1994–1997 to record income tax expense (benefit) and income tax payable (refundable) and the tax effects of the loss carryback and carryforward, assuming that based on the weight of available evidence, it is more likely than not that one-half of the benefits of the carryforward will not be realized.

(b) Prepare the income tax section of the 1996 income statement beginning with the line "Operating loss before income taxes."

(c) Prepare the income tax section of the 1997 income statement beginning with the line "Income before income taxes."

E20-30 (Intraperiod Allocation, Two Rates) In 1996 Theodore Roosevelt Co. has a loss from continuing operations of $2,000,000 and an extraordinary gain of $2,800,000 that is a capital gain for tax purposes. Taxable income and pretax financial income are the same. The tax rate is 40% on ordinary income and 30% on capital gains for all periods.

Instructions

Indicate how income taxes would be reported on the income statement for 1996 by drafting the bottom portion of the statement, beginning with the line "Loss from continuing operations."

PROBLEMS

P20-1 (Four Differences, Beginning Deferred Balance, One Rate) At December 31, 1995, the Versailles Corporation had a temporary difference (related to depreciation) and reported a related deferred tax liability of $40,000 on its balance sheet. At December 31, 1996, Versailles has four temporary differences. An analysis of these reveals the following:

Temporary Difference	Future Taxable (Deductible) Amounts		
	1997	1998	Later Years
1. Use of straight-line depreciation for accounting purposes and accelerated depreciation for tax purposes	$ 80,000	$110,000	$380,000
2. Royalties collected in advance; recognized when earned for accounting purposes and when received for tax purposes	(190,000)	—	—
3. Various expenses accrued when incurred for accounting purposes; recognized for tax purposes when paid	(45,000)	—	—
4. Recognition of gain on installment sales during the period of sale for accounting purposes and during the period of collection for tax purposes	138,000	105,000	—
	$ (17,000)	$215,000	$380,000

The tax rate for all years is 40%. Assume that the company has income taxes of $180,000 due per the tax return for 1996. The installment receivable collectible in 1998 is classified as noncurrent.

Instructions

(a) Indicate the manner in which deferred income taxes should be presented on Versailles Corporation's December 31, 1996, balance sheet.

(b) Compute taxable income for 1996.

(c) Compute pretax financial income for 1996.

(d) Draft the income tax section of the 1996 income statement, beginning with the line "Income before income taxes."

P20-2 (One Temporary Difference, Tracked for 4 Years, One Permanent Difference, Change in Rate) The pretax financial income of Alice Company differs from its taxable income throughout each of 4 years as follows:

Year	Pretax Financial Income	Taxable Income	Tax Rate
1996	$280,000	$180,000	34%
1997	320,000	225,000	40%
1998	350,000	270,000	40%
1999	420,000	580,000	40%

Pretax financial income for each year includes a nondeductible expense of $30,000 (never deductible for tax purposes). The remainder of the difference between pretax financial income and taxable income in each period is due to one depreciation temporary difference. No deferred income taxes existed at the beginning of 1996.

Instructions

(a) Prepare journal entries to record income taxes in all 4 years. Assume that the change in the tax rate to 40% was not enacted until the beginning of 1997.

(b) Draft the income tax section of the income statement for 1997.

P20-3 (Second Year of Depreciation Difference, Two Differences, Single Rate, Extraordinary Item) The following information has been obtained for the Edith Carow Corporation.

1. Prior to 1995, taxable income and pretax financial income were identical.
2. Pretax financial income is $1,700,000 in 1995 and $1,400,000 in 1996.
3. On January 1, 1995, equipment costing $1,000,000 is purchased. It is to be depreciated on a straight-line basis over 5 years for tax purposes and over 8 years for financial reporting purposes. (*Hint:* Use the half-year convention for tax purposes.)
4. Interest of $60,000 was earned on tax-exempt municipal obligations in 1996.
5. Included in 1996 pretax financial income is an extraordinary gain of $200,000, which is fully taxable.
6. The tax rate is 40% for all periods.
7. Taxable income is expected in all future years.

Instructions

(a) Compute taxable income and income tax payable for 1996.

(b) Prepare the journal entry to record 1996 income tax expense, income tax payable, and deferred taxes.

(c) Prepare the bottom portion of Carow's 1996 income statement, beginning with "Income before income taxes and extraordinary item."

(d) Indicate how deferred income taxes should be presented on the December 31, 1996, balance sheet.

P20-4 (Multiple Rates, Future Losses versus Future Income) Panama Co. started operations in 1995. A reconciliation of its pretax financial income to its taxable income for 1995 is as follows:

Pretax financial income	$24,000,000
Litigation accrual for book purposes	8,000,000
Excess depreciation for tax purposes	(3,000,000)
Taxable income	$29,000,000

As of the beginning of 1995, enacted tax rates are 34% for 1995 and 1996, and 40% for all subsequent years. It is estimated that the litigation accrual will be settled in 2000 and that the temporary difference due to the excess depreciation for tax purposes will reverse equally over the 3-year period from 1996 to 1998.

Instructions

(a) Determine the income tax payable, deferred income taxes, and income tax expense to be reported for 1995 assuming that taxable income is expected in all future years.

(b) Classify the deferred income taxes computed in (a) into current and noncurrent components. Explain where the deferred taxes should appear on the balance sheet.

(c) Determine the income tax payable, deferred income taxes, and income tax expense for 1995 assuming that net operating losses are expected to appear on tax returns for 1996 through 2000 and taxable income is very likely for 2001 and later years.

(d) Classify the deferred income taxes computed in (c) into current and noncurrent components. Explain where the deferred taxes should appear on the balance sheet.

P20-5 (Actual NOL Without Valuation Account) William Taft Inc. reported the following pretax income (loss) and related tax rates during the years 1991–1997:

	Pretax Income (loss)	Tax Rate
1991	$ 40,000	30%
1992	25,000	30%
1993	60,000	30%
1994	80,000	45%
1995	(200,000)	50%
1996	60,000	40%
1997	90,000	20%

Pretax financial income (loss) and taxable income (loss) were the same for all years since Taft began business. The taxes from 1994 to 1997 were enacted in 1994.

Instructions

(a) Prepare the journal entries for the years 1995–1997 to record income tax payable (refundable), income tax expense (benefit), and the tax effects of the loss carryback and carryforward. Assume that Taft elects the carryback provision where possible and expects to realize the benefits of any loss carryforward in the year that immediately follows the loss year.

(b) Indicate the effect the 1995 entry(ies) has on the December 31, 1995 balance sheet.

(c) Indicate how the bottom portion of the income statement, starting with "Operating loss before income taxes," would be reported in 1995.

(d) Indicate how the bottom portion of the income statement, starting with "Income before income taxes," would be reported in 1996.

P20-6 (Three Temporary Differences, Multiple Rates, Future Losses Versus Future Income) The following facts apply to the James Sherman Company.

1. 1995 is Sherman's first year of operations.
2. Tax rates enacted by the end of 1995 are as follows:

1995	35%
1996 and 1997	30%
1998 and later	25%

3. For 1995, Sherman has pretax financial income of $80,000 and taxable income of $60,000.
4. Temporary differences existing at the end of 1995 are as follows:

Installment sale difference (taxable in 1996)	$30,000
Depreciation difference (see details below)	10,000
Estimated expenses (deductible in 2001)	(20,000)
Net temporary difference	$20,000

5. The temporary difference related to depreciable assets will result in the following future taxable (deductible) amounts:

1996	$(90,000)
1997	60,000
1998	40,000
	$10,000

Instructions

(a) Assuming Sherman expects to report taxable income in all future years, do the following:
   1. Compute the amount of deferred taxes to appear on the balance sheet at December 31, 1995, and indicate the proper classification(s) (current versus noncurrent and deferred asset versus deferred liability).
   2. Compute the total income tax expense for 1995. Indicate the portion that is current and the portion that is due to deferred tax expense or benefit.
   3. Prepare the journal entry to record income tax payable, deferred taxes, and income tax expense for 1995.

(b) Assuming Sherman expects to report a net operating loss in its 1996 tax return (the benefits of which are expected to be realized through carryback to 1995) and taxable income in 1997 and later years, do the following:
   1. Compute the amount of deferred taxes to appear on the balance sheet at December 31, 1995, and indicate the proper classification(s) (current versus noncurrent and deferred asset versus deferred liability).

2. Compute the total income tax expense for 1995. Indicate the portion that is current and the portion that is due to deferred tax expense or benefit.
3. Prepare the journal entry to record income tax payable, deferred taxes, and income tax expense for 1995.

P20-7 (Two Differences, Two Rates, Future Income Expected) Presented below are two independent situations related to future taxable and deductible amounts resulting from temporary differences existing at December 31, 1995.

1. Helen Herron Co. has developed the following schedule of future taxable and deductible amounts:

	1996	1997	1998	1999	2000
Taxable amounts	$300	$300	$300	$ 300	$300
Deductible amount	—	—	—	(1,400)	—

2. Cherry Blossom Co. has the following schedule of future taxable and deductible amounts:

	1996	1997	1998	1999
Taxable amounts	$300	$300	$ 300	$300
Deductible amount	—	—	(2,000)	—

Both Herron Co. and Blossom Co. have taxable income of $3,000 in 1995 and expect to have taxable income in all future years. The tax rates enacted as of the beginning of 1995 are 30% for 1995–1998 and 40% for years thereafter. All of the underlying temporary differences relate to noncurrent assets and liabilities.

Instructions
For each of these two situations, compute the net amount of deferred income taxes to be reported at the end of 1995 and indicate how it should be classified on the balance sheet.

P20-8 (One Temporary Difference, Tracked Three Years, Change in Rates, Income Statement Presentation) Woodrow Wilson sold an investment on an installment basis. The total gain of $60,000 was reported for financial reporting purposes in the period of sale. The company qualifies to use the installment method for tax purposes. The installment period is three years; one-third of the sale price is collected in the period of sale. The tax rate was 34% in 1995 and 30% in 1996 and 1997. The 30% tax rate was not enacted in law until 1996. The accounting and tax data for the 3 years is shown below.

	Financial Accounting	Tax Return
1995 (34% tax rate)		
Income before temporary difference	$ 70,000	$70,000
Temporary difference	60,000	20,000
Income	$130,000	$90,000
1996 (30% tax rate)		
Income before temporary difference	$ 70,000	$70,000
Temporary difference	–0–	20,000
Income	$ 70,000	$90,000
1997 (30% tax rate)		
Income before temporary difference	$ 70,000	$70,000
Temporary difference	–0–	20,000
Income	$ 70,000	$90,000

Instructions
(a) Prepare the journal entries to record the income tax expense, deferred income taxes, and the income tax payable at the end of each year. No deferred income taxes existed at the beginning of 1995.
(b) Explain how the deferred taxes will appear on the balance sheet at the end of each year. (Assume the Installment Accounts Receivable is classified as a current asset.)
(c) Draft the income tax expense section of the income statement for each year, beginning with the line "Income before income taxes."

P20-9 (Depreciation Difference, Declining Enacted Tax Rates, Future Losses Versus Future Income) Charles Fairbanks Company began operations at the beginning of Year 1. At the beginning of Year 1, Fairbanks Company purchased a truck with a cost of $180,000. For financial reporting purposes, Fairbanks finds it appropriate to depreciate the asset by the straight-line method over a 6-year service life. For tax purposes, Fairbanks uses the MACRS system. The depreciation schedules for both financial reporting and tax purposes follow:

Year	Depreciation for Financial Reporting Purposes	Depreciation for Tax Purposes	Difference
1	$ 30,000	$ 36,000	$ (6,000)
2	30,000	57,600	(27,600)
3	30,000	34,560	(4,560)
4	30,000	20,736	9,264
5	30,000	20,736	9,264
6	30,000	10,368	19,632
	$180,000	$180,000	$ –0–

The difference in depreciation accounting is the only difference Fairbanks has between pretax financial income and taxable income for the six years involved. Tax rates enacted as of the beginning of Year 1 are 40% for Year 1, 30% for Year 2 and Year 3, and 25% for Year 4 and later years.

Instructions

(a) Compute the cumulative temporary difference at the end of each of the six years.

(b) Assuming taxable income of $40,000 for Year 1 and expectations of taxable income for all future years, compute the amount of net deferred taxes to be reported on Fairbanks' balance sheet at the end of Year 1. (Indicate whether the net deferred tax amount is to be classified as an asset or a liability.)

(c) Assuming taxable income for Year 1 of $40,000, expectations of losses for tax purposes for Years 2 and 3 (the benefits of which are expected to be realized through the carryback provision), and expectations of taxable income for Year 4 and later years, compute the amount of net deferred taxes to be reported on Fairbanks' balance sheet at the end of Year 1. (Indicate the proper classification(s) for the deferred taxes calculated.)

(d) Assuming zero taxable income for Year 1, expectations of losses for tax purposes for Years 2 and 3, and expectations of taxable income for Years 4 and later, compute the amount of net deferred taxes to be reported on Fairbanks' balance sheet at the end of Year 1.

P20-10 (Two Differences, 2 Years, Compute Taxable Income and Pretax Financial Income) The following information was disclosed during the audit of Edith Galt Inc.

1.

Year	Amount Due Per Tax Return
1995	$130,000
1996	102,000

2. On January 1, 1995, equipment costing $400,000 is purchased. For financial reporting purposes, the company uses straight-line depreciation over a 5-year life. For tax purposes, the company uses the elective straight-line method over a 5-year life. (*Hint:* For tax purposes, the half-year convention must be used.)

3. In January 1996, $225,000 is collected in advance rental of a building for a 3-year period. The entire $225,000 is reported as taxable income in 1996, but $150,000 of the $225,000 is reported as unearned revenue in 1996 for financial reporting purposes. The remaining amount of unearned revenue is to be earned equally in 1997 and 1998.

4. The tax rate is 40% in 1995 and all subsequent periods. (*Hint:* To find taxable income in 1995 and 1996 the related income tax payable amounts will have to be grossed up.)

5. No temporary differences existed at the end of 1994. Galt expects to report taxable income in each of the next 5 years.

Instructions

(a) Determine the amount to report for deferred income taxes at the end of 1995 and indicate how it should be classified on the balance sheet.

(b) Prepare the journal entry to record income taxes for 1995.

(c) Draft the income tax section of the income statement for 1995 beginning with the line "Income before income taxes." (*Hint:* You must compute taxable income and then combine that with changes in cumulative temporary differences to arrive at pretax financial income.)

(d) Determine the deferred income taxes at the end of 1996 and indicate how they should be classified on the balance sheet.

(e) Prepare the journal entry to record income taxes for 1996.

(f) Draft the income tax section of the income statement for 1996 beginning with the line "Income before income taxes."

CASES

C20-1 (Objectives and Principles for Accounting for Income Taxes) The amount of income taxes due to the government for a period of time is rarely the amount reported on the income statement for that period as income tax expense.

Instructions
- **(a)** Explain the objectives of accounting for income taxes in general purpose financial statements.
- **(b)** Explain the basic principles that are applied in accounting for income taxes at the date of the financial statements to meet the objectives discussed in (a).
- **(c)** List the steps in the annual computation of deferred tax liabilities and assets.

C20-2 (Basic Accounting for Temporary Differences) The A. Lincoln Company appropriately uses the asset-liability method to record deferred income taxes. A. Lincoln reports depreciation expense for certain machinery purchased this year using the modified accelerated cost recovery system (MACRS) for income tax purposes and the straight-line basis for financial reporting purposes. The tax deduction is the larger amount this year.

Lincoln received rent revenues in advance this year. These revenues are included in this year's taxable income. However, for financial reporting purposes, these revenues are reported as unearned revenues, a current liability.

Instructions
- **(a)** What are the principles of the asset-liability approach?
- **(b)** How would Lincoln account for the temporary differences?
- **(c)** How should Lincoln classify the deferred tax consequences of the temporary differences on its balance sheet?

C20-3 (Identify Temporary Differences and Classification Criteria) The asset-liability approach for recording deferred income taxes is an integral part of generally accepted accounting principles.

Instructions
- **(a)** Indicate whether each of the following independent situations should be treated as a temporary difference or a permanent difference and explain why.
  1. Estimated warranty costs (covering a 3-year warranty) are expensed for financial reporting purposes at the time of sale but deducted for income tax purposes when paid.
  2. Depreciation for book and income tax purposes differs because of different bases of carrying the related property, which was acquired in a trade-in. The different bases are a result of different rules used for book and tax purposes to compute the basis of property acquired in a trade-in.
  3. A company properly uses the equity method to account for its 30% investment in another company. The investee pays dividends that are about 10% of its annual earnings.
  4. A company reports a gain on an involuntary conversion of a nonmonetary asset to a monetary asset. The company elects to replace the property within the statutory period using the total proceeds so the gain is not reported on the current year's tax return.
- **(b)** Discuss the nature of the deferred income tax accounts and possible classifications in a company's balance sheet. Indicate the manner in which these accounts are to be reported.

C20-4 (Identify Permanent or Temporary Differences, Future Taxable or Deductible Amounts, Deferred Tax Asset or Liability) Listed below are 16 of the more common items that are treated differently for financial reporting purposes than they are for tax purposes.

1. Excess of charge to accounting records (allowance method) over charge to tax return (direct write-off method) for uncollectible receivables.
2. Excess of accrued pension expense over amount paid.
3. The 80% deduction for dividends received from U.S. corporations.
4. Installment sales of investments are accounted for on the accrual basis for financial reporting purposes and on the installment (cash) basis for tax purposes.
5. Expenses incurred in obtaining tax-exempt income.
6. A trademark acquired directly from the government is capitalized and amortized over subsequent periods for accounting purposes and expensed for tax purposes.
7. Prepaid advertising expense deferred for accounting purposes and deducted as an expense for tax purposes.
8. Premiums paid on life insurance of officers (corporation is the beneficiary).
9. Penalty for filing a late tax return.
10. Proceeds of life insurance policies on lives of officers.
11. Estimated future warranty costs.

12. Fine for polluting.
13. Excess of tax depreciation over accounting depreciation.
14. Tax-exempt interest revenue.
15. Excess of percentage depletion for tax purposes over cost depletion.
16. Estimated gross profit on long-term construction contract is reported in the income statement; some of this gross profit is deferred for tax purposes.

Instructions
For each item above:
  (a) Indicate if it is:
     1. A permanent difference, or
     2. A temporary difference.
  (b) Indicate if it will:
     1. Create future taxable amounts, or
     2. Create future deductible amounts, or
     3. Not affect any future tax returns.
  (c) Indicate if it usually will:
     1. Result in reporting a deferred tax liability, or
     2. Result in reporting a deferred tax asset, or
     3. Not result in reporting any deferred taxes.

C20-5 (Accounting and Classification of Deferred Income Taxes)

Part A
This year Hannibal Hamlin Company has each of the following items in its income statement:

1. Gross profits on installment sales.
2. Revenues on long-term construction contracts.
3. Estimated costs of product warranty contracts.
4. Premiums on officers' life insurance with Hamlin as beneficiary.

Instructions
  (a) Under what conditions would deferred income taxes need to be reported in the financial statements?
  (b) Specify when deferred income taxes would need to be recognized for each of the items above, and indicate the rationale for such recognition.

Part B
Hamlin Company's president has heard that deferred income taxes can be classified in different ways in the balance sheet.

Instructions
Identify the conditions under which deferred income taxes would be classified as a noncurrent item in the balance sheet. What justification exists for such classification?

(AICPA adapted)

C20-6 (Explain Computation of Deferred Tax Liability For Multiple Tax Rates) At December 31, 1996 Mary Todd Corporation has one temporary difference which will reverse and cause taxable amounts in 1997. In 1996 a new tax act set taxes equal to 50% for 1996, 40% for 1997, 35% for 1998 and years thereafter.

Instructions
Explain what circumstances would call for Mary Todd to compute its deferred tax liability at the end of 1996 by multiplying the cumulative temporary difference by:
  (a) 50%.
  (b) 40%.
  (c) 35%.

C20-7 (Explain Future Taxable and Deductible Amounts, How Carryback and Carryforward Affects Deferred Taxes) Andrew Johnson and Eliza McCardle are discussing accounting for income taxes. They are currently studying a schedule of taxable and deductible amounts that will arise in the future as a result of existing temporary differences. The schedule is as follows:

	Current Year	Future Years			
	1996	1997	1998	1999	2000
Taxable income	$700,000				
Taxable amounts		$300,000	$300,000	$ 300,000	$300,000
Deductible amounts				(2,000,000)	
Enacted tax rate	50%	45%	40%	35%	30%

Instructions

(a) Explain the concept of future taxable amounts and future deductible amounts as illustrated in the schedule.

(b) How do the carryback and carryforward provisions affect the reporting of deferred tax assets and deferred tax liabilities?

▶ USING YOUR JUDGMENT ◀

▶ FINANCIAL REPORTING PROBLEM

Refer to the financial statements and other documents of Georgia-Pacific Corporation presented in Appendix 5-A and answer the following questions.

1. In its 1993 Income Statement, Georgia-Pacific reported $41 million of provision for income taxes. This provision was equivalent to a 178.3% effective income tax rate for 1993. What were the factors that affected Georgia-Pacific's effective tax rate to deviate from the statutory federal income tax rate, 35%, for 1993?

2. What were the statements made by Georgia-Pacific in its 1993 annual report regarding the *Statement of Financial Accounting Standards No. 109,* "Accounting for Income Taxes"?

3. Why did Georgia-Pacific report any income tax expense for 1993 when it reported a net loss of $34 million for that year?

▶ WRITING ASSIGNMENT

The pretax financial income (or loss) figures for the Samsonite Company are as follows:

1990	$160,000
1991	250,000
1992	80,000
1993	(160,000)
1994	(380,000)
1995	120,000
1996	80,000

Pretax financial income (or loss) and taxable income (loss) were the same for all years involved. Assume a 50% tax rate for 1990 and 1991 and a 40% tax rate for the remaining years. The client has not yet filed its 1996 federal income tax return.

You are an independent auditor engaged to audit Samsonite's 1996 books. While examining the income tax records, you notice that the controller had recorded a deferred tax asset of $50,000 in 1994. Samsonite was puzzled when the IRS wanted more money in 1995. Samsonite further wished to carry forward the remainder of the tax asset.

Instructions
Find the controller's error by doing the netting process yourself. Then write a short memo explaining what the error is and how it must be corrected. On a second page, provide all journal entries from 1992–1996. Head your work papers with the company's name, the balance sheet date, and a brief description of the memo's contents.

▶ GROUP ASSIGNMENT

(Five Differences, Compute Taxable Income and Deferred Taxes, Draft Income Statement) Pollock Company began operations at the beginning of 1995. The following information pertains to this company.

1. Pretax financial income for 1995 is $100,000.

2. The tax rate enacted for 1995 and future years is 40%.

3. Differences between the 1995 income statement and tax return are listed below:

(a) Warranty expense accrued for financial reporting purposes amounts to $5,000. Warranty deductions per the tax return amount to $2,000.

(b) Gross profit on construction contracts using the percentage-of-completion method for books amounts to $92,000. Gross profit on construction contracts for tax purposes amounts to $62,000.

(c) Depreciation of property, plant, and equipment for financial reporting purposes amounts to $60,000. Depreciation of these assets amounts to $80,000 for the tax return.

(d) A $3,500 fine paid for violation of pollution laws was deducted in computing pretax financial income.

(e) Interest revenue earned on an investment in tax-exempt municipal bonds amounts to $1,400. (Assume (a) is short-term in nature; assume (b) and (c) are long-term in nature.)

4. Taxable income is expected for the next few years.

Instructions

Your instructor will assign one member of the group to serve as recorder and one member to serve as spokesperson. As a group, provide the information for the recorder to prepare responses to the following four requirements. Upon completion of each requirement and before moving on to the next part, the spokesperson will report the group findings to the class.

(a) Compute taxable income for 1995.

(b) Compute the deferred taxes at December 31, 1995, that relate to the temporary differences described above. Clearly label them as deferred tax asset or liability.

(c) Prepare the journal entry to record income tax expense, deferred taxes, and income taxes payable for 1995.

(d) Draft the income tax expense section of the income statement beginning with the line "Income before income taxes."

▶ ETHICS CASE

Sarah Reiter, CPA, is the newly hired director of corporate taxation for Major Electric Incorporated which is a publicly traded corporation. Sarah's first job with ME was the review of the company's accounting practices on deferred income taxes. In doing her review, she noticed differences between tax and book depreciation methods that permitted ME to realize a sizable deferred tax liability on its balance sheet. As a result, ME did not have to report current income tax expenses. Sarah also discovered that ME has an explicit policy of selling off fixed assets before they reversed in the deferred income tax account. This policy, coupled with the rapid expansion of its fixed asset base, allowed ME to "defer" all income taxes payable for several years, even though it has always reported positive earnings and an increasing EPS. Sarah checked with the legal department and found the policy to be legal, but she's uncomfortable with the ethics of it.

Instructions

(a) Why would Major Electric have an explicit policy of selling assets before they reversed in the deferred income tax account?

(b) What are the ethical implications of Major Electric's "deferral" of income taxes?

(c) Who could be harmed by Major Electric's ability to "defer" income taxes payable for several years, despite positive earnings?

(d) As a CPA, what are Sarah Reiter's professional responsibilities in a situation such as this?

CHANGING ACCOUNTING STANDARDS

A visit with
RONALD J. MURRAY

What accounting statements are still with us from the 1970s?

The ones on business combinations, on the equity method of accounting, and a number of others. Prior to *APB 17*, you did not have to amortize goodwill. It was subject to an impairment test, but there was no requirement that you amortize it. *APB 17* put in an amortization period, and as a compromise, settled on not more than 40 years. Today, there are pressures to use shorter periods of time, certainly in high-tech industries. Another one that's still around is *APB 18*, on the equity method of accounting. That one was also fairly controversial. Before that, once your ownership got down below 51%, you were not required to reflect your share of the earnings or losses. *APB 21* dealt with discounting noninterest-bearing receivables and payables. I think today everyone would think that that's axiomatic. What you saw in the statements on the equity method and on discounting was a trend toward recognizing the underlying economics of the transaction.

Inflation was one rule that didn't stick.

There was some concern about whether the inflation statement really reflected the impact of inflation. The question was, if you bought something for $20 and sold it for $25 but then, because of inflation you had to pay $25 to replace it, have you made any money? There were those who said no be-

RONALD J. MURRAY, CPA, is National Director of Accounting and SEC Services for Coopers & Lybrand, one of the "Big Six" accounting firms. He establishes the firm's policy on accounting issues and resolves difficult practice questions from field offices. Murray began his accounting career more than 30 years ago—before the FASB was established. Its predecessor, the Accounting Principles Board, issued general guidelines and met only half a dozen times a year. Murray recalls the establishment of the FASB in 1973 and the controversy it generated—primarily that such a board would become too much of a "think tank," divorced from the business world. That criticism exists to this day.

cause you really ought to measure the cost of the sale at the price it takes to replace what you just sold. Others said if you're in an inflationary period and you can replace the item for $25, then you can probably sell it for $30, so yes, you did make money on the original sale and you're going to make money on the next one. There were disagreements about how the carrying value of assets should be adjusted to reflect inflation.

What were some accounting standards highlights in the 1980s?

There was some attempt to codify foreign currency translation. Let's say you had a German subsidiary and you financed that subsidiary with DM borrowings, and you were in a net asset position, and the value of the DM improved. You were better off economically because you had a net investment in a country whose currency was appreciating in relation to the dollar. But *Statement 8*, the first FASB statement on foreign currency translation, said you had to take a loss even though the economic event you were accounting for was favorable. In 1981, the FASB issued *Statement 52* which remedied the flaws of *Statement 8*.

Accounting for pensions was one of the most controversial statements during that time, wasn't it?

It used to be that the income statement was considered the most important statement. But the matching concept required accruals and deferrals on the balance sheet. The movement has been towards the balance sheet approach, which says we don't want these various accruals and deferrals. The balance sheet should be only real assets and real liabilities—no deferred charges, no accrued liabilities, no attempts to smooth the effect of events that happen in cycles to give you a better measurement of the income statement. The emphasis is moving toward "let's get the right measurement of the financial condition." The balance sheet and the income statement should just be the difference between two successive balance sheets, and if that produces some strange results, then you ought to have some additional disclosure explaining why. With regard to pension accounting, the FASB would have liked to apply a strict balance sheet approach: At any one balance sheet date, you value all the assets in the pension plan, you value your best estimates of your future liabilities; you put that net amount on the balance sheet, do the same thing next year, and the income statement is just the difference. That was too much of a change, and so there is still a lot of smoothing or averaging permitted in measuring pension expense. Not as much as was previously permitted, but a fair amount nevertheless.

In the past few years, we've had income tax accounting, retirement benefits, stock options, and some of these market value issues.

I think the OPEBs (other post-retirement benefits) was something that people should have been accruing all along. *Statement 106* put the accounting for medical benefits on the same footing as the accounting for retirement benefits. You could make an argument that maybe there are some measure-

ment differences, but it's clearly the right accounting.

Income taxes is another good example of the shift from the income statement to the balance sheet. *APB 11*, which was issued in 1970, was clearly income-statement driven. The rule was that you just looked at this year's income statement and figured what your income tax expense would have been had your income statement been your tax return. You provided an amount of deferred taxes, and you left it alone. You didn't try to adjust for changes in tax rates or for any anomalies that this income statement method sometimes created. As the 1980s went on, that was considered to be a real shortcoming, that the number on the balance sheet didn't reflect a real payable or a receivable. *Statement 96* went to the liability approach where you measure what you think your future tax expense will be every year, and your income tax expense doesn't necessarily relate to your operations for the year, but rather the difference between two balance sheets.

Why has accounting trended toward the balance sheet?

My view is that over the course of the past 10–20 years, there has been an increase in the number of business failures, and so it is felt that users of financial statements would be more interested in whether the company could survive. Creditworthiness becomes more important than future stock price. Maybe there is also a feeling that this matching approach allows too much judgment in what is an appropriate accrual or deferral. A balance sheet approach, which has strict definitions of assets and liabilities, takes some of the judgment out of accounting. There's a feeling now that applying judgment is not necessarily a good thing because people don't make their judgments

in the same way, and you get less comparability than if you had a set of prescribed rules.

How do you feel about more prescribed rules as opposed to judgment?

My inclination is towards greater reliance on judgment. I think it's hard to prescribe rules that fit all situations. The more detailed you make the rules, the more the focus is not on complying with the spirit of the rules and on how you can get around the rules.

What are some of the big issues today?

One is the international harmonization of accounting rules. I'm particularly interested in that because I'm on the board of the International Accounting Standards Committee. Business combinations is a good example. There is a wide range of accepted practice. In the U.K. you can write off goodwill on the day of acquisition and not amortize it against income at all. A number of countries do amortize goodwill, over periods that range from 5 to 40 years, and in other countries you don't have to amortize it at all. Looking to the United States, one of the major issues is the accounting for financial instruments and "mark-to-market" accounting. Another one that is getting a lot of attention is restructuring costs. If a company has decided on a course of action that is going to result in the incurrence of restructuring costs that will not have a future benefit, should you record them now? One side would say yes, you should record it at the point of the decision. The other argument, given by the balance sheet people, is that is not enough to make the decision—you have to wait until you have a legal liability.

CHAPTER 21

ACCOUNTING FOR PENSIONS AND POSTRETIREMENT BENEFITS

LEARNING OBJECTIVES

After studying this chapter, you should be able to:

1. Identify types of pension plans and their characteristics.

2. Distinguish between accounting for the employer's pension plan and accounting for the pension fund.

3. Explain alternative measures for valuing the pension obligation.

4. Identify the components of pension expense.

5. Utilize a work sheet for employer's pension plan entries.

6. Describe the amortization of unrecognized prior service costs.

7. Explain the accounting procedure for recognizing unexpected gains and losses.

8. Explain the corridor approach to amortizing unrecognized gains and losses.

9. Explain the recognition of a minimum liability.

10. Describe the reporting requirements for pension plans in financial statements.

*S*ince the late 1800s, many business organizations have been concerned with providing for the retirement of their employees. During recent decades, a marked increase in this concern has resulted in the establishment of private pension plans in most large companies and in many medium- and small-sized ones.

The substantial growth of these plans, both in numbers of employees covered and in dollar amounts of retirement benefits, has increased the significance of pension cost in relation to a company's financial position, results of operations, and cash flows. In 1975, private pension plans covered 27.7 million individuals, paid benefits of $16 billion, and had assets of $211 billion; in 1995, it is estimated, 1.1 million pension plans cover 44.5 million individuals, pay benefits of $106 billion, and have assets in excess of $4 trillion (one-fifth of the total U.S. assets).

Generally accepted accounting principles for accounting by employers for pensions are provided in *FASB Statement No. 87*, "Employers' Accounting for Pension Plans,"[1] issued in 1985. It was one of the most hotly debated subjects that the FASB has examined. The FASB studied the issue for more than 12 years and went down many "blind alleys" before it established a final standard. Although many aspects of the final standard are still controversial, the users of financial statements should benefit from the required information.[2]

INTERNATIONAL INSIGHT

Outside the U.S., private pension plans are less common because many other nations tend to rely on government-sponsored pension plans. Consequently, accounting for defined benefit pension plans is typically a less important issue elsewhere.

---

[1]"Employers' Accounting for Pension Plans," *Statement of Financial Accounting Standards No. 87* (Stamford, Conn.: FASB, 1985).

[2]For an analysis of why pension reform was needed and what the FASB attempted to accomplish through the issuance of *Statement No. 87*, read the article by Paul B. W. Miller, "The New Pension Accounting (Part 1)," *Journal of Accountancy* (January 1987), pp. 98–108.

▶ TYPES OF PENSION PLANS

A **pension plan** is an arrangement whereby an employer provides benefits (payments) to employees after they retire for services they provided while employed. The two most common types of pension arrangements are **defined contribution plans** and **defined benefit plans**.

DEFINED CONTRIBUTION PLAN

In a **defined contribution plan,** the employer agrees to contribute to a pension trust a certain sum each period based on a formula. This formula may consider such factors as age, length of employee service, employer's profits, and compensation level. **Only the employer's contribution is defined;** no promise is made regarding the ultimate benefits paid out to the employees.

The size of the pension benefits that the employee finally collects under the plan depends on the amounts originally contributed to the pension trust, the income accumulated in the trust, and the treatment of forfeitures of funds caused by early terminations of other employees. The amounts originally contributed are usually turned over to an **independent third party trustee** who acts on behalf of the beneficiaries—the participating employees. The trustee assumes ownership of the pension assets and is accountable for their investment and distribution. The trust is separate and distinct from the employer.

The accounting for a defined contribution plan is straightforward. The employee gets the benefit of gain or the risk of loss from the assets contributed to the pension plan. The employer's responsibility is simply to make a contribution each year based on the formula established in the plan. As a result, the employer's annual cost (pension expense) is just the amount that it is obligated to contribute to the pension trust. A liability is reported on the employer's balance sheet only if the contribution has not been made in full, and an asset is reported only if more than the required amount has been contributed.

In addition to pension expense, the only disclosures required by the employer under a defined contribution plan are a plan description, including employee groups covered, the basis for determining contributions, and the nature and effect of significant matters affecting comparability from period to period.[3]

DEFINED BENEFIT PLAN

A **defined benefit plan** defines the benefits that the employee will receive at the time of retirement. The formula that is typically used provides for the benefits to be a function of the employee's years of service and the employee's compensation level when he or she nears retirement. It is necessary to determine what the contribution should be today to meet the pension benefit commitments that will arise at retirement. Many different contribution approaches could be used. Whatever funding method is employed, it should provide enough money at retirement to meet the benefits defined by the plan.

The employees are the beneficiaries of a defined contribution trust, but the employer is the beneficiary of a defined benefit trust. The trust's primary purpose under a defined benefit plan is to safeguard assets and to invest them so that there will be enough to pay the employer's obligation to the employees when they retire. **In form,** the trust is a separate entity; **in substance,** the trust assets and liabilities belong to the employer. That is, **as long as the plan continues, the employer is responsible for the payment of the defined benefits (without regard to what happens in the trust).** Any shortfall in the accumulated assets held by the trust must be made up by the employer. Any excess accumulated in the trust can be recaptured by the employer, either through reduced future funding or through a reversion of funds.

---

[3]"Employers' Accounting for Pension Plans," op cit., pars. 63–66.

The accounting for a defined benefit plan is complex. Because the benefits are defined in terms of uncertain future variables, an appropriate funding pattern must be established to assure that enough funds will be available at retirement to provide the benefits promised. This funding level depends on a number of factors such as turnover, mortality, length of employee service, compensation levels, and interest earnings.

Employers are at risk with defined benefit plans because they must be sure to make enough contributions to meet the cost of benefits that are defined in the plan. The expense recognized each period is not necessarily equal to the cash contribution. Similarly, the liability is controversial because its measurement and recognition relate to unknown future variables. Unfortunately, the accounting issues related to this type of plan are complex. **Our discussion in the following sections primarily deals with defined benefit plans.**[4]

▶ EMPLOYER VERSUS PLAN ACCOUNTING

The subject of pension accounting may be divided and separately treated as **accounting for the employer** and **accounting for the pension fund.** The company or employer is the organization sponsoring the pension plan. It incurs the cost and makes contributions to the pension fund. The fund or plan is the entity that receives the contributions from the employer, administers the pension assets, and makes the benefit payments to the pension recipients (retired employees). The diagram below shows the three entities involved in a pension plan and indicates the flow of cash between them.

OBJECTIVE 2

Distinguish between accounting for employer's pension plan and accounting for the pension fund.

ILLUSTRATION 21-1
Flow of Cash Among Pension Plan Participants

The pension plan above is being **funded:**[5] that is, the employer (company) sets funds aside for future pension benefits by making payments to a funding agency that is responsible for accumulating the assets of the pension fund and for making payments to the recipients as the benefits become due. In an insured plan, the funding agency is an insurance company; in a trust fund plan, the funding agency is a trustee.

Some plans are **contributory;** in these, the employees bear part of the cost of the stated benefits or voluntarily make payments to increase their benefits. Other plans are **noncontributory,** in which the employer bears the entire cost. Companies generally design **qualified pension plans** in accord with federal income tax requirements that permit **deductibility of the employer's contributions to the pension fund and tax-free status of earnings from pension fund assets.**

---

[4]Over a recent one-year period, the IRS issued 370 defined benefit plan approval letters covering 857,000 employees—more than 2,300 employees per plan. In this same period, the IRS issued 11,853 defined contribution plan approval letters covering 1.6 million employees—only 135 employees per plan. The recordkeeping requirements for the defined benefit plans are onerous and, therefore, companies have become more reluctant to use these plans. Also, the benefits in a defined contribution plan are easier for the employee to understand; they tend to prefer them over the defined benefit plan. In terms of total assets, the defined benefit plans have substantially more assets.

[5]When used as a verb, **fund** means to pay to a funding agency (as to fund future pension benefits or to fund pension cost). Used as a noun, it refers to assets accumulated in the hands of a funding agency (trustee) for the purpose of meeting pension benefits when they become due.

The need for proper administration of and sound accounting for pension funds becomes apparent when one appreciates the size of these funds. Listed below are the pension fund assets and related stockholders' equity of four major companies as of December 31, 1993.

ILLUSTRATION 21-2
Big-Company Pension
Fund Assets

Company	Size of Pension Fund	Total Stockholders' Equity
General Motors	$51,025,600,000	$ 5,597,500,000
Eastman Kodak	6,278,000,000	3,356,000,000
Sears Roebuck & Co.	5,618,000,000	11,664,100,000
Campbell Soup	1,035,000,000	1,704,000,000

Pension expense is a substantial percentage of total labor expense for many companies. For example, Bethlehem Steel's percentage at one time was 11.1%, Exxon's 12.8%, and General Motors' 10.8%.[6]

The fund should be a separate legal and accounting entity for which a set of books is maintained and financial statements are prepared. Maintaining books and records and preparing financial statements for the fund, known as "accounting for employee benefit plans," is not the subject of this chapter.[7] Instead this chapter is devoted to the pension accounting and reporting problems of the employer as the sponsor of a pension plan.

▶ THE ROLE OF ACTUARIES IN PENSION ACCOUNTING

Because the problems associated with pension plans involve complicated actuarial considerations, **actuaries** are engaged to ensure that the plan is appropriate for the employee group covered.[8] Actuaries are individuals who are trained through a long and rigorous certification program to assign probabilities to future events and their financial effects. The insurance industry employs actuaries to assess risks and to advise on the setting of premiums and other aspects of insurance policies. Employers rely heavily on actuaries for assistance in developing, implementing, and funding pension plans.

It is actuaries who make predictions (called actuarial assumptions) of mortality rates, employee turnover, interest and earnings rates, early retirement frequency, future salaries, and any other factors necessary to operate a pension plan. They assist by computing the various pension measures that affect the financial statements, such as the pension obligation, the annual cost of servicing the plan, and the cost of amendments to the plan. In summary, accounting for defined benefit pension plans is highly reliant upon information and measurements provided by actuaries.

---

[6]Some have suggested that pension funds are the new owners of America's giant corporations. At the end of 1993, pension funds (private and public) held or owned approximately 25% of the market value of corporate stock outstanding and accounted for 32% of the daily trading volume on the New York Stock Exchange. The enormous size (and the social significance) of these funds is staggering.

[7]The FASB issued a separate standard covering the accounting and reporting for employee benefit plans. "Accounting and Reporting by Defined Benefit Plans," *Statement of Financial Accounting Standards No. 35* (Stamford, Conn.: FASB, 1979).

[8]An actuary's primary purpose is to ensure that the company has established an appropriate funding pattern to meet its pension obligations. This computation entails the development of a set of assumptions and continued monitoring of these assumptions to assure their realism. That the general public has little understanding of what an actuary does is illustrated by the following excerpt from *The Wall Street Journal:* "A polling organization once asked the general public what an actuary was and received among its more coherent responses the opinion that it was a place where you put dead actors."

▶ THE PENSION OBLIGATION (LIABILITY)

In accounting for pension plans, the question eventually arises, "What is the amount of the employer's liability and the amount of the pension obligation that should be reported in the financial statements?" Attempting to answer this question has produced much controversy. Most agree that an employer's **pension obligation** is the deferred compensation obligation it has to its employees for their service under the terms of the pension plan, but there are alternative ways of measuring it.[9]

ALTERNATIVE MEASURES OF THE LIABILITY

One measure of the obligation is to base it only on the benefits vested to the employees. **Vested benefits** are those that the employee is entitled to receive even if the employee renders no additional services under the plan. Under most pension plans, a certain minimum number of years of service to the employer is required before an employee achieves vested benefits status. The **vested benefits obligation** is computed using current salary levels and includes only vested benefits.

OBJECTIVE 3

Explain alternative measures for valuing the pension obligation.

Another measure of the obligation is to base the computation of the deferred compensation amount on all years of service performed by employees under the plan—both vested and nonvested—using **current salary levels.** This measurement of the pension obligation is called the **accumulated benefit obligation.**

A third measure bases the computation of the deferred compensation amount on both vested and nonvested service **using future salaries.** This measurement of the pension obligation is called the **projected benefit obligation.** Because future salaries are expected to be higher than current salaries, this approach results in the largest measurement of the pension obligation.

The choice between these measures is critical because it affects the amount of the pension liability and the annual pension expense reported. The diagram in Illustration 21-3 presents the differences in these three measurements. Regardless of the approach used, the estimated future benefits to be paid are discounted to present value.

Minor changes in the interest rate used to discount pension benefits can dramatically affect the measurement of the employer's obligation. For example, a 1% decrease in the discount rate can increase pension liabilities 15%. Discount rates used to measure the pension liability are required to be changed at each measurement date to reflect current interest rates.

Which of these approaches did the profession adopt? **In general, the profession adopted the projected benefit obligation, which is the present value of vested and nonvested benefits accrued to date based on employees' future salary levels.**[10] As you will learn later, however, the profession uses the accumulated benefit obligation in certain situations.

INTERNATIONAL INSIGHT

Whereas the U.S. requires companies to base pension expense on estimated future compensation levels, Germany and Japan do not.

Those critical of the projected benefit obligation argue that using future salary levels is tantamount to adding future obligations to existing ones. Those in favor of the projected benefit obligation contend that a promise by an employer to pay benefits based on a percentage of the employees' future salary is far different from a promise to pay

---

[9]One measure of the pension obligation is to determine the amount that the Pension Benefit Guaranty Corporation would require the employer to pay if it defaulted (this amount is limited to 30 percent of the employer's net worth). The accounting profession rejected this approach for financial reporting because it is too hypothetical and ignores the going concern concept.

[10]When the term "present value of benefits" is used throughout this chapter, it really means the actuarial present value of benefits. Actuarial present value is the amount payable adjusted to reflect the time value of money **and** the probability of payment (by means of decrements for events such as death, disability, withdrawals, or retirement) between the present date and the expected date of payment. For simplicity, we will use the term "present value" instead of "actuarial present value" in our discussion.

ILLUSTRATION 21-3
Different Measures of the
Pension Obligation

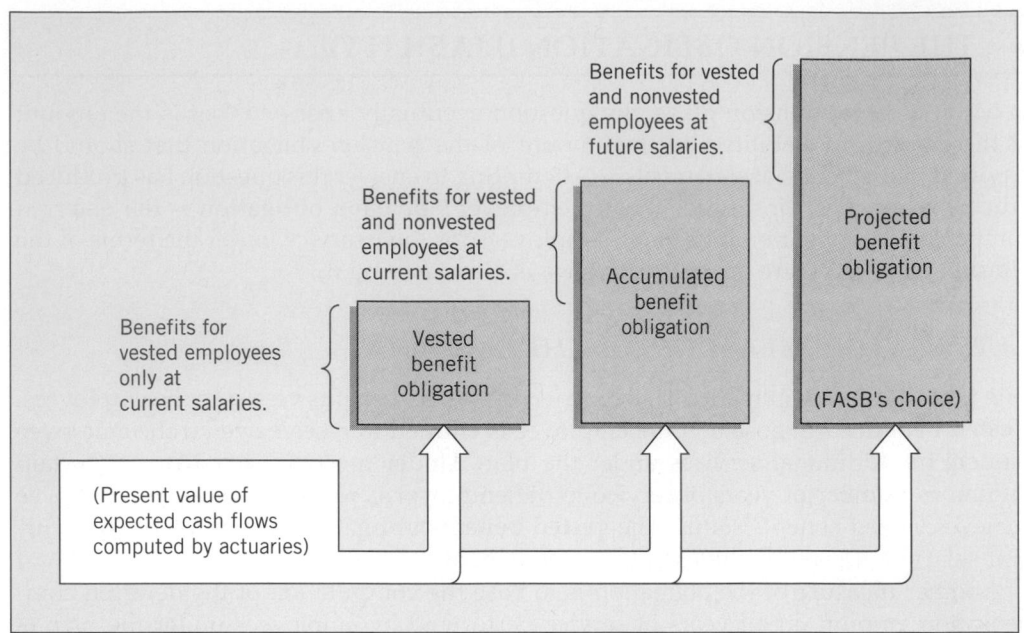

a percentage of their current salary, and such a difference should be reflected in the pension liability and pension expense.

CAPITALIZATION VS. NONCAPITALIZATION

Prior to issuance of *FASB Statement No. 87*, accounting for pension plans followed a **noncapitalization approach.** Noncapitalization, often referred to as **off-balance-sheet financing,** was achieved because the balance sheet reported an asset or liability for the pension plan arrangement only if the amount actually funded during the year by the employer was different from the amount reported by the employer as pension expense for the year. As the employees worked during each year, the employer incurred pension cost and became obligated to fund that amount by making cash payments to the pension fund (viewed as a third-party trust). When the trust paid benefits to retirees, the employer recorded no entries because its own assets or liabilities were not reduced.

The accounting profession has been tending toward a **capitalization approach,** supporting the **economic substance** of the pension plan arrangement over its legal form. Under this view, the employer has a liability for pension benefits that it has promised to pay for employee services already performed. As pension expense is incurred—as the employees work—the employer's liability increases. Funding the plan has no effect on the amount of the liability; only the employer's promises and the employee's services affect the liability. The pension liability is reduced through the payment of benefits to retired employees.

Under a defined benefit plan, if additional funds are necessary to meet the pension obligation, the source is the employer. From the capitalization point of view, under-funding does not increase the liability, and funding more than the amount expensed does not create a prepaid expense. Capitalization means measuring and reporting in the financial statements a fair representation of the employers' pension assets and liabilities.

The FASB in *Statement No. 87* adopted an approach that leans toward capitalization. But, proposals to adopt a full capitalization (total accrual) approach, requiring the recognition of balance sheet items where none existed before, were strongly opposed. *FASB Statement No. 87* **represents a compromise that combines some of the features of capitalization with some of the features of noncapitalization.** As we will learn in more detail later in this chapter, some elements of the pension plan are not recognized in the accounts and the financial statements (that is, not capitalized).

Because of this, the accounting for pensions, outlined in *Statement No. 87* and demonstrated in the balance of this chapter, is not perfectly logical, totally complete, or conceptually sound. The fault is not entirely that of the FASB. Because of the financial complexity of defined benefit pensions, many well-intentioned, competent people cannot agree on the nature of such an arrangement and what exists in it. As a result, they are unlikely to agree on how to account for it. Because of the difficulties in gaining a consensus among the Board members and support from preparers as well as users of financial statements, *Statement No. 87* is riddled with compromises that make it less than an ideal application of the capitalization method. In its defense, however, *Statement No. 87* is a great improvement over previous accounting pronouncements and represents a first step toward a conceptually sound approach to employers' accounting for pension plans.

▶ COMPONENTS OF PENSION EXPENSE

There is broad agreement that pension cost should be accounted for on the **accrual basis.**[11] The profession recognizes that **accounting for pension plans requires measurement of the cost and its identification with the appropriate time periods.** The determination of pension cost, however, is extremely complicated because it is a function of the following components:

OBJECTIVE 4

Identify the components of pension expense.

Service Cost. The expense caused by the increase in pension benefits payable (the projected benefit obligation) to employees because of their services rendered during the current year. Actuaries compute **service cost** as the present value of the new benefits earned by employees during the year.

Interest on the Liability. Because a pension is a deferred compensation arrangement, there is a time value of money factor. As a result, it is recorded on a discounted basis. **Interest expense accrues each year on the projected benefit obligation just as it does on any discounted debt.** The accountant receives help from the actuary in selecting the interest rate, called for this purpose the **settlement rate.**

Actual Return on Plan Assets. The return earned by the accumulated pension fund assets in a particular year is relevant in measuring the net cost to the employer of sponsoring an employee pension plan. Therefore, **annual pension expense should be adjusted for interest and dividends that accumulate within the fund as well as increases and decreases in the market value of the fund assets.**

Amortization of Unrecognized Prior Service Cost. Pension plan amendments (including initiation of a pension plan) often include provisions to increase benefits (in rare situations to decrease benefits) for employee service provided in prior years. Because plan amendments are granted with the expectation that the employer will realize economic benefits in future periods, **the cost (prior service cost) of providing these retroactive benefits is allocated to pension expense in the future, specifically to the remaining service-years of the affected employees.**

Gain or Loss. Volatility in pension expense can be caused by sudden and large changes in the market value of plan assets and by changes in the projected benefit obligation (which changes when actuarial assumptions are modified or when actual experience differs from expected experience). Two items comprise this gain or loss: (1) the difference between the actual return and the expected return on plan assets and (2) amortization of the unrecognized net gain or loss from previous periods. This computation is complex and will be discussed later in the chapter.

UNDERLYING CONCEPT

The matching concept and the definition of a liability justify accounting for pension cost on the accrual basis. This requires recording an expense when the future benefits are earned by the employees and recognizing an existing obligation to pay pensions later based on current services received.

---

[11]Until the mid-1960s, with few exceptions, companies applied the **cash basis** of accounting to pension plans by recognizing the amount paid in a particular accounting period as the pension expense for the period. The problem was that the amount paid or funded in a fiscal period depended on financial management and was too often discretionary. For example, funding could be based on the availability of cash, the level of earnings, or other factors unrelated to the requirements of the plan. Application of the cash basis made it possible to manipulate the amount of pension expense appearing in the income statement simply by varying the cash paid to the pension fund.

In summary, then, the **components of pension expense** and their effect are as follows:

Service cost (increases pension expense).

Interest on the liability (increases pension expense).

Actual return on plan assets (generally decreases pension expense).

Amortization of unrecognized prior service cost (generally increases pension expense).

Gain or loss (decreases or increases pension expense).

The components of pension expense are exhibited in the diagram below.

ILLUSTRATION 21-4
**Components of Annual
Pension Expense**

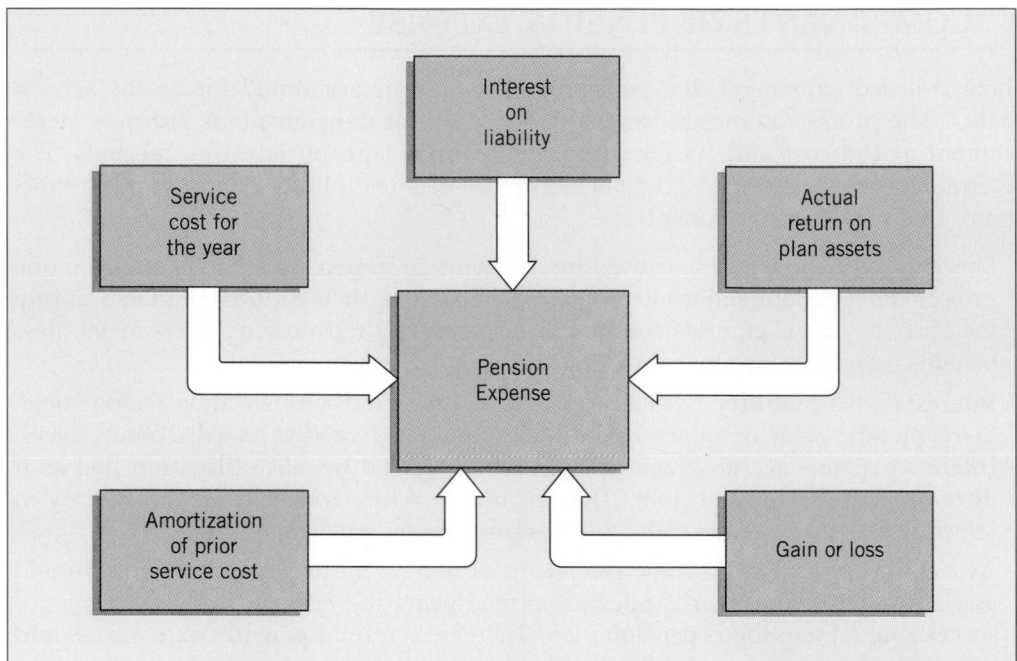

SERVICE COST

In *FASB Statement No. 87,* the Board states that the **service cost** component recognized in a period **should be determined as the actuarial present value of benefits attributed by the pension benefit formula to employee service during the period.** That is, the actuary predicts the additional benefits that must be paid under the plan's benefit formula as a result of the employees' current year's service and then discounts the cost of those future benefits back to their present value.

The Board concluded that **future compensation levels had to be considered in measuring the present obligation and periodic pension expense if the plan benefit formula incorporated them.** In other words, the present obligation resulting from a promise to pay a benefit of 1% of an employee's **final pay** is different from an employer's promise to pay 1% of **current pay.** To ignore this fact would be to ignore an important aspect of pension expense. Thus, the **benefits/years-of-service actuarial method** is the approach adopted by the FASB.

Some object to this determination, arguing that a company should have more freedom to select an expense recognition pattern. Others believe that incorporating future salary increases into current pension expense is accounting for events that have not happened yet. They argue that if the plan were terminated today, only liabilities for accumulated benefits would have to be paid. **Nevertheless the Board indicates that the projected benefit obligation provides a more realistic measure on a going concern basis of the employer's obligation under the plan and, therefore, should be used as the basis for determining service cost.**

INTEREST ON THE LIABILITY

The second component of pension expense is **interest on the liability, or interest expense.** As indicated earlier, a pension is a deferred compensation arrangement under which this element of wages is deferred and a liability is created. Because the liability is not paid until maturity, it is recorded on a discounted basis and accrues interest over the life of the employee. **The interest component is the interest for the period on the projected benefit obligation outstanding during the period.** The FASB did not address the question of how often to compound the interest cost. To simplify our illustrations and problem materials, we use a simple interest computation, applying it to the beginning-of-the-year balance of the projected benefit liability.

How is the interest rate determined? The Board states that the assumed discount rate should **reflect the rates at which pension benefits could be effectively settled (settlement rates).** In determining these rates, it is appropriate to look to available information about rates implicit in current prices of annuity contracts that could be used to effect settlement of the obligation. (Under an annuity contract an insurance company unconditionally guarantees to provide specific pension benefits to specific individuals in return for a fixed consideration or premium.) Other rates of return on high-quality fixed-income investments might also be employed.[12]

ACTUAL RETURN ON PLAN ASSETS

Pension plan assets are usually investments in stocks, bonds, other securities, and real estate that are held to earn a reasonable return, generally at minimum risk. Pension plan assets are increased by employer contributions and actual returns on pension plan assets; they are decreased by benefits paid to retired employees. As indicated, the actual return earned on these assets increases the fund balance and correspondingly reduces the employer's net cost of providing employees' pension benefits. That is, the higher the actual return on the pension plan assets, the less the employer has to contribute eventually and, therefore the less pension expense that needs to be reported.

The actual return on the plan assets is the increase in pension funds from interest, dividends, and realized and unrealized changes in the fair market value of the plan assets. The actual return is computed by adjusting the change in the plan assets for the effects of contributions during the year and benefits paid out during the year. The following equation, or a variation thereof, can be used to compute the actual return:

$$\text{Actual Return} = \left(\begin{array}{c} \text{Plan} \\ \text{Assets} \\ \text{Ending} \\ \text{Balance} \end{array} - \begin{array}{c} \text{Plan} \\ \text{Assets} \\ \text{Beginning} \\ \text{Balance} \end{array} \right) - \Big(\text{Contributions} - \text{Benefits Paid} \Big)$$

ILLUSTRATION 21-5
Equation for Computing Actual Return

Stated another way, the actual return on plan assets is the difference between the **fair value of the plan assets** at the beginning of the period and the end of the period, adjusted for contributions and benefit payments. Computation of the actual return on the basis of the equation above is illustrated below using some assumed amounts:

Fair value of plan assets at end of period		$5,000,000
Deduct: Fair value of plan assets at beginning of period		4,200,000
Increase/decrease in fair value of plan assets		800,000
Deduct: Contributions to plan during period	$500,000	
Less benefits paid during period	300,000	200,000
Actual return on plan assets		$ 600,000

ILLUSTRATION 21-6
Computation of Actual Return on Plan Assets

---

[12]Prior to the implementation of *FASB Statement No. 87*, wide variances in interest rates for pension plans appeared in corporate financial reports. For example, in one year the interest rates used by a number of large companies varied by as much as 9.5%.

If the actual return on the plan assets is positive (gain) during the period, it is subtracted in the computation of pension expense. If the actual return is negative (loss) during the period, it is added in the computation of pension expense.

▶ USING A PENSION WORK SHEET

Before covering in detail the other pension expense components (amortization of unrecognized prior service cost and gains and losses) which seem to get progressively more complex, we will illustrate the basic accounting entries for the first three components: (1) service cost, (2) interest on the liability, and (3) actual return on plan assets.

Important to accounting for pensions under *Statement No. 87* is the fact that **several significant items of the pension plan are unrecognized in the accounts and in the financial statements.** Among the compromises the FASB made in issuing *Statement No. 87* was the nonrecognition (noncapitalization) of the following pension items:

1. Projected benefit obligation.
2. Pension plan assets.
3. Unrecognized prior service costs.
4. Unrecognized net gain or loss.

OBJECTIVE 5

Utilize a work sheet for employer's pension plan entries.

As discussed later, the employer is required to **disclose in notes** to the financial statements all of these four noncapitalized items, but they are not recognized in the body of the financial statements. In addition, the exact amount of these items must be known at all times because they are used in the computation of annual pension expense. Therefore, **in order to track these off-balance-sheet pension items, memo entries and accounts have to be maintained outside the formal general ledger accounting system.** A work sheet unique to pension accounting will be utilized to record both the formal entries and the memo entries to keep track of all the employer's relevant pension plan items and components.[13]

The format of the **pension work sheet** is shown below:

ILLUSTRATION 21-7
Basic Format of Pension Work Sheet

	Pension Work Sheet					
	General Journal Entries				Memo Record	
Items	Annual Pension Expense	Cash	Prepaid/ Accrued Cost		Projected Benefit Obligation	Plan Assets

The left-hand "General Journal Entries" columns of the work sheet record entries in the formal general ledger accounts. The right-hand "Memo Record" columns maintain balances on the unrecognized (noncapitalized) pension items. On the first line of the work sheet, the beginning balances (if any) are recorded. Subsequently, transactions and events related to the pension plan are recorded, using debits and credits and using both sets of records as if they were one for recording the entries. For each transaction or event, the debits must equal the credits. The balance in the Prepaid/Accrued Cost column should equal the net balance in the memo record.

---

[13]The use of this pension entry work sheet is recommended and illustrated by Paul B. W. Miller, "The New Pension Accounting (Part 2)," *Journal of Accountancy* (February 1987), pp. 86–94.

▶ 1995 ENTRIES AND WORK SHEET

To illustrate the use of a work sheet and how it helps in accounting for a pension plan, assume that on January 1, 1995, Zarle Company adopts *FASB Statement No. 87* to account for its defined benefit pension plan. The following facts apply to the pension plan for the year 1995:

Plan assets, January 1, 1995, are $100,000.

Projected benefit obligation, January 1, 1995, is $100,000.

Annual service cost for 1995 is $9,000.

Settlement rate for 1995 is 10%.

Actual return on plan assets for 1995 is $10,000.

Contributions (funding) in 1995 are $8,000.

Benefits paid to retirees in 1995 are $7,000.

Using the data presented above, the work sheet in Illustration 21-8 presents the beginning balances and all of the pension entries recorded by Zarle Company in 1995. The beginning balances for the projected benefit obligation and the pension plan assets are recorded on the first line of the work sheet in the memo record. They are not recorded in the formal general journal and, therefore, are not reported as a liability and an asset in the financial statements of Zarle Company. These two significant pension items are off-balance-sheet amounts that affect pension expense but are not recorded as assets and liabilities in the employer's books.

ILLUSTRATION 21-8
Pension Work Sheet—1995

	Zarle Company				
	General Journal Entries			Memo Record	
Items	Annual Pension Expense	Cash	Prepaid/ Accrued Cost	Projected Benefit Obligation	Plan Assets
Balance, Jan. 1, 1995			—	100,000 Cr.	100,000 Dr.
(a) Service cost	9,000 Dr.			9,000 Cr.	
(b) Interest cost	10,000 Dr.			10,000 Cr.	
(c) Actual return	10,000 Cr.				10,000 Dr.
(d) Contributions		8,000 Cr.			8,000 Dr.
(e) Benefits				7,000 Dr.	7,000 Cr.
Journal entry for 1995	9,000 Dr.	8,000 Cr.	1,000 Cr.*		
Balance, Dec. 31, 1995			1,000 Cr.**	112,000 Cr.	111,000 Dr.

*$9,000 − $8,000 = $1,000.
**$112,000 − $111,000 = $1,000.

Entry (a) records the service cost component, which increases pension expense $9,000 and increases the liability (projected benefit obligation) $9,000. Entry (b) accrues the interest expense component, which increases both the liability and the pension expense by $10,000 (the beginning projected benefit obligation multiplied by the settlement rate of 10%). Entry (c) records the actual return on the plan assets, which increases the plan assets and decreases the pension expense. Entry (d) records Zarle Company's contribution (funding) of assets to the pension fund; cash is decreased $8,000 and plan assets are increased $8,000. Entry (e) records the benefit payments made to retirees, which results in equal $7,000 decreases to the plan assets and the projected benefit obligation.

The "formal journal entry" on December 31, which is the entry made to formally record the pension expense in 1995, is as follows:

1995

Pension Expense	9,000	
Cash		8,000
Prepaid/Accrued Pension Cost		1,000

The credit to Prepaid/Accrued Pension Cost for $1,000 represents the difference between the 1995 pension expense of $9,000 and the amount funded of $8,000. Prepaid/Accrued Pension Cost (credit) is a liability because the plan is underfunded by $1,000. The Prepaid/Accrued Pension Cost account balance of $1,000 also equals the net of the balances in the memo accounts. This reconciliation of the off-balance-sheet items with the prepaid/accrued pension cost reported in the balance sheet is shown in the reconciliation schedule below.

ILLUSTRATION 21-9
Pension Reconciliation
Schedule—December 31,
1995

Projected benefit obligation (Credit)	$(112,000)
Plan assets at fair value (Debit)	111,000
Prepaid/accrued pension cost (Credit)	(1,000)

If the net of the memo record balances is a credit, the reconciling amount in the prepaid/accrued cost column will be a credit equal in amount. If the net of the memo record balances is a debit, the prepaid/accrued cost amount will be a debit equal in amount. The work sheet is designed to produce this reconciling feature which will be useful later in the preparation of the required notes related to pension disclosures.

In this illustration, the debit to Pension Expense exceeds the credit to Cash, resulting in a credit to Prepaid/Accrued Pension Cost—the recognition of a liability. If the credit to Cash exceeded the debit to Pension Expense, Prepaid/Accrued Pension Cost would be debited—the recognition of an asset.

▶ AMORTIZATION OF UNRECOGNIZED PRIOR SERVICE COST (PSC)

OBJECTIVE 6

Describe the amortization of unrecognized prior service costs.

When a defined benefit plan is either initiated (adopted) or amended, credit is often given to employees for years of service provided before the date of initiation or amendment. As a result of prior service credits, the projected benefit obligation is usually greater than it was before. In many cases, the increase in the projected benefit obligation is substantial. One question that arises is whether an expense and related liability for these **prior service costs (PSC)** should be fully reported at the time a plan is initiated or amended. The FASB has taken the position that no expense for these costs and in some cases no liability should be recognized at the time of the plan's adoption or amendment. The Board's rationale is that the employer would not provide credit for past years of service unless it expected to receive benefits in the future. As a result, **the retroactive benefits should not be recognized as pension expense entirely in the year of amendment but should be recognized during the service periods of those employees who are expected to receive benefits under the plan (the remaining service life of the covered active employees).**

The cost of the retroactive benefits (including benefits that are granted to existing retirees) is the increase in the projected benefit obligation at the date of the amendment. The amount of the prior service cost is computed by an actuary. Amortization of the unrecognized prior service cost is an accounting function performed with the assistance of an actuary.

INTERNATIONAL INSIGHT

In the U.S. prior service cost is generally amortized over the average remaining service life of employees. In Germany prior service cost is recognized immediately. In the Netherlands prior service cost may either be recognized immediately or directly charged to shareholders' equity.

The Board prefers a **years-of-service** amortization method that is similar to a units-of-production computation. First, the total number of service-years to be worked by all of the participating employees is computed. Second, the unrecognized prior service cost is divided by the total number of service-years, to obtain a cost per service-year (the unit cost). Third, the number of service-years consumed each year is multiplied by the cost per service-year, to obtain the annual amortization charge.

To illustrate the amortization of the unrecognized prior service cost under the years-of-service method, assume that Zarle Company's defined benefit pension plan covers 170 employees. In its negotiations with its employees, Zarle Company amends its pension plan on January 1, 1996, and grants $80,000 of prior service costs to its employees. The employees are grouped as follows according to expected years of retirement:

Group	Number of Employees	Expected Retirement on Dec. 31
A	40	1996
B	20	1997
C	40	1998
D	50	1999
E	20	2000
	170	

The computation of the service-years per year and the total service-years is shown in the following schedule:

	Service-Years					
Year	A	B	C	D	E	Total
1996	40	20	40	50	20	170
1997		20	40	50	20	130
1998			40	50	20	110
1999				50	20	70
2000					20	20
	40	40	120	200	100	500

ILLUSTRATION 21-10
Computation of Service-Years

Computed on the basis of a prior service cost of $80,000 and a total of 500 service-years for all years, the cost per service-year is $160 ($80,000 ÷ 500). The annual amount of amortization based on a $160 cost per service-year is computed as follows:

Year	Total Service-Years	×	Cost Per Service-Year	=	Annual Amortization
1996	170		$160		$27,200
1997	130		160		20,800
1998	110		160		17,600
1999	70		160		11,200
2000	20		160		3,200
	500				$80,000

ILLUSTRATION 21-11
Computation of Annual Prior Service Cost Amortization

FASB Statement No. 87 allows an alternative method of computing amortization of unrecognized prior service cost; **employers may use straight-line amortization over the average remaining service life of the employees.** In this case, with 500 service years and 170 employees, the average would be 2.94 years (500 ÷ 170). Using this method, the $80,000 cost would be charged to expense at $27,211 ($80,000 ÷ 2.94) in 1996, $27,211 in 1997, and $25,578 ($27,211 × .94) in 1998.

If the Board had adopted full capitalization of all elements of the pension plan, the prior service cost would have been capitalized as an intangible asset—pension goodwill—and amortized over its useful life. The intangible asset (goodwill) comes from the assumption that the cost of additional pension benefits increases loyalty and productivity (and reduces turnover) among the affected employees. However, prior service cost is accounted for off-balance-sheet and is called **unrecognized prior service cost.** Although not recognized on the balance sheet, prior service cost is a factor in computing pension expense.

► 1996 ENTRIES AND WORK SHEET

Continuing the Zarle Company illustration into 1996, we note that a January 1, 1996, amendment to the pension plan grants to employees prior service benefits having a present value of $80,000. The annual amortization amounts, as computed in the previous section using the years-of-service approach ($27,200 for 1996), are employed in this illustration. The following facts apply to the pension plan for the year 1996:

On January 1, 1996, Zarle Company grants prior service benefits having a present value of $80,000.

Annual service cost for 1996 is $9,500.

Settlement rate for 1996 is 10%.

Actual return on plan assets for 1996 is $11,100.

Annual contributions (funding) are $20,000.

Benefits paid to retirees in 1996 are $8,000.

Amortization of prior service cost (PSC) using the years-of-service method is $27,200.

ILLUSTRATION 21-12
Pension Work Sheet—
1996

The following work sheet presents all of the pension entries and information recorded by Zarle Company in 1996.

Zarle Company

	General Journal Entries			Memo Record		
Items	Annual Pension Expense	Cash	Prepaid/ Accrued Cost	Projected Benefit Obligation	Plan Assets	Unrecognized Prior Service Cost
Balance, Dec. 31, 1995			1,000 Cr.	112,000 Cr.	111,000 Dr.	
(f) **Prior service cost**				80,000 Cr.		80,000 Dr.
Balance, Jan. 1, 1996			1,000 Cr.	192,000 Cr.	111,000 Dr.	80,000 Dr.
(g) Service cost	9,500 Dr.			9,500 Cr.		
(h) Interest cost	19,200 Dr.ᵃ			19,200 Cr.		
(i) Actual return	11,100 Cr.				11,100 Dr.	
(j) **Amortization of PSC**	27,200 Dr.					27,200 Cr.
(k) Contributions		20,000 Cr.			20,000 Dr.	
(l) Benefits				8,000 Dr.	8,000 Cr.	
Journal entry for 1996	44,800 Dr.	20,000 Cr.	24,800 Cr.			
Balance, Dec. 31, 1996			25,800 Cr.	212,700 Cr.	134,100 Dr.	52,800 Dr.

ᵃ$19,200 = $192,000 × 10%.

The first line of the work sheet shows the beginning balances of the Prepaid/Accrued Pension Cost account and the memo accounts. Entry (f) records Zarle Company's granting of prior service cost by adding $80,000 to the projected benefit obligation and to the unrecognized (noncapitalized) prior service cost. Entries (g), (h), (i), (k), and (l) are similar to the corresponding entries in 1995. Entry (j) records the 1996 amortization of unrecognized prior service cost by debiting Pension Expense by $27,200 and crediting the new Unrecognized Prior Service Cost account by the same amount.

The journal entry on December 31 to formally record the pension expense—the sum of the annual pension expense column—for 1996 is as follows:

1996

Pension Expense	44,800	
Cash		20,000
Prepaid/Accrued Pension Cost		24,800

Because the expense exceeds the funding, the Prepaid/Accrued Pension Cost account is credited for the $24,800 difference and is a liability. In 1996, as in 1995, the balance of the Prepaid/Accrued Pension Cost account ($25,800) is equal to the net of the balances in the memo accounts as shown in the following reconciliation schedule.

ILLUSTRATION 21-13
Pension Reconciliation
Schedule—December 31,
1996

Projected benefit obligation (Credit)	$(212,700)
Plan assets at fair value (Debit)	134,100
Funded status	(78,600)
Unrecognized prior service cost (Debit)	52,800
Prepaid/accrued pension cost (Credit)	$(25,800)

The reconciliation is the formula that makes the work sheet work. It relates the components of pension accounting, recorded and unrecorded, to one another.

▶ GAIN OR LOSS

OBJECTIVE 7
Explain the accounting procedure for recognizing unexpected gains and losses.

Of great concern to companies that have pension plans are the uncontrollable and unexpected swings in pension expense that could be caused by (1) sudden and large changes in the market value of plan assets and (2) changes in actuarial assumptions that affect the amount of the projected benefit obligation. If these gains or losses were to impact fully the financial statements in the period of realization or incurrence, substantial fluctuations in pension expense would result. Therefore, the profession decided to reduce the volatility associated with pension expense by using **smoothing techniques** that dampen and in some cases fully eliminate the fluctuations.

SMOOTHING UNEXPECTED GAINS AND LOSSES ON PLAN ASSETS

One component of pension expense, actual return on plan assets, reduces pension expense (assuming the actual return is positive). A large change in the actual return can substantially affect pension expense for a year. Assume a company has a 40% return in the stock market for the year. Should this substantial, and perhaps one-time, event affect current pension expense?

Actuaries ignore current fluctuations when they develop a funding pattern to pay expected benefits in the future. They develop an **expected rate of return** and multiply it by an asset value weighted over a reasonable period of time to arrive at an **expected return on plan assets.** This return is then used to determine its funding pattern.

The Board adopted the actuary's approach to dampen wide swings that might occur in the actual return. That is, the expected return on the plan assets is to be included as a component of pension expense, not the actual return in a given year. To achieve this goal, the expected rate of return (the actuary's rate) is multiplied by the fair value of the plan assets or a market-related asset value of the plan assets (throughout our Zarle Company illustrations, market-related value and fair value of plan assets are assumed equal). The **market-related asset value is a calculated value that recognizes changes in fair value in a systematic and rational manner over not more than than 5 years.**[14]

What happens to the difference between the expected return and the actual return, often referred to as the **unexpected gain or loss**—also called **asset gains and losses** by the FASB? Asset gains (occurring when actual return is greater than expected return) and asset losses (occurring when actual return is less than expected return) are recorded in an Unrecognized Net Gain or Loss account and combined with unrecognized gains and losses accumulated in prior years.

To illustrate the computation of an unexpected asset gain or loss and its related accounting, assume that Shierer Company in 1997 has an actual return on plan assets of $16,000 when the expected return is $13,410 (the expected rate of return of 10% times the beginning-of-the-year plan assets). The unexpected asset gain of $2,590 ($16,000 − $13,410) is credited to Unrecognized Net Gain or Loss and debited to Pension Expense.

SMOOTHING UNEXPECTED GAINS AND LOSSES ON THE PENSION LIABILITY

In estimating the projected benefit obligation (the liability), actuaries make assumptions about such items as mortality rate, retirement rate, turnover rate, disability rate, and salary amounts. Any change in these actuarial assumptions changes the amount of the

---

[14]Different ways of calculating market-related value may be used for different classes of assets (for example, an employer might use fair value for bonds and a 5-year-moving-average for equities), but the manner of determining market-related value should be applied consistently from year to year for each asset class.

projected benefit obligation. Seldom does actual experience coincide exactly with the actuarial predictions. These unexpected gains or losses from changes in the projected benefit obligation are called **liability gains and losses.**

Liability gains (resulting from unexpected decreases in the liability balance) and liability losses (resulting from unexpected increases) are deferred (unrecognized). The liability gains and losses are combined in the same Unrecognized Net Gain or Loss account used for asset gains and losses. They are accumulated from year to year, off-balance-sheet, in a memo record account.

CORRIDOR AMORTIZATION

OBJECTIVE 8

Explain the corridor approach to amortizing unrecognized gains and losses.

Because the asset gains and losses and the liability gains and losses can be offsetting, the accumulated total unrecognized net gain or loss may not grow too large. But, it is possible that no offsetting will occur and that the balance in the Unrecognized Net Gain or Loss account will continue to grow. To limit its growth, the FASB invented the **corridor approach** for amortizing the accumulated balance in the Unrecognized Gain or Loss account when it gets too large. **The unrecognized net gain or loss balance is considered too large and must be amortized when it exceeds the arbitrarily selected FASB criterion of 10% of the larger of the beginning balances of the projected benefit obligation or the market-related value of the plan assets.**

To illustrate the corridor approach, assume data on the projected benefit obligation and the plan assets over a period of 6 years as shown in the schedule below.

ILLUSTRATION 21-14
Computation of the Corridor

Beginning-of-the-Year Balances	Projected Benefit Obligation	Market-Related Asset Value	Corridor* +/− 10%
1994	$1,000,000	$ 900,000	$100,000
1995	1,200,000	1,100,000	120,000
1996	1,300,000	1,700,000	170,000
1997	1,500,000	2,250,000	225,000
1998	1,700,000	1,750,000	175,000
1999	1,800,000	1,700,000	180,000

*The corridor becomes 10% of the larger (in boldface) of the projected benefit obligation or the market-related plan asset value.

How the corridor works becomes apparent when the data above are portrayed graphically as in the diagram shown below:

ILLUSTRATION 21-15
Graphic Illustration of the Corridor

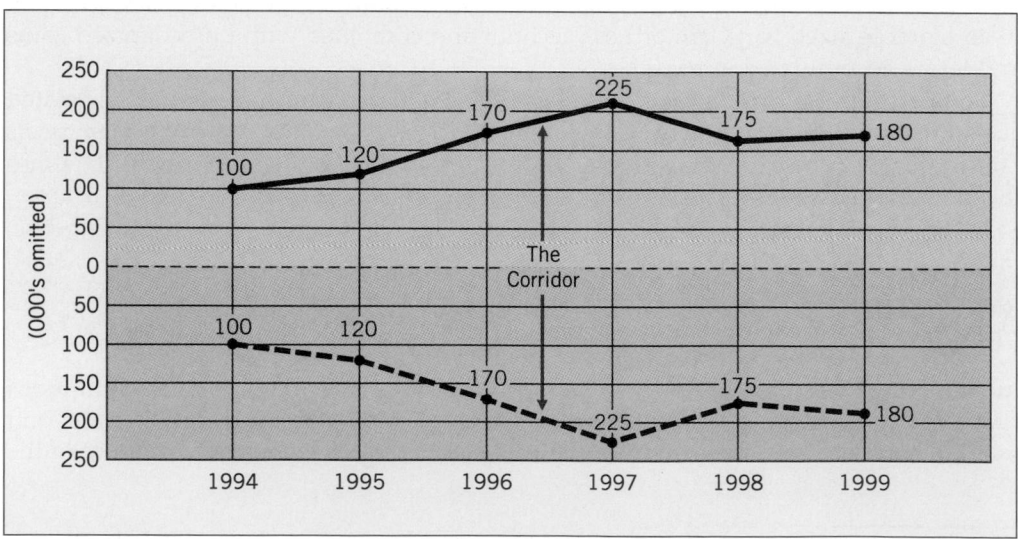

If the balance of the Unrecognized Net Gain or Loss account stays within the upper and lower limits of the corridor, no amortization is required—the unrecognized net gain or loss balance is carried forward unchanged.

If amortization is required, the minimum amortization shall be the excess divided by the average remaining service period of active employees expected to receive benefits under the plan. Any systematic method of amortization of unrecognized gains and losses may be used in lieu of the minimum, provided it is greater than the minimum, is used consistently for both gains and losses, and is disclosed.

Illustration

In applying the corridor, the Board decided that amortization of the excess unrecognized net gain or loss should be included as a component of pension expense only if, at the **beginning of the year,** the unrecognized net gain or loss exceeded the corridor. That is, if no unrecognized net gain or loss exists at the beginning of the period, no recognition of gains or losses can result in that period.

To illustrate the amortization of unrecognized net gains and losses, assume the following information for Soft-White, Inc.:

	1995	1996	1997
		(beginning of the year)	
Projected benefit obligation	$2,100,000	$2,600,000	$2,900,000
Market-related asset value	2,600,000	2,800,000	2,700,000
Unrecognized net loss	–0–	400,000	300,000

If the average remaining service life of all active employees is 5.5 years, the schedule to amortize the unrecognized net loss is as follows:

Year	Projected Benefit Obligation[a]	Plan Assets[a]	Corridor[b]	Cumulative Unrecognized Net Loss[a]	Minimum Amortization of Loss (For Current Year)
1995	$2,100,000	$2,600,000	$260,000	$ –0–	$ –0–
1996	2,600,000	2,800,000	280,000	400,000	21,818[c]
1997	2,900,000	2,700,000	290,000	678,182[d]	70,579[d]

[a]All as of the beginning of the period.
[b]10% of the greater of projected benefit obligation or plan assets market-related value.
[c]$400,000 − $280,000 = $120,000; $120,000 ÷ 5.5 = $21,818
[d]$400,000 − $21,818 + $300,000 = $678,182; $678,182 − $290,000 = $388,182; $388,182 ÷ 5.5 = $70,579.

ILLUSTRATION 21-16
Corridor Test and Gain/Loss Amortization Schedule

As indicated from Illustration 21-16, the loss recognized in 1996 increased pension expense by $21,818. This amount is small in comparison with the total loss of $400,000 and indicates that the corridor approach dampens the effects (reduces volatility) of these gains and losses on pension expense. The rationale for the corridor is that gains and losses result from refinements in estimates as well as real changes in economic value and that over time some of these gains and losses will offset one another. It therefore seems reasonable that gains and losses should not be recognized fully as a component of pension expense in the period in which they arise.

However, gains and losses that arise from a single occurrence not directly related to the operation of the pension plan and not in the ordinary course of the employer's business should be recognized immediately. For example, a gain or loss that is directly related to a plant closing, a disposal of a segment, or a similar event that greatly affects the size of the employee work force, shall be recognized as a part of the gain or loss associated with that event.

At one time, Bethlehem Steel reported a third-quarter loss of $477 million, one of the largest quarterly deficits ever recorded by a U.S. corporation. A great deal of this loss was attributable to future estimated benefits payable to workers who were permanently laid off. In this situation, the loss should be treated as an adjustment to the gain or loss on the plant closing and should not affect pension cost for the current or future periods.

► SUMMARY OF CALCULATIONS FOR ASSET GAIN OR LOSS

The difference between the actual return on plan assets and the expected return on plan assets is the unexpected (deferred) asset gain or loss component. This component defers the difference between the actual return and expected return on plan assets in computing current year pension expense. Thus, after considering this component, **it is really the expected return on plan assets (not the actual return) that determines current pension expense.**

The amortized net gain or loss is determined by amortizing the unrecognized gain or loss at the beginning of the year subject to the corridor limitation. In other words, **if the unrecognized gain or loss is greater than the corridor, these net gains and losses are subject to amortization.** This minimum amortization is computed by dividing the net gains or losses subject to amortization by the average remaining service period. When the unexpected gain or loss is combined with the amortization of prior years' actuarial gains and losses, the net amortized and unexpected gains and losses is determined (often referred to simply as gain or loss). This summary is illustrated graphically below:

ILLUSTRATION 21-17
Graphic Summary of Gain or Loss Computation

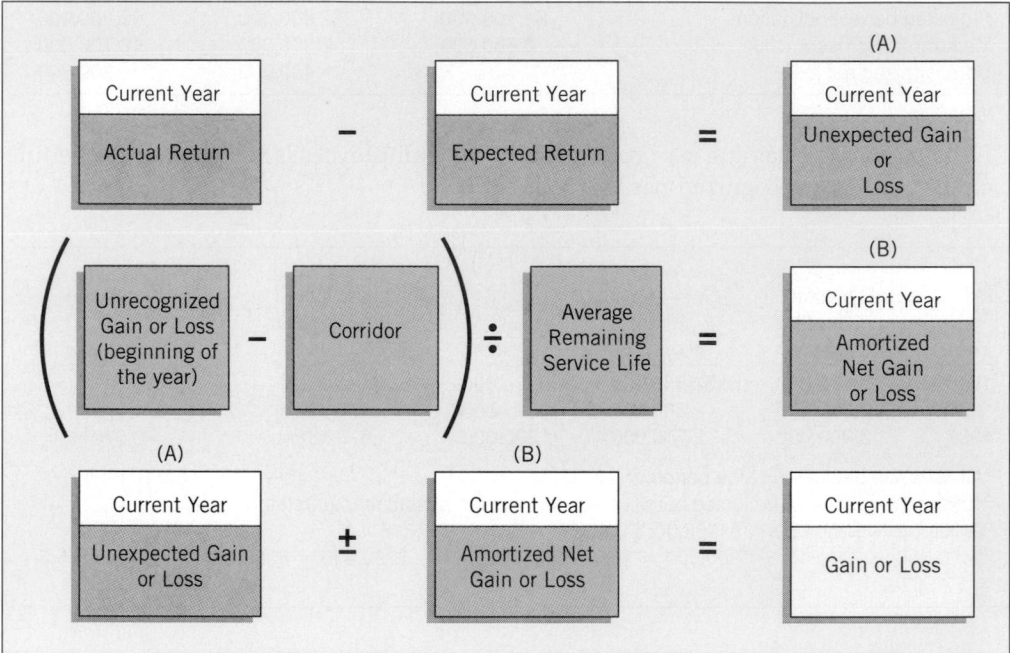

In essence, these gains and losses are subject to triple smoothing. That is, the asset gain or loss is smoothed by using the expected return. Then the unrecognized gain or loss at the beginning of the year is not amortized unless it is greater than the corridor. Finally, the excess is spread over the remaining service life of existing employees.

► 1997 ENTRIES AND WORK SHEET

Continuing the Zarle Company illustration into 1997, the following facts apply to the pension plan:

Annual service cost for 1997 is $13,000.

Settlement rate is 10%; expected earnings rate is 10%.

Actual return on plan assets for 1997 is $12,000.

Amortization of prior service cost (PSC) in 1997 is $20,800.

Annual contributions (funding) are $24,000.

Benefits paid to retirees in 1997 are $10,500.

Changes in actuarial assumptions establish the end-of-year projected benefit obligation at $265,000.

The work sheet shown in Illustration 21-18 presents all of the pension entries and information recorded by Zarle Company in 1997. On the first line of the work sheet are recorded the beginning balances that relate to the pension plan. In this case, the beginning balances for Zarle Company are the ending balances from the 1996 Zarle Company pension work sheet in Illustration 21-12.

ILLUSTRATION 21-18
Pension Work Sheet—1997

	Zarle Company						
	General Journal Entries			**Memo Record**			
Items	Annual Pension Expense	Cash	Prepaid/ Accrued Cost	Projected Benefit Obligation	Plan Assets	Unrecognized Prior Service Cost	Unrecognized Net Gain or Loss
Bal., December 31, 1996			25,800 Cr.	212,700 Cr.	134,100 Dr.	52,800 Dr.	
(m) Service cost	13,000 Dr.			13,000 Cr.			
(n) Interest cost	21,270 Dr.			21,270 Cr.			
(o) Actual return	12,000 Cr.				12,000 Dr.		
(p) **Unexpected loss**	1,410 Cr.						1,410 Dr.
(q) Amortization of PSC	20,800 Dr.					20,800 Cr.	
(r) Contributions		24,000 Cr.			24,000 Dr.		
(s) Benefits				10,500 Dr.	10,500 Cr.		
(t) **Liability increase**				28,530 Cr.			28,530 Dr.
Journal entry for 1997	41,660 Dr.	24,000 Cr.	17,660 Cr.				
Bal., December 31, 1997			43,460 Cr.	265,000 Cr.	159,600 Dr.	32,000 Dr.	29,940 Dr.

Entries (m), (n), (o), (q), (r), and (s) are similar to the corresponding entries previously explained in 1995 or 1996. Entries (o) and (p) are related. Recording the actual return in entry (o) has been illustrated in both 1995 and 1996; it is recorded similarly in 1997. In both 1995 and 1996 it was assumed that the actual return on plan assets was equal to the expected return on plan assets. In 1997 the expected return of $13,410 (the expected rate of return of 10% times the beginning-of-the-year plan assets balance of $134,100) is higher than the actual return of $12,000. To smooth pension expense, the unexpected loss of $1,410 ($13,410 − $12,000) is deferred by debiting the Unrecognized Net Gain or Loss account and crediting Pension Expense. **As a result of this adjustment, the expected return on the plan assets is the amount actually used to compute pension expense.**

Entry (t) records the change in the projected benefit obligation resulting from a change in actuarial assumptions. As indicated, the actuary has now computed the ending balance to be $265,000. Given that the memo record balance at December 31 is $236,470 ($212,700 + $13,000 + $21,270 − $10,500), a difference of $28,530 ($265,000 − $236,470) is indicated. This $28,530 increase in the employer's liability is an unexpected loss that is deferred by debiting it to the Unrecognized Net Gain or Loss account.

The journal entry on December 31 to formally record pension expense for 1997 is as follows:

1997

Pension Expense	41,660	
Cash		24,000
Prepaid/Accrued Pension Cost		17,660

As illustrated in the work sheets of 1995 and 1996, the balance of the Prepaid/Accrued Pension Cost account at December 31, 1997 of $43,460 is equal to the net of the balances in the memo accounts as shown below:

Projected benefit obligation (Credit)	$(265,000)
Plan assets at fair value (Debit)	159,600
Funded status	(105,400)
Unrecognized prior service cost (Debit)	32,000
Unrecognized net loss (Debit)	29,940
Prepaid/accrued pension cost (Credit)	$ (43,460)

ILLUSTRATION 21-19
Pension Reconciliation Schedule—December 31, 1997

▶ MINIMUM LIABILITY

If the FASB had decided to capitalize pension plan assets and liabilities, Zarle Company in our previous illustration would have reported on December 31, 1997, a liability of $265,000, plan assets of $159,600, and unrecognized prior service cost (goodwill) of $32,000 plus an unrecognized net loss of $29,940. Instead it reports only accrued pension cost of $43,460 as a liability. The Board was well aware of this discrepancy. It believed that an employer with a projected benefit obligation in excess of the fair value of pension plan assets has a liability and that an employer with a fair value of plan assets in excess of projected benefit obligation has an asset. Nevertheless, when the Board was faced with the final decision on this matter, it decided that to require the reporting of these amounts in the financial statements would be too great a change in present practice, because up to this point none of these amounts had been reported in the balance sheet.

**UNDERLYING
CONCEPT**

*Recognizing the smaller
benefit obligation ignores the
going concern concept. A
going concern would not
expect to settle the obligation
today at current salaries and
wages. A going concern
would expect to settle the
obligation based upon future
salary levels.*

The Board, therefore, developed a compromise approach that requires immediate recognition of a liability (referred to as the minimum liability) when the accumulated benefit obligation exceeds the fair value of plan assets. The purpose of this minimum liability requirement is to assure that if a significant plan amendment or actuarial loss occurs, a liability will be recognized at least to the extent of the unfunded portion of the accumulated benefit obligation.

Note that the plan assets are compared to the smaller **accumulated** benefit obligation instead of the larger projected benefit obligation. The rationale for using the accumulated benefit obligation is that if the liability were settled today, it would be settled on the basis of current salary rates, not future salary rates. Therefore, it is argued that the accumulated benefit obligation should be used, not the projected benefit obligation. Although the compromise approach frequently ignores a portion of the liability, it does help to report some balance sheet effects when a plan amendment or a large loss occurs. **The Board does not permit the recording of an asset if the fair value of the pension plan assets exceeds the accumulated benefit obligation.**

MINIMUM LIABILITY COMPUTATION

If a liability for accrued pension cost is already reported, only an additional liability to equal the required minimum liability (unfunded accumulated benefit) is recorded. To illustrate, assume that Largent Inc. amends its pension plan on December 31, 1995, giving retroactive benefits to its employees.

**INTERNATIONAL
INSIGHT**

*Only the U.S. requires
companies to revalue their
pension plan obligations each
year. Other nations tend to
require revaluation at
approximately 3-year
intervals.*

Projected benefit obligation	$8,000,000
Accumulated benefit obligation	7,000,000
Plan assets (at fair value)	5,000,000
Market-related asset value	4,900,000
Unrecognized prior service cost	2,500,000
Accrued pension cost	500,000

The unfunded accumulated benefit is computed as follows:

**ILLUSTRATION 21-20
Computation of
Unfunded Accumulated
Benefit**

Accumulated benefit obligation	$7,000,000
Plan assets (at fair value)	5,000,000
Unfunded accumulated benefit obligation (minimum liability)	$2,000,000

Note that the fair value of the plan assets is used, not the market-related asset value, to compute the unfunded accumulated benefit obligation. In this case, an additional $1,500,000 is required to be recorded as a liability and reported on the financial statements. The computation of the **additional liability** is as follows:

Unfunded accumulated benefit obligation (minimum liability)	$2,000,000
Accrued pension cost (balance at December 31, 1995)	500,000
Additional liability required	$1,500,000

ILLUSTRATION 21-21
Computation of Additional Liability Required—Accrued Pension Cost Balance

Largent Inc. would combine the **accrued pension cost** and the additional liability into one amount and report it in the balance sheet as accrued pension cost or pension liability in the amount of $2,000,000.

If Largent Inc. had a **prepaid pension cost** of $300,000 instead of an accrued pension cost of $500,000, an additional liability of $2,300,000 would be recorded as follows:

Unfunded accumulated benefit obligation (minimum liability)	$2,000,000
Prepaid pension cost	300,000
Additional liability required	$2,300,000

ILLUSTRATION 21-22
Computation of Additional Liability Required—Prepaid Pension Cost Balance

The existing balance in the prepaid pension cost (debit) is **combined** with the additional liability (credit) into one amount and reported as accrued pension cost or pension liability in the net amount of $2,000,000.

FINANCIAL STATEMENT PRESENTATION

When it is necessary to adjust the accounts to recognize a minimum liability, the debit should be to an intangible asset that is called Intangible Asset—Deferred Pension Cost. The entry to record the liability and related intangible asset for Largent Inc. (first case) is:

Intangible Asset—Deferred Pension Cost	1,500,000	
Additional Pension Liability		1,500,000

One exception to the general rule of reporting an intangible asset is when the **additional liability exceeds the amount of unrecognized prior service cost.** In this case, the excess is debited to Excess of Additional Pension Liability Over Unrecognized Prior Service Cost. When the additional liability exceeds the unrecognized prior service cost, the excess must have resulted from an actuarial loss, such as an increase in the benefit obligation due to an increase in retiree longevity. The justification for recognizing an intangible asset up to the amount of the unrecognized prior service cost is that an amendment to an existing plan increases goodwill and therefore benefits the company in the future. Such is not the case when the additional liability exceeds the unrecognized prior service cost.

When this excess develops, it should be reported as a contra account in the stockholders' equity section. To illustrate, assume that Largent Inc. has common stock, with a total par value of $1,000,000, additional paid-in capital of $400,000, and retained earnings of $700,000. In addition, it has an additional liability that exceeds the unrecognized prior service cost by $200,000. A condensed version of Largent's stockholders' equity section is provided below:[15]

Stockholders' Equity Section	
Common stock	$1,000,000
Additional paid-in capital	400,000
Total paid-in capital	1,400,000
Retained earnings	700,000
Excess of additional pension liability over unrecognized prior service cost	(200,000)
Total stockholders' equity	$1,900,000

ILLUSTRATION 21-23
Balance Sheet Presentation of Excess of Additional Pension Liability

---

[15]This treatment is similar to the reporting of deferred compensation cost and the unrealized holding loss on available-for-sale securities discussed in earlier chapters.

The amount of the additional liability required should be evaluated each reporting period along with the related intangible asset or contra equity account. At each reporting date, these items above may be increased, decreased, or totally eliminated. Neither the intangible asset nor the contra equity account is amortized from period to period; the balances are merely adjusted up or down.

The minimum liability approach to the Zarle Company pension plan for all three years 1995, 1996, and 1997 is illustrated in the following schedule (values are assumed for the accumulated benefit obligation):

ILLUSTRATION 21-24
Minimum Liability
Computations

Zarle Company

	December 31		
	1995	1996	1997
Accumulated benefit obligation	$(80,000)	$(164,000)	$(240,600)
Plan assets at fair value	111,000	134,100	159,600
Unfunded accumulated benefit obligation (minimum liability)	$ –0–	(29,900)	(81,000)
Accrued pension cost		25,800	43,460
Additional liability		(4,100)	(37,540)
Unrecognized prior service cost*		52,800	32,000
Contra equity charge**		$ –0–	$ (5,540)

*Maximum intangible asset recognizable.
**Difference charged to Excess of Additional Pension Liability Over Unrecognized Prior Service Cost.

In 1995 the fair value of the plan assets exceeds the accumulated benefit obligation; therefore, no additional liability need be reported. **The Board does not permit the recognition of a net investment in the pension plan when the plan assets exceed the pension obligation.**

In 1996, the minimum liability amount ($29,900) exceeds the accrued pension cost liability already recorded ($25,800), so an additional liability of $4,100 ($29,900 − $25,800) is recorded as follows:

December 31, 1996

Intangible Asset—Deferred Pension Cost	4,100	
Additional Pension Liability		4,100

In 1997, the minimum liability ($81,000) exceeds the accrued pension cost liability ($43,460), so an additional liability of $37,540 must be reported at the end of 1997. Since a balance of $4,100 already exists in the Additional Pension Liability account, it is credited for $33,440 ($37,540 − $4,100). Also, since the additional liability exceeds the unrecognized prior service cost by $5,540, the excess is debited to the contra equity account Excess of Additional Pension Liability Over Unrecognized Prior Service Cost. The remainder $27,900 ($33,440 − $5,540) is debited to the Intangible Asset—Deferred Pension Cost. The entry on December 31, 1997, to adjust the minimum liability is as follows:

December 31, 1997

Intangible Asset—Deferred Pension Cost	27,900	
Excess of Additional Pension Liability Over		
Unrecognized Prior Service Cost	5,540	
Additional Pension Liability		33,440

As the additional liability changes, the combined debit balance of the intangible asset and contra equity accounts fluctuates by the same amount.

Zarle Company

Items	General Journal Entries					
	Annual Pension Expense	Cash	Prepaid/ Accrued Cost	**Additional Liability**	**Pension Intangible**	**Contra Equity**
Balance, Dec. 31, 1996			25,800 Cr.	4,100 Cr.	4,100 Dr.	
(m) Service cost	13,000 Dr.					
(n) Interest cost	21,270 Dr.					
(o) Actual return	12,000 Cr.					
(p) Unexpected loss	1,410 Cr.					
(q) Amortization of PSC	20,800 Dr.					
(r) Contributions		24,000 Cr.				
(s) Benefits						
(t) Liability change (Incr.)						
(u) **Minimum liab. adj.**				**33,440 Cr.**	**27,900 Dr.**	**5,540 Dr.**
Journal entry for 1997	41,660 Dr.	24,000 Cr.	17,660 Cr.			
Balance, Dec. 31, 1997			43,460 Cr.	37,540 Cr.	32,000 Dr.	5,540 Dr.

Items	Memo Entries			
	Projected Benefit Obligation	Plan Assets	Unrecognized Prior Service Cost	Unrecognized Net Gain or Loss
Balance, Dec. 31, 1996	212,700 Cr.	134,100 Dr.	52,800 Dr.	
(m) Service cost	13,000 Cr.			
(n) Interest cost	21,270 Cr.			
(o) Actual return		12,000 Dr.		
(p) Unexpected loss				1,410 Dr.
(q) Amortization of PSC			20,800 Cr.	
(r) Contributions		24,000 Dr.		
(s) Benefits	10,500 Dr.	10,500 Cr.		
(t) Liability increase	28,530 Cr.			28,530 Dr.
(u) Minimum liab. adj.				
Journal entry for 1997				
Balance, Dec. 31, 1997	265,000 Cr.	159,600 Dr.	32,000 Dr.	29,940 Dr.

ILLUSTRATION 21-25
Revised Pension Work Sheet—1997, Revised to Include Minimum Liability Computation

WORK SHEET ILLUSTRATION

To illustrate how the pension work sheet is affected by the minimum liability computation, a revised version of the 1997 work sheet of Zarle Company is shown in Illustration 21-25. The boldface items [entry (u)] relate to adjustments caused by recognition of the minimum liability at the end of 1996 and 1997.

As illustrated in prior work sheets, the balance in the Prepaid/Accrued Pension Cost account ($43,460) equals the net of the balances in the memo accounts ($265,000 − [$159,600 + $32,000 + $29,940]). With the Additional Liability amount being combined with the Prepaid/Accrued Pension Cost amount in order to report the minimum pension liability in the balance sheet, the reconciliation at December 31, 1997, as shown below has an added element in it:

ILLUSTRATION 21-26
Reconciliation Schedule—1997, Revised to Show Additional Pension Liability

Projected benefit obligation (Credit)	$(265,000)
Plan assets at fair value (Debit)	159,600
Funded status	(105,400)
Unrecognized prior service cost (Debit)	32,000
Unrecognized net loss (Debit)	29,940
Prepaid/Accrued pension cost (Credit)	(43,460)
Additional liability (Credit)	(37,540)
Accrued pension cost liability recognized in the balance sheet	$ (81,000)

► REPORTING PENSION PLANS IN FINANCIAL STATEMENTS

OBJECTIVE 10

Describe the reporting requirements for pension plans in financial statements.

One might suspect that a phenomenon as significant and complex as pensions would involve extensive reporting and disclosure requirements. We will cover these requirements in two categories: (1) those within the financial statements, and (2) those within the notes to the financial statements.

WITHIN THE FINANCIAL STATEMENTS

If the amount funded (credit to Cash) by the employer to the pension trust is **less than the annual expense** (debit to Pension Expense), a credit balance accrual of the difference arises in the long-term liability section. It might be described as Accrued Pension Cost, Liability for Pension Expense Not Funded, or Due to Pension Fund. A liability is classified as current when it requires the disbursement of cash within the next year.

If the amount funded to the pension trust during the period is **greater than the amount charged to expense,** an asset equal to the difference arises. This asset is reported as Prepaid Pension Cost, Deferred Pension Expense, or Prepaid Pension Expense in the current assets section if it is current in nature, and in the other assets section if it is long-term in nature.

If the **accumulated benefit obligation exceeds the fair value of pension plan assets,** an additional liability is recorded. The debit is either to an Intangible Asset—Deferred Pension Cost or to a contra account to stockholders' equity. If the debit is less than unrecognized prior service cost, it is reported as an intangible asset. If the debit is greater than unrecognized prior service cost, the excess debit is reported as contra equity—Excess of Additional Pension Liability Over Unrecognized Prior Service Cost.

WITHIN THE NOTES TO THE FINANCIAL STATEMENTS

Pension plans are frequently important to an understanding of financial position, results of operations, and cash flows of a company. Therefore, the following information, if not disclosed in the body of the financial statements, should be disclosed in the notes. These notes are particularly important for pensions because of the complexities and compromises that were made in establishing the recognition and nonrecognition of assets and liabilities in *FASB Statement No. 87.* As a result, we have provided a brief rationale for each disclosure. The general disclosures and rationales are as follows:

1. A description of the plan including employee groups covered, type of benefit formula, funding policy, types of assets held, and the nature and effect of significant matters affecting comparability of information for all periods presented.

   Rationale: Because the measurement of pension expense is based on the benefit formula, a description of the plan and the benefit formula is useful. Furthermore, disclosure of funding policies and types of assets held helps determine future cash flows and their likelihood as well as highlights the difference between cash flow and pension expense. Finally, significant events affecting the plan are disclosed so the reader can predict the effect of these events on long-term trends of the plan.

2. The components of net periodic pension cost (pension expense) for the period.

   Rationale: Information on the components helps users better understand how pension expense is determined and why it changes from one period to the next.

3. A schedule reconciling the funded status of the plan with amounts reported in the employer's statement of financial position, showing separately:

   (a) Plan assets available for benefits (at fair value).

   (b) The projected benefit obligation, identifying the accumulated benefit obligation and the vested benefit obligation.

   (c) The amount of unrecognized prior service cost.

   (d) The amount of unrecognized net gain or loss.

   (e) The amount of any remaining net asset or liability existing at transition due to *FASB Statement No. 87.*

(f) The amount of any additional liability recognized.

(g) The amount of prepaid pension cost or accrued pension cost recognized in the balance sheet (which is the net result of combining items (a) through (f) above).

Rationale: The components of the pension obligation are disclosed, including the funded status of the plan. For example, is there an unfunded projected benefit obligation? Furthermore, disclosure of **vested benefits** (for which the employee's right to receive a present or future pension benefit is no longer contingent on remaining in the service of the employer), identifies the "firmness" of a company's liability. Finally, reconciling the plan's funded status to the amount reported on the balance sheet highlights the difference between the funded status and balance sheet presentation.

4. The weighted-average discount rate, the rate of compensation increase used to measure the projected benefit obligation, and the weighted-average expected long-run rate of return on plan assets.

Rationale: Disclosure of these rates permits the reader to determine the reasonableness of the assumptions applied to measuring the liability and certain components of pension expense.

In summary, the disclosure requirements are extensive, and purposely so. One factor that has made pension reporting difficult to understand in the past has been the lack of consistent terminology. Furthermore, a substantial amount of offsetting has been done to arrive at pension expense and the related pension liability. These disclosures should take some of the mystery out of pension reporting.[16]

► ILLUSTRATION OF PENSION NOTE DISCLOSURE

In addition to the detailed description of the pension plan and other disclosures about the operation of the plan during the year, the employer is required to identify the components of pension expense and to reconcile pension plan assets and liabilities recorded in the memo record with asset or liability amounts reported in the financial statements.

COMPONENTS OF PENSION EXPENSE

The Board requires disclosure of the individual pension expense components—(1) service cost, (2) interest cost, (3) actual return on assets, and (4) all other costs combined—so that the more sophisticated readers can understand how pension expense is determined. Using the information from the Zarle Company illustration, the component cost information, taken from the first (left hand) column of the work sheets, for each of the three years, is presented in the following schedule:

Zarle Company Components of Pension Expense			
	1995	1996	1997
Service cost	$ 9,000	$ 9,500	$ 13,000
Interest cost	10,000	19,200	21,270
Actual return on assets	(10,000)	(11,100)	(12,000)
Net deferral and amortization	–0–	27,200	19,390*
Total	$ 9,000	$ 44,800	$ 41,660

*For 1997, the $19,390 of other items is the net of (1) the unexpected loss, $1,410 credit, and (2) the amortization of the past service cost, $20,800 debit.

ILLUSTRATION 21-27
Summary of Pension Expense Components—1995, 1996, 1997

---

[16]An employer that sponsors two or more separate defined benefit pension plans is not permitted in note disclosures to net one against the other unless the assets of one may be used to provide benefits for the other.

RECONCILIATION SCHEDULE

The Board's requirement that off-balance-sheet assets, liabilities, and unrecognized gains and losses be reconciled with the on-balance-sheet asset or liability can be confusing. But, some consider this reconciling schedule the key to understanding *FASB Statement No. 87* and pension plan accounting. The format of this **reconciliation schedule,** as illustrated in *Statement No. 87,* is shown below.

**ILLUSTRATION 21-28
Format of Pension
Reconciliation Schedule**

Pension Reconciliation Schedule	
Actuarial present value of benefit obligations:	
Vested benefit obligation	$ XXX
Accumulated benefit obligation	$ XXX
Projected benefit obligation (end of period)	$(XXXX)
Plan assets at fair value (end of period)	XXX
Projected benefit obligation in excess of plan assets	(XXX)
Unrecognized prior service cost	XX
Unrecognized net gain or loss	XX
Prepaid/accrued pension cost	(XXX)
Adjustment required to recognize minimum liability	(XX)
Prepaid/accrued pension cost recognized in the balance sheet	$ (XXX)

With the exception of the vested benefit obligation and the accumulated benefit obligation included in the reconciliation schedule above, we have illustrated this reconciliation for each of the work sheets presented thus far in the chapter. What we called "additional liability (credit)" in the 1997 revised reconciliation in Illustration 21-26 is called "adjustment required to recognize minimum liability" in *Statement No. 87's* disclosure requirements.

**UNDERLYING
CONCEPT**

*This represents another
compromise between
relevance and reliability. The
listing of the unrecognized
items attempts to balance
these objectives.*

Why is such a detailed listing of these unrecognized items necessary? The FASB gave the following explanation in its "Basis of Conclusions" section: "The Board acknowledges that the delayed recognition included in this statement results in excluding the most current and most relevant information from the employer's statements of financial position. That information is, however, included in the disclosures required, and . . . certain liabilities previously omitted will be recognized."[17]

The reconciliation schedule for Zarle Company, shown below, is prepared from the last line of each of the pension work sheets previously prepared. Only the actuarially provided amounts for vested benefit obligation and accumulated benefit obligation need to be obtained outside the work sheet. (We use assumed values in our illustration.)

**ILLUSTRATION 21-29
Comprehensive Pension
Reconciliation
Schedule—1995, 1996,
1997**

Zarle Company Pension Reconciliation Schedule			
		December 31	
	1995	1996	1997
			Revised
Actuarial present value of benefit obligations:			
Vested benefit obligation (assumed)	$ (50,000)	$(130,000)	$(182,000)
Accumulated benefit obligation (assumed)	$ (80,000)	$(164,000)	$(240,600)
Projected benefit obligation	$(112,000)	$(212,700)	$(265,000)
Plan assets at fair value	111,000	134,100	159,600
Funded status	(1,000)	(78,600)	(105,400)
Unrecognized prior service cost	–0–	52,800	32,000
Unrecognized net gain or loss	–0–	–0–	29,940
Prepaid/accrued pension cost	(1,000)	(25,800)	(43,460)
Adjustment required to recognize minimum liability	–0–	(4,100)	(37,540)
Accrued pension cost liability in balance sheet	$ (1,000)	$ (29,900)	$ (81,000)

---

[17]"Employers' Accounting for Pension Plans," op. cit., par. 104.

The 1995 column reveals that the projected benefit obligation is underfunded by $1,000. The 1996 column reveals that the underfunded liability of $78,600 is reported in the balance sheet at $29,900 because of $52,800 of unrecognized prior service cost and $4,100 of additional liability. The 1997 column reveals that the underfunded liability of $105,400 is reported in the balance sheet at $81,000 because of $32,000 of unrecognized prior service cost; $29,940 of unrecognized net loss; and $37,540 of additional liability.

The note disclosure for pensions provided by Syntex Corporation (a large international health care company) in its 1993 (year-ended July 31) Annual Report is shown in Illustration 21-30 and provides an example of the components of pension expense disclosure and the reconciliation schedule.

UNDERLYING CONCEPT

Does it make a difference to users of financial statements whether pension information is recognized in the financial statements or disclosed only in the notes? The FASB was not sure, so in accord with the full disclosure principle, it decided to provide extensive pension plan disclosures.

ILLUSTRATION 21-30
Note Disclosure for Pensions

Syntex Corporation

Note 8: Retirement Plans

The company's pension plans cover a majority of its employees. Pension costs for fiscal 1993, 1992 and 1991 were $29.2 million, $24.3 million and $18.6 million, respectively. Benefits are based on compensation earned during the years of service immediately preceding retirement. The company's actuarial cost method for its major plan in the United States is the projected unit credit method, and its funding policy for retirement plans is consistent with the relevant government and tax regulations.

Plans' assets consist primarily of stocks, bonds and pooled funds.

Pension cost for the company's benefit plans includes the following components:

($ in millions)	For the Years Ended July 31		
	1993	1992	1991
Significant Plans:			
Service cost—benefits earned during the year	$25.8	$22.0	$18.8
Interest cost on projected benefit obligations	29.5	25.4	20.4
Net increase in fair value of plans' assets	(40.3)	(31.5)	(32.6)
Net amortization and deferral	11.3	5.4	9.2
Net pension cost	26.3	21.3	15.8
Other plans	2.9	3.0	2.8
Total net pension costs	$29.2	$24.3	$18.6

The status of the company's significant plans at July 31, 1993, 1992 and 1991, was as follows:

($ in millions)	Plans in which Assets Exceed Accumulated Benefit Obligations			Plans in Which Accumulated Benefit Obligations Exceed Assets		
	1993	1992	1991	**1993**	1992	1991
Vested benefits	$217.7	$191.3	$161.2	$ 13.5	$ 12.7	$ 10.3
Nonvested benefits	20.5	19.6	18.9	.5	.4	.2
Accumulated benefit obligations	238.2	210.9	180.1	14.0	13.1	10.5
Plan assets at fair value	381.7	336.6	282.6	—	—	—
Plan assets in excess of (less than) accumulated benefit obligations	$143.5	$125.7	$102.5	$(14.0)	$(13.1)	$(10.5)
Total projected benefit obligations	$357.4	$328.7	$282.7	$ 24.8	$ 25.0	$ 15.4
Plan assets at fair value	381.7	336.6	282.6	—	—	—
Projected benefit obligations (in excess of) less than plan assets	24.3	7.9	(.1)	(24.8)	(25.0)	(15.4)
Add (Deduct):						
Unrecognized prior service cost	9.0	8.5	9.1	2.5	2.9	3.2
Unrecognized net (gain) loss	(1.5)	16.6	17.4	3.9	7.5	(.6)
Adjustment to recognize minimum liability	—	—	—	—	(1.1)	(.6)
Unamortized net transition (asset) obligation	(15.4)	(18.1)	(19.1)	2.4	2.6	2.9
Net asset (liability)	$ 16.4	$ 14.9	$ 7.3	$(16.0)	$(13.1)	$(10.5)

For fiscal 1993, 1992 and 1991, the weighted-average discount rate used in determining the projected benefit obligations (PBO) was approximately 8.5 percent; the rate of increase in future compensation levels used in determining the PBO was approximately 7.5 percent; and the weighted-average expected long-term rate of return on the plans' assets was approximately 8.5 percent. Management of the company believes the plans are appropriately funded based on actuarial calculations which include projections of future compensation.

▶ 1998 ENTRIES AND WORK SHEET— A COMPREHENSIVE ILLUSTRATION

Incorporating the corridor computation, the minimum liability recognition, and the required disclosures, the Zarle Company pension plan accounting is continued based on the following facts for 1998:

Service cost for 1998 is $16,000.

Settlement rate is 10%; expected rate of return 10%.

Actual return on plan assets for 1998 is $22,000.

Amortization of unrecognized prior service cost in 1998 is $17,600.

Annual contributions (funding) are $27,000.

Benefits paid to retirees in 1998 are $18,000.

Vested benefit obligation is $195,000 at the end of 1998.

Accumulated benefit obligation is $263,000 at the end of 1998.

Average service life of all covered employees is 20 years.

To facilitate accumulation and recording of the components of pension expense and maintenance of the unrecognized amounts related to the pension plan, the following work sheet is prepared from the basic data presented above. Beginning-of-the-year 1998 account balances are the December 31, 1997, balances from the revised 1997 pension work sheet of Zarle Company in Illustration 21-25.

ILLUSTRATION 21-31 Comprehensive Pension Work Sheet—1998

Zarle Company

General Journal Entries

Items	Annual Pension Expense	Cash	Prepaid/ Accrued Cost	Additional Liability	Pension Intangible	Contra Equity Charge
Balance, Dec. 31, 1997			43,460 Cr.	37,540 Cr.	32,000 Dr.	5,540 Dr.
(aa) Service cost	16,000 Dr.					
(bb) Interest cost	26,500 Dr.					
(cc) Actual return	22,000 Cr.					
(dd) Unexpected gain	**6,040 Dr.**					
(ee) Amortization of PSC	17,600 Dr.					
(ff) Contributions		27,000 Cr.				
(gg) Benefits						
(hh) Unrecog. loss amort.	**172 Dr.**					
(ii) Minimum liab. adj.				25,912 Dr.	20,372 Cr.	5,540 Cr.
Journal entry for 1998	44,312 Dr.	27,000 Cr.	17,312 Cr.			
Balance Dec. 31, 1998			60,772 Cr.	11,628 Cr.	11,628 Dr.	–0–

Memo Entries

Items	Projected Benefit Obligation	Plan Assets	Unrecognized Prior Service Cost	Unrecognized Net Gain or Loss
Balance, Dec. 31, 1997	265,000 Cr.	159,600 Dr.	32,000 Dr.	29,940 Dr.
(aa) Service cost	16,000 Cr.			
(bb) Interest cost	26,500 Cr.			
(cc) Actual return		22,000 Dr.		
(dd) Unexpected gain				**6,040 Cr.**
(ee) Amortization of PSC			17,600 Cr.	
(ff) Contributions		27,000 Dr.		
(gg) Benefits	18,000 Dr.	18,000 Cr.		
(hh) Unrecog. loss amort.				**172 Cr.**
(ii) Minimum liab. adj.				
Journal entry for 1998				
Balance Dec. 31, 1998	289,500 Cr.	190,600 Dr.	14,400 Dr.	23,728 Dr.

WORK SHEET EXPLANATIONS AND ENTRIES

Entries (aa) through (gg) are similar to the corresponding entries previously explained in the prior years' work sheets with the exception of entry (dd). In 1997 the expected return on plan assets exceeded the actual return producing an unexpected loss. In 1998 the actual return of $22,000 exceeds the expected return of $15,960 ($159,600 × 10%), resulting in an unexpected gain of $6,040, entry (dd). By netting the gain of $6,040 against the actual return of $22,000, pension expense is affected only by the expected return of $15,960.

A new entry (hh) in Zarle Company's work sheet results from application of the corridor test on the accumulated balance of unrecognized net gain or loss. Zarle Company begins 1998 with a balance in the unrecognized net loss account of $29,940. The corridor criterion must be applied in 1998 to determine whether the balance is excessive and should be amortized. In 1998 the corridor is 10% of the larger of the beginning-of-the-year projected benefit obligation of $265,000 or the plan asset's market-related asset value (assumed to be fair market value) of $159,600. The corridor for 1998, thus, is $26,500 ($265,000 x 10%). Because the balance in the Unrecognized Net Loss account is $29,940, the excess (outside the corridor) is $3,440 ($29,940 − $26,500). The $3,440 excess is amortized over the average remaining service life of all employees. Using an average remaining service life of 20 years, the amortization in 1998 is $172 ($3,440 ÷ 20). In the 1998 pension work sheet, the $172 is recorded as a debit to Pension Expense and a credit to the Unrecognized Net Loss account. A schedule showing the computation of the $172 amortization charge is presented below:

Zarle Company 1998 Corridor Test	
Unrecognized net (gain) or loss at beginning of year	$29,940
10% of larger of PBO or market-related asset value of plan assets	26,500
Amortizable amount	$ 3,440
Average service life of all employees	20 years
1998 amortization ($3,440 ÷ 20 years)	$172

ILLUSTRATION 21-32
Computation of 1998 Amortization Charge (Corridor Test)

The journal entry to formally record pension expense for 1998 is as follows:

1998

Pension Expense	44,312	
Cash		27,000
Prepaid/Accrued Pension Cost		17,312

The minimum liability, additional liability, and the amount reported as a contra equity charge at the end of 1998 are computed as follows:

Zarle Company	
	December 31, 1998
Accumulated benefit obligation (ABO)	$(263,000)
Plan assets at fair value	190,600
Unfunded accumulated benefit obligation (minimum liability)	(72,400)
Accrued pension cost	60,772
Additional liability	(11,628)
Unrecognized prior service cost	14,400
Contra equity charge	$ –0–

ILLUSTRATION 21-33
Minimum Liability Computation—1998

As indicated in the above computation, the additional liability balance on December 31, 1998, is $11,628. The balance of $37,540 of additional liability carried over from 1997 requires a downward adjustment of $25,912 ($37,540 − $11,628). The balance in the pension intangible account should also be $11,628; it is, therefore, credited for $20,372 to reduce the balance of $32,000 to the desired amount of $11,628. Because the unrecognized prior service cost balance exceeds the additional liability, no contra equity charge is required. The entry to adjust the minimum liability (the three accounts related thereto) at December 31, 1998, is as follows:

	1998	
Additional Pension Liability	25,912	
Intangible Asset—Deferred Pension Cost		20,372
Excess of Additional Pension Liability		
Over Unrecognized Prior Service Cost		5,540

FINANCIAL STATEMENT PRESENTATION

The financial statements of Zarle Company at December 31, 1998, present the following items relative to its pension plan:

ILLUSTRATION 21-34
Balance Sheet
Presentation of Pension
Costs—1998

Zarle Company BALANCE SHEET As of December 31, 1998			
Assets		**Liabilities**	
Intangible assets		Long-term liabilities	
Deferred pension cost	$11,628	Accrued pension cost	$72,400

The prepaid/accrued pension cost balance of $60,772 and the additional liability balance of $11,628 on the work sheet are combined and reported as one pension liability of $72,400 in the balance sheet.

ILLUSTRATION 21-35
Income Statement
Presentation of Pension
Expense—1998

Zarle Company INCOME STATEMENT For the Year Ended December 31, 1998	
Operating expenses	
Pension expense*	$44,312
*Pension expense is frequently reported as "Employee benefits."	

ILLUSTRATION 21-36
Statement of Cash Flows
Presentation of Pension
Liability

Zarle Company STATEMENT OF CASH FLOWS For the Year Ended December 31, 1998		
Cash flow from operating activities		
Net income (assumed)		$905,000
Adjustments to reconcile net income to net		
cash provided by operating activities:		
Increase in accrued pension liability	$17,312	
Note: Significant noncash investing and financing activities		
Decrease of $20,372 in intangible asset and decrease of $5,540 in contra equity due to decrease of $25,912 in minimum liability.		

NOTE DISCLOSURE

The minimum note disclosure by Zarle Company of the pension plan for 1998 is shown in Illustration 21-37.

ILLUSTRATION 21-37
**Minimum Note
Disclosure of Pension
Plan, Zarle Company,
1998**

Notes to the financial statements
Note D. The company has a pension plan covering substantially all of its employees. The plan is contributory and provides pension benefits that are based on the employee's compensation during the three years immediately preceding retirement. The pension plan's assets consist of cash, stocks, and bonds. The company's funding policy is consistent with the relevant government (ERISA) and tax regulations.

Net pension expense for 1998 is comprised of the following components of pension cost:

Service cost	$16,000
Interest on projected benefit obligations	26,500
Actual return on plan assets	(22,000)
Net other components of pension expense	23,812
Net pension expense	$44,312

The following schedule reconciles the funded status of the plan with amounts reported in the company's balance sheet at December 31, 1998:

Actuarial present value of benefit obligations:	
Vested benefit obligation	$ 195,000
Accumulated benefit obligation	$ 263,000
Projected benefit obligation	$(289,500)
Plan assets at fair value	190,600
Projected benefit obligation in excess of plan assets	(98,900)
Unrecognized prior service cost	14,400
Unrecognized net (gain) or loss	23,728
Prepaid/accrued pension cost	(60,772)
Adjustment required to recognize minimum liability	(11,628)
Accrued pension cost liability recognized in the balance sheet	$ (72,400)

The weighted-average discount rate used in determining the 1998 projected benefit obligation was 10%. The rate of increase in future compensation levels used in computing the 1998 projected benefit obligation was 4.5%. The weighted-average expected long-term rate of return on the plan's assets was 10%.

Note that in the reconciliation schedule above, the adjustment required to recognize the minimum liability of $11,628 is included in order to reconcile to the $72,400 accrued pension cost reported in the balance sheet.

▶ THE PENSION REFORM ACT OF 1974

The Employee Retirement Income Security Act of 1974 (ERISA) affects virtually every private retirement plan in the United States. It attempts to safeguard employees' pension rights by mandating many pension plan requirements, including minimum funding, participation, and vesting.

These requirements can influence the employers' costs significantly. Under this legislation annual funding is no longer discretionary; an employer must fund the plan in accordance with an actuarial funding method that over time will be sufficient to pay for all pension obligations. If funding is not carried out in a reasonable manner, fines may be imposed and tax deductions denied.

Plan administrators are required to publish a comprehensive description and summary of their plans and detailed annual reports accompanied by many supplementary schedules and statements. ERISA further mandates that the required reports, statements, and supplementary schedules be subjected to audit by qualified independent public accountants.

Another important provision of the Act is the creation of the Pension Benefit Guaranty Corporation (PBGC). **The PBGC's purpose is to administer terminated plans** and to impose liens on the employer's assets for certain unfunded pension liabilities. If a plan is terminated, the PBGC can effectively impose a lien against the employer's assets for the excess of the present value of guaranteed vested benefits over the pension fund

**UNDERLYING
CONCEPT**

Many plans are underfunded but still quite viable. For example Loews Corp. has a $159 million shortfall. But Loew's had earnings of $594 million in 1993 and a good net worth. Thus, the going concern assumption permits us to ignore these pension underfundings in many cases because in the long run they are not significant.

assets. This lien generally has had the status of a tax lien and, therefore, takes priority over most other creditorship claims. This section of the Act gives the PBGC the power to force an involuntary termination of a pension plan whenever the risks related to nonpayment of the pension obligation seem too great. Because ERISA restricts the lien that the PBGC can impose to 30% of net worth, the PBGC must monitor all plans to ensure that net worth is sufficient to meet the pension benefit obligations.[18]

A large number of terminated plans have caused the PBGC to pay out substantial benefits. Currently the PBGC receives its funding from employers, who contribute a certain dollar amount for each employee covered under the plan (at present more than 38 million employees).

An interesting accounting problem relates to the manner of disclosing the possible termination of a plan. When, for example, should a contingent liability be disclosed, if a company is experiencing financial difficulty and may not be able to meet its pension obligations if its plan is terminated? At present this issue is unresolved, and considerable judgment would be needed to analyze a company with these contingent liabilities.[19]

▶ MULTIEMPLOYER PLANS

Multiemployer pension plans are plans sponsored by two or more different employers. They are often negotiated as part of labor union contracts in the trucking, coal mining, construction, and entertainment industries.

ERISA created an incentive for financially troubled companies to withdraw without penalty from multiemployer plans and shift their liability for paying pension benefits to the federal PBGC. Withdrawal by a substantial number of employers could have triggered widespread bankruptcies of these plans, as the burden of funding them fell on the remaining participating employers.

To remedy this situation, Congress passed the Multiemployer Pension Plan Amendments Act of 1980, which amended ERISA. It provides PBGC coverage only for insolvent plans, not for terminated plans, and it imposes substantial obligations for a part of the plan's unfunded vested benefits on companies that withdraw from multiemployer plans.[20] It is apparent that certain employers' contingent liabilities have significantly increased as a result of this amendment to ERISA.

In *FASB Statement No. 87,* a number of disclosure provisions of multiemployer plans are required:

(a) A description of the multiemployer plan including the employee groups covered, the type of benefit provided (defined benefit or defined contribution), and the nature and effect of significant matters affecting comparability of information for all periods presented.

(b) The amount of cost recognized during the period.

---

[18]The major problems in underfunding are occurring in four labor-intensive industries—steel, autos, rubber, and airlines. General Motors, for example, is two-thirds funded but still has a deficit of over $20 billion.

[19]Pan American is a good illustration of how difficult it is to assess when to terminate. When Pan Am filed for bankruptcy in 1991, it had a pension liability of $900 million. From 1983 to 1991, the IRS gave it six waivers so it did not have to make contributions. When the plan was terminated, there was little net worth upon which a lien could be imposed.

[20]This amendment has come under severe attack by many because it forces unprofitable companies to stay in business against their better judgment. In the trucking industry, at one time many companies wanted to shut down losing operations or liquidate entirely. However, a company that follows one of these options may become liable for a pension liability that exceeds the proceeds it will receive in the liquidation. As an illustration, Republic Industries purchased Johnson Motor Lines in 1979. Subsequently, Johnson Motor Lines closed, making Johnson liable for withdrawal penalties. This resulted in claims from five different multiemployer funds totaling $17.7 million, a figure not only in excess of the net worth of Johnson and Republic but also in excess of the cumulative net income of Johnson since its inception in 1945. See Shirley Hobbs Scheible, "Erisa Eraser," *Barrons*, April 12, 1982.

► PENSION TERMINATIONS

A congressman at one time noted that "employers are simply treating their employee pension plans like company piggy banks, to be raided at will." What this congressman was referring to is the practice by some companies that have pension plan assets in excess of projected benefit obligations of paying off the obligation and pocketing the difference. ERISA prevents companies from recapturing excess assets unless they pay participants what is owed to them and then terminate the plan. As a result, companies are buying annuities to pay off the pension claimants and using the excess funds for other corporate purposes.[21]

For example, pension plan terminations netted $363 million for Occidental Petroleum Corp., $95 million for Stroh's Brewery Co., $58 million for M. W. Kellogg Co., and $29 million for Western Airlines. Since 1980, many large companies have terminated their pension plans and captured billions in surplus assets. All of this is quite legal, but is it ethical? It should be noted that federal legislation recently enacted requires the company to pay an excise tax of anywhere from 20% to 50% on the gains.

The accounting issue that arises from these terminations is whether a gain should be recognized by the corporation when these assets revert back to the company (often called **asset reversion** transactions). The issue is complex because, in some cases, a new defined benefit plan is started after the old one has been eliminated. Therefore some contend that there has been no change in substance, but merely one in form.

Up to this point the profession has required that these gains be reported if the companies switched from a defined benefit plan to a defined contribution plan. Otherwise, the gain is deferred and amortized over at least 10 years in the future. Many questioned this reporting treatment. As a result the FASB issued *FASB Statement No. 88* that requires recognition in earnings of a net gain or loss when the employer settles a pension obligation either by lump-sum cash payments to participants or by purchasing nonparticipating annuity contracts.[22]

► CONCLUDING OBSERVATION

Hardly a day goes by without the financial press analyzing in depth some issues related to pension plans in the United States. This is hardly surprising, since U.S. pension funds now hold over $4 trillion in assets. As should be obvious by now, the accounting issues related to pension plans are complex. *FASB Statement No. 87* clarifies many of these issues and should help users understand the financial implications of a company's pension plans on its financial position, results of operations, and cash flows.

Critics still argue, however, that much remains to be done. One issue in particular relates to the delayed recognition of certain events. Changes in pension plan obligations and changes in the value of plan assets are not recognized immediately but are systematically incorporated over subsequent periods.

---

[21]A real question exists as to whose money it is. Some argue that the excess funds belong to the employees, not the employer. In addition, given that the funds have been reverting to the employer, critics charge that cost-of-living increases and the possibility of other increased benefits are reduced, because companies will be reluctant to use those excess funds to pay for such increases.

[22]"Employers' Accounting for Settlements and Curtailments of Defined Benefit Pension Plans and for Termination Benefits," *Statement of Financial Accounting Standards No. 88* (Stamford, Conn.: FASB, 1985). Some companies have established pension poison pills as an antitakeover measure. These plans require asset reversions from termination of a plan to benefit employees and retirees rather than the acquiring company. For a discussion of pension poison pills, see Eugene E. Comiskey and Charles W. Mulford, "Interpreting Pension Disclosures: A Guide for Lending Officers," *Commercial Lending Review*, Winter 1993–94, Vol. 9, No. 1.

▶ SUMMARY OF LEARNING OBJECTIVES ◀

1. **Identify types of pension plans and their characteristics.** The two most common types of pension arrangements are: (1) *Defined contribution plans:* the employer agrees to contribute to a pension trust a certain sum each period based on a formula. This formula may consider such factors as age, length of employee service, employer's profits, and compensation level. Only the employer's contribution is defined; no promise is made regarding the ultimate benefits paid out to the employees. (2) *Defined benefit plans:* define the benefits that the employee will receive at the time of retirement. The formula typically used provides for the benefits to be a function of the employee's years of service and the employee's compensation level when he or she nears retirement.

2. **Distinguish between accounting for the employer's pension plan and accounting for the pension fund.** The company or employer is the organization sponsoring the pension plan. It incurs the cost and makes contributions to the pension fund. The fund or plan is the entity that receives the contributions from the employer, administers the pension assets, and makes the benefit payments to the pension recipients (retired employees). The fund should be a separate legal and accounting entity for which a set of books is maintained and financial statements are prepared.

3. **Explain alternative measures for valuing the pension obligation.** One measure of the pension obligation bases it only on the benefits vested to the employees. Vested benefits are those that the employee is entitled to receive even if the employee renders no additional services under the plan. The *vested benefits pension obligation* is computed using current salary levels and includes only vested benefits. Another measure of the obligation, called the *accumulated benefit obligation,* bases the computation of the deferred compensation amount on all years of service performed by employees under the plan—both vested and nonvested—using current salary levels. A third measure, called the *projected benefit obligation,* bases the computation of the deferred compensation amount on both vested and nonvested service using future salaries.

4. **Identify the components of pension expense.** Pension expense is a function of the following components: (1) service cost; (2) interest on the liability; (3) actual return on plan assets; (4) amortization of unrecognized prior service cost; and (5) gain or loss.

5. **Utilize a work sheet for pension plan entries.** A work sheet unique to pension accounting may be utilized to record both the formal entries and the memo entries to keep track of all the employer's relevant pension plan items and components.

6. **Describe the amortization of unrecognized prior service costs.** The amount of the prior service cost is computed by an actuary. Amortization of the unrecognized prior service cost is an accounting function performed with the assistance of an actuary. The Board prefers a "years-of-service" amortization method that is similar to a units-of-production computation. First, the total estimated number of service-years to be worked by all of the participating employees is computed. Second, the unrecognized prior service cost is divided by the total number of service-years to obtain a cost per service-year (the unit cost). And third, the number of service-years consumed each year is multiplied by the cost per service-year to obtain the annual amortization charge.

7. **Explain the accounting procedure for recognizing unexpected gains and losses.** In estimating the projected benefit obligation (the liability), actuaries make assumptions about such items as mortality rate, retirement rate, turnover rate, disability rate, and salary amounts. Any change in these actuarial

assumptions changes the amount of the projected benefit obligation. These unexpected gains or losses from changes in the projected benefit obligation are liability gains and losses. Liability gains (resulting from unexpected decreases in the liability balance) and liability losses (resulting from unexpected increases) are deferred (unrecognized). The liability gains and losses are combined in the same Unrecognized Net Gain or Loss account used for asset gains and losses and are accumulated from year to year, off-balance-sheet, in a memo record account.

8. **Explain the corridor approach to amortizing unrecognized gains and losses.** The unrecognized net gain or loss balance is considered too large and must be amortized when it exceeds the arbitrarily selected FASB criterion of 10% of the larger of the beginning balances of the projected benefit obligation or the market-related value of the plan assets. If the balance of the unrecognized net gain or loss account stays within the upper and lower limits of the corridor, no amortization is required.

9. **Explain the recognition of a minimum liability.** Immediate recognition of a liability (referred to as the minimum liability) is required when the accumulated benefit obligation exceeds the fair value of plan assets. The purpose of this minimum liability requirement is to assure that if a significant plan amendment or actuarial loss occurs, a liability will be recognized at least to the extent of the unfunded portion of the accumulated benefit obligation.

10. **Describe the reporting requirements for pension plans in financial statements.** The current financial statement disclosure requirements for pension plans are as follows: (1) A description of the plan including employee groups covered, type of benefit formula, funding policy, types of assets held, and the nature and effect of significant matters affecting comparability of information for all periods presented. (2) The components of net periodic pension expense for the period. (3) A schedule reconciling the funded status of the plan with amounts reported in the employer's statement of financial position. (4) The weighted-average assumed discount rate, the rate of compensation increase used to measure the projected benefit obligation, and the weighted-average expected long-term rate of return on plan assets.

APPENDIX 21-A

ACCOUNTING FOR POSTRETIREMENT BENEFITS

IBM Corporation's adoption of a new accounting standard on postretirement benefits in March 1991 resulted in a $2.3 billion charge and a historical curiosity—IBM's first-ever quarterly loss. General Electric Co. disclosed that its charge for adoption of the same new FASB standard would be $2.7 billion, and in the fourth quarter of 1993, AT&T Co. absorbed a $2.1 billion pretax hit for postretirement benefits. What is this new standard, and how could its adoption have so grave an impact on companies' earnings?

► NEW ACCOUNTING STANDARD

After a decade of study, the FASB in December 1990 issued *Statement No. 106*, "Employers' Accounting for Postretirement Benefits Other Than Pensions." It alone is the cause for those large charges to income. The new standard accounts for health care and other welfare benefits provided to retirees, their spouses, dependents, and beneficiaries.[1] These other welfare benefits include life insurance offered outside a pension plan, dental care as well as medical care, eye care, legal and tax services, tuition assistance, day care, and housing assistance.[2] Because health care benefits are the largest of the other postretirement benefits, this item is used to illustrate accounting for postretirement benefits.

Enactment of *SFAS No. 106* made corporate managers acutely aware of their company's costs of retiree health and medical benefits. In the three years since this statement was issued, health care inflation has fallen from 9.6% to 4.9%. The annual rate of increase in health care costs has not been stopped, but it has been greatly reduced.

For many employers (about 95%) this new standard required a change from the predominant practice of accounting for postretirement benefits on a pay-as-you-go (cash) basis to an accrual basis. Similar to pension accounting, the accrual basis necessitates measurement of the employer's obligation to provide future benefits and accrual of the cost during the years that the employee provides service.

One of the reasons companies have not prefunded these benefit plans is that payments to prefund health care costs, unlike excess contributions to a pension trust, are not tax deductible. Another reason is that postretirement health care benefits were once perceived to be a low-cost employee benefit that could be changed or eliminated at will and, therefore, not a legal liability. Now, the accounting definition of a liability goes beyond the notion of a legally enforceable claim to encompass equitable or constructive obligations as well, making it clear that the postretirement benefit promise is a liability.[3]

► DIFFERENCES BETWEEN PENSION BENEFITS AND HEALTH CARE BENEFITS

OBJECTIVE 11

Identify the differences between pensions and postretirement health care benefits.

The FASB used *Statement No. 87* on pensions as a reference for the accounting prescribed in *Statement No. 106* on health care and other nonpension postretirement benefits.[4] Why didn't the FASB cover both types of postretirement benefits in the earlier pension accounting statement? The apparent similarities between the two benefits mask some significant differences. These differences are shown in Illustration 21A-1.[5]

---

[1]Approximately one-third of all workers in the United States participate in employer health plans that provide for the continuation of health care coverage during the years of retirement. Surprisingly, such coverage translates into a total health care liability estimated at more than $400 billion and perhaps as much as $2 trillion, which is largely unfunded.

[2]"OPEB" is the acronym frequently used to describe postretirement benefits covered by *FASB Statement No. 106*. This term came into being before the scope of the statement was narrowed from "other postemployment benefits" to "other postretirement benefits," thereby excluding postemployment benefits related to severance pay or wage continuation to disabled, terminated, or laid-off employees.

[3]"Elements of Financial Statements," *Statement of Financial Accounting Concepts No. 6* (Stamford, CT: FASB, 1985), page 13, footnote 21.

[4]In November 1992 the FASB issued *Statement of Financial Accounting Standards No. 112*, "Employers' Accounting for Postemployment Benefits," which covers postemployment benefits that are not accounted for under *SFAS No. 87* (pensions), *SFAS No. 88* (settlements, curtailments, and termination benefits), or *SFAS No. 106* (postretirement benefits other than pensions). *SFAS No. 112* requires an employer to recognize the obligation to provide postemployment benefits in accordance with *SFAS No. 43*, similar to accounting for compensated absences (see Chapter 13). These *SFAS No. 112* benefits include, but are not limited to, salary continuation, disability-related benefits, severance benefits, and continuance of health care benefits and life insurance for inactive or former (e.g., terminated, disabled, or deceased) employees or their beneficiaries.

[5]D. Gerald Searfoss and Naomi Erickson, "The Big Unfunded Liability: Postretirement Health Care Benefits," *Journal of Accountancy*, November 1988, pp. 28–39.

Item	Pensions	Health Care Benefits
Funding	Generally funded.	Generally *NOT* funded.
Benefit	Well-defined and level dollar amount.	Generally uncapped and great variability.
Beneficiary	Retiree (maybe some benefit to surviving spouse).	Retiree, spouse, and other dependents.
Benefit Payable	Monthly.	As needed and used.
Predictability	Variables are reasonably predictable.	Utilization difficult to predict. Level of cost varies geographically and fluctuates over time.

ILLUSTRATION 21A-1
Differences Between Pensions and Postretirement Health Care Benefits

Two of the differences presented in the preceding list illustrate why measuring the future payments for health care benefit plans is so much more difficult than for pension plans:

1. Many postretirement plans do not set a limit on health care benefits. No matter how serious the illness or how long it lasts, the benefits continue to flow. (Even if the employer uses an insurance company plan, the premiums will escalate according to the increased benefits provided.)

2. The level of health care benefit utilization and health care costs is difficult to predict. The increased longevity and new, unexpected illnesses (e.g., AIDS) along with new medical technologies (e.g., CAT scans) and cures (e.g., radiation) cause changes in health care utilization.

Additionally, although health care benefits are generally covered by the fiduciary and reporting standards for employee benefit funds under ERISA, the stringent minimum vesting, participation, and funding standards that apply to pensions do not apply to health care benefits. Nevertheless, as you will learn, many of the basic concepts and much of the accounting terminology and measurement methodology applicable to pensions are applicable to other postretirement benefits accounting. Therefore, throughout the following discussion and illustrations, we point out the similarities and differences in the accounting and reporting for these two types of postretirement benefits.

► POSTRETIREMENT BENEFITS ACCOUNTING PROVISIONS

Health care and other postretirement benefits for current and future retirees and their dependents are forms of deferred compensation earned through employee service and subject to accrual during the years an employee is working. The period of time over which the postretirement benefit cost is accrued, called the **attribution period,** is the period of service during which the employee earns the benefits under the terms of the plan. This attribution period (shown in Illustration 21A-2) generally begins when an employee is hired and ends on the date the employee is eligible to receive the benefits and ceases to earn additional benefits by performing service, the vesting date.[6]

---

[6]This is a benefit-years-of-service approach (the projected unit credit actuarial cost method). The FASB found no compelling reason to switch from the traditional pension accounting approach. It rejected the employee's full service period (i.e., to the estimated retirement date) because it was unable to identify any approach that would appropriately attribute benefits beyond the date full eligibility for those benefits is attained. Full eligibility is attained by meeting specified age, service, or age and service requirements of the plan.

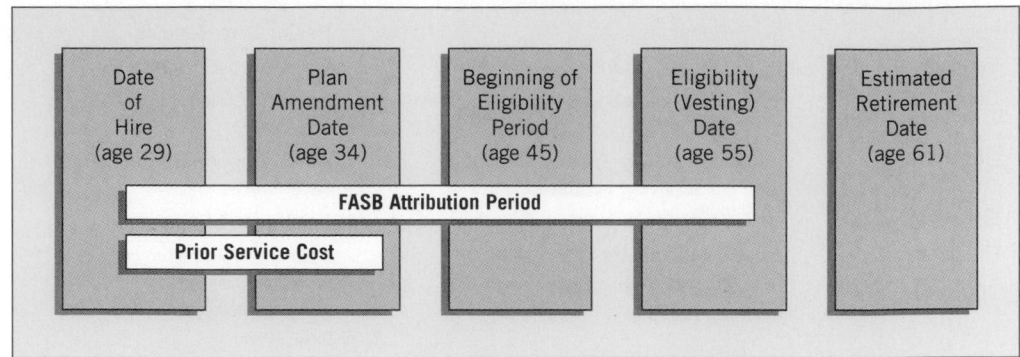

OBLIGATIONS UNDER POSTRETIREMENT BENEFITS

In defining the obligation for postretirement benefits, many concepts similar to pension accounting are maintained, but some new and modified terms are designed specifically for postretirement benefits. Two of the most important are (a) expected postretirement benefit obligation and (b) accumulated postretirement benefit obligation.

Expected Postretirement Benefit Obligation (EPBO). The EPBO is the actuarial present value as of a particular date of **all benefits expected to be paid after retirement to employees and their dependents.** The EPBO is not recorded in the financial statements, but it is used in measuring periodic expense.

Accumulated Postretirement Benefit Obligation (APBO). The APBO is the actuarial present value of **future benefits attributed to employees' services rendered to a particular date.** The APBO is equal to the EPBO for retirees and active employees fully eligible for benefits. Before the date an employee achieves full eligibility, the APBO is only a portion of the EPBO. Or stated another way, the difference between the APBO and the EPBO is the future service costs of active employees who are not yet fully eligible.

The following diagram contrasts the EPBO and the APBO.

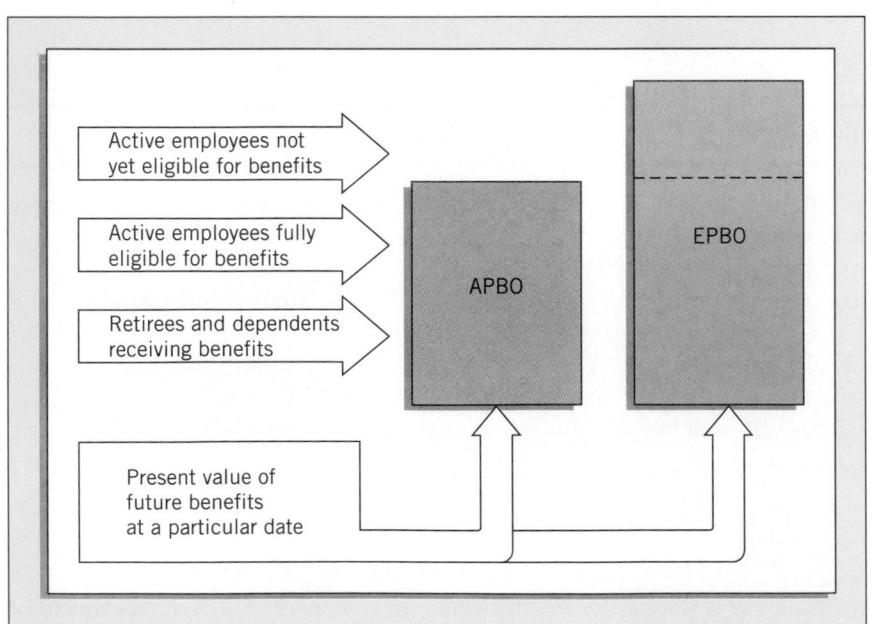

At the date an employee is fully eligible (the end of the attribution period), the APBO and the EPBO relative to that employee are equal.

POSTRETIREMENT EXPENSE

Postretirement expense, also referred to as **net periodic postretirement benefit cost,** is the employer's annual postretirement benefit expense, which consists of many of the familiar components used to compute annual pension expense. The components of net periodic postretirement benefit cost are:[7]

1. **Service Cost.** The portion of the EPBO attributed to employee service during the period.

2. **Interest Cost.** The increase in the APBO attributable to the passage of time. It is computed by applying the beginning-of-the-year discount rate to the beginning-of-the-year APBO, adjusted for benefit payments to be made during the period. The discount rate is based on the rates of return on high-quality, fixed-income investments that are currently available.[8]

3. **Actual Return on Plan Assets.** The change in the fair value of the plan's assets adjusted for contributions and benefit payments made during the period. Because the postretirement expense is credited or charged for the gain or loss on plan assets (the difference between the actual and the expected return), this component is really expected return.

4. **Amortization of Prior Service Cost.** The amortization of the cost of retroactive benefits resulting from plan amendments or a plan initiation that takes place after *Statement No. 106* takes effect. The typical amortization period, beginning at the date of the plan amendment, is the remaining service periods through the full eligibility date.

5. **Gains and Losses.** In general, changes in the APBO resulting from changes in assumptions or from experience different from that assumed. For funded plans, this component also includes the difference between actual return and expected return on plan assets (computed the same as for pensions—actual based on fair value and expected based on market-related value). Gains or losses can be recognized immediately or can be based on a "corridor approach" similar to that used for pension accounting.

6. **Amortization of Transition Obligation.** The straight-line amortization of the unrecognized APBO at the time *FASB Statement No. 106* is adopted. This component of expense is not present if the transition obligation is recognized immediately.

THE TRANSITION AMOUNT

At the beginning of the year of adoption of *FASB Statement No. 106*, a **transition amount** (obligation or asset) is computed as the difference between (1) the APBO and (2) the fair value of the plan assets, plus any accrued obligation or less any prepaid cost (asset). Because most plans are unfunded and most employers are accruing postretirement benefit costs for the first time, large transition obligations occur.

The accounting treatment of this transition amount was one of the most controversial issues in postretirement benefit standard setting. The primary concern of many was that an immediate charge to expense for unrecognized past costs, accompanied by recognition of the total unrecognized liability, would have a large negative impact on reported earnings in the year of the change. Of equal concern to others was that the alternative, deferral and amortization of the expense, accompanied by a rapidly increas-

---

[7]"Employers' Accounting for Postretirement Benefits Other Than Pensions," *Statement of Financial Accounting Standards No. 106* (Norwalk, CT: FASB, 1990), paras. 46–66. And see, James R. Wilbert and Kenneth E. Dakdduk, "The New FASB 106: How to Account for Postretirement Benefits," *Journal of Accountancy*, August 1991, pp. 36–41.

[8]The FASB concluded that the discount rate for measuring the present value of the postretirement benefit obligation and the service cost component should be the same as that applied to pension measurements. It chose not to label it the settlement rate in order to clarify that the objective of the discount rate is to measure the time value of money.

ing liability, would be a drain on reported earnings for many years. And providing the option of immediate writeoff or deferral and amortization was also problematic because of the lack of comparability that would result. Nevertheless, the FASB decided to permit employers to choose between immediate recognition (e.g., the $2.3 billion charge taken by IBM in the first quarter of 1991) and deferral and amortization:

Immediate Recognition. As an immediate writeoff, the transition amount is recognized in the income statement as the "effect of a change in accounting principle" (net of tax)[9] and in the balance sheet as a long-term liability entitled Postretirement Benefit Obligation. Restatement of previously issued annual financial statements is not permitted.[10]

Deferred Recognition. Employers choosing deferred recognition must amortize the transition amount on a straight-line basis over the average remaining service period to expected retirement of the employees in place at the time of transition and expected to receive benefits.[11] If the remaining service period is less than 20 years, the employer may elect a 20-year amortization period. But, the transition amount may not be amortized more slowly than it is paid off (referred to as the "pay-as-you-go constraint").

Once chosen, the method cannot be changed. That is, after once electing to amortize the transition amount, the employer cannot record the remainder of its unamortized transition obligation in a subsequent year under the immediate recognition method.

▶ ILLUSTRATIVE ACCOUNTING ENTRIES

OBJECTIVE 12

Contrast accounting for pensions to accounting for other postretirement benefits.

Like pension accounting, several significant items of the postretirement plan are unrecognized in the accounts and in the financial statements. These off-balance-sheet items are:

1. Expected postretirement benefit obligation (EPBO)
2. Accumulated postretirement benefit obligation (APBO)
3. Postretirement benefit plan assets
4. Unrecognized transition amount
5. Unrecognized prior service cost
6. Unrecognized net gain or loss

The EPBO is not recognized in the financial statements or disclosed in the notes. It is recomputed each year and used by the actuary in measuring the annual service cost. Because of the numerous assumptions and actuarial complexity involved in measuring annual service cost, we have omitted these computations of the EPBO.

All five of the other off-balance-sheet items listed above must be disclosed by the employer in notes to the financial statements. In addition, as in pension accounting, the exact amount of these items must be known because they are used in the computation of postretirement expense. Therefore, in order to track these off-balance-sheet postretirement benefit items, the work sheet illustrated in pension accounting will be utilized to record both the formal general journal entries and the memo entries.

---

[9]The FASB uses the term "effect" rather than "cumulative effect," and because of the unique transition provision and calculations involved, the retroactive effects on prior periods are generally not determinable and therefore pro forma disclosures are not required. The per share effects of the accounting change are required to be shown on the face of the income statement.

[10]In pension accounting, the transition amount must be amortized over the average remaining service life of existing employees or optionally over a 15-year period if the remaining service life is less than 15 years.

[11]For amortization of the transition amount (and for gains and losses as well), the Board chose the longer "retirement date" as opposed to the "full eligibility date" for pragmatic reasons—the magnitude of the transition amount argued for a longer amortization period to minimize the effect on current financial statements.

1995 ENTRIES AND WORK SHEET

To illustrate the use of a work sheet in accounting for a postretirement benefits plan, assume that on January 1, 1995, Quest Company adopts *Statement No. 106* to account for its health care benefit plan. The following facts apply to the postretirement benefits plan for the year 1995:

Plan assets at fair value on January 1, 1995, are zero.

Actual and expected returns on plan assets in 1995 are zero.

APBO, January 1, 1995, is $400,000.

Service cost for 1995 is $22,000.

No prior service cost exists.

Discount rate is 8%.

Contributions (funding) to plan in 1995 are $38,000.

Benefit payments to employees from plan in 1995 are $28,000.

Average remaining service to full eligibility: 21 years.

Average remaining service to expected retirement: 25 years.

Transition amount to be amortized.

Using the preceding data, the following work sheet presents the beginning balances and all of the postretirement benefit entries recorded by Quest Company in 1995.

ILLUSTRATION 21A-4
Postretirement Benefits
Work Sheet—1995

Quest Company

	General Journal Entries			Memo Record		
Items	Annual Postretirement Expense	Cash	Prepaid/ Accrued Cost	APBO	Plan Assets	Unrecognized Transition Amount
Balance, Jan. 1, 1995				400,000 Cr.		400,000 Dr.
(a) Service cost	22,000 Dr.			22,000 Cr.		
(b) Interest cost	32,000 Dr.			32,000 Cr.		
(c) Contributions		38,000 Cr.			38,000 Dr.	
(d) Benefits				28,000 Dr.	28,000 Cr.	
(e) Amortization:						
Transition	16,000 Dr.***					16,000 Cr.
Journal entry for 1995	70,000 Dr.	38,000 Cr.	32,000 Cr.*			
Balance, Dec. 31, 1995			32,000 Cr.**	426,000 Cr.	10,000 Dr.	384,000 Dr.

*$70,000 − $38,000 = $32,000.
**$426,000 − ($10,000 + $384,000) = $32,000
***$400,000 ÷ 25 = $16,000

On the first line of the work sheet, the beginning balances of the APBO and the unrecognized transition amount are recorded in the memo record columns. The transition amount is the difference between the APBO and the fair value of plan assets, in this case $400,000 ($400,000 − $0).

Entry (a) records the service cost component, which increases postretirement expense $22,000 and increases the liability (APBO) $22,000. Entry (b) accrues the interest expense component, which increases both the liability (APBO) and the expense by $32,000 (the beginning APBO multiplied by the discount rate of 8%). Entry (c) records Quest Company's contribution (funding) of assets to the postretirement benefit fund; cash is decreased $38,000 and plan assets are increased $38,000. Entry (d) records the benefit payments made to retirees, which results in equal $28,000 decreases to the plan assets and the liability (APBO). Entry (e) records the amortization of the unrecognized transition amount. It is amortized over the average remaining service to expected retirement, 25 years. The amortized amount of $16,000 ($400,000 ÷ 25) increases postretirement expense and decreases the unrecognized transition amount.

The entry on December 31, which is the adjusting entry made to formally record the postretirement expense in 1995, is as follows:

December 31, 1995

Postretirement Expense	70,000	
Cash		38,000
Prepaid/Accrued Cost		32,000

The credit to Prepaid/Accrued Cost for $32,000 represents the difference between the 1995 postretirement expense of $70,000 and the amount funded of $38,000. The $32,000 credit balance is a liability because the plan is underfunded. The Prepaid/Accrued Cost account balance of $32,000 also equals the net of the balances in the memo accounts. This reconciliation of the off-balance-sheet items with the prepaid/accrued cost reported in the balance sheet is shown below (similar to the pension reconciliation schedule).

ILLUSTRATION 21A-5 Postretirement Benefits Reconciliation Schedule—December 31, 1995

Accumulated postretirement benefit obligation (Credit)	$(426,000)
Plan assets at fair value (Debit)	10,000
Funded status (Credit)	(416,000)
Unrecognized transition amount (Debit)	384,000
Prepaid/accrued cost (Credit)	$ (32,000)

Preparation of this reconciliation schedule is necessary as part of the required note disclosures.

RECOGNITION OF GAINS AND LOSSES

Gains and losses represent changes in the APBO or the value of plan assets resulting either from actual experience different from that expected or from changes in actuarial assumptions. The FASB noted that "recognizing the effects of revisions in estimates in full in the period in which they occur may produce financial statements that portray more volatility than is inherent in the employer's obligation."[12] Therefore, as in pension accounting, gains and losses are not required to be recognized immediately[13] but may be deferred in the period when they occur and amortized in future years.

The Corridor Approach

Consistent with pension accounting, deferred gains and losses are amortized as a component of net periodic expense if, as of the beginning of the period, they exceed a "corridor." The corridor is defined as the greater of 10% of the APBO or 10% of the market-related value of plan assets. The **corridor approach** is intended to reduce postretirement expense volatility by providing a reasonable opportunity for gains and losses to offset over time without affecting net periodic expense.

Amortization Methods

If amortization is required, the **minimum amortization amount** is the excess (beyond the corridor) gain or loss divided by the average remaining service life to expected retirement of all active employees. Any systematic method of amortization may be used provided that (1) the amount amortized in any period is equal to or greater than the minimum amount; (2) the method is applied consistently; and (3) the method is applied similarly for both gains and losses.

---

[12]*FASB Statement No. 106*, par. 293.

[13]If an employer adopts a consistent policy of immediately recognizing gains and losses: (1) the amount of any **net gain** in excess of net losses previously recognized in income would first offset any unamortized **transition obligation;** and (2) the amount of any **net loss** in excess of net gains previously recognized in net income would first offset any unamortized **transition asset** (existence of a transition asset, however, is unlikely).

The amount of unrecognized gain or loss is recomputed each year and amortized over the average remaining service life if the net amount exceeds the "corridor."

1996 ENTRIES AND WORK SHEET

Continuing the Quest Company illustration into 1996 the following facts apply to the postretirement benefits plan for the year 1996:

Actual return on plan assets in 1996 is $600.

Expected return on plan assets in 1996 is $800.

Discount rate is 8%.

Increase in APBO due to change in actuarial assumptions is $60,000.

Service cost for 1996 is $26,000.

Contributions (funding) to plan in 1996 are $50,000.

Benefit payments to employees in 1996 are $35,000.

Average remaining service to full eligibility: 21 years.

Average remaining service to expected retirement: 25 years.

The following work sheet presents all of the pension entries and information recorded by Quest Company in 1996. The beginning balances entered on the first line of the Quest Company work sheet are the ending balances from the 1995 Quest Company postretirement benefits work sheet in Illustration 21A-4.

ILLUSTRATION 21A-6
Postretirement Benefits Work Sheet—1996

	Quest Company						
	General Journal Entries			Memo Record			
Items	Annual Postretirement Expense	Cash	Prepaid/ Accrued Cost	APBO	Plan Assets	Unrecognized Transition Amount	Unrecognized Net Gain or Loss
Balances, Jan. 1, 1996			32,000 Cr.	426,000 Cr.	10,000 Dr.	384,000 Dr.	
(f) Service cost	26,000 Dr.			26,000 Cr.			
(g) Interest cost	34,080 Dr.			34,080 Cr.			
(h) Actual return	600 Cr.				600 Dr.		
(i) Unexpected loss	200 Cr.						200 Dr.
(j) Contributions		50,000 Cr.			50,000 Dr.		
(k) Benefits				35,000 Dr.	35,000 Cr.		
(l) Amortization: Transition	16,000 Dr.					16,000 Cr.	
(m) Inc. in APBO—Loss				60,000 Cr.			60,000 Dr.
Journal entry for 1996	75,280 Dr.	50,000 Cr.	25,280 Cr.*				
Balance, Dec. 31, 1996			57,280 Cr.**	511,080 Cr.	25,600 Dr.	368,000 Dr.	60,200 Dr.

*$75,280 − $50,000 = $25,280
**$511,080 − ($25,600 + $368,000 + $60,200) = $57,280

Entries (f), (g), (j), (k), and (l) are similar to the corresponding entries previously explained in 1995. Entries (h) and (i) are related. The expected return of $800 is higher than the actual return of $600. To smooth postretirement expense, the unexpected loss of $200 ($800 − $600) is deferred by debiting Unrecognized Net Gain or Loss and crediting Postretirement Expense. As a result of this adjustment, the expected return on the plan assets is the amount actually used to compute postretirement expense.

Entry (m) records the change in the APBO resulting from a change in actuarial assumptions. This $60,000 increase in the employer's accumulated liability is an unexpected loss that is deferred by debiting it to Unrecognized Net Gain or Loss.

The journal entry on December 31 to formally record net periodic expense for 1996 is as follows:

December 31, 1996

Postretirement Expense	75,280	
Cash		50,000
Prepaid/Accrued Cost		25,280

The balance of the Prepaid/Accrued Cost account at December 31, 1996, of $57,280 is equal to the net of the balances in the memo accounts as shown in the following reconciliation schedule.

ILLUSTRATION 21A-7
Postretirement Benefits
Reconciliation
Schedule—December 31,
1996

Accumulated postretirement benefit obligation (Credit)	$(511,080)
Plan assets at fair value (Debit)	25,600
Funded status (Credit)	(485,480)
Unrecognized transition amount (Debit)	368,000
Unrecognized net gain or loss (Debit)	60,200
Prepaid/Accrued Cost (Credit)	$ (57,280)

AMORTIZATION OF UNRECOGNIZED NET GAIN OR LOSS IN 1997

Because of the beginning-of-the-year balance in unrecognized net gain or loss, the corridor test for amortization of the balance must be applied at the end of 1997. A schedule showing the computation of the amortization charge for unrecognized net gain or loss is presented below:

ILLUSTRATION 21A-8
Computation of
Amortization Charge
(Corridor Test)—1997

Quest Company	
1997 Corridor Test	
Unrecognized net gain or loss at beginning of year	$60,200
10% of greater of APBO or market-related value of plan assets ($511,080 × .10)	51,108
Amortizable amount	$ 9,092
Average remaining service to expected retirement	25 years
1997 amortization of loss ($9,092 ÷ 25)	$364

▶ DISCLOSURES IN NOTES TO THE FINANCIAL STATEMENTS

The disclosures required for other postretirement benefit plans are similar to and just as detailed and extensive as those required for pensions. The following categories of disclosure are required:

1. Descriptive information about the plan, which is the basis for the accounting.
2. Postretirement expense for the period, separately identifying all components of that cost.
3. A schedule reconciling the funded status of the plan with amounts reported in the employer's balance sheet, separately identifying the reconciling items.
4. The assumptions and rates used in computing the EPBO and APBO, including assumed health care cost trend rates; assumed discount rates; and the effect of a one-percentage-point increase in the assumed health care cost trend rate on the measurement of the APBO, the service cost, and the interest cost.

▶ ACTUARIAL ASSUMPTIONS AND CONCEPTUAL ISSUES

The measurement of the EPBO and the APBO and the net periodic postretirement benefit cost is involved and complex. Due to the uncertainties in forecasting health care costs, rates of utilization, changes in government health programs, and the differences employed in nonmedical assumptions (discount rate, employee turnover, rate of pre-65 retirement, spouse-age difference, etc.), estimates of postretirement benefit costs may have a large margin of error. Is the information, therefore, relevant, reliable, or verifiable? The FASB concluded "that the obligation to provide postretirement benefits meets the definition of a liability, is representationally faithful, is relevant to financial statement users, and can be measured with sufficient reliability at a justifiable cost."[14] Failure to accrue an obligation and an expense prior to payment of benefits is considered to be an unfaithful representation of what financial statements purport to represent.[15]

The FASB took a momentous step by requiring the accrual of postretirement benefits as a liability. Many opposed the requirement warning that the standard would devastate earnings. Others argued that putting "soft" numbers on the balance sheet was inappropriate and, finally, others noted that it would force companies to curtail these benefits to employees.

The authors believe that the FASB deserves special praise for this standard. Because the Board addressed this issue, companies now recognize the magnitude of these costs. This recognition may lead to efforts to control escalating health care costs. As John Ruffle, president of the Financial Accounting Foundation noted, "The Board has done American industry a gigantic favor. Over the long term, industry will look back and say thanks."

▶ SUMMARY OF LEARNING OBJECTIVES FOR APP. 21-A ◀

11. Identify the differences between pensions and postretirement health care benefits. Pension plans are generally funded, but health care benefit plans are not. Pension benefits are generally well-defined and level in amount, but health care benefits are generally uncapped and variable. Pension benefits are payable monthly, but health care benefits are paid as needed and used. Pension plan variables are reasonably predictable, whereas health care plan variables are difficult to predict.

12. Contrast accounting for pensions to accounting for other postretirement benefits. Many of the basic concepts and much of the accounting terminology and measurement methodology applicable to pensions also apply to other postretirement benefit accounting. Because other postretirement benefit plans are unfunded, large transition obligations occur; these may be immediately written off or amortized over 20 years. Two significant concepts peculiar to accounting for other postretirement benefits are (a) expected postretirement benefit obligation (EPBO) and (b) accumulated postretirement benefit obligation (APBO).

KEY TERMS

accumulated postretirement benefit obligation (APBO), 1094

attribution period, 1093

deferred recognition method, 1096

expected postretirement benefit obligation (EPBO), 1094

corridor approach, 1098

immediate recognition method, 1096

minimum amortization amount, 1098

transition amount, 1095

Note: All **asterisked** Questions, Exercises, Problems, and Cases relate to material contained in the appendix to each chapter.

QUESTIONS

1. What is a private pension plan? How does a contributory pension plan differ from a noncontributory plan?

2. Differentiate between a defined contribution pension plan and a defined benefit pension plan. Explain how the employer's obligation differs between the two types of plans.

3. Differentiate between "accounting for the employer" and "accounting for the pension fund."

4. The meaning of the term "fund" depends on the context in which it is used. Explain its meaning when used as a noun. Explain its meaning when it is used as a verb.

5. What is the role of an actuary relative to pension plans? What are actuarial assumptions?

---

[14]*FASB Statement No. 106,* par. 163.

[15]The FASB does not require recognition of a "minimum liability" for postretirement benefit plans. The Board concluded that the postretirement transition provisions that provide for delayed recognition should not be overridden by a requirement to recognize a liability that would accelerate recognition of that obligation in the balance sheet.

6. What factors must be considered by the actuary in measuring the amount of pension benefits under a defined benefit plan?

7. Name three approaches to measuring benefits from a pension plan and explain how they differ.

8. Distinguish between the noncapitalization approach and the capitalization approach with regard to accounting for pension plans. Which approach does *FASB Statement No. 87* adopt?

9. Explain how cash basis accounting for pension plans differs from accrual basis accounting for pension plans. Why is cash basis accounting generally considered unacceptable for pension plan accounting?

10. Identify the five components that comprise pension expense. Briefly explain the nature of each component.

11. What is service cost and what is the basis of its measurement?

12. In computing the interest component of pension expense, what interest rates may be used?

13. What is meant by "prior service cost"? When is prior service cost recognized as pension expense?

14. What are "unexpected gains and losses" as related to pension plans?

15. If pension expense recognized in a period exceeds the current amount funded by the employer, what kind of account arises and how should it be reported in the financial statements? If the reverse occurs—that is, current funding by the employer exceeds the amount recognized as pension expense—what kind of account arises and how should it be reported?

16. Given the following items and amounts, compute the actual return on plan assets: fair value of plan assets at the beginning of the period, $9,200,000; benefits paid during the period, $1,400,000; contributions made during the period, $1,000,000; and fair value of the plan assets at the end of the period, $10,000,000.

17. How does an "asset gain or loss" develop in pension accounting? How does a "liability gain or loss" develop in pension accounting?

18. What is the meaning of "corridor amortization"?

19. Explain the circumstances under which a company may have to recognize a pension liability even though it has been funding its pension plan equal to the amount recognized as pension expense.

20. Explain the nature of a debit to an intangible asset account when an additional pension liability must be recorded. How does the amount of unrecognized prior service cost influence the amount recognized as an intangible asset?

21. At the end of the current period, Warren, Inc. had an accumulated benefit obligation of $400,000, pension plan assets (at fair value) of $300,000, and a balance in prepaid pension cost of $35,000. Assuming that Warren, Inc. follows *FASB Statement No. 87,* what are the accounts and amounts that will be reported on the company's balance sheet as pension assets or pension liabilities?

22. At the end of the current year, Karen Hawkins Co. has unrecognized prior service cost of $9,000,000. In addition, it recognized a minimum liability of $10,500,000 for the year. Where should the unrecognized prior service cost be reported on the balance sheet? Where should the debit related to the establishment of the minimum liability be reported?

23. Determine the meaning of the following terms:
    (a) Contributory plan.
    (b) Vested benefits.
    (c) Retroactive benefits.
    (d) Years-of-service method.

24. One disclosure required by *FASB Statement No. 87* is a "description of the plan, including employee groups covered, type of benefit formula, funding policy, types of assets held and the nature and effect of significant matters affecting comparability of information for all periods presented." What is the rationale for this disclosure?

25. Of what value to the financial statement reader is the schedule reconciling the funded status of the plan with amounts reported in the employer's balance sheet?

26. What is a multiemployer plan? What accounting questions arise when a company is involved with one of these plans?

27. A headline in *The Wall Street Journal* stated "Firms Increasingly Tap Their Pension Funds to Use Excess Assets." What is the accounting issue related to the use of these "excess assets" by companies?

*28. What are postretirement benefits other than pensions?

*29. Why didn't the FASB cover both types of postretirement benefits—pensions and health care—in the earlier pension accounting statement?

*30. What is the transition amount in pension accounting and the transition amount in postretirement benefit accounting? And, how does the accounting treatment for these transition amounts differ under *Statement Nos. 87 and 106*? Why is the accounting for the transition amount so controversial?

*31. What are the major differences between postretirement health care benefits and pension benefits?

*32. What is the difference between the APBO and the EPBO? What are the components of postretirement expense?

EXERCISES

E21-1 (Computation of Pension Expense) Tony Inc. provides the following selected information about its defined benefit pension plan for the year 1996:

Service cost	$ 80,000
Projected benefit obligation at January 1, 1996	700,000
Actual and expected return on plan assets	16,000
Unrecognized prior service cost amortization	10,000
Amortization of unrecognized loss	2,000
Interest/discount (settlement) rate	10%

Instructions
Compute pension expense for the year 1996.

E21-2 (Computation of Pension Expense) Quality Print Company provides the following information about its defined benefit pension plan for the year 1996:

Service cost	$ 90,000
Contribution to the plan	105,000
Prior service cost amortization	10,000
Actual and expected return on plan assets	60,000
Benefits paid	40,000
Accrued pension cost liability at January 1, 1996	7,000
Plan assets at January 1, 1996	643,000
Projected benefit obligation at January 1, 1996	800,000
Unrecognized prior service cost balance at January 1, 1996	150,000
Interest/discount (settlement) rate	10%

Instructions
Compute the pension expense for the year 1996.

E21-3 (Preparation of Pension Work Sheet with Reconciliation) Using the information in E21-2 prepare a pension work sheet inserting January 1, 1996, balances, showing December 31, 1996, balances and the journal entry recording pension expense.

E21-4 (Basic Pension Work Sheet) The following facts apply to the pension plan of Mancuso, Inc. for the year 1996:

Plan assets, January 1, 1996	$490,000
Projected benefit obligation, January 1, 1996	490,000
Settlement rate	8.5%
Annual pension service cost	40,000
Contributions (funding)	30,000
Actual return on plan assets	48,605
Benefits paid to retirees	23,400

Instructions
Using the preceding data, compute pension expense for the year 1996. As part of your solution, prepare a pension work sheet that shows the journal entry for pension expense for 1996 and the year-end balances in the related pension accounts.

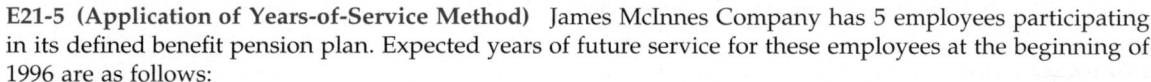 **E21-5 (Application of Years-of-Service Method)** James McInnes Company has 5 employees participating in its defined benefit pension plan. Expected years of future service for these employees at the beginning of 1996 are as follows:

Employee	Future Years of Service
Jim	2
Katie	3
Tom	5
Kathy	5
Joe	5

On January 1, 1996, the company amended its pension plan increasing its projected benefit obligation by $60,000.

Instructions

Compute the amount of prior service cost amortization for the years 1996, 1997, 1998, 1999, and 2000 using the years-of-service method setting up appropriate schedules.

E21-6 (Computation of Actual Return) Jackie Remmers Importers provides the following pension plan information:

Fair value of pension plan assets, January 1, 1996	$2,300,000
Fair value of pension plan assets, December, 31, 1996	2,500,000
Contributions to the plan in 1996	250,000
Benefits paid retirees in 1996	350,000

Instructions

From the data above, compute the actual return on the plan assets for 1996.

E21-7 (Basic Pension Work Sheet) The following defined pension data of J. B. Hobbs Corp. apply to the year 1996:

Projected benefit obligation, 1/1/96 (before amendment)	$548,800
Plan assets, 1/1/96	546,200
Prepaid/accrued pension cost (credit)	2,600
On January 1, 1996, J. B. Hobbs Corp. through plan amendment,	
grants prior service benefits having a present value of	100,000
Settlement rate	9%
Annual pension service cost	58,000
Contributions (funding)	55,000
Actual return on plan assets	52,280
Benefits paid to retirees	40,000
Prior service cost amortization for 1996	17,000

Instructions

For 1996 for J. B. Hobbs Corp., prepare a pension work sheet that shows the journal entry for pension expense and the year-end balances in the related pension accounts.

E21-8 (Application of the Corridor Approach) Ernest Basler Corp. has beginning-of-the-year present values for its projected benefit obligation and market-related values for its pension plan assets:

	Projected Benefit Obligation	Plan Assets Value
1994	$2,000,000	$1,900,000
1995	2,400,000	2,500,000
1996	2,900,000	2,600,000
1997	3,600,000	3,000,000

The average remaining service life per employee in 1994 and 1995 is 10 years and in 1996 and 1997 is 12 years. The unrecognized net gain or loss that occurred during each year is as follows: 1994, $280,000 loss; 1995, $70,000 loss; 1996, $10,000 loss; and 1997, $25,000 gain (in working the solution the unrecognized gains and losses must be aggregated to arrive at year-end balances).

Instructions

Using the corridor approach, compute the amount of unrecognized net gain or loss amortized and charged to pension expense in each of the four years, setting up an appropriate schedule.

E21-9 (Disclosures: Pension Expense and Reconciliation Schedule) David Castle Enterprises provides the following information relative to its defined benefit pension plan:

Balances or values at December 31, 1996	
Projected benefit obligation	$2,733,000
Accumulated benefit obligation	1,980,000
Vested benefit obligation	1,645,852
Fair value of plan assets	2,278,329
Unrecognized prior service cost	205,000
Unrecognized net loss (1/1/96 balance, −0−)	45,680
Accrued pension cost liability	203,991
Other pension plan data:	
Service cost for 1996	$ 90,000
Unrecognized prior service cost amortization for 1996	45,000

Actual return on plan assets in 1996	130,000
Expected return on plan assets in 1996	175,680
Interest on January 1, 1996 projected benefit obligation	253,000
Contributions to plan in 1996	92,329
Benefits paid	140,000

Instructions

(a) Prepare the note disclosing the components of pension expense for the year 1996.

(b) Prepare the required note disclosure schedule reconciling the funded status of the plan with the amounts reported in the December 31, 1996 financial statements.

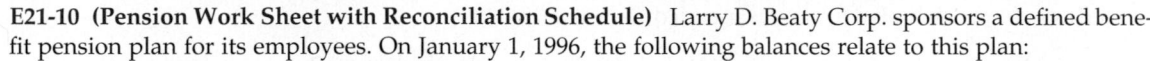 **E21-10 (Pension Work Sheet with Reconciliation Schedule)** Larry D. Beaty Corp. sponsors a defined benefit pension plan for its employees. On January 1, 1996, the following balances relate to this plan:

Plan assets	$480,000
Projected benefit obligation	605,000
Prepaid/accrued pension cost (credit)	25,000
Unrecognized prior service cost	100,000

As a result of the operation of the plan during 1996, the following additional data are provided by the actuary:

Service cost for 1996	$90,000
Settlement rate, 9%	
Actual return on plan assets in 1996	57,000
Amortization of prior service cost	19,000
Expected return on plan assets	52,000
Unexpected loss from change in projected benefit obligation, due to change in actuarial predictions	76,000
Contributions in 1996	99,000
Benefits paid retirees in 1996	85,000

Instructions

(a) Using the data above, compute pension expense for Larry D. Beaty Corp. for the year 1996 by preparing a pension work sheet that shows the journal entry for pension expense and the year-end balances in the related pension accounts.

(b) At December 31, 1996, prepare a schedule reconciling the funded status of the plan with the pension amount reported on the balance sheet.

E21-11 (Computation of Minimum Liability) Jea Nae Wood Company provides the following information relative to its defined benefit pension plan for the years 1995, 1996, and 1997:

	December 31		
	1995	1996	1997
Vested benefit obligation	$ 50,000	$ 65,000	$104,000
Accumulated benefit obligation	105,000	158,000	320,000
Projected benefit obligation	215,000	210,000	340,000
Fair value of plan assets	115,000	170,000	200,000
Unrecognized prior service cost	82,000	65,000	58,000
Accrued pension cost	10,000		60,000
Prepaid pension cost		21,000	
Unrecognized net (gain) or loss	8,000	(4,000)	22,000

Instructions

Compute the amount of additional liability (minimum liability test), if any, that must be reported along with any pension intangible asset or contra equity item for 1995 through 1997.

E21-12 (Pension Expense, Journal Entries, Statement Presentation, Minimum Liability) Rocky Pizza Company sponsors a defined benefit pension plan for its employees. The following data relate to the operation of the plan for the year 1995 in which no benefits were paid:

1. The actuarial present value of future benefits earned by employees for services rendered in 1995 amounted to $50,000.

2. The company's funding policy requires a contribution to the pension trustee amounting to $145,000 for 1995.

3. As of January 1, 1995, the company had a projected benefit obligation of $1,000,000, an accumulated benefit obligation of $800,000, and an unrecognized prior service cost of $400,000. The fair value of pension plan assets amounted to $600,000 at the beginning of the year. The market-related asset value was equal to $600,000. The actual and expected return on plan assets was $54,000. The settlement rate was 9%. No gains or losses occurred in 1995 and no benefits were paid.

4. Amortization of unrecognized prior service cost was $40,000 in 1995; amortization of unrecognized net gain or loss was not required in 1995.

Instructions

(a) Determine the amounts of the components of pension expense that should be recognized by the company in 1995.

(b) Prepare the journal entry or entries to record pension expense and the employer's contribution to the pension trustee in 1995.

(c) Indicate the amounts that would be reported on the income statement and the balance sheet for the year 1995. The accumulated benefit obligation on December 31, 1995, was $830,000.

E21-13 (Pension Expense, Journal Entries, Minimum Liability, Statement Presentation) Vickie Maher Company received the following selected information from its pension plan trustee concerning the operation of the company's defined benefit pension plan for the year ended December 31, 1995:

	January 1, 1995	December 31, 1995
Projected benefit obligation	$2,000,000	$2,075,000
Market-related and fair value of plan assets	800,000	1,130,000
Accumulated benefit obligation	1,600,000	1,715,000
Actuarial (gains) losses (Unrecognized net (gain) or loss)	–0–	(200,000)

The service cost component of pension expense for employee services rendered in the current year amounted to $75,000 and the amortization of unrecognized prior service cost was $115,000. The company's actual funding (contributions) of the plan in 1995 amounted to $250,000. The expected return on plan assets and the actual rate were both 10%; the interest/discount (settlement) rate was 10%. No prepaid/accrued pension cost existed on January 1, 1995. Assume no benefits paid in 1995.

Instructions

(a) Determine the amounts of the components of pension expense that should be recognized by the company in 1995.

(b) Prepare the journal entries to record pension expense and the employer's contribution to the pension plan in 1995.

(c) Indicate the pension-related amounts that would be reported on the income statement and the balance sheet for Vickie Maher Company for the year 1995. (Compute the minimum liability.)

E21-14 (Computation of Actual Return, Gains and Losses, Corridor Test, Prior Service Cost, Minimum Liability, Pension Expense, and Reconciliation) James Reynolds Company sponsors a defined benefit pension plan. The corporation's actuary provides the following information about the plan:

	January 1, 1996	December 31, 1996
Vested benefit obligation	$1,500	$1,900
Accumulated benefit obligation	1,900	2,730
Projected benefit obligation	2,800	3,650
Plan assets (fair value)	1,700	2,600
Settlement rate and expected rate of return		10%
Prepaid/(Accrued) pension cost	–0–	?
Unrecognized prior service cost	1,100	?
Service cost for the year 1996		400
Contributions (funding in 1996)		800
Benefits paid in 1996		200

The average remaining service life per employee is 20 years.

Instructions

(a) Compute the actual return on the plan assets in 1996.

(b) Compute the amount of the unrecognized net gain or loss as of December 31, 1996 (assume the January 1, 1996, balance was zero).

(c) Compute the amount of unrecognized net gain or loss amortization for 1996 (corridor approach).

(d) Compute the amount of prior service cost amortization for 1996.

(e) Compute the minimum liability to be reported at December 31, 1996.

(f) Compute pension expense for 1996.

(g) Prepare a schedule reconciling the plan's funded status with the amounts reported in the December 31, 1996, balance sheet.

E21-15 (Work Sheet for E21-14) Using the information in E21-14 about James Reynolds Company's defined benefit pension plan, prepare a 1996 pension work sheet with supplementary schedules of computations. Prepare the journal entries at December 31, 1996, to record pension expense and any "additional liability." Also, prepare a schedule reconciling the plan's funded status with the pension amounts reported in the balance sheet.

E21-16 (Pension Expense, Journal Entries) Shlomo Crandus Workshop Inc. initiated a noncontributory-defined benefit pension plan for its 50 employees on January 1, 1995. Employment levels have remained constant and are expected to be stable in the future. All these employees are expected to receive benefits under the plan. The total number of service-years is 650 and the service-years attributable to 1996 is 50. On December 31, 1995, the company's actuary submitted the following information:

Present value of future benefits attributed by the pension plan formula to employee services rendered in the current year	$120,000
Accumulated benefit obligation	100,000
Projected benefit obligation (zero balance 1/1/95)	120,000
Employer's funding contribution for 1995 (made on 12/31/95)	130,000
Settlement rate used in actuarial computations	8%
Actual and expected return on plan assets	8%

During 1996, the company amended the pension plan by granting credit for prior services performed prior to January 1, 1996, the date of the plan amendment. The plan amendment increased unrecognized prior service cost by $110,000 which is to be amortized based on the expected future years of service of participants. The company's accountants calculated the pension expense that is to be recognized in 1996 at $167,662.

Instructions
(Round to the nearest dollar)
(a) Calculate the amount of the pension expense to be recognized in 1995. Explain.
(b) Prepare the journal entries to record pension expense and the employer's funding contribution for 1995. (A work sheet need not be prepared to work this exercise.)
(c) Describe how the company's accountants calculated the $167,662 as the pension expense to be recognized in 1996. Indicate each of the five components that make up the total amount to be recognized. (*Hint:* Compute service cost last.) (Market-related asset value and fair value of plan assets are the same.)

E21-17 (Pension Expense, Minimum Liability, Statement Presentation) Lou Brady Foods Company obtained the following information from the insurance company that administers the company's employee-defined benefit pension plan:

	For Year Ended December 31,		
	1995	1996	1997
Plan assets (at fair value)	$280,000	$398,000	$586,000
Accumulated benefit obligation	385,000	512,000	576,000
Pension expense	95,000	128,000	130,000
Employer's funding contribution	110,000	150,000	125,000
Prior service cost not yet recognized in earnings	494,230	451,365	400,438

Prior to 1995, cumulative pension expense recognized equal cumulative contributions. The company has adopted the requirements of the FASB standard on "Employers' Accounting for Pensions." Assume that the market-related asset value is equal to the fair value of plan assets for all three years.

Instructions
(a) Prepare the journal entries to record pension expense, employer's funding contribution, and the adjustment to a minimum pension liability for the years 1995, 1996, and 1997. (Preparation of a pension work sheet is not a requirement of this exercise; insufficient information is given to prepare one.)
(b) Indicate the pension related amounts that would be reported on the company's income statement and balance sheet for 1995, 1996, and 1997.

E21-18 (Minimum Liability, Journal Entries, Balance Sheet Items) Presented below is partial information related to the pension fund of William Monat Inc.

Funded Status (end of year)	1995	1996	1997
Assets and obligations			
Market-related asset value	$1,300,000	$1,650,000	$1,900,000
Plan assets (at fair value)	1,300,000	1,670,000	1,950,000
Accumulated benefit obligation	1,150,000	1,480,000	2,050,000
Projected benefit obligation	1,600,000	1,910,000	2,500,000
Unfunded accumulated benefits			100,000
Overfunded accumulated benefits	150,000	190,000	
Amounts to be recognized			
(Accrued)/prepaid pension cost at beginning of year	$ –0–	$ 15,000	$ 12,000
Pension expense	(250,000)	(268,000)	(300,000)
Contribution	265,000	265,000	275,000
(Accrued)/prepaid pension cost at end of year	$ 15,000	$ 12,000	$ (13,000)

The company's unrecognized prior service cost is $637,000 at the end of 1997.

Instructions
  (a) What pension-related amounts are reported on the balance sheet of William Monat Inc. for 1995, 1996, and 1997?
  (b) What are the journal entries made to record pension expense in 1995, 1996, and 1997?
  (c) What journal entries (if any) are necessary to record a minimum liability for 1995, 1996, and 1997?

E21-19 (Reconciliation Schedule, Minimum Liability, and Unrecognized Loss) Presented below is partial information related to Sharon Costume Company at December 31, 1995.

Market-related asset value	$700,000
Projected benefit obligation	930,000
Accumulated benefit obligation	860,000
Plan assets (at fair value)	700,000
Vested benefits	200,000
Prior service cost not yet recognized in pension expense	120,000
Gains and losses	–0–

Instructions
  (a) Present the schedule reconciling the funded status with the asset/liability reported on the balance sheet. Assume no asset or liability existed at the beginning of period for pensions on Sharon Costume Company's balance sheet.
  (b) Assume the same facts as in (a) except that Sharon Costume Company has an unrecognized loss of $16,000 during 1995.
  (c) Explain the rationale for the treatment of the unrecognized loss and the prior service cost not yet recognized in pension expense.

E21-20 (Amortization of Unrecognized Net Gain or Loss [Corridor Approach], Pension Expense Computation) The actuary for the pension plan of Castle BancGroup Inc. calculated the following net gains and losses:

	Unrecognized Net Gain or Loss

Incurred During the Year	(Gain) or Loss
1995	$300,000
1996	480,000
1997	(210,000)
1998	(290,000)

Other information about the company's pension obligation and plan assets is as follows:

As of January 1,	Projected Benefit Obligation	Plan Assets (market-related asset value)
1995	$4,000,000	$2,400,000
1996	4,520,000	2,200,000
1997	4,980,000	2,600,000
1998	4,250,000	3,040,000

Castle BancGroup Inc. has a stable labor force of 400 employees who are expected to receive benefits under the plan. The total service-years for all participating employees is 5,200. The beginning balance of unrecognized net gain or loss is zero on January 1, 1995. The market-related value and the fair value of plan assets are the same for the four-year period. Use the average remaining service life per employee as the basis for amortization.

Instructions
(Round to the nearest dollar)
Prepare a schedule which reflects the minimum amount of unrecognized net gain or loss amortized as a component of net periodic pension expense for each of the years 1995, 1996, 1997, and 1998. Apply the "corridor" approach in determining the amount to be amortized each year.

E21-21 (Amortization of Unrecognized Net Gain or Loss [Corridor Approach]) Pete Dell Company sponsors a defined benefit pension plan for its 600 employees. The company's actuary provided the following information about the plan:

	January 1,	December 31,	
	1995	1995	1996
Projected benefit obligation	$2,800,000	$3,650,000	$4,400,000
Accumulated benefit obligation	1,900,000	2,430,000	2,900,000
Plan assets (fair value and market related asset value)	1,700,000	2,900,000	2,100,000

Unrecognized net (gain) or loss (for purposes of the corridor calculation)	–0–	101,000	(24,000)
Discount rate (current settlement rate)		11%	8%
Actual and expected asset return rate		10%	10%

The average remaining service life per employee is 10.5 years. The service cost component of net periodic pension expense for employee services rendered amounted to $400,000 in 1995 and $475,000 in 1996. The unrecognized prior service cost on January 1, 1995, was $1,100,000. No benefits have been paid.

Instructions
(Round to the nearest dollar)
- (a) Compute the amount of unrecognized prior service cost to be amortized as a component of net periodic pension expense for each of the years 1995 and 1996.
- (b) Prepare a schedule which reflects the amount of unrecognized gain or loss to be amortized as a component of net periodic pension expense for 1995 and 1996.
- (c) Determine the total amount of net periodic pension expense to be recognized by Pete Dell Company in 1995 and 1996.

*E21-22 (Postretirement Benefit Expense Computation) Toby Coffin Inc. provides the following information related to its postretirement benefits for the year 1997.

Accumulated benefit obligation at January 1, 1997	$810,000
Actual and expected return on plan assets	30,000
Unrecognized prior service cost amortization	21,000
Amortization of transition amount (loss)	3,000
Discount rate	10%
Service cost	88,000

Instructions
Compute postretirement expense for 1997.

*E21-23 (Postretirement Benefit Expense Computation) John Hyatt Co. provides the following information about its postretirement benefit plan for the year 1996.

Service cost	$ 90,000
Prior service cost amortization	3,000
Contribution to the plan	16,000
Actual and expected return on plan assets	62,000
Benefits paid	40,000
Plan assets at January 1, 1996	710,000
Accumulated benefit obligation at January 1, 1996	800,000
Unrecognized prior service cost balance at January 1, 1996	20,000
Amortization of transition amount (Loss)	5,000
Unrecognized transition amount at January 1, 1996	70,000
Discount rate	9%

Instructions
Compute the postretirement expense for 1996.

*E21-24 (Postretirement Benefit Work Sheet) Using the information in *E21-23 prepare a work sheet inserting January 1, 1996, balances, showing December 31, 1996, balances, and the journal entry recording postretirement expense.

*E21-25 (Postretirement Benefit Reconciliation Schedule) Presented below is partial information related to Diane Icke Co. at December 31, 1997.

Accumulated postretirement benefit obligation	$ 960,000
Expected postretirement benefit obligation	1,000,000
Plan assets (at fair value)	650,000
Prior service cost not yet recognized in postretirement expense	60,000
Gain and losses	–0–
Unrecognized transition amount (Loss)	100,000

Instructions
- (a) Present the schedule reconciling the funded status with the asset/liability reported on the balance sheet. Assume no asset or liability existed at the beginning of the period for postretirement benefits on Diane Icke Co.'s balance sheet.
- (b) Assume the same facts as in (a) except that Diane Icke Co. has an unrecognized loss of $20,000 during 1997.

PROBLEMS

P21-1 (Two-Year Work Sheet and Reconciliation Schedule) On January 1, 1996, Kap Shin Company has the following defined benefit pension plan balances:

Projected benefit obligation	$4,200,000
Fair value of plan assets	$4,200,000

The interest (settlement) rate applicable to the plan is 10%. On January 1, 1997, the company amends its pension agreement so that prior service costs of $500,000 are created. Other data related to the pension plan are:

	1996	1997
Service costs	$140,000	$180,000
Unrecognized prior service costs amortization	–0–	90,000
Contributions (funding) to the plan	140,000	184,658
Benefits paid	200,000	280,000
Actual return on plan assets	252,000	260,000
Expected rate of return on assets	6%	8%

Instructions

(a) Prepare a pension work sheet for the pension plan for 1996 and 1997.
(b) As of December 31, 1997, prepare a schedule reconciling the funded status with the reported liability (accrued pension cost).

P21-2 (Three-Year Work Sheet, Journal Entries, and Reconciliation Schedules) Erin Shanahan Company adopts acceptable accounting for its defined benefit pension plan on January 1, 1996, with the following beginning balances: Plan assets, $200,000; projected benefit obligation, $200,000. Other data relating to 3 years' operation of the plan are as follows:

	1996	1997	1998
Annual service cost	$16,000	$ 19,000	$ 26,000
Settlement rate and expected rate of return	10%	10%	10%
Actual return on plan assets	18,000	22,000	24,000
Annual funding (contributions)	16,000	40,000	48,000
Benefits paid	14,000	16,400	21,000
Unrecognized prior service cost (plan amended, 1/1/97)		160,000	
Amortization of unrecognized prior service cost		54,400	41,600
Change in actuarial assumptions establishes			
a December 31, 1998, projected benefit obligation of:			520,000

Instructions

(a) Prepare a pension work sheet presenting all 3 years' pension balances and activities.
(b) Prepare the journal entries (from the work sheet) to reflect all pension plan transactions and events at December 31 of each year.
(c) At December 31 of each year prepare a schedule reconciling the funded status of the plan with the pension amounts reported in the financial statements.

P21-3 (Pension Expense, Journal Entries, Minimum Pension Liability, Amortization of Unrecognized Loss, Reconciliation Schedule) Samuels Company sponsors a defined benefit plan for its 100 employees. On January 1, 1995 (date company starts following *FASB Statement No. 87*), the company's actuary provided the following information:

Unrecognized prior service cost	$150,000
Pension plan assets (fair value and market-related asset value)	200,000
Accumulated benefit obligation	260,000
Projected benefit obligation	350,000

The average remaining service period for the participating employees is 10.5 years. All employees are expected to receive benefits under the plan. On December 31, 1995, the actuary calculated that the present value of future benefits earned for employee services rendered in the current year amounted to $50,000; the projected benefit obligation was $450,000; fair value of pension assets was $275,000; the accumulated benefit obligation amounted to $365,000; and the market-related asset value is $275,000. The expected return on plan assets and the discount rate on the projected benefit obligation were both 10%. The actual return on plan assets is $10,000. The company's current year's contribution to the pension plan amounted to $65,000. No benefits were paid during the year.

Instructions
(Round to the nearest dollar)
  (a) Determine the components of pension expense that the company would recognize in 1995. (With only one year involved, you need not prepare a work sheet.)
  (b) Prepare the journal entries to record the pension expense and the company's funding of the pension plan in 1995.
  (c) Assume Samuels Company elects to recognize the minimum pension liability in its balance sheet for the year ended December 31, 1995. Prepare the journal entry to record the minimum liability.
  (d) Compute the amount of the 1995 increase/decrease in unrecognized gains or losses and the amount to be amortized in 1995 and 1996.
  (e) Prepare a schedule reconciling the funded status of the plan with the pension amounts reported in the financial statement as of December 31, 1995.

P21-4 (Pension Expense, Actual Return Computation, Minimum Liability, Financial Statement Presentation, Computation of Unrecognized Net Gain or Loss, Reconciliation Schedule) Mojave Company sponsors a defined benefit pension plan for its 50 employees. On January 1, 1995, the company's actuary calculated the following:

Projected benefit obligation	$1,200,000
Plan assets (at fair value)	800,000
Unrecognized prior service cost	400,000

(Market-related asset value and fair value of plan assets are the same at the beginning of 1995.) The average remaining service life of the participating employees is 13 years. All employees are expected to receive benefits under the plan. The actuary calculated the present value of future benefits attributed to employees' services in the current year to be $65,000. A 10% interest rate (settlement rate) is assumed for the actuarial computations. The expected return on plan assets is 11%. The company's funding contribution to the pension plan for 1995 was $125,000. The status of the pension plan's operations at December 31, 1995, is as follows:

Projected benefit obligation	$1,310,000
Accumulated benefit obligation (actuarially computed 12/31/95)	1,025,000
Pension plan assets (at fair value)	930,000
Market-related asset value	900,000
Benefit payments	–0–

Instructions
(Round to the nearest dollar; with only one year involved, you need not prepare a work sheet.)
  (a) Determine the amounts of the components of pension expense that should be recognized by the company in 1995. First compute the actual return on plan assets.
  (b) Prepare the journal entries to record pension expense, employer's funding contribution, and the adjustment to the minimum pension liability for 1995.
  (c) Indicate the pension-related amounts that would be reported on the company's income statement and balance sheet for the year 1995.
  (d) Compute the amount of the 1995 increase/decrease in unrecognized gains or losses and the amount to be amortized in 1995 and 1996.
  (e) Prepare a schedule reconciling the funded status of the plan with the pension amounts reported in the financial statements as of December 31, 1995.

P21-5 (Computation of Pension Expense, Amortization of Unrecognized Net Gain or Loss (Corridor Approach), Journal Entries for Three Years, and Minimum Pension Liability Computation) Bluemint Toothpaste Company initiates a defined benefit pension plan for its 50 employees on January 1, 1995. The insurance company which administers the pension plan provided the following information for the years 1995, 1996, and 1997:

	For Year Ended December 31,		
	1995	**1996**	**1997**
Plan assets (fair value)	$50,000	$ 85,000	$170,000
Accumulated benefit obligation	45,000	165,000	292,000
Projected benefit obligation	55,000	200,000	320,000
Unrecognized net (gain) loss (for purposes of corridor calculation)	–0–	(24,500)	84,500
Employer's funding contribution (made at end of year)	50,000	60,000	95,000

There were no balances as of January 1, 1995 when the plan was initiated. The actual and expected return on plan assets was 10% over the three-year period but the settlement rate used to discount the company's pension obligation was 13% in 1995, 11% in 1996, and 8% in 1997. The service cost component of net periodic pension expense amounted to the following: 1995, $55,000; 1996, $85,000; and 1997, $115,000. The average remaining service life per employee is 13 years. No benefits were paid in 1995, $30,000 of benefits were paid in 1996, and $18,500 of benefits were paid in 1997 (all benefits paid at end of year).

Instructions

(Round to the nearest dollar)

(a) Calculate the amount of net periodic pension expense that the company would recognize in 1995, 1996, and 1997.

(b) Prepare the journal entries to record net periodic pension expense, employer's funding contribution, and the adjustment to reflect a minimum pension liability for the years 1995, 1996, and 1997.

P21-6 (Computation of Unrecognized Prior Service Cost Amortization, Pension Expense, Journal Entries, Net Gain or Loss, and Reconciliation Schedule) Pete Hening Inc. has sponsored a noncontributory-defined benefit pension plan for its employees since 1978. Prior to 1995, cumulative net pension expense recognized equaled cumulative contributions to the plan. Management has elected to recognize the minimum pension liability requirement in the balance sheet for the year ending December 31, 1995. Other relevant information about the pension plan on January 1, 1995, is as follows:

1. The company has 200 employees who are expected to receive benefits under the plan. All these employees are expected to receive benefits under the plan. The average remaining service life per employee is 13 years.

2. The projected benefit obligation amounted to $5,000,000 and the fair value of pension plan assets was $3,000,000. The market-related asset value was also $3,000,000. Unrecognized prior service cost was $2,000,000.

On December 31, 1995, the projected benefit obligation and the accumulated benefit obligation were $4,750,000 and $4,000,000, respectively. The fair value of the pension plan assets amounted to $3,900,000 at the end of the year. The market-related asset value was $3,790,000. A 10% settlement rate and a 10% expected asset return rate was used in the actuarial present value computations in the pension plan. The present value of benefits attributed by the pension benefit formula to employee service in 1995 amounted to $200,000. The employer's contribution to the plan assets amounted to $575,000 in 1995. This problem assumes no payment of pension benefits.

Instructions

(Round all amounts to the nearest dollar)

(a) Prepare a schedule, based on the average remaining life per employee, showing the unrecognized prior service cost that would be amortized as a component of pension expense for 1995, 1996, and 1997.

(b) Compute pension expense for the year 1995.

(c) Prepare the journal entries required to report the accounting for the company's pension plan for 1995.

(d) Compute the amount of the 1995 increase/decrease in unrecognized net gains or losses and the amount to be amortized in 1995 and 1996.

(e) Prepare a schedule reconciling the funded status of the plan with the pension amounts reported in the financial statements as of December 31, 1995.

P21-7 (Pension Work Sheet, Minimum Liability) Curt Norton Corp. sponsors a defined benefit pension plan for its employees. On January 1, 1997, the following balances relate to this plan:

Plan assets (fair value)	$520,000
Projected benefit obligation	710,000
Prepaid/accrued pension cost (credit)	18,000
Unrecognized prior service cost	81,000
Unrecognized net gain or loss (debit)	91,000

As a result of the operation of the plan during 1997, the actuary provided the following additional data at December 31, 1997:

Service cost for 1997	$108,000
Settlement rate, 9%; expected return rate, 10%.	
Actual return on assets in 1997	48,000
Amortization of prior service cost	25,000
Market-related asset value at 1/1/97	550,000
Contributions in 1997	138,000
Benefits paid retirees in 1997	85,000
Average remaining service life of active employees	10 years
Accumulated benefit obligation at 12/31/97	651,000

Instructions

Using the preceding data, compute pension expense for Curt Norton Corp. for the year 1997 by preparing a pension work sheet that shows the journal entry for pension expense and any additional pension liability.

(The minimum pension liability must be computed and the corridor approach must be applied to the unrecognized gain or loss.) Use the market related asset value to compute the expected return.

P21-8 (Comprehensive 2-Year Work Sheet) Walt James Company sponsors a defined benefit pension plan for its employees. The following data relate to the operation of the plan for the years 1996 and 1997:

	1996	1997
Projected benefit obligation, January 1	$650,000	
Plan assets (fair value and market related value), January 1	410,000	
Prepaid/Accrued pension cost (credit), January 1	80,000	
Additional pension liability, January 1	12,300	
Intangible asset-deferred pension cost, January 1	12,300	
Unrecognized prior service cost, January 1	160,000	
Service cost	40,000	$ 58,000
Settlement rate	10%	10%
Expected rate of return	10%	10%
Actual return on plan assets	36,000	66,000
Amortization of prior service cost	70,000	55,000
Annual contributions	72,000	81,000
Benefits paid retirees	31,500	54,000
Increase in projected benefit obligation due to changes in actuarial assumptions	87,000	–0–
Accumulated benefit obligation at Dec. 31	721,800	789,000
Average service life of all employees		20 years
Vested benefit obligation at Dec. 31		464,000

Instructions

(a) Prepare a pension work sheet presenting both years 1996 and 1997 and accompanying computations including the computation of the minimum liability (1996 and 1997) and amortization of the unrecognized loss (1997) using the corridor approach.

(b) Prepare the journal entries (from the work sheet) to reflect all pension plan transactions and events at December 31 of each year.

(c) At December 31, 1997, prepare a schedule reconciling the funded status of the pension plan with the pension amounts reported in the financial statements.

P21-9 (Comprehensive Pension Work Sheet) Matt Van Hatten was recently promoted to assistant controller of Haber Corporation, having previously served Haber as a staff accountant. One of the responsibilities of his new position is to prepare the annual pension accrual. Julius Berger, the corporate controller, provided Van Hatten with last year's workpapers and information from the actuary's annual report. The pension worksheet for the prior year is presented below.

	Journal Entry			Memo Records		
	Pension Expense	Cash	Prepaid (accrued) Cost	Projected Benefit Obligation	Plan Assets	Unrecognized Prior Service Cost
6-1-95[1]				$(20,000)	$20,000	
Service cost[1]	$1,800			(1,800)		
Interest[2]	1,200			(1,200)		
Actual return[3]	(1,600)				1,600	
Contribution[1]		$(1,000)			1,000	
Benefits paid[1]				900	(900)	
Prior service cost[4]				(2,000)		$2,000
Journal entry	$1,400	$(1,000)	$(400)			
May 31, 1996 balance			$(400)	$(24,100)	$21,700	$2,000

[1]Per actuary's report.
[2]Beginning projected benefit obligation × settlement rate of 6%.
[3]Expected return was $1,600 (beginning plan assets × expected return of 8%).
[4]A plan amendment that granted employees retroactive benefits for work performed in earlier periods took effect on May 31, 1996. The amendment increased the May 31, 1996, projected benefit obligation by $2,000. No amortization was recorded in the fiscal year ended May 31, 1996.

Pertinent information from the actuary's report for the year ended May 31, 1997, is presented below and on the next page. The report indicated no actuarial gains or losses in the fiscal year ended May 31, 1997.

Contribution	$ 100
Service cost	$ 3,000
Settlement rate	6%
Expected return	8%

Accumulated benefit obligation 5-31-96	$21,000
Accumulated benefit obligation 5-31-97	$27,000
Actual return on plan assets	$ 1,736
Benefits paid	$ 500
Average remaining service life	10 years
Fair value plan assets 5-31-96	$21,700
Fair value plan assets 5-31-97	$23,036

When briefing Van Hatten, Berger indicated that the prior service cost is to be amortized over the average remaining service life. Berger also informed him that, in the current year, there will be an initial adoption of minimum pension liability reporting.

Instructions

(a) Prepare the pension worksheet for Haber Corporation for the year ended May 31, 1997.

(b) Prepare the journal entries required to reflect the accounting for Haber Corporation's pension plan for the year ended May 31, 1997.

(c) If the additional pension liability and the unrecognized prior service cost were $4,800 and $1,700, respectively, at May 31, 1997, explain how Haber Corporation would report the $4,800 in its financial statements.

(CMA adapted)

*P21-10 (Postretirement Benefit Work Sheet with Reconciliation) Jea Nae Foods Inc. sponsors a postretirement medical and dental benefit plan for its employees. The company adopts the provisions of *Statement No. 106* beginning January 1, 1996. The following balances relate to this plan on January 1, 1996:

Plan assets	$ 200,000
Expected postretirement benefit obligation	1,420,000
Accumulated postretirement benefit obligation	860,000
No prior service costs exist.	

As a result of the plan's operation during 1996, the following additional data are provided by the actuary:

Service cost for 1996 is $70,000
Discount rate is 9%
Contributions to plan in 1996 are $60,000
Expected return on plan assets is $9,000
Actual return on plan assets is $15,000
Benefits paid to employees from plan are $44,000
Average remaining service to full eligibility: 20 years
Average remaining service to expected retirement: 22 years
Transition amount to be amortized

Instructions

(a) Using the preceding data, compute the net periodic postretirement benefit cost for 1996 by preparing a work sheet that shows the journal entry for postretirement expense and the year-end balances in the related postretirement benefit memo accounts. (Assume that contributions and benefits are paid at the end of the year.)

(b) At December 31, 1996, prepare a schedule reconciling the funded status of the plan with the postretirement amount reported on the balance sheet.

CASES

C21-1 (Pension Terminology and Theory) Many business organizations have been concerned with providing for the retirement of employees since the late 1800s. During recent decades a marked increase in this concern has resulted in the establishment of private pension plans in most large companies and in many medium- and small-sized ones.

The substantial growth of these plans, both in numbers of employees covered and in amounts of retirement benefits, has increased the significance of pension cost in relation to the financial position, results of operations, and cash flows of many companies. In examining the costs of pension plans, a CPA encounters certain terms. The components of pension costs that the terms represent must be dealt with appropriately if generally accepted accounting principles are to be reflected in the financial statements of entities with pension plans.

Instructions

(a) Define a private pension plan. How does a contributory pension plan differ from a noncontributory plan?

(b) Differentiate between "accounting for the employer" and "accounting for the pension fund."

(c) Explain the terms "funded" and "pension liability" as they relate to:
 1. The pension fund.
 2. The employer.
(d) 1. Discuss the theoretical justification for accrual recognition of pension costs.
 2. Discuss the relative objectivity of the measurement process of accrual versus cash (pay-as-you-go) accounting for annual pension costs.
(e) Distinguish among the following as they relate to pension plans:
 1. Service cost.
 2. Prior service costs.
 3. Actuarial funding methods.
 4. Vested benefits.

C21-2 (Pension Terminology) The following items appear on Marinita Company's financial statements.

1. Under the caption Assets:
 Prepaid pension cost.
 Intangible asset—Deferred pension cost.
2. Under the caption Liabilities:
 Accrued pension cost.
3. Under the caption Stockholders' Equity:
 Excess of additional pension liability over unrecognized prior service cost.
4. On the income statement:
 Pension expense.

Instructions
Explain the significance of each of the items above on corporate financial statements. (*Note:* All items set forth above are not necessarily to be found on the statements of a single company.)

C21-3 (Basic Terminology) In examining the costs of pension plans, Karen Allman, CPA, encounters certain terms. The components of pension costs that the terms represent must be dealt with appropriately if generally accepted accounting principles are to be reflected in the financial statements of entities with pension plans.

Instructions
(a) 1. Discuss the theoretical justification for accrual recognition of pension costs.
 2. Discuss the relative objectivity of the measurement process of accrual versus cash (pay-as-you-go) accounting for annual pension costs.
(b) Explain the following terms as they apply to accounting for pension plans:
 1. Market-related asset value.
 2. Actuarial funding methods.
 3. Projected benefit obligation.
 4. Corridor approach.
(c) What information should be disclosed about a company's pension plans in its financial statements and its notes?

(AICPA adapted)

C21-4 (Basic Concepts of Pension Reporting) Terry Warfield, president of Express Mail Inc., is discussing the possibility of developing a pension plan for its employees with Mark Sullivan, controller, and Iris Butard, assistant controller. Their conversation is as follows:

TERRY WARFIELD: If we are going to compete with our competitors, we must have a pension plan to attract good talent.

MARK SULLIVAN: I must warn you, Terry, that a pension plan will take a large bite out of our income. The only reason why we have been so profitable is the lack of a pension cost in our income statement. In some of our competitors' cases, pension expense is 30% of pretax income.

IRIS BUTARD: Why do we have to worry about a pension cost now anyway? Benefits do not vest until after 10 years of service. If they do not vest, then we are not liable. We should not have to report an expense until we are legally liable to provide benefits.

TERRY WARFIELD: But, Iris, the employees would want credit for prior service with full vesting 10 years after starting service, not 10 years after starting the plan. How would we allocate the large prior service cost?

IRIS BUTARD: Well, I believe that the prior service cost is a cost of providing a pension plan for employees forever. It is an intangible asset that will not diminish in value because it will increase the morale of our present and future employees and provide us with a competitive edge in acquiring future employees.

TERRY WARFIELD: I hate to disagree, but I believe the prior service cost is a benefit only to the present employees. This prior service is directly related to the composition of the employee group at the time the plan is initiated and is in no way related to any intangible benefit received by the company because of the plan's existence. Therefore, I propose that the prior service cost be amortized over the remaining lives of the existing employees.

MARK SULLIVAN (somewhat perturbed): But what about the income statement? You two are arguing theory without consideration of our income figure.

TERRY WARFIELD: Settle down, Mark.

MARK SULLIVAN: Sorry, perhaps Iris's approach to resolving this approach is the best one. I am just not sure.

Instructions
(a) Assuming that Express Mail Inc. establishes a pension plan, how should their liability for pensions be computed in the first year?
(b) How should their liability be computed in subsequent years?
(c) How should pension expense be computed each year?
(d) Assuming that the pension fund is set up in a trusteed relationship, should the assets of the fund be reported on the books of Express Mail Inc.?
(e) What interest rate factor should be used in the present value computations?
(f) How should gains and losses be reported?

C21-5 (Major Pension Concepts) Barlex Corporation is a medium-sized manufacturer of paperboard containers and boxes. The corporation sponsors a noncontributory, defined benefit pension plan that covers its 250 employees. Alex Nowicki has recently been hired as president of Barlex Corporation. While reviewing last year's financial statements with Susan Kimpton, controller, Nowicki expressed confusion about several of the items in the footnote to the financial statements relating to the pension plan. In part, the footnote reads as follows.

> **Note J.** The company has a defined benefit pension plan covering substantially all of its employees. The benefits are based on years of service and the employee's compensation during the last four years of employment. The company's funding policy is to contribute annually the maximum amount allowed under the federal tax code. Contributions are intended to provide for benefits expected to be earned in the future as well as those earned to date.

Effective for the year ending December 31, 1986, Barlex Corporation adopted the provisions of *Statement of Financial Accounting Standard No. 87*—Employer's Accounting for Pensions. The net periodic pension expense on Barlex Corporation's comparative Income Statement was $36,000 in 1996 and $28,840 in 1995.

The following are selected figures from the plan's funded status and amount recognized in the Barlex Corporation's Statement of Financial Position at December 31, 1996 ($000 omitted)

Actuarial present value of benefit obligations:	
Accumulated benefit obligation	
(including vested benefits of $318)	$(435)
Projected benefit obligation	$(600)
Plan assets at fair value	525
Projected benefit obligation in	
excess of plan assets	$ (75)

Given that Barlex Corporation's work force has been stable for the last 6 years, Nowicki could not understand the increase in the net periodic pension expense. Kimpton explained that the net periodic pension expense consists of several elements, some of which may decrease the net expense.

Instructions
(a) The determination of the net periodic pension expense is a function of five elements. List and briefly describe each of the elements.
(b) Describe the major difference and the major similarity between the accumulated benefit obligation and the projected benefit obligation.
(c) 1. Explain why pension gains and losses are not recognized on the income statement in the period in which they arise.
  2. Briefly describe how pension gains and losses are recognized.
(d) Under what conditions must Barlex recognize an additional minimum liability?

(CMA adapted)

C21-6 (Implications of *FASB Statement No. 87*) Sally Groft and Kathy Doll have to do a class presentation on the pension pronouncement "Employers' Accounting for Pension Plans." In developing the class presentation, they decided to provide the class with a series of questions related to pensions and then discuss the answers in class. Given that the class has all read *FASB Statement No. 87,* they felt this approach would provide a lively discussion. Here are the situations:

1. In an article in *Business Week* prior to FASB No. 87, it was reported that the discount rates used by the largest 200 companies for pension reporting ranged from 5 to 11%. How can such a situation exist, and does the new pension pronouncement alleviate this problem?

2. An article indicated that when *FASB Statement No. 87* was issued, it caused an increase in the liability for pensions for approximately 20% of companies. Why might this situation occur?

3. A recent article noted that while "smoothing" is not necessarily an accounting virtue, pension accounting has long been recognized as an exception—an area of accounting in which at least some dampening of market swings is appropriate. This is because pension funds are managed so that their performance is insulated from the extremes of short-term market swings. A pension expense that reflects the volatility of market swings might, for that reason, convey information of little relevance. Are these statements true?

4. Companies as diverse as American Hospital Supply, Ashland Oil, Digital Equipment, GTE, Ralston Purina, and Signal Cos. held assets twice as large as they needed to fund their pension plans at one time. Are these assets reported on the balance sheet of these companies per the pension pronouncement? If not, where are they reported?

5. Understanding the impact of the changes required in pension reporting requires detailed information about its pension plan(s) and an analysis of the relationship of many factors, particularly:
   (a) the type of plan(s) and any significant amendments.
   (b) the plan participants.
   (c) the funding status.
   (d) the actuarial funding method and assumptions currently used.
   What impact does each of these items have on financial statement presentation?

6. An article noted "You also need to decide whether to amortize gains and losses using the corridor method, or to use some other systematic method. Under the corridor approach, only gains and losses in excess of 10 percent of the greater of the projected benefit obligation or the plan assets would have to be amortized." What is the corridor method and what is its purpose?

7. Some companies may have to establish an intangible asset-deferred pension cost if the plan assets at fair value are less than the accumulated benefit obligation. What is the nature of this intangible asset and how is it amortized each period?

8. In its exposure draft on pensions, the Board required a note that discussed the sensitivity of pension expense to changes in the interest rate and the salary progression assumption. This note might read as follows:

At December 31, 1995, the weighted average discount rate and rate of increase in future compensation levels used in determining the actuarial present value of the projected benefit obligation were 9% and 6%, respectively. Those assumptions can have a significant effect on the amounts reported. To illustrate, increasing the discount rate assumption to 10 percent would have decreased the projected benefit obligation and net periodic pension expense by $340,000 and $50,000, respectively, for the year ended December 31, 1995. Increasing the rate of change of future compensation levels to 7 percent would have increased the projected benefit obligation and net periodic pension cost by $180,000 and $30,000, respectively, for the year ended December 31, 1995.

Why do you believe this disclosure was eliminated from the final pronouncement?

Instructions
What answers do you believe Sally and Kathy gave to each of these questions?

*C21-7 (Special Reporting Issues Related to Postretirement Benefits)** A *Wall Street Journal* article discussed a $1.8 billion charge to income made by General Electric for postretirement benefit costs. It was attributed to previously unrecognized health care and life insurance cost. As financial vice president and controller for Alco, Inc., you found this article interesting because the president recently expressed concern about the company's rising health costs. The president was particularly concerned with health care cost premiums being paid for retired employees. He wondered what charge Alco, Inc. will have to take for its postretirement benefit program.

Instructions
As financial vice president and controller of Alco, Inc., explain what the charge was that General Electric made against income and what the options are for Alco, Inc. in accounting for and reporting any transition amount when it adopts *FASB Statement No. 106.*

► FINANCIAL REPORTING PROBLEM

Refer to the financial statements and other documents of Georgia-Pacific Corporation presented in Appendix 5-A and answer the following questions.

1. What kinds of pension plans does Georgia-Pacific offer to its employees? How were the funding policies determined for each of these pension plans?
2. What were the amounts of Georgia-Pacific's prepaid pension cost and accrued pension cost at the end of 1992 and 1993? How did the Corporation report the prepaid and accrued pension cost?
3. What were the amounts of net periodic pension cost for Georgia-Pacific's solely and jointly administered pension plans for the years 1991, 1992, and 1993? What was the discount rate used to determine the projected benefit obligation for 1993? What was the 1993 expected long-term rate of return for plan assets?
4. Georgia-Pacific provides certain health care and life insurance benefits to eligible retired employees. In December 1990, the FASB issued *Statement of Financial Accounting Standards No. 106*, "Employers' Accounting for Postretirement Benefits Other Than Pensions." What were the comments made by Georgia-Pacific regarding *Statement No. 106* in its 1993 Annual Report?

► WRITING ASSIGNMENT

Bryce Sims, accounting clerk in the personnel office of the Paradise Corp., has begun to compute pension expense for 1996 but is not sure whether or not he should include the amortization of unrecognized gains/losses. He is currently working with the following beginning-of-the-year present values for the projected benefit obligation and market-related values for the pension plan:

	Projected Benefit Obligation	Plan Assets Value
1993	$2,200,000	$1,900,000
1994	2,400,000	2,600,000
1995	2,900,000	2,600,000
1996	3,900,000	3,000,000

The average remaining service life per employee in 1993 and 1994 is 10 years and in 1995 and 1996 is 12 years. The unrecognized net gain or loss that occurred during each year is as follows:

1993	$280,000 loss
1994	90,000 loss
1995	12,000 loss
1996	25,000 gain

(In working the solution, you must aggregate the unrecognized gains and losses to arrive at year-end balances.)

Instructions

You are the manager in charge of accounting. Write a memo to Bryce Sims, explaining why in some years he must amortize some of the unrecognized net gains and losses and in other years he does not need to. In order to explain this situation fully, you must compute the amount of unrecognized net gain or loss that is amortized and charged to pension expense in each of the 4 years listed above. Include an appropriate amortization schedule, referring to it whenever necessary.

► GROUP ASSIGNMENT

(2-Year Work Sheet and Reconciliation Schedule) Bogart Co. has the following defined benefit pension plan balances on January 1, 1995:

Projected benefit obligation	$4,500,000
Fair value of plan assets	$4,500,000

The interest (settlement) rate applicable to the plan is 10%. On January 1, 1996, the company amends its pension agreement so that prior service costs of $600,000 are created. Other data related to the pension plan are:

	1995	1996
Service costs	$150,000	$170,000
Unrecognized prior service costs amortization	–0–	90,000
Contributions (funding) to the plan	150,000	184,658
Benefits paid	220,000	280,000
Actual return on plan assets	252,000	250,000
Expected rate of return on assets	6%	8%

Instructions

Your instructor will assign one member of the group to serve as recorder and one member to serve as spokesperson. As a group, provide information for the recorder to prepare responses to the following requirements. Upon completion of each requirement and before moving on to the next part, the spokesperson will report the group findings to the class.

   (a) Prepare a pension work sheet for the pension plan in 1995.

   (b) Prepare any journal entries related to the pension plan that would be needed at December 31, 1995.

   (c) Prepare a pension work sheet for 1996 and any journal entries related to the pension plan as of December 31, 1996.

   (d) As of December 31, 1996, prepare a schedule reconciling the funded status with the reported liability (accrued pension cost).

► ETHICS CASES

EC21-1 (Capitalization vs. noncapitalization of pension accounts) Giant Technology recently merged with University Electronix, a computer graphics manufacturing firm. In performing a comprehensive audit of UE's accounting system, John Wendell, internal audit manager for Giant Technology, discovered that the new subsidiary did not capitalize pension assets and liabilities, subject to the requirements of *FASB Statement No. 87.*

The net present value of UE's pension assets was $15.5 million, the vested benefit obligation was $12.9 million, and the projected benefit obligation was 17.4 million. John reported this audit finding to Jan Arnold, the newly appointed Controller of UE. A few days later, Jan called John for his advice on what to do. Jan started her conversation by stating, "Can't we eliminate the negative income effect of our pension dilemma by simply terminating the employment of nonvested employees before the end of our fiscal year?"

Instruction

How should John Wendell respond to Jan Arnold's remark about firing nonvested employees?

EC21-2 (Cutting postretirement health care benefits) John Gardner, Chief Executive Officer of Apex Dynamics Inc., a large defense-contracting firm, is considering ways to improve the company's financial position after several years of sharply declining profitability. One way to do this is to reduce or completely eliminate AD's commitment to present and future retirees with coverage on full medical and dental benefits. Despite fiscal problems, however, AD is still committed to providing excellent pension benefits.

Instructions

   (a) What factors should John Gardner consider before making his decision to cut postretirement health benefits?

   (b) Does your answer to the above question change if Apex Dynamics was paying John Gardner, CEO, a salary of 50 million dollars per year?

   (c) In your opinion, how did FASB's *Statement No. 106* influence the commitment of many organizations to its employees?

ACCOUNTING FOR LEASES

LEARNING OBJECTIVES

After studying this chapter, you should be able to:

1. Explain the nature, economic substance, and advantages of lease transactions.

2. Describe the accounting criteria and procedures for capitalizing leases by the lessee.

3. Contrast the operating and capitalization methods of recording leases.

4. Identify the classifications of leases for the lessor.

5. Describe the lessor's accounting for direct financing leases.

6. Identify special features of lease arrangements that cause unique accounting problems.

7. Describe the effect of residual values, guaranteed and unguaranteed, on lease accounting.

8. Describe the lessor's accounting for sales-type leases.

9. Describe the lessee's accounting for sale-leaseback transactions.

10. Describe the disclosure requirements for leases.

*O*ver the past two and a half decades, leasing has grown tremendously in popularity and today it is the fastest growing form of capital investment. Instead of borrowing money to buy an airplane, a computer, a nuclear core, or a satellite, a company leases it. Even the gambling casinos lease their slot machines. Airlines and railroads lease huge amounts of equipment; many hotel and motel chains lease their facilities; and most retail chains lease the bulk of their retail premises and warehouses.

A **lease** is a contractual agreement between a **lessor** and a **lessee** that gives the lessee the right to use specific property, owned by the lessor, for a specific period of time in return for stipulated, and generally periodic, cash payments (rents). An essential element of the lease agreement is that the lessor conveys less than the total interest in the property.

Because of the financial, operating, and risk advantages that the lease arrangement provides, many businesses lease substantial amounts of property, both real and personal, as an alternative to ownership. For example, leasing financed more than $125 billion of equipment in 1993. Leasing now provides the funds for about a third of the externally financed capital equipment purchased in the United States.

The increased significance and prevalence of lease arrangements in recent years have intensified the need for uniform accounting and complete informative reporting of these transactions.[1]

▶ LEASE PROVISIONS

OBJECTIVE 1

Explain the nature, economic substance, and advantages of lease transactions.

Because a lease is a contract, the provisions agreed to by the lessor and lessee may vary widely and may be limited only by their ingenuity. The **duration—lease term**—of the lease may be anything from a short period of time to the entire expected economic life of the asset. The **rental payments** may be level from year to year, increasing in amount, or decreasing; they may be predetermined or may vary with sales, the prime interest rate, the consumer price index, or some other factor. In most cases the rent is set to enable the lessor to recover the cost of the asset plus a fair return over the life of the lease.

The **obligations for taxes, insurance, and maintenance** (executory costs) may be assumed by either the lessor or the lessee, or they may be divided. **Restrictions** comparable to bond indentures may limit the lessee's activities regarding dividend payments or the incurrence of further debt and lease obligations in order to protect the lessor from default on the rents. The lease contract may be **noncancelable** or may grant the right to **early termination** on payment of a set scale of prices plus a penalty. In case of **default,** the lessee may be liable for all future payments at once, receiving title to the property in exchange; or the lessor may have the right to sell to a third party and collect from the lessee all or a portion of the difference between the sale price and the lessor's unrecovered cost.

Alternatives of the lessee at termination of the lease may range from none to the right to purchase the leased asset at the fair market value or the right to renew or buy at a nominal price.[2]

▶ ADVANTAGES OF LEASING

Although leasing is not without its disadvantages, the growth in its use suggests that it often has a genuine advantage over owning property. Some of the commonly discussed advantages to the lessee of leasing are:

1. **100% Financing at Fixed Rates.** Leases are often signed without requiring any money down from the lessee, which helps to conserve scarce cash—an especially desirable feature for new and developing companies. In addition, lease payments often remain fixed, which protects the lessee against inflation and increases in the cost of money. The following comment regarding a conventional loan is typical: "Our local bank finally came up to 80% of the purchase price but wouldn't go any higher, and they wanted a floating interest rate. We just couldn't afford the down payment and we needed to lock in a final payment rate we knew we could live with."

2. **Protection against Obsolescence.** Leasing equipment reduces risk of obsolescence to the lessee, and in many cases passes the risk in residual value to the lessor. For example, Syntex Corp. (a pharmaceutical maker) leases computers. Syntex is permitted under the lease agreement to turn in an old computer for a new model at any time, canceling the old lease and writing a new one. The cost of the new lease is added to the balance due on the old lease, less the old computer's trade-in value. As the treasurer of Syntex remarked, "Our instinct is to

---

[1]The popularity of leasing is evidenced by the fact that 534 of 600 companies surveyed by the AICPA in 1992 disclosed either capitalized or noncapitalized lease data (*Accounting Trends and Techniques—1993*).

[2]John H. Myers, "Reporting of Leases in Financial Statements," *Accounting Research Study No. 4* (New York: AICPA, 1964), pp. 10–11.

purchase." But if a new computer comes along in a short time "then leasing is just a heck of a lot more convenient than purchasing."

3. **Flexibility.** Lease agreements may contain less restrictive provisions than other debt agreements. Innovative lessors can tailor a lease agreement to the lessee's special needs. For instance, rental payments can be structured to meet the timing of cash revenues generated by the equipment so that payments are made when the equipment is productive.

4. **Less Costly Financing.** Some companies find leasing cheaper than other forms of financing. For example, start-up companies in depressed industries, or companies in low tax brackets may lease as a way of claiming tax benefits that might otherwise be lost. Depreciation deductions offer no benefit to companies that have little if any taxable income. Through leasing, these tax benefits are used by the leasing companies or financial institutions, which can pass some of these tax benefits back to the user of the asset in the form of lower rental payments.

5. **Alternative Minimum Tax Problems.** As indicated in Chapter 20, all companies are subject to an alternative minimum tax (AMT). Under the AMT rules, a portion of accelerated depreciation deductions are considered tax preference items that are added to a company's regular taxable income to arrive at the alternative minimum taxable income (AMTI). The company must pay whichever is higher—the regular tax or the AMT. Since ownership of equipment can contribute to an increase in AMTI and, ultimately, to an alternative minimum tax liability in excess of the regular tax liability, companies often find leasing a way to avoid the onerous alternative tax provisions.

6. **Off-Balance-Sheet Financing.** Certain leases do not add debt on a balance sheet or affect financial ratios, and they may add to borrowing capacity.[3] "Off-balance-sheet financing" is critical to some companies. For instance, a balance sheet of Chart House, Inc., a restauranteur operating more than 500 restaurants nationwide, showed long-term debt of $127 million and total stockholders' equity of $88 million. Therefore, Chart House's debt-to-equity ratio was a high but manageable 1.4 to 1. But the company also had lease obligations chiefly for restaurant land; the future rental payments related to those noncancelable operating leases was $125 million. If one were to add the capitalized value of these payments to its long-term debt, Chart House's debt-to-equity ratio would climb well over 2 to 1. When Safeway Stores was first required to capitalize lease commitments with a present value of $748 million, its balance sheet previously showed only $131 million in long-term debt. Or, consider what the situation of Glosser Bros., Inc., a retail store chain, would be if it had to capitalize its future minimum lease commitments on noncancelable leases of $70 million on its balance sheet showing less than $4 million of long-term debt and $32 million of equity.

INTERNATIONAL INSIGHT

Some companies double dip. That is, the leasing rules of the lessor's and lessee's countries may be different, permitting both parties to be an owner of the asset. Thus, both lessor and lessee receive the tax benefits related to depreciation. By structuring the lease to take advantage of these international differences, both the lessee and lessor benefit.

► CONCEPTUAL NATURE OF A LEASE

If United Airlines borrows $47 million on a 10-year note from National City Bank to purchase a Boeing 757 jet plane, it is clear that an asset and related liability should be reported on United's balance sheet at that amount. If United purchases the 757 for $47,000,000 directly from Boeing through an installment purchase over 10 years, it is equally clear that an asset and related liability should be reported (i.e., the installment transaction should be "capitalized"). However, if United **leases** the Boeing 757 for 10

---

[3]As demonstrated later in this chapter, certain types of lease arrangements are not capitalized on the balance sheet. The liability section is thereby relieved of large future lease commitments that, if recorded, would adversely affect the debt-to-equity ratio. The reluctance to record lease obligations as liabilities is one of the primary reasons capitalized lease accounting is resisted. For an excellent discussion on the effects of the failure to capitalize long-term lease commitments, see Eugene A. Imhoff, Jr., Robert C. Lipe, and David W. Wright, "Operating Leases: Impact of Constructive Capitalization," *Accounting Horizons*, March, 1991.

years through a noncancelable lease transaction with payments of the same amount as the installment purchase transaction, differences of opinion start to develop over how this transaction should be reported. The various views on **capitalization of leases** are as follows:

Do Not Capitalize Any Leased Assets. Because the lessee does not have ownership of the property, capitalization is considered inappropriate. Furthermore, a lease is an "executory" contract requiring continuing performance by both parties. Because other executory contracts (such as purchase commitments and employment contracts) are not capitalized at present, leases should not be capitalized, either.

Capitalize Those Leases Similar to Installment Purchases. Accountants should report transactions in accordance with their economic substance; therefore, if installment purchases are capitalized, so also should leases that have similar characteristics. For example, United Airlines is committed to the same payments over a 10-year period for either a lease or an installment purchase; lessees make rental payments, whereas owners make mortgage payments. Why shouldn't the financial statements report these transactions in the same manner?

Capitalize All Long-Term Leases. Under this approach, the only requirement for capitalization is the long-term right to use the property. This property-rights approach capitalizes all long-term leases.[4]

Capitalize Firm Leases Where the Penalty for Nonperformance Is Substantial. A final approach is to capitalize only "firm" (noncancelable) contractual rights and obligations. "Firm" means that it is unlikely that performance under the lease can be avoided without a severe penalty.[5]

UNDERLYING CONCEPT

The issue of how to report leases is the classic case of substance versus form. Although technically legal title does not pass in lease transactions, the benefits from the use of the property do transfer.

In short, the various viewpoints range from no capitalization to capitalization of all leases. The FASB apparently agrees with the capitalization approach when the lease is similar to an installment purchase, noting that **a lease that transfers substantially all of the benefits and risks of property ownership should be capitalized.** Transfer of ownership can be assumed only if there is a high degree of permanence to the transfer, that is, the lease is noncancelable. **Noncancelable** means that the lease contract is cancelable only upon the outcome of some remote contingency or that the cancellation provisions and penalties of the contract are so costly to the lessee that cancellation probably will not occur. Only noncancelable leases may be capitalized.

This viewpoint leads to three basic conclusions: (1) The characteristics that indicate that substantially all of the benefits and risks of ownership have been transferred must be identified. (2) The same characteristics should apply consistently to the lessee and the lessor. (3) Those leases that do **not** transfer substantially all the benefits and risks of ownership are operating leases. They should not be capitalized but rather accounted for as rental payments and receipts.

By capitalizing the present value of the future rental payments, **the lessee** records an asset and a liability at an amount generally representative of the asset's market value or purchase price. **The lessor,** having transferred substantially all the benefits and risks of ownership, recognizes a sale by removing the asset from the balance sheet and replacing it with a receivable. The typical journal entries for the lessee and the lessor, assuming equipment is leased and is capitalized, appear as follows:

**ILLUSTRATION 22-1
Journal Entries for
Capitalized Lease**

Lessee			Lessor		
Leased Equipment	XXX		Lease Receivable (net)	XXX	
Lease Obligation		XXX	Equipment		XXX

Having capitalized the asset, the lessee records the depreciation. The lessor and lessee treat the lease rental payments as consisting of interest and principal.

---

[4]See, for example, *Accounting Research Study No. 4,* which advocated this position.

[5]Yuji Ijiri, *Recognition of Contractual Rights and Obligations,* Research Report (Stamford, Conn.: FASB, 1980).

If the lease is not capitalized, no asset is capitalized by the lessee and no asset is removed from the lessor's books. When a lease payment is made, the lessee records rental expense and the lessor recognizes rental revenue.

The remainder of the chapter presents the different types of leases and the specific criteria, accounting rules, and disclosure requirements set forth by the FASB in accounting for leases.

▶ ACCOUNTING BY LESSEES

If at the date of the noncancelable lease agreement (inception of the lease[6]) the lease meets **one or more** of the following four criteria, the lessee shall classify and account for the arrangement as a **capital lease:**

OBJECTIVE 2

Describe the accounting criteria and procedures for capitalizing leases by the lessee.

ILLUSTRATION 22-2
Capitalization Criteria for Lessee

Capitalization Criteria (Lessee)
1. The lease transfers ownership of the property to the lessee.
2. The lease contains a bargain purchase option.[7]
3. The lease term is equal to 75% or more of the estimated economic life of the leased property.
4. The present value of the minimum lease payments (excluding executory costs) equals or exceeds 90% of the fair value of the leased property.[8]

Leases that **do not meet any of the four criteria** are classified and accounted for by the lessee as **operating leases.** Illustration 22-3 shows that a lease meeting any one of the four criteria results in the lessee having a capital lease.

ILLUSTRATION 22-3
Diagram of Lessee's Criteria for Lease Classification

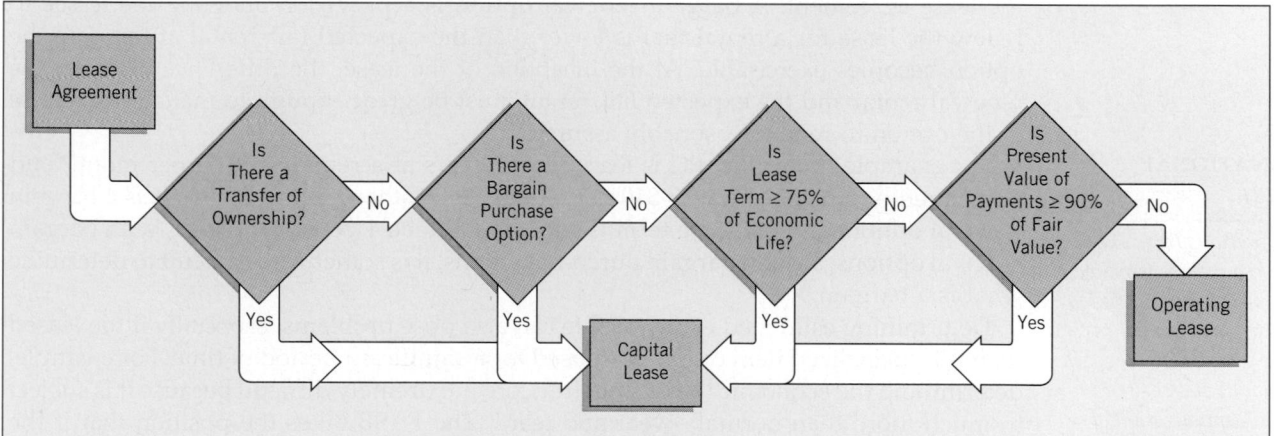

In keeping with the FASB's reasoning that a significant portion of the value of the asset is consumed in the first 75% of its life, neither the third nor the fourth criterion is to be applied when the inception of the lease occurs during the last 25% of the life of the asset.

EXAMINATION OF CAPITALIZATION CRITERIA

The four **capitalization criteria** that apply to lessees are controversial and can be difficult to apply in practice. They are discussed in detail in the following pages.

---

[6]For purposes of classifying the lease transaction, **inception** is the date of the lease agreement or commitment, if earlier. See "Inception of the Lease," *Statement of Financial Accounting Standards No. 23* (Stamford, Conn.: FASB, 1978), par. 7.

[7]A bargain purchase option is defined in the next section.

[8]"Accounting for Leases," *FASB Statement No. 13* as amended and interpreted through May 1980 (Stamford, Conn.: FASB, 1980), par. 7.

Transfer of Ownership Test

If the lease transfers ownership of the asset to the lessee, it is a capital lease. This criterion is not controversial and is easily implemented in practice.

Bargain Purchase Option Test

UNDERLYING
CONCEPT

Capitalization of leases illustrates the necessity for good definitions. The lease fits the definition of an asset, as it gives the lessee the economic benefits that flow from the possession or the use of the asset.

A **bargain purchase option** is a provision allowing the lessee to purchase the leased property for a price that is significantly lower than the property's expected fair value at the date the option becomes exercisable. At the inception of the lease, the difference between the option price and the expected fair market value must be large enough to make exercise of the option reasonably assured.

For example, assume that you were to lease a Honda Accord for $499 per month for 40 months with an option to purchase for $100 at the end of the 40-month period. If the estimated fair value of the Honda Accord is $3,000 at the end of 40 months, the $100 option to purchase is clearly a bargain, and therefore capitalization is required. In other cases, the criterion may not be as easy to apply, and determining now that a certain future price is a bargain can be difficult.

Economic Life Test (75% Test)

If the lease period equals or exceeds 75% of the asset's economic life, it follows that most of the risks and rewards of ownership are transferred to the lessee, and capitalization is therefore appropriate. However, determining the lease term and the economic life of the asset can be troublesome.

The lease term is generally considered to be the fixed, noncancelable term of the lease. However, this period can be extended if a bargain renewal option is provided in the lease agreement. A **bargain renewal option** is a provision allowing the lessee to renew the lease for a rental that is lower than the expected fair rental at the date the option becomes exercisable. At the inception of the lease, the difference between the renewal rental and the expected fair rental must be great enough to make the exercise of the option to renew reasonably assured.

INTERNATIONAL
INSIGHT

In some nations (e.g., Italy, Japan) accounting principles do not specify criteria for capitalization of leases. In others (e.g., Sweden, Switzerland) such criteria exist, but capitalization of the leases is optional.

For example, if an IBM PC is leased for 2 years at a rental of $100 per month and subsequently can be leased for $10 per month for another 2 years, it clearly is a bargain renewal option, and the lease term is considered to be 4 years. However, with bargain renewal options, as with bargain purchase options, it is sometimes difficult to determine what is a bargain.[9]

Determining estimated economic life can also pose problems, especially if the leased item is a specialized item or has been used for a significant period of time. For example, determining the economic life of a nuclear core is extremely difficult because it is subject to much more than normal "wear and tear." The FASB takes the position that if the inception of the lease occurs during the last 25% of the life of the asset, the economic life test cannot be used as a basis to classify a lease as a capital lease.

Recovery of Investment Test (90% Test)

If the present value of the minimum lease payments equals or exceeds 90% of the fair market value of the asset, then the leased asset should be capitalized. The rationale for

---

[9]The original lease term is also extended for leases having the following: substantial penalties for nonrenewal; periods for which the lessor has the option to renew or extend the lease; renewal periods preceding the date a bargain purchase option becomes exercisable; and renewal periods in which any lessee guarantees of the lessor's debt are expected to be in effect or in which there will be a loan outstanding from the lessee to the lessor. The lease term, however, can never extend beyond the time a bargain purchase option becomes exercisable. "Accounting for Leases: Sale-Leaseback Transactions Involving Real Estate; Sales-Type Leases of Real Estate; Definition of the Lease Term; Initial Direct Costs of Direct Financing Leases," *Statement of Financial Accounting Standards No. 98* (Stamford, Conn.: FASB, 1988).

this test is that if the present value of the minimum lease payments is reasonably close to the market price of the asset, the asset is effectively being purchased.

In determining the present value of the minimum lease payments, three important concepts are involved: (1) minimum lease payments, (2) executory costs, and (3) discount rate.

Minimum Lease Payments

These are payments the lessee is obligated to make or can be expected to make in connection with the leased property. **Minimum lease payments** include the following:

Minimum Rental Payments—Minimum payments the lessee is obligated to make to the lessor under the lease agreement. In some cases, the minimum rental payments may be equal to the minimum lease payments. However, the minimum lease payments also may include a guaranteed residual value (if any), penalty for failure to renew, or a bargain purchase option (if any), as noted below.

Guaranteed Residual Value—The residual value is the estimated fair (market) value of the leased property at the end of the lease term. The lessor often transfers the risk of loss to the lessee or to a third party through a guarantee of the estimated residual value. The **guaranteed residual value** is (1) the certain or determinable amount at which the lessor has the right to require the lessee to purchase the asset or (2) the amount the lessee or the third-party guarantor guarantees the lessor will realize. If it is not guaranteed in full, the **unguaranteed residual value** is the estimated residual value exclusive of any portion guaranteed.[10]

Penalty for Failure to Renew or Extend the Lease—The amount payable that is required of the lessee if the agreement specifies that the lease must be extended or renewed and the lessee fails to do so.

Bargain Purchase Option—As indicated earlier, an option given to the lessee to purchase the equipment at the end of the lease term at a price that is fixed sufficiently below the expected fair value, so that, at the inception of the lease, purchase appears to be reasonably assured.

Executory costs (defined below) are not included in the lessee's computation of the present value of the minimum lease payments.

Executory Costs

Like most assets, leased tangible assets require the incurrence of insurance, maintenance, and tax expenses—called **executory costs**—during their economic life. If the lessor retains responsibility for the payment of these "ownership-type costs," a portion of each lease payment that represents executory costs **should be excluded** in computing the present value of the minimum lease payments because it does not represent payment on or reduction of the obligation. If the portion of the minimum lease payments that represents executory costs is not determinable from the provisions of the lease, an estimate of such amount must be made. Many lease agreements, however, specify that executory costs be paid to the appropriate third parties directly by the lessee; in these cases, the rental payment can be used **without adjustment** in the present value computation.

Discount Rate

The lessee computes the present value of the minimum lease payments using the **lessee's incremental borrowing rate,** which is defined as: "The rate that, at the inception of the lease, the lessee would have incurred to borrow the funds necessary to buy the leased asset on a secured loan with repayment terms similar to the payment schedule

---

[10]A lease provision requiring the lessee to make up a residual value deficiency that is attributable to damage, extraordinary wear and tear, or excessive usage is not included in the minimum lease payments. Such costs are recognized as period costs when incurred. "Lessee Guarantee of the Residual Value of Leased Property," *FASB Interpretation No. 19* (Stamford, Conn.: FASB, 1977), par. 3.

called for in the lease."[11] Assume, for example, that Mortenson Inc. decides to lease computer equipment for a 5-year period at a cost of $10,000 a year. To determine whether the present value of these payments is less than 90% of the fair market value of the property, the lessee discounts the payments using its incremental borrowing rate. Determining that rate will often require judgment because it is based on a hypothetical purchase of the property.

However, there is one exception to this rule: If (1) the lessee knows the **implicit interest rate computed by the lessor** and (2) it is less than the lessee's incremental borrowing rate, then the **lessee must use the lessor's implicit rate.** The **interest rate implicit in the lease** is the discount rate that, when applied to the minimum lease payments and any unguaranteed residual value accruing to the lessor, causes the aggregate present value to be equal to the fair value of the leased property to the lessor.[12]

The purpose of this exception is twofold: First, the implicit rate of the lessor is generally a **more realistic rate** to use in determining the amount (if any) to report as the asset and related liability for the lessee. Second, the guideline is provided to ensure that the lessee **does not use an artificially high incremental borrowing rate** that would cause the present value of the minimum lease payments to be less than 90% of the fair market value of the property and thus make it possible to avoid capitalization of the asset and related liability. The lessee may argue that it cannot determine the implicit rate of the lessor and therefore the higher rate should be used. However, in many cases, the implicit rate used by the lessor can be approximated. The determination of whether or not a reasonable estimate could be made will require judgment, particularly where the result from using the incremental borrowing rate comes close to meeting the 90% test. Because **the lessee may not capitalize the leased property at more than its fair value** (as discussed later), the lessee is prevented from using an excessively low discount rate.

ASSET AND LIABILITY ACCOUNTED FOR DIFFERENTLY

In a capital lease transaction, the lessee is using the lease as a source of financing. The lessor finances the transaction (provides the investment capital) through the leased asset, and the lessee makes rent payments, which actually are installment payments. Therefore, over the life of the property rented, **the rental payments to the lessor constitute a payment of principal plus interest.**

Asset and Liability Recorded

Under the capital lease method, the lessee treats the lease transaction as if an asset were being purchased in a financing transaction in which an asset is acquired and an obligation created. Therefore, the lessee records a capital lease as an asset and a liability at the lower of (1) the present value of the minimum lease payments (excluding executory costs) or (2) the fair market value of the leased asset at the inception of the lease. The rationale for this approach is that the leased asset should not be recorded for more than its fair market value.

Depreciation Period

One troublesome aspect of accounting for the depreciation of the capitalized leased asset relates to the period of depreciation. If the lease agreement transfers ownership of the asset to the lessee (Criterion 1) or contains a bargain purchase option (Criterion 2)—the leased asset is depreciated in a manner consistent with the lessee's normal depreciation policy for owned assets, **using the economic life of the asset.** On the other hand, if the lease does not transfer ownership or does not contain a bargain purchase

---

[11]*FASB Statement No. 13,* op. cit., par. 5 (l).

[12]Ibid., par. 5 (k).

option, then it is depreciated over the **term of the lease.** In this case, the leased asset reverts to the lessor after a certain period of time.

Effective Interest Method

Throughout the term of the lease, the **effective interest method** is used to allocate each lease payment between principal and interest. This method produces a constant rate of interest in each period on the obligation's outstanding balance.

The discount rate used by the lessee to determine the present value of the minimum lease payments must be used by the lessee when applying the effective interest method to capital leases.

Depreciation Concept

Although the amounts initially capitalized as an asset and recorded as an obligation are computed at the same present value, the **depreciation of the asset and the discharge of the obligation are independent accounting processes** during the term of the lease. The lessee should depreciate the leased asset by applying conventional depreciation methods: straight-line, sum-of-the-years'-digits, declining-balance, units of production, etc.

The FASB uses the term "amortization" more frequently than "depreciation" to recognize intangible leased property rights. The authors prefer "depreciation" to describe the writeoff of a tangible asset's expired services.

CAPITALIZED LEASE METHOD ILLUSTRATED (LESSEE)

Lessor Company and Lessee Company sign a lease agreement dated January 1, 1996, that calls for Lessor Company to lease equipment to Lessee Company beginning January 1, 1996. The terms and provisions of the lease agreement and other pertinent data are as follows:

1. The term of the lease is 5 years, and the lease agreement is noncancelable, requiring equal rental payments of $25,981.62 at the beginning of each year (annuity due basis).

2. The equipment has a fair value at the inception of the lease of $100,000, an estimated economic life of 5 years, and no residual value.

3. Lessee Company pays all of the executory costs directly to third parties except for the property taxes of $2,000 per year, which are included in the annual payments to the lessor.

4. The lease contains no renewal options, and the equipment reverts to Lessor Company at the termination of the lease.

5. Lessee Company's incremental borrowing rate is 11% per year.

6. Lessee Company depreciates on a straight-line basis similar equipment that it owns.

7. Lessor Company set the annual rental to earn a rate of return on its investment of 10% per year; this fact is known to Lessee Company.[13]

The lease meets the criteria for classification as a capital lease for the following reasons: (1) The lease term of 5 years, being equal to the equipment's estimated economic

---

[13]If Lessee Company had an incremental borrowing rate of, say, 9% (lower than the 10% rate used by Lessor Company) and it did not know the rate used by Lessor Company, the present value computation would have yielded a capitalized amount of $101,675.35 ($23,981.62 × 4.23972). And, because this amount exceeds the $100,000 fair value of the equipment, Lessee Company would have had to capitalize the $100,000 and use 10% as its effective rate for amortization of the lease obligation.

life of 5 years, satisfies the 75% test. (2) The present value of the minimum lease payments ($100,000 as computed below) exceeds 90% of the fair value of the property ($100,000).

The minimum lease payments are $119,908.10 ($23,981.62 × 5), and the amount capitalized as leased assets is computed as the present value of the minimum lease payments (excluding executory costs—property taxes of $2,000) as follows:

ILLUSTRATION 22-4
Computation of
Capitalized Lease
Payments

> Capitalized amount = ($25,981.62 − $2,000) × present value of an annuity due of 1 for
> 5 periods at 10% (Table 6-5)
> = $23,981.62 × 4.16986
> = $100,000

The lessor's implicit interest rate of 10% is used instead of the lessee's incremental borrowing rate of 11% because (1) it is lower and (2) the lessee has knowledge of it.

The entry to record the capital lease on Lessee Company's books on January 1, 1996, is:

Leased Equipment Under Capital Leases	100,000	
Obligations Under Capital Leases		100,000

Note that the preceding entry records the obligation at the net amount of $100,000 (the present value of the future rental payments) rather than at the gross amount of $119,908.10 ($23,981.62 × 5).

The journal entry to record the **first lease payment on January 1, 1996,** is:

Property Tax Expense	2,000.00	
Obligations Under Capital Leases	23,981.62	
Cash		25,981.62

Each lease payment of $25,981.62 consists of three elements: (1) a reduction in the lease obligation, (2) a financing cost (interest expense), and (3) executory costs (property taxes). The total financing cost (interest expense) over the term of the lease is $19,908.10, the difference between the present value of the lease payments ($100,000) and the actual cash disbursed, net of executory costs ($119,908.10). Therefore, the annual interest expense, applying the effective interest method, is a function of the outstanding obligation, as shown in Illustration 22-5:

ILLUSTRATION 22-5
Lease Amortization
Schedule for Lessee—
Annuity Due Basis

LESSEE COMPANY
Lease Amortization Schedule
(Annuity due basis)

Date	Annual Lease Payment	Executory Costs	Interest (10%) on Unpaid Obligation	Reduction of Lease Obligation	Lease Obligation
	(a)	(b)	(c)	(d)	(e)
1/1/96					$100,000.00
1/1/96	$ 25,981.62	$ 2,000	$ −0−	$ 23,981.62	76,018.38
1/1/97	25,981.62	2,000	7,601.84	16,379.78	59,638.60
1/1/98	25,981.62	2,000	5,963.86	18,017.76	41,620.84
1/1/99	25,981.62	2,000	4,162.08	19,819.54	21,801.30
1/1/00	25,981.62	2,000	2,180.32*	21,801.30	−0−
	$129,908.10	$10,000	$19,908.10	$100,000.00	

(a) Lease payment as required by lease.
(b) Executory costs included in rental payment.
(c) Ten percent of the preceding balance of (e) except for 1/1/96; since this is an annuity due, no time has elapsed at the date of the first payment and no interest has accrued.
(d) (a) minus (b) and (c).
(e) Preceding balance minus (d).
*Rounded by 19 cents.

At the end of Lessee Company's fiscal year, December 31, 1996, **accrued interest** is recorded as follows:

Interest Expense	7,601.84	
Interest Payable		7,601.84

Depreciation of the leased equipment over its lease term of 5 years, applying Lessee Company's normal depreciation policy (straight-line method), results in the following entry on December 31, 1996:

Depreciation Expense—Capital Leases	20,000	
Accumulated Depreciation—Capital Leases		20,000
($100,000 ÷ 5 years)		

At December 31, 1996, the assets recorded under capital leases are separately identified on the lessee's balance sheet. Similarly, the related obligations are separately identified. The portion due within one year or the operating cycle, whichever is longer, is classified with current liabilities and the rest with noncurrent liabilities. For example, the current portion of the 12/31/96 total obligation of $76,018.38 in the lessee's amortization schedule is the amount of the reduction in the obligation in 1997, or $16,379.78. The liability section as it relates to lease transactions at 12/31/96 would appear as follows:

Current liabilities	
Interest payable	$ 7,601.84
Obligations under capital leases	16,379.78
Noncurrent liabilities	
Obligations under capital leases	$59,638.60

ILLUSTRATION 22-6
Reporting Current and Noncurrent Lease Liabilities

The journal entry to record the lease payment of January 1, 1997, is as follows:

Property Tax Expense	2,000.00	
Interest Expense (or Interest Payable)	7,601.84	
Obligations Under Capital Leases	16,379.78	
Cash		25,981.62

Entries through 2000 would follow the pattern above. Other executory costs (insurance and maintenance) assumed by Lessee Company would be recorded in a manner similar to that used to record any other operating costs incurred on assets owned by Lessee Company.

Upon expiration of the lease, the amount capitalized as leased equipment is fully amortized and the lease obligation is fully discharged. If not purchased, the equipment would be returned to the lessor, and the leased equipment and related accumulated depreciation accounts would be removed from the books.[14] If the equipment is purchased at termination of the lease at a price of $5,000 and the estimated life of the equipment is changed from 5 to 7 years, the following entry might be made:

Equipment ($100,000 + $5,000)	105,000	
Accumulated Depreciation—Capital Leases	100,000	
Leased Equipment Under Capital Leases		100,000
Accumulated Depreciation—Equipment		100,000
Cash		5,000

OPERATING METHOD (LESSEE)

Under the **operating method,** rent expense (and a compensating liability) accrues day by day to the lessee as the property is used. **The lessee assigns rent to the periods**

---

[14]If the lessee purchases a leased asset **during the term of a "capital lease,"** it is accounted for like a renewal or extension of a capital lease. "Any difference between the purchase price and the carrying amount of the lease obligation shall be recorded as an adjustment of the carrying amount of the asset." See "Accounting for Purchase of a Leased Asset by the Lessee During the Term of the Lease," *FASB Interpretation No. 26* (Stamford, Conn.: FASB, 1978), par. 5.

benefiting from the use of the asset and ignores, in the accounting, any commitments to make future payments. Appropriate accruals or deferrals are made if the accounting period ends between cash payment dates. For example, assume that the capital lease illustrated in the previous section did not qualify as a capital lease and was therefore to be accounted for as an operating lease. The first-year charge to operations would have been $25,981.62, the amount of the rental payment. The journal entry to record this payment on January 1, 1996, would be as follows:

Rent Expense	25,981.62	
Cash		25,981.62

The rented asset, as well as any long-term liability for future rental payments, is not reported on the balance sheet. Rent expense would be reported on the income statement. In addition, **note disclosure is required for all operating leases that have noncancelable lease terms in excess of one year.** An illustration of the type of note disclosure required for an operating lease (as well as other types of leases) is provided in Illustrations 22-32 to 22-35 later in this chapter.

COMPARISON OF CAPITAL LEASE WITH OPERATING LEASE

OBJECTIVE 3

Contrast the operating and capitalization methods of recording leases.

As indicated above, if the lease had been accounted for as an operating lease, the first-year charge to operations would have been $25,981.62, the amount of the rental payment. Treating the transaction as a capital lease, however, resulted in a first-year charge of $29,601.84: depreciation of $20,000 (assuming straight-line), interest expense of $7,601.84 (per Illustration 22-7), and executory costs of $2,000. Illustration 22-7 shows that **while the total charges to operations are the same over the lease term whether the lease is accounted for as a capital lease or as an operating lease, under the capital lease treatment the charges are higher in the earlier years and lower in the later years.**[15]

ILLUSTRATION 22-7
Comparison of Charges to Operations—Capital vs. Operating Leases

	Capital Lease				Operating	
Year	Depreciation	Executory Costs	Interest	Total Charge	Lease Charge	**Difference**
1996	$ 20,000	$ 2,000	$ 7,601.84	$ 29,601.84	$ 25,981.62	$ 3,620.22
1997	20,000	2,000	5,963.86	27,963.86	25,981.62	1,982.24
1998	20,000	2,000	4,162.08	26,162.08	25,981.62	180.46
1999	20,000	2,000	2,180.32	24,180.32	25,981.62	(1,801.30)
2000	20,000	2,000	—	22,000.00	25,981.62	(3,981.62)
	$100,000	$10,000	$19,908.10	$129,908.10	$129,908.10	$ –0–

LESSEE COMPANY
Schedule of Charges to Operations
Capital Lease Versus Operating Lease

If an accelerated method of depreciation is used, the differences between the amounts charged to operations under the two methods would be even larger in the earlier and later years.

In addition, using the capital lease approach would have resulted in an asset and related liability of $100,000 initially reported on the balance sheet; no such asset or liability would be reported under the operating method. Therefore, the following differences occur if a capital lease instead of an operating lease is employed:

1. an increase in the amount of reported debt (both short-term and long-term),

2. an increase in the amount of total assets (specifically long-lived assets), and

[15]The higher charges in the early years is one reason lessees are reluctant to adopt the capital lease accounting method. Lessees (especially those of real estate) claim that it is really no more costly to operate the leased asset in the early years than in the later years; thus, they advocate an even charge similar to that provided by the operating method.

3. a lower income early in the life of the lease and, therefore, lower retained earnings.

Thus, many companies believe that capital leases have a detrimental impact on their financial position as their debt to total equity ratio increases and their rate of return on total assets decreases. As a result, the business community resists capitalizing leases.

Whether their resistance is well founded is a matter of conjecture. From a cash flow point of view, the company is in the same position whether the lease is accounted for as an operating or a capital lease. The reason why managers often argue against capitalization is that it can more easily lead to violation of loan covenants; it can affect the amount of compensation received by owners (for example, a stock compensation plan tied to earnings); and finally, it can lower rates of return and increase debt to equity relationships, thus making the company less attractive to present and potential investors.[16]

▶ ACCOUNTING BY LESSORS

Earlier in this chapter we discussed leasing's advantages to the lessee. Three important benefits are available to the lessor:

1. **Interest Revenue.** Leasing is a form of financing; therefore, financial institutions and leasing companies find leasing attractive because it provides competitive interest margins.

2. **Tax Incentives.** In many cases, companies that lease cannot use the tax benefit, but leasing provides them with an opportunity to transfer such tax benefits to another party (the lessor) in return for a lower rental rate on the leased asset. To illustrate, Boeing Aircraft at one time sold one of its 767 jet planes to a wealthy investor who didn't need the plane but could use the tax benefit. The investor then leased the plane to a foreign airline, for whom the tax benefit was of no use. Everyone gained. Boeing was able to sell its 767, the investor received the tax benefits, and the foreign airline found a cheaper way to acquire a 767.[17]

3. **High Residual Value.** Another advantage to the lessor is the reversion of the property at the end of the lease term. Residual values can produce very large profits. Citicorp at one time assumed that the commercial aircraft it was leasing to the airline industry would have a residual value of 5% of their purchase price. It turned out that they were worth 150% of their cost—a handsome profit. However, 3 years later these same planes slumped to 80% of their cost, but still far more than 5%.

INTERNATIONAL
INSIGHT

In some nations (e.g., France, Italy, Brazil) companies are not permitted to capitalize financing leases.

ECONOMICS OF LEASING

The lessor determines the amount of the rental, basing it on the rate of return—the implicit rate—needed to justify leasing the asset. The key factors considered in establishing the rate of return are the credit standing of the lessee, the length of the lease, and the status of the residual value (guaranteed versus unguaranteed). In the Lessor Company/Lessee Company example on page 1129, the implicit rate of the lessor was 10%, the cost of the equipment to the lessor was $100,000 (also fair market value), and

---

[16]One study indicates that management's behavior did change as a result of *FASB No. 13*. For example, many companies restructure their leases to avoid capitalization; others increase their purchases of assets instead of leasing; and others, faced with capitalization, postpone their debt offerings or issue stock instead. However, it is interesting to note that the study found no significant effect on stock or bond prices as a result of capitalization of leases. A. Rashad Abdel-khalik, ''The Economic Effects on Lessees of FASB Statement No. 13, Accounting for Leases,'' *Research Report* (Stamford, Conn.: FASB, 1981).

[17]Some would argue that there is a loser—the U.S. government. The tax benefits enable the profitable investor to reduce or eliminate taxable income.

the estimated residual value was zero. Lessor Company determined the amount of the lease payment in the following manner:

ILLUSTRATION 22-8
Computation of Lease Payments

Fair market value of leased equipment	$100,000.00
Less present value of the residual value	–0–
Amount to be recovered by lessor through lease payments	$100,000.00
Five beginning-of-the-year lease payments to yield a 10% return ($100,000 ÷ 4.16986[a])	$ 23,981.62

[a]PV of an annuity due of 1 for 5 years at 10% (Table 6-5)

If a residual value were involved (whether guaranteed or not), the lessor would not have to recover as much from the lease payments. Therefore, the lease payments would be less (this situation is shown in Illustration 22-17).

CLASSIFICATION OF LEASES BY THE LESSOR

OBJECTIVE 4

Identify the classifications of leases for the lessor.

From the standpoint of the **lessor,** all leases may be classified for accounting purposes as one of the following:

(a) Operating leases.

(b) Direct financing leases.

(c) Sales-type leases.

If at the date of the lease agreement (inception) the lessor is party to a lease that meets **one or more** of the following Group I criteria (1, 2, 3, and 4) and **both** of the following Group II criteria (1 and 2), the lessor shall classify and account for the arrangement as a direct financing lease or as a sales-type lease.[18] (Note that the Group I criteria are identical to the criteria that must be met in order for a lease to be classified as a capital lease by a lessee, as shown in Illustration 22-2.)

ILLUSTRATION 22-9
Capitalization Criteria for Lessor

INTERNATIONAL INSIGHT

While U.S. GAAP is consistent with International Standard No. 17 (Accounting for Leases), U.S. rules on leases are the most prescriptive and detailed in the world.

Capitalization Criteria (Lessor)

Group I

1. The lease transfers ownership of the property to the lessee.
2. The lease contains a bargain purchase option.
3. The lease term is equal to 75% or more of the estimated economic life of the leased property.
4. The present value of the minimum lease payments (excluding executory costs) equals or exceeds 90% of the fair value of the leased property.

Group II

1. Collectibility of the payments required from the lessee is reasonably predictable.
2. No important uncertainties surround the amount of unreimbursable costs yet to be incurred by the lessor under the lease (lessor's performance is substantially complete or future costs are reasonably predictable).

Why the Group II requirements? The answer is that the profession wants to make sure that the lessor has really transferred the risks and benefits of ownership. If collectibility of payments is not predictable or if performance by the lessor is incomplete, then the criteria for revenue recognition have not been met and it should be accounted for as an operating lease.

Computer leasing companies at one time used to buy IBM equipment, lease it, and remove the leased assets from their balance sheets. In leasing the asset, the computer

---

[18]*FASB Statement No. 13*, op. cit., pars. 6, 7, and 8.

lessors stated that they would be willing to substitute new IBM equipment if obsolescence occurred. However, when IBM introduced a new computer line, IBM refused to sell it to the computer leasing companies. As a result, a number of the lessors could not meet their contracts with their customers and were forced to take back the old equipment. What the computer leasing companies had taken off the books now had to be reinstated. Such a case demonstrates one reason for the Group II requirements.

The distinction for the lessor between a direct financing lease and a sales-type lease is the presence or absence of a manufacturer's or dealer's profit (or loss): A sales-type lease involves a manufacturer's or dealer's profit, and a direct financing lease does not. The profit (or loss) to the lessor is evidenced by the difference between the fair value of the leased property at the inception of the lease and the lessor's cost or carrying amount (book value). Normally, sales-type leases arise when manufacturers or dealers use leasing as a means of marketing their products. For example, a computer manufacturer will lease its computer equipment to businesses and institutions. Direct financing leases generally result from arrangements with lessors that are primarily engaged in financing operations, such as lease-finance companies, banks, insurance companies, and pension trusts. However, a lessor need not be a manufacturer or dealer to recognize a profit (or loss) at the inception of a lease that requires application of sales-type lease accounting.

All leases that do not qualify as direct financing or sales-type leases are classified and accounted for by the lessors as operating leases. The following flowchart shows the circumstances under which a lease is classified as operating, direct financing, or sales-type for the lessor.

ILLUSTRATION 22-10
Diagram of Lessor's Criteria for Lease Classification

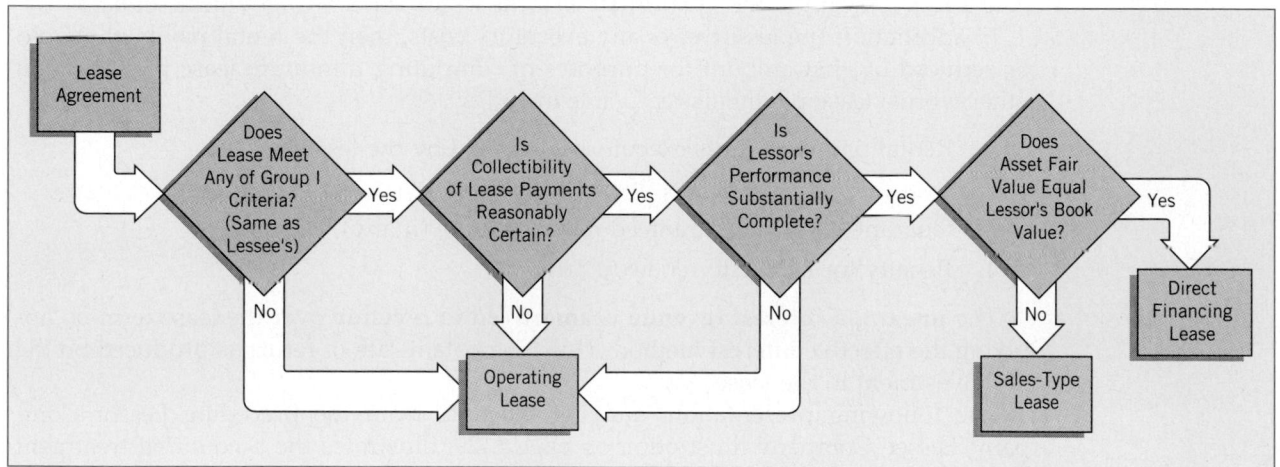

As a consequence of the additional Group II criteria for lessors, it is possible that a lessor having not met both criteria will classify a lease as an **operating** lease but the lessee will classify the same lease as a **capital** lease. In such an event, both the lessor and lessee will carry the asset on their books, and both will depreciate the capitalized asset.

For purposes of comparison with the lessee's accounting, only the operating and direct financing leases will be illustrated in the following section. The more complex sales-type lease will be discussed later in the chapter.

DIRECT FINANCING METHOD (LESSOR)

Leases that are in substance the financing of an asset purchase by a lessee require the lessor to substitute a "lease payments receivable" for the leased asset. The information necessary to record a **direct financing lease** is as follows:

OBJECTIVE 5

Describe the lessor's accounting for direct financing leases.

◄ DIRECT FINANCING TERMS ►

1. **GROSS INVESTMENT ("LEASE PAYMENTS RECEIVABLE").** The minimum lease payments plus the unguaranteed residual value accruing to the lessor at the end of the lease term.[19]

2. **UNEARNED INTEREST REVENUE.** The difference between the gross investment (the receivable) and the fair market value of the property.[20]

3. **NET INVESTMENT.** The gross investment (the receivable) less the unearned interest revenue included therein.

The computation of the gross investment (lease payments receivable) is often confusing because of the uncertainty as to how to account for the residual values. Remember that "minimum lease payments" includes:

1. Rental payments (excluding executory costs).
2. Bargain purchase option (if any).
3. Guaranteed residual value (if any).
4. Penalty for failure to renew (if any).

When "lease payments receivable" is defined as minimum lease payments plus unguaranteed residual value, it means that residual value, both guaranteed (because it is included as part of "minimum lease payments") and unguaranteed (because it is added back in to compute the gross investment), is included as part of lease payments receivable if it is relevant to the lessor (that is, if the lessor expects to get the asset back).

In addition, if the lessor pays any executory costs, then the rental payment should be reduced by that amount for purposes of computing minimum lease payments. In other words, lease payments receivable includes:

1. Rental payments (less executory costs paid by the lessor).
2. Bargain purchase option (if any).
3. Guaranteed or unguaranteed residual value (if any).
4. Penalty for failure to renew (if any).

The **unearned interest revenue is amortized to revenue** over the lease term by applying the effective interest method. Thus, a constant rate of return is produced on the net investment in the lease.

The following presentation, utilizing the data from the preceding Lessor Company/Lessee Company illustration on page 1129, illustrates the accounting treatment accorded a direct financing lease. The information relevant to Lessor Company in accounting for this lease transaction is repeated as follows:

1. The term of the lease is 5 years beginning January 1, 1996, noncancelable, and requires equal rental payments of $25,981.62 at the beginning of each year; payments include $2,000 of executory costs (property taxes).

---

[19]Ibid., par. 17. If the lessee agrees to make up any deficiency below a stated amount that the lessor realizes in residual value at the end of the lease term, that stated amount is the guaranteed residual value.

Initially the unguaranteed residual value could be classified in a separate account. If the unguaranteed residual value is included in the Lease Payments Receivable account, it would be reclassified by the lessor at the end of the lease term if not purchased by the lessee.

[20]In a direct financing lease, the cost or carrying amount of the asset should be used instead of fair market value. In most cases, however, cost or carrying amount is equal to fair market value, so fair market value is used here. The use of fair market value will simplify subsequent discussion in this area. Significant differences between cost or carrying amount and fair market value exist for sales-type leases.

2. The equipment has a cost of $100,000 to Lessor Company, a fair value at the inception of the lease of $100,000, an estimated economic life of 5 years, and no residual value.

3. No initial direct costs were incurred in negotiating and closing the lease transaction.

4. The lease contains no renewable options and the equipment reverts to Lessor Company at the termination of the lease.

5. Collectibility is reasonably assured and no additional costs (with the exception of the property taxes being collected from the lessee) are to be incurred by Lessor Company.

6. Lessor Company set the annual lease payments to insure a rate of return of 10% (implicit rate) on its investment as follows (as shown in Illustration 22-8):

Fair market value of leased equipment	$100,000.00
Less present value of residual value	–0–
Amount to be recovered by lessor through lease payments	$100,000.00
Five beginning-of-the-year lease payments to yield a 10% return ($100,000 ÷ 4.16986[a])	$ 23,981.62

[a]PV of an annuity due of 1 for 5 years at 10% (Table 6–5).

ILLUSTRATION 22-11
Computation of Lease Payments

The lease meets the criteria for classification as a direct financing lease because (1) the lease term exceeds 75% of the equipment's estimated economic life, (2) the present value of the minimum lease payments exceeds 90% of the equipment's fair value, (3) collectibility of the payments is reasonably assured, and (4) there are no further costs to be incurred by Lessor Company. It is not a sales-type lease because there is no difference between the fair value ($100,000) of the equipment and the lessor's cost ($100,000).

The lease payments receivable (gross investment) is calculated as follows:

Lease payments receivable = Minimum lease payments minus executory costs paid by lessor plus unguaranteed residual value
= [($25,981.62 – $2,000) × 5] + $0
= $119,908.10

ILLUSTRATION 22-12
Computation of Lease Payments Receivable

The unearned interest revenue is computed as the difference between the lease payments receivable and the lessor's fair market value of the leased asset:

Unearned interest revenue = Lease payments receivable minus asset's fair market value
= $119,908.10 – $100,000
= $19,908.10

ILLUSTRATION 22-13
Computation of Unearned Interest Revenue

The net investment in direct financing leases is $100,000; that is, the gross investment of $119,908.10 minus the unearned interest revenue of $19,908.10.

The lease of the asset, the resulting receivable, and the unearned interest revenue are recorded January 1, 1996 (the inception of the lease) as follows:

Lease Payments Receivable	119,908.10	
Equipment		100,000.00
Unearned Interest Revenue—Leases		19,908.10

The unearned interest revenue is classified on the balance sheet as a deduction from the lease payments receivable if the receivable is reported gross. Generally, the lease payments receivable, although **recorded** at the gross investment amount, is **reported** in the balance sheet at the "net investment" amount (gross investment less unearned interest revenue) and entitled "Net investment in capital leases." It is classified either as current or noncurrent, depending upon when the net investment is to be recovered.

The leased equipment with a cost of $100,000, which represents Lessor Company's investment, is replaced with a net lease receivable. In a manner similar to the lessee's treatment of interest, Lessor Company applies the effective interest method and recognizes interest revenue as a function of the unrecovered net investment, as illustrated below.

ILLUSTRATION 22-14
Lease Amortization
Schedule for Lessor—
Annuity Due Basis

	LESSOR COMPANY Lease Amortization Schedule (Annuity due basis)				
Date	Annual Lease Payment	Executory Costs	Interest (10%) on Net Investment	Net Investment Recovery	Net Investment
	(a)	(b)	(c)	(d)	(e)
1/1/96					$100,000.00
1/1/96	$ 25,981.62	$ 2,000.00	$ –0–	$ 23,981.62	76,018.38
1/1/97	25,981.62	2,000.00	7,601.84	16,379.78	59,638.60
1/1/98	25,981.62	2,000.00	5,963.86	18,017.76	41,620.84
1/1/99	25,981.62	2,000.00	4,162.08	19,819.54	21,801.30
1/1/00	25,981.62	2,000.00	2,180.32*	21,801.30	–0–
	$129,908.10	$10,000.00	$19,908.10	$100,000.00	

(a) Annual rental that provides a 10% return on net investment.
(b) Executory costs included in rental payment.
(c) Ten percent of the preceding balance of (e) except for 1/1/96.
(d) (a) minus (b) and (c).
(e) Preceding balance minus (d).
*Rounded by 19 cents.

On January 1, 1996, the journal entry to record receipt of the first year's lease payment is as follows:

Cash	25,981.62	
Lease Payments Receivable		23,981.62
Property Tax Expense/Property Taxes Payable		2,000.00

On 12/31/96 the interest revenue earned during the first year is recognized through the following entry:

Unearned Interest Revenue—Leases	7,601.84	
Interest Revenue—Leases		7,601.84

At December 31, 1996, the net investment under capital leases is reported in the lessor's balance sheet among current assets or noncurrent assets, or both. The portion due within one year or the operating cycle, whichever is longer, is classified as a current asset and the rest with noncurrent assets.

The total net investment at 12/31/96 is equal to $83,620.22 (the balance at 1/1/96, $76,018.38 plus interest receivable for 1996 of $7,601.84). The current portion is the net investment to be received in 1997, $16,379.78, plus the interest of $7,601.84. The remainder, $59,638.60 (Lease Payments Receivable of $71,944.86 [$23,981.62 × 3] minus Unearned Interest Revenue of $12,306.26 [$5,963.86 + $4,162.08 + $2,180.32]) should be reported in the noncurrent asset section.

The asset section as it relates to lease transactions at 12/31/96 would appear as follows:

ILLUSTRATION 22-15
Reporting Lease
Transactions by Lessor

Current assets	
Net investment in capital leases	$23,981.62
Noncurrent assets (investments)	
Net investment in capital leases	$59,638.60

The following entries record receipt of the second year's lease payment and recognition of the interest earned:

January 1, 1997

Cash	25,981.62	
Lease Payments Receivable		23,981.62
Property Tax Expense/Property Taxes Payable		2,000.00

December 31, 1997

Unearned Interest Revenue—Leases	5,963.86	
Interest Revenue—Leases		5,963.86

Journal entries through 2000 would follow the same pattern except that no entry would be recorded in 2000 (the last year) for earned interest. Because the receivable is fully collected by 1/1/00, no balance (investment) is outstanding during 2000 to which Lessor Company could attribute any interest. Upon expiration of the lease (whether an ordinary annuity or an annuity due), the gross receivable and the unearned interest revenue would be fully written off. **Lessor Company recorded no depreciation.** If the equipment is sold to Lessee Company for $5,000 upon expiration of the lease, Lessor Company would recognize disposition of the equipment as follows:

Cash	5,000	
Gain on Sale of Leased Equipment		5,000

CLASSIFICATION OF LEASE OBLIGATION/NET INVESTMENT (ORDINARY ANNUITY)

The classification of the lease obligation/net investment was presented in the previous section in an annuity due situation. As indicated in Illustration 22-6, the lessee's current liability is the payment ($23,981.62) to be made on January 1 of the next year. Similarly, as shown in Illustration 22-15, the lessor's current asset is the amount to be collected ($23,981.62) on January 1 of the next year. In both of these annuity due instances, the balance sheet date is December 31 and the due date of the lease payment is January 1 (less than one year), so the present value ($23,981.62) of the payment due the following January 1 is the same as the rental payment ($23,981.62).

What happens if the situation is an ordinary annuity rather than an annuity due situation? For example, assume that the rent is to be paid at the end of the year (December 31) rather than at the beginning (January 1). *FASB Statement No. 13* does not indicate how to measure the current and noncurrent amounts; it requires that for the lessee the "obligations shall be separately identified on the balance sheet as obligations under capital leases and shall be subject to the same considerations as other obligations in classifying them with current and noncurrent liabilities in classified balance sheets."[21] The most common method of measuring the current liability portion in ordinary annuity leases is the change in the present value method.[22]

To illustrate the change in the present value method, assume an ordinary annuity situation with the same facts as the Lessee Company/Lessor Company case, excluding the $2,000 of executory costs. Because the rents are paid at the end of the period instead of at the beginning, the five rents are set at $26,379.73 to have an effective interest rate of 10%. The ordinary annuity amortization schedule appears as follows:

---

[21]"Accounting for Leases," op. cit., par. 16.

[22]For additional discussion on this approach and possible alternatives, see R. J. Swieringa, "When Current is Noncurrent and Vice Versa!" *The Accounting Review* (January 1984), pp. 123–130 and A. W. Richardson, "The Measurement of the Current Portion of the Long-Term Lease Obligations—Some Evidence from Practice," *The Accounting Review* (October 1985), pages 744–752.

ILLUSTRATION 22-16
Lease Amortization
Schedule—Ordinary
Annuity Basis

	LESSEE COMPANY/LESSOR COMPANY Lease Amortization Schedule (Ordinary annuity basis)			
Date	Annual Lease Payment	Interest 10%	Reduction of Principal	Balance of Lease Obligation/ Net Investment
1/1/96				$100,000.00
12/31/96	$ 26,379.73	$10,000.00	$ 16,379.73	83,620.27
12/31/97	26,379.73	8,362.03	18,017.70	65,602.57
12/31/98	26,379.73	6,560.26	19,819.47	45,783.10
12/31/99	26,379.73	4,578.31	21,801.42	23,981.68
12/31/00	26,379.73	2,398.05*	23,981.68	–0–
	$131,898.65	$31,898.65	$100,000.00	

*Rounded by 12 cents.

The current portion of the lease obligation/net investment under the **change in the present value method** as of December 31, 1996, would be $18,017.70 ($83,620.27 − $65,602.57); and as of December 31, 1997, it would be $19,819.47 ($65,602.57 − $45,783.10). The portion of the lease obligation/net investment that is not current is classified as such; that is, $65,602.57 is the noncurrent portion at December 31, 1996.

Thus, both the annuity due and the ordinary annuity situations report the reduction of principal for the next period as a current liability/current asset. In the annuity due situation, interest is accrued during the year but is not paid until the next period. As a result, **a current liability/current asset arises for both the principal reduction and the interest** that was incurred/earned in the preceding period.

In the ordinary annuity situation, the interest accrued during the period is also paid in the same period; consequently, only the principal reduction is shown as a current liability/current asset.

OPERATING METHOD (LESSOR)

Under the **operating method** each rental receipt by the lessor is recorded as rental revenue. The **leased asset is depreciated in the normal manner,** with the depreciation expense of the period matched against the rental revenue. The amount of revenue recognized in each accounting period is a level amount (straight-line basis) regardless of the lease provisions, unless another systematic and rational basis is more representative of the time pattern in which the benefit is derived from the leased asset. In addition to the depreciation charge, maintenance costs and the cost of any other services rendered under the provisions of the lease that pertain to the current accounting period are charged to expense. Costs paid to independent third parties such as appraisal fees, finder's fees, and costs of credit checks are amortized over the life of the lease.

To illustrate the operating method, assume that the direct financing lease illustrated above did not qualify as a capital lease and was therefore to be accounted for as an operating lease. The entry to record the cash rental receipt, assuming the $2,000 was for property tax expense, would be as follows:

Cash	25,981.62	
Rental Revenue		25,981.62

Depreciation is recorded by the lessor as follows (assuming a straight-line method, a cost basis of $100,000, and a 5-year life):

Depreciation Expense—Leased Equipment	20,000	
Accumulated Depreciation—Leased Equipment		20,000

If property taxes, insurance, maintenance, and other operating costs during the year are the obligation of the lessor, they are recorded as expenses chargeable against the gross rental revenues.

If the lessor owned plant assets that it used in addition to those leased to others, **the leased equipment and accompanying accumulated depreciation would be separately classified** in an account such as Equipment Leased to Others or Investment in Leased Property. If significant in amount or in terms of activity, the rental revenues and accompanying expenses are separated in the income statement from sales revenue and cost of goods sold.

▶ SPECIAL ACCOUNTING PROBLEMS

The features of lease arrangements that cause unique accounting problems are:

1. Residual values.
2. Sales-type leases (lessor).
3. Bargain purchase options.
4. Initial direct costs.
5. Sale-leaseback.

OBJECTIVE 6

Identify special features of lease arrangements that cause unique accounting problems.

RESIDUAL VALUES

Up to this point, we have generally ignored discussion of residual values in order that the basic accounting issues related to lessee and lessor accounting could be developed. Accounting for residual values is complex and will probably provide you with the greatest challenge in understanding lease accounting.

Meaning of Residual Value

The residual value is the **estimated fair value** of the leased asset at the end of the lease term. Frequently, a significant residual value exists at the end of the lease term, especially when the economic life of the leased asset exceeds the lease term. If title does not pass automatically to the lessee (criterion 1) and a bargain purchase option does not exist (criterion 2), the lessee returns physical custody of the asset to the lessor at the end of the lease term.[23]

Guaranteed Versus Unguaranteed

The residual value may be unguaranteed or guaranteed by the lessee. If the lessee agrees to make up any deficiency below a stated amount that the lessor realizes in residual value at the end of the lease term, that stated amount is the **guaranteed residual value.**

The guaranteed residual value is employed in lease arrangements for two reasons. The first is a business reason: It protects the lessor against any loss in estimated residual value, thereby ensuring the lessor of the desired rate of return on investment. The second is an accounting benefit that you will learn from the discussion at the end of this chapter.

Lease Payments

A guaranteed residual value—by definition—has more assurance of realization than does an unguaranteed residual value. As a result, the lessor may adjust lease payments because the certainty of recovery has been increased. After this rate is established, however, it makes no difference from an accounting point of view whether the residual value is guaranteed or unguaranteed. The net investment to be recorded by the lessor (once the rate is set) will be the same.

---

[23]When the lease term and the economic life are not the same, the residual value and the salvage value of the asset will probably differ. For simplicity, we will assume that residual value and salvage value are the same, even when the economic life and lease term vary.

Assume the same data as in the Lessee Company/Lessor Company illustrations except that a residual value of $5,000 is estimated at the end of the 5-year lease term. In addition, a 10% return on investment (ROI) is assumed,[24] whether the residual value is guaranteed or unguaranteed. Lessor Company would compute the amount of the lease payments as follows:

ILLUSTRATION 22-17
Lessor's Computation of Lease Payments

LESSOR'S COMPUTATION OF LEASE PAYMENTS (10% ROI) Guaranteed or Unguaranteed Residual Value (Annuity due basis, including residual value)	
Fair market value of leased asset to lessor	$100,000.00
Less present value of residual value ($5,000 × .62092, Table 6–2)	3,104.60
Amount to be recovered by lessor through lease payments	$ 96,895.40
Five periodic lease payments ($96,895.40 ÷ 4.16986, Table 6–5)	$ 23,237.09

Contrast the foregoing lease payment amount to the lease payments of $23,981.62 as computed in Illustration 22-8, where no residual value existed. The payments are less because the lessor's total recoverable amount of $100,000 is reduced by the present value of the residual value.

Lessee Accounting for Residual Value

Whether the estimated residual value is guaranteed or unguaranteed is of both economic and accounting consequence to the lessee. The accounting difference is that the **minimum lease payments,** the basis for capitalization, includes the guaranteed residual value but excludes the unguaranteed residual value.

Guaranteed Residual Value (Lessee Accounting)

OBJECTIVE 7
Describe the effect of residual values, guaranteed and unguaranteed, on lease accounting.

A guaranteed residual value affects the lessee's computation of minimum lease payments and, therefore, the amounts capitalized as a leased asset and a lease obligation. In effect, **it is an additional lease payment that will be paid in property or cash, or both, at the end of the lease term.** Using the rental payments as computed by the lessor above, the minimum lease payments are $121,185.45 ([$23,237.09 × 5] + $5,000). The capitalized present value of the minimum lease payments (excluding executory costs) is computed as follows:

ILLUSTRATION 22-18
Computation of Lessee's Capitalized Amount—Guaranteed Residual Value

LESSEE'S CAPITALIZED AMOUNT (10% RATE) (Annuity due basis; including **guaranteed** residual value)	
Present value of five annual rental payments ($23,237.09 × 4.16986, Table 6–5)	$ 96,895.40
Present value of guaranteed residual value of $5,000 due five years after date of inception: ($5,000 × .62092, Table 6–2)	3,104.60
Lessee's capitalized amount	$100,000.00

Lessee Company's schedule of interest expense and amortization of the $100,000 lease obligation that produces a $5,000 final guaranteed residual value payment at the end of five years is shown in Illustration 22-19.

---

[24]Technically the rate of return demanded by the lessor would be different depending upon whether the residual value was guaranteed or unguaranteed. We are ignoring this difference in subsequent sections to simplify the illustrations.

LESSEE COMPANY
Lease Amortization Schedule
(Annuity due basis, guaranteed residual value—GRV)

Date	Lease Payment Plus GRV	Executory Costs	Interest (10%) on Unpaid Obligation	Reduction of Lease Obligation	Lease Obligation
	(a)	(b)	(c)	(d)	(e)
1/1/96					$100,000.00
1/1/96	$ 25,237.09	$ 2,000	–0–	$ 23,237.09	76,762.91
1/1/97	25,237.09	2,000	$ 7,676.29	15,560.80	61,202.11
1/1/98	25,237.09	2,000	6,120.21	17,116.88	44,085.23
1/1/99	25,237.09	2,000	4,408.52	18,828.57	25,256.66
1/1/00	25,237.09	2,000	2,525.67	20,711.42	4,545.24
12/31/00	5,000.00*		454.76**	4,545.24	–0–
	$131,185.45	$10,000	$21,185.45	$100,000.00	

(a) Annual lease payment as required by lease.
(b) Executory costs included in rental payment.
(c) Preceding balance of (e) × 10%, except 1/1/96.
(d) (a) minus (b) and (c).
(e) Preceding balance minus (d).

*Represents the guaranteed residual value.
**Rounded by 24 cents.

ILLUSTRATION 22-19
Lease Amortization Schedule for Lessee— Guaranteed Residual Value

The journal entries (page 1145) to record the leased asset and obligation, depreciation, interest, and property tax, and lease payments are then made on the basis that the residual value is guaranteed. The format of these entries is the same as illustrated earlier, although the amounts are different because of the guaranteed residual value. The leased asset is recorded at $100,000 and is depreciated over 5 years. To compute depreciation, the guaranteed residual value is subtracted from the cost of the leased asset. Assuming that the straight-line method is used, the depreciation expense each year is $19,000 ([$100,000 − $5,000] ÷ 5 years).

At the end of the lease term, before the lessee transfers the asset to the lessor, the lease asset and obligation accounts have the following balances:

Leased equipment under capital leases	$100,000.00	Interest payable	$ 454.76
Less accumulated depreciation—		Obligations under capital leases	4,545.24
capital leases	95,000.00		
	$ 5,000.00		$5,000.00

ILLUSTRATION 22-20
Account Balances on Lessee's Books at End of Lease Term—Guaranteed Residual Value

If, at the end of the lease, the fair market value of the residual value is less than $5,000, Lessee Company will have to record a loss. Assume that Lessee Company depreciated the leased asset down to its residual value of $5,000 but that the fair market value of the residual value at 12/31/00 was $3,000. In this case, the Lessee Company would have to report a loss of $2,000. The following journal entry would be made, assuming cash was paid to make up the residual value deficiency:

Loss on Capital Lease	2,000.00	
Interest Expense (or Interest Payable)	454.76	
Obligations Under Capital Leases	4,545.24	
Accumulated Depreciation—Capital Leases	95,000.00	
Leased Equipment Under Capital Leases		100,000.00
Cash		2,000.00

If the fair market value exceeds $5,000, a gain may be recognized. Gains on guaranteed residual values may be apportioned to the lessor and lessee in whatever ratio the parties initially agree.

If the lessee depreciated the total cost of the asset ($100,000), a misstatement would occur; that is, the carrying amount of the asset at the end of the lease term would be zero, but the obligation under the capital lease would be stated at $5,000. Thus, if the asset was worth $5,000, the lessee would end up reporting a gain of $5,000 when it transferred the asset to the lessor. As a result, depreciation would be overstated and net income understated in 1996–1999, but in the last year (2000) net income would be overstated.

Unguaranteed Residual Value (Lessee Accounting)

An **unguaranteed residual value** from the lessee's viewpoint is the same as no residual value in terms of its effect upon the lessee's method of computing the minimum lease payments and the capitalization of the leased asset and the lease obligation. Assume the same facts as those above except that the $5,000 residual value is **unguaranteed instead of guaranteed**. The amount of the annual lease payments would be the same, $23,237.09. Whether the residual value is guaranteed or unguaranteed, Lessor Company's amount to be recovered through lease rentals is the same, that is, $96,895.40. The minimum lease payments are $116,185.45 ($23,237.09 × 5). Lessee Company would capitalize the following amount:

ILLUSTRATION 22-21
Computation of Lessee's Capitalized Amount— Unguaranteed Residual Value

LESSEE'S CAPITALIZED AMOUNT (10% RATE) (Annuity due basis, including **unguaranteed** residual value)	
Present value of 5 annual rental payments of $23,237.09 × 4.16986 (Table 6–5)	$96,895.40
Unguaranteed residual value of $5,000 (not capitalized by lessee)	–0–
Lessee's capitalized amount	$96,895.40

The Lessee Company's schedule of interest expense and amortization of the lease obligation of $96,895.40, assuming an unguaranteed residual value of $5,000 at the end of 5 years, is shown in Illustration 22-22.

ILLUSTRATION 22-22
Lease Amortization Schedule for Lessee— Unguaranteed Residual Value

	LESSEE COMPANY Lease Amortization Schedule (10%) (Annuity due basis, **unguaranteed** residual value)				
Date	Annual Lease Payments (a)	Executory Costs (b)	Interest (10%) on Unpaid Obligation (c)	Reduction of Lease Obligation (d)	Lease Obligation (e)
1/1/96					$96,895.40
1/1/96	$ 25,237.09	$ 2,000	–0–	$23,237.09	73,658.31
1/1/97	25,237.09	2,000	$ 7,365.83	15,871.26	57,787.05
1/1/98	25,237.09	2,000	5,778.71	17,458.38	40,328.67
1/1/99	25,237.09	2,000	4,032.87	19,204.22	21,124.45
1/1/00	25,237.09	2,000	2,112.64*	21,124.45	–0–
	$126,185.45	$10,000	$19,290.05	$96,895.40	

(a) Annual lease payment as required by lease.
(b) Executory costs included in rental payment.
(c) Preceding balance of (e) × 10%.
(d) (a) minus (b) and (c).
(e) Preceding balance minus (d).
*Rounded by 19 cents.

The journal entries (page 1145) to record the leased asset and obligation, depreciation, interest, and property tax, and payments on the lease obligation are then made on the basis that the residual value is unguaranteed. The format of these entries is the same as illustrated earlier. Note that the leased asset is recorded at $96,895.40 and is depreciated over 5 years. Assuming that the straight-line method is used, the depreciation expense each year is $19,379.08 ($96,895.40 ÷ 5 years). At the end of the lease term, before the lessee transfers the asset to the lessor, the following balances in the accounts result, as illustrated below.

ILLUSTRATION 22-23
Account Balances on Lessee's Books at End of Lease Term— Unguaranteed Residual Value

Leased equipment under capital leases	$96,895	Obligations under capital leases	$–0–
Less accumulated depreciation— capital leases	96,895		
	$ –0–		

Assuming that the asset had a fair market value of $3,000, no loss would be reported by the lessee. Assuming that the leased asset has been fully depreciated and that the lease obligation has been fully amortized, no entry is required at the end of the lease term, except to remove the asset from the books.

If the lessee depreciated the asset down to its unguaranteed residual value, a misstatement would occur. That is, the carrying amount of the leased asset would be $5,000 at the end of the lease, but the obligation under the capital lease would be stated at zero before the transfer of the asset. Thus, the lessee would end up reporting a loss of $5,000 when it transferred the asset to the lessor. Depreciation would be understated and net income is overstated in 1996–1999, but in the last year (2000) net income would be understated because of the recorded loss.

Lessee Entries Involving Residual Values

The entries by Lessee Company for both a guaranteed and an unguaranteed residual value are shown in Illustration 22-24 in comparative form.

ILLUSTRATION 22-24
Comparative Entries for Guaranteed and Unguaranteed Residual Values, Lessee Company

Guaranteed Residual Value			Unguaranteed Residual Value		
Capitalization of Lease 1/1/96:					
Leased Equipment Under			Leased Equipment Under		
Capital Leases	100,000.00		Capital Leases	96,895.40	
Obligations Under			Obligations Under		
Capital Leases		100,000.00	Capital Leases		96,895.40
First Payment 1/1/96:					
Property Tax Expense	2,000.00		Property Tax Expense	2,000.00	
Obligations Under			Obligations Under		
Capital Leases	23,237.09		Capital Leases	23,237.09	
Cash		25,237.09	Cash		25,237.09
Adjusting Entry for Accrued Interest 12/31/96:					
Interest Expense	7,676.29		Interest Expense	7,365.83	
Interest Payable		7,676.29	Interest Payable		7,365.83
Entry to Record Depreciation 12/31/96:					
Depreciation Expense—			Depreciation Expense—		
Capital Leases	19,000.00		Capital Leases	19,379.08	
Accumulated Deprecia-			Accumulated Depreciation—		
tion—Capital Leases		19,000.00	Capital Leases		19,379.08
([$100,000 − $5,000] ÷ 5 years)			($96,895.40 ÷ 5 years)		
Second Payment 1/1/97:					
Property Tax Expense	2,000.00		Property Tax Expense	2,000.00	
Obligations Under			Obligations Under		
Capital Leases	15,560.80		Capital Leases	15,871.26	
Interest Expense			Interest Expense		
(or Interest Payable)	7,676.29		(or Interest Payable)	7,365.83	
Cash		25,237.09	Cash		25,237.09

Lessor Accounting for Residual Value

As indicated earlier, the net investment to be recovered by the lessor is the same whether the residual value is guaranteed or unguaranteed. The lessor works on the assumption that **the residual value will be realized at the end of the lease term whether guaranteed or unguaranteed.** The lease payments required by the lessor to earn a certain return on investment are the same ($23,237.09) whether the residual value is guaranteed or unguaranteed.

Using the Lessee Company/Lessor Company data and assuming a residual value (either guaranteed or unguaranteed) of $5,000 and classification of the lease as a direct financing lease, the following necessary amounts are computed:

ILLUSTRATION 22-25
Computation of Direct Financing Lease Amounts by Lessor

> Gross investment = ($23,237.09 × 5) + $5,000 = $121,185.45
> Unearned interest revenue = $121,185.45 − $100,000 = $21,185.45
> Net investment = $121,185.45 − $21,185.45 = $100,000

The schedule for amortization with guaranteed or unguaranteed residual value is the same:

ILLUSTRATION 22-26
**Lease Amortization
Schedule, for Lessor—
Guaranteed or
Unguaranteed Residual
Value**

LESSOR COMPANY
Lease Amortization Schedule
(Annuity due basis, **guaranteed** or **unguaranteed** residual value)

Date	Annual Lease Payment Plus Residual Value	Executory Costs	Interest (10%) on Net Investment	Net Investment Recovery	Net Investment
	(a)	(b)	(c)	(d)	(e)
1/1/96					$100,000.00
1/1/96	$ 25,237.09	$ 2,000.00	$ –0–	$ 23,237.09	76,762.91
1/1/97	25,237.09	2,000.00	7,676.29	15,560.80	61,202.11
1/1/98	25,237.09	2,000.00	6,120.21	17,116.88	44,085.23
1/1/99	25,237.09	2,000.00	4,408.52	18,828.57	25,256.66
1/1/00	25,237.09	2,000.00	2,525.67	20,711.42	4,545.24
12/31/00	5,000.00	–0–	454.76*	4,545.24	–0–
	$131,185.45	$10,000.00	$21,185.45	$100,000.00	

(a) Annual lease payment as required by lease.
(b) Executory costs included in rental payment.
(c) Preceding balance of (e) × 10%, except 1/1/96.
(d) (a) minus (b) and (c).
(e) Preceding balance minus (d).
*Rounded by 24 cents.

Using the amounts computed above, the following entries would be made by Lessor Company during the first year for this direct financing lease. Note the similarity to the lessee's entries in Illustration 22-24.

ILLUSTRATION 22-27
**Entries for Either
Guaranteed or
Unguaranteed Residual
Value, Lessor Company**

Inception of Lease 1/1/96:

Lease Payments Receivable	121,185.45	
Equipment		100,000.00
Unearned Interest Revenue—Leases		21,185.45

First Payment Received 1/1/96:

Cash	25,237.09	
Lease Payments Receivable		23,237.09
Property Tax Expense/Property Taxes Payable		2,000.00

Adjusting Entry for Accrued Interest 12/31/96:

Unearned Interest Revenue—Leases	7,676.29	
Interest Revenue—Leases		7,676.29

OBJECTIVE 8

*Describe the lessor's
accounting for sales-type
leases.*

SALES-TYPE LEASES (LESSOR)

As already indicated, the primary difference between a direct financing lease and a **sales-type lease** is the manufacturer's or dealer's gross profit (or loss). A diagram illustrating these relationships is shown in Illustration 22-28.

ILLUSTRATION 22-28
**Direct Financing versus
Sales-Type Leases**

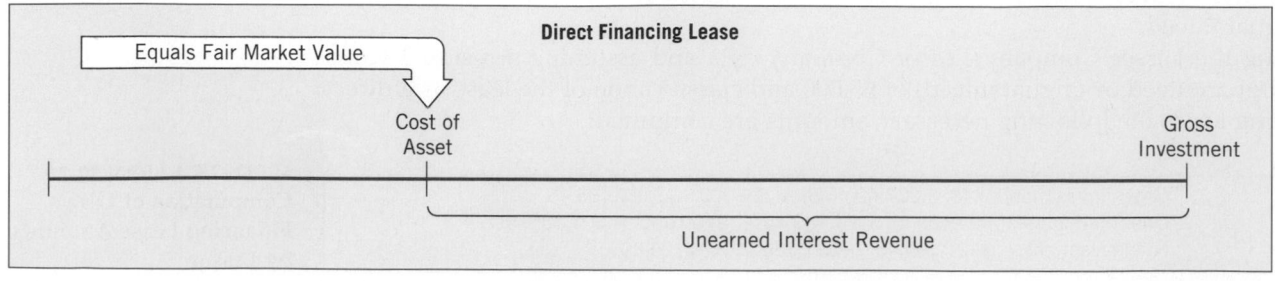

Direct Financing Lease

Equals Fair Market Value

Cost of Asset — Gross Investment

Unearned Interest Revenue

Sales-Type Lease

Does Not Equal Fair Market Value

| Cost of Asset | Sale Price of Asset | Gross Investment |

Gross Profit   Unearned Interest Revenue

ILLUSTRATION 22-28
Continued

The information necessary to record the sales-type lease is as follows:

◄ SALES-TYPE LEASE TERMS ►

1. **GROSS INVESTMENT** (also "**LEASE PAYMENTS RECEIVABLE**"). The minimum lease payments plus the unguaranteed residual value accruing to the lessor at the end of the lease term.

2. **UNEARNED INTEREST REVENUE.** The gross investment less the fair market value of the asset.

3. **SALES PRICE OF THE ASSET.** The present value of the minimum lease payments.

4. **COST OF GOODS SOLD.** The cost of the asset to the lessor, less the present value of any unguaranteed residual value.

The gross investment and the unearned interest revenue are the same whether a guaranteed or an unguaranteed residual value is involved.

When recording sales revenue and cost of goods sold, there is a difference in the accounting for guaranteed and unguaranteed residual values. The guaranteed residual value can be considered part of sales revenue because the lessor knows that the entire asset has been sold. There is less certainty that the unguaranteed residual portion of the asset has been "sold" (i.e., will be realized); therefore, sales and cost of goods sold are recognized only for the portion of the asset for which realization is assured. However, **the gross profit amount on the sale of the asset is the same whether a guaranteed or unguaranteed residual value is involved.**

To illustrate a sales-type lease with a guaranteed residual value and a sales-type lease with an unguaranteed residual value, assume the same facts as in the preceding direct financing lease situation (page 1142). The estimated residual value is $5,000 (the present value of which is $3,104.60), and the leased equipment has an $85,000 cost to the dealer, Lessor Company. Assume that the fair market value of the residual value is $3,000 at the end of the lease term.

The amounts relevant to a sales-type lease are computed as follows:

	Sales-Type Lease	
	Guaranteed Residual Value	Unguaranteed Residual Value
Gross investment	$121,185.45 ([$23,237.09 × 5] + $5,000)	Same
Unearned interest revenue	$21,185.45 ($121,185.45 − $100,000)	Same
Sales price of the asset	$100,000 ($96,895.40 + $3,104.60)	$96,895.40
Cost of goods sold	$85,000	$81,895.40 ($85,000 − $3,104.60)
Gross profit	$15,000 ($100,000 − $85,000)	$15,000 ($96,895.40 − $81,895.40)

ILLUSTRATION 22-29
Computation of Lease Amounts by Lessor Company—Sales-Type Lease

The profit recorded by Lessor Company at the point of sale is the same, $15,000, whether the residual value is guaranteed or unguaranteed, **but the sales revenue and cost of goods sold amounts are different.** The present value of the unguaranteed residual value is deducted from sales revenue and cost of goods sold for two reasons: (1) the criteria for revenue recognition have not been met, and (2) matching expense against revenue not yet recognized is improper. The revenue recognition criteria have not been met **because of the uncertainty surrounding the realization of the unguaranteed residual value.**

ILLUSTRATION 22-30
Entries for Guaranteed and Unguaranteed Residual Values, Lessor Company—Sales-Type Lease

The entries to record this transaction on January 1, 1996, and the receipt of the residual value at the end of the lease term are presented below.

Guaranteed Residual Value			Unguaranteed Residual Value		
To record sales-type lease at inception (January 1, 1996):					
Cost of Goods Sold	85,000.00		Cost of Goods Sold	81,895.40	
Lease Payments			Lease Payments		
Receivable	121,185.45		Receivable	121,185.45	
Sales Revenue		100,000.00	Sales Revenue		96,895.40
Unearned Interest Revenue		21,185.45	Unearned Interest Revenue		21,185.45
Inventory		85,000.00	Inventory		85,000.00
To record receipt of the first lease payment (January 1, 1996):					
Cash	25,237.09		Cash	25,237.09	
Lease Payments Receivable		23,237.09	Lease Payments Receivable		23,237.09
Prop. Tax Exp./Prop. Tax Pay.		2,000.00	Prop. Tax Exp./Prop. Tax Pay.		2,000.00
To recognize interest revenue earned during the first year (December 31, 1996):					
Unearned Interest Revenue	7,676.29		Unearned Interest Revenue	7,676.29	
Interest Revenue		7,676.29	Interest Revenue		7,676.29
(See lease amortization schedule, page 1146.)					
To record receipt of the second lease payment (January 1, 1997):					
Cash	25,237.09		Cash	25,237.09	
Lease Payments Receivable		23,237.09	Lease Payments Receivable		23,237.09
Prop. Tax Exp./Prop. Tax Pay.		2,000.00	Prop. Tax Exp./Prop. Tax Pay.		2,000.00
To recognize interest revenue earned during the second year (December 31, 1997):					
Unearned Interest Revenue	6,120.21		Unearned Interest Revenue	6,120.21	
Interest Revenue		6,120.21	Interest Revenue		6,120.21
To record receipt of residual value at end of lease term (December 31, 2000):					
Inventory	3,000		Inventory	3,000	
Cash	2,000		Loss on Capital Lease	2,000	
Lease Payments Receivable		5,000	Lease Payments Receivable		5,000

The **estimated unguaranteed residual value in a sales-type lease** (and a direct financing-type lease) **must be reviewed periodically.** If the estimate of the unguaranteed residual value declines, the accounting for the transaction must be revised using the changed estimate. The decline represents a reduction in the lessor's net investment and is recognized as a loss in the period in which the residual estimate is reduced. Upward adjustments in estimated residual value are not recognized.

BARGAIN PURCHASE OPTION (LESSEE)

A bargain purchase option allows the lessee to purchase the leased property for a future price that is substantially lower than the property's expected future fair value. The price is so favorable at the lease's inception that the future exercise of the option appears to be reasonably assured. If a bargain purchase option exists, **the lessee must increase the present value of the minimum lease payments by the present value of the option price.**

For example, assume that Lessee Company in the illustration on pages 1142–1143 had an option to buy the leased equipment for $5,000 at the end of the 5-year lease term when the fair value is expected to be $18,000. The significant difference between the option price and the fair value creates a bargain purchase option, the exercise of which is reasonably assured. Four computations are affected by a bargain purchase option in the same manner that they are by a guaranteed residual value: (1) the amount of the five lease payments necessary for the lessor to earn a 10% return on net investment, (2) the amount of the minimum lease payments, (3) the amount capitalized as leased assets and lease obligation, and (4) the amortization of the lease obligation. Therefore, the computations, amortization schedule, and entries that would be prepared for this $5,000 bargain purchase option are identical to those shown on pages 1142–1143 and 1145 for the $5,000 guaranteed residual value.

The only difference between the accounting treatment for a bargain purchase option and a guaranteed residual value of identical amounts and circumstances is in the **computation of the annual depreciation.** In the case of a guaranteed residual value, the lessee depreciates the asset over the lease life, whereas in the case of a bargain purchase option, the lessee uses the **economic life** of the asset.

INITIAL DIRECT COSTS (LESSOR)

Initial direct costs are of two types.[25] The first, **incremental direct costs,** are costs paid to independent third parties, incurred in originating a lease arrangement. Examples would include cost of independent appraisal of collateral used to secure a lease, or the cost of an outside credit check of the lessee or a broker's fee for finding the lessee.

The second type, **internal direct costs,** are the costs directly related to specified activities performed **by the lessor** on a given lease. Examples are evaluating the prospective lessee's financial condition; evaluating and recording guarantees, collateral, and other security arrangements; negotiating lease terms and preparing and processing lease documents; and closing the transaction. The costs directly related to an employee's time spent on a specific lease transaction are also considered initial direct costs.

On the other hand, initial direct costs should **not** include **internal indirect costs** related to activities performed by the lessor for advertising, servicing existing leases, and establishing and monitoring credit policies; nor should they include costs for supervision and administration. In addition, expenses such as rent and depreciation are not considered initial direct costs.

For **operating leases,** the lessor should defer initial direct costs and **allocate them over the lease term** in proportion to the recognition of rental income. In a **sales-type lease** transaction, the lessor expenses the initial direct costs in the year of incurrence; that is, they are **expensed in the period** in which the profit on the sale is recognized.

In a **direct financing lease,** however, initial direct costs are added to the net investment in the lease and **amortized over the life of the lease as a yield adjustment.** In addition, the unamortized deferred initial direct costs that are part of the lessor's investment in the direct financing lease must be disclosed. If the carrying value of the asset in the lease is $4,000,000 and the lessor incurs initial direct costs of $35,000, then the net investment in the lease would be $4,035,000. The yield would be adjusted to ensure proper amortization of this amount over the life of the lease and would be lower than the initial rate of return.

SALE-LEASEBACKS

The term **sale-leaseback** describes a transaction in which the owner of the property (seller-lessee) sells the property to another and simultaneously leases it back from the new owner. The use of the property is generally continued without interruption.

Sale-leasebacks are common. Financial institutions (Bank of America and First Chicago) have used this technique for their administrative offices, public utilities (Ohio Edison and Pinnacle West Corporation) for their generating plants, and airlines (Continental and Alaska Airlines) for their aircraft. The advantages of a sale-leaseback from the seller's viewpoint usually involve two primary considerations.

UNDERLYING
CONCEPT

A sale-leaseback is similar in substance to the parking of inventories discussed in Chapter 8. The ultimate economic benefits remain under the control of the "seller," thus the definition of an asset is satisfied.

---

[25]"Accounting for Nonrefundable Fees and Costs Associated with Originating or Acquiring Loans and Initial Direct Costs of Leases," *Statement of Financial Accounting Standards No. 91* (Stamford, Conn.: FASB, 1987).

1. **Financing**—If the purchase of equipment has already been financed, a sale-leaseback can allow the seller to refinance at lower rates, assuming rates have dropped. In addition, a sale-leaseback can provide another source of working capital, particularly when liquidity is tight.

2. **Taxes**—At the time a company purchased equipment, it may not have known that it would be subject to a minimum tax and that ownership might increase its minimum tax liability. By selling the property, the seller-lessee may deduct the entire lease payment, which is not subject to minimum tax considerations.

Determining Asset Use

To the extent the **seller-lessee's use** of the asset sold continues after the sale, the sale-leaseback is really a form of financing, and therefore **no gain or loss should be recognized** on the transaction. In short, the seller-lessee is simply borrowing funds. On the other hand, if the **seller-lessee gives up the right to the use** of the asset sold, the transaction is in substance a sale, and **gain or loss recognition** is appropriate. Trying to ascertain when the lessee has given up the use of the asset is difficult, however, and complex rules have been formulated to identify this situation.[26] To understand the profession's position in this area, the basic accounting for the lessee and lessor are discussed below.

Lessee

OBJECTIVE 9

Describe the lessee's accounting for sale-leaseback transactions.

If the lease meets one of the four criteria for treatment as a capital lease (see Illustration 22-2), the **seller-lessee accounts for the transaction as a sale and the lease as a capital lease.** Any profit or loss experienced by the seller-lessee from the sale of the assets that are leased back under a capital lease should be **deferred and amortized over the lease term** (or the economic life if either criterion 1 or 2 is satisfied) in proportion to the amortization of the leased assets. If Lessee, Inc. sells equipment having a book value of $580,000 and a fair value of $623,110 to Lessor, Inc. for $623,110 and leases the equipment back for $50,000 a year for 20 years, the profit of $43,110 should be amortized over the 20-year period at the same rate that the $623,110 is depreciated.[27] The $43,110 is credited to **"Unearned Profit on Sale-Leaseback."**

If none of the capital lease criteria are satisfied, **the seller-lessee accounts for the transaction as a sale and the lease as an operating lease.** Under an operating lease, such profit or loss should be deferred and amortized in proportion to the rental payments over the period of time the assets are expected to be used by the lessee.

There are exceptions to these two general rules. They are:

1. **Losses Recognized**—The profession requires that, when the fair value of the asset is **less than the book value** (carrying amount), a loss must be recognized immediately up to the amount of the difference between the book value and fair value. For example, if Lessee, Inc. sells equipment having a book value of $650,000 and a fair value of $623,110, the difference of $26,890 should be charged to a loss account.[28]

2. **Minor Leaseback**—Leasebacks in which the present value of the rental payments are 10% or less of the fair value of the asset are defined as minor leasebacks.

---

[26]Sales and leasebacks of real estate are often accounted for differently. A discussion of the issues related to these transactions is beyond the scope of this textbook. See *Statement of Financial Accounting Standards No. 98*, op. cit.

[27]*Statement of Financial Accounting Standards No. 28*, "Accounting for Sales with Leasebacks" (Stamford, Conn.: FASB, 1979).

[28]There can be two types of losses in sale-leaseback arrangements. One is a **real economic loss** that results when the carrying amount of the asset is higher than the fair market value of the asset. In this case, the loss should be recognized. An **artificial loss** results when the sale price is below the carrying amount of the asset but the fair market value is above the carrying amount. In this case the loss is more in the form of prepaid rent and should be deferred and amortized in the future.

In this case, the seller-lessee gives up most of the rights to the use of the asset sold. Therefore, the transaction is a sale, and full gain or loss recognition is appropriate. It is not a financing transaction because the risks of ownership have been transferred.[29]

Lessor

If the lease meets one of the criteria in Group I and both of the criteria in Group II (see Illustration 22-9), the **purchaser-lessor** records the transaction as a purchase and a direct financing lease. If the lease does not meet the criteria, the purchaser-lessor records the transaction as a purchase and an operating lease.

Sale-Leaseback Illustration

To illustrate the accounting treatment accorded a sale-leaseback transaction, assume that Lessee Corp. on January 1, 1996, sells a used Boeing 747 having a carrying amount on its books of $75,500,000, to Lessor Corp. for $80,000,000 and immediately leases the aircraft back under the following conditions:

1. The term of the lease is 15 years, noncancelable, and requires equal rental payments of $10,487,443 at the beginning of each year.
2. The aircraft has a fair value of $80,000,000 on January 1, 1996, and an estimated economic life of 15 years.
3. Lessee Corp. pays all executory costs.
4. Lessee Corp. depreciates similar aircraft that it owns on a straight-line basis over 15 years.
5. The annual payments assure the lessor a 12% return.
6. The incremental borrowing rate of Lessee Corp. is 12%.

This lease is a capital lease to Lessee Corp. because the lease term exceeds 75% of the estimated life of the aircraft and because the present value of the lease payments exceeds 90% of the fair value of the aircraft to the lessor. Assuming that collectibility of the lease payments is reasonably predictable and that no important uncertainties exist in relation to unreimbursable costs yet to be incurred by the lessor, Lessor Corp. should classify this lease as a direct financing lease.

The typical journal entries to record the transactions relating to this lease for both Lessee Corp. and Lessor Corp. for the first year are presented below.

ILLUSTRATION 22-31
Comparative Entries for Sale-Leaseback for Lessee and Lessor

Lessee Corp.			Lessor Corp.		
Sale of Aircraft by Lessee to Lessor Corp., January 1, 1996:					
Cash	80,000,000		Aircraft	80,000,000	
Aircraft		75,500,000	Cash		80,000,000
Unearned Profit on					
Sale-Leaseback		4,500,000	Lease Payments		
			Receivable	157,311,645	
Leased Aircraft Under			Aircraft		80,000,000
Capital Leases	80,000,000		Unearned Interest		
Obligations Under			Revenue		77,311,645
Capital Leases		80,000,000	($10,487,443 × 15 = $157,311,645)		
First Lease Payment, January 1, 1996:					
Obligations Under			Cash	10,487,443	
Capital Leases	10,487,443		Lease Payments		
Cash		10,487,443	Receivable		10,487,443

---

[29]In some cases the seller-lessee retains more than a minor part but less than substantially all; the computations to arrive at these values are complex and beyond the scope of this textbook.

	Lessee Corp.			Lessor Corp.

Incurrence and Payment of Executory Costs by Lessee Corp. throughout 1996:

Insurance, Maintenance,			(No entry)	
Taxes, etc.	XXX			
Cash or Accounts Payable		XXX		

Depreciation Expense on the Aircraft, December 31, 1996:

Depreciation Expense	5,333,333		(No entry)	
Accumulated Depr.—				
Capital Leases		5,333,333		
($80,000,000 ÷ 15)				

Amortization of Profit on Sale-Leaseback by Lessee Corp., December 31, 1996:

Unearned Profit on			(No entry)	
Sale-Leaseback	300,000			
Depreciation Expense		300,000		
($4,500,000 ÷ 15)				

Note: A case might be made for crediting Revenue instead of Depreciation Expense.

Interest for 1996, December 31, 1996:

Interest Expense	8,341,507ᵃ		Unearned Interest Revenue	8,341,507	
Interest Payable		8,341,507	Interest Revenue		8,341,507ᵃ

ᵃPartial Lease Amortization Schedule:

Date	Annual Rental Payment	Interest 12%	Reduction of Balance	Balance
1/1/96				$80,000,000
1/1/96	$10,487,443	$ –0–	$10,487,443	69,512,557
1/1/97	10,487,443	8,341,507	2,145,936	67,366,621

▶ LEASE ACCOUNTING—THE UNSOLVED PROBLEM

As indicated at the beginning of this chapter, lease accounting is a much abused area in which strenuous efforts are being made to circumvent *Statement No. 13*. In practice, the accounting rules for capitalizing leases have been rendered partially ineffective by the strong desires of lessees to resist capitalization. Leasing generally involves large dollar amounts that when capitalized materially increase reported liabilities and adversely affect the debt-to-equity ratio. Lease capitalization is also resisted because charges to expense made in the early years of the lease term are higher under the capital lease method than under the operating method, frequently without tax benefit. As a consequence, "let's beat *Statement No. 13*" is one of the most popular games in town.[30]

To avoid leased asset capitalization, lease agreements are designed, written, and interpreted so that none of the four capitalized lease criteria are satisfied from the lessee's viewpoint. Devising lease agreements in such a way has not been too difficult when the following specifications have been met.

1. Make certain that the lease does not specify the transfer of title of the property to the lessee.

2. Do not write in a bargain purchase option.

3. Set the lease term at something less than 75% of the estimated economic life of the leased property.

4. Arrange for the present value of the minimum lease payments to be less than 90% of the fair value of the leased property.

---

[30]Richard Dieter, "Is Lessee Accounting Working?" *The CPA Journal* (August 1979), pp. 13–19. This article provides interesting examples of abuses of *Statement No. 13*, discusses the circumstances that led to the current situation, and proposes a solution.

The real challenge lies in disqualifying the lease as a capital lease to the lessee while having the same lease qualify as a capital (sales or financing) lease to the lessor. Unlike lessees, lessors try to avoid having lease arrangements classified as operating leases.[31]

Avoiding the first three criteria is relatively simple, but it takes a little ingenuity to avoid the "90% recovery test" for the lessee while satisfying it for the lessor. Two of the factors involved in this effort are (1) the use of the incremental borrowing rate by the lessee when it is higher than the implicit interest rate of the lessor, by making information about the implicit rate unavailable to the lessee; and (2) residual value guarantees.

The lessee's use of the higher interest rate is probably the more popular subterfuge. While lessees are knowledgeable about the fair value of the leased property and, of course, the rental payments, they generally are not aware of the estimated residual value used by the lessor. Therefore the lessee who does not know exactly the lessor's implicit interest rate might use a different incremental borrowing rate.

The residual value guarantee is the other unique, yet popular, device used by lessees and lessors. In fact, a whole new industry has emerged to circumvent symmetry between the lessee and the lessor in accounting for leases. The residual value guarantee has spawned numerous companies whose principal, or even sole, function is to guarantee the residual value of leased assets. These **third-party guarantors** (insurers), for a fee, assume the risk of deficiencies in leased asset residual value.

Because the guaranteed residual value is included in the minimum lease payments for the lessor, the 90% recovery of fair market value test is satisfied. The lease is a nonoperating lease to the lessor. But because the residual value is guaranteed by a third party, the minimum lease payments of the lessee do not include the guarantee. Thus, by merely transferring some of the risk to a third party, lessees can alter substantially the accounting treatment by converting what would otherwise be capital leases to operating leases.[32]

Much of this circumvention is encouraged by the nature of the criteria, which stem from weaknesses in the basic objective of *Statement No. 13*. Accounting standard-setting bodies continue to have poor experience with arbitrary break points or other size and percentage criteria—that is, rules like "90% of," "75% of," etc. Some accountants believe that a more workable solution would be to require capitalization of all leases that extend for some defined period (such as one year) on the basis that the lessee has acquired an asset (a property right) and a corresponding liability rather than on the basis that the lease transfers substantially all the risks and rewards of ownership.

Three years after it issued *Statement No. 13*, a majority of the FASB expressed "the tentative view that, if *Statement 13* were to be reconsidered, they would support a property right approach in which all leases are included as 'rights to use property' and as 'lease obligations' in the lessee's balance sheet."[33] However, the Board appears reluctant to consider this issue because of its complex nature.

---

[31]The reason is that most lessors are financial institutions and do not want these types of assets on their balance sheets. In fact, banks and savings and loans are not permitted to report these assets on their balance sheets except for relatively short periods of time. Furthermore, the capital lease transaction from the lessor's standpoint provides higher income flows in the earlier periods of the lease.

[32]As an aside, third-party guarantors have experienced some difficulty. Lloyd's of London, for example, insured the fast growing U.S. computer-leasing industry in the amount of $2 billion against revenue losses and losses in residual value if leases were canceled. Because of "overnight" technological improvements and the successive introductions of more efficient and less expensive computers by computer manufacturers, lessees in abundance canceled their leases. As the market for second-hand computers became flooded and residual values plummeted, third-party guarantor Lloyd's of London projected a loss of $400 million. Much of the third-party guarantee business was stimulated by the lessees' and lessors' desire to circumvent *FASB Statement No. 13*.

[33]"Is Lessee Accounting Working?" op. cit., p. 19.

▶ **REPORTING LEASE DATA IN FINANCIAL STATEMENTS**

OBJECTIVE 10

Describe the disclosure requirements for leases.

DISCLOSURES REQUIRED OF THE LESSEE

The FASB requires that the following information with respect to leases be disclosed in the **lessee's** financial statements or in the notes.[34]

(a) For **capital leases:**   i. The gross amount of assets at each balance sheet date categorized by nature or function. This information may be combined with comparable information for owned assets.   ii. Future *minimum lease payments* as of the latest balance sheet date, in the aggregate and for each of five succeeding fiscal years. Separate deductions for *executory costs* included in the *minimum lease payments* and for the amount of imputed interest necessary to reduce net *minimum lease payments* to present value.   iii. Total noncancelable minimum sublease rentals to be received in the future, as of the latest balance sheet date.   iv. Total *contingent rentals*.   v. Assets recorded under capital leases and the accumulated amortization thereon shall be separately identified in the lessee's balance sheet or notes. Likewise, related obligations shall be separately identified as obligations under capital leases. Depreciation on capitalized leased assets should be separately disclosed.

(b) For **operating leases** having initial or remaining noncancelable *lease terms* in excess of one year: i. Future minimum rental payments required as of the latest balance sheet date, in the aggregate and for each of the five succeeding fiscal years.   ii. Total minimum rentals to be received in the future under noncancelable subleases as of the latest balance sheet date.   (c) For **all operating leases,** rental expense for each period with separate amounts for minimum rentals, *contingent rentals,* and sublease rentals. Rental payments under leases with *terms* of a month or less that were not renewed need not be included.   (d) A **general description** of the lessee's arrangements including, but not limited to: i. The basis on which *contingent rental* payments are determined.   ii. The existence and terms of renewal or purchase options and escalation clauses.   iii. Restrictions imposed by lease agreements, such as those concerning dividends, additional debt, and further leasing.

ILLUSTRATION 22-32
Lessee's Disclosures

DISCLOSURES REQUIRED OF THE LESSOR

The FASB requires that **lessors** disclose in the financial statements or in the notes the following information when leasing "is a significant part of the lessor's business activities in terms of revenue, net income, or assets."[35]

ILLUSTRATION 22-33
Lessor's Disclosures

(a) For **sales-type and direct financing leases:**
 i. The components of the net investment in sales-type and direct financing leases as of each balance sheet date:
   a. Future *minimum lease payments* to be received, with separate deductions for (i) *executory costs* and (ii) the accumulated allowance for uncollectible *minimum lease payments* receivable.
   b. The *unguaranteed residual values* accruing to the lessor.
   c. Unearned revenue.
 ii. Future *minimum lease payments* to be received for each of the five succeeding fiscal years.
 iii. The amount of unearned revenue included in income to offset *initial direct costs* charged against income for each

period for which an income statement is presented. (For direct financing leases only.)   iv. Total *contingent rentals* included in income for each period for which an income statement is presented.   (b) For **operating leases:**   i. The cost and carrying amount, if different, of leased property according to nature or function, and total amount of accumulated depreciation.   ii. Minimum future rentals on noncancelable leases as of the latest balance sheet date, in aggregate and for each of five succeeding fiscal years.   iii. Total *contingent rentals* included in income for each period for which an income statement is presented.   (c) A **general description** of the lessor's leasing arrangements.

ILLUSTRATED DISCLOSURES

The financial statement excerpts from the 1992 annual report of The Kroger Co. that follow present the statement and note disclosures typical of a **lessee** having both capital leases and operating leases.

---

[34]"Accounting for Leases," *FASB Statement No. 13,* as amended and interpreted through May 1980 (Stamford, Conn.: FASB, 1980), par. 16.

[35]Ibid., par. 23.

The Kroger Co.
(All dollar amounts in thousands)

	1992	1991
Current liabilities		
Current portion of obligations under capital leases	$ 7,309	$ 6,704
Long-term debt		
Obligations under capital leases	149,028	157,698

Accounting Policies (in part)

Property, Plant and Equipment: Property, plant and equipment are stated at cost. Depreciation and amortization, which includes the amortization of assets recorded under capital leases, are computed principally using the straight-line method over the estimated useful lives of individual assets, composite group lives or the initial or remaining terms of leases. Buildings and land improvements are depreciated based on lives varying from 10 to 40 years and equipment depreciation is based on lives varying from 3 to 15 years. Leasehold improvements are amortized over their useful lives which vary from 4 to 25 years.

Leases: The Company operates primarily in leased facilities. Lease terms generally range from 10 to 25 years with options to renew at varying terms. Certain of the leases provide for contingent payments based upon a percent of sales.

Rent expense (under operating leases) consists of:

	1992	1991	1990
Minimum rentals	$270,763	$253,345	$238,006
Contingent payments	17,350	12,983	14,496
Total	$288,113	$266,328	$252,502

Assets recorded under capital leases consist of:

	1992	1991
Distribution and manufacturing facilities	$ 38,742	$ 46,680
Store facilities	178,502	179,390
Less accumulated amortization	(98,684)	(96,827)
	$118,560	$129,243

Minimum annual rentals for the 5 years subsequent to 1992 and in the aggregate are:

	Capital Leases	Operating Leases
1993	$ 26,679	$ 261,965
1994	26,236	250,205
1995	25,678	237,134
1996	24,881	220,160
1997	24,075	202,487
Thereafter	220,046	1,727,409
	$ 347,595	$2,899,360
Less estimated executory costs included in capital leases	(29,533)	
Net minimum lease payments under capital leases	318,062	
Less amount representing interest	(161,725)	
Present value of net minimum lease payments under capital leases	$ 156,337	

ILLUSTRATION 22-34
Disclosure of Leases by Lessee

The following note from the 1992 annual report of Amdahl Corporation illustrates the disclosures of a **lessor:**

ILLUSTRATION 22-35
Disclosure of Leases by Lessor

Amdahl Corporation
Notes to Consolidated Financial Statements

Note 3: Equipment Leasing

The Company is the lessor of equipment under operating leases for periods generally less than three years. Certain operating leases contain provisions for early termination with a penalty or with conversion to another system. The cost of leased systems is depreciated to a zero value on a straight-line basis over three to four years. Accumulated depreciation on leased systems was $32,530,000 at December 25, 1992 and $29,603,000 at December 27, 1991.

The Company also leases equipment to customers under sales-type leases as defined in Statement of Financial Accounting Standards No. 13. The components of the net investment in sales-type leases were as follows:

**ILLUSTRATION 22-35
Continued**

(In thousands)	1992	1991
Minimum rentals receivable	$142,738	$96,362
Estimated residual values of leased equipment (unguaranteed)	6,988	1,645
Less unearned interest income	(18,458)	(12,610)
Net investment in sales-type leases	$131,268	$85,397

Minimum rentals receivable under existing leases as of December 25, 1992, were as follows:

(In thousands)	Sales-Type	Operating
1993	$ 54,613	$20,729
1994	41,158	12,268
1995	29,591	2,523
1996	13,739	429
1997	3,637	233
Thereafter	—	233
	$142,738	$36,415

▶ ILLUSTRATIONS OF DIFFERENT LEASE ARRANGEMENTS

To illustrate concepts discussed in this chapter, assume that Morgan Bakeries is involved in four different lease situations. Each of these leases is noncancelable and in no case does Morgan receive title to the properties leased during or at the end of the lease term. All leases start on January 1, 1996, with the first rental due at the beginning of the year. The additional information is shown below.

**ILLUSTRATION 22-36
Illustrative Lease
Situations, Lessors**

	Harmon, Inc.	Arden's Oven Co.	Mendota Truck Co.	Appleland Computer
Type of property	Cabinets	Oven	Truck	Computer
Yearly rental	$6,000	$15,000	$5,582.62	$3,557.25
Lease term	20 years	10 years	3 years	3 years
Estimated economic life	30 years	25 years	7 years	5 years
Purchase option	None	$75,000 at end of 10 years $4,000 at end of 15 years	None	$3,000 at end of 3 years, which approximates fair market value
Renewal option	None	5-year renewal option at $15,000 per year	None	1 year at $1,500; no penalty for non-renewal; standard renewal clause
Fair market value at inception of lease	$60,000	$120,000	$20,000	$10,000
Cost of asset to lessor	$60,000	$120,000	$15,000	$10,000
Residual value				
Guaranteed	–0–	–0–	$7,000	–0–
Unguaranteed	$5,000	–0–	–0–	$3,000
Incremental borrowing rate of lessee	12%	12%	12%	12%
Executory costs paid by	*Lessee* $300 per year	*Lessee* $1,000 per year	*Lessee* $500 per year	*Lessor* Estimated to be $500 per year
Present value of minimum lease payments Using incremental borrowing rate of lessee	$50,194.68	$115,153.35	$20,000	$8,224.16
Using implicit rate of lessor	Not known	Not known	Not known	Known by lessee, $8,027.48
Estimated fair market value at end of lease	$5,000	$80,000 at end of 10 years $60,000 at end of 15 years	Not available	$3,000

HARMON, INC.

The following is an analysis of the Harmon, Inc. lease:

1. **Transfer of title?** No.
2. **Bargain purchase option?** No.
3. **Economic life test (75% test).** The lease term is 20 years and the estimated economic life is 30 years. Thus it does **not** meet the 75% test.
4. **Recovery of investment test (90% test):**

Fair market value	$60,000	Rental payments	$ 6,000
Rate	90%	PV of annuity due for	
90% of fair market value	$54,000	20 years at 12%	× 8.36578
		PV of rental payments	$50,194.68

Because the present value of the minimum lease payments is less than 90% of the fair market value, the 90% test is not met. Both Morgan and Harmon should account for this lease as an operating lease, as indicated by the January 1, 1996, entries shown below.

Morgan Bakeries (Lessee)		Harmon, Inc. (Lessor)	
Rent Expense 6,000		Cash 6,000	
Cash	6,000	Rental Revenue	6,000

ILLUSTRATION 22-37
Comparative Entries for Operating Lease

ARDEN'S OVEN CO.

The following is an analysis of the Arden's Oven Co. lease.

1. **Transfer of title?** No.
2. **Bargain purchase option?** The $75,000 option at the end of 10 years does not appear to be sufficiently lower than the expected fair value of $80,000 to make it reasonably assured that it will be exercised. However, the $4,000 at the end of 15 years when the fair value is $60,000 does appear to be a bargain. From the information given, criterion 2 is therefore met. Note that both the guaranteed and the unguaranteed residual values are assigned zero values because the lessor does not expect to repossess the leased asset.
3. **Economic life test (75% test):** Given that a bargain purchase option exists, the lease term is the initial lease period of 10 years plus the 5-year renewal option since it precedes a bargain purchase option. Even though the lease term is now considered to be 15 years, this test is still not met because 75% of the economic life of 25 years is 18.75 years.
4. **Recovery of investment test (90% test):**

Fair market value	$120,000	Rental payments	$ 15,000.00
Rate	90%	PV of annuity due for	
90% of fair market value	$108,000	15 years at 12%	× 7.62817
		PV of rental payments	$114,422.55

PV of bargain purchase option: $a(p_{\overline{n}|i}) = \$4,000(p_{\overline{15}|12\%}) = \$4,000(.18270) = \$730.80$

PV of rental payments	$114,422.55
PV of bargain purchase option	730.80
PV of minimum lease payments	$115,153.35

The present value of the minimum lease payments is greater than 90% of the fair market value; therefore, the 90% test is met. Morgan Bakeries should account for this as a capital lease because both criterion 2 and criterion 4 are met. Assuming that Arden's implicit rate is the same as Morgan's incremental borrowing rate, the following entries are made on January 1, 1996.

ILLUSTRATION 22-38
Comparative Entries for Capital Lease—Bargain Purchase Option

Morgan Bakeries (Lessee)			Arden's Oven Co. (Lessor)		
Leased Asset—Oven 115,153.35			Lease Payments		
Obligation Under			Receivable	229,000*	
Capital Lease		115,153.35	Unearned Interest		
			Revenue		109,000
			Asset—Oven		120,000
			*([$15,000 × 15] + $4,000)		

Morgan Bakeries would depreciate the leased asset over its economic life of 25 years, given the bargain purchase option. Arden's does not use sales-type accounting because the fair market value and the cost of the asset are the same at the inception of the lease.

MENDOTA TRUCK CO.

The following is an analysis of the Mendota Truck Co. lease.

1. **Transfer of title?** No.

2. **Bargain purchase option?** No.

3. **Economic life test (75% test):** The lease term is three years and the estimated economic life is seven years. Thus it does **not** meet the 75% test.

4. **Recovery of investment test (90% test):**

Fair market value	$20,000		Rental payments	$ 5,582.62
Rate	90%		PV of annuity due for	
90% of fair market value	$18,000		3 years at 12%	× 2.69005
			PV of rental payments	$15,017.54

(Note: adjusted for $.01 due to rounding)

PV of guaranteed residual value: $(p_{\overline{n}|i}) = \$7,000(p_{\overline{3}|12\%}) = \$7,000(.71178) = \$4,982.46$

PV of rental payments	$15,017.54
PV of guaranteed residual value	4,982.46
PV of minimum lease payments	$20,000.00

The present value of the minimum lease payments is greater than 90% of the fair market value; therefore, the 90% test is met. Assuming that Mendota's implicit rate is the same as Morgan's incremental borrowing rate, the following entries are made on January 1, 1996.

ILLUSTRATION 22-39
Comparative Entries for Capital Lease

Morgan Bakeries (Lessee)			Mendota Truck Co. (Lessor)		
Leased Asset—Truck 20,000.00			Lease Payments		
Obligation Under			Receivable	23,747.86*	
Capital Lease		20,000.00	Cost of Goods Sold	15,000.00	
			Asset—Truck		15,000.00
			Sales		20,000.00
			Unearned Interest		
			Revenue		3,747.86
			*[($5,582.62 × 3) + $7,000]		

The leased asset is depreciated by Morgan over three years to its guaranteed residual value.

APPLELAND COMPUTER

The following is an analysis of the Appleland Computer lease.

1. **Transfer of title?** No.

2. **Bargain purchase option?** No. The option to purchase at the end of 3 years at approximate fair market value is clearly not a bargain.

3. **Economic life test (75% test):** The lease term is 3 years and no bargain renewal period exists. Therefore the 75% test is **not** met.

4. **Recovery of investment test (90% test):**

Fair market value	$10,000	Rental payments	$3,557.25
Rate	90%	Less executory costs	500.00
90% of fair market value	$ 9,000		3,057.25
		PV of annuity due factor for 3 years at 12%	× 2.69005
		PV of minimum lease payments using incremental borrowing rate	$8,224.16

The present value of the minimum lease payments using the incremental borrowing rate is $8,224.16; using the implicit rate, it is $8,027.48 (see Illustration 22-36). The lessee uses the higher $8,224.16 (lower interest rate when discounting) when comparing with the 90% of fair market value. Because the present value of the minimum lease payments is lower than 90% of the fair market value, the recovery of investment test is **not** met.

The following entries are made on January 1, 1996, indicating an operating lease.

Morgan Bakeries (Lessee)		Appleland Computer (Lessor)	
Rent Expense 3,557.25		Cash 3,557.25	
Cash	3,557.25	Rental Revenue	3,557.25

ILLUSTRATION 22-40
Comparative Entries for Operating Lease

If the lease payments had been $3,557.25 with no executory costs involved, this lease arrangement would have qualified for capital lease accounting treatment.

▶ SUMMARY OF LEARNING OBJECTIVES ◀

1. **Explain the nature, economic substance, and advantages of lease transactions.** A lease is a contractual agreement between a lessor and a lessee that conveys to the lessee the right to use specific property (real or personal), owned by the lessor, for a specified period of time. In return for this right, the lessee agrees to make periodic cash payments (rents) to the lessor. The advantages of lease transactions are: (1) 100% financing; (2) protection against obsolescence, (3) flexibility, (4) less costly financing, (5) possible tax advantage, and (6) off-balance-sheet financing.

2. **Describe the accounting criteria and procedures for capitalizing leases by the lessee.** A lease is a capital lease if one or more of the following criteria are met: (1) the lease transfers ownership of the property to the lessee; (2) the lease contains a bargain purchase option; (3) the lease term is equal to 75% or more of the estimated economic life of the leased property; (4) the present value of the minimum lease payments (excluding executory costs) equals or exceeds 90% of the fair value of the leased property. For a capital lease, the lessee records an asset and a liability at the lower of (1) the present value of the minimum lease payments during the term of the lease or (2) the fair market value of the leased asset at the inception of the lease.

3. **Contrast the operating and capitalization methods of recording leases.** The total charges to operations are the same over the lease term whether the lease is accounted for as a capital lease or as an operating lease; under the capital lease treatment, the charges are higher in the earlier years and lower in the later years. If an accelerated method of depreciation is used, the differences between the amounts charged to operations under the two methods would be even larger in the earlier and later years. The following occurs if a capital lease instead of an operating lease is employed: (1) an increase in the amount of

KEY TERMS

bargain purchase option, 1126

bargain renewal option, 1126

capital lease, 1125

capitalization criteria, 1125

capitalization of leases, 1124

cost of goods sold (sales-type lease), 1147

direct financing lease, 1135

effective interest method, 1129

executory costs, 1127

gross investment, 1147

guaranteed residual value, 1127

implicit interest rate, 1128

incremental borrowing rate, 1128

initial direct costs, 1149

lease, 1121

lease term, 1122

lease payments receivable, 1147

lessee, 1121

lessor, 1121

reported debt (both short-term and long-term), (2) an increase in the amount of total assets (specifically long-lived assets), and (3) a lower income early in the life of the lease and, therefore, lower retained earnings.

4. **Identify the classifications of leases for the lessor.** From the standpoint of the lessor, all leases may be classified for accounting purpose as follows: (1) operating leases, (2) direct financing leases, (3) sales-type leases. The lessor should classify and account for an arrangement as a direct financing lease or a sales-type lease if, at the date of the lease agreement, one or more of the Group I criteria (as shown in learning objective 2 for lessees) are met and both of the following Group II criteria are met. *Group II:* (1) Collectibility of the payments required from the lessee is reasonably predictable; and (2) no important uncertainties surround the amount of unreimbursable costs yet to be incurred by the lessor under the lease. All leases that fail to meet the criteria are classified and accounted for by the lessor as operating leases.

5. **Describe the lessor's accounting for direct financing leases.** Leases that are in substance the financing of an asset purchase by a lessee require the lessor to substitute a "lease payments receivable" for the leased asset. The information necessary to record a direct financing lease is: (1) gross investment ("lease payments receivable"), (2) unearned interest revenue, and (3) net investment. There often is uncertainty as to how to account for the residual values when computing gross investment. When "lease payments receivable" is defined as minimum lease payments plus unguaranteed residual value, it means that residual value, whether guaranteed or unguaranteed, is included as part of lease payments receivable if it is relevant to the lessor (i.e., if the lessor expects to get the asset back).

6. **Identify special features of lease arrangements that cause unique accounting problems.** The features of lease arrangements that cause unique accounting problems are: (1) residual values; (2) sales-type lease (lessor); (3) bargain purchase options; (4) initial direct costs; and (5) sale-leaseback.

7. **Describe the effect of residual values, guaranteed and unguaranteed, on lease accounting.** Whether the estimated residual value is guaranteed or unguaranteed is of both economic and accounting consequence to the lessee. The accounting difference is that the minimum lease payments, the basis for capitalization, includes the guaranteed residual value but excludes the unguaranteed residual value. A guaranteed residual value affects the lessee's computation of minimum lease payments and, therefore, the amounts capitalized as a leased asset and a lease obligation. In effect, it is an additional lease payment that will be paid in property or cash, or both, at the end of the lease term. An unguaranteed residual value from the lessee's viewpoint is the same as no residual value in terms of its effect upon the lessee's method of computing the minimum lease payments and the capitalization of the leased asset and the lease obligation.

8. **Describe the lessor's accounting for sales-type leases.** The information needed to record the sales-type lease is as follows: (1) gross investment (also "lease payments receivable"); (2) unearned interest revenue; (3) sales price of the asset; and (4) cost of goods sold. The gross investment and the unearned interest revenue are the same whether a guaranteed or an unguaranteed residual value is involved. When recording sales revenue and cost of goods sold, there is a difference in the accounting for guaranteed and unguaranteed residual values. The guaranteed residual value can be considered part of sales revenue because the lessor knows that the entire asset has been sold. There is less certainty that the unguaranteed residual portion of the asset has been "sold"; therefore, sales and cost of goods sold are recognized only for the portion of the asset for which realization is assured. However, the gross profit

amount on the sale of the asset is the same whether a guaranteed or unguaranteed residual value is involved.

9. **Describe the lessee's accounting for sale-leaseback transactions.** If the lease meets one of the four criteria for treatment as a capital lease, the seller-lessee accounts for the transaction as a sale and the lease as a capital lease. Any profit or loss experienced by the seller-lessee from the sale of the assets that are leased back under a capital lease should be deferred and amortized over the lease term (or the economic life if either criterion 1 or 2 is satisfied) in proportion to the amortization of the leased assets. If none of the capital lease criteria are satisfied, the seller-lessee accounts for the transaction as a sale and the lease as an operating lease. Under an operating lease, such profit or loss should be deferred and amortized in proportion to the rental payments over the period of time the assets are expected to be used by the lessee.

10. **Describe the disclosure requirements for leases.** The disclosure requirements for the **lessee** are classified as follows: (1) capital leases; (2) operating leases having initial or remaining noncancelable lease terms in excess of one year; (3) all operating leases; and (4) a general description of the lessee's arrangements. The disclosure requirements for the **lessor** are classified as follows: (1) sales-type and direct financing leases; (2) operating leases; and (3) a general description of the lessor's leasing arrangements.

APPENDIX 22-A

REAL ESTATE LEASES AND LEVERAGED LEASES

Presented in this appendix are these additional lease accounting topics: **1.** Leases involving real estate. **2.** Leveraged leases.

▶ LEASES INVOLVING REAL ESTATE[1]

Special problems can arise when leases involve land, land and buildings, and equipment along with real estate.

LAND

If land is the sole item of property leased, the **lessee** should account for the lease as a capital lease if the lease transfers ownership of the property (Criterion 1) or contains a bargain purchase option (Criterion 2). Otherwise it is accounted for as an operating lease. Because ownership of the land is expected to pass to the lessee when the lease is classified as a capital lease, the leased asset is not normally amortized. The **lessor** accounts for a land lease either as a sales-type or direct financing lease,[2] if the lease transfers ownership or contains a bargain purchase option and meets both the collectibility and uncertainties tests. Otherwise the operating method is used.

OBJECTIVE 11

After studying Appendix 22-A, you should be able to: Understand the unique problems of accounting for real estate leases.

---

[1]"Accounting for Leases," *FASB Statement No. 13,* as amended and interpreted through May 1980 (Stamford, Conn.: FASB, 1980), pars. 24–26.

[2]A lease involving real estate may not be classified as a sales-type lease unless the lease agreement provides for the transfer of title to the lessee at or shortly after the end of the lease term. *Statement of Financial Accounting Standards No. 98,* op. cit.

LAND AND BUILDING

If both land and building are involved and the lease transfers ownership or contains a bargain purchase option, the land and the building should be separately classified by the **lessee.** The present value of the minimum lease payments is allocated between land and building in proportion to their fair values at the inception of the lease. The **lessor** accounts for the lease as a single unit either as a sales-type, a direct financing, or an operating lease.

When both land and building are involved and the lease does not transfer ownership or contain a bargain purchase option, the accounting treatment is dependent upon the proportion of land to building. If the fair value of the land is less than 25% of the total fair value of the leased property, both the lessee and the lessor consider the land and the building as a single unit. The land is then amortized along with the building by the lessee. If the fair value of the land is 25% or more of the total fair value, the land and building are considered separately by both the lessee and the lessor. The lessee accounts for the building as a capital lease and the land as an operating lease if one of the two remaining criteria, 3 or 4, is met. If none of the criteria are met, the lessee uses the operating method on the land and building. The lessor accounts for the building as a sales-type or direct financing lease as appropriate and the land element separately as an operating lease.

REAL ESTATE AND EQUIPMENT

If a lease involves both real estate and equipment, the portion of the lease payments applicable to the equipment should be estimated by whatever means are appropriate and reasonable. The equipment then should be treated separately for purposes of applying the criteria and accounted for separately according to its classification by both the lessee and the lessor.

When the leased property is part of a larger whole, for example, an office or a floor of a building or a store in a shopping center, "reasonable estimates of the leased property's fair value might be objectively determined by referring to an independent appraisal of the leased property or to estimated replacement cost information."[3]

▶ LEVERAGED LEASES

OBJECTIVE 12

Understand the leveraged lease arrangement.

Leveraged leasing began in the late 1960s and has grown substantially. It has been estimated that more than $6.5 billion worth of capital equipment is financed annually through the use of leveraged leases. There is every expectation that the use of this type of lease will continue in popularity.

Under a properly structured lease arrangement, the lessor boosts the tax benefits of the asset by **leveraging** the lease. That is, the lessor of the property may come up with a small percentage of the purchase price (with 100% ownership of the asset) and find debt participants who will finance the balance. The **leveraged lease** arrangement generally involves the following:

1. It meets the definition of a direct financing lease, except that the 90% of fair value criterion is not applicable.
2. There are three participants in the lease arrangement:
   a. An owner-lessor (equity participant).
   b. A lessee (user of the asset).
   c. A third-party long-term creditor (debt participant).
3. The owner-lessor provides a portion of the cost of the property to be leased, generally 20% to 40%.

---

[3]"Leases Involving Only Part of a Building," *FASB Interpretation No. 24* (Stamford, Conn.: FASB, 1978), par. 6.

4. Long-term creditors (generally financial institutions) provide the remaining portion (60% to 80%) of the equipment's cost. The amount provided by these third-party creditors is generally called the **leveraged debt.** The leveraged debt is structured **without recourse** to the owner-lessor; it is secured by a pledge of lease payments or by a security interest in the property. For this reason, the interest rate obtained by the long-term creditors for the leveraged debt is based, in part, on the lessee's credit rating.

5. The asset is then purchased from the manufacturer or contractor by the lessor-owner and leased to the lessee. In return, the lessor-owner receives the rental payments, makes debt service payments (principal and interest) to the long-term creditors, and retains any difference. The residual value from the disposition of the asset at the end of the lease term is retained by the lessor. Generally, **the lessor's net investment declines during the early years and rises during the later years of the lease.** The lessor's return and early net cash inflow results from two sources: (1) lease rentals; and (2) income tax benefits such as depreciation (often accelerated) on the total cost of the property, interest expense on the debt, and possibly other expenses.

Illustration 22A-1 shows the relationship of the parties involved in a leveraged lease transaction.

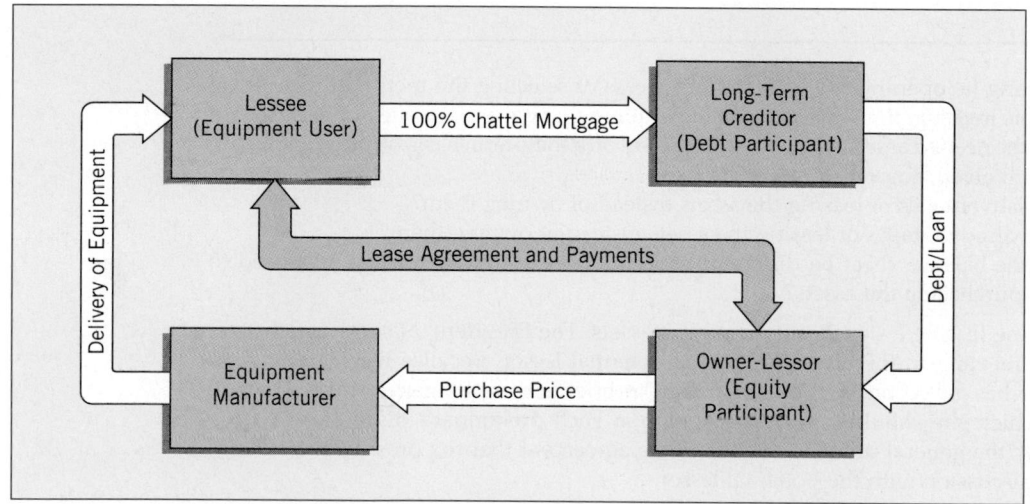

**ILLUSTRATION 22A-1
The Leveraged Lease
Arrangement**[4]

For example, a typical leveraged lease transaction occurred when American Airlines leased seven McDonnell Douglas Super 80s. McDonnell Douglas sold the planes to Bankers Trust Co. and United Parcel Service for $147 million. Bankers Trust and United Parcel borrowed approximately $100 million using a group of investment bankers and came up with the remaining $47 million themselves. Bankers Trust and United Parcel then leased the planes to American Airlines. Through this procedure, it is estimated that American Airlines will save $100 million over the 18-year life of the lease.

The accounting for a leveraged lease by the lessee is not distinguishable from an unleveraged one. The FASB requires that the lessor classify leveraged leases as direct financing leases, with the lessor's liability to the third-party creditor offset against its lease receivables from the lessee. Thus, the lessor reports an asset only if the lease receivable is greater than its debt. And, the lessor reports income from the lease only in those years when the receivable exceeds the debt.

Because the accounting for leveraged leases by lessors can be quite complex and unique to the specific tailored lease, it is not illustrated in this chapter.[5]

---

[4]Taken from "A Straightforward Approach to Leveraged Leasing," by Pierce R. Smith, *The Journal of Commercial Bank Lending* (July 1973), pp. 40–47.

[5]For an illustration of the accounting and financial statement disclosures related to leveraged leases, see *FASB Statement No. 13*, Appendix E, par. 123.

▶ **SUMMARY OF LEARNING OBJECTIVES FOR APP. 22-A** ◀

11. Understand the unique problems of accounting for real estate leases. Lessee and lessor accounting for real estate depends upon whether land is the sole item of property or a building or equipment are also involved.

12. Understand the leveraged lease arrangement. The three participants in a leveraged lease arrangement are: (1) the owner-lessor who is the equity participant; (2) the lessee who is the user of the asset; and (3) the third-party long-term creditor who is the debt participant. A leveraged lease is accounted for by the lessee in the same manner as an unleveraged one. The lessor classifies leveraged leases as direct financing leases, with the lessor's liability to the third-party creditor offset against its lease receivables from the lessee.

Note: All **asterisked** Questions, Exercises, Problems, and Cases relate to material contained in the appendix to each chapter.

QUESTIONS

1. Kosinski Co. is expanding its operations and is in the process of selecting the method of financing this program. After some investigation, the company determines that it may (1) issue bonds and with the proceeds purchase the needed assets, or (2) lease the assets on a long-term basis. Without knowing the comparative costs involved, answer these questions:
   (a) What might be the advantages of leasing the assets instead of owning them?
   (b) What might be the disadvantages of leasing the assets instead of owning them?
   (c) In what way will the balance sheet be differently affected by leasing the assets as opposed to issuing bonds and purchasing the assets?

2. King Corp. is considering leasing a significant amount of assets. The President, Nancy Shanahan, is attending an informal meeting in the afternoon with a potential lessor. Because her legal advisor cannot be reached, she has called on you, the controller, to brief her on the general provisions of lease agreements to which she should give consideration in such preliminary discussions with a possible lessor. Identify the general provisions of the lease agreement that the president should be told to include in her discussion with the potential lessor.

3. Identify the two recognized lease accounting methods for lessees and distinguish between them.

4. W. Higley Company rents a warehouse on a month-to-month basis for the storage of its excess inventory. The company periodically must rent space whenever its production greatly exceeds actual sales. For several years the company officials have discussed building their own storage facility, but this enthusiasm wavers when sales increase sufficiently to absorb the excess inventory. What is the nature of this type of lease arrangement, and what accounting treatment should be accorded it?

5. Why are present-value concepts appropriate and applicable in accounting for financing-type lease arrangements?

6. Differentiate between the "lessee's incremental borrowing rate" and the "lessor's implicit rate" in accounting for leases and indicate when one or the other should be used.

7. Outline the accounting procedures involved in applying the operating method by a lessee.

8. Outline the accounting procedures involved in applying the capital lease method by a lessee.

9. Identify the lease classifications for lessors and the criteria that must be met for each classification.

10. Outline the accounting procedures involved in applying the direct financing method.

11. Outline the accounting procedures involved in applying the operating method by a lessor.

12. Santiago Company is a manufacturer and lessor of computer equipment. What should be the nature of its lease arrangements with lessees if the company wishes to account for its lease transactions as sales-type leases?

13. Okamota Corporation's lease arrangements qualify as sales-type leases at the time of entering into the transactions. How should the corporation recognize revenues and costs in these situations?

14. Ann Torbert, M.D. (lessee) has a noncancelable 20-year lease with Lopez Realty, Inc., (lessor) for the use of a medical building. Taxes, insurance, and maintenance are paid by the lessee in addition to the fixed annual payments, of which the present value is equal to the fair market value of the leased property. At the end of the lease period, title becomes the lessee's at a nominal price. Considering the terms of the lease described above, comment on the nature of the lease transaction and the accounting treatment that should be accorded it by the lessee.

15. The residual value is the estimated fair value of the leased property at the end of the lease term.
    (a) Of what significance is (1) an unguaranteed and (2) a guaranteed residual value in the lessee's accounting for a capitalized lease transaction?
    (b) Of what significance is (1) an unguaranteed and (2) a guaranteed residual value in the lessor's accounting for a direct financing lease transaction?

16. How should changes in the estimated residual value be handled by the lessor?

17. Describe the effect of a "bargain purchase option" on accounting for a capital lease transaction by a lessee.

18. What are "initial direct costs" and how are they accounted for?

19. What is the nature of a "sale-leaseback" transaction?

20. What disclosures should be made by a lessee if the leased assets and the related obligation are not capitalized?

*21. Assume that Mary Sondgeroth leases land for agricultural purposes; what criteria are applied to determine whether capital or operating lease treatment is applied?

*22. What distinguishes a leveraged lease from all other lease arrangements?

*23. What is the cash flow that the lessor realizes in a normal leveraged lease transaction?

EXERCISES

E22-1 (Lessee Entries; Basic Capital Lease) Zephyr Company enters into a lease agreement with Forester Co. on July 1, 1996, to lease a machine to be used in its manufacturing operations. The following data pertain to this agreement:

1. The term of the noncancelable lease is 3 years, with no renewal option and no residual value at the end of the lease term. Payments of $102,356.39 are due on July 1 of each year, beginning July 1, 1996.
2. The fair value of the machine on July 1, 1996 is $300,000. The machine has a remaining economic life of 5 years, with no salvage value. The machine reverts to the lessor upon the termination of the lease.
3. Zephyr Company elects to depreciate the machine on the straight-line method.
4. Zephyr Company's incremental borrowing rate is 10% per year, and it has no knowledge of the implicit rate computed by the lessor.

Instructions
Prepare the journal entries on the books of the lessee that relate to the lease agreement through June 30, 1999. The accounting period of Zephyr Company ends on December 31. (Assume that reversing entries are made.)

E22-2 (Lessee Computations and Entries; Capital Lease with Guaranteed Residual Value) Piper Company leases an automobile with a fair value of $7,850 from Austin Motors, Inc., on the following terms:

1. Noncancelable term of 50 months.
2. Rental of $180 per month (at end of each month; present value at 1% per month is $7,055).
3. Estimated residual value after 50 months is $1,060 (the present value at 1% per month is $645). Piper Company guarantees the residual value of $1,060.
4. Estimated economic life of the automobile is 60 months.
5. Piper Company's incremental borrowing rate is 12% a year (1% a month). Austin's implicit rate is unknown.

Instructions
(a) What is the nature of this lease to Piper Company?
(b) What is the present value of the minimum lease payments?
(c) Record the lease on Piper Company's books at the date of inception.
(d) Record the first month's depreciation on Piper Company's books (assume straight-line).
(e) Record the first month's lease payment.

E22-3 (Lessee Entries; Capital Lease with Executory Costs and Unguaranteed Residual Values) On January 1, 1996, Morrow Paper Co. signs a 10-year noncancelable lease agreement to lease a storage building from Sheffield Storage Company. The following information pertains to this lease agreement:

1. The agreement requires equal rental payments of $70,000.00 beginning on January 1, 1996.
2. The fair value of the building on January 1, 1996 is $440,000.
3. The building has an estimated economic life of 12 years, with an unguaranteed residual value of $10,000. Morrow Paper Co. depreciates similar buildings on the straight-line method.
4. The lease is nonrenewable. At the termination of the lease, the building reverts to the lessor.
5. Morrow Paper's incremental borrowing rate is 12% per year. The lessor's implicit rate is not known by Morrow Paper Co.
6. The yearly rental payment includes $470.51 of executory costs related to taxes on the property.

Instructions
Prepare the journal entries on the lessee's books to reflect the signing of the lease agreement and to record the payments and expenses related to this lease for the years 1996 and 1997. Morrow Paper's corporate year end is December 31.

E22-4 (Lessor Entries; Direct Financing Lease with Option to Purchase) Castle Leasing Company signs a lease agreement on January 1, 1996 to lease electronic equipment to Perry Company. The term of the noncancelable lease is 2 years and payments are required at the end of each year. The following information relates to this agreement:

1. Perry Company has the option to purchase the equipment for $8,000 upon the termination of the lease.
2. The equipment has a cost and fair value of $160,000 to Castle Leasing Company; the useful economic life is 2 years, with a salvage value of $8,000.
3. Perry Company is required to pay $5,000 each year to the lessor for executory costs.
4. Castle Leasing Company desires to earn a return of 10% on its investment.
5. Collectibility of the payments is reasonably predictable, and there are no important uncertainties surrounding the costs yet to be incurred by the lessor.

Instructions
(a) Prepare the journal entries on the books of Castle Leasing to reflect the payments received under the lease and to recognize income for the years 1996 and 1997.
(b) Assuming that Perry Company exercises its option to purchase the equipment on December 31, 1997, prepare the journal entry to reflect the sale on Castle's books.

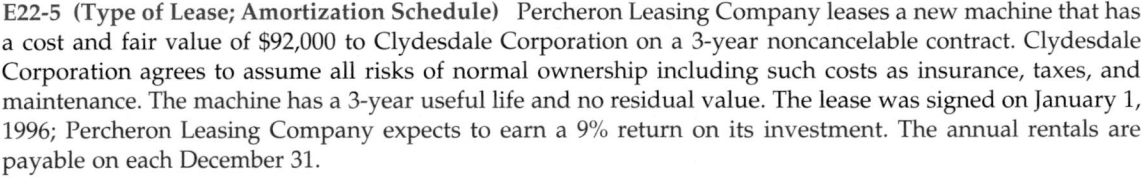 **E22-5 (Type of Lease; Amortization Schedule)** Percheron Leasing Company leases a new machine that has a cost and fair value of $92,000 to Clydesdale Corporation on a 3-year noncancelable contract. Clydesdale Corporation agrees to assume all risks of normal ownership including such costs as insurance, taxes, and maintenance. The machine has a 3-year useful life and no residual value. The lease was signed on January 1, 1996; Percheron Leasing Company expects to earn a 9% return on its investment. The annual rentals are payable on each December 31.

Instructions
(a) Discuss the nature of the lease arrangement and the accounting method each party to the lease should apply.
(b) Prepare an amortization schedule that would be suitable for both the lessor and the lessee and that covers all the years involved.

E22-6 (Lessor Entries; Sales-Type Lease) Dutch Company leases a car at fair value to J. Loriston-Clarke on January 1, 1996. The term of the noncancelable lease is 4 years. The following information about the lease is provided:

1. Title to the car passes to the lessee upon the termination of the lease. Residual value is estimated at $1,000 at the end of the lease.
2. The fair value of the car is $21,188. The car is carried in Dutch's inventory at $17,000. The car has an economic life of 5 years.
3. Dutch Company desires a rate of return of 9% on its investment.
4. Collectibility of the lease payments is reasonably predictable. There are no important uncertainties surrounding the amount of costs yet to be incurred by the lessor.
5. Equal annual lease payments are due at the beginning of each lease year.

Instructions
(a) Prepare a lease amortization schedule for Dutch Company for the 4-year lease term. Round lease payment to the nearest dollar.
(b) What type of lease is this? Discuss.
(c) Prepare the journal entries for 1996, 1997, and 1998 made by Dutch Company to record the lease agreement, the receipt of lease payments, and the recognition of income.

E22-7 (Lessee Entries with Bargain Purchase Option) The following facts pertain to a noncancelable lease agreement between Shetland Leasing Company and Falabella Company, a lessee.

Inception date:	May 1, 1995
Annual lease payment due at the beginning of each year, beginning with May 1, 1995	$20,987.83
Bargain purchase option price at end of lease term	$ 4,000.00
Lease term	5 years
Economic life of leased equipment	10 years
Lessor's cost	$65,000.00
Fair value of asset at May 1, 1995	$90,000.00
Lessor's implicit rate	10%
Lessee's incremental borrowing rate	10%

The collectibility of the lease payments is reasonably predictable, and there are no important uncertainties surrounding the costs yet to be incurred by the lessor. The lessee assumes responsibility for all executory costs.

Instructions

(Round all numbers to the nearest cent.)
  (a) Discuss the nature of this lease to Falabella Company.
  (b) Discuss the nature of this lease to Shetland Company.
  (c) Prepare a lease amortization schedule for Falabella Company for the 5-year lease term.
  (d) Prepare the journal entries on the lessee's books to reflect the signing of the lease agreement and to record the payments and expenses related to this lease for the years 1995 and 1996. Falabella's annual accounting period ends on December 31. Reversing entries are used by Falabella.

E22-8 (Lessor Entries with Bargain Purchase Option) A lease agreement between Shetland Leasing Company and Falabella Company is described in E22-7.

Instructions

(Round all numbers to the nearest cent.)
Refer to the data in E22-7 and do the following for the lessor:
  (a) Compute the amount of gross investment at the inception of the lease.
  (b) Compute the amount of net investment at the inception of the lease.
  (c) Prepare a lease amortization schedule for Shetland Leasing Company for the 5-year lease term.
  (d) Prepare the journal entries to reflect the signing of the lease agreement and to record the receipts and income related to this lease for the years 1995, 1996, and 1997. The lessor's accounting period ends on December 31. Reversing entries are not used by Shetland.

E22-9 (Computation of Rental; Journal Entries for Lessor) Morgan Leasing Company signs an agreement on January 1, 1995, to lease equipment to Shire Company. The following information relates to this agreement.

  1. The term of the noncancelable lease is 6 years with no renewal option. The equipment has an estimated economic life of 6 years.
  2. The cost of the asset to the lessor is $250,000. The fair value of the asset at January 1, 1995, is $250,000.
  3. The asset will revert to the lessor at the end of the lease term at which time the asset is expected to have a residual value of $52,480, none of which is guaranteed.
  4. Shire Company assumes direct responsibility for all executory costs.
  5. The agreement requires equal annual rental payments, beginning on January 1, 1995.
  6. Collectibility of the lease payments is reasonably predictable. There are no important uncertainties surrounding the amount of costs yet to be incurred by the lessor.

Instructions

(Round all numbers to the nearest cent.)
  (a) Assuming the lessor desires a 10% rate of return on its investment, calculate the amount of the annual rental payment required. Round to the nearest dollar.
  (b) Prepare an amortization schedule that would be suitable for the lessor for the lease term.
  (c) Prepare all of the journal entries for the lessor for 1995 and 1996 to record the lease agreement, the receipt of lease payments, and the recognition of income. Assume the lessor's annual accounting period ends on December 31.

E22-10 (Amortization Schedule and Journal Entries for Lessee) Hockney Leasing Company signs an agreement on January 1, 1995, to lease equipment to Cob Company. The following information relates to this agreement.

  1. The term of the noncancelable lease is 5 years with no renewal option. The equipment has an estimated economic life of 5 years.
  2. The fair value of the asset at January 1, 1995, is $80,000.

3. The asset will revert to the lessor at the end of the lease term, at which time the asset is expected to have a residual value of $7,000, none of which is guaranteed.
4. Cob Company assumes direct responsibility for all executory costs, which include the following annual amounts: (1) $1,200 to Rocky Mountain Insurance Company for insurance; (2) $800 to Laclede County for property taxes
5. The agreement requires equal annual rental payments of $18,142.95 to the lessor, beginning on January 1, 1995.
6. The lessee's incremental borrowing rate is 12%. The lessor's implicit rate is 10% and is known to the lessee.
7. Cob Company uses the straight-line depreciation method for all equipment.
8. Cob uses reversing entries when appropriate.

Instructions

(Round all numbers to the nearest cent.)
   (a) Prepare an amortization schedule that would be suitable for the lessee for the lease term.
   (b) Prepare all of the journal entries for the lessee for 1995 and 1996 to record the lease agreement, the lease payments, and all expenses related to this lease. Assume the lessee's annual accounting period ends on December 31.

E22-11 (Accounting for an Operating Lease) On January 1, 1995, Trake Co. leased a building to Suffolk Inc. The relevant information related to the lease is as follows:

1. The lease arrangement is for 10 years.
2. The leased building cost $4,200,000 and was purchased for cash on January 1, 1995.
3. The building is depreciated on a straight-line basis. Its estimated economic life is 50 years.
4. Lease payments are $200,000 per year and are made at the end of the year.
5. Property tax expense of $45,000 and insurance expense of $10,000 on the building were incurred by Trake in the first year. Payment on these two items was made at the end of the year.
6. Both the lessor and the lessee are on a calendar-year basis.

Instructions

   (a) Prepare the journal entries that Trake Co. should make in 1995.
   (b) Prepare the journal entries that Suffolk Inc. should make in 1995.
   (c) If Trake paid $30,000 to a real estate broker on January 1, 1995, as a fee for finding the lessee, how much should be reported as an expense for this item in 1995 by Trake Co.?

E22-12 (Accounting for an Operating Lease) On January 1, 1996, a machine was purchased for $900,000 by Red Mile Co. The machine is expected to have an 8-year life with no salvage value. It is to be depreciated on a straight-line basis. The machine was leased to St. Leger Inc. on January 1, 1996, at an annual rental of $210,000. Other relevant information is as follows:

1. The lease term is for 3 years.
2. Red Mile incurred maintenance and other executory costs of $25,000 in 1996 related to this lease.
3. The machine could have been sold by Red Mile for $940,000 instead of leasing it.
4. St. Leger is required to pay a rent security deposit of $35,000 and to prepay the last month's rent of $17,500.

Instructions

   (a) How much should Red Mile Co. report as income before income tax on this lease for 1996?
   (b) What amount should St. Leger Inc. report for rent expense for 1996 on this lease?

E22-13 (Operating Lease for Lessee and Lessor) On February 20, 1995, Appaloosa Inc., purchased a machine for $1,500,000 for the purpose of leasing it. The machine is expected to have a 10-year life, no residual value, and will be depreciated on the straight-line basis. The machine was leased to Akhal Company on March 1, 1995, for a 4-year period at a monthly rental of $17,500. There is no provision for the renewal of the lease or purchase of the machine by the lessee at the expiration of the lease term. Appaloosa paid $30,000 of commissions associated with negotiating the lease in February 1995.

Instructions

   (a) What expense should Akhal record as a result of the facts above for the year ended December 31, 1995? Show supporting computations in good form.
   (b) What income or loss before income taxes should Appaloosa record as a result of the facts above for the year ended December 31, 1995? (*Hint:* Amortize commissions over the life of the lease.)

(AICPA adapted)

E22-14 (Sale and Leaseback) On January 1, 1995, Breton Corporation sells a computer to Liquidity Finance Co. for $680,000 and immediately leases the computer back. The relevant information is as follows:

1. The computer was carried on Breton's books at a value of $580,000.

2. The term of the noncancelable lease is 10 years; title will transfer to Breton.
3. The lease agreement requires equal rental payments of $110,666.81 at the end of each year.
4. The incremental borrowing rate of Breton Corporation is 12%. Breton is aware that Liquidity Finance Co. set the annual rental to insure a rate of return of 10%.
5. The computer has a fair value of $680,000 on January 1, 1995 and an estimated economic life of 10 years.
6. Breton pays executory costs of $5,000 per year.

Instructions
Prepare the journal entries for both the lessee and the lessor for 1995 to reflect the sale and leaseback agreement. No uncertainties exist, and collectibility is reasonably certain.

E22-15 (Lessee-Lessor, Sale-Leaseback) Presented below are four independent situations:

(a) On December 31, 1996, Hillyard Inc. sold computer equipment to Cowdy Co. and immediately leased it back for 10 years. The sales price of the equipment was $500,000, its carrying amount $400,000, and its estimated remaining economic life 12 years. Determine the amount of deferred revenue to be reported from the sale of the computer equipment on December 31, 1996.

(b) On December 31, 1996, Berber Co. sold a machine to Crown Co. and simultaneously leased it back for one year. The sale price of the machine was $480,000, the carrying amount $435,000, and it had an estimated remaining useful life of 14 years. The present value of the rental payments for the one year is $35,000. At December 31, 1996, how much should Berber report as deferred revenue from the sale of the machine?

(c) On January 1, 1996, Bard Corp. sold an airplane with an estimated useful life of 10 years. At the same time, Bard leased back the plane for 10 years. The sales price of the airplane was $500,000, the carrying amount $390,000, and the annual rental $73,975.22. Bard intends to depreciate the lease asset using the sum-of-the-years'-digits depreciation method. Discuss how the gain on the sale should be reported at the end of 1996 in the financial statements.

(d) On January 1, 1996, Oxford Co. sold equipment with an estimated useful life of 5 years. At the same time, Oxford leased back the equipment for 2 years under a lease classified as an operating lease. The sales price (fair market value) of the equipment was $212,700, the carrying amount was $310,000, the monthly rental under the lease $6,000, and the present value of the rental payments $115,753. For the year ended December 31, 1996, determine which items would be reported on its income statement for the sale-leaseback transaction.

PROBLEMS

P22-1 (Basic Lessee Computations and Entries; Capital Lease) Fell Inc. agrees to rent Country Winery Corporation the equipment that it requires to expand its production capacity to meet customers' demands for its products. The lease agreement calls for five annual lease payments of $90,000 at the end of each year. On the date the capital lease begins, the lessee recognizes the existence of leased assets and the related lease obligation at the present value of the five annual payments discounted at a rate of 12%, $324,430.20. The lessee uses the effective-interest method of reducing lease obligations. The leased equipment has an estimated useful life of 5 years and no residual value; Country Winery uses the sum-of-the-years'-digits method on similar equipment that it owns.

Instructions
(a) What would be the total amount of the reduction in the lease obligation of the lessee during the first year? The second year?
(b) Prepare the journal entry made by Country Winery Corporation (lessee) on the date the lease begins.
(c) Prepare the journal entries to record the lease payment and interest expense for the first year; the second year.
(d) Prepare the journal entry at the end of the first full year to recognize depreciation of the leased equipment.

P22-2 (Operating Lease; Lessee-Lessor Entries) Synergetics Inc. leased a new crane to Alpha Construction under a 5-year noncancelable contract starting January 1, 1996. Terms of the lease require payments of $21,000 each January 1, starting January 1, 1996. Synergetics will pay insurance, taxes, and maintenance charges on the crane, which has an estimated life of 12 years, a fair value of $160,000, and a cost to Synergetics of $160,000. The estimated fair value of the crane is expected to be $45,000 at the end of the lease term. No bargain purchase or renewal options are included in the contract. Both Synergetics and Alpha adjust and close books annually at December 31. Collectibility is reasonably certain and no uncertainties exist relative to unreimbursable lessor costs. Alpha's incremental borrowing rate is 10% and Synergetics' implicit interest rate of 9% is known to Alpha.

Instructions

(a) Identify the type of lease involved and give reasons for your classification. Discuss the accounting treatment that should be applied by both the lessee and the lessor.

(b) Prepare all the entries related to the lease contract and leased asset for the year 1996 for the lessee and lessor, assuming:

1. Insurance $1,700.
2. Taxes $240.
3. Maintenance $650.
4. Straight-line depreciation and salvage value of $10,000.

(c) Discuss what should be presented in the balance sheet and income statement and related notes of both the lessee and the lessor at December 31, 1996.

P22-3 (Lessee-Lessor Entries, Balance Sheet Presentation; Sales-Type Lease) Cascade Industries and Addison Corporation enter into an agreement that requires Addison to build three diesel-electric engines to Cascade's specifications. Upon completion of the engines, Cascade has agreed to lease them for a period of 10 years and to assume all costs and risks of ownership. The lease is noncancelable, becomes effective on January 1, 1996, and requires annual rental payments of $620,000 each January 1, starting January 1, 1996.

Cascade's incremental borrowing rate is 10%, and the implicit interest rate used by Addison and known to Cascade is 8%. The total cost of building the three engines is $3,900,000. The economic life of the engines is estimated to be 10 years with residual value set at zero. Cascade depreciates similar equipment on a straight-line basis. At the end of the lease, Cascade assumes title to the engines. Collectibility is reasonably certain and no uncertainties exist relative to unreimbursable lessor costs.

Instructions

(Round all numbers to the nearest dollar.)

(a) Discuss the nature of this lease transaction from the viewpoints of both lessee and lessor.

(b) Prepare the journal entry or entries to record the transaction on January 1, 1996, on the books of Cascade Industries.

(c) Prepare the journal entry or entries to record the transaction on January 1, 1996, on the books of Addison Corporation.

(d) Prepare the journal entries for both the lessee and lessor to record the first rental payment on January 1, 1996.

(e) Prepare the journal entries for both the lessee and lessor to record interest expense (revenue) at December 31, 1996. (Prepare a lease amortization schedule for 2 years.)

(f) Show the items and amounts that would be reported on the balance sheet (not notes) at December 31, 1996, for both the lessee and the lessor.

P22-4 (Balance Sheet and Income Statement Disclosure—Lessee) The following facts pertain to a noncancelable lease agreement between Omuto Leasing Company and Sylvan Electronics, a lessee, for a computer system.

Inception date:	September 1, 1995
Lease term	6 years
Economic life of leased equipment	6 years
Fair value of asset at September 1, 1995	$200,000.00
Residual value at end of lease term	–0–
Lessor's implicit rate	10%
Lessee's incremental borrowing rate	10%
Annual lease payment due at the beginning of each year, beginning with September 1, 1995	$41,746.77

The collectibility of the lease payments is reasonably predictable, and there are no important uncertainties surrounding the costs yet to be incurred by the lessor. The lessee assumes responsibility for all executory costs, which amount to $4,000 per year and are to be paid each September 1, beginning September 1, 1995. (This $4,000 is not included in the rental payment of $41,746.77.) The asset will revert to the lessor at the end of the lease term. The straight-line depreciation method is used for all equipment.

The following amortization schedule has been prepared correctly for use by both the lessor and the lessee in accounting for this lease. The lease is to be accounted for properly as a capital lease by the lessee and as a direct financing lease by the lessor.

Date	Annual Lease Payment/ Receipt	Interest (10%) on Unpaid Obligation/ Net Investment	Reduction of Lease Obligation/ Net Investment	Balance of Lease Obligation/ Net Investment
10/01/95				$200,000.00
10/01/95	$ 41,746.77		$ 41,746.77	158,253.23
10/01/96	41,746.77	$15,825.32	25,921.45	132,331.78

10/01/97	41,746.77	13,233.18	28,513.59	103,818.19
10/01/98	41,746.77	10,381.82	31,364.95	72,453.24
10/01/99	41,746.77	7,245.32	34,501.45	37,951.79
10/01/00	41,746.77	3,794.98*	37,951.79	–0–
	$250,480.62	$50,480.62	$200,000.00	

*Rounding error is 20 cents.

Instructions

(Round all numbers to the nearest cent.)

(a) Assuming the lessee's accounting period ends on September 30, answer the following questions with respect to this lease agreement:

    (1) What items and amounts will appear on the lessee's income statement for the year ending September 30, 1996?

    (2) What items and amounts will appear where on the lessee's balance sheet at September 30, 1996?

    (3) What items and amounts will appear on the lessee's income statement for the year ending September 30, 1997?

    (4) What items and amounts will appear where on the lessee's balance sheet at September 30, 1997?

(b) Assuming the lessee's accounting period ends on December 31, answer the following questions with respect to this lease agreement:

    (1) What items and amounts will appear on the lessee's income statement for the year ending December 31, 1995?

    (2) What items and amounts will appear where on the lessee's balance sheet at December 31, 1995?

    (3) What items and amounts will appear on the lessee's income statement for the year ending December 31, 1996?

    (4) What items and amounts will appear where on the lessee's balance sheet at December 31, 1996?

P22-5 (Balance Sheet and Income Statement Disclosure—Lessor) Assume the same information as Problem 22-4.

Instructions

(Round all numbers to the nearest cent.)

(a) Assuming the lessor's accounting period ends on September 30, answer the following questions with respect to this lease agreement:

    (1) What items and amounts will appear on the lessor's income statement for the year ending September 30, 1996?

    (2) What items and amounts will appear where on the lessor's balance sheet at September 30, 1996?

    (3) What items and amounts will appear on the lessor's income statement for the year ending September 30, 1997?

    (4) What items and amounts will appear where on the lessor's balance sheet at September 30, 1997?

(b) Assuming the lessor's accounting period ends on December 31, answer the following questions with respect to this lease agreement:

    (1) What items and amounts will appear on the lessor's income statement for the year ending December 31, 1995?

    (2) What items and amounts will appear where on the lessor's balance sheet at December 31, 1995?

    (3) What items and amounts will appear on the lessor's income statement for the year ending December 31, 1996?

    (4) What items and amounts will appear where on the lessor's balance sheet at December 31, 1996?

P22-6 (Lessee Entries with Residual Value) The following facts pertain to a noncancelable lease agreement between Watson Leasing Company and Erwin Company, a lessee.

Inception date:	January 1, 1995
Annual lease payment due at the beginning of each year, beginning with January 1, 1995	$81,915.24
Residual value of equipment at end of lease term, guaranteed by the lessee	$45,000.00
Lease term	6 years
Economic life of leased equipment	6 years
Fair value of asset at January 1, 1995	$400,000.00
Lessor's implicit rate	12%
Lessee's incremental borrowing rate	12%

The lessee assumes responsibility for all executory costs, which are expected to amount to $4,000 per year. The asset will revert to the lessor at the end of the lease term. The lessee has guaranteed the lessor a residual value of $45,000. The lessee uses the straight-line depreciation method for all equipment.

Instructions

(Round all numbers to the nearest cent.)

(a) Prepare an amortization schedule that would be suitable for the lessee for the lease term.

(b) Prepare all of the journal entries for the lessee for 1995 and 1996 to record the lease agreement, the lease payments, and all expenses related to this lease. Assume the lessee's annual accounting period ends on December 31 and reversing entries are used when appropriate.

P22-7 (Lessee Entries and Balance Sheet Presentation; Capital Lease) Kennedy Steel Company as lessee signed a lease agreement for equipment for 5 years, beginning December 31, 1995. Annual rental payments of $32,000 are to be made at the beginning of each lease year (December 31). The taxes, insurance, and the maintenance costs are the obligation of the lessee. The interest rate used by the lessor in setting the payment schedule is 10%; Kennedy's incremental borrowing rate is 12%. Kennedy is unaware of the rate being used by the lessor. At the end of the lease, Kennedy has the option to buy the equipment for $1, considerably below its estimated fair value at that time. The equipment has an estimated useful life of 8 years. Kennedy uses the straight-line method of depreciation on similar owned equipment.

Instructions

(Round all numbers to the nearest dollar.)

(a) Prepare the journal entry or entries, with explanations, that should be recorded on December 31, 1995, by Kennedy. (Assume no residual value.)

(b) Prepare the journal entry or entries, with explanations, that should be recorded on December 31, 1996, by Kennedy. (Prepare the lease amortization schedule for all five payments.)

(c) Prepare the journal entry or entries, with explanations, that should be recorded on December 31, 1997, by Kennedy.

(d) What amounts would appear on the December 31, 1997, balance sheet of Kennedy relative to the lease arrangement?

P22-8 (Lessee Entries and Balance Sheet Presentation; Capital Lease) On January 1, 1996, Mason Holdings Company contracts to lease equipment for 5 years, agreeing to make a payment of $86,000 (including the executory costs of $6,000) at the beginning of each year, starting January 1, 1996. The taxes, the insurance, and the maintenance, estimated at $6,000 a year, are the obligations of the lessee. The leased equipment is to be capitalized at $333,589. The asset is to be amortized on a double-declining-balance basis and the obligation is to be reduced on an effective-interest basis. Mason's incremental borrowing rate is 12%, and the implicit rate in the lease is 10%, which is known by Mason Holdings. Title to the equipment transfers to Mason Holdings when the lease expires. The asset has an estimated useful life of 5 years and no residual value.

Instructions

(Round all numbers to the nearest dollar.)

(a) Explain the probable relationship of the $333,589 amount to the lease arrangement.

(b) Prepare the journal entry or entries that should be recorded on January 1, 1996, by Mason Holdings Company.

(c) Prepare the journal entry to record depreciation of the leased asset for the year 1996.

(d) Prepare the journal entry to record the interest expense for the year 1996.

(e) Prepare the journal entry to record the lease payment of January 1, 1997, assuming reversing entries are not made.

(f) What amounts will appear on the lessee's December 31, 1996, balance sheet relative to the lease contract?

P22-9 (Lessee Entries, Capital Lease with Monthly Payments) Chambers Inc. was incorporated in 1994 to operate as a computer software service firm with an accounting fiscal year ending August 31. Chambers' primary product is a sophisticated on-line inventory-control system; its customers pay a fixed fee plus a usage charge for using the system.

Chambers has leased a large, Alpha-3 computer system from the manufacturer. The lease calls for a monthly rental of $60,000 for the 144 months (12 years) of the lease term. The estimated useful life of the computer is 15 years.

Each scheduled monthly rental payment includes $5,000 for full-service maintenance on the computer to be performed by the manufacturer. All rentals are payable on the first day of the month beginning with August 1, 1995, the date the computer was installed and the lease agreement was signed.

The lease is noncancelable for its 12-year term, and it is secured only by the manufacturer's chattel lien on the Alpha-3 system. Chambers can purchase the Alpha-3 system from the manufacturer at the end of the 12-year lease term for 75% of the computer's fair value at that time.

This lease is to be accounted for as a capital lease by Chambers, and it will be depreciated by the straight-line method with no expected salvage value. Borrowed funds for this type of transaction would cost Chambers 12% per year (1% per month). Following is a schedule of the present value of $1 for selected periods discounted at 1% per period when payments are made at the beginning of each period.

Periods (months)	Present Value of $1 per Period Discounted at 1% per Period
1	1.000
2	1.990
3	2.970
143	76.658
144	76.899

Instructions

Prepare, in general journal form, all entries Chambers should have made in its accounting records during August 1995 relating to this lease. Give full explanations and show supporting computations for each entry. Remember, August 31, 1995, is the end of Chambers' fiscal accounting period and it will be preparing financial statements on that date. Do not prepare closing entries.

(AICPA adapted)

P22-10 (Lessor Computations and Entries; Sales-Type Lease with Unguaranteed RV) Bearden Company manufactures a desk-type computer with an estimated economic life of 12 years and leases it to Sonnet Airlines for a period of 10 years. The normal selling price of the equipment is $210,482, and its unguaranteed residual value at the end of the lease term is estimated to be $20,000. Sonnet will pay annual payments of $30,000 at the beginning of each year and all maintenance, insurance, and taxes. Bearden incurred costs of $180,000 in manufacturing the equipment and $5,000 in negotiating and closing the lease. Bearden has determined that the collectibility of the lease payments is reasonably predictable, that no additional costs will be incurred, and that the implicit interest rate is 10%.

Instructions

(Round all numbers to the nearest dollar.)

(a) Discuss the nature of this lease in relation to the lessor and compute the amount of each of the following items:
1. Gross investment.
2. Unearned interest revenue.
3. Sales price.
4. Cost of sales.

(b) Prepare a 10-year lease amortization schedule.

(c) Prepare all of the lessor's journal entries for the first year.

P22-11 (Lessee Computations and Entries; Capital Lease with Unguaranteed Residual Value) Assume the same data as in Problem 22-10 with Sonnet Airlines Co. having an incremental borrowing rate of 10%.

Instructions

(Round all numbers to the nearest dollar.)

(a) Discuss the nature of this lease in relation to the lessee and compute the amount of the initial obligation under capital leases.

(b) Prepare a 10-year lease amortization schedule.

(c) Prepare all of the lessee's journal entries for the first year.

P22-12 (Lessor Computations; Unearned Revenue Recognized Using Sum-of-Month's-Digits) During 1996, Roth Leasing Co. began leasing equipment to small manufacturers. Below is information regarding leasing arrangement.

1. Roth Leasing Co. leases equipment with terms from 3 to 5 years depending upon the useful life of the equipment. At the expiration of the lease, the equipment will be sold to the lessee at 10% of the lessor's cost, the expected salvage value of the equipment.
2. The amount of the lessee's monthly payment is computed by multiplying the lessor's cost of the equipment by the payment factor applicable to the term of lease.

Term of Lease	Payment Factor
3 years	3.32%
4 years	2.63%
5 years	2.22%

3. The excess of the gross contract receivable for equipment rentals over the cost (reduced by the estimated salvage value at the termination of the lease) is recognized as revenue over the term of the lease under the sum-of-the-year's-digits method computed on a monthly basis.
4. The following leases were entered into during 1996:

Machine	Dates of Lease	Period of Lease	Machine Cost
Die	7/1/96–6/30/00	4 years	$150,000
Press	9/1/96–8/31/99	3 years	$100,000

Instructions

(a) Prepare a schedule of gross contracts receivable for equipment rentals at the dates of the lease for the die and press machines.

(b) Prepare a schedule of unearned lease income at December 31, 1996, for each machine lease.

(c) Prepare a schedule computing the present dollar value of lease payments receivable (gross investment) for equipment rentals at December 31, 1996. (The present dollar value of the "lease receivables for equipment rentals" is the outstanding amount of the gross lease receivables less the unearned lease income included therein.) Without prejudice to your solution to part (b), assume that the unearned lease income at December 31, 1996, was $32,000.

(AICPA adapted)

P22-13 (Basic Lessee Accounting with Difficult PV Calculation) In 1993 UVC Trucking Company negotiated and closed a long-term lease contract for newly constructed truck terminals and freight storage facilities. The buildings were erected to the company's specifications on land owned by the company. On January 1, 1994, UVC Trucking Company took possession of the lease properties. On January 1, 1994 and 1995, the company made cash payments of $1,050,000 that were recorded as rental expenses.

Although the terminals have a composite useful life of 40 years, the noncancelable lease runs for 20 years from January 1, 1994, with a bargain purchase option available upon expiration of the lease.

The 20-year lease is effective for the period January 1, 1994, through December 31, 2013. Advance rental payments of $900,000 are payable to the lessor on January 1 of each of the first 10 years of the lease term. Advance rental payments of $320,000 are due on January 1 for each of the last 10 years of the lease. The company has an option to purchase all of these leased facilities for $1 on December 31, 2013. It also must make annual payments to the lessor of $50,000 for property taxes and $100,000 for insurance. The lease was negotiated to assure the lessor a 6% rate of return.

Instructions

(Round all numbers to the nearest dollar.)

(a) Prepare a schedule to compute for UVC Trucking Company the discounted present value of the terminal facilities and related obligation at January 1, 1994.

(b) Assuming that the discounted present value of terminal facilities and related obligation at January 1, 1994, was $9,000,000, prepare journal entries for UVC Trucking Company to record the:

1. Cash payment to the lessor on January 1, 1996.

2. Amortization of the cost of the leased properties for 1996 using the straight-line method and assuming a zero salvage value.

3. Accrual of interest expense at December 31, 1996.

Selected present value factors are as follows:

Periods	For an Ordinary Annuity of $1 at 6%	For $1 at 6%
1	.943396	.943396
2	1.833393	.889996
8	6.209794	.627412
9	6.801692	.591898
10	7.360087	.558395
19	11.158117	.330513
20	11.469921	.311805

(AICPA adapted)

P22-14 (Lessor Computations and Entries; Sales-Type Lease with Guaranteed Residual Value) Laurel Lake Inc. manufactures an X-ray machine with an estimated life of 12 years and leases it to Regis Medical for a period of 10 years. The normal selling price of the machine is $343,734 and its guaranteed residual value at the end of the lease term is estimated to be $15,000. The hospital will pay rents of $50,000 at the beginning of each year and all maintenance, insurance, and taxes. Laurel Lake Inc. incurred costs of $280,000 in manufacturing the machine and $6,000 in negotiating and closing the lease. Laurel Lake Inc. has determined that the collectibility of the lease payments is reasonably predictable, that there will be no additional costs incurred, and that the implicit interest rate is 10%.

Instructions

(Round all numbers to the nearest dollar.)

(a) Discuss the nature of this lease in relation to the lessor and compute the amount of each of the following items:

1. Gross investment.   3. Sales price.

2. Unearned interest revenue.   4. Cost of sales.

(b) Prepare a 10-year lease amortization schedule.

(c) Prepare all of the lessor's journal entries for the first year.

P22-15 (Lessee Computations and Entries; Capital Lease with Guaranteed Residual Value) Assume the same data as in Problem 22–14 and that Regis Medical has an incremental borrowing rate of 10%.

Instructions
(Round all numbers to the nearest dollar.)
   (a) Discuss the nature of this lease in relation to the lessee and compute the amount of the initial obligation under capital leases.
   (b) Prepare a 10-year lease amortization schedule.
   (c) Prepare all of the lessee's journal entries for the first year.

CASES

C22-1 (Lessee Accounting and Reporting) On January 1, 1996, Grishell Company entered into a noncancelable lease for a machine to be used in its manufacturing operations. The lease transfers ownership of the machine to Evans by the end of the lease term. The term of the lease is 8 years. The minimum lease payment made by Evans on January 1, 1996, was one of eight equal annual payments. At the inception of the lease, the criteria established for classification as a capital lease by the lessee were met.

Instructions
   (a) What is the theoretical basis for the accounting standard that requires certain long-term leases to be capitalized by the lessee? Do not discuss the specific criteria for classifying a specific lease as a capital lease.
   (b) How should Grishell account for this lease at its inception and determine the amount to be recorded?
   (c) What expenses related to this lease will Grishell incur during the first year of the lease, and how will they be determined?
   (d) How should Grishell report the lease transaction on its December 31, 1996, balance sheet?

C22-2 (Lessor and Lessee Accounting and Disclosure) Amirante Inc. entered into a lease arrangement with Beryl Leasing Corporation for a certain machine. Beryl's primary business is leasing and it is not a manufacturer or dealer. Amirante will lease the machine for a period of 3 years, which is 50% of the machine's economic life. Beryl will take possession of the machine at the end of the initial 3-year lease and lease it to another, smaller company that does not need the most current version of the machine. Amirante does not guarantee any residual value for the machine and will not purchase the machine at the end of the lease term.

Amirante's incremental borrowing rate is 16% and the implicit rate in the lease is 14½%. Amirante has no way of knowing the implicit rate used by Beryl. Using either rate, the present value of the minimum lease payments is between 90% and 100% of the fair value of the machine at the date of the lease agreement.

Amirante has agreed to pay all executory costs directly and no allowance for these costs is included in the lease payments.

Beryl is reasonably certain that Amirante will pay all lease payments, and, because Amirante has agreed to pay all executory costs, there are no important uncertainties regarding costs to be incurred by Beryl. Assume that no indirect costs are involved.

Instructions
   (a) With respect to Amirante (the lessee) answer the following:
      1. What type of lease has been entered into? Explain the reason for your answer.
      2. How should Amirante compute the appropriate amount to be recorded for the lease or asset acquired?
      3. What accounts will be created or affected by this transaction and how will the lease or asset and other costs related to the transaction be matched with earnings?
      4. What disclosures must Amirante make regarding this leased asset?
   (b) With respect to Beryl (the lessor) answer the following:
      1. What type of leasing arrangement has been entered into? Explain the reason for your answer.
      2. How should this lease be recorded by Beryl, and how are the appropriate amounts determined?
      3. How should Beryl determine the appropriate amount of earnings to be recognized from each lease payment?
      4. What disclosures must Beryl make regarding this lease?

(AICPA adapted)

C22-3 (Lessee Capitalization Criteria) On January 1, Barnaby Company, a lessee, entered into three noncancelable leases for brand-new equipment, Lease L, Lease M, and Lease N. None of the three leases transfers ownership of the equipment to Barnaby at the end of the lease term. For each of the three leases, the present value at the beginning of the lease term of the minimum lease payments, excluding that portion of the payments representing executory costs such as insurance, maintenance, and taxes to be paid by the lessor, is 75% of the fair value of the equipment.

The following information is peculiar to each lease:

1. Lease L does not contain a bargain purchase option; the lease term is equal to 80% of the estimated economic life of the equipment.
2. Lease M contains a bargain purchase option; the lease term is equal to 50% of the estimated economic life of the equipment.
3. Lease N does not contain a bargain purchase option; the lease term is equal to 50% of the estimated economic life of the equipment.

Instructions
(a) How should Barnaby Company classify each of the three leases above, and why? Discuss the rationale for your answer.
(b) What amount, if any, should Barnaby record as a liability at the inception of the lease for each of the three leases above?
(c) Assuming that the minimum lease payments are made on a straight-line basis, how should Barnaby record each minimum lease payment for each of the three leases above?

(AICPA adapted)

C22-4 (Comparison of Different Types of Accounting by Lessee and Lessor)

Part 1
Capital leases and operating leases are the two classifications of leases described in FASB pronouncements from the standpoint of the **lessee.**

Instructions
(a) Describe how a capital lease would be accounted for by the lessee both at the inception of the lease and during the first year of the lease, assuming the lease transfers ownership of the property to the lessee by the end of the lease.
(b) Describe how an operating lease would be accounted for by the lessee both at the inception of the lease and during the first year of the lease, assuming equal monthly payments are made by the lessee at the beginning of each month of the lease. Describe the change in accounting, if any, when rental payments are not made on a straight-line basis.

Do **not** discuss the criteria for distinguishing between capital leases and operating leases.

Part 2
Sales-type leases and direct financing leases are two of the classifications of leases described in FASB pronouncements from the standpoint of the **lessor.**

Instructions
Compare and contrast a sales-type lease with a direct financing lease as follows:
(a) Gross investment in the lease.
(b) Amortization of unearned interest revenue.
(c) Manufacturer's or dealer's profit.

Do **not** discuss the criteria for distinguishing between the leases described above and operating leases.

(AICPA adapted)

C22-5 (Lessee Capitalization of Bargain Purchase Option) J.K. Albert Corporation is a diversified company with nationwide interests in commercial real estate developments, banking, copper mining, and metal fabrication. The company has offices and operating locations in major cities throughout the United States. Corporate headquarters for J.K. Albert Corporation is located in a metropolitan area of a midwestern state, and executives connected with various phases of company operations travel extensively. Corporate management is currently evaluating the feasibility of acquiring a business aircraft that can be used by company executives to expedite business travel to areas not adequately served by commercial airlines. Proposals for either leasing or purchasing a suitable aircraft have been analyzed, and the leasing proposal was considered to be more desirable.

The proposed lease agreement involves a twin-engine turboprop Viking that has a fair market value of $900,000. This plane would be leased for a period of 10 years beginning January 1, 1996. The lease agreement is cancelable only upon accidental destruction of the plane. An annual lease payment of $127,600 is due on January 1 of each year; the first payment is to be made on January 1, 1996. Maintenance operations are strictly scheduled by the lessor, and J.K. Albert Corporation will pay for these services as they are performed. Estimated annual maintenance costs are $6,200. The lessor will pay all insurance premiums and local property taxes, which amount to a combined total of $3,600 annually and are included in the annual lease payment of $127,600. Upon expiration of the 10-year lease, J.K. Albert Corporation can purchase the Viking for $40,000. The estimated useful life of the plane is 15 years, and its salvage value in the used plane market is estimated to be $100,000 after 10 years. The salvage value probably will never be less than $75,000 if the engines are overhauled and maintained as prescribed by the manufacturer. If the purchase option is not exercised, possession of the plane will revert to the lessor, and there is no provision for renewing the lease agreement beyond its termination on December 31, 2005.

J.K. Albert Corporation can borrow $900,000 under a 10-year term loan agreement at an annual interest rate of 12%. The lessor's implicit interest rate is not expressly stated in the lease agreement, but this rate appears to be approximately 8% based on ten net rental payments of $124,000 per year and the initial market value of $900,000 for the plane. On January 1, 1996, the present value of all net rental payments and the purchase option of $40,000 is $800,000 using the 12% interest rate. The present value of all net rental payments and the $40,000 purchase option on January 1, 1996 is $920,000 using the 8% interest rate implicit in the lease agreement. The financial vice-president of J.K. Albert Corporation has established that this lease agreement is a capital lease as defined in *Statement of Financial Accounting Standards No. 13*, "Accounting for Leases."

Instructions

    (a) What is the appropriate amount that J.K. Albert Corporation should recognize for the leased aircraft on its balance sheet after the lease is signed?

    (b) Without prejudice to your answer in part (a), assume that the annual lease payment is $127,600 as stated in the question, that the appropriate capitalized amount for the leased aircraft is $900,000 on January 1, 1996, and that the interest rate is 9%. How will the lease be reported in the December 31, 1996, balance sheet and related income statement? (Ignore any income tax implications.)

                                          (CMA adapted)

C22-6 (Sale-Leaseback) On January 1, 1995, Simon Company sold equipment for cash and leased it back. As seller-lessee, Simon retained the right to substantially all of the remaining use of the equipment.

The term of the lease is 8 years. There is a gain on the sale portion of the transaction. The lease portion of the transaction is classified appropriately as a capital lease.

Instructions

    a. What is the theoretical basis for requiring lessees to capitalize certain long-term leases? **Do not discuss the specific criteria for classifying a lease as a capital lease.**

    b. 1. How should Simon account for the sale portion of the sale-leaseback transaction at January 1, 1995?

        2. How should Simon account for the leaseback portion of the sale-leaseback transaction at January 1, 1995?

    c. How should Simon account for the gain on the sale portion of the sale-leaseback transaction during the first year of the lease? Why?

                                          (AICPA adapted)

C22-7 (Sale-Leaseback) On December 31, 1995, Lange-Shanahan Co. sold six-month old equipment at fair value and leased it back. There was a loss on the sale. Lange-Shanahan pays all insurance, maintenance, and taxes on the equipment. The lease provides for eight equal annual payments, beginning December 31, 1996, with a present value equal to 85% of the equipment's fair value and sales price. The lease's term is equal to 80% of the equipment's useful life. There is no provision for Lange-Shanahan to reacquire ownership of the equipment at the end of the lease term.

Instructions

    (a) 1. Why is it important to compare an equipment's fair value to its lease payments' present value and its useful life to the lease term?

        2. Evaluate Lange-Shanahan's leaseback of the equipment in terms of each of the four criteria for determination of a capital lease.

    (b) How should Lange-Shanahan account for the sale portion of the sale-leaseback transaction at December 31, 1995?

    (c) How should Lange-Shanahan report the leaseback portion of the sale-leaseback transaction on its December 31, 1996, balance sheet?

▶ USING YOUR JUDGMENT ◀

▶ FINANCIAL REPORTING PROBLEM

Presented in Illustrations 22-34 and 22-35 are the financial statement disclosures for Kroger Co. and Amdahl Corporation.

Instructions
Answer the following questions related to these disclosures.

1. What are the total obligations under capital leases for 1992 for Kroger Co.?
2. What is the book value of the assets under capital lease at the end of 1992 for Kroger Co.? Explain why there is a difference between the amounts reported for assets and liabilities under capital leases.
3. What is the total rental expense reported for leasing activity for Kroger Co. for 1992?
4. Estimate the off-balance sheet liability due to Kroger's operating leases for 1992.
5. What are the minimum lease payments receivable (including residual value) for Amdahl Corporation for 1992? What is its net investment in sales-type leases?
6. Is Amdahl Corporation involved in more capital or operating leases? What are the minimum lease payments receivable by Amdahl Corporation in 1993?

▶ WRITING ASSIGNMENT

You are auditing the December 31, 1996, financial statements of Jeannette Sukley, Inc., manufacturer of novelties and party favors. During your inspection of the company garage, you discovered that a 1995 Yucko automobile not listed in the equipment subsidiary ledger is parked in the company garage. You ask Stacey Dendrinos, plant manager, about the vehicle, and she tells you that the company did not list the automobile because the company was only leasing it. The lease agreement was entered into on January 1, 1996, with Dave Reeder New and Used Cars.

You decide to review the lease agreement to ensure that the lease should be afforded operating lease treatment, and you discover the following lease terms:

1. Noncancelable term of 50 months.
2. Rental of $180 per month (at the end of each month; present value at 1% per month is $7,055).
3. Estimated residual value after 50 months is $1,100 (the present value at 1% per month is $699). Sukley guarantees the residual value of $1,100.
4. Estimated economic life of the automobile is 60 months.
5. Sukley's incremental borrowing rate is 12% per year (1% per month).

Instructions
You are a senior auditor writing a memo to your supervisor, the audit partner in charge of this audit, to discuss the above situation. Be sure to include (a) why you inspected the lease agreement, (b) what you determined about the lease, and (c) how you advised your client to account for this lease. Explain every journal entry that you believe is necessary to record this lease properly on the client's books. (It is also necessary to include the fact that you communicated this information to your client.)

▶ GROUP ASSIGNMENT

GA22-1 (Lease Entries; Capital Lease with Guaranteed RV, Comprehensive) Morgan Dairy leases its milking equipment from S. Zeff Finance Company under the following lease terms:

1. The lease term is 10 years, noncancelable, and requires equal rental payments of $25,250 due at the beginning of each year starting January 1, 1995.
2. The equipment has a fair value and cost at the inception of the lease (January 1, 1995) of $185,078, an estimated economic life of 10 years, and a residual value (which is guaranteed by Morgan Dairy) of $20,000.
3. The lease contains no renewable options and the equipment reverts to S. Zeff Finance Company upon termination of the lease.
4. Morgan Dairy's incremental borrowing rate is 9% per year; the implicit rate is also 9%.
5. Morgan Dairy depreciates similar equipment that it owns on a straight-line basis.
6. Collectibility of the payments is reasonably predictable, and there are no important uncertainties surrounding the costs yet to be incurred by the lessor.

Instructions
Your instructor will assign one member to record your group responses and one member to serve as group spokesperson. As a group, provide the information for the recorder to prepare responses to the following requirements. Upon completion of each requirement and before moving on to the next part, the spokesperson will report the group findings to the class.

(a) Evaluate the criteria for classification of the lease and describe the nature of the lease. In general, discuss how the lessee and lessor should account for the lease transaction.

(b) Prepare the journal entries for the lessee and lessor at January 1, 1995, and December 31, 1995 (the lessee's and lessor's year-end). Assume no reversing entries.

(c) What would have been the amount to be capitalized by the lessee upon the inception of the lease if
   1. The residual value of $20,000 had been guaranteed by a third party, not the lessee?
   2. The residual value of $20,000 had not been guaranteed at all?
(d) On the lessor's books, what would be the amount recorded as the Net Investment at the inception of the lease, assuming
   1. The residual value of $20,000 had been guaranteed by a third party?
   2. The residual value of $20,000 had not been guaranteed at all?
(e) Suppose the useful life of the milking equipment is 20 years. How large would the residual value have to be at the end of 10 years in order for the lessee to qualify for the operating method? (Assume that the residual value would be guaranteed by a third party). (*Hint:* The lessee's annual payments will be appropriately reduced as the residual value increases.)

GA22-2 (Computation of Annual Rentals and Other Amounts for Lessor and Lessee) Buchanan Corporation, a lessor of office machines, purchased a new machine for $600,000 on December 31, 1995, which was delivered the same day (by prior arrangement) to Dunn Company, the lessee. The following information relating to the lease transaction is available:

1. The leased asset has an estimated useful life of 5 years, which coincides with the lease term.
2. At the end of the lease term, the machine will revert to Buchanan, at which time it is expected to have a residual value of $60,000 (none of which is guaranteed by Dunn).
3. Buchanan's implicit interest rate (on its net investment) is 8%, which is known by Dunn.
4. Dunn's incremental borrowing rate is 10% at December 31, 1995.
5. Lease rentals consist of five equal annual payments, the first of which was paid on December 31, 1995.
6. The lease is appropriately accounted for as a direct financing lease by Buchanan and as a capital lease by Dunn. Both lessor and lessee are calendar-year corporations and depreciate all fixed assets on the straight-line basis.

Instructions
Your instructor will assign one member of the group to serve as recorder and one member to serve as spokesperson. As a group, provide the information for the recorder to prepare responses to the following requirements. Upon completion of each requirement and before moving on to the next part, the spokesperson will report the group findings to the class.
(Round all numbers to the nearest dollar.)
(a) Compute the annual rental under the lease.
(b) Compute the amounts of the gross lease rentals receivable and the unearned interest revenue that Buchanan should disclose at the inception of the lease on December 31, 1995.
(c) What expense should Dunn record for the year ended December 31, 1996?
(d) Prepare the journal entries for both the lessor and lessee at inception of the lease and for the first payment

(AICPA adapted)

▶ ETHICS CASE

(Ethical Issue, Lease Agreements) Opcy Corporation entered into a lease agreement for 10 photocopy machines for its corporate headquarters. The lease agreement qualifies as an operating lease in all terms except there is a bargain purchase option. After the 5-year lease term, the corporation can purchase each copier for $1,000, when the anticipated market value is $2,500.

Mark Althaus, the financial vice president, thinks the financial statements must necessarily recognize the lease agreement as a capital lease because of the bargain purchase agreement. The controller, Alicia Greenberg, disagrees: "Although I don't know much about the copiers themselves, there is a way to avoid recording the lease liability." She argues that the corporation might claim that copier technology advances rapidly and that by the end of the lease term the machines will most likely not be worth the $1,000 bargain price.

Instructions
(a) What ethical issue is at stake?
(b) Should the controller's argument be accepted if she does not really know much about copier technology? Would it make a difference if the controller were knowledgeable about the pace of change in copier technology?
(c) What would you do?

CHAPTER 23

ACCOUNTING CHANGES AND ERROR ANALYSIS

LEARNING OBJECTIVES

After studying this chapter, you should be able to:

1. Identify the types of accounting changes.
2. Describe the accounting for changes in accounting principles.
3. Understand how to account for cumulative-effect accounting changes.
4. Understand how to account for retroactive accounting changes.
5. Understand how to account for changes to LIFO.
6. Describe the accounting for changes in estimates.
7. Identify changes in a reporting entity.
8. Describe the accounting for correction of errors.
9. Identify economic motives for changing accounting methods.
10. Analyze the effect of errors.

Readers of the financial press regularly see headlines such as the following which announce accounting changes and related events:

"Accounting Change at Mobil Makes First-Quarter Profit a $145 Million Loss"

"Westvaco Reports Three Accounting Changes"

"Flagstar Restates Financial Results"

"Aeronautical Company Revises Estimates of Service Lives of Boeing 747s"

"J.P. Stevens, Inc. Changes to LIFO Method of Determining Inventory Cost"

Why do these changes in accounting occur? First, the accounting profession may **mandate** the use of a new accounting method or principle. For example, in 1992 the FASB began requiring the recognition of postretirement benefit expenses on an accrual basis. Second, **changing economic conditions** may cause a company to change its methods of accounting. Significant inflation at one time prompted many companies to switch from FIFO to LIFO. Third, **changes in technology** and in operations may require a company to revise the service lives, depreciation method, or the expected salvage value of depreciable assets. AT&T changed its estimates and depreciation methods as a result of changes in its competitive environment and in telecommunications technology.

The accountant also faces the need to make accounting changes when accounting errors are discovered. How should such errors be corrected and disclosed so that the usefulness of the financial information is enhanced? In this chapter we discuss the different types of accounting changes and error corrections and the procedures for handling them in the financial statements.

UNDERLYING CONCEPT

While the qualitative characteristic of **usefulness** *may be enhanced by changes in accounting, the characteristics of* **comparability** *and* **consistency** *may be adversely affected.*

► ACCOUNTING CHANGES

Before the issuance of *APB Opinion No. 20,* "Accounting Changes," companies had considerable flexibility to use alternative accounting treatments for essentially equivalent situations. When steel companies changed their methods of depreciating plant assets from accelerated to straight-line depreciation, the effect of the change was presented in many different ways. The cumulative difference between the depreciation charges that had been recorded and what would have been recorded could have been reported in the income statement of the period of the change. Or, the change could have been ignored, and the undepreciated asset balance simply depreciated on a straight-line basis in the future. Or, companies could have restated the prior periods on the basis that the straight-line approach had always been used.

TYPES OF ACCOUNTING CHANGES

OBJECTIVE 1

Identify the types of accounting changes.

When accounting alternatives exist, comparability of the statements between periods and between companies is diminished and useful historical trend data are obscured. The profession's first step in this area, then, was to establish categories for the different types of changes and corrections that occur in practice.[1] The three types of accounting changes are:

1. **Change in Accounting Principle.** A change from one generally accepted accounting principle to another generally accepted accounting principle: for example, a change in the method of depreciation from double-declining to straight-line depreciation of plant assets.

2. **Change in Accounting Estimate.** A change that occurs as the result of new information or as additional experience is acquired. An example is a change in the estimate of the useful lives of depreciable assets.

3. **Change in Reporting Entity.** A change from reporting as one type of entity to another type of entity: for example, changing specific subsidiaries that constitute the group of companies for which consolidated financial statements are prepared.[2]

A fourth category necessitates changes in the accounting, though it is not classified as an accounting change.

4. **Errors in Financial Statements.** Errors occur as a result of mathematical mistakes, mistakes in the application of accounting principles, or oversight or misuse of facts that existed at the time financial statements were prepared. An example is the incorrect application of the retail inventory method for determining the final inventory value.

Changes were classified in these four categories because the individual characteristics of each category necessitate different methods of recognizing these changes in the financial statements. Each of these items is discussed separately to investigate its unusual characteristics and to determine how each item should be reported in the accounts and how the information should be disclosed in comparative statements.

---

[1]"Accounting Changes," *Opinions of the Accounting Principles Board No. 20* (New York: AICPA, 1971).

[2]*Accounting Trends and Techniques—1993* in its survey of 600 annual reports identified the following specific types of accounting changes reported:

Pension costs (actuarial assumptions)	121
Income taxes (due to issuance of *FASB No. 109*)	244
Reporting entity	5
Inventory method changes	9
Postretirement and postemployment benefits (*FASB No. 112*)	219
Depreciation-related changes	3
Others	17

▶ CHANGES IN ACCOUNTING PRINCIPLE

A change in accounting principle involves a change from one generally accepted accounting principle to another. For example, a company might change the basis of inventory pricing from average cost to LIFO. Or it might change the method of depreciation on plant assets from accelerated to straight-line, or vice versa. Yet another change might be from the completed-contract to percentage-of-completion method of accounting for construction contracts.

A careful examination must be made in each circumstance to ensure that a change in principle has actually occurred. **A change in accounting principle is not considered to result from the adoption of a new principle in recognition of events that have occurred for the first time or that were previously immaterial.** For example, when a depreciation method that is adopted for **newly** acquired plant assets is different from the method or methods used for **previously recorded** assets of a similar class, a change in accounting principle has **not occurred.** Certain marketing expenditures that were previously immaterial and expensed in the period incurred may become material and acceptably deferred and amortized without a change in accounting principle occurring.

Finally, **if the accounting principle previously followed was not acceptable, or if the principle was applied incorrectly, a change to a generally accepted accounting principle is considered a correction of an error.** A switch from the cash or income tax basis of accounting to the accrual basis is considered a correction of an error. If the company deducted salvage value when computing double-declining depreciation on plant assets and later recomputed depreciation without deduction of estimated salvage value, an error is corrected.

Three approaches have been suggested for reporting changes in accounting principles in the accounts:

Retroactively. The cumulative effect of the use of the new method on the financial statements at the beginning of the period is computed. A **retroactive adjustment** of the financial statements is then made, recasting the financial statements of prior years on a basis consistent with the newly adopted principle. Advocates of this position argue that only by restatement of prior periods can changes in accounting principles lead to comparable financial statements. If this approach is not used, the year previous to the change will be on the old method; the year of the change will report the entire cumulative adjustment in income; and the following year will present financial statements on the new basis without the cumulative effect of the change. Consistency is considered essential in providing meaningful earnings-trend data and other financial relationships necessary to evaluate the business.

Currently. The cumulative effect of the use of the new method on the financial statements at the beginning of the period is computed. This adjustment is then reported in the current year's income statement as a **special item** between the captions "Extraordinary items" and "Net income." Advocates of this position argue that restating financial statements for prior years results in a loss of confidence by investors in financial reports. How will a present or prospective investor react when told that the earnings computed 5 years ago are now entirely different? Restatement, if permitted, also might upset many contractual and other arrangements that were based on the old figures. For example, profit-sharing arrangements computed on the old basis might have to be recomputed and completely new distributions made, which might create numerous legal problems. Many practical difficulties also exist; the cost of restatement may be excessive, or restatement may be impossible on the basis of data available.

Prospectively (in the future). Previously reported results remain; no change is made. Opening balances are not adjusted, and no attempt is made to allocate charges or credits for prior events. Advocates of this position argue that once management presents to investors and to others financial statements based on acceptable accounting principles, they are final; management cannot change prior periods by adopting a new principle. According to this line of reasoning, the cumulative adjustment in the current year is not appropriate, because such an approach includes amounts that have little or no relationship to the current year's income or economic events.

Before the adoption of *APB Opinion No. 20,* all three of the approaches above were used. *APB Opinion No. 20,* however, settled this issue by establishing guidelines for changes depending on the type of change in accounting principle involved. We have classified these changes in accounting principle into three categories:

OBJECTIVE 2
Describe the accounting for changes in accounting principles.

INTERNATIONAL INSIGHT

Australia, France, and Japan account for changes in accounting principles by making adjustments to current period income and disclosing the effects of adjustments on current and/or prior period income.

1. Cumulative-effect type accounting change.
2. Retroactive-effect type accounting change.
3. Change to the LIFO method of inventory.

CUMULATIVE-EFFECT TYPE ACCOUNTING CHANGE

The general requirement established by the profession was that the **current, or "catch-up," method should be used to account for changes in accounting principles.** The general requirements are as follows:

1. The current or catch-up approach should be employed. The **cumulative effect** of the adjustment should be reported in the income statement between the captions "extraordinary items" and "net income."

2. Financial statements for prior periods included for comparative purposes should not be restated.

3. Income before extraordinary items and net income, computed on a **pro-forma (as if) basis** should be shown on the face of the income statement for all periods. They are presented **as if the newly adopted principle had been applied during all periods affected.** Related earnings per share data should also be reported. The reader, then, has some understanding of how restated financial statements appear.[3]

Illustration

Assume that Lang Inc. decided at the beginning of 1996 to change from the sum-of-the-years'-digits method of depreciation to the straight-line method for financial reporting for its buildings. For tax purposes, the company has employed the straight-line method and will continue to do so. The assets originally cost $120,000 in 1994 and have an estimated useful life of 15 years. The data assumed for this illustration are:

**ILLUSTRATION 23-1
Data for Change in Depreciation Method**

Year	Sum-of-the-Years'-Digits Depreciation	Straight-Line Depreciation	Difference	Tax Effect 40%	Effect on Income (net of tax)
1994	$15,000[a]	$ 8,000[b]	$ 7,000	$2,800	$4,200
1995	14,000	8,000	6,000	2,400	3,600
	$29,000	$16,000	$13,000	$5,200	$7,800

[a]$120,000 × $\frac{15}{120}$ = $15,000. [b]$120,000 ÷ 15 = $8,000.

Lang Inc. has income before extraordinary items and cumulative effect of changes in accounting principle of $130,000 in 1996 and $111,000 in 1995. Also Lang Inc. has an extraordinary loss (net of tax) of $30,000 in 1996 and an extraordinary gain (net of tax) of $10,000 in 1995.

Journal Entry

Although the journal entry can be made any time during the year, it is effective **as of the beginning of the year.** The entry made to record this change to straight-line depreciation in 1996 should be:

Accumulated Depreciation	13,000	
Deferred Tax Asset		5,200
Cumulative Effect of Change in Accounting Principle—Depreciation		7,800

---

[3]Ibid., par. 21.

The debit of $13,000 to Accumulated Depreciation is the excess of the sum-of-the-years'-digits depreciation over the straight-line depreciation. The credit to the Deferred Tax Asset of $5,200 is recorded to eliminate this account from the financial statements. Prior to the change in accounting principle, sum-of-the-years'-digits was used for book but not tax purposes, which gave rise to a debit balance in the Deferred Tax Asset account of $5,200. The cumulative effect on income resulting from the difference between sum-of-the-years'-digits depreciation and straight-line depreciation is reduced by the tax effect on that difference. Now that the company intends to use the straight-line method for both tax and book purposes, no deferred income taxes related to depreciation should exist and the Deferred Tax Asset account should be eliminated.

Income Statement Presentation

The cumulative effect of the change in accounting principle should be reported on the income statement between the captions "Extraordinary items" and "Net income." The cumulative effect is not an extraordinary item but is reported on a net-of-tax basis similar to that used for extraordinary items. The information is shown in Illustration 23-2.

	1996	1995
Income before extraordinary item and cumulative effect of a		
change in accounting principles	$130,000	$111,000
Extraordinary item, net of tax	(30,000)	10,000
Cumulative effect on prior years of retroactive application of		
new depreciation method, net of tax	7,800	
Net income	$107,800	$121,000
Per share amounts		
Earnings per share (10,000 shares)		
Income before extraordinary item and cumulative effect of		
a change in accounting principle	$13.00	$11.10
Extraordinary item	(3.00)	1.00
Cumulative effect on prior years of retroactive application of		
new depreciation method	.78	
Net income	$10.78	$12.10

ILLUSTRATION 23-2
Income Statement without Pro Forma Amounts

Note that depreciation expense for 1996 is computed on the straight-line basis.

Pro-Forma Amounts

Pro-forma amounts permit financial statements users to determine the net income that would have been shown if the newly adopted principle had been in effect in earlier periods. In other words, how would Lang Inc.'s income be reported if the straight-line method had been used in 1995? To determine this amount, the prior year (1995) is restated, assuming that the straight-line method is used. The computation is as follows:

UNDERLYING CONCEPT

The pro-forma treatment attempts to restore the comparability of the income statements.

Income before extraordinary item (1995) not restated	$111,000
Excess of sum-of-the-years-digits depreciation over straight-line depreciation	3,600
Pro-forma income before extraordinary item (1995)	$114,600

ILLUSTRATION 23-3
Computation of Pro-Forma Income, 1995

This and other information is shown on the face of the income statement as follows:

ILLUSTRATION 23-4
Income Statement with Pro-Forma Amounts

Pro-forma (as if) amounts, assuming retroactive application of new depreciation method:		
	1996	1995
Income before extraordinary item	$130,000	$114,600
Earnings per common share	$13.00	$11.46
Net income	$100,000[a]	$124,600[b]
Earnings per common share	$10.00	$12.46

[a]($130,000 − $30,000 = $100,000)
[b]($114,600 + $10,000 = $124,600)

The $130,000 of 1996 income before extraordinary item needs no restatement like the 1995 income because the new straight-line method of depreciation is used in 1996.

Pro-forma information is useful to individuals interested in assessing the trend of earnings over a period of time. Pro-forma information, which is only shown as supplementary information, may be reported in the income statement, in a separate schedule, or in the notes to the financial statements.

The pro-forma amounts should include both (1) the direct effects of a change and (2) nondiscretionary adjustments in items based on income before taxes or net income (such as profit-sharing expense and certain royalties) that would have been recognized if the newly adopted principle had been followed in prior periods; related income tax effects should be recognized for both (1) and (2). If an income statement is presented for the current period only, the actual and pro-forma amounts (including earnings per share) for the immediately preceding period should be disclosed.

Summary Illustration

Illustration 23-5 indicates how this information is presented on the income statement.[4] The appropriate note disclosure is also provided.

**ILLUSTRATION 23-5
Cumulative-Effect Type
Accounting Change**

CUMULATIVE-EFFECT TYPE ACCOUNTING CHANGE
Reporting the Change in Two-Year Comparative Statements

	1996	1995
Income before extraordinary item and cumulative effect of a change in accounting principles	$130,000	$111,000
Extraordinary item, net of tax	(30,000)	10,000
Cumulative effect on prior years of retroactive application of new depreciation method, net of tax (Note A)	7,800	
Net income	$107,800	$121,000
Per share amounts		
Earnings per share (10,000 shares)		
Income before extraordinary item and cumulative effect of a change in accounting principle	$13.00	$11.10
Extraordinary item	(3.00)	1.00
Cumulative effect on prior years of retroactive application of new depreciation method	.78	
Net income	$10.78	$12.10

Pro-forma (as if) amounts, assuming retroactive application of new depreciation method:

	1996	1995
Income before extraordinary item	$130,000	$114,600
Earnings per common share	$13.00	$11.46
Net income	$100,000	$124,600
Earnings per common share	$10.00	$12.46

Note A: Change in Depreciation Method for Plant Assets. In 1996 depreciation of plant assets is computed by use of the straight-line method. In prior years, beginning in 1994, depreciation of buildings was computed by the sum-of-the-years'-digits method. The new method of depreciation was adopted in recognition of . . . (state justification for the change of depreciation method) . . . and has been applied retroactively to building acquisitions of prior years to determine the cumulative effect. The effect of the change in 1996 was to increase income before extraordinary item by approximately $3,000 (or 30 cents per share). The adjustment necessary for retroactive application of the new method, amounting to $7,800, is included in income of 1996. The pro-forma amounts shown on the income statement have been adjusted for the effect of retroactive application on depreciation, and the pro-forma effect for related income taxes.

---

[4]In practice, three-year comparative income statements are prepared. For reasons of simplicity we have presented two-year comparatives.

RETROACTIVE-EFFECT TYPE ACCOUNTING CHANGE

In certain circumstances, a change in accounting principle may be handled retroactively. Under the retroactive treatment the cumulative effect of the new method on the financial statements at the beginning of the period is computed. A retroactive adjustment of the financial statements presented is made by **recasting the statements of prior years on a basis consistent with the newly adopted principle. Any part of the cumulative effect attributable to years prior to those presented is treated as an adjustment of beginning retained earnings of the earliest year presented.** In such situations, the nature of and justification for the change and the effect on net income and related per share amounts should be disclosed for each period presented. The five situations that require the restatement of all prior period financial statements are:

OBJECTIVE 4
Understand how to account for retroactive accounting changes.

1. A change from the LIFO inventory valuation method to another method.

2. A change in the method of accounting for long-term construction-type contracts.

3. A change to or from the "full-cost" method of accounting in the extractive industries.

4. Issuance of financial statements by a company for the first time to obtain additional equity capital, to effect a business combination, or to register securities. (This procedure may be used only by closely held companies and then only once.)

5. A professional pronouncement recommends that a change in accounting principle be treated retroactively. For example, *FASB No. 11* requires that retroactive treatment be given for changes in "Accounting for Contingencies" and *FASB Statement No. 73* requires retroactive treatment for a change from retirement-replacement-betterment accounting to depreciation accounting.[5]

Why did the profession provide for these exceptions? Though the reasons are varied, the major one is that reporting the cumulative adjustment in the period of the change might have such a large effect on net income that the income figure would be misleading. A perfect illustration is the experience of Chrysler Corporation when it changed its inventory accounting from LIFO to FIFO. If the change had been handled currently, Chrysler would have had to report a $53,500,000 adjustment to net income, which would have resulted in net income of $45,900,000 instead of a net loss of $7,600,000.

As another illustration, in the early 1980s the railroad industry switched from the retirement-replacement method of depreciating railroad equipment to a more generally used method such as straight-line depreciation. Cumulative effect treatment meant that a substantial adjustment would be made to income in the period of change. Many in the railroad industry argued that the adjustment was so large that to include the cumulative effect in the current year instead of restating prior years would distort the information and make it less useful. Such situations lend support to restatement so that comparability is not seriously affected.

To illustrate the retroactive method, assume that Denson Construction Co. has accounted for its income from long-term construction contracts using the completed-contract method. In 1996, the company changed to the percentage-of-completion method because management believes that this approach provides a more appropriate measure of the income earned. For tax purposes (assume a 40% enacted tax rate), the company has employed the completed-contract method and plans to continue using this method in the future.

---

[5]"Accounting for Contingencies—Transition Method," *Statement of the Financial Accounting Standards Board No. 11* (Stamford, Conn.: FASB, 1975); "Reporting a Change in Accounting for Railroad Track Structures," *Statement of the Financial Accounting Standards Board No. 73* (Stamford, Conn.: FASB, 1983); Note that the FASB standard on "Accounting for Income Taxes" permits the company to use either the cumulative effect approach or the retroactive method in changing from the deferred method to the asset-liability method. In addition, if the company elects the cumulative effect approach, pro-forma amounts are not required because of the cost and difficulty of developing this information.

The following information is available for analysis:

ILLUSTRATION 23-6
Data for Change in Accounting for Long-Term Construction Contracts

| | | Pretax Income from | | Difference in Income | | |
		Percentage-of-Completion	Completed-Contract	Difference	Tax Effect 40%	Income Effect (net of tax)
Year						
Prior to	1995	$600,000	$400,000	$200,000	$80,000	$120,000
In	1995	180,000	160,000	20,000	8,000	12,000
Total at beginning of	1996	$780,000	$560,000	$220,000	$88,000	$132,000
In	1996	$200,000	$190,000	$ 10,000	$ 4,000	$ 6,000

The entry to record the change in 1996 would be:

Construction in Process	220,000	
Deferred Tax Liability		88,000
Retained Earnings		132,000

The Construction in Process account is increased by $220,000, representing the adjustment in prior years' income of $132,000 and the adjustment in prior years' tax expense of $88,000. The Deferred Tax Liability account is used to recognize a tax liability for future taxable amounts. That is, in future periods taxable income will be higher than book income as a result of current temporary differences, and, therefore, a deferred tax liability must be reported in the current year.

The bottom portion of the income statement for Denson Construction Co., **before giving effect to the retroactive change in accounting principle,** would be as follows:

ILLUSTRATION 23-7
Income Statement before Retroactive Change

Income Statement	1996	1995
Net income	$114,000[a]	$96,000[a]
Per Share Amounts		
Earnings per share (100,000 shares)	$1.14	$.96

[a]The net income for the two periods is computed as follows:
1996 $190,000 − .40 ($190,000) = $114,000
1995 $160,000 − .40 ($160,000) = $96,000

Assuming a retained earnings balance of $1,600,000 at the beginning of 1995, the retained earnings statement **before giving effect to the retroactive change in accounting principle,** would appear as follows:

ILLUSTRATION 23-8
Retained Earnings Statement before Retroactive Change

STATEMENT OF RETAINED EARNINGS		
	1996	1995
Balance at beginning of year	$1,696,000	$1,600,000
Net income	114,000	96,000
Balance at end of year	$1,810,000	$1,696,000

The bottom portion of the income statement for Denson Construction Co., **after giving effect to the retroactive change in accounting principle,** would be as follows:

ILLUSTRATION 23-9
Income Statement after Retroactive Change

Income Statement	1996	1995
Net income	$120,000[a]	$108,000[a]
Per Share Amounts		
Earnings per share (100,000 shares)	$1.20	$1.08

[a]The net income for the two periods is computed as follows:
1996 $200,000 − .40 ($200,000) = $120,000
1995 $180,000 − .40 ($180,000) = $108,000

Note that the 2-year comparative statement (Illustration 23-9) has a major difference from the earlier 2-year comparative statement (Illustration 23-5). No pro-forma information is necessary when changes in accounting principles are handled retroactively, because the income numbers for previous periods are restated.

The adjustment for the effect of the accounting change would be reported in the statement of retained earnings in comparative form as follows:

STATEMENT OF RETAINED EARNINGS		
	1996	1995
Balance at beginning of year, as previously reported	$1,696,000	$1,600,000
Add adjustment for the cumulative effect on prior years of applying retroactively the new method of accounting for long-term contracts (Note A)	132,000	120,000
Balance at beginning of year, as adjusted	1,828,000	1,720,000
Net income	120,000	108,000
Balance at end of year	$1,948,000	$1,828,000

Note A: Change in Method of Accounting for Long-Term Contracts. The company has accounted for revenue and costs for long-term construction contracts by the percentage-of-completion method in 1996, whereas in all prior years revenue and costs were determined by the completed-contract method. The new method of accounting for long-term contracts was adopted to recognize . . . (state justification for change in accounting principle) . . . and financial statements of prior years have been restated to apply the new method retroactively. For income tax purposes, the completed-contract method has been continued. The effect of the accounting change on income of 1996 was an increase of $6,000 net of related taxes and on income of 1995 as previously reported was an increase of $12,000 net of related taxes. The balances of retained earnings for 1995 and 1996 have been adjusted for the effect of applying retroactively the new method of accounting.

ILLUSTRATION 23-10
Retained Earnings Statement after Retroactive Change

An expanded retained earnings statement is included in this 2-year comparative presentation to indicate the type of adjustment that is needed to restate the beginning balance of retained earnings. In 1995, the beginning balance was adjusted for the excess of the percentage-of-completion income over the completed-contract income prior to 1995 ($120,000). In 1996, the beginning balance was adjusted for the $120,000 cumulative difference plus the additional $12,000 for 1995.

No such adjustments are necessary when the current or catch-up method is employed, because the cumulative effect of the change on net income is reported in the income statement of the current year and no prior period reports are restated. It is ordinarily appropriate to prepare a retained earnings statement when presenting comparative statements regardless of what type of accounting change is involved; an illustration was provided for the retroactive method only to explain the additional computations required.

CHANGE TO LIFO METHOD

The profession generally requires that the cumulative effect of any accounting change should be shown in the income statement between "extraordinary items" and "net income," except for the conditions mentioned in the preceding section. In addition, this rule does not apply when a company changes to the LIFO method of inventory valuation. In such a situation, **the base-year inventory for all subsequent LIFO calculations is the opening inventory in the year the method is adopted. There is no restatement of prior years' income because it is just too impractical.** A restatement to LIFO would be subject to assumptions as to the different years that the layers were established, and these assumptions would ordinarily result in the computation of a number of different earnings figures. The only adjustment necessary may be to restate the beginning inventory to a cost basis from a lower of cost or market approach. This type of adjustment was discussed in Appendix 9-A.

OBJECTIVE 5
Understand how to account for changes to LIFO.

Disclosure then is limited to showing the effect of the change on the results of operations in the period of change. Also the reasons for omitting the computations of the cumulative effect and the pro-forma amounts for prior years should be explained. Finally, the company should disclose the justification for the change to LIFO. The Annual Report of the Quaker Oats Company indicates the type of disclosure necessary.

ILLUSTRATION 23-11
Disclosure of Change
to LIFO

The Quaker Oats Company

Note 1 (In Part): Summary of Significant Accounting Policies

Inventories. Inventories are valued at the lower of cost or market, using various cost methods, and include the cost of raw materials, labor and overhead. The percentage of year-end inventories valued using each of the methods is as follows:

June 30	1989	1988	1987
Average quarterly cost	21%	54%	52%
Last-in, first-out (LIFO)	65%	29%	31%
First-in, first-out (FIFO)	14%	17%	17%

Effective July 1, 1988, the Company adopted the LIFO cost flow assumption for valuing the majority of remaining U.S. Grocery Products inventories. The Company believes that the use of the LIFO method better matches current costs with current revenues. The cumulative effect of this change on retained earnings at the beginning of the year is not determinable, nor are the pro-forma effects of retroactive application of LIFO to prior years. The effect of this change on fiscal 1989 was to decrease net income by $16.0 million, or $.20 per share.

If the LIFO method of valuing certain inventories were not used, total inventories would have been $60.1 million, $24.0 million and $14.6 million higher than reported at June 30, 1989, 1988, and 1987, respectively.

In practice, many companies defer the formal adoption of LIFO until year-end. Management thus has an opportunity to assess the impact that a change to LIFO will have on the financial statements and to evaluate the desirability of a change for tax purposes. As indicated in Chapter 8, many companies change to LIFO because of the advantages of this inventory valuation method in a period of inflation.

► CHANGES IN ACCOUNTING ESTIMATE

OBJECTIVE 6

Describe the accounting for changes in estimates.

The preparation of financial statements requires estimating the effects of future conditions and events. The following are examples of items that require estimates:

1. Uncollectible receivables.
2. Inventory obsolescence.
3. Useful lives and salvage values of assets.
4. Periods benefited by deferred costs.
5. Liabilities for warranty costs and income taxes.
6. Recoverable mineral reserves.

Future conditions and events and their effects cannot be perceived with certainty; therefore, estimating requires the exercise of judgment. Accounting estimates will change as new events occur, as more experience is acquired, or as additional information is obtained.

Changes in estimates must be handled prospectively. That is, no changes should be made in previously reported results. Opening balances are not adjusted, and no attempt is made to "catch-up" for prior periods. Financial statements of prior periods are not restated, and pro-forma amounts for prior periods are not reported. Instead, the effects of all changes in estimate are accounted for in (1) the period of change if the change affects that period only or (2) the period of change and future periods if the change affects both. As a result, changes in estimates are viewed as **normal recurring corrections and adjustments,** the natural result of the accounting process, and retroactive treatment is prohibited.

The circumstances related to a change in estimate are different from those surrounding a change in accounting principle. If changes in estimates were handled on a retroactive basis, or on a cumulative-effect basis, continual adjustments of prior years' income would occur. It seems proper to accept the view that because new conditions or circumstances exist, the revision fits the new situation and should be handled in the current and future periods.

To illustrate, Underwriters Labs, Inc. purchased a building for $300,000 which was originally estimated to have a useful life of 15 years and no salvage value. Depreciation has been recorded for 5 years on a straight-line basis. On January 1, 1996, the estimate of the useful life is revised so that the asset is considered to have a total life of 25 years. Assume that the useful life for financial reporting and tax purposes is the same. The accounts at the beginning of the sixth year are as follows:

INTERNATIONAL INSIGHT

In most nations changes in accounting estimates are treated prospectively. International differences occur in the degree of disclosure required.

Building	$300,000
Less: Accumulated Depreciation—Building (5 × $20,000)	100,000
Book value of building	$200,000

ILLUSTRATION 23-12
Book Value after 5 Years' Depreciation

The entry to record depreciation for the year 1996 is:

Depreciation Expense	10,000	
Accumulated Depreciation—Building		10,000

The $10,000 depreciation charge is computed as follows:

$$\text{Depreciation charge} = \frac{\text{Book value of asset}}{\text{Remaining service life}} = \frac{\$200,000}{25 \text{ years} - 5 \text{ years}} = \$10,000$$

ILLUSTRATION 23-13
Depreciation after Change in Estimate

The disclosure of a change in estimated useful lives and salvage value appeared in the Annual Report of Ampco–Pittsburgh Corporation.

ILLUSTRATION 23-14
Disclosure of Change in Estimated Useful Lives

Ampco–Pittsburgh Corporation

Note 11: Change in Accounting Estimate. Effective January 1, 1992, the Corporation revised its estimate of the useful lives of certain machinery and equipment. Previously, all machinery and equipment, whether new when placed in use or not, were in one class and depreciated over 15 years. The change principally applies to assets purchased new when placed in use. Those lives are now extended to 20 years. These changes were made to better reflect the estimated periods during which such assets will remain in service. The change had the effect of reducing depreciation expense and increasing net income by approximately $991,000 ($.10 per share).

Differentiating between a change in an estimate and a change in an accounting principle is sometimes difficult. Is it a change in principle or a change in estimate when a company changes from deferring and amortizing certain marketing costs to recording them as an expense as incurred because future benefits of the cost have become doubtful? In such a case, **whenever it is impossible to determine whether a change in principle or a change in estimate has occurred, the change should be considered a change in estimate.**

A similar problem occurs in differentiating between a change in estimate and a correction of an error, although the answer is more clear cut. How do we determine whether the information was overlooked in earlier periods (an error) or whether the information is now available for the first time (change in estimate)? Proper classification is important because corrections of errors have a different accounting treatment from that given changes in estimates. The general rule is that **careful estimates that later prove to be incorrect should be considered changes in estimate.** Only when the estimate was obviously computed incorrectly because of lack of expertise or in bad faith should the adjustment be considered an error. There is no clear demarcation line here and the accountant must use good judgment in light of all the circumstances.[6]

▶ REPORTING A CHANGE IN ENTITY

OBJECTIVE 7

Identify changes in a reporting entity.

An accounting change that results in financial statements that are actually the statements of a different entity should be reported by **restating the financial statements of all prior periods presented,** to show the financial information for the new reporting entity for all periods.

Examples of a change in reporting entity are:

1. Presenting consolidated statements in place of statements of individual companies.
2. Changing specific subsidiaries that constitute the group of companies for which consolidated financial statements are presented.
3. Changing the companies included in combined financial statements.
4. Accounting for a pooling of interests.
5. A change in the cost, equity, or consolidation method of accounting for subsidiaries and investments. A change in the reporting entity does not result from creation, cessation, purchase, or disposition of a subsidiary or other business unit.

The financial statements of the year in which the change in reporting entity is made should disclose the nature of the change and the reason for it. The effect of the change on income before extraordinary items, net income, and earnings per share amounts should be reported for all periods presented. These disclosures need not be repeated in subsequent periods' financial statements. The Annual Report of Hewlett-Packard Company illustrates a note disclosing a change in reporting entity.

ILLUSTRATION 23-15
Disclosure of Change in Reporting Entity

Hewlett-Packard Company

Note: Accounting and Reporting Changes (in part)

Consolidation of Hewlett-Packard Finance Company. The company implemented Statement of Financial Accounting Standards No. 94 (SFAS 94), "Consolidation of All Majority-owned Subsidiaries." With the adoption of SFAS 94, the company consolidated the accounts of Hewlett-Packard Finance Company (HPFC), a wholly owned subsidiary previously accounted for under the equity method, with those of the company. The change resulted in an increase in consolidated assets and liabilities but did not have a material effect on the company's financial position. Since HPFC was previously accounted for under the equity method, the change did not affect net earnings. Prior years' consolidated financial information has been restated to reflect this change for comparative purposes.

▶ REPORTING A CORRECTION OF AN ERROR

OBJECTIVE 8

Describe the accounting for correction of errors.

APB Opinion No. 20 also discussed how a **correction of an error** should be handled in the financial statements. (No authoritative guidelines existed previously.) The conclusions of *APB Opinion No. 20* were reaffirmed in *FASB Statement No. 16.*[7] No business,

---

[6]In evaluating reasonableness, the auditor should use one or a combination of the following approaches:

(a) Review and test the process used by management to develop the estimate.
(b) Develop an independent expectation of the estimate to corroborate the reasonableness of management's estimate.
(c) Review subsequent events or transactions occurring prior to completion of fieldwork. "Auditing Accounting Estimates," *Statement on Auditing Standards No. 57* (New York: AICPA, 1988).

[7]"Prior Period Adjustments," *Statement of Financial Accounting Standards No. 16* (Stamford, Conn.: FASB, 1977), p. 5.

large or small, is immune from errors. The risk of material errors, however, may be reduced through the installation of good internal control and the application of sound accounting procedures.

The following are examples of accounting errors:

1. A change from an accounting principle that is **not** generally accepted to an accounting principle that is acceptable. The rationale adopted is that the prior periods were incorrectly presented because of the application of an improper accounting principle. Example: a change from the cash or income tax basis of accounting to the accrual basis.

2. Mathematical mistakes that result from adding, subtracting, and so on. Example: the totaling of the inventory count sheets incorrectly in computing the inventory value.

3. Changes in estimate that occur because the estimates are not prepared in good faith. Example: the adoption of a clearly unrealistic depreciation rate.

4. An oversight, such as the failure to accrue or defer certain expenses and revenues at the end of the period.

5. A misuse of facts, such as the failure to use salvage value in computing the depreciation base for the straight-line approach.

6. The incorrect classification of a cost as an expense instead of an asset and vice versa.

> **INTERNATIONAL INSIGHT**
>
> *Denmark, France, Japan, and the Netherlands account for prior period adjustments in current period income.*

As soon as they are discovered, errors must be corrected by proper entries in the accounts and reported in the financial statements. **The profession requires that corrections of errors be treated as prior period adjustments,** be recorded in the year in which the error was discovered, and be reported in the financial statements as an adjustment to the beginning balance of retained earnings. If comparative statements are presented, the prior statements affected should be restated to correct for the error. The disclosures need not be repeated in the financial statements of subsequent periods.

To illustrate, in 1996 the bookkeeper for Selectric Company discovered that in 1995 the company failed to record in the accounts $20,000 of depreciation expense on a newly constructed building. The depreciation is correctly included in the tax return. Because of numerous temporary differences, reported net income for 1995 was $150,000 and taxable income was $110,000. The following entry was made for income taxes (assume a 40% effective tax rate in 1995):

Income Tax Expense	60,000	
Income Tax Payable		44,000
Deferred Tax Liability		16,000

As a result of the $20,000 omission error in 1995:

Depreciation expense (1995) **was** understated	$20,000
Accumulated depreciation **is** understated	20,000
Income tax expense (1995) **was** overstated ($20,000 × 40%)	8,000
Net income (1995) **was** overstated	12,000
Deferred tax liability **is** overstated ($20,000 × 40%)	8,000

The entry made in 1996 to correct the omission of $20,000 of depreciation in 1995 would be:

1996 Correcting Entry

Retained Earnings	12,000	
Deferred Tax Liability	8,000	
Accumulated Depreciation—Buildings		20,000

The journal entry to record the correction of the error is the same whether single-period or comparative financial statements are prepared; however, presentation on the financial statements will differ. If single-period (noncomparative) statements are presented, the error should be reported as an adjustment to the opening balance of retained earnings of the period in which the error is discovered (see Illustration 23-16).

ILLUSTRATION 23-16
Reporting an Error—
Single-Period Financial
Statement

Retained earnings, January 1, 1996:		
As previously reported		$350,000
Correction of an error (depreciation)	$20,000	
Less applicable income tax reduction	8,000	(12,000)
Adjusted balance of retained earnings, January 1, 1996		338,000
Add net income 1996		400,000
Retained earnings, December 31, 1996		$738,000

If comparative financial statements are prepared, adjustments should be made to correct the amounts for all affected accounts reported in the statements for all periods reported. The data for each year being presented should be restated to the correct basis, and any **catch-up adjustment should be shown as a prior period adjustment to retained earnings** for the earliest period being reported. For example, in the case of Selectric Company, the error of omitting the depreciation of $20,000 in 1995, which was discovered in 1996, results in the restatement of the 1995 financial statements when presented in comparison with those of 1996. The following accounts in the 1995 financial statements (presented in comparison with those of 1996) would have been restated:

ILLUSTRATION 23-17
Reporting an Error—
Comparative Financial
Statements

In the balance sheet:

Accumulated depreciation—buildings	$20,000 increase
Deferred tax liability	$ 8,000 decrease
Retained earnings, ending balance	$12,000 decrease

In the income statement:

Depreciation expense—buildings	$20,000 increase
Tax expense	$ 8,000 decrease
Net income	$12,000 decrease

In the statement of retained earnings:

Retained earnings, ending balance (due to lower net income for the period)	$12,000 decrease

The 1996 financial statements in comparative form with those of 1995 are prepared as if the error had not occurred. As a minimum, such comparative statements in 1996 would include a note in the financial statements calling attention to restatement of the 1995 statements and disclosing the effect of the correction on income before extraordinary items, net income, and the related per share amounts.

▶ SUMMARY OF ACCOUNTING CHANGES AND CORRECTIONS OF ERRORS

The development of guidelines in reporting accounting changes and corrections has helped resolve several significant and long-standing accounting problems. Yet, because of diversity in situations and characteristics of the items encountered in practice, the application of professional judgment is of paramount importance. In applying these guidelines, the primary objective is to serve the user of the financial statements; achieving such service requires accuracy, full disclosure,[8] and an absence of misleading in-

---

[8]A change in accounting principle, a change in the reporting entity (special type of change in accounting principle), and a correction of an error involving a change in accounting principle require an explanatory paragraph in the auditor's report discussing lack of consistency from one period to the next. A change in accounting estimate does not affect the auditor's opinion relative to consistency; however, if the estimate change has a material effect on the financial statements, disclosure may still be required. Error correction not involving a change in accounting principle does not require disclosure relative to consistency.

ferences. The principal distinction and treatments presented in the earlier discussion are summarized below.

ILLUSTRATION 23-18
Summary of Guidelines for Accounting Changes and Errors

1. **Changes in accounting principle.**
   General Rule:
   Employ the current or catch-up approach by:
   a. Reporting current results on the new basis.
   b. Reporting the cumulative effect of the adjustment in the current income statement between the captions "extraordinary items" and "net income."
   c. Presenting prior period financial statements as previously reported.
   d. Presenting pro-forma data on income and earnings per share for all prior periods presented.
   Exceptions:
   Employ the retroactive approach by:
   a. Restating the financial statements of all prior periods presented.
   b. Disclosing in the year of the change the effect on net income and earnings per share for all prior periods presented.
   c. Reporting an adjustment to the beginning retained earnings balance in the statement of retained earnings.
   Employ the change to LIFO approach by:
   a. Not restating prior years' income.
   b. Using opening inventory in the year the method is adopted as the base-year inventory for all subsequent LIFO computations.
   c. Disclosing the effect of the change on the current year, and the reasons for omitting the computation of the cumulative effect and pro-forma amounts for prior years.

2. **Changes in accounting estimate.**
   Employ the current and prospective approach by:
   a. Reporting current and future financial statements on the new basis.
   b. Presenting prior period financial statements as previously reported.
   c. Making no adjustments to current period opening balances for purposes of catch-up, and making no pro-forma presentations.

3. **Changes in reporting entity.**
   Employ the retroactive approach by:
   a. Restating the financial statements of all prior periods presented.
   b. Disclosing in the year of change the effect on net income and earnings per share data for all prior periods presented.

4. **Changes due to error.**
   Employ the retroactive approach by:
   a. Correcting all prior period statements presented.
   b. Restating the beginning balance of retained earnings for the first period presented when the error effects occur in a period prior to that one.

Changes in accounting principle are considered appropriate only when the enterprise demonstrates that the alternative generally accepted accounting principle that is adopted is **preferable** to the existing one. In applying the profession's guidelines, preferability among accounting principles should be determined on the basis of whether the new principle constitutes an **improvement in financial reporting,** not on the basis of the income tax effect alone. But it is not always easy to determine what is an improvement in financial reporting. **How does one measure preferability or improvement?** The Quaker Oats Company, for example, argues that a change in accounting principle to LIFO inventory valuation "better matches current costs and current revenues" (see Illustration 23-11, page 1190). Conversely, another enterprise might change from LIFO to FIFO because it wishes to report a more realistic ending inventory. How does an accountant determine which is the better of these two arguments? The auditor must have some "standard" or "objective" as a basis for determining the preferable method. Because no universal standard or objective is generally accepted, the problem of determining preferability continues to be a difficult one.

Initially the SEC took the position that the auditor should indicate whether a change in accounting principle was preferable. The SEC has since modified this approach, noting that greater reliance may be placed on management's judgment in assessing preferability. Even though the criterion of preferability is difficult to apply, the general guidelines established have acted as a deterrent to capricious changes in accounting

UNDERLYING CONCEPT

This is an example of two widely accepted concepts conflicting. Which is more important, matching (emphasis on the income statement) or qualitative characteristic of representational faithfulness (emphasis on the balance sheet)?

principles.[9] **If an FASB standard creates a new principle or expresses preference for or rejects a specific accounting principle, a change is considered clearly acceptable.** Similarly, other authoritative documents, such as AcSEC's statements of position and AICPA industry audit guides, are considered preferable accounting when a change in accounting principles is contemplated.

▶ MOTIVATIONS FOR CHANGE

Difficult as it is to determine which accounting standards have the strongest conceptual support, other complications make the process even more complex. These complications stem from the fact that managers (and others) have a self-interest in how the financial statements make the company look. Managers naturally wish to show their financial performance in the best light. A favorable profit picture can influence investors, and a strong liquidity position can influence creditors. **Too** favorable a profit picture, however, can provide union negotiators with ammunition during collective bargaining talks. Also, if the federal government has set up a price commission to regulate companies' prices during an inflationary period (as the U.S. government did in the early 1970s), managers might believe that lower-trending profits would persuade the price commission to grant their company a price increase. Hence, managers might have varying profit motives depending on economic times and whom they seek to impress.

Recent research has provided additional insight into why companies may prefer certain accounting methods. Some of these reasons are as follows:

1. **Political Costs.** As companies become larger and more politically visible, politicians and regulators devote more attention to them. Many suggest that these politicians and regulators can "feather their own nests" by imposing regulations on these organizations for the benefit of their own constituents. Thus the larger the firm, the more likely it is to become subject to regulation such as antitrust and the more likely it is to be required to pay higher taxes. Therefore, companies that are politically visible may attempt to report income numbers that are low, to avoid the scrutiny of regulators. Companies thus hope to reduce their exposure to the perception of monopoly power. In addition, other constituents such as labor unions may be less willing to ask for wage increases if reported income is low. Researchers have found that the larger the company, the more likely it is to adopt income decreasing approaches in selecting accounting methods.[10]

2. **Capital Structure.** A number of studies have indicated that the capital structure of the company can affect the selection of accounting methods. For example, a company with a high debt-to-equity ratio is more likely to be constrained by debt covenants. That is, a company may have a debt covenant that indicates that it cannot pay any dividends if retained earnings fall below a certain level. As a result, this type of company is more likely to select accounting methods that will increase net income. For example, one group of writers indicated that a company's capital structure affected its decision whether to expense or capitalize interest.[11] Others indicated that full cost accounting was selected instead of successful efforts by companies that have high debt-to-equity ratios.[12]

---

[9]If management has not provided reasonable justification for the change in accounting principle, the auditor should express a qualified opinion or, if the effect of the change is sufficiently material, the auditor should express an adverse opinion on the financial statements. "Reports on Audited Financial Statements," *Statement on Auditing Standards No. 58* (New York: AICPA, 1988).

[10]Ross L. Watts and Jerold L. Zimmerman, "Positive Accounting Theory: A Ten-Year Perspective," *The Accounting Review* (January 1990).

[11]R. M. Bowen, E. W. Noreen, and J. M. Lacy, "Determinants of the Corporate Decision to Capitalize Interest," *Journal of Accounting and Economics* (August 1981).

[12]See, for example, Dan S. Dhaliwal, "The Effect of the Firm's Capital Structure on the Choice of Accounting Methods," *The Accounting Review* (January 1980); and W. Bruce Johnson and

3. **Bonus Payments.** If bonus payments paid to management are tied to income, it has been found that management will select accounting methods that maximize their bonus payments. Thus, in selecting accounting methods, management does concern itself with the effect of accounting income changes on their compensation plans.[13]

4. **Smooth Earnings.** Substantial increases in earnings attract the attention of politicians, regulators, and competitors. In addition, large increases in income create problems for management because the same results are difficult to achieve the following year. Executive compensation plans would use these higher numbers as a baseline and make it difficult for management to earn bonuses in subsequent years. Conversely, large decreases in earnings might be viewed as a signal that the company is in financial trouble. Furthermore, substantial decreases in income raise concerns on the part of stockholders, lenders, and other interested parties about the competency of management. Thus, companies have an incentive to "manage" or "smooth" earnings. Management therefore believes that a steady 10% growth a year is much better than a 30% growth one year and a 10% decline the next.[14] In other words, management usually prefers a gradually increasing income report (often referred to as income smoothers) and sometimes changes accounting methods to ensure such a result.

Management pays careful attention to the accounting it follows and often changes accounting methods not for conceptual reasons, but rather for economic reasons. As indicated throughout this textbook, such arguments have come to be known as "economic consequences arguments," since they focus on the supposed impact of the accounting method on the behavior of investors, creditors, competitors, governments, or managers of the reporting companies themselves, rather than addressing the conceptual justification for accounting standards.[15]

To counter these pressures, standard setters such as the FASB have declared, as part of their conceptual framework, that they will assess the merits of proposed standards from a position of neutrality. That is, the soundness of standards should not be evaluated on the grounds of their possible impact on behavior. It is not the FASB's place to choose standards according to the kinds of behavior they wish to promote and the kinds they wish to discourage. At the same time, it must be admitted that some standards **will** often have the effect of influencing behavior. Yet their justification should be conceptual and not in terms of their impact.

▶ ERROR ANALYSIS

OBJECTIVE 10
Analyze the effect of errors.

As indicated earlier, material errors are unusual in large corporations because internal control procedures coupled with the diligence of the accounting staff are ordinarily sufficient to find any major errors in the system. Smaller businesses may face a different

---

Ramachandran Ramanan, "Discretionary Accounting Changes from 'Successful Efforts' to 'Full Cost' Methods: 1970–76," *The Accounting Review* (January 1988). The latter study found that firms that changed to full cost were more likely to exhibit higher levels of financial risk (leverage) than firms that retained successful efforts.

[13]See, for example, Mark Zmijewski and Robert Hagerman, "An Income Strategy Approach to the Positive Theory of Accounting Standard Setting/Choice," *Journal of Accounting and Economics* (1985).

[14]O. Douglas Moses, "Income Smoothing and Incentives: Empirical Tests Using Accounting Changes," *The Accounting Review* (April 1987). Findings provide evidence that smoothers are associated with firm size, the existence of bonus plans, and the divergence of actual earnings from expectations.

[15]Lobbyists use economic consequences arguments—and there are many of them—to put pressure on standard setters. We have seen examples of these arguments in the oil and gas industry about successful efforts versus full cost, in the technology area with the issue of mandatory expensing of research and development costs, and so on.

problem. These enterprises may not be able to afford an internal audit staff or to implement the necessary control procedures to ensure that accounting data are always recorded accurately.[16]

In practice, firms do not correct for errors discovered that do not have a significant effect on the presentation of the financial statements. For example, the failure to record accrued wages of $5,000 when the total payroll for the year is $1,750,000 and net income is $940,000 is not considered significant, and no correction is made. Obviously, defining materiality is difficult, and accountants must rely on their experience and judgment to determine whether adjustment is necessary for a given error. **All errors discussed in this section are assumed to be material and to require adjustment.** Also, all of the tax effects are ignored in this section.

The accountant must answer three questions in error analysis:

1. What type of error is involved?
2. What entries are needed to correct for the error?
3. How are financial statements to be restated once the error is discovered?

As indicated earlier, the profession requires that errors be **treated as prior period adjustments and be reported in the current year as adjustments to the beginning balance of Retained Earnings.** If comparative statements are presented, the prior statements affected should be restated to correct for the error.

Three types of errors can occur. Because each type has its own peculiarities, it is important to differentiate among them.

BALANCE SHEET ERRORS

These errors affect only the presentation of an asset, liability, or stockholders' equity account. Examples are the classification of a short-term receivable as part of the investment section; the classification of a note payable as an account payable; and the classification of plant assets as inventory. Reclassification of the item to its proper position is needed when the error is discovered. If comparative statements that include the error year are prepared, the balance sheet for the error year is restated correctly.

INCOME STATEMENT ERRORS

These errors affect only the presentation of the nominal accounts in the income statement. Errors involve the improper classification of revenues or expenses, such as recording interest revenue as part of sales; purchases as bad debt expense; and depreciation expense as interest expense. An income statement classification error has no effect on the balance sheet and no effect on net income. A reclassification entry is needed when the error is discovered, if it is discovered in the year it is made. If the error occurred in prior periods, no entry is needed at the date of discovery because the accounts for the current year are correctly stated. If comparative statements that include the error year are prepared, the income statement for the error year is restated correctly.

BALANCE SHEET AND INCOME STATEMENT EFFECTS

The third type of error involves both the balance sheet and income statement. For example, assume that accrued wages payable were overlooked by the bookkeeper at the end of the accounting period. The effect of this error is to understate expenses, understate liabilities, and overstate net income for that period of time. This type of error affects both the balance sheet and the income statement and is classified in one of two ways—counterbalancing or noncounterbalancing.

---

[16]See Mark L. DeFord and James Jiambalvo, "Incidence and Circumstances of Accounting Errors," *The Accounting Review* (July 1991), for examples of different types of errors and why these errors might have occurred.

Counterbalancing errors are errors that will be offset or corrected over two periods. In the previous illustration, the failure to record accrued wages is considered a counterbalancing error because over a 2-year period the error will no longer be present. In other words the failure to record accrued wages in the previous period means: (1) net income for the first period is overstated; (2) accrued wages payable (a liability) is understated, and (3) wages expense is understated. In the next period, net income is understated; accrued wages payable (a liability) is correctly stated; and wages expense is overstated. For the **2 years combined:** (1) net income is correct; (2) wages expense is correct; and (3) accrued wages payable at the end of the second year is correct. Most errors in accounting that affect both the balance sheet and income statement are counterbalancing errors.

Noncounterbalancing errors are errors that are not offset in the next accounting period, for example, the failure to capitalize equipment that has a useful life of 5 years. If we expense this asset immediately, expenses will be overstated in the first period but understated in the next four periods. At the end of the second period, the effect of the error is not fully offset. Net income is correct in the aggregate only at the end of 5 years, because the asset is fully depreciated at this point. Thus, **noncounterbalancing errors are those that take longer than two periods to correct themselves.**

Only in rare instances is an error never reversed, for example, when land is initially expensed. Because land is not depreciable, theoretically the error is never offset unless the land is sold.

Counterbalancing Errors

The usual types of counterbalancing errors are illustrated on the following pages. In studying these illustrations, a number of points should be remembered. First, determine whether or not the books have been closed for the period in which the error is found:

1. **If the books have been closed:**
   a. If the error is already counterbalanced, no entry is necessary.
   b. If the error is not yet counterbalanced, an entry is necessary to adjust the present balance of retained earnings.

2. **If the books have not been closed:**
   a. If the error is already counterbalanced and the company is in the second year, an entry is necessary to correct the current period and to adjust the beginning balance of Retained Earnings.
   b. If the error is not yet counterbalanced, an entry is necessary to adjust the beginning balance of Retained Earnings and correct the current period.

Second, if comparative statements are presented, restatement of the amounts for comparative purposes is necessary. **Restatement is necessary even if a correcting journal entry is not required.** To illustrate, assume that Sanford's Cement Co. failed to accrue revenue in 1993 when earned, but recorded the revenue in 1994 when received. The error was discovered in 1996. No entry is necessary to correct for this error because the effects have been counterbalanced by the time the error is discovered in 1996. However, if comparative financial statements for 1993 through 1996 are presented, the accounts and related amounts for the years 1993 and 1994 should be restated correctly for financial reporting purposes.

Failure to Record Accrued Wages

On December 31, 1995, accrued wages in the amount of $1,500 were not recognized. The entry in 1996 to correct this error, assuming that the books have not been closed for 1996, is:

Retained Earnings	1,500	
Wages Expense		1,500

The rationale for this entry is as follows: (1) When the accrued wages of 1995 are paid in 1996, an additional debit of $1,500 is made to 1996 Wages Expense. (2) Wages Expense—1996 is overstated by $1,500. (3) Because 1995 accrued wages were not recorded as Wages Expense—1995, the net income for 1995 was overstated by $1,500. (4) Because 1995 net income is overstated by $1,500, the Retained Earnings account is overstated by $1,500 because net income is closed to Retained Earnings.

If the books have been closed for 1996, no entry is made because the error is counterbalanced.

Failure to Record Prepaid Expenses

In January 1995 Hurley Enterprises purchased a 2-year insurance policy costing $1,000; Insurance Expense was debited, and Cash was credited. No adjusting entries were made at the end of 1995.

The entry on December 31, 1996, to correct this error, assuming that the books have not been closed for 1996, is:

Insurance Expense	500	
Retained Earnings		500

If the books have been closed for 1996, no entry is made because the error is counterbalanced.

Understatement of Unearned Revenue

On December 31, 1995, Hurley Enterprises received $50,000 as a prepayment for renting certain office space for the following year. The entry made at the time of receipt of the rent payment was a debit to Cash and a credit to Rent Revenue. No adjusting entry was made as of December 31, 1995. The entry on December 31, 1996, to correct for this error, assuming that the books have not been closed for 1996, is:

Retained Earnings	50,000	
Rent Revenue		50,000

If the books have been closed for 1996, no entry is made because the error is counterbalanced.

Overstatement of Accrued Revenue

On December 31, 1995, Hurley Enterprises accrued as interest revenue $8,000 that applied to 1996. The entry made on December 31, 1995, was to debit Interest Receivable and credit Interest Revenue. The entry on December 31, 1996, to correct for this error, assuming that the books have not been closed for 1996, is:

Retained Earnings	8,000	
Interest Revenue		8,000

If the books have been closed for 1996, no entry is made because the error is counterbalanced.

Understatement of Ending Inventory

On December 31, 1995, the physical count of the inventory was understated by $25,000 because the inventory crew failed to count one warehouse of merchandise. The entry on December 31, 1996, to correct for this error, assuming that the books have not been closed for 1996, is:

Inventory (beginning)	25,000	
Retained Earnings		25,000

If the books have been closed for 1996, no entry is made because the error is counterbalanced.

Overstatement of Purchases

Hurley Enterprises' accountant recorded a purchase of merchandise for $9,000 in 1995 that applied to 1996. The physical inventory for 1995 was correctly stated. The entry on December 31, 1996, to correct for this error, assuming that the books have not been closed for 1996, is:

Purchases	9,000	
Retained Earnings		9,000

If the books have been closed for 1996, no entry is made because the error is counter-balanced.

Overstatement of Purchases and Inventories

Sometimes both the physical inventory and the purchases are incorrectly stated. Assume, as in the previous illustration, that purchases for 1995 are overstated by $9,000 and that inventory is overstated by the same amount. The entry on December 31, 1996, to correct for this error, assuming that the books have not been closed for 1996, is:

Purchases	9,000	
Inventory		9,000[a]

[a]The net income for 1995 is correctly computed because the overstatement of purchases was offset by the overstatement of ending inventory in the cost of goods sold computation.

If the books have been closed for 1996, no entry is made because the error is counterbalanced.

Noncounterbalancing Errors

Because such errors do not counterbalance over a 2-year period, the entries for non-counterbalancing errors are more complex and correcting entries are needed, even if the books have been closed.

Failure to Record Depreciation

Assume that on January 1, 1995, Hurley Enterprises purchased a machine for $10,000 that had an estimated useful life of 5 years. The accountant incorrectly expensed this machine in 1995. The error was discovered in 1996. If we assume that the company desires to use straight-line depreciation on this asset, the entry on December 31, 1996, to correct for this error, given that the books have not been closed, is:

Machinery	10,000	
Depreciation Expense	2,000	
Retained Earnings		8,000[a]
Accumulated Depreciation		4,000[a]

[a]Computations:

Retained Earnings

Overstatement of expense in 1995	$10,000
Proper depreciation for 1995 (20% × $10,000)	(2,000)
Retained earnings understated as of Dec. 31, 1995	$ 8,000

Accumulated Depreciation

Accumulated depreciation (20% × $10,000 × 2)	$ 4,000

If the books have been closed for 1996, the entry is:

Machinery	10,000	
Retained Earnings		6,000[a]
Accumulated Depreciation		4,000

[a]Computations:

Retained Earnings

Retained earnings understated as of Dec. 31, 1995	$ 8,000
Proper depreciation for 1996 (20% × $10,000)	(2,000)
Retained earnings understated as of Dec. 31, 1996	$ 6,000

Failure to Adjust for Bad Debts

Companies sometimes use a specific charge-off method in accounting for bad debt expense when a percentage of sales is more appropriate. Adjustments are often made to change from the specific writeoff to some type of allowance method. For example, assume that Hurley Enterprises has recognized bad debt expense when the debts have actually become uncollectible as follows:

	1995	1996
From 1995 sales	$550	$690
From 1996 sales		700

Hurley estimates that an additional $1,400 will be charged off in 1997, of which $300 is applicable to 1995 sales and $1,100 to 1996 sales. The entry on December 31, 1996, assuming that the **books have not been closed for 1996,** is:

Bad Debt Expense	410[a]	
Retained Earnings	990[a]	
Allowance for Doubtful Accounts		1,400

[a]Computations:

Allowance for doubtful accounts—additional $300 for 1995 sales and $1,100 for 1996 sales.
Bad debts and retained earnings balance:

	1995	1996
Bad debts charged for	$1,240[b]	$ 700
Additional bad debts anticipated in 1997	300	1,100
Proper bad debt expense	1,540	1,800
Charges currently made to each period	(550)	(1,390)
Bad debt adjustment	$ 990	$ 410

[b]$550 + $690 = $1,240

If the **books have been closed for 1996,** the entry is:

Retained Earnings	1,400	
Allowance for Doubtful Accounts		1,400

COMPREHENSIVE ILLUSTRATION: NUMEROUS ERRORS

In some circumstances a combination of errors occurs. A work sheet is therefore prepared to facilitate the analysis. The following problem demonstrates the use of a work sheet. The mechanics of the work sheet preparation should be obvious from the solution format.

The income statements of the Hudson Company for the years ended December 31, 1994, 1995, and 1996 indicate the following net incomes.

1994	$17,400
1995	20,200
1996	11,300

An examination of the accounting records of the Hudson Company for these years indicates that several errors were made in arriving at the net income amounts reported. The following errors were discovered:

1. Wages earned by workers but not paid at December 31 were consistently omitted from the records. The amounts omitted were:

December 31, 1994	$1,000
December 31, 1995	1,400
December 31, 1996	1,600

    These amounts were recorded as expenses when paid in the year following that in which they were earned.

2. The merchandise inventory on December 31, 1994, was overstated by $1,900 as the result of errors made in the footings and extensions on the inventory sheets.

3. Unexpired insurance of $1,200, applicable to 1996, was expensed on December 31, 1995.

4. Interest receivable in the amount of $240 was not recorded on December 31, 1995.

5. On January 2, 1995, a piece of equipment costing $3,900 was sold for $1,800. At the date of sale the equipment had accumulated depreciation of $2,400. The cash

received was recorded as Miscellaneous Income in 1995. In addition, depreciation was recorded for this equipment in both 1995 and 1996 at the rate of 10% of cost.

The first step in preparing the work sheet is to prepare a schedule showing the corrected net income amounts for the years ended December 31, 1994, 1995, and 1996. Each correction of the amount originally reported is clearly labeled. The next step is to indicate the balance sheet accounts affected as of December 31, 1996. The completed work sheet for Hudson Company is as follows:

ILLUSTRATION 23-19
Work Sheet to Correct Income and Balance Sheet Errors

HUDSON COMPANY
WORK SHEET TO CORRECT INCOME AND BALANCE SHEET

	Work Sheet Analysis of Changes in Net Income				Balance Sheet Correction at December 31, 1996		
	1994	1995	1996	Totals	Debit	Credit	Account
Net income as reported	$17,400	$20,200	$11,300	$48,900			
Wages unpaid, 12/31/94	(1,000)	1,000		–0–			
Wages unpaid, 12/31/95		(1,400)	1,400	–0–			
Wages unpaid, 12/31/96			(1,600)	(1,600)		$1,600	Wages Payable
Inventory overstatement, 12/31/94	(1,900)	1,900		–0–			
Unexpired insurance, 12/31/95		1,200	(1,200)	–0–			
Interest receivable, 12/31/95		240	(240)	–0–			
Correction for entry made upon sale of equipment, 1/2/95[a]		(1,500)		(1,500)	$2,400	3,900	Accumulated Depreciation Machinery
Overcharge of depreciation, 1995		390		390	390		Accumulated Depreciation
Overcharge of depreciation, 1996			390	390	390		Accumulated Depreciation
Corrected net income	$14,500	$22,030	$10,050	$46,580			

[a]Cost	$ 3,900
Accumulated depreciation	2,400
Book value	1,500
Proceeds from sale	1,800
Gain on sale	300
Income reported	(1,800)
Adjustment	$(1,500)

Correcting entries **if the books have not been closed** on December 31, 1996, are:

Retained Earnings	1,400	
Wages Expense		1,400
(To correct improper charge to Wages Expense for 1996)		
Wages Expense	1,600	
Wages Payable		1,600
(To record proper wages expense for 1996)		
Insurance Expense	1,200	
Retained Earnings		1,200
(To record proper insurance expense for 1996)		
Interest Revenue	240	
Retained Earnings		240
(To correct improper credit to Interest Revenue in 1996)		
Retained Earnings	1,500	
Accumulated Depreciation	2,400	
Machinery		3,900
(To record writeoff of machinery in 1995 and adjustment of Retained Earnings)		
Accumulated Depreciation	780	
Depreciation Expense		390
Retained Earnings		390
(To correct improper charge for depreciation expense in 1995 and 1996)		

If the books have been closed for 1996, the correcting entries are:

Retained Earnings	1,600	
Wages Payable		1,600
(To record proper wage expense for 1996)		
Retained Earnings	1,500	
Accumulated Depreciation	2,400	
Machinery		3,900
(To record writeoff of machinery in 1995 and adjustment of Retained Earnings)		
Accumulated Depreciation	780	
Retained Earnings		780
(To correct improper charge for depreciation expense in 1995 and 1996)		

PREPARATION OF FINANCIAL STATEMENTS WITH ERROR CORRECTIONS

Up to now, our discussion of error analysis has been concerned with the identification of the type of error involved and the accounting for its correction in the accounting records. The correction of the error should be presented on comparative financial statements. In addition, 5- or 10-year summaries are given for the interested financial reader. The following situation illustrates how a typical year's financial statements are restated given many different errors.

Dick & Wally's Outlet is a small retail outlet in the town of Holiday. Lacking expertise in accounting, they do not keep adequate records. As a result, numerous errors occurred in recording accounting information. The errors are listed below:

1. The bookkeeper inadvertently failed to record a cash receipt of $1,000 on the sale of merchandise in 1996.

2. Accrued wages expense at the end of 1995 was $2,500; at the end of 1996, $3,200. The company does not accrue for wages; all wages are charged to administrative expense.

3. The beginning inventory was understated by $5,400 because goods in transit at the end of last year were not counted. The proper purchase entry had been made.

4. No allowance had been set up for estimated uncollectible receivables. Dick and Wally decided to set up such an allowance for the estimated probable losses as of December 31, 1996 for 1995 accounts of $700, and for 1996 accounts of $1,500. It is also decided to correct the charge against each year so that it shows the losses (actual and estimated) relating to that year's sales. Accounts have been written off to bad debt expense (selling expense) as follows:

	In 1995	In 1996
1995 accounts	$400	$2,000
1996 accounts		1,600

5. Unexpired insurance not recorded at the end of 1995 was $600, and at the end of 1996, $400. All insurance expense is charged to Administrative Expense.

6. An account payable of $6,000 should have been a note payable.

7. During 1995, an asset that cost $10,000 and had a book value of $4,000 was sold for $7,000. At the time of sale Cash was debited and Miscellaneous Income was credited for $7,000.

8. As a result of the last transaction, the company overstated depreciation expense (an administrative expense) in 1995 by $800 and in 1996 by $1,200.

9. In a physical count, the company determined the final inventory to be $40,000.

A work sheet that begins with the unadjusted trial balance of Dick & Wally's Outlet is presented in Illustration 23-20. The correcting entries and their effect on the financial statements can be determined by examining the work sheet.

DICK & WALLY'S OUTLET
WORK SHEET ANALYSIS TO ADJUST FINANCIAL STATEMENTS FOR THE YEAR 1996

	Trial Balance Unadjusted		Adjustments		Income Statement Adjusted		Balance Sheet Adjusted	
	Debit	Credit	Debit	Credit	Debit	Credit	Debit	Credit
Cash	3,100		(1) 1,000				4,100	
Accounts Receivable	17,600						17,600	
Notes Receivable	8,500						8,500	
Inventories, Jan. 1, 1996	34,000		(3) 5,400		39,400			
Property, Plant and Equip.	112,000			(7) 10,000[a]			102,000	
Accumulated Depreciation		83,500	(7) 6,000[a]					75,500
			(8) 2,000					
Investments	24,300						24,300	
Accounts Payable		14,500	(6) 6,000					8,500
Notes Payable		10,000		(6) 6,000				16,000
Capital Stock		43,500						43,500
Retained Earnings		20,000	(4) 2,700[b]	(3) 5,400				17,600
			(7) 4,000[a]	(5) 600				
			(2) 2,500	(8) 800				
Sales		94,000		(1) 1,000		95,000		
Purchases	21,000				21,000			
Selling Expenses	22,000			(4) 500[b]	21,500			
Administrative Expenses	23,000		(2) 700	(5) 400	22,700			
			(5) 600	(8) 1,200				
Totals	265,500	265,500						
Wages Payable				(2) 3,200				3,200
Allowance for Doubtful Accounts				(4) 2,200[b]				2,200
Unexpired Insurance			(5) 400				400	
Inventory, Dec. 31, 1996						(9) 40,000	(9) 40,000	
Net Income					30,400			30,400
Totals			31,300	31,300	135,000	135,000	196,900	196,900

Computations:

[a]Machinery			[b]Bad Debts		1995	1996
Proceeds from sale	$7,000		Bad debts charged for		$2,400	$1,600
Book value of machinery	4,000		Additional bad debts anticipated		700	1,500
Gain on sale	3,000				3,100	3,100
Income credited	7,000		Charges currently made to each year		(400)	(3,600)
Retained earnings adjustment	$4,000		Bad debt adjustment		$2,700	$ (500)

ILLUSTRATION 23-20
Work Sheet to Analyze Effect of Errors in Financial Statements

---

▶ SUMMARY OF LEARNING OBJECTIVES ◀

1. Identify the types of accounting changes. The three different types of accounting changes are: (1) *Change in accounting principle:* a change from one generally accepted accounting principle to another generally accepted accounting principle. (2) *Change in accounting estimate:* a change that occurs as the result of new information or as additional experience is acquired. (3) *Change in reporting entity:* a change from reporting as one type of entity to another type of entity.

2. Describe the accounting for changes in accounting principles. A change in accounting principle involves a change from one generally accepted accounting principle to another. A change in accounting principle is not considered to result from the adoption of a new principle in recognition of events that

KEY TERMS

change in accounting estimate, 1182

change in accounting principle, 1182

change in reporting entity, 1182

correction of an error, 1192

counterbalancing errors, 1199

cumulative effect, 1184

noncounterbalancing errors, 1199

pro-forma, 1184

have occurred for the first time or that were previously immaterial. If the accounting principle previously followed was not acceptable, or if the principle was applied incorrectly, a change to a generally accepted accounting principle is considered a correction of an error.

3. **Understand how to account for cumulative-effect accounting changes.** The general requirement for changes in accounting principle is that the cumulative effect of the change (net of tax) be shown at the bottom of the current year's income statement and that pro-forma net income and earnings per share amounts be reported for all prior periods presented.

4. **Understand how to account for retroactive accounting changes.** A number of accounting principle changes are handled in a retroactive manner; that is, prior years' financial statements are recast on a basis consistent with the newly adopted principle, and any part of the effect attributable to years prior to those presented is treated as an adjustment of the earliest retained earnings presented.

5. **Understand how to account for changes to LIFO.** In changing to LIFO, the base year inventory for all subsequent LIFO calculations is the opening inventory in the year the method is adopted. There is no restatement of prior years' income because it is just too impractical to do so.

6. **Describe the accounting for changes in estimates.** Changes in estimates must be handled prospectively; that is, no changes should be made in previously reported results. Opening balances are not adjusted, and no attempt is made to "catch up" for prior periods. Financial statements of prior periods are not restated, and pro-forma amounts for prior periods are not reported.

7. **Identify changes in a reporting entity.** An accounting change that results in financial statements that are actually the statements of a different entity should be reported by restating the financial statements of all prior periods presented, to show the financial information for the new reporting entity for all periods.

8. **Describe the accounting for correction of errors.** As soon as they are discovered, errors must be corrected by proper entries in the accounts and reported in the financial statements. The profession requires that corrections of errors be treated as prior period adjustments, be recorded in the year in which the error was discovered, and be reported in the financial statements as an adjustment to the beginning balance of retained earnings. If comparative statements are presented, the prior statements affected should be restated to correct for the error. The disclosures need not be repeated in the financial statements of subsequent periods.

9. **Identify economic motives for changing accounting methods.** Managers might have varying profit motives depending on economic times and whom they seek to impress. Some of the reasons of changing accounting methods are: (1) political costs, (2) capital structure, (3) bonus payments, (4) smooth earnings.

10. **Analyze the effect of errors.** Three types of errors can occur: (1) *Balance sheet errors:* affect only the presentation of an asset, liability, or stockholders' equity account. (2) *Income statement errors:* affect only the presentation of the nominal accounts in the income statement. (3) *Balance sheet and income statement effect:* involves both the balance sheet and income statement. Errors are classified into two types: (1) *Counterbalancing errors:* will be offset or corrected over two periods. (2) *Noncounterbalancing errors:* are not offset in the next accounting period and take longer than two periods to correct themselves.

QUESTIONS

1. In recent years, *The Wall Street Journal* has indicated that many companies have changed their accounting principles. What are the major reasons why companies change accounting methods?

2. State how each of the following items is reflected in the financial statements:
   (a) Change from straight-line method of depreciation to sum-of-the-years'-digits.
   (b) Change from FIFO to LIFO method for inventory valuation purposes.
   (c) Charge for failure to record depreciation in a previous period.
   (d) Litigation won in current year, related to prior period.
   (e) Change in the realizability of certain receivables.
   (f) Writeoff of receivables.
   (g) Change from the percentage-of-completion to the completed-contract method for reporting net income.

3. What are the advantages of employing the current or catch-up method for handling changes in accounting principle?

4. Define a change in estimate and provide an illustration. When is a change in accounting estimate affected by a change in accounting principle?

5. Panna Goswami Inc. has followed the practice of capitalizing certain marketing costs and amortizing these costs over their expected life. In the current year, the company determined that the future benefits from these costs were doubtful. Consequently, the company adopted the policy of expensing these costs as incurred. How should this accounting change be reported in the comparative financial statements?

6. Indicate how the following items are recorded in the accounting records in the current year.
   (a) Large writeoff of goodwill.
   (b) A change in depreciating plant assets from accelerated to the straight-line method.
   (c) Large writeoff of inventories because of obsolescence.
   (d) Change from the cash basis to accrual basis of accounting.
   (e) Change from LIFO to FIFO method for inventory valuation purposes.
   (f) Change in the estimate of service lives for plant assets.

7. Kalra Construction Co. had followed the practice of expensing all materials assigned to a construction job without recognizing any salvage inventory. On December 31, 1995, it was determined that salvage inventory should be valued at $59,000. Of this amount, $27,000 arose during the current year. How does this information affect the financial statements to be prepared at the end of 1995?

8. Arun Inc. wishes to change from the sum-of-the-years'-digits to the straight-line depreciation method for financial reporting purposes. The auditor indicates that a change would be permitted only if it is to a preferable method. What difficulties develop in assessing preferability?

9. How should consolidated financial statements be reported this year when statements of individual companies were presented last year?

10. Thomas Vinje controlled four domestic subsidiaries and one foreign subsidiary. Prior to the current year, Vinje had excluded the foreign subsidiary from consolidation. During the current year, the foreign subsidiary was included in the financial statements. How should this change in accounting principle be reflected in the financial statements?

11. Gopal Co., a closely held corporation, is in the process of preparing financial statements to accompany an offering of its common stock. The company at this time has decided to switch from the accelerated depreciation to the straight-line method of depreciation to better present its financial operations. How should this change in accounting principle be reported in the financial statements?

12. Discuss and illustrate how a correction of an error in previously issued financial statements should be handled.

13. Prior to 1996, Nesher Inc. excluded manufacturing overhead costs from work in process and finished goods inventory. These costs have been expensed as incurred. In 1996, the company decided to change its accounting methods for manufacturing inventories to full costing by including these costs as product costs. Assuming that these costs are material, how should this change be reflected in the financial statements for 1995 and 1996?

14. M. Yasin Corp. failed to record accrued salaries for 1993, $2,000; 1994, $2,100; and 1995, $4,200. What is the amount of the overstatement or understatement of Retained Earnings at December 31, 1996?

15. In January, 1995, installation costs of $10,000 on new machinery were charged to Repair Expense. Other costs of this machinery of $30,000 were correctly recorded and have been depreciated using

the straight-line method with an estimated life of 10 years and no salvage value. At December 31, 1996, it is decided that the machinery has a useful life of 20 years, starting with January 1, 1996. What entry(ies) should be made in 1996 to correctly record transactions related to machinery, assuming the machinery has no salvage value? The books have not been closed for 1996 and depreciation expense has not yet been recorded for 1996.

16. On January 2, 1995, $100,000 of 11%, 20-year bonds were issued for $98,000. The $2,000 discount was charged to Interest Expense. The bookkeeper, Girish Bhatt, records interest only on the interest payment dates of January 1 and July 1. What is the effect on reported net income for 1995 of this error, assuming straight-line amortization of the discount? What entry is necessary to correct for this error, assuming that the books are not closed for 1995?

17. An account payable of $11,000 for merchandise purchased on December 23, 1995, was recorded in January 1996. This merchandise was not included in inventory at December 31, 1995. What effect does this error have on reported net income for 1995? What entry should be made to correct for this error, assuming that the books are not closed for 1995?

18. Equipment was purchased on January 2, 1995, for $15,000, but no portion of the cost has been charged to depreciation. The corporation wishes to use the straight-line method for these assets, which have been estimated to have a life of 10 years and no salvage value. What effect does this error have on net income in 1995? What entry is necessary to correct for this error, assuming that the books are not closed for 1995?

EXERCISES

E23-1 (Error and Change in Principle—Depreciation) Jeong Co. purchased a machine on January 1, 1993 for $495,000. At that time it was estimated that the machine would have a 10-year life and no salvage value. On December 31, 1996, the firm's accountant found that the entry for depreciation expense had been omitted in 1994. In addition, management has informed the accountant that they plan to switch to straight-line depreciation, starting with the year 1996. At present, the company uses the sum-of-the-years'-digits method for depreciating equipment.

Instructions
Prepare the general journal entries the accountant should make at December 31, 1996 (ignore tax effects).

E23-2 (Change in Principle and Change in Estimate—Depreciation) Jimenez Inc. acquired the following assets in January of 1993:

Equipment, estimated service life, 5 years; salvage value, $15,000	$525,000
Building, estimated service life, 30 years; no salvage value	$693,000

The equipment has been depreciated using the sum-of-the-years'-digits method for the first 3 years, for financial reporting purposes. In 1996, the company decided to change the method of computing depreciation to the straight-line method for the equipment, but no change was made in the estimated service life or salvage value. It was also decided to change the total estimated service life of the building from 30 years to 45 years, with no change in the estimated salvage value. The building is depreciated on the straight-line method.

The company has 100,000 shares of capital stock outstanding. Results of operations for 1996 and 1995 are shown below:

	1996	1995
Income before cumulative effect of change in computing depreciation for 1996: depreciation for 1996 has been computed on the straight-line basis for both the equipment and building[a]	$385,000	$380,000
Income per share before cumulative effect of change in computing depreciation for 1996	$3.85	$3.80

[a]It should be noted that the computation for depreciation expense for 1996 and 1995 for the building was based on the original estimate of service life of 30 years.

Instructions
(a) Compute the cumulative effect of the change in accounting principle to be reported in the income statement for 1996, and prepare the journal entry to record the change. (Ignore tax effects.)
(b) Present comparative data for the years 1995 and 1996, starting with income before cumulative effect of accounting change. Prepare pro-forma data. Do not prepare the footnote. (Ignore tax effects.)

E23-3 (Change in Principle and Change in Estimate—Depreciation) Joblonsky Corporation owns equipment that originally cost $400,000 and had an estimated useful life of 20 years. The equipment had no expected salvage value.

The two requirements below are independent and must be considered as entirely separate from each other.

Instructions

(a) After using the double-declining balance method for 2 years, the company decided to switch to the straight-line method of depreciation. Prepare the general journal entry(ies) necessary in the third year to properly account for (1) the change in accounting principle and (2) depreciation expense (ignore income tax effects).

(b) After using the straight-line method for 2 years, the company determined that the useful life of the equipment is 27 years (7 more than the original estimate). Prepare the general journal entry(ies) necessary to properly account for the depreciation expense in the third year.

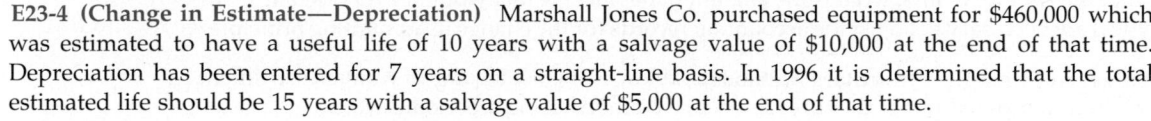 **E23-4 (Change in Estimate—Depreciation)** Marshall Jones Co. purchased equipment for $460,000 which was estimated to have a useful life of 10 years with a salvage value of $10,000 at the end of that time. Depreciation has been entered for 7 years on a straight-line basis. In 1996 it is determined that the total estimated life should be 15 years with a salvage value of $5,000 at the end of that time.

Instructions

(a) Prepare the entry (if any) to correct the prior years' depreciation.

(b) Prepare the entry to record depreciation for 1996.

E23-5 (Change in Principle—Depreciation) Kaalaas Industries changed from the double-declining balance to the straight-line method in 1996 on all its plant assets. For tax purposes, assume that the amount of tax depreciation is higher than the double-declining balance depreciation for each of the 3 years. The appropriate information related to this change is as follows:

Year	Double-Declining Balance Depreciation	Straight-Line Depreciation	Difference
1994	$250,000	$125,000	$125,000
1995	225,000	125,000	100,000
1996	202,500	125,000	77,500

Net income for 1995 was reported at $270,000; net income for 1996 was reported at $300,000, excluding any adjustment for the cumulative effect of a change in depreciation methods. The straight-line method of depreciation was employed in computing net income for 1996.

Instructions

(a) Assuming a tax rate of 30%, what is the amount of the cumulative effect adjustment in 1996?

(b) Prepare the journal entry(ies) to record the cumulative effect adjustment in the accounting records.

(c) Starting with income before cumulative effect of change in accounting principle, prepare the remaining portion of the income statement for 1995 and 1996. Indicate the pro-forma net income that should be reported. Ignore per share computations and note disclosures.

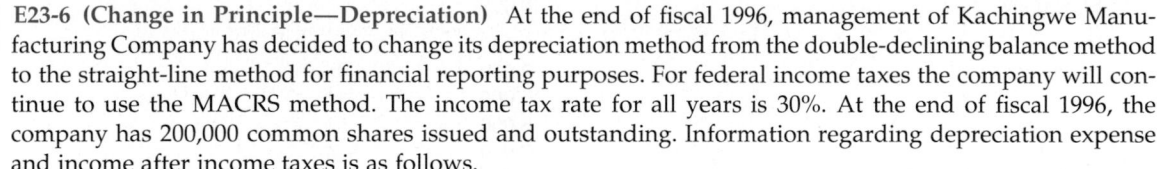 **E23-6 (Change in Principle—Depreciation)** At the end of fiscal 1996, management of Kachingwe Manufacturing Company has decided to change its depreciation method from the double-declining balance method to the straight-line method for financial reporting purposes. For federal income taxes the company will continue to use the MACRS method. The income tax rate for all years is 30%. At the end of fiscal 1996, the company has 200,000 common shares issued and outstanding. Information regarding depreciation expense and income after income taxes is as follows.

Depreciation expense to date under:

	MACRS	Straight-Line	Double-Declining Balance
Pre-1995	$1,000,000	$400,000	$950,000
1995	300,000	150,000	260,000
1996	280,000	160,000	275,000

Reported income after income taxes:

1995	$1,200,000
1996	1,450,000

Instructions

(a) Prepare the journal entries to record the change in accounting method in 1996 and indicate how the change in depreciation method would be reported in the income statement of 1996. Also indicate how earnings per share would be disclosed. (*Hint:* Adjust Deferred Tax Liability account.)

(b) Show the amount of depreciation expense to be reported in 1996.

E23-7 (Change in Principle—Long-term Contracts) Kanwar Construction Company changed from the completed-contract to the percentage-of-completion method of accounting for long-term construction contracts during 1996. For tax purposes, the company employs the completed-contract method and will continue this approach in the future. (*Hint:* Adjust all tax consequences through the Deferred Tax Liability account.) The appropriate information related to this change is as follows:

	Pretax Income from:		
	Percentage-of-Completion	Completed-Contract	Difference
1995	$780,000	$590,000	$190,000
1996	700,000	480,000	220,000

Instructions
(a) Assuming that the tax rate is 40%, what is the amount of net income that would be reported in 1996?
(b) What entry(ies) are necessary to adjust the accounting records for the change in accounting principle?

E23-8 (Various Changes in Principle—Inventory Methods) Below is the net income of Kumar Instrument Co., a private corporation, computed under the three inventory methods using a periodic system.

	FIFO	Average Cost	LIFO
1993	$25,000	$24,000	$20,000
1994	30,000	25,000	21,000
1995	28,000	27,000	24,000
1996	34,000	30,000	26,000

Instructions (Ignore tax considerations)
(a) Assume that in 1996 Kumar decided to change from the FIFO method to the average cost method of pricing inventories. Prepare the journal entry necessary for the change that took place during 1996, and show all the appropriate information needed for reporting on a comparative basis.
(b) Assume that in 1996 Kumar, which had been using the LIFO method since incorporation in 1993, changed to the FIFO method of pricing inventories. Prepare the journal entry necessary for the change, and show all the appropriate information needed for reporting on a comparative basis.

E23-9 (Change in Principle—FIFO to LIFO) Laconta Industries utilizes periodic inventory procedures and on Dec. 31, 1996 decides to change from FIFO to LIFO. The following information is available in the company records:

		Units	Unit Cost
1995:	Beginning Inventory	3,000	$21
	Purchases: #1	5,000	24
	#2	4,000	30
	#3	6,000	32
	#4	5,000	34
	#5	5,000	36
	Ending Inventory	8,000	
1996:	Beginning Inventory	8,000	
	Purchases: #1	2,000	45
	#2	5,000	48
	#3	5,000	50
	#4	7,000	54
	#5	3,000	56
	Ending Inventory	11,000	

Instructions
(a) State the value at which Laconta Industries reports the ending inventory for 1996.
(b) Indicate what additional disclosures are necessary for this change (both within the body of the financial statements and in footnotes). Assume a 40% tax rate.

E23-10 (Error Correction Entries) The first audit of the books of Liu Company was made for the year ended December 31, 1996. In examining the books, the auditor found that certain items had been overlooked or incorrectly handled in the last 3 years. These items are:

1. At the beginning of 1994, the company purchased a machine for $510,000 (salvage value of $30,000) that had a useful life of 6 years. The bookkeeper used straight-line depreciation, but failed to deduct the salvage value in computing the depreciation base for the 3 years.
2. At the end of 1995, the company failed to accrue sales salaries of $42,000.
3. A tax lawsuit that involved the year 1994 was settled late in 1996. It was determined that the company owed an additional $80,000 in taxes related to 1994. The company did not record a liability in 1994 or 1995 because the possibility of loss was considered remote, and charged the $80,000 to a loss account in 1996.

4. Liu Company purchased another company early in 1994 and recorded goodwill of $440,000. Liu had not amortized goodwill because its value had not diminished.

5. In 1996, the company changed its basis of inventory pricing from FIFO to LIFO. The cumulative effect of this change was to decrease net income by $68,000. The company debited this cumulative effect to Retained Earnings. LIFO was used in computing income for 1996.

6. In 1996, the company wrote off $84,000 of inventory considered to be obsolete; this loss was charged directly to Retained Earnings.

Instructions

Prepare the journal entries necessary in 1996 to correct the books, assuming that the books have not been closed. The proper amortization period for goodwill is 40 years. Disregard effects of corrections on income tax.

E23-11 (Change in Principle and Error; Financial Statements) Presented below are the comparative statements for Losoya Inc.

	1996	1995
Sales	$340,000	$270,000
Cost of sales	200,000	142,000
Gross profit	140,000	128,000
Expenses	88,000	50,000
Net income	$ 52,000	$ 78,000
Retained earnings (Jan. 1)	$125,000	$ 72,000
Net income	52,000	78,000
Dividends	(30,000)	(25,000)
Retained earnings (Dec. 31)	$147,000	$125,000

The following additional information is provided:

1. In 1996, Losoya Inc. decided to switch its depreciation method from sum-of-the-years'-digits to the straight-line method. The differences in the two depreciation methods for the assets involved are:

	1996	1995
Sum-of-the-years'-digits	$50,000[a]	$40,000
Straight-line	25,000	25,000

[a]The 1996 income statement contains depreciation expense of $40,000.

2. In 1996, the company discovered that the ending inventory for 1995 was overstated by $28,000; ending inventory for 1996 is correctly stated.

Instructions

(a) Prepare the revised income and retained earnings statement for 1995 and 1996, assuming comparative statements (ignore income tax effects). Do not prepare footnotes or pro-forma amounts.

(b) Prepare the revised income and retained earnings statement for 1996, assuming a noncomparative presentation (ignore income tax effects). Do not prepare footnotes or pro-forma amounts.

E23-12 (Error Analysis and Correcting Entry) You have been engaged to review the financial statements of Miah Corporation. In the course of your examination you conclude that the bookkeeper hired during the current year is not doing a good job. You notice a number of irregularities as follows:

1. Year-end wages payable of $2,300 were not recorded because the bookkeeper thought that "they were immaterial."

2. Accrued vacation pay for the year of $32,600 was not recorded because the bookkeeper "never heard that you had to do it."

3. Insurance for a 12-month period purchased on November 1 of this year was charged to insurance expense in the amount of $2,160 because "the amount of the check is about the same every year."

4. Reported sales revenue for the year is $2,120,000. This includes all sales taxes collected for the year. The sales tax rate is 6%. Because the sales tax is forwarded to the State Department of Revenue, the Sales Tax Expense account is debited because the bookkeeper thought that "the sales tax is a selling expense." At the end of the current year, the balance in the Sales Tax Expense account is $103,400.

Instructions

Prepare the necessary correcting entries (assuming that Miah uses a calendar-year basis).

E23-13 (Error Analysis and Correcting Entry) The reported net incomes for the first 2 years of Ozaki Products, Inc. were as follows: 1995—$147,000; 1996—$185,000. Early in 1997, the following errors were discovered:

1. Depreciation of equipment for 1995 was overstated $9,000.

2. Depreciation of equipment for 1996 was understated $38,500.
3. December 31, 1995, inventory was understated $50,000.
4. December 31, 1996, inventory was overstated $16,200.

Instructions
Prepare the correcting entry necessary when these errors are discovered. Assume that the books are closed. Ignore income tax considerations.

E23-14 (Error Analysis) Mitsdarffer Tool Company's December 31 year-end financial statements contained the following errors:

	December 31, 1995	December 31, 1996
Ending inventory	$9,600 understated	$8,100 overstated
Depreciation expense	$2,300 understated	—

An insurance premium of $60,000 was prepaid in 1995 covering the years 1995, 1996, and 1997. The entire amount was charged to expense in 1995. In addition, on December 31, 1996, fully depreciated machinery was sold for $15,000 cash, but the entry was not recorded until 1997. There were no other errors during 1995 or 1996, and no corrections have been made for any of the errors. Ignore income tax considerations.

Instructions
(a) Compute the total effect of the errors on 1996 net income.
(b) Compute the total effect of the errors on the amount of Mitsdarffer's working capital at December 31, 1996.
(c) Compute the total effect of the errors on the balance of Mitsdarffer's retained earnings at December 31, 1996.

E23-15 (Error Analysis; Correcting Entries) A partial trial balance of Nakaji Corporation is as follows on December 31, 1996:

	Dr.	Cr.
Supplies on hand	$ 2,700	
Accrued salaries and wages		$ 1,500
Interest receivable on investments	5,100	
Prepaid insurance	90,000	
Unearned rental income		–0–
Accrued interest payable		15,000

Additional adjusting data:

1. A physical count of supplies on hand on December 31, 1996 totaled $1,200.
2. Through oversight, the Accrued Salaries and Wages account was not changed during 1996. Accrued salaries and wages on 12/31/96 amounted to $4,200.
3. The Accrued Interest on Investments account was also left unchanged during 1996. Accrued interest on investments amounts to $4,300 on 12/31/96.
4. The unexpired portions of the insurance policies totaled $74,500 as of December 31, 1996.
5. $26,000 was received on January 1, 1996 for the rent of a building for both 1996 and 1997. The entire amount was credited to rental income.
6. Depreciation for the year was erroneously recorded as $2,500 rather than the correct figure of $25,000.
7. A further review of depreciation calculations of prior years revealed that depreciation of $6,200 was not recorded. It was decided that this oversight should be corrected by a prior period adjustment.

Instructions
(a) Assuming that the books have not been closed, what are the adjusting entries necessary at December 31, 1996? Ignore income tax considerations.
(b) Assuming that the books have been closed, what are the adjusting entries necessary at December 31, 1996? Ignore income tax considerations.

E23-16 (Error Analysis) The before tax income for Sujani Co. for 1995 was $98,000 and $75,400 for 1996. However, the accountant noted that the following errors had been made:

1. Sales for 1995 included amounts of $38,200 which had been received in cash during 1995, but for which the related products were delivered in 1996. Title did not pass to the purchaser until 1996.
2. The inventory on December 31, 1995, was understated by $8,640.
3. The bookkeeper in recording interest expense for both 1995 and 1996 on bonds payable made the following entry on an annual basis:

Interest Expense	15,000	
Cash		15,000

The bonds have a face value of $250,000 and pay a stated interest rate of 6%. They were issued at a discount of $15,000 on January 1, 1995, to yield an effective interest rate of 7%. (Assume that the effective yield method should be used.)

4. Ordinary repairs to equipment had been erroneously charged to the Equipment account during 1995 and 1996. Repairs in the amount of $8,500 in 1995 and $9,400 in 1996 were so charged. The company applies a rate of 10% to the balance in the Equipment account at the end of the year in its determination of depreciation charges.

Instructions
Prepare a schedule showing the determination of corrected income before taxes for 1995 and 1996.

E23-17 (Error Analysis) When the records of Chandra Corporation were reviewed at the close of 1996, the errors listed below were discovered. For each item indicate by a check mark in the appropriate column whether the error resulted in an overstatement, an understatement, or had no effect on net income for the years 1995 and 1996.

	1995			1996		
Item	Over-statement	Under-statement	No Effect	Over-statement	Under-statement	No Effect
1. Failure to record amortization of patent in 1996.						
2. Failure to record the correct amount of ending 1995 inventory. The amount was understated because of an error in calculation.						
3. Failure to record merchandise purchased in 1995. Merchandise was also omitted from ending inventory in 1995 but was not yet sold.						
4. Failure to record accrued interest on notes payable in 1995; amount was recorded when paid in 1996.						
5. Failure to reflect supplies on hand on balance sheet at end of 1995.						

PROBLEMS

P23-1 (Change in Estimate, Principle, and Error Correction) Sanborn Company reported net income of $640,000 for 1994. Its preliminary calculation of net income for 1995 shows $900,000. The books are still open for 1995. Additional information is as follows:

1. On January 1, 1994, Sanborn purchased equipment for $880,000. Sanborn estimated its useful life to be 10 years with a zero salvage value. Sanborn uses sum-of-the-years'-digits depreciation. On the basis of new information available at the end of 1995, Sanborn now estimates the asset's useful life should total 8 years. Depreciation expense based on a 10-year useful life has already been recorded in 1995.

2. In reviewing the December 31, 1995, inventory, Sanborn discovered errors in its inventory-taking procedures that have caused inventories for the last 3 years to be incorrect. Inventory at the end of 1993 was overstated $11,000; at the end of 1994, it was overstated $20,000; and at the end of 1995, it was understated $19,000. Sanborn uses a periodic inventory system and does not have a Cost of Goods Sold account. All information used to compute cost of goods sold is compiled in the Income Summary account. At the end of 1995, entries were made to remove the beginning inventory amount from the Inventory account (with a corresponding debit to Income Summary) and to establish the ending in-

ventory amount in the Inventory account (with a corresponding credit to Income Summary). The Income Summary account is still open.

3. Sanborn has failed to accrue wages payable at the end of each of the last 3 years, as follows:

December 31, 1993	$1,600
December 31, 1994	3,000
December 31, 1995	2,400

4. The following change from expensing relining costs to capitalizing them is to be treated as a change in accounting principle.

   a. Sanborn uses two large blast furnaces in its manufacturing process. These furnaces must be periodically relined. Furnace A was relined in January 1989 at a cost of $300,000 and again in January 1994 at a cost of $400,000. Furnace B was relined for the first time in January 1995 at a cost of $450,000. All these costs were charged to Maintenance Expense as incurred.

   b. Since a relining will last for 5 years, a better matching of revenues and expenses would have resulted if the cost of the relining was capitalized and depreciated over 5 years. Sanborn has decided to make a change in accounting principle from expensing relining costs as incurred to capitalizing them and depreciating them over 5 years on a straight-line basis. A full year's depreciation will be taken in the year of relining.

Instructions

(a) Prepare the journal entries necessary at December 31, 1995, to record the corrections and changes above. The books are still open for 1995. Income tax effects may be ignored.

(b) Sanborn plans to issue comparative (1995 and 1994) financial statements. Starting with $900,000 for 1995 and $640,000 for 1994, prepare a schedule to derive the correct net incomes for 1995 and 1994 to be shown in these statements. Income tax effects may be ignored.

(c) What are the pro-forma net incomes for 1995 and 1994 that would be reported in the comparative financial statements? Income tax effects may be ignored.

P23-2 (Comprehensive Accounting Change and Error Analysis Problem) On December 31, 1996, before the books were closed, the management and accountants of Hopkins Inc. made the following determinations about three depreciable assets:

1. Depreciable asset A was purchased January 2, 1993. It originally cost $495,000 and, for depreciation purposes, the straight-line method was originally chosen. The asset was originally expected to be useful for 10 years and have a zero salvage value. In 1996, the decision was made to change the depreciation method from straight-line to sum-of-the-years'-digits, and the estimates relating to useful life and salvage value remained unchanged.

2. Depreciable asset B was purchased January 3, 1992. It originally cost $120,000 and, for depreciation purposes, the straight-line method was chosen. The asset was originally expected to be useful for 15 years and have a zero salvage value. In 1996 the decision was made to shorten the total life of this asset to 9 years and to estimate the salvage value at $3,000.

3. Depreciable asset C was purchased January 5, 1992. The asset's original cost was $70,000, and this amount was entirely expensed in 1992. This particular asset has a 10-year useful life and no salvage value. The straight-line method was chosen for depreciation purposes.

Additional data:

1. Income in 1996 before depreciation expense amounted to $410,000.
2. Depreciation expense on assets other than A, B, and C totaled $55,000 in 1996.
3. Income in 1995 was reported at $380,000.
4. Ignore all income tax effects.
5. 100,000 shares of common stock were outstanding in 1995 and 1996.

Instructions

(a) Prepare all necessary entries in 1996 to record these determinations.

(b) Prepare comparative income statements for Hopkins Inc. for 1995 and 1996, starting with income before the cumulative effects of any change in accounting principle.

(c) Prepare comparative retained earnings statements for Hopkins Inc. for 1995 and 1996. The company had retained earnings of $200,000 at December 31, 1994.

P23-3 (Comprehensive Accounting Change and Error Analysis Problem) Selby Inc. was organized in late 1993 to manufacture and sell hosiery. At the end of its fourth year of operation, the company has been fairly successful, as indicated by the following reported net incomes.

1993	$180,000[a]	1995	$245,000
1994	200,000[b]	1996	316,000

[a]Includes a $12,000 increase because of change in bad debt experience rate.
[b]Includes extraordinary gain of $40,000.

The company has decided to expand operations and has applied for a sizable bank loan. The bank officer has indicated that the records should be audited and presented in comparative statements to facilitate analysis by the bank. Selby, therefore, hired the auditing firm of Check & Doublecheck Co. and has provided the following additional information.

1. In early 1994 Selby changed their estimate from 2% to 1% on the amount of bad debt expense to be charged to operations. Bad debt expense for 1993, if a 1% rate had been used, would have been $12,000. The company, therefore, restated its net income of 1993.
2. In 1996 the auditor discovered that the company had changed its method of inventory pricing from LIFO to FIFO. The effect on the income statements for the previous years is as follows:

	1993	1994	1995	1996
Net income unadjusted-LIFO basis	$180,000	$200,000	$245,000	$316,000
Net income unadjusted-FIFO basis	195,000	205,000	255,000	300,000
	$ 15,000	$ 5,000	$ 10,000	($ 16,000)

3. In 1994, the company changed its method of depreciation from the accelerated method to the straight-line approach. The company used the straight-line method in 1994. The effect on the income statement for the previous year is as follows:

	1993
Net income unadjusted (accelerated method)	$180,000
Net income unadjusted (straight-line method)	187,000
	$ 7,000

4. In 1996, the auditor discovered that:
   a. The company incorrectly overstated the ending inventory by $11,000 in 1995.
   b. A dispute developed in 1994 with the Internal Revenue Service over the deductibility of entertainment expenses. In 1993 the company was not permitted these deductions, but a tax settlement was reached in 1996 that allowed these expenses. As a result of the court's finding, tax expenses in 1996 were reduced by $60,000.

Instructions
(a) Indicate how each of these changes or corrections should be handled in the accounting records. Ignore income tax considerations.
(b) Present comparative income statements for the years 1993 to 1996, starting with income before extraordinary items. Do not prepare pro-forma amounts. Ignore income tax considerations.

P23-4 (Change in Principle (LIFO to Average Cost), Income Statements) The management of Lahey Instrument Company had concluded, with the concurrence of its independent auditors, that results of operations would be more fairly presented if Lahey changed its method of pricing inventory from last-in, first-out (LIFO) to average cost in 1995. Given below is the 5-year summary of income and a schedule of what the inventories might have been if stated on the average cost method.

Lahey Instrument Company
STATEMENT OF INCOME AND RETAINED EARNINGS
For the Years Ended May 31

	1991	1992	1993	1994	1995
Sales—net	$13,964	$15,506	$16,673	$18,221	$18,898
Cost of goods sold					
Beginning inventory	1,000	1,100	1,000	1,115	1,237
Purchases	13,000	13,900	15,000	15,900	17,100
Ending inventory	(1,100)	(1,000)	(1,115)	(1,237)	(1,369)
Total	12,900	14,000	14,885	15,778	16,968
Gross profit	1,064	1,506	1,788	2,443	1,930
Administrative expenses	700	763	832	907	989
Income before taxes	364	743	956	1,536	941
Income taxes (50%)	182	372	478	768	471
Net income	182	371	478	768	470
Retained earnings—beginning	1,206	1,388	1,759	2,237	3,005
Retained earnings—ending	$ 1,388	$ 1,759	$ 2,237	$ 3,005	$ 3,475
Earnings per share	$ 1.82	$ 3.71	$ 4.78	$ 7.68	$ 4.70

		Schedule of Inventory Balances Using Average Cost Method Year Ended May 31			
1990	1991	1992	1993	1994	1995
$950	$1,124	$1,101	$1,270	$1,490	$1,699

Instructions

Prepare comparative statements for the 5 years, assuming that Lahey changed its method of inventory pricing to average cost. Indicate the effects on net income and earnings per share for the years involved. (All amounts except EPS are rounded up to the nearest dollar.)

P23-5 (Financial Statement Effect of Changes in Principle and Estimate) Hendricks Corporation has decided that in the preparation of its 1996 financial statements two changes should be made from the methods used in prior years:

1. **Depreciation.** Hendricks has always used an accelerated method for tax and financial reporting purposes but has decided to change during 1996 to the straight-line method for financial reporting only. Assume that the accelerated method for tax and reporting purposes has been the same in the past. The effect of this change is as follows:

	Excess of Accelerated Depreciation over Straight-line Depreciation
Prior to 1995	$1,365,000
1995	106.050
1996	103,950
	$1,575,000

Depreciation is charged to cost of sales and to selling, general, and administrative expenses on the basis of 75% and 25%, respectively.

2. **Bad debt expense.** In the past Hendricks has recognized bad debt expense equal to 1.5% of net sales. After careful review it has been decided that a rate of 1.75% is more appropriate for 1996. Bad debt expense is charged to selling, general, and administrative expenses.

The following information is taken from preliminary financial statements, prepared before giving effect to the two changes:

Hendricks Corporation
CONDENSED BALANCE SHEET
December 31, 1996
With Comparative Figures for 1995

	1996	1995
Assets		
Current assets	$43,561,000	$43,900,000
Plant assets, at cost	45,792,000	43,974,000
Less accumulated depreciation	23,761,000	22,946,000
	$65,592,000	$64,928,000
Liabilities and Stockholders' Equity		
Current liabilities	$21,124,000	$23,650,000
Long-term debt	15,154,000	14,097,000
Capital stock	11,620,000	11,620,000
Retained earnings	17,694,000	15,561,000
	$65,592,000	$64,928,000

Hendricks Corporation
INCOME STATEMENT
For the Year Ended December 31, 1996
With Comparative Figures for 1995

	1996	1995
Net sales	$80,520,000	$78,920,000
Cost of goods sold	54,847,000	53,074,000
	25,673,000	25,846,000

Selling, general, and administrative expenses	19,540,000	18,411,000
	6,133,000	7,435,000
Other income (expense), net	(1,198,000)	(1,079,000)
Income before income taxes	4,935,000	6,356,000
Income taxes	2,368,800	3,050,880
Net income	$ 2,566,200	$ 3,305,120

There have been no temporary differences between any book and tax items prior to the changes above. The effective tax rate is 48%.

Instructions

For the items listed below compute the amounts that would appear on the comparative (1996 and 1995) financial statements of Hendricks Corporation after adjustment for the two accounting changes. Show amounts for both 1996 and 1995 and prepare supporting schedules as necessary.

(a) Accumulated depreciation.
(b) Deferred liability taxes (cumulative).
(c) Selling, general, and administrative expenses.
(d) Current portion of federal income tax expense.
(e) Deferred portion of federal income tax expense.
(f) Retained earnings.
(g) Pro-forma net income.

P23-6 (Error Corrections) You have been assigned to examine the financial statements of Q. Kellog Company for the year ended December 31, 1996. You discover the following situations:

1. Depreciation of $2,900 for 1996 on delivery vehicles was not recorded.
2. The physical inventory count on December 31, 1995, improperly excluded merchandise costing $18,000 that had been temporarily stored in a public warehouse. Kellog uses a periodic inventory system.
3. The physical inventory count on December 31, 1996, improperly included merchandise with a cost of $7,000 that had been recorded as a sale on December 27, 1996, and held for the customer to pick up on January 4, 1997.
4. A collection of $5,200 on account from a customer received on December 31, 1996, was not recorded until January 2, 1997.
5. In 1996, the company sold for $3,200 fully depreciated equipment that originally cost $22,000. The company credited the proceeds from the sale to the Equipment account.
6. During November 1996, a competitor company filed a patent-infringement suit against Kellog claiming damages of $220,000. The company's legal counsel has indicated that an unfavorable verdict is probable and a reasonable estimate of the court's award to the competitor is $120,000. The company has not reflected or disclosed this situation in the financial statements.
7. Kellog has a portfolio of marketable equity securities which should be reported as a short-term investment at the lower of cost or market. No entry has been made for lower of cost or market. Information on cost and market value is as follows:

	Cost	Market
December 31, 1995	$84,000	$86,000
December 31, 1996	$84,000	$82,000

8. At December 31, 1996, an analysis of payroll information shows accrued salaries of $12,400. The Accrued Salaries Payable account had a balance of $16,000 at December 31, 1996, which was unchanged from its balance at December 31, 1995.
9. A large piece of equipment was purchased on January 3, 1996, for $24,000 and was charged to Repairs Expense. The equipment is estimated to have a service life of 8 years and no residual value. Kellog normally uses the straight-line depreciation method for this type of equipment.
10. A $12,000 insurance premium paid on July 1, 1995, for a policy that expires on June 30, 1998, was charged to insurance expense.
11. A trademark was acquired at the beginning of 1995 for $40,000. No amortization has been recorded since its acquisition. The maximum allowable amortization period is to be used.

Instructions

Assume the trial balance has been prepared but the books have not been closed for 1996. Assuming all amounts are material, prepare journal entries showing the adjustments that are required. Ignore income tax considerations.

P23-7 (Error Corrections and Changes in Principle) Lillie Company is in the process of adjusting and correcting its books at the end of 1996. In reviewing its records, the following information is compiled.

1. On January 1, 1995, Lillie implemented a stock appreciation right (SAR) plan for its top executives. The plan was to run from January 1, 1994, to December 31, 1996. This period was the intended service period and the date of exercise was December 31, 1996. At December 31, 1996 (the measurement date), the executives were to receive in cash the appreciation in the market value of the stock over the 3-year period. Using the market prices of the stock at the end of 1994 and 1995, respectively, Lillie estimated compensation expense of $30,800 for 1994 and $49,700 for 1995. At December 31, however, the market price of the stock was below its price at January 1, 1994.

2. Lillie has failed to accrue sales commissions payable at the end of each of the last 2 years, as follows:

December 31, 1995	$4,000
December 31, 1996	$2,600

3. In reviewing the December 31, 1996, inventory, Lillie discovered errors in its inventory-taking procedures that have caused inventories for the last 3 years to be incorrect, as follows:

December 31, 1994	Understated	$16,000
December 31, 1995	Understated	$21,000
December 31, 1996	Overstated	$ 6,000

Lillie has already made an entry to establish the incorrect December 31, 1996, inventory amount.

4. At December 31, 1996, Lillie decided to change its depreciation method on its office equipment from double-declining balance to straight-line. Assume that tax depreciation is higher than the double-declining depreciation taken for each period. The following information is available (the tax rate is 30%):

	Double-Declining Balance	Straight-Line	Pretax Difference	Tax Effect	Difference, Net of Tax
Prior to 1996	$70,000	$40,000	$30,000	$9,000	$21,000
1996	12,000	10,000	2,000	600	1,400

Lillie has already recorded the 1996 depreciation expense using the double-declining balance method.

5. Before 1996 Lillie accounted for its income from long-term construction contracts on the completed contract basis. Early in 1996 Lillie changed to the percentage-of-completion basis for both accounting and tax purposes. Income for 1996 has been recorded using the percentage-of-completion method. The income tax rate is 30%. The following information is available:

	Pretax Income	
	Percentage of Completion	Completed Contract
Prior to 1996	$150,000	$100,000
1996	60,000	20,000

Instructions
Prepare the journal entries necessary at December 31, 1996, to record the above corrections and changes. The books are still open for 1996. Lillie has not yet recorded its 1996 income tax expense and payable amounts so current year tax effects may be ignored. Prior year tax effects must be considered in items 4 and 5.

P23-8 (Comprehensive Error Analysis) On March 5, 1996, you were hired by Sampsell Inc., a closely held company, as a staff member of its newly created internal auditing department. While reviewing the company's records for 1994 and 1995, you discover that no adjustments have yet been made for the items listed below.

Items

1. Interest income of $13,600 was not accrued at the end of 1994. It was recorded when received in February 1995.

2. A word processor costing $8,000 was expensed when purchased on July 1, 1994. It is expected to have a 4-year life with no salvage value. The company typically uses straight-line depreciation for all fixed assets.

3. Research and development costs of $30,000 were incurred early in 1994. They were capitalized and were to be amortized over a 3-year period. Amortization of $10,000 was recorded for 1994 and $10,000 for 1995.

4. On January 2, 1994, Sampsell leased a building for 5 years at a monthly rental of $8,000. On that date, the company paid the following amounts, which were expensed when paid.

Security deposit	$27,000
First month's rent	8,000
Last month's rent	8,000
	$43,000

5. The company received $33,000 from a customer at the beginning of 1994 for services that it is to perform evenly over a 3-year period beginning in 1994. None of the amount received was reported as unearned revenue at the end of 1994.
6. Merchandise inventory costing $17,500 was in the warehouse at December 31, 1994, but was incorrectly omitted from the physical count at that date.

Instructions

Indicate the effect of any errors on the net income figure reported on the income statement for the year ending December 31, 1994, and the retained earnings figure reported on the balance sheet at December 31, 1995. Assume all amounts are material and ignore income tax effects. Using the following format, enter the appropriate dollar amounts in the appropriate columns. Consider each item independent of the other items. It is not necessary to total the columns on the grid.

	Net Income for 1994		Retained Earnings at 12/31/95	
Item	Understated	Overstated	Understated	Overstated

(CIA adapted)

P23-9 (Error Analysis) Norton Corporation has used the accrual basis of accounting for several years. A review of the records, however, indicates that some expenses and revenues have been handled on a cash basis because of errors made by an inexperienced bookkeeper. Income statements prepared by the bookkeeper reported $31,000 net income for 1995 and $40,000 net income for 1996. Further examination of the records reveals that the following items were handled improperly.

1. Rent was received from a tenant in December 1995; the amount, $1,200, was recorded as income at that time even though the rental pertained to 1996.
2. Wages payable on December 31 have been consistently omitted from the records of that date and have been entered as expenses when paid in the following year. The amounts of the accruals recorded in this manner were:

December 31, 1994	$1,100
December 31, 1995	1,500
December 31, 1996	940

3. Invoices for office supplies purchased have been charged to expense accounts when received. Inventories of supplies on hand at the end of each year have been ignored, and no entry has been made for them.

December 31, 1994	$1,300
December 31, 1995	740
December 31, 1996	1,420

Instructions

Prepare a schedule that will show the corrected net income for the years 1995 and 1996. All items listed should be labeled clearly. Ignore income tax considerations.

P23-10 (Error Analysis and Correcting Entries) Folk Corporation is in the process of negotiating a loan for expansion purposes. Folk's books and records have never been audited and the bank has requested that an audit be performed. Folk has prepared the following comparative financial statements for the years ended December 31, 1996, and 1995:

BALANCE SHEET
As of December 31, 1996, and 1995

	1996	1995
Assets		
Current assets		
Cash	$ 163,000	$ 82,000
Accounts receivable	392,000	296,000
Allowance for doubtful accounts	(37,000)	(18,000)
Marketable securities, at cost	78,000	78,000
Merchandise inventory	207,000	202,000
Total current assets	803,000	640,000
Plant assets		
Property, plant, and equipment	167,000	169,500
Accumulated depreciation	(121,600)	(106,400)
Total fixed assets	45,400	63,100
Total assets	$ 848,400	$703,100

Liabilities and Stockholders' Equity		
Liabilities		
Accounts payable	$ 121,400	$196,100
Stockholders' equity		
Common stock, par value $10, authorized 50,000 shares, issued and outstanding 20,000 shares	260,000	260,000
Retained earnings	467,000	247,000
Total stockholders' equity	727,000	507,000
Total liabilities and stockholders' equity	$ 848,400	$703,100

STATEMENT OF INCOME
For the Years Ended December 31, 1996 and 1995

	1996	1995
Sales	$1,000,000	$900,000
Cost of sales	430,000	395,000
Gross profit	570,000	505,000
Operating expenses	210,000	205,000
Administrative expenses	140,000	105,000
	350,000	310,000
Net income	$ 220,000	$195,000

During the course of the audit, the following additional facts were determined:

1. An analysis of collections and losses on accounts receivable during the past 2 years indicates a drop in anticipated losses due to bad debts. After consultation with management it was agreed that the loss experience rate on sales should be reduced from the recorded 2% to 1%, beginning with the year ended December 31, 1996.

2. An analysis of marketable securities revealed that this investment portfolio consisted entirely of short-term investments in marketable equity securities that were acquired in 1995. The total market valuation for these investments as of the end of each year was as follows:

December 31, 1995	$82,000
December 31, 1996	$65,000

3. The merchandise inventory at December 31, 1995, was overstated by $8,900 and the merchandise inventory at December 31, 1996, was overstated by $13,200.

4. On January 2, 1995, equipment costing $30,000 (estimated useful life of 10 years and residual value of $5,000) was incorrectly charged to operating expenses. Folk records depreciation on the straight-line method. In 1996 fully depreciated equipment (with no residual value) that originally cost $17,500 was sold as scrap for $2,800. Folk credited the proceeds of $2,800 to the equipment account.

5. An analysis of 1995 operating expenses revealed that Folk charged to expense a 4-year insurance premium of $4,240 on January 15, 1995.

Instructions

(a) Prepare the journal entries to correct the books at December 31, 1996. The books for 1996 have not been closed. Ignore income taxes.

(b) Prepare a schedule showing the computation of corrected net income for the years ended December 31, 1996 and 1995, assuming that any adjustments are to be reported on comparative statements for the 2 years. The first items on your schedule should be the net income for each year. Ignore income taxes. (Do not prepare financial statements.)

(AICPA adapted)

P23-11 (Error Analysis and Correcting Entries) You have been asked by a client to review the records of Rudolph Company, a small manufacturer of precision tools and machines. Your client is interested in buying the business, and arrangements have been made for you to review the accounting records.

Your examination reveals the following:

1. Rudolph Company commenced business on April 1, 1993, and has been reporting on a fiscal year ending March 31. The company has never been audited, but the annual statements prepared by the bookkeeper reflect the following income before closing and before deducting income taxes:

Year Ended March 31	Income Before Taxes
1994	$ 73,600
1995	114,400
1996	107,580

2. A relatively small number of machines have been shipped on consignment. These transactions have been recorded as ordinary sales and billed as such. On March 31 of each year, machines billed and in the hands of consignees amounted to:

1994	$6,500
1995	none
1996	5,590

   Sales price was determined by adding 30% to cost. Assume that the consigned machines are sold the following year.

3. On March 30, 1995, two machines were shipped to a customer on a C.O.D. basis. The sale was not entered until April 5, 1995, when cash was received for $6,100. The machines were not included in the inventory at March 31, 1995. (Title passed on March 30, 1995.)

4. All machines are sold subject to a five-year warranty. It is estimated that the expense ultimately to be incurred in connection with the warranty will amount to ½ of 1% of sales. The company has charged an expense account for warranty costs incurred.

   Sales per books and warranty costs were:

Year Ended March 31	Sales	Warranty Expense for Sales Made In			Total
		1994	1995	1996	
1994	$ 940,000	$760			$ 760
1995	1,010,000	360	$1,310		1,670
1996	1,795,000	320	1,620	$1,910	3,850

5. A review of the corporate minutes reveals the manager is entitled to a bonus of ½ of 1% of the income before deducting income taxes and the bonus. The bonuses have never been recorded or paid.

6. Bad debts have been recorded on a direct writeoff basis. Experience of similar enterprises indicates that losses will approximate ¼ of 1% of sales. Bad debts written off were:

	Bad Debts Incurred on Sales Made In			Total
	1994	1995	1996	
1994	$750			$ 750
1995	800	$ 520		1,320
1996	350	1,800	$1,700	3,850

7. The bank deducts 6% on all contracts financed. Of this amount, ½% is placed in a reverse to the credit of Rudolph Company that is refunded to Rudolph as finance contracts are paid in full. The reserve established by the bank has not been reflected in the books of Rudolph. The excess of credits over debits (net increase) to the reserve account with Rudolph on the books of the bank for each fiscal year were as follows:

1994	$ 3,000
1995	3,900
1996	5,100
	$12,000

8. Commissions on sales have been entered when paid. Commissions payable on March 31 of each year were:

1994	$1,400
1995	800
1996	1,120

Instructions

(a) Present a schedule showing the revised income before income taxes for each of the years ended March 31, 1994, 1995, and 1996. Make computations to the nearest whole dollar.

(b) Prepare the journal entry or entries you would give the bookkeeper to correct the books. Assume the books have not yet been closed for the fiscal year ended March 31, 1996. Disregard correction of income taxes.

(AICPA adapted)

CASES

C23-1 (Analysis of Various Accounting Changes and Errors) Nelweem Inc. has recently hired a new independent auditor who says she wants "to get everything straightened out." Consequently, she has proposed the following accounting changes in connection with Nelweem Inc.'s 1996 financial statements:

1. At December 31, 1995, the client had a receivable of $900,000 from KapKim Inc. on its balance sheet. KapKim Inc. has gone bankrupt, and no recovery is expected. The client proposes to write off the receivable as a prior period item.

2. The client proposes the following changes in depreciation policies:
    (a) For office furniture and fixtures it proposes to change from a 10-year useful life to an 8-year life. If this change had been made in prior years, retained earnings at December 31, 1995 would have been $250,000 less. The effect of the change on 1996 income alone is a reduction of $50,000.
    (b) For its manufacturing assets the client proposes to change from double-declining balance depreciation to straight line. If straight-line depreciation had been used for all prior periods, retained earnings would have been $380,800 greater at December 31, 1995. The effect of the change on 1996 income alone is a reduction of $4,800.
    (c) For its equipment in the leasing division the client proposes to adopt the sum-of-the-years'-digits depreciation method. The client had never used SYD before. The first year the client operated a leasing division was 1996. If straight-line depreciation were used, 1996 income would be $90,000 greater.

3. In preparing its 1995 statements, one of the client's bookkeepers overstated ending inventory by $250,000 because of a mathematical error. The client proposes to treat this item as a prior period adjustment.

4. In the past, the client has spread preproduction costs in its furniture division over 5 years. Because its latest furniture is of the "fad" type, it appears that the largest volume of sales will occur during the first 2 years after introduction. Consequently, the client proposes to amortize preproduction costs on a per-unit basis, which will result in expensing most of such costs during the first 2 years after the furniture's introduction. If the new accounting method had been used prior to 1996, retained earnings at December 31, 1995, would have been $400,000 less.

5. For the nursery division the client proposes to switch from FIFO to LIFO inventories because it believes that LIFO will provide a better matching of current costs with revenues. The effect of making this change on 1996 earnings will be an increase of $310,000. The client says that the effect of the change on December 31, 1995, retained earnings cannot be determined.

6. To achieve a better matching of revenues and expenses in its building construction division, the client proposes to switch from the completed-contract method of accounting to the percentage-of-completion method. Had the percentage-of-completion method been employed in all prior years, retained earnings at December 31, 1995, would have been $1,250,000 greater.

Instructions
(a) For each of the changes described above decide whether:
   1. The change involves an accounting principle, accounting estimate, or correction of an error.
   2. Restatement of opening retained earnings is required.
(b) Do any of the changes require presentation of pro-forma amounts?
(c) What would be the proper adjustment to the December 31, 1995, retained earnings? What would be the "cumulative effect" shown separately in the 1996 income statement?

C23-2 (Analysis of Various Accounting Changes and Errors) Various types of accounting changes can affect the financial statements of a business enterprise differently. Assume that the following list describes changes that have a material effect on the financial statements for the current year of your business enterprise.

1. A change from the completed-contract method to the percentage-of-completion method of accounting for long-term construction-type contracts.

2. A change in the estimated useful life of previously recorded fixed assets as a result of newly acquired information.

3. A change from deferring and amortizing preproduction costs to recording such costs as an expense when incurred because future benefits of the costs have become doubtful. The new accounting method was adopted in recognition of the change in estimated future benefits.

4. A change from including the employer share of FICA taxes with Payroll Tax Expenses to including it with "Retirement benefits" on the income statement.

5. Correction of a mathematical error in inventory pricing made in a prior period.

6. A change from prime costing to full absorption costing for inventory valuation.

7. A change from presentation of statements of individual companies to presentation of consolidated statements.

8. A change in the method of accounting for leases for tax purposes to conform with the financial accounting method. As a result, both deferred and current taxes payable changed substantially.
9. A change from the FIFO method of inventory pricing to the LIFO method of inventory pricing.

Instructions

Identify the type of change that is described in each item above and indicate whether the prior year's financial statements should be restated when presented in comparative form with the current year's statements. Ignore possible pro-forma effects.

C23-3 (Analysis of Three Accounting Changes and Errors) Listed below are three independent, unrelated sets of facts relating to accounting changes.

Situation I.

Promila Company is in the process of having its first audit. The company's policy with regard to recognition of revenue is to use the installment method. However, *APB No. 10* states that the installment method of revenue recognition is not a generally accepted accounting principle except in certain circumstances, which are not present here. Promila president, Greg Clem, is willing to change to an acceptable method.

Situation II.

A company decides in January 1996 to adopt the straight-line method of depreciation for plant equipment. The straight-line method will be used for new acquisitions as well as for previously acquired plant equipment for which depreciation had been provided on an accelerated basis.

Situation III.

A company determined that the depreciable lives of its fixed assets are too long at present to fairly match the cost of the fixed assets with the revenue produced. The company decided at the beginning of the current year to reduce the depreciable lives of all of its existing fixed assets by 5 years.

Instructions

For each of the situations described, provide the information indicated below.
 (a) Type of accounting change.
 (b) Manner of reporting the change under current generally accepted accounting principles including a discussion, where applicable, of how amounts are computed.
 (c) Effect of the change on the balance sheet and income statement.

C23-4 (Analysis of Various Accounting Changes and Errors) Katherine Shaw, controller of Lotan Corp., is aware that an opinion on accounting changes has been issued. After reading the opinion, she is confused about what action should be taken on the following items related to Lotan Corp. for the year 1995:

1. In 1995 Lotan decided to change its policy on accounting for certain marketing costs. Previously, the company had chosen to defer and amortize all marketing costs over at least 5 years because Lotan believed that a return on these expenditures did not occur immediately. Recently, however, the time differential has considerably shortened, and Lotan is now expensing the marketing costs as incurred.
2. In 1995 the company examined its entire policy relating to the depreciation of plant equipment. Plant equipment had normally been depreciated over a 15-year period, but recent experience has indicated that the company was incorrect in its estimates and that the assets should be depreciated over a 20-year period.
3. One division of Lotan Corp., Manno Co., has consistently shown an increasing net income from period to period. On closer examination of their operating statement, it is noted that bad debt expense and inventory obsolescence charges are much lower than in other divisions. In discussing this with the controller of this division, it has been learned that the controller has increased his net income each period by knowingly making low estimates related to the writeoff of receivables and inventory.
4. In 1995 the company purchased new machinery that should increase production dramatically. The company has decided to depreciate this machinery on an accelerated basis, even though other machinery is depreciated on a straight-line basis.
5. All equipment sold by Lotan is subject to a 3-year warranty. It has been estimated that the expense ultimately to be incurred on these machines is 1% of sales. In 1995 because of a production breakthrough, it is now estimated that ½ of 1% of sales is sufficient. In 1993 and 1994 warranty expense was computed as $55,000 and $60,000, respectively. The company now believes that these warranty costs should be reduced by 50%.
6. In 1995 the company decided to change its method of inventory pricing from average cost to the FIFO method. The effect of this change on prior years is to increase 1993 income by $60,000 and increase 1994 income by $20,000.

Instructions

Katherine Shaw has come to you, as her CPA, for advice about the situations above. Indicate the appropriate accounting treatment that should be given each of these situations.

C23-5 (Comprehensive Accounting Changes and Error Analysis) Wakino Manufacturing is preparing its year-end financial statements. The controller, Kejia Ho, is confronted with several decisions about statement presentation with regard to the following items:

1. The Vice President of Sales had indicated that one product line has lost its customer appeal and will be phased out over the next 3 years. Therefore, a decision has been made to lower the estimated lives on related production equipment from the remaining 5 years to 3 years.
2. Estimating the lives of new products in the Leisure Products Division has become very difficult because of the highly competitive conditions in this market. Therefore, the practice of deferring and amortizing preproduction costs has been abandoned in favor of expensing such costs as they are incurred.
3. The Hightone Building was converted from a sales office to offices for the Accounting Department at the beginning of this year. Therefore, the expense related to this building will now appear as an administrative expense rather than a selling expense on the current year's income statement.
4. When the year-end physical inventory adjustment was made for the current year, the controller discovered that the prior year's physical inventory sheets for an entire warehouse were mislaid and excluded from last year's count.
5. The method of accounting used for financial reporting purposes for certain receivables has been approved for tax purposes during the current tax year by the Internal Revenue Service. This change for tax purposes will cause both deferred and current taxes payable to change substantially.
6. Management has decided to switch from the FIFO inventory valuation method to the LIFO inventory valuation method for all inventories.
7. Wakino's Custom Division manufactures large-scale, custom-designed machinery on a contract basis. Management decided to switch from the completed-contract method to the percentage-of-completion method of accounting for long-term contracts.

Instructions

(a) *APB Opinion No. 20*, "Accounting Changes," identifies four types of accounting changes—changes in accounting principle, changes in estimates, changes in entity, and changes due to error. For each of these four types of accounting changes:
   1. Define the type of change.
   2. Explain the general accounting treatment required according to *APB Opinion No. 20* with respect to the current year and prior years' financial statements.

(b) For each of the seven changes Wakino Manufacturing has made in the current year, identify and explain whether the change is a change in accounting principle, in estimate, in entity, or due to error. If any of the changes is not one of these four types, explain why.

(CMA adapted)

▶ Using Your Judgment ◀

▶ FINANCIAL REPORTING PROBLEM

Using the financial statements and accompanying notes from Georgia-Pacific Corporation's 1993 Annual Report as presented in Appendix 5-A, answer the following questions or instructions.

1. Identify the changes in accounting principles reported by Georgia-Pacific during the three years covered by its income statement (1991–1993). Describe the nature of the change and the amount and year of the change.
2. For each change in accounting principle, identify, if possible, the cumulative effect, the pro-forma effect of each change on prior years, and the effect on operating results in the year of change.
3. Identify any changes in estimates made by Georgia-Pacific during 1993.
4. Why were the changes made?

▶ WRITING ASSIGNMENT

As a certified public accountant, you have been contacted by Sherry Johnson, CEO of Sports-Pro Athletics, Inc., a manufacturer of a variety of athletic equipment. She has asked you how to account for the following changes:

1. Sports-Pro appropriately changed its depreciation method for its production machinery from the double-declining balance method to the production method effective January 1, 1995.

2. Effective January 1, 1995, Sports-Pro appropriately changed the salvage values used in computing depreciation for its office equipment.
3. On December 31, 1995, Sports-Pro appropriately changed the specific subsidiaries constituting the group of companies for which consolidated financial statements are presented.

Instructions
Write a 1–1.5 page letter to Ms. Johnson explaining how each of the above changes should be presented in the December 31, 1995, financial statements.

▶ GROUP ASSIGNMENT

(Error and Changes in Principle and Estimate—Entries) Presented below is the net income related to Ojeda Inc.:

	1996	1995	1994
	$186,000	$142,000	$224,000

Assume that depreciation entries for 1996 have not been recorded. The following information is also available.

1. Ojeda purchased a truck on January 1, 1993, for $43,000 with a $3,000 salvage value and a 5-year life. The company debited an expense account and credited cash on the purchase date.
2. During 1996 Ojeda changed from the straight-line method of depreciation for its building to the double-declining method. The following computations present depreciation on both bases:

	1996	1995	1994
Straight-line	$30,000	$30,000	$30,000
Double-declining	48,600	54,000	60,000

3. Early in 1996 Ojeda determined that a piece of equipment purchased in January 1993 at a cost of $27,000 with an estimated life of 5 years and salvage of $2,000, is now estimated to continue in use until December 31, 2000, and will have a $1,000 salvage value. Ojeda has been using straight-line depreciation.
4. Ojeda won a court case in 1996 related to a patent infringement in 1993. Ojeda will collect its $20,000 settlement of the suit in 1997. The company had not recorded any entries related to this suit in previous periods.
5. Ojeda, in reviewing its provision for uncollectibles during 1996, has determined that 1% of sales is the appropriate amount of bad debt expense to be charged to operations. The company had used ½ of 1% as its rate in 1995 and 1994 when the expense had been $9,000 and $6,000, respectively. The company would have recorded $8,000 of bad debt expense on December 31, 1996, under the old rate. An entry for bad debt expense in 1996 has not been recorded.

Instructions
Your instructor will assign one member of the group to serve as recorder and one member to serve as spokesperson. For each of the foregoing items, provide the information for the recorder to prepare the journal entry(ies) that Ojeda would have made to record them during 1996; assume the books have not been closed. If no entry is required, briefly explain why. Ignore income tax considerations.

▶ ETHICS CASE

(Ethical Issue: Accounting Change for the Estimated Life of an Asset) Andy Felo is an audit senior of a large public accounting firm who has just been assigned to the Colby Corporation's annual audit engagement, which has been a client of Andy's firm for many years. Colby is a fast-growing business in the commercial construction industry. In reviewing the fixed asset ledger, Andy discovered a series of unusual accounting changes, in which the useful lives of assets, depreciated using the straight-line method, were substantially lowered near the midpoint of the original estimate. For example, the useful life of one dump truck was changed from 10 to 6 years during the fifth year of service. Upon further investigation, Andy was told by Martin Freedman, Colby's accounting manager, "I don't really see your problem. After all, it is perfectly legal to change an accounting estimate. Besides, our CEO likes to see big earnings!"

Instructions
   (a) What are the ethical issues concerning Colby's practice of changing the useful lives of fixed assets?
   (b) Who could be harmed by Colby's unusual accounting changes?
   (c) What should Andy Felo do in this situation?

FINANCIAL ACCOUNTING: A CFO'S VIEWPOINT

A visit with
CLARK JOHNSON

What got you interested in accounting?

I really backed into it. Coming out of high school, I was not able to go full time to college. But I knew Johnson & Johnson, a local company, paid tuition for employees who went to night school. So I went over there and got hired for the mailroom. The first day, they said they had a job in the accounting department as a clerk. Then I walked across the street to Rutgers and registered with the intention of becoming an engineer. They said, "We don't teach engineering at night." So I asked what they did teach and among other things they mentioned accounting. I said, "Well, I'm working in the accounting department, so OK."

How long did it take you to get your degree?

Eight years for my undergrad and four more years for my MBA.

After your bachelor's degree, did you go right into the MBA?

I didn't go back for a number of years. Instead, I got busy with a small J&J start-up, which was probably the secret to getting ahead. I learned a lot very fast. J&J is very decentralized, and I wrote my own chart of accounts, did everything my own way, and had broad responsibility—not only for accounting but for distribution, traffic, purchasing and export sales and marketing. I became CFO there at age 32.

CLARK H. JOHNSON is chief financial officer of Johnson & Johnson (he's no relation), a leading American pharmaceutical corporation based in New Brunswick, New Jersey. He has worked at J&J his entire career, starting in the company's mailroom when he was 17 years old. Mr. Johnson received his bachelor's degree in accounting from Rutgers University and his MBA from Farleigh Dickinson University—attending both at night while he worked at J&J during the day.

You got involved with the CMA program in the early 1970s.

I became one of the first certified management accountants, and that really brought me more to the attention of corporate financial management. The next thing I knew, they asked me to come to corporate to be assistant corporate controller.

The CMA sounds like managerial or cost accounting, though.

Management accounting is not just cost accounting. It includes all corporate accounting and financial management, including preparing financial statements—everything but public accounting.

Why did you do that instead of the CPA?

By the time I got my college degree, I was already at a senior level. Going into public accounting at that point would have been a big step backward. Also, I didn't want to leave J&J.

What was your job when you went to corporate?

My initial assignment was internal reporting from the 200 operating companies to corporate. I traveled the world meeting with the CFOs and controllers of these subsidiaries. I was only in that job for a year before I became general controller. Then, I had public reporting responsibility.

You're very involved in the standard-setting process.

As one of the largest market capitalization (number of shares outstanding × stock price) companies in the United States, we feel an obligation to be involved. I've been on the Financial Accounting Foundation—which sponsors the FASB—for three years. I was chairman of the finance committee that raises funds from industry and public accounting. I have had internal auditors working on a "post audit" of one of the accounting standards—contributing voluntary company time to aid in the oversight of the standard-setting process.

What is industry's concern with the FASB?

Industry's viewpoint, generally speaking, is that accounting standards are much too theoretical and detailed—too cookbookish—and don't allow adequate judgment to reflect individual situations. The auditors would like everything to be spelled out because they figure that the less judgment, the safer they are.

Please comment on the cost of compliance with FASB standards.

Some of them are very expensive. You have to remember that we're in a very competitive society and there's a lot of pressure to reduce costs. And the nature of the FASB is to increase our costs. J&J has 170 subsidiaries outside the United States, and we have to go out and teach these people so it's very complex for us. However, the FASB has shown an open mind to fixing things. For example, *SFAS 96* on income tax accounting was very complex and controversial because it ignored the probability of future tax deductions. *Statement 96* was superceded by *Statement 109*, which was no longer controversial because they made changes that allowed for the recognition of deferred tax assets.

FASB has several new statements in the works. What is your view on stock options?

I'm hoping that the Board will require disclosure only and not require a charge to earnings. But even if they require a charge, it won't affect us too much. Only about 5% of our outstanding stock is in options. The earnings impact per year would be less than 1% for us.

Another proposal concerns segment reporting.

The FASB would ask us to report operating profit on a quarterly basis by segment. Currently, segment reporting is required only annually. Our concern is that such a disclosure would add a lot of volatility to the quarterly reporting. It would make Wall Street's preoccupation with short-term results even worse.

How have you handled the medical and other post-retirement benefits?

We have a substantial reserve, but the numbers are soft. The issue of health care reform recognizes the fact that our medical costs cannot continue to grow at the rate that they have been growing. Yet FASB requires us to accrue costs at the current rate which we know can't continue. The rate at which health care costs are going to grow is still very much an unknown.

You do a lot of acquisitions. How has goodwill accounting changed?

Up until 1994 foreign companies had a big advantage over U.S. companies. Foreign companies could write off goodwill against equity immediately, rather than taking a P&L charge every year. Starting in 1995 goodwill has to be written off over 5–20 years to conform to international accounting standards. That's why, for example, Swiss companies have been so aggressive in 1994 in doing acquisitions. They don't have to take an annual charge for goodwill for any deal done in 1994. Starting in 1995, they will.

What about the pension footnote—*SFAS 87*?

Every year, I go over the pension plan footnote with our outside directors. They all sit there and nod their heads politely, but I know that they don't understand it at all. What they're really interested in is whether we have enough money to fund the obligations, but that's not an accounting question.

As a CFO, what types of ethical questions come up?

As far as Wall Street is concerned, we want to show dependable consistent earnings growth. Where ethics gets involved is doing it without playing games with the numbers. What I always say is that we don't manage earnings—we manage the business.

You spend a lot of time on acquisitions.

That's probably how I got to be CFO, because of my involvement in both buying and selling businesses. We do five or more acquisitions a year totaling up to $500 million. Besides evaluating the transaction from a financial standpoint, one of my roles is to find creative ways to do the transaction. For example, we have a fifty-fifty joint venture with Merck. We have the over-the-counter marketing expertise, and they have the prescription drugs with OTC potential. So, we're combining our marketing and their research.

You can't consolidate sales with a fifty-fifty joint venture.

The U.S. accounting rules don't permit it—although internationally, each partner can take half the sales. However, we came up with a creative way for us to record the sales on our income statement. And that was for the joint venture to subcontract the selling activity to one of our operating companies.

Usually, joint ventures are just disclosed in the footnotes.

We want them on the balance sheet because we have always been quite forthright in disclosing material matters.

It depends on whether you have to undertake a lot of debt. You probably make most of your acquisitions with cash.

We do. We could borrow billions and still maintain a very good credit rating.

CHAPTER 24

STATEMENT OF CASH FLOWS

LEARNING OBJECTIVES

After studying this chapter, you should be able to:

1. Describe the evolution and purpose of the statement of cash flows.

2. Identify the major classifications of cash flows.

3. Differentiate between net income and net cash flows from operating activities.

4. Contrast the direct and indirect methods of calculating net cash flow from operating activities.

5. Determine net cash flows from investing and financing activities.

6. Prepare a statement of cash flows.

7. Identify sources of information for a statement of cash flows.

8. Identify special problems in preparing a statement of cash flows.

9. Explain the use of a work sheet in preparing a statement of cash flows.

*H*ow was Kohlberg Kravis Roberts able to finance its record-shattering $25 billion purchase of RJR Nabisco? How did Atlantic Richfield finance the large investment it made to drill for oil in the North Slope of Alaska? How was Delta Airlines able to purchase 20 new jet planes costing $900 million in a year in which it reported a net loss of $86 million? How much of Marriott's hotel expansion program was financed through net cash flow from operating activities? How much through borrowing? How much through issuance of stock?

Such questions are often asked by investors, creditors, and internal management personnel who are interested in the financial operations of a business enterprise. An examination of the balance sheet, income statement, and statement of retained earnings, however, often fails to provide ready answers to questions of this type. That's why companies are required to prepare a fourth primary financial statement, the **statement of cash flows.**

▶ *SECTION 1 / PREPARATION OF THE STATEMENT OF CASH FLOWS*

▶ **EVOLUTION OF A NEW STATEMENT**

The evolution of the statement of cash flows provides an interesting example of how the needs of financial statement users eventually are met. The statement originated years ago in a simple analysis called the "Where-Got and Where-Gone Statement," which consisted of nothing more than a listing of the increases or decreases in the company's balance sheet items. After some years, the title of this statement was changed

OBJECTIVE 1

Describe the evolution and purpose of the statement of cash flows.

to "the funds statement." In 1961, the AICPA, recognizing the significance of this statement, sponsored research in this area that resulted in the publication of *Accounting Research Study No. 2*, entitled " 'Cash Flow' Analysis and the Funds Statement."[1] This study **recommended** that the funds statement be included in all annual reports to stockholders and that it be covered by the auditor's opinion.

In 1963, *APB Opinion No. 3* was issued to standardize the preparation and presentation of the funds statement. The Board recommended that the name be changed to "Statement of Source and Application of Funds" and that the statement be presented as supplementary information in financial reports. The inclusion of such information was not mandatory, and its coverage by the auditor's report was optional.[2]

The business community, the stock exchanges, and the SEC embraced *APB Opinion No. 3*. As a result, the number of companies presenting funds statements increased sharply. In 1971 *APB Opinion No. 19* **made it mandatory that a "statement of changes in financial position" be presented** as an integral part of the financial statements and that it be covered by the auditor's opinion. The Board concluded that

> . . . information concerning the financing and investing activities of a business enterprise and the changes in its financial position for a period is essential for financial statement users, particularly owners and creditors, in making economic decisions. When financial statements purporting to present both financial position (balance sheet) and results of operations (statement of income and retained earnings) are issued, a statement summarizing changes in financial position should also be presented as a basic financial statement for each period for which an income statement is presented.[3]

The Board recommended that the new title be "Statement of Changes in Financial Position." This title was used exclusively from 1972 through 1987.

Through the 1960s and 1970s, the statements presented the change in working capital as an adequate approximation for cash flow. In the early 1980s, however, the financial reporting environment changed dramatically as companies began taking on increasing amounts of debt. In 1981, the Financial Executives Institute recommended that companies use the cash (or cash and cash equivalents) basis instead of a working capital basis in preparing this statement.[4] Also many practitioners and academics argued for a stronger cash basis orientation to the statement of changes in financial position.[5] In its *Concepts Statement No. 5* (1984), the FASB strongly supported the inclusion in the primary financial statements of a **statement of cash flows** that reflects an entity's cash receipts classified by major sources and its cash payments classified by major uses.[6] In November 1987, the FASB issued *Standard No. 95*, "Statement of Cash Flows," which became effective for annual financial statements for fiscal years ending after July 15, 1988.[7]

---

[1]Perry Mason, " 'Cash Flow' Analysis and the Funds Statement," *Accounting Research Study No. 2* (New York: AICPA, 1961).

[2]"The Statement of Source and Application of Funds," *Opinions of the Accounting Principles Board No. 3* (New York: AICPA, 1963), par. 8.

[3]"Reporting Changes in Financial Position," *Opinions of the Accounting Principles Board No. 19* (New York: AICPA, 1971), par. 7.

[4]Allen H. Seed III, *The Funds Statement—Structure and Use* (Morristown, N.J.: Financial Executives Research Foundation, 1984), p. 3.

[5]For example, one writer had recommended that the statement of changes in financial position as then prepared should be discontinued and replaced with three required statements: a statement of cash receipts and payments, a statement of financing activities, and a statement of investing activities. See Loyd C. Heath, *Accounting Research Monograph No. 3: Financial Reporting and the Evaluation of Solvency* (New York: AICPA, 1978), and Loyd C. Heath, "Let's Scrap the Funds Statement," *The Journal of Accountancy* (October 1978), pp. 94–103. Also see Edward Swanson and Richard Vangermeersch, "Statement of Financing and Investing Activities," *The CPA Journal* (November 1981), pp. 32–40.

[6]"Recognition and Measurement in Financial Statements of Business Enterprises," *Statement of Financial Accounting Concepts No. 5* (Stamford, Conn.: FASB, 1984), pars. 52–54.

[7]"Statement of Cash Flows," *Statement of Financial Accounting Standards No. 95* (Stamford, Conn.: FASB, 1987).

▶ REASONS FOR CHANGE TO THE CASH BASIS

Why the sudden change in the financial reporting environment?[8] One major reason is that investors and analysts are concerned that **accrual accounting has become too far removed from the underlying cash flows of the enterprise.**[9] They contend that accountants are using too many arbitrary allocation devices (deferred taxes, depreciation, amortization of intangibles, accrual of revenues, etc.) and are therefore computing a net income figure that no longer provides an acceptable indicator of the enterprise's earning power. Similarly, **because financial statements take no cognizance of inflation, many interested parties look for a more concrete standard like cash flow to evaluate operating success or failure.** In addition, others contend that the **working capital concept does not provide as useful information about liquidity and financial flexibility as does the cash basis.** Frequently, mismanagement of receivables and inventories leads to a lack of liquidity which a statement focusing on working capital would not uncover.

The classic illustration of such a problem is W. T. Grant, which reported reasonable amounts of working capital provided by operations. However, too much of its working capital was tied up in receivables and inventories. A review of its net cash flow from operating activities would have shown the significant lack of liquidity and financial inflexibility that eventually caused the company's bankruptcy (see Illustration 24-1).

UNDERLYING CONCEPT

The working capital presentation fell short of providing information useful in assessing and reducing the uncertainty of future net cash inflows.

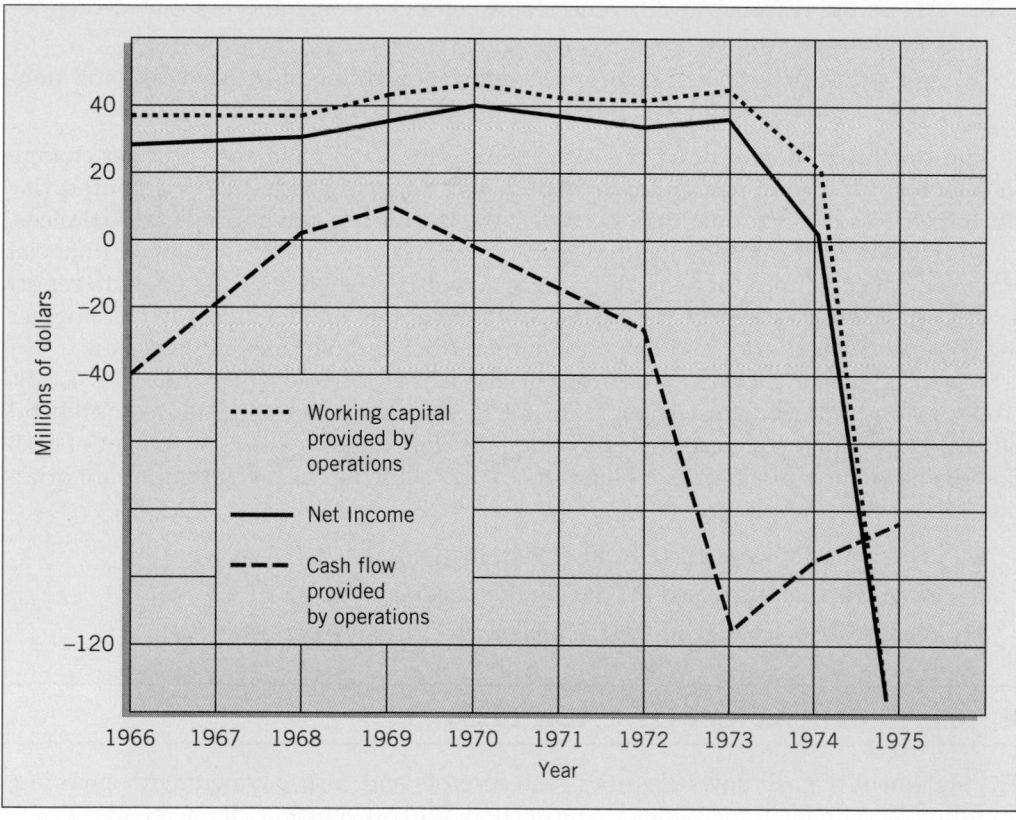

**ILLUSTRATION 24-1
W. T. Grant Company
Net Income, Cash Flow,
and Working Capital
Flow for Years Ending
January 31, 1966 to 1975**

Source: Exhibit 3–1, "Reporting Funds, Flows, Liquidity, and Financial Flexibility," *FASB Discussion Memorandum* (Stamford, Conn.: FASB, 1980), p. 36. Taken from James A. Largay III and Clyde P. Stickney, "Cash Flows, Ratio Analysis and the W. T. Grant Company Bankruptcy," *Financial Analysts Journal* (July–August 1980), p. 51.

---

[8]*Accounting Trends and Techniques—1993* reports that in 1992 all 600 companies surveyed used the cash or cash and cash equivalents basis in measuring changes in financial position. The rapidity of the transition from the working capital basis to the cash basis is evident when the 1992 statistics are compared with those of 1980, when only 59 out of 600 companies used the cash basis.

[9]See "Where's the Cash?" *Forbes* (April 8, 1985), p. 120; three reasons cited for the rising importance of cash flow analysis are: (1) the high and continuing debt levels of many companies, (2) the trend over the past 20 years toward capitalizing and deferring more expenses, and (3) a wave of corporate bankruptcies in the early 1980s.

Finally, a statement of cash flows is useful to management and short-term creditors in **assessing the enterprise's ability to meet cash operating needs.** As Walter Wriston, then Chairman of the Board of Citibank, noted, "Well, assets give you a warm feeling, but they don't generate cash. The first question I would ask any borrower these days, is 'What is your breakeven cash flow?' That's the one thing we can't find out from your audit reports, and it is the single most important question we ask."

▶ PURPOSE OF THE STATEMENT OF CASH FLOWS

The primary purpose of the statement of cash flows is to provide information about an entity's cash receipts and cash payments during a period. A secondary objective is to provide information on a cash basis about its operating, investing, and financing activities. According to the FASB, the information provided in a statement of cash flows, if used with related disclosures and the other financial statements, should help investors, creditors, and others to:

1. Assess the enterprise's ability to generate positive future net cash flows.
2. Assess the enterprise's ability to meet its obligations, its ability to pay dividends, and its needs for external financing.
3. Assess the reasons for differences between net income and associated cash receipts and payments.
4. Assess the effects on an enterprise's financial position of both its cash and non-cash investing and financing transactions during a period.[10]

The statement of cash flows reports cash receipts, cash payments, and net change in cash resulting from operating, investing, and financing activities of an enterprise during a period, in a format that reconciles the beginning and ending cash balances.

The statement of cash flows provides information not available from other financial statements. For example, it helps to indicate how it is possible for a company to report a net loss and still make large capital expenditures or pay dividends. It can tell whether the company issued or retired debt or common stock or both during the period.

Reporting the net increase or decrease in cash is considered useful because investors, creditors, and other interested parties want to know and can generally comprehend what is happening to a company's most liquid resource—its cash. A statement of cash flows is useful because it provides answers to the following simple but important questions about the enterprise:

1. Where did the cash come from during the period?
2. What was the cash used for during the period?
3. What was the change in the cash balance during the period?

▶ CLASSIFICATION OF CASH FLOWS

The statement of cash flows classifies cash receipts and cash payments by operating, investing, and financing activities.[11] Transactions and other events characteristic of each kind of activity are as follows:

---

[10]"The Statement of Cash Flows," pars. 4 and 5.

[11]The basis recommended by the FASB for the statement of cash flows is actually "cash and cash equivalents." **Cash equivalents** are short-term, highly liquid investments that are both: (a) readily convertible to known amounts of cash, and (b) so near their maturity that they present insignificant risk of changes in interest rates. Generally, only investments with original maturities of three months or less qualify under this definition. Examples of cash equivalents are treasury bills, commercial paper, and money market funds purchased with cash that is in excess of immediate needs.

Although we use the term "cash" throughout our discussion and illustrations in this chapter, we mean cash and cash equivalents when reporting the cash flows and the net increase or decrease in cash.

1. **Operating activities** involve the cash effects of transactions that enter into the determination of net income, such as cash receipts from sales of goods and services and cash payments to suppliers and employees for acquisitions of inventory and expenses.

2. **Investing activities** generally involve long-term assets and include (a) making and collecting loans, and (b) acquiring and disposing of investments and productive long-lived assets.[12]

3. **Financing activities** involve liability and stockholders' equity items and include (a) obtaining cash from creditors and repaying the amounts borrowed, and (b) obtaining capital from owners and providing them with a return on, and a return of, their investment.

Illustration 24-2 classifies the typical cash receipts and payments of a business enterprise that are classified according to operating, investing, and financing activities.

Operating
  Cash inflows
    From sales of goods or services.
    From returns on loans (interest) and on equity
      securities (dividends).   ⎱ Income
  Cash outflows   Statement
    To suppliers for inventory.   Items
    To employees for services.
    To government for taxes.
    To lenders for interest.
    To others for expenses.

Investing
  Cash inflows
    From sale of property, plant, and equipment.
    From sale of debt or equity securities of other entities.   ⎱ Generally
    From collection of principal on loans to other entities.   Long-Term
  Cash outflows   Asset Items
    To purchase property, plant, and equipment.
    To purchase debt or equity securities of other entities.
    To make loans to other entities.

Financing
  Cash inflows
    From sale of equity securities.   ⎱ Generally
    From issuance of debt (bonds and notes).   Long-Term
  Cash outflows   Liability
    To stockholders as dividends.   and Equity
    To redeem long-term debt or reacquire capital stock. Items

ILLUSTRATION 24-2
Classification of Typical Cash Inflows and Outflows

INTERNATIONAL INSIGHT

According to International Accounting Standards, as well as some nations such as New Zealand and Canada, "cash and cash equivalents" can be defined as "net monetary assets," that is, "cash and demand deposits and highly liquid investments less short-term borrowings."

Some cash flows relating to investing or financing activities are classified as operating activities. For example, receipts of investment income (interest and dividends) and payments of interest to lenders are classified as operating activities. Conversely, some cash flows relating to operating activities are classified as investing or financing activities. For example, the cash received from the sale of property, plant, and equipment at a gain, although reported in the income statement, is classified as an investing activity, and the effects of the related gain would not be included in net cash flow from operating activities. Likewise, a gain or loss on the payment (extinguishment) of debt would generally be part of the cash outflow related to the repayment of the amount borrowed and therefore is a financing activity.

---

[12]For exceptions to the treatment of purchases and sales of loans and securities by banks and brokers, see *Statement of Financial Accounting Standards No. 102* (February 1989) and "Relevance Gained: FASB Modifies Cash Flow Statement Requirements for Banks," James Don Edwards and Cynthia D. Heagy, *Journal of Accountancy,* June 1991. Banks and brokers are required to classify cash flows from purchases and sales of loans and securities specifically for resale and carried at market value **as operating activities.** This requirement recognizes that for these firms these assets are similar to inventory in other businesses.

▶ FORMAT OF STATEMENT OF CASH FLOWS

The three activities discussed in the preceding paragraphs constitute the general format of the statement of cash flows. The cash flows from operating activities section always appears first, followed by the investing and financing activities sections. The individual inflows and outflows from investing and financing activities are reported separately, that is, they are reported gross, not netted against one another. Thus, cash outflow from the purchase of property is reported separately from the cash inflow from the sale of property. Similarly, the cash inflow from the issuance of debt is reported separately from the cash outflow from its retirement. The net increase or decrease in cash reported during the period should reconcile the beginning and ending cash balances as reported in the comparative balance sheets.

The skeleton format of the statement of cash flows is:

ILLUSTRATION 24-3
Format of Statement of Cash Flows

Company Name STATEMENT OF CASH FLOWS Period Covered		
Cash flows from operating activities		
Net income		XXX
Adjustments to reconcile net income to net cash provided by operating activities:		
(List of individual items)	XX	XX
Net cash flow from operating activities		XXX
Cash flows from investing activities		
(List of individual inflows and outflows)	XX	
Net cash provided (used) by investing activities		XXX
Cash flows from financing activities		
(List of individual inflows and outflows)	XX	
Net cash provided (used) by financing activities		XXX
Net increase (decrease) in cash		XXX
Cash at beginning of period		XXX
Cash at end of period		XXX

▶ PREPARATION OF THE STATEMENT

Unlike the other major financial statements, the statement of cash flows is not prepared from the adjusted trial balance. The information to prepare this statement usually comes from three sources:

Comparative balance sheets provide the amount of the changes in assets, liabilities, and equities from the beginning to the end of the period.

Current income statement data help the reader determine the amount of cash provided by or used by operations during the period.

Selected transaction data from the general ledger provide additional detailed information needed to determine how cash was provided or used during the period.

Preparing the statement of cash flows from the data sources above involves three major steps:

1. **Determine the change in cash.** This procedure is straightforward because the difference between the beginning and the ending cash balance can be easily computed from an examination of the comparative balance sheets.
2. **Determine the net cash flow from operating activities.** This procedure is complex; it involves analyzing not only the current year's income statement but also comparative balance sheets as well as selected transaction data.
3. **Determine cash flows from investing and financing activities.** All other changes in the balance sheet accounts must be analyzed to determine their effect on cash.

▶ FIRST ILLUSTRATION—1994

To illustrate a statement of cash flows, we will use the **first year of operations** for Tax Consultants Inc. The company started on January 1, 1994, when it issued 60,000 shares of $1 par value common stock for $60,000 cash. The company rented its office space and furniture and equipment and performed tax consulting services throughout the first year. The comparative balance sheets at the beginning and end of the year 1994 appear as follows:

Tax Consultants Inc. COMPARATIVE BALANCE SHEETS			
Assets	Dec. 31, 1994	Jan. 1, 1994	Change Increase/Decrease
Cash	$49,000	$-0-	$49,000 Increase
Accounts receivable	36,000	-0-	36,000 Increase
Total	$85,000	$-0-	
Liabilities and Stockholders' Equity			
Accounts payable	$ 5,000	$-0-	5,000 Increase
Common stock ($1 par)	60,000	-0-	60,000 Increase
Retained earnings	20,000	-0-	20,000 Increase
Total	$85,000	$-0-	

ILLUSTRATION 24-4
Comparative Balance Sheets, Tax Consultants Inc., Year 1

The income statement and additional information for Tax Consultants Inc. are as follows:

Tax Consultants Inc. INCOME STATEMENT For the Year Ended December 31, 1994	
Revenues	$125,000
Operating expenses	85,000
Income before income taxes	40,000
Income tax expense	6,000
Net income	$ 34,000
Additional Information	
Examination of selected data indicates that a dividend of $14,000 was paid during the year.	

ILLUSTRATION 24-5
Income Statement, Tax Consultants Inc., Year 1

STEP 1: DETERMINE THE CHANGE IN CASH

To prepare a statement of cash flows, the first step, **determining the change in cash,** is a simple computation. Tax Consultants Inc. had no cash on hand at the beginning of the year 1994, but $49,000 was on hand at the end of 1994; thus, the change in cash for 1994 was an increase of $49,000. The other two steps are more complex and involve additional analysis.

STEP 2: DETERMINE NET CASH FLOW FROM OPERATING ACTIVITIES

A useful starting point in **determining net cash flow from operating activities**[13] is to understand why net income must be converted. Under generally accepted accounting

OBJECTIVE 3

Differentiate between net income and net cash flows from operating activities.

---

[13]"Net cash flow from operating activities" is a generic phrase, which is replaced in the statement of cash flows with either "net cash **provided by** operating activities" if operations increase cash or "net cash **used by** operating activities" if operations decrease cash.

principles, most companies must use the accrual basis of accounting requiring that revenue be recorded when earned and that expenses be recorded when incurred. Net income may include credit sales that have not been collected in cash and expenses incurred that may not have been paid in cash. Thus, under the accrual basis of accounting, net income will not indicate the net cash flow from operating activities.

To arrive at net cash flow from operating activities, it is necessary to report revenues and expenses on a **cash basis. This is done by eliminating the effects of income statement transactions that did not result in a corresponding increase or decrease in cash.** The relationship between net income and net cash flow from operating activities is graphically depicted as follows:

ILLUSTRATION 24-6
Net Income versus Net Cash Flow from Operating Activities

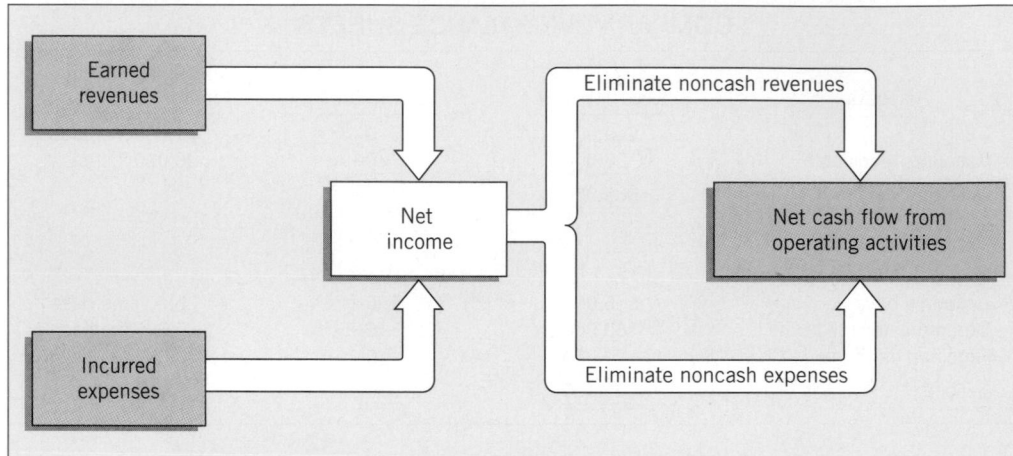

In this chapter, we use the term net income to refer to accrual-based net income. The conversion of net income to net cash flow from operating activities may be done through either a direct method or an indirect method as explained in the following discussion.

Direct Method

OBJECTIVE 4

Contrast the direct and indirect methods of calculating net cash flow from operating activities.

The **direct method** (also called the income statement method) reports cash receipts and cash disbursements from operating activities. The difference between these two amounts is the net cash flow from operating activities. In other words, the direct method deducts from operating cash receipts the operating cash disbursements. The direct method results in the presentation of a condensed cash receipts and cash disbursements statement.

As indicated from the accrual-based income statement, Tax Consultants Inc. reported revenues of $125,000. However, because the company's accounts receivable increased during 1994 by $36,000, only $89,000 ($125,000 − $36,000) in cash was collected on these revenues. Similarly, Tax Consultants Inc. reported operating expenses of $85,000, but accounts payable increased during the period by $5,000. Assuming that these payables related to operating expenses, cash operating expenses were $80,000 ($85,000 − $5,000). Because no taxes payable exist at the end of the year, the $6,000 income tax expense for 1994 must have been paid in cash during the year. Then the computation of net cash flow from operating activities is as follows:

ILLUSTRATION 24-7
Computation of Net Cash Flow from Operating Activities, Year 1—Direct Method

Cash collected from revenues	$89,000
Cash payments for expenses	80,000
Income before income taxes	9,000
Cash payments for income taxes	6,000
Net cash provided by operating activities	$ 3,000

"Net cash provided by operating activities" is the equivalent of cash basis net income ("net cash used by operating activities" would be equivalent to cash basis net loss).

Indirect Method

The **indirect method** (or reconciliation method) starts with net income and converts it to net cash flow from operating activities. In other words, **the indirect method adjusts net income for items that affected reported net income but did not affect cash.** To compute net cash flow from operating activities, noncash charges in the income statement are added back to net income and noncash credits are deducted. Explanations for the two adjustments to net income in this example, namely, the increases in accounts receivable and accounts payable, are as follows.

Increase in Accounts Receivable

When accounts receivable increase during the year, revenues on an accrual basis are higher than revenues on a cash basis because goods sold on account are reported as revenues. In other words, operations of the period led to increased revenues, but not all of these revenues resulted in an increase in cash. Some of the increase in revenues resulted in an increase in accounts receivable. To convert net income to net cash flow from operating activities, the increase of $36,000 in accounts receivable must be deducted from net income.

Increase in Accounts Payable

When accounts payable increase during the year, expenses on an accrual basis are higher than they are on a cash basis because expenses are incurred for which payment has not taken place. To convert net income to net cash flow from operating activities, the increase of $5,000 in accounts payable must be added to net income.

As a result of the accounts receivable and accounts payable adjustments, net cash provided by operating activities is determined to be $3,000 for the year 1994. This computation is shown as follows:

Net income		$34,000
Adjustments to reconcile net income to net cash provided by operating activities:		
Increase in accounts receivable	$(36,000)	
Increase in accounts payable	5,000	(31,000)
Net cash provided by operating activities		$ 3,000

ILLUSTRATION 24-8
Computation of Net Cash Flow from Operating Activities, Year 1— Indirect Method

Note that net cash provided by operating activities is the same whether the direct or the indirect method is used.

STEP 3: DETERMINE NET CASH FLOWS FROM INVESTING AND FINANCING ACTIVITIES

Once the net cash flow from operating activities is computed, the next step is to determine whether any other changes in balance sheet accounts caused an increase or decrease in cash. For example, an examination of the remaining balance sheet accounts shows that both common stock and retained earnings have increased. The common stock increase of $60,000 resulted from the issuance of common stock for cash. The issuance of common stock is a receipt of cash from a financing activity and is reported as such in the statement of cash flows. The retained earnings increase of $20,000 is caused by two items:

OBJECTIVE 5
Determine net cash flows from investing and financing activities.

1. Net income of $34,000 increased retained earnings.
2. Dividends declared of $14,000 decreased retained earnings.

Net income has been converted into net cash flow from operating activities as explained earlier. The additional data indicate that the dividend was paid. Thus, the dividend payment on common stock is reported as a cash outflow, classified as a financing activity.

STATEMENT OF CASH FLOWS—1994

OBJECTIVE 6

Prepare a statement of cash flows.

We are now ready to prepare the statement of cash flows. The statement starts with the operating activities section. Either the direct or indirect method may be used to report net cash flow from operating activities. The FASB **encourages** the use of the direct method over the indirect method. And, if the direct method of reporting net cash flow from operating activities is used, the FASB **requires** that the reconciliation of net income to net cash flow from operating activities be provided in a separate schedule. If the indirect method is used, the reconciliation may be either reported within the statement of cash flows or provided in a separate schedule, with the statement of cash flows reporting only the **net** cash flow from operating activities.[14] Therefore, the indirect method, which is also used more extensively in practice,[15] is used throughout this chapter. In doing homework assignments, you should follow instructions for use of either the direct or indirect method. The advantages and disadvantages of these two methods are discussed later in this chapter.

The statement of cash flows for Tax Consultants Inc. is as follows:

ILLUSTRATION 24-9
**Statement of Cash Flows,
Tax Consultants Inc.,
Year 1**

Tax Consultants Inc. STATEMENT OF CASH FLOWS For the Year Ended December 31, 1994 Increase (Decrease) in Cash		
Cash flows from operating activities		
Net income		$ 34,000
Adjustments to reconcile net income to net cash provided by operating activities:		
Increase in accounts receivable	$(36,000)	
Increase in accounts payable	5,000	(31,000)
Net cash provided by operating activities		3,000
Cash flows from financing activities		
Issuance of common stock	60,000	
Payment of cash dividends	(14,000)	
Net cash provided by financing activities		46,000
Net increase in cash		49,000
Cash, January 1, 1994		–0–
Cash, December 31, 1994		$ 49,000

As indicated, the $60,000 increase in common stock results in a cash inflow from a financing activity. The payment of $14,000 in cash dividends is classified as a use of cash from a financing activity. The $49,000 increase in cash reported in the statement of cash flows agrees with the increase of $49,000 shown as the change in the cash account in the comparative balance sheets.

▶ SECOND ILLUSTRATION—1995

Tax Consultants Inc. continued to grow and prosper during its second year of operations. Land, building, and equipment were purchased, and revenues and earnings increased substantially over the first year. Information related to the second year of operations for Tax Consultants Inc. is presented in Illustrations 24-10 and 24-11.

---

[14]"The Statement of Cash Flows," pars. 27 and 30.

[15]*Accounting Trends and Techniques—1993* reports that in 1992 out of its 600 surveyed companies, 585 (more than 97.5%) used the indirect method while only 15 used the direct method.

ILLUSTRATION 24-10
Comparative Balance
Sheet, Tax Consultants
Inc., Year 2

Tax Consultants Inc.
COMPARATIVE BALANCE SHEET
December 31

Assets	1995	1994	Change Increase/Decrease
Cash	$ 37,000	$49,000	$ 12,000 Decrease
Accounts receivable	26,000	36,000	10,000 Decrease
Prepaid expenses	6,000	–0–	6,000 Increase
Land	70,000	–0–	70,000 Increase
Building	200,000	–0–	200,000 Increase
Accumulated depreciation—building	(11,000)	–0–	11,000 Increase
Equipment	68,000	–0–	68,000 Increase
Accumulated depreciation—equipment	(10,000)	–0–	10,000 Increase
Total	$386,000	$85,000	
Liabilities and Stockholders' Equity			
Accounts payable	$ 40,000	$ 5,000	35,000 Increase
Bonds payable	150,000	–0–	150,000 Increase
Common stock ($1 par)	60,000	60,000	–0–
Retained earnings	136,000	20,000	116,000 Increase
Total	$386,000	$85,000	

ILLUSTRATION 24-11
Income Statement, Tax
Consultants Inc., Year 2

Tax Consultants Inc.
INCOME STATEMENT
For the Year Ended December 31, 1995

Revenues		$492,000
Operating expenses (excluding depreciation)	$269,000	
Depreciation expense	21,000	290,000
Income from operations		202,000
Income tax expense		68,000
Net income		$134,000

Additional Information
(a) In 1995, the company paid an $18,000 cash dividend.
(b) The company obtained $150,000 cash through the issuance of long-term bonds.
(c) Land, building, and equipment were acquired for cash.

STEP 1: DETERMINE THE CHANGE IN CASH

To prepare a statement of cash flows from the available information, the first step is to determine the change in cash. As indicated from the information presented, cash decreased $12,000 ($49,000 − $37,000).

STEP 2: DETERMINE NET CASH FLOW FROM OPERATING ACTIVITIES—INDIRECT METHOD

Using the indirect method, we adjust net income of $134,000 on an accrual basis to arrive at net cash flow from operating activities. Explanations for the adjustments to net income are as follows.

Decrease in Accounts Receivable

When accounts receivable decrease during the period, revenues on a cash basis are higher than revenues on an accrual basis, because cash collections are higher than revenues reported on an accrual basis. To convert net income to net cash flow from operating activities, the decrease of $10,000 in accounts receivable must be added to net income.

Increase in Prepaid Expenses

When prepaid expenses (assets) increase during a period, expenses on an accrual basis income statement are lower than they are on a cash basis income statement. Expenditures (cash payments) have been made in the current period, but expenses (as charges to the income statement) have been deferred to future periods. To convert net income to net cash flow from operating activities, the increase of $6,000 in prepaid expenses must be deducted from net income. An increase in prepaid expenses results in a decrease in cash during the period.

Increase in Accounts Payable

Like the increase in 1994, the 1995 increase of $35,000 in accounts payable must be added to net income to convert to net cash flow from operating activities. A greater amount of expense was incurred than cash disbursed.

Depreciation Expense (Increase in Accumulated Depreciation)

The purchase of depreciable assets is shown as a use of cash in the investing section in the year of acquisition. The depreciation expense of $21,000 (also represented by the increase in accumulated depreciation) is a noncash charge that is added back to net income to arrive at net cash flow from operating activities. The $21,000 is the sum of the depreciation on the building of $11,000 and the depreciation on the equipment of $10,000.

Other charges to expense for a period that do not require the use of cash, such as the amortization of intangible assets and depletion expense, are treated in the same manner as depreciation. Depreciation and similar noncash charges are frequently listed in the statement as the first adjustments to net income.

As a result of the foregoing items, net cash provided by operating activities is $194,000 as computed in the following:

ILLUSTRATION 24-12
Computation of Net Cash Flow from Operating Activities, Year 2—Indirect Method

Net income		$134,000
Adjustments to reconcile net income to		
net cash provided by operating activities:		
Depreciation expense	$21,000	
Decrease in accounts receivable	10,000	
Increase in prepaid expenses	(6,000)	
Increase in accounts payable	35,000	60,000
Net cash provided by operating activities		$194,000

STEP 3: DETERMINE NET CASH FLOWS FROM INVESTING AND FINANCING ACTIVITIES

After you have determined the items affecting net cash provided by operating activities, the next step involves analyzing the remaining changes in balance sheet accounts. The following accounts were revalued:

Increase in Land

As indicated from the change in the land account, land of $70,000 was purchased during the period. This transaction is an investing activity that is reported as a use of cash.

Increase in Building and Related Accumulated Depreciation

As indicated in the additional data, and from the change in the building account, an office building was acquired using cash of $200,000. This transaction is a cash outflow reported in the investing section. The accumulated depreciation account increase of $11,000 is fully explained by the depreciation expense entry for the period. As indicated earlier, the reported depreciation expense has no effect on the amount of cash.

Increase in Equipment and Related Accumulated Depreciation

An increase in equipment of $68,000 resulted because equipment was purchased for cash. This transaction should be reported as an outflow of cash from an investing activity. The increase in Accumulated Depreciation—Equipment was explained by the depreciation expense entry for the period.

Increase in Bonds Payable

The bonds payable account increased $150,000. Cash received from the issuance of these bonds represents an inflow of cash from a financing activity.

Increase in Retained Earnings

Retained earnings increased $116,000 during the year. This increase can be explained by two factors: (1) net income of $134,000 increased retained earnings; (2) dividends of $18,000 decreased retained earnings. Payment of the dividends is a financing activity that involves a cash outflow.

STATEMENT OF CASH FLOWS—1995

Combining the foregoing items, we get a statement of cash flows for 1995 for Tax Consultants Inc., using the indirect method to compute net cash flow from operating activities.

ILLUSTRATION 24-13
Statement of Cash Flows, Tax Consultants Inc., Year 2

Tax Consultants Inc.
STATEMENT OF CASH FLOWS
For the Year Ended December 31, 1995
Increase (Decrease) in Cash

Cash flows from operating activities		
Net income		$134,000
Adjustments to reconcile net income to		
net cash provided by operating activities:		
Depreciation expense	$ 21,000	
Decrease in accounts receivable	10,000	
Increase in prepaid expenses	(6,000)	
Increase in accounts payable	35,000	60,000
Net cash provided by operating activities		194,000
Cash flows from investing activities		
Purchase of land	(70,000)	
Purchase of building	(200,000)	
Purchase of equipment	(68,000)	
Net cash used by investing activities		(338,000)
Cash flows from financing activities		
Issuance of bonds	150,000	
Payment of cash dividends	(18,000)	
Net cash provided by financing activities		132,000
Net decrease in cash		(12,000)
Cash, January 1, 1995		49,000
Cash, December 31, 1995		$ 37,000

▶ THIRD ILLUSTRATION—1996

Our third illustration covering the 1996 operations of Tax Consultants Inc. is slightly more complex; it again uses the indirect method to compute and present net cash flow from operating activities.

Tax Consultants Inc. experienced continued success in 1996 and expanded its operations to include the sale of selected lines of computer software that are used in tax return preparation and tax planning. Thus, inventories is one of the new assets appearing in its December 31, 1996, balance sheet. The comparative balance sheets, income statement, and selected data for 1996 are shown in Illustrations 24-14 and 24-15.

ILLUSTRATION 24-14
Comparative Balance Sheet, Tax Consultants Inc., Year 3

Tax Consultants Inc.
COMPARATIVE BALANCE SHEET
December 31

Assets	1996	1995	Change Increase/Decrease
Cash	$ 54,000	$ 37,000	$ 17,000 Increase
Accounts receivable	68,000	26,000	42,000 Increase
Inventories	54,000	–0–	54,000 Increase
Prepaid expenses	4,000	6,000	2,000 Decrease
Land	45,000	70,000	25,000 Decrease
Buildings	200,000	200,000	–0–
Accumulated depreciation—buildings	(21,000)	(11,000)	10,000 Increase
Equipment	193,000	68,000	125,000 Increase
Accumulated depreciation—equipment	(28,000)	(10,000)	18,000 Increase
Totals	$569,000	$386,000	
Liabilities and Stockholders' Equity			
Accounts payable	$ 33,000	$ 40,000	7,000 Decrease
Bonds payable	110,000	150,000	40,000 Decrease
Common stock ($1 par)	220,000	60,000	160,000 Increase
Retained earnings	206,000	136,000	70,000 Increase
Totals	$569,000	$386,000	

ILLUSTRATION 24-15
Income Statement, Tax Consultants Inc., Year 3

Tax Consultants Inc.
INCOME STATEMENT
For the Year Ended December 31, 1996

Revenues		$890,000
Cost of goods sold	$465,000	
Operating expenses	221,000	
Interest expense	12,000	
Loss on sale of equipment	2,000	700,000
Income from operations		190,000
Income tax expense		65,000
Net income		$125,000

Additional Information
(a) Operating expenses include depreciation expense of $33,000 and amortization of prepaid expenses of $2,000.
(b) Land was sold at its book value for cash.
(c) Cash dividends of $55,000 were paid in 1996.
(d) Interest expense of $12,000 was paid in cash.
(e) Equipment with a cost of $166,000 was purchased for cash. Equipment with a cost of $41,000 and a book value of $36,000 was sold for $34,000 cash.
(f) Bonds were redeemed at their book value for cash.
(g) Common stock ($1 par) was issued for cash.

STEP 1: DETERMINE THE CHANGE IN CASH

The first step in the preparation of the statement of cash flows is to determine the change in cash. As is shown in the comparative balance sheet, cash increased $17,000 in 1996. The second and third steps are discussed on the following pages.

STEP 2: DETERMINE NET CASH FLOW FROM OPERATING ACTIVITIES—INDIRECT METHOD

Explanations of the adjustments to net income of $125,000 are as follows.

Increase in Accounts Receivable

The increase in accounts receivable of $42,000 represents recorded accrual basis revenues in excess of cash collections in 1996; the increase is deducted from net income to convert from the accrual basis to the cash basis.

Increase in Inventories

The increase in inventories of $54,000 represents an operating use of cash for which an expense was not incurred. This amount is therefore deducted from net income to arrive at cash flow from operations. In other words, when inventory purchased exceeds inventory sold during a period, cost of goods sold on an accrual basis is lower than on a cash basis.

Decrease in Prepaid Expenses

The decrease in prepaid expenses of $2,000 represents a charge to the income statement for which there was no cash outflow in the current period. The decrease is added back to net income to arrive at net cash flow from operating activities.

Decrease in Accounts Payable

When accounts payable decrease during the year, cost of goods sold and expenses on a cash basis are higher than they are on an accrual basis, because on a cash basis the goods and expenses are recorded as expense when paid. To convert net income to net cash flow from operating activities, the decrease of $7,000 in accounts payable must be deducted from net income.

Depreciation Expense (Increase in Accumulated Depreciation)

Accumulated Depreciation—Buildings increased $10,000 ($21,000 − $11,000). The Buildings account did not change during the period, which means that $10,000 of depreciation was recorded in 1996.

Accumulated Depreciation—Equipment increased by $18,000 ($28,000 − $10,000) during the year. But Accumulated Depreciation—Equipment was decreased by $5,000 as a result of the sale during the year. Thus, depreciation for the year was $23,000. The reconciliation of Accumulated Depreciation—Equipment is as follows:

Beginning balance	$10,000
Add depreciation for 1996	23,000
	33,000
Deduct sale of equipment	5,000
Ending balance	$28,000

The total depreciation of $33,000 ($10,000 + $23,000) charged to the income statement must be added back to net income to determine net cash flow from operating activities.

Loss on Sale of Equipment

Equipment having a cost of $41,000 and a book value of $36,000 was sold for $34,000. As a result, the company reported a loss of $2,000 on its sale. To arrive at net cash flow from operating activities, it is necessary to add back to net income the loss on the sale of the equipment. The reason is that the loss is a noncash charge to the income statement; it did not reduce cash but it did reduce net income.

From the foregoing items, the operating activities section of the statement of cash flows is prepared as shown in Illustration 24-16.

ILLUSTRATION 24-16
**Operating Activities
Section of Cash Flows
Statement**

Cash flows from operating activities		
Net income		$125,000
Adjustments to reconcile net income to		
net cash provided by operating activities:		
Depreciation expense	$33,000	
Increase in accounts receivable	(42,000)	
Increase in inventories	(54,000)	
Decrease in prepaid expenses	2,000	
Decrease in accounts payable	(7,000)	
Loss on sale of equipment	2,000	(66,000)
Net cash provided by operating activities		59,000

STEP 3: DETERMINE CASH FLOWS FROM INVESTING AND FINANCING ACTIVITIES

By analyzing the remaining changes in the balance sheet accounts, we can identify cash flows from investing and financing activities.

Land

Land decreased $25,000 during the period. As indicated from the information presented, land was sold for cash at its book value. This transaction is an investing activity reported as a $25,000 source of cash.

Equipment

An analysis of the equipment account indicates the following:

Beginning balance	$ 68,000
Purchase of equipment	166,000
	234,000
Sale of equipment	41,000
Ending balance	$193,000

Equipment with a fair value of $166,000 was purchased for cash—an investing transaction reported as a cash outflow. The sale of the equipment for $34,000 is also an investing activity, but one that generates a cash inflow.

Bonds Payable

Bonds payable decreased $40,000 during the year. As indicated from the additional information, bonds were redeemed at their book value. This financing transaction used cash of $40,000.

Common Stock

The common stock account increased $160,000 during the year. As indicated from the additional information, common stock of $160,000 was issued at par. This is a financing transaction that provided cash of $160,000.

Retained Earnings

Retained earnings changed $70,000 ($206,000 − $136,000) during the year. The $70,000 change in retained earnings is the result of net income of $125,000 from operations and the financing activity of paying cash dividends of $55,000.

STATEMENT OF CASH FLOWS—1996

The statement of cash flows as shown in Illustration 24-17 is prepared by combining the foregoing items.

ILLUSTRATION 24-17
**Statement of Cash Flows,
Tax Consultants Inc.,
Year 3**

Tax Consultants Inc. STATEMENT OF CASH FLOWS For the Year Ended December 31, 1996 Increase (Decrease) in Cash		
Cash flows from operating activities		
Net income		$125,000
Adjustments to reconcile net income to net cash provided by operating activities:		
Depreciation expense	$ 33,000	
Increase in accounts receivable	(42,000)	
Increase in inventories	(54,000)	
Decrease in prepaid expenses	2,000	
Decrease in accounts payable	(7,000)	
Loss on sale of equipment	2,000	(66,000)
Net cash provided by operating activities		59,000
Cash flows from investing activities		
Sale of land	25,000	
Sale of equipment	34,000	
Purchase of equipment	(166,000)	
Net cash used by investing activities		(107,000)
Cash flows from financing activities		
Redemption of bonds	(40,000)	
Sale of common stock	160,000	
Payment of dividends	(55,000)	
Net cash provided by financing activities		65,000
Net increase in cash		17,000
Cash, January 1, 1996		37,000
Cash, December 31, 1996		$ 54,000

▶ SOURCES OF INFORMATION FOR STATEMENT OF CASH FLOWS

These are the important points to remember in the preparation of the statement of cash flows.

OBJECTIVE 7
Identify sources of information for a statement of cash flows.

1. Comparative balance sheets provide the basic information from which the report is prepared. Additional information obtained from analyses of specific accounts is also included.

2. An analysis of the Retained Earnings account is necessary. The net increase or decrease in Retained Earnings without any explanation is a meaningless amount in the statement, because it might represent the effect of net income, dividends declared, appropriations of retained earnings, or prior period adjustments.

3. The statement includes all changes that have passed through cash or have resulted in an increase or decrease in cash.

4. Writedowns, amortization charges, and similar "book" entries, such as depreciation of plant assets, are considered as neither inflows nor outflows of cash because they have no effect on cash. To the extent that they have entered into the determination of net income, however, they must be added back to or subtracted from net income to arrive at net cash flow from operating activities.

▶ NET CASH FLOW FROM OPERATING ACTIVITIES— INDIRECT VERSUS DIRECT METHOD

As we discussed previously, the two different methods available to adjust income from operations on an accrual basis to net cash flow from operating activities are the indirect (reconciliation) method and the direct (income statement) method.

The FASB encourages use of the direct method and permits use of the indirect method. Yet, if the direct method is used, the Board requires that a reconciliation of net income to net cash flow from operating activities be provided in a separate schedule. Therefore, under either method the indirect (reconciliation) method must be prepared and reported.

INDIRECT METHOD

For consistency and comparability and because it is the most widely used method in practice, we used the indirect method in the illustrations just presented. We determined net cash flows from operating activities by adding back to or deducting from net income those items that had no effect on cash. The following diagram presents more completely the common types of adjustments that are made to net income to arrive at net cash flow from operating activities.

ILLUSTRATION 24-18 Adjustments Needed to Determine Net Cash Flow from Operating Activities—Indirect Method

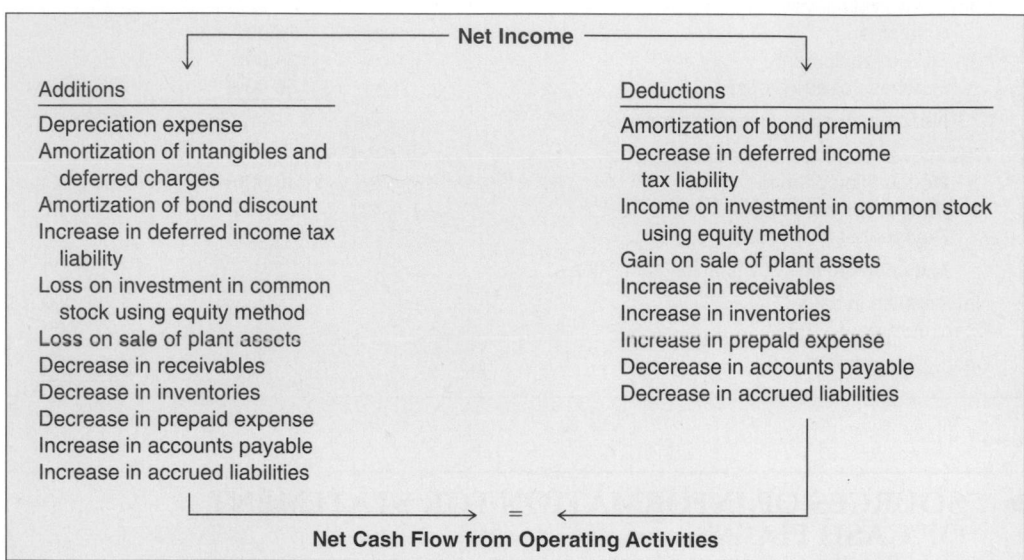

The additions and deductions listed above reconcile net income to net cash flow from operating activities, illustrating the reason for referring to the indirect method as the reconciliation method.

DIRECT METHOD: AN ILLUSTRATION

Under the direct method the statement of cash flows reports net cash flow from operating activities as major classes of operating cash receipts (e.g., cash collected from customers and cash received from interest and dividends) and cash disbursements (e.g., cash paid to suppliers for goods, to employees for services, to creditors for interest, and to government authorities for taxes).

The direct method is illustrated here in more detail to help you understand the difference between accrual-based income and net cash flow from operating activities and to illustrate the data needed to apply the direct method. Emig Company, which began business on January 1, 1996, has the following selected balance sheet information:

ILLUSTRATION 24-19 Balance Sheet Accounts, Emig Co.

	December 31	
	1996	1995
Cash	$159,000	–0–
Accounts receivable	15,000	–0–
Inventory	160,000	–0–
Prepaid expenses	8,000	–0–
Accounts payable	60,000	–0–
Accrued expenses payable	20,000	–0–
Property, plant, and equipment (net)	90,000	–0–

Emig Company's December 31, 1996, income statement and additional information are:

Revenues from sales		$780,000
Cost of goods sold		450,000
Gross profit		330,000
Operating expenses	$160,000	
Depreciation	10,000	170,000
Income before income taxes		160,000
Income tax expense		48,000
Net income		$112,000

Additional Information:
(a) Dividends of $70,000 were declared and paid in cash.
(b) The accounts payable increase resulted from the purchase of merchandise.
(c) Prepaid expenses and accrued expenses payable relate to operating expenses.

ILLUSTRATION 24-20
Income Statement, Emig Co.

Under the **direct method,** net cash provided by operating activities is computed by **adjusting each item in the income statement** from the accrual basis to the cash basis. To simplify and condense the operating activities section, only major classes of operating cash receipts and cash payments are reported. The difference between these major classes of cash receipts and cash payments is the net cash provided by operating activities as shown in Illustration 24-21.

ILLUSTRATION 24-21
Major Classes of Cash Receipts and Payments

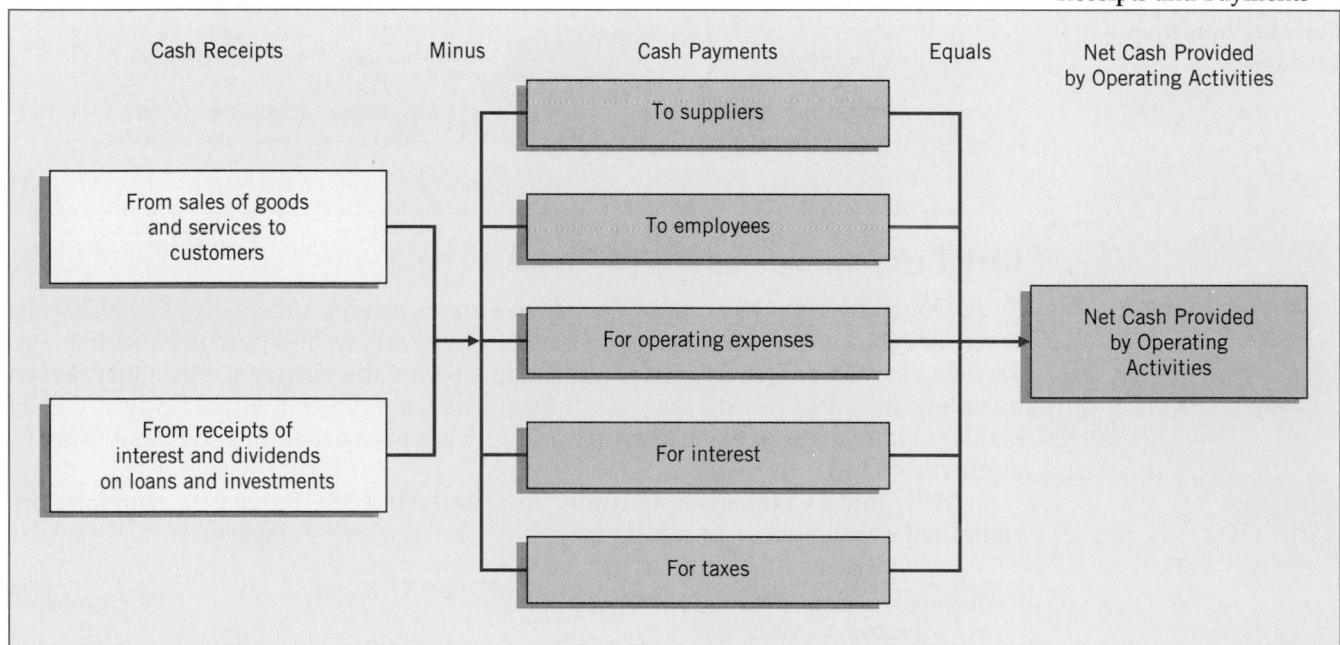

An efficient way to apply the direct method is to analyze the revenues and expenses reported in the income statement in the order in which they are listed. Cash receipts and cash payments related to these revenues and expenses should then be determined. The direct method adjustments for Emig Company in 1996 to determine net cash provided by operating activities are presented in the following sections.

Cash Receipts from Customers

The income statement for Emig Company reported revenues from customers of $780,000. To determine cash receipts from customers, it is necessary to consider the change in accounts receivable during the year. When accounts receivable increase during the year, revenues on an accrual basis are higher than cash receipts from customers. In other words, operations led to increased revenues, but not all of these revenues resulted in cash receipts. To determine the amount of increase in cash receipts, deduct the amount of the increase in accounts receivable from the total sales revenues. Conversely, a decrease in accounts receivable is added to sales revenues, because cash receipts from customers then exceed sales revenues.

For Emig Company, accounts receivable increased $15,000. Thus, cash receipts from customers were $765,000, computed as follows:

Revenues from sales	$780,000
Deduct: Increase in accounts receivable	15,000
Cash receipts from customers	**$765,000**

Cash receipts from customers may also be determined from an analysis of the Accounts Receivable account as shown below.

Accounts Receivable

1/1/96	Balance	–0–	**Receipts from customers**	765,000
	Revenue from sales	780,000		
12/31/96	Balance	15,000		

The relationships between cash receipts from customers, revenues from sales, and changes in accounts receivable are shown in Illustration 24-22.

ILLUSTRATION 24-22
Formula to Compute Cash Receipts from Customers

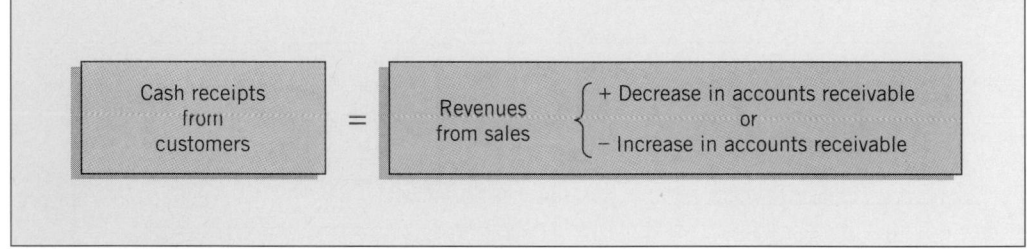

Cash Payments to Suppliers

Emig Company reported cost of goods sold on its income statement of $450,000. To determine cash payments to suppliers, it is first necessary to find purchases for the year. To find purchases, cost of goods sold is adjusted for the change in inventory. When inventory increases during the year, it means that purchases this year exceed cost of goods sold. As a result, the increase in inventory is added to cost of goods sold to arrive at purchases.

In 1996, Emig Company's inventory increased $160,000. Purchases, therefore, are computed as follows:

Cost of goods sold	$450,000
Add: Increase in inventory	160,000
Purchases	**$610,000**

After purchases are computed, cash payments to suppliers are determined by adjusting purchases for the change in accounts payable. When accounts payable increase during the year, purchases on an accrual basis are higher than they are on a cash basis. As a result, an increase in accounts payable is deducted from purchases to arrive at cash payments to suppliers. Conversely, a decrease in accounts payable is added to purchases because cash payments to suppliers exceed purchases. Cash payments to suppliers were $550,000, computed as follows:

Purchases	$610,000
Deduct: Increase in accounts payable	60,000
Cash payments to suppliers	**$550,000**

Cash payments to suppliers may also be determined from an analysis of the Accounts Payable account as shown below.

Accounts Payable				
Payments to suppliers	550,000	1/1/96	Balance	–0–
			Purchases	610,000
		12/31/96	Balance	60,000

The relationships between cash payments to customers, cost of goods sold, changes in inventory, and changes in account payable are shown in Illustration 24-23.

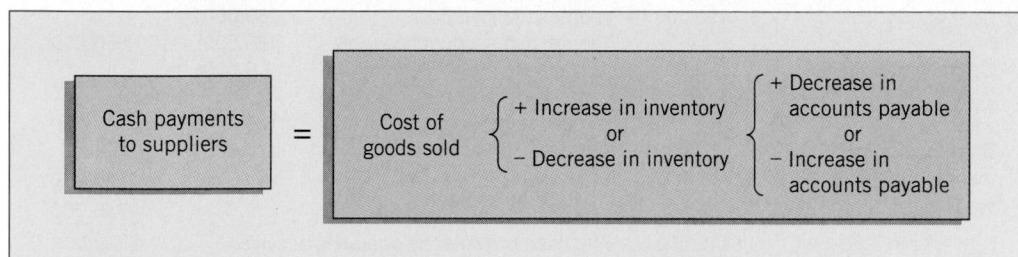

ILLUSTRATION 24-23
Formula to Compute Cash Payments to Suppliers

Cash Payments for Operating Expenses

Operating expenses of $160,000 were reported on Emig's income statement. To determine the cash paid for operating expenses, this amount must be adjusted for any changes in prepaid expenses and accrued expenses payable. For example, when prepaid expenses increased $8,000 during the year, cash paid for operating expenses was $8,000 higher than operating expenses reported on the income statement. To convert operating expenses to cash payments for operating expenses, the increase of $8,000 must be added to operating expenses. Conversely, if prepaid expenses decrease during the year, the decrease must be deducted from operating expenses.

Operating expenses must also be adjusted for changes in accrued expenses payable. When accrued expenses payable increase during the year, operating expenses on an accrual basis are higher than they are in a cash basis. As a result, an increase in accrued expenses payable is deducted from operating expenses to arrive at cash payments for operating expenses. Conversely, a decrease in accrued expenses payable is added to operating expenses because cash payments exceed operating expenses.

Emig Company's cash payments for operating expenses were $158,000, computed as follows:

Operating expenses	$160,000
Add: Increase in prepaid expenses	8,000
Deduct: Increase in accrued expenses payable	(20,000)
Cash payments for operating expenses	$148,000

The relationships among cash payments for operating expenses, changes in prepaid expenses, and changes in accrued expenses payable are shown in the following formula.

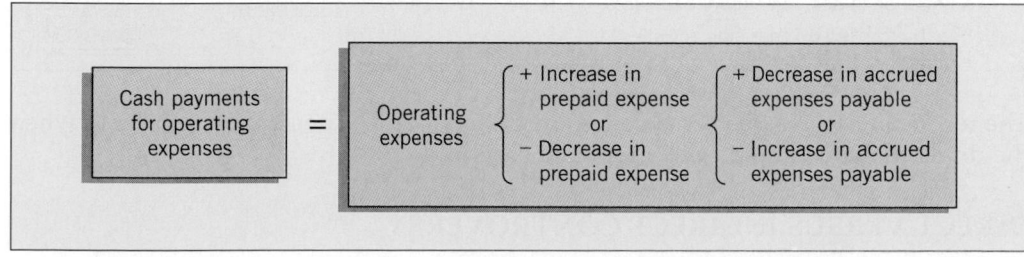

ILLUSTRATION 24-24
Formula to Compute Cash Payments for Operating Expenses

Note that depreciation expense was not considered because it is a noncash charge.

Cash Payments for Income Taxes

The income statement for Emig shows income tax expense of $48,000. This amount equals the cash paid because the comparative balance sheet indicated no income taxes payable at either the beginning or end of the year.

The computations illustrated above are summarized in the following schedule:

ILLUSTRATION 24-25
Accrual Basis to Cash Basis

Accrual Basis		Adjustment	Add (Subtract)	Cash Basis
Revenues from sales	$780,000 −	Increase in accounts receivable	$(15,000)	$765,000
Cost of goods sold	450,000 +	Increase in inventory	160,000	
	−	Increase in accounts payable	(60,000)	550,000
Operating expenses	160,000 +	Increase in prepaid expense	8,000	
	−	Increase in accrued expenses payable	(20,000)	148,000
Depreciation expense	10,000 −	Depreciation expense	(10,000)	−0−
Income tax expense	48,000			48,000
Total expense	668,000			746,000
Net income	$112,000	Net cash provided by operating activities		$ 19,000

Presentation of the direct method for reporting net cash flow from operating activities takes the following form for the Emig Company illustration:

ILLUSTRATION 24-26
Operating Activities Section—Direct Method, 1996

Emig Company STATEMENT OF CASH FLOWS (PARTIAL)		
Cash flows from operating activities		
Cash received from customers		$765,000
Cash payments:		
To suppliers	$550,000	
For operating expenses	148,000	
For income taxes	48,000	746,000
Net cash provided by operating activities		$ 19,000

If Emig Company uses the direct method to present the net cash flows from operating activities, it must provide in a separate schedule the reconciliation of net income to net cash provided by operating activities. The reconciliation assumes the identical form and content of the indirect method of presentation as shown below:

ILLUSTRATION 24-27
Reconciliation of Net Income to Net Cash Provided by Operating Activities

Reconciliation		
Net income		$112,000
Adjustments to reconcile net income to net cash provided by operating activities:		
Depreciation expense	$ 10,000	
Increase in accounts receivable	(15,000)	
Increase in inventory	(160,000)	
Increase in prepaid expenses	(8,000)	
Increase in accounts payable	60,000	
Increase in accrued expense payable	20,000	93,000
Net cash provided by operating activities		$ 19,000

The reconciliation may be presented at the bottom of the statement of cash flows when the direct method is used or in a separate schedule.

DIRECT VERSUS INDIRECT CONTROVERSY

The most contentious decision that the FASB faced in issuing *Statement No. 95* was choosing between the direct method and the indirect method of determining net cash flow from operating activities. Companies lobbied against the direct method, urging adoption of the indirect method. Commercial lending officers expressed a strong preference to the FASB that the direct method be required.

In Favor of the Direct Method

The principal advantage of the direct method is that **it shows operating cash receipts and payments.** That is, it is more consistent with the objective of a statement of cash flows—to provide information about cash receipts and cash payments—than the indirect method, which does not report operating cash receipts and payments.

Supporters of the direct method contend that knowledge of the specific sources of operating cash receipts and the purposes for which operating cash payments were made in past periods is useful in estimating future operating cash flows. Furthermore, information about amounts of major classes of operating cash receipts and payments is more useful than information only about their arithmetic sum (the net cash flow from operating activities). Such information is more revealing of an enterprise's ability (1) to generate sufficient cash from operating activities to pay its debts, (2) to reinvest in its operations, and (3) to make distributions to its owners.[16]

Many corporate providers of financial statements say that they do not currently collect information in a manner that allows them to determine amounts such as cash received from customers or cash paid to suppliers directly from their accounting systems. But supporters of the direct method contend that the incremental cost of assimilating such operating cash receipts and payments data is not significant.

In Favor of the Indirect Method

The principal advantage of the indirect method is that **it focuses on the differences between net income and net cash flow from operating activities.** That is, it provides a useful link between the statement of cash flows and the income statement and balance sheet.

Many providers of financial statements contend that it is less costly to adjust net income to net cash flow from operating activities (indirect) than it is to report gross operating cash receipts and payments (direct). Because the indirect method was used almost exclusively in the former statement of changes in financial position, users are more familiar with it. Supporters of the indirect method also state that the direct method, which effectively reports income statement information on a cash rather than an accrual basis, may erroneously suggest that net cash flow from operating activities is as good as, or better than, net income as a measure of performance.[17]

Special Rules Applying to Direct and Indirect Methods

Companies that use the direct method are required, at a minimum, to report separately the following classes of operating cash receipts and payments:

Receipts
1. Cash collected from customers (including lessees, licensees, etc.).
2. Interest and dividends received.
3. Other operating cash receipts, if any.

Payments
1. Cash paid to employees and suppliers of goods or services (including suppliers of insurance, advertising, etc.).
2. Interest paid.
3. Income taxes paid.
4. Other operating cash payments, if any.

---

[16]"Statement of Cash Flows," pars. 107 and 111.

[17]"Cash Flow: FASB Opens the Floodgates," p. 29.

INTERNATIONAL
INSIGHT

Consolidated statements of funds or cash flows may be of limited use to analysts evaluating multinationals. Without disaggregation, users of such statements are not able to determine "where in the world" the funds are sourced and used.

Companies are encouraged to provide further breakdowns of operating cash receipts and payments that they consider meaningful.

Companies using the indirect method are required to disclose separately changes in inventory, receivables, and payables to reconcile net income to net cash flow from operating activities. In addition, interest paid (net of amount capitalized) and income taxes paid must be disclosed elsewhere in the financial statements or accompanying notes.[18] The FASB requires these separate and additional disclosures so that users may approximate the direct method. Also, an acceptable alternative presentation of the indirect method is to report net cash flow from operating activities as a single line item in the statement of cash flows and to present the reconciliation details elsewhere in the financial statements.

► SPECIAL PROBLEMS IN STATEMENT ANALYSIS

OBJECTIVE 8

Identify special problems in preparing a statement of cash flows.

Some of the special problems related to preparing the statement of cash flows were discussed in connection with the preceding illustrations. Other problems that arise with some frequency in the preparation of this statement may be categorized as follows:

1. Adjustments similar to depreciation.
2. Accounts receivable (net).
3. Other working capital changes.
4. Net losses.
5. Gains.
6. Stock options.
7. Postretirement benefit costs.
8. Irregular items.
9. Significant noncash transactions.

ADJUSTMENTS SIMILAR TO DEPRECIATION

Depreciation expense is the most common adjustment to net income that is made to arrive at net cash flow from operating activities. But there are numerous other noncash expense or revenue items. Examples of expense items that must be added back to net income are the **amortization of intangible assets** such as goodwill and patents, and the **amortization of deferred costs** such as bond issue costs. These charges to expense involve expenditures made in prior periods that are being amortized currently and reduce net income without affecting cash in the current period. Also, **amortization of bond discount or premium** on long-term bonds payable affects the amount of interest expense, but neither changes cash. As a result, amortization of these items should be added back to (discount) or subtracted from (premium) net income to arrive at net cash flow from operating activities.

In a similar manner, **changes in deferred income taxes** affect net income but have no effect on cash. For example, the Kroger Co. at one time experienced an increase in its liability for deferred taxes of approximately $42 million. Tax expense was increased and net income was decreased by this amount, but cash was not affected; therefore, $42 million would be added back to net income on a statement of cash flows. Conversely, General Electric Company at one time had a decrease in its liability for deferred taxes of $171 million. Tax expense decreased and net income increased by this amount, but

---

[18]*Accounting Trends and Techniques—1993* reports that of the 600 companies surveyed in 1992, 354 disclosed interest paid in notes to the financial statements, 219 disclosed interest at the bottom of the statement of cash flows, 17 disclosed interest within the statement of cash flows, and 10 reported no separate amount. Income taxes paid during the year were disclosed in a manner similar to interest payments.

cash flow was unaffected. Therefore, GE subtracted this amount from net income to arrive at net cash flow from operating activities.

Another common adjustment to net income is **a change related to an investment in common stock** when income or loss is accrued under the equity method. For example, General Motors Corporation's equity in undistributed earnings of unconsolidated subsidiaries increased in one year by $111 million. Such an increase, however, is not a cash inflow; hence, it had to be deducted from net income to arrive at net cash flow from operating activities. Dictaphone Corporation's equity in the net losses of its foreign subsidiaries was $132,000, and this amount was added back to net income. If the company receives a dividend from its equity investee, cash provided from a cash dividend is reported as part of net income; no adjustment of net income is necessary for the cash dividend, since this is considered an operating activity cash inflow.

ACCOUNTS RECEIVABLE (NET)

Up to this point, we have assumed that no allowance for doubtful accounts—a contra account—was needed to offset accounts receivable. However, if an allowance for doubtful accounts is needed, how does it affect the determination of net cash flow from operating activities? For example, assume that Redmark Co. reports net income of $40,000 and has the following balances related to accounts receivable:

	1996	1995	Change Increase/Decrease
Accounts receivable	$105,000	$90,000	$15,000 Increase
Allowance for doubtful accounts	10,000	4,000	6,000 Increase
Accounts receivable (net)	$ 95,000	$86,000	9,000 Increase

ILLUSTRATION 24-28
Accounts Receivable Balances, Redmark Co.

The proper reporting treatment using the indirect and direct methods is illustrated in the following sections.

Indirect Method

Because an increase in the Allowance for Doubtful Accounts is caused by a charge to bad debts expense, an increase in the Allowance for Doubtful Accounts should be added back to net income to arrive at net cash flow from operating activities. One method for presenting this information in a statement of cash flows is as follows:

Redmark Co. PARTIAL STATEMENT OF CASH FLOWS For the Year 1996		
Cash flows from operating activities		
Net income		$40,000
Adjustments to reconcile net income to net cash provided by operating activities:		
Increase in accounts receivable	$(15,000)	
Increase in allowance for doubtful accounts	6,000	(9,000)
		$31,000

ILLUSTRATION 24-29
Presentation of Allowance for Doubtful Accounts—Indirect Method

As indicated, the increase in the Allowance for Doubtful Accounts balance is caused by a charge to bad debt expense for the year. Because bad debt expense is a noncash charge, it must be added back to net income in arriving at net cash flow from operating activities.

Instead of separately analyzing the allowance account, a short-cut approach is to net the allowance balance against the receivable balance and compare the change in accounts receivable on a net basis. This presentation would be as follows:

ILLUSTRATION 24-30
Net Approach to
Allowance for Doubtful
Accounts—Indirect
Method

Redmark Co. PARTIAL STATEMENT OF CASH FLOWS For the Year 1996	
Cash flows from operating activities	
Net income	$40,000
Adjustments to reconcile net income to net cash provided by operating activities:	
Increase in accounts receivable (net)	(9,000)
	$31,000

This short-cut procedure works also if the change in the allowance account was caused by a writeoff of accounts receivable. In this case, both the Accounts Receivable and the Allowance for Doubtful Accounts are reduced, and no effect on cash flows occurs. Because of its simplicity, you should use the net approach on your homework assignments.

Direct Method

If the direct method is used, the Allowance for Doubtful Accounts should **not be netted against the Accounts Receivable.** To illustrate, assume that Redmark Co.'s net income of $40,000 comprised the following items:

ILLUSTRATION 24-31
Income Statement,
Redmark Co.

Redmark Co. INCOME STATEMENT For the Year 1996		
Sales		$100,000
Expenses:		
Salaries	$46,000	
Utilities	8,000	
Bad debts	6,000	60,000
Net income		$ 40,000

If the $9,000 increase in accounts receivable (net) is deducted from sales for the year, cash sales would be reported at $91,000 ($100,000 − $9,000) and cash payments for operating expenses at $60,000. Both items are misstated because cash sales should be reported at $85,000 ($100,000 − $15,000), and total cash payments for operating expenses should be reported at $54,000 ($60,000 − $6,000). The proper presentation is as follows:

ILLUSTRATION 24-32
Bad Debts—Direct
Method

Redmark Co. PARTIAL STATEMENT OF CASH FLOWS For the Year 1996		
Cash flows from operating activities		
Cash received from customers		$85,000
Salaries paid	$46,000	
Utilities paid	8,000	54,000
Net cash provided by operating activities		$31,000

An added complication develops when accounts receivable are written off. Simply adjusting sales for the change in accounts receivable will not provide the proper amount of cash sales. The reason is that the writeoff of the accounts receivable is not a cash collection. Thus an additional adjustment is necessary.

OTHER WORKING CAPITAL CHANGES

Up to this point, all of the changes in working capital items (current asset and current liability items) have been handled as adjustments to net income in determining net cash flow from operating activities. You must be careful, however, because **some changes in working capital, although they affect cash, do not affect net income.** Generally, these are investing or financing activities of a current nature. For example, the purchase of **short-term available-for-sale securities** for $50,000 cash has no effect on net income but it does cause a $50,000 decrease in cash.[19] This transaction is reported as a cash flow from investing activities and reported gross as follows:[20]

> Cash flows from investing activities
>> Purchase of short-term available-for-sale securities $(50,000)

Another example is the issuance of a $10,000 **short-term nontrade note payable** for cash. This change in a working capital item has no effect on income from operations but it increases cash $10,000. It is reported in the statement of cash flows as follows:

> Cash flows from financing activities
>> Issuance of short-term note $10,000

Another change in a working capital item that has no effect on income from operations or on cash is a **cash dividend payable.** Although the cash dividends when paid will be reported as a financing activity, the declared but unpaid dividend is not reported on the statement of cash flows.

Because **trading securities** are bought and held principally for the purpose of selling them in the near term, the cash flows from purchases and sales of trading securities should be classified as cash flows from **operating activities.**[21]

NET LOSSES

If an enterprise reports a net loss instead of a net income, the net loss must be adjusted for those items that do not result in a cash inflow or outflow. The net loss after adjusting for the charges or credits not affecting cash may result in a negative **or** a positive cash flow from operating activities. For example, if the net loss was $50,000 and the total amount of charges to be added back was $60,000, then net cash provided by operating activities is $10,000, as shown in this computation:

Net loss		$(50,000)
Adjustments to reconcile net income to net cash provided by operating activities:		
Depreciation of plant assets	$55,000	
Amortization of patents	5,000	60,000
Net cash provided by operating activities		$ 10,000

ILLUSTRATION 24-33
Computation of Net Cash Flow from Operating Activities—Cash Inflow

If the company experiences a net loss of $80,000 and the total amount of the charges to be added back is $25,000, the presentation appears as follows:

Net loss	$(80,000)
Adjustments to reconcile net income to net cash used by operating activities:	
Depreciation of plant assets	25,000
Net cash used by operating activities	$(55,000)

ILLUSTRATION 24-34
Computation of Net Cash Flow from Operating Activities—Cash Outflow

---

[19]If the basis of the statement of cash flows is cash **and cash equivalents** and the short-term investment is considered a cash equivalent, then nothing would be reported in the statement because the balance of cash and cash equivalents does not change as a result of this transaction.

[20]"Accounting for Certain Investments in Debt and Equity Securities," *Statement of Financial Accounting Standards No. 115* (Norwalk, CT: 1993), par. 118.

[21]*Ibid.*, par. 118.

Although it is not illustrated in this chapter, a negative cash flow may result even if the company reports a net income.

GAINS

In the third illustration (1996) of Tax Consultants Inc., the company experiences a loss of $2,000 from the sale of equipment. This loss was added to net income to compute net cash flow from operating activities because **the loss is a noncash charge in the income statement.** If a gain from a sale of equipment is experienced, it too requires that net income be adjusted. Because the gain is reported in the statement of cash flows as part of the cash proceeds from the sale of equipment under investing activities, **the gain is deducted from net income to avoid double counting**—once as part of net income and again as part of the cash proceeds from the sale.

STOCK OPTIONS

If a company has a stock option plan, compensation expense will be recorded during the period(s) in which the employee performs the services. Although compensation expense is debited, stockholders' equity (the paid-in capital accounts) is credited, and cash remains unaffected by the amount of the expense. **Therefore, net income has to be increased by the amount of compensation expense from stock options in computing net cash flow from operating activities.**

POSTRETIREMENT BENEFIT COSTS

If a company has postretirement costs such as an employee pension plan, chances are that the pension expense recorded during a period will either be higher than the cash funded (when there is an unfunded liability) or lower than the cash funded (when there is a deferred or prepaid pension cost). When the expense is higher or lower than the cash paid, **net income must be adjusted by the difference between cash paid and the expense reported** in computing net cash flow from operating activities.

EXTRAORDINARY ITEMS

Cash flows from extraordinary transactions and other events whose effects are included in net income, but which are not related to operations, should be reported **either as investing activities or as financing activities.** For example, if Tax Consultants Inc. had extinguished its long-term bond debt of $40,000 by paying the bondholders $35,000 in cash, it would have recognized a $3,000 extraordinary gain ($5,000 gain less $2,000 of taxes). In the statement of cash flows (indirect method), the $5,000 gain would be deducted from net income in the operating activities section and the $35,000 cash outflow for debt extinguishment would be reported as a financing activity as follows:

Cash flows from financing activities	
Retirement of long-term bonds	$(35,000)

Note that in this example the gain is handled at its gross amount ($5,000), not net of tax. The cash paid to retire the bonds is reported as a financing activity at $35,000, also exclusive of the tax effect. The FASB requires that **all income taxes paid be classified as operating cash outflows.** Some accountants suggested that income taxes paid be allocated to investing and financing transactions. But, the Board decided that allocation of income taxes paid to operating, investing, and financing activities would be so complex and arbitrary that the benefits, if any, would not justify the costs involved. Under both the direct method and the indirect method the total amount of income taxes paid must be disclosed.[22]

SIGNIFICANT NONCASH TRANSACTIONS

Because the statement of cash flows reports only the effects of operating, investing, and financing activities in terms of cash flows, some **significant noncash transactions** and other events that are investing or financing activities are omitted from the body of the statement. Among the more common of these noncash transactions that should be reported or disclosed in some manner are the following:

1. Acquisition of assets by assuming liabilities (including capital lease obligations) or by issuing equity securities.
2. Exchanges of nonmonetary assets.
3. Refinancing of long-term debt.
4. Conversion of debt or preferred stock to common stock.
5. Issuance of equity securities to retire debt.

Prior to the issuance of the new standard on the statement of cash flows, these significant noncash transactions were incorporated in the statement. Now, **these noncash items are not to be incorporated in the statement of cash flows.** If material in amount, these disclosures may be either narrative or summarized in a separate schedule at the bottom of the statement, or they may appear in a separate note or supplementary schedule to the financial statements. The presentation of these significant noncash transactions or other events in a separate schedule at the bottom of the statement of cash flows is shown as follows:

Net increase in cash	$3,717,000
Cash at beginning of year	5,208,000
Cash at end of year	$8,925,000
Noncash investing and financing activities	
Purchase of land and building through issuance of 250,000 shares of	
common stock	$1,750,000
Exchange of Steadfast, NY land for Bedford, PA land	$2,000,000
Conversion of 12% bonds to 50,000 shares of common stock	$ 500,000

ILLUSTRATION 24-35
Schedule Presentation of Noncash Investing and Financing Activities

These noncash transactions might be presented in a separate note as follows:

Note G: Significant noncash transactions. During the year the company engaged in the following significant noncash investing and financing transactions:	
Issued 250,000 shares of common stock to purchase land and building	$1,750,000
Exchanged land in Steadfast, NY for land in Bedford, PA	$2,000,000
Converted 12% bonds due 1998 to 50,000 shares of common stock	$ 500,000

ILLUSTRATION 24-36
Note Presentation of Noncash Investing and Financing Activities

Certain other significant noncash transactions or other events are generally not reported in conjunction with the statement of cash flows. Examples of these types of transactions are **stock dividends, stock splits, and appropriations of retained earnings.**

---

[22]For an insightful article on some weaknesses and limitations in the statement of cash flows caused by implementation of *FASB Statement No. 95*, see Hugo Nurnberg, "Inconsistencies and Ambiguities in Cash Flow Statements Under *FASB Statement No. 95*," *Accounting Horizons*, June 1993, pp. 60–73. Nurnberg identifies the inconsistencies caused by the three-way classification of all cash receipts and cash payments, gross versus net of tax, the ambiguous disclosure requirements for noncash investing and financing transactions, and the ambiguous presentation of third-party financing transactions.

These items, neither financing nor investing activities, are generally reported in conjunction with the statement of retained earnings or schedules and notes pertaining to changes in capital accounts.

► USEFULNESS OF THE STATEMENT OF CASH FLOWS

The information in a statement of cash flows should help investors, creditors, and others to assess the following:

1. **The entity's ability to generate future cash flows.** A primary objective of financial reporting is to provide information that makes it possible to predict the amounts, timing, and uncertainty of future cash flows. By examining relationships between items such as sales and net cash flow from operating activities, or net cash flow from operating activities and increases or decreases in cash, it is possible to make better predictions of the amounts, timing, and uncertainty of future cash flows than is possible using accrual basis data.

2. **The entity's ability to pay dividends and meet obligations.** Simply put, cash is essential. If a company does not have adequate cash, employees cannot be paid, debts settled, dividends paid, or equipment acquired. A statement of cash flows indicates how cash is used and where it comes from. Employees, creditors, stockholders, and customers should be particularly interested in this statement, because it alone shows the flows of cash in a business.

3. **The reasons for the difference between net income and net cash flow from operating activities.** The net income number is important, because it provides information on the success or failure of a business enterprise from one period to another. But some people are critical of accrual basis net income because estimates must be made to arrive at it. As a result, the reliability of the number is often challenged. Such is not the case with cash. Thus, many readers of the financial statement want to know the reasons for the difference between net income and net cash flow from operating activities. Then they can assess for themselves the reliability of the income number.

4. **The cash and noncash investing and financing transactions during the period.** By examining a company's investing activities (purchase and sales of assets other than its products) and its financing transactions (borrowings and repayments of borrowings, investments by owners and distributions to owners), a financial statement reader can better understand why assets and liabilities increased or decreased during the period. For example, the following questions might be answered:

    How did cash increase when there was a net loss for the period?

    How were the proceeds of the bond issue used?

    How was the expansion in the plant and equipment financed?

    Why were dividends not increased?

    How was the retirement of debt accomplished?

    How much money was borrowed during the year?

    Is cash flow greater or less than net income?

► *SECTION 2 / USE OF A WORK SHEET*

OBJECTIVE 9

Explain the use of a work sheet in preparing a statement of cash flows.

When numerous adjustments are necessary, or other complicating factors are present, **many accountants prefer to use a work sheet to assemble and classify the data that will appear on the statement of cash flows.** The work sheet (a **"spreadsheet"** when using computer software) is merely a device that aids in the preparation of the statement; its use is optional. The skeleton format of the work sheet for preparation of the statement of cash flows using the indirect method is shown in the following example.

XYZ COMPANY STATEMENT OF CASH FLOWS For the Year Ended . . .				
Balance Sheet Accounts	End of Last Year Balances	Reconciling Items Debits	Reconciling Items Credits	End of Current Year Balances
Debit balance accounts	XX	XX	XX	XX
	XX	XX	XX	XX
Totals	XXX			XXX
Credit balance accounts	XX	XX	XX	XX
	XX	XX	XX	XX
Totals	XXX			XXX
Statement of Cash Flows Effects				
Operating activities				
Net income		XX		
Adjustments		XX	XX	
Investing activities				
Receipts and payments		XX	XX	
Financing activities				
Receipts and payments		XX	XX	
Totals		XXX	XXX	
Increase (decrease) in cash		(XX)	XX	
Totals		XXX	XXX	

ILLUSTRATION 24-37
Format of Work Sheet for Preparation of Statement of Cash Flows

The following guidelines are important in using a work sheet:

1. In the balance sheet accounts section, **accounts with debit balances are listed separately from those with credit balances.** This means, for example, that Accumulated Depreciation is listed under credit balances and not as a contra account under debit balances. The beginning and ending balances of each account are entered in the appropriate columns. The transactions that caused the change in the account balance during the year are entered as reconciling items in the two middle columns. After all reconciling items have been entered, each line pertaining to a balance sheet account should foot across. That is, the beginning balance plus or minus the reconciling item(s) must equal the ending balance. When this agreement exists for all balance sheet accounts, all changes in account balances have been reconciled.

2. The bottom portion of the work sheet consists of the operating, investing, and financing activities sections. Accordingly, it provides the information necessary to prepare the formal statement of cash flows. **Inflows of cash are entered as debits in the reconciling columns and outflows of cash are entered as credits in the reconciling columns.** Thus, in this section, the sale of equipment for cash at book value is entered as a debit under inflows of cash from investing activities. Similarly, the purchase of land for cash is entered as a credit under outflows of cash from investing activities.

3. **The reconciling items shown in the work sheet are not entered in any journal or posted to any account.** They do not represent either adjustments or corrections of the balance sheet accounts. They are used only to facilitate the preparation of the statement of cash flows.

PREPARATION OF THE WORK SHEET

The preparation of a work sheet involves a series of prescribed steps. The steps in this case are:

1. Enter the balance sheet accounts and their beginning and ending balances in the balance sheet accounts section.

2. Enter the data which explain the changes in the balance sheet accounts (other than cash) and their effects on the statement of cash flows in the reconciling columns of the work sheet.

3. Enter the increase or decrease in cash on the cash line and at the bottom of the work sheet. This entry should enable the totals of the reconciling columns to be in agreement.

To illustrate the preparation and use of a work sheet and to illustrate the reporting of some of the special problems discussed in the prior section, the following comprehensive illustration is presented for Satellite Corporation. Again, the indirect method serves as the basis for the computation of net cash provided by operating activities. The financial statements and other data related to Satellite Corporation are presented with the balance sheet and the statement of income and retained earnings shown on the following pages. Additional explanations related to the preparation of the work sheet are provided throughout the discussion that follows the financial statements.

ILLUSTRATION 24-38
Comparative Balance
Sheets, Satellite
Corporation

Satellite Corporation COMPARATIVE BALANCE SHEETS December 31, 1996 and 1995			
	1996	1995	Difference Incr. or Decr.
Assets			
Cash	$ 59,000	$ 66,000	$ 7,000 Decr.
Accounts receivable (net)	104,000	51,000	53,000 Incr.
Inventories	493,000	341,000	152,000 Incr.
Prepaid expenses	16,500	17,000	500 Decr.
Investments in stock of Porter Co. (equity method)	18,500	15,000	3,500 Incr.
Land	131,500	82,000	49,500 Incr.
Equipment	187,000	142,000	45,000 Incr.
Accumulated depreciation—equipment	(29,000)	(31,000)	2,000 Decr.
Buildings	262,000	262,000	—
Accumulated depreciation—buildings	(74,100)	(71,000)	3,100 Incr.
Goodwill	7,600	10,000	2,400 Decr.
Total assets	$1,176,000	$884,000	
Liabilities			
Accounts payable	$ 132,000	$131,000	1,000 Incr.
Accrued liabilities	43,000	39,000	4,000 Incr.
Income tax payable	3,000	16,000	13,000 Decr.
Notes payable (long-term)	60,000	—	60,000 Incr.
Bonds payable	100,000	100,000	—
Premium on bonds payable	7,000	8,000	1,000 Decr.
Deferred tax liability (long-term)	9,000	6,000	3,000 Incr.
Total liabilities	354,000	300,000	
Stockholders' Equity			
Common stock ($1 par)	60,000	50,000	10,000 Incr.
Additional paid-in capital	187,000	38,000	149,000 Incr.
Retained earnings	592,000	496,000	96,000 Incr.
Treasury stock	(17,000)	—	17,000 Incr.
Total stockholders' equity	822,000	584,000	
Total liabilities and stockholders' equity	$1,176,000	$884,000	

Satellite Corporation
COMBINED STATEMENT OF INCOME AND RETAINED EARNINGS
For the Year Ended December 31, 1996

Net sales		$526,500
Other revenue		3,500
Total revenues		530,000
Expense		
Cost of goods sold		310,000
Selling and administrative expenses		47,000
Other expenses and losses		12,000
Total expenses		369,000
Income before income tax and extraordinary item		161,000
Income Tax		
Current	$47,000	
Deferred	3,000	50,000
Income before extraordinary item		111,000
Gain on condemnation of land (net of $2,000 tax)		6,000
Net income		117,000
Retained earnings, January 1		496,000
Less:		
Cash dividends	6,000	
Stock dividend	15,000	21,000
Retained earnings, December 31		$592,000
Per Share:		
Income before extraordinary item		$2.02
Extraordinary item		.11
Net income		$2.13

Additional Information

(a) Other income of $3,500 represents Satellite's equity share in the net income of Porter Co., an equity investee. Satellite owns 22% of Porter Co.

(b) An analysis of the equipment account and related accumulated depreciation indicates the following:

	Equipment Dr./(Cr.)	Accum. Dep. Dr./(Cr.)	Gain or Loss
Balance at end of 1995	$142,000	$(31,000)	
Purchases of equipment	53,000		
Sale of equipment	(8,000)	2,500	$1,500 L
Depreciation for the period		(11,500)	
Major repair charged to accumulated depreciation		11,000	
Balance at end of 1996	$187,000	$(29,000)	

(c) Land in the amount of $60,000 was purchased through the issuance of a long-term note; in addition, certain parcels of land costing $10,500 were condemned. The state government paid Satellite $18,500, resulting in an $8,000 gain which has a $2,000 tax effect.

(d) The change in the accumulated depreciation—buildings, goodwill, and premium on bonds payable accounts resulted from depreciation and amortization entries.

(e) An analysis of the paid-in capital accounts in stockholders' equity discloses the following:

	Common Stock	Additional Paid-In Capital
Balance at end of 1995	$50,000	$ 38,000
Issuance of 2% stock dividend	1,000	14,000
Sale of stock for cash	9,000	135,000
Balance at end of 1996	$60,000	$187,000

(f) Interest paid (net of amount capitalized) is $9,000; income taxes paid is $62,000.

ANALYSIS OF TRANSACTIONS

The following discussion provides an explanation of the individual adjustments that appear on the work sheet in Illustration 24-40. Because cash is the basis for the analysis, the cash account is reconciled last. Because income is the first item that appears on the statement of cash flows, it is handled first.

Change in Retained Earnings

Net income for the period is $117,000; the entry for it on the work sheet is as follows:

(1)

Operating—Net Income	117,000	
Retained Earnings		117,000

Net income is reported on the bottom section of the work sheet and **is the starting point for preparation of the statement of cash flows (under the indirect method).**

Retained earnings was also affected by a stock dividend and a cash dividend. The retained earnings statement reports a stock dividend of $15,000. The work sheet entry for this transaction is as follows:

(2)

Retained Earnings	15,000	
Common Stock		1,000
Additional Paid-in Capital		14,000

The issuance of stock dividends is not a cash operating, investing, or financing item; therefore, **although this transaction is entered on the work sheet for reconciling purposes, it is not reported in the statement of cash flows.**

The cash dividends paid of $6,000 represents a financing activity cash outflow. The following work sheet entry is made:

(3)

Retained Earnings	6,000	
Financing—Cash Dividends		6,000

The beginning and ending balances of retained earnings are reconciled by the entry of the three items above.

Accounts Receivable (Net)

The increase in accounts receivable (net) of $53,000 represents adjustments that did not result in cash inflows during 1996. As a result, the increase of $53,000 would be deducted from net income. The following work sheet entry is made:

(4)

Accounts Receivable (net)	53,000	
Operating—Increase in Accounts Receivable (net)		53,000

Inventories

The increase in inventories of $152,000 represents an operating use of cash. The incremental investment in inventories during the year reduces cash without increasing the cost of goods sold. The work sheet entry is made as follows:

(5)

Inventories	152,000	
Operating—Increase in Inventories		152,000

Prepaid Expense

The decrease in prepaid expenses of $500 represents a charge in the income statement for which there was no cash outflow in the current period. It should be added back to net income through the following entry:

(6)

Operating—Decrease in Prepaid Expenses	500	
Prepaid Expenses		500

Investment in Stock of Porter Co.

The investment in the stock of Porter Co. increased $3,500, which reflects Satellite's share of the income earned by its equity investee during the current year. Although revenue, and therefore income per the income statement, was increased $3,500 by the accounting entry that recorded Satellite's share of Porter Co.'s net income, no cash (dividend) was provided. The following work sheet entry is made:

(7)

Investment in Stock of Porter Co.	3,500	
Operating—Equity in Earnings of Porter Co.		3,500

Land

Land in the amount of $60,000 was purchased through the issuance of a long-term note payable. This transaction did not affect cash; it is considered a significant noncash investing/financing transaction that would be disclosed either in a separate schedule below the statement of cash flows or in the accompanying notes. The following entry is made to reconcile the work sheet:

(8)

Land	60,000	
Notes Payable		60,000

In addition to the noncash transaction involving the issuance of a note to purchase land, the Land account was decreased by the condemnation proceedings. The work sheet entry to record the receipt of $18,500 for land having a book value of $10,500 is as follows:

(9)

Investing—Proceeds from Condemnation of Land	18,500	
Land		10,500
Operating—Gain on Condemnation of Land		8,000

The extraordinary gain of $8,000 is deducted from net income in reconciling net income to net cash flow from operating activities because the transaction that gave rise to the gain is an item whose cash effect is already classified as an investing cash inflow. The Land account is now reconciled.

Equipment and Accumulated Depreciation

An analysis of Equipment and Accumulated Depreciation shows that a number of transactions have affected these accounts. Equipment in the amount of $53,000 was purchased during the year. The entry to record this transaction on the work sheet is as follows:

(10)

Equipment	53,000	
Investing—Purchase of Equipment		53,000

In addition, equipment with a book value of $5,500 was sold at a loss of $1,500. The entry to record this transaction on the work sheet is as follows:

(11)

Investing—Sale of Equipment	4,000	
Operating—Loss on Sale of Equipment	1,500	
Accumulated Depreciation—Equipment	2,500	
Equipment		8,000

The proceeds from the sale of the equipment provided cash of $4,000. In addition, the loss on the sale of the equipment has reduced net income, but did not affect cash; therefore, it is added back to net income to report accurately cash provided by operating activities.

Depreciation on the equipment was reported at $11,500 and is presented on the work sheet in the following manner:

(12)

Operating—Depreciation Expense—Equipment	11,500	
Accumulated Depreciation—Equipment		11,500

The depreciation expense is added back to net income because it reduced income but did not affect cash.

Finally, a major repair to the equipment in the amount of $11,000 was charged to Accumulated Depreciation—Equipment. Because this expenditure required cash, the following work sheet entry is made:

(13)

Accumulated Depreciation—Equipment	11,000	
Investing—Major Repairs of Equipment		11,000

The balances in the Equipment and related Accumulated Depreciation accounts are reconciled after adjustment for the foregoing items.

Building Depreciation and Amortization of Goodwill

Depreciation expense on the buildings of $3,100 and amortization of goodwill of $2,400 are both expenses in the income statement that reduced net income but did not require cash outflows in the current period. The following work sheet entry is made:

(14)

Operating—Depreciation Expense—Buildings	3,100	
Operating—Amortization of Goodwill	2,400	
Accumulated Depreciation—Buildings		3,100
Goodwill		2,400

Other Noncash Charges or Credits

An analysis of the remaining accounts indicates that changes in the Accounts Payable, Accrued Liabilities, Income Taxes Payable, Premium on Bonds Payable, and Deferred Tax Liability balances resulted from charges or credits to net income that did not affect cash. Each of these items should be individually analyzed and entered in the work sheet. We have summarized in the following compound entry to the work sheet these noncash, income-related items:

(15)

Income Tax Payable	13,000	
Premium on Bonds Payable	1,000	
Operating—Increase in Accounts Payable	1,000	
Operating—Increase in Accrued Liabilities	4,000	
Operating—Increase in Deferred Tax Liability	3,000	
Operating—Decrease in Income Tax Payable		13,000
Operating—Amortization of Bond Premium		1,000
Accounts Payable		1,000
Accrued Liabilities		4,000
Deferred Tax Liability		3,000

Common Stock and Related Accounts

A comparison of the common stock balances and the additional paid-in capital balances shows that transactions during the year affected these accounts. First, a stock dividend of 2% was issued to stockholders. As indicated in the discussion of work sheet entry (2), no cash was provided or used by the stock dividend transaction. In addition to the shares issued via the stock dividend, Satellite sold shares of common stock at $16 per share. The work sheet entry to record this transaction is as follows:

(16)

Financing—Sale of Common Stock	144,000	
Common Stock		9,000
Additional Paid-in Capital		135,000

Also, the company purchased shares of its common stock in the amount of $17,000. The work sheet entry to record this transaction is as follows:

(17)

Treasury Stock	17,000	
Financing—Purchase of Treasury Stock		17,000

Final Reconciling Entry

The final entry to reconcile the change in cash and to balance the work sheet is shown below.

(18)

Decrease in Cash	7,000	
Cash		7,000

The $7,000 amount is the difference between the beginning and ending cash balance.

Once it has been determined that the differences between the beginning and ending balances per the work sheet columns have been accounted for, the reconciling transactions columns can be totaled, and they should balance. The statement of cash flows can be prepared entirely from the items and amounts that appear at the bottom of the work sheet under "Statement of Cash Flows Effects," as shown on the following page.

ILLUSTRATION 24-40
**Completed Work Sheet
for Preparation of
Statement of Cash Flows,
Satellite Corporation**

Satellite Manufacturing Corporation
WORK SHEET FOR PREPARATION OF STATEMENT OF CASH FLOWS
For the Year Ended December 31, 1996

	Balance 12/31/95	Reconciling Items—1996 Debits		Reconciling Items—1996 Credits		Balance 12/31/96
Debits						
Cash	$ 66,000			(18)	$ 7,000	$ 59,000
Accounts receivable (net)	51,000	(4)	$ 53,000			104,000
Inventories	341,000	(5)	152,000			493,000
Prepaid expenses	17,000			(6)	500	16,500
Investment (equity method)	15,000	(7)	3,500			18,500
Land	82,000	(8)	60,000	(9)	10,500	131,500
Equipment	142,000	(10)	53,000	(11)	8,000	187,000
Buildings	262,000					262,000
Goodwill	10,000			(14)	2,400	7,600
Treasury stock		(17)	17,000			17,000
Total debits	$986,000					$1,296,100
Credits		(11)	2,500			
Accum. depr.—equipment	$ 31,000	(13)	11,000	(12)	11,500	$ 29,000
Accum. depr.—buildings	71,000			(14)	3,100	74,100
Accounts payable	131,000			(15)	1,000	132,000
Accrued liabilities	39,000			(15)	4,000	43,000
Income tax payable	16,000	(15)	13,000			3,000
Notes payable	–0–			(8)	60,000	60,000
Bonds payable	100,000					100,000
Premium on bonds payable	8,000	(15)	1,000			7,000
Deferred tax liability	6,000			(15)	3,000	9,000
Common stock	50,000			(2)	1,000	60,000
				(16)	9,000	
Additional paid-in capital	38,000			(2)	14,000	
				(16)	135,000	187,000
Retained earnings	496,000	(2)	15,000	(1)	117,000	592,000
		(3)	6,000			
Total credits	$986,000					$1,296,100

Statement of Cash Flows Effects

		Debits		Credits	
Operating activities					
Net income	(1)	117,000			
Increase in accounts receivable (net)			(4)	53,000	
Increase in inventories			(5)	152,000	
Decrease in prepaid expenses	(6)	500			
Equity in earnings of Porter Co.			(7)	3,500	
Gain on condemnation of land			(9)	8,000	
Loss on sale of equipment	(11)	1,500			
Depr. expense—equipment	(12)	11,500			
Depr. expense—buildings	(14)	3,100			
Amortization of goodwill	(14)	2,400			
Increase in accounts payable	(15)	1,000			
Increase in accrued liabilities	(15)	4,000			
Increase in deferred tax liability	(15)	3,000			
Decrease in income tax payable			(15)	13,000	
Amortization of bond premium			(15)	1,000	
Investing activities					
Proceeds from condemnation of land	(9)	18,500			
Purchase of equipment			(10)	53,000	
Sale of equipment	(11)	4,000			
Major repairs of equipment			(13)	11,000	
Financing activities					
Payment of cash dividend			(3)	6,000	
Issuance of common stock	(16)	144,000			
Purchase of treasury stock			(17)	17,000	
Totals		697,500		704,500	
Decrease in cash	(18)	7,000			
Totals		$704,500		$704,500	

PREPARATION OF STATEMENT

Presented below is a formal statement of cash flows prepared from the data compiled in the lower portion of the work sheet.

ILLUSTRATION 24-41
Statement of Cash Flows, Satellite Corporation

Satellite Corporation
STATEMENT OF CASH FLOWS
For the Year Ended December 31, 1996
Increase (Decrease) in Cash

Cash flows from operating activities		
Net income		$117,000
Adjustments to reconcile net income to net		
cash used by operating activities:		
Depreciation expense	$ 14,600	
Amortization of goodwill	2,400	
Amortization of bond premium	(1,000)	
Equity in earnings of Porter Co.	(3,500)	
Gain on condemnation of land	(8,000)	
Loss on sale of equipment	1,500	
Increase in deferred tax liability	3,000	
Increase in accounts receivable (net)	(53,000)	
Increase in inventories	(152,000)	
Decrease in prepaid expenses	500	
Increase in accounts payable	1,000	
Increase in accrued liabilities	4,000	
Decrease in income tax payable	(13,000)	(203,500)
Net cash used by operating activities		(86,500)
Cash flows from investing activities		
Proceeds from condemnation of land	18,500	
Purchase of equipment	(53,000)	
Sale of equipment	4,000	
Major repairs of equipment	(11,000)	
Net cash used by investing activities		(41,500)
Cash flows from financing activities		
Payment of cash dividend	(6,000)	
Issuance of common stock	144,000	
Purchase of treasury stock	(17,000)	
Net cash provided by financing activities		121,000
Net decrease in cash		(7,000)
Cash, January 1, 1996		66,000
Cash, December 31, 1996		$ 59,000
Supplemental Disclosures of Cash Flow Information:		
Cash paid during the year for:		
Interest (net of amount capitalized)		$ 9,000
Income taxes		$ 62,000
Supplemental Schedule of Noncash Investing and Financing Activities:		
Purchase of land for $60,000 in exchange for a $60,000 long-term note.		

▶ SUMMARY OF LEARNING OBJECTIVES ◀

1. **Describe the evolution and purpose of the statement of cash flows.** With the issuance of *APB Opinion No. 19*, the statement of changes in financial position became an integral part of the financial statements covered by the auditor's opinion. In its *Concepts Statement No. 5*, the FASB strongly supported the inclusion of a statement of cash flows. *FASB Statement No. 95* requires a statement of cash flows in place of a statement of changes in financial position. The primary purpose of the statement of cash flows is to provide information about cash receipts and cash payments of an entity during a period. A second-

ary objective is to report the entity's operating, investing, and financing activities during the period.

2. **Identify the major classifications of cash flows.** The cash flows are classified as: (1) Operating activities—transactions that result in the revenues, expenses, gains, and losses that determine net income. (2) Investing activities—lending money and collecting on those loans, and acquiring and disposing of investments, plant assets, and intangible assets. (3) Financing activities—obtaining cash from creditors and repaying loans, issuing and reacquiring capital stock, and paying cash dividends.

3. **Differentiate between net income and net cash flows from operating activities.** Net income on an accrual basis must be adjusted to determine net cash flow from operating activities because some expenses and losses do not cause cash outflows and some revenues and gains do not provide cash inflows.

4. **Contrast the direct and indirect methods of calculating net cash flow from operating activities.** Under the direct approach, major classes of operating cash receipts and cash disbursements are calculated. The computations are summarized in a schedule of changes from the accrual to the cash basis income statement. Presentation of the direct approach of reporting net cash flow from operating activities takes the form of a condensed cash basis income statement. The indirect method adds back to net income the noncash expenses and losses and subtracts the noncash revenues and gains.

5. **Determine net cash flows from investing and financing activities.** Once the net cash flow from operating activities is computed, the next step is to determine whether any other changes in balance sheet accounts caused an increase or decrease in cash. Net cash flows form investing and financing activities can be determined by examining the changes in noncurrent balance sheet accounts.

6. **Prepare a statement of cash flows.** Preparing the statement involves three major steps: (1) determine the change in cash. This is the difference between the beginning and the ending cash balance shown on the comparative balance sheets. (2) determine the net cash flow from operating activities. This procedure is complex; it involves analyzing not only the current year's income statement but also the comparative balance sheets and the selected transaction data. (3) determine cash flows from investing and financing activities. All other changes in the balance sheet accounts must be analyzed to determine the effects on cash.

7. **Identify sources of information for a statement of cash flows.** The information to prepare the statement usually comes from three sources: (1) comparative balance sheets. Information in these statements indicate the amount of the changes in assets, liabilities, and equities during the period. (2) current income statement. Information in this statement is used in determining the cash provided by operations during the period. (3) selected transaction data. These data from the general ledger provide additional detailed information needed to determine how cash was provided or used during the period.

8. **Identify special problems in preparing a statement of cash flows.** These special problems are: (1) adjustments similar to depreciation; (2) accounts receivable (net); (3) other working capital changes; (4) net losses; (5) gains; (6) stock options; (7) postretirement benefit costs; (8) extraordinary items; and (9) significant noncash transactions.

9. **Explain the use of a work sheet in preparing a statement of cash flows.** When numerous adjustments are necessary, or other complicating factors are present, many accountants prefer to use a work sheet to assemble and classify the data that will appear on the statement of cash flows. The work sheet is merely a device that aids in the preparation of the statement; its use is optional.

⬛⬛⬛⬛⬛

APPENDIX 24-A

THE T-ACCOUNT APPROACH TO PREPARATION OF THE STATEMENT OF CASH FLOWS

Many accountants find the work sheet approach to preparing a statement of cash flows time-consuming and cumbersome. In some cases, the detail of a work sheet is not needed, or there is not enough time to prepare one. Therefore, the **T-account approach** for preparing a statement of cash flows has been devised. This procedure provides a quick and systematic method of accumulating the appropriate information to be presented in the formal statement of cash flows. **The T-accounts used in this approach are not part of the general ledger or any other ledger; they are developed only for use in the process of preparing a statement of cash flows.**

To illustrate the T-account approach, we will use the information of the Satellite Corporation example presented in the comprehensive illustration.

OBJECTIVE 10

After studying Appendix 24-A, you should be able to: Understand the purpose and use of the T-account approach to determine the net change in cash.

▶ T-ACCOUNT ILLUSTRATION

When the T-account approach is employed, the net change in cash for the period is computed by comparing the beginning and ending balances of the cash account. After the net change is computed, a T-account for cash is prepared and the net change in cash is entered at the top of this account on the left if cash increased, and on the right if it decreased. (See illustration of T-account on page 1272).

The cash T-account is then structured into six separate classifications: **Increases**— (1) Operating, (2) Investing, and (3) Financing, on the left; and **Decreases**—(4) Operating, (5) Investing, and (6) Financing, on the right. T-accounts are then set up for all noncash items that have had activity during the period, with the net change entered at the top of each account. The objective of the T-account approach is to explain the net change in cash through the various changes that have occurred in the noncash accounts. The cash T-account acts as a summarizing account. Most of the changes in the noncash items are explained through the cash account. Significant financial transactions that did not affect cash are not recorded in the cash account but are entered in their respective noncash accounts for purposes of reconciling the net changes in those accounts.

To illustrate, a complete version of the T-account approach is presented on the following pages.

The following items caused the change in cash (you should trace each entry by number to the accounts that are presented following the entries):

1. Net income for the period of $117,000 increased retained earnings $117,000. To avoid the detail of noncash revenues and expenses, we employ a short-cut by starting with net income and then in subsequent entries adjust it to reflect net cash flow from operating activities. In general journal form, the entry to record net income would be:

Cash—Operations	117,000	
Retained Earnings		117,000

2. An analysis of the Retained Earnings account also discloses stock dividends of $15,000. Because this transaction does not affect cash and it is not reported on the statement of cash flows, the following entry would be made:

Retained Earnings	15,000	
Common Stock		1,000
Additional Paid-in Capital		14,000

3. Further analysis of the Retained Earnings account indicates that a cash dividend of $6,000 was paid during the current period. The entry to record the transaction would be:

Retained Earnings	6,000	
Cash—Financing		6,000

    Note that the net change in the retained earnings balance of $96,000 is now reconciled. This reconciliation procedure is basic to the T-account approach because it ensures that all appropriate transactions have been considered.

4. The equity in the earnings of Porter Co. must be subtracted from net income because this income item does not increase cash. The journal entry to recognize this equity in the earnings of Porter Co. is as follows:

Investment in Stock of Porter Co.	3,500	
Cash—Operations		3,500

5. A note of $60,000 was issued to purchase land. This transaction did not affect cash; it is a significant financing transaction that should be reported in a separate schedule or note. The following entry would be made:

Land	60,000	
Notes Payable		60,000

6. In addition, land with a book value of $10,500 was condemned. The entry to record this transaction is as follows:

Cash—Investing	18,500	
Land		10,500
Cash—Operations		8,000

    Note that adding the $10,500 book value of this condemnation to the $8,000 extraordinary gain (before tax of $2,000) provides gross proceeds of $18,500 related to the condemnation.

7. Equipment and the related Accumulated Depreciation account indicate that a number of financial transactions affected these accounts. The first transaction is the purchase of equipment, which is recorded as follows:

Equipment	53,000	
Cash—Investing		53,000

8. In addition, equipment with a book value of $5,500 was sold at a loss of $1,500. The entry to record this transaction is as follows:

Cash—Investing	4,000	
Cash—Operations	1,500	
Accumulated Depreciation—Equipment	2,500	
Equipment		8,000

    Note that the loss on the sale of the equipment has reduced net income, but has not affected cash. The loss must therefore be added back to net income to report accurately net cash flow from operating activities.

9. Depreciation on the equipment of $11,500 must be recorded as follows:

Cash—Operations	11,500	
Accumulated Depreciation—Equipment		11,500

10. The major repair reduced cash, so the necessary journal entry is as follows:

Accumulated Depreciation—Equipment	11,000	
Cash—Investing		11,000

    The Equipment account and related Accumulated Depreciation account are now reconciled.

11. Analysis of the remaining **noncurrent accounts** indicates changes in Accumulated Depreciation—Buildings, Premium on Bonds Payable, Goodwill, and Deferred Tax Liability that must be accounted for in determining the net cash flow from operating activities. The compound entry to record these changes is as follows:

Cash—Operations	3,100	
Cash—Operations	2,400	
Cash—Operations	3,000	
Premium on Bonds Payable	1,000	
Accumulated Depreciation—Buildings		3,100
Goodwill		2,400
Deferred Tax Liability		3,000
Cash—Operations		1,000

12. Analysis of the **current accounts** exclusive of cash indicates an increase in Accounts Receivable (net), an increase in Inventories, a decrease in Prepaid Expenses, an increase in Accounts Payable, an increase in Accrued Liabilities, and a decrease in Income Tax Payable. All of these changes must be accounted for in determining the net cash flows from operating activities. The compound entry to record these changes is as follows:

Cash—Operations	500	
Cash—Operations	1,000	
Cash—Operations	4,000	
Accounts Receivable (net)	53,000	
Inventories	152,000	
Income Tax Payable	13,000	
Prepaid Expenses		500
Accounts Payable		1,000
Accrued Liabilities		4,000
Cash—Operations		53,000
Cash—Operations		152,000
Cash—Operations		13,000

13. Examination of the Common Stock account indicates that in addition to the stock dividend (transaction 2), common stock was issued at $16 per share. The entry to record this transaction is as follows:

Cash—Financing	144,000	
Common Stock		9,000
Additional Paid-in Capital		135,000

14. The company also purchased treasury stock, which is recorded as follows:

Treasury Stock	17,000	
Cash—Financing		17,000

After the entries above are posted to the appropriate accounts, the Cash account (Illustration 24A-1) is used as the basis for preparing the statement of cash flows. The debit side of the Cash account contains the cash provided, and the credit side contains the cash used. The difference between the two sides of the Cash account should reconcile to the increase or decrease in cash. The completed statement of cash flows is presented in Illustration 24-41.

ILLUSTRATION 24A-1
T-Account for Cash

	Cash			
Increases		**Decreases**		
		Net change		7,000
Operating Activities:		**Operating Activities:**		
1. Net income	117,000	4. Equity in earnings of Porter Co.		3,500
8. Loss on sale of equipment	1,500	6. Gain on condemnation		8,000
9. Depreciation expense	11,500	11. Bond premium amortization		1,000
11. Depreciation expense	3,100	12. Accounts receivable (net)		53,000
11. Goodwill amortization	2,400	12. Inventories		152,000
11. Deferred tax liability	3,000	12. Income tax payable		13,000
12. Prepaid expenses	500			230,500
12. Accounts payable	1,000			
12. Accrued liabilities	4,000			
	144,000			
Investing Activities:		**Investing Activities:**		
6. Condemnation of land	18,500	7. Purchase of equipment		53,000
8. Sale of equipment	4,000	10. Major repair of equipment		11,000
	22,500			64,000
Financing Activities:		**Financing Activities:**		
13. Sale of common stock	144,000	3. Cash dividends paid		6,000
		14. Purchase of treasury stock		17,000
				23,000

ILLUSTRATION 24A-2
Noncash T-Accounts

	Accounts Receivable (net)		
Net change	53,000		
12. Increase	53,000		
	Inventories		
Net change	152,000		
12. Increase	152,000		
	Prepaid Expenses		
		Net change	500
		12. Decrease	500
	Investment in Stock of Porter Co. (equity method)		
Net change	3,500		
4. Equity in earnings	3,500		
	Land		
Net change	49,500		
5. Purchase of land	60,000	6. Condemnation	10,500
	Equipment		
Net change	45,000		
7. Purchase	53,000	8. Sale of equipment	8,000
	Accumulated Depreciation—Equipment		
Net change	2,000		
8. Sale of equipment	2,500	9. Depreciation expense	11,500
10. Major repair	11,000		
	Accumulated Depreciation—Buildings		
		Net change	3,100
		11. Depreciation expense	3,100
	Goodwill		
		Net change	2,400
		11. Amortization of goodwill	2,400

Accounts Payable		
	Net change	1,000
	12. Increase	1,000

Accrued Liabilities		
	Net change	4,000
	12. Increase	4,000

Income Tax Payable		
Net change	13,000	
12. Decrease	13,000	

Notes Payable		
	Net change	60,000
	5. Issuance of Note	60,000

Premium on Bonds Payable		
Net change	1,000	
11. Bond premium amortization	1,000	

Deferred Tax Liability		
	Net change	3,000
	11. Increase	3,000

Common Stock		
	Net change	10,000
	2. Stock dividend	1,000
	13. Sale of common stock	9,000

Additional Paid-In Capital		
	Net change	149,000
	2. Stock dividend	14,000
	13. Sale of common stock	135,000

Retained Earnings			
		Net change	96,000
2. Stock dividend	15,000	1. Net income	117,000
3. Cash dividend	6,000		

Treasury Stock		
Net change	17,000	
14. Purchase of treasury stock	17,000	

▶ SUMMARY OF T-ACCOUNT APPROACH

Short-cut approaches are often used with the T-account approach. For example, the journal entries may not be prepared because the transactions are few and their effects are obvious. Also, only the noncash T-accounts that have a number of changes, such as Equipment, Accumulated Depreciation—Equipment, and Retained Earnings, need be presented in T-account form. Other more obvious changes in noncash items can be determined simply by examining the comparative balance sheet and other related data.

The T-account approach provides certain advantages over the work sheet method in that (1) a statement of cash flows usually can be prepared much faster using the T-account method, and (2) the use of the T-account method helps in understanding the relationship between cash and noncash items. Conversely, on highly complex problems the work sheet provides a more orderly and systematic approach to preparing the statement of cash flows. In practice the work sheet is used to ensure that all items are properly accounted for.

To summarize, the following steps are used in the T-account approach:

1. Determine the increase or decrease in cash for the period.

2. Post the increase or decrease to the cash T-account and establish six classifications within this account: Increases—Operating, Investing, and Financing, and Decreases—Operating, Investing, and Financing.

3. Determine and post the increase or decrease in each noncash account. Accounts that have no change can be ignored unless two transactions have occurred in the same account of the same amount, which is highly unlikely. A short-cut approach is to prepare T-accounts only for noncash accounts that have a number of transactions. All other changes can be immediately posted to the cash account after examining additional information related to balance sheet changes.

4. Reconstruct entries in noncash accounts and post them to the noncash account affected.

5. Using the postings from the cash T-account, prepare the formal statement of cash flows.

▶ **SUMMARY OF LEARNING OBJECTIVE FOR APP. 24-A** ◀

10. **Understand the purpose and use of the T-account approach to determine the net change in cash.** The purpose of the T-account approach is to determine and explain the net change in cash through the various changes that have occurred in the noncash accounts using the cash T-account as a summarizing account.

QUESTIONS

1. Why has the statement of cash flows become popular and a required financial statement?

2. What is the purpose of the statement of cash flows? What information does it provide?

3. Differentiate between investing activities, financing activities, and operating activities.

4. What are the major sources of cash (inflows) in a statement of cash flows? What are the major uses (outflows) of cash?

5. Unlike the other major financial statements, the statement of cash flows is not prepared from the adjusted trial balance. From what sources does the information to prepare this statement come and what information does each source provide?

6. Why is it necessary to convert accrual-based net income to a cash basis when preparing a statement of cash flows?

7. Differentiate between the direct method and the indirect method by discussing each method.

8. Wyoming Company reported net income of $3.5 million in 1996. Depreciation for the year was $520,000; accounts receivable increased $350,000; and accounts payable increased $500,000. Compute net cash flow from operating activities using the indirect method.

9. Colorado Co. reported sales on an accrual basis of $100,000. If accounts receivable increased $30,000, and the allowance for doubtful accounts increased $12,000 after a writeoff of $8,000, compute cash sales.

10. Your roommate is puzzled. During the last year, the company in which she is a stockholder reported a net loss of $654,127, yet its cash increased $324,585 during the same period of time. Explain to your roommate how this situation could occur.

11. The Board of Directors of Georgia Corp. declared cash dividends of $260,000 during the current year. If dividends payable was $81,000 at the beginning of the year and $70,000 at the end of the year, how much cash was paid in dividends during the year?

12. Mississippi Inc. reported sales of $2 million for 1996. Accounts receivable decreased $308,000 and accounts payable increased $200,000. Compute cash sales assuming that the receivable and payable transactions related to operations.

13. The net income for Dumaine Company for 1996 was $320,000. During 1996 depreciation on plant assets was $90,000, amortization of goodwill was $40,000, and the company incurred a loss on sale of plant assets of $25,000. Compute net cash flow from operating activities.

14. Each of the following items must be considered in preparing a statement of cash flows for Hawkeye Inc. for the year ended December 31, 1996. State where each item is to be shown in the statement, if at all.
    (a) Plant assets that had cost $20,000 6½ years before and were being depreciated on a straight-line basis over 10 years with no estimated scrap value were sold for $6,000.
    (b) During the year, 10,000 shares of common stock with a stated value of $20 a share were issued for $40 a share.
    (c) Uncollectible accounts receivable in the amount of $22,000 were written off against the Allowance for Doubtful Accounts.
    (d) The company sustained a net loss for the year of $50,000. Depreciation amounted to $22,000, and a gain of $7,000 was realized on the sale of marketable equity securities (current) for $38,000 cash.

15. Classify the following items as (1) operating, (2) investing, (3) financing, or (4) significant noncash investing and financing activities (using the direct method).
    (a) Purchase of equipment.
    (b) Redemption of bonds.
    (c) Sale of building.
    (d) Cash payments to suppliers.
    (e) Exchange of equipment for furniture.
    (f) Issuance of capital stock.
    (g) Cash received from customers.
    (h) Purchase of treasury stock.
    (i) Issuance of bonds for land.
    (j) Payment of dividends.
    (k) Cash payments to employees.
    (l) Cash payments for operating expenses.

16. Sally Jo Winslow and Fay Etteville were discussing the presentation format of the statement of cash flows of Dardanelle Co. At the bottom of Dardanelle's statement of cash flows was a separate section entitled "Noncash investing and financing activities." Give three examples of significant noncash transactions that would be reported in this section.

17. During 1996, Maui Company redeemed $2,000,000 of bonds payable for $1,700,000 cash. Indicate how the transaction would be reported on a statement of cash flows, if at all.

18. What are some of the arguments in favor of using the indirect (reconciliation method) as opposed to the direct method for reporting a statement of cash flows?

19. Why is it desirable to use a work sheet when preparing a statement of cash flows? Is a work sheet required to prepare a statement of cash flows?

20. Of what use is the statement of cash flows?

EXERCISES

E24-1 (Classification of Transactions) Jeffries Co. had the following activity in its most recent year of operations:
(a) Purchase of equipment.
(b) Redemption of bonds.
(c) Sale of building.
(d) Depreciation.
(e) Exchange of equipment for furniture.
(f) Issuance of capital stock.
(g) Amortization of intangible assets.
(h) Purchase of treasury stock.
(i) Issuance of bonds for land.
(j) Payment of dividends.
(k) Increase in interest receivable on notes receivable.
(l) Pension expense exceeds amount funded.

Instructions
Classify the items as (1) operating—add to net income; (2) operating—deduct from net income; (3) investing; (4) financing; or (5) significant noncash investing and financing activities (use indirect method).

E24-2 (Statement Presentation of Transactions—Indirect Method) Each of the following items must be considered in preparing a statement of cash flows (indirect method) for Bud Grandgeorge Inc. for the year ended December 31, 1995.
(a) Plant assets that had cost $20,000 6 years before and were being depreciated on a straight-line basis over 10 years with no estimated scrap value were sold for $6,000.
(b) During the year, 10,000 shares of common stock with a stated value of $20 a share were issued for $40 a share.

(c) Uncollectible accounts receivable in the amount of $24,000 were written off against the Allowance for Doubtful Accounts.

(d) The company sustained a net loss for the year of $50,000. Depreciation amounted to $22,000, and a gain of $7,000 was realized on the sale of land for $38,000 cash.

(e) A 3-month U.S. Treasury bill was purchased for $100,000. The company uses a cash and cash-equivalent basis for its cash flow statement.

(f) Goodwill amortized for the year was $9,000.

(g) The company exchanged common stock for a 70% interest in Tabasco Co. for $900,000.

(h) During the year, treasury stock costing $40,000 was purchased.

Instructions

State where each item is to be shown in the statement of cash flows, if at all.

E24-3 (Preparation of Operating Activities Section—Indirect Method) The income statement of Vancover Company is shown below:

Vancover Company
INCOME STATEMENT
For the Year Ended December 31, 1996

Sales		$6,900,000
Cost of goods sold		
Beginning inventory	$1,900,000	
Purchases	4,400,000	
Goods available for sale	6,300,000	
Ending inventory	1,600,000	
Cost of goods sold		4,700,000
Gross profit		2,200,000
Operating expenses		
Selling expenses	450,000	
Administrative expenses	700,000	1,150,000
Net income		$1,050,000

Additional information:

1. Accounts receivable decreased $350,000 during the year.
2. Prepaid expenses increased $150,000 during the year.
3. Accounts payable to suppliers of merchandise decreased $300,000 during the year.
4. Accrued expenses payable decreased $100,000 during the year.
5. Administrative expenses include depreciation expense of $60,000.

Instructions

Prepare the operating activities section of the statement of cash flows for the year ended December 31, 1996, for Vancover Company, using the indirect method.

E24-4 (Preparation of Operating Activities Section—Direct Method) Data for the Vancover Company are presented in E24-3.

Instructions

Prepare the operating activities section of the statement of cash flows using the direct method.

E24-5 (Preparation of Operating Activities Section—Direct Method) Flyer Company's income statement for the year ended December 31, 1995, contained the following condensed information:

Revenue from fees		$840,000
Operating expenses (excluding depreciation)	$624,000	
Depreciation expense	60,000	
Loss on sale of equipment	26,000	710,000
Income before income taxes		130,000
Income tax expense		40,000
Net income		$ 90,000

Flyer's balance sheet contained the following comparative data at December 31:

	1995	1994
Accounts receivable	$37,000	$55,000
Accounts payable	41,000	33,000
Income taxes payable	4,000	9,000

(Accounts payable pertains to operating expenses.)

Instructions

Prepare the operating activities section of the statement of cash flows using the direct method.

E24-6 (Preparation of Operating Activities Section—Indirect Method) Data for Flyer Company are presented in E24-5.

Instructions

Prepare the operating activities section of the statement of cash flows using the indirect method.

E24-7 (Computation of Operating Activities—Direct Method) Presented below are two independent situations:

Situation A:

Olajuwan Co. reports revenues of $200,000 and operating expenses of $110,000 in its first year of operations, 1996. Accounts receivable and accounts payable at year-end were $70,000 and $32,000, respectively. Assume that the accounts payable related to operating expenses. Ignore income taxes.

Instructions

Using the direct method, compute net cash provided by operating activities.

Situation B:

The income statement for Ewing Company shows cost of goods sold $310,000 and operating expenses (exclusive of depreciation) $230,000. The comparative balance sheet for the year shows that inventory increased $6,000, prepaid expenses decreased $8,000, accounts payable (related to merchandise) decreased $7,000, and accrued expenses payable increased $11,000.

Instructions

Compute (a) cash payments to suppliers and (b) cash payments for operating expenses.

E24-8 (Schedule of Net Cash Flow from Operating Activities—Indirect Method) Fargo Co. reported $145,000 of net income for 1996. The accountant, in preparing the statement of cash flows, noted several items that might affect cash flows from operating activities. These items are listed below:

1. During 1996 Fargo purchased 100 shares of treasury stock at a cost of $20 per share. These shares were then resold at $25 per share.
2. During 1996 Fargo sold 100 shares of IBM common at $200 per share. The acquisition cost of these shares was $150 per share. This investment was shown on Fargo's December 31, 1995 balance sheet as a current asset.
3. During 1996 Fargo changed from the straight-line method to the double-declining balance method of depreciation for its machinery. The total Cumulative Effect was for $13,500.
4. During 1996 Fargo revised its estimate for bad debts. Before 1996, Fargo's bad debts expense was 1% of its net sales. In 1996, this percentage was increased to 2%. Net sales for 1996 were $500,000, and net accounts receivable decreased by $12,000 during 1996.
5. During 1996 Fargo issued 500 shares of its $10 par common stock for a patent. The market value of the shares on the date of the transaction was $23 per share.
6. Depreciation expense for 1996 is $38,000.
7. Fargo Co. holds 40% of the Bismarck Company's common stock as a long-term investment. Bismarck Company reported $26,000 of net income for 1996.
8. Bismarck Company paid a total of $2,000 of cash dividends in 1996.
9. During 1996 Fargo declared a 10% stock dividend. One thousand shares of $10 par common stock were distributed. The market price at date of issuance was $20 per share.

Instructions

Prepare a schedule that shows the net cash flow from operating activities using the indirect method. Assume no items other than those listed above affected the computation of 1996 net cash flow from operating activities.

E24-9 (SCF—Direct Method) Flax Corp. uses the direct method to prepare its statement of cash flows. Flax's trial balances at December 31, 1995 and 1994, are as follows:

	December 31	
	1995	1994
Debits		
Cash	$ 35,000	$ 32,000
Accounts receivable	33,000	30,000
Inventory	31,000	47,000
Property, plant, & equipment	100,000	95,000
Unamortized bond discount	4,500	5,000
Cost of goods sold	250,000	380,000
Selling expenses	141,500	172,000
General and administrative expenses	137,000	151,300

	1995	1994
Interest expense	4,300	2,600
Income tax expense	20,400	61,200
	$756,700	$976,100
Credits		
Allowance for doubtful accounts	$ 1,300	$ 1,100
Accumulated depreciation	16,500	15,000
Trade accounts payable	25,000	17,500
Income taxes payable	21,000	27,100
Deferred income taxes	5,300	4,600
8% callable bonds payable	45,000	20,000
Common stock	50,000	40,000
Additional paid-in capital	9,100	7,500
Retained earnings	44,700	64,600
Sales	538,800	778,700
	$756,700	$976,100

Additional information:

1. Flax purchased $5,000 in equipment during 1995.
2. Flax allocated one-third of its depreciation expense to selling expenses and the remainder to general and administrative expenses.

Instructions

Determine what amounts Flax should report in its statement of cash flows for the year ended December 31, 1995, for the following:

1. Cash collected from customers.
2. Cash paid for goods to be sold.
3. Cash paid for interest.
4. Cash paid for income taxes.
5. Cash paid for selling expenses.

E24-10 (Classification of Transactions) Following are selected balance sheet accounts of Zach Corp. at December 31, 1996 and 1995, and the increases or decreases in each account from 1995 to 1996. Also presented are selected income statement information for the year ended December 31, 1996, and additional information.

Selected balance sheet accounts	1996	1995	Increase (Decrease)
Assets			
Accounts receivable	$ 34,000	$ 24,000	$10,000
Property, plant, and equipment	277,000	247,000	30,000
Accumulated depreciation	(178,000)	(167,000)	(11,000)
Liabilities and stockholders' equity			
Bonds payable	49,000	46,000	3,000
Dividends payable	8,000	5,000	3,000
Common stock, $1 par	22,000	19,000	3,000
Additional paid-in capital	9,000	3,000	6,000
Retained earnings	104,000	91,000	13,000

Selected income statement information for the year ended December 31, 1996

Sales revenue	$155,000
Depreciation	33,000
Gain on sale of equipment	13,000
Net income	28,000

Additional information:

1. During 1996, equipment costing $40,000 was sold for cash.
2. Accounts receivable relate to sales of merchandise.
3. During 1996, $20,000 of bonds payable were issued in exchange for property, plant, and equipment. There was no amortization of bond discount or premium.

Instructions

Determine the category (operating, investing, or financing) and the amount that should be reported in the statement of cash flows for the following items:

1. Payments for purchase of property, plant, and equipment.
2. Proceeds from the sale of equipment.
3. Cash dividends paid.
4. Redemption of bonds payable.

E24-11 (SCF—Indirect Method) Condensed financial data of Yarmouth Company for 1996 and 1995 are presented below.

Yarmouth Company
COMPARATIVE BALANCE SHEET DATA
As of December 31, 1996 and 1995

	1996	1995
Cash	$1,800	$1,150
Receivables	1,750	1,300
Inventory	1,600	1,900
Plant assets	1,900	1,700
Accumulated depreciation	(1,200)	(1,150)
Long-term investments	1,300	1,400
	$7,150	$6,300
Accounts payable	$1,200	$ 900
Accrued liabilities	200	300
Bonds payable	1,400	1,500
Capital stock	1,900	1,700
Retained earnings	2,450	1,900
	$7,150	$6,300

Yarmouth Company
INCOME STATEMENT
For the Year Ended December 31, 1996

Sales		$6,900
Cost of goods sold		4,700
Gross margin		2,200
Operating expenses:		
Selling expense	$450	
Administrative expense	650	
Depreciation expense	50	1,150
Net income		1,050
Cash dividends		500
Income retained in business		$ 550

Additional information:

There were no gains or losses in any noncurrent transactions during 1996.

Instructions
Prepare a statement of cash flows using the indirect method.

E24-12 (SCF—Direct Method) Data for Yarmouth Company are presented in E24-11.

Instructions
Prepare a statement of cash flows using the direct method. (Do not prepare a reconciliation schedule.)

E24-13 (SCF—Indirect Method) Condensed financial data of Nantucket Company for the years ended December 31, 1996 and December 31, 1995, are presented below.

Nantucket Company
COMPARATIVE POSITION STATEMENT DATA
As of December 31, 1996 and 1995

	1996	1995
Cash	$160,800	$ 38,400
Receivables	123,200	49,000
Inventories	112,500	61,900
Investments	90,000	97,000
Plant assets	240,000	212,500
	$726,500	$458,800

	1996	1995
Accounts payable	$100,000	$ 67,300
Mortgage payable	50,000	74,900
Accumulated depreciation	30,000	52,000
Common stock	175,000	131,100
Retained earnings	371,500	133,500
	$726,500	$458,800

Nantucket Company
INCOME STATEMENT
For the Year Ended December 31, 1996

Sales	$440,000	
Interest and other revenue	20,000	$460,000
Less:		
Cost of goods sold	130,000	
Selling and administrative expenses	10,000	
Depreciation	42,000	
Income taxes	5,000	
Interest charges	3,000	
Loss on sale of plant assets	12,000	202,000
Net income		258,000
Cash dividends		20,000
Income retained in business		$238,000

Additional information:

New plant assets costing $105,000 were purchased during the year. Investments were sold at book value.

Instructions

Prepare a statement of cash flows using the indirect method.

E24-14 (SCF—Direct Method) Data for Nantucket Company are presented in E24-13.

Instructions

Prepare a statement of cash flows using the direct method. (Do not prepare a reconciliation schedule.)

E24-15 (SCF—Direct Method) Zeeland Inc., a greeting card company, had the following statements prepared as of December 31, 1993:

Zeeland Inc.
COMPARATIVE BALANCE SHEET
As of December 31, 1996 and 1995

	12/31/96	12/31/95
Cash	$ 6,000	$ 7,000
Accounts receivable	62,000	49,000
Short-term investments	35,000	20,000
Inventories	40,000	60,000
Prepaid rent	5,000	4,000
Printing equipment	154,000	130,000
Accumulated depr.—equipment	(35,000)	(25,000)
Goodwill	46,000	50,000
Total assets	$313,000	$295,000
Accounts payable	$ 46,000	$ 40,000
Income taxes payable	4,000	5,000
Wages payable	8,000	4,000
Short-term loans payable	8,000	10,000
Long-term loans payable	60,000	70,000
Common stock, $10 par	100,000	100,000
Contributed capital, common stock	30,000	30,000
Retained earnings	57,000	36,000
Total liabilities & equity	$313,000	$295,000

Zeeland Inc.
INCOME STATEMENT
For the Year Ending December 31, 1996

Sales	$338,150
Cost of goods sold	175,000
Gross margin	163,150
Operating expenses	120,000
Operating income	43,150
Interest expense	9,400
Income before tax	33,750
Income tax expense	6,750
Net income	$ 27,000

Additional information:

1. Dividends in the amount of $6,000 were declared and paid during 1996.
2. Depreciation expense and amortization expense are included in operating expenses.

Instructions
Prepare a statement of cash flows using the direct method. (Do not prepare a reconciliation schedule.)

E24-16 (SCF—Indirect Method) Data for Zeeland Inc. are presented in E24-15.

Instructions
Prepare a statement of cash flows using the indirect method.

E24-17 (SCF—Indirect Method) Presented below are data taken from the records of Wintergreen Company.

	December 31, 1996	December 31, 1995
Cash	$ 15,000	$ 8,000
Current assets other than cash	85,000	55,000
Long-term investments	10,000	58,000
Plant assets	366,000	215,000
	$476,000	$336,000
Accumulated depreciation	$ 20,000	$ 40,000
Current liabilities	35,000	22,000
Bonds payable	80,000	–0–
Capital stock	254,000	254,000
Donated capital	31,000	–0–
Retained earnings	56,000	20,000
	$476,000	$336,000

Additional information:

1. Securities carried at a cost of $48,000 on December 31, 1995, were sold in 1996 for $39,000. The loss (not extraordinary) was incorrectly charged directly to Retained Earnings.
2. Plant assets that cost $50,000 and were 80% depreciated were sold during 1996 for $8,000. The loss (not extraordinary) was incorrectly charged directly to Retained Earnings.
3. Net income as reported on the income statement for the year was $57,000.
4. Dividends paid amounted to $10,000.
5. Depreciation charged for the year was $20,000.
6. Land was donated to Wintergreen Company by the city. The land was worth $31,000. (Assume credit to Donated Capital is correct.)

Instructions
Prepare a statement of cash flows for the year 1996 using the indirect method.

E24-18 (SCF—Indirect Method, and Balance Sheet) Tonopah Inc., had the following condensed balance sheet at the end of operations for 1995.

Tonopah Inc.
BALANCE SHEET
December 31, 1995

Cash	$ 8,500	Current liabilities	$ 15,000
Current assets other than cash	29,000	Long-term notes payable	25,500
Investments	20,000	Bonds payable	25,000
Plant assets (net)	67,500	Capital stock	75,000
Land	40,000	Retained earnings	24,500
	$165,000		$165,000

During 1996 the following occurred:

1. A tract of land was purchased for $4,450.
2. Bonds payable in the amount of $6,000 were retired at par.
3. An additional $10,000 in capital stock was issued at par.
4. Dividends totaling $9,375 were paid to stockholders.
5. Net income for 1996 was $35,250 after allowing depreciation of $11,250.
6. Land was purchased through the issuance of $22,500 in bonds.
7. Tonopah Inc., sold part of its investment portfolio for $12,875. This transaction resulted in a gain of $875 for the firm. The company often sells and buys securities of this nature.
8. Both current assets (other than cash) and current liabilities remained at the same amount.

Instructions
(a) Prepare a statement of cash flows for 1996 using the indirect method.
(b) Prepare the condensed balance sheet for Tonopah Inc. as it would appear at December 31, 1996.

E24-19 (Partial SCF—Indirect Method) The accounts below appear in the ledger of Vegas Company.

Retained Earnings		Dr.	Cr.	Bal.
Jan. 1, 1996	Credit Balance			$ 42,000
Aug. 15	Dividends (cash)	$18,000		24,000
Dec. 31	Net Income for 1996		$12,000	36,000

Machinery		Dr.	Cr.	Bal.
Jan. 1, 1996	Debit Balance			$140,000
Aug. 3	Purchase of Machinery	$62,000		202,000
Sept. 10	Cost of Machinery Constructed	48,000		250,000
Nov. 15	Machinery Sold		$56,000	194,000

Accumulated Depreciation—Machinery		Dr.	Cr.	Bal.
Jan. 1, 1996	Credit Balance			$ 84,000
Apr. 8	Extraordinary Repairs	$21,000		63,000
Nov. 15	Accum. Depreciation on Machinery Sold	25,200		37,800
Dec. 31	Depreciation for 1996		$16,800	54,600

Instructions
From the postings in the accounts above, indicate how the information is reported on a statement of cash flows by preparing a partial statement of cash flows using the indirect method. The loss on sale of equipment (November 15) was $16,800.

E24-20 (Work Sheet Analysis of Selected Accounts) Data for Vegas Company are presented in E24-19.

Instructions
Prepare entries in journal form for all adjustments that should be made on a work sheet for a statement of cash flows.

E24-21 (Work Sheet Analysis of Selected Transactions) The transactions below took place during the year 1996:

1. Convertible bonds payable of a par value of $250,000 were exchanged for unissued common stock of a par value of $250,000. The market price of both types of securities was par.
2. The net income for the year was $60,000.
3. Depreciation charged on the building was $24,000.
4. Organization costs in the amount of $10,000 was written off during the year as a charge to expense.

5. Some old office equipment was traded in on the purchase of some dissimilar office equipment and the following entry was made:

Office Equipment	5,000	
Accum. Depreciation—Office Equipment	3,000	
Office Equipment		4,000
Cash		3,400
Gain on Disposal of Plant Assets		600

The Gain on Disposal of Plant Assets was credited to current operations as ordinary income.

6. Dividends in the amount of $18,000 were declared. They are payable in January of next year.
7. The Appropriations for Bonded Indebtedness in the amount of $400,000 was returned to Retained Earnings during the year, because the bonds were retired during the year.

Instructions

Show by journal entries the adjustments that would be made on a work sheet for a statement of cash flows.

E24-22 (Work Sheet Preparation) Below is the comparative balance sheet for Roanoke Corporation.

	Dec. 31, 1996	Dec. 31, 1995
Cash	$ 16,500	$ 20,000
Short-term investments	25,000	20,000
Accounts receivable	43,000	45,000
Allowance for doubtful accounts	(1,800)	(2,000)
Prepaid expenses	4,200	2,500
Inventories	81,500	65,000
Land	50,000	50,000
Buildings	125,000	73,500
Accumulated depreciation—buildings	(30,000)	(23,000)
Equipment	53,000	47,000
Accumulated depreciation—equipment	(19,000)	(16,500)
Delivery equipment	39,000	39,000
Accumulated depreciation—delivery equipment	(22,000)	(20,500)
Patents	15,000	–0–
	$379,400	$300,000
Accounts payable	$ 26,000	$ 16,000
Short-term notes payable	4,000	6,000
Accrued payables	3,000	5,000
Mortgage payable	73,000	53,000
Bonds payable	50,000	62,500
Capital stock	140,000	102,000
Additional paid-in capital	10,000	4,000
Retained earnings	73,400	51,500
	$379,400	$300,000

Dividends in the amount of $10,000 were declared and paid in 1996.

Instructions

From this information, prepare a work sheet for a statement of cash flows. Make reasonable assumptions as appropriate.

PROBLEMS

P24-1 (SCF—Indirect Method) The following is Omega Corp.'s comparative balance sheet accounts worksheet at December 31, 1996, and 1995, with a column showing the increase (decrease) from 1995 to 1996.

Comparative Balance Sheet			

	1996	1995	Increase (Decrease)
Cash	$ 800,000	$ 700,000	$100,000
Accounts receivable	1,128,000	1,168,000	(40,000)
Inventories	1,850,000	1,715,000	135,000
Property, plant and equipment	3,307,000	2,967,000	340,000
Accumulated depreciation	(1,165,000)	(1,040,000)	(125,000)

	1996	1995	Increase (Decrease)
Investment in Belle Co.	305,000	275,000	30,000
Loan receivable	270,000	—	270,000
Total assets	$6,495,000	$5,785,000	$710,000
Accounts payable	$1,015,000	$ 955,000	$ 60,000
Income taxes payable	30,000	50,000	(20,000)
Dividends payable	80,000	90,000	(10,000)
Capital lease obligation	400,000	—	400,000
Capital stock, common, $1 par	500,000	500,000	—
Additional paid-in capital	1,500,000	1,500,000	—
Retained earnings	2,970,000	2,690,000	280,000
Total liabilities and stockholders' equity	$6,495,000	$5,785,000	$710,000

Additional information:

1. On December 31, 1995, Omega acquired 25% of Belle Co.'s common stock for $275,000. On that date, the carrying value of Belle's assets and liabilities, which approximated their fair values, was $1,100,000. Belle reported income of $120,000 for the year ended December 31, 1996. No dividend was paid on Belle's common stock during the year.
2. During 1996, Omega loaned $300,000 to Chase Co., an unrelated company. Chase made the first semi-annual principal repayment of $30,000, plus interest at 10%, on October 1, 1996.
3. On January 2, 1996, Omega sold equipment costing $60,000, with a carrying amount of $35,000, for $40,000 cash.
4. On December 31, 1996, Omega entered into a capital lease for an office building. The present value of the annual rental payments is $400,000, which equals the fair value of the building. Omega made the first rental payment of $60,000 when due on January 2, 1997.
5. Net income for 1996 was $360,000.
6. Omega declared and paid cash dividends for 1996 and 1995 as follows:

	1996	1995
Declared	December 15, 1996	December 15, 1995
Paid	February 28, 1997	February 28, 1996
Amount	$80,000	$90,000

Instructions

Prepare a statement of cash flows for Omega, Inc. for the year ended December 31, 1996, using the indirect method.

(AICPA adapted)

P24-2 (SCF—Indirect Method) The comparative balance sheets for Vermillion Corporation show the following information:

	December 31	
	1996	1995
Cash	$ 38,500	$13,000
Accounts receivable	12,250	10,000
Inventory	12,000	9,000
Investments	–0–	3,000
Building	–0–	29,750
Equipment	40,000	20,000
Patent	5,000	6,250
Totals	$107,750	$91,000
Allowance for doubtful accounts	$ 3,000	$ 4,500
Accumulated depreciation on equipment	2,000	4,500
Accumulated depreciation on building	–0–	6,000
Accounts payable	5,000	3,000
Dividends payable	–0–	6,000
Notes payable, short-term (nontrade)	3,000	4,000
Long-term notes payable	31,000	25,000
Common stock	43,000	33,000
Retained earnings	20,750	5,000
	$107,750	$91,000

Additional data related to 1996 are as follows:

1. Equipment that had cost $11,000 and was 30% depreciated at time of disposal was sold for $2,500.

2. $10,000 of the long-term note payable was paid by issuing common stock.
3. Cash dividends paid were $6,000.
4. On January 1, 1996, the building was completely destroyed by a flood. Insurance proceeds on the building were $29,750 (net of $2,000 taxes).
5. Investments (long-term) were sold at $3,700 above their cost. The company has made similar sales and investments in the past.
6. Cash of $15,000 was paid for the acquisition of equipment.
7. A long-term note for $16,000 was issued for the acquisition of equipment.
8. Interest of $2,000 and income taxes of $6,500 were paid in cash.

Instructions
Prepare a statement of cash flows using the indirect method. Flood damage is unusual and infrequent in that part of the country.

P24-3 (SCF—Direct Method) Stroudsburg Company has not yet prepared a formal statement of cash flows for the 1996 fiscal year. Comparative balance sheets as of December 31, 1995 and 1996, and a statement of income and retained earnings for the year ended December 31, 1996 are presented below.

Stroudsburg Company
STATEMENT OF INCOME AND RETAINED EARNINGS
Year Ended December 31, 1996
($000 omitted)

Sales		$3,760
Expenses		
Cost of goods sold	$1,100	
Salaries and benefits	725	
Heat, light, and power	75	
Depreciation	80	
Property taxes	18	
Patent amortization	25	
Miscellaneous expenses	10	
Interest	30	2,063
Income before income taxes		1,697
Income taxes		849
Net income		848
Retained earnings—Jan. 1, 1996		310
		1,158
Stock dividend declared and issued		600
Retained earnings—Dec. 31, 1996		$ 558

Stroudsburg Company
BALANCE SHEET
December 31
($000 omitted)

Assets	1996	1995
Current assets		
Cash	$ 383	$ 100
U.S. Treasury notes	0	50
Accounts receivable	740	500
Inventory	720	560
Total current assets	1,843	1,210
Long-term assets		
Land	150	70
Buildings and equipment	940	600
Accumulated depreciation	(200)	(120)
Patents (less amortization)	105	130
Total long-term assets	995	680
Total assets	$2,838	$1,890

Liabilities and Stockholders' Equity

Current liabilities		
Accounts payable	$ 420	$ 340
Income taxes payable	40	20
Notes payable	320	320
Total current liabilities	780	680
Long-term notes payable—due 2001	200	200
Total liabilities	980	880
Stockholders' equity		
Common stock outstanding	1,300	700
Retained earnings	558	310
Total stockholders' equity	1,850	1,010
Total liabilities and stockholders' equity	$2,838	$1,890

Instructions

Prepare a statement of cash flows using the direct method. Changes in accounts receivable and accounts payable relate to sales and cost of sales. Do not prepare a reconciliation schedule.

(CMA adapted)

P24-4 (SCF—Direct Method) Yankton Company had the following information available at the end of 1995:

Yankton Company
COMPARATIVE BALANCE SHEET
As of 12/31/95 and 12/31/94

	12/31/95	12/31/94
Cash	$ 15,000	$ 4,000
Accounts receivable	17,500	12,950
Short-term investments	20,000	30,000
Inventory	42,000	35,000
Prepaid rent	3,000	12,000
Prepaid insurance	2,100	900
Office supplies	1,000	750
Land	125,000	175,000
Building	350,000	350,000
Accumulated depreciation	(105,000)	(87,500)
Equipment	525,000	400,000
Accumulated depreciation	(130,000)	(112,000)
Patent	45,000	50,000
Total assets	$910,600	$871,100
Accounts payable	$ 27,000	$ 32,000
Taxes payable	5,000	4,000
Wages payable	5,000	3,000
Short-term notes payable	10,000	10,000
Long-term notes payable	60,000	70,000
Bonds payable	400,000	400,000
Premium on bonds payable	20,303	25,853
Common stock	240,000	220,000
Paid-in capital in excess of par	20,000	17,500
Retained earnings	123,297	88,747
Total Liabilities and Equity	$910,600	$871,100

Yankton Company
INCOME STATEMENT
For the Year Ended December 31, 1995

Sales revenue		$1,159,248
Cost of goods sold		(747,915)
		411,333
Gross margin		
Operating expenses		
Selling expenses	$ 79,200	

Administrative expenses	156,700	
Depreciation/Amortization expense	40,500	
Total operating expenses		(276,400)
Income from operations		134,933
Other revenues/expenses		
Gain on sale of land	8,000	
Gain on sale of short-term investment	4,000	
Dividend revenue	2,400	
Interest expense	(51,750)	(37,350)
Income before taxes		97,583
Income tax expense		(39,033)
Net income		58,550
Dividends to common stockholders		(24,000)
To retained earnings		$ 34,550

Instructions

Prepare a statement of cash flows for Yankton Company using the direct method accompanied by a reconciliation schedule.

P24-5 (SCF—Indirect Method) El Paso Inc., had the following information available at the end of 1995:

El Paso Inc.
COMPARATIVE BALANCE SHEET
As of December 31, 1995 and 1994

	12/31/95	12/31/94
Cash	$ 46,000	$ 30,000
Accounts receivable	340,000	296,000
Short-term investments	350,000	325,000
Prepaid insurance	16,000	22,000
Merchandise inventory	400,000	350,000
Office supplies	4,000	7,000
Long-term investments (equity)	775,000	700,000
Land	650,000	500,000
Building	1,300,000	1,300,000
Accumulated depreciation—building	(400,000)	(360,000)
Equipment	500,000	550,000
Accumulated depreciation—equipment	(155,000)	(135,000)
Goodwill	63,000	65,000
Total assets	$3,889,000	$3,650,000
Accounts payable	$ 95,000	$ 70,000
Taxes payable	26,000	15,000
Accrued liabilities	47,000	40,000
Dividends payable	–0–	80,000
Long-term notes payable	45,000	50,000
Bonds payable	1,000,000	1,000,000
Discount on bonds payable	(50,750)	(64,630)
Preferred stock	600,000	500,000
Contributed capital, preferred stock	120,000	100,000
Common stock	600,000	600,000
Contributed capital, common stock	550,000	550,000
Retained earnings	876,750	749,630
Treasury stock (common, at cost)	(20,000)	(40,000)
Total liabilities and equity	$3,889,000	$3,650,000

El Paso Inc.
INCOME STATEMENT
For the Year Ended December 31, 1995

Sales revenue	$1,007,500
Cost of goods sold	403,000
Gross profit	604,500

Selling/administrative expenses		222,087
Income from operations		382,413
Other revenues/expenses		
Long-term investment revenue	$115,000	
Short-term investment dividend	15,000	
Gain on sale of equipment	15,000	145,000
Interest expense		(98,880)
Income before taxes		428,533
Income tax expense		(171,413)
Net income		257,120
Dividends (current year)		(130,000)
Increase in retained earnings		$ 127,120

Additional information:

1. In early January, equipment with a book value of $45,000 was sold for a gain.
2. Long-term investments are carried under the equity method; El Paso's share of investee income totaled $115,000 in 1995. El Paso received dividends from its long-term investment totaling $40,000 during 1995.

Instructions
Prepare a statement of cash flows using the indirect method.

P24-6 (SCF—Direct Method) Data for El Paso Inc. are presented in P24-5.

Instructions
Prepare a statement of cash flows using the direct method.

P24-7 (SCF—Indirect Method) You have completed the field work in connection with your audit of Langtry Corporation for the year ended December 31, 1996. The following schedule shows the balance sheet accounts at the beginning and end of the year.

	Dec. 31, 1996	Dec. 31, 1995	Increase or (Decrease)
Cash	$ 267,900	$ 298,000	($30,100)
Accounts receivable	499,424	353,000	146,424
Inventory	741,700	610,000	131,700
Prepaid expenses	12,000	8,000	4,000
Investment in subsidiary	110,500	–0–	110,500
Cash surrender value of life insurance	2,304	1,800	504
Machinery	187,000	190,000	(3,000)
Buildings	535,200	407,900	127,300
Land	52,500	52,500	–0–
Patents	69,000	64,000	5,000
Goodwill	40,000	50,000	(10,000)
Bond discount and expense	4,502	–0–	4,502
	$2,522,030	$2,035,200	$486,830
Accrued taxes payable	$ 95,250	$ 79,600	$ 15,650
Accounts payable	299,280	280,000	19,280
Dividends payable	70,000	–0–	70,000
Bonds payable—8%	125,000	–0–	125,000
Bonds payable—12%	–0–	100,000	(100,000)
Allowance for doubtful accounts	35,300	40,000	(4,700)
Accumulated depreciation—buildings	424,000	400,000	24,000
Accumulated depreciation—machinery	173,000	130,000	43,000
Premium on bonds payable	–0–	2,400	(2,400)
Capital stock—no par	1,176,200	1,453,200	(277,000)
Additional paid-in capital	104,000	–0–	104,000
Appropriation for plant expansion	10,000	–0–	10,000
Retained earnings—unappropriated	10,000	(450,000)	460,000
	$2,522,030	$2,035,200	$486,830

STATEMENT OF RETAINED EARNINGS

January	1, 1996	Balance (deficit)	$(450,000)
March	31, 1996	Net income for first quarter of 1996	25,000
April	1, 1996	Transfer from paid-in capital	425,000
		Balance	–0–
December 31, 1996		Net income for last three quarters of 1996	90,000
		Dividend declared—payable January 21, 1997	(70,000)
		Appropriation for plant expansion	(10,000)
		Balance	$ 10,000

Your working papers contain the following information:

1. On April 1, 1996, the existing deficit was written off against paid-in capital created by reducing the stated value of the no-par stock.
2. On November 1, 1996, 29,600 shares of no-par stock were sold for $252,000. The Board of Directors voted to regard $5 per share as stated capital.
3. A patent was purchased for $15,000.
4. During the year, machinery that had a cost basis of $16,400 and on which there was accumulated depreciation of $5,200 was sold for $7,000. No other plant assets were sold during the year.
5. The 12%, 20-year bonds were dated and issued on January 2, 1984. Interest was payable on June 30 and December 31. They were sold originally at 106. These bonds were retired at 102 (net of $100 tax) plus accrued interest on March 31, 1996.
6. The 8%, 40-year bonds were dated January 1, 1996, and were sold on March 31 at 97 plus accrued interest. Interest is payable semiannually on June 30 and December 31. Expense of issuance was $839.
7. Langtry Corporation acquired 70% control in Amarillo Company on January 2, 1996, for $100,000. The income statement of Amarillo Company for 1996 shows a net income of $15,000.
8. Extraordinary repairs to buildings of $7,200 were charged to Accumulated Depreciation—Buildings.
9. Interest paid in 1996 was $10,500 and income taxes paid were $34,000.

Instructions
From the information above prepare a statement of cash flows using the indirect method. A work sheet is not necessary, but the principal computations should be supported by schedules or skeleton ledger accounts.

P24-8 (SCF—Indirect Method) Presented below are the 1996 financial statements of Gunnison Corporation.

BALANCE SHEETS

	December 31,	
$ in millions	1996	1995
Assets		
Current assets:		
Cash	$ 20.4	$ 7.5
Receivables (net of allowance for doubtful accounts of $5.0 million in 1996 and $4.6 million in 1992)	241.6	213.2
Inventories		
Finished goods	86.7	84.7
Raw materials and supplies	115.7	123.8
Prepaid expenses	6.2	6.7
Total current assets	470.6	435.9
Property, plant, and equipment:		
Plant and equipment	2,358.8	2,217.7
Less—accumulated depreciation	(993.4)	(890.1)
	1,365.4	1,327.6
Timberland—net	166.3	169.5
Total property, plant, and equipment—net	1,531.7	1,497.1
Other assets	74.7	34.7
Total assets	$2,077.0	$1,967.7
Liabilities and stockholders' investment		
Current liabilities:		
Current maturities of long-term debt	$ 13.2	$ 10.5

	1996	1995
Bank overdrafts	25.5	20.2
Accounts payable	102.2	91.3
Accrued liabilities		
Payrolls and employee benefits	73.5	73.9
Interest and other expenses	44.3	29.4
Federal and state income taxes	17.4	12.7
Total current liabilities	276.1	238.0
Long-term liabilities:		
Deferred tax liability	333.6	280.0
4.75% to 11.25% revenue bonds with maturities to 2019	174.6	193.4
Other revenue bonds at variable rates with maturities to 2026	46.3	26.6
7⅞% sinking fund debentures due 2005	19.5	21.0
8.70% sinking fund debentures due 2015	75.0	75.0
9½% convertible subordinated debentures due 2020	—	38.9
9¾% notes due 2002	50.0	50.0
Promissory notes	—	60.2
Mortgage debt and miscellaneous obligations	25.7	21.7
Other long-term liabilities	21.8	—
Total long-term liabilities	746.5	766.8
Stockholders' investment:		
Common stock ($5 par value, 60,000,000 shares authorized, 26,661,770 and 25,265,921 shares outstanding as of December 31, 1996 and 1995)	133.3	126.3
Additional paid-in capital	111.1	70.6
Reinvested earnings	810.0	766.0
Total stockholders' investment	1,054.4	962.9
Total liabilities and stockholders' investment	$2,077.0	$1,967.7

STATEMENT OF INCOME AND REINVESTED EARNINGS

$ in millions, except per share amounts	1996
Income	
Net sales	$2,039.2
Cost of sales	1,637.8
Gross margin	401.4
Selling, general, and administrative expense	(182.6)
Provision for reduced operations	(41.0)
Operating income	177.8
Interest on long-term debt	(33.5)
Other income—net	2.2
Pretax income	146.5
Income taxes	(61.2)
Net income	$ 85.3
Earnings per share	$ 3.20
Reinvested earnings	
Reinvested earnings at beginning of year	$ 766.0
Add—net income	85.3
	851.3
Deduct—dividends:	
Common stock ($1.57 a share in 1996)	41.3
Reinvested earnings at end of year	$ 810.0

Additional information:

1. Depreciation and cost of timberland harvested was $114.6 million.
2. The provision for reduced operations included a decrease in cash of $15.9 million.
3. Purchases of plant and equipment were $176.5 million, and purchases of timberland were $40 million.
4. Sales of plant and equipment resulted in cash inflows of $2.2 million. All sales were at book value.

5. The changes in long-term liabilities are summarized below:

Increase in deferred tax liability	$ 53.6
New borrowings	63.2
Debt retired by cash payments	(86.5)
Debt converted into stock	(37.4)
Reclassification of current maturities	(13.2)
Decrease in long-term liabilities	$(20.3)

6. The increase in common stock and additional paid-in capital results from the issuance of stock for debt conversion, $37.4 million, and stock issued for cash, $10.1 million.
7. Interest paid during 1996 was $21.2 and income tax paid was $2.9.

Instructions

Prepare a statement of cash flows for the Gunnison Corporation using the indirect method.

P24-9 (SCF—Indirect Method, and Net Cash Flow from Operating Activities, Direct Method) Comparative balance sheet accounts of Shenandoah Inc. are presented below:

SHENANDOAH INC.
Comparative Balance Sheet Accounts
December 31, 1996 and 1995

	December 31	
Debit Accounts	**1996**	**1995**
Cash	$ 45,000	$ 33,750
Accounts Receivable	67,500	60,000
Merchandise Inventory	30,000	24,000
Investments (long-term)	22,250	37,500
Machinery	30,000	18,750
Buildings	67,500	56,250
Land	7,500	7,500
Totals	$269,750	$237,750
Credit Accounts		
Allowance for Doubtful Accounts	$ 2,250	$ 1,500
Accumulated Depreciation—Machinery	5,625	2,250
Accumulated Depreciation—Buildings	13,500	9,000
Accounts Payable	30,000	24,750
Accrued Payables	3,375	2,625
Long-Term Note Payable	26,000	30,000
Common Stock, no par	150,000	125,000
Retained Earnings	39,000	42,625
Total	$269,750	$237,750

Additional data: (ignore taxes)

1. Net income for the year was $45,000.
2. Cash dividends declared during the year were $23,625.
3. A 20% stock dividend was declared during the year. $25,000 of retained earnings was capitalized.
4. Investments that cost $20,000 were sold during the year for $23,750.
5. Machinery that cost $3,750, on which $750 of depreciation had accumulated, was sold for $2,200.

Shenandoah's 1996 income statement follows (ignore taxes):

Sales		$540,000
Less cost of goods sold		377,500
Gross margin		162,500
Less operating expenses (includes $8,625 depreciation and $1,000 bad debts)		120,450
Income from operations		42,050
Other: Gain on sale of investments	$3,750	
Loss on sale of machinery	(800)	2,950
Net income		$ 45,000

Instructions

(a) Compute net cash flow from operating activities using the direct method.

(b) Prepare a statement of cash flows using the indirect method.

P24-10 (SCF—Direct and Indirect Methods from Comparative Financial Statements) Fairfax Company, a major retailer of bicycles and accessories, operates several stores and is a publicly traded company. The comparative Statement of Financial Position and Income Statement for Fairfax as of May 31, 1996, are shown below and in the next column. The company is preparing its Statement of Cash Flows.

Fairfax Company
COMPARATIVE STATEMENT OF FINANCIAL POSITION
As of May 31, 1996 and May 31, 1995

	5/31/96	5/31/95
Current assets		
Cash	$ 33,250	$ 20,000
Accounts receivable	80,000	50,000
Merchandise inventory	210,000	250,000
Prepaid expenses	9,000	7,000
Total current assets	332,250	327,000
Plant assets		
Plant assets	600,000	510,000
Less: Accumulated depreciation	150,000	125,000
Net plant assets	450,000	385,000
Total assets	$782,250	$712,000
Current Liabilities		
Accounts payable	$123,000	$115,000
Salaries payable	47,250	72,000
Interest payable	27,000	25,000
Total current liabilities	197,250	212,000
Long-term debt		
Bonds payable	70,000	100,000
Total liabilities	267,250	312,000
Shareholders' equity		
Common stock, $10 par	370,000	280,000
Retained earnings	145,000	120,000
Total shareholders' equity	515,000	400,000
Total liabilities and shareholders' equity	$782,250	$712,000

Fairfax Company
INCOME STATEMENT
For the Year Ended May 31, 1996

Sales	$1,255,250
Cost of merchandise sold	712,000
Total contribution	543,250
Expenses	
Salary expense	252,100
Interest expense	75,000
Other expenses	8,150
Depreciation expense	25,000
Total expenses	360,250
Operating income	183,000
Income tax expense	43,000
Net income	$ 140,000

The following is additional information concerning Fairfax's transactions during the year ended May 31, 1996.

1. All sales during the year were made on account.

2. All merchandise was purchased on account, comprising the total accounts payable account.
3. Plant assets costing $90,000 were purchased by paying $40,000 in cash and issuing 5,000 shares of stock.
4. The "other expenses" are related to prepaid items.
5. All income taxes incurred during the year were paid during the year.
6. In order to supplement its cash, Fairfax issued 4,000 shares of common stock at par value.
7. There were no penalties assessed for the retirement of bonds.
8. Cash dividends of $115,000 were declared and paid at the end of the fiscal year.

Instructions

(a) Compare and contrast the direct method and the indirect method for reporting cash flows from operating activities.

(b) Prepare a Statement of Cash Flows for Fairfax Company for the year ended May 31, 1996, using the direct method. Be sure to support the statement with appropriate calculations. (A reconciliation of net income to net cash is not required.)

(c) Using the indirect method, calculate only the net cash flow from operating activities for Fairfax Company for the year ended May 31, 1996.

CASES

C24-1 (Analysis of Improper SCF) The following statement was prepared by Point Barrow Corporation's accountant:

Point Barrow Corporation
STATEMENT OF SOURCES AND APPLICATION OF CASH
For the Year Ended September 30, 1996

Sources of cash	
Net income	$ 85,000
Depreciation and depletion	70,000
Increase in long-term debt	189,000
Common stock issued under employee option plans	16,000
Changes in current receivables and inventories, less current	
liabilities (excluding current maturities of long-term debt)	14,000
	$374,000
Application of cash	
Cash dividends	$ 50,000
Expenditure for property, plant, and equipment	224,000
Investments and other uses	20,000
Change in cash	80,000
	$374,000

The following additional information relating to Point Barrow Corporation is available for the year ended September 30, 1996:

1. The corporation received $16,000 in cash from its employees on its employee stock option plans, and wage and salary expense attributable to the option plans was an additional $22,000.

2. Expenditures for property, plant, and equipment $250,000
   Proceeds from retirements of property, plant, and equipment 26,000
   Net expenditures $224,000

3. A stock dividend of 10,000 shares of Point Barrow Corporation common stock was distributed to common stockholders on April 1, 1996, when the per-share market price was $7 and par value was $1.

4. On July 1, 1996, when its market price was $6 per share, 16,000 shares of Point Barrow Corporation common stock were issued in exchange for 4,000 shares of preferred stock.

5. Depreciation expense $ 65,000
   Depletion expense 5,000
   $ 70,000

6. Increase in long-term debt $620,000
   Retirement of debt 431,000
   Net increase $189,000

Instructions

(a) In general, what are the objectives of a statement of the type shown above for the Point Barrow Corporation? Explain.

(b) Identify the weaknesses in the form and format of the Point Barrow Corporation's statement of cash flows without reference to the additional information (assume adoption of the indirect method).

(c) For each of the six items of additional information for the statement of cash flows indicate the preferable treatment and explain why the suggested treatment is preferable.

(AICPA adapted)

C24-2 (SCF Theory and Analysis of Improper SCF) Catherine Howard and Henry Darnley are examining the following statement of cash flows for Agincourt's Clothing Store's first year of operations.

Agincourt's Clothing Store
STATEMENT OF CASH FLOWS
For the Year Ended January 31, 1996

Sources of cash	
From sales of merchandise	$362,000
From sale of capital stock	440,000
From sale of investment	80,000
From depreciation	70,000
From issuance of note for truck	30,000
From interest on investments	8,000
Total sources of cash	990,000
Uses of cash	
For purchase of fixtures and equipment	340,000
For merchandise purchased for resale	253,000
For operating expenses (including depreciation)	160,000
For purchase of investment	85,000
For purchase of truck by issuance of note	30,000
For purchase of treasury stock	10,000
For interest on note	3,000
Total uses of cash	881,000
Net increase in cash	$109,000

Catherine claims that Agincourt's statement of cash flows is an excellent portrayal of a superb first year with cash increasing $109,000. Henry replies that it was not a superb first year, that the year was an operating failure, that the statement was incorrectly presented, and that $109,000 is not the actual increase in cash.

Instructions

(a) With whom do you agree, Catherine or Henry? Explain your position.

(b) Using the data provided, prepare a statement of cash flows in proper indirect method form. The only noncash items in income are depreciation and the loss from the sale of the investment (purchase and sale are related).

C24-3 (SCF Theory and Analysis of Transactions) Sedona Company is a young and growing producer of electronic measuring instruments and technical equipment. You have been retained by Sedona to advise it in the preparation of a statement of cash flows using the indirect method. For the fiscal year ended October 31, 1996, you have obtained the following information concerning certain events and transactions of Sedona.

1. The amount of reported earnings for the fiscal year was $800,000, which included a deduction for an extraordinary loss of $85,000 (see item 5 below).

2. Depreciation expense of $325,000 was included in the earnings statement.

3. Uncollectible accounts receivable of $40,000 were written off against the allowance for doubtful accounts. Also, $48,000 of bad debts expense was included in determining income for the fiscal year, and the same amount was added to the allowance for doubtful accounts.

4. A gain of $6,000 was realized on the sale of a machine; it originally cost $75,000, of which $30,000 was undepreciated on the date of sale.

5. On April 1, 1996, lightning caused an uninsured building loss of $85,000 ($140,000 loss, less reduction in income taxes of $55,000). This extraordinary loss was included in determining income as indicated in 1 above.

6. On July 3, 1996, building and land were purchased for $600,000; Sedona gave in payment $75,000 cash, $200,000 market value of its unissued common stock, and signed a $325,000 mortgage note payable.
7. On August 3, 1996, $800,000 face value of Sedona's 10% convertible debentures were converted into $150,000 par value of its common stock. The bonds were originally issued at face value.

Instructions

Explain whether each of the seven numbered items above is a source or use of cash and explain how it should be disclosed in Sedona's statement of cash flows for the fiscal year ended October 31, 1996. If any item is neither a source nor a use of cash, explain why it is not and indicate the disclosure, if any, that should be made of the item in Sedona's statement of cash flows for the fiscal year ended October 31, 1996.

C24-4 (Analysis of Transactions' Effect on SCF) Each of the following items must be considered in preparing a statement of cash flows for Havasu Fashions Inc. for the year ended December 31, 1996.

1. Fixed assets that had cost $20,000 6½ years before and were being depreciated on a 10-year basis, with no estimated scrap value, were sold for $6,250.
2. During the year, goodwill of $10,000 was completely written off to expense.
3. During the year, 500 shares of common capital stock with a stated value of $25 a share were issued for $32 a share.
4. The company sustained a net loss for the year of $2,100. Depreciation amounted to $2,000 and patent amortization was $400.
5. An Appropriation for Contingencies in the amount of $80,000 was created by a charge against Retained Earnings.
6. Uncollectible accounts receivable in the amount of $2,000 were written off against the Allowance for Doubtful Accounts.
7. Investments that cost $12,000 when purchased 4 years earlier were sold for $11,000. The loss was considered ordinary.
8. Bonds payable with a par value of $24,000 on which there was an unamortized bond premium of $2,000 were redeemed at 103. The gain was credited to income as an extraordinary item. Ignore income taxes.

Instructions

For each item, state where it is to be shown in the statement and then how you would present the necessary information, including the amount. Consider each item to be independent of the others. Assume that correct entries were made for all transactions as they took place.

C24-5 (Purpose and Elements of SCF) In 1961 the AICPA recognized the importance of the funds statement by publishing *Accounting Research Study No. 2*, " 'Cash Flow' Analysis and the Funds Statement." Prior to this time, accountants had prepared funds statements primarily as management reports. The Accounting Principles Board responded by issuing *APB Opinion No. 3*, "The Statement of Source and Application of Funds," which recommended that a statement of source and application of funds be presented on a supplementary basis. Because of the favorable response of the business community to this pronouncement, the APB issued *Opinion No. 19*, "Reporting Changes in Financial Position" in 1971. This opinion required that a statement of changes in financial position be presented as a basic financial statement and be covered by the auditor's report.

In 1981 the Financial Accounting Standards Board reconsidered funds flow issues as part of the conceptual framework project. At this time, the Financial Accounting Standards Board decided that cash flow reporting issues should be considered at the standards level. Subsequent deliberations resulted in *Statement of Financial Accounting Standards (SFAS) No. 95*, "Statement of Cash Flows."

Instructions
  (a) By citing problems inherent in the Statement of Changes in Financial Position based on the source and application of funds, explain at least three reasons for developing the statement of cash flows.
  (b) Explain the purposes of the Statement of Cash Flows.
  (c) List and describe the three categories of activities that must be reported in the Statement of Cash Flows.
  (d) Identify and describe the two methods that are allowed for reporting cash flows from operations.
  (e) Describe the financial statement presentation of noncash investing and financing transactions. Include in your description an example of a noncash investing and financing transaction.

▶ USING YOUR JUDGMENT ◀

▶ FINANCIAL REPORTING PROBLEM

Refer to the financial statements and other documents of Georgia-Pacific Corporation presented in Appendix 5-A and answer the following questions.

1. Which method of computing net cash provided by operating activities did Georgia-Pacific use? What were the amounts of cash provided by operations for the years 1992 and 1993? Which item was most responsible for the increase in cash provided by operations in 1993?
2. What was the most significant item in the cash provided by (used for) investment activities section? Which items in the cash provided by (used for) financing activities section were directly related to the item identified above (that is, in the investment activities section)?
3. Where is the "gain on sale of assets" reported in Georgia-Pacific's statement of cash flows? How much is it in 1993, and why does it appear in that section of the statement of cash flows?
4. Where is "deferred income taxes" reported in Georgia-Pacific's statement of cash flows? Why does it appear in that section of the statement of cash flows?
5. Identify at least 3 significant uses of cash by Georgia-Pacific in 1993.

▶ WRITING ASSIGNMENT

Osorio, Inc. had the following condensed balance sheet at the end of operations for 1995.

Osorio Inc.
BALANCE SHEET
December 31, 1995

Cash	$ 10,000	Current liabilities	$ 14,500
Current assets	34,000	Long-term notes payable	30,000
Inventory	40,000	Bonds payable	32,000
Plant assets	57,500	Capital stock	80,000
Land	38,500	Retained earnings	23,500
	$180,000		$180,000

During 1996 the following occurred:

1. Osorio, Inc., sold part of its investment portfolio for $15,500, resulting in a gain of $500 for the firm. The company often sells and buys securities of this nature.
2. Dividends totaling $19,000 were paid to stockholders.
3. A parcel of land was purchased for $5,500.
4. Twenty thousand dollars of capital stock was issued at par.
5. Ten thousand dollars worth of bonds payable were retired at par.
6. Heavy equipment was purchased through the issuance of $32,000 of bonds.
7. Net income for 1996 was $42,000 after allowing depreciation of $13,550.
8. Both current assets (other than cash) and current liabilities remained at the same amount.

Instructions
(a) Prepare a statement of cash flows for 1996 using the indirect method.
(b) Draft a one-page letter to Mr. Peter Osorio, president of Osorio, Inc., briefly explaining the changes within each major cash flow category. Refer to your cash flow statement whenever necessary.

▶ GROUP ASSIGNMENT

(SCF—Indirect Method) Seneca Corporation has contracted with your team to prepare a statement of cash flows. The controller has provided the following information for your task:

	December 31	
	1996	1995
Cash	$ 38,500	$13,000
Accounts receivable	12,250	10,000
Inventory	12,000	9,000
Investments	–0–	3,000
Building	–0–	29,750
Equipment	40,000	20,000
Patent	5,000	6,250
Totals	$107,750	$91,000
Allowance for doubtful accounts	$ 3,000	$ 4,500
Accumulated depreciation on equipment	2,000	4,500
Accumulated depreciation on building	–0–	6,000
Accounts payable	5,000	3,000
Dividends payable	–0–	6,000
Notes payable, short-term (nontrade)	3,000	4,000
Long-term notes payable	31,000	25,000
Common stock	43,000	33,000
Retained earnings	20,750	5,000
	$107,750	$91,000

Additional data related to 1996 are as follows:

1. Equipment that had cost $11,000 and was 40% depreciated at time of disposal was sold for $2,500.
2. $10,000 of the long-term note payable was paid by issuing common stock.
3. Cash dividends paid were $6,000.
4. On January 1, 1996, the building was completely destroyed by a flood. Insurance proceeds on the building were $33,000 (net of $4,000 taxes).
5. Investments (long-term) were sold at $2,500 above their cost. The company has made similar sales and investments in the past.
6. Cash of $15,000 was paid for the acquisition of equipment.
7. A long-term note for $16,000 was issued for the acquisition of equipment.
8. Interest of $2,000 and income taxes of $5,000 were paid in cash.

Instructions

Your instructor will assign one member of the group to serve as recorder and one member to serve as spokesperson. As a group use the indirect method to analyze the above information and provide the information for the recorder to prepare a statement of cash flows for Seneca. Flood damage is unusual and infrequent in that part of the country.

► ETHICS CASE

(Managing Cash Flows) Guthrie Guitar Company is in the business of manufacturing top-quality, steel-string folk guitars. In recent years the company has experienced working capital problems resulting from the procurement of factory equipment, the unanticipated buildup of receivables and inventories, and the payoff of a balloon mortgage on a new manufacturing facility. The founder and president of the company, Jerry Guthrie, has attempted to raise cash from various financial institutions, but to no avail because of the company's poor performance in recent years. In particular, the company's lead bank, First Federal, is especially concerned about Guthrie's inability to maintain a positive cash position. The commercial loan officer from First Federal told Jerry, "I can't even consider your request for capital financing unless I see that your company is able to generate positive cash flows from operations."

Thinking about the banker's comment, Jerry came up with what he believes is a good plan: with a more attractive statement of cash flows, the bank might be willing to provide long-term financing. To "window dress" cash flows, GG can sell its accounts receivables to factors and liquidate its raw material inventories. These rather costly transactions would generate lots of working capital. As the chief accountant for Guthrie Guitar, it is your job to tell Jerry what you think of his plan.

Instructions
   (a) What are the ethical implications of Jerry's idea?
   (b) As the chief accountant of Guthrie Guitar, what would you tell Jerry?

FINANCIAL ACCOUNTING: A FINANCIAL STATEMENT USER'S VIEWPOINT

A visit with
PAT MCCONNELL

You began your career in public accounting. What do you think is the best educational background?

In addition to accounting courses, I would suggest a lot of liberal arts subjects, such as government and history, owing to the globalization of industry. You need a broad perspective in the business world. You have to understand what motivates people.

What's the optimal educational background for Wall Street?

Probably a little more accounting than the average MBA gets. Many MBA candidates haven't gotten as far as intermediate accounting. And tax is a key course. Many transactions are tax motivated. If you're going to be in corporate finance, it's helpful to have a background in the industry in which you're doing transactions. For example, earth sciences would be useful for the natural gas industry.

What would be today's hot topics for investors?

The International Accounting Standard change on goodwill amortization. As of Dec. 1, 1995, anyone who follows international accounting standards must capitalize goodwill and amortize it over a period of 5 to 20 years. The U.S. goodwill rules are 40 years—the U.S. doesn't follow international accounting standards and probably won't.

PATRICIA MCCONNELL, CPA, is one of the most highly respected analysts on Wall Street. As a managing director of Bear, Stearns & Co., she advises money managers throughout the world regarding the implications of accounting and tax developments on their investments. One of her responsibilities is to write an accounting newsletter, called *Accounting Issues*, for Bear Stearns. She also works closely with the firm's investment bankers—making sure they understand the accounting and tax implications of their proposed transactions.

Ms. McConnell majored in accounting and English at Franklin and Marshall College. While working in public accounting, she pursued her MBA at New York University, becoming a graduate assistant to an NYU professor who was a consultant to Bear Stearns. When she finished her degree in 1978, she went to work at Bear Stearns full time.

Doesn't the U.S. lead the world in accounting standards?

Surprise! Not on this one.

How did this change come about?

The International Accounting Standards Committee has been around for about 20 years. They had to homogenize the U.S. rule with the UK and Swiss practice of writing goodwill off immediately. So they decided Solomon-like to split the baby and capitalize and amortize goodwill over 5–20 years.

In general, how do you assess the "quality" of a firm's earnings?

Quality is in the eye of the beholder. Financial analysis is an art, not a science. But, generally, earnings are higher quality if they can be replicated. That is, if the earnings are coming from the company's main business and not from a one-time gain on a sale of assets or early retirement of debt. The other essence of quality is the nearness to cash. The closer the transaction is to the realization of cash, the less risk there is of unpleasant surprises in the future.

How do you tell that?

Days' sales in receivables is one way. Examining the cash flow statement is another.

What's more important to you, cash flow or EPS?

I think they're equally important. True, many investors think cash flow provides a clearer picture than earnings per share. But you'll recall that the reason that accrual accounting was developed was because it was so easy to manipulate transactions done on a cash basis—to shift expenses from one year to the next.

How might the FASB change the EPS calculation?

They're going to simplify the calculation that we do in the U.S. Right now, there are two EPS numbers: primary and fully diluted. They do not represent the ends of the spectrum as the uninitiated might expect. Currently, primary EPS includes in the denominator common stock equivalents such as options that are in the money or a convertible security with an effective yield less than 2/3rds of the AA corporate bond yield. The FASB proposes to eliminate the complication of common stock equivalents. "Basic" EPS would simply be (Net Income − Preferred Dividends)/(weighted average # of shares outstanding).

How will fully diluted EPS change?

Among other things, they're going to eliminate the 3% materiality test. Currently, if fully diluted EPS is lower than primary by 3%, then you don't have to show fully diluted EPS. That will change. Since basic EPS won't have any dilution, the FASB wants to show the entire range of dilution, even if it is smaller than 3%. Every company would be affected by this proposed change. The amount of dilution as measured by the spread in these two new numbers will increase and will surprise some people.

How did you feel about the new liabilities reflecting post-retirement medical and other benefits?

The theory is sound, but I have concerns about the reliability of the measurement—and the ability of companies to manipulate earnings. Most companies that were formed after 1983 were smart enough not to offer these benefits and won't be affected.

How efficient is the market? Does it see through accounting changes and other one-time gains?

Generally yes. The market sees through accounting changes. The accounting standards have helped it do that. They require disclosure of accounting changes and require statements to be done on a comparable basis. However, a couple of new standards—FAS 87 and 106—have transition methodologies that make it more difficult for the market to see through accounting changes. The FASB has muddied the water on these accounting changes by permitting companies to amortize them through earnings for a number of years. Ordinarily, an accounting change comes through in one year, it's disclosed, you see it, you ignore it. In my opinion, they have obscured the impact of the accounting change. *Statement 106* is even worse because it gives companies the option of taking a one-time charge for the transition or amortizing it through—which means that Company A and Company B may not be comparable.

Statement 106 seems to follow a pattern of many pronouncements: You accrue a new liability but there's no impact on the stock. Why is that the case?

Changing the accounting doesn't change the economics of the business.

But you're telling a client that all of a sudden, a company has a $2 billion liability that wasn't there before.

It means something only if the client didn't realize that the company had a retiree health care problem to begin with. Before 106, investors could read about the impact on a pay-as-you-go basis in the footnotes. Investors have been able to see the cash-flow impact and the inflation in that number. They can tell if the number is large or small in relation to revenues and other expenses. However, it is true that the liability itself wasn't actually disclosed.

Tell me what your day is like.

My day is divided fifty-fifty between corporate finance and the typical sell-side equity research activity. I don't actually issue buy or sell recommendations. My responsibility is to be independent and let the client draw their own conclusions.

Most equity research is done in New York and a few other money center cities. Can I still have a career in this industry without relocating to those places?

Well, you're talking about the "sell" side. It's true that most of the jobs on the sell side are in the money centers—though there are a handful of regional firms. But there are a lot more opportunities throughout the country on the "buy" side. Most of the state pension funds have research departments. And, they have their own traders. So do insurance companies and large banks. The accounting background is most helpful in research or corporate finance, but it could also help you be a good broker.

BEAR STEARNS ACCOUNTING ISSUES PAT MCCONNELL

EQUITY RESEARCH

June 13, 1994

Bear, Stearns & Co. Inc.
245 Park Avenue
New York, NY 10167

EPS: TOWARD A COMMON DENOMINATOR

The FASB has reached some important conclusions in its earnings per share (EPS) project. Added to the Board's agenda in March, it deals primarily with the denominator of the EPS calculation. The Board will still require display of two EPS statistics but its decisions to date will cause the spread between the two figures to widen in most cases. The Board will substitute basic earnings per share (BEPS) for primary (PEPS). Basic EPS is net income available to common shareholders divided by the weighted average number of shares outstanding. It will be the same or higher than the current primary number which includes some dilution. Fully diluted earnings per share (FDEPS) generally will be the same or lower than currently calculated. However, in some situations FDEPS may increase. It will be calculated using the "if converted" method for convertible securities and the treasury stock method with period end prices for options and warrants. The modified treasury stock method, currently used when shares under option exceed 20% of shares outstanding, will no longer be allowed. The 3% materiality test that currently limits the presentation of FDEPS to situations where FDEPS is 97% of BEPS is also eliminated. Thus, more companies will have dual presentations. The FASB plans to issue an exposure draft late in 1994 or early in 1995. The impacts will be company specific.

Pat McConnell, CPA
Janet Pegg, CPA

A surprising number of companies have dilution that is not material. For example, a review of the Dow Jones Industrial companies revealed that 20% of them were unambiguously in this position. They are listed in **Exhibit 7** along with the key phrase from their EPS footnote.

Exhibit 7

Dow Jones Industrial Companies with Immaterial EPS Dilution

Allied Signal	No dilution results from outstanding common stock equivalents.
Alcoa	FDEPS is not presented since dilution is not material.
Boeing	There is no material dilutive effect on EPS due to common stock equivalents.
International Paper	The effect of all dilutive securities is immaterial.
McDonalds	The effect of potentially dilutive securities was not material.
Merck	Common stock equivalents do not have a significant dilutive effect.

CHAPTER 25

BASIC FINANCIAL STATEMENT ANALYSIS

LEARNING OBJECTIVES

After studying this chapter, you should be able to:

1. Understand the approach to financial statement analysis.

2. Identify major analytic ratios and describe their calculation.

3. Explain the limitations of ratio analysis.

4. Describe techniques of comparative analysis.

5. Describe techniques of percentage analysis.

What would be important to you in studying a company's financial statements? The answer depends on your particular interest—whether you are a creditor, stockholder, potential investor, manager, government agency, or labor leader. For example, **short-term creditors,** such as banks, are primarily interested in the ability of the firm to pay its currently maturing obligations. In that case, you would examine the current assets and their relation to short-term liabilities to evaluate the short-run solvency of the firm. **Bondholders,** on the other hand, look more to long-term indicators, such as the enterprise's capital structure, past and projected earnings, and changes in financial position. **Stockholders,** present or prospective, also are interested in many of the features considered by a long-term creditor. As a stockholder, you would focus on the earnings picture, because changes in it greatly affect the market price of your investment. You also would be concerned with the financial position of the firm, because it affects indirectly the stability of earnings.

The **management** of a company is concerned about the composition of its capital structure and about the changes and trends in earnings. This financial information has a direct influence on the type, amount, and cost of external financing that the company can obtain. In addition, the company finds financial information useful on a day-to-day operating basis in such areas as capital budgeting, breakeven analysis, variance analysis, gross margin analysis, and for internal control purposes.

The accountant's function is twofold: (1) to measure economic events and transactions and (2) to communicate economic information about them to interested parties. Thus far in this textbook we have discussed the measurement and reporting functions of accounting. But communication in accounting means more than just preparing the reports: communication also presumes understanding. To promote understanding, accountants, as well as other interested parties, analyze and interpret financial statements.

▶ PERSPECTIVE ON FINANCIAL STATEMENT ANALYSIS

OBJECTIVE 1

Understand the approach to financial statement analysis.

Information from financial statements can be gathered by examining relationships between items on the statements and identifying trends in these relationships. The relationships are expressed numerically in ratios and percentages, and trends are identified through comparative analysis. A problem with learning how to analyze statements is that the means may become an end in itself. There are thousands of possible relationships that could be calculated and trends that could be identified. If one knows only how to calculate ratios and trends without understanding how such information can be used, little is accomplished. Therefore, a logical approach to financial statement analysis is necessary. Such an approach may consist of the following steps:

1. **Know the questions for which you want to find answers.** As indicated at the beginning of this chapter, various groups have different types of interest in a company.

2. **Know the questions that particular ratios and comparisons are able to help answer.** These will be discussed in the remainder of this chapter.

3. **Match 1 and 2 above.** By such a matching, the statement analysis will have a logical direction and purpose.

Several caveats must be mentioned. **Financial statements report on the past.** As such, analysis of these data is an examination of the past. Whenever such information is incorporated into a decision-making (future-oriented) process, a critical assumption is that the past is a reasonable basis for predicting the future. This is usually a reasonable approach, but the limitations associated with it should be recognized. Also, ratio and trend analyses will help identify present strengths and weaknesses of a company. They may serve as "red flags" indicating problem areas. In many cases, however, such analyses will not reveal **why** things are as they are. Finding answers about "why" usually requires an in-depth analysis and an awareness of many factors about a company that are not reported in the financial statements—for instance, the impact of inflation, actions of competitors, technological developments, a strike at a major supplier's or buyer's operations, and so on.

Another point is that a **single ratio by itself is not likely to be very useful.** For example, a current ratio of 2 to 1 (current assets are twice current liabilities) may be viewed as satisfactory. However, if the industry average is 3 to 1, such a conclusion may be questioned. Even given this industry average, one may conclude that the particular company is doing well if the ratio last year was 1.5 to 1. Consequently, to derive meaning from ratios, some standard against which to compare them is needed. Such a standard may come from industry averages, past years' amounts, a particular competitor, or planned levels.

Finally, **awareness of the limitations of accounting numbers used in an analysis** is important. We will discuss some of these limitations and their consequences later in this chapter.

▶ RATIO ANALYSIS

Various devices are used in the analysis of financial statement data to bring out the comparative and relative significance of the financial information presented. These devices include ratio analysis, comparative analysis, percentage analysis, and examination of related data. No one device is more useful than another. Every situation faced by the investment analyst is different, and the answers needed are often obtained only upon close examination of the interrelationships among all the data provided. Ratio analysis is the starting point in developing the information desired by the analyst.[1]

---

[1]A fairly comprehensive list and explanation of ratios may be found in the AICPA's *CPA/MAS Technical Consulting Practice Aid No. 3*, "Financial Ratio Analysis," by Joseph E. Palmer (New York: AICPA, 1983), 28 pp.

Ratios (summary indicators) can be classified as follows:[2]

◀ MAJOR TYPES OF RATIOS ▶

LIQUIDITY RATIOS.   Measures of the enterprise's short-run ability to pay its maturing obligations.

ACTIVITY RATIOS.   Measures of how effectively the enterprise is using the assets employed.

PROFITABILITY RATIOS.   Measures of the degree of success or failure of a given enterprise or division for a given period of time.

COVERAGE RATIOS.   Measures of the degree of protection for long-term creditors and investors.[3]

The use of these ratios is illustrated through an actual case example adopted from the annual report of a large chemical concern that we have disguised under the name of Anetek Chemical Corporation.

Anetek Chemical Corporation is a worldwide enterprise offering more than 1,400 products and services. "Anetek" people number some 50,000 in 48 nations. The comparative financial statements of Anetek (shown in Illustrations 25-1 and 25-2) are the basis for all of the ratios. The numbers used in the ratios, like the numbers used in the financial statements, have the last three digits (000) omitted.

ILLUSTRATON 25-1
Income Statement

Anetek Chemical Corporation INCOME STATEMENT For the Year Ended December 31 (000 Omitted)		
	1996	1995
Sales and other revenue		
Net sales	$1,600,000	$1,350,000
Interest revenue	25,000	20,000
Other revenue	50,000	30,000
Total revenue	1,675,000	1,400,000
Cost and other charges		
Cost of goods sold	1,000,000	850,000
Depreciation and amortization	150,000	150,000
Selling and administrative expenses	225,000	150,000
Interest expense	50,000	25,000
Total	1,425,000	1,175,000
Income before taxes	250,000	225,000
Income taxes	100,000	75,000
Net income	$ 150,000	$ 150,000
Earnings per share[a]	$5.00	$5.00

[a]Additional information:
Number of shares outstanding in 1996 is 30 million shares.
Market price of Anetek's stock at end of 1996 is $60.
Cash dividend per share in 1996 is $2.25.
Correction of error in prior period $4.5 million.

---

[2]Summary indicators might be defined as amounts, ratios, or other computations that distill some key information about the business enterprise. For example, a proposed FASB concepts statement used this terminology to describe ratios, and a research report of the FASB uses this term in the same connection. Paul Frishkoff, "Reporting of Summary Indicators: An Investigation of Research and Practice," *Research Report* (Stamford, CT: FASB, 1981).

[3]Other terms may be used to categorize these summary ratios. For example, liquidity ratios are sometimes referred to as solvency ratios; activity ratios as turnover or efficiency ratios; and coverage ratios as leverage or capital structure ratios.

ILLUSTRATION 25-2
Comparative Balance
Sheets

Anetek Chemical Corporation
CONSOLIDATED BALANCE SHEET[a]
December 31
(000 omitted)

	1996	1995
Assets		
Current assets		
Cash	$ 40,000	$ 25,000
Marketable securities	100,000	75,000
Accounts receivable	350,000	300,000
Inventories (at lower of cost or market)	310,000	250,000
Total current assets	800,000	650,000
Investments (at fair value)	300,000	325,000
Fixed assets		
Property, plant, and equipment (at cost)	2,000,000	1,900,000
Less—accumulated depreciation	(900,000)	(800,000)
	1,100,000	1,100,000
Goodwill	50,000	25,000
Total assets	$2,250,000	$2,100,000
Liabilities and Stockholders' Equity		
Current liabilities		
Accounts payable	$ 125,000	$ 100,000
Notes payable	250,000	200,000
Accrued and other liabilities	200,000	150,000
Total current liabilities	575,000	450,000
Long-term debt		
Bonds and notes payable	725,000	782,500
Total liabilities	1,300,000	1,232,500
Stockholders' equity		
Common stock, $5 par	150,000	150,000
Additional paid-in capital	550,000	550,000
Retained earnings	250,000	167,500
Total equity	950,000	867,500
Total debt and equity	$2,250,000	$2,100,000

[a]The notes and some detail that accompanied this statement are excluded for purposes of simplicity and brevity.

LIQUIDITY RATIOS

INTERNATIONAL
INSIGHT

*Applying U.S. techniques of
ratio analysis internationally
can be misleading. Analysts
must understand not only
the accounting principles on
which the statements have
been prepared but also the
business practices and
culture of the foreign
environment.*

The ability of a firm to meet its current debts—**liquidity**—is important in evaluating its financial position. For example, Anetek Chemical has current liabilities of $575,000. Can these current obligations be met when due? Certain basic ratios can be computed that provide some guides for determining the enterprise's short-term debt-paying ability.

1. Current Ratio

The **current ratio** is the ratio of total current assets to total current liabilities. Although the quotient is the dollars of current assets available to cover each dollar of current debt, it is most frequently expressed as a coverage of so many times. Sometimes it is called the **working capital ratio,** because working capital is the excess of current assets over current liabilities. The computation of the current ratio for Anetek is:

$$\text{Current ratio} = \frac{\text{Current assets}}{\text{Current liabilities}} = \frac{\$800,000}{\$575,000} = 1.39 \text{ times}$$

$$\text{Industry average}^4 = 2.30 \text{ times}$$

The current ratio of 1.39 to 1 compared with the industry average of 2.30 to 1 indicates that Anetek's safety factor to meet maturing short-term obligations is noticeably low. Does the relatively low current ratio indicate the existence of a liquidity problem? Or considering that the ratio is greater than 1 to 1, is the situation well in hand? The current ratio is only one measure of determining liquidity, and it does not answer all of the liquidity questions. How liquid are the receivables and inventory? What effect does the omission of the inventory have on the analysis of liquidity? To answer these and other questions, additional analysis of other related data is required.

2. Acid-Test Ratio

A satisfactory current ratio does not disclose the fact that a portion of the current assets may be tied up in slow-moving inventories. With inventories, especially raw material and work in process, there is a question of how long it will take to transform them into the finished product and what ultimately will be realized on the sale of the merchandise. Elimination of the inventories, along with any prepaid expenses, from the current assets might provide better information for the short-term creditor. Many analysts favor a "quick" or "acid-test" ratio that relates total current liabilities to cash, marketable securities, and receivables. The acid-test ratio is computed for Anetek as follows:

$$\text{Acid-test ratio} = \frac{\text{Cash} + \substack{\text{marketable} \\ \text{securities}} + \substack{\text{net} \\ \text{receivables}}}{\text{Current liabilities}} = \frac{\$490,000}{\$575,000} = .85 \text{ times}$$

$$\text{Industry average} = 1.20 \text{ times}$$

The acid-test ratio for Anetek as compared with the industry average is low. This means that Anetek may have difficulty in meeting its short-term needs unless the firm is able to obtain additional current assets through conversion of some of its long-term assets, through additional financing, or through profitable operating results.

3. Defensive-Interval Ratio

Neither the current ratio nor the acid-test ratio gives a complete explanation of the current debt-paying ability of the company. The matching of current assets with current liabilities assumes that the current assets will be employed to pay off the current liabilities. Some analysts argue that a better measure of liquidity is provided by the defensive-interval ratio. The **defensive-interval ratio** measures the time span a firm can operate on present liquid assets without resorting to revenues from next year's sources. This ratio is computed by dividing **defensive assets** (cash, marketable securities, and net receivables) by projected daily expenditures from operations. Projected daily expenditures are computed by dividing cost of goods sold plus selling and administrative expenses and other ordinary cash expenses by 365 days.[5]

---

[4]The industry average ratios are taken from Dun and Bradstreet, Inc., *Key Business Ratios in 25 Lines,* and Leo Troy's *The Almanac of Business and Industrial Financial Ratios.* The standard ratios provide some basis for comparison with other companies in the same industry.

[5]The only necessary adjustments to the total expense figure are deductions of any noncash charges such as depreciation.

The defensive-interval measure for Anetek is:

$$\text{Defensive-interval measure} = \frac{\text{Defensive assets}}{\text{Projected daily operational expenditures (based on past expenditures) minus noncash charges}}$$

$$= \$490,000 \div \frac{\$1,525,000 - \$150,000}{365}$$

$$= 130 \text{ days}$$

$$\text{Industry average} = 80 \text{ days}$$

This ratio does not necessarily provide a better measure of liquidity than the current ratio or acid-test ratio. It does provide another useful tool for analyzing the liquidity position of the enterprise. This ratio establishes a safety factor or margin for the investor in determining the capability of the company to meet its basic operational costs. It would appear that 130 days provides the company with a relatively high degree of protection, and tends to offset the weakness indicated by the low current and acid-test ratios.

ACTIVITY RATIOS

Another way of evaluating liquidity is to determine how quickly certain assets can be turned into cash. How liquid, for example, are the receivables and inventory? In addition, this type of calculation provides information related to how efficiently the enterprise utilizes its assets. Activity ratios are computed for Anetek Chemical on the basis of receivables, inventories, and total assets.

4. Receivables Turnover

The **receivables turnover ratio** is computed by dividing net sales by average receivables outstanding during the year. Theoretically, the numerator should include only net credit sales. This information is frequently not available, however, and if the relative amounts of charge and cash sales remain fairly constant, the trend indicated by the ratio will still be valid. Unless seasonal factors are significant, average receivables outstanding can be computed from the beginning and ending balances of net trade receivables.

$$\text{Accounts receivable turnover} = \frac{\text{Net sales}}{\text{Average trade receivables (net)}}$$

$$= \$1,600,000 \div \frac{\$350,000 + \$300,000}{2}$$

$$= 4.92 \text{ or every 74 days (365 days} \div 4.92)$$

$$\text{Industry average}[6] = 7.15 \text{ or every 51 days}$$

This information provides some indication of the quality of the receivables, and also an idea of how successful the firm is in collecting its outstanding receivables. The faster this turnover, the more credence the current ratio and acid-test ratio have in the financial analysis. If possible, an aging schedule should also be prepared to determine how long the receivables have been outstanding. It is possible that a satisfactory receivables turnover may have resulted because certain receivables were collected quickly though oth-

---

[6]Often the receivables turnover is transformed to **days to collect accounts receivable**—an average collection period. In this case, 4.92 is divided into 365 days to obtain 74 days. Several figures other than 365 could be used here; a most common alternative is 360 days because it is divisable by 30 (days) and 12 (months). Because our industry average was based on 365, we used this figure in our computations.

ers have been outstanding for a relatively long period. An aging schedule would reveal such patterns.

In Anetek's case, the receivables turnover appears low. Dividing 365 days by the turnover provides a measure of the average number of days to collect accounts receivable (74 days for Anetek). The lower the turnover, the longer this period of time. The general rule used is that the time allowed for payment by the selling terms should not be exceeded by more than 10 or 15 days.

5. Inventory Turnover

Inventory turnover measures how quickly inventory is sold. It is computed by dividing the average inventory into the cost of goods sold. Dividing 365 days by the inventory turnover indicates the average number of days it takes to sell inventory (or average number of days' sales for which inventory is on hand). The inventory turnover ratio for Anetek Chemical is:

$$\text{Inventory turnover} = \frac{\text{Cost of goods sold}}{\text{Average inventory}} = \frac{\$1,000,000}{\dfrac{\$310,000 + \$250,000}{2}}$$

$$= 3.57 \text{ times or every 102 days (365 days} \div 3.57)$$

$$\text{Industry average} = 4.62 \text{ or every 79 days}$$

Generally, the higher the inventory turnover, the better the enterprise is performing. It is possible, however, that the enterprise is incurring high "stockout costs" because not enough inventory is available.

This ratio is useful because it provides a basis for determining whether obsolete inventory is present or pricing problems exist. In Anetek's case, the turnover ratio is lower than the industry average, indicating that some slow-moving inventory exists. Remember that this ratio is an average, which means that many goods may be turning over quite rapidly, whereas others may have failed to sell at all. In addition, it was assumed that an average of the beginning and ending inventory was representative of the average for the year. If this situation is not correct, additional computations must be made.

Because inventory is stated at cost, it must be divided into cost of sales (a cost figure) instead of into sales, which includes some margin of profit. Occasionally analysts use sales instead of cost of goods sold as a substitute, but this practice has no theoretical support unless inventories are valued at retail prices.

The method of inventory valuation can affect the computed turnover and the current ratio. The analyst should be aware of the different valuations that can be used in costing inventory (e.g., FIFO, LIFO, etc.) and the effect these different valuation procedures might have on the ratio.

From the accounts receivable and inventory turnover information, a **total conversion period** can be determined. The total conversion period is the average number of days it takes from acquiring inventory to collecting cash from its sale. It is calculated by adding the average number of days it takes to sell inventory (inventory turnover ratio) to the average number of days to collect accounts receivable (receivable turnover ratio). For Anetek, the total conversion period is 176 days (102 + 74). Examining the conversion period and its two components can be useful in identifying differences between companies. It can also be useful in identifying differences between years for the same company, to evaluate the effectiveness of marketing, credit granting, and collection policies.

6. Asset Turnover

The **asset turnover ratio** is determined by dividing average total assets into net sales for the period. The asset turnover for Anetek is:

$$\text{Asset turnover} = \frac{\text{Net sales}}{\text{Average total assets}} = \frac{\$1,600,000}{\dfrac{\$2,250,000 + \$2,100,000}{2}} = .74$$

Industry average = .94

This ratio supposedly indicates how efficiently the company utilizes its assets. If the turnover ratio is high, the implication is that the company is using its assets effectively to generate sales. If the turnover ratio is low, the company either has to use its assets more efficiently or dispose of them.

The problem with this turnover calculation is that it places a premium on using old assets because their book value is low. In addition, this ratio is affected by the depreciation method employed by the company. For example, a company that employs an accelerated method of depreciation will have a higher turnover than a company using straight-line, all other factors being equal. For these reasons, the ratio **should not be the only one considered** in evaluating the efficiency of the company in this area.

PROFITABILITY RATIOS

Profitability ratios indicate how well the enterprise has operated during the year. These ratios answer such questions as: Was the net income adequate? What rate of return does it represent? What is the rate of net income by operating segment or activity? What amount was paid in dividends? What amount was earned by different equity claimants? Generally, the ratios are either computed on the basis of sales or on an investment base such as total assets. Profitability is frequently used as the ultimate test of management effectiveness.

7. Profit Margin on Sales

The **profit margin on sales** is computed by dividing net income by net sales for the period. Anetek's ratio is:

$$\text{Profit margin on sales} = \frac{\text{Net income}}{\text{Net sales}} = \frac{\$150,000}{\$1,600,000} = 9.4\%$$

Industry average = 6%

This ratio indicates that Anetek is achieving an above-average rate of profit on each sales dollar received. It provides some indication of the buffer available in case of higher costs or lower sales in the future.

Employment of this ratio in conjunction with the asset turnover ratio offers an interplay that leads to a **rate of return on total assets.** This relationship is expressed as follows:

$$\text{Rate of return on assets} = \text{Profit margin on sales} \times \text{Asset turnover}$$

$$\text{Rate of return on assets} = \frac{\text{Net income}}{\text{Net sales}} \times \frac{\text{Net sales}}{\text{Average total assets}}$$

$$= \frac{\$150,000}{\$1,600,000} \times \frac{\$1,600,000}{\dfrac{\$2,250,000 + \$2,100,000}{2}}$$

$$= 6.9\%$$

Industry average = 5.6%

The profit margin on sales does not answer the question of how profitable the enterprise was for a given time period. Only by determining how many times the assets turned over during a period of time is it possible to ascertain the amount of net income earned on the total assets.

Many enterprises have a small profit margin on sales and a high turnover. Grocery and discount stores are examples. Other enterprises, such as jewelry and furniture stores, have a relatively high profit margin but a low inventory turnover.

8. Rate of Return on Assets

Rate of return on assets is computed by using as a numerator net income and as a denominator average total assets. The ratio for Anetek is:

$$\text{Rate of return on assets} = \frac{\text{Net income}}{\text{Average total assets}}$$

$$= \$150,000 \div \frac{\$2,250,000 + \$2,100,000}{2}$$

$$= 6.9\%$$

$$\text{Industry average} = 5.6\%$$

Anetek's rate of return is slightly above the average of the industry and is a result of Anetek's relatively high profit margin on sales.

One of the most interesting applications of rate of return is called the du Pont system of financial control. The basic components in the du Pont system are presented in Illustration 25-3.

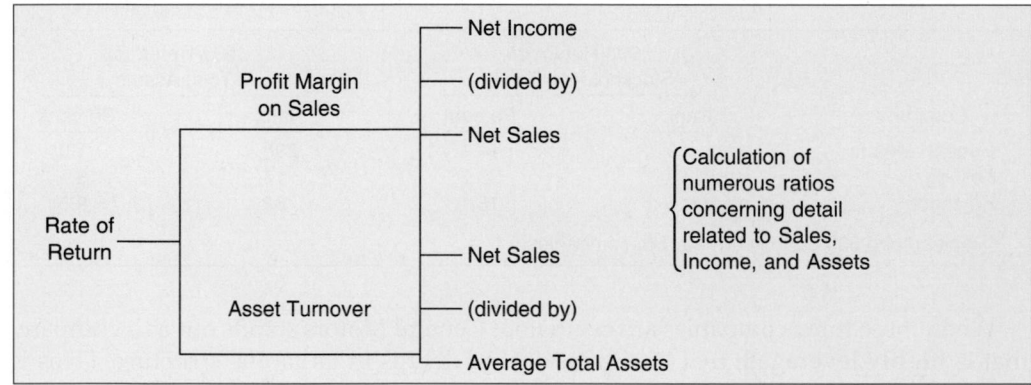

**ILLUSTRATION 25-3
du Pont System of
Financial Control
Illustrated**

In this system, ratios can help explain the different effects leading to the rate of return on assets.

Many contend that a better measure of the rate earned on assets results from using net income before subtraction of the interest charge.[7] This ratio is computed by dividing net income plus interest expense (net of tax effect) by average total assets. Interest expense (net of tax effect), including discount amortization, is added back to income because the interest represents a cost of securing additional assets and, therefore, should not be considered as a deduction in arriving at the amount of return on assets. The ratio for Anetek is:

$$\text{Rate of return on assets} = \frac{\text{Net income} + \text{interest expense} - \text{tax savings}^8}{\text{Average total assets}}$$

$$= \frac{\$150,000 + \$50,000 - .40(\$50,000)}{\dfrac{\$2,250,000 + \$2,100,000}{2}}$$

$$= 8.3\%$$

---

[7]For example, public utilities compute their rate of return using this approach.

[8]The tax savings is computed by multiplying the interest expense by the effective tax rate. The effective tax rate is determined by dividing the provision for income taxes by income before taxes.

9. Rate of Return on Common Stock Equity

This ratio—**rate of return on common stock equity**—is defined as net income after interest, taxes, and preferred dividends divided by average common stockholders' equity. Anetek's ratio is computed in this manner:

$$\text{Rate of return on common stock equity} = \frac{\text{Net income minus preferred dividends}}{\text{Average common stockholders' equity}}$$

$$= \$150{,}000 \div \frac{\$950{,}000 + \$867{,}500}{2}$$

$$= 16.5\%$$

$$\text{Industry average} = 9.5\%$$

When the rate of return on total assets is lower than the rate of return on the common stockholders' investment, the enterprise is said to be trading on the equity at a gain. Trading on the equity increases the company's financial risk, but it enhances residual earnings whenever the rate of return on assets exceeds the cost of debt capital.

Whether the rate of return on total assets or the rate of return on common stock equity is a better measure of performance is difficult to evaluate. At one time when *Forbes* (a popular financial magazine) was asked to provide basic guidelines for profitability, it computed both ratios. The three companies listed below are indicative of differences that arise in rates of return on equity and rates of return on total assets.

ILLUSTRATION 25-4
Comparisons of Different Types of Profitability Indexes

Company	1993 Return on Stockholders' Equity		1993 Return on Total Assets	
	Rank[a]	Percent	Rank	Percent
General Motors	9	44.1	296	1.3
Kellogg	13	39.7	17	16.1
Raytheon	115	16.1	62	9.5

[a]Rank among 500 publicly owned U.S. companies.

When these three companies are evaluated, General Motors stands out as a company that is **highly leveraged;** that is, a great deal of debt is in its capital structure. (This is evidenced by the return on equity being so much higher than the return on assets.) Leveraging per se is not wrong, but in an economic downturn chances are that General Motors would turn less profitable more quickly than the other two companies.

On the other hand, there are companies such as Intel and Tambrands that have little leverage but are very profitable anyway. For example, in 1993 Intel had a rate of return on assets of 20.2% and a rate of return on common equity of 30.6%. Was Intel more or less profitable than General Motors? It is a difficult question to evaluate and both ratios should be considered in the analysis.

Trading on the Equity

The expression **"trading on the equity"** describes the practice of using borrowed money at fixed interest rates or issuing preferred stock with constant dividend rates in hopes of obtaining a higher rate of return on the money used. These issues must be given a prior claim on some or all of the corporate assets. Thus, the advantage to common stockholders of trading on the equity must come from borrowing at a lower rate of interest than the rate of return obtained on the assets borrowed. If this can be done, the capital obtained from bondholders or preferred stockholders earns enough to pay the interest or preferred dividends and to leave a margin for the common stockholders. When this condition exists, trading on the equity is profitable.

A comparison of the rate of return on total assets with the rate paid to other than common stock claimants indicates the profitability of trading on the equity in any given case. To illustrate, Anetek's rate of return on total assets is 6.9%, whereas the rate of return on the stockholders' equity is 16.5%. Anetek traded on the equity at a gain. In essence, the liability claimants were paid a lower rate than 6.9%. Anetek is a very highly leveraged company which has achieved an excellent rate of return on common equity by using its debt effectively. A word of caution—trading on the equity is a two-way street: just as a company's gains can be magnified, so also can losses be magnified.

10. Earnings Per Share

The **earnings per share** figure is one of the most important ratios used by investment analysts, yet it is one of the most deceptive. If no dilutive securities are present in the capital structure, then earnings per share is simply computed by dividing net income minus preferred dividends by the weighted average number of shares of outstanding common stock.[9] The computation for Anetek is:

$$\text{Earnings per share} = \frac{\text{Net income minus preferred dividends}}{\text{Weighted shares outstanding}} = \frac{\$150,000}{30,000} = \$5.00$$

Because no dilutive securities that are common stock equivalents or potentially dilutive securities are present in Anetek's capital structure, primary earnings per share and fully diluted earnings per share amounts need not be reported.

Certain problems exist when the earnings per share ratio is computed. Often earnings per share can be increased simply by reducing the number of shares outstanding through the purchase of treasury stock. In addition, the earnings per share figure fails to recognize the probable increasing base of the stockholders' investment. That is, earnings per share, all other factors being equal, will probably increase year after year if the corporation reinvests earnings in the business, because a larger earnings figure is generated without a corresponding increase in the number of shares outstanding. Even well-informed investors attach importance to earnings per share, but caution must be exercised. The figure should not be given more emphasis than it deserves. The common problem is that the per-share figure draws the investor's attention away from the enterprise as a whole—which involves differing magnitudes of sales, costs, volumes, and invested capital—and concentrates too much attention on the single share of stock.

11. Price Earnings Ratio

The **price earnings (P/E) ratio** is an oft-quoted statistic used by analysts in discussing the investment possibility of a given enterprise. It is computed by dividing the market price of the stock by its earnings per share. For Anetek, the ratio is:

$$\text{Price earnings ratio} = \frac{\text{Market price of stock}}{\text{Earnings per share}} = \frac{\$60}{\$5} = 12.0$$

The average price earnings ratio for the 30 stocks that constitute the Dow Jones industrial average in September 1993 was 20.3. A steady drop in a company's price earnings ratio indicates that investors are wary of the firm's growth potential. Some companies have high P/E ratios (also called "multiples"), while others have low multiples. For instance, Home Depot in 1993 enjoyed a P/E ratio of 36 while Ford Motor had a low P/E ratio of 8. The reason for this difference is linked to several factors: relative risk, stability of earnings, trends in earnings, and the market's perception of the company's growth potential. Analysts who believe a company will be able to gen-

---

[9]If, however, convertible securities, stock options, warrants, or other dilutive securities are included in the capital structure, (1) earnings per common and common equivalent shares and (2) fully diluted earnings per share figures may have to be used. See Chapter 17 for a discussion of how dilutive securities should be handled to compute earnings per share.

erate even higher future earnings may value the stock higher than its present earnings may warrant. The reverse is also true.

12. Payout Ratio

The **payout ratio** is the ratio of cash dividends to net income. If preferred stock is outstanding, this ratio is computed for common stockholders by dividing cash dividends paid to common stock by income available to common stockholders. Assuming that the cash dividends are $67,500, the payout ratio for Anetek is:

$$\text{Payout ratio} = \frac{\text{Cash dividends}}{\text{Net income less preferred dividends}} = \frac{\$67,500}{\$150,000 - 0} = 45\%$$

It is important to many investors that a fairly substantial payout ratio exist; however, speculators view appreciation in the value of the stock as more important. Generally, growth companies are characterized by low payout ratios because they reinvest most of their earnings. Anetek has a rather high payout ratio compared to Dresser Industries, which normally pays out approximately 16% of earnings, but a relatively low payout ratio when compared with Commonwealth Edison Co., which normally pays out 70%.

Another closely related ratio that is often used is the **dividend yield**—the cash dividend per share divided by the market price of the stock. The cash dividend per share for Anetek is $2.25, so the dividend yield is 3.75% ($2.25/$60.00). This ratio affords investors some idea of the rate of return that will be received in cash dividends from their investment. In 1994, Apple Computer stockholders experienced a modest yield of approximately 1%, while Public Service of Colorado stockholders experienced a dividend yield of approximately 7.5%.

COVERAGE RATIOS

The coverage ratios are computed to **help predict the long-run solvency of the firm.** These ratios are of interest primarily to bondholders who need some indication of the measure of protection available to them. In addition, they indicate part of the risk involved in investing in common stock. The more debt that is added to the capital structure, the more uncertain is the return on common stock.

13. Debt to Total Assets

The **debt to total assets ratio** provides the creditors with some idea of the corporation's ability to withstand losses without impairing the interests of creditors. From the creditor's point of view a low ratio of debt to total assets is desirable. The lower this ratio is, the more "buffer" there is available to creditors before the corporation becomes insolvent. The ratio for Anetek is:

$$\text{Debt to total assets} = \frac{\text{Debt}}{\text{Total assets or equities}} = \frac{\$1,300,000}{\$2,250,000} = 58\%$$

Industry average = 38%

INTERNATIONAL INSIGHT

Even after restating the statements of Japanese firms so that they are in compliance with U.S. GAAP, the debt/asset ratios of the Japanese firms still tend to be much higher than those of comparable U.S. firms. Although U.S. analysts would interpret this signal as a "negative," in Japan it would be interpreted positively. A high ratio would indicate that the company is "safe" because the banks have confidence in it.

There are other ways of expressing this ratio, such as the ratio of debt to stockholders' equity and the ratio of stockholders' equity to the sum of debt and stockholders' equity. Essentially, these ratios all provide the same answer to the question: How well protected are the creditors in the case of possible insolvency of the enterprise?[10] These ratios have a very definite effect on the company's ability to obtain additional financing. Anetek is highly leveraged; further growth through debt financing may not be possible.

---

[10]Additional protection, of course, is afforded through specified liens and collateral and through contractual restrictive covenants.

14. Times Interest Earned

The **times interest earned** ratio is computed by dividing income before interest charges and taxes by the interest charge. This ratio stresses the importance of a company **covering all interest charges.** Note that the times interest earned ratio uses income before interest and income taxes because this is the amount of income available to cover interest. The ratio for Anetek is:

$$\text{Times interest earned} = \frac{\text{Income before taxes and interest charges}}{\text{Interest charges}} = \frac{\$300,000}{\$50,000} = 6 \text{ times}$$

In this case Anetek's interest coverage is more than adequate.

If a company pays preferred dividends, the number of times the preferred dividends were earned is computed by dividing the net income for the year by the annual preferred dividend requirements.

15. Book Value Per Share

A much-used basis for evaluating net worth is found in the **book value** or **equity value per share** of stock. Book value per share of stock is the amount each share would receive if the company were liquidated **on the basis of amounts reported on the balance sheet.** The figure loses much of its relevance if the valuations on the balance sheet do not approximate fair market value of the assets. Book value per share is computed by allocating the stockholders' equity items among the various classes of stock and then dividing the total so allocated to each class of stock by the number of shares outstanding.

The book value per common share for Anetek is:

$$\text{Book value per share} = \frac{\text{Common stockholders' equity}}{\text{Outstanding shares}} = \frac{\$950,000}{30,000} = \$31.67$$

Preferred stock is not a part of the capital structure of Anetek. When this type of security is present, an analysis of the covenants involving the preferred shares should be studied. If preferred dividends are in arrears, the preferred stock is participating, or if preferred stock has a redemption or liquidating value higher than its carrying amount, retained earnings must be allocated between the preferred and common stockholders in computing book value.

To illustrate, assume that the following situation exists:

Stockholders' equity	Preferred	Common
Preferred stock, 5%	$300,000.00	
Common stock		$400,000.00
Excess of issue price over par of common stock		37,500.00
Retained earnings		162,582.00
Totals	$300,000.00	$600,082.00
Shares outstanding	3,000	4,000
Book value per share	$100.00	$150.02

ILLUSTRATION 25-5
Computation of Book Value per Share—No Dividends in Arrears

In the computation above it is assumed that no preferred dividends are in arrears and that the preferred is not participating. Now assume that the same facts exist except that the 5% preferred is cumulative, participating up to 8%, and that dividends for three years before the current year are in arrears. The book value of each class of stock is then computed as follows, assuming that no action has yet been taken concerning dividends for the current year:

ILLUSTRATION 25-6
Computation of Book
Value per Share—With
Dividends in Arrears

Stockholders' equity	Preferred	Common
Preferred stock,[11] 5%	$300,000.00	
Common stock		$400,000.00
Excess of issue price over par of common stock		37,500.00
Retained earnings:		
Dividends in arrears (3 years at 5% a year)	45,000.00	
Current year requirement at 5%	15,000.00	20,000.00
Participating—additional 3%	9,000.00	12,000.00
Remainder to common		61,582.00
Totals	$369,000.00	$531,082.00
Shares outstanding	3,000	4,000
Book value per share	$123.00	$132.77

In connection with the book value computation, the analyst must know how to handle the following items: the number of authorized and unissued shares; the number of treasury shares on hand; any commitments with respect to the issuance of unissued shares or the reissuance of treasury shares; and the relative rights and privileges of the various types of stock authorized. Although the book value per share figure is useful in some cases, in some instances it is not meaningful for decision-making purposes—most especially when assets have greatly appreciated in value.

16. Cash Flow Per Share

One of the most popular yet least understood ratios used today is **cash flow per share.** It is computed by dividing net income plus noncash charges (such as depreciation and amortization) by the number of shares of common stock outstanding. The cash flow per share for Anetek is:

$$\text{Cash flow per share} = \frac{\text{Net income + noncash adjustments}}{\text{Outstanding shares}}$$

$$= \frac{\$150,000 + \$150,000}{30,000} = \$10.00$$

This amount represents neither the flow of cash through the enterprise nor the residual of the cash received minus the cash disbursed divided by the outstanding shares of stock. It is frequently used to approximate the amount of cash generated internally.

At present, the profession specifies that cash flow per share may not be presented in annual reports to stockholders.[12] The concern has been that cash flow per share can be misleading and may be used as a measure of profitability. A summary of all the ratios is presented in Illustration 25-7.

---

[11]If the preferred stock has a liquidating preference as to assets, this is considered in determining book value. For example, if the preferred stockholders receive $360,000 at liquidation instead of $300,000, then an additional $60,000 is allocated to the preferred.

[12]"Statement of Cash Flows," *Statement of Financial Accounting Standards No. 95* (Stamford, Conn.: FASB, November, 1987). Note that the cash flow discussed above is highly simplified; it does not adjust for changes in receivables, payables, and other current assets and liabilities affecting operations.

Anetek Chemical Corporation

Ratio	Formula for Computation	Computation
I. Liquidity		
1. Current ratio	$\dfrac{\text{Current assets}}{\text{Current liabilities}}$	$\dfrac{\$800,000}{\$575,000} = 1.39$ times
2. Quick or acid-test ratio	$\dfrac{\text{Cash, marketable securities, and receivables}}{\text{Current liabilities}}$	$\dfrac{\$490,000}{\$575,000} = .85$ times
3. Defensive-interval measure	$\dfrac{\text{Defensive assets}}{\text{Projected daily expenditures minus noncash expenditures}}$	$\dfrac{\$490,000}{\dfrac{\$1,525,000 - \$150,000}{365}} = 130$ days
II. Activity		
4. Receivable turnover	$\dfrac{\text{Net sales}}{\text{Average trade receivables (net)}}$	$\dfrac{\$1,600,000}{\dfrac{\$350,000 + \$300,000}{2}} = 4.92$ times, every 74 days
5. Inventory turnover	$\dfrac{\text{Cost of goods sold}}{\text{Average inventory}}$	$\dfrac{\$1,000,000}{\dfrac{\$310,000 + \$250,000}{2}} = 3.57$ times, every 102 days
6. Asset turnover	$\dfrac{\text{Net sales}}{\text{Average total assets}}$	$\dfrac{\$1,600,000}{\dfrac{\$2,250,000 + \$2,100,000}{2}} = .74$ times
III. Profitability		
7. Profit margin on sales	$\dfrac{\text{Net income}}{\text{Net sales}}$	$\dfrac{\$150,000}{\$1,600,000} = 9.4\%$
8. Rate of return on assets	$\dfrac{\text{Net income}}{\text{Average total assets}}$	$\dfrac{\$150,000}{\dfrac{\$2,250,000 + \$2,100,000}{2}} = 6.9\%$
9. Rate of return on common stock equity	$\dfrac{\text{Net income minus preferred dividends}}{\text{Average common stockholders' equity}}$	$\dfrac{\$150,000}{\dfrac{\$950,000 + \$867,500}{2}} = 16.5\%$
10. Earnings per share	$\dfrac{\text{Net income minus preferred dividends}}{\text{Weighted shares outstanding}}$	$\dfrac{\$150,000}{30,000} = \$5.00$
11. Price earnings ratio	$\dfrac{\text{Market price of stock}}{\text{Earnings per share}}$	$\dfrac{\$60}{\$5} = 12$ times
12. Payout ratio	$\dfrac{\text{Cash dividends}}{\text{Net income}}$	$\dfrac{\$67,500}{\$150,000} = 45\%$
IV. Coverage		
13. Debt to total assets	$\dfrac{\text{Debt}}{\text{Total assets or equities}}$	$\dfrac{\$1,300,000}{\$2,250,000} = 58\%$
14. Times interest earned	$\dfrac{\text{Income before interest charges and taxes}}{\text{Interest charges}}$	$\dfrac{\$300,000}{\$50,000} = 6$ times
15. Book value per share	$\dfrac{\text{Common stockholders' equity}}{\text{Outstanding shares}}$	$\dfrac{\$950,000}{30,000} = \$31.67$
16. Cash flow per share	$\dfrac{\text{Income plus noncash adjustments}}{\text{Outstanding shares}}$	$\dfrac{\$150,000 + \$150,000}{30,000} = \$10.00$

ILLUSTRATION 25-7 Summary of Financial Ratios

▶ LIMITATIONS OF RATIO ANALYSIS

OBJECTIVE 3

Explain the limitations of ratio analysis.

The reader of financial statements must understand the basic limitations associated with ratio analysis. As analytical tools, ratios are attractive because they are simple and convenient. But too frequently, decisions are based on only these simple computations. The ratios are only as good as the data upon which they are based and the information with which they are compared.

One important limitation of ratios is that they are **based on historical cost, which can lead to distortions in measuring performance.** By failing to incorporate changing price information, many believe that inaccurate assessments of the enterprise's financial condition and performance result.

Also, investors must remember that **where estimated items (such as depreciation and amortization) are significant, income ratios lose some of their credibility.** Income recognized before the termination of the life of the business is an approximation. In analyzing the income statement, the user should be aware of the uncertainty surrounding the computation of net income. As one writer aptly noted, "The physicist has long since conceded that the location of an electron is best expressed by a probability curve. Surely an abstraction like earnings per share is even more subject to the rules of probability and risk."[13]

Probably the greatest criticism of ratio analysis is the **difficult problem of achieving comparability among firms in a given industry.** Achieving comparability among firms requires that the analyst (1) identify basic differences existing in their accounting principles and procedures and (2) adjust the balances to achieve comparability.

Basic differences in accounting usually involve one of the following areas:

UNDERLYING CONCEPT

Consistency and comparability are important concepts when financial statement analysis is performed. If the principles and assumptions used to prepare the financial statements are continually changing, it becomes difficult to make accurate assessments of a company's progress.

1. Inventory valuation (FIFO, LIFO, average cost).
2. Depreciation methods, particularly the use of straight-line versus accelerated depreciation.
3. Capitalization versus expense of certain costs, particularly costs involved in developing natural resources.
4. Pooling versus purchase in accounting for business combinations.
5. Capitalization of leases versus noncapitalization.
6. Investments in common stock carried at equity, and fair value.
7. Differing treatments of postretirement benefit costs.
8. Questionable practices of defining discontinued operations, impairments, and extraordinary items.

The use of these different alternatives can make quite a significant difference in the ratios computed. For example, in the brewing industry, at one time Anheuser-Busch noted that if it had used average cost for inventory valuation instead of LIFO, inventories would have increased approximately $33,000,000. Such an increase would have a substantive impact on the current ratio. Several studies have analyzed the impact of different accounting methods on financial statement analysis. The differences in income that can develop are staggering in some cases.[14] The average investor may find it difficult to grasp all these differences, but investors must be aware of the potential pitfalls if they are to be able to make the proper adjustments.

Finally, it must be recognized that a **substantial amount of important information** is not included in a company's financial statements. Events involving such things as industry changes, management changes, competitors' actions, technological developments, government actions, and union activities are often critical to a company's suc-

---

[13]Richard E. Cheney, "How Dependable Is the Bottom Line?" *The Financial Executive* (January 1971), p. 12.

[14]An example of such a descriptive study is: Curtis L. Norton and Ralph E. Smith, "A Comparison of General Price Level and Historical Cost Financial Statements in the Prediction of Bankruptcy," *The Accounting Review* (January 1979), pp. 72–87.

cessful operation. These events occur continuously, and information about them must come from careful analysis of financial reports in the media and other sources. Indeed many argue, under what is known as the **efficient market hypothesis,** that financial statements contain "no surprises" to those engaged in market activities. They contend that the effect of these events is known in the marketplace—and the price of the company's stock adjusts accordingly—well before the issuance of such reports.

▶ REPORTING RATIOS—SOME ISSUES

Rate of return on assets or equity is commonly computed, and therefore some argue that this type of data should be provided in the financial reports. In fact, some believe that the FASB should simply require the reporting of the more common ratios in the financial statements.

Whether the FASB should establish standards for the reporting of ratios is debatable. Some argue that the FASB is already involved in requiring standards in this area, given its requirement that EPS information be disclosed on the face of the income statement for publicly held companies. Furthermore, because EPS is the only ratio required, many believe undue emphasis is given to it. To discourage this emphasis, some argue that additional ratio information should be presented, such as rate of return on assets and equity.

Others, however, believe that the FASB should not be involved in developing standards related to the presentation of ratios. A basic concern expressed by this group is how far the FASB should go. That is, where does financial reporting end and financial analysis begin? Furthermore, we know so little concerning which ratios are used and in what combinations that attempting to require disclosure of certain ratios in this area would not be helpful.[15] One reason for the profession's reluctance to mandate disclosures is that research regarding the use and usefulness of summary indicators is still limited and inconclusive. Some of the major findings to date are as follows:

PREDICTABILITY STUDIES

Because no one knows for certain what an enterprise's future operating and financial results will be, much emphasis is placed on past and current performance as indicators of the future. One interesting approach using financial ratios has been the use of predictive models to determine whether a company is headed for bankruptcy or for increased profitability.

Several studies have been partially successful in using a combination of ratios to predict a possible bankruptcy. One study found the ratio of cash flow to total debt was the best predictor of bankruptcy. It showed that financial ratios can be used to predict failure five years prior to its actual occurrence.[16] A more recent study in this regard highlights the importance of the following ratios as predictors of bankruptcy: return on assets, interest coverage, current assets to current liabilities, and retained earnings to total assets.[17]

---

[15]For an expanded discussion of these points, see Frishkoff, *op. cit.*

[16]William H. Beaver, "Financial Ratios as Predictors of Failure," Empirical Research in Accounting, Selected Studies, 1966, *Journal of Accounting Research,* pp. 71–127; and William H. Beaver, "Alternative Accounting Measures as Predictors of Failures," *The Accounting Review* (January 1968), pp. 113–122. See also E. B. Deakin, "Discriminate Analysis of Predictors of Business Failure," *Journal of Accounting Research* (Spring 1972), pp. 167–179.

[17]See E. I. Altman and J. Spivak, "Predicting Bankruptcy: The Value Line Relative Financial Strength System vs. the Zeta Bankruptcy Classification Approach," *Financial Analysts Journal* (November–December 1983). In addition, see Edward I. Altman, *Corporate Financial Distress and Bankruptcy* (New York: John Wiley & Sons, 1993).

Ratios also have been used to predict other types of events, such as bank lending decisions, credit ratings, mergers and acquisitions, and so on, although success has been limited in these areas. Attempts to predict profitability have met with dismal failure.

SURVEY AND INTERVIEW STUDIES

These studies generally attempt to determine what financial statement users believe are the most appropriate ratios for analysis purposes. One of the most significant studies suggests that information on return on investment, cash flows, changes in financial position, effects of inflation, and components of earnings are more important than earnings per share.[18]

BEHAVIORAL RESEARCH

Experiments that examine the decision-making process given the use of certain information (often referred to as behavioral research) are few and limited in scope. In short, we do not know how information is used, except in a very controlled environment. Some limited evidence on credit granting activities by bank loan officers suggests that reasonable predictions of business failure can be made using only certain key ratios.[19]

Such studies indicate the potential that ratio analysis holds. Although this type of analysis has many limitations, the merits of ratio analysis as a method for analyzing a business situation should be recognized.[20]

▶ COMPARATIVE ANALYSIS

OBJECTIVE 4

Describe techniques of comparative analysis.

In **comparative analysis** the same information is presented for two or more different dates or periods so that like items may be compared. Ratio analysis provides only a single snapshot, the analysis being for one given point or period in time. In a comparative analysis, an investment analyst can concentrate on a given item and determine whether it appears to be growing or diminishing year by year and the proportion of such change to related items. Generally, companies present comparative financial statements.[21]

In addition, many companies include in their annual reports 5- or 10-year summaries of pertinent data that permit the reader to examine and analyze trends. *ARB No. 43* concluded that "the presentation of comparative financial statements in annual and other reports enhances the usefulness of such reports and brings out more clearly the nature and trends of current changes affecting the enterprise." An illustration of a 5-year condensed statement with additional supporting data as presented by Anetek Chemical Corporation is presented in Illustration 25-8.

---

[18]Louis Harris and Associates, Inc., "A Study of the Attitudes Toward an Assessment of the Financial Accounting Standards Board" (Stamford, Conn.: Financial Accounting Foundation, 1980).

[19]See, for example, Robert Libby, "Accounting Ratios and the Prediction of Failure: Some Behavioral Evidence," *Journal of Accounting Research* (Spring 1975), pp. 150–161.

[20]See K. H. Chen and T. A. Shimerda, "An Empirical Analysis of Useful Financial Ratios," *Financial Management*, (Spring 1981), for a codification of the results of numerous studies on the usefulness of various financial ratios.

[21]In 1993 all 600 companies surveyed in *Accounting Trends and Techniques* presented comparative 1991 amounts in their 1992 balance sheets and presented comparative 1990 and 1991 amounts in their 1992 income statements.

Anetek Chemical Corporation CONDENSED COMPARATIVE STATEMENTS (000,000 omitted)							
	1996	1995	1994	1993	1992	10 Years Ago 1986	20 Years Ago 1976
Sales and other revenue:							
Net sales	$1,600.0	$1,350.0	$1,309.7	$1,176.2	$1,077.5	$636.2	$170.7
Other revenue	75.0	50.0	39.4	34.1	24.6	9.0	3.7
Total	1,675.0	1,400.0	1,349.1	1,210.3	1,102.1	645.2	174.4
Costs and other charges:							
Cost of sales	1,000.0	850.0	827.4	737.6	684.2	386.8	111.0
Depreciation and amortization	150.0	150.0	122.6	115.6	98.7	82.4	14.2
Selling and administrative expenses	225.0	150.0	144.2	133.7	126.7	66.7	10.7
Interest expense	50.0	25.0	28.5	20.7	9.4	8.9	1.8
Taxes on income	100.0	75.0	79.5	73.5	68.3	42.4	12.4
Total	1,525.0	1,250.0	1,202.2	1,081.1	987.3	587.2	150.1
Net income for the year	$ 150.0	$ 150.0	$ 146.9	$ 129.2	$ 114.8	$ 58.0	$ 24.3
Other Statistics							
Earnings per share on common stock (in dollars)[a]	$ 5.00	$ 5.00	$ 4.90	$ 3.58	$ 3.11	$ 1.66	$ 1.06
Cash dividends per share on common stock (in dollars)[a]	2.25	2.15	1.95	1.79	1.71	1.11	.25
Cash dividends declared on common stock	67.5	64.5	58.5	64.6	63.1	38.8	5.7
Stock dividend at approximate market value				46.8		27.3	
Taxes (major)	144.5	125.9	116.5	105.6	97.8	59.8	17.0
Wages paid	389.3	325.6	302.1	279.6	263.2	183.2	48.6
Cost of employee benefits	50.8	36.2	32.9	28.7	27.2	18.4	4.4
Number of employees at year end (thousands)	47.4	36.4	35.0	33.8	33.2	26.6	14.6
Additions to property	306.3	192.3	241.5	248.3	166.1	185.0	49.0

[a]Adjusted for stock splits and stock dividends.

ILLUSTRATION 25-8
Condensed Comparative
Financial Information

► PERCENTAGE (COMMON SIZE) ANALYSIS

Analysts also use percentage analysis to help them evaluate and compare companies. **Percentage analysis** consists of reducing a series of related amounts to a series of percentages of a given base. All items in an income statement are frequently expressed as a percentage of sales or sometimes as a percentage of cost of goods sold. A balance sheet may be analyzed on the basis of total assets. This analysis facilitates comparison and is helpful in evaluating the relative size of items or the relative change in items. A conversion of absolute dollar amounts to percentages may also facilitate comparison between companies of different size. To illustrate, here is a comparative analysis of the expense section of Anetek for the last 2 years.

OBJECTIVE 5

Describe techniques of percentage analysis.

ILLUSTRATION 25-9
Horizontal Percentage
Analysis

Anetek Chemical				
	1996	1995	Difference	% Change Inc. (dec.)
Cost of sales	$1,000.0	$850.0	$150.0	17.6
Depreciation and amortization	150.0	150.0	0	0
Selling and administrative expenses	225.0	150.0	75.0	50.0
Interest expense	50.0	25.0	25.0	100.0
Taxes	100.0	75.0	25.0	33.3

This approach, normally called **horizontal analysis,** indicates the proportionate change over a period of time. It is especially useful in evaluating a trend situation, because absolute changes are often deceiving.

Another approach, called **vertical analysis,** is the proportional expression of each item on a financial statement in a given period to a base figure. For example, Anetek Chemical's income statement using this approach appears below.

ILLUSTRATION 25-10
Vertical Percentage Analysis

Anetek Chemical INCOME STATEMENT (000,000 omitted)		
	Amount	Percentage of Total Revenue
Net sales	$1,600.0	96%
Other revenue	75.0	4
Total revenue	1,675.0	100
Less		
Cost of goods sold	1,000.0	60
Depreciation and amortization	150.0	9
Selling and administrative expenses	225.0	13
Interest expense	50.0	3
Income tax	100.0	6
Total expenses	1,525.0	91
Net income	$ 150.0	9%

Reducing all the dollar amounts to a percentage of a base amount is frequently called **common-size analysis** because all of the statements and all of the years are reduced to a common size; that is, all of the elements within each statement are expressed in percentages of some common number and always add up to 100 percent. Common-size (percentage) analysis is the analysis of the composition of each of the financial statements.

In the analysis of the balance sheet, common-size analysis answers such questions as: What is the distribution of equities between current liabilities, long-term debt, and owners' equity? What is the mix of assets (percentage-wise) with which the enterprise has chosen to conduct its business? What percentage of current assets are in inventory, receivables, and so forth?

The income statement lends itself to common-size analysis because each item in it is related to a common amount, usually sales. It is instructive to know what proportion of each sales dollar is absorbed by various costs and expenses incurred by the enterprise.

Common-size statements may be used for comparing one company's statements from different years to detect trends not evident from the comparison of absolute amounts. Also, common-size statements provide intercompany comparisons regardless of size because the financial statements can be recast into a comparable common-size format.

KEY TERMS

▶ **SUMMARY OF LEARNING OBJECTIVES** ◀

1. Understand the approach to financial statement analysis. Basic financial statement analysis involves examining relationships between items on the statements (ratio and percentage analysis) and identifying trends in these relationships (comparative analysis). Analysis is used to predict the future, but ratio analysis is limited because the data are from the past. Also, ratio analysis identifies present strengths and weaknesses of a company but it may not reveal why they are as they are. Although single ratios are helpful, they are not conclusive; they must be compared with industry averages, past years, planned amounts, and the like for maximum usefulness.

2. **Identify major analytic ratios and describe their calculation.** Ratios are classified as liquidity ratios, activity ratios, profitability ratios, and coverage ratios: (1) *Liquidity ratio analysis* measures the short-run ability of the enterprise to pay its currently maturing obligations. (2) *Activity ratio analysis* measures how effectively the enterprise is using its assets. (3) *Profitability ratio analysis* measures the degree of success or failure of an enterprise to generate revenues adequate to cover its costs of operation and provide a return to the owners. (4) *Coverage ratio analysis* measures the degree of protection afforded long-term creditors and investors.

3. **Explain the limitations of ratio analysis.** One important limitation of ratios is that they are based on historical cost, which can lead to distortions in measuring performance. Also, where estimated items (such as depreciation and amortization) are significant, income ratios lose some of their credibility. In addition, difficult problems of comparability develop when changes in principles and procedures occur. Finally, it must be recognized that a substantial amount of important information is not included in a company's financial statements.

4. **Describe techniques of comparative analysis.** Companies present comparative data, which generally includes two years of balance sheet information and three years of income statement information. In addition, many companies include in their annual reports 5- to 10-year summaries of pertinent data that permit the reader to examine and analyze trends.

5. **Describe techniques of percentage analysis.** Percentage analysis consists of reducing a series of related amounts to a series of percentages of a given base. Two approaches are often used. The first, called horizontal analysis, indicates the proportionate change in financial statement items over a period of time; such analysis is most helpful in evaluating trends. Vertical analysis (common-size analysis) is proportional expression of each item on the financial statements in a given period to a base amount. It analyzes the composition of each of the financial statements from different years (a) to detect trends not evident from the comparison of absolute amounts and (b) to make intercompany comparisons of different sized enterprises.

QUESTIONS

1. "The significance of financial statement data is not in the amount alone." Discuss the meaning of this statement.

2. A close friend of yours, who is a history major and who has not had any college courses or any experience in business, is receiving the financial statements from companies in which he has minor investments (acquired for him by his now deceased father). He asks you what he needs to know to interpret and to evaluate the financial statement data that he is receiving. What would you tell him?

3. Distinguish between ratio analysis and percentage analysis relative to the interpretation of financial statements. What is the value of these two types of analysis?

4. The controller of an international transport company has requested you to include in your report certain balance sheet and income statement ratios so that comparisons may be made. Indicate the types or categories of ratios that might be provided and explain their significance.

5. Of what significance is the current ratio? If this ratio is too low, what may it signify? Can this ratio be too high? Explain.

6. How does the acid-test ratio differ from the current ratio? How are they similar? Of what benefit is the defensive interval ratio?

7. Answer each of the questions in the following unrelated situations:
   (a) The current ratio of a company is 5 : 1 and its acid-test ratio is 1 : 1. If the inventories and prepaid items amount to $600,000, what is the amount of current liabilities?

(b) A company had an average inventory last year of $200,000 and its inventory turnover was 5. If sales volume and unit cost remain the same this year as last and inventory turnover is 8 this year, what will average inventory have to be during the current year?

(c) A company has current assets of $90,000 (of which $40,000 is inventory and prepaid items) and current liabilities of $30,000. What is the current ratio? What is the acid-test ratio? If the company borrows $15,000 cash from a bank on a 120-day loan, what will its current ratio be? What will the acid-test ratio be?

(d) A company has current assets of $600,000 and current liabilities of $240,000. The board of directors declares a cash dividend of $180,000. What is the current ratio after the declaration, but before payment? What is the current ratio after the payment of the dividend?

8. Aston Martin Company's budgeted sales and budgeted cost of goods sold for the coming year are $144,000,000 and $90,000,000 respectively. Short-term interest rates are expected to average 10%. If Aston Martin can increase inventory turnover from its present level of nine times a year to a level of 12 times per year, compute its expected cost savings for the coming year.

9. One member of the board of directors suggests that the corporation maximize trading on equity, that is, using stockholders' equity as a basis for borrowing additional funds at a lower rate of interest than the expected earnings from the use of the borrowed funds.
   (a) Explain how a change in income tax rates affects trading on equity.
   (b) Explain how trading on equity affects earnings per share of common stock.
   (c) Under what circumstances should a corporation seek to trade on equity to a substantial degree?

10. In calculating inventory turnover, why is cost of goods sold used as the numerator? As the inventory turnover increases, what increasing risk does the business assume?

11. What is the relationship of the asset turnover ratio to the rate of return on assets?

12. Of what importance are the following ratios in financial analysis?
    (a) Stockholders' equity to total assets or equity.
    (b) Debt to total assets or equity.
    (c) Times interest earned.
    (d) Ratio of plant assets to long-term liabilities.

13. Explain the meaning of the following terms:
    (a) Payout ratio.
    (b) Earnings per share.
    (c) Dividend yield.
    (d) Price-earnings ratio.

14. Ferrari Company's net accounts receivable were $1,000,000 at December 31, 1996 and $1,200,000 at December 31, 1997. Net cash sales for 1997 were $400,000. The accounts receivable turnover for 1997 was 5.0. Determine Ferrari's net sales for 1997.

15. What is meant by book value? Of what significance is preferred stock in the computation of book value?

16. Discuss the inherent limitations of single-year statements for purposes of analysis and interpretation. Include in your discussion the extent to which these limitations are overcome by the use of comparative statements.

17. Comparative balance sheets and comparative income statements that show a firm's financial history for each of the last 10 years may be misleading. Discuss the factors or conditions that might contribute to misinterpretations. Include a discussion of the additional information and supplementary data that might be included in or provided with the statements to prevent misinterpretations.

18. Explain the meaning of the following terms: (a) common-size analysis, (b) vertical analysis, (c) horizontal analysis, (d) percentage analysis.

19. Presently, the profession requires that earnings per share be disclosed on the face of the income statement. What are some disadvantages of reporting ratios on the financial statements?

20. A student who just completed her first finance course commented, "We didn't use ratio analysis; our instructor indicated that ratio analysis was no longer fashionable." Discuss.

EXERCISES

E25-1 (Computation and Analysis of Inventory Turnover) The controller of DaVinci Company finds that, although the company continues to earn about the same net income year after year, the rate of return on stockholders' equity is decreasing. Most of the profits are permitted to remain in the business so that total assets are increasing year by year, but there is very little increase in net income. As the recently hired chief accountant, you are requested to assist the controller in locating the difficulty and to suggest remedial measures.

Among the matters of interest that you find is the following:

	Inventory Dec. 31	Cost of Goods Sold
1993	$456,000	$3,120,000
1994	545,000	2,960,000
1995	601,000	3,000,000
1996	689,000	3,240,000

Instructions

(a) What conclusions can be reached on the basis of this information only?

(b) What further investigation does it suggest? State exactly how you would proceed.

(c) If your conclusions are confirmed in the additional investigation, what recommendations would you make concerning remedial measures?

E25-2 (Trading on the Equity Analysis) Presented below is information related to Salvador Dali Inc.

Operating income	$ 532,150
Bond interest expense	135,000
	397,150
Income taxes	183,432
Net income	$ 213,718
Bonds payable	$1,000,000
Common stock	875,000
Appropriation for contingencies	75,000
Retained earnings, unappropriated	300,000

Instructions

Is Salvador Dali Inc. trading on the equity successfully? Explain.

E25-3 (Ratio Computations and Analysis) Degas Ballet Company's condensed financial statements provide the following information:

BALANCE SHEET

	Dec. 31, 1996	Dec. 31, 1995
Cash	$ 52,000	$ 60,000
Accounts receivable (net)	198,000	80,000
Marketable securities (short-term)	80,000	40,000
Inventories	440,000	360,000
Prepaid expenses	3,000	7,000
Total current assets	$ 773,000	$ 547,000
Property, plant, and equipment (net)	857,000	853,000
Total assets	$1,630,000	$1,400,000
Current liabilities	240,000	160,000
Bonds payable	400,000	400,000
Common stockholders' equity	990,000	840,000
Total liabilities and stockholders' equity	$1,630,000	$1,400,000

INCOME STATEMENT
For the Year Ended 1996

Sales	$1,640,000
Cost of goods sold	(800,000)
Gross profit	840,000
Selling and administrative expense	(440,000)
Interest expense	(40,000)
Net income	$ 360,000

Instructions

(a) Determine the following:
  1. Current ratio at December 31, 1996.
  2. Acid-test ratio at December 31, 1996.
  3. Accounts receivable turnover for 1996.
  4. Inventory turnover for 1996.
  5. Rate of return on assets for 1996.
  6. Rate of return on common stock equity for 1996.

(b) Prepare a brief evaluation of the financial condition of Degas Ballet Company and of the adequacy of its profits.

E25-4 (Ratio Computation and Analysis; Liquidity) As loan analyst for Utrillo Bank, you have been presented the following information:

	Toulouse Co.	Lautrec Co.
Assets		
Cash	$ 120,000	$ 320,000
Receivables	220,000	302,000
Inventories	570,000	518,000
Total current assets	910,000	1,140,000
Other assets	500,000	612,000
Total assets	$1,410,000	$1,752,000
Liabilities and Capital		
Current liabilities	$ 305,000	$ 350,000
Long-term liabilities	400,000	500,000
Capital stock and retained earnings	705,000	902,000
Total liabilities and capital	$1,410,000	$1,752,000
Annual sales	$ 930,000	$1,500,000
Rate of gross profit on sales	30%	40%

Each of these companies has requested a loan of $50,000 for six months with no collateral offered. Inasmuch as your bank has reached its quota for loans of this type, only one of these requests is to be granted.

Instructions
Which of the two companies, as judged by the information given above, would you recommend as the better risk and why? Assume that the ending account balances are representative of the entire year.

E25-5 (Analysis of Given Ratios) Picasso Company is a wholesale distributor of professional equipment and supplies. The company's sales have averaged about $900,000 annually for the 3-year period 1993–1995. The firm's total assets at the end of 1995 amounted to $850,000.

The president of Picasso Company has asked the controller to prepare a report that summarizes the financial aspects of the company's operations for the past 3 years. This report will be presented to the Board of Directors at their next meeting.

In addition to comparative financial statements, the controller has decided to present a number of relevant financial ratios which can assist in the identification and interpretation of trends. At the request of the controller, the accounting staff has calculated the following ratios for the 3-year period 1993–1995:

	1993	1994	1995
Current ratio	1.80	1.89	1.96
Acid-test (quick) ratio	1.04	0.99	0.87
Accounts receivable turnover	8.75	7.71	6.42
Inventory turnover	4.91	4.32	3.42
Percent of total debt to total assets	51	46	41
Percent of long-term debt to total assets	31	27	24
Sales to fixed assets (fixed asset turnover)	1.58	1.69	1.79
Sales as a percent of 1993 sales	1.00	1.03	1.07
Gross margin percentage	36.0	35.1	34.6
Net income to sales	6.9%	7.0%	7.2%
Return on total assets	7.7%	7.7%	7.8%
Return on stockholders' equity	13.6%	13.1%	12.7%

In preparation of the report, the controller has decided first to examine the financial ratios independently of any other data to determine if the ratios themselves reveal any significant trends over the 3-year period.

Instructions

(a) The current ratio is increasing while the acid-test (quick) ratio is decreasing. Using the ratios provided, identify and explain the contributing factor(s) for this apparently divergent trend.

(b) In terms of the ratios provided, what conclusion(s) can be drawn regarding the company's use of financial leverage during the 1993–1995 period?

(c) Using the ratios provided, what conclusion(s) can be drawn regarding the company's net investment in plant and equipment?

(CMA adapted)

E25-6 (Ratio Computations and Effect of Transactions) Presented below is information related to Currier & Ives Inc.:

Currier & Ives Inc.
BALANCE SHEET
December 31, 1996

Cash		$ 45,000	Notes payable (short-term)	$ 50,000
Receivables	$110,000		Accounts payable	32,000
less allowance	15,000	95,000	Accrued liabilities	5,000
Inventories		170,000	Capital stock (par $5)	260,000
Prepaid insurance		8,000	Retained earnings	141,000
Land		20,000		
Equipment (net)		150,000		
		$488,000		$488,000

STATEMENT OF INCOME
Year Ended December 31, 1996

Sales		$1,400,000
Cost of Sales		
Inventory, Jan. 1, 1996	$200,000	
Purchases	790,000	
Cost of goods available for sale	990,000	
Inventory, Dec. 31, 1996	170,000	
Cost of goods sold		820,000
Gross Profit on Sales		580,000
Operating Expenses		170,000
Net Income		$ 410,000

Instructions

(a) Compute the following ratios or relationships of Currier & Ives Inc. Assume that the ending account balances are representative unless the information provided indicates differently.
   1. Current ratio.
   2. Inventory turnover.
   3. Receivables turnover.
   4. Earnings per share.
   5. Profit margin on sales.
   6. Rate of return on common stock equity on December 31, 1996.

(b) Indicate for each of the following transactions whether the transaction would improve, weaken, or have no effect on the current ratio of Currier & Ives Inc. at December 31, 1996.
   1. Write off an uncollectible account receivable, $2,200.
   2. Purchase additional capital stock for cash.
   3. Pay $40,000 on notes payable (short-term).
   4. Collect $23,000 on accounts receivable.
   5. Buy equipment on account.
   6. Give an existing creditor a short-term note in settlement of account.

E25-7 (Computation and Analysis of Ratios) Max Liebermann Co. declared bankruptcy in 1996. The company's financial statements for the three most recent years are as follows:

INCOME STATEMENT

	(figures are in 000s)		
	1993	1994	1995
Sales	$5,000	$5,200	$5,500
Cost of goods sold	3,000	3,100	4,000
Gross profit	2,000	2,100	1,500
Operating expenses	1,150	1,300	1,400
Operating income	850	800	100
Interest expense	150	250	400
Income before taxes	700	550	(300)
Income tax	210	150	–0–
Net income	490	400	(300)
Common stock dividends	$ 200	$ 200	$ –0–

BALANCE SHEET

Assets			
Cash	$ 500	$ 100	$ 10
Marketable securities	400	100	–0–
Accounts receivable	100	300	500
Inventories	300	210	100
Total current assets	1,300	710	610
Land and buildings	2,000	3,000	4,000
Machinery and equipment	500	800	1,500
Other	300	600	500
Less: Accumulated depreciation	1,000	1,400	1,800
Net fixed assets	1,800	3,000	4,200
Total assets	$3,100	$3,710	$4,810
Liabilities and Stockholders' Equity			
Accounts payable	$ 100	$ 50	$ 20
Notes payable	100	150	150
Accruals	200	100	180
Total current liabilities	400	300	350
Long-term debt	1,000	1,510	2,860
Par value of common stock	710	710	710
Paid-in capital in excess of par	300	300	300
Retained earnings	690	890	590
Total stockholders' equity	1,700	1,900	1,600
Total liabilities and stockholders' equity	$3,100	$3,710	$4,810

Instructions

(a) Using the financial statements provided, identify causes of the firm's financial difficulties.

(b) Using the financial statements provided, explain how the company could have either avoided these financial difficulties or resolved the difficulties as they developed.

E25-8 (Ratio Analysis) Edna Millay Inc. is a manufacturer of electronic components and accessories with total assets of $20,000,000. Selected financial ratios for Millay and the industry averages for firms of similar size are presented below.

	Edna Millay			1996 Industry Average
	1994	1995	1996	
Current ratio	2.09	2.27	2.51	2.24
Quick ratio	1.15	1.12	1.19	1.22
Inventory turnover	2.40	2.18	2.02	3.50
Net sales to net worth	2.71	2.80	2.99	2.85
Net income to net worth	0.14	0.15	0.17	0.11
Total liabilities to net worth	1.41	1.37	1.44	0.95

Millay is being reviewed by several entities whose interests vary, and the company's financial ratios are a part of the data being considered. Each of the parties listed below must recommend an action based on its evaluation of Millay's financial position.

Archibald MacLeish Bank. The bank is processing Millay's application for a new 5-year term note. Archibald MacLeish has been Millay's banker for several years, but must reevaluate the company's financial position for each major transaction.

Robert Lowell Company. Lowell is a new supplier to Millay, and must decide on the appropriate credit terms to extend to the company.

Robert Penn Warren. A brokerage firm specializing in the stock of electronics firms that are sold over-the-counter, Robert Penn Warren must decide if it will include Millay in a new fund being established for sale to Robert Penn Warren's clients.

Working Capital Management Committee. This is a committee of Millay's management personnel chaired by the chief operating officer. The committee is charged with the responsibility of periodically reviewing the company's working capital position, comparing actual data against budgets, and recommending changes in strategy as needed.

Instructions
(a) Describe the analytical use of each of the six ratios presented above.
(b) For each of the four entities described above, identify two financial ratios, from those ratios presented, that would be most valuable as a basis for its decision regarding Millay.
(c) Discuss what the financial ratios presented in the question reveal about Millay. Support your answer by citing specific ratio levels and trends as well as the interrelationships between these ratios.

(CMA adapted)

E25-9 (Ratio Computations and Discussion) e. e. cummings Company has been operating for several years, and on December 31, 1996, presented the following balance sheet:

---

e. e. cummings Company
BALANCE SHEET
December 31, 1996

Cash	$ 40,000	Accounts payable	$ 80,000
Receivables	75,000	Mortgage payable	140,000
Inventories	95,000	Common stock ($1.00 par)	150,000
Plant assets (net)	220,000	Retained earnings	60,000
	$430,000		$430,000

The net income for 1996 was $25,000. Projected annual operational expenditures (based on past data) exclusive of depreciation are $45,000. Assume that total assets are the same in 1995 and 1996.

Instructions
Compute each of the following ratios. For each of the five indicate the manner in which it is computed and its significance as a tool in the analysis of the financial soundness of the company.
(a) Current ratio.
(b) Acid-test ratio.
(c) Defensive interval measure.
(d) Debt to total assets.
(e) Rate of return on assets.

E25-10 (Ratio Computation) Financial information for Ogden Nash Company is presented below.

Assets	12/31/96	12/31/95
Cash	$ 140,000	$ 165,000
Receivables (net)	340,000	198,000
Inventories	1,350,000	980,000
Short-term investments	200,000	600,000
Prepaid items	40,000	60,000
Land	580,000	400,000
Building and equipment (net)	2,000,000	1,760,000
	$4,650,000	$4,163,000

Equities	12/31/96	12/31/95
Accounts payable	$ 730,000	$ 543,000
Notes payable	400,000	150,000
Accrued liabilities	100,000	100,000
Bonds payable due 1998	700,000	820,000
Common stock	2,000,000	2,000,000
Retained earnings	720,000	550,000
	$4,650,000	$4,163,000

Ogden Nash Company
COMPARATIVE INCOME STATEMENT
Years Ended December 31, 1996 and 1995

	1996	1995
Sales	$4,400,000	$3,900,000
Cost of goods sold	3,250,000	3,100,000
Gross profit	1,150,000	800,000
Operating expenses	520,000	450,000
Net income	$ 630,000	$ 350,000

Instructions

From these data compute as many ratios presented in the chapter, for both years, as possible. Assume that the ending account balances for 1995 are representative unless the information provided indicates differently. The beginning inventory for 1995 was $720,000.

E25-11 (Comparison of Alternative Forms of Financing) Shown below is the equity section of the balance sheet for James Joyce Company and Marianne Moore Company. Each has assets totaling $4,200,000.

James Joyce Co.		Marianne Moore Co.	
Current liabilities	$ 300,000	Current liabilities	$ 600,000
Long-term debt, 10%	1,200,000	Common stock ($20 par)	2,900,000
Common stock ($20 par)	2,000,000	Retained earnings	700,000
Retained earnings	700,000		
	$4,200,000		$4,200,000

For the last 2 years each company has earned the same income before interest and taxes.

	James Joyce Co.	Marianne Moore Co.
Income before interest and taxes	$1,200,000	$1,200,000
Interest expense	120,000	–0–
	1,080,000	1,200,000
Income taxes (45%)	486,000	540,000
Net income	$ 594,000	$ 660,000

Instructions

(a) Which company is more profitable in terms of return on total assets?
(b) Which company is more profitable in terms of return on stockholders' equity?
(c) Which company has the greater net income per share of stock? Why?
(d) From the point of view of income, is it advantageous to the stockholders of James Joyce Co. to have the long-term debt outstanding? Why?

E25-12 (Ratio Computations) Presented below is information related to Walter de la Mare Company for 1996:

Sales	$440,000	Market price of stock at year end	$28 per share
Net income	34,000	Cash dividend per share	$.50
Average total assets	220,000	Earnings per share	$.84
Average stockholders' equity	50,000		

Instructions

(a) Compute the following ratios for 1996:
1. Profit margin on sales.
2. Rate of return on stockholders' equity.
3. Rate of return on total assets.
4. Price-earnings ratio.

(b) Compute the following for 1997, assuming in each case that all other factors remain constant:
1. Total sales if the profit margin on sales is 10%.
2. Average total assets if the asset turnover is two times.
3. Net income if the earnings per share is $3.50.
4. Rate of return on stockholders' equity, assuming that stockholders' equity increases 10 percent.
5. Asset turnover, assuming that average total assets increase $40,000.

E25-13 (Computation of Book Value per Share) Sylvia Plath Inc. began operations in January 1994 and reported the following results for each of its 3 years of operations:

1994	$260,000 net loss	1995	$40,000 net loss	1996	$800,000 net income

At December 31, 1996, Sylvia Plath Inc. capital accounts were as follows:

8% cumulative preferred stock, par value $100; authorized, issued, and outstanding 5,000 shares	$500,000
Common stock, par value $1.00; authorized 1,000,000 shares; issued and outstanding 750,000 shares	$750,000

Sylvia Plath Inc. has never paid a cash or stock dividend. There has been no change in the capital accounts since Sylvia Plath began operations. The state law permits dividends only from retained earnings.

Instructions
(a) Compute the book value of the common stock and preferred stock at December 31, 1996.
(b) Compute the book value of the common stock and preferred stock at December 31, 1996, assuming that the preferred stock has a liquidating value of $106 per share.

E25-14 (Preparation of Working Capital Section of Balance Sheet from Ratios) You have been engaged to perform management consulting services for D. H. Lawrence Inc. One aspect of the engagement is to project working capital requirements. The sales forecast is $12 million for 1996. Target ratios for this year are as follows:

Cost of sales	55% of sales	Cash	4% of sales
Inventory turnover	6 times	Prepaid expenses	2% of sales
Receivables turnover	10 times	Accrued expenses	3% of sales

Instructions
Prepare the projected working capital section of the balance sheet for 1996. In addition, accounts payable are projected to be $550,000 for 1996. Assume that the beginning and ending accounts receivable and inventory balances have not changed.

PROBLEMS

P25-1 (Ratio Computations and Additional Analysis) Carl Sandburg Corporation was formed 5 years ago through a public subscription of common stock. Robert Frost, who owns 15 percent of the common stock, was one of the organizers of Sandburg and is its current president. The company has been successful, but currently is experiencing a shortage of funds. On June 10, Robert Frost approached the Spokane National Bank, asking for a 24-month extension on two $35,000 notes, which are due on June 30, 1995, and September 30, 1995. Another note of $6,000 is due on December 31, 1996, but he expects no difficulty in paying this note on its due date. Frost explained that Sandburg's cash flow problems are due primarily to the company's desire to finance a $300,000 plant expansion over the next 2 fiscal years through internally generated funds.

The Commercial Loan Officer of Spokane National Bank requested financial reports for the last two fiscal years. These reports are reproduced below.

<table>
<tr><td colspan="3" align="center">Carl Sandburg Corporation
STATEMENT OF FINANCIAL POSITION
March 31</td></tr>
<tr><td>Assets</td><td>1994</td><td>1995</td></tr>
<tr><td>Cash</td><td>$ 12,500</td><td>$ 18,200</td></tr>
<tr><td>Notes receivable</td><td>132,000</td><td>148,000</td></tr>
<tr><td>Accounts receivable (net)</td><td>125,500</td><td>131,800</td></tr>
<tr><td>Inventories (at cost)</td><td>50,000</td><td>95,000</td></tr>
<tr><td>Plant & equipment (net of depreciation)</td><td>1,420,500</td><td>1,449,000</td></tr>
<tr><td>Total assets</td><td>$1,740,500</td><td>$1,842,000</td></tr>
</table>

Liabilities and Owners' Equity

Accounts payable	$ 91,000	$ 69,000
Notes payable	61,500	76,000
Accrued liabilities	6,000	9,000
Common stock (130,000 shares, $10 par)	1,300,000	1,300,000
Retained earnings[a]	282,000	388,000
Total liabilities and owners' equity	$1,740,500	$1,842,000

[a]Cash dividends were paid at the rate of $1.00 per share in fiscal year 1994 and $2.00 per share in fiscal year 1995.

Carl Sandburg Corporation
INCOME STATEMENT
For the Fiscal Years Ended March 31

	1994	1995
Sales	$2,700,000	$3,000,000
Cost of goods sold[a]	1,425,000	1,530,000
Gross margin	$1,275,000	$1,470,000
Operating expenses	780,000	860,000
Income before income taxes	$ 495,000	$ 610,000
Income taxes (40%)	198,000	244,000
Net income	$ 297,000	$ 366,000

[a]Depreciation charges on the plant and equipment of $100,000 and $102,500 for fiscal years ended March 31, 1994 and 1995, respectively, are included in cost of goods sold.

Instructions

(a) Compute the following items for Carl Sandburg Corporation:
   1. Current ratio for fiscal years 1994 and 1995.
   2. Acid test (quick) ratio for fiscal years 1994 and 1995.
   3. Inventory turnover for fiscal year 1995.
   4. Return on assets for fiscal years 1994 and 1995 (assume total assets were $1,688,500 at 3/31/93).
   5. Percentage change in sales, cost of goods sold, gross margin, and net income after taxes from fiscal year 1994 to 1995.
(b) Identify and explain what other financial reports and/or financial analyses might be helpful to the commercial loan officer of Spokane National Bank in evaluating Robert Frost's request for a time extension on Sandburg's notes.
(c) Assume that the percentage changes experienced in fiscal year 1995 as compared with fiscal year 1994 for sales, cost of goods sold, gross margin, and net income after taxes will be repeated in each of the next two years. Is Sandburg's desire to finance the plant expansion from internally generated funds realistic? Discuss.
(d) Should Spokane National Bank grant the extension on Sandburg's notes considering Robert Frost's statement about financing the plant expansion through internally generated funds? Discuss.

(CIA adapted)

P25-2 (Ratio Analysis; Alternative Financing Plans) Harriet Tubman Company is planning to invest $12,000,000 in an expansion program, which is expected to increase income before interest and taxes by $2,200,000. The company currently is earning $2.40 per share on 1,000,000 shares of common stock outstanding. The capital structure prior to the investment is:

Debt	$ 25,000,000
Equity	75,000,000
	$100,000,000

The expansion can be financed by sale of 300,000 shares at $40 net each or by issuing long-term debt at an 8% interest cost. The firm's recent income statement was as follows:

Sales	$100,000,000
Variable cost	$ 65,000,000
Fixed cost	29,000,000
	$ 94,000,000
Income before interest and taxes	$ 6,000,000
Interest	2,000,000

Income before income taxes	$ 4,000,000
Income taxes (40%)	1,600,000
Net income	$ 2,400,000

Instructions

(a) Assuming that the firm maintains its current income and achieves the anticipated income from the expansion, what will be the earnings per share (1) if the expansion is financed by debt? (2) if the expansion is financed by equity?

(b) At what level of income before interest and taxes will the earnings per share under either alternative be the same amount?

(c) The choice of financing alternatives influences the earnings per share. The choice might also influence the earnings multiple used by the "market." Discuss the factors inherent in choice between the debt and equity alternatives that might influence the earnings multiple. Be sure to indicate the direction in which these factors might influence the earnings multiple.

(CMA adapted)

P25-3 (Ratio Analysis; Alternative Financing Plans) Daniel Webster Incorporated has been operating successfully for a number of years. The balance sheet of the company as of December 31 is presented below.

Daniel Webster Incorporated
BALANCE SHEET
December 31, 1996

Assets			**Equities**		
Current assets			Current liabilities		
Cash		$ 50,000	Notes payable		$ 80,000
Accounts receivable (net)		125,000	Accounts payable		97,000
Notes receivable		80,000	Taxes payable		61,000
Inventories		270,000	Total current liabilities		238,000
Prepaid items		20,000			
Total current assets		545,000	Long-term bank loan, due in		
Fixed assets			1999, 10% interest		190,000
Land	$ 30,000		Stockholders' equity		
Building (net)	256,000		Common stock		
Equipment (net)	400,000		($10 par)	$350,000	
Total fixed assets		686,000	Retained		
		$1,231,000	earnings	453,000	803,000
					$1,231,000

This balance sheet indicates that the bulk of the company's growth has been financed by the common stockholders, because $453,000 of past net income of the company has been retained and is now invested in various operating assets. For the last 3 years the company has earned an average net income of $85,000 after interest ($21,000) and taxes ($48,000).

The Board of Directors has been considering an expansion of operations. Estimations indicate that the company can double its volume of operations with an additional investment of about $900,000. Of this amount $600,000 would be used to add to the present building, to purchase new equipment, and to reorganize certain operations. The remaining amount would be needed for working capital—inventories and higher receivables. Competitive conditions are such that the added volume can probably be sold at the existing prices and that income before taxes and interest will total $320,000. The tax rate of about 36% on income after interest will continue.

Three alternative plans for financing the expansion are under consideration:

1. Sell enough additional stock to raise $900,000. For this purpose it is estimated the stock would sell at $30 per share.

2. Sell 20-year bonds at 12% interest, totaling $790,000. In addition, sell 10,000 shares of additional stock at a price of $30 per share. Use part of the proceeds to pay off the present long-term bank loan.

3. Sell 20-year bonds at 12% interest, totaling $900,000. Use part of the proceeds to pay off present long-term bank loans. The remaining funds are to be provided by short-term creditors. The cost of these funds (in interest and discounts not taken) is estimated at $27,000 a year.

Assume that the financing alternative selected will take place immediately.

Instructions

(a) Compute the current ratio under each plan and compare it with the present current ratio.

(b) Compute earnings per share under each plan and compare with the present earnings per share.
(c) Compute the rate of return on common stock equity under each plan and compare with the present return.
(d) Compute the ratio of stockholders' equity to total assets under each plan and compare with present ratio.

P25-4 (Computation of Book Value per Share; Various Assumptions) The stockholders' equity in William Tweed Corp. is as follows:

Preferred stock—9% cumulative, nonparticipating, $50 par			
Authorized 10,000 shares; issued 7,000 shares	$350,000		
Less 500 shares in treasury	25,000		
Outstanding, 6,500 shares	325,000		
Common stock, $1.00 par value			
Authorized 1,000,000 shares; issued 800,000 shares	800,000		
Capital in excess of par	210,000	$1,335,000	
Capital from acquisition of preferred stock below par		3,000	
Retained earnings			
Appropriation for contingencies	46,000		
Appropriation for sinking fund	360,000		
Appropriation for possible inventory decline	75,000		
Unrestricted	284,000	765,000	$2,103,000

Instructions
Compute the book value per share of the common and preferred stock under each of the following conditions:
(a) As stated above, assume that there are no preferred stock dividends in arrears.
(b) Assume the same situation as stated above except that preferred stock dividends are $40,500 in arrears including the current year.
(c) Assume the same situation as in (a) except that the preferred stock is fully participating, based on the ratio of the total par value of the respective stocks outstanding.
(d) Assume the same situation as in (a) except that, instead of retained earnings, the company has a deficit of $525,000.

P25-5 (Ratio Computations) Horace Greeley Corporation's management is concerned about the corporation's current financial position and return on investment. They request your assistance in analyzing their financial statements, and furnish the following statements:

Horace Greeley Corporation
STATEMENT OF WORKING CAPITAL DEFICIT
December 31, 1996

Current liabilities		$224,500
Less current assets:		
Cash	$ 10,000	
Accounts receivable (net)	75,600	
Inventory	117,000	202,600
Working capital deficit		$ 21,900

Horace Greeley Corporation
INCOME STATEMENT
For the Year Ended December 31, 1996

Sales (70,925 units)	$638,325
Cost of goods sold	395,800
Gross profit	242,525
Selling and administrative expenses, including $24,935 depreciation	55,660
Income before income taxes	186,865
Income taxes	82,000
Net income	$104,865

Additional information:

Assets other than current assets consist of land, building, and equipment with a book value of $241,000 on December 31, 1996. Assume that ending account balances are representative of amounts existing throughout the year.

Instructions

Assuming that Horace Greeley Corporation operates 300 days per year, compute the following (use 300 days in all computations):

(a) Accounts receivable turnover.

(b) Inventory turnover.

(c) Number of days' operations (working capital provided by operations) to cover the working capital deficit.

(d) Return on total assets as a product of asset turnover and the profit margin on sales (profit margin ratio).

P25-6 (Ratio Computations) Wheeling Company is listed on the New York Stock Exchange. The market value of its common stock was quoted at $58 per share at December 31, 1996, and 1995. Wheeling Co.'s balance sheet at December 31, 1996, and 1995, and statement of income and retained earnings for the years then ended are presented below:

Wheeling Company
BALANCE SHEET

	December 31, 1996	December 31, 1995
Assets		
Current assets:		
Cash	$ 9,500,000	$ 3,600,000
Available-for-sale securities, at fair value	13,000,000	11,000,000
Accounts receivable, net of allowance for doubtful accounts	123,000,000	141,000,000
Inventories, lower of cost or market	172,000,000	148,000,000
Prepaid expenses	2,500,000	2,400,000
Total current assets	320,000,000	306,000,000
Property, plant, and equipment, net of accumulated depreciation	359,000,000	338,000,000
Investments, at equity	2,000,000	3,000,000
Long-term receivables	14,000,000	18,000,000
Goodwill and patents, net of accumulated amortization	6,000,000	6,500,000
Other assets	7,000,000	8,500,000
Total assets	$708,000,000	$680,000,000
Liabilities and Stockholders' Equity		
Current liabilities:		
Notes payable	$ 10,000,000	$ 20,000,000
Accounts payable	45,000,000	48,000,000
Accrued expenses	31,500,000	27,000,000
Income taxes payable	1,000,000	1,000,000
Payments due within one year on long-term debt	6,500,000	7,000,000
Total current liabilities	94,000,000	103,000,000
Long-term debt	174,000,000	180,000,000
Deferred income taxes	74,000,000	67,000,000
Other liabilities	9,000,000	8,000,000
Stockholders' equity:		
Common stock, par value $1.00 per share; authorized 20,000,000 shares; issued and outstanding 10,000,000 shares	10,000,000	8,000,000
10% cumulative preferred stock, par value $100.00 per share; $100.00 liquidating value; authorized 75,000 shares; issued and outstanding 60,000 shares	6,000,000	6,000,000
Additional paid-in capital	124,000,000	124,000,000
Retained earnings	217,000,000	184,000,000
Total stockholders' equity	357,000,000	322,000,000
Total liabilities and stockholders' equity	$708,000,000	$680,000,000

Wheeling Company
STATEMENT OF INCOME AND RETAINED EARNINGS

	Year ended December 31,	
	1996	1995
Net sales	$800,000,000	$600,000,000
Costs and expenses:		
Cost of goods sold	600,000,000	400,000,000
Selling, general, and administrative expenses	66,000,000	60,000,000
Other, net	7,000,000	6,000,000
Total costs and expenses	673,000,000	466,000,000
Income before income taxes	127,000,000	134,000,000
Income taxes	50,800,000	53,600,000
Net income	76,200,000	80,400,000
Retained earnings at beginning of period	184,000,000	114,200,000
Dividends on common stock	42,600,000	10,000,000
Dividends on preferred stock	600,000	600,000
Retained earnings at end of period	$217,000,000	$184,000,000

Instructions

On the basis of the information above, compute the following for 1996 only:

(a) Current (working capital) ratio.

(b) Quick (acid-test) ratio.

(c) Number of days' sales in average receivables, assuming a business year consisting of 300 days and all sales on account.

(d) Inventory turnover.

(e) Book value per share of common stock, assuming that there is no dividend arrearage on the preferred stock.

(f) Earnings per share on common stock.

(g) Price-earnings ratio on common stock.

(h) Dividend-payout ratio on common stock.

P25-7 (Horizontal and Vertical Analysis) Presented below are comparative balance sheets for the Eola Yevette Company.

Eola Yevette Company
COMPARATIVE BALANCE SHEET
December 31, 1996 and 1995

	December 31	
	1996	1995
Assets		
Cash	$ 180,000	$ 275,000
Accounts receivable (net)	220,000	155,000
Investments	270,000	150,000
Inventories	960,000	980,000
Prepaid expense	25,000	25,000
Fixed assets	2,685,000	1,950,000
Accumulated depreciation	(1,000,000)	(750,000)
	$3,340,000	$2,785,000
Liabilities and Stockholders' Equity		
Accounts payable	$ 50,000	$ 75,000
Accrued expenses	170,000	200,000
Bonds payable	500,000	190,000
Capital stock	2,100,000	1,770,000
Retained earnings	520,000	550,000
	$3,340,000	$2,785,000

Instructions

  (a) Prepare a comparative balance sheet of Yevette Company showing the percent each item is of the total.

  (b) Prepare a comparative balance sheet of Yevette Company showing the dollar change and the percent change for each item.

  (c) Of what value is the additional information provided in part (a)?

  (d) Of what value is the additional information provided in part (b)?

P25-8 (Ratio Computations and Preparation of Statements) Alvarado Corporation has in recent years maintained the following relationships among the data on its financial statements:

1.	Gross profit rate on net sales	30%
2.	Net profit margin on net sales	8%
3.	Rate of selling expenses to net sales	15%
4.	Accounts receivable turnover	8 per year
5.	Inventory turnover	10 per year
6.	Acid-test ratio	2 to 1
7.	Current ratio	3 to 1
8.	Quick asset composition: 8% cash, 27% marketable securities, 65% accounts receivable	
9.	Asset turnover	2 per year
10.	Ratio of total assets to intangible assets	20 to 1
11.	Ratio of accumulated depreciation to cost of fixed assets	1 to 3
12.	Ratio of accounts receivable to accounts payable	2 to 1
13.	Ratio of working capital to stockholders' equity	1 to 1.95
14.	Ratio of total debt to stockholders' equity	1 to 3

The corporation had a net income of $520,000 for 1996, which resulted in earnings of $9.74 per share of common stock. Additional information includes the following:

  1. Capital stock authorized, issued (all in 1988), and outstanding:
      Common, $10 per share par value, issued at 10% premium
      Preferred, 11% nonparticipating, $100 per share par value, issued at a 10% premium

  2. Market value per share of common at December 31, 1996: $119.52

  3. Preferred dividends paid in 1996: $33,000

  4. Times interest earned in 1996: 28.73

  5. The amounts of the following were the same at December 31, 1996, as at January 1, 1996: inventory, accounts receivable, 10% bonds payable—due 1998, and total stockholders' equity

  6. All purchases and sales were "on account."

Instructions

  (a) Prepare in good form the condensed (1) balance sheet and (2) income statement for the year ending December 31, 1996, presenting the amounts you would expect to appear on Alvarado's financial statements (ignoring income taxes). Major captions appearing on Alvarado's balance sheet are: Current Assets, Property, Plant, and Equipment, Intangible Assets, Current Liabilities, Long-Term Liabilities, and Stockholders' Equity. In addition to the accounts divulged in the problem, you should include accounts for Prepaid Expenses, Accrued Expenses, and Administrative Expenses.

  (b) Compute the following for 1996 (show your computations):
    1. Rate of return on common stockholders equity.
    2. Price-earnings ratio for common stock.
    3. Dividends paid per share of common stock.
    4. Dividends paid per share of preferred stock.
    5. Dividend yield on common stock.

(AICPA adapted)

CASES

C25-1 (Ratio Analysis and Limitations) As the CPA for Packard Clipper, Inc., you have been requested to develop some key ratios from the comparative financial statements. This information is to be used to convince creditors that Packard Clipper Inc. is solvent and to support the use of going-concern valuation procedures in the financial statements.

The data requested and the computations developed from the financial statements follow:

	1996	1995
Current ratio	2.6 times	2.1 times
Acid-test ratio	.8 times	1.3 times
Property, plant, and equipment to stockholders' equity	2.5 times	2.2 times
Sales to stockholders' equity	2.4 times	2.7 times
Net income	Up 32%	Down 9%
Earnings per share	$3.30	$2.50
Book value per share	Up 6%	Up 9%

Instructions

(a) Packard Clipper asks you to prepare a list of brief comments stating how each of these items supports the solvency and going concern potential of the business. The company wishes to use these comments to support its presentation of data to its creditors. You are to prepare the comments as requested, giving the implications and the limitations of each item separately, and then the collective inference that may be drawn from them about Packard Clipper's solvency and going-concern potential.

(b) Having done as the client requested in part (a), prepare a brief listing of additional ratio-analysis-type data for this client which you think its creditors are going to ask for to supplement the data provided in part (a). Explain why you think the additional data will be helpful to these creditors in evaluating the client's solvency.

(c) What warnings should you offer these creditors about the limitations of ratio analysis for the purposes stated here?

C25-2 (Theoretical Discussion of Book Value per Share) The owners of Max Inc., a closely held corporation, have offered to sell their 100% interest in the company's common stock at an amount equal to the book value of the common stock. They will retain their interest in the company's preferred stock.

The president of Maurice Sendak Corporation, your client, would like to combine the operations of Max Inc. with the Publishing Division, and she is seriously considering having Maurice Sendak Corporation buy the common stock of Max Inc. She questions the use of "book value" as a basis for the sale, however, and has come to you for advice.

Instructions

Draft a report to your client. Your report should cover the following points:

(a) Define book value. Explain its significance in establishing a value for a business that is expected to continue in operation indefinitely.

(b) Describe the procedure for computing book values of ownership equities.

(c) Why should your client consider the Max Inc. accounting policies and methods in her evaluation of the company's reported book value? List the areas of accounting policy and methods relevant to this evaluation.

(d) What factors, other than book value, should your client recognize in determining a basis for the sale?

(AICPA adapted)

C25-3 (Effect of Transactions on Financial Statements and Ratios) The transactions listed below relate to Botticelli Inc. You are to assume that on the date on which each of the transactions occurred the corporation's accounts showed only common stock ($100 par) outstanding, a current ratio of 2.7 : 1 and a substantial net income for the year to date (before giving effect to the transaction concerned). On that date the book value per share of stock was $151.53.

Each numbered transaction is to be considered completely independent of the others, and its related answer should be based on the effect(s) of that transaction alone. Assume that all numbered transactions occurred during 1996 and that the amount involved in each case is sufficiently material to distort reported net income if improperly included in the determination of net income. Assume further that each transaction was recorded in accordance with generally accepted accounting principles and, where applicable, in conformity with the all-inclusive concept of the income statement.

For each of the numbered transactions you are to decide whether it:

A. Increased the corporation's 1996 net income.
B. Decreased the corporation's 1996 net income.
C. Increased the corporation's total retained earnings directly (i.e., not via net income).
D. Decreased the corporation's total retained earnings directly.
E. Increased the corporation's current ratio.
F. Decreased the corporation's current ratio.
G. Increased each stockholder's proportionate share of total owner's equity.
H. Decreased each stockholder's proportionate share of total owner's equity.
I. Increased each stockholder's equity per share of stock (book value).
J. Decreased each stockholder's equity per share of stock (book value).
K. Had none of the foregoing effects.

Instructions

List the numbers 1 through 10. Select as many letters as you deem appropriate to reflect the effect(s) of each transaction as of the date of the transaction by printing beside the transaction number the letter(s) that identifies that transaction's effect(s).

Transactions

1. Treasury stock originally repurchased and carried at $127 per share was sold for cash at $153 per share.
2. The corporation sold at a profit land and a building that had been idle for some time. Under the terms of the sale, the corporation received a portion of the sales price in cash immediately, the balance maturing at six-month intervals.
3. In January the board directed the writeoff of certain patent rights that had suddenly and unexpectedly become worthless.
4. The corporation wrote off all of the unamortized discount and issue expense applicable to bonds that it refinanced in 1996.
5. The Board of Directors authorized the writeup of certain fixed assets to values established in a competent appraisal.
6. The corporation called in all its outstanding shares of stock and exchanged them for new shares on a 2-for-1 basis, reducing the par value at the same time to $50 per share.
7. The corporation paid a cash dividend which had been recorded in the accounts at time of declaration.
8. Litigation involving Botticelli Inc., as defendant was settled in the corporation's favor, with the plaintiff paying all court costs and legal fees. The corporation had appropriated retained earnings in 1993 as a special contingency appropriation for this court action, and the board directs abolition of the appropriation. (Indicate the effect of reversing the appropriation only.)
9. The corporation received a check for the proceeds of an insurance policy from the company with which it is insured against theft of trucks. No entries concerning the theft had been made previously, and the proceeds reduce but do not cover completely the loss.
10. Treasury stock, which had been repurchased at and carried at $127 per share, was issued as a stock dividend. In connection with this distribution, the Board of Directors of Botticelli Inc., had authorized a transfer from retained earnings to permanent capital of an amount equal to the aggregate market value ($153 per share) of the shares issued. No entries relating to this dividend had been made previously.

(AICPA adapted)

C25-4 (Analysis of Alternative Sources of Funds) The Budget Committee of Donatello Corporation was established to appraise and screen departmental requests for plant expansions and improvements at a time when these requests totaled $11,200,000. The committee then sought your professional advice and help in establishing the minimum performance standards that it should demand of these projects in the way of anticipated rates of return before interest and taxes.

Donatello Corporation is a closely held family corporation in which the stockholders exert an active and unified influence on the management. At this date, the company has no long-term debt and has 1,000,000 shares of common capital stock outstanding which were sold at $20 per share. It is currently earning $5 million (income before interest and taxes) per year. The applicable tax rate is 40%.

If the projects under consideration are approved, management is confident that the $11,200,000 of required funds can be obtained either:

1. By borrowing: via the medium of an issue of $11,200,000, 11%, 20-year bonds.
2. By equity financing: via the medium of an issue of 560,000 shares of common stock to the general public. It is expected and anticipated that the ownership of these 560,000 shares will be widely dispersed and scattered.

The company has been earning a 14% return after taxes. The management and the dominant stockholders consider this rate of earnings to be a fair price-earnings ratio (7 times earnings) as long as the company remains free of long-term debt. A lowering of the price-earnings ratio to 6 times earnings constitutes an adequate adjustment to compensate for the risk of carrying $11,200,000 of long-term debt. They believe that this reflects, and is consistent with, current market appraisals.

Instructions

(a) Prepare columnar schedules comparing minimum returns, considering interest, taxes, and earnings ratio, which should be produced by each alternative to maintain the present capitalized value per share (of $21). (*Hint:* Begin with capitalized value per share and work in reverse to determine earnings.)

(b) What minimum rate of return on new investment is necessary for each alternative to maintain the present capitalized value per share (of $21)?

(AICPA adapted)

▶ FINANCIAL REPORTING PROBLEM

Twin Ricky Inc. (TRI) manufactures a variety of consumer products. The company's founders have run the company for thirty years and are now interested in retiring. Consequently, they are seeking a purchaser who will continue its operations, and a group of investors, Donna Inc., is looking into the acquisition of TRI. To evaluate its financial stability and operating efficiency, TRI was requested to provide the lastest financial statements and selected financial ratios. Summary information provided by TRI is presented below and on the following page.

TRI
STATEMENT OF INCOME
For the Year Ended November 30, 1996
(in thousands)

Sales (net)	$30,500
Interest income	500
Total revenue	31,000
Costs and expenses	
Cost of goods sold	17,600
Selling and administrative expense	3,550
Depreciation and amortization expense	1,890
Interest expense	900
Total costs and expenses	23,940
Income before taxes	7,060
Income taxes	2,900
Net income	$ 4,160

SELECTED FINANCIAL RATIOS

	TRI 1994	TRI 1995	Current Industry Average
Current ratio	1.62	1.61	1.63
Acid-test ratio	.63	.64	.68
Times interest earned	8.50	8.55	8.45
Net profit margin	12.1%	13.2%	13.0%
Total debt to net worth	1.02	.86	1.03
Total asset turnover	1.83	1.84	1.84
Inventory turnover	3.21	3.17	3.18

TRI
STATEMENT OF FINANCIAL POSITION
As of November 30
(in thousands)

	1996	1995
Cash	$ 400	$ 500
Marketable securities (at cost)	500	200
Accounts receivable (net)	3,200	2,900
Inventory	5,800	5,400
Total current assets	9,900	9,000
Property, plant, & equipment (net)	7,100	7,000
Total assets	$17,000	$16,000

	1996	1995
Accounts payable	$ 3,700	$ 3,400
Income taxes payable	900	800
Accrued expenses	1,700	1,400
Total current liabilities	6,300	5,600
Long-term debt	2,000	1,800
Total liabilities	8,300	7,400
Common stock ($1 par value)	2,700	2,700
Paid-in capital in excess of par	1,000	1,000
Retained earnings	5,000	4,900
Total shareholders' equity	8,700	8,600
Total liabilities and shareholders' equity	$17,000	$16,000

Instructions

(a) Calculate a new set of ratios for the fiscal year 1996 for TRI based on the financial statements presented.

(b) Explain the analytical use of each of the seven ratios presented, describing what the investors can learn about TRI's financial stability and operating efficiency.

(c) Identify two limitations of ratio analysis.

(CMA adapted)

► WRITING ASSIGNMENT

As loan analyst for Mark Twain Bank, you have been presented the following information:

Assets

	Henry James Co.	Herman Melville Co.
Cash	$ 120,000	$ 320,000
Receivables	220,000	302,000
Inventories	570,000	518,000
Total current assets	910,000	1,140,000
Other assets	500,000	612,000
Total assets	$1,410,000	$1,752,000

Liabilities and Capital

	Henry James Co.	Herman Melville Co.
Current liabilities	$ 305,000	$ 350,000
Long-term liabilities	400,000	500,000
Capital stock and retained earnings	705,000	902,000
Total liabilities and capital	$1,410,000	$1,752,000
Annual sales	$ 930,000	$1,500,000
Rate of gross profit on sales	30%	40%

Each of these companies has requested a loan of $50,000 for six months with no collateral offered. Inasmuch as your bank has reached its quota for loans of this type, only one of these requests is to be granted.

Instructions

Write a one-page memo to the manager of the loan department, William Dean Howells, recommending one of the companies for the $50,000 loan. In your answer, explain which would be a better credit risk and why. Assume that the ending account balances are representative of the entire year.

► GROUP ASSIGNMENT

(Dividend Policy Analysis) Michaelangelo Inc. went public 3 years ago. The Board of Directors will be meeting shortly after the end of the year to decide on a dividend policy. In the past, growth has been financed primarily through the retention of earnings. A stock or a cash dividend has never been declared. Presented on the following page is a brief financial summary of Michaelangelo Inc. operations.

	1996	1995	($000 omitted) 1994	1993	1992
Sales	$20,000	$16,000	$14,000	$6,000	$4,000
Net income	$ 2,900	$ 1,600	$ 800	$ 900	$ 250
Average total assets	$22,000	$19,000	$11,500	$4,200	$3,000
Current assets	$ 8,000	$ 6,000	$ 3,000	$1,200	$1,000
Working capital	$ 3,600	$ 3,200	$ 1,200	$ 500	$ 400
Common shares:					
Number of shares outstanding (000)	2,000	2,000	2,000	20	20
Average market price	$9	$6	$4	—	—

Instructions

Your instructor will assign one member of the group to serve as recorder and one member to serve as spokesperson. As a group, provide the information for the recorder to prepare responses to the following requirements. Upon completion of each requirement and before moving on to the next part, the spokesperson will report the group findings to the class.

(a) Suggest factors to be considered by the Board of Directors in establishing a dividend policy.

(b) Compute the rate of return on assets, profit margin on sales, earnings per share, price-earnings ratio, and current ratio for each of the 5 years for Michaelangelo Inc.

(c) Comment on the appropriateness of declaring a cash dividend at this time, using the ratios computed in part (b) as a major factor in your analysis.

▶ ETHICS CASE

John C. Calhoun, the financial vice-president, and Henry Clay, the controller, of Americana Manufacturing are reviewing the financial ratios of the company for the years 1994 and 1995. The financial vice-president notes that the profit margin on sales ratio has increased from 6% to 12%, a hefty gain for the two-year period. Calhoun is in the process of issuing a media release that emphasizes the efficiency of Americana Manufacturing in controlling cost. Henry Clay knows that the difference in ratios is due primarily to an earlier company decision to reduce the estimates of warranty and bad debt expense for 1995. The controller, not sure of his supervisor's motives, hesitates to suggest to Calhoun that the company's improvement is unrelated to efficiency in control of cost. To complicate matters: the media release is scheduled in a few days.

Instructions

(a) What, if any, is the ethical dilemma in this situation?

(b) Should Clay, the controller, remain silent? Give reasons.

(c) What stakeholders might be affected by Calhoun's media release?

(d) Give your opinion on the following statement and cite reasons: "Because Calhoun, the vice-president, is most directly responsible for the media release, Clay has no real responsibility in this matter."

CAREERS IN ACCOUNTING

A visit with
JAMES FITZGERALD

What's the best academic background for an accounting career?

In addition to accounting courses, students should get as broad an educational background as possible. Take courses that require reasoning—mathematics, philosophy, etc.

What about writing? Practitioners say CPA's must prepare a great deal of written communication but a lot of students can't do it.

You really hit one of my hot buttons. It's embarassing to see people in their 40s and 50s who can't write a decent letter. Last week, I had to counsel a person who couldn't understand why a four-line sentence is unacceptable. It's absurd. I think we have an enormous problem. The best solution is to have as broadly based an education as possible consistent with being an accounting major.

Isn't the person with the broad background and a "B" average at a disadvantage to the "A" student who takes only accounting courses?

I think that that can be overcome in the job interview. Students should take the time to study the interviewing process as much as they study their courses. Most students don't have the foggiest notion of what they're supposed to say or do in an interview.

What do they do wrong?

Very few students can respond to an inquiry as simple as "Tell me

In the course of your career, you will also come in contact with consultants who specialize in putting employers and potential employees in touch with each other. One such consultant is JAMES F. FITZGERALD, Managing Principal of the Chicago office of Right Associates, the largest U.S. "outplacement" firm.

Career counselors generally agree that accounting is an excellent background for a variety of occupations. By and large, though, most accounting majors seek entry-level positions in either public accounting or corporate accounting departments.

Typically, public accounting firms are the most aggressive recruiters on campus. They are usually categorized in three ways: The "Big Six" worldwide firms, medium-sized regional firms, and local CPA firms.

Some major corporations will recruit on campus for entry-level jobs. There are also many opportunities at companies that prefer you to initiate the contact.

about yourself." They don't prepare. Or make eye contact. Or dress for the role. Make sure that your resume is flawless in terms of its typing. Rehearse your presentation with a friend so that you come across self-assured and confident. Learn from your mistakes in each interview so that you don't repeat them in the next one. After the interview, take some notes about what was discussed. You'll never remember otherwise.

A lot of people coming out of school aren't prepared to deal with the politics of an organization. What advice do you give to college students in this area?

What I wish I knew about the business world when I was 21! Be willing to acknowledge that there might be a different way of doing things than how you did it in a particular accounting class. Survey the environment before you become so steadfast in your position. Learn to be diplomatic. Learn to listen. Don't be too quick to judge.

Isn't the entry level job market tougher in public accounting, what with the consolidation of the Big Eight into the Big Six?

It has encouraged some of the students who otherwise might have gone to work in public accounting to be more willing to go to work for an industrial firm. The CMA (Certified Management Accountant) program is gaining popularity and is certainly well respected.

Some people have the impression that accounting is "fire-proof."

Oh no. I'm not sure that that was ever true. It was very common and still is to this day that public accounting firms terminate some accountants at the conclusion of the busy season. Computers are taking over a lot of the lower-level accounting jobs. You must make a commitment to constantly update your skills throughout your career.

Is public accounting still an "up or out" business?

By and large it is. Typically, an assessment is made after the first or second year that you are or are not cut out for it. It doesn't have anything to do with how intelligent you are. It's a matter of how well you fit. In addition, public accounting is very demanding. There's a sense of urgency. By and large, CPAs in public accounting work longer hours than people do in industry.

The accounting firms recruit heavily on campus. How can they tell if a person can do the work?

They look for more than just academic intelligence. They look for some "street smarts," too—the ability to interact with clients. The recruiters ask themselves whether a candidate six months off of a college campus would be comfortable dealing with someone who's got 5 or 10 years of experience.

OK. Let's assume you get past the first or second busy season. Where's the next hurdle?

A lot of people view themselves as short-termers by design. They're going to be there two or three years, because it's like getting basic training. Maybe they're going for their CPA certificate and want to get enough audit experience to qualify.

The first few years in public accounting provide incredible training in how to communicate, in how to use time effectively, and in how to conduct yourself in business.

But they should pass the CPA exam?

I would encourage anyone to get their certificate because it tends to legitimize that experience. Otherwise, it's like going to grad school but not getting your degree.

Where's the next dropout point?

The next roadblock is the manager level, when they find out whether they are on the partnership track, and that happens after about five or six years.

Why wouldn't they be?

The single most important factor is their ability or lack of ability to generate business. You can tell how well they interact with clients. Are they perceived as just a technocrat? Or do clients rely on their judgment? Have they gotten involved in professional organizations—the Chamber of Commerce or Rotary— that gives evidence that they're into business development?

There could be eight or nine managers in an office competing for two or three partnership slots?

That's about right. It depends on how fast that particular office is growing.

In some smaller cities, they might only admit one partner a year.

So, your advancement is slower. And you might have to transfer to another location. Many people aren't willing or able to do so.

What about a big CPA firm versus a small firm?

I think there's value to both. Now I myself worked for Coopers & Lybrand for 14 years, so it might seem that I'm prejudiced toward a big firm. But some people are just not comfortable with big organizations. Some would argue that in a small firm you're challenged even more because you're expected to do more things. But the markets that these two types of firms serve are starting to merge. It used to be that the big firms only went after the Fortune 1000 type client. Now, they're dealing with a much broader clientele. From a student's point of view, I think they could get an excellent experience with any size CPA firm.

Of course, public accounting isn't the only way to go.

That's true. Accounting, whether in public, industrial, or even governmental, is a real learning experience because it gives you a chance to see how things come together. If you're working in an industrial environment, you should learn about the sales, marketing, inventory, and manufacturing areas as well as finance.

FULL DISCLOSURE IN FINANCIAL REPORTING

LEARNING OBJECTIVES

After studying this chapter, you should be able to:

1. Review the full disclosure principle and describe problems of implementation.

2. Explain the use of notes in financial statement preparation.

3. Describe the disclosure requirements for major segments of a business.

4. Describe the accounting problems associated with interim reporting.

5. Identify the major disclosures found in the auditor's report.

6. Understand other areas of the annual report.

7. Identify issues related to financial forecasts and projections.

8. Describe the profession's response to fraudulent financial reporting.

*A*ccountants have long recognized that attempting to present all essential information about an enterprise in the four basic financial statements—balance sheet, income statement, statement of stockholders' equity, and statement of cash flows—is an extremely difficult task. *FASB Concepts Statement No. 1* notes that although financial reporting and financial statements have essentially the same objectives, some useful information is better provided in the financial statements, and some is better provided by means of financial reporting other than financial statements. For example, earnings and cash flows are readily available in financial statements—but investors might do better to look at comparisons to other companies in the same industry, found in news articles or brokerage house reports.

Financial statements, notes to the financial statements, and supplementary information are areas directly affected by FASB standards. Other types of information found in the annual report, such as management's discussion and analysis, are not subject to FASB standards. See Illustration 26-1 for the types of financial information presented.

▶ FULL DISCLOSURE PRINCIPLE

As indicated in Chapter 2, the profession has adopted a **full disclosure principle** that calls for financial reporting of **any financial facts significant enough to influence the judgment of an informed reader.** In some situations, the benefits of disclosure may be apparent but the costs uncertain, whereas in other instances the costs may be certain but the benefits of disclosure not as apparent.

Recently, the SEC increased the amount of information financial institutions must disclose about their foreign lending practices. With some countries such as Colombia and Argentina in economic straits, the benefits of increased disclosure about the risk of uncollectibility are fairly obvious to the investing public. The exact costs of disclosure in these situations cannot be quantified, though they would appear to be relatively small.

OBJECTIVE 1

Review the full disclosure principle and describe problems of implementation.

On the other hand, the cost of disclosure can be substantial in some cases and the benefits difficult to assess. For example, *The Wall Street Journal* reported that if segment reporting were adopted, a company like Fruehauf would have to increase its accounting staff 50%, from 300 to 450 individuals. In this case, the cost of disclosure is apparent but the benefits are less well defined. Some would even argue that the reporting requirements are so detailed and substantial that users will have a difficult time absorbing the information; they charge the profession with engaging in **information overload.**

The difficulty of implementing the full disclosure principle is highlighted by such financial disasters as Phar-Mor, Miniscribe, Lincoln Savings and Loan, and BCCI. Why were not investors aware of potential problems: Was the information presented about these companies not comprehensible? Was it buried? Was it too technical? Was it properly presented and fully disclosed as of the financial statement date—but the situation later deteriorated? Or was it simply not there? No easy answers are forthcoming.

One problem is that the profession is still in the process of developing the guidelines that tell whether a given transaction should be disclosed and what format this disclosure should take. Different users want different information, and it becomes exceedingly difficult to develop disclosure policies that meet their varied objectives.

ILLUSTRATION 26-1
Types of Financial
Information

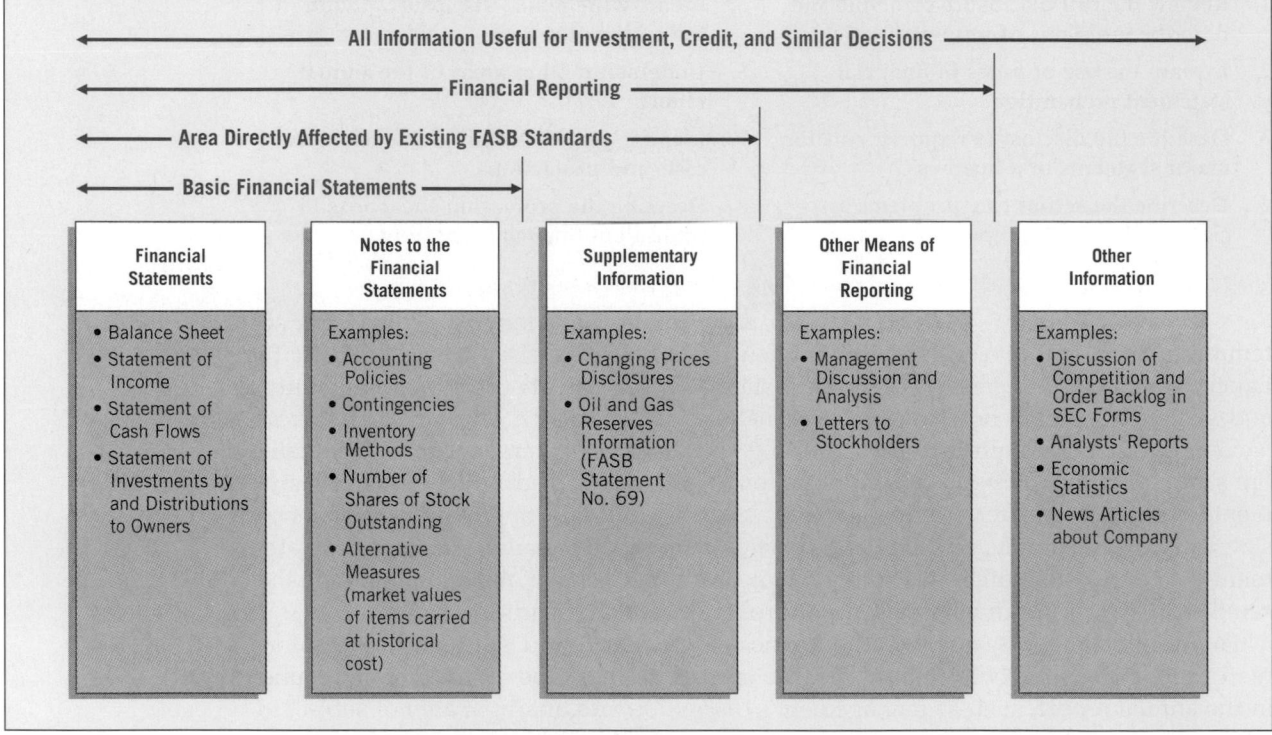

INCREASE IN REPORTING REQUIREMENTS

Disclosure requirements have increased substantially in recent years. One survey showed that in a sample of 25 large, well-known companies, the average number of pages of notes to the financial statements increased from 9 to 17 pages and the average number of pages for management's discussion and analysis from 7 to 12 pages over a recent 10-year period. This result is not surprising because as illustrated throughout this textbook, the FASB has issued many standards in the last 10 years that have substantial disclosure provisions.[1] The reasons for this increase in disclosure requirements are varied. Some of them are:

---

[1]As one writer has noted, rapid growth in additional financial reporting requirements and rapid changes in existing requirements are likely to be permanent features of the financial reporting environment. For the user, the result is a bewildering increase in financial data to interpret. William H. Beaver, *Financial Reporting: An Accounting Revolution* (Englewood Cliffs, N.J.: Prentice-Hall, 1981), pp. 1–2. The survey results were taken from Ray J. Groves, "Financial Disclosure: When More is Not Better," *Financial Executive*, May/June 1994.

Complexity of the Business Environment. The difficulty of distilling economic events into summarized reports has been magnified by the increasing complexity of business operations in such areas as derivatives, leasing, business combinations, pensions, financing arrangements, revenue recognition, and deferred taxes. As a result, **notes to the financial statements** are used extensively to explain these transactions and their future effects.

Necessity for Timely Information. Today, more than ever before, users are demanding information that is current and predictive. For example, more complete **interim data** are required. And published financial forecasts, long avoided and even feared by some accountants, are recommended by the SEC.

Accounting as a Control and Monitoring Device. The government has recently sought more information and public disclosure of such phenomena as management compensation, environmental pollution, related party transactions, errors and irregularities, and illegal activities. An "S&L crisis" concern is expressed in many of these newer disclosure requirements, and accountants and auditors have been selected as the agents to assist in controlling and monitoring these concerns. The "S&L crisis" concern has been deepened by financial scandals involving some major American corporations such as General Electric and General Dynamics which, as the SEC contended, involved "cooked books" or "cute accounting."

DIFFERENTIAL DISCLOSURE

A trend toward **differential disclosure** is also occurring. For example, the SEC requires that certain substantive information be reported to it that is not found in annual reports to stockholders. And the FASB, recognizing that certain disclosure requirements are costly and unnecessary for certain companies, has eliminated reporting requirements for nonpublic enterprises in such areas as earnings per share and segmental reporting.

Some still complain that the FASB has not gone far enough. They note that certain types of companies (small or nonpublic) should not have to follow complex GAAP requirements such as deferred income taxes, leases or pensions. This issue, often referred to as **Big GAAP versus Little GAAP** continues to be controversial. The FASB takes the position that one set of GAAP should be used, except in unusual situations.

▶ NOTES TO THE FINANCIAL STATEMENTS

As you know from your study of this textbook, notes are an integral part of the financial statements of a business enterprise. However, they are often overlooked because they are highly technical and often appear in small print. **Notes are the accountant's means of amplifying or explaining the items presented in the main body of the statements.** Information pertinent to specific financial statement items can be explained in qualitative terms, and supplementary data of a quantitative nature can be provided to expand the information in the financial statements. Restrictions imposed by financial arrangements or basic contractual agreements also can be explained in notes. Although notes may be technical and difficult to understand, they provide meaningful information for the user of the financial statements.

ACCOUNTING POLICIES

Accounting policies of a given entity are the specific accounting principles and methods currently employed and considered most appropriate to present fairly the financial statements of the enterprise. *APB Opinion No. 22,* "Disclosure of Accounting Policies," concluded that information about the accounting policies adopted and followed by a reporting entity is essential for financial statement users in making economic decisions. It recommended that **a statement identifying the accounting policies adopted and followed by the reporting entity should also be presented as an integral part of the financial statements.** The disclosure should be given as the initial note or in a separate

Summary of Significant Accounting Policies section preceding the notes to the financial statements. The Summary of Significant Accounting Policies answers such questions as: What method of depreciation is used on plant assets? What valuation method is employed on inventories? What amortization policy is followed in regard to intangible assets? How are marketing costs handled for financial reporting purposes?

Refer to Appendix 5–A, pages 222–224, for an illustration of note disclosure of accounting policies (Note 1) and other notes accompanying the audited financial statements of Georgia-Pacific Corporation. An illustration from Collaborative Research Incorporated is provided below:

ILLUSTRATION 26-2
Note Disclosure of
Accounting Policies

Collaborative Research Incorporated

Note 1: Summary of Significant Accounting Policies:

Consolidation

The accompanying consolidated financial statements include the accounts of the Company and its subsidiaries. All material intercompany balances and transactions have been eliminated in consolidation.

Research and Development Contract Accounting

The Company participates in both fixed price and cost-plus fixed-fee contracts. Cost-plus contracts and certain fixed price contracts have no stated deliverables associated with them. The Company is, however, required to prepare a scientific report of the Company's research and the results thereof. Revenues under fixed price contracts with stated deliverables are recognized upon completion of each deliverable at contract sales price. Revenues under cost-plus and fixed price contracts with no deliverable requirements are recognized in the proportion that costs incurred bear to total estimated costs. At the Company's option, cost may exceed the amounts funded by these contracts, and the excess is charged to expense. Unbilled costs represent the excess of total expenditures on contracts, plus earned fees thereon, over billings.

Cash Equivalents and Short-Term Investments

Cash equivalents and short-term investments consisting of medium-term notes, treasury notes and money market funds are valued at cost which approximates market value. As of August 31, 1993, the Company has restricted cash of approximately $115,000.

Statements of Cash Flows

The Company considers cash in bank and investments purchased with an original maturity of three months or less to be cash equivalents. Interest and income taxes paid are immaterial in each of the three years ended August 31, 1993. For the years ended August 31, 1993, 1992 and 1991, capital lease obligations of $318,151, $453,169 and $136,087, respectively, were incurred when the Company entered into leases for various equipment. The lease obligations entered into in fiscal 1991 were transferred to Becton Dickinson and Company on August 30, 1991.

Equipment and Leasehold Improvements

Equipment and leasehold improvements are depreciated over their estimated useful lives using the straight-line method. The estimated useful life for leasehold improvements is the lesser of the initial term of the lease plus an extension option period or the estimated useful life of the assets. Equipment and all other depreciable assets' useful lives vary from three to ten years. Expenditures for maintenance and repairs are expensed as incurred.

Service Revenue

Revenues are recognized in the period in which services are rendered. Revenues subject to Medicare or third-party reimbursement are recorded at estimated reimbursable amounts.

Royalty Revenue

Royalty revenue is recorded as earned. Royalties represent receipts from The Dow Chemical Company license agreement for rennin.

Net Loss per Common Share

Net loss per common share has been computed based upon the weighted average number of shares outstanding during each period. Common share equivalents consisting of outstanding stock options have not been used to compute the loss per common share as their effect would be antidilutive.

UNDERLYING
CONCEPT

The AICPA's Special Committee on Financial Reporting states that to meet users' changing needs, business reporting must: (1) Provide more forward-looking information about plans, opportunities, risks, and uncertainties; (2) Focus more on the factors that create longer-term value, including nonfinancial measures indicating how key business processes are performing; and (3) Better align information reported externally with the information reported internally.

Analysts examine carefully the summary of accounting policies section to determine whether the company is using conservative or liberal accounting practices. For example, amortizing intangible assets over 40 years (the maximum) or depreciating plant assets over an unusually long period of time is considered liberal. On the other hand, using LIFO inventory valuation in a period of inflation is generally viewed as following a conservative practice.

OTHER NOTES

Many of the notes to the financial statements have been discussed throughout this textbook. Others will be discussed more fully in this chapter. The more common are as follows:

◀ MAJOR DISCLOSURES ▶

INVENTORY. The basis upon which inventory amounts are stated (lower of cost or market) and the method used in determining cost (LIFO, FIFO, average cost, etc.) should also be reported. Manufacturers should report the inventory composition (finished goods, work in process, raw materials) either in the balance sheet or in a separate schedule in the notes. Unusual or significant financing arrangements relating to inventories that may require disclosure include transactions with related parties, product financing arrangements, firm purchase commitments, involuntary liquidation of LIFO inventories, and pledging of inventories as collateral. Chapter 9 (pages 450–452) illustrates these disclosures.

PROPERTY, PLANT, AND EQUIPMENT. The basis of valuation for property, plant, and equipment should be stated: It is usually historical cost. Pledges, liens, and other commitments related to these assets should be disclosed. In the presentation of depreciation, the following disclosures should be made in the financial statements or in the notes: (1) depreciation expense for the period; (2) balances of major classes of depreciable assets, by nature and function, at the balance sheet date; (3) accumulated depreciation, either by major classes of depreciable assets or in total, at the balance sheet date; and (4) a general description of the method or methods used in computing depreciation with respect to major classes of depreciable assets. Chapter 11 (pages 546–547) illustrates these disclosures.

CREDIT CLAIMS. An investor normally finds it extremely useful to determine the nature and cost of creditorship claims. However, the liability section in the balance sheet can provide the major types of liabilities outstanding only in the aggregate. Note schedules regarding such obligations provide additional information about how the company is financing its operations, the costs that will have to be borne in future periods, and the timing of future cash outflows. Financial statements must disclose for each of the 5 years following the date of the financial statements the aggregate amount of maturities and sinking fund requirements for all long-term borrowings. Chapter 14 (pages 695–696) illustrates these disclosures.

EQUITY HOLDERS' CLAIMS. Many companies present in the body of the balance sheet the number of shares authorized, issued, and outstanding and the par value for each type of equity security. Such data may also be presented in a note. Beyond that, the most common type of equity note disclosure relates to contracts and senior securities outstanding that might affect the various claims of the residual equity holders; for example, the existence of outstanding stock options, outstanding convertible debt, redeemable preferred stock, and convertible preferred stock. In addition, it is necessary to disclose to equity claimants certain types of restrictions currently in force. Generally, these types of restrictions involve the amount of earnings available for dividend distribution. Examples of these types of disclosures are illustrated in Chapter 15 (pages 752, 755–756), Chapter 16 (page 787), and Chapter 17 (pages 831, 845–846).

CONTINGENCIES AND COMMITMENTS. An enterprise may have gain or loss contingencies that are not disclosed in the body of the financial statements. These contingencies include litigation, debt and other guarantees, possible tax assessments, renegotiation of government contracts, sales of receivables with recourse, and so on. In addition, commitments that relate to dividend restrictions, purchase agreements (through-put and take-or-pay), hedge contracts, and

UNDERLYING CONCEPT

The AICPA Special Committee on Financial Reporting notes that standard setters should address disclosures and accounting requirements for off-balance-sheet financial arrangements to ensure that business reporting faithfully reports the risks, opportunities, resources, and obligations that result from those arrangements, consistent with users' needs for information.

UNDERLYING
CONCEPT

*The AICPA Special
Committee on Financial
Reporting indicates that
business reporting has not
kept pace with the
continuing explosion of
innovative financial
instruments such as swaps,
compound options,
swaptions, caps, floors,
collars, and many others. As
a result, users are uncertain
about companies'
involvements with these
instruments and complain
that business reporting is not
answering the questions they
need answered.*

employment contracts are also disclosed. Disclosures of items of this nature are illustrated in Chapter 7 (pages 345–346), Chapter 9 (page 441), Chapter 13 (pages 647–648), and Chapter 14 (pages 695–700).

DEFERRED TAXES, PENSIONS, AND LEASES. Extensive disclosure is required in these three areas. Chapter 20 (pages 1009–1012), Chapter 21 (pages 1080–1083), and Chapter 22 (pages 1154–1156) discuss each of these disclosures in detail. It should be emphasized that notes to the financial statements should be given a careful reading for information about off-balance-sheet commitments, future financing needs, and the quality of a company's earnings.

CHANGES IN ACCOUNTING PRINCIPLES. The profession defines various types of accounting changes and establishes guides for reporting each type. Either in the summary of significant accounting policies or in the other notes, changes in accounting principles (as well as material changes in estimates and corrections of errors) are discussed. See Chapter 23 (pages 1185–1190 and 1191–1194).

SUBSEQUENT EVENTS. Events or transactions that occur subsequent to the balance sheet date but prior to the issuance of the financial statements should be disclosed in the financial statements. Chapter 5 (pages 205–206) sets forth the criteria for the proper treatment of subsequent events.

The disclosures listed above have been discussed in earlier chapters. Three additional disclosures of significance—special transactions or events, segment reporting, and interim reporting—are illustrated in the following sections of this chapter.

▶ DISCLOSURE OF SPECIAL TRANSACTIONS OR EVENTS

Related party transactions, errors and irregularities, and illegal acts pose especially sensitive and difficult problems. The accountant/auditor who has responsibility for reporting on these types of transactions has to be extremely careful that the rights of the reporting company and the needs of users of the financial statements are properly balanced.

INTERNATIONAL
INSIGHT

*In Switzerland there are no
requirements to disclose
related party transactions. In
Italy and Germany related
parties do not include a
company's directors.*

Related party transactions arise when a business enterprise engages in transactions in which one of the transacting parties has the ability to influence significantly the policies of the other, or in which a nontransacting party has the ability to influence the policies of the two transacting parties.[2] Transactions involving related parties cannot be presumed to be carried out on an "arm's-length" basis because the requisite conditions of competitive, free-market dealings may not exist. Transactions such as borrowing or lending money at abnormally low or high interest rates, real estate sales at amounts that differ significantly from appraised value, exchanges of nonmonetary assets, and transactions involving enterprises that have no economic substance ("shell corporations") suggest that related parties may be involved.

The accountant is expected to report the economic substance rather than the legal form of these transactions and to make adequate disclosures. *FASB Statement No. 57* requires the following disclosures of material related party transactions:

1. The nature of the relationship(s) involved.

2. A description of the transactions (including transactions to which no amounts or nominal amounts were ascribed) for each of the periods for which income statements are presented.

---

[2]Examples of related party transactions include transactions between (a) a parent company and its subsidiaries; (b) subsidiaries of a common parent; (c) an enterprise and trusts for the benefit of employees (controlled or managed by the enterprise); and (d) an enterprise and its principal owners, management, or members of immediate families, and affiliates.

3. The dollar amounts of transactions for each of the periods for which income statements are presented.

4. Amounts due from or to related parties as of the date of each balance sheet presented.

Illustration 26-3 is an example of the disclosure of related party transactions taken from the annual report of DEP Corporation.

DEP Corporation
Note 12: Related-Party Transactions Operating expenses for the years ended July 31, 1992, 1991 and 1990 include $372,000, $178,000, and $152,000, respectively, paid or accrued to legal firms affiliated with a director and stockholder of the Company. The Company paid consulting fees of $120,000 for the years ended July 31, 1992 and 1991 to a director and stockholder of the Company.

ILLUSTRATION 26-3
Disclosure of Related Party Transactions

Errors are defined as unintentional mistakes, whereas **irregularities** are intentional distortions of financial statements.[3] As indicated in this textbook, when errors are discovered, the financial statements should be corrected. The same treatment should be given irregularities. The discovery of irregularities, however, gives rise to a whole different set of suspicions, procedures, and responsibilities on the part of the accountant/auditor.[4]

Illegal acts encompass such items as illegal political contributions, bribes, kickbacks, and other violations of laws and regulations.[5] In these situations, the accountant/auditor must evaluate the adequacy of disclosure in the financial statements. For example, if revenue is derived from an illegal act that is considered material in relation to the financial statements, this information should be disclosed. To deter these illegal acts, Congress enacted the Foreign Corrupt Practices Act of 1977. In addition to affecting business practices, this Act has had a significant impact upon the accounting profession by encouraging increased disclosure and tighter controls.

Many companies are involved in related party transactions; errors and irregularities, and illegal acts, however, are the exception rather than the rule. Disclosure plays a very important role in these areas because the transaction or event is more qualitative than quantitative and involves more subjective than objective evaluation. The users of the financial statements must be provided with some indication of the existence and nature of these transactions, where material, through disclosures, modifications in the auditor's report, or in reports of changes in auditors.

▶ REPORTING FOR DIVERSIFIED (CONGLOMERATE) COMPANIES

In the last several decades business enterprises have had, at times, a tendency to diversify their operations. Take the case of conglomerate GenCorp. whose products include tires, Penn tennis balls, parts for the MX missile, and linings for disposable diapers. Its RKO subsidiary owns radio and television stations, makes movies, bottles soda pop, runs hotels, and holds a big stake in an airline. As a result of such diversification efforts, investors and investment analysts have sought more information concerning

OBJECTIVE 3

Describe the disclosure requirements for major segments of a business.

---

[3]"The Auditor's Responsibility to Detect and Report Errors and Irregularities," *Statement on Auditing Standards No. 53* (New York, AICPA, 1988).

[4]The profession became so concerned with certain management frauds that affect financial statements that it established a National Commission on Fraudulent Financial Reporting. The major purpose of this organization was to determine how fraudulent reporting practices can be constrained. Fraudulent financial reporting is discussed later in this chapter.

[5]"Illegal Acts by Clients," *Statement on Auditing Standards No. 54* (New York, AICPA, 1988).

the details behind conglomerate financial statements. Particularly, they want income statement, balance sheet, and cash flow information on the **individual** segments that compose the **total** business income figure.

An illustration of segmentation is presented in the following example of an office equipment and auto parts company.

ILLUSTRATION 26-4
Segmented Income
Statement

Office Equipment and Auto Parts Company INCOME STATEMENT DATA (in millions)			
	Consolidated	Office Equipment	Auto Parts
Net sales	$78.8	$18.0	$60.8
Manufacturing costs:			
Inventories, beginning	12.3	4.0	8.3
Materials and services	38.9	10.8	28.1
Wages	12.9	3.8	9.1
Inventories, ending	(13.3)	(3.9)	(9.4)
	50.8	14.7	36.1
Selling and administrative expense	12.1	1.6	10.5
Total operating expenses	62.9	16.3	46.6
Income before taxes	15.9	1.7	14.2
Income taxes	(9.3)	(1.0)	(8.3)
Net income	$ 6.6	$ 0.7	$ 5.9

If only the consolidated figures are available to the analyst, much information regarding the composition of these figures is hidden in aggregated totals. There is no way to tell from the consolidated data the extent to which the differing product lines **contribute to the company's profitability, risk, and growth potential.** For example, in the illustration above, if the office equipment segment is deemed a risky venture, the segmentation provides useful information for purposes of making an informed investment decision regarding the whole company.

A classic situation that demonstrates the need for segment data involved Caterpillar, Inc. Caterpillar was cited by the SEC because it failed to tell investors that nearly a quarter of its income in 1989 came from a Brazilian unit. This income was nonrecurring in nature. The company knew that different economic policies in the next year would probably greatly affect earnings of the Brazilian unit. But Caterpillar presented its financial results on a consolidated basis, not disclosing the Brazilian's operations. The SEC stated that Caterpillar's failure to include information about Brazil left investors with an incomplete picture of the company's financial results and denied investors the opportunity to see the company "through the eyes of management."

Companies have been somewhat hesitant to disclose segmented data for the reasons listed below.

1. Without a thorough knowledge of the business and an understanding of such important factors as the competitive environment and capital investment requirements, the investor may find the segment information meaningless or may even draw improper conclusions about the reported earnings of the segments.

2. Additional disclosure may harm reporting firms because it may be helpful to competitors, labor unions, suppliers, and certain government regulatory agencies.

3. Additional disclosure may discourage management from taking intelligent business risks because segments reporting losses or unsatisfactory earnings may cause stockholder dissatisfaction with management.

4. The wide variation among firms in the choice of segments, cost allocation, and other accounting problems limits the usefulness of segment information.

5. The investor is investing in the company as a whole and not in the particular segments, and it should not matter how any single segment is performing if the overall performance is satisfactory.

6. Certain technical problems, such as classification of segments and allocation of segment revenues and costs (especially "common costs"), are formidable.

On the other hand, the advocates of segmented disclosures offer these reasons in support of the practice:

1. Segment information is needed by the investor to make an intelligent investment decision regarding a diversified company.
   (a) Sales and earnings of individual segments are needed to forecast consolidated profits because of the differences between segments in growth rate, risk, and profitability.
   (b) Segment reports disclose the nature of a company's businesses and the relative size of the components as an aid in evaluating the company's investment worth.

2. The absence of segmented reporting by a diversified company may put its unsegmented, single product-line competitors at a competitive disadvantage because the conglomerate may obscure information that its competitors must disclose.

The advocates of segmented disclosures appear to have a much stronger case. Many users indicate that segment data are the most useful financial information provided, aside from the basic financial statements. As a result, the FASB has issued extensive reporting guidelines in this area.[6]

PROFESSIONAL PRONOUNCEMENTS

Recognizing the need for guidelines in the area of segment reporting, the profession issued *FASB No. 14*, "Financial Reporting for Segments of a Business Enterprise," and then amended it through the issuance of subsequent standards. The basic requirements related to these pronouncements are discussed below.

Accounting Principle Selection

Segment information that is required to be reported must be prepared on the same accounting basis as that used in the enterprise's consolidated financial statements. An exception is intersegment sales, which are eliminated for consolidated purposes but are shown when individual segments are presented. **Intersegment sales** are transfers of products or services between segments of the enterprise. An example of segment disclosure required by the profession is shown for Tenneco Inc. in Illustration 26-5. Also see Georgia-Pacific's Note 2 on pages 224–225 for its industry segment information.

Note that Tenneco Inc. reports seven major segments (as well as geographical segments). Georgia-Pacific reports two major segments in categorizing its 18 primary product lines. Each segment follows the same accounting principles that are used to prepare the consolidated financial statements. **The profession also requires that the segments' revenues, operating profit (loss), and identifiable assets be reconciled to the consolidated financial statements. In addition, depreciation expense and the amount of capital expenditures must be reported for each segment.**

[6]Professional bodies continue to study this area because of its importance. See, for example, Paul Pacter, "Reporting Disaggregated Information by Business Enterprises," *Invitation to Comment* (Norwalk, Conn.: FASB, 1993); and also John Boersema and Susan Van Weelden, "Financial Reporting for Segments," Research Study (CICA, 1992).

Tenneco Inc.—Segment Information

Note (14): Segment and Geographic Area Information

(Millions)

Segment	Natural Gas Pipelines	Farm and Construction Equipment	Automotive Parts	Shipbuilding	Packaging	Chemicals and Minerals	Other	Reclass. and Elimination	Consolidated
At December 31, and for the Year Then Ended									
Net sales and operating revenues:									
External	$2,459	$5,390	$1,731	$2,113	$1,469	$1,298	$ 51	$ —	$14,511
Intersegment	1	6	—	—	7	—	—	(14)	—
Total	2,460	5,396	1,731	2,113	1,476	1,298	51	(14)	14,511
Operating profit	357	208	222	238	197	167	63	—	1,452
General corporate expenses	(17)	(22)	(9)	(13)	(7)	(7)	(4)	—	(79)
Income before interest expense and federal income taxes	340	186	213	225	190	160	59	—	1,373
Identifiable assets	2,587	9,769	1,090	1,499	1,214	1,409	1,513	(378)	18,703
Investment in affiliated companies	116	48	3	—	18	40	106	—	331
Total assets	2,703	9,817	1,093	1,499	1,232	1,449	1,619	(378)	19,034
Depreciation, depletion and amortization	98	144	48	65	53	61	7	—	476
Capital expenditures	$ 257	$ 140	$ 81	$ 85	$ 140	$ 212	$ 5	$ —	$ 920

(Millions)

Geographic Area	United States	Canada	European Community	Other Foreign	Reclass. and Elimination	Consolidated
At December 31, and for the Year Then Ended						
Net sales and operating revenues:						
External	$ 9,985	$ 798	$3,105	$623	$ —	$14,511
Intergeographic area	495	25	62	26	(608)	—
Total	10,480	823	3,167	649	(608)	14,511
Operating profit	1,129	89	155	79	—	1,452
General corporate expenses	(73)	(1)	(4)	(1)	—	(79)
Income before interest expense and federal income taxes	1,056	88	151	78	—	1,373
Identifiable assets	13,673	1,173	3,879	552	(574)	18,703
Investment in affiliated companies	295	—	13	23	—	331
Total assets	$13,968	$1,173	$3,892	$575	$(574)	$19,034

ILLUSTRATION 26-5
An Example of Segment Disclosure

Selecting Reportable Segments

A number of methods might have been used by Tenneco Inc. and Georgia-Pacific Corporation to identify its industry segments. The Standard Industrial Classification manual identifies and classifies industries. Existing profit centers may be identified as segments, or management may establish segments by relating common risk factors to products or product groups. The FASB concluded that **management should exercise its judgment in determining industry segments.** The FASB, however, did indicate three factors that should be seriously considered:[7]

1. **The Nature of the Product.** Related products or services have similar purposes or end uses. Thus, they may be expected to have similar rates of profitability, similar degrees of risk, and similar opportunities for growth.

2. **The Nature of the Production Process.** Sharing of common or interchangeable production or sales facilities, equipment, labor force, or service group or use of the same or similar basic raw materials may suggest that products or services

---

[7]"Financial Reporting for Segments of a Business Enterprise," *Statement of Financial Accounting Standards No. 14* (Stamford, Conn.: FASB, 1976), par. 100.

are related. Likewise, similar degrees of labor-intensiveness or similar degrees of capital-intensiveness may indicate a relationship among products or services.

3. **Markets or Marketing Methods.** Similarity of geographic marketing areas, types of customers, or marketing methods may indicate a relationship among products or services. The sensitivity of the market to price changes and to changes in general economic conditions may also indicate whether products and services are related or unrelated.

After the company decides on the segments for possible disclosure, a quantitative test is made to determine whether the segment is significant enough to warrant actual disclosure. An industry segment is regarded as significant and therefore identified as a reportable segment if it satisfies **one or more** of the following tests.

1. Its **revenue** (including both sales to unaffiliated customers and intersegment sales or transfers) is 10% or more of the combined revenue (sales to unaffiliated customers and intersegment sales or transfers) of all the enterprise's industry segments.

2. The absolute amount of its **operating profit or operating loss** is 10% or more of the greater, in absolute amount, of
   (a) the combined operating profit of all industry segments that did not incur an operating loss, or
   (b) the combined operating loss of all industry segments that did incur an operating loss.

3. Its **identifiable assets** are 10% or more of the combined identifiable assets of all industry segments.

In applying these tests, two additional factors must be considered. First, segment data must explain a significant portion of the company's business. Specifically, the segmented results must equal or exceed 75% of the combined sales to unaffiliated customers for the entire enterprise. This test prevents a company from providing limited information on only a few segments and lumping all the rest into one category.

Second, the profession recognized that reporting too many segments may overwhelm users with detailed information. Although the FASB did not issue any specific guidelines regarding how many segments are too many, this point is generally considered reached when a company has 10 or more reportable segments.

To illustrate these requirements, assume a company has identified six possible reporting segments (000 omitted):

INTERNATIONAL INSIGHT

Disclosure of segmental information is not required in Brazil, Italy, Korea, Mexico, or Switzerland.

Segments	Total Revenue (Unaffiliated)	Operating Profit (Loss)	Identifiable Assets
A	$ 100	$10	$ 60
B	50	2	30
C	700	40	390
D	300	20	160
E	900	18	280
F	100	(5)	50
	$2,150	$85	$970

ILLUSTRATION 26-6
Data for Different Possible Reporting Segments

The respective tests may be applied as follows:

Revenue test: 10% × $2,150 = $215; C, D, and E meet this test.

Operating profit (loss) test: 10% × $90 = $9 (note that the $5 loss is ignored); A, C, D, and E meet this test.

Identifiable assets test: 10% × $970 = $97; C, D, and E meet this test.

The reportable segments are therefore A, C, D, and E, assuming that these four segments have enough sales to meet the 75% of combined sales test. The 75% test is computed as follows:

75% of combined sales test: 75% × $2,150 = $1,612.50; the sales of A, C, D, and E total $2,000 ($100 + $700 + $300 + $900); therefore, the 75% test is met.

Information to Be Reported

As indicated above, the primary basis for segmenting the results of Tenneco, Inc. was service or product line. The profession requires segmented information on other bases when appropriate. The three general bases are:

1. Service or product line.
2. Foreign operations.
3. Export and major customer.

Foreign operating income, revenues, and identifiable assets are reported when sales of this type are 10% or more of consolidated revenue or when identifiable assets are 10% or more of total assets of the business. Similarly, a 10% guideline exists for separate disclosure of sales to a major customer. Sales, income (loss), and asset information by geographic area is provided to give the reader an understanding of the proportion of sales being made in domestic and foreign markets. This information is extremely useful to investors who are concerned about the political and economic stability of a given geographic area. As the segment information in Illustration 26-5 shows, Tenneco's operations were such that it also had to report segment information on a geographical basis.

Similarly, export sales must be reported when a company derives 10% or more of its revenue from sales from this source. **Export sales** are sales to customers in foreign countries; export sales information provides insight into the stability, risk, and growth potential of this revenue source.

CONTINUING CONTROVERSY

The area of segment reporting is controversial from a number of perspectives. One frequent complaint is that this information is costly to develop. As a result, the Board decided **that nonpublic companies should not be required to disclose segmental data.**[8] Conversely, others argue that segment data information should be expanded or even extended to interim reports (reports that cover periods of less than a year). The following issues, however, are also still being hotly debated.

Definition of a Segment

A general view that seems to prevail among accountants is that the enterprise should be free to select the breakdown that best represents the underlying activities of the business. The problem with using this procedure is that a great deal of subjectivity is involved in selecting the segments, which can lead to a lack of comparability over a period of time.

In addition to the problem of determining the basis for identifying the segments, there is the question of what percentage to use. As indicated earlier, a 10% factor is applied to one of the following items: revenue, income or loss, or identifiable assets. But these criteria are still subject to interpretation. At one time Weyerhaeuser Co. indicated that except for certain real estate ventures, everything else related to paper production, so no additional disclosure was necessary. Other timber companies, including Georgia-Pacific Corporation, have broken down their segments into such categories as pulp and paper, packaging products, and wood products.

Allocation of Common Costs

One of the critical problems in providing segmented income statements for conglomerate companies is the allocation of common costs. **Common costs** are those incurred for the benefit of more than one segment and whose interrelated nature prevents a completely objective division of costs among segments. For example, the company president's salary is very difficult to allocate to various segments. One survey showed that

---

[8]"Suspension of the Reporting of Earnings Per Share and Segment Information by Nonpublic Enterprises," *Statement of Financial Accounting Standards No. 21* (Stamford, Conn.: FASB, 1978).

the average ratio of common costs to net sales is greater than that of net income to net sales.

Many different bases for allocation have been suggested, such as sales, gross profit, assets employed, investment, and marginal income. The choice of basis is important because it can materially influence the relative profitability of the segments.

Transfer Pricing Problems

The practice of charging a price for goods "sold" between divisions or subsidiaries of a company is called **transfer pricing.** A transfer price system is used for several reasons, but the primary objective is to measure the performance and profitability of a given segment of the business in relation to other segments. In addition, a pricing system is needed to ensure control over the flow of goods through the enterprise.

Transfer pricing is not a problem of the same magnitude as common costs, but it still is very significant in many business enterprises. At present, different approaches to transfer pricing are used. Some firms transfer the goods at market prices; others use cost plus a fixed fee; and some use variable cost. In some situations, the company lets the division bargain for the price of the item in question.

In evaluating a specific division, we must consider the transfer pricing problem. If, for example, Division A sells certain goods to Division B using a market price instead of cost, the operating results of both divisions are affected. Transfer pricing in many situations does not occur on an arm's-length basis and, therefore, the final results of a given division must be suspect. The basis of accounting for intersegment sales and transfers should be disclosed.

INTERNATIONAL INSIGHT

In an effort to internationalize accounting standards, the FASB and the standards board of Canada (ACSB) have together issued a document on accounting issues related to segment reporting. It marks the first time the FASB has developed and issued a comment document jointly with another standard-setting body.

▶ INTERIM REPORTS

One further source of information for the investor is interim reports. As noted earlier, **interim reports** are those reports that cover periods of less than one year. At one time, interim reports were referred to as the "forgotten reports"; such is no longer the case. The stock exchanges, the SEC, and the accounting profession have taken an active role in developing guidelines for the presentation of interim information.

The SEC mandates that certain companies file a Form 10Q, which requires a company to disclose quarterly data similar to that disclosed in the annual report. It also requires those companies to disclose selected quarterly information in notes to the annual financial statements. In addition to this requirement, the APB issued *Opinion No. 28,* which attempted to narrow the reporting alternatives related to interim reports.[9] Illustration 26-7 presents the disclosure of selected quarterly data for Electronic Data Systems Corporation.

OBJECTIVE 4
Describe the accounting problems associated with interim reporting.

ILLUSTRATION 26-7
Disclosure of Selected Quarterly Data

Electronic Data Systems Corporation					
	Year Ended December 31, 1993				
(In millions, except per share amounts)	First Quarter	Second Quarter	Third Quarter	Fourth Quarter	Year
Revenues	$2,073.2	$2,090.5	$2,084.3	$2,313.8	$8,561.8
Gross profit from operations	490.1	501.3	525.0	600.3	2,116.7
Income before income taxes	236.6	278.2	299.4	317.1	1,131.3
Separate consolidated net income	151.4	178.1	191.6	202.9	724.0
Earnings attributable to GM Class E					
common stock on a per share basis	0.32	0.37	0.40	0.42	1.51
Stock price range of GM Class E common					
High	35.88	33.38	32.50	31.13	35.88
Low	27.63	28.25	26.00	26.50	26.00
Cash dividends per share of GM					
Class E common	0.10	0.10	0.10	0.10	0.40

---

[9]"Interim Financial Reporting," *Opinions of the Accounting Principles Board No. 28* (New York: AICPA, 1973).

Because of the short-term nature of these reports, however, there is considerable controversy as to the general approach that should be employed. One group (which holds the **discrete view**) believes that each interim period should be treated as a separate accounting period; deferrals and accruals would therefore follow the principles employed for annual reports. Accounting transactions should be reported as they occur, and expense recognition should not change with the period of time covered. Another group (which holds the **integral view**) believes that the interim report is an integral part of the annual report and that deferrals and accruals should take into consideration what will happen for the entire year. In this approach, estimated expenses are assigned to parts of a year on the basis of sales volume or some other activity base. At present, many companies follow the discrete approach for certain types of expenses and the integral approach for others, because the standards currently employed in practice are vague and lead to differing interpretations.

INTERIM REPORTING REQUIREMENTS

The profession indicates that the same accounting principles used for annual reports should be employed for interim reports. Revenues should be recognized in interim periods on the same basis as they are for annual periods. For example, if the installment sales method is used as the basis for recognizing revenue on an annual basis, then the installment basis should be applied to interim reports as well. Also, costs directly associated with revenues (product costs), such as materials, labor and related fringe benefits, and manufacturing overhead should be treated in the same manner for interim reports as for annual reports.

Companies generally should use the same inventory pricing methods (FIFO, LIFO, etc.) for interim reports that they use for annual reports. However, the following exceptions are appropriate at interim reporting periods:

1. Companies may use the gross profit method for interim inventory pricing, but disclosure of the method and adjustments to reconcile with annual inventory are necessary.

2. When LIFO inventories are liquidated at an interim date and are expected to be replaced by year end, cost of goods sold should include the expected cost of replacing the liquidated LIFO base and not give effect to the interim liquidation.

3. Inventory market declines should not be deferred beyond the interim period unless they are temporary and no loss is expected for the fiscal year.

4. Planned variances under a standard cost system which are expected to be absorbed by year end ordinarily should be deferred.

Costs and expenses other than product costs, often referred to as **period costs,** are often charged to the interim period as incurred. But they may be allocated among interim periods on the basis of an estimate of time expired, benefit received, or activity associated with the periods. Considerable latitude is exercised in accounting for these costs in interim periods, and many believe more definitive guidelines are needed.

Regarding disclosure, the following interim data should be reported as a minimum:

1. Sales or gross revenues, provision for income taxes, extraordinary items, cumulative effect of a change in accounting principles or practices, and net income.

2. Primary and fully diluted earnings per share where appropriate.

3. Seasonal revenue, cost, or expenses.

4. Significant changes in estimates or provisions for income taxes.

5. Disposal of a segment of a business and extraordinary, unusual, or infrequently occurring items.

6. Contingent items.

7. Changes in accounting principles or estimates.

8. Significant changes in financial position.

The profession also encourages but does not require companies to publish a balance sheet and a statement of cash flows. When this information is not presented, significant changes in such items as liquid assets, net working capital, long-term liabilities, and stockholders' equity should be disclosed.

UNIQUE PROBLEMS OF INTERIM REPORTING

In *APB Opinion No. 28*, the Board indicated that it favored the integral approach. However, within this broad guideline, a number of unique reporting problems develop related to the following items.

Advertising and Similar Costs

The general guidelines are that costs such as advertising should be **deferred in an interim period if the benefits extend beyond that period; otherwise they should be expensed as incurred.** But such a determination is difficult, and even if they are deferred, how should they be allocated between quarters? Because of the vague guidelines in this area, accounting for advertising varies widely. Some companies in the food industry, such as RJR Nabisco and Pillsbury, charge advertising costs as a percentage of sales and adjust to actual at year end, whereas General Foods and Kellogg's expense these costs as incurred.

The same type of problem relates to such items as social security taxes, research and development costs, and major repairs. For example, should the company expense social security costs (payroll taxes) on highly paid personnel early in the year or allocate and spread them to subsequent quarters? Should a major repair that occurs later in the year be anticipated and allocated proportionately to earlier periods?

Expenses Subject to Year-End Adjustment

Bad debts, executive bonuses, pension costs, and inventory shrinkage are often not known with a great deal of certainty until year end. **These costs should be estimated and allocated in the best possible way to interim periods.** Companies use a variety of allocation techniques to accomplish this objective.

Income Taxes

Not every dollar of corporate taxable income is assessed at the same rate; the tax rate is progressive. This aspect of business income taxes poses a problem in preparing **interim financial statements.** Should the income to date be annualized and the proportionate income tax accrued for the period to date **(annualized approach)**? Or should the first amount of income earned be taxed at the lower rate of tax applicable to such income **(marginal principle approach)**? At one time, companies generally followed the latter approach and accrued the tax applicable to each additional dollar of income.

The marginal principle was especially applicable to businesses having a seasonal or uneven income pattern, because the interim accrual of tax was based on the actual results to date. The profession now, however, uses the annualized approach requiring that "at the end of each interim period the company should make its best estimate of the effective tax rate expected to be applicable for the full fiscal year. The rate so determined should be used in providing for income taxes on income for the quarter."[10]

Because businesses did not uniformly apply this guideline in accounting for similar situations, the FASB issued *Interpretation No. 18*. This interpretation requires that the **estimated annual effective tax rate** be applied to the year-to-date "ordinary" income

---

[10]"Interim Financial Reporting," *Opinions of the Accounting Principles Board No. 28* (New York: AICPA, 1973), par. 19. The estimated annual effective tax rate should reflect anticipated tax credits, foreign tax rates, percentage depletion, capital gains rates, and other available tax planning alternatives.

at the end of each interim period to compute the year-to-date tax. Further, the **interim period tax** related to "ordinary" income shall be the difference between the amount so computed and the amounts reported for previous interim periods of the fiscal period.[11]

Extraordinary Items

Extraordinary items consist of unusual and nonrecurring material gains and losses. In the past, they were handled in interim reports in one of three ways: (1) absorbed entirely in the quarter in which they occurred; (2) prorated over the four quarters; or (3) disclosed only by note. **The required approach is to charge or credit the loss or gain in the quarter that it occurs instead of attempting some arbitrary multiple-period allocation.** This approach is consistent with the way in which extraordinary items are currently handled on an annual basis; no attempt is made to prorate the extraordinary items over several years.

Some accountants favor the omission of extraordinary items from the quarterly net income. They believe that inclusion of extraordinary items that may be large in proportion to interim results distorts the predictive value of interim reports. Many accountants, however, consider such an omission inappropriate because it deviates from actual results.

Changes in Accounting

What happens if a company decides to change an accounting principle in the third quarter of a fiscal year? Should the cumulative effect adjustment be charged or credited to that quarter? Presentation of a cumulative effect in the third quarter may be misleading because of the inherent subjectivity associated with the first two quarters' reported income. In addition, a question arises as to whether such a change might not be used to manipulate a given quarter's income. As a result, *FASB Statement No. 3* was issued indicating that **if a cumulative effect change occurs in other than the first quarter, no cumulative effect should be recognized in those quarters.**[12] **Rather, the cumulative effect at the beginning of the year should be computed and the first quarter restated.** Subsequent quarters would not report a cumulative effect adjustment.

Earnings per Share

Interim reporting of earnings per share has all the problems inherent in computing and presenting annual earnings per share, and then some. If shares are issued in the third period, EPS for the first two periods will not be indicative of year-end EPS. If an extraordinary item is present in one period and new equity shares are sold in another period, the EPS figure for the extraordinary item will change for the year. On an annual basis only one EPS figure is associated with an extraordinary item and that figure does not change; the interim figure is subject to change. **For purposes of computing earnings per share and making the required disclosure determinations, each interim period should stand alone. That is, all applicable tests should be made for that single period.**

Seasonality

Seasonality occurs when sales are compressed into one short period of the year while certain costs are fairly evenly spread throughout the year. For example, the natural gas

---

[11]"Accounting for Income Taxes in Interim Periods," *FASB Interpretation No. 18* (Stamford, Conn.: FASB, March 1977), par. 9. "Ordinary" income (or loss) refers to "income (or loss) from continuing operations before income taxes (or benefits)" excluding extraordinary items, discontinued operations, and cumulative effects of changes in accounting principles.

[12]"Reporting Accounting Changes in Interim Financial Statements," *Statement of the Financial Accounting Standards Board No. 3* (Stamford, Conn.: FASB, 1974). This standard also provides guidance related to a LIFO change and accounting changes made in the fourth quarter of a fiscal year in which interim data are not presented.

industry has its heavy sales in the winter months, as contrasted with the beverage industry, which has its heavy sales in the summer months.

The problem of seasonality is related to the matching concept in accounting. Expenses should be matched against the revenues they create. In a seasonal business, wide fluctuations in profits occur because off-season sales do not absorb the company's fixed costs (for example, manufacturing, selling, and administrative costs that tend to remain fairly constant regardless of sales or production).

To illustrate why seasonality is a problem, assume the following information:

Selling price per unit	$1
Annual sales for the period (projected and actual)	
100,000 units @ $1.00	$100,000
Manufacturing costs:	
Variable	10¢ per unit
Fixed	20¢ per unit or $20,000 for the year
Nonmanufacturing costs:	
Variable	10¢ per unit
Fixed	30¢ per unit or $30,000 for the year

ILLUSTRATION 26-8
Data for Seasonality Example

Sales for four quarters and the year (projected and actual) were:

		Percent of Sales
1st Quarter	$ 20,000	20%
2nd Quarter	5,000	5
3rd Quarter	10,000	10
4th Quarter	65,000	65
Total for the year	$100,000	100%

ILLUSTRATION 26-9
Sales Data for Seasonality Example

Under the present accounting framework, the income statements for the quarters might be as presented as follows:

	1st Qtr	2nd Qtr	3rd Qtr	4th Qtr	Year
Sales	$20,000	$ 5,000	$10,000	$65,000	$100,000
Manufacturing costs					
Variable	(2,000)	(500)	(1,000)	(6,500)	(10,000)
Fixed[a]	(4,000)	(1,000)	(2,000)	(13,000)	(20,000)
	14,000	3,500	7,000	45,500	70,000
Nonmanufacturing costs					
Variable	(2,000)	(500)	(1,000)	(6,500)	(10,000)
Fixed[b]	(7,500)	(7,500)	(7,500)	(7,500)	(30,000)
Net income	$ 4,500	$(4,500)	$ (1,500)	$31,500	$ 30,000

ILLUSTRATION 26-10
Interim Net Income for Seasonal Business— Discrete Approach

[a]The fixed manufacturing costs are inventoried, so that equal amounts of fixed costs do not appear during each quarter.
[b]The fixed nonmanufacturing costs are not inventoried so that equal amounts of fixed costs appear during each quarter.

An investor who uses the first quarter's results can be misled. If the first quarter's earnings are $4,500, should this figure be multiplied by four to predict annual earnings of $18,000? Or, as the analysis suggests, inasmuch as $20,000 in sales is 20% of the predicted sales for the year, net income for the year should be $22,500 ($4,500 × 5). Either figure is obviously wrong, and after the second quarter's results occur, the investor may become even more confused.

The problem with the conventional approach is that the fixed nonmanufacturing costs are not charged in proportion to sales. Some enterprises have adopted a way of avoiding this problem by making all fixed nonmanufacturing costs follow the sales pattern, as shown in Illustration 26-11.

ILLUSTRATION 26-11
Interim Net Income for
Seasonal Business—
Integral Approach

	1st Qtr	2nd Qtr	3rd Qtr	4th Qtr	Year
Sales	$20,000	$5,000	$10,000	$65,000	$100,000
Manufacturing costs					
Variable	(2,000)	(500)	(1,000)	(6,500)	(10,000)
Fixed	(4,000)	(1,000)	(2,000)	(13,000)	(20,000)
	14,000	3,500	7,000	45,500	70,000
Nonmanufacturing costs					
Variable	(2,000)	(500)	(1,000)	(6,500)	(10,000)
Fixed	(6,000)	(1,500)	(3,000)	(19,500)	(30,000)
Net income	$ 6,000	$1,500	$ 3,000	$19,500	$ 30,000

This approach solves some of the problems of interim reporting: sales in the first quarter are 20% of total sales for the year, and net income in the first quarter is 20% of total income. In this case, as in the previous example, the investor cannot rely on multiplying any given quarter by four, but can use comparative data or rely on some estimate of sales in relation to income for a given period.

The greater the degree of seasonality experienced by a company, the greater the possibility of distortion. Because no definitive guidelines are available for handling such items as the fixed nonmanufacturing costs, variability in income can be substantial. To alleviate this problem, the profession recommends that companies subject to material seasonal variations disclose the seasonal nature of their business and consider supplementing their interim reports with information for 12-month periods ended at the interim date for the current and preceding years.

The two illustrations above highlight the difference between the **discrete** and **integral** viewpoint. The fixed nonmanufacturing expenses are expensed as incurred under the discrete viewpoint. They are charged to expense on the basis of some measure of activity under the integral method.

UNDERLYING
CONCEPT

*The AICPA Special
Committee on Financial
Reporting indicates that
users would benefit from
separate fourth-quarter
reporting, including
management's analysis of
fourth-quarter activities and
events—especially year-end
adjustments—to provide
continuity and additional
insight. Also, quarterly
segment reporting is as
important as annual segment
reporting and should be
provided.*

Continuing Controversy

The profession has developed some standards for interim reporting; but much still has to be done. As yet, it is unclear whether the discrete, integral, or some combination of these two methods will be settled on.

Discussion also persists concerning the independent auditor's involvement in interim reports. Many auditors are reluctant to express an opinion on interim financial information, arguing that the data are too tentative and subjective. Conversely, an increasing number of individuals advocate some type of examination of interim reports. A compromise may be a limited review of interim reports that provides some assurance that an examination has been conducted by an outside party and that the published information appears to be in accord with generally accepted accounting principles.[13]

Analysts want financial information as soon as possible, before it's old news. We may not be far from a continuous database system in which corporate financial records can be accessed by microcomputer. Investors might be able to access a company's financial records via computer whenever they wish and put the information in the format they need. Thus, they could learn about sales slippage, cost increases, or earnings changes as they happen, rather than waiting until after the quarter has ended.[14]

---

[13]The AICPA has been involved in developing guidelines for the review of interim reports. "Limited Review of Interim Financial Statements," *Statement on Auditing Standards No. 24* (New York: AICPA, 1979) sets standards for the review of interim reports.

[14]A step in this direction is the SEC's mandate for companies to file their financial statements electronically with the SEC. This system, called EDGAR (electronic data gathering and retrieval) provides interested parties with computer access to financial information such as periodic filings, corporate prospectuses, and proxy materials. By the end of 1993, approximately 2,500 of the largest companies in the United States filed electronically with the SEC. It will not be long before all 11,000 companies that file with the SEC will do so electronically.

A steady stream of information from the company to the investor could be very positive because it might alleviate management's continual concern with short-run interim numbers. Today many contend that U.S. management is too short-run oriented. The truth of this statement is echoed by the words of the president of a large company who decided to retire early: "I wanted to look forward to a year made up of four seasons rather than four quarters."

► **AUDITOR'S REPORT**

Another important source of information that is often overlooked is the **auditor's report.** An **auditor** is an accounting professional who conducts an independent examination of the accounting data presented by a business enterprise. If the auditor is satisfied that the financial statements present the financial position, results of operations, and cash flows fairly in accordance with generally accepted accounting principles, an unqualified opinion is expressed as shown in Illustration 26-12.[15]

OBJECTIVE 5
Identify the major disclosures found in the auditor's report.

To the Shareholders and the Board of Directors of Georgia-Pacific Corporation:

We have audited the accompanying balance sheets of Georgia-Pacific Corporation (a Georgia corporation) and subsidiaries as of December 31, 1993 and 1992 and the related statements of income, shareholders' equity and cash flows for each of the three years in the period ended December 31, 1993. These financial statements are the responsibility of the Corporation's management. Our responsibility is to express an opinion on these financial statements based on our audits.

We conducted our audits in accordance with generally accepted auditing standards. Those standards require that we plan and perform the audit to obtain reasonable assurance about whether the financial statements are free of material misstatement. An audit includes examining, on a test basis, evidence supporting the amounts and disclosures in the financial statements. An audit also includes assessing the accounting principles used and significant estimates made by management, as well as evaluating the overall financial statement presentation. We believe that our audits provide a reasonable basis for our opinion.

In our opinion, the financial statements referred to above present fairly, in all material respects, the financial position of Georgia-Pacific Corporation and subsidiaries as of December 31, 1993 and 1992 and the results of their operations and their cash flows for each of the three years in the period ended December 31, 1993 in conformity with generally accepted accounting principles.

As explained in Note 6 to the financial statements, effective January 1, 1992, the Corporation changed its method of accounting for income taxes. Also as explained in Notes 1 and 7 to the financial statements, effective January 1, 1991, the Corporation changed its methods of accounting for certain manufacturing supplies and for postretirement health care and life insurance benefits.

Arthur Andersen & Co.

Atlanta, Georgia
February 18, 1994

ILLUSTRATION 26-12
Auditor's Report

In preparing this report, the auditor follows these reporting standards:

1. The report shall state whether the financial statements are presented in accordance with generally accepted accounting principles.

2. The report shall identify those circumstances in which such principles have not been consistently observed in the current period in relation to the preceding period.

3. Informative disclosures in the financial statements are to be regarded as reasonably adequate unless otherwise stated in the report.

---

[15]This auditor's report is in exact conformance with the specifications contained in "Reports on Audited Financial Statements," *Statement on Auditing Standards No. 58* (New York: AICPA, 1988).

4. The report shall contain either an expression of opinion regarding the financial statements taken as a whole or an assertion to the effect that an opinion cannot be expressed. When an overall opinion cannot be expressed, the reasons why should be stated. In all cases where an auditor's name is associated with financial statements, the report should contain a clear-cut indication of the character of the auditor's examination, if any, and the degree of responsibility being taken.

In most cases, the auditor issues a standard **unqualified** or **clean opinion;** that is, the auditor expresses the opinion that the financial statements present fairly, in all material respects, the financial position, results of operations, and cash flows of the entity in conformity with generally accepted accounting principles. Certain circumstances, although they do not affect the auditor's unqualified opinion, may require the auditor to add an explanatory paragraph to the audit report. Some of the more important circumstances are as follows:

1. **Uncertainties.** A matter involving an **uncertainty** is one that is expected to be resolved at a future date, at which time sufficient evidence concerning its outcome is expected to become available. In deciding whether an explanatory paragraph is needed, the auditor should consider the likelihood of a material loss resulting from the contingency. If, for example, the possibility that a loss will be incurred is remote, then an explanatory paragraph is not warranted. If the loss is probable but not estimable, or is reasonably possible and material, then an explanatory paragraph is warranted.

2. **Lack of Consistency.** If there has been a change in accounting principles or in the method of their application that has a material effect on the comparability of the company's financial statements, the auditor should refer to the change in an explanatory paragraph of the report. (See, for example, Illustration 26-12.) Such an explanatory paragraph should identify the nature of the change and refer the reader to the note in the financial statements that discusses the change in detail. The auditor's concurrence with a change is implicit unless exception to the change is taken in expressing the auditor's opinion as to fair presentation of the financial statements in conformity with generally accepted accounting principles.

3. **Emphasis of a Matter.** The auditor may wish to emphasize a matter regarding the financial statements, but nevertheless intends to express an unqualified opinion. For example, the auditor may wish to emphasize that the entity is a component of a larger business enterprise or that it has had significant transactions with related parties. Such explanatory information should be presented in a separate paragraph of the auditor's report.

In some situations, however, the auditor is required to (1) express a **qualified** opinion, (2) express an **adverse** opinion, or (3) **disclaim** an opinion. A **qualified opinion** contains an exception to the standard opinion. Ordinarily the exception is not of sufficient magnitude to invalidate the statements as a whole; if it were, an adverse opinion would be rendered. The usual circumstances in which the auditor may deviate from the standard unqualified short-form report on financial statements are as follows:

1. The scope of the examination is limited or affected by conditions or restrictions.
2. The statements do not fairly present financial position or results of operations because of:
   (a) Lack of conformity with generally accepted accounting principles and standards.
   (b) Inadequate disclosure.

If the auditor is confronted with one of the situations noted above, the opinion must be qualified. A qualified opinion states that, except for the effects of the matter to which the qualification relates, the financial statements present fairly, in all material respects, the financial position, results of operations, and cash flows in conformity with generally accepted accounting principles.

An **adverse opinion** is required in any report in which the exceptions to fair presentation are so material that in the independent auditor's judgment a qualified opinion is not justified. In such a case, the financial statements taken as a whole are not presented in accordance with generally accepted accounting principles. Adverse opinions are rare, because most enterprises change their accounting to conform with the auditor's desires.

A **disclaimer of an opinion** is appropriate when the auditor has gathered so little information on the financial statements that no opinion can be expressed.

An example of a report in which the opinion is qualified because of the use of an accounting principle at variance with generally accepted accounting principles follows (assuming the effects are such that the auditor has concluded that an adverse opinion is not appropriate):

Independent Auditor's Report

(*Same first and second paragraphs as the standard report*)

Helio Company has excluded, from property and debt in the accompanying balance sheets, certain lease obligations that, in our opinion, should be capitalized in order to conform with generally accepted accounting principles. If these lease obligations were capitalized, property would be increased by $1,500,000 and $1,300,000, long-term debt by $1,400,000 and $1,200,000, and retained earnings by $100,000 and $50,000 as of December 31, 1996 and 1995, respectively. Additionally, net income would be decreased by $40,000 and $30,000 and earnings per share would be decreased by $.06 and $.04, respectively, for the years then ended.

In our opinion, except for the effects of not capitalizing certain lease obligations as discussed in the preceding paragraph, the financial statements referred to above present fairly, in all material respects, the financial position of Helio Company as of December 31, 1996 and 1995, and the results of its operations and its cash flows for the years then ended in conformity with generally accepted accounting principles.

ILLUSTRATION 26-13
Qualified Auditor's Report

The profession now also requires the auditor to evaluate whether there is substantial doubt about the entity's **ability to continue as a going concern** for a reasonable period of time (not to exceed one year beyond the date of the financial statements). If the auditor concludes that substantial doubt exists, an explanatory note to the auditor's report would be added describing the potential problem.[16]

The audit report should provide useful information to the investor. One investment banker noted, "Probably the first item to check is the auditor's opinion to see whether or not it is a clean one—'in conformity with generally accepted accounting principles'— or is qualified in regard to differences between the auditor and company management in the accounting treatment of some major item, or in the outcome of some major litigation."

▶ **OTHER AREAS IN THE ANNUAL REPORT**

OBJECTIVE 6
Understand other areas of the annual report.

Some other areas that merit special attention are as follows:

1. Management's Discussion and Analysis (MD&A).
2. Management's Responsibilities for Financial Statements.
3. Social Responsibility.

MANAGEMENT'S DISCUSSION AND ANALYSIS

The **management discussion and analysis (MD&A)** section covers three financial aspects of an enterprise's business—liquidity, capital resources, and results of operations. **It requires management to highlight favorable or unfavorable trends and to identify significant events and uncertainties that affect these three factors.** This approach obviously involves a number of subjective estimates, opinions, and soft data. However, the SEC, which has mandated this disclosure, believes the relevance of this information exceeds the potential lack of reliability.

---

[16]"The Auditor's Consideration of an Entity's Ability to Continue as a Going Concern," *Statement on Auditing Standards No. 59* (New York: AICPA, 1988).

The MD&A section (summary only) of Campbell Soup Company's annual report is presented in Illustration 26-14.

Campbell Soup Company

Management's Discussion and Analysis

Summary

Net earnings were reduced to $8 million or $.03 per share by restructuring charges of $300 million and adoption of new accounting standards. Before these special charges, net earnings were a record $574 million, a 17% increase over fiscal 1992 which contained one additional week. Net sales for the year were $6.6 billion, up 5% over last year's sales of $6.3 billion, with acquisitions contributing $212 million.

Three major events affected the Company's results for fiscal 1993: acquisition of a majority stake in Arnotts Limited (Australia's leading biscuit manufacturer), a restructuring program and adoption of new accounting standards. Charges in connection with the restructuring program and accounting changes totaled $2.25 per share and are more fully discussed in the section titled "Special Charges" below.

Worldwide volume in the Company's flagship soup business grew 3% and profitability in international operations improved for the fourth consecutive year. Significant progress was made in the Company's portfolio reconfiguration strategy, including the acquisition of Arnotts.

The MD&A section also must provide information concerning the effects of inflation and changing prices if material to financial statement trends. No specific numerical computations are specified, and companies have provided little analysis on changing prices. The appendix to this chapter illustrates the issues related to accounting for changing prices.

How this section of the annual report can be made even more effective is the subject of continuing questions such as:

1. Is sufficient forward-looking information being disclosed under current MD&A requirements?

2. Should MD&A disclosures be changed to become more of a risk analysis?

3. Should the MD&A be audited by independent auditors?

MANAGEMENT'S RESPONSIBILITIES FOR FINANCIAL STATEMENTS

A recent SEC proposal would require companies to include a report on management's responsibilities including its responsibilities for, and assessment of, the internal control system. Some companies already present this type of information, although the SEC proposal requirements would be more detailed about the internal control procedures used and their effectiveness. An example of the type of disclosure that some companies are now making is as follows:

Pinnacle West Corporation

Report of Management

The primary responsibility for the integrity of the Company's financial information rests with management, which has prepared the accompanying financial statements and related information. Such information was prepared in accordance with generally accepted accounting principles appropriate in the circumstances, based on management's best estimates and judgments and giving due consideration to materiality. These financial statements have been audited by independent auditors and their report is included.

Management maintains and relies upon systems of internal accounting controls, which are periodically reviewed by both the Company's internal auditors and its independent auditors to test for compliance. Reports issued by the internal auditors are released to management, and such reports, or summaries thereof, are transmitted to the Audit Committee of the Board of Directors and the independent auditors on a timely basis.

The Audit Committee, composed solely of outside directors, meets periodically with the internal auditors and independent auditors (as well as management) to review the work of each. The internal auditors and independent auditors have free access to the Audit Committee, without management present, to discuss the results of their audit work.

> Management believes that the Company's systems, policies and procedures provide reasonable assurance that operations are conducted in conformity with the law and with management's commitment to a high standard of business conduct.
>
> *R Snell   Henry Sargent*
>
> Richard Snell
> Chairman & President
>
> Henry B. Sargent
> Executive Vice President & Chief Financial Officer

The proposal to require a management report on its internal controls is in response to a recommendation of the National Commission on Fraudulent Financial Reporting (The Treadway Commission). The purposes of this proposal are (1) to increase the investor's understanding of the roles of management and the auditor in preparation of financial statements and (2) to heighten the awareness of senior management of its responsibilities for the company's financial and internal control system.

SOCIAL RESPONSIBILITY

The social responsibility of business has received a great deal of public attention in recent years. The public and local, state, and federal governments have urged that businesses make a more adequate response to current issues of social concern than they have in the past. For example, the SEC has already required listed corporations to file a report if pollution expenditures have a material effect on their earnings. Some investment funds, such as Pioneer, Dreyfus Third Century Fund, Calvert Social Investment, and Pax World Fund, have been established to invest only in "socially responsible" companies (although the definition of socially responsible varies from fund to fund). What these funds look for are companies with social consciences. As examples, three "good" companies that crop up on some lists are Quaker Oats Co., which makes low-sugar cereals; Dayton Hudson Corp., which uses 5% of its federally taxable income for charitable purposes; and Magma Power Co., a leader in the development of geothermal energy. The Council on Economic Priorities has been established as an independent research organization to inquire into the social activities of private enterprises. The United Church of Christ uses various criteria for determining the social consciousness of a corporation before investing church funds.

The information related to social expenditures as presented in current financial reports is haphazard. Expenditures for the following types of items are generally considered "social awareness expenditures": assistance to educational institutions; grants to hospitals, health, and other community related activities; aid to minority groups or enterprises; contributions to charitable foundations; aid to unemployed and related programs; and assistance in urban development.

General Mills, Inc. for example disclosed the following as one of its expenditures:

INTERNATIONAL INSIGHT

Outside the U.S., especially in Europe, companies tend to disclose more information related to employees. For example, they may disclose the number of employees, as well as data related to their age, training, benefits, and so forth.

ILLUSTRATION 26-16
Social Awareness Expenditures

General Mills, Inc.
(adapted)

Foundation Grants and Corporate Gifts

Direct philanthropy is an important element of corporate citizenship. The General Mills Foundation, the company's major philanthropic arm, made grants during the year that totaled $6.2 million. General Mills, Inc., and its subsidiaries provided an additional $2.1 million in contributions. . . . The Foundation supports the nation's colleges, universities and secondary schools through its employee gift-matching program. During the year, employee gifts to 524 institutions in 45 states were matched by the Foundation for a total contribution of $507,819, a 25 percent increase over last year.

The SEC requires that the following types of environmental information be disclosed in filings with their agency:

1. The material effects that compliance with federal, state, and local environmental protection laws may have upon capital expenditures, earnings, and competitive position.

INTERNATIONAL
INSIGHT

*Firms in Germany,
Scandinavia, and
Switzerland tend to provide
extensive disclosures related
to environmental protection.*

2. Litigation commenced or known to be contemplated against registrants by a government authority pursuant to federal, state, and local environmental regulatory provisions.

3. All other environmental information of which the average prudent investor ought reasonably to be informed.

As yet, no standards or requirements have been proposed by the FASB for the measurement and reporting of the social responsibilities assumed by individual enterprises. To some investors, it is a matter of importance whether a company is adopting affirmative policies with regard to environmental matters or is simply doing the minimum to assure legal compliance. As indicated in Chapter 13, many companies have become concerned about the potentially large contingent liabilities related to hazardous waste because Superfund legislation has been enacted that increases the penalty for improper disposal.

▶ REPORTING ON FINANCIAL FORECASTS AND PROJECTIONS

In recent years, the investing public's demand for more and better information has focused on disclosure of corporate expectations for the future.[17] These disclosures take one of two forms:[18]

OBJECTIVE 7

*Identify issues related to
financial forecasts and
projections.*

Financial Forecast. Prospective financial statements that present, to the best of the responsible party's knowledge and belief, an entity's expected financial position, results of operations, and cash flows. A financial forecast is based on the responsible party's assumptions reflecting conditions it expects to exist and the course of action it expects to take.

Financial Projection. Prospective financial statements that present, to the best of the responsible party's knowledge and belief, given one or more hypothetical assumptions, an entity's expected financial position, results of operations, and cash flows. A financial projection is based on the responsible party's assumptions reflecting conditions it expects would exist and the course of action it expects would be taken, given one or more hypothetical assumptions.

The difference between a financial forecast and a financial projection is that a forecast attempts to provide information on what is expected to happen, whereas a projection may provide information on what is not necessarily expected to happen, but **might** take place.

Financial forecasts are the subject of intensive discussion with journalists, corporate executives, the SEC, financial analysts, accountants and others. Predictably, there are strong arguments on either side. Listed below are some of the arguments.

Arguments for requiring published forecasts:

1. Investment decisions are based on future expectations; therefore, information about the future facilitates better decisions.

2. Forecasts are already circulated informally, but are uncontrolled, frequently misleading, and not available equally to all investors. This confused situation should be brought under control.

---

[17]Some areas in which companies are using financial information about the future are equipment lease-versus-buy analysis, analysis of a company's ability to successfully enter new markets, and examining merger and acquisition opportunities. In addition, forecasts and projections are also prepared for use by third parties in public offering documents (requiring financial forecasts), tax-oriented investments, and financial feasibility studies. Use of forward-looking data has been enhanced by the increased capability of the microcomputer to analyze, compare, and manipulate large quantities of data.

[18]"Financial Forecasts and Projections," *Statement of Standards for Accountants' Services on Prospective Financial Information* (New York: AICPA, October 1985), par. 6.

3. Circumstances now change so rapidly that historical information is no longer adequate for prediction.

Arguments against requiring published forecasts:

1. No one can foretell the future. Therefore forecasts, while conveying an impression of precision about the future, will inevitably be wrong.

2. Organizations will strive only to meet their published forecasts, not to produce results that are in the stockholders' best interest.

3. When forecasts are not proved to be accurate, there will be recriminations and probably legal actions.[19]

4. Disclosure of forecasts will be detrimental to organizations, because it will fully inform not only investors, but also competitors (foreign and domestic).

The AICPA has issued a statement on standards for accountants' services on prospective financial information. This statement established procedures and reporting standards for presenting financial forecasts and projections. It requires accountants to provide (1) a summary of significant assumptions used in the forecast or projection and (2) guidelines for minimum presentation.[20]

To encourage management to disclose this type of information, the SEC has a **safe harbor rule.** This rule provides protection to an enterprise that presents an erroneous forecast as long as the forecast is prepared on a reasonable basis and is disclosed in good faith.[21] However, companies are finding that the safe harbor rule does not work in practice, since it does not cover oral statements, nor has it kept them out of court. As a consequence companies are disclosing less, and therefore the SEC is now looking into ways of strengthening the safe harbor rule.

EXPERIENCE IN GREAT BRITAIN

Great Britain has permitted financial forecasts for years, and the results have been fairly successful. Some significant differences exist between the English and the American business and legal environment,[22] but probably none that could not be overcome if influential interests in this country cooperated to produce an atmosphere conducive to quality forecasting. A typical British forecast adapted from a construction company's report to support a public offering of stock is as follows:

UNDERLYING CONCEPT

The AICPA's Special Committee on Financial Reporting indicates that the current legal environment discourages companies from disclosing forward-looking information. Companies should not have to expand reporting of forward-looking information until there are more effective deterrents to unwarranted litigation.

Profits have grown substantially over the past 10 years and directors are confident of being able to continue this expansion. . . . While the rate of expansion will be dependent on the level of economic activity in Ireland and England, the group is well structured to avail itself of opportunities as they arise, particularly in the field of property development, which is expected to play an increasingly important role in the group's future expansion.

Profits before taxation for the half year ended 30th June 1992 was 402,000 pounds. On the basis of trading experiences since that date and the present level of sales and completions, the directors expect that in the absence of unforeseen circumstances, the group's profits before taxation for the year to 31st December 1992 will be not less than 960,000 pounds.

No dividends will be paid in respect of the year December 31, 1992. In a full financial year, on the basis of above forecasts (not including full year profits) it would be the intention of the board, assuming current rates of tax, to recommend dividends totaling 40% (of after-tax profits), of which 15% payable would be as an interest dividend in November 1993 and 25% as a final dividend in June 1994.

ILLUSTRATION 26-17 Financial Forecast of a British Company

---

[19]The issue is serious. Over the last 3 years, 8 percent of the companies listed on the NYSE have been sued because of an alleged lack of financial disclosure. Companies complain that they are subject to lawsuits whenever the stock price drops. And as one executive noted: You can even be sued if the stock price goes up—because you did not disclose the good news fast enough.

[20]"Financial Forecasts and Projections," op. cit., 44 pages.

[21]"Safe-Harbor Rule for Projections," *Release No. 5993* (Washington: SEC, 1979).

[22]The British system, for example, does not permit litigation on forecasted information, and the solicitor (lawyer) is not permitted to work on a contingent fee basis. See "A Case for Forecasting—The British Have Tried It and Find That It Works," *World* (New York: Peat, Marwick, Mitchell & Co., Autumn 1978), pp. 10–13.

A general narrative-type forecast issued by a U.S. corporation might appear as follows:

ILLUSTRATION 26-18
Financial Forecast for an
American Company

> On the basis of promotions planned by the company for the second half of fiscal 1996, net earnings for that period are expected to be approximately the same as those for the first half of fiscal 1996, with net earnings for the third quarter expected to make the predominant contribution to net earnings for the second half of fiscal 1996.

QUESTIONS OF LIABILITY

What happens if a company does not meet its forecasts? Are the company and the auditor going to be sued? If a company, for example, projects an earnings increase of 15% and achieves only 5%, should the stockholder be permitted to have some judicial recourse against the company? One court case involving Monsanto Chemical Corporation has provided some guidelines. In this case, Monsanto predicted that sales would increase 8 to 9% and that earnings would rise 4 to 5%. In the last part of the year, the demand for Monsanto's products dropped as a result of a business turndown. Therefore, instead of increasing, the company's earnings declined. The company was sued because the projected earnings figure was erroneous, but the judge dismissed the suit because the forecasts were the best estimates of qualified people whose intents were honest.

As indicated earlier, the SEC's safe harbor rules are intended to protect enterprises that provide good-faith projections. However, much concern exists as to how the SEC and the courts will interpret such terms as "good faith" and "reasonable assumptions" when erroneous forecasts mislead users of this information.

► SUMMARY ANNUAL REPORTS

How can annual reports be made more meaningful? Some companies have experimented with the issuance of a **summary annual report (SAR). An SAR contains a condensed financial presentation in a more readable format than that of the traditional annual report.** This approach is based on the concept of "differential disclosure"; that is, certain stockholders need full disclosure, but many need only highly summarized and less technical analysis of financial information.

A small number of companies provided SARs to their stockholders in lieu of the annual report. McKesson Corporation was the first company to adopt this approach. It cut the size of its annual report approximately 40%, and claims that its SAR communicates better the financial condition of the business.

Advocates of the SAR approach note that (1) the structure and the content of the traditional annual report have become too inflexible to meet the needs of all users, and (2) the annual report in the present form is too compliance-oriented to be an effective vehicle for communicating with stockholders. Also, they noted that full audited financial statements and related disclosures are included in proxy materials sent to all stockholders along with the SAR.

Others disagree. They contend that SARs may provide management with the opportunity to emphasize the "good" but not the "bad" conditions that are affecting the company. Furthermore, financial analysts do not seem to favor SARs because the reduced information is not likely to provide the type of information they desire. Finally, some note that nothing prevents a company from sending out a summary package along with more detailed information. This approach would solve all the problems but it would increase costs.

In short, the employment of SARs is debatable. At present, few companies have elected to follow this procedure. Even General Motors, which initiated the idea, opted not to reduce the size of its annual report in the first year that these reports were permitted.

▶ FRAUDULENT FINANCIAL REPORTING

The system of financial reporting in the United States is generally considered the finest in the world. The importance of an effective financial reporting system cannot be underestimated, because it provides the financial information that ensures the proper functioning of the capital and credit markets. Unfortunately, the system does not always work as planned. Evidence of the shortcomings of the system includes financial frauds such as E.S.M. Government Securities, Inc., Home-State Savings and Loan of Ohio, American Savings and Loan Association of Florida, Penn Square Bank, Continental Illinois Bank, Beverly Hills Savings and Loan Association, United American Bank, and Drysdale Government Securities as examples.

OBJECTIVE 8

Describe the profession's response to fraudulent financial reporting.

The case of E.S.M. Government Securities, Inc. (E.S.M.) exemplifies the seriousness of these frauds. E.S.M. was a Fort Lauderdale securities dealer entrusted with monies to invest by municipalities from Toledo, Ohio to Beaumont, Texas.[23] The cities provided the cash to E.S.M. which they thought was collateralized with government securities. Examination of E.S.M.'s balance sheet indicated that the company owed about as much as it expected to collect. Unfortunately, the amount it expected to collect was from insolvent affiliates which, in effect, meant that E.S.M. was bankrupt. In fact, E.S.M. had been bankrupt for more than 6 years, and the fraud was discovered only because a customer questioned a note to the balance sheet! More than $300 million of losses had been disguised.

Although frauds such as these are unusual, they do raise questions about the financial reporting process. As indicated in Chapter 1, Congress continues to examine this process to determine whether improvements can be made. As this textbook is being written, for example, Congress is addressing basic issues such as the following:

1. How well are accounting practices and disclosures serving the public?

2. Are auditors meeting their obligations to the investing public?

3. What are the effects of the SEC's disclosure, compliance, and enforcement policies?

4. Could the effect of these regulatory accounting policies have contributed to these failures?

5. What legislative proposals, if any, are necessary to address perceived weaknesses in accounting and auditing standards and regulatory procedures.

Many other groups have been studying the financial reporting environment. One such group, the National Commission on Fraudulent Financial Reporting, chaired by James C. Treadway, Jr.—hereafter referred to as the **Treadway Commission**—identified causal factors that lead to fraudulent financial reporting and provided steps to reduce its incidence.[24]

The Commission defined **fraudulent financial reporting as "intentional or reckless conduct, whether act or omission, that results in materially misleading financial statements."** It also noted that fraudulent reporting can involve gross and deliberate distortion of corporate records (such as inventory count tags), or misapplication of accounting principles (failure to disclose material transactions).[25]

---

[23]For an expanded discussion of this case, see Robert J. Sack and Robert Tangreti, "ESM: Implications for the Profession," *Journal of Accountancy* (April, 1987).

[24]"Report of the National Commission on Fraudulent Financial Reporting" (Washington, D.C., 1987).

[25]Ibid, page 2. Unintentional errors as well as corporate improprieties (such as tax fraud, employee embezzlements, and so on) which do not cause the financial statements to be misleading are excluded from the definition of fraudulent financial reporting.

CAUSES OF FRAUDULENT FINANCIAL REPORTING

Fraudulent financial reporting usually occurs because of conditions in the internal or external environment.[26] Influences in the **internal environment** relate to poor systems of internal control, management's poor attitude toward ethics, or perhaps a company's liquidity or profitability. Those in the **external environment** may relate to industry conditions, overall business environment, or legal and regulatory considerations.

General incentives for fraudulent financial reporting are the desire to obtain a higher stock price or debt offering, to avoid default on a loan covenant, or to make a personal gain of some type (additional compensation, promotion). Situational pressures on the company or an individual manager also may lead to fraudulent financial reporting. Examples of these situational pressures include:

1. Sudden decreases in revenue or market share. A single company or an entire industry can experience these decreases.

2. Unrealistic budget pressures, particularly for short-term results. These pressures may occur when headquarters arbitrarily determines profit objectives and budgets without taking actual conditions into account.

3. Financial pressure resulting from bonus plans that depend on short-term economic performance. This pressure is particularly acute when the bonus is a significant component of the individual's total compensation.

Opportunities for fraudulent financial reporting are present in circumstances when the fraud is easy to commit and when detection is difficult. Frequently these opportunities arise from:

1. **The absence of a Board of Directors or audit committee** that vigilantly oversees the financial reporting process.

2. **Weak or nonexistent internal accounting controls.** This situation can occur, for example, when a company's revenue system is overloaded as a result of a rapid expansion of sales, an acquisition of a new division, or the entry into a new, unfamiliar line of business.

3. **Unusual or complex transactions** such as the consolidation of two companies, the divestiture or closing of a specific operation, and agreements to buy or sell government securities under a repurchase agreement.

4. **Accounting estimates, requiring significant subjective judgment** by company management, such as reserves for loan losses and the yearly provision for warranty expense.

5. **Ineffective internal audit staffs** resulting from inadequate staff size and severely limited audit scope.

A weak corporate ethical climate contributes to these situations. Opportunities for fraudulent financial reporting also increase dramatically when the accounting principles followed in reporting transactions are nonexistent, evolving, or subject to varying interpretations.

RESPONSE OF THE PROFESSION

The profession is hard at work attempting to find solutions to the problem of fraudulent financial reporting. For example, the Auditing Standards Board of AICPA has issued nine new auditing standards in response not only to the Treadway Commission report, but also to the public's higher expectation of the auditor.[27] These standards address

---

[26]The discussion in this section is taken from the Report of the National Commission on Fraudulent Financial Reporting, pp. 23–24.

[27]Because the profession believes that the role of the auditor is not well understood outside the profession, much attention has been focused on the expectation gap. The **expectation gap** is the gap between (1) the expectation of financial statement users concerning the level of assurance they believe the independent auditor provides and (2) the assurance that the independent auditor actually does provide under generally accepted auditing standards.

three issues: (1) strengthening communications with the audit committee, (2) improving auditor communications with the financial statement users,[28] and (3) enhancing audit procedures.[29]

In addition, the SEC now requires disclosure of a change in a company's independent auditor. Recently, many observers have expressed concern about so-called "opinion shopping" in which companies attempt to find a more favorable accounting approach by asking various auditing firms how they would report a given transaction. Because a great deal of subjectivity may be involved, an auditing firm may provide a more favorable response to the prospective client and therefore eventually be engaged as the auditor. To increase public awareness of possible opinion-shopping situations, the SEC has adopted new disclosure requirements concerning certain consultations between a company and its newly engaged auditor during the company's two most recent fiscal years.

► CRITERIA FOR MAKING ACCOUNTING AND REPORTING CHOICES

Throughout this textbook, and especially in this chapter, we have stressed the need to provide information that is useful to predict the amounts, timing, and uncertainty of future cash flows. To achieve this objective, the accountant must make judicious choices between alternative accounting concepts, methods, and means of disclosure. You are probably surprised by the large number of choices among acceptable alternatives that accountants are required to make.

You should recognize, however, as indicated in Chapter 1, that accounting is greatly influenced by its environment. Because it does not exist in a vacuum, it seems unrealistic to assume that alternative presentations of certain transactions and events will be eliminated entirely. Nevertheless, we are hopeful that the profession, through the development of a conceptual framework, will be able to focus on the needs of financial statement users and eliminate diversity where appropriate. The profession must continue its efforts to develop a sound foundation upon which accounting standards and practice can be built. As Aristotle said: "The correct beginning is more than half the whole."

UNDERLYING CONCEPT

The FASB concept statements on objectives of financial reporting, elements of financial statements, qualitative characteristics of accounting information, and recognition and measurement are important steps in the right direction.

► SUMMARY OF LEARNING OBJECTIVES ◄

1. **Review the full disclosure principle and describe problems of implementation.** The full disclosure principle calls for financial reporting of any financial facts significant enough to influence the judgment of an informed reader. Implementing the full disclosure principle is difficult, because the cost of disclosure can be substantial and the benefits difficult to assess. Disclosure requirements have increased because of (1) the growing complexity of the business environment, (2) the necessity for timely information, and (3) the use of accounting as a control and monitoring device.

2. **Explain the use of notes in financial statement preparation.** Notes are the accountant's means of amplifying or explaining the items presented in the main body of the statements. Information pertinent to specific financial statement items can be explained in qualitative terms, and supplementary data of a quantitative nature can be provided to expand the information in the notes. Com-

KEY TERMS

accounting policies, 1347
adverse opinion, 1364
auditor, 1363
auditor's report, 1363
common costs, 1356
differential
disclosure, 1347
disclaimer of an
opinion, 1365
discrete view, 1358
errors, 1351
export sales, 1356
financial forecast, 1368
financial projection, 1368
fraudulent financial
reporting, 1371

[28]"Communications with Audit Committees," *Statement on Auditing Standards No. 61* (New York, AICPA, 1988).

[29]"The Auditor's Responsibility to Detect and Report Errors and Irregularities," *Statement on Auditing Standards No. 53* (New York, AICPA, 1988).

mon note disclosures relate to such items as the following: accounting policies; inventories; property, plant, and equipment; credit claims; and contingencies and commitments.

3. **Describe the disclosure requirements for major segments of a business.**   If only the consolidated figures are available to the analyst, much information regarding the composition of these figures is hidden in aggregated figures. There is no way to tell from the consolidated data the extent to which the differing product lines contribute to the company's profitability, risk, and growth potential. As a result, segment information is required by the profession in certain situations.

4. **Describe the accounting problems associated with interim reporting.**   Interim reports cover periods of less than one year. Two viewpoints exist regarding interim reports. One view (discrete view) holds that each interim period should be treated as a separate accounting period. Another view (integral view) is that the interim report is an integral part of the annual report and that deferrals and accruals should take into consideration what will happen for the entire year.

   The same accounting principles used for annual reports should be employed for interim reports. A number of unique reporting problems develop related to the following items: (1) advertising and similar costs; (2) expenses subject to year-end adjustment; (3) income taxes; (4) extraordinary items; (5) changes in accounting; (6) earnings per share; and (7) seasonality.

5. **Identify the major disclosures found in the auditor's report.**   If the auditor is satisfied that the financial statements present the financial position, results of operations, and cash flows fairly in accordance with generally accepted accounting principles, an unqualified opinion is expressed. A qualified opinion contains an exception to the standard opinion; ordinarily the exception is not of sufficient magnitude to invalidate the statement as a whole.

   An adverse opinion is required in any report in which the exceptions to fair presentation are so material that a qualified opinion is not justified. A disclaimer of an opinion is appropriate when the auditor has gathered so little information on the financial statements that no opinion can be expressed.

6. **Understand other areas of the annual report.**   Management's discussion and analysis section covers three financial aspects of an enterprise's business: liquidity, capital resources, and results of operations. Management has primary responsibility for the financial statements and this responsibility is often indicated in a letter to stockholders in the annual report. Companies often report on their socially responsible activities. As yet, no standards or requirements have been proposed by the FASB for the measurement and reporting of the social responsibilities assumed by individual enterprises.

7. **Identify issues related to financial forecasts and projections.**   The SEC has indicated that companies are permitted (not required) to include profit forecasts in reports filed with that agency. To encourage management to disclose this type of information, the SEC has issued a "safe harbor" rule. The safe harbor rule provides protection to an enterprise that presents an erroneous forecast as long as the projection was prepared on a reasonable basis and was disclosed in good faith. However, the safe harbor rule has not worked well in practice.

8. **Describe the profession's response to fraudulent financial reporting.**   Fraudulent financial reporting is intentional or reckless conduct, whether act or omission, that results in materially misleading financial statements. Fraudulent financial reporting usually occurs because of poor internal control, management's poor attitude toward ethics, and so on. The profession is hard at work attempting to find solutions, and has issued a number of auditing standards that address part of the problem.

APPENDIX 26-A

ACCOUNTING FOR CHANGING PRICES

One assumption made in accounting is that the monetary unit remains stable over a period of time. But is that assumption realistic? Consider the classic story about the individual who went to sleep and woke up 10 years later. Hurrying to a telephone, he got through to his broker and asked what his formerly modest stock portfolio was worth. He was told that he was a multimillionaire—his General Motors stock was worth $5 million and his AT&T stock was up to $10 million. Elated, he was about to inquire about his other holdings, when the telephone operator cut in with "Your time is up. Please deposit $100,000 for the next three minutes."[1]

What this little story demonstrates is that prices can and do change over a period of time, and that one is not necessarily better off when they do. Although the example above is extreme, consider some more realistic data that compare prices today with what might happen in the future.

	Today	In 10 Years	In 30 Years
Car	$ 20,000	$ 32,282	$ 94,482
Condo	100,000	161,904	472,412
Doctor visit	35	123	2,015
Restaurant dinner	7.50	12	35
Domestic air fare	500	1,178	7,931
Motel room	75	121	354
Monthly electricity bill	125	294	1,982

Normal inflation rate: 5.5%; energy inflation rate: 10%; medical inflation rate: 15%

Despite the inevitability of changing prices during a period of inflation, the accounting profession still follows the stable monetary unit assumption in the preparation of a company's primary financial statements. While admitting that some changes in prices do occur, the profession believes the unit of measure (e.g., the dollar) has remained sufficiently constant over time to provide meaningful financial information.

The profession, however, at one time required and now encourages the disclosure of certain price-level adjusted data in the form of supplemental information. The two most widely used approaches to show the effects of changing prices on a company's financial statements are (1) constant dollar accounting, and (2) current cost accounting.

▶ CONSTANT DOLLAR ACCOUNTING

The real value of the dollar is determined by the goods or services for which it can be exchanged. This real value is commonly called **purchasing power.** As the economy experiences **inflation** (rising price-levels) or **deflation** (falling price-levels), the amount of goods or services for which a dollar can be exchanged changes; that is, the purchasing power of the dollar changes from one period to the next.

Constant dollar accounting restates financial statement items into dollars that have equal purchasing power. As one executive from Shell Oil Company explained, "Constant dollar accounting is a restatement of the traditional financial information into a common unit of measurement." In other words, constant dollar accounting changes the unit of measurement; it does not, however, change the underlying accounting principles used to report historical cost amounts. Constant dollar accounting is cost based.

OBJECTIVE 9

After studying Appendix 26-A you should be able to: Understand and account for changing prices.

**ILLUSTRATION 26A-1
What Things Will Cost**

INTERNATIONAL INSIGHT

Inflation rates vary by countries. Argentina, Brazil, and Russia have had rates exceeding 100 percent per year recently.

---

[1]Adapted from *Barron's*, January 28, 1980, p. 27.

Through constant dollar restatement, financial data are rendered comparable; thus, important trends can be detected. For example, a newspaper article recently lamented the fact that workers in the United States were losing ground economically. The article noted that a family's median after-tax income in 1990 was $41,130, which is exactly the same as the 1986 level adjusted for inflation. This information suggests that the standard of living in the United States has held constant at best.

PRICE-LEVEL INDEXES

To restate financial information into constant dollars, it is necessary to measure a change in the price of a "basket of goods" from one period to the next. Developing this basket of goods is a complex process and involves judgment in selecting the most appropriate items to be part of this market basket. Fortunately, the government puts together a number of different baskets of goods and computes indexes for them. One of the most popular, and the one that accountants use, is the Consumers Price Index for all Urban Consumers (CPI-U). The CPI-U reflects the average change in the retail prices of a fairly broad group of consumer goods.

The procedure for restating reported historical cost dollars, which vary in purchasing power, to dollars of constant purchasing power is relatively straightforward. The restatement is accomplished by multiplying the amount to be restated by a fraction, the numerator of which is the index for current prices and the denominator of which is the index for prices that prevailed at the date related to the amount being restated (as determined from numbers computed by the government). The denominator is often referred to as the base year. The formula is as follows:

ILLUSTRATION 26A-2
Formula for Restating Historical Cost Dollars into Constant Purchasing Power Dollars

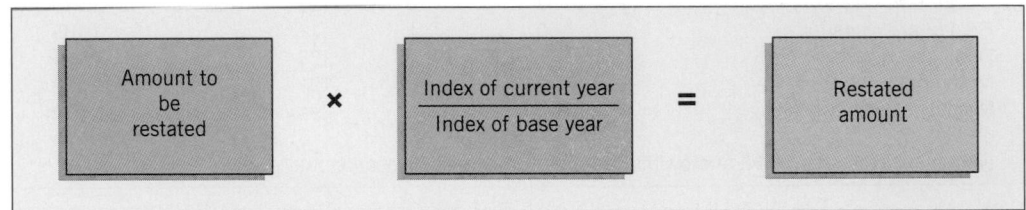

To illustrate how this restatement process works, assume that land was purchased in 1989 for $100,000 and another parcel of land was purchased in 1993 for $80,000. If the price-level index was 100 in 1989, 120 in 1993, and 180 in 1996, the land parcels would be restated to the 1996 price level as follows:

ILLUSTRATION 26A-3
Restatement of Historical Cost

1989 purchase	$\left(\$100{,}000 \times \dfrac{180}{100}\right)$ =	$180,000
1993 purchase	$\left(\$\ 80{,}000 \times \dfrac{180}{120}\right)$ =	120,000
Land as restated		$300,000

The land is restated to $300,000 in terms of 1996 dollars using the 1996 index of 180 as the numerator for both parcels and the base year indexes of 100 and 120 as the denominators. If historical cost dollars are not restated, dollars of different purchasing power are added together, and the total dollar amount is not meaningful.

MONETARY AND NONMONETARY ITEMS

In preparing constant dollar statements, it is essential to distinguish between monetary and nonmonetary items. **Monetary items** are contractual claims to receive or pay a fixed amount of cash. Monetary assets include cash, accounts and notes receivable, and investments that pay a fixed rate of interest and will be repaid at a fixed amount in the future. Monetary liabilities include accounts and notes payable, accruals such as wages and interest payable, and long-term obligations payable in a fixed sum.

All assets and liabilities not classified as monetary items are classified as non-monetary for constant dollar accounting purposes. Nonmonetary items are items whose prices in terms of the monetary unit change in proportion to changes in the general price level. Examples of nonmonetary assets are inventories; property, plant, and equipment; and intangible assets. Most liabilities are monetary items, whereas capital stock equity is usually nonmonetary.

The following chart indicates some major monetary and nonmonetary items.

Monetary Items	Nonmonetary Items
Cash	Inventories
Notes and accounts receivable	Investments in common stock
Investments that pay a fixed rate of interest	Property, plant, and equipment
Notes and accounts payable	Intangible assets
	Capital stock

ILLUSTRATION 26A-4
Major Monetary and Nonmonetary Items

EFFECTS OF HOLDING MONETARY AND NONMONETARY ITEMS

Holders of monetary assets lose during a period of inflation because a given amount of money buys progressively fewer goods and services. Conversely, liabilities such as accounts payable and notes payable held during a period of inflation become less burdensome because they are payable in dollars of reduced general purchasing power. The gains or losses that result from holding monetary items during periods of price changes are often referred to as **purchasing power gains and losses.** As Northwestern National Life Insurance explained in its annual report, "If a company's equity is invested in monetary assets, the purchasing power of its equity is gradually eroded at a rate equal to inflation."

To illustrate the effects of holding monetary and nonmonetary items in a period of inflation, assume that Helio Company has the following balance sheet at the beginning of the year:

Helio Company BALANCE SHEET (Beginning of Period) Price index = 100			
Cash	$1,000	Capital stock	$4,000
Inventory	3,000		
Total assets	$4,000	Total stockholders' equity	$4,000

ILLUSTRATION 26A-5
Balance Sheet (Beginning of Period)—Historical Cost

If the general price-level doubles during the year, and no transactions take place, then for the company to be in the same economic position at the end of the year as it was at the beginning, it should have the balance sheet shown below.

Helio Company BALANCE SHEET (End of Period) Price index = 200			
Cash	$2,000	Capital stock	$8,000
Inventory	6,000		
Total assets	$8,000	Total stockholders' equity	$8,000

ILLUSTRATION 26A-6
Balance Sheet (End of Period)—Historical Cost

As illustrated, all items should have doubled if the company is to be in the same economic position. However, only the inventory and the capital stock can be doubled. Helio still has only $1,000 of cash; therefore, it has experienced a purchasing power loss in holding cash during a period of inflation. Helio's balance sheet presented on a constant dollar basis would appear as follows:

Helio Company BALANCE SHEET (End of Period) Price index = 200			
Cash	$1,000	Capital stock	$8,000
Inventory	6,000	Retained earnings	(1,000)
Total assets	$7,000	Total stockholders' equity	$7,000

As noted, Helio Company has experienced a purchasing power loss of $1,000, which is shown as a reduction of retained earnings.

In summary, because monetary assets and liabilities are already stated in terms of current purchasing power in the historical cost balance sheet, they **appear at the same amounts in statements adjusted for general price-level changes.** The fact that the end-of-the-current-year amounts are the same in historical dollar statements as in constant dollar statements does not obscure the fact that purchasing power gains or losses result from holding them during a period of general price-level change. Conversely, **non-monetary items are reported at different amounts in the constant dollar statements** than they are in the historical cost statements, when there is a change in the general price level. As a result, both the inventory and the capital stock are adjusted to recognize changes in the purchasing power of the dollar.

CONSTANT DOLLAR ILLUSTRATION

To illustrate the preparation of financial statements on a constant dollar basis, assume that Hartley Company starts business on December 31, 1995, by selling $190,000 of capital stock for cash. Land costing $80,000 is purchased immediately. During 1996, the company reports $190,000 of sales, cost of goods sold of $100,000, and operating expenses of $20,000. The income statement for Hartley Company on a historical cost basis is as follows:

Hartley Company INCOME STATEMENT (HISTORICAL COST) For the Year Ended December 31, 1996	
Sales	$190,000
Cost of goods sold	100,000
Gross profit	90,000
Operating expenses	20,000
Net income	$ 70,000

The comparative balance sheets on a historical cost basis are as follows:

Hartley Company BALANCE SHEET (HISTORICAL COST) December 31	1996	1995
Assets		
Cash	$145,000	$110,000
Inventory	35,000	—
Land	80,000	80,000
Total assets	$260,000	$190,000
Liabilities and Stockholders' Equity		
Capital stock	$190,000	$190,000
Retained earnings	70,000	—
Total liabilities and stockholders' equity	$260,000	$190,000

The relevant price indexes for use in preparing constant dollar financial statements are presented below. These price indexes are magnified here to illustrate their effect.

	Price Indexes
December 31, 1995	100
1996 average	160
December 31, 1996	200

ILLUSTRATION 26A-10
Price Indexes

Constant Dollar Income Statement

When a constant dollar income statement is prepared, **revenues and expenses are restated to end-of-year dollars.** The difference between restated revenues and expenses is reported as income (loss) before purchasing power gain (loss). The purchasing power gain (loss) is then added (deducted) to produce "constant dollar net income (loss)."

Revenues and expenses are usually assumed to occur evenly throughout the period. Therefore, the historical dollar amounts are multiplied by the restatement ratio, of which the numerator is the end-of-year index and the denominator is the average index. The constant dollar income statement for Hartley Company is provided below. (The explanations highlighted in color are not part of the formal statement; they are provided to help you understand how the statement is prepared.)

ILLUSTRATION 26A-11
Income Statement—
Constant Dollar Basis

Hartley Company
CONSTANT DOLLAR INCOME STATEMENT
For the Year Ended December 31, 1996

Sales	$237,500	$\left(\$190,000 \times \dfrac{200}{160}\right)$
Cost of goods sold	125,000	$\left(\$100,000 \times \dfrac{200}{160}\right)$
Gross profit	112,500	
Operating expenses	25,000	$\left(\$\,20,000 \times \dfrac{200}{160}\right)$
Income before purchasing power loss	87,500	
Purchasing power loss	(118,750)	(Per computation in Illustration 26A-12.)
Constant dollar net loss	$ (31,250)	

Restatement of the items in Illustration 26A-11 is explained as follows:

Sales. Because sales were spread evenly over the year, the average index is used in the computation to restate sales to end-of-year dollars.

Cost of Goods Sold. The cost of goods sold of $100,000 consists of two amounts, purchases of $135,000 less ending inventory of $35,000. Because the costs of purchases and ending inventories were spread evenly over the year, the average index is used in the computation to restate cost of goods sold to end-of-year dollars.

Operating Expenses. Because operating expenses were spread evenly over the year, the average index is used in the computation to restate operating expenses to end-of-year dollars.

Purchasing Power Loss. Computation of the purchasing power gain (loss) on monetary items requires a reconciliation of the beginning and ending balances of each monetary item for the period. A restatement ratio is then applied to the beginning balance and each reconciling amount. Hartley Company has only one monetary item, cash. Because prices are rising, it will experience a purchasing power loss for 1996. The computation of the loss is shown in Illustration 26A-12.

	1996 Historical	× Restatement Ratio =	Restated to 12/31/96 Dollars
Cash:			
Beginning balance	$110,000	$\frac{200}{100}$	$220,000
Add: Sales	190,000	$\frac{200}{160}$	237,500
Deduct: Purchases	(135,000)	$\frac{200}{160}$	(168,750)
Operating expenses	(20,000)	$\frac{200}{160}$	(25,000)
Total restated dollars			263,750
Ending balance	$145,000		145,000
Purchasing power loss			$(118,750)

The first column of Illustration 26A-12 provides a reconciliation of the beginning and ending cash balances. Note that purchases is determined by adding ending inventory ($35,000) to cost of goods sold ($100,000) for Hartley Company. The restatement ratio for the beginning cash balance is based on the price index at the beginning of the year (100). The other ratios are based on the average price index during the year (160). The totaled restated dollars, $263,750, indicates how much cash the company should have in order to stay even with the price increases that have occurred. This amount is then compared with the historical cost ending balance to determine the amount of the purchasing power gain or loss. In this case, Hartley should have $263,750; it has only $145,000. Therefore, it has experienced a purchasing power loss of $118,750.

Constant Dollar Balance Sheet

When a constant dollar balance sheet is prepared, all monetary items are stated in end-of-year dollars and therefore do not need adjustment. **Nonmonetary items, however, must be restated to end-of-year dollars.** The constant dollar balance sheet for Hartley Company is provided below. (The explanations highlighted in color are not part of the formal statement; they are provided to help you understand how the statement is prepared.)

Hartley Company
CONSTANT DOLLAR BALANCE SHEET
December 31, 1996

Assets		
Cash	$145,000	(Same as historical cost)
Inventory	43,750	$\left(\$35,000 \times \frac{200}{160}\right)$
Land	160,000	$\left(\$80,000 \times \frac{200}{100}\right)$
Total assets	$348,750	
Liabilities and Stockholders' Equity		
Capital stock	$380,000	$\left(\$190,000 \times \frac{200}{100}\right)$
Retained earnings	(31,250)	(See constant dollar income statement)
Total liabilities and stockholders' equity	$348,750	

Restatement of the items in Illustration 26A-13 is explained as follows:

Cash. Cash is a monetary item; therefore, no restatement is necessary.

Inventory. Inventory is a nonmonetary item and therefore it must be restated. Because inventory was purchased evenly throughout the year, the $35,000 must be multiplied by the ratio of the ending index, 200, to the index at the time the inventory was purchased, which was the average for the year of 160.

Land. Land is a nonmonetary item; therefore, it must be restated. Because land was purchased at the end of the preceding year, the $80,000 must be multiplied by the ratio of the ending index to the index at the time the land was purchased, which was 100.

Capital Stock. Capital stock is a nonmonetary item; therefore, restatement is necessary. Because capital stock was issued at the end of the preceding year, the $190,000 must be multiplied by the ratio of the ending index, 200, to the index at the time the capital stock was issued, which was 100.

Retained Earnings. Since no balance existed in retained earnings at the beginning of the year, the retained earnings in constant dollars includes only the constant dollar net loss for the current period of $31,250. Thus, Hartley Company on a constant dollar basis reports a negative retained earnings after its first year of operations.

ADVANTAGES AND DISADVANTAGES OF CONSTANT DOLLAR ACCOUNTING

Constant dollar financial statements have been discussed widely within both the accounting profession and the business and financial community. They are lauded by many as a means of overcoming the reporting problems during periods of inflation or deflation. The following arguments have been submitted in support of preparing such statements:

INTERNATIONAL INSIGHT

Some countries experience hyperinflation. Examples are Argentina, Brazil, and Mexico. Constant-dollar financial statements are a necessity in that environment.

1. Constant dollar accounting provides management with an **objectively** determined quantification of the impact of inflation on its business operations.

2. Constant dollar accounting eliminates the effects of inflation from financial information by requiring each enterprise to follow the same objective procedure and use the same price-level index, thereby **preserving comparability of financial statements between firms.**

3. Constant dollar accounting **enhances comparability between the financial statements of a single firm** by eliminating differences due to price-level changes and thereby improves trend analysis.

4. Constant dollar accounting eliminates the effects of price-level changes without having to develop a new structure of accounting; that is, it **preserves the historical cost-based accounting system** that is currently used and understood.

5. Constant dollar accounting **eliminates the necessity of and attraction to the "piecemeal" approaches** used in combating the effects of inflation on financial statements, namely, LIFO inventory costing and accelerated depreciation of property, plant, and equipment.

However, in spite of widespread publicity, discussion, and authoritative support both inside and outside the accounting profession, the preparation and public issuance of constant dollar financial statements up to this point has been negligible. This result is probably due to the following disadvantages said to be associated with constant dollar financial statements:

1. The additional **cost** of preparing constant dollar statements is not offset by the benefit of receiving sufficient relevant information.

2. Constant dollar financial statements will cause **confusion** and be misunderstood by users.

3. Restating the "value" of nonmonetary items at historical cost adjusted for general

price-level changes **is no more meaningful than historical cost alone,** that is, it suffers all the shortcomings of the historical cost method.

4. The reported purchasing power gain from monetary items is **misleading** because it does not necessarily represent successful management or provide funds for dividends, plant expansion, or other purposes.

5. Constant dollar accounting **assumes that the impact of inflation falls equally** on all businesses and on all classes of assets and costs, which is not true.

Probably the greatest deterrent to adoption of constant dollar accounting in the past has been **what it is not:** constant dollar accounting is not present value, net realizable value, or current cost accounting, and therein lies much of the opposition to its use.

▶ CURRENT COST ACCOUNTING

The price of a specific item may be affected not only by general inflation, but also by individual market forces. For example, in a recent 6-year period, certain items changed more or less than the general price level. To illustrate, during this period of time, the cost of a local telephone call increased 150%, guaranteed overnight mail delivery increased 4,575%, a gallon of gasoline decreased over 30%, and a flawless one-carat diamond decreased over 70%. Thus, changes in the specific price of items may be very different from the change in the general price-level.

A popular means to measure the change in a specific price is current cost. **Current cost** is the cost of replacing the identical asset owned. Current cost may be approximated by reference to current catalog prices or by applying a specific index to the book value of the asset. Unlike the constant dollar approach, which is simply a restatement of historical dollars into constant purchasing power, the current cost approach changes the basis of measurement from historical cost to current value.

CURRENT COST ADJUSTMENTS

When current cost statements are prepared, it is also necessary to distinguish between monetary and nonmonetary items. Monetary items are stated at their current cost in the historical cost financial statements. As a result, no adjustment is necessary to items such as cash, accounts receivable, notes payable, or accounts payable when preparing a current cost balance sheet. A purchasing power gain or loss on the monetary items is not computed under current cost accounting because the measuring unit, the dollar, is not considered to have changed from one period to the next.

Conversely, nonmonetary items as a rule must be adjusted at year-end. The current cost of nonmonetary items tends to change over time. For example, land held over a period of time will usually experience some type of price change. The same is true of other nonmonetary items such as inventory; property, plant, and equipment; and intangible assets.

When a nonmonetary item is restated, a holding gain or loss arises and must be reported on the financial statements. A **holding gain (loss)** is an increase or decrease in an item's value while it is held by the company. For example, if the current cost of land is $20,000 on January 1, 1996, and $32,000 on December 31, 1996, the company has a holding gain on this land of $12,000, computed as follows:

ILLUSTRATION 26A-14
Computation of Holding Gain

Current cost of land, December 31, 1996	$32,000
Current cost of land, January 1, 1996	20,000
Holding gain on land	$12,000

Revenues and expenses appearing on a current cost income statement are the same as the historical cost amounts, because at the time they are earned or incurred they represent current cost. A major exception is the cost of goods sold, which will be explained later.

To illustrate the preparation of financial statements on a current cost basis, assume that Sensor, Inc., starts business on December 31, 1995, by selling $90,000 of capital stock for cash. Land costing $40,000 is purchased immediately. During the next year, the company reports $160,000 of sales revenue, cost of goods sold of $75,000, and operating expenses of $25,000. The income statement for Sensor, Inc., on a historical cost basis is as follows:

Sensor, Inc. INCOME STATEMENT (HISTORICAL COST) For the Year Ended December 31, 1996	
Sales	$160,000
Cost of goods sold	75,000
Gross profit	85,000
Operating expenses	25,000
Net income	$ 60,000

ILLUSTRATION 26A-15
Income Statement—
Historical Cost Basis

The comparative balance sheets on a historical cost basis are as follows:

Sensor, Inc. BALANCE SHEET (HISTORICAL COST) December 31		
	1996	**1995**
Assets		
Cash	$ 30,000	$50,000
Inventory	80,000	—
Land	40,000	40,000
Total assets	$150,000	$90,000
Liabilities and Stockholders' Equity		
Capital stock	$ 90,000	$90,000
Retained earnings	60,000	—
Total liabilities and stockholders' equity	$150,000	$90,000

ILLUSTRATION 26A-16
Comparative Balance
Sheets—Historical Cost
Basis

The relevant current cost amounts for the income statement and balance sheet items for 1996 are as follows:

Income Statement		**Balance Sheet**	
Sales	$160,000	Cash	$ 30,000
Cost of goods sold	95,000	Inventory	105,000
Operating expenses	25,000	Land	48,000
		Capital stock	90,000

ILLUSTRATION 26A-17
Relevant Current Cost
Amounts

CURRENT COST INCOME STATEMENT

In a current cost income statement, two income numbers are reported. The first, **current cost income from operations,** is sales revenues less the current cost of goods sold plus operating expenses. This amount is the **income a company has earned after providing for the replacement of assets used in operations.**

The second income number, **current cost net income,** measures the **total income of a company from one period to the next.** Thus, holding gains (losses) are added (deducted) to current cost income from operations to arrive at this number. The current cost income statement for Sensor, Inc. is provided below. (The explanations highlighted in color are not part of the formal statement; they are provided to help you understand how the statement is prepared.)

ILLUSTRATION 26A-18
Income Statement—
Current Cost Basis

Sensor, Inc. INCOME STATEMENT (CURRENT COST) For the Year Ended December 31, 1996		
Sales	$160,000	(Same as historical cost)
Cost of goods sold	95,000	(Restated to current cost)
Gross profit	65,000	
Operating expenses	25,000	(Same as historical cost)
Current cost income from operations	40,000	
Holding gain	53,000	(Increase in current cost)
Current cost net income	$ 93,000	

The preceding items are explained below.

Sales and Operating Expenses. Sales and operating expenses are already stated at their current cost amounts on historical cost statements; therefore, no adjustment is needed for these items.

Cost of Goods Sold. Goods are sold at varying times of the year. At the time these goods are sold, the current cost of the inventory sold must be determined. The historical cost of goods sold and the current cost of goods sold are usually different.

Total Holding Gain. The holding gain for Sensor comprises three items as shown below.

ILLUSTRATION 26A-19
Computation of Holding
Gain

Current cost of goods sold	$ 95,000	
Historical cost of goods sold	75,000	
		$20,000
Current cost of inventory	105,000	
Historical cost of inventory	80,000	
		25,000
Current cost of land	48,000	
Historical cost of land	40,000	
		8,000
Total holding gain		$53,000

Recall that a holding gain is an increase in an item's value from one period to the next. If the item is sold during the period, however, the holding gain (loss) is computed only to the point of sale. Thus, the inventory sold, as reported in the current cost of goods sold amount, had increased $20,000. Also, inventory on hand and land experienced holding gains of $25,000 and $8,000, respectively. Holding gains or losses indicate how effective management is in acquiring and holding assets.

CURRENT COST BALANCE SHEET

The preparation of a current cost balance sheet is relatively straightforward. Monetary items are not adjusted because they are already stated at current cost. Similarly, **capital stock equity is not adjusted** because its balance represents the current cost of capital stock. All other nonmonetary items must be adjusted to current costs. The current cost balance sheet for Sensor, Inc. is shown in Illustration 26A-20. (The explanations highlighted in color are not part of the formal statement; they are provided to help you understand how the statement is prepared.)

Sensor, Inc. BALANCE SHEET (CURRENT COST) December 31, 1996		
Assets		
Cash	$ 30,000	(Same as historical cost)
Inventory	105,000	(Restated to current cost)
Land	48,000	(Restated to current cost)
Total assets	$183,000	
Liabilities and Stockholders' Equity		
Capital stock	$ 90,000	(Same as historical cost)
Retained earnings	93,000	(From current cost income statement)
Total liabilities and stockholders' equity	$183,000	

As indicated from the statement above, Retained Earnings is determined by adding the current cost net income amount to the beginning balance of retained earnings.

ADVANTAGES AND DISADVANTAGES OF CURRENT COST

A distinct advantage that current cost has over both historical cost and constant dollar accounting is that the **specific changes (up and down) in individual items are considered.** While the general level of prices may be increasing, prices of specific items may be decreasing. Such items as calculators, tennis balls, watches, microwave ovens, and television sets, for example, have decreased in price, whereas the general level of prices has increased. Constant dollar accounting using a general price index does not make an allowance for these changes in prices as effectively as a current cost system does.

The major arguments for the use of a current cost approach are:

1. Current cost provides a **better measure of efficiency.** If, for example, depreciation is based on current costs, not historical costs, a better measure of operating efficiencies is obtained. For example, assume that you are a new manager in an operation that includes a number of assets purchased recently at current prices, and your performance is compared with that of someone in a similar job elsewhere who is using similar assets that were purchased 5 years ago when the price was substantially lower. You probably would contend that the 5-year-old assets should be revalued because the other manager will show a lower depreciation charge and higher net income than you will.

2. Current cost is an **approximation of the service potential** of the asset. It is difficult if not impossible to determine the present discounted values of specific cash flows that will occur from the use of certain assets; but current cost frequently is a reasonable approximation of this value. As the current cost increases, the implication is that the enterprise has a holding gain (an increase from one period to another in the current cost of that item) because the aggregate value of the asset's service potential has increased.

3. Current cost provides for the **maintenance of physical capital.** Assume that an asset is purchased for one dollar, sold for two dollars, and replaced for two dollars. How much income should be reported and how much tax should be paid? Under traditional accounting procedures, one dollar of income would be earned (which is subject to tax and a claim for dividend distribution). If current cost is used, however, no income exists to be taxed and claims for dividend distribution would probably be fewer.

4. Current cost provides an **assessment of future cash flows.** Information on current cost margins may be useful for assessing future cash flows when the selling price of a product is closely related to its current cost. In addition, reporting holding gains (losses) may provide help in assessing future cash flows.

The major arguments against current cost adjustments are:

1. The use of **current cost is subjective** because it is difficult to determine the exact current cost of all items at any point in time. A good second-hand market for all types of assets does not exist. In most cases, the asset is not replaced with an identical asset; it is replaced with a better one, a faster one, an improved one, an altogether different one, or it is not replaced at all.

2. **The maintenance of physical capital is not the accountant's function.** It is generally conceded that it is management's function to ensure that capital is not impaired.

3. **Current cost is not always an approximation of the fair market value.** An asset's value is a function of the future cash flows generated by it. Current cost, however, does not necessarily measure an increase in the service potential of that asset.

One final comment: Many of the arguments above also apply to a **current cost/ constant dollar system** (a full illustration not provided in the chapter). Additional arguments for a current cost/constant dollar system are: (1) It stabilizes the measuring unit and provides current, comparable data, and (2) it provides more information than either other system alone. Holding gains and losses adjusted for inflation or deflation are reported, as well as the purchasing power gain or loss on net monetary items. Its potential disadvantages are its cost to prepare and that more information is not always better information because it may confuse readers or lead to information overload.

▶ PROFESSION'S POSITION ON CHANGING PRICE INFORMATION

In September 1979, the FASB, in response to a perceived need for information on the effects of changing prices on financial statements, required large publicly held companies to disclose certain price-level adjusted financial information. The required price-level adjusted information was provided on an experimental basis and consisted of restated information from the primary financial statements to reflect changes in (1) general price levels (constant dollar data) and (2) specific price levels (current cost data).

An FASB survey of financial statement users, preparers, and auditors revealed that both the number of users and the extent of use of the data were limited. Many respondents commented that the price-level adjusted data did not appear to have been used by the institutional investment community, bankers, or investors in general. Therefore, partly as a result of nonuse and partly as a result of prevailing low inflation rates, the accounting profession in 1987 was persuaded to cease requiring the disclosure of supplementary information on the effects of changing prices. Companies now are only encouraged to disclose price-level adjusted information and are not discouraged from experimenting with different forms of disclosure. Many companies include a discussion of inflation in the Management's Discussion and Analysis section of the annual report.

KEY TERMS

constant dollar
accounting, 1375

current cost, 1382

current cost/constant
dollar systems, 1386

deflation, 1375

holding gain (loss), 1382

inflation, 1375

monetary items, 1376

nonmonetary items, 1377

purchasing power, 1375

purchasing power gains or
losses, 1377

▶ SUMMARY OF LEARNING OBJECTIVE FOR APP. 26-A ◀

9. **Understand and account for changing prices.** The two most widely used approaches to show the effects of changing prices are (1) constant dollar accounting and (2) current cost accounting. Constant dollar accounting restates financial statement items into dollars that have equal purchasing power. Current cost is the cost of replacing the identical asset owned. Companies now are encouraged to disclose price-level-adjusted information and are not discouraged from experimenting with different forms of disclosure. Many companies include a discussion of inflation in the Management's Discussion and Analysis Section of the annual report.

Note: All **asterisked** Questions, Exercises, and Cases relate to materials contained in the appendix to each chapter.

QUESTIONS

1. What are the major advantages of notes to the financial statements? What type of items are usually reported in notes?

2. What is the full disclosure principle in accounting? Why has disclosure increased substantially in the last 10 years?

3. The auditor for Bramhall Inc. is debating whether the major categories of property, plant, and equipment and related accumulated depreciation should be reported in a note or in the summary of significant accounting policies. What would be your recommendation? Why?

4. NRBQ Co. is liable for a 12% mortgage payable of $44,000, secured by land and buildings, which is payable in semiannual installments (including principal and interest) of $6,000. Indicate the balance sheet presentation of long-term debt, current maturities, and indicate in general terms the necessary disclosure.

5. The FASB requires a reconciliation between the effective tax rate and the federal government's statutory rate. Of what benefit is such a disclosure requirement?

6. At the beginning of 1995, Beausoleil Inc. entered into an 8-year nonrenewable lease agreement. Provisions in the lease require the client to make substantial reconditioning and restoration expenditures at the end of the lease. What type of disclosure do you believe is necessary for this type of situation?

7. An annual report of D. Robillard Industries states: "The company and its subsidiaries have long-term leases expiring on various dates after December 31, 1996. Amounts payable under such commitments, without reduction for related rental income, are expected to average approximately $5,711,000 annually for the next three years. Related rental income from certain subleases to others is estimated to average $3,094,000 annually for the next three years." What information is provided by this note?

8. What type of disclosure or accounting do you believe is necessary for the following items:
   (a) Because of a general increase in the number of labor disputes and strikes, both within and outside the industry, there is an increased likelihood that a company will suffer a costly strike in the near future.
   (b) A company reports an extraordinary item (net of tax) correctly on the income statement. No other mention is made of this item in the annual report.
   (c) A company expects to recover a substantial amount in connection with a pending refund claim for a prior year's taxes. Although the claim is being contested, counsel for the company has confirmed the client's expectation of recovery.

9. An annual report of Ford Motor Corporation states: "Net income a share is computed based upon the average number of shares of capital stock of all classes outstanding. Additional shares of common stock may be issued or delivered in the future on conversion of outstanding convertible debentures, exercise of outstanding employee stock options, and for payment of defined supplemental compensation. Had such additional shares been outstanding, net income a share would have been reduced by 10¢ in the current year and 3¢ in the previous year.
   "As a result of capital stock transactions by the company during the current year (primarily the purchase of Class A Stock from Ford Foundation), net income a share was increased by 6¢." What information is provided by this note?

10. The following information was described in a note of Cebar Packing Co. "During August, A. Belew Products Corporation purchased 311,003 shares of the Company's common stock which constitutes approximately 35% of the stock outstanding. A. Belew has since obtained representation on the Board of Directors.
   "An affiliate of A. Belew Products Corporation acts as a food broker for the Company in the greater New York City marketing area. The commissions for such services after August amounted to approximately $20,000." Why is this information disclosed?

11. What approaches might be employed to disclose "social awareness" expenditures?

12. What are diversified companies? What accounting problems are related to diversified companies?

13. Explain the following terms:
    (a) Identifiable assets.
    (b) Intersegment sales.

    (c) Industry segment.

    (d) Common cost.

14. The controller for Fong Sai-Yuk Inc. recently commented: "If I have to disclose our segments individually, the only people who will gain are our competitors and the only people that will lose are our present stockholders." Evaluate this comment.

15. An article in the financial press entitled "Important Information in Annual Reports This Year" noted that annual reports include a discussion and analysis section. What would this section contain?

16. "The financial statements of a company are management's, not the accountant's." Discuss the implications of this statement.

17. Bess Marvin, a student of Intermediate Accounting, was heard to remark after a class discussion on diversified reporting: "All this is very confusing to me. First we are told that there is merit in presenting the consolidated results and now we are told that it is better to show segmental results. I wish they would make up their minds." Evaluate this comment.

18. Nancy Drew, a financial writer, noted recently: "There are substantial arguments for including earnings projections in annual reports and the like. The most compelling is that it would give anyone interested something now available to only a relatively select few—like large stockholders, creditors, and attentive bartenders." Identify some arguments against providing earnings projections.

19. The following recently appeared in the financial press: "Inadequate financial disclosure, particularly with respect to how management views the future and its role in the marketplace, has always been a stone in the shoe. After all, if you don't know how a company views the future, how can you judge the worth of its corporate strategy?" What are some arguments for reporting earnings forecasts?

20. What are interim reports? Why are balance sheets often not provided with interim data?

21. What are the accounting problems related to the presentation of interim data?

22. Mysteries Inc., a closely held corporation, has decided to go public. The controller, C. Keene, is concerned with presenting interim data when a LIFO inventory valuation is used. What problems are encountered with LIFO inventories when quarterly data are presented?

23. What approaches have been suggested to overcome the seasonal problem related to interim reporting?

24. What is the difference between a CPA's unqualified opinion or "clean" opinion and a qualified one?

25. Mary Beidler and Lee Pannebecker are discussing the recent fraud that occurred at Lowrental Leasing, Inc. The fraud involved the improper reporting of revenue to insure that the company would have income in excess of $1 million. What is fraudulent financial reporting and how does it differ from an embezzlement of company funds?

*26. (a) What is meant by constant dollar accounting? (b) What is purchasing power?

*27. Distinguish between monetary items and nonmonetary items. Give two examples of each.

*28. Tod Mullinger, the president of Investor Publications, is confused. He does not understand how a purchasing power gain or loss can exist when monetary assets and liabilities are unadjusted in constant dollar financial statements. Explain why this treatment is proper.

*29. Kimmel Co. purchased equipment in 1989 for $150,000. Kimmel purchased another piece of equipment in 1995 for $70,000. If the price level index was 100 in 1989, 125 in 1995, and 130 in 1996, what would be the restated amount of the equipment in 1996 dollars?

*30. How are income statement items restated on a constant dollar income statement?

*31. What is current cost accounting? How does it differ from constant dollar accounting?

*32. Is both a purchasing power gain or loss and holding gain or loss to be recognized when using current cost accounting? Explain.

*33. A company has land which cost $100,000. It has a current cost of $130,000 on December 31, 1996. The company also had a cash balance of $30,000 throughout the year. What is the holding gain on the land for 1996?

*34. What information does current cost income from operations and current cost net income provide to the financial statement user?

*35. What is the accounting profession's position on reporting changing price information?

EXERCISES

*E26-1 (Constant Dollar Index Use) Kou Fax Co. has made the following purchases of property, plant, and equipment since its formation in 1989:

Year	Price Level Index	Item	Cost
1989	100	Land	$140,000
1989	100	Building	200,000
1989	100	Machinery	80,000
1991	120	Office Equipment	25,000
1993	125	Machinery	30,000
1995	140	Office Equipment	8,000

The price level index for 1996 is 150.

Instructions
Restate the above items in terms of 1996 dollars. (Round to two decimals.)

*E26-2 (Constant Dollar Income Statement) B. Jenner, Inc. had the following income statement data for 1996:

Sales	$250,000
Cost of goods sold	168,000
Gross profit	82,000
Operating expenses	34,000
Net income	$ 48,000

The following price levels were observed during the year:

	Price Index
December 31, 1996	150
1996 average	125
December 31, 1995	100

Instructions
Determine Jenner's constant dollar income before purchasing power gain or loss for 1996.

*E26-3 (Constant Dollar—Purchasing Power Computation) Presented below is comparative financial statement information for Joe Tinker Corp. for the years 1996 and 1995:

	December 31, 1996	December 31, 1995
Cash	$ 78,000	$ 57,000
Inventory	40,000	25,000
Sales	230,000	200,000
Cost of goods sold	150,000	132,000
Operating expenses	44,000	30,000

The following price level indexes were observed during the year:

	Price Index
December 31, 1996	140
1996 average	125
December 31, 1995	100

Instructions
Determine Tinker's purchasing power gain or loss for 1996. Assume all transactions involved cash.

*E26-4 (Constant Dollar Financial Statements) Spitz Corp. in its first year of operations reported the following financial information for the year ended December 31, 1996 before closing:

Cash	$ 90,500	Retained earnings	$ 67,500
Inventory	42,000	Sales	220,000
Land	90,000	Cost of goods sold	122,500
Capital stock	150,000	Operating expenses	25,000

The following price level indexes were observed during the year:

	Price Index
December 31, 1996	121
1996 average	110
January 1, 1996	100

Spitz experienced a purchasing power loss of $15,650 during 1996. Land was purchased and capital stock issued on January 1, 1996. No inventory was on hand at the beginning of the year.

Instructions

Prepare the following financial statements for Spitz Corp.

(a) Constant dollar income statement for the year ended December 31, 1996.

(b) Constant dollar balance sheet on December 31, 1996.

*E26-5 (Current Cost Income Statement) Ames Co. reported the following financial information for 1996, its first year of operations:

Ames Co.
INCOME STATEMENT
For the Year Ended December 31, 1996

Sales	$290,000
Cost of goods sold	196,000
Gross profit	94,000
Operating expenses	41,300
Net income	$ 52,700

Ames Co.
BALANCE SHEET
December 31, 1996

Assets		Liabilities and Stockholders' Equity	
Cash	$ 40,000	Capital stock	$270,000
Inventory	95,000	Retained earnings	40,000
Land	175,000	Total liabilities and stockholders'	
Total assets	$310,000	equity	$310,000

Current cost information for 1996 is as follows:

Sales	$290,000	Inventory	$107,000
Cost of goods sold	215,000	Land	190,000
Operating expenses	41,300	Capital stock	270,000
Cash	40,000		

Instructions

(a) Determine Ames's holding gain or loss for 1996 on a current cost basis.

(b) Prepare Ames's current cost income statement for 1996.

*E26-6 (Determine Current Cost Income Components) Carnelian Chemical, Inc. is experimenting with the use of current costs. In 1996, the company purchased inventory that had a cost of $50,000, of which $30,000 was sold by year end at a sales price of $50,000. It is estimated that the current cost of the inventory at the date of sale was $35,000, and the current cost of the ending inventory at December 31, 1996, is $26,000. Operating expenses are $10,000.

Instructions

(a) Determine current cost income from operations.

(b) Determine current cost net income.

*E26-7 (Constant Dollar Purchasing Power Computation) Assume that Aretha Franklin Company has the following net monetary assets (monetary assets less monetary liabilities) at the beginning and the end of 1996.

	1/1/96	12/31/96
Net monetary assets	$300,000	$200,000

Transactions causing a change in net monetary assets during the period were incurrence and payments of accounts payable, collections of accounts receivable, and purchase and sales of merchandise during the period. All these transactions occurred evenly throughout the year.

Assume the following price-level indexes:

January 1, 1996	125
Average for the year	150
December 31, 1996	175

Instructions

(Round all computations to the nearest dollar.)

(a) What is the amount of purchasing power gain or loss from holding the January 1 balance of net monetary items throughout the year?

(b) What is the amount of purchasing power gain or loss from holding net monetary items?

(c) Explain why the company had a purchasing power gain or loss.

*E26-8 (Constant Dollar Financial Statements) The income statement for 1996 and balance sheet on December 31, 1996 for Carlos Santana Co. appears below:

Carlos Santana Co.
INCOME STATEMENT
For the Year Ended December 31, 1996

Sales	$345,000
Cost of goods sold	246,000
Gross profit	99,000
Operating expenses	30,400
Net income	$ 68,600

Carlos Santana Co.
BALANCE SHEET
December 31, 1996

Assets		Liabilities and Stockholders' Equity	
Cash	$ 59,000	Notes payable	$ 40,400
Accounts receivable	47,100	Accounts payable	61,000
Inventory	75,600	Capital stock	300,000
Land	316,500	Retained earnings	96,800
Total assets	$498,200	Total liabilities and stockholders'	
		equity	$498,200

Additional information:

1. The relevant price indexes are as follows:

January 1, 1991	105
June 30, 1993	112
August 31, 1995	120
December 31, 1996	168
Average for 1996	140

2. The company was founded on January 1, 1991. All capital stock was issued at that time.

3. One-fifth of the land was acquired on August 31, 1995; the remainder of the land was acquired on January 1, 1991.

4. A purchasing power loss of $20,400 was computed for 1996.

Instructions

(a) Prepare a constant dollar income statement for Carlos Santana for the year ended December 31, 1996.

(b) Prepare a constant dollar balance sheet for Carlos Santana on December 31, 1996. (*Hint:* Retained earnings is a balancing item.)

*E26-9 (Current Cost Financial Statements) Ana Linares Co. income statement for 1996 and balance sheet on December 31, 1996, its first year of operations, are presented below.

Ana Linares
INCOME STATEMENT
For the Year Ended December 31, 1996

Sales	$795,000
Cost of goods sold	550,000
Gross profit	245,000
Operating expenses	57,000
Net income	$188,000

Ana Linares Co.
BALANCE SHEET
December 31, 1996

Assets		Liabilities and Stockholders' Equity	
Cash	$ 74,000	Notes payable	$ 42,000
Accounts receivable	91,000	Accounts payable	63,000
Inventory	187,000	Capital stock	559,000
Land	450,000	Retained earnings	188,000
Goodwill	50,000	Total liabilities and stockholders'	
Total assets	$852,000	equity	$852,000

The current cost of the following items on December 31, 1996 is as follows:

Inventory	$200,000
Land	495,000
Goodwill	20,000
Cost of goods sold	585,000

Instructions

(a) Prepare a schedule to show the total holding gain (loss) for Ana Linares for 1996.

(b) Prepare a current cost income statement for Ana Linares for the year ended December 31, 1996.

(c) Prepare a current cost balance sheet for Ana Linares on December 31, 1996.

 *E26-10 (Current Cost Financial Statements) Grupo Rana Enterprises is considering the adoption of a current cost system. Presented below is Rana's balance sheet based on historical cost at the end of its first year of operations.

Grupo Rana Enterprises
BALANCE SHEET
December 31, 1996

Cash	$25,000	Accounts payable	$ 9,000
Inventory	42,000	Capital stock	50,000
Land	16,000	Retained earnings	24,000
	$83,000		$83,000

The following additional information is presented:

1. Cost of goods sold on a historical cost basis is $54,000; on a current cost basis $58,000.
2. No dividends were paid in the first year of operations.
3. Ending inventory on a current cost basis is $46,000; land on a current cost basis is $22,000 at the end of the year.
4. Operating expenses for the first year were $25,000.

Instructions

(a) Prepare an income statement for the current year on a (1) historical cost basis, (2) current cost basis.

(b) Prepare a balance sheet for the current year on a current cost basis.

(c) Assume that the general price level at the beginning of the year was 100; the average for the year was 160; and the ending 200. Also assume that revenues were earned and costs were incurred uniformly during the year. The land was purchased and the capital stock was issued at the beginning of the year.

Determine the following:

1. Income before purchasing power gain or loss on a constant dollar income statement for 1996.
2. Amount reported for land on a constant dollar balance sheet at December 31, 1996.
3. Amount reported for cash on a constant dollar balance sheet at December 31, 1996.

CASES

C26-1 (General Disclosures, Inventories, Property, Plant, and Equipment) Dan D. Lion Corporation is in the process of preparing its annual financial statements for the fiscal year ended April 30, 1995. Because all of Lion's shares are traded intrastate, the company does not have to file any reports with the Securities and

Exchange Commission. The company manufactures plastic, glass, and paper containers for sale to food and drink manufacturers and distributors.

Lion Corporation maintains separate control accounts for its raw materials, work-in-process, and finished goods inventories for each of the three types of containers. The inventories are valued at the lower of cost or market.

The company's property, plant, and equipment are classified in the following major categories: land, office buildings, furniture and fixtures, manufacturing facilities, manufacturing equipment, leasehold improvements. All fixed assets are carried at cost. The depreciation methods employed depend upon the type of asset (its classification) and when it was acquired.

Lion Corporation plans to present the inventory and fixed asset amounts in its April 30, 1995, balance sheet as shown below.

Inventories	$4,814,200
Property, plant, and equipment (net of depreciation)	$6,310,000

Instructions
What information regarding inventories and property, plant, and equipment must be disclosed by Dan D. Lion Corporation in the audited financial statements issued to stockholders, either in the body or the notes, for the 1994–1995 fiscal year?

(CMA adapted)

C26-2 (Disclosures Required in Various Situations) Rem Inc. produces electronic components for sale to manufacturers of radios, television sets, and phonographic systems. In connection with her examination of Rem's financial statements for the year ended December 31, 1996, Maggie Zeen, CPA, completed field work 2 weeks ago. Ms. Zeen now is evaluating the significance of the following items prior to preparing her auditor's report. Except as noted, none of these items have been disclosed in the financial statements or notes.

Item 1
A 10-year loan agreement, which the company entered into 3 years ago, provides that dividend payments may not exceed net income earned after taxes subsequent to the date of the agreement. The balance of retained earnings at the date of the loan agreement was $420,000. From that date through December 31, 1996, net income after taxes has totaled $570,000 and cash dividends have totaled $320,000. On the basis of these data the staff auditor assigned to this review concluded that there was no retained earnings restriction at December 31, 1996.

Item 2
Recently Rem interrupted its policy of paying cash dividends quarterly to its stockholders. Dividends were paid regularly through 1995, discontinued for all of 1996 to finance purchase of equipment for the company's new plant, and resumed in the first quarter of 1997. In the annual report dividend policy is to be discussed in the president's letter to stockholders.

Item 3
A major electronics firm has introduced a line of products that will compete directly with Rem's primary line, now being produced in the specially designed new plant. Because of manufacturing innovations, the competitor's line will be of comparable quality but priced 50% below Rem's line. The competitor announced its new line during the week following completion of field work. Ms. Zeen read the announcement in the newspaper and discussed the situation by telephone with Rem executives. Rem will meet the lower prices that are high enough to cover variable manufacturing and selling expenses but will permit recovery of only a portion of fixed costs.

Item 4
The company's new manufacturing plant building, which cost $2,400,000 and has an estimated life of 25 years, is leased from Ancient National Bank at an annual rental of $600,000. The company is obligated to pay property taxes, insurance, and maintenance. At the conclusion of its 10-year noncancellable lease, the company has the option of purchasing the property for $1.00. In Rem's income statement the rental payment is reported on a separate line.

Instructions
For each of the items above discuss any additional disclosures in the financial statements and notes that the auditor should recommend to her client. (The cumulative effect of the four items should not be considered.)

C26-3 (Correction of Various Notes) You are completing an examination of the financial statements of Fillmore Manufacturing Corporation for the year ended February 28, 1996. Fillmore's financial statements have not been examined previously. The controller of Fillmore has given you the following draft of proposed notes to the financial statements:

Fillmore Manufacturing Corporation
NOTES TO FINANCIAL STATEMENTS
Year Ended February 28, 1996

Note 1. With the approval of the Commissioner of Internal Revenue, the company changed its method of accounting for inventories from the first-in first-out method to the last-in first-out method on March 1, 1995. In the opinion of the company the effects of this change on the pricing of inventories and cost of goods manufactured were not material in the current year but are expected to be material in future years.

Note 2. The investment property was recorded at cost until December, 1995, when it was written up to its appraisal value. The company plans to sell the property in 1996, and an independent real estate agent in the area has indicated that the appraisal price can be realized. Pending completion of the sale the amount of the expected gain on the sale has been recorded in an unearned income account.

Note 3. The stock dividend described in our May 24, 1995, letter to stockholders has been recorded as a 110 for 100 stock split-up. Accordingly, there were no changes in the stockholders' equity account balances from this transaction.

Instructions

For each of the notes above discuss the note's adequacy and needed revisions, if any, of the financial statements or the note.

C26-4 (Disclosures Required in Various Situations) You have completed your audit of Keesha Inc. and its consolidated subsidiaries for the year ended December 31, 1996, and were satisfied with the results of your examination. You have examined the financial statements of Keesha for the past 3 years. The corporation is now preparing its annual report to stockholders. The report will include the consolidated financial statements of Keesha and its subsidiaries and your short-form auditor's report. During your audit the following matters came to your attention:

1. A vice-president who is also a stockholder resigned on December 31, 1996, after an argument with the president. The vice-president is soliciting proxies from stockholders and expects to obtain sufficient proxies to gain control of the board of directors so that a new president will be appointed. The president plans to have a note prepared that would include information of the pending proxy fight, management's accomplishments over the years, and an appeal by management for the support of stockholders.
2. The corporation decides in 1996 to adopt the straight-line method of depreciation for plant equipment. The straight-line method will be used for new acquisitions as well as for previously acquired plant equipment for which depreciation had been provided on an accelerated basis.
3. The Internal Revenue Service is currently examining the corporation's 1993 federal income tax return and is questioning the amount of a deduction claimed by the corporation's domestic subsidiary for a loss sustained in 1993. The examination is still in process, and any additional tax liability is indeterminable at this time. The corporation's tax counsel believes that there will be no substantial additional tax liability.

Instructions

(a) Prepare the notes, if any, that you would suggest for the items listed above.
(b) State your reasons for not making disclosure by note for each of the listed items for which you did not prepare a note.

(AICPA adapted)

C26-5 (Disclosures, Conditional and Contingent Liabilities) Presented below are three independent situations.

Situation I

A company offers a one-year warranty for the product that it manufactures. A history of waranty claims has been compiled and the probable amount of claims related to sales for a given period can be determined.

Situation II

Subsequent to the date of a set of financial statements, but prior to the issuance of the financial statements, a company enters into a contract that will probably result in a significant loss to the company. The amount of the loss can be reasonably estimated.

Situation III

A company has adopted a policy of recording self-insurance for any possible losses resulting from injury to others by the company's vehicles. The premium for an insurance policy for the same risk from an independent insurance company would have an annual cost of $4,000. During the period covered by the financial statements, there were no accidents involving the company's vehicles that resulted in injury to others.

Instructions

Discuss the accrual or type of disclosure necessary (if any) and the reason(s) why such disclosure is appropriate for each of the three independent sets of facts above.

(AICPA adapted)

C26-6 (Segment Reporting—Theory) Presented below is an excerpt from the financial statements of H. J. Heinz Company.

Segment and Geographic Data

The company is engaged principally in one line of business—processed food products—which represents over 90% of consolidated sales. Information about the business of the company by geographic area is presented in the table below.

There were no material amounts of sales or transfers between geographic areas or between affiliates, and no material amounts of United States export sales.

(in thousands of U.S. dollars)	Domestic	United Kingdom	Canada	Foreign Western Europe	Other	Total	Worldwide
Sales	$2,381,054	$547,527	$216,726	$383,784	$209,354	$1,357,391	$3,738,445
Operating income	246,780	61,282	34,146	29,146	25,111	149,685	396,465
Identifiable assets	1,362,152	265,218	112,620	294,732	143,971	816,541	2,178,693
Capital expenditures	72,712	12,262	13,790	8,253	4,368	38,673	111,385
Depreciation expense	42,279	8,364	3,592	6,355	3,606	21,917	64,196

Instructions

(a) Why does H. J. Heinz not prepare segment information on its products or services?

(b) What are export sales and when should they be disclosed?

(c) Why are sales by geographical area important to disclose?

C26-7 (Segment Reporting—Theory) The following article appeared in *The Wall Street Journal:*

WASHINGTON—The Securities and Exchange Commission staff issued guidelines for companies grappling with the problem of dividing up their business into industry segments for their annual reports.

An industry segment is defined by the Financial Accounting Standards Board as a part of an enterprise engaged in providing a product or service or a group of related products or services primarily to unaffiliated customers for a profit.

Although conceding that the process is a "subjective task" that "to a considerable extent, depends on the judgment of management," the SEC staff said companies should consider the nature of the products, the nature of their production and their markets and marketing methods to determine whether products and services should be grouped together or in separate industry segments.

Instructions

(a) What does financial reporting for segments of a business enterprise involve?

(b) Identify the reasons for requiring financial data to be reported by segments.

(c) Identify the possible disadvantages of requiring financial data to be reported by segments.

(d) Identify the accounting difficulties inherent in segment reporting.

C26-8 (Disclosure of Socially Responsible Activities) In an annual report of StateSide Steel, the following was reported:

"In the Cleveland District, a major improvement in air emission control was made possible by the completion of the first phase of construction of a giant suppressed combustion pollution control system for the basic oxygen furnaces."

"The system, believed to be the first of its type ever installed on an existing steelmaking complex, replaces a bank of electrostatic precipitators which will be used to control other emissions that occur in the steelmaking process. The total system is expected to become fully operational this spring."

Instructions

(a) Do you believe that StateSide should disclose information of this nature?

(b) How might an enterprise measure its socially responsible activities?

C26-9 (Interim Reporting) J. J. Kersee Corporation, a publicly traded company, is preparing the interim financial data which it will issue to its stockholders and the Securities and Exchange Commission (SEC) at the end of the first quarter of the 1995–1996 fiscal year. Kersee's financial accounting department has compiled the following summarized revenue and expense data for the first quarter of the year:

Sales	$60,000,000
Cost of goods sold	36,000,000
Variable selling expenses	2,000,000
Fixed selling expenses	3,000,000

Included in the fixed selling expenses was the single lump sum payment of $2,000,000 for television advertisements for the entire year.

Instructions

(a) J. J. Kersee Corporation must issue its quarterly financial statements in accordance with generally accepted accounting principles regarding interim financial reporting.

    1. Explain whether Kersee should report its operating results for the quarter as if the quarter were a separate reporting period in and of itself or as if the quarter were an integral part of the annual reporting period.

    2. State how the sales, cost of goods sold, and fixed selling expenses would be reflected in Kersee Corporation's quarterly report prepared for the first quarter of the 1995–1996 fiscal year. Briefly justify your presentation.

(b) What financial information, as a minimum, must Kersee Corporation disclose to its stockholders in its quarterly reports?

(CMA adapted)

C26-10 (Treatment of Various Interim Reporting Situations) The following statement is an excerpt from Paragraphs 9 and 10 of *Accounting Principles Board (APB) Opinion No. 28*, "Interim Financial Reporting":

Interim financial information is essential to provide investors and others with timely information as to the progress of the enterprise. The usefulness of such information rests on the relationship that it has to the annual results of operations. Accordingly, the Board has concluded that each interim period should be viewed primarily as an integral part of an annual period.

In general, the results for each interim period should be based on the accounting principles and practices used by an enterprise in the preparation of its latest annual financial statements unless a change in an accounting practice or policy has been adopted in the current year. The Board has concluded, however, that certain accounting principles and practices followed for annual reporting purposes may require modification at interim reporting dates so that the reported results for the interim period may better relate to the results of operations for the annual period.

Instructions

Listed below are six (6) independent cases on how accounting facts might be reported on an individual company's interim financial reports. For each of these cases, state whether the method proposed to be used for interim reporting would be acceptable under generally accepted accounting principles applicable to interim financial data. Support each answer with a brief explanation.

    1. B. J. King Company takes a physical inventory at year end for annual financial statement purposes. Inventory and cost of sales reported in the interim quarterly statements are based on estimated gross profit rates, because a physical inventory would result in a cessation of operations. King Company does have reliable perpetual inventory records.

    2. Florence Chadwick Company is planning to report one-fourth of its pension expense each quarter.

    3. N. Lopez Company wrote inventory down to reflect lower of cost or market in the first quarter. At year end the market exceeds the original acquisition cost of this inventory. Consequently, management plans to write the inventory back up to its original cost as a year-end adjustment.

    4. K. Witt Company realized a large gain on the sale of investments at the beginning of the second quarter. The company wants to report one-third of the gain in each of the remaining quarters.

    5. Alice Marble Company has estimated its annual audit fee. They plan to prorate this expense equally over all four quarters.

    6. Lori McNeil Company was reasonably certain they would have an employee strike in the third quarter. As a result, they shipped heavily during the second quarter but plan to defer the recognition of the sales in excess of the normal sales volume. The deferred sales will be recognized as sales in the third quarter when the strike is in progress. McNeil Company management thinks this is more nearly representative of normal second- and third-quarter operations.

C26-11 (Financial Forecasts) An article in *Barron's* noted:

Okay. Last fall, someone with a long memory and an even longer arm reached into that bureau drawer and came out with a moldy cheese sandwich and the equally moldy notion of corporate forecasts. We tried to find out what happened to the cheese sandwich—but, rats!, even recourse to the Freedom of Information Act didn't help. However, the forecast proposal was dusted off, polished up and found quite serviceable. The SEC, indeed, lost no time in running it up the old flagpole—but no one was very eager to salute. Even after some of the more objectionable features—compulsory corrections and detailed explanations of why the estimates went awry—were peeled off the original proposal.

Seemingly, despite the Commission's smiles and sweet talk, those craven corporations were still afraid that an honest mistake would lead down the primrose path to consent decrees and class action suits. To lay to rest such qualms, the Commission last week approved a "Safe Harbor" rule that, providing the forecasts were made on a reasonable basis and in good faith, protected corporations from litigation should the projections prove wide of the mark (as only about 99% are apt to do).

Instructions

    (a) What are the arguments for preparing profit forecasts?

    (b) What is the purpose of the "safe harbor" rule?

    (c) Why are corporations concerned about presenting profit forecasts?

C26-12 (Treatment of Various Interim Reporting Items) Balboa Manufacturing Company, a California corporation listed on the Pacific Coast Stock Exchange, budgeted activities for 1996 as follows:

	Amount	Units
Net sales	$9,000,000	1,000,000
Cost of goods sold	5,400,000	
Gross margin	$3,600,000	
Selling, general, and administrative expenses	2,100,000	
Operating income	$1,500,000	
Nonoperating revenues and expenses	–0–	
Income before income taxes	$1,500,000	
Estimated income taxes (current and deferred)	600,000	
Net income	$ 900,000	
Earnings per share of common stock	$9.00	

Balboa has operated profitably for many years and has experienced a seasonal pattern of sales volume and production similar to those below forecasted for 1996. Sales volume is expected to follow a quarterly pattern of 10%, 20%, 35%, 35%, respectively, because of the seasonality of the industry. Also, owing to production and storage capacity limitations, it is expected that production will follow a pattern of 20%, 25%, 30%, 25%, per quarter, respectively.

At the conclusion of the first quarter of 1996, Vasca DeGama, the controller of Balboa, has prepared and issued the following interim report for public release:

	Amount	Units
Net sales	$ 900,000	100,000
Cost of goods sold	540,000	100,000
Gross margin	$ 360,000	
Selling, general, and administrative expenses	412,500	
Operating loss	$ (52,500)	
Loss from warehouse fire	(262,500)	
Loss before income taxes	$(315,000)	
Estimated income taxes	–0–	
Net loss	$(315,000)	
Loss per share of common stock	$(3.15)	

The following additional information is available for the first quarter just completed, but was not included in the public information released:

1. Assume that the warehouse fire loss met the conditions of an extraordinary loss. The warehouse had an undepreciated cost of $480,000; $217,500 was recovered from insurance on the warehouse. No other gains or losses are anticipated this year from similar events or transactions, and Balboa had no similar losses in preceding years; thus, the full loss will be deductible as an ordinary loss for income tax purposes.

2. The company uses a standard cost system in which standards are set at currently attainable levels on an annual basis. At the end of the first quarter there was underapplied fixed factory overhead (volume variance) of $75,000 that was treated as an asset at the end of the quarter. Production during the quarter was 200,000 units, of which 100,000 were sold.

3. The selling, general, and administrative expenses were budgeted on a basis of $1,350,000 fixed expenses for the year plus 75¢ variable expenses per unit of sales.

4. The effective income tax rate, for federal and state taxes combined, is expected to average 40% of earnings before income taxes during 1996. There are no permanent differences between pretax accounting earnings and taxable income.

5. Earnings per share were computed on the basis of 100,000 shares of capital stock outstanding. Balboa has only one class of stock issued, no long-term debt outstanding, and no stock option plan.

Instructions

    (a) Without reference to the specific situation described above, what are the standards of disclosure for interim financial data (published interim financial reports) for publicly treated companies? Explain.

    (b) Identify the weaknesses in form and content of Balboa's interim report without reference to the additional information.

(c) For each of the five items of additional information, indicate the preferable treatment for each item for interim reporting purposes and explain why that treatment is preferable.

(AICPA adapted)

C26-13 (Disclosures and Auditor's Opinion; Limited Profitability Prospects) Jesse Owens Enterprises acquired a large tract of land in a small town approximately 10 miles from Fleet City. The company executed a firm contract on November 15, 1995, for the construction of a one-mile race track, together with related facilities. The track and facilities were completed December 15, 1996. On December 31, 1996, a 15% installment note of $210,000 was issued along with other consideration in settlement of the construction contract. Installments of $70,000 fall due on December 31 of each of the next 3 years. The company planned to pay the notes from cash received from operations and from sale of additional capital stock.

The company adopted the double-declining balance method of computing depreciation. No depreciation was taken in 1996 because all racing equipment was received in December after the completion of the track and facilities.

The land on which the racing circuit was constructed was acquired at various dates for a total of $81,000, and its approximate market value on December 31, 1996, is $100,000.

Through the sale of tickets to spectators, parking fees, concession income, and income from betting, the company officials anticipated that approximately $275,000 is taken in during the typical year's racing season. Cash expenses for a racing season were estimated at $173,000.

You have made an examination of the financial condition of Owens Enterprises as of December 31, 1996. The balance sheet as of that date and statement of operations follow.

Jesse Owens Enterprises
BALANCE SHEET
December 31, 1996

Assets

Cash		$ 11,000
Accounts receivable		12,000
Prepaid expenses		9,000
Property (at cost)		
Land	$ 81,000	
Grading and track improvements	86,000	
Grandstand	200,000	
Buildings	76,000	
Racing equipment	56,000	499,000
Organization costs		1,000
Total assets		$532,000

Liabilities and Stockholders' Equity

Accounts payable	$ 32,000
Installment note payable—15%	210,000
Stockholders' equity	
Capital stock, par value $1.00 per share, authorized	
200,000, issued and outstanding 121,500 shares	121,500
Capital in excess of par, representing amounts paid	
in over par value of capital stock	188,500
Retained earnings (deficit)	(20,000)
Total liabilities and stockholders' equity	$532,000

Jesse Owens Enterprises
STATEMENT OF INCOME
For the Period from Inception, December 1, 1993
to December 31, 1996

Income	
Profit on sales of land	$10,000
Other	2,000
	12,000
General and administrative expenses	32,000
Net loss for the period	$20,000

On January 15, 1997, legislation that declared betting to be illegal was enacted by the state legislature and was signed by the governor. A discussion with management on January 17 about the effect of the legislation revealed that it is now estimated that revenue will be reduced to approximately $80,000 and cash expenses will be reduced to one-third the original estimate.

Instructions
(Disregard federal income tax implications.)
- **(a)** Prepare the explanatory notes to accompany the balance sheet.
- **(b)** What opinion do you believe the auditor should render? Discuss.

(AICPA adapted)

*C26-14 (Inflation Accounting Methods) A business entity's financial statements could be prepared by using historical cost or current value as a basis. In addition, the basis could be stated in terms of unadjusted dollars or dollars restated for changes in purchasing power. The various permutations of these two separate and distinct areas are shown in the following matrix:

	Unadjusted Dollars	Dollars Restated for Changes in Purchasing Power
Historical cost	1	2
Current value	3	4

Block number 1 of the matrix represents the traditional method of accounting for transactions in accounting today, wherein the absolute (unadjusted) amount of dollars given up or received is recorded for the asset or liability obtained **(relationship between resources)**. Amounts recorded in the method described in block number 1 reflect the original cost of the asset or liability and do not give effect to any change in value of the unit of measure **(standard of comparison)**. This method assumes the validity of the accounting concepts of going concern and stable monetary unit. Any gain or loss (including holding and purchasing power gains or losses) resulting from the sale or satisfaction of amounts recorded under this method is deferred in its entirety until sale or satisfaction.

Instructions
For each of the remaining matrix blocks (2, 3, and 4) respond to the following questions. **Limit your discussion to nonmonetary assets only.**
- **(a)** How will this method of recording assets affect the relationship between resources and the standard of comparison?
- **(b)** What is the theoretical justification for using each method?
- **(c)** How will each method of asset valuation affect the recognition of gain or loss during the life of the asset and ultimately from the sale or abandonment of the asset? Your response should include a discussion of the timing and magnitude of the gain or loss and conceptual reasons for any difference from the gain or loss computed using the traditional method.

(AICPA adapted)

*C26-15 (Accounting for Changing Prices) Carl Lewis Corp., a wholesaler with large investments in plant and equipment, began operations in 1947. The company's history has been one of expansion in sales, production, and physical facilities. Recently, some concern has been expressed that the conventional financial statements do not provide sufficient information for decisions by investors. After consideration of proposals for various types of supplementary financial statements to be included in the 1995 annual report, management has decided to present a balance sheet as of December 31, 1995, and a statement of income and retained earnings for 1995, both restated for changes in the general price level.

Instructions
- **(a)** On what basis can it be contended that Lewis's conventional statements should be restated for changes in the general price level?
- **(b)** Distinguish between financial statements restated for general price-level changes and current value financial statements.
- **(c)** Distinguish between monetary and nonmonetary assets and liabilities as the terms are used in constant dollar accounting. Give examples of each.
- **(d)** Outline the procedures Lewis should follow in preparing the proposed supplementary statements.
- **(e)** Indicate the major similarities and differences between the proposed supplementary statements and the corresponding conventional statements.
- **(f)** Assuming that in the future Lewis will want to present comparative supplementary statements, can the 1995 supplementary statements be presented in 1996 without adjustment? Explain.

(AICPA adapted)

*C26-16 (Accounting for Changing Prices) The general purchasing power of the dollar has declined considerably because of inflation in recent years. To account for this changing value of the dollar, many accountants suggest that financial statements be adjusted for general price-level changes. Three independent, unrelated statements regarding general price-level adjusted financial statements follow. Each statement contains some fallacious reasoning.

Statement I

The accounting profession has not seriously considered price-level adjusted financial statements before because the rate of inflation usually has been so small from year to year that the adjustments would have been immaterial in amount. Price-level adjusted financial statements represent a departure from the historical cost basis of accounting. Financial statements should be prepared on the basis of facts, not estimates.

Statement II

When adjusting financial data for general price-level changes, a distinction must be made between monetary and nonmonetary assets and liabilities, which, under the historical cost basis of accounting, have been identified as "current" and "noncurrent." When using the historical cost basis of accounting, no purchasing power gain or loss is recognized in the accounting process, but when financial statements are adjusted for general price-level changes, a purchasing power gain or loss will be recognized on monetary and nonmonetary items.

Statement III

If financial statements were adjusted for general price-level changes, depreciation charges in the income statement would permit the recovery of dollars of current purchasing power and, thereby, equal the cost of new assets to replace the old ones. General price-level adjusted data would yield statement-of-financial-position amounts closely approximating current values. Furthermore, management can make better decisions if constant dollar financial statements are published.

Instructions

Evaluate each of the independent statements and identify the areas of fallacious reasoning in each and explain why the reasoning is incorrect. Complete your discussion of each statement before proceeding to the next statement.

(AICPA adapted)

▶ USING YOUR JUDGMENT ◀

▶ FINANCIAL REPORTING PROBLEM

Refer to the financial statements and other documents of Georgia-Pacific Corporation presented in Appendix 5-A and answer the following questions.

1. What were the major operations Georgia-Pacific selected to report separately in its Notes to Financial Statements? What were the items reported?
2. Why did Georgia-Pacific not report sales to foreign markets?
3. What were the items disclosed in the interim reports for Georgia-Pacific?

▶ WRITING ASSIGNMENT

You are compiling the consolidated financial statements for Vender Corporation International. The corporation's accountant, Vincent Price, has provided you with the following segment information.

Note 7: Major Segments of Business

VCI conducts funeral service and cemetery operations in the United States and Canada. Substantially all revenues of VCI's major segments of business are from unaffiliated customers. Segment information for fiscal 1995, 1994, and 1993 follows:

	Funeral	Floral	Cemetery	Corporate	Dried Whey	Limousine	Consolidated
				(Thousands)			
Revenues:							
1995	$302,000	$10,000	$ 83,000	$ —	$7,000	$14,000	$416,000
1994	245,000	6,000	61,000	—	4,000	8,000	324,000
1993	208,000	3,000	42,000	—	1,000	6,000	260,000

	Funeral	Floral	Cemetery	(Thousands) Corporate	Dried Whey	Limousine	Consolidated
Operating Income:							
1995	$ 79,000	$ 1,500	$ 18,000	$ (36,000)	$ 500	$ 2,000	$ 65,000
1994	64,000	200	12,000	(28,000)	200	400	48,800
1993	54,000	150	6,000	(21,000)	100	350	39,600
Capital Expenditures[a]:							
1995	$ 26,000	$ 1,000	$ 9,000	$ 400	$ 300	$ 1,000	$ 37,700
1994	28,000	2,000	60,000	1,500	100	700	132,300
1993	14,000	25	8,000	600	25	50	22,700
Depreciation and Amortization:							
1995	$ 13,000	$ 100	$ 2,400	$ 1,400	$ 100	$ 200	$ 17,200
1994	10,000	50	1,400	700	50	100	12,300
1993	8,000	25	1,000	600	25	50	9,700
Identifiable Assets:							
1995	$334,000	$ 1,500	$162,000	$114,000	$ 500	$ 8,000	$620,000
1994	322,000	1,000	144,000	52,000	1,000	6,000	526,000
1993	223,000	500	78,000	34,000	500	3,500	339,500

[a]Includes $4,520,000, $111,480,000, and $1,294,000 for the years ended April 30, 1995, 1994, and 1993, respectively, for purchases of businesses.

Instructions

Determine which of the above segments must be reported separately and which can be combined under the category "Other." Then, write a one page memo to the company's accountant, Vincent Price, explaining the following:

1. What segments must be reported separately and what segments can be combined.
2. What criteria you used to determine reportable segments.
3. What major items for each must be disclosed.

▶ GROUP ASSIGNMENT

(Segment Reporting—Theory) The most recently published statement of consolidated income of Ida Ho Industries, Inc., appears below:

Ida Ho Industries, Inc.
STATEMENT OF CONSOLIDATED INCOME
For the Year Ended March 31, 1995

Net sales	$130,200,000
Other revenue	1,500,000
Total revenue	131,700,000
Cost of products sold	91,520,000
Selling and administrative expenses	28,100,000
Interest expense	1,020,000
Total cost and expenses	120,640,000
Income before income taxes	11,060,000
Income taxes	3,318,000
Net income	$ 7,742,000

Louise E. Anna, a representative of a firm of security analysts, visited the central headquarters of Ho Industries to obtain more information about the company's operations.

In the annual report Ho's president stated that Ho was engaged in the pharmaceutical, food-processing, toy-manufacturing, and metal-working industries. Ms. Anna complained that the published income statement was of limited utility in her analysis of the firm's operations. She said that Ho should have disclosed separately the profit earned in each of its component industries. Further, she maintained that several items appearing on the statement of consolidated retained earnings should have been included on the income statement; a gain of $1,780,000 on the sale of the furniture division in early March of the current year and an assessment for additional income taxes of $495,000 resulting from an examination of the returns covering the years ended March 31, 1995 and 1996 (normally recurring).

Instructions

Your instructor will assign one member of the group to serve as recorder and one member to serve as spokesperson. As a group, provide the information for the recorder to prepare responses to the following requirements. Upon completion of the requirements, the spokesperson will report the group findings to the class.

(a) Explain what is meant by a "conglomerate" company.

(b) 1. Discuss the accounting problems involved in measuring net profit by industry segments within a company.

2. With reference to Ida Ho Industries' statement of consolidated income, identify the specific items where difficulty might be encountered in measuring profit by each of its industry segments, and explain the nature of the difficulty.

(c) 1. What criteria should be applied in determining whether a gain or loss should be excluded from the determination of net income?

2. What criteria should be applied in determining whether a gain or loss that is properly includable in the determination of net income should be included in the results of ordinary operations or shown separately as an extraordinary item after all other items of revenue and expense?

3. How should the gain on the sale of the furniture division and the assessment of additional taxes each be presented in Ho's financial statements?

▶ ETHICS CASE

(Ethical Issue—Full Disclosure) Ken Tucky, the controller of Blue Ridge Furniture Company, and Virg Inia, his assistant, are preparing the year-end financial statements. Inia wants to disclose the cost of available-for-sale securities as a parenthetical note on the balance sheet. Tucky—concerned about the decline in market value compared to cost of these securities—does not want to call attention to this decline. He wants to "bury" the cost information in a note to the financial statements.

Instructions

(a) What ethical issue is posed by the choice between these two forms of disclosure?

(b) Are the interests of different stakeholders in conflict in the choice between the two methods of accounting reports?

(c) Which method would you choose and why?

INDEX

Date Issued		No.	Title
June	1988	No. 98	Accounting for Leases: Sale-Leaseback Transactions Involving Real Estate; Sales-Type Leases of Real Estate; Definition of the Lease Term; Initial Direct Costs of Direct Financing Leases
Sept.	1988	No. 99	Deferral of the Effective Date of Recognition of Depreciation by Not-for-Profit Organizations
Dec.	1988	No. 100	Accounting for Income Taxes—Deferral of the Effective Date of FASB Statement No. 96
Dec.	1988	No. 101	Regulated Enterprises—Accounting for the Discontinuation of Application of FASB Statement No. 71
Feb.	1989	No. 102	Statement of Cash Flows—Exemption of Certain Enterprises and Classification of Cash Flows from Certain Securities Acquired for Resale
Dec.	1989	No. 103	Accounting for Income Taxes—Deferral of the Effective Date of FASB Statement No. 96
Dec.	1989	No. 104	Statement of Cash Flows—Net Reporting of Certain Cash Receipts and Cash Payments and Classification of Cash Flows from Hedging Transactions
Mar.	1990	No. 105	Disclosure of Information About Financial Instruments with Off-Balance-Sheet Risk and Financial Instruments with Concentrations of Credit Risk
Dec.	1990	No. 106	Employers' Accounting for Postretirement Benefits Other Than Pensions
Dec.	1991	No. 107	Disclosures about Fair Value of Financial Instruments
Dec.	1991	No. 108	Accounting for Income Taxes—Deferral of the Effective Date of FASB Statement No. 96
Feb.	1992	No. 109	Accounting for Income Taxes
Aug.	1992	No. 110	Reporting by Defined Benefit Pension Plans of Investment Contracts
Nov.	1992	No. 111	Rescission of FASB Statement No. 32 and Technical Corrections
Nov.	1992	No. 112	Employers' Accounting for Postemployment Benefits
Dec.	1992	No. 113	Accounting and Reporting for Reinsurance of Short-Duration and Long-Duration Contracts
May	1993	No. 114	Accounting by Creditors for Impairment of a Loan
May	1993	No. 115	Accounting for Certain Investments in Debt and Equity Securities
June	1993	No. 116	Accounting for Contributions Received and Contributions Made
June	1993	No. 117	Financial Statements of Not-for-Profit Organizations
Oct.	1994	No. 118	Accounting by Creditors for Impairments of a Loan—Income Recognition and Disclosures
Oct.	1994	No. 119	Disclosure about Derivative Financial Instruments and Fair Value of Financial Instruments
Dec.	1994	No.	Applicability of Generally Accepted Accounting Principles to Mutual Life Insurance Companies and Other Enterprises—Deferral of the Effective Date of FASB Interpretation No. 40.
Dec.	1994	No.	Accounting for Impairments of Long-Lived Assets.

Financial Accounting Standards Board (FASB), Interpretations (1974–1994)

June	1974	No. 1	Accounting Changes Related to the Cost of Inventory (APB Opinion No. 20)
June	1974	No. 2	Imputing Interest on Debt Arrangements Made Under the Federal Bankruptcy Act (APB Opinion No. 21) (superseded)
Dec.	1974	No. 3	Accounting for the Cost of Pension Plans Subject to the Employee Retirement Income Security Act of 1974 (APB Opinion No. 8)
Feb.	1975	No. 4	Applicability of FASB Statement No. 2 to Purchase Business Combinations
Feb.	1975	No. 5	Applicability of FASB St. No. 2 to Development Stage Enterprises (superseded)
Feb.	1975	No. 6	Applicability of FASB Statement No. 2 to Computer Software
Oct.	1975	No. 7	Applying FASB Statement No. 7 in Statements of Established Enterprises
Jan.	1976	No. 8	Classification of a Short-Term Obligation Repaid Prior to Being Replaced by a Long-Term Security (FASB Std. No. 6)
Feb.	1976	No. 9	Applying APB Opinions No. 16 and 17 when a Savings and Loan or Similar Institution is Acquired in a Purchase Business Combination (APB Op. No. 16 & 17)
Sept.	1976	No. 10	Application of FASB Statement No. 12 to Personal Financial Statements (FASB Std. No. 12)
Sept.	1976	No. 11	Changes in Market Value after the Balance Sheet Date (FASB Std. No. 12)
Sept.	1976	No. 12	Accounting for Previously Established Allowance Accounts (FASB Std. No. 12)
Sept.	1976	No. 13	Consolidation of a Parent and Its Subsidiaries Having Different Balance Sheet Dates (FASB Std. No. 12)
Sept.	1976	No. 14	Reasonable Estimation of the Amount of a Loss (FASB Std. No. 5)
Sept.	1976	No. 15	Translation of Unamortized Policy Acquisition Costs by Stock Life Insurance Company (FASB Std. No. 8) (amended and partially superseded)
Feb.	1977	No. 16	Clarification of Definitions and Accounting for Marketable Equity Securities That Become Nonmarketable (FASB Std. No. 12)
Feb.	1977	No. 17	Applying the Lower of Cost or Market Rule in Translated Financial Statements (FASB Std. No. 8) (superseded)
Mar.	1977	No. 18	Accounting for Income Taxes in Interim Periods (APB Op. No. 28)
Oct.	1977	No. 19	Lessee Guarantee of the Residual Value of Leased Property (FASB Std. No. 13)
Nov.	1977	No. 20	Reporting Accounting Changes under AICPA Statements of Position (APB Op. No. 20)
April	1978	No. 21	Accounting for Leases in a Business Combination (FASB Std. No. 13)
April	1978	No. 22	Applicability of Indefinite Reversal Criteria to Timing Differences (APB Op. No. 11 and 23)

Refer to Index for page citations

Date Issued		No.	Title
Aug.	1978	No. 23	Leases of Certain Property Owned by a Governmental Unit or Authority (FASB Std. No. 13)
Sept.	1978	No. 24	Leases Involving Only Part of a Building (FASB Std. No. 13)
Sept.	1978	No. 25	Accounting for an Unused Investment Tax Credit (APB Op. No. 2, 4, 11, and 16)
Sept.	1978	No. 26	Accounting for Purchase of a Leased Asset by the Lessee During the Term of the Lease (FASB Std. No. 13)
Nov.	1978	No. 27	Accounting for a Loss on a Sublease (FASB Std. No. 13 and APB Op. No. 30)
Dec.	1978	No. 28	Accounting for Stock Appreciation Rights and Other Variable Stock Option or Award Plans (APB Op. No. 15 and 25) (amended)
Feb.	1979	No. 29	Reporting Tax Benefits Realized on Disposition of Investments in Certain Subsidiaries and Other Investees (APB Op. No. 23 and 24)
Sept.	1979	No. 30	Accounting for Involuntary Conversions of Nonmonetary Assets to Monetary Assets (APB Op. No. 29)
Feb.	1980	No. 31	Treatment of Stock Compensation Plans in EPS Computations (APB Op. No. 15 and Interp. 28)
Mar.	1980	No. 32	Application of Percentage Limitations in Recognizing Investment Tax Credit (APB Op. No. 2, 4, and 11)
Aug.	1980	No. 33	Applying FASB Statement No. 34 to Oil and Gas Producing Operations (FASB Std. No. 34)
Mar.	1981	No. 34	Disclosure of Indirect Guarantees of Indebtedness of Others (FASB Std. No. 5)
May	1981	No. 35	Criteria for Applying the Equity Method of Accounting for Investments in Common Stock (APB Op. No. 18)
Oct.	1981	No. 36	Accounting for Exploratory Wells in Progress at the End of a Period
July	1983	No. 37	Accounting for Translation Adjustments upon Sale of Part of an Investment in a Foreign Entity (Interprets FASB Statement No. 52)
Aug.	1984	No. 38	Determining the Measurement Date for Stock Option, Purchase, and Award Plans Involving Junior Stock (Interprets APB Opinion No. 25)
Mar.	1992	No. 39	Offsetting of Amounts Related to Certain Contracts (Interprets APB Opinion No. 10 and FASB Statement No. 105)
Apr.	1993	No. 40	Applicability of Generally Accepted Accounting Principles to Mutual Life Insurance and Other Enterprises (Interprets FASB Statements No. 12, 60, 97, and 113)

Financial Accounting Standards Board (FASB), Technical Bulletins (1979–1994)

Dec.	1979	No. 79-1	Purpose and Scope of FASB Technical Bulletins and Procedures for Issuance
Dec.	1979	No. 79-2	Computer Software Costs
Dec.	1979	No. 79-3	Subjective Acceleration Clauses in Long-Term Debt Agreements
Dec.	1979	No. 79-4	Segment Reporting of Puerto Rican Operations
Dec.	1979	No. 79-5	Meaning of the Term 'Customer' as it Applies to Health Care Facilities under FASB Statement No. 14
Dec.	1979	No. 79-6	Valuation Allowances Following Debt Restructuring
Dec.	1979	No. 79-7	Recoveries of a Previous Writedown under a Troubled Debt Restructuring Involving a Modification of Terms
Dec.	1979	No. 79-8	Applicability of FASB Statements 21 and 33 to Certain Brokers and Dealers in Securities
Dec.	1979	No. 79-9	Accounting in Interim Periods for Changes in Income Tax Rates
Dec.	1979	No. 79-10	Fiscal Funding Clauses in Lease Agreements
Dec.	1979	No. 79-11	Effect of a Penalty on the Term of a Lease
Dec.	1979	No. 79-12	Interest Rate Used in Calculating the Present Value of Minimum Lease Payments
Dec.	1979	No. 79-13	Applicability of FASB Statement No. 13 to Current Value Financial Statements
Dec.	1979	No. 79-14	Upward Adjustment of Guaranteed Residual Values
Dec.	1979	No. 79-15	Accounting for Loss on a Sublease Not Involving the Disposal of a Segment
Dec.	1979	No. 79-16	Effect on a Change in Income Tax Rate on the Accounting for Leveraged Leases
Dec.	1979	No. 79-17	Reporting Cumulative Effect Adjustment from Retroactive Application of FASB No. 13
Dec.	1979	No. 79-18	Transition Requirements of Certain FASB Amendments and Interpretations of FASB Statement No. 13
Dec.	1979	No. 79-19	Investor's Accounting for Unrealized Losses on Marketable Securities Owned by an Equity Method Investee
Dec.	1980	No. 80-1	Early Extinguishment of Debt through Exchange for Common or Preferred Stock
Dec.	1980	No. 80-2	Classification of Debt Restructuring by Debtors and Creditors
Feb.	1981	No. 81-1	Disclosure of Interest Rate Futures Contracts and Forward and Standby Contracts
Feb.	1981	No. 81-2	Accounting for Unused Investment Tax Credits Acquired in a Business Combination Accounted for by the Purchase Method
Feb.	1981	No. 81-3	Multiemployer Pension Plan Amendments Act of 1980
Feb.	1981	No. 81-4	Classification as Monetary or Nonmonetary Items
Feb.	1981	No. 81-5	Offsetting Interest Cost to be Capitalized with Interest Income
Nov.	1981	No. 81-6	Applicability of Statement 15 to Debtors in Bankruptcy Situations
Jan.	1982	No. 82-1	Disclosure of the Sale or Purchase of Tax Benefits through Tax Leases
Mar.	1982	No. 82-2	Accounting for the Conversion of Stock Options into Incentive Stock Options as a Result of the Economic Recovery Tax Act of 1981

Refer to Index for page citations